Efallai nad yw'r wybodaeth
sydd yn y rhifyn hwn yn
adlewyrchu
DEDDFWRIAETH
BRESENNOL

Information contained within
this edition may not be
CURRENT LAW

University of South Wales

2065817

BOWSTEAD AND REYNOLDS

ON

AGENCY

VOLUMES IN THE COMMON LAW LIBRARY

Arlidge, Eady & Smith on Contempt
Benjamin's Sale of Goods
Bowstead & Reynolds on Agency
Bullen & Leake & Jacob's Precedents of Pleadings
Charlesworth and Percy on Negligence
Chitty on Contracts
Clerk & Lindsell on Torts
Gatley on Libel and Slander
Goff & Jones, The Law of Restitution
Jackson & Powell on Professional Negligence
McGregor on Damages
Phipson on Evidence

THE COMMON LAW LIBRARY

BOWSTEAD AND REYNOLDS

ON

AGENCY

TWENTY-FIRST EDITION

BY

PETER WATTS QC, LLM (Cantab), FRSNZ

Professor of Law, University of Auckland
Senior Research Fellow, Harris Manchester College, Oxford
GENERAL EDITOR

AND

F.M.B. REYNOLDS QC (Hon), DCL, FBA

Honorary Bencher of the Inner Temple; Professor of Law Emeritus in the
University of Oxford and Emeritus Fellow of Worcester College, Oxford

SWEET & MAXWELL

 THOMSON REUTERS

Published in 2018 by Thomson Reuters, trading as Sweet & Maxwell.
Thomson Reuters is registered in England & Wales. Company number
1679046.
Registered Office and address for service: 5 Canada Square, Canary Wharf,
London, E14 5AQ.

For further information on our products and services, visit *http://
www.sweetandmaxwell.co.uk.*

Computerset by Sweet & Maxwell.
Printed and bound by CPI Group (UK) Ltd, Croydon, CR0 4YY.
No natural forests were destroyed to make this product: only farmed timber
was used and replanted.
A CIP catalogue record for this book is available from the British Library.

ISBN: 978-0-414-06207-8

Thomson Reuters, the Thomson Reuters Logo and Sweet & Maxwell ® are
trademarks of Thomson Reuters.

Crown copyright material is reproduced with the permission of the
Controller of HMSO and the Queen's Printer for Scotland.

All rights reserved. No part of this publication may be reproduced, or
transmitted in any form, or by any means, or stored in any retrieval system of
any nature, without prior written permission, except for permitted fair dealing
under the Copyright, Designs and Patents Act 1988, or in accordance with the
terms of a licence issued by the Copyright Licensing Agency in respect of
photocopying and/or reprographic reproduction. Application for permission for
other use of copyright material, including permission to reproduce extracts in
other published works, should be made to the publishers. Full
acknowledgement of the author, publisher and source must be given.

© 2018 Thomson Reuters

TITLE HISTORY

BOWSTEAD AND REYNOLDS ON AGENCY

First edition	(1896)	By William Bowstead
Second edition	(1898)	By William Bowstead
Third Edition	(1907)	By William Bowstead
Fourth Edition	(1909)	By William Bowstead
Fifth Edition	(1912)	By William Bowstead
Sixth Edition	(1919)	By William Bowstead
Seventh Edition	(1924)	By William Bowstead
Eighth Edition	(1932)	By William Bowstead
Ninth Edition	(1938)	By Arthur H. Forbes
Tenth Edition	(1944)	By Arthur H. Forbes
Eleventh Edition	(1951)	By Peter Allsop
Twelfth Edition	(1959)	By E.J. Griew
Thirteenth Edition	(1968)	By F.M.B. Reynolds and B.J. Davenport
Fouteenth Edition	(1976)	By F.M.B. Reynolds and B.J. Davenport
Fifteenth Edition	(1985)	By F.M.B. Reynolds
Sixteenth Edition	(1996)	By F.M.B. Reynolds
Seventeenth Edition	(2001)	By F.M.B. Reynolds
Eighteenth Edition	(2006)	By F.M.B. Reynolds
Nineteenth Edition	(2010)	By Peter Watts and F.M.B. Reynolds
Twentieth Edition	(2014)	By Peter Watts and F.M.B. Reynolds
Twenty-First Edition	(2018)	By Peter Watts and F.M.B. Reynolds

PREFACE

While only three years have intervened since the previous edition of this work, there have been plenty of developments, mainly in case law, to take into account. An opportunity has also been taken to review, and where necessary, to revise the treatment of a range of topics within the work. Some new subject matter has also been introduced. In the result, every chapter of the work has required attention in some degree. Over 100 new cases have been integrated into the book. A fairly comprehensive approach has been taken to cases from England and Wales (omitting those where the application of principle has been routine), with more discrimination for cases from elsewhere in the Commonwealth. Agency law remains a subject where there is considerably more uniformity of content and cross-citation around the common law world than with many other subjects.

In Chapter 1 (nature of agency), minor revisions have been made to the discussion of the nature of the agency relationship (emphasising the voluntariness of the conferral of authority), and more substantial revisions to the treatment of the significance of agency law for companies (taking into account, *Bilta (UK) Ltd v Nazir (No.2)* [2015] UKSC 23). Otherwise, there are many new cases that have been integrated into the footnotes of the chapter.

Chapter 2 (creation of agency) has new material on the capacity of agents to self-deal and a new paragraph on dual agency, some of which ties into revisions to Chapter 6, discussed below. More has been said too on the capacity of corporations. Questions relating to the authority to act illegally have been re-addressed, taking into account *Patel v Mirza* [2016] UKSC 42. New cases on ratification have been integrated into that part of the chapter.

Chapter 3 (authority) has new material and illustrations on the conferral of authority (including the onus of proof), and on the ability of a principal to reserve the power to act personally. The paragraphs on the effect dishonesty has on an agent's authority have been recast, with the long-controversial decision in *Hambro v Burnand* [1904] 2 KB 10 reassessed.

Chapters 4 and 5 can be taken together. Only very minor updating has been needed for chapter 4 (agency of necessity). Chapter 5 on sub-agency has also needed little attention, but there is minor revision to the equitable duties sub-agents can owe principals, and some case law has been added (including *Involnert Management Inc v Aprilgrange Ltd* [2015] EWHC 2225 (Comm)).

There is considerable new material throughout Chapter 6 (duties of agents to their principals). Much of the material on restorative and compensatory remedies for breach of trust has been rewritten not just to take account of *AIB Group (UK) Plc v Mark Redler & Co Solicitors* [2014] UKSC 58 but also subsequent academic scholarship (see paras 6–003 and 6-043). In particular, it seems premature to assume that a general remedy of equitable compensation will be able to do all the work that the older equitable accounting action and the action for money had and received performed. Reconstitutive or restitutionary remedies seem to have been neglected in *Redler*, but there are signs of survival (*Main v Giambrone & Law (a firm)* [2017] EWCA Civ 1193), and those remedies remain very much alive in other jurisdictions. The material on proprietary remedies has been revised to take account of *Angove's Pty Ltd v Bailey* [2016] UKSC 47. The duties applying to self-dealing and fair-dealing have also been given revised treatment, tying in with modifications to Chapter 2.

Chapter 7 (rights of agents) on the rights of agents has new material on rights to remuneration. There is also further discussion of forfeiture of agent's remuneration. In that regard, the decision in *Imageview Management Ltd v Jack* [2009] EWCA Civ 963 has continued to be problematic, producing some eight subsequent cases. It would be preferable to revert to the position when forfeiture was largely just a matter of the law of contract; the questions being, has the agent's conduct meant that, where remuneration has already been paid, there has been a total failure of consideration, and where not paid, has the conduct justified termination of the agency with concomitant discharge of the duty to pay remuneration.

Chapter 8 (relations between principals and third parties) covers many of the central problems of agency law. There have been a number of revisions to the section on apparent authority, including the apparent authority of Crown agents, and taking account of such developments as unauthorised applications of electronic signatures. A significant reassessment of the book's position on the lingering apparent authority of agents whose actual authority has ceased or has been markedly reduced has also been undertaken in Chapter 10. Commentary has been added on the relevance of an agent's subjective intentions when acting for more than one undisclosed or unidentified principal, in response to dicta in *Magellan Spirit ApS v Vitol SA (Magellan Spirit)* [2016] EWHC 454 (Comm). Account has been taken of recent decisions of the Court of Appeal on the role of agency law in the law of negligent misstatement (*Foster v Action Aviation Ltd* [2014] EWCA Civ 1368; *Playboy Club London Ltd v Banca Nazionale del Lavoro SpA* [2016] EWCA Civ 457 (now under appeal to the Supreme Court). Other revisions have been made to the section on tortious liability to address recent case law on vicarious liability, non-delegable duties, and the role of agents in pleas of contributory negligence (including *Cox v Ministry of Justice* [2016] UKSC 10; and *Woodland v Essex CC* [2013] UKSC 66). The subject of imputed knowledge continues to undergo development, and substantial revisions have been needed, not least to take account of *Bilta (UK) Ltd*, above.

Chapter 9 (relations between agents and third parties) incorporates a number of new cases on the liability of agents to third parties, either as parties to the principal contract (*Rabiu v Marlbray Ltd* [2016] EWCA Civ 476; *Savills (UK) Ltd v Blacker* [2017] EWCA Civ 68) or as a party to a warranty of authority (*Zoya Ltd v Sheikh Nasir Ahmed (t/a Property Mart)* [2016] EWHC 2249 (Ch); *Re Sherlock Holmes International Society Ltd* [2016] EWHC 1392 (Ch)). The legal position of agents who act for principals who are impersonating a third party is also discussed in the light of recent authority (in particular, *P&P Property Ltd v Owen White & Catlin LLP* [2016] EWHC 2276 (Ch)). The material on the restitutionary liability of agents has had some revision. The liability of agents in tort has had a degree of reworking, as has the material on the liability of agents for equitable wrongs.

The most significant changes to Chapter 10 (termination of authority) stem from *Angove's Pty Ltd v Bailey* [2016] UKSC 47, where Lord Sumption's dicta on when authority can be made irrevocable expressly departed from the existing treatment in this work. But having thrown doubt on the existing tests, his Lordship did not go on to provide a substitute principle or set of principles. Otherwise, there has been a reworking of some of the material on lasting powers of attorney, the recall by corporations of resolutions conferring authority, and (as reported above) a revision of the approach to the question when an agent's apparent authority can no longer be assumed to continue. New illustrations have also been added.

As regards Chapter 11, a group of significant cases on commercial agents appeared just before the copy was prepared. *Monk v Largo Foods Ltd* [2016] EWHC 1837 (Comm) concerns termination of an agent's contract that had been "subject to successful review", and contains discussion of damages and compensation also; *Nagel v Pluczenik Diamond Co NV* [2017] EWHC 1750 (Comm) contains consideration, among various other matters, of the meaning of "commodity market"; and *ERGO Poist'ovna a.s.* (C-48/16) concerns extinction of the right to commission on partial inexecution, and the meaning of "reasons for which the principal is not to blame", both in connection with reg.11(1) of the Commercial Agents Regulations.

The text of Chapter 12 has been reconsidered, but there are no special cases to which attention should be drawn. Brief reference is made to the problems of bonds issued by the Ukrainian Government to the Russian government in *Law Debenture Trust Corp Plc v Ukraine* [2017] EWHC 655 (Comm).

Once again, I have relied on Francis Reynolds to revise and update Chapters 11 and 12. He has also made a number of useful suggestions for change in other chapters of the work. I am most grateful for his continuing support and instruction. I am pleased to acknowledge the work of a former student, Callum Burnett, in updating the multitude of references to other textbooks throughout the book. And I remain greatly indebted to my family for their forbearance and support through the never-ending task of keeping *Bowstead & Reynolds* up to date.

The cut-off date for this edition was 31 July 2017, but where judgments have appeared on an appeal from a case already in the manuscript (such as *Armes v Nottinghamshire CC* [2017] UKSC 60) I have endeavoured to incorporate at least notice of their existence.

Peter Watts
Bankside Chambers, Auckland, and Fountain Court Chambers, London
6 November 2017

STANDARD ABBREVIATIONS

Books on the Law of Agency

As with previous editions, certain standard works are referred to throughout this book without further description.

Bennett	H. Bennett, *Principles of the Law of Agency*, Hart Publishing, 2013.
Dal Pont	G.E. Dal Pont, *Law of Agency*, 3rd edn, LexisNexis, 2013.
Fridman	G.H.L. Fridman, *Canadian Agency Law*, 3rd edn, LexisNexis, 2017.
Macgregor	L. Macgregor, *The Law of Agency in Scotland*, W. Green, 2013.
Munday	R. Munday, *Agency—Law and Principles*, 3rd edn, OUP, 2016.
Powell	Raphael Powell, *The Law of Agency*, 2nd edn, Pitman, 1961.
Restatement	*Restatement of the Law 3rd, Agency*, American Law Institute, 2007.
Stoljar	S.J. Stoljar, *The Law of Agency*, Sweet & Maxwell, 1961.
Tan	Tan Cheng Han, *The Law of Agency*, 2nd edn, Academy Publishing, 2017.

Books on the Commercial Agents Regulations 1993

There are now several specialised works dealing with these Regulations. They are listed in the first footnote of Chapter 11, which deals with the Regulations, and within that chapter, reference back to a work by name is to that footnote. The Chapter also continues a short bibliography of some relevant continental European books.

The American Restatements

The American Restatements consist of formulations of legal principle in the style of a code ("blackletter") accompanied by comments interleaved with illustrations, and Reporter's notes, which refer to relevant case law. They are published by the American Law Institute, a prestigious body with its headquarters in Philadelphia, and have been formulated by a Reporter, subjected to various forms of consultation and finally approved at a meeting of the members of the Institute itself as representing the Institute's position. They have in general no legal status, but are available as influential guidance for lawyers and courts, by which they are frequently cited.

The first *Restatement of Agency* was published in 1933. The first Reporter was Professor Floyd R. Mechem of the University of Chicago, and he was succeeded, before publication of the final version, by Professor Warren Seavey of the Harvard Law School. Mechem had been the author of *A Treatise on the Law of Agency*, published in 1889 (a few years before the present work) and succeeded by a second edition in 1914, which was lengthy and very much in the style of *Pomeroy's Equity Jurisprudence* (1881) and Williston's later (1920) treatise on contract. He also wrote a shorter book, *Outlines of the Law of Agency*, which was after his death edited by his son Professor Philip Mechem of the University of Pennsylvania. At any rate in its 4th edition of 1952, the only one available to us, this was a perceptive work. But after 1914 no treatise of any comparable size was published in the United States, and it can be said that the *Restatement* itself represented from 1933 an authoritative treatise. A very substantial second version, *Restatement, Second*, serving the same purpose, was published in 1957. The Reporter was again Professor Seavey, and the whole document is strongly influenced by his views (which never outside of this document became the subject of a systematic book, though he published frequent articles and comments).

Restatement, Third, was published in 2007. The Reporter is Professor Deborah DeMott of Duke University, North Carolina. This aims partly to produce something considerably less detailed than *Restatement, Second*, which occupies three heavy volumes and (to take an example) had separate treatment for each topic in the contexts of disclosed principal and of undisclosed principal. *Restatement, Third* seeks to set out many fewer, and more generalised principles, and also to pay more attention to the significance of statutes in agency law, and to agents acting for organisational principals, whether corporate or not.

It is obviously intended that *Restatement, Third* should supersede *Restatement, Second*, completely, just as that superseded the first *Restatement*. It can provide guidance outside the United States too. In this book therefore the main statements of issues of general principle are accompanied by footnote citations to *Restatement, Third* (as was true of *Restatement, Second* in the previous five editions). However, for the purposes of a book on English law (referring also to material in other common law systems outside the United States) it has proved undesirable to omit all references to *Restatement, Second*. An obvious purpose for citing it is to emphasise changes in approach which are to be found in *Restatement, Third*: most conspicuously, in the selection of the word "manifestation" for certain basic propositions regarding an agent's authority, and also because the new version makes no use of Seavey's notion of "inherent agency power", a controversial way of dealing with certain difficult decisions which do not readily yield to orthodox analysis. But *Restatement, Second* also expressed specific views on a large number of detailed points on which guidance, at any rate outside the United States, may still be found to be of value. In the end it has seemed inadvisable to delete all reference to all of them, even if pursuing the *Restatement* into a superseded version is likely to be an activity for researchers only.

Modern European "Codes"

There have been produced in Europe in the last decade or so a number of sets of non-statutory "codes". The first two listed below were produced for the purposes of a putative European law, and the third as a guiding law for international arbitration. All have short sections on Agency and for a common lawyer are useful not only as formulations (rather like the *Restatements*) but also as giving indications of the sort of propositions that may be regarded as generally acceptable to continental European legal systems. On Agency they differ between themselves in significant respects. In particular, the Principles of European Contract Law ("PECL") and the Draft Common Frame of Reference ("DCFR") make use of the distinction between direct and indirect representation, which the UNIDROIT Principles seek specifically to avoid. The PECL and the UNIDROIT Principles are confined to agency in contract law, but the scope of the DCFR is wider, albeit that agency and representation appear in connection with contract. Only DCFR deals in detail with the internal relationship between principal and agent.

PECL   *The Principles of European Contract Law* (ed. Lando and Beale, Kluwer, 2000).

DCFR   Draft Common Frame of Reference. The Outline version of the text of this can be downloaded free from *http://www.storme.be/ 2009_02_DCFR_OutlineEdition.pdf*. The six volume commentary that accompanies the code is published as *Principles, Definitions and Model Rules of European Private Law* (ed. Von Bar and Clive, OUP, 2010).

Unidroit Principles   UNIDROIT Principles of International Commercial Contracts (UNIDROIT, 2004).

Commonwealth Case Law Abbreviations

The citations to cases from the United Kingdom use standard abbreviations, which it is not necessary to set out herein. However, it may be useful for the reader to have an explanation of some of those used for Commonwealth cases. All recent Australian and New Zealand cases that are cited are available free at *http:// www.austlii.edu.au*. Many Singapore cases are available free at *http:// www.commonlii.org/* and Hong Kong cases at *http://legalref.judiciary.gov.hk/lrs/ common/ju/judgment.jsp*. Abbreviations with points refer to report series; those without are neutral citations.

A.C.L.C.	Australian Company Law Cases
A.C.S.R.	Australian Company and Securities Reports
A.L.R.	Australian Law Reports
A.T.R.	Australian Tax Reports
A.N.Z. Conv.R.	Australian and New Zealand Conveyancing Reports
B.P.R.	Butterworths Property Reports
C.L.R.	Commonwealth Law Reports
D.L.R.	Dominion Law Reports
FCAFC	Federal Court of Australia Full Court
F.C.R.	Federal Court Reports
F.L.R.	Federal Law Reports
G.L.R.	Gazette Law Reports (New Zealand)
HCA	High Court of Australia
H.K.C.F.A.R.	Hong Kong Court of Final Appeal Reports
HKCU	Hong Kong Cases Unreported
H.K.L.R.	Hong Kong Law Reports
H.K.L.R.D.	Hong Kong Law Reports & Digest
NSWCA	New South Wales Court of Appeal
NSWSC	New South Wales Supreme Court

N.Z.C.L.C.	New Zealand Company Law Cases
N.Z.C.P.R.	New Zealand Conveyancing and Property Reports
NZHC	New Zealand High Court
N.Z.L.R.	New Zealand Law Reports
NZSC	New Zealand Supreme Court
P.R.N.Z.	Procedure Reports of New Zealand
QSC	Queensland Supreme Court
QCA	Queensland Court of Appeal
SCC	Supreme Court of Canada
S.L.R.	Singapore Law Reports
VCA	Court of Appeal of Victoria
V.R.	Victorian Reports
VSC	Supreme Court of Victoria
W.A.R.	Western Australia Reports

TABLE OF CONTENTS

Preface vii
Standard Abbreviations xi
Table of Cases xxi
Table of Statutes cliii
Table of Statutory Instruments clix

1. NATURE OF THE SUBJECT

    Article 1   Agency and Authority 1-001
    Article 2   Further Definitions 1-039

2. CREATION OF AGENCY

   1.   General 2-001

    Article 3   How Agency Arises 2-001
    Article 4   Capacity to Act as Principal 2-006
    Article 5   Capacity to Act as Agent 2-011
    Article 6   Acts Which May Be Done By Means of an Agent .. 2-017

   2.   Agency Arising by Conferral of Authority 2-027

    Article 7   Express Agreement to Confer Authority 2-027
    Article 8   Implied Agreement 2-029
    Article 9   Formalities for Appointment 2-035
    Article 10   Authority to Execute a Deed 2-040
    Article 11   Co-agents 2-043
    Article 12   Co-principals 2-045

   3.   Ratification 2-047

    Article 13   General Principle 2-047
    Article 14   What Acts May Be Ratified 2-054
    Article 15   Who may Ratify 2-062
    Article 16   Knowledge Necessary for Ratification 2-071
    Article 17   What Constitutes Ratification 2-074
    Article 18   Events Not Preventing Ratification 2-084
    Article 19   Limits on Ratification 2-089
    Article 20   Effect of Ratification 2-095

   4.   Estoppel from Denying Existence of Agency Relationship 2-101

    Article 21   Estoppel from Denying Existence of Agency
                       Relationship 2-101

3. AUTHORITY OF AGENTS

   1.   Actual and Apparent Authority 3-001

    Article 22   General Principles 3-001
    Article 23   No Authority to Act Other Than for Principal's
                       Benefit 3-010

   2.   Express Actual Authority 3-013

Article 24 Construction of Powers of Attorney 3-013
Article 25 Construction of Authority Not Given By Deed 3-016
Article 26 Authority Given in Ambiguous Terms 3-019

3. Implied Actual Authority 3-021

Article 27 To Do What is Necessary for, or Incidental to,
              Effective Execution of Express Authority
              (Incidental Authority) 3-021
Article 28 Authority to Receive Payment of Money 3-024
Article 29 Managerial Agents: Implied Authority Where
              Employed to Conduct Trade or Business or Act
              Generally in Certain Matters (Usual Authority) .. 3-027
Article 30 Professional Agents: Implied Authority Where
              Employed in the Course of Business as Agent
              (Usual Authority) 3-030
Article 31 Authority Implied from Special Usages
              (Customary Authority) 3-033
Article 32 Authority Implied from Course of Dealing and
              Circumstances of Case 3-041

4. Presumed Authority 3-043

4. AGENCY OF NECESSITY

Article 33 Doctrine of Agency of Necessity 4-001

5. SUB-AGENCY

Article 34 When Agent May Delegate Authority 5-001
Article 35 Relation Between Principal and Sub-agent 5-008

6. DUTIES OF AGENTS TOWARDS THEIR PRINCIPALS

1. Duties of Performance 6-002

Article 36 Agent's Duty to Perform Undertaking 6-002
Article 37 Contractual Agent's Duty to Obey Further
              Instructions Given by Principal 6-008
Article 38 Ambiguous Instructions 6-010
Article 39 Contractual Agent's Duties of Diligence 6-012
Article 40 Contractual Agent's Duty to Exercise Skill and
              Care 6-017
Article 41 Not Liable to Principal in Respect of Contracts
              Entered into on Principal's Behalf 6-025
Article 42 Liability of Gratuitous Agents 6-027

2. Fiduciary and Other Equitable Duties 6-032

Article 43 Agents' Equitable Duties—General Matters 6-033
Article 44 Duty to Avoid Conflicts of Interest, Unless with
              Consent 6-046
Article 45 Agent Dealing with Principal 6-062
Article 46 Agent's Duty Not to Profit from Position 6-073
Article 47 Agent Using Principal's Property and Confidential
              Information 6-075

Article 48 Agent Acquiring Benefits in Breach of Duty 6-079
Article 49 Liability of Agents in Respect of Bribes and Secret
Commissions 6-084
Article 50 Duty to Keep Property of Principal Separate and
Deliver Business Records and Correspondence .. 6-090
Article 51 Duty to Account 6-094
Article 52 Common Law Duty to Pay Over Money Held for
Principal 6-099
Article 53 Liability for Interest 6-102

3. Estoppel as to Principal's Title 6-110

Article 54 Agent's Estoppel as to Principal's Title 6-110

7. RIGHTS OF AGENTS AGAINST THEIR PRINCIPALS

1. Remuneration 7-003

Article 55 Whether Agent Entitled to Any Remuneration 7-003
Article 56 Agents' Remuneration Due Upon the Happening of
an Event 7-013
Article 57 Whether Agent Is Effective Cause of Transaction ... 7-027
Article 58 Agent Prevented By Principal from Earning
Remuneration 7-033
Article 59 Specific Enforcement of Agency Contract 7-045
Article 60 No Remuneration for Unauthorised Transactions or
in Cases of Misconduct or Breach of Duty 7-048
Article 61 No Remuneration in Respect of Unlawful
Transactions 7-052

2. Reimbursement and Indemnity 7-057

Article 62 Reimbursement of Expenses and Indemnity from
Liabilities Incurred in Course of Agency 7-057
Article 63 Cases Where Reimbursement or Indemnity Not
Available 7-063

3. Lien 7-071

Article 64 Definitions of General and Particular Possessory
Liens 7-071
Article 65 Possessory Lien of Agents 7-074
Article 66 Confined to Rights of Principal, Except in the Case
of Money or Negotiable Securities 7-087
Article 67 How Lien Extinguished or Lost 7-090
Article 68 Lien of Sub-Agents 7-095

4. Other Miscellaneous Rights 7-100

Article 69 Rights in Respect of Goods Bought in Own Name . 7-100
Article 70 Right to Interplead 7-103

8. RELATIONS BETWEEN PRINCIPALS AND THIRD PARTIES

1. Contract 8-001

Article 71 Disclosed Principal: General Rule 8-001
Article 72 Apparent (or Ostensible) Authority 8-010

Article 73 No Unauthorised Act Binding with Respect to
Persons with Notice 8-047

Article 74 Fraud of Agent is Not Incompatible with Apparent
Authority 8-062

Article 75 Disclosed Principal Not Bound by Acts Outside
Actual or Apparent Authority 8-065

Article 76 Undisclosed Principal: Rights and Liabilities 8-068
Article 77 Deeds 8-083
Article 78 Bills, Notes and Cheques 8-089
Article 79 Defences to Action by or against Principal 8-094
Article 80 Settlement Between Principal and Agent Affecting
Recourse to Principal 8-100

Article 81 Settlement with or Set-off Against Agent Affecting
Rights of Principal 8-107

Article 82 Merger and Election: Release of Principal 8-113

2. Dispositions of Property and Restitutionary Claims 8-125

Article 83 Dispositions of Principal's Property By Agent
Acting Within Actual or Apparent Authority 8-125

Article 84 Doctrine of Apparent Ownership 8-129
Article 85 Dispositions By Agents Entrusted with Indicia of
Property 8-134

Article 86 Dealings with Money and Negotiable Securities 8-139
Article 87 Dispositions Protected By the Factors Act 1889 8-143
Article 88 Principal's Rights to Recover Property and
Money—Restitutionary Claims 8-159

Article 89 Dispositions and Payments to Agent 8-168

3. Wrongs 8-176

Article 90 Liability of Principal for Torts Committed By
Agent 8-177

Article 91 Misrepresentations by Agent as to Credit of Third
Parties 8-197

Article 92 Money, etc., Misappropriated by Agent 8-199
Article 93 Money Applied by Agent for Benefit of Principal ... 8-202

4. Notification to and Knowledge Acquired through Agent 8-205

Article 94 Notification to Agent 8-205
Article 95 Knowledge Acquired through Agent 8-208

5. Interference with Agent By Third Party and Involvement in
Agent's Breach of Duty 8-218

Article 96 Rights of Principal Where Third Party Implicated
in Agent's Breach of Duties 8-218

9. Relations between Agents and Third Parties

1. Contract 9-001

Article 97 General Rule 9-001
Article 98 When Agent Has Rights and Liabilities 9-004
Article 99 Written Contracts 9-036
Article 100 Admissibility of Extrinsic Evidence 9-039

Article 101 Oral Contracts 9-043
Article 102 Deeds 9-047
Article 103 Bills, Notes and Cheques 9-050
Article 104 Merger and Election: Release of Agent 9-057
Article 105 Warranty of Authority 9-060
Article 106 Measure of Damages for Breach of Warranty of
               Authority 9-077
Article 107 Principal Fictitious or Non-existent 9-084
Article 108 Agent Shown to Be the Real Principal 9-088
Article 109 No Right of Action for Promised Bribes or Secret
               Commissions 9-098

2.   Restitution 9-099

Article 110 Right of Agent to Sue for Money Paid By Mistake,
               Etc 9-099
Article 111 Duty of Agent to Repay Money Received for Use
               of Principal 9-101
Article 112 Money Held to Use of Third Parties 9-110

3.   Torts 9-115

Article 113 Agent Personally Liable for Torts and Other
               Wrongs 9-115
Article 114 Conversion By Innocent Agent 9-126
Article 115 Agent Not Liable for Wrongs of Co-agents or Sub-
               agents Working for Principal 9-132

4.   Equity 9-134

Article 116 Accessory Liability to Breach of Trust or Fiduciary
               Obligation and Knowing Receipt of Property
               Subject to Trust or Fiduciary Obligation 9-134

10.   TERMINATION OF AUTHORITY

Article 117 Termination of Actual Authority 10-002
Article 118 When Authority Cannot Be Terminated
               (Irrevocable Authority) 10-006
Article 119 Termination of Authority by Death, Mental
               Incapacity or Insolvency 10-015
Article 120 Termination of Authority by Notice of Revocation
               or Renunciation 10-023
Article 121 Apparent Authority Where Actual Authority
               Terminated 10-030
Article 122 Statutory Protection of Third Parties and Agents in
               Respect of Acts Done Under Powers of
               Attorney 10-034
Article 123 Compensation at Common Law on Termination of
               Authority 10-038

11.   COMMERCIAL AGENTS

1.   Introduction 11-001
2.   The Commercial Agents Regulations 11-003
3.   Application of the Regulations 11-005

4. Relations Between Agent and Principal 11-024
5. Remuneration and Commission 11-027
6. Termination of the Agency 11-037

12. CONFLICT OF LAWS

APPENDIX THE COMMERCIAL AGENTS (COUNCIL DIRECTIVE) REGULATIONS
1993 777

Index 787

TABLE OF CASES

Paragraph references in bold indicate that the case is referred to in an illustration.

UNITED KINGDOM

A/S Dan Bunkering Ltd v F G Hawkes (Western) Ltd [2009] EWHC 3141 (Comm) 3-042
A/S Hansen Tangens Rederi III v Total Transport Corp; The Sagona [1984] 1 Lloyd's Rep.
   194... 9-046
A/S Rendal v Arcos Ltd (1937) 106 L.J.K.B. 756; 157 L.T. 485; 53 T.L.R. 953; [1937] 3
   All E.R. 577; 81 S.J. 733; 43 Com.Cas. 1; 58 Lloyd's L.R. 287 HL 8-206
A&J Fabrications (Batley) Ltd v Grant Thornton (A Firm) (No.2) [1997] T.L.R. 588;
   [2000] B.P.I.R. 1; [1999] Lloyd's Rep. P.N. 863; [1999] P.N.L.R. 811; (1999) 96(31)
   L.S.G. 41; (1999) 143 S.J.L.B. 213 Ch.. 9-117
Aas v Benham [1891] 2 Ch. 44; 65 L.T. 25 .... 6-074, 6-081
Abbey National Building Society v Cann [1991] 1 A.C. 56; [1990] 2 W.L.R. 833; [1990] 1
   All E.R. 1085; [1990] 2 F.L.R. 122; (1990) 22 H.L.R. 360; (1990) 60 P. & C.R. 279 HL 8-134
Abbey National Plc v Tufts [1999] 2 F.L.R. 399; [1999] Fam. Law 542; [1999] E.G. 24
   (C.S.) CA 8-214
Abbott v Condici Ltd [2005] 2 Lloyd's Rep. 450 CC (Central London) 11-042, 11-057
Abel v Sutton (1800) 3 Esp. 108 .... **3-018**
Aberdeen Railway Co v Blaikie Bros (1854) 1 Macq. 461; 2 Eq. Rep. 1281; 23 L.T. (O.S.)
   315.. 1-028, 6-036, **6-061**, 6-065
Abigail v Lapin [1934] A.C. 491 .... 8-133, 8-135
Abou-Rahmah v Abacha [2006] EWCA Civ 1492; [2007] Bus. L.R. 220; [2007] 1 All
   E.R. (Comm) 827; [2007] 1 Lloyd's Rep. 115; [2007] W.T.L.R. 1; (2006–07) 9
   I.T.E.L.R. 401 .... 9-107, 9-135
Abraaj Investment Management Ltd v Bregawn Jersey Ltd [2010] EWHC 630 (Ch) 6-100
Abrahams v Deakin [1891] 1 Q.B. 516; 60 L.J.K.B. 238; 63 L.T. 690; 7 T.L.R. 117; 55 J.P.
   212; 39 W.R. 183.................................... 3-029, 8-192
Abrahams v Spitz (1963) 107 S.J. 113 CA 3-023
Abu Dhabi National Tanker Co v Product Star Shipping; The Product Star [1992] 2 All
   E.R. 20; [1991] 2 Lloyd's Rep. 508 QBD (Comm)........................ 8-081, 9-010
Acatos v Burns (1878) 3 E. & D. 282; 47 L.J.K.B. 566; 26 W.R. 624 CA 4-004
Accentuate Ltd v Asigra Inc [2009] EWHC 2655 (QB); [2009] 2 Lloyd's Rep. 599; [2010]
   Eu. L.R. 260 .... 11-006, 11-007, 11-010
Accidia Foundation v Simon C Dickinson Ltd [2010] EWHC 3058 (Ch) 3-033, 3-035, 5-011,
                                                                 6-092, 6-108, 7-009
Acey v Fernie (1840) 7 M. & W. 151; 10 L.J.Ex. 9 .... **3-029**, 8-067
Ackroyd & Sons v Hasan [1960] 2 Q.B. 144; [1960] 2 W.L.R. 810; [1960] 2 All E.R. 254;
   104 S.J. 388 CA.................................... 7-019, 7-023
Actavis Group hf v Eli Lilly & Co [2013] EWCA Civ 517; [2013] R.P.C. 37 1-023
Acute Property Developments Ltd v Apostolou [2013] EWHC 200 (Ch); [2013] Bus. L.R.
   D22 .... **3-029**, 8-012, 8-021, 8-049, 8-061
Adair v Young (1879) 12 Ch.D. 13; 41 L.T. 361; 28 W.R. 85 .... **9-125**
Adams v Atlas International Property Services Ltd [2016] EWHC 2680 (QB); [2017] Bus.
   L.R. 287... 8-119
Adams v Buckland (1705) 2 Vern. 514 10-016
Adams v Cape Industries Plc [1990] Ch. 433; [1990] 2 W.L.R. 657; [1991] 1 All E.R. 929;
   [1990] B.C.C. 786; [1990] B.C.L.C. 479 CA....................................... 1-030
Adams v Ford [2012] EWCA Civ 544; [2012] 1 W.L.R. 3211; [2012] 3 All E.R. 247;
   [2012] C.P. Rep. 31... 2-094
Adams v Hall (1877) 37 L.T. 70; 3 Asp. M.L.C. 496 9-090
Adams v Morgan & Co Ltd [1924] 1 K.B. 751; [1923] All E.R. Rep. 189; 93 L.J.K.B.
   382; 130 L.T. 792; 40 T.L.R. 70; 68 S.J. 348 CA 7-059, 7-060, **7-062**
Adamson v Jarvis (1829) 4 Bing 66; 12 Moore C.P. 241 .... 7-068, **7-070**, 8-191
Addison v Gandassequi (1812) 4 Taunt. 574 .... 8-073, 8-120
Adelbert (Prinz), The [1917] A.C. 586 PC 7-101

[xxi]

Adler v Ananhall Advisory & Consultancy Services Ltd [2009] EWCA Civ 586; [2009]
 N.P.C. 80 . . . . 7-018, 7-039
Aerostar Maintenance International Ltd v Wilson [2010] EWHC 2032 (Ch) . . . 6-042, 6-080, 8-221
Agip (Africa) Ltd v Jackson [1991] Ch. 547; [1991] 3 W.L.R. 116; [1992] 4 All E.R. 451;
 (1991) 135 S.J. 117 CA. 6-003, 8-161, 8-162, 8-166, **8-167**, 9-100, 9-102, 9-106, 9-135, 9-136
Agnew v Inland Revenue Commissioner. *See* Brumark Investments Ltd, Re 7-077
Agra Bank Ex p., Re Worcester (1868) L.R. 3 Ch.App. 555; 37 L.J.Bcy 23; 18 L.T. 866 8-217
Ahlers v Broome & Greene Ltd (1938) 62 Ll.Rep. 163 7-082
AIB Group (UK) Plc v Mark Redler & Co Solicitors [2014] UKSC 58; [2015] A.C. 1503;
 [2014] 3 W.L.R. 1367; [2015] 1 All E.R. 747; [2015] 2 All E.R. (Comm) 189; [2015]
 P.N.L.R. 10; [2015] W.T.L.R. 187; 18 I.T.E.L.R. 216; (2014) 158(43) S.J.L.B. 49. . . . 3-030, 6-003,
 6-007, 6-043
Aiken v Caledonian Railway Co 1913 S.C. 66; 50 S.C.L.R. 45; 1912 2 S.L.T. 314 8-196
Aiken v Stewart Wrightson Members Agency Ltd [1995] 1 W.L.R. 1281 . . . . 5-010, 5-016
Ainsworth v Creeke (1868) L.R. 4 C.P. 476 . . . . 2-057, 2-091
AJU Remicon Co Ltd v Alida Shipping Co Ltd [2007] EWHC 2246 (Comm) . 2-103, **3-040**, 5-015,
 8-019, 8-021, 8-023
Akita Holdings Ltd v Attorney General of Turks and Caicos Islands [2017] UKPC 7;
 [2017] 2 W.L.R. 1153 . . . . 6-042, 6-068, 6-080, 9-136
Al Khudairi v Abbey Brokers Ltd [2010] EWHC 1486 (Ch); [2010] P.N.L.R. 32 6-100
AL Underwood Ltd v Bank of Liverpool [1924] 1 K.B. 775 3-011
Al-Kandari v Brown (JR) & Co [1988] Q.B. 665; [1988] 2 W.L.R. 671; [1988] 1 All E.R.
 833; (1988) 132 S.J. 462; (1988) 138 N.L.J. 62; (1988) Fam.Law. 382; [1988] L.S.Gaz.
 April 13, 1988 CA 6-028, 9-117, **9-125**
Alan (WJ) & Co Ltd v El Nasr Export & Import Co [1972] 2 Q.B. 189; [1972] 2 W.L.R.
 800; 116 S.J. 139; [1972] 2 All E.R. 127; [1972] 1 Lloyd's Rep. 313 CA. 7-094
Alan Ramsay Sales & Marketing Ltd v Typhoo Tea Ltd [2016] EWHC 486 (Comm);
 [2016] 4 W.L.R. 59. . . . . 11-051, 11-056, 11-057
Albacruz (Cargo Owners) v Albazero, The (Owners) [1977] A.C. 774; [1976] 3 W.L.R.
 419; [1976] 3 All E.R. 129; [1976] 2 Lloyd's Rep. 467; 120 S.J. 570 HL 2-067, 9-013
Albazero, The. *See* Albacruz (Cargo Owners) v Albazero, The (Owners) 2-067, 9-013
Albemarle Supply Co Ltd v Hind & Co [1928] 1 K.B. 307; 97 L.J.K.B. 25; 138 L.T. 102;
 43 T.L.R. 783; 71 S.J. 77 CA 1-033, 7-091, 7-094
Albion, The (1872) 27 L.T. 723 . . . . **7-094**
Albon (t/a NA Carriage Co) v Naza Motor Trading Sdn Bhd [2007] EWHC 9 (Ch); [2007]
 1 W.L.R. 2489; [2007] 2 All E.R. 719; [2007] 1 All E.R. (Comm) 795; [2007] 1 Lloyd's
 Rep. 297; [2007] Bus. L.R. D87 12-003
Albright & Wilson UK Ltd v Biachem Ltd [2002] UKHL 37; [2002] 2 All E.R. (Comm)
 753; [2003] 1 C.L.C. 637; (2002) 146 S.J.L.B. 241 8-047
Alchemy (International) Ltd v Tattersalls Ltd [1985] 2 E.G.L.R. 17; (1985) 276 E.G. 675;
 (1985) 276 E.G. 793 QBD 6-024
Alder v Boyle (1847) 4 C.B. 635; 16 L.J.C.P. 232; 9 L.T.(O.S.) 246; 11 Jur. 591 . . . . . 7-004, 7-014,
 7-018
Aldermore Bank Plc v Rana [2015] EWCA Civ 1210; [2016] 1 W.L.R. 2209 2-033
Alexander & Co v Wilson Holgate & Co (1923) 14 Ll.Rep. 538 6-024
Alexander v Automatic Telephone Co [1900] 2 Ch. 56; 69 L.J.Ch. 428; 82 L.T. 400; 16
 T.L.R. 339; 44 S.J. 407; 48 W.R. 546 6-039
Alexander v Davis & Son (1885) 2 T.L.R. 142 10-042
Alexander v Sizer (1869) L.R. 4 Ex. 102; 38 L.J.Ex. 38 . . . . **9-056**
Alexander v Southey (1821) 5 B. & A. 247 . . . . **9-131**
Alexander v Webber [1922] 1 K.B. 642; 91 L.J.K.B. 320; 126 L.T. 512; 38 T.L.R. 42 KBD . . 8-221
Alfred McAlpine Construction Ltd v Panatown Ltd (No.1); sub nom. Panatown Ltd v
 Alfred McAlpine Construction Ltd [2001] 1 A.C. 518; [2000] 3 W.L.R. 946; [2000] 4
 All E.R. 97; [2000] C.L.C. 1604; [2000] B.L.R. 331; (2000) 2 T.C.L.R. 547; 71 Con.
 L.R. 1; [2000] E.G.C.S.102; (2000) 97(38) L.S.G. 43; (2000) 150 N.L.J. 1299; (2000)
 144 S.J.L.B. 240; [2000] N.P.C. 89 HL 2-067, 9-011, 9-013, 9-014
Algemeene Bankvereeniging v Langton (1935) 40 Com. Cas. 247; 51 Ll. L. Rep. 275 2-059
Ali v Caton [2014] EWCA Civ 1313; [2015] P.I.Q.R. Q1 10-020
Alicia Hosiery Ltd v Brown Shipley & Co Ltd; sub nom. Alicia Hosiery v Brown Shipley
 & Co, and Allied Shippers [1970] 1 Q.B. 195; [1969] 2 W.L.R. 1268; [1969] 2 All E.R.
 504; 113 S.J. 466; [1969] 2 Lloyd's Rep. 179 8-173
Allam & Co Ltd v Europa Poster Services Ltd [1968] 1 W.L.R. 638; [1968] 1 All E.R.
 826; 112 S.J. 86 . . . . 5-001, 5-007

Allan v Leo Lines Ltd [1957] 1 Lloyd's Rep. 127 . . . . 7-029, 7-030, **7-032**
Allan v Sundius (1862) 1 H. & C. 123; 31 L.J.Ex. 307; 6 L.T. 359; 10 W.R. 648 7-004
Allanfield Property Insurance Services Ltd v Aviva Insurance Ltd [2015] EWHC 3721
(Ch); [2016] Lloyd's Rep. I.R. 217. 6-060
Allard v Bowne (1863) 15 C.B.(N.S.) 468; 3 New Rep. 42 2-083
Allaway v Duncan (1867) 16 L.T. 264; 15 W.R. 711 9-038
Allen (Hugh V) & Co v Holmes (A); Same v Holmes [1969] 1 Lloyd's Rep. 348 CA 7-004
Allen & Co v Whiteman (1920) 89 L.J.Ch. 534; 123 L.T. 773; 64 S.J. 727 3-032
Allen v O'Hearn (F) & Co [1937] A.C. 213; 106 L.J.P.C. 14; 156 L.T. 149; 53 T.L.R. 176 . . 8-069,
9-011, 9-013
Alley v Hotson (1815) 4 Camp. 325 10-006
Allfiled UK Ltd v Eltis [2015] EWHC 1300 (Ch); [2016] F.S.R. 11 6-077
Alliance & Leicester Building Society v Edgestop [1993] 1 W.L.R. 1462; [1994] 2 All
E.R. 38; [1993] N.P.C. 79; [1993] E.G.C.S. 92. . . . . 8-048, 8-063
Allison v Clayhills (1907) 97 L.T. 709 . . . . 6-064, 6-067
Allkins v Jupe (1876–77) L.R. 2 C.P.D. 375; 46 L.J.K.B. 824 CPD 7-052
Alpha Lettings Ltd v Neptune Research & Development Inc [2003] EWCA Civ 704;
(2003) 147 S.J.L.B. 627 CA. 10-042
Alpha Trading Ltd v Dunnshaw-Patten [1981] Q.B. 290; [1981] 2 W.L.R. 169; [1981] 1
All E.R. 482; (1980) 124 S.J. 827; [1981] 1 Lloyd's Rep. 122 CA 7-018, 7-041, **7-044**, 10-042
Alpstream AG v PK Airfinance [2013] EWHC 2370 (Comm); [2014] 1 All E.R. (Comm)
441 . . . . 9-121, 9-135
Alsop v Sylvester (1823) 1 C. & P. 107 6-025
Altair, The. See Ministry of Trade of Iraq v Tsavliris Salvage (International) Ltd (The
Altair) 4-009
Aluminium Industrie Vaassen BV v Romalpa Aluminium Ltd [1976] 1 W.L.R. 676; [1976]
2 All E.R. 552; 120 S.J. 95; [1976] 1 Lloyd's Rep. 443 CA. 1-035
Amalgamated Industrials v Johnson & Firth Brown *Times*, April 15, 1981 6-085
Amalgamated Investment & Property Co Ltd (in liquidation) v Texas Commerce
International Bank Ltd [1982] Q.B. 84; [1981] 3 W.L.R. 565; [1981] 3 All E.R. 577;
(1981) 125 S.J. 623; [1981] Com.L.R. 236 CA 2-059, 6-029, 9-030
Amalgamated Metal Corp Plc v Wragge & Co (A Firm) [2011] EWHC 887 (Comm);
[2011] P.N.L.R. 24. . . . . 6-003, 6-004
Amazonia, The. See Furness Withy (Australia) Ltd v Metal Distributors (UK) Ltd (The
Amazonia) Amazonia, The 12-016
AMB Generali Holding AG v SEB Trygg Liv Holding AB [2005] EWCA Civ 1237;
[2006] 1 W.L.R. 2276; [2006] 1 All E.R. 437; [2006] 2 All E.R. (Comm) 38; [2006] 1
Lloyd's Rep. 318; [2006] 1 C.L.C. 849; (2005) 102(45) L.S.G. 28; (2005) 155 N.L.J.
1781 . . . . 2-050, 2-072, 2-078, 3-005, **3-029**, 8-028, 9-067, **9-076**, 10-031, 12-002, 12-023
AMB Imballaggi Plastici Srl v Pacflex Ltd [1999] 2 All E.R. (Comm) 249; [1999] C.L.C.
1391; [2000] E.C.C. 381; [1999] Eu. L.R. 930; (1999) 18 Tr. L.R. 153; (1999) 96(27)
L.S.G. 34 CA 1-036, 11-013, 11-015, 11-021, 11-026, 11-027
Amber Size and Chemical Co Ltd v Menzel [1913] 2 Ch. 239; 82 L.J.Ch. 573; 109 L.T.
520; 29 T.L.R. 590; 57 S.J. 627; 310 R.P.C. 433 6-077
Ambrose v Kerrison (1851) 10 C.B. 776; 20 L.J.C.P. 135; 17 L.T. (O.S.) 41 4-010
Americano's Ltd v State Insurance Ltd (1999) 6 N.Z. Business L.C. 102, 892 1-029
Amoutzas v Tattersalls [2010] EWHC 1696 (QB) 5-001
Anangel Atlas Compania Naviera SA v Ishikawajima-Harima Heavy Industries Co Ltd
[1990] 1 Lloyd's Rep. 167 QBD (Comm). 6-085, 8-222
Ancona v Marks (1862) 7 H. & N. 686; 31 L.J.Ex. 163; 5 L.T. 753; 8 Jur. (N.S.) 516; 10
W.R. 251 . . . . 2-061, 2-091
Anderson (WB) & Sons v Rhodes (Liverpool) Ltd [1967] 2 All E.R. 850, Assizes
(Liverpool). 8-186, 8-198
Anderson Antiques (UK) Ltd v Anderson Wharf (Hull) Ltd [2007] EWHC 2086 (Ch) 9-120
Anderson v Erlanger [1980] C.L.Y. 133 4-006
Anderson v Sutherland (1897) 13 T.L.R. 163; 41 S.J. 226; 2 Com.Cas. 65 . . . . 3-026, 3-036, 3-037
Andrew v Robinson (1812) 3 Camp. 199 6-100
Andrews v Ramsay & Co [1903] 2 K.B. 635; 72 L.J.K.B. 865; 89 L.T. 450; 19 T.L.R. 620;
47 S.J. 728; 52 W.R. 126 . . . . 7-050, **7-051**
Anglia Television Ltd v Reed [1972] 1 Q.B. 60; [1971] 3 W.L.R. 528; [1971] 3 All E.R.
690; 115 S.J. 723 CA 9-081

Anglo African Merchants Ltd v Bayley; Exmouth Clothing Co Ltd v Bayley [1970] 1 Q.B.
311; [1969] 2 W.L.R. 686; [1969] 2 All E.R. 421; [1969] 1 Lloyd's Rep. 268; 113 S.J.
281 QBD (Comm). 2-013, 3-035, 6-048, 6-057
Anglo Overseas Transport Co Ltd v Titan Industrial Corp (United Kingdom) Ltd [1959] 2
Lloyd's Rep. 152 QBD (Comm). 3-033, **7-062**, 9-016, 9-042
Anglo-African Shipping Co, New York Inc v Mortner (J) Ltd [1962] 1 Lloyd's Rep. 610
CA 1-022, 1-036, 7-101, 8-071, 9-008, 9-020, 9-021, 12-029
Anglo-American Asphalt Co Ltd v Crowley Russell & Co Ltd [1945] 2 All E.R. 524; 173
L.T. 228 6-098
Anglo-Maltese Hydraulic Dock Co Ltd, Re (1885) 54 L.J.Ch. 730; 52 L.T. 841; 1 T.L.R.
392; 433 W.R. 652 . . . . **7-089**
Anglo-Scottish Beet Sugar Corp Ltd v Spalding UDC [1937] 2 K.B. 607; 106 L.J.K.B.
885; 157 L.T. 450; 53 T.L.R. 822; [1937] 3 All E.R. 335; 81 S.J. 734 . . . . 8-166, 8-185
Angove's Pty Ltd v Bailey [2016] UKSC 47; [2016] 1 W.L.R. 3179 . . . 3-008, 6-041, 6-045, 7-046,
8-163, 10-002, 10-006, 10-007, 10-011
Anguilla v Estate and Trust Agencies Ltd [1938] A.C. 624 (PC) 6-003
Angus v McLachlan (1883) 23 Ch.D. 330; 52 L.J.Ch. 587; 48 L.T. 863; 31 W.R. 641 . . . . **7-094**
Annesley v Muggeridge (1816) 1 Madd. 593; 56 E.R. 218 9-026
Anscombe & Ringland v Watson [1991] 2 E.G.L.R. 28; [1991] 38 E.G. 230 7-030
Antonio Gramsci Shipping Corp v Stepanovs [2011] EWHC 333 (Comm); [2012] 1 All
E.R. (Comm) 293; [2011] 1 Lloyd's Rep. 647; [2012] B.C.C. 182; [2012] 1 B.C.L.C.
561; [2011] 1 C.L.C. 396; [2011] Bus. L.R. D117 . . . . 6-042, 8-116
Antrobus v Wickens (1865) 4 F. & F. 291 7-032
Applebee v Percy (1874) L.R. 9 C.P. 647; 43 L.J.C.P. 365; 30 L.T. 785; 38 J.P. 567; 22
W.R. 704 . . . . **8-217**
Applegate v Moss; sub nom. Archer v Moss [1971] 1 Q.B. 406; [1971] 2 W.L.R. 541;
[1971] 1 All E.R. 747; 3 B.L.R. 1; (1970) 114 S.J. 971 CA **2-026**
Appleton v Binks (1804) S.East 148; 1 Smith 361 . . . . 8-087, **9-049**
Apthorp v Nevill & Co (1907) 23 T.L.R. 575 . . . . 2-025, 8-217
Aqualon (UK) Ltd v Vallana Shipping Corp [1994] 1 Lloyd's Rep. 669 QBD (Comm) 9-024
Arab Bank Plc v Zurich Insurance Co [1999] 1 Lloyd's Rep. 262; [1998] C.L.C. 1351 8-212,
8-214
Arab Monetary Fund v Hashim (No.9) [1996] 1 Lloyd's Rep. 589 CA 8-218
Arbiter Group Plc v Gill Jennings & Every [2001] R.P.C. 67; [2000] Lloyd's Rep. P.N.
669; [2000] P.N.L.R. 680 CA 6-024
Arbitration between Deb Chemical Proprietaries Ltd and Dreumex Chemie BV, Re QBD
Nov 2, 1979. 6-015
Archer v Stone (1898) 78 L.T. 34 . . . . 8-080, 8-096
Archer's Case [1892] 1 Ch. 322; 61 L.J.Ch. 129; 65 L.T. 800; 8 T.L.R. 90; 36 S.J. 91; 40
W.R. 212 6-089
Architects of Wine Ltd v Barclays Bank Plc [2007] EWCA Civ 239; [2007] 2 All E.R.
(Comm) 285; [2007] 2 Lloyd's Rep. 471; (2007) 151 S.J.L.B. 431; [2007] Bus. L.R.
D37 3-011
Arctic Shipping Co Ltd v Mobilia AB; The Tatra [1990] 2 Lloyd's Rep. 511 QBD (Comm) . . 8-024
Argos (Cargo Ex), The. See Gaudet v Brown; Brown v Gaudet; Geupel v Cornforth Cargo
ex Argos; Hewsons, The 4-008
Argyll (Duchess) v Argyll (Duke) [1967] Ch. 302; [1965] 2 W.L.R. 790; [1965] 1 All E.R.
611 Ch D. 6-077
Argyll (Duchess) v Beuselinck [1972] 2 Lloyd's Rep. 172 Ch D 6-019, 6-021
Aries Tanker Corp v Total Transport Ltd; The Aries [1971] 1 W.L.R. 185; [1977] 1 All
E.R. 398; (1977) 121 S.J. 117; [1977] 1 Lloyd's Rep. 334 HL 6-100
Arklow Investments Ltd v Maclean [2000] 1 W.L.R. 594; (2000) 144 S.J.L.B. 81 PC (NZ) . . 6-034,
6-038, 6-077, 6-080
Armagas Ltd v Mundogas SA; The Ocean Frost [1986] A.C. 717; [1986] 2 W.L.R. 1063;
[1986] 2 All E.R. 385; (1986) 130 S.J. 430; [1988] 2 Lloyd's Rep. 109; (1986) 83
L.S.Gaz. 2002 HL. . . 1-026, 4-007, 8-010, 8-014, 8-017, 8-020, 8-021, 8-028, **8-067**, 8-098, 8-176,
8-180, 8-182, **8-196**, 8-221, 8-223, 8-224
Armitage v Nurse [1998] Ch. 241; [1997] 3 W.L.R. 1046; [1997] 2 All E.R. 705; (1997)
74 P. & C.R. D13 CA. 6-056, 6-058
Armour v Duff & Co 1912 S.C. 120 9-038
Armstrong Brands Ltd, Re [2015] EWHC 3303 (Ch) 8-040

Armstrong DLW GmbH v Winnington Networks Ltd [2012] EWHC 10 (Ch); [2013] Ch.
  156; [2012] 3 W.L.R. 835; [2012] 3 All E.R. 425; [2012] Bus. L.R. 1199; (2012) 109(5)
  L.S.G. 20; (2012) 162 N.L.J. 181; [2012] Env. L.R. D4 9-136
Armstrong v Jackson [1917] 2 K.B. 822; 86 L.J.K.B. 1375; 117 L.T. 479; 33 T.L.R. 444;
  61 S.J. 631 . . . . 6-068, 6-071
Armstrong v Stokes (1872) L.R. 7 Q.B. 598; 41 L.J.Q.B. 253; 26 L.T. 872; 21 W.R. 52 1-021,
                        1-022, 1-046, 8-069, 8-071, 8-073, 8-104, 8-105, 8-106, 9-016, 9-020, 12-029
Armstrong v Strain [1952] 1 K.B. 232; [1952] 1 T.L.R. 82; [1952] 1 All E.R. 139 CA 8-185,
                                                                                          8-186, **8-196**
Arnhem Technology v Dudley Joiner January 31, 2001 Ch D 9-109
Arnold v Cheque Bank (1876) 1 C.P.D. 578; 45 L.J.Q.B. 562; 34 L.T. 729; 40 J.P. 711; 24
  W.R. 759 9-130
Arnot v Briscoe (1748) 1 Ves. 95 . . . . **9-125**
Arthur JS Hall & Co v Simons [2002] 1 A.C. 615 . . . . 6-018, 6-028
Ashbury Railway Carriage and Iron Co v Riche; sub nom. Riche v Ashbury Railway
  Carriage & Iron Co Ltd (1875) L.R. 7 H.L. 653; 44 L.J.Ex. 185; 33 L.T. 450; 24 W.R.
  794. 8-032
Ashford Shire Council v Dependable Motors Pty Ltd [1961] A.C. 336; [1960] 3 W.L.R.
  999; [1961] 1 All E.R. 96; 104 S.J. 1055 PC 2-030, 2-031, **3-029**
Ashmore Benson Pease & Co Ltd v AV Dawson Ltd [1973] 1 W.L.R. 828; [1973] 2 All
  E.R. 856; [1973] 2 Lloyd's Rep. 21; [1973] R.T.R. 473; (1973) 117 S.J. 203 CA. 2-025
Ashmore v Corp of Lloyd's (No.2) [1992] 2 Lloyd's Rep. 620 QBD (Comm) 7-001
Ashton v Spiers & Pond (1893) 9 T.L.R. 606 . . . . **3-029**
Ashton, Re; Ex p. McGowan (1891) 64 L.T. 28; 7 T.L.R. 207; 8 Morr. 72; 39 W.R. 320 . . . . . **8-217**
Aspen Underwriting Ltd v Kairos Shipping Ltd [2017] EWHC 1904 (Comm) 8-079
Association of British Travel Agents Ltd v British Airways Plc [2000] 2 All E.R. (Comm)
  204; [2000] 2 Lloyd's Rep. 209 CA 6-009
Aste v Montague (1858) 1 F. & F. 264 . . . . 8-211, 10-030, 10-033
Astex Therapeutics Ltd v Astrazeneca AB [2017] EWHC 1442 (Ch) 8-166
Astilleros Canarios SA v Cape Hatteras Shipping Co Inc; The Cape Hatteras [1982] 1
  Lloyd's Rep. 518 QBD (Comm). **9-038**
Astley Industrial Trust Ltd v Miller [1968] 2 All E.R. 36, Assizes (Liverpool) . 8-133, 8-147, 8-153
Aston v Kelsey [1913] 3 K.B. 314; 82 L.J.K.B. 817; 108 L.T. 750; 29 T.L.R. 530; 18
  Com.Cas. 257 7-070
Astra Trust v Adams and Williams [1969] 1 Lloyd's Rep. 81 QBD (Comm) 7-017
Asty Maritime Co v Rocco Guiseppe & Figli; The Astynax [1985] 2 Lloyd's Rep. 109 CA . . 8-071,
                                                                                                    8-078
Astynax, The. See Asty Maritime Co v Rocco Guiseppe & Figli; Astynax, The 8-071, 8-078
Atkins v Rowe (1728) Mos. 39 6-082
Atkinson v Cotesworth (1825) 3 B. & C. 647; 3 L.J.(O.S.) K.B. 104; 1 C. & P. 516; 5
  Dow. & Ry. K.B. 552. . . . . 9-003, 9-010
Atkyns and Batten v Amber (1796) 2 Esp. 493 . . . . **9-035**
Atlantic Emperor, The. See Marc Rich & Co AG v Societa Italiana Impianti pA (The
  Atlantic Emperor) (No.1) 12-016
Atlantic Mutual Insurance Co v Huth (1880) 16 Ch.D. 474; 44 L.T. 67; 29 W.R. 387; 4
  Asp.M.L.C. 369 CA. 4-004, 4-005
Atlantic Underwriting Agencies Ltd and David Gale (Underwriting) Ltd v Compania di
  Assicurazione di Milano SpA [1979] Lloyd's Rep. 240 QBD (Comm) 7-047, 10-004, 10-045,
                                                                                                    11-057
Atlas Maritime Co SA v Avalon Maritime Ltd; The Coral Rose (No.1) [1991] 4 All E.R.
  769; [1991] 1 Lloyd's Rep. 563 CA 1-012, 1-030, 1-037, 8-071
Atlas Wright (Europe) Ltd v Wright [1999] B.C.C. 163; [1999] 2 B.C.L.C. 301; (1999)
  96(8) L.S.G. 29 1-028
Attenborough v St. Katharine Docks Co (1878) 3 C.P.D. 450; 47 L.J.Q.B. 763; 38 L.T.
  404; 26 W.R. 583 7-103
Atterbury v Wallis (1856) 25 L.J.Ch. 792; 8 De G.M. & G. 454; 27 L.T.(O.S.) 301; 2 Jur.
  (N.S.) 1177; 4 W.R. 734. . . . . 8-210, 8-214, **8-217**
Attorney General (Ceylon) v Silva (AL) [1953] A.C. 461; [1953] 2 W.L.R. 1185; 97 S.J.
  384; [1953] 1 Lloyd's Rep. 563 PC (Cey) 3-005, 8-020, 8-042, 8-058
Attorney General (Hong Kong) v Reid [1994] 1 A.C. 324; [1993] 3 W.L.R. 1143; [1994] 1
  All E.R. 1; (1993) 137 S.J.(L.B.) 251; [1993] NPC 144; (1993) 143 N.L.J. 1569 (NZ). 5-012,
                                                                                    6-042, 6-080, 6-085, 6-087

Attorney General ex rel Cooperative Retail Services Ltd v Taff-Ely BC; Cooperative
   Retail Services Ltd v Taff-Ely BC (1981) 42 P. & C.R. 1 HL 8-042
Attorney General of Belize v Belize Telecom Ltd [2009] UKPC 10; [2009] 1 W.L.R.
   1988; [2009] Bus. L.R. 1316; [2009] 2 All E.R. 1127; [2009] 2 All E.R. (Comm) 1;
   [2009] B.C.C. 433; [2009] 2 B.C.L.C. 148 PC (Belize) 6-001, 7-001
Attorney General of Zambia v Meer Care & Desai (a firm) [2007] EWHC 952 (Ch) 9-135
Attorney General v Alford (1854) 2 Sim. & G. 488; 23 L.T. (O.S.) 226; 18 Jur. 592; 2
   W.R. 580; 65 E.R. 494; (1855) 4 De G.M. & G. 843 LC 6-103
Attorney General v Blake [2001] 1 A.C. 268; [2000] 3 W.L.R. 625; [2000] 4 All E.R. 385;
   [2000] 2 All E.R. (Comm) 487; [2001] I.R.L.R. 36; [2000] E.M.L.R. 949; (2000)
   23(12) I.P.D. 23098; (2000) 97(32) L.S.G. 37; (2000) 150 N.L.J. 1230; (2000) 144
   S.J.L.B. 242 HL 6-034, 6-039
Attorney General v Cape (Jonathan); Attorney General v Times Newspapers [1976] Q.B.
   752; [1975] 3 W.L.R. 606; [1975] 3 All E.R. 484; 119 S.J. 696 QBD 6-077
Attorney General v Corporation of London (1850) 2 Mac. & G. 24; 19 L.J.Ch. 314; 14
   L.T. (O.S.) 501; 14 Jur. 205. 6-111
Attorney General v Drapers' Company (1869) L.R. 9 Eq. 69; 21 L.T. 651 7-005
Attorney General v Earl of Chesterfield (1854) 18 Beav. 596; 23 L.T. (O.S.) 153; 18 Jur.
   686; 2 W.R. 499; 52 E.R. 234 5-016
Attorney General v Goddard (1929) 98 L.J.K.B. 743; 45 T.L.R. 609; 73 S.J. 514 . . . . . 6-083, 6-087
Attorney General v Guardian Newspapers Ltd (No.2); Attorney General v Observer Ltd
   (No.2); Attorney General v Times Newspapers Ltd (No.2) [1990] 1 A.C. 109; [1988] 3
   W.L.R. 776; [1988] 3 All E.R. 545; [1989] 2 F.S.R. 181; (1988) 85(42) L.S.G. 45;
   (1988) 138 N.L.J. Rep. 296; (1988) 132 S.J. 1496. 6-077
Attorney General v Leicester Corp (1844) 7 Beav. 176 9-140
Attorney General v Nissan; Nissan v Attorney General [1970] A.C. 179; [1969] 2 W.L.R.
   926; [1969] 1 All E.R. 629; 113 S.J. 207 HL 9-124
Attorney General v Trueman (1843) 11 Mow. 694; 13 L.J.Ex. 70; 8 J.P. 443; 152 E.R. 983 . . . 7-087
Attorney General's Reference (No.1 of 1985), Re [1986] Q.B. 491; [1986] 2 W.L.R. 733;
   (1986) 150 J.P. 242; [1986] 2 All E.R. 219; (1986) 130 S.J. 299; (1986) 83 Cr.App.R.
   70; [1986] Crim.L.R. 476; (1986) 83 L.S.Gaz. 1226; (1986) 150 J.P.N. 287 CA 8-077
Attorney General's Reference (No.2 of 1999), Re [2000] Q.B. 796; [2000] 3 W.L.R. 195;
   [2000] 3 All E.R. 182; [2001] B.C.C. 210; [2000] 2 B.C.L.C. 257; [2000] 2 Cr. App. R.
   207; [2000] I.R.L.R. 417; [2000] Crim. L.R. 475; (2000) 97(9) L.S.G. 39 CA 1-029
Attwood (G) Holdings Ltd v Woodward [2009] EWHC 1083 (Ch) 6-054
Attwood v Munnings (1827) 7 B. & C. 278; 1 Man. & Ry. K.B. 66; 6 L.J. (O.S.) K.B. 9 3-013
Aubanel and Alabaster Ltd v Aubanel (1949) 66 R.P.C. 343 . . . . 6-034, 6-061
Audley (Lord) v Pollard (1597) Cro. Eliz. 561 2-089
Austin v Chambers (1838) 6 C. & F. 1 . . . . 6-064, 6-082
Australasian Steam Navigation Co v Morse (1872) L.R. 4 P.C. 222; 8 Moo.P.C.C. (N.S.)
   482; 27 L.T. 357; 20 W.R. 728; 1 Asp.M.L.C. 407 . . . . 4-004, 4-005
Australia & New Zealand Bank Ltd v Colonial & Eagle Wharves Ltd [1960] 2 Lloyd's
   Rep. 241 QBD (Comm Ct) 8-213
Australia and New Zealand Bank Ltd v Ateliers de Constructions Electriques de Charleroi
   [1967] 1 A.C. 86; [1966] 2 W.L.R. 1216; 110 S.J. 467; [1966] 2 Lloyd's Rep. 463 PC
   (Aus) 3-015
Australia, The (1859) 13 Moo.P.C. 132; Swab. 480; 7 W.R. 718 . . . . 2-078, 4-004, 4-005
Australian Bank of Commerce v Perel [1926] A.C. 737; 95 L.J.P.C. 185; 135 L.T. 586 8-024
Auty v Hutchinson (1848) 6 C.B. 266; 17 L.J.C.P. 304; 12 Jur. 962 . . . . **9-034**
Avery (WT) Ltd v Charlesworth (1914) 31 T.L.R. 52 9-038
Avinue Ltd v Sunrule Ltd [2003] EWCA Civ 1942; [2004] 1 W.L.R. 634; [2004] C.P. Rep.
   19; (2004) 101(2) L.S.G. 30 2-024
Aviva Life & Pensions UK Ltd v Strand Street Properties Ltd [2010] EWCA Civ 444 2-028,
   2-077, 3-042
Avonwick Holdings Ltd v Shlosberg [2016] EWCA Civ 1138 6-050
Avrahami v Biran [2013] EWHC 1776 (Ch) 7-050
Avrora Fine Arts Investment Ltd v Christie, Manson & Woods Ltd [2012] EWHC 2198
   (Ch); [2012] P.N.L.R. 35. 9-117
AXA Corporate Solutions SA v National Westminster Bank Plc [2010] EWHC 1915
   (Comm); [2010] 2 C.L.C. 149; [2011] Lloyd's Rep. I.R. 438 . . . . **8-207**
AXA Sun Life Services Plc v Campbell Martin Ltd [2011] EWCA Civ 133; [2012] Bus.
   L.R. 203; [2011] 2 Lloyd's Rep. 1; [2011] 1 C.L.C. 312; 138 Con. L.R. 104 7-001
Axon v Ministry of Defence [2016] EWHC 787 (QB); [2016] E.M.L.R. 20 . . . . 8-178, 8-190

Azov Shipping Co v Baltic Shipping Co (No.3) [1999] 2 All E.R. (Comm) 453; [1999] 2
    Lloyd's Rep. 159; [1999] C.L.C. 1425 QBD (Comm) 12-016, 12-020
Babury Ltd v London Industrial Plc (1989) 139 N.L.J. 1596 QBD 9-063, 9-066, 9-076
Bacmeister v Fenton Levy & Co (1883) C. & E. 121 . . . . 9-016, 9-042
Bacon v Dubarry (1697) 1 Salk. 70; Carth. 412; 12 Mod.Rep. 129; Comb. 439; Holt K.B.
    78; 1 Ld. Raym. 246; 3 Ld. Raym. 241; Skin 679; 91 E.R. 65. 9-049
Baden Delvaux v Sociètè Gènèrale pour Favoriser le Developpement du Commerce et de
    l'Industrie en France SA [1985] B.C.L.C. 258 . . . . 8-048, 9-135, 9-1369, 9-141, **9-142**
Badgerhill Properties Ltd v Cottrell [1991] B.C.L.C. 805; [1991] B.C.C. 463; 54 B.L.R.
    23 CA 9-034, 9-037, **9-038**, 9-055
Bagnall v Carlton (1877) 6 Ch. D. 371 CA 6-035
Bahia and San Francisco Railway Co Ltd, Re (1868) L.R. 3 Q.B. 584; 9 B. & S.844; 37
    L.J.Q.B. 176; 18 L.T. 467; 16 W.R. 862. 8-173
Bailey & Whites Ltd v House (1915) 31 T.L.R. 583 8-044
Bailey Hay & Co, Re [1971] 1 W.L.R. 1357; [1971] 3 All E.R. 693; (1971) 115 S.J. 639 1-028
Bailey v de Kerangat December 7, 1993 CA **9-049**
Bailey v Rawlins (1829) 7 L.J.(O.S.) K.B. 208 3-038
Bain Clarkson Ltd v Owners of Sea Friends; The Friends [1991] 2 Lloyd's Rep. 322 CA 7-084
Bain v Fothergill (1874) L.R. 7 H.L. 158; 43 L.J.Ex. 243; 31 L.T. 387; 39 J.P. 228; 23
    W.R. 261 9-083
Bainbridge v Postmaster General [1906] 1 K.B. 178; 75 L.J.K.B. 366; 94 L.T. 120; 22
    T.L.R. 70; 54 W.R. 221 CA. 8-042
Bairstow Eves London Central Ltd v Smith [2004] EWHC 263; [2004] 2 E.G.L.R. 25;
    [2004] 29 E.G. 118 QBD 7-008
Bairstow v Queens Moat Houses Plc; Marcus v Queens Moat Houses Plc; Hersey v
    Queens Moat Houses Plc; Porter v Queens Moat Houses Plc [2001] EWCA Civ 712;
    [2002] B.C.C. 91; [2001] 2 B.C.L.C. 531 CA 6-043
Baker v Courage & Co [1910] 1 K.B. 56; 79 L.J.K.B. 313; 101 L.T. 854 6-100
Baker v Gibbons [1972] 1 W.L.R. 693; [1972] 2 All E.R. 759; 116 S.J. 313 . . . . 6-077, 6-078
Baker v Nottingham & Nottinghamshire Banking Co Ltd (1891) 60 L.J.Q.B. 542; 7 T.L.R.
    235. 7-089
Baldry v Bates (1885) 52 L.T. 620; 1 T.L.R. 558 . . . . 3-028, 3-032, 8-014
Baldwin v BK Books Ltd [2010] EWCA Civ 1440 9-121
Baldwin v Casella (1872) L.R. 7 Ex. 325; 41 L.J.Ex. 167; 26 L.T. 707; 21 W.R. 16 . . . 8-213, **8-217**
Balfe v West (1853) 13 C.B. 466; 22 L.J.C.P. 175; 21 L.T.(O.S.) 90; 1 W.R. 335; 1 C.L.R.
    225. 6-029
Ball v Dunsterville (1791) 4 T.R. 313 2-041
Balsamo v Medici [1984] 1 W.L.R. 951; [1984] 2 All E.R. 304; (1984) 81 L.S.G. 2700;
    (1984) 128 S.J. 500 Ch D. 5-004, 5-011, **5-016**
Balston Ltd v Headline Filters Ltd (No.2) [1990] F.S.R. 385 . . . . 6-034, 6-054, 6-081
Bamford v Bamford [1970] Ch. 212; [1969] 2 W.L.R. 1107; [1969] 1 All E.R. 969; 113
    S.J. 123 CA 2-061, 8-221
Bamford v Shuttleworth (1840) 11 A. & E. 926; 113 E.R. 666 9-109
Banbury v Bank of Montreal [1918] A.C. 626; 87 L.J.K.B. 1158; 119 L.T. 446; 62 S.J.
    665; 34 T.L.R. 518 HL 8-198
Bank Melli Iran v Barclays Bank (Dominion Colonial & Overseas) [1951] 2 Lloyd's Rep.
    367; [1951] 2 T.L.R. 1057 KBD **2-034**, 2-078
Bank of America v Arnell [1999] Lloyd's Rep. Bank. 399 QBD (Comm Ct) 8-162, 9-135
Bank of Baroda v Vysya Bank Ltd [1994] 2 Lloyd's Rep. 87; [1994] 3 Bank. L.R. 216
    QBD (Comm Ct). 12-003
Bank of Bengal v Fagan (1849) 5 Moo.Ind.App. 27; 7 Moo. P.C.C. 61 . . . . 3-011, **3-015**
Bank of Bengal v James William Macleod (1849) 5 Moo. Ind. App. 1; 18 E.R. 795 PC
    (India) 3-015
Bank of Credit and Commerce International (Overseas) Ltd (In Liquidation) v Price
    Waterhouse (No.2) [1998] Lloyd's Rep. Bank. 85; [1998] B.C.C. 617; [1998] E.C.C.
    410; [1998] P.N.L.R. 564; (1998) 95(15) L.S.G. 32; (1998) 142 S.J.L.B. 86 CA 9-117
Bank of Credit and Commerce International (Overseas) Ltd v Chief Labode Onadimaki
    Akindele [2001] Ch. 437; [2000] 3 W.L.R. 1423; [2000] 4 All E.R. 221; [2000] Lloyd's
    Rep. Bank. 292; [2000] B.C.C. 968; (2000) 1 W.T.L.R. 1049; (2000) 97(26) L.S.G. 36;
    (2000) 150 N.L.J. 950 CA 9-136
Bank of Credit and Commerce International SA (In Liquidation) (No.15), Re Morris v
    Bank of India [2005] EWCA Civ 693; [2005] B.C.C. 739; [2005] 2 B.C.L.C. 328;
    [2005] B.P.I.R. 1067 . . . . 8-214, 8-215

Bank of Credit and Commerce International SA v Aboody [1990] 1 Q.B. 923; [1989] 2
    W.L.R. 759; [1992] 4 All E.R. 955; [1990] 1 F.L.R. 354; [1989] C.C.L.R. 63; [1989]
    Fam. Law 435; (1988) 132 S.J. 1754 . . . . 8-098, 8-211, 8-213, 8-214
Bank of Ireland v Evans' Trustees (1855) 5 H.L.C. 389; 25 L.T. (O.S.) 272; 3 W.R. 573; 3
    C.L.R. 1066 . . . . 2-059, 8-130
Bank of Ireland v Jaffery [2012] EWHC 1377 (Ch) 6-085, 7-050
Bank of New South Wales v Goulburn Valley Butter Co Pty [1902] A.C. 543; 71 L.J.P.C.
    112; 87 L.T. 88; 18 T.L.R. 735; 51 W.R. 367 PC (Aus) **3-029**, 9-142
Bank of New South Wales v Owston (1879) 4 App.Cas. 270; 48 L.J.P.C. 25; 40 L.T. 500;
    43 J.P. 476; 14 Cox.C.C. 267. . . . . **3-029**, 8-192
Bank of Nova Scotia v Hellenic Mutual War Risk Association (Bermuda) Ltd; The Good
    Luck [1992] 1 A.C. 233; [1991] 2 W.L.R. 1279; [1991] 3 All E.R. 1; [1991] 2 Lloyd's
    Rep. 191; (1991) 141 N.L.J. 779 HL 2-107
Bank of Scotland v Alfred Truman (A Firm) [2005] EWHC 583 (QB) 9-026
Bank of Scotland v Dominion Bank (Toronto) [1891] A.C. 592 HL **3-023**
Bank of Scotland v Qutb (Costs) [2012] EWCA Civ 1661; [2013] C.P. Rep. 14 . . . . . 9-067, 10-016
Bank of Scotland v Watson (1813) 1 Dow. 40 3-032
Bank voor Handel en Scheepvaart NV v Slatford (No.2); Bank voor Handel en
    Scheepvaart NV v Administrator of Hungarian Property [1954] A.C. 584; [1954] 2
    W.L.R. 867; [1954] 1 All E.R. 969; 47 R. & I.T. 373; 35 T.C. 311; (1954) 33 A.T.C.
    102; [1954] T.R. 115; 98 S.J. 301 HL. 8-190
Bannatyne & D&C McIver [1906] 1 K.B. 103; 75 L.J.K.B. 120; 94 L.T. 150; 54 W.R. 293
    CA 8-203, 8-204
Banner Homes Holdings Ltd (formerly Banner Homes Group Plc) v Luff Developments
    Ltd (No.2) [2000] Ch. 372; [2000] 2 W.L.R. 772. 6-083
Banque Belge pour l'Etranger v Hambrouck [1921] 1 K.B. 321; 90 L.J.K.B. 322; 37
    T.L.R. 76; 65 S.J. 74; 26 Com.Cas. 72 CA 8-141, 8-161, 8-167
Banque des Marchands de Moscou (Koupetschesky) (No.1), Re; Royal Exchange
    Assurance v Liquidator; Wilenkin v Liquidator (No.1) [1952] 1 All E.R. 1269; [1952] 1
    T.L.R. 739; [1952] W.N. 151 Ch D 4-005, 9-085
Banque Financiere de la Cite SA (formerly Banque Keyser Ullmann SA) v Westgate
    Insurance Co (formerly Hodge General & Mercantile Co Ltd) [1991] 2 A.C. 249;
    [1990] 3 W.L.R. 364; [1990] 2 All E.R. 947; [1990] 2 Lloyd's Rep. 377; (1990) 87(35)
    L.S.G. 36; (1990) 140 N.L.J. 1074; (1990) 134 S.J. 1265 HL 8-212
Banque Jacques Cartier v Banque d' Epargne de Montreal (1887) 13 App.Cas. 111; 57
    L.J.P.C. 42. 2-048
Bao Xiang International Garment Centre v British Airways Plc [2015] EWHC 3071 (Ch);
    [2016] C.P. Rep. 8. 12-025
Barber v Taylor (1839) 5 M. & W. 527; 9 L.J.Ex. 21 . . . . 6-003, 6-012, **6-016**
Barclay & Co Ltd v Malcolm & Co (1925) 133 L.T. 512; 41 T.L.R. 518; 69 S.J. 675 9-100
Barclay Pharmaceuticals Ltd v Waypharm LP [2012] EWHC 306 (Comm); (2012)
    109(26) L.S.G. 19. . . . . 2-025, 8-189, 9-119
Barclay v Harris & Cross (1915) 85 L.J.K.B. 115; 112 L.T. 1134; 31 T.L.R. 213 6-108
Barclays Bank Ltd v O'Brien [1994] 1 A.C. 180; [1993] 3 W.L.R. 786; [1993] 4 All E.R.
    417; (1993) 137 S.J. (LB) 240; [1993] E.G.C.S.169; [1993] N.P.C. 135; (1993) 143
    N.L.J. 1511 HL 1-027, 2-014
Barclays Bank Ltd v Quincecare Ltd [1992] 4 All E.R. 363 9-142
Barclays Bank Ltd v Quistclose Investments Ltd. See Quistclose Investments v Rolls
    Razor Ltd 6-040, 6-041
Barclays Bank Ltd v Thomson [1997] 4 All E.R. 816; [1996] 5 Bank. L.R. 402; [1997] 1
    F.L.R. 156; [1997] 1 F.C.R. 541; (1998) 75 P. & C.R. 5; [1997] Fam. Law 245; (1996)
    146 N.L.J. 1778; [1996] N.P.C. 155; (1997) 73 P. & C.R. D21 8-216
Barclays Bank Ltd v TOSG Trust Fund Ltd [1984] A.C. 626; [1984] 2 W.L.R. 650; [1984]
    1 All E.R. 1060; (1984) 81 L.S.G. 1360; (1984) 134 N.L.J. 656; (1984) 128 S.J. 261 HL. . . . 8-037,
    8-154
Barclays Bank Ltd v Williams (1971) 115 S.J. 674 8-117
Barclays Bank Ltd v WJ Simms Son & Cooke (Southern) Ltd [1980] Q.B. 677 6-003
Barclays Bank Plc v Kalamohan [2010] EWHC 1383 (Ch) 3-043
Barclays Bank v Roberts [1954] 1 W.L.R. 1212; [1954] 3 All E.R. 107; 98 S.J. 589 CA 2-070,
    8-196
Bardiger v Halberg Spedition Aps October 26, 1990 QBD (Comm) 9-024
Baring v Corrie (1818) 2 B. & A. 137 . . . . . 1-039, 1-046, 7-082, 8-054, 8-073, 8-109, 8-110, 9-016

Baring v Furlong [1891] 2 Ch. 172; 60 L.J.Ch. 368; 64 L.T. 411; 7 T.L.R. 406; 39 W.R.
621 . . . . 9-129, 9-131
Baring v Highley (1863) 16 C.B.(N.S.) 27; 2 New Rep. 489; 32 L.J.C.P. 270; 9 L.T. 228;
10 Jur. (N.S.) 391; 11 W.R. 968; 1 Mar.L.C. 383 3-029
Baring v Stanton (1876) 3 Ch.D. 502; 35 L.T. 652; 25 W.R. 237; 3 Asp.M.L.C. 294   . . 6-089, 6-097,
7-004
Barker Sportcraft Ltd's Agreements, Re (1947) 177 L.T. 420   10-042
Barker v Greenwood (1837) 2 Y. & C. Ex. 414; 160 E.R. 458   . . . . **3-026**, 8-108
Barker v Harrison (1846) 2 Coll. 546; 63 E.R. 854   6-068
Barker v Levinson [1951] 1 K.B. 342; 66 T.L.R. (Pt. 2) 717; 114 J.P. 545; [1950] 2 All
E.R. 825; 94 S.J. 688; 49 L.G.R. 110 KBD 8-064
Barlow Clowes International Ltd (In Liquidation) v Eurotrust International Ltd [2005]
UKPC 37; [2006] 1 W.L.R. 1476; [2006] 1 All E.R. 333; [2006] 1 All E.R. (Comm)
478; [2006] 1 Lloyd's Rep. 225; [2005] W.T.L.R. 1453; (2005–06) 8 I.T.E.L.R. 347;
(2005) 102(44) L.S.G. 32; [2006] 1 P. & C.R. DG16 9-135
Barlow Clowes International Ltd (In Liquidation) v Vaughan; Vaughan v Barlow Clowes
International Ltd [1992] 4 All E.R. 22; [1992] B.C.L.C. 910 CA 8-167
Barnard v Hunter (1856) 2 Jur. (N.S.) 1213   . . . . 6-063, 6-069
Barnett Fashion Agency Ltd v Nigel Hall Menswear Ltd [2011] EWHC 978 (QB)   11-057
Barnett Hoares & Co v South London Tramways Co (1887) 18 Q.B.D. 815 CA 8-046, **8-067**
Barnett v Brown (1890) 6 T.L.R. 463   . . . . 7-030, 7-032
Barnett v Creggy [2014] EWHC 3080 (Ch); [2015] P.N.L.R. 13; [2016] W.T.L.R. 17   6-092
Barnett v Crystal Palace Co (1861) 4 L.T. 403   8-189
Barnett v Isaacson (1888) 4 T.L.R. 645   . . . . 7-004, 7-024, **7-032**
Barns v Guardians of St. Mary, Islington (1911) 76 J.P. 11   2-056
Baron Investments (Holdings) Ltd, Re [2000] 1 B.C.L.C. 272 Ch D   6-052
Barratt v Gough-Thomas [1951] Ch. 242; [1950] 2 All E.R. 1048; 94 S.J. 760 CA   7-082
Barrett v Bem [2012] EWCA Civ 52; [2012] Ch. 573; [2012] 3 W.L.R. 330; [2012] 2 All
E.R. 920; [2012] W.T.L.R. 567; (2012) 156(5) S.J.L.B. 31 . . . . 1-047, 2-014, 2-022, 6-037
Barrett v Deere (1828) Moo. & M. 200   . . . . **8-043**
Barrett v Gilmour & Co (1901) 17 T.L.R. 292; 6 Com.Cas. 72   7-042
Barrington v Lee [1972] 1 Q.B. 326; [1971] 3 W.L.R. 962; [1971] 3 All E.R. 1231; 115
S.J. 833 CA 8-013, 8-117, **8-124**, 9-026, 9-109
Barron v Fitzgerald (1840) 6 Bing.N.C. 201   . . . . **7-070**
Barrow & Bros v Dyster, Nalder & Co (1884) 13 Q.B.D. 635; 51 L.T. 573; 33 W.R. 199   . . . . **9-042**
Barry v Davies (t/a Heathcote Ball & Co); sub nom. Heathcote Ball & Co (Commercial
Auctions) Ltd v Barry; Barry v Heathcote Ball & Co (Commercial Auctions) Ltd [2000]
1 W.L.R. 1962; [2001] 1 All E.R. 944; [2000] 3 E.G.L.R. 7; [2000] 47 E.G. 178; (2000)
97(39) L.S.G. 41; (2000) 150 N.L.J. 1377; (2000) 144 S.J.L.B. 249 CA 9-023, 9-034
Barry v Longmore (1840) 12 A. & E. 639; Arn. & H. 14; 4 Per. & Dav 344   . . . . **7-089**
Bart v British West Indian Airways Ltd [1967] 1 Lloyd's Rep. 239 CA (Guy) 1-033, 8-079
Bartlett v Barclays Bank Trust Co Ltd (No.2) [1980] Ch. 515; [1980] 2 W.L.R. 430;
[1980] 2 All E.R. 92; (1980) 124 S.J. 221 Ch D 6-043
Bartlett v Cole [1963] E.G.D. 452; 188 E.G. 397 CA 7-030, **7-032**
Bartlett v Pickersgill (1785) 4 East 577n; 1 Cox. 15; 1 Eden 515; 4 East 576n 2-037, 6-082
Barton Thompson & Co v Vigers Bros (1906) 19 Com.Cas. 175   9-035
Bartram & Sons v Lloyd (1904) 90 L.T. 357; 20 T.L.R. 281 CA 6-048, 6-086, 8-223
Barwell v Parker (1751) 2 Ves. 364   6-109
Barwick v English Joint Stock Bank (1867) L.R. 2 Ex. 259; 36 L.J.Ex. 147; 16 L.T. 461;
15 W.R. 877 . . . . 8-176, 8-185, 8-189
Baschet v London Illustrated Standard Co [1900] 1 Ch. 73; 69 L.J.Ch. 35; 44 S.J. 42; 81
L.T. 509; 48 W.R. 56 . . . . **9-125**
Base Metal Trading Ltd v Shamurin [2004] EWCA Civ 1316; [2005] 1 W.L.R. 1157;
[2005] 1 All E.R. (Comm) 17; [2005] B.C.C. 325; [2005] 2 B.C.L.C. 171; [2004] 2
C.L.C. 916; (2004) 148 S.J.L.B. 1281 . . . . 1-028, 12-008
Basma (Abdul Karim) v Weekes [1950] A.C. 441; [1950] 2 All E.R. 146; 66 T.L.R. (Pt. 1)
1047 PC (West Africa) 8-003, 9-006
Bassano v Toft [2014] EWHC 377 (QB); [2014] E.C.C. 14; [2014] C.T.L.C. 117; [2014]
Bus. L.R. D9 8-126
Bateman v Phillips (1812) 15 East 272   8-003
Bates v Pilling (1826) 6 B. & C. 38; 9 Dow. & Ry. K.B. 44; 5 L.J.(O.S.) K.B. 40   8-196
Bath v Standard Land Co [1911] 1 Ch. 618; 80 L.J.Ch. 426; 55 S.J. 482; 104 L.T. 867; 27
T.L.R. 393; 18 Mans. 258 . . . . 5-012, **5-016**, 6-070, 6-097, 6-100, 7-006, 9-138

Battams v Tompkins (1892) 8 T.L.R. 707 7-032
Battersby v Smyth (1818) 3 Madd. 110 .... 6-098, 6-100
Baturina v Chistyakov [2017] EWHC 1049 (Comm) 8-211
Bauerman v Radenius (1792) 7 T.R. 663 9-010
Bauman v Hulton Press Ltd [1952] 2 All E.R. 1121; [1952] W.N. 556 QBD 10-042, 10-045
Baumwoll Manufactur Von Carl Scheibler v Furness; Baumvoll Manufactur Von Scheibler
   v Gilchrist & Co; Baumvoll Manufactur Von Scheibler v Gilchrest & Co [1893] A.C. 8;
   62 L.J.Q.B. 201; 68 L.T. 1; 9 T.L.R. 71; 7 Asp.M.L.C. 263; 1 R. 59 HL................. 8-045
Bavins & Sims v London & South Western Bank Ltd [1900] 1 Q.B. 270; 69 L.J.K.B. 164;
   81 L.T. 655; 16 T.L.R. 61; 5 Com.Cas. 1; 48 W.R. 210 CA.................... 9-107
Bawden v London, Edinburgh and Glasgow Assurance Co [1892] 2 Q.B. 534; 61 L.J.Q.B.
   792; 8 T.L.R. 566; 57 J.P. 116; 36 S.J. 502 CA **8-217**
Baxendale v Bennett (1878) 3 Q.B.D. 525; 47 L.J.Q.B. 624; 40 L.T. 23; 26 W.R. 899; 42
   J.P. 677 8-045
Bayley v Chadwick (1878) 39 L.T. 429; 4 Asp.M.L.C. 59 7-032
Bayley v Wilkins (1849) 7 C.B. 886; 18 L.J.C.P. 273; 13 L.T.(O.S.) 234; 13 Jur. 883 .. 3-021, **3-023**
Baylis v Bishop & London [1913] 1 Ch. 127; 82 L.J.Ch. 61; 57 S.J. 96; 107 L.T. 750; 29
   T.L.R. 59 CA.. 9-104
Baylis v Dineley (1815) 3 M. & S.477 2-065
Bayntun v Cattle (1833) 1 Moo. & R. 265 6-100
BCM Group Ltd v Visualmark [2008] EWHC 1831 (QB) 11-058
BDG Roof Bond Ltd (In Liquidation) v Douglas [2000] 1 B.C.L.C. 401; [2000] B.C.C.
   770; [2000] Lloyd's Rep. P.N. 273; [2000] P.N.L.R. 397 Ch D.................... 9-117
Beable v Dickerson (1885) 1 T.L.R. 654 .... 7-032, 7-050
Beadon v Capital Syndicate (1912) 28 T.L.R. 427; 56 S.J. 536 8-117
Beal v South Devon Railway Co (1864) 3 H. & C. 337; 11 L.T. 184; 12 W.R. 115 6-019
Beale, Re; Ex p. Durrant (1888) 5 Morr. 37 .... 7-030, **7-032**
Bear v Stevenson (1874) 30 L.T. 177 9-133
Beard v London General Omnibus Co [1900] 2 Q.B. 530; [1900-1903] All E.R.Rep. 112;
   69 L.J.Q.B. 895; 83 L.T. 362; 48 W.R. 658; 16 T.L.R. 499 CA.................... 8-192
Beattie v Ebury (1872) L.R. 7 H.L. 102 .... 9-060, 9-069, 9-070, **9-076**, 9-087
Beaufort (Duke of) v Neeld (1845) 12 C. & F. 248; 9 Jur. 813 .... 3-022, **8-045**
Beaumont v Boultbee (1800) 5 Ves. Jun 485 6-098
Beaumont v Boultbee (1802) 7 Ves. Jun. 599 6-095
Becerra v Close Brothers Corporate Finance Ltd [1999] EWHC 289 (Comm) 7-009
Bechuanaland Exploration Co v London Trading Bank Ltd [1898] 2 Q.B. 658; 67 L.J.Q.B.
   986; 79 L.T. 270; 14 T.L.R. 587; 3 Com.Cas.285 QBD (Comm)...................... 8-142
Becker v Riebold (1913) 30 T.L.R. 142 .... 2-056, 2-073
Becket, Re; sub nom. Purnell v Paine [1918] 2 Ch. 72; 87 L.J.Ch. 457; 119 L.T. 108; 34
   T.L.R. 389 CA.. 5-002, 5-007
Bedford Insurance Co Ltd v Instituto de Resseguros do Brasil [1985] Q.B. 966; [1984] 3
   W.L.R. 726; [1984] 3 All E.R. 766; [1984] 1 Lloyd's Rep. 210; [1985] Fin. L.R. 49;
   (1985) 82 L.S.G. 37; (1984) 134 N.L.J. 34; (1984) 128 S.J. 701 QBD (Comm)...... 2-053, 2-060,
                                                           2-061, 2-071, 2-092
Behzadi v Shaftesbury Hotels Ltd [1992] Ch. 1; [1991] 2 W.L.R. 1251; [1991] 2 All E.R.
   477; (1991) 62 P. & C.R. 163; [1990] E.G.C.S.111; (1990) 140 N.L.J. 1385 CA.......... 6-013
Beigtheil & Young v Stewart (1900) 16 T.L.R. 177 .... 8-120, 8-121, 9-060
Beldon v Campbell (1851) 6 Exch. 886; 20 L.J.Ex. 342; 17 L.T.(O.S.) 257 4-005
Beliard, Crighton (Belgium) & Co Ltd v Charles Lowe & Partners Ltd (1922) 13
   Ll.L.Rep. 567... 8-120, 9-046
Bell and Head v Nixon and Davison (1832) 9 Bing. 393 .... **2-044**
Bell Electric Ltd v Aweco Appliance Systems GmbH & Co KG [2002] EWCA Civ 1501;
   [2003] 1 All E.R. 344; [2003] C.P. Rep. 18 CA.......................... 11-015, 11-057
Bell v Balls [1897] 1 Ch. 663; 66 L.J.Ch. 397; 76 L.T. 254; 13 T.L.R. 274; 45 W.R. 378;
   41 S.J. 331; [1895–9] All E.R.Rep. 733 .... 2-014, 3-032, **5-007**, **10-005**
Bell v Lever Brothers Ltd; Lever Bros Ltd v Bell [1932] A.C. 161; 101 L.J.K.B. 129; 146
   L.T. 258; 48 T.L.R. 133; 76 S.J. 50; 37 Com.Cas.98 HL........................... 6-054
Bell v London & Northern Western Ry Co (1852) 15 Beav. 548; 19 L.T.(O.S.) 292 9-114
Bell v Marsh [1903] 1 Ch. 528; 72 L.J.Ch. 360; 88 L.T. 605; 51 W.R. 325; 47 S.J. 296 CA .. 6-111,
                                                                          8-130
Bell's Indenture, Re; sub nom. Bell v Hickley [1980] 1 W.L.R. 1217; [1980] 3 All E.R.
   425; (1979) 123 S.J. 322 Ch D.................................... 9-140
Belleli SpA v AIG (Europe) May 22, 1996 QBD 9-006

Bellis v Challinor. *See* Challinor v Juliet Bellis & Co (A Firm) . . 1-028, 2-091, 6-041, 8-182, 9-106
Bellman v Northampton Recruitment Ltd [2016] EWHC 3104 (QB); [2017] I.C.R. 543 8-178
Belmont Finance Corp v Williams Furniture Ltd (No.2) [1980] 1 All E.R. 393 CA . . . 2-025, 8-211,
                 8-215, **8-217**, 8-221, 9-136, 9-141, 9-142
Belmont Finance Corp v Williams Furniture Ltd [1979] Ch. 250; [1978] 3 W.L.R. 712;
 [1979] 1 All E.R. 118; 122 S.J. 743 CA. 2-025, 8-208, 8-214
Belvoir Finance Co Ltd v Cole (Harold G) & Co Ltd [1969] 1 W.L.R. 1877; [1969] 2 All
 E.R. 904 QBD 8-145, 8-147
Benedetti v Sawiris [2013] UKSC 50; [2014] A.C. 938; [2013] 3 W.L.R. 351; [2013] 4 All
 E.R. 253; [2013] 2 All E.R. (Comm) 801; 149 Con. L.R. 1 . . . . 7-009, 7-014
Benham v Batty (1865) 12 L.T. 266; 6 New Rep. 42; 13 W.R. 636 . . . . **2-083**
Benhams Ltd v Kythira Investments Ltd [2004] EWHC 2973 QBD 7-004, 7-007, 7-020, 7-056
Beningfield v Kynaston (1887) 3 T.L.R. 279 7-018
Benjamin v Barnett (1903) 19 T.L.R. 564; 8 Com.Cas. 244 . . . . 3-036, 3-037, **3-040**
Benjamin v Clothier (1969) 210 E.G. 29 5-002
Benmag Ltd v Barda [1955] 2 Lloyd's Rep. 354 . . . . 1-021, **3-023**
Bennett & Partners v Millett [1949] 1 K.B. 362; [1949] L.J.R. 1050; 64 T.L.R. 612; [1948]
 2 All E.R. 929; 92 S.J. 675 KBD 7-019
Bennett v Bayes, Pennington & Harrison (1860) 5 H. & N. 391; 29 L.J.Ex. 224; 2 L.T.
 156; 24 J.P. 294; 8 W.R. 320 . . . . 9-116, **9-125**
Bennett, Walden & Co v Wood [1950] W.N. 329; 66 T.L.R. (Pt. 2) 3; [1950] 2 All E.R.
 134 CA 7-019
Bennetts v McIlwraith [1896] 2 Q.B. 464; 65 L.J.Q.B. 632; 75 L.T. 145; 54 W.R. 17; 12
 T.L.R. 616; 8 Asp.M.L.C. 176; 1 Com.Cas. 441 9-075
Benourad v Compass Group Plc [2010] EWHC 1882 (QB) 1-030, 7-009, 7-028, 10-031
Benson v Heathorn (1842) 1 Y. & C.Ch.Cas. 326 . . . . 6-039, 6-068, 8-220
Bentall, Horsley & Baldry v Vicary [1931] 1 K.B. 253; 100 L.J.K.B. 201; 144 L.T. 365;
 47 T.L.R. 99; 74 S.J. 862 KBD 1-036, 7-024, 7-037
Bentinck v London Joint Stock Bank [1893] 2 Ch. 120; 62 L.J.Ch. 358; 68 L.T. 315; 9
 T.L.R. 262; 42 W.R. 140; 3 R. 120 . . . . **8-128**, 8-142
Bentley v Craven (1853) 18 Beav. 75 . . . . 6-065, 6-068, 6-082
Bentley v Gaisford [1997] Q.B. 627; [1997] 2 W.L.R. 401; [1997] 1 All E.R. 842; (1996)
 146 N.L.J. 1615 CA 7-093
Bentley v Griffin (1814) 5 Taunt. 3356 8-120
Benton v Campbell, Parker & Co [1925] 2 K.B. 410; 94 L.J.K.B. 881; 134 L.J. 60; 89 J.P.
 187; 69 S.J. 842; 41 T.L.R. 662. . . . . 1-041, 8-117, 8-120, 9-023, 9-034
Beresford (Lady) v Driver (1852) 16 Beav. 134; 22 L.J.Ch. 407; 51 E.R. 728 6-093
Berezovsky v Edmiston & Co Ltd [2011] EWCA Civ 431 . . . . 5-011, 7-005, 7-030
Berkeley Applegate (Investment Consultants) Ltd, Re; Harris v Conway [1989] Ch. 32;
 [1988] 3 W.L.R. 95; [1988] 3 All E.R. 71; (1988) 4 B.C.C. 274; [1989] B.C.L.C. 28;
 [1989] P.C.C. 261; (1988) 132 S.J. 896 Ch D 4-010, 6-080
Berkeley Community Villages Ltd v Pullen [2007] EWHC 1330 (Ch); [2007] 3 E.G.L.R.
 101; [2007] 24 E.G. 169 (C.S.); [2007] N.P.C. 71 . . . . 7-013, 7-024
Berkeley v Hardy (1826) 5 B. & C. 355; 8 D. & R.K.B. 102; 4 L.J. (O.S.) K.B. 184 . . 2-040, **8-088**
Berkshire, The [1974] 1 Lloyd's Rep. 185 QBD (Admlty) 5-001
Berney v Saul (t/a Thomas Saul & Co) [2013] EWCA Civ 640; [2013] P.N.L.R. 26; (2013)
 157(23) S.J.L.B. 31. 6-018
Berry Estates v Burgess (1949) 153 E.G. 343 7-019
Berryland Books Ltd v BK Books Ltd [2009] EWHC 1877 (Ch); [2009] 2 B.C.L.C. 709 6-054
Bertram, Armstrong & Co v Godfrey (1830) 1 Knapp. 381 . . . . **3-020**, **6-007**, 6-010
Best v Hayes (1863) 1 H. & C. 718; 32 L.J.Ex. 129; 11 W.R. 71; 158 E.R. 1073 . . . . . 7-103, **7-104**
Beswick v Beswick [1968] A.C. 58; [1967] 3 W.L.R. 932; [1967] 2 All E.R. 1197; 111 S.J.
 540 HL 8-086
Betts & Drewe v Gibbins (1834) 2 A. & E. 57; 4 L.J.K.B. 1; 4 Nev & M.K.B. 64 7-068
Betts v Neilson; Betts v De Vitre; sub nom. Neilson v Betts; sub nom. De Vitre v Betts
 (1868) 3 Ch.App. 429; 37 L.J.Ch. 325; 18 L.T. 165; 32 J.P. 547; 16 W.R. 529 CA;
 (1871) L.R. 5 H.L. 1 HL; (1873) L.R. 6 H.L. 319 HL **8-196**
Bevan v Webb [1901] 2 Ch. 59; 70 L.J.Ch. 536; 17 T.L.R. 440; 45 S.J. 465; 84 T.L. 609;
 49 W.R. 548 . . . . 2-017, **2-026**
Beverley Acceptances Ltd v Oakley [1982] R.T.R. 417 CA 1-025, 8-130, **8-133**, 8-146, 8-147,
                         8-149, 8-152, **8-158**
Bexhill UK Ltd v Razzaq [2012] EWCA Civ 1376 9-008

Beyer v Adams; Re Law; Arkell's Claim (1857) 26 L.J.Ch. 841; 30 L.T.(O.S.) 8; 3 Jur. (N.S.) 709; 5 W.R. 795 6-100
Bhoomidas v Port of Singapore Authority [1978] 1 W.L.R. 189; [1978] 1 All E.R. 956; [1978] 1 Lloyd's Rep. 330 PC (Sing) 8-179
Bhullar (Karuppan) v Bhullar; sub nom. Bhullar Bros Ltd, Re [2003] EWCA Civ 424; [2003] B.C.C. 711; [2003] 2 B.C.L.C. 241; [2003] W.T.L.R. 1397; (2003) 147 S.J.L.B. 421; [2003] N.P.C. 45 CA... 6-081
Bickerton v Burrell (1816) SM. & S.383 9-094
Bickley v Browning, Todd & Co (1913) 30 T.L.R. 134 7-042
Biddle v Bond (1865) 6 B. & S.225; 5 New. Rep. 485; 34 L.J.Q.B. 137; 12 L.T. 178; 11 Jur. (N.S.) 425; 13 W.R. 561; 29 J.P. 565.. 6-111, **6-112**
Bieber v Teathers Ltd (In Liquidation) [2012] EWCA Civ 1466; [2013] 1 B.C.L.C. 248; [2013] W.T.L.R. 1; 15 I.T.E.L.R. 492; [2013] 1 P. & C.R. DG11 .... 3-011, 3-016, 6-041
Biffa Waste Services Ltd v Maschinenfabrik Ernst Hese GmbH [2008] EWCA Civ 1257; [2009] Q.B. 725; [2009] 3 W.L.R. 324; [2009] Bus. L.R. 696; [2009] B.L.R. 1; 122 Con. L.R. 1; [2009] P.N.L.R. 12; (2008) 152(45) S.J.L.B. 25................... 8-179, 8-184
Bigg v Strong (1858) 4 Jur. (N.S.) 983; 32 L.T.(O.S.) 98; 6 W.R. 536 2-079
Biggar v Rock Life Ass.Co [1902] 1 K.B. 516; 71 L.J.K.B. 79; 85 L.T. 636; 46 S.J. 105; 18 T.L.R. 119 8-217
Biggerstaff v Rowatt's Wharf Ltd [1896] 2 Ch. 93; 65 L.J.Ch. 536; 74 L.T. 473; 44 W.R. 536 .... **3-029**, 8-039, **8-046**
Biggs v Evans [1894] 1 Q.B. 88; 10 T.L.R. 59; 69 L.T. 723; 58 J.P. 84 8-153
Bilbee v Hasse & Co Times, January 16, 1890 7-042
Bilta (UK) Ltd v Nazir (No.2) [2015] UKSC 23; [2016] A.C. 1; [2015] 2 W.L.R. 1168; [2015] 2 All E.R. 1083; [2015] 2 All E.R. (Comm) 281; [2015] 2 Lloyd's Rep. 61; [2015] B.C.C. 343; [2015] 1 B.C.L.C. 443; [2015] B.V.C. 20... 1-028, 1-029, 2-025, 6-023, 8-208, 8-209, 8-214
Bingham v Allport (1833) 1 N. & M. 398; 2 L.J.Q.B. 86 8-045
Binstead v Buck (1776) 2 Wm.Bl. 1117 4-010
Bird v Boulter (1833) 4 B. & Ad. 443; 1 Nev & M. 313 .... 2-014, 5-007
Bird v Brown (1850) 4 Exch. 786; 19 L.J.Ex. 154; 14 Jur. 132 .. 2-047, 2-048, 2-054, 2-091, **2-094**, 2-095, **2-100**
Bird v M'Gahey (1849) 2 C. & K. 707 7-012
Birdseye v Roythorne & Co [2015] EWHC 1003 (Ch); [2015] W.T.L.R. 961 2-021
Birt, Re; Birt v Burt (1883) 22 Ch.D. 604; 52 L.J.Ch. 397; 48 L.T. 67; 31 W.R. 334 6-080
Bishop v Jersey (Courts) (1854) 2 Drew. 143; 2 Eq.Rep. 545; 23 L.J.Ch. 483; 22 L.T. (O.S.) 326; 18 Jur. 765; 2 W.R. 247 8-201
Bishop v Shillito (1819) note to 2 Barn. & Ald. 327 6-003
Bishopsgate Investment Management Ltd (In Liquidation) v Maxwell (No.1) [1994] 1 All E.R. 261; [1993] B.C.C. 120; [1993] B.C.L.C. 1282 CA 6-034, 6-043, 8-220
Bishopsgate Investment Management Ltd v Homan [1995] Ch. 211; [1994] 3 W.L.R. 1270; [1995] 1 All E.R. 347; [1994] B.C.C. 868; (1994) 91(36) L.S.G. 37; (1994) 138 S.J.L.B. 176 CA... 6-040, 8-162
Biss, Re; sub nom. Biss v Biss [1903] 2 Ch. 40; 72 L.J.Ch. 473; 88 L.T. 403; 51 W.R. 504; 47 S.J. 383 CA 6-080
Bissill v Bradford & District Tramway Co Ltd (1893) 9 T.L.R. 337 7-094
Black King Shipping Corp v Massie; The Litsion Pride [1985] 1 Lloyd's Rep. 437; (1984) 134 New J.J. 887 QBD (Comm).. 8-182
Blackburn and District Benefit Building Society v Cunliffe Brooks & Co. See Cunliffe, Brooks & Co v Blackburn and District Benefit Building **7-089**
Blackburn Building Society Cunliffe, Brookes & Co (1882) 22 Ch.D. 61; 52 L.J.Ch. 92; 48 L.T. 33; 31 W.R. 98 8-203
Blackburn Low & Co v Haslam (1888) 21 Q.B.D. 144; 57 L.J.Q.B. 479; 59 L.T. 407; 4 T.L.R. 577; 36 W.R. 855; 6 Asp.M.L.C. 326.. 8-212, 8-217
Blackburn Low & Co v Vigors (1887) 12 App.Cas. 531; 57 L.J.K.B. 114; 57 L.T. 730; 3 T.L.R. 835; 36 W.R. 449; 6 Asp.M.L.C. 216 .... 6-021, 8-211, 8-213, **8-217**
Blackburn v Mason (1893) 68 L.T. 510; 9 T.L.R. 286; 37 S.J. 283; 4 R. 297 ... 3-026, 3-037, 5-010
Blackburn v Scholes (1810) 2 Lamp. 341 .... 8-109, **10-005**
Blackpool Corp v Locker [1948] 1 K.B. 349; [1948] L.J.R. 847; 112 J.P. 130; [1948] 1 All E.R. 85; 46 L.G.R. 88 CA.. 2-057
Blades v Free (1829) 9 B. & C. 167; 4 Man. & Ry. K.B. 282; 7 L.J.(O.S.) K.B. 211 ...... **10-022**, 10-032, **10-033**
Blake & Co v Sohn [1969] 1 W.L.R. 1412; [1969] 3 All E.R. 123; 113 S.J. 690 QBD 7-018

Blaker v Hawes and Brown (1913) 109 L.T. 320; 29 T.L.R. 609 7-070
Blanc Canet v Europcar France [2005] E.C.C. 34 11-013
Blandy Bros & Co Ltd v Nello Simoni Ltd [1963] 2 Lloyd's Rep. 393 CA **3-032**, 3-035
Blankley v Central Manchester and Manchester Children's University Hospitals NHS
    Trust [2015] EWCA Civ 18; [2015] 1 W.L.R. 4307; [2015] 1 Costs L.R. 119 . 2-009, 9-063, 10-020
Blaustein v Maltz, Mitchell & Co [1937] 2 K.B. 142; 106 L.J.K.B. 471; 53 T.L.R. 397;
    81S.J. 177; [1937] 1 All E.R. 497 . . . . 6-099, 6-110, 6-111, **6-112**
Bligh v Davies (1860) 28 Beav. 211 7-090
Bloom v Yefet [1982] 2 E.G.L.R. 30; (1982) 264 E.G. 142 CA 7-030
Bloomenthal v Ford; Veuve Monnier et Ses Fils Ltd (In Liquidation), Re; Veuve Monnier
    et Ses Fils Ltd Ex p. Bloomenthal, Re [1897] A.C. 156; 66 L.J.Ch. 253; 76 L.T. 205; 13
    T.L.R. 240; 45 W.R. 449; 4 Mans. 156 . . . . 8-024, 8-050
Bloomsbury International Ltd, Re [2010] EWHC 1150 (Ch) 6-051
Blore v Sutton (1817) 3 Mer. 237 . . . . **5-007**
Bloye's Trust, Re (1849) 1 Mac. & G. 488; 2 H. & T.W. 140; 15 L.T. (O.S.) 517; 19
    L.J.Ch. 89; 14 Jur. 49 . . . . **6-070**
Blucher, (Prince), Re; Ex p. Debtor [1931] 2 Ch. 70; 47 T.L.R. 19; 74 S.J. 735 2-022
Blumberg v Life Interests and Reversionary Securities Corp [1898] 1 Ch. 27 CA 3-025
Blundell, Re; Blundell v Blundell (1888) 40 Ch.D. 370; 57 L.J.Ch. 730; 58 L.T. 933; 4
    T.L.R. 506; 36 W.R. 770; [1886-90] All E.R. Rep. 837 . . . . **9-142**
Blunden v Desart (1842) (Ir.) 59 R.R. 753; 2 Dr. & War. 405 . . . . 7-088, **7-089**
Blyth v Fladgate; Morgan v Blyth; Smith v Blyth [1891] 1 Ch. 337; 60 L.J.Ch. 66; 63 L.T.
    546; 7 T.L.R. 29; 39 W.R. 422. . . . . 9-140, 9-142
Blyth v Whiffin (1872) 27 L.T. 330 6-100
Boardman v Phipps; sub nom. Phipps v Boardman [1967] 2 A.C. 46; [1966] 3 W.L.R.
    1009; [1966] 3 All E.R. 721; 110 S.J. 853 HL 6-047, 6-074, 6-076, 6-077, 6-080, 6-081, **6-083**
Boardman v Sill (1808) 1 Camp. 410n 7-094
Bock v Gorrissen (1860) 2 De. G.F. & J. 434; 30 L.J.Ch. 39; 3 L.T. 424; 7 Jur. (N.S.) 81; 9
    W.R. 209. . . . . 7-073, 7-074, 7-086
Bocking Garage v Mazurk *Times*, February 4, 1954 8-043
Boden v French (1851) 10 C.B. 886; 20 L.J.C.P. 143; 17 L.T. (O.S.) 77 . . . . . . **3-018**, 3-025, 6-010
Bolkiah v KPMG; sub nom. HRH Prince Jefri Bolkiah v KPMG [1999] 2 A.C. 222;
    [1999] 2 W.L.R. 215; [1999] 1 B.C.L.C. 1; [1999] P.N.L.R. 220; (1999) 149 N.L.J. 16;
    (1999) 143 S.J.L.B. 35 HL. 6-034, 6-038, 6-044, 6-051, 6-060, 6-077
Bolton Partners v Lambert (1889) 41 Ch. D. 295; 58 L.J.Ch. 425; 60 L.T. 687; 37 W.R.
    434; 5 T.L.R. 357 CA 2-055, 2-084, 2-087, **2-088**, 2-090, 2-091, 2-092, 8-030
Bonaparte, The (1853) 8 Moo. P.C. 459 4-004
Bond Worth Ltd, Re [1980] Ch. 228; [1979] 3 W.L.R. 629; [1979] 3 All E.R. 919; (1979)
    123 S.J. 216 Ch D 1-035
Bondina Ltd v Rollaway Shower Blinds Ltd; Bondina Ltd v Ward; Bondina Ltd v
    McMahon [1986] 1 W.L.R. 517; [1986] 1 All E.R. 564; [1986] P.C.C. 325; [1986]
    E.C.C. 260; [1986] F.L.R. 266; (1986) 83 L.S.G. 36; (1986) 136 N.L.J. 116; (1985) 130
    S.J. 264 CA. 9-056
Bone v Ekless (1860) SM. & N. 925; 29 L.J.Ex. 438 6-100
Bonita, The; Charlotte, The (1861) Lush. 252; 30 L.J.P.M. & A. 145; S.L.T. 141; 1
    Mar.L.C. 145 . . . . **2-073**, 2-083
Bonsor v Musicians' Union [1956] A.C. 104; [1955] 3 W.L.R. 788; [1955] 3 All E.R. 518;
    99 S.J. 814 HL **2-034**
Bonzi v Stewart (1842) 5 Scott N.R. 1; 4 M. & G. 295; 11 L.J.C.P. 228; 3 L.T.(O.S.) 301 . . . . **6-101**
Boorman v Brown (1842) 3 Q.B. 511; 2 Gal. & Dav. 793; 11 L.J.Ex. 437 6-019
Booth v Hodgson (1795) 6 T.R. 405 6-100
Boots v Christopher (E.) & Co [1952] 1 K.B. 59; [1951] 2 T.L.R. 1169; [1951] 2 All E.R.
    1045; 95 S.J. 788 CA. 7-018, 7-024
Borag, The. *See* Compania Financiera Soleada SA, Netherlands Antilles Ships
    Management Corp 6-035, 6-043, 7-076
Borden (UK) Ltd v Scottish Timber Products Ltd [1981] Ch. 25; [1979] 3 W.L.R. 672;
    [1979] 3 All E.R. 961; [1980] 1 Lloyd's Rep. 160; 123 S.J. 688 CA. 1-035
Borries v Imperial Ottoman Bank (1873) L.R. 9 C.P. 38; 43 L.J.CP. 3; 29 L.T. 689; 22
    W.R. 92 . . . . 8-053, 8-073, 8-109, 8-110
Borvigilant, The. *See* Owners of the Borvigilant v Owners of the Romina G; sub nom.
    Borkan General Trading Ltd v Monsoon Shipping Ltd . . 2-077, 2-090, 2-091, 2-092, 2-093, **2-094**
Boschsek Pty Co Ltd etc. v Fuke [1906] 1 Ch. 148; 75 L.J.Ch. 261; 94 L.T. 398; 22 T.L.R.
    196; 54 W.R. 359; 50 S.J. 170; 13 Mans. 100. 2-069

Boston Deep Sea Fishing and Ice Co v Ansell (1888) 39 Ch.D. 339; 59 L.T. 345 . . . . 2-087, 6-087, **6-089**, 6-108, 7-050, 11-039

Boston Deep Sea Fishing and Ice Co v Farnham [1957] 1 W.L.R. 1051; [1957] 3 All E.R. 204; 101 S.J. 834; [1957] 2 Lloyd's Rep. 238; [1957] T.R. 243; 50 R. & I.T. 675; 37 T.C. 505; 30 A.T.C. 211 Ch D 2-010, **2-070**

Boston Fruit Co v British & Foreign Marine Insurance Co [1906] A.C. 336; 75 L.J.K.B. 537; 94 L.T. 806; 54 W.R. 557; 22 T.L.R. 571; 10 Asp.M.L.C. 260; 11 Com.Cas.196 2-067

Boswell v Coaks. *See* Coaks v Boswell 6-070

Bottomley v Nuttall (1858) 5 C.B. (N.S.) 122; 28 L.J.C.P. 110; 32 L.T. (O.S.) 222; 5 Jur. (N.S.) 315 8-120

Boughton v Knight (1873) L.R. 3 P. & D. 64; 42 L.J.P. 4 M. 41; 29 L.T. 43; 37 J.P. 647 10-020

Boulton v Reynolds (1859) 2 E. & E. 369; 29 L.J.Q.B. 11; 1 L.T. 166; 24 J.P. 53; Jur. (N.S.) 46; 8 W.R. 62 3-032

Bourne, Re; Ex p. Bird (1851) 4 De G. & S. 273; 20 L.J.Bcy 16; 17 L.T. (O.S.) 303; 15 Jur. 894. . . . . 9-106, **9-109**

Boursot v Savage (1866) L.R. 2 Eq. 134; 35 L.J.Ch. 627; 14 L.T. 299; 14 W.R. 565; 30 J.P. 484. . . . . 8-208, 8-210, 8-211, 8-214, 8-217

Bousfield v Hodges (1863) 33 Beav. 90 3-032

Bousfield v Wilson (1846) 16 M. & W. 185; 4 Ry. & Can.Cas. 687; 16 L.J.Ex. 44; 8 L.T. (O.S.) 194 6-100

Boverman, Re; Ex p. Vining (1836) 1 Deac. 555; 5 L.J.Bcy 44 8-120

Bovine Ltd v Dent & Wilkinson (1904) 21 T.L.R. 82 10-019

Bovis International Inc (formerly L/M International Construction Inc) v Circle Ltd Partnership (1995) 49 Con. L.R. 12; [1995] N.P.C. 128 CA 1-022, 9-013, 9-014

Bow (R&J) Ltd v Hill (1930) 37 Ll.L.Rep. 46 9-034

Bow's Emporium Ltd v AR Brett & Co Ltd [1928] 44 T.L.R. 194 7-030

Bower v Jones (1831) 8 Bing. 65; 1 Moo. & S.140; 1 L.J.C.P. 31 . . . . **7-012**

Bowers (Maghull) Ltd v Morton (1940) 67 Ll.L.Rep. 1 . . . . **2-034**

Bowes, Re; Strathmore v Vane (1886) 33 Ch.D. 5 & 6; 56 L.J.Ch. 143; 55 L.T. 260; 35 W.R. 166. . . . . **7-086**

Bowlby v Bell (1846) 3 C.B. 284; 4 Ry. & Can.Cas.692; 16 L.J.C.P. 18; 7 L.T. (O.S.) 300; 10 Jur. 669. 7-058

Bowles' Mortgage Trust, Re (1874) 31 L.T. 365 3-015

Bowmaker Ltd v Wycombe Motors Ltd [1946] 1 K.B. 505; [1946] 2 All E.R. 113; 115 J.L.K.B. 411; 175 L.T. 133; 62 T.L.R. 437; 90 S.J. 407 1-033

Bowman v Secular Society Ltd [1917] A.C. 406 HL 2-025

Bowthorpe Holdings Ltd v Hills [2002] EWHC 2331 (Ch); [2003] 1 B.C.L.C. 226 1-028

Bowyer, Philpott & Payne Ltd v Mather [1919] 1 K.B. 419; 88 L.J.K.B. 377; 120 L.T. 346; 83 J.P. 50; [1918-19] All E.R.Rep. 579; 17 L.G.R. 222 2-057

Box v Midland Bank Ltd [1979] 2 Lloyd's Rep. 391 8-186

Boyce v Rendells [1983] E.G.D. 26 6-003

Boyd & Forrest v Glasgow & SW Railway Co 1915 S.C. (HL) 20; 52 S.L.R. 205; 1915. 1 S.L.T. 114. . . . . 7-009, 8-185

Boyd v Tovil Paper Co Ltd (1884) 4 T.L.R. 332 7-032

Boyter v Thomson [1995] 2 A.C. 628; [1995] 3 W.L.R. 36; [1995] 3 All E.R. 135; 1995 S.C. (HL) 15; 1995 S.L.T. 875; 1995 S.C.L.R. 1009; (1995) 145 N.L.J. 922; (1995) 139 S.J.L.B. 174 HL. 8-068, 8-155

BP Oil International Ltd v Target Shipping Ltd [2012] EWHC 1590 (Comm); [2012] 2 Lloyd's Rep. 245; [2012] 2 C.L.C. 336 . . . . 3-040, 8-019, 8-166

BPE Solicitors v Hughes-Holland [2017] UKSC 21; [2017] 2 W.L.R. 1029 . . . . 3-016, 6-043

Brace v Calder [1895] 2 Q.B. 253; 64 L.J.Q.B. 582; 72 L.T. 829; 59 J.P. 693; 11 T.L.R. 450; 14 R. 473 . . . . 10-019, 10-042

Bradford & Bingley v Cutler [2008] EWCA Civ 74 2-026

Bradford & Sons v Price Brothers (1923) 92 L.J.K.B. 871; 129 L.T. 408; 39 T.L.R. 272 3-025

Bradford Third Equitable Benefit Building Society v Borders [1941] 2 All E.R. 205; 110 L.J.Ch. 123; 57 T.L.R. 616 . . . . 8-098, 8-182

Bradley Egg Farm Ltd v Clifford [1943] 2 All E.R. 378 9-087

Bradley v Riches (1878) 9 Ch.D. 189 8-214

Bradshaw v Beard (1862) 12 C.B.(N.S.) 344; 31 L.J.C.P. 273; 6 L.T. 458; 8 Jur. (N.S.) 1288; 26 J.P. 630; 142 E.R. 1175 4-010

Brady v Todd (1861) 9 C.B.(N.S.) 592; 30 L.J.C.P. 223; 4 L.T. 212; 25 J.P. 598; 7 Jur. (N.S.) 827; 9 W.R. 483. . . . . 1-045, 3-028, **3-032**

Bramwell v Spiller (1870) 21 L.T. 672; 18 W.R. 316 . . . . 1-042, 9-002, 9-009, 9-022, 9-035

Brand Studio Ltd v St John Knits Inc [2015] EWHC 3143 (QB); [2015] Bus. L.R. 1421;
 [2016] 1 Lloyd's Rep. 179; [2016] E.C.C. 1 11-041
Brandao v Barnett (1846) 12 C. & F. 787; 3 C.B. 519; 7 L.T.(O.S.) 525 HL . . . 7-081, 7-082, **7-086,**
7-089
Brandeis (Brokers) Ltd v Black [2001] 2 Lloyd's Rep. 359 . . . . 6-056, 6-081
Brandt (HO) & Co v HN Morris & Co Ltd [1917] 2 K.B. 784; 87 L.J.K.B. 101; 117 L.T.
 196. . . . . 9-006, 9-020, 9-035, 9-038
Brandt's (William) Sons & Co v Dunlop Rubber Co [1905] A.C. 454; 74 L.J.K.B. 898; 93
 L.T. 495; 21 T.L.R. 710; 11 Com.Cas.1 9-112
Branwhite v Worcester Works Finance Ltd [1969] 1 A.C. 552; [1968] 3 W.L.R. 760;
 [1968] 3 All E.R. 104; 112 S.J. 758 HL. . . . . 1-026, 2-030— **2-034,** 8-201
Bray v Ford [1896] A.C. 44; 65 L.J.Q.B. 213; 73 L.T. 609; 12 T.L.R. 119 . . . . 6-046, 6-080
Bray v Hine & Fox (1818) 6 Price 203 7-099
Braymist Ltd v Wise Finance Co Ltd; sub nom. Wise Finance Ltd v Braymist Ltd [2002]
 EWCA Civ 127; [2002] Ch. 273; [2002] 3 W.L.R. 322; [2002] 2 All E.R. 333; [2002]
 B.C.C. 514; [2002] 1 B.C.L.C. 415; [2002] 9 E.G.C.S.220; (2002) 99(13) L.S.G. 25;
 (2002) 146 S.J.L.B. 60; [2002] N.P.C. 25 CA 8-004, 9-086, 9-094, 9-096
Brazil v Durant International Corp [2015] UKPC 35; [2016] A.C. 297; [2015] 3 W.L.R.
 599; [2016] 1 All E.R. (Comm) 722; [2015] 2 Lloyd's Rep. 460; [2015] Lloyd's Rep.
 F.C. 593; [2015] W.T.L.R. 1323; 18 I.T.E.L.R. 334; [2015] 2 P. & C.R. DG24. 8-162
Brebner v Henderson 1925 S.C. 643 . . . . **8-093, 9-056**
Breitenfeld UK Ltd v Harrison [2015] EWHC 399 (Ch); [2015] 2 B.C.L.C. 275 . . . . . 6-015, 6-034,
6-047
Breming v Mackie (1862) 3 F. & F. 197 . . . . **3-026**
Breslauer v Barwick (1876) 36 L.T. 52; 24 W.R. 901; 3 Asp.M.L.C. 355; 3 Char.Pr.Cas. 56 . . 9-040
Brewer v Sparrow (1827) 7 B. & C. 310; 1 Man. & Ry. K.B. 2; 6 L.J.(O.S.) K.B. 1 . . . . **2-083**
Brewery Assets Corp., Re Truman's Case [1894] 3 Ch. 272 . . . . **8-207**
Brewin v Briscoe (1859) 2 E. & E. 116; 28 L.J.Q.B. 329; 5 Jur. (N.S.) 1206 . . . . **8-217**
Brice v Bannister (1878) 3 Q.B.D. 569; 47 L.J.Q.B. 722; 38 L.T. 739; 26 W.R. 670 9-112
Brickles v Snell [1916] 2 A.C. 599; 86 L.J.P.C. 22; 115 L.T. 568 6-013
Bridger v Savage (1855) 15 Q.B.D. 363; 54 L.J.Q.B. 464; 53 L.T. 129; 1 T.L.R. 585; 33
 W.R. 891; 49 J.P. 725 6-100
Bridges & Salmon Ltd v Owner of The Swan; The Swan; Marine Diesel Service
 (Grimsby) Ltd v Owner of The Swan [1968] 1 Lloyd's Rep. 5; (1968) 118 N.L.J. 182,
 PDAD 9-002, 9-005, 9-006, **9-034,** 9-036, 9-038, 9-044
Bridges v Garrett (1870) L.R. 5 C.P. 451; 39 L.J.C.P. 251; 22 L.T. 448; 18 W.R. 815 3-025
Briess v Woolley; sub nom. Briess v Rosher [1954] A.C. 333; [1954] 2 W.L.R. 832;
 [1954] 1 All E.R. 909; 98 S.J. 286; HL. 2-013, 2-056, 2-072, 6-035, 8-098, 8-185, **8-196**
Briggs v Jones (1870) L.R. 10 Eq. 92; 23 L.T. 212 8-135
Bright Ex p.; Re Smith (1879) 10 Ch.D. 566; 48 L.J.Bcy 81; 39 L.T. 649; 27 W.R. 385 1-036
Brind v Hampshire (1836) 1 M. & W. 365; 2 Gale 33; Tyr. & Gr. 790; S.L.J.Ex. 197 9-114
Brink's Global Services Inc v Igrox Ltd [2010] EWCA Civ 1207; [2011] I.R.L.R. 343 8-178
Brinks Ltd v Abu-Saleh (No.3) [1996] C.L.C. 133 Ch D 9-135
Brinks-Mat Ltd v Noye [1991] 1 Bank L.R. 68 8-214
Brinsmead v Harrison (1872) L.R. 7 C.P. 547; 41 L.J.C.P. 190; 27 L.T. 99; 20 W.R. 784 8-191,
8-223
Brinson v Davies (1911) 105 L.T. 134; 27 T.L.R. 442; 44 S.J. 501 . . . . 3-007, 7-035
Bristol (Earl) v Wilsmore (1823) 1 B. & C. 514; 2 Dow. & Ry. K.B.; 1 Dow. & Ry. M.C.
 407; 1 L.J. (O.S.) K.B. 178. 7-093
Bristol Alliance Nominee (No.1) Ltd v Bennett [2013] EWCA Civ 1626; [2014] 1 P. &
 C.R. DG15 9-026
Bristol and West Building Society v Fancy & Jackson [1997] 4 All E.R. 582; [1997]
 N.P.C. 109 Ch D 9-065
Bristol and West Building Society v May May & Merrimans (No.1) [1996] 2 All E.R. 801;
 [1996] P.N.L.R. 138; [1996] E.G.C.S.69; (1996) 93(19) L.S.G. 30; (1996) 146 N.L.J.
 625; (1996) 140 S.J.L.B. 110 Ch D 6-043
Bristol and West Building Society v Mothew (t/a Stapley & Co); sub nom. Mothew v
 Bristol and West Building Society [1998] Ch. 1; [1997] 2 W.L.R. 436; [1996] 4 All E.R.
 698; [1997] P.N.L.R. 11; (1998) 75 P. & C.R. 241; [1996] E.G.C.S.136; (1996) 146
 N.L.J. 1273; (1996) 140 S.J.L.B. 206; [1996] N.P.C. 126 CA . . . 2-028, 6-003, 6-034, 6-043, **6-045,**
6-048, 6-050, 6-056, 6-062, 6-064, 6-065, 9-135
Bristow and Porter v Taylor (1817) 2 Stark. 50 . . . . 10-006, 10-028

Bristow v Whitimore (1861) 9 H.L. Cas. 391; L.J.Ch. 467; 4 L.T. 622; 8 Jur. (N.S.) 291; 9
   W.R. 621; 1 Mar.L.C. 95 . . . . 2-074, **2-100**
Britannia Electric Lamp Works v Mandler (D) & Co Ltd [1939] 2 K.B. 129; 108 L.J.K.B.
   823; 160 L.T. 587; 55 T.L.R. 655; [1939] 2 All E.R. 469 . . . . 8-092, 8-093, 9-054, 9-056
Britannia Steamship Insurance Association v Ausonia Assicurazioni SpA [1984] 2 Lloyd's
   Rep. 98 CA 12-016, 12-025
British America Elevator Co Ltd v Bank of British North America [1919] A.C. 658 (PC)   . . . 6-003,
   6-043
British American Continental Bank v British Banking Foreign Trade [1926] 1 K.B. 328;
   95 L.J.K.B. 326; 134 L.T. 472; 42 T.L.R. 202 9-107
British Bank of Foreign Trade Ltd v Novinex [1949] 1 K.B. 623; [1949] L.J.R. 658;
   [1949] 1 All E.R. 155; 93 S.J. 146 7-009
British Bank of the Middle East v Sun Life Assurance Co of Canada (UK) Ltd [1983] 2
   Lloyd's Rep. 9; [1983] 2 Lloyd's Rep. 9; [1983] Co. L.R. 187; 133 N.L.J. 575 HL . . . 1-026, 8-015,
                                              8-019, 8-021, 8-039, 8-060, **8-067**, 8-077
British Energy Power & Energy Trading Ltd v Credit Suisse [2008] EWCA Civ 53; [2008]
   2 All E.R. (Comm) 524; [2008] 1 Lloyd's Rep. 413 . . . . 1-032, 9-036
British Marine Mutual Insurance Co v Jenkins [1900] 1 Q.B. 299; 69 L.J.Q.B. 177; 82
   L.T. 297; 9 Asp.M.L.C. 26; 5 Com.Cas. 143 8-082
British Midland Tool Ltd v Midland International Tooling Ltd [2003] EWHC 466 (Ch);
   [2003] 2 B.C.L.C. 523 . . . . 6-034, 6-054, 6-080
British Racing Drivers Club Ltd v Hextall Erskine & Co [1996] 3 All E.R. 667; [1997] 1
   B.C.L.C. 182; [1996] B.C.C. 727; [1996] P.N.L.R. 523 Ch D 8-188
British Russian Gazette Ltd v Associated Newspapers Ltd [1933] 2 K.B. 616; 102
   L.J.K.B. 775; 149 L.T. 545 . . . . 9-064, 9-066, 9-080, 9-083
British Syphon Co v Homewood [1956] 1 W.L.R. 1190; [1956] 2 All E.R. 897; 100 S.J.
   633; [1956] R.P.C. 225, 330 6-081
British Thomson Houston Co Ltd v Sterling Accessories Ltd [1924] 2 Ch. 33   9-120
British Thomson-Houston Co Ltd v Federated European Bank Ltd [1932] 2 K.B. 176; 101
   L.J.K.B. 690; 147 L.T. 345 8-039
Brittain v Brown & Millar (1871) 24 L.T. 504 . . . . 8-211, 8-217
Brittain v Lloyd (1845) 14 M. & W. 762; 15 L.J.Ex. 43   . . . . 7-059, 7-06
Broad v Thomas (1830) 7 Big. 99; 4 C. & P. 338; 4 Moo. & P. 732; 9 L.J. (O.S.) C.P. 32   7-004,
   7-012
Broadbent v Barlow (1861) 3 De G.F. & J. 570; 30 L.J.Ch. 569; 4 L.T. 193; 7 Jur. (N.S.)
   479 . . . . **8-167**
Brocklebank v Lancashire & Yorkshire Railway Co (1887) 3 T.L.R. 575   7-005
Brocklesby v Temperance Building Society [1895] A.C. 173; 64 L.J.Ch. 433; 72 L.T. 477;
   56 J.P. 676; 43 W.R. 606; 11 T.L.R. 297; 11 R. 159 . . . . 3-005, 8-130, 8-134, 8-135, **8-138**
Brodard v Pilkington [1953] C.P.L. 275; 161 E.G. 436 CA   9-109
Brogden, Re (1886) 38 Ch.D. 546   6-043
Bronester Ltd v Priddle [1961] 1 W.L.R. 1294; [1961] 3 All E.R. 471; 105 S.J. 683 CA   7-025
Brook v Bool [1928] 2 K.B. 578   9-120
Brook v Hook (1871) L.R. 6 Ex. 89; 40 L.J.Ex. 50; 24 L.T. 34; 19 W.R. 508   . . . . 2-059, **2-061**
Brooks v Hassall (1883) 49 L.T. 569   . . . . 3-004, 3-028, **3-032**
Brooks's Wharf & Bull Wharf Ltd v Goodman Bros [1937] 1 K.B. 534; 106 L.J.K.B. 437;
   156 L.T. 4; 53 T.L.R. 126; 80 S.J. 991; 42 Com.Cas. 99; [1963] 3 All E.R. 696 7-060
Broom v Hall (1859) 7 C.B.(N.S.) 503; 34 L.T.(O.S.) 66   7-062
Broomhead, Re (1847) 5 D. & L. 52; 16 L.J.Q.B. 355   7-090
Brotherton, Widow v Hatt, Widow, Martha Coy, Sir Edward Hungerford & Al', & e contra
   23 E.R. 973; (1706) 2 Vern. 574 . . . . 8-211, 8-213
Broun v Kennedy (1864) 4 De G.J. & S. 217; 33 L.J.Ch. 342; 9 L.T. 736; 10 Jur. (N.S.)
   141; 12 W.R. 360; 46 E.R. 901 . . . . 6-069, 7-006
Brouncker v Scott (1811) 4 Taunt. 1   . . . . **9-003**
Brown & Co v Bedford Pantechnicon Co (1889) 5 T.L.R. 449   8-147
Brown & Gracie Ltd v Green (FW) & Co Pty Ltd. *See* Green (FW) & Co Ltd v Brown &
   Gracie Ltd 1-022, 1-036, 3-020, 6-010, 7-101
Brown v Andrew (1849) 18 L.J.Q.B. 153; 12 L.T.(O.S.) 398; 13 Jur. 938   . . . . 2-043, **2-044**
Brown v Bennett [1999] 1 B.C.L.C. 649; [1999] B.C.C. 525 CA   9-135
Brown v Boorman (1844) 11 Cl. & F. 1; 8 E.R. 1003 HL 6-003, 6-007
Brown v Farebrother (1888) 58 L.J. Ch. 3; 59 L.T. 822   6-100
Brown v Hickinbotham (1881) 50 L.J.Q.B. 426   9-131
Brown v InnovatorOne Plc [2012] EWHC 1321 (Comm) 2-071, 2-072, 2-077, 2-078, 3-013

Brown v IRC [1965] A.C. 244; [1964] 3 W.L.R. 511; [1964] 3 All E.R. 119; 1964 S.C.
(H.L.) 180; 1964 S.L.T. 302; 42 T.C. 42; (1964) 43 A.T.C. 244; [1964] T.R. 269; 108
S.J. 636 HL 6-041, 6-103, 6-105, **6-109**
Brown v Law (1895) 72 L.T. 779; 11 T.L.R. 395; 8 Asp.M.L.C. 230 9-064
Brown v Michaels (1949) 153 E.G. 511 7-019
Brown v Robinson [2004] UKPC 56 PC (Jam) 8-192
Brown v Staton (1816) 2 Chit. 353 6-024
Brown v Tombs [1891] 1 Q.B. 253; 60 L.J.K.B. 38; Fox & S.Reg. 196; 64 L.T. 114; 55
J.P. 359; 7 T.L.R. 49 QBD 5-007
Brown v Westminster Bank Ltd [1964] 2 Lloyd's Rep. 187 2-061
Browne (Henry) & Sons Ltd v Smith [1964] 2 Lloyd's Rep. 476 QBD 9-034
Browne v Barber [1913] 2 K.B. 553 CA 7-056
Browne v Southouse (1790) 3 Bro.C.C. 107 . . . . **6-109**
Browning v Provincial Insurance Co of Canada (1873) L.R. 5 P.C. 263; 28 L.T. 853;
21 W.R. 587; 2 Asp.M.L.C. 35 . . . . 8-068, 8-073, 8-098
Brumark Investments Ltd, Re; sub nom. Inland Revenue Commissioner v Agnew; Agnew
v Inland Revenue Commissioner [2001] UKPC 28; [2001] 2 A.C. 710; [2001] 3 W.L.R.
454; [2001] Lloyd's Rep. Bank. 251; [2001] B.C.C. 259; [2001] 2 B.C.L.C. 188 (NZ) 7-077
Brumder v Motornet Service and Repairs Ltd [2013] EWCA Civ 195; [2013] 1 W.L.R.
2783; [2013] 3 All E.R. 412; [2013] B.C.C. 381; [2013] 2 B.C.L.C. 58; [2013] I.C.R.
1069; [2013] P.I.Q.R. P13; (2013) 157(38) S.J.L.B. 41 1-028
Brummell v M'Pherson (1828) 5 Russ. 263; 7 L.J. (O.S.) Ch. 1 10-029
Brunton v Electrical Engineering Corp [1892] 1 Ch. 434; 61 L.J.Ch. 356; 65 L.T. 745; 8
T.L.R. 158 . . . . **7-089**
Brutton v Alfred Savill Curtis & Henson [1971] E.G.D. 497; (1970) 218 E.G. 1417 6-024
Bryans v Nix (1839) 4 M. & W. 775; 1 Horn. & H. 480; 8 L.J.Ex. 137 . . . . 7-073, 7-078
Bryant v Flight (1839) 5 M. & W. 114; 2 Horn & H. 84; 3 Jur. 681 . . . . **7-012**
Bryant, Powis and Bryant Ltd v Banque du Peuple; Bryant, Powis and Bryant Ltd v
Quebec Bank [1893] A.C. 170; 62 L.J.P.C. 68; 68 L.T. 546; 41 W.R. 600; 9 T.L.R. 322;
1 R. 336 PC (Can) 3-013, 3-015, 8-056, **8-056**, 8-063
BSM Marketing Ltd v Take Ltd [2009] EWCA Civ 45 6-034
Buchanan v Findlay (1829) 9 B. & C. 738; 4 Man. & Ry. K.B. 593; 7 L.J. (O.S.) K.B. 314 . . 7-086
Buckland and Garrard v Pawson & Co (1890) 6 T.L.R. 421 7-005
Budberg v Jerwood & Ward (1934) 51 T.L.R. 99; 78 S.J. 878 8-145
Bulfield v Fournier (1895) 11 T.L.R. 282 6-087
Bull v Price (1831) 5 M. & P. 2; 7 Bing. 237; 9 L.J.(O.S.) C.P. 78 7-018
Buller v Harrison (1777) 2 Camp. 565 . . . . 9-102, 9-106, 9-107
Bultfontein Sun Diamond Mine Ltd, Re; Ex p. Cox, Hughes and Norman (1897) 75 L.T.
669; 13 T.L.R. 156 10-014
Bunge Corp v Tradax Export SA [1981] 1 W.L.R. 711; [1981] 2 All E.R. 540; (1981) 125
S.J. 373; [1981] Lloyd's Rep. 1 HL 6-013
Burbidge v Morris (1865) 3 H. & C. 664; 34 L.J.Ex. 131; 12 L.T. 426; 13 W.R. 921 8-045
Burchell v Gowrie and Blockhouse Collieries Ltd [1910] A.C. 614; 80 L.J.P.C. 41; 103
L.T. 325 PC (Can) 7-028, 7-030
Burdick v Garrick (1870) L.R. 5 Ch.App. 233; 39 L.J.Ch. 369; 18 W.R. 387 . . 6-041, **6-045**, 6-091,
6-103, 6-105, 6-107, **6-109**
Burge, Woodall & Co, Re; Ex p. Skyrne [1912] 1 K.B. 393; 81 L.J.K.B. 721; 106 L.T. 47;
20 Mans. 11 8-167
Burgis v Constantine [1908] 2 K.B. 484; 77 L.J.K.B. 1045; 99 L.T. 490; 24 T.L.R. 682; 11
Asp.M.L.C. 130; 13 Com.Cas. 299 CA 8-131
Burkinshaw v Nicolls (1878) 3 App. Cas. 1004 HL 8-040
Burland v Earle [1902] A.C. 83; 71 L.J.P.C. 1; 85 L.T. 553; 18 T.L.R. 41; 50 W.R. 241; 9
Mans. 17 PC (Can) 6-056, 6-068
Burn v Brown (1817) 2 Stark **7-086**
Burn v Carvalho (1839) 4 Myl. & C. 690; 9 L.J.Ch. 65; 3 Jur. 1141 . . . . **9-113**
Burnaby v Equitable Reversionary Interest Society (1885) 28 Ch.D. 416; 54 L.J.Ch. 466;
52 L.T. 350; 33 W.R. 639 2-008
Burnand Ex p. Baker Sutton & Co, Re [1904] 2 K.B. 68; 20 T.L.R. 377; 52 W.R. 437; 48
S.J. 368; 73 L.J.K.B. 413; 11 Mans. 113; 91 L.T. 46 CA 6-090
Burnden Holdings (UK) Ltd v Fielding [2016] EWCA Civ 557; [2017] 1 W.L.R. 39;
[2016] C.P. Rep. 41 . . . . 6-040, 8-214, 9-136
Burnett v Bouch (1840) 9 C. & P. 620 7-004
Burney v London Mews Co Ltd [2003] EWCA Civ 766 CA 7-032

Burns v Coomber [1966] E.G.D. 110 . . . . 7-030, 7-032

Burnside v Dayrell (1849) 3 Exch. 224; 6 Ry. & Can.Cas.67; 19 L.J.Ex. 46; 12 L.T. (O.S.) 312. 2-031

Burrell v Jones (1819) 3 B. & Ald. 47 . . . . **9-038**

Burrell v Mossop (1888) 4 T.L.R. 270 6-080

Burridge v MPH Soccer Management Ltd [2011] EWCA Civ 835 1-036

Burrough v Skinner (1770) 5 Burr. 2639 . . . . **9-109**

Burrough's Adding Machine Ltd v Aspinall (1925) 41 T.L.R. 276 7-004

Burt v Cousins (Claude) & Co Ltd [1971] 2 Q.B. 426; [1971] 2 W.L.R. 930; [1971] 2 All E.R. 611; (1971) 115 S.J. 207 CA. 8-013, 9-006, 9-026, **9-109**

Burton v Denman (1848) 2 Exch. 167 . . . . **2-053**, 9-124

Burton v Hughes (1885) 1 T.L.R. 207 . . . . 7-030, 7-032

Butler v Knight (1867) L.R. 2 Ex. 109; 36 L.J.Ex. 66; 15 L.T. 621; 15 W.R. 407 . . . . 6-003, **10-005**

Butwick v Grant [1924] 2 K.B. 483; 93 L.J.K.B. 972; 131 L.T. 476 . . . . **3-023**, 3-032, **8-112**

Buxton v Baughan (1834) 6 C. & P. 674 1-033

Byas v Miller (1897) 3 Com.Cas. 39 2-067

C Inc Plc v L [2001] 2 All E.R. (Comm) 446; [2001] 2 Lloyd's Rep. 459; [2001] C.L.C. 1054; (2001) 151 N.L.J. 535. 8-113

Cable & Wireless Plc v Muscat [2006] EWCA Civ 220; [2006] I.C.R. 975; [2006] I.R.L.R. 354; (2006) 103(12) L.S.G. 30; (2006) 150 S.J.L.B. 362. 1-034

Cadogan Finance v Lavery & Fox [1982] Com. L.R. 248 8-133

Cadogan Petroleum Plc v Tolly [2011] EWHC 2286 (Ch); [2012] 1 P. & C.R. DG5 . . . 6-042, 6-087

Caine v Horsefall (1847) 1 Exch. 519; 2 Car. & Kir. 349; 17 L.J.Ex. 25; 10 L.T.(O.S.)169 . . . 7-004, 7-012

Calder v Dobell (1871) L.R. 6 C.P. 486; 40 L.J.C.P. 224; 25 L.T. 129; 19 W.R. 978 . . 8-003, 8-120, 8-121, **8-124**, 9-006

Caldwell v Sumpters [1972] Ch. 478; [1972] 2 W.L.R. 412; [1972] 1 All E.R. 567; (1971) 116 S.J. 15 CA. 7-093, **7-094**

Calico Printers Assn. Ltd v Barclays Bank Ltd (1931) 145 L.T. 51; 36 Com.Cas. 197 CA . . . 5-008, 5-010, 5-011, 5-016

Caliendo v Mishcon De Reya (A Firm) [2016] EWHC 150 (Ch) 6-018

Callaghan and Hedges v Thompson [2000] C.L.C. 360; [2000] Lloyd's Rep. I.R. 125 QBD (Comm). 2-016

Calland v Lloyd (1840) 6 M. & W. 16; 9 L.J.Ex. 56 8-161

Callander v Oelrichs (1838) 5 Bing.N.C. 58; 1 Arn. 401; 6 Scott 761; 8 L.J.C.P. 25; 2 Jur. 967. . . . . 6-012, **6-016**

Callot v Nash (1923) 39 T.L.R. 291 . . . . 3-043, 8-120

Callow v Kelson (1862) 10 W.R. 193 . . . . **8-133**

Calyon v Wytwornia Sprzetu Komunikacynego PZL Swidnik SA [2009] EWHC 1914 (Comm); [2009] 2 All E.R. (Comm) 603 12-002

Cameron v Nystrom [1893] A.C. 308; 62 L.J.P.C. 85; 68 L.T. 772; 57 J.P. 550; 7 Asp.M.L.C. 320; 1 R. 362 PC (NZ) 8-179

Cammell v Sewell (1860) 5 Hurl. & N. 728; 157 E.R. 1371 12-032

Campanari v Woodburn (1854) 15 C.B. 400; 3 C.L.R. 140; 24 L.J.C.P. 13; 24 L.T.(O.S.) 95; 1 Jur. (N.S.) 17; 3 W.R. 59. . . . . **7-051**, **10-022**

Campbell v Hassel (1816) 1 Stark. 223 . . . . **3-026**

Campbell v Hicks (1858) 28 L.J.Ex. 70 8-103

Campbell v Larkworthy (1894) 9 T.L.R. 528 7-060

Campbell v M'Creath 1975 S.C. 81; 1975 S.L.T. (Notes) 5, OH **8-217**

Campbell v Paddington Corp; sub nom. Campbell v Mayor, Aldermen, & Councillors of the Metropolitan Borough of Paddington [1911] 1 K.B. 869 KBD 2-025, 8-189

Campbell v Peter Gordon Joiners Ltd [2016] UKSC 38; [2016] A.C. 1513; [2016] 3 W.L.R. 294; [2017] 2 All E.R. 161; 2017 S.C. (U.K.S.C.) 13; 2016 S.L.T. 887; 2016 S.C.L.R. 434; [2016] 2 B.C.L.C. 287; [2016] I.C.R. 862; [2016] Lloyd's Rep. I.R. 591; [2016] P.I.Q.R. P15; 2016 G.W.D. 21-380 9-115

Campbell v Thompson [1953] 1 Q.B. 445; [1953] 2 W.L.R. 656; [1953] 1 All E.R. 831; 97 S.J. 229 QBD 9-087

Campbell v Walker; subsequent proceedings; sub nom. Sanderson v Walker (1800) 5 Ves. 678; (1807) 13 Ves.601. 6-064

Campden Hill Ltd v Chakrani [2005] EWHC 911; [2005] N.P.C. 65 Ch D 8-167, 8-204

Canadian Pacific Railway Co v Lockhart [1942] A.C. 591; 111 L.P.C. 113; 167 L.T. 231; [1942] 2 All E.R. 464 PC (Can). 8-178, **8-193**

Cane v Allen (1814) 2 Dow. 290 6-070

Cane v Jones [1980] 1 W.L.R. 1451; [1981] 1 All E.R. 533; (1980) 124 S.J. 542 ..... 1-028, 8-037
Caparo Industries Plc. v Dickman [1990] 2 A.C. 605; [1990] 2 W.L.R. 358; [1990] 1 All
   E.R. 568; (1990) 134 S.J. 494; [1990] B.C.C. 164; [1990] B.C.L.C. 273; [1990] E.C.C.
   313 HL..6-029, 8-183
Cape Breton Co, Re. *See* Cavendish-Bentinck v Fenn 6-035, 6-068, **6-071**
Cape Distribution Ltd v Cape Intermediate Holdings Plc (No.1) [2016] EWHC 1119 (QB) .. 7-066
Cape Distribution Ltd v Cape Intermediate Holdings Plc (No.2) [2016] EWHC 1786 (QB) .. 7-059
Cape v Thames Haven Dock, etc., Co (1849) 3 Exch. 841 2-038
Capel & Co v Sim's Composition Co (1888) 58 L.T. 808 8-050
Capel v Thornton (1828) 3 C. & P. 352 3-023
Capita Plc v Darch [2017] EWHC 1248 (Ch); [2017] I.R.L.R. 718 6-093
Capital Fire Ins.Assn., Re; sub nom. Re Capital Fire Insurance Association Ltd Ex p. Beall
   (1838) 24 Ch.D. 408; 49 L.T. 697; 32 W.R. 260; 53 L.J.Ch. 71.....................**7-089**
Capp v Topham (1805) 6 East 392; 2 Smith K.B. 443 ....**7-070**
Cardigan v Moore [2012] EWHC 1024 (Ch); [2012] W.T.L.R. 931; 14 I.T.E.L.R. 967;
   [2012] 2 P. & C.R. DG8 6-064
Carew's Estate Act, Re (1862) 31 Beav. 39 8-217
Cargill v Bower (1878) 10 Ch.D. 502; 47 L.J.Ch. 649; 38 L.T. 779; 26 W.R. 716 ..... 1-028, 9-133
Carl Zeiss Stiftung v Rayner & Keeler Ltd (Directions: Existence of East Germany);
   Rayner & Keeler Ltd v Courts & Co [1965] Ch. 525; [1964] 3 W.L.R. 905; [1964] 3 All
   E.R. 326; 108 S.J. 672 CA 9-142
Carliles Steamship Co v Simpson, Spence & Young (1926) 25 Ll.L.Rep. 278 6-019
Carlill v Carbolic Smoke Ball Co [1893] 1 Q.B. 256 CA 9-062, 9-065
Carltona Ltd v Commissioner of Works [1943] 2 All E.R. 560 5-006
Carnell v Harrison [1916] 1 Ch. 328; [1916-17] All E.R. Rep. 827; 85 L.J.Ch. 321; 114
   L.T. 478; 60 S.J. 290...2-008
Carr v Jackson (1852) 7 Exch. 382; 21 L.J.Ex. 137; 18 L.T.(O.S.) 279 9-090
Carr v L&NW Railway (1875) L.R. 10 C.P. 310 8-029
Carr v Levingston (1865) 35 Beav. 41 10-015
Carreras Rothmans Ltd v Freeman Matthews Treasure Ltd [1985] Ch. 207; [1984] 3
   W.L.R. 1016; [1985] 1 All E.R. 155; [1985] P.C.C. 222; (1984) 81 L.S.G. 2375; (1984)
   128 S.J. 614 Ch D..6-041
Carter v Palmer (1842) 8 C. & F. 657; 1 I.Eq.R. 289; 1 Dr. & Wal. 22 6-067
Carter v St. Mary Abbotts, Kensington Vestry (1900) 64 J.P. 548 ....2-056, **2-083**
Carter v White (1883) 25 Ch.D. 666; 54 L.J.Ch. 138; 50 L.T. 670; 32 W.R. 692 10-006
Carter, Re; Carter v Carter (1885) 55 L.J.Ch. 230; 53 L.T. 630; 34 W.R. 57 ....7-090, 7-093
Caruthers v Graham (1811) 14 East 578 7-014
Cary v Webster (1721) 1 Str. 480 9-106
Cascades and Quayside Ltd v Cascades Freehold Ltd [2007] EWCA Civ 1555; [2008] L.
   & T.R. 23...2-022
Casio Computer Ltd v Sayo [2001] EWCA Civ 661 QBD; [2001] I.L.Pr. 43 9-135
Cass v Rudele (1672) 2 Vern. 280; 1 Eq.Cas.Abr. 25 ....**9-049**
Cassaboglou v Gibb (1883) 11 Q.B.D. 797; 52 L.J.Q.B. 538; 48 L.T. 850; 32 W.R. 138 1-021,
                                        1-022, 1-036, 6-012, 7-100, 7-101, **7-102**
Cassils & Co and Sassoon & Co v Holden Wood Bleaching Co Ltd (1914) 112 L.T. 373;
   112 L.T. 373..1-033, 7-095
Casson Beckman & Partners v Papi [1991] B.C.C. 68; [1991] B.C.L.C. 299 CA 6-035
Castle v Duke (1832) 5 C. & P. 359 9-043
Caterpillar (NI) Ltd (formerly FG Wilson (Engineering) Ltd) v John Holt & Co
   (Liverpool) Ltd [2013] EWCA Civ 1232; [2014] 1 All E.R. 785; [2014] 1 All E.R.
   (Comm) 393; [2014] 1 Lloyd's Rep. 180; [2013] 2 C.L.C. 501; [2014] B.L.R. 1038 1-035
Caterpillar Logistics Services (UK) Ltd v Huesca de Crean [2012] EWCA Civ 156; [2012]
   3 All E.R. 129; [2012] C.P. Rep. 22; [2012] I.C.R. 981; [2012] F.S.R. 33 ....6-051, 6-077
Catlin v Bell (1815) 4 Camp. 183 ....**5-007**, 6-100
Catterall v Hindle (1867) L.R. 2 C.P. 368 3-026
Cave v Mackenzie (1871) 46 L.J.Ch. 564; 37 L.T. 218 ....2-037, 6-082
Cave v Mills (1862) 7 H. & N. 913; 31 L.J.Ex. 265; 6 L.T. 650; 8 Jur. (N.S.) 363; 10 W.R.
   471...6-097
Cavell USA Inc v Seaton Insurance Co [2009] EWCA Civ 1363; [2009] 2 C.L.C. 991;
   [2010] Lloyd's Rep. F.C. 197 ....6-087, 8-223
Cavendish-Bentinck v Fenn; sub nom. Re Cape Breton Co (1887) 12 App.Cas.652 .. 6-035, 6-068,
                                                                     6-071

Cawdery Kaye Fireman & Taylor (A Firm) v Minkin [2012] EWCA Civ 546; [2012] 3 All
    E.R. 1117; [2012] 4 Costs L.R. 650; [2013] 2 F.C.R. 125; [2012] P.N.L.R. 26; [2012] 19
    E.G. 94 (C.S.); (2012) 162 N.L.J. 681; (2012) 156(18) S.J.L.B. 31. 7-050
Cawood, Wharton & Co Ltd v Samuel Williams & Sons Ltd; The Cawood III [1951] P.
    270; [1951] 1 Lloyd's Rep. 350; [1951] 1 T.L.R. 924; 95 S.J. 337 PDAD 8-217
Cawthorn v Trickett (1864) 15 C.B. (N.S.) 754; 3 New Rep. 383; 33 L.J.C.P. 182; 9 L.T.
    609; 12 W.R. 311; 1 Mar.L.C. 414 9-003
Caxton Publishing Co Ltd v Sutherland Publishing Co Ltd (No.1); Sutherland Publishing
    Co Ltd v Caxton Publishing Co Ltd; Caxton Publishing Co Ltd v Sutherland Publishing
    Co Ltd (No.2) [1939] A.C. 178; [1938] 4 All E.R. 389 HL 9-126, 9-129
CBS Songs Ltd v Amstrad Consumer Electronics Plc [1988] A.C. 1013; [1988] 2 W.L.R.
    1191; [1988] 2 All E.R. 484; [1988] 2 F.T.L.R. 168; [1988] R.P.C. 567; (1988) 132 S.J.
    789. 9-120
CCC Films (London) Ltd v Impact Quadrant Films Ltd [1985] Q.B. 16; [1984] 3 W.L.R.
    245; [1984] 3 All E.R. 298; (1984) 81 L.S.G. 1046; (1984) 134 N.L.J. 657; (1984) 128
    S.J. 297 QBD 9-081
Cemp Properties (UK) Ltd v Dentsply Research and Development Corp [1989] 2 E.G.L.R.
    196; [1991] 34 E.G. 62 CA 8-182, **8-196**
Central Bank of Ecuador v Conticorp SA [2015] UKPC 11; [2016] 1 B.C.L.C. 26; [2015]
    Bus. L.R. D7 9-135
Central Newbury Car Auctions Ltd v Unity Finance Ltd, Mercury Motors (Third Parties)
    [1957] 1 Q.B. 371; [1956] 3 W.L.R. 1068; [1956] 3 All E.R. 905; 100 S.J. 927 CA. . . 8-126, 8-130,
                                                                            8-133, 8-149
Centre Reinsurance International Co v Freakley [2006] UKHL 45; [2007] Bus. L.R. 284;
    [2006] 1 W.L.R. 2863; [2006] 4 All E.R. 1153; [2006] 2 All E.R. (Comm) 943; [2006]
    B.C.C. 971; [2007] 1 B.C.L.C. 85; [2006] B.P.I.R. 1405; [2007] Lloyd's Rep. I.R. 32;
    (2006) 103(41) L.S.G. 35; (2006) 156 N.L.J. 1613; (2006) 150 S.J.L.B. 1395 10-018
Century Insurance Co Ltd v Northern Ireland Road Transport Board [1942] A.C. 509;
    [1942] 1 All E.R. 491; (1942) 72 Ll. L. Rep. 119 HL (NI) 8-179, **8-192**
Cerascope Ltd v Todagres SA [2008] EWHC 1502 (Ch) 11-046
CF Asset Finance Ltd v Okonji [2014] EWCA Civ 870; [2014] E.C.C. 23; [2014] C.T.L.C.
    218. . . . . 2-034, 8-207
CGL Group Ltd v The Royal Bank of Scotland Plc [2017] EWCA Civ 1073 . . 6-029, 8-180, 8-183,
                                                                            9-117
Chadburn v Moore (1892) 61 L.J.Ch. 674; 67 L.T. 257; 41 W.R. 39; 36 S.J. 666 3-032
Chadwick v Maden (1851) 9 Hare 188; 21 L.J.Ch. 876 9-034
Challinor v Juliet Bellis & Co (A Firm) [2015] EWCA Civ 59; [2016] W.T.L.R. 43; [2015]
    2 P. & C.R. DG3 . . . . 1-028, 2-091, 6-041, 8-182, 9-106
Champion v Rigby (1840) 9 L.J.(O.S.) Ch. 211 6-068
Chancery Client Partners Ltd v MRC 957 Ltd [2016] EWHC 2142 (Ch) 8-221
Chandler v Bradley [1897] 1 Ch. 315; 66 L.J.Ch. 214; 75 L.T. 581; 45 W.R. 296; 41 S.J.
    157. 8-223
Chandler v Cape Plc [2012] EWCA Civ 525; [2012] 1 W.L.R. 3111 . . . . 1-030, 8-183
Chaney v Maclow [1929] 1 Ch. 461; 98 L.J.Ch. 345; 140 L.T. 312; 45 T.L.R. 135; 73 S.J.
    26 . . . . 2-014, 3-032, 10-012
Chantrey Martin v Martin [1953] 2 Q.B. 286; [1953] 3 W.L.R. 459; [1953] 3 W.L.R. 459;
    [1953] 2 All E.R. 691; 97 S.J. 539; 46 R.A.I.T. 516 CA 6-093
Chapleo v Brunswick Building Society (1881) 6 Q.B.D. 696; 50 L.J.K.B. 372; 44 L.T.
    449; 29 W.R. 529. . . . . 2-020, **9-076**
Chaplin v Frewin (Leslie) (Publishers) Ltd [1966] Ch. 71; [1966] 2 W.L.R. 40; [1965] 3
    All E.R. 764; 109 S.J. 871 CA 2-008
Chapman v Smethurst [1909] 1 K.B. 927; 78 L.J.K.B. 654; 100 L.T. 465; 25 T.L.R. 383;
    53 S.J. 340; 14 Com.Cas.94; 16 Mans. 171. . . . . **8-093, 9-056**
Chapman v Smith [1907] 2 Ch. 97 . . . . **9-049**
Chapman v Walton (1833) 10 Bing. 57; 3 Moo. & S.389; 2 L.J.C.P. 910 . . . . **6-024**
Chapman v Winson (1904) 91 L.T. 17; 53 W.R. 19; 20 T.L.R. 663 7-018
Chappell v Bray (1860) 6 H. & N. 145; 30 L.J.Ex. 24; 3 L.T. 278; 9 W.R. 17 10-010
Chappell v Poles (1837) 2 H. & W. 867; Murp. & H. 262; 6 L.J.M.C. 157; 1 J.P. 171 9-105
Chappell v Times Newspapers Ltd [1975] 1 W.L.R. 482; [1975] 2 All E.R. 233; [1975]
    I.C.R. 145; [1975] I.R.L.R. 90; 18 Man. Law 5; 119 S.J. 82 CA **2-034**, 7-046
Charan Singh v Sardar Investments Ltd [2002] EWCA Civ 1706; [2002] N.P.C. 134 CA 9-080

Charge Card Services Ltd, Re [1989] Ch. 497; [1988] 3 W.L.R. 764; [1988] 3 All E.R. 702; (1988) 4 B.C.C. 524; [1988] B.C.L.C. 711; [1988] P.C.C. 390; [1988] Fin. L.R. 308; (1989) 8 Tr. L.R. 86; (1988) 85(42) L.S.G. 46; (1988) 138 N.L.J. Rep. 201; (1988) 132 S.J. 1458 CA 3-025
Charles Terence Estates Ltd v Cornwall CC [2012] EWCA Civ 1439; [2013] 1 W.L.R. 466; [2013] P.T.S.R. 175; [2013] H.L.R. 12; [2013] B.L.G.R. 97 . . . . . . 1-028, 8-032, 8-042, 8-221
Charrington Fuel Oils Ltd v Parvant Co Times, December 28, 1988 CA 8-043
Charter v Trevelyan (1844) 11 C. & F. 714; 8 Jur. 1015 . . . . 6-062, 6-065
Chase Manhattan Bank NA v Israel British Bank Ltd (London) [1981] Ch. 105; [1980] 2 W.L.R. 202; [1979] 3 All E.R. 1025; (1979) 124 S.J. 99 Ch D 8-162
Chasen Ryder & Co Hedges [1993] 1 E.G.L.R. 47; [1993] 08 E.G. 119; [1993] N.P.C. 6 CA. 7-030
Chatenay v Brazilian Submarine Telegraph Co Ltd [1891] 1 Q.B. 79 CA . . 12-004, 12-010, 12-013, 12-017, 12-018, 12-030
Chatteris Ex p. (1874) 22 W.R. 289 7-032
Chattock v Muller (1878) 8 Ch.D. 177 . . . . **6-083**
Chaudhry v Prabakhar [1989] 1 W.L.R. 29; (1989) 133 S.J. 82 CA 6-029
Chedworth v Edwards (1802) 8 Ves. 46 . . . . 6-092, 6-109
Cheese v Keen [1908] 1 Ch. 245; 77 L.J.Ch. 163; 98 L.T. 316; 24 T.L.R. 138 6-098
Cheesman v Exall (1851) 6 Exch. 341; 20 L.J.Ex. 209 6-111
Chellaram (K) & Sons (London) Ltd v Butlers Warehousing and Distribution Ltd [1978] 2 Lloyd's Rep. 412 CA. 7-082, 7-095, 7-099
Chelmsford Auctions Ltd v Poole [1973] Q.B. 542; [1973] 2 W.L.R. 219; [1973] 1 All E.R. 810; (1972) 117 S.J. 219 CA 3-032, 9-005, 9-023, **9-035**
Cherney v Deripaska [2007] EWHC 965 (Comm); [2007] 2 All E.R. (Comm) 785; [2007] I.L.Pr. 49 . . . . **3-032**
Cherney v Neuman [2011] EWHC 2156 (Ch) 6-003
Cherry & M'Dougall v Colonial Bank of Australasia; sub nom. Colonial Bank of Australasia v Cherry & McDougall (1869) L.R. 3 P.C. 24; 38 L.J.P.C. 49; 6 Moo.P.C.C.(N.S.) 235; 17 W.R. 1029. . . . . **9-076**
Cherry v Allied Insurance Brokers Ltd [1978] 1 Lloyd's Rep. 274 QBD 6-024
Cherry v Anderson (1876) I.R. 10 C.L. 204 9-023
Cheshire (Thomas) & Co v Vaughan Bros & Co [1920] 3 K.B. 240; 89 L.J.K.B. 1168; 123 L.T. 487; 84 J.P. 233; 15 Asp.M.L.C. 69; 25 Com.Cas. 242. . . . . 5-010, 5-011, 6-009, 6-023
Cheshire v Bailey [1905] 1 K.B. 237 8-194
Chesterfield & Baythorpe Colliery Co v Black (1877) 37 L.T. 740; 26 W.R. 207 6-071
Chesterfield & Co Ltd v Zahid [1989] 2 E.G.L.R. 24; 4 N. 7 M.K.B. 195; 111 E.R. 50 7-030
Chestertons v Barone [1987] 1 E.G.L.R. 15; (1987) 282 E.G. 87 CA 8-119, 8-121
Chillingworth v Esche [1924] 1 Ch. 97; 93 L.J.Ch. 129; 129 L.T. 808; 40 T.L.R. 23; 68 S.J. 80 . . . . 7-017, 9-026
China Pacific S.A. v Food Corp of India; The Winson [1982] A.C. 939; [1981] 3 W.L.R. 860; [1981] 3 All E.R. 688; (1981) 125 S.J. 808; [1982] 1 Lloyd's Rep. 117 HL 4-004, 4-005, 4-006, 4-007, 4-008, 4-010, **4-013**, 12-032
Chinnock v Sainsbury (1860) 30 L.J.Ch. 409; 3 L.T. 258; 6 Jur. (N.S.) 1318; 9 W.R . . 7-037, 7-046
Chitholie v Nash & Co (1993) 229 E.G. 786 . . . . 9-077, 9-083
Choko Star, The. See Industrie Chimiche Italia Centrale and Cerealfin SA v Tsavliris (Alexander) Maritime Co; Panchvisto Shipping Co SA and Bula Shipping Corp; Choko Star, The 4-005, 4-007, 4-008, 4-009, **4-013**, 12-032
Chown v Parrott; sub nom. Choun v Parrott (1863) 14 C.B. (N.S.) 74; 2 New Rep. 127; 32 L.J.C.P. 197; 9 Jur. (N.S.) 1290; 11 W.R. 668; 8 L.T. 391 6-020
Chris Hart (Business Sales) Ltd v Mitchell 1996 S.L.T. (Sh Ct) 132; 1996 S.C.L.R. 68, Sh Pr. 7-008
Christie & Co v Jones [1966] E.G.D. 439 7-032
Christie & Vesey v Maatschappij Tot Exploitatie van Schepen en Andere Zaken, Helvetia NV [1960] 1 Lloyd's Rep. 540 QBD (Comm) 7-044, 10-042
Christie Owen & Davies Plc v RAOBGLE Trust Corp [2011] EWCA Civ 1151; [2011] N.P.C. 104. 7-018
Christie Owen & Davies Plc v Ryelance [2005] 18 E.G.C.S. 148, CC (Liverpool) 7-030
Christie Owen & Davis Plc v King 1998 S.C.L.R. 786; 1998 G.W.D. 22-1103, IH (2 Div) . . 7-030, 7-032
Christie Owen & Davis v Stockton [1953] 1 W.L.R. 1353; [1953] 2 All E.R. 1149; 97 S.J. 781 QBD. 7-019
Christoforides v Terry [1924] A.C. 566 6-070

Christopher (C) (Hove) Ltd v Williams [1936] 3 All E.R. 68; 80 S.J. 853 8-121
Christopher (C) & Co v Essig [1948] W.N. 461; 92 S.J. 675 7-037
Church of Scientology v Kaufman (No.2) [1973] R.P.C. 635 6-077
Churchill & Sim. v Goddard [1937] 1 K.B. 92; 105 L.J.K.B. 571; 154 L.T. 586; 52 T.L.R.
  356; [1936] 1 All E.R. 675; 80 S.J. 285; 41 Com.Cas. 309; 54 Ll.L.Rep. 279 . . 1-042, 9-022, **9-035**
Cia de Seguros Imperio v Heath (REBX) Ltd (formerly CE Heath & Co (America) Ltd);
  sub nom. Companhia de Seguros Imperio v Heath (REBX) Ltd [2001] 1 W.L.R. 112;
  [2000] 2 All E.R. (Comm) 787; [2000] C.L.C. 1543; [2001] Lloyd's Rep. I.R. 109;
  [2000] Lloyd's Rep. P.N. 795 CA.. 6-043
CIBC Mortgages v Pitt [1994] 1 A.C. 200; [1993] 3 W.L.R. 802; [1993] 4 All E.R. 433;
  [1994] 1 F.L.R. 17; [1994] 1 F.C.R. 374; (1994) 26 H.L.R. 90; (1994) 13 Tr. L.R. 180;
  [1994] C.C.L.R. 68; [1993] Fam. Law 79; [1993] E.G.C.S. 174; (1993) 143 N.L.J.
  1514; (1993) 137 S.J.L.B. 240; [1993] N.P.C. 136 HL 6-065
Cifal Groupe SA v Meridian Securities (UK) Ltd (formerly Ginger Investment
  Management SAS) [2013] EWHC 3553 (Comm) 9-005
Citibank NA v QVT Financial LP [2007] EWCA Civ 11; [2007] 1 All E.R. (Comm) 475;
  [2008] 1 B.C.L.C. 376; [2007] 1 C.L.C. 113 6-056
Citizen's Life Assurance Co Ltd v Brown [1904] A.C. 423; 73 J.L.P.C. 102; 90 L.T. 739;
  53 W.R. 176; 20 T.L.R. 497.. 1-028, 8-196
Citizens' Banking Lousiana v First National Bank (1874) L.R. 6 H.L. 352; 43 L.J.Ch. 269;
  22 W.R. 194.. 9-112
City Equitable Fire Insurance Co, Re [1925] Ch. 407; 94 L.J.Ch. 445; 133 L.T. 520; 40
  T.L.R. 853; [1925] B.A.C.R. 109 9-133
City Index Ltd v Gawler [2007] EWCA Civ 1382; [2008] Ch. 313; [2008] 2 W.L.R. 950;
  [2008] 3 All E.R. 126; [2008] 2 All E.R. (Comm) 425; [2007] 2 C.L.C. 968; [2008]
  P.N.L.R. 16; [2008] W.T.L.R. 1773; (2008) 105(2) L.S.G. 27 9-135
Claramoda Ltd v Zoomphase Ltd (t/a Jenny Packham) [2009] EWHC 2857 (Comm);
  [2010] 1 All E.R. (Comm) 830; [2010] E.C.C. 1 11-046
Clarence House Ltd v National Westminster Bank Plc [2009] EWCA Civ 1311; [2010] 2
  All E.R. 201; [2010] L. & T.R. 1; [2010] 8 E.G. 106; [2009] 50 E.G. 66 (C.S.); [2009]
  N.P.C. 141.. 6-041
Clarion Ltd v National Provident Institution [2000] 1 W.L.R. 1888; [2000] 2 All E.R. 265
  Ch D 7-001
Clark Boyce v Mouat [1994] 1 A.C. 428; [1993] 3 W.L.R. 1021; [1993] 4 All E.R. 268;
  (1993) 137 S.J. (LB) 231; [1993] NPC 128; (1993) 143 N.L.J. 1440 PC 6-003, 6-035, 6-048
Clark v Cutland [2003] EWCA Civ 810; [2004] 1 W.L.R. 783; [2003] 4 All E.R. 733;
  [2004] B.C.C. 27; [2003] 2 B.C.L.C. 393; [2003] O.P.L.R. 343; [2003] Pens.L.R. 179;
  [2004] W.T.L.R. 629; [2003] W.T.L.R. 1413; (2003) 147 S.J.L.B. 781 CA 8-162, 8-221
Clark v Hoskins (1868) 37 L.J.Ch. 561; 10 L.T. 331; 16 W.R. 1159 9-125
Clark v Urquhart [1930] A.C. 28; 99 L.J.P.C. 1; 141 L.T. 641 8-117
Clarke v Marlborough Fine Art (London) Ltd (Constructive Trusts) *Times,* July 5, 2001 Ch
  D 6-043
Clarke v Palmer; sub nom. Re Palmer; Clarke v Palmer (1882) 21 Ch.D. 124; 48 L.T. 857;
  51 L.J.Ch. 634.. 8-135
Clarke v Shee & Johnson (1774) 1 Comp. 197 8-141
Clarke v Tipping (1846) 9 Beav. 284 .... 6-090, 6-098
Clarkson Booker Ltd v Andjel [1964] 2 Q.B. 775; [1964] 3 W.L.R. 466; [1964] 3 All E.R.
  26; 108 S.J. 580.. 8-119, 8-121, **9-059**, 9-060
Clauss v Pir [1988] Ch. 267; [1987] 3 W.L.R. 493; [1987] 2 All E.R. 752; (1987) 131 S.J.
  1087; (1987) 84 L.S.Gaz. 2767.. 2-021
Clay & Newman v Southern (1852) 7 Exch. 717; 21 L.J.Ex. 202; 19 L.T.(O.S.) 67; 16 Jur.
  1074.. 9-035
Clay Hill Brick & Tile Co Ltd v Rawlings [1938] 4 All E.R. 100; 159 L.T. 482; 82 S.J.
  909.. 3-025, 8-039
Clayton Newbury Ltd v Findlay [1953] 1 W.L.R. 1194; [1953] 2 All E.R. 826; 97 S.J. 589
  KBD 7-025
Cleadon Trust Ltd, Re [1939] Ch. 286; 108 L.J.Ch. 81; 160 L.T. 45; 55 T.L.R. 154; 82 S.J.
  1030; [1938] 4 All E.R. 518 8-203
Cleave v Moore (1857) 3 Jur. (N.S.) 48; 28 L.T.(O.S.) 255; 5 W.R. 234 9-023
Clef Aquitaine Sarl v Laporte Materials (Barrow) Ltd [2001] Q.B. 488; [2000] 3 W.L.R.
  1760; [2000] 3 All E.R. 493 CA.. 9-120
Cleveland Manufacturing Co v Muslim Commercial Bank Ltd [1981] 2 Lloyd's Rep. 646;
  [1981] Com.L.R. 247 QBD (Comm) **3-023**, 8-015, 8-024, **8-067**

Cleverton v Uffernel (1887) 3 T.L.R. 509 8-217
Clissold v Cratchley [1910] 2 K.B. 244; 79 L.J.K.B. 635; 102 L.T. 520; 26 T.L.R. 409; 54
    S.J. 442 ....8-196, 9-125
Close v Wilson [2011] EWCA Civ 5 ....6-023, 6-098
Clough Mill Ltd v Martin [1985] 1 W.L.R. 111; [1984] 3 All E.R. 982; (1984) 128 S.J. 850
    CA...1-035
Club Speciality (Overseas) Inc v United Marine(1939) Ltd [1971] 1 Lloyd's Rep. 482
    QBD 6-024
Clutterbuck v Coffin (1842) 3 M. & G. 842; 1 Dowl. (N.S.) 479; 4 Scott N.R. 509; 11
    L.J.C.P. 65; 6 Jur. 131...**9-034**
Clydesdale Bank Ltd v Paton [1896] A.C. 381; 65 L.J.P.C. 73; 74 L.T. 738 HL 8-197
CMS Dolphin Ltd v Simonet [2002] B.C.C. 600; [2001] 2 B.C.L.C. 704; [2001] Emp.
    L.R. 895...6-038, 6-042
Co-operative Insurance Society Ltd v Argyll Stores (Holdings) Ltd [1998] A.C. 1; [1997]
    2 W.L.R. 898; [1997] 3 All E.R. 297; [1997] C.L.C. 1114; [1997] 1 E.G.L.R. 52; [1997]
    23 E.G. 141; [1997] E.G.C.S.81; (1997) 94(26) L.S.G. 30; (1997) 147 N.L.J. 845;
    (1997) 141 S.J.L.B. 131; [1997] N.P.C. 79 HL............................7-046
Co-operative Retail Services Ltd v Taff-Ely BC. *See* Attorney General ex rel Cooperative
    Retail Services Ltd v Taff-Ely BC 8-042
Coaks v Boswell (1886) 11 App. Cas. 232 HL 6-070
Coates v Lewes (1808) 1 Camp. 444 8-109
Coates, Son & Co v Pacey 8 T.L.R. 474 3-038
Cobb v Becke (1845) 6 Q.B. 930; 14 L.J.Q.B. 108; 4 L.T. (O.S.) 394; 9 Jur. 439 .....5-012, **5-016**
Cobbetts LLP v Hodge [2009] EWHC 786 (Ch); (2009) 153(17) S.J.L.B. 29 ..6-039, 6-074, 6-080
Cobbs Property Services Ltd v Liddell-Taylor [1990] 1 E.G.L.R. 49 7-030
Cobridge SS Co Ltd v Bucknall SS Lines Ltd (1910) 15 Com.Cas.138 CA 6-010, 6-020
Cochrane v Rymill (1879) 40 L.T. 744; 43 J.P. 572; 27 W.R. 776 ....9-129, **9-131**
Cockburn v Edwards (1880–81) 18 Ch. D. 449; 51 L.J.Ch. 46; 45 L.T. 500; 30 W.R. 446
    CA..6-072
Cocker v Quayle (1830) 1 Russ. & M. 535 6-043
Cockerell v Aucompte (1857) 2 C.B.(N.S.) 440; 26 L.J.C.P. 194; 3 Jur. (N.S.) 844; 5 W.R.
    633...9-087
Cockran v Irlam (1813) 2 M. & S.301 5-002
Cocks v Bruce, Searl and Good; sub nom. Cocks v BSAG (1904) 21 T.L.R. 62; 49 S.J. 69 ...9-003
Coco v AN Clark (Engineers) Ltd [1969] R.P.C. 41; [1968] F.S.R. 415 Ch D 6-077
Coggs v Bernard (1703) 2 Ld. Raym. 909; Com. 133; 1 Salk. 26; 3 Salk. 11; Holt K.B. 13 ...6-031
Cohen v Kittell (1889) 22 Q.B.D. 680; 58 L.J.Q.B. 241; 60 L.T. 932; 53 J.P. 469; 37 W.R.
    400; 5 T.L.R. 345 6-009
Cohen v Kuschke & Co and Koenig (1906) 83 L.T. 102; 16 T.L.R. 489 8-223
Cohen v Paget (1814) 4 Camp. 96 7-004
Coldman v Hill [1919] 1 K.B. 443; 88 L.J.K.B. 491; 120 L.T. 412; 35 T.L.R. 146; 63 S.J.
    166...1-033, 4-006
Coldunell Ltd v Gallon [1986] Q.B. 1184; [1986] 2 W.L.R. 466; [1986] 1 All E.R. 429;
    (1986) 130 S.J. 88; [1986] FLR 183; (1986) 82 L.S.Gaz. 520 CA....................1-027
Cole v North Western Bank (1872) L.R. 10 C.P. 354; 44 L.J.C.P. 233; 32 L.T. 733 ...8-126, 8-144,
    8-145, 8-147
Coleman Taymar Ltd v Oakes [2001] 2 B.C.L.C. 749; (2001) 98(35) L.S.G. 32; (2001)
    145 S.J.L.B. 209 ....6-034, 6-081
Coleman v Bucks and Oxon Union Bank [1897] 2 Ch. 243; 66 L.J.Ch. 564; 76 L.T. 684;
    41 S.J. 491; 45 W.R. 616...9-141, 9-142
Coleman v Mellersh (1850) 2 Mac. & G. 309; L.T. (O.S.) 45 6-098
Coles v Bell (1808) 1 Camp. 478n 2-091
Coles v Enoch [1939] 3 All E.R. 327; 83 S.J. 603 ....**7-032**
Coles v Trecothick (1804) 9 Ves. 234; 1 Smith K.B. 223 ....2-036, 5-002
Colget v Norris (1886) 2 T.L.R. 471 8-217
Collen v Gardner (1856) 21 Beav. 540 ....3-021, 3-028, **3-029**, 8-014
Collen v Wright (1857) 8 E. & B. 647; 27 L.J.Q.B. 215; 30 L.T.(O.S.) 209; 4 Jur. (N.S.)
    357; 6 W.R. 123 ....9-060, 9-061, 9-066, 9-081, 9-083, 9-085, 9-090
Colley v Overseas Exporters [1921] 3 K.B. 302; 90 L.J.K.B. 1301; 126 L.T. 58; 37 T.L.R.
    797; 26 Com. Cas. 325; 8 Ll.L.Rep. 127 7-041
Collie, Re, Ex p. Adamson (1878) 8 Ch.D. 807 ....6-003, 6-043
Collingridge v Gladstone (1890) 7 T.L.R. 60 9-087

Collins v Associated Greyhound Racecourse [1930] 1 Ch. 1; 99 L.J.Ch. 52; 141 L.T. 529;
  45 T.L.R. 519 . . . . 8-079, 8-099
Collins v Brebner [2000] Lloyd's Rep. P.N. 587 CA 6-043
Collins v Brook (1860) 5 H. & N. 700; 29 L.J.Ex. 255; 6 Jur. 999 . . . . 5-012, 5-016
Collins v Hare (1928) 2 Bli. (N.S.) 106; 1 Dow. & Cl. 139 6-062
Collins v Howell-Jones (1980) 259 E.G. 331; [1981] E.G.D. 207 . . . . 3-032, 8-061, 8-217
Collins v Stimson (1882–83) L.R. 11 Q.B.D. 142; 52 L.J.Q.B. 440; 48 L.T. 828; 47 J.P.
  439; 311 W.R. 920 9-026
Collyer v Dudley (1823) T. & R. 421; 2 L.J. (O.S.) Ch. 15 6-090
Colonial Bank v Cady and Williams (1890) 15 App.Cas. 267; 60 L.J.Ch. 131; 63 L.T. 27;
  6 T.L.R. 329; 39 W.R. 17 . . . . 8-020, 8-053, 8-130, 8-161
Colonial Bank v Exchange Banking of Yarmouth Nova Scotia (1885) 11 App.Cas. 84; 55
  L.J.P.C. 14; 54 L.T. 256; 34 W.R. 417 . . . . 9-099, 9-100
Colonial Bank v Hepworth (1887) 36 Ch. D. 36 . . . . 2-014, 6-037
Colyer v Finch; sub nom. Finch v Shaw; Colver v Finch (1856) 5 H.L. Cas. 905; 26
  L.J.Ch. 65; 28 L.T.(O.S.) 27; 3 Jur. (N.S.) 25 8-135
Combe v Lord Swaythling [1947] Ch. 625; [1947] 1 All E.R. 838; [1948] L.J.R. 392; 177
  L.T. 76 Ch D 9-025
Combe's Case (1613) 9 W. Rep. 75a 8-084
Comber v Anderson (1808) 1 Camp. 523 . . . . 3-019, 6-003, 6-010
Comet Group plc v British Sky Broadcasting Ltd Times, April 26, 1991 QBD 10-046
Commercial & Estates Co of Egypt v Board of Trade [1925] 1 K.B. 271; 94 L.J.K.B. 50;
  132 L.T. 516 9-124
Commercial Banking Co of Sydney v Mann [1961] A.C. 1; [1960] 3 W.L.R. 726; [1960] 3
  All E.R. 482; 104 S.J. 846 PC (Aus) 2-083
Commerzbank Aktiengesellschaft v IMB Morgan Plc [2004] EWHC 2771; [2005] 1
  Lloyd's Rep. 298; [2005] 1 P. & C.R. DG17 Ch D 8-167
Commission for the New Towns v Cooper (Great Britain) Ltd (formerly Coopind UK);
  Milton Keynes Development Corp v Cooper (Great Britain) [1995] Ch. 259; [1995] 2
  W.L.R. 677; [1995] 2 All E.R. 929; (1996) 72 P. & C.R. 270; [1995] 2 E.G.L.R. 113;
  [1995] E.G.C.S.30; (1995) 139 S.J.L.B. 87; [1995] N.P.C. 34; (1995) 69 P. & C.R. D40
  CA 8-004
Commission of Crown Lands v Page [1960] 2 Q.B. 274; [1960] 3 W.L.R. 446; [1960] 2
  All E.R. 726; 104 S.J. 642 8-042
Commissioner of Police of the Metropolis v Charles (Derek Michael); sub nom. R. v
  Charles (Derek Michael) [1977] A.C. 177; [1976] 3 W.L.R. 431; [1976] 3 All E.R. 112;
  (1976) 63 Cr. App. R. 252; [1977] Crim. L.R. 615; 120 S.J. 588 HL . . . 6-005, 8-010, 8-028, 9-061
Commissioners for Revenue and Customs v InsuranceWide.com Services Ltd [2010]
  EWCA Civ 422; [2010] S.T.C. 1572; [2011] Lloyd's Rep. I.R. 120; [2010] B.V.C. 606;
  [2010] S.T.I. 1474 1-023
Commissioners of Customs & Excise v Pools Finance Ltd [1952] 1 All E.R. 775 2-033
Commonwealth Oil & Gas Co Ltd v Baxter [2009] CSIH 75; 2010 S.C. 156; 2009 S.L.T.
  1123; 2009 S.C.L.R. 898; 2009 G.W.D. 35-592 8-221
Commonwealth Portland Cement Co Ltd v Weber Lohmann & Co Ltd [1905] A.C. 66; 74
  L.J.P.C. 25; 91 L.T. 813; 53 W.R. 337; 31 T.L.R. 149; 10 Asp.M.L.C. 27 . . . . 6-019, **6-024**
Commonwealth Trust v Akotey [1926] A.C. 72; 94 L.J.P.C. 167; 134 L.T. 33; 41 T.L.R.
  641 8-130
Compania Financiera Soleada SA v Hamoor Tanker Corp Inc; The Borag [1981] 1 W.L.R.
  274; [1981] 1 All E.R. 856; [1981] 1 Lloyd's Rep. 483; [1981] Com. L.R. 29; 125 S.J.
  185 CA 6-035, 6-043, 7-076
Compania Naviera Vasconzada v Churchill & Sim [1906] 1 K.B. 237; 75 L.J.K.B. 94; 94
  L.T. 59; 54 W.R. 406; 22 T.L.R. 85; 50 S.J. 76; 10 Asp.M.L.C. 177; 11 Com.Cas. 49 8-044
Competitive Insurance Co Ltd v Davis Investments Ltd [1975] 1 W.L.R. 1240; [1975] 3
  All E.R. 354; 119 S.J. 559 Ch D 9-142
Computastaff Ltd v Ingledew Brown Bennison & Garrett (1989) 268 E.G. 906 9-117
Concordia Chemische Fabrik Auf Actien v Squire (1876) 34 L.T. 824 9-037
Concourse Initiatives Ltd v Maiden Outdoor Advertising Ltd [2005] EWHC 2995 QBD
  (Comm) 10-042
Condliffe v Sheingold [2007] EWCA Civ 1043 6-043
Condy v Blaiberg (1891) 55 J.P. 580; 7 T.L.R. 424 8-196
Connell Estate Agents v Begej [1993] 39 E.G. 125; [1993] 2 E.G.L.R. 35; [1993] N.P.C.
  47 CA 7-030, 7-056
Connolly v Brown [2006] CSOH 187; 2007 S.L.T. 778; 2007 G.W.D. 9-155, OH 6-067

Connolly-Martin v Davis; sub nom. Connolly-Martin v D [1999] Lloyd's Rep. P.N. 790;
   [1999] P.N.L.R. 826; (1999) 96(23) L.S.G. 35 CA....................................9-117
Conservative and Unionist Central Office v Burrell [1982] 1 W.L.R. 522; [1982] 2 All
   E.R. 1; [1985] 55 T.C. 671; [1982] S.T.C. 317; [1981] T.R. 543 CA....................1-027
Consolidated Co v Curtis & Son [1892] 1 Q.B. 495; 61 L.J.Q.B. 325; 56 J.P. 565; 8 T.L.R.
   403; 36 S.J. 328; 36 S.J. 328; 40 W.R. 426 ....9-128, 9-129, **9-131**
Consolidated Finance Ltd v Collins [2013] EWCA Civ 475; [2013] E.C.C. 21; [2013]
   B.P.I.R. 543; [2013] C.T.L.C. 121 6-056
Consolidated Gold Fields of South Africa v E. Spiegel & Co (1909) 100 L.T. 351; 25
   T.L.R. 275; 53 S.J. 245; 14 Com.Cas. 61 3-040
Consort Deep Level Gold Mines Ltd, Re; Ex p. Stark [1897] 1 Ch. 575; 66 L.J.Ch. 297;
   76 L.T. 300; 45 W.R. 420; 13 T.L.R. 265 10-014
Const v Harris 37 E.R. 1191; (1824) Turn. & R. 496 1-028
Contex Drouzhba Ltd v Wiseman [2007] EWCA Civ 1201; [2008] B.C.C. 301; [2008] 1
   B.C.L.C. 631; (2007) 157 N.L.J. 1695 ....8-198, 9-118
Continental Caoutchouc & Gutta Percha Co v Kleinwort & Sons & Co (1904) 90 L.T.
   474; 52 W.R. 489; 20 T.L.R. 403; 48 S.J. 383; 9 Com.Cas. 240..............9-104, 9-106
Conway v Wimpey (George) & Co (No.2) [1951] 2 K.B. 266; [1951] 1 T.L.R. 587; [1951]
   1 All E.R. 363; 95 S.J. 156 CA..**8-193**
Cook v Addison (1869) L.R. 7 Eq. 466; 38 L.J.Ch. 322; 20 L.T. 212; 17 W.R. 480 6-040
Cook v Deeks [1916] 1 A.C. 554; 85 L.J.P.C. 161; 114 L.T. 636 ....6-039, 6-080, 6-081, **6-083**
Cook v Lister (1863) 13 C.B. N.S.543 10-013
Cook v Williams (1897) 14 T.L.R. 31 9-070
Cooke & Sons v Eshelby (1887) 12 App.Cas. 271; 56 L.J.Q.B. 505; 56 L.T. 673; 35 W.R.
   629; 3 T.L.R. 481.................8-054, 8-069, 8-073, 8-109, 8-110, 8-111, **8-112**, 9-016
Cooke v Hopper [2012] EWCA Civ 175 7-012
Cooke v Wilson (1856) 1 C.B.(N.S.) 153; 26 L.J.C.P. 15; 28 L.T.(O.S.) 103; 2 Jur. (N.S.)
   1094; 5 W.R. 24...**9-035**, 9-038
Cooker v Child; sub nom. Coker v Child (1673) 2 Lev. 74; 3 Keb. 115 8-084
Coomber, Re; Coomber v Coomber [1911] 1 Ch. 723; 80 L.J.Ch. 399; 104 L.T. 517 CA 6-037
Cooper (Brian) & Co v Fairview Estates (Investments) Ltd [1987] 1 E.G.L.R. 18; (1987)
   282 E.G. 1131 CA.....................................7-021, 7-028, 7-030, 7-032
Cooper v De Tastet (1829) Tamlyn 177 6-110
Cooper v PRG Powerhouse Ltd [2008] EWHC 498 (Ch); [2008] 2 All E.R. (Comm) 964;
   [2008] B.C.C. 588; [2008] B.P.I.R. 492; [2008] 2 P. & C.R. DG4.....................6-041
Cooper v Pure Fishing (UK) Ltd (formerly Outdoor Technology Group (UK) Ltd) [2004]
   EWCA Civ 375; [2004] 2 Lloyd's Rep. 518; [2004] 2 C.L.C. 412; [2005] E.C.C. 6;
   [2004] Eu. L.R. 664 CA..11-043, 11-056
Cooper v Stoneham [1893] 68 L.T. 18 9-140
Cooper v Strauss & Co (1898) 14 T.L.R. 233 8-111
Coore v Callaway (1794) 1 Esp. 115 2-091
Cooter & Green Ltd v Tyrrell [1962] 2 Lloyd's Rep. 377 CA 2-034
Copland v Stein (1799) 8 T.R. 199 7-079
Copp v Lynch (1882) 26 S.J. 348 6-089
Coral (UK) Ltd v Rechtman and Altro Mozart Food Handels GmbH [1996] 1 Lloyd's Rep.
   235 QBD (Comm Ct) 9-085, 9-086
Coral Rose, The (No.1). See Atlas Maritime Co SA v Avalon Maritime Ltd; The Coral
   Rose (No.1) 1-012, 1-030, 1-037, 8-071
Corbin v Stewart (1911) 28 T.L.R. 99 7-004
Corfield v Grant 59 B.L.R. 102; 29 Con. L.R. 58; [1992] E.G.C.S.36 QBD 9-013
Corlett v Gordon (1813) 3 Camp. 472 ....**6-007**
Cornfoot v Fowke (1840) 6 M. & W. 358; 9 L.J.Ex. 297; 4 Jur. 919 ....8-185, 9-120
Cornford v Carlton Bank [1899] 1 Q.B. 392; 68 L.J.Q.B. 196; 80 L.T. 121; 15 T.L.R. 156 ...8-189
Cornhill Management Ltd v Commission of Customs and Excise [1991] 1 VATTR 1 1-036
Cornish v Abington (1859) 4 H. & N. 549; 28 L.J.Ex. 262; 7 W.R. 504 8-024
Cornwal v Wilson (1750) 1 Ves. 510 ....**2-083**, **2-100**
Corona Energy Unreported 1977 7-084
Corporacion Nacional del Cobre de Chile v Sogemin Metals Ltd [1997] 1 W.L.R. 1396;
   [1997] 2 All E.R. 917; [1997] C.L.C. 435; (1996) 93(46) L.S.G. 29; (1997) 167 N.L.J.
   161 Ch D 6-043, 9-135
Corporation Agencies Ltd v Home Bank of Canada [1927] A.C. 318 PC (Canada) 3-029
Cortis v Kent Waterworks Co (1827) 7 B. & C. 314; 5 L.J.(O.S.) M.C. 106 2-043
Cory (W) & Son Ltd v Lambton and Hetton Collieries (1916) 86 L.J.K.B. 401 ......7-058, 7-060,

7-066, 7-068

Cory Brothers Shipping Ltd v Baldan Ltd [1997] 2 Lloyd's Rep. 58, CC (Central London) . . 9-016, 9-024

Cothay v Fennell (1830) 10 B. & C. 671; 8 L.J. (O.S.) K.B. 302 8-082

Cotronic (UK) Ltd v Dezonie [1991] B.C.L.C. 721 9-086

Cotter v Bank of England (1833) 3 Moo. & S. 180; 2 Dowl. 728; 2 L.J.C.P. 158 7-103

Cottey v National Provincial Bank Ltd (1904) 20 T.L.R. 607; 48 S.J. 589 8-135

Cotton, Re; Ex p. Cooke (1913) 103 L.T. 310; 57 S.J. 343 . . . . 6-041, 8-167

Coughlan (JJ) Ltd v Ruparelia [2003] EWCA Civ 1057; [2004] P.N.L.R. 4; (2003) 100(37) L.S.G. 34; (2003) 147 S.J.L.B. 905 CA 8-178

Coulthard v Disco Mix Club Ltd [2000] 1 W.L.R. 707; [1999] 2 All E.R. 457; [1999] E.M.L.R. 434; [1999] F.S.R. 900; Ch D 6-043

Coulthart v Clementson (1879) 5 Q.B.D. 42 10-016

Coulthurst v Sweet (1866) L.R. 1 C.P. 649 . . . . 8-174, **8-175**

County Homesearch Co (Thames & Chilterns) Ltd v Cowham [2008] EWCA Civ 26; [2008] 1 W.L.R. 909; [2008] 1 E.G.L.R. 24; [2008] 15 E.G. 178; [2008] N.P.C. 10 7-028

Coupe v Collyer (1890) 62 L.T. 927 3-026

Coupers Partnership Ltd v Basarik (t/a Uppers Bistro) [2007] EWCA Civ 40; [2007] R.V.R. 116; [2007] 6 E.G. 164 (C.S.); (2007) 151 S.J.L.B. 195 . . . . 7-014, 7-041

Courtauld v Saunders (1867) 16 L.T. 562; 15 W.R. 906 9-056

Courtney & Fairbairn Ltd v Tolaini Brothers (Hotels) Ltd; Courtney & Fairburn v Tolaini Bros (Hotels) [1975] 1 W.L.R. 297; [1975] 1 All E.R. 716; 2 B.L.R. 97; (1974) 119 S.J. 134 CA 7-009

Cousins v International Brick Co Ltd [1931] 2 Ch. 90 . . . . **3-009**, 10-027

Cousins, Re (1886) 31 Ch.D. 671; 55 L.J.Ch. 662; 54 L.T. 376; 34 W.R. 393 8-216

Coutts & Co v Irish Exhibition in London (1891) 7 T.L.R. 313 9-087

Couturier v Hastie (1852) 8 Exch. 40; 22 L.J.Ex. 97 1-042

Coventry v Lawrence (No.2) [2014] UKSC 46; [2015] A.C. 106; [2014] 3 W.L.R. 555; [2014] 4 All E.R. 517; [2014] P.T.S.R. 1014; [2014] 5 Costs L.O. 759; [2014] H.L.R. 42; [2014] 2 P. & C.R. 19; [2015] L. & T.R. 2; [2014] 3 E.G.L.R. 71 9-120

Coventry, Sheppard & Co v GE Railway Co (1883) 11 Q.B.D. 776 8-173

Cowan de Groot Properties Ltd v Eagle Trust plc [1992] 4 All E.R. 700; [1991] B.C.L.C. 1045 . . . . 6-047, 9-136

Cowdry v Day (1859) 1 Giff. 316; 29 L.J.Ch. 39; 1 L.T. 88; 5 Jur. (N.S.) 1199; 8 W.R. 55 . . . **6-072**

Cowell v Simpson (1809) 16 Ves. 275 . . . . **7-094**

Cowern v Neild [1912] 2 K.B. 419; [1911–13] All E.R.Rep. 425; 81 L.J.K.B. 865; 106 L.T. 984; 28 T.L.R. 423; 56 S.J. 552 2-015

Cowie v Witt (1874) 23 W.R. 76 9-040

Cox v Midland Railway Co (1849) 3 Exch. 268; 5 Ry. & CoCas.583; 18 L.J.Ex. 65; 12 L.J.(O.S.) 403; 12 Jur. 65; 12 J.P.J. 820 . . . . **3-029**

Cox v Ministry of Justice [2016] UKSC 10; [2016] A.C. 660; [2016] 2 W.L.R. 806; [2016] I.R.L.R. 370 . . . . 8-178, 8-190

Cox v Prentice (1815) 3 M. & S. 344 9-106

Cox v Sorrell [1960] 1 Lloyd's Rep. 471 9-020

Cox, Patterson & Co v Bruce & Co (1886) 18 Q.B.D. 147; 56 L.J.Q.B. 121; 57 L.T. 128; 35 W.R. 207; 3 T.L.R. 167; 6 Asp.M.L.C. 152 . . . . **8-067**

Crabb v Arun DC [1976] Ch. 179; [1975] 3 W.L.R. 847; [1975] 3 All E.R. 865; (1976) 32 P. & C.R. 70; 119 S.J. 711 CA 8-015

Craddock v Rogers (1884) 53 L.J.Ch. 968 6-072

Cradock v Piper (1846) 15 Sim. 301 7-006

Craig & Co v Blackater 1923 S.C. 472 9-013

Cramaso LLP v Viscount Reidhaven's Trustees [2014] UKSC 9; [2014] A.C. 1093; [2014] 2 W.L.R. 317; [2014] 2 All E.R. 270; [2014] 1 All E.R. (Comm) 830; 2014 S.C. (U.K.S.C.) 121; 2014 S.L.T. 521; 2014 S.C.L.R. 484; (2014) 158(7) S.J.L.B. 37 . . . . . 8-025, 8-098, 8-183

Cramb v Goodwin (1919) 35 T.L.R. 477; 63 S.J. 496 7-042

Crane v Sky In-Home Service Ltd [2007] EWHC 66 (Ch); [2007] 2 All E.R. (Comm) 599; [2007] 1 C.L.C. 389; [2007] E.C.C. 25; [2007] Eu. L.R. 549; [2007] Bus. L.R. D47; further proceedings [2008] EWCA Civ 978 . . . . 6-006, 11-013, 11-020, 11-022, 11-024, 11-056

Cranleigh Precision Engineering Ltd v Bryant [1965] 1 W.L.R. 1293; [1964] 3 All E.R. 289; 109 S.J. 830; [1966] R.P.C. 81 QBD 6-077, 7-047

Craven-Ellis v Canons Ltd [1936] 2 K.B. 403; 105 L.J.K.B. 767; 155 L.T. 376; 52 T.L.R. 657; [1936] 2 All E.R. 1066; 80 S.J. 652 . . . . 7-009, 7-060

Crawshay v Homfray (1820) 4 B. & Ald. 50 7-076
Crédit Agricole Corp and Investment Bank v Papadimitriou [2015] UKPC 13; [2015] 1
    W.L.R. 4265; [2015] 2 All E.R. 974; [2015] 2 All E.R. (Comm) 646; [2015] Lloyd's
    Rep. F.C. 301; [2016] W.T.L.R. 109; [2015] 2 P. & C.R. DG7 .... 3-011, 8-162, 9-136
Credit Agricole Indosuez v Muslim Commercial Bank Ltd [2000] 1 All E.R. (Comm) 172;
    [2000] 1 Lloyd's Rep. 275; [2000] Lloyd's Rep. Bank. 1; [2000] C.L.C. 437 CA 2-034
Credit Lyonnais Bank Nederland NV (now Generale Bank Nederland NV) v Export
    Credits Guarantee Department; sub nom. Generale Bank Nederland NV (formerly
    Credit Lyonnais Bank Nederland NV) v Export Credits Guarantee Department [2000] 1
    A.C. 486; [1999] 2 W.L.R. 540; [1999] 1 All E.R. 929; [1999] 1 Lloyd's Rep. 563;
    [1999] C.L.C. 823; (1999) 96(10) L.S.G. 30; (1999) 143 S.J.L.B. 89 HL 8-185, 9-121
Credit Suisse International v Stichting Vestia Groep [2014] EWHC 3103 (Comm); [2015]
    Bus. L.R. D5 .... 12-017, 12-020
Creggy v Barnett [2016] EWCA Civ 1004; [2017] 2 W.L.R. 1054 6-043
Crema v Cenkos Securities Plc [2010] EWCA Civ 1444; [2011] Bus. L.R. 943; [2010] 2
    C.L.C. 963; [2011] C.I.L.L. 2980 .... 7-017, 7022, 7-032
Crest Nicholson (Londinium) Ltd v Akaria Investments Ltd [2010] EWHC 243 (Ch) 2-077
Criterion Properties Plc v Stratford UK Properties LLC [2004] UKHL 28; [2004] 1
    W.L.R. 1846; [2004] B.C.C. 570; (2004) 101(26) L.S.G. 27; (2004) 148 S.J.L.B. 760;
    [2004] N.P.C. 96 HL.. 3-011, 8-220, 8-225
CRJ Services Ltd v Lanstar Ltd (t/a CSG Lanstar) [2011] EWHC 972 (TCC) 8-044
Crocker Hurlock Ltd v Lang (B) & Co Ltd [1949] 1 All E.R. 526; [1949] W.N. 97 7-042
Crocs Europe BV v Anderson (t/a Spectrum Agencies (A Partnership)) [2012] EWCA Civ
    1400; [2013] 1 Lloyd's Rep. 1; [2013] E.C.C. 1............................ 7-050, 11-039
Cropper v Cook (1868) L.R. 3 C.P. 194; 17 L.T. 603; 16 W.R. 596 ..... **3-040**, 6-100, **7-062**, 9-016
Cross & Co v Matthews and Wallace (1904) 91 L.T. 500; 20 T.L.R. 603 .... 8-117, 8-118
Cross v Williams (1862) 31 L.J.Ex. 145; 6 L.T. 434; 26 J.P. 423; 10 W.R. 302; 158 E.R.
    641... 9-087
Crossco No.4 Unlimited v Jolan Ltd [2011] EWCA Civ 1619; [2012] 2 All E.R. 754;
    [2012] 1 P. & C.R. 16; [2012] 1 E.G.L.R. 137; 14 I.T.E.L.R. 61 .... 8-209, 8-215
Crossley v Magniac [1893] 1 Ch. 594; 67 L.T. 798; 41 W.R. 598; 9 T.L.R. 126; 3 R. 202 3-026
Crowe v Ballard (1790) 2 Cox. Eq.Cas. 253; 3 Bro.C.C. 117; 1 Ves. 215 .... 6-068, 6-070
Crowfoot v Gurney (1832) 9 Bing. 372; 2 Moo. A.S.473; 2 L.J.C.P. 21 .... **9-113, 9-114**
Crowson Fabrics Ltd v Rider [2007] EWHC 2942 (Ch); [2008] I.R.L.R. 288; [2008]
    F.S.R. 17 .... 6-078, 6-083
Crowson v HSBC Insurance Brokers Ltd Unreported, January 26, 2010, Ch.D 9-117
Cunliffe-Owen v Teather & Greenwood; Cunliffe Owen v Schaverien Habermann, Simon
    & Co; Cunliffe Owen v LA Seligmann & Co [1967] 1 W.L.R. 1421; [1967] 3 All E.R.
    561; 111 S.J. 866 Ch D 3-034, 3-035, 3-036, 6-009, 8-006
Cunliffe, Brooks & Co v Blackburn and District Benefit Building Society (1884) 9
    App.Cas. 857; 54 L.J.Ch. 376; 52 L.T. 225; 33 W.R. 309 .... **7-089**
Cunningham v Collier [1785] 4 Doug. 233; 99 E.R. 857 9-034
Cureton v Mark Insulations Ltd [2006] EWHC 2279 (Admin) 11-056
Curlewis v Birkbeck (1863) 3 F. & F. 894 .... 8-061, 8-109, 8-112, 10-030, 10-031
Curtis v Barclay (1826) 5 B. & C. 141; 7 Dow. & Ry. K.B. 539; 4 L.J.(O.S.) K.B. 82 . 6-100, **7-062**
Curtis v Nixon (1871) 24 L.T. 706 .... 7-030, **7-032**
Curtis v Pulbrook [2009] EWHC 782 (Ch) 6-039
Curtis v Williamson (1874) L.R. 10 Q.B. 57; 44 L.J.Q.B. 27; 31 L.T. 678; 23 W.R. 236 .... **8-082**,
                                                            8-104, 8-119, 8-121, **8-124**
Curwen v Milburn (1889) 42 Ch.D. 432 7-090
Customs and Excise Commissioners v Barclays Bank Plc [2006] UKHL 28; [2007] 1 A.C.
    181; [2006] 3 W.L.R. 1; [2006] 4 All E.R. 256; [2006] 2 All E.R. (Comm) 831; [2006] 2
    Lloyd's Rep. 327; [2006] 1 C.L.C. 1096; (2006) 103(27) L.S.G. 33; (2006) 156 N.L.J.
    1060; (2006) 150 S.J.L.B. 859 .... 6-029, 8-180, 8-183, 9-117
Customs and Excise Commissioners v Johnson [1980] S.T.C. 624 .... 1-002, 1-036
Customs and Excise Commissioners v Music & Video Exchange Ltd; Music & Video
    Exchange Ltd v Customs and Excise Commissioners [1992] S.T.C. 220, DC............. 1-036
Customs and Excise Commissioners v National Westminster Bank Plc (Authorisation:
    Mistake) [2002] EWHC 2204 (Ch); [2003] 1 All E.R. (Comm) 327; (2002) 99(48)
    L.S.G. 27.. 9-100
Customs and Excise Commissioners v Paget [1989] S.T.C. 773, DC 1-036
Cuthbert v Robarts, Lubbock & Co [1909] 2 Ch. 226; 78 L.J.Ch. 529; 100 L.T. 796; 25
    T.L.R. 583; 53 S.J. 559 7-087

Cutts v Salmon (1852) 21 L.J.Ch. 750; 19 L.T.(O.S.) 53; 16 Jur. 623 6-064
Cyril Lord (Carpet Sales) v Browne (1966) 111 S.J. CA 8-117, 8-118
Czarnikow (C) v Koufos. *See* Koufos v Czarnikow (C) 9-077
D'Angibau, Re; Andrews v Andrews (1880) 15 Ch.D. 236 2-012
D&C Builders v Rees [1986] 2 Q.B. 617; [1966] 2 W.L.R. 288; [1965] 3 All E.R. 837; 109
   S.J. 971; [1965] C.L.Y. 1486 CA 3-025
D&D Wines International Ltd (In Liquidation), Re [2014] EWCA Civ 215; [2015] 1 All
   E.R. (Comm) 36; [2014] 2 B.C.L.C. 129; [2014] B.P.I.R. 902. 10-011
Dadswell v Jacobs (1887) 34 Ch.D. 278; 56 L.J.Ch. 857; 35 W.R. 261 6-090
Dails v Lloyd (1848) 12 Q.B. 531; 17 L.J.Q.B. 247; 5 Ry. & Can.Cas. 572; 11 L.T.(O.S.)
   327; 12 Jur. 827. 6-097
Daimler Co Ltd v Continental Tyre & Rubber Co (Great Britain) Ltd; Continental Tyre &
   Rubber Co (Great Britain) Ltd v Daimler Co Ltd; Continental Tyre & Rubber Co (Great
   Britain) Ltd v Thomas Tilling Ltd [1916] 2 A.C. 307; 85 L.J.K.B. 1333; 114 L.T. 1049;
   32 T.L.R. 624; 60 S.J. 602; 22 Com.Cas.32 . . . . 3-029, 10-003
Dalby v Pullen (1830) 1 Russ. & M. 296 . . . . **2-034**
Dale & Co Ex p. *See* West of England & South Wales District Bank Ex p. 6-041
Dale v Humfrey (1858) E.B. & E. 1004 8-003
Dale v Humfrey sub nom. Humphrey v Dale & Morgan (1858) E.B. & E. 1004; 6 W.R.
   854; 120 E.R. 783; 27 L.J.Q.B. 390; 31 L.T.(O.S.) 328; 5 Jur. (N.S.) 191 . . . . . 9-016, 9-041, 9-042
Dale v Sollet (1767) 4 Burr. 2133 . . . . 6-097, 6-100
Dally v Wonham (1863) 33 Beav. 154; 32 L.J.Ch. 790; 9 L.T. 75; 9 Jur. (N.S.) 980; 11
   W.R. 1000 . . . . 6-064, 6-070
Daly v Lime Street Underwriting Agencies Ltd [1987] 2 F.T.L.R. 277 . . . . 10-010, 10-011
Dampskibsselskab Halla v Catsell & Co (1928) 30 Ll.L.Rep. 284 . . . . 6-019, 6-021
Danby v Coutts & Co (1885) 29 Ch.D. 500; 54 L.J.Ch. 577; 52 L.T. 401; 33 W.R. 559; 1
   T.L.R. 313 . . . . **3-015**, 10-002
Daniel v Adams (1764) Ambl. 495; 27 E.R. 322 . . . . **3-032**
Daniell v Sinclair (1881) 6 App.Cas.181; 50 L.J.P.C. 50; 44 L.T. 257; 29 W.R. 569 6-098
Daniels v Trefusis [1914] 1 Ch. 788; 83 L.J.Ch. 579; 58 S.J. 271; 109 L.J. 922 2-019
Danish Mercantile Co v Beaumont [1951] Ch. 680; [1951] 1 All E.R. 925; 95 S.J. 300 CA . . 2-059,
                                                                                       2-061, 2-091
Danziger v Thompson [1944] K.B. 654; 113 L.J.K.B. 539; 170 L.T. 424; 60 T.L.R. 425;
   [1944] 2 All E.R. 151; 88 S.J. 247 . . . . 8-074, 8-078, **8-082**
Darlington BC v Wiltshier Northern Ltd [1995] 1 W.L.R. 68; [1995] 3 All E.R. 895; 69
   B.L.R. 1; (1995) 11 Const. L.J. 36; (1994) 91(37) L.S.G. 49; (1994) 138 S.J.L.B. 161
   CA 9-013
Dashwood (formerly Kaye) v Fleurets Ltd [2007] EWHC 1610 (QB); [2007] 2 E.G.L.R.
   7; [2007] 34 E.G. 84; [2007] 28 E.G. 120 (C.S.) 7-028, 7-032
Daulia Ltd v Four Millbank Nominees Ltd [1978] Ch. 231; [1978] 2 W.L.R. 621; [1978] 2
   All E.R. 557; 121 S.J. 851; (1977) 36 P. & C.R. 244 CA 7-039, 10-043
Daun v Simmins (1879) 41 L.T. 783; 44 J.P. 264; 28 W.R. 129 . . . . **8-067**, 8-077
Davenport v Whitmore (1836) 2 My. & Cr. 177; Donnelly 166; 6 L.J.Ch. 58 6-100
David Moore Builders Ltd v Preddy Unreported October 24, 1995 CA 9-006
Davies v Barnes Webster & Sons Ltd [2011] EWHC 2560 (Ch); [2012] B.P.I.R. 97 9-087
Davies v Collins [1945] 1 All E.R. 247; 114 L.J.K.B. 199; 172 L.T. 155; 61 T.L.R. 218; 89
   S.J. 152 2-019
Davies v Jenkins (1843) 11 M. & W. 745; 1 D. & L. 321; 1 L.T.(O.S.) 290; 7 Jur. 801 . . . . . **9-125**
Davies v Sweet [1962] 2 Q.B. 300; [1962] 2 W.L.R. 525; [1962] 1 All E.R. 92; 105 S.J.
   1083 CA 8-003
Davis (B.) Ltd v Tooth & Co Ltd [1937] 4 All E.R. 118; 81 S.J. 881 . . . . 1-035, 6-015
Davis (Godfrey) Ltd v Culling & Hecht [1962] 2 Lloyd's Rep. 349; 106 S.J. 918 CA 2-034
Davis v Anthony unreported 5 July 1995 CA 2-018
Davis v Artingstall (1880) 49 L.J.Ch. 609; 42 L.T. 507; 29 W.R. 137 . . . . **9-131**
Davis v Bowsher (1794) 5 T.R. 488 7-086
Davis v James (1770) 5 Burr. 2680; 98 E.R. 407 9-010
Davis v Trollope & Sons [1943] 1 All E.R. 501 7-030
Davis, Re; Davis v Davis [1902] 2 Ch. 314; 71 L.J.Ch. 539; 86 L.T. 523; 51 W.R. 8 6-103
Davison v Donaldson (1882) 9 Q.B.D. 623; 47 L.T. 564; 31 W.R. 277; 4 Asp.M.L.C. 601 . . . 8-101,
                                                                                8-103, 8-104, 8-105, **8-106**, 8-119
Davisons Solicitors (a firm) v Nationwide Building Society [2012] EWCA Civ 1626 6-003
Davy v Waller (1899) 81 L.T. 107 . . . . **8-045**, 8-126

Davys v Richardson (1888) 21 Q.B.D. 202; 57 L.J.Q.B. 409; 59 L.T. 765; 4 T.L.R. 608; 36
  W.R. 728 9-106
Dawson (Ship Stores) v Atlantica Co Ltd (1931) 40 Ll.Rep. 63 . . . . 8-120, 9-038
Dawson Line Ltd v Aktiengesellschaft f,r Chemische Industrie of Berlin [1932] 1 K.B.
  433; [1931] All E.R.Rep. 546; 101 L.J.K.B. 57; 146 L.T. 187; 37 Com.Cas. 28 3-032
Day v Day [2013] EWCA Civ 280; [2014] Ch. 114; [2013] 3 W.L.R. 556; [2013] 3 All
  E.R. 661; [2013] W.T.L.R. 817; [2013] 2 P. & C.R. DG1 . . . . 2-009, 3-019, 6-009
Day v Harris [2013] EWCA Civ 191; [2014] Ch. 211; [2013] 3 W.L.R. 1560; [2013]
  W.T.L.R. 591; 16 I.T.E.L.R. 111; (2013) 157(12) S.J.L.B. 35 3-014
Day v Harris. *See* Day v Royal College of Music 10-009
Day v Royal College of Music [2013] EWCA Civ 191; [2014] Ch. 211; [2013] 3 W.L.R.
  1560; [2013] W.T.L.R. 591; 16 I.T.E.L.R. 111; (2013) 157(12) S.J.L.B. 35 10-009
De Bussche v Alt (1878) 8 Ch.D. 286; 47 L.J.Ch. 381; 38 L.T. 370; 3 Asp.M.L.C. 584 2-048,
              4-007, 5-001, 5-002, **5-007**, 5-008, 5-010, 5-012, **5-016**, **6-061**, 6-064, 6-068
De Comas v Prost (1865) 3 Moo.P.C.(N.S.) 158; 12 L.T. 682; 11 Jur. (N.S.) 417; 13 W.R.
  595. 10-014
De Franco v Commissioner of Police for the Metropolis *Times,* May 8, 1987 6-111
De Gorter v Attenborough & Son (1904) 21 T.L.R. 19 . . . . 8-063, 8-153
De Mattos v Benjamin (1894) 63 L.J.Q.B. 248; 70 L.T. 560; 10 T.L.R. 221; 42 W.R. 284;
  38 S.J. 238; 10 R. 103 . . . . 6-023, 6-100
De Montmorency v Devereux (1840) 7 C. & F. 188; West 64; 1 Dr. & Wal. 119; 2 Dr. &
  Wal. 410; 4 Jur. 403 6-068
De Tchihatchef v Salerni Coupling Ltd [1932] 1 Ch. 330; 101 L.J.Ch. 209; 146 L.T. 505 8-020,
                                                                                           8-022
Dean v Allin & Watts [2001] EWCA Civ 758; [2001] 2 Lloyd's Rep. 249 CA . 6-019, 8-182, 9-117,
                                                                                       9-125
Debenham Tewson & Chinnocks v Rimington [1990] 2 E.G.L.R. 21; [1990] 34 E.G. 55
  CA. 7-012
Debenham v King's College Cambridge (1884) 1 Cab. & El. 438; 1 T.L.R. 170 7-005
Debenham v Mellon (1880) 6 App.Cas. 24; 50 L.J.Q.B. 155; 43 L.T. 673; 29 W.R. 141; 45
  J.P. 252 . . . . 3-044, **8-045**, 10-030
Debenhams Ltd v Perkins (1925) 133 L.T. 252 8-117
Debs v Sibec Developments Ltd [1990] R.T.R. 91 8-133
Debtor, Re A (No.229 of 1927) [1927] 2 Ch. 367; 96 L.J.Ch. 381; 137 L.T. 507; [1927] B.
  & C.R. 127 CA 2-013, 6-048, 6-086, 8-223
Decro-Wall International SA v Practitioners in Marketing Ltd; sub nom. Decro-Wall
  International SA v Practitioners in Marketing [1971] 1 W.L.R. 361; [1971] 2 All E.R.
  216; (1970) 115 S.J. 171 CA 6-001, 7-046, 7-047, 10-025, 10-042
Dee Estates Ltd, Re; Wright v Dee Estates Ltd [1911] 2 Ch. 85; 80 L.J.Ch. 461; 104 L.T.
  903; 55 S.J. 424; 18 Mans. 247. 7-089
Dellafiora v Lester; Lester v Barr (Adrian) & Co [1962] 1 W.L.R. 1208; [1962] 3 All E.R.
  393; 106 S.J. 570 CA 7-019
Demco Investment and Commercial SA v Interamerican Life Assurance (International)
  Ltd [2012] EWHC 2053 (Comm). 2-059
Demerara Bauxite Co v Hubbard [1923] A.C. 673; 92 L.J.P.C. 148; 129 L.T. 517 . . . . 6-062, 6-064,
                                                                                            6-067
Denew v Daverell (1813) 3 Camp. 451 . . . . 7-050, **7-051**
Denham & Co, Re (1883) 25 Ch.D. 752; 50 L.T. 523; 32 W.R. 487 . . . . 2-020, 9-133
Denham v Midland Employers Mutual Ass. Ltd [1955] 2 Q.B. 437; [1955] 3 W.L.R. 84;
  [1955] 2 All E.R. 561; 99 S.J. 417; [1955] 1 Lloyd's Rep. 467 CA. 8-179
Denmark Productions Ltd v Boscobel Productions Ltd [1969] 1 Q.B. 699; [1968] 3
  W.L.R. 841; [1968] 3 All E.R. 513 CA 7-046, 7-047
Dennard v PricewaterhouseCoopers LLP [2010] EWCA Civ 1437 6-047
Dennis (AR) & Co v Campbell [1978] Q.B. 365; [1978] 2 W.L.R. 429; [1978] I.C.R. 862;
  [1978] 1 All E.R. 1215; (1977) 121 S.J. 790 CA 6-100
Dennison v Jeffs [1896] 1 Ch. 611; 65 L.J.Ch. 435; 74 L.T. 270; 44 W.R. 476; 40 S.J. 335;
  12 T.L.R. 251 2-036
Derry v Peek (1889) 14 App.Cas. 337; 58 L.J.Ch. 864; 61 L.T. 265; 5 T.L.R. 625; 38 W.R.
  33; 54 J.P. 148; 1 Meg. 292 HL 8-185
Deslandes v Gregory (1860) 30 L.J.Q.B. 36; 2 E. & E. 610; 2 L.T. 634; 6 Jur. (N.S.) 651;
  8 W.R. 585. . . . . **9-038**
Det Danske Hedelskabet v KDM International Plc [1994] 2 Lloyd's Rep. 534 QBD
  (Comm Ct) 8-213

Deutsche Bank AG v Asia Pacific Broadband Wireless Communications Inc [2008]
    EWCA Civ 1091; [2009] 2 All E.R. (Comm) 129; [2008] 2 Lloyd's Rep. 619; [2008] 2
    C.L.C. 520; [2009] I.L.Pr. 36 . . . . 3-012, 8-021, 8-039
Deutsche Ruckversicherung Aktiengesellschaft v Walbrook Ins Co Ltd. *See* Group Josi Re
    Co SA v Walbrook Insurance Co Ltd 1-029, 8-212, 8-214
Deverell v Lord Bolton (1812) 18 Ves. 505 2-036
Dey v Pullinger Engineering Co [1921] 1 K.B. 77; 89 L.J.K.B. 1229; 124 L.T. 534; 37
    T.L.R. 10 . . . . **3-029**
Diamantis v JP Morgan Chase Bank [2005] EWCA 1612 1-030
Diamond v Bank of London and Montreal Ltd [1979] Q.B. 333; [1979] 2 W.L.R. 228;
    [1979] 1 All E.R. 561; (1978) 122 S.J. 814; [1979] 1 Lloyd's Rep. 335 CA 8-198
Dibbens (E) & Sons (In Liquidation), Re [1990] B.C.L.C. 577 Ch D 9-011
Dibbins v Dibbins [1896] 2 Ch. 348; 65 L.J.Ch. 724; 75 L.T. 137; 44 W.R. 595; 40 S.J.
    599 . . . . 2-065, **2-094**
Dicas v Stockley (1836) 7 C. & P. 5 & 7 . . . . 7-073, 7-093, **7-099**
Dickinson v Lilwall (1815) 4 Camp. 279; 1 Stark. 128 . . . . **10-005**
Dickinson v Naul (1833) 4 B. & Ad. 638; 1 N. & M.K.B. 721 . . . . 9-029, **9-035**
Dickinson v Valpy (1829) 10 B. & C. 128; L. & W. 6; 5 Man. & Ry. K.B. 126; 8 L.J.(O.S.)
    K.B. 51 . . . . 8-024, 8-130
Dickson (AA) & Co O'Leary (1979) 254 E.G. 731; 124 S.J. 48 CA 7-019
Dickson v Reuter's Telegram Co Ltd (1877) 3 C.P.D. 1; 47 L.J.Q.B. 1; 37 L.T. 370; 42 J.P.
    308; 26 W.R. 23 9-062
Dietrichsen v Cabburn (1846) 2 Ph. 52 10-025
Diggle v Higgs (1877) 2 Ex.D. 422; 46 L.J.Q.B. 721; 37 L.T. 27; 42 J.P. 345; 25 W.R. 777 . 10-029
Digicel (St Lucia) Ltd v Cable & Wireless Plc [2010] EWHC 774 (Ch 9-119, 9-120
Diment v NH Foot Ltd [1974] 1 W.L.R. 1427; [1974] 2 All E.R. 785; (1974) 28 P. & C.R.
    163; 118 S.J. 810 Ch D 8-217
Dingle v Hare (1859) 7 C.B.(N.S.) 145; 29 L.J.C.P. 143; 1 L.T. 38; 6 Jur. (N.S.) 679 . . 3-022, **3-040**
Diplock v Blackburn (1811) 3 Camp. 43 . . . . **6-078**
Diplock, Re. *See* Ministry of Health v Simpson 8-162, 8-167
Diptford Parish Lands, Re [1934] Ch. 151 2-022
Director General of Fair Trading v Pioneer Concrete (UK) Ltd [1995] 1 A.C. 456; [1994]
    3 W.L.R. 1249; [1995] 1 All E.R. 135; [1995] I.C.R. 25; (1995) 92(1) L.S.G. 37; (1995)
    145 N.L.J. 17; [1995] 139 S.J.L.B. 14 2-025
Director General of Fair Trading v Smiths Concrete; sub nom. Supply of Ready Mixed
    Concrete, Re [1992] Q.B. 213; [1991] 3 W.L.R. 707; [1991] 4 All E.R. 150; [1992]
    I.C.R. 229 CA 1-026
Dixon Ex p.; Re Henley (1876) 4 Ch.D. 133; 46 L.J.Bcy 20; 35 L.T. 644; 25 W.R. 105 8-071,
    8-073, 8-109, 8-111
Dixon v Blindley Heath Investments Ltd [2015] EWCA Civ 1023 3-003
Dixon v Broomfield (1814) 2 Chit. 205 . . . . 2-031, **2-034**
Dixon v Hamond (1819) 2 B. & A. 310 . . . . 6-111, **6-112**
Dixon v Stansfield (1850) 10 C.B. 398; 16 L.T. (O.S.) 150 . . . . 7-080, **7-086**
Dixon v Winch [1900] 1 Ch. 736; 69 L.J.Ch. 465; 82 L.T. 437; 48 W.R. 612; 16 T.L.R.
    276; 44 S.J. 327 8-217
Docker v Somes (1834) 2 My. & K. 655; 3 L.J.Ch. 200; 39 E.R. 1095, L.C 6-040, 6-097
Dodd v Amalgamated Marine Workers' Union [1924] 1 Ch. 116 2-026
Doe d. Lyster v Goldwin (1841) 2 Q.B. 143; 10 L.J.Q.B. 275; 1 Gal. & Dav 463 . . . . . 2-091, **2-094**
Doe d. Mann v Walters (1830) 10 B. & C. 626; 5 Man. & Ry. K.B. 357; [1822-34] All
    E.R.Rep. 428; 8 L.J.(O.S.) K.B. 297; 109 E.R. 583 . . . . 2-091, 2-094
Doe d. Prior v Ongley (1850) 10 C.B. 25; 20 L.J.C.P. 26; 15 L.T.(O.S.) 434; 138 E.R. 11 2-018
Doe d. Rhodes v Robinson (1837) 3 Bing.N.C. 677; 3 Hodg. 84; 4 Scott 396; 6 L.J.C.P.
    235; 1 Jur. 356; 132 E.R. 571 . . . . **5-007**
Doe d. Thomas v Robert (1847) 16 M. & W. 778; 153 E.R. 1404 2-008
Doe d. Willis v Martin (1790) 4 T.R. 39 8-214
Doey v L&NW Ry Co [1919] 1 K.B. 623; 88 L.J.K.B. 737; 120 L.T. 612; 35 T.L.R. 290 8-055
Doherty v Allman (1878) 3 App.Cas. 709 10-025
Dolphina, The [2011] SGHC 273; [2012] 1 Lloyd's Rep. 304 HC (Singapore) 8-215
Domb v Isoz [1980] Ch. 548; [1980] 2 W.L.R. 565; [1980] 1 All E.R. 942; (1980) 40 P. &
    C.R. 516; (1979) 123 S.J. 838 CA **3-032**
Domsalla (t/a Domsalla Building Services) v Dyason [2007] EWHC 1174 (TCC); [2007]
    B.L.R. 348; [2007] T.C.L.R. 5; 112 Con. L.R. 95; [2007] C.I.L.L. 2501 9-005

Don King Productions Inc v Warren (No.1) [2000] Ch. 291; [1999] 3 W.L.R. 276; [1999]
    2 All E.R. 218; [1999] 1 Lloyd's Rep. 588; [2000] 1 B.C.L.C. 607; [1999] E.M.L.R.
    402 CA. 6-080, 6-081
Donaldson v Haldane (1840) 7 C. & F. 762 . . . . 6-028, **6-032**
Donegal International Ltd v Zambia [2007] EWHC 197 (Comm); [2007] 1 Lloyd's Rep.
    397. . . . . 2-071, 6-085, 6-086, 8-042, 8-223, 12-002, 12-016, 12-022
Donelly v Popham (1807) 1 Taunt. 1 CCP **2-100**
Donnell v Bennett (1883) 22 Ch.D. 835; 52 L.J.Ch. 414; 98 L.T. 68; 47 J.P. 342; 31 W.R.
    316. 7-046
Donoghue v Stevenson [1932] A.C. 562; 101 L.J.P.C. 119; 147 L.T. 281; 48 T.L.R. 494;
    76 S.J. 396; 37 Com.Cas. 850 HL. 5-011
Donovan v Invicta Airways Ltd [1970] 1 Lloyd's Rep. 486 CA 6-009
Dooby v Watson (1888) 39 Ch.D. 178; 57 L.J.Ch. 865; 58 L.T. 943; 36 W.R. 764; 4 T.L.R.
    584. 6-041
Dorf v Neumann, Luebeck & Co (1924) 40 T.L.R. 405 6-100
Douglas Norman & Co, Re [1898] 1 Ch. 199 7-094
Douglas v Archbutt (1850) 2 De. G. & J. 148; 27 L.J.Ch. 271; 31 L.T.(O.S.) 4; 4 Jur.
    (N.S.) 315; 6 W.R. 306; 44 E.R. 944, L.JJ 7-006
Douglass Re Ex p. Cotterill (1837) 3 Mont. & Ayr. 376; 3 Deac. 12; 7 L.J.Bcy 2; 1 Jur.
    825. 9-113
Dovey v Cory; sub nom. National Bank of Wales Ltd, Re [1901] A.C. 477; 70 L.J.Ch.
    753; 85 L.T. 257; 17 T.L.R. 732; 50 W.R. 65; 8 Mans. 346 HL. 9-133
Doward, Dickson & Co v Williams & Co (1890) 6 T.L.R. 316 . . . . 10-007, 10-024, 10-029
Downman v Williams; sub nom. Downman v Jones (1845) 7 Q.B. 103; 14 L.J.Q.B. 226;
    S.L.T.(O.S.) 77; 9 Jur. 454 . . . . 9-037, **9-038**, 9-061, 9-090
Dowson & Mason Ltd v Potter [1986] 1 W.L.R. 1419; [1986] 2 All E.R. 418; (1986) 130
    S.J. 841; (1986) 83 L.S.Gaz. 3429 CA 6-077
Dowson and Jenkins' Contract, Re [1904] 2 Ch. 219; 73 L.J.Ch. 684; 91 L.T. 121 . . . . **3-014**, 3-015
Doyle v Olby (Ironmongers) Ltd [1969] 2 Q.B. 158; [1969] 2 W.L.R. 673; [1969] 2 All
    E.R. 119; 113 S.J. 128 CA 9-078
DPP v Kent Sussex Contractors Ltd [1944] K.B. 146; [1944] 1 All E.R. 119; 113 L.J.K.B.
    88; 170 L.T. 41; 108 J.P. 1; 60 T.L.R. 175; 88 S.J. 59; 42 L.G.R. 10, DC 1-029
Drakeford v Piercy (1866) 7 B. & S. 515; 14 L.T. 403 . . . . 3-023, 8-109
Dramburg v Pollitzer (1873) 28 L.T. 470; 21 W.R. 682 . . . . 8-120, 9-020, **9-034**
Dranez Anstalt v Hayek [2002] 1 B.C.L.C. 693 6-081
Draper v Earl Manvers (1892) 9 T.L.R. 73 8-043
Draycott v Hannells Letting Ltd (t/a Hannells Letting Agents) [2010] EWHC 217 (QB);
    [2011] 1 W.L.R. 1606; [2010] 3 All E.R. 411; [2010] H.L.R. 27; [2010] L. & T.R. 12;
    [2010] N.P.C. 18 9-025
Dresser v Norwood (1864) 17 C.B.(N.S.) 466; 4 New Rep. 376; 34 L.J.C.P. 48; 11 L.T.
    111; 10 Jur. (N.S.) 851; 12 W.R. 1030 . . . . 8-110, **8-112**, 8-211, 8-212, **8-217**
Drew v Josolyne (1888) 4 T.L.R. 717 7-005
Drew v Nunn (1879) 4 Q.B.D. 661; 48 L.J.Q.B. 591; 40 L.T. 671; 43 J.P. 541; 27 W.R.
    810. 2-009, **8-045**, 9-071, 10-016, 10-020, 10-031, 10-032, **10-033**
Drew, Wood & Son v Heath (1899) 8 T.L.R. 111 9-087
Drewery and Drewery v Ware-Lane [1960] 1 W.L.R. 1204; [1960] 3 All E.R. 529; 104 S.J.
    933; CA. 7-021
Drexel Burnham Lambert International N.V v El Nasr [1986] 1 Lloyd's Rep. 356 . . . . 3-034, 6-024
Drinkwater v Goodwin (1775) 1 Cowp. 251 . . . . 1-046, **8-112**, **9-035**, 10-010
Drughorn v Rederiaktiebolaget Transatlantic [1919] A.C. 203; 88 L.J.K.B. 233; 120 L.T.
    70; 35 T.L.R. 73; 63 S.J. 99; 14 Asp.M.L.C. 400; 24 Com.Cas. 45 HL. 8-078
Drummond (Robert) v Mangles [1981] E.G.D. 265 7-032
Dry Bulk Handy Holding Inc v Fayette International Holdings Ltd [2013] EWCA Civ
    184; [2013] 1 W.L.R. 3440; [2013] 2 All E.R. (Comm) 295; [2013] 2 Lloyd's Rep. 38;
    [2013] 1 C.L.C. 535 10-027
Dryden v Frost (1837) 3 M. & C. 670; 8 L.J.Ch. 235; 1 Jur. 330 . . . . 2-014, 8-217
Du Boulay v Raggett (1988) 58 P. & C.R. 138; [1989] 1 E.G.L.R. 229, DC 2-037
Du Jardin v Beadman Bros [1952] 2 Q.B. 712; [1952] 1 T.L.R. 1601; [1952] 2 All E.R.
    160; 96 S.J. 414 QBD 8-146
Dubai Aluminium Co Ltd v Salaam; Dubai Aluminium Co Ltd v Amhurst; Dubai
    Aluminium Co Ltd v Amhurst Brown Martin & Nicholson [2002] UKHL 48; [2003] 2
    A.C. 366; [2002] 3 W.L.R. 1913; [2003] 1 All E.R. 97; [2003] 2 All E.R. (Comm) 451;

[2003] 1 Lloyd's Rep. 65; [2003] 1 B.C.L.C. 32; [2003] 1 C.L.C. 1020; [2003] I.R.L.R.
608; [2003] W.T.L.R. 163; (2003) 100(7) L.S.G. 36; (2002) 146 S.J.L.B. 280 HL 6-035, 8-176,
8-178, 8-180, 8-191, 8-218, 9-135, 9-138, 9-140
Dublin City Distillery Ltd v Doherty [1914] A.C. 823; 83 L.J.P.C. 265; 111 L.T. 81; 58
S.J. 413 HL 8-172
Ducarrey v Gill (1830) M. & M. 450; 4 C. & P. 121 . . . . **8-093**
Dufresne v Hutchinson (1810) 3 Taunt. 117 6-007
Dugdale v Lovering (1875) L.R. 10 C.P. 186; 44 L.J.C.P. 197; 32 L.T. 155; 23 W.R. 391 7-058,
7-060, 7-068
Duggan v Full Sutton Prison Governor [2004] EWCA Civ 78; [2004] 1 W.L.R. 1010;
[2004] 2 All E.R. 966; (2004) 101(9) L.S.G. 31; (2004) 148 S.J.L.B. 232 CA 6-041
Duke of Norfolk's Settlement Trusts, Re [1982] Ch. 61; [1981] 3 W.L.R. 455; [1981] 3 All
E.R. 220; (1981) 125 S.J. 554 CA 6-080
Dun & Bradstreet Software Services (England) Ltd v Provident Mutual Life Assurance
Association [1998] 2 E.G.L.R. 175; [1997] E.G.C.S.89; [1997] N.P.C. 91 CA 1-045, 2-026
Duncan v Hill; Duncan v Beeson (1873) L.R. 8 Ex. 242; 42 L.J.Ex. 179; 29 L.T. 268; 21
W.R. 797 . . . . 7-066, **7-070**
Dunford & Elliott Ltd v Johnson & Firth Brown Ltd [1977] 1 Lloyd's Rep. 505; [1978]
F.S.R. 143; (1976) 121 S.J. 53 6-077
Dunhill v Burgin [2014] UKSC 18; [2014] 1 W.L.R. 933; [2014] 2 All E.R. 364; [2014]
R.T.R. 16; [2014] P.I.Q.R. P13; (2014) 164(7599) N.L.J. 20; (2014) 158(12) S.J.L.B. 41 1-047,
2-009, 10-020
Dunlop & Sons v De Murrieta & Co (1886) 3 T.L.R. 166 5-004
Dunlop Haywards (DHL) Ltd (formerly Dunlop Heywood Lorenz Ltd) (In Liquidation) v
Barbon Insurance Group Ltd (formerly Erinaceous Insurance Services Ltd (formerly
Hanover Park Commercial Ltd)) [2009] EWHC 2900 (Comm); [2010] Lloyd's Rep.
I.R. 149 6-018
Dunlop Haywards (DHL) Ltd (formerly Dunlop Heywood Lorenz Ltd) v Erinaceous
Insurance Services Ltd (formerly Hanover Park Commercial Ltd) [2009] EWCA Civ
354; [2009] Lloyd's Rep. I.R. 464 . . . . 5-011, 8-183
Dunlop Lambert (1839) 6 Cl. & F. 600; Mad. & Rob. 663; 7 E.R. 824 HL 9-010
Dunlop Pneumatic Tyre Co v Selfridge & Co Ltd [1915] A.C. 847; 84 L.J.K.B. 1680; 113
L.T. 386; 31 T.L.R. 399; 59 S.J. 439 9-122
Dunlop Rubber Co Ltd v Haigh & Sons [1937] 1 K.B. 347; [1936] 3 All E.R. 381; 106
L.J.K.B. 166; 155 L.T. 579; 53 T.L.R. 98; 80 S.J. 933; [1936-37] B. & C.R. 149 . . . . **8-044**
Dunn v Macdonald [1897] 1 Q.B. 555 CA 9-074
Dunn v Newton (1884) C. & E. 278 8-121
Dunn v Ocean Accident & Guarantee Ltd (1933) 50 T.L.R. 32; 47 Ll.L.Rep. 129 8-217
Dunn v Shanks [1932] N.I. 66 8-043
Dunne v English (1874) L.R. 18 Eq. 524; 31 L.T. 75 . . . . 6-039, 6-064, **6-070**
Dunton Properties Ltd v Coles; Knapp & Kennedy (1959) 174 E.G. 723 CA 6-021
Duomatic Ltd, Re [1969] 2 Ch. 365; [1969] 2 W.L.R. 114; [1969] 1 All E.R. 161; (1968)
112 S.J. 922 1-028
Durrant v Holdsworth (1886) 2 T.L.R. 763 . . . . **8-045**
Durrell v (1862) 1 H. & C. 174; 31 L.J.Ex. 337; 7 L.T. 97; 9 Jur. (N.S.) 104; 10 W.R. 665 . . . 2-014
Dutton v Marsh (1871) L.R. 6 Q.B. 361; 40 L.J.K.B. 175; 24 L.T. 470; 19 W.R. 754 . . . . **9-056**
DVB Bank SE v Isim Amin Ltd [2014] EWHC 2156 (Comm) 10-018
Dyer v Munday [1895] 1 Q.B. 742; 64 L.J.Q.B. 448; 59 J.P. 276; 43 W.R. 440; 11 T.L.R.
282; 14 R. 306 . . . . **8-192**
Dyer v Pearson (1824) 3 B. & C. 38; 4 Dow. & Ry. K.B. 648 8-130
Dyster v Randall & Sons [1926] Ch. 932; 95 L.J.Ch. 504; 135 L.T. 596; 70 S.J. 797;
[1926] B. & C.R. 113 . . . . 8-071, 8-080, **8-082**
E (Enduring Power of Attorney), Re [2001] Ch. 364; [2000] 3 W.L.R. 1974; [2000] 3 All
E.R. 1004; [2000] 1 F.L.R. 882; [2000] 3 F.C.R. 320; [2000] W.T.L.R. 383; [2000] Fam.
Law 469 10-027
E Hannibal & Co Ltd v Frost (1988) 4 B.C.C. 3 2-025
E Surv Ltd v Goldsmith Williams Solicitors [2015] EWCA Civ 1147; [2016] 4 W.L.R. 44;
[2016] P.N.L.R. 11 6-021
E v English Province of Our Lady of Charity [2012] EWCA Civ 938; [2013] Q.B. 722;
[2013] 2 W.L.R. 958; [2012] 4 All E.R. 1152; [2013] P.T.S.R. 565; [2012] I.R.L.R. 846;
[2012] P.I.Q.R. P19 8-178
E-Clear (UK) Plc (In Liquidation) v Elia [2013] EWCA Civ 1114; [2013] 2 B.C.L.C. 455;
[2014] 1 P. & C.R. DG4 6-061

Eagle Star Insurance Co Ltd v Spratt [1971] 2 Lloyd's Rep. 116 CA   . . . 2-013, 3-005, 6-048, 8-048
Eagle Trust Plc v SBC Securities Ltd (No.2); sub nom. Eagle Trust Plc v SBCI Swiss
    Bank Corp Investment Banking Ltd [1996] 1 B.C.L.C. 121; [1995] B.C.C. 231 Ch D. 9-136
Eagle Trust Plc v SBC Services Ltd [1993] 1 W.L.R. 484; [1992] 4 All E.R. 488; [1991]
    B.C.L.C. 438 Ch D 9-136
Eaglesfield v Londonderry (1876) 38 L.T. 303   . . . . 6-099, 6-111, **6-112**
East India Co v Blake (1673) C.Temp.F. 117   6-097
East v Henchman; sub nom. Henchman v East India Co (1797) Bro.Parl.Cas. 85   6-020
East v Mainston (1676) 2 Cas. in. Cha. 218   6-098
East v Smith (1847) 16 L.J.Q.B. 292   2-091
Eastern Construction Co v National Trust Co [1914] A.C. 197 PC (Canada)   . . 2-056, 2-063, 2-067,
                                                                                                        2-071, 6-111
Eastern Counties Railway Co v Broom (1851) 6 Exch. 314; 6 Ry. & Can.Cas.743; 16
    L.T.(O.S.) 465; 15 Jur. 297; 20 L.J.Ex. 196. . . . . 2-056, **2-061**, 8-189
Eastern Distributors Ltd v Goldring (Murphy, Third Party) [1957] 2 Q.B. 600; [1957] 3
    W.L.R. 237; [1957] 2 All E.R. 525; 101 S.J. 553 CA. 8-127, 8-130, **8-133**, 8-135
Eastman v Harry (1875) 33 L.T. 800; 3 Asp.M.L.C. 117   . . . . 8-120, 8-121, 9-046
Easyair Ltd (t/a Openair) v Opal Telecom Ltd [2009] EWHC 339 (Ch)   7-001
EBM Co Ltd v Dominion Bank [1937] 3 All E.R. 555 (PC)   3-011
Eccles v Bryant [1948] Ch. 93; [1948] L.J.R. 418; 177 L.T. 247; [1947] 2 All E.R. 865 CA   . . 7-017
Eclairs Group Ltd v JKX Oil & Gas Plc [2015] UKSC 71; [2015] Bus. L.R. 1395; [2016]
    B.C.C. 79; [2016] 1 B.C.L.C. 1 8-220
Ecossaise S.S. Co Ltd v Lloyd, Low. Co (1890) 7 T.L.R. 76   . . . . 5-010, 5-011
Edelstein v Schuler [1902] 2 K.B. 144; 71 L.J.K.B. 572; 87 L.T. 204; 50 W.R. 493; 18
    T.L.R. 597; 46 S.J. 500; 7 Com.Cas.172 8-142
Eden v Ridsdales Railway Lamp & Lighting Co Ltd (1889) 23 Q.B.D. 368; 58 L.J.Q.B.
    579; 61 L.T. 444; 54 J.P. 20; 38 W.R. 55. . . . . 6-087, 6-089
Edenwest Ltd v CMS Cameron McKenna [2012] EWHC 1258 (Ch); [2013] B.C.C. 152;
    [2013] 1 B.C.L.C. 525; (2012) 109(22) L.S.G. 20 9-002
Edgell v Day (1865) L.R. 1 C.P. 80; 35 L.J.C.P. 7; 13 L.T. 328; 12 Jur. (N.S.) 27; 14 W.R.
    87 . . . . 6-099, 6-100, 6-108
Edmond De Rothschild Securities (UK) Ltd v Exillon Energy Plc [2014] EWHC 2165
    (Comm); [2014] 5 Costs L.O. 749 7-028
Edmunds v Bushell and Jones (1865) L.R. 1 Q.B. 97; 4 F. & F. 1044; 35 L.J.Q.B. 20; 30
    J.P. 694; 12 Jur. (N.S.) 332 . . . . 8-077, **8-082**
Edwards Ex p. Chapman, Re (1884) 13 Q.B.D. 747; 51 L.T. 881; 33 W.R. 268; 1 Morr.
    238 . . . . 9-105, **9-109**
Edwards Ex p.; sub nom. Re Johnson Ex p. Edwards (1881) 8 Q.B.D. 262; 45 L.T. 578   . . . . . **5-016,**
                                                                                                                 7-099
Edwards Karwacki Smith & Co Pty Ltd v Jacka Nominees Pty Ltd (1994) 15 A.C.S.R.
    502. 8-188
Edwards v Carter [1893] A.C. 360   2-008
Edwards v Hodding (1814) 5 Taunt. 815; 1 Marsh. 377   9-109
Edwards v International Connection (UK) Ltd [2006] EWCA Civ 662   . . . . 11-022, 11-031
Edwards v London North Western Railway (1869) L.R.S.C.P. 445; 39 L.J.C.P. 241; 22
    L.T. 656; 18 W.R. 834. . . . . 2-056, 2-072
Edwards v Meyrick (1842) 2 Hare 60; 12 L.J.Ch. 49; 6 Jur. 924   6-067
Edwards v Porter [1925] A.C. 1; 94 L.J. K.B. 65; 132 L.T. 496; 41 T.L.R. 57; 69 S.J. 87   9-062
Edwards v Society of Graphical and Allied Trades [1971] Ch. 354; [1970] 3 W.L.R. 713;
    [1970] 3 All E.R. 689; 8 K.I.R. 1 CA. 2-024
Edwards v Southgate (1862) 10 W.R. 528   7-073
Ee v Kakar (1979) 40 P. & C.R. 223; 124 S.J. 327; 255 E.G. 879 Ch D   7-017
Efploia Shipping Corp Ltd v Canadian Transport Co Ltd (The Pantanassa) Pantanassa,
    The [1958] 2 Lloyd's Rep. 449. 8-209
Egan Lawson Ltd v Standard Life Assurance Co; sub nom. Standard Life Assurance Co v
    Egan Lawson Ltd [2001] 1 E.G.L.R. 27; [2001] 08 E.G. 168; [2000] N.P.C. 128CA . . 7-030, 7-032
Egger v Chelmsford (Viscount); sub nom. Egger v Davies [1965] 1 Q.B. 248; [1964] 3
    W.L.R. 714; [1964] 3 All E.R. 406; 108 S.J. 619 CA. 8-185, 8-196, 9-116, 9-120
Eggington v Reader [1936] 1 All E.R. 7   . . . . 8-182, **8-192**
Egyptian International Foreign Trade Co v Soplex Wholesale Supplies and PS Refson &
    Co; The Raffaella. See Soplex Wholesale Supplies and Refson (PS) & Co v Egyptian
    International Foreign Trading Co 8-015, 8-017, 8-018, 8-028, **8-044**, 8-050, 8-067, 9-106
Ehrensperger v Anderson (1848) 3 E. & Ch. 148; 18 L.J. Ex. 132; 12 L.T. (O.S.) 292   6-100

EIC Services Ltd v Phipps [2003] EWHC 1507 (Ch); [2003] 1 W.L.R. 2360; [2003] 3 All
E.R. 804; [2003] B.C.C. 931. 6-039
EIC Services Ltd v Phipps [2004] EWCA Civ 1069; [2005] 1 W.L.R. 1377; [2005] 1 All
E.R. 338; [2004] B.C.C. 814; [2004] 2 B.C.L.C. 589; (2004) 148 S.J.L.B. 1118 CA 8-037
Eichengruen v Mond [1940] Ch. 785; 109 L.J. Ch. 468; 163 L.T. 219; 56 T.L.R. 845; 84
S.J. 426; [1940] 3 All E.R. 148. 10-003
Eide UK Ltd v Lowndes Lambert Group Ltd [1999] Q.B. 199; [1998] 3 W.L.R. 643;
[1998] 1 All E.R. 946; [1998] 1 Lloyd's Rep. 389; [1998] C.L.C. 266; (1998) 95(4)
L.S.G. 34; (1998) 148 N.L.J. 86 CA 7-077, 7-088, 7-098
El Ajou v Dollar Land Holdings Plc [1994] 2 All E.R. 685; [1994] B.C.C. 143; [1994] 1
B.C.L.C. 464; [1993] N.P.C. 165 CA 1-029, 8-162, 8-206, 8-208, 8-209, 8-210, 8-211, 8-212,
8-215, **8-217**, 9-136
El Biret Cie SA v Yukiteru Kaiun KK; The Sun Happiness [1984] 1 Lloyd's Rep. 381
QBD (Comm) 9-006, 9-038
Elbinger Aktien-Gesellschaft v Claye (1873) L.R. 8 Q.B. 313; 42 L.J.Q.B. 151; 28 L.T.
405. . . . . 1-022, 8-071, 9-006, 9-020, 12-029
Elder Dempster & Co Ltd v Paterson Zochonis & Co Ltd. *See* Paterson Zochonis & Co
Ltd v Elder Dempster & Co Ltd 9-122
Electrosteel Castings (UK) Ltd v Metalpol Ltd [2014] EWHC 2017 (Ch) 7-050, 8-225
Electrosteel Castings Ltd v Scan Trans Shipping & Chartering Sdn Bhd [2002] EWHC
1993; [2002] 2 All E.R. (Comm) 1064; [2003] 1 Lloyd's Rep. 190; 87 Con. L.R. 50
QBD (Comm) 9-038, 9-089
Elidor Investments SA v Christie's, Manson Woods Ltd [2009] EWHC 3600 (QB) 6-020
Elikon, The. *See* Internaut Shipping GmbH v Fercometal Sarl 9-038
Elim Court RTM Company Ltd v Avon Freeholds Ltd [2017] EWCA Civ 89; [2017]
H.L.R. 18. 2-022
Elkington & Co v Hirter [1892] 2 Ch. 452; 61 L.J. Ch. 514; 66 L.T. 764 9-076
Elliott (Michael) & Partners Ltd v UK Land Plc [1991] 1 E.G.L.R. 39; [1991] 08 E.G.
123; [1990] E.G.C.S.98 QBD. 7-012
Elliott v Bax-Ironside [1925] 2 K.B. 301; 94 L.J.K.B. 807; 133 L.T. 624; 41 T.L.R. 631 9-054,
9-056, 9-085
Elliott v Ince (1857) 7 De G.M. & G. 475; 26 L.J.Ch. 821; 30 L.T.(O.S.) 92; 3 Jur. (N.S.)
597; 5 W.R. 465 2-009
Ellis (Richard) v Pipe-Chem (Holdings) Ltd [1981] E.G.D. 222; (1980) 258 E.G. 329, DC . . 7-021
Ellis (WA) Services Ltd v Wood (Stuart) [1993] 2 E.G.L.R. 43; [1993] 31 E.G. 78 Ch D 7-017,
7-075
Ellis & Co's Trustee v Watsham (1923) 155 L.T.Jo. 365 6-071
Ellis & Ellis, Re [1900] W.N. 215; 2 S.T.L.R. 38 6-090
Ellis v Goulton [1893] 1 Q.B. 350; 62 L.J.Q.B. 232; 68 L.T. 144; 41 W.R. 411; 9 T.L.R.
223; 4R. 267 . . . . 9-025, 9-102, 9-103, **9-109**
Ellis v May & Co (1960) 110 L.J. 140 7-032
Ellis v National Free Labour Association (1905) 7 F. 629; 42 Sc.L.R. 495; 13 S.L.T. 70 8-196
Ellis v Pond [1898] 1 Q.B. 426; 67 L.J.Q.B. 345; 78 L.T. 125; 14 T.L.R. 152 CA 7-066
Ellis v Sheffield Gas Consumers Co (1853) 2 E. & B. 767 9-120
Elmville, The [1904] P. 319; 73 L.J.P. 104; 91 L.T. 151; 9 Asp. M.L.C. 606 . . . . **9-056**
Elpis Maritime Co v Marti Chartering Co; The Maria D [1992] 1 A.C. 21; [1991] 3 W.L.R.
330; [1991] 3 All E.R. 758; [1991] 2 Lloyd's Rep. 311; (1991) 135 S.J. (LB) 100;
[1991] 141 N.L.J. 1109 HL. 9-038
Else v Barnard Ex p. Courtauld (1860) 28 Beav. 228; 29 L.J.Ch. 729; 2 L.T. 203; 6 Jur.
(N.S.) 621; 54 E.R. 353. 3-032
Ely, Re Ex p. Trustee (1900) 48 W.R. 693; 44 S.J. 483 . . . . **9-125**
Emerald Supplies Ltd v British Airways Plc [2015] EWCA Civ 1024; [2016] Bus. L.R.
145. 9-120
Emeraldian Ltd Partnership v Wellmix Shipping Ltd (The Vine) [2010] EWHC 1411
(Comm); [2011] 1 Lloyd's Rep. 301; [2010] 1 C.L.C. 993 12-002
Emile Elias & Co Ltd v Attorney General of Trinidad & Tobago [2011] UKPC 19 PC
(Trinidad and Tobago). 2-031, 2-033
Emma Silver Mining Co v Lewis & Sons (1879) 4 C.P.D. 396; 40 L.T. 749; 27 W.R. 836 6-035
Emmanuel v DBS Management Plc [1999] Lloyd's Rep P.N. 593 8-178
Emmerson v Heelis (1809) 2 Taunt. 38 . . . . 2-013, 2-014, **3-032**, 5-007
Empress Engineering Co, Re (1880) 16 Ch.D. 125; 43 L.T. 742; 29 W.R. 342 2-064
Enderby Town Football Club Ltd v Football Association Ltd [1971] Ch. 591; [1970] 3
W.L.R. 1021; [1971] 1 All E.R. 215; (1970) 114 S.J. 827 CA 2-024

ENE 1 Kos Ltd v Petroleo Brasileiro SA Petrobras (The Kos) [2012] UKSC 17; [2012] 2
    A.C. 164; [2012] 2 W.L.R. 976; [2012] 4 All E.R. 1; [2013] 1 All E.R. (Comm) 32;
    [2012] 2 Lloyd's Rep. 292; [2013] 1 C.L.C. 1; 149 Con. L.R. 76; (2012) 162 N.L.J. 680 4-008
English & Colonial Produce Co, Re [1906] 2 Ch. 435; 75 L.J.Ch. 831; 95 L.T. 580; 22
    T.L.R. 669; 50 S.J. 595; 13 Mans. 387 2-064
English v Dedham Vale Properties Ltd; sub nom. English v Denham Vale Properties
    [1978] 1 W.L.R. 93; [1978] 1 All E.R. 382; (1978) 35 P. & C.R. 148; 245 E.G. 747;
    [1978] J.P.L. 315; 121 S.J. 320 Ch D 6-076, 6-077, 6-080, **6-083**
English v English [2010] EWHC 2058 (Ch); (2010) 107(32) L.S.G. 14 .... 2-059, 2-061, 2-103
Enron (Thrace) Exploration & Production BV v Clapp (No.2) [2005] EWHC 401 (Comm) .. 1-030
Entick v Carrington (1765) 19 St.Tr. 1029; 2 Wils 275 9-124
Epps v Rothnie [1945] K.B. 562 8-078
Equitas Ltd v Horace Holman & Co Ltd [2007] EWHC 903 (Comm); [2007] Lloyd's Rep.
    I.R. 567 .... 6-092, 6-093, 6-098
Equitas Ltd v Walsham Bros & Co Ltd [2013] EWHC 3264 (Comm); [2014] P.N.L.R. 8;
    [2014] Bus. L.R. D7 .... 6-012, 6-018, 6-019, 6-100
Eric v Stansfield v South East Nursing Home Services Ltd [1986] 1 E.G.L.R. 29 7-051
Erlanger v New Sombrero Phosphate Co; sub nom. New Sombrero Phosphate Co v
    Erlanger (1878) 3 App.Cas. 1218; 39 L.T. 269; 27 W.R. 65; 48 L.J.Ch. 73............... 6-035
Errington v Errington and Woods [1952] 1 K.B. 290; [1952] 1 T.L.R. 231; [1952] 1 All
    E.R. 149; 96 S.J. 119 CA 10-043
Erskine, Oxenford & Co v Sachs [1901] 2 K.B. 504; 70 L.J.K.B. 978; 85 L.T. 385; 17
    T.L.R. 636 .... **6-070**
Esdaile v La Nauze (Lanage) (1835) 1 Y. & C. Ex 394; 4 L.J.Eq. 46 3-015
Esmail v Bank of Scotland 1999 S.L.T. 1289; 1999 G.W.D. 22-1026 OH 3-015
Espin v Pemberton (1859) 3 De G. & J. 547; 28 L.J.Ch. 311; 32 L.T.(O.S.) 345; 5 Jur.
    (N.S.) 157; 7 W.R. 221 .... 2-014, 8-210, 8-214, **8-217**
Essfood v Crown Shipping (Ireland) Ltd [1991] 1 L.R.M. 97 8-020
Esso Petroleum Co Ltd v Mardon [1970] Q.B. 801; [1976] 2 W.L.R. 583; [1976] 2 All
    E.R. 5; 120 S.J. 131; [1976] 2 Lloyd's Rep. 305 CA.................... 8-186, 9-117, 9-121
Estafnous v London & Leeds Business Centres Ltd [2011] EWCA Civ 1157 .. 7-018, 7-028, **7-032**
Estate of FC Jones & Sons v Jones. See Trustee of the Property of FC Jones & Sons (A
    Firm) v Jones 8-066, 8-161, 10-021
Eurasian Natural Resources Corp Ltd v Judge [2014] EWHC 3556 (QB) 6-077
Euromaster Ltd, Re [2012] EWHC 2356 (Ch); [2013] Bus. L.R. 466; [2012] B.C.C. 754;
    [2013] 1 B.C.L.C. 273 2-012
European Asian Bank A.G. v Punjab and Sind Bank (No.2) [1983] 1 W.L.R. 652; [1983] 2
    All E.R. 508; (1983) 127 S.J. 379; [1983] 1 Lloyd's Rep. 611; [1983] Com.L.R. 128 CA ... 2-034,
                                                                                   3-019, 6-011
European Bank, Re, Ex p. Oriental Commercial Bank (1870) L.R. 5 Ch.App. 358; 39
    L.J.Ch. 588; 22 L.T. 422; 18 W.R. 474 .... **8-142**, 8-214
European Bank, Re; Agra Bank Claim (1872) L.R. 8 Ch.App. 41 7-086
European International Reinsurance Co Ltd v Curzon Insurance Ltd [2003] EWCA Civ
    1074; [2003] Lloyd's Rep. I.R. 793; (2003) 100(36) L.S.G. 43; (2003) 147 S.J.L.B. 906
    CA.. 9-117
Euroption Strategic Fund Ltd v Skandinaviska Enskilda Banken AB [2012] EWHC 584
    (Comm); [2013] 1 B.C.L.C. 125; [2013] Bus. L.R. D67 6-020
Eurymedon, The. See Satterthwaite (AM) & Co v New Zealand Shipping Co Ltd 7-036
Evans (C) & Sons Ltd v Spritebrand Ltd [1985] 1 W.L.R. 317; [1985] 1 All E.R. 415;
    (1985) 29 S.J. 189; [1985] PCC 109; [1985] F.S.R. 267; (1985) 82 L.S.Gaz. 606 CA . 8-177, 9-120,
                                                                                   9-125
Evans (J) & Sons (Portsmouth) Ltd v Merzario (Andrea) Ltd [1976] 1 W.L.R. 1078;
    [1976] 2 All E.R. 930; 120 S.J. 734; [1976] 2 Lloyd's Rep. 165 CA.................... 9-024
Evans & Evans v Nichol & Nichol; sub nom. v Nichol & Ludlow (1841) 3 M. & G. 614; 4
    Scott N.R. 43; 5 Jur. 1110; 11 L.J.C.P. 6................................... 7-078
Evans & Reid Coal Co v McNabb Rougier & Co Ltd (1924) 18 Ll.Rep. 471 .... 8-120, 9-046
Evans Marshall & Co v Bertola SA (No.2) [1976] 2 Lloyd's Rep. 17 HL 7-046, 10-025
Evans v Employers Mutual Life Assn. Ltd [1936] 1 K.B. 505 8-215
Evans v Evans (1834) 3 A. & E. 132; 1 Har. & W. 239; 111 E.R. 363 9-023
Evans v Forster (1830) 1 B. & Ad. 118; L. & Welsh 285; 8 L.J.(O.S.) K.B. 348; 109 E.R.
    731.. 9-003
Evans v Hooper (1875) 1 Q.B.D. 45; 45 L.J.Q.B. 306; 33 L.T. 374; 24 W.R. 226 .... **9-003**

Evans v James [2001] C.P. Rep. 36; [2003] C.P.L.R. 163; [2000] 3 E.G.L.R. 1; [2000] 42
  E.G. 173; [2000] E.G. 95 (C.S.); [2000] N.P.C. 85; (2000) 80 P. & C.R. D39. 10-020
Evans v Kymer (1830) 1 B. & Ad. 528; 9 L.J.(O.S.) K.B. 92   . . . . **8-061**
Evans v Smallcombe (1868) L.R. 3 H.L. 249 HL   1-028
Evans, Re, Ex p. Barber (1843) 3 M.D. De G. 174   7-078
Ever Success, The; sub nom. Crew Members of the Ever Success v Owners of the Ever
  Success [1999] 1 Lloyd's Rep. 824 QBD (Adm Ct). 7-084
Everett v Collins (1810) 2 Comp. 515   . . . . 8-106, 8-121
Everett v Hogg, Robinson & Gardner Mountain (Insurance) Ltd [1973] 2 Lloyd's Rep.
  217. 6-009
Ewbank v Nutting (1849) 7 C.B. 797; 13 L.T. (O.S.) 94   . . . . 8-176, **8-196**
Excel Securities Plc v Masood Mercantile Court, Manchester, June 10, 2009   9-065
Excess Life Insurance Co Ltd v Fireman's Insurance Co of Newark New Jersey [1982] 2
  Lloyd's Rep. 599 QBD (Comm). 1-045
Explora Group Plc v Hesco Bastion Ltd [2005] EWCA Civ 646; (2005) 149 S.J.L.B. 924   . . . 7-042,
                                                                                                                        11-035
Explora Group Plc v Hesco Bastion Ltd; Explora Group Ltd v Trading Force Ltd [2005]
  EWCA Civ 646 CA. 7-042, 11-033
Express Engineering Works Ltd Re [1920] 1 Ch. 466; 89 L.J. Ch. 379; 122 L.T. 790; 36
  T.L.R. 275. 2-069
Exsus Travel Ltd v Turner [2014] EWCA Civ 1331; [2015] C.P. Rep. 7   6-096
Eyre v Hughes (1876) 2 Ch.D. 148; 45 L.J.Ch. 395; 34 L.T. 211; 24 W.R. 597; 2
  Char.Pr.Cas. 33. 6-072
Eyre v Lovell (1782) 3 Doug. 66; 99 E.R. 541   3-008
F v West Berkshire HA; sub nom. F (Mental Patient: Sterilisation), Re [1990] 2 A.C. 1;
  [1989] 2 W.L.R. 1025; [1989] 2 All E.R. 545; [1989] 2 F.L.R. 376; (1989) 139 N.L.J.
  789; (1989) 133 S.J. 785 HL. 4-005
F&C Alternative Investments (Holdings) Ltd v Barthelemy [2011] EWHC 1731 (Ch);
  [2012] Ch. 613; [2012] 3 W.L.R. 10; [2012] Bus. L.R. 891. . . . . 2-031, 2-033, 6-034, 6-035
Faccenda Chicken Ltd v Fowler; Fowler v Faccenda Chicken [1987] Ch. 117; [1986] 3
  W.L.R. 288; [1986] 1 All E.R. 617; (1986) 130 S.J. 573; [1986] I.C.R. 297; [1986]
  I.R.L.R. 69; [1986] F.S.R. 291 CA 6-077, 6-078
Facer v Vehicle & General Insurance Co Ltd [1965] 1 Lloyd's Rep. 113 QBD   8-217
Fadallah v Pollak [2013] EWHC 3159 (QB) 8-145, 8-147, 8-152, 8-156
Fairfax Gerrard Holdings Ltd v Capital Bank Plc [2007] EWCA Civ 1226; [2008] 1 All
  E.R. (Comm) 632; [2008] 1 Lloyd's Rep. 297; [2007] 2 C.L.C. 896; [2008] B.P.I.R. 332. . . . 1-035,
                                                                                                          8-145, 8-152, 8-154
Fairfield Shipbuilding & Engineering Co Ltd v Gardner Mountain & Co Ltd (1911) 104
  L.T. 288; 27 T.L.R. 281; 11 Asp.M.L.C. 594 7-099
Fairlie v Fenton (1870) L.R. 5 Ex. 169; 39 L.J.Ex. 107; 22 L.T. 373; 18 W.R. 700   . . . **9-003**, 9-005,
                                                                                                                        9-009
Fairline Shipping Corp v Adamson [1975] Q.B. 180; [1974] 2 W.L.R. 824; [1974] 2 All
  E.R. 967; (1973) 118 S.J. 406; [1974] 1 Lloyd's Rep. 133. . . . . 9-117, **9-125**
Fairstar Heavy Transport NV v Adkins [2013] EWCA Civ 886; [2013] 2 C.L.C. 272;
  [2014] E.M.L.R. 12; [2014] F.S.R. 8; [2014] Bus. L.R. D2 . . . . 6-093, 11-024
Fairvale Ltd v Sabharwal [1992] 2 E.G.L.R. 27   . . . . 7-004, 7-012, 7-024
Falcke v Scottish Imperial Insurance Co (1886) 34 Ch.D. 234; 56 L.J.Ch. 707; 56 L.T.
  220; 35 W.R. 143; 3 T.L.R. 141 4-010
Falk v Fletcher (1865) 18 C.B. (N.S.) 403; 2 New Rep. 272; 34 L.J.C.P. 146; 11 Jur. (N.S.)
  176; 13 W.R. 346   7-101
Famatina Development Corp Ltd, Re [1914] 2 Ch. 271; 84 L.J.Ch. 48; 30 T.L.R. 696   7-062
Far East Chartering Ltd (formerly Visa Comtrade Asia Ltd) v Great Eastern Shipping Co
  Ltd [2012] EWCA Civ 180; [2012] 2 All E.R. (Comm) 707; [2012] 1 Lloyd's Rep. 637;
  [2012] 1 C.L.C. 427 9-122
Faraday v Tamworth Union (1917) 86 L.J.Ch. 436; 81 J.P. 81; 15 L.G.R. 258   . . 7-005, 7-009, **7-012**
Faramus v Film Artistes Association [1964] A.C. 925; [1964] 2 W.L.R. 126; [1964] 1 All
  E.R. 25; 108 S.J. 13 HL   2-024
Farebrother v Simmons (1822) 5 B. & A. 333   2-014
Farepak Food and Gifts Ltd (In Administration), Re [2006] EWHC 3272 (Ch); [2008]
  B.C.C. 22; [2007] 2 B.C.L.C. 1; [2007] W.T.L.R. 1407. 6-041
Farley Health Products v Babylon Trading Co [1987] C.L.Y. 1126   9-083
Farmer v Russell (1798) 1 B. & P. 296   6-100
Farncombe v Sperling (1922) 66 S.J. 312   . . . . 9-037, 9-040

Farquhar v East India Co (1845) 8 Beav. 260 6-098
Farquharson Bros & Co v King & Co [1902] A.C. 325; 71 L.J.K.B. 667; 86 L.T. 810; 51
   W.R. 94; 18 T.L.R. 665; 46 S.J. 584. 2-102, 8-023, 8-024, 8-063, 8-126, 8-130, **8-133**, 8-158, 8-161
Farrar v Definne (1844) 1 Car. & K. 580 10-031
Farrer v Lacy, Hartland & Co (1888) 31 Ch.D. 42; 55 L.J.Ch. 149; 53 L.T. 515; 34 W.R. 2
   T.L.R. 11 .... 3-025, 3-026
Farrow v Wilson (1860) L.R. 4 C.P. 744; 38 L.J.C.P. 326; 20 L.T. 810; 18 W.R. 43 . 10-015, 10-016
Farrow's Bank Ltd, Re [1923] 1 Ch. 41 CA 10-011
Farthing v Tomkins (1893) 9 T.L.R. 566 7-005
Faruk v Wyse [1988] 2 E.G.L.R. 26 6-024
Faulkner v Cooper & Co Ltd (1899) 4 Com.Cas. 213 7-042
Favermead Ltd v FPD Savills Ltd [2005] EWHC 626 Ch D 7-028
Fawcett v Whitehouse (1829) 1 Russ. & M. 132; 39 E.R. 51 .... 6-085, 6-087
Fawcus, Re, Ex p. Buck (1876) 3 Ch.D. 795; 34 L.T. 807 7-082
Fawkes v Lamb (1862) 31 L.J.Q.B. 98; 8 Jur. (N.S.) 385; 10 W.R. 348 .... **9-003**, 9-005
Fay v Miller, Wilkins & Co [1991] Ch. 360; [1941] 2 All E.R. 18; 85 S.J. 213; 110 L.J.Ch.
   124; 166 L.T. 33; 57 T.L.R. 423................................... 8-020, 8-045, 9-080
Federal Supply and Cold Storage of South Africa v Angehrn & Piel (1910) 80 L.J.P.C. 1;
   103 L.T. 150; 26 T.L.R. 626 .... 6-086, 6-087
Feise v Wray (1802) 3 East 93 .... **7-101**
Fell v Parkin (1882) 52 L.J.Q.B. 99; 47 L.T. 350 .... 8-119, 8-121
Fellowes v Gwydyr (Lord) (1829) 1 Russ & M. 83 9-094
Fenton v Browne; Browne v Fenton (1807) 14 Ves. 144; 33 E.R. 476 9-026
Fenwick, Stobart & Co, Re; Deep Sea Fishery Co's claim [1902] 1 Ch. 507 Ch D 8-215
Ferguson Associates v Sohl 62 B.L.R. 95 CA 7-025
Ferguson v Dawson (John) & Partners (Construction) Ltd [1976] 1 W.L.R. 1213; [1976] 3
   All E.R. 817; 120 S.J. 603; [1976] 2 Lloyd's Rep. 669; [1976] I.R.L.R. 346; [1978]
   J.B.L. 247; CA 1-034
Ferguson v Wilson (1866) L.R. 2 Ch.App. 77; 36 L.J. Ch. 67; 15 L.T. 230; 30 J.P. 788; 12
   Jur. (N.S.) 912; 15 W.R. 27 .... 1-028, 9-055
Fern Computer Consultancy Ltd v Intergraph Cadworx & Analysis Solutions Inc [2014]
   EWHC 2908 (Ch); [2014] Bus. L.R. 1397; [2015] 1 Lloyd's Rep. 1; [2014] 2 C.L.C.
   326 .... 11-006, 11-016, 11-040
FernÈe v Gorlitz [1915] 1 Ch. 177; 84 L.J.Ch. 404; 112 L.T. 283 .... 9-066, 9-081
Ferrera v Hardy [2013] EWHC 4164 (Ch) 6-041
Ferrers v Robins (1835) 2 C.M. & R. 152; 1 Gale 70; 5 Tyr. 705; 4 L.J. Ex. 178 .... **6-007**
Ferryways NV v Associated British Ports (The Humber Way) Humber Way, The [2009]
   EWCA Civ 189; [2009] 1 Lloyd's Rep. 595 .... **8-082**, 9-016
Feuer Leather Corp v Frank Johnston & Sons Ltd [1981] Com.L.Rep. 251; [1983]
   Com.L.R. 12 CA 8-048, **8-061**
FG Wilson (Engineering) Ltd v John Holt & Co (Liverpool) Ltd [2013] EWCA Civ 1232;
   [2014] 1 W.L.R. 2365; [2014] 1 All E.R. 785; [2014] 1 All E.R. (Comm) 393; [2014] 1
   Lloyd's Rep. 180; [2013] 2 C.L.C. 501; [2014] B.L.R. 103; [2014] B.P.I.R. 1104 1-035
FHR European Ventures LLP v Cedar Capital Partners LLC [2014] UKSC 45; [2015] A.C.
   250; [2014] 3 W.L.R. 535; [2014] 4 All E.R. 79; [2014] 2 All E.R. (Comm) 425; [2014]
   2 Lloyd's Rep. 471; [2014] 2 B.C.L.C. 145; [2014] Lloyd's Rep. F.C. 617; [2014] 3
   E.G.L.R. 119; [2014] W.T.L.R. 1135; [2015] 1 P. & C.R. DG1 . . 5-012, 6-039, 6-040, 6-042, **6-045**,
                                                  6-048, 6-080, 6-081, 6-085—6-087, 6-089
Fidcott v Friesner (1895) 11 T.L.R. 187 7-018
Field v Allen (1842) 9 M. & W. 694 .... 6-100, 6-111
Fielden v Christie-Miller [2015] EWHC 87 (Ch); [2015] W.T.L.R. 1165; 18 I.T.E.L.R.
   369; [2015] 2 P. & C.R. DG5 2-021
Filby v Hounsell [1896] 2 Ch. 737; 65 L.J.Ch. 852; 75 L.T. 270; 12 T.L.R. 612; 40 S.J.
   703; 45 W.R. 232 8-003
Filmer v Lynn (1835) SN. & M. 559; 1 Har. & W. 59 8-045
Financial Conduct Authority v Da Vinci Invest Ltd [2015] EWHC 2401 (Ch); [2016] Bus.
   L.R. 274; [2015] Lloyd's Rep. F.C. 540 1-028
Financings Ltd v Stimson [1962] 1 W.L.R. 1184; [1962] 3 All E.R. 386 CA **2-034, 8-026**
Finburgh v Moss Empires Ltd 1908 S.C. 928 8-196
Finch v Boning (1879) 4 C.P.D. 143; 40 L.T. 484; 43 J.P. 527; 27 W.R. 872 8-045
Finkielkraut v Monahan; sub nom. sub nom. Finkielkraut v Monohan [1949] W.N. 298;
   [1949] L.J.R. 1378; 93 S.J. 433; [1949] 2 All E.R. 234 6-013

Finlay, Re; Wilson (C.S.) & Co v Finlay [1913] 1 Ch. 565; 82 L.J.Ch. 295; 108 L.T. 699;
    29 T.L.R. 436; 57 S.J. 444 6-070
Finmoon Ltd v Baltic Reefers Management Ltd [2012] EWHC 920 (Comm); [2012] 2
    Lloyd's Rep. 388; [2012] 1 C.L.C. 813 8-076
Finn (Malcolm) & Co v Hoyle (1893) 63 L.J.Q.B. 1 9-020
Finzel, Berry & Co v Eastcheap Dried Fruit Co [1962] 2 Lloyd's Rep. 11 CA 8-078, 8-079
Fiona Trust & Holding Corp v Privalov [2007] UKHL 40; [2007] 4 All E.R. 951; [2007] 2
    All E.R. (Comm.) 1053 . . . . 3-012, 6-087, 8-023
Fiona Trust & Holding Corp v Privalov [2010] EWHC 3199 (Comm); (2011) 108(3)
    L.S.G. 17. . . . . 5-008, 6-085, 6-086, 6-087
Fiona Trust & Holding Corp v Skarga [2013] EWCA Civ 275 12-034
Fiona Trust Holding Corp v Privalov [2007] EWHC 1217 (Comm) 6-042
Firbank's Exors v Humphreys (1886) 18 Q.B.D. 54; 56 L.J.Q.B. 57; 56 L.T. 36; 35 W.R.
    92; 3 T.L.R. 49 . . . . 9-064, **9-076**, 9-078, 9-079
Firm of Solicitors, Re [2000] 1 Lloyd's Rep. 31 . . . . 6-050, 6-051
Firma C-Trade SA v Newcastle Protection and Indemnity Association; The Fanti; Socony
    Mobil Oil Inc v West of England Shipowners Mutual Insurance Association; The Padre
    Island (No.2) [1991] 2 A.C. 1; [1990] 3 W.L.R. 78; [1990] 2 All E.R. 705; (1990) 134
    S.J. 833; [1990] B.C.L.C. 625; [1990] 2 Lloyd's Rep. 191 HL 7-059
First Energy (UK) Ltd v Hungarian International Bank Ltd [1993] 2 Lloyd's Rep. 194;
    [1993] B.C.C. 533; [1993] B.C.L.C. 1409; [1993] N.P.C. 34 CA. 1-026, 2-051, 8-021, 8-039,
                                                                                                      8-044, 8-067
First Sport Ltd v Barclays Bank Plc 1993] 1 W.L.R. 1229; [1993] 3 All E.R. 789; (1993)
    12 Tr. L.R. 69 CA **8-043**
First Subsea Ltd v Balltec Ltd [2017] EWCA Civ 186 . . . . 6-034, 6-038, 6-040
Firth v Hylane Ltd [1959] E.G.D. 212 7-024
Firth v Staines [1897] 2 Q.B. 70; 66 L.J.Q.B. 510; 76 L.T. 496; 13 T.L.R. 394; 61 J.P. 452;
    45 W.R. 575; 41 S.J. 494 . . . . 2-047, 2-057, 2-062
Fish & Fish Ltd v Sea Shepherd UK [2015] UKSC 10; [2015] A.C. 1229; [2015] 2 W.L.R.
    694; [2015] 4 All E.R. 247; [2015] 2 All E.R. (Comm) 867; [2015] 1 Lloyd's Rep. 593. 8-195,
                                                                                                      9-120, 9-121
Fish v Kempton (1849) 7 C.B. 687; 18 L.J.C.P. 206; 13 L.T. (O.S.) 72; 13 Jur. 750 . . . 8-073, 8-109
Fisher v Drewett (1878) 48 L.J. Ex 32; L.T. 253; 27 W.R. 12 . . . . 7-014, 7-035
Fisher v Marsh (1865) 6 B. & S.411; 34 L.J.Q.B. 177; 12 L.T. 604; 29 J.P. 646; 11 Jur.
    (N.S.) 795; 13 W.R. 834. . . . . 9-005, 9-023, 9-035
Fisher v Smith (1878) 4 App.Cas.1; 48 L.J.Q.B. 411; 39 L.T. 430; 27 W.R. 113 . . . . . 7-076, 7-082,
                                                                                                      7-086, 7-099
Fitzalan-Howard v Hibbert [2009] EWHC 2855 (QB); [2010] P.N.L.R. 11 9-135
Fitzmaurice v Bayley (1860) 9 H.L.Cas.78; 3 L.T. 69; 6 Jur. (N.S.) 1215; 8 W.R. 750 . 2-073, 2-081
Fitzpatrick (t/a James F Fitzpatrick and Co Solicitors) v Allan Associates Architects Ltd
    [2015] NIQB 41 5-011
Fitzroy Bessemer Steel Co Ltd, Re (1884) 50 L.T. 144; 32 W.R. 475 . . . . 8-206, 8-214, 8-217
Flatau, Dick & Co v Keeping (1931) 39 Ll.L.Rep. 42; 36 Com.Cas. 243 9-035
Fleet Disposal Services Ltd, Re; sub nom. Spratt v AT&T Automotive Services Ltd [1995]
    1 B.C.L.C. 345; [1995] B.C.C. 605 Ch D. 6-041
Fleet v Murton (1871) L.R. 7 Q.B. 126; 41 L.J.Q.B. 49; 26 L.T. 181; 20 W.R. 97 . . . . 8-117, 9-006,
                                                                                                      9-016, **9-042**
Fleming v London Produce Co; Inland Revenue Commissioners v London Produce Co
    [1968] 1 W.L.R. 1013; [1968] 2 All E.R. 975; 44 T.C. 582; [1968] T.R. 97; (1968) 112
    S.J. 356 Ch D. 1-021, 1-022
Flemyng v Hector (1836) 2 M. & W. 172; 2 Gale 189; 8 L.J. Ex. 43 9-087
Flint v Woodin (1852) 9 Hare 618; 22 L.J.Ch. 92; 19 L.T. (O.S.) 240; 16 Jur. 719 6-068
Flitcroft's case; Re Exchange Banking Co (1882) 21 Ch.D. 519; 52 L.J.Ch. 217; 48 L.T.
    86; 31 W.R. 174 6-041
Floydd v Cheney; Cheney v Floydd [1970] Ch. 602; [1970] 2 W.L.R. 314; [1970] 1 All
    E.R. 446; 114 S.J. 70 Ch D 6-093
FNCB Ltd (formerly First National Commercial Bank Plc) v Barnet Devanney (Harrow)
    Ltd (formerly Barnet Devanney & Co Ltd); sub nom. FNCB Ltd v Barnet Devanney &
    Co Ltd [1999] 2 All E.R. (Comm) 233; [1999] Lloyd's Rep. P.N. 908; [2000] P.N.L.R.
    248; (1999) 96(28) L.S.G. 28 CA 6-024
Foalquest Ltd v Roberts [1990] 1 E.G.L.R. 50 CA 9-006
Fogg v Gaulter and Blane (1960) 110 L.J. 718 6-092
Foley v Classique Coaches Ltd [1934] 2 K.B. 1; 103 L.J.K.B. 550; 151 L.T. 242 7-009

Foley v Hill (1848) 2 H.L. Cas. 28 6-095
Folkes v King [1923] 1 K.B. 282; 92 L.J.K.B. 125; 12 L.T. 405; 39 T.L.R. 77; 67 S.J. 227;
    28 Com.Cas.110; 86 J.P.J. 552. . . . . 8-146, 8-153
Foord v Morley (1859) 1 F. & F. 496 7-004
Football Association Premier League Ltd v QC Leisure [2008] EWHC 1411 (Ch); [2008]
    U.K.C.L.R. 329; [2008] 3 C.M.L.R. 12; [2008] Info. T.L.R. 159; [2008] F.S.R. 32 9-120
Footner v Joseph (1860) 5 L.C.J. 225; 11 C.L.R. 94 7-005
Ford v Polymer Vision Ltd [2009] EWHC 945 (Ch); [2009] 2 B.C.L.C. 160 8-037
Fordham v Christie, Manson & Woods [1977] E.G.D. 94; (1977) 121 S.J. 529; (1977) 244
    E.G. 213 6-024
Fore Street Warehouse Co Ltd v Durrant & Co (1883) 10 Q.B.D. 471 10-020
Foreman v Great Western Railway (1878) 38 L.T. 851; 42 J.P. 648 2-016
Forman & Co Pty Ltd v Liddesdale, The [1900] A.C. 190; 69 L.J.P.C. 44; 82 L.T. 331; 9
    Asp.M.L.C. 45 PC (Aus) 2-077, 2-078, 2-083, 8-055
Format International Security Printers Ltd v Mosden [1975] 1 Lloyd's Rep. 37 QBD . 8-120, 9-006,
                                                                                    9-034, 9-060
Formby Brothers v Formby (1910) 102 L.T. 116; 54 L.J. 269 8-078
Forsikringsaktieselskapet Vesta v Butcher [1989] A.C. 852 HL 6-018
Forsta AP-Fonden v Bank of New York Mellon SA/NV [2013] EWHC 3127 (Comm) 3-016,
                                                                                    6-043, 6-056
Forth v Simpson (1849) 13 Q.B. 680; 18 L.J.Q.B. 263; 13 L.T.(O.S.) 187; 13 Jur. 1024 7-094
Fortis Bank SA NV v Indian Overseas Bank [2011] EWHC 538 (Comm); [2012] 1 All
    E.R. (Comm) 41. . . . . 1-012, 1-031
Foskett v McKeown [2001] 1 A.C. 102; [2000] 2 W.L.R. 1299; [2000] 3 All E.R. 97;
    [2000] Lloyd's Rep. I.R. 627; (2000) 1 W.T.L.R. 667; (2000) 97(23) L.S.G. 44 HL . . 6-040, 8-159,
                                                                                    8-162
Foster Bryant Surveying Ltd v Bryant [2007] EWCA Civ 200; [2007] Bus. L.R. 1565;
    [2007] B.C.C. 804; [2007] 2 B.C.L.C. 239; [2007] I.R.L.R. 425; [2007] 12 E.G. 154
    (C.S.); (2007) 104(13) L.S.G. 24 6-054
Foster v Action Aviation Ltd [2014] EWCA Civ 1368 . . . . 8-079, 8-180, 9-117, 9-119
Foster v Bates (1843) 12 M. & W. 226; 1 D. & L. 400; 13 L.J.Ex. 88; 2 L.T.(O.S.) 150; 7
    Jur. 1093 . . . . 2-070, 2-088, 10-017, 10-022
Foster v Fyfe; sub nom. Le Neve Foster v Fyfe [1896] 2 Q.B. 104; 65 L.J.M.C. 184; 74
    L.T. 784; 60 J.P. 423; 18 Cox.C.C. 364; 44 W.R. 524; 12 T.L.R. 433; 40 S.J. 546 2-026
Foster v Green (1862) 7 H. & N. 881; 31 L.J.Ex. 158 8-096
Foster v Pearson (1835) 1 C.M. & R. 849; 5 Tyr. 255; 4 L.J.Ex. 120 3-040
Foster's Agency Ltd v Romaine (1916) 32 T.L.R. 545 7-018
Fountaine v Carmarthen Railway Co (1868) L.R. 5 Eq. 316 . . . . 2-020, 2-021
Fowler v Bratt [1950] 2 K.B. 96; 66 T.L.R. (Pt. 1) 889; [1950] 1 All E.R. 662; 94 S.J. 269
    CA. 7-018
Fowler v Hollins; sub nom. Hollins v Fowler (1875) L.R. 7 H.L. 757; 44 L.J.Q.B. 169; 33
    L.T. 73; 40 J.P. 53 . . . . 1-039, 9-131
Fox v Hawks (1879) 13 Ch.D. 822; 49 L.J.Ch. 579; 42 L.T. 622; 28 W.R. 656 . . . . 8-135, 8-138
Fox v Martin (1895) 64 L.J.Ch. 473 . . . . 8-130, 8-135, 8-138, 8-161
Fox Walker & Co Ex p. Bishop, Re (1880) 15 Ch. D. 400; 50 L.J.Ch. 18; 43 L.T. 165; 29
    W.R. 144 CA. 7-062
Foxton v Manchester and Liverpool District Banking Co (1881) 44 L.T. 406 9-141
Foxtons Ltd v Bicknell [2008] EWCA Civ 419; [2008] 2 E.G.L.R. 23; [2008] 24 E.G.
    142; [2008] 17 E.G. 163 (C.S.); (2008) 105(18) L.S.G. 24; (2008) 152(17) S.J.L.B. 28;
    [2008] N.P.C. 52 . . . . 7-007, 7-017, 7-030, 7-038
Foxtons Ltd v Thesleff [2005] EWCA Civ 514; [2005] 21 E.G. 140; [2005] 17
    E.G.C.S.122 CA; [2005] 2 E.G.L.R. 29. . . . . 7-020, 7-021, 9-005
Framlington Group Plc v Anderson [1995] B.C.C. 611; [1995] 1 B.C.L.C. 475 6-054
France v Clark (1884) 26 Ch.D. 257; 58 L.J.Ch. 585; 50 L.T. 1; 32 W.R. 466 . . . . 8-130, 8-161
France v Dutton [1891] 2 Q.B. 208; 60 L.J.Q.B. 488; 64 L.T. 793; 39 W.R. 716 2-022
Francis v Francis (1854) 5 De G.M. & G. 108; 43 E.R. 811 7-089
Francis v Kuala Lumpur Councillors [1962] 1 W.L.R. 1411; [1962] 3 All E.R. 633; 106
    S.J. 833 PC (FMS) 7-047
Franklyn v Lamond (1847) 4 C.B. 637; 16 L.J.C.P. 221; 9 L.T. (O.S.) 246; 11 Jur. 780 9-034
Frape v Emreco International Ltd 2002 S.L.T. 371; 2001 S.C.L.R. 997; [2002] Eu. L.R.
    10; 2001 G.W.D. 26-993, OH 11-043
Fraser v Equitorial Shipping Co Ltd and Equitorial Lines Ltd; The Ijaolo [1979] 1 Lloyd's
    Rep. 103 QBD (Comm). 7-062, 7-075, 9-020, 9-038, 9-045

Fraser v Evans [1969] 1 Q.B. 349; [1968] 3 W.L.R. 1172; [1969] 1 All E.R. 8; 112 S.J.
   805 CA 6-077
Fraser v Furman (BN) (Productions) Ltd [1967] 1 W.L.R. 898; [1967] 3 All E.R. 57;
   [1967] 2 Lloyd's Rep. 1; 2 K.I.R. 483; (1967) 111 S.J. 471 CA 6-009
Fraser v Mudge [1975] 1 W.L.R. 1132; [1975] 2 All E.R. 78; 119 S.J. 508 CA 2-024
Fraser v Thames Television Ltd [1984] Q.B. 44; [1983] 2 W.L.R. 917; [1983] 2 All E.R.
   101; (1983) 133 N.L.J. 281; (1983) 127 S.J. 379 QBD. 6-077, 9-089
Fraser-Johnston Engineering, etc, Co v Sam Isaacs (Aberdeen) Ltd (1922) 12 Ll.Rep. 233 . . 8-120,
   9-046
Fray v Voules (1859) 1 E. & E. 839 6-003
Frazer's Patent, Re [1981] R.P.C. 53, Pat. Ct 1-038
Freedman (t/a John Freedman & Co) v Union Group Plc [1997] E.G.C.S.28 CA 7-028, 7-032
Freeman & Lockyer v Buckhurst Park Properties (Mangal) Ltd [1964] 2 Q.B. 480; [1964]
   2 W.L.R. 618; [1964] 1 All E.R. 630; 108 S.J. 96 CA . . . 1-006, 1-028, 2-009, 2-028, 2-032, 2-102,
        3-003, 3-004, 3-005, 3-011, 3-016, 3-029, 3-041, 3-042, 8-002, 8-010, 8-011, 8-014, 8-015,
              8-020, 8-023, 8-024, 8-031, 8-033, 8-034, 8-039, **8-046**, 8-069
Freeman v Appleyard (1862) 33 L.J.Ex. 175; 1 New Rep. 30; 7 L.T. 282 8-148
Freeman v Cooke (1848) 2 Exch. 654; 6 Dow. & L. 187; 18 L.J.Ex. 114; 12 L.T.(O.S.) 66;
   12 Jur. 777 . . . . 8-010, 8-024, 8-029
Freeman v Jeffries (1869) L.R. 4 Ex. 189; 38 L.J.Ex. 116; 20 L.T. 533 6-100
Freeman v Rosher (1849) 13 Q.B. 780; 18 L.J.Q.B. 340; 13 Jur. 881 . . . . **2-073**
Freeman v Sovereign Chicken Ltd [1991] I.C.R. 853; [1991] I.R.L.R. 408, EAT 3-032
Freimuller (J) (Ships Stores) Ltd v Ocean Carriers (London) Ltd [1961] 2 Lloyd's Rep.
   309 . . . . 8-120, 9-046
French (L) & Co Ltd v Leeston Shipping Co Ltd [1922] 1 A.C. 451; 91 L.J.K.B. 655; 127
   L.T. 169; 38 T.L.R. 459; 15 Asp.M.L.C. 544; 27 Com.Cas. 257; 10 Ll.L.Rep. 448. . . **7-044**, 10-042
French v Carter Lemon Camerons LLP [2012] EWCA Civ 1180; [2012] 6 Costs L.O. 879;
   [2013] P.N.L.R. 2; (2012) 162 N.L.J. 1155; (2012) 156(34) S.J.L.B. 27 . . . . 7-050, 7-083
French v Howie [1906] 2 K.B. 674; 75 L.J.K.B. 980; 95 L.T. 274 8-117
Friend v Young; sub nom. Re Friend; Friend v Friend (Young) [1897] 2 Ch. 421; 66
   L.J.Ch. 737; 77 L.T. 50; 46 W.R. 139; 41 S.J. 607 Ch D 10-016, 10-019
Frith v Cartland (1865) 34 L.J.Ch. 301; 2 Hem. & M. 417; 12 L.T. 175; 11 Jur. (N.S.) 283;
   13 W.R. 493. . . . . **8-167**
Frith v Frith [1906] A.C. 254; 75 L.J.P.C. 50; 94 L.T. 383; 54 W.R. 618; 22 T.L.R. 388 10-006,
   10-024, 10-029
Frixione v Tagliaferro & Sons (1856) 10 Moo. P.C. 175; 27 L.T.(O.S.) 21; 4 W.R. 373 . . . . . **2-100**,
   7-062, 7-063
Frontin v Small (1726) 2 Ld. Raym. 1418; 4 Stra. 765 . . . . 8-084, 8-087
Fruhling v Schroder (1835) 7 C. & P. 103; 2 Bing N.C. 77; 1 Hodg. 105; 2 Scott 135; 4
   L.J.C.P. 169 9-114
Fry & Mason v Smellie & Taylor [1912] 3 K.B. 282; 81 L.J.K.B. 1003; 106 L.T. 404 8-126,
   8-134, 8-135, **8-138**
Fry v Tapson (1884) 28 Ch.D. 268; 54 L.J.Ch. 224; 51 L.T. 326; 33 W.R. 113 . . . . 2-021, 5-010
FSS Travel & Leisure Systems Ltd v Johnson [1997] EWCA Civ. 2759; [1998] I.R.L.R.
   382; [1999] I.T.C.L.R. 218; [1999] F.S.R. 505. 6-038
Fuentes v Montis (1868) L.R. 4 C.P. 93; 38 L.J.C.P. 95; 19 L.T. 364; 17 W.R. 208 8-147
Fuller v Benett (1843) 2 Hare 394; 67 E.R. 162 . . . . 8-211, 8-213
Fuller v Eames (1892) 8 T.L.R. 278 . . . . 7-014, 7-035
Fuller v Glyn, Mills, Currie & Co [1914] 2 K.B. 168; 83 L.J.K.B. 764; 110 L.T. 318; 30
   T.L.R. 162; 58 S.J. 235; 19 Com.Cas.186 . . . . 8-126, 8-130, 8-138
Fullwood v Hurley [1928] 1 K.B. 498; 96 L.J.K.B. 976; 138 L.T. 49; 43 T.L.R. 609; 73
   S.J. 514 . . . . 2-013, 6-048
Fung Kai Sun v Chen Fui Hing [1951] A.C. 489; [1951] 2 T.L.R. 47; 95 S.J. 431 PC (HK) . . 2-059,
   8-041, 8-128
Furlong v Howard (1804) 2 Sch. & Lef. 115 7-089
Furness Withy (Australia) Ltd v Metal Distributors (UK) Ltd (The Amazonia) Amazonia,
   The [1990] 1 Lloyd's Rep. 236 CA 12-016
Furnivall v Hudson [1893] 1 Ch. 335; 62 L.J.Ch. 178; 68 L.T. 378; 41 W.R. 358; 3 R. 230 . . **2-026**
Furtadou v Lumley (1890) 6 T.L.R. 168; 54 J.P. 407 . . . . 9-025, 9-109
Fyffes Group Ltd v Templeman [2000] 2 Lloyd's Rep. 643; (2000) 97(25) L.S.G. 40 QBD
   (Comm Ct) 6-087, 8-225, 9-135
G (A) v G (T) [1970] 2 Q.B. 643; [1970] 3 W.L.R. 132; [1970] 3 All E.R. 546; (1970) 114
   S.J. 493 CA. 2-008

G-Star Raw CV v Rhodi Ltd [2015] EWHC 216 (Ch) 8-209
Gabriel (Thomas) & Sons v Churchill & Sim [1914] 3 K.B. 1272; 84 L.J.K.B. 233; 111
    L.T. 933; 30 T.L.R. 658; 58 S.J. 740; 19 Com.Cas. 411 . . . . 1-042, 9-022
Gabriel v Little [2013] EWCA Civ 1513; 16 I.T.E.L.R. 567 3-016
Gadd v Houghton (1876) 1 Ex.D. 357; 46 L.J.Q.B. 71; 35 L.T. 222; 24 W.R. 975 . . . . 9-006, 9-037,
                                                                                                        9-038
Gailey v Environmental Waste Controls [2004] Eu.L.R. 423; 2003 G.W.D. 40-1068, OH . . . 11-022
Galaxy Aviation v Sayegh Group Aviation [2015] EWHC 3478 (Comm) 8-024, 9-094
Galbraith & Grant v Bloch [1922] 2 K.B. 155; 91 L.J.K.B. 649; 127 L.T. 521; 38 T.L.R.
    669; 66 S.J. 596. 8-043
Gale (Martin) & Wright v Buswell [1961] E.G.D. 418 7-019
Galinski v McHugh [1989] 1 E.G.L.R. 109 2-026
Galland v Hall (1888) 4 T.L.R. 761 . . . . 9-106, **9-109**
Gallie v Lee. *See* Saunders (Executrix of the Estate of Rose Maud Gallie) v Anglia
    Building Society 2-107, 8-130
Galvin (GF) (Estates) Ltd v Hedigan [1985] I.L.R.M. 295 7-037
Gamatronic (UK) Ltd v Hamilton [2016] EWHC 2225 (QB) 6-015, 6-054, 6-068, 7-050
Garden Gully United Quartz Mining Co v McLister (1875) 1 App. Cas. 39 (PC) 2-038
Gardener Steel Ltd v Sheffield Bros (Profiles) Ltd [1978] 1 W.L.R. 916; [1978] 3 All E.R.
    399; (1978) 122 S.J. 488 CA 6-108
Gardiner v Heading [1928] 2 K.B. 284; 97 L.J.K.B. 766; 139 L.T. 449 . 8-120, 9-006, 9-044, 9-090,
                                                                                                        9-091, 9-092
Gardner v Lachlan 41 E.R. 51; (1838) 4 My. & C. 129 . . . . **9-113**
Gardner v McCutcheon (1842) Beav. 534 6-078
Garforth v Esam (1892) 56 J.P. 521; 8 T.L.R. 243 2-026
Garland v Pay (Ralph) & Ransom (1984) 271 E.G. 106, 116 9-117
Garnac Grain Co Inc v HMF Faure & Fairclough Ltd; Bunge Corp v HMF Faure &
    Fairclough Ltd [1968] A.C. 1130; [1967] 3 W.L.R. 143; [1967] 2 All E.R. 353; [1967] 1
    Lloyd's Rep. 495; 111 S.J. 434 HL . 1-012, 1-022, 1-026, 1-036, 2-030, 2-031, 2-032, 8-080, 8-096
Garrard v Southey (AE) & Co (Davey Estates, Third Party) [1952] 2 Q.B. 174; [1952] 1
    T.L.R. 630; [1952] 1 All E.R. 597; 96 S.J. 166. 8-179
Garrett v Handley (1825) 4 B. & C. 664; 7 Dow. & Ry. K.B. 144; 107 E.R. 1208 8-003
Gator Shipping Corp v Trans-Asiatic Oil SA and Occidental Shipping Etablissement SA;
    The Odenfeld [1978] 2 Lloyd's Rep. 357 QBD (Comm) 2-107, 8-130
Gaudet v Brown; Brown v Gaudet; Geipel v Cornforth Cargo Ex. Argos; The Hewsons
    (1873) L.R. 5 P.C. 134, P.C. 4-008
Gaussen v Morton (1830) 10 B. & C. 731; 5 Mar. & Ry. K.B. 613; 8 L.J.(O.S.) K.B. 313 . . . **10-014**
Gavaghan v Edwards [1961] 2 Q.B. 220; [1961] 2 W.L.R. 948; [1961] 2 All E.R. 477; 105
    S.J. 405 CA **2-016**, 3-023
Gaydamak v Leviev [2012] EWHC 1740 (Ch) 8-049
Gelley v Shephard [2013] EWCA Civ 1172; [2014] 1 P. & C.R. DG5 2-091
Gencor ACP Ltd v Dalby [2000] 2 B.C.L.C. 734 Ch D 9-135
General Accident Fire & Life Assurance Corp Ltd v Midland Bank Ltd [1940] 2 K.B. 388 . . . 8-200
General Accident Fire & Life Assurance Corp Ltd v Tanter; The Zephyr [1985] 2 Lloyd's
    Rep. 529 CA 6-028, 6-029
General Aviation Service (UK) Ltd v TGWU [1976] I.R.L.R. 224 HL 2-034
General Finance Facilities Ltd v Hughes (1966) 110 S.J. 847 8-045
General Legal Council (on the application of Whitter) v Frankson [2006] UKPC 42;
    [2006] 1 W.L.R. 2803 PC (Jamaica) 2-021, 2-022
General Publicity Services Ltd v Best's Brewery Co Ltd [1951] W.N. 507; [1951] 2 T.L.R.
    875; 95 S.J. 670 CA 10-042
General Reinsurance Corp v Forsakringsaktiebolaget Fenna Patria [1983] Q.B. 856;
    [1983] W.L.R. 318; [1983] 2 Lloyd's Rep. 287; (1983) 127 S.J. 389 CA. 3-034
Generics (UK) Ltd v Yeda Research and Development Co Ltd [2012] EWCA Civ 726;
    [2013] Bus. L.R. 777; [2012] C.P. Rep. 39; [2013] F.S.R. 13. . . . . 6-034, 6-051
Geniki Investments International Ltd v Ellis Stockbrokers Ltd [2008] EWHC 549 (QB);
    [2008] 1 B.C.L.C. 662 . . . . 2-072, 2-080, 2-103
Geoffrey Silver & Drake v Baines (t/a Wetherfield Baines & Baines) [1971] 1 Q.B. 396;
    [1971] 2 W.L.R. 187; [1971] 1 All E.R. 473; (1970) 114 S.J. 865 CA. 9-034
George v Clagett (1797) 7 T.R. 359; Peake, Add. Cas.131; 2 Esp. 557 8-109
Georgian American Alloys Inc v White and Case LLP [2014] EWHC 94 (Comm) 6-051
Gerard v Penswick (1818) 1 Swan. 533; 1 Wils. Ch. 222 6-092
Gething v Keighley (1878) 9 Ch.D. 547; 48 L.J.Ch. 45; 27 W.R. 283 6-098

Gewa Chartering BV v Remco Shipping Lines; The Remco [1984] 2 Lloyd's Rep. 205
    QBD (Comm) 9-094, **9-097**
GHLM Trading Ltd v Maroo [2012] EWHC 61 (Ch); [2012] 2 B.C.L.C. 369   . 6-004, 6-039, 6-054,
    6-096, 8-221
Giancarlo Zeta, The [1966] 2 Lloyd's Rep. 317, Ex Ct (Can) 2-013
Gibbon v Budd (1863) 2 H. & C. 92 7-004
Gibbon v Pease [1905] 1 K.B. 810; 74 L.J. K.B. 502; 92 L.T. 433; 69 J.P. 209; 53 W.R.
    417; 21 T.L.R. 365; 49 S.J. 382; 3 L.G.R. 461 . . . . 6-093, 7-005
Gibbs v Daniel (1862) 4 Giff. 1; 7 L.T. 27; 9 Jur. (N.S.) 636; 10 W.R. 688 . . . . **6-070**
Giblin v McMullen (1869) L.R. 2 P.C. 317; 5 Moo. P.C.(N.S.) 434; 38 L.J.P.C. 25; 21 L.T.
    214; 17 W.R. 445 6-031
Gibson v Jeyes (1801) 6 Ves. 266 . . . . 6-064, 6-065
Gibson v Minet (1824) 9 Moo. C.P. 31; 2 Bing. 7; 2 L.J.(O.S.) C.P. 99 . . . . 9-110, **10-029**
Gibson v Winter (1833) S.B. & Ad. 96; 2 N.A.M.K.B. 737; 2 L.J.K.B. 130 9-029
Giddys v Horsfall [1947] 1 All E.R. 460; 63 T.L.R. 160 7-019
Gidley v Palmerston (1822) 3 B. & B. 275; 1 State Tr.(N.S.) 1263; 7 Moore C.P. 91 9-028
Gidman v Barron [2003] EWHC 153 (Ch) 6-039
Giles (CH) & Co Ltd v Morris [1972] 1 W.L.R. 307; [1972] 1 All E.R. 960; (1971) 116
    S.J. 176 Ch D 7-046
Giles v Taff Vale Railway (1853) 2 E. & B. 822; 23 L.J.Q.B. 43; 22 L.T. 157; 18 Jur. 510;
    2 C.L.R. 132 8-189
Gillard v Wise (1826) 5 B. & C. 134; 7 Dow. & Ry. K.B. 523; 4 L.J.(O.S.) K.B. 88; 108
    E.R. 49 3-025
Gillett v Peppercorne (1840) 3 Beav. 78 . . . . **6-071**
Gillow & Co v Lord Aberdare (1892) 9 T.L.R. 12 . . . . 7-051, **10-005**
Gilman v Robinson (1825) 1 Ry. & M. 266; 1 C. & P. 642 8-044
Gissing v Gissing [1971] A.C. 886; [1970] 3 W.L.R. 255; [1970] 2 All E.R. 780; (1970) 21
    P. & C.R. 702; (1970) 114 S.J. 550 HL. 8-050
Gladman Commercial Properties v Fisher Hargreaves Proctor [2013] EWCA Civ 1466;
    [2014] C.P. Rep. 13; [2013] 47 E.G. 128 (C.S.) 8-182, 8-191
Gladman v Johnson (1867) 36 L.J.C.P. 153; 15 L.T. 476; 15 W.R. 313 . . . . **8-217**
Gladstone v Birley (1817) 2 Mer. 401 7-073
Gladstone v King (1813) 1 M. & S.35 . . . . 8-213, **8-217**
Glasgow Corp v Lorimer; sub nom. Glasgow Corp v Riddell [1911] A.C. 209; 80 L.J.P.C.
    175; 104 L.T. 534 8-196
Glasgow, The (1856) Swab. 145 4-004
Glaxo Wellcome UK Ltd (t/a Allen & Hanburys) v Sandoz Ltd [2017] EWCA Civ 227 9-120
Gledhill v Bentley Designs (UK) Ltd [2010] EWHC B8 . . . . 10-042, 11-056
Glencore International AG v MSC Mediterranean Shipping Co SA [2015] EWHC 1989
    (Comm); [2015] 2 Lloyd's Rep. 508 . . . . 8-209, 8-217
Glenester v Hunter (1831) S.C. & P. 62 . . . . **8-043**
Glengal (Earl of) v Barton (1836) 1 Keen 769 3-032
Glentree Estates Ltd v Favermead Ltd [2010] EWCA Civ 1473; [2011] 1 E.G.L.R. 23;
    [2011] 11 E.G. 104; [2011] 1 P. & C.R. DG20 . . . . 7-021, 7-030
Glentree Estates Ltd v Gee [1981] E.G.D. 235 7-032
Glentree Estates Ltd v Holbeton Ltd [2011] EWCA Civ 755; [2011] 28 E.G. 74 (C.S.);
    [2011] 2 P. & C.R. DG19 7-030
Global Container Lines Ltd v Bonyad Shipping Co (No.1) [1998] 1 Lloyd's Rep. 528
    QBD (Comm Ct). 6-035
Global Energy Horizons Corp v Gray [2015] EWHC 2232 (Ch) 6-040, 6-042
Gloucester Municipal Election Petition, 1900, Re; Ford v Newth [1901] 1 K.B. 683; 70
    L.J.K.B. 459; 84 L.T. 354; 65 J.P. 391; 17 T.L.R. 325; 49 W.R. 345. . . . . 2-057, 2-095, 2-097
Glover v Langford (1892) 8 T.L.R. 628 . . . . 9-020, 9-038
Gluckstein v Barnes; sub nom. Olympia Ltd, Re [1900] A.C. 240; 69 L.J. Ch. 385; 82 L.T.
    393; 16 T.L.R. 321; 7 Mans. 321 . . . . 6-035, 6-039, 6-071
Godfrey v Furzo (1733) 3 P. Wms.186 8-167
Godin v London Assurance Co (1758) 1 W.Bl. 103; 1 Burr. 489; 2 Keny. 254; 97 E.R. 419 . . 7-082
Goding v Frazer [1967] 1 W.L.R. 286; [1966] 3 All E.R. 234; 199 E.G. 127; (1966) 110
    S.J. 870 9-026
Godwin v Francis (1870) L.R. 5 C.P. 295; 39 L.J. C.P. 121; 22 L.T. 338 . . . . 9-081, 9-083
Gokal Chand-Jagan Nath v Nand Ram Das-Atma Ram [1939] A.C. 106; 108 L.J.P.C. 9; 55
    T.L.R. 15; 82 S.J. 888; [1938] 4 All E.R. 407. . . . . 3-022, 3-025, 4-007, 6-020
Gold v Essex CC [1942] 2 K.B. 293; [1942] 2 All E.R. 237; 112 L.J.K.B. 1; 86 S.J. 295 9-116

Gold v Life Assurance Company of Pennsylvania [1971] 2 Lloyd's Rep. 164 7-042
Goldcorp Exchange Ltd (In Receivership), Re; Kensington v Unrepresented Non-
    Allocated Claimants; Goldcorp Finance Ltd, Re [1995] 1 A.C. 74; [1994] 3 W.L.R. 199;
    [1994] 2 All E.R. 806; [1994] 2 B.C.L.C. 578; (1994) 13 Tr. L.R. 434; (1994) 91(24)
    L.S.G. 46; (1994) 144 N.L.J. 792; (1994) 138 S.J.L.B. 127 (NZ) 6-035, 6-040
Golden Ocean Group Ltd v Salgaocar Mining Industries Pvt Ltd [2012] EWCA Civ 265;
    [2012] 1 W.L.R. 3674; [2012] 3 All E.R. 842; [2012] 2 All E.R. (Comm) 978; [2012] 1
    Lloyd's Rep. 542; [2012] 1 C.L.C. 497; [2012] C.I.L.L. 3161; (2012) 162 N.L.J. 425. 2-019, 2-023,
                                                                        8-060, 12-017, 12-020, 12-026
Golding v Royal London Auxiliary Insurance Co Ltd (1914) 30 T.L.R. 350 8-217
Goldrei Foucard & Sun v Russian Chamber of Commerce [1918] 1 K.B. 180; [1916-17]
    All E.R. Rep. 898; 87 L.J.K.B. 267 8-117
Goldsmith Williams Solicitors v E Surv Ltd. *See* E Surv Ltd v Goldsmith Williams
    Solicitors 6-021
Gomer v Pitt & Scott (1922) 12 Ll.Rep. 115 . . . . 6-028, **6-032**
Gompertz v Cook (1903) 20 T.L.R. 106 8-161
Goodacre v Meyer [2002] EWHC 1785 (Ch) 9-121
Goodall v Lowndes (1844) 6 Q.B. 464; 8 J.P. 771; 9 Jur. 177 9-109
Goodey and Southwold Trawlers v Garriock, Mason and Millgate [1972] 2 Lloyd's Rep.
    369 QBD 8-117, 8-118, 9-109
Goodman v Harvey (1836) 4 A. & E. 870; 6 New & N.K.B. 372; 6 L.J.K.B. 63, 260 8-140
Goodwin v Francis (1870) L.R. 5 C.P. 295 . . . . 9-079, **9-083**
Goodwin v Robarts (1876) 1 App. Cas. 476; 45 L.J.Q.B. 748; 35 L.T. 179; 24 W.R. 987 . . . . **8-142**
Goose v Wilson Sandford & Co (No.2) [2001] Lloyd's Rep. P.N. 189 CA 9-135
Gordon Hill Trust Ltd v Segall [1941] 2 All E.R. 379; 85 S.J. 191 8-185
Gordon v Selico Co Ltd [1980] 1 E.G.L.R. 71; (1986) 18 H.L.R. 219; (1986) 278 E.G. 53
    CA 8-064
Gore v Van Der Lann; sub nom. Gore v Van der Lann Corp of Liverpool (Interveners)
    [1961] 2 Q.B. 31; [1967] 2 W.L.R. 358; [1967] 1 All E.R. 360; 110 S.J. 928; [1967] 1
    Lloyd's Rep. 145; [1966] C.L.Y. 1167 CA 9-122
Goshawk Dedicated Ltd v Tyser & Co Ltd [2006] EWHC Civ 54 . . . . 2-016, 3-035, 6-048
Gosling v Anderson (1972) 223 E.G. 1743 . . . . 8-186, 9-117
Gosling v Gaskell [1897] A.C. 575 1-037
Goulandris Bros Ltd v Goldman & Sons [1958] 1 Q.B. 74; [1957] 3 W.L.R. 596; [1957] 3
    All E.R. 100; 101 S.J. 762; [1957] 2 Lloyd's Rep. 207 7-066
Gould v South Eastern and Chatham Railway [1920] 2 K.B. 186; 89 L.J.K.B. 700; 123
    L.T. 256 3-020
Governor and Company of The Bank of Scotland v Alfred Truman (A Firm) [2005]
    EWHC 583 (QB) 6-104
Gowers v Lloyds, etc., Foreign Bank [1938] 1 All E.R. 766 . . . . 9-106, **9-109**
Graanhandel T. Vink BV v European Grain & Shipping Ltd [1989] 2 Lloyd's Rep. 531 4-005
Grace v Biagioli [2005] EWCA Civ 1222; [2006] B.C.C. 85; [2006] 2 B.C.L.C. 70; (2005)
    102(48) L.S.G. 18 6-054
Graham & Baldwin v Taylor, Sun & Davis (1965) 109 S.J. 793; 196 E.G. 305 7-005
Graham & Scott (Southgate) Ltd v Oxlade [1950] 2 K.B. 257; 66 T.L.R. (Pt. 1) 808;
    [1950] 1 All E.R. 856; 94 S.J. 209 CA 7-019
Graham v Ackroyd (1853) 10 Hare 192; 22 L.J.Ch. 1046; 17 Jur. 657; 1 W.R. 107 1-042
Graham v Musson (1839) 5 Bing. N.C. 603; 7 Scott 769; 8 L.J.C.P. 324; 3 Jur. 483 . . . 2-019, 2-023
Graham v Public Works Commrs. [1901] 2 K.B. 781; 70 L.J.K.B. 860; 85 L.T. 96; 65 J.P.
    677; 50 W.R. 122; 17 T.L.R. 540; 45 S.J. 538 . . . . **9-034**
Grahame (John W) (English Financiers) Ltd v Ingram [1955] 1 W.L.R. 563; [1955] 2 All
    E.R. 320; 99 S.J. 336 CA 2-018
Gran Gelato Ltd v Richcliff (Group) Ltd [1992] Ch. 560; [1992] 2 W.L.R. 867; [1992] 1
    All E.R. 865; [1992] 1 E.G.L.R. 297; [1991] E.G.C.S.136; (1992) 142 N.L.J. 51 Ch D 8-182,
                                                                        8-196, 9-117, **9-125**
Grand Trunk Railway Co of Canada v Robinson [1915] A.C. 740, Privy Council (Canada) . . 2-103,
                                                                        8-211
Grant v Fletcher (1826) 5 B. & C. 436; 8 Dow. & Ry., K.B. 59 . . . . 6-019, 6-024
Grant v Gold Exploration & Development Syndicate Ltd [1900] 1 Ch. 233; 69 L.J.Q.B.
    150; 82 L.T. 5; 48 W.R. 280; 16 T.L.R. 86; 44 S.J. 100 . . . . 6-085, 8-222, 8-223
Grant v Norway (1851) 10 C.B. (N.S.) 665; 20 L.J.C.P. 135; 60 L.J.(O.S.) 504; 15 Jur. 296 . . 8-067

Grant v U.K. Switchback Railway Co; sub nom. Grant v Thompson's Patent Gravity
 Switchback Rys (1880) 40 Ch.D. 135; 60 L.T. 525; 5 T.L.R. 92; 1 Meg. 117; 58 L.J.Ch.
 211; 37 W.R. 312. 2-069
Gratitudine, The (1801) 3 Ch. Rob. 240 4-004
Gray v Gutteridge (1828) 3 C. & P. 40; 6 C.J. (O.S.) K.B. 154; 1 Man. & Ry. K.B. 614 9-109
Gray v Haig (1855) 20 Beav. 219 . . . . 6-090, 6-092
Gray v Johnston (1868) L.R. 3 H.L. 1; 16 W.R. 842 . . . . 9-141, 9-142
Gray v Kirby (1834) 2 Dowl. 601 . . . . **5-016**
Gray v Pearson (1870) L.R. 5 C.P. 568; 23 L.T. 416 9-003
Gray v Raper (1861) L.R. 1 C.P. 694; Har. & Ruth. 794; 14 W.R. 780 . . . . **9-056**
Gray v Smith [2013] EWHC 4136 (Comm); [2014] 2 All E.R. (Comm) 359 . . . 6-082, 8-072, 8-162
Great Atlantic Insurance Co v Home Insurance Co; Great Atlantic Insurance Co v
 American Foreign Insurance Association; Great Atlantic Insurance Co v CE Heath &
 Co (International); Great Atlantic Insurance Co v Frank Elger & Co [1981] 1 W.L.R.
 529; [1981] 2 All E.R. 485; [1981] 2 Lloyd's Rep. 138; 125 S.J. 203 CA. 6-005
Great Britain 100 A1 Steamship Insurance Association v Wyllie (1889) L.R. 22 Q.B.D.
 710. 8-082
Great Estates Group Ltd v Digby [2011] EWCA Civ 1120; [2012] 2 All E.R. (Comm) 361;
 [2011] 3 E.G.L.R. 101; [2011] 43 E.G. 104 (C.S.); [2011] N.P.C. 102; [2012] 1 P. &
 C.R. DG7 . . . . 7-007, 7-038, 7-042
Great Northern Railway Co v Swaffield (1874) L.R. 9 Ex. 132; 43 L.J. Ex. 89; 30 L.T. 562 . 4-004,
 4-005, 4-006
Great Southern Mysore Gold Mining Co, Re (1882) 48 L.T. 11 2-021
Great Western Insurance Co of New York v Cunliffe (1874) L.R. 9 Ch. App. 525; 43
 L.J.Ch. 741; 30 L.T. 661 . . . . 6-086, **6-089**, 7-004
Greatorex & Co v Shackle [1895] 2 Q.B. 249; 64 L.J.Q.B. 634; 72 L.T. 897; 44 W.R. 47;
 39 S.J. 602; 15 R. 501 . . . . 7-030, **7-104**
Green (E) & Son Ltd v Tughan (G) & Co (1913) 30 T.L.R. 64 6-089
Green (FW) & Co Ltd v Brown & Gracie Ltd [1960] 1 Lloyd's Rep. 289; 1960 S.L.T.
 (Notes) 43 HL 1-022, 1-036, 3-020, 6-010, 7-101
Green (Tranckle's Trustee) v Bramston (Kingshouse Developments Ltd's Liquidator)
 [2010] EWHC 3106 (Ch); [2011] B.P.I.R. 44. 4-010
Green v Bartlett (1863) 14 C.B.(N.S.) 681; 2 New Rep. 279; 32 L.J.C.P. 261; 8 L.T. 503;
 10 Jur. (N.S.) 78; 11 W.R. 834. . . . . 7-030, **7-032**
Green v Elgie (1843) 5 Q.B. 99; Dar. & Mer. 199; 14 L.J.Q.B. 162; 8 J.P. 133; 8 Jur. 187 . . . **9-125**
Green v Kopke (1856) 18 C.B. 549; 25 L.J.C.P. 297; 27 L.T.(O.S.) 172; 2 Jur. (N.S.) 1049;
 4 W.R. 598. 9-038
Green v Lucas (1876) 33 L.T. 584; 40 J.P. 390 . . . . 7-014, 7-035
Green v Mules (1861) 30 L.J.C.P. 343 . . . . 7-004, **7-012**, 7-032
Green v Skandia Life Assurance Co Ltd [2006] EWHC 1626 (Ch) 7-039
Green v Wroe [1877] W.N. 130 2-056
Greene v All Motors Ltd [1917] 1 K.B. 625; 86 L.J.K.B. 590; 116 L.T. 189 1-033
Greener Solutions Ltd v HMRC [2012] UKUT 18 (TCC); [2012] S.T.C. 1056; [2012]
 Lloyd's Rep. F.C. 235; [2012] B.V.C. 1551 8-214
Greenglade Estates Ltd v Chana [2012] EWHC 1913 (Ch); [2012] 3 E.G.L.R. 99; [2012]
 42 E.G. 138; [2012] 29 E.G. 85 (C.S.) 9-081, 9-083
Greenway v Atkinson (1881) 29 W.R. 560 9-114
Greenway v Fisher (1824) 1 C. & P. 190 9-129
Greenway v Hurd (1792) 4 T.R. 553 9-106
Greenwood v Martins Bank Ltd [1933] A.C. 51 HL **2-059**, 2-061, 8-041, 8-091, 8-128, 9-066
Greer v Downs Supply Co [1927] 2 K.B. 28; 96 L.J.K.B. 534; 137 L.T. 174 . . 8-050, 8-073, 8-079,
 8-110, 8-111, 8-155
Gregory v Ford [1951] 1 All E.R. 121 Assizes (Nottingham) 7-063
Gregory v Turner; R. (on the application of Morris) v North Somerset Council [2003]
 EWCA Civ 183; [2003] 1 W.L.R. 1149; [2003] 2 All E.R. 1114; [2003] C.P. Rep. 40;
 [2003] 3 E.G.L.R. 129 CA 2-024
Gregson v HAE Trustees Ltd [2008] EWHC 1006 (Ch); [2009] Bus. L.R. 1640; [2009] 1
 All E.R. (Comm) 457; [2008] 2 B.C.L.C. 542; [2008] Pens. L.R. 295; [2008] W.T.L.R.
 1; [2008] 2 P. & C.R. DG9. . . . . 5-012, 9-135, 9-138
Gresley v Mousley (1862) 31 L.J.Ch. 537; 3 De G.F. & J. 433; 6 L.T. 86; 8 Jur. (N.S.)
 320; 10 W.R. 222 6-064
Gribbon v Lutton [2001] EWCA Civ 1956; [2002] Q.B. 902; [2002] 2 W.L.R. 842; [2002]
 Lloyd's Rep. P.N. 272; [2002] P.N.L.R. 19; [2002] 2 E.G.C.S.100; [2002] N.P.C. 2 CA 9-026

Grice v Kenrick (1870) L.R. 5 Q.B. 340; 39 L.J.Q.B. 175; 22 L.T. 743; 18 W.R. 1155 ...... **9-035**
Griffin v UHY Hacker Young & Partners (A Firm) [2010] EWHC 146 (Ch) 6-023
Griffin v Weatherby (1868) L.R. 3 Q.B. 753; 9 B. & S.726; 37 L.J.Q.B. 280; 18 L.T. 881;
  17 W.R. 8 .... 9-113, 10-010
Griffiths Cycle Corp Ltd v Humber & Co Ltd [1899] 2 Q.B. 414; 68 L.J.Q.B. 959; 81 L.T.
  310. 2-019
Grindell v Bass [1920] 2 Ch. 487; 89 L.J.Ch. 591; 124 L.T. 211; 36 T.L.R. 867 2-019
Grindley v Barker (1798) 1 B. & P. 229 2-043
Grissell v Bristowe (1868) L.R. 4 C.P. 36 .... 8-117, 9-023
Grogan v Smith (1890) 7 T.L.R. 132 7-035
Gross Fine & Krieger Chalfen v Clifton (1974) 223 E.G. 837 7-004
Gross, Re, Ex p. Kingston (1871) L.R. 6 Ch.App. 632; 40 L.J. Bcy 61; 25 L.T. 250; 19
  W.R. 910 7-088
Grosvenor Casinos Ltd v National Bank of Abu Dhabi [2008] EWHC 511 (Comm);
  [2008] 2 All E.R. (Comm) 112; [2008] 2 Lloyd's Rep. 1; [2008] 1 C.L.C. 399; [2008]
  Bus. L.R. D95 5-008
Ground Gilbey Ltd v Jardine Lloyd Thompson UK Ltd [2011] EWHC 124 (Comm);
  [2012] Lloyd's Rep. I.R. 12; [2011] P.N.L.R. 15 .... **6-024**
Group Josi Re Co SA v Walbrook Insurance Co Ltd; Group Josi Re (formerly Group Josi
  Reassurance SA) v Walbrook Insurance Co Ltd; Deutsche Ruckversicherung AG v
  Walbrook Insurance Co Ltd [1996] 1 W.L.R. 1152; [1996] 1 All E.R. 791; [1996] 1
  Lloyd's Rep. 345; [1996] 5 Re. L.R. 91 CA 1-029, 8-212, 8-214
Grupo Torras SA v Al-Sabah (No.5); Al-Sabah v Grupo Torras SA; Bonafonte v Grupo
  Torras SA [2001] Lloyd's Rep. Bank. 36; [2001] C.L.C. 221; [2001] Lloyd's Rep. P.N.
  117 CA 8-218, 9-135, 12-025
Guaranty Trust Co of New York v Hannay & Co [1918] 2 K.B. 623; [1914-15] All E.R.
  Rep. 24; 84 L.J.K.B. 1465; 113 L.T. 98; 21 Com.Cas.67 .... 7-060, 9-034, 9-066
Gudermes, The. *See* Mitsui & Co v Novorossiysk Shipping Co; Gudermes, The 8-217, 9-125
Guest v Smythe (1870) L.R. 5 Ch.App. 551; 39 L.J.Ch. 536; 22 L.T. 563; 34 J.P. 676; 18
  W.R. 742, L.J 6-070
Guinness Plc v Saunders [1990] 2 A.C. 663; [1990] 2 W.L.R. 324; [1990] 1 All E.R. 652;
  (1990) 134 S.J. 457; [1990] B.C.C. 205; [1990] B.C.L.C. 402 HL..... 6-080, 6-083, 7-004, 8-066,
  8-067, 8-221
Gullischen v Stewart Bros (1884) 13 Q.B.D. 317; 53 L.J.Q.B. 173; 50 L.T. 47; 32 W.R.
  763; 5 Asp. M.L.C. 200. .... 6-080, 6-083, 7-004, 8-068, 8-069, 8-221, 9-096
Gunn v Bolckow, Vaughan & Co (1875) L.R. 10 Ch.App. 491; 44 L.J.Ch. 732; 32 L.T.
  781; 23 W.R. 739 .... **7-094**
Gunn v Roberts (1873–74) L.R. 9 C.P. 331, CCP 2-072, 4-004
Gunn v Showell's Brewery Co Ltd (1902) 18 T.L.R. 659; 46 S.J. 584 .... 7-021, 7-028, **7-032**
Gunton v Richmond-upon-Thames LBC [1981] Ch. 448; [1980] 3 W.L.R. 714; [1980] 3
  All E.R. 577; [1980] I.C.R. 755; [1980] I.R.L.R. 321; 79 L.G.R. 241; 124 S.J. 792 CA 7-047
Gurney v Womersley (1854) 4 E. & B. 133; 24 L.J.Q.B. 46; 24 L.T. (O.S.) 71; 1 Jur.
  (N.S.) 328; 3 C.L.R. 3 .... 9-043, **9-109**
Gurtner v Beaton [1993] 2 Lloyd's Rep. 369 .... 2-025, 8-015, **8-043**, 8-077
Guthrie v Armstrong (1822) 5 B. & A. 628; 1 Dow. & Ry. K.B. 248 .... **2-044**
Gwatkin v Campbell (1854) 1 J.W.(N.S.) 131 6-020
Gwembe Valley Development Co Ltd (In Receivership) v Koshy. See DEG-Deutsche
  Investitions- und Entwicklungsgesellschaft mbH v Koshy (Account of Profits:
  Limitations)
Gwilliam v Twist [1895] 2 Q.B. 84; 64 L.J.Q.B. 474; 72 L.T. 579; 59 J.P. 484; 43 W.R.
  566; 11 T.L.R. 415; 14 R. 461 .... 4-005, 4-010, 5-001
Habas Sinai Ve Tibbi Gazlar Istihsal Endustrisi v VSC Steel Co Ltd [2013] EWHC 4071
  (Comm); [2014] 1 Lloyd's Rep. 479 .... 12-016, 12-017, 12-020
Habton Farms v Nimmo; sub nom. Nimmo v Habton Farms [2003] EWCA Civ 68; [2004]
  Q.B. 1; [2003] 3 W.L.R. 633; [2003] 1 All E.R. 1136; [2003] 2 All E.R. (Comm) 109;
  [2003] 2 C.L.C. 353; (2003) 147 S.J.L.B. 176 CA 9-080, **9-083**
Hackett v Advanced Medical Computer Systems Ltd [1999] C.L.C. 160 QBD 11-046
Hackney v Knight (1891) 7 T.L.R. 254 8-200
Hagedorn v Oliverson (1814) 2 M. & S.485 2-093
Haines v Busk (1814) 5 Taunt 521; 1 Marsh. 191 .... **7-056**
Hair & Skin Trading Co Ltd v Norman Airfreight Carriers Ltd and World Transport
  Agencies [1974] 1 Lloyd's Rep. 443 9-024
Halbot v Lens [1901] 1 Ch. 344; 70 L.J.Ch. 125; 83 L.T. 702; 49 W.R. 214; 45 S.J. 15 9-060,

9-070, **9-076**
Halesowen Presswork and Assemblies Ltd v Westminster Bank Ltd [1972] A.C. 785;
  [1972] 2 W.L.R. 455; [1972] 1 All E.R. 641; [1972] 1 Lloyd's Rep. 101; (1972) 116 S.J.
  138 HL 7-077
Halewood International Ltd v Addleshaw Booth & Co [2000] Lloyd's Rep. P.N. 298;
  [2000] P.N.L.R. 788 Ch D. 6-051
Halifax Mortgage Services Ltd (formerly BNP Mortgages Ltd) v Stepsky [1996] Ch. 207;
  [1996] 2 W.L.R. 230; [1996] 2 All E.R. 277; [1996] 1 F.L.R. 620; [1996] 2 F.C.R. 97;
  (1996) 28 H.L.R. 522; [1996] Fam. Law 279; (1996) 93(1) L.S.G. 21; (1996) 140
  S.J.L.B. 9; [1995] N.P.C. 184 CA. 8-216
Hall Ex p.; Re Whitting; sub nom. Re Whitting Ex p. Rowell (1879) 10 Ch.D. 619 9-112
Hall v Ashurst (1883) 1 C. & M. 714; 3 Tyr. 420; 2 L.J.Ex. 295 . . . . 9-006, **9-038**
Hall v Benson (1836) 7 C. & P. 711 7-004
Hall v Hallett (1784) 1 Cox Eq.Cas. 134 6-068
Hall v Laver (1842) 1 Hare 571 . . . . **2-100**, 7-089
Hall v North Eastern Railway Co (1875) L.R. 10 Q.B. 437; 44 L.J.Q.B. 164; 33 L.T. 306;
  36 J.P. 724; 23 W.R. 860. 9-122
Hallett & Co, Re; Ex p. Blane [1894] 2 Q.B. 237; 63 L.J.Q.B. 573; 40 T.L.R. 287; 42 W.R.
  305; 1 Mans. 25; 9 R. 278. 8-167
Hallett's Estate, Re; Knatchbull v Hallett (1880) 13 Ch.D. 696; 49 L.J.Ch. 415; 42 L.T.
  421; 28 W.R. 732. . . . . 8-162, **8-167**
Halton International Inc (Holdings) Sarl v Guernroy Ltd [2006] EWCA Civ 801; [2006]
  W.T.L.R. 1241 . . . . 6-043, 9-135
Hambro v Burnand [1903] 2 K.B. 399 3-011
Hambro v Burnand [1904] 2 K.B. 10; 73 L.J.K.B. 669; 90 L.T. 803; 52 W.R. 583; 20
  T.L.R. 398; 48 S.J. 369; 9 Com. Cas. 251. . . . . 3-005, 3-011, 8-052, **8-064**
Hamburg, The (1864) 2 Moo.P.C.(N.S.) 289 4-004
Hamer v Sharp (1874) L.R. 19 Eq. 108; 44 L.J.Ch. 53; 31 L.T. 643; 23 W.R. 158 . . . . **3-032**
Hamid (t/a Hamid Properties) v Francis Bradshaw Partnership [2013] EWCA Civ 470;
  [2013] B.L.R. 447; 148 Con. L.R. 205. . . . . 9-006, 9-037, 9-055
Hamilton v Spottiswoode (1849) 4 Exch. 200; 18 L.J.Ex. 393; 14 L.T.(O.S.) 108 . . . . . **9-113**, 9-114
Hamilton v Wright (1842) 9 Cl. & Fin. 111 (HL) 6-034
Hamilton v Young (1881) 7 L.R.Ir. 289 . . . . 3-034, 3-037, **3-040**, 6-057, **6-061**
Hamlyn & Co v Wood & Co [1891] 2 Q.B. 488; 60 L.J.Q.B. 734; 65 L.T. 286; 40 W.R.
  24; 7 T.L.R. 731 10-042
Hamlyn v Houston (John) & Co [1901] 1 K.B. 81; 72 L.J.K.B. 72; 87 L.T. 500; 51 W.R.
  99; 19 T.L.R. 66; 47 S.J. 90 CA 8-192, 8-224
Hammond & Co v Bussey (1887) 20 Q.B.D. 79; 57 L.J.Q.B. 58; 4 T.L.R. 95 9-081
Hammond v Schofield [1891] 1 Q.B. 453; 60 L.J.Q.B. 539; 7 T.L.R. 300 8-118
Hammonds v Barclay (1802) 2 East 227 . . . . 7-071, 7-078
Hamond v Holiday (1824) 1 C. & P. 384 7-050
Hampden v Walsh (1876) 1 Q.B.D. 189; 45 L.J.Q.B. 238; 33 L.T. 852; 24 W.R. 607 . . . . **10-029**
Hampshire Land Co (No.2), Re; sub nom. Re Hampshire Land Co Ltd Ex p. Portsea
  Island Building Society [1891] 2 Ch. 743; 75 L.T. 181; 12 T.L.R. 517; 45 W.R. 136; 40
  S.J. 654; 3 Mans. 269; 65 L.J.Ch. 860. . . . . 8-214, 8-215, **8-217**
Hampton & Sons v Chapman [1952] C.P.L. 24 7-037
Hampton v George [1939] 3 All E.R. 627 . . . . 7-037, 10-045
Hampton v Trade and General Securities Ltd (1978) 250 E.G. 451 7-012
Hanak v Green [1958] 2 Q.B. 9; [1958] 2 W.L.R. 755; [1958] 2 All E.R. 141; 102 S.J. 329
  CA. 6-100
Hancock v Smith (1889) Ch.D. 456; 58 L.J.Ch. 725; 61 L.T. 341; 5 T.L.R. 459 . . . . . . 6-041, 8-167
Hancocks v Leblache (1878) 3 C.P.D. 197 9-017
Hangkam Kwingtong Woo v Liu Lan Fong (alias Liu Ah Lan) [1951] A.C. 707; [1951] 2
  T.L.R. 442; [1951] 2 All E.R. 567; 95 S.J. 544 PC (HK) 2-010, 10-003
Hankinson v Vickers [1931] E.G.D. 16 7-035
Hanley v Cassam (1847) 11 Jur. 1088; 2 New Pr.Cas. 431; 10 L.T. (O.S.) 189 . . . . **5-016**
Hanna v Imperial Life Assurance Co of Canada [2007] UKPC 29 PC (Bahamas) 1-034
Hannaford v Syms (1898) 79 L.T. 30; 14 T.L.R. 530 5-016
Hannan's Empress Gold Mining & Development Co, Re; Carmichael's Case [1896] 2 Ch.
  643; 65 L.J.Ch. 902; 75 L.T. 45. . . . . 10-007, **10-014**
Hannibal (E.) & Co Ltd v Frost (1988) 4 B.C.C. 3 CA **3-029**, 8-224
Hanson v Lorenz & Jones [1987] 1 F.T.L.R. 23; (1986) 136 N.L.J. 1088 CA 6-062
Hanson v Roberdeau (1792) Peake 163 9-034

Hanstown Properties Ltd v Green (1977) 246 E.G. 917 CA 8-082
Happy Day, The; Glencore Grain Ltd v Flacker Shipping Ltd; sub nom. Flacker Shipping
  Ltd v Glencore Grain Ltd; Happy Day, The [2002] EWCA Civ 1068; [2002] 2 All E.R.
  (Comm) 896; [2002] 2 Lloyd's Rep. 487; [2003] 1 C.L.C. 537 CA 1-023, 3-032
Harben v Phillips (1883) 23 Ch. D. 14 CA 2-018
Hardie Polymers Ltd v Polymerland Ltd 2002 S.C.L.R. 64; 2001 G.W.D. 35-1338, OH 11-044
Harding Maughan Hambly Ltd v Compagnie Europeenne de Courtage d'Assurances et de
  Reassurances SA [2000] 1 All E.R. (Comm) 225; [2000] 1 Lloyd's Rep. 316; [2000]
  C.L.C. 524; [2000] Lloyd's Rep. I.R. 293 QBD (Comm Ct)............... 7-004, 7-030, 7-032
Hardman v Bellhouse (1842) 9 M. & W. 596; 11 L.J.Ex. 135 6-100
Hardman v Booth (1863) 1 H. & C. 803; 1 New Rep. 240; 32 L.J.Ex. 105; 7 L.T. 638; 9
  Jur. (N.S.) 81; 11 W.R. 239 .... 9-094, 9-095
Hardwick (Earl) v Vernon (1808) 14 Ves. 504 6-098
Hardy v Caley (1864) 33 Beav. 365 9-140
Hare v Nicoll; sub nom. Hare v Nichol [1966] 2 Q.B. 130; [1966] 2 W.L.R. 441; [1966] 1
  All E.R. 285; 110 S.J. 11 CA 6-013
Hargreaves v Rothwell 48 E.R. 265; (1836) 1 Keen 154 8-211
Harington v Hoggart (1830) 1 B. & Ad. 577; 9 L.J.(O.S.) K.B. 14 .... 6-104, 9-025, 9-026
Harker v Edwards (1887) 57 L.J.Q.B. 147; 4 T.L.R. 92 .... 3-033, 3-036, 3-037
Harley & Co v Nagata (1917) 34 T.L.R. 124; 23 Com. Cas.121 .... 7-004, 7-012
Harlow & Jones Ltd v PJ Walker Shipping & Transport Ltd [1986] 2 Lloyd's Rep. 141
  QBD (Comm) 6-001, 9-024
Harmer v Armstrong [1934] Ch. 65; 103 L.J.Ch. 1; 149 L.T. 579 ...... 8-083, 8-085, 8-087, **8-088**
Harmond Properties Ltd v Gajdzis [1968] 1 W.L.R. 1858; [1968] 3 All E.R. 263; 112 S.J.
  762; 19 P. & C.R. 718 CA... 2-026
Harper & Co v Vigers Bros [1909] 2 K.B. 549; 78 L.J.K.B. 867; 100 L.T. 887; 25 T.L.R.
  627; 53 S.J. 780; 11 Asp. M.L.C. 275; 14 Com. Cas.213 .... 9-095, 9-096
Harper & Sons v Keller, Bryant and Co Ltd (1915) 84 L.J.K.B. 1696; 113 L.T. 175; 31
  T.L.R. 284; 13 Asp. M.L.C. 98; 20 Com. Cas.291 9-020
Harper v Godsell (1870) L.R. 5 Q.B. 422; 39 L.J.Q.B. 185; 18 W.R. 954 3-015
Harper v Granville-Smith (1891) 7 T.L.R. 284 .... 8-043, 9-087
Harper v Williams (1843) 4 Q.B. 219; 12 L.J.Q.B. 227 .... 9-037, 9-038
Harrington v Victoria Graving Dock Co (1878) 3 Q.B.D. 549; 47 L.J.Q.B. 594; 39 L.T.
  120; 42 J.P. 744; 26 W.R. 740.............................. 6-086, 7-052, 7-054, 9-098
Harris (LS) Trustees (t/a Harris & Co) v Power Packing Services (Hermit Road) [1970] 2
  Lloyd's Rep. 65 QBD 6-003, 7-050
Harris v Fiat Motors Ltd (1907) 23 T.L.R. 504 5-001
Harris v Nickerson (1873) L.R. 8 Q.B. 286; 42 L.J.Q.B. 171; 28 L.T. 410; 37 J.P. 536; 21
  W.R. 635... 9-034
Harris v Richard Lawson Autologistics Ltd [2002] EWCA Civ 442; [2002] I.C.R. 765;
  [2002] I.R.L.R. 476; (2002) 99(18) L.S.G. 36; (2002) 146 S.J.L.B. 99 CA.............. 2-034
Harrison (JJ) (Properties) Ltd v Harrison [2001] EWCA Civ 1467; [2002] B.C.C. 729;
  [2002] 1 B.C.L.C. 162; [2001] W.T.L.R. 1327 CA............ 6-040, 6-062, 6-070, 8-221, **8-226**
Harrison Ex p.; Re Bentley & Co v Yorkshire Breweries Ltd (1893) 69 L.T. 204 .... **8-045**
Harrison v Michelin Tyre Co Ltd [1985] 1 All E.R. 918; [1985] I.C.R. 696 QBD 8-178
Harrisons & Crosfield Ltd v L&NW Ry Co Ltd [1917] 2 K.B. 755; 86 L.J.K.B. 1461; 33
  T.L.R. 517; 61 S.J. 647.. 2-078
Harrods Ltd v Geneen [1938] 4 All E.R. 493; 55 T.L.R. 139; 82 S.J. 1009 CA 7-035
Harrods v Lemon [1931] 2 K.B. 157; 100 L.J.K.B. 219; 144 L.T. 657; 47 T.L.R. 248; 75
  S.J. 11 CA... 6-048, 6-050, **7-051**
Harsant v Blaine, Macdonald & Co (1887) 56 L.J.Q.B. 511; 3 T.L.R. 689 .... 5-012, 6-099, 6-100,
                                                                          6-108
Hart (Chris) (Business Sales) Ltd v Currie 1992 S.L.T. 544; 1991 S.C.L.R. 534, IH (1 Div) .. 7-021
Hart & Hodge v Frame, Son & Co (1839) 6 C. & F. 193; Mad. & Rob. 595; 3 Jur. 547 6-019
Hart v O'Connor [1985] A.C. 1000; [1985] 3 W.L.R. 214; [1985] 2 All E.R. 880; [1985] 1
  N.Z.L.R. 159; (1985) 82 L.S.G. 2658; (1985) 129 S.J. 484 PC (New Zealand) 2-009
Hartas v Ribbons (1889) 22 Q.B.D. 254; 58 L.J.Q.B. 187; 37 W.R. 278; 5 T.L.R. 200 2-096
Hartnell v Taylor, Cook & Bromwich [1982] E.G.D. 436 CA 7-032
Hartop Ex p. (1806) 12 Ves.Jun. 349; 33 E.R. 132 9-002
Hartwells of Oxford Ltd v British Motor Trade Association [1951] Ch. 50; 66 T.L.R. (Pt.
  2) 483; [1950] 2 All E.R. 705; 94 S.J. 505 CA................................. 6-013
Harvey v O'Dell (RG); Galway, Third Party [1958] 2 Q.B. 78; [1958] 2 W.L.R. 473;
  [1958] 1 All E.R. 657; 102 S.J. 196; [1958] 1 Lloyd's Rep. 273 8-191

Haseler v Lemoyne (1858) 5 C.B.(N.S.) 530; 28 L.J.C.P. 103; 22 J.P. 788; 14 Jur. (N.S.)
   1279; 7 W.R. 14 . . . . 2-056, **2-073**, 8-196
Haslam and Hier-Evans, Re [1902] 1 Ch. 765; 71 L.J.Ch. 374; 86 L.T. 663; 50 W.R. 444;
   18 T.L.R. 461; 46 S.J. 381 . . . . 6-048, 6-086, **6-089**
Hastings Ltd v Pearson [1893] 1 Q.B. 62; L.J.Q.B. 75; 67 L.T. 553; 57 J.P. 70; 41 W.R.
   127; 9 T.L.R. 18; 36 S.J. 866; 5 R. 26. 8-145
Hastingwood Property Ltd v Saunders Bearman Anselm [1991] Ch. 114; [1990] 3 W.L.R.
   623; (1990) 134 S.J. 1153; (1990) 140 N.L.J. 817 Ch D 9-026
Hatch v Hale (1850) 15 Q.B. 10; 19 L.J.Q.B. 289; 15 L.T.(O.S.) 65; 14 Jur. 459 . . . . **3-032**
Hatch v Searles (1854) 24 L.J.Ch. 22; 24 L.T.(O.S.) 122; 2 Sm. & G. 147; 2 W.R. 49 . . . . . . **8-045**
Hatch v Taylor 10 N.H. 538 (1840) 1-045
Hathesing v Laing (1873) 17 Eq. 92; 43 L.J.Ch. 233; 29 L.T. 734 . . . . 7-094, 7-101
Hatsall v Griffith (1834) 2 Cr. & M. 679; 4 Tyr. 487; 3 L.J.Ex. 191 2-046
Hatton v Car Maintenance Co Ltd [1915] 1 Ch. 621; 84 L.J.Ch. 847; 110 L.T. 765; 30
   T.L.R. 275; 58 S.J. 361 . . . . 7-078, 7-094
Haugesund Kommune v Depfa ACS Bank [2010] EWCA Civ 579; [2012] Q.B. 549;
   [2012] 2 W.L.R. 199; [2011] 1 All E.R. 190; [2011] 1 All E.R. (Comm) 985; [2012]
   Bus. L.R. 1; [2010] 1 C.L.C. 770 . . . . 12-002, 12-020
Hawkes v Cuddy [2009] EWCA Civ 291; [2009] 2 B.C.L.C. 427 . . . . 2-031, 2-033
Hawkes v Dunn (1831) 1 C. & J. 519; 1 Tyr. 413; 9 L.J.(O.S.) Ex. 184 7-101
Hawkesley v Outram [1892] 3 Ch. 359 3-015
Hawkins v Kemp (1803) 3 East 410 2-021
Hawkins v Pearse (1903) 9 Com.Cas. 87 6-009
Hawksford v Hawksford (2005) 191 F.L.R. 173 3-007
Hawtayne v Bourne (1841) 7 N. & W. 595; 10 L.J.Ex. 224; 5 Jur. 118; 151 E.R. 905 . . 4-003, 4-006
Hay's Case; Re Canadian Oil Works Corp (1875) L.R. 10 Ch.App. 593; 44 L.J.Ch. 721;
   33 L.T. 466; 24 W.R. 191 . . . . 6-087, **6-089**
Haycraft Gold Reduction and Mining Co Ltd, Re [1900] 2 Ch. 230 . . . . **3-029**
Hayim v Citibank N.A. [1987] A.C. 730; [1987] 3 W.L.R. 83; (1987) 131 S.J. 660; (1987)
   84 L.S.Gaz. 1573, P.C. 6-056
Hayle, The [1929] P. 275 8-217
Hayman & Son v M'Lintock; sub nom. Hayman & Son v M'lintock 1907 S.C. 936; 44
   S.C.L.R. 691; 15 S.L.T. 63 8-173
Headway Construction Co Ltd v Downham (1974) 233 E.G. 675 . . . . . . 6-064, 6-068, **6-071**, 7-051
Heald v Kenworthy (1855) 10 Exch. 739; 24 L.J.Ex. 76; 24 L.T.(O.S.) 260; 1 Jur. (N.S.)
   70; 3 W.R. 176; 3 C.L.R. 612. . . . . 8-101, 8-103, 8-104
Heane v Rogers (1820) 9 B. & C. 577; 40 Man. & Ry. K.B. 486; 7 L.J.(O.S.) K.B. 285;
   109 E.R. 215 8-126
Heap v Motorists Advisory Agency Ltd [1923] 1 K.B. 577; 92 L.J.K.B. 553; 129 L.T. 146;
   39 T.L.R. 150; 67 S.J. 300 . . . . 8-145, 8-153, 8-154
Heard v Pilley (1869) L.R. 4 Ch.App. 548; 38 L.J.Ch. 718; 21 L.T. 68; 33 J.P. 628; 17
   W.R. 750 . . . . 2-036, 2-037
Heath Lambert Ltd v Sociedad de Corretaje de Seguros [2004] EWCA Civ 792; [2004] 1
   W.L.R. 2820 CA 5-016
Heath v Chilton (1844) 12 M. & W. 632; 13 L.J.Ex. 225; 2 L.T. (O.S.) 424 2-070
Heath v Parkinson (1926) 136 L.T. 128; 42 T.L.R. 693; 70 S.J. 798 . . . . **7-051**
Heatons Transport (St. Helens) v Transport and General Workers Union; Craddock
   Brothers v Same; Panalpina Services v Same [1973] A.C. 15; [1972] 3 W.L.R. 431;
   [1972] 3 All E.R. 101 HL 1-026, **2-034**, 8-176, 8-180, 10-027
Hedley Byrne & Co Ltd v Heller & Partners Ltd [1964] A.C. 465; [1963] 3 W.L.R. 101;
   [1963] 2 All E.R. 575; [1963] 1 Lloyd's Rep. 485, HL . . 6-030, 6-043, 8-183, 8-186, 9-061, 9-083,
                                                                  9-117
Heinl v Jyske Bank (Gibraltar) Ltd [1999] Lloyd's Rep. Bank. 511; (1999) 96(34) L.S.G.
   33 CA. 3-011, 8-219
Heisch v Carrington (1833) 5 C. & P. 471 3-026
Helmet Integrated Systems Ltd v Tunnard [2006] EWCA Civ 1735; [2007] I.R.L.R. 126;
   [2007] F.S.R. 16. . . . . 6-038, 6-054
Hely-Hutchinson v Brayhead Ltd [1968] 1 Q.B. 549; [1967] 3 W.L.R. 1408; [1967] 3 All
   E.R. 98; 111 S.J. 830 CA . . . 3-003, 3-004, 3-005, 3-028, **3-029**, 3-041, 3-042, 4-008, 6-068, 8-010,
                                          8-015, 8-020, 8-031, 8-034, 8-039, 8-221
Helyear v Hawke (1803) 5 Esp. 72 . . . . **3-018**
Hemming v Hale (1859) 7 C.B. (N.S.) 487; 29 L.J.C.P. 137; 6 Jur. (N.S.) 554; 8 W.R. 46 . . . 5-001,
                                                                5-009

Henderson & Co v Williams [1895] 1 Q.B. 521; 64 L.J.Q.B. 308; 72 L.T. 98; 43 W.R.
  274; 11 T.L.R. 148; 14 R. 375. 8-130
Henderson v Barnewall (1827) 1 Y. & J. 387 5-002
Henderson v Merrett Syndicates Ltd [1995] 2 A.C. 145; [1994] 3 All E.R. 506 . . . . . . 5-008, 5-011,
                     5-016, 6-013, 6-018, 6-029, 6-035, 6-043, 6-058, 7-001, 8-183, 9-117
Henderson v Prosser [1982] C.L.Y. 21 . . . . 8-045, 8-147
Henley v Soper (1928) 8 B. & C. 16; Dan. & Ll. 38; 2 Man. & Ry. K.B. 153; 6 L.T. (O.S.)
  K.B. 210 . . . . **3-015**
Henry v Gregory (1905) 22 T.L.R. 53 7-018
Henry v Hammond [1913] 2 K.B. 515; 82 L.J.K.B. 575; 108 L.T. 729; 29 T.L.R. 340; 57
  S.J. 358; 12 Asp. M.L.C. 332 . . . . 6-041, **6-045**, 6-091
Henry v Lowson (1885) 2 T.L.R. 199 10-042
Hepworth Group Ltd v Stockley [2006] EWHC 3626 (Ch); [2007] 2 All E.R. (Comm) 82 . . . 9-100
Hermione, The; sub nom. The HMS Daffodil [1922] P. 162; 91 L.J.P. 136; 126 L.T. 701;
  15 Asp. M.L.C. 493; 38 T.L.R. 381 6-003
Hern v Nichols (1701) 1 Salk. 289; Holt K.B. 462 8-185
Hersom v Bernett [1955] 1 Q.B. 98; [1954] 3 W.L.R. 737; [1954] 3 All E.R. 370; 98 S.J.
  805 QBD 1-041, 9-017, 9-092
Heskell v Continental Express Ltd [1950] W.N. 210; [1950] 1 All E.R. 1033; 94 S.J. 339;
  83 Ll.L.Rep. 438 . . . . 9-061, 9-064, 9-066, 9-080, 9-081, **9-083**
Hesse v Briant (1856) 6 De G.M. & G. 623; 43 E.R. 1375 6-050
Heugh v Abergavenmy (Earl of) and Delves (1874) 23 W.R. 40 9-116
Heugh v Garrett (1875) 44 L.J.Ch. 305; 32 L.T. 45 6-092
Hewison v Guthrie (1836) 2 Bing. N.C. 755; 2 Hodg. 51; 3 Scott 298; 5 L.C.J.P. 283 7-094
Hewitt v Bonvin [1940] 1 K.B. 188; 109 L.J.K.B. 223; 161 L.T. 360; 56 T.L.R. 43; 83 S.J.
  869. 1-034
Hewitt v Loosemoore (1851) 9 Hare 449; 2 L.J.Ch. 69; 18 L.T.(O.S.) 133; 15 Jur. 1097 8-217
Hewitt v Spiers & Pond (1896) 13 T.L.R. 64 8-196
Hexstone Holdings Ltd v AHC Westlink Ltd [2010] EWHC 1280 (Ch); [2010] L. & T.R.
  22; [2010] 2 E.G.L.R. 13; [2010] 32 E.G. 62 . . . . 1-045, 2-094
Heyman v Flewker (1863) 13 C.B.(N.S.) 519; 1 New Rep. 479; 32 L.J.C.P. 132; 9 Jur.
  (N.S.) 895 . . . . 8-144, 8-145
Heys v Tindall (1861) 1 B. & S.296; 30 L.J.Q.B. 362; 4 L.T. 403; 9 W.R. 664 . . . . . . 6-019, **6-024**
HIB Ltd v Guardian Insurance Co Inc [1997] 1 Lloyd's Rep. 412 12-003
Hibblewhite v M'Morine (1840) 6 M. & W. 200; previous proceedings (1839) 5 M. & W.
  462; 8 L.J.Ex. 271; 3 Jur. 509. 2-041
Hichens, Harrison Woolston & Co v Jackson & Sons [1943] A.C. 266; [1943] 1 All E.R.
  128; 112 L.J.K.B. 88; 168 L.T. 128; 59 T.L.R. 112; 87 S.J. 7 . . . . **9-034**
Hick v Tweedy (1890) 63 L.T. 765; 7 T.L.R. 114; 6 Asp.M.L.C. 599 9-038
Hickey v McGowan [2017] IESC 6 8-178
Higgins v Senior (1841) 8 M. & W. 834; 11 L.J.Ex. 199 . . . . 8-003, 9-006, 9-039, 9-040, **9-042**
HIH Casualty & General Insurance Ltd v Chase Manhattan Bank; Chase Manhattan Bank
  v HIH Casualty & General Insurance Ltd [2003] UKHL 6; [2003] 1 All E.R. (Comm)
  349; [2003] 2 Lloyd's Rep. 61; [2003] 1 C.L.C. 358; [2003] Lloyd's Rep. I.R. 230;
  (2003) 147 S.J.L.B. 264 HL 6-056, 8-185
HIH Casualty & General Insurance Ltd v JLT Risk Solutions Ltd (formerly Lloyd
  Thompson Ltd) [2007] EWCA Civ 710; [2008] Bus. L.R. 180; [2007] 2 All E.R.
  (Comm) 1106; [2007] 2 Lloyd's Rep. 278; [2007] 2 C.L.C. 62; [2007] Lloyd's Rep. I.R.
  717; [2008] P.N.L.R. 3; (2007) 104(30) L.S.G. 35. . . . . **2-016**, 6-015, 6-024, 6-048
Hilberry v Hatton (1864) 2 H. & C. 822; (1862) 2 H. & C. 822; 3 New Rep. 671; 33 L.J.
  Ex. 190; 10 L.T. 39; 2 Mar.L.C. 31 . . . . 2-056, **2-061**, **2-073**
Hill S.S. Co Ltd v Hugo Stinnes Ltd 1941 S.C. 324 . . . . 9-095, 9-096
Hill Street Services Co Ltd v National Westminster Bank Plc [2007] EWHC 2379 (Ch) **3-009**,
                                                                                   6-009, 8-038
Hill v Curtis (1865) L.R. 1 Eq. 90; 35 L.J.Ch. 133; 13 L.T. 584; 12 Jur. (N.S.) 4; 14 W.R.
  125. 9-125
Hill v Customs and Excise Commissioners v Paget [1988] S.T.C. 424, DC 1-036
Hill v Featherstonhough (1831) 7 Bing. 569; 5 Moo. & P. 541 7-050
Hill v Harris [1965] 2 Q.B. 601; [1965] 2 W.L.R. 1331; [1965] 2 All E.R. 358; 109 S.J.
  333 CA **3-032**
Hill v Parsons (CA) & Co Ltd [1972] 1 Ch. 305; [1971] 3 W.L.R. 995; [1971] 3 All E.R.
  1345; 115 S.J. 868 CA. 7-046, 10-025
Hill v Royds (1869) L.R. 8 Eq. 290; 38 L.J.Ch. 538; 20 L.T. 842 9-114

Hill v Smith (1844) 12 M. & W. 618; 13 L.J.Ex. 243; 2 L.T. (O.S.) 424; 8 Jur. 179 6-100
Hillas & Co Ltd v Arcos Ltd (1932) 38 Com.Cas. 23; 147 L.T. 503; 43 Ll.L.Rep. 359 7-009
Hillen & Pettigrew v ICI Alkali Ltd [1936] A.C. 65; 104 L.J.K.B. 473; 153 L.T. 403; 51
    T.L.R. 532; 41 Com.Cas.29 8-176
Hilmi & Associates Ltd v 20 Pembridge Villas Freehold Ltd [2010] EWCA Civ 314;
    [2010] 1 W.L.R. 750; [2010] 3 All E.R. 391; [2010] N.P.C. 42 CA 1-029, 1-047, 2-022
Hilton v Barker Booth & Eastwood [2005] UKHL 8; [2005] 1 W.L.R. 567; [2005] 1 All
    E.R. 651; [2005] P.N.L.R. 23; [2005] 6 E.G.C.S.141; (2005) 102(14) L.S.G. 27; (2005)
    155 N.L.J. 219; (2005) 149 S.J.L.B. 179; [2005] N.P.C. 14 HL . 2-013, 6-015, 6-021, 6-043, 6-048,
                                                                          6-050
Hindle v Brown (1908) 98 L.T. 791 9-035
Hine Brothers v Steamship Insurance Syndicate Ltd; Netherholme, Glen Holme & Rydal
    Holme, The (1895) 72 L.T. 79; 11 T.L.R. 224; 7 Asp.M.L.C. 558; 11 R. 777 . . . . **3-026**
Hippisley v Knee Bros [1905] 1 K.B. 1; 74 L.J.K.B. 68; 92 L.T. 20; 21 T.L.R. 5; 49 S.J. 15 . 6-087,
                                                                          6-089, 7-050, **7-051**
Hirachand Punamchand v Temple; sub nom. Punamchand Shrichand & Co v Temple
    [1911] 2 K.B. 330; 80 L.J. K.B. 1155; 105 L.T. 277; 27 T.L.R. 430; 55 S.J. 519 CA 9-122
Hirschfeld v London, Brighton & South Coast Railway Co (1876) 2 Q.B.D. 1 9-069
Hirst v Etheringtons [1999] Lloyd's Rep. P.N. 938; (1999) 96(31) L.S.G. 42; (1999) 149
    N.L.J. 1110 CA 4-007, 8-021, 8-044, 8-048
Hirst v West Riding Union Banking Co Ltd [1901] 2 K.B. 560; 70 L.J.K.B. 828; 85 L.T. 3;
    49 W.R. 715; 17 T.L.R. 629; 45 S.J. 614 8-198
His Royal Highness Okpabi v Royal Dutch Shell Plc [2017] EWHC 89 (TCC); [2017]
    B.L.R. 136. 1-030
Hivac Ltd v Park Royal Scientific Instruments Ltd [1946] Ch. 169; [1946] 2 All E.R. 350;
    115 L.J.Ch. 241; 174 L.T. 422; 62 T.L.R. 231; 90 S.J. 175 CA 6-015, 6-061
HLB Kidsons (A Firm) v Lloyd's Underwriters (Costs) [2007] EWHC 2699 (Comm);
    [2008] 3 Costs L.R. 427 8-207
HLB Kidsons (A Firm) v Lloyd's Underwriters [2007] EWHC 1951 (Comm); [2008] 1 All
    E.R. (Comm) 769; [2008] Lloyd's Rep. I.R. 237; [2008] Bus. L.R. D28 8-207
HLB Kidsons (A Firm) v Lloyd's Underwriters [2008] EWCA Civ 1206; [2009] Bus. L.R.
    759; [2009] 2 All E.R. (Comm) 81; [2009] 1 Lloyd's Rep. 8; [2008] 2 C.L.C. 617;
    [2009] Lloyd's Rep. I.R. 178. . . . . 8-206, 8-207
Ho Tung v Man On Insurance Co Ltd [1902] A.C. 232 PC (Hong Kong) 1-028
Hoare v Niblett [1891] 1 Q.B. 781; 60 L.J.Q.B. 565; 64 L.T. 659; 55 J.P. 664; 39 W.R. 491 . . 9-006
Hobbs, Re (1887) 36 Ch.D. 553; 57 L.J.Ch. 184; 58 L.T. 9; 36 W.R. 445 6-111
Hobday v Peters (No.1) (1860) 28 Beav. 349; 29 L.J.Ch. 780; 2 L.T. 590; 6 Jur. (N.S.)
    794; 8 W.R. 512; 54 E.R. 400. 6-064
Hobhouse v Hamilton (1826) 1 Hog. 401 (Ir.) 9-034
Hocker v Waller (1929) 29 Com. Cas.296 . . . . **7-032**
Hoddell v Smith [1976] E.G.D. 217; (1975) 240 E.G. 295 CA 7-012, 7-030
Hodges & Sons v Hackbridge Park Residential Hotel Ltd [1940] 1 K.B. 404; 109 L.J.K.B.
    190; 56 T.L.R. 128; [1939] 4 All E.R. 347; 83 S.J. 941; 162 L.T. 74. . . . . **7-032**
Hodgkinson v Kelly (1868) L.R. 6 Eq. 496; 37 L.J.Ch. 837; 16 W.R. 1078 3-040
Hodgson v Anderson (1825) 3 B. & C. 842; 5 Dow. & Ry. K.B. 735 . . . . **9-113**
Hogarth v Wherley (1875) L.R. 10 C.P. 630; 44 L.J.C.P. 330; 32 L.T. 800 3-026
Hogg v Cramphorn [1967] Ch. 254; [1966] 3 W.L.R. 995; [1966] 3 All E.R. 420; (1966)
    110 S.J. 887. 8-226
Hogg v Snaith (1808) 1 Tant. 347 . . . . **3-015**
Holder v Holder [1968] Ch. 353; [1968] 2 W.L.R. 237; [1968] 1 All E.R. 665; (1967) 112
    S.J. 17 CA 6-064, 6-068
Holderness v Collinson (1827) 7 B. & C. 212; 1 Mar. & Ry. K.B. 55; 6 L.J.(O.S.) K.B. 17 . . 7-074,
                                                                          7-082
Holding Oil Finance Inc v Marc Rich & Co AG [1996] C.L.Y. 1085 9-121
Holding v Elliott (1860) 5 H. & N. 117; 29 L.J.Ex. 134; 1 L.T. 381; 8 W.R. 192 . . . . . 9-040, **9-046**
Holdnerness v Goslin [1975] 2 N.Z.L.R. 46 8-178
Holdsworth v Glasgow (City of) Bank (1880) 5 App.Cas. 317 8-176
Holdsworth v Lancashire & Yorkshire Insurance Company (1907) 23 T.L.R. 521 8-217
Holland Ex p. Warren, Re (1884) 15 Q.B.D. 48; (1885) 1 T.L.R. 430 CA **8-207**
Holland v King (1848) 6 C.B. 727 2-094
Holland v Russell (1863) 4 B. & S.14; 2 New Rep. 188; 32 L.J.Q.B. 297; 8 L.T. 468; 11
    W.R. 757 . . . . 9-107, **9-109**
Holland, Re, Ex p. Alston (1868) L.R. 4 Ch.App. 168; 19 L.T. 542; 17 W.R. 266 8-167

Hollandia, The. *See* Owners of Cargo on Board the Morviken v Owners of the Hollandia;
The Hollandia and the Morviken 11-006
Hollebone's Agreement, Re; sub nom. Hollebone v WJ Hollebone & Sons [1959] 1
W.L.R. 536; [1959] 2 All E.R. 152; 103 S.J. 349; [1959] T.R. 147 CA 7-062
Hollins v Fowler (1874) L.R. 7 H.L. 757; 44 L.J.Q.B. 169; 33 L.T. 73; 40 J.P. 53 . . . . 9-125, 9-129,
9-131
Hollis v Claridge (1813) 5 Taunt. 807   . . . . **7-089**
Hollman v Pullin (1884) C. & E. 254   . . . . 9-085, **9-087**
Holman v Loynes (1854) 4 De G.M. & G. 270; 2 Eq. Rep. 715; 23 L.J.Ch. 529; 22
L.T.(O.S.) 296; 18 Jur. 839; 2 W.R. 205 6-064
Holmes v Kennard (H.) & Son (A Firm) (1984) 44 P. & C.R. 202; 128 S.J. 854; CA   3-032
Holmes v Tutton (1855) 5 E. & B. 65; 24 L.J.Q.B. 346; 25 L.T. (O.S.) 177; 1 Jur. (N.S.)
975; 3 C.L.R. 1343 9-035
Holt & Moseley v Cunningham & Partners (1949) 83 Ll.Rep. 141   9-020
Holt v Ely (1853) 1 E. & B. 795; 17 Jur. 892; 1 C.L.R. 420   . . . . 8-167, 9-099
Homburg Houtimport BV v Agrosin Private Ltd; The Starsin; sub nom. Owners of Cargo
Lately Laden on Board the Starsin v Owners of the Starsin; Hunter Timber Ltd v
Agrosin Private Ltd [2003] UKHL 12; [2004] 1 A.C. 715; [2003] 2 W.L.R. 711; [2003]
2 All E.R. 785; [2003] 1 All E.R. (Comm) 625; [2003] 1 Lloyd's Rep. 571; [2003] 1
C.L.C. 921; 2003 A.M.C. 913; (2003) 100(19) L.S.G. 31 HL 8-021, 8-029, 8-067, 9-006
Honduras Inter-Oceanic Railway Co v Lefevre & Tudor (1877) 2 Ex.D. 301; 46 L.J.Q.B.
391; 36 L.T. 46; 25 W.R. 310 9-075
Hone v Going Places Leisure Travel Ltd [2001] EWCA Civ 947 CA 1-038, 9-033
Honeywell International Middle East Ltd v Meydan Group LLC [2014] EWHC 1344
(TCC); [2014] 2 Lloyd's Rep. 133; [2014] B.L.R. 401; 154 Con. L.R. 113; [2014] Bus.
L.R. D13 8-223
Honeywill & Stein Ltd v Larkin Bros (London's Commercial Photographers) Ltd [1934] 1
K.B. 191; 103 L.J.K.B. 74; 150 L.T. 71; 50 T.L.R. 56 1-034
Hood v West End Motor Car Packing Co [1917] 2 K.B. 38; 86 L.J.K.B. 831; 116 L.T. 365;
61 S.J. 252; 14 Asp.M.L.C. 12 6-016
Hooper v Kerr, Stuart & Co Ltd (1901) 83 L.T. 729; 17 T.L.R. 162; 45 S.J. 139   . . . . . 2-061, 2-069,
2-087, 2-091, **2-100**
Hooper v Lane (1857) 6 H.L. Cas.443; 27 L.J.Q.B. 75; 30 L.T. (O.S.) 33; 3 Jur. (N.S.)
1026; 3 W.R. 146; 10 E.R. 1368 8-196
Hooper v Treffry (1847) 1 Exch. 17; 16 L.J.Ex. 233; 9 L.T. (O.S.) 200   . . . . **7-062**
Hoover Plc v George Hulme (Stockport) Ltd [1982] Com. L.R. 195; [1982] 3 C.M.L.R.
186; [1982] F.S.R. 565 Ch D 9-120
Hope (John D) & Co v Glendinning [1911] A.C. 419; 80 L.J.C.P. 193   7-082
Hopkins v TL Dallas Group Ltd; Hopkins v TL Dallas & Co Ltd [2004] EWHC 1379;
[2005] 1 B.C.L.C. 543 Ch D 3-010, 3-011, 8-050
Hopkins v Ware (1869) L.R. 4 Ex. 268; 38 L.J.Ex. 147; 20 L.T. 668   . . . . 8-103, **8-106**
Horcal Ltd v Gatland [1983] I.R.L.R. 459 CA   6-054
Horder v Scott (1880) 5 Q.B.D. 552; 49 L.J.M.C. 78; 42 L.T. 660; 44 J.P. 520; 28 W.R.
918. 2-026
Horford v Wilson (1807) 1 Taunt. 12; 127 E.R. 733   7-014
Horler v Rubin [2012] EWCA Civ 4; [2013] 1 B.C.L.C. 1; [2012] B.P.I.R. 749 6-020
Hornby v Lacy (1817) 6 H.M. & S.166 1-039
Horsfall v Fauntleroy (1830) 10 B. & C. 755; L. & Welsh. 340; 5 Man. & Ry. K.B. 635; 8
L.J. (O.S.) K.B. 259 8-103
Horsfall v Handley (1818) 8 Taunt. 136; 2 Moore C.P. 5; 129 E.R. 334   9-106
Hosking v Marathon Asset Management LLP [2016] EWHC 2418 (Ch); [2017] Ch. 157   7-050
Hough & Co v Manzanos & Co (1874) 4 Ex.D. 104; 48 L.J.Q.B. 398; 27 W.R. 536   9-038
Hough v Bolton (1885) 1 T.L.R. 606 8-226
Hough v Guardian Fire & Life Ass.Co (1902) 18 T.L.R. 273   8-217
Houghton & Co v Nothard, Lowe & Wills [1928] A.C. 1; [1927] 1 K.B. 246   . . 3-029, 8-034, 8-039,
8-046, 8-050, 8-214
Houghton v Fayers [2000] Lloyd's Rep. Bank. 145; [2000] 1 B.C.L.C. 511; (1999–2000) 2
I.T.E.L.R. 512 8-221
Houghton v Matthews (1803) 3 B. & P. 485   . . . . 3-025, 7-073, 7-080, **7-086**
Houghton v Pilkington [1912] 3 K.B. 308; 82 L.J.K.B. 79; 107 L.T. 235; 28 T.L.R. 492;
56 S.J. 633. 3-029
Houlder (Howard) & Partners Ltd v Manx Islands S.S. Co [1923] 1 K.B. 110; 92 L.J.K.B.
233; 38 T.L.R. 757; 66 S.J. 682; 128 L.T. 347; 16 Asp.M.L.C. 95; 28 Com.Cas.15 . . . 7-004, 7-014,

7-024, 7-030, 7-032, 10-042
Houlgate (Frank) Investment Co Ltd v Biggart Baillie LLP [2011] CSOH 160; 2012
S.L.T. 256; [2012] P.N.L.R. 2; 2011 G.W.D. 36-735 9-068
Houstoun v Robertson (1816) 6 Taunt. 448; 2 Marsh 138 10-015
Hovenden & Sons v Millhoff (1900) 83 L.T. 41; 16 T.L.R. 506 . . . . 6-085, 6-086, 6-087, 8-223
How v Kirchner; sub nom. The Alan Ker; How v Kirchner (1857) 11 Moo. P.C. 21; 6 W.R.
198; 30 L.T.(O.S.) 296 7-090
Howard Marine and Dredging Co Ltd v Ogder (A) & Sons (Excavations) Ltd [1978] Q.B.
574; [1978] 2 W.L.R. 515; [1978] 2 All E.R. 1134; (1977) 122 S.J. 48; [1978] 1 Lloyd's
Rep. 334; CA 8-186
Howard Smith Ltd v Ampol Petroleum Ltd [1974] A.C. 821; [1974] 2 W.L.R. 689; [1974]
1 All E.R. 1126; 118 S.J.L.B. 330; (1974) 118 S.J. 330 PC (Australia) 8-220, **8-226**
Howard v Baillie (1726) 2 H.Bl. 618 . . . . 3-013, 3-022
Howard v Chapman (1831) 4 C. & P. 508 3-026
Howard v Hudson (1853) 2 E. & B. 1; 1 C.L.R. 267; 22 L.J.Q.B. 341; 21 L.T.(O.S.) 88; 17
J.P. 630; 17 Jur. 855; 1 W.R. 325 8-024
Howard v Patent Ivory Co; Re Ivory Manufacturing Co (1888) 38 Ch.D. 156; 57 L.J.Ch.
878; 58 L.T. 395; 36 W.R. 801 . . . . 2-064, 8-039
Howard v Sheward (1866) L.R. 2 C.P. 148; 36 L.J.C.P. 42; 15 L.T. 183; 12 Jur. (N.S.)
1015; 15 W.R. 45. . . . . 3-028, **3-032**
Howard v Tucker (1831) 1 B. & Ad. 712; 9 L.J. (O.S.) K.B. 108 . . . . **8-044**
Howell Ex p.; Re Williams (1865) 12 L.T. 785 . . . . 3-033, 3-034
Howell v Batt (1833) 5 B & Ad. 504; 3 L.J.K.B. 49; 3 Nev & M.K.B. 381 9-114
Howell v Falmouth Boat Construction Co [1951] A.C. 837; [1951] 2 All E.R. 278; [1951]
2 Lloyd's Rep. 45; [1951] 2 T.L.R. 151; 95 S.J. 413 HL 8-042
Howitt Transport Ltd v Transport and General Workers Union [1973] I.C.R. 1; [1972]
I.R.L.R. 93, NIRC. 2-034
Hubbard v Vosper [1972] 2 Q.B. 84; [1972] 2 W.L.R. 389; [1972] 1 All E.R. 1023; (1971)
116 S.J. 95 CA 6-077
Hubbart v Phillips (1845) 13 M. & W. 702; 153 E.R. 294 . . . . **9-076**
Hudgell Yeates & Co v Watson [1978] Q.B. 451; [1978] 1 W.L.R. 661; [1978] 2 All E.R.
363; 121 S.J. 831 CA 7-056
Hudson Bay Apparel Brands LLC v Umbro International Ltd [2010] EWCA Civ 949;
[2011] 1 B.C.L.C. 259; [2010] E.T.M.R. 62 . . . . 1-030, 3-007
Hudson v Granger (1821) 5 B. & A. 27 . . . . **8-112**, 10-021
Hughes v Graeme (1864) 33 L.J.Q.B. 335; 4 New Rep. 190; 12 W.R. 857 . . . . . **9-076**, 9-081, **9-083**
Hughes v Hughes (1971) 115 S.J. 911 CA **2-083**
Hughes v Liverpool Victoria Legal Friendly Society [1916] 2 K.B. 482 CA 8-098
Hughes v NM Superannuation Pty Ltd (1993) 29 N.S.W.L.R. 653 3-029
Hughes-Holland v BPE Solicitors [2017] UKSC 21; [2017] 2 W.L.R. 1029 . . . . 6-019, 8-207
Hughmans Solicitors v Central Stream Services Ltd (In Liquidation) [2012] EWCA Civ
1720; [2013] B.P.I.R. 322; [2013] 1 E.G.L.R. 27; [2013] 12 E.G. 80; [2013] W.T.L.R.
239; [2013] 3 E.G. 86 (C.S.); (2013) 163 N.L.J. 20; [2013] 1 P. & C.R. DG15 6-041
Hull v Pickersgill (1819) 1 B. & B. 282; 3 Moo. P.C. 612 . . . . . . 2-056, 2-061, 2-070, 2-088, 2-100,
9-125
Hulse v Hulse (1856) 17 C.B. 711; 25 L.J.C.P. 177; 4 W.R. 239 7-004
Hulton, Re; Ex p. Manchester & County Bank (1891) 39 W.R. 303; 8 Morr. 69 8-167
Humble v Hunter (1848) 12 Q.B. 310; 17 L.J.Q.B. 350; 11 L.T. (O.S.) 265; 12 Jur. 1021 8-078,
8-082
Hunt v Elmes (1861) 30 L.J.Ch. 255; 2 De G.F. & J 578; 3 L.T. 796; 7 Jur. (N.S.) 200; 9
W.R. 362 8-135
Hunt v Hosking [2013] EWCA Civ 1408; [2014] 1 B.C.L.C. 291; [2014] B.P.I.R. 285 1-032
Hunter v Atkins (1834) 3 Myl & K. 113 6-069
Hunter v Belcher (1864) 2 De. G.J. & S.194; 10 L.T. 548; 10 Jur. (N.S.) 663; 12 W.R. 782 . . 6-092,
6-098
Hunter v Parker (1840) 7 M & W. 322; 10 L.J. Ex. 281; 9 L.T. 53 . . . . . 2-072, 2-073, **2-074**, 2-082,
2-083
Hunter v Walters; Curling v Walters; Darnell v Hunter (1871) 7 Ch.App. 75; 41 L.J.Ch.
175; 25 L.T. 765; 20 W.R. 218 8-135
Hunter v Welsh (1816) 1 Stark. 224 6-100
Huntley v Bulwer (1839) 6 Bing N.C. 111; 8 Scott 325; 3 J.P. 787; 3 Jur. 1105 7-050
Huntsman, The [1894] P. 214; 70 L.T. 386; 7 Asp. M.L.C. 431; 6 R. 698 . . . . . **3-029**, 8-120, 8-121

Hurlingham Estates Ltd v Wilde & Partners [1997] 1 Lloyd's Rep. 525; [1997] S.T.C. 627;
   [1997] B.T.C. 240; (1997) 147 N.L.J. 453 6-019
Hurry v Richman and Sutcliffe (1831) 1 M. & Rob. 126 .... **8-196**
Hurst v Bryk [2002] 1 A.C. 185; [2000] 2 W.L.R. 740; [2000] 2 All E.R. 193; [2000] 2
   B.C.L.C. 117; [2000] E.G.C.S.49; (2000) 97(17) L.S.G. 35; (2000) 150 N.L.J. 511;
   (2000) 144 S.J.L.B. 189 HL 10-019
Hurst v Holding (1810) 3 Taunt. 32 .... 7-050, 7-066
Hurst v Picture Theatres Ltd [1915] 1 K.B. 1; [1914–15] All E.R. Rep. 836; 83 L.J.K.B.
   1937; 111 L.T. 972; 30 T.L.R. 642; 58 S.J. 739 CA 10-025
Hurstanger Ltd v Wilson [2007] EWCA Civ 299; [2007] 1 W.L.R. 2351; [2008] Bus. L.R.
   216; [2007] 4 All E.R. 1118; [2007] 2 All E.R. (Comm) 1037; (2007) 104(16) L.S.G.
   23; (2007) 157 N.L.J. 555; (2007) 151 S.J.L.B. 467; [2007] N.P.C. 41 . 3-011, 6-039, 6-068, 6-086,
                                                   6-089, 8-221, 8-223
Husband v Davis (1851) 10 C.B. 645 .... 2-046, 6-100
Hut Group Ltd v Nobahar-Cookson [2016] EWCA Civ 128 .... 8-209, 8-214
Hutcheson v Eaton (1884) 13 Q.B.D. 861; 51 L.T. 846 9-037
Hutchings v Nunes (1863) 1 Moo. P.C. (N.S.) 243; 9 L.T. 125; 10 Jur. (N.S.) 109 .... 2-048, 2-091
Hutchinson v Colorado United Mining Co & Hamill; Hamill v Lilley (1886) 3 T.L.R. 265 .. 8-130,
                                               8-135, 8-138, 8-161
Hutchinson v Heyworth (1838) 9 A. & E. 375; 1 Per. & Dav 266; 1 W.W. & H. 730; 8
   L.J.Q.B. 17 .... **9-113**
Hutchinson v Tatham (1873) L.R. 8 C.P. 482; L.J.C.P. 260; 29 L.T. 103; 22 W.R. 18 . 9-016, **9-042**,
                                                      9-090
Huth v Clarke (1890) 25 Q.B.D. 391; 59 L.J.M.C. 120; 63 L.T. 348; 55 J.P. 86; 38 W.R.
   655; 6 T.L.R. 373 10-024
Huth, Exp.; Pemberton, Re (1840) Mont. & C. 667; & Deac. 294 .... **6-070**
Hutton v Bulloch (1874) L.R. 9 Q.B. 572; 30 L.T. 648; 22 W.R. 956 .. 1-022, 8-071, 9-020, 12-029
Hyde v Johnson (1836) 2 Bing. N.C. 776 2-022
Ian Greenhill Residential Ltd v Asfari [2007] EWHC 1491 (QB) 7-004, 7-007, 7-024
IBM United Kingdom Holdings Ltd v Dalgleish [2017] EWCA Civ 1212 1-030
Ideal Films Ltd v Richards [1929] 1 K.B. 374; [1926] 1 All E.R. Rep.; 96 L.J.K.B. 161;
   136 L.T. 295; 43 T.L.R. 7; 70 S.J. 1138 CA 9-087
Ilkiw v Samuels [1963] 1 W.L.R. 991; [1963] 2 All E.R. 879; 107 S.J. 680 CA 8-192
Imageview Management Ltd v Jack [2009] EWCA Civ 63; [2009] Bus. L.R. 1034; [2009]
   2 All E.R. 666; [2009] 1 All E.R. (Comm) 921; [2009] 1 Lloyd's Rep. 436; [2009] 1
   B.C.L.C. 724 .... 6-048, 6-080, **6-083**, 6-087, 7-042, 7-050, **7-051**
Imeson v Lister (1920) 149 L.T.Jo. 446 6-064
Imperial Bank of Canada Ltd v Begley [1936] 2 All E.R. 367 .... 2-048, 2-059
Imperial Bank v London St. Katharine Docks Co (1877) 5 Ch.D. 195; 46 L.J.Ch. 335; 36
   L.T. 233 .... 7-101, **7-102**, 8-117, 9-006, 9-016, **9-042**
Imperial Loan Co v Stone [1892] 1 Q.B. 599; 61 L.J.Q.B. 449; 66 L.T. 556; 8 T.L.R. 408;
   56 J.P. 436 2-009
Imperial Mercantile Credit Association Co v Coleman (1873) L.R. 6 H.L. 189 ...... 6-039, **6-071**
Imperial Smelting Corp Ltd v Joseph Constantine Steamship Line Ltd [1942] A.C. 154;
   [1941] 2 All E.R. 165; (1941) 70 Ll. L. Rep. 1 HL 6-004
In Plus Group Ltd v Pyke [2002] EWCA Civ 370; [2003] B.C.C. 332; [2002] 2 B.C.L.C.
   201 CA 6-015, 6-038, 6-067
Inchbald v Western Neilgherry Coffee, Tea and Cinchona Plantation Co Ltd (1864) 17
   C.B. (N.S.) 733; 5 New Rep. 52; 34 L.J.C.P. 15; 11 L.T. 345; 10 Jur. (N.S.) 1129; 13
   W.R. 95 7-041
Indata Equipment Supplies Ltd (t/a Autofleet) v ACL Ltd (1997) [1998] 1 B.C.L.C. 412;
   [1998] F.S.R. 248; (1997) 141 S.J.L.B. 216 CA 6-077
Indian Oil Corp Ltd v Greenstone Shipping Co SA (Panama); The Ypatianna; Greenstone
   Shipping Co SA v Indian Oil Corp Ltd [1988] Q.B. 345; [1987] 3 All E.R. 893; [1987]
   2 Lloyd's Rep. 286; [1987] 2 F.T.L.R. 95; (1987) 84 L.S.G. 2768; (1987) 131 S.J. 1121
   QBD (Comm) 6-040
Industrial Development Consultants Ltd v Cooley [1972] 1 W.L.R. 443; [1972] 2 All E.R.
   162; (1971) 116 S.J. 255, Assizes (Birmingham)..................... 6-080, 6-081, **6-083**
Industrie Chimiche Italia Centrale and Cerealfin SA v Alexander G Tsavliris & Sons
   Maritime Co; The Choko Star; Industrie Chimiche Italia Centrale v Pancristo Shipping
   Co SA; Industrie Chimiche Italia Centrale v Bula Shipping Corp [1990] 1 Lloyd's Rep.
   516 .... 4-005, 4-007, 4-008, 4-009, **4-013**, 12-032

Industries and General Mortgage Co v Lewis [1949] W.N. 333; [1949] 2 All E.R. 573; 93
   S.J. 577 KBD 6-085, 6-086, 8-223
Infiniteland Ltd v Artisan Contracting Ltd [2005] EWCA Civ 758; [2006] 1 B.C.L.C. 632   . . . 8-028
Ing Re (UK) Ltd v R&V Versicherung AG [2006] EWHC 1544 (Comm); [2006] 2 All
   E.R. (Comm) 870; [2007] 1 B.C.L.C. 108; [2006] Lloyd's Rep. I.R. 653 . . . . . 2-072, 2-079, 2-096,
                                                                   3-005, 5-015, 6-005, 8-024
Ingham v Walker (1887) 3 T.L.R. 448   7-104
Ingram (Executors of the Estate of Lady Ingram) v Inland Revenue Commissioners [2000]
   1 A.C. 293; [1999] 2 W.L.R. 90; [1999] 1 All E.R. 297; [1999] S.T.C. 37; [1999] L. &
   T.R. 85; [1998] B.T.C. 8047; [1998] E.G.C.S.181; (1999) 96(3) L.S.G. 33; (1999) 143
   S.J.L.B. 52; [1998] N.P.C. 160 HL 1-032
Ingram v Ingram (1740) 2 Atk. 88   2-021
Ingram v Inland Revenue Commissioners [2000] 1 A.C. 293   2-014
Ingram v Little [1961] 1 Q.B. 31; [1960] 3 W.L.R. 504; [1960] 3 All E.R. 332; 104 S.J.
   704 CA 8-146
Initial Services Ltd v Putterill [1968] 1 Q.B. 396; [1967] 3 W.L.R. 1032; [1967] 3 W.L.R.
   1032; [1967] 3 All E.R. 145; 111 S.J. 541 CA 6-077
Innes v Stephenson (1831) 1 M. & R. 145   6-100
Integral Petroleum SA v SCU-Finanz AG [2015] EWCA Civ 144; [2016] 1 All E.R.
   (Comm) 217; [2015] Bus. L.R. 640; [2015] 1 Lloyd's Rep. 545; [2015] I.L.Pr. 50. 12-020
Interactive Technology Corp Ltd v Ferster [2016] EWHC 2896 (Ch)   3-029
International Contract Co, Re; Pickering's Claim (1871) L.R. 6 Ch.App. 525; 24 L.T. 178   . . . **8-088**
International Railway v Niagara Parks Commission [1941] A.C. 328; 111 L.J.C.P. 55; 57
   T.L.R. 462; [1941] 2 All E.R. 456 . . . . 9-006, 9-028
International Sales and Agencies Ltd v Marcus [1982] 3 All E.R. 551; [1982] 2 C.M.L.R.
   46. 8-037
International Sponge Importers Ltd v Watt (Andrew) & Sons [1911] A.C. 279; 81 L.J.P.C.
   12; 27 T.L.R. 364; 55 S.J. 422; 16 Com.Cas.224 . . . . **3-023**, 3-025, 8-014, 8-044, **8-112**
Internaut Shipping GmbH v Fercometal Sarl The Elikon [2003] EWCA Civ 812; [2003] 2
   All E.R. (Comm) 760; [2003] 2 Lloyd's Rep. 430 CA 9-038
Interoven Stove Co Ltd v Hibbard etc. [1946] 1 All E.R. 263   9-125
Interprods Ltd v De La Rue International Ltd [2014] EWHC 68 (Comm); [2014] 1 Lloyd's
   Rep. 540 3-012
Investment Trust Companies v Revenue and Customs Commissioners [2017] UKSC 29;
   [2017] 2 W.L.R. 1200; [2017] 3 All E.R. 113; [2017] S.T.C. 985; [2017] B.V.C. 16;
   [2017] S.T.I. 1041 . . . . 8-161, 9-106
Invicta UK v International Brands Ltd [2013] EWHC 1564 (QB); [2013] E.C.C. 30   11-018,
                                                                11-019, 11-022, 11-051, 11-057
Invideous Ltd v Thorogood [2013] EWHC 3015 (CH)   6-081
Involnert Management Inc v Aprilgrange Ltd [2015] EWHC 2225 (Comm); [2016] 1 All
   E.R. (Comm) 913; [2015] 2 Lloyd's Rep. 289; [2015] Lloyd's Rep. I.R. 661 . . . . 5-011, 6-021
Irani v Southampton and South West Hampshire Health Authority [1985] I.C.R. 80;
   [1985] I.R.L.R. 203; (1985) 82 L.S.Gaz. 1167 7-046
IRC v Graham's Trustees 1971 S.C. (H.L.) 1; 1971 S.L.T. 46; [1970] T.R. 343 HL   10-011
IRC v Ufitec Group Ltd [1977] 3 All E.R. 924; [1977] S.T.C. 363 DC   8-015
Ireland v Livingston (1872) L.R. 5 H.L. 395; 41 L.J.Q.B. 201; 27 L.T. 79; 1 Asp. M.L.C.
   389 . . . . 1-021, 1-022, 1-036, 3-016, 3-018, 3-019, **3-020**, 6-010, 7-101, 8-071, 12-029
Irvine & Co v Watson & Sons (1880) 5 Q.B.D. 414; 49 L.J.Q.B. 531; 42 L.T. 800   . . . 8-101, 8-103,
                                                                   8-104, 8-105, **8-106**
Irvine v Union Bank of Australia (1877) 2 App.Cas. 366 PC (Ind) **2-100**
Irvings v Motly (1831) 7 Bing. 543; 5 Moo. A.P. 380; 9 L.J. (O.S.) C.P. 161   2-061
Isaacs & Sons v Salbstein [1916] 2 K.B. 139; 85 L.J.K.B. 1433; 114 L.T. 924; 32 T.L.R.
   370; 60 S.J. 444. 8-117
Islamic Republic of Iran Shipping Lines v Zannis Compania Naviera SA; The Tzelepi
   [1991] 2 Lloyd's Rep. 265 QBD (Comm) 7-059
Island Export Finance Ltd v Umunna [1986] B.C.L.C. 460   . . . . 6-081, 6-083
Ismail v Polish Ocean Lines; The Ciechnocinek [1976] Q.B. 893; [1976] 2 W.L.R. 477;
   [1976] 1 All E.R. 902; 120 S.J. 168; [1976] 1 Lloyd's Rep. 489 CA 3-032
Israel v Douglas (1789) 1 H.Bl. 239   9-113
Issacs, Re, Ex p. Miles (1885) 15 Q.B.D. 39; 54 L.J.Q.B. 566 CA   7-101
IT Human Resources Plc v Land [2014] EWHC 3812 (Ch); [2016] F.S.R. 10   6-054

Item Software (UK) Ltd v Fassihi; sub nom. Fassihi v Item Software (UK) Ltd [2004]
    EWCA Civ 1244; [2004] B.C.C. 994; [2005] 2 B.C.L.C. 91; [2005] I.C.R. 450; [2004]
    I.R.L.R. 928; (2004) 101(39) L.S.G. 34; (2004) 148 S.J.L.B. 1153 CA 6-054
Itex Itagrani Export SA v Care Shipping Corp; The Cebu (No.2) [1993] Q.B. 1; [1991] 3
    W.L.R. 609; [1992] 1 All E.R. 91; [1990] 2 Lloyd's Rep. 316 QBD (Comm). 7-077
Iveson v Conington (1823) 1 B. & C. 160; 1 L.J. (O.S.) K.B. 71; 2 Dow & Ry. KB. 307   9-006
J&H Ritchie Ltd v Lloyd Ltd [2007] UKHL 9; [2007] Bus. L.R. 944; [2007] 1 W.L.R.
    670; [2007] 2 All E.R. 353; [2007] 1 All E.R. (Comm) 987; [2007] 1 Lloyd's Rep. 544;
    2007 S.C. (H.L.) 89; 2007 S.L.T. 377; [2007] 1 C.L.C. 208; (2007) 157 N.L.J. 403;
    (2007) 151 S.J.L.B. 397; 2007 G.W.D. 9-171 6-001
Jack and Willows v HBS (Trust) Ltd [1952] E.G.D. 443 7-028
Jackson & Co v Napper (1886) 35 Ch.D. 162; 56 L.J.Ch. 406; 55 L.T. 836; 35 W.R. 228; 3
    T.L.R. 238. 2-017
Jackson v Dear [2013] EWCA Civ 89; [2014] 1 B.C.L.C. 186   1-028
Jackson v Royal Bank of Scotland [2000] C.L.C. 1457 CA   1-036
Jacobs v Batavia & General Plantations Trust Ltd [1924] 1 Ch. 287   9-040
Jacobs v Latour (1828) 5 Bing. 130; 2 Moo & P. 201; 6 L.J. (O.S.) C.P. 243   . . . . **7-094**
Jacobs v Morris [1902] 1 Ch. 816; 71 L.J.Ch. 363; 86 L.T. 275; 50 W.R. 371; 18 T.L.R.
    384; 46 S.J. 315. . . . . **3-015**, 8-052, **8-061**, 12-016
Jacobus Marler Estates Ltd v Marler (1916) 85 L.J.P.C. 167n; 114 L.T. 640 PC 6-035, 6-068,
                                                                                                                                          6-071
Jafari-Fini v Skillglass Ltd (In Administration) [2007] EWCA Civ 261   . 8-209, 8-215, 8-215, **8-217**
James & Co Scheepvaart en Handelmij BV v Chinecrest Ltd [1979] 1 Lloyd's Rep. 126
    CA. 6-100
James Ex p. (1803) 8 Ves. 337   . . . . 6-064, 6-070
James v Smith (1892) 65 L.T. 544   . . . . 2-037, 6-082, 7-018
Jameson v Union Bank of Scotland (1913) 109 L.T. 850   . . . . 8-126, 8-135
Janesich v Attenborough & Son (1910) 102 L.T. 605; 26 T.L.R. 278   8-153
Jani-King (GB) Ltd v Pula Enterprises Ltd [2007] EWHC 2433 (QB); [2008] 1 All E.R.
    (Comm) 451 7-001
Janred Properties Ltd v Ente Nazionale Italiano per il Turismo (ENIT) (No.2) [1989] 2 All
    E.R. 444; [1987] 2 F.T.L.R. 179 CA 12-020, 12-022
Janus Capital Management LLC v Safeguard World International Ltd [2016] EWHC 1355
    (Ch). 1-038
Japan Leasing (Europe) Plc, Re [1999] B.P.I.R. 911; [2000] W.T.L.R. 301   6-041
Jaques v George (Lloyd D) Partners Ltd (1968) 1 W.L.R. 625; [1968] 2 All E.R. 187;
    (1968) 112 S.J. 211 CA 7-009, 7-017, 7-021
Jardine v Leathley (1863) 3 B. & S.700; 1 New Rep. 394; 32 L.J.Q.B. 132; 7 L.T. 783; 9
    Jur. (N.S.) 1035; 11 W.R. 432; 1 Mar L.C. 288. . . . . 2-091, 2-093
Jarmain v Hooper (1843) 6 Man. & G. 827; 1 Dow & L. 769; 7 Scott N.R. 663; 13
    L.J.C.P. 63; 2 L.T. (O.S.) 209; 8 Jur. 127 8-196
Jarvis & Sons Ltd v Castle Wharf Developments Ltd; J Jarvis & Sons Ltd v Gleeds
    Management Services Ltd; J Jarvis & Sons Ltd v Franklin Ellis Architects Ltd; Castle
    Wharf Developments Ltd v J Jarvis & Sons Ltd [2001] EWCA Civ 19; [2001] Lloyd's
    Rep. P.N. 308; [2001] N.P.C. 15 CA 9-117
Jarvis, Re; Edge v Jarvis [1958] 1 W.L.R. 815; [1958] 2 All E.R. 336; 102 S.J. 546 Ch D   6-080
Jawara v Gambian Airways [1992] E.G.C.S.54; [1992] NPC 61 PC (Gam) 3-026, 3-032
JD Wetherspoon Plc v Van de Berg & Co Ltd [2009] EWHC 639 (Ch); [2009] 16 E.G. 138
    (C.S.). 5-012, 6-015, 6-039, 6-080, 6-081, 9-135, **9-142**
Jebara v Ottoman Bank [1928] A.C. 269   . . . . 2-010, 4-005, 4-010, 10-003
Jefferson v Derbyshire Farmers Ltd; sub nom. Jeffries & Atkey (AR) & Co Ltd v
    Derbyshire Farmers Ltd [1921] 2 K.B. 281; 90 L.J.K.B. 1361; 124 L.T. 775 8-192
Jeffery (Michael) & Co v Bamford [1921] 2 K.B. 351   6-023
Jeffryes v Agra & Masterman's Bank (1866) L.R. 2 Eq. 674; 35 L.J.Ch. 686; 14 W.R. 889   . . . 7-088
Jenkins v Gould (1827) 3 Russ.385   6-092
Jenkins v Hutchinson (1849) 13 Q.B. 744; 18 L.J.Q.B. 274; 13 L.T. (O.S.) 401; 13 Jur.
    763 . . . . 9-037, 9-061, 9-090
Jenkins v Tucker (1788) 1 H.Bl. 90; 126 E.R. 55   4-010
Jenkyns v Brown (1849) 14 Q.B. 496; 19 L.J.Q.B. 286; 14 L.T. (O.S.) 395; 14 Jur. 505   7-101
Jenkyns v Usborne (1844) 7 M. & G. 678; 8 Scott N.R. 505; 13 L.J.C.P. 196; 3 L.T. (O.S.)
    300; 8 Jur. 1139. 7-101
Jennings, Executor of Carew Guidott v Adrian Moore, Blincorne (1709) 2 Bro. P.C. 278
    (HL). 8-208, 8-211, 8-213, 8-214

Jeremy D Stone Consultants Ltd v National Westminster Bank Plc [2013] EWHC 208
 (Ch). 9-106
Jerome v Bentley [1952] W.N. 357; [1952] 2 T.L.R. 58; [1952] 2 All E.R. 114; 96 S.J. 463 . . 8-077,
 8-126, 8-130, 8-135
Jesson v Solly (1811) 4 Taint 52; 128 E.R. 247 9-003
Jetivia SA v Bilta (UK) Ltd (In Liquidation) [2015] UKSC 23; [2016] A.C. 1 1-029
Jetley v Hill (1884) C. & E. 239 . . . . **8-045**
Jewry v Busk (1814) S.Taunt. 302 7-012
Jewsbury v Newbold (1851) 26 L.J.Ex. 247; 29 L.T. (O.S.) 128 8-120
JL Builders & Son v Naylor and Naylor [2008] EWCA Civ 1621 8-207
Joblin v Watkins & Roseveare Motors Ltd [1949] 1 All E.R. 47; 64 T.L.R. 464 8-149
John D Wood & Co (Residential & Agricultural) Ltd v Craze [2007] EWHC 2658 (QB);
 [2008] 1 E.G.L.R. 17; [2008] 6 E.G. 132; [2007] 50 E.G. 108 (C.S.); [2007] N.P.C. 130;
 [2008] 1 P. & C.R. DG14. . . . . 7-018, 7-021, 7-041
John D Wood & Co (Residential & Agricultural) Ltd v Knatchbull [2002] EWHC 2822;
 [2003] P.N.L.R. 17; [2003] 1 E.G.L.R. 33; [2003] 08 E.G. 131; (2003) 19 Const. L.J.
 339 QBD 6-021, 6-024
John D Wood & Co v Dantata; Beauchamp Estates v Same [1987] 2 E.G.L.R. 23 . . . . 7-018, 7-030
John v Dodwell and Co Ltd [1918] A.C. 563; 87 L.J.P.C. 92; 118 L.T. 661; 34 T.L.R. 261 . . . 8-064,
 8-066
John Youngs Insurance Services Ltd v Aviva Insurance Service UK Ltd [2011] EWHC
 1515 (TCC); [2012] 1 All E.R. (Comm) 1045 . . . . 6-035, 6-037, 6-063, 6-095
Johnson v CrÈdit Lyonnais (1877) 3 C.P.D. 32; 47 L.J.Q.B. 241; 37 L.T. 657; 42 J.P. 548;
 26 W.R. 195. 8-126
Johnson v EBS Pensioner Trustees Ltd [2002] EWCA Civ 164; [2002] Lloyd's Rep. P.N.
 309. 6-068
Johnson v Emerson & Sparrow (1871) L.R. 6 Ex. 329; 40 L.J.Ex. 201; 25 L.T. 337 . . . . **9-125**
Johnson v Gore Wood & Co. [2002] A.C. 1; [2001] 2 W.L.R. 72; [2001] 1 All E.R. 481;
 [2001] C.P.L.R. 49; [2001] P.N.L.R. 18 1-030
Johnson v Kearley [1908] 1 K.B. 514; 77 L.J.K.B. 904; 99 L.T. 506; 24 T.L.R. 729 . . . 6-021, 7-070
Johnson v Robarts (1875) L.R. 10 Ch.App. 505; 44 L.J.Ch. 678; 33 L.T. 138; 23 W.R. 763 . . 7-089,
 9-114
Johnston v Boyes [1899] 2 Ch. 73; 68 L.J.Ch. 425; 80 L.T. 488; 47 W.R. 517; 43 S.J. 457 . . . 9-034
Johnston v Kershaw (1867) L.R. 2 Ex. 82; 36 L.J.Ex. 44; 15 L.T. 485; 15 W.R. 354 . . 1-036, **3-018**
Johnston v Reading (1893) 9 T.L.R. 200 8-077
Johnstone v Pedlar [1921] 2 A.C. 262; 90 L.J.P.C. 181; 125 L.T. 809; 37 T.L.R. 870; 65
 S.J. 679; 27 Cox. C.C. 68 9-124
Jones (RE) Ltd v Waring & Gillow Ltd [1926] A.C. 670; 95 L.J.K.B. 913; 135 L.T. 548;
 42 T.L.R. 644; 70 S.J. 756; 32 Com.Cas. 8 . . . . 2-102, 8-130
Jones and Roberts, Re 74 L.J.Ch. 458 7-099
Jones v Churcher [2009] EWHC 722 (QB); [2009] 2 Lloyd's Rep. 94 . . . . 8-200, 9-107
Jones v Gordon; sub nom. Gomersall, Re (1877) 2 App.Cas. 616; 47 L.J. Bcy 1; 37 L.T.
 477; 26 W.R. 172 8-140
Jones v Gurney [1913] W.N. 72 9-010
Jones v Hope (1880) 3 T.L.R. 247n 2-063, **2-070**, 9-085, **9-087**
Jones v Lowe [1945] K.B. 73; 114 L.J.K.B. 164; 172 L.T. 18; 61 T.L.R. 57; [1945] 1 All
 E.R. 194; 87 S.J. 46 . . . . 7-004, 7-018
Jones v Manchester Corp [1952] 2 Q.B. 852; [1952] 1 T.L.R. 1589; 116 J.P. 412; [1952] 2
 All E.R. 125 CA 8-177, 8-191
Jones v Peppercorne (1858) John. 430; 28 L.J.Ch. 158; 32 L.T. (O.S.) 240; 5 Jur. (N.S.)
 140; 7 W.R. 103 . . . . 7-082, **7-086**, **7-089**
Jones v Phipps (1868) L.R. 3 Q.B. 567; 37 L.J.Q.B. 198; 9 B. & S.761; 18 L.T. 813; 33
 J.P. 229; 16 W.R. 1044. . . . . **2-026**, 3-029
Jones v Rhind; Rhind v Jones (1869) 17 W.R. 1091 8-135
Jones v Southwark LBC [2016] EWHC 457 (Ch); [2016] H.L.R. 14 1-036
Jones v Thomas (1837) 2 Y. & C.Ex. 498; 3 Per. & Dav. 91 6-062
Jones v Williams 53 E.R. 274; (1857) 24 Beav. 47 . . . . 3-011, 8-052
Jonmenjoy Coondow v Watson (1884) 9 App.Cas. 561; 50 L.T. 411 . . . . **3-015**
Jordan v Norton (1838) 4 M. & W. 155; 1 Horn & H. 234; 7 L.J.Ex. 281 . . . . **8-061**
Jorden v Money (1854) 5 H.L. Cas. 185 PC (United Kingdom); 10 E.R. 868 8-050
Jordeson & Co & Kahn v London Hardwood Co (1913) 11 O.L.T. 666; 19 Com.Cas.164 9-035
Jordy v Vanderpump (1920) 64 S.J. 324 6-086
Joseph v Knox (1813) 3 Camp. 320 9-010

Josephs v Pebrer (1825) 3 B. & C. 639; 1 C. & P. 507; 5 Dow. & Ry. K.B. 542; 3 L.T.
(O.S.) K.B. 102 . . . . 3-038, **7-056**
Jowitt & Sons v Union Cold Storage Co [1913] 3 K.B. 1; 82 L.J.K.B. 890; 108 L.T. 724;
29 T.L.R. 477; 57 S.J. 560; 18 Com.Cas.185 7-082
Joynson v Hunt & Son (1905) 93 L.T. 470; 21 T.L.R. 692 10-043
JSC BTA Bank v Ablyazov [2013] EWHC 510 (Comm) 8-214
Jubilee Cotton Mills v Lewis; sub nom. Jubilee Cotton Mills Ltd, Re [1924] A.C. 958; 93
L.J.Ch. 414; 40 T.L.R. 621; 68 S.J. 663; [1925] B. & C.R. 16; 131 L.T. 579 6-035
Jugoslavenska Linijska Plovidba v Hulsman (t/a Brusse & Sippel Import-Export); The
Primorje [1980] 2 Lloyd's Rep. 74 QBD (Comm) 9-038
Jung v Phosphate of Lime Co Ltd (1868) L.R. 3 C.P. 139; 37 L.J.C.P. 73; 17 L.T. 541 9-008
K v S [2015] EWHC 1945 (Comm); [2015] 2 Lloyd's Rep. 363 9-039
Kˆnig v Brandt (1901) 84 L.T. 748; 9 Asp. M.L.C. 199 7-086
Kabel v Ronald Lyon Espanola S.A. (1968) 208 E.G. 265 8-196
Kahler v Midland Bank Ltd [1950] A.C. 24; [1949] 2 All E.R. 621; 65 T.L.R. 663; [1949]
L.J.R. 1687 HL 5-008, 6-111
Kahn v Aircraft Industries Corp Ltd [1937] 3 All E.R. 476; 81 S.J. 610 7-035
Kallang Shipping SA Panama v AXA Assurances Senegal (The Kallang) [2008] EWHC
2761 (Comm); [2009] 1 Lloyd's Rep. 124 8-176
Kaltenbach Fischer & Co v Lewis & Peat; sub nom. Kaltenbach v Lewis (1884–85) 10
App. Cas.617 HL 8-071, **8-112**, 8-150
Kammins Ballroom Co Ltd v Zenith Investment (Torquay) Ltd [1971] A.C. 850; [1970] 3
W.L.R. 287; [1970] 2 All E.R. 871; 114 S.J. 590; 22 P. & C.R. 74 HL 2-050, 8-121
Kanchenjunga, The. See Motor Oil Hellas (Corinth) Refineries SA v Shipping Corp of
India (The Kanchenjunga) 2-050
Karak Rubber Co Ltd v Burden (No.2) [1972] 1 W.L.R. 602; [1972] 1 All E.R. 1210;
(1971) 115 S.J. 888; [1972] 1 Lloyd's Rep. 73 . . . . 9-141, 9-142
Kay v ITW Ltd [1968] 1 Q.B. 140; [1967] 3 W.L.R. 695; [1967] 3 All E.R. 22; 111 S.J.
351; 3 K.I.R. 18 CA **8-192**
Kaye v Brett (1850) 5 Exch. 269; 19 L.J. Ex. 346; 15 L.T. (O.S.) 185 . . . . **3-023**
Kayford Ltd (In Liquidation), Re [1975] 1 W.L.R. 279; [1975] 1 All E.R. 604; (1974) 118
S.J. 752 Ch D 6-041
Keay v Fenwick (1876) 1 C.P.D. 745 . . . . 2-046, **2-083**, 2-096, 5-004, 5-010, 7-048
Keech v Sandford (1726) Sel.Cas.Ch. 61; 2 Eq.Cas.Abr. 741 . . . . 6-080, 6-081
Keegan v Palmer [1961] 2 Lloyd's Rep. 449 9-105
Keeling v Pearl Life Assurance Co Ltd (1923) 129 L.T. 573 8-217
Keen v Mear [1920] 2 Ch. 574; 89 L.J.Ch. 513; 124 L.T. 19 . . . . **3-032**
Keene v Thomas [1905] 1 K.B. 136; 74 L.J.K.B. 21; 92 L.T. 19; 53 W.R. 336; 21 T.L.R. 2;
48 S.J. 815 1-033
Keighley Maxsted & Co v Durant [1901] A.C. 240; 70 L.J.K.B. 662; 84 L.T. 777; 17
T.L.R. 527; 45 S.J. 536 . . . . 2-048, 2-070, 2-091, 8-069, 8-070, 8-072, 8-135
Kelly v Cooper [1993] A.C. 205; [1992] 3 W.L.R. 936; (1992) 136 S.J. (LB) 303; [1992]
EGCS 119; [1992] NPC 134 PC 1-015, 6-015, 6-035, **6-045**, 6-048, 6-052, 6-056, 7-050
Kelly v Enderton [1913] A.C. 191; 82 L.J.P.C. 57; 107 L.T. 781 . . . . 1-036, 6-066
Kelly v Fraser [2012] UKPC 25; [2013] 1 A.C. 450; [2012] 3 W.L.R. 1008; [2013] 1 All
E.R. (Comm) 296; [2012] I.C.R. 1408; [2012] Pens. L.R. 405 PC (Jamaica) . . **3-029**, 8-019, 8-020,
8-024, 8-039
Kelly's Directories Ltd v Gavin & Lloyds [1902] 1 Ch. 631 9-125
Kelner v Baxter (1866) L.R. 2 C.P. 174; 36 L.J.C.P. 94; 15 L.T. 213; 12 Jur. (N.S.) 1016;
15 W.R. 278 . . . . 2-062, 2-064, 2-067, **2-070**, **9-084**, 9-085, **9-087**
Kemeh v Ministry of Defence [2014] EWCA Civ 91; [2014] I.C.R. 625; [2014] I.R.L.R.
377; [2014] Eq. L.R. 259 . . . . 1-023, 2-025
Kempler v Bravington (1925) 41 T.L.R. 519; 133 L.T. 680; 69 S.J. 639 8-157
Kendall v Hamilton (1879) 4 App.Cas. 504; 48 L.J.Q.B. 705; 41 L.T. 418; 28 W.R. 97 8-076,
8-116
Keningtons v Regional Properties Ltd [1946] E.G.D. 86; 201 L.T. 311 7-019
Kennedy v Broun and Wife (1863) 13 C.B. N.S. 677; 143 E.R. 268 7-006
Kennedy v De Trafford [1897] A.C. 180; 66 L.J.Ch. 413; 76 L.T. 427; 45 W.R. 671 . . 1-032, 2-031,
2-032
Kennedy v Green (1834) 3 Ry. & K 699 . . . . 8-210, 8-214, 8-217
Kenney v Hall, Pain & Foster [1976] E.G.D. 629; 239 E.G. 355 . . . . 6-013, **6-024**
Kenneys v Proctor (1820) 1 Jac. & W. 350 3-032

Kensington International Ltd v Congo [2007] EWCA Civ 1128; [2008] 1 W.L.R. 1144;
  [2008] 1 All E.R. (Comm) 934; [2008] 1 Lloyd's Rep. 161; [2008] C.P. Rep. 6; [2007] 2
  C.L.C. 791; [2008] Lloyd's Rep. F.C. 107; (2007) 104(45) L.S.G. 31 . . . . 6-087, 8-223
Kent v Ward (1894) 70 L.T. 612; 38 S.J. 401; 9 R. 593 . . . . **7-056**
Keown v Nahoor [2015] EWHC 3418 (Ch) 6-092
Keppel Bus Co Ltd v Sa'ed Bin Ahmad [1974] 1 W.L.R. 1082; [1974] 2 All E.R. 700; 118
  S.J. 531; 17 K.I.R. 90; [1974] R.T.R. 504, P.C. 8-192
Keppel v Wheeler [1927] 1 K.B. 577; 96 L.J.K.B. 433; 136 L.T. 203   . . 6-021, 6-037, 6-068, 7-050,
  7-051
Ker v Dungannon; sub nom. Dungannon (Lord) v Smith (Lord) (1846) 12 Cl. & Fin 546;
  10 Jur. 721. 6-072
Kerrison v Glyn Mills, Currie & Co (1911) 81 L.J.K.B. 465; 105 L.T. 721; 28 T.L.R. 106;
  17 Com.Cas. 41 . . . . 9-102, 9-106
Kettle v Dunster and Wakefield (1927) 43 T.L.R. 770; 138 L.T. 158 9-056
Kettlewell v Watson (1882) 21 Ch. D. 685 . . . . 8-210, 8-214
Khans Solicitors v Chifuntwe [2013] EWCA Civ 481; [2014] 1 W.L.R. 1185; [2013] 4 All
  E.R. 367; [2013] 4 Costs L.R. 564; [2013] P.N.L.R. 29; (2013) 157(19) S.J.L.B. 35 7-083
Khouj v Acropolis Capital Partners Ltd [2016] EWHC 2120 (Comm) 6-092
Kidderminster Corp v Hardwicke (1873) L.R. 9 Ex. 13; 43 L.J.Ex. 9; 29 L.T. 611; 22 W.R.
  160 . . . . 2-038, 2-074, 2-087
Kiddill v Farnell (1857) 3 Sn. & G. 428; 26 L.J.Ch. 818; 29 L.T. (O.S.) 324; 3 Jur. (N.S.)
  786; 5 W.R. 324 10-010
Kilgour v Finlayson (1789) 1 H.Bl. 155 . . . . **3-018**
Killick & Co v Price & Co & Lingfield SS Co Ltd (1896) 12 T.L.R. 263 8-078
Kimber Coal Co v Stone & Rolfe Ltd [1926] A.C. 414; 95 L.J.K.B. 601; 135 L.T. 161; 42
  T.L.R. 430; 31 Com.Cas. 333; 17 Asp. M.L.C. 37 9-038
Kimber v Barber (1872) L.R. 8 Ch.App. 56 6-062
Kimber v Barber (1872) L.R. 8 Ch.App. 56; 27 L.T. 526; 21 W.R. 65 . . . . 6-068, 6-085
Kinahan & Co v Parry [1911] 1 K.B. 459 . . . . 8-077, **8-082**
King v Anderson (1874) 8 I.R. Eq. 625 . . . . 6-064, **6-070**
King v Hutton (1860) 83 L.T. 68; 2 Q.B. 504; 69 L.J.Q.B. 786; 7 Mans. 393 CA 6-041, 6-078,
  8-167
King v Parsons (Victor) & Co [1973] 1 W.L.R. 29; [1973] 1 All E.R. 206; 116 S.J. 901;
  [1973] 1 Lloyd's Rep. 189 CA 2-026
King v Stewart (1892) 66 L.T. 339 9-104
King v T Tunnock Ltd 2000 S.C. 424; 2000 S.L.T. 744; [2001] E.C.C. 6; [2000] Eu. L.R.
  531; [2000] I.R.L.R. 569; 2000 G.W.D. 12-408 Ex Div 11-051, 11-057
King Viall & Benson v Howell (1910) 27 T.L.R. 114 6-071
Kings North Trust Ltd v Bell [1986] 1 W.L.R. 119; [1986] 1 All E.R. 423; (1985) 17
  H.L.R. 352; [1985] Fam. Law 225; (1985) 82 L.S.G. 1329; (1986) 130 S.J. 88 1-027
Kingscroft Insurance Co Ltd v HS Weavers (Underwriting Agencies Ltd [1993] 1 Lloyd's
  Rep. 187 . . . . 6-041, 7-077, 9-141
Kinloch v Craig (1789) 3 T.R. 119 7-078
Kinsella v Hamilton (1890) 26 L.R.Ir. 671 2-081
Kirkham v Peel (1880) 44 L.T. 195 . . . . 1-021, 6-041, **6-045**, **6-083**
Kirton v Braithwaite (1836) 1 B. & W. 310; 5 L.J.Ex. 165; 15 Dowl. 101; 2 Gale 48; Tyr.
  & Gr. 945 8-045
Kitson v King (S) & Son Ltd (1919) 36 T.L.R. 162 1-036
Kleinwort Benson Ltd v Lincoln City Council; Kleinwort Benson Ltd v Birmingham City
  Council; Kleinwort Benson Ltd v Southwark LBC; Kleinwort Benson Ltd v Kensington
  and Chelsea RLBC [1999] 2 A.C. 349; [1998] 3 W.L.R. 1095; [1998] 4 All E.R. 513;
  [1998] Lloyd's Rep. Bank. 387; [1999] C.L.C. 332; (1999) 1 L.G.L.R. 148; (1999) 11
  Admin. L.R. 130; [1998] R.VR. 315; (1998) 148 N.L.J. 1674; (1998) 142 S.J.L.B 279;
  [1998] N.P.C. 145 HL 8-022, 9-040
Kleinwort v Dunlop Rubber Co (1907) 99 L.T. 263; 23 T.L.R. 696; 51 S.J. 672   . . . . . 9-102, 9-106,
  9-107
Kleinwort, Cohen & Co v Cassa Maritima of Genoa (1877) 2 App.Cas. 156; 36 L.T. 118;
  25 W.R. 608; 3 Asp. M.L.C. PC 4-004
Kleinwort, Sons Co v Associated Automatic Machine Corp (1934) 50 T.L.R. 244; 151 L.T.
  1; 78 S.J. 153; 39 Com.Cas. 189 . . . . 8-046, 8-180
Knight Frank LLP v Du Haney [2011] EWCA Civ 404; [2011] 16 E.G. 78 (C.S.); (2011)
  108(17) L.S.G. 15; [2011] N.P.C. 40 . . . . 9-066, 9-067, 9-092
Knight v Bulkeley (1859) 5 Jur. (N.S.) 817; 5 Jur. (N.S.) 817 10-006

Knight v Fitch (1855) 15 C.B. 566; 3 C.L.R. 567; 24 L.J.C.P. 121; 1 Jur. (N.S.) 525 7-055
Knight v Frost [1999] B.C.C. 819; [1999] 1 B.C.L.C 364 6-039
Knight, Frank & Rutley v Gordon (1923) 39 T.L.R. 399 7-018
Knight, Frank and Rutley v Fraser 1974 S.L.T. 50 . . . . 7-019, 7-030
Knights v Wiffen (1870) L.R. 5 Q.B. 660; 40 L.J.Q.B. 51; 23 L.T. 610; 19 W.R. 244 8-173
Knott v Cottee (1852) 16 Beav. 77 6-043
Knowles v Haughton (1805) 11 Ves. 168 . . . . 6-098, 6-100
Knowles v Scott [1891] 1 Ch. 717 10-018
Koch (John) Ltd v C. & H. Products Ltd [1956] 1 Lloyd's Rep. 59 CA 6-012, **7-062**
Koch v Dicks [1933] 1 K.B. 307 CA 6-037
Koenigsblatt v Sweet [1923] 2 Ch. 314; 92 L.J.Ch. 598; 129 L.T. 659; 39 T.L.R. 576; 67
S.J. 638 . . . . 2-048, 2-074, 2-087
Kofi Sunkersette Obu v Strauss (A) & Co [1951] A.C. 243; 95 S.J. 137, P.C 7-004, **7-012**
Kolfor Plant Ltd v Tilbury Plant Ltd (1971) 121 S.J. 390, D.C 4-010
KOO Golden East Mongolia v Bank of Nova Scotia [2007] EWCA Civ 1443; [2008] Q.B.
717; [2008] 2 W.L.R. 1160; [2008] Bus. L.R. 744; [2008] 2 All E.R. (Comm) 314 9-116
Kooragang Investments Pty v Richardson & Wrench Ltd [1982] A.C. 462; [1981] 3
W.L.R. 493; [1981] 3 All E.R. 65, P.C 1-026, 8-018, 8-063, **8-064**, 8-077, 8-178, 8-180, 8-183,
8-193
Koufos v Czarnikow (C); sub nom. Koufos v Czarnikow (C); The Heron II; sub nom.
Czarnikow (C) v Koufos [1969] 1 A.C. 350; [1967] 3 W.L.R. 1491; 111 S.J. 848; [1967]
3 All E.R. 686; [1967] 2 Lloyd's Rep 457 HL 9-077
Koursk, The [1924] P. 140; (1924) 18 Ll. L. Rep. 228 CA 9-120
Kreditbank Cassel GmbH v Schenkers [1927] 1 K.B. 826; [1927] All E.R. Rep. 421; 96
L.J.K.B. 501; 136 L.T. 716; 43 T.L.R. 237; 7 S.J. 141; 32 Com.Cas. 197 . . . . 8-039, 8-041
Kronprinzessin Cecilie, The (1917) 33 T.L.R. 292 1-035
Kruger v Wilcox (1755) Amb. 252; 1 Kenv. 32; Dick 269 . . . . 7-078, 7-082, 7-090
Kuddus v Chief Constable of Leicestershire [2001] UKHL 29; [2002] 2 A.C. 122; [2001]
2 W.L.R. 1789; [2001] 3 All E.R. 193; (2001) 3 L.G.L.R. 45; [2001] Po. L.R. 181;
(2001) 98(28) L.S.G. 43; (2001) 151 N.L.J. 936; (2001) 145 S.J.L.B. 166 8-177
Kuenigl v Donnersmarck [1955] 1 Q.B. 515; [1955] 2 W.L.R. 82; [1955] 1 All E.R. 46; 99
S.J. 60 . . . . 2-012, 2-065, 10-003
Kuhlirz v Lambert Brothers (1913) 18 Com.Cas 217; 108 L.T. 565 6-065
Kum v Wah Tat Bank [1971] 1 Lloyd's Rep. 439 3-035
Kuwait Asia Bank EC v National Mutual Life Nominees Ltd [1991] 1 A.C. 187; [1990] 3
W.L.R. 297; [1990] 3 All E.R. 404; [1990] 2 Lloyd's Rep. 95; [1990] B.C.C. 567;
[1990] B.C.L.C. 868 PC (New Zealand) 2-031, 2-033, 8-178
Kuwait Oil Tanker Co SAK v Al Bader [2000] 2 All E.R. (Comm) 271 9-120
Kwei Tek Chao (Trading as Zung Fu Co) v British Tractors and Shippers, NV
Handelsmaatschappi J. Smits Import-Export Third Party (No.2); sub nom. Chao v
British Traders and Shippers [1954] 2 Q.B. 459; [1954] 3 W.L.R. 496; 98 S.J. 592;
[1954] 3 All E.R. 165; [1954] 2 Lloyd's Rep. 114 8-063
Kwei Tek Chao v British Traders and Shippers Ltd [1954] 2 Q.B. 459 . . 8-182, 8-185, 8-214, 9-078
Kymer v Suwercropp (1807) 1 Camp. 109 . . . . 8-101, 8-103, 8-106
Lacey (William) (Hounslow) Ltd v Davis [1957] 1 W.L.R. 932; [1957] 2 All E.R. 712;
101 S.J. 629 7-009
Lacey v Hill; Crowley's Claim (1874) L.R. 18 Eq. 182; 43 L.J.Ch. 551; 30 L.T. 484; 22
W.R. 586 . . . . 7-059, 7-060, **7-062**
Lacey, Exp. (1802) 6 Ves. 625 6-064
Lady Forrest (Murchison) Gold Mine, Re [1901] 1 Ch. 582; 70 L.J.Ch. 275; 84 L.T. 559;
17 T.L.R. 198; 45 S.J. 222; 8 Mans. 438 6-035
Lady Manor Ltd v Fat Cat Cafe Bars Ltd [2001] 2 E.G.L.R. 1; [2001] 33 E.G. 88; [2001]
23 E.G.C.S.156, CC (West London) 7-004
Laemthong International Lines Co Ltd v Artis; The Laemthong Glory (No.2); sub nom.
Laemthong International Lines Co Ltd v Abdullah Mohammed Fahem & Co [2005]
EWCA Civ 519; [2005] 1 Lloyd's Rep. 688 CA 1-023, 9-122
Lagunas Nitrate Co Ltd v Schroeder & Co (1901) 85 L.T. 22 10-028
Lagunas Nitrate v Lagunas Syndicate [1899] 2 Ch. 392; 68 L.J.Ch. 699; 81 L.T. 334; 48
W.R. 74; 15 T.L.R. 436; 43 S.J. 622; 7 Mans. 165 . . . . 6-020, 6-035, 6-043
Laidlaw (James) & Son v Griffin 1968 S.L.T. 278 9-013
Lake v Simmons [1927] A.C. 487 . . . . 8-077, 8-146
Lakeman v Mountstephen; sub nom. Mountstephen v Lakeman (1874) L.R. 7 H.L. 17 9-043

Lamb (W.T.) & Sons v Goring Brick Co [1932] 1 K.B. 710; 101 L.J.K.B. 214; 416 L.T.
 318; 48 T.L.R. 160; 37 Com.Cas. 73 . . . . 1-035, 1-036, 7-001, 7-037
Lamb v Attenborough (1862) 1 B. & S.831; L.J.Q.B. 41; 8 Jur. (N.S.) 280; 10 W.R. 211 8-145
Lamb v Evans [1893] 1 Ch. 218; 62 L.J.Ch. 404; 68 L.T. 131; 41 W.R. 405; 9 T.L.R. 87; 2
 R. 189. . . . . 6-035, 6-077, **6-078**, 7-001, **8-157**
Lambert (t/a Lambert Commercials) v Fry [2000] C.L.Y. 113 4-010
Lambert v G&C Finance Corp (1963) 107 S.J. 666 8-153
Lamont v Hamilton 1907 S.C. 628 . . . . 8-120, 9-046
Landes v Bradwell (1909) T.L.R. 478 9-056
Landless v Wilson (1880) 8 R. 289; 18 S.L.R. 206 7-004
Lands Allotment Co v Broad (1895) 13 R. 699; 2 Man. 470 8-223
Lands Allotment Co, Re [1894] 1 Ch. 616 CA 6-003
Lang v Smyth (1831) 7 Bing 284; 5 Moo. A.P. 78; 9 L.J. (O.S.) C.P. 91 8-161
Langan v Great Western Railway Co (1873) 30 L.T. 173 . . . . 3-029, 4-007
Langley, Beldon & Gaunt Ltd v Morley [1965] 1 Lloyd's Rep. 297 . . . . 7-074, 7-082
Langsam v Beachcroft LLP [2012] EWCA Civ 1230 . . . . 6-020, 7-009
Langston v Corney (1815) 4 Comp. 176 9-114
Langstroth v Toulmin (1822) 3 Stark 145 9-099
Langton v Waite (1869) L.R. 4 Ch.App. 402 6-078
Lanphier v Phipos (1838) 8 C.P. 475 6-019
Lantic Sugar Ltd v Baffin Investments Ltd [2009] EWHC 3325 (Comm) 3-032
Lanyon v Blanchard (1811) 2 Camp. 597 8-020
Lara v Hill (1863) 15 C.B. (N.S.) 45 7-014
Larsen v Anglo American Oil Co Ltd (1924) 20 Ll L. Rep. 40 6-010
Lascelles v Rathburn (1919) 35 T.L.R. 347; 63 S.J. 410 CA 9-087
Launchbury v Morgans [1973] A.C. 127; [1972] 2 W.L.R. 1217; [1972] 2 All E.R. 606;
 116 S.J. 396. 8-187
Laurence, Re; Ex p. M'Kenna; City Bank Case; sub nom. Streatfield, Lawrence & Co Re,
 Ex p. Mackenna; City Bank Case; sub nom. Mortimore, Re; Ex p. M'Kenna (1861) 3
 De G.F. & T 629; 4 L.T. 164; 7 Jur. (N.S.) 588; 9 W.R. 490 7-086
Lauritzencool AB v Lady Navigation Inc; Lady Navigation Inc v Lauritzen Cool AB
 Reported [2005] EWCA Civ 579; [2005] 1 W.L.R. 3686; [2005] 2 All E.R. (Comm)
 183; [2005] 2 Lloyd's Rep. 63; [2005] 1 C.L.C. 758 CA. 10-025
Law Debenture Trust Corporation Plc v Ukraine [2017] EWHC 655 (Comm); [2017] 3
 W.L.R. 667 . . . . 2-020, 3-005, 8-042, 12-020, 12-022, 12-025
Law Society of England and Wales v Habitable Concepts Ltd [2010] EWHC 1449 (Ch) 9-135,
 9-199
Lawrance v Galsworthy (1857) 3 Jur. (N.S.) 1049; 30 L.T. (O.S.) 112 6-070
Lawrance, Re; Bowker v Austin [1894] 1 Ch. 556; 63 L.J.Ch. 205; 70 L.T. 91; 42 W.R.
 265; 8 R. 102. . . . . **7-094**
Lawrence Chemical Co Ltd v Rubinstein [1982] 1 W.L.R. 284; [1982] 1 All E.R. 653;
 (1982) 126 S.J. 71 CA. **2-026**
Lawrence v Fletcher (1879) 12 Ch.D. 858; 41 L.T. 207; 27 W.R. 937 . . . . **7-099**
Lawrie v Lees (1880) 14 Ch.D. 249 8-084
Lawson v Hosemaster Co Ltd [1966] 1 W.L.R. 1300; [1966] 2 All E.R. 944; 110 S.J. 407
 CA 2-068, 2-096
Laycock v Pickles (1863) 4 B. & S. 497; 3 New Rep. 73; 33 L.J.Q.B. 43; 9 L.T. 378; 10
 Jur. (N.S.) 336; 12 W.R. 76. 6-098
Lazarus v Cairn Line Ltd (1912) 106 L.T. 378; 28 T.L.R. 244; 17 Com.Cas. 107; 56 S.J.
 345. 10-042
LBI HF v Stanford [2014] EWHC 3921 (Ch) 8-198
Le Neve v Le Neve (1747) 1 Ves. Sen. 64; 27 E.R. 893; (1748) 3 Atk. 646 . . . . 8-208, 8-211, 8-213,
 8-214, 8-216, **8-217**
Lea Bridge District Gas Co v Malvern [1917] 1 K.B. 803; 86 L.J.K.B. 553; 116 L.T. 311;
 81 J.P. 141; 15 L.G.R. 412 8-120
Leadbitter v Farrow (1816) 5 M. & S.345 . . . . 8-093, 9-052, **9-056**
Leak v Charles & Sons Ltd (1948) 92 S.J. 1543 10-042
Learoyd v Whiteley; sub nom. Whiteley v Learoyd, Re (1887) 12 App.Cas. 727; 57
 L.J.Ch. 390; 58 L.T. 93; 36 W.R. 721; 3 T.L.R. 813. 2-021
Lease Management Services v Purnell Secretarial Services; sub nom. Purnell Secretarial
 Services v Lease Management Services [1994] C.C.L.R. 127; (1994) Tr.L.Rep. 337 CA 8-043,
 8-077

Lebon v Aqua Salt Co Ltd [2009] UKPC 2; [2009] B.C.C. 425; [2009] 1 B.C.L.C. 549 PC
    (Mauritius) 1-029, 8-214, 8-215, 8-217
Leckenby v Wolman [1921] W.N. 100 .... **3-023**
Lee (David) (Lincoln) Ltd v Coward Chance (A Firm) Supasave Retail v Coward Chance
    (A Firm) [1991] Ch. 259; [1990] 3 W.L.R. 1278; [1991] 1 All E.R. 668; (1990) 134 S.J.
    1403; [1990] B.C.L.C. 519 Ch D 6-051
Lee v Bayes and Robinson (1856) 18 C.B. 599; 26 L.T. (O.S.) 221; 2 Jur. (N.S.) 1093 9-131
Lee v Everest (1857) 2 H. & N. 285; 26 L.J.Ex. 334; 29 L.T. (O.S.) 263; 22 J.P. 55; 5 W.R.
    759. 9-003
Lee v Lee's Air Farming Ltd [1961] A.C. 12 2-014
Lee v Rumilly (1891) 55 J.P. 519; 7 T.L.R. 303 8-196
Lee v Sankey (1873) L.R. 15 Eq. 204; 27 L.T. 809; 21 W.R. 286 ...... 2-046, 6-100, 9-137, 9-140
Lee v Walker (1872) L.R. 7 C.P. 121; 41 L.J.C.P. 91; 26 L.T. 70 .... 6-019, **6-024**
Lee, Re, Ex p. Neville (1868) L.R. 4 Ch.App. 43; 19 L.T. 435; 17 W.R. 108 .... 6-090, 7-050
Leeds & Hanley Theatres of Varieties, Re [1902] 2 Ch. 809; 72 L.J.Ch. 1; 87 L.T. 488; 51
    W.R. 5; 46 S.J. 648; 10 Mans.72. 6-035
Leeds and Holbeck Building Society v Arthur & Cole [2001] Lloyd's Rep. P.N. 649;
    [2002] P.N.L.R. 4 6-056
Lees v Nuttall (1834) 2 My. & K. 819 .... 6-077, 6-082
Leesh River Tea Co v British India Steam Navigation Co [1967] 2 Q.B. 250; [1966] 3
    W.L.R. 642; [1966] 3 All E.R. 593; 110 S.J. 633; [1966] 2 Lloyd's Rep. 193 CA 8-063
Leete v Wallace (1888) 58 L.T. 577 6-089
Legge v Byas, Mosley & Co (1901) 7 Com.Cas. 16; 18 T.L.R. 137 3-026
Lehman Bros International (Europe) v CRC Credit Fund Ltd [2012] UKSC 6; [2012] 3 All
    E.R. 1; [2012] Bus. L.R. 667; [2012] 1 B.C.L.C. 487; [2012] W.T.L.R. 1355; (2012)
    162 N.L.J. 364 .... 6-040, 6-041, 6-060
Leicestershire CC v Faraday (Michael) & Partners [1941] 2 K.B. 205; [1941] 2 All E.R.
    483; 110 L.J.K.B. 511; 105 J.P. 348; 57 T.L.R. 572; 40 L.G.R. 82 6-093
Leif Hoegh & Co A/S v Petrolsea Inc; The World Era [1992] 1 Lloyd's Rep. 45 QBD
    (Comm Ct) 9-013
Leigh and Sillavan Ltd v Aliakmon Shipping Ltd; The Aliakmon [1986] A.C. 785; [1986]
    2 W.L.R. 902; [1986] 2 All E.R. 145; (1986) 130 S.J. 357; [1986] 2 Lloyd's Rep. 1 HL 9-089
Lemenda Trading Co Ltd v African Middle East Petroleum Co Ltd [1988] Q.B. 448;
    [1988] 2 W.L.R. 735; [1988] 1 All E.R. 513; (1988) 132 S.J. 538; [1988] 1 F.T.L.R.
    123; [1988] 1 Lloyd's Rep. 361 QBD (Comm). 8-218, 9-098
Lennard v Robinson (1855) S.E. & B. 125; 24 L.J.Q.B. 275; 1 Jur. (N.S.) 853; 3 C.L.R.
    1363. .... 9-037, 9-038
Lennard's Carrying Co v Asiatic Petroleum Co Ltd; sub nom. Asiatic Petroleum Co Ltd v
    Lennard's Carrying Co Ltd [1915] A.C. 705; 84 L.J.K.B. 1281; 113 L.T. 195; 31 T.L.R.
    294; 59 S.J. 411; 13 Asp. M.L.C. 81; 20 Com.Cas. 283. 1-029
Lennox (Hendy) (Industrial Engines) Ltd v Puttick (Grahame) Ltd [1984] 1 W.L.R. 485;
    [1984] 2 All E.R. 152; (1984) 128 S.J. 220; [1984] 2 Lloyd's Rep. 422 6-037
Leon, The. See Ridgeway Maritime Inc v Beulah Wings Ltd; The Leon 9-121
Lepage v San Paulo Copper Estates Ltd (1917) 33 T.L.R. 457; 61 S.J. 612 2-010
Lepard v Vernon (1813) 2 V. & B. 51 10-006
Les Affreteurs Reunis SA v Leopold Walford (London) Ltd [1919] A.C. 801; 88 L.J.K.B.
    861; 121 L.T. 393; 35 T.L.R. 542; 14 Asp. M.L.C. 451; 24 Com.Cas. 268. ..... 2-031, 2-033, 7-022
Leslie (R) Ltd v Sheill [1914] 3 K.B. 607; [1914–15] All E.R. 511; 83 L.J.K.B. 1145; 111
    L.T. 106; 30 T.L.R. 460; 58 S.J. 453. 2-015
Lester v Balfour Williamson & Co, Merchant Shippers [1953] 2 Q.B. 168; [1953] 2
    W.L.R. 1068; 117 J.P. 308; [1953] 1 All E.R. 1146; 97 S.J. 353; [1953] 2 Lloyd's Rep.
    13, D.C 9-038
Lettice v Judkins (1840) 9 L.J.Ex. 142 .... **3-023**
Lever (Finance) Ltd v Westminster Corp; Lever (Finance) Ltd v Westminster LBC [1971]
    1 Q.B. 222; [1970] 3 W.L.R. 732; [1970] 3 All E.R. 496; 68 L.G.R. 757; (1970) 21 P. &
    C.R. 778; [1971] J.P.L. 115; 114 S.J. 651 CA 8-042
Lever (Mark) & Co Ltd v Wingate (W) & Johnston (Cox & King's (Agents) Third Parties)
    (1950) 84 H.L. Rep. 156. 6-012
Lever v Goodwin (1887) 36 Ch.D. 1; 57 L.T. 583; 36 W.R. 177; 3 T.L.R. 650; 4 R.P.C.
    492. 6-077
Levers v Dunsdon [1968] E.G.D. 280 .... 7-028, 7-032
Levitt v Hamblet [1901] 2 K.B. 53; 70 L.J.K.B. 520; 84 L.T. 638; 17 T.L.R. 307; 6
    Com.Cas. 79 8-006

Levy v Barnard (1818) 8 Taunt. 149; 2 Moo. C.P. 34 .... 7-093, 7-098
Levy v Goldhill [1917] 2 Ch. 297; 86 L.J.Ch. 693; 117 L.T. 442; 33 T.L.R. 479; 61 S.J.
   630... 7-042, 10-043
Levy v Richardson (1890) 5 T.L.R. 236 8-054
Lewcock v Bromley (1920) 37 T.L.R. 48; 127 L.T. 116; 65 S.J. 75 3-032
Lewes Sanitary Steam Laundry v Bardey & Co Ltd (1906) 22 T.L.R. 737; 95 L.T. 444;
   11Com.Cas.255... 8-130
Lewes v Morgan (1817) 5 Price 421; 46 E.R. 530 6-098
Lewis & Graves v Harper (1978) 250 E.G. 1287 CA 7-012
Lewis & Tucker v Lee (1949) 153 E.G. 342 7-019
Lewis v Hillman; sub nom. Bloye's Trust, Re (1852) 3 H.L.Cas. 607; 19 L.T. (O.S.) 329 6-070
Lewis v Nicholson (1852) 18 Q.B. 503; 21 L.J.Q.B. 311; 19 L.T. (O.S.) 122; 16 Jur. 1041 .. 9-037,
   9-038, 9-061, 9-090
Lewis v Ramsdale (1886) 55 L.T. 179; 35 W.R. 8; 2 T.L.R. 691 3-015
Lewis v Read (1845) 12 M. & W. 834; 14 L.J.Ex. 295; 4 L.T. (O.S.) 116 .... **2-073**
Lewis v Samuel (1846) 8 Q.B. 685; 1 New Pract. Cas.424; 15 L.J.Q.B. 218; 7 L.T. (O.S.)
   60; 10 Jur. 429.. **7-070**
Lewis v Yeeles [2010] EWCA Civ 326 9-121
Lewisham London Borough v Leslie & Co Ltd (1978) 250 E.G. 1289; (1978) 12 Build.
   L.R. 22 CA 2-026
Lexi Holdings (In Administration) v Pannone & Partners [2009] EWHC 2590 (Ch) .. 3-005, **3-029**,
   8-048, 8-053, 8-063
Lexington Insurance Co v Multinacional de Seguros SA [2008] EWHC 1170 (Comm);
   [2009] 1 All E.R. (Comm) 35; [2009] Lloyd's Rep. I.R. 1......................... 12-001
Liberian Insurance Agency Inc v Mosse [1977] 2 Lloyd's Rep. 560 7-060
Lichtenstein (Jacques) v Clube Atletico Mineiro [2005] EWHC 1300 QBD 5-001, 7-030
Lickborrow v Mason; sub nom. Mason v Lickbarrow (1790) 1 Hy. Bl. 357 8-130
Lienard v Dresslar (1862) 3 F. & F. 212 .... **3-040**
Liggett (B) Liverpool v Barclays Bank [1928] 1 K.B. 48; 97 L.J.K.B. 1; 137 L.T. 443; 43
   T.L.R. 449... 8-039
Light v Ty Europe Ltd [2003] EWCA Civ 1238; [2004] 1 Lloyd's Rep. 693; [2004] 1
   C.L.C. 71; [2004] E.C.C. 39; [2003] Eu. L.R. 858; (2003) 100(38) L.S.G. 33 CA .. 11-014, 11-043
Lightfoot v Keane (1836) 1 M. & W. 745; 2 Gale 138; Tyr. & Gr. 1004; 5 L.J.Ex. 257 ... 7-089
Liles v Terry [1895] 2 Q.B. 679; 65 L.J.Q.B. 34; 73 L.T. 428; 44 W.R. 116; 12 T.L.R. 26;
   40 S.J. 53.. 6-069
Lilly v Hays (1836) 5 A. & E. 548; 2 Har. & W. 338; 1 Nev & P.K.B. 26; 6 L.J.K.B. 5 9-113
Lilly, Wilson & Co v Smales, Ecles & Co [1892] 1 Q.B. 456; 40 W.R. 544; 8 T.L.R. 410 .... **9-076**
Limako BV v Hentz & Co Inc [1979] 2 Lloyd's Rep. 23 CA 1-022, 3-040, **6-070**
Limpus v London General Omnibus Co (1862) 1 H. & C. 526; 32 L.J. Ex. 34; 7 L.T. 641;
   27 J.P. 147; 9 Jur. (N.S.) 333; 11 W.R. 149 .... 8-176, **8-193**
Linck, Moeller & Co v Jameson & Co (1885) 2 T.L.R. 206 .... 1-046, **8-112**
Linden Gardens Trust Ltd v Lenesta Sludge Disposal Ltd; St Martins Property Corp Ltd v
   Sir Robert McAlpine & Sons [1994] 1 A.C. 85; [1993] 3 W.L.R. 408; [1993] 3 All E.R.
   417; 63 B.L.R. 1; 36 Con. L.R. 1; [1993] E.G.C.S.139; (1993) 143 N.L.J. 1152; (1993)
   137 S.J.L.B. 183 HL... 9-013
Lindgren v L&P Estates Co [1968] Ch. 572; [1968] 2 W.L.R. 562; [1968] 1 All E.R. 917;
   (1967) 204 E.G. 15 CA.. 6-080
Lindsay & Son v Scholefield (1897) 24 R. (Ct. of Sess.) 530; 34 Sc.L.R. 404; 4 S.L.T. 291 .. 3-032
Lindsay v O'Loughnane [2010] EWHC 529 (QB) 2-023, 8-197, 9-118
Linford v Provincial etc, Insurance Co (1864) 34 Beav. 291; 5 New Rep. 29; 11 L.T. 330;
   28 J.P. 803; 10 Jur. (N.S.) 1066.. 8-067
Linford v Provincial, etc., Ins.Co (1864) 34 Beav. 291; 11 L.T. 330; 28 J.P. 803; 10 Jur.
   (N.S.).. **3-029, 8-067**
Linklaters v HSBC Bank Plc [2003] EWHC 1113; [2003] 2 Lloyd's Rep. 545; [2003] 2
   C.L.C. 162 QBD (Comm) 7-060, 7-063, 7-066
Lion Laboratories Ltd v [1985] Q.B. 526; [1984] 3 W.L.R. 539; [1984] 2 All E.R. 417;
   (1984) 128 S.J. 533 CA.. 6-077
Lipkin Gorman v Karpnale Ltd [1991] 2 A.C. 548; [1991] 3 W.L.R. 10; [1992] 4 All E.R.
   512 HL.................................... 8-141, 8-161, **8-167**, 9-102, 9-107, 9-136
Lister & Co v Stubbs (1890) 45 Ch.D. 1; 59 L.J.Ch. 570; 63 L.T. 75; 38 W.R. 548; 6
   T.L.R. 317.. 6-042, 6-087
Lister v Hesley Hall Ltd [2001] UKHL 22; [2002] 1 A.C. 215; [2001] 2 W.L.R. 1311;
   [2001] 2 All E.R. 769; [2001] I.C.R. 665; [2001] I.R.L.R. 472; [2001] Emp. L.R. 819;

[2001] 2 F.L.R. 307; [2001] 2 F.C.R. 97; (2001) 3 L.G.L.R. 49; [2001] E.L.R. 422; [2001] Fam. Law 595; (2001) 98(24) L.S.G. 45; (2001) 151 N.L.J. 728; (2001) 145 S.J.L.B. 126; [2001] N.P.C. 89 HL 8-178

Lister v Romford Ice and Cold Storage Co Ltd; Romford Ice & Cold Storage Co v Lister [1957] A.C. 555; [1957] 2 W.L.R. 158; [1957] 1 All E.R. 125; [1956] 2 Lloyd's Rep. 505; 121 J.P. 98; 101 S.J. 106 HL 7-001, 8-191

Litsion, The. *See* Black King Shipping Corp v Massie 8-182

Litster v Forth Dry Dock & Engineering Co Ltd [1990] 1 A.C. 546; [1989] 2 W.L.R. 634; [1989] I.C.R. 341; [1989] 1 All E.R. 1134; (1989) 133 S.J. 455; [1989] 1 RLR 161; [1989] 2 C.M.L.R. 194 HL 8-035, 11-004

Little v Spreadbury [1910] 2 K.B. 658; 79 L.J.K.B. 119; 102 L.T. 829; 26 T.L.R. 552; 54 S.J. 618 . . . . 2-031, 3-032

Littlewood v Williams (1815) 6 Taunt. 277 6-041

Liverpool City Council v Irwin [1977] A.C. 239; (1976) 238 E.G. 879; (1984) 13 H.L.R. 38 HL 4-008, 6-001, 7-001, 7-039

Liverpool Household Stores, Re (1890) 59 L.J.Ch. 616 . . . . **2-044**

Liversidge v Broadbent (1859) 4 H. & N. 603; 28 L.J.Ex. 332; 33 L.T. (O.S.) 226; 7 W.R. 615 9-113

Livingstone v Ross [1901] A.C. 327; 70 L.J.P.C. 58; 85 L.T. 382 1-036

Llanelly Railway and Dock Co v London & North Western Railway Co (1875) L.R. 7 H.L. 550 HL 10-042

Llewellin, Re; sub nom. A Solicitor, Re [1891] 3 Ch. 145; 60 L.J.Ch. 732; 65 L.T. 249; 39 W.R. 713; 7 T.L.R. 742 . . . . **7-089**

Lloyd v Grace, Smith & Co [1912] A.C. 716; 81 L.J.K.B. 1140; 107 L.T. 531; 28 T.L.R. 547; 58 S.J. 723 . . . . 8-028, 8-063, 8-098, 8-176, 8-180, 8-188, **8-194**, 8-214

Lloyd v Sigourney (1829) 5 Bing. 525; 3 Y. & J. 220; 3 Moo. & P. 229; 130 E.R. 1164 . . . . . **8-061**

Lloyd v Stanbury [1971] 1 W.L.R. 535; [1971] 2 All E.R. 267; (1970) 115 S.J. 264; 22 P.& C.R. 432 9-081

Lloyd's v Harper (1880) 16 Ch.D. 290; [1874–80] All E.R. Rep. Ext. 1337; 50 L.J.Ch. 140; 43 L.T. 481; 29 W.R. 452 CA 9-011

Lloyds & Scottish Finance v Williamson [1965] 1 W.L.R. 404; [1965] 1 All E.R. 641; 109 S.J. 10 CA 8-109, 8-130, 8-135, 8-153

Lloyds Bank Ltd v Bank of America National Trust and Savings Association [1938] 2 K.B. 147; 107 L.J.K.B. 538; 158 L.T. 301; 54 T.L.R. 599; [1938] 2 All E.R. 63; 82 S.J. 312; 43 Com.Cas.209 . . . . 8-135, 8-146, **8-158**

Lloyds Bank Plc v Independent Insurance Co Ltd [2000] Q.B. 110; [1999] 2 W.L.R. 986; [1999] 1 All E.R. (Comm.) 8; [1999] Lloyd's Rep. Bank. 1; [1999] C.L.C. 510; (1999) 96(3) L.S.G. 31 CA 2-102, 8-028

Lloyds TSB Bank Plc v Markandan & Uddin (A Firm) [2012] EWCA Civ 65; [2012] 2 All E.R. 884; [2012] P.N.L.R. 20; (2012) 162 N.L.J. 328 . . . . 6-003, 6-043

Lloyds v Bullock [1896] 2 Ch. 193; 65 L.J.Ch. 680; 74 L.T. 687; 44 W.R. 633; 12 T.L.R. 435; 40 S.J. 545 8-135

Lloyds v Chartered Bank of India, Australia & China [1929] 1 K.B. 40; 97 L.J.K.B. 609; 139 L.T. 126; 44 T.L.R. 534; 33 Com.Cas. 306 8-063

Lloyds v Cooke [1907] 1 K.B. 794; 76 L.J.K.B. 666; 96 L.T. 715; 23 T.L.R. 429 . . . . **8-045**, 8-130, 8-134

Lloyds v Swiss Bank Bankverein (1912) 107 L.T. 309 . . . . 8-077, 8-141, 8-142

LNOC Ltd v Watford Association Football Club Ltd [2013] EWHC 3615 (Comm) . . 3-016, 8-040, 8-049

Lo v Russell [2016] VSCA 323 3-032

Lock v Bell [1931] 1 Ch. 35; 100 L.J.Ch. 22; 144 L.T. 108 6-013

Lockett v Norman-Wright [1925] Ch. 56 . . . . **3-032**

Lockwood v Abdy (1845) 14 Sim 437; 5 L.T. (O.S.) 122; 5 Jur. 267 . . . . **5-016**

Lockwood v Levick (1860) 8 C.B. (N.S.) 603; 29 L.J.C.P. 340; 2 L.T. 357; 7 Jur. (N.S.) 102; 8 W.R. 583 7-014

Lodgepower Ltd v Taylor; Taylor v Lodgepower Ltd [2004] EWCA Civ 1367; [2005] 1 E.G.L.R. 1; [2005] 08 E.G. 192; [2004] 44 E.G.C.S.152; [2004] N.P.C. 156 CA 10-015

Lofts v Bourke (1884) 1 T.L.R. 58 7-032

Loftus v Roberts (1902) 18 T.L.R. 532 7-009

Logicrose Ltd v Southend United Football Club (No.2) [1988] 1 W.L.R. 1256 . 6-087, **6-089**, 8-221, 8-222, 8-223, 8-225, **8-226**

London & Colonial Co Re, Ex p. Clark (1869) L.R. 7 Eq. 550; 38 L.J.Ch. 562; 20 L.T. 774 10-042

London & Globe Finance Corp, Re [1902] 2 Ch. 416; 71 L.J.Ch. 893; 87 L.T. 49; 18
   T.L.R. 679. . . . . 7-081, 7-082, 7-086
London & Mediterranean Bank Re, Ex p. Birmingham Banking Co (1868) L.R. 3 Ch.App.
   651; 37 L.J.Ch. 905; 19 L.T. 193; 16 W.R. 1003 . . . . **5-007**
London and County Banking Co Ltd v Ratcliffe (1881) 6 App.Cas. 722; 51 L.J.Ch. 28; 45
   L.T. 322; 30 W.R. 109. . . . . **7-089**
London Borough of Bromley v Ellis [1971] 1 Lloyd's Rep. 97; (1970) 114 S.J. 906 CA **6-032**
London Borough of Southwark v IBM UK Ltd [2011] EWHC 549 (TCC)   11-016
London Chartered Bank of Australia v White (1879) 4 App.Cas. 413; 48 L.J.P.C. 75   . . 7-081, 7-082
London County Council v Agricultural Food Products; Same v Vitamins [1955] 2 Q.B.
   218; [1955] 2 W.L.R. 925; [1955] 2 All E.R. 229; 99 S.J. 305; 59 L.G.R. 350 CA 2-022, **2-026**
London County Council v Cattermoles (Garages) Ltd [1953] 1 W.L.R. 997; [1953] 2 All
   E.R. 582; 97 S.J. 505; [1953] S.L.T. 185 CA 8-193
London County Freehold & Leasehold Properties Ltd v Berkeley Property & Investment
   Co Ltd [1936] 2 All E.R. 1039; 155 L.T. 190; 80 S.J. 652. 8-185
London Export Corp v Jubilee Coffee Roasting Co [1958] 1 W.L.R. 661; 102 S.J. 452;
   [1958] 2 All E.R. 411; [1958] 1 Lloyd's Rep. 367; 74 L.Q.R. 471 3-035
London General Omnibus Co Ltd v Pope (1922) 38 T.L.R. 270 9-058
London International Trust Ltd v Barclays Bank Ltd [1980] 1 Lloyd's Rep. 241   3-009
London Joint Stock Bank v Simmons [1892] A.C. 201; 61 L.J.Ch. 732; 66 L.T. 625; 56
   J.P. 644; 41 W.R. 108; 8 T.L.R. 478; 36 S.J. 396. . . . . 8-048, **8-142**
London Mews Co v Burney. *See* Burney v London Mews Co   7-032
London School Board v Northcroft (1892) Hudson's Building and Engineering Contracts
   (12th ed.), para.2.235. . . . . 6-085, 6-093
London Transport Executive v Clarke [1981] I.C.R. 355; [1981] I.R.L.R. 166; (1981) 125
   S.J. 306 CA 7-047
London v Hobbis (1897) 7 S.L.T. 688; 61 J.P. 85; 45 W.R. 270; 41 S.J. 143   2-021
Long (Peter) & Partners v Burns [1956] 1 W.L.R. 1083; [1956] 3 All E.R. 207; 100 S.J.
   619 CA 7-018
Longman v Hill (1891) 7 T.L.R. 639   8-117
Longstaff v Birtles [2001] EWCA Civ 1219; [2002] 1 W.L.R. 470; [2001] 34 E.G. 98
   (C.S.); (2001) 98(34) L.S.G. 43; (2001) 145 S.J.L.B. 210; [2001] N.P.C. 128. . . . . 6-038, 6-067
Lonsdale v Howard & Hallam Ltd [2007] UKHL 32; [2007] 1 W.L.R. 2055; [2008] Bus.
   L.R. 788; [2007] 4 All E.R. 1; [2007] 2 All E.R. (Comm) 621; [2008] 1 Lloyd's Rep.
   78; [2007] 2 C.L.C. 1; [2008] E.C.C. 11; [2007] Eu. L.R. 799; [2007] I.C.R. 1338;
   [2007] I.R.L.R. 825; (2007) 151 S.J.L.B. 922. . . . . 11-051—11-053
Lord v Hall (1848) 2 C. & K. 698; 8 C.B. 627; 19 L.J.C.P. 47; 14 L.T. (O.S.) 253   5-007
Lordsgate Properties Ltd v Balcombe [1985] 1 E.G.L.R. 20; (1985) 274 E.G. 493   . . . 7-021, 7-030,
   7-032
Lorenz Consultancy Ltd v Fox-Davies Capital Ltd [2011] EWHC 574 (Ch); [2011] 12
   E.G. 115 (C.S.) 1-012
Loring v Davis (1886) 32 Ch.D. 625; 55 L.J.Ch. 725; 54 L.T. 899; 34 W.R. 701; 2 T.L.R.
   645. . . . . 3-020, 6-010
Lothian v Jenolite Ltd 1969 S.C. 111   . . . . 6-015, 6-037
Lott v Outhwaite (1893) 10 T.L.R. 76   . . . . 7-004, 7-018, 7-024
Lovesy v Palmer [1916] 2 Ch. 233; 85 L.J.Ch. 481; 114 L.T. 1033 . . . . 8-003, 9-041
Lovett v Carson Country Homes Ltd [2009] EWHC 1143 (Ch); [2009] 2 B.C.L.C. 196   8-014,
   8-040, 8-041, 8-044
Low v Bouverie [1891] 3 Ch. 82 CA 2-106, 8-029
Lowe v Dorling [1906] 2 K.B. 772   . . . . **9-125**
Lowther v Harris [1927] 1 K.B. 393; 96 L.J.K.B. 170; 136 L.T. 377; 43 T.L.R. 24   . . . 8-145, 8-147,
   8-158
Lowther v Lowther (1866) 13 Ves.95   6-064
LSC Finance Ltd v Abensons Law Ltd (t/a Abensons Solicitors) [2015] EWHC 1163 (Ch)   . . . 9-068
Luanda Exportadora SARL v Wahbe Tamari & Sons Ltd; Akkawi Trading Co v Luanda
   Exportadora SARL [1967] 2 Lloyd's Rep. 353 QBD (Comm) 7-009
Lucas v Mason (1875) L.R. 10 Ex. 251; 44 L.J.Ex. 145; 33 L.T. 13; 39 J.P. 663; 23 W.R.
   924. 8-195
Lucifero v Castel (1887) 3 T.L.R. 371   6-065
Luckombe v Ashton (1862) 2 F. & F. 705 8-043
Luddy's Trustees v Peard (1886) 33 Ch.D. 500; 55 L.J.Ch. 884; 55 L.T. 137; 35 W.R. 44;
   2 T.L.R. 841 . . . . **6-070**
Ludgater v Love (1881) 44 L.T. 694; 45 J.P. 600   . . . . 8-096, 8-185

Ludsin Overseas Ltd v Eco3 Capital Ltd [2013] EWCA Civ 413 9-119
Lumley v Nicholson (1886) 34 W.R. 716; 2 T.L.R. 711 . . . . **7-032**
Lumsden & Co v London Trustee Savings Bank [1971] 1 Lloyd's Rep. 114 QBD (Comm) . . 9-130
Lund (JO) Ltd v Anglo Overseas Transport Co Ltd [1955] 1 Lloyd's Rep. 142 QBD 7-066
Lupton v White (1808) 15 Ves. Jun. 432 8-162
Lupton v White 33 E.R. 817; (1808) 15 Ves. Jun. 432 . . . . 6-040, 6-042
Lutscher v Comptoir d' Escompte de Paris (1876) 1 Q.B.D. 709; 34 L.T. 798; 3
   Asp.M.L.C. 209 7-078
Luxmoore May v Messenger May Baverstock [1990] 1 W.L.R. 1009; [1990] 1 All E.R.
   1067; [1990] 07 E.G. 61 CA 6-022, **6-024**
Luxor (Eastbourne) Ltd v Cooper [1941] A.C. 108; 110 L.J.K.B. 131; 164 L.T. 313; 57
   T.L.R. 213; [1941] 1 All E.R. 33; 85 S.J. 105; 46 Com.Cas. 120 . . . . . . 3-007, 3-008, 7-001, 7-014,
                  7-015, 7-016, 7-017, 7-018, 7-019, 7-035, 7-036, 7-041, **7-044**, 10-043, 10-045
Lyddon v Moss (1859) 4 De G. & J. 104; 33 L.T.(O.S.) 170; 5 Jur. (N.S.) 637; 7 W.R. 433 . . . 6-068
Lyde v Barnard (1836) 1 M. & W. 101; 1 Gale 388; Tyr. & Gr. 250; 5 L.J.Ex. 117; 150
   E.R. 363 8-197
Lydney and Wigpool Ore Co v Bird (1886) 33 Ch.D. 85; 55 L.J.Ch. 875; 55 L.T. 558; 34
   W.R. 749; 2 T.L.R. 722 6-035
Lyell v Kennedy (1899) 14 App.Cas. 437; 59 L.J.K.B. 268; 62 L.T. 77; 38 W.R. 353 . **2-026**, 2-067,
                                                             2-070, 2-083, 6-111, **6-112**
Lyon (JN) & Co Ltd v Fuchs (N) (1920) 2 Ll.Rep. 333 1-022
M v Hendron [2007] CSIH 27 8-178
M'Auliffe v Bicknell (1835) 2 Cr.M. & R. 263; 1 Gale 232; 5 Tyr. 1035; 4 L.J.Ex. 225;
   150 E.R. 114 8-079
M'Kenzie v British Linen Co (1881) 6 App.Cas. 82; 44 L.T. 431; 29 W.R. 477 . . . . . . 2-059, **2-061**,
                                                                       8-041, 8-128
Maanss v Henderson (1801) 1 East 335 . . . . 7-099, 8-110
Macbeath v Haldimand (1786) 7 T.R. 172 9-028
MacClure v Schemeil (1871) 20 W.R. 168 . . . . 8-103, **8-106**, 8-119, 8-121
Macfarlane v Giannacopulo (1858) 3 H. & N. 860; 28 L.J.Ex. 72; 32 L.T. (O.S.) 133 8-101
MacFisheries Ltd v Harrison (1924) 93 L.J.K.B. 811; 132 L.T. 22; 88 J.P. 154; 40 T.L.R.
   709; 69 S.J. 89 . . . . 8-024, **8-043**
Mackay v Commercial Bank of New Brunswick (1874) L.R. 5 P.C. 394; 43 L.J.P.C. 31; 30
   L.T. 180; 38 J.P. 296; 22 W.R. 473 . . . . 2-025, 8-098, 8-185, 8-189
Mackay v Dick (1881) 6 App.Cas. 251; 29 W.R. 541 7-041
Mackenzie v Johnston (1819) 4 Madd. 373; 56 E.R. 742 6-095
Mackersy v Ramsay, Bonars & Co (1843) 9 C. & F. 818 . . . . 5-004, 5-011
Maclean v Dunn (1828) 4 Bing. 722; 1 Moo. & P. 761; 6 L.T. (O.S.) C.P. 184 . **2-053**, 2-074, 2-082
Macleod v Jones (1883) 24 Ch.D. 289; 53 L.J.Ch. 145; 49 L.T. 321; 32 W.R. 43 . . . . **6-072**
Maclure Ex p. (1870) L.R. 5 Ch.App. 737 10-042
Maclure v Fortescue [1907] 2 K.B. 1; 76 L.J.K.B. 393; 96 L.T. 444; 23 T.L.R. 292; 51 S.J.
   245 . . . . 6-019, **8-045**, 9-034, 9-070, 9-071
MacMillan Inc v Bishopsgate Investment Trust (No.3) [1996] 1 W.L.R. 387; [1996] 1 All
   E.R. 585; [1996] B.C.C. 453; (1995) 139 S.J.L.B. 225 . . . . 3-011, 8-135
Macmillan Inc v Bishopsgate Investment Trust Plc (No.1) [1993] 1 W.L.R. 837; [1993] 4
   All E.R. 99; [1993] I.C.R. 385; [1993] I.R.L.R. 393 8-048
Macoun v Erskine, Oxenford & Co [1901] 2 K.B. 493; 70 L.J.K.B. 973; 85 L.T. 372 . . . . . **6-070**
MacPherson v European Strategic Bureau Ltd [2002] B.C.C. 39; [2000] 2 B.C.L.C. 683;
   (2000) 97(35) L.S.G. 36 CA **6-061**
Madden v Kempster (1807) 1 Camp. 12 7-079
Maddick v Marshall (1864) 17 C.B.(N.S.) 829; 5 New Rep. 250; 11 L.T. 611; 10 Jur.
   (N.S.) 1201; 13 W.R. 205 . . . . **8-045**
Madoff Securities International Ltd v Raven [2011] EWHC 3102 (Comm) 1-028
Madoff Securities International Ltd v Raven [2013] EWHC 3147 (Comm) 6-003
Maga v Birmingham Roman Catholic Archdiocese Trustees [2010] EWCA Civ 256;
   (2010) 107(13) L.S.G. 15 8-178
Magee v Atkinson (1837) 2 M. & W. 440; Murph. & H. 115; 6 L.J.Ex. 115 9-039
Magellan Spirit ApS v Vitol SA [2016] EWHC 454 (Comm) 2-067, 8-071, 8-072
Magnus v Queensland National Bank (1888) 37 Ch.D. 466 6-043
Maharaj v Johnson [2015] UKPC 28; [2015] P.N.L.R. 27 . . . . 3-015, 6-018
Mahesan S/O Thambiah v Malaysian Government Officers' Co-operative Housing Society
   [1979] A.C. 374; [1978] 2 W.L.R. 444; [1978] 2 All E.R. 405; (1978) 122 S.J. 31, P.C. 6-084,
                                                             6-087, **6-089**, 8-218, 8-223

Mahkutai, The [1996] A.C. 650; [1996] 3 W.L.R. 1; [1996] 3 All E.R. 502; [1996] 2
    Lloyd's Rep. 1; [1996] C.L.C. 799; (1996) 146 N.L.J. 677; (1996) 140 S.J.L.B. 107
    (HK) 9-122
Mahmud v Bank of Credit and Commerce International SA. *See* Malik v Bank of Credit
    and Commerce International SA... 7-001
Mahony v East Holyford Mining Co (1875) L.R. 7 H.L. 869; 33 L.T. 383 ..... 3-029, 8-034, 8-039
Mahony v Kekuli (1854) 14 C.B. 390; 23 L.J.C.P. 54; 22 L.T.(O.S.) 224; 18 Jur. 313; 2
    W.R. 155; 2 C.L.R. 343.. 9-038
Maile v Mann (1848) 2 Exch. 608; 6 Dow. & L. 42; 17 L.J.Ex. 336; 12 J.P. 647 9-003
Main v Giambrone & Law (a firm) [2017] EWCA Civ 1193 .... 6-003, 6-043
Mair v Rio Grande Rubber Estates 1913 S.C.(H.L.) 74 .... 8-098, 8-185
Majrowski v Guy's and St Thomas's NHS Trust [2006] UKHL 34; [2007] 1 A.C. 224;
    [2006] 3 W.L.R. 125; [2006] 4 All E.R. 395; [2006] I.C.R. 1199; [2006] I.R.L.R. 695;
    (2006) 91 B.M.L.R. 85; (2006) 156 N.L.J. 1173; (2006) 150 S.J.L.B. 986 .... 8-176, 8-178
Malcolm v Scott (1850) 5 Exch. 601 9-114
Malhi v Abbey Life Assurance Co [1996] L.R.L.R. 237; [1994] C.L.C. 615; [1995] 4 Re.
    L.R. 305 8-215
Malhotra v Dhawan [1997] EWCA Civ 1096 6-092
Malik v Bank of Credit and Commerce International SA (In Liquidation); sub nom.
    Mahmud v Bank of Credit and Commerce International SA (In Liquidation); BCCI SA,
    Re [1998] A.C. 20; [1997] 3 W.L.R. 95; [1997] 3 All E.R. 1; [1997] I.C.R. 606; [1997]
    I.R.L.R. 462; (1997) 94(25) L.S.G. 33; (1997) 147 N.L.J. 917 HL 7-001
Mallozzi v Carapelli SpA [1976] 1 Lloyd's Rep. 407 CA 7-009
Maloney v Hardy and Moorsehead (1970) 216 E.G. 1582 CA ... 5-002, 5-004, 5-009, 9-026, **9-109**
Man Nutzfahrzeuge AG v Ernst & Young [2007] EWCA Civ 910; [2007] B.C.C. 986;
    [2008] 2 B.C.L.C. 22... 2-013, 8-215
Man v Shiffner (1802) 2 East 523; 102 E.R. 469 7-099
Manby and Richards v Scott (1660) 1 Lev. 4; 1 Mod. Rep. 124; O. Bridg. 229; 1 Sid. 109 ... 3-043
Manchester Trust v Furness; sub nom. Manchester Trust Ltd v Turner, Withy & Co Ltd
    [1895] 2 Q.B. 539; 73 L.T. 110; 44 W.R. 178; 8 Asp.M.L.C. 57; 1 Com.Cas.39; 14 R.
    739; 64 L.J.Q.B. 766; 11 T.L.R. 530 .... **8-045**, 8-048, 8-110
Mangena v Moyatusi [1918] App.D. 650 6-111
Manifest Shipping Co Ltd v Uni-Polaris Insurance Co Ltd (The Star Sea) [2001] UKHL 1;
    [2003] 1 A.C. 469; [2001] 2 W.L.R. 170; [2001] 1 All E.R. 743; [2001] 1 All E.R.
    (Comm) 193; [2001] 1 Lloyd's Rep. 389; [2001] C.L.C. 608; [2001] Lloyd's Rep. I.R.
    247.. 8-223
Manley & Sons Ltd v Berkett [1912] 2 K.B. 329; 81 L.J.K.B. 1232 9-035
Mann v Forrester (1814) 4 Camp. 60 .... 7-082, **7-099**, 8-109
Mann v Shell Petroleum Ltd [1961] C.L.Y. 1440 7-012
Manners v Mew (1885) 29 Ch.D. 725; 54 L.J.Ch. 909; 53 L.T. 84; 1 T.L.R. 421 8-135
Mansell v Clements (1874) L.R. 9 C.P. 139 .... 7-030, **7-032**
Manson v Baillie (1855) 2 Macq. 80; 26 L.T.(O.S.) 24 7-004
Manton v Brighton Corp [1951] 2 K.B. 393; [1951] 1 T.L.R. 1105; 115 J.P. 377; [1951] 2
    All E.R. 101; 95 S.J. 369 10-024
Manzanilla Ltd v Corton Property & Investments Ltd (No.1) Unreported November 13,
    1996 CA 6-104
Mar-Train Heavy Haulage Ltd v Shipping.DK Chartering A/S (t/a Frank & Tobiesen A/S)
    [2014] EWHC 355 (Comm) 11-027
Marathon Asset Management LLP v Seddon [2017] EWHC 300 (Comm) 6-077
Marbrook Freight Ltd v K.M.I. (London) Ltd [1979] 2 Lloyd's Rep. 341 CA **6-024**
Marc Rich & Co AG v Societa Italiana Impianti pA (The Atlantic Emperor) (No.1) [1989]
    1 Lloyd's Rep. 548; [1991] I.L.Pr. 562................................. 12-016
Marcan Shipping (London) Ltd v Polish S.S. Co [1989] 2 Lloyd's Rep. 138 CA 7-044
Marchant v Morton, Down & Co [1901] 2 K.B. 829; 70 L.J.K.B. 820; 85 L.T. 169; 17
    T.L.R. 640... 2-042
Marcq v Christie Manson & Woods Ltd (t/a Christie's); Christie Manson & Woods Ltd (t/a
    Christies) v Marcq [2003] EWCA Civ 731; [2004] Q.B. 286; [2003] 3 W.L.R. 980;
    [2003] 3 All E.R. 561; (2003) 100(27) L.S.G. 38; (2003) 147 S.J.L.B. 662 CA 9-129, **9-131**
Marcus (Bernard) & Co v Ashraf [1988] 1 E.G.L.R. 7 .... 7-012, 7-021, 7-030
Mardorf Peach & Co v Attica Sea Carriers Corp of Liberia; The Laconia [1977] A.C. 850;
    [1977] 2 W.L.R. 286; [1977] 1 All E.R. 545; (1977) 121 S.J. 134; [1977] 1 Lloyd's Rep.
    315 HL 3-032

Marina Shipping Ltd v Laughton; The Antama [1982] Q.B. 1127; [1982] 2 W.L.R. 569; [1982] I.C.R. 215; [1982] 1 All E.R. 481; (1982) 126 S.J. 207; [1982] I.R.L.R. 20; [1982] Com.L.R. 36; [1982] 2 Lloyd's Rep. 112 CA 9-046
Marine Blast Ltd v Targe Towing Ltd; sub nom. Targe Towing Ltd v Marine Blast Ltd [2004] EWCA Civ 346; [2004] 1 Lloyd's Rep. 721; [2004] 1 C.L.C. 1082 CA 2-030
Maritime Stores Ltd v Marshall (H.P.) & Co Ltd [1963] 1 Lloyd's Rep. 602 .... 9-005, 9-020
Marjandi Ltd v Bon Accord Glass Ltd 2008 G.W.D. 5-80; 2007 WL 4947410 Sheriff Court (Grampian, Highland and Islands) 11-016
Markel International Insurance Co Ltd v Surety Guarantee Consultants Ltd [2009] EWCA Civ 790 .... 5-008, 5-012, **5-016**, 6-003, 9-135
Marks & Spencer Plc v Freshfields Bruckhaus Deringer [2004] EWCA Civ 741; [2005] P.N.L.R. 4; (2004) 148 S.J.L.B. 788 CA 6-052
Marks and Spencer Plc v BNP Paribas Securities Services Trust Co (Jersey) Ltd [2015] UKSC 72; [2016] A.C. 742.. 7-001
Markwick v Hardingham (1880) 15 Ch.D. 339; 43 L.T. 647; 29 W.R. 361 6-111
Marlow v Pitfield (1719) 1 P.Wms.558; 2 Eq.Cas.Abr. 516 8-203
Marsden v City & County Ass.Co (1865) L.R. 1 C.P. 232; Har. & Ruth. 53; 35 L.J.C.P. 60; 13 L.T. 465; 12 Jur. (N.S.) 76; 14 W.R. 106 .... 8-207, **10-033**
Marseilles Extension Railway Co Ex p. Credit Foncier and Mobilier of England, Re (1871–72) L.R. 7 Ch. App. 161 .... 2-020, 8-215
Marsfield Automotive Inc v Siddiqi [2017] EWHC 187 (Comm) 8-174, 9-102
Marsh v Conquest (1864) 17 C.B. 418; 4 New Rep. 282; 33 L.J.C.P. 319; 10 L.T. 717; 10 Jur. (N.S.) 989; 12 W.R. 1006; 144 E.R. 169 8-195
Marsh v Jelf (1862) 3 F. & F. 234 .... 3-032, **7-051**
Marsh v Joseph [1897] 1 Ch. 213; 66 L.J.Ch. 128; 75 L.T. 558; 45 W.R. 209; 13 T.L.R. 136; 41 S.J. 171 .... 2-056, 2-071, 2-072
Marsh v Keating (1834) 1 Bing. N.C. 198; 8 Bli. (N.S.) 651; 2 Cl. & Fin. 250; 1 Mont. & A. 582; 1 Scott 5 .... 8-161, 8-167
Marsh v Pedder (1815) 4 Camp. 257; Holt N.P. 72 8-121
Marshall (Thomas) (Exports) Ltd v Guinle [1979] Ch. 227; [1978] 3 W.L.R. 116; [1978] I.C.R. 905; [1978] 3 All E.R. 193; (1978) 122 S.J. 295; [1979] F.S.R. 208; [1978] I.R.L.R. 174.. 10-004, 10-045
Marshall v Glanvill [1917] 2 K.B. 87; 86 L.J.K.B. 767; 116 L.T. 560; 33 T.L.R. 301 . 7-042, 10-003
Marshall v National Provincial Bank (1892) 61 L.J.Ch. 465; 66 L.T. 525; 40 W.R. 328; 36 S.J. 294 .... **8-133**
Marshall v Parsons (1841) 9 Car. & P. 656; 173 E.R. 998 7-004
Marshall, Re Ex p. Sutton (1788) 2 Cox 84 .... **5-007**
Marston Excelsior Ltd v Arbuckle Smith & Co Ltd [1971] 2 Lloyd's Rep. 306; 115 S.J. 654 CA 9-024
Martin P, The [2003] EWHC 3470; [2004] 1 Lloyd's Rep. 389 2-074
Martin v Britannia Life Ltd [2000] Lloyd's Rep. P.N. 412 8-018
Martin v JRC Commercial Mortgages Plc [2012] EWCA Civ 63; [2012] P.N.L.R. 18 6-001
Martin v Perry and Daw [1931] 2 K.B. 310; 100 L.J.K.B. 582; 145 L.T. 455; 47 T.L.R. 377; 75 S.J. 259... 7-018
Martin v Tucker (1885) 1 T.L.R. 655 .... 7-018, 7-024
Martin v Watson [1996] A.C. 74; [1995] 3 W.L.R. 318; [1995] 3 All E.R. 559; (1995) 145 N.L.J. 1093; (1995) 139 S.J.L.B. 190 HL.................................... 8-192
Martin-Baker Aircraft Co Ltd v Canadian Flight Equipment Ltd; Martin-Baker Aircraft Co v Murison [1955] 2 Q.B. 556; [1955] 3 W.L.R. 212; [1955] 2 All E.R. 722; 99 S.J. 472; 72 R.P.C. 236 .... 1-035, 7-001, 10-042
Martin-Smith v Williams [1999] E.M.L.R. 571 CA 6-034, 7-039, 7-044
Martinez v Cooper (1826) 2 Russ. 198 8-135
Martinson v Clowes (1885) 52 L.T. 706 6-070
Marubeni Hong Kong & South China Ltd v Mongolia (Jurisdiction); sub nom. Marubeni Hong Kong and South China Ltd v Ministry of Finance of Mongolia [2002] 2 All E.R. (Comm) 873 QBD (Comm) 3-005
Marubeni Hong Kong and South China Ltd v Mongolia [2005] EWCA Civ 395; [2005] 1 W.L.R. 2497; [2005] 1 C.L.C. 540 CA.................... 8-042, 12-002, 12-016, 12-022
Mashonaland Exploration Co Ltd v New Mashonaland Exploration Co Ltd [1891] W.N. 165. 6-015
Mason and Taylor, Re (1878) 10 Ch.D. 729; 48 L.J.Ch. 193; 27 W.R. 311 7-094
Mason v Clarke [1955] A.C. 778 2-020
Mason v Clifton (1863) 3 F. & F. 899 .... 2-096, 5-004, 5-011, 5-015

Mason v Hamilton (1831) 5 Sim. 19 . . . . **7-104**
Mason v Morley (No.1) (1865) 34 Beav. 471; 34 L.J.Ch. 422; 12 L.T. 414; 11 Jur. (N.S.)
   459; 13 W.R. 669; 55 E.R. 717 7-094
Maspons y Hermano v Mildred, Goyeneche & Co. *See* Mildred, Goyeneche & Co v
   Maspons 1-022, **7-099**, 8-071, 8-073, 8-110, **8-112**, 8-156, 12-028, 12-029, 12-030
Massey v Banner (1820) 1 Jac. & W. 241 6-029
Massey v Davies (1794) 2 Ves. 317 . . . . 6-065, 6-068
Massey v Heynes (1888) 21 Q.B.D. 330; 57 L.J.Q.B. 468; 59 L.T. 470; 26 W.R. 834 9-075
Mather Ex p. (1797) 3 Ves. 373 . . . . **7-070**
Mathew v Brise (1851) 14 Beav. 341; 17 L.T.(O.S.) 249 6-041
Matthews v Gibbs (1860) 30 L.J.Q.B. 55; 3 L.T. 551; 7 Jur. (N.S.) 186; 9 W.R. 200; 1
   Mar.L.C. 14. 8-219
Matthews v Haydon (1786) 2 Esp. 509 5-011
Matveieff & Co v Crosfield (1903) 51 W.R. 365; 19 T.L.R. 182; 47 S.J. 258; 8
   Com.Cas.120. 3-026
Maund v Monmouthshire Canal Co (1842) 4 Man. & G. 452; Car. & M. 606; 2 Dowl.
   (N.S.) 113; 3 Ry. & Can.Cas.159; 2 Scott N.R. 457; 11 L.J.C.P. 317; 6 Jur. 932. 8-189
Mawcon Ltd, Re [1969] 1 W.L.R. 78; [1969] 1 All E.R. 188; (1968) 112 S.J. 1004 . . 2-074, 10-018
Mawson, Re, Ex p. Hardcastle (1881) 44 L.T. 523; 29 W.R. 615 8-167
Maxfield v Burton (1873) L.R. 17 Eq. 15; 43 L.J.Ch. 46; 29 L.T. 571; 22 W.R. 148 8-216
Maxform SpA v Mariani and Goodville [1981] 2 Lloyd's Rep. 54 CA 8-117, 9-050
Maxted v Paine (1871) L.R. 6 Ex. 132; (1929) 39 Yale L.J. 265 . . . . 8-117, 9-023
May & Butcher v R. (1929) reported [1934] 2 K.B. 17n; 103 L.J.K.B. 556n.; 151 L.T.
   246n. 7-009
Mayberry v Mansfield (1846) 9 Q.B. 754; 16 L.J.Q.B. 102; 8 L.T.(O.S.) 158; 11 Jur. 60 9-003
Maynard v West Midlands Regional Health Authority [1984] 1 W.L.R. 632; [1985] 1 All
   E.R. 635; 128 S.J. 317; (1983) 133 N.L.J. 641; (1984) 81 L.S.Gaz. 1926 HL. 6-019
MCA Records Inc v Charly Records Ltd (No.5) [2001] EWCA Civ 1441; [2002] B.C.C.
   650; [2003] 1 B.C.L.C. 93; [2002] E.C.D.R. 37; [2002] E.M.L.R. 1; [2002] F.S.R. 26 9-120
McAdam v Boxpak Ltd 2005 S.L.T. (Sh Ct) 47; 2005 G.W.D. 9-127, Sh Pr 11-022
McCall v Australian Meat Co Ltd (1870) 19 W.R. 188 10-021
McCallum v Hicks [1950] 2 K.B. 271; 66 T.L.R. (Pt. 1) 747; [1950] 1 All E.R. 864; 94
   S.J. 210 . . . . 7-018, 7-019
McCann (John) & Co v Pow [1974] 1 W.L.R. 1643; [1975] 1 All E.R. 129; 118 S.J. 717
   CA 5-002, 5-004, 7-050, 7-051
McCarthy v Colvin (1839) 9 A. & E. 609; 8 L.J.Q.B. 158; 1 Per. & Dav 429 . . . . 6-100, 9-107
McCollin v Gilpin (1881) 6 Q.B.D. 516; 44 L.T. 914; 45 J.P. 828; 29 W.R. 408 . . . . . . 9-037, **9-038**
McCombie v Davis (1805) 7 East 5; 3 Smith K.B. 3 . . . . 7-078, 7-093
McCowin Lumber and Export Co v Pacific Marine Insurance Co (1922) 38 T.L.R. 901; 12
   Ll.L.Rep. 496 3-026
McCullagh v Lane Fox and Partners Ltd 49 Con. L.R. 124; [1996] P.N.L.R. 205; [1996] 1
   E.G.L.R. 35; [1996] 18 E.G. 104; [1995] E.G.C.S.195; [1995] N.P.C. 203 CA . 8-182, 9-117, 9-125
McEntire v Potter & Co (1889) 22 Q.B.D. 438; 60 L.T. 600; 37 W.R. 607 . . . . **9-131**
McEvoy v Belfast Bank of Co Ltd [1935] A.C. 24; 103 L.J.C.P. 137; 151 L.T. 501; 40
   Com.Cas.1. 2-085
MCI WorldCom International Inc v Primus Telecommunications Inc; sub nom. Primus
   Telecommunications Inc v MCI Worldcom International Inc [2004] EWCA Civ 957;
   [2004] 2 All E.R. (Comm) 833; [2004] Info. T.L.R. 250 CA 8-185, 8-186, 9-117, 9-125
McInerny v Lloyd's Bank Ltd [1974] 1 Lloyd's Rep. 246 CA 8-186
McKay's Case (1875) 2 Ch.D. 1; 45 L.J.Ch. 148; 33 L.T. 517; 24 W.R. 49 . . . . 6-087, **6-089**
McKellar v Wallace (1853) 8 Moo. P.C. 378; 5 Moo.Ind.App. 372; 1 Eq.Rep. 309; (1854)
   22 L.T.(O.S.) 309 6-098
McLaren (JD) & Co v Nomikos [1961] 1 Lloyd's Rep. 318 9-046
McLarty v Middleton (1858) 6 W.R. 379; 9 W.R. 861; 4 L.T. 852; 1 Mar.L.C. 114 6-100
McLaughlin v Duffill [2008] EWCA Civ 1627; [2010] Ch. 1; [2009] 3 W.L.R. 1139;
   [2009] 34 E.G. 80 8-004
McLaughlin v Solloway. *See* Solloway v McLaughlin 6-003, 6-078, 7-066
McLean's Case (1885) 55 L.J.Ch. 36; 53 L.T. 250; 1 T.L.R. 660 .6-089
McMaster v Byrne [1952] 1 All E.R. 1362; [1952] W.N. 239; 96 S.J. 325 . . . . 6-051, 6-064, 6-066,
   6-070
McNaughton (James) Paper Group Ltd v Hicks Anderson & Co [1991] 2 Q.B. 113; [1991]
   2 W.L.R. 641; [1991] 1 All E.R. 134; [1991] B.C.L.C. 235; [1990] B.C.C. 891; [1991]
   E.C.C. 186; [1955–95] P.N.L.R. 574; (1990) 140 N.L.J. 1311 CA 9-117

McNealey v Pennine Insurance Co Ltd [1978] 2 Lloyd's Rep. 18; (1978) 122 S.J. 229;
  [1978] R.T.R. 285 CA.. 6-024
McNicholas Construction Co Ltd v Customs and Excise Commissioners [2000] S.T.C.
  553; [2000] B.T.C. 5225; [2000] B.V.C. 255; [2000] S.T.I. 889 8-214
MCP Pension Trustees Ltd v Aon Pension Trustees Ltd [2010] EWCA Civ 377; [2012]
  Ch. 1 8-206
McPherson v Watt (1877) 3 App.Cas. 254 .... 6-063, 6-064, **6-070**
McQuillan v McCormick [2010] EWHC 1112 (QB) 11-011, 11-031, 11-040, 11-051, 11-053
McWilliam v Norton Finance (UK) Ltd (t/a Norton Finance) [2015] EWCA Civ 186;
  [2015] 1 All E.R. (Comm) 1026; [2015] 2 B.C.L.C. 730; [2015] P.N.L.R. 22; [2015]
  C.T.L.C. 60 6-086
Meacock (John) & Co v Abrahams, Loescher (Third Party) [1956] 1 W.L.R. 1463; [1956]
  3 All E.R. 660; 100 S.J. 837 CA 7-009, **7-012**
Mead v SE Ry (1870) 18 W.R. 735 9-010
Meadow Schama & Co v Mitchell C & Co Ltd (1973) 228 E.G. 1511 .... 6-085, 6-087, 9-098
Mediterranean Salvage & Towage Ltd v Seamar Trading & Commerce Inc (The Reborn)
  Reborn, The [2009] EWCA Civ 531; [2010] 1 All E.R. (Comm) 1; [2009] 2 Lloyd's
  Rep. 639; [2009] 1 C.L.C. 909; (2009) 159 N.L.J. 898 6-001
Mediterranean Shipping Co SA v Cottonex Anstalt [2015] EWHC 283 (Comm); [2015] 1
  Lloyd's Rep. 359... 11-025
Medsted Associates Ltd v Canaccord Genuity Wealth (International) Ltd [2017] EWHC
  1815 (Comm)... 6-039, 6-086, 8-223
Meek v Wendt (1881) 21 Q.B.D. 176; 59 L.T. 558; 4 T.L.R. 582; 6 Asp.M.L.C. 331 .... **9-083**
Meekins v Henson [1964] 1 Q.B. 472; [1962] 3 W.L.R. 299; [1962] 1 All E.R. 899; 106
  S.J. 571 8-196
Meering v Graham-White Aviation Co Ltd (1919) 122 L.T. 44 CA 8-192
Megevand, Re, Ex p. Delhasse (1878) 7 Ch.D. 511; 47 L.J.Bcy. 65; 38 L.T. 106; 26 W.R.
  338... 2-031
Melhado v Porto Alegre, etc., Railway Co (1874) L.R. 9 C.P. 503 2-064
Mendelssohn v Normand Ltd [1970] 1 Q.B. 177; [1969] 3 W.L.R. 139; [1969] 2 All E.R.
  1215; (1969) 113 S.J. 263 CA................................... 2-109, 8-043, 8-061, 8-194
Mendoza & Co v Bell (1952) 159 E.G. 372; [1952] C.P.L. 334 7-037
Menelaou v Bank of Cyprus UK Ltd [2015] UKSC 66; [2016] A.C. 176; [2015] 3 W.L.R.
  1334; [2015] 2 Lloyd's Rep. 585; [2016] 1 B.C.L.C. 335 8-160
Merak, The. *See* Varverakis v Compagnia de Navegacion Artico SA; Merak, The 7-017
Mercantile Bank of India Ltd v Central Bank of India Ltd [1938] A.C. 287; [1938] 1 All
  E.R. 52; 107 L.J.P.C. 25; 158 L.T. 269; 54 T.L.R. 208; 81 S.J. 1020 ... 2-102, 8-039, 8-126, 8-130,
                                                                                      8-133
Mercantile Bank of India Ltd v Chartered Bank of India, Australia and China [1937] 1 All
  E.R. 231 .... **8-046**
Mercantile Credit Co v Garrod [1962] 3 All E.R. 1103 8-176
Mercantile Credit Co v Hamblin [1965] 2 Q.B. 242; [1964] 3 W.L.R. 798; [1964] 3 All
  E.R. 592; 108 S.J. 674 CA 2-102, 8-130, 8-133, 8-135
Mercantile International Group Plc v Chuan Soon Huat Industrial Group Plc [2002]
  EWCA Civ 288; [2002] 1 All E.R. (Comm) 788; [2002] C.L.C. 913; [2003] E.C.C. 28;
  [2002] Eu. L.R. 314 CA...................... 1-036, 11-013, 11-017, 11-026, 11-027
Mercer v Wright, Graham & Co (1917) 33 T.L.R. 343 9-038
Merchant International Co Ltd v Natsionalna Aktsionerna Kompaniia Naftogaz Ukrainy
  [2014] EWCA Civ 1603; [2015] 1 C.L.C. 1................................ 9-026
Merchants of Staple v Bank of England (1888) 21 Q.B.D. 160; 57 L.J.Q.B. 418; 52 J.P.
  580; 36 W.R. 880; 4 T.L.R. 46 8-130
Meretz Investments NV v ACP Ltd [2007] EWCA Civ 1303; [2008] Ch. 244; [2008] 2
  W.L.R. 904 9-120
Meridian Global Funds Management Asia Ltd v Securities Commission [1995] 2 A.C.
  500; [1995] 3 W.L.R. 413; [1995] 3 All E.R. 918; [1995] B.C.C. 942; [1995] 2 B.C.L.C.
  116; (1995) 92(28) L.S.G. 39; (1995) 139 S.J.L.B. 152 (NZ).............. 1-028, 8-209, 8-215
Merrett v Babb [2001] EWCA Civ 214; [2001] Q.B. 1174; [2001] 3 W.L.R. 1; [2001]
  B.L.R. 483; (2001) 3 T.C.L.R. 15; 80 Con. L.R. 43; [2001] Lloyd's Rep. P.N. 468;
  [2001] P.N.L.R. 29; [2001] 1 E.G.L.R. 145; [2001] 8 E.G.C.S.167; (2001) 98(13)
  L.S.G. 41; (2001) 145 S.J.L.B. 75 CA 9-117
Merrill Lynch Capital Services Inc v Municipality of Piraeus (No.2) [1997] 6 Bank. L.R.
  241; [1997] C.L.C. 1214 .... 12-002, 12-022, 12-025
Merrill Lynch Futures Inc v York House Trading (1984) 81 L.S.G. 2544 CA 6-024

Merry v Abney the Father, and Abney the Son, and Kendal 22 E.R. 682; (1663) 1 Ch. Cas.
   38 . . . . 8-208, 8-217
Merryweather v Moore [1892] 2 Ch. 518; 61 L.J.Ch. 505; 66 L.T. 719; 40 W.R. 540; 8
   T.L.R. 539; 36 S.J. 488 6-077
Merryweather v Nixan (1799) 8 T.R. 186 . . . . 7-068, 8-191
Mersey Docks and Harbour Board Ex p. [1899] 1 Q.B. 546; 68 L.J.Q.B. 540; 80 L.T. 143;
   47 W.R. 306; 15 T.L.R. 199 . . . . 7-103, 7-104
Mersey v Coggins & Griffiths (Liverpool) [1947] A.C.I.; 115 L.J.K.B. 465; 175 L.T. 270;
   62 T.L.R. 533; [1946] 2 All E.R. 345 HL 8-179
Metall und Rohstoff AG v Donaldson Lufkin & Jenrette Inc [1990] 1 Q.B. 391; [1989] 3
   W.L.R. 563; [1989] 3 All E.R. 14; (1989) 133 S.J. 1200 CA 9-135
Metcalfe v Shaw (1811) 3 Camp. 22 8-120
Metropolitan Asylums Board v Kingham & Sons (1890) 6 T.L.R. 217 . . . . 2-087, 2-092, **2-094**
Metropolitan Electric Supply Co Ltd v Ginder [1901] 2 Ch. 799; 70 L.J.Ch. 682; 84 L.T.
   818; 65 J.P. 519; 49 W.R. 508; 17 T.L.R. 435; 45 S.J. 467 7-046
Meyer v Charters (1918) 34 T.L.R. 589 8-216
Meyerstein v Eastern Agency Co Ltd (1885) 1 T.L.R. 595 5-011
Meynell v Angell (1863) 32 L.J.Q.B. 14; 8 Jur. 1211; 11 W.R. 122 7-103
MGB Printing & Design Ltd v Kall Kwik UK Ltd [2010] EWHC 624 (QB) 7-001
Michael Wilson & Partners Ltd v Sinclair [2012] EWHC 2560 (Comm); [2013] 1 All E.R.
   (Comm) 476 6-087
Michelin Tyre Co Ltd v McFarlane (Glasgow) Ltd (1917) 55 S.L.R. 35; 2 S.L.T. 205 . 1-036, 1-043
Micklefield v SAC Technology Ltd [1990] 1 W.L.R. 1002; [1991] 1 All E.R. 275; [1990]
   I.R.L.R. 218 . . . . 7-044, 10-040
Mid-Kent Fruit Factory, Re [1896] 1 Ch. 567; 65 L.J.Ch. 250; 74 L.T. 22; 44 W.R. 284; 40
   S.J. 211; 3 Mans. 59 7-057
Middle East Tankers & Freighters Bunker Services SA (Offshore) v Abu Dhabi Container
   Lines PJSC [2002] EWHC 957; [2002] 2 Lloyd's Rep. 643 QBD (Comm) 9-006, 9-034
Middleton v Welles; sub nom. Welles v Middleton (1785) 4 Bro.P.C. 245 6-069
Midgley Estates Ltd v Hand [1952] 2 Q.B. 432; [1952] 1 T.L.R. 1452; [1952] 1 All E.R.
   1394; 96 S.J. 375 . . . . 7-017, 7-021
Midland Bank Ltd v Reckitt [1933] A.C. 1; 102 L.J.K.B. 297; 148 L.T. 374; 48 T.L.R.
   271; 76 S.J. 165; 37 Com.Cas.202 . . . . 2-049, **3-015**, **3-029**, 8-053, **8-064**
Midland Bank Plc v Cox McQueen (A Firm) [1999] Lloyd's Rep. Bank. 78; [1999] 1
   F.L.R. 1002; [1999] Lloyd's Rep. P.N. 223; [1999] P.N.L.R. 593; [1999] Fam. Law 310;
   [1999] E.G. 12 (C.S.); (1999) 96(6) L.S.G. 36; (1999) 149 N.L.J. 164; [1999] N.P.C. 11
   CA 9-065
Midland Bank Trust Co Ltd v Hett, Stubbs, & Kemp [1979] Ch. 384; [1978] 3 W.L.R.
   167; [1978] 3 All E.R. 571; (1977) 121 S.J. 830 . . . . 6-018, 9-117
Midland Business Agency v Apted (1971) 218 E.G. 1727 7-037
Mildner (F) & Sons v Noble [1956] C.L.Y. 32 . . . . 8-018, **8-043**
Mildred, Goyaneche & Co v Maspons (1883) 8 App.Cas. 874; 53 L.J.Q.B. 33; 49 L.T.
   685; 32 W.R. 125; 5 Asp.M.L.C. 182 HL . 1-022, **7-099**, 8-071, 8-073, 8-110, **8-112**, 8-156, 12-028,
                                                                           12-029, 12-030
Miles Ex p. *See* Isaacs, Re, Ex p. Miles 7-101
Miles v Haslehurst & Co (1906) 12 Com.Cas. 83; 23 T.L.R. 142 . . . . 3-019, 6-010, 6-011
Miles v McIlwraith (1833) 8 App.Cas. 120; 52 L.J.P.C. 17; 48 L.T. 689; 31 W.R. 591 3-005,
                                                                      8-042, 8-077
Millar, Son & Co v Radford (1903) 19 T.L.R. 575 . . . . 7-028, 7-032
Miller v Beale (1879) 27 W.R. 403 . . . . 7-004, **7-012**
Miller v Douglas (1886) 56 L.J.Ch. 91; 55 L.T. 583; 35 W.R. 122 8-103
Miller v Race (1758) 1 Burr. 452; 2 Keny. 189 8-141
Miller, Gibb & Co v Smith & Tyrer Ltd [1917] 2 K.B. 141; 86 L.J.K.B. 1259; 116 L.T.
   753; 33 T.L.R. 295; 22 Com.Cas.320 . . . . 9-020, 9-038, **9-042**
Millwall, The [1905] P. 155; 74 L.J.P. 61, 82; 93 L.J. 426; 53 W.R. 471; 21 T.L.R. 346; 10
   Asp.M.L.C. 110 CA 7-062
Milner (JH) & Son v Bilton (Percy) [1966] 1 W.L.R. 1582; [1966] 2 All E.R. 894; 110 S.J.
   635 7-035
Milroy v Lord (1862) 4 De G.F. & J. 264; 45 E.R. 1185 . . . . 2-014, 10-010
Milsom v Bechstein (1898) 14 T.L.R. 159 7-037
Milvain v Perez (1861) 3 E. & E. 495; 30 L.J.Q.B. 90; 3 L.T. 736; 7 Jur. (N.S.) 336; 9
   W.R. 269; 1 Mar.L.C. 32 9-027

Ministry of Health v Simpson; Diplock's Estate, Re; Diplock v Wintle; Simpson v Lilburn
  [1951] A.C. 251; [1950] 2 All E.R. 1137; 66 T.L.R. (Pt. 2) 1015; 94 S.J. 777 HL 8-162, 8-167
Ministry of Housing and Local Government v Sharp [1970] 2 Q.B. 223; [1970] 2 W.L.R.
  802; [1970] 1 All E.R. 1009; 114 S.J. 109; 68 L.G.R. 187; 21 P. & C.R. 166 CA 8-186
Ministry of Trade of Iraq v Tsavliris Salvage (International) Ltd (The Altair) [2008]
  EWHC 612 (Comm); [2008] 2 All E.R. (Comm) 805; [2008] 2 Lloyd's Rep. 90; [2008]
  1 C.L.C. 592 4-009
Mir Steel UK Ltd v Morris [2012] EWCA Civ 1397; [2013] 2 All E.R. (Comm) 54; [2013]
  C.P. Rep. 7; [2013] 2 B.C.L.C. 76 9-121
Mirror Group Newspapers Plc v Maxwell (No.1) [1998] B.C.C. 324; [1998] 1 B.C.L.C.
  638 . . . . 7-004, 7-006, 7-066
Misa v Currie (1876) 1 App.Cas. 554   . . . . 7-077, 7-082, **7-089**
Miss Gray Ltd v Cathcart (Earl) (1922) 38 T.L.R. 562   3-043
Mitcalfe's Case (1879) 13 Ch.D. 169   6-089
Mitchell v Hayne (1824) 2 Sim & S. 63   . . . . 7-103, 7-104
Mitchell, Re (1884) L.J.Ch. 342; 52 L.T. 178; T.L.R. 153   5-011
Mitchell, The Margaret (1858) Sw. 382   10-024
Mitsui & Co Ltd v Marpro Industrial Ltd [1974] 1 Lloyd's Rep. 386   9-071
Mitsui OSK Lines Ltd v Salgaocar Mining Private Ltd [2015] EWHC 565 (Comm);
  [2015] 2 Lloyd's Rep. 518 3-007
Mitsui v Novorossiysk Shipping Co; Kilmun, The [1983] 1 Lloyd's Rep. 311   . . . . 8-217, 9-125
Mobile Sourcing Ltd v Revenue and Customs Commissioners [2016] UKUT 274 (TCC);
  [2016] B.V.C. 524 . . . . 8-209, 8-210, 8-214
Moffat v Bateman (1869) L.R. 3 P.C. 115; 6 Moo. P.C.C. (N.S.) 369; 22 L.T. 140; 34 J.P.
  275. 6-031
Moffat v Parsons (1814) 1 Marsh. 55; 5 Taunt. 307   . . . . **8-045**
Mohamud v Wm Morrison Supermarkets Plc [2016] UKSC 11; [2016] A.C. 677; [2016] 2
  W.L.R. 821; [2016] I.R.L.R. 362 8-178
Mole v Parkdean Holiday Parks Ltd [2017] EWHC B10 (Costs)   10-020
Molony v Kernan (1842) 2 Dr. & War. (Ir.) 31   . . . . 6-062, 6-072
Molton v Camroux (1849) 4 Exch. 17   2-009
Mona Oil Equipment Supply Co Ltd v Rhodesia Railways Ltd [1950] W.N. 10; [1949] 2
  All E.R. 1014; 83 Ll.L.Rep. 178 . . . . 7-001, 7-041
Monaghan v Taylor (1886) 2 T.L.R. 685   . . . . **8-195**
Moneypenny v Hartland (1824) 1 C. & P. 352   7-050
Monk v Largo Foods Ltd [2016] EWHC 1837 (Comm) 11-025, 11-032, 11-051
Monkland v Jack Barclay Ltd [1951] 2 K.B. 252; [1951] 1 T.L.R. 763; [1951] 1 All E.R.
  714; 95 S.J. 236 CA 6-013
Monkwearmouth Flow Mill Co Ltd v Lightfoot (1897) 13 T.L.R. 327; 41 S.J. 407   6-100
Montagu v Forwood [1893] 2 Q.B. 350; 69 L.T. 371; 42 W.R. 124; 9 T.L.R. 634; 37 S.J.
  700; 4 R. 579 . . . . 7-098, **7-099**, 8-111, **8-112**
Montagu's Settlement Trusts, Re; Duke of Manchester v National Westminster Bank
  [1987] Ch. 264; [1987] 2 W.L.R. 1192; (1987) 131 S.J. 411; (1987) 84 L.S.Gaz. 1057. 8-163,
  8-209, 9-136
Montague Stanley & Co v Solomon (J.C.) Ltd [1932] 2 K.B. 287   1-042
Montaignac v Shitta (1890) 15 App.Cas. 357   . . . . 4-007, **8-045**
Montesquieu v Sandys (1811) 18 Ves. 302   . . . . 6-063, 6-067
Montgomerie v United Kingdom Mutual Steamship Assn. [1891] 1 Q.B. 370; 60 L.J.Q.B.
  429; 64 L.T. 323; 39 W.R. 351; 7 T.L.R. 203; 7 Asp.M.L.C. 19 . 1-021, 8-069, 8-082, 8-099, 8-109,
  9-002, 9-005, 9-006, 9-012
Montreal and St Lawrence Light & Power Co v Robert [1906] A.C. 196 PC (Canada)   . 3-029, 8-039
Moody v Cox and Hatt [1917] 2 Ch. 71; 86 L.J.Ch. 424; 116 L.T. 740; 61 S.J. 398   . . . 2-013, 2-014,
  6-048, 6-050, 6-052, 6-064
Moody v Pall Mall Deposit & Forwarding Co Ltd (1917) 33 T.L.R. 306   8-147
Moody v Spencer (1822) 2 D. & R. 6; 1 L.J.(O.S.) K.B. 1   7-099
Moon v Towers (1860) 8 C.B.(N.S.) 611   2-056
Moons v De Barnales (1826) 1 Russ. 301; 38 E.R. 117   6-103
Moor Line Ltd v Louis Dreyfus & Co [1918] 1 K.B. 89; 87 L.J.K.B. 126; 118 L.T. 87; 14
  Asp.M.L.C. 185 7-004
Moorcock, The (1889) 14 P.D. 64; 58 L.J.P. 73; 60 L.T. 654; 37 W.R. 439; 5 T.L.R. 316; 6
  Asp.M.L.C. 373 CA 10-042

Moore Stephens (A Firm) v Stone & Rolls Ltd (In Liquidation) [2008] EWCA Civ 644;
    [2008] 3 W.L.R. 1146; [2008] Bus. L.R. 1579; [2008] 2 Lloyd's Rep. 319; [2008] 2
    B.C.L.C. 461; [2008] Lloyd's Rep. F.C. 426; [2008] P.N.L.R. 36; (2008) 105(25) L.S.G.
    26 . . . . 8-214, 8-215
Moore v Bresler Ltd [1944] 2 All E.R. 515 . . . . 1-029, 8-063
Moore v Bushell (1857) 27 L.J.Ex. 3 . . . . **9-114**
Moore v Flanagan [1920] 1 K.B. 919; 89 L.J.K.B. 417; 122 L.T. 739 . . . . 8-114, 8-117, 8-124
Moore v Hotelplan Ltd (t/a Inghams Travel) [2010] EWHC 276 (QB) 1-038
Moore v Mourgue (1776) 2 Coup. 479 . . . . 3-019, 6-020
Moore v Peachey [1891] 2 Q.B. 707; (1891) 7 T.L.R. 748 2-032
Moore v Piretta PTA Ltd [1999] 1 All E.R. 174; [1998] C.L.C. 992; [1998] E.C.C. 392;
    [1999] Eu. L.R. 32; (1998) 17 Tr. L.R. 161 QBD 11-003, 11-004, 11-030, 11-044, 11-051
Moore v Ullcoats Mining Co Ltd [1908] 1 Ch. 575; (1907) 97 L.T. 845; 77 L.J.Ch. 282;
    24 T.L.R. 54 2-043
Moore v Usher (1835) 7 Sim 383; 4 L.J.Ch. 205 7-103
Moore v Wilson (1787) 1 T.R. 659; 99 E.R. 1306 9-010
Moores v Hopper (1807) 2 B. & P.N.R. 411; 127 E.R. 688 9-010
Moorgate Mercantile Co Ltd v Twitchings [1977] A.C. 890; [1975] 3 W.L.R. 386; [1975]
    3 All E.R. 314; 119 S.J. 559; [1975] R.T.R. 528 . . 1-026, 2-103, 2-102, 2-107, 8-077, 8-126, 8-130,
    8-133, 8-149
Moran Yacht & Ship Inc v Pisarev [2016] EWCA Civ 317; [2016] 1 Lloyd's Rep. 625 7-009
Morel Bros & Co Ltd v Earl of Westmorland [1904] A.C. 11; 73 L.J.K.B. 93; 89 L.T. 702;
    52 W.R. 353; 20 T.L.R. 38 . . . . 2-074, 8-114, 8-117, **8-124**, 9-006
Morgan v Elford (1876) 4 Ch.D. 352; 25 W.R. 136 CA 8-223
Morgan v Manser [1948] 1 K.B. 184; [1947] 2 All E.R. 666 10-003
Morgan v Minnett (1877) 6 Ch.D. 638; 36 L.T. 948; 25 W.R. 744 6-069
Morgan v Stephens (1861) 3 Giff. 226; 4 L.T. 614; 7 Jur. (N.S.) 701; 66 E.R. 392 9-140
Moriarty v Various Customers of BA Peters Plc [2008] EWCA Civ 1604; [2009] B.P.I.R.
    248 8-162
Morison v Kemp (1912) 29 T.L.R. 70 3-015
Morison v Thompson (1874) L.R. 9 Q.B. 480; 43 L.J.Q.B. 215; 30 L.T. 869; 38 J.P. 695;
    22 W.R. 859 6-087
Morrell v Studd and Millington [1913] 2 Ch. 648; 83 L.J.Ch. 114; 109 L.T. 628; 58 S.J. 12 . . 2-092
Morrell v Workers Savings & Loan Bank [2007] UKPC 3; [2007] Bus. L.R. D57 PC
    (Jamaica) 3-009, 6-009
Morrell v Wotten (1852) 16 Beav. 197; 51 E.R. 753 9-114
Morris (BO) Ltd v Perrott and Bolton [1945] 1 All E.R. 567; 172 L.T. 234 8-117
Morris v Cleasby (1816) 4 M. & S. 566; 105 E.R. 943 1-039
Morris v Hunt & Co (1896) 12 T.L.R. 187 7-042
Morris v Kanssen; sub nom. Kanssen v Rialto (West End) Ltd [1946] A.C. 459; 1 All E.R.
    586; 115 L.J.Ch. 177; 174 L.T. 353; 62 T.L.R. 306 . . . . 8-037, 8-038, 8-039, 8-050
Morris v Martin (CW) & Sons Ltd [1966] 1 Q.B. 716; [1965] 3 W.L.R. 276; [1965] 2 All
    E.R. 725; 109 S.J. 451; [1965] 2 Lloyd's Rep. 63 CA 8-023, 8-063, 8-176, 8-194, 9-122
Morris v Salberg (1889) 22 Q.B.D. 614; 58 L.J.Q.B. 275; 61 L.T. 283; 53 J.P. 772; 37
    W.R. 469; 5 T.L.R. 376 . . . . 2-070, 8-196, 9-125
Morris v Wilson (1859) 5 Jur. (N.S.) 168; 33 L.T.(O.S.) 56 8-003
Morris, Re [1908] 1 K.B. 473; 77 L.J.K.B. 265; 98 L.T. 500; 52 S.J. 78 . . . . **7-094**
Morrison Kekewich & Co v Mendel (1888) 5 T.L.R. 153 8-006
Morten v Hilton, Gibbes & Smith (1908) reported in [1937] 2 K.B. 176n 6-020, **6-024**
Mortgage Express Ltd v Bowerman & Partners [1996] 2 All E.R. 836 . . . . 6-021, 6-024
Mortgage Express v Sawali [2010] EWHC 3054 (Ch); [2011] P.N.L.R. 11; [2011] 1
    E.G.L.R. 58; [2011] 7 E.G. 98; [2010] N.P.C. 114 10-010
Mortimer v Beckett [1920] 1 Ch. 571; 89 L.J.Ch. 245; 123 L.T. 27; 64 S.J. 341 7-037
Mortimer v M'Callan; sub nom. M'Callan v Mortimer (1841) 7 M. & W. 20; (1842) 9 M.
    & W. 636 8-120
Mostyn v West Mostyn Coal & Iron Co (1876) 1 C.P.D. 145; 45 L.J.Q.B. 401; 34 L.T.
    325; 40 J.P. 455; 24 W.R. 401; 2 Char.Pr.Cas. 43 9-040
Motion v Michaud (1892) 8 T.L.R. 253 . . . . 10-042, 10-043
Moto Vespa SA v MAT (Britannia Express) Ltd and Mateu & Maten SA and Vincente
    Belloch Galvez; Same v Mateu & Mateu SA and Vincente Belloch Galvez [1979] 1
    Lloyd's Rep. 175 8-068
Motor Oil Hellas (Corinth) Refineries SA v Shipping Corp of India (The Kanchenjunga)
    [1990] 1 Lloyd's Rep. 391 HL 2-050

Motor Union Insurance Co Ltd v Mannheimer Versicherungs Gesellschaft [1933] 1 K.B. 812; 102 L.J.K.B. 671; 149 L.T. 94; 48 T.L.R. 522; 76 S.J. 495; 37 Com.Cas. 407; 18 Asp.M.L.C. 345 2-031
Moukataff v B.O.A.C. [1967] 1 Lloyd's Rep. 396 . . . . 8-042, 8-190
Moundreas (George) & Co S.A. v Navimpex Centrala Navala [1985] 2 Lloyd's Rep. 515 . . . 7-044
Mountford v Scott (1818) 3 Madd. 34 8-211
Movitex Ltd v Bulfield [1988] B.C.L.C. 104 6-056
Moxham v Grant [1900] 1 Q.B. 88 2-020
Mozeley v Cowie (1877) 47 L.J.Ch. 271; 38 L.T. 908; 26 W.R. 854 6-098
MPT Group Ltd v Peel [2017] EWHC 1222 (Ch) 6-054
MSM Consulting Ltd v Tanzania [2009] EWHC 121 (QB); 123 Con. L.R. 154 . . . . . . 7-009, 7-028
Muduroglu v Reddish LLP [2015] EWHC 1044 (Ch) 8-189
Muir v Fleming (1822) D. & R.N.P. 29 . . . . **7-086**
Mullens v Miller (1882) 22 Ch.D. 194; 52 L.J.Ch. 380; 48 L.T. 103; 31 W.R. 559 . . . . **3-032**, 8-096
Multinational Gas & Petrochemical Co v Multinational Gas & Petrochemical Services Ltd [1983] Ch. 258; [1983] 3 W.L.R. 492; [1983] 2 All E.R. 563; (1983) 127 S.J. 562 CA 1-028
Mumtaz Properties Ltd, Re, Wetton v Ahmed [2011] EWCA Civ 610; [2012] 2 B.C.L.C. 109. 6-096
Munro v Wilmott [1949] 1 K.B. 295; [1949] L.J.R. 471; 64 T.L.R. 627; [1948] 2 All E.R. 983; 92 S.J. 662 . . . . 4-006, 4-010
Munro, Re; Ex p. Singer [1981] 1 W.L.R. 1358 . . . . **3-032**
Murad v Al-Saraj; Murad v Westwood Business Inc [2005] EWCA Civ 959; [2005] 1 W.T.L.R. 1573 CA 6-034, 6-039, 6-042, 6-080, **6-083**
Murdoch Lownie v Newman [1949] W.N. 423; 65 T.L.R. 717; [1949] 2 All E.R. 783; 93 S.J. 711 7-019
Murphy v Boese (1875) L.R. 10 Ex. 126; 44 L.J.Ex. 40; 32 L.T. 122; 23 W.R. 474 2-014
Murphy v Brentwood DC [1991] 1 A.C. 398; [1990] 3 W.L.R. 414; [1990] 2 All E.R. 908 HL. 9-116
Murphy v Howlett (Jonathan) (A Firm) [1960] E.G.D. 231 . . . . 6-041, 9-023
Murphy v O'Shea (1845) 8 I.Eq.R. 329; 2 Jo. & Lat. 422 6-070
Murray v Currie (1836) 7 C. & P. 584 7-030
Murray v East India Co (1821) 5 B. & A. 204 3-015
Murray v Mann (1848) 2 Exch. 538 17 L.J.Ex. 256; 12 Jur. 634 . . . . 6-100, **6-101**, 6-111
Murray Vernon Holdings Ltd v Hassall [2010] EWHC 7 (Ch) 6-043
Mussen v Van Diemen's Land Co [1938] Ch. 252; 107 L.J.Ch. 136; 158 L.T. 40; 54 T.L.R. 225; [1938] 1 All E.R. 210; 82 S.J. 35 6-013
Mustad (O) & Son v Dosen (1928) [1964] 1 W.L.R. 109n; [1963] 3 All E.R. 416; [1963] R.P.C. 41 6-077
Mustafa v Palos (K.G.) [1972] E.G.D. 797 CA 7-017, 7-021
Mutton v Peat [1900] 2 Ch. 79 8-142
Mutual Aid Permanent Benefit BS, Re, Ex p. James (1883) L.T. 530; 48 J.P. 54 5-004
Mutual Life & Citizens Assurance Co v Evatt [1971] A.C. 793; [1971] 2 W.L.R. 23; [1971] 1 All E.R. 150; [1970] 2 Lloyd's Rep. 441; 114 S.J. 932; [1969] 1 Lloyd's Rep. 535; (1968) 42 A.L.J.R. 316 HC (Aus) 8-186, 9-117
Mutzenbecher v La Aseguradura Espanola SA [1906] 1 K.B. 254; 75 L.J.K.B. 172; 94 L.T. 127; 54 W.R. 207; 22 T.L.R. 175 CA 10-042
Myers v Elman; sub nom. Myers v Rothfield [1940] A.C. 282; 109 L.J.K.B. 105; 162 L.T. 113; 56 T.L.R. 177; [1939] 4 All E.R. 484; 84 S.J. 184 8-194
Myers v Watson (1851) 1 Sim. (N.S.) 523 8-096
Mynn v Joliffe (1834) 1 Moo. & Rob. 326 . . . . **3-032**
NA v Nottinghamshire CC [2015] EWCA Civ 1139; [2016] 1 F.C.R. 419; [2016] Fam. Law 171 8-178
Nahum v Royal Holloway and Bedford New College [1999] E.M.L.R. 252; (1998) 95(46) L.S.G. 33; (1998) 142 S.J.L.B. 286 CA 7-030, **7-032**
Nakanishi Marine Co Ltd v Gora Shipping Ltd [2012] EWHC 3383 (Comm) 8-207
Nandrame v Ramsaran [2015] UKPC 20 . . . . 3-004, 3-032
Nant-y-glo and Blaina Iron Co v Grave (1878) 12 Ch.D. 738; 38 L.T. 345; 36 W.R. 504 . . . . 6-087, **6-089**
Napier and Ettrick (Lord) v Kershaw (R.F.) [1993] A.C. 713; [1993] 2 W.L.R. 42; [1993] 1 All E.R. 385; (1993) 137 S.J. (LB) 44; [1993] 1 Lloyd's Rep. 197 HL 6-041
Narandas-Girdhar v Bradstock [2016] EWCA Civ 88; [2016] B.P.I.R. 428 2-079
Nash v Dix (1898) 78 L.T. 445 . . . . 8-071, 8-080, **8-082**

Natal Land, etc., Co v Pauline, etc., Syndicate [1904] A.C. 120; 73 L.J.P.C. 22; 89 L.T.
  678; 11 Mans. 29. 2-064
National Bank of Lahore v Sohan Lal, A.I.R. 1965 S.C. 1663 8-200
National Bolivian Navigation Co v Wilson (1880) 5 App.Cas. 176; 43 L.T. 60 8-052
National Coal Board v Galley [1958] 1 W.L.R. 16; [1958] 1 All E.R. 91; 102 S.J. 31 CA 7-009
National Coffee Palace Co, Re, Ex p. Panmure (1883) 24 Ch.D. 367; 53 L.J.Ch. 57; 50
  L.T. 38; 32 W.R. 236. . . . . 9-079, **9-083**
National Crime Agency v Robb [2014] EWHC 4384 (Ch); [2015] Ch. 520; [2015] 3
  W.L.R. 23; [2015] Lloyd's Rep. F.C. 161. 8-162
National Employers Mutual General Insurance Assn. Ltd v Elphinstone [1929] W.N. 135 . . . 5-004,
                                                                                              5-011
National Employers Mutual General Insurance Association v Jones; sub nom. NEMG
  Insurance Association v Jones [1990] 1 A.C. 24; [1988] 2 W.L.R. 952; [1988] 2 All E.R.
  425; [1988] R.T.R. 289; (1989) 8 Tr. L.R. 43; (1988) 138 N.L.J. 118; (1988) 132 S.J.
  658 HL 8-152
National Grid Electricity Transmission Plc v McKenzie [2009] EWHC 1817 (Ch) 6-042
National Home Loans Corp Plc v Giffen Couch & Archer [1998] 1 W.L.R. 207 6-021
National Mercantile Bank v Rymill (1881) 44 L.T. 767 . . . . 9-129, **9-131**
National Oilwell (UK) Ltd v Davy Offshore Ltd [1993] 2 Lloyd's Rep. 582 . . 2-067, 2-093, 8-072,
                                                                                              9-011
National Provincial Bank v Jackson (1886) 33 Ch.D. 1; 55 L.T. 458; 34 W.R. 597 . . . . 8-135, 8-028
National Trust for Places of Historic Interest v Birden [2009] EWHC 2023 (Ch) 6-081
National Union of Mineworkers v Scargill [2012] EWHC 3750 (Ch) 2-071, 12-075
National Westminster Bank Plc v Morgan [1985] A.C. 686; [1985] 2 W.L.R. 588; [1985] 1
  All E.R. 821; (1985) 129 S.J. 205 HL 6-069
Nationwide Building Society v Balmer Radmore [1999] Lloyd's Rep. P.N. 241; [1999]
  Lloyd's Rep. P.N. 558 Ch D 6-043, 6-048
Nationwide Building Society v Dunlop Haywards Ltd [2007] EWHC 1374 (Comm) . 8-211, 8-214,
                                                                                              8-217
Nationwide Building Society v Goodwin Harte [1999] Lloyd's Rep. P.N. 338 6-056
Navarro v Moregrand Ltd [1951] 2 T.L.R. 674; [1951] W.N. 335; 95 S.J. 367 CA . . . 8-028, **8-064**,
                                                                                        8-176, 8-180, **8-196**
Naviera Mogor SA v Societe Metallurgique de Normandie; The Nogar Marin [1988] 1
  Lloyd's Rep. 412; [1988] 1 F.T.L.R. 349 CA. 7-060
Navulshaw v Brownrigg (1852) 2 De. G.M. & G. 441; 21 L.J.Ch. 908; 20 L.T. (O.S.) 25;
  16 Jur. 979. 6-095
Naylor v Mangles (1794) 1 Esp. 109 7-082
Nayyar v Denton Wilde Sapte [2009] EWHC 3218 (QB); [2010] P.N.L.R. 15 . 3-021, 6-023, 8-223,
                                                                                              8-224
NBH Ltd v Hoare [2006] EWHC 73 (Ch); [2006] 2 B.C.L.C. 649 6-065
Ndole Assets Ltd v Designer M&E Services UK Ltd [2017] EWHC 1148 (TCC) 2-024
Nea Tyhi, The [1982] 1 Lloyd's Rep. 606; [1982] Com.L.R. 9 QBD (Admlty) . 8-044, 8-067, 8-115
Neale v Gordon Lennox (Lady) [1902] A.C. 465; [1900–3] All E.R. Rep. 622; 71 L.J.K.B.
  939; 87 L.T. 341; 66 J.P. 757; 51 W.R. 140; 18 T.L.R. 791; 46 S.J. 319 HL 6-003
Near East Relief v King Chasseur & Co Ltd [1930] 2 K.B. 40; 99 L.J.K.B. 522; 35
  Com.Cas. 104 . . . . 7-093, 7-098
Neilson v James (1882) 9 Q.B.D. 546; 51 L.J.Q.B. 369; 46 L.T. 791 . . . . 3-038, 6-019
Nelmes v NRAM Plc [2016] EWCA Civ 491; [2016] C.T.L.C. 106 8-223
Nelson (EP) & Co v Rolfe [1950] 1 K.B. 139; [1949] 2 All E.R. 584; 93 S.J. 576 CA 7-019
Nelson (EP) v Lyons (1949) 154 E.G. 376 . . . . 7-019, 10-027
Nelson (James) & Sons Ltd v Nelson Line (Liverpool) Ltd [1906] 2 K.B. 217; 75 L.J.K.B.
  895; 95 L.T. 180; 22 T.L.R. 630; 54 W.R. 546; 10 Asp.M.L.C. 265; 11 Com.Cas. 228. 9-010
Nelson v Aldridge (1818) 2 Stark. 435 . . . . **3-032**
Nelson v Larholt [1948] 1 K.B. 339; [1948] L.J.R. 340; 64 T.L.R. 1; [1947] 2 All E.R. 751
  KBD. 8-064, 8-141
Nelson v Nelson [1997] 1 W.L.R. 233; [1997] 1 All E.R. 970; [1997] B.P.I.R. 702; [1997]
  P.N.L.R. 413; (1997) 94(2) L.S.G. 26; (1997) 147 N.L.J. 126; (1997) 141 S.J.L.B. 30
  CA. 9-066, 9-067, 9-076, 10-021
Nelson v Powell (1784) 3 Doug. 410 8-119
Nelson v Raphael [1979] R.T.R. 437 CA 8-182, 8-192
Nelthorpe v Holgate (1844) 1 Col.C.C. 203; 8 Jur. 551 8-079
Nesbitt Ex p. (1805) 2 Sch.& Lef. 279 7-089

Neste Oy v Lloyds Bank Plc; The Tiiskeri, The Nestegas and The Enskeri [1983] 2
  Lloyd's Rep. 658; [1983] Com. L.R. 145; (1983) 133 N.L.J. 597 QBD (Comm) 1-032, 5-012,
                                                                  6-041, **6-045**, 6-091, 9-141
Netz v Ede; sub nom. Netz v Home Secretary [1946] Ch. 224; [1946] 1 All E.R. 628; 174
  L.T. 363; 90 S.J. 187; 115 L.J.Ch. 197 9-124
Nevill v Fine Art Assurance Co; sub nom. Nevill v Fine Arts and General Insurance Co
  Ltd [1897] A.C. 68 8-196
Neville v C&A Modes Ltd 1945 S.C. 175; 1945 S.L.T. 189, IH (1 Div) **8-192**
New Brunswick Railway v Conybeare (1862) 9 H.L. Cas. 711; 11 E.R. 907 8-098
New Cedos Engineering Co Ltd, Re [1994] 1 B.C.L.C. 797 1-028
New Falmouth Resorts Ltd v International Hotels Jamaica Ltd [2013] UKPC 11 PC
  (Jamaica) 2-069, 8-038
New Zealand & Australian Land Co v Watson (1881) 7 Q.B.D. 374; 50 L.J.Q.B. 433; 44
  L.T. 675; 29 W.R. 694 . . . . 1-021, 5-008, 5-012, 5-013, **5-016**, 6-041, 7-099, 8-071, 8-112
New Zealand Netherlands Society "Oranje" v Kuys [1973] 1 W.L.R. 1126; [1973] 2 All
  E.R. 1222; [1974] R.P.C. 272; 117 S.J. 565 PC (NZ) 6-037, 6-039, 6-080
New Zealand Shipping Co Ltd v Satterthwaite (A.M.) & Co Ltd; sub nom. New Zealand
  Shipping Co v Satterthwaite (A.M.) & Co; The Eurymedon [1975] A.C. 154; [1974] 2
  W.L.R. 865; [1974] 1 All E.R. 1015; 118 S.J. 387; [1974] 1 Lloyd's Rep. 534, P.C 9-122
Newall v Tomlinson (1871) L.R. 6 C.P. 405; 25 L.T. 382 . . . . **9-109**
Newbold v Coal Authority [2013] EWCA Civ 584; [2014] 1 W.L.R. 1288 . . . . 2-018, 2-022
Newborne v Sensolid (Great Britain) Ltd [1954] 1 Q.B. 45; [1953] 2 W.L.R. 596; [1953] 1
  All E.R. 708; 97 S.J. 209 CA 1-029, 9-034, 9-037, 9-066, 9-085, **9-087**, 9-092, 9-095, 9-096
Newcastle International Airport Ltd v Eversheds LLP [2013] EWCA Civ 1514; [2014] 1
  W.L.R. 3073; [2014] 2 All E.R. 728; [2015] B.C.C. 794; [2014] P.N.L.R. 13 . . **3-029**, **6-024**, **8-046**,
                                                                                       8-049
Newcastle United Plc v Revenue and Customs Commissioners [2007] EWHC 612 (Ch);
  [2007] S.T.C. 1330; [2007] B.T.C. 5481; [2007] B.V.C. 449; [2007] S.T.I. 1050 . . . . . 2-013, 2-031,
                                                                                       2-033
Newen, Re; Carruthers v Newen [1903] 1 Ch. 812; 72 L.J.Ch. 356; 88 L.T. 264; 51 W.R.
  297; 19 T.L.R. 247; 47 S.J. 300 . . . . 3-032, **5-007**, 10-005
Newgate Stud Co v Penfold [2004] EWHC 2993; [2008] 1 B.C.L.C. 46 . . . . 6-047, 6-065
Newlands v National Employer's Accident Association Ltd (1885) 54 L.J.Q.B. 428; 53
  L.T. 242; 49 J.P. 628 . . . . **8-067**
Newman (R.S.) Ltd, Re; Raphael's Claim [1916] 2 Ch. 309; 85 L.J.Ch. 625; 115 L.T. 134;
  60 S.J. 585; H.B.R. 129 10-042
Newman v Payne (1793) 2 Ves. 199; 4 Bro.C.C. 350 6-098
Newsholme Bros v Road Transport & General Ins. Co Ltd [1929] 2 K.B. 356; 98 L.J.K.B.
  751; 141 L.T. 570; 45 T.L.R. 573; 73 S.J. 465; 34 Com.Cas. 330 . . . . 2-013, 2-014, **8-217**
Newton v Chambers (1844) 13 L.J.Q.B. 141; 2 L.T.(O.S.) 351; 8 Jur. 244 . . . . **9-003**
Newton v Erickson (1951) 157 E.G. 414 7-037
Newtons of Wembley Ltd v Williams [1965] 1 Q.B. 560; [1964] 3 W.L.R. 888; [1964] 3
  All E.R. 532; 108 S.J. 619 CA 8-153, 8-156
Nicholas Prestige Homes v Neal (2010) 107(48) L.S.G. 14 7-037
Nichols v Clent (1817) 3 Price 547 . . . . 7-078, 7-079
Nicholson Re; Ex p. Quinn (1883) 53 L.J.Ch. 302; 49 L.T. 811; 32 W.R. 296 . . . . **7-094**
Nicholson v Chapman (1793) 2 H.Bl. 254 4-010
Nicholson v Mansfield (J) & Co (1901) 17 T.L.R. 259 . . . . 6-071, 6-087
Nickolson v Knowles (1820) 5 Madd. 47 6-099
Nicrotherm Electrical Co, AG Cox, AE Drew and LEG Francis v GA Percy (JR) and
  Harvey & Co (London) [1957] R.P.C. 207 CA 6-077
Nigel Fryer Joinery Services Ltd v Ian Firth Hardware Ltd [2008] EWHC 767 (Ch);
  [2008] 2 Lloyd's Rep. 108 . . . . 11-018, 11-056
Nightingale v Parsons [1914] 2 K.B. 621; 83 L.J.K.B. 742; 110 L.T. 806 . . . . 7-029, 7-032
Nippon Yusen Kaisha v International Import and Export Co; The Elbe Maru [1978] 1
  Lloyd's Rep. 206 QBD (Comm) 9-122
Nissan v Attorney General. *See* Attorney General v Nissan 9-124
Nisshin Shipping Co Ltd v Cleaves & Co Ltd [2003] EWHC 2602; [2004] 1 All E.R.
  (Comm) 481; [2004] 1 Lloyd's Rep. 38; [2003] 2 C.L.C. 1097; (2003) 153 N.L.J. 1705
  QBD (Comm) 7-001
Nitedals Taendstikfabrik v Bruster [1906] 2 Ch. 671; 75 L.J.Ch. 798; 22 T.L.R. 724 . . . . **7-051**
Nobel's Explosives Co v Jones & Co (1882) 8 App.Cas. 5 . . . . **9-125**
Noble v National Discount Co (1860) 5 H. & N. 225; 29 L.J.Ex. 210 9-114

Nocton v Ashburton (Lord) [1914] A.C. 398; 83 L.J.Ch. 784; 111 L.T. 641; 30 T.L.R. 602 .. 6-043, **6-045**

Nocton v Lord Ashburton [1914] A.C. 932; [1914–15] All E.R. Rep. 45 HL 6-068

Noel v Poland [2001] 2 B.C.L.C. 645; [2002] Lloyd's Rep. I.R. 30 QBD (Comm) 9-117

Nordisk Insulinlaboratorium v Gorgate Products; Nordisk Insulinlaboratorium v CL Bencard Ltd [1953] Ch. 430; [1953] 2 W.L.R. 879; [1953] 1 All E.R. 986; 97 S.J. 298 CA 2-010, 6-067, **6-070**, 6-081, 10-003

Nordman v Rayner and Sturges (1916) 33 T.L.R. 87 10-003

Norey v Keep [1909] 1 Ch. 561; 78 L.J.Ch. 334; 100 L.T. 322; 25 T.L.R. 289 .... **2-026**

Norfolk (Duke of) v Worthy (1808) 1 Camp. 337 .... 8-068, **8-082**, 9-100, 9-103

Norfolk County Council v Secretary of State for the Environment [1973] 1 W.L.R. 1400; [1973] 3 All E.R. 673; 117 S.J. 650; 26 P. & C.R. 23; 72 L.G.R. 44 QBD 8-024, 8-042

Norfolk County Trading Standards Service v Bycroft (t/a Charles Bycroft & Co) [2012] EWHC 4417 (Admin); [2012] 45 E.G. 95 (C.S.) 9-117

Norreys v Hodgson (1897) 13 T.L.R. 421 6-089

North American Land and Timber Co v Watkins [1904] 2 Ch. 233 .... 6-041, **6-045**, 6-089

North and South Trust Co v Berkeley; Berkeley v North and South Trust Co; sub nom. North and South Trust Co v Berkeley [1971] 1 W.L.R. 470; [1971] 1 All E.R. 980; [1970] 2 Lloyd's Rep. 467; (1970) 115 S.J. 244 .. 2-013, **2-016**, 3-035, 6-048, 6-050, 6-057, 6-080, 6-093

North Eastern Timber Importers v Ch. Arendt & Sons and Impresa Cerrito [1952] 2 Lloyd's Rep. 513 9-106

North v Loomes [1919] 1 Ch. 378; [1918-19] All E.R. 936; 88 L.J.Ch. 217; 120 L.T. 533 ... 2-019

North Western Bank Ltd v Poynter, Son & Macdonalds [1895] A.C. 56; 64 L.J.P.C. 27; 72 L.T. 93; 11 R. 125 .... **7-094**

North Western Rubber Co Ltd and H¸ttenbach & Co, Re [1908] 2 K.B. 907; 78 L.J.K.B. 51; 99 L.T. 680 3-034

North-West Transportation Ltd v Beatty (1887) 12 App.Cas. 589 6-056

Northampton Regional Livestock Centre Co Ltd v Cowling [2015] EWCA Civ 651; [2016] 1 B.C.L.C. 431; [2015] 4 Costs L.O. 477; [2016] P.N.L.R. 5 ... 6-015, 6-039, 6-042, 6-048, 6-056, 8-178

Northcote's Will Trusts, Re; Northcote v Northcote [1949] W.N. 69; 1 All E.R. 442 7-006

Northern Counties Insurance Co v Whipp (1884) 26 Ch.D. 482; 53 L.J.Ch. 629; 51 L.T. 806; 32 W.R. 626 8-135

Northey v Trevillion (1902) 7 Com.Cas. 201; 18 T.L.R. 648 .... 10-002, 10-042

Northgate, The. See Ocean Pride Maritime Ltd Partnership v Qingdao Ocean Shipping Co (The Northgate) Northgate, The 3-032

Northside Developments Pty Ltd v Registrar-General (1990) 170 C.L.R. 146 3-029

Northumberland Avenue Hotel Co; Re; sub nom. Re Northumberland Avenue Hotel Co; Sully's Case (1886) 33 Ch.D. 16 2-064

Norton v Herron (1825) 1 C. & P. 648; Ry. & M. 229 .... **9-038**

Norwegian American Cruises A/S v Paul Munday Ltd; The Vistafjord [1988] 2 Lloyd's Rep. 343 CA 8-205, 8-206

Norwich and Peterborough Building Society v Steed (No.2) [1993] Ch. 116; [1992] 3 W.L.R. 669; [1993] 1 All E.R. 330; [1992] N.P.C. 33 CA 2-012

Norwich Union Life & Pensions Ltd v Strand Street Properties Ltd [2009] EWHC 1109 (Ch). 2-072, **3-023**, 5-001

Nosotti v Auerbach (1899) 15 T.L.R. 140 7-035

Nottinghamshire Healthcare NHS Trust v Prison Officers Association. See Prison Officers Association v Nottinghamshire Healthcare NHS Trust 2-091

Nouvelles Huileries Anversoises SA v Mann (H.C.) & Co (1924) 40 T.L.R. 804 ..... 1-042, 2-031

Novoship (UK) Ltd v Mikhaylyuk [2014] EWCA Civ 908; [2015] Q.B. 499; [2015] 2 W.L.R. 526; [2014] W.T.L.R. 1521; (2014) 158(28) S.J.L.B. 37 . 6-039, 6-042, 6-085, 8-225, 9-135

Novus Aviation Ltd v Onur Air Tasimacilik AS [2009] EWCA Civ 122; [2009] 1 Lloyd's Rep. 576; [2009] 1 C.L.C. 850 12-002

NRAM Plc v Steel [2016] CSIH 11; 2016 S.C. 474; 2016 S.L.T. 285; 2016 S.C.L.R. 736; [2016] P.N.L.R. 20; 2016 G.W.D. 6-136 .... 8-182, 9-117

Nutt v Easton [1900] 1 Ch. 29 .... **6-070**

NYK Bulkship (Atlantic) NV v Cargill International SA [2016] UKSC 20; [2016] 1 W.L.R. 1853 1-023

NZ Guardian Trust v Brooks [1995] 1 W.L.R. 96; [1995] B.C.C. 407; [1995] 2 B.C.L.C. 242; (1995) 92(1) L.S.G. 36; (1994) 138 S.J.L.B. 240 PC (NZ). 8-182, 8-191

O'Brien v Lewis (1863) 32 L.J.Ch. 569; 8 L.T. 179; 27 J.P. 244; 9 Jur. (N.S.) 528; 11 W.R.
   318. 6-069
O'Connor v B.D.B. Kirby & Co; sub nom. O'Connor v D.B.D. Kirby & Co v Kirby
   [1972] 1 Q.B. 90; [1971] 2 W.L.R. 1233; [1971] 2 All E.R. 1415; 115 S.J. 267; [1971]
   R.T.R. 440; [1971] 1 Lloyd's Rep. 454 CA. 6-024, 8-217
O'Donnell v Shanahan [2009] EWCA Civ 751; [2009] B.C.C. 822; [2009] 2 B.C.L.C. 666 . . 6-081
O'Hagan v Body Corp 189855 [2010] 3 N.Z.L.R. 445 8-188
O'Herlihy v Hedges (1803) 1 Sch.& Lef. 123 . . . . 8-069, 8-076, 8-099, 9-012
O'Keefe v London & Edinburgh Insurance Insurance Co Ltd [1927] N.I. 85 . . . . 5-009, 8-211
O'Kelly v Trusthouse Forte Plc [1984] Q.B. 90; [1983] 3 W.L.R. 605; [1983] I.C.R. 728;
   [1983] 3 All E.R. 456; (1983) 127 S.J. 632; [1983] I.R.L.R. 369 CA 1-034
O'Sullivan v Management Agency and Music Ltd [1985] Q.B. 428; [1984] 3 W.L.R. 448;
   [1985] 3 All E.R. 351; (1984) 128 S.J. 548 CA. 6-069, 6-080, 6-107
O/Y Wasa S.S.Co & N.V Stoomschip Hannah v Newspaper Pulp & Wood Export (1949)
   82 Ll.L.Rep. 936. 8-078
Oates v Hudson (1851) 6 Exch. 346; 20 L.J.Ex. 284 . . . . 9-105, 9-109
Oatway, Re [1903] 2 Ch. 356; 72 L.J.Ch. 575; 88 L.T. 622 . . . . 6-040, 8-167
OBG Ltd v Allan [2007] UKHL 21; [2008] 1 A.C. 1; [2007] 2 W.L.R. 920; [2007] Bus.
   L.R. 1600; [2007] 4 All E.R. 545; [2008] 1 All E.R. (Comm) 1; [2007] I.R.L.R. 608;
   [2007] E.M.L.R. 12; [2007] B.P.I.R. 746; (2007) 30(6) I.P.D. 30037; [2007] 19 E.G.
   165 (C.S.); (2007) 151 S.J.L.B. 674; [2007] N.P.C. 54. . . . . . 6-003, 6-005, 8-038, 9-120, 9-135
Occidental Worldwide Investment Corp v Skibs A/S Avanti; The Siboen and The Sibotre
   [1976] 1 Lloyd's Rep. 293 QBD (Comm Ct) 8-185
Ocean Iron Steamship Insurance Association v Leslie (1889) 22 Q.B.D. 722n; 57 L.T.
   722; 6 Asp.M.L.C. 226 . . . . **8-082**
Ocean Pride Maritime Ltd Partnership v Qingdao Ocean Shipping Co (The Northgate)
   Northgate, The [2007] EWHC 2796 (Comm); [2008] 2 All E.R. (Comm) 330; [2008] 1
   Lloyd's Rep. 511. 3-032
Odell v Cormack Brothers (1887) 19 Q.B.D. 223 3-018
Odessa Tramways Co v Mendel (1878) 8 Ch.D. 235; 47 L.J.Ch. 505; 38 L.T. 731; 26 W.R.
   887. 8-221
Odyssey Entertainment Ltd (In Liquidation) v Kamp [2012] EWHC 2316 (Ch) 6-034
Odyssey Re (London) Ltd v OIC Run Off Ltd [2001] L.R.L.R. 1; (2000) 144 S.J.L.B. 142
   CA. 1-029
Oelkers v Ellis [1914] 2 K.B. 139; 83 L.J.K.B. 658; 110 L.T. 332 6-071
OEM Plc v Schneider [2005] EWHC 1072 (Ch) 9-104
Office of Fair Trading v Foxtons Ltd [2009] EWCA Civ 288; [2010] 1 W.L.R. 663; [2010]
   Bus. L.R. 228; [2009] 3 All E.R. 697; [2010] 1 All E.R. (Comm) 497; [2009] 3
   C.M.L.R. 6; [2009] 14 E.G. 87 (C.S.); (2009) 159 N.L.J. 553 . . . . 6-001, 6-059
Official Assignee of Madras v Mercantile Bank of India Ltd [1935] A.C. 53 8-172
Official Manager of the Athenaeum Life Assurance Society v Pooley (1858) 28 L.J. (N.S.)
   Ch. 119; (1858) 3 De G. & J. 294; 44 E.R. 1281 3-011
Ogden v Hall (1879) 40 L.T. 751 9-038
Oglesby v Yglesias (1858) E.B. & E. 930; 27 L.J.Q.B. 356; 31 L.T.(O.S.) 234; 6 W.R. 690 . . 9-027,
   9-096
Ojelay v Neosale Ltd [1987] 2 E.G.L.R. 167 CA 9-025, 9-026, 9-109
Okura & Co Ltd v Forsbacka Jernverks A/B [1914] 1 K.B. 715; 83 L.J.K.B. 561; 110 L.T.
   464; 30 T.L.R. 242; 58 S.J. 232 CA 1-020
Oldendorff GmbH & Co KG v Sea Powerful Ii Special Maritime Enterprises (The Zagora)
   [2016] EWHC 3212 (Comm); [2017] 1 Lloyd's Rep. 194. 2-033
Oliver v Bank of England [1902] 1 Ch. 610 . . . . 9-076, 9-081
Oliver v Court (1820) 8 Price 127; Dan. 301 . . . . **6-070**
Oliver v Woodroffe (1839) 4 M. & W. 650; 7 Dowl. 166; 1 Horn. & H. 474; 3 J.P. 85; 3
   Jur. 59; 150 E.R. 158. 2-008
Olympia & York Canary Wharf Ltd (No.2), Re; Bear Stearns International v Adamson
   [1993] B.C.C. 159. 6-013
Olympic Reinsurance Co, Re; Pole's Case [1920] 2 Ch. 341; 89 L.J.Ch. 544; 123 L.T.
   786; 36 T.L.R. 691 10-014
Omnium Electric Palaces Ltd v Baines [1914] 1 Ch. 332; 83 L.J.Ch. 372; 109 L.T. 964; 30
   T.L.R. 213; 58 S.J. 218; 21 Mans. 94 6-035
OMV Petrom SA v Glencore International AG [2016] EWCA Civ 778 . . . . 1-021, 8-214
One Mail Money Ltd v RIA Financial Services [2015] EWCA Civ 1084 6-015

Onward, The (1873) L.R. 4 A. & E. 38; 42 L.J.Adm. 61; 28 L.T. 204; 21 W.R. 601; 1
    Asp.M.L.C. 540 4-004
Oppenheimer v Attenborough & Son [1908] 1 K.B. 221   . . . . . . 8-063, 8-145, 8-153, 8-155, **8-158**
Oppenheimer v Frazer & Wyatt [1907] 2 K.B. 50; 76 L.J.K.B. 806; 97 L.T. 3; 23 T.L.R.
    410; 51 S.J. 373; 12 Com.Cas. 147. 8-154
Orakpo v Manson Investments Ltd [1977] 1 W.L.R. 347; [1977] 1 All E.R. 666; 121 S.J.
    256 CA 8-203
Oricon Waren-Handels GmbH v Intergraan NV [1967] 2 Lloyd's Rep. 82   3-035
Orient Overseas Management and Finance Ltd v File Shipping Co Ltd; The Energy
    Progress [1993] 1 Lloyd's Rep. 355 QBD (Comm) 7-044
Oriental Bank Corp, Re; Ex p. Guillemin (1884) 28 Ch.D. 634   10-027
Orme v Wright (1839) 3 Jur. 19   6-070
Oshkosh B'Ghosh Inc v Dan Marbel Inc Ltd [1989] B.C.L.C. 507; 4 B.C.C. 795; 1989
    P.C.C. 320; [1989] 1 C.M.L.R. 94 CA 9-086
Osman v Moss (J Ralph) Ltd [1970] 1 Lloyd's Rep. 313 CA   6-024
Otkritie International Investment Management Ltd v Urumov [2014] EWHC 191 (Comm)   . . 6-085,
                                                                    6-086, 8-222, 9-135
Ottoman Bank v Jebara. See Jebara v Ottoman Bank 2-010, 4-005, 4-010, 10-003
Overbrooke Estates Ltd v Glencombe Properties Ltd [1974] 1 W.L.R. 1335; [1974] 3 All
    E.R. 511; 118 S.J. 775 Ch D 3-032, **8-061**, 8-185, 8-217
Overend, Gurney & Co v Gibb (1872) L.R. 5 H.L. 480; 42 L.J.Ch. 67   . . . . **6-007**
Overton v Hewett (1887) 3 T.L.R. 246   9-087
Overweg, Re; Haas v Durant [1900] 1 Ch. 209; 69 L.J.Ch. 255; 81 L.T. 776; 16 T.L.R. 70   . . **10-022**
Ovington v Bell (1812) 3 Camp. 237   6-098
Owen (Christie) & Davies Ltd v Rapacioli [1974] Q.B. 781; [1974] 2 W.L.R. 723; [1974]
    2 All E.R. 311; 118 S.J. 167 CA 7-019, 7-021
Owen & Co v Cronk [1895] 1 Q.B. 265; 64 L.J.Q.B. 288; 11 T.L.R. 76; 2 Mans. 115; 14
    R. 229. . . . . 9-105, 9-106
Owen v Gooch (1797) 2 Esp. 567   9-092
Owen v Tate [1976] Q.B. 402; [1975] 3 W.L.R. 369; [1975] 2 All E.R. 129; (1974) 119
    S.J. 575 CA 7-060
Owens v Kirby (1861) 30 Beav. 31   6-097
Owners of Cargo on Board the Morviken v Owners of the Hollandia; The Hollandia and
    the Morviken [1983] 1 A.C. 565; [1982] 3 W.L.R. 1111; [1982] 3 All E.R. 1141; [1983]
    1 Lloyd's Rep. 1; [1983] Com. L.R. 44; 126 S.J. 819 HL 11-006
Owners of the Borvigilant v Owners of the Romina G; sub nom. Borkan General Trading
    Ltd v Monsoon Shipping Ltd [2003] EWCA Civ 935; [2003] 2 All E.R. (Comm) 736;
    [2003] 2 Lloyd's Rep. 520; [2004] 1 C.L.C. 41 CA 2-077, 2-090, 2-091, 2-092, 2-093, **2-094**
Oxford Corp v Crow [1893] 3 Ch. 535; 69 L.T. 228; 42 W.R. 200; 8 R. 279   . . . . 2-074, 2-087
Oxted Motor Co Re [1921] 3 K.B. 32   2-069
P&P Property Ltd v Owen White & Catlin LLP [2016] EWHC 2276 (Ch); [2016] Bus.
    L.R. 1337; [2017] P.N.L.R. 3; [2017] 1 P. & C.R. DG6. . . . . 9-068, 9-076, 9-117
Pa Mar, The. See Tsavliris Salvage (International) Ltd v Guangdong Shantou Overseas
    Chinese Materials Marketing Co 4-008
Pacific & General Insurance Co Ltd v Hazell; Pacific & General Insurance Co Ltd v Home
    & Overseas Insurance Co Ltd [1997] L.R.L.R. 65; [1997] B.C.C. 400; [1997] 6 Re.
    L.R. 157 QBD (Comm Ct) 10-010, 10-018
Pacific Coast Coal Mines Ltd v Arbuthnot [1917] A.C. 607 (PC)   2-038
Pacific Motor Auctions Pty Ltd v Motor Credits (Hire Finance) Ltd [1965] A.C. 867;
    [1965] 2 W.L.R. 881; [1965] 2 All E.R. 105; 109 S.J. 210 PC (Aus) 8-147, 8-156
Pacol Ltd v Trade Lines Ltd; The Henrik Sif [1982] 1 Lloyd's Rep. 456; [1982] Com. L.R.
    92; 126 S.J. 312 QBD (Comm). 9-030
Padget v Priest (1787) 2 T.R. 97   . . . . 9-109, 9-125
Padwick v Hurst (1854) 18 Beav. 575; 2 Eq.Rep. 1071; 23 L.J.Ch. 657; 23 L.T.(O.S.) 240;
    18 Jur. 763; 2 W.R. 501; 52 E.R. 225 7-001
Padwick v Stanley (1852) 9 Hare 627; 22 L.J.Ch. 184; 19 L.T.(O.S.) 293; 16 Jur. 586; 68
    E.R. 664 7-001
Page One Records Ltd v Britton [1968] 1 W.L.R. 157; [1967] 3 All E.R. 822; 111 S.J. 944,
    Ch. 7-037, 7-046
Paget v Paget (1882) 11 L.R.Ir. 26   2-008
Pagnan S.p.A. v Feed Products Ltd [1987] 2 Lloyd's Rep. 601 CA   2-078
Paice v Walker (1870) L.R. 5 Ex. 173; 39 L.J.Ex. 109; 22 L.T. 547; 18 W.R. 789   . . . . . 9-037, 9-038

Painter v Abel (1863) 2 H. & C. 113; 2 New Rep. 83; 33 L.J.Ex. 60; 8 L.T. 287; 9 Jur.
    (N.S.) 549; 11 W.R. 651 . . . . **8-138**
Palgrave, Brown & Son Ltd v S.S. Turid; sub nom. The Turid [1922] 1 A.C. 397; 91 L.J.P.
    81; 66 S.J. 349; 27 Com.Cas. 216; 127 L.T. 42; 38 T.L.R. 423; 15 Asp.M.L.C. 538; 10
    Ll.L.Rep. 375 3-035
Pallant v Morgan [1953] Ch. 43; [1952] 2 T.L.R. 813; [1952] 2 All E.R. 951 6-083
Palmer v Hutchinson (1881) 6 App.Cas. 619; 50 L.J.P.C. 62; 45 L.T. 180 9-028
Panama & South Pacific etc v India Rubber, Gutta Percha & Telegraph Works Co (1875)
    L.R. 10 Ch.App. 515; 45 L.J.Ch. 121; 32 L.T. 517; 23 W.R. 583 . . . . . . 8-218, 8-221, 8-223, **8-226**
Pangood Ltd v Barclay Brown & Co Ltd [1999] 1 All E.R. (Comm.) 460; [1999] Lloyd's
    Rep. I.R. 405; [1999] Lloyd's Rep. P.N. 237; [1999] P.N.L.R. 678 CA 5-011
Panorama Developments (Guildford) Ltd v Fidelis Furnishing Fabrics Ltd [1971] 2 Q.B.
    711; [1971] 3 W.L.R. 440; [1971] 3 All E.R. 16; 115 S.J. 483 CA **3-029**, 8-039, **8-046**, 8-067
Pantland Hick v Raymond & Reid [1893] A.C. 22 6-013
Pape v Westacott [1894] 1 Q.B. 272; 63 L.J.Q.B. 222; 70 L.T. 18; 42 W.R. 130; 10 T.L.R.
    51; 38 S.J. 39; 9 R. 35 . . . . 3-025, 6-005
Papillon v Brunton (1860) 5 H. & N. 29 L.J.Ex. 265; 2 L.T. 326 . . . . **3-029**
Paquin Ltd v Beauclerk [1906] A.C. 148; 75 L.J.K.B. 395; 94 L.T. 350; 54 W.R. 521; 22
    T.L.R. 395; 50 S.J. 358 9-002
Paragon Finance Plc v Thakerar & Co; Paragon Finance Plc v Thimbleby & Co [1999] 1
    All E.R. 400; (1998) 95(35) L.S.G. 36; (1998) 142 S.J.L.B. 243 CA . . . 2-037, 6-040, 6-041, 6-043,
                                                                        6-091, 6-096
Pariente v Lubbock (1856) 8 De G.M. & G. 5 . . . . 3-019, 6-010
Park v Hammond (1816) 6 Taunt. 495; 2 Marsh 189; 4 Camp. 344 . . . . 6-019, **6-024**
Park's of Hamilton (Holdings) Ltd v Campbell [2014] CSIH 36; 2014 S.C. 726; 2015
    S.C.L.R. 17; 2014 G.W.D. 18-338 . . . . 1-030, 6-035, 6-039
Parkdale, The [1897] P. 53; 66 L.J.P. 10; 75 L.T. 597; 45 W.R. 368; 13 T.L.R. 82; 8
    Asp.M.L.C. 211 . . . . 6-085, **6-089**
Parker (Harry) Ltd v Mason [1940] 2 K.B. 590; 109 L.J.K.B. 985; 164 L.T. 164; 57 T.L.R.
    35; [1940] 4 All E.R. 199 6-100
Parker & Cooper Ltd v Reading [1926] Ch. 975 1-028
Parker v Ibbetson (1858) 4 C.B.(N.S.) 346; 27 L.J.C.P. 236; 31 L.T.(O.S.) 101; 22 J.P.
    659; 4 Jur. (N.S.) 536; 6 W.R. 519 7-004
Parker v McKenna (1874) L.R. 10 Ch.App. 96; 44 L.J.Ch. 425; 31 L.T. 739; 23 W.R. 271 . . 6-062,
                                                                                6-080
Parker v Rolls (1854) 14 C.B. 691 . . . . **6-024**
Parker v Winslow (1857) 7 E. & B. 942; 27 L.J.Q.B. 49 . . . . 9-006, **9-038**
Parker, Re (1882) 21 Ch.D. 408 CA **7-070**
Parkes v Prescott (1869) L.R. 4 Ex. 169; 38 L.J.Ex. 105; 20 L.T. 537; 17 W.R. 773 . . . . **8-195**
Parkinson v Hanbury (1867) L.R. 2 H.L. 1; 36 L.J.Ch. 292; 16 L.T. 243; 15 W.R. 642 6-098
Parks v Esso Petroleum Co Ltd; Parkes v Esso Petroleum Co Ltd [2000] E.C.C. 45; [2000]
    Eu. L.R. 25; (1999) 18 Tr. L.R. 232 CA 11-018, 11-019
Parouth, The [1982] 2 Lloyd's Rep 351 12-016
Parry v Roberts (1835) 3 A. & E. 118; 5 Nev. & M.K.B. 669; 4 L.J.K.B. 189 6-100
Parsons v Thompson (1790) 1 Hy.Bl. 322 7-056
Parti v Al Sabah [2007] EWHC 1869 (Ch) 3-011
Partington v Hawthorne (1888) 52 I.P. 807 8-118
Passingham v King (1898) 14 T.L.R. 392 7-04
Patel v Mirza [2014] EWCA Civ 1047; [2015] Ch. 271; [2015] 2 W.L.R. 405; [2015] 1 All
    E.R. 326; [2015] 2 All E.R. (Comm) 1; [2015] 1 B.C.L.C. 256; [2014] Lloyd's Rep.
    F.C. 561; [2014] W.T.L.R. 1567; [2015] L.L.R. 133 . . . . 2-025, 6-100, 7-054
Patent Floor Cloth Co Ltd, Re; Dean & Gilbert's Claim (1872) 41 L.J.Ch. 476; 26 L.T.
    467. 10-042
Paterson v Gandasequi (1812) 15 East 62 . . . . 8-073, 8-120, 9-020
Paterson Zochonis & Co Ltd v Elder Dempster & Co Ltd; Paterson Zochnois & Co Ltd v
    Elder Dampster & Co Ltd; Elder Dempster & Co Ltd v Paterson Zochonis & Co Ltd;
    Griffiths Lewis Steam Navigation Co Ltd v Paterson Zochonis & Co Ltd [1924] A.C.
    522; (1924) 18 Ll. L. Rep. 319 HL. 9-122
Paton v Rosesilver Group Corp [2017] EWCA Civ 158 . . . . 6-039, 6-047
Pauling's Settlement Trusts, Re; Younghusband v Coutts & Co [1964] Ch. 303; [1963] 2
    W.L.R. 742; [1963] 3 All E.R. 1; 107 S.J. 492 CA. 6-039
Pavy's Patent Felted Fabric Co, Re (1876) 1 Ch.D. 631; 45 L.J.Ch. 318; 24 W.R. 507 7-086
Pawle v Gunn (1838) 4 Bing. N.C. 445; 1 Arn. 200; 6 Scott 286; 7 L.J.C.P. 206 . . . . . . 7-058, 7-059

Payne David & Co Ltd, Re; Young v David Payne & Co Ltd [1904] 2 Ch. 608; [1903–7]
    All E.R. Rep. Ext. 1051; 73 L.J.Ch. 849; 91 L.T. 777; 20 T.L.R. 590; 48 S.J. 572; 11
    Mans. 437 . . . . 2-020, 8-215, 8-217
Payne v Leconfield (Lord) (1882) 51 L.J.Q.B. 642; 30 W.R. 814 3-032
PCW Syndicates v PCW Reinsurers [1996] 1 W.L.R. 1136; [1996] 1 All E.R. 774; [1996]
    1 Lloyd's Rep. 241 CA 8-212, 8-214
Peachdart Ltd, Re [1984] Ch. 131; [1983] 3 W.L.R. 878; [1983] 3 All E.R. 204; (1983)
    127 S.J. 839; (1984) 81 L.S.Gaz. 204 1-035
Peacock v Freeman (1888) 4 T.L.R. 541 . . . . 7-014, 7-024
Peacock v Peacock (1809) 2 Camp. 45; 16 Ves. 49 7-012
Pearse v Boulter (1860) 2 F. & F. 133 . . . . **3-029**
Pearse v Green (1819) 1 J. & W. 135 . . . . 6-090, 6-092, 6-108
Pearson (S) & Son Ltd v Dublin Corp [1907] A.C. 351; 77 L.J.P.C. 1; 97 L.T. 645 . . . 6-056, 8-185
Pearson and I'Anson, Re [1899] 2 Q.B. 618; 68 L.J.Q.B. 878; 81 L.T. 289; 63 J.P. 677; 48
    W.R. 154; 15 T.L.R. 452 . . . . **3-029**
Pearson v Benson (1860) 28 Beav. 598 6-072
Pearson v Cardon (1831) 2 Russ. & M. 606 7-104
Pearson v Lehman Brothers Finance SA [2011] EWCA Civ 1544; [2012] 2 B.C.L.C. 151 . . . 6-041
Pearson v Nell (1860) 12 L.T. 607; 13 W.R. 967; 2 Mar.L.C. 213 8-120
Pearson v Rose & Young Ltd (Little, Third Party; Marshall, Fourth Party) [1951] 1 K.B.
    275; 66 T.L.R. (Pt. 2) 886; [1950] 2 All E.R. 1027; 94 S.J. 778 CA 8-146, 8-147, 8-148, 8-149,
                                                                                                                                        8-153
Pearson v Scott (1878) 9 Ch.D. 198; 47 L.J.Ch. 705; 38 L.T. 747; 26 W.R. 796 . . . . . 3-025, **3-026**,
                                                                                                                            3-037, 5-012, 5-013, 8-108
Pearson's Case, Re; Caerphilly Colliery Co (1877) 5 Ch.D. 336; 46 L.J.Ch. 339; 25 W.R.
    618 . . . . 6-087, 6-089
Peatfield v Barlow (1869) L.R. 8 Eq. 61; 38 L.J.Ch. 310; 20 L.T. 217; 17 W.R. 516 7-099
PEC Ltd v Asia Golden Rice Co Ltd [2014] EWHC 1583 (Comm) 2-105, 8-042, 8-044, 8-049,
                                                                                                                        8-215, 12-016, 12-017
Peekay Intermark Ltd v Australia & New Zealand Banking Group Ltd [2006] EWCA Civ
    386; [2006] 2 Lloyd's Rep. 511; [2006] 1 C.L.C. 582 8-050
Peel Developments (South) Ltd v Siemens plc [1992] 2 E.G.L.R. 83 3-029
Peers v Sneyd (1853) 17 Beav. 151 3-029
Pelham v Hilder (1841) 1 Y. & C.Ch.Cas. 3; 62 E.R. 765 3-025
Pelly v Wathen (1851) 1 De G.M. & G. 16 7-089
Penkivil v Connell (1850) 5 Exch. 381; 1 L.M. & P. 398; 19 L.J.Ex. 305; 15 L.T.(O.S.)
    207 . . . . **9-056**
Penn v Bristol and West Building Society; sub nom. Brill & Co v Penn [1997] 1 W.L.R.
    1356; [1997] 3 All E.R. 470; [1997] 3 F.C.R. 789; [1997] P.N.L.R. 607; (1997) 74 P. &
    C.R. 210; [1997] E.G.C.S.54; (1997) 94(18) L.S.G. 32; (1997) 141 S.J.L.B. 105; [1997]
    N.P.C. 58 CA 9-065
Pennell v Alexander (1854) 3 E. & B. 283; 23 L.J.Q.B. 171; 22 L.T.(O.S.) 274; 18 Jur.
    627; 118 E.R. 1146 8-120
Pennell v Stephens (1849) 7 C.B. 987; 18 L.J.C.P. 291; 13 L.T.(O.S.) 257; 13 Jur. 766 8-217
Pennington v Reliance Motor Works Ltd [1923] 1 K.B. 127; [1922] All E.R. 466; 92
    L.J.K.B. 202; 128 L.T. 384; 38 T.L.R. 670; 66 S.J. 667 1-033
Pennwell Publishing (UK) Ltd v Ornstien [2007] EWHC 1570 (QB); [2008] 2 B.C.L.C.
    246; [2007] I.R.L.R. 700 6-054
Pennyfeathers Ltd v Pennyfeathers Property Co Ltd [2013] EWHC 3530 (Ch) 6-081
Peppy, The. See Stewart Chartering Ltd v Owners of the Ship Peppy 6-074, 7-051
Percival v Wright [1902] 2 Ch. 421; 71 L.J.Ch. 846; 51 W.R. 31; 18 T.L.R. 697; 46 S.J.
    616; 9 Mans. 443 6-035
Performing Rights Society Ltd v Ciryl Theatrical Syndicate Ltd [1924] 1 K.B. 1 . . . . . 8-195, 9-120
Perishables Transport Co Ltd v Spyropoulos (N.) (London) Ltd [1964] 2 Lloyd's Rep. 379 . . 7-062,
                                                                                                                                9-016, 9-042
Perry v Barnett (1885) 15 Q.B.D. 388; 54 L.J.Q.B. 466; 53 L.T. 585; 1 T.L.R. 580 3-037
Perry v Holl (1860) 2 De G.F. & J. 38; 29 L.J.Ch. 677; 2 L.T. 585; 6 Jur. (N.S.) 661; 8
    W.R. 570 3-013
Perry-Herrick v Attwood (1857) 2 De G. & J. 21; 27 L.J.Ch. 121; 30 L.T.(O.S.) 267; 4 Jur.
    (N.S.) 101; 6 W.R. 204 . . . . 8-134, 8-135
Personal Touch Financial Services Ltd v Simplysure Ltd [2016] EWCA Civ 461; [2016]
    Bus.L.R. 1049 7-042

Personnel Hygiene Services Ltd v Rentokil Initial UK Ltd (t/a Initial Medical Services) [2014] EWCA Civ 29 6-077
Peter Pan Manufacturing Corp Ltd v Corsets Silhouette Ltd [1964] 1 W.L.R. 96; [1963] 3 All E.R. 402; 108 S.J. 97; [1963] R.P.C. 45 . . . . 6-077, **6-078**
Peterson Farms Inc v C&M Farming Ltd; sub nom. Petersen Farms Inc v C&M Farming Ltd [2004] EWHC 121; [2004] 1 Lloyd's Rep. 603; [2004] N.P.C. 13 QBD (Comm). . 1-030, 8-071
Peto v Blades (1814) 5 Taunt. 657 9-023
Petrofina (UK) Ltd v Magnaload Ltd [1984] Q.B. 127; [1983] 3 W.L.R. 805; [1983] 3 All E.R. 35; (1983) 127 S.J. 729; [1983] 2 Lloyd's Rep. 91 . . . . 2-067, 9-011
Petrotrade Inc v Smith [2000] 1 Lloyd's Rep. 486; [2000] C.L.C. 916 QBD (Comm Ct) 6-087, 8-223, 8-225, 9-135
Pett v Greyhound Racing Association Ltd (No.2) [1970] 1 Q.B. 46; [1969] 2 W.L.R. 1228; [1969] 2 All E.R. 221; 113 S.J. 166 2-024
Pettigrew v George Wimpey UK Ltd [2007] EWHC 2559 (QB) 7-029
Pettitt v Pettitt [1970] A.C. 777; [1969] 2 W.L.R. 966; [1969] 2 All E.R. 385; (1969) 20 P. & C.R. 991; (1969) 113 S.J. 344 HL 9-065
Pettman v Keble (1850) 9 C.B. 701; 19 L.J.C.P. 325; 15 Jur. 38 . . . . **7-062**
Peyman v Lanjani [1985] Ch. 457; [1985] 2 W.L.R. 154; [1984] 3 All E.R. 703; (1984) 128 S.J. 853; (1984) 48 P. & C.R. 398 CA 6-068, 8-121
Pharmed Medicare Private Ltd v Univar Ltd [2002] EWCA Civ 1569; [2003] 1 All E.R. (Comm) 321; (2002) 146 S.J.L.B. 254 CA 8-014, 8-044, 8-050
Phelps, James & Co v Hill [1891] 1 Q.B. 605; 60 L.J.Q.B. 382; 64 L.T. 610; 7 T.L.R. 319; 7 Asp.M.L.C. 42 4-005
Phillipps v Briard (1856) 25 L.J.Ex. 233 7-004
Phillips v Butler [1945] Ch. 358; [1945] 2 All E.R. 258; 114 L.J.Ch. 327; 173 L.T. 224; 61 T.L.R. 477; 89 S.J. 403 10-012
Phillips v Duke of Bucks (1683) 1 Vern. 226 . . . . 8-079, 8-080
Phillips v Homfray; Fothergill v Phillips (1871) L.R. 6 Ch.App. 770 2-079
Phillips v Jones (1888) 4 T.L.R. 401 10-015
Phillips, (WA) Anderson & Co v Euxine Shipping Co [1955] 2 Lloyd's Rep. 512 . . . . **6-089**
Phipps v Boardman. *See* Boardman v Phipps 6-047, 6-074, 6-076, 6-077, 6-080, 6-081, **6-083**
Phoenix General Insurance Co Greece SA v Administratia Asigurarilor de Stat; Same v Halvanon Insurance; Same v Administration Asiguraliror de Stat [1988] Q.B. 216; [1987] 2 W.L.R. 512; [1987] 2 All E.R. 152; (1987) 131 S.J. 257; [1987] FLR 48; [1986] 2 Lloyd's Rep. 552 CA 2-061, 7-053
Phoenix Properties Ltd v Wimpole Street Nominees Ltd [1992] B.C.L.C. 737 2-041
Phonogram Ltd v Lane [1982] Q.B. 938; [1981] 3 W.L.R. 736; [1981] 3 All E.R. 182; (1981) 125 S.J. 527; [1982] C.M.L.R. 615; [1981] Com.L.R. 228 CA . . 1-029, 9-085, 9-086, **9-087**
Phonographic Performance Ltd v CGK Trading Ltd [2016] EWHC 2642 (Ch) 9-120
Phosphate of Lime Co v Green (1871–72) L.R. 7 C.P. 43 1-028
Phosphate Sewage Co v Hartmont (1877) 5 Ch.D. 394; 46 L.J.Ch. 661; 37 L.T. 9 8-223
Photo Production Ltd v Securicor Transport Ltd [1980] A.C. 827; [1980] 2 W.L.R. 283; [1980] 1 All E.R. 556; (1980) 124 S.J. 147; [1980] 1 Lloyd's Rep. HL. 2-050
Picea Holdings v London Rent Assessment Panel; R. v London Rent Assessment Panel Ex p. Picea Holdings [1971] 2 Q.B. 216; [1971] 2 W.L.R. 1374; [1971] 2 All E.R. 805; (1971) 22 P. & C.R. 681; 115 S.J. 265 QBD 2-043
Pickard v Sears (1837) 6 A. & E. 469; 2 N. & P.K.B. 488; W.N. & D. 678 . . . . 8-010, 8-024, 8-029, 8-130
Pickering v Busk (1812) 15 East 38 . . . . 3-004, 8-010, 8-028, 8-127, **8-129**, 8-130
Pike v Ongley (1887) 18 Q.B.D. 708; 56 L.J.Q.B. 373; 35 W.R. 534; 3 T.L.R. 549 . . . 9-016, **9-042**, 9-090
Pike v Stephens (1848) 12 Q.B. 465; 17 L.J.Q.B. 282; 12 L.T. (O.S.) 145; 12 Jur. 746 8-217
Pillott v Wilkinson (1864) 3 H. & C. 345 9-131
Pilot v Craze (1888) 52 J.P. 311; 4 T.L.R. 453 8-043
Pindaros, The [1983] 2 Lloyd's Rep. 635 7-060
Pioneer Container, The [1994] 2 A.C. 324; [1994] 3 W.L.R. 1; [1994] 2 All E.R. 250; [1994] 1 Lloyd's Rep. 593; (1994) 138 S.J. (LB) 85 9-122
Pipe (PJ) and Valve Co Ltd v Audco India Ltd [2005] EWHC 1904 QBD; [2006] Eu L.R. 383 . . . . 11-018, 11-027
Piraeus, The [1974] 2 Lloyd's Rep. 266 9-062
Pisani v Attorney General for Gibraltar (1874) L.R. 5 P.C. 516; 30 L.T. 516; 30 L.T. 729; 22 W.R. 900. 6-064
Pitt Ex p. (1923) 40 T.L.R. 5 CA 8-121

Planche v Colburn (1831) 8 Bing. 14; 1 Moo. & S.51; 1 L.J.C.P. 7 7-024
Plant Engineers (Sales) Ltd v Davies (1969) 113 S.J. 484 9-047
Platt v Depree (1893) 9 T.L.R. 194 7-014
Playboy Club London Ltd v Banca Nazionale del Lavoro SpA [2016] EWCA Civ 457;
    [2016] 1 W.L.R. 3169; [2017] 1 All E.R. (Comm) 309; [2016] 2 B.C.L.C. 442. . . . . . 8-079, 8-180
Plevin v Paragon Personal Finance Ltd [2014] UKSC 61; [2014] 1 W.L.R. 4222; [2015] 1
    All E.R. 625; [2015] 1 All E.R. (Comm) 1007; [2014] Bus. L.R. 1257; [2015] E.C.C. 2;
    [2015] Lloyd's Rep. I.R. 247 . . . . 1-004, 1-012, 1-023, 2-033
PLG Research Ltd v Ardon International Ltd [1995] F.S.R. 116; [1995] R.P.C. 287 CA 9-120
Plumb v Cobden Flour Mills Co Ltd [1914] A.C. 62; 83 L.J.K.B. 197; 109 L.T. 759; 30
    T.L.R. 174; 58 S.J. 184; 7 B.W.C.C. 1 8-178
Plumbly v BeatthatQuote.com Ltd [2009] EWHC 321 (QB) 6-015
PM Law Ltd & Motorplus Ltd [2016] EWHC 193 (QB); [2016] 1 Costs L.R. 143 9-010
PNC Telecom Plc v Thomas [2007] EWHC 2157 (Ch); [2008] 2 B.C.L.C. 95 . . . . 6-043, **6-061**
Poland v Parr (John) & Sons Ltd [1927] 1 K.B. 236 8-178
Pole v Leask (1863) 33 L.J.Ch. 155; 8 L.T. 645; 9 Jur. (N.S.) 829 HL . . 1-012, 1-045, 2-031, 3-007,
    3-016, 3-021, 3-042, 8-014, 8-029, 10-030, 10-031
Polhill v Walter (1832) 3 B. & Ad. 114; 1 L.J.K.B. 92 . . . 8-089, 8-092, **8-093**, 9-053, 9-061, 9-117
Polish S.S. Co v Williams (AJ) Fuels (Overseas Sales) Ltd, The Suwalki [1989] 1 Lloyd's
    Rep. 511 QBD (Comm) 3-007, 3-040, 8-024
Pollard v Bank of England (1871) L.R. 6 Q.B. 623; 40 L.J.Q.B. 233; 25 L.T. 415; 19 W.R.
    1168. 9-106
Pollock v Stables (1848) 12 Q.B. 765; 5 Ry. & Can.Cas. 352; 17 L.J.Q.B. 352; 12 Jur.
    1043. . . . . **3-040**
Pollway Ltd v Abdullah [1974] 1 W.L.R. 493; [1974] 2 All E.R. 381; 118 S.J. 277 CA 9-023,
    9-035
Polly Peck International Plc v Nadir (No.2) [1992] 4 All E.R. 769; [1992] 2 Lloyd's Rep.
    238; [1993] B.C.L.C. 187; (1992) 142 N.L.J. 671, 1992 CA. 8-162
Pontin v Wood [1962] 1 Q.B. 737; [1962] 2 W.L.R. 258; [1962] 1 All E.R. 294; 105 S.J.
    1105 CA. 2-059, 2-091
Pool v Pool (1889) 58 L.J.P. 67; 61 L.T. 401 . . . . **10-022**
Poole v Clarke & Co [1945] 2 All E.R. 445 7-018
Pooley's Trustee v Whetham (1886) 2 T.L.R. 808; 33 Ch.D. 76 6-072
Pople v Evans [1969] 2 Ch. 255; [1968] 3 W.L.R. 97; [1968] 2 All E.R. 743; 112 S.J. 441 . . . 1-032,
    8-069
Port Jackson Stevedoring Pty v Salmond & Spraggon (Australia) Pty; The New York Star;
    Salmond & Spraggon (Australia) Pty v Joint Cargo Services Pty [1981] 1 W.L.R. 138;
    [1980] 3 All E.R. 257; [1980] 2 Lloyd's Rep. 317; 124 S.J. 756 PC (Aus) 7-036, 9-122
Port Swettenham Authority v TW Wu & Co [1979] A.C. 580 6-031
Portalis v Tetley (1867) L.R. 5 Eq. 140; 37 L.J.Ch. 139; 17 L.T. 344; 16 W.R. 503; 3
    Mar.L.C. 34. 8-147
Portman Building Society v Hamlyn Taylor Neck [1998] 4 All E.R. 202; [1998] P.N.L.R.
    664; (1999) 77 P. & C.R. 66; [1998] 2 E.G.L.R. 113; [1998] 31 E.G. 102 CA . 8-174, 9-103, 9-106,
    9-107
Portuguese Consolidated Copper Mines Ltd, Re; Ex p. Badman (1890) 45 Ch.D. 16; 63
    L.T. 423; 39 W.R. 25; 2 Meg. 249 . . 1-028, 2-038, 2-050, 2-059, 2-061, 2-068, 2-087, 2-089, **2-094**
Posner v Scott-Lewis [1987] Ch. 25 7-046
Potel v IRC [1971] 2 All E.R. 504; 46 T.C. 658; [1970] T.R. 325 10-028
Potter (PAR) v Customs and Excise Commissioners [1985] S.T.C. 45; (1984) 81 L.S.Gaz.
    3342 CA 1-036
Potter v Equitable Bank (1921) 8 Ll.L.Rep. 291 6-012
Potter v Fowler (1837) 6 L.J.Ch. 273 6-100
Potters (A Firm) v Loppert [1973] Ch. 399; [1973] 2 W.L.R. 469; (1972) 116 S.J. 862;
    [1973] 1 All E.R. 658; (1972) 25 P. & C.R. 82 Ch D. 6-041, 6-104, 9-026
Poulter v Dogget (1964) 115 L.J. 76 . . . . 7-028, 7-030
Povey v Taylor (1966) 116 N.L.J. 1656 8-043
Pow v Davies (1861) 1 B. & S.220; 30 L.J.Q.B. 257; 4 L.T. 399; 25 J.P. 662; 7 Jur. (N.S.)
    1010; 9 W.R. 611; 121 E.R. 697 . . . . 9-080, 9-081
Powell & Thomas v Jones (Evan) & Co [1905] 1 K.B. 11; 74 L.J.K.B. 115; 92 L.T. 430;
    53 W.R. 277; 21 T.L.R. 55; 10 Com.Cas. 36. . . . . 5-008, 5-012, **5-016**, 6-064, 6-087
Powell v Braun; sub nom. Powell v Gilmore [1954] 1 W.L.R. 401; [1954] 1 All E.R. 484;
    98 S.J. 144; CA 7-004, 7-012

Powell v Brodhurst [1901] 2 Ch. 160; 70 L.J.Ch. 587; 84 L.T. 620; 49 W.R. 532; 17 T.L.R.
   501; 45 S.J. 502...2-046
Powell v Hoyland (1851) 6 Exch. 67; 20 L.J.Ex. 82; 16 L.T.(O.S.) 369 9-126
Powell v Lee (1908) 99 L.T. 284 10-028
Powell v Lloyd's Bowmaker Ltd 1996 S.L.T. (Sh Ct) 117; [1996] C.C.L.R. 50, Sh Ct
   (Lothian)...2-034
Powell v London and Provincial Bank [1893] 2 Ch. 555; 62 L.J.Ch. 795; 69 L.T. 421; 41
   W.R. 545; 9 T.L.R. 446; 37 S.J. 476; 2 R. 482...2-041
Powell v Smith (1872) L.R. 14 Eq. 85; 41 L.J.Ch. 734; 26 L.T. 754; 20 W.R. 602 ....2-071, 2-072
Powles v Page (1846) 3 C.B. 16; 15 L.J.C.P. 217; 7 L.T. (O.S.) 257; 10 Jur. 526 .....8-214, **8-217**
Prager v Blatspiel, Stamp & Heacock Ltd [1924] 1 K.B. 566; 93 L.J.K.B. 410; 130 L.T.
   672; 40 T.L.R. 287; 68 S.J. 460...4-005, 4-010
Prebble (PG) & Co v West (1969) 211 E.G. 831 ....6-013, 6-024
Preedy v Dunne [2015] EWHC 2713 (Ch); [2015] W.T.L.R. 1795; [2016] 1 P. & C.R.
   DG7...2-021
Premier Motorauctions Ltd v Pricewaterhousecoopers LLP [2016] EWHC 2610 (Ch);
   [2017] Bus. L.R. 490...8-215
Premium Nafta Products Ltd v Fili Shipping Co Ltd [2007] UKHL 40; [2007] Bus. L.R.
   1719; [2007] 4 All E.R. 951; [2007] 2 All E.R. (Comm) 1053; [2008] 1 Lloyd's Rep.
   254; [2007] 2 C.L.C. 553; 114 Con. L.R. 69; [2007] C.I.L.L. 2528; (2007) 104(42)
   L.S.G. 34; (2007) 151 S.J.L.B. 1364...2-005, 8-021
Prentis Donegan & Partners Ltd v Leeds & Leeds Co Inc [1998] 2 Lloyd's Rep. 326;
   [1998] C.L.C. 1132 QBD (Comm Ct)..5-010, 5-011, **5-016**
Presentaciones Musicales SA v Secunda [1994] Ch. 271; [1994] 2 W.L.R. 660; [1994] 2
   All E.R. 737; (1994) 138 SJ (LB) 4......................2-061, 2-087, 2-091, **2-094**, 12-025
President of India v La Pintada Compania Navigacion SA; The La Pintada [1985] A.C.
   104; [1984] 3 W.L.R. 10; [1984] 2 All E.R. 773; 128 S.J. 414; [1984] 2 Lloyd's Rep. 9
   HL..6-108
Prest v Petrodel Resources Ltd [2013] UKSC 34; [2013] 2 A.C. 415; [2013] 3 W.L.R. 1;
   [2013] 4 All E.R. 673; [2013] B.C.C. 571; [2014] 1 B.C.L.C. 30; [2013] 2 F.L.R. 732;
   [2013] 3 F.C.R. 210; [2013] W.T.L.R. 1249; [2013] Fam. Law 953; (2013) 163(7565)
   N.L.J. 27; (2013) 157(24) S.J.L.B. 37...1-028, 1-030
Preston v Tubbin 23 E.R. 474; (1684) 1 Vern. 286 8-211
Price v Metropolitan House Investments and Agency Co Ltd (1902) 23 T.L.R. 630 ...6-019, 7-050
Price, Davies & Co v Smith (1929) 141 L.T. 490; 45 T.L.R. 542; 73 S.J. 401 ..7-017, 7-018, 7-028,
   7-032
Prickett v Badger (1856) 1 C.B.(N.S.) 296; 26 L.J.C.P. 33; 3 Jur. (N.S.) 66; 5 W.R. 117 7-035
Priestly v Fernie (1863) 3 Hurl. & C. 977; 34 L.J.Ex. 172; 13 L.T. 208; 11 Jur. (N.S.) 813;
   13 W.R. 1089; 2 Mar.L.C. 281 ....8-116, 8-117, 8-119, **8-124**
Primlake Ltd (In Liquidation) v Matthews Associates [2006] EWHC 1227 (Ch); [2007] 1
   B.C.L.C. 666 ....7-004, 8-161, 8-162
Prince v Clark (1823) 1 B. & C. 186; 2 Dow. & Ry. K.B. 266; 1 L.J. (O.S.) K.B. 69 ..2-078, **2-083**,
   6-012
Printers and Finishers Ltd v Holloway (No.2) [1965] 1 W.L.R. 1; [1964] 3 All E.R. 731;
   [1965] R.P.C. 239; 109 S.J. 47 6-077
Prior v Moore (1887) 3 T.L.R. 624 3-032
Prison Officers Association v Nottinghamshire Healthcare NHS Trust; sub nom.
   Nottinghamshire Healthcare NHS Trust v Prison Officers Association [2003] I.C.R.
   1192 EAT 2-091
Proactive Sports Management Ltd v Rooney [2011] EWCA Civ 1444; [2012] 2 All E.R.
   (Comm) 815; [2012] I.R.L.R. 241; [2012] F.S.R. 16.....................3-007, 6-001, 7-009, 7-042
Produce Brokers Co Ltd v Olympia Oil & Cake Co Ltd [1916] 1 A.C. 314; 85 L.J.K.B.
   160; 114 L.T. 94; 32 T.L.R. 115; 60 S.J. 74; 21 Com.Cas. 320 3-034
Prometheus, The (1949) 82 Ll.Rep. 859 9-074
Protheroe v Protheroe [1968] 1 W.L.R. 519; [1968] 1 All E.R. 1111; 112 S.J. 151; 19 P. &
   C.R. 396 CA...6-080
Proudfoot v Montefiore (1867) L.R. 2 Q.B. 511; 8 B. & S.510; 36 L.J.Q.B. 225; 16 L.T.
   585; 15 W.R. 920; 2 Mar.L.C. 512...6-021, 8-213, **8-217**
Provincial Insurance Co of Canada v Leduc (1874) L.R. 6 P.C. 224; 43 L.J.P.C. 49; 31
   L.T. 142; 22 W.R. 929; 2 Asp.M.L.C. 538 9-011
Punjab National Bank v de Boinville [1992] 1 W.L.R. 1138; [1992] 3 All E.R. 104; [1992]
   1 Lloyd's Rep. 7 CA......................................**6-024**, 8-182, **9-038**, 9-117

Purrunsing v A'Court & Co (a firm) [2016] EWHC 789 (Ch); [2016] 4 W.L.R. 81; [2016]
    E.C.C. 32; [2016] Lloyd's Rep. F.C. 310; [2016] P.N.L.R. 26; [2016] W.T.L.R. 1027;
    [2016] 2 P. & C.R. DG14 . . . . 6-003, 9-137, 9-140
Pye Ex p. (1811) 18 Ves. Jun. 140; 34 E.R. 2718 10-010
Pyrene Co Ltd v Scindia Navigation Co Ltd [1954] 2 Q.B. 402; [1954] 2 W.L.R. 1005;
    [1954] 2 All E.R. 158; [1954] 98 S.J. 354; [1954] 1 Lloyd's Rep. 321 9-122
Pyxis Special Shipping Co Ltd v Dritsis & Kaylis Bros Ltd; The Scaplake [1978] 2
    Lloyd's Rep. 380 . . . . 8-073, 8-121, 9-038
QBE Management Services (UK) Ltd v Dymoke [2012] EWHC 80 (QB); [2012] I.R.L.R.
    458; (2012) 162 N.L.J. 180 . . . . 6-044, 6-054
Quarman v Burnett (1840) 6 M. & W. 499 8-178
Quarter Master UK Ltd (In Liquidation) v Pyke [2004] EWHC 1815 (Ch); [2005] 1
    B.C.L.C. 245 6-042
Quebec & Richmond Railway Co v Quinn (1858) 12 Moo.P.C. 232; 33 L.T. (O.S.) 68 5-001
Queen of Spain v Parr (1869) 39 L.J.Ch. 73; 21 L.T. 555; 18 W.R. 110 6-089
Queensland Investment Co v O'Connell & Palmer (1896) 12 T.L.R. 502; 40 S.J. 621 6-026
Quinn v CC Automotive Group Ltd (t/a Carcraft) [2010] EWCA Civ 1412; [2011] 2 All
    E.R. (Comm) 584 . . . . 8-049, **8-061**, 8-126, 8-180
Quistclose Investments v Rolls Razor Ltd [1970] A.C. 567; [1968] 2 W.L.R. 478; 112 S.J.
    85 . . . . 6-040, 6-041
R. (on the application of Jet Services Ltd) v Civil Aviation Authority; sub nom. R. v Civil
    Aviation Authority Ex p. Jet Services Ltd; Civil Aviation Authority v Jet Services Ltd
    [2001] EWCA Civ 610; [2001] 2 All E.R. (Comm) 769; (2001) 98(24) L.S.G. 44;
    (2001) 145 S.J.L.B. 127 CA 1-036
R. v Barber (1887) 3 T.L.R. 491 6-088
R. v Bedwelty UDC Ex p. Price [1934] 1 K.B. 333; 103 L.J.K.B. 152; 150 L.T. 180; 98
    J.P. 25; 50 T.L.R. 91; 31 L.G.R. 430 2-026
R. v Board of Visitors of the Maze Prison Ex p. Hone; sub nom. Hone and McCartan's
    Application, Re; R. v Board of Visitors of the Maze Prison Ex p. McCartan [1988] A.C.
    379; [1988] 2 W.L.R. 177; [1988] 1 All E.R. 321; (1988) 132 S.J. 158 HL 2-024
R. v Bottrill Ex p. Kuechenmeister [1947] K.B. 41; 115 L.J.K.B. 500; 175 L.T. 232; 62
    T.L.R. 570; [1946] 2 All E.R. 434 9-124
R. v Chapman Ex p. Arlidge [1918] 2 K.B. 298; 87 L.J.K.B. 1142; 119 L.T. 59; 82 J.P.
    229; 16 L.G.R. 525 . . . . 2-048, 2-057
R. v Charles. *See* Commissioner of Police of the Metropolis v Charles (Derek Michael)   6-005,
                                                                            8-010, 8-028, 9-061
R. v De Kromme (1892) 66 L.T. 301; 56 J.P. 682; 8 T.L.R. 325; 17 Cox.C.C. 492 6-088
R. v ICR Haulage Ltd [1944] K.B. 551 1-029
R. v J [2013] EWCA Crim 2287; [2014] 1 W.L.R. 1857; [2014] 1 Cr. App. R. 21; [2014]
    Lloyd's Rep. F.C. 87; [2014] Crim. L.R. 534 6-088
R. v John Wait (1823) 11 Price 518; 147 E.R. 551 10-024
R. v Kent JJ (1873) L.R. 8 Q.B. 305; 42 L.J.M.C. 112; 37 J.P. 644; 21 W.R. 635 . . . . . 2-017, 2-022
R. v Longnor (Inhabitants) (1833) 4 B. & Ad. 647; 1 Ner. & M.K.B. 576; 1 Ner. &
    M.M.C. 128; 2 L.P.M.C. 62 . . . . 2-008, 2-041
R. v Secretary of State for the Home Department Ex p. Tarrant; R. v Board of Visitors of
    Albany Prison, Ex p. Leyland; R. v Board of Visitors of Wormwood Scrubs Prison Ex
    p. Tangney, Clark Anderson [1985] Q.B. 251; [1984] 2 W.L.R. 613; [1984] 1 All E.R.
    799; (1984) S.J. 223; (1984) 81 L.S.Gaz. 1045, D.C 2-024
R. v South Devon Railway Co (1850) 15 Q.B. 1043; 20 L.J.Q.B. 145; 16 L.T.(O.S.) 149;
    15 Jur. 464; 117 E.R. 754 7-075
R. v St Mary Abbotts (Kensington) Assessment Committee [1891] 1 Q.B. 378 . . . . . . 2-017, 2-024
R. v Vincent (1852) 16 Jur. 457 8-161
R. v Whitaker [1914] 3 K.B. 1283; 84 L.J.K.B. 224; 112 L.T. 41; 79 J.P. 28; 30 T.L.R.
    627; 58 S.J. 707; 24 Cox.C.C. 472; 10 Cr.App.R. 245 6-088
Rabiu v Marlbray Ltd [2016] EWCA Civ 476; [2016] 1 W.L.R. 5147; [2016] 2 P. & C.R.
    DG21 9-006
Rabone v Williams (1785) 7 T.R. 360 . . . . 8-098, 8-109
Racing UK Ltd v Doncaster Racecourse Ltd [2005] EWCA Civ 999 8-025
Raclaw v Fay, Conmy & Co 668 N.E.2d 114 (1996) 2-109
Rahimtoola v Nizam of Hyderabad; sub nom. Nizam of Hyderabad and State of
    Hyderabad v Jung [1958] A.C. 379; [1957] 3 W.L.R. 884; [1957] 3 All E.R. 441; 101
    S.J. 901 HL 9-106
Rahme v Smith & Williamson Trust Corp Ltd [2009] EWHC 911 (Ch) 7-050, 7-051

Railton v Hodgson (1804) 4 Taunt. 576n 9-090, 9-091
Rainbow v Howkins & Sons [1904] 2 K.B. 322; 73 L.J.K.B. 641; 91 L.T. 149; 53 W.R.
    46; 20 T.L.R. 508; 48 S.J. 494 .... 6-019, **8-045**, 9-034, 9-071
Raineri v Miles; Wjejski (Third Party) [1981] A.C. 1050; [1980] 2 W.L.R. 847; [1980] 2
    All E.R. 145; (1980) 124 S.J. 328; (1980) 41 P. & C.R. 71 HL 6-013
Rainham Chemical Works Ltd (In Liquidation) v Belvedere Fish Guano Co Ltd; sub nom.
    Belvedere Fish Guano Co Ltd v Rainham Chemical Works Ltd; Ind Coope & Co v
    Rainham Chemical Works Ltd [1921] 2 A.C. 465 HL 1-030, 9-120
Rainy Sky SA v Kookmin Bank [2011] UKSC 50; [2011] 1 W.L.R. 2900; [2012] 1 All
    E.R. 1137; [2012] 1 All E.R. (Comm) 1; [2012] Bus. L.R. 313; [2012] 1 Lloyd's Rep.
    34; [2011] 2 C.L.C. 923; [2012] B.L.R. 132; 138 Con. L.R. 1; [2011] C.I.L.L. 3105 8-050
Raja v Rollerby Ltd [1997] E.G.C.S.79; [1997] N.P.C. 76; (1997) 74 P. & C.R. D25 CA   7-021,
                                                                                            7-028
Rakusens Ltd v Baser Ambalaji Plastik Sanayi Ticaret AS [2001] EWCA Civ 1820; [2002]
    1 B.C.L.C. 104 1-020
Raleigh v Atkinson (1840) 6 M. & W. 670; 9 L.J. Ex. 206   10-014
Raleigh v Goschen [1898] 1 Ch. 73; 67 L.J.Ch. 59; 77 L.T. 429; 46 W.R. 90; 14 T.L.R. 36;
    42 S.J. 46. 8-042
Rama Corp Ltd v Proved Tin and General Investments Ltd [1952] 2 Q.B. 147; [1952] 1
    All E.R. 554; [1952] 1 T.L.R. 709; 96 S.J. 197 QBD 2-102, 3-004, 8-024, 8-028, 8-033, 8-039
Ramazotti v Bowring (1859) 7 C.B.(N.S.) 851; 29 L.J.C.P. 30; 6 Jur. (N.S.) 172; 8 W.R.
    114. 8-109
Ramcoomarsingh v Administrator General [2002] UKPC 67; [2003] W.T.L.R. 291; (2003)
    147 S.J.L.B. 354 PC (Trinidad and Tobago). 6-069
Ramsay v Love [2015] EWHC 65 (Ch) 1-047, 2-022, 2-023, 8-126
Ramsden v Dyson (1866) L.R. 1 H.L. 129   2-103
Randall v Trimen (1856) 18 C.B. 786; 25 L.J.C.P. 307   .... 9-061, 9-063, **9-083**, 9-117
Randhawa v Hardy [2017] EWCA Civ 1201   1-028
Ranger v Great Western Railway Co (1854) 5 H.L. Cas. 72; 24 L.T.(O.S.) 22; 18 Jur. 795   ... 1-028,
                                                                                            8-189
Ranson v Customer Systems Plc [2012] EWCA Civ 841; [2012] I.R.L.R. 769; (2012)
    156(26) S.J.L.B. 31 .... 1-028, 6-054
Raphael v Bank of England (1855) 17 C.B. 161; 25 L.J.C.P. 33; 26 L.T.(O.S.) 60; 4 W.R.
    10. .... 8-140, 8-141
Raphael v Goodman (1838) 8 A. & E. 565; 3 N. & P.K.B. 547; 1 W.W. & H. 363; 7
    L.J.Q.B. 200 8-096
Rapid Road Transit Co, Re [1909] 1 Ch. 96; 78 L.J.Ch. 132; 99 L.T. 774; 53 S.J. 83; 16
    Mans. 289 7-089
Rashdall v Ford (1866) L.R. 2 Eq. 750; 35 L.J.Ch. 769; 14 L.T. 790; 14 W.R. 950   .... **9-076**
Rasnoimport V/O v Guthrie & Co [1966] 1 Lloyd's Rep. 1   .... 8-173, 9-062, 9-064, 9-065, 9-070,
                                                                            9-071, **9-076**, 9-083
Ratiu v Conway [2005] EWCA Civ 1302; [2006] 1 All E.R. 571; [2006] 1 E.G.L.R. 125;
    [2006] W.T.L.R. 101; [2005] 46 E.G. 177 (C.S.). 1-030, 6-035, 6-038
Rayner (J.H.) (Mincing Lane) v Department of Trade and Industry, Maclaine Watson v
    Department of Trade and Industry; Maclaine Watson v International Tin Council; sub
    nom. International Tin Council, Re [1990] 2 A.C. 418; [1989] 3 W.L.R. 969; [1989] 3
    All E.R. 523 HL 8-079
Rayner v Grote (1846) 15 M. & W. 359; 16 L.J.Ex. 79; 8 L.T. (O.S.) 474   ..... 9-094, 9-096, **9-097**
Rayner v Paskell and Cann (1948) 152 E.G. 270   9-109
Rayner v Sturges (1916) 33 T.L.R. 87   2-012
Re-use Collections Ltd v Sendall [2014] EWHC 3852 (QB); [2015] I.R.L.R. 226   6-034
Rea v Bell (1852) 18 L.T. (O.S.) 312   6-068
Read v Anderson (1884) 13 Q.B.D. 779; 53 L.J.Q.B. 532; 51 L.T. 55; 49 J.P. 4; 32 W.R.
    950. .... 3-038, 7-055, 10-010, 10-026
Read v Rann (1830) 10 B. & C. 438; L. & Welsh 121; 8 L.J.(O.S.) K.B. 144   .... 7-004, 7-012
Readdy v Pendergast (1887) 56 L.T. 790; varying (1886) 55 L.T. 767   .... **6-072**
Reading v Attorney General [1951] A.C. 507; [1951] 1 T.L.R. 480; [1951] 1 All E.R. 617;
    95 S.J. 155. .... **6-083**
Ready Mixed Concrete (East Midlands) Ltd v Yorkshire Traffic Area Licensing Authority
    [1970] 2 Q.B. 397; [1970] 2 W.L.R. 627; 114 S.J. 111; [1970] R.T.R. 141, D.C. 8-179
Ready Mixed Concrete (South East) Ltd v Minister of Pensions and National Insurance;
    sub nom. Ready Mixed Concrete (South East) v Minister of Pensions and National
    Insurance; Minister of Social Security v Greenham Ready Mixed Concrete; Minister of

Social Security v Ready Mixed Concrete (South East) [1968] 2 Q.B. 497; [1968] 2
    W.L.R. 775; [1968] 1 All E.R. 433; 4 K.I.R. 132 1-034
Real Estate Opportunities Ltd v Aberdeen Asset Managers Jersey Ltd [2007] EWCA Civ
    197; [2007] Bus. L.R. 971; [2007] 2 All E.R. 791; [2008] 2 B.C.L.C. 116 . . . . . 8-208, 8-209, 8-215
Reardon Smith Line Ltd v Cayzer, Irvine & Co Ltd (1929) 35 Com.Cas.270; 46 T.L.R.
    146. 8-117
Reckitt v Barnett, Pembroke & Slater Ltd [1929] A.C. 176; 98 L.J.K.B. 136; 140 L.T. 208;
    45 T.L.R. 36; 34 Com.Cas. 126 . . . . 3-011, **3-015**
Rederiaktiebolaget Argonaut v Hani [1918] 2 K.B. 247; 87 L.J.K.B. 991; 118 L.T. 176; 14
    Asp.M.L.C. 310 8-078
Redgrave v Hurd (1881) 20 Ch.D. 1 CA 8-050
Redpath v Wigg (1866) L.R. 1 Ex. 335; 4 H. & C. 432; 35 L.J.Ex. 211; 14 L.T. 764; 12
    Jur. (N.S.) 903; 14 W.R. 866. . . . . **9-038**
Reed (Dennis) Ltd v Goody [1950] 2 K.B. 277; 66 T.L.R. (Pt. 1) 918; [1950] 1 All E.R.
    919; 94 S.J. 270 CA 7-017, 7-018, 7-019
Reed (Dennis) Ltd v Nicholls; Dennis Reed Ltd v Goody [1948] 2 All E.R. 914 7-019
Reeve v Reeve (1858) 1 F. & F. 280 7-004
Refuge Assurance Co Ltd v Kettlewell; sub nom. Kettlewell v Refuge Ass Co Ltd [1908]
    1 K.B. 545 . . . . 8-064, 8-098, 8-203
Regal (Hastings) Ltd v Gulliver [1967] 2 A.C. 134; [1962] 1 All E.R. 378 . . . . 5-012, 6-074, 6-081,
    6-083
Regent International Hotels (UK) Ltd v Pageguide Ltd *Times,* May 13, 1985 CA 10-025
Regent Leisuretime Ltd v NatWest Finance Ltd [2003] EWCA Civ 391 8-215
Regier v Campbell-Stuart [1939] Ch. 766; 108 L.J.Ch. 321; 161 L.T. 30; 55 T.L.R. 798;
    [1939] 3 All E.R. 235; 83 S.J. 497. . . . . 6-037, 6-067, 6-068, **6-071**, 6-082
Reid v Dreaper (1861) 6 H. & N. 813; 30 L.J.Ex. 268; 4 L.T. 650; 7 Jur. (N.S.) 1125 9-016
Reid v Rigby & Co [1894] 2 Q.B. 40; 63 L.J.Q.B. 451; 10 T.L.R. 418; 10 R. 280 . . . . **8-204**
Reid-Newfoundland Co v Anglo-American Telegraph Co Ltd [1912] A.C. 555; 81 L.J.P.C.
    224; 106 L.T. 691; 28 T.L.R. 385 . . . . **6-078**
Reif Diner & Co v Catalytic International Inc [1978] 246 E.G. 743 . . . . 7-012, 7-024
Reigate v Union Manufacturing Co (Ramsbottom) Ltd [1918] 1 K.B. 592; 87 L.J.K.B.
    724; 118 L.T. 479 CA 10-042, 10-045
Relfo Ltd (In Liquidation) v Varsani [2014] EWCA Civ 360; [2015] 1 B.C.L.C. 14 . . . 3-010, 8-161
Renault UK Ltd v Fleetpro Technical Services Ltd [2007] EWHC 2541 (QB); [2008] Bus.
    L.R. D17 8-214
Renpor, The (1883) 8 P.D. 115; 52 L.J.P. 49; 48 L.T. 887; 31 W.R. 640; 5 Asp.M.L.C. 117 . . . 4-004
Repetto v Millar's Karri and Jarrah Forests Ltd [1901] 2 K.B. 306; 70 L.J.K.B. 561; 84
    L.T. 836; 49 W.R. 526; 17 T.L.R. 421; 9 Asp. M.L.C. 215; 6 Com.Cas.129 . . . . **9-003**
Republic of Chili v London and River Plate Bank (1894) 10 T.L.R. 658 10-032
Republic of Peru v Peruvian Guano Co (1887) 36 Ch.D. 489; 56 L.J.Ch. 1081; 57 L.T.
    337; 36 W.R. 217; 3 T.L.R. 848 2-074
Resolute Maritime Inc v Nippon Kaiji Kyokai; The Skopas [1983] 1 W.L.R. 857; [1983] 2
    All E.R. 1; (1983) 127 S.J. 491; [1983] 1 Lloyd's Rep. 431 . . . . 9-117, **9-125**
Reuter v Electric Telegraph Co (1856) 6 E. & B. 341; 26 L.J.Q.B. 46; 27 L.T. (O.S.) 167;
    2 Jur. (N.S.) 1245; 4 W.R. 564. . . . . 1-028, 2-069
Revenue and Customs Commissioners v Holland [2010] UKSC 51; [2010] 1 W.L.R. 2793;
    [2011] 1 All E.R. 430; [2011] Bus. L.R. 111; [2011] S.T.C. 269; [2011] B.C.C. 1; [2011]
    1 B.C.L.C. 141; [2011] B.P.I.R. 96; [2010] S.T.I. 3074 . . . . 5-012, 6-003
Revenue and Customs Commissioners v Secret Hotels2 Ltd (formerly Med Hotels Ltd)
    [2014] UKSC 16; [2014] 2 All E.R. 685; [2014] S.T.C. 937; [2014] B.V.C. 9; [2014]
    S.T.I. 864. 1-023
Revenue and Customs Commissioners v Total Network SL [2008] UKHL 19; [2008] 1
    A.C. 1174; [2008] 2 W.L.R. 711; [2008] 2 All E.R. 413; [2008] S.T.C. 644; [2008]
    Lloyd's Rep. F.C. 275; [2008] B.P.I.R. 699; [2008] B.T.C. 5216; [2008] B.V.C. 340;
    [2008] S.T.I. 938; (2008) 152(12) S.J.L.B. 29 9-120
Reversion Funds Insurance Co v Maison Cosway Ltd [1913] 1 K.B. 364; 82 L.J.K.B. 512;
    108 L.T. 87; 57 S.J. 144; 20 Mans.194 . . . . 8-203, **8-204**
Reynell v Lewis (1846) 15 M. & W. 517; 4 Ry. & Can.Cas. 351; 16 L.J.Ex. 25; 8 L.T.
    (O.S.) 167; 10 J.P. 775; 10 Jur. 1097 . . . . 2-030, 3-007, 8-010
Reynolds v Smith; sub nom. Smith v Reynolds (1893) 9 T.L.R. 474 . . . . 3-036, 3-037
Rhodes v Bate (1866) L.R. 1 Ch.App. 252; 35 L.J.Ch. 267; 13 L.T. 778; 12 Jur. (N.S.)
    178; 14 W.R. 292 6-069
Rhodes v Fielder, Jones and Harrison (1919) 89 L.J.K.B. 15; 148 L.T.J. 158 . . 7-059, **7-062**, 10-010

Rhodes v Forwood (1876) 1 App.Cas. 256; 47 L.J.Q.B. 396; 34 L.T. 890; 24 W.R. 1078 . . . 10-002, 10-042, **10-046**

Rhodes v Macalister (1923) 29 Com.Cas. 19 7-050

Rhodian River Shipping Co SA v Holla Maritime Corp; The Rhodian River & Rhodian Sailor [1984] 1 Lloyd's Rep. 373 8-077

Ricci Burns Ltd v Toole [1989] 1 W.L.R. 993; [1989] 3 All E.R. 478 CA 8-015

Rice v Chute (1801) 1 East 579 9-034

Rice v Rice (1854) 2 Draw. 73; 2 Eq. Rep. 341; 23 L.J.Ch. 289; 22 L.T. (O.S.) 208; 2 W.R. 139. 8-135

Richard Buxton Solicitors v Mills-Owens [2010] EWCA Civ 122; [2010] 1 W.L.R. 1997; [2010] 4 All E.R. 405; [2010] C.P. Rep. 26; [2010] 3 Costs L.R. 421; [2010] 2 E.G.L.R. 73; [2010] 17 E.G. 96; [2010] 9 E.G. 166 (C.S.); (2010) 107(10) L.S.G. 15; (2010) 154(8) S.J.L.B. 29; [2010] N.P.C. 21. . . . . 7-050, 10-023

Richards v Jenkins (1887) 18 Q.B.D. 451; 56 L.J.Q.B. 293; 56 L.T. 591; 35 W.R. 355; 3 T.L.R. 425 8-126

Richards v Johnston (1859) 4 H. & N. 660; 28 L.J.Ex. 322; 33 L.T.(O.S.) 206; 5 Jur. (N.S.) 520; 157 E.R. 1000. 8-126

Richards v Law Society [2009] EWHC 2087 (Admin) 6-067, 6-038

Richards v Phillips [1969] 1 Ch. 39; [1968] 3 W.L.R. 33; [1968] 2 All E.R. 859; (1968) 112 S.J. 460 CA 9-034

Richards v West Middlesex Waterworks Co (1885) 15 Q.B.D. 660; 54 L.J.Q.B. 551; 49 J.P. 631; 33 W.R. 902 . . . . **8-196**

Richardson v Goss (1802) 3 B. & P. 119 . . . . **7-089**

Richardson v Oxford (1861) 2 F. & F. 449 2-086

Richardson v Williamson (1871) L.R. 6 B.Q. 276; 40 L.J.Q.B. 145; 35 J.P. 728 . . . . . **9-076**, 9-079, **9-083**

Richmond Gate Property Co Ltd, Re [1965] 1 W.L.R. 335; [1964] 3 All E.R. 936 . . . . 7-004, 7-012

Richmond Shipping Ltd v D/S and A/S Vestland; The Vestland [1980] 2 Lloyd's Rep. 171 . . . 7-077

Rickards (Charles) Ltd v Oppenhaim [1950] 1 K.B. 616; 66 T.L.R. (Pt. 1) 435; [1950] 1 All E.R. 420; 94 S.J. 161 CA 6-013

Riddick v Thames Board Mills Ltd [1971] Q.B. 881; [1977] 3 W.L.R. 63; [1977] 3 All E.R. 677; (1977) 121 S.J. 274 CA 8-180

Ridgeway Maritime Inc v Beulah Wings Ltd; The Leon [1991] 2 Lloyd's Rep. 611 QBD (Comm Ct) 9-121

Ridgway v Ley (1856) 25 L.J.Ch. 584 7-075

Ridyard v Roberts Unreported, May 16, 1980 CA 4-006

Right d. Fisher, Nash and Hyrons v Cuthell (1804) 5 East 491; 2 Smith K.B. 33 . . . . . 2-091, 2-094

Riley v Packington (1867) L.R. 2 C.P. 536; 36 L.J.C.P. 204; 16 L.T. 382; 15 W.R. 746 8-045

Rimmer v Knowles (1874) 30 L.T. 496; 22 W.R. 574 7-014

Rimmer v Webster [1902] 2 Ch. 163; 71 L.J.Ch. 561; 86 L.T. 491; 50 W.R. 517; 18 T.L.R. 548. . . . . 8-130, **8-133**, 8-134, 8-135, 8-138

Rimpacific Navigation Inc v Daehan Shipbuilding Co [2009] EWHC 2941 (Comm); [2010] 2 All E.R. (Comm) 814; [2010] 2 Lloyd's Rep. 236; [2010] Bus. L.R. D61; further proceedings [2011] EWHC 2618 . . . . 3-029, 12-002, 12-016, 12-020

Ringham v Hackett [1980] C.L.Y. 158 9-055

Risbourg v Bruckner (1858) 3 C.B.(N.S.) 812; 27 L.J.C.P. 90; 30 L.T.(O.S.) 258; 6 W.R. 215. . . . . **2-100**, 6-025

Riverstone Meat Co Pty Ltd v Lancashire Shipping Co Ltd; The Muncaster Castle [1961] A.C. 807; [1961] 2 W.L.R. 269; [1961] 1 All E.R. 495; [1961] 1 Lloyd's Rep. 57; 105 S.J. 148 HL 8-184

Rivoli Hats Ltd v Gooch [1953] 1 W.L.R. 1190; [1953] 2 All E.R. 823; 97 S.J. 589 QBD 7-025

Riyad Bank v Ahli United Bank (UK) Plc [2005] EWHC 279 QBD (Comm) 5-011

RMKRM (A Firm) v MRMVL (A Firm); sub nom. RMKRM (A Firm) v MRMVL (A Firm), RMKRM Somasundarum Chetty v MRMVL Supramanian Chetty [1926] A.C. 761; 135 L.T. 645; 95 L.J.C.P. 197; 42 T.L.R. 686 . . . . 8-117, **8-124**

Roadchef (Employee Benefits Trustees) Ltd v Hill [2014] EWHC 109 (Ch) 8-220, 9-135

Robb v Green [1895] 2 Q.B. 315; 64 L.J.Q.B. 593; 73 L.T. 15; 59 J.P. 695; 44 W.R. 25; 11 T.L.R. 517; 39 S.J. 653; 14 R. 580 . . . . 6-061, 6-077

Robbins v Fennell; sub nom. Robins v Fennell (1847) 11 Q.B. 248; 2 New Pr.Cas. 426; 17 L.J.Q.B. 77; 12 Jur. 157; (1847) 10 L.T. (O.S.) 246 . . . . 5-012, **5-016**

Robbins v Heath (1848) 11 Q.B. 257n.; 2 New Pr.Cas.433; 10 L.T.(O.S.) 371; 12 Jur. 158 . . 5-012, 5-016

Roberts v Barnard (1884) 1 Cab. & El. 336 7-035

Roberts v Elwells Engineers Ltd [1972] 2 Q.B. 586; [1972] 3 W.L.R. 1; [1972] 2 All E.R.
890; 116 S.J. 431; [1973] 1 Lloyd's Rep. 153 CA 7-037, 7-042, 7-047, 10-045
Roberts v Ogilby (1821) 9 Price 269 .... 2-032, 6-100, 6-111, **6-112**
Roberts v Smith (1859) 4 H. & N. 315; 28 L.J.Ex. 164; 32 L.T. (O.S.) 320 7-012
Robertson v Fauntleroy (1823) 8 Moo.C.P. 10; 1 L.J.(O.S.) C.P. 55 .... **9-114**
Robertson v Minister of Pensions [1949] 1 K.B. 227; [1949] L.J.R. 323; 64 T.L.R. 526;
[1948] 2 All E.R. 767; 92 S.J. 603 8-042
Robins v Bridge (1837) 3 M. & W. 114; 6 Dowl. 140; Murph & H. 357; 7 L.J.Ex. 49; 2
Jur. 19 .... **9-003**
Robinson v Gleadow (1835) 2 Bing.N.C. 156; 1 Hodg. 245; 2 Scott 250 ...... 2-067, 2-079, **3-029**
Robinson v Jenkins (1890) 24 Q.B.D. 275; 59 L.J.Q.B. 147; 62 L.T. 439; 38 W.R. 360; 6
T.L.R. 158 .... **7-104**
Robinson v Mollett (1875) L.R. 7 H.L. 802; 44 L.J.C.P. 362; 33 L.T. 544 HL   . 1-021, 1-022, 3-033,
3-037, **3-040**, 6-057, 6-071, 7-101, 8-071
Robinson v Montgomeryshire Brewery Co Ltd [1896] 2 Ch. 841; 65 L.J.Ch. 915; 3 Mans.
279 .... 8-126, 8-135
Robinson v PE Jones (Contractors) Ltd [2011] EWCA Civ 9; [2012] Q.B. 44; [2011] 3
W.L.R. 815; [2011] B.L.R. 206; 134 Con. L.R. 26; [2011] 1 E.G.L.R. 111; (2011) 27
Const. L.J. 145; [2011] C.I.L.L. 2972; [2011] 4 E.G. 100 (C.S.)..................... 8-183
Robinson v Randfontein [1921] App.D. 168 6-068
Robinson v Read (1829) 9 B. & C. 449; 4 Man. & Ry. K.B. 349; 7 L.J.(O.S.) K.B. 236 8-121
Robinson v Rutter (1855) 4 E. & B. 954; 24 L.J.Q.B. 250; 25 L.T.(O.S.) 127; 1 Jur. (N.S.)
823; 3 W.R. 405; 3 C.L.R. 1195 .... 7-086, **9-035**
Robson v Kemp (1802) 4 Esp. 233 10-010
Rochefoucauld v Boustead [1897] 1 Ch. 196; 66 L.J.Ch. 74; 75 L.T. 502; 45 W.R. 272; 13
T.L.R. 118; 41 S.J. 156 .... 2-037, 6-082
Rockeagle Ltd v Alsop Wilkinson [1992] Ch. 47; [1991] 3 W.L.R. 573; [1991] 4 All E.R.
659 CA.. 7-083, 7-088, 9-026
Roder UK Ltd v West [2011] EWCA Civ 1126; [2012] Q.B. 752; [2012] 3 W.L.R. 469;
[2012] 1 All E.R. 1305; [2012] 1 All E.R. (Comm) 659; (2011) 161 N.L.J. 1450; [2011]
N.P.C. 101 8-198
Rodick v Gandell (1852) 1 De G.M. & G. 763 .... 9-112, 9-114
Rodmell v Eden (1859) 1 F. & F. 542 2-078
Roe d. Rochester (Dean & Chapter) v Pierce (1809) 2 Camp. 96 .... **3-029**
Roe v Birkenhead, etc. Railway (1851) 7 Exch. 36; 6 Ry. & Can. Cas.795; 21 L.J.Ex. 9;
155 E.R. 845... 2-056
Rogers v Hadley (1821) 2 H. & C. 227; 32 L.J.Ex. 241; 9 L.T. 292; 9 Jur. (N.S.) 898; 11
W.R. 1074... 9-012, 9-040, 9-094
Rogers v Kennay (1846) 9 Q.B. 592; 15 L.J.Q.B. 381; 11 Jur. 14 7-073
Rogers v Price (1829) 3 Y. & J. 28 4-010
Rogers, Son & Co v Lambert & Co [1891] 1 Q.B. 318; 60 L.J.Q.B. 187; 64 L.T. 406; 55
J.P. 452; 39 W.R. 114; 7 T.L.R. 69..................................... 6-111, 6-112
Rolfe (FP) & Co v George [1969] E.G.D. 331 7-030
Rolfe, Lubell & Co v Keith [1979] 1 All E.R. 860; (1978) 123 S.J. 32; [1979] 2 Lloyd's
Rep. 75.. 9-050, 9-056
Rolland v Hart (1871) L.R. 6 Ch.App. 678; 40 L.J.Ch. 701; 25 L.T. 191; 19 W.R. 962 8-208,
8-210, 8-211, 8-213, 8-214, **8-217**
Rolled Steel Products (Holdings) Ltd v British Steel Corp [1986] Ch. 246; [1985] 2
W.L.R. 908; [1985] 3 All E.R. 1; (1984) 128 S.J. 629 CA...... 1-028, 2-020, 3-011, 8-032, **8-046**,
8-050, 8-066, 8-203, 8-219, 8-221, 12-020
Rolls Razor Ltd v Cox [1967] 1 Q.B. 552; [1967] 2 W.L.R. 241; [1967] 1 All E.R. 397;
110 S.J. 943 CA................................... 1-039, 1-046, 7-082, 7-086, 8-144
Rolls Royce Power Engineering Plc v Ricardo Consulting Engineers Ltd [2003] EWHC
2871; [2004] 2 All E.R. (Comm) 129; 98 Con. L.R. 169 QBD (TCC) 8-072, 8-079, 9-013
Rooke v Kensington (Lord) (1856) 2 K. & J. 753 .... **3-015**
Rootkin v Kent C.C. [1981] 1 W.L.R. 1186; [1981] 2 All E.R. 227; [1980] 125 S.J. 496;
[1982] 80 L.G.R. 201 CA... 8-042
Roper v Public Works Commrs. [1915] 1 K.B. 45; 84 L.J.K.B. 219; 111 L.T. 630 9-034
Roscoe (James) (Bolton) Ltd v Winder [1915] 1 Ch. 62; 84 L.J.Ch. 286; 112 L.T. 121;
(1915) H.B.R. 61 .... 6-040, **8-167**
Rose v CMS Operations Ltd [2002] EWHC 59 (Ch) 7-078, 7-094
Rose v McGivern [1998] 2 B.C.L.C. 593 2-038

Rose v Plenty; sub nom. Rose v Plenty and Co-operative Retail Services [1976] 1 W.L.R.
141; [1975] I.C.R. 430; [1976] 1 All E.R. 97; 119 S.J. 592; [1976] I.R.L.R. 60; [1976] 1
Lloyd's Rep. 263 CA 8-176
Rose, Re, Ex p. Hasluck & Garrard (1894) 1 Manson 218; 10 R. 262 10-014
Rosenbaum v Belson [1900] 2 Ch. 267; 69 L.J.Ch. 569; 82 L.T. 658; 48 W.R. 522; 44 S.J.
485 .... **3-023, 3-032**
Ross River Ltd v Cambridge City Football Club Ltd [2007] EWHC 2115 (Ch); [2008] 1
All E.R. 1004; [2008] 1 All E.R. (Comm) 1028; 117 Con. L.R. 129; [2007] 41 E.G. 201
(C.S.); (2007) 157 N.L.J. 1507 .... 6-086, 6-087
Ross River Ltd v Waveley Commercial Ltd [2013] EWCA Civ 910; [2014] 1 B.C.L.C.
545 .... 5-012, 6-035, 6-043, 6-092, 6-096
Ross v Edwards & Co (1895) 73 L.T. 100; 11 R. 574 .... 6-111, 6-112
Rossetti Marketing Ltd v Diamond Sofa Co Ltd [2012] EWCA Civ 1021; [2013] 1 All
E.R. (Comm) 308; [2013] Bus. L.R. 543; [2012] C.P. Rep. 45 .... 6-015, 6-039, 6-045, 11-013,
11-024, 11-056, 11-057
Rossiter v Trafalgar Life Ass.Assn. (1859) 27 Beav. 377 5-001
Rothschild v Brookman (1831) 2 Dow. & Cl. 188; 5 Bli (N.S.) 165; 5 E.R. 273 ..... 6-061, 6-064,
6-065, 6-071, 6-080
Rothschild v Brookman (1831) 5 Bli. (NS) 165 6-068
Rothwell v Timbrell (1842) 1 Dowl. (N.S.) 778; 6 Jur. 691 8-217
Routh v Thompson (1811) 13 East 274; 104 E.R. 375 .... 2-067, 2-093
Rover International Ltd v Cannon Film Sales Ltd (No.3) [1989] 1 W.L.R. 912; [1988]
B.C.L.C. 710; [1989] 3 All E.R. 423 CA 2-064, 9-086
Rover International Ltd v Cannon Film Sales Ltd [1987] 1 W.L.R. 1597; [1987] 3 All E.R.
986; (1987) 131 S.J. 1591; (1987) 3 B.C.C. 369; [1987] B.C.L.C. 540 9-086
Row, Ex parte South, Re (1818) 3 Swans. 392; 36 E.R. 907 9-114
Rowe v London Pianoforte Co Ltd (1876) 34 L.T. 450; 13 Cox.C.C. 211 2-056
Rowe v May (1854) 18 Beav. 613; 52 E.R. 241 9-026
Rowland v Chapman (1901) 17 T.L.R. 669 6-086
Rowlandson v National Westminster Bank Ltd [1978] 1 W.L.R. 798; [1978] 3 All E.R.
370; (1977) 122 S.J. 347; [1978] 1 Lloyd's Bank 523 9-142
Rowles v Senior (1846) 8 Q.B. 677; 15 L.J.Q.B. 231; 10 Jur. 354 .... **9-125**
Rowley Homes & Co v Barber [1977] 1 W.L.R. 371 2-014
Roxburghe v Cox (1881) 17 Ch.D. 520; 50 L.J.Ch. 772; 45 L.T. 225; 30 W.R. 74 .... 6-100, 9-112,
9-114
Roy v MR Pearlman Ltd 1999 S.C. 459; 2000 S.L.T. 727; 1999 S.C.L.R. 803; [1999] 2
C.M.L.R. 1155; 1999 G.W.D. 11-486 OH 11-038, 11-057
Royal & Sun Alliance Insurance Plc v MK Digital FZE (Cyprus) Ltd [2006] EWCA Civ
629; [2006] 2 All E.R. (Comm) 145; [2006] 2 Lloyd's Rep. 110; [2006] 1 C.L.C. 787;
[2007] I.L.Pr. 3 .... 9-024, 11-019
Royal Albert Hall Corp v Winchilsea (1891) 7 T.L.R. 362 ...... 2-048, 2-071, 2-074, 8-043, 9-087
Royal Bank of Scotland Plc v Bannerman Johnstone Maclay 2005 S.L.T. 579; [2005] S.C.
437, IH (2 Div) 8-179
Royal Bank of Scotland Plc v Etridge (No.2); Barclays Bank Plc v Coleman; Barclays
Bank Plc v Harris; Midland Bank Plc v Wallace; National Westminster Bank Plc v Gill;
UCB Home Loans Corp Ltd v Moore; Bank of Scotland v Bennett; Kenyon-Brown v
Desmond Banks & Co (Undue Influence) (No.2) [2001] UKHL 44; [2002] 2 A.C. 773;
[2001] 3 W.L.R. 1021; [2001] 4 All E.R. 449; [2001] 2 All E.R. (Comm) 1061; [2002] 1
Lloyd's Rep. 343; [2001] 2 F.L.R. 1364; [2001] 3 F.C.R. 481; [2002] H.L.R. 4; [2001]
Fam. 880; [2001] 43 E.G.C.S.184; (2001) 151 N.L.J. 1538; [2001] N.P.C. 147; [2002] 1
P. & C.R. DG14 HL 1-027
Royal British Bank v Turquand (1856) 6 E. & B. 327; 25 L.J.Q.B. 317; 2 Jur. (N.S.) 663 .. 8-034,
8-046, 8-050
Royal Brunei Airlines Sdn Bhd v Tan; sub nom. Royal Brunei Airlines Sdn Bhd v Philip
Tan Kok Ming [1995] 2 A.C. 378; [1995] 3 W.L.R. 64; [1995] 3 All E.R. 97; [1995]
B.C.C. 899; (1995) 92(27) L.S.G. 33; (1995) 145 N.L.J. 888; [1995] 139 S.J.L.B. 146
(Bru) 8-221, 8-225, 9-135, 9-136
Royal Exchange Ass.v Moore (1863) 8 L.T. 242; 3 New Rep. 63; 11 W.R. 592 9-109
Royal Mail Estates Ltd v Maple Teesdale [2015] EWHC 1890 (Ch); [2016] 1 W.L.R. 942;
[2015] B.C.C. 647 9-086
Royal Norwegian Government v Constant & Constant and Calcutta Marine Engineering
Co Ltd [1960] 2 Lloyd's Rep. 431 .... 6-041, 6-104

Royal Products Ltd v Midland Bank Ltd [1981] 2 Lloyd's Rep. 194; [1981] Com.L.R. 93 . . . 5-011, 5-012

Royle v Busby (1880) 6 Q.B.D. 171; 50 L.J.Q.B. 196; 43 L.T. 717; 29 W.R. 315 . . . . **9-003**

RTA (Business Consultants) Ltd v Bracewell [2015] EWHC 630 (QB); [2015] Bus. L.R. 800; [2015] Lloyd's Rep. F.C. 357; [2015] C.T.L.C. 221 . . . . 2-025, 7-052

Ruben & Ladenburg v Great Fingall Consolidated [1906] A.C. 439; 75 L.J.K.B. 843; 95 L.T. 214; 22 T.L.R. 712; 13 Mans. 248 . . . . 8-046, 8-063, 8-067

Ruby SS Corp v Commercial Union Assurance Ltd (1933) 39 Com. Cas. 48 . . . . . . 12-001, 12-018

Rucker v Lunt (1863) 3 F. & F. 959 7-004

Ruddy v Marco [2008] CSIH 47; 2008 S.C. 667; 2008 S.L.T. 855; 2008 G.W.D. 29-442, IH 9-002

Rumball v Metropolitan Bank (1877) 2 Q.B.D. 194; 46 L.J.Q.B. 346; 36 L.T. 240; 25 W.R. 366 8-142

Ruscoe Ltd (In Liquidation), Re August 7, 2012 6-043

Rushforth v Hadfield (1805) 6 East 519 . . . . 7-073, 7-074

Rusholme & Bolton & Roberts Hadfield v Read (S.G.) & Co [1955] 1 W.L.R. 146; [1955] 1 All E.R. 180; 99 S.J. 132 . . . . 1-021, 1-042, 9-020, 9-021, 9-022

Russell v Northern Bank Development Corp Ltd [1992] 1 W.L.R. 588; [1992] 3 All E.R. 161; [1992] B.C.L.C. 1016; [1992] B.C.C. 578; (1992) 89(27) L.S.G. 33; (1992) 136 S.J.L.B. 182 HL 10-040

Russian & English Bank v Baring Bros & Co Ltd [1935] Ch. 120; 103 L.J.Ch. 111; 150 L.T. 353; 77 S.J. 913. 9-066

Russo-Chinese Bank v Li Yau Sam [1910] A.C. 174; 79 L.J.P.C. 60; 101 L.T. 689; 26 T.L.R. 203. . . . . 8-055, 8-200, 8-201

Ryan v Fildes [1938] 3 All E.R. 517 8-191

Ryan v Pilkington [1959] 1 W.L.R. 403; [1959] 1 All E.R. 689; 103 S.J. 310 CA 3-004, 3-022, 8-013, 8-028

Ryan v Sams (1848) 12 Q.B. 460; 17 L.J.Q.B. 271; 11 L.T. (O.S.) 221; 12 Jur. 745 . . **8-045**, 10-030

Ryde Holdings Ltd v Rainbow Corp Ltd [1993] UKPC 40 6-042

S v Attorney General [2003] 3 N.Z.L.R. 450 8-178

SA d'Intermediaries Luxembourgeois v Farex Gie [1995] L.R.L.R. 116 . . . . 8-212, 8-214

Sabaf SpA v MFI Furniture Centres Ltd [2002] EWCA Civ 976; [2003] R.P.C. 14 2-025

Sachs v Miklos [1948] 2 K.B. 23; [1948] L.J.R. 1012; 64 T.L.R. 181; [1948] 1 All E.R. 67 CA 4-005, 4-006, 4-010

Sadler v Evans (1766) 4 Burr. 1984 9-103

Sadler, Re, Ex p. Davies (1881) 19 Ch.D. 86; 45 L.T. 632; 30 W.R. 237 . . . . 6-111, 7-103

Safeway Stores Ltd v Twigger [2010] EWCA Civ 1472; [2011] 2 All E.R. 841; [2011] Bus. L.R. 1629; [2011] 1 Lloyd's Rep. 462; [2011] 1 C.L.C. 80; [2011] U.K.C.L.R. 339 . . . . 2-025, 6-023

Saffron Walden Second Benefit Building Society v Rayner (1877) 14 Ch.D. 406; (1877) 14 Ch.D. 406; 49 L.J.Ch. 465; 43 L.T. 3; 28 W.R. 681 CA **8-207**, 9-069

Sagal (t/a Bunz UK) v Atelier Bunz GmbH [2009] EWCA Civ 700; [2009] Bus. L.R. 1527; [2009] 4 All E.R. 1253; [2010] 1 All E.R. (Comm) 104; [2009] 2 Lloyd's Rep. 303; [2009] 2 C.L.C. 1; [2009] E.C.C. 30; (2009) 153(27) S.J.L.B. 28. . . . . 11-013, 11-018, 11-019

Said v Butt [1920] 3 K.B. 497; 90 L.J.K.B. 239; 124 L.T. 413; 36 T.L.R. 762 . 8-069, 8-079, **8-082**, 9-121

Sainsbury's Supermarkets Ltd v Condek Holdings Ltd [2014] EWHC 2016 (TCC); [2014] B.L.R. 574. 8-176

Salaman v Secretary of State for India [1906] 1 K.B. 613; 75 L.J.K.B. 418; 94 L.T. 858 9-124

Salford Corp v Lever [1891] 1 Q.B. 168; 60 L.J.Q.B. 39; 63 L.T. 658; 55 J.P. 244; 39 W.R. 85; 7 T.L.R. 18. . . . . 6-087, 8-223

Salkeld Investments Ltd v West One Loans Ltd [2012] EWHC 2701 (QB) 8-209

Salomon v Salomon & Co Ltd [1897] A.C. 22 HL 1-028

Salomons v Pender (1865) 3 H. & C. 639; 6 New Rep. 34 L.J.Ex. 95; 12 L.T. 267; 29 J.P. 295; 11 Jur. (N.S.) 432; 13 W.R. 637. . . . . 2-014, **6-061**, 6-062, 6-064, 6-068, 7-049— **7-051**

Salsi v Jetspeed Sir Services Ltd [1977] 2 Lloyd's Rep. 57 . . . . 9-006, 9-024

Saltman Engineering Co, Ferotel and Monarch Engineering Co (Mitcham) v Campbell Engineering Co (1948) [1963] 3 All E.R. 413n; 65 R.P.C. 203 CA. 6-077

Salton v New Beeston Cycle Co [1900] 1 Ch. 43; 69 L.J.Ch. 20; 81 L.T. 437; 48 W.R. 92; 16 T.L.R. 25; 7 Mans. 74 . . . . 9-063, 10-018, **10-022**

Salvesen & Co v Rederi A/B Nordstjernan [1905] A.C. 302; 74 L.J.P.C. 96; 92 L.T. 575 . . . . 6-012, 9-064, 9-078

Sampson v Wilson [1996] Ch. 39; [1995] 3 W.L.R. 455; (1997) 29 H.L.R. 18; (1995) 70 P.
  & C.R. 359 CA 5-010
Samson v Frazier Jelke & Co [1937] 2 K.B. 170; [1937] 2 All E.R. 588; 106 L.J.K.B. 854;
  157 L.T. 530; 81 S.J. 398 6-024
Samuel (No.2) Re; sub nom. Re Samuel; Trustee v Kerman [1945] Ch. 408; [1945] 2 All
  E.R. 437n.; 114 L.J.Ch. 318; 173 L.T. 390; 61 T.L.R. 581; 89 S.J. 446 . . . . 9-129, **9-131**
Samuel (P) & Co Ltd v Dumas [1923] 1 K.B. 592 2-067
Samuel & Co v Sanders Bros (1886) 3 T.L.R. 145 7-018
Samuel Bros Ltd v Whetherly [1908] 1 K.B. 184; 77 L.J.K.B. 69; 98 L.T. 169; 24 T.L.R.
  160; 52 S.J. 112. 9-087
Sanders (Ernest A) Ltd [1974] 1 C.R. 565; [1974] 3 All E.R. 327; [1974] I.T.R.
  395; [1975] K.I.R. 77; [1974] I.R.L.R. 236, N.I.R.C 7-046, 7-047
Sanders v Parry [1967] 1 W.L.R. 753; [1967] 2 All E.R. 803; 111 S.J. 296 . . . . **6-061**
Sanderson v Bell (1833) 2 C. & M. 304; 4 Tyr. 244; 3 L.J.Ex. 66 . . . . **3-023**
Sanderson v Blyth Theatre Co [1903] 2 K.B. 533 9-075
Sandiford (No.2), Re; Halo-Canadian Corp Ltd v Sandiford [1935] Ch. 681; 104 L.J.Ch.
  335; 154 L.T. 7 7-006
Santa Carina, The. *See* Vlassopulos (N&T) Ltd v Ney Shipping Ltd; Santa Carina, The 1-046,
                                                                 8-026, 9-006, 9-016, 9-034, **9-046**
Santander UK Plc v National Westminster Bank Plc [2014] EWHC 2626 (Ch) 9-102, 9-017
Santander UK Plc v Royal Bank of Scotland Plc [2015] EWHC 2560 (Ch) 9-017
Santander UK v RA Legal Solicitors [2014] EWCA Civ 183; [2014] Lloyd's Rep. F.C.
  282; [2014] P.N.L.R. 20; [2014] W.T.L.R. 813; [2014] 2 P. & C.R. DG6 6-003
Sargent (J) (Garages) Ltd v Motor Auctions (West Bromwich) Ltd [1971] R.T.R. 121,CA . . . 8-127,
                                                                   8-130, 8-133, 8-149
Sargent v Morris (1820) 3 B. & Ald. 277; 106 E.R. 665 9-012
Sarginson Bros v Moulton (Keith) & Co (1942) 73 Ll.L.Rep. 104 . . . . **6-024**
Satnam Investments Ltd v Dunlop Heywood & Co Ltd [1999] 3 All E.R. 652; [1999] 1
  B.C.L.C 385; [1999] F.S.R. 722; [1999] Lloyd's Rep. P.N. 201; [1998] E.G. 190 (C.S.);
  (1999) 96(6) L.S.G. 33; (1999) 96(2) L.S.G. 30; [1998] N.P.C. 169 CA 8-221, 9-135
Satterthwaite (AM) & Co v New Zealand Shipping Co Ltd; The Eurymedon [1975] A.C.
  154; [1974] 2 W.L.R. 865; [1974] 1 All E.R. 1015; [1974] 1 Lloyd's Rep. 534; 118 S.J.
  387 PC (NZ) 7-036
Satyam Computer Services Ltd v Upaid Systems Ltd [2008] EWCA Civ 487; [2008] 2 All
  E.R. (Comm) 465; [2008] 2 C.L.C. 864; [2008] Bus. L.R. D131 8-185
Saunders (Executrix of the Estate of Rose Maud Gallie) v Anglia Building Society
  (formerly Northampton Town and County Building Society) (Costs); sub nom. Gallie v
  Lee [1971] A.C. 1039; [1971] 2 W.L.R. 349; [1971] 1 All E.R. 243; 22 P. & C.R. 300;
  (1970) 115 S.J. 112 HL 2-107, 8-130
Saunders v Anglia Building Society (formerly Northampton Town and County Building
  Society) [1971] A.C. 1004; [1970] 3 W.L.R. 1078; [1970] 3 All E.R. 961; (1971) 22 P.
  & C.R. 300; (1970) 114 S.J. 885 HL 2-009
Saunders v Soper [1975] A.C. 239; [1974] 3 W.L.R. 777; [1974] 3 All E.R. 1025; 118 S.J.
  863 HL 7-053
Saunderson v Glass (1742) 2 Atk. 296 6-069
Saunderson v Griffiths (1826) S.B. & C. 909; 8 Dow. A. Ry. K.B. 643; 4 L.J. (O.S.) K.B.
  318. . . . . **2-070**
Savash v CIS General Insurance Ltd [2014] EWHC 375 (TCC); [2014] Lloyd's Rep. I.R.
  471. 8-097
Savery v King (1856) 5 H.L. Cas.627; 25 L.J.Ch. 482; 27 L.T. (O.S.) 145; 2 Jur. (N.S.)
  503; 4 W.R. 571 . . . . 2-072, 6-062, 6-064
Savills (UK) Ltd v Blacker [2017] EWCA Civ 68 . . . . 7-037, **9-006**, 9-034
Savills v Scott [1988] 1 E.G.L.R. 20; [1988] 12 E.G. 115, DC 9-061
Saxon v Blake (1861) 29 Beav. 438 9-034
Sayers Ex p. (1800) 5 Ves. 169 8-167
Scally v Southern Health and Social Services Board [1992] 1 A.C. 294; [1991] 3 W.L.R.
  778; [1991] 4 All E.R. 563; [1991] I.C.R. 771; [1991] I.R.L.R. 522; (1991) 141 N.L.J.
  1482; (1991) 135 S.J. 172 HL. 7-001
Scammel (Robinson) & Co v Ansell [1985] 2 E.G.L.R. 41 . . . . **7-051**
Scammell (G) & Nephew Ltd v Hurley [1929] 1 K.B. 419; 98 L.J.K.B. 98; 140 L.T. 236;
  93 J.P. 99; 27 L.G.R. 53, L.A 9-121
Scammell v Ouston [1941] A.C. 251; 110 L.J.K.B. 197; 164 L.T. 379; 57 T.L.R. 280;
  [1941] 1 All E.R. 14; 85 S.J. 224; 46 Com.Cas. 190 7-009

Scarf v Jardine (1882) 7 App.Cas. 345; 51 L.J.Q.B. 612; 47 L.T. 258; 30 W.R. 893 . . . 2-050, 8-119,
                                                              8-121, 10-030, 10-031
Scarfe v Morgan (1838) 4 M. & W. 270; 1 Horn & H. 292; 7 L.J.Ex. 324; 2 Jur. 569; 150
   E.R. 1430 7-092
Scarisbrick v Parkinson (1869) 20 L.T. 175; 17 W.R. 467 7-005
Schack v Anthony (1813) 1 M. & S. 573 . . . . **8-088**
Scheggia v Gradwell; sub nom. Sheggia v Gradwell [1963] 1 W.L.R. 1049; [1963] 3 All
   E.R. 114; 107 S.J. 572 CA 7-021
Schering Chemicals Ltd v Falkman Ltd [1982] Q.B. 1; [1981] 2 W.L.R. 848; [1981] 2 All
   E.R. 321; (1981) 125 S.J. 342 CA 6-077, **6-078**
Schindler v Brie [2003] EWHC 1804; [2003] W.T.L.R. 1361; (2003–04) 6 I.T.E.L.R. 157
   Ch D 10-014
Schmaling v Tomlinson (1815) 6 Taunt. 147; 1 Marsh 500 . . . . 5-004, 5-011, 5-015, 5-015
Schmaltz v Avery (1851) 16 Q.B. 655; 20 L.J.Q.B. 228; 17 L.T. (O.S.) 27; 15 Jur. 291 8-078,
                                                             9-095, 9-096, **9-097**
Schneider v Eisovitch [1960] 2 Q.B. 430; [1960] 2 W.L.R. 169; [1960] 1 All E.R. 169;
   104 S.J. 89 QBD 4-010, 7-059
Scholes & Sons Re (1886) 32 Ch.D. 245; 55 L.J.Ch. 626; 54 L.T. 466; 34 W.R. 515; 2
   T.L.R. 476 5-007
Schostall v Johnson (1919) 36 T.L.R. 75 . . . . 2-012, 10-003
Schuster v McKellar (1857) 7 E. & B. 704; 26 L.J.Q.B. 281; 29 L.T. (O.S.) 225; 3 Jur.
   (N.S.) 1320; 5 W.R. 656 7-101
Schwensen & Ellinger Heath, Western & Co (1949) 83 Ll.L.Rep. 79 . . . . 5-008, 5-010
Scotland v British Credit Trust Ltd [2014] EWCA Civ 790; [2015] 1 All E.R. 708; [2015]
   1 All E.R. (Comm) 401; [2014] Bus. L.R. 1079; [2015] C.T.L.C. 25 2-034
Scott (Ian) & Co v Medical Installations Co Ltd [1981] E.G.D. 228; (1981) 256 E.G. 556 . . . 7-050
Scott and Horton v Godfrey [1901] 2 K.B. 76; 70 L.J.K.B. 954; 85 L.T. 415; 50 W.R. 61;
   17 T.L.R. 633; 45 S.J. 640; 6 Com.Cas. 226 . . . . 3-040, 6-019
Scott v Ebury (1867) L.R. 2 C.P. 255 . . . . **9-087**
Scott v Livingston (J.B.) & Nicol 1990 S.L.T. 305 . . . . 9-066, 9-068, 9-085
Scott v Porcher (1817) 3 Meriv. 652 9-114
Scott v Surman (1742) Willes 400 . . . . 8-161, **8-167**
Scottish & Newcastle International Ltd v Othon Ghalanos Ltd [2008] UKHL 11; [2008]
   Bus. L.R. 583; [2008] 2 All E.R. 768; [2008] 2 All E.R. (Comm) 369; [2008] 1 Lloyd's
   Rep. 462; [2008] 1 C.L.C. 186; [2008] I.L.Pr. 30; (2008) 158 N.L.J. 334; (2008) 152(8)
   S.J.L.B. 32 9-006
Scottish Metropolitan Assurance Co Ltd v P Samuel & Co Ltd [1923] 1 K.B. 348; 92
   L.J.K.B. 218; 128 L.T. 445; 38 T.L.R. 847; 16 Asp. M.L.C. 105 KBD 9-107
Scottish Power Energy Retail Ltd v Taskforce Contracts Ltd [2008] CSOH 110; 2009
   S.C.L.R. 137; [2009] Eu. L.R. 62; 2008 G.W.D. 30-454 11-040
Scrace v Whittington (1823) 2 B. & C. 11; 3 Dow. & Ry. K.B. 221 . . . . **9-003**
Scragg (Ernest) & Son Ltd v Perserverance Banking and Trust Co Ltd [1973] 2 Lloyd's
   Rep. 101 CA 9-037
Scrimshire v Alderton (1743) 2 Str. 1182 . . . . 1-022, 8-071
Scriven v Scriven [2015] EWHC 1690 (Ch) 1-030
Scruttons Ltd v Midland Silicones Ltd; sub nom. Midland Silicones Ltd v Scruttons Ltd
   [1962] A.C. 446; [1962] 2 W.L.R. 186; [1962] 1 All E.R. 1; [1961] 2 Lloyd's Rep. 365;
   106 S.J. 34 HL 9-122
Sea Emerald SA v Prominvestbank - Joint Stockpoint Commercial Industrial &
   Investment Bank [2008] EWHC 1979 (Comm) 2-079, 2-017, 3-028, 3-031, 12-002, 12-016,
                                                                           12-017, 12-018, 12-025
Seaboard Offshore Ltd v Secretary of State for Transport [1994] 1 W.L.R. 541; (1994) 138
   S.J. (LB) 86; [1994] 1 Lloyd's Rep. 589 1-029
Seager v Copydex Ltd [1967] 1 W.L.R. 923; [1967] 2 All E.R. 415; 2 K.I.R. 828; [1967]
   F.S.R. 211; [1967] R.P.C. 349; 111 S.J. 335 CA 6-077
Seagram v Tuck (1881) 18 Ch.D. 296; 50 L.J.Ch. 572; 44 L.T. 800; 29 W.R. 784 6-041
Seakom Ltd v Knowledgepool Group Ltd [2013] EWHC 4007 (Ch) 7-029
Seascope Capital Services Ltd v Anglo Atlantic S.S. Co Ltd [2002] EWHC 1277; [2002] 2
   Lloyd's Rep. 611 QBD (Comm) 7-030
Seatrade Groningen BV v Geest Industries Ltd; The Frost Express [1996] 2 Lloyd's Rep.
   375 CA 9-016, 9-037, **9-038**
SEB Trygg Liv Holding AB v Manches. *See* AMB Generali Holding AG v SEB Trygg Liv
   Holding AB 2-050, 2-072, 2-078, 3-005, **3-029**, 8-028, 9-067, **9-076**, 10-031, 12-002, 12-023

Sebright v Hanbury [1916] 2 Ch. 245; 85 L.J.Ch. 748; 115 L.T. 75 . . . . 9-015, 9-017
Secretary of State for Employment v Associated Society of Locomotive Engineers and
    Firemen (No.2); sub nom. Secretary of State for Employment v ASLEF (No.2) [1972] 2
    Q.B. 455; [1972] 2 W.L.R. 1370; [1972] 2 All E.R. 949; [1972] I.C.R. 19; 13 K.I.R. 1;
    116 S.J. 467 CA 7-041
Secretary of State for India v Bank of India Ltd [1938] 2 All E.R. 797 7-058
Secretary of State for India v Kamachee Boye Sahaba (1859) 7 Moo. Ind. App. 476; 13
    Moo. P.C. 22; 7 W.R. 722 2-053
Secretary of State for Justice v Topland Group Plc [2011] EWHC 983 (QB) . . . 6-086, 6-089, 8-225
Seddon (James), The (1866) L.R. 1 A. & E. 62; 35 L.J. Adm 117; 15 L.T. 636; 12 Jur.
    (N.S.) 609; 2 Mar. L.C. 443 7-062
Selangor United Rubber Estates Ltd v Cradock (No.3) [1968] 1 W.L.R. 1555; [1968] 2 All
    E.R. 1073; 112 S.J. 744; [1968] 2 Lloyd's Rep 289 Ch D 9-135, 9-141, **9-142**
Seller v Work (1801) Marsh Ins.305 6-029
Sellers v London Counties Newspapers [1951] 1 K.B. 784; [1951] 1 All E.R. 544; 95 S.J.
    252 CA 7-042
Selsey v Rhoades (1827) 2 Bl. (N.S.) 1 . . . . 6-064, **6-072**
Semenza v Brinsley (1865) 18 C.B. (N.S.) 467; 34 L.J.C.P. 161; 12 L.T. 265; 11 Jur.
    (N.S.) 409; 13 W.R. 634 . . . . 8-073, 8-109, 8-110, 8-111
Sempra Metals Ltd (formerly Metallgesellschaft Ltd) v Inland Revenue Commissioners
    [2007] UKHL 34; [2008] 1 A.C. 561; [2007] 3 W.L.R. 354; [2008] Bus. L.R. 49; [2007]
    4 All E.R. 657; [2007] S.T.C. 1559; [2008] Eu. L.R. 1; [2007] B.T.C. 509; [2007] S.T.I.
    1865; (2007) 104(31) L.S.G. 25; (2007) 157 N.L.J. 1082; (2007) 151 S.J.L.B. 985 6-107
Semtex v Gladstone [1954] 1 W.L.R. 945; [1954] 2 All E.R. 206; 98 S.J. 438 8-191
Senex Holdings Ltd (In Liquidation) v National Westminster Bank Plc [2012] EWHC 131
    (Comm); [2012] 1 All E.R. (Comm) 1130 . . . . 3-011, 8-220, 8-226
Serious Fraud Office v Lexi Holdings Plc (In Administration) [2008] EWCA Crim 1443;
    [2009] Q.B. 376; [2009] 2 W.L.R. 905; [2009] Bus. L.R. 647; [2009] 1 All E.R. 586;
    [2009] 1 Cr.App.R. 23; [2008] Lloyd's Rep. F.C. 489; [2008] B.P.I.R. 1598 6-040
Seton v Slade (1801) 7 Ves. 265; 32 E.R. 108 . . . . **3-032**
Seymour v Bridge (1885) 14 Q.B.D. 460; 54 L.J.Q.B. 347; 1 T.L.R. 236 . . . . 3-038, 10-010
Seymour v Kingscote (1922) 38 T.L.R. 586 . . . . 3-043, **8-045**
Seymour v Pychlau (1817) 1 B. & A. 14 7-101
Shackell v Rosier (1836) 2 Bing. N.C. 634; 2 Hodg. 17; 3 Scott 59; 5 L.J.C.P. 193 7-068
Shackleton Aviation Ltd v Maitland Drewery Aviation Ltd [1964] Lloyd's Rep. 293 QBD . . 10-042
Shaffer (James) Ltd v Findlay Durham & Brodie [1953] 1 W.L.R. 106; 97 S.J. 26 CA 6-015
Shah v HSBC Private Bank (UK) Ltd [2010] EWCA Civ 31; [2010] Lloyd's Rep. F.C. 276 . . 6-021
Shah v HSBC Private Bank (UK) Ltd [2012] EWHC 1283 (QB); [2013] 1 All E.R.
    (Comm) 72; [2012] Lloyd's Rep. F.C. 507; [2013] Bus. L.R. D38 6-021
Shallcross v Oldham (1862) 2 Johns & H. 609; 5 L.T. 824; 10 W.R. 291 . . . . **6-078**
Shallcross v Wright (1850) 12 Beav. 558; 19 L.J.Ch. 443; 16 L.T. (O.S.) 257; 14 Jur. 1037 . . 4-010
Shalson v Russo (Tracing Claims); sub nom. Mimran v Russo [2003] EWHC 1637;
    [2005] Ch. 281; [2005] 2 W.L.R. 1213; [2003] W.T.L.R. 1165; (2003) 100(35) L.S.G.
    37 Ch D 2-025, 8-161
Shamia v Joory [1958] 1 Q.B. 448; [1958] 2 W.L.R. 84; [1958] 1 All E.R. 111; 102 S.J. 70
    QBD 9-113, **9-114**
Shand v Grant (1863) 15 C.B. (N.S.) 324; 9 L.T. 390; 1 Mar. L.C. 396 9-109
Sharab v Prince Al-Waleed Bin Tala Bin Abdal-Aziz-Al-Saud [2008] EWHC 1893 (Ch) 1-038
Sharland v Mildon, Sharland v Loosemore (1846) 5 Hare 469; 15 L.J.Ch. 434; 7 L.T.
    (O.S.) 223; 10 Jur. 771 . . . . 9-109, **9-125**
Sharma v Sharma [2013] EWCA Civ 1287; [2014] B.C.C. 73; [2014] W.T.L.R. 111 6-039
Sharma v Top Brands Ltd [2015] EWCA Civ 1140; [2016] B.C.C. 1; [2016] Lloyd's Rep.
    F.C. 1; [2016] B.P.I.R. 111; [2016] P.N.L.R. 12 6-023
Sharman v Brandt (1871) L.R. 6 Q.B. 720; 40 L.J.Q.B. 312; 19 W.R. 936 . . . . . 2-014, 9-035, 9-096
Sharp v Taylor (1849) 2 Ph. 801; 14 L.T. (O.S.) 1; 41 E.R. 1153, L.C 6-100
Sharpe v Foy (1868) L.R. 4 Ch.App. 35; 17 W.R. 65; 19 L.T. 541 . . . . 8-206, 8-214
Shaw v Commissioner of Police of the Metropolis [1987] 1 W.L.R. 1332; [1987] 2 All
    E.R. 405; (1987) 131 S.J. 1357; [1988] T.L.R. 33 CA 8-126, 8-133
Shaw v Dartnall (1826) 6 B. & C. 56; 9 Dow. & Ry. K.B. 54; 5 L.T. (O.S.) K.B. 35 6-097
Shaw v Neale (1858) 6 H.L. Cas.581; 27 L.J.Ch. 444; 31 L.T. (O.S.) 190; 4 Jur. (N.S.)
    605; 6 W.R. 635 7-078
Shaw v Picton (1825) 4 B. & C. 715; 7 Dow. & Ry. K.B. 201; 4 L.J. (O.S.) K.B. 29 . . 6-097, **6-101**

Shaw v Woodcock (1827) 7 B. & C. 73; 9 Dow. & Ry. K.B. 889; 5 L.J. (O.S.) K.B. 294 .... 1-042, 6-097

Shearman (t/a Charles Shearman Agencies) v Hunter Boot Ltd [2014] EWHC 47 (QB); [2014] E.C.C. 12 .... 11-041, 11-045

Shearson Lehman BrosInc v Maclaine Watson & Co Ltd [1988] 1 W.L.R. 16; [1988] 1 All E.R. 116; (1988) 85(2) L.S.G. 35; (1987) 131 S.J. 1658 HL 8-018, 8-126

Shearson Lehman Hutton Inc v Maclaine Watson & Co Ltd [1989] 1 All E.R. 1056; [1989] 2 Lloyd's Rep 570 2-109

Sheffield Corp v Barclay [1905] A.C. 392; 74 L.J.K.B. 747; 93 L.T. 83; 69 J.P. 385; 54 W.R. 49; 21 T.L.R. 642; 49 S.J. 617; 10 Com.Cas. 287; 3 L.G.R. 992; 12 Mans. 248 . 7-058, 7-060, 9-066

Sheffield v London Joint Stock Bond Ltd (1888) 13 App.Cas. 333; 57 L.J.Ch. 986; 58 L.T. 735; 37 W.R. 33; 4 T.L.R. 389 .... 8-053, 8-142

Sheldon v Cox (1764) 2 Eden 224; Amb. 624 .... 8-210, 8-217

Shell Co of Australia Ltd v NAT Shipping and Bagging Services Ltd; Kilmun The [1988] 2 Lloyd's Rep. 1 CA 1-023, 2-078

Shenstone & Co v Hilton [1894] 2 Q.B. 452; 63 L.J.Q.B. 584; 71 L.T. 339; 10 T.L.R. 557; 10 R. 390 9-128

Shephard v Cartwright; sub nom. Shephard, Re [1955] A.C. 431; [1954] 3 W.L.R. 967; [1954] 3 All E.R. 649; 98 S.J. 868 HL 2-008

Shepherds Investments Ltd v Walters [2006] EWHC 836 (Ch); [2007] 2 B.C.L.C. 202; [2007] I.R.L.R. 110; [2007] F.S.R. 15; (2006) 150 S.J.L.B. 536 6-054

Sherborne Park Residents Co Ltd, Re [1987] B.C.L.C. 82; (1986) 2 B.C.C. 99528 8-220

Sheriff v Axe (1827) 4 Russ. 33 7-006

Sherlock Holmes International Society Ltd, Re [2016] EWHC 1392 (Ch); [2016] 4 W.L.R. 173; [2017] 2 B.C.L.C. 38; [2016] P.N.L.R. 31 .... 9-067, 9-070

Shiells v Blackburne (1789) 1 Hy.Bl. 158 .... **6-032**

Shindler v Northern Raincoat Co Ltd [1960] 1 W.L.R. 1038; [1960] 2 All E.R. 239; 104 S.J. 806 10-040

Shipping Co Uniform Inc v Inc Transport Workers' Federation Allen, Ross and Davies; The Uniform Star [1985] 1 Lloyd's Rep. 173; [1985] 1 C.R. 245; [1985] 1 I.R.L.R. 71 QBD (Comm) 9-046

Shipway v Broadwood [1899] 1 Q.B. 369; 68 L.J.Q.B. 360; 80 L.T. 11; 15 T.L.R. 145 ..... 6-086, 8-222, 8-223, **8-226**

Shogun Finance Ltd v Hudson; sub nom. Hudson v Shogun Finance Ltd [2003] UKHL 62; [2004] 1 A.C. 919; [2003] 3 W.L.R. 1371; [2004] 1 All E.R. 215; [2004] 1 All E.R. (Comm) 332; [2004] 1 Lloyd's Rep. 532; [2004] R.T.R. 12; (2003) 100(46) L.S.G. 25; (2003) 153 N.L.J. 1790; (2003) 147 S.J.L.B. 1368 HL 2-034, 8-126

Shoolbred Ex p. (1880) 28 W.R. 339 .... **8-204**

Short v Spackman (1851) 2 B. & Ad. 962 .... 9-008, **9-035**

Shropshire Union Railways and Canal Co v R; sub nom. R. v Shropshire Union Co; Robson v Shropshire Union Railways & Canal Co (1875) L.R. 7 H.L. 496; 45 L.J.Q.B. 31; 32 L.T. 283; 23 W.R. 709 8-131

Sibel v Springfield (1863) 8 New Rep. 36; 9 L.T. 324; 12 W.R. 73 7-073

Siboen, The and Sibotre, The. See Occidental Worldwide Investment Corp v Skibs A/S Avanti 8-185

Sickens v Irving (1858) 29 L.J.C.P. 25; 7 C.B. (N.S.) 165; 6 Jur. (N.S.) 200 3-032

Sidney Bolsom Investment Trust Ltd v E Karmios & Co (London) Ltd [1956] 1 Q.B. 529; [1956] 2 W.L.R. 625; [1956] 1 All E.R. 536; [1956] J.P.L. 45; (1956) 100 S.J. 169 CA 8-050

Siffken & Feize v Wray (1805) 6 East 371; 2 Smith K.B. 480 7-101

Sika Contracts Ltd v Gill (BL) and Closeglen Properties (1978) 9 Build. L.R. 11 .... 9-005, 9-037, **9-038**, 9-039

Sill v Thomas (1839) 8 C. & P. 762 6-021

Silver v Ocean Steamship Co Ltd [1930] 1 K.B. 416; 99 L.J.K.B. 104; 142 L.T. 244; 46 T.L.R. 78; 73 S.J. 849; 35 Com.Cas.140; 18 Asp. M.L.C. 74; 35 H.L. Rep. 49 .... 8-024, 8-044

Simaan General Contracting Co v Pilkington Glass Ltd (No.2) [1988] Q.B. 758; [1988] 2 W.L.R. 761; [1988] 1 All E.R. 791; (1988) 132 S.J. 463 CA 5-011

Simmons v Liberal Opinion Ltd, Re, Dunn [1911] 1 K.B. 966; 80 L.J.K.B. 617; 104 L.T. 264; 27 T.L.R. 278; 55 S.J. 315 .... 9-066, 9-076

Simmons v Pennington [1955] 1 W.L.R. 183; [1955] 1 All E.R. 240; 99 S.J. 146 CA **6-024**

Simner v New India Ass.Co Ltd Times, July 21, 1994 8-213

Simons v Patchett (1857) 7 R. & B. 568; 26 L.J.Q.B. 195; 29 L.T. (O.S.) 88; 3 Jur. (N.S.) 742; 5 W.R. 500 .... 9-079, **9-083**

Simpole v Chee [2013] EWHC 4444 (Ch) 2-083
Simpson and Miller v British Industries Trust Lyd (1923) 39 T.L.R. 286 7-062
Simpson v Eggington (1855) 10 Exch. 845; 24 L.J.Ex. 312; 19 J.P. 776 . . . . 2-084, 2-085
Simpson v Grant & Bowman Ltd [2006] Eu. L.R. 933 11-025
Simpson v Swan (1812) 3 Camp. 291 7-062
Sims & Co v Midland Ry Co [1913] 1 K.B. 103; 82 L.J.K.B. 67; 107 L.T. 700; 29 T.L.R.
    81; 18 Com.Cas.44. . . . . 4-004, 4-006, 6-013
Sims v Bond (1833) S B & Ad. 389; 2 N. & M.K.B. 608 . . . . 8-068, 8-098
Sims v Brittain (1832) 4 B. & Ad. 375; 1 N. & M.K.B. 594 5-012
Sims v Landray [1894] 2 Ch. 318; 63 L.J.Ch. 535; 70 L.T. 530; 42 W.R. 621; 8 R. 582 2-014
Sinclair Goldsmith v Minero Peru Comercial [1978] E.G.D. 194; (1978) 248 E.G. 1015 . . . . **7-012**,
                                                                                            7-024
Sinclair Investment Holdings SA v Versailles Trade Finance Ltd (In Administrative
    Receivership) [2007] EWHC 915 (Ch); [2007] 2 All E.R. (Comm) 993; (2007–08) 10
    I.T.E.L.R. 58 . . . . 8-225, 9-135
Sinclair Investments (UK) Ltd v Versailles Trade Finance Ltd (In Administration) [2011]
    EWCA Civ 347; [2012] Ch. 453; [2011] 3 W.L.R. 1153; [2011] 4 All E.R. 335; [2011]
    Bus. L.R. 1126; [2011] 2 B.C.L.C. 501; [2011] W.T.L.R. 1043; [2011] 2 P. & C.R. DG6 5-012,
                                                             6-042, **6-045**, 6-080, 6-085, 6-087
Sinclair Investments (UK) Ltd v Versailles Trade Finance Ltd [2010] EWHC 1614 (Ch) 6-042
Sinclair v Brougham [1914] A.C. 398 . . . . 2-020, 3-011
Sinclair v Broughton and Government of India (1882) 47 L.T. 170, P.C 9-124
Sinfra Aktiengesellscheft v Sinfra Ltd [1939] 2 All E.R. 675 . . . . . . 1-006, 10-024, 12-013, 12-017,
                                                                                            12-024
Singer Mfg. Co v London & South Weestern Ry [1894] 1 Q.B. 833; 63 L.J.Q.B. 411; 70
    L.T. 172; 42 W.R. 347; 10 T.L.R. 246; 38 S.J. 238; 10 R. 152. 1-033
Singla v Stockler [2012] EWHC 1176 (Ch); [2012] B.P.I.R. 1061; (2012) 162 N.L.J. 713 . . . 6-051
Singularis Holdings Ltd v Daiwa Capital Markets Europe Ltd [2017] EWHC 257 (Ch);
    [2017] 1 Lloyd''s Rep. 226. 8-214
Sino Channel Asia Ltd v Dana Shipping and Trading PTE Singapore [2016] EWHC 1118
    (Comm); [2016] 2 Lloyd's Rep. 97. . . . . 2-079, 3-032
Siqueira v Noronha [1934] A.C. 332; 103 L.J.P.C. 63; 151 L.T. 6 6-098
Siu Yin Kwan v Eastern Insurance Co Ltd [1994] 2 A.C. 199; [1994] 2 W.L.R. 370; [1994]
    1 All E.R. 213; [1994] 1 Lloyd's Rep. 616; [1994] C.L.C. 31; (1994) 144 N.L.J. 87;
    (1994) 138 S.J.L.B. 26 . . . . 8-068, 8-069, 8-072, 8-079, **8-082**, 8-094, 8-098, 8-109, 9-016
Sivewright v Richardson (1852) 19 L.T. (O.S.) 10 6-024
Skelton v Wood (1894) 71 L.T. 616; 15 R. 130 . . . . 6-065, 6-071
Skelwith (Leisure) Ltd v Armstrong [2015] EWHC 2830 (Ch); [2016] Ch. 345; [2016] 2
    W.L.R. 144 8-087
Skinner & Co v Weguelin, Eddowes & Co (1882) C. & E. 12 5-011
Skinner v Andrews & Hall (1910) 26 T.L.R. 340; 54 S.J. 340 7-014
Skinner v Trustee of the Property of Reed; sub nom. sub nom. Skinner v Vick and Partners
    [1967] Ch. 1194; [1967] 3 W.L.R. 871; [1967] 2 All E.R. 1286; (1967) 111 S.J. 477. . 7-086, 9-025,
                                                                                            9-026
Sky Petroleum Ltd v VI.P. Petroleum Ltd [1974] 1 W.L.R. 576; [1974] 1 All E.R. 954;
    (1973) 118 S.J. 311. 7-046
Skylight Maritime SA v Ascot Underwriting Ltd [2005] EWHC 15 (Comm); [2005]
    P.N.L.R. 25; (2005) 155 N.L.J. 139. . . . . 9-076, 9-079
Skyring v Greenwood (1825) 4 B. & C. 281; 6 Dow. & Ry. K.B. 401 6-097
Slingsby v District Bank Ltd [1932] 1 K.B. 544; 101 L.J.K.B. 281; 146 L.T. 377; 48
    T.L.R. 114; 37 Com.Cas.39 CA 8-044
Smally v Smally (1700) 1 Eq.Ca.Abr. 6 . . . . 2-011, 2-012
Smart v Sandars (1846) 3 C.B. 380; 136 E.R. 152 . . . . 1-046, 7-073
Smart v Sandars (1848) 5 C.B. 895; 136 E.R. 1132 . . . . 1-046, 10-007, **10-014**
SMC Electronics v Akhter Computers Ltd [2001] 1 B.C.L.C. 433 3-021
Smethurst v Mitchell (1859) 1 E. & E. 623; 28 L.J.Q.B. 241; 33 L.T. (O.S.) 9; 5 Jur. (N.S.)
    978; 7 W.R. 226. . . . . 8-103, 8-104, 8-119, 8-121
Smith (WH) & Son v Clinton & Harris (1908) 99 L.T. 840; 25 T.L.R. 34 7-068
Smith v Baker (1873) L.R. 8 C.P. 350; 42 L.J.C.P. 155; 28 L.T. 637; 37 J.P. 567 2-083
Smith v Bennett (1874) 30 L.T. 100 . . . . 6-111, 6-112
Smith v Bush (Eric S); Harris v Wyre Forest District Council [1990] 1 A.C. 831; [1989] 2
    W.L.R. 790; (1989) 133 S.J. 597; [1989] 2 All E.R. 574 HL 6-029, 6-030, 6-058, 9-117
Smith v Butler [2012] EWCA Civ 314; [2012] Bus. L.R. 1836; [2012] B.C.C. 645 . . . . **3-029**

Smith v Chadwick (1884) 9 App. Cas. 187 HL 8-050
Smith v Cologan (1788) 2 T.R. 188n 2-096, 6-020
Smith v Cox [1940] 2 K.B. 558; [1940] 3 All E.R. 546; 109 L.J.K.B. 732; 163 L.T. 330;
    56 T.L.R. 899; 84 S.J. 598 2-062
Smith v Ferrand (1827) 7 B.C. 191; 9 Dow & Ry. K.B. 803; 5 L.J. (O.S.) K.B. 335 .. 8-103, **8-106**,
    8-121
Smith v General Motor Cab Co Ltd; sub nom. Bates-Smith v General Motor Cab Co Ltd
    [1911] A.C. 188; 80 L.J.K.B. 839; 105 L.T. 113; 27 T.L.R. 370; 55 S.J. 439; 4 B.W.C.C.
    249. 1-033
Smith v Hamilton [1951] Ch. 174; 66 T.L.R. (Pt. 2) 937; [1950] 2 All E.R. 928; 94 S.J.
    724. 9-026
Smith v Hammond (1833) 6 Sim 10 .... **7-104**
Smith v Henniker-Major & Co [2002] EWCA Civ 762; [2003] Ch. 182; [2002] 3 W.L.R.
    1848; [2002] B.C.C. 768; [2002] 2 B.C.L.C. 655; (2002) 99(37) L.S.G. 36 CA...... 2-081, 2-090,
    2-091, 2-092, 8-037
Smith v Hughes (1870–71) L.R. 6 Q.B. 597; [1861-73] All E.R. Rep. 632; (1871) 19 W.R.
    1059. 8-050
Smith v Hull Glass Co (1852) 11 C.B. 897; 7 Ry. & Com.Cas.287; 21 L.J.C.P. 106; 16 Jur.
    595. .... **2-083**
Smith v Jenning's Case (1610) Case 97 10-027
Smith v Keal (1882) 9 Q.B.D. 340; 47 L.T. 142; 46 J.P. 615; 31 W.R. 76 .... 8-196, 9-125
Smith v Land and House Property Corp (1884) 28 Ch.D. 7 .... **3-032**
Smith v Lascelles (1788) 2 T.R. 187 .... 6-003, 6-007, 6-012, 6-029
Smith v Lindo (1858) 5 C.B. (N.S.) 587; 27 L.J.C.P. 335; 32 L.T. (O.S.) 62; 4 Jur. (N.S.)
    974; 6 W.R. 748 .... **7-070**
Smith v Lyon (1813) 3 Camp. 465 9-010
Smith v M'Guire (1858) 3 H. & N. 554; 1 F. & F. 199; 27 L.J.Ex. 465; 31 L.T. (O.S.) 248;
    6 W.R. 726. .... 1-045, **3-023**, 3-028, 8-010, 8-029, 8-043, 8-053
Smith v MacGowan [1938] 3 All E.R. 447; 159 L.T. 278; 82 S.J. 605 3-023
Smith v Plummer (1818) 1 B. & A. 575; 106 E.R. 212 .... 9-003, 10-007
Smith v Price (1862) 2 F. & F. 748 6-012
Smith v Prosser [1907] 2 K.B. 735; 77 L.J.K.B. 71; 97 L.T. 155; 23 T.L.R. 597; 51 S.J.
    551 .... 8-018, 8-045, 8-130
Smith v Redford (1872) 19 Grant 274 6-098
Smith v Reed (1886) 2 T.L.R. 442 9-076
Smith v Reliance Water Controls Ltd [2003] EWCA Civ 1153; [2004] E.C.C. 38; [2003]
    Eu. L.R. 874 CA 11-015
Smith v Sleap (1844) 12 M. & W. 585 .... 9-105, **9-109**
Smith v Sorby (1875) 3 Q.B.D. 552n.; 30 J.P.J. 100 .... 8-221, **8-226**
Smith v Webster (1876) 3 Ch.D. 49; 45 L.J.Ch. 528; 35 L.T. 44; 40 J.P. 805; 24 W.R. 894 ... 3-023
Smith v Wheatcroft (1878) 9 Ch.D. 223; 39 L.T. 103; 27 W.R. 42 .... 8-079, 8-080
Smith-Bird v Blower [1939] 2 All E.R. 406 8-003
Smout v Ilbery 152 E.R. 357; (1842) 10 M. & W. 1 9-063
Smyth v Anderson (1849) 7 C.B. 21; 18 L.J.C.P. 109; 12 L.T. (O.S.) 450; 13 Jur. 211 . 8-103, 8-104,
    8-106, 9-020
Snell, Re (1877) 6 Ch.D. 105; 46 L.J.Ch. 627; 37 L.T. 350; 25 W.R. 823 7-094
Snelling v Snelling (John G.) Ltd [1973] Q.B. 87; [1972] 2 W.L.R. 588; [1972] 1 All E.R.
    79; 116 S.J. 217. 9-122
Snook v Davidson (1809) 2 Camp. 218 7-099
Snook v London & West Riding Investments Ltd [1967] 2 Q.B. 786; [1967] 2 W.L.R.
    1020; [1967] 1 All E.R. 518; 111 S.J. 71 CA 8-133
Snowdon v Davis (1808) 1 Taunt. 359 .... 9-105, **9-109**
So v HSBC Bank Plc [2009] EWCA Civ 296; [2009] 1 C.L.C. 503; [2009] Lloyd's Rep.
    F.C. 338. .... 1-026, 2-107, 8-180, 9-117
Soames v Spencer (1822) 1 D. & R. 32 .... 2-053, 2-074, 2-082, 2-084, 2-085
Soar v Ashwell [1893] 2 Q.B. 390; 69 L.T. 585; 42 W.R. 165; 4 R. 602 .... 9-140, **9-142**
Sobell Industries Ltd v Cory Bros & Co (Sachkogin Bros., Third Parties) [1955] 2 Lloyd's
    Rep. 82 .... 9-021, 9-022, **9-034**, 9-039
Soblomsten, The (1866) L.R. 1 A. & E. 293; 36 L.J. Adm. 5; 15 L.T. 393; 15 W.R. 591; 2
    Mar. L.C. 436 4-004
Societa Esplosivi Industriali SpA v Ordnance Technologies (UK) Ltd (formerly SEI (UK)
    Ltd) [2007] EWHC 2875 (Ch); [2008] 2 All E.R. 622; [2008] 2 B.C.L.C. 428; [2008]
    R.P.C. 12; [2008] Bus. L.R. D37 9-120

Societe Generale (London Branch) v Geys [2012] UKSC 63; [2013] 1 A.C. 523; [2013] 2
    W.L.R. 50; [2013] 1 All E.R. 1061; [2013] I.C.R. 117; [2013] I.R.L.R. 122....... 10-004, 10-045,
    11-042, 11-057
Societe Generale de Paris v Walker (1886) 11 App.Cas.20 HL **8-217**
Societe Italo-Belge Pour le Commerce et l'Industrie SA (Antwerp) v Palm and Vegetable
    Oils (Malaysia) Sdn Bhd; The Post Chaser [1982] 1 All E.R. 19; [1981] 2 Lloyd's Rep.
    695; [1981] Com. L.R. 249.. 8-114
Society of Lloyd's v Leighs, Society of Lloyd's v Lyon; Society of Lloyd's v Wilkinson
    [1997] C.L.C. 1398; [1997] 6 Re. L.R. 289 CA.................................... 10-011
Socimer International Bank Ltd (In Liquidation) v Standard Bank London Ltd (No.2)
    [2008] EWCA Civ 116; [2008] Bus. L.R. 1304; [2008] 1 Lloyd's Rep. 558.............. 6-020
Software Incubator UK Ltd v Computer Association UK Ltd [2016] EWHC 1587 (QB);
    [2017] Bus. L.R. 245... 11-016
Solicitor, Re A [1975] Q.B. 475; [1975] 2 W.L.R. 105; [1974] 3 All E.R. 853; 118 S.J.
    737, D.C 6-069
Solicitors' Estate Agency (Glasgow) Ltd v MacIver 1993 S.L.T. 23; 1992 S.C.L.R. 804
    (2nd Div)... **7-056**
Solley v Wood (1852) 16 Beav. 370 .... **5-007**
Solloway v McLaughlin [1938] A.C. 247; [1937] 4 All E.R. 328; 107 L.J.P.C. 1; 54 T.L.R.
    69 .... 6-003, 6-078, 7-066
Solly v Rathbone (1814) 2 M. & S.298 .... 5-002, 5-004, **7-099**
Solly v Weiss (1818) & Taunt. 371; 2 Moore C.P. 420 7-014
Solomon v Barker (1862) 2 F. & F. 726; 11 W.R. 375 .... 6-019, **6-024**
Solomons v Bank of England (1791) 13 East 135n; 104 E.R. 319 .... **7-089**
Solomons v Dawes (1794) 1 Esp. 83 2-091
Soods Solicitors v Dormer [2010] EWHC 502 (QB) 8-214
Soplex Wholesale Supplies and Refson (PS) & Co v Egyptian International Foreign
    Trading Co; The Raffaella [1985] F.L.R. 123; [1985] 2 Lloyd's Rep. 36 CA .. 8-015, 8-017, 8-018,
    8-028, **8-044**, 8-050, 8-067, 9-106
Sorrell v Finch [1977] A.C. 728; [1976] 2 W.L.R. 833 HL 1-026, 3-004, 3-022, **3-032**, 8-013,
    8-067, 8-117, 8-124, **8-201**, 9-026, 9-101, **9-109**
Sorrell v Paget [1950] 1 K.B. 252; 65 T.L.R. 595; [1949] 2 All E.R. 609; 93 S.J. 631 CA 4-010
South Yorkshire Railway and River Dun Co v Great Northern Railway (1853) 9 Ex. 55 8-040
Southampton (Lord) v Brown (1827) 6 B. & C. 718; 5 L.J. (O.S.) K.B. 253 8-088
Southampton, Re; Isle of Wight & Portsmouth Improved Steam Boat Co Ltd; Bird's Case;
    sub nom. Southampton, Re, Isle of Wight & Portsmouth Improved Steam Boat Co Ex p.
    Southampton, Isle of Wight & Portsmouth Improved Steam Boat Co (1864) 4 De G.J.
    & S.200; 33 L.J. Bcy. 69; 9 L.T. 669; 10 Jur. (N.S.) 138; 12 W.R. 321 .... **9-034**
Southend-on-Sea Corp v Hodgson (Wickford) Ltd [1962] 1 Q.B. 416; [1961] 2 W.L.R.
    806; 125 J.P. 348; [1961] 2 All E.R. 46; 105 S.J. 181; 12 P. & C.R. 165; 59 L.G.R. 193
    DC.. 8-042
Southern Foundries (1926) Ltd and Federated Foundries Ltd v Shirlaw [1940] A.C. 701;
    [1940] 2 All E.R. 445; 109 L.J.K.B. 164; L.T. 251; 56 T.L.R. 637; 84 S.J. 464 HL 10-040
Southern Pacific Personal Loans Ltd, Re [2013] EWHC 2485 (Ch) 1-028
Southern v Watson [1940] 3 All E.R. 439 1-030
Southport & West Lancashire Banking Co, Re (1885) 1 T.L.R. 204 .... **8-067**
Southwark LBC v Mills [2001] 1 A.C. 1 9-120
Southwell v Bowditch (1876) 1 C.P.D. 374; 45 L.J.Q.B. 630; 35 L.T. 196; 24 W.R. 838 9-016,
    9-037, **9-038**
Sovereign Life Assce. Co, Re; Salter's Claim (1891) 7 T.L.R. 602 .... 7-014, 7-024
Sovfracht, etc. v Van Udens [1943] A.C. 203; [1943] 1 All E.R. 76; 112 L.J.K.B. 32;
    168L.T. 323; 59 T.L.R. 101; 86 S.J. 376..................................... 2-010, 10-003
Sowerby v Butcher (1834) 4 Tyr. 320; 2 Cr. & M. 368; 3 L.J.Ex. 80 9-056
Sowler v Potter [1940] 1 K.B. 271; [1939] 4 All E.R. 478; 109 L.J.K.B. 177; 162 L.T. 12;
    56 T.L.R. 142; 84 S.J. 115.. 9-095
Space Investments Ltd v Canadian Imperial Bank of Commerce Trust Co (Bahamas) Ltd
    [1986] 1 W.L.R. 1072; [1986] 3 All E.R. 75; (1986) 130 S.J. 612; (1986) 83 L.S.Gaz.
    2567.. 6-040
Spackman v Evans; sub nom. Agriculturist Insurance Co, Re; Spackman's Case (1868)
    L.R. 3 H.L. 171; 37 L.J.Ch. 752; 19 L.T. 151 .... 2-059, 2-069, 2-072
Spalding v Ruding (1846) 15 L.J.Ch. 374 .... **7-086**

Spar Shipping AS v Grand China Logistics Holding (Group) Ltd [2015] EWHC 718
(Comm); [2015] 1 All E.R. (Comm) 879; [2015] 2 Lloyd's Rep. 407; [2015] 1 C.L.C.
356 . . . . 3-007, 12-002, 12-016
Spears v Hartly (1800) 3 Esp. 81 . . . . 7-082, 7-090
Spector v Ageda [1973] 1 Ch. 30; [1971] 3 W.L.R. 498; [1971] 3 All E.R. 417; 115 S.J.
426; 22 P. & C.R. 1002 . . . . 2-013, 2-014, 6-052, 6-064
Spedding v Nevell (1869) L.R. 4 C.P. 212; 38 L.J.C.P. 133 . . . . 9-079, 9-081, **9-083**
Speed Seal Products Ltd v Paddington [1985] 1 W.L.R. 1327 6-077
Speight v Gaunt; sub nom. Re Speight; Speight v Gaunt (1883) 9 App.Cas.1; 53 L.J.Ch.
419; 50 L.T. 330; 48 J.P. 84; 32 W.R. 435 2-021
Spence (Vic) Associates v Balchin 1990 S.L.T. 10 . . . . 9-038, 9-086
Spencer v Topham (1856) 22 Beav 573; 28 L.T. (O.S.) 56; 2 Jur. (N.S.) 865 6-064
Spencer, Re; Spencer v Hart (1881) 51 L.J.Ch. 271; 45 L.T. 645; 30 W.R. 296 5-016
Sphere Drake Insurance Ltd v Euro International Underwriting Ltd [2003] EWHC 2376;
[2003] Lloyd's Rep. I.R. 525 QBD (Comm) 3-011
Spiess v Taylor (1984) 271 E.G. 196; (1984) 128 S.J. 448; (1984) 81 L.S.Gaz. 1676 CA 7-030,
7-050
Spiro v Lintern [1973] 1 W.L.R. 1002; [1973] 3 All E.R. 319; 117 S.J. 584 . . . 2-059, 2-080, 2-103,
2-109, 3-032, 8-004, 8-041, 8-128, 12-016
Spittle v Lavender (1821) 5 Moo. C.P. 270; 2 Brod. & Bing. 452 9-038
SPL Private Finance (PF1) IC Ltd v Arch Financial Products LLP [2014] EWHC 4268
(Comm) 9-121
Spooner v Browning [1898] 1 Q.B. 528; 67 L.J.Q.B. 339; 78 L.T. 98; 46 W.R. 369; 14
T.L.R. 245 . . . . **8-014, 8-021,** 8-044, **8-067**
Spooner v Sandilands (1842) Y. & C.Ch.Cas.390 10-006
Sport International Bussum B.V v Inter-Footwear Ltd [1984] 1 W.L.R. 776; [1984] 2 All
E.R. 321; (1984) 128 S.J. 383 HL 7-047, 10-042
Spread Trustee Co Ltd v Hutcheson [2011] UKPC 13; [2012] 2 A.C. 194; [2012] 2 W.L.R.
1360; [2012] 1 All E.R. 251; [2012] P.N.L.R. 1; [2012] W.T.L.R. 317; 14 I.T.E.L.R. 37
PC (Guernsey) 6-056, 6-058
Spring v Guardian Assurance Plc [1995] 2 A.C. 296; [1994] 3 W.L.R. 354; [1994] 3 All
E.R. 129; [1994] I.C.R. 596; [1994] IRLR 460; (1994) 138 S.J. (LB) 193; (1994) 144
N.L.J. 971 . . . . 6-029, 9-117
Springer v Great Western Railway Co [1921] 1 K.B. 257; 89 L.J.K.B. 1010; 124 L.T. 79;
15 Asp. M.L.C. 86 . . . . 4-004, 4-005, 4-006
Sproule v Triumph Cycle Co Ltd [1927] N.I. 83 . . . . 1-035, 1-036
Spurr v Cass; Cass v Spurr (1870) L.R. 5 QB 656; 39 L.J.Q.B. 249; 23 L.T. 409 . . . . **8-082**
St Albans City and District Council v International Computers Ltd [1996] 4 All E.R. 481;
[1997-98] Info. T.L.R. 58; [1997] F.S.R. 251; (1996) 15 Tr. L.R. 444; [1998] Masons
C.L.R. Rep. 98; (1997) 20(2) I.P.D. 20020 CA 11-016
St. Leonard's Vestry v Holmes (1885) 50 J.P. 132 2-057
Stackpole v Earle (1761) 2 Wil.K.B. 133 . . . . **7-056**
Stadium Finance Ltd v Robbins [1962] 2 Q.B. 664; [1962] 3 W.L.R. 453; [1962] 2 All
E.R. 633; 106 S.J. 369 CA 8-146, 8-147, 8-148, 8-153, 8-154
Stafford v Conti Commodity Services Ltd [1981] 1 All E.R. 691; [1981] 1 Lloyd's Rep.
466; [1981] Com. L.R. 10 6-024
Staffordshire Area Health Authority v South Staffordshire Waterworks Co [1978] 1
W.L.R. 1387; [1978] 3 All E.R. 769; (1978) 122 S.J. 331; (1978) 77 L.G.R. 17 CA 10-042
Staffs Motor Guarantee Ltd v British Motor Wagon Co Ltd [1934] 2 K.B. 305; 103
L.J.K.B. 613; 151 L.T. 396 8-147
Stag Line Ltd v Board of Trade (1950) 83 Ll.L.Rep. 356 3-035
Stag v Tyne Shiprepair Group Ltd; The Zinnia [1984] 2 Lloyd's Rep. 211; (1985) 4 Tr.L.
33 . . . . 9-006, 9-034, 9-037
Stainton v Carron Co (1857) 24 Beav. 346; 27 L.J.Ch. 89; 30 L.T. (O.S.) 299; 23 Jur.
(N.S.) 1235 6-098
Stait v Fenner [1912] 2 Ch. 504 Ch D 1-032
Standard Bank v Bank of Tokyo [1995] 2 Lloyd's Rep. 169 8-048
Standard Chartered Bank v Ceylon Petroleum Corp [2012] EWCA Civ 1049 . . . . . 12-002, 12-016,
12-017, 12-020
Standard Chartered Bank v Pakistan National Shipping Corp (No.1) [1998] 1 Lloyd's Rep.
656 CA 9-117
Standard Chartered Bank v Pakistan National Shipping Corp (No.2); Standard Chartered
Bank v Mehra [2002] UKHL 43; [2003] 1 A.C. 959; [2002] 3 W.L.R. 1547; [2003] 1

All E.R. 173; [2002] 2 All E.R. (Comm) 931; [2003] 1 Lloyd's Rep. 227; [2002] B.C.C. 846; [2003] 1 B.C.L.C. 244; [2002] C.L.C. 1330; (2003) 100(1) L.S.G. 26; (2002) 146 S.J.L.B. 258 HL 1-028, 6-003, 6-043, 8-050, 8-180, 9-119, 9-120, 9-125, 9-135
Standard Life Assurance Ltd v Oak Dedicated Ltd [2008] EWHC 222 (Comm); [2008] 2 All E.R. (Comm) 916; [2008] 1 C.L.C. 59; [2008] Lloyd's Rep. I.R. 552; [2008] P.N.L.R. 26 6-016
Standard Life Health Care Ltd v Gorman [2009] EWCA Civ 1292; [2010] I.R.L.R. 233 . . . . 7-039, 7-046
Stange & Co v Lowitz (1898) 14 T.L.R. 468 . . . . 6-071, 6-087
Staniar v Staniar (1886) 3 T.L.R. 215; 34 Ch.D. 470; 56 L.J.Ch. 581; 56 L.T. 87; 35 W.R. 286. . . . . **7-089**
Starglade Properties Ltd v Nash [2010] EWCA Civ 1314; [2011] Lloyd's Rep. F.C. 102; [2011] 1 P. & C.R. DG17 9-135
Starkey v Bank of England [1903] A.C. 114; 72 L.J.Ch. 402; 88 L.T. 244; 51 W.R. 513; 19 T.L.R. 312; 8 Com.Cas.142. . . . . 9-063, 9-064, 9-065, **9-076**, 9-081
Starlight Shipping Co v Allianz Marine and Aviation Versicherungs AG [2014] EWHC 3068 (Comm); [2015] 2 All E.R. (Comm) 747; [2014] 2 Lloyd's Rep. 579; [2014] 2 C.L.C. 503; [2015] Lloyd's Rep. I.R. 54. . . . . 8-191, 9-122
Starsin, The. See Homburg Houtimport BV v Agrosin Private Ltd 8-021, 8-029, 8-067, 9-006
State of Wyoming Syndicate, Re [1901] 2 Ch. 431; 70 L.J.Ch. 727; 84 L.T. 868; 49 W.R. 650; 17 T.L.R. 631; 45 S.J. 656; 8 Mans. 311 2-061
Statek Corp v Alford [2008] EWHC 32 (Ch); [2008] B.C.C. 266; [2008] Lloyd's Rep. F.C. 127; [2008] W.T.L.R. 1089 . . . . 6-043, 9-135
Staton v National Coal Board [1957] 1 W.L.R. 893; [1957] 2 All E.R. 667; 101 S.J. 592 8-192
Stavely v Uzielli 175 E.R. 945; (1860) 2 F. & F. 30 . . . . 10-030, **10-031**, 10-033
Stead v Thornton (1832) 3 B. & Ad. 357n; 1 L.J.K.B. 74; 110 E.R. 134 2-009
Stedman v Baker & Co (1896) 12 T.L.R. 451 . . . . **3-029**
Steedman v Drinkle [1916] 1 A.C. 275; 85 L.J.P.C. 79; 114 L.T. 248; 32 T.L.R. 231 6-013
Steele v Gourley (1887) 3 T.L.R. 772 . . . . **9-087**
Steele v M'Kinlay (1880) 5 App.Cas. 754; 43 L.T. 358; 29 W.R. 17 . . . . 8-089, 8-092, 9-053
Steele v Williams (1853) 8 Exch. 625; 22 L.J.Ex. 225; 21 L.T. (O.S.) 106; 17 J.P. 378; 17 Jur. 464; 1 C.L.R. 258. 9-105
Steere v Smith (1885) 2 T.L.R. 131 . . . . 7-030, 7-032
Steiglitz v Eglinton (1815) Holt N.P. 141 2-040
Stenning, Re [1895] 2 Ch. 433; 73 L.T. 207; 13 R. 807 . . . . **8-167**
Stephens v Badcock (1832) 3 B. & Ad. 354 . . . . 5-012, 6-112
Stephens v Elwall (1815) 4 M. & S.259 . . . . **9-125**, 9-129
Stevens v Biller (1883) 25 Ch.D. 31; 53 L.J.Ch. 249; 50 L.T. 36; 32 W.R. 419 . 1-039, 1-046, **7-086**
Stevens v Hill (1805) 5 Esp. 247 . . . . **9-114**
Stevens v Legh (1853) 2 C.L.R. 251; 22 L.T. (O.S.) 84; 2 W.R. 16 . . . . 6-100, 8-096
Stevens v Midland Counties Railway Co (1854) 10 Exch. 352; 2 C.L.R. 1300; 23 L.J.Ex. 328; 23 L.T. (O.S.) 70; 18 J.P. 713; 18 Jur. 932 9-125
Stevenson (Hugh) & Sons Ltd v Aktiengesellschaft f,r Cartonnagen Industrie [1918] A.C. 239; 87 L.J.K.B. 416; 118 L.T. 126; 34 T.L.R. 206; 62 S.J. 290. . . . . 2-010, 10-003
Stevenson v Mortimer (1778) Camp. 805 . . . . **8-167**, 9-099
Stevenson v Singh [2012] EWHC 2880 (QB) **9-076**, 9-078, 9-121
Stewart Chartering Ltd v Owners of the Ship Peppy; Stewart Offshore Services (Jersey) Ltd v Silan Maritime Co Ltd [1997] 2 Lloyd's Rep. 722 QBD (Adm Ct) 6-074, 7-051
Stewart v Aberdein (1838) 4 M. & W. 211; 1 Morn. & H. 284; 7 L.J.Ex. 292; 7 L.T. 46 . . . . . 3-026, 8-108
Stewart v Reavell's Garage [1952] 2 Q.B. 545; [1952] 1 T.L.R. 1266; [1952] 1 All E.R. 1191; 96 S.J. 314 . . . . 2-019, 5-011
Stewarts & Lloyds Ltd v Zoess *Times*, July 5, 1955 7-028
Stickney v Keeble [1915] A.C. 386; 84 L.J.Ch. 259; 112 L.T. 664 6-013
Stiedl v Enyo Law LLP [2011] EWHC 2649 (Comm); [2012] P.N.L.R. 4 6-050
Stiftung (Carl Zeiss) v Herbert Smith & Co (No.2) [1969] 2 Ch. 276; [1969] 2 W.L.R. 427; [1969] 2 All E.R. 367; (1968) 112 S.J. 1021 CA 8-154, **9-142**
Stiles v Cardiff Steam Navigation Co (1864) 33 L.J.Q.B. 310; 10 Jur. (N.S.) 1199; 12 W.R. 1080 . . . . **8-217**
Stockton v Mason [1978] 2 Lloyd's Rep. 430; [1979] R.T.R. 130 CA 2-016, 8-067
Stocznia Gdanska S.A. v Latvian Shipping Co [2001] 1 Lloyd's Rep. 537 9-121
Stolos Cia. S.A. v Ajax Insurance Co Ltd; The Admiral C [1981] 1 Lloyd's Rep. 9; [1980] Com. L.R. 4 CA 3-026

Stolt Loyalty, The [1995] 1 Lloyd's Rep. 598 CA **2-109**, 9-030
Stone & Rolls Ltd v Moore Stephens [2009] UKHL 39; [2009] 1 A.C. 1391; [2009] 3
    W.L.R. 455; [2009] 4 All E.R. 431; [2010] 1 All E.R. (Comm) 125; [2009] Bus. L.R.
    1356; [2009] 2 Lloyd's Rep. 537; [2009] 2 B.C.L.C. 563; [2009] 2 C.L.C. 121; [2009]
    Lloyd's Rep. F.C. 557; [2009] B.P.I.R. 1191; [2009] P.N.L.R. 36; (2009) 159 N.L.J.
    1218; (2009) 153(31) S.J.L.B. 28 .... 1-029, 2-025, 8-031, 8-214
Stone v Cartwright (1795) 6 Term Rep. 411; 101 E.R. 622 9-133
Stone v Reliance Mutual Insurance Society Ltd [1972] 1 Lloyd's Rep. 469 CA 8-217
Stoneham v Wyman (1901) 6 Com.Cas. 174; 17 T.L.R. 562 8-120
Stoneleigh Finance Ltd v Phillips [1965] 2 Q.B. 537; [1965] 2 W.L.R. 508; [1965] 1 All
    E.R. 513; 109 S.J. 68 CA 8-130, 8-133, 8-214
Strachan, Re, Ex p. Cooke (1876) 4 Ch.D. 123; 46 L.J. Bcy. 52; 35 L.T. 649; 41 J.P. 180;
    25 W.R. 171. .... **8-167**
Strong v Hart (1827) 6 B. & C. 160; Dow. & Ry. K.B. 189; 5 L.J. (O.S.) K.B. 82 8-121
Strongman v Sincock [1955] 2 Q.B. 525 6-023
Strover v Harrington [1988] Ch. 390; [1988] 2 W.L.R. 572; [1988] 1 All E.R. 769; (1988)
    132 S.J. 416; (1988) 56 P. & C.R. 302; [1988] 09 E.G. 61. .... **3-023**, 8-182, 8-196, **8-207**
Stubbs v Slater [1910] 1 Ch. 632; 79 L.J.Ch. 520; 102 L.T. 444 7-004
Stumore v Campbell & Co [1892] 1 Q.B. 314; 61 L.J.Q.B. 463; 66 L.T. 218; 40 W.R. 101;
    8 T.L.R. 99; 36 S.J. 90 7-057
Stupples v Stupples & Co (High Wycombe) Ltd [2012] EWHC 1226 (Ch); [2013] 1
    B.C.L.C. 729. 7-050
Style Financial Services Ltd v Bank of Scotland (No.2) 1998 S.L.T. 851; 1997 S.C.L.R.
    633; 1997 G.W.D. 7-255, OH. 6-041
Suart v Haigh (1893) 9 T.L.R. 488 .... **9-076**
Suart v Welch (1839) 4 Myl. & Cr. 305; 3 Jur. 237 .... 6-100, 6-111, **7-104**
Sudarshan Chemical Industries Ltd v Clariant Produkte (Deutschland) GmbH [2013]
    EWCA Civ 919; [2014] R.P.C. 6 1-029
Sudbrook Trading Estate Ltd v Eggleton [1983] 1 A.C. 444; [1982] 3 W.L.R. 315; [1982]
    3 All E.R. 1; (1982) 126 S.J. 512; (1982) 44 P. & C.R. 153 HL. 7-012, 7-046
Suleman v Havard [2011] EWCA Civ 764; [2011] 2 Lloyd's Rep. 283 .... 8-153, 8-154
Suleman v Shahsavari [1988] 1 W.L.R. 1181; (1988) 132 S.J. 1243; (1988) 138 N.L.J.
    241, DC 9-065, **9-083**
Summers v Solomon (1857) 7 E. & B. 579; 26 L.J.Q.B. 301; 3 Jur. (N.S.) 962; 5 W.R. 660 . **10-033**
Sun Alliance Pensions Life & Investments Services Ltd v RJL; Sun Alliance Pensions Life
    & Investments Services Ltd v Anthony Webster [1991] 2 Lloyd's Rep. 410 QBD 7-044, 9-038
Sun Life Assurance Co of Canada v CX Reinsurance Co Ltd (formerly CNA Reinsurance
    Co Ltd) [2003] EWCA Civ 283; [2004] Lloyd's Rep I.R. 58. 8-021
Suncorp Insurance & Finance v Milano Assicurazioni SpA [1993] 2 Lloyd's Rep. 225 2-068,
    2-071, 2-074, 2-078, 2-080, 2-096, 3-007, 6-005, 8-052
Sunderland Marine Insurance Co v Kearney (1851) 16 Q.B. 925; 20 L.J.Q.B. 417; 18 L.T.
    (O.S.) 33; 15 Jur. 1006 8-084
Sunrise Brokers LLP v Rodgers [2014] EWCA Civ 1373; [2015] I.C.R. 272; [2015]
    I.R.L.R. 57 6-015
Supply of Ready Mixed Concrete, Re. *See* Director General of Fair Trading v Smiths
    Concrete 1-026
Surrey Breakdown Ltd v Knight [1999] R.T.R. 84 CA 4-010
Surrey Shipping Co Ltd v Cie Continentale (France) SA; The Shackleford [1978] 1
    W.L.R. 1080; (1978) 122 S.J. 555; [1978] 2 Lloyd's Rep. 154 CA 3-032
Sutton & Co v Grey [1894] 1 Q.B. 285; 63 L.J.Q.B. 633; 69 L.T. 673; 42 W.R. 195; 10
    T.L.R. 96; 38 S.J. 77; 9 R. 106 1-042
Sutton v Tatham (1839) 10 A. & E. 27; 2 Per. & Dav. 308; 8 L.J.Q.B. 210 3-033
Swain (Frank) v Whitfield Corp Ltd (1962) 183 E.G. 479 7-005
Swain v Law Society [1983] 1 A.C. 598; [1982] 3 W.L.R. 261; [1981] 2 All E.R. 827;
    (1982) 126 S.J. 464 HL. 6-042, 6-048
Swale v Ipswich Tannery Co Ltd (1906) 11 Com.Cas. 88 .... 6-039, 6-087
Swan & Edgar Ltd v Mathieson (1910) 103 L.T. 832; 27 T.L.R. 153 .... **8-045**
Swan v North British Australasian Co Ltd (1863) 2 Hurl. & C. 175 .... 2-104, 8-130
Swan, The. *See* Bridges & Salmon Ltd v Owner of The Swan; The Swan 9-002, 9-005, 9-006,
    9-034, 9-036, 9-038, 9-044
Sweet & Pym (1800) 1 East 4 .... **7-094**
Sweeting v Pearce (1861) 9 C.B. (N.S.) 534; 30 L.J.C.P. 1095; L.T. 79; 7 Jur. (N.S.) 800; 9
    W.R. 343; 1 Mar L.C. 134; 142 E.R. 210, Ex Ch. 3-025, **3-026**, 3-037, 3-039, **3-040**, 3-069

Sweeting, Re [1898] 1 Ch. 268; 67 L.J.Ch. 159; 78 L.T. 6; 14 T.L.R. 171; 46 W.R. 242 7-056
Swift v Jewsbury and Goddard (1874) L.R. 9 Q.B. 301; 43 L.J.Q.B. 56; 30 L.T. 31; 22
   W.R. 319. . . . . 8-098, 8-198, **9-125**
Swindle v Harrison [1997] 4 All E.R. 705; [1997] P.N.L.R. 641; [1997] N.P.C. 50 CA 6-043,
   6-045
Swinfen v Chelmsford (Lord) (1860) S.H. & N. 890; 29 L.J. Ex. 382; 2 L.T. 406; 6 Jur.
   (N.S.) 1035; 8 W.R. 545 6-003
Swire v Francis (1877) 3 App.Cas. 106; 47 L.J.P.C. 18; 37 L.T. 554 . . . . 5-011, 8-176, 8-200, **8-201**
Swiss Air Transport Co Ltd v Palmer [1976] 2 Lloyd's Rep. 604 QBD 8-044
Swotbooks.com Ltd v Royal Bank of Scotland Plc [2011] EWHC 2025 (QB) 2-077
Swycher v Vakil [2002] EWCA Civ 1668 6-038
Sybron Corp v Rochem Ltd [1984] Ch. 112; [1983] 1 C.R. 80; [1983] 3 W.L.R. 713;
   [1983] 2 All E.R. 767; (1983) 127 S.J. 391; [1983] I.R.L.R. 253 CA 6-034, 6-054, **6-061**
Sycamore Bidco Ltd v Breslin [2012] EWHC 3443 (Ch) 8-215
Sykes (F&G) (Wessex) Ltd v Fine Fare Ltd [1967] 1 Lloyd's Rep. 53 CA 7-009
Sykes v Beadon (1879) 11 Ch.D. 170; 48 L.J.Ch. 522; 40 L.T. 243; 27 W.R. 464 . . . . . 6-098, 6-100
Sykes v Giles (1839) 5 M. & W. 645; 9 L.J.Ex. 106 . . . . 3-026, 3-032
Sykes v Sykes (1869–70) L.R. 5 C.P. 113 . . . . **9-125**
Synergy Health (UK) Ltd v CGU Insurance Plc (t/a Norwich Union) [2010] EWHC 2583
   (Comm); [2011] Lloyd's Rep. I.R. 500. 6-024
Tadcaster Tower Brewery v Wilson [1897] 1 Ch. 705 6-013
Tai Hing Cotton Mill Ltd v Liew Chong Hing Bank Ltd [1986] A.C. 80; [1985] 3 W.L.R.
   317; [1985] 2 All E.R. 947; [1986] F.L.R. 14; [1985] 2 Lloyd's Rep. 313 PC. 7-001
Take v BSM Marketing [2006] EWHC 1085 (QB) 6-034, 6-043
Talbot Underwriting Ltd v Nausch Hogan & Murray Inc (The Jascon 5) [2006] EWCA
   Civ 889; [2006] 2 All E.R. (Comm) 751; [2006] 2 Lloyd's Rep. 195; [2006] 1 C.L.C.
   1138; [2006] Lloyd's Rep. I.R. 531 8-079
Talbot v General Television Corp Pty Ltd [1981] R.P.C. 1, Sup Ct (Vic) 6-077
Tallentire v Ayre (1884) 1 T.L.R. 143 3-020
Tallerman v Rose (1886) 15 L.T. 450 6-012
Tamarind International Ltd v Eastern Natural Gas (Retail) Ltd [2000] C.L.C. 1397; [2000]
   Eu. L.R. 708; (2000) 97(26) L.S.G. 35 QBD (Comm Ct). 11-011, 11-016, 11-021, 11-022
Tamvaco v Simpson (1866) L.R. 1 C.P. 363; Har. & Ruth 374; 35 L.J.C.P. 196; 14 T.L.R.
   893; 13 W.R. 376; 2 Man. L.C. 383 7-094
Tanham v Nicholson (1872) L.R. 5 H.L. 561 . . . . 2-026, 8-205, 8-206, **8-207**
Tank Express A/S v Cie Financiere Belge des Petroles S.A. [1949] A.C. 76; [1949] L.J.R.
   170; [1948] 2 All E.R. 939; 93 S.J. 26; 82 Ll.L.Rep. 43 3-025
Tanner v Christian (1855) 4 E. & B. 591; 24 L.J.Q.B. 91; 1 Jur. (N.S.) 519; 3 W.R. 204; 3
   C.L.R. 1366 . . . . 9-006, 9-038
Tanner v European Bank; sub nom. Re Tanner v European Bank; Bowen v European Bank
   (1866) LR 1 Ex. 261; 4 H. & C. 398; 35 L.J.Ex. 151; 12 Jur. (N.S.) 414; 14 W.R. 675;
   14 L.T. 414. . . . . 7-103, **7-104**
Taplin v Barrett (1889) 6 T.L.R. 30 . . . . **7-032**
Taplin v Florence (1851) 10 C.B. 744; L.J.C.P. 137; 17 L.T. (O.S.) 63; 15 Jur. 402 . . . . **10-014**
Tappenbeck, Re, Ex p. Banner (1876) 2 Ch.D. 278; 45 L.J. Bcy. 73; 34 L.T. 199; 24 W.R.
   476. 7-101
Tappenden v Artus [1964] 2 Q.B. 185; [1963] 3 W.L.R. 685; [1963] 3 All E.R. 213; 107
   S.J. 572 CA. 1-033, **3-023**, 4-007, 4-008, 7-095, **7-102**
Tarbuck v Bispham (1836) 2 M. & W. 2; 6 L.J.Ex. 49; 150 E.R. 643 2-009
Targe Towing Ltd v Marine Blast Ltd. See Marine Blast Ltd v Targe Towing Ltd 2-030
Target Holdings Ltd v Redferns (No.1) [1996] A.C. 421; [1995] 3 W.L.R. 352; [1995] 3
   All E.R. 785; (1995) 139 S.J.L.B. 195; [1995] N.P.C. 136 HL 6-003, 6-043, **6-045**, 9-135
Tarn v Scanlan (Surveyor of Taxes); sub nom. WH Muller & Co (London) Ltd v Lethem
   (Inspector of Taxes) Nielsen Andersen & Co v Collins (Inspector of Taxes); WH Muller
   & Co (London) Ltd v Inland Revenue Commissioners; Tarn v Scanlan (Surveyor of
   Taxes) [1928] A.C. 34; (1927–28) 29 Ll. L. Rep. 93 HL 5-016
Tasker v Shepherd (1861) 6 H. & N. 575; 30 L.J.Ex. 207; 4 L.T. 19; 9 W.R. 476 . . . 10-019, 10-042
Tate & Sons v Hyslop (1884–85) 15 Q.B.D. 368 CA **8-207**
Taylor Fashions Ltd v Liverpool Victoria Trustee Co Ltd; Old & Campbell v Same [1981]
   Q.B. 133; [1981] 2 W.L.R. 576; [1981] 1 All E.R. 897; [1981] Com. L.R. 34; (1979)
   251 E.G. 159. 9-030
Taylor v Bowers (1876) 1 Q.B.D. 291; 46 L.J.Q.B. 39; 34 L.T. 938; 24 W.R. 499 6-100
Taylor v Brewer (1813) 1 M. & S.290 7-012

Taylor v Kymer (1832) 3 B. & Ad. 320; 1 L.J.K.B. 114 . . . . 1-022, **7-099**
Taylor v Lendey (1807) 9 East 49 . . . . **10-029**
Taylor v London & County Banking Co; London & County Banking Co v Nixon [1901] 2
   Ch. 231; 70 L.J.Ch. 477; 84 L.T. 397; 49 W.R. 451; 17 T.L.R. 413; 45 S.J. 394 8-216
Taylor v Metropolitan Railway Co [1906] 2 K.B. 55 9-106
Taylor v Plumer (1815) 3 M. & S. 562; Rose 457 . . . . 8-161, **8-167**
Taylor v Robinson (1818) 2 Moo. 730; 8 Taunt. 648 . . . . 7-078, **7-086**
Taylor v Salmon (1838) 4 Myl. & Cr. 134 6-082
Taylor v Sheppard (1835) 1 Y. & C.Ex. 271; 4 L.J.Ex.Eq. 7 8-119
Taylor v Walker [1958] 1 Lloyd's Rep. 490 . . . . . . 2-009, 2-013, 6-085, 6-087, 8-221, 8-222, **8-226**
Taylor, Stileman & Underwood, Re; sub nom. Re Taylor, Stileman & Underwood Ex p.
   Payne Collier [1891] 1 Ch. 590; 60 L.J.Ch. 525; 7 T.L.R. 262; 64 L.T. 605; 39 W.R. 417 7-094
TCB Ltd v Gray [1987] Ch. 458; [1987] 3 W.L.R. 1144; [1988] 1 All E.R. 108; [1988]
   B.C.L.C. 281; [1988] F.L.R. 116; (1987) 3 B.C.C. 503 CA 2-042
Teheran-Europe Co Ltd v Belton (ST) (Tractors) Ltd [1968] 2 Q.B. 545; [1968] 3 W.L.R.
   205; [1968] 2 All E.R. 886; (1968) 122 S.J. 501; [1968] 2 Lloyd's Rep. 37 CA 1-021, 1-041,
                            8-073, 8-078, 8-079, 9-002, 9-006, 9-016, 9-020, 9-096
Telemetrix Plc v Modern Engineers of Bristol (Holdings) Plc [1985] B.C.L.C. 213 9-121
Telewest Communications Plc v Customs and Excise Commissioners [2005] EWCA Civ
   102; [2005] S.T.C. 481; [2005] B.T.C. 5125; [2005] B.V.C. 156; [2005] S.T.I. 220;
   (2005) 102(17) L.S.G. 33 CA 1-030
Tellrite Ltd v London Confirmers Ltd [1962] 1 Lloyd's Rep. 236 . . . . 7-080, 7-082
Temperley v Black Rod Mfg. Co Ltd (1967) 71 J.P. 341 . . . . 6-086, 6-087, 6-089
Temple Legal Protection Ltd v QBE Insurance (Europe) Ltd [2009] EWCA Civ 453;
   [2010] 1 All E.R. (Comm) 703; [2009] 1 C.L.C. 553; [2009] Lloyd's Rep. I.R. 544;
   (2009) 153(14) S.J.L.B. 27 . . . . 5-011, 9-005, 10-007, 10-010, 10-011, 10-023
Templeton Insurance Ltd v Motorcare Warranties Ltd [2010] EWHC 3113 (Comm) 6-041
Tenant v Elliot (1797) 1 B. & P. 3 6-100
Tesco Supermarkets Ltd v Nattrass [1972] A.C. 153; [1971] 2 W.L.R. 1166; [1971] 2 All
   E.R. 127; 115 S.J. 285 HL 1-028, 1-029
Tetley & Co v British Trade Corp (1922) 10 Ll.L. Rep. 678 . . . . 4-005, 4-006, 4-010
Tetley v Shand (1871) 25 L.T. 658; 20 W.R. 206 . . . . 6-057, 6-065, 7-101, **7-101**
Th'l v Leask (1855) 10 Exch. 704; 24 L.J.Ex. 142; 24 L.T. (O.S.) 262; 1 Jur. (N.S.) 117; 3
   C.L.R. 317 9-017
Thacker v Hardy (1878) 4 Q.B.D. 685; 48 L.J.Q.B. 289; 39 L.T. 595; 43 J.P. 221; 25 W.R.
   158 . . . . 7-058, 7-063, 7-068
Thackwell v Barclays Bank Plc [1986] 1 All E.R. 676 9-130
Thames Valley Housing Association Ltd v Elegant Homes (Guernsey) Ltd [2011] EWHC
   1288 (Ch); [2011] 22 E.G. 102 (C.S.); [2011] N.P.C. 54 9-121
Thermascan Ltd v Norman [2009] EWHC 3694 (Ch); [2011] B.C.C. 535 6-081
Thomas v Da Costa (1818) 8 Taunt. 345; 2 Moore C.P. 386 6-100
Thomas v Edwards (1836) 2 M. & W. 215; Tyr. & Gr. 872 8-120
Thomas v Hewes (1834) 2 C. & M. 519; 4 Tyr. 335 . . . . 9-061, 9-090
Thomas v Lewis; sub nom. Thomas v Oxley (1878) 4 Ex.D. 18; 48 L.J.Q.B. 7; 39 L.T.
   669; 43 J.P. 56; 4 Asp. M.L.C. 51; 27 W.R. 111 . . . . **3-029**
Thomas v Pearce [2000] F.S.R. 718 CA 9-135
Thompson v Bell (1854) 10 Exch. 10; 23 L.J.Ex. 321; 23 L.T. (O.S.) 178; 2 W.R. 559; 2
   C.L.R. 1212 . . . . 8-200, **8-201**
Thompson v British Berna Motor Lorries Ltd (1917) 33 T.L.R. 187 7-032
Thompson v Cartwright; sub nom. Re Cartwright, Thompson v Cartwright (1863) 2 De
   G.J.A. Sm. 10; 2 New Rep. 549 8-214
Thompson v Finden (1829) 4 C. & P. 158 8-120
Thompson v Meade (1891) 7 T.L.R. 698 6-066
Thompson v Palmer (1933) 49 C.L.R. 507 2-106
Thompson v Renwick Group Plc [2014] EWCA Civ 635; [2014] 2 B.C.L.C. 97; [2014]
   P.I.Q.R. P18 . . . . 1-030, 2-031, 2-033
Thompson, Ripon & Co v Thomas (1896) 11 T.L.R. 304 . . . . 7-030, 7-032
Thompson's Trustee in Bankruptcy v Heaton [1974] 1 W.L.R. 605; [1974] 1 All E.R.
   1239; (1974) 118 S.J. 295 6-081
Thomson (DC) & Co Ltd v Deakin [1952] Ch. 646; [1952] 2 T.L.R. 105; [1952] 2 All E.R.
   361; CA 9-121
Thomson v Clydesdale Bank [1893] A.C. 282; 62 L.J.P.C. 91; 69 L.T. 156; 1 R. 255 9-142

Thomson v Davenport (1829) 9 B. & C. 78 Dan. & Ll 278; 4 Man. & Ry. K.B. 110; 7 LJ
    (O.S.) K.B. 134. . . . . 8-068, 8-104, 8-105, 8-120, 8-121, 9-016
Thomson v Thomson (1802) 7 Ves.470 6-100
Thomson, Re; Thomson v Allen [1930] 1 Ch. 203; 99 L.J.Ch. 156; 142 L.T. 253 6-081
Thorndike v Hunt; Browne v Butter (1859) 3 De G. & J. 563; 28 L.J.Ch. 417; 32 L.T.
    (O.S.) 346; 5 Jur. (N.S.) 879; 7 W.R. 246. 8-162
Thorne v Deas 4 Johns N.Y.R. 84 (1809) 6-029
Thorne v Heard & Marsh [1895] A.C. 495; 64 L.J.Ch. 652; 73 L.T. 291; 44 W.R. 155; 11
    T.L.R. 464; 11 R. 254 2-026
Thornton Hall v Wembley Electrical Appliances Ltd [1947] 2 All E.R. 630 CA **6-061**, 7-050,
                                                                                          8-223
Thornton Springer v NEM Insurance Co Ltd [2000] 2 All E.R. 489; [2000] 1 All E.R.
    (Comm) 486; [2000] C.L.C. 975; [2000] Lloyd's Rep. I.R. 590; (2000) 97(13) L.S.G.
    42; (2000) 144 S.J.L.B. 1478 8-050
Thornton v Fehr & Co (1935) 51 Ll.Rep. 330 . . . . 1-041, 9-016
Thornton-Smith v Motor Union Insurance Co Ltd (1913) 30 T.L.R. 139 8-217
Thorpe (Bernard) & Partners v Flannery (1977) 244 E.G. 129 CA 7-061
Thurman v Best (1907) 97 L.T. 239 3-032
Tickel v Short (1751) 2 Ves.Sen. 239 6-098
Tiedemann and Ledermann FrÈres, Re [1899] 2 Q.B. 66; 68 L.J.Q.B. 852; 81 L.T. 191 2-063,
                                                                           2-070, 2-084, 9-091
Tigana v Decoro Ltd [2003] EWHC 23; [2003] E.C.C. 23; [2003] Eu. L.R. 189 QBD 11-032,
                                                                                          11-043
Tigress, The (1863) B. & L. 38; 32 L.J.P.M. & A. 97; 8 L.T. 117; 11 W.R. 538; 1 Mar. L.C.
    323; 1 New Rep. 449; 9 Jur. (N.S.) 361 7-101
Tigris International NV v China Southern Airlines Co Ltd [2014] EWCA Civ 1649 . . . 6-038, 8-223
Tilley v Thomas (1867) L.R. 3 Ch.App. 61; 17 L.T. 422; 32 J.P. 180; 16 W.R. 166 6-013
Tilley's Will Trusts, Re [1967] Ch. 1179; [1967] 2 W.L.R. 1533; [1967] 2 All E.R. 303;
    111 S.J. 237. 6-040
Times Travel (UK) Ltd Nottingham Travel (UK) Ltd v Pakistan International Airlines
    Corp [2017] EWHC 1367 (Ch). 7-009
Tindall v Powell (1858) 32 L.T. (O.S.) 8; 4 Jur. (N.S.) 944; 6 W.R. 850 6-092
Tingley v Miller [1917] 2 Ch. 144; 86 L.J.Ch. 625; 116 L.T. 482; 33 T.L.R. 369; 61 S.J.
    478. 10-003
Titan Steel Wheels Ltd v Royal Bank of Scotland Plc [2010] EWHC 211 (Comm) 6-058
Tito v Waddell (No.2) Tito v Attorney General [1977] Ch. 106; [1977] 2 W.L.R. 496;
    [1977] 3 All E.R. 129 . . . . 6-062, 6-063, 6-065, 7-046
Titshall v Qwerty Travel Ltd [2011] EWCA Civ 1569; [2012] 2 All E.R. 627; [2012] 2 All
    E.R. (Comm) 347; [2011] C.T.L.C. 219 . . . . 1-038, 9-033
Tobin v Broadbent (1947) 75 C.L.R. 378 3-011
Todd v Emly (1841) 8 M. & W. 505; H. & W. 144; 10 L.J.Ex. 161; 151 E.R. 1832 9-087
Todd v Robinson (1825) 1 Ry. & M. 217 . . . . **8-044**
Toepfer v Warinco A.G. [1978] 2 Lloyd's Rep. 569 . . . . **3-032**
Tom Hoskins Plc v EMW Law (A Firm) [2010] EWHC 479 (Ch); (2010) 160 N.L.J. 584 . . . 6-012,
                                                                                          6-024
Tomlinson (A.) (Hauliers) Ltd v Hepburn [1966] A.C. 451; [1966] 2 W.L.R. 453; [1966] 1
    All E.R. 418; [1966] 1 Lloyd's Rep. 309 HL. 2-067, 8-072, 9-011
Tomson v Judge (1885) 3 Drew 306; 3 Eq. Rep. 850; 24 L.J.Ch. 785; 25 L.T. (O.S.) 233; 1
    Jur. (N.S.) 583; 3 W.R. 561. 6-069
Tonge v Ward (1869) 21 L.T. 480 . . . . **8-196**
Toplis v Grane (1839) 5 Bing N.C. 636; 7 Arn. 110; 7 Scott 620; 9 L.J.C.P. 180 . . . . . . 7-059, 7-068
Toppin v Healey (1863) 11 W.R. 466; 1 New Rep. 326 . . . . **7-051**
Torre Asset Funding Ltd v Royal Bank of Scotland Plc [2013] EWHC 2670 (Ch); (2013)
    157(35) S.J.L.B. 41 . . . . 1-047, 6-001, 6-020, 6-021, 6-056
Torrington (Viscount) v Lowe (1868) L.R. 4 C.P. 26; 38 L.J. 121; 19 L.T. 316; 17 W.R. 78 . . **8-088**
Touche v Metropolitan Railway Warehousing Co (1871) L.R. 6 Ch.App. 671; 40 L.J.Ch.
    496. 2-064
Toulmin v Millar (1887) 58 L.T. 96; 3 T.L.R. 836 . . . . 7-029, **7-032**, 7-036
Tower Hamlets LBC v British Gas Corp *Times*, December 14, 1984 CA 10-042
Towers v Premier Waste Management Ltd [2011] EWCA Civ 923; [2012] B.C.C. 72;
    [2012] 1 B.C.L.C. 67; [2012] I.R.L.R. 73. 6-087
Townsends Carriers Ltd v Pfizer Ltd (1977) 33 P. & C.R. 361; (1977) 121 S.J. 375; (1977)
    242 E.G. 813. . . . . 2-026, 3-029, 8-207

Townson v Wilson (1808) 1 Camp. 396 9-105
Trading and General Investment Corp v Gault, Armstrong & Kemble Ltd; The Okeanis
   [1986] 1 Lloyd's Rep. 195 . . . . 3-026, 5-004, 5-011
Transcontinental Underwriting Agency S.R.L. v Grand Union Ins.Co Ltd [1987] 2 Lloyd's
   Rep. 409; [1987] 1 F.T.L.R. 35. . . . . 9-011, 9-037, 9-039
Transplanters (Holdings Co) Ltd, Re [1958] 1 W.L.R. 822; [1958] 2 All E.R. 711; 102 S.J.
   547 . . . . 2-026, **2-034**
Transvaal Delagoa Bay Investment Co v Atkinson [1944] 1 All E.R. 579 . . . . . 8-068, 9-102, 9-104,
                                                                                              9-106
Transvaal Lands Co v New Belgium (Transvaal) Land and Development Co [1914] 2 Ch.
   488; 84 L.J.Ch. 94; 112 L.T. 965; 31 T.L.R. 1; 59 S.J. 27; 21 Mans. 364 6-065
Tranton v Astor (1917) 33 T.L.R. 383 9-006
Trench v Harrison (1849) 17 Sim. 111 6-082
Trevelyan v White (1839) 1 Beav. 588 6-068
Tribe v Taylor (1876) 1 C.P.D. 505 . . . . **7-032**
Trickett v Tomlinson (1863) 13 C.B. (N.S.) 663; 1 New Rep. 273; 7 L.T. 678 . . . . **8-045**
Triffit Nurseries v Salads Etcetera Ltd [2000] 1 All E.R. (Comm) 737; [2000] 2 Lloyd's
   Rep. 74; [2000] 1 B.C.L.C. 761 CA 1-021, 1-022, 8-167, 10-002, 10-011
Trimble v Goldberg [1906] A.C. 494 PC (Transvaal) 6-081
Trimble v Hill (1879) 5 App.Cas. 342; 49 L.J.P.C. 49; 42 L.T. 103; 28 W.R. 479 PC 10-029
Trinder (John E) & Partners v Haggis [1951] W.N. 416; 95 S.J. 546; (1951) 158 E.G. 4
   CA 7-019, 7-036
Triplex Safety Glass Co Ltd v Scorah [1938] Ch. 211; [1937] 4 All E.R. 693; 107 L.J.Ch.
   91; 157 L.T. 576; 54 F.L.R. 90; 81 S.J. 982; 55 R.P.C. 21 6-077
Trollope (G.) & Sons v Caplan [1936] 2 K.B. 382; 105 L.J.K.B. 819; 155 L.T. 365; 52
   T.L.R. 630; [1936] 2 All E.R. 842; 41 Com.Cas. 325 . . . . 7-035, 10-045
Trollope (G.) & Sons v Martyn Bros [1934] 2 K.B. 436 7-035
Tronson v Dent (1853) 8 Moo. P.C. 419 . . . . 4-004, 4-005
Trott v National Discount Co (1900) 17 T.L.R. 37 8-200
Trueman v Loder (1840) 11 A. & E. 589; 3 Per. & Dav. 267; 9 L.J.Q.B. 165; 4 Jur. 934 10-033
Trustee of the Property of FC Jones & Sons (A Firm) v Jones [1997] Ch. 159; [1997] 1
   W.L.R. 51; [1996] 3 W.L.R. 703; [1996] 4 All E.R. 721; [1996] B.P.I.R. 644; (1996)
   93(19) L.S.G. 29; (1996) 140 S.J.L.B. 123 CA 8-066, 8-161, 10-021
Trustor AB v Smallbone (No.4) [2001] 1 W.L.R. 1177; [2001] 3 All E.R. 987; [2002]
   B.C.C. 795; [2001] 2 B.C.L.C. 436; (2001) 98(20) L.S.G. 40; (2001) 151 N.L.J. 457;
   (2001) 145 S.J.L.B. 99. . . . . 1-030, 6-042
Tsang Chuen v Li Po Kwai [1932] A.C. 715 8-135
Tsavliris Salvage (International) Ltd v Guangdong Shantou Overseas Chinese Materials
   Marketing Co; The Pa Mar; sub nom. Guangdong Shantou Overseas Chinese Materials
   Marketing Co v Tsavliris Salvage (International) Ltd [1999] 1 Lloyd's Rep. 338 QBD
   (Adm Ct). 4-008
Tucker v Linger (1883) 8 App.Cas. 508 3-035
Tudor Marine Ltd v Tradax Export SA; The Virgo [1976] 2 Lloyd's Rep. 135 CA 9-016, **9-038**
Tudor v Hamid [1988] 1 E.G.L.R. 251; (1987) 137 N.L.J. 79 CA 9-025, **9-109**
Tufnell v Costain (Richard) Ltd (1968) 209 E.G. 705 7-032
Tufton Associates v Dilmun Shipping [1992] 1 Lloyd's Rep. 71 7-030
Tugwell v Heyman (1812) 3 Camp. 298 4-010
Tupper v Foulkes (1861) 9 C.B. (N.S.) 797; 2 F. & F. 166; 30 L.J.C.P. 214; 3 L.T. 741; 7
   Jur. (N.S.) 709; 9 W.R. 349. 2-082
Turnbull v Garden (1869) 38 L.J.Ch. 331; 20 L.T. 218 . . . . 6-029, 6-085, 6-085, **6-089**
Turner v Burkinshaw (1867) L.R. 2 Ch.App. 488; M.L.T. 83; 15 W.R. 753 . . . . 6-090, 6-092, 6-103
Turner v Deane (1849) 3 Ebl. 836; 6 Dow. & L. 669; 18 L.J.Ex. 343 . . . . **7-089**
Turner v Goldsmith [1891] 1 Q.B. 544; 60 L.J.Q.B. 247; 64 L.T. 301; 39 W.R. 547; 7
   T.L.R. 233 . . . . 10-042, **10-046**
Turner v Hockey (1887) 56 L.J.Q.B. 301 9-129
Turner v Letts (1855) 20 Beav. 185 . . . . **7-089**
Turner v Reeve (1901) 17 T.L.R. 592 . . . . 7-004, 7-005
Turner v Sampson (1911) 27 T.L.R. 200 . . . . 8-147, 8-153, **8-158**
Turner v Thomas (1871) L.R. 6 C.P. 610; 40 L.J.C.P. 271; 24 L.T. 879; 19 W.R. 1170 8-109
Turpin v Bilton (1843) Man. & G. 455; 6 Scott N.R. 447; 12 L.J.C.P. 167; 7 Jur. 950 . 6-012, **6-024**
Turton v London & North Western Railway (1850) 15 L.T. (O.S.) 92 8-212
Turvey v Dentons (1923) Ltd [1953] 1 Q.B. 218; [1952] 2 T.L.R. 996; [1952] 2 All E.R.
   1025; 96 S.J. 852; [1952] T.R. 471; 45 R.A.I.T. 772; 31 A.T.C. 470 8-166

Twentieth Century Fox Film Corp v Newzbin Ltd [2010] EWHC 608 (Ch); [2010] E.C.C.
   13; [2010] E.C.D.R. 8; [2010] E.M.L.R. 17; [2010] F.S.R. 21; (2010) 154(14) S.J.L.B.
   30; [2011] Bus. L.R. D49 9-120
Twentieth Century Fox Film Corp v Sky UK Ltd [2015] EWHC 1082 (Ch) 9-120
Twine v Bean's Express Ltd [1946] 1 All E.R. 202; 62 T.L.R. 458; 175 L.T. 131 8-193
Twinsectra Ltd v Yardley [2002] UKHL 12; [2002] 2 A.C. 164; [1999] Lloyd's Rep. Bank.
   438; [2000] Lloyd's Rep. P.N. 239; (2000) 1 W.T.L.R. 527 CA 8-162, 9-135
Tyler v Dairy Supply Co (1908) 98 L.T. 867; 72 J.P. 132; 21 Cox C.C. 612; 6 L.G.R. 422 . . . **2-026**
Tyler, Re; Graves v King; sub nom. Tyler's Fund Trusts Re; Graves v King [1967] 1
   W.L.R. 1269; 111 S.J. 794; [1967] 3 All E.R. 389 6-069
Tyrrell v Bank of London (1862) 10 H.L. Cas. 26; 31 L.J.Ch. 369; 6 L.T.; 8 Jur. (N.S.)
   849; 10 W.R. 359 . . . . 6-042, 6-068, 6-081, 6-082
UBAF Ltd v European American Banking Corp; The Pacific Colocotronis [1984] Q.B.
   713; [1984] 2 W.L.R. 508; [1984] 2 All E.R. 226; (1984) 128 S.J. 243; [1984] 1 Lloyd's
   Rep. 258 CA. 1-029, 2-023, 8-198
UBS AG (London Branch) v Kommunale Wasserwerke Leipzig GmbH [2014] EWHC
   3615 (Comm). 6-039, 8-185, 8-208, 8-214, 8-223, 8-224
UCB Home Loans Corp Ltd v Soni [2013] EWCA Civ 62 8-024
Udell v Atherton (1861) 7 H. & N. 172; 30 L.J.Ex. 337; 4 L.T. 797; 7 Jur. (N.S.) 777 8-185
Ultra Processor, The (1983) Lloyd's Maritime Law Newsletter, September 15, 1983 6-024
Ultraframe (UK) Ltd v Fielding [2005] EWHC 1638; [2006] F.S.R. 17 . 6-038, 6-042, 6-043, 9-135
Umbro International Ltd v Revenue and Customs Commissioners [2009] EWHC 438
   (Ch); [2009] S.T.C. 1345 . . . . 1-036, 11-013
Unaoil Ltd v Amona Ranhill Consortium Sdn Bhd [2012] EWHC 1595 (Comm) 3-016
Underwood (AL) Ltd v Bank of Liverpool; Same v Barclays Bank [1924] 1 K.B. 775; 93
   L.J.K.B. 690; 131 L.T. 271; 40 T.L.R. 302; 68 S.J. 716; 29 Com.Cas. 182 . . . . 3-011, 8-023, 8-039,
   8-050, 8-063, 8-077
Underwood v Nicholls (1855) 17 C.B. 239; 25 L.J.C.P. 79; 26 L.T. (O.S.) 106; 4 W.R. 153 . . 3-025,
   3-026
Underwood, Son & Piper v Lewis [1894] 2 Q.B. 306; 64 L.J.Q.B. 60; 70 L.T. 833; 42
   W.R. 517; 10 T.L.R. 465; 38 S.J. 479; 9 R. 440 7-050
Unilever Plc v Chefaro Proprietaries Ltd (Discovery) [1994] F.S.R. 135 CA 9-120
Union Accident Insurance Co, Re (Costs) [1972] 1 W.L.R. 640; [1972] 1 All E.R. 1105;
   [1972] 1 Lloyd's Rep. 340 10-018
Union Bank of Australia v McClintock [1922] 1 A.C. 240; 91 L.J.P.C. 108; 126 L.T. 588 . . . . **2-083**
Union Carbide Corp v Naturin Ltd [1987] F.S.R. 538 CA 6-077
Union Corp Ltd v Charrington & Brodrick (1902) 19 T.L.R. 129; 8 Com.Cas. 99 3-036
Union Credit Bank Ltd v Mersey Docks and Harbour Board [1899] 2 Q.B. 205; 68
   L.J.Q.B. 842; 81 L.T. 44; 4 Com.Cas. 227 . . . . 8-130, 8-135, 9-126, 9-129
Union Transport Finance Ltd v British Car Auctions Ltd [1978] 2 All E.R. 385; (1977)
   246 E.G. 131 CA. 9-129, 9-131
Union v Murray Aynsley [1898] A.C. 693; 67 L.J.P.C. 123 9-142
Unique Mariner, The [1978] 1 Lloyd's Rep. 438 . . . . **3-029**, 4-004, 4-008, **4-013**, **8-045**
United Africa Co Ltd v Saka Owoade [1955] A.C. 130; [1955] 2 W.L.R. 13; [1957] 3 All
   E.R. 216; 99 S.J. 26; [1954] 2 Lloyd's Rep. 607, P.C. **8-194**
United Australia Ltd v Barclays Bank Ltd [1941] A.C. 1; [1940] 4 All E.R. 20; 109
   L.J.K.B. 919; 164 L.T. 139; 57 T.L.R. 13; 46 Com.Cas. 1 . . . . . . 2-050, 2-056, 8-112, 8-119, 8-223
United Bank of Kuwait Ltd v Hammoud [1988] 1 W.L.R. 1051; [1988] 3 All E.R. 418;
   (1988) 132 S.J. 1388 CA. 3-022, 3-031, 4-007, 8-021, **8-044**
United Dominions Trust Ltd v Western; Romanay (BS) (Trading as Romanay Care Sales),
   Third Party [1976] Q.B. 513; [1976] 2 W.L.R. 64; [1975] 3 All E.R. 1017; 119 S.J. 792
   CA 8-130
United Kingdom Mutual Steamship Assurance Association v Nevill (1887) 19 Q.B.D.
   110; 56 L.J.Q.B. 522; 35 W.R. 746; 2 T.L.R. 658; 6 Asp. M.L.C. 226n 8-079, **8-082**
United Pan Europe Communications NV v Deutsche Bank AG [2000] 2 B.C.L.C. 461 CA . . 6-042,
   6-077, 6-080
United Scientific Holdings Ltd v Burnley BC; Cheapside Land Development Co Ltd v
   Messels Service Co [1978] A.C. 904; [1977] 2 W.L.R. 806; [1977] 2 All E.R. 62; 75
   L.G.R. 407; (1977) 33 P. & C.R. 220; (1977) 243 E.G. 43; 121 S.J. 223 HL 6-013
United Sterling Corp Ltd v Felton and Mannion [1973] F.S.R. 409; [1974] R.P.C. 162;
   [1974] I.R.L.R. 314 Ch D 6-077
Universal Steam Navigation Co v McKelvie [1923] A.C. 492; 92 L.J.K.B. 647; 129 L.T.
   395; 39 T.L.R. 480; 67 S.J. 593; 16 Asp.M.L.C. 184; 28 Com.Cas. 353 . 9-036, 9-037, **9-038**, 9-096

University of Nottingham v Fishel [2000] EWHC 2221 (QB); [2000] I.C.R. 1462; [2000]
I.R.L.R. 471; [2001] R.P.C. 22; [2000] Ed. C.R. 505; [2000] E.L.R. 385; (2001) 24(2)
I.P.D. 24009 QBD 6-034, 6-074, 6-080
Universo Insurance Co of Milan v Merchants Marine Insurance Co [1897] 2 Q.B. 93; 66
L.J.Q.B. 564; 76 L.T. 748; 45 W.R. 625; 13 T.L.R. 432; 8 Asp. M.L.C. 279; 2 Com.Cas.
180. 6-026
Unwin v Wolseley (1787) 1 T.R. 674; 99 E.R. 1314 9-034
Uppington v Bullen (1842) 2 Dr. & War. 184; 1 Com. & L. 291 6-070
Upsdell v Stewart (1793) Peake 255 7-005
Uxbridge Permanent Benefit Building Society v Pickard [1939] 2 K.B. 248; [1939] 2 All
E.R. 344; 108 L.J.K.B. 757; 160 L.T. 407; 55 T.L.R. 579; 83 S.J. 297 . . 8-063, 8-176, 8-182, **8-194**
Uzinterimpex JSC v Standard Bank Plc [2008] EWCA Civ 819; [2008] Bus. L.R. 1762;
[2008] 2 Lloyd's Rep. 456; [2008] 2 C.L.C. 80 . . . . 9-136, 9-141
Vale (J) & Co v Van Oppen & Co Ltd (1921) 37 T.L.R. 367 3-020
Vale of Neath and South Wales Brewery Company, Re Morgan's Case (1849) 1 De G. &
Sm. 750; 63 E.R. 1280 1-028
Valpy v Sanders (1848) 5 C.B. 887; 17 L.J.C.P. 249; 11 L.T. (O.S.) 20; 12 Jur. 483 2-083
Van Praagh v Everidge [1903] 1 Ch. 434 . . . . 3-023, 3-032, 10-007, 10-012
Vane v Vane (1872–73) L.R. 8 Ch.App. 383 8-210
Varden v Parker (1798) 2 Esp. 710 . . . . 6-012, 6-025, 6-100
Various Claimants v Barclays Bank Plc [2017] EWHC 1929 (QB) 8-178
Various Claimants v Institute of the Brothers of the Christian Schools [2012] UKSC 56;
[2013] 2 A.C. 1; [2012] 3 W.L.R. 1319; [2013] 1 All E.R. 670; [2013] I.R.L.R. 219;
[2013] E.L.R. 1; [2013] P.I.Q.R. P6; (2012) 162 N.L.J. 1505; (2012) 156(45) S.J.L.B.
31 . . . . 8-178, 8-179
Varverakis v Compagnia de Navegacion Artico SA; The Merak [1976] 2 Lloyd's Rep. 250
CA 7-017
Vaughan v Moffatt (1868) 38 L.J.Ch. 144 . . . . **8-158**
Vehicle and General Insurance Co Ltd v Elmbridge Insurances [1973] 1 Lloyd's Rep. 325,
MCLC. 6-048
Velos Group Ltd v Harbour Insurance Services Ltd [1997] 2 Lloyd's Rep. 461, CC
(Central London). 5-016
Venning v Bray (1862) 2 B. & S. 502; 31 L.J.Q.B. 181; 6 L.T. 327; 26 J.P. 364; 8 Jur.
(N.S.) 1039; 10 W.R. 561 . . . . **10-029**
Verderame v Commercial Union Ass.Co *Times,* April 2, 1992 CA 6-028
Verschures Creameries Ltd v Hull & Netherlands SS Co Ltd [1921] 2 K.B. 608; 91
L.J.K.B. 39; 125 L.T. 165 . . . . 2-056, 2-074, **2-100**, 8-114
Versloot Dredging BV v HDI Gerling Industrie Versicherung AG [2014] EWCA Civ 1349;
[2015] Q.B. 608; [2015] 2 W.L.R. 1063; [2015] 1 Lloyd's Rep. 32; [2014] 2 C.L.C.
590; [2015] Lloyd's Rep. I.R. 115. . . . . 8-050, 8-097
Vestergaard Frandsen S/A (now called MVF3 APS) v Bestnet Europe Ltd [2013] UKSC
31; [2013] 1 W.L.R. 1556; [2013] 4 All E.R. 781; [2013] I.C.R. 981; [2013] I.R.L.R.
654; [2013] E.M.L.R. 24; [2013] R.P.C. 33; (2013) 157(21) S.J.L.B. 31 6-038
Viasystems (Tyneside) Ltd v Thermal Transfer (Northern) Ltd [2005] EWCA Civ 1151;
[2005] 4 All E.R. 181; [2005] I.R.L.R. 983 8-179
Vick v Vogle-Gapes Ltd [2006] EWHC 1665 (QB); (2006) 150 S.J.L.B. 917 . . . . . . 11-051, 11-056
Vine v National Dock Labour Board [1957] A.C. 488; [1957] 2 W.L.R. 106; [1956] 3 All
E.R. 939; 101 S.J. 86; [1956] 2 Lloyd's Rep 567 HL. 7-047
Vinogradoff, Re; Allen v Jackson [1935] W.N. 68; 179 L.T.J. 274 2-015
Vistafjord, The. *See* Norwegian American Cruises v Paul Mundy; Visafjord, The 8-205, 8-206
Vlassopulos (N&T) Ltd v Ney Shipping Ltd; The Santa Carina [1977] 1 Lloyd's Rep. 478
CA 1-046, 8-026, 9-006, 9-016, 9-034, **9-046**
VLM Holdings Ltd v Ravensworth Digital Services Ltd [2013] EWHC 228 (Ch); [2014]
F.S.R. 9 . . . . 2-103, 8-029, 8-130
Vogel v Kohnstamm (R. & A.) Ltd [1973] Q.B. 133; [1971] 3 W.L.R. 537; [1971] 2 All
E.R. 1428; 115 S.J. 773 . . . . 1-020, 1-035
Von Essen Hotels 5 Ltd v Vaughan [2007] EWCA Civ 1349 . . . . 3-032, 8-207
Von Traubenberg v Davies, Turner & Co Ltd [1951] 2 Lloyd's Rep. 462 CA **6-024**
VSH Ltd v BKS Air Transport Ltd and Stevens [1964] 1 Lloyd's Rep. 460 9-038
VTB Capital Plc v Nutritek International Corp [2013] UKSC 5; [2013] 2 A.C. 337; [2013]
2 W.L.R. 398; [2013] 1 All E.R. 1296; [2013] 1 All E.R. (Comm) 1009; [2013] 1
Lloyd's Rep. 466; [2013] B.C.C. 514; [2013] 1 B.C.L.C. 179; [2013] 1 C.L.C. 15 . . . 1-028, 6-042,
8-069

Vulcan Car Agency Ltd v Fiat Motors Ltd (1915) 32 T.L.R. 73 7-014
Vynior's Case (1609) 8 Co. Rep. 81b; 77 E.R. 597 10-024
W Nagel (a firm) v Pluczenik Diamond Company NV [2017] EWHC 1750 (Comm);
    [2017] 2 Lloyd's Rep. 215 . . . . . . 10-042, **10-045**, 11-013, 11-017, 11-019, 11-022, 11-023, 11-051
Waddington & Sons v Neale & Sons (1907) 96 L.T. 786; 23 T.L.R. 464 . . . . 8-151, 9-128
Wah Tat Bank Ltd v Chan Cheng Kum; sub nom. Wah Tat Bank Ltd and Oversea-Chinese
    Banking Corp Ltd v Chan Cheng Kum [1975] A.C. 507; [1975] 2 W.L.R. 475; [1975] 2
    All E.R. 257; [1975] 2 Lloyd's Rep. 62; 119 S.J. 151 PC (Sing) 9-120
Wake v Harrop (1862) 1 H. & C. 202; 31 L.J. Ex. 451; 7 L.T. 96; 8 Jur. (N.S.) 845; 10
    W.R. 626; 1 Mar. L.C. 247; 158 E.R. 859. 9-040
Wakefield v Duckworth [1915] 1 K.B. 218; 84 L.J.K.B. 335; 112 L.T. 130; 31 T.L.R. 40;
    59 S.J. 91. 9-003
Wakefield v Newbon (1844) 6 Q.B. 276; 13 L.J.Q.B. 258; 3 L.T. (O.S.) 160; 8 Jur. 735 7-089,
                                                                                            9-104, 9-105
Waldo v Martin (1825) 4 B. & C. 319; 2 C. & P. 1; 6 Dow. & Ry. K.B. 364 7-056
Waldy v Gray (1875) L.R. 20 Eq. 238; 44 L.J.Ch. 394; 32 L.T. 531; 23 W.R. 676 . . . . 8-214, 8-217
Walker and Gould v King (1897) 13 T.L.R. 270 6-070
Walker Crips Stockbrokers Ltd v Savill [2007] EWHC 2598 (QB) 1-042
Walker v Baird [1892] A.C. 491; 61 L.J.P.C. 92; 67 L.T. 513 9-124
Walker v Birch (1795) 6 T.R. 258 . . . . **7-086**
Walker v Great Western Railway Co L.R. 2 Ex. 228; 36 L.J. Ex. 123; 16 L.T. 327; 15 W.R.
    769 . . . . **3-029**, 4-007
Walker v Nightingale; sub nom. Walker v Gascoigne (1726) 4 Bro. P.C. 193; 2
    Eq.Cas.Abr. 161 . . . . **7-056**
Walker v Rostron (1842) 9 M. & W. 411; 11 L.J.Ex. 173 . . . . **9-113**, **9-114**, 10-010
Walker v South Eastern Railway; Smith v South Eastern Railway (1870) L.R. 5 C.P. 640;
    39 L.J.C.P. 346; 23 L.T. 14 2-056
Walker v Stones [2001] 2 W.L.R. 623; [2000] 4 All E.R. 412 CA 6-056, 6-058
Walker, Fraser and Steele v Fraser's Trustees 1910 S.C. 222 . . . . 7-030, 7-032
Walker, Re [1905] 1 Ch. 160; 74 L.J.Ch. 86; 91 L.T. 713 CA 2-009
Wallace v Kelsall (1840) 7 M. & W. 264; 8 Dow. 1. 849; H. & W. 25; 10 L.J.Ex. 12; 4 Jur.
    1064; 151 E.R. 765 2-046
Wallace v Tellfair (1786) 2 T.R. 188n 6-029
Wallace v Woodgate (1824) R. & M. 193; 1 C. & P. 575 7-093
Wallace, Re; Ex p. Wallace (1884) 14 Q.B.D. 22; 54 L.J.Q.B. 293; 51 L.T. 551; 1 Morr.
    246; 22 W.R. 66; 1 T.L.R. 17 . . . . **3-015**
Waller v Holmes; sub nom. Waller v Holmes; Re Mead & Daubeny (1860) 1 John. & H.
    239; 30 L.J.Ch. 24; 25 J.P. 483; 6 Jur. (N.S.) 1367; 9 W.R. 32; 3 L.T. 289 7-099
Wallersteiner v Moir; Moir v Wallersteiner (No.2) [1975] Q.B. 373; [1975] 2 W.L.R. 389;
    [1975] 1 All E.R. 849; 119 S.J. 97 CA 6-107, 6-108, 7-060, 7-062
Walsh v Shanahan [2013] EWCA Civ 411; [2013] 2 P. & C.R. DG7 . . . . 6-038, 6-077
Walsh v Whitcomb (1797) 2 Esp. 565 . . . . 10-007, 10-024
Walsham v Stainton (1863) 1 De G.J. & S.678; 3 New Rep. 56; 33 L.J.Ch. 68; 9 L.T. 357;
    9 Jur (N.S.) 1261; 12 W.R. 63 . . . . 6-042, 6-098
Walter v James (1871) L.R. 6 Ex. 124; 40 L.J.Ex. 104; 24 L.T. 188; 19 W.R. 472 . . . . 2-087, **2-088**,
                                                                                            9-100
Ward (Alexander) & Co Ltd v Samyang Navigation Co Ltd [1975] 1 W.L.R. 673; [1975] 2
    All E.R. 424; 119 S.J. 319; [1975] 2 Lloyd's Rep. 1 HL 2-061, 2-091, 10-017, 10-021
Ward v Carttar (1865) 14 App.Cas. 437 6-111
Ward v Carttar (1865) L.R. 1 Eq. 29; 25 Beav. 171; 55 E.R. 860 . . . . **6-112**
Ward v Sharp (1884) 53 L.J.Ch. 313; 50 L.T. 557; 32 W.R. 584 . . . . 6-062, 6-064, 6-098
Warehousing and Forwarding Co of East Africa Ltd v Jafferali & Sons [1964] A.C. 1;
    [1963] 3 W.L.R. 489; [1963] 3 All E.R. 571; 107 S.J. 700 PC. 2-051, 2-078, 2-084, 2-087
Waring v Favenck (1807) 1 Camp. 85 . . . . 8-101, 8-104
Warlow v Harrison (1859) 1 E. & E. 309; [1843-60] All E.R. Rep. 620; 29 L.J.Q.B. 14; 1
    L.T. 211; 6 Jur. (N.S.) 66; 8 W.R. 95; 120 E.R. 925, Ex.Ch. 7-062, **9-034**, 10-010, **10-029**
Warmingtons v McMurray (1937) 52 T.L.R. 381 7-050
Warner v M'Kay (1836) 1 M. & W. 591; 2 Gale 86; Tyr. & Cr. 965; 5 L.J.Ex. 276 8-112
Warr v Jones (1876) 24 W.R. 695 9-080
Warren (t/a On-line Cartons and Print) v Drukkeri Flack BV [2014] EWCA Civ 993 11-051
Warren & Co v Agdeshman (1922) 38 T.L.R. 588 10-042
Warren v Henlys [1948] W.N. 449; [1948] 2 All E.R. 935; 92 S.J. 706 8-192
Warren v Sutton (Henry) & Co [1976] 2 Lloyd's Rep. 276 CA 6-024

Warrick v Warrick (1745) 3 Atk. 291 . . . . 8-209, 8-211
Warwick Rural DC v Miller-Mead; sub nom. Miller-Mead v Warwick Rural DC [1962]
   Ch. 441; [1962] 2 W.L.R. 284; [1962] 1 All E.R. 212; 126 J.P. 143; 60 L.G.R. 29; 105
   S.J. 1124 CA 2-057, 2-061
Warwick v Slade (1811) 3 Camp. 127 . . . . **7-070**
Waters v Monarch Fire and Life Ins.Co (1856) S.E. & B. 870; 25 L.J.Q.B. 102; 26 L.T.
   (O.S.) 217; 2 Jur. (N.S.) 375; 4 W.R. 245; 119 E.R. 705 9-011
Waters v Shaftesbury (1866) 14 L.T. 184 . . . . 6-062, 6-072
Watersheds Ltd v Simms [2009] EWHC 713 (QB) 7-028
Watson v Davies [1931] 1 Ch. 455; 100 L.J.Ch. 87; 144 L.T. 545 . . . . . . 2-051, 2-084, 2-087, **2-088**
Watson v King (1815) 4 Camp. 272; 1 Stark 121 . . . . 10-007, 10-032
Watson v Lyon (1855) 7 De G.M. & G. 299; 24 L.J.Ch. 754; 25 L.T. (O.S.) 230; 3 W.R.
   543 . . . . 7-088, **7-094**
Watson v Rodwell (1879) 11 Ch.D. 150; 48 L.J.Ch. 209; 39 L.T. 614; 43 J.P. 542; 27 W.R.
   265. 6-098
Watson v Swann (1862) 11 C.B. (N.S.) 756; 31 L.J.C.P. 210 . . . . 2-062, 2-067
Watt v Grove (1805) 2 Sch.& Lef. 492 6-072
Watteau v Fenwick [1893] 1 Q.B. 346; 67 L.T. 831; 56 J.P. 839; 41 W.R. 222; 9 T.L.R.
   133; 37 S.J. 117; 5 R. 143 . . . . 3-005, 8-043, 8-068, 8-077, **8-082**, 8-136
Watts v Christie (1849) 11 Beav. 546; 18 L.J.Ch. 173; 13 L.T. (O.S.) 297; 13 Jur. 845 7-089
Waugh v Clifford (HB) & Sons Ltd [1982] Ch. 374; [1982] 2 W.L.R. 679; [1982] 1 All
   E.R. 1095 CA 1-025, 3-004, **3-032**, 8-015, 8-021, 8-028, **8-045**, 8-048, 8-053
Wauton v Coppard [1899] 1 Ch. 92; 79 L.T. 467; 47 W.R. 72; 43 S.J. 28 8-096
Way & Waller Ltd v Ryde [1944] 1 All E.R. 9 7-036
Way & Waller Ltd v Verrall [1939] 3 All E.R. 533; 161 L.T. 86; 83 S.J. 675 7-035
Way v Latilla [1937] 3 All E.R. 759; 81 S.J. 786 . . . . 7-004, 7-005, **7-012**
Weall, Re (1889) 42 Ch.D. 674; 58 L.J.Ch. 713; 61 L.T. 238; 37 W.R. 779; 5 T.L.R. 681 5-010
Weare v Brimsdown Lead Co (1910) 103 L.T. 429 7-042
Webb v Smith (1885) 30 Ch.D. 192; 55 L.J.Ch. 343; 53 L.T. 737; 1 T.L.R. 235 . . . . . . 7-086, **9-114**
Webb, Re [1894] 1 Ch. 73; 63 L.J.Ch. 145; 70 L.T. 318 6-098
Webster v British Empire Mutual Life Assurance Co (1880) 15 Ch.D. 169; 49 L.J.Ch. 769;
   43 L.T. 229; 28 W.R. 818 6-108
Weddall v Barchester Healthcare Ltd [2012] EWCA Civ 25; [2012] I.R.L.R. 307 8-178
Wedderburn v Wedderburn (1838) 4 My. & Cr. 41 6-097
Wedlake v Hurley (1830) 1 C. & J. 83; L. & Welsh 330 . . . . 6-112, 9-114
Weeks v Goode; sub nom. Wicks v Good (1859) 6 C.B. (N.S.) 367; 33 L.T. (O.S.) 93 . . . . . . **7-094**
Weeks v Propert (1873) L.R. 8 C.P. 427; 42 L.J.C.P. 129; 21 W.R. 676 . . . . 9-069, **9-076**, 9-079
Weidner v Hoggett (1876) 1 C.P.D. 533; 35 L.T. 368 . . . . 9-037, 9-038
Weigall & Co v Runciman & Co (1916) 85 L.J.K.B. 1187; 115 L.T. 61; 13 Asp. M.L.C.
   463 . . . . **3-020**, 6-010
Weiner v Gill; Same v Smith [1906] 2 K.B. 574 . . . . 8-126, 8-157
Weiner v Harris [1910] 1 K.B. 285; 79 L.J.K.B. 342; 101 L.T. 647; 26 T.L.R. 96; 54 S.J.
   81; 15 Com.Cas. 39. . . . . 1-036, 8-145, **8-157**, 8-158
Weir v Bell; sub nom. Weir v Barnett, Bell, etc (1878) 3 Ex.D. 238; 47 L.J.Q.B. 704; 38
   L.T. 929; 26 W.R. 746 . . . . 8-098, 9-133
Weir, Re; Hollingworth v Willing (1888) 58 L.T. 792 8-217
Welburn v Dibb Lupton Broomhead [2002] EWCA Civ 1601; [2003] B.P.I.R. 768; [2003]
   P.N.L.R. 28 CA 9-013
Welch v Bank of England [1955] Ch. 508; [1955] 2 W.L.R. 757; [1955] 1 All E.R. 811; 99
   S.J. 236 . . . . 2-059, 8-041
Weld-Blundell v Stevens [1920] A.C. 956; 89 L.J.K.B. 705; 123 L.T. 593; 36 T.L.R. 640;
   64 S.J. 529. 6-019
Wellesley Partners LLP v Withers LLP [2015] EWCA Civ 1146; 163 Con. L.R. 53; [2016]
   P.N.L.R. 19; [2016] C.I.L.L. 3757 6-018
Wells & Croft Re, Ex p. Official Receiver (1895) 72 L.T. 359; 11 T.L.R. 300; 2 Mans. 41;
   15 R. 169. 7-062
Wells v Devani [2016] EWCA Civ 1106; [2017] 2 W.L.R. 1391 . . . . 7-004, 7-007
Wells v Minister of Housing and Local Government [1967] 1 W.L.R. 1000; 131 JJ.P. 431;
   [1967] 2 All E.R. 1041; 111 S.J. 519 CA 8-042
Wells v Smith [1914] 3 K.B. 722; 83 L.J.K.B. 1614; 111 L.T. 809; 30 T.L.R. 623 . . . . 8-214, 8-217
Wells v Wells [1914] P. 157; 83 L.J.P. 81; 111 L.T. 399; 30 T.L.R. 545; 58 S.J. 555 7-006
Welsh Development Agency v Export Finance Co Ltd [1992] B.C.L.C. 148; [1992] B.C.C.
   270 CA 1-037, 8-069, 9-121

Welsh Irish Ferries Ltd; The Ugland Trailer, Re [1986] Ch. 471; [1985] 3 W.L.R. 610;
  1985 P.C.C. 303; (1985) 129 S.J. 683; [1985] 2 Lloyd's Rep. 372 7-077
Welstead v Levy (1831) 1 M. & Rob. 138 9-010
Wemys v Greenwood, Cox and Hammersley (1827) 5 L.J. (O.S.) K.B. 257 6-100
Wentworth v Lloyd (1863) 32 Beav. 467 . . . . 6-068, 6-070
Wessex Dairies Ltd v Smith [1935] 2 K.B. 80; 104 L.J.K.B. 484; 153 L.T. 185; 51 T.L.R.
  439 . . . . 6-034, 6-038, 6-061
West London Commercial Bank v Kitson (1883) 12 Q.B.D. 157; (1884) 13 Q.B.D. 360
  CA 9-061, 9-064, 9-117
West London Commercial Bank v Kitson (1884) 13 Q.B.D. 360; 53 L.J.K.B. 345; 50 L.T.
  656; 32 W.R. 757 CA 9-069
West of England & South Wales District Bank Ex p. Dale & Co (1879) 11 Ch.D. 772; 48
  L.J.Ch. 600; 40 L.T. 712; 27 W.R. 815 6-041
West of England Bank v Batchelor (1882) 51 L.J.Ch. 199; 46 L.T. 132; 30 W.R. 364 7-088
West of England Ship Owners Mutual Protection and Indemnity Association
  (Luxembourg) v Hellenic Industrial Development Bank SA [1999] 1 Lloyd's Rep. 93;
  [1998] C.L.C. 1431 3-022
West Yorkshire Darracq Agency Ltd (In Liquidation) v Coleridge [1911] 2 K.B. 326 KBD . . 10-013
Westdeutsche Landesbank Girozentrale v Islington LBC Kleinwort Benson Ltd v
  Sandwell BC [1996] A.C. 669; [1996] 2 W.L.R. 802; [1996] 2 All E.R. 961; [1996] 5
  Bank. L.R. 341; [1996] C.L.C. 990; (1996) 160 J.P. Rep. 1130; (1996) 146 N.L.J. 877;
  (1996) 140 S.J.L.B. 136 HL 5-012, 6-107
Wester Moffat Colliery v Jeffrey 1911 S.C. 346 8-111
Western Digital Corp v British Airways Plc [2000] 2 Lloyd's Rep. 142 1-036
Western Fish Products Ltd v Penwith D.C. [1981] 2 All E.R. 204; (1978) 122 S.J. 471;
  (1978) 38 P. & C.R. 7 CA 8-042
Weston's Case, Re West Jewell Tin Mining Co (1879) 10 Ch.D. 579; 48 L.J.Ch. 425; 40
  L.T. 43; 27 W.R. 310 . . . . **6-089**
Westport (No.3), The [1966] 1 Lloyd's Rep. 342; 116 N.L.J. 754 7-084
Westwood v Bell (1815) 4 Camp. 349; Holt N.P. 122 . . . . 7-082, 7-098, 7-099
Whaley Bridge Calico Printing Co v Green (1879) 5 Q.B.D. 109; 49 L.J.Q.B. 326; 41 L.T.
  674; 44 J.P. 185; 28 W.R. 351 . . . . 6-035, 8-223
Wharton v Walker (1825) 4 B. & C. 163; 6 Dow. & Ry. K.B. 288; 3 L.J. (O.S.) K.B. 183 9-113
Wheeler (Arthur) & Co Re; Trustee v Kirby & Grainger (1933) 102 L.J.Ch. 341; [1933]
  B. & C.R. 124 . . . . 6-041, 8-167
Wheeler & Wilson Mfg. Co v Shakespear (1869) 39 L.J.Ch. 36 1-036
Wheen v Smithmann European Homes Ltd June 20, 2000 CA 7-050
Whitcomb v Minchin (1820) 5 Madd. 91 . . . . **6-070**
White Ex p.; Re Neville; sub nom. Towle (John) & Co v White (1873) 29 L.T. 78 . . . . 1-036, 1-043
White Horse Distillers Ltd v Gregson Associates Ltd [1984] R.P.C. 61 Ch D 9-120
White v Bayley (1861) 10 C.B. (N.S.) 227; previous proceedings 2 F.&F. 385 6-111
White v Benekendorff (1873) 29 L.T. 475 7-101
White v Cuyler (1795) 6 T.R. 176; 1 Esp. 200 8-084
White v Jones [1995] 2 A.C. 207; [1995] 2 W.L.R. 187; [1995] 1 All E.R. 691; [1995] 3
  F.C.R. 51; (1995) 145 N.L.J. 251; (1995) 139 S.J.L.B. 83; [1995] N.P.C. 31 HL 6-024, 6-029,
                                                                             6-034
White v Lincoln (Lady) (1803) 8 Ves. 363 . . . . 6-092, 7-050
White v Proctor (1811) 4 Taunt. 209 . . . . 2-014, 3-032, **5-007**
White v Turnbull Martin & Co (1898) 3 Com.Cas.183; 78 L.T. 726; 14 T.L.R. 401; 8 Asp.
  M.L.C. 406 CA 7-044
Whitechurch (George Ltd v Cavanagh; sub nom. Cavanagh v Whitechurch (George) Ltd
  [1902] A.C. 117; 71 L.J.K.B. 400; 85 L.T. 349; 50 W.R. 218; 17 T.L.R. 746; 9 Mans.
  351 . . . . 8-021, 8-024
Whitcomb v Jacob (1710) 1 Salk. 160 8-167
Whitehaven Joint Stock Banking Co v Reed (1886) 2 T.L.R. 353; 54 L.T. 360 . . . . 9-076, 9-079
Whitehead (Patrick Whitehead Partnership) v Jenks & Cattell Engineering Ltd [1999] Eu.
  L.R. 827 QBD 11-043
Whitehead & Co Ltd v Watt [1902] 1 Ch. 835 9-025
Whitehead v Howard (1820) 2 B. & B. 372; 5 Moore C.P. 105 6-100
Whitehead v Lord (1852) 7 Exch. 691; 21 L.J.Ex. 239; 19 L.T. (O.S.) 113 10-022
Whitehead v Taylor (1839) 10 A. & E. 210; 2 Per. & Dow. 367; 9 L.J.Q.B. 65; 4 Jur. 247 . . . **2-061**,
                                                                       2-088, 2-100
Whitehead v Tuckett (1812) 15 East 400 8-024

Whitehom Bros v Jordan [1981] 1 W.L.R. 246; [1981] 1 All E.R. 267; (1980) 125 S.J. 167
  HL 6-019
Whitehorn Bros v Davison [1911] 1 K.B. 463; 80 L.J.K.B. 425; 104 L.T. 234 .... 8-146, 8-154
Whiteley Insurance Consultants (A Firm), Re [2008] EWHC 1782 (Ch); [2009] Bus. L.R.
  418; [2009] Lloyd's Rep. I.R. 212 9-085
Whitfield v South Eastern Railway (1858) E.B. & E. 115; 27 L.J.Q.B. 229; 31 L.T. (O.S.)
  113; 4 Jur. (N.S.) 688; 6 W.R. 545 8-196
Whitley Partners Ltd, Re (1886) 32 Ch.D. 337; 55 L.J.Ch. 540; 54 L.T. 912; 34 W.R. 505;
  2 T.L.R. 541 .... 2-017, 2-022, 2-036, 8-087
Whitmar Publications Ltd v Gamage [2013] EWHC 1881 (Ch) 6-077
Whittaker v Forshaw [1919] 2 K.B. 419; 88 L.J.K.B. 989; 121 L.T. 320; 83 J.P. 210; 35
  T.L.R. 487; 63 S.J. 608; 17 L.G.R. 457; 26 Cox. C.C. 475 .... **3-023**
Whittle Movers Ltd v Hollywood Express Ltd [2009] EWCA Civ 1189; [2009] 2 C.L.C.
  771; [2010] C.I.L.L. 2804; (2009) 153(44) S.J.L.B. 33 7-009
Whitwell v Perrin; sub nom. The Feliza; Whitwell v Perren (1858) 4 C.B. (N.S.) 412; 31
  L.T. (O.S.) 134; 7 L.T. 509 .... 8-120, 9-046
Whurr v Devenish (1904) 20 T.L.R. 385 8-096
Wickham v Wickham (1855) 2 K. & J. 478 1-042
Wickman Machine Tool Sales Ltd v Schuler (L) AG [1974] A.C. 235; [1973] 2 W.L.R.
  683; [1973] 2 All E.R. 39; 117 S.J. 340; [1973] 2 Lloyd's Rep. 53 .... 6-001, 10-042
Wilde v Gibson (1848) 1 H.L.Cas.605; 12 Jur. 527 8-096
Wilder v Pilkington [1956] J.P.L. 739 9-109
Wilkie v Scottish Aviation Ltd 1956 S.C. 198 .... 7-005, **7-012**
Wilkinson (AL) Ltd v Brown [1966] 1 W.L.R. 194; [1966] 1 All E.R. 509; 109 S.J. 955;
  [1965] C.L.Y. 26 CA 7-019, 7-021
Wilkinson v Alston (1879) 48 L.J.Q.B. 733; 41 L.T. 394; 44 J.P. 35; 4 Asp. M.L.C. 191
  CA 7-032
Wilkinson v Coverdale (1793) 1 Esp. 74 6-028
Wilkinson v General Accident Fire and Life Insurance Co Ltd [1967] 2 Lloyd's Rep. 182,
  Assizes (Manchester) **3-029, 8-067**, 8-217
Wilkinson v Martin 173 E.R. 373; (1837) 8 Car. & P. 1 Assizes **7-032**
Wilkinson v North Suburban Properties Ltd [1959] E.G.D. 218 CA 6-100
Wilkinson v O'Neil (1961) 181 E.G. 137 CA 7-019
Wilkinson v West Coast Capital [2005] EWHC 3009 (Ch); [2007] B.C.C. 717 6-081
Wilks v Back (1802) 2 East 142 8-084
Williams v Allsup (1861) 10 C.B. (N.S.) 417; 30 L.J.C.P. 353; 4 L.T. 550; 8 Jur. (N.S.) 57;
  1 Mar L.C. 87 8-133
Williams v Barton [1927] 2 Ch. 9; [1927] All E.R. Rep. 751; 71 S.J. 370; 96 L.J.Ch. 355;
  137 L.T. 294; 43 T.L.R. 446 7-006
Williams v Central Bank of Nigeria [2014] UKSC 10; [2014] A.C. 1189; [2014] 2 W.L.R.
  355; [2014] 2 All E.R. 489; [2014] W.T.L.R. 873; 16 I.T.E.L.R. 740; (2014) 164(7596)
  N.L.J. 16 .... 6-040, 6-043, 9-135
Williams v Evans (1866) L.R. 1 Q.B. 352; 35 L.J.Q.B. 111; 13 L.T. 753; 30 J.P. 692; 14
  W.R. 330 .... **3-026**, 6-007
Williams v Everett (1811) 14 East. 582 .... **9-114**
Williams v Lister & Co (1913) 109 L.T. 699 7-062
Williams v Mason (1873) 28 L.T. 232; 37 J.P. 264; 21 W.R. 386 8-198
Williams v Millington (1788) 1 H.Bl. 81 .... **7-086, 9-035**
Williams v Natural Life Health Foods Ltd [1998] 1 W.L.R. 830; [1998] 2 All E.R. 577;
  [1998] B.C.C. 428; [1998] 1 B.C.L.C. 689; (1998) 17 Tr. L.R. 152; (1998) 95(21)
  L.S.G. 37; (1998) 148 N.L.J. 657; (1998) 142 S.J.L.B. 166 HL . 1-028, 6-029, 8-176, 8-180, 8-182,
                                                     9-117, 9-119, 9-120
Williams v North China Insurance Co (1876) 1 C.P.D. 757; 35 L.T. 884; 3 Asp. M.L.C.
  342 .... 2-053, 2-091—2-093
Williams v Pott (1871) L.R. 12 Eq. 149; 40 L.J.Ch 775 .... 6-110, 6-111, **6-112**
Williams v Redcard Ltd [2011] EWCA Civ 466; [2011] 4 All E.R. 444; [2011] Bus. L.R.
  1479; [2013] B.C.C. 689; [2011] 2 B.C.L.C. 350; [2011] 2 E.G.L.R. 67; [2011] 25 E.G.
  106; [2011] 19 E.G. 96 (C.S.); (2011) 161 N.L.J. 635; [2011] 2 P. & C.R. DG11 1-029
Williams v Stevens (1866) L.R. 1 P.C. 352; 12 Jur. (N.S.) 952 6-080
Williams v Trye (1854) 18 Beav. 366; 2 Eq. Rep. 766; 23 L.J.Ch. 860; 18 Jur. 442; 2 W.R.
  314 6-098
Williams v Williams (1881) 17 Ch. D. 437 9-142
Williams v Williams and Nathan [1937] 2 All E.R. 559; 81 S.J. 435 .... 2-070, 8-196

Williams, Re; Williams v Ball [1917] 1 Ch. 1; 86 L.J.Ch. 36; 115 L.T. 689; 61 S.J. 42 10-010
Williams, Torrey & Co Knight [1894] P. 342; 64 L.J.P. 15; 71 L.T. 92; 7 Asp. M.L.C. 500;
 11 R. 736. 7-062
Williamson v Barbour (1877) 9 Ch.D. 529; 50 L.J.Ch. 147; 37 L.T. 698; 27 W.R. 284n 6-098,
 8-211
Williamson v Barton (1862) 7 H. & N. 899; 31 L.J.Ex. 170; 5 L.T. 800; 8 Jur. (N.S.) 341;
 10 W.R. 321. . . . . 8-120, **9-034**
Williamson v Hine Bros [1891] 1 Ch. 390 7-004
Willis & Co v Baddeley [1982] 2 Q.B. 324; 61 L.J.Q.B. 769; 67 L.T. 206; 40 W.R. 577; 36
 S.J. 592 9-010
Willis Faber & Co Ltd v Joyce (1911) L.T. 576; 27 T.L.R. 388; 55 S.J. 443; 11 Asp.
 M.L.C. 601; 16 Com.Cas.190 . . . . 10-030, 10-031, 10-032
Willis Ltd v Jardine Lloyd Thompson Group Plc [2015] EWCA Civ 450; [2015] I.R.L.R.
 844. 6-034
Willis v Barron; sub nom. Barron v Willis [1902] A.C. 271; 71 L.J.Ch. 609; 86 L.T. 805;
 18 T.L.R. 602 6-069
Willis v Maritin (1790) 4 T.R. 39 . . . . 8-208, 8-211, 8-213, 8-214
Willis v Palmer (1859) 7 C.B. (N.S.) 340; 29 L.J.C.P. 194; 2 L.T. 626; 6 Jur. (N.S.) 732; 8
 W.R. 295; 141 E.R. 847 3-015
Wilson, Re [1916] 1 K.B. 382 . . . . **2-026**
Wilson v Anderton (1830) 1 B. & Ad. 450; 9 L.J. (O.S.) K.B. 48 9-131
Wilson v Avec Audio-Visual Equipment Ltd [1974] 1 Lloyd's Rep. 81 CA ... 6-026, 7-062, 9-006,
 9-016, 9-042, 9-045
Wilson v Barker (1833) 4 B. & Ad. 614; 1 N. & M.K.B. 409 2-063
Wilson v Barthrop (1837) 2 M. & W. 863; Murp & H. 81; 6 L.J.Ex. 251; 1 Jur. 949 . . . . **9-056**
Wilson v Brett (1843) 11 M. & W. 113; 12 L.J.Ex. 264 6-031
Wilson v Harper, Son & Co [1908] 2 Ch. 370; 77 L.J.Ch. 607 10-016
Wilson v Hart (1817) 1 Moo. C.P. 45; 7 Taunt. 295 8-078
Wilson v Kymer (1813) 1 M. & S.157 7-093
Wilson v Lombank [1963] 1 W.L.R. 1294; [1963] 1 All E.R. 740 6-111
Wilson v Moore (1834) 1 Myl. & K. 126 . . . . **9-142**
Wilson v Poulter (1724) 2 Str. 859; 1 Barn. K.B. 118 . . . . **2-083**
Wilson v Salamandra Ass.Co of St Petersburg (1903) 88 L.T. 96; 19 T.L.R. 229; 9 Asp.
 M.L.C. 370; 8 Com.Cas.129. 8-217
Wilson v Short (1848) 6 Hare 366; 17 L.J.Ch. 289; 10 L.T. (O.S.) 519; 12 Jur. 301 . . . . **6-071**
Wilson v St Helen's BC; sub nom. British Fuels Ltd v Baxendale; Meade v British Fuels
 Ltd; Baxendale v British Fuels Ltd [1999] 2 A.C. 52; [1998] 3 W.L.R. 1070; [1998] 4
 All E.R. 609; [1999] 1 C.M.L.R. 918; [1998] I.C.R. 1141; [1998] I.R.L.R. 706; (1999) 1
 L.G.L.R. 123; [1999] B.L.G.R. 255 HL 7-047
Wilson v Tunman and Fretson (1843) 6 M. & G. 236; 6 Scott N.R. 894; 1 Dow. & L. 513;
 12 L.J.C.P. 306; 1 L.T. (O.S.) 256. . . . . 2-047, 2-054, 2-056, **2-070**, 2-095, 6-005, **9-125**
Wilson v Wallani (1880) 5 Ex.D. 155 2-022
Wilson v West Hartlepool Railway & Harbour Co (1865) 2 De G.J. & S.475; 5 New Rep.
 289; 34 L.J.Ch. 241; 11 L.T. 692; 11 Jur. (N.S.) 124; 13 W.R. 361 2-069
Wilson & Co v Baker Lees & Co (1901) 17 T.L.R. 473 9-087
Wilson & Meeson v Pickering [1946] K.B. 422; 1 All E.R. 394 . . . . 2-102, 8-024, 8-130, 8-134
Wilson & Sons v Pike [1949] 1 K.B. 176; [1949] L.J.R. 17; 64 T.L.R. 566; [1948] 2 All
 E.R. 267; 92 S.J. 513 CA 2-014
Wilsons & Clyde Coal Co Ltd v English [1938] A.C. 57; [1937] 3 All E.R. 628; 1937 S.C.
 (H.L.) 46; 1937 S.L.T. 523 HL. 8-184
Wilsons and Furness-Leyland Line v British and Continental Shipping Co (1907) 23
 T.L.R. 397. . . . . 6-045, 8-167
Wiltshire v Sims (1808) 1 Camp. 258 3-022
Wimpey Construction UK Ltd v Poole [1984] 2 Lloyd's Rep. 499; (1984) 128 S.J. 969;
 (1985) 27 Build. L.R. 58. . . . . 6-019, 6-021
Winch v Winchester (1812) 1 Ves. & B. 375 8-096
Windle (Jack) Ltd v Brierley [1952] 1 All E.R. 398 . . . . 7-028, 7-032
Windsor Refrigerator Co v Branch Nominees Ltd [1961] Ch. 375; [1961] 2 W.L.R. 196;
 [1961] 1 All E.R. 277; 105 S.J. 205 CA 2-041, 2-042
Wing v Harvey (1854) 5 De G.M. & G. 265; 2 Eq. Rep. 533; 23 L.J.Ch. 511; 23 L.T.
 (O.S.) 120; 18 Jur. 394; 2 W.R. 370 . . . . **8-044**
Winson, The. *See* China Pacific SA v Food Corp of India; Winson, The 4-004, 4-005, 4-006,
 4-007, 4-008, 4-010, **4-013**, 12-032

Winter Garden Theatre (London) Ltd v Millennium Productions Ltd [1948] A.C. 173;
    [1947] L.J.R. 1422; 177 L.T. 349; 63 T.L.R. 529; [1947] 2 All E.R. 331; 91 S.J. 504 HL . . . 10-025,
    10-042
Winter v Bancks (1901) 84 L.T. 504; 65 J.P. 468; 49 W.R. 574; 17 T.L.R. 446; 19 Cox.
    C.C. 587 9-131
Winters v Mishcon de Reya [2008] EWHC 2419 (Ch); (2008) 158 N.L.J. 1494 6-051
Wintle v Nye [1959] 1 W.L.R. 284 6-064
Wise v Jimenez [2014] W.T.L.R. 163; [2014] 1 P. & C.R. DG9 1-030
Wise v Perpetual Trustee Co Ltd [1903] A.C. 139; 72 L.J.P.C. 37; 87 L.T. 569; 51 W.R.
    241; 19 T.L.R. 125 PC 9-087
Wishart v Credit & Mercantile Plc [2015] EWCA Civ 655; [2016] B.P.I.R. 209; [2015] 2
    P. & C.R. 15 8-135
Withers LLP v Langbar International Ltd [2011] EWCA Civ 1419; [2012] 1 W.L.R. 1748;
    [2012] 2 All E.R. 616; [2011] 2 Lloyd's Rep. 126; [2012] 2 Costs L.O. 114; [2012]
    B.P.I.R. 246; [2012] P.N.L.R. 10; (2012) 109(1) L.S.G. 14; (2011) 161 N.L.J. 1742 . . 7-079, 7-082,
    7-086
Withington v Herring (1829) 5 Bing. 442; 3 Moo. & P. 30; 7 L.T. (O.S.) C.P. 172 . . . . 3-013, 3-015
Witt & Scott Ltd v Blunmenreich [1949] N.Z.L.R. 806 . . . . 1-021, 7-101
Witt, Re, Ex p. Shubrook (1876) 2 Ch.D. 489; 45 L.J. Bcy 118; 34 L.T. 785; 24 W.R. 891 . . . 7-082
WLR Traders (London) Ltd v British & Northern Shipping Agency and Leftley Ltd [1955]
    1 Lloyd's Rep. 554 . . . . **6-024**
Wolfe v Findlay (1847) 6 Hare 66; 16 L.J.Ch. 241; 8 L.T. (O.S.) 408; 11 Jur. 82 6-108
Wolfe, Re; Heller v Wolfe [1952] 2 All E.R. 545; [1952] 2 T.L.R. 388; [1952] W.N. 427 7-005,
    7-012
Wolff v Horncastle (1798) 1 B. & P. 316 . . . . **2-053, 2-100**
Wollenberg v Casinos Austria International Holding GmbH [2011] EWHC 103 (Ch) . 6-063, 6-067
Wolstenholm v Sheffield Union Banking Co Ltd; sub nom. Wolstenholm v Sheffield
    Union Banking Co Ltd (1886) 54 L.T. 746; 2 T.L.R. 472 . . . . **7-086**
Wong Mee Wan v Kwan Kin Travel Services Ltd [1996] 1 W.L.R. 38; [1995] 4 All E.R.
    745; (1996) 93(3) L.S.G. 28; (1995) 139 S.J.L.B. 246 PC 1-038, 8-184
Wood (Harold) Brick Co v Ferris [1935] 2 K.B. 198; 104 L.J.K.B. 533; 153 L.T. 241; 79
    S.J. 502 6-013
Wood v Baxter (1883) 49 L.T. 45 . . . . **9-034**
Wood v Leadbitter (1845) 13 M. & W. 838 10-007
Wood, Re, Ex p. Boden (1873) 28 L.T. 174 . . . . 8-161, 8-167
Woodar Investment Development Ltd v Wimpey Construction UK Ltd [1980] 1 W.L.R.
    277; [1980] 1 All E.R. 571; (1980) 124 S.J. 184 HL 9-011
Woodhouse AC Israel Cocoa Ltd SA v Nigerian Produce Marketing Co Ltd [1972] A.C.
    741; [1972] 2 W.L.R. 1090; [1972] 2 All E.R. 271; 116 S.J. 329; [1972] 1 Lloyd's Rep.
    439 HL 3-019, 6-011
Woodin v Burford (1834) 2 Cr. & M. 391; 4 Tyr. 264; 3 L.J.Ex. 75 3-023
Woodland v Essex CC [2013] UKSC 66; [2014] A.C. 537; [2013] 3 W.L.R. 1227; [2014]
    1 All E.R. 482; [2014] E.L.R. 67; (2013) 16 C.C.L. Rep. 532; [2014] P.I.Q.R. P6;
    (2013) 163(7582) N.L.J. 15; (2013) 157(41) S.J.L.B. 39 8-184
Woodland v Swimming Teachers Association [2013] UKSC 66; [2014] A.C. 537; [2013] 3
    W.L.R. 1227; [2014] 1 All E.R. 482; [2014] E.L.R. 67; (2013) 16 C.C.L. Rep. 532;
    [2014] P.I.Q.R. P6; (2013) 163(7582) N.L.J. 15; (2013) 157(41) S.J.L.B. 39 . . . . 8-178, 8-184
Woodstock Shipping Co v Kyma Compania Naviera SA (The Wave) [1981] 1 Lloyd's
    Rep. 521; [1981] Com. L.R. 185 3-040
Woodward v Wolferstans [1997] N.P.C. 51 Ch D 9-117
Woodworth v Conroy; Conroy v Woodworth [1976] Q.B. 884; [1976] 2 W.L.R. 338;
    [1976] 1 All E.R. 107; (1975) 119 S.J. 810 CA 7-075
Wookey v Pole (1820) 4 B. & Ald. 1 8-141
Woolcott v Excess Insurance Co Ltd and Miles, Smith Anderson & Game Ltd (No.1)
    [1979] 1 Lloyd's Rep. 231 CA 8-217
Woolfe v Horne (1877) 2 Q.B.D. 355; 46 L.J.Q.B. 534; 36 L.T. 705; 41 J.P. 501; 25 W.R.
    728 . . . . **9-034**
Woollen v Wright (1862) 1 H. & C. 554; 31 L.J.Ex 513; 10 W.R. 715; 7 L.T. 73 2-070
Worboys v Carter [1987] 2 E.G.L.R. 1; (1987) 283 E.G. 307 CA 2-080, 2-108, 2-109, 8-128
Worcester Works Finance Ltd v Cooden Engineering Co Ltd [1972] 1 Q.B. 210; [1971] 3
    W.L.R. 661; [1971] 3 All E.R. 708; 115 S.J. 605 CA 8-151
World Transport Agency Ltd v Royte (England) Ltd [1957] 1 Lloyd's Rep. 381 . . . . . 6-012, 6-024,
    7-062

Worrall v Harford (1802) 8 Ves. 4 7-089
Worsley v Earl of Scarborough (1746) 3 Atk. 392 .... 8-209, 8-211
Woyka & Co v London & Northern Trading Co (1922) 10 Ll.Rep. 110 8-185
Wragg v Lovett [1948] W.N. 455; [1948] 2 All E.R. 968 CA 3-032
Wray v Kemp (1884) 26 Ch.D. 169; 53 L.J.Ch. 1020; 50 L.T. 552 .... **5-007**
Wreford, Re; Carmichael v Rudkin (1897) 13 T.L.R. 153 .... 6-041, 8-167
Wrexham Associated Football Club Ltd v Crucialmove Ltd [2006] EWCA Civ 237;
    [2008] 1 B.C.L.C. 508... 3-011, 8-037, 8-039, 8-050
Wright v Carter [1903] 1 Ch. 27; 72 L.J.Ch. 138; 87 L.T. 624; 51 W.R. 196; 19 T.L.R. 29 ... 6-063,
                                                                                6-064, 6-069
Wright v Dannah (1809) 2 Camp. 203 2-014
Wright v Freeman (1879) 40 L.T. 358 7-104
Wright v Glyn [1902] 1 K.B. 745; 71 L.J.K.B. 497; 86 L.T. 373; 40 W.R. 402; 78 T.L.R.
    404... 3-028
Wright v Pepin [1954] 1 W.L.R. 635; [1954] 2 All E.R. 52; 98 S.J. 252 .... 2-019, **2-026**
Wright v Proud (1806) 13 Ves. 136 6-069
Wright (AR) and Son Ltd v Romford BC [1957] 1 Q.B. 431; [1956] 3 W.L.R. 896; 121
    J.P. 44; [1956] 3 All E.R. 785; 100 S.J. 859; 54 L.G.R. 647 2-038
Wright Hassall LLP v Horton Jr [2015] EWHC 3716 (QB) 7-050
Wrout v Dawes (1858) 25 Beav. 369; 27 L.J.Ch. 135; 31 L.T. (O.S.) 261; 4 Jur. (N.S.) 396 .. 3-026
WS Tankship II BV v Kwangju Bank Ltd [2011] EWHC 3103 (Comm); [2012] C.I.L.L.
    3155... 2-023
Wyatt v Hertford (1802) 3 East 147 .... 8-103, 8-104, **8-106**
Wyllie v Pollen (1863) 32 L.J.Ch. 782; 3 De G.J. & Sm 596; 2 New Rep. 500; 9 L.T. 71;
    11 W.R. 1081.. **8-217**
Wythes v Labouchere (1859) 3 De G. & J. 593; 33 L.T. (O.S.) 30; 5 Jur. (N.S.) 499; 7
    W.R. 271... 8-217
Xenos v Wickham (1866) L.R. 2 H.L. 296; 36 L.J.C.P. 313; 16 L.T. 800; 16 W.R. 38; 2
    Mar. L.C. 537 HL.. **8-067**
Yarborough v Governor and Company of The Bank of England (1812) 16 East 6 .... 1-028, 1-029,
                                                                                8-189
Yasuda Fire & Marine Insurance Co of Europe Ltd v Orion Marine Insurance
    Underwriting Agency [1995] Q.B. 174; [1995] 2 W.L.R. 49; [1995] 3 All E.R. 211;
    [1995] 1 Lloyd's Rep. 525; [1995] 4 Re. L.R. 217 QBD (Comm) 1-006, 6-035, 6-044, 6-092,
                                                                        10-010, 10-045, 11-036
Yates (Peter) & Co v Bullock [1990] 2 E.G.L.R. 24 .... 7-018, 7-021, 7-030, 7-032
Yates v Finn (1880) 13 Ch.D. 839; 49 L.J.Ch. 188; 28 W.R. 387 6-080
Yates v Hoppe (1850) 9 C.B. 541; 19 L.J.C.P. 180; 15 L.T. (O.S.) 25; 14 Jur. 372 10-010
Yenula Properties Ltd v Naidu; sub nom. Naidu v Yenula Properties Ltd [2002] EWCA
    Civ 719; [2003] H.L.R. 18; [2003] L. & T.R. 9; [2002] 3 E.G.L.R. 28; [2002] 42 E.G.
    162; [2002] 23 E.G.C.S.121; (2002) 99(27) L.S.G. 34 CA 2-026
Yeung Kai Yung v Hong Kong and Shanghai Banking Corp [1981] A.C. 787, D.C.; [1980]
    3 W.L.R. 950; [1980] 2 All E.R. 599; (1980) 124 S.J. 591, D.C . 7-060, 7-068, 9-002, 9-006, **9-034**,
                                                                                9-066
Yona International Ltd v La R'eunion Francaise SA D'Assurances et de Reassurances
    [1996] 2 Lloyd's Rep. 84 QBD (Comm Ct)............................ 2-068, 2-074, 2-079
Yonge v Toynbee [1910] 1 K.B. 215; 79 L.J.K.B. 208; 102 L.T. 57; 26 T.L.R. 211 ... 2-009, 9-060,
                                            9-062, 9-063, 9-066, 9-071, **9-076**, 9-081, 10-016, 10-020, 10-032
York Buildings v MacKenzie (1795) 8 Bro. P.C. 42 .... 6-035, 6-062, 6-080
Youell v Bland Welch & Co Ltd Superhulls (No.2) [1990] 2 Lloyd's Rep. 431 QBD
    (Comm)... 6-012, 6-016, 6-018, **6-024**, 6-028
Young & Co v White (1911) 28 T.L.R. 87; 76 J.P. 14 .... 8-120, 8-121
Young v Box (Edward) & Co [1951] 1 T.L.R. 789 CA 8-176, 8-193
Young v Cole (1837) 3 Bing N.C. 724; 4 Scott. 489; 6 L.J.C.P. 201; 1 Jur. 22 .... **3-040**
Young v English (1843) 7 Beav. 10; 13 L.J.Ch. 76 .... 7-088, **7-089**
Young v Ladies' Imperial Club Ltd [1920] 2 K.B. 525 2-038
Young v Robson Rhodes (A Firm) [1999] 3 All E.R. 524; [1999] Lloyd's Rep. P.N. 641Ch
    D 6-051
Young v Schuler (1883) 11 Q.B.D. 651; 49 L.T. 546 .... 8-117, 9-006, 9-037, **9-038**
Young v White (1844) 7 Beav. 506; 13 L.J.Ch. 418; 3 L.T. (O.S.) 339; 8 Jur. 654 8-108
Yuille v B&B Fisheries (Leigh) Ltd; The Radiant [1958] 2 Lloyd's Rep. 596, PDAD 9-120

Yukong Line Ltd of Korea v Rendsburg Investments Corp of Liberia; The Rialto [1998] 1
 W.L.R. 294; [1998] 4 All E.R. 82; [1998] 1 Lloyd's Rep. 322; [1998] 2 B.C.L.C. 485;
 [1998] B.C.C. 870; (1997) 94(39); L.S.G. 39; (1997) 141 S.J.L.B. 212............1-030, 8-071
Zoha Ltd v Ahmed [2016] EWHC 1981 (Ch); [2017] 2 W.L.R. 773 3-007
Zouch d. Abbot and Hallett v Parsons (1765) 3 Burr. 1794; 1 Wm.Bl. 575; 97 E.R. 1103 2-008
Zoya Ltd v Ahmed (Sheikh Nasir) (t/a Property Mart) [2016] EWHC 2249 (Ch); [2016] 4
 W.L.R. 174; [2017] 2 Costs L.O. 133 ....9-062, 9-065, 9-067, 9-070, 9-076
Zulueta v Vinent (1852) 1 De G.M. & G. 315; 19 L.T. (O.S.) 330; 42 E.R. 573 ....**6-112**
Zurich Australian Insurance Ltd v Withers [2016] NZCA 618; [2017] 2 N.Z.L.R. 745 8-188

INTERNATIONAL CASES

AFRICA

Gundle (Isaac) v Mohanlal Sunderji (1939) 18 K.L.R. 137 ....1-021, 9-021
Parkar's Music & Sprots House v Motorex Ltd [1959] E.A.L.R. 534 1-036
Victory Shiphandlers v Leslie & Anderson Ltd [1972] E.A.L.R. 42 9-046

AUSTRALIA

ACCC v Flight Centre Travel Group Ltd [2016] HCA 49 ....3-008, 6-015
ACN 007528207 Pty Ltd v Bird Cameron (2005) 54 A.C.S.R. 505 ....1-012, 1-035
Adams v Bank of New South Wales [1984] 1 N.S.W.L.R. 285 9-139
Aequitas Ltd v Sparad No.100 Ltd (2001) 19 A.C.L.C. 1006 6-068
Agricultural Land Management Ltd v Jackson (No .2) [2014] WASC 102; (2014) 285
 F.L.R. 121...6-043
Air Tahiti Nui Pty Ltd v McKenzie [2009] NSWCA 429 9-006
Alexander v Perpetual Trustees WA Ltd [2004] HCA 7; (2004) 216 C.L.R. 109 ......6-003, 6-043
Alfred v Wakelin (No.2) [2008] FCA 1543 8-176
Allco Finance Group Ltd v Gothard [2014] FCAFC 6 8-020
Alliance Acceptance Co Ltd v Oakley (1987) 45 S.A.S.R. 148 9-040
Alliance Craton Explorer Pty Ltd v Quasar Resources Pty Ltd [2013] FCAFC 29 ....1-004, 1-018,
 1-034, 1-038, 6-056
Ardlethan Options Ltd v Easdown (1915) 20 C.L.R. 285 6-087
Ariston Products Pty Ltd v Egan (1971) 3 A.C.L.R. 418 7-075
Armor Coatings (Marketing) Pty Ltd v General Credits (Finance) Pty Ltd (1978) 17
 S.A.S.R. 259..6-037
Atlas Steels (Australia) Pty Ltd v Atlas Steels Ltd (1948) 49 S.R. (N.S.W.) 157 7-046
Attorney General v Wylde (1946) 47 S.R. (N.S.W.) 99 2-062
Australia and New Zealand Banking Group Ltd v Frenmast Pty Ltd [2013] NSWCA 459 ...8-020,
 8-039
Australia and New Zealand Banking Group Ltd v Westpac Banking Corp (1988) 164
 C.L.R. 662 ....9-102, 9-106, 9-107
Australia Robinson v Abbott (1894) 20 V.L.R. 346 6-043
Australian Agricultural Co v Oatmont Pty Ltd (1992) 8 A.C.S.R. 255 2-025
Australian Careers Institute Pty Ltd v Australian Institute of Fitness Pty Ltd [2016]
 NSWCA 34; (2017) 340 A.L.R. 580..8-225
Australian Competition and Consumer Commission v Radio Rentals Ltd (2006) 146
 F.C.R. 292...8-209
Australian Metropolitan Life Assurance Co Ltd v Ure (1923) 33 C.L.R. 199 8-220
Australian Mutual Provident Society v Chaplin (1978) 18 A.L.R. 385 1-034
Australian Securities and Investments Commission v Citigroup Global Markets Australia
 Pty Ltd (2007) 62 A.C.S.R. 427 (Fed. Ct.)...6-056
Australian Tallow and Agriculture Commodities Pty Ltd v Malaysian International
 Shipping Corp (2001) 50 N.S.W.L.R. 576 9-024
Australian Trade Commission v Goodman Fielder Industries (1992) 36 F.C.R. 517 9-002
Australian Workers' Union v Leighton Contractors Pty Ltd [2013] FCAFC 4 2-077
Aztech Science Pty Ltd v Atlanta Aerospace (Woy Woy) Pty Ltd (2005) 55 A.C.S.R. 1
 (NSWCA)...2-078
Badenach v Calvert [2016] HCA 18; (2016) 257 C.L.R. 440 6-029
Bain Securities Ltd v Curmi (1990) 1 A.C.S.R. 794 ....8-114, 8-119
Barker v Burns, Philp & Co Ltd (1944) 45 S.R. (N.S.W.) 1 4-005

Barkley v Barkley Brown [2009] NSWSC 76 6-092
Barrow v Bank of New South Wales [1931] V.R. 323 8-203
Beach Petroleum NL v Johnson (1993) 115 A.L.R. 411 . . . . 8-209, 8-214
Beach Petroleum NL v Kennedy (1999) 48 N.S.W.L.R. 1 . . . . 6-039, 6-048
Bell Group Ltd v Herald and Weekly Times [1985] V.R. 613 3-036
Bennett v Goodwin (2005) 62 A.T.R. 515 6-003
Bennett v Strauss [2016] NSWCA 324 . . . . 2-063, 2-070
Berry v Hodson [1989] 1 Qd. R. 361 9-026
Birtchnell v Equity Trustee, Executor and Agency Co Ltd (1929) 42 C.L.R. 384 6-037
Black v Smallwood (1966) 117 C.L.R. 52 . 9-037, 9-061, 9-066, 9-084, 9-085, **9-087**, 9-090, 9-092
Blackham v Haythorpe (1917) 23 C.L.R. 156 6-068
Bosanquet v Mofflin (1906) S.R. (N.S.W.) 617 . . . . 1-021, 1-036
Breen v Williams (1996) 186 C.L.R. 71 . . . . 6-036, 6-039
Brick and Pipe Industries Ltd v Occidental Life Nominees Pty Ltd (1991) 6 A.C.S.R. 464 . . . 1-028
Brick and Pipe Industries Ltd v Occidental Life Nominees Pty Ltd [1992] 2 V.R. 279 3-041
Brockway v Pando (2000) 22 W.A.R. 405 8-182
Brookton Co-op Society Ltd v FCT (1981) 147 C.L.R. 441 . . . . 3-003, 10-028
Brownett v Newton (1941) 64 C.L.R. 439; 47 A.L.R. 146; 15 A.L.J. 29; 58 W.N. 127; 14
    S.R. (N.S.W.) 107 9-066
Brunninghausen v Glavanics (1999) 46 N.S.W.L.R. 538 6-035
Buckingham v Trotter (1901) 1 S.R. (N.S.W.) 253 . . . . 8-118, 8-119
Buckley and Bienefelt Re (1976) 13 A.L.R. 291 8-045
Bucknell v O'Donnell (1922) 31 C.L.R. 40 8-117
Bugge v Brown (1919) V.L.R. 264; (1919) 26 C.L.R. 110 8-178
Bunnings Group Ltd v CHEP Australia Ltd [2011] NSWCA 342 8-215
Butcher v Lachlan Realty Pty Ltd (2004) 218 C.L.R. 592 9-117
Butler v Duckett (1891) 17 V.L.R. 439 2-042
Cachia v Isaacs (1985) 3 N.S.W.L.R. 366 7-050
Caldwell v Treloar (1982) 30 S.A.S.R. 202 7-050
CAN074971109 v National Mutual Life Association of Australasia Ltd (2008) 69
    A.C.S.R. 118 2-106
Canberra Residential Developments Pty Ltd v Brendas (No.5) [2009] FCA 34 6-081
Capital Management Corp v Hackett Development (1971) 18 F.L.R. 362 7-021
Carberry v Gardiner (1936) 36 S.R.(N.S.W.) 559 8-082
Carlton Cricket and Football Social Club v Joseph [1970] V.R. 487 9-087
Carminco Gold & Resources Ltd v Findlay & Co Stockbrokers (Underwriters) Pty Ltd
    [2007] F.C.A.F.C. 194 . . . . 9-005, 9-008, **9-035**, 9-095
Carrington Slipways Pty Ltd v Patrick Operations Pty Ltd (1991) 24 N.S.W.L.R. 745 9-024
Cassegrain v Gerard Cassegrain & Co Pty Ltd [2015] HCA 2; (2015) 316 A.L.R. 111 . 8-209, 8-211
Celthene Pty Ltd v W.J.K. Hauliers Pty Ltd [1981] 1 N.S.W.L.R. 606 . . . . 2-074, 2-089, 2-092
Central Darling Shire Council v Greeney [2015] NSWCA 51 8-184
Chan (Kak Loui) v Zacharia (1984) 154 C.L.R. 178 . . . . 6-034, 6-036, 6-080, 6-083
Chen v Marcolongo (2009) 260 A.L.R. 353 6-064
Chomley v Union Bank of Australia Ltd [1951] S.A.S.R. 152 8-130
Christie v Permewan, Wright & Co Ltd (1904) 1 C.L.R. 693 2-017
Christie v Robinson (1907) 4 C.L.R. 1338 9-026
Citigroup Pty Ltd v National Australia Bank Ltd [2012] NSWCA 381; (2012) 82
    N.S.W.L.R. 391 . . . . 9-107, 9-109
City Bank of Sydney v Barden (1908) 9 S.R. (N.S.W.) 41 8-150
Clayton Robard Management Ltd v Siu (1988) 6 A.C.L.C. 5 2-103
Coachcraft Ltd v SVP Fruit Co Ltd (1980) 28 A.L.R. 319 . . . . 6-035, 6-037
Cohen v Cohen (1929) 42 C.L.R. 91 6-041
Coleman, Re (1929) 24 Tas.L.R. 77 10-020
Colin R Price & Associates Pty Ltd v Four Oaks Pty Ltd [2017] FCAFC 75 3-029
Colonial Mutual Life Assurance Society Ltd v Producers and Citizens Co-operative
    Assurance Co of Australia (1931) 46 C.L.R. 41; A.L.J. 355; 38 A.L.R. 73 . . . . 1-038, 8-176, 8-182,
        8-196
Colyer Fehr Tallow Pty Ltd v KNZ Australia Pty Ltd [2011] NSWSC 457 . . . . 6-015, 6-081
Combulk Pty Ltd v TNT Management Pty Ltd (1993) 113 A.L.R. 214 . . . . 8-047, 8-048
Commissioner of Taxation v Byrne Hotels Queensland Pty Ltd [2011] FCAFC 127 6-024
Commonwealth Bank of Australia v Hamilton [2012] NSWSC 242 . . . . 9-062, 9-076
Commonwealth Bank of Australia v Kojic [2016] FCAFC 186 8-209
Commonwealth Bank of Australia v Perrin [2011] QSC 274 . . . . 2-059, 2-079

Commonwealth of Australia v Verwayen (1990) 170 C.L.R. 394 8-029
Commonwealth v Crothall Hospital Services (Aust.) Ltd (1981) 54 F.L.R. 439 8-042
Con-Stan Industry of Australia Pty Ltd v Norwich Winterthur Insurance (Australia) Ltd
   (1986) 160 C.L.R. 226 . . . . 3-035, 8-114, 8-121
Constitution Road Pty Ltd v Downey (2008) 68 A.C.S.R. 118 2-046
Construction Engineering Aust. Pty Ltd v Hexyl Pty Ltd (1985) 155 C.L.R. 541 . . . . . 8-077, 8-079
Construction Forestry Mining and Energy Union (1994) 181 C.L.R. 539 2-091
Cook v Rodgers (1946) 46 S.R.(N.S.W.) 229 8-152
Cornwall v Rowan (2004) 90 S.A.S.R. 268 8-182
Coshott v Barry [2016] FCAFC 173 . . . . 7-090, 7-091, 7-094
Cox v Goldcrest Developments (N.S.W.) Pty (2000) 1 N.S.W.L.R. 76 . . . . 2-045, 2-046
Crabtree-Vickers Pty Ltd v Australian Direct Mail Advertising & Addressing Pty Ltd
   (1975) 133 C.L.R. 72 . . . . 2-103, 8-019, 8-039
Crawford Fitting Co v Sydney Valve and Fittings Pty Ltd (1988) 14 N.S.W.L.R. 438 10-042
Curtis v Perth & Fremantle Bottle Exchange Co Ltd (1914) 18 C.L.R. 17 8-126
Custom Credit Corp v Lynch [1993] 2 V.R. 469 . . . . 2-031, 2-033, 2-034
Daily Telegraph Newspaper Co Ltd v McLaughlin [1904] A.C. 776 PC 2-009
Dalgety & Co v Gray (1919) 26 C.L.R. 249 PC 6-066
Daly v Sydney Stock Exchange Ltd (1986) 160 C.L.R. 371 . . . . 6-034, 6-040
Daniels v Anderson (1995) 37 N.S.W.L.R. 438 8-188
Dargusch v Sherley Investments Pty Ltd [1970] Qd.R. 338 . . . . 6-048, 7-051
Darlington Futures Ltd v Delco Australia Pty Ltd (1986) 161 C.L.R. 500 6-005
Davies (Paul A) (Australia) Pty Ltd v Davies [1983] 1 N.S.W.L.R. 440 6-080
Davison v Vickery's Motors Ltd (1925) 37 C.L.R. 1 2-087
Dawson (dec'd), Re [1966] 2 N.S.W.R. 211 . . . . 6-003, 6-043
Day v Bank of New South Wales (1978) 19 A.L.R. 32 3-015
Day v The Ocean Beach Hotel Shellharbour Pty Ltd [2013] NSWCA 250 8-179
Deatons Pty Ltd v Flew (1949) 79 C.L.R. 370 8-192
Deaves v CML Fire & General Insurance Co Ltd (1978) 143 C.L.R. 24 8-217
Del Casale v Artedomus (Aust) Pty Ltd (2007) 73 I.P.R. 326 6-077
Delco Australia Pty Ltd v Darlington Finance Ltd (1986) 161 C.L.R. 500 2-096
Dellas v Kourtessis [1962] V.R. 456 . . . . 9-113, 9-114
Derham v Amev Life Insurance Co Ltd (1981) 56 F.L.R. 34 . . . . 8-018, 8-117, 8-182, 8-196
Despot v Registrar-General of NSW [2013] NSWCA 313 . . . . 3-011, 3-015, 9-136, 10-007
Di Dio Nominees Pty Ltd v Mark (Brian) Real Estate Pty Ltd [1992] 2 V.R. 732 . . . . . 7-021, 7-032
Director of Posts and Telegraphs v Abbott (1974) 22 F.L.R. 157 8-042
Dominion Factors Pty Ltd v Hooker (L.J.) Ltd [1963] N.S.W.L.R. 573 7-104
Donnellan v Watson (1990) 21 N.S.W.L.R. 335 3-032
Doyle v Mr Kidston Mining and Exploration Pty Ltd [1984] 2 Qd.R. 386 . . . . 7-028, 7-030
Doyle v White City Stadium Ltd [1935] 1 K.B. 110 CA 2-008, 3-036
Dwyer v Lippiatt (2004) 50 A.C.S.R. 333 6-081
Edwards Karwacki Smith & Co Pty v Kacka Nominees Pty (1994) 15 A.C.S.R. 502 8-188
Eisentrager v Lyneham [1952] S.R.Qd. 232 6-099
Elder Smith Goldsbrough Mart Ltd v McBride [1976] 2 N.S.W.L.R. 631 . . . . . 9-023, **9-034**, 9-035
Equiticorp Finance Ltd v Bank of New Zealand (1993) 32 N.S.W.L.R. 50 3-041
Eric Preston Pty Ltd v Euroz Securities Ltd [2011] FCAFC 11 6-003
Essington Investments Pty Ltd v Regency Property Pty Ltd [2004] NSWCA 375 . . . . . 2-102, 2-109
Farah Constructions Pty Ltd v Say-Dee Pty Ltd [2007] HCA 22; (2007) 230 C.L.R. 89 6-039,
                                                                                    8-211, 8-221, 9-136
Farrow Finance Co Ltd v Farrow properties Pty Ltd (1998) 26 A.C.S.R. 544 8-215
Flexirent Capital Pty Ltd v EBS Consulting Pty Ltd [2007] VSC 158 . . 2-016, 2-017, 3-011, 5-015,
                                                                                    8-060
Forestview Nominees Pty v Perron Investments Pty (1999) 93 F.C.R. 117 8-182
Forsyth v Blundell (1973) 129 C.L.R. 477 8-210
Freehold Land Investments Ltd v Queensland Estates Pty Ltd (1920) 123 C.L.R. 418 1-020
FTV Holdings Cairns Pty Ltd v Smith [2014] QCA 217 9-113
Gadsden (J) Pty v Strider 1, AES Express, The (1990) 20 N.S.W.L.R. 57 4-010
Gallimore v Moore (1867) 6 S.R. (N.S.W.) 388 1-033
Gardiner v Grigg (1938) 38 S.R. (N.S.W.) 524 . . . . 2-083, 3-032
Geddes v M'Donnell (1896) 22 V.L.R. 330 8-126
General Distributors Ltd v Paramotors Ltd [1962] S.A.S.R. 1 8-127
Gerlach v Pearson [1950] V.L.R. 321 7-019
Gibbons v Wright (1904) 91 C.L.R. 423 . . . . 2-008, 2-009

Gothard v Davey [2010] FCA 1163 8-073
Grant v O'Leary (1955) 93 C.L.R. 587 9-026
Gray v Dalgety & Co Ltd (1916) 21 C.L.R. 309 6-072
Great Investments Ltd v Warner [2016] FCAFC 85 . . . . 3-013, 3-015
Green & Clara Pty Ltd v Bestobell Industries Pty Ltd [1982] W.A.R. 1 6-083
Greenwood v Harvey [1965] N.S.W.R. 1489 7-050
Griffin v Clark (1940) 40 S.R. (N.S.W.) 409 10-006
Grimaldi v Chameleon Mining NL (No. 2) (2012) 287 A.L.R. 22 . . . . 6-042, 8-214, 8-215
Haines Bros Earthmoving Pty Ltd v Rosecell Pty Ltd [2016] NSWCA 112 . . . . 2-028, 8-130
Hancock Family Memorial Foundation Ltd v Porteous (2000) 22 W.A.R. 198 6-040
Hannaford v Australian Farmlink Pty Ltd [2008] FCA 1591 1-036
Harkness v Commonwealth Bank of Australia Ltd (1993) 32 N.S.W.L.R. 543 8-211
Harris v Digital Pulse Pty Ltd (2003) 56 N.S.W.L.R. 298 6-036
Harvey v Phillips (1956) 95 C.L.R. 235 . . . . 3-004, 6-003
Harvey v State of New South Wales [2006] NSWSC 1436 8-018
Hawkins v Clayton [1988] HCA 15; 164 C.L.R. 539 6-032
Hawksford v Hawksford (2005) 191 F.L.R. 173 3-007
Hawksford v Hawksford [2005] NSWSC 463 3-029
Hawthorne Bros v Reilly [1949] V.L.R. 137 8-045
Haywood v Roadknight [1927] V.L.R. 512; 49 A.L.T. 29; 33 Arg. L.R. 331 6-070
Henry (Keith) & Co Pty Ltd v Walker (Stuart) & Co Pty Ltd (1958) 100 C.L.R. 342 6-037
Heperu Pty Ltd v Belle (2009) 258 A.L.R. 727; [2009] NSWCA 252 . . . . 8-200, **8-201**, 9-136
Heperu Pty Ltd v Morgan Brooks Pty Ltd (No.2) [2009] NSWCA 84 . . 1-035, 8-018, 8-045, 8-130
Herrod v Johnston [2013] 2 Qd.R. 102 6-107
Hewett v Court (1983) 149 C.L.R. 639 7-077
Hill v van Erp (1997) 188 C.L.R. 159 . . . . 6-018, 6-029
Hoare v McCarthy (1916) 22 C.L.R. 296 3-007
Hollis v Vabu Pty Ltd (2001) 207 C.L.R. 21 8-178
Homecare Direct Shopping Pty Ltd v Gray [2008] VSCA 111 5-008
Hooker (LJ) Ltd v Adams (WJ) Estates Pty Ltd (1977) 138 C.L.R. 52; 51 A.L.J.R. 413 7-001,
7-030, **7-032**, 7-036
Horsell International Pty Ltd v Divetwo Pty Ltd [2013] NSWCA 368 . . . . 6-011, 6-024
Hospital Products Ltd v US Surgical Corp (1984) 156 C.L.R. 41; (1984) 58 A.L.J.R. 587 . . . 1-035,
6-015, 6-035, 6-036, 6-037, 7-001
Howard v Commissioner of Taxation [2014] HCA 21; (2014) 253 C.L.R. 83 6-081
Hughes v NM Superannuation Pty Ltd (1993) 29 N.S.W.L.R. 653 2-094
Hydrocool Pty Ltd v Hepburn (No.4) [2011] FCA 495; (2011) 83 A.C.S.R. 652 6-043
Icon Property Pty Ltd v Wood [2008] VSCA 123 . . . . **7-012**
Imaje Events Pty Ltd v Taylor [2007] VSC 390 . . . . **7-062**
Interfirm Comparison (Australia) Pty Ltd v Law Society of NSW [1975] 2 N.S.W.L.R.
104. 6-077
International Harvester Co of Australia Pty Ltd v Carrigan's Hazeldene Pastoral Co (1958)
100 C.L.R. 644 . . . . 1-004, 1-036
International Paper Co v Spicer (1906) 4 C.L.R. 739 . . . . 3-020, 6-010, 8-010, 8-021, 8-044, 8-077
IVI Pty Ltd v Baycrown Pty Ltd [2005] QCA 205 . . . . 3-032, 8-207, 9-015
Johnson Matthey (Australia) v Dascorp Pty Ltd (2003) 9 V.R. 171 . . . . 8-023, 8-130, 9-121
Jones v Canavan [1972] 2 N.S.W.L.R. 236 . . . . 3-040, 6-048, 6-057, 6-066, 6-070, 7-051
Jones v Moffett (1846) 3 J. & L. 636 6-098
JR Consulting & Drafting Pty Ltd v Cummings [2016] FCAFC 20 9-120
Jumna Khan v Bankers and Traders Insurance Co Ltd (1925) 37 C.L.R. 451; 43
N.S.W.W.N. 98 8-217
Kendirjian v Lepore [2017] HCA 13 6-003
Keogh v Dalgety & Co Ltd (1916) 22 C.L.R. 402 6-080
Kilcran v Gothard [2014] FCAFC 6 8-021
Knights Capital Group Ltd v Bajada and Associates Pty Ltd [2016] WASC 69 9-121
Korda v Australian Executor Trustees (SA) Ltd [2015] HCA 6; (2015) 255 C.L.R. 62;
(2015) 317 A.L.R. 225 6-041
Krakowski v Eurolynx Properties Ltd (1995) 183 C.L.R. 563 8-209
Langlands Foundry Co v Worthington Pumping Engine Co (1896) 22 V.L.R. 144 2-081
Langmead v Thyer Rubber Co Ltd [1947] S.A.S.R. 29 8-156
Leahy (David) (Aust.) Pty Ltd v McPherson's Ltd [1991] 2 V.R. 362 . . . . 7-028, **7-032**
Learmouth v Bailey (1875) 1 V.L.R. 122 6-067
Ledir Enterprises Pty Limited, Re [2013] NSWSC 1332; (2013) 96 A.C.S.R. 1 5-002

Leggo v Brown & Dureau Ltd (1923) 32 C.L.R. 95 . . . . 9-062, 9-065, 9-070
Legione v Hateley (1983) 152 C.L.R. 406 8-021
Leonard v Ielassi (1987) 46 S.A.S.R. 495 . . . . 8-130, 8-133
Lep International Pty Ltd v Atlantrafic Express Service Inc (1987) 10 N.S.W.L.R. 614 5-001
Life Savers (Australasia) Ltd v Frigmobile Pty Ltd [1983] 1 N.S.W.L.R. 431 . . 2-074, 2-089, 2-092
Lifeplan Australia Friendly Society Ltd v Ancient Order of Foresters in Victoria Friendly
    Society Ltd [2017] FCAFC 74 8-225
Lift Capital Partners Pty Ltd v Merrill Lynch International (2009) 73 N.S.W.L.R. 404 2-041
Lincolne v Williams [2008] TASSC 41 7-004
Links Golf Tasmania Pty Ltd v Sattler [2012] FCA 634; (2012) 292 A.L.R. 382 . . . . . 6-015, **6-083**
Lloyd v Borg [2013] NSWCA 245 8-187
LMI Australasia Pty Ltd v Baulderstone Hornibrook Pty Ltd [2003] NSWCA 74 . . . . 2-031, 2-033,
                                                                                                          9-121
Lo v Russell [2016] VSCA 323 8-012
Lomax v Dankel (1981) 29 S.A.S.R. 68 . . . . 9-066, 9-085
Lord v Trippe (1977) 51 A.L.J.R. 574 . . . . 7-018, 7-032
Lucke v Cleary (2011) 111 S.A.S.R. 134 3-032
Lundie v Rowena Nominees Pty Ltd (2007) 32 W.A.R. 404 . . . . 2-042, 8-089, 9-016, 9-048, 9-089
Lunghi v Sinclair [1966] W.A.R. 172 . . . . 6-064, 6-068
Lyons (HJ) & Sando Ltd v Hulson [1963] S.A.S.R. 29 . . . . 9-034, 9-046
Lysaght & Co Ltd v Falk (1905) 2 C.L.R. 421 3-011
Lysaght Bros & Co Ltd v Falk (1905) 2 C.L.R. 421 . . . . 3-007, 3-011, 8-047
MacCormac v Bradford [1927] S.A.S.R. 152 9-096
Magnusson v Flanagan [1981] 2 N.S.W.L.R. 926 8-153
Magripilis v Baird [1926] St.R.Qd. 89 8-015
Maguire v Makaronis (1997) 188 C.L.R. 449 . . . . 6-036, 6-039, 6-044, 6-045, 6-068, **6-072**
Majeau Carrying Co Pty Ltd v Coastal Rutile Ltd (1973) 129 C.L.R. 48 7-082
Mallesons Stephen Jaques v KPMG Peat Marwick (1990) 4 W.A.R. 357 6-051
Manduoit v Ross (1884) 10 V.L.R. 264 2-056
Mantonella Pty Ltd v Thompson (2009) 255 A.L.R. 367 6-043
Marginson v Potter (Ian) & Co (1976) 136 C.L.R. 161; (1976) 50 A.L.J.R 8-003, 8-116
Marsh & McLennan Pty Ltd v Stanyers Transport Pty Ltd [1994] 2 V.R. 232 . . . . 1-041, 9-016
Marshall v Prescott [2015] NSWCA 110 6-051
Marzo v Land and Homes (W.A.) Ltd (1931) 34 W.A.L.R. 62 9-096
Matthews v SPI Electricity Pty Ltd [2011] VSC 167; (2011) 34 V.R. 560 2089
Maynegrain Pty Ltd v Compafina Bank (1984) 58 A.L.J.R. 389 PC 8-171, 8-172, **8-175**, 9-012
MBF Australia Ltd v Malouf [2008] NSWCA 214 8-210
McBride v Christie's Australia Pty Ltd [2014] NSWSC 1729 9-017
McHugh v Eastern Star Gas Ltd [2012] NSWCA 169 . . . . 2-057, 2-078
McIntosh v Linke Nominees Pty Ltd [2008] QCA 275 9-078
McKeand v Thomas (2006) 12 B.P.R. 23 . . . . **3-029**
McKenzie v McDonald [1927] V.L.R. 134 6-064
McLauchlan-Troup v Peters [1983] V.R. 53 2-077
McLaughlin v Darcy (1918) 18 S.R. (N.S.W.) 585 2-008
McLean Bros & Rigg Ltd v Grice (1906) 4 C.L.R. 835 2-071
McRae v Commonwealth Disposals Commission (1951) 84 C.L.R. 377 7-006
McRae v Coulton (1986) 7 N.S.W.L.R. 644 . . . . 2-017, 2-022, 2-023
Mega-Top Cargo Pty Ltd v Moneytech Services Pty Ltd [2015] NSWCA 402 7-063
Metropolitan Waste Disposal Authority v Willoughby Waste Disposals Ltd (1987) 9
    N.S.W.L.R. 7 . . . . **3-023**
MF (Australia) Ltd v Meadow Springs Fairway Resort Ltd [2009] FCAFC 9 4-010
Miller Associates (Australia) Pty Ltd v Bennington Pty Ltd (1975) 7 A.L.R. 144 9-085
Moneywood Pty v Salamon Nominees Pty [2001] H.C.A. 2; (2001) 202 C.L.R. 351 7-030
Mooney v Williams (1905) 3 C.L.R. 1 . . . . 8-069, 8-107
Mordecai (1988) 12 N.S.W.L.R. 58 6-034
Morgan v Babcock & Wilcox Ltd (1929) 43 C.L.R. 163 . . . . 2-025, 3-029
Morlend Finance Corp (Vic.) Pty Ltd v Westendorp [1993] 2 V.R. 284 . . . . **2-034**
Mortgage Loan & Finance Co of Australia Ltd v Richards (1932) 32 S.R. (N.S.W.) 50 8-145
Motel Marine Pty Ltd v IAC Finance Pty Ltd (1964) 110 C.L.R. 9 1-029
Motor Credits (Hire Finance) Ltd v Pacific Motor Auctions Pty [1965] A.C. 867 . . . . 8-127, 8-130,
                                                                                                          8-153
Motor Finance and Trading Co Ltd v Brown [1928] S.A.S.R. 153 8-130
MYT Engineering Pty Ltd v Mulcon Pty Ltd (1999) C.L.R. 636 2-042

National Australia Bank Ltd v Dionys [2016] NSWCA 242 2-079
National Commercial Banking Corp of Australia Ltd v Batty (1986) 160 C.L.R. 251 8-200
National Mutual Holdings Pty v Sentry Corp (1987) 87 A.L.R. 539 6-051
National Roads and Motorists' Assocation v Whitlam (2007) 25 A.C.L.C. 688 NSWCA 7-057,
    7-062
Nationwide News Pty Ltd v Naidu (2007) 71 N.S.W.L.R. 471 . . . . **8-217**
Netline Pty Ltd v Qav Pty Ltd (No.2) [2015] WASC 113 7-046
New South Wales v Ibbett (2006) 231 A.L.R. 485 HCA 8-177, 8-190, **8-192**
New South Wales v Lepore (2003) 212 C.L.R. 511 8-178
Nicholson v Morgan (No.3) [2013] WASC 110 9-141
Nielsen v Capital Finance Australia Ltd [2014] QCA 139; [2014] 2 Qd R. 459 . . . . 2-022, 2-024
NIML Ltd v Man Financial Australia Ltd (2006) 15 V.R. 156, Vic. CA **8-064**, 8-209
NMFM Property Pty Ltd v Citibank (2000) 107 F.C.R. 270 2-034
Noranda Australia v Lachlan Resources NL (1988) 14 N.S.W.L.R. 1 6-056
North v Marra Developments Ltd (1981) 148 C.L.R. 42 . . . . 7-052, 7-056
Northside Development Pty Ltd v Registrar-General (1990) 170 C.L.R. 146 . . 2-059, 8-034, 8-040,
    8-041, 8-050, 8-126
Norwest Refrigeration Services Pty Ltd v Bain Dawes (WA) Pty Ltd (1984) 157 C.L.R.
   149; (1984) 58 A.L.J.R. 521 . . . . 6-028, **6-032**
Nowrani Pty Ltd v Brown [1989] 2 Qd.R. 582 3-032
O'Brien v Dawson (1942) 66 C.L.R. 18 9-121
Ogden (Claude R) & Co Pty Ltd v Reliance Fire Sprinkler Co Pty (First Third Party);
   Stenhouse (N.S.W.) (Second Third Party) [1975] 1 Lloyd's Rep. 52 N.S.W. Supreme Ct 6-024
Ogden v McLaughlin (1909) 9 C.L.R. 615 . . . . 2-065, 2-079, 2-103, 8-203
Owens v Harris Bros (1932) 34 W.A.L.R. 110 8-111
P&O SN Co v Johnson (1938) 60 C.L.R. 189 . . . . 6-068, 6-086, 6-087
P&V Industries Pty Ltd v Porto (2006) 14 V.R. 1 . . . . 6-039, 6-054
Pacific Carriers Ltd v BNP Paribas (2004) 218 C.L.R. 451 . . . . 2-106, **2-109**, 8-017
Paget v Pearson (1949) 49 S.R. (N.S.W.) 235 3-023
Palette Shoes Pty Ltd v Krohn (1937) 58 C.L.R. 1 . . . . 6-041, 6-090
Pascoe v Lucas (2000) 33 A.C.S.R. 357 1-028
Pavlovic v Universal Music Australia Pty Ltd [2015] NSWCA 313; (2015) 90 N.S.W.L.R.
   605 . . . . 3-007, 3-032
Peckham v Moore [1975] 1 N.S.W.L.R. 353 9-087
Permanent Building Society v Wheeler (1994) 14 A.C.S.R. 109 . . . . 6-043, **6-045**
Permanent Custodians Ltd v Geagea [2014] NSWSC 562 9-062
Permanent Trustee Australia Co v FAI General Insurance Co (2003) 214 C.L.R. 514 . 8-211, 8-212,
    8-213
Permanent Trustee Co Ltd v O'Donnell [2011] NSWCA 389 . . . . 2-031, 8-214, 8-215
Perpetual Trustee Co Ltd v Aroney (1944) 44 S.R. (N.S.W.) 313; 61 W.N. 177 10-003
Perpetual Trustee Co Ltd v Burniston (No.2) [2012] WASC 383 5-009
Perpetual Trustee Co Ltd v El-Bayeh [2010] NSWSC 1487 8-200
Perpetual Trustee Co Ltd v Nebo Road Pty Ltd [2011] QSC 283 9-008
Perpetual Trustees Victoria Ltd v Cox [2014] NSWCA 328 2-079
Petersen v Moloney (1951) 84 C.L.R. 91 . . . . 2-077, 3-032, 8-114, 8-117, 8-118, 8-119
Phillipson v Indus Realty Pty Ltd (2004) 8 V.L.R. 446 7-018
Pilmer v Duke Group Ltd (2001) 75 A.L.J.R. 1067 6-036
Pinata Pty Limited (In Liquidation), Re [2012] NSWSC 162 2-007
Pioneer Mortgage Services Pty Ltd v Columbus Capital Pty Ltd [2016] FCAFC 78 8-180
Polkinghorne v Holland (1934) 51 C.L.R. 143; [1934] S.A.S.R. 475; 40 Arg. L.R. 353;
   S.A.L.J. 140 8-063
Pourzand v Telstra Corp Ltd [2014] WASCA 14 . . . . 8-012, 8-018, 8-050
Powercor Australia Ltd v Pacific Power Ltd [1999] VSC 110 2-056
Premier Building and Consulting Pty Ltd v Spotless Group Ltd (2008) 64 A.C.S.R. 114 1-030
Presser v Caldwell Estates Pty Ltd [1971] 2 N.S.W.L.R. 471 . . . . 3-032, 9-117
Prince Alfred College Inc v ADC [2016] HCA 37 8-178
Propell National Valuers (WA) Pty Ltd v Australian Executor Trustees Ltd [2012] FCAFC
   31 9-117
Provincial Insurance Australia Pty Ltd v Wood Products Ltd (1991) 25 N.S.W.L.R. 541 6-024
Public Trustee v Taylor [1978] V.R. 289 8-073
Queensland Mines Ltd v Hudson (1978) 18 A.L.R. 1 PC 6-039, **6-083**
Quikfund (Australia) Pty Ltd v Chatswood Appliance Spare parts Pty Ltd [2013] NSWSC
   646 8-018

Quikfund (Australia) Pty Ltd v Prosperity Group International Pty Limited (In Liquidation) [2013] FCAFC 5 2-034
R. v Board of Appeal Ex p. Kay (1916) 22 C.L.R. 183 2-024
R. v Visiting Justice at JM Prison, Pentridge [1975] V.R. 883 2-024
Raffoul v Esanda Ltd [1970] 3 N.S.W.R. 8 .... 8-126, 8-153
Raleigh v McGarth (1877) 3 V.L.R. 250 6-082
Residues Treatment & Trading Co Ltd v Southern Resources Ltd (No.4) (1989) 14 A.C.L.R. 569. 8-221
Richardson v Landecker (1950) 50 S.R. (N.S.W.) 250 2-036
Roache v Australian Mercantile Land & Finance Co Ltd (No.2) [1966] 1 N.S.W.L.R. 384 ... 8-151
Robash Pty Ltd v Gladstone Pacific Nickel Pty Ltd (2012) 86 A.C.S.R. 432 6-081
Robertson (JS) (Australia) Pty Ltd v Martin (1956) 94 C.L.R. 30 .... 1-021, 7-101, 9-034
Robinson v Tyson (1888) 9 L.R. (N.S.W.) 297 8-010
Rochfort v Trade Practices Commission (1982) 153 C.L.R. 134; (1981) 37 A.L.R. 439 . 8-170
Root Quality Pty Ltd v Root Control Technologies Pty Ltd (2001) 177 A.L.R. 231 ... 9-120
Roots v Oentory Pty Ltd [1983] 2 Qd.R. 745 9-117
Rowe v B. & R. Nominees Pty Ltd [1964] V.R. 477 .... 2-059, 8-041
Royal Globe Life Assurance Co Ltd v Kovacevic (1979) 22 S.A.S.R. 78 8-201
Russell Gould Pty Ltd v Ramangkura (No.2) [2015] NSWCA 14 8-014
Rutherford v Poole [1953] V.L.R. 130 9-121
Saad v Doumeny Holdings Pty Ltd [2005] NSWSC 893 .... 3-011, 5-002
Salim v Ingham Enterprises (1998) 55 N.S.W.L.R. 7 9-091
Schlieske v Overseas Construction Co Pty Ltd [1960] V.R. 195 ...... 9-063, 9-066, 9-070, 9-083
Scots Church Adelaide Inc v Fead [1951] S.A.S.R. 41 2-079
Scott v Bagshaw (1999) 92 F.C.R. 424 2-077
Scott v Davis (2000) 204 C.L.R. 333 .... 1-004, 8-178, 8-187, 8-196
Scott v Geoghegan & Sons Pty Ltd (1969) 43 A.L.J.R. 243 9-021
Scott v Scott (1963) 109 C.L.R. 649; (1963) 37 A.L.J. 345 6-040
Seiwa Australia Pty Ltd v Beard (2010) 75 N.S.W.L.R. 74 ...... 3-007, 3-031, **3-032**, 8-015
Selfe v Colonial Ice Co (1894) 10 W.N. (N.S.W.) 153 10-018
Serventy v Commonwealth Bank of Australia (No.2) [2016] WASCA 223 1-004
Shepherd v Felt and Textiles of Australia Ltd (1931) 45 C.L.R. 359 7-050
Siahos v JP Morgan Trust Australia Ltd [2009] NSWCA 20 3-015
Slatter v Railway Commissioners (New South Wales) 1931 45 C.L.R. 68 10-006
Smith (Howard) & Co Ltd v Varawa (1907) 5 C.L.R. 68 2-062
Smith v Peter & Diana Hubbard Pty Ltd [2006] NSWCA 109 .... 3-022, 3-032, 8-050
Smits v Roach (2006) 228 A.L.R. 262 HCA **8-217**
Soblusky v Egan (1960) 103 C.L.R. 215 8-187
South Sydney District Rugby League Football Club v News (2003) 215 C.L.R. 563 .. 1-004, 1-018, 2-031
South Sydney DRLFC v News Ltd (2000) 177 A.L.R. 611 2-033
Spangaro Corporate Investment Funds Management Ltd (2003) 47 A.C.S.R. 285 ... 8-161
Spedley Securities Ltd v Greater Pacific Investments Pty Ltd (1992) 7 A.C.S.R. 155 ... 3-029
Spellson v George (1992) 26 N.S.W.L.R. 666 6-039
Spina v Permanent Custodians Ltd [2008] NSWSC 561 3-014
State of South Australia v Clark (1996) S.A.S.R. 199 8-220
State Rail Authority of NSW v Heath Outdoor Pty Ltd (1986) 7 N.S.W.L.R. 170 ..... 3-032, 8-021
Stephens Travel Service Inc Pty Ltd v Qantas Airways Ltd (1988) 13 N.S.W.L.R. 331 6-041
Stevens v Brodribb Sawmilling Co Pty Ltd (1986) 160 C.L.R. 16 8-178
Stewart v Layton (1992) 111 A.L.R. 687 6-050
Stott Land Development Corp v Dean [1967] W.A.R. 86 9-085
Stunzi Sons Ltd v House of Youth Pty Ltd [1966] S.R. (N.S.W.) 220 9-021
Summergreene v Parker (1950) 80 C.L.R. 304 9-085
Sweeney v Boylan Nominees Pty Ltd [2006] HCA 19; (2006) 226 C.L.R. 161 8-182
Sweeney v Howard [2007] NSWSC 852 .... 3-010, 3-013, 3-015
Swindle v Knibb (1929) 29 S.R. (N.S.W.) 325; 46 N.S.W.N. 102 9-026
Sze Tu v Lowe [2014] NSWCA 462 6-042
Taheri v Vitek [2014] NSWCA 209; (2014) 320 A.L.R. 555 3-014
Tasita Pty Ltd v Sovereign State of Papua New Guinea (1991) 34 N.S.W.L.R. 691 8-042
Taylor v Smith (1926) 38 C.L.R. 48 .... 2-071, 2-078, 8-167
Technology Leasing Ltd v Lennmar Pty Ltd [2012] FCA 709 .... 2-031, 8-024
Telstra Corp Ltd v Ivory [2008] Q.S.C. 123 .... **3-029**

Thomas Australia Wholesale Vehicle Trading Co Pty Ltd v Marac Finance Australia Ltd
  (1985) 3 N.S.W.L.R. 452 8-130
Thompson (Geo) (Austr) Pty Ltd v Vitadello [1978] V.R. 199 8-093
Thompson v Henderson & Partners Pty Ltd (1989) 51 S.A.S.R. 43 8-196
Thornley v Tilley (1925) 36 C.L.R. 1; 42 N.S.W.W.N. 70; 31 Arg. L.R. 291 .... 3-040, **6-078**
Tibmor Pty Ltd v Nashlyn Pty Ltd [1989] 1 Q. & R. 610 7-090
Timms v Carofaro (1989) 53 S.A.S.R. 572 7-018
Tina Motors Pty Ltd v ANZ Banking Group Ltd [1971] V.R. 205 2-061
Tipperary Developments Pty Ltd v The State of Western Australia (2009) W.A.R. 488 8-042
Tobin v Broadbent (1947) 75 C.L.R. 378 .... 3-015, 8-126, 8-128, 8-130, 8-133, 8-135, 8-138
Toll (FGCT) Pty Ltd v Alphapharm Pty Ltd (2004) 219 C.L.R. 165 .... **3-029**, 8-050
Tonto Home Loans Australia Pty Ltd v Tavares [2011] NSWCA 389 .... 1-012, 2-033, 2-034
Toycorp Ltd v Milton Bradley Australia Pty Ltd [1992] 2 V.R. 572 1-035
Tracy v Mandalay Pty Co (1953) 88 C.L.R. 215 .... 6-035, 6-068
Traderight (NSW) Pty Ltd v Bank of Queensland Ltd [2015] NSWCA 94 7-001
Trident General Ins.Co Ltd v McNiece Bros Pty Ltd (1988) 165 C.L.R. 107 .. 2-067, **2-070**, 2-074,
                                                         2-089, 2-092, 2-093
Tweedvale Investments Pty Ltd v Thiran (1996) 14 W.A.R. 109 6-068
Unioil International Pty Ltd v Deloitte Touche Tohmatsu (1997) 17 W.A.R. 98 6-051
Union Bank of Australia v Rudder (1911) 13 C.L.R. 152 2-096
Union Fidelity Trustee Co of Australia Ltd v Gibson [1971] V.R. 573 6-069
Universal Guarantee Pty Ltd v Metters Ltd [1966] W.A.R. 74 .... 8-147, 8-158
Utz v Carver [1972] 1 N.S.W.L.R. 407 6-090
Van Rassel v Kroon (1953) 87 C.L.R. 298; [1953] A.L.R. 190; 27 A.L.J. 75 6-040
Veljkovic v Vrybergen [1985] V.R. 419 .... 3-019, 3-020, 6-011, 6-028
Vella v Permanent Mortgages Pty Ltd [2008] NSWSC 505 .... 2-040, 3-032, 9-109
Vickery v Woods (1952) 85 C.L.R. 336 9-085
Vitek v Estate Homes Pty Ltd [2013] NSWSC 1764 3-014
Wagdy Hanna and Associates Pty Ltd v National Library of Australia (2004) 185 F.L.R.
  367. 6-051
Waimond Pty Ltd v Byrne (1989) 18 N.S.W.L.R. 642 6-021
Walden Properties Ltd v Beaver Properties Pty Ltd (1973) 2 N.S.W.L.R. 81 .... 6-068, 6-071
Walker v Corboy (1990) 19 N.S.W.L.R. 382 .... 6-041, 6-091
Walters v Crisp (John) Pty Ltd (1982) 64 F.L.R. 299 7-019
Waltons Stores (Interstate) Ltd v Maher (1988) 164 C.L.R. 387 .... 6-029, 8-021
Wandel and Goltermann GmbH v Wandel Global Services Pty Ltd [2002] FCA 1609 3-004
Warman International Pty Ltd v Dwyer (1995) 182 C.L.R. 544 . 6-034, 6-040, 6-076, 6-077, 6-080,
                                                    6-096
Wheatley v Bell [1982] 2 N.S.W.L.R. 544; [1984] F.S.R. 16 6-077
White v Baycorp Advantage Business Information Services Ltd (2006) 200 F.L.R. 125 8-078,
                                                     8-079
Whitehouse v Carlton Hotel Pty Ltd (1987) 162 C.L.R. 285 8-226
Williams Group Australia Pty Ltd v Crocker [2016] NSWCA 265 .... 2-059, 8-018, 8-023
Williams v Bulat [1992] 2 Qd.R. 566 8-082
Wingecarribee Shire Council v Lehman Brothers Australia Ltd [2012] FCA 1028; (2013)
  301 A.L.R. 1 .... **6-024**, 6-035
Woolworths Ltd v Kelly (1991) 22 N.S.W.L.R. 189 6-039
Wright v Gasweld Pty Ltd (1991) 22 N.S.W.L.R. 317 .... 2-014, 6-037
Wright v Madden [1992] 1 Qd.R. 343 9-034
Youyang Pty Ltd v Minter Ellison Morris Fletcher [2003] W.T.L.R. 751; (2003) 212
  C.L.R. 484, HC (Aus). 6-036, 6-043
Yu v Brownvalley Investments Pty Ltd [2010] NSWSC 253 8-126
ZBB (Australia) Ltd v Allen 91991) 4 A.C.S.R. 495 8-215

CANADA

1196303 Inc v Glen Grove Suites Inc 2015 ONCA 580 8-117
Aaran Acceptance Corp v Adam (1987) 37 D.L.R. (4th) 733 6-064
Abbey Glen Property Corp v Stumborg (1978) 85 D.L.R. (3d) 35 6-083
Advanced Realty Funding Corp v Bannink (1979) 106 D.L.R. (3d) 137 6-048
Alberta v Elder Advocates of Alberta Society 2011 SCC 24 6-035
Alessio v Jovica (1973) 42 D.L.R. (3d) 242 9-117
Alvin's Auto Service v Clew Holdings (1997) 3 B.L.R. (2d) 11 .... 9-079, 9-085

Attorney General (Nova Scotia) v Christian (1974) 49 D.L.R. (3d) 742 . . . . **8-226**
Austin v Real Estate Listing Exchange (1912) 2 D.L.R. 324 9-070
Automobile Renault Canada Ltd v Maritime Import Autos Ltd (1961) 31 D.L.R. (2d) 592 . . . 9-037
Avery v Salie (1972) 25 D.L.R. (3d) 495 . . . . 6-028, 9-117
B&M Readers' Service Ltd v Anglo Canadian Publishers Ltd [1950] O.R. 159 1-022
Bango v Holt (1971) 21 D.L.R. (3d) 66 9-117
Bank of Montreal v Young (1966) 60 D.L.R. (2d) 220 8-180
Barry v Stoney Point Canning Co (1917) 55 S.C.R. 51 8-224
BC Timber Industries Journal v Black [1934] 3 D.L.R. 31 . . . . **6-078**
Becherer v Asher (1896) 23 Ont. App. Rep. 202; 23 A.R. 202 8-077
Beer v Lea (1913) 29 O.L.R. 255 6-066
Bentley v Nasmith (1912) 46 S.C.R. 477 6-066
Berryere v Firemans Fund Insurance Co (1965) 51 D.L.R. (2d) 603 8-021
Blackwater v Plint (2005) 258 D.L.R. (4th) 275 8-177
Blanchette v CIS Ltd [1973] S.C.R. 833 8-217
Block Bros Kealty Ltd v Viktora (1974) 42 D.L.R. (3d) 474 7-017
Blueberry River Indian Band v R [1995] 2 S.C.R. 344; (1996) 130 D.L.R. (4th) 193 6-036
BMP Global Distribution Inc v Bank of Nova Scotia [2009] 1 S.C.R. 504; (2009) 304
    D.L.R. (4th) 292 9-106
Boyle v Maritime Travel Inc 2014 NSCA 44 3-007
Bradley-Wilson (1954) Ltd v Canyon Gardens Ltd (1965) 53 W.W.R. 413; (1965) 52
    D.L.R. (2d) 717 7-037
Brennen (M) & Sons Mfg Co Ltd v Thompson (1915) 33 Ont. L.R. 465; 8 O.W.N. 206 8-116,
    8-117, 8-118
Burns Fry Ltd v Khurana (1985) 20 D.L.R. (4th) 245 7-036
Burns v Peters (Kelly) & Associates Ltd (1987) 41 D.L.R. (4th) 571 6-056
Cadbury Schweppes Inc v FBI Foods Ltd [1999] 1 S.C.R. 142; (1999) 167 D.L.R. (4th)
    577 . . . . 1-035, 6-015, 6-036, 6-037, 6-077
Campbell v National Trust Co Ltd [1931] 1 W.W.R. 465; [1931] 1 D.L.R. 705 PC 7-004
Campbellville Gravel Supply Ltd v Cook Paving Co Ltd (1968) 70 D.L.R. (2d) 354 8-079
Canada v Merchant Law Group 2010 FCA 206 (Can. Fed. CA) 1-023
Canadian Aero Services Ltd v O'Malley [1974] S.C.R. 592; (1973) 40 D.L.R. (3d) 371 6-081,
    6-083
Canadian Laboratory Supplies Ltd v Engelhard Industries of Canada [1979] 2 S.C.R. 787;
    (1979) 97 D.L.R. (3d) 1; (1977) 78 D.L.R. (3d) 232 . . . . 2-083, 8-019, 8-020, 8-030, 8-060, 8-063,
    8-133
Canadian Pacific Airlines Ltd v Canadian Imperial Bank of Commerce (1990) 71 Q.R.
    (2d) 63 6-041
Canson Enterprises Ltd v Boughton & Co [1991] 3 S.C.R. 534 . . . . 6-036, **6-045**
Carey v Laiken 2015 SCC 17; [2015] 2 S.C.R. 79 9-116
Cash v Dundas (George) Realty Ltd [1976] 2 S.C.R. 796; (1975) 59 D.L.R. (3d) 605 7-021
Cec. McManus Realty Ltd v Bray (1970) 14 D.L.R. (3d) 56 . . . . 6-048, 6-057, 6-087, 7-050
Central Trust Co v Rafuse [1986] 2 S.C.R. 147 6-018
CFTO TV Ltd v Mr Submarine Ltd (1997) 151 D.L.R. (4th) 382 . . . . 1-018, 9-006
Chand v Sabo Bros Realty Ltd (1979) 96 D.L.R. (3d) 445 9-117
Chartwell Shipping Ltd v Q.N.S. Paper Co Ltd [1989] 2 S.C.R. 683 . . . . 9-016, 9-037, **9-038**
Christie v McCann (1972) 27 D.L.R. (3d) 544 . . . . 6-064, 6-086
Citadel General Assurance Co v Lloyd's Bank Canada [1997] 3 S.C.R. 805; (1997) 152
    D.L.R. (4th) 411 9-136
Comeau v Province of New Brunswick (1973) 36 D.L.R. (3d) 763 8-042
Commerce Realty Ltd v Olenyk (1957) 8 D.L.R. (2d) 60 6-007
Commonwealth Trust Co v De Witt (1973) 40 D.L.R. (3d) 113 8-074
Crampsey v Deveney [1968] S.C.R. 267; (1968) 2 D.L.R. (3d) 161 2-062
Cypress Disposal Ltd v Inland Kenworth Sales (Nanaimo) Ltd (1975) 54 D.L.R. (3d) 598 . . . 8-021
Dairy Supplies Ltd v Fuchs (1959) 18 D.L.R. (2d) 408 9-085
Dale v Government of Manitoba (1997) 147 D.L.R. (4th) 605 8-021
Deacon (RH) & Co Ltd v Varga 41 D.L.R. (3d) 767 . . . . 6-003, 6-016, 6-037, 6-066
Delta Construction Co Ltd v Lidstone (1979) 46 D.L.R. (3d) 457 . . . . 9-066, 9-080, 9-085
Deutsch, Re (1976) 82 D.L.R. (3d) 567 5-001
Dodds v Dodds and Millman (1964) 45 D.L.R. (2d) 472 9-117
Durham v Asser (1968) 67 D.L.R. (2d) 574 8-153
Evans v Anderson (1977) 76 D.L.R. (3d) 482 . . . . 6-081, 6-083
Felty v Ernst & Young LLP [2015] BCCA 445 9-005

Fidelity Trust Co v Rudy (1957) 23 W.W.R. 668 7-037
Fine's Flowers Ltd v General Accident Ass.Co of Canada (1977) 81 D.L.R. (3d) 139 . 6-012, **6-016**, 6-024
Frame v Smith [1987] 2 S.C.R. 99 6-036
Friedmann Equity Developments Inc v Final Note Ltd [2000] 1 S.C.R. 842; (2000) 188 D.L.R. (4th) 265 8-084
Funduk and Horncastle, Re (1973) 39 D.L.R. (3d) 94 .... 8-061, 8-154
Galambos v Perez [2009] 3 S.C.R. 247; (2009) 312 D.L.R. (4th) 220 SCC 7-001
Galan v Alekno [1950] 3 D.L.R. 9 7-037
Gebhard Hoelzler Construction Ltd v Seidler [2008] B.C.C.A. 77 2-034
General Motors Acceptance Corp of Canada Ltd v Weisman (1979) 96 D.L.R. (3d) 159 9-085
Glendinning v Cavanagh (1908) 40 S.C.R. 414 7-032
Globex Foreign Exchange Corp v Launt 2011 NSCA 67 .... 1-030, 3-017
Goodison Thresher Co v Doyle (1925) 57 O.L.R. 300 2-087
Gray v New Augarita Porcupine Mines [1952] 3 D.L.R. 1 .... 6-039, 6-065, 6-068, 6-083
Groves v Stirling Bonding Co [1935] 3 D.L.R. 481 10-046
Guaranty Trust Co v Richardson (James) & Son (1963) 39 D.L.R. (2d) 517 7-058
Guerin v R. [1984] 2 S.C.R. 335 .... 1-015, 6-036, 6-043
Hartt Group and Land Securities Ltd, Re (1984) 7 D.L.R. (4th) 89 10-006
Hawrelak v City of Edmonton (1975) 54 D.L.R. (3d) 45 6-083
Hayes v Standard Bank of Canada [1928] 2 D.L.R. 898 3-015
Hazlewood v West Coast Securities Ltd (1976) 68 D.L.R. (3d) 172 .... 8-203, 8-204
Hodgkinson v Simms [1994] 3 S.C.R. 377; (1994) 117 D.L.R. (4th) 161 ...... 6-036, 6-043, 6-045
Houston v Houston 2012 BCCA 300; [2012] 12 W.W.R. 215 10-027
Howard v Carline (1956) 7 D.L.R.(2d) 324 2-109
Indutech Canada Ltd v Gibbs Pipe Sales Ltd [2011] 8 W.W.R. 60 5-008
Investors Syndicate Ltd v Versatile Investments Ltd (1983) 149 D.L.R. (3d) 46 ...... 6-077, 6-078
Jackson v Packham Real Estate Ltd (1980) 109 D.L.R. (3d) 277 6-037
Jensen v South Trail Mobile Ltd (1972) 28 D.L.R. (3d) 233 8-021
Jirna Ltd v Mister Donut of Canada Ltd (1973) 40 D.L.R. (3d) 303 .... 6-037, 7-001
Keshen v Lipsky (S) Co Ltd (1956) 3 D.L.R. (2d) 438 10-043
Knoch Estate v Picken (John) Ltd (1991) 83 D.L.R. (4th) 447 .... 6-037, 6-048
Kohn v Devon Mortgage Ltd (1985) 20 D.L.R. (4th) 480 .... 3-032, 8-118
Komarniski v Marien (1979) 100 D.L.R. (3d) 81 9-117
Lang Transport v Plus Factor International Trucking (1997) 143 D.L.R. (4th) 672 (Ontario Ct. of Appeal) 8-114, 8-117, 8-118
Liebig (HW) & Co v Leading Investments Ltd [1987] 1 S.C.R. 70 .... 7-017, 7-018, 7-019
London Drugs Ltd v Kuehne & Nagel International Ltd [1992] 3 S.C.R. 299 .... 9-117, 9-122
Lowe v Rutherford Thompson McRae Ltd (1970) 14 D.L.R. (3d) 772 10-043
M (K) v M (H) [1992] 3 S.C.R. 6; (1992) 96 D.L.R. (4th) 289 6-036
Markal Investments Ltd v Morley Shafron Agencies Ltd (1987) 44 D.L.R. (4th) 745 6-024
Martin (LB) Construction Ltd v Gagliardi [1979] 1 W.W.R. 171; (1978) 91 D.L.R. (3d) 393.. 6-009
Martin v Artyork Investments Ltd [1997] 2 S.C.R. 290 8-012
Matheson v Smiley [1932] 2 D.L.R. 787 4-010
McBrayne v Imperial Loan Co (1913) 13 D.L.R. 448 7-032
McDonald Estate v Martin; sub nom. Martin v Gray [1990] 3 S.C.R. 1235; (1990) 77 D.L.R. (4th) 249 6-051
McGraw-Edison (Canada) Ltd v Direct-Winters Tpt. Ltd [1969] 1 O.R. 663 3-025
McKeag Harris Realty & Development Co Ltd v Builders' Mutual Assets Ltd (1968) 66 W.W.R. 512.. 7-030, 7-032
McLaughlin v Gentles (1919) 51 D.L.R. 383; 46 O.L.R. 477; 17 O.W.N. 245 8-077
McLellan Properties Ltd v Roberge [1947] S.C.R. 561 2-021
McLeod and More v Sweezey [1944] 2 D.L.R. 145 .... 6-067, **6-083**
McManus v Eastern Ford Sales Ltd (1981) 128 D.L.R. (3d) 246 .... 8-133, 8-147
Mentmore Manufacturing Co Ltd v National Merchandising Co Ltd (1978) 89 D.L.R. (3d) 195.. 9-120
Mid-Western News Agency Ltd v Vanpinxteren (1975) 62 D.L.R. (3d) 555 .... 6-081, 6-083
Morgan v Lifetime Building Supplies Ltd (1967) 61 D.L.R. (2d) 178 .... 8-119, 10-030
Mortimer-Rae v Barthel (1979) 105 D.L.R. (3d) 289 8-153
Moxness v Co-operative Fire and Casualty Co (1979) 95 D.L.R. (3d) 365 8-217
Murray v Delta Copper Co Ltd [1925] 4 D.L.R. 1061 .... 8-117, 8-120
Norberg v Wynrib [1992] 2 S.C.R. 226 6-036

O'Connor Real Estate Ltd v Flynn (1969) 3 D.L.R. (3d) 345 7-032
Ocean City Realty Ltd v A & M Holdings Ltd (1987) 36 D.L.R. (4th) 94 . . . . 6-021, 7-050
Olsen v Poirier (1978) 91 D.L.R. (3d) 123 9-117
Ontario Marble Co Ltd v Creative Memorials Ltd (1964) 45 D.L.R. (2d) 244 9-038
Palinko v Bower [1976] 4 W.W.R. 118 6-064
Papers Sales Corp Ltd v Miller Bros Co (1982) Ltd (1975) 55 D.L.R. (3d) 492 10-042
Parks, Re (1956) 8 D.L.R. (2d) 155 10-032
Pasen v Dominion Herb Distributors Inc 69 D.L.R. (2d) 651 7-046
Paxton v Spira (1965) 54 D.L.R. (2d) 627 7-046
Peso Silver Mines Ltd v Cropper [1966] S.C.R. 673; (1966) 58 D.L.R. (2d) 1 . . . . . . 6-081, **6-083**
RBC Dominion Securities Inc v Merrill Lynch Canada Inc [2008] 3 S.C.R. 79 . . . . . . 6-034, 6-054
Roberts v Montex Development Corporation 100 D.L.R. (3d) 660 9-117
Rockland Industries Inc v Amerada Minerals Corp of Canada Ltd [1980] 2 S.C.R. 2 10-031,
     10-033
Royal Securities Corp Ltd v Montreal Trust Co (1967) 63 D.L.R. (2d) 15 . . . . 2-013, 2-031, 2-033,
     9-099
Rungay v Forrester (1967) 63 D.L.R. (2d) 338 7-032
Salter v Cormie (1993) 108 D.L.R. (4th) 372 9-066
Schafhauser v Shaffer and National Finance Co [1943] 3 D.L.R. 656 8-147
Sharbern Holding Inc v Vancouver Airport Centre Ltd [2011] 2 S.C.R. 175; (2011) 331
     D.L.R. (4th) 1 . . . . 6-038, 6-039, 6-047, 6-063, **6-071**
Sign-o-Lite Plastics Ltd v Metropolitan Life Insurance Co (1990) 73 D.L.R. (4th) 541 8-077
Simpson (Robert) & Co v Godson [1937] 1 D.L.R. 454 . . . . 8-008, 10-027
Soulos v Korkontzilas [1997] 2 S.C.R. 217; (1997) 146 D.L.R. (4th) 214 6-036
Standard Investments Ltd v Canadian Imperial Bank of Commerce (1985) 22 D.L.R. (4th)
     410. 6-050
State Vacuum Stores v Phillips [1954] 3 D.L.R. 621 6-061
Stratton v Vachan and Wilson (1911) 44 S.C.R. 395 7-032
Strother v 3464920 Canada Inc [2007] 2 S.C.R. 177; (2007) 281 D.L.R. (4th) 640 . . . 6-036, 6-081
Styles v Rogers Realty Ltd (1987) 43 D.L.R. (4th) 629 . . . . 6-024, 7-050
Swanton Seed Service Ltd v Kulba (1968) 68 D.L.R. (2d) 38 . . . . 8-117, 9-006
Tedrick v Big T Restaurants of Canada [1983] 2 W.W.R. 135 8-120
Terry Martel Real Estate Ltd v Lovette Investments Ltd (1981) 123 D.L.R. (3d) 387 7-030
Thiessen v Clarica Law Reinsurance Co (2002) 219 D.L.R. (4th) 98 8-182
Thoresen v Capital Credit Corp Ltd (1964) 43 D.L.R. (2d) 94 . . . . 8-145, 8-150
Travelers Guarantee Co of Canada v Farajollahi [2012] B.C.S.C. 1283 2-012
Trident Holdings Ltd v Danand Investments Ltd (1988) 49 D.L.R. (4th) 1 1-032
Turner v Laurentide Financial Realty Corp (Western) Ltd (1979) 97 D.L.R. (3d) 429 . 6-048, 7-051
Verreault (JE) et Fills Ltèe v Attorney General for Quebec [1977] 1 S.C.R. 41 8-042
Volkers v Midland Doherty (1985) 17 D.L.R. (4th) 343 . . . . 6-003, 6-012, **6-016**, 6-037
Western Radio Group Ltd v McIsaac (1989) 63 D.L.R. (4th) 433 9-085
Wickberg v Shatsky (1969) 4 D.L.R. (3d) 540 9-085
Wolfe Stevedores (1968) Ltd v Salter's (Joseph) Sons Ltd (1971) 16 D.L.R. (3d) 334 9-006
Worrall v Peters (1902) 32 S.C.R. 52; 35 N.S.R. 26 6-097

EUROPE

Agro Foreign Trade Agency v Petersime NV (Case C-507/15) 11-006
Arcado SPRL v Haviland SA (9/87) [1988] E.C.R. 1539; [1989] E.C.C. 1 11-040
Bellone v Yokohama SpA (C215/97) [1998] E.C.R. I-2191; [1998] 3 C.M.L.R. 975 ECJ . . . 11-002,
     11-026, 11-035
Caprini v Conservatore Camera di Commercio Industria Artigianato e Agricoltura; sub
     nom. Caprini v Conservatore del Registro Delle Imprese di Trento (C-485/02) [2003]
     E.C.R. I-2371 ECJ. 11-002
Centrosteel Srl v Adipol GmbH (C-456/98) [2000] E.C.R. I-6007; [2000] 3 C.M.L.R. 711;
     [2000] C.E.C. 527 ECJ 11-001, 11-002
Chevassus-Marche v Groupe Danone (C-19/07) [2008] 2 All E.R. (Comm.) 1093 . . 11-025, 11-031
Commission v Italy (C7/68) [1968] E.C.R. 423; [1969] C.M.L.R. 1 ECJ 11-016
ERGO Poist'ovna a.s. (C-48/16) CJEU, May 17, 2017 . . . . 11-033, 11-034
Etablissements Somafer SA v Saar-Ferngas AG (33/78) [1978] E.C.R. 2183; [1979] 1
     C.M.L.R. 490 12-005
Fadin Habitat (Société) v Constructions Traditionelles du Val de Loire [2015] E.C.C.27 . . . 11-039,
     11-042

Ferro v Santoro (Case C-273/01) [2002] OJ C-323/24 .... 11-013, 11-018
GO Poist'ovna a.s. (Case C-48/16) CJEU, May 17, 2017 11-034
Honyvem Informazioni Commerciali v Mariellad de Zotti (C-465/04) [2006]
    E.C.R.I-02879 .... 11-044, 11-051
Ingmar GB Ltd v Eaton Leonard Technologies Inc (C381/98) [2000] E.C.R. I-9305;
    [2001] All E.R. (EC) 57; [2001] 1 All E.R. (Comm) 329; [2001] 1 C.M.L.R. 9 ECJ (5th
    Chamber) 11-006, 11-007, 11-010, 11-035, 11-041
Intercontainer Interfrigo SC (ICF) v Balkenende Oosthuizen BV (C-133/08) [2010] All
    E.R. (EC) 1; [2010] 1 All E.R. (Comm) 613; [2010] C.E.C. 310; [2010] I.L.Pr. 3 ECJ 12-003,
                                                                                   12-013
Jakob Handte & Co GmbH v Traitements Mecano-Chimiques des Surfaces SA (TMCS)
    (C-26/91) [1992] E.C.R. I-3967; [1993] I.L.Pr. 5 ECJ.............................. 12-004
Kontogeorgas v Kartonpak AE (C104/95) [1996] E.C.R. I-6643; [1997] 1 C.M.L.R. 1093
    ECJ (5th Chamber) 11-031, 11-035
Laboratoires Arkopharma SA v Gravier [2003] E.C.C. 333 11-056
Lawlor v Sandvik Mining and Construction Mobile Crushers and Screens Ltd [2012]
    EWHC 1188 (QB); [2012] 2 Lloyd's Rep. 25; [2012] I.L.Pr. 31 .... 11-006, 12-003
Marchon Germany GmbH v Karaskiewicz (Case C-315/14) [2016] Bus.L.R. 694 11-044
Marleasing SA v La Comercial Internacional de Alimentacion SA (C106/89) [1990]
    E.C.R. I-4135; [1993] B.C.C. 421; [1992] 1 C.M.L.R. 305 ECJ (6th Chamber) 8-035, 11-004
Mavrona & Sia OE v Delta Etaireia Symmetochon AE (Case C-85/03) [2004] E.C.R.
    I-1573.. 11-013, 11-019
Poseidon Chartering BV v Marianne Zeeschip VOF (Case C-3/04) [2006] 2 Lloyd's Rep.
    105.. 11-017
Quenon K SPRL v Citibank Belgium SA (C-338/14) EU:C:2015:795; [2016] Bus. L.R.
    264.. 11-047
Semen v Deutsche Tamoil GmbH (C-348/07) [2009] 2 All E.R. (Comm) 243; [2009] 1
    Lloyd's Rep. 653; [2009] E.C.R. I-2341; [2009] 3 C.M.L.R. 12; [2009] C.E.C. 1008
    ECJ 11-044
United Antwerp Maritime Agencies (Unamar) NV v Navigation Maritime Bulgare
    (C-184/12) [2014] 1 All E.R. (Comm) 625; [2014] 1 Lloyd's Rep. 161 11-006
Volvo Car Germany GmbH v Autohof Weidensdorf GmbH (C-203/09) [2011] 1 All E.R.
    (Comm) 906; [2012] Bus. L.R. D13 .... 11-044, 11-056
Von Colson and Kamann v Land Nordrhein-Westfahlen (No.14/83); Harz v Deutsche
    Tradax GmbH (No. 79/83) [1984] E.C.R. 1891; [1986] 2 C.M.L.R. 430 ECJ............. 11-004
Wood Floor Solutions Andreas Domberger GmbH v Silva Trade SA (C-19/09) [2010] 1
    W.L.R. 1900; [2010] Bus. L.R. 1050; [2010] 2 Lloyd's Rep. 114; [2010] I.L.Pr. 21 ECJ ... 11-006,
                                                                                   12-003

HONG KONG

Akai Holdings Ltd v Thanakhorn Kasikorn Thai Chamchat ("Akai"). See Thanakharn
    Kasikorn Thai Chamchat v Akai Holdings Ltd (In Liquidation) . 3-011, 3-029, 8-024, 8-049, 8-050,
                                                                                   9-136
Dragages et Travaux Publics v Gladhover Ltd [1988] 1 H.K.L.R. 298 9-038
Ellis (Richard) Ltd v Van Hong-Tuan [1988] 1 H.K.L.R. 169 2-013
First Laser Ltd v Fujian Enterprises (Holdings) Co Ltd [2012] H.K.E.C. 946 HKCFA 12-016
Goei Tsusho Co Ltd v Leader Engineering & Construction Ltd [2010] 2 H.K.L.R.D. 1084 ... 9-006
Hall v Libertarian Investments Ltd [2013] HKCFA 94; 16 H.K.C.F.A.R. 681 6-003
HKSAR v Luk Kin [2016] HKCFA 81 .... 1-030, 6-080, 8-166, 8-209
Hobbins v Royal Skandia Life Assurance Ltd [2012] HKCU 62 6-089
Lai Wo Heung v Cheung Kong Fur Pty Co Ltd [2004] 1 H.K.L.R.D. 959 .... 2-067, 8-072
Libertarian Investments Ltd v Hall [2013] H.K.C.F.A. 93 .... 6-043, 6-096, 6-107
Montrio Ltd v Tse Ping Shun David [2012] H.K.E.C. 1781 2-103
Moulin Global Eyecare Holdings Ltd, Active Base Ltd v Sutton [2009] HKCFA 14 .... **8-061**
Moulin Global Eyecare Trading Ltd v CIR [2014] HKCFA 22 .... 1-028, 8-209, 8-214, 8-215
PCCW-HKT Telephone Ltd v Aitken [2009] HKCFA 11 .... 6-044, 6-051
Poon Ka Man v Cheng Wai Tao [2016] HKCFA 23 .... 6-015, 6-081
Probus Ltd v Treble & Triple Ltd [2010] CACV270/2010 10-020
Secretary for Justice v Chan Chi Wan [2017] HKCFA 15 6-085
Tang Ying Ip v Tang Ying Loi [2017] HKCFA 3 2-014
Tang Ying Loi v Tang Ying Ip [2017] HKCFA 3 .... 6-040, 6-068

Thanakharn Kasikorn Thai Chamchat v Akai Holdings Ltd (In Liquidation) (2010) 13
  H.K.C.F.A.R. 479 . . . . 3-011, 3-029, 8-024, 8-049, 8-050, 9-136
Vastfame Camera Ltd v Birkart Globistics [2005] 4 H.K.C. 117 9-024
Wise Think Global Ltd v Finance Worldwide Ltd [2013] H.K.E.C. 1790 3-032
Wisecal Ltd v Conwell International Ltd [2011] H.K.L.R.D. 27 . . . . 3-007, 3-032
Wong Wai Hing v Hui Wei Lee [2001] 1 H.K.L.R.D. 736 8-196
Yu Hing Tong Ltd v Fung Hing Chiu [2016] HKCFI 1798 2-018

INDIA

Cowasjee Nanabhoy v Lallbhoy (1876) L.R. 3 Ind.App. 200 10-042

IRELAND

Allied Irish Bank v Maguire & Co [2016] IESC 57 6-003
Antisell v Doyle [1899] 2 I.R. 275 . . . . **3-032**
Athy Guardians v Murphy [1986] 1 I.R. 65 . . . . 2-074, 2-087
Barrett v Irvine [1907] 2 I.R. 462 . . . . 1-045, 2-083, 3-028
Brandon v Hanna [1907] 2 I.R. 212 . . . . 7-030, 7-032
Brennan v O'Connell [1980] I.R. 13 . . . . **2-073**
Bunbury v Hibernian Bank [1908] 1 I.R. 261 8-214
Emerald Meat Ltd v Minister of Agriculture (No.2) [1997] 1 I.R. 1 1-004
Fitzsimons v Duncan and Kemp & Co [1908] 2 I.R. 483 8-196
Hilton v Helliwell [1894] 2 I.R. 94 7-042
Kearney v Cullen [1955] I.R. 18 3-025
Kenny v Cosgrave [1926] I.R. 51 . . . . 9-028, 9-074
Kenny v Ireland Roc Ltd 2005 I.E.H.C. 241; [2006] Eu. L.R. 368 11-018
Lavan v Walsh [1964] I.R. 87 . . . . 9-006, 9-034, 9-037, 9-038
Law v Roberts (Robert) & Co [1964] I.R. 292 3-032
McDonnell v McGuinness [1939] I.R. 223 9-083
Murphy Buckley, Keogh Ltd v Pye (Ireland) Ltd [1971] I.R. 57 7-037
Porter v Kirtlan [1917] 2 I.R. 138; 51 I.L.T. 101 9-003
Rutherford v Ounan [1913] 2 I.R. 265 . . . . 8-117, 9-006
Sheridan v Higgins [1971] I.R. 291 . . . . 2-053, 2-074
Sullivan v Sullivan [1912] 2 I.R. 116 . . . . 8-117, 8-124
Taylor v Yorkshire Insurance Co Ltd [1913] 2 Ir. R. 1 . . . . 8-206, 8-208, 8-211, 8-212
Williamson v Rover Cycle Co Ltd [1901] 2 I.R. 189 1-035

MALAYSIA

Chua Yew Phong v AS Yeo [1966] 2 M.L.J. 257 5-009
Lim Eng Chuan Sdn Bhd v United Malayan Banking Corp [2011] 1 M.L.J. 486 CA 10-006
Wotherspoon (JM) & Co Ltd v Henry Agency House (1961) 28 M.L.J. 86 1-042

NEW ZEALAND

Adlam v Savage [2016] NZCA 454; [2017] 2 N.Z.L.R. 309 6-074
Akel v Turner [1926] G.L.R. 574 . . . . 2-074, 2-085
Allen v Anderson [1969] N.Z.L.R. 951 . . . . 7-028, 7-030
Allied Finance and Investments Ltd v Haddow & Co [1983] N.Z.L.R. 22 . . . . 9-117, **9-125**
Amaltal Corp v Maruha Corp [2007] 3 N.Z.l.R. 192 . . . . 1-015, 6-034, **6-045**, 6-097
Aotearoa International Ltd v Westpac Banking Corp [1984] 2 N.Z.L.R. 34 2-071
Apatu v Peach Prescott & Jamieson [1985] 1 N.Z.L.R. 50 6-003
Aquaculture Corp v New Zealand Green Mussel Co Ltd [1990] 3 N.Z.L.R. 299 6-036
Ararimu Holdings Ltd, Re [1989] 3 N.Z.L.R. 487 6-041
Artifakts Design Group Ltd v Rigg (N.P.) Ltd [1993] 1 N.Z.L.R. 196 6-015
Atkinson v Brown [1963] N.Z.L.R. 775 2-043
Auckland Workingmen's Club v Rennie [1976] 1 N.Z.L.R. 278 8-192
Awaroa Holdings Ltd v Commercial Securities & Finance Ltd [1976] 1 N.Z.L.R. 19 8-185
Baby Hammock Co Ltd v AJ Park Law [2011] NZHC 686 6-051
Bambury v Jensen [2015] NZHC 2384 6-041
Bank of New Zealand v Elders Pastoral Ltd [1992] 1 N.Z.L.R. 536 8-162
Bank of New Zealand v New Zealand Guardian Trust Co [1999] 1 N.Z.L.R. 213; [1999] 1
  N.Z.L.R. 664 . . . . 6-036, 6-043

Barfoot & Thompson Ltd v Real Estate Agents Authority [2016] NZCA 105 6-055
Barrett v West (J.R.) Ltd [1970] N.Z.L.R. 789 9-117
Batham Ex p (1888) 6 N.Z.L.R. 342 8-214
Black v Taylor [1993] 3 N.Z.L.R. 403 6-051
Blackley v National Mutual Life Association of Australasia Ltd [1972] N.Z.L.R. 1038 8-205,
8-206, **8-207**
Blair v Martin [1929] N.Z.L.R. 225 6-064
Blake v Melrose [1950] N.Z.L.R. 781 9-043
Body Corporate 202254 v Taylor [2009] 2 N.Z.L.R. 17 . . . . 9-116, 9-119
Body Corporate 366611 v Wu [2014] NZSC 137; [2015] 1 N.Z.L.R. 215 . . . . 8-195, 9-120
Body Corporate 398983 v Zurich Australian Insurance Ltd [2014] NZSC 147 8-212
Bolus & Co Ltd v Inglis Bros Co Ltd [1924] N.Z.L.R. 164 . . . . 1-021, 7-101, 9-021
Bromley Industries Ltd v Martin & Judith Fitzsimons Ltd [2009] NZHC 1992 9-121
BS Developments No.12 Ltd v PB & SF Properties Ltd (2006) 7 N.Z.C.P.R. 603 . . . . 2-013, 2-031,
2-033
Burnard v Lysnar [1927] N.Z.L.R. 757 . . . . 8-211, 8-217
Butler's (London) Ltd v Roope [1922] N.Z.L.R. 549 . . . . 1-021, 1-036
Ceres Orchard Partnership v Fiatagri Australia Pty Ltd [1995] 1 N.Z.L.R. 112 . . . . 8-153, 8-154
Chamberlains v Lai [2006] NZSC 70; [2007] 2 N.Z.L.R. 7 6-028
Chief Executive of the New Zealand Customs Service v Nike New Zealand Ltd [2004] 1
N.Z.L.R. 238 1-030
Chirnside v Fay [2007] 1 N.Z.L.R. 433 (NZSC) 6-036, 6-081, 6-083
Chuan Wu v Body Corporate 366611 [2014] NZSC 137; [2015] 1 N.Z.L.R. 215 . . . . . 8-195, 9-120
Clark v Libra Developments Ltd [2007] 2 N.Z.L.R. 709 (NZCA) 2-083
Coleman v Myers [1977] 2 N.Z.L.R. 225 6-035
Commerce Commission v Vero Insurance New Zealand Ltd (2006) 8 N.Z.C.L.C. 101 1-023
Cook Strait Skyferry Ltd v Thompson (Dennis) International Ltd [1993] 2 N.Z.L.R. 72 9-121
Cook v Evatt (No.2) [1992] 1 N.Z.L.R. 676 . . . . 6-036, 6-068, 6-081
Credit Services Investments Ltd v [1974] 2 N.Z.L.R. 603 . . . . 8-064, 8-196
Cromwell Corp Ltd v Sofrana Immobilier (NZ) Ltd (1992) N.Z.C.L.C. 67 . . . . 1-030, 2-031, 2-032,
8-019
Cromwell Corporation Ltd v Sofrana Immobilier (NZ) Ltd (1992) 6 N.Z. Company L.C.
67,997 2-033
Croskery v Gee [1957] N.Z.L.R. 586 4-010
Cullen v R [2015] NZSC 73; [2015] 1 N.Z.L.R. 715 1-025
Dairy Containers Ltd v NZI Bank Ltd [1995] 2 N.Z.L.R. 30 8-188
Davey v Paine Bros (Motors) Ltd [1954] N.Z.L.R. 1122 . . . . 8-145, 8-153
Davis v Capel [1959] N.Z.L.R. 825 8-079
Day v Mead [1987] 2 N.Z.L.R. 443 . . . . 6-036, 6-050
Diamond Stud Ltd v New Zealand Bloodstock Finance Lts [2010] NZCA 423 . . . . 8-078, 8-079
Dillon v Macdonald (1902) 21 N.Z.L.R. 45 9-070
Dobson v Holderness [1975] 2 N.Z.L.R. 749 8-182
Dollars & Sense Finance Ltd v Nathan [2008] 2 N.Z.L.R. 557 . . . . 1-027, 3-011, 5-001, 8-214
Downie Bros v Oakley (Henry) & Sons [1923] N.Z.L.R. 734 . . . . 1-021, 1-036, 9-021
Dunphy v Sleepyhead Manufacturing Co Ltd [2007] 3 N.Z.L.R. 602, CA 1-028, 6-009, 10-018
Dyas v Diel [2013] NZHC 2645 5-012
Estate Realties Ltd v Wignall (No.2) [1992] 2 N.Z.L.R. 431 6-068
Estate Realties Ltd v Wignall [1992] 2 N.Z.L.R. 615 6-080
FAME Ins.Co Ltd v Spence [1958] N.Z.L.R. 735 8-215
Farrington v Rowe McBride & Partners [1985] 1 N.Z.L.R. 83 6-050
Fawcett v Star Car Sales Ltd [1960] N.Z.L.R. 406 8-078
Fenwick v Naera [2015] NZSC 68 6-068
Field v R [2012] 3 N.Z.L.R. 1 . . . . 6-085, 6-088
Fortex Group Ltd v Macintosh [1998] 3 N.Z.L.R. 471 . . . . 6-040, **6-045**
Fowler (LC) & Sons Ltd v St. Stephen's College Board of Governors [1991] 3 N.Z.L.R.
304 . . . . 8-114, 8-117, 8-120, 8-121, **8-124**
Franicevich v Strong [1997] 1 N.Z.L.R. 460 7-089
Fraser v Dalgety & Co Ltd [1953] N.Z.L.R. 126 . . . . 9-023, 9-029, 9-034
Galloway v Pedersen (1915) 34 N.Z.L.R. 513 . . . . 8-221, 8-226
Gannow Engineering Co Ltd v Richardson [1920] N.Z.L.R. 361 1-036
Gathergood v Blundell & Brown Ltd [1991] 1 N.Z.L.R. 405 6-064
Gathergood v Blundell & Brown Ltd [1992] 3 N.Z.L.R. 643 9-142

General Communications Ltd v Development Finance Corp of New Zealand [1990] 3
   N.Z.L.R. 406...6-041
Gilbert v Shanahan [1998] 3 N.Z.L.R. 528 6-043
Giltrap City Ltd v The Commerce Commission [2004] 1 N.Z.L.R. 608 ....2-025, 8-176
Godfrey v Marshall [2017] NZHC 420 ....3-015, 10-009
Gu v Du [2011] NZCA 577 10-023
Haddow Nominees Ltd v Rarawa Farm Ltd [1981] 2 N.Z.L.R. 16 ....1-028, 2-042
Haira v Burbery Mortgage Finance and Savings [1995] 3 N.Z.L.R. 396 6-003
Hawke's Bay Milk Corp Lyd v Watson [1974] 1 N.Z.L.R. 236 ....9-066, 9-085, 9-087
Herbert Equities Ltd v Mamfredos [2009] NZHC 128 6-107
Heslop v Cousins [2007] 3 N.Z.L.R. 679 7-089
Hickman v Turn and Wave Ltd [2013] 1 N.Z.L.R. 741 8-211
IH Wedding & Sons Ltd v Buy-Sell Realty NZ Ltd [2009] NZHC 1717 ....**8-061**
Jeanswest Corp (New Zealand) Ltd v G-Star Raw CV [2015] NZCA 14 8-209
Jeffcott v Andrew Motors Ltd [1960] N.Z.L.R. 721 8-156
Jessett Properties Ltd v UDC Finance Ltd [1992] 1 N.Z.L.R. 138 ....8-211, 8-212
Jiao v Barge (2006) 18 Procedure R.N.Z. 396 (NZSC) 2-037, 2-042
Johnston v Schurr [2015] NZSC 82; [2016] 1 N.Z.L.R. 403 10-020
Jones v Still [1965] N.Z.L.R. 1071 ....9-064, 9-117
JS Brooksbank & Co (Australasia) Ltd v EXFTX Ltd (2009) 10 N.Z. C.L.C. 264 ....6-003, 8-161,
                                                                                8-167
Kavanagh v Continental Shelf (No.46) Ltd [1993] 2 N.Z.L.R. 517 9-061
KBL Investments Ltd v KBL Courtenay Ltd [2016] NZCA 227 6-067
Kiriwai Consultants Ltd v Holmes [2015] NZCA 149 ....6_035
Knight v Matson & Co (1902) 22 N.Z.L.R. 293 ....8-053, **8-061**, 8-073, 8-109, 8-112
L v Robinson [2000] 3 N.Z.L.R. 499 6-036
Levin v Rastkar [2011] NZCA 233 ....**3-015**
Livingstone v Elmslie (1902) 21 N.Z.L.R. 640 6-100
Lower Hutt City v Attorney General [1965] N.Z.L.R. 65 1-034
Lowther v Kim [2003] 1 N.Z.L.R. 327 2-137
Madden v UDC Finance Ltd PC 71/1996, 30 October 1997 2-014
Maheno, The [1977] 1 Lloyd's Rep. 81, N.Z. Sup. Ct 9-024
Maketu Estates Ltd v Robb [2014] NZHC 2664 7-050
Marblestone Industries Ltd v Fairchild [1975] 1 N.Z.L.R. 529 ....9-084, 9-085, 9-087
Marchand v Jackson [2012] NZHC 2893 6-016
Marr v Arabco Traders Ltd 91987) 1 N.Z. Business L.C. 102,732 8-215
Martin v Pont [1993] 3 N.Z.L.R. 25 ....6-003, 6-099, 6-100, **6-101**
Mathews v CD Realty (PN) Ltd [2010] NZHC 1881 ....**9-083**
McDonnell v Barton Realty Ltd [1992] 3 N.Z.L.R. 418 6-048
McKaskell v Benseman [1989] 1 N.Z.L.R. 75 6-021
McKittrick v Jordan Sandman Smythe Ltd [1991] NZCA 16 3-007
McNamara v Auckland City Council [2012] 3 N.Z.L.R. 701 NZSC 8-209
Messenger v Stanaway Real Estate Ltd [2015] NZHC 1795; (2015) 16 N.Z. Conv. P.R.
   335...6-024
Mike Pero Mortgages Ltd v Pero [2015] 3 N.Z.L.R. 246 6-052
Mineaplenty Pty Ltd v Trek 31 Oty Ltd (2007) A.N.Z. Conveyancing R. 123 ....**2-026**
Moneyworld NZ 2000 Ltd v Lee (2005) N.Z. Business L.C. 101,638 8-018
Murphy v Rae [1967] N.Z.L.R. 103 8-078
Napier v Torbay Holdings Ltd [2016] NZCA 608 ....6-100, 8-161
Nash v Barnes [1922] N.Z.L.R. 303 8-153
Nathan v Dollars & Sense Ltd [2008] 2 N.Z.L.R. 557 8-214
National Australia Finance Ltd v Fahey [1990] 2 N.Z.L.R. 482 ....**8-207**
New Zealand Farmers Co-operative Distributive Co Ltd v National Mortgage and Agency
   Co of New Zealand Ltd [1961] N.Z.L.R. 969...........................6-019, **7-070**
New Zealand Insurance Co Ltd v Tyneside Pty Ltd [1917] N.Z.L.R. 569 ....**2-100**
New Zealand Needle Manufacturers Ltd v Taylor [1975] 2 N.Z.L.R. 33 6-077
New Zealand Tenancy Bonds Ltd v Mooney [1986] 1 N.Z.L.R. 280 ...**3-026**, 3-032, 8-020, 8-021
Nguyen v SM & T Homes Ltd [2016] NZCA 581 10-012
Nicholls v Peers (1993) 4 N.Z.B.L.C. 103,313 ....**6-032**
Nimmo v Westpac Banking Corp [1993] 3 N.Z.L.R. 218 9-142
Northwestern Autoservices Ltd [1980] 2 N.Z.L.R. 302 8-038
O'Hagan v Body Corp 189855 [2010] 3 N.Z.L.R. 445 8-188
Official Assignee v Dowling [1964] N.Z.L.R. 578 9-121

Ogilvy & Mather (N Z) v Turner [1996] 1 N.Z.L.R. 641 10-042
Owen v Trickett (1908) 27 N.Z.L.R. 950 6-048
P v Bridgecorp Ltd [2013] NZSC 152 2-014
P v P [1957] N.Z.L.R. 854 8-042
P v P (No.2) [1958] N.Z.L.R. 349 8-042
Pacifica Shipping Co Ltd v Anderson [1986] 2 N.Z.L.R. 328 6-081
Paper Reclaim Ltd v Aotearoa International Ltd [2007] 3 N.Z.L.R. 169 NZSC 7-001, 7-047,
                                                                                      10-004, 10-045
Paris v Goodwin [1954] N.Z.L.R. 823 8-148
Parkin v Williams [1986] 1 N.Z.L.R. 294 . . . . 5-001, **5-007**
Pascoe Properties Ltd v Att.-Gen. [2014] NZCA 616 . . . . 2-109, 8-042
Pemberton v Action Realty Ltd [1986] 1 N.Z.L.R. 286 7-017
Pendergrast v Chapman [1988] 2 N.Z.L.R. 177 9-035
Peninsular Real Estate Ltd v Harris [1992] 2 N.Z.L.R. 216 6-077
Pettersson v Royal Oak Hotel Ltd [1948] N.Z.L.R. 136 8-192
Powierza v Daley [1985] 1 N.Z.L.R. 558 . . . . 2-033, **2-034**
Powierza v Daley [1985] 1 N.Z.L.R. 558 3-032
Premier Products Ltd, Re [1965] N.Z.L.R. 50 10-042
Premium Real Estate Ltd v Stevens [2009] 2 N.Z.L.R. 384 . . . . 6-015, 6-021, 6-034, 6-037, 6-043,
                                                                    6-047, 6-048, 7-050, **7-051**
Progressive Enterprises Ltd v Commerce Commission (2009) 9 N.Z. Business L.C.
    102,485 8-028
Prudential Assurance Co Ltd v Rodriguez [1982] 2 N.Z.L.R. 54 7-025
Public Trustee v Guardian Trust & Executors Co of New Zealand Ltd [1942] N.Z.L.R. 115
    PC 8-209
Rama v Millar [1996] 1 N.Z.L.R. 257 PC 6-043
Rawleigh v Tait [2009] N.Z. Family L.R. 802 6-043
Richardson v Smith (Norris) Real Estate Ltd [1971] 1 N.Z.L.R. 152 9-117
Rita Joan Dairies Ltd v Thompson [1974] 1 N.Z.L.R. 285 9-087
Rohr v Kennedy [2010] NZHC 772 7-063
Rothmans Industries Ltd v Floral Holdings Ltd [1986] 2 N.Z.L.R. 480 2-087
Russell McVeagh McKenzie Bartleet & Co v Tower Corp [1998] 3 N.Z.L.R. 641 6-051
S v Attorney General [2003] 3 N.Z.L.R. 450 . . . . 1-027, 6-036, 8-177
Savill v Chase Holdings (Wellington) Ltd [1989] 1 N.Z.L.R. 257 8-021
Shaw Savill & Albion Co v Timaru Harbour Board (1890) 15 App.Cas. 429 2-091
Sheehan v Watson [2011] 1 N.Z.L.R. 314 9-122
Shell (Petroleum Mining) Co Ltd v Todd Petroleum Mining Co Ltd [2008] 2 N.Z.L.R.
    418, NZCA 7-046, 10-025
Shing v Ashcroft [1987] N.Z.L.R. 154 9-117
Smith (GE) Ltd v Smith [1952] N.Z.L.R. 470 6-081
Sopwith Aviation & Engineering Co Ltd v Magnus Motors Ltd [1928] N.Z.L.R. 433;
    [1928] G.L.R. (N.Z.) 380. . . . . 1-021, 8-105
Southbourne Investments Ltd v Greenmount Manufacturing Ltd [2008] 1 N.Z.L.R. 30
    NZSC 3-025, 3-032, **8-207**
Steel Co Ltd v Pipes NZ Ltd [2016] NZCA 175 8-211
Stevenson Brown Ltd v Montecillo Trust [2017] NZCA 57 8-212
Sunnyvale Property Trust v Liu [2015] NZHC 2804 9-038
Szembrener v Pepper (New Zealand) Custodians Ltd [2014] NZHC 324 8-045
Temarama 2004 Ltd (In Liquidation) v McRobie [2011] NZHC 1456 3-043
Thomas Borthwick & Sons v SOFCO [1978] N.Z.L.R. 538 10-025
Thompson v Howley [1977] 1 N.Z.L.R. 16 . . . . 3-032, 6-005, 8-045
Tingey (RE) & Co Ltd v Chambers (John) & Co Ltd [1967] N.Z.L.R. 785 . . . . 3-025, 8-153
Toll Logistics (NZ) Ltd v McKay [2011] 2 N.Z.L.R. 601 7-082
Torchlight Fund No .1 LP v NZ Credit Fund (GP) 1 Ltd [2014] NZHC 2552 6-051
Totara Investments Ltd v Crismac Ltd [2010] NZSC 36; [2010] 3 N.Z.L.R. 285 3-015
Trengrouse & Co v Official Assignee of Steeds (1896) 14 N.Z.L.R. 636 5-011
Trevor Ivory Ltd v Anderson [1992] 2 N.Z.L.R. 517 9-119
Turnbull & Jones Ltd v Amner & Sons [1923] N.Z.L.R. 673 . . . . 9-009, 9-035
Turton & Co Ltd (In Liquidation) v Kerslake & Partners [2000] Lloyd's Rep. P.N. 967 CA
    (NZ). 6-018
Union SS Co Of New Zealand Ltd v CIR [1962] N.Z.L.R. 656 8-042
US International Marketing Ltd v National Bank of New Zealand Ltd [2004] 1 N.Z.L.R.
    589. . . . . 9-135, 9-141

Vernon v Public Trustee [2016] NZCA 388 . . . . 3-011, 3-015, 8-163
Waiwera Co-operative Dairy Co Ltd v Wright, Stephenson & Co Ltd [1917] N.Z.L.R. 178 . . 2-074
Waller v Davies [2007] 2 N.Z.L.R. 508 8-211
Watson v Dolmark Industries Ltd [1992] 3 N.Z.L.R. 311 . . . . 6-037, 9-120
Wellington Steam Ferry Co Ltd (In Liquidation) v Wellington Deposit, Mortgage, and
    Building Assoc. Ltd (1915) 34 N.Z.L.R. 913 . . . . 10-006, 10-015
West v Dillicar [1920] N.Z.L.R. 139 . . . . 2-108, 2-109, **8-128**
Westerman realty Ltd v McKinstry (2007) 8 N.Z.C.P.R. 553 6-007
Westminster Chemical NZ Ltd v McKinley [1973] 1 N.Z.L.R. 659 6-077
Westpac Banking Corp v Savin [1985] 2 N.Z.L.R. 41 . . . . 6-041, 9-141, 9-142
Westpac New Zealand Ltd v Map & Associates Ltd [2011] 3 N.Z.L.R. 751 NZSC 6-009
Wilson v New Brighton Panelbeaters [1989] 1 N.Z.L.R. 74 . . . . 9-125, 9-129
Xie v Huang [2012] NZHC 960; (2012) N.Z.C.P.R. 239 . . . . 3-015, 8-052
Zhong v Wang (2007) N.Z.C.P.R. 488 . . . . 6-041, 6-100

SINGAPORE

Alrich Development Pte v Rafiq Jumabhoy [1994] 3 S.L.R. 1 6-051
Banque National de Paris v Credit Agricole Indosuez [2001] 1 S.L.R. 300 9-135
Bunga Melati 5, The [2016] SGCA 20 2-080
Chua Chye Leong Alan v Grand Plance De-luxe Nite Club Pte Ltd [1993] 3 S.L.R. 449 8-179
Family Food Court v Seah Boon Lock [2008] S.G.C.A. 31 9-013
Fong Maun Yee v Yoong Weng Ho [1997] 2 S.L.R. 297 9-061
Goh Lay Khim v Isabel Redrup Agency Pte Ltd [2017] SGCA 11 7-030
Hinckley Singapore Trading Pte Ltd v Sogo Department Stores (S) Pte Ltd (Under
    Judicial Management) (2001–02) 4 I.T.E.L.R. 301; [2001] 4 Singapore L.R. 154 CA 6-041
Ho Kang Peng v Scintronix Corp Ltd [2014] SGCA 22 8-224
HSBC Ltd v Jurong Engineering Ltd [2000] 2 S.L.R. 54 8-021
Kok Seng Chong v Bukit Turf Club [1993] 2 S.L.R. 388 2-024
Liu Wing Ngai v Lui Kok Wai [1996] 3 Singapore L.R. 508 . . . . 1-036, 4-006
Ng Eng Ghee v Mamata Kapildev Dave [2009] SGCA 14 . . . . **6-061**
Ng Hock Kon v Sambawang Capital Pte Ltd [2010] 1 S.L.R. 307 . . . . 3-043, 8-206
Ohm Mariana, The [1993] 2 S.L.R. 698 7-085
Ong Kee Ming v Quek Yong Kang [1991] 3 M.L.J. 294 7-032
Pan-Electric Industries Ltd v Sim Lim Finance Ltd [1993] 3 S.L.R. 242 8-130
Pearlson Enterprises Ltd v Hong Leong Co Ltd [1968] 1 M.L.J. 24 1-036
Skandinaviska Enskilda Banken v Asia Pacific Breweries (Singapore) Pte Ltd [2011]
    SGCA 22 . . . . 8-041, 8-048, 8-180
Thomson Hill Pte Ltd v Chang Erh [1992] 2 S.L.R. 769 9-026
Yong Kheng Leong v Panweld Trading Pte Ltd [2012] SGCA 59 6-040

SOUTH AFRICA

Colonial Mutual Life Assurance Society Ltd v Macdonald [1931] A.D. 412 . . . . 8-182, **8-196**
Davie v Sachs [1911] C.P.D. 992 6-111
De Coning v Monror Estate and Investment Co (Pty) Ltd 1974 (3) S.A. 72 7-037
Esterhuyse v Selection Cartage (Pty.) Ltd 1965 (1) S.A. 360 3-025
Lucke v Cleary (2011) S.A.S.R. 134 3-032
Mineworkers' Union v Brodrick 1948 (2) S.A. 959 . . . . 2-096, 6-005
Osry v Hirsch [1922] C.P.D. 531 6-068
Union Government v Chappell [1918] C.P.D. 462 6-083
Wylde (DC) & Co v Sparg 1977 (2) S.A.L.R. 75 . . . . 7-018, 7-030

UNITED STATES OF AMERICA

Black v Shearson, Hammill & Co 72 Cal. Rptr. 157 (1968) 6-052
Butler v Maples 76 U.S. 822 (1869) 1-045
Chilsan Merchant Marine Co Ltd v M/V K Fortune 110 F.Supp. 2d 492; 497 (E.D.La.
    2000) 2-032
Crown Controls Inc v Smiley 756 P.2d 717 (Wash., 1988) 8-116
Dempsey v Chambers 154 Mass.330; 28 N.E. 279 (1891) 2-056
Engelstat v Cargill Inc 336 N.W.2d 284 (Minn., 1983) 8-116
Equitable Variable Life Insurance Co v Wood 362 S.E. 2d 741 (Va.,1987) 8-029

Grinder v Bryans Road Building and Supply Co 432 A.2d 453 (Ct.App.Md., 1981) . . . 8-115, 8-116
Havas v Carter 515 P. 2d 397 (1975) 6-012
Hoddesdon v Koos Bros 135 A.2d 702 (N.J., 1957) **2-109**, 8-043
Home Owners Loan Corp v Thornburgh 106 P.(2d.) 511; 512 (S.C. Okl., 1940) 8-024
Hunt v Rousmanier's Administrators 21 U.S. 174 (1823) 10-007
Jenson (A Gay) Farms Co v Cargill Inc 309 N.W.2d 285 (Minn.1981) 1-037
Kelly Asphalt Block Co v Ashphalt Paving Co 105 N.E. 88 (Ct.App.N.Y. 1914) 8-080
King v Bankerd 492 A 2d 608 (Ct. App. Md., 1985) 3-015
Kirschner v KPMG LLP (2010) 15 N.Y. 3d 446 8-214
Lake Charles Stevedores v M/V Professor Vladimir Popov 199 F. 3d 220 (3rd Cir., 1999) . . . 8-026
Lamb v Scott 643 So.2d 972 (S.C.Ala 1994) 3-015
Laughland v Millar (1904) 6 F. 413 9-098
Luken v Buckeye Parking Corp 68 N.E.2d 217 (Ohio, 1945) 2-109, 8-043
MacAndrews & Forbes Co v United States 23 F. 2d 667 (1928) 2-102
Meinhard v Salmon 164 N.E. 545 (1928) 6-079
New Georgia National Bank v Lippmann 249 N.Y. 307; 164 N.E. 108 (1928) 9-064
Norfolk Southern Railway Co v James N Kirby Pty Ltd 125 S.Ct. 385 (2004) 9-024
Northeast General Corp v Wellington Advertising Inc 604 N.Y.S. (2d) 1 (Ct.App.1993) 1-020
Novick v Gouldsberry 173 F. (2d) 496 (1949) 2-056
Opp v Wheaton Van Lines 231 F.2d 1060 (10th Cir., 2000) 2-032
Ruggles v American Central Insurance Co of St. Louis 114 N.Y. 415; 76 N.Y. Supp. 787
   (1889) 2-032
Tower Cranes of America v Public Service Co 702 F.Supp.371 (D.N.H., 1988) 8-116
Turner v Webster 24 Kan. 38 (1880) 7-009

TABLE OF STATUTES

Access to Medical Reports Act 1988 (c.28)
  s.8 11-036
Accommodation Agencies Act 1953 (1 & 2 Eliz.
  2, c.23) 7-053
Administration of Estates Act 1925
  s.2(2) 2-021
Administration of Justice Act 1982 (c.53)
  s.15 6-108
Animals Act 1971 (c.22)
  s.2(2) 8-217
Banking Companies (Shares) Act 1867 (30 & 31
  Vict., c.109) 3-038, 9-109
Bankruptcy Act 1914 (4 & 5 Geo. 5, c.59)
  s.16(1) 2-022
Bills of Exchange Act 1882 (45 & 46 Vict., c.61)
  9-052
  s.17 8-092
  (1) 8-089, 9-050, 9-053
  s.20 .... 8-045, 8-130
  (1) 2-014
  s.23 .... 8-089, 8-092, 9-050
  (1) 9-055
  (2) 9-055
  s.24 8-091
  s.25 .... 8-056, 8-091
  s.26 8-091
  (1) 9-053, 9-056
  (2) 8-092, 9-050, 9-056
  s.27(1) 8-140
  (3) 7-088, 7-089
  s.29 .... 7-088, 7-089, 8-059
  (1)—(3) 8-140
  s.35 8-061
  s.38 8-140
  s.60 8-140
  ss.65—68 .... 4-003, 8-089, 9-050
  s.80 8-140
  s.81 8-140
  s.81A 8-140
  s.82 .... 8-064, 8-140, 9-130
  s.89 .... 8-089, 9-050
  s.90 8-140
  s.91 2-023
  (1) 2-022, 8-089
Bills of Exchange (Crossed Cheques) Act 1906
  (6 Edw. 7, c.17) 9-130
Bills of Lading Act 1855 (18 & 19 Vict., c.111)
  9-010
Bribery Act 2010 (c.23) 6-087, 6-088
  s.1 6-088
  s.2 6-088
  s.3 6-088
  s.4 6-088
  s.6 6-088
  s.7 .... 2-025, 6-088
Building Societies Act 1986 (c.53)
  s.87(1) 2-022

Carriage of Goods by Sea Act 1971 (c.19)
  s.1(2) 11-006
  Sch. art.IV bis2 1-023
Carriage of Goods by Sea Act 1992 (c.50)
  9-010
  s.4 .... 8-021, 8-067, 9-076
Chancery Amendment Act 1858 (Lord Cairns'
  Act) (21 & 22 Vict., c. 27) 9-077
Charities Act 1993 (c.10)
  s.63 8-031
  s.65 8-031
  s.67 8-031
  s.68 8-031
Cheques Act 1957 (5 & 6 Eliz. 2 c.36)
  9-130
  s.4 .... 8-064, 8-140, 9-130
  (2) 9-130
  (3) 9-130
Cheques Act 1992 (c.32) 8-140
Civil Evidence Act 1995 (c.38) 8-205
Civil Liability (Contribution) Act 1978 (c.47)
  .... 7-060, 7-063, 8-117, 9-135
  s.1 8-191
  (1) 7-068
  s.2 8-191
  s.3 .... 8-114, 8-116, 9-006
  s.5 8-191
  s.7(3) 8-191
Companies Act 1862 (25 & 26 Vict., c.89)
  10-014
Companies Act 1948 (11 & 12 Geo.6, c.38)
  Table A 7-004
Companies Act 1985 (c.6) 8-036
  s.35 8-035
  s.36 12-016
  s.36A 8-040
  s.36C(1) 9-084
  s.292 8-038
  s.349 9-055
  s.322A 8-037
  s.695(2) 1-020
Companies Act 1989 (c.40)
  s.108 2-058
  s.130(4) 9-084
Companies Act 2006 (c.46) 6-063, 8-035,
                                   8-059
  Pt 10 Ch.2 6-033
  Ch.4 1-028
  Pt 18 9-141
  Pt 31 Ch.3 10-018
  s.8 2-022
  s.16 2-064
  s.17 8-037
  s.29 8-037
  s.35(3) 2-058
  s.39 ..... 2-025, 2-058, 2-069, 8-035, 8-189,
                                  12-020

Companies Act 2006 (c.46)—*cont.*
s.40 ..... 2-058, 2-069, 8-036, 8-037, 8-038,
 8-039, 8-189, 12-020
 (1) 8-035, 8-037
 (2) 8-037
  (b) 8-037
 (3) 8-037
 (4) 8-035, 8-037
 (5) 8-035
s.41 .... 8-037, 12-020
s.42 .... 8-031, 8-035
s.43 .... 2-038, 12-020
 (1)(b) 12-017, 12-020
 (2)(a) 12-020
s.44 ..... 1-029, 8-040, 8-041, 8-126, 12-020
 (2) 2-022, 8-040, 8-040
 (4) 12-020
 (5) 8-041, 12-020
s.45 8-126
s.46 12-020
s.48 .... 8-040, 12-020
s.51 .... 1-029, 8-004, 9-084, 9-087
 (1) 9-086
s.52 8-092
s.70(3) 6-033
ss.82—84 .... 9-050, 9-055
s.113 7-089
s.114 7-089
s.157 2-012
s.160 8-038
s.161 .... 2-012, 8-038
s.170(3) 6-034
s.171 6-002
s.172 6-054
s.175 .... 6-054, 6-081
s.177(6)(a) 6-047
s.324 2-018
s.601 1-028
s.694 1-028
s.1045 8-040
s.1139 1-020
s.1157 6-003
Consumer Credit Act 1974 (c.39) 2-018
s.56 2-034
s.57 2-034
s.69 2-034
s.102 2-034
s.140A 2-223
Consumers, Estate Agents and Redress Act 2007
 (c.17)
s.54 6-092
Sch.6 .... 6-001, 9-117
Consumer Protection Act 1987 (c.43) 1-036
Consumer Rights Act 2015 (c.15) 6-059
Pt 2 6-059
s.62 6-063
Contracts (Applicable Law) Act 1990 (c.36)
 .... 12-001, 12-026
Contracts (Rights of Third Parties) Act 1999
 (c.31) .. 1-023, 1-031, 7-001, 8-083, 8-086,
 9-011, 9-122
s.1 .... 8-083, 8-089
 (1) 9-122

 (1)—(3) 5-011
 (3) 9-122
 (7) 9-122
s.6(1) 8-089
s.7(1) 8-086
Conveyancing Act 1881 (44 & 45 Vict., c.41)
s.46 8-087
Conveyancing Act 1882 (45 & 46 Vict., c.39)
s.3 8-216
Corporate Bodies' Contracts Act 1960 (8 & 9
 Eliz. 2, c.46) 2-038
s.1(1) 2-038
Corporate Manslaughter and Corporate
 Homicide Act 2007 (c.19)
s.1 2-025
County Courts Act 1984 (c.28)
s.69(1) 6-108
Crown Proceedings Act 1947 (10 & 11 Geo. 6,
 c.44) 8-190, 9-028, 9-124
s.1 8-042
s.2(1)(a) 8-176
 (b) 8-190
s.38(2) 8-190
Data Protection Act 1998 (c.29) 1-028
Defamation Act 1952 (15 & 16 Geo. 6 & 1 Eliz.
 2, c.66)
s.11 7-068
Enduring Powers of Attorney Act 1985 (c.29)
 10-009
s.2(1) 2-033
s.9 10-009
Enterprise Act 2002 (c.40) 1-032, 6-001
Estate Agents Act 1979 (c.38) 1-032, 6-001,
 7-056, 7-077
s.1 .... 6-104, 7-007, 7-020, 7-038
s.12 6-104
s.13 .... 6-091, 6-104
 (3) 6-104
ss.13—16 6-041
s.14 6-104
s.15 6-104
s.18 .... 6-055, 7-007
 (5) 6-055, 7-020, 7-038, 7-056, 7-067
s.21 9-033
s.21A 6-092
ss.23A—23C 9-117
s.30 .... 7-007, 7-038
 (1) 7-020
European Communities Act 1972 (c.68)
s.2(2) 1-044, 11-003
s.9(1) 8-035, 8-036
 (2) 1-029, 9-086, 9-087
Factors Act 1889 (52 & 53 Vict., c.45)
 .... 1-025, 1-046, 7-087, 8-126, 8-144
s.1(1) 8-145
 (2) 8-147
 (3) 8-148
 (4) 8-149
s.2 .... 8-059, 8-135, 8-156
 (1) 8-143
 (2) 8-146, 10-030
 (3) 8-146
 (4) 8-146

Factors Act 1889 (52 & 53 Vict., c.45)—*cont.*
  s.7 8-156
  s.9 8-156
  s.12(3) 3-032
Family Law Act 1996 (c.27) 3-043
Financial Services Act 1986 (c.60) 6-060
  s.132 2-061
Financial Services Act 2012 (c.21) 6-060
  s.24 6-041
Financial Services and Markets Act 2000 (c.8)
  .... 7-069, 11-001
  Pt VI 9-138
  Pt IXA 6-060
  s.90A 2-025
  s.137A 6-060
  s.137B 6-060
  s.137H 6-060
  s.137P 6-060
  s.138 6-060
  s.139 6-041
  s.147 6-060
  s.247(1)(b) 6-060
  s.262(2)(e) 6-060
  s.412 7-069
Forgery and Counterfeiting Act 1981 (c.45)
  s.1 8-063
  s.2 8-063
  s.3 8-063
  s.4 8-063
  s.5 8-063
  s.9(1) 2-059
Gaming Act 1845 (8 & 9 Vict.10, c.109)
  .... 7-055, 7-069
  s.18 .... 3-038, 7-069
Gaming Act 1892 (55 & 56 Vict., c.9) ... 3-038,
                 7-055, 7-069, 10-029
  s.1 7-055
Gambling Act 2005 (c.19) . 3-038, 6-100, 7-055,
                             7-069
  Pt 17 7-069
Housing Act 2004 (c.34)
  ss.214—215 9-025
Insolvency Act 1986 (c.45) 7-006
  s.113 10-021
  s.283 10-021
  (3) 8-164
  s.284(1) 10-021
  (4) 10-021
  s.306 10-021
  s.307 10-021
  (4) 10-021
  s.315 10-021
  s.388 11-023
  s.436 10-021
Insurance Act 2015 (c.4) 8-212, 8-213
  ss.3—6 8-217
Insurance Companies Act 1982 (c.50)
  s.2 6-052
Interpretation Act 1889 (52 & 53 Vict., c.63)
  s.38(2) 3-043
Landlord and Tenant (Rent Control) Act 1949
  (12, 13 & 14 Geo. 6, c.40)
  s.2(5) 8-064

Late Payment of Commercial Debts (Interest)
  Act 1998 (c.20) 6-108
Law of Distress (Amendment) Act 1908 (8 Edw.
  7, c.53) 2-026
  s.2 9-125
Law of Property Act 1925 (15 & 16 Geo. 5,
  c.20)
  s.7(2) 8-087
  (3) 8-087
  s.20 2-015
  s.40 ..... 2-014, 8-003, 8-004, 8-005, 8-075
  s.41 6-013
  s.53 2-036
  s.54 2-036
  s.56 .... 8-086, 8-088
  (1) 8-083
  s.74 8-087
  (3) 8-087
  (4) 8-087
  s.94 7-089
  s.123 9-048
  (1) 8-087
  s.124 10-035
  s.125(1) 8-052
  s.127 10-035
  s.128 10-035
  s.199(1) 8-048
  (II) 8-124
  (2) 8-211, 8-216
  s.205(1)(xx) 8-216
Law of Property Amendment Act 1859 (22 & 23
  Vict., c. 35) 10-032
  s.26 9-063
Law of Property (Miscellaneous Provisions) Act
  1989 (c.34) ... 2-019, 8-071, 9-048, 9-080
  s.1 .... 8-083, 8-087
  (1) 2-041
  (3) 2-040, 2-041
  (c) 2-082
  s.2 . 2-014, 2-016, 2-053, 3-023, 3-032, 5-007,
        8-004, 8-005, 8-075, 9-086, 10-005
  (5)(b) 8-005, 10-012
  (8) 8-005
  Sch.1 .... 2-023, 2-042
  Sch.2 2-023
Law Reform (Contributory Negligence) Act
  1945 (8 & 9 Geo.6, c.28) 9-130
Law Reform (Enforcement of Contracts) Act
  1954 (2 & 3 Eliz. 2, c.34) 2-019
Law Reform (Married Women and Tortfeasors)
  Act 1935 (25 & 26 Geo. 5, c.30) ... 3-043,
                         8-191, 8-223
  s.2 8-191
  (1) 7-068
  s.4 8-191
  s.6 .... 7-068, 8-191
  s.7(3) 7-068
Leasehold Reform, Housing and Urban
  Development Act 1993 (c.28) 1-029,
                       1-047, 2-022
Legal Services Act 2007 (c.29) 2-024
Limitation Act 1980 (c.58)
  s.2 6-016

Limitation Act 1980 (c.58)—*cont.*
s.21(1) 6-043
 (b) 6-040
s.23 6-096
s.30(2) 2-026
s.32(1) 2-026
s.35(1) 6-043
Lodgers' Goods Protection Act 1871 (34 & 35
 Vict., c.29) 9-125
Marine Insurance Act 1906 (6 Edw. 7, c.41)
s.18 8-213
s.19 . . . . 6-021, 8-212
s.53 . . . . 7-098, 9-041
 (2) 7-098, 7-099
s.54 9-041
Matrimonial and Family Proceedings Act 1984
 (c.42) 3-043
Matrimonial Causes Act (c.18) 1973
Pt II 3-043
s.54 3-043
Sch.3 3-043
Matrimonial Proceedings and Property Act 1970
 (c.45)
s.41 3-043
 (1) 3-043
Mental Capacity Act 2005 (c.9) . . 2-009, 2-032,
                 4-012, 8-052, 10-006, 10-009, 10-020,
                             10-032, 12-032
s.1 10-009
ss.1—3 10-009
ss.1—4 10-020
s.2 10-009
s.4 10-009
s.5 . . . . 4-012, 10-009
s.6 . . . . 4-012, 10-009
s.7 10-009
s.8 . . . . 4-012, 10-009
s.9 . . . . 2-009, 10-009
 (2)(b) 10-009
ss.9—29 10-009
s.10 2-043
s.11 10-009
s.12 10-009
s.13 10-021
 (1) 10-009
 (1)—(4) 10-009
 (2) 10-009
 (3) 10-009
 (4) 10-009
 (5)—(11) 10-009
s.14 . . . . 2-009, 10-009
 (1) 10-037
 (3) 10-037
 (5) 10-037
ss.15—21 2-009
s.16 10-009
ss.22—23 10-009
s.42 10-009
s.43 10-009
s.63 . . . . 12-023, 12-032
s.66(3) 10-009
Sch.1 . . . . 2-033, 10-009
Sch.3 . . . . 12-023, 12-032

Sch.4 . . . . 2-043, 10-009
Mental Health Act 1983 (c.20) 2-009
Mental Health Act 2007 (c.12) 10-009
Merchant Shipping Act 1894 (57 & 58 Vict.,
 c.60)
s.502 1-029
Merchant Shipping Act 1995 (c.21)
s.41 7-084
s.224(1) 4-009
Sch.11 4-009
Metalliferous Mines Regulation Act 1872 (35 &
 36 Vict., c.77) 2-026
Minors Contracts Act 1987 (c.13)
s.3(1) 2-015
Misrepresentation Act 1967 (c.7) . . 8-050, 9-117
s.2 8-186
 (1) 8-176, 8-182, 8-196, 8-197, 8-198,
                 8-207, 9-117, 9-125
s.3 . . . . 6-058, 8-061, 8-217
Moneylenders Act 1927 (17 & 18 Geo. 5, c.21)
 2-018
Partnership Act 1890 (53 & 54 Vict., c.39)
 1-025
s.5 . . . . 3-004, 8-015, 8-029, 8-031, 8-047
s.6 8-092
s.7 8-065
s.8 3-004
s.9 . . . . 2-045, 8-117, 9-006
s.10 . . . . 8-176, 8-177, 8-178
s.11 . . . . 8-199, 8-200
s.14 . . . . 3-004, 8-015
 (1) 8-020, 8-024
 (2) 10-032
s.16 8-215
s.24(9) 2-026
s.36 10-031
 (1) 10-030
 (3) 10-032
s.38 10-011
Powers of Attorney Act 1971 (c.27) 1-032,
                                 2-009
s.1 . . . . 2-008, 2-040
 (1) 10-008
s.2 . . . . 2-042, 8-052
s.3 2-042
s.4 . . . . 10-007, 10-008
 (1) 10-006
 (2) 10-006
s.5 . . . . 2-009, 10-009
 (1) 2-009, 9-071, 10-034, 10-035
 (2) 2-009, 9-071, 10-034
 (3) 10-034
 (4) 10-034, 10-035
 (5) 10-036
 (7) 10-035
s.6 10-034
s.7 . . . . 2-023, 2-040, 10-007
 (1) 2-019, 8-083, 8-086, 8-087, 9-048
s.10 2-042
 (1) 2-017, 2-043
Sch.1 . . . . 2-042, 2-043
Prevention of Corruption Act 1906 (6 Edw. 7,
 c.34) 6-088

Prevention of Corruption Act 1906 (6 Edw. 7, c.34)—*cont.*
Prevention of Corruption Act 1916 (6 & 7 Geo. 5, c.64) 6-088
Proceeds of Crime Act 2002 (c.29)
  s.333 6-021
Property Misdescriptions Act 1991 (c.29)
  9-117
Protection of Animals Act 1911 (1 & 2 Geo. 5, c.27)
  s.7 .... 4-006, 4-010
Public Bodies Corrupt Practices Act 1889 (52 & 53 Vict., c. 69) 6-088
  s.2(b) 6-087
Public Health Act 1875 (38 & 39 Vict., c.55)
  s.247(4) 2-026
Public Interest Disclosure Act 1998 (c.23)
  6-077
Recognition of Trusts Act 1987 (c.14) .. 12-036
Rent Act 1977 (c.42)
  s.41(2) 2-018
  s.151(1) 2-018
Sale of Goods Act 1893 (56 & 57 Vict., c.71)
  s.14 3-029
  s.25(1) 8-147
Sale of Goods Act 1979 (c.54) 8-150, 8-127
  s.1(5) 8-150
  s.2 8-150
  s.3 8-150
  s.4 8-150
  s.5 .... 8-150, 8-151
  s.6 .... 8-153, 8-156
  s.10 6-013
  s.11 8-150
  s.12(1) 8-156
    (2) 8-156, 8-158
    (3) 8-156, 8-158
  s.13 8-156
  s.14(5) 8-068
  s.16 8-170
  s.17 .... 8-170, 8-171
  s.21 .... 1-025, 8-127, 8-130
    (1) 8-126
  s.23 8-154
  s.24 ...... 1-025, 7-087, 8-147, 8-150, 8-156
  s.25 ...... 1-025, 7-087, 8-059, 8-150, 8-156
    (1) 8-152, 8-156
  s.26 .... 7-087, 8-059
  s.38(2) 7-100, 7-101
  s.43(1)(c) 7-090
  s.48(3) 4-006
  s.61(3) 8-154
  s.62(2) 8-125
Sale of Goods (Amendment) Act 1994 (c.32)
  8-144
Sale of Goods (Amendment) Act 1995 (c.28)
  .... 8-170, 8-173
Senior Courts Act 1981 (c.54)
  s.20(2)(p) 7-085
  s.35A 6-108

  s.49 9-040
Solicitors Act 1974 (c.47) 7-053
  s.1 7-056
  s.25(1) 7-056
    (2) 7-056, 7-067
  s.32 .... 6-091, 6-105
  s.33 .... 6-091, 6-105
    (3) 6-105
  s.73 7-083
  s.87(1) 7-056
Statute Law Revision Act 1893 (56 & 57 Vict., c.14) 3-038
Statute Law Revision Act 1966 (c.5) 3-038, 9-109
Statute of Frauds 1677 (29 Car. 2, c.3)
  .... 2-014, 8-075, 8-078, 9-066
  s.4 .... 1-042, 2-019, 8-003
Statute of Frauds Amendment Act 1828 (9 Geo. 4, c.14) 8-197, 8-198
  s.6 .... 2-019, 8-197, 9-118
Supply of Goods and Services Act 1982 (c.29)
  s.15 7-004
Torts (Interference with Goods) Act 1977 (c.32)
  s.8 6-112
    (1) 6-110, 6-111, 7-103
    (2) 6-111
  s.11(1) 9-130
  s.12 4-006
  s.13 4-006
Trade Union and Labour Relations (Consolidation) Act 1992 (c.52)
  s.236 7-046
Tribunals, Courts and Enforcement Act 2007 (c.15)
  s.71 .... 2-061, 2-100, 8-160, 8-196
  Sch.23 2-026
Trustee Act 1925 (15 & 16 Geo. 5, c.19)
  1-032
  s.25 .... 2-036, 8-052
  s.27 8-206
  s.61 6-003
Trustee Act 2000 (c.29) 1-032
  ss.11—23 .... 2-021, 5-002
Trustee Delegation Act 1999 (c.15) 1-032, 2-021, 5-002
  s.1 3-013
  s.5 2-038
  s.10 3-013
Unfair Contract Terms Act (c.50) 1977
  6-058
  s.2(2) 6-030
  s.3 6-058
    (2)(b)(i) 6-058
  Sch.1 6-058
Unsolicited Goods and Services Act 1971 (c.30)
  4-006
Welfare Reform and Pensions Act 1999 (c.30)
  3-043
Wills Act 1837 (7 Will 4 & 1 Vict., c.26)
  s.9 2-022

TABLE OF STATUTORY INSTRUMENTS

Civil Procedure Rules 1998 (SI 1998/3132)
.... 2-009, 10-020
Pt 6 .... 11-006, 11-040
r.6.20(5) 11-006
r.21.2 2-009
r.21.10 2-009
r.25.1 6-040
Pt 40 PD40D 7-012
Sch.1 RSC Ord.17 7-102
Commercial Agents (Council Directive)
(Amendment) Regulations 1993 (SI 1993/
3173) 1-044, 11-003, 11-056
Commercial Agents (Council Directive)
(Amendment) Regulations 1998 (SI 1998/
2868) 1-044, 11-003, 11-006, 11-044
Commercial Agents (Council Directive)
Regulation (Northern Ireland) 1993 (SR
1993/483) ... 1-044, 1-050, 11-003, 11-006
Commercial Agents (Council Directive)
Regulations 1993 (SI 1993/3053)
. 1-032, 1-044, 6-006, 7-002, 7-011, 7-026,
7-031, 7-043, 11-003, 11-006
Pt III 11-027, 11-028
reg.1(2) 11-005, 11-006
(3) 11-006
(a) 11-006, 11-007, 11-008, 11-009
(b) 11-006, 11-008, 11-009
reg.2(1) 1-039, 11-006, 11-013, 11-028,
11-058
(i)—(iii) 11-023
(2) 11-023, 11-027
(3) 11-023
(4) 11-020
reg.3 .... 11-025, 11-035
(1) 6-006, 11-024
(2) 6-006
reg.4 11-035
(1) 7-002, 11-025
(2) 11-009, 11-025
(3) 11-025
reg.5(1) 11-024, 11-025
(2) 11-024, 11-038
reg.6 11-027
(1) 7-011
(3) 11-020, 11-027
reg.7 .... 11-032, 11-034, 11-035
(1) 7-031, 11-029
(a) 11-035
(b) 11-030, 11-032, 11-035
(2) 11-031, 11-032, 11-035
regs 7—9 11-037
regs 7—12 .... 7-026, 11-027
reg.8 .... 7-043, 11-032, 11-034, 11-035
(a) 11-053
(b) 11-032
reg.9 .... 11-032, 11-034, 11-035
reg.10 11-035

(1) 11-033
(2) 11-033, 11-034
(3) 11-033
(4) 11-033
reg.11 11-035
(1) 11-034, 11-035, 11-056
(2) 11-034
(3) 11-034
reg.12 11-036
(1)—(4) 11-036
reg.13 .... 11-014, 11-026, 11-037
(2) 11-037
reg.14 .... 11-035, 11-037, 11-043
reg.15 .... 11-037, 11-039
(1) 11-038
(2) 11-037, 11-038
(3) 11-035
(5) 11-035
reg.16 .... 11-004, 11-039, 11-041
reg.17 ..... 11-037, 11-040, 11-041, 11-043,
11-048
(1) 11-014, 11-040, 11-041, 11-043
(2) 11-044
(a) 11-044
(3) 11-050
(a) 11-030
(b) 11-042
(4) 11-044
(5) 11-047, 11-053
(6) 11-043, 11-048
(7) 11-049
(8) 11-042
(9) 11-046, 11-054
reg.18 ...... 11-004, 11-037, 11-041, 11-056
(a) 11-056
(b) 11-056
(i) 11-039
(ii) 11-042
reg.19 ..... 11-037, 11-041, 11-045, 11-048,
11-054
reg.20 .... 11-035, 11-058
reg.22 ...... 11-025, 11-026, 11-036, 11-038
reg.23 11-003
Sch.1 .... 11-020, 11-021
para.2 .... 11-020, 11-021
para.3 .... 11-020, 11-021, 11-022
para.4 .... 11-020, 11-021
Companies (Model Articles) Regulations 2008
(SI 2008/3229) 2-043
Estate Agents (Accounts) Regulations 1981 (SI
1981/1520)
reg.7 6-104
Estate Agents (Provision of Information)
Regulations 1991 (SI 1991/859) ... 7-020,
7-028, 7-038
reg.3 .... 7-020, 7-038
(1) 7-007

Estate Agents (Provision of Information) Regulations 1991 (SI 1991/859)—*cont.*
reg.4 7-007
reg.5 . . . . 7-020, 7-038
 (1) 7-020, 7-038
 (2) 7-020, 7-038
 (3) 7-020, 7-038
Sch. 7-020, 7-028
Estate Agents (Undesirable Practices) (No.2) Order 1991 (SI 1991/1032) 9-033
art.2 6-055
Sch.1 para.2 6-055
Sch.3 para.2 . . . . 6-021, 7-051
Land Registration (Powers of Attorney) Rules 1986 (SI 1986/1537) 2-042
Lasting Powers of Attorney, Enduring Powers of Attorney and Public Guardian Regulations 2007 (SI 2007/1253) 10-009
reg.22 10-009
Limited Liability Partnerships (Application of Companies Act 2006) Regulations 2009 (SI 2009/1804) 12-020
Mental Capacity Act 2005 (Commencement No. 1) (England and Wales) Order 2007 (SI 2007/563) 10-009

Mental Capacity Act 2005 (Commencement No. 2) Order 2007 (SI 2007/1897) 10-009, 12-023, 12-032
Money Laundering Regulations 2007 (SI 2007/2157) 7-052
Overseas Companies (Execution of Documents and Registration of Charges) Regulations 2009 (SI 2009/1917) 8-040, 12-017, 12-020
Package Travel, Package Holidays and Package Tours Regulations 1992 (SI 1992/3288) 1-034, 9-033
Police (Conduct) Regulations 2012 (SI 2012/2632)
reg.7 2-024
Rules of the Supreme Court 1965 (SI 1965/1776)
Ord.11 r.1(f) 9-062
 (g) 9-062
Ord.14 . . . . 8-117, 8-121
Unfair Terms in Consumer Contracts Regulations 1999 (SI 1999/2083) 6-001, 7-008
reg.6(2) 7-008

CHAPTER 1

NATURE OF THE SUBJECT

Article 1

AGENCY AND AUTHORITY

(1) Agency is the fiduciary relationship which exists between two persons, one of   **1-001**
   whom expressly or impliedly manifests assent that the other should act on his
   behalf so as to affect his relations with third parties, and the other of whom
   similarly manifests assent so to act or so acts pursuant to the manifestation.
   The one on whose behalf the act or acts are to be done is called the principal.
   The one who is to act is called the agent. Any person other than the principal
   and the agent may be referred to as a third party.[1]
(2) In respect of the acts to which the principal so assents, the agent is said to have
   authority to act; and this authority constitutes a power to affect the principal's
   legal relations with third parties.[2]
(3) Where the agent's authority results from a manifestation of assent that he
   should represent or act for the principal expressly or impliedly made by the
   principal to the agent himself, the authority is called actual authority, express
   or implied. But the agent may also have authority resulting from such a
   manifestation made by the principal to a third party; such authority is called
   apparent authority.[3]
(4) A person may have the same fiduciary relationship with a principal where he
   acts on behalf of that principal but has no authority to affect the principal's
   relations with third parties. Because of the fiduciary relationship such a person
   may also be called an agent.[4]

Comment

1. Theoretical basis of agency in the common law

Purpose of definition   It is customary to begin a systematic treatise with some sort   **1-002**
of definition of its subject-matter. The definition given here is partly based on that
in the American *Restatement*, and it is hoped that it may provide a useful starting
point to an area of law where concepts have been "peculiarly troublesome".[5]

   Definitions such as that above serve two purposes. They may, first, simply form
an introduction to the subject-matter following. But recourse may also be had to

---

[1] *Restatement, Third*, § 1.01.
[2] *Restatement, Third*, §§ 2.01, 2.03 and Comment c to § 1.01.
[3] *Restatement, Third*, § 2.01 and 2.03. And see in general Conant, "Proposed Code of Agency
   Contracts" (1971) 13 Mal. L.R. 98.
[4] See below, para.1-020.
[5] Müller-Freienfels, in *Civil Law in the Modern World* (Yiannopoulos ed., 1965), 77 at 79.

such a definition when general words such as (in this context) "agent" and "agency" appear in propositions of law, particularly in statutes and other formal documents. What meaning should be attributed to these terms in such contexts is discussed later.[6] A major problem in the application of the law in this area is that questions are frequently asked of lawyers in forms such as "Is A an agent?", "Is A B's agent or C's agent?", as if a clear all-purpose answer could be given for the purposes of resolving a dispute. Any useful response must be couched in a much more restricted form, for agency is a relative notion and there are many acceptable uses of the term which do not always coincide with each other.

It must be stressed at the outset therefore that the definition given above is intended to be read as a whole. No single sentence should be treated as encapsulating the whole notion of agency. The first of the above propositions, (1), is no more than the first of four. Taken by itself it is very wide, as Woolf J noted in a case involving the distinction between sale and agency for the purpose of a taxing statute.[7] For the purposes of most legal usage, (2) and (3) provide an essential restriction, in limiting the central use of the term to cases where the agent has authority to affect the principal's legal position. The proposition in (4) adds for completeness another situation (referred to below as that of the "canvassing" or "introducing" agent[8]) where the terms "agent" and "agency" may be not inappropriately used.

1-003 **Limits on definition** But in any case definitions are, however commonplace, of limited utility in law as elsewhere; in particular, reasoning based on presupposed definitions is often suspect. A longer explanation is usually required than can be encapsulated in the definitional form. No one has the monopoly of the "correct" use of this or any other term. The word "agency", to a common lawyer, refers in general to a branch of the law under which one person, the agent, may directly affect the legal relations of another person, the principal, as regards yet other persons, called third parties, by acts which the agent is said to have the principal's authority to perform on his behalf and which when done are in some respects treated as the principal's acts. These acts are probably thought of as most likely to occur in connection with the formation and discharge of contracts and in the disposition of property, but the same idea appears, sometimes in modified form, in many other parts of the law. Even in this context, the term "agency" may be used to refer to: the relationship between the principal and the agent; to the function of the agent with respect to the outside world; or to the sum total of all legal relations involving principal, agent and third parties arising in such situations.[9] But these are only some possibilities: even in legal terminology the term may be used in other senses, and lay usage of the words "agency" and "agent" provides further variations. The definition given in (1) above selects as the initial referent of the term "agency" the internal relationship between principal and agent which, since it involves the reposing of special trust and confidence, is a fiduciary one. In view of the other relationships which are also involved this selection may appear somewhat arbitrary. But in what follows it will be argued that that relationship is fundamental to this whole

---

[6] See below, para.1-023.
[7] *Customs and Excise Commissioners v Johnson* [1980] S.T.C. 624 at 629 (though the formulation there referred to is that of the 15th edition of this work: the present formulation is narrower). The definition in the *Restatement, Third* is much wider: see below, para.1-004.
[8] See below, para.1-020.
[9] Powell, pp.31–32.

branch of the law, since it provides the paradigm situation and justification for the application of the typical rules regarding the agent's power to affect the principal's legal position vis-à-vis third parties, which in fact then dominate the subject.

Affecting principal's relations with third parties This definition not only requires that the agent act on the principal's behalf; it also requires that the acting be "so as to affect [the principal's] relations with third parties". This is a narrowing of the definition, and necessitates another provision, Rule (4), which then extends the term to the position of certain persons who act for others but do not necessarily act in such a way. The *Restatement*, on the other hand, simply refers to a person who acts "on the principal's behalf",[10] which is very much wider and can be taken to include agents of the sort just referred to without a special exception, and also can more easily encompass other phenomena of agency reasoning such as its application in tort, or as regards the acquisition of notice—though of course it encounters reciprocal difficulties as to how to limit the phrase "on behalf of".[11]

    The choice of the principal definition selected here is largely a matter of exposition: it has then to be supplemented by exceptions. But the special features of an agent, in particular the fiduciary duties, derive from the power that some agents have to affect their principal's legal position. It seems best, therefore, to stress this aspect of agency, that is to say, its fiduciary nature and its application to contract and transfers of property. "The term 'agency' is best used ... 'to connote an authority or capacity in one person to create legal relations between a person occupying the position of principal and third parties.' Usually the legal relations so created will be contractual in nature."[12] Where these criteria are met, the normal incidents of agency are, prima facie, likely to apply even if the parties' contract expressly disavows one being the "agent" of the other.[13] Nonetheless, it is one thing to find that a disavowal is not conclusive, it is another for a court to find an agency for purely instrumental reasons without regard to the fact that the relationship of agency is fundamentally an intentional and voluntary one.[14] Equally, the mere use of a label such as agent or "manager" may not attract the incidents of agency, if there is no authority to alter the other's legal position conferred.[15]

Fundamental role of consensual agency The basic notion behind the common law of agency can be explained along the following lines. The mature law recognises that a person need not always do things that change his legal relations himself: he may utilise the services of another to change them, or to do something

1-004

1-005

---

10 § 1.01.

11 See, e.g. *Emerald Meat Ltd v Minister of Agriculture (No.2)* [1997] 1 I.R. 1 (person obtaining import licence "on behalf of" may be the importer); *Plevin v Paragon Personal Finance Ltd* [2014] UKSC 61; [2014] 1 W.L.R. 4222 at [30], where Lord Sumption says that the ordinary and natural meaning of the term "on behalf of" imports agency.

12 *Scott v Davis* (2000) 204 C.L.R. 333 at [227], per Gummow J, citing the judgment of the High Court of Australia delivered by Dixon J in *International Harvester Co of Australia Pty Ltd v Carrigan's Hazeldene Pastoral Co* (1958) 100 C.L.R. 644 at 652.

13 See *Sydney District Rugby League Football Club Ltd v News Ltd* (2000) 177 A.L.R. 611 at [131] onwards; affd (2003) 215 C.L.R. 563. For a useful consideration of indicia of agency, see *Serventy v Commonwealth Bank of Australia (No.2)* [2016] WASCA 223 at [29]–[37]. For the converse situation (parties use word "agent" but no agency found), see below, para.1-035.

14 For further discussion, see below, para.1-026.

15 See *Alliance Craton Explorer Pty Ltd v Quasar Resources Pty Ltd* [2013] FCAFC 29 (no entitlement of one party to a joint venture to demand access to business papers of the other). See too *UBS AG (London Branch) v Kommunale Wasserwerke Leipzig GmbH* [2017] EWCA Civ 1567 at [91].

during the course of which they may be changed. Thus, where one person, the principal, requests or authorises another, the agent, to act on his behalf, and the other agrees or does so, the law recognises that the agent has power to affect the principal's legal position by acts which, though performed by the agent, are to be treated in certain respects as if they were acts of the principal. The conferral of authority is voluntary. This result is not confined to cases where the agent simply has specific instructions to do one thing, e.g. to hand over, or perhaps sign, a document. A person who acts in such a way (sometimes called a *nuntius* or messenger) performs no more than a ministerial function, which is attributable to the person for whom he acts without much stretching of elemental notions.[16] Any developed system must also recognise the more advanced notion of permitting a person to give to another a general authority to act according to his own discretion within certain limits.

1-006 **Basis in unilateral manifestation of will** The basic justification for the agent's power as so far explained seems to be the idea of a unilateral manifestation by the principal of willingness to have his legal position changed by the agent.[17] To this any contract between principal and agent is secondary,[18] though there will usually be one, which often provides the reason for the conferral and indeed may contain it. The phrase "consensual agency" used in the previous paragraph and below,[19] and "agency by agreement" used later in this book,[20] are to be understood in this sense and not as relating to any supporting contract. There is certainly no conceptual reason which requires a contract between principal and agent to achieve this creation of power, and it is indeed clear that no contract is necessary, for a person without juristic capacity may be an agent.[21] Nor need the agent undertake to act as such. It is sufficient if the principal manifests to the agent that he is willing for the agent to act, and the agent does so in circumstances indicating that his acts arise from the principal's manifestation.[22] This is not dissimilar from the formation of a contract, but is notionally separate, as the example of a power of attorney shows. In common with other situations where in the civil law it is important to derive a party's intention, the principal's manifestation of will is generally determined on an objective basis, whether or not the conferral of power meets the requirements of the law of contract.[23]

1-007 The phrase "manifestation of assent" is selected by *Restatement, Third* instead of "manifestation of consent" in *Restatement, Second*, seemingly to stress the objective nature of the inquiry.

---

[16] See further below, para.1-047.
[17] Montrose (1938) 16 Can.B.R. 757 at 779; Müller-Freienfels (1964) 13 Am.J.Comp.L. 193 at 203. See also *Sinfra A-G. v Sinfra Ltd* [1939] 2 All E.R. 675 at 682 (power of attorney a "one-sided instrument").
[18] See *HKSAR v Luk Kin* [2016] HKCFA 81 at [29] per Lord Hoffmann. This point is most obviously exposed in the context of the conflict of laws: see below, para.12-009. It is also noticeable in connection with revocation of authority, which is effective even if it constitutes a breach of any attendant contract: see below, para.10-004.
[19] See below, paras 1-012 and 1-025.
[20] See Ch.2, Section 2.
[21] See Article 5; *Yasuda Fire and Marine Ins. Co v Orion Marine Ins. Underwriting Agency Ltd* [1995] Q.B. 174.
[22] See Comment to Article 8 for discussion of the specific question whether the *agent* needs to know of the principal's manifestation or whether the manifestation, assuming that it can be proved, is sufficient.
[23] See *Freeman & Lockyer v Buckhurst Park Properties (Mangal) Ltd* [1964] 2 Q.B. 480 at 502.

"A manifestation is conduct by a person, observable by others, that expresses meaning. It is a broader concept than communication. The relevant state of mind is that of the person who observes or otherwise learns of the manifestation."[24]

Extensions of reasoning   The basic idea is extended to cases where the words and conduct of one person towards another are such that the law treats that other as entitled to regard himself as authorised in certain respects, even though the first person cannot be shown to have had, and may indeed not have had, a specific intention of conferring authority; and to cases where the first person subsequently approves an act done by another on his behalf though he had not previously authorised it. The paradigm situation, in which the principal intends to confer authority, is in this book referred to as agency by express agreement.[25] The first extension set out above is called agency by implied agreement[26]; and the second is dealt with under the heading of ratification.[27]   **1-008**

No requirement that agent purport to act for principal   In some legal systems such reasoning would normally only be accepted in the case of an agent who when acting purported, or at least was understood, to do so on behalf of, or "in the name of", a principal, though usually the principal need not actually be named.[28] The common law, however, has no such requirement: if there is preceding authority to act for the principal, the rules so far set out, other than those as to ratification, will apply despite the fact that the existence of the principal, or his connection with the transaction, is unknown to the third party. Where his existence or connection with the transaction is not known, the principal is referred to as undisclosed,[29] and the rules then applicable are referred to as the doctrine of the undisclosed principal, which can be regarded as a unique feature of common law (though some civil law systems now approach some of its results, and such results were earlier known to the *ius commune*). In addition to the exclusion of ratification, however, the doctrine is limited by other safeguards appropriate to the fact that it in substance involves intervention on a contract by one not contemplated as a party to it.   **1-009**

No requirement that agent pursue recognised commercial function   Although the main operation of agency principles is in the commercial sphere, they are in fact absolutely general and may apply to domestic and other non-commercial situations. There is no requirement that the agent pursue a commercial function at all, and certainly none that he pursue a commercial function of a recognised type.   **1-010**

Apparent authority   By a further extension, the law may treat a third party dealing with a person who appears to have authority from a principal as entitled, by virtue of the principal's manifestations to him by words or conduct, to assume that the person in question has such authority, regardless of whether anything has occurred from which the law would draw that conclusion if the matter were in issue only between the supposed agent and the supposed principal. This reasoning takes effect in the doctrine of apparent authority. This applies both where the supposed   **1-011**

---

[24] *Restatement, Third*, § 1.031 Comment b.
[25] Articles 7 and 24–26.
[26] Articles 8 and Articles 27–32.
[27] Articles 13–20.
[28] See, e.g. French CC, arts 1119 and 1984. There may be exceptions in some systems for situations where the agent is a "man of straw".
[29] See Article 76.

agent is not authorised to act at all, and also where he appears to have a greater authority than was actually conferred on him. It is said in the English cases that this reasoning depends on estoppel. But it is suggested below that it is a very weak form of estoppel, and to be distinguished from other agency-related situations where the principles of estoppel as normally stated more obviously apply.[30] The doctrine operates regardless of whether the agent himself believed that he was authorised, provided that he reasonably appeared to the third party to be authorised. But the basis of the doctrine makes it essential that he has purported to act on the principal's behalf. Because the full consequences of the basic agency relationship are not applicable, the general doctrine of apparent authority is not fully discussed until the section dealing with the relations between the principal and third parties,[31] though certain problems of estoppel are briefly treated at an earlier stage[32] in Chapter 2.

1-012 **Consensual agency as paradigm case** Under the above explanation, the basic situation of agency is treated as being that in which the principal agrees that the agent should act for him and the agent expressly or impliedly agrees to do so. This is the paradigm, and it is from their similarity in various respects to this situation that the others derive their legal force. It is for this reason that the term "agency" is assigned to this relationship in the wording of Article 1(1). The other cases may fairly be regarded as derivatives. Ratification cases can, but only with difficulty, be assimilated into the paradigm situation; and in English law at any rate apparent authority cases only affect third parties in the first instance, so do not give rise to the full range of results flowing from the paradigm situation.

This account conforms with the approach taken by the English cases. In 1863 Lord Cranworth said that: "No one can become the agent of another person except by the will of that other person"[33]; more than 100 years later the same starting point was selected by Lord Pearson when he said: "The relationship of principal and agent can only be established by the consent of the principal and the agent".[34] Although the notions of "will" and "consent" are objectively determined, they clearly remain fundamental. Mere economic interdependence between two parties does not create one the agent of the other.[35]

1-013 **Authority as the basis of power** The technical description of the results which the law puts on the agency situations described is, however, to say that in all of them

---

[30] See below, para.8-029.
[31] Articles 72 and 83.
[32] Article 21.
[33] *Pole v Leask* (1863) 33 L.J. Ch. 155 at 161 (a dissenting speech).
[34] *Garnac Grain Co Inc v H.M.F. Faure & Fairclough Ltd* [1968] A.C. 1130 fn. at 1137; see also *Atlas Maritime Co SA v Avalon Maritime Ltd (The Coral Rose) (No.1)* [1991] 4 All E.R. 769 at 774–775, 779; *ACN 007528207 Pty Ltd v Bird Cameron* (2005) 54 A.C.S.R. 505 at [96] (accountancy firm creates company, using a variant of the firm name, and hives off to it some of its accounting services—company found not to be agent of firm, there being no intention to create an agency); *Fortis Bank SA NV v Indian Overseas Bank* [2011] EWHC 538 (Comm); [2012] 1 All E.R. (Comm) 41 (consignee not principal of shipper though named in bill of lading); *The Lorenz Consultancy Ltd v Fox-Davies Capital Ltd* [2011] EWHC 574 (Ch) (leasing agent could not look to nominee tenant for commission when contract was only with nominator).
[35] See *Tonto Home Loans Australia Pty Ltd v Tavares* [2011] NSWCA 389 at [194]; *UBS AG (London Branch) v Kommunale Wasserwerke Leipzig GmbH* [2017] EWCA Civ 1567 at [100]. See too *Plevin v Paragon Personal Finance Ltd* [2014] UKSC 61; [2014] 1 W.L.R. 4222 at [33].

the agent has a power to affect the principal's legal relations[36]: and this terminology has already been used above. It is nevertheless more commonly said that the agent has authority. When examined, this authority amounts to no more than a power of a special sort, a power by doing an act to affect the principal's legal relations as if he had done the act himself. But the notions of authority and power are different.[37] Where such a power is voluntarily conferred by one person on another (the paradigm case), the person on whom it is conferred is said to "be authorised" by the other, or to "have his authority". But, as can be seen from what is said above, the power may exist in a person upon whom it cannot be said to have been voluntarily conferred. In the common law, such cases seem exceptional, and it is said that there is only "agency by estoppel" or "apparent authority". Yet the power is the same: there is no temptation to talk of "apparent power". "Authority", like "possession", carries the image of a paradigm case justifying a legal result: "power" is neutral and simply states the result regardless of the justifications for it.

Actual and apparent authority The placing of actual and apparent authority together in the definition in Article 1(3) can therefore be criticised, for actual authority arises where the principal agrees that the agent shall act for him (the paradigm case), whereas apparent authority can be said to be no authority at all, in that the principal has not authorised the agent to act, even if a third party is entitled to assume that he has. But the two types of authority are frequently spoken of together, and both create a power in the agent: it seems important, therefore, to reflect this usage at the outset. This scheme can also be justified on the basis that in both cases the authority stems from the principal's objectively determined assent, the difference being that in one case the assent is manifested to the agent and in the other to the third party. The wording of Article 1(3) reflects this reasoning,[38] though the notion of manifestation to the third party is frequently an artificial one and involves considerable difficulties.[39]
1-014

Fiduciary relationship between agent and principal Since the paradigm agent has conferred on him special powers which enable him to change the legal position of another, the law also imposes on him special duties of a fiduciary nature towards that other.[40] These duties are not necessarily contractual (though of course they may be) for it is not necessary that there be any contract between principal and agent. Rather, they originate from equity, and are connected with the duties imposed by equity on express trustees. Consequently, their application is not confined to agents.[41] It has been said in the Privy Council that:
1-015

---

[36] Hohfeld, *Fundamental Legal Conceptions as Applied in Judicial Reasoning* (4th printing, 1966), p.52; Montrose (1938) 16 Can.B.R. 757.

[37] Powell, p.6; Corbin (1925) 34 Yale L.J. 788 at 794; Montrose, above, at p.763; Falconbridge (1939) 17 Can.B.R. 248 at 251–252; Dowrick (1954) 17 M.L.R. 24 at 37; McMeel (2000) 116 L.Q.R. 387; Tiberg, in *Lex Mercatoria* (Rose ed., 2000), Ch.4.

[38] cf. *Restatement, Second*, §§ 26 and 27; Abbott (1896) 9 Harvard L.R. 507; Montrose, above.

[39] See below, para.8-029.

[40] Articles 43–53; Dowrick (1954) 17 M.L.R. 24; *Guerin v R.* [1984] 2 S.C.R. 335 at 383–385, 394; (1984) 13 D.L.R. (4th) 321 at 339–341, 348–349; *Amaltal Corp Ltd v Maruha Corp* [2007] 3 N.Z.L.R. 192 at [22]; Illustration 14 to Article 43.

[41] See *Guerin v R.*, above.

"agency is a contract made between principal and agent ... like every other contract, the rights and duties of the principal and agent are dependent upon the terms of the contract between them, whether express or implied".[42]

This approach is discussed later,[43] where it is submitted that the statement should be treated with reserve, not least because agency need not be contractual. For the present it is sufficient to say that though the fiduciary duties can be modified by contract, they are nevertheless a sufficiently prominent part of the agent's position to be incorporated within the original definition and noted at the outset.

1-016   **Other features: remuneration on commission**   The fiduciary duties lead to another feature of agency. It is inconsistent with those duties that an agent should act in respect of his relationship with the principal for his own profit (unless he discloses this to the principal and the principal consents). His relationship with his principal is commercially related rather than commercially adverse. Thus, he should be remunerated by commission in respect of the services he has rendered, and not take his own undisclosed profit as an independent intermediary. The commission need not however be related to the value of the transaction: it can be by a mark-up. But the essence of the payment received by the agent is that it is not an independent profit taken by the agent, but rather a fee paid to him by the principal in return for acting on his behalf.[44]

1-017   **Duty of due diligence**   There is a further feature of the relationship between principal and agent which may be taken as typical. It is that the agent owes to the principal, unless there are other indications, only a duty to use due diligence, or, if appropriate, his best endeavours to achieve the result required. He does not owe the strict duties customarily imposed on, for instance, a seller, who has an adverse commercial relationship with his buyer.[45] To some extent this is of course a feature of contracts for services, as opposed to contracts for the transfer of property, in general; but though no doubt an agent *can* undertake strict liability in some respect,[46] the duty of due diligence is, when combined with the features already referred to, also a typical indication of agency.

1-018   **Control**   It is common to regard control by the principal as a defining characteristic of agency. Thus, *Restatement, Third*, defines agency in terms of acting "on the principal's behalf and subject to the principal's control".[47] This notion has obvious relevance in employment law, where it can be treated as an identifying characteristic of the employment relationship, and hence to the vicarious liability of an employer for an employee. In agency in general however it plays a more limited role.[48] A distinction between agent and trustee, and between agent and some bailees, is that control cannot in general be exercised by beneficiaries over trustees, nor by many

---

[42]   *Kelly v Cooper* [1993] A.C. 205 at 213–214, per Lord Browne-Wilkinson.
[43]   See below, para.6-034.
[44]   Articles 45 and 46.
[45]   See below, para.1-035.
[46]   e.g. a *del credere* agent: see below, para.1-042.
[47]   This feature is, contrary to the approach here adopted, made much of in *Restatement, Third*: see § 1.01, Comments f, g and corresponding reporter's notes.
[48]   See *South Sydney District Rugby League Football Club Ltd v News Ltd* (2000) 177 A.L.R. 611, at [131] onwards, actual decision affd (2003) 215 C.L.R. 563.

bailors over their bailees.[49] The same is true of lenders who take powers to act in their own interests in ways which affect the borrower's position.[50] But agents will often not accept control by their principals as to the manner in which they act, and some will only accept instructions to act in accordance with usages of their own market. Others may be authorised only to do specific things. In many such situations the principal's only control lies in his power to revoke the authority, a power which agency law assumes that he has at all times.[51] It might seem therefore that control is not a significant feature of the internal relationship, except in so far as the relationship by definition posits a person, the principal, giving authority, and the agent's duty to obey instructions if he wishes to continue as agent. Nevertheless, if the principal gives up all control of his supposed agent the relationship is only doubtfully one of agency.[52] The idea of control may also be relevant where it is contended that a company is an agent of its parent.[53] For this reason the idea requires mention; but if the central notion of agency is not required, as it is not on the explanation given in this book, to extend to tort, the idea of control does not seem sufficiently important to be inserted into the formal definition.

Internal and external aspects of agency   The full reasoning above has been developed to meet the case of a person who may be called an agent in a strict sense, who has the power to affect his principal's legal relations. To such an agent legal rules attach which require the drawing of a distinction between what may be called the internal and external aspects of agency. The *external* aspect is that under which the agent has powers to affect the principal's legal position in relation to third parties. The *internal* aspect is the relationship between principal and agent, which imposes on the agent special duties vis-à-vis the principal, appropriate to the powers which he can exercise on the principal's behalf. These may arise in connection with an accompanying contract, but may arise only from the agent's fiduciary liability. They follow from the need to control the agent's opportunities to exploit his position. To an agent in the fullest sense, both aspects are relevant. Some persons may, however, be described as agents by virtue of the internal relationship but have no external powers, as appears below.

1-019

Incomplete agency: internal relationship only—the "canvassing" or "introducing" agent   Article 1(4) seeks to achieve completeness by taking in a well-established type of intermediary who makes no contracts and disposes of no property, but is simply hired,[54] whether as an employee or independent contractor, to introduce parties desirous of contracting and leaves them to contract between themselves. In effecting such introductions he is remunerated by commission, which he may sometimes take from both parties.[55] Such a person is a common figure in most western legal systems and may well be referred to as an agent. The most obvi-

1-020

---

[49]   See below, paras 1-032 and 1-033.
[50]   See Article 118.
[51]   See Article 120. This point is further developed in the Comment to Article 37.
[52]   This makes some of the usages of Lloyd's difficult to account for. See *CFTO-TV Ltd v Mr Submarine Ltd* (1994) 108 D.L.R. (4th) 517; affd (1997) 151 D.L.R. (4th) 382; *Alliance Craton Explorer Pty Ltd v Quasar Resources Pty Ltd* [2013] FCAFC 29 at [74].
[53]   See the *South Sydney* case, above, at [137].
[54]   A fiduciary relationship, central to this category, would be difficult to attribute without a contract between principal and agent.
[55]   As has been pointed out (see above, para.1-004), a wider definition of agency such as that adopted in *Restatement, Third*, does not require an exception for this type of agent: but it creates its own difficulties.

ous example of such an intermediary in the English cases is the estate agent, who introduces purchasers to vendors and tenants to lessors of houses, and vice versa.[56] Such persons are sometimes also referred to as brokers, and indeed in some English-speaking countries the estate agent is referred to as a "real estate broker": but this may be misleading since the current practice, at any rate in England, is to use the term "broker" for persons who go beyond introductions and certainly do make contracts for their principals, e.g. commodity brokers, insurance brokers and stockbrokers. Canvassing agents are on the fringe of the central agency principles used by the common law, since their powers to alter their principals' legal relations are at best extremely limited.[57] They often, however, have authority to receive and communicate information on their principals' behalf, and in so doing have the capacity to alter their principals' legal position. They also usually act in a capacity which may involve the repose of trust and confidence, and hence may be subject in some respects to the fiduciary duties of agents towards their principals.[58] They are also subject of typical rules, largely developed in estate agent cases, as to entitlement to commission, which are normally regarded as part of agency law and are relied on also by agents who have greater powers to bind their principals.[59] They may sometimes hold money (e.g. deposits) for their principals.[60] The rules applicable to the internal relationship between principal and agent will therefore apply as appropriate, and for this reason such persons should certainly be treated in a work on agency even though they lack the external powers of the agent. It is an advantage of the formulation of basic agency principle in Article 1, which selects the internal relationship between principal and agent as a distinguishing feature of agency, that it can be taken to cover such persons. Canvassing agents are persons to whom the internal parts of agency law may apply, but who, because of the limited nature of their external powers to affect their principals' legal positions, are not agents in the full sense of the word.[61] They may therefore be said to provide an example of "incomplete agency".

1-021   **Indirect representation**[62]   There is another situation that can be said to amount to "incomplete agency": that which may be called indirect representation. In commercial spheres a method of dealing can be adopted whereby a principal appoints

---

[56] There is an elaborate discussion of a statutory definition of a "real estate agent" in *Freehold Land Investments Ltd v Queensland Estates Pty Ltd* (1970) 123 C.L.R. 418.
[57] See Article 30, Illustration 6.
[58] See Article 45, Illustrations 16 and 17. But cf. *Northeast General Corp v Wellington Advertising Inc*, 604 N.Y.S. (2d) 1 (Ct.App.1993) ("Non-exclusive independent investment broker and business consultant for the purposes of finding and presenting candidates for purchase, sale, merger or other business combination" held not to owe fiduciary duty to disclose information regarding persons introduced).
[59] Articles 56–58.
[60] See Comment to Article 52.
[61] For a useful general survey see Yiannopoulos (1959) 19 La.L.Rev. 777 especially at p.799 onwards. In *Vogel v R. & A. Kohnstamm Ltd* [1973] Q.B. 133 an introducer of business was held not to be an agent for the purposes of enforcement of a foreign judgment: see pp.136–137 and 147; and in *Rakusens Ltd v Baser Ambalaj Plastik Sanayi Ticaret AS* [2001] EWCA Civ 1820; [2002] 1 B.C.L.C. 104 the office of such a representative was held not to be the company's "place of business" for the purposes of s.695(2) of the Companies Act 1985 (now Companies Act 2006 s.1139). See also *Okura & Co Ltd v Forsbacka Jernverks A/B* [1914] 1 K.B. 715.
[62] See Busch, *Indirect Representation in European Contract Law* (The Hague: Kluwer Law International, 2005); Kortmann and Kortmann, in Busch, Macgregor and Watts (eds), *Agency Law in Commercial Practice* (Oxford: Oxford University Press, 2016), Ch.6.

a person, who may be called an agent, to deal (especially to buy[63]) on his behalf, on the understanding that when dealing with any third party the agent will deal in his own name as principal. As between principal and agent, however, the relationship is one of agency[64]; viz. the agent does not promise to achieve a result but only to use his best endeavours; he does not answer to his principal on the strict basis appropriate to seller or buyer[65] (though he may have some of the rights of a seller, e.g. a lien[66]); he is normally remunerated by commission; he owes fiduciary duties and thus may not without disclosure take commission from the other party; and he is in a sense under his principal's control. Here, again, the internal aspect of agency is found but not the external. This arrangement is sometimes referred to in civil law countries as indirect representation, and intermediaries operating on such a basis, often by virtue of their professions (such as freight forwarders), may be referred to as operating under a contract of *commission* or the equivalent in other languages (the title referring to the task entrusted to the agent rather than, as might seem more natural to a common lawyer, the method of remuneration).[67] In many such situations the third party may infer, often from the nature of the agent's profession, or may even know that a principal is involved: he may even know the principal's name. Its recognition can lead to a method of expounding agency law on the basis that a person wishing to appoint a representative has the choice of two methods, direct or indirect representation: such an approach is in fact adopted in the PECL and indeed the DCFR, for which a measure of universality is claimed, though the UNIDROIT Principles have abandoned it as a classification.[68] The notion of authority can also be employed in both contexts, in the sense that the indirect agent can be said to be "authorised" to deal in his own name, but for the account and at the risk of the principal.[69] This can be pressed so as to consider other doctrines of direct

---

[63] For analogous arrangements regarding selling, see *Kirkham v Peel* (1880) 44 L.T. 195; *New Zealand and Australian Land Co v Watson* (1881) 7 Q.B.D. 374; and cases on factors generally (below, para.1-046); *Bosanquet v Mofflin* (1906) S.R. (N.S.W.) 617; *Benmag Ltd v Barda* [1955] 2 Lloyd's Rep. 354; *Fleming v London Produce Co Ltd* [1968] 1 W.L.R. 1013.

[64] See *Ireland v Livingston* (1872) L.R. 5 H.L. 395 at 407–409; *Armstrong v Stokes* (1872) L.R. 7 Q.B. 598; *Robinson v Mollett* (1875) L.R. 7 H.L. 802 at 809–810; *Cassaboglou v Gibb* (1883) 11 Q.B.D. 797 at 803–804; *Montgomerie v UK Mutual SS Assn* [1891] 1 Q.B. 370 at 372; *Butlers (London) Ltd v Roope* [1922] N.Z.L.R. 549; *Downie Bros v Henry Oakley & Sons* [1923] N.Z.L.R. 734; *Bolus & Co Ltd v Inglis Bros Ltd* [1924] N.Z.L.R. 164 at 175; *Sopwith Aviation & Engineering Co Ltd v Magnus Motors Ltd* [1928] G.L.R. (N.Z.) 380; *Isaac Gundle v Mohanlal Sunderji* (1939) 18 Kenya L.R. 137; *Witt & Scott Ltd v Blumenreich* [1949] N.Z.L.R. 806; *Rusholme & Bolton & Roberts Hadfield Ltd v S.G. Read & Co* [1955] 1 W.L.R. 146 at 152; *J.S. Robertson (Australia) Pty Ltd v Martin* (1956) 94 C.L.R. 30; *Teheran-Europe Co Ltd v ST Belton (Tractors) Ltd* [1968] 2 Q.B. 53 at 59–60; affd [1968] 2 Q.B. 545; Hill [1964] J.B.L. 304; [1967] J.B.L. 122; (1968) 31 M.L.R. 623; (1972) 3 J. Maritime Law & Commerce 307; Schmitthoff, 1970 I *Hague Recueil des Cours* 115 at 151–154; Lando [1965] J.B.L. 179 at 374; [1966] J.B.L. 82. For a more modern example, see *Triffit Nurseries v Salads Etcetera Ltd* [1999] 1 All E.R. (Comm) 110 at 115; affd [2000] 1 All E.R. (Comm) 737, where such reasoning seems essential and below, para.10-010; and *OMV Petrom SA v Glencore International AG* [2015] EWHC 666 (Comm) at [138] (indirect principal able to plead deceit made to agent).

[65] See below, para.1-036.

[66] See the important material collected in Article 69.

[67] See, e.g. Hamel, *Le Contrat de Commission* (Paris, 1949); Cohn, *Manual of German Law* (2nd edn), Vol.2, p.40 onwards; Horn, Kötz and Leser, *German Private and Commercial Law* (1982), pp.232–234; Schmitthoff, 1970 I *Hague Recueil des Cours* 115, 122–125; Müller-Freienfels (1955) 18 M.L.R. 33 at 36–38; Busch, fn.62 above.

[68] See above, p.xvii.

[69] See Busch, fn.62 above, pp.11 and 14.

agency, especially apparent authority and ratification, in the context of indirect representation.[70]

On some views the idea of indirect representation is also applicable where the agent has authority to create direct representation, but for some reason (whether the principal's or his own) does not indicate that he is doing so.[71] This is nearer to the common law doctrine of the undisclosed principal, a much narrower doctrine which common lawyers treat as an unusual form of *direct* representation.[72] In civil law countries the "principal" of the indirect agent (or *commissionnaire*) is not usually liable to the third party, though he may be in special situations, and he may rather more easily be able to sue.[73] Where he is, the case for applying doctrines by analogy applicable to direct agency obviously becomes stronger.

1-022   **Is indirect representation accepted at common law?**   This dichotomy between direct and indirect representation is unlikely to be attractive to common law systems, which tend to reach the result of direct representation with more facility than the civil law. But this apart, it is difficult to see any doctrinal objection at common law to the setting-up of a situation of indirect representation. Indeed, something like this seems to have been the mode of operation of the nineteenth-century factor,[74] who received goods on consignment and sold them without always making clear whether he sold his own goods or those of another. A commercial intermediary operating on this basis is sometimes even referred to in nineteenth-century cases as a "commission agent" or "commission merchant"[75]; and the cases on the old "foreign principal" rule[76] refer to this method of operation. It was most clearly enunciated by Blackburn J when he said:

> "Any person, if he chooses, may give an order to an agent to buy as his agent, not only with an express dispensation from any obligation to establish privity of contract between him and the person from whom the agent buys, but even expressly refusing authority to the agent to establish such privity.
>
> This is the ordinary authority given to a foreign commission merchant who (on account of the great inconvenience which would result from establishing privity of contract between the foreign producer and the home merchant) is not allowed (far less required)

---

[70] See Busch, passim.

[71] See Busch, fn.62 above, pp.13, 23–26, 231 and 234.

[72] See below, Article 76.

[73] In Dutch law the principal is in certain cases liable and entitled: see Busch, pp.44–48; as to German law, see Busch, p.93 onwards.

[74] See below, para.1-046.

[75] As to commission agents, see the leading case of *Ireland v Livingston* (1872) L.R. 5 H.L. 395 at 408; *Armstrong v Stokes* (1872) L.R. 7 Q.B. 598; Story, *Agency* (1839), § 33. The term "commission agent" or "commission merchant" appears in *Taylor v Kymer* (1832) 3 B. & Ad. 320; *Armstrong v Stokes* (1872) L.R. 7 Q.B. 598, Illustration 7 to Article 80; *Elbinger Actien-Gesellschaft v Claye* (1873) L.R. 8 Q.B. 313; *Hutton v Bulloch* (1874) L.R. 9 Q.B. 572; *Maspons y Hermano v Mildred, Goyeneche & Co* (1882) 9 Q.B.D. 530; affd (1883) 8 App.Cas. 874; *Cassaboglou v Gibb* (1883) 11 Q.B.D. 797 at 804; *J. N. Lyon & Co Ltd v N. Fuchs* (1920) 2 Lloyd's Rep. 333. See also *Fleming v London Produce Co Ltd* [1968] 1 W.L.R. 1013 as to the term "general commission agent" in connection with tax legislation. See in general Munday (1977) 6 Anglo-Am. L.Rev. 221, esp. at p.232 onwards.

[76] See below, para.8-071; Busch, *Indirect Representation in European Contract Law* (2005), pp.168–173.

to establish privity of contract between them. This, however, in no way interferes with the existence of a fiduciary relation."[77]

But by a unique development of the common law, the factor's principal was held entitled to intervene not only to sue, but also to be liable on the factor's contracts. This is said to be the origin of the common law doctrine of the undisclosed principal, though the case law on that doctrine appears to confine it to situations where the agent has authority to create privity of contract without disclosing that he is doing so.[78] Such an intermediary may therefore sometimes in English law be regarded as creating *direct* representation, at least where he gives no indication that he is acting for a principal and perhaps on occasion even where he does give such indication.[79] This seems to have led to an assimilation of this special arrangement with normal agency. Several cases seem therefore to assume, without the point being properly argued, one of two possible interpretations to such a situation. The first is that the intermediary is a normal agent of an undisclosed principal, and that the undisclosed principal rules therefore apply with the result that the principal is liable and entitled whatever the intentions of the parties.[80] The second is that because the agent in such a situation has no external authority to create privity of contract between his principal and the third party, the undisclosed principal rules do not apply at all and the agent must himself alone be a party to the contract of sale, carriage, or whatever transaction he has performed for the principal, and deal with his principal as principal.[81] If the approach to be derived from such cases is correct, however, this is an area where the breadth of common law agency principles, which normally produce a more flexible result, act as a limiting factor and exclude the recognition of such an arrangement.[82] There seems no obvious reason why this should be so, unless it be thought undesirable that a principal should be able, by agreement with the agent, to determine his liability to third parties. Indeed, such a situation may arise even now where, under the undisclosed principal doctrine, the intervention of a third party is excluded.[83]

---

[77] *Robinson v Mollett* (1875) L.R. 7 H.L. 802 at 809–810 (a dissenting speech). See also his famous speech in *Ireland v Livingston* (1872) L.R. 5 H.L. 395.

[78] See Comment to Article 76.

[79] See, e.g. *Maspons y Hermano v Mildred, Goyeneche & Co* (1882) 9 Q.B.D. 530 (holding the foreign principal rule inapplicable); affd on other grounds (1883) 8 App.Cas. 874.

[80] See, e.g. the *Maspons* case, above; and see *Brown & Gracie Ltd v F.W. Green & Co Pty Ltd* [1960] 1 Lloyd's Rep. 289; Reynolds [1983] *Current Legal Problems* 119. It could be said that *Scrimshire v Alderton* (1743) 2 Strange 1182 is an early example of such judicial analysis; see Stoljar, pp.207–208; Chorley (1929) 45 L.Q.R. 221 at 224–225.

[81] See, e.g. the dissenting judgment of Diplock LJ in *Anglo-African Shipping Co of New York Inc v J. Mortner Ltd* [1962] 1 Lloyd's Rep. 610 (which, it is respectfully submitted, presents an analysis which does not accord with commercial reality). See also the same judge in *Garnac Grain Co Inc v H.M.F. Faure & Fairclough Ltd* [1966] 1 Q.B. 650 at 684; affd [1968] A.C. 1130; *Limako BV v Hentz & Co Inc* [1979] 2 Lloyd's Rep. 23; *B. & M. Readers' Service Ltd v Anglo Canadian Publishers Ltd* [1950] O.R. 159 (subscription to magazine). But cf. *L/M International Construction Inc (now Bovis International Inc) v The Circle Ltd Partnership* (1995) 49 Con.L.R. 12; and *Triffit Nurseries v Salads Etcetera Ltd* [2000] 1 All E.R. (Comm) 737, in both of which the "indirect representation" reasoning may assist the analysis.

[82] It is possible to identify situations of a different type where a person who may be called a representative acts as principal but accounts on an agency basis: e.g. the position of an issuing and correspondent bank in documentary credits (as to which see, e.g. *Benjamin's Sale of Goods* (9th edn), para.23-029 onwards). But this does not involve an act which the principal could do himself, and hence is not easily regarded as agency.

[83] See below, para.8-079.

1-023   Meaning of term "agent" in the abstract   When it is necessary, as in statutory interpretation, to attribute a meaning to the word "agent", it may be said that the central significance of the term agent refers to a person who attracts both the external and internal aspects of agency, for it is here that the complete complex of rules is most fully worked out, and it is because of the external powers that the internal duties are imposed. And where the term agent is used in a statute or formal document, it has been said that it may be presumed that the word is used in this, its proper legal connotation, unless there are strong contrary indications.[84] But there is certainly no rule to that effect, and the term is often used of any form of intermediary, or of persons who simply perform functions for others.[85] Similarly, the word "authority" in a statute may not require actual authorisation by the principal, but extend to acts, authorised or not, occurring in the performance of authorised tasks.[86]

1-024   Essence of agency   Should the essence of agency then be regarded as the internal or external aspect of the concept, or as both? In the fullest sense it requires both; and the internal aspect follows the external, i.e. as stated above, it is because the agent has the power to alter the principal's position that the fiduciary duties are imposed on him. In another sense, however, it is the internal conferring of the power that justifies that power, and such reasoning would make the internal aspect primary. However this question is viewed, it is useful to note the typical features of the internal position which distinguish agency from other relationships: the agent undertakes to use due diligence on behalf of another, rather than undertake strict duties to another in a situation commercially adverse to that other; he is subject to fiduciary duties; and he is remunerated by commission or an equivalent rather than by taking his own profit. Though any of these three features can be modified in an appropriate case, they nevertheless remain typical.[87]

1-025   "Externalised" theories   The explanation of the common law of agency offered

---

[84]   *Shell Co of Australia Ltd v Nat Shipping and Bagging Services Ltd (The Kilmun)* [1988] 2 Lloyd's Rep. 1 at 16, per Sir Denys Buckley (in a dissenting judgment); *Canada v Merchant Law Group* 2010 FCA 206 (Can. Fed. CA) at [17] (incidence of goods and services tax); *Plevin v Paragon Personal Finance Ltd* [2014] UKSC 61; [2014] 1 W.L.R. 4222 at [30].

[85]   See, e.g. *Laemthong International Lines Co Ltd v Artis (The Laemthong Glory)* [2005] EWCA Civ 519; [2005] 1 Lloyd's Rep. 688 (promise to indemnify "you, your servants or agents" considered in the context of the Contracts (Rights of Third Parties) Act 1999: shipowner held "agent" of charterer for delivering cargo and so able to sue). Another example is the reference to "servants or agents" in Art.IV bis 2 of the Hague-Visby Rules scheduled to the Carriage of Goods by Sea Act 1971: see *Carver on Bills of Lading* (4th edn), para.9-303. See further *The Happy Day* [2002] EWCA Civ 1068; [2002] 2 Lloyd's Rep. 487 (agency of receiver for charterer); *Commerce Commission v Vero Insurance New Zealand Ltd* (2006) 8 N.Z.C.L.C. 101, 871 (possession of apparent authority enough to meet the operative provision of a statute that a person be an agent); *Commissioners for Revenue and Customs v Insurancewide.Com Services Ltd* [2010] EWCA Civ 422; [2010] S.T.C. 1572 at [87] (exemption from VAT for insurance brokers and agents); *Revenue and Customs v Secret Hotels2 Ltd* [2014] UKSC 16; [2014] S.T.C. 937 (VAT intermediaries); *Actavis Group hf v Eli Lilly & Co* [2013] EWCA Civ 517; [2013] R.P.C. 37 at [57] (business carried on through an agent); *NYK Bulkship (Atlantic) NV v Cargill International SA* [2016] UKSC 20; [2016] 1 W.L.R. 1853 (only irrelevant functions of sub-charterers were those of "agent" and otherwise they were independent parties).

[86]   See *Kemeh v Ministry of Defence* [2014] EWCA Civ 91; [2014] I.C.R. 625 at [11] (racial discrimination). Sed quaere when defences to principal in relation to employees not available in relation to agents.

[87]   As to the significance of the right of control, see above, para.1-018.

above can, however, be subjected to fundamental criticisms. A simple version of such criticisms is to say that it is the law that imposes certain consequences on the facts in all these cases; thus all agency arises by operation of law, and the insistence on consent in the internal relationship as the ground base of agency is misplaced.[88] This view can fairly easily be said to fail to attach sufficient importance to the paradigm case, the degree of similarity to which renders appropriate or inappropriate the use of the sort of reasoning to which that situation gives rise. The controversy is similar to that as to whether there is a distinction between "possession in fact" and "possession in law", or whether all possession, being attributed by the law, should be treated as possession in law.[89] Admittedly there are few limits on the situations where the law can regard someone as possessing: but the paradigm case where there is physical control or something very near to it nevertheless regulates to some extent what are thought to be acceptable uses of the term "possession", in whatever context. Hence the notion of "possession in fact" is contrasted with "possession in law". The same is true of the notion of authority as opposed to that of power.

More elaborately, but to similar effect, it may be argued that cases of genuine express conferring of authority are in fact the exception rather than the rule, at least where disputes arise, and that the external power conferred by the law on the agent, which applies also in situations of apparent authority, is so clearly predominant that it, and not subjective consent, should be emphasised and analysed as the connecting link between cases of agency.[90] Agency situations should therefore be viewed in the first place from the point of view of the third party, and apparent authority should, again, be an application of the normal rules rather than an exception accommodated by elaborate explanations. In some continental European legal systems a distinction sharper than would be appropriate to common law authority is made between the internal relationship of principal and agent and the general external power of the agent. This seems to be particularly so in German law, and systems influenced by it, where the distinction achieved prominence following a famous article by Paul Laband published in 1866.[91] It leads to greater emphasis on the external aspect of agency situations than the approach set out in Article 1: the conferring of power may in all cases be regarded as a unilateral act in the law directed from the principal not to the agent, but rather to the third party.[92]

The contrast between such an approach and that of the common law as here explained can be likened to the conflict of principle frequently recognised in the law of property between security of title and security of transactions. In some jurisdictions the approach that prefers the value of protecting apparently valid transac-

---

[88] See, e.g. Salmond and Winfield, *Law of Contracts* (1927), p.340: "An agent may be defined as a person who is authorised by law to exercise on behalf of another person ... any power possessed by that other person of entering into a contract or other agreement, or of doing any other act in law"; Dowrick (1954) 17 M.L.R. 24 at 35–38.

[89] This is rather a dated controversy. See Salmond, *Jurisprudence* (12th edn), Ch.9.

[90] Seavey (1920) 29 Yale L.J. 859 at 872 onwards; Fridman (1968) 84 L.Q.R. 224 at 228–231.

[91] Die Stellvertretung bei dem Abschluss von Rechtsgeschäften nach dem Allgemeinen Deutschen Handelsgesetzbuch (1866) 10 *Zeitschrift für Handelsrecht* 183. See Müller-Freienfels (1964) 13 Am.J.Comp.L. 193 at 197–202; Schmitthoff 1970 I *Hague Recueil des Cours* 115 at 120 onwards; Schlesinger, *Comparative Law* (6th edn), p.854 onwards; Tiberg, in *Lex Mercatoria* (Rose ed., 2000), Ch.4. It appears that the approach of French law is somewhat nearer the English approach. For a recent comparative study of the question in various European jurisdictions, see Busch and Macgregor (eds), *The Unauthorised Agent* (2009). See too Macgregor, Ch.2.

[92] It has some similarity with the reasoning used of general agents, and agents of specific types (e.g. factors) in England in the nineteenth century. See Brown [2004] J.B.L. 391.

tions predominates. At common law, or at any rate in the English common law, the predominant principle is, however, that a person does not lose his ownership except by his own voluntary act. Significant exceptions are created only by statute (principally the Factors Act 1889[93]) and under the doctrine of estoppel.[94] The same is true of contractual obligations: a person cannot be subjected to a contractual obligation through another except by his own volition. Exceptions can in general only be created by statute (the most obvious being the Partnership Act 1890[95]) and under the doctrine of apparent authority, which can be said to be based on estoppel, though there are difficulties with this view.[96]

It seems that common law unaided is almost bound to arrive at the particular balance, which it does, since it must proceed by the use of commonly accepted lines of reasoning. The principles concerning loss of property or imposition of obligations seem an inevitable starting point, even if their results are later to be modified by secondary doctrines. With one possible exception, to be discussed below, no other reasoning seems readily available for initial use. Therefore agency depends on the assent of the principal except where corrective (apparent authority) reasoning can be found or the result is modified by statute, as in the Factors Act. To achieve a completely different emphasis would require a general statute, or at least the acceptance of a technique of judicial reasoning which can derive general policies from particular statutes.[97] The German doctrinal separation referred to above was in fact derived from the *Prokura*, a general authority in commercial matters created by the Commercial Code of 1861.[98] Reasoning by analogy from statutes has not been a feature of the English common law.[99]

But even the most extreme externalised theories are in fact likely to derive the agent's power ultimately from such an internal starting point, for example, creation of *Prokura*, or appointment to a specific position, which the principal need not have made, and may, with appropriate publicity, cancel.[100] Indeed, on one view his main protection lies in this possibility of cancelling the authority completely by removing his agent.

When this is borne in mind, common law is not so different as may appear. It has been said that its approach to agency, as outlined above, fails to make the proper

---

[93] Article 87; see also Sale of Goods Act 1979 ss.24 and 25 (derived from the Factors Act).

[94] Articles 83 and 85; see also Sale of Goods Act 1979 s.21.

[95] ss.5 and 10.

[96] Articles 21 and 72. The requirements for an estoppel are less stringent in the area of obligations than in that of property to such an extent that it can be doubted whether estoppel is in truth the basis of the results reached in the law of obligations. This is not surprising, for it has long been established that obligations can be imposed on the basis of objective appearances: but it perhaps indicates that the rules protecting against loss of ownership are too severe. See below, para.8-028.

[97] See Tiberg, in *Lex Mercatoria* (Rose ed., 2000), Ch.4, esp. at p.61. ("Thus, the 'dependent' or 'mandate' power which is the exception in Nordic and Continental law is 'actual authority' and the rule in English law, while the independent powers that are the rule in Continental law are the exceptions ('apparent authority') in English law").

[98] HGB, para.49; see Müller-Freienfels (1964) 13 Am.J.Comp.L. 193 at 207 onwards and 341–346.

[99] But see *Beverley Acceptances Ltd v Oakley* [1982] R.T.R. 417 at 426, per Lord Denning MR (dissenting); "This means that we need no longer interpret the Factors Acts by the letter. We can go by spirit which lies behind them. Modern law has made them a particular application of general principle." See also Beatson (2001) 117 L.Q.R. 247.

[100] See Grönfors (1962) 6 *Scandinavian Studies in Law* 95 (in English), referring to s.10(2) of the Uniform Scandinavian Contracts Act of 1915. The same writer's *Ställningsfullmakt och Bulvanskap* (Stockholm, 1961) contains an exhaustive international bibliography to that date. It was reviewed by Müller-Freienfels (1963) 12 Am.J.Comp.L. 272 (together with Stoljar's *Law of Agency* (1961)). See further Tiberg, above.

distinction between the internal relation between principal and agent and the external relation between the agent and third parties, but simply derives the one from the other.[101] But although there are certainly dicta which can be taken to support such a view, it has been submitted above that there is an essential difference between the conferring of authority, which is a unilateral act of will even if like a contract it is to be justified by the consent of the parties, and an accompanying contract, if there is one. In so far as there is a genuine difference of approach, each generates its own difficulties. The common law approach has some difficulty in completely explaining the basis of apparent authority[102]: but its concentration on the conferring of authority enables it (for better or worse) to accommodate the rights and liabilities of the undisclosed principal.[103] The "external" approach certainly protects innocent third parties dealing with the agent, and no doubt many more claims are in practice based on apparent than on actual authority. But the protection can perhaps be excessive: for it can (unless other, corrective doctrines can be invoked) lead to the conclusion that third parties are entitled to rely on the appearance of agency even though they have reason to know that the agent was not in fact authorised.[104] It appears also to be associated with a tendency to isolate numerous different types of agent, each with its own special rules; though this is more probably a legacy of the Romanistic notion of nominate contracts.[105]

The tort approach From time to time a different approach to agency problems **1-026** has been urged by common law writers, an approach quite separate from the "externalised" theories referred to above. It has been argued that traditional agency reasoning, which requires authority or its appearance for one person to alter the legal position of another, is inadequate, and that recourse should be had to a line of reasoning which seeks more generally to place responsibility on the instigator or beneficiary of the enterprise in relation to which a person acts.[106] Sometimes it has been suggested that a principle similar to that of vicarious liability in the law of torts should be adopted in place of normal agency reasoning.[107] A suggestion for the adoption of such an approach was put forward by Lord Wilberforce:

"It may be that some wider conception of vicarious responsibility other than that of agency, as normally understood, may have to be recognised in order to accommodate some of the more elaborate cases which now arise when there are two persons who become mutually involved or associated in one side of a transaction."[108]

The case itself involved the potential liability of a finance company for the representations of a car dealer who assisted his buyers in obtaining finance from the

[101] See Müller-Freienfels (1957) 6 Am.J.Comp.L. 165 at 170–173; cf. the same writer in *Civil Law in the Modern World*, (Yiannopoulos ed., 1965), 77 at 86–89. A similar point can be made of French law: see Müller-Freienfels (1964) 13 Am.J.Comp.L. 341 at 346–349; Graziadei, Mattei and Smith, *Commercial Trusts in European Private Law* (Cambridge: Cambridge University Press, 2015) pp.48–52.
[102] See Comment to Article 72.
[103] See above, para.1-009; Article 76.
[104] Müller-Freienfels (1964) 13 Am.J.Comp.L. 193 at 211 onwards.
[105] See Schmitthoff, 1970 I *Hague Recueil des Cours* 115 at 123–124 (listing 13 types of intermediary known to German law); Bonell [1984] Uniform L.Rev. 52.
[106] Seavey (1920) 29 Yale L.J. 859, esp. at pp.883–885.
[107] See, e.g. Wright (1936) 1 U. Toronto L.J. 17 at 40 onwards; Mearns (1962) 48 Va.L.Rev. 50; Brown [2004] J.B.L. 391.
[108] *Branwhite v Worcester Works Finance Ltd* [1969] 1 A.C. 552 at 587. See also *First Energy (UK) Ltd v Hungarian International Bank Ltd* [1993] 2 Lloyd's Rep. 194 at 196, 204, per Steyn LJ.

company for their purchases from him—a common enough situation. If it was sought to generalise on this situation alone, it might perhaps be possible to develop a doctrine that where two parties are in a business association of some sort, the nature of which is unclear to the outside world, the burden should rather be on the party who appears to be the instigator of, or possibly even merely a participator in, the combined business to show that there was not and would not reasonably be expected to have been authority in the other party, rather than the reverse. Lord Wilberforce had said earlier in his speech:

"Thus there are two rival views as to the manner in which a typical hire purchase transaction should be regarded. That expressed by Holroyd Pearce L.J. and by Pearson L.J. involves an analysis without any initial presumption of each individual transaction, on the available documents and evidence, in order to see whether, in any respect, the finance company (or, if that is relevant, the hirer) should be held to have conferred authority (actual or apparent) upon the dealer to act as his agent. That of Lord Denning M.R. and Donovan L.J. takes as a starting point the established mercantile background of hire-purchase transactions, as known to and accepted by all three parties, takes that as establishing in general the basis for an agency relationship, and finally considers, against that background, any individual features of the particular case to see whether they confirm or weaken the agency inference. My Lords, for my part I think that the latter approach is now to be preferred."[109]

This was however a dissenting speech; the majority of the House of Lords decided the question in issue against liability by the application of normal agency principles, and Lord Wilberforce himself was able also to justify the (minority) result which he reached in favour of liability on the basis of orthodox doctrine. Subsequently it was held that a person employing the services of an estate agent to sell his house was not liable when the agent without authority took deposits from a number of people, who were thereby defrauded[110]; that a finance company was not bound by the representations of a hire-purchase information service, set up by finance companies as an independent, non-profit-making organisation, as to whether a particular vehicle was the subject of a hire-purchase agreement[111]; that an insurance company was not liable for representations made by a branch manager (an employee who was more or less a canvassing agent or a controller of canvassing agents[112]) which were neither actually nor apparently authorised[113]; and that a company was not liable in tort for fraudulent misrepresentations by a manager not within the scope of his apparent authority.[114] Such decisions tend against any generalised approach of the sort mentioned,[115] which is in any case directed towards the principal's *duties*. Orthodox agency law gives him rights also.

---

[109] At 585–586.

[110] *Sorrell v Finch* [1977] A.C. 728, Illustration 4 to Article 92: see Articles 92 and 111.

[111] *Moorgate Mercantile Co v Twitchings* [1977] A.C. 890, Illustration 7 to Article 84. Both the above two cases are criticised by Fridman (1982) 20 U. of W.Ont.L.Rev. 23.

[112] As to canvassing agents see above, para.1-020.

[113] *British Bank of the Middle East v Sun Life Assurance Co of Canada (UK) Ltd* [1983] 2 Lloyd's Rep. 9, Illustration 10 to Article 77 (noted [1982] J.B.L. 496; [1983] J.B.L. 409).

[114] *Armagas Ltd v Mundogas SA (The Ocean Frost)* [1986] A.C. 717. But as to vicarious liability for the negligent misstatements of employees, see now *So v HSBC Bank Plc* [2009] EWCA Civ 296; and below, para.8-180.

[115] See Fridman (1983) 13 Manitoba L.J. 1. But see the observations in the difficult and specialised case of *Heatons Transport (St Helens) Ltd v Transport and General Workers' Union* [1973] A.C. 15 at 99–100, which suggests a similarity between authority and scope of employment; *Re Supply of Ready Mixed Concrete* [1992] Q.B. 213; *First Energy (UK) Ltd v Hungarian International Bank Ltd* [1993] 2 Lloyd's Rep. 194, Illustration 12 to Article 72.

A more drastic use of such reasoning might seek to make the principal liable regardless even of whether he was known by the third parties to be connected with the transaction. This, which is again a liability doctrine only, might for agency law be justified as an extension of the undisclosed principal doctrine[116]; but it would more probably require to be based on reasoning similar to that now used in tort cases, where the recent tendency has been to invoke principles for vicarious liability much broader than those formerly employed.[117] In the speech of Lord Wilberforce quoted above he later suggested[118] that this was the true matter in issue in *Garnac Grain Co Inc v HMF Faure & Fairclough Ltd*,[119] where it was sought to say that a commercial concern which sold goods and at the same time secretly contracted to repurchase them from a sub-sub-buyer was liable to the sub-buyer as an undisclosed principal of the sub-sub-buyer. The argument in that case was unsuccessful, however; and more recently a company was held not liable for the act of an employee (a true agent) who caused the loss to third parties by a negligent valuation set out on the principal's notepaper, effected contrary to his instructions and in such a way that the third parties did not know who had prepared the valuation.[120] The trend of decisions again suggests, therefore, that the orthodox basis of agency law, which requires some indication of authority or of the appearance of it, will still be followed.[121] That is not to say, however, that the use made of agency doctrine may not vary from time to time, and case to case, for the doctrine is a flexible one.[122] Vicarious liability is indeed connected with agency law historically, and in practice governs certain of the principal's tort liabilities, which cannot necessarily be readily separated from his contractual position. The doctrine of apparent authority is also in some ways similar to vicarious liability in tort, since (in English law) it involves liability only. In the United States it was at one time fashionable to seek to link agency reasoning in contract and property with vicarious liability in tort with a view to the development of more general principles.[123] But it seems that such schemes are now less in fashion, and if this is so it can be justified.[124] For a tort situation is in general not one voluntarily entered into by the aggrieved party, whereas an agency situation is. This means that the duty to compensate in tort may be more readily imposed than a similar duty in contractual situations. Although it is now recognised that the boundary between contract and tort is more fluid than may sometimes have been thought in the past, the distinction between the two types of obligation still seems a valid one and no satisfactory organising technique based on different notions has yet been propounded. Furthermore, a major reason for the imposition of liability on one person for the torts of another is the degree of control exercised over him: the main instance of vicarious liability is that of a master for

---

[116] See Comment to Article 22; Montrose (1937) 17 Can.B.R. 224.

[117] See Article 90.

[118] [1969] 1 A.C. at 587.

[119] [1968] A.C. 1130n.

[120] *Kooragang Investments Pty Ltd v Richardson & Wrench Ltd* [1982] A.C. 462.

[121] But see below, para.8-180 for consideration of *So v HSBC Bank Plc* [2009] EWCA Civ 296; [2009] 1 C.L.C. 503.

[122] This, it is suggested, is the answer to the points made by Fridman in (1982) 20 U. of W.Ont.L.Rev. 23.

[123] See Conard (1949) 1 J. Legal Ed. 540; Mechem (1949) 2 J. Legal Ed. 203; Street, *Foundations of Legal Liability* (1906), Vol. 2, Pt. IV; and *Restatement, Second.* (*Restatement, Third* is more limited.) See also Wyse (1979) 40 Mont. L.Rev. 31.

[124] See Ferson (1951) 4 Vand.L.Rev. 260; Müller-Freienfels in *Civil Law in the Modern World* (Yiannopoulos ed., 1965), 77 at 107–108, 117–120.

the torts of his servant. But, although an agent may be an employee, the typical agent is not, and acts in an independent manner. Finally, in agency disputes the question is not, as it is usually in tort, merely one of liability of the instigator of an enterprise: a person designated as principal to a transaction will also be able to sue, except in situations of pure apparent authority—and even here there may be ratification. Agency is therefore more instructively viewed as a notion facilitating commerce rather than as part of a generalised area of law providing compensation for the acts of others; and for these reasons it is submitted that the approach adopted and developed over the past century remains correct.

One question that has not so far been fully addressed in the case law is whether restitutionary liability of a principal for the statements and other acts of agents turns on the authority, actual or apparent, of the agent: see the discussion in Article 79.

1-027 **Diverse use of agency reasoning** The ruling notion of agency law may be said to be that the acts of a person (the agent) authorised, or to be treated as authorised, by another are in certain circumstances to be treated as having the same legal effect as if the had been done by that other (the principal).[125] This is sometimes expressed by the idea that the agent's acts *are* those of the principal—*qui facit per alium facit per se*, though such a complete identification is usually regarded as inappropriate. Reasoning along these lines may be found in the spheres of contract, property, tort, restitution, criminal law, evidence, administrative law, taxation,[126] labour law and elsewhere. But though this approach has value in imposing some unity on the law applicable to situations where one party represents or acts for another, it should not be taken too literally. It is misleading to assume that a single set of principles, valid for the whole law, relating to the representation of one person by another can be evolved under the title of agency.[127] The main application of such reasoning is in the law of contract, where it is obviously desirable for rules to exist under which a person may make a contract for another, and such reasoning was necessary to render the principal liable in *assumpsit*. Different policies may regulate the considerations applicable in the law of property, of restitution, of tort and elsewhere. Nor is it possible exhaustively to analyse agency principles separately in each branch of the law, since the boundaries between the branches are too fluid. Finally, agency principles in English law evolve from disparate sources: from common law as to master and servant, from Admiralty cases concerned with shipmasters, from equity and the law of trusts, from cases on deeds, and from the action of account.[128] Agency reasoning should therefore be regarded as a tool to be picked up as and when it may be useful.[129] The study and separate treatment of agency as a subject is valuable, but no hidden key is to be found thereby. Indeed in the vast majority of cases problems of agency arise as questions of fact only: and perhaps the majority of cases on agency are useful not as laying down rules, but as providing examples of views that may be taken of facts.

That does not mean, however, that all applications of agency reasoning are

---

[125] See further below, Article 6.
[126] Some interesting reasoning can be found in *Conservative and Unionist Central Office v Burrell* [1982] 1 W.L.R. 522; see Emery (1983) 133 N.L.J. 87.
[127] See the first *Restatement* criticised on these grounds by Miller (1936) 20 Marquette L.Rev. 141.
[128] Holdsworth, *H.E.L.* VIII, pp.222–229 and 248–254; Pollock and Maitland, *H.E.L.*, Vol. 2, p.225 onwards; Holmes, 3 *Select Essays in Anglo-American Legal History* (1909), p.368; Stoljar, pp.14–17; Simpson, *History of the Common Law of Contract* (1975), pp.552–557.
[129] cf. the difficulties put forward by Fridman (1968) 84 L.Q.R. 224; (1982) 20 U.W.Ont. L.Rev. 23.

acceptable. The basic notion is that the agent acts on behalf of another. This makes the use of agency terminology in creating irrevocable authority[130] and assignment inappropriate (though use of representation in the latter context goes back to Roman law). Its use (as "agency of necessity") in the context of conferring of benefits now appears inappropriate also,[131] and to be the result of the lack of any concept of *negotiorum gestio* in common law. Agency reasoning is rarely an appropriate solution to problems of subsidiary companies, where a better inquiry addresses problems of "piercing the veil"[132]; or of undue influence exercised over the guarantor or mortgagor by a third party to a guarantee or mortgage.[133] Its use in creating or protecting security over chattels also causes unintended repercussions.[134] The use of the concept of agency to denote the relationship between the Crown and foster parents in charge of children subject to state care has also proved problematic.[135]

2. Agency law and companies[136]

Attributing acts, omissions and states of mind to companies   A company (as   **1-028** with other corporations) can operate only through individuals, but in relation to the rules of the common law (including equity) the rules of agency and vicarious liability suffice to enable a company to be held liable and entitled in respect of acts performed, and the states of mind held, by its agents and employees in the same way as a human principal. No special rules are needed. The position was well stated by Lord Diplock in *Tesco Supermarkets Ltd v Nattrass*[137]:

> "A corporation is an abstraction. It is incapable itself of doing any physical act or being in any state of mind. Yet in law it is a person capable of exercising legal rights and of being subject to legal liabilities which may involve ascribing to it not only physical acts which are in reality done by a natural person on its behalf but also the mental state in which that person did them. In civil law, apart from certain statutory duties, this presents no conceptual difficulties. Under the law of agency the physical acts and state of mind of the agent are in law ascribed to the principal, and if the agent is a natural person it matters not whether the principal is also a natural person or a mere legal abstraction. Qui facit per alium facit per se: qui cogitat per alium cogitat per se."

However, in relation to drafted rules (such as those created by statutes) that are directed at owners of businesses, including companies, it is always a question of construction as to whose acts, omissions and states of mind the drafter intended be

---

[130] See Article 118 and Comment.
[131] See Article 33 and Comment.
[132] See above, para.1-028.
[133] See, e.g. *Coldunell Ltd v Gallon* [1986] Q.B. 1184; *Kings North Trust Ltd v Bell* [1986] 1 W.L.R. 119. A different approach to such questions was established (though not without difficulty) in *Barclays Bank Plc v O'Brien* [1994] 1 A.C. 180 and *Royal Bank of Scotland Plc v Etridge (No.2)* [2001] UKHL 44; [2002] 2 A.C. 773. But cf. *Dollars & Sense Finance Ltd v Nathan* [2008] 2 N.Z.L.R. 557 at [25].
[134] The "Romalpa" clause (below, para.8-165) often seeks to use agency terminology. For a striking nineteenth-century example of such misclassification, see the "attornment of money" cases discussed under Article 112.
[135] See *S. v Att.-Gen.* [2003] 3 N.Z.L.R. 450. cf. *Armes v Nottinghamshire CC* [2017] UKSC 60.
[136] See Müller-Freienfels in *Civil Law in the Modern World* (Yiannopoulos edn, 1965), 77 at 90–92; *Gower's Principles of Modern Company Law* (10th edn), Ch.7; Watts (2000) 116 L.Q.R. 525; Worthington (2017) 133 L.Q.R. 118.
[137] *Tesco Supermarkets Ltd v Nattrass* [1972] A.C. 153 at 198–199; *Bilta (UK) Ltd v Nazir (No.2)* [2015] UKSC 23; [2016] A.C. 1 at [181] and [205] per Lords Toulson and Hodge.

attributed to the owner.[138] Sometimes the drafter may have intended to draw on the common law concepts of attribution, but in others special rules may be required to give effect to the relevant provision. This point is elaborated upon in the next paragraph. Even at common law, the rules by which the acts and states of mind of agents are attributed to their principals must remain sensitive to the legal question that is engaged by the facts.[139] In particular, a principal will not usually be precluded from suing an agent for a breach of duty owed the principal, including as a result of the agent having exposed the principal to liability to a third party, on the basis of an agent's argument that his actions or knowledge are attributed to the principal.[140] Similarly, the agent may not be able to initiate action against the principal in respect of conduct for which the agent is factually responsible simply on the basis that for other purposes the principal is prima facie answerable for it.[141] Again, these principles are as applicable to companies as any other principal, and do not cease to apply merely because the agents in question are directors or otherwise have control of the company's affairs. In general, it is useful to conceive of the company as in exactly the same position as an absentee human owner of a business who has no direct knowledge of its affairs and whose participation is otherwise always remote. In general, therefore, it is useful to conceive of the company as in exactly the same position as an absentee human owner of a business who has no direct knowledge of its affairs and whose participation is otherwise always remote.[142]

In *Meridian Global Funds Management Asia Ltd v Securities Commission*,[143] Lord Hoffmann drew a distinction between the primary rules for attributing the acts of humans to a company, such as the rule that decisions of the board bind the company, and the general rules for attributing conduct to another that apply both to corporations and individuals, namely the principles of the law of agency. However, Lord Hoffmann did not go so far as to state that the bodies of persons who engage the primary rules are not agents, and Lord Diplock's dictum, above, together with the weight of authority, clearly takes the view that they are.[144] The primary rules of attribution are best seen, it is suggested, as simple sources of actual author-

---

[138] *Meridian Global Funds Management Asia Ltd v Securities Commission* [1995] 2 A.C. 500 at 507 and 511–512.

[139] *Bilta (UK) Ltd v Nazir (No.2)* [2015] UKSC 23; [2016] A.C. 1 at [9], [41], [181], [191] and [202]. See below, para.8-208.

[140] *Bilta (UK) Ltd v Nazir (No.2)* [2015] UKSC 23; [2016] A.C. 1 at [42]–[45], [129], and [208]; *HKSAR v Luk Kin* [2016] HKCFA 81 at [41].

[141] See *Brumder v Motornet Service and Repairs Ltd* [2013] EWCA Civ 195; [2013] 1 W.L.R. 2783.

[142] See, e.g. *Williams v Natural Life Health Foods Ltd* [1998] 1 W.L.R. 830 at 835; *Standard Chartered Bank v Pakistan National Shipping Corp (Nos 2 and 4)* [2003] 1 A.C. 959 at [23]; *Prest v Petrodel Resources Ltd* [2013] UKSC 34; [2013] 2 A.C. 415 at [31]; *Bilta (UK) Ltd v Nazir (No.2)* [2015] UKSC 23; [2016] A.C. 1 at [205]; *Financial Conduct Authority v Da Vinci Invest Ltd* [2015] EWHC 2401 (Ch); [2016] Bus L.R. 274. See too *Moulin Global Eyecare Trading Ltd v CIR* [2014] HKCFA 22 at [106].

[143] [1995] 2 A.C. 500 at 506.

[144] Recognition that bodies corporate primarily operate through the concept of agency dates back at least as far as *Yarborough v Governor and Company of The Bank of England* (1812) 16 East 6 at 7, per Lord Ellenborough. See also *Ranger v Great Western Ry Co* (1854) 5 H.L.C. 73; *Ferguson v Wilson* (1866) L.R. 2 Ch.App. 77 at 89, per Cairns LJ; and *Citizen's Life Assurance Co Ltd v Brown* [1904] A.C. 423 (PC) at 426, per Lord Lindley; *Cargill v Bower* (1878) 10 Ch.D. 502 at 513; *Rolled Steel (Holdings) Ltd v British Steel Corp* [1986] Ch. 246 at 304; *Charles Terence Estates Ltd v Cornwall Council* [2012] EWCA Civ 1439; [2013] 1 W.L.R. 466 at [46]; *Ranson v Customer Systems Plc* [2012] EWCA Civ 841 at [20]; *VTB Capital Plc v Nutritek International Corp* [2013] UKSC 5; [2013] 2 A.C. 337 at [138]; *Petrodel Resources Ltd v Prest* [2012] EWCA Civ 1395; [2013] Fam

ity vested usually in the board of directors, but sometimes in shareholders. The point was put in the following way by Diplock LJ in *Freeman & Lockyer v Buckhurst Park Properties (Mangal) Ltd*[145]:

> "Such 'actual' authority may be conferred by the constitution of the corporation itself, as, for example, in the case of a company, upon its board of directors."

On this basis, the board of directors when acting to bind the company, or to authorise others to bind the company, operates as a body of co-agents.[146] Equally, to the extent that some of the functions of shareholders in general meeting involve participating in decision-making on the company's behalf with a view to altera-tion in the company's legal position, they act as co-agents. The source of their authority is the incorporation statute and the company's constitutional documents.[147] It would not follow, however, that everything shareholders or directors do is as agent for the company; sometimes, for instance, directors may act on behalf of shareholders rather than the company (such as when acting for shareholders who have received a takeover offer), and it is also the case that in exercising some func-tions shareholders act solely in their own interests as principals (for example, in changing the constitution).

Normally, directors and shareholders will have actual authority, as opposed to ap-parent authority, only when they make their decisions in accordance with the procedures established by the statute and constitution.[148] However, both in rela-tion to directors and shareholders the courts recognised early on that these groups could also bind their company informally, so long as it could be established that all directors,[149] or all shareholders,[150] as the case may be, assented unanimously to the decision being made on the company's behalf.[151] In respect of shareholders, Lord

---

Law 150 at [105] (reversed on other grounds [2013] UKSC 34; [2013] 2 A.C. 415); *Bilta (UK) Ltd v Nazir (No.2)* [2015] UKSC 23; [2016] A.C. 1 at [183].

[145] *Freeman & Lockyer v Buckhurst Park Properties (Mangal) Ltd* [1964] 2 Q.B. 480 at 505.

[146] See *Aberdeen Railway Co v Blaikie Bros* (1854) 1 Macq. 461 at 471, per Lord Cranworth LC: "The directors are a body to whom is delegated the duty of managing the general affairs of the company. A corporate body can only act by agents". See Watts in Busch, Macgregor and Watts (eds), *Agency Law in Commercial Practice* (2016), Ch.7. As to co-agency in general, see Article 11.

[147] In some circumstances, it may be necessary for both the board and the general meeting to resolve upon a matter before actual authority exists. In the Companies Act 2006, see, e.g. Pt 10, Ch.4 (transactions with directors requiring approval of members); s.601 (agreement to transfer of non-cash assets made by public company with subscriber to the memorandum of association); s.694 (ap-proval of off-market purchases by company of its own shares).

[148] *Rolled Steel Products (Holdings) Ltd v British Steel Corp* [1986] 1 Ch. 246 at 304. For the usual authority of individual directors, see below, para.3-029.

[149] *Reuter v Electric Telegraph Co* (1856) 6 E. & B. 341; *Re Portuguese Consolidated Copper Mines Ltd Ex p. Badman* (1890) 45 Ch.D. 16; *Haddow Nominees Ltd v Rarawa Farm Ltd* [1981] 2 N.Z.L.R. 16; *Base Metal Trading Ltd v Shamurin* [2004] EWCA Civ 1316; [2005] 1 All E.R. (Comm) 17.

[150] The concept of informal unanimous assent seems to have its origins in an implication into the deeds of partnerships: see *Const v Harris* (1824) T. & R. 496 at 522, per Lord Eldon LC; and *Re Vale of Neath and South Wales Brewery Co, Morgan's Case* (1849) 1 De G. & S. 750 at 776 (joint stock company). The assent need be only of voting shareholders: *Jackson v Dear* [2012] EWHC 2060 (Ch) at [68]; reversed on other issues [2013] EWCA Civ 89; [2014] 1 B.C.L.C. 186. Difficult issues arise, however, where the assent is only of the beneficial owner of shares: see Watts (2006) 122 L.Q.R. 15; and *Challinor v Juliet Bellis & Co* [2013] EWHC 347 (Ch) at [622]; reversed on other points, sub nom. *Bellis v Challinor* [2015] EWCA Civ 59.

[151] *Meridian Global Funds Management Asia Ltd v Securities Commission* [1995] 2 A.C. 500 at 506; approving *Multinational Gas and Petrochemical Co v Multinational Gas and Petrochemical Services Ltd* [1983] Ch. 258. Other leading cases include *Salomon v Salomon & Co Ltd* [1897] A.C. 22 at

Hoffmann in the *Meridian* case approved the formulation of the concept of informal unanimous assent as follows[152]:

"... the unanimous decision of all the shareholders in a solvent company about anything which the company under its memorandum of association has power to do shall be the decision of the company".

Assent must be proven, but may be tacit and need not be manifested in concert,[153] and may occur before or after the events in question have taken place.[154] Informal unanimous assent cannot, however, be used to do anything that could not be achieved by formal resolution.[155]

Liquidators, administrators and receivers of companies can also be regarded as agents of the affected company for many, if not all, purposes,[156] although special rules apply to them, including as to the revocability of their authority. Reference should be made to specialist works on these topics.[157]

1-029   Directing mind and will—a tool of construction   In construing statutes, contracts, or other documents intended to have legal effect, it will frequently be necessary to consider how the text applies to the owners of businesses who rely on agents to run the business, as all companies must. Usually, there will be little difficulty in assuming that the drafter intended the acts, omissions, and states of mind of appropriate agents to be attributed to the owner. Occasionally, however, commonly as a result of the drafter's oversight, a rule may be drafted on the basis that an act or state of mind must be that of the principal personally. Such drafting is problematic for companies (and often absentee human owners of businesses as well). A court may have to conclude that the relevant rule does not apply to companies at all.[158] But it may also be necessary, in order to make the provision work with companies, to make a distinction between "mere" agents, and a person who is so centrally concerned with the company's operations, its "directing mind and will",[159] that his acts may be regarded as those of the company itself. Artifice is involved. Thus, it may be necessary by the use of such reasoning to determine

---

57; *Ho Tung v Man On Insurance Co Ltd* [1902] A.C. 232; *Re Duomatic Ltd* [1969] Ch. 975; *Cane v Jones* [1981] 1 All E.R. 533; and *Atlas Wright (Europe) Ltd v Wright* [1999] 2 B.C.L.C. 30; *Randhawa v Turpin* [2017] EWCA Civ 1201. For further discussion, see *Gower's Principles of Modern Company Law*, above, at paras 15-15–15-21; Watts, *Directors' Powers and Duties* (2nd edn, 2015), p.42 onwards.

[152] [1995] 2 A.C. 500 at 506. See also *Bilta (UK) Ltd v Nazir (No.2)* [2015] UKSC 23; [2016] A.C. 1 at [187].

[153] See *Evans v Smallcombe* (1868) L.R. 3 H.L. 249; *The Phosphate of Lime Co Ltd v Green* (1871) L.R. C.P. 43; *Re Bailey, Hay & Co Ltd* [1971] 1 W.L.R. 1357; *Pascoe Ltd v Lucas* (2000) 33 A.C.S.R. 357 at [264]; *Parker & Cooper Ltd v Reading* [1926] 1 Ch. 975; *Brick & Pipe Industries Ltd v Occidental Life Nominees Pty Ltd* (1990) 3 A.C.S.R. 649 at 684–689; affd (1991) 6 A.C.S.R. 464.

[154] *Bowthorpe Holdings Ltd v Hills* [2002] EWHC 2331 (Ch); [2003] 1 B.C.L.C. 226 at [54]. See further below, para.2-067.

[155] *Re New Cedos Engineering Co Ltd* [1994] 1 B.C.L.C. 797 at 814; *Madoff Securities International Ltd v Raven* [2011] EWHC 3102 (Comm) at [111] (no shareholder ratification of fraud).

[156] See, e.g. *Re Southern Pacific Personal Loans Ltd* [2013] EWHC 2485 (Ch); [2014] 1 Ch. 246 at [24] (liability under Data Protection Act 1998); *Dunphy v Sleepyhead Manufacturing Co Ltd* [2007] 3 N.Z.L.R. 602 (NZCA) at [22]. See also Wee and Tan, Busch, Macgregor and Watts (eds), *Agency Law in Commercial Practice* (2016), Ch.8.

[157] See *Palmer's Corporate Insolvency* (looseleaf); Goode, *Principles of Corporate Insolvency* (4th edn); Lightman and Moss, *Law of Administrators and Receivers of Companies* (5th edn).

[158] See, for example, *Motel Marine Pty Ltd v IAC Finance Pty Ltd* (1964) 110 C.L.R. 9.

[159] *Lennard's Carrying Co v Asiatic Petroleum Co Ltd* [1915] A.C. 705 at 713–714, per Viscount Haldane LC; *Bilta (UK) Ltd v Nazir (No.2)* [2015] UKSC 23; [2016] A.C. 1 at [40]. Ideally, the

whether there is "actual fault or privity" in the company itself[160]; and in criminal law it may be necessary to attribute mens rea to the company itself.[161] In *Meridian* it was held, again in a statutory context, that the person concerned need not be the central directing mind and will, but may instead be the person whose functions within the company lead to the conclusion that his or her act must be regarded as that of the company for the purposes of the relevant provision.[162] This development in "identifying" certain conduct as the company's has been referred to in the context of perjury by a company as a "liberating principle",[163] but others have expressed caution in broadening the classes of person whose conduct is directly attributed to the company, at least in the context of criminal law.[164] Most of the cases that have required resort to direct attribution have concerned statutes, but there are also examples involving contracts.[165]

The distinction between direct corporate action and that via agents has also manifested itself in other ways. So, some statutes require personal signature, rather than that of an agent. To apply such a provision to a company, the signature must purport to be that of the company itself[166]; this is essentially a conceit.

The directing-mind-and-will concept has on occasion been extended beyond the resolution of problems in the construction of text, into the ordinary civil law,[167] usually on the basis of some perceived difficulty in using the general principles of the law of agency. However, these extensions are open to criticism on the basis that, in some instances, the rule that was said to preclude the use of agency law was misunderstood,[168] and, in others, the relevant rule of the law of agency was misstated.[169] The result, it has been argued, has been unhelpful distinctions in the common law between incorporated and unincorporated businesses, and the

---

statute itself will advert to how it is to apply to companies.

[160] *Lennard's Carrying Co v Asiatic Petroleum Co Ltd*, above (on Merchant Shipping Act 1894 s.502).

[161] See, e.g. *DPP v Kent & Sussex Contractors Ltd* [1944] K.B. 146; *R. v ICR Haulage Ltd* [1944] K.B. 551; *Moore v Bresler Ltd* [1944] 2 All E.R. 515; *Tesco Supermarkets Ltd v Nattrass* [1972] A.C. 153; *Seaboard Offshore Ltd v Secretary of State for Transport* [1994] 1 W.L.R. 541 (HL).

[162] [1995] 2 A.C. 500. See also *Sudarshan Chemical Industries Ltd v Clariant Produkte (Deutschland) GmbH* [2013] EWCA Civ 919; [2014] R.P.C. 6 at [132].

[163] *Odyssey Re (London) Ltd v OIC Run-Off Ltd* [2001] L.R.L.R. 1 at 64, per Brooke LJ.

[164] [2001] L.R.L.R. 1 at 64, per Buxton LJ. See also *Attorney-General's Reference (No.2 of 1999)* [2000] Q.B. 796; *Cullen v R* [2015] NZSC 73; [2015] 1 N.Z.L.R. 715.

[165] See, e.g. *Americano's Ltd v State Insurance Ltd* (1999) 6 N.Z. Business L.C. 102, 892; *Bilta (UK) Ltd v Nazir (No.2)* [2015] UKSC 23; [2016] A.C. 1 at [198]. *Group Josi Re v Walbrook Insurance Co Ltd* [1996] 1 W.L.R. 1152 can be viewed as another instance: see Watts (2001) 117 L.Q.R. 300 at 326–328.

[166] *Newborne v Sensolid (Great Britain) Ltd* [1954] 1 Q.B. 45; *Hilmi & Associates Ltd v 20 Pembridge Villas Freehold Ltd* [2010] EWCA Civ 314; [2010] 1 W.L.R. 2750 (Leasehold Reform Housing and Urban Development Act 1993); *Williams v Redcard Ltd* [2011] EWCA Civ 466; [2011] 2 B.C.L.C. 350 (execution in two capacities under Companies Act 2006 s.44). But this distinction has no significance in connection with Companies Act 2006 s.51 (see below, paras 9-085 and 9-086): *Phonogram Ltd v Lane* [1982] Q.B. 938, a case under the original provision, s.9(2) of the European Communities Act 1972, which casts some doubt on the distinction in general); *UBAF Ltd v European American Banking Corp* [1984] Q.B. 713. See further below, para.8-197.

[167] See *El Ajou v Dollar Land Holdings Ltd* [1994] 2 All E.R. 685; *Odyssey Re (London) Ltd v OIC Run-Off Ltd* [2001] L.R.L.R. 1 and *Stone & Rolls Ltd v Moore Stephens Ltd* [2009] UKHL 39; [2009] 1 A.C. 1391.

[168] *Odyssey Re*, above (rescission of judgment on the basis of perjury); and *Stone & Rolls*, above (application of maxim ex turpi causa non oritur actio).

[169] *El Ajou*, above; *Lebon v Aqua Salt Co Ltd* [2009] UKPC 2; [2009] 1 B.C.L.C. 549 (imputation of agent's knowledge acquired before appointment); cf. *Bilta (UK) Ltd v Nazir (No.2)* [2015] UKSC 23; [2016] A.C. 1 at [197] per Lords Toulson and Hodge. See further below, paras 8-180 and 8-188.

introduction of unnecessary complexity.[170] In one case, the Court of Appeal found itself having to disapply the notion of the 'directing-mind-and-will' when, as the Supreme Court subsequently found, it was not necessary in the first place to impute the conduct to the company for the purposes of an action by the company against its controllers.[171] It is indeed arguable that no rule of the common law or equity requires the deployment of special rules for companies. One possible candidate is the rule that a deed must be signed personally or by power of attorney (itself signed personally).[172] Corporations cannot sign anything personally. Either the designated signatories for a corporation must be directly identified with the company or they remain agents and provide an exception to the general rule that deeds must be signed personally. The latter view has some very old support, see *Yarborough v Governor and Company of The Bank of England* per Lord Ellenborough[173]:

"As a corporation, they can do no act, not even affix their corporate seal to a deed, but through the instrumentality and agency of others."

1-030   **Agency of companies for each other or for shareholders**   It may appear tempting to regard a subsidiary company as agent for the principal company; or even the principal as agent for the subsidiary. This would have the effect of circumventing (rather than piercing) the corporate veil. English courts have not looked favourably on such arguments, and situations where there is such agency would be required to be proved by normal criteria,[174] as where a trader converted his business into a limited company and it was specifically provided that the new company would perform sale contracts entered into by the previous company as agent for the vendor.[175] Similarly, courts will not lightly find that companies, or their directors, are agents for their human shareholders, but cases will arise where this is the correct conclusion.[176] Sometimes too the facts may support a conclusion that a director or employee of a parent company has authority, actual or apparent, to bind or

---

[170] See Watts (2000) 116 L.Q.R. 525; Campbell and Armour [2003] C.L.J. 290; and Watts (2010) 126 L.Q.R. 14; see now *Bilta (UK) Ltd v Nazir (No.2)* [2015] UKSC 23; [2016] A.C. 1 at [41].
[171] See *Jetivia SA v Bilta (UK) Ltd* [2013] EWCA Civ 968; [2014] Ch. 52; discussed in Watts [2014] J.B.L. 162, upheld on different grounds in [2015] UKSC 23; [2016] A.C. 1.
[172] See below, para.2-040.
[173] *Yarborough v The Governor and Company of the Bank of England* (1812) 16 East 6 at 7.
[174] See *Adams v Cape Industries Plc* [1990] Ch. 439 (doing business for purpose of jurisdiction as relevant to enforcement of foreign judgment); *Scriven v Scriven* [2015] EWHC 1690 (Ch) at [269]. See too *Telewest Communications Plc v Customs and Excise Commissioners* [2005] EWCA Civ 102; [2005] S.T.C. 481; *Premier Building and Consulting Pty Ltd v Spotless Group Ltd* (2008) 64 A.C.S.R. 114 at [339]. cf. *Globex Foreign Exchange Corp v Launt* 2011 NSCA 67.
[175] *Southern v Watson* [1940] 3 All E.R. 439. See also *Rainham Chemical Works Ltd v Belvedere Fish Guano Co Ltd* [1921] 2 A.C. 465 (newly formed company in possession of land as agent of the vendor); *Chief Executive of the New Zealand Customs Service v Nike New Zealand Ltd* [2004] 1 N.Z.L.R. 238 (parent company held buying agent of subsidiary); *Chandler v Cape Plc* [2011] EWHC 951 (QB) at [75]; affd [2012] EWCA Civ 525; [2012] 1 W.L.R. 3111 (parent company undertaking responsibility for health and safety issues for subsidiaries in the group). cf. *Thompson v Renwick Group Plc* [2014] EWCA Civ 635; noted Day [2014] L.M.C.L.Q. 454; *His Royal Highness Okpabi v Royal Dutch Shell Plc* [2017] EWHC 89 (TCC); [2017] B.L.R. 136.
[176] See *Prest v Petrodel Resources Ltd* [2013] UKSC 34; [2013] 2 A.C. 415 at [32]–[33], explaining *Trustor AB v Smallbone (No.2)* [2001] 1 W.L.R. 1177; *Park's of Hamilton's (Holdings) Ltd v Campbell* [2014] CSIH 36; 2014 S.C. 726 (directors as negotiating agent for shareholders in takeover); *Wise v Jimenez* [2014] 1 P. & C.R. DG9 (company mere conduit for money provided by shareholder).

otherwise act on behalf of a subsidiary, or vice versa.[177] Otherwise, it is recognised that:

"In commercial terms the creation of a corporate structure is by definition designed to create separate legal entities for entirely legitimate purposes which would often if not usually be defeated by any general agency relationship between them."[178]

The question of when the corporate veil may be pierced is a matter for company law.[179]

3. Agency distinguished from other relationships

The nature of agency is sometimes further elucidated by comparing it with other legal relationships. It is common, for instance, for someone to contract, or otherwise act, as principal, and not as an agent, even though he manifests an intention that another will benefit from the contract or other action. This is true even where, under modern law, that other party may sue on the contract pursuant to the Contracts (Rights of Third Parties) Act 1999.[180]   **1-031**

Agent and trustee[181]   Agents and trustees have many similarities, for both are   **1-032**
persons who act on behalf of others and, though agency is essentially a common law notion, much of the law of agency is derived from, or is connected with, the law of trusts, which is of course equitable.[182] But the two roles, though they have considerable overlap, are conceptually different. An agent acts for another; a trustee holds property for another as principal, not as agent, but subject to equitable obligations.[183]

Thus a *trustee* holds money or property for another, to which he has the legal title, but which belongs in equity to the beneficiary and to whom, accordingly, the trustee owes a number of obligations. The property may well be vested in the trustee by a

---

[177] See, e.g. *Enron (Thrace) Exploration and Production BV v Clapp* [2005] EWHC 401 (Comm) at [92]; *Cromwell Corp Ltd v Sofrana Immobilier (NZ) Ltd* (1992) N.Z.C.L.C. 67, 997; *HKSAR v Luk Kin* [2016] HKCFA 81 at [33]. A director who ceases to be an executive director of the parent company and moves to become an executive director of a subsidiary normally ceases to have actual authority to bind the parent, though apparent authority may linger: see *Benourad v Compass Group Plc* [2010] EWHC 1882 (QB) at [113]. See too *Hudson Bay Apparel Brands LLC v Umbro International Ltd* [2010] EWCA Civ 949; [2011] 1 B.C.L.C. 259 (managing director of subsidiary with authority to administer US licences had no authority on behalf of parent company to vary those licences).

[178] *Peterson Farms Inc v C&M Farming Ltd* [2004] EWHC 21 (Comm); [2004] 1 Lloyd's Rep. 603 at [62], per Langley J (arbitrators had awarded damages for "parent losses"). See also *The Coral Rose* [1991] 1 Lloyd's Rep. 563 (borrower not agent); *Yukong Lines v Rendsburg Investment Corp (The Rialto) (No.2)* [1998] 1 Lloyd's Rep. 322 ("owners" of company not undisclosed principals of company as named charterer); *IBM United Kingdom Holdings Ltd v Dalgleish* [2017] EWCA Civ 1212 at [372] (motives of senior employee of parent company not attributed to subsidiary). See also Harris (2005) 23 Coy & Securities, L.J. 7.

[179] As to which see *Gower's Principles of Modern Company Law* (10th edn), p.197 onwards; and *Prest v Petrodel Resources Ltd* [2013] UKSC 34; [2013] 2 A.C. 415. Fiduciary duties, or duties in negligence, can sometimes be owed to the company or person "behind" a company: see *Johnson v Gore Wood & Co* [2002] 2 A.C. 1; *Ratiu v Conway* [2005] EWCA Civ 1302; cf. *Diamantis v JP Morgan Chase Bank* [2005] EWCA Civ 1612.

[180] *Fortis Bank SA NV v Stemcor UK Ltd* [2011] EWHC 538; [2012] 1 All E.R. (Comm) 41 at [65].

[181] Street (1892) 8 L.Q.R. 220; *Restatement, Third*, § 8 and comment; *Restatement, Third, Trusts*, § 6 and comment; *Scott on Trusts* (5th edn), § 2.3.4.

[182] See Dowrick (1954) 17 M.L.R. 24 at 28–32.

[183] See, e.g. *Hunt v Hosking* [2013] EWCA Civ 1408 at [37].

person who is not the beneficiary. As such, a trustee may have no agency functions at all. Furthermore, a trustee's duty is to carry out the terms of the trust; he is not (unless there is express provision to that effect) subject to control by the beneficiary, nor to revocation by him of the trust. Lastly, the position of express trustee is a well-recognised and specialised one to which various forms of statutory regulation apply.[184]

An *agent*, on the other hand, may often hold no money or property for his principal at all; if he does receive money from or for his principal, he may merely be in the position of debtor to his principal in respect of it,[185] and if he receives goods he may hold them as bailee only.[186] As such, therefore, an agent may have no trustee functions or liabilities at all. He may well be subject to some degree of control by his principal, and his authority can normally be revoked.[187] His function is far too varied in the many spheres in which it may operate to be the subject of general statutory regulation, though statutes may affect particular types of agent or agency situation.[188]

But of course a trustee *may* also in appropriate circumstances have agency powers. This may particularly be so when there are two or more trustees, and the issue arises whether one trustee becomes an agent for the others. Although the starting assumption of equity is that trustees are expected to act unanimously, in relation to any legal property (or rights recognised at law) that the trustees may hold together, each trustee would have the powers at law of any other co-owner, and co-owners may generally confer agency powers on others, including their colleagues.[189] This is so even if the delegation were to involve a breach of trust. Equally, where the express or implied terms of the trust permit delegation of one or more tasks involving alteration of the trustees' legal relations, then the delegate, even if one of the trustees, would be an agent. By the same token, an agent *may* hold money or property as trustee, whether express or constructive[190]: the principal may well seek to secure this in order to achieve protection should the agent become insolvent.[191] Sometimes agents hold as bare trustees: in such cases the agency function predominates.[192] And an agent is subject to fiduciary duties which usually lead also to money which he receives improperly being regarded as money of the principal held upon constructive trust, and hence subject to a proprietary claim.[193]

Thus the two functions, though conceptually distinct, may be difficult to differentiate: one person may have both capacities in relation to another.[194]

---

[184] Trustee Act 1925; Trustee Delegation Act 1999; Trustee Act 2000.
[185] e.g. *Neste Oy v Lloyd's Bank Plc* [1983] 2 Lloyd's Rep. 658, below, para.6-041.
[186] e.g. a factor: below, para.1-046.
[187] See Article 120.
[188] e.g. Powers of Attorney Act 1971; Estate Agents Act 1979 (as amended by Enterprise Act 2002); Commercial Agents (Council Directive) Regulations 1993.
[189] See further below, para.2-022. See, Watts, in Davies and Penner (eds), *Equity, Trusts and Commerce* (2017), Ch.2. Note that co-owners are not automatically agents of one another: see *Kennedy v De Trafford* [1897] A.C. 180 at 188.
[190] Or he may hold under a *Quistclose* trust: see Lewin, *Trusts* (19th edn), para.8-040 onwards.
[191] See Comment to Article 43; Articles 49 and 51.
[192] e.g. *Trident Holdings Ltd v Danand Investments Ltd* (1988) 49 D.L.R. (4th) 1, where it was held that a bare trustee subject to the control of beneficiaries was their agent and could bind them by contract. But see *Ingram v IRC* [2000] 1 A.C. 293 at 305.
[193] Articles 43–53.
[194] See also *Pople v Evans* [1969] 2 Ch. 255, where it was held that an agent who sued on behalf of an undisclosed principal was not a trustee for the purposes of estoppel *per rem judicatam*. The

Agent and bailee[195]   Like a trustee, a bailee holds for another, but he only holds   **1-033**
as possessor, and ownership remains in the bailor. The notion of bailment is
moreover restricted to chattels, and does not of itself involve control by the bailor.
An agent may hold no property for his principal at all; or he may hold property as
trustee. Equally, a bailee as such may have no agency powers.[196] However, an agent
may hold his principal's chattels as bailee: this was the practice, for example, of the
nineteenth-century factor.[197] And a bailee *may* sometimes be regarded as having
agency powers to do such things as are reasonably incidental to his use of the goods
which he holds, e.g. have them repaired, in which connection an artificer's lien created by him may be valid against his principal.[198] The authority may, in accordance with normal principles, be actual, express or implied,[199] or apparent[200]: in the
latter case limitations on authority may be ineffective against a third party who did
not know of them.[201] Again, the categories are not mutually exclusive: one person
may have both capacities in relation to another, and indeed that of trustee also. Thus
a commercial intermediary may be a bailee of goods, an agent to sell them and a
trustee of the proceeds of sale.

Agent and servant; agent and independent contractor   The dichotomy of serv-   **1-034**
ant (or employee) and independent contractor stems from the law of tort: a person
is more readily liable for the torts of his servants than for those of his independent
contractors. The difference turns on the degree of control exercised. A servant has
been defined as a:

"person employed by another to do work for him on terms that he, the servant, is to be
under the control and directions of his employer in respect of the manner in which his
work is to be done."[202]

An independent contractor has been defined as:

"one who undertakes to produce a given result, but so that in the actual execution of the

---

beneficiary of a bare trust is not an agent of the trustee: *Stait v Femner* [1912] 2 Ch. 504 at 511. See
British Energy Power & Trading Ltd v Credit Suisse [2008] EWCA Civ 53; [2008] 2 All E.R.
(Comm) 524; [2008] 1 Lloyd's Rep. 413 ("as agent and security trustee" in context of syndicated
loan agreement).
[195] Fridman (1964) 114 L.J. 265.
[196] See *Buxton v Baughan* (1834) 6 C. & P. 674; *Cassils & Co. v Holden Wood Bleaching Co* (1914)
112 L.T. 373; *Pennington v Reliance Motor Works Ltd* [1923] 1 K.B. 127; cf. *Smith v General Motor Cab Co Ltd* [1911] A.C. 188. See also *Bart v British West Indian Airways Ltd* [1967] 1 Lloyd's
Rep. 239 (person collecting and forwarding football pool coupons not agent of investors to make
contract with carrier).
[197] See below, para.1-046. Another example is an auctioneer.
[198] *Tappenden v Artus* [1964] 2 Q.B. 185. See also *Coldman v Hill* [1919] 1 K.B. 443 at 456. cf. *Gallimore v Moore* (1867) 6 S.C.R. (N.S.W.) 388.
[199] *Singer Mfg. Co v L. & S.W. Ry Co* [1894] 1 Q.B. 833; *Keene v Thomas* [1905] 1 K.B. 136; *Greene
v All Motors Ltd* [1917] 1 K.B. 625. See Articles 24 onwards.
[200] *Albemarle Supply Co Ltd v Hind & Co* [1928] 1 K.B. 307; *Bowmaker Ltd v Wycombe Motors Ltd*
[1946] 1 K.B. 505 at 509.
[201] See cases cited above, fn.198; Articles 72 and 83.
[202] Salmond and Heuston, *Torts* (21st edn), p.434; wording approved in *Hewitt v Bonvin* [1940] 1 K.B.
188 at 191. See also *Ready Mixed Concrete (South East) Ltd v Minister of Pensions and National
Insurance* [1968] 2 Q.B. 497. The substance overrides the form: a person who purports to be, or to
be employed as, "labour only subcontractor" may be a servant or employee: see *Ferguson v John
Dawson & Partners (Construction) Ltd* [1976] 1 W.L.R. 1213; *O'Kelly v Trusthouse Forte Plc*
[1984] Q.B. 90. See also *Australian Mutual Provident Society v Chaplin* (1978) 18 A.L.R. 385. As
to vicarious liability, see Article 90.

work he is not under the orders or control of the person for whom he does it, and may use his discretion in things not specified beforehand."[203]

Much space has been devoted in books to considering the relationship between these figures and the agent.[204] It is submitted that the controversy is somewhat sterile. Some employees have agency powers, and these may be (as in the case of a manager) very wide; in other cases (e.g. a domestic employee) they may be very limited. Others have no agency powers. Many agents (e.g. brokers) could be called independent contractors; other independent contractors (e.g. repairers) are unlikely to have agency powers. An independent contractor who has authority to alter another's legal relations is likely to be an agent, and one who does not is unlikely to be treated as an agent.[205] Persons may exercise agency powers who fall into neither category: an obvious example is a gratuitous agent. Though there are interactions, both historical and practical, it is unlikely that the terminology can be reduced to a satisfactory scheme.

1-035   **Distributors, concessionnaires and franchisees**[206]   A supplier of the goods of a manufacturer, whether on a retail or wholesale basis, who has some form of concession as a regular stockist, distributor or franchisee is often described as "agent", "selling agent", "main agent" and the like, for the manufacturer of the goods which he supplies. Although it is possible that he is an agent in the common law sense,[207] it is nowadays much more likely that he actually buys from the manufacturer and resells to his own customer. In one case his typical position was made very clear by a clause reading:

> "The term 'agent' is used in a complimentary sense only, and those firms whom we style our agents are not authorised to advertise, incur any debts, or transact any business whatever on our account, other than the sale of goods which they may purchase from us; nor are they authorised to give any warranty or make any representation on our behalf other than those contained in the above guarantee."[208]

---

[203] Pollock, *Torts* (15th edn), p.63. See also *Honeywill & Stein Ltd v Larkin Bros Ltd* [1934] 1 K.B. 191 at 196.

[204] Powell, pp.7–24; Fridman, para.1.28–1.30; Stoljar, pp.3–5; *Restatement, Third*, Reporter's Notes to § 1.01. See also *Lower Hutt City v Att.-Gen.* [1965] N.Z.L.R. 65. An agent can still be an employee though he is rewarded principally by commissions: *Hanna v Imperial Life Assurance Co of Canada* [2007] UKPC 29 (insurance agent required to work full-time for principal, eligible for company's pension plan, all equipment provided by principal, seconded to a management role for a period). Similarly, the fact that a contractor is described as such and is paid by an employment agency does not preclude his being an employee of the party for whom he performs services: *Cable & Wireless Plc v Muscat* [2006] EWCA Civ 220; [2006] I.C.R. 975.

[205] See *Alliance Craton Explorer Pty Ltd v Quasar Resources Pty Ltd* [2013] FCAFC 29 at [72]–[74].

[206] The topic of franchising is a specialised one. See, e.g. Pratt, *Franchising: Law and Practice* (looseleaf); Mendelsohn, *Guide to Franchising* (7th edn); Mendelsohn, *Franchising Law* (2nd edn); Adams, Hickey and Prichard-Jones, *Franchising* (5th edn). For a case where a franchising company was held to have ordered goods as agent for its franchisee, see *Toycorp Ltd v Milton Bradley Australia Pty Ltd* [1992] 2 V.R. 572.

[207] This seems to have been a practice more favoured some time ago. See *Williamson v Rover Cycle Co Ltd* [1901] 2 I.R. 189 at 615; *Sproule v Triumph Cycle Co Ltd* [1927] N.I. 83.

[208] *Sproule v Triumph Cycle*, above (where the distributor was nevertheless held an agent). Such clauses are not uncommon. In *Vogel v R. & A. Kohnstamm Ltd* [1973] Q.B. 133 at 136 such a concern was said (in the context of enforcement of a foreign judgment) to be "in no legal sense of the word an agent at all". See also *The Kronprinzessin Cecilie* (1917) 33 T.L.R. 292; *W.T. Lamb & Son v Goring Brick Co Ltd* [1932] 1 K.B. 710; *B. Davis Ltd v Tooth & Co Ltd* [1937] 4 All E.R. 118; *Martin-Baker Aircraft Co Ltd v Canadian Flight Equipment Ltd* [1955] 2 Q.B. 556 ("selling agents").

Such a person or concern may have limited agency functions such as those of guarantee referred to, or as to transmission of complaints and rectification of faults. But in general the relationship is an adverse commercial relationship quite different from agency and is therefore not treated in this book except for the purpose of distinguishing it from agency. In continental European countries and elsewhere, the protection given to commercial agents[209] may sometimes be extended to distributors and the like. The EC Directive on this subject is, however, confined to commercial agents, and in the United Kingdom there has therefore been no reason to extend it further. The analogy of agency is not normally followed where a purchase for resale is identified: the contract is one of sale. Any additional relationship between the parties to a distributorship agreement turns on the terms of the particular contract and such contracts therefore require careful drafting.

There is however overlap between such distributors and true agents in that the contracts under which both act may be affected by mandatory general rules such as those of EC competition law[210] and those relating to restraint of trade.[211] Indeed, the restrictions contractually imposed on distributors, such as requirements not to compete, sometimes place them under the manufacturer's control in a way that makes the analogy of agency not inappropriate. Thus in an important case the High Court of Australia were split by three to two on the question whether a particular distributorship contract gave rise to fiduciary duties.[212] Such distributors may also hold goods as bailees only, and in general their contracts may contain reservation of title clauses, so-called "*Romalpa*" clauses,[213] which in authorising the distributor to resell goods on which the seller has reserved title may use expressly or by implication the terminology of agency. The question whether a power of resale is exercised as agent would affect the liability and rights on that sale of the original seller and/or his right to the proceeds of sale.[214] Comparable principles for determining whether a trader operates independently or as an agent apply to franchisees of services as to franchisees of goods.[215]

It is always a question of fact whether someone is a franchisee or an agent. The mere use of the language of "licensee" will not preclude there being an agency, if in fact the licensee is intended to find customers who will have direct links with the "licensor".[216]

---

[209] See Ch.11.

[210] See, e.g. Bellamy and Child, *The Common Market Law of Competition* (6th edn), especially Ch.7; Whish, *Competition Law* (7th edn), pp.621–623.

[211] See, e.g. Chitty, *Contracts* (32nd edn), Vol. 1, para.16-085 onwards.

[212] *Hospital Products Ltd v US Surgical Corp* (1984) 156 C.L.R. 41. See also *Cadbury Schweppes Inc v FBI Foods Ltd* [1999] 1 S.C.R. 142; (1999) 167 D.L.R. (4th) 577 (product licensing agreement).

[213] See *Aluminium Industrie Vaassen BV v Romalpa Aluminium Ltd* [1976] 1 W.L.R. 676; *Re Bond Worth Ltd* [1980] Ch. 228; *Borden (UK) Ltd v Scottish Timber Products Ltd* [1981] Ch. 25; *Re Peachdart Ltd* [1984] Ch. 131; *Clough Mill Ltd v Martin* [1985] 1 W.L.R. 111; *Fairfax Gerrard Holdings Ltd v Capital Bank Plc* [2007] EWCA Civ 1226; [2008] 1 Lloyd's Rep. 297 (party had actual authority to pass title to goods, which was effective even though acquirer could not establish apparent authority or one of the exceptions to the *nemo dat* principle); *FG Wilson (Engineering) Ltd v John Holt & Co (Liverpool) Ltd* [2013] EWCA Civ 1232; [2014] 1 W.L.R. 2365, discussed Gullifer [2014] L.M.C.L.Q. 564; *Unitherm Heating Systems Ltd v Wallace* [2015] IECA 191. See below, para.8-165; and Chitty, *Contracts* (32nd edn), Vol.2, para.44-171 onwards.

[214] Reynolds (1978) 94 L.Q.R. 224 at 235–238; Watts (1986) 6 O.J.L.S. 456.

[215] *ACN 007528207 Pty Ltd v Bird Cameron* (2005) 54 A.C.S.R. 505 (see above, fn.34).

[216] *Heperu Pty Ltd v Morgan Brooks Pty Ltd (No.2)* [2007] NSWSC 1438; reversed on other points [2009] NSWCA 84 (mortgage broker operated offices using independent agents, called licensees; the licensees were held to be agents).

1-036 **Agent and seller; agent and buyer** The above discussion raises the distinction between agency and sale. These relationships, unlike the others dealt with above, are mutually exclusive: in respect of a particular transaction a person cannot be acting as agent if (without appropriate disclosure[217]) he is a buyer or seller to his principal and vice versa.[218] Sale is a commercially adverse relationship; agency involves a fiduciary relationship of trust and confidence. The solution to commercial disputes may frequently turn on whether the parties are to be regarded as parties to one or the other relationship. Thus a manufacturer may contract not to market his goods through anyone but a particular supplier, who is said to be "sole" or "exclusive agent". If the supplier is on the true construction of the agreement a buyer from the manufacturer, the manufacturer may be in breach of contract if he sells the goods himself[219]; but if the supplier is a true agent the manufacturer will usually be entitled to sell personally as well.[220] If the supplier buys from the manufacturer and resells, it is he who answers to the ultimate buyer for the quality of the goods, and the manufacturer is liable, in the absence of other indications, in tort or by statute only.[221] If the supplier is the manufacturer's agent, his liability to the ultimate buyer may turn on whether or not he is what is above described as a commission agent.[222] If he is, he may likewise answer as seller for quality, but will have the agent's rights of reimbursement and indemnity against his principal.[223] If he is not, it is the manufacturer who is the seller and he, and not (normally[224]) the agent, must answer for quality of the goods.[225] If the supplier buys from the manufacturer and resells, money paid or due to him from the ultimate buyer may be part of his assets in bankruptcy: if he is an agent, it may not.[226] Similar issues

---

[217] See Articles 43–48.
[218] The question has arisen in the specialised context of value added tax. See *Customs and Excise Commissioners v Johnson* [1980] S.T.C. 624 (provision of educational courses); *Potter v Customs and Excise Commissioners* [1985] S.T.C. 45 ("Tupperware" sold at specially convened functions); *Hill v Customs and Excise Commissioners* [1989] S.T.C. 424 (craft pottery); *Customs and Excise Commissioners v Paget* [1989] S.T.C. 773 (school photographs sold to parents); *Cornhill Management Ltd v Commissioners of Customs and Excise* [1991] 1 VA.T.T.R. 1 (fund managers); *Customs and Excise Commissioners v Music and Video Exchange Ltd* [1992] S.T.C. 220 (profit on resale as commission); *Umbro International Ltd v Revenue and Customs Commissioners* [2009] EWHC 438 (Ch); [2009] S.T.C. 1345. See also *AMB Imballaggi v Pacflex Ltd* [1999] 2 All E.R. (Comm) 249; *Mercantile International Group Plc v Chuan Soon Huai Industrial Group Plc* [2002] EWCA Civ 288; [2002] 1 All E.R. (Comm) 788 (Commercial Agents Regulations); *R. (Jet Services Ltd) v Civil Aviation Authority* [2001] EWCA Civ 610; [2001] 2 All E.R. (Comm) 769.
[219] *W.T. Lamb & Sons v Goring Brick Co* [1932] 1 K.B. 710. It may, however, be that today the question might turn on whether the word "exclusive" had been used rather than "sole". See below, para.7-036.
[220] See *Bentall, Horsley & Baldry v Vicary* [1931] 1 K.B. 253 (an estate agent case); Article 58.
[221] *Sproule v Triumph Motor Cycle Co* [1927] N.I. 83; *International Harvester Co of Australia Pty Ltd v Carrigan's Hazeldene Pastoral Co* (1958) 100 C.L.R. 644; and see *Wheeler & Wilson Mfg. Co v Shakespear* (1869) 39 L.J.Ch. 36; *Pearlson Enterprises Ltd v Hong Leong Co Ltd* [1968] 1 Malaya L.J. 24 (where agent buys for resale, price increase imposed by manufacturer subsequent to resale contract may not be passed on). The statutory liability could be under the Consumer Protection Act 1987.
[222] See above, para.1-021.
[223] See, e.g. *Liu Wing Ngai v Lui Kok Wai* [1996] 3 Singapore L.R. 508.
[224] But see Article 98: the agent may sometimes be liable in addition.
[225] e.g. *Parkar's Music & Sports House v Motorex Ltd* [1959] E. Africa L.Rep. 534.
[226] *Ex p. White, re Neville* (1871) L.R. 6 Ch.App. 397, affd sub. nom. *John Towle & Co v White* (1873) 29 L.T. 78 (a case on *del credere* agency: below, para.1-042).

arise in determining whether a party has assigned a debt or has simply given a mandate to collect payment of the debt as the party's agent.[227]

The distinction between agent and buyer for resale normally turns on whether the person concerned acts for himself to make such profit as he can, or is remunerated by pre-arranged commission.[228] A supplier who himself fixes the resale price is likely to be a buyer for resale[229]: but the fact that the resale price is fixed by the manufacturer does not necessarily make the supplier an agent,[230] for resale prices are frequently fixed by manufacturers. Exceptionally a buyer for resale may also be paid commission,[231] or an agent remunerated by being allowed to keep the excess over and above a stipulated price.[232] But the making of such a profit by an agent would normally be improper.[233]

Conversely, there may be difficulty in deciding whether a person who has agreed to procure goods for another is acting as that other's agent or selling to him. Again, the first question is to ask whether he takes a profit on the resale which will make him a seller, or a commission, in which case he is likely to be an agent and indeed the making of any further profit would usually be improper. But here another criterion also is relevant. If he is selling, he normally undertakes absolutely to supply the goods on the terms agreed: but an agent prima facie only binds himself to use his best endeavours to make a contract or procure the goods, depending on whether he is a genuine agent or what is above described as a commission agent.[234] Thus a seller answers for defects in description and quality: an agent may not do so at all, because he is not a party to the contract,[235] or if he is a commission agent may only answer for failure to carry out his instructions as closely as is practicable.[236]

There may also in either situation be repercussions as regards the damages obtainable: the measure of damages appropriate to a breach of a contract of sale may not be applicable to breach of the agent's duty.[237] Questions of the passing of property also may depend on how the case is analysed.[238]

Each transaction must be examined on its facts, considering the extent to which an agent's duties are appropriate. Much turns on the extent to which the principal can call for an account, for the duty to account is a typical feature of the agent's

---

[227] See *Burridge v MPH Soccer Management Ltd* [2011] EWCA Civ 835.
[228] See *Weiner v Harris* [1910] 1 K.B. 285; *Restatement*, § 14 J (listing relevant factors); *Bosanquet v Mofflin* (1906) 6 S.R. (N.S.W.) 617; *AMB Imballaggi v Pacflex Ltd* [1999] 2 All E.R. (Comm) 249; *Jackson v Royal Bank of Scotland* [2000] C.L.C. 1457; *Hannaford v Australian Farmlink Pty Ltd* [2008] FCA 1591; cf. above, para.1-016.
[229] *Ex p. White, re Neville*, above; *Jones v Southwark LBC* [2016] EWHC 457 (Ch) at [52].
[230] *Michelin Tyre Co Ltd v McFarlane (Glasgow) Ltd* (1917) 55 Sc.L.Rep. 35 (a House of Lords case containing a full review of the authorities, and again on *del credere* agency: below, para.1-042).
[231] *Kelly v Enderton* [1913] A.C. 191; *Gannow Engineering Co Ltd v Richardson* [1930] N.Z.L.R. 361. cf. *Kitson v P.S. King & Son Ltd* (1919) 36 T.L.R. 162 (publishing).
[232] *Ex p. Bright, re Smith* (1879) 10 Ch.D. 566 at 570; *Western Digital Corp v British Airways Plc* [2000] 2 Lloyd's Rep. 142 at 148; *Mercantile International Group Plc v Chuan Soon Huat Industrial Group Plc* [2002] EWCA Civ 288; [2002] 1 All E.R. (Comm) 788.
[233] Articles 45–48.
[234] See *Anglo-African Shipping Co of New York Inc v J. Mortner Ltd* [1962] 1 Lloyd's Rep. 610; above, para.1-021.
[235] See *Ireland v Livingston* (1872) L.R. 5 H.L. 395; *Brown & Gracie v F.W. Greene & Co Pty Ltd* [1960] 1 Lloyd's Rep. 289.
[236] See *Johnston v Kershaw* (1867) L.R. 2 Ex. 82; *Butlers (London) Ltd v Roope* [1922] N.Z.L.R. 549; *Downie Bros v Henry Oakley & Sons* [1923] N.Z.L.R. 734.
[237] *Cassaboglou v Gibb* (1883) 1 Q.B.D. 797, Illustration 4 to Article 69.
[238] See Article 69.

position.[239] The ways in which the parties describe themselves are not conclusive. "There is no magic in the word 'agency.' It is often used in commercial matters where the real relationship is that of vendor and purchaser."[240] There may indeed be reasons for principal and agent adopting the relationship of vendor and purchaser, for example, to avoid tax, exchange control rules or trade embargoes. It is also the case that the trading functions of intermediaries may imperceptibly alter over a period.[241]

1-037   **Agent and borrower**   A person may act as agent and as such use money stemming from his principal: this money he may hold on trust for the principal, or receive it as his own subject to a duty to return or account for it.[242] Alternatively, he may borrow from another on a commercial basis and hence receive money not as agent at all, even though he may appear to be conducting business for that other. This distinction may be important in the case of subsidiary companies.[243] Sometimes however there may be provisions in contracts which protect creditors' interests. They will not usually make the debtor the creditor's agent.[244] Questions can also arise as to whether a person providing finance for another has a charge over that other's property or whether he buys it from that other, who then resells as his agent.[245]

1-038   **Agent and person supplying services**   An agent obviously supplies services. Most persons supplying services, however, do so on a commercially adverse basis: that is to say, as in the case of sellers, they supply their services for the best price that they can obtain. This is true of, for example, a repairer or a portrait painter. The mere fact, therefore, that one person undertakes work at the other's request and for his benefit is insufficient to establish agency.[246] Such a person normally owes a duty of best endeavours only, but he is not usually remunerated on commission and owes no fiduciary duties. An agent offers services of a personal and confidential type: as such he is subject to fiduciary duties also. There is, however, an intermediate category. Some persons offering personal services, such as solicitors, charge fees rather than commission (though their fees may in some way be controlled); but in so far as they give advice and may have agency powers they are under fiduciary duties not as regards profits made from the exercise of their profession, but in respect of information held and profits made from their special positions vis-à-vis their

---

[239] *Michelin Tyre Co Ltd v McFarlane (Glasgow) Ltd* (1917) 55 Sc.L.Rep. 35; Article 52.

[240] *Ex p. White, re Neville* (1871) L.R. 6 Ch.App. 397 at 399. cf. *Weiner v Harris* [1910] 1 K.B. 285, where a person buying on sale or return was held an agent. See also *Livingstone v Ross* [1901] A.C. 327; *Garnac Grain Co Inc v H.M.F. Faure & Fairclough Ltd* [1968] A.C. 1130n.

[241] See Hill, "The Broker and the Commodity Markets" in *New Directions in International Trade Law* (UNIDROIT, 1977), Vol.2, p.523 onwards.

[242] See below, para.6-041.

[243] For an example of the second situation, see *Atlas Maritime Corp v Avalon Maritime Ltd (The Coral Rose) (No.1)* [1991] 4 All E.R. 796. Related problems occur in connection with receivers appointed by debenture holders: e.g. *Gosling v Gaskell* [1897] A.C. 575; see Goode, *Principles of Corporate Insolvency Law* (4th edn), paras 10-01 and 10-41 onwards.

[244] But see *A. Gay Jenson Farms Co v Cargill Inc* 309 N.W. 2d 285 (Minn. 1981); see further Hynes (1991) 58 Tenn.L.Rev. 635.

[245] See *Welsh Development Agency v Export Finance Co Ltd* [1992] B.C.L.C. 148.

[246] See *Colonial Mutual Life Assurance Society Ltd v Producers and Citizens Co-operative Assurance Co of Australia Ltd* (1931) 46 C.L.R. 41 at 48–49; *Alliance Craton Explorer Pty Ltd v Quasar Resources Pty Ltd* [2013] FCAFC 29 at [72]; *Janus Capital Management LLC v Safeguard World International Ltd* [2016] EWHC 1355 (Ch) at [245].

clients.[247] This is true also of others, who if their work is directed towards a fixed target which may be valued may actually be remunerated by commission also, such as patent agents,[248] travel agents,[249] or even persons assisting in the preparation of a contractual offer or bid.[250] All these, other than those who render commercial services on a purely commercial basis, may attract some, but not all, of the features of agency law.

Article 2

FURTHER DEFINITIONS

(1) A disclosed principal, for the purposes of this book, is a principal, whether identified or unidentified, whose interest in the transaction as principal is known to the third party at the time of the transaction in question.[251]   **1-039**

(2) An identified principal, for the purposes of this book, is a disclosed principal whose name is known to the third party at that time.[252]

(3) An unidentified principal, for the purposes of this book, is a disclosed principal whose name is not known, but who could if necessary be identified, at that time.[253]

(4) An undisclosed principal, for the purposes of this book, is a principal whose existence as such is not known to the third party at the time of the transaction in question.[254]

(5) A *del credere* agent is an agent who, in consideration of extra remuneration, which may be called a *del credere* commission, guarantees to his principal that third parties with whom he enters into contracts on behalf of the principal will duly pay any sums becoming due under those contracts.[255]

(6) A commercial agent is a self-employed intermediary who has continuing authority to negotiate the sale or purchase of goods on behalf of another person (the "principal"), or to negotiate and conclude the sale or purchase of goods on behalf of and in the name of that principal.[256]

(7) A general agent is an agent who has authority to act for his principal in all matters concerning a particular trade or business, or of a particular nature; or

---

[247] Articles 44–48.

[248] See *Re Frazer's Patent* [1981] R.P.C. 53, where a solicitor failed to pay the renewal fee for a patent, with the result that it lapsed. The solicitor may have been negligent, but it was held that the proprietor of the patent was not: the solicitor was merely the system set up by him for renewal, which was reasonable even though it had failed on the particular occasion.

[249] Nelson-Jones and Stewart, *A Practical Guide to Package Holiday Law and Contracts* (3rd edn) However, some travel agents and tour operators may in effect supply services as principal and not merely as an agent: see *Wong Mee Wan v Kwan Kin Travel Services Ltd* [1996] 1 W.L.R. 38; *Moore v Hotelplan Ltd (t/a Inghams Travel)* [2010] EWHC 276 (QB). Package Travel, Package Holidays and Package Tours Regulations 1992 (SI 1992/3288, as amended); *Hone v Going Places Leisure Travel Ltd* [2001] EWCA Civ 947; *Titshall v Qwerty Travel Ltd* [2011] EWCA Civ 1569 at [16].

[250] For an example of a claim on such a contract, see *Sharab v HRH Prince Al-Waleed bin Talal* [2008] EWHC 1893 (Ch); affd [2009] EWCA Civ 353.

[251] See Comment.

[252] See Comment.

[253] See Comment.

[254] See Comment.

[255] *Morris v Cleasby* (1816) 4 M. & S. 566; *Hornby v Lacy* (1817) 6 M. & S. 166: see Comment.

[256] Commercial Agents (Council Directive) Regulations 1993 reg.2(1): see Comment and Ch.11.

to do some act in the ordinary course of his trade, profession or business as an agent, on behalf of his principal.[257]

(8) A special agent is an agent who has only authority to do some particular act, or to represent his principal in some particular transaction, such act or transaction not being in the ordinary course of his trade, profession or business as an agent.[258]

(9) A factor is an agent whose ordinary course of business is to sell or dispose of goods, of which he is entrusted with the possession or control by his principal.[259]

(10) A broker is an agent whose ordinary course of business is to negotiate and make contracts for the sale and purchase of goods and other property, of which he is not entrusted with the possession or control.[260]

(11) A nuntius, or messenger, is a person who undertakes a specific task for the principal under close direction of the principal and sometimes in the principal's presence. Other labels are also sometimes applied, such as amanuensis, or conduit, depending on the task involved.

Comment

1-040   Many of the terms here defined are terms of art and are found in legal sources. Some are of limited contemporary significance, but their appearance in some of the leading cases warrants brief explanation here.

1-041   **Disclosed principal (identified or unidentified); undisclosed principal**   It should be noted that the usage in this book does not entirely accord with that found in the cases. As stated, a principal is referred to in this book as disclosed in all situations where the third party knows that there is a principal involved, and it does not matter whether the principal is named to, or even identifiable by, the third party so long as the third party realises that there is a principal involved and does not at the time of the transaction in question think that he is dealing with the agent alone. The term "disclosed principal" therefore includes both identified and unidentified[261] principals.[262] The term "undisclosed principal" is reserved for cases where the third party does not intend to deal with a principal at all and intends to deal with the agent personally: these cases are regulated by special rules, and raise different equities. There are however difficult marginal cases where the existence of a principal was suspected or even known, but because the third party intended to deal with the agent, the undisclosed principal rules have been applied; and there are also cases which clearly involve unnamed but disclosed principals, where the term "undisclosed" has been used.[263] The matter is discussed under the heading of

---

[257] See Comment; Articles 29 and 30.

[258] See Comment.

[259] *Baring v Corrie* (1818) 2 B. & A. 137 at 143; *Stevens v Biller* (1883) 25 Ch.D. 31 at 37; *Rolls Razor Ltd v Cox* [1967] 1 Q.B. 552 at 568. See Comment.

[260] (1818) 2 B. & A. 137 at 143, above; *Fowler v Hollins* (1872) L.R. 7 Q.B. 616. See Comment.

[261] i.e. principals whose identity is known to the third party at the time of the transaction, and principals whose identities are not known, though it is known that there is a principal involved.

[262] See *Restatement, Third*, § 1.04. In earlier editions of this book the words "named" and "unnamed" were used, but these have been altered to conform with the *Restatement*. The change reflects the fact that an unnamed principal may nevertheless be identified.

[263] See, e.g. *Benton v Campbell, Parker & Co* [1925] 2 K.B. 410 at 414; *Thornton v Fehr & Co* (1935)

undisclosed principal,[264] where it will be seen that it is in fact not clear in exactly what circumstances a person may rank as an "undisclosed principal".

Del credere agent[265] A *del credere* agent is an agent who for a special commission undertakes in effect the liability of a surety to his principal for the due performance, by the persons with whom he deals, of contracts made by him with them on his principal's behalf.[266] His obligation is confined to answering for the failure of the other contracting parties, owing to insolvency or the like, to pay any ascertained sums which may become due from them as debts (largely in respect of the price of goods bought).[267] The principal is therefore not entitled to litigate with a *del credere* agent any disputes arising out of contracts made by him, nor is such an agent responsible to the third party for the due performance of the principal's contract.[268] In this respect the *del credere* agent is the antithesis of the commission agent, whose function is effectively the reverse.[269] A *del credere* agency may in principal be inferred from the course of conduct between the parties,[270] though such inference would nowadays be rare.[271] An agreement by an agent to act on a *del credere* commission is not a promise to answer for the debt, default or miscarriage of another person within the meaning of s.4 of the Statute of Frauds but a contract of indemnity, and it is therefore not necessary that such an agreement should be evidenced in writing.[272]

1-042

A *del credere* agency would often in modern conditions involve liabilities which an ordinary commercial agent acting for commission would be reluctant to undertake, and has been largely superseded by documentary credits, credit guarantees, confirmations and similar methods of securing payment from overseas buyers undertaken by institutions with special expertise.[273] But it seems that such arrangements are still made in certain contexts, for example dealings with numerous and unknown buyers, or with parties in undeveloped countries.

---

51 Ll.Rep. 330; *Hersom v Bernett* [1955] 1 Q.B. 98; *Teheran-Europe Co Ltd v S.T. Belton (Tractors) Ltd* [1968] 2 Q.B. 545; *Marsh & McLennan Pty Ltd v Stanyers Transport Pty Ltd* [1994] 2 V.R. 232.

[264] See Article 76.

[265] Chorley (1929) 45 L.Q.R. 221; (1930) 46 L.Q.R. 11. See also Schmitthoff, 1970 I *Hague Recueil des Cours* 115 at 162–165; Hill (1968) 31 M.L.R. 623 at 639, fn.64; Derham, *Law of Set-Off* (4th edn), paras 13-112–13-114; below, para.9-022.

[266] i.e. he does not deal as principal with his principal: see cases cited at fn.255 above. He cannot sue for advances made to his principal which are covered by sums due to the principal the payment of which he has guaranteed: *Graham v Ackroyd* (1853) 10 Hare 192. See also *Bramwell v Spiller* (1870) 21 L.T. 672.

[267] *Thomas Gabriel & Sons v Churchill & Sim* [1914] 3 K.B. 1272; *Rusholme & Bolton & Roberts Hadfield v S.G. Read & Co* [1955] 1 W.L.R. 146. Indeed, the principal would have to sue the third party to quantify the damages arising from the third party's insolvency: see at p.151. The execution of a deed of assignment does not establish a loss: *Montague Stanley & Co v J.C. Solomon Ltd* [1932] 2 K.B. 287.

[268] *Churchill & Sim v Goddard* [1937] 1 K.B. 92.

[269] See above, para.1-021.

[270] *Shaw v Woodcock* (1827) 7 B. & C. 73.

[271] *Nouvelles Huileries Anversoises SA v H.C. Mann & Co* (1924) 40 T.L.R. 804 (mere description in contract of agents as *del credere* agents did not constitute them such): *J.M. Wotherspoon & Co Ltd v Henry Agency House* (1961) 28 M.L.J. 86 (no *del credere* agency where no special commission paid).

[272] *Couturier v Hastie* (1852) 8 Exch. 40; *Wickham v Wickham* (1855) 2 K. & J. 478; *Sutton & Co v Grey* [1894] 1 Q.B. 285; *Walker Crips Stockbrokers Ltd v Savill* [2007] EWHC 2598 (QB).

[273] See further below, para.9-022.

1-043   **Distinction between del credere agent and buyer**   Problems as to the distinction between agent and buyer arise conspicuously in the case of *del credere* agents. The general topic is discussed above,[274] but it should be noted that some of the leading cases have involved this type of agent.[275]

1-044   **Commercial agent**   The term "commercial agent" stems from continental European legal systems and is not known to the common law. It is significant in English law now because of the EC Directive on Self-Employed Commercial Agents,[276] which regulates the relations between commercial agents and their principals, and in particular gives them special rights on termination of their agency. Such rights have long been known to continental legal systems, but were unknown to the common law. The Directive was implemented in Great Britain[277] by the Commercial Agents (Council Directive) Regulations 1993,[278] made under s.2(2) of the European Communities Act 1972 and effective on January 1, 1994. The rules for commercial agents as defined are therefore somewhat different from the general rules of agency law described in this book. They are dealt with together as a unit in Chapter 11, where the definition given above is further expanded. They are also referred to at the relevant points in the description of the general rules of English law.

The remaining distinctions are mainly significant in the understanding of old cases.

1-045   **General agent, special agent**   This distinction, an obvious and common sense one, is relevant to the question of the nature and extent of the authority conferred on the agent, and was principally significant in the early development of the doctrine of apparent authority. It was a general agent who had such authority and might bind his principal by an act which he had been forbidden to do.[279] Similar reasoning appears to have been used in the civil law to fix the principal with liability for the agent's unauthorised acts.[280] But the doctrine of apparent authority is nowadays in England normally explained without reference to the distinction, but rather by invocation of the notion of estoppel or similar reasoning.[281] Therefore, though the

---

[274] See above, para.1-035 onwards.

[275] *Ex p. White, re Neville* (1871) L.R. 6 Ch.App. 397; affd sub nom. *John Towle & Co v White* (1873) 29 L.T. 78; *Michelin Tyre Co Ltd v Macfarlane (Glasgow) Ltd* (1917) 55 Sc.L.Rep. 35.

[276] Directive 86/653 [1986] OJ L382/17.

[277] As to Northern Ireland, see Commercial Agents (Council Directive) Regulations (Northern Ireland) (SR 1993 No.483).

[278] SI 1993/3053, as amended by SI 1993/3173 and SI 1998/2868.

[279] See *Smith v M'Guire* (1858) 3 H. & N. 554; *Brady v Todd* (1861) 9 C.B. (N.S.) 592; *Butler v Maples* 76 U.S. 822 (1869). A dramatic example is *Hatch v Taylor* 10 N.H. 538 (1840) (complicated instructions regarding sale of a team of horses). See also Stoljar, pp.77–80. The meaning of "general agent" in the context of an insurance policy is considered in *Excess Life Assurance Co Ltd v Fireman's Insurance Co Ltd* [1982] 2 Lloyd's Rep. 599. In *Barrett v Irvine* [1907] 2 I.R. 462 it was held that a multiplicity of separately authorised transactions does not constitute a general agency (as to which also see *Pole v Leask* (1863) 33 L.J. Ch. 155 at 162).

[280] Müller-Freienfels (1964) 13 Am.J.Comp.L. 193 at 341; Schmitthoff, 1970 I *Hague Recueil des Cours* 115.

[281] See Comment to Article 72. The notion of usual authority can however be related to the concept of the general agent.

distinction between general and special agents is a well-established one, it is doubtful whether it is of much utility in English law at the present day.[282]

Factor, broker[283]   The distinction between these was again of great importance in the nineteenth century, when many of the cases from which our present rules are derived were decided.[284] Some knowledge of the commercial practices of that time helps in understanding those cases. The distinction concerned commercial sales, but within that area of activity was general and not confined to particular trades. A factor was an agent for sale, often of goods sent from another country which he held on consignment: he had possession or control of the goods he sold and usually sold in his own name without disclosing the name of his principal.[285] Indeed, he might not indicate whether he was dealing on behalf of a principal or on his own account. Such a person would readily be held to have apparent authority to sell the goods, or even to have apparent ownership of them, so that his dispositions might be valid even if unauthorised. Payment to a factor was a good discharge even to a buyer who knew of the agency, and where he sold in his own name the factor had the right to sue for the price.[286] The broker is a figure who emerges later than the factor, a person who negotiates and makes contracts between buyers and sellers of goods which he may never see: of him the above propositions are not therefore necessarily true. He should not sell in his own name[287] and payment to him would not be a good discharge,[288] though these were only prima facie rules. The distinction was far from clear. Thus a factor might act also as an independent merchant; and one person might act as both factor and broker. An understanding of the distinction is however essential for the reading of many nineteenth century cases: for example, several decisions are based on the notion that a person dealing with a broker must have known that he had a principal whether he said so or not, but would not necessarily know this of a factor.[289] Indeed, there was at that time the beginnings of an approach to agency which addressed nominate types of agent. But the term "factor" is little used in the above sense today (indeed it is used in other senses, e.g. that of

1-046

---

[282] See also Müller-Freienfels (1964) 13 Am.J.Comp.L. 193 at 341; Seavey (1955) 1 Howard L.J. 79, where he approves the distinction on the ground that it facilitates the wider liability of an undisclosed principal; he had expressed a similar view in (1920) 29 Yale L.J. 859 at 882; Comment to Article 29. Contrast "The most useful thing that can be said about a special agent is that he is one who falls outside the ambit of any useful generalisation": Mechem, *Outlines of Agency* (4th edn), p.46. The notion of general agent is however utilised in the context of landlord and tenant in *Dun & Bradstreet Software Services Ltd v Provident Mutual Life Assurance Assn* [1998] 2 E.G.L.R. 175; cf. *Hexstone Holdings Ltd v AHC Westlink Ltd* [2010] EWHC 1280 (Ch); [2010] 32 E.G. 62; [2010] 2 E.G.L.R. 13 at [37]. But for a view that it provides a better route to liability for agents than the uncertainties of apparent authority see Brown [2004] J.B.L. 391.

[283] See in general Munday (1977) 6 Anglo-Am.L.Rev. 221 (a valuable survey).

[284] See Stoljar, pp.242–247.

[285] *Baring v Corrie* (1818) 2 B. & A. 137 at 143; *Rolls Razor Ltd v Cox* [1967] 1 Q.B. 552 at 568. But he may do: cf. *Stevens v Biller* (1883) 25 Ch.D. 31. An interesting explanation is given in The Matchless (1822) 1 Hagg. 97. As to his discretion, see *Smart v Sandars* (1846) 3 C.B. 380 (see also (1848) 5 C.B. 895). See as to the general trade background Miller (1957) 24 U.Chi.L.Rev. 256.

[286] *Drinkwater v Goodwin* (1775) 1 Cowp 251 at 255–256. As to the ways in which this could be explained in modern terminology see below, para.9-009.

[287] *Baring v Corrie*, above.

[288] *Linck, Moeller & Co v Jameson & Co* (1885) 2 T.L.R. 206.

[289] e.g. *Baring v Corrie*, above; *Armstrong v Stokes* (1872) L.R. 7 Q.B. 598 at 610. For a modern example see *N. & J. Vlassopulos Ltd v Ney Shipping Ltd (The Santa Carina)* [1977] 1 Lloyd's Rep. 478.

credit factoring[290]); and the term "broker" has been applied to many more types of activity than the commodity broker referred to above, and is often applied to intermediaries whom the definition given does not fit at all, e.g. insurance brokers, mortgage brokers, shipbrokers. Further, the Factors Act 1889, the culmination of legislation formulating and extending the special rules applicable to unauthorised dispositions by factors and protecting those who dealt with them, introduced a new term for its purposes, that of "mercantile agent": this is discussed elsewhere.[291] The general distinction is therefore out of date, but important for the comprehension of early case law.

1-047   **Nuntius and other ministerial agents**   Sometimes a person may be asked to undertake a specific task on behalf of a principal under close direction of the principal and sometimes in the principal's presence. The task may be no more than to deliver a document, or orally communicate the principal's decision, when delivery or communication, as the case may be, is likely to change the principal's legal position. Such a person may be called a nuntius, or messenger. The term is not, however, one of art, and there are various other cognates, such as amanuensis, functionary, ministerial agent, and conduit,[292] depending on the task. So, an amanuensis may be asked to sign a document for the principal, who perhaps because of physical disability may not be able to sign personally.[293] Another context is the courtroom, where a barrister in some circumstances may be no more than the mouthpiece of the client, having taken specific instructions from the client, perhaps at the request of the tribunal in order immediately to convey the answer to the tribunal.[294] It may be argued that a person performing such tasks is not an agent at all, not least because in the absence of discretion there will be limited place for the application of fiduciary duties.[295] Nonetheless, the participation of the nuntius or other ministerial agent may have been critical in effecting a change in the principal's legal position, one of the key features of agency. The issue whether or not a nuntius is an agent is likely to be significant only for a rule of law that requires personal action; the conclusion being that the proscription of delegation does not necessarily prohibit the use of a nuntius. In such cases, the relevant act is treated as effected by, as opposed to on behalf of, the principal. Such a rule is more likely to be statutory,[296] or created by a contract, since the normal position of the common law is that whatever can be done personally can be done by an agent.[297] But the rule, for example, that requires a deed to be executed by the party making the deed (un-

---

[290] See Ruddy, Mills and Davidson, *Salinger on Factoring* (5th edn). See also Steffen and Danziger, "The Rebirth of the Commercial Factor" (1936) 36 Col.L.Rev. 745.

[291] Article 87.

[292] See below, para.9-129 (ministerial agents not liable for conversion).

[293] See, e.g. *Barrett v Bem* [2012] EWCA Civ 52; [2012] Ch. 573 (signing will by direction of testator); *Ramsay v Love* [2015] EWHC 65 (Ch) at [7] (operation of signature machine by another).

[294] See the oblique reference to this idea in *Dunhill v Burgin* [2014] UKSC 18; [2014] 1 W.L.R. 933 at [31].

[295] See, e.g. *Torre Asset Funding Ltd v The Royal Bank of Scotland Plc* [2013] EWHC 2670 (Ch) at [30] (limited agency of lead bank for syndicated lenders, but more than mere postal service). See further below, para.6-037.

[296] See, e.g. *Hilmi & Associates Ltd v 20 Pembridge Villas Freehold Ltd* [2010] EWCA Civ 314; [2010] 1 W.L.R. 2750 (Leasehold Reform Housing and Urban Development Act 1993), and fn.166, above.

[297] See below, para.2-017. See too para.2-023.

less an attorney is authorised by a separate deed to do so) can be met by the use of an amanuensis, with the principal present.[298]

---

[298] See below, Article 10.

CHAPTER 2

CREATION OF AGENCY

1. GENERAL

Article 3

HOW AGENCY ARISES

(1) The relationship of principal and agent may be constituted— **2-001**
  (a) by the conferring of authority by the principal on the agent, which may be express, or implied from the conduct or situation of the parties[1];
  (b) retrospectively, by subsequent ratification by the principal of acts done on his behalf.[2]
(2) A person may be liable under the doctrine of apparent authority in respect of another who is not his agent at all[3]; or may be estopped as against a third party from denying the existence of an agency relationship.[4]

Comment

This general statement seeks only to give an indication of the ways in which the **2-002** relationship of principal and agent can arise in the full sense, creating internal rights and duties between principal and agent and giving the agent external authority to affect the principal's legal relations with third parties. Sometimes however the issue may be entirely an internal one between principal and agent; and sometimes, when only apparent authority or estoppel is relevant, the issue may, at least initially, be an external one only. In such situations its relevance may be limited.[5]

Relevance of contract   It has been explained in Chapter 1 that the essence of **2-003** agency must lie in a unilateral manifestation of will, but that very often arises from, or is accompanied by, a contract between principal and agent.[6] If there is no such contract there is still an internal relationship, though a non-contractual one. These features make it appropriate to attribute in exposition a fundamental role to consensual agency.

Ratification   In a second group of cases, a principal may ratify the unauthorised **2-004**

---

[1]   Section 2 of this chapter.
[2]   Section 3.
[3]   See Article 72.
[4]   Article 21.
[5]   cf. Article 1.
[6]   See above, paras 1-005 and 1-006.

acts of a person who purported to act for him while having no actual authority. This in general retrospectively creates the relationship of principal and agent, and the full consequences of such relationship, but although the analogy of authority having been initially conferred is in many respects followed, the relationship cannot easily be said to arise by agreement. Further, certain special rules are found in this area to prevent the retroactivity from operating unfairly.[7] This, therefore, must be treated as a separate type of case. The doctrine of ratification applies also, and perhaps more commonly, to situations where the person who acts is already an agent, but exceeds his authority. Since however it can also create agency it is most conveniently taken in this chapter.

2-005 **Apparent authority and estoppel** There is also a way in which some of the consequences of agency can arise, under the doctrine of apparent authority. Under this, the principal may as against a third party be unable to deny that a person is or was his agent. The principal is here bound by the acts of his apparent agent: but the full relationship of principal and agent does not arise between him and such person, the legal position between them being governed by rules which start from the assumption that there is no agreement between them, at least in respect of the transaction in question. Apparent authority is therefore referred to above as a way in which a person not already an agent can bind a principal.[8] But since its main application is to persons already agents, and only operates between principal and third party, discussion is deferred till Chapter 8, which deals with that relationship.[9] Reference is also made in Article 21 below to cases where a person is estopped by conduct, prior or subsequent, from disputing the validity of an unauthorised transaction entered into on his behalf. An agent may also be found to have sufficient apparent authority to bind his purported principal to a collateral contract of arbitration, or to a collateral contract designating a jurisdiction for determining disputes, without necessarily having such authority to conclude the main contract.[10]

Article 4

CAPACITY TO ACT AS PRINCIPAL

2-006 Capacity to contract or do any other act by means of an agent is co-extensive with the capacity of the principal himself to make the contract or do the act which the agent is authorised to make or do.[11]

Comment

2-007 "It would seem that the proper view should be that anyone may be a principal who has the mental power to act at all, and that if he is a person of no, or limited, contractual power,

---

[7] Articles 16–19.
[8] See Article 3(2).
[9] See Article 72.
[10] See *Premium Nafta Products Ltd v Fili Shipping Co Ltd* [2007] UKHL 40; [2008] 1 Lloyd's Rep. 254 (arbitration clause); and *Deutsche Bank AG v Asia Pacific Broadband Wireless Communications Inc* [2008] EWCA Civ 1091; [2008] 2 Lloyd's Rep. 619 at [25] (jurisdiction clause). See further below, para.3-012.
[11] See further Article 6, below.

his incapacity should be reflected solely in the contract made for him by his agent, which contract would stand on the same footing as if he had made it in person."[12]

Such a simple approach, which is also formulated in this Article, cannot however be left without further comment, for where, as often, incapacity leads to voidable transactions, a more complex analysis may be necessary. As with most principles, there are likely also to be some exceptional cases.[13] It seems right to confirm, however, a general principle that if the would-be principal cannot bring about a legal result personally, it cannot be effected by an agent.[14]

Minors   In old cases it is suggested that minors cannot appoint agents at all.[15] The   **2-008** dicta were wider than was necessary for the decisions in connection with which they were uttered,[16] and are nowadays interpreted restrictively. The following judicial statement may provide a better guide: "Whenever a minor can lawfully do an act on his own behalf, so as to bind himself, he can instead appoint an agent to do it for him".[17] This to some extent follows from the general principle that whatever a person may himself do he may do through an agent.[18] Thus a minor may by an agent enter into a contract that binds him in accordance with the general law[19]; and it has been held that a minor may authorise another to make admissions, even contrary to his interest.[20] On the other hand, contracts which would not otherwise bind a minor will not do so merely because made through an adult agent; and a minor cannot by an agent, any more than he can personally, make an irrevocable disposition taking effect by deed, for such a disposition is avoidable by the minor within a reasonable time of coming of age,[21] and the interposition of an agent should make no difference. This latter proposition probably does not, however, extend to dispositions of property taking effect otherwise than by deed, e.g. by writing or delivery, though the matter is not clear.[22]

It is frequently said that a minor cannot execute a power of attorney appointing an agent. The cases cited, however, mostly concern warranty of attorney in litigation,[23] where a minor is only permitted to act by his next friend or guardian ad litem. The true proposition may rather be that any deed disposing of a minor's property

---

[12]   Mechem, *Outlines of Agency* (4th edn), p.9. See also *Restatement, Third*, § 3.04.
[13]   See Article 6.
[14]   So, for example, if a partner cannot sue his partners in relation to moneys lent to or invested in the partnership except as part of an equitable accounting, neither can a receiver appointed to the affairs of the partner: see *Re Pinata Pty Ltd* [2012] NSWSC 162 at [52].
[15]   *Zouch d. Abbot and Hallett v Parsons* (1765) 3 Burr. 1794 at 1804; *Doe d. Thomas v Robert* (1847) 16 M. & W. 778.
[16]   See *Chaplin v Leslie Frewin (Publishers) Ltd* [1966] Ch. 71 at 96–97.
[17]   *G. (A.) v G. (T.)* [1970] 2 Q.B. 643 at 652, per Lord Denning MR, limiting earlier dicta of his own in *Shephard v Cartwright* [1953] Ch. 728 at 735; affd on another point [1955] A.C. 431.
[18]   Article 6.
[19]   See *R. v Longnor (Inhabitants)* (1833) 4 B. & Ad. 647; *Doyle v White City Stadium Ltd* [1935] 1 K.B. 110.
[20]   *G. (A.) v G. (T.)*, above, (where it was held that in the event there had been no authority).
[21]   *Edwards v Carter* [1893] A.C. 360; *Paget v Paget* (1882) 11 L.R.Ir. 26; *Burnaby v Equitable Reversionary Interest Society* (1885) 28 Ch.D. 416 at 424; unless, presumably, the disposition is in pursuance of a contract which is in law binding on him. See also *Carnell v Harrison* [1916] 1 Ch. 328; Chitty, *Contracts* (32nd edn), para.9-036 onwards.
[22]   See *Chaplin v Leslie Frewin (Publishers) Ltd* [1966] 1 Ch. 71 at 90, 93, 94, 97. Sometimes of course the disposition may be in pursuance of a contract which is itself voidable: *Chaplin*, above.
[23]   e.g. *Oliver v Woodroffe* (1839) 4 M. & W. 650. See also *Zouch d. Abbot and Hallett v Parsons* (1765) 3 Burr. 1794; *Gibbons v Wright* (1904) 91 C.L.R. 423 at 447; Alcock, *Powers of Attorney* (1935), pp.63–64; Aldridge, *Powers of Attorney* (10th edn), pp.26–27.

executed by an agent appointed by means of such a power would be voidable by the minor as if he had executed it himself: "an infant cannot appoint an agent to make a disposition of his property so as to bind him irrevocably".[24] But where the power of attorney is executed in deed form, which is now requisite,[25] it may be possible to argue that the deed itself is caught by this rule: that not only is the power revocable for the future, but the deed itself is also voidable. It seems that the contract (if there is a contract) with the agent is to be treated like a contract of service, and binding on the minor if it is for his benefit[26]: the effect of this contract is of course a separate question from that of the validity of the agent's acts.[27]

2-009   **Mentally incapacitated persons**[28]   The general principle of the common law is that transactions entered into by a mentally incapacitated person are prima facie effective, and, in relation to transactions other than gifts, cannot be set aside unless the person with whom the transaction was entered into knew, or ought to have known, of the incapacity.[29] This principle is consistent with the higher level general principle that intention in the formation of contracts and other transactions is judged objectively. However, in cases of extreme incapacity, or where it can be established that for other reasons an actor had no appreciation whatsoever of the document to which he is said to have given consent, the transaction may be a nullity under the non est factum doctrine.[30] The incapacity in such a case will usually be apparent to the world, and the beneficiary of the document will often be aware of it too.

Although the case law on the topic is surprisingly thin, it is suggested that these principles apply to the creation of authority, actual or apparent, in an agent.[31] Hence, mental incapacity in a principal will not preclude his conferring actual authority on an agent when the agent had no reason to know of the incapacity, and such authority will endure until the agent becomes aware of the incapacity (or the agency otherwise terminates under general principles).[32] There would, however, be no need for the principal, or someone on his behalf, to take steps to terminate the mandate once the agent becomes aware of the incapacity. It ought not to matter whether or not the agent is appointed under a contract.[33] The same principles should apply to the existence of apparent authority, the incapacity of the principal not preventing

---

[24]   *G. (A.) v G. (T.)*, above, at p.652, per Lord Denning MR. See Megarry and Wade, *Law of Real Property* (8th edn, Harpum edn), para.36-012.

[25]   Powers of Attorney Act 1971 s.1.

[26]   *Chaplin v Leslie Frewin (Publishers) Ltd*, above. See further Webb (1955) 18 M.L.R. 461; *McLaughlin v Darcy* (1918) 18 S.R.(N.S.W.) 585.

[27]   See O'Hare (1970) 3 U.Tas.L.Rev. 312.

[28]   This paragraph replaced the text on this subject that appeared from the 13th edn (1968) to the 19th edn (2010), but is consistent with such material as there was on the subject in all editions before the 13th. For elaboration of the points made in this paragraph, see Watts [2015] C.L.J. 140. cf. Varney (2017) 37 Leg. Stud. 493.

[29]   *Molton v Camroux* (1849) 4 Exch. 17 at 19–20; *Imperial Loan Co v Stone* [1892] 1 Q.B. 599; *Daily Telegraph Newspaper Co Ltd v McLaughlin* (1904) 1 C.L.R. 243 at 272–273; affd [1904] A.C. 776 (PC); *Hart v O'Connor* [1985] A.C. 1000. As to gifts, see *Day v Day* [2013] EWCA Civ 280; [2014] Ch. 114 (principal sane, but mistaken gift made through innocent attorney was subject to rectification).

[30]   See *Saunders v Anglia Building Society* [1971] A.C. 1004.

[31]   That the conferral of actual authority is judged objectively is confirmed by *Freeman & Lockyer v Buckhurst Park Properties Ltd* [1964] 2 Q.B. 480 at 502–503.

[32]   See too *Restatement, Third*, § 3.08 and § 3.11. In the absence of apparent authority, the third party's position in relation to the principal is dependent on the agent's actual authority, again in accordance with general principle.

[33]   In *Blankley v Central Manchester and Manchester Children's University Hospitals NHS Trust* [2015]

any representation made by him to the third party as to the agent's authority from being effective, unless the third party is aware of the incapacity.[34] There is insufficient reason for treating representations of authority made to the third party by the principal differently from communications which would be sufficient to create a contract directly between those parties. Where mental incapacity occurs after the grant of authority, or the holding out of authority, the relevant authority will terminate only once known (or it ought to have been known) to the agent or third party, as the case may be.[35]

The fullest judicial discussion is in *Daily Telegraph Newspaper Co Ltd v McLaughlin*,[36] where, however, the High Court of Australia was relieved from ruling on the principles by its conclusion that the relevant power of attorney was caught by the non est factum doctrine and void on that ground. The court otherwise appeared to favour the view that the general principles, above, apply to the creation of actual authority in an agent.[37] Older cases sometimes cited for automatic voidness of an appointment of an agent by an incapax principal do not on analysis support that conclusion.[38] There are, in addition, some obiter dicta that suggest that a power of attorney granted by an incapax person is automatically void.[39] This view is also hard to justify, except perhaps on an argument that the open-ended nature of the mandate often granted by such documents exposes the donor to too much risk. The better view, apparently favoured in *Daily Telegraph*,[40] is that there is no such exception.

Statutory provisions now add an overlay to the common law on powers of attorney. These provisions may have been drafted on an assumption of automatic voidness, but such an assumption could not be determinative of the relevant common law. So, where an instrument is registered as a lasting power of attorney under the Mental Capacity Act 2005 but was not in fact validly created, the Act gives protection to the donee of the power and to third parties who deal with the donee, so long as, in each case, they did not know of the invalidity at the time of the

---

EWCA Civ 18; [2015] 1 W.L.R. 4307 at [36], a case concerned with supervening incapacity (as to which, see below, para.10-020) the Court of Appeal favoured a review of the case law that suggests that incapacity automatically terminates an agent's actual authority, and indicated support for a view that the agent's state of knowledge of the incapacity ought to be relevant to the issue.

[34] *Drew v Nunn* (1879) 4 Q.B.D. 661. Brett LJ in this case appears to have thought that it was significant that the incapacity was supervening, but Bramwell LJ, and possibly Cotton LJ, took a broader view.
[35] *Drew v Nunn* (1879) 4 Q.B.D. 661. See further below, paras 10-020 and 10-032. The position may be different if the terms of appointment expressly provide for automatic termination of the agency upon the principal's becoming mentally incapable. For the position where the agent is unaware of the incapacity, but the third party is aware, see below, para.8-008.
[36] (1904) 1 C.L.R. 243 affd [1904] A.C. 776. See also *Taylor v Walker* [1958] 1 Lloyd's Rep. 490 at 514 where, however, the principal signed the relevant compromise.
[37] (1904) 1 C.L.R. 243 at 272 and 276. But cf. at 275.
[38] *Stead v Thornton* (1832) 3 B. & Ad. 357 and *Tarbuck v Bispham* (1836) 2 M. & W. 2 are both cases where the insanity was known to the agent; *Elliot v Ince* (1857) 7 De G.M. & G. 475 was decided on the basis that the disposition under the power of attorney was voluntary. In *Yonge v Toynbee* [1910] 1 K.B. 215 it was assumed, without argument, that incapacity automatically terminated the authority of a solicitor to continue to defend court proceedings; the question of liability for costs plainly raised no issue of the validity of a contract or other transaction. See too *Evans v James* [2000] 3 E.G.L.R. 1 (stroke victim, but illness known to agent). The issues arising were expressly left open by the Supreme Court in *Dunhill v Burgin* [2014] UKSC 18; [2014] 1 W.L.R. 933 at [31].
[39] *Gibbons v Wright* (1954) 91 C.L.R. 423 at 444–445 and 448. This was not a case involving agents, and the court seems to have misread its earlier decision in the *Daily Telegraph* case.
[40] (1904) 1 C.L.R. 243 at 276. See too V. St Clair Mackenzie, *The Law of Powers of Attorney and Proxies* (2nd edn, 1913), pp.4–5, 92–94.

dealing.[41] Similarly, the Powers of Attorney Act 1971 gives protection against later revocation of a power of attorney, including on the grounds of incapacity, again so long as the donee or third party, as the case may be, did not know of the revocation at the time of the relevant transaction.[42] Other provisions permit, in certain circumstances, a power of attorney to continue in operation where supervening incapacity occurs even where the agent knows of the incapacity.[43]

There are other legislative provisions that may bear on the application of the common law, including those that result in an incapax person being the subject of formal orders under the Mental Capacity Act 2005,[44] and the Civil Procedure Rules that apply to compromises of court proceedings.[45] In respect of the latter, it has been held that the failure to appoint a litigation friend where one is required by the CPR and then to obtain the court's approval of any compromise invalidates the compromise even if the incapax person was legally represented and the third party was unaware of the mental incapacity.[46]

2-010   **Alien enemies**   An alien enemy probably cannot appoint an agent, at any rate if the transaction involved would be of benefit to the enemy country.[47]

Article 5

CAPACITY TO ACT AS AGENT

2-011   (1)   All persons including minors and other persons with limited or no capacity to contract on their own behalf, but excluding the profoundly insane, are competent to act or contract as agents.

      (2)   But the personal liability of the agent upon any contract of agency, and upon any contract entered into by him with a third party, is dependent on his capacity to contract on his own behalf.[48]

---

[41]   Mental Capacity Act 2005 s.14.

[42]   Powers of Attorney Act 1971 s.5(1) and (2). See below, para.10-034.

[43]   Mental Capacity Act 2005 s.9 (see below, para.10-009) and Powers of Attorney Act 1971 s.5 (see below, para.10-008).

[44]   The contracts of a person found to be of unsound mind by inquisition were void even if made during a lucid interval: *Re Walker* [1905] 1 Ch. 160. The same rule presumably applies where a person's property is under present legislation under the control of the court (see Mental Capacity Act 2005 ss.15–21; and see Mental Health Act 1983 as amended). But it is not clear whether the principle applies only to contracts relating to property. See Treitel, *Law of Contract* (14th edn), paras 12-058–12-061.

[45]   See CPR rr.21.2, 21.10.

[46]   *Dunhill v Burgin* [2014] UKSC 18; [2014] 1 W.L.R. 933.

[47]   *Stevenson & Sons Ltd v Aktiengesellschaft für Cartonnagen-Industrie* [1918] A.C. 239; *Ottoman Bank v Jebara* [1928] A.C. 269; *Sovfracht, etc. v Van Udens* [1943] A.C. 203; *Nordisk Insulinlaboratorium v Gorgate Products Ltd* [1953] Ch. 430 (on termination of agency); *Boston Deep Sea Fishing & Ice Co v Farnham* [1957] 1 W.L.R. 1051 (on ratification). cf. *Lepage v San Paulo Copper Estates Ltd* (1917) 33 T.L.R. 457 (administrator-sequestrator appointed by French court to act for enemy alien may claim dividends due to alien); *Hangkam Kwingtong Woo v Liu Lan Fong* [1951] A.C. 707 (application of rule when territory occupied by enemy). See also Article 119.

[48]   *Smally v Smally* (1700) 1 Eq.Ca.Abr. 6. See *Restatement, Third*, § 3.05.

Comment

Rule (1)   The rationale of this seems to be that the agent is a mere instrument and **2-012**
that it is the principal who bears the risk of inadequate representation.[49] An early
example was the married woman, who could act as agent, though she had no
contractual capacity till 1882: indeed it was her lack of capacity that led to her being held to be an agent for her husband.[50] Thus a minor may act as agent provided
that he has sufficient understanding to consent to the agency and to do the act
required.[51] A person who cannot read may be an agent to sign a written contract.[52]
A person lacking all understanding of what he is doing cannot act as agent, but a
lesser degree of mental incapacity would not preclude the conferral of actual authority, even if the principal were unaware of the incapacity.[53] Agency by an alien enemy
would often be void on grounds of public policy.[54]

Statutes sometimes require certain qualifications in persons who act as agents,
e.g. solicitors, and company directors.[55] When this is so, persons who act without
such qualifications may commit offences by doing so, and may not be entitled to
remuneration, reimbursement or indemnity; the matter is discussed under Articles
61 and 63. But they will nevertheless bind their principals unless the statute also
expressly or impliedly invalidates their acts.[56]

Agent acting for both parties to a transaction   The agent of one party is not **2-013**
incompetent to act as agent of the other. Thus solicitors frequently act for both the
buyer and the seller of a house, though there are many judicial warnings as to the
dangers of this practice.[57] It is perhaps more likely that an agent can acceptably
acquire the second capacity after the relevant contract has been made.[58] Although
there may not be an implied term of the traditional sort in the contract of agency

---

[49] Müller-Freienfels (1957) 6 Am.J.Comp.L. 165 at 180–181; (1964) 13 Am.J.Comp.L. 193 at 204; *Norwich and Peterborough B.S. v Steed* [1993] Ch. 116 at 128. As to the bankruptcy of an agent, see para.10-021.
[50] See below, para.3-043.
[51] *Smally v Smally*, above; *Re D'Angibau* (1880) 15 Ch.D. 228 at 246; *Travelers Guarantee Co of Canada v Farajollahi* [2012] B.C.S.C. 1283 (son signs indemnity for father). See *Restatement, Third*, Comment to § 3.05, giving the example of a child ordering books for a parent through the internet.
[52] Illustration 1.
[53] See *Norwich and Peterborough B.S. v Steed*, above, at 128 (but dictum addressed only to situation where the principal was aware of the agent's incapacity).
[54] See Articles 4 and 117; *Kuenigl v Donnersmarck* [1955] 1 Q.B. 515; *Rayner v Sturges* (1916) 33 T.L.R. 87; *Schostall v Johnson* (1919) 36 T.L.R. 75 (friendly enemy aliens resident in England).
[55] See Companies Act 2006 s.157 (minimum age of 16).
[56] In respect of directors, see the express preservation of authority in Companies Act 2006 s.161. See further below, para.8-037. For general illustration, see *Re Euromaster Ltd* [2012] EWHC 2356 (Ch); [2013] Bus. L.R. 466 (appointment of administrator outside statutory period not invalid).
[57] See *Moody v Cox and Hatt* [1917] 2 Ch. 71 at 91; *Spector v Ageda* [1973] Ch. 30 at 47; below, para.6-048. For other examples of agents acting for both parties see *Emmerson v Heelis* (1809) 2 Taunt. 38 (auctioneer); *Newsholme v Road Transport Insurance Co*, Illustration 2 to Article 95 (insurance agent); *Briess v Woolley* [1954] A.C. 333 (director); *The Giancarlo Zeta* [1966] 2 Lloyd's Rep. 317 (freight broker) (Can.); *BS Developments No.12 Ltd v PB & SF Properties Ltd* (2006) 7 N.Z. Conveyancing and Property R. 603 (real estate agent found to act for both sides); *Newcastle United Plc v Revenue and Customs Commissioners* [2007] EWHC 612 (Ch); [2007] S.T.C. 1330 (sports agent acting for two parties). For further discussion, see below, para.2-031.
[58] See Story, *Agency* (1839), § 31, and *Royal Securities Corp Ltd v Montreal Trust Co* (1966) 59 D.L.R. (2d) 666; affd (1967) 63 D.L.R. (2d) 15.

that would preclude the agent's acting for the other party,[59] the rules of equity will apply to the situation, and equity presumes that a person in a fiduciary position must avoid conflicts of interest unless the parties assent to the conflict.[60] Equity may intervene with an injunction in appropriate cases.[61] Otherwise, an agent who acts for both parties runs grave risks of finding himself in a position in which his duty to one party is inconsistent with his duty to the other, for example as regards information coming into his possession. In such a case he will be in breach of his duty to his first principal, and liable accordingly, unless that principal has given his informed consent to the transaction with the other principal.[62] Where the agent's acts result in a transaction with a third party who knew of the agent's dual capacity, that transaction may be voidable.[63] But in other cases an action taken by the agent on behalf of his other principal may be valid in itself, though wrongful.[64] In a slightly different context, the employee of one party can in principle be agent for another.[65]

2-014   **One party to a transaction as agent of the other**   Similarly, one party is not in principle incompetent to act as agent for the other party to a transaction. This can occur not merely where the third party performs only some functions as agent for the principal, but also where the agent actually makes a contract with himself on behalf of the principal.[66] An agent cannot, however, contract with his principal on behalf of his principal so as to make his principal not himself liable to sue and be sued on the contract; there must be two parties to a contract.[67]

Capacity is one thing, authority is another.[68] The common law has not produced much modern case law on the circumstances in which there might be implied limitations on an agent's authority to contract with himself on behalf of the principal. It has largely been left to equity to address self-dealing, which rules make a transaction prima facie voidable whatever authority the agent might have. Protections of "fair dealing" also apply even where the agent deals with the principal in person. For example, an agent will be in breach of his duty if while agent he fails to disclose his interest on the other side of the contract (e.g. as undisclosed principal of the third party),[69] and the transaction is in such a case likely to be voidable.[70] But there will be cases where a finding of lack of authority is appropriate, and in which case there

---

[59] *Newcastle United Plc v Revenue and Customs Commissioners* [2007] EWHC 612 (Ch); [2007] S.T.C. 1330 at [29].

[60] See below, Article 44, and in particular para.6-048.

[61] See below, para.6-044.

[62] *Fullwood v Hurley* [1928] 1 K.B. 498 at 502; *Anglo-African Merchants Ltd v Bayley* [1970] 1 Q.B. 311 (insurance broker); *Eagle Star Insurance Co Ltd v Spratt* [1971] 2 Lloyd's Rep. 116 at 133; *Richard Ellis Ltd v Van Hong-tuan* [1988] 1 H.K.L.R. 169; *Hilton v Barker Booth and Eastwood* [2005] UKHL 8; [2005] 1 W.L.R. 567. See further below, para.6-039.

[63] *Re a Debtor* [1927] 2 Ch. 367; *Taylor v Walker* [1958] 1 Lloyd's Rep. 490; *North and South Trust Co v Berkeley* [1971] 1 W.L.R. 470 at 485. See further Article 96.

[64] See Illustration 3.

[65] *Man Nutzfahrzeuge AG v Ernst & Young* [2005] EWHC (Comm) 2347 at [99], per Moore-Bick J; though in general not at the same time and in relation to the same transaction; affd on other points [2007] EWCA Civ 910.

[66] See *Rowley Homes & Co v Barber* [1977] 1 W.L.R. 371; *Lee v Lee's Air Farming Ltd* [1961] A.C. 12. For a comparative study of the power of an agent to contract on behalf of his principal with himself, see Badr (1982) 30 Am.J.Comp.L. 255.

[67] *Ingram v Inland Revenue Commissioners* [1997] 4 All E.R. 395 at 423, per Millett LJ (dissenting, but approved on appeal: [2000] 1 A.C. 293 at 305).

[68] See *Tang Ying Ip v Tang Ying Loi* [2017] HKCFA 3 at [19].

[69] See Articles 45 and 96.

[70] e.g. *Moody v Cox and Hatt* [1917] 2 Ch. 71; *Spector v Ageda* [1973] Ch. 30 (solicitors).

would be no contract at all. There are older cases involving self-dealing where the court concluded that the transaction was void for want of authority.[71] And in the case of the Statute of Frauds, there is a rule of actual competence: it has long been established that a party to a contract is not competent to sign a contract or a note or memorandum thereof, as agent of the other party.[72] The reasoning is based on the purpose of the statute, and it is submitted that it should also be applied to s.2 of the Law of Property (Miscellaneous Provisions) Act 1989, which now requires the actual contract to be in writing. However, one party can authorise the agent of the other party to sign, though it may be difficult to establish that he has in fact given such authority[73]: thus the signature of an auctioneer to a contemporary memorandum or contract of sale operated as the signature of both parties within s.40 of the Law of Property Act 1925,[74] provided that the auctioneer was not himself the claimant.[75] If he was the claimant, however, he was suing on a contract made with himself and could not claim to have signed as agent for the other party. But the signature of his clerk (if authorised) might suffice[76]; or even in one case the signature of the employee, himself a licensed auctioneer, who conducted the auction (and who had prima facie authority to sign).[77] Contracts made in the course of public auctions are exempted from s.2 of the 1989 Act referred to above, with the result that these cases may on their facts be no longer relevant. They are, however, retained as examples of general principle, and as being still relevant to contracts of guarantee, the only type of contract still covered by the Statute of Frauds. It is also at least arguable that the requirements of the 1989 Act can be met where a person makes a contract with a company, and signs for himself and the company.

Other examples can be found of situations where the third party performs only some functions as agent for the counter-party. These include where one party signs a bill of exchange in blank,[78] or signs a contract leaving the other party to complete gaps in it; in completing the document on behalf of the former, the latter acts as agent to the extent that he thereby alters the legal position of the former.[79] It was also at one time assumed that a party purchasing land from a solicitor engaged the solicitor as his agent for the purposes of performing the standard duty to make

---

[71] See, e.g. *Salomons v Pender* (1865) 3 H. & C. 639 at 642. See further below, Article 45.
[72] *Wright v Dannah* (1809) 2 Camp. 203; *Farebrother v Simmons* (1882) 5 B. & A. 333; *Sharman v Brandt* (1870–71) L.R. 6 Q.B. 720.
[73] *Bird v Boulter* (1833) 4 B. & Ad. 443; *Durrell v Evans* (1862) 1 Hurl. & C. 174; cf. *Murphy v Boese* (1874–75) L.R. 10 Ex. 126.
[74] *Emmerson v Heelis* (1809) 2 Taunt. 38; *White v Proctor* (1811) 4 Taunt. 209; *Chaney v Maclow* [1929] 1 Ch. 461.
[75] *Farebrother v Simmons*, above.
[76] *Bird v Boulter*, above; *Sims v Landray* [1894] 2 Ch. 318. But an auctioneer's clerk had no prima facie authority to sign; *Bell v Balls* [1897] 1 Ch. 663. And see Article 8, Illustration 1.
[77] *Wilson & Sons v Pike* [1949] 1 K.B. 176.
[78] See Bills of Exchange Act 1882 s.20(1); and commentary in *Chalmers and Guest on Bills of Exchange* (17th edn), para.2-131. See also *Colonial Bank v Hepworth* (1884) 36 Ch.D. 36 (share certificates in blank with authority to complete).
[79] See *Wright v Gasweld Pty Ltd* (1991) 22 N.S.W.L.R. 317 at 323; *Madden v UDC Finance Ltd* [1996] 1 N.Z.L.R. 542, CA (affd PC 71/1996, 30 October 1997). See also the controversial case, *Newsholme Bros v Road Transport & General Insurance Co Ltd* [1929] 2 K.B. 356, Illustration 2 to Article 95 and note thereto. See too the discussion of *Milroy v Lord* (1862) 4 De G.F. & J. 264, below, para.10-010; and *Barrett v Bem* [2011] EWHC 1247 (Ch); [2011] 3 W.L.R. 1193; reversed on facts [2012] EWCA Civ 52; [2012] Ch. 573 (beneficiary under will was not incompetent to sign will by direction of testator present at the time); *P v Bridgecorp Ltd* [2013] NZSC 152; [2014] 1 N.Z.L.R. 195 at [104] (debtor authorises creditor to file admission of liability).

inquiries as to title if he had no other solicitor acting for him, an assumption no longer made.[80]

2-015   **Rule (2)**   A minor's liability to his principal, or on the contract which he has made with a third party (where this involves his personal liability[81]) is regulated by his capacity to contract. Where the agency is not contractual, the minor may nevertheless be subject to the non-contractual rights and duties of an agent.[82] The extent to which an agent who is a minor would be subject to fiduciary duties is beyond the scope of this book. A minor cannot be an express trustee[83]: but it has been held that a minor can be a resulting trustee of personalty,[84] and there seems no reason why he should not be a constructive trustee. It has been held that a restitutionary claim against a minor is controlled by his contractual capacity.[85] Whether this is good law or not, an equitable claim, whether in rem or in personam, may not be so controlled,[86] and there is also a statutory jurisdiction to order the minor to transfer property where it is just and equitable to do so.[87] A minor is liable in tort provided that the tortious action is not merely a way of evading a contractual immunity.[88]

Illustrations

2-016   (1)   A farmer sends cattle by rail: his drover, who cannot read, signs a consignment note containing contractual terms. The farmer is bound.[89]

(2)   The buyer and seller of a house sign a printed form of contract which covers all details except date of completion. The seller's solicitor is instructed to act for the buyer. The seller tells the solicitor the date subsequently agreed for completion, and being asked by the solicitor to confirm this, the buyer does so. The solicitor is authorised to create an additional memorandum binding the buyer.[90]

(3)   Lloyd's brokers, who act as agents for the assured,[91] are instructed by the underwriters to obtain an assessor's report in connection with a claim made by the brokers' principals. The brokers obtain such a report and in the course of litigation refuse to show it to their principals. Any custom of Lloyd's by

---

[80]   See, e.g. *Dryden v Frost* (1838) 3 My. & Cr. 670 from where earlier cases can be traced. The change of approach commenced with *Espin v Pemberton* (1859) 3 De G. & J. 547. See also *Barclays Bank Plc v O'Brien* [1994] 1 A.C. 180 at 195.

[81]   See Article 98.

[82]   Article 42.

[83]   Law of Property Act 1925 s.20.

[84]   *Re Vinogradoff* [1935] W.N. 68.

[85]   *Cowern v Nield* [1912] 2 K.B. 419; criticised, Goff and Jones, *Law of Unjust Enrichment* (9th edn), paras 24-13–24-27 and 34-13–34-17.

[86]   But see *R. Leslie Ltd v Sheill* [1914] 3 K.B. 607; criticised, Goff and Jones, above.

[87]   Minors' Contracts Act 1987 s.3(1).

[88]   See Treitel, *Law of Contract* (14th edn), paras 12-033–12-035. For discussion of the possibility of a minor's tortious liability to a principal where as agent he exceeds his mandate, see Watts (2009) 17 Torts L.J. 100 at 103.

[89]   *Foreman v G.W. Ry Co* (1878) 38 L.T. 851.

[90]   *Gavaghan v Edwards* [1961] 2 Q.B. 220. The analysis of this situation would now be different by virtue of s.2 of the Law of Property (Miscellaneous Provisions) Act 1989, but the reasoning still seems valid.

[91]   This is the standard position: see *HIH Casualty & General Insurance Ltd v JLT Risk Solutions Ltd* [2007] EWCA Civ 710; [2007] 2 Lloyd's Rep. 278; [2007] 2 All E.R. (Comm) 1106 at [60]; *Flexirent Capital Pty Ltd v EBS Consulting Pty Ltd* [2007] VSC 158 at [211].

which brokers act also for the underwriters is unreasonable[92] and the brokers are in breach of duty to their principals: but their principals are nevertheless not entitled to see the report, which the brokers obtained while acting for the underwriters.[93]

Article 6

ACTS WHICH MAY BE DONE BY MEANS OF AN AGENT

An agent may execute a deed, or do any other act on behalf of the principal, which the principal might himself execute, make or do; except for the purpose of executing a right, privilege or power conferred, or of performing a duty imposed, on the principal personally, the exercise or performance of which requires discretion or special personal skill, or for the purpose of doing an act which the principal is required, by or pursuant to any statute or other relevant rule, to do in person.[94]   **2-017**

Comment

The authorities cited for the proposition contained in this Article indicate that it is a general rule of common law which will apply unless displaced. The idea behind the proposition can be traced back as least as far as *Coke on Littleton*:   **2-018**

> "Here it appeareth that where the servant doth all that which he is commanded, and which his master ought to doe, there it is as sufficient as if his master did it himselfe: for the rule is, *Qui per alium facit, per se ipsum facere videtur*."[95]

Similar considerations operate in the reverse situation, viz. where it is sought to use the rule against a principal. Thus it has been held that a notice to quit may be served on an agent.[96] In contrast, a memorandum under the Moneylenders Act may not be furnished to an agent,[97] and it was held at common law that a member of a corporation could not vote at meetings by proxy or other agent unless the incorporating statute or the constitution of the organisation provided for that.[98] Court proceed-

---

[92] See Article 31.
[93] *North and South Trust Co v Berkeley* [1971] 1 W.L.R. 470. See (1972) 35 M.L.R. 78 and the explanation of this case in *Callagan and Hedges v Thompson* [2000] Lloyd's Rep. I.R. 125 at 132. cf. *Goshawk Dedicated Ltd v Tyser & Co Ltd* [2006] EWCA Civ 54; [2007] Lloyd's Rep. I.R. 224. In *Stockton v Mason* [1978] 2 Lloyd's Rep. 430 a broker was held to have authority to issue temporary cover. It is also arguable that he in many cases has authority to receive premiums on behalf of the underwriter.
[94] *R. v Kent JJ.* (1872–73) L.R. 8 Q.B. 305; *Re Whitley Partners Ltd* (1886) 32 Ch.D. 337; *Jackson & Co v Napper* (1886) 35 Ch.D. 162 at 172; *R. v Assessment Committee of St Mary Abbotts, Kensington* [1891] 1 Q.B. 378; *Bevan v Webb* [1901] 2 Ch. 59 at 77; *Christie v Permewan, Wright & Co Ltd* (1904) 1 C.L.R. 693 at 700; *McRae v Coulton* (1986) 7 N.S.W.L.R. 644 at 663–664. See too Powers of Attorney Act 1971 s.10(1).
[95] *Coke on Littleton*, Section 434. See also Story, *Agency* (1839), § 2; *Newbold v Coal Authority* [2013] EWCA Civ 584; [2014] 1 W.L.R. 1288 at [58].
[96] *Doe d. Prior v Ongley* (1850) 10 C.B. 25 at 34; and statutes frequently provide for service on agents, e.g. Rent Act 1977 ss.41(2) and 151(1).
[97] *John W. Grahame (English Financiers) Ltd v Ingram* [1955] 1 W.L.R. 563. The Moneylenders Act 1927 was repealed by the Consumer Credit Act 1974.
[98] *Harben v Phillips* (1883) 23 Ch.D. 14. A right to appoint one or more proxies in relation to companies is now provided for by the Companies Act 2006 s.324. See further, Ahern and Maher

ings cannot usually be commenced in the name of an agent, including under a power of attorney; the principal must be the party named.[99]

2-019　**Contracts and deeds**　In general a person may make any contract through an agent. He can also perform a contract through an agent unless it is a contract that involves his own personal attributes or otherwise expressly or impliedly excludes vicarious performance.[100] But this is not an assignment of the burden of the contract and the principal remains liable personally.[101] An agent may sign in his own name a memorandum of a guarantee within the requirements of the Statute of Frauds s.4,[102] since it refers to a person "thereunto lawfully authorised"[103]: there is no requirement that he state for whom he acts, and he need not be specifically authorised, nor (necessarily) intend to bind his principal by contract[104], or memorandum of contract.[105] An agent may likewise sign a contract for the sale or other disposition of an interest in land for the purposes of the Law of Property (Miscellaneous Provisions) Act 1989; but here, since the document constitutes the contract, an intention to bind by contract is required.[106]

　A deed may be executed through an agent provided that the agent is duly authorised by deed.[107] An individual authorised to act by power of attorney may execute an instrument in his own name.[108]

2-020　**Corporations**　Corporations can act only through agents,[109] so there can be no question of the capacity of a corporation to appoint agents. But what the corporation itself has the capacity to do turns at common law on the source of its incorporation. This is a complex topic beyond the scope of this work,[110] but in general it can be noted that a corporation the existence of which turns on a statute has only such capacity as the statute expressly or impliedly permits. A charter corporation, on the other hand, has unlimited capacity. No agent can have actual authority to do what the corporation does not have capacity to do. It is frequently suggested that an act that is ultra vires is a nullity whatever the state of innocence

---

[2011] J.B.L. 125.

99　*Davis v Anthony* (Unreported 5 July 1995, English Court of Appeal); *Yu Hing Tong Ltd v Fung Hing Chiu* [2016] HKCFI 1798.

100　See *Davies v Collins* [1945] 1 All E.R. 247; Chitty, *Contracts* (32nd edn), para.19-082 onwards.

101　*Stewart v Reavell's Garage* [1952] 2 Q.B. 545. Nor can the agent be sued in contract by the other party to the contract, unless, of course, the principal has acted as agent for the purpose of setting up contractual relations between his agent and the other party.

102　As amended by the Law Reform (Enforcement of Contracts) Act 1954.

103　It seems that he can sign his own name or his principal's name: *Graham v Musson* (1839) 5 Bing.N.C. 603. But as to forms of signature see below, para.2-023.

104　*Griffiths Cycle Corp Ltd v Humber & Co Ltd* [1899] 2 Q.B. 414; *Daniels v Trefusis* [1914] 1 Ch. 788; *North v Loomes* [1919] 1 Ch. 378; *Grindell v Bass* [1920] 2 Ch. 487; *Wright v Pepin* [1954] 1 W.L.R. 635. Liability for representations as to credit under s.6 of the Statute of Frauds Amendment Act 1828 (Lord Tenterden's Act) does not arise if the representation is merely signed by an agent, except in the case of a limited company: see Article 91.

105　*Golden Ocean Group Ltd v Salgaocar Mining Industries PVT Ltd* [2011] EWHC 56 (Comm); [2011] 1 W.L.R. 2575 at [94]; affd [2012] EWCA Civ 265; [2012] 1 W.L.R. 3674 at [35]. The agent who signs a memorandum, so long as authorised to do so, need not be the agent who made the contract: [2011] EWHC 56 (Comm) at [85].

106　See below, para.2-037.

107　See Article 10.

108　Powers of Attorney Act 1971 s.7(1); below, para.2-039.

109　See above, para.1-028.

110　See *Halsbury's Laws of England*, Vol.9(2), paras 1230 and 1231.

of the outside party.[111] However, it is arguable that this overstates the general position. The cases point in different directions. What is clear is that all persons are deemed to know the statutory or constitutional limits of the powers of the corporation (unless the statute otherwise provides). But where the lack of capacity turns on facts which were not apparent on the face of the transaction, the act may still be valid unless the outside party knows or ought to have known of those facts.[112] In this regard, there are compelling reasons for thinking that corporations are in no more secure position than a human who lacks capacity.[113] In relation to companies incorporated under general companies legislation, the foregoing position has been much modified, and is discussed below.[114]

Delegation: sub-agency, and delegations by trustees and other holders of discretionary powers   A person who is given a power of a discretionary nature must as a rule exercise it in person. However, the power to delegate is very context-specific and turns on the consent of the principal rather than issues of capacity. It will frequently be implicit that an agent will be able to employ other persons to help him perform the tasks undertaken for the principal. The question of sub-agency is dealt with in Chapter 5. For some officeholders the question of delegation turns on the express or implied terms of their appointment. Thus where the consent of a particular person was required for the execution of a power of appointment, it was held that he had no power to appoint an agent to consent for him.[115] Trustees are in general in the same position and cannot delegate their duties: *delegatus non potest delegare*. But there were exceptions to this[116] and they have been extended and modified by statute.[117] Moreover, the mere fact that a trustee wrongly delegates powers to a colleague or to another agent will not entail that at law the agent has no authority, including, for instance, the power to pass title to property owned at law by the trustee.[118] The third party in such a case would get good title, but would take subject to the trust if possessed of notice of the trust and the identity of its trustees.

2-021

---

[111] See, e.g. *Law Debenture Trust Corp Plc v Ukraine* [2017] EWHC 655 (Comm) at [108] (foreign states inherently have unlimited capacity).

[112] See *Re Marseilles Extension Railway Co, Ex p. Credit Foncier and Mobilier of England* (1871) L.R. 7 Ch. App. 161, where the borrowing was for a purpose that was not only ultra vires but illegal, yet held valid when lender did not know of the purpose; *Re David Payne & Co Ltd* [1904] 2 Ch. 608. The latter case was analysed as involving directors' authority rather than corporate capacity in *Rolled Steel Products (Holdings) Ltd v British Steel Corp* [1986] Ch. 246, but this is not consistent with the reasoning in *David Payne* nor *Sinclair v Brougham* [1914] A.C. 398 and cannot provide the explanation of the *Marseilles* case (see Watts [1986] N.Z.L.J. 270). See also the need for knowledge before shareholders can be required to return ultra vires dividends: *Re Denham & Co* (1883) 25 Ch.D. 752; *Moxham v Grant* [1900] 1 Q.B. 88. cf. *Fountaine v Carmarthen Railway Co* (1868) L.R. 5 Eq. 316; *Chapleo v Brunswick Permanent Building Society* (1881) 6 Q.B.D. 696 (where, however, it was suggested there was a duty of inquiry that had not been met by the outside party).

[113] See above, para.2-009. See also *Mason v Clarke* [1955] A.C. 778 at 794 (voidness for illegality).

[114] See below, para.8-031.

[115] *Hawkins v Kemp* (1803) 3 East 410. See also *Ingram v Ingram* (1740) 2 Atk. 88 (special power of appointment). Aliter, if the duty is merely ministerial: *LCC v Hobbis* (1897) 75 L.T. 688.

[116] *Speight v Gaunt* (1883–84) 9 App.Cas. 1; *Fry v Tapson* (1885) 28 Ch.D. 268; *Learoyd v Whiteley* (1887) 12 App.Cas. 727. cf. the position of executors, any one of whom can generally bind the others in relation to the affairs of an estate: *Birdseye v Roythorne & Co* [2015] EWHC 1003 (Ch).

[117] Trustee Delegation Act 1999; Trustee Act 2000 ss.11–23; Snell, *Equity* (33rd edn), paras 28-016–28-025; Lewin, *Trusts* (19th edn), para.29-093 onwards.

[118] See *McLellan Properties Ltd v Roberge* [1947] S.C.R. 561 (ratification by trustee); *Fielden v Christie-Miller* [2015] EWHC 87 (Ch); *Preedy v Dunne* [2015] EWHC 2713 (Ch).

Historically, individual executors (and it appears administrators), in contrast to trustees, can act alone without the consent of their colleagues in the disposition of personalty, and can also delegate their powers to one of their number.[119] This power of delegation has been extended by statute.[120]

It has been held that an affidavit verifying documents cannot be sworn by the holder of a power of attorney,[121] and where Chitty J delegated the appointment of the official liquidator of a company to his chief clerk, the appointment was held invalid.[122]

2-022   **Signature by proxy**   As a general rule, "at common law a person sufficiently 'signs' a document if it is signed in his name and with his authority by somebody else".[123] An indication that the signature is *per procurationem* is desirable but not essential.[124] Thus it was held that an agent might subscribe the name of his principal to the memorandum of association of a company,[125] or the instrument of dissolution of a building society,[126] and such a signature still seems sufficient compliance with the similar wording of the present Companies Act 2006 s.8, and the Building Societies Act 1986 s.87(1), respectively. But there may be cases where a statute requires personal signature: thus it was held that an agent could not sign a proposal for a scheme of composition under the Bankruptcy Act 1914 s.16(1).[127] There is conflicting authority as to whether a statute requiring signature "under the hand of" a person permits signature by an agent.[128] The better view seems to be that it does not. In relation to companies, where a statute requires signature in person, it is likely

---

[119] See *Fountain Forestry Ltd v Edwards* [1975] Ch. 1; *Birdseye v Roythorne & Co* [2015] EWHC 1003 (Ch); [2015] W.T.L.R. 961.

[120] Administration of Estates Act 1925 s.2(2).

[121] *Clauss v Pir* [1988] Ch. 267. *Clauss v Pir* was distinguished in *General Legal Council Ex p. Whitter v Frankson* [2006] UKPC 42; [2006] 1 W.L.R. 2803 at [10] where the affidavit was designed to function as a statement of complaint rather than as evidence (son held entitled to make affidavit on behalf of mother).

[122] *Re Great Southern Mysore Gold Mining Co* (1882) 48 L.T. 11.

[123] *LCC v Agricultural Foods Products Ltd* [1955] 2 Q.B. 218 at 223–224, per Romer LJ. See also *R. v Kent JJ.* (1872–73) L.R. 8 Q.B. 305 (notice of appeal); *France v Dutton* [1891] 2 Q.B. 208 (solicitor's claim for costs); Bills of Exchange Act 1882 s.91(1); *Tennant v LCC* (1957) 121 J.P. 428 (notice to terminate tenancy); *Barrett v Bem* [2012] EWCA Civ 52; [2012] Ch. 573 (signing of will on behalf of testator under Wills Act 1837 s.9, not established on facts); *Newbold v Coal Authority* [2013] EWCA Civ 584; [2014] 1 W.L.R. 1288 at [58]; *Ramsay v Love* [2015] EWHC 65 (Ch) at [7]; *Elim Court RTM Company Ltd v Avon Freeholds Ltd* [2017] EWCA Civ 89; [2017] H.L.R. 18 at [48] (not fatal that authorised signatory purported to sign in another capacity).

[124] *LCC v Agricultural Food Products Ltd*, above, at p.223. cf. *Nielsen v Capital Finance Australia Ltd* [2014] QCA 139; [2014] 2 Qd R. 459 (execution by attorney in own name using power of attorney acceptable where not a deed).

[125] *Re Whitley Partners Ltd* (1886) 32 Ch.D. 337.

[126] *Dennison v Jeffs* [1896] 1 Ch. 611.

[127] *Re Prince Blücher Ex p. Debtor* [1931] 2 Ch. 70. This case has now been disapproved in *General Legal Council, Ex p. Whitter v Frankson* [2006] UKPC 42; [2006] 1 W.L.R. 2803 at [7]. For examples where it was concluded that the drafting required personal signature, see, *Cascades and Quayside Ltd v Cascades Freehold Ltd* [2007] EWCA Civ 1555; [2008] L. & T.R. 23; *Hilmi & Associates Ltd v 20 Pembridge Villas Freehold Ltd* [2010] EWCA Civ 314; [2010] 1 W.L.R. 2750 (Leasehold Reform Housing and Urban Development Act 1993).

[128] *Wilson v Wallani* (1880) 5 Ex.D. 155; but cf. *Re Diptford Parish Lands* [1934] Ch. 151. See also *Hyde v Johnson* (1836) 2 Bing. N.C. 776 ("signed by the party chargeable thereby").

that compliance with the execution provisions of s.44(2) of the Companies Act 2006 will be required.[129]

Form of signature The reference above to signature "in his name" can be taken   **2-023**
to suggest that the agent should write the principal's name first, adding, if he desires, his own signature below, and there is further support for such a requirement in the case cited.

"On this view if Richard Roe wished to sign as agent for John Doe he can sign John Doe by his agent Richard Roe, but he cannot sign Richard Roe as agent for John Doe."[130]

This would be the rule unless there was an indication in the relevant wording that the agent could sign his own name first, indicating if desired the person for whom he had signed. The latter procedure is justified, for example, in the case of the Statute of Frauds, which contemplated signature by an agent "thereunto lawfully authorised"[131] and by the Powers of Attorney Act 1971,[132] which refers in s.7 to signature and other acts by the agent "in his own name". However, despite the above dicta, the inflexibility of such reasoning (the burden of which would be quite unknown to most signers who had not taken legal advice and to many who had) may be doubted: it has been said in the Australian decisions[133] that such requisites for ordinary signature by an agent should not be rigidly insisted on, at least unless the wording of the enabling provision appears to require it.[134] The crucial question must surely be whether signature by an agent is permissible: so long as the purport of such a signature is clear, it is difficult to see that the form should be of particular consequence. It seems also that an electronic signature may suffice for the purposes of the Statute of Frauds and its amending Acts.[135]

Right to be represented before courts and tribunals The right to be represented   **2-024**
in court, and restrictions on the use of agents to carry out "restricted legal activities", is settled by statute.[136] Converse difficulties can arise where a person seeks to be legally (or otherwise) represented before a domestic or statutory tribunal before which he is entitled or bound to appear, but which by its rules, or in the exercise of its discretion to control its own proceedings, does not wish to permit legal (or any) representation. There is some authority for applying the general

---

[129] See *Hilmi & Associates Ltd v 20 Pembridge Villas Freehold Ltd* [2010] EWCA Civ 314; [2010] 1 W.L.R. 2750 at [31]. As to the requirements of the Companies Act 2006 s.44, and the application of that section where there is a lack of actual authority, see below, para.8-039.
[130] *McRae v Coulton* (1989) 7 N.S.W.L.R. 644 at 664, per Hope JA. See also *UBAF Ltd v European American Banking Corp* [1982] Q.B. 713; Article 91.
[131] *Graham v Musson* (1839) 5 Bing. N.C. 603.
[132] As amended by Law of Property (Miscellaneous Provisions) Act 1989 Schs 1 and 2.
[133] See *McRae v Coulton*, above, at 666; *Nielsen v Capital Finance Australia Ltd* [2014] QCA 139.
[134] See 664. An example is s.91 of the Bills of Exchange Act 1882, which provides that it is "sufficient if his signature is written thereon by some other person or under his authority".
[135] *Lindsay v O'Loughnane* [2010] EWHC 529 (QB); [2012] B.C.C. 153 at [95]; *Golden Ocean Group Ltd v Salgaocar Mining Industries PVT Ltd* [2012] EWCA Civ 265; [2012] 1 W.L.R. 3674 at [32]; affg [2011] EWHC 56 (Comm); [2011] 1 W.L.R. 2575 at [95]; *WS Tankship II BV v The Kwangju Bank Ltd* [2011] EWHC 3103 (Comm) at [155]; *Ramsay v Love* [2015] EWHC 65 (Ch) at [7].
[136] Legal Services Act 2007: see *Gregory v Turner* [2003] EWCA Civ 183; [2003] 1 W.L.R. 1149; and *Avinue Ltd v Sunrule Ltd* [2003] EWCA Civ 1942; [2004] 1 W.L.R. 634; *Ndole Assets Ltd v Designer M&E Services UK Ltd* [2017] EWHC 1148 (TCC). As to making an affidavit by an agent, see above, para.2-021.

private law principles of agency to such cases.[137] Viewed from the standpoint of public law, on the other hand, it may be said that the requirements of natural justice do not often demand professional representation or even representation at all[138] and that a tribunal may have perfectly good reasons for seeking to exclude such representation (though exclusion of professional representation is easier to justify than exclusion of all representation). It may be suggested that agency reasoning is not really relevant: the matter is one of contract and natural justice.[139] In the case of a domestic tribunal, although contractual terms contrary to the requirements of natural justice are probably unenforceable,[140] a clear contractual provision or rule excluding representation would normally not contravene those requirements and so would be valid[141]: but in the control of its own proceedings the tribunal may not adopt an absolute rule of no representation[142] and should retain a discretion to allow or disallow representation for good reason.[143] In the case of a statutory tribunal the matter is frequently settled by statute or delegated legislation.[144] In the absence of such guidance, it seems again that general agency reasoning is not relevant, and that there is no right to representation even where the facts under investigation may constitute a crime.[145]

2-025 **Authority to act illegally** An issue that has not received much attention is whether a principal can expressly authorise an agent to act illegally.[146] In principle, there is no reason why such authority cannot be given as a matter of law, and in practice it must be a common occurrence.[147] Actual authority to act illegally will

---

[137] *R. v Assessment Committee of St Mary Abbotts, Kensington* [1891] 1 Q.B. 378; *R. v Board of Appeal Ex p. Kay* (1916) 22 C.L.R. 183; *Pett v Greyhound Racing Association Ltd* [1969] 1 Q.B. 125.
[138] *Pett v Greyhound Racing Association Ltd (No.2)* [1970] 1 Q.B. 46; *Enderby Town Football Club Ltd v Football Association Ltd* [1971] Ch. 591.
[139] *Kok Seng Chong v Bukit Turf Club* [1993] 2 Singapore L.R. 388.
[140] See *Faramus v Film Artistes Association* [1964] A.C. 925 at 941; *Edwards v SOGAT* [1971] Ch. 354 at 376, 381; *Enderby Town Football Club Ltd v Football Association Ltd*, above, at 606.
[141] *Enderby Town Football Club Ltd v Football Association*, above. But Lord Denning MR thought that an absolute exclusion without the possibility of exceptions might be invalid: at 607.
[142] Save for obvious cases such as representation by a "manifestly improper person": see *R. v Assessment Committee of St Mary Abbotts, Kensington* [1891] 1 Q.B. 378.
[143] See *Enderby Town Football Club Ltd v Football Association Ltd*, above, at 605–606, suggesting that where serious consequences are in issue, representation may be more appropriate; *R. v Visiting Justice at H.M. Prison, Pentridge* [1975] V.R. 883.
[144] e.g. the Police (Conduct) Regulations 2012 (SI 2012/2632) reg.7.
[145] *R. v Board of Visitors of H.M. Prison, The Maze* [1988] A.C. 379, following *Fraser v Mudge* [1975] 1 W.L.R. 1132 and *R. v Secretary of State for the Home Department Ex p. Tarrant* [1985] Q.B. 251. See also *R. v Visiting Justice of H.M. Prison, Pentridge* [1975] V.R. 883; *Kok Seng Chong v Bukit Turf Club* [1993] 2 Singapore L.R. 388; Craig, *Administrative Law* (7th edn), para.12-027 onwards.
[146] See the more detailed treatment of the issues in Watts [2011] J.B.L. 213.
[147] It seems that, at least under companies statutes which confer unlimited capacity on companies, it would be intra vires the board of directors to commit the company to illegal action: see *Morgan v Babcock & Wilcox Ltd* (1929) 43 C.L.R. 163 at 173–174; *Australian Agricultural Co v Oatmont Pty Ltd* (1992) 8 A.C.S.R. 255 at 265; *Sabaf SpA v MFI Furniture Centres Ltd* [2002] EWCA Civ 976; [2003] R.P.C. 264. The Companies Act 2006 s.39 does not go as far as other jurisdictions in expressly conferring capacity on companies (see, e.g. Corporations Act 2001 (Aust.) s.124; Companies Act 1993 (NZ) s.16). See too *Bowman v Secular Society* [1917] A.C. 406 at 438–439 (but cf. Lord Sumner at 454); *Campbell v Paddington Corp* [1911] 1 K.B. 869 at 878. As to the possibility of a company's engaging in a conspiracy to act illegally with its officers and employees, see *Barclay Pharmaceuticals Ltd v Waypharm LP* [2012] EWHC 306 (Comm) at [229] (for criticism, see Watts, in Busch, Macgregor and Watts (eds), *Agency Law in Commercial Practice* (2016), Ch.5).

not usually be implied.[148] However, the authority of a board of directors of a company to act illegally on its behalf and to authorise delegates to act illegally can probably be taken to be implied. At least before the judgments of the Supreme Court in *Patel v Mirza*,[149] the issue of actual authority or lack of it in relation to a principal's rights and duties under a contract affected by illegality would be of little relevance; where the illegality was known to the third party,[150] no rights or duties would generally arise under an illegal contract, whether that contract was between the principal and agent,[151] or one between principal and third party.[152] On the other hand, authorisation of fraud would not preclude a contract arising between the principal and third party; the contract might be voidable at the option of the defrauded party.[153] The majority judgments in *Patel* now support a more flexible approach to the enforceability of contracts affected by illegality. In these circumstances, it may become important for a principal faced with a claim to enforce a contract that might formerly have been treated as illegal to take the point that there was no contract, not because of illegality, but because the relevant agents had no authority to make it. Arguments of this sort have always had potential relevance where what is being sought is recovery of money or other property transferred under a contract affected by illegality. If the principal did not authorise the actual or proposed illegal action, in principle his rights to recover property (purportedly) transferred by the agent should not be affected by the maxim ex turpi causa non oritur actio.[154] In relation to restitutionary claims, *Patel* has now adopted an approach which presumptively gives a party to an illegal transaction (at least where the transaction has not been executed) a right to recover money or other property. Even so, to the extent that this regime does give an automatic right of recovery, it may remain important for a principal to take the point that the activity was not in any event authorised if in fact that was true. Equally, a principal who did authorise illegal action will not be able straightforwardly to disown it.[155]

A principal's liability in tort does not usually turn on whether or not the agent's conduct was expressly authorised (apart perhaps from those torts requiring an assumption of responsibility). Hence the question whether the principal authorised illegal activity which causes damage to the claimant may be sufficient for liability but will not usually be necessary, at least where the agent is an employee and vicari-

[148] *Mackay v Commercial Bank of New Brunswick* (1874) L.R. 5 P.C. 394 at 411. As to unlawful customs, see below, para.3-038. The payment of bribes is normally outside the actual or apparent authority of an agent: see *E. Hannibal & Co Ltd v Frost* (1988) 4 B.C.C. 3, Illustration 4 to Article 29.
[149] *Patel v Mirza* [2016] UKSC 42; [2017] A.C. 467.
[150] Where the illegality was unknown to the third party, the agent may have apparent authority to make the contract: see *Gurtner v Beaton* [1993] 2 Lloyd's Rep. 369.
[151] See, e.g. *RTA (Business Consultants) Ltd v Bracewell* [2015] EWHC 630 (QB); [2015] Bus. L.R. 800. As to an agent's duty to account to the principal for money received in relation to illegal activity, see below, para.6-099, and as to the effect of illegality on rights to commission, para.7-051.
[152] See in general, Chitty, *Contracts* (32nd edn), Ch.16. See also *Safeway Stores Ltd v Twigger* [2010] EWHC 11 (Comm); [2010] 2 Lloyd's Rep. 39 at [71]–[72]; reversed on other issues [2010] EWCA Civ 1472; [2011] 1 Lloyd's Rep. 462 (discussed Watts [2011] J.B.L. 214).
[153] *Shalson v Russo* [2005] Ch. 281 at 316.
[154] See, e.g. *Belmont Finance Corp Ltd v Williams Furniture Ltd* [1979] Ch. 250 at 261; and *Belmont Finance Corp v Williams (No.2)* [1980] 1 All E.R. 393 (also explicable as a case where the relevant statutory provision was designed to protect the company from the conduct in question). As to rights to recover property wrongly disposed of by an agent, see below, Articles 88 and 96.
[155] *Bilta (UK) Ltd v Nazir (No.2)* [2015] UKSC 23; [2016] A.C. 1 at [29], [48]–[49], disapproving dicta to the opposite effect in *Stone & Rolls Ltd v Moore Stephens* [2009] UKHL 39; [2009] 1 A.C. 1391 at [8], [27]–[28].

ous liability is in play.[156] Where it is a question whether a principal is liable to some criminal or civil penalty for illegal conduct committed by an agent, the liability of the principal will usually turn on the construction of the relevant statute.[157]

Illustrations

2-026 (1) A bill of sale may be executed by an attorney on behalf of the grantor, and the grantee of the bill of sale is not necessarily incapable of acting as such attorney.[158]

(2) An agent may be appointed to execute a deed of arrangement.[159]

(3) A partner may exercise his right to inspect and take copies from partnership books under s.24(9) of the Partnership Act 1890 by means of an agent to whom no reasonable objection could be taken by his co-partners.[160]

(4) Where the rules of a trade union provided that its books should be open to the inspection of all the members, the members might inspect the books by means of an accountant, the accountant undertaking to use the information obtained only to inform his clients of the results of the inspection.[161] Similarly, a "person interested" under the Public Health Act 1875 s.247(4), was entitled to inspect the books and accounts of a local authority by means of an accountant.[162]

(5) A tenancy agreement provided that if the landlords, the LCC, wished to determine the tenancy, it must be by "a written notice signed by the valuer to the council". The name of the valuer to the council appeared as signatory to a notice to quit, but his name had been written on the document by an assistant valuer, and there was no indication that the signature was by proxy. Held, the signature was valid provided the valuer had authorised the signature.[163]

(6) A "sampling officer" under food and drugs legislation may purchase or take a sample by means of an agent, and lay an information in his own name in respect of an analysis of the sample so procured.[164]

(7) An acknowledgment or part payment under the Limitation Act may be made by or to an agent duly authorised[165]; a right of action may be concealed by

---

156 See para.2-056 and Article 90.

157 See, e.g. *Director General of Fair Trading v Pioneer Concrete (UK) Ltd* [1995] 1 A.C. 456; *Giltrap City Ltd v The Commerce Commission* [2004] 1 N.Z.L.R. 608; *Kemeh v Ministry of Defence* [2014] EWCA Civ 91; [2014] I.C.R. 625. Some statutory regimes expressly define whose acts count as the principal's, see Financial Services and Markets Act 2000 s.90A; Corporate Manslaughter and Corporate Homicide Act 2007 s.1; and Bribery Act 2010 s.7.

158 *Furnivall v Hudson* [1893] 1 Ch. 335.

159 *Re Wilson* [1916] 1 K.B. 382.

160 *Bevan v Webb* [1901] 2 Ch. 59; *Dodd v Amalgamated Marine Workers' Union* [1923] 2 Ch. 236; affd [1924] 1 Ch. 116.

161 *Norey v Keep* [1909] 1 Ch. 561; *Dodd v Amalgamated Marine Workers' Union*, above.

162 *R. v Bedwelty UDC Ex p. Price* [1934] 1 K.B. 333.

163 *LCC v Agricultural Food Products Ltd* [1955] 2 Q.B. 218.

164 See *Tyler v Dairy Supply Co* (1908) 98 L.T. 867; *Garforth v Esam* (1892) 56 J.P. 521; *Horder v Scott* (1880) 5 Q.B.D. 552. The relevant provision is now the Food Safety Act 1990. And see *Foster v Fyfe* [1896] 2 Q.B. 104, a case on the Metalliferous Mines Regulation Act 1872.

165 Limitation Act 1980 s.30(2); see *Wright v Pepin* [1954] 1 W.L.R. 635 (solicitor: authorised); *Re Transplanters (Holding Co) Ltd* [1958] 1 W.L.R. 822 (auditor: not authorised); *Bradford & Bingley Plc v Cutler* [2008] EWCA Civ 74 (Government Benefits Agency pays interest on outstanding mortgage).

fraud for the purposes of the same Act where the fraud is that of an agent[166]; and land may be adversely possessed through an agent.[167]

(8) A notice to quit may be given by and served on an agent.[168]

(9) A declaration under the Law of Distress (Amendment) Act 1908 (repealed as of April 6, 2014[169]) may be signed by an agent.[170]

(10) An option may take effect by an agent giving notice of its exercise.[171]

2. AGENCY ARISING BY CONFERRAL OF AUTHORITY

Article 7

EXPRESS AGREEMENT TO CONFER AUTHORITY

Where there is an express agreement between principal and agent for the confer‑ ral of authority, this will constitute the relationship of principal and agent, and the assent of both parties will be contained in it.

2-027

Comment

This Article commences the working out of the notion of assent stated in Article 1. The simplest way in which agency arises, both between principal and agent and as regards third parties, is by an express appointment whether written or oral, by the principal,[172] and acquiescence by the agent, or person similarly empowered to act for him.

2-028

> "An 'actual' authority is a legal relationship between principal and agent created by a consensual agreement to which they alone are parties. Its scope is to be ascertained by ap‑ plying ordinary principles of construction of contracts, including any proper implica‑ tions from the express words used, the usages of the trade, or the course of business between the parties."[173]

The agreement may be accompanied by or even contained in a contract, to which the normal rules as to offer and acceptance, consideration, mistake, misrepresenta‑ tion,[174] duress,[175] illegality, etc., apply, and the relations between principal and agent are regulated by the normal law of contract. But the conferral of authority is not

---

[166] Limitation Act 1980 s.32(1); see *Applegate v Moss* [1971] 1 Q.B. 406 (concealment by builder act‑ ing as independent contractor to developer); *King v Victor Parsons & Co* [1973] 1 W.L.R. 29; *Lewisham LBC v Leslie & Co Ltd* (1978) 250 E.G. 1289; cf. *Thorne v Heard* [1895] A.C. 495.

[167] *Lyell v Kennedy* (1889) L.R. 14 App.Cas. 437. See in general Prime and Scanlan, *Modern Law of Limitation* (2nd edn), Ch.3; Oughton, Lowry and Merkin, *Limitation of Actions* (1998).

[168] *Jones v Phipps* (1867–68) L.R. 3 Q.B. 567; *Harmond Properties Ltd v Gajdzis* [1968] 1 W.L.R. 1858; *Townsends Carriers Ltd v Pfizer Ltd* (1977) 33 P. & C.R. 361; *Tanham v Nicholson* (1871– 72) L.R. 5 H.L. 561; *Galinski v McHugh* [1989] 1 E.G.L.R. 109; *Dun & Bradstreet Software Services (England) Ltd v Provident Mutual Life Assurance Assn* [1998] 2 E.G.L.R. 175; *Yenula Properties Ltd v Naidu* [2002] EWCA Civ 719; [2002] 3 E.G.L.R. 28.

[169] See Tribunals, Courts and Enforcement Act 2007 Sch.23.

[170] *Lawrence Chemical Co. Ltd v Rubinstein* [1982] 1 W.L.R. 284.

[171] *Mineaplenty Pty Ltd v Trek 31 Pty Ltd* (2007) A.N.Z. Conveyancing R. 123 at [38].

[172] See Article 9 as to formalities.

[173] *Freeman & Lockyer v Buckhurst Park Properties (Mangal) Ltd* [1964] 2 Q.B. 480 at 502, per Diplock LJ. For informal extension of initial authority, see *Aviva Life & Pensions UK Ltd v Strand Street Properties Ltd* [2010] EWCA Civ 444.

[174] See *Bristol and West Building Society v Mothew* [1998] Ch. 1 at 22.

itself contractual, and it will not be where there is no consideration, or the agent lacks contractual capacity.[176] Sometimes there will be neither conferral nor contract, e.g. where so much coercion is applied to the principal that there is no real consent to the agency.[177]

Many illustrations will be found in Chapter 3, which deals with the agent's authority, for, as throughout the law of agency, there is much overlap between the question whether a person is agent of another, and whether he has the authority of that other.

Article 8

IMPLIED AGREEMENT

2-029   Agreement between principal and agent for the conferral of authority may be implied in a case where one party has conducted himself towards another in such a way that it is reasonable for that other to infer from that conduct assent to an agency relationship.

Comment

2-030   No special rules of law peculiar to agency are involved here: this Article simply represents, in the sphere of agency, the obvious proposition that contracts are not always expressly made, but often inferred by the court from the circumstances.[178] The same principle applies to non-contractual liability.

> "While agency must ultimately derive from consent, the consent need not necessarily be to the relationship of principal and agent itself (indeed the existence of it may be denied) but it may be to a state of fact upon which the law imposes the consequences which result from agency."[179]

In accordance with the usage in *Restatement, Third*, "consent" is replaced by "assent".[180]

The principle stated in this Article must not be confused with the notions of apparent authority and applications of estoppel, whereby a third party is in certain cases entitled to assume, from the conduct of the principal, that the agent has author-

---

[175] See *Haines Bros Earthmoving Pty Ltd v Rosecell Pty Ltd* [2016] NSWCA 112 (no authority where de facto controller of company had taken over its affairs as a result of physical duress applied to its shareholder and director).

[176] See Articles 4 and 5 as to capacity; Article 42 as to gratuitous agents.

[177] See *Haines Bros Earthmoving Pty Ltd v Rosecell Pty Ltd* [2016] NSWCA 112, above.

[178] See *Garnac Grain Co Inc v HMF Faure and Fairclough Ltd* [1968] A.C. 1130n at 1137; *Ashford Shire Council v Dependable Motors Pty Ltd* [1961] A.C. 336 at 349–350; *Reynell v Lewis* (1846) 15 M. & W. 517. The distinction between express contract and implied contract is of doubtful utility. "A contract implied in fact is like any other contract in legal effect: it differs from an express contract only in that the promise is expressed, wholly or in part, by conduct rather than by words": Mechem, *Outlines of Agency* (4th edn), p.28. In *Targe Towing Ltd v Marine Blast Ltd* [2004] EWCA Civ 346; [2004] 1 Lloyd's Rep. 721 the Court of Appeal disapproved a formulation that for implied agreement the relevant act must be necessarily incident to the commercial venture upon which the parties were to engage.

[179] *Branwhite v Worcester Works Finance Ltd* [1969] 1 A.C. 552 at 587, per Lord Wilberforce (dissenting). See further Fridman (1968) 84 L.Q.R. 224.

[180] See above, para.1-006.

ity, even where this is not so.[181] The reasonable interpretation must in the present case be applied to determine whether it is reasonable for the agent to think that he has been appointed or authorised, and likewise as regards the principal in respect of the agent: not, as in the case mentioned above, whether the third party is entitled to assume that the agent has authority. In some cases, of course, the court is not considering whether relations exist between principal and agent, nor even whether relations exist between principal and third party, but merely whether a person is an "agent" for the purpose of some statute: in this inquiry the two considerations mentioned may, but need not, be determinative.

Assent of the principal Assent of the principal may be implied when he places   **2-031**
another in such a situation that, according to ordinary usage, that person would understand himself to have the principal's authority to act on his behalf[182]: or where the principal's words or conduct, coming to the knowledge of the agent, are such as to lead to the reasonable inference that he is authorising the agent to act for him.[183] But where one person purports to act on behalf of another, the assent of that other will not be presumed merely from his silence, unless there is further indication that he acquiesces in the agency.[184] The substance of the matter is more important than the form: a contract describing the parties as principal and agent is not conclusive that they are such,[185] and conversely there may be an agency relationship though the agreement creating it purports to exclude the possibility.[186] It will be rare, however, that it would be appropriate to ignore an express denial of agency, at least outside a statutory or regulatory context, since agency is in general a voluntary relationship.

Assent of the agent It is traditional to state that the agent's assent (or consent)   **2-032**
is required,[187] and to discuss the ways in which this can be implied from acts or waived by the principal. Consent is certainly relevant to the relationship between principal and agent: only mutual consent will give rise to a contract, rendering the agent liable for non-performance of what he has undertaken; and the duties arising in non-contractual agency would normally only do so if there was consent to the relationship. But as regards the position between principal and third party, the relevant act is the conferring of authority.[188] It is suggested above that the basis of agency is a unilateral manifestation of will: a power of attorney, for instance, does

---

[181] Articles 21 and 72.
[182] See *Pole v Leask* (1863) 33 L.J.Ch. 155 at 161–162; see too *Technology Leasing Ltd v Lennmar Pty Ltd* [2012] FCA 709 at [158].
[183] *Little v Spreadbury* [1910] 2 K.B. 658; *Ashford Shire Council v Dependable Motors Pty Ltd*, above, at p.349; *Restatement, Third*, § 3.01 ("manifestation").
[184] *Dixon v Broomfield* (1814) 2 Chit. 205; *Burnside v Dayrell* (1849) 3 Exch. 224. As to ratification by silence, see below, para.2-079.
[185] *Nouvelles Huileries Anversoises SA v HC Mann & Co* (1924) 40 T.L.R. 804; *Motor Union Insurance Co. Ltd v Mannheimer Versicherungs Gesellschaft* [1933] 1 K.B. 812; *Kennedy v De Trafford* [1897] A.C. 180 at 188. See also above, paras 1-004 and 1-036.
[186] *Re Megevand Ex p. Delhasse* (1878) 7 Ch.D. 511; *Garnac Grain Co Inc v H.M.F. Faure and Fairclough Ltd* [1968] A.C. 1130n at 1137; *South Sydney DRLFC v News Ltd* (2000) 177 A.L.R. 611 at 645 onwards (a useful discussion of the general principles by Finn J).
[187] See, e.g. *Garnac Grain Co Inc v HMF Faure and Fairclough Ltd* [1968] A.C. 1130n at 1137; *Freeman & Lockyer v Buckhurst Park Properties (Mangal) Ltd* [1964] 2 Q.B. 480 at 501.
[188] cf. Müller-Freienfels (1964) 13 Am.J.Comp.L. 193 at 203.

not require acceptance by the donee of the power.[189] When all that is in issue is whether the supposed agent's act was authorised, it may not be necessary that the agent's assent should have been manifested at all, provided the authority has clearly been conferred. Thus when the principal confers authority on the agent, and the agent purports to act on the principal's behalf, he is not permitted to deny that it was on the principal's behalf that he acted.[190] On the other hand the agent must have purported to act for the principal: he will not be regarded as doing so merely because he does what was authorised or requested without other indications.[191] The idea that the conferring of authority is a unilateral act could be argued to have the further consequence that provided it is proved that the principal has conferred authority (as for example where he tells someone else that he is doing or has done so) the agent is authorised though there is no manifestation to him at all. For example, the principal may grant authority by renewing or extending an existing authority, and the agent may act on the principal's behalf without knowing of this, perhaps because the communication has not reached him,[192] because he has forgotten that his authority has lapsed,[193] because he wrongly thinks that his existing authority covers the matter in question,[194] or simply because he decides to take a risk. It is arguable that in such situations the agent should be regarded as authorised. Such reasoning is certainly accepted where what the principal does is ratify the agent's act: there is no need that the ratification be communicated to the agent.[195] Both *Restatement, Second* and *Restatement, Third* are clear however that in such circumstances the agent is not to be regarded as authorised by virtue of such facts alone: a manifestation by the principal to the agent is required for actual authority, and one by the principal to the third party for apparent authority.[196] It may then be asked why this is not so for ratification, which in many respects is likened to a conferring of prior authority. The answer may be that a consent to future acts is a serious enough matter to require communication, because *ex hypothesi* the exact nature of the future acts may not be known, and also because the agent may need to act on the communication in the future; whereas an adoption of something known already to have been done only requires proof that the principal "has exercised choice and has consented" to what is *ex hypothesi* known about, and, further, has no significance as to the future.[197] The view that if it can be established that an act was authorised even though neither the agent nor the relevant third party was told, this is enough to hold the principal, is not however without merit. It would of course frequently be possible in such a case to prove ratification, or sufficient manifestation to a third party to create apparent authority.

---

[189] See above, para.1-006. This is not, however, true of a lasting power of attorney under the Mental Capacity Act 2005, which requires execution by donor and attorney (Sch.1, replacing Enduring Powers of Attorney Act 1985 s.2(1)). See further below, para.10-009.
[190] See *Roberts v Ogilby* (1821) 9 Price 269; *Moore v Peachey* (1891) 7 T.L.R. 748 (receipt of money by agent).
[191] See *Kennedy v De Trafford* [1897] A.C. 180; Powell, p.297. See too *Cromwell Corporation Ltd v Sofrana Immobilier (NZ) Ltd* (1992) 6 N.Z. Company L.C. 67,997 (company director of parent company not intending to bind wholly-owned subsidiary).
[192] As in *Ruggles v American Central Insurance Co of St Louis* 114 N.Y. 415, 76 N.Y. Supp.787 (1889).
[193] See *Restatement, Third*, Illustration 3 to § 2–01.
[194] See *Opp v Wheaton Van Lines* 231 F.3d 1060 (10th Cir. 2000); *Chilsan Merchant Marine Co Ltd v M/V K.Fortune* 110 F.Supp.2d 492 at 497 (E.D.La. 2000).
[195] See below, para.2-076.
[196] See *Restatement, Second*, § 26, Comment a; *Restatement, Third*, §§ 2.01 and 3.01 (note the discussion of the *Ruggles* case, above, in reporter's note b).
[197] See *Restatement, Third*, § 4.01, Comment d.

Dual agency   It has already been seen (above, para.2-013) that there is no outright   **2-033**
bar on an agent acting for more than one party to a contract or other transaction,
including where the parties have opposing interests. Usually, a dual appointment
will be manifested by express agreement. However, dual agency can arise by
implied agreement. While industry practice and previous judicial decisions may create something like a presumption that a person is the agent of one side to a common commercial relationship rather than the other, or agent for both, each case must
ultimately be decided on its facts.[198] A statement in a contract negotiated by an agent
between one party and another that the agent acts for one of the parties is not
conclusive that he only does so, if in some respects he in fact acts for the other.[199]
The fact that commission is paid by one party is not necessarily inconsistent with
the agent's acting for the other party: the source of commission or payments is
relevant but not conclusive in determining an agency relationship.[200] The presence
of a detailed contract between the third party and the agent of the other party may
indicate a dual agency, but is again unlikely to be decisive unless the contract
provides for the third party to be able to direct the agent how to act.[201]

Issues of dual agency can arise in a number of settings. Dual agency is likely to
be particularly relevant when questions of a party's knowledge of potential defects
in the other party's coming to contract are at issue.[202] The fact that an agent is acting in a dual capacity can also be of importance in determining when acceptance
of an offer has been communicated to the offeror, or when an offer has been
revoked.[203] Otherwise, nice questions can arise as to on whose behalf an agent with
multiple principals acts when performing certain acts under the relevant
transaction.[204] So, where an agent dishonestly runs off with the funds intended for
the transaction, it can become important to know in what capacity the dual agent
had possession of the funds.[205] Difficulties in determining the capacity in which an
agent acts can also arise where an agent shares dual roles within a group of
companies. An employee of a parent company, for instance, who is appointed a
director of a subsidiary is not normally assumed to be acting as agent of the parent

---

[198] *Branwhite v Worcester Works Finance Ltd* [1969] 1 A.C. 552 at 573 and 586–587. See further, the
useful discussion in Dal Pont, paras 1.31 and 1.51.

[199] *Commissioners of Customs & Excise v Pools Finance Ltd* [1952] 1 All E.R. 775; *Newcastle United
Plc v Revenue and Customs Commissioners* [2007] EWHC 612 (Ch); [2007] S.T.C. 1330. See also
above, para.2-013.

[200] *Royal Securities Corp v Montreal Trust Co* (1967) 59 D.L.R. (2d) 666; affd (1967) 63 D.L.R. (2d)
15; cf. *Les Affréteurs, etc. v Leopold Walford (London) Ltd* [1919] A.C. 801; *BS Developments No.12
Ltd v PB & SF Properties Ltd*, (2006) 7 N.Z. Conveyancing and Property R. 603; and *Custom Credit
Corp v Lynch* [1993] 2 V.R. 469 (mortgage broker agent for borrower not lender notwithstanding
lender pays commission to broker); *Plevin v Paragon Personal Finance Ltd* [2014] UKSC 61; [2014]
1 W.L.R. 4222 at [33].

[201] See *Tonto Home Loans Australia Pty Ltd v Tavares* [2011] NSWCA 389; *UBS AG (London Branch)
v Kommunale Wasserwerke Leipzig GmbH* [2017] EWCA Civ 1567 at [100]. cf. *South Sydney
DRLFC v News Ltd*, (2000) 177 A.L.R. 611 at [155]–[156].

[202] See below, para.8-209.

[203] *Powierza v Daley* [1985] 1 N.Z.L.R. 558, Illustration 10; *BS Developments No.12 Ltd v PB & SF
Properties Ltd* (2006) 7 N.Z. Conveyancing and Property R. 603 (vendor's estate agent held agent
for purchaser also, and had authority from purchaser to give written notice to solicitor for vendor
of purchaser's decision to terminate agreement). See too Dal Pont, at paras 1.51 to 1.55.

[204] See, e.g. *Oldendorff GmbH & Co KG v Sea Powerful Ii Special Maritime Enterprises (The Zagora)*
[2016] EWHC 3212 (Comm); [2017] 1 Lloyd's Rep. 194 at [23] (delivery of cargo to shipping agent
which held appointments from both the shipowner and the buyer).

[205] See *Aldermore Bank Plc v Rana* [2015] EWCA Civ 1210; [2016] 1 W.L.R. 2209.

when making decisions in his capacity as a director,[206] but regard must always be had to the particular circumstances.[207] Equally, the fact that one of the directors of a debtor is also a director of the creditor would not automatically confer authority on the director to communicate acknowledgement of the debt by the debtor.[208]

Illustrations

2-034 (1) A called at B's office and orally agreed to be responsible for the price of certain goods to be supplied by B to a third person. B's clerk, in A's presence, made and signed a memorandum of the agreement. Held, that the clerk had no implied authority to sign as A's agent, and that there was not a sufficient memorandum in writing of the agreement to satisfy s.4 of the Statute of Frauds.[209]

(2) Property is sold under a decree. The solicitor having the management of the sale is, in the conduct of it, deemed to be the agent of all the parties to the suit, as between them and the purchaser.[210]

(3) Where a letter of credit is opened, the issuing bank and the confirming bank are in the positions, at any rate in some respects, of principal and agent respectively.[211]

(4) Auditors are not agents of the company whose accounts they audit for the purposes of making an acknowledgment under the Limitation Act.[212]

(5) A dealer selling goods on credit may by statute act in the capacity of agent of the finance company which finances the arrangement, as regards antecedent negotiations[213] and for the purpose of receiving notice of withdrawal, cancellation and rescission.[214] He may sometimes be its agent in other respects at common law, e.g. to deliver the goods,[215] and to receive notice of revocation of an offer in circumstances where the statutory regulation does not apply.[216] To some extent the question may turn on whether the payments are to be collected directly by the company, or whether the dealer is to collect them. But while he may be agent for certain purposes, there is no general agency relationship and he acts primarily on his own behalf.[217]

---

[206] See *Kuwait Asia Bank EC v National Mutual Life Nominees Ltd* [1991] 1 A.C. 187 (PC); *LMI Australasia Pty Ltd v Baulderstone Hornibrook Pty Ltd* [2003] NSWCA 74; *Hawkes v Cuddy* [2009] EWCA Civ 291; [2009] 2 B.C.L.C. 427; *F&C Alternative Investments (Holdings) Ltd v Barthelemy* [2011] EWHC 1731 (Ch); [2012] Ch. 613 (directors of limited liability partnership); *Thompson v Renwick Group Plc* [2014] EWCA Civ 635.

[207] *Cromwell Corporation Ltd v Sofrana Immobilier (NZ) Ltd* (1992) 6 N.Z. Company L.C. 67,997.

[208] *Emile Elias and Co Ltd v Attorney General of Trinidad and Tobago* [2011] UKPC 19.

[209] *Dixon v Broomfield* (1814) 2 Chit 205.

[210] *Dalby v Pullen* (1830) 1 Russ. & M. 296.

[211] *Bank Melli Iran v Barclays Bank* [1951] 2 T.L.R. 1057; *European Asian Bank AG v Punjab and Sind Bank (No.2)* [1983] 1 W.L.R. 642; *Credit Agricole Indosuez v Muslim Commercial Bank Ltd* [2000] 1 Lloyd's Rep. 275. See further *Benjamin's Sale of Goods* (9th edn), para.23–029 onwards.

[212] *Re Transplanters (Holding Co) Ltd* [1958] 1 W.L.R. 822.

[213] Consumer Credit Act 1974 s.56. See *Scotland v British Credit Trust Ltd* [2014] EWCA Civ 790; [2014] Bus. L.R. 1079 at [65].

[214] Consumer Credit Act 1974 ss.57, 69 and 102.

[215] *Branwhite v Worcester Works Finance Ltd* [1969] 1 A.C. 552 at 573; *Shogun Finance Ltd v Hudson* [2003] UKHL 62; [2004] 1 A.C. 919 at [52].

[216] *Financings Ltd v Stimson* [1962] 1 W.L.R. 1184; *CF Asset Finance Ltd v Okonji* [2014] EWCA Civ 870 at [22].

[217] *Branwhite v Worcester Works Finance Ltd* [1969] 1 A.C. 552; but the dissenting opinion (on this point) of Lord Wilberforce repays study. See also *Powell v Lloyds Bowmaker Ltd* 1996 S.L.T. (Sh.

(6)   Agents of insurance companies frequently act as agents for persons making insurance proposals to such companies by filling in the forms for them.[218]

(7)   A car is damaged in an accident. The insurers instruct a garage to effect repairs. It is a question of fact whether they do so on their own account or as agent of the assured. Similar rules apply where the assured orders the repairs. The normal interpretation of such a situation seems to be that the repairers contract with the insurers.[219]

(8)   Shop stewards may act as agents for a trade union in negotiation, and in taking industrial action, even contrary to the advice of union officials, provided that they act within union rules or policy.[220] This authority derives from all the members: thus the union also may sometimes act as agent for the members in doing the same.[221] But an official of a trade union who expels a member does not act as that member's agent so as to prevent the member suing for wrongful expulsion.[222]

(9)   A mortgage broker normally acts as agent for borrowers in procuring loans.[223]

(10)   A purchaser's agent who has been instructed to find a suitable commercial property approaches a vendor who also appoints him agent by written mandate. The purchaser makes an offer which is followed by a counter-offer by the vendor, the documents being carried between the parties by the agent. This counter-offer is initially rejected by the purchaser but is then accepted, initialled and given to the agent. Before the vendor is made aware of this outcome, the vendor agrees to sell the property to a third party at a higher price and tells the agent he has done so before the agent is able to inform him of the purchaser's acceptance. The vendor is held liable to the purchaser. It was too late for the vendor to revoke the counter-offer, acceptance of the counter-offer having been communicated to the vendor's agent who had authority to receive it.[224]

Ct.) 117; *Quikfund (Australia) Pty Ltd v Prosperity Group International Pty Limited (In Liquidation)* [2013] FCAFC 5 at [86].

[218] See Article 95, Illustration 2. But insurance brokers act for the assured in placing insurance: see above, para.2-016.

[219] See *Bowers (Maghull) Ltd v Morton* (1940) 67 Lloyd's Rep. 1; *Godfrey Davis Ltd v Culling & Hecht* [1962] 2 Lloyd's Rep. 349; *Cooter & Green Ltd v Tyrrell* [1962] 2 Lloyd's Rep. 377. But cf. *Gebhard Hoelzler Construction Ltd v Seidler* [2008] B.C.C.A. 77.

[220] *Heaton's Transport (St Helens) Ltd v Transport and General Workers' Union* [1973] A.C. 15; *Howitt Transport Ltd v TGWU* [1973] I.C.R. 1; cf. *General Aviation Service (UK) Ltd v TGWU* [1976] I.R.L.R. 224.

[221] See *Chappell v Times Newspapers Ltd* [1975] 1 W.L.R. 482 at 500; *Harris v Richard Lawson Autologistics Ltd* [2002] EWCA Civ 442; [2002] I.C.R. 765.

[222] *Bonsor v Musicians' Union* [1956] A.C. 104. These cases, which were famous when decided, are retained as illustrations of ways in which agency reasoning can be deployed in the area of labour law, and because the general dicta in some of them might on occasion be of use. They should not, however, be regarded as significant authorities on general agency principle; and as to the law now governing the contexts in which they were decided, reference should be made to up-to-date works on labour law.

[223] *Morlend Finance Corp (Vic.) Pty Ltd v Westendorp* [1993] 2 V.R. 284 at 308; *Custom Credit Corp v Lynch* [1993] 2 V.R. 469; *NMFM Property Pty Ltd v Citibank* (2000) 107 F.C.R. 270; *Tonto Home Loans Australia Pty Ltd v Tavares* [2011] NSWCA 389.

[224] *Powierza v Daley* [1985] 1 N.Z.L.R. 558.

Article 9

2-035   Subject to the provisions of Article 10, and except where otherwise expressly provided by or pursuant to any statute, or by the terms of the power or authority (if any) under which the agent is appointed, an agent may be appointed and authority conferred by deed, by writing, or by word of mouth.

Comment

2-036   In general no formalities are required for the creation of agency and the conferral of authority. This is normally so even where the agent is authorised to enter into a contract that is required to be in writing or evidenced in writing, or to sign a memorandum of such a contract.[225] The approach of English law contrasts with that of some other countries, which may require the same form for authorisation as that necessary for the act authorised, or special forms for powers of a general nature.[226] Thus it has been held that authority to subscribe the name of the principal to the memorandum of association of a company, or to the instrument of dissolution of a building society, may be given orally.[227] But some appointments are required by statute to be in writing,[228] and some must be by deed.[229] The most conspicuous example of the latter requirement is a power of attorney.[230]

2-037   **Agent for the purchase of land**   A contract for the purchase of land made by an agent as such (whether his principal is disclosed or undisclosed) vests the equitable estate in the principal, and the contract may be enforced by the principal against both the vendor and the agent, even if the agent was appointed orally, provided that the legal estate has not been conveyed to the agent.[231] When the land has actually been conveyed to the agent so as to vest the legal estate in him, he is trustee for the principal and is not entitled to take advantage of the Law of Property Act 1925 s.53, which provides that a declaration of trust respecting land or any interest therein must be evidenced by writing, because to allow this would be to permit the statute to be used as an instrument of fraud.[232]

2-038   **Exercise of authority on behalf of corporations**   Until 1960 the basic rule was

---

[225] *Coles v Trecothick* (1804) 9 Ves. 234 at 250; *Deverell v Lord Bolton* (1812) 18 Ves. 505 at 509; *Heard v Pilley* (1868–69) L.R. 4 Ch. App.548. Assuming that the writing can be executed through an agent: see Article 6. For "equal dignity" requirements in the United States see *Restatement, Third*, § 2.02, Comment b.

[226] See Müller-Freienfels, in *Civil Law in the Modern World* (Yiannopoulos edn, 1965), 77 at 108–111 (citing comparative material). See also below, para.11-013 as to commercial agents.

[227] *Re Whitley Partners Ltd* (1886) 32 Ch.D. 337; *Dennison v Jeffs* [1896] 1 Ch. 611; above, para.2-022.

[228] e.g. Law of Property Act 1925 ss.53 and 54, which require an agent signing certain types of instrument relating to land to be "lawfully authorised in writing," with certain alternatives. See *Richardson v Landecker* (1950) 50 S.R. (N.S.W.) 250, where it was held in connection with a section similar to s.53 that a company manager had signed as the company, not as its agent, and did not therefore require written authorisation.

[229] e.g. Trustee Act 1925 s.25, as substituted by Trustee Delegation Act 1999 s.5.

[230] See below, para.2-039.

[231] *Heard v Pilley* (1868–69) L.R. 4 Ch.App. 548; *Cave v Mackenzie* (1877) 46 L.J.Ch. 564; *Lowther v Kim* [2003] 1 N.Z.L.R. 327; *Jiao v Barge* (2006) 18 Procedure R.N.Z. 396 (NZSC). See further para.8-004.

[232] *Rochefoucauld v Boustead* [1897] 1 Ch. 196; disapproving the earlier view shown in *Bartlett v*

that a corporation must contract under seal[233]: thus a corporation could only contract using agents who had themselves been appointed under seal. But the rule had many exceptions and was abolished completely by the Corporate Bodies Contracts Act 1960, whereby a corporation can make contracts by means of any person acting under its authority, express or implied, in the same manner as a private person.[234] Thus a corporation can appoint an agent by parol where a private person could do so, by means of any person acting under its authority, express or implied.[235] Companies formed under the relevant companies legislation had long been subject to much more informal requirements, and that generally remains the case under the Companies Act 2006.[236] In circumstances, where authority must be exercised by a board or other committee, normally the board will have actual authority only where the decision results from a properly called and held meeting.[237] Similarly, if the matter requires prior approval by shareholders, normally a resolution will have validity only where the relevant meeting was properly called and held.[238]

Powers of attorney   A power of attorney is "a formal instrument by which one person empowers another to represent him, or act in his stead for certain purposes".[239] It may confer general or particular powers. Before 1971 it was not necessary that such an instrument be a deed, though an unsealed document might not often be called a power of attorney[240] and if the authority to execute deeds was to be conferred it would require to be conferred by deed under the rule stated in the next Article. Now, however, the Powers of Attorney Act 1971 s.1(1), as amended by the Law of Property (Miscellaneous Provisions) Act 1989, requires that instruments creating powers of attorney be executed as deeds: the requirements are given in the next Article. The Act does not define the term "power of attorney": presumably what is referred to is a formal grant of power, especially of general power to represent a person in all matters. It is difficult to believe that it is intended to affect any conferring of authority which could previously have been effected without a deed. Nor does the Act state what is to happen if a power of attorney is executed other than by deed. But where an appointment purports to be by deed, and the document is for some reason ineffective as a deed, the appointment may sometimes be valid as an appointment in writing.[241]

2-039

Pickersgill (1785) 4 East 577n. and *James v Smith* [1891] 1 Ch. 384; *Heard v Pilley*, above, at 553; *Du Boulay v Raggett* (1989) 58 P. & C.R. 138. The trust is said to be constructive in *Paragon Finance Plc. v D.B. Thackerar & Co.* [1999] 1 All E.R. 399 at 408. See Megarry and Wade, *Law of Real Property* (8th edn), para.11–043. See also Article 53.

[233] *Kidderminster Corp v Hardwicke* (1873–74) L.R. 9 Ex. 13; *Cape v Thames Haven Dock, etc., Co* (1849) 3 Exch. 841; *A.R. Wright & Son Ltd v Romford BC* [1957] 1 Q.B. 431.

[234] See s.1(1).

[235] The statute itself should be regarded as the source of the authority of the person appointing the agent.

[236] See s.43.

[237] See *Re Portuguese Consolidated Copper Mines Ltd* (1889) 42 Ch.D. 160; *Young v Ladies' Imperial Club Ltd* [1920] 2 K.B. 525.

[238] *Garden Gully United Quartz Mining Co v McLister* (1875) 1 App.Cas. 39 (PC); *Pacific Coast Coal Mines Ltd v Arbuthnot* [1917] A.C. 607 (PC); *Rose v McGivern* [1998] 2 B.C.L.C. 593.

[239] Jowitt, *Dictionary of English Law* (3rd edn, 2010). See also below, para.3-011.

[240] See Alcock, *Powers of Attorney* (1935), pp.1–2.

[241] See cases cited at fn.253 below.

Article 10

AUTHORITY TO EXECUTE A DEED

2-040   Where an agent is authorised to execute a deed on behalf of his principal, his authority must be given in a deed,[242] except where the deed is signed at the direction and in the presence of the principal and of two witnesses who each attest the signature.[243]

Comment

2-041   Certain acts must by law be performed by deed, notably conveyances and many leases. In these cases authority to an agent to execute such a deed must itself be given by deed, usually called a power of attorney. This formerly applied not only to authority to execute a deed, but also to authority to fill up a deed partly executed,[244] or to deliver a deed already sealed,[245] for it was "well-known law that an agent cannot execute a deed, or do any part of the execution which makes it a deed, unless he is appointed under seal".[246] It is not, however, now necessary that deeds be sealed at all; and authority (given, e.g. to a solicitor) to deliver a deed need no longer be given by deed.[247] It has long been established also that a deed may be executed for another in his presence by an amanuensis[248]; and this practice now has statutory authority, requiring the attestation of two witnesses instead of the one normally required.[249]

2-042   **Powers of attorney**   By virtue of the Powers of Attorney Act 1971, as amended,[250] s.1, an instrument creating a power of attorney[251] must be executed as a deed by, or by direction and in the presence of, the donor of the power; in the first case one and in the latter two witnesses are required to attest the instrument. Under s.25 of the Trustee Act 1925 (as substituted by s.5 of the Trustee Delegation Act 1999) a trustee may under certain conditions delegate his powers by power of attorney.[252]

   Where an agent not appointed by deed purports to execute a deed, the document may be taken to have a lesser effect if the intended result could in fact be

---

[242] *Steiglitz v Eglinton* (1815) Holt N.P. 141; *Berkeley v Hardy* (1826) 5 B. & C. 355; Powers of Attorney Act 1971 ss.1 and 7. See also *Vella v Permanent Mortgages Pty Ltd* [2008] NSWSC 505 at [206].

[243] Law of Property (Miscellaneous Provisions) Act 1989 s.1(3).

[244] *Hibblewhite v M'Morine* (1840) 6 M. & W. 200.

[245] *Windsor Refrigerator Co v Branch Nominees Ltd* [1961] Ch. 88.

[246] *Powell v London and Provincial Bank* [1893] 2 Ch. 555 at 563, per Bowen LJ. See also *Phoenix Properties Ltd v Wimpole Street Nominees Ltd* [1992] B.C.L.C. 737; *Lift Capital Partners Pty Ltd v Merrill Lynch International* (2009) 73 N.S.W.L.R. 404 at [37].

[247] Law of Property (Miscellaneous Provisions) Act 1989 s.1(1).

[248] *R. v Longnor (Inhabitants)* (1833) 4 B. & Ad. 647; *Ball v Dunsterville* (1791) 4 T.R. 313.

[249] Law of Property (Miscellaneous Provisions) Act 1989 s.1(3).

[250] By Law of Property (Miscellaneous Provisions) Act 1989 Sch.1.

[251] As to the meaning of this term, see Comment to Article 9.

[252] The Act also makes provision for proof of powers of attorney (s.3), and provides a form of general power of attorney (s.10 and Sch.1). Depositing or filing of instruments creating powers of attorney is not necessary: s.2. The donee may normally execute any instrument, sign or do any act in his own name; s.7. See in general *Law Com. No.30*, Cmnd. 4473 (1970); (1971) New L.J. 746 at 751, 764, 771, 795; (1971) 115 S.J. 596; (1971) 35 Conv (N.S.) 310; (1971) 68 L.S.Gaz. 434 at 437; Land Registration (Powers of Attorney) Rules 1986 (SI 1986/1537); Aldridge, *Powers of Attorney* (10th edn); Thurston, *Powers of Attorney: a Practical Guide* (8th edn).

achieved without a deed: thus an invalid appointment by deed may take effect as an appointment in writing.[253] It was held that a party might be estopped from denying that a document was sealed[254]; but now that sealing is no longer required a similar estoppel would be more difficult to establish, except perhaps as to delivery. A purported exercise of power under an invalid power of attorney may not preclude a contract arising between the agent and the third party.[255]

Article 11

CO-AGENTS

(1) Where an authority is given to two or more persons, it is presumed to be given to them jointly,[256] unless a contrary intention appears from the nature or terms of the authority, or from the circumstances of the particular case.[257]   **2-043**

(2) Where an authority is given to two or more persons severally, or jointly and severally, any one or more of them may execute it without the concurrence of the others.[258]

(3) All the co-agents must concur in the execution of a joint authority in order to bind the principal, unless there is a provision that a certain number shall form a quorum,[259] or there is provision for majority decision-making. But where the authority is of a public nature, and the matter to be determined is of public concern, and the persons in whom it is invested meet for the purpose of executing it, the act of the majority is for this purpose deemed to be the act of the whole body, unless a contrary intention is to be collected from the nature of the power and the duty to be performed under it.[260]

Illustrations

(1) A provisional committee appointed eight specified persons to act as a managing committee on their behalf. Six of such persons gave an order within the   **2-044**

---

[253] *Windsor Refrigerator Co Ltd v Branch Nominees Ltd* [1961] Ch. 375; *Hunter v Parker* (1840) 7 M. & W. 322 at 343–344 (sale of ship); *Marchant v Morton, Down & Co* [1901] 2 K.B. 829 (assignment); *Butler v Duckett* (1891) 17 V.L.R. 439. See also *Haddow Nominees Ltd v Rarawa Farms Ltd* [1981] 2 N.Z.L.R. 16; *MYT Engineering Pty Ltd v Mulcon Pty Ltd* (1999) 195 C.L.R. 636; *Jiao v Barge* (2006) 18 Procedure R.N.Z. 396 (NZSC) (power of attorney alleged to be invalid, but Court finding appointment of agent can be oral for the purposes of signature to contract for the sale of land).

[254] *TCB Ltd v Gray* [1986] Ch. 821 (and see [1987] Ch. 458n).

[255] See *Lundie v Rowena Nominees Pty Ltd* (2007) 32 W.A.R. 404 at [53] (see further below, para.9-016).

[256] Illustrations 1 to 3.

[257] See *Moore v Ullcoats Mining Co Ltd* (1907) 97 L.T. 845 (power to inspect a mine). For the statutory form of power of attorney conferring joint and several authority see Powers of Attorney Act 1971 s.10(1), Sch.1. As to joint and joint and several authority under the Mental Capacity Act 2005, see s.10 and Sch.4. See further below, para.10-009.

[258] Illustration 4.

[259] *Brown v Andrew* (1849) 18 L.J.Q.B. 153, Illustration 1. This is commonly provided for in the case of companies, in relation both to the board of directors and the shareholders in general meeting (see, e.g. Companies (Model Articles) Regulations 2008 (SI 2008/3229).

[260] *Grindley v Barker* (1798) 1 B. & P. 229; *Cortis v Kent Waterworks Co* (1827) 7 B. & C. 314; Judicial Committee of the Privy Council's Report on the Irish Boundary Commission (1924) 59 L.J. 517; *Atkinson v Brown* [1963] N.Z.L.R. 755; *Picea Holdings Ltd v London Rent Assessment Panel* [1971] 2 Q.B. 216. This is really a matter of public law.

scope of the authority conferred. Held, that the provisional committee were not bound by the order.[261]

(2)   Two persons filled the office of clerk to the trustees of a road. Held, that they must contract jointly in order to bind the trustees.[262]

(3)   The directors of a company, being duly authorised in that behalf, resolved that all their powers, except their power to make calls, should be delegated to three of their number as a committee. Held, that at a meeting of the committee for the purpose of exercising such powers, all the members of the committee must be present.[263]

(4)   A power of attorney was given to 15 persons, "jointly or severally to execute such policies as they or any of them should jointly or severally think proper." Held, that a policy executed by four of such persons was binding on the principal.[264]

Article 12

CO-PRINCIPALS

2-045   Where two or more persons give authority to an agent, it is presumed that the authority is to act for their joint account only, unless a contrary intention appears from the nature of the terms of the authority, or from the circumstances of the particular case.[265]

Comment

2-046   The prima facie rule is that the obligation arising from a contract made by two or more persons on one side is joint.[266] Thus where two or more persons give authority to an agent, the presumption is that they are authorising him to act only in such matters as concern them jointly, e.g. their joint property, and not in matters concerning one or the other alone.[267] But there may be indications to the contrary: and of course the contractual liability (if there is a contract) of the co-principals may be held to be joint and several rather than joint, in appropriate cases.[268] An agent acting for joint principals is not bound to account to one alone.[269] Payment to or release by one of joint creditors may however discharge a debt under the rules for joint obligations, even where the person concerned is not authorised to receive pay-

[261] *Brown v Andrew* (1849) 18 L.J.Q.B. 153.
[262] *Bell and Head v Nixon and Davison* (1832) 9 Bing. 393.
[263] *Re Liverpool Household Stores* (1890) 59 L.J.Ch. 616. But the articles will usually deal with this problem.
[264] *Guthrie v Armstrong* (1822) 5 B. & A. 628.
[265] cf. *Restatement, Third*, § 3.16; Partnership Act 1890 s.9; Glanville Williams, *Joint Obligations* (1949), pp.35–37; *Cox v Goldcrest Developments (NSW) Pty Ltd* (2000) 50 N.S.W.L.R. 76 (evidence of subsequent conduct admitted); see also Treitel, *Law of Contract* (14th edn), Ch.13.
[266] See above.
[267] e.g. *Keay v Fenwick* (1876) 1 C.P.D. 745; *Constitution Road Pty Ltd v Downey* (2008) 68 A.C.S.R. 118 (statutory demand on joint debt must be authorised by both creditors).
[268] Glanville Williams, above, at 38–39.
[269] *Hatsall v Griffith* (1834) 2 Cr. & M. 679. See also below, para.6-100.

ment or release the debt[270]: but these rules have exceptions.[271] Where one co-principal dies, if the authority is joint it is not terminated by the death.[272]

3. Ratification

Article 13

General Principle

Where an act is done purportedly in the name or on behalf of another by a person who has no actual authority to do that act, the person in whose name or on whose behalf the act is done may, if the third party had believed the act to be authorised, by ratifying the act, make it as valid and effectual, subject to the provisions of Article 14 to 20, as if it had been originally done by his authority, whether the person doing the act was an agent exceeding his authority, or was a person having no authority to act for him at all.[273]

2-047

Comment

This Article sets out by way of introduction the general principle of ratification, which is that it is "equivalent to an antecedent authority".[274] The whole notion is much criticised and is often treated as exceptional,[275] mainly in the context of contract because of the lack of reciprocity: the third party may be in the power of the principal while the latter decides whether or not to ratify. It is submitted, however, that in typical contract situations ratification is not anomalous. The primary application of the doctrine is indeed in the law of contract, where it fills a practical need in validating the acts of agents who act outside their authority in circumstances where it appears advisable to do so. As the comment to *Restatement, Second* says, "It operates normally to cure minor defects in an agent's authority, minimising technical defences and preventing unnecessary lawsuits".[276] In such a case, as between principal and third party, where the principal seeks to intervene and enforce the contract, the third party is getting exactly what he bargained for. Where the third party seeks to enforce the contract against a ratifying principal he

2-048

---

[270] *Wallace v Kelsall* (1840) 7 M. & W. 264 at 274; *Husband v Davis* (1851) 10 C.B. 645; *Powell v Brodhurst* [1901] 2 Ch. 160 at 164.

[271] e.g. joint banking accounts: *Husband v Davis*, above, at 650. See also *Lee v Sankey* (1872–73) L.R. 15 Eq. 204 (trustees).

[272] See *Cox v Goldcrest Developments (NSW) Pty Ltd* (2000) 50 N.S.W.L.R. 76.

[273] *Wilson v Tunman and Fretson* (1843) 6 M. & G. 236 at 242; *Bird v Brown* (1850) 4 Exch. 786 at 798; *Firth v Staines* [1897] 2 Q.B. 70; *Restatement, Third*, Ch.4; and see below, para.2-050. As to the distinction between agency doctrine and use of the term "ratification" in connection with the release of directors from liability in company law, see *Gower and Davies' Principles of Modern Company Law* (7th edn), pp.437–442 (not carried forward in subsequent editions).

[274] *Koenigsblatt v Sweet* [1923] 2 Ch. 314 at 325, per Lord Sterndale MR.

[275] Powell, pp.121–122 and 138–139; Seavey (1920) 29 Yale L.J. 859, especially at 891; (1954) 21 U.Chi.L.Rev. 248. cf. Krebs, in Burrows and Peel (eds), *Contract Formation and Parties* (2010), Ch.10; Munday, Ch.6; Krebs, in Busch, Macgregor and Watts (eds), *Agency Law in Commercial Practice* (2016), Ch.2; Schultz (2014) 20 Auckland Univ. L.R. 20.

[276] § 82, comment d. Lord Macnaghten called the doctrine "a wholesome and convenient fiction": *Keighley, Maxsted & Co v Durant* [1901] A.C. 240 at 247. A simple example is that if there is no actual authority, and there is uncertainty as to whether apparent authority can be established, a valid ratification puts the matter beyond doubt.

cannot possibly be prejudiced, and the principal is simply held to the transaction which he chose to adopt. Since a master can be liable even for forbidden acts done by an employee in the scope of his employment, it is not surprising that a principal can sometimes be liable for what he has actually ratified.[277] It would seem that ratification should be regarded as providing a normal case of agency, but one where the intention of the parties is given effect to retrospectively.

The position between principal and agent requires slightly more careful formulation. In many cases it is possible to say that the agent, by purporting to act on the principal's behalf, makes an offer to the principal to act as his agent (though not necessarily as his contractual agent), or (where he is already an agent) as his agent in respect of the act concerned, which the principal accepts by ratifying. But the acting outside authority may be a breach of contract; and it seems that there may be cases where the principal ratifies but nevertheless reserves his right to treat the agent as liable to him for the cost of so doing.[278]

Overall it is also true that the potentially retrospective nature of the doctrine of ratification requires special rules to prevent its application having oppressive results, and this makes it a topic requiring special treatment. It does not follow that it is anomalous; and it is certainly convenient:

"The various requirements of ratification, as given in the books, sound largely in terms of a principal who wishes in cold blood to become bound on a contract made in his name but by a purported agent who lacked authority. This is quite unrealistic. Rarely indeed is the principal trying to ratify: he is trying to escape from ratification."[279]

As stated above, the doctrine is primarily applicable to contract, and the tendency is largely to think of it in this connection. However, the term, and the general notion, are used in other parts of the law also. Different considerations arise in different cases, and it is misleading to think that there is any set of rules for ratification applicable to all parts of the law.[280] Many of the cases where the general notion of ratification is invoked are properly to be classified as involving questions of restitution, conversion, formation or performance of contract, novation, waiver, estoppel, notification or notice. Indeed, it may be that such cases form the majority, and that situations of deliberate ratification of unauthorised acts are rare.[281] Cases where the general notion of ratification is employed should therefore be examined carefully in order to ascertain exactly what is in issue.[282]

Ratification of itself only creates agency in respect of the transaction ratified, though a ratification may sometimes be used as evidence of already existing authority,[283] and a series of ratifications may on the facts be held to confer authority for the future, or to generate apparent authority.[284] For this reason it is to be distinguished from the other examples of creation of agency contained in this

---

[277] See Stoljar, pp.177–178; Twerski (1968) 42 Temple L.Q. 1.
[278] See below, para.2-096.
[279] Mechem, *Outlines of Agency* (4th edn), § 197.
[280] *Bird v Brown* (1850) 4 Exch. 786 at 799; cf. Stoljar, p.178.
[281] Mechem, above, § 198.
[282] See, e.g. *Imperial Bank of Canada Ltd v Begley* [1936] 2 All E.R. 367 at 374–375, (misappropriation of proceeds of cheque); *Banque Jacques Cartier v Banque d'Epargne de Montreal* (1888) 13 App.Cas. 111 (liquidator acquiescences in false accounts); *De Bussche v Alt* (1878) 8 Ch.D. 286 at 312–315 (sub-delegation by agent); *Royal Albert Hall Corp v Winchilsea* (1891) 7 T.L.R. 362 (use of hall justified quantum meruit). See also Procaccia (1978) 4 Tel Aviv U. Studies in Law 9.
[283] See *Hutchings v Nunes* (1863) 1 Moo.P.C.(N.S.) 243.
[284] cf. *Restatement*, § 43(2). As to apparent authority, see Article 72.

chapter. Like apparent authority it can apply where the person whose act is ratified is already an agent, and where he is not an agent at all, though cases of the second type are rarer.[285]

Ratification in advance of act ratified Powers of attorney and other docu-   **2-049** ments frequently contain clauses whereby the principal purports to ratify in advance acts which the attorney may do. Such a clause cannot constitute ratification. It operates, if anything, as a grant of authority; as creating apparent authority; possibly as a contractual offer, whether to agent or third party, which may be accepted by some form of action in reliance; if consideration can be found, as part of a contract; or as evidence supporting an alleged subsequent ratification.[286]

Juristic nature of ratification[287] Ratification seems to be a notion sui generis. It   **2-050** involves the idea that in certain circumstances a person can by expression of will adopt a transaction entered into by another on his behalf on which he is not liable or entitled so as to become liable and/or entitled as if he had made it at the time. It requires no consideration; and a novation would be juristically different.[288] In so far as it depends on the choice of the person concerned, it can be said to be an application of the doctrine of election. But in the case of election to treat a contract as discharged, there is a choice of remedies in respect of a legal relationship already existing: the innocent party to a breach of contract can choose to treat it as discharged, but if he does not do so the contract continues.[289] The other form of election normally cited is that between inconsistent existing rights.[290] In both these cases it is usually said that the election must be communicated to the other party involved, and that it is irrevocable once made.[291] It would appear, however, that ratification need not be communicated to anyone if it can be established by probative material[292]; that a party who initially refused to ratify may in some circumstances later do so[293]; and that the doctrine overlaps with estoppel and restitutionary doctrine, which is manifested especially in the case of ratification by acquiescence or inactivity.[294]

Ratification in the Restatements In *Restatements, Second* and *Third* it appears   **2-051** that the role left for ratification is rather different from its function in English law. First, *Restatement, Third* gives as its sphere of application "acts done without actual or apparent authority".[295] In this it follows *Restatement, Second*, which refers to

---

[285] But see *Bird v Brown*, above; also the dissenting judgment of Atkin J in *R. v Chapman Ex p. Arlidge* [1918] 2 K.B. 298.
[286] See *Midland Bank Ltd v Reckitt* [1933] A.C. 1, Illustration 7 to Article 24.
[287] See the valuable discussion by Seavey in *Restatement, Second*, Appendix, reporter's notes to § 94 (also printed in (1954) 103 U.Pa. L.Rev. 30).
[288] *Re Portuguese Consolidated Copper Mines Ltd* (1890) 45 Ch.D. 16 at 34.
[289] *Photo Production Ltd v Securicor Transport Ltd* [1980] A.C. 827 at 849.
[290] *Scarf v Jardine* (1882) 7 App.Cas. 345; *United Australia Ltd v Barclays Bank Ltd* [1941] A.C. 1.
[291] *The Kanchenjunga* [1990] 1 Lloyd's Rep. 391 at 397–399; see also *Kammins Ballroom Co Ltd v Zenith Investment (Torquay) Ltd* [1971] A.C. 850 at 883.
[292] See below, para.2-078.
[293] Article 18.
[294] Article 18. This paragraph is considered by the Court of Appeal in *AMB Generali Holdings AG v SEB Trygg, etc.* [2005] EWCA Civ 1237; [2006] 1 Lloyd's Rep. 318 at [46].
[295] § 4.01.

ratification as "affirmance by a person of an act which did not bind him",[296] and clearly proceeds on the basis of the view of Professor Seavey, the Reporter, that where there is apparent authority the principal is not only bound but also entitled.[297] This leaves a very limited role for ratification. In particular, it appears to mean that the safeguards against unfair ratification do not apply against a principal who seeks to enforce a contract under which he would be liable under the doctrine of apparent authority only, for he is not ratifying but enforcing an existing contract. Thus it would appear to mean that a third party who discovers that the agent had no actual authority could not on that ground alone withdraw from the contract, despite the uncertainties of establishing apparent authority. This is an unattractive proposition. Ratification in the *Restatements* therefore appears to be confined to situations where there is no apparent authority because the third party's belief in the agent's authority was unreasonable, or where the third party actually knew or had reason to know that the agent had no authority or that the agent was genuinely uncertain as to the extent of his authority, yet in either case did not expressly contract subject to ratification.[298] It is indeed expressly stated in the Comment to *Restatement, Third*, that "Ratification is effective even when the third party knew that the agent lacked authority to bind the principal but nonetheless dealt with the agent".[299]

This leads to a second point, under which ratification in the *Restatements* appears by contrast to have a wider operation than it would in English common law. In English law it is submitted that a transaction with an agent known to have no authority would be a complete nullity, a contract with the agent himself, or what might be called a transaction "subject to ratification". The last mentioned would actually be no more than an offer by or to the third party to be bound on certain terms.[300] The third party might be regarded as promising the agent to keep an offer open or to accept an offer made to him. Consideration might be found in some promise by the agent to seek his principal's adoption of the transaction. But the result of such reasoning is that if the third party withdraws before the principal has adopted the contract, his liability if any is to the agent only and recourse to ratification doctrine is unnecessary and inappropriate.[301]

2-052   **European sources**[302]   Since quite an important point of principle is involved, it seems appropriate to go further. The UNIDROIT *Principles of International Com-*

---

[296] *Restatement, Second*, § 82.

[297] See *Restatement, Second*, § 8, Comment d, and below, para.8-029.

[298] See *Restatement, Second*, § 85, Comment e, 92(f) and Comment.

[299] See *Restatement, Third*, § 4.01, Comment b. The case given as example, however, simply concerns a contract made for a company not yet formed, and holds the transaction adopted.

[300] See the firm statement in *Watson v Davies* [1931] 1 Ch. 455 at 468–469; *Warehousing and Forwarding Co of East Africa Ltd v Jafferali & Sons* [1964] A.C. 1, where a distinction is taken between contracting subject to ratification and negotiating subject to approval. The point seems to be that in the latter case the agent may not have enough authority even to formulate an offer which the third party might make. There are more uncertainties, opportunities for misunderstanding, and possible differences of analysis in this area than may initially appear. An example is *First Energy (UK) Ltd v Hungarian International Bank Ltd* [1993] 2 Lloyd's Rep. 194, below, para.8-021, where considerations such as those above were raised by the facts but did not need to be considered.

[301] See also below, para.2-087.

[302] For identificatory details, see the *Standard Abbreviations*, above, p.xvii. For commentary, see Busch and Macgregor (eds), *The Unauthorised Agent* (2009), Chs 11 and 12; Vogenauer and Kleinhesterkamp (eds), *Commentary on the UNIDROIT PICC* (2009), Ch.2, Section 2; and DeMott (2009) 6 *European Review of Private Law* 987; Reynolds, *ICC International Court of Arbitration Bulletin* (2005) at 9.

mercial Contracts appear to apply ratification to cases of lack of actual authority[303]; but they seem also to contemplate it where the third party knows that the agent is unauthorised, for they give such a third party the right to specify a reasonable time for ratification; though if he did not know of the lack of authority, they also allow him to withdraw from the transaction when he discovers the fact. The *Principles of European Contract Law* and the *Draft Common Frame of Reference* appear to take the same approach.[304] Of course, the problem of the revocability of an offer is a common law one and not necessarily to be taken account of in such international codifications. However, the approach taken in this book is to confine the special ratification rules, with their retroactivity and consequent protective features, to situations where the third party believed the agent to have authority: it is only to such situations that the rather rough and ready rationale of ratification, that the third party gets what he expected,[305] applies. The text of Article 13 has been modified to make this clear.[306]

Illustrations

(1) A entered into and signed a written contract on behalf of B, without authority. A memorandum of the contract was required by statute to be in writing. B subsequently ratified the contract. Not only was the contract itself effective, but A was also deemed to have been B's duly authorised agent to sign the memorandum.[307]   **2-053**

(2) An agent, without authority, insures goods on behalf of his principal. The principal ratifies the policy. The policy is as valid as if the agent had been expressly authorised to insure the goods.[308]

(3) An agent of the Crown does an act, which would normally be a tort, outside the realm and in excess of his authority. The Crown ratifies the act. The act is deemed to be an act of state and the agent is not liable for it.[309]

---

[303] They apply ratification to acts of an agent who acts without authority or exceeds his authority (§ 2.2.9), and the wording of § 2.2.5 and other wording suggests that what is referred to is actual authority, since apparent authority is presented merely as a case where the principal may not invoke the lack of authority of the agent.

[304] See PECL arts 3:201(1) and (3), 3:204(1) and 3:207: but their interrelationship is not entirely clear; and DCFR, II, 6:111.

[305] See above, para.2-048. *Restatement, Third*, however, also allows ratification by an undisclosed principal: see below, para.2-063: the justification would not apply to that either.

[306] By the insertion of the words "if the third party had believed the act to be authorised". Contra, Seavey in *Restatement, Second, Appendix*, pp.148–149.

[307] *Maclean v Dunn* (1828) 4 Bing. 722; *Soames v Spencer* (1822) 1 D. & R. 32; *Koenigsblatt v Sweet* [1923] 2 Ch. 314; *Sheridan v Higgins* [1971] I.R. 291. There seems no reason why the same reasoning should not apply where the contract is required to be in writing, as now under the Law of Property (Miscellaneous Provisions) Act 1989 s.2.

[308] *Wolff v Horncastle* (1798) 1 B. & P. 316; *Williams v North China Insurance Co.* (1876) 1 C.P.D. 757; *Bedford Insurance Co. Ltd v Instituto de Resseguros do Brasil* [1985] Q.B. 966, Illustration 6 to Article 14. See further Article 18.

[309] *Burton v Denman* (1848) 2 Exch. 167; *Secretary of State for India v Kamachee Boye Sahaba* (1859) 7 Moo.Ind.App. 476. See further Article 113. In such cases, it may well be said that the doctrine is oppressive to third parties despite the principle of Article 19.

Article 14

WHAT ACTS MAY BE RATIFIED

2-054   Every unauthorised act, whether lawful or unlawful,[310] which is capable of being done by means of an agent (except an act which is in its inception void[311]) is capable of ratification by the person in whose name or on whose behalf it was purportedly done.[312]

Comment

2-055   **Lawful or unlawful: contracts**   As indicated in the Comment to Article 13, the doctrine, and therefore this Article, applies primarily to transactions, normally contracts. The making of a contract on behalf of another without authority could perhaps be described as unlawful, but such a contract can certainly be ratified. Even a contract induced by a fraudulent, and therefore tortious, profession of agency can be ratified, though the agent might be liable to the principal. The right to rescind for misrepresentation, whether fraudulent or innocent, is clearly extinguished.[313]

2-056   **Torts**   The words "lawful or unlawful" are included primarily to indicate that the doctrine can apply to torts. From them it would follow that a principal by ratification may retrospectively turn what was previously an act wrongful against the principal, e.g. an unauthorised sale by the agent, or against a third party, e.g. a wrongful distress, into a legitimate one; or become liable for the tort of another by ratifying. The first proposition is clearly valid: ratification can make an unlawful act lawful ex post facto.[314] But as regards liability, the importance of ratification in the law of torts generally is nowadays, except as regards conversion and trespass to goods, open to question.[315] For the cases giving the widest operation to the doctrine of ratification in tort represent an attempt to extend the notion of command to commit a tort, and originate before the establishment of a general doctrine of vicarious liability.[316] Since the acceptance of a general doctrine, these cases will not usually be relevant, save possibly where the act ratified is not within the course of the servant's employment, or where the tortfeasor is not a servant: and even here the doctrine of casual delegation may cover the situation.[317] It may obviously, furthermore, be extremely difficult to determine what constitutes ratification in non-proprietary torts.[318] It may therefore be suggested that the doctrine of ratification, in so far as it makes one person liable for the torts of another (as opposed to provid-

---

[310] See below, para.2-053; Illustrations 1 to 3; *Wilson v Tunman and Fretson* (1843) 6 M. & G. 236 at 242; *Bird v Brown* (1850) 4 Exch. 786 at 799.
[311] See below, para.2-058.
[312] See Article 15.
[313] See, e.g. *Bolton Partners v Lambert* (1889) 41 Ch.D. 295, Illustration 1 to Article 18.
[314] Illustration 3; *Hull v Pickersgill* (1819) 1 B. & B. 282.
[315] See the valuable discussion in Stoljar, pp.179–182; Tedeschi (1969) 4 Israel L.Rev. 1.
[316] See 4 Co. Inst 317, referred to in *Eastern Counties Ry Co v Broom* (1851) 6 Exch. 314, Illustration 2.
[317] See below, para.8-187. If the tortfeasor is not a servant, it may in any case be held that his act cannot be ratified: see *Wilson v Tunman and Fretson* (1843) 6 M. & G. 236, Illustration 1 to Article 15. See too *Powercor Australia Ltd v Pacific Power Ltd* [1999] VSC 110 at [1274].
[318] See *Moon v Towers* (1860) 8 C.B.(N.S.) 611 at 614 (a case of trespass and false imprisonment): Stoljar, pp.179–180. A case often cited in the books is *Novick v Gouldsberry* 173 F. 2d 496 (1949) ("If I had been there I would have broke your God damn neck" held ratification of assault). See also

ing a defence to an action in tort), normally applies only to conversion, and possibly also to trespass to goods, where the fields of contract, tort and property overlap[319] and liability is strict; and that in torts requiring personal fault it should not be regarded as significant.

Even in the restricted field suggested it will rarely be crucial to the result, since many of the cases can be explained alternatively on the basis of contract, in that they deal with principals who by accepting goods ratify unauthorised contracts[320]; and further, an act said to be a ratification of a conversion may itself be regarded as a conversion.[321] The cases that depend most obviously on the doctrine of ratification are those envisaging ratification of unlawful distress levied by a bailiff[322]; but most are cases of trespass or conversion, and in many of them liability was denied on the grounds that there was no acting for the supposed principal, or that the supposedly ratifying principal did not know the facts. In some cases the possibility of ratifying other torts has been considered,[323] but the decision has usually been that there was no ratification.

However, other situations can be envisaged where the doctrine of ratification could arise incidentally in a tort case. Thus a coach proprietor might ratify an unauthorised hiring of one of his coaches in order to demand payment for the hire, thereby rendering himself liable for negligence causing damage during the journey: and the owner of a car might ratify unauthorised use of it in order to take advantage of the insurance policy.[324]

Notices and court filings   The notion of ratification arises also in other contexts,   **2-057**
such as that of the unauthorised commencement of court proceedings,[325] and the validity of a notice issued by a person who was at the time of issue unauthorised, but whose act was subsequently ratified.[326] Where the notice affects property rights, as in the case of a notice to quit, ratification may not be permitted.[327] Other cases

---

Manduoit v Ross (1884) 10 V.L.R. 264; and *Barns v Guardians of St Mary, Islington* (1911) 76 J.P. 11.

[319] See, e.g. Illustration 1.

[320] i.e. the tort ceases to exist. See *United Australia Ltd v Barclays Bank Ltd* [1941] A.C. 1 at 28; *Verschures Creameries Ltd v Hull & Netherlands SS Co Ltd* [1921] 2 K.B. 608, Illustration 6 to Article 20.

[321] See the explanation of *Hilberry v Hatton* (1864) 2 H. & C. 822, Illustration 1, given in Powell, p.122; Stoljar, p.179.

[322] See Powell, p.122; Article 16, Illustrations 1, 2 and 3; *Haseler v Lemoyne* (1858) 5 C.B.(N.S.) 530; *Green v Wroe* [1877] W.N. 130; *Carter v St Mary Abbotts, Kensington, Vestry* (1900) 64 J.P. 548, Illustration 5 to Article 17; *Becker v Riebold* (1913) 30 T.L.R. 142, Illustration 3; Clerk and Lindsell, *Torts* (21st edn), paras 6-83–6-85; Atiyah, *Vicarious Liability in the Law of Torts* (1967), Chs 14, 28.

[323] e.g. Illustration 2; *Roe v Birkenhead, etc., Ry* (1851) 7 Exch. 36; *Moon v Towers* (1860) 8 C.B.(N.S.) 611 (trespass and false imprisonment); *Marsh v Joseph* [1897] 1 Ch. 213; *Briess v Woolley* [1954] A.C. 333 (fraud); *Edwards v L & NW Ry* (1869–70) L.R. 5 C.P. 445; *Walker v South Eastern Ry* (1869–70) L.R. 5 C.P. 640 at 643; *Rowe v London Pianoforte Co Ltd* (1876) 34 L.T. 450 (false imprisonment). As to trespass to goods, see *Eastern Construction Co v National Trust Co* [1914] A.C. 197; *Manduoit v Ross* (1884) 10 V.L.R. 264.

[324] cf. *Dempsey v Chambers*, 154 Mass. 330, 28 N.E. 279 (1891), cited by Stoljar, pp.181–182.

[325] See the cases discussed in para.2-091, below; and *McHugh v Eastern Star Gas Ltd* [2012] NSWCA 169.

[326] See Illustration 4.

[327] See below, para.2-091; Article 19, Illustration 1.

arise in a public law context and may turn on the interpretation of statutes or otherwise raise special considerations.[328]

2-058 **Void acts: companies** The proposition that a nullity cannot be ratified is in principle uncontroversial. However, much turns on what is meant by "nullity" or "void act". An unauthorised act could in some contexts be regarded as void, but the starting point of ratification is that such an act can be ratified. There are in fact few situations where such a principle is significant. The main context for its application was formerly that of ultra vires acts of companies. But even if the notion of ratification was relevant in this context, the changes to the ultra vires rule made by the companies legislation[329] actually permit ratification,[330] so that the point ceases to require discussion in this context.

2-059 **Forgeries** It has been held that a forgery cannot be ratified, and the reason given that a forgery is a nullity. The leading case[331] seeks to make a distinction between voidable acts, which can be ratified, and void acts, such as forgery, which cannot. As a general criterion, however, this is unsatisfactory. It is certainly true that in the case of some voidable acts, e.g. the contract of a mentally incapable person, the terminology of ratification has been used.[332] But acts done without authority, e.g. the unauthorised issue of a writ, are not appropriately called voidable. If anything, they could be called void; but they can often be regarded as simply suffering from a defect that can be cured.[333] As regards forgery, it is submitted that the true reason why there can normally be no ratification is that the forger who counterfeits a signature or seal makes no profession of being an agent, so that agency doctrines do not apply to him.[334] An unauthorised signature or affixing of a seal for another may also, however, constitute a forgery[335]; and in such a case it seems that there can be ratification.[336]

---

[328] *St Leonard's Vestry v Holmes* (1885) 50 J.P. 132; *Firth v Staines* [1897] 2 Q.B. 70; *R. v Chapman, Ex p. Arlidge* [1918] 2 K.B. 298; *Blackpool Corp v Locker* [1948] 1 K.B. 349 (requisitioning); *Warwick RDC v Miller-Mead* [1962] Ch. 441 (statutory notices to abate nuisances); *Bowyer, Philpott & Payne Ltd v Mather* [1919] 1 K.B. 419 (institution of proceedings under Public Health Act); *Ainsworth v Creeke* (1868–69) L.R. 4 C.P. 476 (insertion on list of ratepayers); *Re Gloucester Municipal Election Petition, Ford v Newth* [1901] 1 Q.B. 683 (disqualification of councillor); Lanham (1981) 5 Otago L.Rev. 35.

[329] See now Companies Act 2006 ss.39 and 40; see below, para.8-030 onwards.

[330] Companies Act 2006 s.35(3). As to ratification of pre-incorporation contracts see below, para.2-062.

[331] *Brook v Hook* (1870–71) L.R. 6 Ex. 89, Illustration 5.

[332] See below, para.2-065.

[333] See the judgments in *Danish Mercantile Co. v Beaumont* [1951] Ch. 680, Illustration 4; *Pontin v Wood* [1962] 1 Q.B. 737; *Spackman v Evans* (1868) L.R. 3 H.L. 171 at 244; *Re Portuguese Consolidated Copper Mines Ltd* (1890) 45 Ch.D. 16 at 30; below, para.2-091.

[334] Treitel, *Law of Contract* (14th edn), paras 16–046–16–050; *Brook v Hook*, above, at 100; *Greenwood v Martins Bank Ltd* [1932] 1 K.B. 371 at 378–379; affd [1933] A.C. 51; *Algemeene Bankvereeniging v Langton* (1935) 40 Com.Cas. 247; 51 Ll. List Rep. 275; *Imperial Bank of Canada v Begley* [1936] 2 All E.R. 367 at 374–375; *Rowe v B. & R. Nominees Pty Ltd* [1964] V.R. 477; *Demco Investment & Commercial SA v Interamerican Life Assurance (International) Ltd* [2012] EWHC 2053 (Comm) at [122]; *Commonwealth Bank of Australia v Perrin* [2011] QSC 274 at [144]; *Williams Group Australia Pty Ltd v Crocker* [2016] NSWCA 265 at [137] (unauthorised use of electronic signature but issue left undetermined). But cf. *English v English* [2010] EWHC 2058 (Ch) (where the rule appears to have been overlooked).

[335] Forgery and Counterfeiting Act 1981 s.9(1).

[336] See Campbell (1960) 76 L.Q.R. at p.130 onwards; *Bank of Ireland v Evans' Trustees* (1855) 5 H.L.C.

This proposition is sometimes criticised as being over-technical.[337] It is submitted, however, that it is correct: a forger who counterfeits a signature or seal no more professes agency than does a person who disguises himself as another. The reason why the notion of ratification is invoked in these cases is that an adoption of a forgery would often be treated as a promise requiring consideration.[338] Nevertheless, the proper solution to the problem of the adoption of forgeries must, as in many other cases where ideas of ratification, adoption and acquiescence are invoked, lie within the areas of formation of contract, waiver, estoppel, and perhaps the rules as to gifts. Thus it has been held that an estoppel can be raised against a person who induces a third party to believe that a signature is his, if the third party acts on the representation.[339]

Illegality   It has been said that "life cannot be given by ratification to prohibited   **2-060**
transactions"[340]; and in that case ratification of a prohibited insurance contract was refused validity. The extent to which it is correct to regard a transaction affected by illegality as actually void will, however, turn on the nature of the illegality, the wording of any relevant statute, and the extent of the illegality. The law is far from clear. A detailed treatment is beyond the scope of this book.[341]

Illustrations

(1)   A, on B's behalf but without his authority, purchases from C a chattel which   **2-061**
C has no right to sell, under such circumstances that the purchase of the chattel is a conversion. B ratifies the purchase. B is guilty of converting the chattel.[342]

(2)   A, an agent of a corporation, assaults B on its behalf. The corporation ratifies the assault. The corporation is civilly liable to B for the assault. Sed quaere.[343]

(3)   A distrains B's goods in the name of B's landlord, but without the landlord's authority. The landlord may ratify the distress, and it is then deemed to have been levied by his authority.[344]

(4)   The managing director of a company, without having authority to do so,

---

389 at 414; *M'Kenzie v British Linen Co* (1881) 6 App.Cas. 82 at 99–100; *Rowe v B. & R. Nominees Pty Ltd*, above; *Northside Development Pty Ltd v Registrar-General* (1990) 170 C.L.R. 146 at 184–185, 200, 207–208; *Demco Investment & Commercial SA v Interamerican Life Assurance (International) Ltd* [2012] EWHC 2053 (Comm) at [123].

[337] Stoljar, pp.185–186; Atiyah, *Vicarious Liability in the Law of Torts* (1967), p.315. In the United States ratification is made effective by UCC s.3–403(a).

[338] In *Brook v Hook*, above, itself, the consideration was the suppression of a prosecution and so illegal.

[339] *Greenwood v Martins Bank Ltd* [1933] A.C. 51, Illustration 5 (criticised by Stoljar, pp.185–186, on the basis that there was no detriment: sed quaere); *M'Kenzie v British Linen Co*, above; *Fung Kai Sun v Chan Fui Hing* [1951] A.C. 489 (setting rather strict limits); *Rowe v B. & R. Nominees Pty Ltd*, above; *English v English* [2010] EWHC 2058 (Ch) at [59]. See also *Welch v Bank of England* [1955] Ch. 508; *Spiro v Lintern* [1973] 1 W.L.R. 1002; *Amalgamated Investment & Property Co. Ltd v Texas Commerce International Bank Ltd* [1982] Q.B. 84; below, para.8-040. A different view is taken in *Restatement, Third*, § 4.03, Comment c.

[340] *Bedford Insurance Co. Ltd v Instituto de Resseguros do Brasil* [1985] Q.B. 966 at 986, per Parker J (Illustration 6).

[341] See the brief treatment in para.2-025; and Chitty, *Contracts* (32nd edn), Ch.16.

[342] *Hilberry v Hatton* (1864) 2 H. & C. 822. And see *Irvings v Motly* (1831) 7 Bing. 543.

[343] *Eastern Counties Ry v Broom* (1851) 6 Exch. 314. This proposition might be correct if based on the general rules of vicarious liability, but it seems out of date on the point of ratification, and rests on obiter dicta only, since it was held that there was no ratification. See Clerk and Lindsell, *Torts* (21st edn), para.6-76.

[344] *Whitehead v Taylor* (1839) 10 A. & E. 210. The common law of distraint in relation to commercial

instructed solicitors to commence an action in the name of the company. An order for the winding-up of the company having been made, the liquidator adopted the action. A motion to strike out the name of the plaintiff company failed; for, although not properly constituted when commenced (so that the defendant acting promptly could have obtained a stay), the action was not a nullity, and the subsequent ratification cured the defect in the proceedings as originally constituted.[345]

(5) A signs an instrument in B's name without his authority and with intent to defraud. B cannot ratify the signature.[346] But if B, knowing of the forgery, by his conduct induces a third person to believe that the signature is his, and if such third person acts on that belief to his detriment, B will be estopped from denying that it is his signature in any action between him and such third person[347]; as he will be if, knowing of the forgery, he delays in repudiating the signature, so that the third person's chance of recovering from the forger is materially prejudiced.[348]

(6) B in Hong Kong authorises A in London to write marine insurance risks on his behalf, subject to financial limitations as to the size of the risk. He also has an open cover reinsurance policy. A exceeds the limits in writing risks on B's behalf and declares the risks to the reinsurers. The insurances are void and unenforceable by statute because B is not authorised to carry on insurance business in Great Britain. Claims are made under the insurances. B ratifies the insurances and claims on the reinsurance policy. The original insurances are void whether made with B's authority or not and so cannot be ratified. There is thus no claim on the reinsurance policy.[349]

Article 15

WHO MAY RATIFY

2-062 The only person who has power to ratify an act is the person in whose name or on whose behalf the act was purported to be done,[350] and it is necessary that he

---

tenancies has been abolished and replaced as from April 6, 2014 pursuant to Tribunals, Courts and Enforcement Act 2007 s.71. See also *Hull v Pickersgill* (1819) 1 B. & B. 282 (seizure of bankrupt's property ratified by assignee). For consideration of this problem in connection with liability in tort, see Atiyah, *Vicarious Liability in the Law of Torts* (1967), pp.314–316.

[345] *Danish Mercantile Co Ltd v Beaumont* [1951] Ch. 680. See also *Ancona v Marks* (1862) 7 H. & N. 686; *Hooper v Kerr, Stuart & Co Ltd* (1901) 83 L.T. 729, Illustration 2 to Article 20; *Presentaciones Musicales SA v Secunda* [1994] Ch. 271 at 280, Illustration 6 to Article 19. cf. *Re State of Wyoming Syndicate* [1901] 2 Ch. 431. And see *Re Portuguese Consolidated Copper Mines* (1890) 45 Ch.D. 16 (allotment of shares by irregular meeting); *Warwick RDC v Miller-Mead* [1962] Ch. 441 (local authority); *Bamford v Bamford* [1970] Ch. 12 (but may not be on ratification); *Alexander Ward & Co Ltd v Samyang Navigation Co Ltd* [1975] 1 W.L.R. 673 (arrest of ship in Scotland *ad fundandam jurisdictionem*: see (1976) 39 M.L.R. 327); Article 20, Illustration 10.

[346] *Brook v Hook* (1870–71) L.R. 6 Ex. 89; but see Comment, above.

[347] *M'Kenzie v British Linen Co* (1881) 6 App.Cas. 82; *English v English* [2010] EWHC 2058 (Ch).

[348] *Greenwood v Martins Bank Ltd* [1933] A.C. 51; *Brown v Westminster Bank Ltd* [1964] 2 Lloyd's Rep. 187; *Tina Motors Pty Ltd v ANZ Banking Group Ltd* [1977] V.R. 205.

[349] *Bedford Insurance Co Ltd v Instituto de Resseguros do Brasil* [1985] Q.B. 966, approved on the illegality issue in *Phoenix General Ins. Co of Greece SA v Halvanon Ins. Co Ltd* [1988] Q.B. 216 (effect reversed by Financial Services Act 1986 s.132, now repealed).

[350] Illustrations 1–4; *Watson v Swann* (1862) 11 C.B.(N.S.) 756; *Smith v Cox* [1940] 2 K.B. 558 (pay-

should have been in existence at the time when the act was done,[351] and competent at that time and at the time of ratification to be the principal of the person doing the act[352]; but it is not necessary that at the time the act was done he was known, either personally or by name, to the third party.[353] Ratification can be effected on the principal's behalf by an agent or agents who had actual authority to do the act in question.[354]

Comment

Person acted for: agent must purport to have authority to bind principal It   **2-063** is clear that ratification only applies where the person whose act is in question professed or purported at the time of acting to do so as agent and to have authority to bind the principal.[355] Although if the agent had authority at that time, an undisclosed principal could take the benefit of the contract and likewise would be liable to be sued,[356] it has been held that an undisclosed principal cannot ratify. The reason given in the leading case of *Keighley, Maxsted & Co v Durant*[357] is that "civil obligations are not to be created by, or founded upon, undisclosed intentions".[358] It is however difficult to see that this is not exactly what happens under the doctrine of the undisclosed principal. A more general reason sometimes given is that to allow ratification in such a case would be to allow too easy intervention upon a contract by a person not in truth connected with it. In one sense this is obvious: the doctrine of ratification would not be appropriately invoked to allow intervention by a person, uncontemplated by the purported agent, who simply found it convenient to ratify the transaction. This would, indeed, not be ratification by an undisclosed principal. But *Keighley Maxsted*'s case did not involve such a situation. The person whose acts were purportedly ratified was already an agent, and had merely exceeded his authority in respect of the price at which he agreed to buy. Furthermore, the principal chose to ratify and it was the third party who, in suing the principal, sought to rely on the ratification. He was not permitted to do so. It is arguable therefore that at the very least a principal who ratifies should be held liable in the situation where a person who is already an agent exceeds his authority; and possibly should be able to sue in such a case, the third party being adequately protected by the normal restrictions against unfair results of ratification.[359] The decision is however clear that ratification in such a case is ineffective, and is one of the House of Lords.[360]

---

ment of rent by stranger); *Att.-Gen. v Wylde* (1946) 47 S.R.(N.S.W.) 99 (ratification of act of Crown agent by another officer of the Crown); *Howard Smith & Co Ltd v Varawa* (1907) 5 C.L.R. 68 at 82; *Crampsey v Deveney* [1968] S.C.R. 267, (1968) 2 D.L.R. (3d) 161; *Restatement, Second*, §§ 85 and 87 (not followed by *Restatement, Third*, which allows ratification by an undisclosed principal: see § 4.03).

[351] *Kelner v Baxter* (1866–67) L.R. 2 C.P. 174, Illustration 6; *Restatement, Third*, § 4.04(1).
[352] *Firth v Staines* [1897] 2 Q.B. 70 at 75; and see Illustrations.
[353] See Comment.
[354] See below, paras 2-068 and 2-069.
[355] See, e.g. *Bennett v Strauss* [2016] NSWCA 324, Illustration 10.
[356] Article 76.
[357] [1901] A.C. 240, Illustration 3. See Rochvarg (1989) 34 McGill L.J. 286.
[358] Per Lord Macnaghten at p.247.
[359] Article 19.
[360] *Restatement, Third*, abandons the rule altogether: see § 4.03 and Comment *b*. But see the defence of the rule by Krebs, in Busch, Macgregor and Watts, *Agency Law in Commercial Practice* (2016) Ch.2.

Conversely, however, where the agent purports to act for a principal but actually intends to act for himself the principal can ratify.[361] And where the agent purports to act for one person, no other person can ratify[362]:

"If there is one legal principle better established than another it is this, that nobody can ratify a contract purporting to be made by an agent except the party on whose behalf the agent purported to act."[363]

It is under this principle that some forgeries cannot be ratified, for a forger does not usually purport to act for someone else but as someone else.[364] In tort cases, it is clear that in principle there can be no ratification of a tort unless the tortfeasor has in some way purported to act for the party who subsequently ratifies[365] but exactly what interpretation is to be given to the idea of "purporting to act" in this context is a difficult matter.[366]

2-064   **In existence when act done**   The requirement that the principal exist at the time of the alleged contract arises most commonly in relation to contracts made on behalf of companies not yet registered.[367] Where the promoters of a prospective company enter into a contract on its behalf before its incorporation, the company cannot after incorporation ratify the contract, because it was not in existence at the time when the contract was made and so could not have made the contract at that time.[368] The company may make a new contract on the same terms as the old,[369] and this may be proved by part performance,[370] but it cannot ratify the contract with retrospective effect. Other remedies have sometimes been found in respect of pre-incorporation contracts[371]; but it has also been held that a company is not bound in equity to pay for work done before its formation, even though it has taken the benefit of the work.[372] Such results have proved inconvenient in practice and in some jurisdictions are changed by statute.[373] Issues relating to the existence of the principal also arise with unidentified principals and are discussed below.[374]

2-065   **Competent at the time when the act was done**   Again, a person cannot ratify an

[361] *Re Tiedemann and Ledermann Frères* [1899] 2 Q.B. 66, Illustration 4.
[362] Illustrations 1 and 2.
[363] *Jones v Hope* (1880) 3 T.L.R. 247n. at 251, per Brett LJ (Illustration 5).
[364] See above, para.2-059.
[365] See, e.g. *Wilson v Barker* (1833) 4 B. & Ad. 614; *Eastern Construction Co Ltd v National Trust Co Ltd* [1914] A.C. 197 at 213. See Atiyah, *Vicarious Liability in the Law of Torts* (1967), pp.314–316.
[366] See Seavey, 21 U.Chi.L.Rev. 248 (1954); cf. Twerski, 42 Temple L.Q. 1 (1968).
[367] See Companies Act 2006 s.16.
[368] *Kelner v Baxter* (1866–67) L.R. 2 C.P. 174, Illustration 6; *Re Empress Engineering Co* (1880–81) 16 Ch.D. 125; *Re Northumberland Avenue Hotel Co* (1886) 33 Ch.D. 16; *Melhado v Porto Alegre, etc., Ry Co* (1873–74) L.R. 9 C.P. 503; *Natal Land, etc., Co v Pauline, etc., Syndicate* [1904] A.C. 120. But the person acting for the company may be personally liable: see Article 107.
[369] *Howard v Patent Ivory Co* (1888) 38 Ch.D. 156; cf. *Touche v Metropolitan Ry Warehousing Co* (1870–71) L.R. 6 Ch.App. 671.
[370] *Howard v Patent Ivory Co* (1888) 38 Ch.D. 156; cf. *Touche v Metropolitan Ry Warehousing Co* (1870–71) L.R. 6 Ch.App. 671.
[371] See *Re Empress Engineering Co*, above; *Re Dale & Plant* (1889) 61 L.T. 206; *Rover International Ltd v Cannon Film Sales Ltd (No.3)* [1989] 1 W.L.R. 912; *Gower's Principles of Modern Company Law* (10th edn), paras 5-24–5-28.
[372] *Re English & Colonial Produce Co* [1906] 2 Ch. 435.
[373] e.g. Companies Act 1981 (Australia) s.81; Companies Act (Singapore), cap. 50 s.41; Companies Act 1993 (NZ) ss.182–185. See Hambrook (1982) 8 Adelaide L.Rev. 119.
[374] See below, para.2-067.

act which he was not competent to do at the time it was done: an example appears in Illustration 9. Apart from alien enemies, with whom Illustration 9 is concerned,[375] the main case for considering this requirement is that of minors. Where a contract made for a minor would, if made by the minor himself, be valid,[376] it can presumably be ratified in the normal way. Other contracts are void against the minor but bind the other party: they can be "ratified" by the minor after reaching full age. If entered into through an agent, they can likewise presumably be ratified by the minor personally or through an agent: except that it was long ago held that a penal bond could not be ratified.[377] The distinction between void and voidable acts may regulate the ratification by mentally incapable persons of contracts made on their behalf: they can ratify, when of sound mind, acts which if effected by themselves would have been voidable.[378]

Competent at the time of ratification   A minor clearly cannot ratify a contract that would not bind him, while still under age, nor a mentally incapable person while still incapable (at least unless he appeared to be sane to the party to whom the ratification was communicated), nor a person who is an alien enemy, even if he was not such when the act was done.[379]   **2-066**

Unidentified principal   In general, as will be seen from the above rules regarding the existence and competence of the principal, the rules for ratification follow those for initial authority: the test is to inquire whether the principal could have entered into such a transaction at the time when the agent originally acted. If this analogy is followed, since an agent need not always name his principal but may and often does act for a completely unidentified principal (e.g. "bought for our principals"), ratification should be possible in such a case also. If the third party is willing to deal on this basis, he should arguably be bound under the doctrine of ratification just as under the normal principles of authority. A number of dicta however suggest that the principal must be known or ascertainable by the third party at the time of contracting. Thus in one case it was said that: **2-067**

> "The law obviously requires that the person for whom the agent professes to act must be a person capable of being ascertained at the time. It is not necessary that he should be named; but there must be such a description of him as shall amount to a reasonable designation of the person intended to be bound by the contract."[380]

An example of the latter category is that of an agent who acts for the heirs of property, whoever they are.[381] Such dicta would, if applied as a rule, restrict the scope of ratification. If there is any policy reason for doing this, it is that the ability to ratify where the principal was completely unidentified and undescribed will depend on the agent having had a particular person in mind; and this may ef-

---

[375] And see *Kuenigl v Donnersmarck* [1955] 1 Q.B. 515 at 539.
[376] e.g. a contract for necessaries, or a beneficial contract of service.
[377] *Baylis v Dineley* (1815) 3 M. & S. 477. It may be regarded as a nullity.
[378] *City Bank of Sydney v McLaughlin* (1909) 9 C.L.R. 615. See Comment to Article 4. In *Dibbins v Dibbins* [1896] 2 Ch. 348, Illustration 3 to Article 19, it was assumed that the ratification would have been valid had it been effected in time.
[379] See Comment to Article 117.
[380] *Watson v Swann* (1862) 11 C.B.(N.S.) 756 at 771, per Willes J. See also *Kelner v Baxter* (1866–67) L.R. 2 C.P. 174 at 184; *Eastern Construction Co Ltd v National Trust Co Ltd* [1914] A.C. 197 at 213.
[381] *Lyell v Kennedy* (1889) 14 App.Cas. 437, Illustration 7.

fectively permit him at a later stage to choose the person who is to ratify by declaring that this was the person whom he had originally had in mind. This is not, at least in theory, true in ordinary dealings on behalf of unidentified principals, where actual authority would in the event of dispute need to be proved. Even in such cases however there may be an element of choice, for agents may have identical instructions from several principals and thus be free in practice to choose to which principal a particular contract should be allocated. There is also some possibility of such choice where the question of the intervention or liability of an undisclosed principal arises.[382] Such uncertainties are not therefore unknown to agency law. The dicta quoted come from a nineteenth-century case on insurance, where the difficulty of distinguishing between identifying the person who can sue on the policy as principal and identifying the interests covered by the policy is notorious.[383]

A carefully reasoned judgment of Colman J confirms the above view.[384] It also states (in wording appropriate to its context, that of insurance) that:

"Evidence as to whether in any particular case the principal assured or other contracting party did have the relevant intention may be provided by the terms of the policy itself, by the terms of any contract between the principal assured or other contracting party and the alleged co-assured or by any other admissible material showing what was subjectively intended by the principal assured."[385]

Although this decision and these dicta seem, with respect, correct, they do raise considerable problems of evidence, whether within or outside the context of insurance. Where an agent has no principal in mind at the time of the act, but proposes to "allocate" the contract, there can in principle be no ratification. Where he has a principal in mind, there can. The two situations may be difficult to distinguish.

A related point arises from the fact that policies of marine insurance on goods have long been taken out for the benefit of "all those to whom they do, may or shall appertain", or similar wording; and it has often been assumed that beneficiaries of such policies may sue on them. It seems that in such a case the understanding is that the agent who procures the insurance need not at the moment have in mind any particular person or persons as the intended principal or principals, provided that there is some general contemplation as to the person or persons intended to benefit.[386] Although there are dicta to the contrary it is submitted that, as regards agency reasoning, a person who had no interest at the time of the insurance should

---

[382] See below, para.8-072.
[383] See below; Arnould, *Marine Insurance* (18th edn) (9 and 10 British Shipping Laws), paras 8-26–8-27 and 8-29–8-32. See also *The Albazero* [1977] A.C. 774.
[384] *National Oilwell (UK) Ltd v Davy Offshore Ltd* [1993] 2 Lloyd's Rep. 582; Powell, pp.125–126; Reynolds, in *Consensus ad Idem* (Rose edn, 1997), pp.80–83; Reynolds, "Unidentified Principals in Common Law", in Busch, Macgregor and Watts (eds), *Agency Law in Commercial Practice* (2016), Ch.4.
[385] [1993] 2 Lloyd's Rep. 582 at 597, per Colman J. The judgment contains authority for this proposition and consideration of such evidence. See too *Lai Wo Heung v Cheung Kong Fur Pty Co Ltd* [2004] 1 H.K.L.R.D. 959 (subjective intention of agent important). In *Magellan Spirit ApS v Vitol SA* [2016] EWHC 454 (Comm) at [19] Leggatt J said that he had "serious doubts as to whether this proposition is correct": but gave no specific reasons.
[386] See *Boston Fruit Co v British & Foreign Marine Insurance Co* [1906] A.C. 336 at 389 (insurance by shipowner could not benefit charterer); *P. Samuel & Co Ltd v Dumas* [1923] 1 K.B. 592; [1924] A.C. 431; *Routh v Thompson* (1811) 13 East 274; *Robinson v Gleadow* (1835) 2 Bing. N.C. 156; cf. *Watson v Swann* (1862) 11 C.B.(N.S.) 756; *Byas v Miller* (1897) 3 Com.Cas. 39. See also *Alfred McAlpine Construction Ltd v Panatown Ltd* [2001] 1 A.C. 518 at 582.

not in principle be able to ratify, and therefore should not be able to sue on such a policy as principal. The analogy of authorised contracts should again be followed, and a contract could not be validly made on behalf of a person who might at a future time acquire a particular qualification.[387] Trust reasoning is not so limited. It is possible for a policy on goods to be taken out which covers the interests of such persons; and the person who takes it out may have an insurable interest to do so and be able to recover an indemnity in respect of loss incurred by such persons, which he would hold in trust.[388] Equally such a policy may be assigned; and in an appropriate case such a policy might be held to convey a contractual offer to persons later acquiring the qualification mentioned. It is submitted that it is on this basis that such provisions should be explained, and that their efficacy in favour of future beneficiaries cannot satisfactorily be based on reasoning that there is agency for a person not at the time ascertainable.[389]

Ratification by agents   Ratification can clearly be effected by an agent, subject   **2-068**
to the normal principles of authority.[390] The agent who ratifies requires only authority to ratify, not authority to have performed the act ratified.[391] The authority may in appropriate cases be apparent.

Ratification by companies   An act or transaction done or entered into on behalf   **2-069**
of a company may be ratified by the directors, if they have power to do or enter into such an act or transaction on behalf of the company[392]: and a ratification by the directors may be implied from part performance made or permitted by the company.[393] Where an act or transaction is beyond the powers of the directors, it can only be effectively ratified by the shareholders.[394] An act done by the directors in excess of their powers, but within the scope of the articles of association, may be ratified by ordinary resolution of the shareholders,[395] or by an informal meeting of all the shareholders.[396] A number of cases go further and indicate that a ratification by the shareholders may be implied if they can be regarded as having acquiesced in such an act with knowledge of the circumstances, even in the absence

---

[387]   See *Kelner v Baxter* (1866–67) L.R. 2 C.P. 174 at 184.

[388]   *A. Tomlinson (Hauliers) Ltd v Hepburn* [1966] A.C. 451. See also *Petrofina (UK) Ltd v Magnaload Ltd* [1983] 2 Lloyd's Rep. 91.

[389]   This reasoning was accepted in the Court of Appeal of New South Wales in *Trident General Ins. Co Ltd v McNiece Bros Pty Ltd* (1987) 8 N.S.W.L.R. 270 at 276–277, Illustration 8 (affd on other grounds (1988) 165 C.L.R. 107: but see p.113).

[390]   *Suncorp Insurance and Finance v Milano Assecurazioni SpA* [1993] 2 Lloyd's Rep. 225 at 235; *Yona International Ltd v La Réunion Française SA d'Assurances* [1996] 2 Lloyd's Rep. 84 at 103; *Lawson v Hosemaster Co Ltd* [1966] 1 W.L.R. 1300; see also *Restatement, Third*, § 4.01, Comment *e*.

[391]   *Re Portuguese Consolidated Copper Mines Ltd* (1890) 45 Ch.D. 16.

[392]   *Reuter v Electric Telegraph Co* (1856) 6 E. & B. 341; *Wilson v West Hartlepool Ry & Harbour Co* (1865) 2 De G.J. & S. 475; *Hooper v Kerr, Stuart & Co Ltd* (1901) 83 L.T. 729; *New Falmouth Resorts Ltd v International Hotels Jamaica Ltd* [2013] UKPC 11.

[393]   *Reuter v Electric Telegraph Co*, above; *Wilson v West Hartlepool Ry & Harbour Co*, above; Illustration 7 to Article 17.

[394]   *Spackman v Evans* (1868) L.R. 3 H.L. 171.

[395]   *Grant v UK Switchback Ry Co* (1888) 40 Ch.D. 135. cf. *Boschoek Pty Co Ltd, etc. v Fuke* [1906] 1 Ch. 148.

[396]   *Re Express Engineering Works Ltd* [1920] 1 Ch. 466; *Re Oxted Motor Co* [1921] 3 K.B. 32.

of a formal meeting.[397] In some circumstances, the third party will be protected by statute against unauthorised acts of directors.[398]

Illustrations

2-070 (1) A sheriff, acting under a valid writ of execution, wrongfully seizes goods which are not the property of the debtor. The execution creditor does not, by becoming a party to an interpleader issue or otherwise, ratify the act of the sheriff so as to render himself liable for the wrongful seizure, because the act was not done by the sheriff on his behalf, but in performance of a public duty.[399]

(2) A enters into an agreement professedly on behalf of B's wife and C. B cannot ratify the agreement so as to give himself a right to sue upon it jointly with his wife and C.[400]

(3) A is authorised to buy wheat on the joint account of himself and B, with a certain limit as to price. A, intending to buy on the joint account of himself and B, and expecting that B will ratify the contract, but not disclosing such intention to the seller, enters into a contract in his own name to buy at a price which is above the limit. B ratifies, but later refuses to take the wheat. He cannot be sued by the seller.[401]

(4) A sells wheat to X on P's behalf, and repurchases it himself. He then purports to sell it to Q, R and S on P's behalf, knowing that Q, R and S would not deal with him personally. He really intends to carry through the whole transaction on his own behalf. Q, R and S repudiate the transaction. P may ratify.[402]

(5) A contracts on behalf of a volunteer corps with B, both parties thinking that the corps as an entity may be bound. The corps as an entity cannot be bound. The contract cannot be ratified by individual members of the corps, because it was not made on their behalf as individuals.[403]

(6) A contract for the supply of goods is made by "A, B and C on behalf of" a company not yet formed. This company cannot when formed render itself liable by ratification for the price of the goods.[404]

(7) A person may act on behalf of an heir, or an administrator, or the owner of particular property, whoever he may be, though unascertained and unknown to him, and the person on whose behalf the act was done may ratify it.[405]

(8) A policy of insurance is taken out describing the assured as "X, all its subsidiary associated and related companies, all contractors and subcontractors and/or suppliers". A subcontractor appointed in the following year cannot

[397] See para.1-028; and *Gower's Principles of Modern Company Law* (10th edn), paras 14-11–14-14 and 15-15–15-21.
[398] Companies Act 2006 ss.39 and 40: below, para.8-033 onwards.
[399] *Wilson v Tunman and Fretson* (1843) 6 M. & G. 236; *Woollen v Wright* (1862) 1 H. & C. 554; *Williams v Williams and Nathan* [1937] 2 All E.R. 559; *Barclays Bank v Roberts* [1954] 1 W.L.R. 1212. cf. *Morris v Salberg* (1889) 22 Q.B.D. 614.
[400] *Saunderson v Griffiths* (1826) 5 B. & C. 909; *Heath v Chilton* (1844) 12 M. & W. 632.
[401] *Keighley, Maxsted & Co v Durant* [1901] A.C. 240.
[402] *Re Tiedemann & Ledermann Frères* [1899] 2 Q.B. 66.
[403] *Jones v Hope* (1880) 3 T.L.R. 247n.
[404] *Kelner v Baxter* (1866–67) L.R. 2 C.P. 174. See also Article 107.
[405] *Lyell v Kennedy* (1889) 14 App.Cas. 437; *Foster v Bates* (1843) 1 D. & L. 400. See also *Hull v Pickersgill* (1819) 1 B. & B. 282.

ratify the contract so as to sue on it as a party to it by virtue of the law of agency.[406]

(9)   A trawler owned by a French company is at an English port when, as a result of enemy occupation of France, the company becomes an alien enemy. While this state of affairs continues, A, without the company's authority, acts as manager of the trawler. A's conduct cannot subsequently be ratified by the company, which was not at the time of A's acts competent to be A's principal.[407]

(10)   A daughter purporting to act on behalf of her mother in respect of the prospective sale of the latter's interest in land orally indicates she will need to get her mother's consent to proposed terms but indicates that her mother would be likely to accept her recommendation. Mother later signs a receipt for part-payment of the purchase price. Ratification was not available because the daughter did not purport to have present authority to bind her mother, and the receipt was not unequivocal evidence that her mother understood what was alleged to have been agreed.[408]

Article 16

KNOWLEDGE NECESSARY FOR RATIFICATION

In order that a person may be held to have ratified an act done without his authority, it is necessary that, at the time of the ratification, he should have full knowledge of all the material circumstances in which the act was done,[409] unless he intended to ratify the act and take the risk whatever the circumstances may have been.[410] But knowledge of the legal effect of the act may be imputed to him,[411] and it is not necessary that he should have notice of collateral circumstances affecting the nature of the act.[412]

2-071

---

[406] *Trident General Ins. Co Ltd v McNiece Bros Pty Ltd* (1987) 8 N.S.W.L.R. 270 at 276–277 (affd on other grounds (1988) 165 C.L.R. 107, but see p.113).

[407] *Boston Deep Sea Fishing & Ice Co v Farnham* [1957] 1 W.L.R. 1051.

[408] *Bennett v Strauss* [2016] NSWCA 324.

[409] *Suncorp Insurance and Finance v Milano Assecurazioni SpA* [1983] 2 Lloyd's Rep. 225; see Illustrations 1, 2 and 6. It seems clear that the knowledge of the agent should not in such a case be imputed to him; see Corbin (1906) 15 Yale L.J. 331. See also *Royal Albert Hall Corp v Winchilsea* (1891) 7 T.L.R. 362; *Eastern Construction Co Ltd v National Trust Co Ltd* [1914] A.C. 197 at 213; *McLean Bros & Rigg Ltd v Grice* (1906) 4 C.L.R. 835; *Taylor v Smith* (1926) 38 C.L.R. 48; *Bedford Insurance Co Ltd v Instituto de Resseguros do Brasil* [1985] Q.B. 966 at 987; *Aotearoa International Ltd v Westpac Banking Corp* [1984] 2 N.Z.L.R. 34; *National Union of Mineworkers v Scargill* [2012] EWHC 3750 (Ch) at [159]; *Restatement, Third,* § 4.06.

[410] Illustrations 3 and 5; *Marsh v Joseph* [1897] 1 Ch. 213; *Restatement, Third,* § 4.06. See also *Donegal International Ltd v Republic of Zambia* [2007] EWHC 197 (Comm); [2007] 1 Lloyd's Rep. 397 at [454].

[411] *Powell v Smith* (1872) L.R. 14 Eq. 85; *Brown v Innovatorone Plc* [2012] EWHC 1321 (Comm) at [858]: see Comment. See also *Restatement, Third*, § 4.06 Comment *d*: "A factfinder may conclude that the principal has made such a choice when the principal is shown to have knowledge of facts that would lead a reasonable person to investigate, but the principal ratified without further investigation"; Corbin (1906) 15 Yale L.J. 331.

[412] Illustration 4.

Comment

2-072   This proposition has appeared in all editions of this work, and it is therefore preserved as a general guide. It is a rule protecting the principal against being found to have ratified sooner than is appropriate. It is obvious that some sort of rule to this effect is appropriate, both for ratification and for situations where similar reasoning is employed.[413] Although most rules relating to ratification are directed towards protecting the third party against unfair results, this rule protects the principal against being too easily treated as having ratified. But it is in fact doubtful whether any satisfactory formulation can in fact be found for all the different circumstances in which such reasoning is encountered.

Many of the clearest cases from which this rule is to be derived concern unlawful distress, and conclude that there was no ratification. It has already been argued that the doctrine of ratification has only limited application to torts.[414] In so far as ratification is applicable to make a person liable in tort, it would seem that the requirement of knowledge should be more strictly interpreted in that branch of the law,[415] whereas in a contractual situation a "blanket ratification" (as by receipt of goods) should be more easily able to be established. The objective interpretation of contractual situations, and the related notion that a person may be taken to know matters of which he might be expected to be aware,[416] may obviously allow the inference of ratification where this would not be permissible in a tort case, and it is right that it should.[417] Thus where a person ratified a lease negotiated by an agent under a misapprehension as to its provisions which would not have affected the validity of the contract had the parties made it without an intermediary, he was held bound by it.[418] But where a person to whom a duty of disclosure was owed purported to ratify a transaction (not effected through an agent) which was to his prejudice and voidable as such, this was held inoperative since he did not know that the transaction was voidable.[419] The burden of proof is on the person alleging ratification.[420] Where the principal is aware of the agent's acts and the terms of the purported contract, it appears not to be necessary that the principal had realised, perhaps because of lack of internal records, that the agent had exceeded his authority.[421] Assent may otherwise be manifested by the principal's commencing to perform the contract, and where, to the principal's knowledge, the third party commences to act on it, the principal may become estopped from disowning it.[422] Ordinarily, the knowledge of a director of the relevant facts may be sufficient to

---

[413] See above, para.2-048.

[414] See Comment to Article 14; Atiyah, *Vicarious Liability in the Law of Torts* (1967), pp.316–318.

[415] cf. *Marsh v Joseph*, above, at pp.246–247; see also *Edwards v L & NW Ry Co* (1869–70) L.R. 5 C.P. 445; *Briess v Woolley* [1954] A.C. 333 at 344. But a general ratification of an employer-employee relationship may perhaps involve implied ratification of torts committed by the employee: Atiyah, above, pp.316–318.

[416] See Comment to Article 73.

[417] Mechem, *Outlines of Agency* (4th edn), pp.206–211.

[418] *Powell v Smith*, above; but this is not in fact an agency case: see *AMB Generali Holdings AG v SEB Trygg, etc.* [2005] EWCA Civ 1237; [2006] 1 Lloyd's Rep. 318 at [42]. See also *Hunter v Parker* (1840) 7 M. & W. 322, Illustration 6.

[419] *Savery v King* (1856) 5 H.L. Cas. 627. See also *Spackman v Evans* (1868) L.R. 3 H.L. 171.

[420] *Gunn v Roberts* (1874) L.R. 9 C.P. 331 at 335; *Marsh v Joseph* [1897] 1 Ch. 213 at 246–247.

[421] *Ing Re (UK) Ltd v R & V Versicherung AG* [2006] EWHC 1544 (Comm); [2006] Lloyd's Rep. I.R. 653 at [155]; *Brown v Innovatorone Plc* [2012] EWHC 1321 (Comm) at [858].

[422] See *Geniki Investments International Ltd v Ellis Stockbrokers Ltd* [2008] EWHC 549 (QB); [2008] 1 B.C.L.C. 662 at [46]. See further below, para.2-103.

bind his company,[423] though quaere when the decision to ratify is made by a different person.[424]

Illustrations

(1) An agent wrongfully distrains goods which were neither on the debtor's land nor his property, without the authority of the principal, and pays over the proceeds to the principal. The principal is not deemed to have ratified the wrongful distress by receiving the proceeds, unless he received them with knowledge of the irregularity, or intended without inquiry to take the risk upon himself.[425] **2-073**

(2) An agent, with authority to distrain for rent, wrongfully seized and sold a fixture, and paid the proceeds to the principal, who received them without notice that it was a fixture which had been sold. Held, that the principal had not ratified the trespass.[426]

(3) An agent, without authority, signed a distress warrant and, after the distress, informed his principal, who said that he should leave the matter in the agent's hands. Held, that this was a ratification of the whole transaction, though there had been irregularities in levying the distress of which the principal had no knowledge.[427]

(4) An agent purchased a chattel on his principal's behalf from a person who had no right to sell it, and the principal ratified the purchase. Held, that the principal was guilty of a conversion of the chattel, though he had no knowledge at the time of the ratification that the sale was unlawful. Here, the circumstances rendering the transaction a conversion were collateral to, and did not form part of, the contract ratified. The ratification of the purchase as such was however sufficient to make the principal liable for conversion, liability for which is strict.[428]

(5) An agent entered into an unauthorised contract for the purchase of land on behalf of his principal. A letter from the principal, saying that he did not know what the agent had agreed to, but that he must support him in all he had done, was held to be sufficient ratification of the agreement, whatever it might be.[429]

(6) The master of a ship sells it in circumstances where no agency of necessity arises. The owner receives the proceeds of the sale by bills of exchange, believing that a situation of necessity had in fact arisen. On hearing the true facts he arrests the ship, presents the bills for payment and pays the money into court. He has not ratified the sale.[430] But he may be held to have done so if in similar circumstances the only irregularity unknown to him was as to the procedure by which the sale was effected.[431]

(7) An estate agent makes a contract to sell his principal's land. The principal rati-

---

[423] *Norwich Union Life & Pensions Ltd v Strand Street Properties Ltd* [2009] EWHC 1109 (Ch) at [243].
[424] See further below, para.8-214.
[425] *Lewis v Read* (1845) 13 M. & W. 834.
[426] *Freeman v Rosher* (1849) 13 Q.B. 780.
[427] *Haseler v Lemoyne* (1858) 5 C.B.(N.S.) 530. See also *Becker v Riebold* (1913) 30 T.L.R. 142.
[428] *Hilberry v Hatton* (1864) 2 H. & C. 822. See Powell, p.122; Stoljar, p.179. The distinction between these cases and Illustrations 1 and 2 is perhaps that in those Illustrations the principal did not know of the act constituting the conversion at all.
[429] *Fitzmaurice v Bayley* (1856) 6 E. & B. 868 (see also (1860) 9 H.L.C. 78).
[430] *The Bonita, The Charlotte* (1861) Lush. 252.
[431] *Hunter v Parker* (1840) 7 M. & W. 322.

fies, not knowing that the estate agent has subsequently received an inquiry about the land from someone else. The ratification is effective.[432]

Article 17

WHAT CONSTITUTES RATIFICATION

2-074 (1) Ratification may be express or by conduct.

(2) An express ratification is a manifestation by one on whose behalf an unauthorised act has been done that he treats the act as authorised and becomes a party to the transaction in question.[433] It need not be communicated to the third party or the agent.[434]

(3) Ratification will be implied whenever the conduct of the person in whose name or on whose behalf the act or transaction is done or entered into is such as to amount to clear evidence that he adopts or recognises such act or transaction[435]: and may be implied from the mere acquiescence or inactivity of the principal.[436]

(4) The adoption of part of a transaction operates as a ratification of the whole.[437]

(5) It is not necessary that the ratification of a written contract should be in writing,[438] but the execution of a deed can only be ratified by deed.[439]

Comment

2-075 **Rule (1)** Just as a grant of authority may be express or implied, so may ratification. Thus suing on a transaction, or basing a defence on it, will (subject to any rules as to ratifications which come too late[440]) often amount to an implied ratification of it.[441] So also receipt or retention of money with knowledge of the circumstances of a contract under which it is paid will normally constitute ratifica-

---

[432] *Brennan v O'Connell* [1980] I.R. 13.

[433] See *Restatement, Third*, § 4.01(2): "A person ratifies an act by (a) manifesting assent that the act shall affect the person's legal relations; or (b) conduct that is justifiable only on the assumption that the person so consents."

[434] See below, para.2-078.

[435] Illustrations 1–7; Illustration 12; *Waiwera Co-operative Dairy Co Ltd v Wright, Stephenson & Co Ltd* [1917] N.Z.L.R. 178 (ratification of contract by sending goods forward); *Akel v Turner* [1926] G.L.R. 574 (NZ) (ratification of sale of partnership business to company by acting as manager of company); Atiyah, *Vicarious Liability in the Law of Torts* (1967), p.318 onwards.

[436] *Suncorp Insurance and Finance v Milano Assecurazioni SpA* [1993] 2 Lloyd's Rep. 225 at 234; *Yona International Ltd v La Réunion Française SA d'Assurances* [1996] 2 Lloyd's Rep. 84 at 103, 106; Illustration 9; and see Comment.

[437] Illustrations 2, 3, 10 and 11; see also *Bristow v Whitimore* (1861) 9 H.L.Cas. 391; *Republic of Peru v Peruvian Guano Co* (1887) 36 Ch.D. 489; *Re Mawcon Ltd* [1969] 1 W.L.R. 78; *Restatement, Third*, § 4.07 (ratification not effective unless it encompasses "the entirety of an act, contract or other single transaction").

[438] *Maclean v Dunn* (1828) 4 Bing. 722; *Soames v Spencer* (1822) 1 D. & R. 32; *Koenigsblatt v Sweet* [1923] 2 Ch. 314; *Sheridan v Higgins* [1971] I.R. 291.

[439] See *Hunter v Parker* (1840) 7 M. & W. 322; *Kidderminster Corp v Hardwicke* (1873) L.R. 9 Ex. 13; *Oxford Corp v Crow* [1893] 3 Ch. 535; *Athy Guardians v Murphy* [1986] 1 I.R. 65. But see Comment.

[440] Article 19.

[441] e.g. Illustration 6; *Verschures Creameries Ltd v Hull & Netherlands SS Co Ltd* [1921] 2 K.B. 608, Illustration 6 to Article 20; *Celthene Pty Ltd v WJK Hauliers Pty Ltd* [1981] 1 N.S.W.L.R. 606 at 615; *Life Savers (Aust.) Pty Ltd v Frigmobile Pty Ltd* [1983] 1 N.S.W.L.R. 431 at 438; *Trident General Ins. Co Ltd v McNiece Bros Pty Ltd* (1987) 8 N.S.W.L.R. 270 at 280, Illustration 8 to Article

tion of that contract,[442] as will use or disposal of goods received under it,[443] unless the supposed principal did not assent to the transaction and had no alternative but to receive them and use them as they were, e.g. where they were already his own.[444] It is clear therefore that ratification of an executed contract will be easier to establish than ratification of an executory contract, for there are few cases where a person can keep another's property, or benefit otherwise at the expense of another, without paying, unless he is unaware of the circumstances.[445] However, where the principal was unaware of the circumstances of receipt of property, liability, if any, may more appropriately be founded in conversion or in the law of restitution, than in contract. Such cases are different from those in which inactivity is no more than evidence of a voluntary ratification.[446]

Rule (2): Express ratification   This needs no explanation: it is obvious that if the principle of ratification is accepted at all, an express statement will constitute its prime example. It would seem that a conditional ratification would, if the condition was as to a future event, take effect only as a promise to ratify, and only bind if supported by consideration or the requirements of estoppel.   **2-076**

Rule (3): Implied ratification   Express ratification will however be comparatively rare, and a ratification will more often be implied from words or conduct.[447] Such words or conduct must be unequivocal: they must not be such that they could be accounted for by other interpretations,[448] e.g. that the principal is simply resuming possession of his own property.[449] Such reasoning is necessary to protect the principal against too easily being held liable as having ratified. Ratification can, however, be implied from a position taken in litigation.[450]   **2-077**

Ratification need not be communicated, so long as manifested   There is in principle no necessity for the ratification to be communicated to the other party: it seems long established that it operates, if proved, as a unilateral manifestation of   **2-078**

15; affd on other grounds (1988) 165 C.L.R. 107.

[442] Illustrations 1 and 3; *Restatement, Third*, § 4.01 Comment *g*.

[443] Illustrations 2, 4 and 7.

[444] Illustration 8. See also *The Martin P* [2003] EWHC 3470; [2004] 1 Lloyd's Rep. 389 at [129] (approving cancellation of unauthorised contract not a ratification).

[445] See, e.g. *Royal Albert Hall Corp v Winchilsea* (1891) 7 T.L.R. 362. But the situation may be otherwise where the principal does not use the goods personally, e.g. in a husband and wife case like *Morel Bros & Co Ltd v Earl of Westmorland* [1904] A.C. 11.

[446] *Restatement, Second*, Appendix, reporter's note to § 94 at pp.178–180 (also printed in (1954) 103 U. Pa. L.Rev. 30).

[447] See, e.g. *Crest Nicholson (Londinium) Ltd v Akaria Investments Ltd* [2010] EWHC 243 (Ch) at [72]; *Aviva Life & Pensions UK Ltd v Strand Street Properties Ltd* [2010] EWCA Civ 444; *Brown v Innovatorone Plc* [2012] EWHC 1321 (Comm) at [863] (submitting tax return and claiming tax relief on basis that had joined partnership was ratification of partnership).

[448] *Petersen v Moloney* (1951) 84 C.L.R. 91 at 101; *McLauchlan-Troup v Peters* [1983] V.R. 53 (receipt of rent through agent whose authority was withdrawn, explicable on basis that he acted as agent for payer); *Swotbooks.com Ltd v Royal Bank of Scotland Plc* [2011] EWHC 2025 (QB) at [46] (inconsistent entries in principal's own records); *National Union of Mineworkers v Scargill* [2012] EWHC 3750 (Ch) at [160].

[449] *Forman & Co Pty Ltd v The Liddesdale* [1900] A.C. 190, Illustration 8.

[450] e.g. Illustrations 6 and 7. See also *Scott v Bagshaw* (1999) 92 F.C.R. 424; *The Borvigilant* [2003] EWCA Civ 935; [2003] 2 Lloyd's Rep. 520 at [59]–[61] (letter before action); *Australian Workers' Union v Leighton Contractors Pty Limited* [2013] FCAFC 4 at [96].

will.[451] It will normally be communicated, or at least manifested, to the agent, or sometimes to the third party only: but in principle it would seem that it need not be communicated to either or at all so long as it is manifested in some way.[452] On this basis, it would seem that where the manifestation is to the third party it might operate as a form of estoppel, should, for instance, there have been an inconsistent communication to the agent. In accordance with general principles, it is objective appearances that matter not the internal intentions of the principal:

"It seems to me that it should not be open to a principal, who to the outside world by his conduct, or that of his duly authorised agents, appears to have adopted a transaction to be able to prove subjectively that in fact he had not."[453]

2-079 **Ratification by inactivity and acquiescence**[454]   The issue whether ratification can be inferred from inactivity or acquiescence is more likely to arise with executory contracts, since in the cases of executed contracts it will be difficult to remain totally inactive, except in the case of unasked-for improvements to one's own property[455] (though, as seen, the possibility of an analysis based on conversion or the law of restitution may also be preferable in some such cases[456]). If inactivity of the principal can be taken as manifesting assent, it may constitute ratification.[457] Several cases involving executory contracts have been explained in this way.[458] However, it is also true that "silence or inaction may simply reflect an unwillingness or in-

---

[451] See *Harrisons & Crosfield Ltd v L & NW Ry Co Ltd* [1917] 2 K.B. 755 at 758; *Pagnan SpA v Feed Products Ltd* [1987] 2 Lloyd's Rep. 601 at 613; *Shell Co of Australia Ltd v Nat Shipping and Bagging Services Ltd (The Kilmun)* [1988] 2 Lloyd's Rep. 1 at 11, 14; *AMB Generali Holdings AG v SEB Trygg, etc.* [2005] EWCA Civ 1237; [2006] 1 Lloyd's Rep. 318 at [37] onwards; *Brown v Innovatorone Plc* [2012] EWHC 1321 (Comm) at [856]; *McHugh v Eastern Star Gas Ltd* [2012] NSWCA 169 at [58] (signing of board minutes ratifies court proceedings). In the case of a contract made "subject to ratification", however, the situation is different, for what is in issue is formation of the contract, not ratification of it. Hence notice would normally be required unless the offeror had waived notice of acceptance. See *Warehousing and Forwarding Co of East Africa Ltd v Jafferali & Sons* [1964] A.C. 1 at 9–10; above, para.2-050, below, para.2-087.
[452] Mechem, *Principles of Agency* (4th edn), § 216; *Restatement, Second*, §§ 92(g), 93(1) and 95; *Restatement, Third*, § 4.01 Comment *d*; UNIDROIT Principles art.2.2.9, Comment 1. In the context of a statutory provision extending the concept of ratification to pre-incorporation contracts, it has been held that ratification by the company post-incorporation need not be communicated to the other party to be effective, even though the parties must have been aware that there would be no contract with the company until ratification: *Aztech Science Pty Ltd v Atlanta Aerospace (Woy Woy) Pty Ltd* (2005) 55 A.C.S.R. 1 (NSWCA).
[453] *Suncorp Insurance and Finance v Milano Assecurazioni SpA* [1993] 2 Lloyd's Rep. 225 at 235.
[454] See *Restatement, Second*, Appendix, reporter's note to § 94 (also printed in (1954) 103 U.Pa.L.Rev. 30).
[455] *Forman & Co Pty v The Liddesdale* [1900] A.C. 190, Illustration 8; *Prince v Clark* (1823) 1 B. & C. 186, Illustration 9; *Rodmell v Eden* (1859) 1 F. & F. 542; *The Australia* (1859) 13 Moo.P.C. 132; *City Bank of Sydney v McLaughlin* (1909) 9 C.L.R. 615; *Bank Melli Iran v Barclays Bank Ltd* [1951] 2 T.L.R. 1057; cf. *Taylor v Smith* (1926) 38 C.L.R. 48.
[456] See above, para.2-075.
[457] *City Bank of Sydney v McLaughlin* (1909) 9 C.L.R. 615; *Bank Melli Iran v Barclays Bank Ltd* [1951] 2 T.L.R. 1057 at 1063; *Yona International Ltd v La Réunion Française SA d'Assurances* [1996] 2 Lloyd's Rep. 84 at 106: ratification can be inferred from silence where the principal "allows a state of affairs to come about which is inconsistent with treating the transaction as unauthorised", per Moore-Bick J; *National Australia Bank Ltd v Dionys* [2016] NSWCA 242 at [127]; *Narandas-Girdhar v Bradstock* [2016] EWCA Civ 88 at [31].
[458] *Robinson v Gleadow* (1835) 2 Bing. N.C. 156; *Bigg v Strong* (1858) 4 Jur.(N.S.) 983; *Phillips v Homfray* (1871) L.R. 6 Ch.App.770; *Scots Church Adelaide Inc v Fead* [1951] S.A.S.R. 41.

ability on the part of the principal to commit himself",[459] and there can be a range of other explanations for inactivity that make a finding of an intention to ratify unproven.[460] It has been held that to the extent that silence can amount to ratification, the third party cannot assume assent without allowing at least a reasonable period for (assumed) deliberation to pass.[461]

Past inactivity in respect of what was done by agents may also be held to confer actual or apparent authority[462]: a person who acts by representatives runs risks in doing so, and may owe a duty to make his position clear where a person acting alone would not. In all these cases, the principal is more likely to be bound where the person concerned is already an agent than when he is not.[463]

Estoppel   Ratification merges almost imperceptibly into estoppel.[464] When the silence or inactivity is known to and relied on by the third party, an estoppel may in appropriate cases arise against the principal, who may be estopped from saying that he has not ratified.[465] This will be different from an implied ratification if it comes as later and unrelated conduct, or if there is some difficulty as to the ratification, e.g. in respect of form or capacity.[466] Conversely, an estoppel may arise if the principal leads the third party to believe that he will not ratify, or does not do so within a reasonable time.[467]   **2-080**

Rule (4)   The principal cannot adopt the favourable parts of a transaction and disaffirm the rest: he cannot approbate and reprobate, for this would enable him to effect a transaction into which the third party had never intended to enter.[468] He must therefore adopt or reject the transaction in toto, and where it can be said that this has not been done, the conclusion may be drawn that there was no ratification[469] (though where an agent has effected several separate transactions, the principal may   **2-081**

---

[459] *Yona International Ltd v La Réunion Française S.A. d'Assurances*, above, at 106; *Ing Re (UK) Ltd v R & V Versicherung AG* [2006] EWHC 1544 (Comm); [2006] Lloyd's Rep. I.R. 653 at [162]; *Sea Emerald SA v Prominvestbank-Joint Stockpoint Commercial Industrial and Investment Bank* [2008] EWHC 1979 (Comm) at [105]. See above, para.2-072.

[460] See *Commonwealth Bank of Australia v Perrin* [2011] QSC 274 at [146]; *Perpetual Trustees Victoria Ltd v Cox* [2014] NSWCA 328 (no ratification by borrower of broker's dishonest drawdown purportedly on borrower's behalf merely by borrower receiving notice from lender); *Sino Channel Asia Ltd v Dana Shipping and Trading PTE Singapore* [2016] EWHC 1118 (Comm); [2016] 2 Lloyd's Rep. 97 at [60] (no duty actively to repudiate being made party to arbitration proceedings).

[461] *Ing Re (UK) Ltd v R & V Versicherung AG* [2006] EWHC 1544 (Comm); [2006] Lloyd's Rep. I.R. 653 at [155]. It was for this reason that the plea of ratification failed on the facts.

[462] *City Bank of Sydney v McLaughlin* (1909) 9 C.L.R. 615 at 625. This could also be relevant if other requirements for ratification were not present, e.g. capacity or form. See below, paras 8-043 and 8-045.

[463] As with apparent authority: see Comment to Article 21.

[464] See the discussion by Waller J in *Suncorp Insurance and Finance v Milano Assecurazioni SpA* [1993] 2 Lloyd's Rep. 225 at 234–235; and also *Geniki Investments International Ltd v Ellis Stockbrokers Ltd* [2008] EWHC 549 (QB); [2008] 1 B.C.L.C. 662 at [46]. cf. *The Bunga Melati 5* [2016] SGCA 20 at [12].

[465] cf. *Spiro v Lintern* [1973] 1 W.L.R. 1002, Illustration 3 to Article 21; *Worboys v Carter* [1987] 2 E.G.L.R. 1.

[466] See *Restatement, Third*, § 4.08.

[467] Article 19.

[468] See Illustration 11; cases cited at fn.437 above. But cf. *Langlands Foundry Co Ltd v Worthington Pumping Engine Co* (1896) 22 V.L.R. 144.

[469] *Smith v Henniker-Major & Co* [2002] EWCA Civ 762; [2003] Ch. 182 at [56].

ratify certain transactions individually and refuse to ratify others[470]). This does not, however, mean that there are no circumstances whatever where he may ratify a transaction for one purpose while rejecting it for another. Thus in *Harrisons & Crossfield Ltd v London and North Western Ry Co*[471] a principal whose servant had, while on sick leave, stolen, before the commencement of transit, consignments which the principal had been employed to carry, ratified the transaction to the extent of laying the possession in himself for the purpose of the law of larceny. It was held that he had not ratified so as to vest possession in himself under the contract of carriage, so as to make him liable as a common carrier for non-delivery.

2-082   **Rule (5)**   Since authority to execute a contract required to be in writing, or to be evidenced in writing, need not be in writing,[472] it follows that ratification need not be in writing either.[473] But authority to execute a deed must be conferred by deed,[474] and hence ratification of such an action must equally be by deed.[475] But what appears to be a parol ratification may in fact amount to a second delivery[476]; and if a deed was not necessary for the transaction, the document executed may be treated as a written instrument so that a parol ratification of it is valid.[477]

Illustrations

2-083   (1)   A shipmaster without authority of the owner sells his ship. The owners receive the purchase money with full knowledge of the circumstances in which the ship was sold. The receipt of the purchase money is a ratification of the sale.[478]

(2)   A is a bankrupt. B, at the request of A's wife, purchases certain bonds with A's money, and hands them to her. The trustee in bankruptcy seizes some of the bonds as part of A's estate. The trustee in bankruptcy has ratified the act of B, and thereby discharged him from liability in respect of money used for purchasing the other bonds.[479]

(3)   A is a bankrupt. B wrongfully sells part of A's property. The trustee in bankruptcy accepts the proceeds or part of them, or otherwise recognises B as his agent in the transaction. B is deemed to have been duly authorised by the trustee to sell the property.[480]

(4)   An agent purchases goods on behalf of his principal at a price exceeding his

---

[470] See *Fitzmaurice v Bayley* (1860) 9 H.L.Cas. 78 at 112; Illustration 10.
[471] [1917] 2 K.B. 755. See also *Kinsella v Hamilton* (1890) 26 L.R.Ir. 671 (ratification of distress does not ratify homicide committed in course of it).
[472] Article 9.
[473] *Soames v Spencer* (1822) 1 D. & R. 32; *Maclean v Dunn* (1828) 4 Bing. 722; *Sheridan v Higgins* [1971] I.R. 291.
[474] Article 10. But authority to deliver a deed need no longer be given by deed: Law of Property (Miscellaneous Provisions) Act 1989 s.1(3)(c).
[475] See cases cited at fn.437 above. They are not conclusive, but the proposition seems correct in principle.
[476] *Tupper v Foulkes* (1861) 9 C.B.(N.S.) 797.
[477] *Hunter v Parker* (1840) 7 M. & W. 322; cf. above, para.2-042.
[478] *Hunter v Parker*, above; cf. *The Bonita, The Charlotte* (1861) Lush. 252; Illustration 6 to Article 16. See also *Simpole v Chee* [2013] EWHC 4444 (Ch) at [29].
[479] *Wilson v Poulter* (1724) 2 Str. 859.
[480] *Brewer v Sparrow* (1827) 7 B. & C. 310; *Smith v Baker* (1872-73) L.R. 8 C.P. 350; cf. *Valpy v Sanders* (1848) 5 C.B. 887. See also *Gardiner v Grigg* (1938) 38 S.R.(N.S.W.) 524 (adoption of sale by auctioneer with unauthorised warranty renders principal liable on warranty unless it was collateral); *Clark v Libra Developments Ltd* [2007] 2 N.Z.L.R. 709 (NZCA) at [166] (company which rendered invoices was held thereby to have ratified contract made by purporting agent); *Simpole v*

limit. The principal objects to the contract, but disposes of some of the goods as his own. He is deemed to have ratified the contract, and is bound by it.[481]

(5) A employs a broker to execute a distress warrant. The broker, in executing the warrant, illegally seizes goods belonging to B. In answer to a letter from B demanding compensation, A writes that he is at a loss to understand the threat of proceedings, but that his solicitor will accept service of any process B thinks proper to issue. This reply is evidence of a ratification by A of the wrongful seizure.[482]

(6) A receives the rents of certain property for many years without the authority of the owner (who is unknown, it not being clear who inherited the land on the death of the previous owners). The owner sues A for possession, and for an account of the rents and profits. The action is a sufficient ratification to render A the agent of the owner from the commencement.[483]

(7) The chairman and deputy-chairman of directors, and the secretary, of a manufacturing company, respectively, ordered goods which were necessary for the purposes of the business of the company, and the goods were supplied and used therein. Held, that though the goods were ordered without authority, the directors must be taken to have known that they had been supplied and used in the business, and that therefore the company was liable for the price.[484]

(8) A contracts to do certain specified repairs to a ship. An agent of the shipowner, whose authority is to the knowledge of A limited to the repairs so specified, sanctions certain variations in the work, and the repairs are executed according to the contract as varied. The shipowner sells the ship as repaired. The sale is not a ratification of the unauthorised variations.[485]

(9) A ships goods to Calcutta and entrusts them to the captain of the ship to dispose of them as best he can in the interest of A, and to invest the proceeds in certain specified articles, or in bills at the exchange of the day. The captain sells the goods and invests the proceeds in unauthorised goods. A, on hearing of this, does nothing for ten weeks, after which he attempts to repudiate the captain's act. A is bound by the sale.[486]

(10) D, the managing owner of a ship, sells it, through a broker, without authority. The other owners formally ratify the sale and receive their shares of the purchase money. They are liable to the selling agent for commission, the employment of a broker being an essential part of the whole transaction.[487] But ratification by a joint owner of the sale of a house may not constitute ratification of the contract with the estate agent who effects the sale, for the house need not have been sold through such an agent and there is therefore no need to regard the acquiescence in one contract as covering the other.[488]

(11) A, who was B's manager, fraudulently and without authority obtained from

---

Chee [2013] EWHC 4444 (Ch).

[481] *Cornwal v Wilson* (1750) 1 Ves. 510.

[482] *Carter v St Mary Abbotts, Kensington, Vestry* (1900) 64 J.P. 548. cf. *Barrett v Irvine* [1907] 2 I.R. 462 (negotiation for a compromise does not amount to ratification).

[483] *Lyell v Kennedy* (1889) 14 App.Cas. 437.

[484] *Smith v Hull Glass Co* (1852) 11 C.B. 897; *Allard v Bowne* (1863) 15 C.B.(N.S.) 468.

[485] *Forman & Co Pty Ltd v The Liddesdale* [1900] A.C. 190.

[486] *Prince v Clark* (1823) 1 B. & C. 186.

[487] *Keay v Fenwick* (1876) 1 C.P.D. 745.

[488] *Hughes v Hughes* (1971) 115 S.J. 911.

B's bankers, in exchange for cheques drawn by B upon the bankers, drafts drawn by the bankers upon themselves, payable to bearer and crossed "not negotiable". A paid these drafts into an account which he had with the C Bank, and the C Bank collected the amounts. In an action by B against the C Bank for conversion of the drafts it was held that B must, in order to have a title to sue, ratify A's act in obtaining the drafts; but that B could not ratify this act without also ratifying A's payment of the drafts into his account with the C Bank, for the form of the drafts necessitated payment into some bank for collection; and that the action therefore failed.[489]

(12) D instructs an estate agent to act in the sale of a house, no.17. No.7 is also on the agent's books. A purchaser wishing to acquire no.7 is persuaded to sign a contract relating to no.17 and to pay a deposit, on the agent's representation that the properties are the same. D objects to some of the terms of the contract and refuses to sign it. The agent refuses to return the deposit without an order from D. D by letter requests the agent to return the deposit but the agent again refuses. There is evidence from which it could be determined that D has ratified the agent's receipt of it and may be liable to repay it.[490]

Article 18

EVENTS NOT PREVENTING RATIFICATION

2-084 Ratification is effective—

(1) although the person ratifying had refused at first to recognise the act,[491] unless to allow ratification would unfairly prejudice the third party[492];

(2) although proceedings have been commenced against the person purporting to act as agent[493];

(3) of a contract, notwithstanding that the third party has given notice to the principal of his withdrawal from it,[494] unless the contract was made by the agent expressly or impliedly subject to ratification, in which case the offer or purported acceptance may be withdrawn at any time before ratification.[495]

Comment

2-085 **Rule (1)** It has been held that where the principal refused to ratify but, being nevertheless urged to do so, eventually did, he could sue the third party[496]: but that where he indicated that he would not do so, and the third party acted to his prejudice

---

[489] *Union Bank of Australia v McClintock* [1922] 1 A.C. 240; *Commercial Banking Co of Sydney v Mann* [1961] A.C. 1. But see Hornby (1961) 24 M.L.R. 271; Megrah [1961] J.B.L. 35; *Canadian Laboratory Supplies Ltd v Engelhard Industries of Canada Ltd* (1977) 78 D.L.R. (3d) 232, 236–237, 247; [1979] 2 S.C.R. 787 at 801–804; (1979) 97 D.L.R. (3d) 1 at 11–14.
[490] *Benham v Batty* (1865) 12 L.T. 266.
[491] *Soames v Spencer* (1822) 1 D. & R. 32; *Simpson v Eggington* (1855) 10 Exch. 845; see Comment.
[492] See Comment.
[493] Illustration 4.
[494] *Bolton Partners v Lambert* (1889) 41 Ch.D. 295, Illustration 1; *Re Tiedemann & Ledermann Frères* [1899] 2 Q.B. 66, Illustration 4 to Article 15.
[495] *Watson v Davies* [1931] 1 Ch. 455, Illustration 3; *Warehousing & Forwarding Co of East Africa v Jafferali & Sons* [1964] A.C. 1: see Comment.
[496] *Soames v Spencer* (1822) 1 D. & R. 32. See also *Akel v Turner* [1926] G.L.R. 574 (NZ).

on that basis, the principal could not subsequently ratify.[497] It has also been held that an *uncommunicated* refusal to ratify can be reversed, so that the principal can take advantage of the act ratified.[498] In general it seems, therefore, that the rule is correctly expressed as above: a ratification may be effective against the principal though originally he refused to ratify, and also in his favour unless the third party has relied on a previous refusal in a way that would make a subsequent ratification unfairly prejudicial. These conclusions seem better based on the rules as to limits on ratification than an estoppel, since there may be difficulties concerning representations of intention as founding estoppel. The reasoning seems best based on an analogy with the grant of preceding authority, which cannot be withdrawn as regards the transaction authorised once acted on: since the agent's action has already taken place, a ratification cannot without the consent of the other party be withdrawn. A refusal to ratify, on the other hand, is merely equivalent to a refusal to grant authority: this does not prevent a subsequent grant of authority, subject to the doctrine of estoppel. The other limitations on the power to ratify are of course also applicable.[499]

Rule (2)   This proposition covers cases where ratification renders lawful an act which was initially a tort, notwithstanding that proceedings have been instituted against the agent prior to ratification: an example appears in Illustration 4. In the case of contract, there is authority that where proceedings have been commenced against a *principal*, he may ratify thereafter and so render himself liable.[500] But a purported ratification by the principal after the commencement of proceedings against the agent would sometimes not be within a reasonable time[501] and so inoperative against a third party who did not wish to take advantage of it.[502]   **2-086**

Rule (3)   This proposition is a conspicuous and controversial application of the technical notion that ratification creates authority which relates back to the time of the act ratified. It is often referred to as the rule in *Bolton Partners v Lambert*,[503] a leading case which appears as Illustration 1. Such a rule is rejected in *Restatement, Third*,[504] and the case has been criticised by distinguished writers as giving an inappropriately full effect to the doctrine of relation back.[505] The third party, though he may not know it, is in the power of the principal, not merely as to whether he has made a contract, but also as to whether he must already answer for breach of it. Furthermore, when the third party discovers before any ratification that the agent is unauthorised (which was not the case in *Bolton Partners v Lambert*), it may   **2-087**

---

[497] See *McEvoy v Belfast Banking Co Ltd* [1935] A.C. 24 at 45.
[498] *Simpson v Eggington* (1855) 10 Exch. 845.
[499] e.g. that the ratification must be within a reasonable time: though this may also be based in estoppel. See in general Comment to Article 19.
[500] *Richardson v Oxford* (1861) 2 F. & F. 449.
[501] See Article 19.
[502] Except as regards the rules relating to mitigation of damages.
[503] (1889) 41 Ch.D. 295, Illustration 1. See also *Re Portuguese Consolidated Copper Mines Ltd* (1890) 45 Ch.D. 16, Illustration 4 to Article 19; *Hooper v Kerr, Stuart & Co Ltd* (1901) 83 L.T. 729, Illustration 2 to Article 20; *Koenigsblatt v Sweet* [1923] 2 Ch. 314.
[504] § 4.05.
[505] Wambaugh (1895) 9 Harvard L.Rev. 60; Fry, *Specific Performance* (6th edn), Additional Note A; Seavey (1920) 29 Yale L.J. 859 at 890–891; Tamaki (1941) 19 Can.B.R. 733; Pappas (1948) 2 Vand.L.Rev. 100; Hambrook (1982) 8 Adelaide L.Rev. 119 at 134–140; *Restatement, Third*, § 4.05(1) and Comment *c*; Dal Pont, para.5-40 onwards; Krebs, in Busch, Macgregor and Watts (eds), *Agency Law in Commercial Practice*, pp.28–32.

well be argued that he should be able to escape from the transaction rather than have to wait, if only for a reasonable time, to see if he has a contract. In *Fleming v Bank of New Zealand*[506] the Privy Council reserved the right to reconsider the case. It is certainly true that the judgments in *Bolton Partners v Lambert* itself consist largely of assertion. It is also true that the rule can only work fairly if it is made the subject of exceptions, discussed in the next Article, which are extremely difficult to formulate. This difficulty casts some doubt on the initial rule. The rule has however been assumed to be binding on the Court of Appeal.[507] Perhaps the rule's strongest rationale is that the third party's inability to withdraw is the consideration for the agent's warranty of authority; "I will warrant my authority so long as you permit the principal to ratify if I am wrong". If this is right, it ought to follow that if the agent consents to the third party's withdrawal from the contract, the principal ceases to be able to ratify.

If the English courts had a free hand, however, it is unlikely that many would disagree with the proposition that if a third party at the time of contracting believes an agent to be authorised, and subsequently finds that this was not so, he should, if he wishes, be able to withdraw from the transaction on that ground alone, and should not remain potentially bound until the principal decides whether or not to ratify. But the matter is less clear if the third party, not knowing of the lack of authority and believing himself to be bound, simply repudiates the contract, i.e. refuses or can be shown to be unable to perform, even if he uses the word "withdraw" to refer to his conduct—and it is this which appears to have been *Bolton Partners v Lambert* itself (with the added feature that the third party there apparently "withdrew" because he believed that the negotiations had not reached the stage at which he was bound at all). If one assumes that such a third party would normally have believed on reasonable grounds that the agent had authority, he can rely on the doctrine of apparent authority (or even ratification) and sue the principal for non-performance. In such a situation it is therefore the supposed principal, if he cannot ratify, who is potentially bound until the third party decides whether or not to proceed against him. *Restatement, Third* rejects the reasoning behind *Bolton Partners v Lambert* completely and treats the third party as being able to "withdraw" in this second situation also[508]; but the scope of ratification in the Restatements is in some respects different from that under English common law.[509] It is not clear that a party who believed himself bound, and therefore breaching his contractual obligations, and able to sue even only if he establishes apparent authority (or ratification), is fairly released by the fact that unknown to him the person with whom he had dealt had no actual authority. Perhaps his release could be based for English law on the known rule that a party who gives one reason justifying what appears to be a repudiation of contract may subsequently give another if it was in existence at the time of the original repudiation.[510] But as stated above, the *Bolton Partners* case, whatever it stands for, is binding on any court other than the Supreme Court.

It is in any case clear that where a contract is made expressly or impliedly subject

---

[506] [1900] A.C. 577 at 587. See the elaborate dissenting judgment of Isaacs J in *Davison v Vickery's Motors Ltd* (1925) 37 C.L.R. 1 and cases and dicta there cited.
[507] *Presentaciones Musicales S.A. v Secunda* [1994] Ch. 271 at 280 (Illustration 6 to Article 19).
[508] See *Restatement, Third*, § 4-05(1).
[509] See above, para.2-050.
[510] *Boston Deep Sea Fishing and Ice Co v Ansell* (1888) 39 Ch.D. 339.

to ratification, it is not binding at all and there is nothing to ratify.[511] Such an interpretation can be put on most cases where the third party is aware of the lack of authority, whatever the reasons for it. The purported ratification, would in fact simply create the contract, unless the other party had previously withdrawn. The case is the same as that where the agent does not purport to have authority.[512] The third party's promise is at best one made to the agent, not to withdraw from the transaction, and unless there is independent consideration does not bind him. Although it is possible to enter into a contract which binds in the sense that neither party may withdraw from the moment of agreement, but the main obligation does not come into operation unless certain events occur,[513] it is difficult to see that such a contract can be found to exist where the condition relates to the question whether one purported party is bound at all.

It seems also that the rule in *Bolton Partners v Lambert* is one of agency law only and to be restricted to cases of lack of authority. If the original agreement is ineffective for any other reason (e.g. lack of a deed) there is no contract to withdraw from and the doctrine of relation back does not apply.[514]

It has further been held that where the act the subject of purported ratification ceases to be operative before ratification, there is nothing to ratify.[515] The case in question involved unauthorised payment of a debt, and it was said that in such a case the party to whom the debt was paid was entitled to return the money on discovering that the payment had been unauthorised, and apply to his debtor for payment.[516]

Illustrations

(1) A made an offer to B, the managing director of a company, and it was accepted by him on the company's behalf. B had no authority to accept the offer. Not knowing of the lack of authority, but on the basis of disagreement in subsequent negotiations, which appear to have led him to assume that he was not yet bound, A gave the company notice that he withdrew his offer. The company subsequently ratified B's unauthorised acceptance. Held, that the ratification dated back to the time of the acceptance, rendering the purported withdrawal of the offer a breach. Specific performance was decreed against A.[517] **2-088**

(2) A, without B's authority, pays a debt owed by B. The creditor, upon discover-

---

[511] *Watson v Davies* [1931] 1 Ch. 455, Illustration 3; *Warehousing and Forwarding Co of East Africa v Jafferali & Sons* [1964] A.C. 1; *Rothmans Industries Ltd v Floral Holdings Ltd* [1986] 2 N.Z.L.R. 480 (contract "subject to approval of shareholders", a nullity). See also above, para.2-050. The judgment in *Jafferali*'s case is not easy to follow. It distinguishes between negotiating subject to approval and contracting subject to ratification. Obviously in the first case the details of the proposed agreement may be vaguer, but in neither case is there any transaction binding the third party.

[512] Contra, Seavey (1954) 21 U.Chi.L.Rev. 248; cf. Twerski (1948) 42 Temple L.Q. 1. See *Goodison Thresher Co v Doyle* (1925) 57 O.L.R. 300.

[513] See Treitel, *Law of Contract* (14th edn), para.2-102 onwards.

[514] *Kidderminster Corp v Hardwick* (1873) L.R. 9 Ex. 13 at 22 (followed in *Oxford v Crow* [1893] 3 Ch. 535) as explained in *Athy Guardians v Murphy* [1896] 1 I.R. 65. However, *Kidderminster Corp v Hardwick* was not referred to in *Bolton Partners v Lambert* and the approaches of the two cases are not easily reconciled. If the reasoning in *Athy Guardians v Murphy* is correct, it could also be used to explain *Metropolitan Asylums Board v Kingham & Sons*, below, Illustration 5 to Article 19.

[515] *Walter v James* (1870–71) L.R. 6 Ex. 124, Illustration 2; see *Birks and Beatson* (1976) 92 L.Q.R. 188 esp. at p.190 onwards.

[516] At p.127.

[517] *Bolton Partners v Lambert* (1889) 41 Ch.D. 295. A had also later claimed misrepresentation.

ing that A was not authorised to pay the debt, returns the money to him. B cannot subsequently ratify or take advantage of the payment.[518]

(3) A offers land to a charity at a certain price. The chairman and 14 of the 18 members of the board of the charity visit the property. They tell A that they have all made up their minds to purchase it and that a board meeting to be summoned to approve the purchase will be a mere formality. A may withdraw before the meeting, and a purported ratification by the meeting is ineffective, there being no initial agreement which can be ratified.[519]

(4) An agent, after the death of his principal, distrained in the principal's name for rent due. Held, that the executor might ratify the distress, and so justify the agent, although an action was at the time of the ratification pending against the agent for the trespass, and although the distress was levied before probate.[520]

Article 19

LIMITS ON RATIFICATION

2-089   Ratification is not effective where to permit it would unfairly prejudice a third party, and in particular—

(1) where it is essential to the validity of an act that it should be done within a certain time, the act cannot be ratified after the expiration of that time, to the prejudice of any third party[521];

(2) ratification may not be recognised if it will affect proprietary rights in either real or personal property, including intellectual property rights, which have arisen in favour of the third party or others claiming through him since the act of the unauthorised agent[522];

(3) the ratification of a contract can only be relied on by the principal if effected within a time after the act ratified was done which is reasonable in all the circumstances.[523]

Comment

2-090   It is clear that although the principle of ratification is convenient it could operate unfairly on the third party, particularly if it is given full retroactive effect, as in *Bolton Partners v Lambert*.[524] This Article seeks to formulate limits on the efficacy, and in particular on the retroactivity, of ratification. However, the basic rule is that first stated, that the ratification must not cause unfair prejudice: this has been

---

[518] *Walter v James*, above. But see as to this case Birks and Beatson (1976) 92 L.Q.R. 188, especially at p.190 onwards; Watts [1993] N.Z. Recent L.R. 248. As to the position in Scotland, see Macgregor and Whitty (2010) 15 Edin. L.R. 57.

[519] *Watson v Davies* [1931] 1 Ch. 455.

[520] *Whitehead v Taylor* (1839) 10 A. & E. 210; see also *Foster v Bates* (1843) 12 M. & W. 226; *Hull v Pickersgill* (1819) 1 B. & B. 282.

[521] Illustrations 1–3; *Lord Audley v Pollard* (1597) Cro.Eliz. 561; *Restatement, Third*, § 4.05(2).

[522] See Comment.

[523] *Re Portuguese Consolidated Copper Mines Ltd* (1890) 45 Ch.D. 16, Illustration 4; *Celthene Pty Ltd v WKJ Hauliers Pty Ltd* [1981] 1 N.S.W.L.R. 606 at 615; *Life Savers (Australasia) Ltd v Frigmobile Pty Ltd* [1983] 1 N.S.W.L.R. 431 at 438; *Trident General Insurance Co v McNiece Bros Pty Ltd* (1987) 8 N.S.W.L.R. 270 at 282; affd on other grounds (1988) 165 C.L.R. 107.

[524] (1889) 41 Ch.D. 295, Illustration 1 to Article 18; see Comment to Article 18.

accepted twice recently in the Court of Appeal.[525] The more detailed formulations which follow are therefore to be read subject to this.

Rules (1) and (2)   The strongest examples of this exception concern property   **2-091** rights. In what is often treated as the leading case, *Bird v Brown*,[526] goods were stopped in transit by an agent who had no authority to do so. They were formally demanded on behalf of the consignee, whose property they were and who tendered the freight. The consignor later ratified the stoppage. It was held that this was ineffective to affect the proprietary right which had vested in the consignee, and the agent was liable in conversion. It was said in *Bolton Partners v Lambert* itself that "an estate once vested cannot be divested by the doctrine of ratification".[527] A similar interpretation could be given to *Dibbins v Dibbins*,[528] in which it was held that where an option was exercised within its time limit by an agent who had no authority, its exercise could not be ratified outside that time. There are also cases holding ineffective ratification of unauthorised notices to quit after their operative date[529] which should perhaps be brought within this reasoning, in that the leasehold interest terminates on the expiry of the period set by a valid notice.[530] It cannot in fact be doubted that the doctrine cannot change property rights.

Bird v Brown is also frequently cited outside the context of property reasoning, but it does not of itself solve the contractual issues. In the case of an option, even though the ratification might not alter the equitable property rights involved, if property is the only exception it could be that ratification would render the holder of the property concerned nevertheless liable in contract to the person ratifying.[531] The reasoning of *Dibbins v Dibbins* nevertheless indicates that ratification is not possible even as regards the contractual liability. There are other cases where ratification is not permitted outside a time limit for the doing of the act: in particular, service of a notice to quit, already referred to in connection with pure property reasoning, could be brought within this wider rubric. Some rule regarding time limits is therefore needed. It may therefore be that outside property reasoning the cases should be approached on the basis that there is a simple rule preventing ratification outside time limits set for the doing of an act. This is supported by *Bird v Brown* also, where it was said that the right of stoppage can only be exercised during the transit. In *Presentaciones Musicales SA v Secunda*,[532] dealing with ratification of an unauthorised writ outside the limitation period, such a view was taken

---

[525] *Smith v Henniker-Major & Co* [2003] EWCA Civ 762; [2003] Ch. 182 (see Robert Walker LJ at [71]); and *The Borvigilant* [2003] EWCA Civ 935; [2003] 2 Lloyd's Rep. 520, Illustration 7 (see Clarke LJ at [70]). See also *Restatement, Third*, § 4.05(3).

[526] (1850) 4 Exch. 786, Illustration 2; cf. *Hutchings v Nunes* (1863) 1 Moo.P.C.(N.S.) 243, where the court apparently held that an agent already had general authority, despite a purported ratification after the end of the transit. There are animadversions on some of the reasoning in *Bird v Brown* in *Keighley, Maxsted & Co v Durant* [1901] A.C. 240 at 247–248.

[527] (1889) 41 Ch.D. at 307.

[528] [1896] 2 Ch. 348, Illustration 3.

[529] e.g. *Right d. Fisher, Nash and Hyrons v Cuthell* (1804) 5 East 491; and the argument of Coleridge J in *Doe d. Mann v Walters* (1830) 10 B. & C. 626 at 627–631; *Doe d. Lyster v Goldwin* (1841) 2 Q.B. 143. See Illustration 1.

[530] *Ancona v Marks* (1862) 7 H.&N. 686 at 697.

[531] See Tan Cheng-Han (2001) 117 L.Q.R. 626 at 630–634.

[532] [1994] Ch. 271, Illustration 6. See Brown (1994) 111 L.Q.R. 531. In addition to the cases there cited see *Shaw Savill & Albion Co v Timaru Harbour Board* (1888) 6 N.Z.L.R. 456; affd on other grounds (1890) 15 App.Cas. 429 (see argument).

by two members of the Court of Appeal,[533] though the third[534] restricted the limit on ratification to situations involving property rights in a broad sense. The majority view has been justified by an assertion that the principal can only ratify where he could have performed the act at the time of ratification.[535] This however does not square with the rule that a principal can ratify an insurance contract after loss,[536] which would require to be explained as an exception. It is also difficult to reconcile with *Bolton Partners v Lambert*[537] itself, where no such rule was referred to.

A viable "time limits" rule would however require some reference to the purpose of the limit in question. In this context reference to the notion of validity is sometimes suggested. It can be said that where it is essential to the validity of an act that it should be done within a certain time, it cannot be ratified after that time to the prejudice of the third party (though the third party can always accept the ratification). In *Presentaciones Musicales SA v Secunda* it was in fact held that since a writ issued without authority was not a complete nullity[538] it could be ratified after the expiry of the limitation period.

But the workability of a rule that void acts cannot be ratified has already been doubted,[539] and it may be better simply to proceed on the basis that certain acts are by their context required to be valid and effective when done,[540] lest a time limit be extended or the party affected be in a state of uncertainty. Such a rule would require discrimination between situations. Thus although the unauthorised issue of a writ can apparently be ratified[541] (at least before entry of judgment in favour of the defendant[542]), an assignment probably cannot after action on the right assigned has been commenced by the purported assignee,[543] nor a demand for payment or delivery,[544] a notice of abandonment in marine insurance,[545] a notice of dishonour of a negotiable instrument[546] or a notice to quit.[547] It may be possible to say that a ratification will be given retrospective effect unless there are cogent reasons why to give it such effect would contravene the purpose of any time element involved

---

[533] Dillon and Nolan LJJ; particular reliance was placed on *Ainsworth v Creeke* (1868–69) L.R. 4 C.P. 476, a case on a borough poor-rate.

[534] Roch LJ. But see Robert Walker LJ in *Smith v Henniker-Major & Co* [2003] EWCA Civ 762; [2003] Ch. 182.

[535] *Bird v Brown* (1850) 4 Exch. 786 at 799; *Ainsworth v Creeke*, above, at 486 and 487; *Williams v North China Insurance Co* (1875–76) 1 C.P.D. 757 at 764 (arguendo), 766. But the argument was rejected in *Hooper v Kerr, Stuart & Co Ltd* (1900) 83 L.T. 729, Illustration 2 to Article 20.

[536] See below, para.2-093.

[537] Illustration 1 to Article 18; see Comment to Article 18.

[538] On the ground that adoption or ratification does not require any application to the court: [1994] Ch. 271 at 279–280.

[539] See Article 14 and Comment.

[540] See *Re Construction Forestry Mining and Energy Union* (1994) 181 C.L.R. 539 at 545.

[541] *Presentaciones Musicales SA v Secunda*, Illustration 6; *Nottinghamshire NHS Trust v Prison Officers Assn* [2003] I.C.R. 1192 (complaint of unfair dismissal after expiry of time limit: useful discussion). *Danish Mercantile Co Ltd v Beaumont* [1951] Ch. 680, Illustration 4 to Article 14; *Alexander Ward & Co Ltd v Samyang Navigation Co Ltd* [1975] 1 W.L.R. 673; and see *Pontin v Wood* [1962] 1 Q.B. 594; *Matthews v SPI Electricity Pty Ltd* [2011] VSC 167; (2011) 34 V.R. 560 at [65] (nominal plaintiff able to ratify representative proceedings).

[542] See *Gelley v Shepherd* [2013] EWCA Civ 1172 at [73].

[543] See Mechem, *Law of Agency* (2nd edn), § 530 (deprivation of defence).

[544] See *Solomons v Dawes* (1794) 1 Esp. 83; *Coore v Callaway* (1794) 1 Esp. 115; *Coles v Bell* (1808) 1 Camp. 478n.

[545] See *Jardine v Leathley* (1863) 3 B. & S. 700 at 708.

[546] *East v Smith* (1847) 16 L.J.Q.B. 292.

[547] See cases cited at fn.529 above.

or otherwise be unfair to the third party. The third party can always however accept the ratification if he pleases.

Rule (2) is taken from the judgment of Roch LJ in the *Presentaciones Musicales* case, and represents a passage favourably referred to in the other two principal recent decisions by Robert Walker LJ in *Smith v Henniker-Major & Co*[548] and by Clarke LJ in *The Borvigilant*.[549] In particular, Robert Walker LJ said that the "deprivation of an accrued right" was "an important example of the general rationale identified in ... Article 19, that is, unfair prejudice".[550] It may be assumed that interests in real and personal property cannot, at any rate normally, and certainly not against a third party, be divested by ratification.[551] The words used in Rule (2) however permit the extension of such reasoning to other occurrences which could be regarded as analogous, such as an accrued right of action: but, it would appear, not in all cases. For the *Presentaciones Musicales* case holds that immunity from suit by reason of limitation is not automatically barred and can, at least sometimes, be extinguished by ratification, and *The Borvigilant* that a right of action in tort can be extinguished or limited by ratification of a contract containing an applicable exclusion of liability clause (which it must always have been assumed would be operative). It seems therefore that the rule is being clarified as a flexible one; but it is also a "judgmental application of principle ... not ... an exercise of judicial discretion, though for practical purposes the two are closely akin".[552]

Rule (3): reasonable time   There is a dictum by Fry LJ that "if the ratification is   **2-092**
to bind it must be made within a reasonable time after acceptance by an authorised person".[553] Fry LJ went on, however, to say that "such a reasonable time can never extend after the time at which the contract is to commence". This part of the dictum has been disapproved[554] and cannot now be regarded as valid.[555] The first part of the dictum seems, however, an appropriate restriction on ratification; but that not all delay makes ratification too late is shown by the fact that a letter before action may amount to ratification.[556] It is probably best based on a wider principle, such as that suggested in *Restatement, Third*,[557] that:

"A ratification of a transaction is not effective unless it precedes the occurrence of circumstances that would cause the ratification to have adverse and inequitable effects on the rights of third parties".[558]

In different words, the rule is one for the protection of the third party against whom

---

[548] [2002] EWCA Civ 762; [2003] Ch. 182.
[549] [2003] EWCA Civ 935; [2003] 2 Lloyd's Rep. 520, Illustration 7. See also *Challinor v Juliet Bellis & Co* [2013] EWHC 347 (Ch) at [643]; reversed on other points, sub nom. *Bellis v Challinor* [2015] EWCA Civ 59.
[550] At [71].
[551] See Clarke LJ in *The Borvigilant*, above, at [84]–[86].
[552] *Smith v Henniker-Major & Co*, above, at [82] per Robert Walker LJ.
[553] *Metropolitan Asylums Board v Kingham & Sons* (1890) 6 T.L.R. 217 at 218 (Illustration 5).
[554] *Celthene Pty Ltd v WKJ Hauliers Pty Ltd* [1981] 1 N.S.W.L.R. 606 at 615; *Life Savers (Aust.) Pty Ltd v Frigmobile Pty Ltd* [1983] 1 N.S.W.L.R. 431 at 438; *Bedford Insurance Co Ltd v Instituto de Resseguros do Brasil* [1983] Q.B. 966 at 987. See also *Morrell v Studd and Millington* [1913] 2 Ch. 648.
[555] It is extremely difficult to reconcile with *Bolton Partners v Lambert* itself. Fry LJ was a declared opponent of the rule in any case: see Fry, *Specific Performance* (6th edn), Additional Note A.
[556] As in *The Borvigilant* [2003] EWCA Civ 935: [2003] 2 Lloyd's Rep. 520, Illustration 7.
[557] § 4.05.
[558] Tan Cheng-Han (2001) 117 L.Q.R. 626, suggests that this rule can solve the retroactivity problems

the ratification might be invoked. If the principal ratifies and the third party actually wishes to rely on this, he should be entitled to do so. Where the third party wishes to resist ratification, the mere lapse of time may often make it inequitable,[559] particularly when "a modest degree of prejudice is magnified by delay".[560] But there may be other circumstances which do so. For a start, the third party who discovers that the agent was unauthorised may be put in a state of uncertainty in which a rapid indication by the principal of his position is required: it would then behove the principal to ratify quickly or not at all. And it is sometimes said that if an agent contracts without authority to sell property to another, and the property is then destroyed without anyone's fault, the principal can no longer ratify.[561]

2-093 Ratification of policies of insurance after loss It has, however, long been established that a policy of marine insurance may be ratified after loss[562]: this was justified on the basis that:

> "where an agent effects an insurance subject to ratification, the loss insured against is very likely to happen before ratification, and it must be taken that the insurance so effected involves that possibility as the basis of the contract."[563]

It had been controversial whether this principle applies to other insurances also, but it now seems clear that it does,[564] and this seems correct. If the commercial background dictates that policies are entered into on this basis, it is not inequitable to hold the insurer liable.[565]

Illustrations

2-094   (1) A, without the authority of the landlord, gives a tenant notice to quit. The notice cannot be made binding on the tenant by the landlord's ratification after the time for giving notice has expired.[566]

   (2) The agent of a consignor of goods, without the authority of his principal, gave notice of stoppage in transit on the principal's behalf. The goods afterwards arrived at their destination, and were formally demanded by the trustee in bankruptcy of the consignee. It was held that the consignor could not subsequently ratify the stoppage in transit and so divest the property in the

---

discussed above, para.2-091. It seems doubtful however whether the rule can bear such a weight of specific criteria as are needed.

[559] In *Trident General Insurance Co Ltd v McNiece Bros Pty Ltd* (1987) 8 N.S.W.L.R. 270 at 282–283 it was held that ratification against an insurer was not valid seven years after the making of the policy. The case was affirmed on other grounds, (1988) 165 C.L.R. 107.

[560] See *Smith v Henniker-Major & Co* [2002] EWCA Civ 762; [2003] Ch. 162 at [73].

[561] See *Williams v North China Insurance Co* (1876) 1 C.P.D. 757 at 770; but cf. Stoljar, p.196.

[562] *Routh v Thompson* (1811) 13 East 275; *Hagedorn v Oliverson* (1814) 2 M. & S. 485; *Jardine v Leathley* (1863) 3 B. & S. 700.

[563] *Williams v North China Insurance Co* (1876) 1 C.P.D. 757 at 764–765; see also 770.

[564] *Trident General Insurance Co v McNiece Bros Pty Ltd* (1987) 8 N.S.W.L.R. 270 at 280–281; (decision affirmed on other grounds (1988) 165 C.L.R. 107); and see *National Oilwell (UK) Ltd v Davy Offshore Ltd* [1993] 2 Lloyd's Rep. 582; *The Borvigilant* [2003] EWCA Civ 935; [2003] 2 Lloyd's Rep. 520; *MacGillivray on Insurance Law* (13th edn), para.1-198.

[565] cf. *Restatement, Second*, § 89, Comment c.

[566] *Doe d. Mann v Walters* (1830) 10 B. & C. 626; *Doe d. Lyster v Goldwin* (1841) 2 Q.B. 143; *Right d. Fisher, Nash and Hyrons v Cuthell* (1804) 5 East 491; *Hexstone Holdings Ltd v AHC Westlink Ltd* [2010] EWHC 1280 (Ch); [2010] 32 E.G. 62; [2010] 2 E.G.L.R. 13 at [32].

goods, which had in the meantime vested in the consignee's trustee in bankruptcy.[567]

(3) It is agreed between A and B, who are partners, that on the death of either of them the survivor shall have the option of purchasing the share of the deceased upon giving notice to the executors within three months after the death. A dies, and within three months after his death, C, on B's behalf, but without his authority, gives notice to the executors of B's intention to exercise the option. Such notice cannot be ratified after the expiration of the three months so as to bind the executors.[568]

(4) Directors of a company purport to allot shares by procedures which are not valid. The allottees complain but do not repudiate the allotments. In the circumstances, ratification of the allotments by the company several months later may be valid.[569]

(5) A corporation advertises for tenders for the supply of eggs for six months from September 30. K puts in a tender, and on September 22 the board of the corporation resolves to accept it and notifies K. On September 24 K writes that he had made a mistake in drawing up his tender and inserted the wrong price. On October 6 the corporation ratifies the acceptance by affixing its common seal. The ratification is ineffective.[570]

(6) A solicitor issues a writ without authority, within the period of limitation applicable for the proceedings in question. The person on whose behalf the writ was issued ratifies the issue of the writ after the period of limitation has expired. The ratification is effective.[571]

(7) A shipowner entering port is required to sign a contract for tug service which provides that the port operator is not liable in respect of the service and that this immunity is extended to the tug owner. The tug collides with the ship. Tug and ship sue each other. The port operator had implied authority to sign a contract on behalf of the tug owner containing the exemption from liability; but if this is not so, a letter before action sent by the tug owner ranks as ratification and is not unfair, even though there was by that time an accrued cause of action.[572]

Article 20

EFFECT OF RATIFICATION

(1) The effect of ratification is to invest the person on whose behalf the act ratified was done, the person who did the act, and third parties, with the same rights, duties, immunities and liabilities in all respects as if the act had been done with the previous authority of the person on whose behalf it was done[573];

2-095

---

[567] *Bird v Brown* (1850) 4 Exch. 786; see Comment.
[568] *Dibbins v Dibbins* [1896] 2 Ch. 348; *Hughes v NM Superannuation Pty Ltd* (1993) 29 N.S.W.L.R. 653. See also *Holland v King* (1848) 6 C.B. 727.
[569] *Re Portuguese Consolidated Copper Mines* (1890) 45 Ch.D. 16.
[570] *Metropolitan Asylums Board v Kingham & Sons* (1890) 6 T.L.R. 217; see Comment.
[571] *Presentaciones Musicales SA v Secunda* [1994] Ch. 271; *Adams v Ford* [2012] EWCA Civ 544; [2012] 1 W.L.R. 3211; see Comment.
[572] *The Borvigilant* [2003] EWCA Civ 935; [2003] 2 Lloyd's Rep. 520.
[573] See *Wilson v Tunman and Fretson* (1843) 6 M. & G. 236; *Bird v Brown* (1850) 4 Exch. 786; Illustrations 1–5; *Restatement, Third*, § 4.02.

subject to the agent's liability to the third party for any loss caused by his breach of the warranty of authority, and to his principal for loss caused by his breach of duty except in so far as this has been waived as between them.[574]

(2) But the doctrine of ratification may not be invoked to divest or affect prejudicially any proprietary or possessory right vested in any third party at the time of the ratification.[575]

(3) Ratification does not of itself give any new authority to the person whose act is ratified.[576]

(4) A ratification once effected cannot be withdrawn without the consent of the third party.[577]

Comment

2-096   Rule (1)   Rule (1) is a general statement of the effect of a valid ratification and to a certain extent overlaps with the introductory Article 13. Thus where A, on behalf of P, but without authority, makes a contract with T, and P ratifies the contract, the normal effects of such ratification will be as follows:

(i) P and T can enforce the contract against each other as though it had been originally authorised, even though T has meanwhile purported to withdraw from the contract.[578]

(ii) Although in general A remains liable to T for any breach of warranty of authority, it will not normally be possible for T to prove damages[579]: A is thus no longer liable to T unless he contracted personally.[580] If, however, he has caused loss to the third party, e.g. because the third party has taken advice as to, or even instituted proceedings against him, A might be liable to that extent, subject to the possible duty of the third party to mitigate his damages on ratification, if the ratification was not too late.[581]

(iii) In general it may be said that A is not liable to P for exceeding his authority,[582] for the doctrine of ratification normally contemplates a principal who is glad to waive the technical irregularity and adopt the transaction. This may however not always be so; a principal may ratify a transaction for convenience, or to preserve his commercial reputation, or even from commercial necessity. It is necessary therefore:

"to consider the matter in two stages. First, is there ratification of the contract which the agent purported to make. Secondly, has the principal waived the breach of duty if any vis-à-vis the agent. Often the facts will lead to ratification and exoneration, but not always."[583]

---

[574] See Comment.

[575] See above, para.2-091; Illustration 9; *Re Gloucester Municipal Election Petition, 1900, Ford v Newth* [1901] 1 K.B. 683.

[576] Illustration 10.

[577] See Comment.

[578] See above, para.2-087.

[579] Article 106.

[580] See Article 98.

[581] Article 98.

[582] *Smith v Cologan* (1788) 2 T.R. 188n.; Illustrations 6 and 7; *Union Bank of Australia Ltd v Rudder* (1911) 13 C.L.R. 152, below, para.6-005.

[583] *Suncorp Insurance and Finance v Milano Assicurazioni SpA* [1993] 2 Lloyd's Rep. 225 at 234–235, per Waller J. See also *Restatement*, § 416; Mechem, *Treatise on the Law of Agency* (2nd edn),

(iv) Equally, in many cases, by ratifying, P may be regarded as accepting an offer by the agent to act as his agent in a manner not previously authorised, on the normal basis as to remuneration, reimbursement and indemnity. Hence P may be liable to pay A such sum in respect of remuneration as A would have been entitled to had the contract been authorised[584] and must reimburse and indemnify A in respect of the transaction.[585] Conversely, A also becomes a fiduciary retrospectively if he was not previously so. But again, where P's ratification is not voluntary, it is submitted that he may ratify but not waive the agent's breach or accept any offer by the agent. In such a case the agent may by virtue of the terms of his contract or because of the gravity of his breach be entitled to no payments at all, and the principal may have a valid claim in damages.

(v) Any title acquired by P relates back to the moment of ratification.[586]

Rule (2) Rule (2) has already been considered in connection with time limits. Where an act to be effective must be done within a certain time (e.g. the exercise of an option, or of the right of stoppage in transit), to allow a ratification to operate after that time would be to prejudice rights vested in the other party, or in third parties. But the principle as stated here is wider and can apply to proprietary rights vested in persons not connected with the instant transaction at all,[587] or cases where the right is hardly of a proprietary nature, such as the interests of electors or candidates in avoiding corruption in local elections.[588] Such cases will, however, be rare.   **2-097**

Rule (3) Rule (3) may seem obvious: it confines ratification to the act done, though doubtless ratification may be evidence of some other authority.[589] It is this rule which makes it difficult to say loosely that ratification creates agency, for it is clear that if it did, an authority would be set up that might thereafter need revocation.   **2-098**

Rule (4) Once a contract is validly ratified, it is binding. The third party may agree to rescind it, but the ratifying principal has no unilateral power to dissolve the contract once he has affirmed it. There is no analogy with the withdrawal of authority, for that relates to the future. But it may be that where the ratification has been induced by a misrepresentation by the third party, the contract may be rescinded.[590] Similar reasoning will apply in other situations of ratification.   **2-099**

---

§§ 492-493; *Mineworkers' Union v Brodrick* 1948 (2) S.A.L.R. 959, 979; *Delco Australia Pty Ltd v Darlington Futures Ltd* (1986) 43 S.A.S.R. 519, reversed on other grounds (1986) 161 C.L.R. 500; *Ing Re (UK) Ltd v R & V Versicherung AG* [2006] EWHC 1544 (Comm); [2006] 2 All E.R. (Comm) 870; [2006] Lloyd's Rep. I.R. 653; [2007] 1 B.C.L.C. 108 at [152] (suggesting that a more complete knowledge of the facts may be required before exoneration is found).

[584] *Keay v Fenwick* (1876) 1 C.P.D. 745, Illustration 10 to Article 17; *Mason v Clifton* (1863) 3 F. & F. 899.

[585] Illustrations 3, 7 and 8; *Hartas v Ribbons* (1889) 22 Q.B.D. 254; Article 62.

[586] *Lawson v Hosemaster Co Ltd* [1966] 1 W.L.R. 1300 at 1314 (shares and dividends).

[587] Illustration 9.

[588] *Re Gloucester Municipal Election Petition, 1900, Ford v Newth* [1901] 1 K.B. 683; this is perhaps a doubtful case.

[589] See above, para.2-049.

[590] See *Restatement, Third*, § 4.02(2)(a) (any situation that would make a contract voidable).

Illustrations

2-100   (1)   A, on B's behalf, but without his authority, distrains goods belonging to C. B ratifies the distress. If B had a right to distrain, A is discharged from liability, then the ratification having a retroactive effect, and rendering the distress lawful ab initio[591] if B had no right to distrain, A and B are jointly and severally liable as trespassers.[592]

(2)   The secretary of a company, without the authority of the directors, sends out a notice purporting to have been issued by order of the board, convening an extraordinary general meeting, a requisition for such meeting having been duly served on the company in accordance with the articles of association. At a board meeting held two days before the date for which the general meeting is called, the directors resolve to ratify and confirm the issuing of the notice by the secretary. The notice is thereby rendered valid, and the meeting is duly summoned.[593]

(3)   A insures goods, in which he has no insurable interest, on behalf of B. B, who has an insurable interest in goods, ratifies the insurance. The insurable interest of B is sufficient to support an action by A on the policy,[594] and B is liable for the premium.[595]

(4)   A factor contracts to purchase goods on his principal's behalf at a price exceeding his limit. The principal ratifies the contract by disposing of the goods. He must pay the factor the full price.[596]

(5)   A buys goods from T on behalf of P without authority. P pays A and ratifies the transaction. It turns out that the goods had been fraudulently disposed of prior to the transaction by the captain of the ship on which they had been. P may not sue A.[597]

(6)   A firm of carriers, employed to deliver goods to A, delivers them to B. The senders invoice the goods to B, sue him for the price, recover judgment and take bankruptcy proceedings against him. They may not subsequently sue the carriers for misdelivery.[598]

(7)   A shipmaster entered into contracts with the Admiralty for the transport of troops, and paid and incurred various sums and liabilities to enable him to perform the contracts, the shipowner being bankrupt and having mortgaged the vessel. Held, that the master had a right to be repaid the expenses and indemnified against the liabilities, out of the freight due from the Admiralty, the assignees in bankruptcy and mortgagees not being entitled to take the

---

[591] *Whitehead v Taylor* (1839) 10 A. & E. 210; *Hull v Pickersgill* (1819) 1 B. & B. 282.

[592] See *Bird v Brown* (1850) 4 Exch. 786 at 799. The common law of distraint in relation to commercial tenancies has been abolished and replaced as from April 6, 2014 pursuant to Tribunals, Courts and Enforcement Act 2007 s.71.

[593] *Hooper v Kerr, Stuart & Co Ltd* (1901) 83 L.T. 729.

[594] *Wolff v Horncastle* (1798) 1 B. & P. 316.

[595] *New Zealand Insurance Co Ltd v Tyneside Pty Ltd* [1917] N.Z.L.R. 569.

[596] *Cornwal v Wilson* (1750) 1 Ves. Sen. 510. And see *Brice v Wilson* (1834) 8 A. & E. 349 (relatives of deceased order extravagant funeral: ratifying executor personally liable); cf. *Lucy v Walrond* (1837) 3 Bing. N.C. 841.

[597] *Risbourg v Bruckner* (1858) 3 C.B.(N.S.) 812. The case is complicated by the foreign principal rule (below, para.9-020); and there may have been prior authority.

[598] *Verschures Creameries Ltd v Hull & Netherlands SS Co* [1921] 2 K.B. 608; see explanation in *United Australia Ltd v Barclays Bank Ltd* [1941] A.C. 1 at 31 and criticism in Goff and Jones, *Law of Restitution* (4th edn) p.733, fn.38 (not in later editions).

benefit of the contract, unless they also adopted the burdens connected therewith.[599]

(8) An agent who is personally liable unsuccessfully defends an action brought against him for breach of an unauthorised contract entered into by him on behalf of his principal. The principal ratifies what he has done. The principal must indemnify the agent against the damages and costs recovered by the plaintiff in the action.[600] So, where a person is made a party to an action without his authority, he cannot avail himself of the benefit of the action, unless he pays the costs of conducting it.[601]

(9) A commodore in the navy, without authority to do so, appointed a captain. Held, that even if the Crown ratified the appointment, that would not give the commodore the right to share as a commodore with a captain under him, in prizes taken before the date of the ratification, because the rights to the various shares in those prizes would then be already vested.[602]

(10) The directors of a company borrow money in excess of the amount which they have power to borrow. This may be ratified by a simple majority of the shareholders at an extraordinary meeting. But such a ratification confers no further power to borrow in excess of the directors' powers: such power would require a vote of more than one half of the shareholders in accordance with the terms of the articles.[603]

4. ESTOPPEL FROM DENYING EXISTENCE OF AGENCY RELATIONSHIP

Article 21

ESTOPPEL FROM DENYING EXISTENCE OF AGENCY RELATIONSHIP

A person may be held liable as principal where it cannot be said that he has made a manifestation or representation as to the authority of another to that other or to a third party as required in Articles 7, 8, 72 or 83, but he is affected in an agency context by the operation of the doctrine of estoppel.[604]   **2-101**

Comment

Estoppel as creating agency In most situations where the question of estoppel arises in respect of an agent's authority, the relevant agent will have possessed some actual authority but has proceeded to exceed it. This topic is considered in detail in Chapter 8, under the heading of "Apparent Authority".[605] But some reference to the establishment of a relationship of agency ab initio is appropriate in a chapter   **2-102**

---

[599] *Bristow v Whitmore* (1861) 9 H.L.Cas. 391.

[600] *Frixione v Tagliaferro & Sons* (1856) 10 Moo.P.C. 175. But in this case there may have been prior authority. Quaere as to the extent to which this result would apply where the principal ratified a contract in respect of which the agent had already incurred expenditure in defending an action for breach of warranty of authority. There seems no reason why it should unless the principal was in some way in breach of his duty to the agent in not ratifying earlier.

[601] *Hall v Laver* (1842) 1 Hare 571.

[602] *Donelly v Popham* (1807) 1 Taunt. 1.

[603] *Irvine v Union Bank of Australia* (1877) 2 App.Cas. 366. Though the third party lender would normally be protected by s.40 of the Companies Act 2006. See below, para.8-036.

[604] See Comment; and the Comments to the related Articles 72 and 83.

[605] Article 72.

on "Creation of Agency" even if most of the law concerned is to be found in cases on apparent authority (and even though the full relationship of agency, including the principal's right to sue, and that between principal and agent, was not created in such situations). Any difference of terminology could be given some slight justification on the basis that stronger evidence would usually be required to support the authority of one who had not previously been in an agency relationship with the principal than would be required where the person concerned already had agency powers; but this was misleading.[606]

This arrangement of the book could have been, and was,[607] taken to mean that in situations of the first type referred to above (no initial authority at all) the operative reasoning was based on estoppel; but that this was not or might not be so of cases of the second type (some but insufficient authority). A highly relevant question is therefore whether the operative reasoning for both situations is indeed based on estoppel. Although a judicial statement by Slade J that all apparent authority is based on estoppel,[608] though often cited, was perhaps not strong authority, the same attribution was made by Diplock LJ in the leading case of *Freeman & Lockyer v Buckhurst Park Properties (Mangal) Ltd*.[609] However, it is pointed out in the discussion of apparent authority in Article 72 that in many or even most cases of such authority the full requirements of estoppel as normally explained are not really satisfied, and it is there suggested that it is probably appropriate to regard the estoppel as a special one with weak requirements, special to agency. This explanation must apply to cases of both types.

Restatement, Third, however, takes a different approach and bases all apparent authority, of both types, on the objective interpretation normally applied to contractual situations.[610] (This technique of interpretation was indeed also at one time attributed, at any rate in England, to estoppel,[611] but such an explanation would not now be thought appropriate.) This enables the *Restatement* to mark off what may be called "true" estoppel cases from cases of apparent authority.[612]

The *Restatement*'s explanation of apparent authority is not accepted in this book.[613] But there is no doubt that agency situations can give rise to estoppel under the general law, in situations where the full, normally stated requirements of clear manifestation, causal connection and detrimental reliance are in fact satisfied. The present function of this Article is therefore a different one: leaving apparent authority and its basis completely aside, to draw attention to the possibility of the application of orthodox estoppel doctrines in the agency context where it may be difficult to say that the normal principles of apparent authority, whether by way of extending authority or of creating it in a person who never had authority, apply.

2-103   **Estoppel in agency situations**   *Restatement, Third* (from which the title, though not the wording, of this Article is taken) gives two types of such situation where a third party is induced to make a detrimental change in position because a transac-

---

[606] See DeMott, in Busch, Macgregor and Watts (eds), *Agency Law in Commercial Practice* (2016), Ch.3.
[607] See Spencer Bower, *Reliance-Based Estoppel* (5th edn), para.9.3 fn.3.
[608] *Rama Corp v Proved Tin and General Investments* [1952] 2 Q.B. 147 at 149–150. See also *Lloyd's Bank Plc v Independent Insurance Co Ltd* [2000] Q.B. 110 at 122.
[609] [1964] 2 Q.B. 480, 503. See below, para.8-011.
[610] See § 2.03, Comment c and below, para.8-028 onwards.
[611] See Hughes (1930) 54 L.Q.R. 370.
[612] § 2.05.
[613] See below, para.8-029.

tion into which he has entered is believed to be on account of another, but no manifestation by the principal can be detected under ordinary principles. The first is that in which the "principal", while making no manifestation of authority, by conduct (usually before the operative transaction) intentionally or carelessly caused belief that the agent was authorised. The second is that where, having notice of such a belief and that it might induce others to change their position, the "principal" did not take (often after the operative transaction) easily taken steps to notify those others of the facts.[614] So, an estoppel by acquiescence will arise where the putative principal is aware that an agent is purporting to act as such but fails to take steps to intervene when those could readily have been taken.[615] In each case it must be assumed that there is no possibility of explaining the case on the basis that a representation was made by a person authorised by the principal.[616]

First category   In some cases of the first category mentioned above such an estop-   **2-104** pel can be regarded as an example of estoppel by representation.[617] When the representation was negligent it may raise questions not only of causation and detrimental reliance, but also the initial question whether a duty of care is owed to the particular claimant: in this context it seems that the duty can be owed to quite a wide class of persons.[618] The courts have also, however, sometimes been willing to see an estoppel based merely on the breach of duty of care by the negligence of a person in facilitating, or failing to take reasonable steps to prevent, situations in which a third party might be led to assume that a person was authorised, even though there was no manifestation that this was so. An Australian decision in a contract context which may be explicable on this basis appears in Illustration 2 below. There is however very little other authority applying such reasoning in contract situations. There is slightly more in connection with property, largely in connection with the doctrine of apparent ownership; but there are also many authoritative dicta that persons owe no general duty to look after their own property,[619] and it is fairly clear that (for example) giving another a blank signed

---

[614] See § 2.05. A fairly clear case is *Spiro v Lintern* [1973] 1 W.L.R. 1002, Illustration 3. See too *Ramsden v Dyson* (1866) L.R. 1 H.L. 129 at 158; *Grand Trunk Railway Co of Canada v Robinson* [1915] A.C. 740 at 747–748; *Geniki Investments International Ltd v Ellis Stockbrokers Ltd* [2008] EWHC 549 (QB); [2008] 1 B.C.L.C. 662 at [46], and above, para.2-077. Cf. *English v English* [2010] EWHC 2058 (Ch) (mother failing to reveal son's forgery of her signature, and herself making payments referable to purported contract).

[615] *City Bank of Sydney v McLaughlin* (1909) 9 C.L.R. 615 at 625; *Clayton Robard Management Ltd v Siu* (1988) 6 A.C.L.C. 57 at 60; *AJU Remicon Co Ltd v Alida Shipping Co Ltd* [2007] EWHC 2246 (Comm) at [15]; *VLM Holdings Ltd v Ravensworth Digital Services Ltd* [2013] EWHC 228 (Ch) at [70]. In some markets, it may not be reasonable to require putative principals to prevent persons from purporting to act as their agents (but the position will be different if they adopt the benefit of the intervenor's actions): *Montrio Ltd v Tse Ping Shun David* [2012] HKEC 1781.

[616] This possibility was rejected in the leading property case of *Moorgate Mercantile Co Ltd v Twitchings* [1977] A.C. 890, Illustration 7 to Article 84. See also *Crabtree-Vickers Pty Ltd v Australian Direct Mail Advertising Co Pty Ltd* (1975) 133 C.L.R. 72.

[617] See a useful discussion in Spencer Bower, *Reliance-Based Estoppel* (5th edn), para.3.27 onwards.

[618] See *Swan v North British Australasian Co Ltd* (1863) 2 Hurl. & C. 175 at 182; *RE Jones Ltd v Waring & Gillow Ltd* [1926] A.C. 670 at 693; *Mercantile Bank of India v Central Bank of India Ltd* [1938] A.C. 287 at 298–299; *Wilson & Meeson v Pickering* [1946] K.B. 422 at 425; *Mercantile Credit Co Ltd v Hamblin* [1965] 2 Q.B. 242 at 271; *Moorgate Mercantile Co Ltd v Twitchings* [1977] A.C. 890. See also Comment to Article 84.

[619] e.g. *Farquharson Brothers & Co v King & Co* [1902] A.C. 325 at 332; see Comment to Article 84.

document is not necessarily a breach of duty owed to third parties.[620] In general it seems doubtful whether such an estoppel construction should often be put on facts which create no right of action under any other head.[621] There is no general obligation in the common law not to cause another's economic loss, and the starting point is that individuals should protect themselves in attempting to contract with others. To impose liability would further require the making of what may be rather an arbitrary choice between the negligence of the plaintiff and that of the defendant, without any possibility of apportioning blame as might be possible in a negligence claim in tort. The general argument for a contract analysis would sometimes have to be the rather dubious one, by no means always accepted by the law, that a person whose chooses to act through others must take the risk of the ways in which those others act.[622]

2-105 **Second category** Cases in the second category are easier to explain. They are cases where there is no manifestation of authority, but the principal is in full possession of the facts and has stood by allowing the agent to overstate his authority; an example appears in Illustration 3 below. The law must, however, be careful not to impose inconvenience on the principal in requiring intervention to correct the false impression gained by the third party. The position was persuasively stated in *City Bank of Sydney v McLaughlin*[623]:

> "In general a man is not bound actively to repudiate or disaffirm an act done in his name but without his authority. But this is not the universal rule. The circumstances may be such that a man is bound by all rules of honesty not to be quiescent, but actively to dissent, when he knows that others have for his benefit put themselves in the position of disadvantage, from which, if he speaks or acts at once, they can extricate themselves, but from which, after a lapse of time, they can no longer escape."

The inactivity must be of the principal or of persons who would have had authority to do what the more junior agent is purporting to have done. Where there is co-agency, and there has been no holding out, it is possible that even the inactivity of a majority of their number cannot create the estoppel if their actual authority turns on compliance with rules for group decision-making.[624]

2-106 **Contractual operation of estoppel** Although this can be said to be a straightforward example of estoppel, the way in which it operates in this context is to ground contract liability. The prevailing view in the United States seems to be that estoppel reasoning is related to tort,[625] and it is certainly true that the requirements for negligence liability (in particular a duty of care to the person or persons affected) apply in some degree. But in the context of contract it seems that damages are to be calculated on the basis that the contract had been authorised, and need not be

---

[620] See Comment to Article 84.

[621] See Spencer Bower, *Reliance-Based Estoppel* (5th edn), paras 3-50–3.51.

[622] An example where the court falls back on this is the American case of *MacAndrews & Forbes Co v United States* 23 F. 2d 667 (1928) (where a delivery order was left in a drawer). See *Reliance-Based Estoppel*, above, paras 5.23–5.24; cf. *Essington Investments Pty Ltd v Regency Property Pty Ltd* [2004] NSWCA 375. See too Watts (2005) 26 Aust. Bar Rev. 185.

[623] (1909) 9 C.L.R. 615 at 625.

[624] See *PEC Ltd v Asia Golden Rice Co Ltd* [2014] EWHC 1583 (Comm) at [58] (majority of board knew junior agent had been purporting to exercise unusual powers only open to the board, but minority did not).

[625] See *Restatement, Third*, § 2-05, Comment d.

based on the reliance interest appropriate to tort claims.[626] The use of such reasoning seems historically to have gone some distance towards filling the gap in misrepresentation liability caused by the narrow view taken of the scope of the tort of deceit in *Derry v Peek*.[627] It seems possible that the second category of estoppel could also be used to justify a rescission of any relevant contract on the basis of misrepresentation.[628]

Possibility of tort action   Where the negligence has arisen in an estoppel context,   **2-107**
the courts have, as stated above, looked for a duty of care towards the third party. It is not clear whether the criteria applied are the same as those required for a tort action for pure economic loss, which is what is normally caused in such cases. The better view seems to be that they are[629]; and that the other requirements of estoppel (clarity of representation (where relevant), causation and reliance) will also be required.[630] Hence it may be asked whether an action in tort based only on the duty of care (and matters of causation) would sometimes be an alternative way of proceeding.[631] Even if it were available, the contract action, supported by an estoppel, will usually be better because it will attract the contract rules for assessment of damages on the basis that the transaction was authorised, and hence loss of profit, where the tort rules would only give loss caused.

Ratification   The conduct of the supposed principal may often instead be   **2-108**
interpreted as a ratification.[632] This does not require that the third party acted on the ratification, nor even (probably) that it be communicated to the third party at all.[633] But it requires that the principal has been known at the time of the act ratified: an undisclosed principal cannot ratify.[634]

Illustrations

(1)   A goes into a spacious furniture shop and is approached by a person with grey-   **2-109**
ing hair whose dress and manner suggest that he is a senior salesman. A selects a mirror and bedroom furniture. The supposed salesman calculates the total price on a notepad which he produces. A is told that the goods will be delivered in two weeks. She pays cash but is not given a receipt. The supposed salesman was an impostor who keeps the money and is not seen again. There is

---

[626]   e.g. *Pacific Carriers Ltd v BNP Paribas* (2004) 218 C.L.R. 451, Illustration 2 below. But cf. *ACN074971109 v National Mutual Life Association of Australasia Ltd* (2008) 69 A.C.S.R. 118 at [171] (estoppel as to authority only justified a remedy less than full expectation damages).

[627]   See the leading estoppel case of *Low v Bouverie* [1891] 3 Ch. 82. (The other route was by the notion of warranty.) See also a valuable exposition of when estoppel operates by Dixon J in *Thompson v Palmer* (1933) 49 C.L.R. 507 at 547.

[628]   See further para.8-065 below.

[629]   See Hobhouse J at first instance in *Bank of Nova Scotia v Hellenic Mutual War Risks Assn (Bermuda) Ltd (The Good Luck)* [1988] 1 Lloyd's Rep. 514 at 547–548, basing himself on *Moorgate Mercantile Co Ltd v Twitchings* [1977] A.C. 890 (not raised in the appeals culminating in [1992] 1 A.C. 233). See also *The Odenfeld* [1978] 1 Lloyd's Rep. 357 at 375–378 per Kerr J. But cf. *Saunders v Anglia BS* [1971] A.C. 1004 at 1038.

[630]   See *Reliance-Based Estoppel*, above, para.3.32 onwards.

[631]   See *So v HSBC Bank Plc* [2009] EWCA Civ 296; and below, para.8-180.

[632]   For a case where it was not, with the results that estoppel as to past events had to be relied on, see *Worboys v Carter* [1987] 2 E.G.L.R. 1.

[633]   See Article 17.

[634]   See above, para.2-063. This was the first point considered in *Spiro v Lintern and West v Dillicar* [1920] N.Z.L.R. 139, Illustration 3 below.

nothing indicating a manifestation by the owner of the shop, but if the facts permit, it may perhaps be held that he has been negligent towards the customer in having arrangements in place which permit such activity of an impostor on the shop floor, and hence is estopped from saying that it is not bound by the purported sale and the payment made under it.[635]

(2) The Documentary Credit Manager of a bank has actual authority to sign letters of credit and authentications of signature, but not to sign guarantees of letters of indemnity against delivery of goods without a bill of lading. She signs such a guarantee (in fact on an inappropriate form) illegibly, not making clear what her status is, and stamps it with the bank's rubber stamp which she is allowed to use for purposes within her authority. In reliance on the document the carrier delivers without bill of lading, is thereby landed with liability to the true receiver and sues the bank on the guarantee. In view of the illegibility of the signature and lack of indication of the signer's identity or status it cannot be said that there was any manifestation of authority by the bank conferring apparent authority, and the carrier relying on the document (as faxed to it) had no other contact with the bank at all, as its issue had been procured by the shipper of the goods. The question of the usual authority of such an official is not considered. There are no or inadequate procedures laid down by the bank for control of signatures or use of the stamp. The bank had been held in a lower court not liable in negligence, but was nevertheless held liable in contract on the guarantee.[636]

(3) A husband who owns a house asks his wife to put it into the hands of estate agents, and this she does. An offer is made to the agents, who telephone the wife. She instructs them to accept it, and authorises them over the telephone to sign a contract, which they do. She has no authority on her husband's behalf to contract to sell, nor purports to act for him. Later the purchasers become aware that the house belongs to the husband. However, the husband subsequently behaves as if he had authorised the transaction, as by receiving visits from the purchasers and allowing repairs. He gives his wife a power of attorney to transfer the house and goes abroad. She subsequently conveys the house to another purchaser. The husband is estopped from saying that she had had no authority, and the first contract is binding on him.[637]

---

[635] *Hoddesdon v Koos Bros* 135 A.2d 702 (1957), where a new trial was ordered on just this issue. Similar situations can arise in connection with supposed car salesman: see *Luken v Buckeye Parking Corp* 68 N.E.2d 217 (1945); or supposed car park attendants or "parking jockeys": see *Mendelsohn v Normand Ltd* [1970] 1 Q.B. 177; or persons allowed the use of offices: *Howard v Carline* (1956) 7 D.L.R.(2d) 324. See also *Raclaw v Fay, Conmy & Co* 668 N.E.2d 114 at 118 (1996).

[636] *Pacific Carriers Ltd v BNP Paribas* (2004) 218 C.L.R. 451. In view of the lack of contact between the parties, and the obscurity of the signature, this decision of the High Court of Australia goes further than might be expected and should be received with caution. See Reynolds (2004) 121 L.Q.R. 55; Watts (2005) 26 Aust. Bar Rev. 185; Peden and Carter (2005) 21 J.C.L. 172 (considering the application of the principles of contractual construction to the decision). For similar reasoning, see *Essington Investments Pty Ltd v Regency Property Pty Ltd* [2004] NSWCA 375, also considered by Watts, above. See also the criticism of the *Pacific Carriers* decision by Fridman (2006) 22 J.Contract.L. 105. For judicial recognition that Australian courts seem to be adopting a broader approach to the concept of a holding out of authority than in the United Kingdom, see *Flexirent Capital Pty Ltd v EBS Consulting Pty Ltd* [2007] VSC 158 at [221]. cf. *Sea Emerald SA v Prominvestbank-Joint Stockpoint Commercial Industrial and Investment Bank* [2008] EWHC 1979 (Comm) at [109].

[637] *Spiro v Lintern* [1973] 1 W.L.R. 1002; see also *West v Dillicar* [1920] N.Z.L.R. 139, Illustration 3 to Article 83; *Worboys v Carter* [1987] 2 E.G.L.R. 1; *Pascoe Properties Ltd v Att.-Gen.* [2014]

(4) The solicitors of a claimant pursuing a claim on a bill of lading seek from the agents of the P&I insurers an extension of time in respect of the time bar of Article III.6 of the Hague Rules. They ask for this extension from the "owners". The ship is under demise charter and the appropriate defendants, from whom extension should have been sought via the same agents, are the demise charterers. The agents grant an extension on behalf of the "owners", who would not be liable. The demise charterers, who are the appropriate defendants, later allege that this was not granted on their behalf and that the claim against them is therefore time-barred. They are estopped from doing so, as if the extension was really to be interpreted as granted on their behalf, the agents must have been aware of the mistake and it was unconscionable to take advantage of it.[638]

NZCA 616 at [54] (Crown estopped by conduct of ministry official).

[638] *The Stolt Loyalty* [1993] 2 Lloyd's Rep. 281 (affd without reference to this point [1995] 1 Lloyd's Rep. 598), doubting dicta in *Shearson Lehman Hutton Inc v Maclaine Watson & Co* [1989] 2 Lloyd's Rep. 570 at 596.

CHAPTER 3

AUTHORITY OF AGENTS

1. ACTUAL AND APPARENT AUTHORITY

Article 22

GENERAL PRINCIPLES

(1) The authority of an agent may be— **3-001**
    (a) actual (express or implied) where it results from a manifestation of assent that he should represent or act for the principal expressly or impliedly made by the principal to the agent himself; or
    (b) apparent, where it results from such a manifestation made by the principal to third parties.[1]
(2) The burden of establishing a conferral of authority rests on the party asserting its existence.
(3) A conferral of authority does not remove the principal's privilege to perform the same tasks personally.

The propositions contained in Articles 23 to 32 relate directly to actual authority only; but they may also be relevant to the ascertainment of apparent authority.

Comment

The notion of authority is explained in Article 1 and this Article broadly fol- **3-002**
lows the scheme there adopted. It has already been pointed out that the placing together of the concepts of actual and apparent authority can easily be criticised,[2] and this point is now due for further discussion. This chapter deals primarily with actual authority, and the rules for determining what is and what is not to be regarded as actually authorised. The scope of an agent's authority may require to be investigated from the point of view of any of three relationships: (i) that of principal and third party dealing with the agent, (ii) that of principal and agent, and (iii) that of agent and third party. Thus where there is actual authority, the principal will prima facie be liable to, and entitled to sue, the third party on the agent's transactions; the principal may be liable to indemnify and reimburse the agent and/or entitled to proceeds received by the agent; and the agent will be free from liability for breach of warranty of authority to the third party. In this chapter no distinction is expressly made between these three relationships, to all of which the agent's

---

[1] See Comment and Article 1. As to apparent authority, see especially Articles 72 and 83.
[2] See above, para.1-014. See Falconbridge (1939) 17 Can. B.R. 248 at 251–252; Seavey (1920) 29 Yale L.J. 859; Corbin (1934) 34 Yale L.J. 788.

actual authority may be relevant. Other general aspects of authority, including the fact that a conferral of authority is not usually to the exclusion of the principal's own powers, and the issue of the onus of proving a conferral of authority, are dealt with in the following paragraphs.

3-003   **Actual authority**   Actual authority is the authority which the principal has given the agent wholly or in part by means of words or writing (called here express authority) or is regarded by the law as having given him because of the interpretation put by the law on the relationship and dealings of the two parties. Although founded in the principal's assent, the conferral of authority is judged objectively:

> "An 'actual' authority is a legal relationship between principal and agent created by a consensual agreement to which they alone are parties. Its scope is to be ascertained by applying ordinary principles of construction of contracts, including any proper implications from the express words used, the usages of the trade, or the course of business between the parties. To this agreement the contractor is a stranger: he may be totally ignorant of the existence of any authority on the part of the agent. Nevertheless, if the agent does enter into a contract pursuant to the 'actual' authority, it does create contractual rights and liabilities between the principal and the contractor."[3]

Note that it is implicit in the foregoing quotation that actual authority is effective only once acted upon by the agent in relation to a third party. It follows that a principal can withdraw actual authority before the third party has obtained any rights.[4] In the context of companies, a board may by resolution confer actual authority for a transaction, but then cancel that resolution which would terminate any actual authority in a delegate if the resolution had not already been acted upon.[5] It is common to distinguish express actual authority from implied actual authority. The most obvious case of express authority is a power of attorney. In a commercial setting, express authority can also arise when the principal authorises the agent to do something "by express words, such as when a board of directors pass a resolution which authorises two of their members to sign cheques".[6] Letters conferring authority are also common. The most obvious cases of implied authority arise in the forms of incidental authority (implied authority to do whatever is necessarily or normally incidental to the activity expressly authorised[7]), usual authority (implied authority to do whatever an agent of the type concerned would usually have authority to do[8]) and customary authority (implied authority to act in accordance with such applicable business customs as are reasonable[9]); there is a further general category of implied authority arising from the course of dealing between the parties and the circumstances of the case.[10] But where the express authority is not clear the court will interpret it, and in this and other situations, whether the authority is to be regarded as express or implied is obviously a question susceptible of argument.

3-004   **Apparent authority**   The placing of apparent authority beside actual authority in

---

[3]   *Freeman & Lockyer v Buckhurst Park Properties (Mangal) Ltd* [1964] 2 Q.B. 480 at 502, per Diplock LJ. See further Article 8, above.
[4]   See further below, Article 120.
[5]   *Brookton Co-operative Society Ltd v FCT* (1979) 24 A.L.R. 547; *Dixon v Blindley Heath Investments Ltd* [2015] EWCA Civ 1023 at [110].
[6]   *Hely-Hutchinson v Brayhead Ltd* [1968] 1 Q.B. 549 at 583.
[7]   Article 27.
[8]   Articles 29 and 30.
[9]   Article 31.
[10]   Article 32.

this rule can easily be criticised, for the reasoning behind the doctrine of apparent authority involves the assumption that there is in fact no authority at all. Under this doctrine, where a principal represents, or is regarded by the law as manifesting, that another has authority, he may be bound as against a third party by the acts of that other person within the authority which that person appears to have, though he had not in fact given that person such authority or had limited the authority by instructions not made known to the third party.[11] "Ostensible or apparent authority is the authority of an agent as it *appears* to others."[12]

On the other hand, the term "apparent authority" is very frequently used, and a chapter on authority that did not mention it alongside actual authority would be misleading. It should, however, be remembered that, at any rate on the approach taken in the English cases,[13] the idea is significantly different from that of actual authority. The notion of apparent authority is essentially confined to the relationship between principal and third party: the principal may under it be bound by unauthorised acts of the agent. He cannot sue unless he ratifies; and consideration of the other two relationships in cases where there is apparent authority proceeds from the starting-point that there is no actual authority. Therefore apparent authority is primarily dealt with in Chapter 8 on the relationship between principal and third party. The cases cited in this chapter are nevertheless relevant, as the authority which the third party is entitled to assume the agent has is in most situations the authority which would normally be implied between principal and agent in the circumstances. The actual and apparent authority will therefore normally coincide,[14] and it will often not matter which of the two notions is relied on: indeed, some of the cases cited in this chapter are decisions on apparent authority. In many nineteenth century cases, it is not possible to tell upon which doctrine the court bases its decision, and even in the cases that are clearly based on what is now called apparent authority, the authority is sometimes referred to as implied.[15] The isolation of the doctrine of apparent authority is not of long standing: it is only comparatively recently that a sharp distinction has been made in the English cases.[16]

The difference between them occurs in two main situations. First, there may be cases where there is an actual manifestation by the principal to the third party upon which the apparent authority is based, which may indicate something different from the authority which the agent would on general criteria impliedly have. Secondly, there may be apparent authority even though in fact as between principal and agent the agent does not have the implied authority which would be normal in the circumstances, either because the principal has, unknown to the third party, forbidden the act in question, or because of facts known to the agent which negate such

---

[11] Article 72; *Freeman & Lockyer v Buckhurst Park Properties (Mangal) Ltd* [1964] 2 Q.B. 480 at 503.
[12] *Hely-Hutchinson v Brayhead Ltd* [1968] 1 Q.B. 549 at 583, per Lord Denning MR. "Apparent authority, which negatives the existence of actual authority" (*Rama Corp v Proved Tin & General Investments* [1952] 2 Q.B. 147 at 149, per Slade J) is, however, too extreme a statement. So, but in the other direction, at any rate if taken out of context, is "The apparent authority is the real authority" (*Pickering v Busk* (1812) 15 East 38 at 43, per Lord Ellenborough CJ; it appears that what he meant was that the authority actually conferred in the case was that which the agent would normally have conferred.)
[13] See below, para.8-029.
[14] *Freeman & Lockyer v Buckhurst Park Properties (Mangal) Ltd* [1964] 2 Q.B. 480 at 502.
[15] e.g. *Brooks v Hassall* (1883) 49 L.T. 569.
[16] See, e.g. *Ryan v Pilkington* [1959] 1 W.L.R. 403, criticised by Powell, pp.51–52 and finally disapproved by the House of Lords in *Sorrell v Finch* [1977] A.C. 728. Clear examples of the two being by modern standards run together are to be found in the Partnership Act 1890: see esp. ss.5, 8 and 14.

authority. Thus it is said that a solicitor normally has implied authority to compromise a suit, and hence apparent authority to do so.[17] It could be offensive on the part of the other party's solicitor to demand evidence of authority: yet the first solicitor may have been told specifically not to act in this way, or may have knowledge of his client's finances which would negate any possibility of his having implied authority to act in this way.[18]

3-005   **Usual authority**   A case can be made out for adding a third type of authority, usual authority.[19] This has been defined by one writer as "the authority which a person normally possesses in certain circumstances to act on behalf of another person, whether or not he is actually authorised so to act".[20]

The expression "usual authority" is referred to in three contexts[21]:

(i)   *As a type of implied authority.* Many cases show that where an agent is put in a position which normally carries with it certain authority, he impliedly has such authority unless it is withdrawn from him.[22] Examples appear below. A person can in such circumstances be said to have "usual authority".

(ii)   *As a type of apparent authority.* Apparent authority seems to involve two types of case[23]: cases where there can be said to be something like a specific representation by the principal of the agent's authority, on which the third party relied, which could be called cases of "genuine apparent authority"; and cases where the only representation made by the principal lies in putting the agent in a position carrying with it a usual authority as described above.[24] In both cases the principal is liable despite reservations in the authority uncommunicated to the third party: but the two could be differentiated as "apparent" and "usual" authority respectively. In this sense usual authority would have affinities with the "externalised" theories of civil law discussed earlier, under which the principal may be liable simply because he has permitted another to assume a recognised type of

---

17 *Waugh v H.B. Clifford & Sons Ltd* [1982] Ch. 374; and see Article 30, Illustration 5.
18 *Waugh v H.B. Clifford & Sons Ltd,* above, at p.387. This is a well-reasoned modern case; but cf. *Nandrame v Ramsaran* [2015] UKPC 20, and para.3-032 below. But it was decided before the days of most recent communications technology, and it is doubtful whether a solicitor would be regarded as so authorised today, and whether it would be "officious", as suggested in the case, to inquire further. See Foskett, *Law and Practice of Compromise* (6th edn), para.29-11. This would affect his apparent authority also. The court may sometimes in such cases refuse to give effect to the compromise: *Harvey v Phillips* (1956) 95 C.L.R. 235; *Wandel and Goltermann GmbH v Wandel Global Services Pty Ltd* [2002] FCA 1609.
19 See especially Powell, Ch.II; Treitel, *Law of Contract* (14th edn), paras 16-030–16-031.
20 Powell, p.37.
21 For its recognition in the first two categories, see *Hely-Hutchinson v Brayhead Ltd* [1968] 1 Q.B. 549 at 583; *ING Re (UK) Ltd v R&V Versicherung AG* [2006] EWHC 1544 (Comm); [2006] 2 All E.R. (Comm) 870 at [125]. In *Law Debenture Trust Plc v Ukraine* [2017] EWHC 655 (Comm) at [156]–[157] usual authority is separated from ostensible authority, whereas in fact it is a subcategory of both actual and ostensible or apparent authority.
22 Articles 29 and 30.
23 See Comment to Article 72.
24 The difference is accepted by Buxton LJ in *AMB Generali Holding AG v SEB Trygg Liv, etc.* [2005] EWCA Civ 1237; [2006] 1 Lloyd's Rep. 318 at [32]; see also *Marubeni Hong Kong and South China Ltd v Mongolian Government* [2002] 2 All E.R. (Comm) 873 at [46]. It is however rejected by Dal Pont, p.524, fn.75. For an example, see *Lexi Holdings Plc v Pannone & Partners* [2009] EWHC 2590 (Ch).

position in regard to him.[25] The common law approach remains one based on a representation of assent by the principal to the agent's action.

(iii) *As an independent type of authority.* There is a small number of cases in which an *undisclosed* principal has been held liable on a contract made by his agent within such powers as would usually be possessed by a person in such a position, where that authority had in fact been withdrawn. The leading case is *Watteau v Fenwick*,[26] where Wills J said:

> "The principal is liable for all the acts of his agent which are within the author-ity usually confided to an agent of that character, notwithstanding limitations, as between the principal and the agent, put upon such authority. It is said that this is only so where there has been a holding out of authority ... But I do not think so."

In view of the fact that the agent's authority was limited, these cases cannot be treated as based on actual authority: but since the principal was undisclosed, he can have made no representation to the third party, therefore the authority could not have been apparent. The cases can simply be criticised as incorrect[27] and may well be so. If however, they are to be supported on agency grounds they must either be treated as exceptional or as indicating an independent notion which could be called "usual authority". It might then be possible to build on these cases to erect such a third type of authority, and to say that a principal is bound by the acts of his agent when that agent acts, not only within his actual or his apparent authority, but also when he acts within his usual authority.[28] This would provide perhaps the readiest framework for seeking to emancipate the principal's liability from notions of authorisation and reliance, a matter discussed earlier.[29] The extension would largely be in the area of undisclosed principals, but it is said that cases where the liability of a disclosed principal could be extended can be envisaged.

> "P appoints A as his general manager for the purchase of houses in Leeds, instructing A, however, not to disclose the existence of the agency and not to purchase except on a surveyor's report. A discloses his position to T, withholding, however, the requirement of a surveyor's report, and purchases houses in Leeds from T as agent for P without a surveyor's report."

The writer's assumption seems to be that only an independent doctrine of usual authority would sustain liability.[30]

Restatement, Second, the Reporter for which was Professor Seavey, provided in a somewhat vaguer way for the liability of a principal beyond the actual and apparent authority:

> "The liability of a principal to a third person upon a transaction conducted by an agent, or the transfer of his interests by an agent, may be based upon the fact that: (a) the agent was authorised; (b) the agent was apparently authorised; or (c) the agent had a power aris-ing from the agency relation and not dependent upon authority or apparent authority."[31]

The notion referred to under (c) is elsewhere described as "inherent agency power"

---

25   See above, para.1-025.
26   [1893] 1 Q.B. 346, discussed below, para.8-077.
27   See below, para.8-077.
28   cf. Powell, p.73 onwards; Montrose (1939) 17 Can. B.R. 693; Treitel, above.
29   See above, para.1-025.
30   Montrose, above, p.711.
31   § 140.

and explained as follows[32]:

> "Inherent agency power is a term used in the restatement of this subject to indicate the power of an agent which is derived not from authority, apparent authority or estoppel, but solely from the agency relation and exists for the protection of persons harmed by or dealing with a servant or other agent."[33]

This approach would accommodate not only the supposed doctrine of *Watteau v Fenwick*[34] but also other intractable cases which a doctrine of usual authority would not, viz. cases where an agent has actual authority to effect a disposition of property but does so in a manner different from that authorised,[35] cases where the agent acts within his authority but for his own benefit,[36] and cases of apparent ownership.[37] It can be likened to the "external" view of civil law,[38] but occurring as an exception rather than as a rule.[39] But though this approach was welcomed and approved by some writers[40] and may have provided a convenient receptacle into which to consign difficult decisions and fact situations, it is submitted that the cases it covers are too disparate, and it is too vague to serve as a systematic basis for the formation and prediction of legal decisions.[41] Not only are some of the existing exceptional cases difficult to justify, including *Watteau v Fenwick*, but others are better supported on more specific rationales than by a concept of usual authority.[42] The Reporter for *Restatement, Third*, Professor DeMott, makes no use of it.[43]

On the current trend of English case law,[44] it is clear that there is little support for any generalised form of liability of the principal beyond the agent's actual or apparent authority. Not much weight can be put on the dictum of Lord Wilberforce referred to in Chapter 1[45] and the dubious decision in *Watteau v Fenwick*.[46] Recent judicial statements of the basic principles of agency are clearly based on the assumption that the principal is only bound where the agent had actual or apparent authority.[47] References to any notion of usual authority should therefore be made and interpreted with caution. As regards usual authority as a form of implied author-

---

[32] § 8A.
[33] See comments to these sections and reporter's notes to § 161; Seavey (1948) 1 U.Okla.L. Rev. 1; *Studies in Agency* (1949), p.181.
[34] [1893] 1 Q.B. 346. Seavey said that the case was "based upon the theory that the principal is the principal and that because the agent is doing his work the principal ought to be liable": (1933) 13 Nebraska L. Bull. 55 at 63.
[35] The supposed doctrine of *Brocklesby v Temperance Building Society* [1895] A.C. 173: see Article 85 and Comment.
[36] See *Hambro v Burnand* [1904] 2 K.B. 10, Illustration 1 to Article 74.
[37] See Article 86. Also the old cases on agency of necessity: see Article 33.
[38] See above, para.1-025.
[39] See Tiberg, in *Lex Mercatoria* (Rose ed., 2000), Ch.4.
[40] *Wright* (1936) 1 U. Toronto L.J. 17 at 40 onwards; Falconbridge (1939) 17 Can.B.R. 248 at 252 onwards (more equivocal); Montrose, above, 693; Munro (1958) 20 U. Pittsburgh L. Rev. 33; Mearns (1962) 48 Va.L.Rev. 50; Bester (1972) 89 S.A.L.J. 49.
[41] cf. Conant (1968) 47 Neb.L.Rev. 678 at 686: "so vague it can cause more analytical problems that it can solve".
[42] Watts (2002) 2 O.U. Commonwealth L.J. 93, discusses a number of the exceptional cases, but does not argue for any overarching concept of inherent agency power.
[43] See *Restatement, Third*, Comment to § 2.01; DeMott (2014) U. Illinois L.R. 1813.
[44] See above, para.1-026. Dicta from older cases to a different effect can of course be found, for as in other areas, nineteenth-century cases contain many lines of reasoning, not all of which were eventually settled on as being acceptable.
[45] See above, para.1-026.
[46] See above.
[47] See above, para.1-026.

ity, it covers two different types of situation which, it is submitted, should be distinguished.[48] As to apparent authority, the two types referred to above, of specific and general representations,[49] are in the cases both subsumed under the same heading and treated together,[50] sometimes being connected with estoppel: the "usual authority" cases are not separated off.[51] Further, to treat a type of actual authority and a type of apparent authority together may cause confusion.[52]

The notion of usual authority is nevertheless one that should be borne in mind; for the distinction between the two types of apparent authority is a significant one which illuminates various points of difficulty in the cases.

Authority of necessity Emergencies may sometimes enlarge the implied authority of an agent. To some extent cases of such extended authority can be subsumed under the accepted heads of implied authority. But many old cases relating to the authority of an agent to act in an emergency contain highly specific requirements linking them with a special but limited doctrine of agency of necessity, whereby a person not previously an agent is by an emergency constituted an agent. The cases are dealt with together under that head in Chapter 4, where it is submitted that the category should now be assimilated into normal principles of implied authority.

3-006

Onus of proof The onus of proving authority, actual or apparent, lies on the party asserting it against the principal, whether the third party or the agent.[53] The principal may, however, be obliged to plead lack of authority.[54] If a principal makes a written statement as to the putative agent's lack of authority but then declines to make himself available for cross-examination, adverse inferences may be drawn against him.[55] It is relatively rare for a third party to wish to deny a putative agent's authority to act (as opposed to be asserting that there is authority) and if the third party does so it may find in any event that the principal ratifies the agent's actions. There is little case law authority on where the burden of proof lies where it is the third party who is asserting that there is no authority. It seems that where the third party

3-007

---

[48] See Article 29, 30.
[49] And see below, para.8-015.
[50] *Freeman & Lockyer v Buckhurst Park Properties (Mangal) Ltd* [1964] 2 Q.B. 480 at 502–504; *Hely-Hutchinson v Brayhead Ltd* [1968] 1 Q.B. 549. The same assumption is made in *Miles v McIlwraith* (1833) 8 App.Cas. 120; *Att.-Gen. for Ceylon v Silva* [1953] A.C. 461; and in *Eagle Star Insurance Co Ltd v Spratt* [1971] 1 Lloyd's Rep. 295; [1971] 2 Lloyd's Rep. 116.
[51] See below, para.8-028.
[52] See *Freeman & Lockyer v Buckhurst Park Properties (Mangal) Ltd*, above, at p.503.
[53] Third party: *Reynell v Lewis* (1846) 15 M. & W. 517 at 526; *Pole v Leask* (1863) L.J. 33 Ch. 155 at 162; *Lysaght Bros v Falk* (1905) 2 C.L.R. 421; *Hoare v McCarthy* (1916) 22 C.L.R. 296 at 303; *Polish SS Co v A.J. Williams Fuels (Overseas Sales) Ltd, The Suwalki* [1981] 1 Lloyd's Rep. 511 at 514; *Suncorp Insurance & Finance v Milano Assecurazioni SpA* [1993] 2 Lloyd's Rep. 225 at 233; *Hudson Bay Apparel Brands LLC v Umbro International Ltd* [2010] EWCA Civ 949; [2011] 1 B.C.L.C. 259 at [48]; *Seiwa Australia Pty Ltd v Beard* (2010) 75 N.S.W.L.R. 74 at [248] (onus of proving apparent authority of a partner); *Pavlovic v Universal Music Australia Pty Ltd* [2015] NSWCA 313; (2015) 90 N.S.W.L.R. 605 at [8]; *Boyle v Maritime Travel Inc* 2014 NSCA 44 at [14]. Agent: *McKittrick v Jordan Sandman Smythe Ltd* [1991] NZCA 16. As to allegations by a principal that the agent has exceeded mandate, or that the agent's authority has been terminated, see below, para.6-004, and para.10-027. As to assertions of lack of authority by a third party in an action for breach of warranty of authority, see below, para.9-066. As to admissibility of evidence of appointment of same agent in unrelated proceedings, see *Mitsui OSK Lines Ltd v Salgaocar Mining Private Ltd* [2015] EWHC 565 (Comm); [2015] 2 Lloyd's Rep. 518 at [31].
[54] See *Wisecal Ltd v Conwell International Ltd* [2011] H.K.L.R.D. 27.
[55] *Spar Shipping AS v Grand China Logistics Holding (Group) Co Ltd* [2015] EWHC 718 (Comm) at [81].

is challenging an agent's authority to commence litigation in the principal's name and the principal is represented by a solicitor, the onus does lie on the third party to establish that the solicitor was improperly instructed.[56] In other circumstances, once the defendant puts in issue the agent's authority to act, it is at least arguable that the burden lies on the agent to show that he was authorised. A principal who asserts that he was an undisclosed principal would have the onus of proving the conferral of actual authority on the agent.

3-008 **Principal retains right to act personally** A principal's conferral of authority on an agent will not usually be to the exclusion of the principal's own powers to act. Much will turn on the context, but one would normally expect clear agreement before it would be concluded that a principal had surrendered the privilege to act himself. Many of the leading cases involve commission agencies, and the judgments are often directed to claims by agents for lost commission when the principal acts himself.[57] However, the issue of retention by a principal of his freedom to act personally (and in priority to the agent) is a more general one, and arises in many contexts.[58] Lord Wright put the point clearly when he said that it is difficult to imply a term "restricting in the interests of an agent the freedom of a principal to deal with his own property or business according to his own judgment".[59]

Illustrations

3-009 (1) The dean and canons of a Cathedral each have power to appoint one of their number as proxy and a canon does so. The fact that the canon then attends in person does not revoke the proxy for later occasions.[60]

(2) A shareholder of a company who grants a proxy attends a company meeting and asserts the right to vote in person. The power of the proxy in such circumstances is superseded, or suspended if not confined to the particular meeting.[61]

(3) A bank's written mandate is to make payments on behalf of a company on the direction of certain named persons. It is protected if the company's sole director, not a notified signatory, authorises payment.[62]

---

[56] See *Hawksford v Hawksford* (2005) 191 F.L.R. 173 at [55]; and *Zoha Ltd v Ahmed* [2016] EWHC 1981 (Ch); [2017] 2 W.L.R. 773.

[57] See *Brinson v Davies* (1911) 105 L.T. 134 at 135; *Luxor (Eastbourne) Ltd v Cooper* [1941] A.C. 108 at 143–145. Even agencies that are expressly made exclusive may be challenged if they are in (unreasonable) restraint of trade: see *Proactive Sports Management Ltd v Rooney* [2011] EWCA Civ 1444; [2012] 2 All E.R. (Comm) 815.

[58] See Illustrations. See also *Angove's Pty Ltd v Bailey* [2016] UKSC 47; [2016] 1 W.L.R. 3179 at [16] (agent's right to collect in price did not exclude principal's right to collect price directly); and *ACCC v Flight Centre Travel Group Ltd* [2016] HCA 49 (travel agents in competition with airlines for the sale of air tickets).

[59] *Luxor (Eastbourne) Ltd v Cooper* [1941] A.C. 108 at 145. As to the principal's right to give further instructions, see below, para.6-009. As to termination of an exclusive agency, see below, Article 120.

[60] *Eyre v Lovell* (1782) 3 Doug. 66; 99 E.R. 541.

[61] *Cousins v International Brick Co* [1931] 2 Ch. 90.

[62] *Hill Street Services Co Ltd v National Westminster Bank Plc* [2007] EWHC 2379 (Ch) at [17]. See too *London International Trust Ltd v Barclays Bank Ltd* [1980] 1 Lloyd's Rep. 241 at 248–249; *Morrell v Workers Savings & Loan Bank* [2007] UKPC 3 at [10] (dictum that conferral on party holding power of attorney or other agent of power to operate bank account did not preclude bank acting directly on instructions from the account holder).

Article 23

NO AUTHORITY TO ACT OTHER THAN FOR PRINCIPAL'S BENEFIT

Authority to act as agent includes only authority to act honestly in pursuit of the interests of the principal.[63]   **3-010**

Comment

It is implicit in a conferral of authority that the principal intends the agent to exercise the relevant powers in the interests of the principal. An agent who deliberately or recklessly exercises powers against the interests of the principal must know that he acts without his principal's consent, and therefore acts without authority. A clear statement of the principle can be found in *Lysaght & Co Ltd v Falk*[64]:   **3-011**

> "Every authority conferred upon an agent, whether express or implied, must be taken to be subject to a condition that the authority is to be exercised honestly and on behalf of the principal. That is a condition precedent to the right of exercising it, and, if that condition is not fulfilled, then there is no authority, and any act purporting to have been done under it, unless in dealing with innocent parties, is void."

It might be noted that the passage contains the qualification "unless in dealing with innocent parties", but this is, it is suggested, an allusion to the concept of apparent authority rather than a true rider to the concept of actual authority. If actual authority all turned on the state of innocence or otherwise of the third party it would not be accurate to say that honesty is a condition precedent to the exercise of actual authority. But it would be odd to have the conferral of authority turn on the state of knowledge of the third party, and it is well established that the third party's state of knowledge is irrelevant to the concept of actual authority. The concept is solely focused on the relationship between principal and agent, to which the third party "is a stranger".[65]

The *Restatement, Third* contains a comparable principle, as follows:

> "An agent acts with actual authority when, at the time of taking action that has legal consequences for the principal, the agent reasonably believes, in accordance with the principal's manifestations to the agent, that the principal wishes the agent so to act."[66]

---

[63] See Comment. The approach taken here was approved in *Hopkins v T.L. Dallas Group Ltd* [2004] EWHC 1379; [2005] 1 B.C.L.C. 543 at [89]; and *Sweeney v Howard* [2007] NSWSC 852 at [56] (power of attorney did not extend to borrowing on mortgage for the purpose of on-lending the funds for the attorney's own ends). See too *Relfo Ltd v Varsani* [2012] EWHC 2168 (Ch) at [86]; affd [2014] EWCA Civ 360.

[64] *Lysaght & Co Ltd v Falk* (1905) 2 C.L.R. 421 at 439, per O'Connor J (see too at 430, per Griffith CJ). The reference to innocent parties should be taken as a reference to there being apparent authority. See also *Architects of Wine Ltd v Barclays Bank Plc* [2006] EWHC 1648 (QB); [2007] 1 Lloyd's Rep. 55, reversed on other grounds [2007] EWCA Civ 239; [2007] 2 All E.R. (Comm) 285 (quaere whether mere fraud on a company's creditors ought to deprive directors of authority); *Parti v Al Sabah* [2007] EWHC 1869 (Ch) at [50]; *Flexirent Capital Pty Ltd v EBS Consulting Pty Ltd* [2007] VSC 158 at [166]; *Thanakharn Kasikorn Thai Chamchat v Akai Holdings Ltd (In Liquidation)* (2010) 13 H.K.C.F.A.R. 479 at [77], per Lord Neuberger NPJ.

[65] See *Freeman and Lockyer v Buckhurst Park Properties (Mangal) Ltd* [1964] 2 Q.B. 480 at 502.

[66] *Restatement, Third*, § 2.01.

This is reinforced by other provisions.[67] This formulation may go too far, insofar as it requires the agent's belief to be reasonable. In this context, however, it may be that what is intended is "rationally believes" rather than "competently believes". A rule that an agent lacks authority merely because he incompetently thought his decision was in his principal's interests would prove problematic for the principal, let alone the agent and third parties.[68] For one thing, a forensic decision as to "reasonableness" would be needed before it were known whether it were necessary for a principal who had not disowned the decision to have ratified it.

An agent who is acting dishonestly in relation to his principal may still, of course, have apparent authority.[69] But where a transaction is transparently not in the principal's interests, the agent is also unlikely to have apparent authority. The body of case law that affirms that there is no apparent authority where the third party ought to have realised that the agent was acting for his own benefit[70] inferentially also affirms the general principle that an agent who acts dishonestly lacks actual authority.

The substance of Article 23 did not appear before the 17th edition, and earlier editions contained a general statement in the chapter on relations between principal and third parties that:

> "An act of an agent within the scope of his actual or apparent authority does not cease to bind the principal merely because the agent was acting fraudulently and in furtherance of his own interests."[71]

That earlier proposition was clearly based on a case at the turn of the twentieth century, *Hambro v Burnand*.[72] In *Macmillan Inc v Bishopsgate Investment Trust Plc (No.3)* at first instance,[73] Millett J cited the statement with approval, saying also that English law distinguishes between the act and the motive with which it was done; and that English law recognises the distinction between want of authority and abuse of authority. However, it is submitted, with respect, that so long as the concept of *actual* authority turns on consent, as it does, it is not possible, in determining the scope of the mandate intended to be conferred, to exclude the purpose for which a power is given, whether express[74] or implied, such as the purpose of promoting the

---

[67] § 2.02, Comment *h:* "acts that create no prospect of economic advantage for a principal ... require specific authorisation"; § 8.10: "An agent has a duty "to refrain from conduct that is likely to damage the principal's enterprise".

[68] *Bieber v Teathers Ltd* [2012] EWHC 190 (Ch) at [86]; affd [2012] EWCA Civ 1466; [2012] 2 B.C.L.C. 585 ("an investor cannot say that the stockbroker is authorised only to make successful investments"). See further below, para.3-016.

[69] See below, Article 74.

[70] See, e.g. *Reckitt v Barnett, Pembroke and Slater Ltd* [1929] A.C. 176 at 189, Illustration 6 to Article 24; *Rolled Steel (Holdings) Ltd v British Steel Corp* [1986] Ch. 246 at 306–307, per Browne-Wilkinson LJ; *Heinl v Jyske Bank (Gibraltar) Ltd* [1999] Lloyd's Rep. Bank. 511 at 521; per Nourse LJ; *Wrexham Ass. Football Club Ltd v Crucialmove Ltd* [2006] EWCA Civ 237; [2008] 1 B.C.L.C. 508.

[71] Article 76 in the 16th edition. For a defence of this approach, see Worthington (2017) 133 L.Q.R. 118. But cf. Watts [2017] J.B.L. 269.

[72] [1904] 2 K.B. 10, Illustration 1 to Article 74 (where more literature is cited).

[73] [1995] 1 W.L.R. 978 at 984; affd without reference to this point [1996] 1 W.L.R. 387.

[74] An exemplar of express purposes are those formerly found in memoranda of association of companies: see, for example, *Sinclair v Brougham* [1914] A.C. 398 (building society had power to borrow but only in the pursuit of the business of a building society).

interests of the principal is. The weight of authority also supports the current proposition.[75]

As to *Hambro v Burnand*, the case concerned a member of Lloyd's authorised to write insurance for others who did so in the ordinary course of business, but for improper motives. It was held that his principals were bound. The judgments were plainly concerned to protect the innocent third party, and the case was decided at a time before the distinction between actual and apparent authority was perceived as clearly as it is now. There seems little doubt that his principals did not *actually* authorise him to act in the way he did; indeed, no premiums were paid and he did not enter the policies in his books nor introduce them into the accounts rendered to his principals, and he intercepted letters addressed to his principals.[76] To modern eyes the case might have been founded on *apparent* authority: to the third party, he was acting in the ordinary course of business, it would have been odd to ask for evidence of his authority and even had he shown it he would still have appeared authorised.[77] But in fact, it appears from the report of the case at first instance, that the claimants had not only not seen the document of appointment but they had had no direct dealings with the principals, and their counsel expressly disowned any reliance on apparent authority.[78]

Even in its own terms, *Hambro* does not establish that purpose is altogether irrelevant to the scope of authority since it appears that if the third party had known of the agent's mismotivation the transaction would have been treated as unauthorised, rather than simply affected by breach of fiduciary duty.[79] The case seems to turn on the proposition that where what the agent is doing is so routinely attached to his usual instructions that had the third party inquired of the principal the latter would have confirmed the agent's mandate, there is no need to inquire. It is not clear, however, that this notion can be squared with older authority,[80] and the reasoning in the case remains problematic.[81]

It may also be that if an agent is directed to do exactly what is done, rather than given a discretion, it may not matter that the agent realises that the instructions are contrary to his principal's interests and proceeds anyway. This may have been the case in *Macmillan v Bishopsgate* itself, where the person concerned (Mr Robert Maxwell) was authorised as a result of a specific resolution of the executive com-

---

[75] See *Official Manager of the Athenaeum Life Insurance Co v Pooley* (1858) 28 L.J. (N.S.) Ch. 119 at 129–130 (contract void for agent's fraud on principal, and innocent assignee could not sue on it); *Reckitt v Barnett, Pembroke and Slater Ltd* [1929] A.C. 176 (agent authorised to draw cheques "without restriction": no authority to do so for paying private debts); *A.L. Underwood Ltd v Bank of Liverpool* [1924] 1 K.B. 775; *EBM Co Ltd v Dominion Bank* [1937] 3 All E.R. 555 (PC) at 568–569; *Hopkins v T.L. Dallas Group Ltd* [2004] EWHC 1379; [2005] 1 B.C.L.C. 543; *Parti v Al Sabah* [2007] EWHC 1869 (Ch) at [49]; *Saad v Doumeny Holdings Pty Ltd* [2005] NSWSC 893 at [24] (holder of power of attorney purports to allot shares for the purpose of diluting principal's shareholding); *Despot v Registrar-General of NSW* [2013] NSWCA 313 at [55] (power of attorney used to pay debts owed to donee's companies)); *Vernon v Public Trustee* [2016] NZCA 388 at [37] (fiduciary duties of attorney).

[76] See [1904] 2 K.B. 10 at 15.

[77] See Article 74. Alternatively, the case can be viewed as exceptional: see Watts (2002) 2 O.U. Commonwealth L.J. 93 at 96–98.

[78] *Hambro v Burnand* [1903] 2 K.B. 399.

[79] See too *Reckitt v Barnett, Pembroke and Slater Ltd* [1929] A.C. 176; *Tobin v Broadbent* (1947) 75 C.L.R. 378.

[80] *Jones v Williams* (1857) 24 Beav. 47 at 62. See too *A.L. Underwood Ltd v Bank of Liverpool* [1924] 1 K.B. 775 at 789; and *Crédit Agricole Corp and Investment Bank v Papadimitriou* [2015] UKPC 13; [2015] 1 W.L.R. 4265.

[81] See further, Watts [2017] J.B.L. 269 at 277–278.

mittee to effect a transfer of shares to a nominee company (Bishopsgate) and did so, though intending subsequently to use them for his own benefit.[82] On the other hand, if the very acting is contrary to the principal's interests, it cannot be regarded as authorised unless expressly.[83] An example where the agent does exactly what is authorised could be where an agent for sale becomes aware of poor quality in his principal's goods the significance of which the principal may not realise, but continues with sales because he is at that time on bad terms with his principal and wishes to do him harm—or indeed simply to increase his commission. It would be otherwise if he had actively concealed defects. This should also be so of an agent in the insurance market knowingly accepting losing risks.[84]

It is important to note that the result of the foregoing reasoning is that the transaction is, as regards the principal, void as being unauthorised. This is quite independent of the possibility of setting the transaction aside, or giving other relief, in equity. This may also exist.[85] Equity too may recognise a broader range of improper purposes than the common law.[86] In such cases, the agent's honesty will mean that he still has actual authority at common law, even if a challenge to the resulting transaction might be mounted in equity against a third party with knowledge of the breach of equitable duty.[87]

3-012   **Arbitration clauses and jurisdiction clauses**   Contracts containing arbitration and jurisdiction clauses raise particular issues where the defendant asserts that its agent, purporting to make the contract, was not acting in the defendant's interests, and that the contract was on that basis unauthorised. In *Premium Nafta Products Ltd v Fili Shipping Co Ltd*,[88] the House of Lords held that the fact that a contract had been procured by bribing the promisor's agents would not entail that an arbitration clause in the contract was ineffective. This conclusion is unproblematic where all that is at issue is bribe-taking. An agent who takes a bribe may nonetheless believe that the relevant contract is still in his principal's interests, and thereby act within authority. There, the resulting contract will be voidable only. Where, however, the bribe-taker both makes the contract and knows that the contract is contrary to his principal's interests, he is, under the above Article, likely to be act-

---

[82] cf. *Bank of Bengal v Fagan* (1849) 7 Moo.P.C. 61 at 74, per Lord Brougham: "[indorser's purpose] only refers to the use of the funds to be made from the indorsement, not to the power".

[83] This point appears to have been misunderstood in *Dollars & Sense Ltd v Nathan* [2008] 2 N.Z.L.R. 557 (NZSC) at [42]. For an example of express instructions contrary to the principal's interest see Article 39, Illustration 4; cf. Article 39, Illustration 9.

[84] See *Sphere Drake Insurance Ltd v Euro International Underwriting* [2003] EWHC 2376; [2003] Lloyd's Rep. I.R. 525 at [49].

[85] See commentary to Article 96; and *Criterion Properties Plc v Stratford UK Properties LLC* [2004] UKHL 28; [2004] 1 W.L.R. 1846 (Illustration 10 to Article 96). *Heinl v Jyske Bank (Gibraltar) Ltd* [1999] Lloyd's Rep. Bank. 511 at 521. For full discussion see Stevens [2004] L.M.C.L.Q. 421; Prentice and Payne [2005] L.M.C.L.Q. 447; Watts (2005) 121 L.Q.R. 4, arguing that some dicta in *Criterion Properties* too readily assimilated equitable grounds of intervention within that of lack of authority.

[86] See commentary to Article 96; Watts (2005) 121 L.Q.R. 4. See too, *Hurstanger Ltd v Wilson* [2007] EWCA Civ 299; [2007] 1 W.L.R. 2351: [2007] 4 All E.R. 1118, note to para.8-219 below.

[87] See, e.g. *Senex Holdings Ltd v National Westminster Bank Plc* [2012] EWHC 131 (Comm); [2012] 1 All E.R. (Comm) 1130.

[88] [2007] UKHL 40; [2007] 4 All E.R. 951; [2007] 2 All E.R. (Comm) 1053 (affirming the Court of Appeal, sub nom. *Fiona Trust and Holding Corp v Privalov* [2007] EWCA Civ 20; [2007] 2 Lloyd's Rep. 267; [2007] 1 All E.R. (Comm) 891); *Interprods Ltd v De La Rue International Ltd* [2014] EWHC 68 (Comm) at [7].

ing beyond his authority, and any purported contract will be void.[89] *Premium Nafta* was decided on procedural issues and it is not clear that the bribe-taker actually made the contracts, though it does appear that the relevant contracts were very unfavourable to the principal. It is a fair inference that the House considered that an arbitration clause would remain effective even where the agent had exceeded his authority. So long as the relevant agent would have had authority to enter into an arbitration contract, independent of the particular contract in respect of which there is a dispute, the arbitration clause would be effective.[90] Lord Hoffmann, who gave the leading judgment, did accept that if the agent had no authority whatever to enter into arbitration agreements then the clause would be ineffective.[91] The reasoning is said to be based on the intention of the parties, but given that the principal will not usually have anticipated the wrong and the agent has acted without authority, a strong element of pragmatism seems to be involved. Nonetheless, similar reasoning has since been applied in testing the validity of jurisdiction clauses.[92]

2. EXPRESS ACTUAL AUTHORITY

Article 24

CONSTRUCTION OF POWERS OF ATTORNEY

Powers of attorney are strictly construed and are interpreted as giving only such authority as they confer expressly or by necessary implication.[93] The following are the most important rules of construction: **3-013**

(1) The operative part of a deed is controlled by the recitals where there is ambiguity.[94]
(2) Where authority is given to do particular acts, followed by general words, the general words are restricted to what is necessary for the proper performance of the particular acts.[95]
(3) General words do not confer general powers, but are limited to the purpose for which the authority is given, and are construed as enlarging the special powers only when necessary for that purpose.[96]

---

[89] A point apparently accepted by Longmore LJ in the Court of Appeal in *Fiona Trust and Holding Corp v Privalov*, above, at [26].

[90] *Corp v Privalov*, above, at [18].

[91] *Corp v Privalov*, above, at [17].

[92] See *Deutsche Bank AG v Asia Pacific Broadband Wireless Communications Inc* [2008] EWCA Civ 1091; [2008] 2 Lloyd's Rep. 619 at [25].

[93] *Bryant, Powis & Bryant v La Banque du Peuple* [1893] A.C. 170 at 177; *Withington v Herring* (1829) 5 Bing. 442 at 458; *Sweeney v Howard* [2007] NSWSC 852 at [54] (power to grant mortgage not conferring power to on-lend proceeds for purposes unrelated to donor of power of attorney); *Great Investments Ltd v Warner* [2016] FCAFC 85 at [92]. See also Dal Pont, in *Agency Law in Commercial Practice* (Busch, Macgregor and Watts (eds) (2016)), Ch.12. As to execution of deeds under powers of attorney, see Article 77. The Trustee Delegation Act 1999 s.10, somewhat enlarges the scope of powers concerning land unless a contrary intention appears. See also s.1, which authorises an attorney to exercise trustee functions of the donor in certain circumstances.

[94] Illustration 1.

[95] *Perry v Holl* (1860) 2 De G.F. & J. 38 at 48; Illustrations 2 and 3.

[96] *Attwood v Munnings* (1827) 7 B. & C. 278 at 284; Illustrations 4, 5 and 7. But cf. *Brown v Innovatorone Plc* [2012] EWHC 1321 (Comm) at [809] (context remains important in construing power of attorney).

(4)   A deed must be construed so as to include all incidental powers necessary for the effective execution of the power it confers.[97]

Comment

3-014   The term "power of attorney" is usually applied to a formal grant of power to act made by deed or contained in a deed relating also to other matters. There was in fact no rule that agency must be created by deed, except where the agent himself is to be empowered to execute a deed, and it seems that such a power could at common law be granted by simple writing.[98] However the Powers of Attorney Act 1971 s.1 requires that powers of attorney be executed by deed. The term "power of attorney" is not defined, but presumably means a formal grant of agency powers, often of a general nature. To such deeds the strict rules stated above apply: but to other conferring of authority, even where written, the laxer rules given in the following Articles apply.

It is worth noting that the basic rule here given for powers of attorney is even contrary to the normal rule for deeds, which is that they are construed against the grantor.[99] A reason given is "because the rights of other persons may be affected",[100] though this does not seem very convincing since the rule will usually operate to the prejudice of those other persons. However, the normal rule favouring the grantee has behind it the idea of non-derogation from grant, a principle of the law of property which is not necessarily appropriate in situations of representation. As such the above rule has parallels with the specific requirements which exist in some countries that there be an express authorising clause for certain acts such as alienation of land, mortgage, etc.[101] The comparison should not however be pressed too far, for these rules may operate on agency powers of potentially greater generality than may be required in common law systems, which can make use of the trust to transfer powers. In any case, the rule here seems well established in nineteenth-century cases, though the notion of protecting the principal as opposed to the third party, which seems to lie behind it, may be regarded now as being somewhat unfashionable, especially in the commercial sphere. The whole idea of strict construction is, indeed, inconsistent with the doctrine of apparent authority, which is now so prominent in the law of agency.[102] Many powers of attorney are however used in non-commercial situations such as absence abroad, illness or debility of the principal. It may be right in such circumstances to place a duty of inquiry on the third party.[103] And in the commercial sphere, powers of attorney tend to be drawn by lawyers and use technical wording which may be assumed to have been carefully chosen. Where an absolutely general power is required, doubts can be avoided by using the form provided by s.10 of the Powers

---

[97] *Howard v Baillie* (1726) 2 H.Bl. 618 at 619; Illustrations 6 and 8. See in general Aldridge, *Powers of Attorney* (10th edn), para.2-16 onwards; Thurston, *Powers of Attorney* (8th edn), Ch.7; Dal Pont, *Powers of Attorney* (2nd edn).
[98] See Articles 9 and 10. See also the definition above, para.2-039.
[99] See Stoljar, pp.91–92.
[100] *Re Dowson and Jenkins' Contract* [1904] 2 Ch. 219 at 223.
[101] e.g. French CC, art.1988. See Müller-Freienfels in *Civil Law in the Modern World* (Yiannopoulos ed., 1965), 77 at 100–102.
[102] See Stoljar, pp.92–95.
[103] For a survey of the use of powers of attorney in international practice see Eder (1950) 98 U.Pa.L.Rev. 840, who puts forward the view that "the burden of a badly drafted power of attorney should be cast on the principal, not on the third party" (p.857).

of Attorney Act 1971 (as amended), which confers authority to do on behalf of the donor anything which he can lawfully do by attorney.[104]

Extrinsic evidence that the agent was not intended to have these powers, or to have additional powers, will not normally be accepted. This is the more so since powers of attorney are required to be conferred by deed. Such evidence may however be admissible where the wording is ambiguous, or to prove custom.[105] It is also possible that an attorney may have authority conferred by the principal independently of the power of attorney, which the agent can rely upon without calling in aid the power of attorney.[106]

Illustrations

Rule (1)

(1) A power of attorney recited that the principal was going abroad, and the opera- **3-015**
tive part gave authority in general terms. Held, that the authority subsisted only during the principal's absence abroad.[107] But where the operative words are clear, they will prevail over a recital.[108]

Rule (2)

(2) Power was given:

> "to demand and receive all moneys due to the principal on any account whatsoever and to use all means for the recovery thereof, to appoint attorneys to bring actions, and to revoke such appointments, and to do all other business."

Held, that "all other business" must be construed to mean all other business necessary for the recovery of the moneys, or in connection with it; and that the power of attorney gave the agent no authority to indorse a bill of exchange received by him under it.[109]

(3) X, who carried on business in Australia, gave an agent in England a power of attorney to purchase goods in connection with the business, either for cash or on credit, and where necessary in connection with any such purchases, or in connection with the business, to make, draw, sign, accept or indorse for him and on his behalf any bills of exchange or promissory notes which should be requisite or proper. It was held that the power of attorney gave no power to borrow money, and the agent, purporting to act in pursuance of the power, having given bills of exchange in respect of a loan, and misapplied the money, that X was not liable on the bills.[110]

---

[104] *Spina v Permanent Custodians Ltd* [2008] NSWSC 561 (power of attorney permitting self-benefit is effective for the purpose of determining scope of authority, whether or not self-benefit would put the attorney in breach of fiduciary duty); *Taheri v Vitek* [2014] NSWCA 209; (2014) 320 A.L.R. 555.
[105] See Article 31.
[106] See *Day v Harris* [2013] EWCA Civ 191; [2014] Ch. 211. See also below, paras 6-009 and 10-009.
[107] *Danby v Coutts & Co* (1885) 29 Ch.D. 500.
[108] *Rooke v Lord Kensington* (1856) 2 K. & J. 753 at 769.
[109] *Hogg v Snaith* (1808) 1 Taunt. 347. See also *Esdaile v La Nauze* (1835) 1 Y. & C.Ex. 394; *Murray v East India Co* (1821) 5 B. & A. 204; *Harper v Godsell* (1870) L.R. 5 Q.B. 422; *Totara Investments Ltd v Crismac Ltd* [2010] NZSC 36; [2010] 3 N.Z.L.R. 285.
[110] *Jacobs v Morris* [1902] 1 Ch. 816. See also *Esmail v Bank of Scotland* (1999) S.L.T. 1289 (power referring to "his" accounts did not refer to joint accounts).

Rule (3)

(4)   A power of attorney:

"to recover and receive all sums of money owing … by virtue of any security … and to give, sign, and execute receipts, releases, or other discharges for the same, … and to sell any real or personal property … belonging" to the principal, does not authorise the agent to exercise the statutory power of sale of real property vested in the principal as a mortgagee."[111]

(5)   A power of attorney "from time to time to negotiate, make sale, dispose of, assign and transfer" gives no authority to pledge.[112] But a power "to sell, indorse and assign" authorises an indorsement to a bank as security for a loan to the agent; such a power being construed as giving (i) authority to sell, (ii) authority to indorse and (iii) authority to assign.[113]

(6)   A power of attorney to manage the principal's affairs while he is abroad, amplified by a letter from the principal to his bankers stating that he wished the power to cover the drawing of cheques upon the bank without restriction, does not authorise the attorney to draw cheques in payment of his own private debts.[114]

(7)   A clause in a power of attorney, whereby the principal agrees to ratify and confirm whatsoever the attorney shall do or purport to do by virtue of the power, does not extend the authority given by the power.[115]

(7a)   A power of attorney given over the whole of the donor's property did not entitle the attorney to exercise donor's powers as director of a company.[116]

---

[111] *Re Dowson and Jenkins' Contract* [1904] 2 Ch. 219. See also *Re Bowles' Mortgage Trust* (1874) 31 L.T. 365; *Lewis v Ramsdale* (1886) 55 L.T. 179; *Hawkesley v Outram* [1892] 3 Ch. 359; *Bryant, Powis & Bryant v La Banque du Peuple* [1893] A.C. 170; *Xie v Huang* [2012] NZHC 960; (2012) N.Z. Conveyancing P.R. 239 at [28] (power to manage properties did not extend to a power of sale).

[112] *Jonmenjoy Coondoo v Watson* (1884) 9 App.Cas. 561; *Tobin v Broadbent* (1947) 75 C.L.R. 378.

[113] *Bank of Bengal v Macleod* (1849) 5 Moo.Ind.App.1; *Bank of Bengal v Fagan* (1849) 5 Moo.Ind.App. 27.

[114] *Reckitt v Barnett, Pembroke & Slater Ltd* [1929] A.C. 176 (a famous case which is noted at (1929) 45 L.Q.R. 6; (1929) 3 C.L.J. 445; (1929) 17 Calif.L.Rev. 258; (1929) 77 U.Pa.L.Rev. 271); *Midland Bank Ltd v Reckitt* [1933] A.C. 1. See also *Morison v Kemp* (1912) 29 T.L.R. 70; *Hayes v Standard Bank of Canada* [1928] 2 D.L.R. 898. cf. *Australia and New Zealand Bank Ltd v Ateliers de Constructions Electriques de Charleroi* [1967] 1 A.C. 86 (authority to indorse principal's cheque and pay into own bank account necessary to give business effect to transactions authorised), distinguished in *Day v Bank of New South Wales* (1978) 19 A.L.R. 32. Wide wording would not normally authorise an agent to make gifts to or transfer to himself. See *King v Bankerd* 492 A 2d 608 (Ct.App.Md., 1985); *Lamb v Scott* 643 So.2d 972 (S.C.Ala 1994), cited in Hynes and Loewenstein, *Agency, Partnership and the LLC* (7th edn, 2007) pp.276–277; *Sweeney v Howard* [2007] NSWSC 852 at [56]; *Siahos v JP Morgan Trust Australia Limited* [2009] NSWCA 20; *Despot v Registrar-General of NSW* [2013] NSWCA 313; *Great Investments Ltd v Warner* [2016] FCAFC 85 at [84] (authorisation of conflict of interest does not license appropriation by donee of donor's property); *Vernon v Public Trustee* [2016] NZCA 388 at [37].

[115] *Midland Bank Ltd v Reckitt* [1933] A.C. 1. Nor can it amount to ratification, since it comes before the act. See above, para.2-049.

[116] *Levin v Rastkar* [2011] NZCA 210 at [46]; *Godfrey v Marshall* [2017] NZHC 420 (powers of donor not extending to power as trustee). cf. *Maharaj v Johnson* [2015] UKPC 28; [2015] P.N.L.R. 553 at [13] (in obiter, power of attorney by necessary implication extending to powers of donor in capacity as executor).

Rule (4)

(8) A partner gave his son a power of attorney "to act on his behalf in dissolving the partnership, with authority to appoint any other person as he might see fit". Held, this gave the son power to submit the partnership accounts to arbitration.[117]

(9) A power of attorney:

> "to commence and carry on, or to defend at law or in equity, all actions, suits, or other proceedings touching anything in which the principal or his ships or other personal estate may be in anywise concerned"

authorises the attorney to sign on behalf of the principal a bankruptcy petition against a debtor of the principal.[118]

Article 25

CONSTRUCTION OF AUTHORITY NOT GIVEN BY DEED

Where the authority of an agent is given by an instrument not under seal, or is given orally, it is construed liberally, with regard to the object of the authority and to the usages of trade or business.[119] Courts will assume that a principal has not made the existence of an agent's authority turn on impractical or impossible conditions. Hence, an agent may warrant success to his principal, but his possession of authority could not be made to turn on his committing his principal only to profitable transactions.[120]

3-016

Comment

The rules for the construction of documents other than deeds are clearly very much laxer, and it was said at first instance in the leading case of *Pole v Leask*[121] that where authority is general it will be construed liberally. It is presumably often, though not necessarily, true that a deed is more carefully drawn than a less formal document, and so should be more strictly construed: and powers of attorney may often be executed to establish an agency against a non-commercial background,

3-017

---

[117] *Henley v Soper* (1928) 8 B. & C. 16. See also *Withington v Herring* (1829) 5 Bing. 442; *Willis v Palmer* (1859) 7 C.B.(N.S.) 340.

[118] *Re Wallace Ex p. Wallace* (1884) 14 Q.B.D. 22.

[119] *Pole v Leask* (1860) 28 Beav. 562 at 574; affd (1863) 33 L.J.Ch. 155; *Ireland v Livingston* (1872) L.R. 5 H.L. 395; *Freeman and Lockyer v Buckhurst Park Properties (Mangal) Ltd* [1964] 2 Q.B. 480 at 502; *Unaoil Ltd v Amona Ranhill Consortium Sdn Bhd* [2012] EWHC 1595 (Comm) at [58] (usual approaches to contract construction applied).

[120] *Bieber v Teathers Ltd* [2012] EWHC 190 (Ch) at [86]; affd [2012] EWCA Civ 1466; [2012] 2 B.C.L.C. 585; *Forsta AP-Fonden v Bank of New York Mellon SA/NV* [2013] EWHC 3127 (Comm) at [105]; *LNOC Ltd v Watford Association Football Club Ltd* [2013] EWHC 3615 (Comm) at [64] (negligence does not remove actual authority); *Gabriel v Little* [2013] EWCA Civ 1513 at [57] (affd on different points sub nom. *BPE Solicitors v Hughes-Holland* [2017] UKSC 21; [2017] 2 W.L.R. 1029).

[121] (1860) 28 Beav. 562 at 574; affd (1863) 33 L.J.Ch. 155. The judgment of Lord Romilly MR should, however, be read with caution, as it does not clearly distinguish between (what would now be called) actual and apparent authority: see the case on appeal (1863) 33 L.J.Ch. 155, especially the speech of Lord Cranworth.

which would also make strict interpretation appropriate.[122] Be that as it may, in the commercial sphere the interpretation of documents and correspondence concerning the agency relationship is plainly far more liberal where no formal power of attorney by deed has been executed, as can be seen from the cases cited. Reference should also be made to subsequent Articles, for most of the cases there cited concern instructions given in writing.[123] The rule applies a fortiori to authority given orally, and indeed *Pole v Leask*[124] itself was a case of oral authority. The interpretation of both written and oral authority is a matter of law: but in the latter case questions of fact as to what was said and done may make law and fact difficult to distinguish. Furthermore, in both cases questions of the normal course of business, and of trade customs, may arise, which are questions of fact.[125]

Illustrations

3-018 (1) An agent was instructed to sell goods at such a price as would realise 15s. per ton, net cash. He sold them at 15s. 6d. per ton, subject to two months' credit. Held, that the instructions might fairly be construed as meaning *15s. net* cash, or such a price as would eventually realise 15s. after allowing for interest, or a *del credere* commission; that the contract might be presumed to have reference to some well-known usage of the coal trade; and that the sale was within his authority.[126]

(2) 100 bales of cotton are ordered by a Liverpool merchant from a merchant at Pernambuco. The Pernambuco merchant buys 94 bales. There is evidence to show that it is not normally possible to purchase 100 bales at Pernambuco. The purchase is authorised.[127]

(3) A is authorised to sell and warrant certain goods. He cannot bind his principal by a warranty given at any other time than at the sale of his goods.[128]

(4) On the dissolution of a partnership, authority is given to one of the partners by his co-partners (i) to settle the partnership affairs,[129] or (ii) to receive all debts owing to, and to pay all debts owing by, the firm.[130] In neither case has the authority to draw, accept or indorse bills of exchange in the name of the firm.

Article 26

AUTHORITY GIVEN IN AMBIGUOUS TERMS

3-019 Where the authority of an agent is conferred in such ambiguous terms, or the instructions given to him are so uncertain, as to be fairly capable of more than one construction, an act reasonably done by him in good faith which is justified by any

---

[122] Stoljar, pp.91–92.
[123] See especially Article 26.
[124] Above.
[125] See Articles 27–32; though what constitutes a custom is a question of law: see Article 31. See *Globex Foreign Exchange Corp v Launt* 2011 NSCA 67 at [19].
[126] *Boden v French* (1851) 10 C.B. 886.
[127] *Johnston v Kershaw* (1867) L.R. 2 Ex. 82; *Ireland v Livingston* (1872) L.R. 5 H.L. 395, Illustration 1 to Article 26.
[128] *Helyear v Hawke* (1803) 5 Esp. 72.
[129] *Abel v Sutton* (1800) 3 Esp. 108. See also *Odell v Cormack Brothers* (1887) 19 Q.B.D. 223; cf. *Smith v Winter* (1838) 4 M. & W. 454.
[130] *Kilgour v Finlyson* (1789) 1 H.Bl. 155.

of those constructions is deemed to have been duly authorised, though the construction adopted and acted upon by him was not that intended by the principal.[131] But with modern communications it may be possible to obtain clarification, and an agent may not act reasonably if he does not do so.[132] Where a principal makes a mistake in giving instructions to an agent, including one acting under a power of attorney, and the agent in response conveys an interest in property by way of gift to a third party, the principal may still be able to have the conveyance rectified if it was not the principal's intention to make a gift.[133]

Illustrations

(1) A commission agent in Mauritius was authorised to buy and ship 500 tons of sugar (subject to a certain limit in price, to cover cost, freight and insurance), 50 tons more or less of no moment, if it enabled him to secure a suitable vessel. The principal stated that he would prefer the option of sending the vessel to London, Liverpool or the Clyde, but that if that was not possible the goods might be shipped to Liverpool or London. Held that a shipment of 400 tons in a vessel carrying other cargo direct to London and thus not amenable to orders was a good execution of the authority, it being doubtful what the instructions meant.[134]   **3-020**

(2) An agent undertook to sell and transfer certain stock when funds should be at 85 or over. Held, that he was bound to sell when the funds reached 85, and had no discretion to wait until they went higher than that price.[135]

(3) A shipowner by telegram requests shipbrokers to "fix steamer" on certain terms. The brokers take this as an instruction to let out one of the shipowner's vessels, to be named subsequently, on such terms. The owner intended them to obtain a ship on charter. The brokers' interpretation is justified.[136]

---

[131] *Ireland v Livingston* (1872) L.R. 5 H.L. 395, Illustration 1. See above, para.1-021.

[132] See *Woodhouse AC Israel Cocoa Ltd SA v Nigerian Produce Marketing Co Ltd* [1972] A.C. 741 at 772; *European Asian Bank AG v Punjab and Sind Bank (No.2)* [1983] 1 W.L.R. 642 at 655, saying that the principle is "only available in very limited circumstances"; *Veljkovic v Vrybergen* [1985] V.R. 419. See also cases cited under Article 25; Article 38; *Moore v Mourgue* (1776) 2 Cowp. 479; *Comber v Anderson* (1808) 1 Camp. 523; *Pariente v Lubbock* (1856) 8 De G.M. & G. 5; *Miles v Haslehurst* (1906) 23 T.L.R. 142.

[133] *Day v Day* [2013] EWCA Civ 280; [2014] Ch. 114; noted Dawson (2014) 130 L.Q.R. 356.

[134] *Ireland v Livingston*, above. See also *Loring v Davis* (1886) 32 Ch.D. 625; *International Paper Co v Spicer* (1906) 4 C.L.R. 739; *Gould v South Eastern and Chatham Ry* [1920] 2 K.B. 186; *J. Vale & Co v Van Oppen & Co Ltd* (1921) 37 T.L.R. 367; *Brown and Gracie v F.W. Green & Co Pty Ltd* [1960] 1 Lloyd's Rep. 289; and see a useful discussion in *Veljkovic v Vrybergen*, above.

[135] *Bertram, Armstrong & Co v Godfray* (1830) 1 Knapp. 381. See also *Tallentire v Ayre* (1884) 1 T.L.R. 143.

[136] *Weigall & Co v Runciman & Co* (1916) 85 L.J.K.B. 1187. As to the legal position of shipbrokers in general, see *H. Edwin Anderson III* (2000) 31 J.M.L.C. 89.

3. IMPLIED ACTUAL AUTHORITY

Article 27

TO DO WHAT IS NECESSARY FOR, OR INCIDENTAL TO, EFFECTIVE EXECUTION OF EXPRESS AUTHORITY (INCIDENTAL AUTHORITY)

3-021 An agent has implied authority to do whatever is necessary for, or ordinarily incidental to, the effective execution of his express authority in the usual way.[137]

Comment

3-022 This Article only refers to actual authority. A good statement of the notion behind it is that:

> "an authority of this nature necessarily includes medium powers, which are not expressed. By medium powers I mean all the means necessary to be used in order to obtain the accomplishment of the object of the principal power ...".[138]

But a similar notion is relevant to apparent authority, and statements of the rule appear in this context[139]: indeed in many cases it is unnecessary and even impossible to decide whether the decision rests on implied or on apparent authority.[140] By way of example, it is said that an agent has authority, unless there are special circumstances, to disclose the existence of the agency, the identity of his principal, his relationship with his principal,[141] and documents evidencing his authority which his principal might reasonably expect that third parties would wish to see for their own protection.[142] On the other hand, a recurring theme is that authority to do an act does not necessarily involve authority to receive payment in relation to it.[143] Some cases usually associated with the notion of agency of necessity could also be regarded as examples of incidental authority.[144]

Illustrations

3-023 (1) A is authorised to enter into a binding contract relating to land. He has implied authority to sign a memorandum thereof to satisfy the Law of Property Act 1925 s.40.[145] But it must relate to the contract authorised; and where solicitors, acting upon instructions, bid for three separate lots of property at an auc-

---

[137] *Pole v Leask* (1860) 28 Beav. 562 at 574–575 (affd (1863) 33 L.J.Ch. 155); *SMC Electronics v Akhter Computers Ltd* [2001] 1 B.C.L.C. 433; *Bayley v Wilkins* (1849) 7 C.B. 886; *Collen v Gardner* (1856) 21 Beav. 540; *Nayyar v Sapte* [2009] EWHC 3218 (QB); [2010] P.N.L.R. 15 at [132]; and see Illustrations.

[138] *Howard v Baillie* (1796) 2 H.Bl. 618 at 619, per Eyre CJ. See too *The West of England Ship Owners Mutual P. & I. Assoc. v Hellenic Industrial Development Bank SA* [1999] 1 Lloyd's Rep. 93.

[139] e.g. *Beaufort v Neeld* (1845) 12 C. & F. 248; *Dingle v Hare* (1859) 7 C.B.(N.S.) 145; *Wiltshire v Sims* (1808) 1 Camp. 258.

[140] cf. above, para.3-005. See *Ryan v Pilkington* [1959] 1 W.L.R. 403; criticised by Powell, pp.51–52 and finally disapproved by the House of Lords in *Sorrell v Finch* [1977] A.C. 728.

[141] *United Bank of Kuwait Ltd v Hammoud* [1988] 1 W.L.R. 1051 at 1066–1067.

[142] Powell, p.46.

[143] See Illustrations 2 and 10; and *Smith v Peter & Diana Hubbard Pty Ltd* [2006] NSWCA 109.

[144] e.g. *Gokal Chand-Jagan Nath v Nand Ram Das-Atma Ram* [1939] A.C. 106; see below, para.4-007.

[145] *Rosenbaum v Belson* [1900] 2 Ch. 267; the relevant provision is now s.2 of the Law of Property

tion and the property was knocked down to them, it was held that they had no authority to sign one indivisible agreement to purchase all the lots.[146]

(2)   An assistant in a shop normally has authority to receive payment for goods sold in the shop, but not necessarily to receive it elsewhere[147] or in other circumstances outside the ordinary course of business.[148] A person delivering goods may have no such authority,[149] and a traveller taking orders for the purchase of goods may have no authority to receive the price,[150] though there may be a course of dealing or of business whereby payment to such a traveller is normal.[151]

(3)   A is authorised to buy certain shares. He has implied authority to do everything in the usual course of business necessary to complete the bargain, e.g. reimburse the seller for payment on a call.[152]

(4)   An agent is authorised to institute proceedings for liquidation of a company. He has authority to give a notice of demand on behalf of the creditor.[153]

(5)   An agent is employed to obtain payment of a bill of exchange from the acceptor. He has no implied authority to receive payment subject to a condition that the acceptor shall not be liable for the expenses of protesting the bill for nonpayment.[154]

(6)   An agent is employed to sell a consignment of goods by description while afloat. He has no implied authority to warrant them to be of any particular condition or quality.[155]

(7)   An agent authorised to deliver a horse has no authority to give a warranty,[156] and an agent authorised to deliver milk has no authority to sell it to someone other than the person to whom it is being sent.[157] A furniture salesman may have authority to cancel the sale.[158]

(8)   A bailee for use may have authority to part with possession of the goods when it is reasonably incidental to the reasonable use of them to do so. Thus if he delivers goods for repair, the repairer may acquire a valid lien over them.[159]

(Miscellaneous Provisions) Act 1989. And see *Gavaghan v Edwards* [1961] 2 Q.B. 220; Article 6.

[146]   *Smith v MacGowan* [1938] 3 All E.R. 447. See also *Smith v Webster* (1876) 3 Ch.D. 49; *Van Praagh v Everidge* [1902] 2 Ch. 266, reversed on other grounds [1903] 1 Ch. 434. But sales by auction no longer require a memorandum, nor to be in writing: Law of Property (Miscellaneous Provisions) Act 1989 s.2.

[147]   *Kaye v Brett* (1850) 5 Exch. 269 at 274.

[148]   See *Sanderson v Bell* (1833) 2 C. & M. 304.

[149]   *Lettice v Judkins* (1840) 9 L.J.Ex. 142.

[150]   *Butwick v Grant* [1924] 2 K.B. 483, Illustration 1 to Article 81. See also *Drakeford v Piercy* (1866) 7 B. & S. 515.

[151]   *International Sponge Importers Ltd v Andrew Watt & Sons* [1911] A.C. 279, Illustration 2 to Article 81; *Capel v Thornton* (1828) 3 C. & P. 352. See further Articles 28 and 81.

[152]   *Bayley v Wilkins* (1849) 7 C.B. 886.

[153]   *Metropolitan Waste Disposal Authority v Willoughby Waste Disposals Ltd* (1987) 9 N.S.W.L.R. 7. See also *Paget v Pearson* (1949) 49 S.R. (N.S.W.) 235 (authority to obtain possession of premises included authority to sign notice to quit).

[154]   *Bank of Scotland v Dominion Bank (Toronto)* [1891] A.C. 592.

[155]   *Benmag Ltd v Barda* [1955] 2 Lloyd's Rep. 354 at 357 (but on the facts of the case such authority could be inferred from the conduct of the parties); cf. *Abrahams v Spitz* (1963) 107 S.J. 113 (agent to sell car had authority to warrant that it was insured).

[156]   *Woodin v Burford* (1834) 2 Cr. & M. 391.

[157]   *Whittaker v Forshaw* [1919] 2 K.B. 419.

[158]   *Leckenby v Wolman* [1921] W.N. 100.

[159]   *Tappenden v Artus* [1964] 2 Q.B. 185. See further cases cited above, para.1-033.

(9)   A solicitor handling a conveyancing transaction after "subject to contract" agreement has authority to receive all relevant information from the other party.[160]

(10)   A person engaged in freight forwarding, and in particular in preparing documents for presentation under a letter of credit, has no authority to receive the payment under the credit.[161]

(11)   An agent appointed as project manager for a land development is given authority to appoint planning professionals and consultants for the project. It has implied authority to agree the fees that should be paid to those persons.[162]

Article 28

AUTHORITY TO RECEIVE PAYMENT OF MONEY

3-024   An agent who is authorised to receive payment of money has prima facie no authority to receive payment otherwise than in cash, unless it is in the normal course of business to do so, or it is usual or customary in the particular business to receive payment in some other form, and such usage or custom is reasonable or known to the principal at the time when he confers the authority.[163]

Comment

3-025   Many agents have no authority to receive payment at all.[164] Where they have, nineteenth-century cases reiterate a basic rule that there is normally no authority to accept payment except in cash.[165] Under this rule an agent has prima facie no authority to give credit,[166] nor to accept a cheque. Although business practices have changed, it seems worth retaining the collection of cases and the statement of the rule, for care over payment is plainly to be required of any agent. But the rule is conditioned by the general principles as to the authority of agents, under which agents are normally authorised to do whatever is usual in the course of business.[167] It is thus not necessary to establish an actual custom that the agent need not receive cash, though it is obviously permissible to do so[168]: and this is important because customs are difficult to prove.[169] Therefore it has long been fairly easy to establish

---

[160] *Strover v Harrington* [1988] Ch. 390 at 409–410.
[161] *Cleveland Mfg. Co Ltd v Muslim Commercial Bank Ltd* [1981] 1 Lloyd's Rep. 646.
[162] *Norwich Union Life & Pensions Ltd v Strand Street Properties Ltd* [2009] EWHC 1109 (Ch) at [231].
[163] See Comment and Illustrations. See also Comment to Article 81; Article 27, Illustration 2; Article 30, Illustrations 6 and 7.
[164] See further above, para.3-022.
[165] *Sweeting v Pearce* (1859) 7 C.B.(N.S.) 449 at 480, 484; affd (1861) 9 C.B.(N.S.) 534, Illustration 4; *Farrer v Lacy, Hartland & Co* (1885) 31 Ch.D. 42; *Papé v Westacott* [1894] 1 Q.B. 272; *Blumberg v Life Interests and Reversionary Securities Corp Ltd* [1897] 1 Ch. 171; [1898] 1 Ch. 27; *Southbourne Investments Ltd v Greenmount Manufacturing Ltd* [2008] 1 N.Z.L.R. 30 (NZSC) at [19] (solicitor has no implied authority to accept payment of deposit by cheque in relation to land transaction).
[166] Though if he does he may be estopped against the principal from saying that he has not received the money: *Gillard v Wise* (1826) 5 B. & C. 134.
[167] See Articles 25, 27, 29 and 30.
[168] See Article 31.
[169] See Comment to Article 31.

implied authority to sell on credit.[170] As to cheques, a cheque is usually regarded not as a separate form of payment but as conditional payment,[171] and no problem arises when it is duly met on presentation, for it is then equivalent to payment in cash even where it is in the agent's favour.[172] Disputes can however arise as to whether a cheque is a valid tender,[173] whether an agent is in breach of his duty in accepting a cheque,[174] and whether an agent has actual or apparent authority to transfer property or release goods (which may, for instance, be subject to a lien) against a cheque rather than cash. Though the basic rule doubtless remains, it seems likely that a practice of accepting payment by cheque (especially if supported by some form of bank card), whether in favour of agent or principal, will fairly readily be recognised nowadays as being in the normal course of business, and hence within the scope of an agent's authority without proof of special usage.[175] The same is true (probably even more so as usage of cheques declines) of payment by credit card, which may rank as absolute payment.[176] It will not however prima facie be within the agent's authority to accept abnormal forms of payment, such as an adjustment of the account between agent and third party. "The payer who knows he is paying an agent must pay in such a manner as to facilitate and encourage the agent to pay it to his principal."[177] Here it may be necessary to prove an actual custom permitting such payment, and, if the custom is held unreasonable, knowledge of it.[178] But where the debtor to the principal is financially embarrassed, the agent's duty may be to do his best to collect all that he can in the circumstances, and "the onus is on the [principal] in such a case to prove that the [agent] has failed in that duty".[179] In such a case the agent may have discharged his duty by getting what cash he can and giving credit for the rest.[180]

Illustrations

(1) It is provided by the conditions of a sale by auction that the purchase-money **3-026**

---

[170] See *Houghton v Matthews* (1803) 3 B. & P. 485 at 489; *Pelham v Hilder* (1841) 1 Y. & C.C.C. 3; *Boden v French* (1851) 10 C.B. 886; *Papé v Westacott*, above, at 278; *R. & E. Tingey & Co Ltd v John Chambers & Co Ltd* [1967] N.Z.L.R. 785.

[171] *D. & C. Builders Ltd v Rees* [1966] 2 Q.B. 617.

[172] *Bridges v Garrett* (1870) L.R. 5 C.P. 451; *International Sponge Importers Ltd v Andrew Watt & Sons* [1911] A.C. 279; *Papé v Westacott*, above; *Bradford & Sons v Price Brothers* (1923) 92 L.J.K.B. 871 (authorities reviewed); *Clay Hill Brick & Tile Co Ltd v Rawlings* [1938] 4 All E.R. 100.

[173] *Blumberg v Life Interests and Reversionary Securities Corp Ltd*, above.

[174] *Farrer v Lacy, Hartland & Co*, above; *Papé v Westacott*, above; *Kearney v Cullen* [1955] I.R. 18 (solicitor).

[175] See *Underwood v Nicholls* (1855) 17 C.B. 239 at 244; *Papé v Westacott*, above, at 278, 283 (estate agent); *Farrer v Lacy, Hartland & Co*, above (auctioneer). In many transactions the supporting of a cheque by a cheque card or credit card may be normal. As to notification that only certain forms of cheque are acceptable, see *International Sponge Importers Ltd v Andrew Watt & Sons*, above; *Bradford & Sons v Price Brothers*, above. As to payment by cheque under a stipulation for payment in cash, see *Tankexpress A/S v Cie. Financière Belge des Petroles SA* [1949] A.C. 76. Where the delivery of goods has the effect of releasing a lien, it may be held that a mere driver, for instance, is not authorised to deliver against a cheque, which may not be met: see *Esterhuyse v Selection Cartage (Pty) Ltd* (1965) 1 S.A. 360; *McGraw-Edison (Canada) Ltd v Direct-Winters Tpt. Ltd* [1969] 1 O.R. 663. See further van Zyl (1974) 91 S.A.L.J. 337 (on South African cases).

[176] *Re Charge Card Services Ltd* [1989] Ch. 497.

[177] *Pearson v Scott* (1878) 9 Ch.D. 198 at 205, per Fry J; and see in general Illustrations.

[178] See Article 31; *Sweeting v Pearce* (1859) 7 C.B.(N.S.) 449; affd (1861) 9 C.B.(N.S.) 534, Illustration 4.

[179] *Gokal Chand-jagan Nath v Nand Ram Das-Atma Ram* [1939] A.C. 106 at 113, per Lord Wright.

[180] *Gokal Chand-jagan Nath v Nand Ram Das-Atma Ram* [1939] A.C. 106 at 113, per Lord Wright.

shall be paid to the auctioneer. The auctioneer has no authority to receive a bill of exchange in payment, and if his authority to receive payment is revoked during the currency of the bill, such a payment does not discharge the purchaser.[181] So, an insurance broker has no authority to take a bill of exchange in payment of a claim in respect of which he is authorised to receive payment.[182]

(2) An agent is authorised to receive payment of an account, and to retain part of the amount in discharge of a debt due to him from the principal. He has authority, to the extent of his debt, to settle in his own way with the debtor of his principal.[183]

(3) A authorises B, a country stockbroker, to receive money due from C, a London stockbroker. B has no authority to settle with C by way of set-off, and a custom permitting such settlement is unreasonable.[184]

(4) A authorises B, an insurance broker, to receive the amount due from the underwriters under a policy of insurance. The underwriters in good faith settle with B by setting off a debt due to them from him, and their names are struck out of the policy. By a custom at Lloyd's, a set-off is considered equivalent to payment as between broker and underwriter. If A is aware of the custom when he authorises B to receive payment, he is bound by the settlement. Otherwise he is not bound, because the custom is unreasonable.[185]

(5) An agent authorised to receive money has prima facie no authority to receive payment before it is due, and if his authority is revoked before that time, the debtor is not discharged by such payment[186]; he may have no authority to receive payment after it is due,[187] nor to accept it on terms different in some other respect from those prescribed by the contract.[188]

---

[181] *Williams v Evans* (1866) L.R. 1 Q.B. 352; *Sykes v Giles* (1839) 5 M. & W. 645. See also *Hogarth v Wherley* (1875) L.R. 10 C.P. 630; *Howard v Chapman* (1831) 4 C. & P. 508 (no authority to accept payment in goods). cf. *Farrer v Lacy, Hartland & Co* (1888) 31 Ch.D. 42 (cheque).

[182] *Hine Brothers v Steamship Insurance Syndicate Ltd (The Netherholme)* (1895) 72 L.T. 79 (but facts rather special).

[183] *Barker v Greenwood* (1837) 2 Y. & C. Ex. 414.

[184] *Pearson v Scott* (1878) 9 Ch.D. 198; *Blackburn v Mason* (1893) 68 L.T. 510; *Crossley v Magniac* [1893] 1 Ch. 594; *Anderson v Sutherland* (1897) 13 T.L.R. 163 (all stockbroker cases). As to custom, see Article 31. See also *Underwood v Nicholls* (1855) 17 C.B. 239; *Wrout v Dawes* (1858) 25 Beav. 369; *Coupe v Collyer* (1890) 62 L.T. 927 (solicitors).

[185] *Sweeting v Pearce* (1859) 7 C.B.(N.S.) 449; affd (1861) 9 C.B.(N.S.) 534; *Stewart v Aberdein* (1838) 4 M. & W. 211; *Legge v Byas, Mosley & Co* (1901) 7 Com.Cas. 16; *Matveieff & Co v Crosfield* (1903) 51 W.R. 365; *McCowin Lumber and Export Co v Pacific Marine Insurance Co* (1922) 38 T.L.R. 901; *Stolos Cia. SA v Ajax Insurance Co Ltd (The Admiral C)* [1981] 1 Lloyd's Rep. 9. But see *Trading & General Investment Co v Gault Armstrong & Kemble Ltd (The Okeanis)* [1986] 1 Lloyd's Rep. 196 at 200 where reference is made to evidence given that certain accounts of the customs of insurance companies were "completely out of date". See in general Hodgin, *Insurance Intermediaries: Law and Practice* (1992).

[186] *Breming v Mackie* (1862) 3 F. & F. 197. But there may be a custom permitting this: *Catterall v Hindle* (1867) L.R. 2 C.P. 368; *Heisch v Carrington* (1833) 5 C. & P. 471; see Article 31.

[187] See Article 29, Illustration 7 (insurance agent); *New Zealand Tenancy Bonds Ltd v Mooney* [1986] 1 N.Z.L.R. 280 (estate agent); cf. *Jawara v Gambian Airways* [1992] E.G.C.S. 54 (PC) (lawyer).

[188] *Campbell v Hassel* (1816) 1 Stark. 233. But a contract can be varied by custom: see Article 31.

Article 29

MANAGERIAL AGENTS: IMPLIED AUTHORITY WHERE EMPLOYED TO CONDUCT TRADE OR BUSINESS OR ACT GENERALLY IN CERTAIN MATTERS (USUAL AUTHORITY)

An agent who is authorised to conduct a particular trade or business or gener-　**3-027**
ally to act for his principal in matters of a particular nature, or to do a particular class
of acts, has implied authority to do whatever is incidental to the ordinary conduct
of such trade or business,[189] or of matters of that nature, or is within the scope of
that class of acts,[190] and whatever is necessary for the proper and effective
performance of his duties[191]: but not to do anything that is outside the ordinary scope
of his employment and duties.[192]

Comment

The authority referred to here is that which arises from appointment to a　**3-028**
particular managerial post. When the board of directors appoint one of their number
to be managing director, for example, "they thereby impliedly authorise him to do
all such things as fall within the usual scope of that office".[193]

Many of the cases refer to an agent of this type as a general agent, as
distinguished from a special agent. Much use is made of the distinction in
nineteenth-century English cases, mainly in the context of what is now called apparent authority[194]: and it has sometimes been referred to in more recent times.[195]
But it is submitted that the distinction should now be regarded in England as no
more than a rather specific example of the obvious fact that, from the point of view
of implied authority, a person made agent with general authority to do acts of various types or to negotiate a number of transactions of the same type is likely to have
a wider authority than one appointed with limited authority to do acts of a particular
class or to negotiate a particular transaction. The borderline between general and
special agents is so indistinct that it is unwise to regard the test as a definitive one.[196]

The authority here discussed is an example of what can be called usual
authority.[197] It should be noted, as with other Articles in this chapter, that the
principle here cited is relevant not only to actual authority but also to apparent
authority, in that in many cases the normal implied authority was negatived as
between the parties by the circumstances, yet the third party was held entitled to
assume that it existed, since the authority concerned would regularly be implied.
The "general agent" cases are in fact, as stated above, in the main relevant to the
development of the doctrine of apparent authority. However, they can, of course,
support the proposition that implied authority will normally extend thus far.[198] It

---

[189] Illustrations 1 and 4.
[190] Illustrations 2, 4, 5 and 9.
[191] Illustrations 3, 6, 10 and 11.
[192] Illustrations 2, 3, 7 and 10.
[193] *Hely-Hutchinson v Brayhead Ltd* [1968] 1 Q.B. 549 at 583, per Lord Denning MR. See further Illustration 4.
[194] See, e.g. *Smith v M'Guire* (1858) 3 H. & N. 554; see Article 72.
[195] e.g. *Barrett v Irvine* [1907] 2 I.R. 462.
[196] See above, para.1-045.
[197] As to this term see above, para.3-005.
[198] e.g. *Collen v Gardner* (1856) 21 Beav. 540, Illustration 2; *Wright v Glyn* [1902] 1 K.B. 745 (coach-

would be unusual for a general manager to have greater implied authority to make contracts with foreign parties than with domestic ones.[199]

Many of the examples relate to ways of living and trading which no longer exist; their value is simply as providing examples of the typical reasoning used, and analogies.

Illustrations

3-029 (1) A is the manager of an estate. He has implied authority to contract for the usual and customary leases,[200] and to give and receive notice to quit to and from tenants[201] and to enter into agreements with tenants authorising them to change the mode of cultivation, and providing for the basis on which compensation for improvements shall be payable on the determination of the tenancy.[202]

(2) A rent collector has no implied authority, as such, to receive a notice to quit from a tenant.[203] A steward has such implied authority,[204] but not to grant leases for terms of years.[205]

(3) A is the managing owner of a ship. He has implied authority to pledge the credit of his co-owners for all such things, including repairs, as are necessary for the usual or suitable employment of the ship.[206] But he has no authority as such to insure the vessel on behalf of his co-owners,[207] or to agree to pay a sum of money for the cancellation of a charter party made by him on their behalf.[208]

(4) Individual directors of companies, at least those without an executive role, have little usual authority to bind the company.[209] The managing director of a company has a broad authority (subject to the company's constitution) to make decisions for the company in the ordinary course of business,[210] includ-

---

man); *Hely-Hutchinson v Brayhead Ltd* [1968] 1 Q.B. 549 at 583. See also *Brady v Todd* (1861) 9 C.B.(N.S.) 592; *Howard v Sheward* (1866) L.R. 2 C.P. 148; *Brooks v Hassall* (1883) 49 L.T. 560; *Baldry v Bates* (1885) 52 L.T. 620. These are cases where the usual authority of the agent is relied on, and therefore the representation giving rise to apparent authority would be very general indeed: see Comment to Article 72.

[199] *Sea Emerald SA v Prominvestbank-Joint Stockpoint Commercial Industrial and Investment Bank* [2008] EWHC 1979 (Comm) at [70].
[200] *Peers v Sneyd* (1853) 17 Beav. 151.
[201] *Papillon v Brunton* (1860) 5 H. & N. 518; *Jones v Phipps* (1868) L.R. 3 Q.B. 567; *Townsends Carriers Ltd v Pfizer Ltd* (1977) 33 P. & C.R. 361; *Peel Developments (South) Ltd v Siemens Plc* [1992] 2 E.G.L.R. 85.
[202] *Re Pearson and I'Anson* [1899] 2 Q.B. 618.
[203] *Pearse v Boulter* (1860) 2 F. & F. 133.
[204] *Roe d. Rochester (Dean & Chapter) v Pierce* (1809) 2 Camp. 96.
[205] *Collen v Gardner* (1856) 21 Beav. 540.
[206] *The Huntsman* [1894] P. 214; *Barker v Highley* (1863) 15 C.B.(N.S.) 27.
[207] *Robinson v Gleadow* (1835) 2 Bing. N.C. 156.
[208] *Thomas v Lewis* (1878) 4 Ex.D. 18. See Scrutton, *Charterparties* (17th edn), Article 16 (omitted in later eds). Quaere as to the present day.
[209] *Re Haycraft Gold Reduction and Mining Co Ltd* [1900] 2 Ch. 230; *Houghton & Co v Nothard Lowe & Wills Ltd* [1927] 1 K.B. 246 at 267; *Northside Developments Pty Ltd v Registrar-General* (1990) 170 C.L.R. 146 at 205; *Hughes v NM Superannuation Pty Ltd* (1993) 29 N.S.W.L.R. 653 (chairperson of directors); *Colin R Price & Associates Pty Ltd v Four Oaks Pty Ltd* [2017] FCAFC 75 at [150].
[210] *Hely-Hutchinson v Brayhead Ltd* [1968] 1 Q.B. 549; *Rimpacific Navigation Inc v Daehan Shipbuilding Co Ltd* [2009] EWHC 2941 (Comm); [2010] 2 Lloyd's Rep. 236.

ing to sign cheques and bills of exchange,[211] borrow money and give security over the company's property,[212] guarantee loans made by a subsidiary of the company and agree to indemnify other guarantors,[213] and authorise the commencement of legal proceedings.[214] He may reimburse himself for expenses on the company's behalf,[215] but should do so by payment through a bank account and not by using company money to pay for private items of consumption.[216] He may direct the method of discharge of debts owed to the company, but not by directing payment to a family member.[217] A managing director may have usual authority to instruct solicitors as to the drafting of his own remuneration contract.[218] A managing director would not have usual authority to make extraordinary decisions (those would normally need to be taken by the board of directors),[219] such as the sale or termination of the company's business.[220] He has no authority to bribe representatives of other companies,[221] but would have authority to cause the company to breach a contract.[222] A managing director has no authority to use his powers to suspend employees in order to suspend the chairman of directors in that role, even though the latter is an employee.[223]

(5)   A company secretary has authority to order cars to meet visitors at airports, and in general to make contracts in connection with the administration of the company's affairs.[224] Similarly, a corporate "general counsel" might be expected to have authority to instruct solicitors to oppose an application to wind up the company.[225] A company secretary would normally also have usual

---

[211] *Dey v Pullinger Engineering Co* [1921] 1 K.B. 77.

[212] *Biggerstaff v Rowatt's Wharf Ltd* [1896] 2 Ch. 93.

[213] *Hely-Hutchinson v Brayhead Ltd* [1968] 1 Q.B. 549.

[214] *AMB Generali Holding AG v SEB Trygg Liv, etc.* [2005] EWCA Civ 1237; [2006] 1 Lloyd's Rep. 318 at [32]; *Hawksford v Hawksford* (2005) 191 F.L.R. 173.

[215] *Bank of New South Wales v Goulburn Valley Butter Co Pty Ltd* [1902] A.C. 543 (PC); *Corporation Agencies v Home Bank of Canada* [1927] A.C. 318 (PC).

[216] See *Midland Bank Ltd v Reckitt* [1933] A.C. 1.

[217] *Acute Property Developments Ltd v Apostolou* [2013] EWHC 200 (Ch) at [40].

[218] *Newcastle International Airport Ltd v Eversheds LLP* [2012] EWHC 2648 (Ch); [2013] P.N.L.R. 5 at [111]; affd on this point [2013] EWCA Civ 1514; [2014] 1 W.L.R. 3073 at [76] (but finding of express authority).

[219] See *Freeman & Lockyer v Buckhurst Park Properties (Mangal) Ltd* [1964] 2 Q.B. 480 at 509; *Smith v Butler* [2012] EWCA Civ 314; [2012] Bus. L.R. 1836 at [30]; *Spedley Securities Ltd v Greater Pacific Investments Pty Ltd* (1992) 7 A.C.S.R. 155 at 16; *Thanakharn Kasikorn Thai Chamchat v Akai Holdings Ltd (In Liquidation)* (2010) 13 HKCFAR 479 at [110]. It is doubtful whether a board of directors would any longer be expected to delegate total management power to a managing director: the broad dicta in *Biggerstaff v Rowatt's Wharf Ltd* [1896] 2 Ch. 93 at 102, 106, should be viewed in the light of later authorities.

[220] *Interactive Technology Corp Ltd v Ferster* [2016] EWHC 2896 (Ch) at [188].

[221] *E. Hannibal & Co Ltd v Frost* (1988) 4 B.C.C. 3. But cf. *Morgan v Babcock & Wilcox Ltd* (1929) 43 C.L.R. 163. See further Watts [2011] J.B.L. 214 at 215.

[222] *Lexi Holdings Plc v Pannone & Partners* [2009] EWHC 2590 (Ch).

[223] *Smith v Butler* [2012] EWCA Civ 314; [2012] Bus. L.R. 1836 at [31].

[224] *Panorama Developments (Guildford) Ltd v Fidelis Furnishing Fabrics Ltd* [1971] 2 Q.B. 711, recognising the change in the function of company secretaries since the early years of that century. As to a secretary's usual authority to communicate board decisions, see *Mahony v East Holyford Mining Co* (1875) L.R. 7 H.L. 869 at 887 and 902; *Montreal and St Lawrence Light and Power Co v Robert* [1906] A.C. 196 at 203 (joint representation of president and secretary). See too *Daimler Co Ltd v Continental Tyre & Rubber Co* [1916] 2 A.C. 307 at 323 (but cf. p.326).

[225] *Telstra Corp Ltd v Ivory* [2008] QSC 123 at [89].

authority to communicate the decisions of the board of the company, and to authenticate documents which record what the board has decided.[226]

(6)   The general manager of a railway company has implied authority to order medical attendance for an employee of the company.[227] But a station-master has no implied authority to pledge the credit of the railway company for medical attendance to an injured passenger.[228]

(7)   A is the agent of an insurance company, and has authority to receive the payment of premiums within 15 days of their becoming due. He has no implied authority to accept payment after the expiration of that time.[229] So, a local agent of an insurance company, employed to introduce business, has as a rule no implied authority to grant, or contract to grant, policies on behalf of the company, that being outside the ordinary scope of his employment and duties,[230] though he may be authorised to grant temporary cover.[231]

(8)   The master of a stranded ship has in the absence of express instructions authority to bind his owners or demise charterers by entering into a reasonable salvage contract.[232]

(9)   The engineer of a local authority has authority to specify the purpose for which goods are required by the authority, for the purposes of the Sale of Goods Act 1893 s.14.[233]

(10)   Authority to arrest or give persons into custody is normally implied when the duties of the agent could not efficiently be performed without such authority. A bank manager has no implied authority to arrest or prosecute supposed offenders on behalf of the bank.[234] The manager of a restaurant has implied authority to give into custody persons behaving in a riotous manner,[235] but not persons who refuse to pay a disputed bill.[236]

(11)   A manager of a building project, even where the husband of the owner, has no usual authority to grant an easement to a neighbour in return for the latter's co-operation with the project.[237]

(12)   An importer engages an agent to arrange for the receipt, storage and subsequent carriage of its products. The agent signs a standard-form carriage contract without reading its terms which include a broad exclusion

---

[226] *Kelly v Fraser* [2012] UKPC 25; [2013] 1 A.C. 450 at [13].

[227] *Walker v Great Western Ry Co* (1867) L.R. 2 Ex. 228.

[228] *Cox v Midland Ry Co* (1849) 3 Exch. 268. See also *Houghton v Pilkington* [1912] 3 K.B. 308; cf. *Langan v Great Western Ry Co* (1873) 30 L.T. 173. See also Article 33.

[229] *Acey v Fernie* (1840) 7 M. & W. 151. See *MacGillivray on Insurance Law* (12th edn), para.7-72 onwards.

[230] *Linford v Provincial, etc., Ins Co* (1864) 34 Beav. 291. See Article 77, Illustrations 8, 9 and 10.

[231] *Wilkinson v General Accident Fire and Life Insurance Co Ltd* [1967] 2 Lloyd's Rep. 182.

[232] *The Unique Mariner* [1978] 1 Lloyd's Rep. 438; but see below, para.4-008.

[233] *Ashford Shire Council v Dependable Motors Pty Ltd* [1961] A.C. 336.

[234] *Bank of New South Wales v Owston* (1879) 4 App.Cas. 270, where there is a full review of the authorities; *Abrahams v Deakin* [1891] 1 Q.B. 516. But many of the old cases on false imprisonment may be out of date in England at least. Whereas in former times a person was "given in charge", the increased speed of communications today means that police officers are normally able to arrive soon enough to effect arrests on their own responsibility. See Atiyah, *Vicarious Liability in the Law of Torts* (1967), pp.266–267.

[235] *Ashton v Spiers & Pond* (1893) 9 T.L.R. 606.

[236] *Stedman v Baker & Co* (1896) 12 T.L.R. 451.

[237] *McKeand v Thomas* (2006) 12 B.P.R. 23, 593 at [74] (NSWSC).

clause. The agent's actions held to be within the scope of its actual authority.[238]

Article 30

PROFESSIONAL AGENTS: IMPLIED AUTHORITY WHERE EMPLOYED IN THE COURSE OF BUSINESS AS AGENT (USUAL AUTHORITY)

An agent who is authorised to do any act in the course of his trade, profession or business as an agent has implied authority to do whatever is normally incidental, in the ordinary course of such trade, profession or business, to the execution of his express authority,[239] but not to do anything which is unusual in such trade, profession or business, or which is neither necessary for nor incidental to the execution of his express authority.[240]

3-030

Comment

In this case the implied authority arises, not from the managerial nature of the post to which the agent has been appointed, as in the previous Article, but from the nature of the general occupation which he carries on apart from this particular agency. Agents of this type also are sometimes referred to as general agents, though as has already been stated, the utility of this term is doubtful.[241] The examples given here are for illustrative purposes, but more specific information should be sought in specialist works dealing with the authorities of those practising the various types of trade and profession. Expert evidence as to current practice is more likely to be relevant than old illustrations: as Staughton LJ said in connection with the authority of a solicitor, "I prefer to have regard to the expert evidence of today in deciding what is the ordinary authority".[242]

3-031

This proposition is again an example of what may be called usual authority.[243] As in the previous Articles, the primary reference is to actual authority, but the reasoning will apply also to apparent authority: indeed many of the cases relate to apparent authority, since the notion of general agency was primarily relevant to what is now called apparent authority.[244]

Illustrations

(1) A bailiff is authorised to distrain for rent. He has implied authority to receive

3-032

---

[238] *Toll (FGCT) Pty Ltd v Alphapharm Pty Ltd* (2004) 219 C.L.R. 165.
[239] Illustrations 1, 2 and 7. See too *AIB Group (UK) Plc v Mark Redler & Co (A Firm)* [2012] EWHC 35 (Ch) at [21]–[22]; affd on different grounds [2014] UKSC 58; [2015] A.C. 1503 (solicitor's usual authority in disbursing client moneys).
[240] Illustrations 3–6.
[241] See above, para.3-028.
[242] *United Bank of Kuwait Ltd v Hammoud* [1988] 1 W.L.R. 1051 at 1063; *Sea Emerald SA v Prominvestbank-Joint Stockpoint Commercial Industrial and Investment Bank* [2008] EWHC 1979 (Comm) at [108] (experts should give evidence of their experience not just opinion); *Seiwa Australia Pty Ltd v Beard* (2010) 75 N.S.W.L.R. 74 at [269] onwards (deprecating use of judicial notice in this context). See also Illustration 5.
[243] See above, para.3-005.
[244] See above, para.3-028.

the rent and expenses due, and a tender thereof to him operates as a tender to the landlord.[245]

(2) A horse-dealer is authorised to sell a horse. He has implied authority to warrant it.[246] So also has his employee. But the employee of a private seller has not[247] unless he sells in circumstances where custom requires a warranty.[248]

(3) An architect was employed to make plans for building certain houses. He instructed a quantity surveyor to take out quantities, and then invited tenders, all of which exceeded the limits of the building-owner's proposed expenditure. The quantity surveyor sued the building-owner for his fees, relying on an alleged custom in the building trade, by which the liability for such fees was thrown on the building-owner where no tender was accepted. The jury having found that there was no custom by which an architect was authorised to employ a surveyor without the sanction of the building-owner, and the owner not having expressly authorised the employment, it was held that the defendant was not liable.[249]

(4) A ship's agent has implied authority to arrange and pay for the stowage of cargo.[250] A loading superintendent employed by a f.o.b. buyer has no authority to waive a term of the contract as to description: but failure by him to object to goods which do not conform with the contract description may be attributed to the buyer for the purpose of the buyer's duty to mitigate damages.[251]

(5) A solicitor entrusted with the conduct of litigation has authority to agree to a settlement of it provided that the settlement does not concern matters collateral to the action.[252] He has in general no implied authority to accept notices

---

[245] *Hatch v Hale* (1850) 15 Q.B. 10. Tender to a man left in possession by the bailiff is ineffective: *Boulton v Reynolds* (1859) 2 E. & E. 369.

[246] *Howard v Sheward* (1866) L.R. 2 C.P. 148; *Baldry v Bates* (1885) 52 L.T. 620. See also *Bank of Scotland v Watson* (1813) 1 Dow. 40 at 45. But this question is now of less importance in view of warranties implied by statute.

[247] *Brady v Todd* (1861) 9 C.B.(N.S.) 592.

[248] *Brooks v Hassall* (1883) 49 L.T. 569; see Article 31.

[249] *Antisell v Doyle* [1899] 2 I.R. 275.

[250] *Blandy Bros & Co Ltd v Nello Simoni Ltd* [1963] 2 Lloyd's Rep. 393. cf. *Sickens v Irving* (1858) 29 L.J.C.P. 25 (no authority to make substantially new contract); *Lindsay & Son v Scholefield* (1897) 24 R. (Ct. of Sess.) 530. See in general as to ship's agents Trappe [1978] L.M.C.L.Q. 595; Morris [1982] L.M.C.L.Q. 218; also *Intermediaries in Shipping* (Grönfors ed., Gothenburg Maritime Law Association, 1990). As to agency in chartering, see Anderson (2000) 31 J.M.L.C. 89.

[251] *Toepfer v Warinco AG* [1978] 2 Lloyd's Rep. 569. See further as to authority to waive contract terms *Dawson Line Ltd v Aktiengesellschaft für Chemische Industrie* [1932] 1 K.B. 433; *Ismail v Polish Ocean Lines* [1976] Q.B. 893; *Mardorf Peach & Co Ltd v Attica Sea Carriers Corp (The Laconia)* [1977] A.C. 850 (authority of bank to accept late payment); *Surrey Shipping Co Ltd v Cie. Continentale (France) SA (The Shackleford)* [1978] 1 W.L.R. 1080 (receiver of goods had authority to waive defects in notice of readiness); *The Happy Day* [2002] EWCA Civ 1068; [2002] 2 Lloyd's Rep. 487 (receivers' agents); *The Northgate* [2007] EWHC 2796; [2008] 2 All E.R. (Comm) 330 at [108] (implied power to waive in relation to notice of readiness); *State Rail Authority of NSW v Heath Outdoor Pty Ltd* (1986) 7 N.S.W.L.R. 170 at 194 (advertising manager had authority to indicate circumstances in which employer would terminate advertising contract, but not to vary contract); *Nowrani Pty Ltd v Brown* [1989] 2 Qd.R. 582 (solicitor had no authority to insert term into sale of land). See further *Restatement, Third*, § 6.08 and Comment.

[252] *Waugh v H.B. Clifford & Sons Ltd* [1982] Ch. 374 (authorities reviewed); *Lucke v Cleary* (2011) 111 S.A.S.R. 134; *Nandrame v Ramsaran* [2015] UKPC 20; *Pavlovic v Universal Music Australia Pty Ltd* [2015] NSWCA 313; (2015) 90 N.S.W.L.R. 605 at [7]. But cf. *Re Newen* [1903] 1 Ch. 812; *Little v Spreadbury* [1910] 2 K.B. 658; *Thompson v Howley* [1977] 1 N.Z.L.R. 16; *Holmes v Kennard & Son* (1984) 44 P. & C.R. 202 (solicitor for purchaser had no authority to cancel notice on land

on behalf of his clients.[253] Agents, including employees and solicitors, have no implied authority to receive service of court proceedings in circumstances where personal service on a party is required. Subsequent delivery of the documents by the agent to the principal will not in itself be service.[254]

(6) A solicitor negotiating the sale of land on a "subject to contract" basis has no usual authority to sign the contract, nor otherwise to make a contract,[255] but would have usual authority to deliver and receive signed counterparts to a contract.[256]

(7) An estate agent in England has normally no authority to sell land: even though he is instructed as to the price at which the vendor will sell, his function is to solicit offers and transmit them to his principal.[257] But he may be authorised expressly or impliedly to sell[258] though in such circumstances he normally has no authority to sign anything but an open contract.[259] In any case he is prima facie authorised to describe the property and state to an intending purchaser circumstances which may affect its value[260]; but not to accept a deposit on such terms as will make the prospective vendor liable in respect of it[261]; to receive payment[262]; to warrant that the property may legally be used for a particular

---

register); *Donnellan v Watson* (1990) 21 N.S.W.L.R. 335 (no authority to agree to different compromise from that authorised); Cordery, *Solicitors* (8th edn), p.80 (not reproduced in later editions); Fridman (1987) 36 U. New Brunswick L.J. 9. cf. above, para.3-005. It has been held that a Citizens' Advice Bureau worker had a somewhat wider authority: *Freeman v Sovereign Chicken Ltd* [1991] I.C.R. 853.

[253] *Re Munro Ex p. Singer* [1981] 1 W.L.R. 1358; *IVI Pty Ltd v Baycrown Pty Ltd* [2005] QCA 205 at [33] (notice of revocation of offer given to purchaser's solicitor held ineffective where negotiations had principally been face-to-face). cf. *Von Essen Hotels 5 Ltd v Vaughan* [2007] EWCA Civ 1349 at [36] (see below, para.8-206). See further Article 94.

[254] *Cherney v Deripaska* [2007] EWHC 965 (Comm); [2007] 2 All E.R. (Comm) 785; *Lantic Sugar Ltd v Baffin Investments Ltd* [2009] EWHC 3325 (Comm); [2010] 2 Lloyd's Rep. 141 at [44]; *Sino Channel Asia Ltd v Dana Shipping and Trading PTE Singapore* [2016] EWHC 1118 (Comm); [2016] 2 Lloyd's Rep. 97 at [49].

[255] *Lockett v Norman-Wright* [1925] Ch. 56; *James v Evans* [2000] 3 E.G.L.R. 1; *Vella v Permanent Mortgages Pty Ltd* [2008] NSWSC 505 at [207]; *Pavlovic v Universal Music Australia Pty Ltd* [2015] NSWCA 313; (2015) 90 N.S.W.L.R. 605 at [6].

[256] *Domb v Isoz* [1980] 1 Ch. 548. See also *Wise Think Global Ltd v Finance Worldwide Ltd* [2013] H.K.E.C. 1790 (authority to receive deposit). cf. *Southbourne Investments Ltd v Greenmount Manufacturing Ltd* [2008] 1 N.Z.L.R. 30 (NZSC) at [19] (no authority to receive deposit in form of cheque).

[257] *Hamer v Sharp* (1874) L.R. 19 Eq. 108; *Prior v Moore* (1887) 3 T.L.R. 624; *Chadburn v Moore* (1892) 61 L.J.Ch. 674; *Thurman v Best* (1907) 97 L.T. 239; *Lewcock v Bromley* (1920) 37 T.L.R. 48; *Keen v Mear* [1920] 2 Ch. 574; *Wragg v Lovett* [1948] 2 All E.R. 968; (but cf. *Jawara v Gambian Airways* [1992] E.G.C.S. 54, PC); *Law v Robert Roberts & Co* [1964] I.R. 292 (authorities reviewed). He is a "canvassing" or "introducing" agent: above, para.1-020. This does not exclude the possibility of other usages in other countries, e.g. *Powierza v Daley* [1985] 1 N.Z.L.R. 558.

[258] *Rosenbaum v Belson* [1900] 2 Ch. 267; *Allen & Co v Whiteman* (1920) 89 L.J.Ch. 534; *Wragg v Lovett*, above; *Spiro v Lintern* [1973] 1 W.L.R. 1002.

[259] *Keen v Mear*, above; *Wragg v Lovett*, above. cf. *Wisecal Ltd v Conwell International Ltd* [2011] 4 H.K.L.R.D. 275 at [22].

[260] *Mullens v Miller* (1882) 22 Ch.D. 194. But cf. *Overbrooke Estates Ltd v Glencombe Properties Ltd* [1974] 1 W.L.R. 1335; *Presser v Caldwell Estates Pty Ltd* [1971] 2 N.S.W.L.R. 471.

[261] *Sorrell v Finch* [1977] A.C. 728. See Articles 92 and 111. See also *New Zealand Tenancy Bonds Ltd v Mooney* [1986] 1 N.Z.L.R. 280 (no authority to accept late payment of deposit); cf. *Kohn v Devon Mortgage Ltd* (1985) 20 D.L.R. (4th) 480 (mortgage broker had authority to receive capital).

[262] See *Mynn v Joliffe* (1834) 1 Moo. & Rob. 326; *Petersen v Moloney* (1951) 84 C.L.R. 91; *Smith v Peter & Diana Hubbard Pty Ltd* [2006] NSWCA 109; cf. *Butwick v Grant* [1924] 2 K.B. 483.

purpose[263]; it seems, to receive notice of cancellation of the contract under a statutory cooling-off provision.[264]

(8) An auctioneer has authority not only to sell but also at the time of the sale to sign a contract or memorandum of the sale for both vendor and purchaser.[265] In general there is no authority to receive payment,[266] but authority to describe the property[267] and receive a post-contract deposit may be usual,[268] and, except in the case of land, authority to receive the whole price may likewise be usual.[269] An auctioneer has normally no authority to rescind a sale,[270] to warrant,[271] to negotiate terms[272] or to sell by private contract after the auction, even where the public sale proves abortive and he is offered more than the reserve price.[273]

(9) Evidence of industry practice would be needed to show that it was within the usual authority of a firm of accountants to be holding and operating custodial (non-trust) accounts in off-shore tax havens on behalf of clients.[274]

Article 31

AUTHORITY IMPLIED FROM SPECIAL USAGES (CUSTOMARY AUTHORITY)

3-033 (1) An agent has implied authority to act, in the execution of his express authority, according to the usages and customs of the particular place, market or business in which he is employed.[275]

(2) But an agent has no implied authority to act in accordance with any usage or custom which is unreasonable, unless the principal had actual notice of such

---

[263] *Hill v Harris* [1965] 2 Q.B. 601.

[264] *Lo v Russell* [2016] VSCA 323 at [37].

[265] *Emmerson v Heelis* (1809) 2 Taunt. 38; *White v Proctor* (1811) 4 Taunt. 209; *Kenneys v Proctor* (1820) 1 Jac. & W. 350; *Earl of Glengal v Barton* (1836) 1 Keen 769 at 788; *Bell v Balls* [1897] 1 Ch. 663; *Chaney v Maclow* [1929] 1 Ch. 461. cf. *Van Praagh v Everidge* [1903] 1 Ch. 434. By virtue of s.2 of the Law of Property (Miscellaneous Provisions) Act 1989 the contract must now be in writing; but this does not apply in public auctions, which now require neither writing nor memorandum. Quaere whether an auctioneer has authority to sign a written contract. See Murdoch, *Law of Estate Agency* (5th edn), p.174 onwards.

[266] See *Mynn v Joliffe*, above; cf. *Butwick v Grant*, above.

[267] See, e.g. *Smith v Land and House Property Corp* (1884) 28 Ch.D. 7. But cf. *Overbrooke Estates Ltd v Glencombe Properties Ltd* [1974] 1 W.L.R. 1335 and *Collins v Howell-Jones* (1980) 259 E.G. 331, where this authority was excluded.

[268] See *Sykes v Giles* (1830) 5 M. & W. 645; Murdoch, above, p.229 onwards.

[269] cf. Factors Act 1889 s.12(3); *Chelmsford Auctions Ltd v Poole* [1973] Q.B. 542.

[270] *Nelson v Aldridge* (1818) 2 Stark. 435.

[271] *Payne v Lord Leconfield* (1882) 51 L.J.Q.B. 642; *Gardiner v Grigg* (1938) 38 S.R.(N.S.W.) 524.

[272] *Seton v Slade* (1802) 7 Ves. 265 at 276.

[273] *Daniel v Adams* (1764) Ambl. 495; *Marsh v Jelf* (1862) 3 F. & F. 234. cf. *Else v Barnard* (1860) 28 Beav. 228; *Bousfield v Hodges* (1863) 33 Beav. 90. See in general Murdoch, *Law of Estate Agency* (5th edn), Ch.3.

[274] *Seiwa Australia Pty Ltd v Beard* (2010) 75 N.S.W.L.R. 74 at [310] (general discussion of usual authority of accountants).

[275] Illustrations 1–7; *Sutton v Tatham* (1839) 10 A. & E. 27; *Ex p. Howell, re Williams* (1865) 12 L.T. 785. There is a useful discussion of the requirement and effects of custom in Law Com. C.P. No. 124, *Fiduciary Duties and Regulatory Rules* (1992), pp.63–76.

usage or custom at the time when he conferred the authority[276]; or to act in accordance with any usage or custom which is unlawful.[277]

(3) The question whether any usage or custom is unreasonable or unlawful is a question of law. In particular, a usage or custom inconsistent with the intrinsic character of the contract of agency,[278] or a usage or custom whereby an agent who is authorised to receive payment of money may require payment by way of set-off, or by way of settlement of accounts between himself and the person from whom he is authorised to receive payment,[279] is unreasonable.

Comment

General rule   This Article embodies the general rule that an agent is authorised   **3-034**
to act in accordance with the commercial customs in the sphere in which he operates, e.g. a stock or commodity exchange. The rule is, however, of limited application. The rules concerning proof of custom are strict, for their effect in the general law is to imply terms into contracts, which is not normally permitted unless they are to be derived from the nature of the transaction or essential to give it business efficacy.

Accordingly, proof of custom is notoriously difficult:

"In the mind of a layman there is often a confusion between custom and that which is customarily done, and he wrongly imagines that the latter amounts to a legal custom."[280]

The latter would of course be evidence of what authority is reasonably to be implied, or, in other contexts, of what is reasonably to be expected of principal or agent in the circumstances.[281] This Article therefore only applies to generally recognised and established customs in markets or the like, and not to mere customary courses of dealing between agent and third party, or between agents of the particular type and third parties.[282] Evidence of such courses of dealing may be well relevant to establish some other form of implied authority.

Custom   The burden of proving the existence of a custom or usage is a heavy one.   **3-035**
It is not normally one that can be discharged by evidence given on affidavit if that

---

[276] *Robinson v Mollett* (1874) L.R. 7 H.L. 802, Illustration 8.

[277] *Harker v Edwards* (1887) 57 L.J.Q.B. 147; and see Comment. Rules (1) and (2) were cited with approval in *Anglo Overseas Transport (United Kingdom) Ltd v Titan Industrial Corporation (United Kingdom) Ltd* [1959] 2 Lloyd's Rep. 152 at 160.

[278] Illustrations 8 and 9. See also *Accidia Foundation v Simon C. Dickinson Ltd* [2010] EWHC 3058 (Ch) at [75] (appointment of art sales sub-agent on terms that contemplated suppression of terms of remuneration).

[279] Illustration 10.

[280] *Re North Western Rubber Co Ltd and Hüttenbach & Co* [1908] 2 K.B. 907 at 919, per Fletcher Moulton LJ. The case itself was overruled in *Produce Brokers Co Ltd v Olympia Oil & Cake Co Ltd* [1916] 1 A.C. 314, which contains a detailed consideration of much of this topic. See also *Drexel Burnham Lambert International NV v El Nasr* [1986] 1 Lloyd's Rep. 356 at 365, per Staughton LJ: "What has to be shown by evidence is that the custom is recognised as imposing a binding obligation".

[281] See Articles 27–30.

[282] See *Hamilton v Young* (1881) 7 L.R.Ir. 289; *Ex p. Howell, Re Williams* (1865) 12 L.T. 785; *Cunliffe-Owen v Teather & Greenwood* [1967] 1 W.L.R. 1421 at 1438; *General Reinsurance Corp v Forsakringsaktiebolaget Fenna Patria* [1983] Q.B. 856.

evidence is challenged.[283] In order to establish the existence of a custom or usage the plaintiff must show that the alleged custom is (i) reasonable[284]; (ii) universally accepted by the particular trade or profession or at the particular place; (iii) certain; (iv) not unlawful; and (v) not inconsistent with the express or implied terms of the contract.[285] Therefore, even if a custom is proved to exist, the court will ignore it if it is expressly or impliedly excluded. But where the custom does exist and is not excluded, it is:

"to be considered as part of the agreement: and if the agreement be in writing, though the custom is not written it is to be treated exactly as if that unwritten clause had been written out at length."[286]

3-036 **Rules** The position as regards rules, e.g. of a market or organisation, as opposed to customs, seems, despite suggestions to the contrary,[287] to be the same.[288] It is however obvious that special problems may arise when rules are changed. It has been held that a resolution of a regulatory body passed after a transaction cannot bind the principal or alter the contract between the parties,[289] though it may validly decide a dispute between the parties.[290]

3-037 **Unreasonable customs** There was much authority for applying the criterion of reasonableness to usages and customs, and especially to the rules of the Stock Exchange,[291] though the law does not normally protect contracting parties from unreasonable terms with much tenderness. But the situations referred to in Rule (3) of this Article are better regarded as sui generis rather than examples of unreasonable arrangements[292]: they were held to be actually inconsistent with the nature of the contract of agency, and were in the first edition of this work treated as in

---

[283] *Stag Line Ltd v Board of Trade* (1950) 83 Lloyd's Rep. 356 at 360. See also *Blandy Bros v Nello Simoni* [1963] 2 Lloyd's Rep. 24 at 29; [1963] 2 Lloyd's Rep. 393 at 400, 404.

[284] Thus in *Anglo-African Merchants Ltd v Bayley* [1970] 1 Q.B. 311 at 323 Megaw J said that the court would not uphold a custom which contradicted the principle that an agent might not serve both parties simultaneously. This was followed in *North and South Trust Co v Berkeley* [1971] 1 W.L.R. 470, Illustration 3 to Article 5; but cf. *Goshawk Dedicated Ltd v Tyse & Co Ltd* [2006] EWCA Civ 54. And see Article 44, Illustration 5.

[285] These well-known principles were accepted in *Oricon Waren-Handels GmbH v Intergraan NV* [1967] 2 Lloyd's Rep. 82 at 96 and in *Cunliffe-Owen v Teather & Greenwood* [1967] 1 W.L.R. 1421 at 1439. See also *Con-Stan Industry of Australia Pty Ltd v Norwich Winterthur Insurance (Australia) Ltd* (1986) 160 C.L.R. 226. As to (v) see further *Palgrave, Brown & Son Ltd v SS Turid* [1922] 1 A.C. 397 at 406; *London Export Corp v Jubilee Coffee Roasting Co* [1958] 1 W.L.R. 661 at 675; *Kum v Wah Tat Bank* [1971] 1 Lloyd's Rep. 437; *Accidia Foundation v Simon C. Dickinson Ltd* [2010] EWHC 3058 (Ch) at [69] and [71] (art agent not authorised to appoint sub-agent on terms that the latter could keep as commission any sums in excess of floor price).

[286] *Tucker v Linger* (1883) 8 App.Cas. 508 at 511, per Lord Blackburn.

[287] *Benjamin v Barnett* (1903) 19 T.L.R. 564.

[288] *Harker v Edwards* (1887) 57 L.J.Q.B. 147; *Cunliffe-Owen v Teather & Greenwood* [1967] 1 W.L.R. 1421. But see *Anderson v Sutherland* (1897) 13 T.L.R. 163.

[289] *Union Corp Ltd v Charrington & Brodrick* (1902) 19 T.L.R. 129; *Benjamin v Barnett* (1903) 19 T.L.R. 564. And see, on the changing of rules, *Doyle v White City Stadium Ltd* [1935] 1 K.B. 110.

[290] *Harker v Edwards* (1887) 57 L.J.Q.B. 147; *Reynolds v Smith* (1893) 9 T.L.R. 474; *Bell Group Ltd v Herald and Weekly Times* [1985] V.R. 613.

[291] e.g. *Pearson v Scott* (1878) 9 Ch.D. 198, Illustration 3 to Article 28; *Blackburn v Mason* (1893) 9 T.L.R. 286; *Anderson v Sutherland* (1897) 13 T.L.R. 163; *Sweeting v Pearce* (1861) 9 C.B.(N.S.) 534; *Hamilton v Young* (1881) 7 L.R.Ir. 289; *Harker v Edwards*; *Benjamin v Barnett*; *Reynolds v Smith*, above.

[292] The matter is exhaustively discussed in *Robinson v Mollett* (1874) L.R. 7 H.L. 802. But in *Perry v Barnett* (1885) 15 Q.B.D. 388 the two grounds are treated as the same: see 393–394.

themselves a ground for the non-operation of custom. In all these cases the agent has no authority unless the principal knew of the custom when he gave or confirmed the authority for the particular transaction.

Unlawful customs   Knowledge of an unreasonable custom may import assent to it. But it is difficult to see how the law can permit a principal to assent to a custom which is actually unlawful.[293] Nevertheless, a different conclusion could be derived from a group of cases relating to the former custom of the Stock Exchange to disregard Leeman's Act,[294] under which contracts for the sale of shares in banking companies were void if they did not contain certain information. In *Perry v Barnett*[295] it was held that this custom did not bind persons without notice,[296] but it was implied that it might, like an unreasonable custom, bind someone who had notice.[297] In *Seymour v Bridge*[298] it had been held that this custom could bind a plaintiff who was at the time unaware of the existence of the Act: the case was explained in *Perry v Barnett* as referring to a situation where there was notice of the usage, even if not of the Act. *Seymour v Bridge* followed *Read v Anderson*,[299] where it was held that a principal might come under an obligation to indemnify an agent for paying lost bets, and could not revoke the authority to do so, though the bets were themselves void.[300] However, the payment of a lost bet is in the nature of a gift, and while there is no reason why an agent should not be employed to make gratuitous payments (though revocation of authority would normally be a simple matter[301]), whether an agent can validly be employed to act in such a way as to contravene a statute is more doubtful. The purpose of the Gaming Act 1845 s.18, was simply to render void and unenforceable wagering transactions: but that of Leeman's Act was:

3-038

> "to make Provision for the Prevention of Contracts for the Sale and Purchase of Shares and Stock in Joint Stock Banking Companies of which the Sellers are not possessed or over which they have no Control."[302]

The particular problem is now obsolete, not least because of the repeal of Leeman's Act,[303] but it is submitted that much will turn on the nature of the illegality when it is sought to determine whether a principal can assent to an unlawful custom.

Burden of proof   Although the question is one of fact, it seems that the person alleging that there was knowledge of the custom must establish that fact.[304] There

3-039

---

[293] See *Bailey v Rawlins* (1829) 7 L.J.(O.S.) K.B. 208; *Josephs v Pebrer* (1825) 3 B. & C. 639, Illustration 3 to Article 61, where it was held that an agent was not entitled to reimbursement for illegal transactions.
[294] Banking Companies (Shares) Act 1867; repealed by Statute Law Revision Act 1966.
[295] (1885) 15 Q.B.D. 388.
[296] Following *Neilson v James* (1882) 9 Q.B.D. 546. And see *Coates v Pacey* (1892) 8 T.L.R. 351.
[297] At 394, 395 and 397–398.
[298] (1885) 14 Q.B.D. 460.
[299] (1884) 13 Q.B.D. 779.
[300] This result was reversed by the Gaming Act 1892; and the whole problem has been removed by the Gambling Act 2005.
[301] See *Read v Anderson* (1884) 13 Q.B.D. 779 at 783.
[302] Preamble (though this was deleted by the Statute Law Revision Act 1893).
[303] Above.
[304] See *Sweeting v Pearce* (1859) 7 C.B.(N.S.) 449 at 481–482, 484 and 486; affd (1861) 9 C.B.(N.S.) 534.

may, however, be occasions when judicial notice is taken of a custom that is very well known.

Illustrations

3-040
(1) A was authorised to sell manure. The jury found that it was customary to sell manure with a warranty. Held, that A had implied authority to give a warranty on a sale of the manure.[305]

(2) An agent buys tallow for a foreign principal, undertaking, in accordance with custom, personal liability. The principal becomes insolvent without having paid the agent, who is liable for the price. The agent sells the tallow. If this is the customary procedure in such a situation, the agent is not liable for doing so.[306]

(3) A stockbroker, employed to transact business at a particular place, has implied authority to act in accordance with the reasonable usages of that place, and if he incurs liability when his principal defaults and the vendor, in accordance with local custom, resells the shares, he can recover from his principal.[307]

(4) A broker, a member of the Stock Exchange, when authorised to sell certain bonds, had implied authority, if it was discovered that the bonds were not genuine, to rescind the sale and repay the purchaser the price, in accordance with the usage of the Stock Exchange.[308]

(5) A stockbroker, authorised to buy or sell or carry over shares or stock, had implied authority, according to usage, to execute the order by means of several contracts, or to execute any portion or portions of it.[309]

(6) A bill-broker in London was entrusted with bills for discounting. The jury found that it was usual for bill-brokers in London to raise money by depositing their customers' bills en bloc, the brokers alone being looked to by the customers, and that the parties contracted in reference to such usage. Held, that the broker had implied authority to pledge their bills together with bills of his own and those of other customers.[310]

(7) A broker is authorised to buy wool in the Liverpool market. By a custom of that market, a broker so authorised may buy either in his own name or in the name of his principal, without giving the principal notice whether or not he has bought in his own name. Such a custom is not unreasonable, and the principal is bound by a contract made in the name of the broker, though he had no notice of the custom or of the fact that the contract was made by the broker in his own name.[311]

(8) A broker is authorised to buy 50 tons of tallow. It is customary in the tallow trade for a broker to make a single contract in his own name for the purchase of a sufficiently large quantity of tallow to supply the orders of several principals, and to parcel it out amongst them. The broker has no implied authority to purchase a larger quantity than 50 tons and allocate 50 tons of it

---

[305] *Dingle v Hare* (1859) 7 C.B.(N.S.) 145. Most of the following Illustrations are out of date; but they represent useful examples of principle.

[306] *Lienard v Dresslar* (1862) 3 F. & F. 212.

[307] *Pollock v Stables* (1848) 12 Q.B. 765; *Hodgkinson v Kelly* (1868) L.R. 6 Eq. 496.

[308] *Young v Cole* (1837) 3 Bing.N.C. 724.

[309] *Benjamin v Barnett* (1903) 19 T.L.R. 564.

[310] *Foster v Pearson* (1835) 1 C.M. & R. 849.

[311] *Cropper v Cook* (1868) L.R. 3 C.P. 194.

to the principal, unless the principal was aware of the usage at the time when he gave the authority, because the effect of such a usage is to change the intrinsic character of the contract of agency by turning the agent into a principal, and thus giving him an interest at variance with his duty.[312]

(9) A broker is authorised to sell stock. All alleged custom of the Stock Exchange, whereby he is himself permitted to take over the stock at the price of the day, if he is unable to find a purchaser, is unreasonable, and such a transaction is not binding on the principal unless he had notice of the custom.[313]

(10) An insurance broker is authorised to receive from the underwriters payment of money due under a policy. A custom at Lloyd's whereby the broker may settle with the underwriters by way of set-off is unreasonable, and the principal is not bound by such a settlement unless he was aware of the custom when he authorised the broker to receive payment.[314] The same rule has been applied to stockbrokers settling with country brokers, solicitors or other agents.[315]

(11) A shipping broker has not customary authority to conclude a charterparty.[316]

Article 32

Authority Implied from Course of Dealing and Circumstances of Case

An agent has, in addition to the forms of authority indicated in Articles 27 to 31, such authority as is to be inferred from the conduct of the parties and the circumstances of the case.[317] **3-041**

Comment

The types of authority indicated in Articles 27 to 31 do not exhaust the notion of implied authority, for it is clear that over and above authority to do incidental acts, the acts usually performed by a person holding the position in question, the acts usually performed by a person following the agent's particular profession or occupation, and authority to follow usages customary in the place, market or busi- **3-042**

---

[312] *Robinson v Mollett* (1874) L.R. 7 H.L. 802 (but the dissenting opinion of Blackburn J has much force: cf. above, para.1-022). For a case where the principal was held to have accepted a usage of similar effect see *Limako BV v Hentz & Co Inc* [1978] 1 Lloyd's Rep. 400. *Robinson v Mollett* was distinguished in cases concerning the right of stockbrokers to buy quantities of shares in a single contract and allocate quantities to particular clients: e.g. *Scott & Horton v Godfrey* [1901] 2 K.B. 76; *Consolidated Gold Fields of South Africa v E. Spiegel & Co* (1909) 100 L.T. 351. As to "marrying" of buying and selling transactions by a broker, see *Jones v Canavan* [1972] 2 N.S.W.L.R. 236 (custom to do so in Sydney and Brisbane held reasonable).

[313] *Hamilton v Young* (1881) 7 L.R.Ir. 289. See also *Thornley v Tilley* (1925) 36 C.L.R. 1 (custom that broker can deal on his own behalf with shares bought for principal unreasonable).

[314] See Article 28, Illustration 4.

[315] See Article 28, Illustration 3.

[316] *AJU Remicon Co Ltd v Alida Shipping Co Ltd* [2007] EWHC 2246 (Comm) at [11], following *Polish SS Co v A.J. Williams Fuels (Overseas Sales) Ltd, The Suwalki* [1981] 1 Lloyd's Rep. 511. But cf. *Woodstock Shipping Co v Kyma Compania Naviera SA (The "Wave")* [1981] 1 Lloyd's Rep. 521; *BP Oil International Ltd v Target Shipping Ltd* [2012] EWHC 1590 (Comm) at [221].

[317] *Hely-Hutchinson v Brayhead Ltd* [1968] 1 Q.B. 549 at 583; *Freeman & Lockyer v Buckhurst Park Properties (Mangal) Ltd* [1964] 2 Q.B. 480 at 502; *Brick and Pipe Industries Ltd v Occidental Life Nominees Pty Ltd* [1992] 2 V.R. 279 at 362; *Equiticorp Finance Ltd v Bank of New Zealand* (1993) 32 N.S.W.L.R. 50.

ness concerned, an agent may have an authority peculiar to himself implied from the circumstances of the particular case. The question as to implication does not stop at the matters previously mentioned, but goes on to involve consideration of the whole circumstances of the agent's position. This may lead to the agent's having a wider authority initially, or to his authority being enlarged by his principal's acquiescence in his assuming further powers.[318] Thus in *Hely-Hutchinson v Brayhead Ltd*[319] the chairman of a company acted as de facto managing director and chief executive of it, and entered into larger transactions on its behalf which he would sometimes merely report to the board without seeking prior authority or subsequent ratification. The Board acquiesced in this course of dealing. The chairman was held to have had actual authority equivalent to that of a managing director, though he was acting beyond the normal powers of a chairman.

This type of implied authority corresponds to the implied appointment of an agent dealt with in Article 8. It results from the application of the general rules as to interpretation and construction of contracts and agreements. There may of course also be cases where such facts may merely be taken, as a matter of evidence, to point to the fact that express authority was actually conferred.[320] For the relevance of a course of dealing to the concept of apparent authority, see below, para.8-014.

4. PRESUMED AUTHORITY

3-043 **Position of wife** In the 13th edition of this book it was stated that:

> "what is sometimes called presumed authority is not a type of authority at all: the phrase simply refers to the fact that the existence of actual authority may sometimes be presumed subject to rebuttal."[321]

The main case of presumed authority is that arising, usually in a wife, from cohabitation, which was in the first 13 editions of this book treated in a special chapter on the agency of married women. Such a chapter was appropriate because the position of married women for long provided the focus for the intersection of a number of agency rules of different kinds of which a presumed authority arising from cohabitation was only one. Her special position was caused by two factors: her husband's obligation to support her, and her inability until the late nineteenth century to own separate property and thus to be liable on contracts.[322]

The latter inability has been long removed[323]; and the most specialised set of rules involved, those as to the powers of a deserted wife to pledge her husband's credit for necessaries, was abolished by statute in 1970.[324] The law as to the agency of a

---

[318] *Hely-Hutchinson v Brayhead Ltd*, above; *Pole v Leask* (1860) 28 Beav. 560; affd (1864) 33 L.J.Ch. 155.

[319] Above. Perhaps the court in *Freeman & Lockyer v Buckhurst Park Properties (Mangal) Ltd* [1964] 2 Q.B. 480 was too cautious in rejecting on the facts a finding of actual authority by acquiescence.

[320] Mechem, *Outlines of Agency* (4th edn), pp.30–31. See, e.g. *A/S Dan Bunkering Ltd v F.G. Hawkes (Western) Ltd* [2009] EWHC 3141 (Comm) (evidence on discovery that agent had been undertaking similar transactions without objection from principal for some time); *Aviva Life & Pensions UK Ltd v Strand Street Properties Ltd* [2010] EWCA Civ 444.

[321] At p.65.

[322] See the leading case of *Manby v Scott* (1660) 1 Lev. 4; 2 Sm.L.C. 417.

[323] The last main statute on this topic was the Law Reform (Married Women and Tortfeasors) Act 1935.

[324] Matrimonial Proceedings and Property Act 1970 s.41(1). Section 41 of the 1970 Act was repealed by the Matrimonial Causes Act 1973 s.54 and Sch.3, but not so as to revive the doctrine: Interpreta-

deserted wife, a full account of which was given in the 13th edition,[325] is no longer treated here; and consequently the position of a wife in the law of agency no longer requires a separate chapter. On the other hand the rules as to presumed authority in the case of cohabitation had a status of their own which could conceivably still be relevant, and it seemed proper to consider them in the chapter on authority. Therefore, though it is true that the phrase "presumed authority" does not refer so much to a type of authority as to a situation where authority may be presumed, the cases can be isolated as a category.

It is however obvious that social habits have changed since the various times at which these cases were decided, and will continue to do so. In most consumer transactions today, the supplier will look to the person placing the order rather than to another person with whom that person is living; and the use of credit cards makes supply of goods on ordinary retailer's credit less common, though services are not infrequently supplied in this way. Discussion of this curious and intriguing group of cases, many of which concern clothing charged to a husband,[326] is therefore omitted from this edition despite its interest as social history. A full account appears in the 17th edition of 2001. In general, one spouse has no usual authority to bind the other in contract,[327] or to receive notices,[328] although, of course, it is common for one spouse to have actual authority to act for the other, and a person who receives money or other value through the agency of a spouse may be burdened with the latter's knowledge.[329]

Classification of presumed authority This type of authority could be said to be   **3-044**
an example of implied authority: indeed it was sometimes so described in nineteenth-century cases, which contain many attempts to set the doctrines in order in different ways. But the most authoritative statement of the applicable rule suggests that there is or was a rebuttable presumption of fact,[330] viz. that from the mere fact of cohabitation and the absence of contrary indications, the finders of fact may, but need not, draw the inference that authority had actually been granted.[331] This differs from implied authority in four ways. First, the accepted categories of implied authority do not cover this case.[332] Secondly, implied authority affects apparent authority: a third party is normally entitled to assume that a person has such author-

---

tion Act 1889 s.38(2). cf. (1973) 36 M.L.R. at 642. Powers were conferred by the 1970 Act on the court to make orders in cases of divorce, nullity and judicial separation with respect to financial provision for the wife and children of the marriage, and in cases of wilful neglect to maintain: these could be made for the purpose of covering liabilities or expenses reasonably incurred before the making of the application. These powers now derive from Pt II of the Matrimonial Causes Act 1973 (a consolidation) as amended principally by Matrimonial and Family Proceedings Act 1984, and the Family Law Act 1996. The powers are extended by the Welfare Reform and Pensions Act 1999.
[325] Articles 37–41. For a somewhat more recent account see Hardingham (1980) 54 A.L.J. 661 (discussing also Commonwealth authorities).
[326] Three that may be mentioned are *Miss Gray Ltd v Earl Cathcart* (1922) 38 T.L.R. 562; *Seymour v Kingscote* (1922) 38 T.L.R. 586; and *Callot v Nash* (1923) 39 T.L.R. 291 ("the dress of women has been ever the mystery and sometimes the calamity of the ages").
[327] See *Temarama 2004 Ltd (In Liquidation) v McRobie* [2011] NZHC 1456 (husband no actual or apparent authority to bind wife to joint borrowing).
[328] See *Ng Hock Kon v Sambawang Capital Pte Ltd* [2010] 1 S.L.R. 307.
[329] See, e.g. *Barclays Bank Plc v Kalamohan* [2010] EWHC 1383 (Ch) at [82].
[330] *Debenham v Mellon* (1880) 6 App.Cas. 24 (the leading case).
[331] See in general Phipson, *Evidence* (18th edn), para.6-16 onwards.
[332] See Articles 27–32.

ity as would normally be implied.[333] But it is clear that the presumed agency from cohabitation was quite separate from apparent authority.[334] Thirdly, the presumed authority was confined to necessaries. Fourthly, it is possible to say that *implication* of authority is a question of law.[335] But the difference in practice, after such cases ceased to be tried by jury, was likely to be slight.

---

[333] See above, para.3-005.
[334] See *Debenham v Mellon*, above, at 32.
[335] See *Phipson on Evidence* (18th edn), para.6-16 onwards.

CHAPTER 4

AGENCY OF NECESSITY

Article 33

DOCTRINE OF AGENCY OF NECESSITY

(1) A person may have authority to act on behalf of another in certain cases where **4-001** he is faced with an emergency in which the property or interests of that other are in imminent jeopardy and it becomes necessary, in order to preserve the property or interests, so to act.

(2) In some cases this authority may entitle him to affect his principal's legal position by making contracts or disposing of property. In others it may merely entitle him to reimbursement of expenses or indemnity against liabilities incurred in so acting, or to a defence against a claim that what he did was wrongful as against the person for whose benefit he acted.[1]

Comment

Introduction   The term "agency of necessity" is used to indicate a general no-   **4-002** tion derived from a group of cases in which a person is regarded as justified in taking action for the benefit of another in an emergency. They are said to create a special category of agency which arises by operation of law in such situations. In earlier editions these cases were treated in Chapter 2 under the heading of "Creation of Agency". They cannot, however, be classified entirely as creating agency, for although some can be regarded as recognising agency powers in persons who had none before the event concerned, the majority refer to a person who is already an agent, but is by this doctrine given greater powers. This, together with the fact that it is highly doubtful whether any coherent doctrine is to be derived from them for the modern law, makes it appropriate now to place the topic apart in its own chapter.

The cases from which the doctrine stems seem to be analytically of two quite different types, and treating these two groups of cases as components of a single doctrine has caused confusion. The two types of cases have been treated together because it is said that similar specific rules regarding the emergency requisite to trigger off certain legal results apply to both; and that these are rules which create a special form of agency or authority by operation of law. It is suggested below that

---

[1] See Comment. See also Powell, Ch.IX; Treitel (1954) 3 U. Western Australia L.Rev. 1; W.B. Williston (1944) 22 Can. Bar Rev. 492; Wade (1966) 19 Vanderbilt L.Rev. 1183; Birks [1971] *Current Legal Problems* 110; Hunter (1974) 23 U.New Brunswick L.J. 5; Marasinghe (1976) 8 Ottawa L.Rev. 573; McCamus (1979) 11 Ottawa L.Rev. 297; Matthews [1981] C.L.J. 340; Rose (1989) 9 O.J.L.S. 167; Brown (1992) 55 M.L.R. 414; McMeel (2000) 116 L.Q.R. 387 at 408–410; Goff and Jones, *Law of Unjust Enrichment* (8th edn), Ch.18; Burrows, *Law of Restitution* (3rd edn), Ch.18; Virgo, *Principles of the Law of Restitution* (3rd edn, 2015), Ch.11. But the relevance of discussion in books and articles on the law of restitution to pure agency issues is doubtful: see Comment.

the first proposition does not now appear to be true: that the emergency rules do not apply to all the cases. It is also suggested that even if the second proposition was formerly regarded as true, the notion of a special type of authority by operation of law is in this context at the present time no longer necessary or appropriate.

4-003   **The traditional cases: the shipmaster and the acceptor for honour**   The two traditional cases from which the concept of agency of necessity derives are those of the shipmaster, who has wide powers to bind by contract his owner, and also sometimes the cargo owners, in situations of emergency[2]; and the person who accepts a bill of exchange for honour and succeeds to the rights of the holder against the person for whom he accepts.[3] The second case appears to originate from the law merchant[4] and is now statutory[5]: it may in effect confer a right to reimbursement on the acceptor but its relation to agency is tenuous from the start. The dissimilarity between these two cases is enough to indicate immediately that a category comprising them both is unlikely to be a satisfactory one.

4-004   **First category: the shipmaster**   The first category, based on the case of the shipmaster, creates full agency in that it involves both the external and the internal aspects of the agency relationship. As to the external aspect, the master can create contracts binding and conferring rights on his principal (usually the shipowner or demise charterer), make dispositions of his principal's property and receive money and property for his principal also. He has also the internal entitlement to reimbursement and indemnity against his principal in respect of what he has done[6]; even if that is not needed, he has a defence to any action brought against him by his principal in respect of his acts. And the act will be valid where validity is in issue. Thus there is old authority that the master can sell[7] or hypothecate[8] the ship, enter into a salvage agreement regarding it[9] and contract for the cargo to be transhipped and carried forward.[10] He can also sell or hypothecate the cargo, whether together with or separately from the ship,[11] and enter into a salvage agreement regarding it.[12] There are a few cases suggesting that these powers may apply also to land carriers.[13] The actual decisions concerning the latter type of carrier involve only claims to reimbursement and indemnity between principal and agent and so may only be

---

[2]   See below, para.4-004.

[3]   Bills of Exchange Act 1882, ss.65–68; and see *Hawtayne v Bourne* (1841) 7 M. & W. 595 at 599.

[4]   See *Hawtayne v Bourne*, above, at 599.

[5]   See fn.3 above.

[6]   See Article 62.

[7]   *The Glasgow* (1856) Swab. 145; *The Australia* (1859) Swab. 480; *Atlantic Mutual Insurance Co v Huth* (1880) 16 Ch.D. 474.

[8]   *The Gratitudine* (1801) 3 Ch. Rob. 240; *The Bonaparte* (1853) 8 Moo.P.C. 459; *The Hamburg* (1864) 2 Moo.P.C.(N.S.) 289; *The Onward* (1873) L.R. 4 A. & E. 38; *Gunn v Roberts* (1874) L.R. 9 C.P. 331 at 337; *Kleinwort, Cohen & Co. v Cassa Maritima of Genoa* (1877) 2 App.Cas. 156 (cases of bottomry, viz. hypothecating the cargo also).

[9]   *The Renpor* (1883) 8 P.D. 115; *The Unique Mariner* [1978] 1 Lloyd's Rep. 438, Illustration 3, discussed also below.

[10]   See *The Soblomsten* (1866) L.R. 1 A. & E. 293; Scrutton, *Charterparties* (22st edn), Arts 137–139.

[11]   As to sale, see *Tronson v Dent* (1853) 8 Moo.P.C. 419; *Australasian S.N. Co v Morse* (1872) L.R. 4 P.C. 222; *Acatos v Burns* (1878) 3 Ex. D. 282; *Atlantic Mutual Insurance Co v Huth*, above. As to hypothecation, see cases cited in fn.8 above.

[12]   *The Winson* [1982] A.C. 939, Illustration 1. See below, para.4-008.

[13]   *Great Northern Ry Co v Swaffield* (1874) L.R. 9 Ex. 132 (stabling uncollected horse); *Sims & Co v Midland Ry Co* [1913] 1 K.B. 103 (sale of uncollected goods); cf. *Springer v Great Western Ry Co* [1921] 1 K.B. 257.

examples of the second category: they are further referred below in that connection. It is there submitted, however, that they should in fact be attributed to the first category if that category can be enlarged and re-explained on a broader basis than that of agency by operation of law.

In respect of the shipmaster selling, hypothecating or contracting for salvage of the ship, this can be treated as involving no more than the extension of the authority of one who is already an agent in the full sense, for the master obviously has already in many situations actual authority, express or implied, from the shipowner (or demise charterer) to make normal trading contracts. However, where the action taken relates to the *cargo*, the master as such has no legal relationship with the cargo owner; and it can therefore be said that the master is by the emergency created an agent where he was not before, and that this requires special rules. Yet he is still agent for the shipowner, who is bailee of the cargo: and although the shipowner may well have had no agency powers prior to the emergency, his position as bailee means that he has a legal relationship with the cargo owner which is in principle capable of giving rise to such powers, which can be exercised through the master, who is his agent. So the significance of the distinction between ship and cargo is doubtful.

Rules determining necessity The traditional rules applicable to the exercise of this authority may be stated as follows. They derive largely from the shipmaster case, and it will be obvious later that they are in large measure inapplicable to the second category. Indeed in *The Winson*,[14] discussed below, Lord Diplock said that they should be confined to cases of the first category.[15]   **4-005**

(a) It must be impossible, or at any rate impracticable, for the agent to communicate with the principal. Some cases imply that communication must be impossible,[16] but this seems too strict: as long ago as 1851 Parke B spoke of the principal's being unable to be "conveniently communicated with",[17] and in 1895 Lord Esher MR of an "opportunity to consult".[18] In *Springer v Great Western Railway Co* Bankes LJ approved the phrase "practically impossible"[19] and Scrutton LJ spoke of communication as being "commercially impossible".[20] This would include situations where there are too many principals to consult (e.g. owners of cargo shipped under bills of lading on liner terms[21]).

(b) The action taken must be necessary[22] for the benefit of the principal.[23] The agent's opinion as to the necessity is irrelevant. It is, however, sufficient if

---

[14] *China Pacific SA v Food Corp of India (The Winson)* [1982] A.C. 939, Illustration 1, also discussed below.

[15] At 958.

[16] e.g. *Prager v Blatspiel, Stamp & Heacock Ltd* [1924] 1 K.B. 566 at 571.

[17] *Beldon v Campbell* (1851) 6 Exch. 886 at 890. See also *Australasian S.N. Co v Morse* (1872) L.R. 4 P.C. 222.

[18] *Gwilliam v Twist* [1895] 2 Q.B. 84 at 87.

[19] [1921] 1 K.B. 257 at 265.

[20] [1921] 1 K.B. 257 at 268. And see *Barker v Burns, Philp & Co Ltd* (1944) 45 S.R. (N.S.W.) 1 (communication possible despite wartime conditions); *Sachs v Miklos* [1948] 2 K.B. 23.

[21] See *The Choko Star* [1990] 1 Lloyd's Rep. 516, Illustration 2, also discussed below.

[22] For the meaning of "necessary", see *Prager v Blatspiel, Stamp & Heacock Ltd* [1924] 1 K.B. 566 at 571–572; *The Australia* (1859) Swab. 480; *Australasian S.N. Co v Morse* (1872) L.R. 4 P.C. 222; *Atlantic Mutual Ins. Co v Huth* (1879) 16 Ch.D. 474. And see *Phelps, James & Co v Hill* [1891] 1 Q.B. 605.

a reasonable person would think there was a necessity.[24] Mere inconvenience does not create necessity.[25] The necessity must of course be for the protection of the interests of the principal, not of the agent.

(c) The agent must have acted bona fide in the interests of the principal.[26]

(d) The person in whose interest the agent is acting must be competent: for example, a dissolved corporation,[27] or an alien enemy,[28] cannot be a principal under these rules. This limitation is inevitable if the doctrine is one of agency, but its results can be criticised.[29]

(e) It would also seem that in both types of situation the authority could not prevail against express instructions to the contrary: this follows from the fact that it does not operate where the principal can be consulted.[30] The inference is that the principal could forbid the action at the time: if so, he can do so in advance.[31]

4-006 **Second category: the acceptor for honour** The second type of case involves situations where a person who acts for another in an emergency seeks only reimbursement or indemnity from the person benefited, or to defend himself in respect of what he has done in an action for breach of contract (if there is a contract) or in tort (usually conversion, which he might otherwise have committed by his dealing with property of the principal). No issue arises as regards third parties: if this is an example of agency reasoning, it involves only the internal relationship between principal and agent. Although in 1841 Parke B said that the acceptor for honour was, after the shipmaster, the only other example of agency of necessity,[32] it is clear that the second category is not in fact confined to the acceptor for honour. Thus it has been held that a carrier may make a contract for the stabling of an uncollected horse and recover the charges from the consignor[33]; that he is justified in selling perishable goods which remain uncollected and are deteriorating[34]; and that a salvor may warehouse goods on behalf of their owner at the termination of the salvage service and recover the cost of doing so.[35] These cases may in fact be examples of the first category: it may be that these carriers made or could have made

---

[23] See *Burns, Philp & Co Ltd v Gillespie Bros Pty Ltd* (1947) 74 C.L.R. 148 (doctrine inapplicable where measures undertaken (in wartime) for security of ship and cargo considered as one adventure).

[24] *Tetley & Co v British Trade Corp* (1922) 10 Ll. Rep. 678.

[25] *Sachs v Miklos* [1948] 2 K.B. 23.

[26] *Prager v Blatspiel, Stamp & Heacock Ltd*, above, at 570; *Tronson v Dent* (1853) 8 Moo.P.C. 419 at 449–452; *The Winson* [1982] A.C. 959, Illustration 1, discussed also below; *Re F (Mental Patient: Sterilisation)* [1990] 2 A.C. 1 at 75, per Lord Goff of Chieveley.

[27] *Re Banque des Marchands de Moscou* [1952] 1 T.L.R. 739.

[28] *Jebara v Ottoman Bank* [1927] 2 K.B. 254; reversed [1928] A.C. 269.

[29] See Goff and Jones, *Law of Restitution* (7th edn), para.17-006 (not carried forward in subsequent editions).

[30] See Illustrations 1 and 2. See also Goddard [1984] L.M.C.L.Q. 255; but cf. *Great Northern Ry Co v Swaffield* (1874) L.R. 9 Ex. 132.

[31] But in *Graanhandel T. Vink BV v European Grain & Shipping Ltd* [1989] 2 Lloyd's Rep. 531 at 533, Evans J said that there could be circumstances where "it might well be argued that the seller's refusal to acknowledge these facts would not prevent the buyer from alleging that the agency did exist". The deserted wife's agency of necessity, now obsolete, applied even though the husband had forbidden the act: see below, para.4-011.

[32] *Hawtayne v Bourne* (1841) 7 M. & W. 595 at 597.

[33] *Great Northern Ry Co v Swaffield* (1874) L.R. 9 Ex. 132.

[34] *Sims & Co v Midland Ry Co* [1913] 1 K.B. 103; cf. *Springer v Great Western Ry Co* [1921] 1 K.B. 257.

[35] *The Winson* [1982] A.C. 939, Illustration 1: see below.

contracts binding the goods owners to third parties. The actual decisions, however, relate only to the internal relationship between principal and agent. It has also been held that an agent for sale was justified in shipping the goods elsewhere, even contrary to instructions, where they were in danger because of potentially hostile conditions.[36] On the other hand it has been held that a bailee of furniture was liable in conversion when he sold it after fruitless attempts to contact the owner: though in this case it appears that necessity, as opposed to inconvenience, had not arisen.[37] It should be noted that in these cases the supposed agent may have no prior relationship with the principal, as in the leading case of the acceptor for honour: but equally he may already be an agent, and is at any rate likely to have some relationship with the person for whom he acts, such as that of bailee.

Since cases in the second category only give rise to internal rights, duties and defences between the person acting and the person benefited, they are not dissimilar to the *negotiorum gestio* of Roman law, which is a quasi-contractual institution entitling the *gestor*, a person intervening in situations of necessity, to reimbursement and also making him liable for acting inappropriately.[38] As such they seem in the modern law more appropriately dealt with as part of the law of restitution. The second category in fact contains a limited number of rather miscellaneous situations where the law of agency was pressed into service long ago to provide a way of dealing with problems which probably ought nowadays to be approached differently. The cases usually involve an inappropriate use of agency reasoning, as in another context does the use of a notion of irrevocable agency to create what are really property or security interests.[39] The problems of this category should nowadays, therefore, be considered against the background not of agency but of a possible general principle of necessitous intervention within the law of restitution.[40]

Only first category a true example of agency Thus only the first category is a   **4-007**
true example of agency reasoning, and only that category is therefore really relevant for discussion in this book. It is also much less significant than it was, for modern communications will normally make dramatic actions by shipmasters, or indeed others, unnecessary even in remote places: even in maritime salvage situations a master may often be in touch by radio. Situations can obviously still arise, however, where communication is impossible or impracticable; and as regards cargo, where the ship contains goods covered by many bills of lading it may be impracticable to trace and/or communicate with all the cargo owners.[41] Cases may also arise where

[36] *Tetley & Co v British Trade Corp* (1922) 10 Ll. Rep. 678. See too *Liu Wing Ngai v Lui Kok Wai* [1996] 3 Singapore L.R. 508.
[37] *Sachs v Miklos* [1948] 2 K.B. 23; followed in *Anderson v Erlanger* [1980] C.L.Y. 133. See also *Munro v Wilmott* [1949] 1 K.B. 295 (similar facts). In *Ridyard v Roberts* Unreported May 16, 1980, CA a bailee of ponies was held justified in selling them when the owner in breach of contract failed to remove them. In *Coldman v Hill* [1919] 1 K.B. 443 at 456 Scrutton LJ suggested that a bailee of cattle from whom they are stolen ought, if he cannot contact the owner, to "act as agent of necessity on behalf of and at the expense of the owner". Sometimes statute gives a power of sale: e.g. unpaid seller's right to resell: Sale of Goods Act 1979 s.48(3); Protection of Animals Act 1911 s.7; Unsolicited Goods and Services Act 1971 as amended; Torts (Interference with Goods) Act 1977 ss.12 and 13.
[38] See Buckland, *Textbook of Roman Law* (3rd edn), pp.537–538.
[39] See Article 118.
[40] See Goff and Jones, fn.1 above.
[41] See *The Choko Star* [1990] 1 Lloyd's Rep. 516, Illustration 2, also discussed below.

the cargo owner does not answer, or does not answer clearly, requests for instructions.[42]

This type of agency of necessity seems in origin to be a primitive example of what would now be regarded as vicarious liability reasoning. To impose liability on the principal in such cases was more important than to think of any correlative rights for him. A justification given in 1808 was that the master "is seldom of ability to make good a loss of any considerable amount"[43]: hence the owner should be liable. The idea of authority arising in specified circumstances by operation of law is not, however, so satisfactory as the combination of the more general rules of implied and apparent authority, which (particularly the latter) have been developed subsequently to the old cases. For the old rules require that the third party dealing with the agent take the risk as to whether the circumstances creating authority by operation of law have arisen—whether there really is an emergency and whether it really is impracticable for the agent to communicate with his principal. Furthermore, if it is correct, as is suggested above, that there is no possibility of authority if the principal has been communicated with and has forbidden the act in question, this also is not easy to reconcile with the idea of authority by operation of law. Yet as the law at present stands, if the full requirements are not complied with, the agency power does not exist, whatever the appearance to the third party. Such an approach is much less sensitive to the merits of the cases than the normal rules of implied and apparent authority.[44] It is true that under the doctrine of apparent authority the third party cannot rely merely on the statement of the agent that he has authority, so that if the requirements for operation of the doctrine have not arisen but the master says that they have, the third party will not on that ground alone be protected.[45] But if there was an appearance of authority, modern doctrine would make the shipowner liable in some cases where old cases would not—for example, where it appeared that the act was justified; where the act had been forbidden by the principal but this was not known to the third party; and perhaps where the agent gave the impression that the principal could not be consulted.[46]

The old English rules were much more elaborately worked out than the corresponding law in the United States, which has been content with the idea of implied (incidental) authority to act in emergency.[47] There is, however, some other English case law which approaches the question of emergency powers simply on the basis of implied (and hence in appropriate cases apparent) authority, suggesting that the authority of an agent may be enlarged in situations of emergency. This reasoning has been used to justify delegation by an agent of his powers,[48] lending

---

[42] As in *The Winson* [1982] A.C. 939, Illustration 1, also discussed below.
[43] Abbott, *Merchant Ships and Seaman* (3rd edn), cited in Holdsworth, H.E.L. VIII, p.250.
[44] See in general below, para.4-008. The same can in fact be said of the Factors Acts: see Article 89.
[45] *Armagas Ltd v Mundogas SA (The Ocean Frost)* [1986] A.C. 717.
[46] cf. *United Bank of Kuwait Ltd v Hammoud* [1988] 1 W.L.R. 1051, where a solicitor was held liable on an unauthorised and fraudulent transaction by an assistant where the transaction could have been authorised had a certain background of facts existed: the third party was entitled to assume from the conduct of the agent that it did. "The bank, knowing that [X] was a practising solicitor with established firms, were entitled to assume the truth of what he said unless alerted to the fact that the contrary might be the case"—per Lord Donaldson of Lymington MR at 1066. But cf. *Hirst v Etherington* [1999] Lloyd's Rep. P.N. 938 and below, para.8-021.
[47] See *Restatement, Third*, § 2.02, Comments e, f.
[48] *De Bussche v Alt* (1878) 8 Ch.D. 286, Illustration 7 to Article 34. See also *Walker v G.W. Ry Co* (1867) L.R. 2 Ex. 228; *Langan v G.W. Ry Co* (1873) 30 L.T. 173 (railway officials ordering medical attention for passengers: company liable: but here the emergency is not that of the principal, the company).

[164]

on unusual terms[49] and giving credit in circumstances where this would not be normal.[50] It is submitted that this is the correct approach. If it is correct, it entails that the person acting already has a legal relationship with the principal. It is necessary, however, to add to it the proposition, to be derived from *Tappenden v Artus* and *The Winson*, discussed below, that a person already in some other legal relationship with the principal which is not one of agency (such as a bailee) may likewise have agency powers in certain situations, some of which may involve emergencies. If such an approach is followed, the supposedly separate notion of agency of necessity, or at any rate much of it, could, and, it is submitted, should be absorbed into the general law relating to implied and apparent authority.

Salvage contracts: an opportunity for improved analysis   In the case of salvage   **4-008** agreements, where rapid decisions may be required, the advantages of detaching from the ancient, strict rules and subsuming the problem under the general rules of authority can readily be seen. The first step in doing so was taken by Brandon J in *The Unique Mariner*,[51] where in a salvage situation he held owners bound by the master's signature on Lloyd's Open Form on the basis of apparent authority, without reference to the old rules (which probably were not satisfied, because the master had already been in touch with the owners at the time). The case only concerned salvage in respect of the *ship*, for whose owner the master is certainly agent. Subsequently however in *The Choko Star*[52] the Court of Appeal applied the ancient case law to hold that the master's signature to a Lloyd's Open Form did not bind *cargo* unless it had been impracticable to consult cargo (which was not so).

The main reason given was that though he is agent of the *owner*, the master is not an agent for *cargo*, and so cannot act for it except when the special rules of agency of necessity are complied with. There are certainly abundant old dicta to that effect against the background of shipping operations in the nineteenth century. Against this it may be said, as has been suggested above, that the master acts for the shipowner, and the shipowner as bailee may be regarded as having implied and therefore normally also apparent authority to do what is necessary to preserve the cargo during the voyage. This argument was rejected on the basis that there were no grounds for implying such a power (beyond what the agency of necessity doctrine permits) into the contract of carriage between cargo owner and shipowner. The rules regarding the implication of terms into contracts are of course strict[53]: perhaps too much so. But even if those rules are accepted, despite suggestions that "[a]gency of necessity is traditionally regarded as part of the law of contract",[54] it is not clear that questions of authority are always to be determined by reference to implied terms of the contract between the supposed principal and the supposed agent. Particular relationships, such as that of bailor and bailee, may carry their own

---

[49]   *Montaignac v Shitta* (1890) 15 App.Cas. 357, Illustration 15 to Article 72.
[50]   *Gokal Chand-Jagan Nath v Nand Ram Das-Atma Ram* [1939] A.C. 106.
[51]   [1978] 1 Lloyd's Rep. 438, Illustration 3.
[52]   [1990] 1 Lloyd's Rep. 516, Illustration 2; noted [1991] L.M.C.L.Q. 1; (1992) 55 M.L.R. 414; followed in *The Pa Mar* [1999] 1 Lloyd's Rep. 338.
[53]   See *Liverpool City Council v Irwin* [1977] A.C. 239.
[54]   Goff and Jones, *Law of Restitution* (7th edn), para.17-006 (not carried forward in subsequent editions), citing *Notara v Henderson* (1872) L.R. 7 Q.B. 225 and *Cargo ex Argos* (1873) L.R. 5 P.C. 134. It is not clear exactly what this means. If it indicates that it stems from an extension of authority granted by contract, this may be so in most cases, but agency can be gratuitous (as indeed the text goes on to point out).

implications of implied, and hence apparent, authority. Implied *authority* is inferred "from the conduct of the parties and the circumstances of the case",[55] which is quite different reasoning from that relating to implied *terms of contracts*.

In the third of the three principal recent cases on the doctrine, *The Winson*,[56] a salvor procured the warehousing of the goods salved, after completion of the salvage service, and claimed reimbursement of the cost of so doing. This was therefore a case in the second, not the first, category. The full requirements for the operation of traditional agency of necessity were not operative, for the salvor was able to communicate with the cargo owners (who did not give a clear answer) and was in any case acting partly for his own benefit (to preserve his lien). But he was held able to recover, Lord Diplock saying that the strict requirements were inapplicable to the second (*negotiorum gestio*) category.[57] It was said that the salvor was under a duty to the goods owner to care for the goods, and that he had "a correlative right to charge the owner of the goods with the expenses reasonably incurred".[58] But with subsequent development of principle, it may be argued that the strict rules are not needed in the first category either. It can then be argued that the bailment relationship is sufficient to give the bailee authority not only to do things entitling him to reimbursement but also to entitle him to make contracts binding on the principal. On this basis the principal might in an appropriate case have been liable directly to the warehouse proprietor. (Though in this particular situation, if the salvor warehoused to protect his lien, he would be unlikely to do so on behalf of another.) Thus in *Tappenden v Artus*[59] it was held that the bailee of a car could leave it for repair in circumstances creating a lien against the owner. The case is not directly in point, because the decision was based on the bailee's right to use the goods, and hence to keep them in a usable state: but the reasoning is relevant.

The statement by Lord Diplock in *The Winson* that the strict rules should be eliminated from the assessment of cases of the second category is therefore to be welcomed in so far as it provides support for the detachment of the second category from the first. But it does not follow that all the cases where the only questions that have arisen were as to the internal relationship between principal and agent, and in particular the case of the bailee who makes a contract in respect of the goods bailed, are really no more than examples of the second category. Some may in fact be real agency cases, attributable to the first category, and now to be explained on the basis of implied or apparent authority. It has already been suggested that this is true of the land carrier decisions. It is submitted therefore that the old strict rules should no longer have any part to play in cases of the first category any more than in the second; and that the substance of all cases in the first category should be assimilated to the general rules as to implied and apparent authority. On this basis a master may be held to have a general implied authority (under the category of incidental authority) to sign a salvage agreement for ship and (because of the bailment reasoning above) cargo, except perhaps where consultation is practicable and expected; and hence apparent authority even in some circumstances where the implied authority is not applicable (e.g. because the owner has forbidden the contract, or could easily have been consulted). As for the more drastic acts of sell-

[55] *Hely-Hutchinson v Brayhead Ltd* [1968] 1 Q.B. 549 at 583.
[56] [1982] A.C. 939, Illustration 1. See too *Brasileiro SA (Petrobas)* [2012] UKSC 17; [2012] 2 A.C. 164.
[57] At 958.
[58] At 960.
[59] [1964] 2 Q.B. 185.

ing or hypothecating ship or cargo, this would normally require consultation, and it may well be that the third party's belief that the master's act is justified is less likely to appear reasonable under the doctrine of apparent authority.

The present law as to the first category   As regards salvage contracts, the mat-   **4-009**
ter is now settled by statute. Article 6 of the International Convention on Salvage of 1989, now law under the Merchant Shipping Act 1995,[60] gives the master or owner the power to sign a salvage contract for cargo. But although the Court of Appeal in *The Choko Star*[61] had thought this topic an unsuitable one for judicial development, it is submitted that the Supreme Court should, if the opportunity arises, take the opportunity to bring the case law on situations of necessity into line so far as possible with present-day thinking on agency authority, which no longer needs a special and rather rigid notion of agency by operation of law, a notion which antedates the development of the doctrine of apparent authority, and even the full development of that of implied authority, and depends on the existence of facts which may not be known or even knowable to the third party.

Development of the second category: restitutionary doctrine   In this area, the   **4-010**
analogy of agency is a mistaken one, perhaps caused by the lack of the civil law concept of *negotiorum gestio*. If any wider principle in respect of necessitous intervention is to emerge from the cases in the second category, however, creative development of a different order within the principles of restitution would be required. In 1924 McCardie J, in a case of the first category, spoke strongly in favour of enlarging the whole doctrine of agency of necessity, and was prepared in principle to apply it to an agent for purchase who was unable because of wartime conditions to forward goods purchased to his principal in Romania and resold them in England.[62] The dicta were, however, doubted by Scrutton LJ three years later in a case of the second category,[63] and other dicta against extension of the reasoning can be cited.[64] Proper analysis has been hampered by the running together of the two categories. Any attempt at development within the second category has to contend initially with the dictum of Bowen LJ in 1886 that "work or labour done or money expended by one man to preserve or benefit the property of another do not according to English law create any lien upon the property saved, nor even, if standing alone, create any obligation to repay the expenditure".[65] Nevertheless, though they were said by Bowen LJ to be a special exception, the rules of maritime salvage,[66] including the decision in *The Winson*, can be used to justify movement towards generalisation; as can certain cases concerning the payment of funeral

---

[60]   s.224(1) and Sch.11. See this provision applied in *The Altair* [2008] EWHC 612 (Comm); [2008] 2 All E.R. (Comm) 805.
[61]   [1990] 1 Lloyd's Rep. 516, Illustration 2. The judgment of Sheen J at first instance repays study.
[62]   *Prager v Blatspiel, Stamp & Heacock Ltd* [1924] 1 K.B. 566. In this category, extension in cases where the principal has forbidden the act might be easier: cf. *Tetley & Co v British Trade Corp* (1922) 10 Lloyd's Rep. 678; above, para.4-006.
[63]   *Jebara v Ottoman Bank* [1927] 2 K.B. 254 at 270–271; reversed [1928] A.C. 269) (selling goods overseas after outbreak of war).
[64]   *Gwilliam v Twist* [1895] 2 Q.B. 84 at 87, per Lord Esher MR (substitute driver where official driver drunk); *Sachs v Miklos* [1948] 2 K.B. 23 at 35–36, per Lord Goddard CJ.
[65]   *Falcke v Scottish Imperial Insurance Co* (1886) 34 Ch.D. 234 at 248. See Birks, *Introduction to the Law of Restitution* (1989), p.194 onwards.
[66]   See Goff and Jones, *Law of Unjust Enrichment* (9th edn), Ch.18.

expenses of a deceased person[67]; and an established line of cases remunerating liquidators and other insolvency practitioners for work done in preserving and realising property belonging to others but in the possession of the company or other insolvent person.[68] On the other hand it has been held that no lien arises in favour of a person who succours a stray animal,[69] or conveys timber on the bank of a river to a place of safety.[70] Though writers strongly advocate the development of generalised principle, the picture remains unclear and the case law very limited indeed.[71] Other doctrines may sometimes secure a similar result by different means. Thus where there is an established cause of action, the damages awarded may cover expenses incurred in emergencies[72]; and a person who seeks to recover property may sometimes be able to do so only if he pays for work done on it.[73] But the appropriate reasoning for cases of necessitous intervention in general must be found outside the law of agency, and further discussion is beyond the scope of this work.[74]

4-011   **Agency of deserted wives**   Until comparatively recently a line of cases whereby a deserted wife was regarded as having, even if forbidden to do so, authority to pledge her husband's credit for necessaries was said to be a further instance of agency of necessity, and of agency by operation of law. These cases made any general principle behind the notion even more difficult to extract, for the necessity in such cases was that of the agent and not of the principal. This seems another example of agency law being deployed to achieve a desired result which did not at the time seem attainable by other means. This method of protecting deserted wives has, however, been superseded by other institutions for that purpose, and the doctrine inherent in the cases has in consequence been abolished in England by

---

[67] *Jenkins v Tucker* (1788) 1 H.Bl. 90; *Tugwell v Heyman* (1812) 3 Camp. 298; *Rogers v Price* (1829) 3 Y. & J. 28; *Ambrose v Kerrison* (1851) 10 C.B. 776; *Shallcross v Wright* (1850) 12 Beav. 558; *Bradshaw v Beard* (1862) 12 C.B.(N.S.) 344; *Rees v Hughes* [1946] K.B. 517; *Croskery v Gee* [1957] N.Z.L.R. 586. See also *Matheson v Smiley* [1932] 2 D.L.R. 787 (medical expenses).

[68] See *Re Berkeley Applegate (Investment Consultants) Ltd* [1989] Ch. 32; *Green v Bramston* [2010] EWHC 3106 (Ch). See too *MF (Australia) Ltd v Meadow Springs Fairway Resort Ltd* [2009] FCAFC 9.

[69] *Binstead v Buck* (1776) 2 Wm. Bl. 1117. But there may in appropriate cases be distress damage feasant. See *Sorrell v Paget* [1950] 1 K.B. 252, where both matters are discussed. See also Protection of Animals Act 1911 s.7.

[70] *Nicholson v Chapman* (1793) 2 H.Bl. 254. See also *J. Gadsden Pty Ltd v Strider 1 Ltd (The AES Express)* (1990) 20 N.S.W.L.R. 57 (carriage of goods after termination of time charter).

[71] For example, as to the relevance of the fault of the person concerned in getting into the situation of emergency, it has been held that a car recovery company instructed by the police to remove an abandoned stolen car did not act as agent of necessity for the owner: *Surrey Breakdown Ltd v Knight* [1999] R.T.R. 84, CA; and see *Lambert v Fry* [2000] C.L.Y. 113. The *Surrey Breakdown* case is doubtful authority, as it appears to proceed on the basis that the company was agent for the owner (with whom it had no prior connection), and was claiming reimbursement of expenses under the second category of agency of necessity. The argument had been however that the *police* were agent for the owner to make a contract with the company, which sued for its normal charges: i.e. a first category situation. In this category the police, having no prior relationship with the owner, have by private law at least no authority to make such a contract for another. See Kortmann, *Altruism in Private Law* (2005), pp.167–169.

[72] *Schneider v Eisovitch* [1960] 2 Q.B. 430 (tort); *Kolfor Plant Ltd v Tilbury Plant Ltd* (1977) 121 S.J. 390 (sale of rejected goods).

[73] *Munro v Wilmott* [1949] 1 K.B. 295; *Greenwood v Bennett* [1973] 1 Q.B. 195.

[74] See Goff and Jones, *Law of Restitution* (7th edn, not carried forward in subsequent editions), para.17-009 onwards (which, since it approaches the law from a different angle, should be taken into account by any reader of this chapter); Birks, *Introduction to the Law of Restitution* (1989), p.193 onwards.

statute.[75] Discussion of these cases is therefore omitted: a full account appeared in the thirteenth edition of this work.

Mentally incapacitated persons   The Mental Capacity Act 2005 creates what **4-012** may be called a statutory form of agency of necessity. It permits a person intervening on behalf of a mentally incapacitated person to pledge that person's credit and use that person's money for acts in connection with his or her care or treatment: the person intervening may also be entitled to indemnity for expenditure incurred.[76] This does not affect any power or any other power which a person may have who has lawful control of the mentally incapacitated person's property or power to spend money for his or her benefit.[77]

Illustrations

(1)   A salvor, after the completion of the salvage operation, warehouses salved **4-013** goods at a nearby port, principally to preserve them but partly with a view to preserving his lien. He asks the cargo owner to make arrangements to accept the goods at that port. The cargo owner does not respond. The salvor was bailee of the cargo owner from the time the goods were put into the vessels which he provided, and even if the salvage service was finished when the vessels arrived at the port, he remained bailee of the cargo owner thereafter. As such he had a duty to the cargo owner to take reasonable measures to preserve the cargo, and a correlative right to charge its owner with the warehousing expenses, which had been reasonably incurred in fulfilling that duty.[78]

(2)   A ship strands in the River Paraná in Argentina. The master signs a salvage agreement on Lloyd's Open Form with Greek salvors, though local salvors are available. There is only one cargo owner, who could have been consulted but was not. The master has no authority to sign for cargo (as opposed to the ship itself) except under the agency of necessity rules, which are not satisfied because of the lack of consultation, quite apart from the question whether the act of the master was reasonable or the third party was aware of the lack of consultation.[79]

(3)   A ship strands. The master contacts his owners, who notify him that a tug will be sent. By chance the captain of another tug with different owners is completing a salvage service nearby. He notices the stranded ship, goes to it and offers his services. The master takes this to be the tug sent by his owners and signs a salvage agreement. As his owners are already sending another tug, he is not authorised to do so, and the agency of necessity rules do not apply: but his owners are nevertheless liable under the doctrine of apparent authority.[80]

---

[75]   See above, para.3-041.

[76]   See Mental Capacity Act 2005 ss.5, 6 and 8. The Act also provides for the appointment of a "deputy" who may have more extensive powers.

[77]   As under a lasting power of attorney, created by the 2005 Act.

[78]   *China Pacific SA v Food Corp of India (The Winson)* [1982] A.C. 939. Quaere, however, whether the salvage service was really terminated: if it had not been, the case would have been more easily solved.

[79]   *Industrie Chimiche Italia v Alexander G. Tsavliris & Sons Maritime Co (The Choko Star)* [1990] 1 Lloyd's Rep. 516. But see Comment above.

[80]   *The Unique Mariner* [1978] 1 Lloyd's Rep. 438.

CHAPTER 5

SUB-AGENCY

Article 34

WHEN AGENT MAY DELEGATE AUTHORITY

(1) An agent may not delegate his authority in whole or in part except with the **5-001** express or implied authority of the principal, or the delegation may be ratified by the principal.[1]
(2) The authority of the principal is implied in the following cases:
  (a) Where the principal knows and accepts, at the time of the agent's appointment, that the agent intends to delegate his authority.[2]
  (b) Where the authority conferred is of such a nature as to necessitate its execution wholly or in part by means of a sub-agent.[3]
  (c) Where the employment of a sub-agent is justified by the usage of the particular trade or business in which the agent is employed, provided that such usage is not unreasonable, and not inconsistent with the express terms of the agent's authority.[4]
  (d) Where in the course of the agent's employment unforeseen circumstances arise which render it necessary for the agent to employ a sub-agent.[5]
  (e) Where, from the conduct of the principal or of the principal and the agent, it may reasonably be presumed to have been intended that the agent should have power to employ a sub-agent.[6]
(3) The above principles are inapplicable where the act done or to be done is purely ministerial and does not involve confidence or discretion.[7]

---

[1] *De Bussche v Alt* (1878) 8 Ch.D. 286 at 310–311 (Illustration 5). It seems that the converse position is taken by French CC, art.1994. As to apparent authority see Comment; as to ratification, see Articles 13–20. See in general *Restatement, Third*, § 3.15, especially Comment *c*.
[2] *Quebec & Richmond Railway Co v Quinn* (1858) 12 Moo.P.C. 232 at 265 (English contractor employed to construct railroad in Canada); *Jacques Lichtenstein v Clube Atletico Mineiro* [2005] EWHC 1300 (QB) (football agent sues "football consultant"). Jack J said that such a commercial agreement of a general nature can be performed through the actions of another; *Norwich Union Life & Pensions Ltd v Strand Street Properties Ltd* [2009] EWHC 1109 (Ch) at [223].
[3] *Quebec & Richmond Railroad Co v Quinn*, above.
[4] *De Bussche v Alt*, above. See also Article 31.
[5] *De Bussche v Alt*, above; cf. *Gwilliam v Twist* [1895] 2 Q.B. 84; *Harris v Fiat Motors Ltd* (1906) 22 T.L.R. 556; reversed on other grounds (1907) 23 T.L.R. 504). See also Ch.4.
[6] *De Bussche v Alt*, above. See also *Re Deutsch* (1976) 82 D.L.R. (3d) 567 (consul as administrator of estate had power to delegate); *Dollars & Sense Finance Ltd v Nathan* [2008] 2 N.Z.L.R. 557 at [28].
[7] See Illustration 5; *Rossiter v Trafalgar Life Ass. Assn* (1859) 27 Beav. 377 (insurance proposal); *Hemming v Hale* (1859) 7 C.B. (N.S.) 487 (attorney's clerk); *Allam & Co Ltd v Europa Poster Services Ltd* [1968] 1 W.L.R. 638 (solicitor acting for agent gave notice to terminate licence agreement); *The Berkshire* [1974] 1 Lloyd's Rep. 185 at 188; *Lep International Pty Ltd v Atlanttrafic Express Service Inc* (1987) 10 N.S.W.L.R. 614 (signature of bill of lading); *Parkin v Williams* [1986]

Comment

5-002   **General rule of no delegation**   The general rule is that an agent may not delegate the discretions to act for another which are reposed in him: *delegatus non potest delegare*. This maxim is founded on the confidential nature of the contract of agency: whenever authority is coupled with a discretion or confidence it must, as a rule, be exercised by the agent in person[8]:

> "The reason is fairly obvious: the risks of agency are substantial, and a person has a right not to be represented, save at his own election and by an agent of his own choice."[9]

Thus auctioneers,[10] factors,[11] directors,[12] liquidators,[13] brokers,[14] estate agents,[15] solicitors,[16] etc., have normally no implied authority to employ deputies or subagents to exercise their agency powers.[17] But this is no more than a general starting-point and its significance should not be overstated.[18] Plainly, where a principal appoints a company as agent, it must be envisaged that at least the company's directors, and probably its employees, will carry out the tasks requested. Appointment of other large employers as agent will often also carry an implication that employee sub-agents may be used.

5-003   **Ministerial acts**   On the other hand an agent may delegate the performance of purely ministerial or ancillary acts, unless there are statutory or other provisions to the contrary or evidence of usage not permitting this[19]; and in general other, non-fiduciary functions of persons who have agency powers may be performed vicariously in accordance with normal contractual principles. This is not delegation.

5-004   **Effect of unauthorised delegation**   Where the agent is not authorised to delegate and does so, acts performed by a purported sub-agent will not be valid, where validity is in question, nor bind or entitle the principal[20]; payment to such sub-agent will not rank as payment to the principal[21]; the principal is not, of course, liable to the sub-agent for commission[22]; the sub-agent has no lien against the principal[23]; and

---

1   N.Z.L.R. 294, Illustration 4 (Statute of Frauds); *Amoutzas v Tattersalls Ltd* [2010] EWHC 1696 (QB) at [128].
8   *De Bussche v Alt* (1878) 8 Ch.D. 286.
9   Mechem, *Outlines of Agency* (4th edn), p.50.
10   *Coles v Trecothick* (1804) 9 Ves.Jun. 234.
11   *Solly v Rathbone* (1814) 2 M. & S. 298.
12   *Saad v Doumeny Holdings Pty Ltd* [2005] NSWSC 893 at [17] (holder of power of attorney could not act as director); *Re Ledir Enterprises Pty Ltd* [2013] NSWSC 1332; (2013) 96 A.C.S.R. 1.
13   Illustration 5.
14   *Cockran v Irlam* (1813) 2 M. & S. 301; *Henderson v Barnewall* (1827) 1 Y. & J. 387.
15   *John McCann & Co v Pow* [1974] 1 W.L.R. 1643. See also *Benjamin v Clothier* (1969) 210 E.G. 29; *Maloney v Hardy and Moorsehead* (1970) 216 E.G. 1582.
16   *Re Becket, Purnell v Paine* [1918] 2 Ch. 72. But see Illustration 6 as to London agents.
17   Delegation by trustees is a specialised topic. See Trustee Delegation Act 1999; Trustee Act 2000 ss.11–23.
18   See fn.2 above.
19   See Illustrations 4 and 5, and other authorities cited in fn.7 above.
20   Illustrations 3 and 5.
21   *Dunlop & Sons v De Murrieta & Co* (1886) 3 T.L.R. 166 (shipping agent acting for shipbrokers); *Maloney v Hardy and Moorsehead* (1970) 216 E.G. 1582; *John McCann & Co v Pow* [1974] 1 W.L.R. 1643.
22   *Schmaling v Tomlinson* (1815) 6 Taunt. 147; *Mason v Clifton* (1863) 3 F. & F. 899.

the agent may be liable in respect of money received by such a person[24] and in general for wrongful execution of his authority.[25] But an agent may be expressly authorised to delegate; he may have implied authority to do so in the situations specified in this Article; or his act in doing so may be ratified.[26]

Apparent authority   The principle here stated is one of actual authority, but the   **5-005** rules of apparent authority may also apply where third parties are involved, and to these the Article is also relevant. There may be a specific representation or conduct by the principal from which the third party will be entitled to assume that the agent had the authority to delegate where such authority to do so would normally be implied. In such a case he will be entitled to make that assumption even though the authority to delegate had actually been negatived between principal and agent, provided that he did not know of this.[27]

Administrative law   The same maxim *delegatus non potest delegare* is often   **5-006** invoked in administrative law to declare invalid the exercise of powers by persons other than those to whom they have been entrusted. Some cases purport to distinguish between delegation and appointment of an agent, on the basis that the second is permitted but the first is not; other cases treat the two notions as the same. It is doubtful whether private law agency terminology assists in clarifying or solving these problems of public law, which is itself moving towards considering such issues under the heading of "legitimate expectation". An account of the topic is beyond the scope of this work and should be sought in specialised books.[28] One point may however be noted: that a Government Minister may normally act through departmental officials without infringing the maxim.[29]

Illustrations

(1)   A shipmaster was authorised to sell certain goods. He was held to have no   **5-007** implied authority to send them on to another person for sale when he could not himself find a purchaser, and hence was liable in respect of them.[30]

(2)   A notice to quit given by the agent of an agent is not sufficient without further evidence of authority or ratification.[31]

(3)   An agent buys property at a sale by auction, and the auctioneer enters his name as buyer without objection by the principal, who is present at the sale. The entry is sufficient memorandum of the contract as against the principal.[32] But entry by the auctioneer's clerk would not suffice unless there was other

---

[23]   *Solly v Rathbone* (1814) 2 M. & S. 298; see Article 70.

[24]   *Mackersy v Ramsay, Bonars & Co* (1843) 9 C. & F. 818; *Re Mutual Aid Permanent Benefit B.S.* (1883) 49 L.T. 530; *National Employers Mutual General Insurance Assn Ltd v Elphinstone* [1929] W.N. 135; *Balsamo v Medici* [1984] 1 W.L.R. 951; *Trading and General Investment Corp v Gault, Armstrong & Kemble Ltd (The Okeanis)* [1986] 1 Lloyd's Rep. 195.

[25]   e.g. Illustration 1.

[26]   e.g. *Keay v Fenwick* (1876) 1 C.P.D. 745. See Articles 13–20.

[27]   See Article 72.

[28]   e.g. Wade and Forsyth, *Administrative Law* (11th edn), p.281 onwards; Craig, *Administrative Law* (8th edn), Ch.22.

[29]   *Carltona Ltd v Commissioner of Works* [1943] 2 All E.R. 560 at 563.

[30]   *Catlin v Bell* (1815) 4 Camp. 183.

[31]   *Doe d. Rhodes v Robinson* (1837) 3 Bing.N.C. 677. But cf. *Allam & Co v Europa Poster Services Ltd* [1968] 1 W.L.R. 638 (notice given by solicitor of company).

[32]   *White v Proctor* (1811) 4 Taunt. 209; *Emmerson v Heelis* (1809) 2 Taunt. 38.

evidence of authority.[33] And where a tenant for life had power to lease, and a memorandum of the contract for a lease was signed by his agent's clerk with the approval of the agent and in the ordinary course of business it was held that the memorandum was not sufficient to satisfy the Statute of Frauds, not having been proved to have been signed by a duly authorised agent within the meaning of that statute.[34]

(4) Attorneys under a power of attorney may delegate the signature of an agreement for sale to the auctioneer.[35]

(5) An agent has authority to draw bills of exchange in the principal's name. Signature by the agent's clerk is sufficient if it is in accordance with the usual practice.[36] So, an authority given to an agent to indorse a particular bill in the principal's name may be delegated, because such acts are purely ministerial and involve no discretion. Where four liquidators had no power to authorise one of their number to accept bills of exchange on behalf of them all, it was held that they might authorise him to accept a particular bill on their behalf, because the execution of the former authority would involve discretion, whereas the latter was an authority to do a purely ministerial act.[37]

(6) A country solicitor has implied authority to act through his London agent when necessary or usual in the ordinary course of business: thus the issue of proceedings by his London agent acting as such is valid.[38] Where a London agent has the general conduct of an action, he has the same general authority in conducting it, including authority to compromise, as the country solicitor employing him, in the absence of any express limits on such general authority.[39] But a solicitor cannot delegate his entire employment to his London agent so as to make the agent his client's solicitor: a retainer to a country solicitor does not justify an action in which the London agents are the solicitors on the record.[40]

(7) A shipowner employed merchants carrying on business at Hong Kong, Shanghai and Yokohama to sell a ship at any port where the ship might happen to be from time to time in the course of employment under charter. The merchants had authority to appoint a sub-agent with branches at Nagasaki and other Japanese ports.[41]

---

[33] *Bell v Balls* [1897] 1 Ch. 663; *Bird v Boulter* (1833) 4 B. & Ad. 443.

[34] *Blore v Sutton* (1817) 3 Mer. 237. These questions would not now arise in the same form because of the different requirements of the Law of Property (Miscellaneous Provisions) Act 1989 s.2. The cases are retained as illustrations of principle.

[35] *Parkin v Williams* [1986] 1 N.Z.L.R. 294.

[36] *Re Marshall Ex p. Sutton* (1788) 2 Cox 84. See also *Lord v Hall* (1848) 2 C. & K. 698; *Brown v Tombs* [1891] 1 Q.B. 253.

[37] *Re London and Mediterranean Bank Ex p. Birmingham Banking Co* (1868) L.R. 3 Ch.App. 651 at 653–654.

[38] *Solley v Wood* (1852) 16 Beav. 370. See Article 35, Illustrations 3 and 4.

[39] *Re Newen, Carruthers v Newen* [1903] 1 Ch. 812.

[40] *Wray v Kemp* (1884) 26 Ch.D. 169; *Re Scholes & Sons* (1886) 32 Ch.D. 245; see also *Re Beckett, Purnell v Paine* [1918] 2 Ch. 72. These cases also are largely out of date but are retained as good examples of principle.

[41] *De Bussche v Alt* (1878) 8 Ch.D. 286. But see further discussion of this case below.

Article 35

Relation Between Principal and Sub-agent

(1) Acts done on the principal's behalf by a sub-agent whose appointment was authorised or ratified by the principal bind the principal as if they had been performed by the agent himself.[42]

(2) The relation of principal and agent may be established by an agent between his principal and a sub-agent if the agent is expressly or impliedly authorised to constitute such relation, or if his act is ratified, and it is the intention of the agent and of such sub-agent that such relation should be constituted.[43]

(3) But there is no privity of contract between a principal and a sub-agent as such merely because the delegation was effected with the authority of the principal; and in the absence of such privity the rights and duties arising out of any contracts between the principal and the agent, and between the agent and the sub-agent, respectively, are only enforceable by and against the immediate parties to those contracts.[44] However, the sub-agent in the latter case may in some circumstances be liable to the principal as a fiduciary, in tort, and possibly to account generally.[45] A sub-agent may also implicate himself in a breach of duty by the agent, and be liable for dishonest assistance in a breach of the former's duty.[46]

5-008

Comment

Rule (1) The acts of an authorised sub-agent bind the principal. This is not because the sub-agent is the principal's agent:

5-009

> "it is rather that he is bound by the act of his own agent, who, in this instance, is (properly) doing the act through the sub-agent."[47]

Thus he may receive notification or be held to have acquired knowledge through a sub-agent[48]; signature by a sub-agent may bind him[49]; issue of process by a sub-

---

[42] See Comment. As to apparent authority, see below, para.5-015.

[43] *De Bussche v Alt* (1878) 8 Ch.D. 286, Illustration 5. Alternatively, it may be found that, properly construed, there was no intermediate agency but a direct agency made through one of the principal's agents: *Homecare Direct Shopping Pty Ltd v Gray* [2008] VSCA 111.

[44] *New Zealand & Australian Land Co v Watson* (1881) 7 Q.B.D. 374, Illustration 1; *Calico Printers Assn. Ltd v Barclays Bank Ltd* (1931) 145 L.T. 51; *Schwensen v Ellinger, Heath, Western & Co* (1949) 83 Ll. L.Rep. at 81; *Kahler v Midland Bank Ltd* [1950] A.C. 24; *Grosvenor Casinos Ltd v National Bank of Abu Dhabi* [2008] EWHC 511 (Comm); [2008] 2 Lloyd's Rep. 1; [2008] 2 All E.R. (Comm) 112 at [157]; noted by Bennett (2008) 124 L.Q.R. 532. This statement was approved in *Henderson v Merrett Syndicates Ltd* [1995] 2 A.C. 145 at 202.

[45] *Powell & Thomas v Evan Jones & Co* [1905] 1 K.B. 11; *Henderson v Merrett Syndicates Ltd*, above; *Markel International Insurance Co Ltd v Surety Guarantee Consultants Ltd* [2008] EWHC 1135 (Comm) at [225], Illustration 11; affd [2009] EWCA Civ 790. See Comment.

[46] *Markel International Insurance Co Ltd v Surety Guarantee Consultants Ltd* [2008] EWHC 1135 (Comm) at [237]; *Indutech Canada Ltd v Gibbs Pipe Sales Ltd* [2011] 8 W.W.R. 60 at [411]; *Fiona Trust & Holding Corporation v Privalov* [2010] EWHC 3199 (Comm) at [66]. See further below, para.9-135.

[47] Mechem, *Outlines of Agency* (4th edn), p.51.

[48] See Article 95, Illustration 16; cf. Article 95, Illustration 10. The position is otherwise, it seems, where the sub-agency was unauthorised, at least where the principal cannot be said to be approbating and reprobating the actions of the sub-agent: *O'Keefe v London and Edinburgh Insurance Co*

agent may be valid[50]; he may be bound by a contract made by a sub-agent[51]; and payment to a sub-agent may rank as payment to the principal.[52] These propositions are obvious where the sub-agent is in privity of contract with the principal, but it is clear that the same results obtain where he is not; for example, an insurance policy obtained through a sub-agent, giving the insured rights against the insurer.[53]

The consequences of authorised sub-delegation between principal and subagent depend on the way in which this was effected. There are two possibilities.

5-010   Rule (2): Privity of contract   The agent may appoint another agent for the principal, whether in substitution for,[54] or in addition to,[55] himself. Complete handing-over of functions is obviously unlikely to be authorised, except as regards particular geographical locations,[56] a specific time or in abnormal circumstances.[57] This may create privity of contract between the principal and the new agent, and the full consequences of agency ensue. Since this all may occur where the new agent is to perform different functions from those performed by the appointing agent (e.g. where a manager hires staff), and where the appointing agent has no agency relationship with the person appointed, there will be many cases where the terms "sub-agency" and "delegate" will be inappropriate, and it has been suggested that such a person should not be called a sub-agent at all.[58] He is in fact a co-agent. But usage in the cases is indiscriminate.

There may be express authority to delegate by this means, or there may be ratification.[59] But it seems that such authority will not readily be implied.[60] Indeed, it has been said that the influence of the leading authority where direct privity was found, *De Bussche v Alt*,[61] "seems to have waned".[62] However, where it does exist, the duty of the appointing agent to his principal is normally no more than to exercise due care in making the appointment,[63] and he does not, without further

---

Ltd [1927] N.I. 85; *Perpetual Trustee Co Ltd v Burniston (No.2)* [2012] WASC 383 at [241].

[49]   See Article 34, Illustrations 3 and 5.
[50]   See Article 34, Illustration 6.
[51]   Illustration 5.
[52]   *Hemming v Hale* (1859) 7 C.B.(N.S.) 487; *Maloney v Hardy and Moorsehead* (1970) 216 E.G. 1582 at 1586; but cf. p.1583.
[53]   *Chua Yew Phong v A.S.Yeo* [1966] 2 M.L.J. 257.
[54]   e.g. *Schwensen v Ellinger, Heath, Western & Co* (1949) 83 Ll. L.Rep. 79 (wartime conditions): but in this case it seems that the principal himself appointed the new agent.
[55]   See Illustration 5; *Ecossaise SS Co Ltd v Lloyd, Low & Co* (1890) 7 T.L.R. 76.
[56]   e.g. *De Bussche v Alt* (1878) 8 Ch.D. 286, Illustration 5.
[57]   e.g. *Schwensen v Ellinger, Heath, Western & Co*, above.
[58]   *Restatement, Second*, Appendix, reporter's note to § 5.
[59]   e.g. *Keay v Fenwick* (1876) 1 C.P.D. 745.
[60]   See *Calico Printers Assn Ltd v Barclays Bank Ltd* (1931) 145 L.T. 51. But cf. *De Bussche v Alt* (1878) 8 Ch.D. 286, Illustration 5; *Keay v Fenwick*, above; *Ecossaise SS Co Ltd v Lloyd, Low & Co*, above. Country solicitors did not normally have the power to create such privity between their clients and their London agents: see Article 34, Illustration 6. But compare the position of solicitors or stockbrokers employing stockbrokers; *Blackburn v Mason* (1893) 68 L.T. 510. See Article 28, Illustration 3.
[61]   (1878) 8 Ch.D. 286, Illustration 5.
[62]   *Prentis Donegan & Partners Ltd v Leeds & Leeds Co Inc* [1998] 2 Lloyd's Rep. 326 at 331, per Rix J (Illustration 9).
[63]   See *Thomas Cheshire & Co v Vaughan Bros & Co* [1920] 3 K.B. 240 at 259; *Ecossaise SS Co Ltd v Lloyd Low & Co* (1890) 7 T.L.R. 76; *Fry v Tapson* (1884) 28 Ch.D. 268; *Re Weall* (1889) 42 Ch.D. 674.

circumstances (e.g. if he is a *del credere* agent or undertakes a duty of supervision), undertake that the appointed agent will perform the work adequately.[64]

Rule (3): No privity of contract The agent may equally appoint his own agent **5-011**
to do the requisite work; again, authority may be express or implied or there may
be ratification. The prima facie rule seems to be that a delegation has been effected by this means[65]: this is not surprising as it retains the responsibility of the
person in whom trust is reposed by the principal. Thus, for the default of such a sub-agent the agent is normally responsible[66]; and if such person receives money for the
principal, that is sufficient to charge the agent with its receipt.[67]

The full position of such a person, who may genuinely be called a sub-agent, is
not, however, fully worked out in English law. The tacit assumption in cases seems
to be that if the sub-agent is not appointed to be in privity with the principal, he is
only in privity with the agent and owes common law and equitable duties only to
the agent.

It is arguable, however, that the very fact that such a sub-agent binds the principal
when acting in connection with the principal's affairs shows that he is at least in
some respects to be regarded as an agent of the principal, and that there will be
circumstances when he should be also directly liable to the principal. In a sense, this
is a contract for the benefit of a third party, and in the United States[68] reasoning
along such lines made it possible for Seavey to write in 1955 that a:

"sub-agent is liable to the principal for negligence in performing or failing to perform duties undertaken for the principal. He is also under a duty to account for anything received
for the principal, and is liable as a fiduciary for any breach of a fiduciary duty."[69]

Under this approach the principal may also be liable to indemnify the subagent.[70]
These propositions do not rest on contract: indeed the sub-agent is not liable to the
principal for breach of contract, for he normally has no contract with him, nor is
the principal liable to the sub-agent for remuneration.[71]

The position in England, where the authorities are, as always, more limited, cannot be stated so clearly because of the existence of old case law which has not been

[64] *Sampson v Wilson* [1996] Ch. 39; *Aiken v Stewart Wrightson Members Agency Ltd* [1995] 1 W.L.R.
1281. There are also cases on the liability of directors for acts of co-directors. And see Article 115.
[65] *Calico Printers Assn Ltd v Barclays Bank Ltd* (1931) 145 L.T. 51; *Royal Products Ltd v Midland
Bank Ltd* [1981] 2 Lloyd's Rep. 194; *Prentis Donegan & Partners Ltd v Leeds & Leeds Co Inc*
[1998] 2 Lloyd's Rep. 326. See also *Trengrouse & Co v Official Assignee of Steeds* (1896) 14
N.Z.L.R. 636.
[66] *Re Mitchell* (1884) L.J.Ch. 342; *Meyerstein v Eastern Agency Co Ltd* (1885) 1 T.L.R. 595; *Ecossaise
SS Co Ltd v Lloyd, Low & Co* (1890) 7 T.L.R. 76; *Stewart v Reavell's Garage* [1952] 2 Q.B. 545;
Swire v Francis (1877) 3 App.Cas. 106. But cf. *Thomas Cheshire & Co v Vaughan Bros & Co*, above.
This would apply even where the delegation was unauthorised.
[67] *Matthews v Haydon* (1786) 2 Esp. 509; *Mackersy v Ramsays, Bonars & Co* (1843) 9 C. & F. 818;
Skinner & Co v Weguelin, Eddowes & Co (1882) C. & E. 12; *National Employers' Mutual General
Insurance Assn Ltd v Elphinstone* [1929] W.N. 135; *Trading and General Investment Corp v Gault,
Armstrong & Kemble Ltd (The Okeanis)* [1986] 1 Lloyd's Rep. 195. This would apply even where
the delegation was unauthorised: see above, para.5-004.
[68] Seavey (1955) 68 HarvL.Rev. 658 at 666–667; also printed as *Restatement, Second*, Appendix,
reporter's note to § 5 (a valuable article). The provision in *Restatement, Third*, is more general: see
§ 3.15, especially Comment *d*.
[69] (1955) 68 HarvL.Rev. at 666–667.
[70] (1955) 68 HarvL.Rev. at 669.
[71] (1955) 68 HarvL.Rev. at 667.

reconsidered.[72] There can however be said to be some movement in the same direction. Although it was held in 1931 that the sub-agent could not be liable to the principal in tort for negligently performing the work,[73] this is not an absolute rule. Where it can be shown that the sub-agent has assumed a legal responsibility to the principal (usually in addition to the contractual duties owed the agent) a duty in tort may arise, as was affirmed in 1995 in *Henderson v Merrett Syndicates Ltd*.[74] The facts of the case indicated quite close relations between principal and sub-agent which will not be found in all other situations of sub-agency: it was stressed that the persons concerned:

> "hold themselves out as possessing a special expertise ... the Names ... placed implicit reliance on that expertise."[75]

It was said that in other cases an action in tort might be:

> "short circuiting the contractual structure ... put in place by the parties. It cannot therefore be inferred from the present case that other sub-agents will be held directly liable to the agent's principal in tort."[76]

As mentioned earlier, it may also be possible in some cases to regard the contract between agent and sub-agent as one for the benefit of a third party, the principal. Where it is possible to say that a term in the contract purports to confer a benefit on the principal and envisages the principal's being able to enforce that term, the principal might have a right of action under the Contracts (Rights of Third Parties) Act 1999.[77] This would be subject to defences, in particular in this context set-offs, available against the agent.[78]

When one turns to consider the rights of sub-agent against principal, while no one suggests that the principal should be liable to the sub-agent for remuneration in the absence of a contract,[79] restitutionary reasoning can sometimes also be used to justify a right of reimbursement for expenses and liabilities incurred: although

---

[72] [1932] A.C. 562.
[73] *Calico Printers Assn Ltd v Barclays Bank Ltd* (1931) 145 L.T. 51, still however a significant case because of its analysis of the legal position in such situations. See also *Involnert Management Inc v Aprilgrange Ltd* [2015] EWHC 2225 (Comm); [2016] 1 All E.R. (Comm) 913 at [291].
[74] [1995] 2 A.C. 145. See also *Riyad Bank v Ahli United Bank* [2005] EWHC 279; [2005] 2 Lloyd's Rep. 409 at [64], per Moore-Bick J. See also *Dunlop Haywards Ltd v Erinaceous Insurance Services Ltd* [2008] EWHC 520 (Comm) at [66], reversed on other points [2009] EWCA Civ 354.
[75] At 182, per Lord Goff of Chieveley.
[76] At 195, citing as an example *Simaan Contracting Co v Pilkington Safety Glass Ltd (No.2)* [1988] Q.B. 758 (a case on construction sub-contracts). A case where a sub-agent had earlier been held not liable in tort is *Balsamo v Medici* [1984] 1 W.L.R. 951, Illustration 7. It is submitted that the decision in that case was correct but much of the reasoning extremely doubtful even at the time, and certainly in the light of subsequent developments. See Whittaker (1985) 48 M.L.R. 86. A sub-agent (a Lloyd's broker) was held not liable in *Pangood Ltd v Barclay Brown & Co Ltd* [1999] P.N.L.R. 678.
[77] s.1(1)(2); subject to the requirement of identification in s.1(3). A rights-of-third-parties clause is not conclusive against there being a contractual relationship between principal and sub-agent: *Temple Legal Protection Ltd v QBE Insurance (Europe) Ltd* [2008] EWHC 843 (Comm); [2008] Lloyd's Rep. I.R. 643 at [110]; affd on other grounds [2009] EWCA Civ 453; [2009] 1 All E.R. (Comm) 703.
[78] s.3.
[79] See *Schmaling v Tomlinson* (1815) 6 Taunt: 147; *Mason v Clifton* (1863) 3 F.&F. 899 (subject to the 1999 Act, above); *Berezovsky v Edmiston & Co Ltd* [2010] EWHC 1883 (Comm) at [69] (reversed on one issue [2011] EWCA Civ 431). But cf. *Accidia Foundation v Simon C. Dickinson Ltd* [2010] EWHC 3058 (Ch) at [94] (remuneration of sub-agent by equitable allowance in an account by that sub-agent, but to be met out of commission that might otherwise have gone to the head agent).

these can usually be justified on the basis of contract,[80] the restitutionary explanation now available outside contract gives a scope which is not so limited, though narrower in that it is confined to the extent of any benefit conferred on the principal.[81] Otherwise, it is always possible for a principal to undertake contractual obligations in favour of the sub-agent, in addition to or in substitution for the agent.[82]

Equitable liability   The position in English law of the sub-agent in respect of the various forms of equitable liability is not much clearer. A sub-agent who knowingly misapplies the property of the principal will undoubtedly be liable in equity to the principal for such actions, but so too would most third parties who implicate themselves in such events.[83] On the other hand, an innocent, even negligent, misapplication of funds or other failure by the subagent to comply with the principal's instructions, at least where the sub-agent did not benefit therefrom, would not necessarily expose the sub-agent to liability to the principal in equity.[84] This would be so even where the sub-agent's actions caused the agent to be liable to the principal, including for breach of trust.[85]

5-012

The legal position where the sub-agent makes profits which could not have been made but for the agent's position as such, or where the sub-agent engages in a transaction where he can be said to have interests conflicting with those of the principal, is unsettled. It was held in 1905 that the sub-agent might be liable to the principal in respect of a secret profit[86]: the view was expressed that there was a contract between principal and sub-agent, but that ground was not the basis of the decision. Such reasoning would in fact have solved the earlier case of *De Bussche v Alt*,[87] where the issue was again one of a (considerable) secret profit, but the problem was solved by finding privity of contract between principal and sub-agent. The sub-agent would be liable to the agent for such profits, and the latter, at least once the sub-agent had accounted to him, would usually be liable to the principal, but direct liability to the principal seems also tenable.

---

[80] See Comment to Article 62.

[81] See Comment to Article 62; Goff and Jones, *Law of Unjust Enrichment* (9th edn), Chs 19–20.

[82] See e.g. *Prentis Donegan & Partners Ltd v Leeds & Leeds Co Inc* [1998] 2 Lloyd's Rep. 326, Illustration 9: see 334; *Fitzpatrick v Allan Associates Architects Ltd* [2015] NIQB 41 (solicitors seeking fees from ultimate principal). But cf. *Temple Legal Protection Ltd v QBE Insurance (Europe) Ltd* [2009] EWCA Civ 453 at [26].

[83] See *Bath v Standard Land Co Ltd* [1911] 1 Ch. 618 at 626, Illustration 10; *Ross River Ltd v Waveley Commercial Ltd* [2013] EWCA Civ 910 at [59]. See further below, Articles 96 and 116.

[84] *Gregson v HAE Trustees Ltd* [2008] EWHC 1006 (Ch); *Revenue and Customs Commissioners v Holland* [2010] UKSC 51; [2010] 1 W.L.R. 2793, noted Watts (2011) 127 L.Q.R. 162; Ferran [2011] C.L.J. 321; Ji Lian Yap [2012] J.B.L. 57 (director of incorporated director not a de facto director of head company and hence not liable for honest misapplication of company property). Not all breaches of trust involve breaches of fiduciary duty: see Rt Hon. Lord Millett (1998) 114 L.Q.R. 399 at 405 and 417.

[85] See *Bath v Standard Land* [1911] 1 Ch. 618 at 627 and 637; *Revenue and Customs Commissioners v Holland* [2010] UKSC 51; [2010] 1 W.L.R. 2793.

[86] *Powell & Thomas v Evan Jones & Co* [1905] 1 K.B. 11, Illustration 6; *Markel International Insurance Co Ltd v Surety Guarantee Consultants Ltd* [2008] EWHC 1135 (Comm), Illustration 11; but cf. *New Zealand & Australian Land Co v Watson* (1881) 7 Q.B.D. 374; *Royal Products Ltd v Midland Bank Ltd* [1981] 2 Lloyd's Rep. 194. See further Finn, *Fiduciary Obligations* (1977), pp.177–178 and 202–203.

[87] (1878) 8 Ch.D. 286, Illustration 5.

In *Bath v Standard Land Co Ltd*[88] a majority of the Court of Appeal took the view that the directors of a company that was itself an agent of the claimant did not owe fiduciary duties to the claimant. However, that was a case where the claimant, on the basis of conflict of interest, was attempting to deny the relevant directors any remuneration at all for valuable services they had performed in an external capacity for the company, and thereby the claimant. The decision may have been different if the relevant contracts had been unexecuted and the claimant had been simply seeking to have them rescinded, or, if executed, the claimant had been willing to seek rescission on terms that the directors were to receive reasonable remuneration. Buckley LJ, one of the majority judges, indicated that a sub-agent who buys from or sells to a trustee or principal would be subject to the same constraints in respect of conflict of interest as the agent.[89] It has since been held that a sub-agent may take upon himself fiduciary duties to the principal, and can therefore be directly liable for diverting business opportunities to a competitor of the principal.[90] But the mere existence of a conflict of interest, or simple profiting from position, where there is no suggestion that the principal was harmed by the sub-agent's actions, may be capable of being excused by the agent, properly informed of the circumstances.[91]

Whether there can be said to be a general duty in a sub-agent to account to the principal, as was argued by Seavey in 1955[92] and more recently again suggested,[93] remains uncertain, though it seems desirable. It may first be noted that there are undoubtedly cases where the sub-agent may hold property on trust for the principal, including the fruits of bribes and secret commissions received by the sub-agent.[94] But there can also be other situations.[95] Any further argument for such a right would need to overcome the nineteenth-century cases, mostly but not all on solicitors, relying on the lack of privity of contract between sub-agent and principal.[96] It is true that other cases might appear to take a different line[97]; but where a duty to account has been found it is usually not clear whether or not the court has proceeded on the basis that there is a contract between principal and sub-agent. If there is, the problem of course vanishes; and some cases may have taken this approach in order to secure

---

[88] [1911] 1 Ch. 618.
[89] [1911] 1 Ch. 618 at 644. In some jurisdictions, statutory provisions may expressly regulate the conflicts of interest of sub-agents: see, e.g. *Dyas v Diel* [2013] NZHC 2645 (employees of real estate agent).
[90] *JD Wetherspoon Plc v Van De Berg & Co Ltd* [2009] EWHC 639 (Ch) at [77].
[91] In *Regal (Hastings) Ltd v Gulliver* [1967] 2 A.C. 134n the directors of the claimant company were held capable of condoning a profit made by the company's solicitor, even though they could not retain their own profits.
[92] See Seavey (1955) 68 Harv.L.Rev. 658.
[93] Tettenborn (1999) 115 L.Q.R. 655. It is however not easy to accept all the explanations of the cases discussed in this article.
[94] *Att.-Gen. for Hong Kong v Reid* [1994] 1 A.C. 324. *FHR European Ventures LLP v Cedar Capital Partners LLC* [2014] UKSC 45; [2014] 3 W.L.R. 535. See further below, para.6-042.
[95] Money received was held not impressed with a trust in *New Zealand & Australian Land Co v Watson* (1881) 7 Q.B.D. 374; but this can be true of property held by an agent: see, e.g. *Neste Oy v Lloyd's Bank Plc* [1983] 2 Lloyd's Rep. 658; see below, para.6-042; also Tettenborn (1999) 115 L.Q.R. 655 at 657–658.
[96] *Robbins v Fennell* (1847) 11 Q.B. 248, Illustration 3; *Cobb v Becke* (1845) 6 Q.B. 930, Illustration 4; *Stephens v Badcock* (1832) 3 B. & Ad. 354; *Sims v Brittain* (1832) 4 B. & Ad. 375; but cf. *Robbins v Heath* (1848) 11 Q.B. 257n; *Collins v Brook* (1860) 5 H. & N. 700.
[97] See *Pearson v Scott* (1878) 9 Ch.D. 198, Illustration 3 to Article 28; *Harsant v Blaine McDonald & Co* (1887) 56 L.J.Q.B. 511, cited by Tettenborn (1999) 115 L.Q.R. 655.

an appropriate result. This is arguably what happened in the leading case of *De Bussche v Alt*.[98]

Set-off, etc   Failure of the intermediary agent features in many of the cases.[99] A   **5-013**
major reason for argument by the sub-contractor that his contract is with the agent
rather than the principal is that he may have paid, or have a set-off against, or
otherwise be able to adjust his accounts with the agent, and this has been relevant
in several cases.[100] Even where there is actual privity of contract with the principal,
however, the sub-agent, who cannot of course in such a case set off in the strict
sense a debt owed to him by the agent,[101] may seek to argue that he has in effect
paid the agent by retaining money in adjustment of the financial position between
them. This last argument can sometimes be met by saying that unless there are other
indications the agent normally has no authority to accept payment other than in
cash.[102]

Lien   The question of the sub-agent's lien involves special considerations, since   **5-014**
a lien is a property interest. It is therefore dealt with elsewhere.[103]

Apparent authority   This Article again deals with actual authority. But it should   **5-015**
be remembered that the principles of apparent authority still apply where third parties are involved. Thus a person appointed as sub-agent to the principal by another
agent may be able to rely on the apparent authority of the appointing agent if there
was some specific representation by the principal, or if the case is one where authority to delegate would normally be implied, despite instructions not to delegate given
by the principal to his agent but unknown to the appointed agent. And a person dealing with an agent so appointed may be able to rely on the principal's holding out
such person as his agent, or on the apparent authority of the appointing agent to
make the appointment. So also a person may be able to rely on apparent authority
to appoint him a sub-agent, e.g. where he wishes to exercise the lien of a sub-
agent. It seems that where the agent who appoints the sub-agent has only apparent
authority to make the appointment, third parties who deal with the sub-agent
(whether disclosed or not) need not establish that they knew of the original holding out. The principal is precluded from denying the sub-agent's actual authority
to bind, so long at least as there has been no communication otherwise. Otherwise,
the sub-agent would unjustly be exposed to an action for breach of warranty of
authority at the third party's hands.[104] The position will be different where the sub-
agent himself exceeds the scope of his delegated authority; there it may be necessary for the third party to show that he relied on the chain of representations.[105]
Where the appointment of the sub-agent is without actual authority, and there is no

---

[98]   (1878) 8 Ch.D. 286, Illustration 5. The case could also be explained on the basis of secret profit,
       whether there was privity or not.
[99]   See Article 98.
[100] A leading example is *New Zealand & Australian Land Co v Watson* (1881) 7 Q.B.D. 374, Illustra-
       tion 1.
[101] See Article 81.
[102] See, e.g. *Pearson v Scott* (1878) 9 Ch.D. 198; Article 28, Illustrations 3 and 4.
[103] See Article 68.
[104] *AJU Remicon Co Ltd v Alida Shipping Co Ltd* [2007] EWHC 2246 (Comm) at [18].
[105] See *Ing Re (UK) Ltd v R & V Versicherung AG* [2006] EWHC 1544 (Comm); [2006] 2 All E.R.
       (Comm) 870; [2006] Lloyd's Rep. I.R. 653; [2007] 1 B.C.L.C. 108 at [100]; *Flexirent Capital Pty
       Ltd v EBS Consulting Pty Ltd* [2007] VSC 158 at [213].

apparent authority, the principal will not in general be bound by the acts of such a sub-agent.[106]

Illustrations

5-016 (1) A factor was employed to sell goods on a *del credere* commission. The factor, with the principal's authority, employed a broker on an ordinary commission to sell the goods. The broker sold the goods and received the proceeds, and made payments on account to the factor from time to time. While the balance of the proceeds was still in the hands of the broker, the factor, being then indebted to the broker in respect of other independent transactions, became bankrupt. Held, (i) that there was no privity of contract between the principal and the broker; (ii) that the broker was not liable to account to the principal for the proceeds of the goods sold; and (iii) that the principal was not entitled to recover the balance of the proceeds from the broker in the factor's name without allowing the amount due from the factor to the broker in respect of other transactions to be set off, though the broker had reason to believe that the factor was acting as an agent.[107]

(2) An agent, being expressly authorised to do so, appointed a solicitor as sub-agent to manage the principal's affairs. The sub-agent took over their entire management, and communicated with the principal direct. Held, that the subagent was not liable to render an account of his agency to the principal.[108]

(3) The London agent of a country solicitor, in the ordinary course of business, receives, as such, the proceeds of a cause in which he is engaged. There is no privity of contract between the client and the London agent, and the client cannot recover the proceeds from him as money received to the client's use.[109] So, a London agent, in the ordinary course of business, gives credit to the country solicitor and not to the client, and has no remedy, except his lien, against the client for costs, and such lien, as against the client, is limited to the amount due from the client to the country solicitor.[110] The court may, however, in exercise of its summary jurisdiction over its own officers, order a London agent to pay over to the client money received, the agent claiming to retain the amount in satisfaction of a debt due to him from the country solicitor,[111] or having received it without the authority of either the country solicitor or the client.[112]

(4) A client gives money to his solicitor to pay a debt and costs. The solicitor remits the amount, by means of his own cheque, to his London agent for the purpose of paying such debt and costs. The agent retains the amount in satisfaction of a debt due to him from the solicitor. The agent is not liable to

---

[106] See *Schmaling v Tomlinson* (1815) 6 Taunt. 147; *Mason v Clifton* (1863) 3 F. & F. 899.

[107] *New Zealand & Australian Land Co v Watson* (1881) 7 Q.B.D. 374.

[108] *Lockwood v Abdy* (1845) 14 Sim. 437. And see *Att.-Gen. v Earl of Chesterfield* (1854) 18 Beav. 596; *Re Spencer* (1881) 51 L.J.Ch. 271.

[109] *Robbins v Fennell* (1847) 11 Q.B. 248. And see *Hannaford v Syms* (1898) 79 L.T. 30; cf. *Collins v Brook* (1860) 5 H. & N. 700. See in general Cordery, *Solicitors* (8th edn), p.279–281 onwards (not reproduced in the current (looseleaf) edition). These cases are largely out of date, but are retained as relevant examples of principle.

[110] *Ex p. Edwards* (1881) 8 Q.B.D. 262; affirming 7 Q.B.D. 155. See further Article 70, Illustration 3.

[111] *Ex p. Edwards*, above; *Hanley v Cassam* (1847) 11 Jur. 1088.

[112] *Robbins v Fennell* (1847) 11 Q.B. 248; but cf. *Robbins v Heath* (1848) 11 Q.B. 257n.

the client in an action for money had and received to the client's use.[113] So, if a London agent receives money improperly, the remedy of the client is against his own solicitor, not against the agent.[114]

(5)   A ship was consigned to A, an agent in China, for sale, a minimum price being fixed. A employed B to sell the ship in circumstances in which he had authority to do so.[115] B, being unable to find a purchaser, bought the ship himself at the minimum price, and subsequently resold it at a large profit. It was held that privity of contract existed between the principal and B, and that B was liable to account to the principal for the profit made on the resale.[116]

(6)   Shipowners employ agents to obtain for them a loan secured by means of debentures on their ships. The agents, with the shipowners' consent, employ a sub-agent, who negotiates such a loan but accepts a commission from the lender. The shipowners can recover this sum from the sub-agent, whether or not they are in privity of contract with him.[117] The sub-agent cannot, however, be compelled to enforce the contract for the commission for the benefit of the principal.

(7)   The Italian owner of a vintage car asks a friend to sell it for him in England and remit the proceeds to the owner's mother-in-law in England. The friend sells the car but has to return to Italy before the proceeds have been received. Without the owner's knowledge he asks an English associate to receive and transmit the money. By his own negligence the associate is tricked out of the money. The associate is not liable in tort to the owner.[118]

(8)   "Names" investing in the Lloyd's market entrust their business to "members' agents". These agents further entrust the business to "managing agents". The managing agents handle the investors' funds negligently. They have no privity of contract with the names, only with the managing agents. They are liable in tort directly to the names.[119]

(9)   American insurance brokers approach Lloyd's brokers for marine insurance. The slip is written "Account: Offshore Service (U.K.) Ltd" (a managing company for the owners of the ship insured). The insurance is effected and the Lloyd's brokers pay premiums. Being not reimbursed by the American brokers they sue the brokers, who argue that the only contract is between the assured (as principal) and the Lloyd's brokers. The Lloyd's brokers have a contract with the American brokers, who are liable.[120]

(10) A landowner in financial difficulties agrees to the appointment of a company as managing agent. The company's articles of association permit its direc-

[113] *Cobb v Becke* (1845) 6 Q.B. 930. See, however, *Ex p. Edwards*, above.
[114] *Gray v Kirby* (1834) 2 Dowl. 601. See, however, *Robbins v Fennell*, above; *Robbins v Heath*, above.
[115] See Article 34, Illustration 7.
[116] *De Bussche v Alt.* (1878) 8 Ch.D. 286; see also *Tarn v Scanlan* [1928] A.C. 34. But see above, text to fn.81.
[117] *Powell & Thomas v Evan Jones & Co* [1905] 1 K.B. 11. See further below, para.6-042.
[118] *Balsamo v Medici* [1984] 1 W.L.R. 951. But see fn.76 above. A similar decision was reached in a more substantial banking case, *Calico Printers Assn v Barclays Bank Ltd* (1931) 145 L.T. 51. See above, para.5-012.
[119] *Henderson v Merrett Syndicates Ltd* [1995] 2 A.C. 145. See also *Aiken v Stewart Wrightson Agency* [1995] 1 W.L.R. 1281.
[120] *Prentis Donegan & Partners Ltd v Leeds & Leeds Co Inc* [1998] 2 Lloyd's Rep. 326, distinguishing *Velos Group Ltd v Harbour Insurance Services Ltd* [1977] 2 Lloyd's Rep. 461. See also *Heath Lambert Ltd v Sociedad de Corretaje de Seguros* [2003] EWHC 2269 (Comm); [2004] 1 Lloyd's Rep. 495.

tors to provide services to the company in their professional capacities for reward. Four directors (a solicitor, an auctioneer, an accountant, and a pit manager) provide services under contract in the operation of the landowner's estate. The landowner unsuccessfully seeks to deny the directors any remuneration for their services.[121]

(11) The claimant insurance company appoints a corporate underwriting agent to write surety bonds on its behalf. The appointment designates the defendants (officers and employees of the agent) as approved personnel to conduct the business. The defendants dishonestly write bonds that do not conform to the instructions, thereby exposing the claimant to losses, and also obtain for the agent secret commissions on the unauthorised business. The defendants are held to be sub-agents, and liable directly for breach of fiduciary duty. Alternatively, they are liable for dishonestly procuring breaches of duty by their company.[122]

[121] *Bath v Standard Land Co Ltd* [1911] 1 Ch. 618.
[122] *Markel International Insurance Co Ltd v Surety Guarantee Consultants Ltd* [2008] EWHC 1135 (Comm), affd [2009] EWCA Civ 790.

CHAPTER 6

DUTIES OF AGENTS TOWARDS THEIR PRINCIPALS

INTRODUCTORY NOTE

In legal systems where agency is fragmented into certain typical sorts of activity, it may be possible to lay down fairly detailed rules as to the duties of agents towards their principals. The immense breadth of the agency concept at common law means that it is not easy to do so in a general work on agency.[1] Many agents work under written contracts which contain detailed provisions as to the agent's duties, and perhaps specify the circumstances in which the principal can terminate the contract for breach by the agent. They may contain provisions which require to be measured against the rules relating to contracts in restraint of trade, and also considered in the light of EC law.[2] The same is true of distributorship contracts.[3] Some agents, such as estate agents, are subject to a degree of statutory regulation.[4] Other persons exercising agency powers may be parties to contracts of employment and entitled to the protections of employment law.[5] Beyond this, the question is one of interpretation. Where the contract is silent, the court may be willing to find implied terms: although the English courts are traditionally reluctant to do this, there are circumstances where they will do so.[6] But often the question is one of interpretation of an oral transaction. And some agents, e.g. canvassing agents, undertake no duties. They are simply entitled to certain contractual rights if they do certain things, though they may be liable for various forms of misconduct.[7] Again, some persons to whom the term "agent" may be applied act gratuitously: there may be difficulties in ascribing a liability to them for acting in a way which is unsatisfactory to the principal, and even more in holding them liable when they have undertaken to act but have not done so.

All this means that the common law duties of an agent can only be referred to in very general terms, which indicate the sorts of way in which an agent may be

6-001

---

[1] *Torre Asset Funding Ltd v The Royal Bank of Scotland Plc* [2013] EWHC 2670 (Ch) at [147].
[2] For international agents, see R. Christou, *International Agency, Distribution and Licensing Agreements* (6th edn, 2011).
[3] See, e.g. *Decro-Wall International SA v Practitioners in Marketing Ltd* [1971] 1 W.L.R. 361; *Wickman Machine Tool Sales Ltd v L. Schuler A.G.* [1974] A.C. 235; *Proactive Sports Management Ltd v Rooney* [2011] EWCA Civ 1444 (exclusive image-marketing agency of eight years' duration at 20 per cent commission found void on grounds of restraint of trade).
[4] See the Estate Agents Act 1979 (as amended by Enterprise Act 2002); and the Consumers, Estate Agents and Redress Act 2007 Sch.6. See too the Unfair Terms in Consumer Contracts Regulations 1999, as applied in *Office of Fair Trading v Foxtons Ltd* [2009] EWCA Civ 288; [2010] 1 W.L.R. 663.
[5] See Freedland (ed), *The Contract of Employment* (2016).
[6] See *Liverpool City Council v Irwin* [1977] A.C. 239; *J. & H. Ritchie Ltd v Lloyd Ltd* [2007] UKHL 9; [2007] 1 Lloyd's Rep. 544; *Att.-Gen. of Belize v Belize Telecom Ltd* [2009] UKPC 10; [2009] 1 W.L.R. 1988; and *Mediterranean Salvage & Towage Ltd v Seamar Trading & Commerce Inc* [2009] EWCA Civ 531. Chitty, *Contracts* (32nd edn), Ch.14; below, para.7-001.
[7] See above, para.1-020 onwards; below, para.7-016.

held in breach of duty. An obvious example is the duty not to exceed authority, where the agent is under a duty to make good to the principal loss caused by so doing. Generally speaking, an agent is expected to know the scope of his mandate and adhere to it. Otherwise, however, the agent does not normally warrant success in what he does, but only to use reasonable endeavours; but there can be cases where strict liability is undertaken.[8] In one area a specialised body of law has developed, and is still developing. This is the law relating to the fiduciary obligations of agents, which connects with the rules of equity applicable to express trustees. The principles of fiduciary obligation are not confined to agents, but apply to agents among others, because of the special trust which is reposed in them. It is only in this area that it can be said that special rules on the duties of agents towards their principals can be identified. Sometimes the fiduciary obligations give rise to implied terms in the contract. But often they are to be regarded as operating independently of contract.

1. DUTIES OF PERFORMANCE

Article 36

AGENT'S DUTY TO PERFORM UNDERTAKING

6-002   An agent is bound to act in accordance with the terms of his authority.[9]

Comment

6-003   This rule is certainly fundamental to every contractual agency. Subject as always to the express provisions of the contract, an agent appointed under contract must comply with the terms of what he has agreed to do, and is in breach of contract if he exceeds his authority on the one hand, or fails to carry it out on the other.[10] But even agents who act gratuitously are expected to adhere to their instructions, and may be found to have assumed a legal responsibility to their principal to do so. So, they may be liable for money had and received if they disperse the principal's money without mandate,[11] or otherwise liable in tort, as discussed below. Where the agent has been entrusted with his principal's money and holds it as trustee then any disbursement that is inconsistent with his mandate will normally also involve a breach of trust.[12] Equity provides its own remedies for breach of trust, but these in many respects parallel those of contract.

---

[8] e.g. *Harlow & Jones Ltd v P.J. Walker Shipping and Transport Ltd* [1986] 2 Lloyd's Rep. 141 (freight forwarder warrants freight rate). cf. *Martin v JRC Commercial Mortgages Plc* [2012] EWCA Civ 63 (fixed-fee mortgage broker undertook duty of care but did not warrant success in obtaining a mortgage for client).

[9] cf. *Restatement, Third*, §§ 8.07 and 8.09; see too DeMott, in Gold and Miller (eds), *Philosophical Foundations of Fiduciary Law* (2014), Ch.16. As to a company director's duty to act in accordance with a company's constitution, see Companies Act 2006 s.171.

[10] See Illustrations; *Smith v Lascelles* (1788) 2 T.R. 187; *Comber v Anderson* (1808) 1 Camp. 523; *Barber v Taylor* (1839) 5 M. & W. 527; *L.S. Harris Trustees Ltd v Power Packing Services (Hermit Road) Ltd* [1970] 2 Lloyd's Rep. 65; *Restatement, Third*, § 8.07.

[11] *Martin v Pont* [1993] 3 N.Z.L.R. 25.

[12] See *Re Collie, Ex p. Adamson* (1878) 8 Ch.D. 807 at 819; *British America Elevator Co Ltd v Bank of British North America* [1919] A.C. 658 (PC); *Anguilla v Estate and Trust Agencies Ltd* [1938] A.C. 624 (PC) at 637; *Re Dawson (dec'd)* [1966] 2 N.S.W.R. 211 at 244; *Alexander v Perpetual Trustees WA Ltd* (2003) 216 C.L.R. 109 at [44], [47] and [59]; *Madoff Securities International Ltd*

Failure to adhere to instructions is by definition a breach of duty and in principle results in strict liability for resulting loss. How such liability is worked out in terms of remedy is somewhat controversial. Recent case law at equity has concluded that if the principal would have suffered the same or other loss had the instructions been correctly carried out, this may result in no recovery.[13] It remains arguable that these cases are explicable on their facts, and in a clear case of deviation involving the expenditure of the principal's money, a principal may simply be able to call for the return of the money, in an action for money had and received or for an account at equity.[14] Were, for instance, an agent to send his principal's money to the wrong person, it would ordinarily be inappropriate to permit the agent to attempt to show that the money would have been lost even had it been sent to the correct person. Where the agent uses his own money in misconceived pursuit of the principal's affairs, the principal may simply be able to disown the agent's action.[15] A principal who finds his agent has deviated from instructions may nonetheless have to take the point early and not wait to see how things turn out—such a failure occurred in what is now the leading case in this area, *AIB Group (UK) Plc v Mark Redler & Co Solicitors*.[16] A failure to adhere to instructions may also be capable of being cured if the agent can rescue the situation before the principal terminates the agent's mandate and calls for return of any money provided the agent.[17] It is further possible that upon construction of the agency contract an apparently absolute obligation may be found to be one only to exercise reasonable care and skill.[18]

By way of example of the foregoing principles, a solicitor who is retained to conduct an action and instructed not to compromise it will be in breach of contract if he does compromise it without his client's instructions, although both he and counsel may consider that a settlement is in the client's best interests and strongly advise in favour of such a course.[19] Barristers are in a similar position.[20] On the other hand, even if the principal's instructions are foolhardy, the agent must carry out what he has agreed to do.[21] He may sometimes be under a duty to warn and advise,[22]

---

v Raven [2013] EWHC 3147 (Comm) at [291]; *Libertarian Investments Ltd v Hall* [2013] HKCFA 94; 16 H.K.C.F.A.R. 681 at [168]; *Allied Irish Bank v Maguire & Co* [2016] IESC 57. See also Rt Hon. Lord Millett (1998) 114 L.Q.R. 214 at 226–227; Watts [2016] L.M.C.L.Q. 118; Penner (2014) 8 J. Eq. 202; Conaglen (2016) 40 Melb. U.L.R. 126. For further discussion of the position in equity see below, para.6-043.

[13] *Target Holdings Ltd v Redferns* [1996] A.C. 421; *AIB Group (UK) Plc v Mark Redler & Co Solicitors* [2014] UKSC 58; [2015] A.C. 1503.

[14] See, e.g. *Main v Giambrone & Law (a firm)* [2017] EWCA Civ 1193.

[15] *Barclays Bank Ltd v WJ Simms Son & Cooke (Southern) Ltd* [1980] Q.B. 677; *Agip (Africa) Ltd v Jackson* [1990] Ch. 265 at 283–294, per Millett J; [1991] Ch. 547 (CA) at 561–562.

[16] *AIB Group (UK) Plc v Mark Redler & Co Solicitors* [2014] UKSC 58; [2015] A.C. 1503, Illustration 5.

[17] See *Target Holdings Ltd v Redferns* [1996] A.C. 421.

[18] *Bristol and West Building Society v Mothew* [1998] Ch. 1 at 24; *Davisons Solicitors (a firm) v Nationwide Building Society* [2012] EWCA Civ 1626 at [57].

[19] *Fray v Voules* (1859) 1 E. & E. 839; *Butler v Knight* (1867) L.R. 2 Ex. 109; *The Hermione* [1922] P. 162; *Apatu v Peach Prescott & Jamieson* [1985] 1 N.Z.L.R. 50 at 64; *Amalgamated Metal Corp Plc v Wragge & Co (A Firm)* [2011] EWHC 887 (Comm); [2011] P.N.L.R. 24 (damages awarded on loss of chance of better settlement). As to a solicitor's apparent authority to compromise a suit, see Article 30, Illustration 5.

[20] *Swinfen v Lord Chelmsford* (1860) 5 H. & N. 890; *Neale v Gordon Lennox* [1902] A.C. 465; cf. *Harvey v Phillips* (1956) 95 C.L.R. 235. See too *Kendirjian v Lepore* [2017] HCA 13 at [15].

[21] See *R.H. Deacon & Co Ltd v Varga* (1972) 30 D.L.R. (3d) 653; affd. 41 D.L.R. (3d) 767n (stockbroker); Illustration 4; *Volkers v Midland Doherty* (1985) 17 D.L.R. (4th) 343, Illustration 4 to Article 39.

but if such advice is ignored, he is bound to carry out the terms of the agency contract and may be liable to his principal for breach of contract if he does not do so.[23]

In some circumstances at least, an agent may also be liable to his principal in tort if he commits the principal to a contract or other obligation without, or in excess of, authority. In *OBG Ltd v Allan*,[24] Lord Hoffmann in dicta was of the opinion that liability could arise only in contract in such circumstances. However, it seems likely that those who assume the role of agent without having a contract with the principal (such as minors, gratuitous agents (dealt with below), and dismissed former agents) could be liable to their principals in tort for acting without or beyond mandate.[25] Contractual agents may not automatically be immune from the same liability. Many of the details of such liability remain to be worked out. Where, for example, an ex-agent deliberately exploits lingering apparent authority it seems likely that any carelessness on the principal's part in allowing an appearance of authority could not reduce the extent of the defendant's liability.[26] Where the agent purports to pass title to the principal's property in breach of instructions, even if only by mistake, he and the recipient may be liable in conversion,[27] and, in the case of money, in breach of trust.[28]

6-004   **Onus of proof**   The question as to who as between principal and (putative) agent bears the onus of proving absence, or breach, of mandate is unclear. The general principle is that the party asserting a proposition bears the onus of proof,[29] but it is arguable that proof that one's legal position has been changed coupled with an al-

---

[22] Especially where there is a fiduciary obligation (see Article 43): *Clark Boyce v Mouat* [1994] 1 A.C. 428 at 437; *Haira v Burbery Mortgage Finance and Savings Ltd* [1995] 3 N.Z.L.R. 396 at 406. Frequently, however, it will be concluded that giving advice is not part of the agent's undertaking: see e.g. *Eric Preston Pty Ltd v Euroz Securities Ltd* [2011] FCAFC 11 at [160] (stockbroker no duty to advise); *Cherney v Neuman* [2011] EWHC 2156 (Ch) at [108] (solicitor no duty to advise on commercial merits of transaction, but duty to reveal known facts relevant to transaction that client had entered into).

[23] See *Boyce v Rendells* [1983] E.G.D. 26 at 37.

[24] *OBG Ltd v Allan* [2007] UKHL 21; [2008] 1 A.C. 1 at [93]. See Watts (2007) 123 L.Q.R. 519. cf. *Brown v Boorman* (1844) 11 Cl. & Fin. 1 (broker handing over goods without securing payment, in breach of instructions, is held liable in tort)); *Kendirjian v Lepore* [2017] HCA 13 at [15].

[25] For the range of torts potentially applicable in this context, see Watts (2009) 17 Torts L.J. 100 at 120. See too *Markel International Insurance Co Ltd v Surety Guarantee Consultants Ltd* [2008] EWHC 1135 (Comm); affd [2009] EWCA Civ 790 (liability of sub-agents for conspiracy to defraud in writing contracts in excess of authority). As to the possibility of tortious liability for lack of care and skill in the exercise of due authority, see below, para.6-018.

[26] See *Standard Chartered Bank v Pakistan National Shipping Corp (No.2)* [2002] UKHL 43; [2003] 1 A.C. 959.

[27] *Bishop v Shillito* (1819) note to 2 Barn. & Ald. 327; *Solloway v McLaughlin* [1938] A.C. 247; *Bennett v Goodwin* (2005) 62 A.T.R. 515; *J.S. Brooksbank & Co (Australasia) Ltd v EXFTX Ltd* (2009) 10 N.Z.C.L.C. 264,520 (goods mistakenly released by agent in breach of instructions).

[28] See, e.g. *Lloyds Tsb Bank Plc v Markandan & Uddin (A Firm)* [2012] EWCA Civ 65; [2012] 2 All E.R. 884 (solicitor, victim of fraud, commits breach of trust in releasing funds in breach of mandate); *AIB Group (UK) Plc v Mark Redler & Co Solicitors* [2014] UKSC 58; [2015] A.C. 1503. *Re Lands Allotment Co* [1894] 1 Ch. 616 at 638 (director who innocently pay dividends in breach of dividend rules strictly liable); *H.M. Revenue and Customs v Holland* [2010] UKSC 51; [2010] 1 W.L.R. 2793 at [45]. In some circumstances, relief from liability may be available under s.61 of the Trustee Act 1925: see *Davisons Solicitors (a firm) v Nationwide Building Society* [2012] EWCA Civ 1626; *Santander UK Plc v R.A. Legal Solicitors* [2014] EWCA Civ 183; *Purrunsing v A'Court & Co (a firm)* [2016] EWHC 789 (Ch) or under the Companies Act 2006 s.1157. See further, para.6-043; and Watts [2016] L.M.C.L.Q. 118.

[29] *Joseph Constantine Steamship Line Ltd v Imperial Smelting Corp Ltd* [1942] A.C. 154 at 174; and

legation that the defendant effected the change without authority is sufficient to shift the burden to the defendant to prove authority to do so. Where the agent has paid out the principal's money, again the onus is on the agent properly to account for such dispositions.[30]

Exceeding authority: apparent authority and ratification Sometimes an **6-005** unauthorised act of the agent may bind the principal. This occurs where the agent has apparent, though no actual, authority, viz. he appears to a reasonable third party to have authority[31]; and when the principal chose to ratify an act done on his behalf without authority.[32] In such cases the question may arise as to whether the agent is liable to the principal for exceeding his authority. In the case of apparent authority the matter seems fairly clear in relation to contractual agencies; on principle, if the agent has caused loss to the principal by exceeding his authority, he must answer for it.[33] As seen above, liability may also arise in tort and equity.

The second case, that of ratification, is perhaps more arguable, inasmuch as the principal has chosen to ratify when he need not have done so, and there is authority by way of general dicta that ratification validates an unauthorised act for all purposes.[34] There can however obviously be circumstances where a principal ratifies, not because he wishes to do so but because he finds it commercially expedient or even essential. In such a case it must be asked whether, while ratifying the contract, the principal has waived the agent's breach of duty. "Often the facts will lead to both ratification and exoneration, but not always."[35]

Commercial agents The Commercial Agents (Council Directive) Regulations **6-006** 1993 lay down duties for commercial agents as there defined. In particular, a commercial agent must in performing his duties "look after the interests of his principal and act dutifully and in good faith".[36] The Regulations are dealt with in Chapter 11.

---

see *Amalgamated Metal Corp Plc v Wragge & Co (A Firm)* [2011] EWHC 887 (Comm) at [90] where it was assumed that the principal bore the burden of proving lack of mandate in a solicitor.

[30] *GHLM Trading Ltd v Maroo* [2012] EWHC 61 (Ch). See further, Article 51. In relation to the onus of proof of loss following a breach of trust or breach of fiduciary obligation, see below, para.6-043.

[31] See Article 72.

[32] See Articles 13–20.

[33] cf. *Papé v Westacott* [1894] 1 Q.B. 272; *Thompson v Howley* [1977] 1 N.Z.L.R. 16; *Restatement, Third*, § 8.09. He may also sometimes commit a crime by so doing: see *R. v Charles* [1977] A.C. 177. The view to the contrary expressed in *Great Atlantic Insurance Co v Home Insurance Co* [1981] 2 Lloyd's Rep. 219 at 222; noted [1982] J.B.L. 39, was strongly criticised by Mance LJ, dissenting, in *OBG Ltd v Allan* [2005] EWCA Civ 106; [2005] Q.B. 762 at [88].

[34] e.g. *Wilson v Tunman and Fretson* (1843) 6 M. & G. 236 at 242.

[35] *Suncorp Insurance and Finance v Milano Assacurazioni SpA* [1993] 2 Lloyd's Rep. 225 at 235, per Waller J.; *Ing Re (UK) Ltd v R & V Versicherung AG* [2006] EWHC 1544 (Comm); [2006] 2 All E.R. (Comm) 870 at [152]. See above, para.2-094. See also Mechem, *Treatise on the Law of Agency* (2nd edn), §§ 492–493; *Mineworkers' Union v Brodrick* 1948 (2) S.A.L.R. 959 at 979. See also Comment to Article 20. Sometimes the agent may be protected by an exclusion clause. In *Darlington Futures Ltd v Delco Australia Pty Ltd* (1986) 161 C.L.R. 500 an agent who by unauthorised commodity transactions caused loss to the client was not protected by one form of words in the contract but under another could limit his liability to $100. The general statements in the case merit approval, but the final result seems surprising.

[36] reg.3(1); see also reg.3(2) (duties regarding the transactions entrusted to him, supplying information to the principal and compliance with instructions); *Crane v Sky In-Home Service Ltd* [2007] EWHC 66 (Ch); [2007] 2 All E.R. (Comm) 599 at [86] (agent passing off separate service business as associated with his principal's).

Illustrations

6-007 (1) A was instructed by P to sell certain shares when the funds reached 85 or more. It was held that he was bound to sell when the funds reached 85, and had no discretion to wait until they went higher.[37]

(2) A, an auctioneer, was instructed by P to sell some furniture for ready money only. A sold the furniture to X, taking a bill of exchange from him. A was liable to P for the proceeds of sale on X's default.[38]

(3) A foreign merchant (P) sent a bill of lading to his English correspondent (A) with instructions to insure the goods and sell them for P's account. A did not wish to accept P's instructions, but, with the intention of safeguarding P's interests by getting the goods insured, indorsed the bill of lading over to X, who insured the goods. A was held liable to P, because, having accepted the bill of lading by indorsing it, he was bound to carry out P's instructions in full.[39]

(4) A company was formed for the purpose of purchasing the goodwill and assets of a partnership. At the time the partnership was deeply in debt, and shortly after the purchase the whole business failed. The company brought proceedings against one of its directors for negligence in purchasing the partnership when he knew it was in difficulties. Held, an agent who was expressly authorised to do an act which was itself imprudent, and one which the principal ought not, as a matter of prudence, to have authorised, was not liable for the consequences of doing it. The director, as an agent of the company, had been expressly authorised to buy the partnership, and was not liable for having done so.[40]

(5) Solicitors acting for a lender are instructed to pay off an existing mortgage before releasing the balance of the £3.3 million loan to the borrower. They overlook a debt of £300,000 secured by the existing mortgage, and thereby fail to obtain a first mortgage for the lender. The lender is made aware of the error. The borrower subsequently defaults on the whole loan and the security proves very inadequate. The solicitors are not liable for all the lender's loss even though none of the funds should have been released without a first mortgage being in place. They are liable for approximately £300,000.[41]

Article 37

CONTRACTUAL AGENT'S DUTY TO OBEY FURTHER INSTRUCTIONS GIVEN BY PRINCIPAL

6-008 (1) Subject to any special circumstances indicating the contrary, the agent is bound to obey all lawful and reasonable instructions of his principal in relation to the manner in which the agent carries out his duties.

(2) In determining what is reasonable the court will have regard to all the

---

[37] *Bertram, Armstrong & Co v Godfray* (1830) 1 Knapp 381. See also *Dufresne v Hutchinson* (1810) 3 Taunt. 117.

[38] *Ferrers v Robins* (1835) 2 C.M. & R. 152. See also *Brown v Boorman* (1844) 11 Cl. & Fin. 1; *Williams v Evans* (1866) L.R. 1 Q.B. 352; and *Westerman Realty Ltd v McKinstry* (2007) 8 N.Z.C.P.R. 553 (auctioneer sells on a tax-inclusive basis when instructions were tax-exclusive).

[39] *Corlett v Gordon* (1813) 3 Camp. 472. See also *Smith v Lascelles* (1788) 2 T.R. 187.

[40] *Overend, Gurney & Co v Gibb* (1872) L.R. 5 H.L. 480; and see *Commerce Realty Ltd v Olenyk* (1957) 8 D.L.R. (2d) 60.

[41] *AIB Group (UK) Plc v Mark Redler & Co Solicitors* [2014] UKSC 58; [2015] A.C. 1503.

circumstances of the case, including the nature of the agency and the customs, practices and ethics of the business to be undertaken by the agent.[42]

Comment

Wording to similar effect as the above has appeared in all previous editions of this work, and from the time of the introduction of Comments to the Articles it has been said that although there is little authority for the proposition contained in the Article, it is almost self-evident.[43] In some ways it must be; but the lack of illustrative case law perhaps derives from the limited ways in which issues are likely to arise. The internal agency relationship, usually but not always a contract, is based on the grant of authority to the agent, accompanied by a duty to indemnify and reimburse the agent against the consequences of so doing (as explained in Article 62, though not necessarily based on a contractual implication). This is the only implication in an arrangement for representation that has no further features. The principal's control over the agent is based on his powers not to grant authority, to limit the authority and to withdraw or revoke authority (as explained in Article 118). In general there is no other implication as regards authority in such a bare agency arrangement, and this right is reciprocal to the agent's duty not to exceed his authority, which (subject to any contract term) can be translated into a duty to compensate the principal for loss caused if he does (as explained in Article 36). **6-009**

It has been held that a principal can give directions to an agent in relation to a specific matter notwithstanding that the agent holds a broad power of attorney.[44] Similarly, it has been held that the sole director of a company can orally override general instructions to a bank that it is to act only on written instructions.[45]

Whether or not an agent must obey new instructions in other respects, for example as regards the method by which he carries out his duties, cannot always be determined by considering whether his authority has been modified or withdrawn.[46] Any further duty to accept instructions outside the sphere of existing authority must be based on the interpretation of some other relationship that may exist between agent and principal, for example a contract of employment, or, to take a random example in the sphere of independent contractors, a contract made by a shipper with a freight forwarder.[47] Even in that context, instructions which involve the performance of an illegal or void act normally need not be obeyed.[48] However, an agent would not normally be excused from carrying out the principal's directions on the basis of a mere suspicion that the principal is engaged in furthering an

---

[42] cf. *Restatement, Third*, § 8.09.

[43] DeMott, in Gold and Miller eds, *Philosophical Foundations of Fiduciary Law* (2014).

[44] *Morrell v Workers Savings & Loan Bank* [2007] UKPC 3 at [10]; *Day v Day* [2013] EWCA Civ 280; [2014] Ch. 114 at [26]. See further para.3-009, above.

[45] *Hill Street Services Co Ltd v National Westminster Bank Plc* [2007] EWHC 2379 (Ch) at [17].

[46] For the general significance of control, see above, para.1-018. As to the difference between agents and trustees on this issue, see above, para.1-029.

[47] See cases on serious breach by an agent, below, para.7-050, and in general above, para.1-018.

[48] See e.g. *Cohen v Kittell* (1889) 22 Q.B.D. 680 (failure to make bets): *Donovan v Invicta Airways Ltd* [1970] 1 Lloyd's Rep. 486; *Association of British Travel Agents Ltd v British Airways Plc* [2000] 1 Lloyd's Rep. 169. If the instructions involve performing an illegal act, the agent may not be liable if he carries them out negligently: *T. Cheshire v Vaughan Bros & Co* [1920] 3 K.B. 240, where an agent instructed to effect a ppi policy failed to disclose a material fact. But see *Fraser v B.N. Furman (Productions) Ltd* [1967] 1 W.L.R. 898; *Everett v Hogg, Robinson & Gardner Mountain (Insurance) Ltd* [1973] 2 Lloyd's Rep. 217; *L.B. Martin Construction Ltd v Gagliardi* (1978) 91 D.L.R. (3d) 393. See further below, para.6-023.

illegal object; some agents, such as banks in relation to the operation of their customers' accounts, may have even less discretion to decline to follow instructions.[49] In the case of a professional person the agent will be bound to a considerable extent by the rules and ethical standards of the profession and could not be required to perform an act which was contrary to those rules or standards.[50]

Article 38

AMBIGUOUS INSTRUCTIONS

6-010   Where the principal's instructions are ambiguous (viz. capable of bearing two or more interpretations), if the agent fairly and honestly assumes them to bear one of those interpretations and acts accordingly, he will not be in breach of contract by so acting.[51]

Comment

6-011   This is certainly a general principle of the law of agency, and can be applied elsewhere.[52] But it must necessarily have limits. If the agent realised or ought to have realised that the instructions were ambiguous, he ought, if the circumstances so permit, to seek clarification from his principal before starting to act.[53]

Article 39

CONTRACTUAL AGENT'S DUTIES OF DILIGENCE

6-012   (1) Subject to circumstances indicating the contrary, a term will normally be implied into a contract of agency that the agent should carry out his obligations with reasonable dispatch. What is reasonable will depend on all the circumstances of the case.[54] In relation to agents who are not employees, a

---

[49] *Westpac New Zealand Ltd v Map & Associates Ltd* [2011] 3 N.Z.L.R. 751 (NZSC) (bank wrongly declining to transfer funds to customer's order).

[50] Thus a stockbroker was only required to carry out a sale of shares in accordance with the rules of the Stock Exchange and could not be required to act other than in accordance with those rules: *Hawkins v Pearse* (1903) 9 Com.Cas. 87; *Cunliffe-Owen v Teather & Greenwood* [1967] 1 W.L.R. 1421. A company liquidator is similarly an agent subject to external duties: *Dunphy v Sleepyhead Manufacturing Co Ltd* [2007] 3 N.Z.L.R. 602 at [22].

[51] *Ireland v Livingston* (1872) L.R. 5 H.L. 395, Illustration 1 to Article 24; *Comber v Anderson* (1808) 1 Camp. 523; *Bertram, Armstrong & Co v Godfrey* (1830) 1 Knapp. 381, Illustration 1 to Article 36; *Boden v French* (1851) 10 C.B. 886; *Cobridge SS Co Ltd v Bucknall SS Lines Ltd* (1910) 15 Com.Cas. 138; *Weigall & Co v Runciman & Co* (1916) 85 L.J.K.B. 1187, Illustration 3 to Article 26; *Pariente v Lubbock* (1856) 8 De G.M. & G. 5; *Lindsay, Gracie & Co v Barter & Co* (1885) 2 T.L.R. 4; *Loring v Davis* (1886) 32 Ch.D. 5; *Miles v Haslehurst & Co* (1906) 12 Com.Cas. 83; *International Paper Co v Spicer* (1906) 4 C.L.R. 739 at 751; *Larsen v Anglo-American Oil Co Ltd* (1924) 20 Lloyd's Rep. 40 at 67; *Brown & Gracie Ltd v F.W. Green & Co Pty Ltd* [1960] 1 Lloyd's Rep. 289. And see in general Article 26.

[52] See *Woodhouse A.C. Israel Cocoa Ltd SA v Nigerian Produce Marketing Co* [1972] A.C. 741; *Miles v Haslehurst & Co*, above; *Veljkovic v Vrybergen* [1985] V.R. 419 at 424.

[53] See the *Woodhouse A.C. Israel Cocoa* case, above, at 772; *European Asian Bank AG v Punjab and Sind Bank* [1983] 1 W.L.R. 652 at 656; *Veljkovic v Vrybergen*, above (request to "get insurance"); *Horsell International Pty Ltd v Divetwo Pty Ltd* [2013] NSWCA 368 at [238].

[54] *Varden v Parker* (1798) 2 Esp. 710; *Barber v Taylor* (1839) 5 M. & W. 527, Illustration 1; *Turpin v*

similar implied term may arise under the Supply of Goods and Services Act 1982 s.14.[55]

(2) If an agent appointed by a contract cannot, or will not, carry out his orders when instructed or within a reasonable time he must inform his principal.[56]

Comment

The principle expressed in this Article is part of the agent's duty to exercise the **6-013** required degree of care in and about the performance of his duties. It is also a general rule of contract that where no time for performance is stated, the contract must be performed within a reasonable time having regard to all the circumstances of the case.[57] It has been said that a stipulation as to the time of performance will prima facie not be held to be of the essence of a contract.[58] These and similar expressions do not mean that a time stipulation is merely a target date: if it is appropriately expressed, failure to comply would give rise to an action in damages.[59] The expression simply means that the contract cannot be treated as discharged for breach of that term as such. And the contract may expressly state[60] or be interpreted on the basis[61] that time is of the essence. Finally, in the case of the obligation to complete in transactions regarding land, and perhaps other obligations, and possibly outside land transactions also, one party can give notice requiring performance within a reasonable time, and failure to comply with this may entitle him to treat the contract as discharged.[62]

Bilton (1843) 5 M. & G. 455; *Potter v Equitable Bank* (1921) 8 Ll. L.Rep. 291 at 332; *World Transport Agency Ltd v Royte (England) Ltd* [1957] 1 Lloyd's Rep. 381; *Tom Hoskins Plc v EMW Law (A Firm)* [2010] EWHC 479 (Ch) (liability for consequential business losses as well as losses on transaction); *Equitas Ltd v Walsham Brothers & Co Ltd* [2013] EWHC 3264 (Comm) at [47] (duty to account timeously for moneys received).

[55] *Equitas Ltd v Walsham Brothers & Co Ltd* [2013] EWHC 3264 (Comm) at [51].

[56] *Smith v Lascelles* (1788) 2 T.R. 187; *Prince v Clark* (1823) 1 B. & C. 186; *Callander v Oelrichs* (1838) 5 Bing.N.C. 58, Illustration 2; *Smith v Price* (1862) 2 F. & F. 748; *Cassaboglou v Gibb* (1883) 11 Q.B.D. 797; *Tallerman v Rose* (1886) 15 L.T. 450; *Salvesen & Co v Rederi A/B Nordstjernan* [1905] A.C. 302; *Mark Lever & Co Ltd v W. Wingate & Johnson Ltd* (1950) 84 Lloyd's Rep. 156; *John Koch Ltd v C. & H. Products Ltd* [1956] 1 Lloyd's Rep. 59; *Havas v Carter*, 515 P. 2d 397 (1975); *Fine's Flowers Ltd v General Accident Ass. Co of Canada* (1977) 81 D.L.R. (3d) 139 at 149 (Illustration 3); *Volkers v Midland Doherty* (1985) 17 D.L.R. (4th) 393, Illustration 4; *Youell v Bland Welch & Co Ltd (the Superhulls Cover case) (No.2)* [1990] 2 Lloyd's Rep. 431 at 446–447.

[57] See, e.g. *Pantland Hick v Raymond & Reid* [1893] A.C. 22; *Sims & Co v Midland Ry Co* [1913] 1 K.B. 103; *Hartwells of Oxford Ltd v BMTA* [1951] Ch. 50; *Monkland v Jack Barclay Ltd* [1951] 2 K.B. 252.

[58] *United Scientific Holdings Ltd v Burnley BC* [1978] A.C. 904 at 940; Law of Property Act 1925 s.41. See Chitty, *Contracts* (32nd edn), para.21-011 onwards; Treitel, *Law of Contract* (14th edn), paras 18-086–18-099.

[59] *Raineri v Miles* [1981] A.C. 1050.

[60] *Steedman v Drinkle* [1916] 1 A.C. 275; *Brickles v Snell* [1916] 2 A.C. 599; *Harold Wood Brick Co v Ferris* [1935] 2 K.B. 198; *Mussen v Van Diemen's Land Co* [1938] Ch. 253.

[61] See, e.g. *Tilley v Thomas* (1867) L.R. 3 Ch.App. 61; *Tadcaster Tower Brewery v Wilson* [1897] 1 Ch. 705 at 710; *Lock v Bell* [1931] 1 Ch. 35; *Hare v Nicoll* [1966] 2 Q.B. 130. Stipulations as to time in mercantile contracts may well be of the essence: *Bunge Corp v Tradax Export SA* [1981] 1 W.L.R. 711 at 725; but stipulations as to the time of payment are not of the essence in a contract for the sale of goods unless a contrary intention appears from the contract: Sale of Goods Act 1979 s.10.

[62] See, e.g. *Stickney v Keeble* [1915] A.C. 386; *Finkielkraut v Monohan* [1949] 2 All E.R. 234; *Behzadi v Shaftesbury Hotels Ltd* [1992] Ch. 1; but cf. *Re Olympia & York Canary Wharf Ltd (No.2)* [1993] B.C.C. 159. As to other contracts see *Charles Rickards Ltd v Oppenhaim* [1950] 1 K.B. 616; Treitel, *Law of Contract* (14th edn), para.18-101 onwards.

6-014   **Estate and other canvassing agents**   On the traditional analysis, the normal contract of an estate agent is unilateral, i.e. the agent only earns commission by performing the act entitling him to it. Until then he is under no duty to act. He is only under such a duty if a bilateral contract can be inferred, which will normally be so if he is a "sole" or "exclusive" agent.[63] The same reasoning may be applied to other canvassing agents acting on commission. If this analysis is correct, the estate agent acting, or failing to act, in respect of such a contract cannot be liable under the reasoning given in this and the Article immediately following. An assertion of this sort was described in one case as "startling",[64] but no other reasoning was offered and the proposition is consistent with the assumptions behind this type of contract. But such an agent may be liable if a collateral contract can be inferred and the omission or conduct in question is a breach of it; or in tort, as where he gives negligent advice or a negligent valuation,[65] or if he can be regarded as having assumed responsibility and not carried through what he assumed[66] (as is also true in the case of gratuitous agents[67]); or sometimes for breach of fiduciary duty.[68]

6-015   **Dealing for competitors**   Whether an agent has undertaken to work full time and solely for his principal plainly turns on the terms of his appointment. More difficulty arises as to whether an agent can work for a competitor of his principal. This question also turns on the terms, express or implied, of the contract of appointment. There may be room too for the operation of equitable principles in this context[69]; including the issuing of an injunction prohibiting an employee from working for a competitor.[70] The issues that arise are not peculiar to agents. So, it frequently arises in connection with distributorship contracts whether the distributor is entitled to deal on behalf of the supplier's competitors, and this field is the source of considerable case law. Usually, the matter turns on an express contractual provision, or the inference to be drawn from other contractual provisions. Thus a promise to "push the sale" of a brand of whisky was not complied with by inaction and merely not preferring other brands, and was also broken in the circumstances by soliciting orders for other brands.[71] Where there were no clear terms, the Court of Session held that there is no principle that the agent will not "even in an outside matter" act in such a way as to bring his interests in conflict with those of his principal: thus an agent (perhaps a distributor) was entitled to deal also in competing products.[72] But an exclusive licensing and distributorship agreement requiring the agent to "make every endeavour" has been held terminable on the grounds that the agent sold similar products of competitors.[73] In a leading Australian case it was held that there was no term to be implied that a distributor would not do anything "inimical" to the

---

[63]   See Comment to Article 56.

[64]   *Prebble & Co v West* (1969) 211 E.G. 831 at 832, per Edmund Davies LJ.

[65]   *Kenney v Hall, Pain & Foster* [1976] E.G.D. 629, Illustration 6 to Article 40.

[66]   See *Henderson v Merrett Syndicates Ltd* [1995] 2 A.C. 145, per Lord Goff of Chieveley. But this reasoning may not easily extend to pure nonfeasance: below, para.6-029.

[67]   Article 42.

[68]   See Articles 44–49.

[69]   See *Hospital Products Ltd v United States Surgical Corp* (1984) 156 C.L.R. 41, per Mason J; cf. *Cadbury Schweppes Inc v FBI Foods Ltd* [1999] 1 S.C.R. 142; (1999) 167 D.L.R. (4th) 577; and see Article 43 onwards.

[70]   See *Sunrise Brokers LLP v Rodgers* [2014] EWCA Civ 1373; [2015] I.C.R. 272.

[71]   *B. Davis Ltd v Tooth & Co Ltd* [1937] 4 All E.R. 118. And see *James Shaffer Ltd v Findlay Durham & Brodie* [1953] 1 W.L.R. 106.

[72]   *Lothian v Jenolite Ltd* 1969 S.C. 111.

[73]   *Re Arbitration between Deb Chemical Proprietaries Ltd and Dreumex Chemie BV*, QBD, November

market for the manufacturer's products, since a "best efforts" obligation to distribute them made this unnecessary. But it was also held that it was a breach of contract to defer fulfilling orders for the manufacturer's products in anticipation of fulfilling them himself.[74]

In relation to agents, it has recently been held that the starting point is that agents appointed to sell a type of product are not expected to be acting for competing principals in the same market.[75] On the other hand, in the case of estate agents[76] and travel agents,[77] it may be expected that they will be acting for competing principals in the same market. However, a principal should not have to anticipate that an agent might wish to act for parties with opposed interests in the same transaction, and the agent's consequent failure to do his best for a principal is likely to lead to liability in contract, negligence and, at least where disloyalty is present, in equity.[78] It is an unsettled issue whether non-executive company directors may, in the absence of express prohibition, hold office with competing businesses.[79] Executive directors would normally be expected to devote all their time to the one company, and certainly not work for competitors.[80] The duties of disclosure that can arise when certain types of agent are planning to resign and compete with their principal are dealt with elsewhere.[81]

Illustrations

(1) P instructed A to purchase 150 bales of cotton for P's account and to send him **6-016** the bill of lading. A failed to release the bill of lading to P for some days after the arrival of the goods in the United Kingdom. He was held to have been in

2, 1979; European Law Letter, Feb. 1980, p.4.
[74] *Hospital Products Ltd v United States Surgical Corp* (1984) 156 C.L.R. 41; but cf. *Artifakts Design Group Ltd v N.P. Rigg Ltd* [1993] 1 N.Z.L.R. 196.
[75] See *Rossetti Marketing Ltd v Diamond Sofa Co Ltd* [2012] EWCA Civ 1021; [2013] 1 All E.R. (Comm) 308 at [20]; *The Northampton Regional Livestock Centre Co Ltd v Cowling* [2014] EWHC 30 (QB) at [178], varied on other points [2015] EWCA Civ 651. cf. *One Mail Money Ltd v RIA Financial Services* [2015] EWCA Civ 1084 at [5] (restraint of trade doctrine can in rare circumstances protect liberty of someone still employed by the promisee).
[76] *Kelly v Cooper* [1993] A.C. 205 (PC), Illustration 9 to Article 43; *Colyer Fehr Tallow Pty Ltd v KNZ Australia Pty Ltd* [2011] NSWSC 457 (purchasing agent). See further below, para.6-048. But cf. *JD Wetherspoon Plc v Van De Berg & Co Ltd* [2009] EWHC 639 (Ch) (purchaser's agent found to be precluded from acting for competitors).
[77] See *ACCC v Flight Centre Travel Group Ltd* [2016] HCA 49 (in fact concerned with the principal's rights to compete with its agents in the sale of tickets).
[78] *Hilton v Barker, Booth & Eastwood (a firm)* [2005] 1 W.L.R. 567; *HIH Casualty & General Insurance Ltd v JLT Risk Solutions Ltd* [2007] EWCA Civ 710; [2007] 2 Lloyd's Rep. 278; [2007] 2 All E.R. (Comm) 1106; and *Premium Real Estate Ltd v Stevens* [2009] 2 N.Z.L.R. 384; *The Northampton Regional Livestock Centre Co Ltd v Cowling* [2015] EWCA Civ 651; [2016] 1 B.C.L.C. 431. See further below, para.6-048.
[79] Compare *Mashonaland Exploration Co Ltd v New Mashonaland Exploration Co Ltd* [1891] W.N. 165 with *In Plus Group Ltd v Pyke* [2002] EWCA Civ 370; [2002] 2 B.C.L.C. 201. See too *Links Golf Tasmania Pty Ltd v Sattler* [2012] FCA 634; (2012) 292 A.L.R. 382 at [575] (potential breach recognised but director had resigned before competing business commenced earning revenue); and *Poon Ka Man v Cheng Wai Tao* [2016] HKCFA 23 at [104].
[80] *Hivac v Park Royal Scientific Instruments Ltd* [1946] Ch. 169; *Breitenfeld UK Ltd v Harrison* [2015] EWHC 399 (Ch); [2015] 2 B.C.L.C. 275 at [90] (employees diverting work to their own new business). As to what is a competitor in this context, see *Plumbly v Beatthatquote.com Ltd* [2009] EWHC 321 (QB) at [118]; *Gamatronic (UK) Ltd v Hamilton* [2016] EWHC 2225 (QB) at [95].
[81] See below, para.6-054.

breach of contract in failing to send the bill to P within a reasonable time, which was within 24 hours of the arrival of the goods.[82]

(2) P, a merchant in England, instructed A, his correspondent in America, to effect an insurance on certain special terms upon a cargo of wheat to be shipped by P from London to Baltimore. A tried in vain to effect an insurance on the special terms requested and eventually, without informing P, insured on the usual terms. Held that A was in breach of duty in failing to tell P that he could not carry out P's instructions relating to special insurance.[83]

(3) An insurance broker is instructed to obtain "full coverage". He obtains cover for a number of risks but not for those which in fact occurred. He is liable for failure to obtain the cover promised; or alternatively, for failure to warn that he had not obtained it.[84]

(4) A representative of a firm of stockbrokers is instructed at 4.30 p.m. to buy a quantity of designated stock "at the market price first thing in the morning". He accepts the instructions but does not carry them out when he arrives at 7 a.m. because he thinks it more prudent to wait for the arrival of the representative who usually deals with that customer. That representative arrives between 8.30 and 9 a.m., at which time the order is referred to him. But at 8.45 a.m. dealings in the shares are suspended, and when they are resumed the shares have doubled in price. The firm is liable to the client for loss of profits.[85]

Article 40

CONTRACTUAL AGENT'S DUTY TO EXERCISE SKILL AND CARE

6-017   Every agent acting for reward is bound to exercise such skill, care and diligence in the performance of his undertaking as is usual or necessary in or for the ordinary or proper conduct of the profession or business in which he is employed, or is reasonably necessary for the proper performance of the duties undertaken by him.[86]

Comment

6-018   **Contract, tort or both?**   A gratuitous agent's liability, if any, cannot lie in contract and must clearly lie in tort.[87] Where the agency is contractual, however, it is obvious that the primary action is one for breach of contract. Where what is alleged is negligence, as it often is, the question then arises whether it is possible to sue in tort instead of contract. There may be advantages in doing so, particularly in connec-

---

[82]   *Barber v Taylor* (1839) 5 M. & W. 527.

[83]   *Callander v Oelrichs* (1838) 5 Bing.N.C. 58 (but see the criticism of the case on the question of damages in Duer, *Law and Practice of Marine Insurance* (1845), Vol. 2, pp.222–225). See also *Hood v West End Motor Car Parking Co* [1917] 2 K.B. 38 at 47: "When a person is instructed to procure an insurance he is bound to use reasonable care and skill to effect the policy. If he is unable to procure the policy, he must at once inform his principal of his inability to do so".

[84]   *Fine's Flowers v General Accident Co of Canada* (1977) 81 D.L.R. (3d) 139; see also *Youell v Bland Welch & Co Ltd (the Superhulls Cover case) (No.2)* [1990] 2 Lloyd's Rep. 431 (failure to inform assured that reinsurance subject to 48-month cut-off); *Standard Life Assurance Ltd v Oak Dedicated Ltd* [2008] EWHC 222 (Comm); [2008] 2 All E.R. (Comm) 916 at [102] (proffering inadequate wording to underwriter); *Marchand v Jackson* [2012] NZHC 2893.

[85]   *Volkers v Midland Doherty* (1985) 17 D.L.R. (4th) 343. See also *R.H. Deacon & Co v Varga* (1972) 30 D.L.R. (3d) 653; affd (1973) 41 D.L.R. (4th) 767n.

[86]   cf. *Restatement, Third*, § 8.08.

[87]   See Article 42.

tion with the running of limitation periods. For in contract time runs from the moment of the breach (but the position is different if there is an ongoing duty of performance); in tort, since the gist of the action is damage, it runs from when damage is suffered.[88] The matter has been one of dispute for a considerable time in common law jurisdictions. For England, it is clear that an action in tort may concurrently lie in some circumstances,[89] with the incidental advantages that this may bring.[90]

Degree of skill and care The degree of skill and care which may be expected of **6-019** an agent acting for reward has been stated many times.[91] It is objective but its content and scope are governed by the particular responsibility assumed by the agent.[92] An agent employed for the purpose of effecting a contract between the principal and a third party must use due skill and care in making that contract. Thus, a broker is under a duty not to sell goods at less than the best obtainable price[93] and an estate agent must use reasonable care to ascertain the general solvency of tenants.[94] Agents must use proper care to ensure that contracts they make are binding in law.[95] An agent does not, however, guarantee the contract; his duty is to exercise reasonable care in making it.

Many agents for reward will be professional agents. They must show the skill and care to be expected of those engaged in such a profession.[96] Not only must they be adequately qualified; they must take reasonable care to keep themselves up to date

---

[88] Some relief is provided by Limitation Act 1980 s.2.

[89] *Henderson v Merrett Syndicates Ltd* [1995] 2 A.C. 145. See also *Midland Bank Trust Co Ltd v Hett, Stubbs & Kemp* [1979] Ch. 384, holding a solicitor liable in contract and tort, the reasoning of which was approved in the *Henderson* case; *Equitas Ltd v Walsham Brothers & Co Ltd* [2013] EWHC 3264 (Comm) at [57]; *Berney v Saul (t/a Thomas Saul & Co)* [2013] EWCA Civ 640 (limitation issues); *Maharaj v Johnson* [2015] UKPC 28 (solicitors' negligence); *Central Trust Co v Rafuse* [1986] 2 S.C.R. 147; (1986) 31 D.L.R. (4th) 481 (Canada); *Hill v van Erp* (1997) 188 C.L.R. 159 (Australia); *R.M. Turton & Co v Kerslake & Partners* [2000] 3 N.Z.L.R. 406 (New Zealand); *Wellesley Partners LLP v Withers LLP* [2015] EWCA Civ 1146; *Caliendo v Mishcon De Reya (a firm)* [2016] EWHC 150 (Ch) (solicitor assumed limited duties of care to shareholder of client company). See too *Arthur JS Hall & Co v Simons* [2002] 1 A.C. 615 at 688. As to tortious liability for exceeding mandate, see above, para.6-005.

[90] As to the pleading of contributory negligence in contract cases see Treitel, *Law of Contract* (14th edn), para.20-126 onwards; Chitty, *Contracts* (32nd edn), para.26-077; *Forsikringsaktieselskapet Vesta v Butcher* [1986] 2 All E.R. 488; affd on other grounds [1989] A.C. 852; *Youell v Bland Welch & Co Ltd (the Superhulls Cover case) (No.2)* [1990] 2 Lloyd's Rep. 431; and *Dunlop Haywards (DHL) Ltd v Barbon Insurance Group Ltd* [2009] EWHC 2900 (Comm); [2010] Lloyd's Rep I.R. 149 (not established against principal, but established by sub-agent against agent).

[91] See, e.g. *Beal v South Devon Ry Co* (1864) 3 H. & C. 337 at 341 for the classical statement which forms the basis of this Article. See also *Boorman v Brown* (1842) 3 Q.B. 511; *Price v Metropolitan House Investment and Agency Co Ltd* (1907) 23 T.L.R. 630; *Commonwealth Portland Cement Co Ltd v Weber, Lohmann & Co Ltd* [1905] A.C. 66, Illustration 8; *Weld-Blundell v Stevens* [1920] A.C. 956; *Whitehouse v Jordan* [1981] 1 W.L.R. 246; *Maynard v West Midlands RHA* [1984] 1 W.L.R. 632.

[92] See *Hughes-Holland v BPE Solicitors* [2017] UKSC 21; [2017] 2 W.L.R. 1029 at [20].

[93] *Solomon v Barker* (1862) 2 F. & F. 726. For other cases see Stoljar, p.274, fn.31.

[94] *Heys v Tindall* (1861) 1 B. & S. 296, Illustration 5. See also *Carlile Steamship Co v Simpson, Spence & Young* (1926) 25 Lloyd's Rep. 278; *Dampskibsselskab Halla v Catsell & Co* (1928) 30 Lloyd's Rep. 284.

[95] *Grant v Fletcher* (1826) 5 B. & C. 436; *Neilson v James* (1882) 9 Q.B.D. 546; *Scott and Horton v Godfrey* [1901] 2 K.B. 726; *Rainbow v Howkins & Sons* [1904] 2 K.B. 322; *McManus v Fortescue* [1907] 2 K.B. 1.

[96] *Lanphier v Phipos* (1838) 8 C. & P. 475; *Hart and Hodge v Frame, Son & Co* (1839) 6 C. & F. 193; *Lee v Walker* (1872) L.R. 7 C.P. 121; *New Zealand Farmers Cooperative Ltd v National Mortgage*

with current developments in their profession.[97] Their duty is not, however, to make no mistakes; it is only to use the required degree of care. In the case of agents other than employees, an implied obligation of care and skill may arise under the Supply of Goods and Services Act 1982 s.13.[98]

6-020   **Discretion**   If the agent has a discretion to exercise he must, in general, use proper care and skill in doing so. Thus a solicitor may compromise a case in the absence of instructions to the contrary from his principal, but he must exercise proper care and skill in arranging the compromise.[99] A similar situation may arise where an agent cannot obtain instructions from his principal but some action has to be taken by him. If he acts in a way which he reasonably considers to be in the principal's best interests and exercises the proper degree of care he will not be liable.[100] Where the terms of appointment expressly confer on an agent a "complete discretion" in making decisions as to when and how powers are to be exercised, the terms are generally construed as leading to liability only where the agent has acted with "arbitrariness, capriciousness, perversity [or] irrationality".[101] Similarly, a company's constitution may provide that any validly appointed proxy is entitled to vote on resolutions at the relevant meeting as he thinks fit unless the appointing shareholder expressly directs how the proxy should vote.[102] Where the relevant powers of action of the agent arise upon default by the principal in its obligations to the agent, again it may be inappropriate to imply duties of care and skill in the exercise of those powers.[103]

6-021   **Information**[104]   An agent is, in general,[105] under a duty to keep his principal informed about matters which are of his concern.[106] Thus, a solicitor must inform

---

     and Agency Co of New Zealand Ltd [1961] N.Z.L.R. 969; *Duchess of Argyll v Beuselinck* [1972] 2 Lloyd's Rep. 172; *Wimpey Construction UK Ltd v Poole* [1984] 2 Lloyd's Rep. 499. See further Article 30.

[97] See *Park v Hammond* (1816) 6 Taunt. 495, Illustration 2; a fortiori a solicitor must take reasonable care to keep himself abreast with changes in the law; *Hurlingham Estates Ltd v Wilde & Partners* [1997] 1 Lloyd's Rep. 525; *Dean v Allin & Watts* [2001] 2 Lloyd's Rep. 249.

[98] *Equitas Ltd v Walsham Brothers & Co Ltd* [2013] EWHC 3264 (Comm) at [51].

[99] *Chown v Parrott* (1863) 14 C.B.(N.S.) 74; *Langsam v Beachcroft LLP* [2012] EWCA Civ 1230 at [84]. See above, para.6-003; Article 30, Illustration 5.

[100] *Moore v Mourgue* (1776) 2 Cowp. 479; *Smith v Cologan* (1786) 2 T.R. 188n.; *East India Co v Henchman* (1791) 1 Ves.Jun. 287; *Gwatkin v Campbell* (1854) 1 Jur.(N.S.) 131; *Lagunas Nitrate v Lagunas Syndicate* [1899] 2 Ch. 392; *Morten v Hilton, Gibbes & Smith* (1908), reported in [1937] 2 K.B. 176n. (HL), Illustration 9; *Re Cobridge and Bucknall SS Lines Ltd* (1910) 15 Com.Cas. 138; *Gokal Chand-Jagan Nath v Nand Ram Das-Atma Ram* [1939] A.C. 106.

[101] See *Elidor Investments SA v Christie's, Mansons Woods Ltd* [2009] EWHC 3600 (QB), citing *Socimer International Bank Ltd v Standard Bank London Ltd* [2008] EWCA Civ 116; [2008] 1 Lloyd's Rep. 558 at [66] (advertising for auction); *Torre Asset Funding Ltd v The Royal Bank of Scotland Plc* [2013] EWHC 2670 (Ch) at [37].

[102] *Horler v Rubin* [2012] EWCA Civ 4 at [21].

[103] *Euroption Strategic Fund Ltd v Skandinaviska Enskilda Banken AB* [2012] EWHC 584 (Comm) at [129].

[104] cf. *Restatement, Third*, § 8.11.

[105] For one potential exception, see the Proceeds of Crimes Act 2002 s.333, in relation to moneylaundering, briefly discussed in *Shah v HSBC Private Bank (UK) Ltd* [2010] EWCA Civ 31 at [37]–[39]; *Shah v HSBC Bank (UK) Ltd* [2012] EWHC 1283 (QB); [2012] 1 All E.R. (Comm) 72 at [172].

[106] See *Ocean City Realty Ltd v A & M Holdings Ltd* (1987) 36 D.L.R. (4th) 94 at 98; *John D Wood & Co (Residential & Agricultural) Ltd v Knatchbull* [2002] EWHC 2822; [2003] 1 E.G.L.R. 33 (Illustration 6); *Premium Real Estate Ltd v Stevens* [2009] 2 N.Z.L.R. 384.

his client of any overtures of settlement[107] and a broker must inform his principal of any contracts made on his behalf.[108] An estate agent must notify his principal of offers received up to the time of exchange of contracts.[109] A ship's agent must likewise inform his principal of any facts which the principal ought to know in order to make full disclosure to underwriters.[110] Moreover, an insurance broker owes a special duty of disclosure, not only to his principal but to the underwriters. This duty, for breach of which he may be liable to his principal, arises from the nature of the insurance contract, which is uberrimae fidei.[111] A solicitor or other agent in a position of conflict of interest cannot normally use the conflict as an excuse for not passing on information relevant to the retainer to a principal.[112] As always, the scope of an agent's duties is governed by the terms and context of any contract between the principal and agent, and there will be cases where mere neglect to pass on information will not create liability.[113] As to duties to keep records of transactions, see below, para.6-093, and as to equitable duties of disclosure, see para.6-054.

Special skill   Some agents may be regarded as holding themselves out as possessed of special skills. In such cases it would seem that the standard of care which they owe should be higher. Thus in one case where a provincial auctioneer was held not liable for failure to recognise pictures possibly by Stubbs, the decision was affected by the fact that they were described "general practitioners"[114]: it would seem that a person offering more specialised skills should be liable if they are not exercised.[115]   **6-022**

Illegal conduct   Difficult issues arise where an agent has acted illegally. It will be   **6-023** rare that an agent will have implied authority to act illegally,[116] and without authority the agent may be liable to compensate the principal where the principal is not directly complicit in the illegality but suffers loss as a result of the conduct.[117] The mere fact that the principal is attributed with responsibility for the agent's illegal-

---

[107] *Sill v Thomas* (1839) 8 C. & P. 762. For more recent examples see *McKaskell v Benseman* [1989] 1 N.Z.L.R. 75 (offensive letter from solicitors acting for other side); *Waimond Pty Ltd v Byrne* (1989) 18 N.S.W.L.R. 642 (failure to guard interests of client when they were prejudiced by another client).

[108] *Johnson v Kearley* [1908] 2 K.B. 514. See also *Dampskibsselskab Halla v Catsell & Co* (1928) 30 Lloyd's Rep. 284; *Dunton Properties Ltd v Coles, Knapp & Kennedy* (1959) 174 E.G. 723.

[109] *Keppel v Wheeler* [1927] 1 K.B. 577, Illustration 6 to Article 60; see also Estate Agents (Undesirable Practices) (No.2) Order 1991 (SI 1991/1032) Sch.3 para.2.

[110] *Proudfoot v Montefiore* (1867) L.R. 2 Q.B. 511.

[111] See Marine Insurance Act 1906 s.19, and *Blackburn Low & Co v Vigors* (1887) 12 App.Cas. 531 at 537, 541. A broker may also owe a duty to its client to inform the client of its duties of disclosure to the insurer: *Involnert Management Inc v Aprilgrange Ltd* [2015] EWHC 2225 (Comm) at [318].

[112] *Hilton v Barker Booth & Eastwood* [2005] UKHL 8; [2005] 1 W.L.R. 567; *Mortgage Express Ltd v Bowerman & Partners* [1996] 2 All E.R. 836; *Goldsmith Williams Solicitors v E.Surv Ltd* [2015] EWCA Civ 1147; [2016] 4 W.L.R. 44. See further below, para.6-048.

[113] See, e.g. *National Home Loans Corp Plc v Giffen Couch & Archer* [1998] 1 W.L.R. 207 (default on existing mortgage not reported to client lender but existing credit performance of debtor not within instructions); *Torre Asset Funding Ltd v The Royal Bank of Scotland Plc* [2013] EWHC 2670 (Ch) at [156] (agent in syndicated lending had assumed limited duties, and was not required to assess whether an event of default by a borrower had occurred in order to inform principals).

[114] *Luxmoore-May v Messenger May Baverstock* [1990] 1 W.L.R. 1009 at 1020.

[115] See *Duchess of Argyll v Beuselinck* [1972] 2 Lloyd's Rep. 172 at 183–184; but cf. *Wimpey Construction UK Ltd v Poole* [1984] 2 Lloyd's Rep. 499 at 506.

[116] See further above, para.2-026.

[117] See *Bilta (UK) Ltd v Nazir* [2015] UKSC 23; [2016] A.C. 1 at [42]–[43], [130], [160] and [191]. See too *Safeway Stores Ltd v Twigger* [2010] EWHC 11 (Comm) (action against directors and

ity for some purposes ought not to preclude the principal's suing the agent for breach of mandate or other breach of contract. Even where there is evidence that a principal has in fact given some discretion to act illegally, the exercise of the discretion without due cause may not preclude an action by the principal against the agent. In cases, however, where there was some colour of right to the action taken by the agent, there may not be the want of due care necessary for liability. A principal may also be taken to have warranted that his instructions are lawful.[118] Further, where the principal or a duly authorised senior agent expressly authorised, or acquiesced in, the agent's illegal conduct then it is unlikely that the agent will be liable for breach of contract because there will not have been a breach. It is possible too that any action brought by the principal against the agent could be barred by the ex turpi maxim.[119] In some circumstances too it may be contrary to the policy of the particular rule infringed for the principal to be compensated for loss.[120] Authority, however, holds that an agent who is given money by a principal for the purpose of illegal gaming remains accountable for any winnings.[121] The fact that former agents of the principal have caused it to engage in, and be responsible for, unlawful activity cannot excuse a later agent's unconnected acts of negligence or other breaches of duty.[122]

Where the principal is a company, the company will not automatically be treated as knowing and condoning illegal conduct even where its senior management is apprised of it, especially where the question is the liability to the company of that senior management for engaging in the conduct.[123]

Illustrations

6-024   (1)   "[A solicitor's liability] is the same as anybody else's liability; having regard to the degree of skill held out to the public by solicitors, does the conduct of the solicitor fall short of the standard which the public had been led to expect of the solicitor?"[124] A solicitor "is bound to bring a fair and reasonable amount of skill to the performance of his professional duty".[125] A solicitor who is being instructed to draft a contract by an agent of the client should bring to the

---

[118] employees for causing company to engage in unlawful competitive action), reversed on point of statutory construction: [2010] EWCA Civ 1472; [2011] 1 Lloyd's Rep. 462.

[118] See *Strongman v Sincock* [1955] 2 Q.B. 525. See also above, para.6-009.

[119] See, e.g. *Nayyar v Sapte* [2009] EWHC 3218 (QB) (principal authorises and funds agent to pay bribe). As to the agent's rights against the principal, see Article 61.

[120] See *Safeway Stores Ltd v Twigger* [2010] EWCA Civ 1472; [2011] 1 Lloyd's Rep. 462 (this surprising result is discussed in Watts [2011] J.B.L. 213). cf. *Griffin v Uhy Hacker Young & Partners (a firm)* [2010] EWHC 146 (Ch) (accountants). See further, paras 3-035 and 6-009.

[121] *De Mattos v Benjamin* (1894) 63 L.J.Q.B. 248; *Cheshire (Thomas) & Co v Vaughan Bros & Co* [1920] 3 K.B. 240; *Jeffrey v Bamford* [1921] 2 K.B. 351; *Close v Wilson* [2011] EWCA Civ 5. The position may be otherwise where the claimant needs to rely on a contractual claim, the contract being illegal: *Close v Wilson*, above.

[122] *Sharma v Top Brands Ltd* [2015] EWCA Civ 1140; [2016] P.N.L.R. 12 (liquidator of company the business of which largely involved VAT fraud not excused for negligence in paying away remaining funds).

[123] *Bilta (UK) Ltd v Nazir* [2015] UKSC 23; [2016] A.C. 1 at [42]–[43], [130], [160] and [191].

[124] *Simmons v Pennington* [1955] 1 W.L.R. 183 at 188, per Hodson LJ, citing with approval this dictum from a judgment of Harman J (unreported). See too *Tom Hoskins Plc v EMW Law (a firm)* [2010] EWHC 479 (Ch).

[125] *Parker v Rolls* (1854) 14 C.B. 691 at 695, per Talfourd J. See in general Cordery, *Solicitors*, Ch.6. A solicitor may be liable to others than his client: *White v Jones* [1995] 2 A.C. 207 (prospective beneficiary); and if he acts for those on both sides of a transaction (e.g. a conveyance) he may owe duties to both: *Mortgage Express Ltd v Bowerman & Partners* [1996] 2 All E.R. 836.

client's notice provisions in respect of which the agent has a conflict of interest.[126]

(2)   An insurance broker is bound to exercise reasonable and proper care, skill and judgment in obtaining a policy to cover his principal's interests and protecting his principal generally in relation to the underwriters.[127] The expert evidence of other brokers may be called to prove what is the requisite standard of care. A broker is bound to keep himself up to date on the current developments of the law relating at least to that part of the business of insurance with which he is concerned.[128] If he does give advice on points of insurance law generally he must take reasonable care to ensure that such advice is correct.[129] He must act with due speed in obtaining insurance cover[130] and if he cannot obtain such cover he must at once inform his principal.[131] He may be liable if he erroneously and negligently informs his principal that cover is unobtainable, with the result that the principal does not make further attempts to obtain it.[132] He may also be liable in tort to others than his client.[133] A broker may be found to have undertaken ongoing duties to advise as to the suitability of cover earlier obtained if relevant facts come to light.[134] Similar duties are owed by investment brokers who advise and act for clients in the acquisition of investments.[135]

(3)   A patent agent is "bound to bring reasonable and ordinary care and

---

[126] *Newcastle International Airport Ltd v Eversheds LLP* [2013] EWCA Civ 1514 at [80].

[127] *Chapman v Walton* (1833) 10 Bing. 57; *Osman v J. Ralph Moss Ltd* [1970] 1 Lloyd's Rep. 313; *Claude R. Ogden & Co Pty Ltd v Reliance Fire Sprinkler Co Pty Ltd* [1975] 1 Lloyd's Rep. 52; *Fine's Flowers v General Accident Assurance Co of Canada* (1977) 81 D.L.R. (3d) 139; *Warren v Henry Sutton & Co* [1976] 2 Lloyd's Rep. 276; *Cherry v Allied Insurance Brokers Ltd* [1978] 1 Lloyd's Rep. 274; *McNealy v Pennine Insurance Co Ltd* [1978] 2 Lloyd's Rep. 18; cf. *O'Connor v B.D. Kirby & Co* [1972] 1 Q.B. 90; *Provincial Insurance Australia Pty Ltd v Wood Products Pty Ltd* (1991) 25 N.S.W.L.R. 541 at 556 ("go through with the insured the list of exceptions in the policy secured"); *FNCB Ltd v Barnet Devanney & Co Ltd* [1999] 2 All E.R. (Comm) 233; *Ground Gilbey Ltd v Jardine Lloyd Thompson UK Ltd* [2011] EWHC 124 (Comm); [2011] P.N.L.R. 15; [2012] Lloyd's Rep. I.R. 12 at [73]; *Synergy Health (UK) Ltd v CGU Insurance Plc (t/a Norwich Union)* [2010] EWHC 2583 (Comm); [2011] Lloyd's Rep I.R. 500 at [204] (duty to advise principal as to what types of information must be disclosed to insurer to avoid rescission for non-disclosure); *Horsell International Pty Ltd v Divetwo Pty Ltd* [2013] NSWCA 368 at [235]. A broker cannot be excused from his duty to advise by reason of a conflict of interest: *HIH Casualty & General Insurance Ltd v JLT Risk Solutions Ltd* [2007] EWCA Civ 710; [2007] 2 Lloyd's Rep. 278; [2007] 2 All E.R. (Comm) 1106 (see below, para.6-048).

[128] *Park v Hammond* (1816) 6 Taunt. 495; *The Ultra Processor* (1983) Lloyd's Maritime Law Newsletter, September 15, 1983 (SC, BC); *Provincial Insurance Australia Pty Ltd v Consolidated Wood Products Pty Ltd*, above, at 556 ("pointing out legal pitfalls").

[129] *Sarginson Bros v Keith Moulton & Co* (1942) 73 Ll.Rep. 104. See too *Horsell International Pty Ltd v Divetwo Pty Ltd* [2013] NSWCA 368 at [238].

[130] *Turpin v Bilton* (1843) 5 M. & G. 455. See further above, para.6-014.

[131] See Article 61. See also *Youell v Bland Welch & Co Ltd (the Superhulls Cover case) (No.2)* [1990] 2 Lloyd's Rep. 431 at 445. As to insurance brokers generally see *MacGillivray on Insurance Law* (13th edn), Chs 36 and 37; Clarke, *Law of Insurance Contracts* (6th edn), Ch.9; Hodgin, *Insurance Intermediaries: Law and Regulation* (1992).

[132] *Sarginson Bros v Keith Moulton & Co*, above; *Markal Investments Ltd v Morley Shafron Agencies Ltd* (1987) 44 D.L.R. (4th) 745.

[133] *Punjab National Bank v de Boinville* [1992] 1 W.L.R. 1138 (to assignee of policy).

[134] *Ground Gilbey Ltd v Jardine Lloyd Thompson UK Ltd* [2011] EWHC 124 (Comm); [2011] P.N.L.R. 15; [2012] Lloyd's Rep. I.R. 12 at [73].

[135] *Wingecarribee Shire Council v Lehman Brothers Australia Ltd* [2012] FCA 1028; (2013) 301 A.L.R. 1 at [787]–[789].

knowledge to the performance of his duty as such skilled agent".[136] He is bound to know and keep abreast of the most recent decisions of the courts relating to the business of obtaining patents.[137]

(4) Brokers who are employed to sell goods are bound to employ due care and diligence in obtaining the best available price.[138]

(5) An estate agent was employed to let houses and was paid a commission of 5 per cent for doing so. It was held that he was bound to use reasonable care to ascertain the solvency of the tenants[139]:

> "The house agent must use reasonable care and diligence in ascertaining the condition of a person before he introduces him to the landlord as a tenant. It cannot be supposed that the commission of 5 per cent is to be paid for only putting the name of the owner and the particulars of the premises upon the house agent's books for the information of those who may come to make inquiries at his office."[140]

(6) An estate agent suggests a "reasonable asking price" of £100,000 to a prospective seller of land. He is then asked to act for the seller and does not suggest any change to the asking price. The advice was negligent. He is liable for negligent valuation when the seller buys another property at a price which proves ruinous when the original land can only be sold for £36,000.[141]

(7) In the case of an ordinary commercial transaction a freight forwarder will not be negligent if he fails to insure the goods.[142] But in the case of a transaction involving a private individual where the goods are known to be valuable the agent may be negligent if he neither insures the goods nor refers immediately to his principal for instructions.[143] In the former instance he may expect his principals to have made their own arrangements for insurance. In the latter case the principal may well not have made any such arrangements. The agent may well also be liable if he fails to make appropriate claims against the carrier.[144]

---

[136] *Lee v Walker* (1872) L.R. 7 C.P. 121 at 125, per Brett J. See *Arbiter Group Plc v Gill Jennings & Every* [2001] R.P.C. 67.

[137] *Lee v Walker*, above.

[138] *Solomon v Barker* (1862) 2 F. & F. 726. See also *Grant v Fletcher* (1826) 5 B. & C. 436; *Sivewright v Richardson* (1852) 19 L.T.(O.S.) 10; *Alexander & Co v Wilson Holgate & Co* (1923) 14 Ll.Rep. 538.

[139] *Heys v Tindall* (1861) 1 B. & S. 296; and see *P.G. Prebble & Co v West* (1969) 211 E.G. 831; *Brutton v Alfred Savill, Curtis & Henson* [1971] E.G.D. 497; *Faruk v Wyse* [1988] 2 E.G.L.R. 26; *Messenger v Stanaway Real Estate Ltd* [2015] NZHC 1795; (2015) 16 N.Z. Conv. P.R. 335 (failure to draft for security on sale of land with deferred payment).

[140] *Heys v Tindall*, above, at 298, per Cockburn CJ arguendo. As to the liability of an exclusive agent for not trying hard enough, see *Styles v Rogers Realty Ltd* (1987) 43 D.L.R. (4th) 629; *Commissioner of Taxation v Byrne Hotels Queensland Pty Ltd* [2011] FCAFC 127 at [113]. See further as to estate agents Murdoch, *Law of Estate Agency* (5th edn), p.52 onwards.

[141] *Kenney v Hall, Pain & Foster* [1976] E.G.D. 629; see Brazier (1977) 41 Conv. 233. The "asking price" may also be too low: *John D. Wood & Co v Knatchbull* [2002] EWHC 2822; [2003] 1 E.G.L.R. 33 (reasonable when set, but agent should have advised of subsequent change in market).

[142] *W.L.R. Traders (London) Ltd v British & Northern Shipping Agency and Leftley Ltd* [1955] 1 Lloyd's Rep. 554; *Club Speciality (Overseas) Inc v United Marine (1939) Ltd* [1971] 1 Lloyd's Rep. 482. See also Hill, *Freight Forwarders* (1974); *British Shipping Laws*, Vol.13, 635–656; Scrutton, *Charterparties* (23rd edn), pp.93–96, *Contracts for Carriage of Goods* (Yates ed., 1993), Ch.7, "Freight Forwarders"; Bugden, *Goods in Transit* (3rd edn).

[143] *Von Traubenberg v Davies, Turner & Co Ltd* [1951] 2 Lloyd's Rep. 462.

[144] *Marbrook Freight Ltd v K.M.I. (London) Ltd* [1979] 2 Lloyd's Rep. 341.

(8)   A contracted to lighter and load certain machinery, and pass it through the customhouse. It was common knowledge that import duties were about to be imposed on machinery, and A might have cleared it in time to escape the taxation, but did not do so, though he cleared it within the time prescribed by the customs regulations. In an action against A for the amount of the duty paid, it was held that there was no evidence to go to the jury of any negligence or breach of duty for which he would be liable.[145]

(9)   Stockbrokers who were speculating on P's instructions had to know from P before the end of the accounting period which of P's accounts to close and which to leave open. They were unable to obtain instructions from P and so they closed some and left others open, exercising their discretion in what they considered to be in P's interests. In fact it would have been better to have closed all the accounts, and P sued them for negligence. Held, that they had acted reasonably and in P's best interests[146]:

> "I think brokers so situated were not only entitled but bound to carry through the transaction in the reasonable way they honestly thought most to the advantage of their principal and themselves, and that they did so. These considerations dispose of the case."[147]

(10) An auctioneer who sells goods has no duty to get in the price, even though he has the right to sue for it.[148] An auctioneer asked to express a view on the sale of pictures is liable for the negligence of a valuer whose advice he seeks and transmits to the client; but the formation of a wrong view may not be negligent.[149]

Article 41

Not Liable to Principal in Respect of Contracts Entered into on Principal's Behalf

An agent is in general not liable to his principal on contracts made by him   **6-025**
between his principal and third parties.[150]

Comment

This is the general rule for contracts: an authorised contract is that of the   **6-026**
principal. But just as the agent may in some case be liable to, and entitled to sue,

---

[145] *Commonwealth Portland Cement Co v Weber, Lohmann & Co Ltd* [1905] A.C. 66. See also *World Transport Agency Ltd v Royte (England) Ltd* [1957] 1 Lloyd's Rep. 381.

[146] *Morten v Hilton, Gibbes & Smith (1908)* [1937] 2 K.B. 176n. (HL). See also *Samson v Frazier Jelke & Co* [1937] 2 K.B. 170; *Stafford v Conti Commodity Services Ltd* [1981] 1 All E.R. 691; *Merrill Lynch Futures Inc v York House Trading Ltd, The Times,* May 24, 1984 (losses on commodity market are not of themselves evidence of negligence by broker); *Drexel Burnham Lambert Ltd NV v El Nasr* [1986] 1 Lloyds Rep. 356 at 366–367 (commodity broker).

[147] *Morten v Hilson, Gibbes & Smith*, above, at 178, per Lord Loreburn LC.

[148] *Fordham v Christie, Manson & Woods* [1977] E.G.D. 94. cf. *Brown v Staton* (1816) 2 Chit. 353.

[149] *Luxmoore-May v Messenger May Baverstock* [1990] 1 W.L.R. 1009. As to the duties of auctioneers see further *Alchemy (International) Ltd v Tattersalls Ltd* [1985] 2 E.G.L.R. 17; Murdoch, *Law of Estate Agency and Auctions* (4th edn), Ch.2 (see also more specifically on auctioneers 3rd edn, Ch.9).

[150] *Varden v Parker* (1798) 2 Esp. 710; *Alsop v Sylvester* (1823) 1 C. & P. 107; *Risbourg v Bruckner* (1858) 3 C.B.(N.S.) 812.

the third party,[151] so also he may be liable to his principal, by express or implied agreement or by usage. This may occur, for example, when he is a *del credere* agent,[152] or where he in some other way agrees to answer to his principal in respect of transactions which he negotiates; where he in some respects deals as principal with a person for whom he is in other respects an agent (e.g. an insurance broker[153]); or where he acts also as agent for the third party and undertakes liability to his first principal as such agent.[154] And of course the entering into of the transaction may be a breach of duty under the principles stated in the previous Articles.

Article 42

LIABILITY OF GRATUITOUS AGENTS

6-027   A gratuitous agent will be liable to his principal if in carrying out the work he fails to exercise the degree of care which may reasonably be expected of him in all the circumstances.[155]

Comment

6-028   **Liability in tort**   There is no general requirement in the law of agency that an agent has a contract with his principal, and the external position between principal and third party can certainly be changed by a gratuitous agent.[156] The internal position between principal and agent however, is, in such a case only imperfectly enforceable. Where there is no contract between principal and agent, it would seem that the alleged agent cannot be liable for pure failure to do what he undertook to do without consideration. However, where he assumed responsibility to exercise care and skill, he can be liable in tort for negligently failing to complete, or to complete with due care, work which he has undertaken and upon which he has embarked. He must also take care to adhere to the mandate given him.[157] Thus a person who gratuitously agrees to procure insurance for another may owe a duty of care in respect of the manner in which he does so.[158] Not all the cases which can be cited as instances of such a duty are necessarily to be regarded as true cases of gratuitous agency—some involve at the very least a strongly commercial background, in that the agent is a professional person who anticipates being remunerated or has already earned commission (as where he obtains insurance and subsequently undertakes gratuitously to change it).[159] In some he is already agent

---

[151] See Articles 98–103 and 107–109.

[152] See above, para.1-040.

[153] *Universo Insurance Co of Milan v Merchants Marine Insurance Co* [1897] 2 Q.B. 93; *MacGillivray on Insurance Law* (13th edn), para.36-008 onwards; and see *Wilson v Avec Audio-Visual Equipment Ltd* [1974] 1 Lloyd's Rep. 81. See also Hon. Mrs Justice Gloster [2007] L.M.C.L.Q. 302.

[154] e.g. *Queensland Investment Co v O'Connell* (1896) 12 T.L.R. 502 (stockbroker).

[155] See Comment. For the position of minors as agents, see above, para.2-015.

[156] See Article 3.

[157] See further above, para.6-003.

[158] *Wilkinson v Coverdale* (1793) 1 Esp. 74; *Norwest Refrigeration Services Pty Ltd v Bain Dawes (W.A.) Pty Ltd* (1984) 157 C.L.R. 149 at 168–170 (Illustration 6); *Veljkovic v Vrybergen* [1985] VR. 419; *Youell v Bland Welch & Co Ltd (the Superhulls Cover case) (No.2)* [1990] 2 Lloyd's Rep. 431. But when his principal is a company, he does not necessarily owe a duty to its directors personally: *Verderame v Commercial Union Ass. Co, The Times,* April 2, 1992.

[159] See *General Accident Fire & Life Assurance Corp Ltd v Tanter (The Zephyr)* [1985] 2 Lloyd's Rep.

for the other side to the transaction.[160] However, the proposition itself seems clearly established.[161]

Non-feasance The dividing line between not carrying out the work at all and car- **6-029**
rying it out negligently, or negligently failing to carry out part of it, whether as a
gratuitous agent or not, can be fine in some instances. Some time ago it was suggested that where a gratuitous agent has undertaken to do a particular task, he owes
a duty of care to his principal if he knows that, because he has accepted the
undertaking, the principal has refrained from instructing anyone else to do the work
or otherwise acted in reliance. At least, it was suggested, the agent must inform his
principal if he is not going to perform the task undertaken, and he must do so in time
to enable the principal not to suffer damage by having insufficient time to instruct
anyone else.[162] However, authority justifying liability in tort for pure failure to act
is difficult to find. Thus in one case an insurance broker acting who, having placed
all risks insurance with underwriters, gratuitously undertook to a reinsurance
underwriter in respect of the same risks to obtain further signatures on a slip and
failed to do so, causing loss to the reinsurer, was held at first instance liable in tort[163];
but the Court of Appeal was able to detect an implied contractual promise to justify
the liability, and doubt was expressed as to the appropriateness of a tort action.[164]
Although the House of Lords formerly cast doubt on the significance of the notion
of assumption of responsibility as a basis of negligence liability,[165] there has been
a movement back towards such reasoning,[166] which indeed stems directly from
Hedley Byrne & Co Ltd v Heller & Partners Ltd[167] itself. But these cases involve
misfeasance, and it is not easy to justify a tort liability on facts indicating no more
than a failure to do an act promised.[168] However, the line between this and failure
to go through with a responsibility undertaken is a fine one.

529 at 537, per Mustill LJ. This could be true of *Gomer v Pitt & Scott* (1922) 12 Ll. L.Rep. 115,
Illustration 5, and many insurance broker cases. As to barristers, see *Arthur JS Hall & Co v Simons*
[2002] 1 A.C. 615 (as to the ability of barristers now to sue for fees, see below, para.7-006);
Chamberlains v Lai [2006] NZSC 70; [2007] 2 N.Z.L.R. 7.

[160] As in *Donaldson v Haldane* (1840) 7 C. & F. 762, Illustration 4; *Al-Kandari v J.R. Brown & Co*
[1987] Q.B. 514, Illustration 13 to Article 113; and in various other cases where the agent of one
party is held to owe a duty to the other, as to which see *Avery v Salie* (1972) 25 D.L.R. (3d) 495 and
Article 113.

[161] It is clearly accepted in *Chaudhry v Prabakhar* [1989] 1 W.L.R. 29, though see discussion of this
case below. See also *Wallace v Tellfair* (1786) 2 T.R. 188n.; *Smith v Lascelles* (1788) 2 T.R. 187;
Seller v Work (1801) Marsh. Ins. 305; *Thorne v Deas* (1809) 4 Johns N.Y.R. 84; *Massey v Banner*
(1820) 1 Jac. & W. 241; *Balfe v West* (1853) 13 C.B. 466; *Turnbull v Garden* (1869) 38 L.J. Ch. 331.

[162] See Powell, p.303; Seavey, *Studies in Agency* (1949), pp.395–400; (1951) 64 HarvL.R. 913; Prosser,
Selected Topics on the Law of Torts (1953), p.380; *Wallace v Tellfair*, above.

[163] *General Accident Fire and Life Ass. Corp Ltd v Tanter (The Zephyr)* [1984] 1 Lloyd's Rep. 58.

[164] [1985] 2 Lloyd's Rep. 529: see p.538, where Mustill LJ refers to negligence liability as applicable
to an "obligation to avoid doing something, or to avoid doing something badly". He also says that
"doing something badly may often involve a neglect to carry out an act which would turn bad
performance into adequate performance".

[165] *Smith v Eric S. Bush* [1990] 1 A.C. 831; *Caparo Industries Plc v Dickman* [1990] 2 A.C. 605.

[166] *Spring v Guardian Assurance Plc* [1995] 2 A.C. 296 (negligent letter of reference); *Henderson v
Merrett Syndicates Ltd* [1995] 2 A.C. 145 (negligent management by sub-agent); *Williams v Natural
Life Health Foods Ltd* [1998] 1 W.L.R. 830; cf. *Customs and Excise Commissioners v Barclays Bank
Plc* [2006] UKHL 28; [2007] 1 A.C. 181 (no liability on bank for negligently breaching freezing
order over customer's funds); and *CGL Group Ltd v The Royal Bank of Scotland Plc* [2017] EWCA
Civ 1073.

[167] [1964] A.C. 435.

[168] See *Restatement, Third*, § 378: "When the gratuitous agent has not entered upon performance, it is

In jurisdictions willing to recognise an estoppel liability based on reliance only, it might be possible to hold the gratuitous agent who completely fails to act liable on this basis to a person who acted or refrained from acting on the basis of the agent's undertaking.[169]

6-030   **Exclusions of liability**   A person may in principle limit what he undertakes by some form of disclaimer or exclusion clause.[170] Although it is arguable that such reservations are not exclusions of liability at all, but rather determine the scope and degree of the tortious duty undertaken, they have often been treated as exclusions, and hence subject to s.2(2) of the Unfair Contract Terms Act 1977, which imposes a requirement of reasonableness on exclusions of liability for loss caused by negligence.[171]

6-031   **Standard of care**   It was formerly customary to state, and old editions of this work did state, that the duty of care owed by a gratuitous agent was one of such skill and care as persons ordinarily exercise in their own affairs. This idea, which is similar to the *diligentia quam suis rebus* of Roman law (where different contracts had different prescribed levels of care), was derived in English law from old cases on bailment, which suggested (in like manner) that whereas a contractual bailee was liable for negligence, a gratuitous bailee was only liable for gross negligence.[172] But as Rolfe B remarked in 1843,[173] gross negligence can be said to be no more than negligence with a vituperative epithet; and the determination of fixed standards for different types of case is not a technique now used by English law. Ormerod LJ said in 1962[174]:

> "It seems to me that to try and put a bailment, for instance, into a watertight compartment—such a gratuitous bailment on the one hand, and bailment for reward on the other—is to overlook the fact that there might well be an infinite variety of cases, which might come into one or the other category. The question that we have to consider in a case of this kind, if it is necessary to consider negligence, is whether in the circumstances of this particular case a sufficient standard of care has been observed by the defendants or their servants."

This view was subsequently specifically accepted for gratuitous agency. In *Chaudhry v Prabakhar*[175] a person undertook to find a suitable second-hand car for a friend to buy, and negligently recommended a car which had been in an accident.

---

not clear that liability will be imposed". A solicitor was held liable to the intended beneficiary under a will when he took no steps to carry out instructions from the testator, who died, in *White v Jones* [1995] 2 A.C. 207; but the "disappointed beneficiary" cases are probably sui generis. cf. *Hill v van Erp* (1997) 188 C.L.R. 159; *Badenach v Calvert* [2016] HCA 18; (2016) 257 C.L.R. 440. See Clerk and Lindsell, *Torts* (21st edn), para.10-109 onwards; and Gordley (1995) 83 Calif L Rev. 547 at pp.582–584.

169 See *Waltons Stores (Interstate) Ltd v Maher* (1988) 164 C.L.R. 387; *Amalgamated Investment and Property Co Ltd v Texas Commerce International Bank Ltd* [1982] Q.B. 84.

170 As in the leading case of *Hedley Byrne & Co Ltd v Heller & Partners Ltd* [1964] A.C. 465 itself.

171 See, e.g. *Smith v Eric S. Bush*, above.

172 See *Coggs v Bernard* (1703) 2 Ld.Raym. 909; see also *Wilson v Brett* (1843) 11 M.&W. 113; *Giblin v McMullen* (1869) L.R. 2 P.C. 317; *Moffat v Bateman* (1869) L.R. 3 P.C. 115. But cf. *Port Swettenham Authority v T.W.Wu & Co* [1979] A.C. 580.

173 *Wilson v Brett*, above, at 115.

174 *Houghland v R.R. Low (Luxury Coaches) Ltd* [1962] 1 Q.B. 694 at 698; see also *Grill v General Iron Screw Collier Co* (1866) L.R. 1 C.P. 694 at 698.

175 [1989] 1 W.L.R. 29.

He was held liable in tort. The case was argued as turning on the duty owed by a gratuitous agent, though it is not clear that the defendant was in inspecting the car appropriately described as an agent[176]; indeed it is not clear that he should have been regarded as undertaking any duty at all, though this was expressly conceded and the case decided on the basis of the concession.[177] In substance accepting the view put forward[178] in the Comment (but not the Article itself) in a previous edition of this work, the Court of Appeal can be said to have taken the overall view that the agent's duty is "that which may be reasonably expected of him in all the circumstances".[179] Factors relevant to the determination of the standard owed are whether the agent is paid, and if so whether he exercises any trade, profession or calling; and where he is unpaid, the skill and experience which he has or represents himself as having.[180]

Illustrations

(1) A gratuitously undertakes to arrange an insurance policy on P's cargo. He then changes his mind and decides not to do so. P's cargo is lost, but it has been said that P has no claim against A.[181] Sed quaere. If A started to make the necessary arrangements but negligently failed to answer letters from the underwriters so that no policy was effected, or if A obtained a policy but negligently failed to obtain cover against the usual risks, semble, P would have a claim against A for the loss he suffered. **6-032**

(2) E purchased a motor car from X. It was agreed that X's insurance would be transferred to E. E then arranged with X's insurance brokers for them to arrange the transfer. The insurers were not satisfied with the information given them by the brokers relating to E and in default of any answer to their questions cancelled the temporary insurance which they had granted. The brokers failed to inform E, who later had an accident. Held, the brokers were liable to indemnify E against the sums he had to pay in consequence of the accident. They were liable for their negligence notwithstanding that they were acting gratuitously.[182]

(3) A general merchant undertakes, without reward, to enter a parcel of P's goods at the custom-house together with a parcel of his own. By mistake he enters both parcels under the wrong denomination of goods, and both parcels are, in consequence, seized. He has not held himself out as having any special skill in this respect (i.e. he is not a broker or customs clerk) and is therefore not liable to P, because he has taken as much care with P's goods as with his own.[183]

(4) A writer to the signet was employed to invest money for a client and did so

---

[176] He subsequently took a cheque for part of the purchase price and passed it to the seller, so could perhaps be regarded as having negotiated, or at least introduced, the sale.
[177] A concession doubted by May LJ at pp.38–39.
[178] In a passage originally written by Mr Brian Davenport QC.
[179] See Stuart-Smith LJ at p.34; see also Stocker LJ at p.37.
[180] See p.34.
[181] See Duer, *Law and Practice of Marine Insurance* (1845), Vol. 2, pp.128–130, who comments unfavourably on the hardship inflicted on P, who has trusted A to carry out his promise.
[182] *London Borough of Bromley v Ellis* [1971] 1 Lloyd's Rep. 97.
[183] *Shiells v Blackburne* (1789) 1 Hy.Bl. 158.

without obtaining adequate security. He charged no fee for his services but was held liable to the lenders for his negligence.[184]

(5) P asked A, a shipping agent, to check with P's bank to ensure that the marine insurance policy on certain of P's goods covered a voyage to Lisbon. A acted gratuitously in accepting this request. He obtained an oral assurance from the bank but did not look at the terms of the policy itself (although he had been requested by P to "see the policy"). A was liable, since he had not shown that care which a reasonably careful man of business would have exercised in his own affairs.[185]

(6) The owner of a fishing vessel is required by his banker to get it insured. He contacts the manager of a fisherman's co-operative which he has recently joined, and which has said that it can obtain insurance for members at a reduced rate. The vessel is added to the co-operative's fleet policy, but the manager fails to tell the owner that the insurance is inoperative if the vessel does not have a certificate of survey. A loss occurs and the insurers repudiate liability because of the absence of such a certificate. The co-operative is liable.[186]

(7) Solicitors make a will for a testatrix and retain it. On her death they make no effort to locate the executor and notify him of the will for six years, during which time the main asset, a house, lies vacant and falls into decay. The solicitors are liable to the executor.[187]

(8) An accountant volunteers to be appointed joint signatory on a bank account operated by an attorney for the claimants. The attorney fraudulently procures the accountant's signature in blank on cheques and proceeds to misappropriate funds from the account. The accountant is liable to the claimants.[188]

2. FIDUCIARY AND OTHER EQUITABLE DUTIES

Article 43 provides an overview of the subject matter of an agent's fiduciary and other equitable duties. Succeeding Articles provide a more detailed treatment of various aspects of those duties.

Article 43

AGENTS' EQUITABLE DUTIES—GENERAL MATTERS

6-033   An agent owes to his principal a duty of loyalty, a duty that attracts fiduciary obligations.[189]

---

[184] *Donaldson v Haldane* (1840) 7 C. & F. 762. See also *Dartnall v Howard & Gibbs* (1825) 4 B. & C. 345; *Whitehead v Greetham* (1825) 2 Bing. 464.
[185] *Gomer v Pitt & Scott* (1922) 12 Ll. L.Rep. 115.
[186] *Norwest Refrigeration Services Pty Ltd v Bain Dawes (W.A.) Pty Ltd* (1984) 157 C.L.R. 149.
[187] *Hawkins v Clayton* (1988) 164 C.L.R. 539.
[188] *Nicholls v Peers* (1993) 4 N.Z.B.L.C. 103,313.
[189] The literature on this topic is enormous and constantly increasing. See, Conaglen, *Fiduciary Loyalty* (2010); *Meagher, Gummow and Lehane's Equity Doctrines and Remedies* (5th edn), Ch.5; Finn, *Fiduciary Obligations* (1977), Pt II; *Equity and Commercial Relationships* (Finn ed., 1987), Chs 6, 7; Glover, *Commercial Equity: Fiduciary Relationships* (1995); Snell, *Equity* (33rd edn), Ch.7; Worthington, *Equity* (2nd edn), p.127 onwards; *Equity in Commercial Law* (Degeling and Edelman eds, 2005); *Contract, Status, and Fiduciary Law* (Miller and Gold, eds, 2016); and other material cited in the following pages.

Comment

The duties of a fiduciary   Most of the material in this Article, and those that im-   **6-034**
mediately follow it, is concerned with fiduciary duties. It should be noted, however,
that the meaning of the expression "fiduciary duties" and its connections to other
concepts remain contentious in many respects. It is common, for instance, for courts
to refer to the duty of loyalty owed by trustees, agents and other "fiduciaries" as a
fiduciary duty, whereas some commentators argue that only those sub-duties which
reinforce the duty of loyalty should be termed fiduciary.[190] Others draw a distinction between a simple breach of trust and a breach of fiduciary duty, the former, but
not the latter, extending to entirely innocent misapplications of the principal's
property in breach of instructions.[191] A third troublesome issue is the relationship
between fiduciary duties and duties not to disclose confidential information, now,
in England anyway, treated as discrete sets of obligation.[192] A fourth area of difficulty is the relationship between fiduciary duties and the duty of fidelity said to
be owed by all employees to their employers.[193] Finally, there is the relationship
between fiduciary duties and the concept of undue influence, the latter concept
particularly affecting some types of agent, such as solicitors, and possibly having
operation before the contract of retainer is entered into, and extending after the
retainer has ceased.[194]

The essence of the duties owed by a fiduciary has been expressed in the following statement:

> "A person will be a fiduciary in his relationships with another when and in so far as that
> other is entitled to expect that he will act in that other's interests or (as in a partnership)
> in their joint interests, to the exclusion of their several interests."[195]

In a leading case, *Bristol and West Building Society v Mothew*,[196] Millett LJ stated:

> "A fiduciary is someone who has undertaken to act for or on behalf of another in a
> particular matter or circumstances which give rise to a relationship of trust and
> confidence."

Millett LJ went on to say:

---

[190] See Flannigan (2004) 83 Can. Bar Rev. 35; Conaglen (2005) 121 L.Q.R. 452; Flannigan (2008) 124 L.Q.R. 274.

[191] See the Rt Hon. Lord Millett (1998) 114 L.Q.R. 399 at 403–406.

[192] See *Prince Jefri Bolkiah v KPMG* [1999] 2 A.C. 222 at 235; *Arklow Investments Ltd v Maclean* [2000] 1 W.L.R. 594 (PC). cf. *Att.-Gen. v Blake* [1998] Ch. 439 at 454; *University of Nottingham v Fishel* [2000] EWHC 2221 (QB); [2000] I.C.R. 1462; *Generics (UK) Ltd v Yeda Research & Development Co Ltd* [2012] EWCA Civ 726; [2013] F.S.R. 13 at [48]. cf. Rt Hon. Lord Millett (1998) 114 L.Q.R. 214. See further below, paras 6-051 and 6-077.

[193] See *University of Nottingham v Fishel* [2000] EWHC 2221 (QB); [2000] I.C.R. 1462; *Helmet Integrated Systems Ltd v Tunnard* [2006] EWCA Civ 1735; [2007] F.S.R. 16 at [26]–[27] and [37]; *Ranson v Customer Systems Plc* [2012] EWCA Civ 841; [2012] I.R.L.R. 769; *Generics (UK) Ltd v Yeda Research & Development Co Ltd* [2012] EWCA Civ 726; [2013] F.S.R. 13 at [79] onwards; *Re-use Collections Ltd v Sendall* [2014] EWHC 3852 (QB); [2015] I.R.L.R. 226 at [153] (employee recruiting colleagues to leave). cf. Flannigan [2015] J.B.L. 189; Frazer (2015) 131 L.Q.R. 53.

[194] See below, Article 45.

[195] Finn, in *Commercial Aspects of Trusts and Fiduciary Obligations* (McKendrick ed., 1992), p.9.

[196] [1998] Ch. 1 at 18. See *Restatement, Third*, § 8.01: "An agent has a fiduciary duty to act loyally for his principal's benefit in all matters connected with the agency relationship". See also Lord Browne-Wilkinson in *White v Jones* [1995] 2 A.C. 207 at 231.

"The distinguishing obligation of a fiduciary is the obligation of loyalty. The principal is entitled to the single-minded loyalty of his fiduciary. This core liability has several facets. A fiduciary must act in good faith; he must not make a profit out his trust; he may not act for his own benefit or the benefit of a third person without the informed consent of his principal".[197]

The dictum opens by referring to a general obligation of loyalty, in respect of which the particular fiduciary duties not to profit from position and not to place oneself in a position of conflict of interest are manifestations. Those duties, including an agent's liability for self-dealing, are dealt with in detail in Articles 44 to 48. They are designed to remove any temptation in the fiduciary to act disloyally, and hence operate whether or not the fiduciary is in fact disloyal.[198] Actual disloyalty, on the other hand, can take a myriad of forms, from deliberately misapplying the principal's funds, accepting bribes, soliciting (before termination of the agency) colleagues and customers to cease to work for and do business with the principal,[199] to conduct that is malicious or spiteful,[200] and to a bad faith omission to act.[201] It is also disloyal for an agent consciously to mislead his principal.[202] Breach of fiduciary duty can, it seems, also found the illegality necessary for liability in conspiracy.[203]

Whether or not one regards the paradigm fiduciary as the express trustee, with the duties of agents and others as an extension of the trustee's duties,[204] or whether one says that a trustee is a special sort of fiduciary holding property,[205] is probably no longer of relevance. The attribution of such duties forms a significant area where the common law techniques of strict interpretation of contract, and reluctance to imply terms which the parties did not choose to make express, are modified by dif-

---

197 *Bristol and West BS v Mothew* [1998] 1 Ch. 1 at 18, per Millett LJ. As to duties of a manager towards a music group see: *Martin-Smith v Williams* [1999] E.M.L.R. 571.

198 *Hamilton v Wright* (1842) 9 Cl. & Fin. 111 at 123–124 (HL).

199 *Wessex Dairies Ltd v Smith* [1935] 2 K.B. 80; *Aubanel & Alabaster Ltd v Aubanel* (1949) 66 R.P.C. 343 at 347; *Sybron Corp v Rochem Ltd* [1984] Ch. 112; *Balston Ltd v Headline Filters Ltd* [1990] F.S.R. 385 at 417; *Coleman Taymar Ltd v Oakes* [2001] 2 B.C.L.C. 749; *Také Ltd v BSM Marketing Ltd* [2006] EWHC 1085 (QB) and subsequent damages appeal at [2009] EWCA Civ 45; *Willis Ltd v Jardine Lloyd Thompson Group Plc* [2015] EWCA Civ 450 (interim injunction against manager on "gardening leave" soliciting employees to leave and compete); *Breitenfeld UK Ltd v Harrison* [2015] EWHC 399 (Ch); [2015] 2 B.C.L.C. 275 at [77] (assisting competitor to be ready for business). See too *Warman International Ltd v Dwyer* (1995) 182 C.L.R. 544; *RBC Dominion Securities Inc v Merrill Lynch Canada Inc* [2008] 3 S.C.R. 79.

200 See *Mordecai v Mordecai* (1988) 12 N.S.W.L.R. 58 (company directors running down company business to leave nothing for estranged wife and child of deceased shareholder). cf. *Bishopsgate Investment Management Ltd v Maxwell (No.2)* [1994] 1 All E.R. 261 at 264.

201 *British Midland Tool Ltd v Midland International Tooling Ltd* [2003] EWHC 466 (Ch); [2003] 2 B.C.L.C. 523 (company director fails to reveal that former colleague is recruiting key company staff because he too is planning to leave and join colleague); *Chan v Zacharia* (1984) 154 C.L.R. 178 (partner's refusal to renew lease so that available for self). See further below, para.6-080.

202 *Murad v Al-Saraj* [2005] EWCA Civ 959; 1 W.T.L.R. 1573; *Daly v Sydney Stock Exchange Ltd* (1986) 160 C.L.R. 371; *Amaltal Corp Ltd v Maruha Corp* [2007] 3 N.Z.L.R. 192, Illustration 14 to Article 43; and *Premium Real Estate Ltd v Stevens* [2009] 2 N.Z.L.R. 384 (estate agent misleads vendor principal as to intentions of purchaser). See too *Odyssey Entertainment Ltd v Kamp* [2012] EWHC 2316 (Ch) at [234] (director intentionally misleads colleagues with unduly pessimistic advice on profitability of projects).

203 See *First Subsea Ltd v Balltec Ltd* [2014] EWHC 866 (Ch).

204 See Maitland, *Equity* (1936 edn), pp.81–82 and 230–232; Worthington, *Equity* (2nd edn), pp.129–130.

205 See *Restatement, Third, Trusts*, T.D.No.1, § 2.

ferent techniques.[206] These fiduciary duties apply whether or not the agency is gratuitous: they do not depend on the fact that the principal is paying for the agent's services.

The fiduciary, and other, duties of directors of companies are now governed by statute, in the form of the Companies Act 2006 Pt 10 Ch.2. These provisions have replaced their common law and equitable equivalents.[207]

Agent as fiduciary   An agent in the strict sense of the word holds a power to af-   **6-035**
fect the legal relations of his principal.[208] This power is conferred by the law in the implementation of the supposed intentions of the parties; but it is not surprising that the law also imposes controls on the way in which the holder of such a strong power may behave towards the person who conferred it. This is not a situation like the more usual one regulated by the law in which the parties are in an adverse commercial relationship, for example a simple hire of services. Agency services are services of a special kind. Even when no such power to affect legal relations was conferred, as in the "incomplete agency" case of the canvassing agent,[209] the relationship of the parties still imports an undertaking by one to act in the interests of the other rather than his own, and this likewise, though to a lesser extent, justifies the law's intervention.

It has however been said in the context of an agent's fiduciary obligations that:

"Agency is a contract made between principal and agent ... like every other contract, the rights and duties of the principal and agent are dependent upon the terms of the contract between them, whether express or implied."[210]

Although older dicta of a similar nature can be cited,[211] not everyone may agree with the emphasis inherent in this statement. Agency need not be contractual; and although there is much overlap with common law duties[212] the notion of fiduciary obligation is independent of contract. It is submitted that the law's control over the agent's exercise of his powers of intervention is not to be derived from contract terms alone. As was said in a subsequent case: "The essence of a fiduciary obligation is that it creates obligations of a different character from those deriving from the contract itself".[213] The role itself will, however, usually be one that is voluntarily assumed by the fiduciary.[214]

---

[206]   See Goodhart and Jones (1980) 43 M.L.R. 489.

[207]   Companies Act 2006 s.170(3). See *Palmer's Company Law* (2007); *Company Directors: Duties, Liabilities and Remedies* (Mortimore, ed., 3rd edn); Keay, *Directors' Duties* (2nd edn); Watts, *Directors' Powers and Duties* (2nd edn, 2015). As to the application of fiduciary principles between members of limited liability partnerships, see *F&C Alternative Investments (Holdings) Ltd v Barthelemy* [2011] EWHC 1731 (Ch).

[208]   See Article 1.

[209]   See above, para.1-020.

[210]   *Kelly v Cooper* [1993] A.C. 205 at 213–214 (PC), per Lord Browne-Wilkinson (Illustration 9). See also *Clark Boyce v Mouat* [1994] 1 A.C. 428 at 437; *Henderson v Merrett Syndicates Ltd* [1995] 2 A.C. 145 at 204–205; *Global Container Lines Ltd v Bonyad Shipping Co* [1998] 1 Lloyd's Rep. 528 (joint venture); *F&C Alternative Investments (Holdings) Ltd v Barthelemy* [2011] EWHC 1731 (Ch) at [223].

[211]   e.g. *Lamb v Evans* [1893] 1 Ch. 218, per Bowen LJ.

[212]   See below, para.6-043.

[213]   *Re Goldcorp Exchange Ltd* [1995] 1 A.C. 74 at 98, per Lord Mustill. See also *Casson Beckman & Partners v Papi* [1991] B.C.L.C. 299 at 313, per Sir Denys Buckley: "The existence of a fiduciary duty to account would eliminate or negative any need to imply anything". See also *Yasuda Fire and*

Even where the relationship is contractual (as it normally will be), the matter is too important to be left entirely to the agreement of the parties and the interpretation of that agreement. This is an area where the vulnerability of the principal has for more than two centuries[215] been recognised as requiring a degree of supervision. The relief is principally given by the application of fiduciary duties, though other equitable (or partly equitable) doctrines such as duress or undue influence and the special rules for confidential information may on occasion be relevant. The agreement of the parties or the background of the case may however establish either that the relationship is not one of agency[216] or that the fiduciary duties have been modified from the normal standards[217]; but equally a fiduciary relationship may, while consistent with them, increase the contract duties.[218] The long-standing application of fiduciary duties to company promoters, who may have had no appointment, contractual or otherwise, with the claimant company, and who sometimes show little conscious regard for the interests of investors, is an example of the reach of equitable doctrine.[219] Similar considerations apply to those, admittedly circumscribed, cases where company directors have been found to have assumed a responsibility to advise shareholders.[220]

Marine Ins. Co of Europe Ltd v Orion Marine Ins. Underwriting Agency Ltd [1995] Q.B. 174 at 186, per Colman J: "The rights and obligations arising as a matter of law from the existence of duty creating relationships, such as bailment, are not in principle displaced by contractual rights and obligations unless the contract provides that such rights and obligations are to be excluded or includes remedies which are inconsistent with the duties attributable as a matter of law to the relationship"; *Wingecarribee Shire Council v Lehman Bros Australia Ltd* (2013) 301 A.L.R. 1 at [731]. See too DeMott (2007) 58 Alabama L.R. 1049; Conaglen (2013) 7 J.Eq. 105; L. Smith in *Contract, Status, and Fiduciary Law* (Miller and Golds, eds, 2016) Ch.5. cf. Edelman (2010) 126 L.Q.R. 302; and (2013) 7 J.Eq. 128.

214 *Alberta v Elder Advocates of Alberta Society* 2011 SCC 24 at [30], noted Flannigan (2011) 127 L.Q.R. 505; *Dubai Aluminium Co Ltd v Salaam* [2002] UKHL 48; [2003] 2 A.C. 366 at [128]; *Ross River Ltd v Waveley Commercial Ltd* [2012] EWHC 81 (Ch) at [256], affirmed on these issues in [2013] EWCA Civ 910. See too Rt Hon. Lord Millett (1998) 114 L.Q.R. 399 at 404–405.

215 See *York Buildings v MacKenzie* (1795) 8 Bro. P.C. 42. See further, Getzler, in Gold and Miller (eds), *Philosophical Foundations of Fiduciary Law* (2014), Ch.2.

216 See *Coachcraft Ltd v SVP Fruit Co Ltd* (1980) 28 A.L.R. 319 at 328–329 (PC) (proxy with no obligations to vote as shareholder directed).

217 See *Hospital Products Ltd v US Surgical Corp* (1984) 156 C.L.R. 41 at 96–97, per Mason J; below, para.6-056.

218 See Mason J in the *Hospital Products* case, above, at 99; *Conway v Ratiu* [2005] EWCA Civ 1302; [2006] 1 All E.R. 571 at [74]; *Cia. Fianciera "Soleada" SA v Hamoor Tanker Corp Inc (The Borag)* [1980] 1 Lloyd's Rep. 111 (reversed on a different point [1981] 1 W.L.R. 274) (unusual terms imposed higher duty of loyalty); *John Youngs Insurance Services Ltd v Aviva Insurance Service UK Ltd* [2011] EWHC 1515 (TCC) at [120] (duty to account survives termination of contract).

219 See *Erlanger v New Sombrero Phosphate Co* (1878) 3 App.Cas. 1218; *Gluckstein v Barnes* [1900] A.C. 240. See also *Bagnall v Carlton* (1877) 6 Ch.D. 371; *Emma Silver Mining Co v Lewis & Sons* (1879) 4 C.P.D. 396; *Emma Silver Mining Co v Grant* (1879) 11 Ch.D. 918; *Whaley Bridge Calico Printing Co v Green* (1879) 5 Q.B.D. 109; *Lydney and Wigpool Ore Co v Bird* (1886) 33 Ch.D. 85; *Re Cape Breton Co* (1885) 29 Ch.D. 795; affd sub nom. *Cavendish-Bentinck v Fenn* (1887) 12 App.Cas. 652; *Lagunas Nitrate Co v Lagunas Syndicate* [1899] 2 Ch. 392; *Re Lady Forrest (Murchison) Gold Mine* [1901] 1 Ch. 582; *Re Leeds & Hanley Theatres of Varieties* [1902] 2 Ch. 809; *Omnium Electric Palaces Ltd v Baines* [1914] 1 Ch. 332; *Jacobus Marler Estates Ltd v Marler* (1916) 85 L.J.P.C. 167n.; *Jubilee Cotton Mills v Lewis* [1924] A.C. 958; *Tracy v Mandelay Pty Ltd* (1953) 88 C.L.R. 215.

220 *Briess v Woolley* [1954] A.C. 333; *Coleman v Myers* [1977] 2 N.Z.L.R. 225; *Brunninghausen v Glavanics* (1999) 46 N.S.W.L.R. 538; noted by Goddard (2000) 116 L.Q.R. 197; *Park's of Hamilton (Holdings) Ltd v Campbell* [2014] CSIH 36; 2014 SC 726 at [27]; *Kiriwai Consultants Ltd v Holmes* [2015] NZCA 149. cf. *Percival v Wright* [1902] 2 Ch. 421.

Development of doctrine   The duties of fiduciaries such as agents have been   **6-036**
developed over the last two centuries to accommodate the difference between
express trustees and others who hold special powers similar in varying degrees to
those of the trustee. In particular, the position of company promoters and directors
was at one time a focal point of such development; hence cases on promoters and
directors figure prominently in the older illustrations to this part of the book. The
full trust analogy has however long appeared less cogent, and a whole separate area
of the law has been developed (or perhaps rediscovered) with broader usage and
less stringent controls. The immediate origins in nineteenth century trust law must
nevertheless be borne in mind when old cases are read, which apply harsher rules
to trustees than those appropriate to agents as a class,[221] and abound in cautionary
statements[222]; and they often have fairly easy recourse to notions such as that of trust
property when speaking of property in the hands of agents, and of "breach of trust"
when referring to even innocent deviation from instructions.

Fiduciary reasoning has been much developed in other common law jurisdictions, perhaps most conspicuously in Canada[223]; but is under discussion
everywhere.[224] It should not however be taken too far; and it may be that the dictum
of Lord Browne-Wilkinson quoted above is best interpreted as a warning against
excessive use of such reasoning.[225] It is sometimes imprecisely and mistakenly
invoked to justify results which would be more appropriately attributed to express

---

[221]   e.g. as to purchase of the trust property: Lewin, *Trusts* (19th edn), para.20-98 onwards and as to rights
to remuneration, see below, Article 1. As to the earlier history of fiduciary obligations, see Getzler,
in *Mapping the Law* (Burrows and Lord Rodger of Earlsferry eds, 2006), Ch.31.

[222]   e.g. *Aberdeen Ry Co v Blaikie Bros* (1854) 1 Macq. 461 at 471, per Lord Cranworth LC. It has been
said that such statements "are to be explained by judicial acceptance of the inability of the courts
'in much the greater number of cases' to ascertain the precise effect which the existence of a conflict
with personal interest has had upon the performance of fiduciary duty": *Chan v Zacharia* (1984) 154
C.L.R. 178 at 204, per Deane J.

[223]   e.g. *Canson Enterprises Ltd v Boughton & Co* [1991] 3 S.C.R. 534; (1991) 85 D.L.R. (4th) 129, Illustration 8 (solicitor); *Strother v 3464920 Canada Inc* [2007] 2 S.C.R. 177; (2007) 281 D.L.R. (4th)
640 (solicitor); *Hodgkinson v Simms* [1994] 3 S.C.R. 377; (1995) 117 D.L.R. (4th) 161 (accountant); *Soulos v Korkontzilas* [1977] 2 S.C.R. 217; (1997) 146 D.L.R. (4th) 214 (real estate broker)
(noted by L.D. Smith (1998) 114 L.Q.R. 14); *Cadbury Schweppes Inc v FBI Foods Ltd* [1999] 1
S.C.R. 142; (1999) 167 D.L.R. (4th) 577 (no fiduciary relationship in product licensing agreement).
See also *Guerin v R.* [1984] 2 S.C.R. 335; (1984) 13 D.L.R. (4th) 321; *Blueberry River Indian Band
v R.* [1995] 2 S.C.R. 344; (1996) 130 D.L.R. (4th) 193 (public law); *Frame v Smith* [1987] 3 S.C.R.
99; (1987) 42 D.L.R. (4th) 81, per Wilson J (refusal of access to children); *Norberg v Wynrib* [1992]
2 S.C.R. 226; (1992) 92 D.L.R. (4th) 449 (doctor and patient); *M. (K.) v M. (H.)* [1992] 3 S.C.R. 6;
(1992) 96 D.L.R. (4th) 289 (parent and child); Shepherd, *Law of Fiduciaries* (1981); Rotman, *Fiduciary Law* (2005); *Waters on Trusts* (4th edn), Ch.19.

[224]   As to Australia see *Hospital Products Ltd v US Surgical Corp* (1984) 156 C.L.R. 41 (distributor: no
fiduciary relationship); *Breen v Williams* (1996) 186 C.L.R. 71 (doctor and patient: no fiduciary
relationship) (noted by Nolan (1997) 113 L.Q.R. 220); *Maguire v Makaronis* (1997) 188 C.L.R. 449
(solicitor: fiduciary relationship: rescission); *Pilmer v Duke Group Ltd* (2001) 207 C.L.R. 165;
Youyang Pty. Ltd v Minter Ellison Morris Fletcher (2003) 212 C.L.R. 484; *Harris v Digital Pulse
Pty. Ltd* (2003) 56 N.S.W.L.R. 298 (no exemplary damages). As to New Zealand see *Bank of New
Zealand v New Zealand Guardian Trust Co Ltd* [1999] 1 N.Z.L.R. 213; affd [1999] 1 N.Z.L.R. 664
(bank and trust company: no breach of fiduciary duty); *L. v Robinson* [2000] 3 N.Z.L.R. 499 (doctor and patient: not fiduciary relationship); cf. *S. v Att.-Gen.* [2003] 3 N.Z.L.R. 450 (foster parents
agents of Crown). There are also significant cases in the area of remedies, e.g. *Day v Mead* [1987]
2 N.Z.L.R. 443 (contributory negligence); *Aquaculture Corp v New Zealand Green Mussel Co Ltd*
[1990] 3 N.Z.L.R. 299; *Cook v Evatt (No.2)* [1992] 1 N.Z.L.R. 676 (see Watts [1992] L.M.C.L.Q.
439) (exemplary damages); *Chirnside v Fay* [2007] 1 N.Z.L.R. 433.

[225]   See below, at the end of para.6-043. See also the Rt Hon. Lord Millett (1998) 114 L.Q.R. 214;
Davies, in *Consensus ad Idem* (Rose ed., 1996), pp.170–174.

or implied contract terms, or to breach of the common law duty of care in tort; and there have been warnings against invoking such reasoning simply to justify particular remedies, especially the constructive trust.[226] But other available doctrines are duress, undue influence, unconscionability or even, if such could be developed, a requirement of good faith in commercial transactions.[227] Also of potential importance is the equitable concept of "fraud on a power". This concept has had particular application to trustees and company directors, and has not so far been a prominent feature of the general law of agency. Where it applies, it does not require disloyalty in the actor, and it operates independently of the strictly fiduciary duties. An outline of its operation is given in Chapter 8.[228]

6-037   Are all agents always fiduciaries?[229]   Turning first to the question of how the incidence of the duties should be explained, it will be noted that the formulations in Article 1 and in the present Article treat the relationship of principal and agent as by definition a fiduciary one, and therefore in effect say that every agent is a fiduciary and hence owes fiduciary duties. This can be criticised on the basis that not every person who can be described by the word "agent" is subject to fiduciary duties; and that a person who certainly is so to be described may owe such duties in some respects and not in others.[230] Hence it is said that there may be a "non-fiduciary agent", and that in some functions an acknowledged agent may not act as fiduciary at all.[231] Rather than talk of a "non-fiduciary agent" it seems better to say that where an agent does not act in a fiduciary capacity (e.g. because he simply carries out specific instructions), this is a reflection of the scope of his duties and the boundaries of the equitable rules.

Another view is that the approach should rather be to identify the general circumstances in which a fiduciary duty may arise of itself and note these as situations in which agents may sometimes, but do not always, find themselves. Thus in *Phipps v Boardman*,[232] Lord Upjohn said:

"The facts and circumstances must be carefully examined to see whether in fact a purported agent and even a confidential agent is in a fiduciary relationship to his principal. It does not necessarily follow that he is in such a position (see *In Re Coomber*)."

And in the case referred to, *Re Coomber*,[233] Fletcher Moulton LJ said, in a much quoted passage[234]:

"It is said that the son was the manager of the stores and therefore was in a fiduciary relationship to his mother. This illustrates in a most striking form the danger of trusting to verbal formulae. Fiduciary relations are of many different types; they extend from the

---

[226] See *Breen v Williams*, above, at 110.
[227] See Finn in *Equity, Fiduciaries and Trusts* (Youdan ed., 1989), Ch.1; cf. Conaglen (2005) 121 L.Q.R. 452 at 456.
[228] See below, para.8-219.
[229] See *Meagher, Gummow and Lehane's Equity Doctrines and Remedies* (5th edn), para.5-210 onwards.
[230] *John Youngs Insurance Services Ltd v Aviva Insurance Service UK Ltd* [2011] EWHC 1515 (TCC) at [98] (defendant was agent in placing repair work on behalf of insurer, but not in so far as defendant also undertook repair work itself for the insurer under detailed contractual provisions).
[231] *Coachcraft Ltd v SVP Fruit Co Ltd* (1980) 28 A.L.R. 319 at 328–329 (PC) (proxy but with no obligations to vote as shareholder directed).
[232] [1967] 2 A.C. 46 at 127; followed in *Hendy Lennox (Industrial Engines) Ltd v Grahame Puttick Ltd* [1984] 1 W.L.R. 485. See also Article 48.
[233] [1911] 1 Ch. 723.
[234] At pp.728–729.

relation of myself to an errand boy who is bound to bring me back my change up to the most intimate and confidential relations which can possibly exist between one party and another where the one is wholly in the hands of the other because of his infinite trust in him. All these are cases of fiduciary relations, and the Courts have again and again, in cases where there has been a fiduciary relation, interfered and set aside acts which, between persons in a wholly independent position, would have been perfectly valid. Thereupon in some minds there arises the idea that if there is any fiduciary relation whatever any of these types of interference is warranted by it. They conclude that every kind of fiduciary relation justifies every kind of interference. Of course that is absurd. The nature of the fiduciary relation must be such that it justifies the interference. There is no class of case in which one ought more carefully to bear in mind the facts of the case, when one reads the judgment of the Court on those facts, than cases which relate to fiduciary and confidential relations and the action of the Court with regard to them. In my opinion there was absolutely nothing in the fiduciary relations of the mother and the son with regard to this house which in any way affected this transaction."

It is certainly true that fiduciary relationships arise in situations other than those of agency. Nevertheless, it is submitted that the fact that an agent in the strictest sense of the word has a power to alter his principal's legal position makes it appropriate and salutary to regard the fiduciary duty as a typical feature of the paradigm agency relationship. To do so will not mislead so long as two things are borne in mind.

The first is that the word "agent" can be used in varying senses, and not all persons to whom the word is applied are agents in the full (or sometimes, any) legal sense. A canvassing, or introducing agent,[235] for instance, may do no more than bring two parties together and thus may in many situations do little involving the incidence of fiduciary responsibilities at all; though equally he can, as has been stated above, in some circumstances become liable for breach of such duties, as when he conceals from his principal the existence of further offers.[236] Further, even canvassing agents usually have authority to make and receive communications on behalf of their principals, and can be expected to act loyally in exercising those powers. A distributor or franchisee, though sometimes called an agent, is in most respects in a position commercially adverse, rather than fiduciary, to the person whose goods he distributes: he buys and resells.[237] But again it is conceivable that circumstances might give him knowledge of and power over his principal's affairs which could justify the imposition of some fiduciary duties[238]; and this is quite apart from the possibility that he may also in some circumstances exercise true agency functions, for example as regards complaints concerning the goods, and be subject to fiduciary duties in that respect.

---

[235] See above, para.1-020.

[236] *Keppel v Wheeler* [1927] 1 K.B. 577, Illustration 6 to Article 60; *Jackson v Packham Real Estate Ltd* (1980) 109 D.L.R. (3d) 277; and see *Regier v Campbell-Stuart* [1939] Ch. 766, Illustration 16 to Article 45; *Premium Real Estate Ltd v Stevens* [2009] N.Z.L.R. 384. Or if he gives information to third parties about those he has introduced. But cf. *Knoch Estate v John Picken Ltd* (1991) 83 D.L.R. (4th) 447.

[237] See *Jirna Ltd v Mister Donut of Canada Ltd* (1971) 22 D.L.R. (3d) 639; affd (1973) 40 D.L.R. (3d) 303; see also *Keith Henry & Co Pty Ltd v Stuart Walker & Co Pty Ltd* (1958) 100 C.L.R. 342; *Lothian v Jenolite Ltd* 1969 S.C. 11; *Hospital Products Ltd v US Surgical Corp* (1984) 156 C.L.R. 41 (a leading case on this point, where the court was divided)—see in this context the judgment of Mason J; cf. *Watson v Dolmark Industries Ltd* [1992] 3 N.Z.L.R. 311. See also *Cadbury Schweppes Inc v FBI Foods Ltd* [1999] 1 S.C.R. 142; (1999) 167 D.L.R. (4th) 577; above, paras 1-032 and 6-015.

[238] This might even be so of the franchisor's position vis-à-vis the franchisee: cf. the *Mister Donut* case, above.

The second matter which should be borne in mind is that the extent of an agent's equitable duties (a phrase that embraces more than the strictly fiduciary duties to avoid conflicts of interest and not to profit) and also common law duties may vary from situation to situation. For example, a person who is certainly an agent in general, but who is authorised on a particular occasion to carry out an exactly specified act, may on the occasion act in no more than a ministerial capacity, even though he affects his principal's legal position.[239] Nevertheless, even a messenger may have to decide what to do if the person to whom he is sent is not there. To take another example, a person otherwise at arm's length with a claimant with whom he is proposing to contract may have a limited authority to act for the claimant, for example in filling out the blanks in the document recording the contract.[240] In so doing he may be required both to adhere to the mandate given and to exercise it in good faith. In many situations the duty may be, by virtue of the circumstances, limited; or restricted or even excluded by contract. "The precise scope of [the obligation] must be moulded according to the nature of the relationship."[241]

6-038 **When do fiduciary duties start and end?** A subject not without difficulty is when, in relation to an agent, fiduciary duties (and the underlying duty of loyalty) begin and cease to operate? The issues are, in part at least, a reflection of the difficulties that have already been noted in differentiating fiduciary duties from other equitable controls on conduct.

The basic principle, at least in English law, seems to be that fiduciary duties commence[242] and end[243] with the relationship of agency, which may or may not coincide with any contract between the parties. It will be rare that fiduciary duties cease to operate before any contractual relationship or officeholding terminates. It has been held that in a case of total exclusion from participation as a director, some aspects at least of the director's fiduciary duties can cease to operate.[244] Once an agent's appointment has ceased, he is in general free to compete with, or work for a competitor of, his former principal.[245] A useful modern statement of the position, addressed to the case of directors, is that of Lawrence Collins J in *CMS Dolphin Ltd v Simonet*[246]:

"In English law a director's power to resign from office is not a fiduciary power. A direc-

---

[239] See, e.g. *Volkers v Midland Doherty* (1985) 17 D.L.R. (4th) 343, Illustration 4 to Article 39; see also *R.H. Deacon & Co v Varga* (1972) 30 D.L.R. (3d) 653; affd (1973) 41 D.L.R. (4th) 767n.

[240] For the engagement of agency law in such circumstances, see *Colonial Bank v Hepworth* (1884) 36 Ch.D. 36; *Koch v Dicks* [1933] 1 K.B. 307; *Armor Coatings (Marketing) Pty Ltd v General Credits (Finance) Pty Ltd* (1978) 17 S.A.S.R. 259; and *Wright v Gasweld Pty Ltd* (1991) 22 N.S.W.L.R. 317. See too *Barrett v Bem* [2012] EWCA Civ 52; [2012] Ch. 573 (signature of will on behalf of testator).

[241] *New Zealand Netherlands Society "Oranje" Inc v Kuys* [1973] 1 W.L.R. 1126 at 1130, per Lord Wilberforce. See also *Birtchnell v Equity Trustee, Executor and Agency Co Ltd* (1929) 42 C.L.R. 384 at 408.

[242] See *Arklow Investments Ltd v Maclean* [2000] 1 W.L.R. 594 at 599–600 (PC). See too *Sharbern Holding Inc v Vancouver Airport Centre Ltd* [2011] 2 S.C.R. 175; (2011) 331 D.L.R. (4th) 1 at [144].

[243] See *Prince Jefri Bolkiah v KPMG* [1999] 2 A.C. 222 at 235–236; *Walsh v Shanahan* [2013] EWCA Civ 411 at [38]. But cf. *Ratiu v Conway* [2005] EWCA Civ 1302; [2006] 1 All E.R. 571 at [72].

[244] See *In Plus Group Ltd v Pyke* [2002] EWCA Civ 370; [2002] 2 B.C.L.C. 210. cf. *First Subsea Ltd v Balltec Ltd* [2017] EWCA Civ 186 at [23].

[245] *Wessex Dairies Ltd v Smith* [1935] 2 K.B. 80; *FSS Travel and Leisure Systems Ltd v Johnson* [1997] EWCA Civ 2759, [1998] I.R.L.R. 382 at 385; *Ultraframe (UK) Ltd v Fielding* [2005] EWHC 1638 (Ch) at [1309]; *Helmet Integrated Systems Ltd v Tunnard* [2006] EWCA Civ 1735, [2007] I.R.L.R. 126; *Vestergaard Frandsen A/S v Bestnet Europe Ltd* [2013] UKSC 31; [2013] 1 W.L.R. 1556 at [44] (employees).

[246] [2001] 2 B.C.L.C. 704 at 733.

tor is entitled to resign even if his resignation might have a disastrous effect on the business and reputation of the company. So also in English law, at least in general, a fiduciary obligation does not continue after the determination of the relationship which gives rise to it."

In *Longstaff v Birtles*,[247] on the other hand, it was held that a solicitor continued to owe the duties of trust and confidence of a fiduciary even though the particular matter for which he had been engaged had come to an end. In the case, the solicitor, immediately after his client had told him in his offices that the client was not proceeding with the relevant transaction, raised with the client the possibility of the client's investing in a similar business in which the solicitor had a personal interest. The solicitor was found to have had a conflict of interest, which ultimately led to a liability in damages (a remedy which may not have been available if only undue influence were the basis of the complaint).

Other controls on conduct may commence to operate before, and continue to operate after, the end of the agent's retainer. Hence, duties to uphold confidences (including trade secrets) will usually start with the imparting of the confidential information, which may be before any agency arises, and will continue until the information ceases to be confidential or the party receiving the information is released from the obligation. Some types of agent, most conspicuously solicitors, may be subject to particularly exacting duties in relation to confidential information that endure after the retainer,[248] and can also be subject to a presumption of influence in relation to transactions (both gifts and contracts), taking place both during and after the retainer (quaere in relation to the terms of the retainer itself, where professional regulation may also operate).[249] As will be seen below, an agent who attempts to profit from position or who is under a duty to pursue for the principal relevant business opportunities, cannot free himself from those duties by simply resigning.[250]

Disclosure and consent[251] The fiduciary duties not to profit and to avoid conflicts   **6-039**
have been said to be purely negative duties.[252] They forbid the agent from having a conflict and from profiting from position, but impose no positive obligations. However, as a matter of practicalities, it will often be in the principal's interests as much as the agent's that the conflict exists or the profiting takes place. In such circumstances, it becomes essential that the agent fully informs the principal of all relevant facts and then obtains consent to the conflict or profiting. Those duties of disclosure and consent, albeit arising only secondarily, are positive duties. In other words, the fiduciary duties are not outright prohibitions, but merely proscribe profit-

[247] [2001] EWCA Civ 1219; [2002] 1 W.L.R. 470; criticised Conaglen, *Fiduciary Loyalty* at 192–193. See also *Ratiu v Conway* [2005] EWCA Civ 1302; [2006] 1 All E.R. 571; *Richards v Law Society* [2009] EWHC 2087 (Admin). cf. *Swycher v Vakil* [2002] EWCA Civ 1668.
[248] See below, para.6-051.
[249] See below, paras 6-067 and 6-069.
[250] See paras 6-067, 6-077 and 6-081. See also *Tigris International NV v China Southern Airlines Co Ltd* [2014] EWCA Civ 1649 at [163].
[251] See *Restatement, Third*, § 8.06(1); *Meagher, Gummow and Lehane's Equity Doctrines and Remedies* (5th edn), paras 5-130 and 5-135; Payne, 'Consent' in *Breach of Trust* (Birks and Pretto eds, 2002), Ch.10.
[252] See, e.g. *Breen v Williams* (1996) 186 C.L.R. 71 at 95 and 113; noted by Nolan (1997) 113 L.Q.R. 220; *Att. Gen. v Blake* [1998] Ch. 439 at 455; *P & V Industries Pty Ltd v Porto* (2006) 14 V.R. 1 at [24].

ing and conflicts that have not been consented to by the principal.[253] What constitutes a fully informed consent is a question of fact and "there is no precise formula which will determine all cases".[254] Consent must be positively shown, but it can be inferred if the principal is plainly fully aware of all the facts and raises no objection.[255] The burden of proving full disclosure of a conflict of interest and of obtaining consent lies on the agent.[256] It is not sufficient for him merely to disclose that he has an interest[257] or to make such statements as would put the principal on inquiry[258] nor is it a defence to assert that had he asked for permission it would have been given.[259] It is possible that the consent itself may be recalled if obtained by undue influence,[260] duress or misrepresentation. Consent may be given in advance or retrospectively. In some circumstances it may not be necessary for the agent to give details of the amount of a commission being paid by a third party where the principal knows that the remuneration will be received and the commission is at a rate standard in the industry.[261] It is not always necessary that the principal understand that without consent there would be a breach of fiduciary duty, but usually the principal should be aware that his consent is being sought.[262]

In the case of company directors, equity took the stance that in relation to conflicts of interest, disclosure to the principal, the company, could not be ef-

---

[253] *New Zealand Netherlands Society "Oranje" Inc v Kuys* [1973] 1 W.L.R. 1126.
[254] *Maguire v Makaronis* (1997) 188 C.L.R. 449 at 466; *Farah Constructions Pty Ltd v Say-Dee Pty Ltd* (2007) 230 C.L.R. 89; *Beach Petroleum NL v Kennedy* (1999) 48 N.S.W.L.R. 1; *Sharbern Holding Inc v Vancouver Airport Centre Ltd* [2009] BCCA 224; affd [2011] 2 S.C.R. 175; (2011) 331 D.L.R. (4th) 1. As to the possibility of an estoppel against a principal who is aware of all the facts, see *Rossetti Marketing Ltd v Diamond Sofa Co Ltd* [2012] EWCA Civ 1021; [2013] 1 All ER (Comm) 308 at [41]; *Northampton Regional Livestock Centre Co Ltd v Cowling* [2015] EWCA Civ 651 at [77]; [2016] 1 B.C.L.C. 431. As to the stricter approach applicable to trustees, see Lewin, *Trusts* (19th edn), para.20-098 onwards; *Spellson v George* (1992) 26 N.S.W.L.R. 666.
[255] *Paton v Rosesilver Group Corp* [2017] EWCA Civ 158 at [34].
[256] *Dunne v English* (1874) L.R. 18 Eq. 524; *Hurstanger v Wilson* [2007] 1 W.L.R. 2351 at [36]; *JD Wetherspoon Plc v Van De Berg & Co Ltd* [2009] EWHC 639 (Ch) at [68]; *Cobbetts LLP v Hodge* [2009] EWHC 786 (Ch) at [108]. On the analogy of concurrence with breach of trust, it should not be necessary to show that the principal knew that what he was consenting to was a breach of duty, so long as he knew clearly what the facts were: *Re Pauling's Settlement Trusts* [1962] 1 W.L.R. 86 at 108.
[257] *Imperial Mercantile Credit Association Co v Coleman* (1873) L.R. 6 H.L. 189; *Alexander v Automatic Telephone Co* [1900] 2 Ch. 56; *Gluckstein v Barnes* [1900] A.C. 240; *Gray v New Augarita Porcupine Mines* [1952] 3 D.L.R. 1 (PC); *Cobbetts LLP v Hodge* [2009] EWHC 786 (Ch) at [110]; *FHR European Ventures LLP v Mankarious* [2011] EWHC 2308 (Ch) at [78], reversed on other points at [2014] UKSC 45; [2015] A.C. 250; *Medsted Associates Ltd v Canaccord Genuity Wealth (International) Ltd* [2017] EWHC 1815 (Comm) at [97].
[258] *Dunne v English*, above; *Novoship (UK) Ltd v Mikhaylyuk* [2012] EWHC 3586 (Comm) at [83] affd on this point [2014] EWCA Civ 908. cf. *Swale v Ipswich Tannery Co Ltd* (1906) 11 Com.Cas. 88 at 86–97. The mere fact that a solicitor acting for both agent and principal in a transaction is aware of an agent's undisclosed personal benefit, is not disclosure to the principal by the agent: *Park's of Hamilton (Holdings) Ltd v Campbell* [2014] CSIH 36; 2014 SC 726 at [28].
[259] *Murad v Al-Saraj* [2005] EWCA Civ 959; 1 W.T.L.R. 1573, Illustration 12 to Article 48; *Gidman v Barron* [2003] EWHC 153 (Ch) at [126]; *FHR European Ventures LLP v Mankarious* [2011] EWHC 2308 (Ch) at [79], reversed on other points at [2014] UKSC 45; [2015] A.C. 250.
[260] *Curtis v Pulbrook* [2009] EWHC 782 (Ch) (donee of power of attorney in respect of donor, his father).
[261] See below, para.6-086, and the cases cited in fn.721.
[262] *Knight v Frost* [1999] B.C.C. 819 at 828; *EIC Services Ltd v Phipps* [2003] EWHC 1507 (Ch); [2003] B.C.C. 931 at [133]; *Sharma v Sharma* [2013] EWCA Civ 1287; [2014] B.C.C. 73 at [47].

fected by a director simply disclosing to his colleagues on the board,[263] but rather required disclosure to shareholders. Further, in relation to at least some cases of interception by a director of corporate opportunities (as to which, see below, para.6-081), consent even of a majority of shareholders may be insufficient; only unanimity will suffice.[264] These rules, however, have been modified by the Companies Act 2006. Authorisation may now be given by directors so long as the affected director is not counted as part of the quorum and does not vote, and in the case of public companies, the constitution provides for directors to give the relevant dispensation.[265]

Similar issues could arise where an agent has joint principals, where disclosure to one principal may not be sufficient.[266]

As for modification by consent of the fiduciary duties themselves, see below, para.6-056. As for positive duties of disclosure that may be imposed on at least some types of agent, see below, para.6-054.

Remedies: proprietary or personal?   Turning to the question of remedies, an   **6-040** important question to ask is when the principal's remedies against the agent are proprietary and when they are personal. A proprietary remedy for breach of fiduciary duty is an application of a main technique of equity, of requiring the legal owner of money or other property to hold it as trustee; it involves the notion that the agent holds such money or property on constructive trust. The money or property belongs in equity to the principal. A personal remedy on the other hand holds him liable to pay money to the principal as upon an obligation. As has been stated above, such obligations can often in agency situations be derived from common law independently of the fiduciary duties, being formulated by way of breach of implied terms of a contract, or a claim in restitution or tort.

The main advantages of a proprietary remedy from the point of view of the principal are that (i) the principal is generally entitled to any profits made with his money or property[267]; (ii) if the agent mixes the money with his own, the principal will be entitled to the contents of the mixture, or anything acquired by expenditure from the mixture, up to the value of his input[268]; (iii) the property will not in general

---

[263] *Benson v Heathorn* (1842) 1 Y. & C. Ch. Cas. 326; *Woolworths Ltd v Kelly* (1991) 22 N.S.W.L.R. 189 at 207. But cf. *Queensland Mines Ltd v Hudson* (1978) 18 A.L.R. 1 (PC); and *New Zealand Netherlands Society "Oranje" Inc v Kuys* [1973] 1 W.L.R. 1126; *GHLM Trading Ltd v Maroo* [2012] EWHC 61 (Ch) at [200].

[264] *Cook v Deeks* [1916] 1 A.C. 554.

[265] See Companies Act 2006 s.175. See too ss.177 and 182. As to the possibility of ratification after the event, see s.239. However, s.239(7) provides that the statutory procedure for ratification does not affect any rule of law imposing additional requirements for ratification. See *Sharma v Sharma* [2013] EWCA Civ 1287.

[266] See *FHR European Ventures LLP v Mankarious* [2011] EWHC 2308 (Ch) at [84] (disclosure to one co-principal only would turn on actual or apparent authority to do so), reversed on other grounds at [2014] UKSC 45; [2015] A.C. 250.

[267] *Docker v Somes* (1834) 2 My. & K. 655; *Foskett v McKeown* [2000] 1 A.C. 102; Goff and Jones, *Law of Unjust Enrichment* (9th edn), para.37-02 onwards. See Finn, *Fiduciary Obligations* (1977), Ch.18. This may include interest (see Article 52); an account attributing the profits in a mixed fund to the constituent elements of it: see *Scott v Scott* (1963) 109 C.L.R. 649; *Re Tilley's Will Trusts* [1967] Ch. 1179; Article 51; and sometimes an award in respect of savings effected for the trustee by the use of the property: see Finn, op cit., pp.127–129.

[268] *Lupton v White* (1808) 15 Ves. 432; *Cook v Addison* (1868) L.R. 7 Eq. 466; *Re Oatway* [1903] 2 Ch. 356; *James Roscoe (Bolton) Ltd v Winder* [1915] 1 Ch. 62; *Indian Oil Corp Ltd v Greenstone Shipping SA* [1988] Q.B. 345; *Bishopsgate Investment Management Ltd v Homan* [1995] Ch. 211:

be available to the agent's creditors in his bankruptcy[269]; (iv) the principal may be able to trace the money, not only against the agent but also into the hands of third parties other than bona fide purchasers for value[270]; (v) there may be no limitation period applicable in relation to recovery of the property as a result of relevant provisions of the Limitation Act[271]; (vi) the principal may be able to obtain an order for the return of specific property and an interim order for its preservation pending trial.[272] It seems that the claimant may elect whether to take the asset in specie or to seek merely an order for the payment of its value.[273] The claimant will also be able to elect whether to claim the asset or its value (whether or not the defaulting party can show that he could, if desired, have acquired it using his own money) or to reject the expenditure and claim the original sum taken plus interest.[274]

It is generally accepted, however, that it would be inappropriate for a breach of fiduciary duty to create proprietary rights in assets that were not the principal's apart from the breach or that have not been derived from the breach.[275]

6-041   **Remedies: agent holding money for principal**[276]   It is convenient first to consider situations where the agent simply holds for his principal without any issue of breach of fiduciary obligation. The analogy with trust might be taken to suggest first, that when an agent holds title to money or other property for his principal, he always does so (in situations where the principal does not himself own it) as trustee. This would often be impractical and has never been the rule. It is perfectly possible for property so held, especially money, to be the agent's own, and mixed with his own assets subject only to a duty to transfer or account for it to his principal. Equally however he may certainly hold as trustee.

Often the answer turns on the contract between principal and agent. It is clear in

---

see also *Re Tilley's Will Trusts* [1967] Ch. 1179. But the matter is sometimes put on the basis that the defendant can prove that something is his: see *Van Rassel v Kroon* (1953) 87 C.L.R. 298 (lottery ticket); *Warman International Ltd v Dwyer* (1995) 182 C.L.R. 544 at 561–562.

[269]   *Barclays Bank Ltd v Quistclose Investments* [1970] A.C. 567.

[270]   See Article 91.

[271]   Limitation Act 1980, s.21(1)(b); older cases, of course, related to earlier legislation. See e.g. Illustrations 1 and 3. See now *Williams v Central Bank of Nigeria* [2014] UKSC 10; [2014] A.C. 1189; *Burnden Holdings (UK) Ltd v Fielding* [2016] EWCA Civ 557; [2017] 1 W.L.R. 39; *First Subsea Ltd v Balltec Ltd* [2017] EWCA Civ 186 and the discussion of trusteeship in this context by Millett LJ in *Paragon Finance Plc v D.B. Thakerar & Co* [1999] 1 All E.R. 400; *J.J. Harrison (Properties) Ltd v Harrison* [2001] EWCA Civ 1467; [2002] 1 B.C.L.C. 162; *Yong Kheng Leong v Panweld Trading Pte Ltd* [2012] SGCA 59 at [42] onwards. See further Lewin, *Trusts* (19th edn), Ch. 44, paras 44-004—44-017; 44-040 and 44-049—44-051; also para.7-008 onwards.

[272]   Now fused into "Interim Remedies" (together with freezing injunctions) in CPR 25.1.

[273]   See *FHR European Ventures LLP v Cedar Capital Partners LLC* [2014] UKSC 45; [2015] A.C. 250 at [7]; *Global Energy Horizons Corp v Gray* [2015] EWHC 2232 (Ch) at [139]–[143].

[274]   See *Scott v Scott* (1963) 109 C.L.R. 649 at 660 and 662; *Tang Ying Ip v Tang Ying Loi* [2017] HKCFA 3 at [27], per Lord Millett.

[275]   See *Daly v Sydney Stock Exchange Ltd* (1986) 160 C.L.R. 371; *Hancock Family Memorial Foundation Ltd v Porteous* (2000) 22 W.A.R. 198; *Fortex Group Ltd v Macintosh* [1998] 3 N.Z.L.R. 471 (Illustration 6). Dicta to the contrary in *Space Investments Ltd v Canadian Imperial Bank of Commerce Trust Co (Bahamas) Ltd* [1988] 1 W.L.R. 1072 have not been followed: see *Re Goldcorp Exchange Ltd* [1995] 1 A.C. 74; *Serious Fraud Office v Lexi Holdings Plc* [2008] EWCA Crim 1443; [2009] Q.B. 376; *Lehman Brothers International (Europe) v CRC Credit Fund Ltd & Ors* [2009] EWHC 3228 (Ch) at [192] (ultimately reversed on basis of statutory provisions: [2012] UKSC 6; [2012] 3 All E.R. 1). See also the Rt Hon. Lord Millett [1993] Restitution L.Rev. 7; (1998) 114 L.Q.R. 214 at 225–227.

[276]   The text of this paragraph received general approval in *Pearson v Lehman Brothers Finance SA* [2010] EWHC 2914 (Ch) at [253], affd [2011] EWCA Civ 1544.

this context and in general that the existence of a contractual relationship of debtor and creditor between the parties does not prevent the existence of a simultaneous trust relationship, or a fiduciary relationship of a less onerous nature, involving nevertheless that certain money or property is held on trust.[277] Thus it may be provided expressly between principal and agent that money received is so held. At other times the intention to create a trust may be inferred; the matter turns on the objective interpretation, according to general principles, of the intentions of the parties.[278] Equally, it is possible that a person may be appointed agent to collect moneys owed a principal, such as rent, but then have the express right to have recourse to those funds for discharge of obligations owed by the principal to the agent (whether or not those obligations relate to the agency relationship).[279]

It is sometimes said that there is a prima facie duty on an agent to keep the principal's money and property separate[280]; but it seems likely that this is overstated.[281] Earlier editions of this book suggested that the situations where a trust has been held to exist largely fall into two broad categories: (i) where money or property has been specifically entrusted to the agent by the principal to hold for his benefit or to use for a specific purpose[282]; and (ii) where money or property has been handed to the agent by a third party to hold or convert into a specific property for the benefit of the principal.[283] Another relevant consideration is whether money or property was received in pursuance of a single transaction for which the agent was appointed, or as part of a group of transactions in respect of which a general account was to be rendered later or periodically. No implication of a personal right to use agency moneys would normally be appropriate where the agent was of a type who is not expected to handle money for his principal at all. These are all useful indications, though the cases are not all easily reduced to such form.[284]

The present trend seems to be to approach the matter more functionally and to

---

[277] See *Barclays Bank Ltd v Quistclose Investments Ltd* [1970] A.C. 567 (giving rise to the so-called "Quistclose trust": see Lewin, *Trusts* (19th edn), para.8-040 onwards); *Re Kayford* [1975] 1 W.L.R. 279; *Carreras Rothmans Ltd v Freeman Matthews Treasure Ltd* [1985] Ch. 207; *General Communications Ltd v Development Finance Corp of New Zealand* [1990] 3 N.Z.L.R. 406; *Pearson v Lehman Brothers Finance SA* [2011] EWCA Civ 1544 at [68] (trust sustained even though identification of varying beneficial ownership of assets would be complex); *Hughmans Solicitors v Central Stream Services Ltd* [2012] EWCA Civ 1720 at [21]; *Bambury v Jensen* [2015] NZHC 2384; *Lehman Bros International (Europe) v CRC Credit Fund Ltd* [2012] UKSC 6; [2012] 3 All E.R. 1 at [194]. (solicitor's client account held on trust even though no certainty as to who was beneficiary of the funds).
[278] See *Scott and Ascher on Trusts* (5th edn), Vol.1 § 2.3.8.1.
[279] See *Clarence House Ltd v National Westminster Bank Plc* [2009] EWCA Civ 1311 at [35]. cf. *Ferrera v Hardy* [2013] EWHC 4164 (Ch) at [18].
[280] See Article 50; *Palette Shoes Pty Ltd v Krohn* (1937) 58 C.L.R. 1 at 30; *Westpac Banking Corp v Savin* [1985] 2 N.Z.L.R. 41 at 49. See also *Cohen v Cohen* (1929) 42 C.L.R. 91 at 101–102.
[281] See the valuable discussion by the Court of Appeal of New South Wales in *Walker v Corboy* (1990) 19 N.S.W.L.R. 382; Article 50.
[282] e.g. *Burdick v Garrick* (1870) L.R. 5 Ch.App. 233, Illustration 1; *Flitcroft's case* (1882) 21 Ch.D. 519; *Dooby v Watson* (1888) 39 Ch.D. 178; *North American Land and Timber Co Ltd v Watkins* [1904] 2 Ch. 233, Illustration 3; *Royal Norwegian Government v Calcutta Marine Engineering Co Ltd* [1960] 2 Lloyd's Rep. 431 (but compare this case with *Potters (A Firm) v Loppert* [1973] Ch. 399; and see Article 53); *Cooper v PRG Powerhouse Ltd* [2008] EWHC 498 (Ch); [2008] B.P.I.R. 492; [2008] 2 All E.R. (Comm) 964.
[283] e.g. *Littlewood v Williams* (1815) 6 Taunt. 277; *Mathew v Brise* (1851) 14 Beav. 341; *Seagram v Tuck* (1881) 18 Ch.D. 296; *Brown v IRC* [1965] A.C. 244, Illustration 1 to Article 53. cf. *Ex p. Dale & Co* (1879) 11 Ch.D. 772.
[284] e.g. as to stockbrokers: *Hancock v Smith* (1889) 41 Ch.D. 456; *Re Wreford* (1897) 13 T.L.R. 153 (trustee of client account); see also *Re Fleet Disposal Services Ltd* [1995] 1 B.C.L.C. 345 (selling

ask whether the trust relationship is appropriate to the commercial relationship in which the parties find themselves[285]; whether it was appropriate that money or property should be, and whether it was, held separately, or whether it was contemplated that the agent should use the money, property or proceeds of the property as part of his normal cash flow in such a way that the relationship of debtor and creditor is more appropriate.[286] There are a great number of cases.[287] At the same time, there is no absolute rule that the absence of a duty to keep the principal's property separate is fatal to there being a trust. Such a trust would have to be over a mixed fund,[288] and there would also have to be a personal duty on the agent to maintain the balance of the fund at or above the amounts owed the principal.

Further, even where an agent does not hold money provided by his principal for specific purposes, there may be a duty to use it only for purposes relevant to the agency, with the consequence that if the money is used for non-agency purposes, any asset acquired with it is held on trust.[289] Sometimes the position is secured by statute or regulation providing that particular types of functionary (e.g. estate agents and solicitors) hold clients' money on trust, pay into client accounts and keep trust accounts.[290]

---

agent a trustee); *Re Ararimu Holdings Ltd* [1989] 3 N.Z.L.R. 487; cf. *King v Hutton* (1860) 83 L.T. 68 (not a trustee); and auctioneers: *Re Cotton Ex p. Cooke* (1913) 103 L.T. 310 (trustee); cf. *Murphy v Howlett* [1960] E.G.D. 231 (not a trustee).

[285] See *New Zealand and Australian Land Co v Watson* (1881) 7 Q.B.D. 374 at 382; *Templeton Insurance Ltd v Motorcare Warranties Ltd* [2010] EWHC 3113 (Comm) at [194]; *Bieber v Teathers Ltd* [2012] EWHC 190 (Ch) at [25], affd [2012] EWCA Civ 1466; [2012] 2 B.C.L.C. 585 (no trust where impossible to carry out instructions if keep moneys separate).

[286] This passage as it appeared in the 15th edition of this book was approved by Lord Goff of Chieveley in the context of equitable lien in *Lord Napier and Ettrick v Hunter* [1993] A.C. 713 at 744. As to such liens, see Phillips, in *Interests in Goods* (Palmer and McKendrick, eds, 2nd edn), Ch.39.

[287] See *King v Hutton*, above; *Henry v Hammond* [1913] 2 K.B. 515, Illustration 4; *Neste Oy v Lloyd's Bank Plc* [1983] 2 Lloyd's Rep. 658, Illustration 5; *Stephens Travel Service Inc Pty Ltd v Qantas Airways Ltd* (1988) 13 N.S.W.L.R. 331 (distinguished in *Canadian Pacific Airlines Ltd v Canadian Imperial Bank of Commerce* (1987) 42 D.L.R. (4th) 375; affd (1990) 71 Q.R. (2d) 63); *Walker v Corboy* (1990) 19 N.S.W.L.R. 382; *Kingscroft Insurance Co Ltd v H.S. Weavers (Underwriting Agencies) Ltd* [1993] 1 Lloyd's Rep. 187; *Style Financial Services Ltd v Bank of Scotland (No.2)* 1998 S.L.T. 851; *Paragon Finance Plc v D.B. Thackerar & Co* [1999] 1 All E.R. 400 at 415; *Hinckley Singapore Trading Pte Ltd v Sogo Department Stores (S) Pte Ltd* [2001] 4 Singapore L.R. 154 (concessionaire agreement); *Duggan v Governor of Full Sutton Prison* [2004] EWCA Civ 78; [2004] 1 W.L.R. 1010 (prisoners depositing cash); *Pearson v Lehman Bros Finance SA* [2011] EWCA Civ 1544; *Bellis v Challinor* [2015] EWCA Civ 59; *Korda v Australian Executor Trustees (SA) Ltd* [2015] HCA 6; (2015) 255 C.L.R. 62 at [111]. See too *Re Farepak Food & Gifts Ltd* [2006] EWHC 3272 (Ch); [2007] 2 B.C.L.C. 1 (alleged agent held agent only for seller and not buyer, and no duty to keep proceeds separate). For the position in relation to travel agents and air tickets, see Smith, in *Commercial Trusts in European Private Law* (Graziadei, Mattei and Smith eds, 2005), p.294.

[288] See *Lehman Brothers International (Europe) Ltd v CRC Credit Fund Ltd* [2012] UKSC 6; [2012] 3 All E.R. 1 at [194]; *Bambury v Jensen* [2015] NZHC 2384 at [119].

[289] *Zhong v Wang* (2007) N.Z.C.P.R. 488. See too *Lehman Bros International (Europe) v CRC Credit Fund Ltd* [2009] EWHC 3228 (Ch) at [151] (power to maintain mixed fund of client and personal moneys, but duty to maintain buffer to cover amount owed clients), ultimately reversed on some issues [2012] UKSC 6; [2012] 3 All E.R. 1.

[290] Estate Agents Act 1979 ss.13–16 (in fact, persons engaged in "estate agency work") (see Murdoch, *Law of Estate Agency* (5th edn), p.233 onwards; Murdoch, *The Estate Agents and Property Misdescriptions Acts* (3rd edn), Ch.3D); see also Solicitors Act 1974 s.32 as amended; Financial Services and Markets Act 2000 s.139 and regulations thereunder, as construed in *Re Lehman Bros International (Europe) (In Administration)* [2012] UKSC 6; [2012] 3 All E.R. 1 (subsequently amended by Financial Services Act 2012 s.24). See further *Walker v Corboy*, above. As to interest, see Article 53.

Many disputes over an agent's obligations in relation to moneys or other property in his hands do not surface until the agent has become insolvent. There had been longstanding authority, albeit at first instance, that where money received from, or due to, the principal came into the agent's hands only after the agent had become insolvent, such that the agent was never going to be in a position to execute his undertakings to the principal, equity could impose a constructive trust over the money in the principal's favour, independently of any express or implied agreement for this result.[291] The approach taken in these cases has now been disapproved of by the Supreme Court, albeit in what strictly were obiter dicta.[292] On this approach, any trust must arise by express or implied agreement, and not be constructed by the court.

Remedies: profits made in breach of duty to principal Turning now to breach **6-042** of duty, perhaps the most specific of the agent's fiduciary duties is that not to make a profit at his principal's expense.[293] There is no doubt that a fiduciary is not permitted to profit from use of position, without the fully-informed consent of the principal. There is also no doubt that the remedy of account of profits is available to remove those profits. There has until recently been much less certainty about whether the agent holds any specific assets obtained from a breach of duty on trust for the principal. Assets derived from the misapplication of money or other property belonging legally or beneficially to the principal have consistently been found to be held on constructive trust for the principal (it is irrelevant that the agent could have used personal moneys to acquire the asset). Where an asset was not so derived but is of a type the acquisition of which would be beneficial to the principal's business, and the agent's tasks include obtaining such assets, or assisting in obtaining such assets, for the principal, then the asset will also be held on constructive trust for the principal.[294] This is so even if, had the agent not acquired the asset at all, there would not have been any breach of duty on the part of the agent. But the position where an agent obtains money or other property from the simple use of his position, such as by taking a secret commission or bribe, which should never have been obtained at all, has been much less clear. However, the longstanding uncertainty has been settled by the Supreme Court in *FHR European Ventures LLP v Cedar Capital Partners LLC*.[295] In this important decision the Court held that all money and other property constituting a bribe or secret commission, and any fruits derived therefrom, will be held on constructive trust for the principal. It seems, in fact, that any identifiable property derived by an agent from a breach of fiduciary duty, innocent or not, will be held on constructive trust.[296] In so ruling, the Court disapproved the contrary ruling of the House of Lords in *Tyrrell v Bank of*

---

[291] *Neste Oy v Lloyd's Bank Plc* [1983] 2 Lloyd's Rep. 658; *Re Japan Leasing (Europe) Plc* [1999] B.P.I.R. 911.
[292] See *Angove's Pty Ltd v Bailey* [2016] UKSC 47; [2016] 1 W.L.R. 3179 at [31]; noted Watts (2017) 133 L.Q.R. 11.
[293] As to the detail of the duty not to profit without consent, see Articles 46 to 49.
[294] See below, Article 48.
[295] [2014] UKSC 45; [2015] A.C. 250; noted Gummow (2015) 131 L.Q.R. 21; Conaglen [2014] C.L.J. 490; Campbell (2015) 39 Aust. Bar Rev. 320.
[296] [2014] UKSC 45 at [35]; *Akita Holdings Ltd v Attorney General of Turks and Caicos Islands* [2017] UKPC 7; [2017] A.C. 590 at [16]. *Sinclair Investments Ltd v Versailles Trade Finance Ltd* [2012] Ch. 453, which involved only indirect profiting from position, was expressly overruled in *FHR European*, above at [50], although only insofar as the case founded itself on cases on secret commissions. It is assumed that the proviso is intended to keep alive any holdings that do not relate to proprietary remedies.

London,[297] and overruled several decisions of the Court of Appeal.[298] The Court saw itself as bringing the law of England and Wales into line with leading Commonwealth authorities.[299] It is clear that the trust remedy will apply even where the principal has rescinded any contract with a third party infected by the agent's breach of duty, and has hence avoided any loss. Nor will the fact that the principal has not suffered any loss prevent his prevailing over a party who has innocently taken an equitable security over the trust property, or over the agent's general creditors in an insolvency.[300] Where any gain has ceased to be identifiable, the principal will retain a personal claim against the agent, including in any insolvency of the agent, again without regard to whether any loss has been suffered or to the innocence of the breach. Once the claimant has established relevant breaches of fiduciary duty and a plausible connection to a profit made by the agent (including a particular asset if a constructive trust is being sought), the agent will bear the burden of proving that there was no causative connection between the breach and the profit (or acquisition of the asset).[301] Similar principles apply where a fiduciary has mixed his principal's property with his own in determining the extent of the principal's proprietary claim on the mixture.[302]

There remains some uncertainty whether an agent can be made accountable for profits not derived personally, but diverted by the agent to a third party.[303] Where the third party is a company wholly owned by the agent, it may be possible to treat the company as identified with the agent,[304] although that will not normally be necessary.

---

[297] (1862) 10 H.L. Cas. 26. *Tyrrell*, however, remains a sound authority as to the general fiduciary duties of solicitors and in its affirmation of a constructive trust over business opportunities: see the full discussion of the case in Watts, (2013) 129 L.Q.R. 526.

[298] Including *Metropolitan Bank v Heiron* (1880) 5 Ex.D. 319; *Lister & Co v Stubbs* (1890) 45 Ch.D. 1; and *Sinclair Investments Ltd v Versailles Trade Finance Ltd* [2012] Ch. 453.

[299] In particular, *Att.-Gen. for Hong Kong v Reid* [1994] 1 A.C. 324; and *Grimaldi v Chameleon Mining NL (No. 2)* (2012) 287 A.L.R. 22 at [576].

[300] See *FHR European*, above at [43].

[301] *Ryde Holdings Ltd v Rainbow Corp Ltd* [1993] UKPC 40; *United Pan-Europe Communications NV v Deutsche Bank AG* [2000] 2 B.C.L.C. 461 at [34]; *Murad v Al-Saraj* [2005] EWCA Civ 959 at [77]. cf. *Global Energy Horizons Corp v Gray* [2015] EWHC 2232 (Ch) at [135] (burden of proof often not determinative). See also below, para.6-077.

[302] *Lupton v White* (1808) 15 Ves. Jun. 432; *Sze Tu v Lowe* [2014] NSWCA 462. See further, para.8-162.

[303] Support for the view that a company director can be accountable for gains made by third parties as a result of the director's breach of duty can be found in *CMS Dolphin Ltd v Simonet* [2001] 2 B.C.L.C. 704. See too *Walsham v Stainton* (1863) 1 De G.J. & S. 678. But cf. *Ultraframe (UK) Ltd v Fielding* [2005] EWHC 1638 (Ch) at [1575]–[1576]; *Fiona Trust Holding Corp v Privalov* [2007] EWHC 1217 (Comm) at [29]; *National Grid Electricity Transmission Plc v McKenzie Harbour Management Resources Ltd* [2009] EWHC 1817 (Ch) at [118] (indicating special rules where the defaulting agent is a member of a partnership which derives the resulting gains); *Aerostar Maintenance International Ltd v Wilson* [2010] EWHC 2032 (Ch) at [204]; *Novoship (UK) Ltd v Mikhaylyuk* [2012] EWHC 3586 (Comm) at [99] (issue not addressed on appeal: [2014] EWCA Civ 908; [2015] Q.B. 499). See too *Northampton Regional Livestock Centre Co Ltd v Cowling* [2015] EWCA Civ 651; [2016] 1 B.C.L.C. 431 at [96] (partner liable for improper profit derived by colleague in the course of partnership).

[304] See *Trustor AB v Smallbone (No.2)* [2001] 1 W.L.R. 1177; and *Quarter Master UK Ltd v Pyke* [2005] 1 B.C.L.C. 245. See too *Antonio Gramsci Shipping Corp v Stepanovs* [2011] EWHC 333 (Comm); [2011] C.L.C. 396 at [21] and [26] (both puppet company and puppeteer might be liable); *Akita Holdings Ltd v Attorney General of Turks and Caicos Islands* [2017] UKPC 7; [2017] A.C. 590 at [16]. But cf. *VTB Capital Plc v Nutritek International Corp* [2013] UKSC 5; [2013] 2 A.C. 337 at [147]; and *Prest v Petrodel Resources Ltd* [2013] UKSC 34; [2013] 2 A.C. 415. For discussion, see Glister, in Davis and Penner (eds) *Equity, Trusts and Commerce* (2017), Ch.12.

Losses caused: equitable restitution and compensation[305] The prophylactic **6-043**
nature of the fiduciary duties, operating whether or not any harm has been done to
the beneficiary of the duties, has encouraged a focus on remedies such as rescission of transactions where the fiduciary has a conflict of interest and on the account of profits where the fiduciary has profited from position. However, there has
always been a range of situations where restorative (restitutionary) and compensatory remedies (comparable to damages for loss caused) have been available at
equity. Hence, trustees (and other fiduciaries) can be liable for misapplying trust
property, failing to invest, and exercising a discretion negligently.[306] Many of the
trustee cases relate to application of the trust property inconsistently with the trust
deed (honesty not being a defence).[307] The principles of these cases have also been
applied to agents, but, as has been seen above, spending a principal's money in
breach of mandate is likely also to lead to liability at common law, in particular to
an order for money had and received, or for damages for breach of contract.[308]
Equity has also long awarded compensation for loss resulting from a trustee's or
agent's active disloyalty. For example, an agent who disloyally encourages his
principal's suppliers to supply other traders, and who secretly encourages his
principal's customers to cease to deal with him will be liable for ensuing loss to the
principal, which can include compensation for loss of a chance of continuing business with the customers.[309]

It has been less clear whether the mere failure to disclose a conflict of interest
(having not avoided the conflict in the first place) can support a duty on an honest
fiduciary to pay compensation at equity,[310] as opposed to merely assisting to
evidence a breach of a duty of care, which duty might for an agent arise in equity,
contract or tort.[311]

Traditionally, equity distinguished between actions seeking to have lost trust
capital restored and claims for consequential losses.[312] So, where the complaint was
that the trustee had wrongly disbursed trust capital, whether through stepping

---

[305] See Snell, *Equity* (33rd edn), Ch.20; *Meagher, Gummow and Lehane's Equity Doctrines and
Remedies* (5th edn), Ch.24; Conaglen (2003) 119 L.Q.R. 246; Conaglen (2010) 126 L.Q.R. 72;
Conaglen, *Fiduciary Loyalty* (2010), Ch.6; Degeling and Varuhas (eds) *Equitable Compensation and
Disgorgement of Profit* (2017).

[306] See Lewin, *Trusts* (19th edn), para.39-001 onwards.

[307] See, e.g. *Re Dawson* [1966] 2 N.S.W.R. 211; *AIB Group (UK) Plc v Mark Redler & Co (A Firm)*
[2014] UKSC 58; [2015] A.C. 1503 at [19] (solicitor disbursing client funds without authority). For
further authority see above, para.6-003.

[308] See above, Article 36.

[309] See e.g. *Také Ltd v BSM Marketing Ltd* [2006] EWHC 1085 (QB), and subsequent damages appeal
at [2009] EWCA Civ 45; *Premium Real Estate Ltd v Stevens* [2009] 2 N.Z.L.R. 384; *Hydrocool Pty
Ltd v Hepburn (No.4)* [2011] FCA 495; (2011) 83 A.C.S.R. 652 (director puts own job protection
ahead of company's interest in negotiating sale of business). cf. *Rama v Millar* [1996] 1 N.Z.L.R.
257 (PC) where no disloyalty was found. See too Glister (2014) 8 J.Eq. 235.

[310] For argument, and supporting authorities, that mere breach of fiduciary duty can sustain damages
where causation is established, see Conaglen (2003) 119 L.Q.R. 246; and (2010) 126 L.Q.R. 72. See
too *Hodgkinson v Simms* [1994] 3 S.C.R. 377; (1994) 117 D.L.R. (4th) 161; *Gwembe Valley
Development Co Ltd v Koshy (No.3)* [2003] EWCA Civ 1048; [2004] 1 B.C.L.C. 131 at [159] (but
causation not established); *PNC Telecom Plc v Thomas* [2007] EWHC 2157 (Ch); [2008] 2 B.C.L.C.
95.

[311] See e.g. *Hilton v Barker Booth & Eastwood* [2005] UKHL 8; [2005] 1 W.L.R. 567 (claim pleaded
and decided on the basis of negligence in performance of duties).

[312] For an enlightening discussion, see Conaglen (2016) 40 Melb.U.L.R. 126. Cases include *Cocker v
Quayle* (1830) 1 Russ. & M. 535; *Re Collie, Ex p. Adamson* (1878) 8 Ch.D. 807 at 819; *Magnus v
Queensland National Bank* (1888) 37 Ch.D. 466; *British America Elevator Co Ltd v Bank of Brit-
ish North America* [1919] A.C. 658 (PC) at 666; *Re Dawson* [1966] 2 N.S.W.R. 211; *Main v

outside the terms of the trust or by the careless exercise of discretion, equity responded through the beneficiaries bringing an action for an account in common form (different from an account of profits).[313] The trustee was required "to effect a restitution to the estate".[314] This did not entail that liability was in all cases strict. Strict liability did apply to failure to comply with the terms of the trust (the parallel position to the common law where an agent fails to adhere to instructions), but usually carelessness would be needed where it was a discretionary decision relating to the management of the trust property that was being challenged. However, in all cases the restitutionary action was not generally governed by the common law principles of damages regarding time of assessment, causation, remoteness, contributory negligence and so forth.[315] In such proceedings, defaults in the disposition of trust property have simply not been recognised as having any validity as far as the trustee is concerned[316]; the transactions are said to be "falsified" and the trustee left to ensure that the trust assets that were formerly there are made available when called for. The trustee has not been permitted to argue that had there been no breach, loss would have occurred anyway. If, however, the beneficiaries' claim was for more than reconstitution of lost capital, such as for consequential losses as a result of a "wilful default", then principles of causation did become applicable.[317] Reconstitution of capital is one thing, assessing what the claimant's financial position might have been had the trustee performed his duties is another. Neither type of claim was conceived of as a damages claim in the common law sense.

Much of this learning, in England, seems to be in the process of being swept away, and replaced by a general concept of equitable compensation.

The modern origin of such a remedy is usually supported by reference to the speech of Lord Haldane in *Nocton v Ashburton*,[318] though what is said in that case is not easy to follow.[319] However, since the decision of the House of Lords in *Target Holdings Ltd v Redferns*,[320] the concept of damages in equity has become generalised, almost to the point where the stricter approach taken in the account-

---

Giambrone & Law (a firm) [2017] EWCA Civ 1193 at [62].
[313] See below, Article 51.
[314] *Re Dawson* [1966] 2 N.S.W.R. 211 at 214–216, per Street J; *Bristol and West BS v Mothew* [1998] Ch. 1 at 18; *Lloyds TSB Bank Plc v Markandan & Uddin (A Firm)* [2012] EWCA Civ 65 at [54]; *Re Ruscoe Ltd* Unreported August 7, 2012 Ch.D.; *Libertarian Investments Ltd v Hall* [2013] HKCFA 93 at [168]; *Creggy v Barnett* [2016] EWCA Civ 1004; [2017] 2 W.L.R. 1054 at [45] (where, however, the particular claimant was not a beneficiary and had only a damages claim). See *Heydon* (1997) 113 L.Q.R. 8.
[315] See the Hon. Justice Gummow in *Equity, Fiduciaries and Trusts* (Youdan ed., 1989), Ch.2; *Meagher, Gummow and Lehane's Equity Doctrines and Remedies* (5th edn), Ch.24; Davidson (1982) Melb.U.L. Rev. 349; Davies, in *Equity, Fiduciaries and Trusts* (Waters ed., 1993), Ch.14; Edelman and Elliott (2003) 119 L.Q.R. 545; (2004) Trusts Law Int. 116; the Rt Hon. Lord Millett, in *Commercial Law: Principles and Practice* (2006), para.1.44 onwards; McDermott, *Equitable Damages* (1994); Penner (2014) 8 J.Eq. 202; Shaw-Mellors [2015] J.B.L. 165; Watts [2016] L.M.C.L.Q. 118; Conaglen (2016) 40 Melb.U.L.R. 126.
[316] *Knott v Cottee* (1852) 16 Beav. 77 at 79–80; *Ultraframe (UK) Ltd v Fielding* [2005] EWHC 1638(4) (Ch) at [1513]; *Libertarian Investments Ltd v Hall* [2013] HKCFA 93 at [169].
[317] See *Re Brogden* (1886) 38 Ch.D. 546; *Bartlett v Barclays Bank Trust Co Ltd (No.2)* [1980] Ch. 515 at 545.
[318] *Nocton v Ashburton* [1914] A.C. 398, Illustration 7. For cases before *Nocton*, see Conaglen (2016) 40 Melb. U.L.R. 126 at 146–150. cf. *Henderson v Merrett Syndicates Ltd* [1995] 2 A.C. 145 at 204–205, per Lord Browne-Wilkinson. See Gummow, above; cf. Getzler, in *Restitution and Equity* (Birks and Rose, eds, 2000), Vol.1, p.251.
[319] See *Hedley Byrne & Co Ltd v Heller & Partners Ltd* [1964] A.C. 465 at 530.
[320] *Target Holdings Ltd v Redferns* [1996] A.C. 421.

ing process has been supplanted. The court there favoured an approach analogous to that taken to damages in tort, looking to see what position the beneficiary would have been in had no breach of trust occurred.[321] If the beneficiary would have suffered the same loss even had there been no breach there would be no liability. Lord Browne-Wilkinson stated:

"Equitable compensation for breach of trust is designed to achieve exactly what the word compensation suggests: to make good a loss in fact suffered by the beneficiaries and which, using hindsight and common sense, can be seen to have been caused by the breach."[322]

In fact, Lord Browne-Wilkinson did not altogether rule out the older restitutionary approach.[323] The facts of the case, a case of a bare trust of intended loan moneys where the moneys had been released by the trustee (the lender's solicitor) without the required mortgage being in place, fitted with the older remedy of the common account. But, that remedy ceased to be applicable, his Lordship said, when the trustee had got in the required mortgage after the event. That may have been all that was needed for deciding the case.[324] However, the broader approach, based on analogies with common law damages, which formed the heart of his judgment, has now been taken up and affirmed by the Supreme Court in *AIB Group (UK) Plc v Mark Redler*,[325] a case on similar facts to *Target Holdings*. Lord Toulson, who gave the lead judgment, favoured a broad remedy of equitable compensation being available for all honest breaches of trust, one that mimicked the expectation remedy in contract.[326] Lord Reed's judgment was more cautious about assimilating remedies for breach of trust with tort or contract damages, but accepted much of the reasoning of *Target Holdings*, including the notion that equitable remedies are designed to put the beneficiaries in the position they would have been in had the trustee correctly performed his duties.[327] As with *Target Holdings*, it is probable that the same result could have been reached in *AIB Group* using the older learning. While this was not a case where the solicitors' breach of instructions was cured, it was arguable that the client had ratified what had happened (without prejudice to a claim for damages) and therefore could not falsify the disbursal of the loan.[328]

It appears that some other jurisdictions, most notably Australia and Hong Kong, are not yet willing to abandon the older, stricter, approach where what is in question is the disbursal by a trustee of trust funds in breach of instructions or in the exercise of a discretion incautiously exercised.[329] The force of the older view is most compelling in cases where the conditions for releasing funds were simply not met

---

[321] At 432.

[322] At 439, per Lord Browne-Wilkinson, following dicta of McLachlin J in *Canson Enterprises Ltd v Boughton & Co* [1991] 3 S.C.R. 335. See also *Beach Petroleum NV v Kennedy* (1999) 48 N.S.W.L.R. 1 at 91–94.

[323] At 436.

[324] See the Rt Hon. Lord Millett (1998) 114 L.Q.R. 214; Conaglen (2010) 4 J.Eq. 288 (trustee's continuing authority to act as such is key to ability to rectify earlier wrongful disbursement).

[325] *AIB Group (UK) Plc v Mark Redler* [2014] UKSC 58; [2015] A.C. 1503; noted Hon. W. Gummow (2015) 41 Aust. Bar Rev. 5; Rt Hon. Lord Millett (2015) UK Supreme Ct Yearbook 193; Turner [2015] C.L.J. 188; Davies (2015) 78 M.L.R. 681.

[326] At [71].

[327] At [134].

[328] For elaboration, see Watts [2016] L.M.C.L.Q. 118.

[329] See *Youyang Pty Ltd v Minter Ellison Morris Fletcher* (2003) 212 C.L.R. 484 at [39] and [42]; *Alexander v Perpetual Trustees WA Ltd* [2004] HCA 7; (2004) 216 C.L.R. 109 at [46] and [59]; *Agricultural Land Management Ltd v Jackson (No.2)* [2014] WASC 102; (2014) 285 F.L.R. 121 at

at the time of the release. It has been noted earlier (above, para.6-003) that even at common law it is not usually a defence for an agent to say that had the conditions been met the money would still have been lost. Within the general law of contract, a promisee is not confined to expectation damages but can call for restitution when there has been a total failure of consideration. It might be thought remarkable, for instance, if a solicitor holding trust moneys earmarked for a loan accidentally released them to a complete stranger and was then permitted to set up an argument that even had he sent them to the correct borrower they would not have been recoverable.[330] Such a solicitor may have been authorised to send the funds to the insolvent borrower but could not vis-à-vis the client claim a *right* to do so.

Where what is at issue is loss caused by breach of fiduciary duty unrelated to misapplication of the principal's moneys, issues of causation do become relevant, as they do with the account on the basis of wilful default.[331] Further restraints on recovery may result if the loss was not within the risk created by the default, or was caused by the claimant himself.[332] But where actual disloyalty has been proven, the fiduciary can be liable for resulting loss even if a careful and loyal agent might have made the same choice of action,[333] and the onus of proving that loss would have resulted irrespective of the agent's action is likely to lie on the agent.[334] The general position has been stated as follows:

"the Court should assess the compensation in a robust manner, relying on the presumption against wrongdoers, the onus of proof, and resolving doubtful questions against the party whose actions have made an accurate determination so problematic."[335]

Nothing in the foregoing addresses the situation where an agent acts carelessly in a way which does not involve the handling of trust moneys. In such case the duties of care may arise only at common law, or if they arise in equity they are

---

[344] and [368]; *Libertarian Investments Ltd v Hall* [2013] HKCFA 93 at [90] and [168].

[330] See *Main v Giambrone & Law (a firm)* [2017] EWCA Civ 1193.

[331] See *Swindle v Harrison* [1997] 4 All E.R. 705, Illustration 12; *Nationwide BS v Balmer Radmore* [1999] Lloyd's Rep. P.N. 241; *Collins v Brebner* [2000] Lloyd's Rep. P.N. 587. But cf. *Bristol & West BS v May, May & Merrimans* [1996] 2 All E.R. 801, where there were positive misrepresentations by the fiduciary. See also *Gilbert v Shanahan* [1998] 3 N.Z.L.R. 528; *Mantonella Pty Ltd v Thompson* (2009) 255 A.L.R. 367; *Rawleigh v Tait* [2008] NZCA 525; [2009] N.Z. Family L.R. 802. For discussion of Swindle and later cases, see Conaglen (2010) 126 L.Q.R. 72 at 81–86.

[332] See e.g. *BPE Solicitors v Hughes-Holland* [2017] UKSC 21; [2017] 2 W.L.R. 1029 (contractual negligence). In so far as a breach of duty is deliberate, it does not seem appropriate to permit a contributory negligence argument: see the *Nationwide* case, above, at 281, per Blackburne J. See too Conaglen, above at 96–100. Contributory negligence cannot be pleaded against fraud: *Standard Chartered Bank v Pakistan National Shipping Corp (No.4)* [2002] UKHL 43; [2003] 1 A.C. 959.

[333] See *Bishopsgate Investment Management Ltd v Maxwell (No.2)* [1994] 1 All E.R. 261; *Permanent Building Society v Wheeler* (1994) 14 A.C.S.R. 109 (Illustration 13); *Bairstow v Queens Moat Houses Plc* [2001] EWCA Civ 712; [2001] 2 B.C.L.C. 531 (recovery from directors of amount of improper dividend dishonestly paid, whether or not a lawful dividend could have been properly authorised at the time). But cf. *Murray Vernon Holdings Ltd v Hassall* [2010] EWHC 7 (Ch) at [65] (director acted honestly and dividend could lawfully have been made, hence no causation).

[334] *Bank of New Zealand v New Zealand Guardian Trust Co Ltd* [1999] 1 N.Z.L.R. 664 at 687. See too *Condliffe v Sheingold* [2007] EWCA Civ 1043 at [23] (measure of value of mis-sold goodwill belonging to claimant company); *Ross River Ltd v Waveley Commercial Ltd* [2013] EWCA Civ 910 at [94]; *Libertarian Investments Ltd v Hall* [2013] HKCFA 93; (2013) 16 H.K.C.F.A.R. 681 at [93] (agent who misspends funds given him for the purpose of buying shares bears onus of proving that it was not possible to acquire the shares); noted Turner [2014] C.L.J. 257.

[335] *Houghton v Immer* (1997) 44 N.S.W.L.R. 46, per Handley JA. See too *Libertarian Investments Ltd v Hall* [2013] HKCFA 93 at [139].

governed by similar principles.[336] Attempts to label a breach of a duty of care as a breach of fiduciary duty in order to argue for the special equitable rules, whatever they may be, whether as to damages, or limitation of actions (where the Limitation Act does not apply to claims for money held on trust[337]) have generally met with little sympathy from English courts,[338] and the common law rules have been applied where they would justify the claim. In the area of confidential information considerable flexibility has been employed in the award of remedies, and there seems to be some tendency to extend this to the area of breach of fiduciary duty generally.[339]

Other remedies: rescission, injunction, and declaration   The principal other remedy is rescission of the transaction with the agent (as where he deals with the principal without disclosing that he is doing so[340]); or, where a third party is involved in the transaction, against the third party, as in the case of transactions obtained by bribery or other conflict of interest on the part of the agent.[341] But other remedies such as declaration and injunction are possible.[342] The injunction is often used to prevent agents, particularly solicitors, from continuing to act where there is a conflict of interest or risk of disclosure of confidential information.[343]

      6-044

Illustrations

(1)   An agent in London had a power of attorney from his principal in America   **6-045**
to sell his English property and invest the proceeds as he thought fit. The agent, who was a solicitor, paid the interest received from the investments into the account of his firm. Held, he was a trustee of the profits and must ac-

---

[336] See, e.g. *Lagunas Nitrate Co v Lagunas Syndicate* [1899] 2 Ch. 392 at 435–437; *The Borag* [1980] 1 Lloyd's Rep. 111 at 125; *Bristol and West BS v Mothew* [1998] Ch. 1, Illustration 11; *Nationwide BS v Balmer Radmore*, above; *Bank of New Zealand v New Zealand Guardian Trust Co Ltd* [1999] 1 N.Z.L.R. 213; *Forsta AP-Fonden v Bank of New York Mellon SA/NV* [2013] EWHC 3127 (Comm) at [185]. For a contrary view, see Heydon, in *Equity in Commercial Law* (Degeling and Edelman eds, 2005), Ch.9; and *Youyang Pty Ltd v Minter Ellison Morris Fletcher* (2003) 212 C.L.R. 484 at [39].

[337] s.21(1). The doctrine of laches would still apply. But the Act may in any case apply by analogy to certain types of constructive trustee: see s.35(1) and *Cia de Seguros Imperio v Heath (REBX) Ltd* [2001] 1 W.L.R. 113, where the equitable claims were identical with common law claims in tort or contract: following *Coulthard v Disco Mix Club Ltd* [2000] 1 W.L.R. 707. See also *Clarke v Marlborough Fine Art (London) Ltd, The Times*, July 5, 2001 and in general Lewin, *Trusts* (19th edn), para.44-037 onwards, especially para.44-039.

[338] See the cases cited above and *Paragon Finance Plc v D.B. Thakerar & Co* [1999] 1 All E.R. 400 (amendment of pleadings); *Williams v Central Bank of Nigeria* [2014] UKSC 10; [2014] A.C. 1189. See too *Halton International Inc v Guernroy Ltd* [2006] EWCA Civ 801.

[339] See below, para.6-077; Abdullah and Tey (1999) 115 L.Q.R. 376; *Corp Nacional del Cobre de Chile v Sogemin Metals Ltd* [1997] 1 W.L.R. 1396.

[340] e.g. *Maguire v Makaronis* (1997) 188 C.L.R. 449. For more detailed discussion, see Article 45 and para.6-068 in particular.

[341] See Articles 49.

[342] In *Yasuda Fire and Marine Insurance Ltd v Orion Marine Insurance Underwriting Ltd* [1995] Q.B. 174 declarations and an order of specific performance were granted to permit the principal to inspect the agent's records. As to the injunction, see *QBE Management Services (UK) Ltd v Dymoke* [2012] EWHC 80 (QB) (injunction to prevent competition by former management employees who, amongst other breaches of duty, solicited colleagues to join them in leaving to compete with their employer).

[343] *Prince Jefri Bolkiah v KPMG* [1999] 2 A.C. 222 at 235–236 (the case itself is concerned with confidential information). See too *PCCW-HKT Telephone Ltd v Aitken* [2009] HKCFA 11.

count for them. Accordingly the Statute of Limitations did not run against the principal.[344]

(2)   A selling agent agrees to sell goods in India against an advance. He pays 85 per cent of the price to the principal and then sells the goods. He uses the balance of the price to buy goods in India and sell them in England, which is very profitable to him. Held, the agent does not have to account to the principal for the profit but only for the balance of the price, since he is not in a fiduciary position in relation to the money.[345]

(3)   An agent was employed to buy timber lands for a company. All these had already been bought up and he recommended the company to buy prairie land instead. The company agreed and sent the agent money for that specific purpose. It was later discovered that the agent had charged the company more than he had himself paid for the land. Held, as the money had been sent to the agent for investment in a specified manner, he was a trustee of the improper profit and so could not plead the Statute of Limitations.[346]

(4)   An agent is employed to sell cargo from a wrecked ship for average adjusters. After deducting claims for salvage and other expenses, £96 remains in his hands. He is not bound to keep the proceeds of sale of the cargo in a separate fund, and he is not a trustee of the £96 but only a debtor to his principal.[347]

(5)   Shipping agents are placed in funds by shipowners from time to time to enable them to discharge jetty and river dues, pilotage and towage, berth fees and similar expenses on ships which visit the local port, and for their agency fee. They do not hold the money in trust, but in their insolvency and in respect of claims by their bank to set off other debts they are simply debtors to the shipowners in respect of money received and not disbursed.[348]

(6)   A company had authority to make deductions from its employees' wages to be paid to a trustee of the staff superannuation fund. It made the deductions but used the credit to reduce its own bank account which at all times was in overdraft. The company was in breach of its duties as agent but the employees were not entitled to any proprietary interest in the company's other assets.[349]

(7)   A solicitor is associated with a client in transactions relating to the development of land. He persuades the client to release part of a mortgage over land on which he (the solicitor) has a second mortgage; this advances the solicitor's security and leaves the client with insufficient security. The solicitor does not explain to the client the advantage which the solicitor gains from this, nor fully explains other matters relating to the release. The solicitor is liable for the loss caused to the client.[350]

(8)   A solicitor acts for the purchaser of land. He does not disclose that between the apparent vendor of the land and the purchaser there is an intermediate vendor, for whom he has acted, who bought from the original vendor and

---

[344] *Burdick v Garrick* (1870) L.R. 5 Ch. App. 233.
[345] *Kirkham v Peel* (1880) 43 L.T. 171; affd (1880) 44 L.T. 195.
[346] *North American Land and Timber Co v Watkins* [1904] 1 Ch. 242; [1904] 2 Ch. 233.
[347] *Henry v Hammond* [1913] 2 K.B. 515. See also *Wilsons and Furness-Leyland Line v British and Continental Shipping Co* (1907) 23 T.L.R. 397.
[348] *Neste Oy v Lloyd's Bank Plc* [1983] 2 Lloyd's Rep. 658, following *Henry v Hammond*, above; one particular payment was held on trust, but this holding has in effect been overruled in *Angove's Pty Ltd v Bailey* [2016] UKSC 47; [2016] 1 W.L.R. 3179.
[349] *Fortex Group Ltd v MacIntosh* [1998] 3 N.Z.L.R. 471.
[350] *Nocton v Ashburton* [1914] A.C. 398.

resold at a profit; and he conveys the property direct from the original vendor to the ultimate purchaser and bills the entire cost of the transaction to the purchaser. Subsequently a warehouse is built on the acquired land, but because of the negligence of the engineer and the pile-driving contractor the purchaser suffers loss, not all of which he recovers from the contractors concerned. The solicitor is liable for the profit made by the intermediate purchaser, but not for the subsequent losses.[351]

(9)   An estate agent acts for the vendor of land and negotiates a sale of it "subject to contract". She is subsequently asked by the prospective purchaser if she can assist in obtaining a sale to him of the adjacent land, for the owner of which she has previously acted unsuccessfully. She approaches that second owner and gives minimal advice in respect of the price; she does not disclose that the offeror has just entered into a "subject to contract" arrangement in relation to the adjacent land. The information would have been of consequence to the second vendor, as the purchaser desired to secure a "family compound" of the two properties. The second vendor sells the property. The estate agent is not liable for loss (in so far as provable) suffered by the second vendor, and is not disentitled to commission, for there is:

> "an implied term of the contract with such an agent that he is entitled to act for other principals selling competing properties and to keep confidential the information obtained from each of his principals".[352]

(10) Solicitors acting for purchasers of land receive money lent by mortgagees, for whom they are also acting, and release it to the purchaser without authority before the mortgage security is executed. The security is later executed. The borrower defaults and the property is repossessed and sold for less than the mortgage debt. The solicitors are liable, not to replace the trust estate, but to compensate the mortgagee for loss which he would not have suffered but for the breach of duty.[353]

(11) A solicitor acts for a husband and wife in the purchase of a house, and also for the mortgage lender. The lender offers to lend on the express basis that the rest of the price is provided by the purchasers without resort to further borrowing. The solicitor knows that the purchasers are arranging for an existing loan to be secured by a second mortgage on the property, but by an oversight tells the lenders that their requirements are complied with. The purchase is completed but the purchasers default and the house is sold by the lenders on a fallen market. The solicitor's negligence is unconnected with the fact that he is acting for both parties to the transaction. He is liable on a com-

---

[351] *Canson Enterprises Ltd v Boughton & Co* [1991] 3 S.C.R. 534; (1991) 85 D.L.R. (4th) 129; cf. *Hodgkinson v Simms* [1994] 3 S.C.R. 377; (1994) 117 D.L.R. (4th) 161 (accountant).

[352] *Kelly v Cooper* [1993] A.C. 205 (PC): as to the implied term see p.214, per Lord Browne-Wilkinson. Sed quaere in view of the fact that advice was given and because the reasoning relies on the proposition that all agency is contractual. The decision may be correct for estate agents, who are only imperfectly agents (above, para.1-020) and are known to act for many principals. It is doubtful whether its reasoning should be generalised. Both parties would have benefited from disclosure by the agent. The fiduciary duties were treated as affected, not by the express terms of any contract, but by an implied term that they did not apply. See [1994] J.B.L. 147; and further as to estate agents in this context Murdoch, *Law of Estate Agency* (5th edn), p.62 onwards. See now *Rossetti Marketing Ltd v Diamond Sofa Co Ltd* [2012] EWCA Civ 1021 at [27].

[353] *Target Holdings Ltd v Redferns* [1996] A.C. 421.

mon law basis for loss attributable to his negligence, but not for the whole sum lost by the lender on the transaction.[354]

(12) A solicitor acts for a purchaser of a restaurant, who already has a loan on the security of her own house for the purchase, but needs further money which is not forthcoming. He makes to the purchaser a bridging loan secured by a first charge, without disclosing that he is making a small profit on it and that he had been aware that other finance would not be available. The purchaser defaults on the mortgage of her own house and the lender takes possession of it. Later the solicitor sues for possession of the restaurant. The non-disclosure was a breach of fiduciary duty to her, but the circumstances were such that she would have had to accept the loan anyway. The loss which she suffered was not caused by the non-disclosure, but by the risk taken by her in mortgaging her home.[355]

(13) Directors of the claimant building society commit it to a purchase of commercial land, a transaction outside its normal business, at a price found to be reasonable. A number of the defendant directors who had promoted the transaction did so for improper reasons (there was an undisclosed side deal between them and the vendor). Another director was aware of this improper motivation but kept silent about it. A yet further director was innocent of the impropriety. There is a downturn in the property market and the claimant loses money on the land. The improperly motivated directors are liable for the loss on the basis of breach of fiduciary duty, as is the director who condoned their actions. The innocent director is not liable because he committed no breach of fiduciary duty and the transaction was one which a reasonable director might have supported not knowing of the corruption of his colleagues.[356]

(14) An agreement between the two shareholders in a company, X and Y, provided for X to undertake the necessary accounting and tax functions for the company and the shareholders, which task was contemplated as possibly requiring the parties to make capital payments to keep the company in sufficient funds. X in keeping the accounts misled Y into making larger capital contributions than were necessary, and later siphoned off the excess. X was held to be the agent of Y and in breach of fiduciary duty, and accountable to Y for the excess payments.[357]

(15) Company A is established to receive investments from the public to be on-lent to company B for its business, ostensibly a type of factoring business. Company B is the wholly owned subsidiary of company C which is listed on the stock exchange. D is a director of company A, and a major shareholder in company C. In fact, company B has no legitimate business, but is engaged, in D's hands, in an elaborate "ponzi scheme", involving massive movements of money between parties but no genuine trading transactions. The appearance of a successful business leads to the shares in company C trading very well, and D makes a £28 million profit by selling his shares. Once the scheme collapses, company A brings proceedings alleging that the profits

[354] *Bristol & West BS v Mothew* [1998] Ch. 1.
[355] *Swindle v Harrison* [1997] 4 All E.R. 705 (see Tjio and Yeo (1998) 114 L.Q.R.181); cf. *Maguire v Makaronis* (1997) 188 C.L.R. 449.
[356] *Permanent Building Society v Wheeler* (1994) 14 A.C.S.R. 109.
[357] *Amaltal Corp v Maruha Corp* [2007] 3 N.Z.L.R. 192 (NZSC).

made by D resulted from his breaches of his director's duties to company A, and that the land and other assets acquired by D from those profits are held on trust for company A. Held, D is accountable for his gains.[358]

(16) A company, D, is appointed agent to the claimant consortium (of which it is also potentially a member) to assist in the purchase of a Monaco hotel for the best price obtainable. D also enters into a sole-agency agreement with the owner of the shares in the hotel under which it is to receive a â10 million commission if a sale occurs within the period of the agency. D reveals some but insufficient details of this arrangement to the claimants. When the purchase goes through D receives its commission. It is held that the commission contract and the resulting payment were held on constructive trust for the claimants.[359]

Article 44

DUTY TO AVOID CONFLICTS OF INTEREST, UNLESS WITH CONSENT[360]

An agent may not put himself in a position or enter into a transaction in which his personal interest, or his duty to another principal, may conflict with his duty to his principal, unless his principal, with full knowledge of all the material circumstances and of the nature and extent of the agent's interest, consents.[361]   **6-046**

Comment

The foregoing statement is derived from Lord Herschell's judgment in *Bray v Ford*. Equally well known is Lord Cranworth LC's dictum in *Aberdeen Railway Co v Blaikie Bros*[362]:   **6-047**

"No one having [fiduciary] duties to discharge, shall be allowed to enter into engagements in which he has, or can have, a personal interest conflicting, or which may possibly conflict, with the interests of those whom he is bound to protect."

While it is clear from this that potential conflicts of interest are within the proscription, there must be "a real sensible possibility of conflict" before equity's rules commence to operate.[363]

Whether there is a material conflict of interest will always be fact sensitive and a matter of judgement. So, the fact that an agent is owed a debt in his personal

---

[358] *Sinclair Investments (UK) Ltd v Versailles Trade Finance Group Plc* [2011] EWCA Civ 347; [2012] Ch. 453. This case is assumed to be overruled in *FHR European*, below, on the issue of the form of remedy.

[359] *FHR European Ventures LLP v Cedar Capital Partners LLC* [2014] UKSC 45; [2015] A.C. 250.

[360] See, in general, Hollander and Salzedo, *Conflicts of Interest and Chinese Walls* (3rd edn); Conaglen, *Fiduciary Loyalty* (2010), Chs 5 and 6.

[361] See *Bray v Ford* [1896] A.C. 44 at 51. See the very much simpler provisions in Article 3:205 of PECL and art.2.2.7 of the UNIDROIT Principles. The attention paid to the origins of doctrine in (some) common law countries creates more complexity, but also greater sensitivity to fact situations. The operation of the above provisions would require considerable working out.

[362] (1854) 1 Macq. 461 at 471, Illustration 2.

[363] *Phipps v Boardman* [1967] 2 A.C. 46 at 124, per Lord Upjohn; *Paton v Rosesilver Group Corp* [2017] EWCA Civ 158 at [33]. See too *Sharbern Holding Inc v Vancouver Airport Centre Ltd* [2011] 2 S.C.R. 175; (2011) 331 D.L.R. (4th) 1 at [151] and [160], suggesting that the principal must establish the materiality of an alleged conflict (unless, presumably, it is self-evident).

capacity by the third party would not automatically entail that the agent had a conflict in dealing on his principal's behalf with the third party, but it might do if it was known that the transaction was likely materially to assist the third party to discharge its debts.[364]

Most commonly, a conflict of interest will involve financial considerations, either relating to the agent's own position (or that of his relatives)[365] or to that of another party for whom the agent is also acting. It is possible, however, that a conflict might arise on other grounds. To take a hypothetical example, an agent might commit his principal to a transaction as part of an understanding, or even a hope, that the third party will not as a result commence a prosecution against the agent.

Again, in the usual case the conflicts principle will be concerned with some aspect of the exercise by the agent of the powers conferred by the principal. It is possible, however, that a conflict, actual or potential, might also affect a personal undertaking, whether or not legally binding, given by the agent *not* to exercise his powers.

The liability of an agent to account for profits made as a result of placing himself in a position of conflicting interests is treated in Article 48.

There has been little judicial discussion of what equitable controls may be necessary to govern what might loosely be called "future client" conflicts. It seems that, ordinarily, an agent will not be taken to have a conflict of interest merely because there is evidence that he entertains hopes of obtaining business in the future from a current counterparty of his principal; doing a good job for his existing principal may be the best way of obtaining that business.[366] However, disloyalty would be established if there were evidence that the prospect of such business actually motivated the agent in his actions on the principal's behalf.[367] The prospect of such future business may also have some evidential role to play in an allegation of negligence against the agent.

6-048   Conflict of duty and duty[368]   One manifestation of the agent's fiduciary duty to avoid conflicts is that he must not serve two principals whose interests may conflict. So he may not act for both parties to a transaction unless he ensures that he fully discloses all the material facts to each party and obtains their informed consent to his so acting.[369] In this situation the agent does not prefer his own interest, but equally may not act entirely in the interests of either single principal. There may also be breach of the duty of loyalty in the sense that the loyalty must be

---

[364] *Cowan de Groot Properties Ltd v Eagle Trust Plc* [1991] B.C.L.C. 1045. See now Companies Act 2006 s.177(6)(a).

[365] As to which, see *Newgate Stud Co v Penfold* [2004] EWHC 2993; [2008] 1 B.C.L.C. 46, the holding in which is noted below, para.6-065; *Breitenfeld UK Ltd v Harrison* [2015] EWHC 399 (Ch); [2015] 2 B.C.L.C. 275.

[366] See *Dennard v PricewaterhouseCoopers LLP* [2010] EWHC 812 (Ch) at [218]; affd [2010] EWCA Civ 1437.

[367] See *Premium Real Estate Ltd v Stevens* [2009] 2 N.Z.L.R. 384 (see below, fn.385).

[368] See Conaglen (2009) 125 L.Q.R. 111. See also *Restatement, Third*, § 8.06(2); Snell, *Equity* (33rd edn), para.7-036 onwards.

[369] This passage was cited with approval by Megaw J in *Anglo-African Merchants Ltd v Bayley* [1970] 1 Q.B. 311 at 323 and by Douglas J in *Dargusch v Sherley Investments Pty Ltd* [1970] Qd.R. 338 at 347; see also *Eagle Star Insurance Co Ltd v Spratt* [1971] 2 Lloyd's Rep. 116 at 133; *McDonnell v Barton Realty Ltd* [1992] 3 N.Z.L.R. 418. cf. *Swain v Law Society* [1983] 1 A.C. 598 (statutory scheme for solicitors' insurance).

undivided.[370] In such cases he may cause loss to one by failure to disclose information acquired in connection with the other—information, indeed, the disclosure of which would be a breach of duty to the first.[371]

Thus, a solicitor who is a trustee of trust property which is for sale should not act as solicitor for the purchaser and may be liable in respect of non-disclosure of information known to him as trustee if he does[372]; an agent who is employed by a borrower to negotiate a loan may not receive a commission from the lender[373]; a hotel broker who is acting for the vendor of a hotel may not also claim commission from the purchaser[374]; a sports agent who represents a player should not, without consent, also act for the sports club in obtaining a work permit for the player[375]; and an insurance broker (who is the assured's agent) may not act as agent for underwriters in obtaining an assessor's report, because such report may be adverse to the assured's claim against the underwriters.[376] In general, a custom to the contrary will not be upheld.[377] It is not material that the agent is acting gratuitously for one or both parties; the mere fact of being agent for two or more parties who may have adverse interests is improper unless all principals have given their informed consent.

The foregoing states the general position. Perhaps where it is notorious that agents do act for both sides to a transaction, and where the agent explains all the circumstances fully to the principal and the principal consents to the agent receiving two commissions, he cannot subsequently call the agent to account for the commission paid by the other party,[378] nor can he himself refuse to pay his own commission.[379] Even if the agent is improperly acting for two opposing principals, the court will not normally make an order on the application of one of the principals which will result in the agent breaking his confidence towards his other principal, at least where that other principal has acted in good faith.[380]

In the best-known case, *Kelly v Cooper*, where an estate agent acted for the

---

[370] *Beach Petroleum NL v Kennedy* (1999) 48 N.S.W.L.R. 1. See Snell, *Equity* (33rd edn), para.7-036.
[371] See also *Bristol and West BS v Mothew* [1998] Ch. 1 at 18–20.
[372] *Moody v Cox and Hatt* [1917] 2 Ch. 71; cf. *Clark Boyce v Mouat* [1994] 1 A.C. 428. For a recent reconsideration of the problem see *Hilton v Barker Booth and Eastwood* [2005] UKHL 8; [2005] 1 W.L.R. 567: the breach does not lie in failing to terminate the retainer, but in not informing the client of the relevant facts (even though to do so would have been a breach to the other client).
[373] *Re a Debtor* [1927] 2 Ch. 367; *Advanced Realty Funding Corp v Bannink* (1979) 106 D.L.R. (3d) 137. cf. *Turner v Laurentide Financial Realty Corp (Western) Ltd* (1979) 97 D.L.R. (3d) 429.
[374] *Fullwood v Hurley* [1928] 1 K.B. 498; *FHR European Ventures LLP v Cedar Capital Partners LLC* [2014] UKSC 45; [2015] A.C. 250. cf. *Foster v Reaume* [1924] 2 D.L.R. 951.
[375] *Imageview Management Ltd v Jack* [2009] EWCA Civ 63; [2009] 2 All E.R. 666 (see further below, para.7-050).
[376] *Anglo-African Merchants Ltd v Bayley* [1970] 1 Q.B. 311; *North and South Trust Co v Berkeley* [1971] 1 W.L.R. 470, Illustration 3 to Article 5: cf. *Goshawk Dedicated Ltd v Tyser & Co Ltd* [2006] EWCA Civ 54 (insurance broker must reveal documents relating to placing, claims and premium accounting).
[377] *Bartram & Sons v Lloyd* (1903) 88 L.T. 286; reversed on other grounds (1904) 90 L.T. 357; *Fullwood v Hurley* [1928] 1 K.B. 498; *Cec. McManus Realty Ltd v Bray* (1970) 14 D.L.R. (3d) 564 at 568; and compare *Jones v Canavan* [1971] 2 N.S.W.L.R. 243. See also *Knoch Estate v Jon Picken Ltd* (1991) 83 D.L.R. (4th) 447.
[378] *Re Haslam and Hier-Evans* [1902] 1 Ch. 765, Illustration 7 to Article 49. This reasoning would presumably cover the "buyer's premium" charged by some auctioneers. As to auctioneers bidding for third parties, see Murdoch, *Law of Estate Agency and Auctions* (4th edn), pp.66–70.
[379] *Harrods Ltd v Lemon* [1931] 2 K.B. 157, Illustration 8 to Article 60; cf. *Owen v Trickett* (1908) 27 N.Z.L.R. 950.
[380] *North and South Trust Co v Berkeley* [1971] 1 W.L.R. 470, Illustration 3 to Article 5; but see (1972) 35 M.L.R. 78; Rider (1978) 42 Conv. 114. See also *Vehicle and General Insurance Co Ltd v*

vendors of adjacent or nearby properties she was held entitled to do so on the basis that the normal fiduciary duty was impliedly excluded in the circumstances.[381] But this was a case not of an agent acting for both sides, but for competing principals,[382] and a more recent decision regarding a solicitor handling business between two clients, who did not disclose to one that the other had criminal convictions, while in a different context, prompts caution about reading too much into the first decision.[383] So, while acting for competing sellers in the same market might be an acceptable implication,[384] it is unlikely that an entitlement to act for both buyer and seller (with or without a formal appointment), or indeed any two parties with opposed interests, would be acceptable.[385] In general, the implication of a term excluding fiduciary duties, or particular fiduciary duties, is not easy to justify.

Where there is a duty, its breach may be remediable by way of an action for breach of contract, and in some cases in tort by way of negligence, or deceit. But the duty may also derive from equity:

> "Fully informed consent apart, an agent cannot lawfully place himself in a position in which he owes a duty of care to another which is inconsistent with his duty to his principal."[386]

In particular, any affected transaction is likely to be rescindable at the principal's behest.

6-049 **Application of conflict of interest rules, including to companies and partnerships** The principles stated above were developed largely in the context of individual agents and individual principals, though there were some cases involving partnerships. Their application to companies, and even to large partnerships, has yet to be fully worked out. Thus an individual agent is not permitted to act on both sides of the same transaction without disclosure; but different parts of a company,

---

Elmbridge Insurances [1973] 1 Lloyd's Rep. 325, where effect was (surprisingly) given to a clause by which an insurance broker agreed to hold money received from clients in trust for the insurance company.

[381] [1993] A.C. 205, Illustration 9 to Article 43. This case, which was welcomed among legal advisers in the financial markets, is the source of Lord Browne-Wilkinson's dictum on the primacy of contract considered above, para.6-034.

[382] See further on this topic above, para.6-015.

[383] *Hilton v Barker Booth & Eastwood* [2005] UKHL 8; [2005] 1 W.L.R. 567, noted by Getzler (2006) 122 L.Q.R. 1. See also *Nationwide BS v Radmore* [1999] Lloyd's Rep. P.N. 237; and *HIH Casualty & General Insurance Ltd v JLT Risk Solutions Ltd* [2007] EWCA Civ 710; [2007] 2 Lloyd's Rep. 278; [2007] 2 All E.R. (Comm) 1106 where an insurance broker, acting both for the insured and the claimant reinsured on income insurance policies in the film industry, was found in breach of a duty of care to the reinsured by failing to inform it of various post-contract breaches of warranty by the insured. The broker's potentially inconsistent contractual duties did not excuse it from performing its duty to the claimant. On the facts, however, the claimant was unable to establish that the breach caused its loss.

[384] In *Kelly v Cooper* the claimant, surprisingly, conceded that the agent owed a duty to the other vendor-principal to keep confidential the fact of his treating with the purchaser. Arguably, the two vendors had a common interest which the agent failed to pursue, to the benefit of the purchaser to whom the agent owed no duties. On the topic of acting for competing principals, see further above, para.6-015.

[385] See *Premium Real Estate Ltd v Stevens* [2009] 2 N.Z.L.R. 384 (estate agent failing to reveal to its vendor principal its connections to buyer and misleading the vendor as to the buyer's intentions in relation to the house); *The Northampton Regional Livestock Centre Co Ltd v Cowling* [2015] EWCA Civ 651; [2016] 1 B.C.L.C. 431.

[386] *North & South Trust Co v Berkeley* [1971] 1 W.L.R. 470 at 484–485, per Donaldson J.

or of solicitors' or accountants' firms, may do so at the same time in absolute good faith, without the company or firm necessarily being even aware that this is happening. This has been called a "same matter" conflict.[387] A company or firm may act for a client in respect of a particular matter, and subsequently act for another client who is on the other side of the dispute: this may be called a "former client" conflict. A company or firm may acquire knowledge from a client in respect of one matter, and an employee or partner may then move employment and subsequently act for another client in another matter to which information gained in connection with the first matter may be relevant: this may be called a "separate matter" conflict. Finally, part of a company or firm may appear to act in an agency or at least advisory capacity for a client while another part is acting in a different capacity in respect of the same client, for example as a seller or market-maker. This may be called a "fair dealing" conflict; such conflicts are not confined to conglomerates, though in modern conditions are more likely to arise in that context. It may be sought to address these conflicts by the creation of so-called "Chinese (or Ethical) Walls", that is, by arrangements which seek to isolate the business activities of different parts of firms from each other.

Of these conflicts the first three raise general questions of agency law, and stem from the agent's duty of loyalty. There is likely to be a conflict between the right of one client (principal) that information regarding his business is not disclosed to anyone else, and the right of another that the agent, as fiduciary, make available to him all knowledge that he has and does not conceal relevant information. On the other hand, the case law, which has become very complex and even contradictory, does suggest that much may turn on the nature of the duties particular classes of agent (and indeed individual agents) have undertaken. Many of the cases involve solicitors where particularly high standards of conduct may be expected, for example in the maintenance of confidentiality, and managerial agents, such as company directors, may be subject to similar standards. There has also, as already noted, been a movement to separate the obligation not to disclose confidential information from general fiduciary doctrine,[388] the implications of which are not yet fully worked out.

Situation 1: "same matter" conflicts This situation concerns companies and firms which, for example through different departments or partners, are simultaneously involved as agents on the two sides of a transaction or dispute. Against the background of the situation of the single agent, it is clear that this would, if not disclosed, involve a breach of duty to each party.[389] The agent must therefore in such a situation disclose to each party the extent of his double employment,[390] so that that party can decide for himself whether to continue using the services of the agent. Furthermore, he must make further disclosure if an actual conflict of interests **6-050**

---

[387] Much of what follows draws heavily on the essay by Finn, "Fiduciary Law and the Modern Commercial World", in *Commercial Aspects of Trusts and Fiduciary Obligations* (McKendrick ed., 1992), Ch.1, pp.19–36. See also Finn, "Conflicts of Interest and Professionals" in *Professional Responsibility* (Legal Research Foundation, 1987), Ch.1; Law Com.C.P. No.124, *Fiduciary Duties and Regulatory Rules* (1992); and Hollander and Salzedo, *Conflicts of Interest and Chinese Walls* (3rd edn). See too the Solicitors' Code of Conduct 2007, Rule 3.

[388] See above, para.6-034.

[389] See *North & South Trust Co v Berkeley* [1971] 1 W.L.R. 470, Illustration 3 to Article 5. See also above, para.2-013; below, para.6-060; *Restatement, Third*, § 8.03.

[390] *Moody v Cox and Hatt* [1917] 2 Ch. 71 (solicitor). See too *Hesse v Briant* (1856) 6 G.M. & G. 623 (solicitor); *Harrods Ltd v Lemon* [1931] 2 K.B. 157 (estate agent).

between clients arises[391]; and if at that point he has information acquired on behalf of one party which would be relevant to the other, his position is extremely difficult, for an unauthorised disclosure would be a breach of duty to the first party, and a concealment of the information a breach towards the second. In the corporate context it seems unlikely that, absent statutory provision, the law will accept either ignorance of the conflict or Chinese Walls as a defence to proceedings for breach of duty in such cases.[392] The agent should avoid the conflict arising in the first place, but if it arises he has little option but to cease to act for one party and sometimes for both.[393]

Sometimes confidential or privileged information relevant to litigation is accidentally disclosed to an opposing party's solicitor. Where this happens, the court must decide whether justice requires an order that the latter cease to act, rather than merely not make use of the confidential information.[394]

6-051   **Situation 2: "former client" conflicts**[395]   The problems here have usually arisen in connection with solicitors, and have mostly focused on issues of confidential information. In general, the equitable restrictions on solicitors and other litigation advisers are more extensive than those that apply to former employees and other agents who have not been involved in providing litigation support to a former employer or client.[396] The position of in-house solicitors and patent attorneys in relation to their former employer is uncertain, and has been the subject of divided judgments in the Court of Appeal.[397] In many cases there will be no doubt that in-house counsel are in possession of confidential information about relevant litigation, and subject to injunctive relief if they commence working for a party with adverse interests.

In the standard fact pattern, a partner or employee of one law firm who has knowledge of or access to a client's affairs moves to another firm which is acting against, or more generally, in a manner adverse to that client; or it is simply sought to employ another part of the same firm against the client after the firm's retainer with the client has been terminated. This has been authoritatively held to be a problem of confidential information, not of fiduciary duty,[398] on the basis that the fiduciary relationship ends with the retainer; a client cannot be taken to have purchased the solicitor's loyalty forever. It can be noted, however, that some cases,

---

[391] See *Hilton v Barker Booth and Eastwood* [2005] UKHL 8; [2005] 1 W.L.R. 567; *Farrington v Rowe McBride & Partners* [1985] 1 N.Z.L.R. 83; *Day v Mead* [1987] 2 N.Z.L.R. 443; *Stewart v Layton* (1992) 111 A.L.R. 687.

[392] See *Harrods Ltd v Lemon* [1931] 2 K.B. 157, Illustration 8 to Article 60; *Standard Investments Ltd v Canadian Imperial Bank of Commerce* (1985) 22 D.L.R. (4th) 410. But cf. *In re a Firm of Solicitors* [2000] 1 Lloyd's Rep. 31.

[393] *Bristol & West Building Society v Mothew* [1998] Ch. 1 at 19.

[394] *Stiedl v Enyo Law LLP* [2011] EWHC 2649 (Comm); [2012] P.N.L.R. 4 at [42]; *Avonwick Holdings Ltd v Shlosberg* [2016] EWCA Civ 1138 at [92].

[395] See McVea [2000] C.L.J. 370.

[396] See *PCCW-HKT Telephone Ltd v Aitken* (2009) 12 H.K.C.F.A.R. 114 (noted by Nolan (2009) 125 L.Q.R. 374); *Caterpillar Logistics Services (UK) Ltd v de Crean* [2012] EWCA Civ 156; [2012] F.S.R. 33 at [60].

[397] *Generics (UK) Ltd v Yeda Research & Development Co Ltd* [2012] EWCA Civ 726; [2013] F.S.R. 13 (the court's decision was, however, unanimous).

[398] *Prince Jefri Bolkiah v KPMG* [1999] 2 A.C. 222 (litigation accountant conceded to be in similar position to solicitor); *PCCW-HKT Telephone Ltd v Aitken* [2009] HKCFA 11; *The Baby Hammock Co Ltd v AJ Park Law* [2011] NZHC 686 (patent attorneys able to act successively for clients with potentially competing products but no clash of patents). cf. *McMaster v Byrne* [1952] 1 All E.R. 1362, Illustration 8 to Article 45. See too Flannigan (2014) 130 L.Q.R. 498.

particularly in Australia and New Zealand, manifest a reluctance to confine the former solicitor's duties only to maintaining confidential information, or at least take a stricter view of what is confidential as between solicitor and client than might be taken with other parties.[399] The solicitor's knowledge of the client's business habits and disposition is said to make it inappropriate for him to be acting adversely to the client. On the other hand, where a solicitor has acted for two parties in an earlier matter with their consent, a restraint against later acting for only one of them would not normally succeed.[400]

The first question that arises is the extent to which knowledge from previous employment is to be inferred. Should knowledge of relevant information be presumed? And should it be imputed to all partners or employees involved in the first firm or department?[401] The second is the extent to which the relevant person or firm is to be restrained from acting in the matter: for if strict controls are imposed, the choice of the second client of legal representation may become much restricted, especially in communities where there are not many lawyers, or law firms with suitable resources, available. The case law so far suggests that once the former client convinces the court that his former solicitor or firm of solicitors possesses relevant confidential information the interest of the first client in confidence will normally prevail over those of the second in being able to choose a lawyer; and that the relevant party will be restrained from acting unless the court is satisfied that there is no risk of disclosure.[402] The value of a Chinese Wall, i.e. an administrative arrangement which should exclude the person concerned from either receiving or imparting the relevant information, has been viewed with some scepticism by the courts, albeit in the context of solicitors, to whom special considerations concerned with the administration of justice apply.[403]

Situation 3: "separate matter" conflicts These raise straight conflicts between the duty of a firm to provide skill and knowledge to a client on one matter and to

6-052

---

[399] See *Black v Taylor* [1993] 3 N.Z.L.R. 403 at 406; *Wagdy Hanna and Associates Pty Ltd v National Library of Australia* (2004) 185 F.L.R. 367 at [55]. This broader view of "former client" conflicts was adverted to in *Winters v Mishcon De Reya* [2008] EWHC 2419 (Ch) at [93]. For the mass of case law on this issue in Australia, see Conaglen, *Fiduciary Loyalty* (2010), p.194. See too para.6-067.

[400] See *Singla v Stockler* [2012] EWHC 1176 (Ch) at [10]; *Marshall v Prescott* [2015] NSWCA 110 (information acquired while acting for two parties available to both even after they fall into dispute).

[401] See *Mallesons Stephen Jaques v KPMG Peat Marwick* (1990) 4 W.A.R. 357; but the same judge modified his view in *Unioil International Pty Ltd v Deloitte Touche Tohmatsu* (1997) 17 W.A.R. 98.

[402] *Prince Jefri Bolkiah v KPMG* [1999] 2 A.C. 222, per Lord Millett, approving *McDonald Estate v Martin* [1990] 3 S.C.R. 1235, sub nom. *Martin v Gray* (1990) 77 D.L.R. (4th) 249, where the Supreme Court of Canada by a majority preferred a rebuttable presumption that information would be imparted and required that all reasonable measures had been taken to ensure that no disclosure would occur (Lord Millett preferred "effective" to "reasonable"); *Georgian American Alloys Inc v White & Case LLP* [2014] EWHC 94 (Comm).This approach was regarded as too strict in Singapore: *Alrich Development Pte Ltd v Rafiq Jumabhoy* [1994] 3 Singapore L.R. 1, and a less restrictive approach has been taken in New Zealand: see *Russell McVeagh McKenzie Bartleet & Co v Tower Corp* [1998] 3 N.Z.L.R. 641 (expressly disapproved in *Bolkiah*). cf. *Torchlight Fund No.1 LP v NZ Credit Fund (GP) 1 Ltd* [2014] NZHC 2552. See also *National Mutual Holdings Pty v Sentry Corp* (1987) 87 A.L.R. 539.

[403] *David Lee (Lincoln) Ltd v Coward Chance* [1991] Ch. 259; *Re a Firm of Solicitors* [1997] Ch. 1; *Prince Jefri Bolkiah v KPMG*, above; *Newman v Phillips Fox* (1999) 21 W.A.R. 309; cf. *Young v Robson Rhodes* [1999] 3 All E.R. 524 and *Halewood International Ltd v Addleshaw Booth & Co* [2000] Lloyd's Rep. P.N. 298, where precautions and undertakings were accepted; *Bloomsbury International Ltd v Holyoake* [2010] EWHC 1150 (Ch) at [55] (accounting firm with sufficiently discrete departments). See also Law Com. C.P. No.124, pp.144–149.

do so for another client in another matter. There is a danger that the loyalties may clash. As Megarry VC said in connection with a solicitor:

"A solicitor must put at his client's disposal not only his skill but also his knowledge, so far as it is relevant; and if he is unwilling to reveal his knowledge to his client, he should not act for him. What he cannot do is to act for the client and at the same time withhold from him any relevant knowledge that he has."[404]

Similar reasoning can be applied to other professionals.

There can be no doubt that the disclosure of the first client's information will (unless specifically authorised) be a breach of contract towards that client; no development of rules to cover such situations is likely to change this. It can be argued that the information which the second client "buys" is limited to that held by the fiduciary independently of that acquired through his client or clients, with the result that there need be no breach of duty at all. It has been so held, in effect, in the case of an estate agent who did not disclose information coming to her when acting for an adjacent proprietor.[405] But failure to disclose known facts to the second client may make other statements fraudulent; or it may falsify advice given and so cause avoidable and foreseeable loss to the second client.[406] The grant of relief requires a "reasonable apprehension of potential conflict (not a mere theoretical possibility)".[407] This postulates "some reasonable relation between the two matters".[408] In this situation it may be that a Chinese Wall defence would be more acceptable, if it indicated that the precautions taken were such as effectively to prevent the knowledge from the first transaction being available to those handling the second.[409] However, there may be problems when a person with oversight of two departments is aware of the conflict or its possibility; or if one department is aware that information may be available elsewhere in the firm. If the problem has been foreseen and provided for, the terms on which the agent accepts engagement from the second client may afford protection, subject to the difficulties discussed below.

Separate matter conflicts could concern matters other than knowledge. To take a hypothetical example, a firm could find itself compromised by acting for an employee in an employment dispute if at the same time it were tendering for business work for the employer.[410]

6-053 **Situation 4: "fair dealing" conflicts** The fourth situation raises the problems created by the abolition of "single capacity" rules in some stock and other markets, including the securities markets of the United Kingdom. The functions previously performed by persons and organisations which were certainly agents (e.g. stockbrokers) may now be performed by parts of multi-function companies which advise clients, undertake execution of orders and may then sell securities which they themselves hold, or have purchased for the purpose, or in which they have an

[404] *Spector v Ageda* [1973] Ch. 30 at 48.
[405] *Kelly v Cooper* [1993] A.C. 205, Illustration 9 to Article 43.
[406] "We have been given no sufficient reason for permitting a person to avoid one fiduciary obligation by accepting another which conflicts with it": *Black v Shearson, Hammill & Co* 72 Cal.Rptr. 157 at 161 (1968); and see *Moody v Cox and Hatt* [1917] 2 Ch. 71.
[407] *Re Baron Investment (Holdings) Ltd* [2000] 1 B.C.L.C. 272.
[408] *Marks & Spencer Plc v Freshfields Bruckhaus Deringer* [2004] EWHC 1337; [2004] 1 W.L.R. 2331 (conflict of interest and confidential information).
[409] They were held insufficient in the *Marks & Spencer* case, above.
[410] See, e.g. *Mike Pero Mortgages Ltd v Pero* [2015] 3 N.Z.L.R. 246 (solicitor attempting to act both for and against client in separate matters).

interest.[411] Chinese Walls have no relevance here; indeed the problem could arise with a sole trader. In view of the stringency of the duties which can be imposed by fiduciary law, organisations which act in such markets in a potentially fiduciary capacity must seek to define the scope of their duties by way of contract terms, quite regardless of the requirements of specific forms of regulation. The most obvious example is that of providers of financial services, who may well appear to act as (what would previously have been called) agents, or at least advisers, but also may now act, sometimes by way of a different part of the organisation, in ways which are potentially adverse to any fiduciary responsibilities which they may have: examples have already been given.

Such changes in the patterns of dealing have been followed by the making, by delegated legislation, of principles, rules and codes for the proper conduct of business, of which the most relevant in the United Kingdom are those made under the Financial Services and Markets Act 2000. There have been iterations of regulation under this Act.[412] It is important here for the law to maintain the strength of fiduciary duties and to recognise that a person engaged to act on another's behalf is undertaking thereby to prefer that other's interests to his own and must be held to his undertaking. At the same time it must be recognised that commercial patterns change, and that as in other areas of activity some of those who were formerly intermediaries may adopt a new role as independent traders. Further, it is important not to set requirements such that financial services become impossible to carry out to the standards set by the law, for this would be subverting the mechanisms established under the aegis of statute by those authorised to establish them. These mechanisms may sometimes indeed be stronger and more effective than the rules of the general law, because they cover situations to which fiduciary duties might not apply, and also because they may be more specific and addressed to identified forms of dealing. For example, the so-called "riskless principal" who buys on specific instructions and immediately sells to his client is not unlike an agent in doing so and may be required to disclose his mark-up.

Positive obligation to inform—duties of fidelity?   It has been seen that fiduci-   **6-054**
ary duties are frequently said to be proscriptive not prescriptive; they do not impose positive obligations but rather state what must *not* be done.[413] This view may be true of fiduciary duties in the narrow or strict sense (the duties to avoid conflicts of interest and not to profit from position), but it does not follow that positive obligations on an agent to communicate information to a principal cannot otherwise exist. Plainly, a duty of disclosure arises if an agent wishes safely to continue to act notwithstanding the conflict of interest. But other positive duties can arise. One source of such obligations would be the contract of agency.[414] Equitable obligations of good faith may also impose positive obligations. However, it seems unlikely

---

[411] As to the general principles concerning agents dealing with their principals, see Article 45.

[412] Further change, including some directed to conflicts of interest, will occur when the Markets in Financial Instruments Directive II (MiFID II) comes into force, projected to be January 3, 2018. The impact of "Brexit" on this is unknown at the time of writing. For an analysis of the conflict of interest provisions of MiFID II, see Busch, in *Agency Law in Commercial Practice* (Busch, Macgregor and Watts, eds, 2016), Ch.9.

[413] See above, para.6-039.

[414] See above, para.6-019.

that, in contrast to the position with the core fiduciary duties, uniform rules of disclosure applicable to all agents can be arrived at.[415]

Hence, until recently the leading case of *Bell v Lever Bros Ltd*[416] was taken to establish that an employee, and on that account other agents, were under no duty to disclose their own past breaches of duty. This seems to be true as regards disclosure by an employee negotiating a severance payment, which is what the case concerns.[417] But it has now been held that, at least where a breach has ongoing implications for the principal's business, an employee is normally required to disclose breaches of duty by other employees even if this involves disclosing his own,[418] and in general there may be a duty on the employee, under his general obligation of fidelity and care, to disclose other wrongdoing at the time (as opposed to on severance negotiations) if it concerns some matter which the employer should know about in order to take appropriate action.[419]

Bell v Lever did not involve directors: the persons concerned were employees of Lever Bros appointed to act as directors of a subsidiary, and the non-disclosure was also at the time of severance negotiations. It was recognised in the case that the position might be different for directors, and it has indeed been held by the Court of Appeal in *Item Software (UK) Ltd v Fassihi*[420] that a director is liable for not disclosing his breaches of duty that have ongoing relevance, as well as any such breaches by his colleagues and employees.[421]

Another issue that has received consideration is the circumstances in which an agent might come under a positive obligation to reveal to his principal an intention to terminate the agency in order to compete with the principal. Again, authority now supports the view that company directors owe such a duty—there is in such circumstances a conflict of interest between the director's duty to do his best for his company and his interest in promoting the interests of his prospective employer.[422] Note that there is no duty not to leave, but rather a positive duty to reveal that one

---

[415] cf. *Restatement, Third*, § 8.11. See too R Lee [2009] Conv. 236.

[416] [1932] A.C. 161. The case was of course finally decided on grounds of mistake. See a valuable historical account of the case by MacMillan in (2003) 119 L.Q.R. 625.

[417] See further *Horcal Ltd v Gatland* [1984] B.C.L.C. 549.

[418] *Sybron Corp v Rochem Ltd* [1984] Ch. 112, Illustration 6. cf. *PennWell Publishing (UK) Ltd v Ornstien* [2007] EWHC 1570 (QB); [2008] 2 B.C.L.C. 246 at [65] (no duty on employee to report misdeeds of more senior staff).

[419] See a valuable discussion of *Bell v Lever* at first instance in *Item Software (UK) Ltd v Fassihi* [2003] EWHC 3116 (Ch); [2003] 2 B.C.L.C. 1, especially at [51].

[420] [2004] EWCA Civ 1244; [2005] 2 B.C.L.C. 91. See Watts (2007) 123 L.Q.R. 21, and Ho and Lee [2007] C.L.J. 348. For criticism, see Berg (2005) 121 L.Q.R. 213. See too *GHLM Trading Ltd v Maroo* [2012] EWHC 61 (Ch) at [192] onwards; *IT Human Resources Plc v Land* [2014] EWHC 3812 (Ch) at [121] (supplying copyright material to a competitor).

[421] *British Midland Tool Ltd v Midland International Tooling Ltd* [2003] EWHC 466 (Ch); [2003] 2 B.C.L.C. 523; *QBE Management Services (UK) Ltd v Dymoke* [2012] EWHC 80 (QB) at [169]. But an implied duty to disclose one's own breaches does not, it seems, attach to employees, at least those not serving in a management role: *Ranson v Customer Systems Plc* [2012] EWCA Civ 841; [2012] I.R.L.R. 769 at [55].

[422] *Foster Bryant Surveying Ltd v Bryant* [2007] EWCA Civ 200; [2007] 2 B.C.L.C. 239 (where the duty of disclosure was met); *British Midland Tool Ltd v Midland International Tooling Ltd* [2003] EWHC 466 (Ch); [2003] 2 B.C.L.C. 523; *Shepherds Investments Ltd v Walters* [2006] EWHC 836 (Ch); [2007] F.S.R. 15; [2007] 2 B.C.L.C. 202, not following dicta in *Balston Ltd v Headline Filters Ltd* [1990] F.S.R. 385, and *Framlington Group Plc v Anderson* [1995] 1 B.C.L.C. 475. See too *Berryland Books Ltd v BK Books Ltd* [2009] EWHC 1877 (Ch) at [23]; *G. Attwood Holdings Ltd v Woodward* [2009] EWHC 1083 (Ch); *Gamatronic (UK) Ltd v Hamilton* [2016] EWHC 2225 (QB) at [88] and [151]. *Grace v Biagioli* [2005] EWCA Civ 1222; [2006] 2 B.C.L.C. 70 at [69]–[70] suggests also that where the director's intention becomes apparent, the company may remove the direc-

is planning to, once a firm decision to do so has been formed. It has also been held that employees who are not managers do not owe such duties.[423] Such employees may not be obliged to answer truthfully questions about what they are going to do once their employment ceases,[424] at least where their intentions are not hampering the performance of their duties before their departure.

Statutory requirements Sometimes disclosure of a conflict is required by statute **6-055** or statutory instrument. Thus persons engaged in estate agency work are in some circumstances required to disclose to their clients services which they or persons connected with them offer to purchasers[425]; or that they or persons connected with them are seeking to acquire an interest in the land concerned.[426] Statutory requirements would usually be taken as supplemental to, rather than a replacement for, equity's requirements unless the statute were clear on the point.[427]

Modification of duties by contract: common law[428] Some persons exercising **6-056** pure agency functions in the old sense may remain in this sphere of activity, but wish to modify the equitable duties that would otherwise apply to them. Yet others who normally act as principals may undertake agency functions, or something like them, but wish to make clear that they do not intend the ordinary incidents of agency to apply to them. An appropriate professional description or contract clause can be used to seek to make clear that, for instance, a securities firm, or a joint venture party, is not an agent, but rather a financial adviser and/or dealer. Although certain fiduciary duties may perhaps attach to them as advisers, these will be more limited than those attaching to pure agents[429]; and of course a dealer would not prima facie be under fiduciary duties at all.

Otherwise, contract terms can purport in some way to exclude or restrict the fiduciary duties which might otherwise arise. It is plain that a fiduciary could not exclude his own liability for fraud (including fraudulent non-disclosure) or deliberate breach of contract[430] though he might, if the wording was clear enough, exclude liability for the fraud of his agent.[431] Furthermore, in the absence of the clearest language, it is unlikely that a court would find that a clause permitting a conflict was

tor from office or require him to stand down. See also Companies Act 2006 ss.172 and 175; and *Company Directors: Duties, Liabilities and Remedies* (Mortimore, ed, 3rd edn); Watts (2007) 123 L.Q.R. 21.
[423] *Helmet Integrated Systems Ltd v Tunnard* [2006] EWCA Civ 1735; [2007] I.R.L.R. 126. See too *RBC Dominion Securities Inc v Merrill Lynch Canada Inc* [2008] 3 S.C.R. 79; Brodie (2012) 16 Edinburgh L.R. 198; and *Ranson v Customer Systems Plc* [2012] EWCA Civ 841; [2012] I.R.L.R. 769 at [68].
[424] See *MPT Group Ltd v Peel* [2017] EWHC 1222 (Ch) at [86].
[425] Estate Agents (Undesirable Practices) (No.2) Order 1991 (SI 1991/1032) (made under Estate Agents Act 1979 s.18), reg.2; see Murdoch, *The Estate Agents and Property Misdescriptions Acts* (3rd edn), Ch.3A; *Law of Estate Agency* (5th edn), p.290 onwards. The civil remedy is that the contract may be unenforceable: Estate Agents Act 1979 s.18(5).
[426] Estate Agents (Undesirable Practices) (No.2) Order 1991, above, Sch.1 para.2; see Murdoch, above, pp.212–213.
[427] See *Barfoot & Thompson Ltd v Real Estate Agents Authority* [2016] NZCA 105.
[428] See Bean, *Fiduciary Obligations and Joint Ventures* (1995), p.84 onwards.
[429] See *Burns v Kelly Peters & Associates Ltd* (1987) 41 D.L.R. (4th) 577; *Alliance Craton Explorer Pty Ltd v Quasar Resources Pty Ltd* [2013] FCAFC 29; Finn, in *Commercial Aspects of Trusts and Fiduciary Obligations* (McKendrick ed., 1992), pp.7 and 10–11.
[430] *S. Pearson & Son Ltd v Dublin Corp* [1907] A.C. 351 at 355 and 362; Treitel, *Law of Contract* (14th edn), para.7-042.
[431] *HIH Casualty and General Insurance Ltd v Chase Manhattan Bank* [2003] UKHL 6; [2003] 1 All

intended to permit the agent actively to prefer one party over the other, as opposed to attempting to act even-handedly. In *Bristol and West BS v Mothew* Millett LJ referred to what he called the "no inhibition principle",[432] that requires an agent acting with consent for both parties to refrain from putting himself in a position where he feels inhibited about doing his best for both parties. Liability for damages might ensue where this principle is not adhered to,[433] and almost certainly will where the fiduciary actively promotes the interests of one party over the other.

As for the general approach to attempts to modify what would otherwise be fiduciary duty, it is usually necessary for there to be an express term to that effect. However, we have seen that recent dicta of high authority suggesting that all agency is contractual and that the rights and duties of the parties to such a contract stem entirely from the contract between them,[434] may be taken to suggest that the background against which intermediaries act, and the general understandings in the type of business, may establish that there are no fiduciary duties, or very limited duties, in certain situations. The principles of interpretation and implied terms may be adequate without express exclusion clauses. It has earlier been noted, however, that this purely contractual approach is not beyond question, certainly as a reason for inferring that obligations implied by law are inapplicable.[435] It was, for example, long ago held in *Robinson v Mollett*[436] that a usage of the market which allowed an agent to buy to become a seller to his principal was inconsistent with the relationship of agency and so invalid against a principal unless he was aware of it.

As for express terms, there are some precedents but the case law has until recently been relatively thin.[437] Recent important cases upholding exclusion clauses in respect of the duties of trustees could prima facie be extended to the duties of agents.[438]

This paragraph is principally directed to modification of fiduciary duties in advance of action. Generally speaking, a principal is also able, retrospectively, to excuse what would otherwise have been a breach of duty. In relation to company

---

E.R. (Comm) 349, requiring express reference to fraud or very similar wording. But see the Hon. Justice K.R. Handley (2003) 119 L.Q.R. 537.

[432] [1998] Ch.1 at 19; *Consolidated Finance Ltd v Collins* [2013] EWCA Civ 475 at [59]; *Northampton Regional Livestock Centre Co Ltd v Cowling* [2015] EWCA Civ 651; [2016] 1 B.C.L.C. 431 at [77]. For discussion, see Conaglen (2009) 125 L.Q.R. 111 at 127–140.

[433] *Leeds and Holbeck Building Society v Arthur and Cole* [2002] P.N.L.R. 78; *Nationwide Building Society v Goodwin Harte* [1999] Lloyd's Rep. P.N. 338 at 345.

[434] *Kelly v Cooper* [1993] A.C. 205 at 213–214 (Illustration 9 to Article 43); *Torre Asset Funding Ltd v The Royal Bank of Scotland Plc* [2013] EWHC 2670 (Ch) at [143]; *AP-Fonden v Bank of New York Mellon SA/NV* [2013] EWHC 3127 (Comm) at [177]; cf. above, para.6-034.

[435] See above, para.6-034.

[436] (1874) L.R. 7 H.L. 802, Illustration 8 to Article 31. See too *Brandeis (Brokers) Ltd v Black* [2001] 2 Lloyd's Rep. 359.

[437] cf. *Hayim v Citibank NA* [1987] A.C. 730 (clause reducing duties of executor of will towards beneficiaries); *Movitex Ltd v Bulfield* [1988] B.C.L.C. 104 (modification of self-dealing rules in company's articles); see also *Noranda Australia Ltd v Lachlan Resources NL* (1988) 14 N.S.W.L.R. 1.

[438] *Armitage v Nurse* [1998] Ch. 241; *Walker v Stones* [2001] Q.B. 902; Law Com. C.P. No.171 (2003); *Citibank NA v QVT Financial LP* [2007] EWCA Civ 11; [2007] 1 All E.R. (Comm) 475; *Spread Trustee Co Ltd v Hutcheson* [2011] UKPC 13; [2012] 2 A.C. 194. See also *Australian Securities and Investments Commission v Citigroup Global Markets Australia Pty Ltd* (2007) 62 A.C.S.R. 427 (Fed. Ct) (contractual provision avoided any conflict-of-interest disabilities that might have arisen from the fact that one division of the defendant was advising a client on its takeover offer for a company at the same time as another division was independently buying up shares in the company); noted by Getzler (2008) 124 L.Q.R. 15; Tuch (2007) 7 J. Corp Leg. Stud. 51.

directors, waiver of breach is referred to as "ratification" (a different usage to that used in agency law in general).[439] Such ratification is now governed by the Companies Act 2006 s.239. As for consent to what would otherwise be a breach of fiduciary duty, see above, para.6-039.

Custom or usage A custom or usage which converts an agent into a principal or otherwise gives him an interest at variance with his duty is prima facie unreasonable,[440] and will therefore be ineffective unless known of and consented to by the principal.[441]   **6-057**

Unfair Contract Terms Act 1977[442] A contract clause seeking to make clear that a person who might be an agent is not, or might in some circumstances not be acting as such, may also be caught by the Unfair Contract Terms Act 1977, which could require it to be assessed against the "requirement of reasonableness". Here, however, conceptual problems may arise.[443] The relevant provision will normally be s.3, which operates where one party deals "as consumer or on the other's written standard terms of business". One of these two requirements may often be satisfied; but then the wording of the section is entirely geared to exclusions or restrictions of "breach of contract", "contractual performance" and "contractual obligation". The section therefore seems to apply only to such duties as can be regarded as contractual and normal to the type of transaction; and we are therefore remitted to the problem, discussed above,[444] as to the extent to which the agent owes fiduciary duties and the extent to which, in so far as he does, these are contractual.[445] If the duties arise outside the contract, the Act may not affect such duties at all. Equally, it could be argued that a clause establishing the nature of the function of a person in question is not an exclusion clause within the Act at all, and so is immune from the requirement of reasonableness. Reasoning of this type was rejected, albeit in a slightly different context, by the House of Lords, but may have recently become more acceptable.[446]   **6-058**

In response to either argument, the strongest part of s.3 is s.3(2)(b)(i), which does not rely on the idea of existing contractual obligations at all: under it a person cannot "claim to be entitled to render a contractual performance substantially different from that which was reasonably expected of him", except in so far as the clause is reasonable under the Act. It is this provision which gets nearest to approaching

---

[439] See, e.g. *North-West Transportation Ltd v Beatty* (1887) 12 App.Cas. 589; *Burland v Earle* [1902] A.C. 83 (PC).

[440] *Robinson v Mollett* (1875) L.R. 7 H.L. 802, Illustration 8 to Article 31; *Hamilton v Young* (1881) 7 L.R.Ir. 289, Illustration 5; *Tetley v Shand* (1871) 25 L.T. 658; *Anglo-African Merchants Ltd v Bayley* [1970] 1 Q.B. 311; *North and South Trust Co v Berkeley* [1971] 1 W.L.R. 470; *Cec. McManus Realty Ltd v Bray* (1970) 14 D.L.R. (3d) 564 at 568; cf. *Jones v Canavan* [1971] 2 N.S.W.L.R. 243.

[441] See Article 31.

[442] See in general Chitty, *Contracts* (32nd edn), para.15-062 onwards. Exclusion of liability for misrepresentation is covered by s.3 of the Misrepresentation Act 1967.

[443] Sch. 1 cl.1(e) to the Act excludes from its scope "any contract so far as it relates to the creation or transfer of securities or of any right or interest in securities". This appears on its face to relate to provisions concerning the transfer of the securities themselves and not to the function performed by the person effecting the transfer.

[444] See above, para.6-034.

[445] See above, para.6-034.

[446] *Smith v Eric S. Bush* [1990] 1 A.C. 831; cf. *Henderson v Merrett Syndicates Ltd* [1995] 2 A.C. 145; *Titan Steel Wheels Ltd v Royal Bank of Scotland Plc* [2010] EWHC 211 (Comm); [2010] 2 Lloyd's Rep. 92.

the problems outlined above and it may accordingly prove to be of most value where the exclusions used by a person who might be taken to be offering agency or similar functions are such that a reasonable person using that person's services would not have anticipated their effect.

A different issue is raised by clauses which seek to limit liability to fraud or gross negligence or the like.[447] As applied to agents, these would normally be subject to the Act's provisions.

The financial market in the United Kingdom is, as has already been stated, regulated by techniques laid down by statute, now the Financial Services and Markets Act 2000.[448] In so far as the 1977 Act, and its "requirement of reasonableness", is applicable, it seems likely that compliance with such provisions would be strong, but should not be conclusive, evidence of the reasonableness of a particular contract term.

6-059 **Consumer Rights Act 2015**[449]   A contract by a private person with a professional agent may involve the supply of services to a consumer and hence be caught by Part 2 of the Consumer Rights Act 2015. The provisions do not apply to the fairness of a term to the extent that the term specifies the main subject matter of the contract.[450] Otherwise, the Act could be used to address modifications or exclusions of what would otherwise be equity's control of conflicts of interest or other incidents of the fiduciary relationship. The control is exercised where a term "contrary to the requirement of good faith causes a significant imbalance to the parties' rights and obligations under the contract to the detriment of the consumer".[451] Such terms are not enforceable, but the rest of the contract normally remains.

6-060 **Public law: the Financial Services and Markets Act 2000**[452]   The Financial Services and Markets Act 2000, as substantially amended by the Financial Services Act 2012, rationalised the legislative framework governing banks, building societies, investment firms, insurance companies as well as several other types of regulated financial services entity. Under the legislation, the Financial Conduct Authority ("FCA", replacing the earlier Financial Services Authority) operates as the UK's single statutory financial services regulator.

The Act authorises the making of rules by the FCA which may potentially affect fiduciary duties. Thus, Part 9A (replacing earlier s.138) contains powers for the FCA to make rules applying to the activities of regulated firms which are necessary or expedient for protecting the interests of consumers. Rules made under this section would include requirements for firms to disclose to their customers details

---

[447] See *Armitage v Nurse* [1998] Ch. 241; *Walker v Stones* [2001] 2 Q.B. 902; *Spread Trustee Co Ltd v Hutcheson* [2011] UKPC 13; [2012] 2 A.C. 194.

[448] See below.

[449] Formerly, the Unfair Terms in Consumer Contracts Regulations 1999. See Chitty, *Contracts* (32nd edn), Ch.38; Treitel, *Law of Contract* (14th edn), para.7-093 onwards.

[450] SI 1999/2083, replacing earlier regulations of 1994, SI 1994/3159.

[451] See s.62. The former Regulations have been treated as potentially applicable to renewal and commission terms in management contracts between real estate agents and landlords in *Office of Fair Trading v Foxtons Ltd* [2009] EWCA Civ 288; [2010] 1 W.L.R. 663.

[452] The Act is a specialised topic which has generated its own literature. See, for example, Sweet & Maxwell's *Encyclopaedia of Financial Services Law* (Lomnicka and Powell eds); Butterworths *Financial Services Law and Practice* (looseleaf); and Blackstone's *Guide to the Financial Services and Markets Act 2000*.

of charges, remuneration and commission.[453] The general rulemaking power in s.137A is supplemented by various other sections. So, for example, additional provision is made in relation to client money (s.137B) and as to the rights and duties of participants in authorised unit trust schemes and openended investment companies (ss.247(1)(b) and 262(2)(e)). Most conspicuous is s.147, which allows for the making of so-called "control of information" rules which relate to "the disclosure and use of information held by an authorised person ('A')". Section 137P (replacing earlier s.147) provides that control of information rules may:

"(a)   require the withholding of information which A would otherwise be required to disclose to a person ("B") for or with whom A does business in the course of carrying on any regulated or other activity;

(b)   specify circumstances in which A may withhold information which A would otherwise be required to disclose to B;

(c)   require A not to use for the benefit of B information—
   (i)   which is held by A, and
   (ii)   which A would otherwise be required to use for the benefit of B;

(d)   specify circumstances in which A may decide not to use for the benefit of B information within paragraph (c)."

The section is taken to refer to the setting up of Chinese, or "Ethical", Walls for which rules then provide the details.

The view can be taken that rules so made can alter the rights and duties of the parties as they would otherwise be determined by the rules of private law[454] in the particular context of financial services, for example in the first three conflict situations referred to above. Equally, rules made under s.147(2) might affect situations of the fourth type. Indeed, the UK Government took this view when introducing the Act. It stated that, in light of recent case law[455]:

"It is the Government's firm belief that the courts would be unlikely to hold that someone could successfully sue an authorised person for breach of fiduciary duties where the authorised person has complied with FCA rules, which, of course, are made under Parliament's delegated statutory powers."[456]

It seems very doubtful, however, whether the power to alter basic protective rules of law could be conferred on a rule-making body in this way and by such general wording. Compliance with such standards might, however, as indicated above, be evidence of statutory reasonableness; or be a guide to the extent of the fiduciary obligation; to trade usage; or more simply as to the understandings of the parties to a contract. The provisions as to clients' money, on the other hand, raise no such problems, for the way in which a fiduciary holds money is in any case variable in accordance with the context. In many circumstances, claimants will prefer to use the statutory provisions, the remedies for which are very flexible.[457]

---

[453] See s.137H onwards.

[454] Law Com. C.P. No.124, p.176 onwards.

[455] This was primarily a reference to *Prince Jefri Bolkiah v KPMG* [1999] 2 A.C. 222.

[456] *Hansard*, H.L., col.1409, May 9, 2000, per Lord McIntosh of Haringey.

[457] See above, para.6-041. And in relation to the remedies under the statute, *Re Lehman Bros International (Europe) Ltd (in administration)* [2012] UKSC 6; [2012] 3 All E.R. 1; *Allanfield Property Insurance Services Ltd v Aviva Insurance Ltd* [2015] EWHC 3721 (Ch); [2016] Lloyd's Rep. I.R. 217.

Illustrations

6-061 (1) An agent for sale sells to a company of which he is a director and large shareholder. The sale is not binding on the principal.[458]

(2) A director of a company may not sell to his company articles which he, or a firm in which he has an interest, manufactures. Any such contract is voidable by the company, quite apart from the question of its fairness, since a director is not permitted to enter into transactions in which his own interest is in conflict with his duty to promote the interests of the company.[459]

(3) Factory owners employed a surveyor to prepare a specification of repairs for submission to the War Damage Commission and to supervise the repair work as it was done by a building company. After the preparation of a specification, but before any repair work was done, the surveyor became the managing director of the building company and told the factory owners of his new position. The surveyor placed himself in a position where his duty and interest conflicted and this was a breach of his contract. But he was entitled to recover his fees since the factory owners had acquiesced in his continuance as their agent.[460]

(4) A solicitor engaged an assistant to undertake, among other business, the work of an important client. During his employment, the assistant agreed with the client to leave the employment of the solicitor in order to set up in practice on his own. The client agreed that, if he did so, the client would transfer his work to the assistant. Held, in so acting, the assistant was in breach of the implied term of his agreement to serve the plaintiff with good faith and fidelity. He was, accordingly, liable in damages to his principal.[461]

(5) A broker was authorised to sell certain shares, and pay himself certain advances out of the proceeds. A custom whereby he might himself take over the shares at the price of the day, in the event of him being unable to find a purchaser at an adequate price, was unreasonable, and such a transaction was not binding on the principal unless he had notice of the custom at the time when he gave the broker the authority, even if a forced sale of the shares would inevitably have realised less than the price given by the broker.[462] So a custom whereby an agent for sale of a ship may himself purchase at the minimum price if he cannot find a purchaser was held to be unreasonable.[463]

(6) The European zone controller of an international chemical company engages with other employees in setting up and operating rival businesses in competition with the company. He is in breach of duty in not disclosing the misconduct of the other employees, and on the terms of the company's pension scheme the company need not make certain payments to him and can recover sums paid.[464]

---

[458] *Salomons v Pender* (1865) 3 H. & C. 639, although the case was primarily reasoned on the basis of the agent selling to the principal (as to which see below, para.6-065).

[459] *Aberdeen Ry Co v Blaikie Bros* (1854) 1 Macq. 461.

[460] *Thornton Hall v Wembley Electrical Appliances Ltd* [1947] 2 All E.R. 630.

[461] *Sanders v Parry* [1967] 1 W.L.R. 753. See also *Robb v Green* [1895] 2 Q.B. 315 at 320. This expression is also to be found in *Wessex Dairies Ltd v Smith* [1935] 2 K.B. 80; *Hivac Ltd v Park Royal Scientific Instruments Ltd* [1946] Ch. 169; *Aubanel and Alabaster Ltd v Aubanel* (1949) 66 R.P.C. 343; *State Vacuum Stores v Phillips* [1954] 3 D.L.R. 621.

[462] *Hamilton v Young* (1881) 7 L.R.Ir. 289; *Rothschild v Brookman* (1831) 2 Dow. & Cl. 188. But cf. Article 45, Illustration 9.

[463] *De Bussche v Alt* (1878) 8 Ch.D. 286.

[464] *Sybron Corp v Rochem Ltd* [1984] Ch. 112.

(7) Two members of a committee appointed to sell residential units on behalf of joint principals, including themselves, promote a rapid sale, deliberately failing to pursue other potential offers, in order to be able to meet debt obligations on personal loans they had taken out to acquire some of their units. Since the purchaser was aware of the conflict of interest, the sale agreement was set aside.[465]

(8) The outgoing chief executive of a company, X, agrees a remuneration package with an incoming executive director, Y, which is very generous including in its severance entitlements. X had sold Y his shares in the company albeit at no more than market value. Y is later made redundant and invokes the severance terms. X had a conflict of interest and is liable to compensate the company for the severance costs.[466] Similar consequences attach to a director who at a time when his company is insolvent takes steps to ensure that the company discharges a debt to him ahead of paying the company's other creditors.[467]

Article 45

AGENT DEALING WITH PRINCIPAL[468]

(1) Where an agent purports to enter into a contract or transaction with himself on behalf of the principal he will need express authority to do so. In the absence of such authority, the dealing may be void at law[469] and will be voidable *ex debito justitiae* at equity.[470]   **6-062**

(2) Where an agent enters into any other contract or transaction with his principal, or with his principal's representative in interest, he must act with perfect good faith, and make full disclosure of all the material circumstances, and of everything known to him respecting the subject-matter of the contract or transaction which would be likely to influence the conduct of the principal or his representative.[471]

---

[465] *Ng Eng Ghee v Mamata Kapildev Dave* [2009] SGCA 14.

[466] *PNC Telecom Plc v Thomas* [2007] EWHC 2157 (Ch); [2008] 2 B.C.L.C. 95.

[467] *MacPherson v European Strategic Bureau Ltd* [2000] 2 B.C.L.C. 683; *E-Clear (UK) Plc v Elia* [2013] EWCA Civ 1114 at [33].

[468] See generally Snell, *Equity* (33rd edn), paras 7-020 and 7-021; Conaglen [2006] C.L.J. 366; Edelman, in Glister and Ridge (eds) *Fault Lines in Equity* (2012), Ch.5.

[469] See, e.g. *Salomons v Pender* (1865) 3 H. & C. 639 at 642 (a case denying the agent any commission, when arguably it was not in any event earned on a sale to oneself).

[470] See *Tito v Waddell (No.2)* [1977] Ch. 106 at 241; *York Buildings v MacKenzie* (1795) 8 Bro. P.C. 42; *Kimber v Barber* (1872) L.R. 8 Ch. App. 56. For a collection of other cases, see Conaglen, *Fiduciary Loyalty*, p.126.

[471] *Collins v Hare* (1828) 2 Bli.(N.S.) 106; *Jones v Thomas* (1837) 2 Y. & C.Ex. 498; *Molony v Kernan* (1842) 2 Dr. & War. (Ir.) 31; *Charter v Trevelyan* (1844) 11 C. & F. 714; *Savery v King* (1856) 5 H.L.Cas. 627; *Waters v Shaftesbury* (1866) 14 L.T. 184; *Parker v McKenna* (1874) L.R. 10 Ch.App. 96; *Ward v Sharp* (1884) 53 L.J.Ch. 313; *Demerara Bauxite Co v Hubbard* [1923] A.C. 673; *J.J. Harrison (Properties) Ltd v Harrison* [2001] EWCA Civ 1467; [2002] 1 B.C.L.C. 162; but cf. *Hanson v Lorenz & Jones* [1987] 1 F.T.L.R. 23 (agent enters joint venture with principal). And see Illustrations; Finn, *Fiduciary Obligations* (1977), Ch.20 and pp.223–228; Meagher, Gummow and Lehane's *Equity Doctrines and Remedies* (5th edn), para.5-180 onwards. The problem of "self-contracting" raises in civil law jurisdictions theoretical problems to which the common law, largely concerned with protection of the principal, has paid little attention. See Badr (1982) 30 Am.J.Comp.L. 255.

(3)   Where any question arises as to the validity of any such contract or transaction, or of any gift made by a principal to his agent, the burden of proving that no advantage was taken by the agent of his position, or of the confidence reposed in him, and that the transaction was fair, and entered into in perfect good faith and after full disclosure, lies upon the agent.[472]

Comment

6-063   **Basis of principles**   The foregoing principles reflect what are often called the "self-dealing" and the "fair-dealing" rules. The two concepts are not always kept distinct, but in the context of agency, the former is certainly the appropriate term where the agent purports to make a contract with himself on behalf of the principal, or where he is a co-agent and participates in the decision to make the contract.[473] The fair-dealing rule governs where the principal acts in person but is negotiating a contract with his agent. To the extent that self-dealing transactions may be unauthorised at law it is not necessary to have recourse to the fiduciary duties to avoid conflicts of interest and not to profit from position. The relationship of the fair-dealing rule with those duties is, however, not altogether clear.[474] In part this reflects the fact that fact patterns do not fall into neat categories. Particularly where an agent is buying property from his principal, the agent may have received information about the property in his capacity as agent that means he could be profiting from position. In other cases, there could be such a marked degree of confidence reposed by the principal in the agent that a relationship of undue influence exists or can be presumed[475]; this would not be the case with all agency relationships. It seems, however, that the fair-dealing rule, as with the self-dealing rule, does not turn on proof of use of position or on the existence of a relationship of influence, but does require that the dealing be one that has a connection with the subject-matter of the agency. A transaction between principal and agent that relates, for instance, to property which has no connection to the mandate that the agent has, or has had, from the principal would not be caught by the fair-dealing rule, even if in some cases it might otherwise be subject to challenge for undue influence.[476] On this basis, it has been argued that the fair-dealing rule is simply part of the conflicts rule affecting all fiduciaries.[477]

Another difficult topic is whether duties of disclosure and fair dealing arise while negotiating the terms of appointment of the agency; in short, is the contract of appointment one uberrimae fidei? It has been suggested that until the agency is cre-

---

[472]   See *Bristol and West BS v Mothew* [1998] Ch.1 at 18, per Millett LJ; and see material cited in fn.471 above.

[473]   As to the capacity and the authority of an agent to contract with himself on behalf of his principal, see above, para.2-014.

[474]   See Conaglen [2006] C.L.J. 366, a most useful analysis.

[475]   *Barnard v Hunter* (1856) 2 Jur. (N.S.) 1213; *Wright v Carter* [1903] 1 Ch. 27 (solicitors). See further below, para.6-069.

[476]   *Montesquieu v Sandys* (1811) 18 Ves. 302 at 313; *McPherson v Watt* (1877) 3 App.Cas. 254 at 270–271; *John Youngs Insurance Services Ltd v Aviva Insurance Service UK Ltd* [2011] EWHC 1515 (TCC) at [98] (see further above, para.6-036); *Wollenberg v Casinos Austria International Holding GmbH* [2011] EWHC 103 (Ch) (solicitor enters into business arrangement with former client on basis of share of profits). See further Conaglen [2006] C.L.J. 366 at 381–382.

[477]   Conaglen [2006] C.L.J. 366, critically analysing a much cited dictum of Megarry VC in *Tito v Waddell (No. 2)* [1977] Ch. 106 at 341.

ated the parties are at arm's length and must look after their own interests,[478] subject
again to the law of undue influence and any statutory regulation that might exist.[479]

Purchase from principal   A long-established line of cases indicates that a person   **6-064**
who stands in a position of a confidential character in respect of the property of
another, which would include many types of agent, cannot purchase it for himself
without full and fair disclosure of all the facts to the principal.[480] The onus in such
a case is on the agent to show that the price was adequate, that the sale was as
advantageous to his principal as any other sale he could have obtained from a third
party, and that he disclosed all the relevant facts to his principal before the purchase
and that the principal gave his informed consent.[481] The rule extends to sub-
agents, who may themselves be fiduciaries.[482] It also applies to agents who take
leases from their principals.[483] In this respect an agent may differ in some degree
from a trustee, because a purchase of the trust property by a trustee is voidable at
the instance of any beneficiary unless very stringent rules are complied with.[484]
Where a solicitor purchases from a client, it is important (if not essential) that the
client should have had independent advice; otherwise, the solicitor will have difficulty in showing that the transaction was a fair one.[485] Such advice may be appropriate in other relationships of presumptive undue influence also.

---

[478] *Sharbern Holding Inc v Vancouver Airport Centre Ltd* [2011] 2 S.C.R. 175; (2011) 331 D.L.R. (4th)
1 at [144].

[479] See, for instance, Consumer Rights Act 2015 s.62; and in relation to directors, Companies Act 2006
Ch.4 (transactions with directors requiring approval of members).

[480] *Gibson v Jeyes* (1801) 6 Ves. 266; *Lowther v Lowther* (1806) 13 Ves. 95; *Austin v Chambers* (1838)
6 C. & F. 1, 37; *Rothschild v Brookman* (1831) 2 Dow. & Cl. 188; *Dally v Wonham* (1863) 33 Beav.
154; *Salomons v Pender* (1865) 3 H. & C. 639; *Dunne v English* (1874) L.R. 18 Eq. 524, Illustration 4; *McPherson v Watt* (1877) 3 App.Cas. 254, Illustration 3; *Imeson v Lister* (1920) 149 L.T.Jo.
446; *McKenzie v McDonald* [1927] V.L.R. 143; *Christie v McCann* (1972) 27 D.L.R. (3d) 544;
Lunghi v Sinclair [1966] W.A.R. 172; *Headway Construction Co Ltd v Downham* (1974) 233 E.G.
675, Illustration 17; *Gathergood v Blundell & Brown Ltd* [1991] 1 N.Z.L.R. 405; *Chen v Marcolongo*
(2009) 260 A.L.R. 353.

[481] *Gibson v Jeyes*, above; *Holman v Loynes* (1854) 4 De G.M. & G. 270; *Savery v King* (1856) 5
H.L.Cas. 627 at 655–656; *Spencer v Topham* (1856) 22 Beav. 573; *Gresley v Mousley* (1862) 31
L.J.Ch. 537; *Pisani v Att.-Gen. for Gibraltar* (1874) L.R. 5 P.C. 516; *Ward v Sharp* (1883) 53 L.J.Ch.
313; *Wright v Carter* [1903] 1 Ch. 27; *Moody v Cox & Hatt* [1917] 2 Ch. 71; *Demerara Bauxite Co
Ltd v Hubbard* [1923] A.C. 673; *Christie v McCann*, above; *Bristol and West BS v Mothew* [1998]
Ch. 1 at 18 ("he must prove affirmatively that the transaction is fair", per Millett LJ). Such is the
authority. But another approach would be to look to the disclosure: if a fully informed principal
wishes to deal on terms adverse to himself, he should be allowed to do so-for case law support for
this view, see Conaglen [2006] C.L.J. 366.

[482] *Ex p. James* (1803) 8 Ves. 337; *Hobday v Peters* (1860) 28 Beav. 349; *De Bussche v Alt* (1878) 8
Ch.D. 286; *Powell & Thomas v Evan Jones & Co* [1905] 1 K.B. 11; *Blair v Martin* [1929] N.Z.L.R.
225; *Christie v McCann* (1972) 27 D.L.R. (3d) 544; *Palinko v Bower* [1976] 4 W.W.R. 118; Finn,
Fiduciary Obligations (1977), pp.177–178 and 202–203; and see Article 35.

[483] *Selsey v Rhoades* (1824) 2 S. & St. 41; affd (1827) 2 Bli. (N.S.) 1, Illustration 20. See also *Aaran
Acceptance Corp v Adam* (1987) 37 D.L.R. (4th) 133 (loan).

[484] *Ex p. Lacey* (1802) 6 Ves. 625; *Ex p. James*, above; *Campbell v Walker* (1800) 5 Ves. 678; (1807)
13 Ves. 601; *Cardigan v Moore* [2012] EWHC 1024 (Ch). But cf. *Holder v Holder* [1968] Ch. 353,
an unusual case; as to which see Goff and Jones, *Law of Unjust Enrichment* (9th edn) paras 8-175–
8-180. See Lewin, *Trusts* (19th edn), para.20-186 onwards; Finn, *Fiduciary Obligations* (1977),
pp.182–185, suggesting that there is little difference.

[485] *Allison v Clayhills* (1907) 97 L.T. 709; *McMaster v Byrne* [1952] 1 All E.R. 1362, Illustration 8;
Wintle v Nye [1959] 1 W.L.R. 284. See also *Cutts v Salmon* (1852) 21 L.J.Ch. 750; *King v Anderson*
(1874) 8 I.R.Eq. 625; *Spector v Ageda* [1973] Ch. 30, where Megarry J said that a solicitor should
in ordinary circumstances refuse to act for a client in relation to a transaction when he is himself a
party with an adverse interest in that same transaction.

6-065 **Sale to principal** Similarly, an agent may not sell his own property to his principal without full and fair disclosure and the obtaining of his principal's informed consent[486]; nor may he lease his own property to his principal without full disclosure. He must also prove that the transaction was fair.[487] But however fair the transaction may be, it can still be set aside by the principal if there has not been full disclosure.[488] Cases suggesting a more lenient rule have not been followed.[489] However, it has been held that a sale to an agent's wife is not automatically void-able, unless the agent was also her agent, but the fairness of the transaction is open to scrutiny.[490]

6-066 **Agent with specific instructions** Where, however, the agent has specific instructions to buy or sell at a particular price and no element of advice or discretion is involved, there may be cases where he is free to sell his own property to the principal or buy the principal's property himself, there being no possibility of conflicting interest.[491]

6-067 **Person who has ceased to be agent** Difficult questions arise if the agent deals with his principal after he has ceased to be an agent. It appears that the duty to disclose can continue, but whether it does so in any particular case in fact will depend on all the circumstances of the case. For example, if the confidence created by the agency relationship still exists at the time of the transaction,[492] or if the agent has a personal ascendancy over his principal, and certainly if he has acquired special knowledge during his employment relating to the subject-matter of the transaction, a court will be inclined to hold that the duty of disclosure is still binding on the agent.[493] Thus a solicitor's duty to disclose may last longer than the duty

---

[486] *Massey v Davies* (1794) 2 Ves. 317; *Gibson v Jeyes* (1801) 6 Ves. 266; *Rothschild v Brookman* (1831) 2 Dow. & Cl. 188; *Bentley v Craven* (1853) 18 Beav. 75; *Lucifero v Castel* (1887) 3 T.L.R. 371; *Tetley v Shand* (1871) 25 L.T. 658; *Skelton v Wood* (1894) 71 L.T. 616; *Kuhlirz v Lambert Brothers* (1913) 18 Com.Cas. 217; *Tito v Waddell (No. 2)* [1977] Ch. 106 at 240–244. See too *NBH Ltd v Hoare* [2006] EWHC 73 (Ch); [2006] 2 B.C.L.C. 649 (informal unanimous assent by company's shareholders precluded later complaint by company about sale to it made by director).

[487] *Bristol and West BS v Mothew* [1998] Ch. 1 at 18.

[488] *Aberdeen Ry Co v Blaikie Bros* (1854) 1 Macq. 461, Illustration 2 to Article 44; *Transvaal Lands Co v New Belgium (Transvaal) Land and Development Co* [1914] 2 Ch. 488; *Gray v New Augarita Porcupine Mines* [1952] 3 D.L.R. 1 (PC); *Maguire v Makaronis* (1997) 188 C.L.R. 449 (mortgage).

[489] e.g. *Charter v Trevelyan* (1844) 11 C. & F. 714 at 732. Distinguish the doctrine of undue influence, as to which see Snell, *Equity* (33rd edn), para.8-009 onwards. But see also *CIBC Mortgages Plc v Pitt* [1994] 1 A.C. 200 at 209, per Lord Browne-Wilkinson. See further below, para.6-069.

[490] *Newgate Stud Co v Penfold* [2004] EWHC 2993 (Ch); [2008] 1 B.C.L.C. 46.

[491] See *Kelly v Enderton* [1913] A.C. 191; *Dalgety & Co v Gray* (1919) 26 C.L.R. 249, 265 (PC) (loan to principal); *Jones v Canavan* [1972] 2 N.S.W.L.R. 236 (stockbroker); *R.H. Deacon & Co v Varga* (1972) 30 D.L.R. (3d) 653; affd (1973) 41 D.L.R. (3d) 767 (stockbroker); cf. *Thompson v Meade* (1891) 7 T.L.R. 698 (stockbroker); cf. also *Beer v Lea* (1913) 29 O.L.R. 255; *Bentley v Nasmith* (1912) 46 S.C.R. 477; *McMaster v Byrne* [1952] 1 All E.R. 1362, Illustration 8. And see Finn, Commercial Aspects of Fiduciary Obligations (McKendrick ed., 1992), Ch.1, pp.37–39.

[492] *Carter v Palmer* (1842) 8 C. & F. 657. But cf. *Connolly v Brown* 2007 S.L.T. 778 (fiduciary duty had on the facts terminated); *Wollenberg v Casinos Austria International Holding GmbH* [2011] EWHC 103 (Ch) (commercial client of solicitor and no need to advise to take independent advice); *KBL Investments Ltd v KBL Courtenay Ltd* [2016] NZCA 227 at [64] (mortgage broker becomes purchaser from client).

[493] *Allison v Clayhills* (1907) 97 L.T. 709; *Demerara Bauxite Co v Hubbard* [1923] A.C. 673. See also *Edwards v Meyrick* (1842) 2 Hare 60; *Montesquieu v Sandys* (1811) 18 Ves. 302; *Learmonth v Bailey* (1875) 1 V.L.R. 122.

of a less confidential agent, e.g. a stockbroker.[494] An agent who resigns in order to exploit an appropriate opportunity remains subject to fiduciary obligations at any rate in respect of that matter. An agent cannot, of course, claim that his own breach of duty terminates his agency and that therefore he is no longer bound to make full disclosure in any transaction that afterwards takes place between himself and his principal.[495]

Remedies of principal   A number of remedies can arise out of self-dealing and fair-dealing. While most of the relevant case law is at equity, in some cases of self-dealing, at least, the transaction will be unauthorised and treated both at law and equity as a nullity.[496] As to equity, a principal who finds, for instance, that his agent has purported to borrow the principal's money without consent may disown the loan, and either seek an account of the money or treat any asset bought with the money as belonging to the principal.[497] Otherwise, the principal may, in general, rescind any contract affected by the self-dealing and fair-dealing rules.[498] Rescission in equity is, however, a discretionary remedy, it seems, and a court may withhold it, including on the ground that the principal is not fully disowning the transaction.[499] The remedy may otherwise be unavailable,[500] but, it normally does not matter that the contract has been executed or that the property has meanwhile decreased in value.[501] The principal must take proceedings within a reasonable time after discovering the truth about the transaction or he may be taken to have acquiesced or affirmed.[502] Otherwise, the principal can elect to affirm,[503] but where there is doubt, the onus is on the agent to show that the principal has affirmed.[504] He will also usually be able to claim the profit any agent has made, for it is deemed

6-068

---

[494]   Compare Illustrations 8 and 9; and see *Longstaff v Birtles* [2001] EWCA Civ 1219; [2002] 1 W.L.R. 471; *Richards v Law Society* [2009] EWHC 2087 (Admin) at [45].
[495]   *Regier v Campbell-Stuart* [1939] Ch. 766, Illustration 16; *McLeod & More v Sweezey* [1944] 2 D.L.R. 145. Quaere whether, if the principal is in breach of duty, the agent's obligation can continue. In some cases it may not: see In *Plus Group Ltd v Pyke* [2002] EWCA Civ 370; [2002] 2 B.C.L.C. 201. If the principal becomes an alien enemy, it may well be that the agent's duties of loyalty come to an end: *Nordisk Insulinlaboratorium v Gorgate Products Ltd* [1953] Ch. 430 at 442, Illustration 11.
[496]   See *Rothschild v Brookman* (1831) 5 Bli. (NS) 165 at 191–192 and at 282; *Salomons v Pender* (1865) 3 H. & C. 639.
[497]   See *Tang Ying Loi v Tang Ying Ip* [2017] HKCFA 3.
[498]   *Maguire v Makaronis* (1997) 188 C.L.R. 449 (mortgage set aside on terms).
[499]   *Johnson v EBS Pensioner Trustees Ltd* [2002] EWCA Civ 164; [2002] Lloyd's Rep P.N. 309; *Hurstanger Ltd v Wilson* [2007] EWCA Civ 299; [2007] 1 W.L.R. 2351; [2007] 4 All E.R. 1118 at [50]; *Fenwick v Naera* [2015] NZSC 68; [2016] 1 N.Z.L.R. 354 at [122]; *Gamatronic (UK) Ltd v Hamilton* [2016] EWHC 2225 (QB) at [218].
[500]   e.g. because the property has already been conveyed to a sub-purchaser. For sub-purchases pendente lite, see *Trevelyan v White* (1839) 1 Beav. 588.
[501]   *Armstrong v Jackson* [1917] 2 K.B. 822.
[502]   *De Montmorency v Devereux* (1840) 7 C. & F. 188; *Champion v Rigby* (1830) 1 Russ. & M. 539; aff'd (1840) 9 L.J.(O.S.) Ch. 211; *Flint v Woodin* (1852) 9 Hare 618; *Lyddon v Moss* (1859) 4 De G. & J. 104; *Clanricarde v Henning* (1861) 30 Beav. 175; *Wentworth v Lloyd* (1863) 32 Beav. 467.
[503]   *Bentley v Craven* (1853) 18 Beav. 75; *Rea v Bell* (1852) 18 L.T.(O.S.) 312; *Gray v New Augarita Porcupine Mines* [1952] 3 D.L.R. 1 (PC); *Hely-Hutchinson v Brayhead Ltd* [1968] 1 Q.B. 549; *Robinson v Randfontein* [1921] App.D. 168 at 178.
[504]   *Cavendish-Bentinck v Fenn* (1887) 12 App.Cas. 652 at 666, Illustration 15. The principal must know the full facts, including the fact that he could rescind the transaction if he so wished: *Crowe v Ballard* (1790) 2 Cox Eq.Cas. 253; *Osry v Hirsch* [1922] Cape P.D. 531; *Holder v Holder* [1968] Ch. 353; *Peyman v Lanjani* [1985] Ch. 457.

to have been made on his behalf.⁵⁰⁵ Recent authority further suggests that the principal might, where there is a sale at an undervalue, treat the agent (and affected third parties) as holding the asset on constructive trust for the principal in proportion that the price paid by the agent bears to the true value of the asset purchased.⁵⁰⁶ The resulting remedy might be proprietary or personal. Alternatively, if the complaint is of loss he may claim damages for breach of contract, or conceivably equitable compensation under the principle of *Nocton v Ashburton*.⁵⁰⁷ Thus, where an agent has bought his principal's property, the principal can claim any profit on a resale⁵⁰⁸ or the difference between the value of the property and the price the agent gave.⁵⁰⁹

However, where the agent sells his property to the principal, it seems that a distinction is to be drawn between the situation in which the agent is instructed to find a seller but secretly buys property which he then sells to the principal, making a profit for himself, and the situation in which the agent sells property which was his own before the agency was created. In the first situation the agent will be liable to account for any profit he has made from the transaction, since he will be presumed to have bought on his principal's behalf and to have been holding on trust for him.⁵¹⁰ But in the second situation he was not acting on the principal's behalf and the orthodox view is that he will not be accountable for profits made: the usual remedy will be rescission, for no profit has been made within the scope of the agency.⁵¹¹ If this remedy is lost for any reason, e.g. because restitutio in integrum is impossible, it seems that the only right is to damages or compensation as above.⁵¹² That right, too, may be lost if the contract is affirmed in such a manner as to show that the principal does not intend to pursue his rights against the agent.⁵¹³ In any case the agent's right to commission on the transaction is lost.⁵¹⁴

---

⁵⁰⁵ For an example of calculation see *Estate Realties Ltd v Wignall (No.2)* [1992] 2 N.Z.L.R. 615; Watts [1992] L.M.C.L.Q. 439.
⁵⁰⁶ *Akita Holdings Ltd v Attorney General of Turks and Caicos Islands Is* [2017] UKPC 7; [2017] A.C. 590.
⁵⁰⁷ [1914] A.C. 932; above para.6-042. See Conaglen (2003) 119 L.Q.R. 246.
⁵⁰⁸ *Barker v Harrison* (1846) 2 Coll. 546; *De Bussche v Alt* (1878) 8 Ch.D. 286; *Blackham v Haythorpe* (1917) 23 C.L.R. 156; *Headway Construction Co Ltd v Downham* (1974) 233 E.G. 675, Illustration 17.
⁵⁰⁹ *Hall v Hallett* (1784) 1 Cox Eq.Cas. 134.
⁵¹⁰ *Massey v Davies* (1794) 2 Ves. 317; *Benson v Heathorn* (1842) 1 Y. & C.Ch.Cas. 326; *Tyrrell v Bank of London* (1862) 10 H.L.Cas. 26; *Kimber v Barber* (1872) L.R. 8 Ch.App. 56; *Regier v Campbell-Stuart* [1939] Ch. 766, Illustration 16; *Tweedvale Investments Pty Ltd v Thiran* (1996) 14 WAR 109.
⁵¹¹ *Re Cape Breton Co* (1885) 29 Ch.D. 795; affirmed sub nom. *Cavendish-Bentinck v Fenn* (1887) 12 App.Cas. 652, Illustration 15 (see discussion by Conaglen, above, at 249–250); *Burland v Earle* [1902] A.C. 83; *Robinson v Randfontein* [1921] App.D. 168 at 179; *Cook v Evatt (No.2)* [1992] 1 N.Z.L.R. 676; (noted by Watts [1992] L.M.C.L.Q. 439).
⁵¹² *Jacobus Marler Estates Ltd v Marler* (1913) 85 L.J.P.C. 167n; *P. & OSN Co v Johnson* (1938) 60 C.L.R. 189 at 213. This topic is discussed in *Walden Properties Ltd v Beaver Properties Pty Ltd* [1973] 2 N.S.W.L.R. 815 at 835–837; and in *Aequitas Ltd v Sparad No.100 Ltd* (2001) 19 A.C.L.C. 1006 at [430]. It is strongly argued by Conaglen above, that equitable compensation should be available. See discussion of the *Marler* case at 253–254; but cf. Meagher, *Gummow and Lehane's Equity Doctrines and Remedies* (5th edn), para.5-180.
⁵¹³ This would appear to be the effect of *Re Cape Breton Co*, above, as approved by the PC in *Burland v Earle* [1902] A.C. 83. See also *Cook v Deeks* [1916] 1 A.C. 554; *Tracy v Mandalay Pty Co* (1953) 88 C.L.R. 215; Sealy [1963] C.L.J. 119 at 132–135. But see Finn, *Fiduciary Obligations* (1977), p.225.
⁵¹⁴ *Salomons v Pender* (1865) 3 H. & C. 639; *Keppel v Wheeler* [1927] 1 K.B. 577 at 592; *Lunghi v Sinclair* [1966] W.A.R. 172; Article 60.

Gifts The nature of the relationship between a particular principal and agent may   **6-069**
lead to the application of a different, but related, rule, the presumption of undue
influence, to a gift received by an agent from his principal,[515] and indeed to other
transactions between them. On this basis the gift may be set aside unless it can be
proved that undue influence was not exercised. The rule has often been applied
between solicitor and client or counsel and lay client.[516] Any gift made by a client
to his solicitor is presumed to have been made under undue influence and his
presumption is not rebutted merely because the client has employed a completely
separate and independent solicitor to advise about the gift.[517] This presumption will
be applied although the solicitor-client relationship has come to an end, provided
that there is still a relationship of confidence and trust between the parties. But a
gift can be supported if the court is satisfied that it is perfectly fair and proper in
all the circumstances:

"The court, in dealing with such a transaction, starts with the presumption that undue influence exists on the part of the donee, and throws upon him the burden of satisfying the court
that the gift was uninfluenced by the position of the solicitor. Secondly, this presumption
is not a presumption which is entirely irrebuttable, though it is one which is extremely difficult to be rebutted."[518]

The rule will apply to gifts to near relatives of the solicitor,[519] but it does not apply
to trifling gifts.[520] The rule may be applied somewhat less strictly to gifts by will
but the solicitor must ensure that the client receives independent legal advice and
is fully capable of understanding what he is doing.[521] The desirability of independent advice can apply to other relationships also.[522]

Illustrations

Purchase from principal

(1)   A solicitor purchases property from his client's trustee in bankruptcy. He must   **6-070**
make a full disclosure of all the knowledge acquired by him respecting such
property during the time when he was acting as solicitor for the bankrupt.[523]
(2)   A solicitor purchased property from a former client, and concealed a mate-

---

[515] *Hunter v Atkins* (1834) 3 Myl. & K. 113; *Barnard v Hunter* (1856) 2 Jur. (N.S.) 1213; *Union Fidelity Trustee Co of Australia Ltd v Gibson* [1971] V.R. 573. See in general *National Westminster Bank
Plc v Morgan* [1985] A.C. 686; Snell, *Equity* (33rd edn), para.8-009 onwards; Finn, above, Ch.16.
[516] *Broun v Kennedy* (1864) 4 De G.J. & S. 217.
[517] *Morgan v Minnett* (1877) 6 Ch.D. 638; *Saunderson v Glass* (1742) 2 Atk. 296; *Middleton v Welles*
(1785) 4 Bro.P.C. 245; *Wright v Proud* (1806) 13 Ves. 136; *Tomson v Judge* (1885) 3 Drew. 306;
O'Brien v Lewis (1863) 32 L.J.Ch. 569; *Liles v Terry* [1895] 2 Q.B. 679; *Wright v Carter* [1903] 1
Ch. 27. For a solicitor to accept a gift without ensuring that his client has received independent legal
advice can amount to professional misconduct: *Re a Solicitor* [1975] Q.B. 475.
[518] *Wright v Carter* [1903] 1 Ch. 27 at 57, per Stirling LJ.
[519] See, e.g. *Willis v Barron* [1902] A.C. 271.
[520] *Rhodes v Bate* (1866) L.R. 1 Ch.App. 252; *Wright v Carter*, above.
[521] See for a discussion of this topic, see Cordery, *Solicitors* (8th ed), pp.17–18, and *Ramcoomarsingh
v Administrator-General* [2002] UKPC 67; cf. *Re Tyler* [1967] 1 W.L.R. 1269 at 1276, where it is
said that the court will require evidence which will satisfy it beyond doubt. Because the burden of
proof in a civil case is never more than the balance of probabilities, this must mean that the presumption to be displaced is a heavy one.
[522] See, e.g. *O'Sullivan v Management Agency and Music Ltd* [1985] Q.B. 428 (musician and manager).
[523] *Luddy's Trustees v Peard* (1886) 33 Ch.D. 500. See also *Boswell v Coaks* (1884) 27 Ch.D. 424
(reversed on the evidence, sub nom. *Coaks v Boswell* (1886) 11 App.Cas. 232).

rial fact. Another solicitor acted for the client in this transaction, but he did not possess all the necessary information and somewhat neglected his duty. The transaction was set aside.[524]

(3) A Scottish attorney purchased four houses from his clients, doing so in the name of his brother. He did not disclose that he was the real purchaser of two of the houses. The House of Lords refused to order specific performance of the contract.[525]

(4) Two persons become partners to sell a mine. One represents to the other that he has found a purchaser. Actually he has arranged to share with the purchaser in the profits made by floating a company to buy and work the mine. He must share the profit he makes with the other.[526]

(5) An auctioneer, who was employed to sell an estate, purchased it himself. The transaction was set aside, after an interval of 13 years.[527] So, an agent of a trustee for sale or of a mortgagee selling under his power of sale, who is employed as agent in the matter of the sale,[528] cannot purchase the property sold[529]; and a solicitor who conducts a sale of property must not purchase it without a full explanation to the vendor.[530]

(6) A broker is employed to sell goods. He sells them ostensibly to A, really to A and himself jointly. While the goods are still in possession of the broker, he becomes bankrupt, A also being insolvent. The principal may repudiate the contract and recover the goods specifically from the trustee in bankruptcy of the broker.[531]

(7) An agent for the management of trust property purchased part of such property from the cestui que trust. Held, that the circumstances being highly disadvantageous to the seller, the burden lay on the agent to prove that the transaction was right and honest, and that in the circumstances the lack of disinterested advice was fatal.[532]

(8) M owned shares in a Canadian company. He granted X an option to purchase them for $30,000. X assigned the option to B, who was the solicitor to the company and had until recently been solicitor to M. B exercised the option. At that time active negotiations for the take-over of the company were taking place and that fact was known to B when he exercised the option. As a result of the take-over B later sold the shares for $127,000. Held, although B was no longer M's solicitor, the confidential relationship between them still

[524] *Gibbs v Daniel* (1862) 4 Giff. 1; cf. *Guest v Smythe* (1870) L.R. 5 Ch.App. 551 (solicitor's name appeared on particulars of sale only).

[525] *McPherson v Watt* (1877) 3 App.Cas. 254. See also *Lewis v Hillman* (1852) 3 H.L.Cas. 607; *Cane v Allen* (1814) 2 Dow. 289; *Uppington v Bullen* (1842) 2 Dr. & War. 184; *Murphy v O'Shea* (1845) 8 I.Eq.R. 329; *Crowe v Ballard* (1790) 2 Cox.Eq.Cas. 253.

[526] *Dunne v English* (1874) L.R. 18 Eq. 524.

[527] *Oliver v Court* (1820) 8 Price 127. See also *Haywood v Roadknight* [1927] V.L.R. 512. But laches may afford a defence: see *Wentworth v Lloyd* (1863) 32 Beav. 467.

[528] See *Nutt v Easton* [1899] 1 Ch. 873; aff'd on other grounds [1900] 1 Ch. 29.

[529] *Whitcomb v Minchin* (1820) 5 Madd. 91; *Martinson v Clowes* (1882) 21 Ch.D. 857; *Lawrance v Galsworthy* (1857) 3 Jur.(N.S.) 1049; cf. *Bath v Standard Land Co* [1911] 1 Ch. 618 and *Orme v Wright* (1839) 3 Jur. 19; *Nuna v Easton* above, at 972.

[530] *Re Bloye's Trust* (1849) 1 Mac. & G. 488; *Ex p. James* (1803) 8 Ves. 337.

[531] *Ex p. Huth, re Pemberton* (1840) Mont. & C. 667.

[532] *King v Anderson* (1874) 8 I.R.Eq. 625. See also *Dally v Wonham* (1863) 33 Beav. 154.

subsisted and B was under a duty to make full disclosure to M before he purchased the shares from him.[533]

(9)   A stockbroker is commissioned to buy for a client. The client is unable to meet the amount due on settlement. In accordance with normal procedures the broker sells the shares. This is a valid closing of the account and he is entitled to indemnity.[534] He also repurchases them himself. This is legitimate[535] unless the repurchase is sufficiently a part of the same transaction that he secures a preferential price because the market-maker does not have to carry the shares. In the latter case the broker may be liable for a secret profit.[536]

(10)   Dealers employ agents to grant future options in cocoa. The agents do so and then take the options themselves. They fail to notify the dealers that the options have been declared. This is not merely a breach of their duties as agents, but rather, since their own taking of the options was valid, the options in respect of which no declarations were made by them lapse.[537]

(11)   A Danish corporation deposited insulin in an English bank shortly before the outbreak of war. When the Germans invaded Denmark the corporation became an alien enemy and the property vested in the Custodian of Enemy Property, who sold it to the defendants. The defendants had been the English selling agents of the corporation before the war; they now resold the insulin at a profit. Held, as the defendants had not acquired any special or secret knowledge about the insulin while they were the corporation's agents, they were under no fiduciary duty regarding it and were not accountable for the profit they made on resale.[538]

Sale to principal

(12)   A firm of brokers were authorised to purchase goods. They delivered bought notes to the principal which purported to be notes of a contract of which the brokers guaranteed performance, but which did not disclose the sellers. The principal paid the brokers their commission and a deposit, and subsequently discovered that one of the brokers intended to perform the contract himself. The principal was held to be entitled to repudiate the contract, and the brokers were ordered to repay the deposit and commission, with interest, since no agent can become a principal and deal on that footing without full and fair disclosure.[539]   **6-071**

(13)   A stockbroker was employed to purchase certain shares. He purchased the

---

[533]   *McMaster v Byrne* [1952] 1 All E.R. 1362. See also *J.J. Harrison (Properties) Ltd v Harrison* [2001] EWCA Civ 1467; [2002] 1 B.C.L.C. 162, Illustration 7 to Article 96.

[534]   *Macoun v Erskine, Oxenford & Co* [1901] 2 K.B. 493; *Walter and Gould v King* (1897) 13 T.L.R. 270; *Christoforides v Terry* [1924] A.C. 566. But a direct purchase by the broker himself would be voidable: *Re Finlay* [1913] 1 Ch. 565. See also *Jones v Canavan* [1972] 2 N.S.W.L.R. 236 (custom of "marrying" buying and selling transactions held reasonable).

[535]   See cases cited above.

[536]   *Erskine, Oxenford & Co v Sachs* [1901] 2 K.B. 504.

[537]   *Limako BV v Hentz & Co Inc* [1979] 2 Lloyd's Rep. 23.

[538]   *Nordisk Insulinlaboratorium v Gorgate Products Ltd* [1953] Ch. 430.

[539]   *Wilson v Short* (1848) 6 Hare 366. See also *Robinson v Mollett* (1874) L.R. 7 H.L. 802, Illustration 8 to Article 31; *Skelton v Wood* (1894) 71 L.T. 616; *Stange & Co v Lowitz* (1898) 14 T.L.R. 468; *Nicholson v J. Mansfield & Co* (1901) 17 T.L.R. 259. cf. *Ellis & Co's Trustee v Watsham* (1923) 155 L.T.Jo. 363 ("bought of ourselves as principals"—held sufficient disclosure).

shares from his own trustee without informing the principal of the fact. The transaction was set aside, after an interval of many years, without inquiry whether or not a fair price was charged.[540]

(14) A director proposes to contract with his company, it being provided by the articles of association that directors may contract with the company on disclosing their interest. It is his duty to declare the full extent and exact nature of his interest.[541]

(15) A company was formed to purchase certain coal areas in Newfoundland. It purchased these areas from A, who was a trustee for B and had been so for some time before the formation of the company. B was one of the directors of the company but did not disclose that he was beneficially interested in the coal areas. When the company was wound up, the shareholders, with full knowledge of the circumstances, decided to sell the coal areas. They realised a smaller sum than expected, but rescission of the original contract of purchase was now impossible. Held, any claim to damages had been forfeited by the affirmation of the contract, and any claim to B's profit was unsustainable as B had not acquired the property with a view to selling it to the company but owned it already.[542]

(16) A, an estate agent, agreed with B that A would furnish B with particulars of houses which A might think suitable for purchase by B. A, having found a suitable house, procured C to purchase it for £2,000, the purchase money being provided by A; and thereupon purported to buy it from C for £4,500. A then informed B that he had purchased the house for £4,500, and offered it to B for £5,000, representing that this price would allow a profit to A of £500. B purchased the house from A for £5,000. Held, that A was the agent of B for the purpose of furnishing particulars of suitable houses; that though an agent might terminate the relationship of principal and agent by selling to his principal property which belonged to himself, it was his duty to act honestly and faithfully, and, if he concealed material facts, the relationship was not terminated by such a transaction; and that A, having concealed the true nature of the transaction, was liable to account to B for all profits obtained by A without B's knowledge and consent.[543]

(17) P engaged A to ascertain the owners of properties adjacent to a site he was developing. A did so but dishonestly told P that he had failed. A then made an agreement with P whereby he agreed for a commission to acquire the properties for P. He then formed a company and acquired the properties for £42,000. This company then sold the properties to P for £57,000. Held, A was liable to P for the profit of £15,000 and damages of £3,000 for loss of the chance to acquire the properties for less than £42,000. P was entitled to avoid

---

[540] *Gillett v Peppercorne* (1840) 3 Beav. 78. See also *Rothschild v Brookman* (1831) 2 Dow. & Cl. 188; *King, Viall & Benson v Howell* (1910) 27 T.L.R. 114; *Oelkers v Ellis* [1914] 2 K.B. 139; *Armstrong v Jackson* [1917] 2 K.B. 822.

[541] *Imperial Mercantile Credit Co v Coleman* (1873) L.R. 6 H.L. 189; *Gluckstein v Barnes* [1900] A.C. 240. cf. *Chesterfield & Baythorpe Colliery Co v Black* (1877) 37 L.T. 740.

[542] *Re Cape Breton Co* (1885) 29 Ch.D. 795; affd sub nom. *Cavendish-Bentinck v Fenn* (1887) 12 App.Cas. 652. See also *Jacobus Marler Estates Ltd v Marler* (1913) 85 L.J.P.C. 167n (on both cases see Conaglen (2003) 119 L.Q.R. 246 at 249 onwards); *Walden Properties Ltd v Beaver Properties Pty Ltd* [1973] 2 N.S.W.L.R. 815 at 836.

[543] *Regier v Campbell-Stuart* [1939] Ch. 766. See Murdoch, *Law of Estate Agency and Auctions* (4th edn), p.63 onwards.

the contract with A and was not liable to A for commission in respect of other transactions.[544]

(18) An airport company, X Ltd, develops two hotels and markets units in each of them. The contracts of sale of units in respect of each hotel provide for X Ltd to be the managing agent of the hotels, but on different terms as to remuneration. The fact that there were those differences was not disclosed to investors. Whatever other rules might govern the situation, there was no breach of the fair dealing rules because the terms of the contracts pre-dated the creation of the agency relationship.[545]

Other dealings by agent with principal

(19) If a solicitor takes a mortgage from his client, the transaction may be rescinded.[546] The court will not enforce any unusual stipulations in the mortgage disadvantageous to the client,[547] and will restrain the solicitor from exercising his rights as mortgagee in an unfair or inequitable manner.[548] Where a power of sale exercisable at any time was inserted in such a mortgage without the usual proviso requiring interest to be in arrear or notice to be given, and the solicitor sold the property under the power, he was held liable to the client in damages as for an improper sale, it not being shown that he had explained to the client the unusual nature of the power.[549] **6-072**

(20) A steward contracts with his employer for a lease. He must show that he is giving as high a rent as it would have been his duty to obtain from a third party and that his employer was fully informed of every circumstance affecting the value of the property which was, or ought to have been, within the steward's knowledge.[550]

Article 46

AGENT'S DUTY NOT TO PROFIT FROM POSITION

An agent must not profit from his position as agent, except with the principal's consent. **6-073**

---

[544] *Headway Construction Co Ltd v Downham* (1974) 233 E.G. 675.
[545] *Sharbern Holding Inc v Vancouver Airport Centre Ltd* [2011] 2 S.C.R. 175; (2011) 331 D.L.R. (4th) 1.
[546] *Maguire v Makaronis* (1997) 188 C.L.R. 449 (set aside on terms).
[547] *Cowdry v Day* (1859) 1 Giff. 316; *Eyre v Hughes* (1876) 2 Ch.D. 148. See also *Gray v Dalgety & Co Ltd* (1916) 21 C.L.R. 509.
[548] *Macleod v Jones* (1883) 24 Ch.D. 289; *Pearson v Benson* (1860) 28 Beav. 598.
[549] *Readdy v Pendergast* (1887) 56 L.T. 790; *Cockburn v Edwards* (1881) 18 Ch.D. 449; *Craddock v Rogers* (1884) 53 L.J.Ch. 968. cf. *Pooley's Trustee v Whetham* (1886) 2 T.L.R. 808. See in general Cordery, *Solicitors* (8th edn), p.13 onwards.
[550] *Selsey v Rhoades* (1824) 2 S. & St. 41; affd (1827) 1 Bli.(N.S.) 1. See also *Watt v Grove* (1805) 2 Sch. & Lef. 492; *Waters v Shaftesbury* (1866) 14 L.T. 184; *Molony v Kernan* (1842) 2 Dr. & War. 31; *Ker v Lord Dungannon* (1841) 1 Dr. & War. (Ir.) 509.

Comment

6-074   This is a principle applicable to all fiduciaries. One of its classic expositions is that of Lord Russell of Killowen in *Regal (Hastings) Ltd v Gulliver*[551]:

> "The rule of equity which insists on those, who by use of a fiduciary position make a profit, being liable to account for that profit, in no way depends on fraud, or absence of bona fides; or upon such questions or considerations as whether the profit would or should otherwise have gone to the plaintiff, or whether the profiteer was under a duty to obtain the source of the profit for the plaintiff, or whether he took a risk or acted as he did for the benefit of the plaintiff, or whether the plaintiff has in fact been damaged or benefited by his action. The liability arises from the mere fact of a profit having, in the stated circumstances, been made. The profiteer, however honest and well-intentioned, cannot escape the risk of being called upon to account."

Lord Russell's compact exposition makes a number of points directed to the stringency of the obligation not to profit, including the fact that honesty in the fiduciary is no defence nor the fact that the principal may have suffered no loss. More detail on these aspects will be found in the succeeding paragraphs.[552]

Commonly, the profit will be derived from use of the principal's property or confidential information, but it need not be so derived, at least directly. In one of the most famous illustrations, *Phipps v Boardman*,[553] it is possible to regard the relevant profit as being derived indirectly from the use of the clients' property, but it is simpler to see it as derived from the defendant solicitor's use of his position as representative of his clients (trustees of a trust) in respect of their shareholding in a company. In that capacity he attended company meetings, pressured the directors to provide information, and over a three-year period carried on negotiations with the directors and the shareholders of the company in relation both to changing the company's operations and to the acquisition of their shares in the company. Ultimately, he was able, through his own and his clients' shareholding, to have himself appointed director, whereupon he set about further rationalising the company's business assets. By these methods he became privy to confidential information in relation to the company, but that information belonged to the company not to his clients. He was held accountable to his clients (along with a second defendant who also could be said to have used the clients' status) for the profit made on his own shares. Lord Cohen, in particular, rested his judgment on use of position rather than use of confidential information,[554] an analysis found also in the dissenting judgments of Viscount Dilhorne and Lord Upjohn, and less decisively in the judgment of Lord Hodson. The fifth member of the court, Lord Guest, does seem to have considered that liability rested on use of confidential information.

Complications can arise from the principle that a mere use of position is sufficient for accountability. In particular, it is possible that the agent's profiting might also involve improperly using the property of a third party, or leveraging the position that the agent has with a separate principal. *Boardman*, as noted, was potentially

---

[551] [1967] 2 A.C. 134n at 144–145. For discussion of the traditionally strict approach of equity in this field, see Samet (2008) 28 O.J.L.S. 768.

[552] See especially, Article 48.

[553] [1967] 2 A.C. 46. For further detail of the facts see Illustration 4 to Article 48. See too *The Peppy* [1997] 2 Lloyd's Rep. 722; *Cobbetts LLP v Hodge* [2009] EWHC 786 (Ch) (employee solicitor taking shares in client of firm arising out of work done by the firm for the client).

[554] [1967] 2 A.C. 46 at 102.

a case of this sort, since the inside information acquired by the defendant belonged to the company not the claimant trustees. Where the agent has already had to account to the third party, the costs of so doing would be taken into account in measuring the account of profits to the principal. Otherwise, the principal who has obtained a full account may need to be joined to proceedings if the agent is later sued by the third party.[555]

Broad though the concept of profiting-from-position is, it has limits. Hence, the mere fact that the agent learns something while acting for the principal would not make the agent liable for exploiting that information, if the information was not confidential but publicly available and the resulting opportunity for profit had no connection to the principal's lines of business.[556] For what is required for consent to be given to profiting see above, para.6-039, and for modification of fiduciary duties, see above, para.6-056.

The application of the principle to use of property and confidential information is dealt with in Article 47, where it will be seen that other remedies such as injunction and compensation for loss can also arise. Other aspects of the duty not to profit from position are then addressed in subsequent Articles.

Article 47

AGENT USING PRINCIPAL'S PROPERTY AND CONFIDENTIAL INFORMATION

An agent may not, without the informed consent of his principal, use his principal's property, or confidential information acquired during the course of the agency, to acquire a benefit (i.e. a secret profit).[557] **6-075**

Comment

Property It has long been established that if the agent makes any secret profit **6-076**
from the use of his principal's property, he is accountable to his principal for that profit, unless the principal with full knowledge of the circumstances consents to the retention of it by the agent:

> "It is quite clear that if an agent uses property, with which he has been entrusted by his principal, so as to make a profit for himself out of it, without his principal's consent, then he is accountable for it to his principal ... Likewise with information or knowledge which he has been employed by his principal to collect or discover, or which he has otherwise acquired, for use of his principal, then again if he turns it to his own use, so as to make a profit by means of it for himself, he is accountable ...".[558]

The fact that the agent's liability can be based on his holding identifiable property of the principal makes this an obvious example where the duties of a trustee can be said to be extended to the agent. But it can also be regarded as a simple example of the general principle stated in Article 46, that the agent must not without

---

[555] See *Adlam v Savage* [2016] NZCA 454; [2017] 2 N.Z.L.R. 309 at [48].
[556] *Aas v Benham* [1891] 2 Ch. 244 at 255–256; *Phipps v Boardman* [1967] 2 A.C. 46 at 100; *Nottingham University v Fishel* [2000] I.C.R. 146 (university academic not accountable for income from private consulting, but accountable for arranging for other employees to work on his external projects). For other authorities on this point, see below, para.6-081.
[557] See Comment.
[558] *Phipps v Boardman* [1965] Ch. 992 at 1030, per Pearson LJ.

disclosure make a profit from his position. It is not, of course, any use by the agent of his principal's property which attracts this liability: in many circumstances some form of use is contemplated. It is use leading to an undisclosed profit to which the rule applies.

Under this principle can also be brought the case where an agent is treated as holding in trust money he has received from his principal, with the result that he is liable for interest on it or may be required to account for profits.[559] Such profits would not of course be secret. Where the agent has recourse to his principal's money without authority, the principal can elect as of right to take ownership of any assets bought with it.[560] All these liabilities appear to attract a proprietary remedy; but courts often speak of an account of profits, which is personal.[561]

A person who acts as agent without authority may also be liable under this principle.[562] See further above, para.6-068.

6-077   **Confidential information**[563]   There is also no doubt that if an agent uses confidential information acquired as a result of his agency he may be liable to his principal in respect of it.[564] On one view, this is explicable on the basis that such information is property.[565] But:

> "perhaps the most sterile of the debates which have arisen around the subject of information received in confidence is whether or not such information should be classified as property."[566]

For it is only in certain circumstances, difficult of definition, that information is protected, and the criteria for ascertaining this are not the same as those used to determine whether property reasoning is inherently appropriate:

> "If only some information is described as property, i.e. information protected by the courts, to call that information property is merely to add yet another consequence to a decision taken for reasons quite unrelated to property considerations."[567]

The principle is not, however, peculiar to the law of agency; if any fiduciary exploits confidential information which he acquires in the course of his relationship with his beneficiary, he is in breach of his fiduciary duty and if, as is usually the case with an agent, he has a contract with his principal, he will probably be in breach of

---

[559] See above, para.6-041.

[560] See above, para.6-040.

[561] See *Warman International Ltd v Dwyer* (1995) 182 C.L.R. 544 at 556 onwards; above, paras 6-042 and 6-043; below, paras 6-079, 6-094.

[562] *English v Dedham Vale Properties Ltd* [1978] 1 W.L.R. 93.

[563] See *Restatement, Third*, § 8.05; Finn, *Fiduciary Obligations* (1977), Ch. 19; Jones (1970) 86 L.Q.R. 463; Snell, *Equity* (33rd edn), paras 7-068–7-072 and 18-021. The *Law Commission (No.110, Cmnd. 8388 (1981))* recommended the creation of statutory tort liability. This would have left much of the liability arising from fiduciary relationships as a separate area of law. There may sometimes be a defence to disclosure under the Public Interest Disclosure Act 1998.

[564] *Phipps v Boardman* [1967] 2 A.C. 46, Illustration 4 to Article 48; *Peter Pan Manufacturing Corporation v Corsets Silhouette Ltd* [1964] 1 W.L.R. 96, Illustration 6; *Att.-Gen. v Guardian Newspapers Ltd (No.2)* [1990] 1 A.C. 109 at 288; Jones [1989] C.L.P. 49.

[565] See *Phipps v Boardman*, above, at 89–90, 107 and 115; cf. 102, 127–128; but this was not the basis of the decision, which may simply have been the use by the defendant of his position.

[566] Finn, above, p.131. See also The Rt Hon. Lord Millett [1993] Restitution L.Rev. 7 at 11: "owes more to metaphor than to legal reality".

[567] Finn, above, p.132.

contract also.[568] But the duty may be independent of contract or even of a standing relationship. If any person receives information which he knows or ought to know[569] is confidential and uses that information for his own profit, he is so liable whether there is any previous relationship between him and the plaintiff or not, although the remedy for breach will depend on the circumstances[570]:

> "The law on this subject does not depend on any implied contract. It depends on the broad principle of equity that he who has received information in confidence shall not take unfair advantage of it. He must not make use of it to the prejudice of him who gave it without obtaining his consent."[571]

The mere receipt of confidential information does not of itself create a fiduciary relationship.[572] It may therefore be said that the rule is not a special one applicable to fiduciaries, but rather that the receipt of confidential information may impose an obligation not to misuse it.[573] Confidential information can be any non-public information expressly or impliedly imparted in confidence. It can extend beyond trade secrets[574] to such things as lists or databases of customers of the principal.[575]

Once the information is readily available to the public it has ceased to be confidential. It will then no longer be a breach of confidence for the agent to make use of it.[576] However, even in those circumstances, the other duties of some agents, including those relating to the pursuit of business opportunities,[577] may constrain the agent from exploiting the information. Similarly, while the agent remains engaged, damaging and unnecessary dispersal of non-confidential information held

---

[568] *Lamb v Evans* [1893] 1 Ch. 218, Illustration 5; *Robb v Green* [1895] 2 Q.B. 315; *Duchess of Argyll v Duke of Argyll* [1967] Ch. 302; *Westminster Chemical NZ Ltd v McKinley* [1973] 1 N.Z.L.R. 659; *New Zealand Needle Manufacturers Ltd v Taylor* [1975] 2 N.Z.L.R. 33; *Investors Syndicate Ltd v Versatile Investments Ltd* (1983) 149 D.L.R. (3d) 46; *Prince Jefri Bolkiah v KPMG* [1999] 2 A.C. 222; *Cadbury Schweppes Inc v FBI Foods Ltd* [1999] 1 S.C.R. 142; (1999) 167 D.L.R. (4th) 577; cf. *Arklow Investments Ltd v Maclean* [2000] 1 W.L.R. 594 (PC) (no proof of misuse). See Abdullah and Tey (1995) 115 L.Q.R. 376.

[569] *Coco v A.N. Clark (Engineers) Ltd* [1969] R.P.C. 41 at 48; and see *Printers and Finishers Ltd v Holloway* [1965] R.P.C. 239 at 252; *Att.-Gen. v Jonathan Cape Ltd* [1976] Q.B. 752; cf. *United Sterling Corp Ltd v Felton* [1974] R.P.C. 162. See also *Union Carbide Corp v Naturin Ltd* [1987] F.S.R. 538; *Att.-Gen. v Guardian Newspapers Ltd (No.2)* [1990] 1 A.C. 109 at 281.

[570] *Saltman Engineering Co Ltd v Campbell Engineering Co* (1948) [1963] 3 All E.R. 413n.; *Talbot v General Television Corp Pty Ltd* [1981] R.P.C. 1; *Fraser v Thames Television Ltd* [1984] Q.B. 44.

[571] *Seager v Copydex Ltd* [1967] 1 W.L.R. 923 at 931, per Lord Denning MR. The liability extends to persons to whom information is further transmitted. See Finn, *Fiduciary Obligations* (1977), pp.152–156; *Schering Chemicals Ltd v Falkman Ltd* [1982] Q.B. 1, Illustration 7; *Wheatley v Bell* [1982] 2 N.S.W.L.R. 544. But different considerations may arise where information is received in confidence which ought in the public interest to be disclosed to one who has a proper interest to receive it: *Initial Services Ltd v Putterill* [1968] 1 Q.B. 396; *Fraser v Evans* [1969] 1 Q.B. 349; *Hubbard v Vosper* [1972] 2 Q.B. 84; *Church of Scientology v Kaufman* [1973] R.P.C. 635; cf. *Schering Chemicals Ltd v Falkman Ltd*, above; *Lion Laboratories Ltd v Evans* [1985] Q.B. 526.

[572] *Indata Equipment Supplies Ltd v ACL Ltd* [1998] 1 B.C.L.C. 412; *Arklow Investments Ltd v Maclean* [2000] 1 W.L.R. 594 (PC); *Walsh v Shanahan* [2013] EWCA Civ 411 at [38].

[573] cf. above, para.6-061.

[574] See *Faccenda Chicken Ltd v Fowler* [1987] 1 Ch. 117; *Del Casale v Artedomus (Aust) Pty Ltd* (2007) 73 I.P.R. 326.

[575] *Baker v Gibbons* [1972] 1 W.L.R. 693; *Peninsular Real Estate Ltd v Harris* [1992] 2 N.Z.L.R. 216; *Whitmar Publications Ltd v Gamage* [2013] EWHC 1881 (Ch) at [58].

[576] *O Mustad & Son v Dosen (1928)* [1964] 1 W.L.R. 109n.; *Cranleigh Precision Engineering Ltd v Bryant* [1965] 1 W.L.R. 1293 at 1314–1319; *Speed Seal Products Ltd v Paddington* [1985] 1 W.L.R. 1327; *Att.-Gen. v Guardian Newspapers (No.2)* [1990] 1 A.C. 109, esp. at 285.

[577] See below, para.6-081.

on behalf of the principal could conceivably be a breach of an agent's duties of care and skill.

A principal whose confidential information has been used by his agent, or his former agent, has various remedies open to him.[578] It seems indeed that remedies are particularly flexible in this area. It is not impossible that this flexibility may in due course be extended to breach of fiduciary duty in general. The principal may seek an injunction to restrain the agent from making any further use of the information[579]; he may sue for damages for breach of contract in an appropriate case. Where a contractual action is not available, there is authority that damages may be awarded in equity to cover the price which the owner would have charged for the information,[580] and it seems that this award may be independent of damages in lieu of injunction under Lord Cairns' Act.[581] The principal may also sue for an account of the profits made by the agent from his use of the confidential information,[582] and where the agency relationship is still subsisting at the time of exploitation an account of profits would usually be granted.[583] The onus of proving that a profit has been derived without the use of confidential information lies on the fiduciary.[584] It seems however that the court will determine the appropriate remedy rather than permit the plaintiff to elect.[585] Finally, whether or not the information can properly be described as the property of the principal, it seems that an agent who has made profits for himself by making use of it is a trustee of those profits for the principal,[586] though where no fiduciary is involved and the recourse is simply to general principle the matter is more arguable, for the action for an account of profits is in principle in personam.[587] An injunction against a former employee, even a senior one, to prevent him working for a competitor (as opposed to an injunction against

---

[578] See Finn, *Fiduciary Obligations* (1977), p.163 onwards; Davies, in *Consensus ad Idem* (Rose ed., 1996), pp.163–165; Abdullah and Tey (1999) 115 L.Q.R. 376.

[579] *Merryweather v Moore* [1892] 2 Ch. 518; *Lamb v Evans* [1893] 1 Ch. 218, Illustration 5; *Robb v Green* [1895] 2 Q.B. 315; *Peter Pan Manufacturing Co Ltd v Corsets Silhouette Ltd* [1964] 1 W.L.R. 96, Illustration 6; *Coco v A.N. Clark (Engineers) Ltd* [1969] R.P.C. 41; *Dunford & Elliott Ltd v Johnson & Firth Brown Ltd* [1977] 1 Lloyd's Rep. 505; cf. *Amber Size and Chemical Co Ltd v Menzel* [1913] 2 Ch. 239; *Baker v Gibbons* [1972] 1 W.L.R. 693. The grant of an injunction is of course discretionary: see *Att.-Gen. v Guardian Newspapers Ltd (No.2)* [1990] 1 A.C. 109.

[580] *Saltman Engineering Co Ltd v Campbell Engineering Co* (1948) [1963] 3 All E.R. 413n. *Seager v Copydex Ltd* [1967] 1 W.L.R. 923 at 932, where Lord Denning MR says that there is to be an inquiry as to damages as "it may not be a case for an injunction"; for the principle upon which the damages were to be assessed see *Seager v Copydex Ltd (No.2)* [1969] 1 W.L.R. 809; *Interfirm Comparison (Australia) Pty Ltd v Law Society of NSW* [1975] 2 N.S.W.L.R. 104; *Dowson & Mason Ltd v Potter* [1986] 1 W.L.R. 1419. cf. *Marathon Asset Management LLP v Seddon* [2017] EWHC 300 (Comm) at [235]. And see Illustration 4.

[581] See *Nicrotherm Electrical Co Ltd v Percy* [1956] R.P.C. 272; [1957] R.P.C. 207; *Seager v Copydex Ltd*, above. But see *English v Dedham Vale Properties Ltd* [1978] 1 W.L.R. 93 at 111–112.

[582] *Peter Pan Manufacturing Corp Ltd v Corsets Silhouette Ltd* [1964] 1 W.L.R. 96, Illustration 6; cf. *Lever v Goodwin* (1887) 36 Ch.D. 1; *Att.-Gen. v Guardian Newspapers Ltd (No.2)* [1990] 1 A.C. 109 at 288; *Dart Industries Inc v Decor Corp Pty Ltd* (1993) 179 C.L.R. 101; *Hoechst Celanese International Corp v BP Chemicals Ltd* [1999] R.P.C. 203 (all profits treated as made on claimants' behalf).

[583] *Walsh v Shanahan* [2013] EWCA Civ 411 at [68].

[584] *United Pan-Europe Communications NV v Deutsche Bank AG* [2000] 2 B.C.L.C. 461 at [34].

[585] *English v Dedham Vale Properties Ltd*, above; *Walsh v Shanahan* [2013] EWCA Civ 411 at [66].

[586] *United Pan-Europe Communications NV v Deutsche Bank AG* [2000] 2 B.C.L.C. 461.

[587] See *Lees v Nuttall* (1829) 1 Russ. & M. 53; affd (1834) 2 My. & K. 819; *Triplex Safety Glass Co Ltd v Scorah* [1938] Ch. 211; *Boardman v Phipps* [1965] Ch. 992; [1967] 2 A.C. 46; the *Lac Minerals* case, above, para.6-042; *Warman International Ltd v Dwyer* (1995) 182 C.L.R. 544 at 556–557; above, paras 6-042 and 6-043; below, para.6-094.

using the confidential information itself[588]) would not usually be given in the absence of a restraint of trade clause.[589] A principal cannot automatically obtain against a former agent an order for delivery up of all copies of written confidential information held by the agent.[590]

Illustrations

(1) The master of a ship was authorised to employ the vessel to the best advantage; **6-078** he could not procure remunerative freight and so loaded her with cargo of his own. Held, he must account to the owners for the profit to be made on the sale of the cargo and not merely for a reasonable freight.[591]

(2) A telegraph company erected and maintained a "special wire" alongside a railway line in Newfoundland. The railway company were by contract entitled to use the wire in and about their railway business but were not entitled to transmit any commercial messages except for the account of the telegraph company. In fact they used it in part for their shipping business and other commercial undertakings. Held, they were accountable to the telegraph company for all the profits made and that they held these profits in trust for the company.[592]

(3) A client instructs a stockbroker to buy a certain quantity of stock in a company and "carry at 8%". The stockbroker deals with the shares so bought on his own account. He must account for his profits.[593]

(4) B is managing director of a company publishing a trade journal for the timber industry. With the company's consent, he is also manager and principal shareholder of another company which publishes a "Lumberman's Atlas". He inserts in the journal free advertisements for the Atlas. He must refund to his employer company a reasonable charge for doing so.[594]

(5) The proprietor of a trade directory employed canvassers to obtain advertisements from traders for insertion in the directory. He discovered that the canvassers were proposing to assist a rival publication with similar advertisements after their agreement with his had come to an end. Held, the canvassers were not entitled to use material or information obtained while in the plaintiff's employment for the purpose of this publication.[595]

(6) English licensees of the patents for brassières were shown in confidence new designs not yet on the market. They made use of this information to design

---

[588] *Personnel Hygiene Services Ltd v Rentokil Initial UK Ltd* [2014] EWCA Civ 29; *Allfiled UK Ltd v Eltis* [2015] EWHC 1300 (Ch) (interim injunction).

[589] *Caterpillar Logistics Services (UK) Ltd v de Crean* [2012] EWCA Civ 156; [2012] F.S.R. 33.

[590] *Eurasian Natural Resources Corp Ltd v Judge* [2014] EWHC 3556 (QB) at [75].

[591] *Shallcross v Oldham* (1862) 2 Johns. & H. 609. See also *Gardner v M'Cutcheon* (1842) 4 Beav. 534; *Diplock v Blackburn* (1811) 3 Camp. 43.

[592] *Reid-Newfoundland Co v Anglo-American Telegraph Co Ltd* [1912] A.C. 555. See as to this unusual case Finn, *Fiduciary Obligations* (1977), p.99. The wire remained the property of the company.

[593] *Thornley v Tilley* (1925) 36 C.L.R. 1; see also *Langton v Waite* (1868) L.R. 6 Eq. 165 (reversed on other grounds (1869) L.R. 4 Ch.App. 402); *McLaughlin v Solloway* [1936] S.C.R. 127; [1938] A.C. 247; cf. *King v Hutton* [1900] 2 Q.B. 504.

[594] *B.C. Timber Industries Journal v Black* [1934] 3 D.L.R. 31.

[595] *Lamb v Evans* [1893] 1 Ch. 218. For the extent to which names and addresses not in a written list may be confidential information which a defendant may be restrained from using, see *Baker v Gibbons* [1972] 1 W.L.R. 693; *Investors Syndicate Ltd v Versatile Investments Inc* (1983) 149 D.L.R. (3d) 46. See also *Faccenda Chicken Ltd v Fowler* [1987] Ch. 117; *Crowson Fabrics Ltd v Rider* [2007] EWHC 2942 (Ch); [2008] I.R.L.R. 288; [2008] F.S.R. 17.

their own brassi'eres and then terminated their licence from the plaintiffs. Held, the plaintiffs were entitled: (a) to an injunction restraining the defendants from making and selling brassieres made from the new designs; (b) to an account of the profits from the brassieres already sold; and (c) to an order for delivery-up or destruction of the offending goods.[596]

(7) A drug company, to combat unfavourable publicity as to the side effects of one of its drugs, engages a specialist in television training to train its executives to put the company's point of view effectively when interviewed on television. The person engaged himself engages an experienced broadcaster to assist. During the courses the latter acquires information which he subsequently uses in making a documentary film in conjunction with a television company. The showing of the film is a breach of confidence and may be restrained by injunction.[597]

Article 48

AGENT ACQUIRING BENEFITS IN BREACH OF DUTY

6-079 An agent may not in breach of duty acquire for himself a benefit from a third party without his principal's consent. He must account to his principal for any benefit so obtained.[598]

Comment

6-080 **Scope of principle** On the account here given of the fiduciary duties of an agent, this is a residual principle, insofar as it does not rely on the notion of using the principal's property, information or other attributes, though it can be taken to suggest that acquisitions *become* the principal's property. In part, it addresses the first limb, the "conflicts rule", in the following well-known description of the fiduciary's liability to account for profits, found in the judgment of Deane J in *Chan v Zacharia* (the second limb being the subject of Articles 46 and 47)[599]:

> "Stated comprehensively in terms of the liability to account, the principle of equity is that a person who is under a fiduciary obligation must account to the person to whom the obligation is owed for any benefit or gain (i) which has been obtained or received in circumstances where a conflict or significant possibility of conflict existed between his fiduciary duty and his personal interest in the pursuit or possible receipt of such a benefit or gain or (ii) which was obtained or received by use or by reason of his fiduciary position or of opportunity or knowledge resulting from it."

It is important to note that the principle covers profits derived from the agent's hav-

---

[596] *Peter Pan Manufacturing Corp Ltd v Corsets Silhouette Ltd* [1964] 1 W.L.R. 96.
[597] *Schering Chemicals Ltd v Falkman Ltd* [1982] Q.B. 1.
[598] See Comment and Illustrations; *Restatement, Third*, § 8.02; *Meinhard v Salmon* 164 N.E. 545 (1928), per Cardozo CJ. For the possibility of the agent's being accountable for benefits derived by third parties as a result of the agent's breach of duty, see above, para.6-042.
[599] (1984) 154 C.L.R. 178 at 198–199, per Deane J, quoted with approval in *Don King Productions Inc v Warren* [2000] Ch. 291. See also *Rothschild v Brookman* (1831) 2 Dow. & Cl. 188; *Parker v McKenna* (1874) L.R. 10 Ch.App. 96 at 118; *Re Birt* (1883) 22 Ch.D. 604; *Bray v Ford* [1896] A.C. 44 at 51–52; *Lindgren v L.&P. Estates Ltd* [1968] Ch. 572; *North and South Trust Co v Berkeley* [1971] 1 W.L.R. 470; the Rt Hon. Lord Millett [1993] Restitution L.Rev. 7 at 16: "A fiduciary will not be allowed to retain any advantage acquired in violation of the rule".

ing placed himself in a position where his interests *potentially* conflict with his principal's,[600] as well as cases where there is *actual* conflict and the agent has clearly been disloyal in his actions.[601] The taking of bribes and secret commissions, covered by this principle, is elaborated in Article 49, below. Note that the duty of loyalty is usually applied to the positive exercise of powers conferred on the agent by the principal, but a conflict of interest can arise in relation to an omission to exercise those powers.[602]

The principle also makes accountable those agents whose functions include locating assets or business opportunities (either particular or of a class) for their principals, or who have assumed management functions in the principal's business affairs, who proceed to acquire assets or opportunities (often termed "corporate opportunities" or "business opportunities") in their own right which should have been pursued, if at all, for the principal. It is not altogether clear whether this aspect of the principle is merely a particular example of the duty to avoid conflicts of interest, or an independent head of liability. While all fiduciaries have an obligation to avoid conflicts of interest, not all agents have the function of acquiring assets or business opportunities. The reconciliation might be, however, that the application of the conflicts rule can only be determined in each case by identifying the tasks that the relevant agent has undertaken to perform for the principal.

The detail of the relevant case law is treated separately in the succeeding paragraphs, but the body of law can be traced back to *Keech v Sandford*.[603] Here, property was leased to a trust, and when the lease determined the trustee renewed it for his own personal benefit. It was held that the trustee held the benefit of the lease on trust for his beneficiaries. The rule as to renewals has been held to extend also to purchases of the reversion.[604] But the presumption may sometimes be rebuttable.[605] It undoubtedly performs a cautionary role. "I very well see" said Lord King LC "if a trustee on refusal to renew might have a lease to himself, few trust estates would be renewed to cestui que use".[606] As elsewhere, full disclosure of all the material facts and consent by the principal will displace liability that would otherwise ensue.[607] However, a plea that the principal would have consented to the fiduciary's conduct if asked is unlikely to be countenanced by the court.[608]

The principle the subject of this Article is a strict one, and all profits must be ac-

---

[600] *Imageview Management Ltd v Jack* [2009] EWCA Civ 63; [2009] 2 All E.R. 666 (Illustration 13); *Keogh v Dalgety & Co Ltd* (1916) 22 C.L.R. 402 (defendants appointed agent to procure mortgage loan for claimant, but arrange one whereby, without disclosure, they obtain a commission from the mortgagee for giving a guarantee of the mortgage).

[601] *JD Wetherspoon Plc v Van De Berg & Co Ltd* [2009] EWHC 639 (Ch) (diversion of opportunity to acquire properties to self and subsequent on-sale to competitor of the principal; defendant disguised conflict by inserting an intermediary in his transactions with principal).

[602] e.g. *British Midland Tool Ltd v Midland International Tooling Ltd* [2003] EWHC 466 (Ch); [2003] 2 B.C.L.C. 523; *Chan v Zacharia* (1984) 154 C.L.R. 178 (refusal to renew lease).

[603] (1726) Sel.Cas.Ch. King 61; But cf. Hicks [2010] C.L.J. 287. For the application of *Keech v Sandford* to agents, see *York Buildings v Mackenzie* (1795) 8 Bro. P.C. 42 at 63–64. See too *Chan v Zacharia* (1984) 154 C.L.R. 178 at 201, 203.

[604] *Protheroe v Protheroe* [1968] 1 W.L.R. 519.

[605] See *Re Biss* [1903] 2 Ch. 40; *Chan v Zacharia*, above, at pp.201–205; Lewin, *Trusts* (18th edn), para.20-02 onwards; Finn, *Fiduciary Obligations* (1977), Ch.23; *Meagher, Gummow and Lehane's Equity Doctrines and Remedies* (5th edn), para.5-055.

[606] See also *Bray v Ford* [1896] A.C. 44 at 51–52; *Chan v Zacharia*, above.

[607] *New Zealands Netherlands Society "Oranje" Inc v Kuys* [1973] 1 W.L.R. 1126. For further detail, see above, para.6-039. As to modification of fiduciary duties by contract, see above, para.6-056.

[608] *Murad v Al-Saraj* [2005] EWCA Civ 959; [2005] 1 W.T.L.R. 1573. See too *United Pan-Europe Communications BV v Deutsche Bank AG* [2000] 2 B.C.L.C. 461 at [47].

counted for even if, in acquiring them, the agent has incurred a risk of loss,[609] and the principal could not himself have made the profit, has suffered no injury or has even made a profit himself.[610] However, the court may make an allowance to the fiduciary for his skill and expenditure in making the profit[611]; and sometimes this appears to approach a share in the profit.[612]

A claim made under the principle set out in this Article is often, of course, advanced in conjunction with a claim that the agent has used property or information belonging to his principal to acquire a benefit for himself[613]: but the present principle is wider, since it is not confined to situations where trust property can be readily identified. Since there is, until it is generated, no property to which the right can attach, it can be said that the only remedy is a duty to account, which is personal[614]; but where an identifiable asset is acquired in most cases the principal will have a proprietary claim.[615] The case for a proprietary remedy is most compelling where the agent was under a positive duty to obtain the asset for the principal.[616]

A person who acts as agent without authority may also be liable under this principle, although this is an unusual situation.[617]

6-081 **"Business (or corporate) opportunities"**[618]   The body of law dealing with liability for diverting business opportunities is in modern times commonly associated with company directors, in which context it is usual to refer to "corporate opportunities", but it is by no means so confined. It applies to any agent who has undertaken, not necessarily as a matter of contract, to locate, or assist in the acquisition of, business opportunities for his principal, or who has assumed management functions in relation to the principal's business affairs.[619] The agent will be held accountable for pursuing opportunities in his own right which should have been

---

[609] See e.g. *Burrell v Mossop* (1888) 4 T.L.R. 270; *Williams v Stevens* (1866) L.R. 1 P.C. 352.

[610] *Parker v McKenna* (1874) L.R. 10 Ch.App. 96; *Phipps v Boardman* [1967] 2 A.C. 46, Illustration 4, a case where the principal acquired great benefit as a result of the fiduciaries' action: *Industrial Development Consultants Ltd v Cooley* [1972] 1 W.L.R. 443, Illustration 7; *Warman International Ltd v Dwyer* (1995) 182 C.L.R. 544; *Akita Holdings Ltd v Attorney General of Turks and Caicos Islands* [2017] UKPC 7; [2017] A.C. 590.

[611] *Phipps v Boardman*, above; but cf. *Guinness Plc v Saunders* [1990] 2 A.C. 663; *Imageview Management Ltd v Jack* [2009] EWCA Civ 63; [2009] 2 All E.R. 666; *Cobbetts LLP v Hodge* [2009] EWHC 786 (Ch) at [118]. See also *Yates v Finn* (1880) 13 Ch.D. 839; *Re Jarvis* [1958] 1 W.L.R. 815; *Paul A. Davies (Australia) Pty Ltd v Davies* [1983] 1 N.S.W.L.R. 440; *Nottingham University v Fishel* [2000] I.C.R. 146. See further Watts (2009) 125 L.Q.R. 369 at 374.

[612] See *O'Sullivan v Management Agency and Music Ltd* [1985] Q.B. 428; *Re Duke of Norfolk's Settlement Trusts* [1962] Ch. 61; *Re Berkeley Applegate (Investment Consultants) Ltd* [1989] Ch. 32; *Estate Realties Ltd v Wignall* [1992] 2 N.Z.L.R. 615; *Warman International Ltd v Dwyer*, above.

[613] e.g. *Phipps v Boardman*, above; see Article 47.

[614] *Warman International Ltd v Dwyer*, above, at 557. See above, para.6-041; below, para.6-094. See also paras 6-051, 6-052, 6-075 and 6-094.

[615] See *FHR European Ventures LLP v Cedar Capital Partners LLC* [2014] UKSC 45; [2015] A.C. 250.

[616] e.g. *Cook v Deeks* [1916] 1 A.C. 554; *Aerostar Maintenance International Ltd v Wilson* [2010] EWHC 2032 (Ch) at [193].

[617] *English v Dedham Vale Properties Ltd* [1978] 1 W.L.R. 93. As to "self-appointed" agents: see Beatson, *Use and Abuse of Unjust Enrichment* (1991), pp.241–243; (1978) 94 L.Q.R. 347; (1978) 41 M.L.R. 474; and DeMott in *Agency Law in Commercial Practice* (Busch, Macgregor and Watts, eds, 2016), Ch.3. See also *HKSAR v Luk Kin* [2016] HKCFA 81 at [34]. cf. *Arklow Investments Ltd v Maclean* [2000] 1 W.L.R. 594 (PC).

[618] See *Gower's Principles of Modern Company Law* (10th edn), Chs 5 and 16; Worthington (2000) 116 L.Q.R. 638 at 662 onwards; Kershaw (2005) 25 O.J.L.S. 603.

[619] e.g. *Cook v Deeks* [1916] 1 A.C. 554 (company director); *Thompson's Trustee in Bankruptcy v Heaton* [1974] 1 W.L.R. 605 (partnership); *Don King Productions Inc v Warren* [2000] Ch. 291;

pursued, if at all, for the principal. As remarked already, some examples also involve the agent in using his principal's property, confidential information or other attributes.[620] However, it is not necessary to show that there has been any use of position, property or information; indeed, the agent may have learned of the opportunity casually in "his own time".[621]

Where such an undertaking exists, to divert such opportunities will usually be disloyal conduct, though dishonesty is not necessary. Liability for profits arises even if no liability would have arisen had the agent simply failed to have pursued the opportunity at all[622]—so, non-executive directors may have no positive obligation to pursue a relevant opportunity for their company, but would nonetheless be precluded from pursuing it for themselves, or it may be that the third party is only interested in dealing with the agent.[623] The agent may be liable even though by the time he makes the profit he has ceased to act as agent for the principal; indeed, the person concerned may often have resigned as agent precisely in order to pursue the profit.[624] Nor does it matter if the parties have been negotiating to terminate their relationship when the opportunity arises.[625]

Some authority appears to support the view that it is only "maturing opportunities", namely those that the principal had already identified for pursuit, that cannot be exploited by the agent, or former agent, for himself.[626] Other cases conclude that accountability cannot be so confined.[627] Much turns on the scope of the tasks that the agent has undertaken to perform, and the closeness of the connection of the opportunity to the principal's existing business or businesses. The principle may, however, extend to opportunities that have a close fit with a dormant part of the principal's business,[628] or which relate to new lines of business in which the principal has indicated a firm interest.[629] The mere possibility that the agent might at some time in the future be called on to act for the principal in the relevant matter is, on some authority, sufficient to impose liability on him even though when he makes the profit he has not been so called on.[630] This however is open to doubt, unless he is under a pre-existing duty to act in that way.[631]

Chirnside v Fay [2007] 1 N.Z.L.R. 433 (NZSC) (informal joint venture); *Brandeis Brokers Ltd v Black* [2001] 2 Lloyd's Rep. 359 at 368 (broker); *JD Wetherspoon Plc v Van De Berg & Co Ltd* [2009] EWHC 639 (Ch) (purchaser's agent); *Cook v Evatt (No.2)* [1992] 1 N.Z.L.R. 676 (investment adviser); *FHR European Ventures LLP v Cedar Capital Partners* [2014] UKSC 45; [2015] A.C. 250. As to company directors, see now Companies Act 2006 s.175; and above, para.6-080.

[620] e.g. *Regal (Hastings) Ltd v Gulliver* [1967] 2 A.C. 134n (directors' combining personal capital with that of company capital to obtain shared ownership of assets relevant to company's business). As to use of property and confidential information in general, see Article 47.

[621] e.g. *Bhullar v Bhullar* [2003] 2 B.C.L.C. 241; cf. *Wilkinson v West Coast Capital Ltd* [2005] EWHC 3009 (Ch); [2007] B.C.C. 717 at [306].

[622] Perhaps implicit in *Keech v Sandford* (1726) Sel.Cas.Ch. 61 itself, per Lord King LC.

[623] *Industrial Development Consultants Ltd v Cooley* [1972] 1 W.L.R. 443; *G.E. Smith Ltd v Smith* [1952] N.Z.L.R. 470.

[624] See Illustrations 7 and 8.

[625] *Bhullar v Bhullar* [2003] 2 B.C.L.C. 241; *Pennyfeathers Ltd v Pennyfeathers Property Co Ltd* [2013] EWHC 3530 (Ch) at [58].

[626] See *Island Export Finance Ltd v Umunna* [1986] B.C.L.C. 460 at 482; *Balston Ltd v Headline Filters Ltd* [1990] F.S.R. 385 at 412; *Dranez Anstalt v Hayek* [2002] 1 B.C.L.C. 693 at [76].

[627] *Bhullar v Bhullar* [2003] 2 B.C.L.C. 241; *Canadian Aero Service Ltd v O'Malley* (1973) 40 D.L.R. (3d) 371 at 391; *Pacifica Shipping Co Ltd v Anderson* [1986] 2 N.Z.L.R. 328 at 334.

[628] *Coleman Taymar Ltd v Oakes* [2001] 2 B.C.L.C. 749; *Bhullar v Bhullar* [2003] 2 B.C.L.C. 241.

[629] *Dwyer v Lippiatt* (2004) 50 A.C.S.R. 333.

[630] See *Phipps v Boardman* [1967] 2 A.C. 46 where it was said that the solicitor might at some time be

Conversely, accountability will not extend to opportunities that are not part of the principal's business,[632] or which clearly do not arise until after the agent's appointment has ceased.[633] One case has suggested that for all but partners the corporate opportunity doctrine does not require a connection between the lines of the principal's business and the profit,[634] but the case is readily, and better, explained as involving exploitation of the fiduciary's position, for which there need not be any connection to the business.

In a controversial decision,[635] a majority of the Supreme Court of Canada extended the corporate opportunity doctrine to a person who was a mere adviser of the principal. The solicitor there had a duty to inform the claimant of the availability of a *type* of tax driven scheme, but, as the majority accepted, his undertaking did not preclude him from informing any other client of specific opportunities or from exploiting them himself (putting aside the fact that his colleagues had directed him not to get involved with clients in a scheme). Because he had failed to inform the claimant of the tax opportunity the court held him accountable for all the profits he derived from his own participation in such schemes during the period that the claimant was a client of the firm. This seems wrong. There was insufficient connection between the profits made and the breach of duty. The profits were not a result of an undisclosed conflict (he did not need the client's consent to make them), there was no use of fiduciary position, and he had given no undertaking to direct opportunities the claimant's way. The award was, therefore, punitive. It may have been acceptable to award "springboard damages" to remove any advantage the solicitor gained from suppressing from his client the availability of the schemes, but not more.

The liability to account for the taking of corporate opportunities is, in accordance with principle, subject to there having been no disclosure to, and consent by, the principal to the agent's action.[636] In some cases, it has been held that that consent can be given to a company director by the other directors,[637] but it is not clear that a director's colleagues are the appropriate persons to be giving such an indulgence.

---

called on to advise whether to apply to the court for permission for the trust to increase its holding in the company. However, liability in this case arose even without this consideration.

[631] See *Tyrrell v Bank of London* (1862) 10 H.L. Cas. 26; *Re Thomson* [1930] 1 Ch. 203; *British Syphon Co v Homewood* [1956] 1 W.L.R. 1190; Finn, *Fiduciary Obligations* (1977), pp.244–246.

[632] See Illustrations 1, 6, 9 and 15. See too *Aas v Benham* [1891] 2 Ch. 244; *Trimble v Goldberg* [1906] A.C. 494 (partner's purchase of land from company in which partnership held shares not a breach of duty); *Wilkinson v West Coast Capital* [2005] EWHC 3009 (Ch); [2007] B.C.C. 717 at [284]; *Canberra Residential Developments Pty Ltd v Brendas (No.5)* [2009] FCA 34; *Howard v Commissioner of Taxation* [2014] HCA 21; (2014) 253 C.L.R. 83 at [37].

[633] *Nordisk Insulinlaboratorium v Gorgate Products Ltd* [1953] Ch. 430; *National Trust for Places of Historic Interest v Birden* [2009] EWHC 2023 (Ch); *Thermascan Ltd v Norman* [2009] EWHC 3694 (Ch) at [16] (relevant contracts made with former regular customers of principal, but not initiated until after agent's resignation).

[634] *O'Donnell v Shanahan* [2009] EWCA Civ 751; [2009] 2 B.C.L.C. 666 at [55] (criticised Lim (2013) 129 L.Q.R. 242); *Invideous Ltd v Thorogood* [2013] EWHC 3015 (Ch). cf. *Poon Ka Man v Cheng Wai Tao* [2016] HKCFA 23 at [85] (not following *O'Donnell*).

[635] *Strother v 3464920 Canada Inc* [2007] 2 S.C.R. 177; criticised by Edelman (2008) 124 L.Q.R. 21; Duggan, in Bant and Harding (eds), *Exploring Private Law* (2010), Ch.12. cf. *Colyer Fehr Tallow Pty Ltd v KNZ Australia Pty Ltd* [2011] NSWSC 457 (buying agent held not liable because undertook no implied obligation not to buy for others or for own account).

[636] See above, para.6-039. See also *Robash Pty Ltd v Gladstone Pacific Nickel Pty Ltd* (2012) 86 A.C.S.R. 432.

[637] *Peso Silver Mines Ltd v Cropper* [1966] S.C.R. 673; (1966) 58 D.L.R. (2d) 1, a controversial case: see (1967) 30 M.L.R. 450; Beck (1971) 49 Can.B.R. 80; Prentice (1972) 50 Can.B.R. 623. See also

Agent acquiring specific asset in own name   If an agent who agrees to acquire,   **6-082**
to assist in the acquisition of, land or another asset on behalf of his principal
acquires it in his own name or on his own behalf he becomes a trustee of it for his
principal.[638] The principle is not limited to purchases; it applies, for example, to
leases. Thus, where an agent took a lease in his own name which he had been
instructed to take jointly for himself and his principal, it was decided that he held
it on trust for the benefit of both himself and his principal.[639]

At least in relation to land, the intervention of equity in this context can be
explained by the fact that neither a disclosed nor an undisclosed principal can claim
that conveyance to the agent vests property in the principal. In the case of chattels,
a disclosed principal will often be able to claim that title vested directly in him. It
is also possible that an undisclosed principal may sometimes claim that property
is by transfer to his agent vested in him, rather than held on trust,[640] but often
recourse to equity would be needed.

If the agent purports to sell to the principal the property which he has acquired
in his own name (and which he therefore holds on trust), the sale is of no effect in
equity, since the agent is already holding it on trust for his principal. Accordingly,
the principal can recover from the agent anything he has paid in excess of the price
paid by the agent for the property. It also follows that the agent holds this excess
on trust for the principal until it is claimed from him.[641]

Illustrations

(1)   Commission agents who were also merchants were employed to ship and sell   **6-083**
goods abroad. They did so and purchased other goods with the proceeds. They
were not bound to account for the profit on the sale of the goods bought with
the proceeds, because such profit was not made in the course of or by means
of the agency. They were only bound to account for the proceeds of the goods
sold on the principal's behalf.[642]
(2)   Three directors of a company which carried on the business of railway
construction contractors obtained for themselves a contract to build a railway
line to the exclusion of the company. They concealed this from the fourth
director until the contract was obtained. Held, they held the benefit of the
contract on behalf of the company.[643]
(3)   A company wished to purchase the leases of two cinemas from X which, with

---

Mid-Western News Agency Ltd v Vanpinxteren (1975) 62 D.L.R. (3d) 555; *Evans v Anderson* (1977)
76 D.L.R. (3d) 482; and the cases cited above, para.6-039.
[638] *Lees v Nuttall* (1829) 1 Russ. & M. 53; (1834) 2 Myl. & K. 819; *Austin v Chambers* (1837) 6 C. &
F. 1 at 36–40; *Tyrrell v Bank of London* (1862) 10 H.L. Cas. 26 (discussed in detail in Watts (2013)
129 L.Q.R. 526). In *Bartlett v Pickersgill* (1760) 1 Cox 15 and *James v Smith* [1891] 1 Ch. 384; affd
(1892) 65 L.T. 544, there was held to be a trust in favour of the principal, but one which he could
not enforce as it did not comply with s.7 of the Statute of Frauds. In *Rochefoucauld v Boustead*
[1897] 1 Ch. 196 this limitation was overruled but the cases are still authority for the principle
expressed in the Article. See also *Taylor v Salmon* (1838) 4 Myl. & Cr. 134 at 139; *Trench v Harrison* (1849) 17 Sim. 111; *Cave v Mackenzie* (1877) 46 L.J.Ch. 564; *Gray v Smith* [2013] EWHC
4136 (Comm); [2014] 2 All E.R. (Comm) 359 at [35]. See further Comment to Article 9; Youdan
[1984] C.L.J. 306.
[639] *Atkins v Rowe* (1728) Mos. 39; *Taylor v Salmon*, above; *Raleigh v McGrath* (1877) 3 V.L.R. 250.
[640] See Article 89.
[641] cf. *Regier v Campbell-Stuart* [1939] Ch. 766, Illustration 16 to Article 45, and *Bentley v Craven*
(1853) 18 Beav. 75.
[642] *Kirkham v Peel* (1881) 44 L.T. 195; cf. *Union Government v Chappell* [1918] Cape P.D. 462.
[643] *Cook v Deeks* [1916] 1 A.C. 554.

a cinema it already owned, were to be transferred to a subsidiary company and then sold to a third party. The intention was that the company should own all the shares in the subsidiary. X required personal guarantees of the rent so long as the subscribed capital of the subsidiary was below a certain amount. It being difficult to secure such guarantees, and the company not having the money to subscribe further, the directors of the company and their solicitor personally subscribed for the remainder of the capital. When the directors sold their shares they made a profit which they could not keep for themselves but held for the benefit of their company, even after the company had been sold. The solicitor was however unaffected.[644]

(4)   A will created a trust which included a shareholding in a private company. X, the solicitor who had been acting for the trust, and Y, a beneficiary, decided that the best way to protect the interests of the trust was to gain control of the company and this they did by purchasing sufficient extra shares in the company with their own money. By holding themselves out as acting on behalf of the trust, they acquired both the opportunity to bid for the further shares and also confidential information which satisfied them that the purchase of the shares would be a good investment. As a result of the changes in control of the company, X and Y and the trust made considerable profits. They had made formal disclosure to two trustees but not to the third; and later, when the estate had been administered, disclosure to the beneficiaries had not been complete. Held, X and Y were accountable to the trust for the profit made on the shares which they had purchased with their own money, as they had used their position to make a profit for themselves as well as the trust. X and Y could, however, claim remuneration for their expenses and labour in taking over the company.[645]

(5)   Two mine prospectors employed X to stake asbestos mineral claims for them in Manitoba. X received information about the area from them, explored the area and reported that there was no asbestos there. However, in the course of his prospecting he discovered that there were other valuable minerals in the area. Shortly afterwards he staked claims to these minerals for himself and made a considerable profit. Held, he was under a duty to disclose all he had learnt about the area to his principals and he must account for the profits made within the area he agreed to explore.[646]

(6)   The board of directors of a mining company considers a proposition put up by an outsider for mining in an area near to the company's holdings, and reject it. Individual directors contact the outsider and put up the money for

---

[644] *Regal (Hastings) Ltd v Gulliver* [1967] 2 A.C. 134n.
[645] *Phipps v Boardman* [1967] 2 A.C. 46. This is a stern decision, and there is considerable force in the dissenting judgment of Lord Upjohn. A crucial reason seems to have been that X and Y purported, at any rate initially, to be acting for the trust: there was certainly no pre-existing agency relationship. The company was also a private one and information could not be obtained from its public documents. The trust could not have purchased shares in the company without leave of the court and in some speeches reliance is placed, perhaps questionably, on the fact that it was possible that at some time in the future the solicitor would be asked to advise in this respect; on the question of remuneration cf. *Guinness Plc v Saunders* [1990] 2 A.C. 663. See Finn, *Fiduciary Obligations* (1977), p.242 onwards; *Chan v Zacharia* (1984) 154 C.L.R. 178 at 204–205, per Deane J.
[646] *McLeod and More v Sweezey* [1944] 2 D.L.R. 145.

the venture, taking advice from the company's consulting geologist. They are not liable to account for profits.[647]

(7) C was managing director of the plaintiffs, a company which carried on business as construction consultants. As such, he was negotiating with E for a contract. E made it clear to him that he had no intention of contracting with the plaintiffs but indicated that he might be prepared to contract with C personally. At a subsequent interview with the chairman of the plaintiffs, C did not tell him of E's offer but falsely told him that he was seriously ill. For this reason he was given permission by the plaintiffs to resign at once instead of working out his contractual period of notice. Having resigned from the plaintiff's employment C at once made a contract with E. Held, C had allowed his personal interest to conflict with his duty as a director of the plaintiffs. Notwithstanding that the plaintiffs had sustained no loss (because E was not willing to contract with them) C was ordered to account to the plaintiffs for all his profits from his contract with E.[648]

(8) The executive president and vice-president of a company engage in preliminary prospecting towards an extensive aerial mapping project to be paid for by a government. They subsequently form a separate company and obtain the contract in competition with their previous company. They must account for profits.[649]

(9) The managing director of a company formed to exploit mining licences is poised to exploit successful negotiations. The collapse of one of the company's shareholders leaves it without working capital. The managing director takes the licences in his own name, resigns as managing director (but not as a director) and forms his own company to exploit the concession. He explains the full position and the inherent risks to the board, which decides to pursue the concession no further and permit him to do what he wants with the licence. He is not liable to account.[650]

(10) The prospective purchaser of property applies for planning permission in respect of it in the vendor's name without telling the vendor. He must account for profits made as the result of the application.[651]

(11) A sergeant in the Army stationed at Cairo, while in uniform, accompanied civilian lorries containing illicit goods through Cairo, enabling them to pass the civilian police without inspection. He was paid large sums of money for his services. The military authorities took possession of the money, and the sergeant petitioned the Crown for its return. Held, he could not recover the money. He had obtained the money by reason of his employment, but in

---

[647] *Peso Silver Mines Ltd v Cropper* [1966] S.C.R. 673; (1966) 58 D.L.R. (2d) 1, a controversial case: see (1967) 30 M.L.R. 450; Beck (1971) 49 Can.B.R. 80; Prentice (1972) 50 Can.B.R. 623. See also *Mid-Western News Agency Ltd v Vanpinxteren* (1975) 62 D.L.R. (3d) 555; *Evans v Anderson* (1977) 76 D.L.R. (3d) 482.

[648] *Industrial Development Consultants Ltd v Cooley* [1972] 1 W.L.R. 443. See also *Green & Clara Pty Ltd v Bestobell Industries Pty Ltd* [1982] W.A.R. 1; *Crowson Fabrics Ltd v Rider* [2007] EWHC 2942 (Ch); [2008] I.R.L.R. 288; [2008] F.S.R. 17.

[649] *Canadian Aero Service Ltd v O'Malley* [1974] S.C.R. 592; (1973) 40 D.L.R. (3d) 371. See also *Abbey Glen Property Corp v Stumborg* (1978) 85 D.L.R. (3d) 35; (1979) 42 M.L.R. 215; and in general as to those cases *Gower's Principles of Modern Company Law* (10th edn), para.16-84 onwards.

[650] *Queensland Mines Ltd v Hudson* (1978) 52 A.L.J.R. 399 (PC); see (1979) 42 M.L.R. 711. See also *Island Export Finance Ltd v Umunna* [1986] B.C.L.C. 460.

[651] *English v Dedham Vale Properties Ltd* [1978] 1 W.L.R. 93. For comment on this case, see above, notes to para.6-080.

dereliction of his duty—by using his position as a sergeant and the uniform to which his rank entitled him; the Crown could retain the money—at least against the sergeant— even though it was earned by a criminal act.[652]

(12) A enters into a joint venture with B and C to buy a hotel for £4.1 million. It is understood that A will contribute £500,000 and B and C together £1 million; the remainder will be borrowed from a bank. In breach of his fiduciary duty A conceals the fact that his contribution is largely by way of deductions to the price in respect of the introduction. Had they known this B and C would have gone ahead, but allowing a smaller profit share to A. The hotel is sold for a profit of £2 million. A must account to B and C for the whole of the profit less the small amount of money genuinely put in by him, subject to an allowance for skill and effort.[653]

(13) A sports agent undertakes to provide advice to and representation for a professional footballer for a two-year period, in return for a commission on salary payable under any resulting employment contracts. The agent procures for the player a position with a Club. At the same time, at the Club's request and for a fee, the agent provides services in obtaining a work permit for the player. Some time into his contract with the Club, the player subsequently disowns the contract with the agent on the basis of the non-disclosure of the work undertaken for the Club, reclaiming all commission, and claiming an account of the fee paid by the Club. Held, the agent must not only account for the fee but must also refund the commission received from the player and forfeit any right to ongoing commission under the Club contract.[654]

(14) A agrees with B to bid at an auction for property which they both want and promises that if he acquires it he will cede part to B. A holds that part on trust for B and cannot claim to own the whole.[655]

(15) An owner of land sells part of it to a company for a golf course and becomes a director, and for a time CEO, of that company. He commences to develop another golf course on his remaining land. He is not obliged to offer this new business to the company. His involvement in managing two competing businesses could in principle involve an actionable conflict of interest, but not where he had resigned from the company before the new business commenced trading.[656]

[652] *Reading v Att.-Gen.* [1951] A.C. 507; but care must be taken in applying the principles of fiduciary obligation in public law situations: see Finn, *Fiduciary Obligations* (1977), pp.214–215. See also *Att.-Gen. v Goddard* (1929) 98 L.J.K.B. 743; *Hawrelak v City of Edmonton* (1975) 54 D.L.R. (3d) 45.

[653] *Murad v Al-Saraj* [2005] EWCA Civ 959; [2005] 1 W.T.L.R. 1573. See also *Gray v New Augarita Porcupine Mines Ltd* [1952] 3 D.L.R. 1 (PC); cf. *Chirnside v Fay* [2007] 1 N.Z.L.R. 433.

[654] *Imageview Management Ltd v Jack* [2009] EWCA Civ 63; [2009] 2 All E.R. 666; noted Watts (2009) 125 L.Q.R. 369; and Oram [2010] L.M.C.L.Q. 95. For doubt about whether forfeiture of remuneration was appropriate here, see below para.7-050.

[655] *Chattock v Muller* (1878) 8 Ch.D. 177; applied in *Pallant v Morgan* [1953] Ch. 43; considered in *Banner Homes Group Plc v Luff Developments Ltd* [2000] Ch. 372. See also *Chirnside v Fay* [2007] 1 N.Z.L.R. 433.

[656] *Links Golf Tasmania Pty Ltd v Sattler* [2012] FCA 634; (2012) 292 A.L.R. 382.

Article 49

LIABILITY OF AGENTS IN RESPECT OF BRIBES AND SECRET COMMISSIONS

When an agent receives or arranges to receive any money or property by way of **6-084**
bribe or secret commission in the course of his agency from a person who deals or
seeks to deal with his principal, the agent is liable to his principal jointly and severally with that person—

(1) in restitution for the amount of the bribe or secret commission; or
(2) in tort or contract, for any loss suffered by the principal from entering into
the transaction in respect of which the bribe or secret commission was given
or promised.[657]

Comment

Bribes[658]   A bribe is a type of secret profit, and a clear breach of fiduciary duty.   **6-085**
However, the rules for bribes have special features, and the area has its own
specialised group of cases. Courts generally eschew attaching rigid definitions to
common law concepts, and this is true of the concept of a bribe. However, two
formulations much referred to in other cases follow, the latter more apposite to the
broader concept of a secret commission:

> "If a gift be made to a confidential agent with the view of inducing the agent to act in
> favour of the donor in relation to transactions between the donor and the agent's principal
> and that gift is secret as between the donor and the agent—that is to say, without the
> knowledge and consent of the principal—then the gift is a bribe in the view of the law":
> *Hovenden & Sons v Millhoff*, per Romer LJ.[659]

> "[F]or the purpose of the civil law a bribe means a payment of a secret commission, which
> only means (i) that the person making the payment makes it to the agent of the other
> person with whom he is dealing; (ii) that he makes it to that person knowing that the
> person is acting as the agent of the other person with whom he is dealing; and (iii) that
> he fails to disclose to the other person with whom he is dealing that he has made that pay-
> ment to the person whom he knows to be the other person's agent": *Industries and General
> Mortgage Co Ltd v Lewis*, per Slade J.[660]

Where the payment is not for a corrupt purpose, a corrupt purpose being one
intended to influence the agent in the performance of his tasks in favour of the payer
or some other outside party, it is more appropriate to refer to the arrangement as a
secret commission. The reasoning applies also to commissions given by way of
discount on payment.[661] It is generally as problematic for the third party to promise
a secret commission as to pay it, although inducement will need to be proven by

---

[657] *Mahesan v Malaysia Government Officers Co-operative Housing Society Ltd* [1979] A.C. 374, Illustration 8. See further Article 96 as to the position between principal and third party.
[658] See Berg [2001] L.M.C.L.Q. 27 (a valuable article).
[659] *Hovenden & Sons v Millhoff* (1900) 83 L.T. 41 at 43, per Romer LJ. See too *Novoship (UK) Ltd v
Mikhaylyuk* [2012] EWHC 3586 (Comm) at [106] reversed on other issues [2014] EWCA Civ 908.
[660] [1949] 2 All E.R. 573 at 575. See also *Taylor v Walker* [1958] 1 Lloyd's Rep. 490, Article 96, Illustration 4; *Anangel Atlas Cia. Naviera SA v Ishikawajima-Harima Heavy Industries Co Ltd* [1990]
1 Lloyd's Rep. 167 at 171, per Leggatt J: "More succinctly it may be said that a bribe consists in a
commission or other inducement which is given by the third party to an agent as such, and which is
secret from the principal".
[661] e.g. *Turnbull v Garden* (1869) 38 L.J.Ch. 331, Illustration 2. Sometimes such transactions can be
treated as a sale by the agent to his principal: see *Kimber v Barber* (1872) L.R. 8 Ch.App. 56; Article
45.

the principal (actual payment supplies it own proof).[662] Older cases did not necessarily regard such commissions as bribes but might simply treat the agent as bound to account to his principal on the ground that the money or property had been received for him.[663] It is now clear however that the agents are liable in respect of bribes and secret commissions in restitution or in tort.[664] It is now also clear that a bribe which comprises money or other property is held on trust for the principal.[665] But liability does not attach to small gifts made after the conclusion of a transaction related to services performed by the agent himself,[666] unless it appears that such gifts were expected when the transaction was entered into, or are intended to affect future transactions[667]; nor to discounts obtained on transactions independent of the agency relationship.[668] Bribes may be offered by the third party or sought by the agent,[669] can frequently be in kind (including an offer of future employment),[670] and can be paid to relatives of, trustees for, or otherwise at the direction of, the agent.[671] It is not necessary that the bribe relate to a particular transaction, and the validity of all subsequent transactions may be affected.[672] On the other hand, not all undisclosed profiting from position would amount to a bribe or secret commission. Some gains which an agent might make will be from activities that do not relate directly to the services he performs for the principal and their receipt could not realistically be considered as likely to influence those services. The agent may be accountable in equity for having derived such incidental benefits (because his fiduciary position was sufficiently connected to their derivation), without the benefits being considered commissions or bribes.[673]

---

[662] *Grant v Gold Exploration & Development Syndicate Ltd* [1900] 1 Ch. 233; though the agent can only be liable in restitution where he has received the money; *Donegal International Ltd v Republic of Zambia* [2007] EWHC 197 (Comm); [2007] 1 Lloyd's Rep. 397 at [274]–[275]; *Otkritie International Investment Management Ltd v Urumov* [2014] EWHC 191 (Comm) at [68] (corrupt purpose need not be proved).

[663] e.g. *Fawcett v Whitehouse* (1829) 1 Russ. & M. 132; *Turnbull v Garden*, above.

[664] *Mahesan's case* [1979] A.C. 374 above, at 383.

[665] *FHR European Ventures LLP v Cedar Capital Partners LLC* [2014] UKSC 45; [2015] A.C. 250. See further para.6-087.

[666] *The Parkdale* [1897] P. 53, Illustration 1. See also *Meadow Schama & Co v C. Mitchell & Co Ltd* (1973) 228 E.G. 1511 (sum promised after commission earned: not a bribe). See too *Donegal International Ltd v Republic of Zambia* [2007] EWHC 197 (Comm); [2007] 1 Lloyd's Rep. 397 at [277]; *Bank of Ireland v Jaffery* [2012] EWHC 1377 (Ch) at [392] (side deals but for full value and not intended as inducements).

[667] See *Fiona Trust Holding Corp v Privalov* [2010] EWHC 3199 (Comm) at [73] and [1392] ("sufficient to create a 'real possibility' of a conflict between interest and duty"); *Field v R.* [2012] 3 N.Z.L.R. 1 (MP criminally liable for having received free labour on house following assistance to immigrants in electorate). See also Article 96, Illustration 1.

[668] See *London School Board v Northcroft (1892), Hudson's Building and Engineering Contracts* (12th edn), para.2.235.

[669] *Novoship (UK) Ltd v Mikhaylyuk* [2012] EWHC 3586 (Comm) at [106] (issue not addressed on appeal: [2014] EWCA Civ 908).

[670] See the cases cited below, para.6-087; and *Amalgamated Industrials Ltd v Johnson & Firth Brown Ltd, The Times,* April 15, 1981 (offer of future employment).

[671] *Novoship (UK) Ltd v Mikhaylyuk* [2012] EWHC 3586 (Comm) at [107] (issue not addressed on appeal: [2014] EWCA Civ 908).

[672] *Novoship (UK) Ltd v Mikhaylyuk* [2012] EWHC 3586 (Comm) at [109] affd [2014] EWCA Civ 908 at [54]; *Otkritie International Investment Management Ltd v Urumov* [2014] EWHC 191 (Comm) at [70].

[673] For an example in the context of the criminal law, see *Secretary for Justice v Chan Chi Wan* [2017] HKCFA 15.

Disclosure Active concealment is not necessary: it is sufficient that the principal **6-086** did not know of the bribe.[674] Furthermore, to free the agent from liability, the disclosure must be such as to enable the principal to understand the implications of the arrangement: thus a partial disclosure may be insufficient.[675] That the principal is aware that his agent is receiving some sort of commission from the third party may preclude his rescinding the transaction with the third party, but leave the agent accountable for incomplete disclosure.[676]

If the relevant elements are proved, it is irrelevant to show that the agent has not in fact been influenced or departed from his duty to his principal,[677] for the acceptance of or agreement to receive a bribe is of itself a breach of his general fiduciary duty, as giving him an interest contrary to his duty to his principal.[678]

If however the principal knows that the agent has been paid such a commission and consents, he cannot afterwards claim against the agent[679]; similarly, where he leaves the agent to look to the other party for his remuneration or knows that he will receive something from the other party, he cannot object on the ground that he did not know the precise particulars of the amount paid. Such situations often occur in connection with usage and custom of trades and markets.[680] The courts are generally most reluctant to recognise any custom or market practice that is asserted in relation to undisclosed benefits received by an agent,[681] but nonetheless the existence of the practice may provide some circumstantial evidence of consent on the part of the principal.[682]

Where the principal is a company and the recipient of the bribe is a director, disclosure by that director to a colleague, rather than to the board as a whole (or

---

[674] *Temperley v Blackrod Mfg. Co Ltd* (1907) 71 J.P. 341; *Fiona Trust & Holding Corp v Privalov* [2010] EWHC 3199 (Comm) at [1388]. cf. *Rowland v Chapman* (1901) 17 T.L.R. 669 (knowledge of solicitor).

[675] *Bartram & Sons v Lloyd* (1904) 90 L.T. 357; *McWilliam v Norton Finance (UK) Ltd (t/a Norton Finance)* [2015] EWCA Civ 186; [2015] 1 All E.R. (Comm) 1026 at [49] (credit broker receives commission from both parties). See also *Christie v McCann* (1972) 27 D.L.R. (3d) 544. The onus is on the agent: *Jordy v Vanderpump* (1920) 64 S.J. 324; *FHR European Ventures LLP v Cedar Capital Partners LLC* [2014] UKSC 45; [2015] A.C. 250; *Medsted Associates Ltd v Canaccord Genuity Wealth (International) Ltd* [2017] EWHC 1815 (Comm) at [97].

[676] *Hurstanger Ltd v Wilson* [2007] EWCA Civ 299; [2007] 1 W.L.R. 2351; [2007] 4 All E.R. 1118 (lender pays finder's fee to borrower's agent; loan not rescindable, but agent accountable to borrower).

[677] *Harrington v Victoria Graving Dock Co* (1878) 3 Q.B.D. 549; *Shipway v Broadwood* [1899] 1 Q.B. 369; *Re a Debtor* [1927] 2 Ch. 367; *Donegal International Ltd v Republic of Zambia* [2007] EWHC 197 (Comm); [2007] 1 Lloyd's Rep. 397 at [275]; *Fiona Trust & Holding Corp v Privalov* [2010] EWHC 3199 (Comm) at [72]; *Otkritie International Investment Management Ltd v Urumov* [2014] EWHC 191 (Comm) at [164].

[678] *Shipway v Broadwood*, above, at 373. Statements that the recipient is conclusively presumed to have been influenced (e.g. *Hovenden v Millhoff* (1900) 83 L.T. 41; *Industries and General Mortgage Co v Lewis* [1949] 2 All E.R. 573 at 578), are therefore beside the point: the Rt Hon. Lord Millett [1993] Restitution L.Rev. 7 at 13, fn.42.

[679] *Great Western Insurance Co of New York v Cunliffe* (1874) L.R. 9 Ch.App. 525; *Re Haslam and Hier-Evans* [1902] 1 Ch. 765; *P&O SN Co v Johnson* (1938) 60 C.L.R. 189; cf. *Federal Supply and Cold Storage of South Africa v Angehrn & Piel* (1910) 80 L.J.P.C. 1 (in which an acceptance of an agent's denial that he had received a bribe was held not to be condonation or consent, where he had in fact done so).

[680] See Illustration 9.

[681] See *McWilliam v Norton Finance (UK) Ltd (t/a Norton Finance)* [2015] EWCA Civ 186; [2015] 1 All E.R. (Comm) 1026 at [54]; and the cases cited in *Secretary of State for Justice v Topland Group Plc* [2011] EWHC 983 (QB), and above, para.6-057.

[682] *Secretary of State for Justice v Topland Group Plc* [2011] EWHC 983 (QB) at [69].

the shareholders, which may be necessary in some cases), is insufficient disclosure.[683] Where the issue is notification to the company by the third party that it has given a commission to the director, then it may be sufficient for notice to be given to the managing director (or other independent director), or to the company's solicitors.[684]

6-087 **Remedies** The principal has various remedies open to him when he discovers that his agent has been bribed. If the bribe has been paid and is in money, he can sue the agent for its amount[685] in an action which was in earlier cases regarded as lying in equity[686] but was subsequently treated as an action in restitution at common law[687]; and this regardless of whether he affirms or disaffirms the contract with the third party.[688] A sub-agent is similarly liable despite the absence of privity of contract.[689] In this action the person who gave the bribe is also liable jointly and severally.[690] If the bribe is given in property, older cases say that the agent is liable for the value of the property at the highest value which it had while in his possession.[691] Interest is payable from the date when the bribe was received.[692] The Supreme Court has now determined that the proceeds of bribetaking, where identifiable, are held on constructive trust for the principal.[693] This brings English law into line with other common law jurisdictions.[694] This topic is dealt with in more detail above.[695]

In addition, the agent and the person giving the bribe are jointly and severally liable in deceit for any loss suffered.[696] This action will be preferable to the restitutionary and proprietary claims where the loss suffered exceeds the amount

---

[683] *Ross River Ltd v Cambridge City Football Club Ltd* [2007] EWHC 2115 (Ch); [2008] 1 All E.R. 1004 at [213].

[684] *Ross River Ltd*, above at [214].

[685] *Morison v Thompson* (1874) L.R. 9 Q.B. 480; *Hay's Case* (1875) L.R. 10 Ch.App. 593; *Boston Deep Sea Fishing and Ice Co v Ansell* (1888) 39 Ch.D. 339; *Lister & Co v Stubbs* (1890) 45 Ch.D. 1; *Att.-Gen. v Goddard* (1929) 98 L.J.K.B. 743 (but see Article 48, Illustration 11); *Ardlethan Options Ltd v Easdown* (1916) 20 C.L.R. 285 at 292.

[686] *Fawcett v Whitehouse* (1829) 1 Russ. & M. 132.

[687] *Mahesan v Malaysia Government Officers' Co-operative Housing Society Ltd* [1979] A.C. 374, Illustration 8.

[688] *Logicrose Ltd v Southend United Football Club Ltd* [1988] 1 W.L.R. 1256 at 1263.

[689] *Att.-Gen. v Goddard*, above; *Powell & Thomas v Evan Jones & Co Ltd* [1905] 1 K.B. 11, Illustration 6 to Article 35.

[690] *Mahesan's* case [1979] A.C. 374; see Article 78.

[691] *McKay's Case* (1878) 2 Ch.D. 1; *Pearson's Case* (1877) 5 Ch. D. 336; *Nant-y-glo and Blaina Iron Co v Grave* (1878) 12 Ch.D. 738; *Eden v Ridsdales Railway Lamp & Lighting Co Ltd* (1889) 23 Q.B.D. 368; see Illustration 4. It is not clear on what basis a bribe in services would be quantified. An agent will, it seems, be accountable for the market value of a bribe in kind even if the agent asserts that he would not have been willing to pay for the benefit: *Towers v Premier Waste Management Ltd* [2011] EWCA Civ 923 at [48] (use of dumper and excavator on director's private property). See also *Fiona Trust & Holding Corp v Privalov* [2010] EWHC 3199 (Comm) at [1387] (free holiday).

[692] *Nant-y-glo and Blaina Iron Co v Grave*, above; *Boston Deep Sea Fishing and Ice Co v Ansell* (1888) 39 Ch.D. 339 at 353 and 372 (Illustration 3).

[693] *FHR European Ventures LLP v Cedar Capital Partners LLC* [2014] UKSC 45; [2015] A.C. 250.

[694] See *Att.-Gen. for Hong Kong v Reid* [1994] 1 A.C. 324; *Grimaldi v Chameleon Mining NL (No.2)* (2012) 27 A.L.R. 22.

[695] See above, para.6-042.

[696] *Mahesan's case* [1979] A.C. 374; *Fyffes Group Ltd v Templeman* [2000] 2 Lloyd's Rep. 643; Article 96; (1978) 41 M.L.R. 603; (1978) 94 L.Q.R. 344; Needham (1979) 95 L.Q.R. 536. In *Petrotrade Inc v Smith* [2000] 1 Lloyd's Rep. 486 at [19] David Steel J considered that the action was one in fraud rather than deceit, but see *Kensington International Ltd v Republic of Congo* [2007] EWCA

of the bribe, or the bribe has decreased in value; and as regards the action against the agent, where the bribe has not yet been paid. The agent who makes a lossmaking contract for his principal is also likely to be liable for breach of the contract of agency. The principal cannot however recover under all heads and must elect before judgment.[697]

An agent who takes a bribe or secret commission may also forfeit his right to commission or remuneration that he would have otherwise received[698]; he may also lose his right to indemnity.[699] The principal is justified in terminating without notice the contract of any agent who accepts a bribe in the course of his agency[700] and such a termination will still be justifiable, even if the bribery is not discovered until after the agent has been dismissed.[701]

Where the bribed agent knows that the proposed contract is contrary to his principal's interests, or is reckless on that issue, he acts dishonestly, and thereby without authority. The contract is likely to be void in such circumstances, and not merely voidable. It would seem, however, that an arbitration clause in such a contract may nonetheless remain valid.[702] In other cases, the contract with the third party will be voidable at the option of the principal.[703] A bribe paid in relation to one contract, however, will not usually give a right in the principal to rescind both that contract and an independent, though related, agreement with the third party made before the inducement occurred.[704] The liability of the agent persists even if the contract is disowned, and where the principal has recovered the bribe money he is entitled to keep it and need not give credit for it in the rescission.[705]

Criminal law   Corrupt dealings with agents are a criminal offence. The Bribery Act 2010 replaces existing offences in this area, both common law and statutory (principally, at common law, criminal conspiracy,[706] and, in statute, the Prevention of Corruption Act 1906, the Public Bodies Corrupt Practices Act 1889 and the Prevention of Corruption Act 1916).   **6-088**

It is beyond the scope of this work to give a detailed treatment of the 2010 Act,

Civ 1128; [2008] 1 Lloyd's Rep. 161 at [62]–[63]; and *Cavell USA Inc v Seaton Insurance Co* [2009] EWCA Civ 1363 at [25].

[697] *Mahesan's* case, above, not following dicta in *Salford Corp v Lever* [1891] 1 Q.B. 168 and *Hovenden & Sons v Millhoff* (1900) 83 L.T. 41. See Tettenborn (1979) 95 L.Q.R. 68.

[698] See Article 55 and *Cec. McManus Realty Ltd v Bray* (1970) 14 D.L.R. (3d) 564; *Meadow Schama & Co v C. Mitchell & Co Ltd* (1973) 228 E.G. 1511; *Imageview Management Ltd v Jack* [2009] EWCA Civ 63; [2009] 2 All E.R. 666. But not necessarily in respect of other transactions: cf. *Hippisley v Knee Bros* [1905] 1 K.B. 1; *P & OSN Co v Johnson* (1938) 60 C.L.R. 189 at 216–217. And see Article 60.

[699] *Stange & Co v Lowitz* (1898) 14 T.L.R. 468; *Nicholson v J. Mansfield & Co* (1901) 17 T.L.R. 259. See Article 65.

[700] *Bulfield v Fournier* (1895) 11 T.L.R. 282; *Swale v Ipswich Tannery Ltd* (1906) 11 Com. Cas. 88; *Temperley v Blackrod Manufacturing Co Ltd* (1907) 71 J.P. 341; *Federal Supply and Cold Storage Co of South Africa v Angehrn & Piel* (1910) 80 L.J.P.C. 1.

[701] *Boston Deep Sea Fishing & Ice Co v Ansell* (1888) 39 Ch.D. 339, Illustration 3.

[702] *Fiona Trust and Holding Corp v Privalov* [2007] EWCA Civ 20; [2007] 2 Lloyd's Rep. 267 at [26]; affd sub nom. *Premium Nafta Products Ltd v Fili Shipping Co Ltd* [2007] UKHL 40; [2007] 4 All E.R. 951; [2007] 2 All E.R. (Comm) 1053. See further above, para.3-012 and below, para.8-021.

[703] See *Taylor v Walker* [1958] 1 Lloyd's Rep. 490; Article 96.

[704] *Ross River Ltd v Cambridge City Football Club Ltd* [2007] EWHC 2115 (Ch); [2008] 1 All E.R. 1004 at [228].

[705] *Logicrose v Southend United Football Club* [1988] 1 W.L.R. 1256.

[706] *R. v Barber* (1887) 3 T.L.R. 491. See also *R. v Whitaker* [1914] 3 K.B. 1283; *R. v De Kromme* (1892) 66 L.T. 301 (incitement to conspire).

and only a bare outline is provided.[707] The Act creates four offences: the paying of bribes (s.1); the receiving of bribes (s.2); the bribery of foreign public officials (s.6); and the failure of commercial organisations to prevent bribery (s.7). The last of these has no counterpart in the prior law and has far-reaching implications for businesses.

In paraphrase, the first offence turns on the offering, promising or giving of "financial or other advantages" to another, either knowing or believing that acceptance would involve the "improper performance" of "a relevant function or activity", or intending to induce or reward such improper performance. The second offence makes provision for four alternative types of comparable conduct by any party who requests, agrees to receive or accepts such advantages. The concept of "function or activity" embraces functions of a public nature, any activity connected with business or any activity performed in the course of employment or on behalf of a body of persons (corporate or unincorporate), so long as the relevant person is expected to perform it in good faith or impartially, or is otherwise in a position of trust in performing it (s.3). Improper performance is to be judged by the expectations of a reasonable person in the United Kingdom, irrespective of where the conduct takes place (ss.4 and 5), unless relevant written law of the foreign jurisdiction permits it.

The offence of bribery of foreign public officials in large part overlaps with the first offence, given the extraterritorial application of both offences. Bribery, as defined, is an offence where the defendant intends thereby to obtain or retain business, or an advantage in the conduct of business.

The offence of failing to prevent bribery can be committed only by commercial organisations (business incorporations or partnerships) that are formed in the United Kingdom or which carry on business in the United Kingdom. Liability potentially arises whenever an "associated person" of the defendant commits an offence under s.1 or s.6 (whether or not that person has been prosecuted). An associated person is a person who, in any capacity (including without limitation, an employee, agent or subsidiary of the defendant), performs services for or on behalf of the defendant. The offence is one of strict liability, subject only to a defence that the organisation had in place adequate procedures designed to prevent offences under ss.1 and 6.

Illustrations

6-089 (1) The master of a ship receives three payments totalling £45 by way of gratuity for efficient discharge of cargo. This is not a bribe and he may retain the money.[708]

(2) A requested B to provide an outfit for A's son. B did so, and obtained certain discounts, but charged A the full prices. The discounts were disallowed, although B did not charge any commission as an agent.[709]

(3) A director of a company who was a shareholder in two other companies ac-

---

[707] For more detail, see *Blackstone's Guide to the Bribery Act 2010* (2011); Shea, *The Bribery Act 2010* (2011). For the philosophical background, see Horder (2011) 127 L.Q.R. 37; Arnell and Evans [2015] Jur. Rev. 167. As to the concept of "corruption" that was central to the former legislation, see *R v J* [2013] EWCA Crim 2287; *Field v R.* [2012] 3 N.Z.L.R. 1 (SC), and for earlier authorities the nineteenth edition of this work.
[708] *The Parkdale* [1897] P. 53.
[709] *Turnbull v Garden* (1869) 38 L.J.Ch. 331. See also *Hippisley v Knee Bros* [1905] 1 K.B. 1, Illustration 5 to Article 60; *North American Land and Timber Co Ltd v Watkins* [1904] 1 Ch. 242; [1904] 2 Ch. 233, Illustration 3 to Article 29.

cepted bonuses from such other companies, in consideration of his giving them orders on behalf of the first company. He also took a commission, which was unknown to his company, on a contract for the building of a number of boats. The articles of association provided that the directors might contract with the company. Held, that he was accountable to the company for the bonuses and the secret commission with interest; and that the bribery justified the dismissal of the director, although it was not discovered until after the dismissal.[710]

(4)   The secretary of a company, when making a contract on behalf of the company with the vendor, stipulated that he should receive, and subsequently did receive, from the vendor 600 fully paid-up shares. Held, that he must account to the company for the highest value borne by the shares during the time they were held by him, which in this case was assumed to be the nominal value.[711]

(5)   A director of a company, before the transactions between the promoter and the company had been finally completed, accepted his qualification shares from the promoter. The director had to account to the company for the highest value attributable to the shares during the time they were held by him, with interest on such value from the date the shares were transferred to him to the date of the action.[712] So, if a director receives the money to pay for his qualification shares, he must account for the amount received, with interest from the date of its receipt.[713] Where a promoter sold shares to a director, the director was compelled to account for the difference between the nominal value of the shares and the price he paid for them.[714]

(6)   A assisted B in the negotiations for the building of a ship by C for B, B agreeing to pay A a sum for his services. The negotiations with C were conducted through D, a shipbroker, who was to receive commission from C. Unknown to B, A and D arranged that A should take half of D's commission. Held, B could recover from A the latter's share of the commission.[715]

(7)   A solicitor, who was retained by A to act for him in negotiation for the purchase of a patent, had previously received a commission note from the owner of the patent agreeing to pay him commission in the event of a purchaser being found. A purchased the patent and the solicitor, with A's knowledge, received the commission from the seller. Held, that he was not accountable to A for the commission, having made full disclosure.[716]

(8)   The agent of a housing society, for a bribe of $122,000 arranges that a third party should buy land at a low price and sell it to the society at a profit. The third party buys the land for $456,000 and sells it to the society for $944,000. The society recovers the $122,000 from the agent and also sues him for

[710] *Boston Deep Sea Fishing & Ice Co v Ansell* (1888) 39 Ch.D. 339; see also *Temperley v Blackrod Manufacturing Co Ltd* (1907) 71 J.P. 341.
[711] *McKay's Case* (1875) 2 Ch.D. 1.
[712] *Nant-y-glo & Blaina Iron Co v Grave* (1878) 12 Ch.D. 738; *Pearson's Case* (1877) 5 Ch.D. 336; *Eden v Ridsdale's Railway Lamp & Lighting Co Ltd* (1889) 58 L.J.Q.B. 579; *Mitcalfe's Case* (1879) 13 Ch.D. 169.
[713] *Hay's Case* (1875) L.R. 10 Ch.App. 593; *McLean's Case* (1885) 55 L.J.Ch. 36; cf. *Archer's Case* [1892] 1 Ch. 322.
[714] *Weston's Case* (1879) 10 Ch.D. 579.
[715] *W.A. Phillips, Anderson & Co v Euxine Shipping Co* [1955] 2 Lloyd's Rep. 512.
[716] *Re Haslam and Hier-Evans* [1902] 1 Ch. 765.

$443,000, being the third party's net profit. The society must elect between one claim and the other before judgment is entered.[717]

(9)   It was usual for underwriters to allow all intermediaries, for punctual payment of premiums, a percentage as discount, or 12 per cent calculated on the yearly profits, in addition to the ordinary commission of 5 per cent on each reinsurance. A company, having made no inquiry as to the remuneration paid by the underwriters, and not being aware of the 12 per cent allowance, employed Baring Bros as agent to negotiate business. After the agent (who received no remuneration from the company) had been paid the usual allowance of 12 per cent for more than eight years, the company discovered it and claimed to have it paid over to them as secret profit. It was held that they were not entitled to recover.[718]

(10)   An agent accepts a bribe in connection with the grant of a concession. The facts are discovered and the agent accounts for most of the bribe to his principal. The principal rescinds the concession. He may keep the bribe: if he has not received it he can still recover it from the agent. He is under no obligation to give credit for it to the third party in the rescission.[719]

Article 50

DUTY TO KEEP PROPERTY OF PRINCIPAL SEPARATE AND DELIVER BUSINESS RECORDS AND CORRESPONDENCE

6-090   It is the duty of an agent—

(1)   where he holds money or property belonging to his principal, to keep it separate from his own and from that of other persons[720];

(2)   to preserve and be constantly ready with correct accounts of all his dealings and transactions in the course of his agency[721];

(3)   to produce to the principal upon request, or to a proper person appointed by the principal, all books, correspondence and documents (including emails and other electronic material) under his control relating to the principal's affairs.[722]

Comment

6-091   **(1) Separation of property**   If an agent is entrusted with the money or property of his principal, he must keep it separate from his own. If he is sued for an account

---

[717] *Mahesan v Malaysia Government Officers' Co-operative Housing Society Ltd* [1979] A.C. 374.
[718] *Great Western Insurance Co of New York v Cunliffe* (1874) L.R. 9 Ch.App. 525; see also *Leete v Wallace* (1888) 58 L.T. 577; *Norreys v Hodgson* (1897) 13 T.L.R. 421, where an agent who was instructed to procure a loan from an insurance company which required a policy on the life of the principal was held entitled to retain the commission on the policy; *Baring v Stanton* (1876) 3 Ch.D. 502; cf. *Queen of Spain v Parr* (1869) 39 L.J.Ch. 73; *E. Green & Son Ltd v G. Tughan & Co* (1913) 30 T.L.R. 64; cf. *Copp v Lynch* (1882) 26 S.J. 348; *Hurstanger Ltd v Wilson* [2007] EWCA Civ 299; [2007] 1 W.L.R. 2351; [2007] 4 All E.R. 1118 at [36]; *FHR European Ventures LLP v Mankarious* [2011] EWHC 2308 (Ch) at [81]; reversed on other points [2014] UKSC 45; [2015] A.C. 250; *Secretary of State for Justice v Topland Group Plc* [2011] EWHC 983 (QB) at [65]; *Hobbins v Royal Skandia Life Assurance Ltd* [2012] HKCFI 10.
[719] *Logicrose v Southend United Football Club* [1988] 1 W.L.R. 1256.
[720] *Gray v Haig* (1855) 20 Beav. 219; *Clarke v Tipping* (1846) 9 Beav. 284; *Palette Shoes Pty Ltd v*

and has failed to keep his principal's property separate, he will be liable for the contents of the mixture or anything acquired by expenditure from it, up to the value of the input.[723] This obligation only arises, however, in connection with money or property which is beneficially owned by the principal; in such a case the agent will be in the position of a trustee.[724] In other cases however the court will infer that the parties intended the relationship of debtor and creditor, on the ground that a duty to keep money separate would be an unintended restriction on the agent's commercial activity.[725]

(2) Accounts   An agent is under an obligation to keep an accurate account of all   **6-092**
transactions entered into on his principal's behalf[726] and he must be ready at all time to produce it to his principal.[727] If he fails to keep and preserve correct accounts, everything is presumed against him:

> "In such a case ... I am compelled to ... presume everything most unfavourable to him, which is consistent with the rest of the facts which are admitted or proved."[728]

The agent need not, however, produce records of transactions which do not concern the principal[729] (but the position is otherwise, it seems, when the agent has made it

---

Krohn (1937) 58 C.L.R. 1 at 30; cf. above, para.6-041.

[721] *Gray v Haig*, above; *Clarke v Tipping*, above; *Pearse v Green* (1819) 1 J. & W. 135; *Turner v Burkinshaw* (1867) L.R. 2 Ch.App. 488; *Collyer v Dudley* (1823) T. & R. 421; *Utz v Carver* [1972] 1 N.S.W.L.R. 407; cf. *Re Lee Ex p. Neville* (1868) L.R. 4 Ch.App. 43.

[722] *Restatement, Third*, § 8.12; *Dadswell v Jacobs* (1887) 34 Ch.D. 278; *Re Burnand Ex p. Baker, Sutton & Co* [1904] 2 K.B. 68 (bankruptcy of agent); *Re Ellis & Ellis* [1908] W.N. 215; 25 T.L.R. 38 (bankruptcy of principal).

[723] See material cited above, para.6-040.

[724] See, e.g. *Burdick v Garrick* (1870) L.R. 5 Ch.App. 233, Illustration 1 to Article 43. The Estate Agents Act 1979 s.13, requires clients' money to be held on trust (but see Article 53 as to interest). The same is the case with solicitors: Solicitors Act 1974 ss.32–33. See above, paras 6-040–6-041; also Murdoch, *The Estate Agents and Property Misdescriptions Acts* (3rd edn); Cordery, *Solicitors*, Division K.

[725] See *Henry v Hammond* [1913] 2 K.B. 515; *Neste Oy v Lloyd's Bank Plc* [1983] 2 Lloyd's Rep. 658; *Walker v Corboy* (1990) 19 N.S.W.L.R. 398; *Paragon Finance Plc v D.B. Thackerar & Co* [1999] 1 All E.R. 400 at 415; and generally above, para.6-041; Article 43, Illustrations 1–5.

[726] *Chedworth v Edwards* (1802) 8 Ves. 46; *White v Lincoln* (1803) 8 Ves. 363; *Tindall v Powell* (1858) 32 L.T.(O.S.) 8; and cases cited at fn.720 above. Some agents are under a statutory obligation to keep special forms of accounts and other records, e.g. solicitors under the Solicitors' Accounts Rules 1998; and estate agents under Estate Agents Act 1979 s.21A, as added by Consumers, Estate Agents and Redress Act 2007 s.54. It may be a breach of duty wrongfully to disclose the account to third parties: see *Fogg v Gaulter and Blane* (1960) 110 L.J. 718; *Yasuda Fire and Marine Ins. Co of Europe Ltd v Orion Marine Ins. Underwriting Agency Ltd* [1995] Q.B. 174 (right still existed though contract terminated by repudiatory breach); *Khouj v Acropolis Capital Partners Ltd* [2016] EWHC 2120 (Comm) at [46] and [76] (no need for contract between agent and principal).

[727] *Pearse v Green* (1819) 1 J. & W. 135; *Turner v Burkinshaw* (1867) L.R. 2 Ch.App. 488; *Equitas Ltd v Horace Holman & Co Ltd* [2007] EWHC 903 (Comm) at [27]; *Barkley v Barkley Brown* [2009] NSWSC 76; *Accidia Foundation v Simon C. Dickinson Ltd* [2010] EWHC 3058 (Ch) at [88] (duty to inform principal of gross sale price). A sub-agent must account in the usual way to the head agent, even where the latter had no legal or beneficial interest in the funds handled by the sub-agent: *Barnett v Creggy* [2014] EWHC 3080 (Ch) at [66].

[728] *Gray v Haig* (1855) 20 Beav. 219 at 226, per Romilly MR; see also *Jenkins v Gould* (1827) 3 Russ. 385; *Malhotra v Dhawan* [1997] EWCA Civ 1096; *Ross River Ltd v Waveley Commercial Ltd* [2013] EWCA Civ 910 at [94]; *Keown v Nahoor* [2015] EWHC 3418 (Ch).

[729] *Gerard v Penswick* (1818) 1 Swan. 533; *Heugh v Garrett* (1875) 44 L.J.Ch. 305.

not possible to extricate those relating to the principal from those of other clients[730]), nor need he produce detailed items which his principal has agreed expressly or impliedly not to require of him.[731]

6-093   **(3) Documents and electronic records and correspondence**   The principal is prima facie entitled to have delivered up to him upon request, and at the termination of the agency, all documents and electronic records and correspondence (together "records") concerning his affairs which have been prepared by the agent in the course of the agency and are retained.[732] It is not necessary for the principal to prove that he owns the records,[733] although where he does not own particular records it seems likely that only a copy need be furnished. In each case it is necessary (unless, as may be the case, the right to the documents is settled by the contract between the parties) to decide whether the document in question came into existence for the purpose of the agency relationship or for some other purpose, e.g. in pursuance of a duty to give professional advice. Thus land agents have been ordered to hand over memorandum books, a private rental and cash book and a field book[734]; an architect was ordered to deliver up the plans of a house after the work had been completed and paid for.[735] Both the land agents and the architect were considered to be acting as agents. But memoranda prepared by quantity surveyors for their own use in measuring up buildings were held to be their own property[736]; and documents, books, maps and plans prepared by rating valuers employed to give advice and assistance to a county council remained the property of the valuers.[737] In one case[738] the Court of Appeal held that working papers, draft and final accounts, notes and calculations and draft tax computations, brought into being by chartered accountants in the course of auditing a company's accounts, were the property of the accountants, the relationship being that of professional person and client; while correspondence between the accountants and the Inland Revenue relating to the company's tax liability was conducted by the accountants as the company's agents, so that original and copy letters comprising such correspondence belonged to the company. Where a document was prepared by the agent for the third party, the agent, though in breach of his duty to his principal in preparing it, was held not bound or entitled to give his principal inspection or possession of it.[739]

What the duties of agents are to preserve records as they arise is a separate question on which there is little authority. Plainly, Rule (2) of Article 50 asserts an obligation to preserve the basic records of all dealings and transactions. Beyond that, it is suggested that an agent should take reasonable steps to maintain records (including copies of correspondence) that might reasonably be expected to be

---

[730] *Equitas Ltd v Horace Holman & Co Ltd* [2007] EWHC 903 (Comm) at [27].
[731] *Hunter v Belcher* (1864) 2 De G.J. & S. 194.
[732] *Fairstar Heavy Transport NV v Adkins* [2013] EWCA Civ 886; [2014] F.S.R. 8.
[733] *Fairstar Heavy Transport NV v Adkins*, above. Normally, emails and other correspondence created in the course of the agency would be accessible to the principal but would not be "owned" by him: *Capita Plc v Darch* [2017] EWHC 1248 (Ch); [2017] I.R.L.R. 718 at [70].
[734] *Beresford v Driver* (1851) 14 Beav. 387.
[735] *Gibbon v Pease* [1905] 1 K.B. 810, in which the Court of Appeal held that a custom to the contrary would be unreasonable.
[736] *London School Board v Northcroft* (1889), Hudson's *Building and Engineering Contracts* (12th edn), para.2.235.
[737] *Leicestershire CC v Michael Faraday & Partners* [1941] 2 K.B. 205.
[738] *Chantrey Martin v Martin* [1953] 2 Q.B. 286; and see *Floydd v Cheney* [1970] Ch. 602; *Equitas Ltd v Horace Holman & Co Ltd* [2007] EWHC 903 (Comm) at [28].
[739] *North and South Trust Co v Berkeley* [1971] 1 W.L.R. 470, Illustration 3 to Article 5.

relevant to the ongoing business of the principal, including in relation to disputes with third parties.

The agent may sometimes exercise a lien over documents and other records.[740]

Article 51

DUTY TO ACCOUNT

An agent may be required to account in equity to his principal.   6-094

Comment

The action of account: history   The action of account was an ancient common   6-095
law action first used against bailiffs and receivers.[741] It fell gradually into disuse
when the Court of Chancery began to exercise jurisdiction in matters of account:
the Chancery procedure could be used to compel a defendant to make discovery on
oath and so was superior. It became settled that the action was available not only
against trustees but also against other fiduciaries such as agents[742] (but not in favour
of agents against their principals[743]).

Before the fusion of law and equity there were various rules to determine when
an action of account lay in equity. Thus if there was a fiduciary situation between
the principal and his agent, or if there was a suspicion of fraud, or if the accounts
were complicated, the agent could be compelled to account in equity: otherwise,
the principal could only bring his action in the courts of common law.[744] Since the
Judicature Acts, however, any division of the High Court has the jurisdiction
originally vested in the previous courts of Common Law and Chancery. By virtue
of s.61 of and Sch.1 to the Senior Courts Act 1981, actions for an account are usually to be assigned to the Chancery Division.[745]

Substantive significance   The duty to account is in this sense simply a liability   6-096
to the exercise of certain sorts of procedures used in courts of equity for the
ascertainment of the true position between trustee or other fiduciary and beneficiary.
As such it can be regarded as no more than a procedure ancillary to the ascertainment of other rights[746]: though the remedy does of course provide a sanction for,
and hence the basis of, the duty to keep accounts and make them available to the
principal.[747] However, the liability to account in equity has also a certain substantive significance in that it may lead to a judgment of the court for payment of the

---

[740] Article 65.
[741] See Fifoot, *History and Sources of the Common Law* (1952), pp.268–277; Jackson, *History of Quasi-Contract* (1936), pp.9–17; Stoljar, pp.299–300; (1964) 80 L.Q.R. 203.
[742] See in general Snell, *Equity* (33rd edn), para.20-003 onwards; *Meagher, Gummow and Lehane's Equity Doctrines and Remedies* (5th edn), Ch.26. See too *John Youngs Insurance Services Ltd v Aviva Insurance Service UK Ltd* [2011] EWHC 1515 (TCC).
[743] *Beaumont v Boultbee* (1802) 7 Ves. 599; *Mackenzie v Johnston* (1819) 4 Madd. 373.
[744] See especially *Foley v Hill* (1848) 2 H.L.Cas. 28; *Navulshaw v Brownrigg* (1852) 2 De G.M. & G. 441.
[745] And see *Civil Procedure* (2005), Vol.1, 25.1.38, Vol.2, [1-88].
[746] This is borne out by the wording of s.23 of the Limitation Act 1980, which refers to the "claim which is the basis of the duty to account". See *Libertarian Investments Ltd v Hall* [2013] HKCFA 93 at [167]–[168], per Lord Millett. See also Conaglen (2016) 40 Melb. U.L.R. 126.
[747] Article 50.

money shown to be due on the account, whether arising from liabilities for breach of trust, constructive trust, contract etc., or on other grounds such as tracing. Further, when the agent cannot explain exactly what has happened to money or property, presumptions may be made against him which will lead to substantive liabilities in him.[748] It is also frequently said that the agent has a general fiduciary obligation to account for profits. Although on orthodox doctrine claims in pursuance of such an obligation are traditionally regarded as proprietary, and amount to claims to profits attributable to what has been designated as the principal's property,[749] a more general and less precise notion of accounting (which is particularly relied on in some cases relating to confidential information[750]) has assisted also in the development of an equitable action in personam against the agent, which does not carry the sometimes inappropriate consequences on bankruptcy of the agent which would follow from a true proprietary claim.[751]

6-097   **The account**   The actual taking of accounts can be a long and complex matter, and it has been said in the context of dissolution of partnership that such a judgment may be "often oppressive".[752]

An agent will usually be held to be bound by his own accounts; thus if they show that he has credited his principal with money received, the agent will be presumed to have received that money and will be liable for it to his principal.[753] But the agent will not be liable if the account shows that the money has not, in fact, been received,[754] or if the principal's accounts show that the agent has not received the money.[755] Similarly, if the agent, after submitting an account which shows money in his hands, later corrects the accounts and the principal does not disagree with such correction,[756] or if the agent shows he has made a mistake, he will not be accountable to his principal.[757]

In an action of account the agent will be allowed to deduct all reasonable expenses incurred on his principal's behalf,[758] unless such deduction is contrary to

---

[748] See *GHLM Trading Ltd v Maroo* [2012] EWHC 61 (Ch) at [148]; *Re Mumtaz Properties Ltd, Wetton v Ahmed* [2011] EWCA Civ 610 at [16]; *Ross River Ltd v Waveley Commercial Ltd* [2013] EWCA Civ 910 at [94]. cf. *Exsus Travel Ltd v Turner* [2014] EWCA Civ 1331 at [24] (account should not be an instrument of oppression of agent).

[749] See above, para.6-042.

[750] See above, paras 6-077 and 6-079.

[751] See above, paras 6-077 and 6-079; *Warman International Pty Ltd v Dwyer* (1995) 182 C.L.R. 544 at 556–557; *Paragon Finance Plc v D.B. Thackerar & Co* [1999] 1 All E.R. 400 at 416. See further the explanation put forward by the Rt Hon. Lord Millett (1998) 114 L.Q.R. 214 at 225–227; but cf. Getzler, in *Restitution and Equity* (Birks and Rose eds, 2000), pp.248–250. See also above, paras 6-040 and 6-041.

[752] *Lindley and Banks on Partnership* (19th edn), para.25-30. See also *Docker v Somes* (1834) 2 My. & K. 655 at 673; *Wedderburn v Wedderburn* (1838) 4 My. & Cr. 41.

[753] *Shaw v Picton* (1825) 4 B. & C. 715. See also *Shaw v Woodcock* (1827) 7 B. & C. 73 (where the submission of accounts showing amounts received and allowing the principal to draw on the agent for the amounts was held sufficient evidence to go to the jury to establish a personal obligation on the agent to pay); *Skyring v Greenwood* (1825) 4 B. & C. 281; *Owens v Kirby* (1861) 30 Beav. 31; *Cave v Mills* (1862) 7 H. & N. 913.

[754] *Shaw v Dartnall* (1826) 6 B. & C. 56 at 65.

[755] *Shaw v Dartnall*, above, at pp.65–66.

[756] *Shaw v Dartnall*, above, at pp.65–66.

[757] *Shaw v Picton* (1825) 4 B. & C. 715; *Dails v Lloyd* (1848) 12 Q.B. 531; cf. *Worrall v Peters* (1902) 32 S.C.R. 52.

[758] *Dale v Sollet* (1767) 4 Burr. 2133 (expenses of fighting an action for principal); *East India Co v Blake*

the terms of the agency agreement.[759] An account will also take account of any benefits derived by the principal from the agent's activities, but the onus rests on the agent to establish that the principal did derive a benefit.[760]

Account stated   If an account is agreed, the principal can sue on an account stated. **6-098** This may be a mere acknowledgment of a debt, and in that case the agent may show that no such debt in fact existed; or it may be an account containing debts on both sides in which the parties have agreed that the debts of one should be set against the debts of the other and only the balance paid. In the latter case the agent may only dispute the account where there are items which, if paid, would be recoverable by him on the basis of a total failure of consideration.[761] This second form of account stated is also called a settled account. It is not always clear when an account will be held a settled account. There must be mutual debts, since if all the accounting has to be done by one party, there cannot be a settling of accounts.[762] Once the principal has approved the accounts, they are settled,[763] and if the principal enters the account as agreed in his books and either pays the balance or recognises in some other way that the account is correct, there is also a settled account.[764] It has been held that a principal who received an account and kept it for two years without objection could not later maintain it was not a settled account.[765] But there will not be a settled account where a principal allows part of his agent's claim but is silent as to the rest.[766]

The general rule is that settled accounts will not be reopened,[767] but the principal may be given leave to surcharge and falsify them, if they are drawn up under a mistake.[768] Thus, where a partnership account recorded £1,950 as lent to the plaintiff, whereas only £1,000 was in fact advanced, it was held that the amount could be corrected without the whole account being reopened.[769]

But where the agent has been guilty of fraud (whether legal or equitable)[770] or the accounts have been settled under undue influence,[771] the accounts may be reopened from the commencement of the agency. In such cases lapse of time is no defence and proof of one fraudulent overcharge has been held sufficient to entitle

---

[759] (1673) C.Temp.F. 117 (entertainment expenses); cf. *Baring v Stanton* (1876) 3 Ch.D. 502.

See *Bath v Standard Land Co Ltd* [1911] 1 Ch. 618.

[760] *Amaltal Corp Ltd v Maruha Corp* [2007] 3 N.Z.L.R. 192 at [30], Illustration 14 to Article 43.

[761] *Siqueira v Noronha* [1934] A.C. 332; *Laycock v Pickles* (1863) 4 B. & S. 497.

[762] *Anglo-American Asphalt Co Ltd v Crowley Russell & Co Ltd* [1945] 2 All E.R. 324; *Equitas Ltd v Horace Holman & Co Ltd* [2007] EWHC 903 (Comm) at [91].

[763] *East India Co v Mainston* (1676) 2 Cas. in Cha. 218.

[764] *Ovington v Bell* (1812) 3 Camp. 237; *Hunter v Belcher* (1864) 2 De G.J. & S. 194; *McKellar v Wallace* (1853) 8 Moo.P.C. 378.

[765] *Tickel v Short* (1751) 2 Ves.Sen. 239; but see the Canadian case of *Smith v Redford* (1872) 19 Grant 274.

[766] *Farquhar v East India Co* (1845) 8 Beav. 260.

[767] *Parkinson v Hanbury* (1867) L.R. 2 H.L. 1.See also *Re Webb* [1894] 1 Ch. 73.

[768] *Mozeley v Cowie* (1877) 47 L.J.Ch. 271; *Hardwicke v Vernon* (1798–99) 4 Ves. 411; *Gething v Keighley* (1878) 9 Ch.D. 547; *Cheese v Keen* [1908] 1 Ch. 245; the Rt Hon. Lord Millett (1998) 114 L.Q.R. 214 at 225–227.

[769] *Gething v Keighley* (1878) 9 Ch.D. 547; cf. *Daniell v Sinclair* (1881) 6 App.Cas. 181.

[770] *Beaumont v Boultbee* (1800) 5 Ves. 485; *Clarke v Tipping* (1846) 9 Beav. 284, as mentioned by Jessel MR in *Williamson v Barbour* (1877) 9 Ch.D. 529; *Hardwicke v Vernon* (1808) 14 Ves. 504; *Walsham v Stainton* (1863) 1 De G.J. & S. 678.

[771] *Watson v Rodwell* (1879) 11 Ch.D. 150; *Coleman v Mellersh* (1850) 2 Mac. & G. 309; *Lewes v Morgan* (1817) 5 Price 42; *Jones v Moffett* (1846) 3 J. & L. 636; *Ward v Sharp* (1883) 53 L.J.Ch. 313.

the principal to have the agent's accounts reopened for a period of 20 years.[772] When accounts have been drawn up between fiduciaries and their beneficiaries, the courts have been astute to reopen them if there is any suspicion of underhand dealing.[773] So, where there were incorrect entries, and amounts unexplained and unaccounted for in the accounts of a deceased agent of a company, who was also a large shareholder in the company, his accounts were reopened after his death for a period of 25 years.[774]

The illegality of a transaction entered into by an agent is not a bar to an action by the principal for an account,[775] unless the contract of agency is itself illegal, in which case money paid to the agent may be irrecoverable.[776]

Article 52

COMMON LAW DUTY TO PAY OVER MONEY HELD FOR PRINCIPAL

6-099 Subject to the provisions of Article 70, an agent who holds or receives money for his principal is bound to pay over or account for that money at the request of his principal, notwithstanding claims made by third persons, even if the money has been received in respect of a void or illegal transaction.[777]

Comment

6-100 The principle expressed in this Article is a principle of common law which applies wherever an agent holds money for his principal. Thus if the agent has received money on his principal's behalf, or receives it for a particular purpose which he does not carry out, the principal can sue the agent in restitution.[778] Further, if the principal has entrusted money to his agent for a particular purpose which the agent has not carried out, the principal can recover that money on the same basis.[779] When available, such common law actions in restitution have long been alterna-

---

[772] *Williamson v Barbour* (1877) 9 Ch.D. 529; *Coleman v Mellersh* (1850) 2 Mac. & G. 309.

[773] *Williamson v Barbour*, above; *Re Webb* [1894] 1 Ch. 73; *Cheese v Keen* [1908] 1 Ch. 245; cf. *Newman v Payne* (1793) 2 Ves. 199; *Equitas Ltd v Horace Holman & Co Ltd* [2007] EWHC 903 (Comm) at [92].

[774] *Stainton v Carron Co* (1857) 24 Beav. 346.

[775] *Williams v Trye* (1854) 18 Beav. 366; *Close v Wilson* [2011] EWCA Civ 5.

[776] *Knowles v Haughton* (1805) 11 Ves. 168; *Battersby v Smyth* (1818) 3 Madd. 110; *Sykes v Beadon* (1879) 11 Ch.D. 170; and see Article 52.

[777] See this Article discussed in *Martin v Pont* [1993] 3 N.Z.L.R. 25, Illustration 4; *Edgell v Day* (1865) L.R. 1 C.P. 80; *Blaustein v Maltz Mitchell & Co* [1937] 2 K.B. 142, Illustration 7 to Article 56; *Eames v Hacon* (1881) 18 Ch.D. 347, Illustration 6 to Article 54; *Nickolson v Knowles* (1820) 5 Madd. 47; *Harsant v Blaine, Macdonald & Co* (1887) 56 L.J.Q.B. 511; *Eisentrager v Lyneham* [1952] St. R. Qd. 232.

[778] See Powell, pp.324–326. Article 48. See, e.g. *Al Khudairi v Abbey Brokers Ltd* [2010] EWHC 1486 (Ch) at [117]; [2010] P.N.L.R. 32 (misapplication by mortgage broker of moneys received for principal).

[779] *Parry v Roberts* (1835) 3 A. & E. 118; *Hill v Smith* (1844) 12 M. & W. 618; *Martin v Pont*, above; *Napier v Torbay Holdings Ltd* [2016] NZCA 608 at [20]. cf. *Thomas v Da Costa* (1818) 8 Taunt. 345, *Livingstone v Elmslie* (1902) 21 N.Z.L.R. 640 (money paid by husband to be paid to wife on her obtaining a divorce could not be recovered); *Abraaj Investment Management Ltd v Bregawn Jersey Ltd* [2010] EWHC 630 (Comm). Probably an action in restitution will not lie against an agent entrusted with money for a particular purpose until the agent violates his duty by applying it for some other purpose, or otherwise shows an intention not to be bound by his obligation: *Hardman v Bellhouse* (1842) 9 M. & W. 596; *Ehrensperger v Anderson* (1848) 3 Exch. 148; *Whitehead v*

tives to an account.[780] Where the money can be regarded as held in trust, however, a proprietary remedy will be available, and may be more advantageous.[781] Liability to account is prima facie strict, and does not turn on proof of want of care,[782] but a reasonable time to effect payment over may need to be allowed for. Liability in tort on the basis of an assumption of responsibility may in some cases provide an alternative claim.[783] It has been held that, in some circumstances at least, the duty to account is a continuing one, with in consequence a moving limitation date.[784]

The principal cannot make his claim in restitution until the agent has either received the money[785]; or has been credited with it in his own account with a third party.[786] This does not mean that the principal must wait until the agent admits he has received the money; if, for example, the principal employs an agent to sell goods for him and the agent does not account to the principal within a reasonable time, it may be presumed in the absence of evidence to the contrary that the agent has received money for the goods.[787] It is not settled whether demand has to be made by the principal for his money before he can start his action against the agent, but on general principles it seems that the right to money held to the principal's use accrues as soon as it comes into the agent's hands and that no demand should be necessary.[788] It may be, however, that a claim for interest on such a claim will only run from the date of a demand for payment and its refusal.[789] At the same time, an implied term to account promptly will often be appropriate, for breach of which damages may be available.[790]

An agent usually discharges his liability by handing over the money or property he has received to his principal, but he may also pay a third party in accordance with the principal's instructions[791]; he will also be discharged if he pays a third party in obedience to the instructions of the court.[792] Furthermore, an agent, in accounting for money received for his principal, is entitled to set off all just allowances and any sums expended by him in that connection with the authority of the principal,[793] even

---

Howard (1820) 2 B. & B. 372. See too *Zhong v Wang* (2007) N.Z.C.P.R. 488.
[780] Stoljar, pp.301–302.
[781] See above, paras 6-040 and 6-041.
[782] *Equitas Ltd v Walsham Brothers & Co Ltd* [2013] EWHC 3264 (Comm) at [49].
[783] *Equitas Ltd v Walsham Brothers & Co Ltd* above, at [58].
[784] *Equitas Ltd v Walsham Brothers & Co Ltd* above, at [71], perhaps a rather surprising conclusion, outside cases involving breach of trust.
[785] *Varden v Parker* (1798) 2 Esp. 710.
[786] *Andrew v Robinson* (1812) 3 Camp. 199; but if the principal and the third party have a common agent, an entry in the books of such agent will not be conclusive: see *McLarty v Middleton* (1858) 6 W.R. 379; 9 W.R. 861.
[787] *Hunter v Welsh* (1816) 1 Stark. 224.
[788] There are confusing dicta in actions for money paid under a mistake of fact: see *Freeman v Jeffries* (1869) L.R. 4 Ex. 189; *Baker v Courage & Co* [1910] 1 K.B. 56.
[789] See, e.g. *Edgell v Day* (1865) L.R. 1 C.P. 80; *Harsant v Blaine, Macdonald & Co* (1887) 56 L.J.Q.B. 511. See also Article 52.
[790] See *Equitas Ltd v Walsham Brothers & Co Ltd* [2013] EWHC 3264 (Comm) at [47] and [125].
[791] *McCarthy v Colvin* (1839) 9 A. & E. 607; *Blyth v Whiffin* (1872) 27 L.T. 330 at 333.
[792] *Brown v Farebrother* (1888) 58 L.J.Ch. 3.
[793] *Dale v Sollett* (1767) 4 Burr. 2133; *Curtis v Barclay* (1826) 5 B. & C. 141; *Wemys v Greenwood, Cox and Hammersley* (1827) 5 L.J.(O.S.) K.B. 257; *Potter v Fowler* (1837) 6 L.J.Ch. 273; *Cropper v Cook* (1868) L.R. 3 C.P. 194; *Roxburghe v Cox* (1881) 17 Ch.D. 520; cf. *Monkwearmouth Flour Mill Co Ltd v Lightfoot* (1897) 13 T.L.R. 327; *Dorf v Neumann, Luebeck & Co* (1924) 40 T.L.R. 405; *Bath v Standard Land Co Ltd* [1911] 1 Ch. 618. The agent cannot retain money where his right to do so has not yet accrued: *Wilkinson v North Surburban Properties Ltd* [1959] E.G.D. 218. In contracts for work and labour the defendant may have the right to make deductions in respect

if they were spent for an unlawful purpose[794]; but if the authority to deal with the money in an unlawful manner is revoked before the agent has used the money, the principal can recover.[795]

Even though the agent receives money for his principal in respect of a transaction which is void or illegal, the principal can sue his agent in restitution. Thus if an agent was employed to make bets and he won money, he was under a duty to pay it over to the principal, although the betting transactions were themselves void[796]; similarly, if an agent is employed to sell shares, he cannot retain the money he receives by saying that the sale is illegal by Act of Parliament.[797] Even if the contract between the principal and agent is itself illegal, then the principal may be able to recover any money received by the agent. Formerly, the money would have been irrecoverable under the ex turpi causa principle, but the law has now been changed.[798]

Where money is wrongfully obtained by an agent or is paid to him under a mistake of fact he can resist an action by his principal on the grounds that he has repaid it to the person who paid it to him[799]; and where money is paid to an agent in respect of a voidable contract, he can show that the contract has been rescinded and the money repaid, even where the contract was rescinded solely on the ground of his own fraud.[800]

Where an agent is appointed by two or more persons jointly, he is not discharged unless he accounts to them all, except where the principals are partners.[801] But an agent who has been severally appointed by one person cannot refuse to account separately to him on the ground that others are jointly interested in the money in the agent's hands.[802]

Illustrations

6-101 (1) B granted an annuity to C and D guaranteed the payment of the instalments. B was in arrears with his instalments and at the same time owed money for another reason to C's agent, E. E made an application to B and D for the payment of the instalments and as a result of this application and D's insistence

---

of defective performance of contractual services: see, e.g. *Hanak v Green* [1958] 2 Q.B. 9. Such deductions cannot be made in respect of a claim for marine freight: *Aries Tanker Corp v Total Transport Ltd (The Aries)* [1977] 1 W.L.R. 185; and this exception has been held to apply also to a claim against an agent for freight: *James & Co v Chinecrest Ltd* [1979] 1 Lloyd's Rep. 126.

[794] *Bayntun v Cattle* (1833) 1 Moo. & R. 265.

[795] *Bone v Ekless* (1860) 5 H. & N. 925; *Taylor v Bowers* (1876) 1 Q.B.D. 291.

[796] *De Mattos v Benjamin* (1894) 63 L.J.Q.B. 248, Illustration 3; *Bridger v Savage* (1885) 15 Q.B.D. 363; overruling *Beyer v Adams* (1857) 26 L.J.Ch. 841. But cf. *A.R. Dennis & Co v Campbell* [1978] Q.B. 365. The basis of these cases is removed by the validation of betting and gaming transactions by the Gambling Act 2005.

[797] *Bousfield v Wilson* (1846) 16 M. & W. 185; *Tenant v Elliot* (1797) 1 B. & P. 3; *Farmer v Russell* (1798) 1 B. & P. 296; *Sharp v Taylor* (1849) 2 Ph. 801; see also *Sykes v Beadon* (1879) 11 Ch.D. 170; *Thomson v Thomson* (1802) 7 Ves. 470.

[798] See now *Patel v Mirza* [2016] UKSC 42; [2017] A.C. 46. For the earlier position, see *Booth v Hodgson* (1795) 6 T.R. 405; *Catlin v Bell* (1815) 4 Camp. 183; *Knowles v Haughton* (1805) 11 Ves. 168; *Battersby v Smyth* (1818) 3 Madd. 110, with which cf. *Davenport v Whitmore* (1836) 2 My. & Cr. 177; *Harry Parker Ltd v Mason* [1940] 2 K.B. 590; and, Illustration 2.

[799] See Article 111 and Comment.

[800] *Murray v Mann* (1848) 2 Exch. 538, Illustration 2; cf. *Stevens v Legh* (1853) 2 C.L.R. 251 and *Field v Allen* (1842) 9 M. & W. 694.

[801] *Lee v Sankey* (1872) L.R. 15 Eq. 204; *Innes v Stephenson* (1831) 1 M. & R. 145; for authority to the contrary see *Husband v Davis* (1851) 10 C.B. 645. See Article 11.

[802] *Roberts v Ogilby* (1821) 9 Price 269; and see *Suart v Welch* (1839) 4 Myl. & Cr. 305; Article 54.

B paid a sum of money to E. Held, E could not keep the money as payment for his own debt but had received it on C's behalf and must account for it to C.[803]

(2) An agent sells a horse and receives the purchase money. The sale is subsequently rescinded on the ground of the agent's fraud, and the purchase money is repaid. The agent is not liable to the principal for the amount of the purchase money.[804]

(3) A factor raises money by wrongfully pledging the goods of his principal. The principal may adopt the transaction, and treat the money raised as money had and received to his use.[805]

(4) P gives money to an accountant to invest. The accountant's daughter misappropriates it. The accountant is liable for its return.[806]

Article 53

LIABILITY FOR INTEREST

(1) Where an agent holds money which belongs in law or equity to his principal, any interest earned in respect of that money belongs to the principal, and the agent must account to him for it.[807]   **6-102**

(2) Subject to the discretion of the court under s.35A of the Senior Courts Act 1981 an agent who receives money in breach of his fiduciary duties, or who fails to pay his principal on demand, must pay interest on it from the date of his default.

Comment

Rule (1) If the agent holds money as trustee for his principal, he may not keep   **6-103**
for himself anything earned with that money.[808] The claim for interest is alternative to a proprietary claim for profits[809] and sometimes merely interest is claimed because of the difficulty of establishing what the profits are, or because the result has been not to make a profit but to effect a saving. When the agent is under a duty to invest and does not do so, he may under this head be liable for the interest which should have been received.[810] It is not, however, clear exactly when such a duty arises; there are dicta suggesting that a holder of trust money is always liable for interest if he knows that the money has this character,[811] but there are cases holding that there is no liability where it is proved that no profit was made.[812]

---

[803] *Shaw v Picton* (1825) 4 B. & C. 715.
[804] *Murray v Mann* (1848) 2 Exch. 538.
[805] *Bonzi v Stewart* (1842) 5 Scott N.R. 1 at 26; 4 M. & G. 295.
[806] *Martin v Pont* [1993] 3 N.Z.L.R. 25: see Stevens [2005] L.M.C.L.Q. 101 at 118.
[807] See a critical analysis by Elliott [2001] Conv. 313.
[808] See *Att.-Gen. v Alford* (1855) 4 De G.M. & G. 843; *Brown v IRC* [1965] A.C. 244; above, para.6-040 onwards.
[809] *Re Davis* [1902] 2 Ch. 314.
[810] *Burdick v Garrick* (1870) L.R. 5 Ch.App. 233, Illustration 2. As to the amount of interest see Snell, *Equity* (33rd edn), para.30-020.
[811] *Moons v De Barnales* (1826) 1 Russ. 301; *Att.-Gen. v Alford*, above, at p.851; and see Finn, *Fiduciary Obligations* (1977), pp.114–115.
[812] e.g. *Turner v Burkinshaw* (1867) L.R. 2 Ch.App. 488.

6-104   **Stakeholders**   In *Potters (A Firm) v Loppert*[813] Pennycuick VC held that an estate agent was under no obligation to account for the interest earned by him on a sum deposited with him to hold as stakeholder. The decision related to a precontract deposit, but the reasoning applies equally to contract deposits. The basis of the decision was that the agent was not a trustee and was liable only in contract or restitution. A better reason for the rule might be that although the agent holds as trustee, there is a usage that he is entitled to the income in return for his services in holding the deposit.[814] The rule is of ancient origin[815] and it is open to question whether such a rule is appropriate to modern times, particularly in view of the size of some deposits on commercial and other property. In relation to estate agents, it is now however provided by the Estate Agents Act 1979 that money received in the course of estate agency work by way of pre-contract or contract deposit is held on trust[816] and must be paid into a client account[817]; there is provision for the making of accounts regulations requiring payment of interest.[818] These detailed requirements supersede the normal consequences of a trusteeship in such cases[819]; but the regulations made do not in fact require payment of interest on money received as stakeholder.[820]

6-105   **Solicitors**   A solicitor may hold property on trust, depending on the circumstances.[821] In many cases however money held for clients is paid into general client account. In *Brown v IRC*[822] it was held that the solicitor had no right to the interest earned on such money, whatever the difficulty of accounting as between the clients concerned. The matter was subsequently regulated by statute[823] under which rules may be made providing for payment of interest on client accounts[824]: beyond this no interest is due.[825] It is apparently assumed that these rules are not applicable to money received as stakeholder.

---

[813] [1973] Ch. 399; *Manzanilla Ltd v Corton Property and Investments Ltd* Unreported November 13, 1996, CA, per Millett LJ); *The Governor and Company of The Bank of Scotland v Truman* [2005] EWHC 583 (QB).

[814] See Goode (1976) 92 L.Q.R. at 371, fn.44.

[815] Pennycuick VC followed *Harrington v Hoggart* (1830) 1 B. & Ad. 577, a case concerning an auctioneer decided in the Court of King's Bench which was a claim in assumpsit not based upon principles of equity. However, the court cited an unreported dictum of Lord Eldon and upon this basis said that their decision was not at variance with any rule of equity. (Yet the case had been argued partly on the basis that the agent was a trustee and therefore not obliged to obey the instructions of the vendor to put the money out to earn interest). The defendant auctioneer was treated as if he were a banker and his position was contrasted with that of an agent. See also below, Illustrations 1–3 to Article 111; *Royal Norwegian Government v Calcutta Marine Engineering Co Ltd* [1960] 2 Lloyd's Rep. 431.

[816] ss.12 and 13. "Estate agency work" is defined in s.1 and applies only to some of the work performed by estate agents. See in general Murdoch, *The Estate Agents and Property Misdescriptions Acts* (3rd edn), Ch.13D; *Law of Estate Agency* (5th edn), Ch.6.

[817] s.14.

[818] s.15.

[819] s.13(3).

[820] See Estate Agents (Accounts) Regulations 1981 (SI 1981/1520) reg.7.

[821] See, e.g. *Burdick v Garrick* (1870) L.R. 5 Ch.App. 233, Illustration 2.

[822] [1965] A.C. 244, Illustration 1.

[823] See Solicitors Act 1974 ss.32 and 33 as amended.

[824] Solicitors' Accounts Rules 1998.

[825] Solicitors Act 1974 s.33(3).

Financial services   For details on this topic the reader is referred to specialised   **6-106**
works.[826]

Rate of interest   The rate of interest may vary in accordance with whether the   **6-107**
agent has, or may be presumed to have, made more money by his breach, or
whether the misconduct is serious, as where there is fraud or breach of fiduciary
duty.[827] Old cases used 4 per cent on the basic simple interest rate, with 5 per cent
and compound interest for the special cases. However, more recently, and not
surprisingly, higher rates have been ordered.[828]

Rule (2)   In general there was no right to interest on money received for a principal   **6-108**
and not held in trust unless the agent was guilty of a breach of fiduciary obligation
or refused to pay his principal on demand. In these latter cases there was such a right
in equity though not at common law,[829] and the same considerations as those
mentioned above were applicable in calculating the rate of interest. The decisions
on this point were largely rendered obsolete by s.3 of the Law Reform (Miscellaneous Provisions) Act 1934, which gave the court a wide discretion to award interest
on all or any part of any debt or damages for which judgment is given at such rate
as it thinks fit for the whole or any part of the period between the date when the
cause of action arose and judgment. These powers are now contained in the Senior
Courts Act 1981 as amended.[830] The 1934 provision used the words "proceedings
tried" and thus did not apply to a default judgment, nor perhaps to certain other
situations. In such cases it was sometimes still necessary to rely on the equitable
rather than on the statutory jurisdiction.[831] The wording of the (amended) Senior
Courts Act, referring simply to "proceedings … before the High Court", is wider.[832]

Illustrations

(1)   A solicitor held sums of money on deposit in his clients' account. This ac-   **6-109**
      count earned interest which, in accordance with common practice, the solici-
      tor kept for himself as part of the profits of his firm. Held, the solicitor was in
      a fiduciary position in relation to his clients and that the interest accordingly

---

[826] See above, para.6-060.
[827] See *Burdick v Garrick* (1870) L.R. 5 Ch.App. 233 at 241–242; *Wallersteiner v Moir (No.2)* [1975]
Q.B. 373 at 397; *Westdeutsche Landesbank Girozentrale v Islington LBC* [1996] A.C. 669; *Herbert
Equities Ltd v Mamfredos* [2009] NZHC 128; *Herrod v Johnston* [2013] 2 Qd R. 102 at [50];
Libertarian Investments Ltd v Hall [2013] HKCFA 93 at [141] (simple interest only). Snell, *Equity*
(33rd edn), para.30-020; Finn, *Fiduciary Obligations* (1977), pp.115–117.
[828] *Wallersteiner v Moir (No. 2)*, above. And see *O'Sullivan v Management Agency and Music Ltd*
[1985] Q.B. 428; and *Sempra Metals Ltd v IRC* [2007] UKHL 34; [2008] 1 A.C. 561.
[829] See e.g. *Pearse v Green* (1819) 1 J. & W. 135; *Wolfe v Findlay* (1847) 6 Hare 66; *Edgell v Day* (1865)
L.R. 1 C.P. 80; *Harsant v Blaine, Macdonald & Co* (1887) 56 L.J.Q.B. 511; *Boston Deep Sea Fishing and Ice Co v Ansell* (1888) 39 Ch.D. 339; *Barclay v Harris* (1915) 85 L.J.K.B. 115; *Webster v
British Empire Mutual Life Assurance Co* (1880) 15 Ch.D. 169; *Accidia Foundation v Simon C.
Dickinson Ltd* [2010] EWHC 3058 (Ch) at [97] (compound interest).
[830] s.35A, inserted by Administration of Justice Act 1982 s.15. See also County Courts Act 1984 s.69(1),
as amended.
[831] See *Wallersteiner v Moir (No.2)* [1975] Q.B. 373; *Gardener Steel Ltd v Sheffield Bros (Profiles) Ltd*
[1978] 1 W.L.R. 916.
[832] *President of India v La Pintada Compania Navigacion SA (The La Pintada)* [1985] A.C. 104; cf.
Hungerfords v Walker (1989) 171 C.L.R. 125. Interest may sometimes also be due under the Late
Payment of Commercial Debts (Interest) Act 1998.

belonged to them. The practice of the solicitor retaining the interest for himself could not be permitted.[833]

(2) A solicitor was authorised by power of attorney to sell certain property and invest the proceeds. He paid the proceeds into the account of his firm, who made use of the money. Held, that he must pay interest at the rate of 5 per cent.[834]

(3) An agent, who undertook to invest his principal's money in the funds, kept large balances in his hands. Held, that he must pay interest on such balances.[835]

3. ESTOPPEL AS TO PRINCIPAL'S TITLE

Article 54

AGENT'S ESTOPPEL AS TO PRINCIPAL'S TITLE

6-110 (1) Where an agent is in possession of property in his capacity as agent, he is estopped from asserting that he has a better title to it than his principal, for his possession is deemed to be that of his principal.[836]

(2) An agent is estopped from asserting that a third party has a better right than his principal to receive money held by him as agent for or on account of his principal or owed by him as agent to his principal.[837]

(3) But an agent who is a bailee of chattels from his principal as bailor may in an action by his principal for wrongful interference with them show that a third party has a better right than his principal as respects all or any part of the interest claimed by the principal or in right of which he sues.[838]

Comment

6-111   Although the word "estoppel" is not much used in the cases relating to these propositions, the first and second constitute situations where an agent is not allowed to make such allegations against his principal, and they can conveniently be regarded as based on a form of estoppel. The third was formerly a case where estoppel reasoning was articulately applied: but this has been reversed by statute.

An agent who is in possession of property in his capacity as agent cannot acquire title against his principal under the Limitation Act, for he is estopped from denying that his possession is that of the principal[839]:

---

[833] *Brown v IRC* [1965] A.C. 244. The problems presented to solicitors by this case are met in part by the Solicitors' Accounts Rules 1998.
[834] *Burdick v Garrick* (1870) L.R. 5 Ch.App. 233. cf. *Chedworth v Edwards* (1802) 8 Ves. Jun. 48.
[835] *Browne v Southouse* (1790) 3 Bro.C.C. 107; *Barwell v Parker* (1751) 2 Ves. 364.
[836] *Cooper v De Tastet* (1829) Tamlyn 177 at 179; *Williams v Pott* (1871) L.R. 12 Eq. 149 at 151.
[837] *Blaustein v Maltz, Mitchell & Co* [1937] 2 K.B. 142, Illustration 7.
[838] Torts (Interference with Goods) Act 1977 s.8(1).
[839] *Ward v Carttar* (1865) L.R. 1 Eq. 29, Illustration 2; *Smith v Bennett* (1874) 30 L.T. 100; *Lyell v Kennedy* (1889) 14 App.Cas. 437, Illustration 1. He must possess as agent and not in any other capacity, but it is for the agent to prove that he was not acting as agent, and the burden of proof is heavy: *White v Bayley* (1861) 10 C.B.(N.S.) 227; *Markwick v Hardingham* (1880) 15 Ch.D. 339; *Re Hobbs* (1887) 36 Ch.D. 553; *Bell v Marsh* [1903] 1 Ch. 528.

"An agent cannot well get an adverse title, unless he can very distinctly shew that what he has done is in respect of title, and not in respect of his agency".[840]

Moreover, an agent may not set up his own title as true owner against a prescriptive title acquired by his principal through him. Thus, where an agent received rents for 25 years and paid them to his principal, it was the principal who acquired the statutory title by limitation, since the agent was not permitted to deny that the principal acquired it through him.[841]

Again, if the agent has received money for his principal as a result of his agency he cannot assert that a third party has a better right to receive it than his principal[842]:

"The law is perfectly clear that an agent receiving money rightfully for his principal is not liable in respect of that money to the owner of the money even where the principal, upon receiving it, would be bound to pay it over to the owner."[843]

This rule applies where the relationship between principal and agent is merely that of creditor and debtor. A fortiori the agent cannot assert a third party's rights to money which he holds as trustee for his principal.

There was long a third rule whereby an agent was prevented from making a claim adverse to his principal, and here the term estoppel was more frequently used.[844] Where the agent was also a bailee of his principal, he was bound by a rule that a bailee may not assert that a third party has a better right to the property than has the bailor.[845] There were exceptions to this: a bailee might rely on a third party's title if he had handed the goods over to him or if he defended the bailor's claim by authority of and on behalf of the third party.[846] The exceptions did not apply if the bailee had accepted the bailment or attorned to the bailor with knowledge of the third party's claim.[847]

But by virtue of section 8(1) of the Torts (Interference with Goods) Act 1977:

"in any action for wrongful interference with goods the defendant is entitled to show, in accordance with rules of court, that a third party has a better right than the plaintiff as respects all or part of the interest claimed by the plaintiff or in right of which he sues, and any rule of law (sometimes called jus tertii) to the contrary is abolished."

---

[840] *Att.-Gen. v Corporation of London* (1850) 2 Mac. & G. 247 at 259, per Lord Cottenham LC.
[841] *Williams v Pott* (1871) L.R. 12 Eq. 149, Illustration 3.
[842] *Dixon v Hamond* (1819) 2 B. & A. 310, Illustration 5; *Roberts v Ogilby* (1821) 9 Price 269, Illustration 5; *Suart v Welch* (1839) 4 Myl. & Cr. 305; *Eames v Hacon* (1881) 18 Ch.D. 347, Illustration 6; *Davie v Sachs* [1911] Cape P.D. 992; *Mangena v Moyatusi* [1918] App.D. 650; *Blaustein v Maltz, Mitchell & Co* [1937] 2 K.B. 142, Illustration 7. However, it seems that the agent may deny his principal's title to money (or chattels) received by the agent as a result of the principal's fraud on a third party: *Field v Allen* (1842) 9 M. & W. 694; *Murray v Mann* (1848) 2 Exch. 538; *Cheesman v Exall* (1851) 6 Exch. 341. See too the rules about receipt by an agent of money paid by a third party under mistake, discussed below, Article 111.
[843] *Blaustein v Maltz, Mitchell & Co*, above, at 156, per Scott LJ. Sed quaere: see Article 113.
[844] See, e.g. *Kahler v Midland Bank Ltd* [1950] A.C. 24 at 38.
[845] Clerk and Lindsell, *Torts* (21st edn), para.17-82; Palmer, *Bailment* (3rd edn), para.4-026 onwards; Spencer Bower, *Reliance-Based Estoppel* (5th edn), paras 9.54 and 9.58–9.61.
[846] *Biddle v Bond* (1865) 6 B. & S. 225; *Rogers, Sons & Co v Lambert & Co* [1891] 1 Q.B. 318; *Ross v Edwards & Co* (1895) 73 L.T. 100; *Kahler v Midland Bank Ltd* [1950] A.C. 24.
[847] *Re Sadler Ex p. Davies* (1881) 19 Ch.D. 86; *Eastern Construction Co Ltd v National Trust Co* [1914] A.C. 197 at 210; *Wilson v Lombank* [1963] 1 W.L.R. 1294 at 1297.

The purpose of this legislation was in general to end multiplicity of actions[848]; and to that end the defendant's proper course is to apply for joinder of the named third party.[849]

Illustrations

6-112 (1) A receives the rents of certain properties as an agent, and pays them into a separate account at his own bank. The principal dies intestate. A continues to receive the rents for more than 12 years after the death of the principal, stating to several of the tenants that he is acting for the heir, whoever he may be. Thirteen years afterwards, a purchaser from the heir brings an action against A, claiming possession of the property and an account of the rents and profits. A claims the property as his own, and pleads the Statute of Limitations. The plaintiff is entitled to possession of the property, and an account of all the rents and profits received by A, which were held in trust.[850]

(2) A solicitor paid off a mortgage debt due from a client, and entered into possession of the mortgaged property. Held, that he must be taken to have acted as the agent of the client, and therefore (a) was not a mortgagee in possession, and (b) was not entitled to set up the Statute of Limitations in an action by the client for redemption.[851]

(3) A receives the rents of certain property as B's agent for more than 12 years, and duly pays them over to B. B thereby acquires a good prescriptive title to the property, in the absence of fraud, even if A was the true owner.[852]

(4) A makes advances for the purpose of a mine, in order to obtain ore, which he consigns to B for sale, B undertaking to account to him for the proceeds. B cannot set up any paramount title to the ore, or dispute A's right to the proceeds, on the ground that there are rights of third persons existing independently of the contract between A and B.[853]

(5) A ship which is the property of A is transferred to B as security for a debt. B insures the ship for and on behalf of A & Co, and charges them with the premiums. The ship is lost, and B receives the insurance money. B must pay over the money, after deducting the amount of his debt, to A & Co, and cannot set up A's title, having insured for and on behalf of A & Co[854] So an insurance broker who receives money under a policy cannot dispute the claim of his principal on the ground that other persons are interested in the subject-matter of the insurance.[855]

(6) E died intestate in Ireland and letters of administration were granted to P. Part of E's assets were in India and P sent a power of attorney to F & Co, who obtained letters of administration for the benefit of P. They collected his Indian

---

[848] See Law Reform Committee, 18th Report, Cmnd. 4774 (1971), paras 51–78; Clerk and Lindsell, *Torts* (21st edn), para.17-84; Palmer, *Bailment* (3rd edn), para.4-058 onwards. See also *De Franco v Commissioner of Police for the Metropolis, The Times,* May 8, 1987.

[849] See s.8(2) of the Act.

[850] *Lyell v Kennedy* (1889) 14 App.Cas. 437. And see *Smith v Bennett* (1874) 30 L.T. 100.

[851] *Ward v Carttar* (1865) L.R. 1 Eq. 29.

[852] *Williams v Pott* (1871) L.R. 12 Eq. 149.

[853] *Zulueta v Vinent* (1852) 1 De G.M. & G. 315. But see Illustration 8.

[854] *Dixon v Hamond* (1819) 2 B. & A. 310.

[855] *Roberts v Ogilby* (1821) 9 Price 269. But if money is paid by B to A to hold for P, it cannot be claimed by P until A has acknowledged the agency: *Wedlake v Hurley* (1830) 1 C. & J. 83; *Stephens v Badcock* (1832) 3 B. & Ad. 354; Article 112.

assets, paid his debts and sent the assets to A, their English agents. A refused to hand the assets over to P without the concurrence of E's next of kin. Held (the next of kin making no claim), A could not set up any third party's title against P.[856]

(7) B was engaged to Miss J. Her father, J, gave him a cheque for £172.10s., the amount of the deposit on the intended matrimonial home, as a gift conditional on the marriage taking place. B paid the cheque into his bank account and sent his own cheque for the same sum to the estate agent, B then instructed M (who was J's son-in-law) to act for him as solicitor in the purchase of the house. The engagement between B and Miss J was broken off and B instructed M to reclaim the deposit, which he did. M refused to pay B the amount of the deposit since J had ordered him not to do so and had told M to account to J for it. Held, (i) the relationship between B and M was that of principal (creditor) and agent (debtor); (ii) the principle of jus tertii as applied to bailments had no application to a sum of money; and (iii) M could not plead J's orders and must account to B for the money.[857]

(8) A wrongfully distrains B's goods and delivers them to C, an auctioneer, for sale, C having at the time no knowledge of B's adverse claim. B subsequently gives notice of his title to C, and claims the proceeds.[858] C may now, if sued by A, apply for B to be joined as a party.[859]

---

[856] *Eames v Hacon* (1881) 18 Ch.D. 347.
[857] *Blaustein v Maltz, Mitchell & Co* [1937] 2 K.B. 142.
[858] cf. *Biddle v Bond* (1865) 6 B. & S. 225; *Rogers Son & Co v Lambert & Co* [1891] 1 Q.B. 318; *Ross v Edwards & Co* (1895) 73 L.T. 100.
[859] Torts (Interference with Goods) Act 1977 s.8; see Comment.

CHAPTER 7

RIGHTS OF AGENTS AGAINST THEIR PRINCIPALS

INTRODUCTORY NOTE

Duties of co-operation   Legal systems which categorise types of agent and seek   **7-001**
to lay down the incidents of the various legal relationships may well prescribe duties of principals towards their agents just as they prescribe duties of agents towards
their principals. English law however has traditionally viewed the principal as the
person requiring protection, against wrongful use of the agent's powers, and have
paid little attention to the position of the agent. Thus it was long ago held that the
principal was under no duty to account on a fiduciary basis to the agent[1]; and in
general the view that the principal has fiduciary duties towards the agent is not one
that is often put forward. Equally, the limited body of law relating to the common
law duties owed by agents towards their principals has no obvious counterpart
concerning duties owed towards agents by their principals.

The fiduciary duties of an agent are however acknowledged to be manifestations of a wider principle which is not confined to agents, and there can be no
general reason why a principal should not find himself under a fiduciary responsibility towards his agent, even if the situation would be rarer than those imposing
fiduciary responsibilities on the agent.[2] So also there can be no objection to a
principal being liable to his agent in tort: the existence of a contractual action
between them may regulate or modify the duties owed, but does not exclude tort
liability based on general principles.[3] As to contract, however, parties drafting
agency contracts (or related contracts such as distributorship contracts) are well
advised to deal specifically with the duties of the principal. The rules as to implication of terms at common law are strict: a brief indication is that terms can only be
implied to implement the general nature of a recognised type of relationship or

---

[1]   *Padwick v Stanley* (1852) 9 Hare 627; cf. *Padwick v Hurst* (1854) 18 Beav. 575; *Paper Reclaim Ltd
v Aotearoa International Ltd* [2007] 3 N.Z.L.R. 169 (NZSC) (principals do not, in general, owe
fiduciary duties to agents); *Galambos v Perez* [2009] 3 S.C.R. 247 (SCC).
[2]   Fiduciary duties in a franchisor were denied in *Jirna v Mister Donut of Canada Ltd* (1973) 40 D.L.R.
(3d) 303; criticised by Shepherd (1981) 97 L.Q.R. 51 at 59; and see Brown (1971) 49 Tex.L.Rev
650, suggesting that franchising should be regarded as creating a fiduciary relationship. But see
Hospital Products Ltd v US Surgical Corp (1984) 156 C.L.R. 41, per Mason and Deane JJ (on duties of a distributor). See also *Jani-King (GB) Ltd v Pula Enterprises Ltd* [2007] EWHC 2433; [2008]
1 All E.R. (Comm) 451 (no implied term of trust and confidence in favour of franchisee); cf. above,
para.6-015. *Restatement, Third*, § 8.15 provides for a duty to act "fairly and in good faith, including a duty to provide the agent about risks of physical harm or pecuniary loss" that may affect the
agent's work; and a franchisor has been held liable to the franchisee for negligent advice concerning the franchise: *MGB Printing & Design Ltd v Kall Kwik UK Ltd* [2010] EWHC 624 (QB);
Traderight (NSW) Pty Ltd v Bank of Queensland Ltd [2015] NSWCA 94 (alleged inaccurate projections of revenue to prospective agent).
[3]   *Henderson v Merrett Syndicates Ltd* [1995] 2 A.C. 145, explaining *Tai Hing Cotton Mill Ltd v Liu
Chong Hing Bank Ltd* [1986] A.C. 80.

transaction (such as employer and employee, landlord and tenant), or to give business efficacy to a particular transaction.[4]

The relevant cases do not cite the principal/agent relationship as coming within the first category of implication, and perhaps indeed could not because the varied ways in which agency relationships arise do not easily generate a "particular generic type of contract".[5] But, there has recently been a tendency to imply terms more readily into the related contract of employer and employee. Thus in *Mahmud v Bank of Credit and Commerce International SA*[6] the House of Lords approved the existence of an implied term that "the employer shall not, without reasonable and proper cause, conduct itself in a manner calculated and likely to destroy or seriously damage the relationship of confidence and trust between employer and employee"[7]; from this statement conclusions as to implication of terms can be drawn. There are also cases discussing the basic nature of particular types of agency transactions.[8] It may well be therefore that the courts will not be unwilling under the first category of implication to find certain elemental duties of co-operation by a principal with his agent,[9] at least in those situations which involve a fiduciary relationship between the parties.[10] In cases of a more obviously commercial nature, such as distributorship, they may be more cautious.[11] An obvious example is the implication that the principal will reimburse and indemnify the agent against expenses incurred, stated in Article 62, though this may not always be contractual. A number of cases, not easy to reconcile, discuss the implication of terms in connection with the termination of the agent's authority.[12] Other cases consider more generally when a term will be implied that the principal will not prevent the agent from earning commission.[13] Except where the analogy of employment contracts is available[14] both groups use the second of the techniques above mentioned, viz. they deny the possibility of a general implication and only find terms when this is necessary to give business efficacy to a transaction. There is therefore nothing in the law sufficiently specific to make the formulation of a general Article on the principal's inherent duties towards

---

[4] See *Liverpool City Council v Irwin* [1977] A.C. 239; cf. *Att.-Gen. of Belize v Belize Telecom Ltd* [2009] UKPC 10; [2009] 1 W.L.R. 1988. See now *Marks and Spencer Plc v BNP Paribas Securities Services Trust Co (Jersey) Ltd* [2015] UKSC 72; [2016] A.C. 742 and Chitty, *Contracts* (32nd edn), Ch.14; Treitel, *Law of Contract* (14th edn), para.6-032 onwards.

[5] See *Clarion Ltd v National Provident Institution* [2000] 1 W.L.R. 1888 at 1897, per Rimer J; *Ashmore v Corporation of Lloyd's (No.2)* [1992] 2 Lloyd's Rep. 620 at 626 onwards.

[6] [1998] A.C. 20.

[7] At p.45 per Lord Steyn. See also *Lister v Romford Ice and Cold Storage Co Ltd* [1957] A.C. 555, esp. at 576 and 594; *Scally v Southern Health Board* [1992] 1 A.C. 294; *Spring v Guardian Assurance Plc* [1995] 2 A.C. 296.

[8] e.g. the normal estate agent's contract, discussed in *Luxor (Eastbourne) Ltd v Cooper* [1941] A.C. 108, esp. at 137 onwards and *L.J. Hooker Ltd v W.J. Adams Estates Pty Ltd* (1977) 138 C.L.R. 52, esp. at 73 onwards See also *W.T. Lamb & Sons v Goring Brick Co Ltd* [1932] 1 K.B. 710 ("sole selling agents": distributorship).

[9] See in general Burrows (1968) 31 M.L.R. 390; Lücke (1973) 5 Adelaide L.Rev. 32; Kerr (1980) 97 S.A.L. Rev. 550; Brodie (1996) 25 I.L.J. 121; (2001) 117 L.Q.R. 604. As to the application of exclusion clauses in relation to duties of co-operation, see *Axa Sun Life Services Plc v Campbell Martin Ltd* [2011] EWCA Civ 133; [2011] 2 Lloyd's Rep. 1; [2011] 1 C.L.C. 312.

[10] cf. *Lamb v Evans* [1893] 1 Ch. 218, per Bowen LJ.

[11] See *Hospital Products Ltd v United States Surgical Corp* (1984) 156 C.L.R. 41 (as to the duties of distributors); cf. *Mona Oil Equipment Supply Co Ltd v Rhodesia Railways Ltd* [1949] 2 All E.R. 1014.

[12] See Comment to Article 123.

[13] Article 58.

[14] See *Martin-Baker Aircraft Co Ltd v Canadian Flight Equipment Ltd* [1955] 2 Q.B. 556; below, para.10-040.

the agent appropriate. *Restatement, Second,*[15] listed certain general duties in this connection; these included a duty not to interfere unreasonably with agent's work, to give relevant information, to keep and render accounts (so as, e.g. to enable the amount of commission payable to be calculated[16]), and

> "to conduct himself so as not to harm the agent's reputation, nor to make it impossible for the agent, consistently with his reasonable self-respect or personal safety, to continue in the employment."

While these may be useful reminders of suitable standards, it is submitted that they were (and are) no more than that. It remains appropriate therefore to list as the basic rights of an agent only those which follow.

The duties discussed in this chapter concern the internal relationship between principal and agent; and the best examples actually concern "canvassing" or "soliciting" agents, who have no authority to contract on behalf of their principals.[17] Hence many of the cases discussed concern estate agents, who are a primary example in this category.

The rights of an agent are normally based on a contract between agent and principal. The agent may sometimes however be entitled under the Contracts (Rights of Third Parties) 1999: for example, a duty to pay commission to a broker is often contained in a charterparty.[18]

Commercial agents   The Commercial Agents (Council Directive) Regulations   **7-002** 1993, however, lay down duties for the principals of commercial agents as there defined. In particular, a principal must act towards the agent "dutifully and in good faith".[19] The Regulations are dealt with in Chapter 11.

1.   REMUNERATION

Article 55

WHETHER AGENT ENTITLED TO ANY REMUNERATION

(1)   An agent is only entitled to remuneration for his services as agent if either the   **7-003** express or implied terms of the agency contract, if any, so provide or he has a right in restitution to claim on a quantum meruit.

(2)   Where the contract contains express terms providing for remuneration to be paid, the agent cannot normally claim remuneration other than in accordance with those terms. In the absence of such express terms the right to claim any remuneration, and the amount and terms of payment of such remuneration, are determined by such terms as may be implied into the contract.

(3)   In deciding what terms are to be implied the court will have regard to all the circumstances of the case, including the nature and length of the services, the

---

[15]   §§ 432–437. But *Restatement, Third* simply provides for a duty to deal fairly and in good faith: see fn.2 above.

[16]   See the inconclusive discussion in *Easyair Ltd (t/a Openair) v Opal Telecom Ltd* [2009] EWHC 339 (Ch) at [47].

[17]   See above, para.1-020.

[18]   See *Nisshin Shipping Co Ltd v Cleaves & Co* [2003] EWHC 2602 (Comm); [2004] 1 All E.R. (Comm) 481 (holding that the third party in effect becomes a statutory assignee of the promisee's right of action and hence is subject to a requirement of arbitration as the promisee would be).

[19]   reg.4(1).

express terms of the contract and the customs, usages and practices of the particular area of activity. In the absence of any factors to the contrary, a term will be implied that the agent is entitled to reasonable remuneration.[20]

Comment

7-004 **Contractual claim** Apart from claims in restitution, the rendering of services to another, however long continued, creates no right to remuneration unless the agency contract expressly or impliedly makes provision for such payments.[21] If there are no express terms relating to remuneration, terms providing for remuneration will only be implied where the circumstances are such as to indicate that the parties intended that there should be remuneration.[22] In general, however, the mere employment of a professional person raises a presumption that it was intended that he should be remunerated unless there are circumstances indicating the contrary.[23] The position is different with company directors, who are entitled to remuneration only if express provision is made therefor.[24] Consistently with the foregoing principles, it is unlikely that a court would imply a right to remuneration in favour of a relative or friend of the donor under a power of attorney; the relationship would generally be non-contractual.[25] The position would likely be different where the attorney appointed was a professional person.

In respect of some contracts, failure to agree on the price would be a strong indication that no contract had been concluded. In the case of the contract of agency, however, the question of the agent's remuneration is less central, and if it is found that remuneration was intended, its amount can be determined by reference to scales or even by what is reasonable.[26] However, if the parties have not settled the event which triggers the right to commission—a highly variable element in agency contracts—it is unlikely that any contract can be established.[27]

What terms may be implied into the contract will depend upon the normal rules for the implication of terms into contracts.[28] In particular, no terms may be implied which would be inconsistent with the express terms.[29] Thus, if the express terms provide for remuneration which seems unduly low, no term may be implied which

---

[20] See Comment.
[21] Of course if there is no agency contract at all, there is no duty to pay commission (though there may be restitutionary consequences): see *Lady Manor Ltd v Fat Cat Café Bars Ltd* [2001] 2 E.G.L.R. 1 ("cold calling" by estate agents).
[22] *Reeve v Reeve* (1858) 1 F. & F. 280; *Foord v Morley* (1859) 1 F. & F. 496. See also *Hulse v Hulse* (1856) 17 C.B. 711. See *Benhams Ltd v Kythira Investments Ltd* [2004] EWHC 2973 (QB); *Ian Greenhill Residential Ltd v Asfari* [2007] EWHC 1491 (QB) at [106]; cf. *Primlake Ltd v Matthews Associates* [2006] EWHC 1227 (Ch); [2007] 1 B.C.L.C. 666.
[23] *Miller v Beale* (1879) 27 W.R. 403, Illustration 6; *Manson v Baillie* (1855) 2 Macq. 80; *Gibbon v Budd* (1863) 2 H. & C. 92; *Landless v Wilson* (1880) 8 R. 289; *Turner v Reeve* (1901) 17 T.L.R. 592; *Corbin v Stewart* (1911) 28 T.L.R. 99 (the former) practice of one doctor charging no fee for attendance on the children of another doctor was a circumstance displacing the general rule); *Way v Latilla* [1937] 3 All E.R. 759, Illustration 3; Supply of Goods and Services Act 1982 s.15.
[24] See *Guinness Plc v Saunders* [1990] 2 A.C. 663.
[25] See *Lincolne v Williams* [2008] TASSC 41 at [15].
[26] cf. Supply of Goods and Services Act 1982 s.15. See *Ian Greenhill Residential Ltd v Asfari* [2007] EWHC 1491 (QB) at [96].
[27] See *Wells v Devani* [2016] EWCA Civ 1106; [2017] 2 W.L.R. 1391.
[28] See above, para.7-001.
[29] *Broad v Thomas* (1830) 7 Bing. 99; *Read v Rann* (1830) 10 B. & C. 438; *Phillipps v Briard* (1856) 25 L.J.Ex. 233; *Alder v Boyle* (1847) 4 C.B. 635; *Green v Mules* (1861) 30 L.J.C.P. 343, Illustration 8; *Barnett v Isaacson* (1888) 4 T.L.R. 645; *Lott v Outhwaite* (1893) 10 T.L.R. 76; *Harley & Co*

will give a more reasonable remuneration.[30] But if the agent performs services at the request of the principal which are outside the duties for which the contract expressly provides for remuneration, a term may exceptionally be implied that a reasonable sum shall be paid for such services.[31] If the contract provides that the amount of remuneration shall be in the discretion of the principal, the court may not decide what sum should be paid; to do so would be to re-write the contract and usurp the principal from the function which the parties agreed should be his.[32] But if the contract expressly or impliedly provides that a reasonable sum shall be payable, the court will determine what is a reasonable sum and the terms on which it should be paid.[33] In the absence of a contrary indication as to the amount payable, the term which will be implied is for a reasonable sum on reasonable terms. What is reasonable will depend upon all the circumstances of the case.[34] When an agent is charging on an hourly basis, it will often be relevant to consider whether the ends to be obtained justify the hours spent.[35]

Scales: implied terms and custom[36]   The fact that a professional person normally   **7-005**
charges on a fixed scale, such as a scale of charges laid down by his professional body which provides for a varying percentage of the total sum involved, does not ipso facto entitle him to remuneration according to that scale. He must show that the scale was incorporated into the contract either by express term or otherwise. If it is not incorporated expressly he may show that the scale is to be implied by custom; but the custom must, of course, be reasonable if it is to bind the other party.[37] In the absence of express or implied incorporation of a scale, the implied term will be that the professional person is only entitled to a reasonable sum, although the scale may provide the measure of or an indication of what a reasonable sum might be.[38] The court may have regard to the negotiations of the parties

---

v Nagata (1917) 34 T.L.R. 124; Moor Line Ltd v Louis Dreyfus & Co [1918] 1 K.B. 89; Howard Houlder & Partners Ltd v Manx Islands SS Co [1923] 1 K.B. 110; Burrough's Adding Machine Ltd v Aspinall (1925) 41 T.L.R. 276; Jones v Lowe [1945] K.B. 73; Fairvale Ltd v Sabharwal [1992] 2 E.G.L.R. 27. But a trade custom or usage may be used to interpret a contract, provided that it is not inconsistent with the express terms: Caine v Horsefall (1847) 1 Exch. 519; Allan v Sundius (1862) 1 H. & C. 123; Parker v Ibbetson (1858) 4 C.B.(N.S.) 346.

[30] Kofi Sunkersette Obu v Strauss & Co [1951] A.C. 243, Illustration 1.

[31] Marshall v Parsons (1841) 9 C. & P. 656; Williamson v Hine Bros [1891] 1 Ch. 390.

[32] fn.30 above; Re Richmond Gate Property Co Ltd [1965] 1 W.L.R. 335, where the articles of a company provided (from Table A in the Companies Act 1948) for "such remuneration as the directors may determine". This was held to exclude any implied term because the contract provided expressly for the directors to determine the sum payable and any implied term would have been contrary to the express terms.

[33] Way v Latilla [1937] 3 All E.R. 759, Illustration 3; Powell v Braun [1954] 1 W.L.R. 401; Gross Fine & Krieger Chalfen v Clifton (1974) 223 E.G. 837; Harding Maughan Hambly Ltd v CECAR [2000] 1 Lloyd's Rep. 316.

[34] As to the amount, see Cohen v Paget (1814) 4 Camp. 96; Rucker v Lunt (1863) 3 F. & F. 959; Great Western Insurance Co v Cunliffe (1874) L.R. 9 Ch.App. 525; Baring v Stanton (1876) 3 Ch.D. 502; Stubbs v Slater [1910] 1 Ch. 632; Campbell v National Trust Co Ltd [1931] 1 D.L.R. 705 (PC); Hugh V. Allen & Co v A. Holmes Ltd [1969] 1 Lloyd's Rep. 348; Harding Maughan Hambly Ltd v C.E.C.A.R., above. As to the conditions, see Broad v Thomas (1830) 7 Bing. 99; Hall v Benson (1836) 7 C. & P. 711; Burnett v Bouch (1840) 9 C. & P. 620.

[35] See Mirror Group Newspapers Plc v Maxwell (No.2) [1998] 1 B.C.L.C. 638.

[36] For a full discussion of this topic in connection with estate agents, see Murdoch, Law of Estate Agency (5th edn), p.134 onwards.

[37] See Article 31.

[38] Upsdell v Stewart (1793) Peake 255 (in which a surveyor attempted to prove a trade custom that he

in order to ascertain the value which each of them put upon the services.[39] It has been suggested that where the agent performs services which are not geared to producing particular results, the sum should be ascertained on the basis of time and trouble, unless a custom incorporating a scale can be established; but that where an agent employed to achieve results achieves those results, assessment of a reasonable sum by reference to a scale may be more appropriate.[40]

7-006   **Fiduciaries**   The fiduciary nature of the agent's functions may mean that he cannot charge for other services without the informed consent of the person or persons to whom the fiduciary duty is owed.[41] There are equitable[42] and statutory[43] exceptions to this rule, often concerning solicitors. Until 2013, barristers had no legal right to receive remuneration for services rendered in an official capacity.[44] Where an agent's remuneration turns on variable factors, such as number of hours worked, then equity will exercise supervision over the agent's rendering of costs to the principal.[45]

7-007   **Estate agents**   Under s.18 of the Estate Agents Act 1979 a person who enters into a contract with another under which the agent will engage in estate agency work must give the client certain information regarding the remuneration payable and other sums (such as advertising and other expenses) which may become payable.[46] If he does not do so, the contract is unenforceable except pursuant to an order of

---

was entitled to 5 per cent of the cost of the works. Of this custom, Lord Kenyon said: "as to the custom offered to be proved, the course of robbery on Bagshot Heath might as well be proved in a court of justice"); *Footner v Joseph* (1859) 3 L.C.J. 233; affd 5 L.C.J. 225 (Canada); *Debenham v King's College, Cambridge* (1884) 1 T.L.R. 170; *Brocklebank v Lancashire & Yorkshire Ry Co* (1887) 3 T.L.R. 575; *Drew v Josolyne* (1888) 4 T.L.R. 717 (in which Lord Coleridge said that he would never sanction surveyors being paid not with reference to the work done but on a percentage of the amount involved. A similar view was expressed by Younger J in *Faraday v Tamworth Union* (1917) 86 L.J.Ch. 436, Illustration 5); *Farthing v Tomkins* (1893) 9 T.L.R. 566; *Wilkie v Scottish Aviation Ltd* 1956 S.C. 198, Illustration 4. See also *Gibbon v Pease* [1905] 1 K.B. 810 (custom that architect can retain plans after payment unreasonable); *Att.-Gen. v Drapers' Company* (1869) L.R. 9 Eq. 69; *Buckland and Garrard v Pawson & Co* (1890) 6 T.L.R. 421; *Turner v Reeve* (1901) 17 T.L.R. 592; *Re Wolfe* [1952] 2 All E.R. 545; *Frank Swain v Whitfield Corp Ltd* (1962) 183 E.G. 479; *Graham & Baldwin v Taylor, Son & Davis* (1965) 109 S.J. 793.

39   *Way v Latilla* [1937] 3 All E.R. 759, Illustration 3, following *Scarisbrick v Parkinson* (1869) 20 L.T. 175; *Berezovsky v Edmiston & Co Ltd* [2011] EWCA Civ 431 at [53].

40   *Murdoch* [1981] Conv 424, doubting the cases cited at Illustration 10.

41   e.g. *Sheriff v Axe* (1827) 4 Russ. 33 (commission agent became executor); *Williams v Barton* [1927] 2 Ch. 9 (stockbroker's clerk was trustee); cf. *Douglas v Archbutt* (1858) 2 De G. & J. 148 (trustee acted as auctioneer); and see *Bath v Standard Land Co Ltd* [1911] 1 Ch. 618; *Re Northcote's Will Trusts* [1949] 1 All E.R. 442 (charge for getting in foreign assets allowable by foreign law). See in general Articles 43–48; Finn, *Fiduciary Obligations* (1977), pp.206–208.

42   The rule in *Cradock v Piper* relating to solicitor trustees: see Snell, *Equity* (33rd edn), para.7-028; Cordery, *Solicitors* (8th edn), pp.177–178.

43   Rules made under the Insolvency Act 1986.

44   See *Kennedy v Broun* (1863) 13 C.B.(N.S.) 677; *Broun v Kennedy* (1864) 4 De G.J. & S. 217, affirming 33 Beav. 133; *Re May* (1858) 4 Jur.(N.S.) 1169; *Wells v Wells* [1914] P. 157; *Re Sandiford (No.2)* [1935] Ch. 681. See now Standard Contractual Terms for the Supply of Legal Services by Barristers to Authorised Persons 2012, and the Code of Conduct of the Bar of England and Wales.

45   See *Mirror Group Newspapers Plc v Maxwell (No.2)* [1998] 1 B.C.L.C. 638. See also Article 51.

46   "Estate agency work" is defined in s.1; it only covers some of the functions normally performed by estate agents. The notice must be in writing: Estate Agents (Provision of Information) Regulations 1991 (SI 1991/859) reg.4 (made under s.30 of the Act). See *Foxtons Ltd v Bicknell* [2008] EWCA Civ 419; [2008] 24 E.G. 142; [2008] N.P.C. 52 (noted Watts [2009] J.B.L. 268).

the court.[47] The time at which the information must be given is specified by regulation.[48] This legislative scheme has generated a body of case law which is not fully analysed in this work.[49] There are some uncertainties with it. Hence, it is not altogether clear how the scheme applies to the classic estate agent's agreement, which involves a unilateral offer by the client, and under which the agent enters into no contract until he earns his commission by introducing a purchaser or something similar.[50] The Act contemplates a contract being made before the agent commences work.

Unfair Terms in Consumer Contracts Regulations 1999[51]   Some commission agreements in consumer contracts may be caught by these, for example if a higher sum is due on late payment.[52]

7-008

Quantum meruit where no contractual right   If services are rendered by the agent not pursuant to a contract, but they were freely accepted by the principal with full knowledge, or (perhaps) from which he incontrovertibly benefits, the courts may, on principles of restitution, award a reasonable sum to the agent as remuneration on a quantum meruit.[53] The leading case is now *Benedetti v Sawiris*,[54] confirming that the basis of the action is unjust enrichment, even if it is arguable that the rejection in this context of the older approach based on implied contract is doctrinaire. Recourse to the law of restitution is likely if the contract under which the services were rendered was a nullity or was subsequently rescinded[55] or made

7-009

---

[47] As to the court's discretion see: *Benhams Ltd v Kythira Investments Ltd* [2004] EWHC 2973; *Great Estates Group Ltd v Digby* [2011] EWCA Civ 1120; [2012] 2 All E.R. (Comm) 361; *Wells v Devani* [2016] EWCA Civ 1106; [2017] 2 W.L.R. 1391. In *Ian Greenhill Residential Ltd v Asfari* [2007] EWHC 1491 (QB) at [96] it was held that the 1979 Act was not inconsistent with the existence of an implied term as to remuneration, but the agreement would not be enforceable without the court's consent. On the facts no agreement as to remuneration was established.

[48] Estate Agents (Provision of Information) Regulations 1991 reg.3(1): "when communication commences between the estate agent and the client or as soon as is reasonably practicable thereafter provided it is at a time before the client is committed to any liability towards the estate agent".

[49] See in general Murdoch, *The Estate Agents and Property Misdescriptions Acts 1979* (3rd edn); *Law of Estate Agency* (5th edn); below, paras 7-020 and 7-038.

[50] See below, para.7-015.

[51] SI 1999/2083.

[52] *Bairstow Eves London Central Ltd v Smith* [2004] EWHC 263; [2004] 2 E.G.L.R. 25. But the basic commission charge would not be so subject, by virtue of cl.6(2) of the Regulations. For an example of a penal provision before the Regulations see *Chris Hart (Business Sales) Ltd v Mitchell* 1996 S.C.L.R. 68.

[53] See *Benedetti v Sawiris* [2013] UKSC 50; [2014] A.C. 938; noted Virgo [2013] C.L.J. 508; McInnes (2014) 130 L.Q.R. 8; Mitchell [2013] L.M.C.L.Q. 436. See, more generally, Goff and Jones, *Law of Unjust Enrichment* (9th edn), para.1-06, and Ch.17. In some of the authorities quantum meruit is used to describe a claim in contract for a reasonable sum due under an implied term of that contract. It is probably preferable to avoid this terminology, which may lead to confusion between a claim under a contract and a claim in restitution where no contract exists and may, further, cause the normal principles for the implication of terms into a contract to be overlooked. cf. below, para.7-024. See also *Accidia Foundation v Simon C. Dickinson Ltd* [2010] EWHC 3058 (Ch) (remuneration to sub-agent by way of equitable allowance in an account).

[54] *Benedetti v Sawiris* [2013] UKSC 50; [2014] A.C. 938.

[55] *Faraday v Tamworth Union* (1917) 86 L.J.Ch. 436, Illustration 5. This case may be difficult to reconcile with the earlier Scottish case of *Boyd & Forrest v Glasgow & SW Ry Co*, 1915 S.C. 20 (HL) (reported also as a note in [1915] A.C. 526). See also *Proactive Sports Management Ltd v Rooney* [2011] EWCA Civ 1444 at [122] (agency contract void as being in restraint of trade of the principal; quantum meruit not governed by the contractual rate); *Times Travel (UK) Ltd Not-*

without authority (ratification being impossible),[56] or it contained terms so vague or uncertain as to make it unenforceable,[57] or the parties provided that remuneration shall be such as they shall subsequently agree but they thereafter fail to reach agreement.[58] However, agency services performed in the simple hope that a contract on commission may eventuate will not normally meet the requirements for a quantum meruit.[59] Nor will a quantum meruit be awarded when to do so would undermine statutory policy.[60] The starting point for setting the rate of remuneration under a quantum meruit is the reasonable or market value of the services. In some circumstances, it might be possible for the recipient of the services to devalue that rate, but it will be rare for above-market rates to be awarded even if there is evidence that under some circumstances, such as a now abandoned contract, the recipient might have been prepared to pay more than market rate[61]; those other circumstances may have reflected bad judgement on the recipient's part, and if the provider of the services has not cemented the terms in contract he has not secured the windfall.

7-010 **Contractual right** This situation must, of course, be distinguished from that in which P asks A to perform a service and A does so. Request and performance will normally create a contract and, subject to the considerations discussed above, reasonable remuneration will be payable pursuant to an implied term of that contract rather than give rise to a claim upon a quantum meruit in restitution. Equally, the contract may itself provide for reasonable remuneration where for some reason commission is not earned.[62]

7-011 **Commercial agents** The Commercial Agents (Council Directive) Regulations

---

tingham Travel (UK) Ltd v Pakistan International Airlines Corp [2017] EWHC 1367 (Ch) at [262] (variation of travel agents' commission contract voidable for economic duress).

[56] *Craven-Ellis v Canons Ltd* [1936] 2 K.B. 403. See also *William Lacey (Hounslow) Ltd v Davis* [1957] 1 W.L.R. 932.

[57] See *Turner v Webster*, 24 Kan. 38 (1880) for a clear illustration of this principle, which was considered in a wider context in *Scammell v Ouston* [1941] A.C. 251. See also *Jaques v Lloyd D. George & Partners Ltd* [1968] 1 W.L.R. 625, where the contract was void for uncertainty and no remuneration was payable, and *John Meacock & Co v Abrahams* [1956] 1 W.L.R. 1463, Illustration 9.

[58] *Loftus v Roberts* (1902) 18 T.L.R. 532; *Benourad v Compass Group Plc* [2010] EWHC 1882 (QB) at [132] (insufficient evidence of value adduced). The courts will be keen to find a contract if they can by implying reasonable terms, especially when the parties have proceeded a long way under the supposed contract: *F. & G. Sykes (Wessex) Ltd v Fine Fare Ltd* [1967] 1 Lloyd's Rep. 53. But cf. *Courtney & Fairbairn Ltd v Tolaini Bros (Hotels) Ltd* [1975] 1 W.L.R. 297; *Mallozzi v Carapelli SpA* [1975] 1 Lloyd's Rep. 229; *Whittle Movers Ltd v Hollywood Express Ltd* [2009] EWCA Civ 1189 at [15]. See also *Hillas & Co Ltd v Arcos Ltd* (1932) 38 Com.Cas. 23; *May & Butcher v R.* (1929) reported [1934] 2 K.B. 17n.; *Foley v Classique Coaches Ltd* [1934] 2 K.B. 1; *British Bank of Foreign Trade Ltd v Novinex* [1949] 1 K.B. 623; *National Coal Board v Galley* [1958] 1 W.L.R. 16; *Luanda Exportadora v Wahbe Tamari* [1967] 2 Lloyd's Rep. 353 at 361.

[59] *MSM Consulting Ltd v United Republic of Tanzania* [2009] EWHC 121 (QB); *Becerra v Close Brothers Corporate Finance Ltd* [1999] EWHC 289 (Comm); *Moran Yacht & Ship Inc v Pisarev* [2014] EWHC 1098 (Comm); [2014] 2 Lloyd's Rep. 88 at [91]; affd [2016] EWCA Civ 317; [2016] 1 Lloyd's Rep. 625 (claimant attempting to assist defendant sell yacht so latter would be in position to buy other yacht for which claimant had an agency). cf. *Cooke v Hopper* [2012] EWCA Civ 175 (investigatory work collateral to otherwise gratuitous assistance awarded quantum meruit).

[60] See *Langsam v Beachcroft LLP* [2011] EWHC 1451 (Ch) at [253] (appealed on other points, [2012] EWCA Civ 1230).

[61] *Benedetti v Sawiris* [2013] UKSC 50; [2014] A.C. 938.

[62] See Illustration 10; below, para.7-024.

1993 provide in some detail for remuneration of commercial agents in the absence of agreement.[63] The Regulations are discussed in Chapter 11.

Illustrations

(1) A company engaged A to act as its agent for the purchase and shipment of rubber to the company. The contract of engagement provided that:

> "the company has agreed to remunerate my services with a monthly sum of fifty pounds ... A commission is also to be paid to me ... which I have agreed to leave to the discretion of the company."

7-012

A claimed a commission on all rubber purchased by him for the company. The Privy Council held that it could not determine the basis and rate of commission and that to do so would be to vary the existing contract by transferring to the court the exercise of a discretion vested in the company.[64]

(2) A entered into an agreement which provided:

> "I hereby agree to enter your service as a weekly manager, and the amount of payment I am to receive I leave entirely for you to determine."

He served in that capacity for six weeks. It was held that he was entitled, in an action on a quantum meruit, to recover such an amount as the employer, acting in good faith, ought to have awarded.[65]

(3) A alleged that he had agreed with P that he should send P information relating to gold mines and concessions in Africa and that P should give him a reasonable share in the same and pay a reasonable sum for the information. Held, there was no concluded contract between the parties as to the amount of the share and the court could not complete the contract for the parties, but that there was an employment contract between the parties which clearly indicated that A was not to work gratuitously; a term would be implied under which A was entitled to reasonable remuneration. In fixing the amount, the court could have regard to the negotiations between the parties in order to ascertain what value they had themselves placed upon the service.[66]

(4) W was employed by S to act as valuer, adviser and witness in arbitration proceedings. No provision was made for his fees. After the work was completed W prepared a bill of charges, made up in accordance with the Scale of Professional Charges of the Royal Institution of Chartered Surveyors, amounting to £3,009. S paid him £1,000 and he sued for the balance. Held, fees would be payable according to the Scale if it was customary to pay according to the Scale and if the resulting fee was reasonable. If W could not

---

[63] reg.6(1).
[64] *Kofi Sunkersette Obu v Strauss & Co* [1951] A.C. 243. See also *Taylor v Brewer* (1813) 1 M. & S. 290; *Roberts v Smith* (1859) 4 H. & N. 315; *Mann v Shell Petroleum Ltd* [1961] C.L.Y. 1440; *Re Richmond Gate Property Co Ltd* [1965] 1 W.L.R. 335. But cf. *Sudbrook Trading Estate Ltd v Eggleton* [1983] 1 A.C. 444.
[65] *Bryant v Flight* (1839) 5 M. & W. 114. The basis of the decision is obscure. See also *Peacock v Peacock* (1809) 2 Camp. 45; *Jewry v Busk* (1814) 5 Taunt. 302; *Bird v M'Gahey* (1849) 2 C. & K. 707; *Powell v Braun* [1954] 1 W.L.R. 401 where it was clear that the parties intended a reasonable sum to be paid.
[66] *Way v Latilla* [1937] 3 All E.R. 759.

prove the incorporation of the Scale by custom the court would fix a reasonable fee.[67]

(5) F was employed by the defendants to act as surveyor for them in connection with an arbitration. The contract provided that he should be paid a percentage fee on Ryde's Scale of Professional Charges, but as a result of an innocent misrepresentation by the defendants, F thought that his percentage would be based on the entire amount in issue whereas the contract provided that it should be based only on the defendants' share. Held, (i) the contract could be rescinded by F for the defendants' innocent misrepresentation; (ii) F was entitled to reasonable remuneration on a quantum meruit; (iii) such remuneration was to be fixed in accordance with the work actually done and not on a percentage of values. Ryde's Scale was therefore ignored.[68]

(6) A engages an auctioneer to sell property on his behalf. It is implied that A is to pay the auctioneer the usual and reasonable commission.[69]

(7) A contract provided that an agent should receive commission on all sales effected or orders executed by him. By a custom of the trade, no commission was payable in respect of bad debts. It was held that the agent was entitled to commission on all sales effected by him, including those resulting in bad debts, the trade custom being inconsistent with the express terms of the contract.[70]

(8) P employed A to find a purchaser or mortgagee for property. A introduced N to P and negotiations started between them. These negotiations flagged and P agreed with A that A should write N a letter and that if N made an advance or purchased *in consequence* of the letter P would pay A £100. N purchased but gave evidence that he was not influenced by the letter. It was held that A was entitled to no remuneration since (i) the subsequent agreement had replaced the original agreement; (ii) the terms of the subsequent agreement left no room for a claim on a quantum meruit; and (iii) the event specified in the subsequent agreement had not taken place.[71]

(9) P, a second mortgagee, gave A instructions to sell the property by auction. The contract between P and A provided that if a sale was effected between the date of receipt of instructions and the date of the auction, commission was payable on the same scale as for a sale by auction. On the day before the auction the mortgagor redeemed the mortgages and sold the property himself. Held, (i) A was not entitled to commission since the event on which commission was due had not taken place; (ii) no claim on a contractual quantum meruit lay because P had received no advantage and the contract provided for the events on which payment became due.[72]

(10) An agent introduces suitable purchasers to a prospective vendor, but takes no

---

[67] *Wilkie v Scottish Aviation Ltd* 1956 S.C. 198.
[68] *Faraday v Tamworth Union* (1917) 86 L.J.Ch. 436.
[69] *Miller v Beale* (1879) 27 W.R. 403. As to the remuneration of auctioneers on a sale by the court, and the relevant practice, see *Re Wolfe, Heller v Wolfe* [1952] 2 All E.R. 545 and CPR 40 PD 40D.
[70] *Bower v Jones* (1831) 8 Bing. 65; cf. *Caine v Horsefall* (1847) 1 Exch. 519; and see *Read v Rann* (1830) 10 B. & C. 438; *Broad v Thomas* (1830) 7 Bing. 99; *Harley v Nagata* (1917) 34 T.L.R. 124. And see Article 58.
[71] *Green v Mules* (1861) 30 L.J.C.P. 343. This decision may today be regarded as somewhat harsh.
[72] *John Meacock & Co v Abrahams* [1956] 1 W.L.R. 1463. See also *Fairvale Ltd v Sabharwal* [1992] 2 E.G.L.R. 27; cf. *Bernard Marcus & Co v Ashraf* [1988] 1 E.G.L.R. 7; Murdoch, *Law of Estate Agency and Auctions* (4th edn), pp.144–147.

part in negotiations. The relevant scale provides commission for "seeking and negotiating" but not for seeking and finding without negotiating. It also provides for quantum meruit on "abortive work". Remuneration may be assessed on the basis of trouble taken, at considerably less than the scale fee.[73]

(11) An agent entitled to, and paid, commission upon a binding contract being made irrespective of completion, which contract fell through, was not entitled to a further commission when he effected a second sale, since there was no fresh written contract for the second sale as required by local law.[74]

Article 56

AGENTS' REMUNERATION DUE UPON THE HAPPENING OF AN EVENT

(1) Where an agent is entitled to his remuneration upon the happening of a future event, his entitlement does not arise until that event has occurred.   **7-013**

(2) The event upon which the agent's entitlement to remuneration arises is to be ascertained from the terms of the agency contract.

(3) Where the event upon which the agent's entitlement to remuneration arises does not occur, the agent will not be entitled to receive remuneration on a quantum meruit unless provision for this is expressly made in the agency contract, or unless a term to such effect can be implied into the agency contract in order to give it business efficacy or otherwise to give effect to the intentions of the parties.[75]

Comment

General rule   This Article should be read in conjunction with Articles 57 and 58.   **7-014** The rule stated above is fundamental to the remuneration of the large number of agents who are paid by way of a commission on transactions which they bring about for their principals. The commission may be payable on many separate transactions, as in the case of a selling agent,[76] or it may be payable on a single transaction, as in the case of an estate agent acting for a private vendor. The principle stated is, however, of general application.[77] The agent must prove that the event has oc-

---

[73] *Sinclair Goldsmith v Minero Peru Comercial* [1978] E.G.D. 194, following *Reif Diner & Co v Catalytic International Inc* (1978) 246 E.G. 743. See also *Hoddell v Smith* [1976] E.G.D. 217; *Hampton & Sons v Trade and General Securities Ltd* (1978) 250 E.G. 451; *Lewis & Graves v Harper* (1978) 250 E.G. 1287. But see Murdoch [1981] Conv. 424 and *Law of Estate Agency* (5th edn), p.124 onwards; above, para.7-005. See further *Debenham Tewson & Chinnocks v Rimington* [1990] 2 E.G.L.R. 21; *Michael Elliott & Partners Ltd v UK Land Plc* [1991] 1 E.G.L.R. 39; *Cooke v Hopper* [2012] EWCA Civ 175 at [42].

[74] *Icon Property Pty Ltd v Wood* [2008] VSCA 123.

[75] See Comment. The Article was cited with approval in *Berkeley Community Villages Ltd v Pullen* [2007] EWHC 1330 (Ch); [2007] N.P.C. 71 at [106].

[76] See, e.g. *Lockwood v Levick* (1860) 8 C.B.(N.S.) 603. *Del credere* commission is due and payable, in the absence of any special terms to the contrary, as soon as the contract is made in respect of which it is claimed: *Solly v Weiss* (1818) 8 Taunt. 371; *Caruthers v Graham* (1811) 14 East 578.

[77] *Lara v Hill* (1863) 15 C.B.(N.S.) 45; *Alder v Boyle* (1847) 4 C.B. 635; *Horford v Wilson* (1807) 1 Taunt. 12; *Platt v Depree* (1893) 9 T.L.R. 194; *Passingham v King* (1898) 14 T.L.R. 392; *Re Sovereign Life Assce. Co, Salter's Claim* (1891) 7 T.L.R. 602; *Skinner v Andrews & Hall* (1910) 26 T.L.R. 340; but cf. *Peacock v Freeman* (1888) 4 T.L.R. 541. Many of the early cases must be regarded with caution in view of the leading decision in *Luxor (Eastbourne) Ltd v Cooper* [1941] A.C. 108, e.g. *Fisher v Drewett* (1878) 48 L.J.Ex. 32; *Fuller v Eames* (1892) 8 T.L.R. 278; *Green v*

curred upon which remuneration becomes due. What that event is is a question of law to be determined from the construction of the terms of agency contract.

> "It is a settled rule for the construction of commission notes and the like documents which refer to the remuneration of an agent that a plaintiff cannot recover unless he shows that the conditions of the written bargain have been fulfilled. If he proves fulfilment he recovers. If not, he fails. There appears to be no halfway house, and it matters not that the plaintiff proves expenditure of time, money and skill."[78]

In most instances the question whether the event has occurred presents no great difficulties. For example, if the agent is engaged to bring about a contract for his principal his entitlement to commission will arise if and when the contract is made. He has then done what he was engaged to do. However, owing largely to the number of stages involved in a contract for the purchase of real property, the commission of an estate agent has been the subject of many decisions in the courts; the estate agent frequently wishes to earn his commission at a stage earlier than at which his principal enters into the contract the agent was engaged to bring about. Rule (3) may not apply where principal and agent effectively enter upon a new engagement, to which the former arrangements for commission are not applicable.[79]

7-015 **Estate agents**[80]   Much of the law on entitlement to commission derives from cases of the 1950s and 1960s relating to estate agents. But "commission contracts are subject to no peculiar rules or principles of their own; the law which governs them is the law which governs all contracts and all questions of agency".[81] There are, therefore, no special rules of law relating to estate agents' contracts although the application to these of some of the basic principles of the law of contract has given rise to a considerable body of case law which can, making due allowances, be applied also in other contexts.

7-016 **Nature of estate agent's contract**   The nature of the estate agent's contract was analysed by Lord Russell of Killowen in *Luxor (Eastbourne) Ltd v Cooper*.[82] He said that:

> "contracts by which owners of property, desiring to dispose of it, put it in the hands of agents on commission terms, are not (in default of specific provisions) contracts of employment in the ordinary meaning of those words. No obligation is imposed on the agent to do anything. The contracts are merely promises binding on the principal to pay a sum of money upon the happening of a specified event, which involves the rendering of some service by the agent. There is no real analogy between such contracts, and

---

Lucas (1876) 33 L.T. 584; *Vulcan Car Agency Ltd v Fiat Motors Ltd* (1915) 32 T.L.R. 73; and the dicta on substantial performance in *Rimmer v Knowles* (1874) 30 L.T. 496.

[78]   *Howard Houlder & Partners Ltd v Manx Isles SS Co* [1923] 1 K.B. 110 at 113–114, per McCardie J; *Coupers Partnership Ltd v Basarik* [2007] EWCA Civ 40; [2007] R.V.R. 116.

[79]   See, e.g. *Benedetti v Sawiris* [2013] UKSC 50; [2014] A.C. 938.

[80]   See Murdoch, *Law of Estate Agency* (5th edn), Ch.3 (also discussing commission and remuneration of auctioneers). The nature of the estate agent's contract was considered in detail, and the then relevant cases reviewed, in Ash, *Willing to Purchase* (1963).

[81]   *Luxor (Eastbourne) Ltd v Cooper* [1941] A.C. 108 at 124, per Lord Russell of Killowen (Illustration 1 to Article 58).

[82]   Above.

contracts of employment by which one party binds himself to do certain work, and the other binds himself to pay remuneration for the doing of it."[83]

The normal estate agent's contract is therefore said to be a unilateral contract, the agent not being bound to do anything if he does not wish to do so. A "sole" or "exclusive" agency agreement is however said to raise a bilateral contract. There are difficulties of analysis which are discussed below.[84]

Entitlement to commission Whenever an estate agent claims his remuneration   **7-017**
the court must determine, as a matter of construction of the particular agency contract concerned, whether the event has occurred upon which the agent's entitlement to remuneration accrues:

> "No general rule can be laid down by which the rights of the agent or the liability of the principal under commission contracts are to be determined. In each case these must depend upon the exact terms of the contract in question, and upon the true construction of those terms."[85]

A useful statement of the relevant principles is that of Jenkins LJ in *Midgley Estates Ltd v Hand*[86]:

> "So far as any general principle is deducible from the authorities, their effect may, I think, be thus summarised: The question depends on the construction of each particular contract, but prima facie the intention of the parties to a contract of this type is likely to be that the commission stipulated for should only be payable in the event of an actual sale resulting ... That is, broadly, speaking, the intention which, as a matter of probability, the court should be disposed to impute to the parties. It follows that general or ambiguous expressions, purporting, for instance, to make the commission payable in the event of the agent 'finding a purchaser' or ... 'selling the property,' have been construed as meaning that the commission is only to be payable in the event of an actual and completed sale resulting, or, at least, in the event of the agent succeeding in introducing a purchaser who is able and willing to purchase the property. That is the broad general principle in the light of which the question of construction should be approached; but this does not mean that the contract, if its terms are clear, should not have effect in accordance with those terms, even if they do involve the result that the agent's commission is earned and becomes payable although the sale in respect of which it is claimed, for some reason or another, turns out to be abortive."

Clear and unambiguous words must, therefore, be used if the commission is to be payable without an actual sale taking place,[87] since it is "the common understanding of men ... that the agent's commission is payable out of the purchase price".[88] A comparable understanding may make a sub-agent's entitlement to commission

---

[83] [1941] A.C. 108 at 124.
[84] See Comment to Article 58.
[85] *Luxor (Eastbourne) Ltd v Cooper* [1941] A.C. 108 at 124, per Lord Russell of Killowen.
[86] [1952] 2 Q.B. 432 at 435–436.
[87] See also *Luxor (Eastbourne) Ltd v Cooper* [1941] A.C. 108 at 129. The contra proferentem rule was applied in *Price, Davies & Co v Smith* (1929) 141 L.T. 490 at 494; *Jaques v Lloyd D. George & Partners Ltd* [1968] 1 W.L.R. 625 at 632; *Block Bros Realty Ltd v Viktora* (1974) 42 D.L.R. (3d) 474. See also *Mustafa v K.G. Palos* [1972] E.G.D. 797.
[88] *Dennis Reed Ltd v Goody* [1950] 2 K.B. 277 at 284, per Denning LJ; *H.W. Liebig & Co v Leading Investments Ltd* [1986] 1 S.C.R. 70 at 79–82; (1985) 25 D.L.R. (4th) 161 at 176–179. (But an argument, based on this statement, that a contract contained an implied term that the estate agent was entitled to commission from the purchase money held by the vendor's solicitor was rejected in *W.A. Ellis Services Ltd v Stuart Wood* [1993] 2 E.G.L.R. 43.) See also *Jaques v Lloyd D. George*, above,

contingent on the agent's entitlement, or even actual collection by the agent of commission from the principal, though express words would be needed to achieve a pay-if-paid result.[89] A similarly narrow approach to the question whether agents' services *caused* a sale has recently been taken by the Court of Appeal.[90]

But as fast as the courts have held that one particular formula will not entitle the agent to commission before the contract of sale is made, so have estate agents devised new formulae in an endeavour to achieve this result. The reported cases are therefore no more than illustrations of the strict criteria which the courts have applied, and many of the contractual formulae used in them must be regarded as obsolete in so far as they clearly will not achieve what the agent generally desires to do, viz., to secure his right to commission as soon as he produces someone who shows a serious interest in buying the property. It must also be remembered that in the purchase of real property in England and Wales the contractual arrangements have, unlike a normal commercial contract, traditionally fallen into three distinct stages:

(1) *Agreement "subject to contract"*. The third party makes an offer "subject to contract" or "subject to survey" and, if this is accepted, pays a deposit to the estate agent. This transaction is not normally, in law, a contract to purchase the property and either party is free to withdraw from further negotiations for any, or even no, reason.[91]

(2) *Contract*. The parties sign and, normally through their solicitors, exchange contracts. From the moment of exchange of contracts, but not until then, they are contractually bound to each other[92] (subject to the ordinary rules, such as those relating to void and voidable contracts).

(3) *Completion*. This is normally effected through solicitors. The vendor's solicitor transmits the title deeds to the purchaser's solicitor in exchange for a banker's draft for the balance of the purchase price with an adjustment for outgoings from the date of contract.

The estate agent generally wants to be entitled to his commission at stage (1); the courts have rarely held that he is entitled to it before stage (2) and sometimes even not until stage (3).

In a work of this nature it is not appropriate to consider every reported case in which an estate agent has claimed commission and, indeed, there is a very large

---

where Lord Denning MR said that if the agency contract provided for payment of commission other than on the conclusion of business, it was the agent's duty to inform his principal; if not, the agent might be unable to recover. This statement goes further than other cases and may be difficult to reconcile with the general principle that a person is presumed to have read his contract. The contract provided that commission was payable if the agent should be "instrumental in introducing a person willing to sign a document capable of becoming a contract to purchase at a price which at any stage of the negotiations has been agreed" by the prospective vendor. The court held that these words were too vague to be enforceable: they could cover signature of a blank piece of paper.

[89] *Crema v Cenkos Securities Plc* [2010] EWCA Civ 1444; [2011] 1 W.L.R. 2066, reversing [2010] EWHC 461 (Comm).

[90] *Foxtons Ltd v Bicknell* [2008] EWCA Civ 419; [2008] 24 E.G. 142; [2008] N.P.C. 52, noted by Watts [2009] J.B.L. 268. See further Article 57.

[91] *Chillingworth v Esche* [1924] 1 Ch. 97; *Eccles v Bryant* [1948] Ch. 93. But as to "subject to survey" and "subject to satisfactory survey", see *Astra Trust v Adams* [1969] 1 Lloyd's Rep. 81, doubted in *The Merak* [1976] 2 Lloyd's Rep. 250 at 254; *Ee v Kakar* (1979) 40 P. & C.R. 223; and in general Treitel, *Law of Contract* (14th edn), paras 2-087–2-088.

[92] *Eccles v Bryant*, above.

number of such cases.[93] All that is possible is to consider some of the leading cases in which forms of wording then common were used, in order thereby to illustrate the general principle. This Article is therefore not accompanied by Illustrations: it has seemed better to incorporate them into the exposition. It should be noted also that differences and developments in conveyancing practice, and in the functions of an estate agent, lead to differences between jurisdictions. For example, in some countries an estate agent may be expected to procure a purchaser's signature to the contract and take a deposit.[94]

Introduction of a "purchaser"　　The simplest practical form of estate agent's **7-018** contract provides that commission shall be payable on the "introduction of a purchaser".[95] Sometimes the agent is merely asked to "find a purchaser"[96] or to "find someone to buy".[97] In these cases there must, it seems, be a binding contract to purchase before there can be any question of entitlement to commission.[98] Moreover, if after contract and before completion the purchaser withdraws for any reason, the agent's entitlement will (unless specific performance is obtained[99]) be lost because the person introduced was not a "purchaser".[100] On the other hand, if the *vendor* defaults after contract but before completion, the agent's entitlement is normally not lost; the vendor may not rely upon the fact that it was his own wrong vis-à-vis the person introduced which prevented the contract from proceeding to

---

[93]　See Murdoch (1982) 264 E.G. 419 at 513. Almost all the older cases of importance were examined in Ash, *Willing to Purchase* (1963). For another account of the modern law see Murdoch, *Law of Estate Agency* (5th edn), p.83 onwards.

[94]　See, e.g. *Pemberton v Action Realty Ltd* [1986] 1 N.Z.L.R. 286.

[95]　*Jones v Lowe* [1945] K.B. 73. As to the meaning of "introduce", see *D.C. Wylde & Co v Sparg* 1977 (2) S.A.L.R. 75: in the context the word meant: "to direct the attention of a person who has not applied his mind in that direction to the fact that a property is for sale, or to a material element of the sale not previously appreciated by him". See also *John D. Wood & Co v Dantata* [1987] 2 E.G.L.R. 23 at 25, per Nourse LJ ("the leading or bringing in of the purchaser to that transaction"); *Peter Yates & Co v Bullock* [1990] 2 E.G.L.R. 24; *Estafnous v London & Leeds Business Centres Ltd* [2009] EWHC 1308 (Ch) at [53]; affd [2011] EWCA Civ 1157 (introduction does not require personal contact between vendor and purchaser) A clause entitling to commission on introduction will not in the absence of other indications entitle to commission on introductions effected before the making of the contract providing for commission: *Samuel & Co v Sanders Bros* (1886) 3 T.L.R. 145.

[96]　*Fowler v Bratt* [1950] 2 K.B. 96.

[97]　*McCallum v Hicks* [1950] 2 K.B. 271. See also *Alder v Boyle* (1847) 4 C.B. 635; *Lott v Outhwaite* (1893) 10 T.L.R. 76; *Chapman v Winson* (1904) 91 L.T. 17; *Henry v Gregory* (1905) 22 T.L.R. 53; *Timms v Carofaro* (1989) 53 S.A.S.R. 572 ("effect a sale … substantially the transaction contemplated by the contract").

[98]　See *McCallum v Hicks*, above; *James v Smith* (1921) [1931] 2 K.B. 317n; *Blake & Co v Sohn* [1969] 1 W.L.R. 1412; *Phillipson v Indus Realty Pty. Ltd* (2004) 8 V.L.R. 446 ("subject to completion of sale"). But the right to commission is not lost because the parties later vary the contract: *Lord v Trippe* (1977) 51 A.L.J.R. 574.

[99]　See *Boots v E. Christopher & Co* [1952] 1 K.B. 89 at 98 where Denning LJ also suggests that if the vendor sues, and obtains full damages including commission payable to the agent, commission would be due. In *H.W. Liebig & Co v Leading Investments Ltd* [1986] 1 S.C.R. 70 at 86; (1985) 25 D.L.R. (4th) 161 at 181–182 LaForest J suggests that the agent may in such a case be entitled to some form of restitutionary award. But the vendor is not bound to sue and may settle the case: ibid.

[100]　*James v Smith*, above; *Martin v Perry and Daw* [1931] 2 K.B. 310; *Poole v Clarke & Co* [1945] 2 All E.R. 445. If the contract expressly or impliedly provides that commission is to be paid out of the purchase price, no commission will be due if the purchase price is not paid: *Bull v Price* (1831) 5 M. & P. 2; *Martin v Tucker* (1885) 1 T.L.R. 655; *Beningfield v Kynaston* (1887) 3 T.L.R. 279; *Knight, Frank & Rutley v Gordon* (1923) 39 T.L.R. 399; *Price, Davies & Co v Smith* (1929) 141 L.T. 490; *Boots v E. Christopher & Co* [1952] 1 K.B. 89. See also *Fidcott v Friesner* (1895) 11 T.L.R. 187; *Foster's Agency Ltd v Romaine* (1916) 32 T.L.R. 545.

completion.[101] If a purchaser withdraws from a contract owing to the vendor's misrepresentation, the agent, it seems, will not normally be entitled to commission due solely upon a binding contract being made,[102] but the vendor may be liable to the agent for damages for breach of an implied term in the contract of appointment that he will not make fraudulent misrepresentations to the purchaser.[103] Many forms of commission contract provide extending definitions of the word "purchaser" to include direct and indirect links between the person introduced and the actual purchasers.[104]

7-019   Introduction of a person "ready, willing and able to purchase"   Use of the above expressions was unsatisfactory to those agents who wanted to be entitled to their commission at an earlier stage than exchange of contracts. Accordingly, some agents provided that their commission was to be earned on the introduction of a person who was "ready, willing and able to purchase".[105] Sometimes one or more of the adjectives was dropped (e.g. a person "willing and able to purchase"[106]). It does not matter what adjectives are used; the principle which the courts have applied in the construction of such contracts is the same. The agent must prove that the person he introduced fulfilled the qualifications provided in the contract.

At first, commission was fairly readily awarded to the agent on such wording,[107] but in the 1950s it became clear that the courts would apply a strict test to decide whether the agent's entitlement had arisen. In *Graham and Scott (Southgate) Ltd v Oxlade*[108] the Court of Appeal held that if a prospective purchaser made an offer which was subject to any conditions, such as "subject to contract" or "subject to survey", this showed that he was not "willing to purchase" because he had reserved for himself a *locus poenitentiae*. Only an unqualified offer, capable of acceptance by the vendor, would show that the prospective purchaser was "willing". Shortly afterwards, in *Dennis Reed Ltd v Goody*,[109] the Court of Appeal repeated its decision in *Oxlade*'s case, holding that a person who made a conditional offer

---

[101] *Luxor (Eastbourne) Ltd v Cooper* [1941] A.C. 108 at 126, 142; *Dennis Reed Ltd v Goody* [1950] 2 K.B. 277 at 285. See also *Alpha Trading Ltd v Dunnshaw-Patten Ltd* [1981] Q.B. 290, Illustration 3 to Article 58. But cf. *Adler v Ananhall Advisory & Consultancy Services Ltd* [2009] EWCA Civ 586; [2009] N.P.C. 80 (commission only upon completion).

[102] *Peter Long & Partners v Burns* [1956] 1 W.L.R. 1083; *John D. Wood & Co (Residential and Agricultural) Ltd v Craze* [2007] EWHC 2658 (QB); [2008] 1 E.G.L.R. 17: [2008] 6 E.G. 132; [2007] 50 E.G. 108 (C.S.); [2007] N.P.C. 130.

[103] *John D. Wood & Co (Residential and Agricultural) Ltd v Craze*, above (noted by Watts [2009] J.B.L. 268).

[104] See, e.g. *Christie Owen & Davies Plc v Raobgle Trust Corp* [2011] EWCA Civ 1151.

[105] See, e.g. *Keningtons v Regional Properties Ltd* [1946] E.G.D. 86; *Dennis Reed Ltd v Nicholls* [1948] 2 All E.R. 914; *Lewis & Tucker v Lee* (1949) 153 E.G. 342; *Bennett & Partners v Millett* [1949] 1 K.B. 362; *Berry Estates v Burgess* (1949) 153 E.G. 343; *Brown & Co v Michaels* (1949) 153 E.G. 511; *E.P. Nelson & Co v Rolfe* [1950] 1 K.B. 139; *E.P. Nelson v Lyons* (1949) 154 E.G. 376; *Murdoch Lownie v Newman* [1949] 2 All E.R. 783; *Dennis Reed Ltd v Goody* [1950] 2 K.B. 277.

[106] *Graham & Scott (Southgate) Ltd v Oxlade* [1950] 2 K.B. 257.

[107] See, e.g. *Dennis Reed Ltd v Nicholls* [1948] 2 All E.R. 914; *Bennett & Partners v Millett* [1949] 1 K.B. 362; *Knight, Frank and Rutley v Fraser* 1974 S.L.T. 50.

[108] [1950] 2 K.B. 257. This involved overruling *Giddys v Horsfall* [1947] 1 All E.R. 460; *Bennett & Partners v Millett* [1949] 1 K.B. 362; and probably by implication disapproving of some of the reasoning in *Dennis Reed Ltd v Nicholls* [1948] 2 All E.R. 914. This latter case was regarded as overruled by Denning LJ in *Dennis Reed Ltd v Goody* [1950] 2 K.B. 277 at 289. Another inconsistent decision, *E.P. Nelson & Co v Rolfe* [1950] 1 K.B. 139 was explained as having turned on a concession.

[109] [1950] 2 K.B. 277. A month later the Court of Appeal held in *Bennett, Walden & Co v Wood* [1950] 2 All E.R. 134 that an offer "subject to contract" did not entitle the agent to commission when the

to purchase was not shown to be "willing" to purchase. This strict approach was subsequently followed. In *Dellafiora v Lester*[110] where, after contract, the vendor's landlord refused to consent to the assignment of the lease to the person introduced and the parties did not proceed further, the Court of Appeal held that this showed that the person introduced was not "able" to purchase and the agent was therefore not entitled to commission. In *Christie, Owen & Davies v Stockton*[111] the contract provided that commission should be payable if, inter alia, the vendor withdrew "after having accepted an offer to purchase by a person able and willing to enter into a formal contract". The agents introduced a person and a price was agreed "subject to contract". During negotiations the vendor withdrew. Slade J held that the agent was not entitled to commission. The language was not clear and unequivocal and there were no agreed terms since the whole matter was "subject to contract". Under these circumstances the principle of *Oxlade*'s case applied. A rather similar attempt to claim commission failed in *A.L. Wilkinson Ltd v Brown*.[112] Commission was due on the introduction of a person "prepared to enter into a contract to purchase" at an agreed price. A person was introduced and a price "agreed" but the offer to purchase was conditional on the potential purchaser selling his own house. Before contract the vendor sold elsewhere. The Court of Appeal held that there was only an expectancy that a contract would be signed and that there was therefore no introduction of a suitably qualified person.

In the above cases the agent failed because the event upon which the commission became due had not occurred. That event was defined by the contract as being the introduction of a person having certain qualifications ("ready, willing and able to purchase"). The person introduced did not have those qualifications and the commission thus had not become due. Whether the person introduced did have those qualifications is a question of fact and if the agent does introduce such a person, he is entitled to his commission even if no sale contract is thereafter concluded because the potential vendor declines to enter into a contract with that person. Thus in *Christie Owen & Davies Ltd v Rapacioli*[113] the defendant instructed the plaintiff agents to help him find a purchaser of his business and to quote a price of £20,000. The agency contract provided that commission was payable in the event of the plaintiffs "effecting an introduction either directly or indirectly of a person ... ready able and willing to purchase [for £20,000] or any other price". The plaintiffs introduced a person who was prepared to purchase for £17,700 and this offer was accepted "subject to contract". The parties' solicitors thereafter negotiated and a draft contract was prepared, engrossed and signed by the potential purchaser. The defendant then decided to proceed no further with the sale. The

---

agency contract provided that commission was due when the agent "secured an offer".

[110] [1962] 1 W.L.R. 1208. The form of wording in the case was unusual, but the case was decided on whether the potential purchaser was "able". The Court of Appeal expanded the definition given in earlier cases in which it had suggested that the ability to purchase related to financial ability; the potential purchaser must be "able" in every way.

[111] [1953] 1 W.L.R. 1353.

[112] [1966] 1 W.L.R. 194. See also *Gerlach v Pearson* [1950] V.L.R. 321 ("secure a purchaser": offer "subject to finance": no commission due).

[113] [1974] Q.B. 781. The court followed *A.L. Wilkinson Ltd v O'Neil* (1961) 181 E.G. 137. See also John E. Trinder & Partners v Haggis (1951) 158 E.G. 4 (not cited in the *Christie* case but decided on similar principles). The court declined to follow *Martin, Gale & Wright v Buswell* [1961] E.G.D. 418 in view of the different grounds of decision given by the court. See also *Walters v John Crisp Pty Ltd* (1982) 64 F.L.R. 299 (Aus.) ("if you or anyone else obtains a person who is ready, willing and able to purchase the property ... a full fee is payable to the listing agent").

Court of Appeal held that the plaintiffs were entitled to succeed in their claim to commission. The person whom they had introduced was willing to contract with the defendant in terms acceptable to him until the moment of his withdrawal. The court expressly approved a passage from the judgment of Bucknill LJ in *Dennis Reed Ltd v Goody*,[114] who said:

> "... the plaintiffs' claim to commission is not established merely by showing that the person whom they introduced was able and willing to purchase the property at any one particular moment of time: they must prove that he was ready, able and willing to purchase up to the time when either an enforceable contract for the purchase of the house is made between the parties or, alternatively, up to the time when the vendor refuses to enter into such a contract on terms on which the purchaser is willing to purchase and the vendor was at one time willing to sell."[115]

It should be noted that the wording of the contract in *Rapacioli*'s case was particularly precise. Although there were suggestions in the judgments that some of Lord Denning's earlier dicta may have gone too far, it is not clear that this is so.[116]

The problem raised by this case is that the prospective purchaser's willingness must be measured against some terms on which he is to be "willing to purchase". In theory it might be possible to specify in the agency contract all the terms which the prospective purchaser must be willing to accept; only if he agreed to those terms would he be a "willing" purchaser for the purposes of the agency contract. But in practice this would be unacceptable in view of the fact that negotiations between prospective purchaser and prospective vendor are inevitable. Furthermore, neither party would be willing to accept such provisions before the market has been tested. The prospective purchaser's willingness has therefore been tested by the courts against the terms on which the prospective vendor is prepared to sell. The difficulty is that the "subject to contract" situation is not a simple offer and acceptance situation; at any time until exchange of contracts the prospective vendor can change the terms on which he is prepared to sell and his willingness is thus only a temporary willingness until that time. The most that can be said is that until exchange of contracts the prospective vendor has expressed the view that in due course he will be willing to sell on certain terms provided that he does not change his mind thereafter. In holding that the prospective purchaser's willingness may be tested against terms which at one time the prospective vendor was prepared to accept, the court was referring only to this temporary manifestation of preparedness to accept which could at any time be altered vis-à-vis the prospective purchaser. A conclusive willingness can only be tested at the moment of exchange of contracts because it is only at this moment that it is known what the prospective vendor's terms are, and thus whether the prospective purchaser is "willing to purchase" on those terms. The Court of Appeal was therefore prepared to look for a willingness on the part of the prospective vendor for the purposes of the agency contract which was not yet a willingness to sell for the purposes of the sale contract.

These difficulties had been foreseen by Denning LJ (as he then was) in *McCallum v Hicks*.[117] He said:

> "A person may not properly be said to be 'willing' to purchase, so as to entitle the agent

---

[114] [1950] 2 K.B. 277.
[115] [1950] 2 K.B. 277 at 283.
[116] See *H.W. Liebig & Co v Leading Investments Ltd* [1987] 1 S.C.R. 70 at 82; (1986) 25 D.L.R. (4th) 161 at 179, per LaForest J.
[117] [1950] 2 K.B. 277.

to commission, unless he is irrevocably willing, that is, unless he has given irrevocable proof of his willingness by entering into a binding contract to purchase."[118]

Only then could the prospective purchaser be said to be "willing to purchase" on terms acceptable to the prospective vendor. This remark of Denning LJ was expressly disapproved by the Court of Appeal in *Christie Owen & Davies Ltd v Rapacioli*,[119] as was a similar statement by the same judge in *Dennis Reed Ltd v Goody*.[120] A problem of a similar nature had also arisen indirectly in *Ackroyd & Sons v Hasan*[121]: the agents' contract there provided that their commission was due in the event of their introducing "a party prepared to enter into a contract to purchase [on certain terms set out in the agency contract] or on such other terms to which [the vendor might] assent". The terms of sale were agreed "subject to contract" between the potential purchaser's and the potential vendor's solicitors, but the vendor had not yet agreed to what her solicitors had negotiated. She withheld this agreement and no contract was ever made. The Court of Appeal held that, on the facts, the agents had failed to prove that the vendor had assented to the terms. At first instance, Winn J had said[122] that in his view "assent" meant legally binding assent. In the Court of Appeal Upjohn and Ormerod LJJ expressed their strong disagreement with this view.[123] Upjohn LJ said that whether the vendor had assented[124] was "purely a question of fact" and that, for example, it could be strongly argued that a vendor could be shown to assent by having signed his part of the contract notwithstanding that he withdrew before exchange. Sellers LJ,[125] however, was not satisfied that Winn J's view was wrong or that commission could be due where the assent of the vendor fell short of communicated assent so as to conclude a contract. He reserved consideration of this question until it might arise on another set of facts. The view of the majority of the court was that which was later accepted in *Christie Owen & Davies v Rapacioli*.[126] The court in that case recognised that a situation might well arise where the potential vendor might well have to pay two commissions, one to the agent who introduced a person who was willing to purchase on terms on which the principal had at one time been willing to sell but from which he had withdrawn, and another to the agent through whom he finally sold. Such a conclusion in this

---

[118] [1950] 2 K.B. 277 at 276.
[119] [1974] Q.B. 781 at 787, 790, 791. But see *H.W. Liebig & Co v Leading Investments Ltd*, above.
[120] [1950] 2 K.B. 277 at 287–288.
[121] [1960] 2 Q.B. 144.
[122] [1959] 1 W.L.R. 706 at 712: " ... in that context the word assent means: finally 'assent' at the last moment of time at which you, the property owner, will be entitled, when the negotiations have proceeded to that final stage, to say: 'These are the terms precisely to which I give my concluded and considered assent'. I do not think it permissible to construe in favour of the estate agent and against the property owner in such a contract as this the word 'assent' as meaning: 'give a half-considered assent on the basis that it seems at the moment to be all right, but possibly with a mental reservation, due to advice received from the solicitor, that there is no final commitment on this matter until the time comes for exchanging the formal contracts'."
[123] [1960] 2 Q.B. 144 at 156 (Upjohn LJ), 162 (Ormerod LJ).
[124] In *Martin Gale & Wright v Buswell* [1961] E.G.D. 418 Upjohn LJ made it clear that what the vendor's solicitor had "agreed" with the potential purchaser's solicitor was not the "assent" which had to be proved since the solicitor, in the absence of express authority could not bind his client. What had to be proved was that the vendor assented to the draft contract prepared by the solicitor.
[125] [1960] 2 Q.B. 144 at 166–167.
[126] *Christie Owen & Davies v Rapacioli* [1974] Q.B. 781.

context seems however at variance with the statement of Lord Wright in *Luxor (Eastbourne) Ltd v Cooper*[127] that:

> "the commission agreement is, however, subordinate to the hoped for principal agreement of sale. It would be strange if what was preliminary or accessory should control the freedom of action of the principal in regard to the main transaction which everyone contemplates might never materialise."

Where however the agent does introduce a person who signs an offer to purchase, but at the time he does so the principal has already accepted an offer from another buyer introduced by another agent, it has been held that no commission is due, on the basis that the right to commission is subject to an implied restriction that the property has not already been sold. This implication is a natural one for most transactions.[128]

7-020 Estate Agents (Provision of Information) Regulations 1991[129] By these Regulations, an estate agent using in the course of estate agency work[130] the phrase "ready, willing and able purchaser" must explain the intention and effect of these words in writing in a way described in the Regulations.[131] Failure to comply with this obligation makes the contract unenforceable except by order of the court.[132] The explanation required is as follows:

> "A purchaser is a 'ready, willing and able' purchaser if he is prepared and is able to exchange unconditional contracts for the purchase of your property.
>   You will be liable to pay remuneration to us, in addition to any other costs or charges agreed, if such a purchaser is introduced by us in accordance with your instructions and this must be paid even if you subsequently withdraw and unconditional contracts for sale are not exchanged, irrespective of your reasons."[133]

Where the contract wording varies, the explanation must be given with appropriate modifications.[134] It may be that this requirement, in calling for clearer drafting, will avoid in the future some of the difficulties of the past. The older cases must, however, be noted as examples of the problems to be avoided. It should be noted that the explanation given by the regulations, while inappropriate to estate agents seeking *tenants*, is more favourable to the estate agent than some of the judicial decisions on similar wording.[135]

7-021 Other types of estate agent contracts Some of the difficulties discussed above

---

127 [1941] A.C. 108 at 138–139.
128 *A.A. Dickson & Co v O'Leary* (1979) 254 E.G. 731, following *E.P. Nelson & Co v Rolfe* [1950] 1 K.B. 139 on this point. But it is certainly possible for a vendor to be liable for two commissions: below, para.7-029.
129 SI 1991/859, made under s.30(1) of the Estate Agents Act 1979.
130 As to which see Estate Agents Act 1979 s.1; Murdoch, *Law of Estate Agency and Auctions* (4th edn), p.266 onwards; and in general Murdoch, *The Estate Agents and Property Misdescriptions Acts* (3rd edn).
131 reg.5.
132 Estate Agents Act 1979 s.18(5). Such a contract was enforced in *Benhams Ltd v Kythira Investments Ltd* [2004] EWHC 2973.
133 Regulations 1991 Schedule. The definition clause defines "purchaser" as "a person to whom an interest in land is transferred or in whose favour it was created". In *Foxtons Ltd v Thesleff* [2005] EWCA Civ 514; [2005] 2 E.G.L.R. 29 it was held that this covered a person who contracted unconditionally to buy, and also that the Regulations could not affect the proper meaning of the contract entered into.
134 reg.5(1) (2). As to the time at which notice must be given, see regs 3, 5(3).
135 It does not require that the transaction proceeds as far as the exchange of contracts. See Murdoch,

have been avoided where the agent has stipulated for his commission upon the introduction by him of a person who signs or enters into a legally binding contract to purchase. The event here is clearly defined, even if it may not be sufficiently advanced in time to please all estate agents. Thus, in *Midgley Estates Ltd v Hand*[136] and *Scheggia v Gradwell*[137] the agents were held entitled to their commission although, in the former case, the purchaser withdrew after contract and, in the latter, the contract that was signed would not have been enforced by specific performance. In each case the event, the signature of a legally binding contract, had occurred. On the other hand, in *Peter Long & Partners v Burns*[138] the agents' claim to commission failed because the contract was voidable due to an innocent misrepresentation. They had therefore not introduced a person who had entered into a legally binding contract. Another format entitles the agent to commission if he introduces a person "with whom we have not been in prior communication, and who subsequently completes" a contract. This avoids problems of effective cause[139] and appears effective.[140] Where commission contracts with different terms are used, this may result in two commissions being payable.[141] Where the person or group introduced subsequently completes the transaction by means of a newly formed company, subsidiary or syndicate, it may be held that the person introduced has completed the purchase, though by means of others,[142] subject to considerations of effective cause.[143]

The most satisfactory way for the agent to ensure that he becomes entitled to his commission upon an introduction seems to be to avoid all references to the ultimate contract or to purchasers. Thus in *Drewery and Drewery v Ware-Lane*[144] the agents' contract provided that commission was to be due when a "prospective purchaser" signed the agents' "purchaser's agreement" and the vendor signed the agents' "vendor's agreement" (both supplied by the agents). Both these documents were "subject to contract" but both were signed. The Court of Appeal held that the agents

---

Law of Estate Agency and Auctions (3rd edn), pp.205–206.

[136] [1952] 2 Q.B. 432; and see *Foxtons Ltd v Thesleff* [2005] EWCA Civ 514; [2005] 2 E.G.L.R. 29.

[137] [1963] 1 W.L.R. 1049. In *A.L. Wilkinson Ltd v Brown* [1966] 1 W.L.R. 194 at 202–203. Salmon LJ described the *Scheggia* type of contract as "a ridiculous bargain" and said that the scope of that decision ought not to be extended. See also *Jaques v Lloyd D. George & Partners Ltd* [1968] 1 W.L.R. 625 at 632; para.7-017, above.

[138] [1956] 1 W.L.R. 1083; cf. *Chris Hart (Business Sales) Ltd v Currie* 1992 S.L.T. 544 (concluded contract conditional on transfer of licence of public house by licensing board; licence not transferred; commission due). Even a vendor's fraudulent misrepresentation will not entitle the agent to commission on an otherwise unconditional contract. The vendor may, however, be liable to the agent for damages on an implied term: *John D. Wood & Co (Residential and Agricultural) Ltd v Craze* [2007] EWHC 2658 (QB); [2008] 1 E.G.L.R. 17; [2008] 6 E.G. 132; [2007] 50 E.G. 108 (C.S.); [2007] N.P.C. 130 (noted [2009] J.B.L. 268).

[139] See Article 57.

[140] *Brian Cooper & Co v Fairview Estates (Investments) Ltd* [1987] 1 E.G.L.R. 18. See also *Raja v Rollerby Ltd* (1997) 74 P. & C.R. D25 ("in case of selling the above properties to your clients at the sum of £750,000 your commission will be 2 per cent. This offer is valid until the end of this week"); *Glentree Estates Ltd v Favermead Ltd* [2010] EWCA Civ 1473 at [17] (express entitlement to commission even if vendor himself finds purchaser implies that no need for agent to be effective cause of sale when the agent effects an introduction).

[141] See, e.g. *Lordsgate Properties Ltd v Balcombe* [1985] 1 E.G.L.R. 20; *Bernard Marcus & Co v Ashraf* [1988] 1 E.G.L.R. 7 (auctioneer); *Peter Yates & Co v Bullock* [1990] 2 E.G.L.R. 24. It is also possible that there may be two effective causes: *Lordsgate Properties Ltd v Balcombe*, above: see below, para.7-029.

[142] *Di Dio Nominees Pty Ltd v Brian Mark Real Estate Pty Ltd* [1992] 2 V.R. 732.

[143] *Gunn v Showell's Brewery Co Ltd* (1902) 50 W.R. 659, Illustration 12 to Article 57.

[144] [1960] 1 W.L.R. 1204.

were entitled to their commission notwithstanding that the prospective purchaser was unable to obtain a mortgage and so never entered into a contract to purchase. The court held that the expression "prospective purchaser" did not require that the person introduced must be ready, willing or able but simply that he must bona fide contemplate purchasing.[145] This condition had been fulfilled. But in *Mustafa v K.G. Palos*[146] the contract provided that commission was payable to a mortgage broker in the event of "an offer of mortgage" on terms set out in the agency contract. The agent found a building society which offered to grant a mortgage but the prospective vendor then withdrew from the sale negotiations. The Court of Appeal held that commission was not due because an "offer of mortgage" meant an offer which actually led to a mortgage.

7-022   **Custom**[147]   Just as custom cannot entitle an agent to commission where it is unreasonable or contrary to the express terms of the contract,[148] it also cannot debar an agent from commission where it is unreasonable, or where the terms of the contract entitle the agent to commission.[149]

7-023   **Conclusion**   The cases discussed in this Comment are no more than illustrations of the criteria applied. It cannot be too strongly emphasised that each case falls to be decided with reference to the general principles:

> "first, when an agent claims that he has earned the right to commission, the test is whether upon the proper interpretation of the contract between the principal and agent the event has happened upon which commission is to be paid. Secondly, there are no special principles of construction applicable to commission contracts with estate agents. Thirdly, contracts under which a principal is bound to pay commission for an introduction which does not result in a sale must be expressed in clear language."[150]

7-024   **Claims for work done when commission not earned**   In the nineteenth century it was commonly thought that if an agent was prevented from earning his commission he was nevertheless entitled to receive a reasonable sum on a quantum meruit[151]; but, as was frequently also pointed out,[152] such suggestions were contrary to principle. A claim for a contractual quantum meruit of the type envisaged must

---

[145] Even this difficulty could, it seems, have been overcome by substituting "person" in the agency contract for "prospective purchaser".

[146] [1972] E.G.D. 797. The principles expressed in this case seem entirely at variance with those expressed in *Christie Owen & Davies Ltd v Rapacioli* [1974] Q.B. 781 although the two cases can, perhaps, be reconciled on their particular facts and contractual terms. On "obtain an offer", see *Cash v George Dundas Realty Ltd* [1976] 2 S.C.R. 796; (1975) 59 D.L.R. (3d) 605; on "arrange a mortgage", see *Capital Management Corp v Hackett Development* (1971) 18 F.L.R. 362; and on "subject to our offer being accepted", see *Richard Ellis v Pipe-Chem (Holdings) Ltd* [1981] E.G.D. 222.

[147] See Article 31.

[148] See above, para.3-037.

[149] *Les Affréteurs Reunis Société Anonyme v Leopold Walford (London) Ltd* [1919] A.C. 801. See too *Crema v Cenkos Securities Plc* [2010] EWHC 461 (Comm).

[150] *Ackroyd & Sons v Hasan* [1960] 2 Q.B. 144 at 154, per Upjohn LJ.

[151] The expression quantum meruit is used in at least two different senses in the cases: (i) to describe a claim in restitution: see above, para.7-009; (ii) to describe a claim in contract for a reasonable sum. Such a claim must be based on an express or implied term in the agency contract. In many of the older authorities no distinction is made between the two different uses of the expression and it is often not clear to which the court intended to refer. The matter is further complicated because the courts have sometimes been referring to the principle expressed in *Planché v Colburn* (1831) 8 Bing. 14 that in certain circumstances, where an innocent party has rendered services under a contract which

be based on an implied contractual term that a reasonable sum is payable in the circumstances. Where the contract expressly provides for remuneration on the happening of an event, any such implication would be contrary to this express term and so could not be made. "It was said that there was an implied contract to pay the agent a quantum meruit for his services. The answer was that there could be no implied contract when there was an express contract".[153] The principle is, perhaps, most clearly to be found in *Howard Houlder & Partners Ltd v Manx Isles SS Co*[154] and *Bentall, Horsley & Baldry v Vicary*.[155] In the latter case an estate agent claimed on a quantum meruit when the vendor sold the property himself, although the agent had been appointed the sole agent. McCardie J held that the principal was not in breach of contract. Of the agent's claim on a quantum meruit he said[156]:

> "Undoubtedly ... [the agent] did work and incurred expense. But this is quite a usual feature of an estate agent's vocation when he works under a commission note which only gives him a right to recover commission when he fulfils the terms of the note. He runs the risk of losing his labour and expense unless he can comply with the conditions of the bargain. There is no scope in the present case for the operation of the doctrine of quantum meruit."

It may, however, be that the intention of the parties was that the principal should pay the agent a reasonable sum if the event upon the happening of which remuneration was due did not occur. The contract may make express provision to this effect.[157] Alternatively, the implication of a term to this effect might be necessary to give business efficacy to the contract or otherwise to effect the clear intention of the parties. But it is clear that such an implication would only be made in the most exceptional cases.[158]

Overpaid commission   Sometimes advance payments of commission exceed the   **7-025**
amounts actually due when the contract is terminated. In such a case it is a matter

---

has been terminated by him because of the other party's breach, he may waive the claim for breach of contract and sue in restitution on a quantum meruit to recover a reasonable sum for his services: cf. Goff and Jones, *Law of Unjust Enrichment* (9th edn), para.5-40. Because the principle depends essentially on breach of contract and termination, it is doubtful whether it can have any application to the typical estate agent's contract, which is unilateral.

[152] See, e.g. *Martin v Tucker* (1885) 1 T.L.R. 655; *Peacock v Freeman* (1888) 4 T.L.R. 541; *Barnett v Isaacson* (1888) 4 T.L.R. 645; *Re Sovereign Life Assce. Co, Salter's Claim* (1891) 7 T.L.R. 602; *Lott v Outhwaite* (1893) 10 T.L.R. 76.

[153] *Lott v Outhwaite*, above, at p.141, per Lindley LJ.

[154] [1923] 1 K.B. 110.

[155] [1931] 1 K.B. 253. *Berkeley Community Villages Ltd v Pullen* [2007] EWHC 1330 (Ch); [2007] N.P.C. 71 at [104] onwards.

[156] [1931] 1 K.B. at 262. See also for more modern examples *Fairvale Ltd v Sabharwal* [1992] 2 E.G.L.R. 27; and *Ian Greenhill Residential Ltd v Asfari* [2007] EWHC 1491 (QB).

[157] See, e.g. *Sinclair Goldsmith v Minero Peru Comercial* [1978] E.G.D. 194; *Reif Diner & Co v Catalytic International Co* (1978) 246 E.G. 743, Illustration 10 to Article 55. For the amount payable see para.7-005, above.

[158] See, e.g. *Firth v Hylane Ltd* [1959] E.G.D. 212. The agency contract there provided that if the agent could find a purchaser willing to purchase the property for £35,000 he would receive £1,000 commission. This figure for commission was admitted to be high and in the nature of a bonus. The property was eventually sold for £31,000 to a person introduced by the agent. The Court of Appeal said it did not make sense for the agent to be paid nothing if the property fetched less than £35,000 and held that the parties had merely defined how the commission was to be quantified. They had, therefore, not excluded payment of a reasonable sum for work done by the agent at the principal's request. The court awarded £450 plus £100 expenses. See also *Boots v E. Christopher & Co* [1952] 1 K.B. 89 at 98–99; Article 58.

of interpretation of each contract whether there is or is not an implication that such overpayments must be repaid.[159]

7-026 **Commercial agents** The Commercial Agents (Council Directive) Regulations 1993 contain provisions as to entitlement to commission.[160] These are discussed in Chapter 11.

Article 57

WHETHER AGENT IS EFFECTIVE CAUSE OF TRANSACTION

7-027 Subject to any special terms or other indications in the contract of agency, where the remuneration of an agent is a commission on a transaction to be brought about, he is not entitled to such commission unless his services were the effective cause of the transaction being brought about.[161]

Comment

7-028 The principle stated in this Article is no more than a particular example of the wider principle stated in the preceding Article, and it has recently been stressed that there are contracts to which it does not apply.[162] But there exists a body of cases on the notion of "effective cause" which is sufficiently discrete to require segregation. Where the agent is to be remunerated upon the happening of an event, the question whether that event has occurred depends upon the facts of the case and the express or implied terms of the agency contract. Many agents are employed upon terms that if a certain transaction is brought about, they will be entitled to a commission calculated by reference to the amount of the consideration passing in that transaction or to a stated fee. Sometimes the transaction is carried out but has not been brought about as a result of the agent's efforts. Sometimes the agent has played a part in bringing about the transaction but only a small part, or he has only achieved a partial success.

Sometimes the principal has carried out a different transaction from the one the agent was employed to bring about but the substitute transaction was nevertheless the result of the agent's efforts. For example, an agent may have been employed to find a purchaser for a house. He introduces a person who is only willing to take a long lease of the house and the principal thereafter decides to grant such a lease rather than sell. Has the agent earned his commission? The matter may take a more complicated form. For example, an agent is employed to find a purchaser for part of the business being carried on by the principal. He introduces a potential purchaser, but after direct negotiations between the principal and the potential purchaser, the two of them agree to establish a new company with the principal as minority shareholder and transfer the business to that company in exchange for

---

[159] See *Rivoli Hats Ltd v Gooch* [1953] 1 W.L.R. 1190; *Clayton Newbury, Ltd v Findlay* [1953] 1 W.L.R. 1194 (Note); *Bronester Ltd v Priddle* [1961] 1 W.L.R. 1294; *Prudential Assurance Co Ltd v Rodriguez* [1982] 2 N.Z.L.R. 54. See *D.O. Ferguson & Associates v Sohl* (1992) 62 Build.L.R. 95; Birks, in *Consensus ad Idem* (Rose ed., 1996), p.199.

[160] regs 7–12.

[161] See Comment, esp. para.7-029 as to "the" or "an"; *Murdoch* (1985) 276 E.G. 742 and 877.

[162] *Freedman v Union Group Plc* [1997] E.G.C.S. 28; *Raja v Rollerby Ltd* (1997) 74 P. & C.R. D25, per Evans LJ; *Watersheds Ltd v Simms* [2009] EWHC 713 (QB); *Edmond De Rothschild Securities (UK) Ltd v Exillon Energy Plc* [2014] EWHC 2165 (Comm) at [25].

shares. The final transaction is different in substance from the sale the agent was employed to achieve but was carried out in substitution for that sale without the agent having caused or even been aware of the change. Has the agent earned his commission?

The answers to these questions depend upon the express or implied terms of the relevant agency contract. But a large number of them interpret the agent's contract in connection with a sale on the basis that to be entitled to commission the agent must be the, or at least an, effective cause of the sale. This seems to result:

"from the use in the agency agreements of expressions such as 'find a purchaser' or 'introduce a purchaser' … It would have been quite artificial to suppose that the parties intended that the agent should earn his commission simply by finding an individual who, independently of any further action by the agent, later agreed to buy the subject property."[163]

Where the contract is in such terms as "You are employed to find a purchaser of the property," the above result flows as a result of a constructional implication.[164] Where there is no such term, the implication will only be made to give business efficacy to the contract.[165] Where the ultimate transaction is different from and carried out in substitution for the contract which the agent was employed to bring about, the same implication will be made and the court will ask whether the agent was the effective cause of the particular transaction which the principal entered into.[166] The fact of a substitute transaction may be evidence of a break in the chain of causation. But it should be noted that in some cases the terms of the contract or the nature of the transaction mean that there is no room for this implication.[167]

An agency involving "sole selling rights" within the Estate Agents (Provision of Information) Regulations 1991 Schedule, does not require that the agent has been an effective cause of the transaction before being entitled to commission.[168]

---

[163] *Doyle v Mr. Kidston Mining and Exploration Pty Ltd* [1984] 2 Qd.R. 386 at 392, per McPherson J; *MSM Consulting Ltd v United Republic of Tanzania* [2009] EWHC 121 (QB) at [139]; *Benourad v Compass Group Plc* [2010] EWHC 1882 (QB) at [123]. In *The County Homesearch Co (Thames & Chilterns) Ltd v Cowham* [2008] EWCA Civ 26; [2008] 1 W.L.R. 909 at [16], per Longmore LJ it was tentatively accepted that the presumption of the need for cause may be weaker where the agent is acting for a purchaser. Sed quaere; see Watts [2009] J.B.L. 268.

[164] This is probably the explanation of *Favermead Ltd v FPD Savills* [2002] EWHC 626 (Ch), though the implication was described as an implied term. A winding-up petition by estate agents claiming commission was restrained by injunction on the basis that the question whether there was such an implication was arguable.

[165] See above, para.7-001.

[166] *Gunn v Showell's Brewery Co Ltd* (1902) 18 T.L.R. 659, Illustration 12; *Burchell v Gowrie and Blockhouse Collieries Ltd* [1910] A.C. 614; *Price Davies & Co v Smith* (1929) 141 L.T. 490; *Stewarts & Lloyds Ltd v Zoess, The Times,* July 5, 1955 (HL); *Jack Windle Ltd v Brierley* [1952] 1 All E.R. 398 (doubted [1981] E.G.D. at 245); *Chamberlain and Willows v HBS (Trust) Ltd* [1952] E.G.D. 443; *Poulter v Doggett* (1964) 115 L.J. 76; *Allen v Anderson* [1969] N.Z.L.R. 951; *Levers v Dunsdon* [1968] E.G.D. 280. But cf. *Estafnous v London & Leeds Business Centres Ltd* [2011] EWCA Civ 1157, Illustration 13.

[167] See *David Leahy (Aust.) Pty Ltd v McPhersons Ltd* [1991] 2 V.R. 367, Illustration 18; *Brian Cooper Ltd v Fairview Estates (Investments) Ltd* [1987] 1 E.G.L.R. 18. Also the definition of "sole selling rights" in the Estate Agents (Provision of Information) Regulations 1991 Schedule, does not seem to require effective cause.

[168] *Dashwood v Fleurets Ltd* [2007] EWHC 1610 (QB) at [43].

7-029   **General principle**   This is well stated in *Millar, Son & Co v Radford*[169] where the defendant employed the plaintiff to find a purchaser of property or, failing that, a tenant. A tenant was found and commission was paid. Fifteen months later the tenant purchased the property and the plaintiff claimed commission on the sale although he had not been concerned with the property since the letting. In holding that the plaintiff was not entitled to commission Collins MR said[170]:

> "It is important to point out that the right to commission does not arise out of the mere fact that agents had introduced a tenant or purchaser. It is not sufficient to show that the introduction was a causa sine qua non. It is necessary to show that the introduction was an efficient[171] cause in bringing about the letting or the sale. Here the plaintiffs fail to establish what is a condition precedent to their right to commission—viz., that they have brought about the sale. It is open to the defendant[172] in an action like this to say either that, though the plaintiffs effected a sale, they were not his agents, or that, though they were his agents, they had not effected the sale. If the defendant proves either the one or the other, the plaintiffs fail to make out their case."[173]

7-030   **"The" or "an"?**   There is doubt as to whether the rule is more helpfully formulated by requiring that the agent's act be "the effective cause" or merely "an effective cause". The word "the" is used in this Article: but it should be noted that in various places, including the passage quoted in the paragraph above, the indefinite article "an" is used.[174] It is certainly true that the agent can be entitled to his commission though there are other events which could be called causes of the transaction. In some cases the introduction is crucial.[175] Thus if the agent introduces a person who becomes the purchaser "it is nothing to the point … that that person would have become the purchaser without the intervention of the agent, or that the principal's own efforts were also an effective cause of the sale".[176] But it is submitted that it is the word "effective" which is the most significant.

> "'Effective cause' means more than simply 'cause'. The inquiry is whether the actions of the agent really brought about the relation of buyer and seller, and it is seldom conclusive

---

[169] (1903) 19 T.L.R. 575. For cases on almost identical facts, see *Toulmin v Millar* (1887) 58 L.T. 96, Illustration 4; *Nightingale v Parsons* [1914] 2 K.B. 621. See too *Seakom Ltd v Knowledgepool Group Ltd* [2013] EWHC 4007 (Ch) at [96].

[170] (1903) 19 T.L.R. 575 at 576.

[171] The word "efficient" has changed its meaning since 1903. The modern equivalent is "effective" (see, e.g. *Allan v Leo Lines Ltd* [1957] 1 Lloyd's Rep. 127 at 133).

[172] The burden of proving entitlement to commission rests on the agent throughout. By using the expression "it is open to the defendant" Collins MR can mean no more than that the defendant may assert; the plaintiff agent must, of course, disprove the assertions. See *Pettigrew v George Wimpey UK Ltd* [2007] EWHC 2559 (QB) at [48] (onus on claimant to show effective cause of sale).

[173] The passage has, for the sake of clarity, been altered from the indirect speech of the original report to direct speech.

[174] See also *Burchell v Gowrie and Blockhouse Colleries Ltd* [1910] A.C. 614 at 624, where both phrases are used.

[175] See *Allan v Leo Lines Ltd* [1957] 1 Lloyd's Rep. 127 per Devlin J.

[176] *L.J. Hooker Ltd v W.J. Adams Estates Pty Ltd* (1977) 138 C.L.R. 52 at 58, per Barwick CJ. For an example see *Doyle v Mt. Kidston Mining & Exploration Pty Ltd* [1984] 2 Qd.R. 386. Both cases are discussed by Waller LJ in *Nahum v Royal Holloway, etc., College* [1999] E.M.L.R. 252, Illustration 20; *Seascape Capital Services Ltd v Anglo-Atlantic SS Co Ltd* [2002] EWHC (Comm) 1277; [2002] 2 Lloyd's Rep. 611. But cf. *Lichtenstein v Clube Atletico Mineiro* [2005] EWHC 1300 (Q.B.).

that there were other events which could each be described as a cause of the ensuing sale. The factual inquiry is whether a sale is really brought about by the act of the agent."[177]

In a more recent case where a submission was made that the better usage was "*an* effective cause", Woolf LJ said that this could create problems where there are "two or more effective causes, each of which could be the object of a claim for commission".[178] A situation of two genuinely effective causes of equal potency is possible, though unlikely,[179] and recent judicial authority prefers "an".[180] But a vendor may more easily become liable for two (or more) commissions on the same sale by virtue of the specific terms of two (or more) agency contracts.[181]

Apart from the general principle that in the absence of other indications the agent must be the effective cause of the transaction taking place, no clear principles can be easily derived from the many cases on this topic. No precise definition of "effective cause" in this context has yet been given by an English court.[182] Accordingly, any conclusions to be drawn from these cases must be advanced with hesitation. The agent will normally be entitled to his commission if he causes a person to negotiate with his principal and contract, no substantial break in the negotiations having taken place.[183] It appears that the agent does not have to complete or even take part in the negotiations,[184] nor arrange any meeting,[185] nor persuade either party to enter into the contract. Further, he is still entitled to his com-

---

[177] ibid., at 86, per Jacobs J. See also *Tufton Associates v Dilmun Shipping* [1992] 1 Lloyd's Rep. 71 at 78 ("cause which had the greatest efficacy" not the last).

[178] *Brian Cooper & Co v Fairview Estates (Investments) Ltd* [1987] 1 E.G.L.R. 18 at 20.

[179] It occurred in *Lordsgate Properties Ltd v Balcombe* [1985] 1 E.G.L.R. 20, Illustration 19; but many cases simply decide between rival claims to be effective cause, e.g. *Bloom v Yefet* [1982] 2 E.G.L.R. 30; *Anscombe & Ringland Ltd v Watson* [1991] 2 E.G.L.R. 28.

[180] In *Nahum v Royal Holloway, etc., College*, above, Waller LJ used "an" while saying that he doubted whether there was any difference except possibly where "there are two agents with agreements that they are entitled to commission if they introduce a purchaser". "An" was also preferred in *Harding Maughan Hambly Ltd v CECAR* [2000] 1 Lloyd's Rep. 316 at 335, in the context of insurance brokers.

[181] See *Bernard Marcus & Co v Ashraf* [1988] 1 E.G.L.R. 7 (auctioneer); *Peter Yates & Co v Bullock* [1990] 2 E.G.L.R. 24; above, para.7-021.

[182] *Restatement, Second*, § 448, states that: "an agent is an 'effective cause' ... when his efforts have been sufficiently important in achieving a result for the accomplishment of which the principal has promised to pay him, so that it is just that the principal should pay the promised compensation to him." This definition is open to the objection that it begs the question. But see *Harding Maughan Hambly Ltd v CECAR* [2000] 1 Lloyd's Rep. 316 at 334; *Goh Lay Khim v Isabel Redrup Agency Pte Ltd* [2017] SGCA 11 at [37]. Discussion of the earning of commission is omitted from *Restatement, Third* as being a matter of general contract law.

[183] It seems that merely sending out particulars may rank as introduction: *Christie Owen & Davies Plc v Ryelance* [2005] EWHC 148; (2005) 18 E.G. 148 (C.S.); *Christie Owen & Davies Plc v King* 1998 S.C.L.R. 786; Murdoch (2005) E.G. (No.154) 177.

[184] *Re Beale Ex p. Durrant* (1888) 5 Morr. 37, Illustration 8; *Green v Bartlett* (1863) 14 C.B.(N.S.) 681, Illustration 9; *Mansell v Clements* (1874) L.R. 9 C.P. 139; *Barnett v Brown & Co* (1890) 6 T.L.R. 463; *Steere v Smith* (1885) 2 T.L.R. 131; *Burton v Hughes* (1885) 1 T.L.R. 207; *Thompson, Rippon & Co v Thomas* (1896) 11 T.L.R. 304; *Brandon v Hanna* [1907] 2 I.R. 212; *Walker, Fraser and Steele v Fraser's Trustees*, 1910 S.C. 222; *Burchell v Gowrie and Blockhouse Collieries Ltd* [1910] A.C. 614; *Howard Houlder & Partners Ltd v Manx Isles SS Co Ltd* [1923] 1 K.B. 110; *Bow's Emporium Ltd v A.R. Brett & Co Ltd* (1928) 44 T.L.R. 194; *Bartlett v Cole* [1963] E.G.D. 452, Illustration 15; *Burns v Coomber* [1966] E.G.D. 110; *F.P. Rolfe & Co v George* [1969] E.G.D. 331; *McKeag Harris Realty & Development Co Ltd v Builders' Mutual Assets Ltd* (1968) 66 W.W.R. 512; *Knight, Frank & Rutley v Fraser* 1974 S.L.T. 50; *Berezovsky v Edmiston & Co Ltd* [2010] EWHC 1883 (Comm) at [41] (reversed on one issue, [2011] EWCA Civ 431). But if he simply advises his principal, he may not be the effective cause: *Hoddell v Smith* [1976] E.G.D. 217.

[185] See, e.g. *Green v Bartlett* (1863) 14 C.B.(N.S.) 681, Illustration 9.

mission if the principal contracts at a lower price or on other terms than the agent was authorised to offer, provided that the agent was the effective cause and the express or implied terms of the agency contract are such as to show that the remuneration was payable upon the happening of the transaction which actually resulted.[186]

The agent will not normally be entitled to his commission if the third party who ultimately contracts has his attention drawn to the possibility of contracting by means other than those intended by the agent to bring about the contract.[187] Moreover, the fact that one agent introduces a person who ultimately purchases after a later introduction by another agent will not necessarily entitle the first agent to commission.[188] In such a case the court must determine which of the two agents was the effective cause of the transaction taking place.[189] On the whole, it may be said that the first introducer has more often succeeded. But it is possible that a sale might have two effective causes.[190]

7-031 **Commercial agents** The Commercial Agents (Council Directive) Regulations 1993 contain provisions on entitlement to commission which parallel the "effective cause" rule.[191] The Regulations are discussed in Chapter 11.

Illustrations

7-032 (1) A employs B, a broker, to procure a charter for a ship. B introduces C, who is also a broker, C introduces D, who negotiates for but does not enter into a charterparty. D informs E that the ship is available and E charters her from A. B is not entitled to commission, the transaction being too remote a consequence of his introduction.[192]

(2) A employs B to find a purchaser for a ship. B, acting on behalf of A, contracts with C that C will receive a commission if he finds a purchaser. X, acting through D, asks C to find a ship for purchase and C gives X the name of A's

---

[186] *Allan v Leo Lines Ltd* [1957] 1 Lloyd's Rep. 127, Illustration 2; *Poulter v Dogget* (1964) 115 L.J. 76; *Allen v Anderson* [1969] N.Z.L.R. 951. See also *Spiess v Taylor* (1984) 271 E.G. 196 (no effective cause where property offered at wrong price: sed quaere); *Connell Estates v Begej* [1993] 2 E.G.L.R. 35 (commission on sale by part exchange); *Moneywood Pty Ltd v Salamon Nominees Pty Ltd* (2001) 202 C.L.R. 351 (part of land only) (see Fridman (2002) 76 A.L.J. 195); *Glentree Estates Ltd v Favermead Ltd* [2010] EWCA Civ 1473 at [23].

[187] Illustrations 9, 13 and 16. See also *D.C. Wylde & Co v Sparg* 1977 (2) S.A.L.R. 75 (eventual purchaser knew about property already); *Lichtenstein v Clube Atletico Mineiro* [2005] EWHC 1300 (QB) (football agent authorised to interest clubs in player; club which bought player had previously been interested). But cf. *Cobbs Property Services Ltd v Liddell-Taylor* [1990] 1 E.G.L.R. 49.

[188] *Murray v Currie* (1836) 7 C. & P. 584; *Barnett v Brown* (1890) 6 T.L.R. 463; *Curtis v Nixon* (1871) 24 L.T. 706, Illustration 3; *Davis v Trollope & Sons* [1943] 1 All E.R. 501; *Bartlett v Cole* [1963] E.G.D. 452, Illustration 15; *Chesterfield & Co Ltd v Zahid* [1989] 2 E.G.L.R. 24; *Egan Lawson Ltd v Standard Life Assurance Co* [2001] 1 E.G.L.R. 27; *Foxtons Ltd v Bicknell* [2008] EWCA Civ 419; [2008] 24 E.G. 142; [2008] N.P.C. 52; *Glentree Estates Ltd v Holbeton Ltd* [2011] EWCA Civ 755. Sometimes the matter may turn on who "introduced": e.g. *Terry Martel Real Estate Ltd v Lovette Investments Ltd* (1981) 123 D.L.R. (3d) 387.

[189] *John D. Wood & Co v Dantata* [1987] 2 E.G.L.R. 23. See also *Chasen Ryder & Co v Hedges* [1993] 1 E.G.L.R. 47. If two different agents are claiming commission from the principal he cannot normally interplead: *Greatorex & Co v Shackle* [1895] 2 Q.B. 249. See also Article 70.

[190] *Lordsgate Properties Ltd v Balcombe* [1985] 1 E.G.L.R. 20, Illustration 19.

[191] reg.7(1).

[192] *Wilkinson v Martin* (1837) 8 C. & P. 1. And see *Ellis v May & Co* (1960) 110 L.J. 140 (introduction of mortgage broker: no commission for "arranging mortgage"); cf. *Crema v Cenkos Securities Plc* [2010] EWHC 461 (Comm).

ship. Various offers and counter-offers are passed through C, the last being rejected by A. Shortly afterwards A sells the ship to X privately. C is entitled to his commission, the introduction of X being the effective cause of the sale. The fact that the final sale was at a different figure from any that passed through C did not mean that C was not the real cause of the sale taking place at all.[193]

(3)   An estate agent lets a house for a term of years, the tenant having the option of taking it for a further term. The tenant declines to exercise this option but agrees to take the house for a further term at a lower rent. The first agent is not entitled to commission on the further term since he was not the proximate cause of the reletting.[194]

(4)   An agent is employed to let an estate and procures a tenant. The tenant subsequently buys the estate without any further communication with the agent. The agent is not entitled to commission on the sale.[195]

(5)   An agent employed to sell property on commission is not entitled to commission if he and the principal agree together that he shall be the purchaser himself, unless they expressly agree that commission shall be payable on such a sale.[196]

(6)   An agent, employed to find a purchaser of property at a specified price, brings it to the notice of a government department which, after negotiations to purchase fail, compulsorily acquires it at a lower price and against the wishes of the principal. The agent is not entitled to commission. He was employed only to find a ready and willing purchaser at a price which the principal voluntarily accepts.[197]

(7)   A entered into an agreement with B in the following terms:

> "In case of your introducing a purchaser [of a certain business] of whom I approve, or capital which I should accept, I could pay you 5 per cent commission, provided no one else is entitled to commission in respect of the same introduction."

B introduced C, who advanced £10,000 by way of loan, and B was duly paid his commission in respect of that advance. Some months afterwards, A and C entered into an agreement for a partnership, C advancing a further £4,000 by way of capital. Held, that B was not entitled to commission on the £4,000, that

---

[193] *Allan v Leo Lines Ltd* [1957] 1 Lloyd's Rep. 127. The facts have been slightly simplified for the sake of clarity.

[194] *Curtis v Nixon* (1871) 24 L.T. 706. See also *Ex p. Chatteris* (1874) 22 W.R. 289; *Lofts v Bourke* (1884) 1 T.L.R. 58.

[195] *Toulmin v Millar* (1887) 58 L.T. 96 (reported on another point (1887) 12 App.Cas. 746). The test there laid down by Lord Watson that "in order to found a legal claim for commission there must not only be a causal, there must also be a contractual relation between the introduction and the ultimate transaction of sale" is difficult to understand and does not seem in practice to have been applied. See also *Millar, Son & Co v Radford* (1903) 19 T.L.R. 575 and *Nightingale v Parsons* [1914] 2 K.B. 621 for cases on almost identical facts.

[196] *Hocker v Waller* (1929) 29 Com.Cas. 296. See also *Barnett v Isaacson* (1888) 4 T.L.R. 645, Illustration 14.

[197] *Hodges & Sons v Hackbridge Park Residential Hotel Ltd* [1940] 1 K.B. 404. See also *Battams v Tompkins* (1892) 8 T.L.R. 707; *Beable v Dickerson* (1885) 1 T.L.R. 654; *Thompson v British Berna Motor Lorries Ltd* (1917) 33 T.L.R. 187; cf. *Price, Davies & Co v Smith* (1929) 141 L.T. 490 and *O'Connor Real Estate Ltd v Flynn* (1969) 3 D.L.R. (3d) 345.

amount having been advanced in consequence of the negotiations between A and C for a partnership, with which B had nothing to do.[198]

(8)   A, who was employed by B to find a purchaser for certain property, introduced C to B, but C could not accept B's terms. Shortly afterwards B became bankrupt. Further negotiations took place between C and B's trustee in bankruptcy, resulting in a sale of the property three weeks after the original introduction. Held, A's introduction brought about the sale and he was entitled to prove in the bankruptcy for his commission.[199]

(9)   A, an auctioneer and estate agent, was employed by P to sell the island of Herm by auction or otherwise. He put it up for auction and the reserve price was not reached. Afterwards T, who had attended the auction, asked A for and was given P's name. T then approached P direct and eventually purchased the island from him. Shortly before the sale P wrote to A withdrawing A's authority to sell. Held, A was the *causa causans* of the sale and was entitled to commission.[200]

(10)   A employed B to sell an estate in lots. C bought certain lots and B received commission on them. At this stage C refused to buy further lots. A then withdrew B's authority, and 27 months later C bought the remaining lots by private contract. Held, that the jury were entitled to find that the ultimate sale was not due to B's intervention.[201]

(11)   An estate agent, A, was instructed by P to offer a house for sale. It was agreed that he should receive two-and-a-half per cent commission if he found a purchaser or a guinea for his services if the house was sold without his intervention. T called on A and received a card to view the house. T viewed it and after negotiations through a friend of P, he ultimately bought it. Held, there was evidence for the jury that the house was sold through the intervention of A so as to entitle him to commission.[202]

(12)   Two brewery companies agreed to pay A a commission on all licensed properties or businesses they might purchase through his introduction. A submitted a brewery for their consideration. The companies decided that the most advantageous course was for them to promote a new company to buy the brewery. Held, the position was the same as if the companies had bought the brewery themselves and sold it to the new company. A was accordingly entitled to his commission.[203]

---

[198] *Tribe v Taylor* (1876) 1 C.P.D. 505. See also *Boyd v Tovil Paper Co Ltd* (1884) 4 T.L.R. 332.

[199] *Re Beale Ex p. Durrant* (1888) 5 Morr. 37; cf. *Egan Lawson Ltd v Standard Life Assurance Co* [2001] 1 E.G.L.R. 27.

[200] *Green v Bartlett* (1863) 14 C.B.(N.S.) 681. See also *Bayley v Chadwick* (1878) 39 L.T. 429; *Wilkinson v Alston* (1879) 48 L.J.Q.B. 733; *Ong Kee Ming v Quek Yong Kang* [1991] 3 M.L.J. 294; *Dashwood v Fleurets Ltd* [2007] EWHC 1610 (QB) at [51].

[201] *Lumley v Nicholson* (1886) 34 W.R. 716. Compare *Jack Windle Ltd v Brierley* [1952] 1 All E.R. 398; *Christie Owen & Davis Plc v King* 1998 S.C.L.R. 786 ("introduced to you").

[202] *Mansell v Clements* (1874) L.R. 9 C.P. 139. See also *Barnett v Brown* (1890) 6 T.L.R. 463; *Steere v Smith* (1885) 2 T.L.R. 131; *Burton v Hughes* (1885) 1 T.L.R. 207; *Thompson, Ripon & Co v Thomas* (1896) 11 T.L.R. 304; *Brandon v Hanna* [1907] 2 I.R. 212; *Howard Houlder & Partners Ltd v Manx Isles SS Co* [1923] 1 K.B. 110; *Burns v Coomber* [1966] E.G.D. 110; *McKeag Harris Realty & Development Co Ltd v Builders Mutual Assets Ltd* (1968) 64 W.W.R. 208; affd (1968) 66 W.W.R. 512.

[203] *Gunn v Showell's Brewery Co Ltd & Crosswell's Ltd* (1902) 50 W.R. 659 (see also at first instance (1901) 17 T.L.R. 563); *Di Dio Nominees Pty Ltd v Brian Mark Real Estate Pty Ltd* [1992] 2 VR. 732. See also *Glendinning v Cavanagh* (1908) 40 S.C.R. 414; *Stratton v Vachan and Wilson* (1911)

(13) A company agrees to pay a commission upon the introduction of a buyer for a property. Instead, the potential buyer buys the shares in the vendor. Held, that while the agency contract might have impliedly extended to a sale of shares where the vendor owned the company that owned the property, it did not extend to a sale of the shares in the vendor itself.[204]

(14) A introduced T to P, his principal, as a possible purchaser of certain property belonging to P, but no agreement between them was reached. P subsequently sold the property by auction, T being the purchaser. Held, A was not entitled to his commission.[205]

(15) A agreed to pay B a commission of £5,000 in the event of B introducing a purchaser of A's business. B failed to find a purchaser, but introduced C, an accountant, as a person who might be able to introduce a purchaser. C eventually himself bought the property at the proposed price after deducting the commission which he was to have been paid in the event of his finding a purchaser. Held, that there was no evidence that B had introduced a purchaser of the business, he having introduced C, not as a purchaser, but as an agent to find a purchaser, and that B could not recover either the agreed commission or a quantum meruit, the claim for a quantum meruit being excluded by the express terms of the contract.[206]

(16) A employed B to sell his café. B introduced C, who wanted to buy but could not without a loan, and who eventually went to new agents for a lower-priced business. The new agents also had A's business on their books, and assured C of finance, advising him to employ a solicitor for the purchase. The new agents' finance fell through but C's solicitor found finance and C bought. Held, the removal of the financial problem made B's introduction which had otherwise been successful the effective cause of the purchase. Semble, if the new agents had been able to supply finance they would have been the effective cause.[207]

(17) P, who was the owner of a shop suitable for a pin-table arcade, arranged with A to pay him a commission if A could find a tenant. A telephoned C, a manufacturer of pin-tables, and told him of the shop. C said he wanted to consult his partner. T overheard the telephone conversation and asked C for the address. C merely said it was "in Victoria". T went to Victoria, found the shop, and arranged a lease direct with P. Held, A was not entitled to commission. The deliberate withholding of the address by C broke the chain

44 S.C.R. 395; *McBrayne v Imperial Loan Co* (1913) 13 D.L.R. 448; *Levers v Dunsdon* [1968] E.G.D. 280; *L.J. Hooker Ltd v W.J. Adams Estates Pty Ltd* (1977) 138 C.L.R. 52; Illustration 17; *Lord v Trippe* (1977) 51 A.L.J.R. 574. See also *Freedman v Union Group Plc* [1997] E.G.C.S. 28.

[204] *Estafnous v London & Leeds Business Centres Ltd* [2011] EWCA Civ 1157.

[205] *Taplin v Barrett* (1889) 6 T.L.R. 30. See also *Green v Mules* (1861) 30 L.J.C.P. 343, Illustration 8 to Article 55; *Lofts v Bourke* (1884) 1 T.L.R. 58; *Coles v Enoch* [1939] 3 All E.R. 327, Illustration 16; cf. *Walker, Fraser and Steele v Fraser's Trustees* 1910 S.C. 222.

[206] *Barnett v Isaacson* (1888) 4 T.L.R. 645; cf. *Burney v London Mews Co Ltd* [2003] EWCA Civ 766, where the agent gave the particulars to another agent, who introduced a purchaser.

[207] *Bartlett v Cole* [1963] E.G.D. 452; cf. *Robert Drummond v Mangles* [1981] E.G.D. 265; *Hartnell v Taylor, Cook v Bromwich* [1982] E.G.D. 436. See also *Rungay v Forrester* (1967) 63 D.L.R. (2d) 338; *Tufnell v Richard Costain Ltd* (1968) 209 E.G. 705; *Christie & Co v Jones* [1966] E.G.D. 439; *Glentree Estates Ltd v Gee* [1981] E.G.D. 235; cf. *Jack Windle Ltd v Brierley* [1952] 1 All E.R. 398 as a case where the finance was provided by the seller; doubted in *Glentree Estates Ltd v Gee*, above; *Peter Yates & Co v Bullock* [1990] 2 E.G.L.R. 24.

of causation and A was not the direct or efficient cause of T becoming the tenant.[208]

(18) An agent is engaged to locate a satisfactory purchaser for land at a satisfactory price. The agent introduces two persons, L and H, who conduct real property development operations though a number of companies including A Co L makes several unsuccessful offers. The vendor had independently been in touch with another development company of which B Co was a subsidiary. A Co and B Co enter into a joint venture agreement; B Co buys the land and makes an allotment of shares to A Co The agent had played no part in introducing either company and did not know of the joint venture. He is not entitled to commission.[209]

(19) A "business broker" states terms to company X upon which it will act in the acquisition of other businesses. A fee is payable if a company or business submitted by the broker is acquired by the company. In 1982 the broker introduces a business. Negotiations ensue but are abandoned. In 1985 the business is transferred to a public listed company. In 1987 company X effects a takeover of the listed company. The broker's fee is due.[210]

(20) X engages the services of two agents, each of which introduces the same prospective purchaser. X's son tells the second agents that he has an offer through the first agents, and the second agents tell this to the prospective purchaser, who raises his offer, neither he nor the second agent realising that he is bidding against himself. The two agents are both effective causes of the eventual sale.[211]

(21) A is asked to find a buyer for paintings. He introduces a buyer for one. The second is later sold to the same buyer, but the buyer's agent attempts to cut A out and A plays little role in the sale. He is held entitled to commission in respect of both paintings.[212]

Article 58

AGENT PREVENTED BY PRINCIPAL FROM EARNING REMUNERATION

7-033   The principal will only be liable for preventing the agent from earning his remuneration when the implication of a promise that he will not do so is necessary to give business efficacy to the contract, or otherwise to effect the intention of the parties.[213]

---

[208] *Coles v Enoch* [1939] 3 All E.R. 327. See also *Antrobus v Wickens* (1865) 4 F. & F. 291.
[209] *L.J. Hooker Ltd v W.J. Adams Estates Pty Ltd* (1977) 138 C.L.R. 52. (The judgments in this case repay study.) See too *Aboulsaud v Aboukhater* [2007] EWHC 2122 (QB).
[210] *David Leahy (Aust.) Pty Ltd v McPherson's Ltd* [1991] 2 V.R. 362. See also *Brian Cooper Ltd v Fairview Estates (Investments) Ltd* [1987] 1 E.G.L.R. 18 ("introduce a tenant ... with whom we have not been in previous communication and who subsequently completes a lease"). See also *Harding Maughan Hambly Ltd v CECAR* [2000] 1 Lloyd's Rep. 316 (agent's services dispensed with after most of placing work done: effective cause).
[211] *Lordsgate Properties Ltd v Balcombe* [1985] 1 E.G.L.R. 20.
[212] *Nahum v Royal Holloway and Bedford New College* [1999] E.M.L.R. 252.
[213] See Comment.

Comment

If the agent claims that he is entitled to damages because his principal has wrong- **7-034**
fully deprived him of the opportunity to earn his remuneration, he must be able to
show some contractual promise of which the principal is in breach. Where there is
an express promise on which the agent can rely, no difficulty will arise. But where
there is no express promise the question will arise whether any, and if so what,
promise can be implied.

Earlier case law   For many years it was thought that the principal was under a **7-035**
duty not to deprive the agent of the opportunity of earning his commission. This
view was first expressed in *Prickett v Badger*.[214] A series of confused cases followed,[215] the basis of the supposed principle never being fully worked out. Most of
the cases concerned agents, e.g. estate agents, who were entitled to receive a commission if they brought about a certain transaction for their principals. It was
realised, however, that the principal could not be held liable in the context of sale
of land when he did *any* act which had the effect of preventing the agent from earning commission; for the vendor may be taken normally to wish to retain some element of discretion. The supposed rule became therefore more and more tenuous.
In *G. Trollope & Sons v Martyn Bros*[216] the Court of Appeal held that the principal
of an estate agent would be liable in damages to the agent if (but only if) he
unreasonably withdrew from negotiations with the potential purchaser with the
result that the agent could not earn his commission. However, the dissenting judgment of Scrutton LJ revealed the fallacies in the reasoning of the majority of the
court, and in *Luxor (Eastbourne) Ltd v Cooper*[217] the House of Lords expressly
overruled *G. Trollope & Sons v Martyn Bros*.

Estate agent's contract   In *Luxor*'s case the House made a detailed examination **7-036**
of the estate agent's contract. The peculiarity of the usual version of this arrangement is that the agent is not under an obligation to do anything.[218] Hence in the typical situation the principal makes a continuing or single offer of a unilateral contract
only, which the agent accepts by introducing a purchaser or whatever else is
required by the terms of the particular offer.[219] Sometimes a letter following the
engagement may contain wording purporting to create a bilateral contract, inasmuch

---

[214] (1856) 1 C.B.(N.S.) 296.
[215] These are considered in detail in Ash, *Willing to Purchase* (1963). They include *Green v Lucas*
(1875) 33 L.T. 584; *Fisher v Drewett* (1878) 48 L.J.Q.B. 32; *Roberts v Barnard* (1884) 1 Cab. &
El. 336; *Grogan v Smith* (1890) 7 T.L.R. 132; *Fuller v Eames* (1892) 8 T.L.R. 278; *Nosotti v
Auerbach* (1899) 15 T.L.R. 140; *Brinson v Davies* (1911) 105 L.T. 134; *Hankinson v Vickers* [1931]
E.G.D. 16.
[216] [1934] 2 K.B. 436. This case was followed in *G. Trollope & Sons v Caplan* [1936] 2 K.B. 382; *Kahn
v Aircraft Industries Corp Ltd* [1937] 3 All E.R. 476; *Harrods Ltd v Geneen* [1938] 4 All E.R. 493;
Way & Waller Ltd v Verrall [1939] 3 All E.R. 533.
[217] [1941] A.C. 108, Illustration 1. Most of the cases cited in fnn.215 and 216 above must now be taken
to have been wrongly decided, or at least decided on the wrong principles. In general, any case on
this topic before *Luxor*'s case should be regarded with caution. It is suggested that the statement in
J.H. Milner & Son v Percy Bilton [1966] 1 W.L.R. 1582 at 1588 that "the estate agent who has been
employed to sell a particular house can sue for damages if his authority is withdrawn" is now out
of date, especially since the judge relied upon *G. Trollope & Sons v Martyn Bros*.
[218] See Comment to Article 56.
[219] *L.J. Hooker Ltd v W.J. Adams Estates Pty Ltd* (1977) 138 C.L.R. 52 at 73. A different type of
analysis, which tends to discount the conceptual difference between unilateral and bilateral contracts,
is however suggested by Lord Wilberforce in *A.M. Satterthwaite & Co v New Zealand Shipping Co*

as it contains undertakings that the agent will use his best endeavours and so forth.[220] Although there can be no objection in principle to a new contract being subsequently formed in this way, or indeed to the initial contract being a bilateral one, the authoritative way in which the normal agency contract is analysed in *Luxor's* case means that such an interpretation of the facts, which might force a bilateral contract on one who has made a unilateral one, would be difficult to establish.

On the unilateral analysis, the next question is whether the principal is to be regarded as promising not to deprive the agent of commission. Although the speeches in the case speak of implied *terms*, it is submitted that if the contract is truly unilateral, the requirement would be for the implication of an implied collateral *contract*.[221] However this be, the House, having interpreted the nature of the transaction, treated the question of implication as a question of business efficacy and held that such implication was not appropriate. It was improbable that the principal would wish to fetter his freedom of choice by binding himself vis-à-vis his agent not to withdraw unreasonably from negotiations when he was free vis-à-vis the potential purchaser to withdraw at any time for any reason. Furthermore, the agent earns a considerable commission if successful: he likewise takes the business risk that if his efforts are unsuccessful he earns nothing.[222]

7-037 **"Sole" and "exclusive" agency** Where the agent is appointed "sole" agent, however, it is established that if the principal then employs a second agent who earns the commission on the transaction which the first agent should have earned, the first agent is entitled to damages.[223] The normal view of such a transaction is that it is a bilateral contract, the consideration for the principal's promise not to sell through another agent being the agent's undertaking to use his best endeavours to sell the property.[224] Alternatively, it could be said that the contract is still unilateral, but that this is a case where a collateral contract not to revoke will readily be

---

Ltd (The Eurymedon) [1975] A.C. 154 at 167–168; followed by Barwick CJ in *Port Jackson Stevedoring Pty Ltd v Salmond & Spraggon (Australia) Pty Ltd (The New York Star)* [1979] 1 Lloyd's Rep. 298 at 305–306, whose judgment was endorsed by the Privy Council [1981] 1 W.L.R. 138 at 148.

[220] See Murdoch, *Law of Estate Agency* (5th edn), pp.141–144; (1977) 242 E.G. 609; cf. McConnell (1983) 265 E.G. 547. In two cases the confirming letter appears to have been treated as effective: *Way & Waller Ltd v Ryde* [1944] 1 All E.R. 9 and *John E. Trinder & Partners v Haggis* (1951) 158 E.G. 4. Murdoch, above, suggests that they are inconsistent with *Toulmin v Millar* (1887) 58 L.T. 96, Illustration 4 to Article 57.

[221] Contra, Treitel, *Law of Contract* (14th edn), para.2-053. And see fn.218 above.

[222] See also *Burns Fry Ltd v Khurana* (1985) 20 D.L.R. (4th) 245.

[223] *Milsom v Bechstein* (1898) 14 T.L.R. 159; *Hampton & Sons Ltd v George* [1939] 3 All E.R. 627; *Newton v Erickson* (1951) 157 E.G. 414; *Nicholas Prestige Homes v Neal* [2010] EWCA Civ 1552. Where the agent was employed to effect a single transaction the damages will be calculated by reference to the sum at which it is proved that the plaintiff agent could have found a purchaser: *Hampton & Sons Ltd v George*, above; *De Coning v Monror Estate and Investment Co (Pty) Ltd* 1974 (3) S.A. 72. Where the agent was employed generally, the damages will, on the principles expressed in *Roberts v Elwells Engineers Ltd* [1972] 2 Q.B. 586, be what he has lost in consequence of breach, i.e. what he would have been expected to earn, less any saved expenses. An account is not the appropriate relief. Nor, under this reasoning, is commission due: but see below, para.7-038.

[224] *C. Christopher & Co v Essig* [1948] W.N. 461; *Mendoza & Co v Bell* (1952) 159 E.G. 372; *Hampton & Sons v Chapman* [1952] C.P.L. 24; *Galan v Alekno* [1950] 3 D.L.R. 9; *Fidelity Trust Co v Rudy* (1957) 23 W.W.R. 668; *Bradley-Wilson (1954) Ltd v Canyon Gardens Ltd* (1965) 53 W.W.R. 413; cf. *Midland Business Agency v Apted* (1971) 218 E.G. 1727, where the supposed consideration was illusory.

implied, which would not be the case in the first and more general situation.[225] This seems however a more artificial interpretation and where an ordinary bilateral contract can be found it is probably better to use this analysis rather than have recourse to collateral contracts. Normally however the principal will still not be in breach of contract by negotiating the sale of the property himself, for the mere appointment of a sole agent does not imply any prohibition on the principal from so acting.[226] Some agency contracts may, however, expressly prohibit the principal from selling, or at least require the payment of commission on sale, other than through the agent during the period of the sole agency[227]: these are sometimes called "exclusive" or "sole selling" agency contracts.[228] Equally, provision may be made that commission must nevertheless be paid to the agent though the principal sells the property himself.[229] It would seem, however, that the principal can still *withdraw* the property.[230] The question of commission if the principal refuses to sell to a particular buyer, or chooses one over another, is solved by the interpretation of the contract term under which commission is due.[231] Similar problems arise with distributorship contracts, though here a prohibition on the principal selling himself may more easily be inferred.[232] But in all cases the interpretation of the whole contract is crucial: decisions cannot be based entirely on the phrase used.[233]

Estate Agents (Provision of Information) Regulations 1991[234]   Where the terms   **7-038**
"sole selling rights" or "sole agency" are used in the course of estate agency work[235] the estate agent must give an explanation of their meaning in the way described in the regulations.[236] Failure to do so makes the estate agency contract unenforceable, except pursuant to an order of the court.[237] It should be noted that the forms prescribed in the Regulations[238] entitle the estate agent to actual commission rather than, as under the common law, to damages for breach of the special contract term.

---

[225] Murdoch (1975) 91 L.Q.R. 357.
[226] *Bentall, Horsley & Baldry v Vicary* [1931] 1 K.B. 253; *Sadler v Whittaker* (1953) 162 E.G. 404.
[227] See, e.g. *Snelgrove v Ellringham Colliery Co* (1881) 45 J.P. 408; *Chamberlain & Willows v Rose* [1924] E.G.D. 356; *Property Choice Ltd v Fronda* [1991] 2 E.G.L.R. 249; *Harwood v Smith* [1998] 1 E.G.L.R. 5 (interpreting such a provision). They are common in auctioneers' contracts: see *Bernard Marcus & Co v Ashraf* [1988] 1 E.G.L.R. 7. See also *Chinnock v Sainsbury* (1860) 30 L.J.Ch. 409; *Lamb & Sons v Goring Brick Co Ltd* [1932] 1 K.B. 710.
[228] *Brodie Marshall & Co (Hotel Division) v Sharer* [1988] 1 E.G.L.R. 21 at 22.
[229] See, e.g. *Tredinnick v Browne* (1921), cited in *Bentall, Horsley & Baldry v Vicary* [1931] 1 K.B. 253 at 260; *Savills (UK) Ltd v Blacker* [2017] EWCA Civ 68.
[230] See Murdoch, *Law of Estate Agency* (5th edn), pp.127–128.
[231] See above, para.7-029.
[232] *W.T. Lamb & Sons v Goring Brick Co Ltd* [1932] 1 K.B. 710: see above, para.1-033.
[233] *Murphy Buckley & Keogh Ltd v Pye (Ireland) Ltd* [1971] I.R. 57; *G.F. Galvin (Estates) Ltd v Hedigan* [1985] I.L.R.M. 295 at 300, where it was apparently argued that "sole selling agency" allowed the vendor to sell personally, but "exclusive selling rights" did not.
[234] SI 1991/859, made under s.30 of the Estate Agents Act 1979.
[235] As to which, see Estate Agents Act 1979 s.1; Murdoch, *Law of Estate Agency and Auctions* (4th edn), p.266 onwards; and in general Murdoch, *The Estate Agents and Property Misdescriptions Acts* (3rd edn).
[236] reg.5.
[237] Estate Agents Act 1979 s.18(5). As to the exercise of the court's discretion, see *Great Estates Group Ltd v Digby* [2011] EWCA Civ 1120.
[238] In the Schedule. They are as follows.
   "Sole selling rights.
   You will be liable to pay remuneration to us, in addition to any other costs or charges agreed, in each of the following circumstances—
   •   if unconditional contracts for the sale of the property are exchanged, in the period dur-

Where a contract does not, however, provide for commission in circumstances where damages would still be available at common law for breach by a vendor of a term as to sole agency, it seems that the right to damages must also be spelt out in the contract in order to comply with the Regulations.[239] It has been held that the word "purchaser" in the phrase "a purchaser introduced by us during the period of our sole agency" means a purchaser who becomes a purchaser as a result of the introduction, thereby engaging something like the "effective cause" requirement that is ordinarily implied as a prerequisite to commission.[240] Where the contract wording varies, the explanation must be given with appropriate modifications.[241]

7-039 Principles of general application It would seem that the principles referred to above are of general application in connection with agents remunerated by commission. Where the transaction is interpreted as a unilateral contract, and the agent has no duty to do anything, the agent could only be protected by an implied collateral contract not to revoke, and although there are dicta in another context that a promise not to revoke the offer of such a contract will in general be implied,[242] it is submitted that these are too wide. Where the contract is bilateral, the question is one of implication of terms. Since the contract for an agent working for commission seems to be too varied to rank as one of which general incidents are worked out,[243] in both cases there will only be implications on the basis of "business efficacy"[244]; and such implications have hitherto been rare.[245] It may however be that the implication of a *term* is easier than the implication of a *contract*, since the latter is to some extent inconsistent with, or at least modifies the nature of the transaction as already determined.

7-040 Dismissal and termination of authority The most obvious way of preventing

---

ing which we have sole selling rights, even if the purchaser was not found by us but by another agent or by any other person, including yourself;
* if unconditional contracts for the sale of the property are exchanged after the expiry of the period during which we have sole selling rights but to a purchaser who was introduced to you during that period or with whom we had negotiations about the property during that period."

"Sole agency.
You will be liable to pay remuneration to us, in addition to any other costs or charges agreed, if at any time unconditional contracts for the sale of the property are exchanged—
* with a purchaser introduced by us during the period of our sole agency or with whom we had negotiations about the property during that period; or
* with a purchaser introduced by another agent during that period."

[239] *Great Estates Group Ltd v Digby* [2011] EWCA Civ 1120 (Rix and Toulson LJJ.; Lloyd LJ dissenting); noted Murdoch (2012) 1203 E.G. 87.
[240] *Foxtons Ltd v Bicknell* [2008] EWCA Civ 419; [2008] 24 E.G. 142; [2008] N.P.C. 52.
[241] regs 5(1) (2). As to the time at which notice must be given, see regs 3, 5(3).
[242] *Daulia Ltd v Four Millbank Nominees Ltd* [1978] Ch. 231 at 239, per Goff LJ.
[243] Under the principles laid down in *Liverpool City Council v Irwin* [1977] A.C. 239; see above, para.7-001.
[244] See ibid; below, para.7-041.
[245] See above, para.7-002 and *Martin-Smith v Williams* [1999] E.M.L.R. 571, where in the present context Mummery LJ said that the cases cited "are only illustrations of a more general principle that a term will be implied in a contract when it is necessary to do so to give it business efficacy."; *Green v Skandia Life Assurance Co Ltd* [2006] EWHC 1626 (Ch) at [30]–[31] (no duty to ensure insurance agent earned commission); *Adler v Ananhall Advisory & Consultancy Services Ltd* [2009] EWCA Civ 586; [2009] N.P.C. 80 (no implied term for commission upon cancellation by principal of contract where commission earned only if contract "completed"). But cf. *Standard Life Health Care Ltd v Gorman* [2009] EWCA Civ 1292; [2010] I.R.L.R. 233 at [21] per Waller LJ (where agent employed on commission basis, obligation on principal not to prevent earning of commission).

the agent from earning his commission is by terminating his authority or dismissing him. Whether or not this constitutes a breach of contract at all turns on the interpretation of the contract (if any) and in particular on its provisions (if any) relating to appointment for a specified period and to termination by either party; or on the interpretation of an offer of a unilateral contract, and any additional promises that may be implied with such an offer. The matter is dealt with under "Termination of authority" in Article 123.

Prevention by other means Terms may by the same techniques be implied against prevention by other means. The nature of the promise will vary from case to case. The term sometimes[246] might be that the principal will not do *anything* to prevent the agent from earning the commission as contemplated. Or it might be that there are certain things which the principal must not do. It has been held that a term was to be implied to prevent a vendor from "playing a dirty trick on the agent ... a term which prevents the vendor from acting unreasonably to the possible gain of the vendor and the loss of the agent"; as by breaking the contract on performance of which the agent is entitled to commission.[247] In another case a term that the vendor will not make fraudulent misrepresentation to the purchaser, which thereby allowed the contract to be cancelled, was implied.[248]

7-041

A further implication might be that if the principal does prevent the agent from earning commission on the happening of an event but, as contemplated by the contract, the agent has had to spend money and undertake work, the principal will pay him on a quantum meruit for what he has already done.[249] It is clear from *Luxor*'s case that such a contractual promise will not normally be implied into an estate agent's engagement in general, and it is probable that such an implication will be made only in an exceptional case. Where the agent cannot perform his duties under the agency contract without the active cooperation of his principal, a promise can sometimes be implied that such cooperation will be forthcoming.[250] This implication is an example of the general rule and can again only be made in so far as it is necessary "to make the contract workable".[251]

Remuneration after termination Sometimes the question will arise whether the agent is entitled to remuneration after the contract has been terminated. This remuneration will usually take the form of commission on business introduced

7-042

---

[246] But not in an estate agent situation: above, para.7-036.
[247] *Alpha Trading Ltd v Dunnshaw-Patten Ltd* [1981] Q.B. 290 at 306, per Templeman LJ (Illustration 3). See further cases cited at Illustration 3. See also *John D. Wood & Co (Residential and Agricultural) Ltd v Craze* [2007] EWHC 2658 (QB); [2007] 50 E.G. 108 (C.S.); [2007] N.P.C. 130, and above, para.7-018.
[248] *John D. Wood & Co (Residential and Agricultural) Ltd v Craze*, above (but see note, Watts [2009] J.B.L. 268).
[249] This is, perhaps, the most satisfactory explanation of *Inchbald v Western Neilgherry Coffee, Tea and Cinchona Plantation Co Ltd* (1864) 17 C.B.(N.S.) 733. In *Luxor (Eastbourne) Ltd v Cooper* [1941] A.C. 108 at 147, Lord Wright said that he could not understand Inchbald's case unless it was treated as analogous to a case of wrongful dismissal. Its authority must be regarded as doubtful.
[250] *Mona Oil Equipment & Supply Co Ltd v Rhodesia Railways Ltd* [1949] 2 All E.R. 1014. See also *Luxor (Eastbourne) Ltd v Cooper* [1941] A.C. 108 at 118, 148; *Mackay v Dick* (1881) 6 App.Cas. 251; *Colley v Overseas Exporters* [1921] 3 K.B. 302. See also Burrows (1968) 31 M.L.R. 390; Lücke (1973) 5 Adelaide L.Rev. 32.
[251] *Mona Oil Equipment & Supply Co Ltd v Rhodesia Railways Ltd*, above, at 1018, per Devlin J; and see *Secretary of State for Employment v Associated Society of Locomotive Engineers and Firemen (No.2)* [1972] 2 Q.B. 455; *Coupers Partnership Ltd v Basarik* [2007] EWCA Civ 40; [2007] R.V.R. 116 at [23].

before the contract was terminated. Usually the solution is found by interpreting the contract; but sometimes questions of implied terms arise.

If the fact which renders the commission earned occurs before the termination of the contract, whether the contract is terminated for breach or otherwise,[252] and no matter by which party, the commission has become due and is still payable. So if the contract on its true construction so provides, commission may be earned by a mere introduction effected before termination. This is so even though the contract provides that the agent is actually to be paid on receipt, acceptance or execution of the order, and this occurs after termination.[253]

There may be more difficulty if the commission is, despite an earlier introduction, only earned, on the true interpretation of the contract, by receipt, acceptance, or execution of the order,[254] and this occurs after the termination of the contract. Here, after the initial question of interpretation, if the termination occurs without breach (e.g. by effluxion of time, or by the exercise of a power by principal or agent), the issue may be as to whether the contract is to be regarded as containing an implied term that commission is to remain payable after termination where the business was introduced before termination.[255] To determine this it is "legitimate to have regard to the course of dealing to supplement the express terms".[256] The same inquiry could be relevant if the agent was in breach in terminating, though it is unlikely here that he would be protected by an implied term. If the principal was in breach in terminating, the appropriate course is to sue him for depriving the agent of the opportunity to earn commission.[257]

Similar reasoning should be applied where the contract provides for commission on "repeat orders". If it does not do so expressly, an implied term to that effect is unlikely.[258] It may be that on interpretation an entitlement to commission on repeat orders will be found to exist only on orders that come in while the agency subsisted.[259] But if this is not so, and the initial introduction occurred before termination, and the repeat orders came in later, a question may arise as to whether there is an implied term that the repeat order provision should survive termination.[260] If the termination occurs without breach, this could be so.[261] If it is

---

[252] But no commission on a transaction will be payable, it seems, if the contract is terminated for the agent's failure to disclose a conflict of interest in respect of that transaction: *Imageview Management Ltd v Jack* [2009] EWCA Civ 63; [2009] 2 All E.R. 666. See, further Article 76, below.

[253] *Sellers v London Counties Newspapers* [1951] 1 K.B. 784; *Gold v Life Assurance Co of Pennsylvania* [1971] 2 Lloyd's Rep. 164; *Explora Group Plc v Hesco Bastion Ltd* [2005] EWCA Civ 646 at [64], per Rix LJ; *Proactive Sports Management Ltd v Rooney* [2011] EWCA Civ 1444 at [45].

[254] As in *Hilton v Helliwell* [1894] 2 I.R. 94.

[255] See *Explora Group Plc v Hesco Bastion Ltd* [2005] EWCA Civ 646 at [126]–[128], per Longmore LJ; *Bilbee v Hasse & Co* (1889) 5 T.L.R. 677, affd *The Times,* January 16, 1890; *Levy v Goldhill* [1917] 2 Ch. 297.

[256] *Explora,* above, at [67], per Rix LJ.

[257] See *Roberts v Elwells Engineers Ltd* [1972] 2 Q.B. 586; *Faulkner v Cooper & Co Ltd* (1889) 4 Com.Cas. 213; *Great Estates Group Ltd v Digby* [2011] EWCA Civ 1120 (Lloyd LJ dissenting).

[258] The question of commission on repeat orders is considered in detail in Powell, pp.364–369. See *Weare v Brimsdown Lead Co* (1910) 103 L.T. 429.

[259] *Crocker Horlock & Co Ltd v B. Lang & Co Ltd* [1949] 1 All E.R. 526. See also *Morris v Hunt & Co* (1896) 12 T.L.R. 187; *Barrett v Gilmour & Co* (1901) 17 T.L.R. 292; *Cramb v Goodwin* (1919) 35 T.L.R. 477; also *Bickley v Browning, Todd & Co* (1912) 30 T.L.R. 134 ("half-commission man").

[260] As in *Sellers v London Counties Newspapers* [1951] 1 K.B. 784.

[261] As in *Levy v Goldhill* [1917] 2 Ch. 297; cf. *Marshall v Glanvill* [1917] 2 K.B. 87.

the agent who terminates, the implication of a term that commission on repeat orders continues is less likely.[262]

If it is the principal who terminates and such an interpretation is appropriate, the remedy is again an action for damages for loss of opportunity of earning commission rather than a declaration as to the right to commission.[263]

Commercial agents   The Commercial Agents (Council Directive) Regulations   **7-043**
1993 contain provisions regarding remuneration after termination.[264] They are discussed in Chapter 11.

Illustrations

(1) An agent indicates willingness to introduce a purchaser for two cinemas if paid   **7-044**
commission. He introduces a prospective purchaser but the vendor decides not to proceed with the sale. The agent is not entitled to commission.[265]
(2) Shipbrokers procured a charter of a vessel for 18 months which provided for a commission of two-and-a-half per cent on hire paid under it and any continuation of it. After four months the owners sold the vessel. The brokers were unable to recover commission for the remainder of the charter period.[266]
(3) Agents introduced buyers to sellers, who entered into a contract of sale. A contract between agents and sellers provided, in consideration for the introduction, for commission calculated per metric ton sold on performance of the sale contract, and for certain other payments in connection with the demurrage payable at the port of discharge. The sellers failed to perform the contract, forfeited a performance bond and settled additionally with the buyers. Held, a term was to be implied that:

> "the vendors will not deprive the agents of their commission by committing a breach of the contract between the vendors and the purchaser which releases the purchaser from its obligation to pay the purchase price."[267]

---

[262] See Longmore LJ in *Explora Group Plc v Hesco Bastion Ltd* [2005] EWCA Civ 646; (2005) 149 S.J.L.B. 924 at [125]; *Personal Touch Financial Services Ltd v Simplysure Ltd* [2016] EWCA Civ 461; [2016] Bus.L.R. 1049 at [47].
[263] See cases cited in fn.257 above.
[264] reg.8.
[265] *Luxor (Eastbourne) Ltd v Cooper* [1941] A.C. 108.
[266] *L. French & Co Ltd v Leeston Shipping Co Ltd* [1922] 1 A.C. 451. See this case explained by Bingham LJ in *Marcan Shipping (London) Ltd v Polish SS Co* [1989] 2 Lloyd's Rep. 138. See also Article 123 and Illustrations; *Sun Alliance, etc., Ltd v Webster* [1991] 2 Lloyd's Rep. 410.
[267] *Alpha Trading Ltd v Dunnshaw-Patten Ltd* [1981] Q.B. 290 (see (1982) 45 M.L.R. 220); followed in *Martin-Smith v Williams* [1999] E.M.L.R. 571 (waiver by principal of future royalties on which agent would have earned commission); *George Moundreas & Co SA v Navimpex Centrata Navata* [1985] 2 Lloyd's Rep. 515; *Orient Overseas Management and Finance Ltd v File Shipping Co Ltd (The Energy Progress)* [1993] 1 Lloyd's Rep. 355; cf. *Marcan Shipping (London) Ltd v Polish SS Co*, above; *Sun Alliance Pensions Life and Investments Services Ltd v Webster* [1991] 2 Lloyd's Rep. 410; *Micklefield v SAC Technology Ltd* [1990] 1 W.L.R. 1002. Sometimes such events are specifically provided for: see *Christie & Vesey Ltd v Maatschappij, etc., Helvetia NV (The Helvetia-S)* [1960] 1 Lloyd's Rep. 540; cf. *White v Turnbull Martin & Co* (1898) 3 Com.Cas. 183.

Article 59

SPECIFIC ENFORCEMENT OF AGENCY CONTRACT

7-045   The performance of a contract of agency will not normally be enforced by an order for specific performance or other similar order.[268]

Comment

7-046   **Specific performance exceptional**   A contract of agency is by its nature a personal contract; the relationship between the parties is of a fiduciary character and depends upon mutual confidence. It has long been established that the courts will not normally enforce the continuation of such a contract, whether directly by an order for specific performance or indirectly by injunction.[269] The normal remedy for breach of contract by the principal is therefore an action for damages. But because these specific remedies are equitable they are discretionary and it is therefore not possible to state that the principle has no exceptions. In this context the contract of agency has many similarities with the contract of employment: indeed some agents may be employees. In *Hill v C.A. Parsons & Co Ltd*[270] the Court of Appeal gave an interim injunction to an employee to restrain his employers from dismissing him.[271] The court made clear the wholly exceptional nature of the case[272]: the employers had full confidence in the employee and were being forced to dismiss him in breach of contract under pressure from a trade union. However, some cases have indicated a greater readiness to enforce performance.[273] The continuation of confidence is clearly a factor of importance, especially in what may be called the field of pure agency where the agent represents the principal vis-à-vis third parties and can bring him into contractual relationship with them.[274] Where the agent is a sole agent, it is particularly hard to envisage the contract being specifically enforced;

---

[268] See in general Chitty, *Contracts* (32nd edn), Ch.27; Treitel, *Law of Contract* (14th edn), para.21-016 onwards; Meagher, *Gummow and Lehane's Equity Doctrines and Remedies* (5th edn), Ch.20; Spry, *Equitable Remedies* (9th edn); Sharpe, *Injunctions and Specific Performance* (4th edn); Jones and Goodhart, *Specific Performance* (2nd edn).

[269] See Fry, *Specific Performance* (6th edn), p.50; *Chinnock v Sainsbury* (1860) 30 L.J.Ch. 409 (auctioneer); *Mortimer v Beckett* [1920] 1 Ch. 571; *Page One Records Ltd v Britton* [1968] 1 W.L.R. 157; *Denmark Productions Ltd v Boscobel Productions Ltd* [1969] 1 Q.B. 699; *Netline Pty Ltd v Qav Pty Ltd (No.2)* [2015] WASC 113. The leading case is now *Co-operative Insurance Society Ltd v Argyll Stores (Holdings) Ltd* [1998] A.C. 1, which though in a different context may perhaps be taken as authority for a stricter approach to specific enforcement than has sometimes been adopted.

[270] [1972] 1 Ch. 305. See also *Tito v Waddell (No.2)* [1977] Ch. 106 at 321–322; *Posner v Scott-Lewis* [1987] Ch. 25; *Irani v Southampton, etc., Health Authority* [1985] I.C.R. 80.

[271] s.236 of the Trade Union and Labour Relations (Consolidation) Act 1992 prohibits a court, whether by an order for specific performance or an injunction, from compelling an employee to do any work or attend at any place for the doing of any work.

[272] The exceptional nature of the relief granted in *Hill v C.A. Parsons & Co Ltd* was emphasised in *Sanders v Ernest A. Neale Ltd* [1974] I.C.R. 565 and *Chappell v Times Newspapers Ltd* [1975] 1 W.L.R. 482. But see Freedland, below.

[273] See *C.H. Giles & Co Ltd v Morris* [1972] 1 W.L.R. 307, esp. at 318; *Sky Petroleum Ltd v V.I.P. Petroleum Ltd* [1974] 1 W.L.R. 576; *Sudbrook Trading Estate Ltd v Eggleton* [1983] 1 A.C. 444; Freedland, *The Personal Employment Contract* (2006), p.372 onwards (stressing that many cases involve public authorities).

[274] The importance of continued confidence was stressed in *Page One Records Ltd v Britton* [1968] 1 W.L.R. 157 where the manager of a very successful group of young musicians was refused an injunction which would have had the effect of enforcing his agency contract. See too *Angove's Pty Ltd v Bailey* [2016] UKSC 47; [2016] 1 W.L.R. 3179 at [6].

in that event the principal would be obliged to cease carrying on the business in question or to continue it through the agency of someone in whom he may have lost confidence and against whom he is currently engaged in litigation. In other cases the principal may have a right to terminate the contract,[275] or the agent himself may have only limited rights, e.g. because his contract is unilateral.[276] But a distributorship or franchising contract, and other contracts which may be said to involve a joint venture rather than pure agency, may perhaps more readily be specifically enforced, or at least supported by an injunction against dealing with others.[277]

Subsistence of contract It was formerly considered that, contrary to the principles of the general law of contract, a contract of employment could be unilaterally terminated by either party[278] and that a court would therefore not grant a declaration that such a contract still subsisted. But in *Francis v Kuala Lumpur Councillors*[279] the Privy Council said that in exceptional circumstances such a declaration might be made, and in *Decro-Wall International SA v Practitioners in Marketing Ltd*[280] a majority of the Court of Appeal expressed the view that an employment contract could not be unilaterally terminated by one party and that such a contract was therefore not an exception to the general principles of the law of contract in this respect. The latter case concerned not a contract of employment but a distributorship contract; and it has been held that the reasoning applies to pure agency.[281] Many difficulties however remain unresolved.[282] A declaration that a contract still subsists is a discretionary remedy and it is clear that it will not easily be granted. The points here made impact on the question of the revocability of the agent's authority, which is considered under Article 120.

7-047

---

275 See Article 123.

276 As in the case of an estate agent: see above, para.7-035. See also *Chinnock v Sainsbury* (1860) 30 L.J.Ch. 409 (auctioneer); *Metropolitan Electric Supply Co Ltd v Ginder* [1901] 2 Ch. 799.

277 See, e.g. *Decro-Wall International SA v Practitioners in Marketing Ltd* [1971] 1 W.L.R. 361; *Evans Marshall & Co v Bertola SA* [1973] 1 W.L.R. 349, esp. at 379 (injunction cases); but cf. *Co-operative Insurance Co Ltd v Argyll Stores (Holdings) Ltd* [1998] A.C. 1. See also *Donnell v Bennett* (1883) 22 Ch.D. 835; *Atlas Steels (Australia) Pty Ltd v Atlas Steels Ltd* (1948) 49 S.R. (N.S.W.) 157; *Pasen v Dominion Herb Distributors Inc* (1968) 67 D.L.R. (2d) 405; affd 69 D.L.R. (2d) 651. cf. *Paxton v Spira* (1965) 54 D.L.R. (2d) 627; *Shell (Petroleum Mining) Co Ltd v Todd Petroleum Mining Co Ltd* [2008] 2 N.Z.L.R. 418 (NZCA) (injunction against action that involved repudiation of agency agreement, where agent a joint venture company). See also *Standard Life Health Care Ltd v Gorman* [2009] EWCA Civ 1292; [2010] I.R.L.R. 233.

278 e.g. *Vine v National Dock Labour Board* [1957] A.C. 488; *Cranleigh Precision Engineering Ltd v Bryant* [1965] 1 W.L.R. 1293; *Denmark Productions Ltd v Boscobel Productions Ltd* [1969] 1 Q.B. 699; *Roberts v Elwells Engineers Ltd* [1972] Q.B. 586; *Sanders v Ernest A. Neale Ltd* [1974] I.C.R. 565.

279 [1962] 1 W.L.R. 1411 at 1417–1418.

280 [1971] 1 W.L.R. 361. See also *Gunton v Richmond-upon-Thames LBC* [1981] Ch. 448; *London Transport Executive v Clarke* [1981] I.C.R. 355. cf. *Sport International Bussum BV v Inter-Footwear Ltd* [1984] 1 W.L.R. 776 (no relief against forfeiture); *Wilson v St Helen's BC* [1999] 2 A.C. 52 at 77.

281 *Atlantic Underwriting Agencies Ltd v Cia. di Assicurazione di Milano SpA* [1979] 2 Lloyd's Rep. 240; *Paper Reclaim Ltd v Aotearoa International Ltd* [2007] 3 N.Z.L.R. 169 (NZSC) at [19] (repudiation by principal of agency agreement to market its products had the effect of determining the agency but not the contract itself until the repudiation had been accepted; the duty to mitigate will frequently lead to acceptance of the repudiation).

282 See Kerr (1984) 47 M.L.R. 30; Treitel, *Law of Contract* (14th edn), para.18-006; Chitty, *Contracts* (32nd edn), paras 40-183 and 40-192 onwards.

Article 60

NO REMUNERATION FOR UNAUTHORISED TRANSACTIONS OR IN CASES OF MISCONDUCT OR BREACH OF DUTY

7-048   An agent is not entitled to remuneration—

(1)   in respect of any unauthorised transaction[283] which is not ratified by the principal[284];

(2)   in respect of transactions in relation to which he is in breach of his duties as agent, such breach going to the root of the contract or otherwise justifying the principal's repudiation of the liability to pay.[285]

Comment

7-049   **Unauthorised transactions**   Commission is by its nature only payable in respect of transactions expressly or impliedly authorised or ratified. A transaction made by an agent with himself without the consent of his principal may be unauthorised.[286] Where authority is wrongfully withdrawn, however, there may be an action for breach of contract.

7-050   **Breach of duty by agent**   Where the agent is in serious breach of his duty to his principal, the principal may be justified in refusing to pay commission in respect of the transaction as to which the agent is in breach[287]: further, if the agent is appointed by the principal for a fixed time in circumstances entitling him to notice[288] the principal may terminate his employment or other contract summarily and decline to pay any remuneration that is not due and payable at the date of dismissal.[289] But commission earned, and retainer, salary or wages already due, at the time of the breach must normally be paid.[290] This is simply an application of the law as to discharge of contract by breach.[291]

A breach of duty such as to warrant the withholding of remuneration, and in some cases the recovery of remuneration already paid, may be justified in various ways. In some cases it may be sufficient to say that commission has not been earned, without reference to discharge of the contract of agency, if any: this reasoning has been used where the agent has wrongfully delegated his duties[292] or stated a wrong asking price for the property leading to its sale at less than the vendor intended.[293] But in other cases it may be appropriate to say more generally that the agent's

---

[283] Illustrations 1–42.
[284] As in *Keay v Fenwick* (1876) 1 C.P.D. 745. See Articles 13–20.
[285] See Comment.
[286] *Salomons v Pender* (1865) 3 H. & C. 639, Illustration 4.
[287] *Andrews v Ramsay & Co* [1903] 2 K.B. 635, Illustration 4; *Rhodes v Macalister* (1923) 29 Com.Cas. 19.
[288] See Comment to Article 123.
[289] *Boston Deep Sea Fishing & Ice Co v Ansell* (1888) 39 Ch.D. 339; *Rhodes v Macalister*, above, at 29; *Shepherd v Felt and Textiles of Australia Ltd* (1931) 45 C.L.R. 359. See further Article 48.
[290] ibid.
[291] See Chitty, *Contracts* (32nd edn), Ch.24; Treitel, *Law of Contract* (14th edn), Chs 17 and 18. See too *Crocs Europe BV v Anderson (t/a Spectrum Agencies)* [2012] EWCA Civ 1400; [2013] 1 Lloyd's Rep. 1 at [24] (not all breaches of fiduciary duty will warrant termination of agency).
[292] *Beable v Dickerson* (1885) 1 T.L.R. 654; *John McCann & Co v Pow* [1974] 1 W.L.R. 1643.
[293] *Spiers v Taylor* (1984) 271 E.G. 196.

breach goes to the root of the contract,[294] or that his dereliction of duty is itself a repudiation of his obligations which may be accepted by the principal.[295]

A breach by the agent of the obligations arising from his fiduciary character, e.g. where the agent accepts a bribe, or himself purchases (without disclosure) his principal's property, can be regarded as fatal to a right to remuneration,[296] and may be described as a breach going to the root of the contract[297]; though in some such cases it may also be said that an agent so acting is not acting as agent at all but as buyer, or generally not within the scope of his authority.[298] In other cases, especially of professional agents, it may be said that he has been guilty of gross neglect or misconduct,[299] or lack of due diligence,[300] or dishonesty[301]; or again that his acts have by his own default been entirely valueless and useless to his principal and do not therefore qualify him for commission.[302] Again a slight breach of duty or omission may bar him from remuneration if the obligation is treated as entire, for such an obligation cannot be sued upon by an agent until he has completely performed it.[303]

In a recent case, *Imageview Management Ltd v Jack*,[304] forfeiture of an agent's entire remuneration was upheld even though there was no finding of dishonesty in the agent, and even though the services conformed to what was requested and there was no suggestion that their value had been affected by the breach of duty. The

---

[294] *Thornton Hall & Partners v Wembley Electrical Appliances Ltd* [1947] 2 All E.R. 630 at 634; cf. *Keppel v Wheeler* [1927] 1 K.B. 577 at 592.
[295] *Boston Deep Sea Fishing & Ice Co v Ansell* (1888) 39 Ch.D. 339 at 365. And see *Hurst v Holding* (1810) 3 Taunt. 32 (agent himself prevented performance); *Styles v Rogers Realty Ltd* (1987) 43 D.L.R. (4th) 629 (exclusive agent did not use reasonable efforts to sell land).
[296] *Boston Deep Sea Fishing & Ice Co v Ansell; Salomons v Pender* (1865) 3 H. & C. 639, Illustration 4; *Andrews v Ramsay & Co* [1903] 2 K.B. 635, Illustration 4; *Rhodes v Macalister* (1923) 29 Com.Cas. 19; *Price v Metropolitan House Investment Agency Co Ltd* (1907) 23 T.L.R. 630; *L.S. Harris Trustees Ltd v Power Packing Services (Hermit Road) Ltd* [1970] 2 Lloyd's Rep. 65 (breach of confidence); *Greenwood v Harvey* [1965] N.S.W.R. 1489; *Cec. McManus Realty Ltd v Bray* (1970) 14 D.L.R. (3d) 564; *Ian Scott & Co v Medical Installations Co Ltd* [1981] E.G.D. 228 (attempt to extract extra commission); *Ocean City Realty Ltd v A. & M. Holdings Ltd* (1987) 36 D.L.R. (4th) 94; *Wheen v Smithmann European Homes*, CA June 20, 2000 (where Article 60 was cited by the court). But this is not always so: cf. *Hippisley v Knee Bros* [1905] 1 K.B. 1, Illustration 5; *Keppel v Wheeler*, above, at 592.
[297] *Thornton Hall & Partners v Wembley Electrical Appliances Ltd* [1947] 2 All E.R. 630 at 634.
[298] *Salomons v Pender*, above; *Andrews v Ramsay*, above.
[299] *White v Lady Lincoln* (1803) 8 Ves. 363 (failure by solicitor to keep accounts; but the principle of this case does not apply when the solicitor is not the general agent of the client: *Re Lee Ex p. Neville* (1868) L.R. 4 Ch.App. 43); *Huntley v Bulwer* (1839) 6 Bing.N.C. 111.
[300] *Moneypenny v Hartland* (1824) 1 C. & P. 352.
[301] *Rhodes v Macalister* (1923) 29 Com.Cas. 19; *Andrews v Ramsay & Co* [1903] 2 K.B. 635, Illustration 4.
[302] *Huntley v Bulwer* (1839) 6 Bing.N.C. 111; *Denew v Daverell* (1813) 3 Camp. 451, Illustration 10; *Hamond v Holiday* (1824) 1 C. & P. 384 (shipbroker); *Hill v Featherstonhaugh* (1831) 7 Bing. 569 (attorney); *Maketu Estates Ltd v Robb* [2014] NZHC 2664.
[303] Such may be the case with solicitors' retainers to conduct actions: *Underwood, Son & Piper v Lewis* [1894] 2 Q.B. 306; *Cachia v Isaacs* (1985) 3 N.S.W.L.R. 366; *Richard Buxton (Solicitors) v Mills-Owens* [2010] EWCA Civ 122; [2010] 1 W.L.R. 1997; *French v Carter Lemon Camerons LLP* [2012] EWCA Civ 1180 at [26]. But cf. *Warmingtons v McMurray* (1937) 52 T.L.R. 381; *Caldwell v Treloar* (1982) 30 S.A.S.R. 202; *Cawdery Kaye Fireman & Taylor v Minkin* [2012] EWCA Civ 546; [2012] 3 All E.R. 1117 (client ends solicitor's retainer).
[304] [2009] EWCA Civ 63; [2009] 2 All E.R. 666, Illustration 11; See too *Rahme v Smith & Williamson Trust Corp Ltd* [2009] EWHC 911 (Ch) at [141]; *Stupples v Stupples & Co (High Wycombe) Ltd* [2012] EWHC 1226 (Ch); [2013] 1 B.C.L.C. 729 at [25]; *Avrahami v Biran* [2013] EWHC 1776 (Ch) at [345] (project manager misappropriates sums throughout period of project).

reasoning in this case has since been applied to forfeit the profit share of a partner in a limited partnership when the partner had disloyally been seeking to persuade some employees to leave and start a new business with him.[305] It is strongly arguable that the reasoning in *Imageview* (and in some cases before *Imageview*) is inconsistent with both common law and equitable principle, since, where there has been no failure of performance nor any dishonesty, and any collateral profit has (rightly) already been stripped, forfeiture of remuneration is penal. Perhaps only the Supreme Court could now undertake a principled reconsideration of the law. But some recent cases show judges finding the means to take a more restrained approach to forfeiture, looking for a breach which goes to the root of the agency contract,[306] and otherwise not forfeiting remuneration where to do so would be "disproportionate and inequitable".[307]

There can obviously however be cases where the agent effects severable transactions, and in these cases the rule depriving him of commission will only apply to those in respect of which he is in breach of duty[308]; or where the breach does not go to the whole contract.[309] There has also been some tendency to hold commission recoverable when the agent makes an honest mistake, even if that mistake renders him liable in damages.[310] And there may be a waiver of the agent's breach[311]: but this is not implied from the fact that the principal takes the benefit of the transaction negotiated by the agent,[312] nor from the fact that he recovers a bribe from the agent.[313]

Illustrations

7-051 (1) A is employed on commission to procure a loan upon certain terms. Before anything is done the principal varies the terms. A is unable to procure the loan on the terms as varied, but obtains an offer on the original terms, which the principal refuses to accept. A is not entitled to any commission, though he may be entitled to damages for breach of contract.[314]

(2) An agent is employed on commission to sell certain property. His authority is revoked by the death of the principal, but he subsequently sells the property, and the principal's executors confirm the sale. The agent is not entitled to recover the agreed commission from the executors unless they recognise the terms of his employment, but he may be entitled upon a quantum meruit.[315]

[305] See *Hosking v Marathon Asset Management LLP* [2016] EWHC 2418 (Ch); [2017] Ch. 157.
[306] For relatively recent dicta, see *Kelly v Cooper* [1993] A.C. 205 at 216; and *Premium Real Estate Ltd v Stevens* [2009] 2 N.Z.L.R. 384 at [90], Illustration 12, where emphasis is put on the agent's bad faith; *Wright Hassall LLP v Horton Jr* [2015] EWHC 3716 (QB) at [61]. For discussion of these and older cases, see Watts (2009) 125 L.Q.R. 369; Macgregor (2010) 14 Edinburgh L.R. 121; Oram [2010] L.M.C.L.Q. 95.
[307] See *Bank of Ireland v Jaffery* [2012] EWHC 1377 (Ch) at [373]; *Gamatronic (UK) Ltd v Hamilton* [2016] EWHC 2225 (QB) at [171].
[308] Illustration 5.
[309] See Illustrations 5 and 6. See also *Bank of Ireland v Jaffery* [2012] EWHC 1377 (Ch) at [372]; *Electrosteel Castings (UK) Ltd v Metalpol Ltd* [2014] EWHC 2017 (Ch) at [64].
[310] See Illustrations 6 and 7.
[311] Illustration 8; *Thornton Hall & Partners v Wembley Electrical Appliances Ltd* [1947] 2 All E.R. 630.
[312] *Salomons v Pender* (1865) 3 H. & C. 639; *Rhodes v Macalister* (1923) 29 Com.Cas. 19; *Imageview Management Ltd v Jack* [2009] EWCA Civ 63; [2009] 2 All E.R. 666.
[313] *Andrews v Ramsay & Co* [1903] 2 K.B. 635.
[314] *Toppin v Healey* (1863) 11 W.R. 466.
[315] *Campanari v Woodburn* (1854) 15 C.B. 400. As to quantum meruit see above, paras 7-009 and 7-024.

(3)   An auctioneer, who is employed to sell property by auction, sells it by private contract. He is not entitled to commission.[316]

(4)   An agent, who is employed to sell certain land, sells it to a company in which he is a director and large shareholder. He is not entitled to commission upon the sale, even if it is adopted and confirmed by the principal.[317] This can be explained on the basis that the agent had no authority to sell to himself or a party in which he held a substantial equity interest. In other cases, the explanation can be that because of the agent's breach of duty, the principal received no benefit from the transaction. So, if an agent for sale fraudulently takes a secret commission from the purchaser, he is not only accountable to the principal for the secret commission, but is not entitled to remuneration from the seller; and if the seller pays him commission in ignorance of the facts, he is entitled to recover it.[318]

(5)   An auctioneer, employed to sell property on the terms that he should be paid a certain commission and out-of-pocket expenses, received discounts from printers and advertisers, and charged the principal in full without deducting the discounts, in the honest belief that he was entitled to retain them. It was held that, though he must account for the discounts, he was entitled to commission, as he had not acted fraudulently, and as the receipt of the discount was incidental to his main duty of selling the goods.[319] So, where a commission agent fraudulently overcharged his principal in respect of some transactions, but acted honestly in other separate and distinct transactions, it was held that he was entitled to commission on the transactions in which he had acted honestly.[320]

(6)   An agent, employed to find a purchaser, procured an offer, which the vendor accepted, subject to contract. Subsequently, a higher offer was made by another party to the agent, which, in the bona fide belief that he had fulfilled his duty, he failed to communicate to the vendor, and the vendor concluded a contract with the person whose offer had been accepted. The vendor recovered as damages from the agent the difference between the price fixed by the concluded contract and the higher offer. The agent would have been entitled to commission on the price so fixed and this sum was therefore to be deducted from the damages.[321]

(7)   An agent firm introduces purchasers whose offer is accepted subject to contract. The agents' branch manager hears of difficulties which the vendors are having concerning the house to which they hope to move. He thinks it his duty to tell the prospective purchasers and does so. The sale nearly falls through, but the vendors terminate the agents' instructions and sell the property to the same purchasers directly: they move into rented

[316] *Marsh v Jelf* (1862) 3 F. & F. 234; *Gillow & Co v Lord Aberdare* (1892) 9 T.L.R. 12.
[317] *Salomons v Pender* (1865) 3 H. & C. 639.
[318] *Andrews v Ramsay & Co* [1903] 2 K.B. 635. cf. *Turner v Laurentide Financial Realty Corp (Western) Ltd* (1979) 97 D.L.R. (3d) 429. See also Articles 48 and 96.
[319] *Hippisley v Knee Bros* [1905] 1 K.B. 1; applied in *The Peppy* [1997] 2 Lloyd's Rep. 722. See (1905) 21 L.Q.R. 102.
[320] *Nitedals Taendstikfabrik v Bruster* [1906] 2 Ch. 671. But cf. *Headway Construction Co Ltd v Downham* (1974) 233 E.G. 675 (whole commission agreement voidable for fraud).
[321] *Keppel v Wheeler* [1927] 1 K.B. 577. See also Murdoch (1974) 232 E.G. 1021, criticising *John McCann & Co v Pow* [1974] 1 W.L.R. 1643. See also Estate Agents (Undesirable Practices) (No.2) Order 1991 (SI 1991/1032) Sch.3 para.2.

accommodation. The agents are entitled to commission, though they would
have been liable in damages had loss resulted to the vendor.[322]

(8) The estate department of a company acting for the vendor of a house
introduced a purchaser, and, in ignorance of the agency, the building department of the company acted for the purchaser and made a report on the house
which had the effect of reducing the price. Subsequently the company
discovered that they had been acting in this way and made an offer to the
vendor to invite the purchaser to obtain an independent report on the house.
The vendor refused and completed the sale at a reduction of the agreed price,
the reduction being due to the work required to be done as a result of the
report. Held, that although the company had committed a breach of their duty
as agents, since the principal with full knowledge of this breach had
completed the sale at the reduced price, he had affirmed the transaction and
the agent was entitled to commission.[323]

(9) An agent was employed by a lessee to find a purchaser of leasehold premises
which were subject to a covenant prohibiting the carrying on of any business other than that of a music seller without the consent of the lessor. Several
tailors made offers to the lessee to buy the premises for £2,500, but the lessee, believing that the lessor would not consent, did not approach him upon
the matter. The agent, having an offer from a tailor of £2,250, and having
obtained an assurance from the lessor that he would consent to a tailor's business being carried on upon the premises, concealed from the lessee the fact
that the lessor had so assured his consent and the nature of the business of the
person making the offer, and induced the lessee to accept £2,250. Held, that
the agent was not entitled to any commission.[324]

(10) An auctioneer employed to sell an estate negligently omitted to insert in the
conditions of sale a proviso usually inserted in them, and in consequence of
the omission the sale was rendered nugatory. Held, that he was not entitled
to any compensation or remuneration for his services, although the particulars
of the sale had been submitted to the principal and were not objected to by
him.[325]

(11) A sports agent under a two-year contract with a professional footballer obtains
for him a position with a club, taking a commission on his salary. The agent
also receives a fee from the club for procuring a work permit for the player,
which fee is not revealed to the player. Held, on account of the failure to
disclose the conflict of interest, that the agent both forfeited his commission
(even though the principal had no objection to the contract obtained for him
by the agent and continued to play for the club) and was accountable for the
fee received from the club.[326]

(12) A real estate agency appointed by the vendor leads the vendor to believe that
the proposing purchaser intends to live in the house, when it knows that the

[322] *Robinson Scammell & Co v Ansell* [1985] 2 E.G.L.R. 41; see also *Eric V Stansfield v South East Nursing Home Services Ltd* [1986] 1 E.G.L.R. 29.
[323] *Harrods Ltd v Lemon* [1931] 2 K.B. 157. See also *Dargusch v Sherley Investments Pty Ltd* [1970] Qd.R. 338. cf. *Jones v Canavan* [1972] 2 N.S.W.L.R. 236.
[324] *Heath v Parkinson* (1926) 136 L.T. 128.
[325] *Denew v Daverell* (1813) 3 Camp. 451.
[326] *Imageview Management Ltd v Jack* [2009] EWCA Civ 63; [2009] 2 All E.R. 666. See too *Rahme v Smith & Williamson Trust Corporation Ltd* [2009] EWHC 911 (Ch) at [141].

purchaser is a property developer intent on on-selling the house, a fact that would have been material to the vendor in its negotiating position and who would not have sold to the developer had he known the facts. The agency regularly also acts for the purchaser, and so acts in the subsequent sale of the property at a profit. Held, that the agency was not entitled to any commission on the sale.[327]

Article 61

No Remuneration in Respect of Unlawful Transactions

(1) An agent may be debarred from recovering remuneration for his services if at the time when the services were rendered he was not legally qualified to act in the capacity in which he claims the remuneration, or if the enforcement of his contract of agency is affected in some other way by statute or statutory instrument.[328]   **7-052**

(2) An agent cannot recover any remuneration in respect of any transaction which is obviously, or to his knowledge, unlawful,[329] or unlawful by virtue of legislation which is to be interpreted as affecting contracts which involve the doing of acts prohibited by it.

Comment

Rule (1): Incapacity to act   There are frequently statutory or other requirements regarding capacity to act in certain professional and similar activities. An obvious example is the Solicitors Act 1974, referred to in Illustration 1. So also in Australia, New Zealand and elsewhere real estate agents may require licences.[330] Unqualified persons cannot normally recover remuneration. But the exact result must in each case turn on the terms of the legal provisions imposing the requirement of qualification. Sometimes the very acting as agent for the particular person in certain ways is unlawful.[331] Some statutes prevent persons exercising agency functions from suing on the agency contract in certain circumstances.[332] Other statutes simply prescribe penalties.   **7-053**

Rule (2): Illegal transactions   This rule is an application of the common law principles as to illegal contracts, which should be considered, as developed by cases most of which are not relevant to agency, in each situation individually.[333] The   **7-054**

---

[327] *Premium Real Estate Ltd v Stevens* [2009] 2 N.Z.L.R. 384.
[328] Illustrations 1 and 2; and see Comment.
[329] Illustrations 3, 4 and 5; and see Comment. See also *Allkins v Jupe* (1877) 2 C.P.D. 375 (illegal insurance); *Harrington v Victoria Graving Dock Co* (1878) 3 Q.B.D. 549 (corrupt contract, see further below); *North v Marra Developments Ltd* (1981) 148 C.L.R. 42; *RTA (Business Consultants) Ltd v Bracewell* [2015] EWHC 630 (QB) (Money Laundering Regulations 2007).
[330] e.g. Auctioneers and Agents Act 1971 (Qld); Real Estate Agents Act 2008 (NZ).
[331] e.g. Accommodation Agencies Act 1953; see *Saunders v Soper* [1975] A.C. 239; Partington (1975) 125 New L.J. 148; Cartwright (1979) 123 S.J. 577; Szekely (1984) 12 Aus. Bus. Law Rev. 408. See also *Phoenix General Ins. Co of Greece SA v Halvanon Ins. Co* [1988] Q.B. 216 (Insurance Companies Act 1982 s.2, now repealed).
[332] See Illustrations 1 and 2.
[333] See Chitty, *Contracts*, (32nd edn), Ch.16; Treitel, *Law of Contract* (14th edn), Ch.11.

formulation in the Article gives no more than the most general of guidelines. Older cases will need to be reconsidered in the light of *Patel v Mirza*.[334]

7-055 **Wagering transactions**   It seems that before 1892 commission was recoverable by agents employed to make wagers[335] just as indemnity was recoverable.[336] But this was reversed by the Gaming Act 1892, which by s.1 provided that:

> "any promise, express or implied ... to pay any sum of money by way of commission, fee, reward or otherwise, in respect of any contract or agreement [rendered null and void by the Gaming Act 1845], or of any services in relation thereto or connection therewith, shall be null and void, and no action shall be brought or maintained to recover any such sum of money."[337]

The main difficulties occurred in connection with speculative transactions on the Stock Exchange.[338] But the 1892 Act is repealed by the Gambling Act 2005, under which wagers are enforceable.

Illustrations

7-056 (1) No costs are recoverable in respect of anything done by any unqualified person acting as a solicitor.[339]
(2) An estate agent who enters into a contract with another under which he will engage in estate agency work and who fails to supply to his client information as required by the Estate Agents Act 1979 or statutory instrument made under it cannot enforce the contract, whether by legal action or the exercise of a lien over the client's money, except pursuant to an order of the court.[340]
(3) An action was brought for work done and money expended in buying shares in a company which affected to act as a body corporate without authority by charter or statute and was therefore illegal. Held, that the action was not maintainable because it arose out of an unlawful transaction.[341]
(4) Commission was claimed by a broker for procuring freight. Held, that the fact that the charterparty in respect of which commission was claimed would be illegal unless the charterer obtained certain licences was no answer to the ac-

---

[334] *Patel v Mirza* [2016] UKSC 42; [2017] A.C. 467. Quaere, e.g. whether *Harrington v Victoria Graving Dock Co* (1878) 3 Q.B.D. 549 would be decided the same way (agreement to employ agent with corrupt intention in relation to his principal but agent not in fact corrupted and unsuccessfully seeking remuneration).

[335] *Knight v Fitch* (1855) 15 C.B. 566.

[336] *Read v Anderson* (1884) 13 Q.B.D. 779.

[337] Note that it is only money that is referred to.

[338] Especially contracts for "differences".

[339] Solicitors Act 1974 s.25(1). "Costs" includes fees, charges, disbursements, expenses and remuneration: Solicitors Act 1974 s.87(1). For "unqualified person" see Solicitors Act 1974 s.87(1) as amended and s.1. See also Solicitors Act 1974 s.25(2); *Kent v Ward* (1894) 70 L.T. 612; *Re Sweeting* [1898] 1 Ch. 268; *Browne v Barber* [1913] 2 K.B. 553; *Hudgell Yeates & Co v Watson* [1978] Q.B. 451; Cordery, *Solicitors* (8th edn), p.35.

[340] Estate Agents Act 1979 s.18(5); above, paras 7-007 and 7-037; *Solicitors' Estate Agency (Glasgow) Ltd v MacIver* 1993 S.L.T. 23; *Connell Estate Agents v Begej* [1993] 2 E.G.L.R. 35; Murdoch, *Law of Estate Agency* (5th edn), p.288 onwards; Murdoch, *The Estate Agents and Property Misdescriptions Acts* (3rd edn). As to lien, see Articles 64–68. For an example of court approval despite there being no such information supplied, see *Benhams Ltd v Kythira Investments Ltd* [2004] EWHC 2973 (QB).

[341] *Josephs v Pebrer* (1825) 3 B. & C. 639.

tion, it not being part of the broker's duty to see that the licences were obtained.[342]

(5) Claims for remuneration for attending auctions for the purpose of "puffing" prices,[343] and claims for remuneration for procuring the sale of public offices,[344] are unenforceable.

2. REIMBURSEMENT AND INDEMNITY

Article 62

REIMBURSEMENT OF EXPENSES AND INDEMNITY FROM LIABILITIES INCURRED IN COURSE OF AGENCY

Subject to the provisions of Article 63, every agent has a right against his **7-057** principal to be reimbursed all expenses and to be indemnified against all losses and liabilities incurred by him in the execution of his authority[345]: and where the agent is sued for money due to his principal, he has a right to set off the amount of any such expenses, losses or liabilities,[346] unless the money due to the principal is held on trust.[347] There is, it seems, no implied indemnity in respect of loss suffered by an agent from torts committed against him by third parties in the course of the agency.[348]

Comment

The rule here given is normally stated in such general terms,[349] but its juristic **7-058** basis may require attention. In the nineteenth century, actions at law were based on the common count for money paid, and it was not often necessary to distinguish between contractual and what would now be called restitutionary claims.[350] At the present day it could matter how the claim was classified in a particular case.

Contract Where the agency agreement is contractual, the agreement to reimburse **7-059** and indemnify in return for what has been requested, if not express,[351] can be

---

[342] *Haines v Busk* (1814) 5 Taunt. 521.
[343] *Walker v Nightingale* (1726) 4 Bro.P.C. 193. See too *North v Marra Developments Ltd* (1981) 148 C.L.R. 42.
[344] *Stackpole v Earle* (1761) 2 Wil.K.B. 133; *Parsons v Thompson* (1790) 1 Hy.Bl. 322; *Waldo v Martin* (1825) 4 B. & C. 319.
[345] See Comment and Illustrations; *Restatement, Third* § 8.14; Ch.3 above as to authority. See Illustrations 11 and 12 of para.7-062 below.
[346] Illustrations 4 and 5.
[347] See *Stumore v Campbell & Co* [1892] 1 Q.B. 314; *Re Mid-Kent Fruit Factory* [1896] 1 Ch. 567; above, para.6-040 onwards.
[348] *National Roads and Motorists' Association v Whitlam* (2007) 25 A.C.L.C. 688 (NSWCA) at [94], Illustration 11.
[349] See, e.g. *Thacker v Hardy* (1878) 4 Q.B.D. 685 at 687. The principle is also stated in even wider terms that do not confine it to agency: see *Dugdale v Lovering* (1875) L.R. 10 C.P. 196; *Sheffield Corp v Barclay* [1905] A.C. 392; *Secretary of State for India v Bank of India Ltd* [1938] 2 All E.R. 797; *Guaranty Trust Co v James Richardson & Son* (1963) 39 D.L.R. (2d) 517. But cf. *Cory & Son Ltd v Lambton & Hetton Collieries Ltd* (1916) 86 L.J.K.B. 401.
[350] See Stoljar, *Law of Quasi-Contract* (2nd edn), p.152 onwards; *Bowlby v Bell* (1846) 3 C.B. 284; *Pawle v Gunn* (1838) 4 Bing.N.C. 445.
[351] As in *Toplis v Grane* (1839) 5 Bing.N.C. 636; *Moore v Moore* (1611) 1 Bulst. 169.

regarded as an implied term of the contract that operates unless clearly excluded.[352] There is thus no difficulty in such cases in holding that the principal is liable to reimburse and indemnify the agent for all payments made and liabilities incurred within the agent's express or implied authority.[353] This would include not only payments that the principal is legally bound to make, but also payments which the agent is legally bound to make though the principal would not be liable for them,[354] cases where the agent is bound by the usage of a market,[355] cases where the agent makes an authorised but gratuitous payment on the principal's behalf,[356] cases where the agent makes a payment which could not have been enforced but which there is a strong and legitimate pressure to make,[357] cases where the agent, though under a liability, has as yet not had to meet it,[358] and cases where a payment is reasonably but mistakenly made by the agent.[359] Cases where the agent acts beyond his instructions,[360] or interferes without request, would not however be included.

7-060 **Restitution** But where the agency is not contractual and the law of contract cannot be relied on, the agent's claim is only restitutionary[361] and confined to the reimbursement of payments made by the agent under compulsion, in respect of which the ultimate liability is on the principal, and the benefit of which the principal obtains.[362] It does not, therefore, extend to the full indemnity which the contractual right might give. Normally speaking, agency is contractual: but circumstances can arise where it is not, e.g. because one of the parties is a minor, or because the agent has not been properly appointed.[363] In some cases there may still be room for the implication of an independent contract to indemnify, created by the request of one party to another to do something, accompanied by a promise to indemnify against

---

[352] Since agency is probably not a generic contract such as to attract the implications developed for such contracts, it is probably a "business efficacy" implied term, perhaps more satisfactorily coming under the wording of the "officious bystander" test. See above, para.7-001. It could also be based on interpretation of the consideration offered. Where there is a separate implied contract, these difficulties disappear.

[353] As to whether the right of indemnity can arise before the agent has suffered loss by meeting the liability, see *Firma C-Trade SA v Newcastle P & I Assn (The Fanti and The Padre Island)* [1991] 2 A.C. 1; *McIntosh v Dalwood (No.4)* (1930) 4 S.R. (N.S.W.) 415.

[354] *Adams v Morgan & Co* [1924] 1 K.B. 751, Illustration 6; *Brittain v Lloyd* (1845) 14 M. & W. 762.

[355] See Illustration 11; there were many old cases on the usage of the London Stock Exchange, but most are now obsolete. As to customs and usages of markets, see Article 31.

[356] *Brittain v Lloyd*, above, at 773; *Pawle v Gunn* (1838) 4 Bing.N.C. 445 at 448–449.

[357] *Rhodes v Fielder, Jones and Harrison* (1919) 89 L.J.K.B. 15, Illustration 10; *Schneider v Eisovitch* [1960] 2 Q.B. 430.

[358] *Lacey v Hill, Crowley's Claim* (1874) L.R. 18 Eq. 182, Illustration 7. cf. *Cape Distribution Ltd v Cape Intermediate Holdings Plc (No.2)* [2016] EWHC 1786 (QB) at [111] (consideration of when limitation period runs in relation to right to indemnity). Where the agent has incurred a liability, his right to indemnity has arisen, and a purported revocation of his authority to discharge it is ineffective. See below, para.10-010.

[359] See Illustration 8.

[360] *Islamic Republic of Iran Shipping Lines v Zannis Cia. Naviera SA (The Tzelepi)* [1991] 2 Lloyd's Rep. 265.

[361] See Goff and Jones, *Law of Unjust Enrichment* (9th edn), para.19-17 onwards taking a distinction between reimbursement and indemnity, and attributing a special restitutionary meaning to the former.

[362] See *Brook's Wharf & Bull Wharf Ltd v Goodman Bros* [1937] 1 K.B. 534; *Owen v Tate* [1976] Q.B. 402; *Liberian Insurance Agency Inc v Mosse* [1977] 2 Lloyd's Rep. 560; *The Pindaros* [1983] 2 Lloyd's Rep. 635; Goff and Jones, above.

[363] cf. *Craven-Ellis v Canons Ltd* [1936] 2 K.B. 403.

loss incurred by so doing. A widely stated principle permits this[364]; though in the agency context it is doubtful whether it extends to gratuitous agents.[365] But in other cases it may be necessary to rely on the restitutionary remedy, which will normally (though not always, because not limited by the scope of the agent's authority) be narrower in scope. However, the right of indemnity exists also in equity, and where the agent can invoke the assistance of equity,[366] e.g. as trustee[367] or surety,[368] the limitations imposed by the common law rules of restitution will not apply: the right may therefore be wider.

Right of reimbursement superseded by remuneration   It should be borne in   **7-061**
mind that in many cases the right of reimbursement of *expenses* will not apply, because any expense incurred is taken to be covered by the remuneration. Thus in some areas estate agents do not seek to recover the cost of advertising, for this is taken to be included in their commission, if earned, and if no commission is earned the expenditure is a business loss in respect of which no reimbursement can be claimed.[369] Many office and professional expenses are likewise taken to be covered by the remuneration payable.

Illustrations

(1)   A employs B to find a purchaser for certain bark. C agrees with B to purchase   **7-062**
the bark, subject to its being equal to sample. B, being offered a *del credere* commission by A, accepts A's draft for the price of the bark, and in due course pays the amount of the draft. C then refuses the bark, which is not equal to sample. B is entitled to recover from A the amount of the draft paid by him.[370]

(2)   An auctioneer is instructed to sell certain property, and after he has incurred liabilities in reference to his employment, his authority is revoked by the principal. The principal must indemnify him against the liabilities.[371]

(3)   An accommodation bill is drawn and accepted for the purpose of raising money for the benefit of the drawer and acceptor. The drawer instructs a bill broker to get the bill discounted. It is the common practice for bill brokers to give a general guarantee to the bankers who discount their bills, and not to indorse each bill discounted on behalf of their customers. The bill is

---

[364]   See *Dugdale v Lovering* (1875) L.R. 10 C.P. 196; *Sheffield Corp v Barclay* [1905] A.C. 392; *Yeung Kai Yung v Hong Kong and Shanghai Banking Corp* [1981] A.C. 787; *Naviera Mogar SA v Soc. Metallurgique de Normandie (The Nogar Marin)* [1988] 1 Lloyd's Rep. 412 (implication turns on form of individual case); *Linklaters v HSBC Bank Plc* [2003] EWHC 1113 (Comm); [2003] 2 Lloyd's Rep. 545; cf. *Guaranty Trust Co of New York v Hannay & Co* [1918] 2 K.B. 623. There are even dicta in these cases suggesting that the obligation is wider than a contractual obligation. But in Yeung Kai Yeung's case it was suggested (at pp.799–800) that the rule in the Sheffield case might be too wide, and require reconsideration in view of the division of responsibility permitted by the Civil Liability (Contribution) Act 1978: below, para.7-068.

[365]   See *W. Cory & Son Ltd v Lambton and Hetton Collieries* (1916) 86 L.J.K.B. 401 at 405–406.

[366]   See *Lacey v Hill, Crowley's Claim* (1874) L.R. 18 Eq. 182, Illustration 7; *Wallersteiner v Moir (No.2)* [1975] Q.B. 373 (minority shareholder suing on behalf of company).

[367]   cf. *Adams v Morgan & Co* [1924] 1 K.B. 751, Illustration 6; *Campbell v Larkworthy* (1894) 9 T.L.R. 528.

[368]   See Snell, *Equity* (33rd edn), para.45-020.

[369]   But see *Bernard Thorpe & Partners v Flannery* (1977) 244 E.G. 129, where such expenses were recoverable on the terms of the contract. It is usually said that neither auctioneers nor estate agents are normally entitled to expenses: see Murdoch, *Law of Estate Agency* (5th edn), pp.150–151.

[370]   *Hooper v Treffry* (1847) 1 Exch. 17; but distinguish *Simpson v Swan* (1812) 3 Camp. 291.

[371]   *Warlow v Harrison* (1859) 1 E. & E. 309 at 317; *Brittain v Lloyd* (1845) 14 M. & W. 762.

dishonoured, and the broker becomes liable to the bankers upon such a guarantee. The broker is entitled to recover from the acceptor the amount that he is compelled to pay in pursuance of such guarantee, with interest, it being a liability incurred in the execution of his authority in the ordinary course of his business as a bill broker.[372]

(4)   A broker, in accordance with a reasonable custom of the particular market in which he was employed, rendered himself personally responsible for the price of goods bought on behalf of his principal, and duly paid for the goods. Held, that he was entitled to set off the amount so paid, in an action by the principal's trustee in bankruptcy for money due to the principal.[373]

(5)   An agent, who had general authority to receive and sell goods on behalf of the principal, in good faith brought an action against a third person who wrongfully withheld possession of the goods. In an action by the principal for the proceeds of the goods it was held that the agent was entitled to set off the amount of the costs incurred by him in the proceedings to recover the goods.[374]

(6)   The seller of a business carries it on between the date of contract and the date of completion on the buyer's account, a clause in the contract expressly providing for indemnity. He may obtain indemnity for supertax which he is obliged to pay, even though the buyer, being a corporation, would not be liable for supertax.[375]

(7)   A stockbroker incurred liabilities on the Stock Exchange on behalf of his principal. The stockbroker subsequently paid a composition on the amount of his debts (including such liabilities), and by a rule of the Stock Exchange he could not be sued for the balance of such debts without the permission of the committee. The principal was bound to indemnify him to the full extent of the liabilities incurred on his behalf.[376]

(8)   An agent incurs damages and expenses in defending an action on behalf of his principal. He is entitled to reimbursement of such damages and expenses if he was acting within the scope of his authority in defending the action, and the loss was not caused by his own default.[377] Where an agent, exercising his best judgment, compromised an action brought against him in respect of a contract made on behalf of the principal, who had notice of the action, and had not given any instructions as to the course to be pursued, it was held that the agent was entitled to indemnity, although the plaintiff could not, in the circumstances, have succeeded in the action.[378]

---

[372] *Re Fox, Walker & Co Ex p. Bishop* (1880) 15 Ch.D. 400.

[373] *Cropper v Cook* (1868) L.R. 3 C.P. 194. And see *Anglo-Overseas Transport Co Ltd v Titan Industrial Corp (United Kingdom)* [1959] 2 Lloyd's Rep. 152; *Perishables Transport Co Ltd v N. Spyropoulos (London) Ltd* [1964] 2 Lloyd's Rep. 379.

[374] *Curtis v Barclay* (1826) 5 B. & C. 141; *Williams, Torrey & Co v Knight* [1894] P. 342 at 349.

[375] *Adams v Morgan & Co* [1923] 2 K.B. 234; [1924] 1 K.B. 751. cf. *Re Hollebone's Agreement* [1959] 1 W.L.R. 536.

[376] *Lacey v Hill, Crowley's Claim* (1874) L.R. 18 Eq. 182; *Fraser v Equitorial Shipping Co Ltd (The Ijaolo)* [1979] 1 Lloyd's Rep. 103.

[377] *Frixione v Tagliaferro & Sons* (1856) 10 Moo.P.C. 175; *The James Seddon* (1866) L.R. 1 A. & E. 62; *Re Wells & Croft Ex p. Official Receiver* (1895) 72 L.T. 359; *Williams v Lister & Co* (1913) 109 L.T. 699; *Re Famatina Development Corp Ltd* [1914] 2 Ch. 271; *Simpson and Miller v British Industries Trust Ltd* (1923) 39 T.L.R. 286.

[378] *Pettman v Keble* (1850) 9 C.B. 701. See also *Broom v Hall* (1859) 7 C.B.(N.S.) 503; *The Millwall* [1905] P. 155 at 174; *Wallersteiner v Moir (No.2)* [1975] Q.B. 373.

(9)   A acted as B's agent for the purchase of goods from C. The terms included immediate payment, made by A, of £1,000, which would be forfeited if the contract were cancelled. Subsequently, believing that B would not be able to perform the contract, A without authority cancelled the contract, and the £1,000 was forfeited. A claimed to be reimbursed by B in respect of the £1,000 paid out. Held, that although the cancellation by A was a breach of the contract of agency for which B might obtain damages (though none could be shown here, for, on the facts, the £1,000 would have been lost in any case), yet the £1,000 had been paid by A, and his right to reimbursement accrued when it was paid, before the breach; and the £1,000 was therefore recoverable.[379]

(10)   A country solicitor requests his London agent to instruct counsel. The litigation is successful, but some of the costs are disallowed. The country solicitor purports to revoke the authority of the London solicitor to pay fees to counsel. The London solicitor nevertheless pays. Counsel could not have sued for the fees, but the London agent might have been guilty of professional misconduct had he not paid them. He is entitled to an indemnity in respect of the fees paid out, and may retain money in his hands for this purpose.[380]

(11)   A freight forwarder is by custom of the market obliged to undertake personal liability for dead freight when his customer provides insufficient cargo. He may recover the sum paid from his customer.[381] A corporate officer in his capacity as such gives a media interview, which he alleges was later distorted by the media in a way that defamed him. It was held that the director had no implied right to be indemnified by the corporation against the losses caused by the defamation.[382]

(12)   P requests a travel agent to buy 42 tickets for international travel on Ansett Airlines. Agent pays for tickets, having first obtained credit card indemnity by P. Airline goes into financial collapse and ceases operations. P cancels credit card payment. Held that the agent retained its right to indemnity from P.[383]

Article 63

CASES WHERE REIMBURSEMENT OR INDEMNITY NOT AVAILABLE

Subject to contrary agreement and to context: 7-063

(1)   An agent may be debarred from recovering reimbursement or indemnity if at the time when the services were rendered he was not legally qualified to act in the capacity in which he claims the reimbursement or indemnity, or

---

[379] *John Koch Ltd v C. & H. Products Ltd* [1956] 2 Lloyd's Rep. 59; cf. *World Transport Agency v Royte (England) Ltd* [1957] 1 Lloyd's Rep. 381.

[380] *Rhodes v Fielder, Jones and Harrison* (1919) 89 L.J.K.B. 15.

[381] *Anglo Overseas Transport Co Ltd v Titan Industrial Corp (United Kingdom) Ltd* [1959] 2 Lloyd's Rep. 152; *Perishables Transport Co Ltd v N. Spyropoulos (London) Ltd* [1964] 2 Lloyd's Rep. 379; cf. *Wilson v Avec Audio-Visual Equipment Ltd* [1974] 1 Lloyd's Rep. 81 (insurance broker not personally liable to insurance company so not entitled to indemnity).

[382] *National Roads and Motorists' Association v Whitlam* (2007) 25 A.C.L.C. 688.

[383] *Imaje Events Pty Ltd v Taylor* [2007] VSC 390.

if the enforcement of his contract of agency is in some other way affected by statute or statutory instrument.

(2) An agent is not entitled to reimbursement of expenses incurred by him, nor to indemnity against losses or liabilities—

    (a) in respect of any unauthorised act or transaction which is not ratified by the principal, except where the agent has a right of action in restitution[384];

    (b) incurred solely[385] in consequence of his own negligence, default, insolvency or breach of duty[386];

    (c) in respect of any act or transaction which is obviously, or to his knowledge, unlawful,[387] or unlawful by virtue of legislation which is to be interpreted as affecting contracts which involve the doing of acts prohibited by it; except where he is entitled to contribution towards damages for which he is liable in tort[388];

    (d) where the contract of agency expressly precludes a right to indemnity.[389]

Comment

7-064   **Rule (1)**   The statutory provisions which prevent certain agents and others acting in certain capacities from recovering commission normally apply also to reimbursement and indemnity, at least in so far as claims for these arise in contract.[390]

7-065   **Rule (2): Unauthorised acts**   It is obvious that the contractual duty to reimburse and indemnify cannot operate where the act is unauthorised and not ratified[391]; there may however be cases where, though it is not possible to rely on the contractual right, an action in restitution is available.[392]

7-066   **Where agent at fault**   Where the expenses and liabilities only arise because of the agent's fault, including by excessive employment of solicitors and other advisers,[393] it is obvious that there will usually be no liability to indemnify[394]: and this is true also where the liability cannot be said to arise from the performance of the

---

[384] See Comment; Illustrations 1, 2; *Frixione v Tagliaferro & Sons* (1856) 10 Moo.P.C. 175 at 196.

[385] This word has been added pursuant to dicta in *Linklaters v HSBC Bank* [2003] EWHC 1113 (Comm); [2003] 2 Lloyd's Rep. 545 at [36], and in conformity with *Restatement, Second*, § 440. On this case however see Ellinger (2004) 120 L.Q.R. 226. See too *Rohr v Kennedy* [2010] NZHC 772 (solicitor in course of acting for client by mistake exposed himself to liability to beneficiary of estate in respect of which he successfully claimed indemnity from his client who would have had the ultimate liability to the beneficiary).

[386] *Thacker v Hardy* (1878) 4 Q.B.D. 685 at 687; *Frixione v Tagliaferro & Sons*, above; Illustrations 3 and 4; and see *Gregory v Ford* [1951] 1 All E.R. 121: there may be circumstances in which an agent can recover his losses by a different cause of action (employee not to be required to do unlawful act).

[387] See Comment; Illustrations 5–9; below, para.7-067.

[388] Under the Civil Liability (Contribution) Act 1978: see Comment.

[389] See *Mega-Top Cargo Pty Ltd v Moneytech Services Pty Ltd* [2015] NSWCA 402.

[390] See Article 61, Illustrations 2 and 3.

[391] See Comment to Article 62.

[392] See above, para.7-060.

[393] See *Mirror Group Newspapers Plc v Maxwell (No.2)* [1998] 1 B.C.L.C. 638 (court-appointed receivers' spending on legal services).

[394] See Illustration 3. But cf. *Cape Distribution Ltd v Cape Intermediate Holdings Plc (No.1)* [2016] EWHC 1119 (QB) at [87] (subsidiary agent for parent company).

act requested.[395] It should be noted that the reasoning covers liability arising from the agent's bankruptcy, where the bankruptcy was not occasioned by the agent's activities on behalf of the principal.[396] Where the expenses and liabilities do not so arise, but the agent is in repudiatory breach of his duties as agent, contractual indemnity may be refused on grounds similar to those relating to refusal of remuneration discussed under Article 62.[397] The principal may sometimes, however, incur a liability in restitution as indicated under Article 64.

Unlawful transactions   Here again, as in Article 63, the wording gives only the most general indication of the applicable rules: too much turns on the nature of the illegality for a more precise formulation to be possible.[398] But it should be noted that provisions forbidding unqualified persons from recovering remuneration may not apply to mere reimbursement and indemnity.[399]   **7-067**

Joint tortfeasors   The old rule was that a tortfeasor could recover neither contribution nor indemnity from the person at whose request or on whose behalf the tort was committed,[400] and this was based on the maxim ex turpi causa non oritur actio. But: **7-068**

> "where one person requests another to commit or where they jointly commit an indifferent act, of which the illegality does not appear, but which may subsequently be proved to be tortious, the contractual relation may arise; and where one party induces another party by fraud to commit a tortious act, and that other party does not in fact know and need not be presumed to know that he was doing an unlawful act, he may have redress or contribution."[401]

And even where the act is obviously unlawful, contribution may now be recoverable by statute. By the Civil Liability (Contribution) Act 1978 s.1(1),[402] any person liable in respect of damage suffered by another person may recover contribution from any other person liable in respect of the same damage, whether jointly with him or otherwise. Nothing in the Act however affects express or implied contractual

---

[395] See *W. Cory & Son Ltd v Lambton and Hetton Collieries* (1916) 86 L.J.K.B. 401 as explained in *Linklaters v HSBC Banks Plc* [2003] EWHC 1113 (Comm); [2003] 2 Lloyd's Rep. 545 at [36].

[396] *Duncan v Hill* (1873) L.R. 8 Ex. 242, Illustration 4.

[397] See, e.g. *Hurst v Holding* (1810) 3 Taunt. 32 (agent prevented goods reaching principal); *Ellis v Pond* [1898] 1 Q.B. 426 (wrongful sale by stockbroker); *Solloway v McLaughlin* [1938] A.C. 247 (fraud of agent). It can also be said that a person cannot claim an indemnity in respect of the consequences of his own wrong; or that the allowing of an indemnity would promote circuity of action. See *Goulandris Bros Ltd v Goldman & Sons* [1958] 1 Q.B. 74, esp. at 94–98; Comment to Article 60; cf. *J.O. Lund Ltd v Anglo Overseas Transport Co Ltd* [1955] 1 Lloyd's Rep. 142.

[398] See, e.g. Illustration 6.

[399] See Solicitors Act 1974 s.25(2); Cordery, *Solicitors* (8th edn), pp.91–92. But cf. Estate Agents Act 1979 s.18(5).

[400] *Merryweather v Nixan* (1799) 8 T.R. 186; *Shackell v Rosier* (1836) 2 Bing.N.C. 634; *W.H. Smith & Son v Clinton & Harris* (1908) 99 L.T. 840.

[401] *W.H. Smith & Son v Clinton & Harris*, above, at 841 (and see Defamation Act 1952 s.11). See *Adamson v Jarvis* (1827) 4 Bing. 66, Illustration 9; *Betts & Drewe v Gibbins* (1834) 2 A. & E. 57; *Toplis v Grane* (1839) 5 Bing.N.C. 636 (cf. *Cory & Son Ltd v Lambton & Hetton Collieries Ltd* (1916) 86 L.J.K.B. 401); *Dugdale v Lovering* (1875) L.R. 10 C.P. 196; *Thacker v Hardy* (1878) 4 Q.B.D. 685 at 687.

[402] Replacing Law Reform (Married Women and Tortfeasors) Act 1935 s.6. See Clerk & Lindsell, *Torts* (21st edn), para.4-12 onwards.

or other right to indemnity.[403] The amount of contribution is such as the court may find just and equitable having regard to that person's extent of responsibility for the damage; and the court has power to exempt from liability or direct a complete indemnity.[404] But the Act does not render enforceable any agreement for indemnity which would not have been enforceable apart from it.[405] The ready implication of a promise to indemnify by one who requests another to act[406] may sometimes exclude these provisions, and it has been suggested that the cases on such implication may require reconsideration because of the advantages of permitting the court to divide responsibility.[407]

7-069 **Wagering transactions** From the early eighteenth century there have been legal restrictions on gaming and wagering: in particular, the Gaming Act 1845 s.18, provided that all suits by way of gaming or wagering should be null and void. In the context of agency the Gaming Act 1892 excluded the principal's obligation to indemnify by providing that any promise to pay any person any sum of money paid by him under or in respect of any contract or agreement rendered null and void by the Act of 1845 should itself be null and void. Apart from its central context, this caused difficulties in respect of speculative financial transactions. All this legislation was repealed by the Gambling Act 2005.[408] Part 17 of the Act deals with the legality and enforceability of gambling contracts. Gambling contracts are no longer void, but the Gambling Commission is given powers to avoid particular bets. The financial transactions context is dealt with by the Financial Services and Markets Act 2000.[409]

Illustrations

7-070 (1) A authorises B, a broker, to effect a marine insurance policy. After the underwriters have signed the slip, but before a binding contract is made, A revokes B's authority. B, nevertheless, effects the policy, and pays the premiums. B cannot recover the premiums from A, having acted without authority.[410]

(2) A authorises B and C to insure his life in their names. They insure in the names of B, C and D, and pay the premiums. They are not entitled to recover the amount of the premiums from A, not having strictly pursued their authority.[411]

(3) A solicitor undertook a prosecution for perjury, and agreed that he would only charge out-of-pocket expenses. The prosecution failed in consequence of the negligent way in which the indictment was drawn. Held, that the solicitor was not entitled to recover his disbursements.[412] So, an auctioneer is not entitled to be indemnified against a loss incurred by him in consequence of his own

---

[403] s.7(3).
[404] s.2(1).
[405] s.7(3).
[406] See above, para.7-060.
[407] *Yeung Kai Yung v Hong Kong and Shanghai Banking Corp* [1981] A.C. 787 at 799–800.
[408] The Act was brought fully into force on September 1, 2007.
[409] See s.412 (which is amended by the Gambling Act 2005 to remove references to the old legislation).
[410] *Warwick v Slade* (1811) 3 Camp. 127.
[411] *Barron v Fitzgerald* (1840) 6 Bing.N.C. 201. As to instructions given to stockbrokers, see *Johnson v Kearley* [1908] 2 K.B. 514; *Aston v Kelsey* [1913] 3 K.B. 314; *Blaker v Hawes and Brown* (1913) 109 L.T. 320.
[412] *Lewis v Samuel* (1846) 8 Q.B. 685.

mistake on a point of law as to which he ought to have been competent.[413] And where the manager of the stud stock department of a company conducting activities connected with agriculture is asked to buy "top rams" and because of lack of knowledge of terms used by sheep breeders buys rams which are not "tops" no reimbursement is due.[414]

(4) A stockbroker is instructed by his principal to carry over stock to the next settlement. Before the next settling day the broker becomes insolvent and is declared a defaulter, in consequence of which the stock is sold at a loss. The principal is not bound to indemnify the broker, the loss having been caused by the broker's insolvency.[415]

(5) A purchased shares as a broker, not being duly licensed as the law then required. Held, that he was entitled to recover from the principal the price of the shares, which he was compelled to pay, such payment not being an essential part of the duty of a broker, although, in consequence of not being licensed, he could not recover any commission or remuneration.[416]

(6) A broker effects an illegal insurance on behalf of his principal, and pays the premium. He is not entitled to recover from the principal the amount of the premium, or any other payments made by him in respect of such insurance.[417]

(7) An election agent made payments which were illegal under the Corrupt Practices Acts. He could not recover the amount of any such payments from the candidate employing him.[418]

(8) A employs B to purchase smuggled goods. B purchases the goods and pays for them. B cannot recover the price from A, even if A obtains possession of the goods.[419]

(9) A instructs B, an auctioneer, to sell goods of which A has no right to dispose, B having no knowledge of any defect in A's title. B sells the goods, and duly pays over the proceeds to A. B is afterwards compelled to pay to the true owner the value of the goods. A must indemnify B, the transaction not being obviously, or to B's knowledge, unlawful.[420]

3. LIEN

Article 64

DEFINITIONS OF GENERAL AND PARTICULAR POSSESSORY LIENS

(1) A possessory lien is the right of a person who has possession of goods or chattels belonging to another to retain possession of them until the satisfaction of some debt or obligation by the owner of the goods or chattels.[421]   **7-071**

[413] *Capp v Topham* (1805) 6 East 392.
[414] *New Zealand Farmers Co-operative Distributing Co Ltd v National Mortgage and Agency Co of New Zealand Ltd* [1961] N.Z.L.R. 969.
[415] *Duncan v Hill* (1873) L.R. 8 Ex. 242. This case is retained here on account of the general significance of the reasoning.
[416] *Smith v Lindo* (1858) 5 C.B.(N.S.) 587.
[417] *Ex p. Mather* (1797) 3 Ves. 373.
[418] *Re Parker* (1882) 21 Ch.D. 408.
[419] *Ex p. Mather*, above.
[420] *Adamson v Jarvis* (1827) 4 Bing. 66.
[421] See *Hammonds v Barclay* (1802) 2 East 227 at 235.

(2) Where the right is to retain possession in respect of a general balance of account, or until the satisfaction of debts or obligations incurred independently of the goods or chattels subject to the right, it is called a general lien. Where the right is confined to debts and obligations incurred in respect of the goods and chattels subject to the right, it is called a particular lien.

Comment

7-072 **Introduction** The cases collected in this section go beyond agency law as such; and many of them are old and reflect practices that may no longer obtain. It seems, however, worth preserving the collection and updating it, for they remain the only authority on many of the matters which they decide, and excellent illustrations from which the principles may be understood.

7-073 **Liens** A possessory lien involves the right to retain goods only[422]: it does not involve the right to sell the them except in special circumstances,[423] e.g. where trade usage or statute permit. Indeed, a person who sells thereby destroys his lien and becomes liable in conversion.[424] But such a lien confers not only a defence against the principal (who cannot sue in conversion since he has not the immediate right to possess), but also the right to sue in conversion, where the goods are wrongfully removed, against the principal or third parties, for it involves possession and may confer an immediate right to possession.[425]

Strictly speaking, liens are given by law only; but an analogous right can be regarded as arising by contract,[426] and it is a right of this latter type that an agent has. Particular liens are favoured by the law, but general liens are "founded in custom only, and are therefore to be taken strictly".[427]

Article 65

POSSESSORY LIEN OF AGENTS

7-074 (1) An agent has a possessory lien on the goods and chattels of his principal in respect of all lawful claims he may have as such agent against the principal, for remuneration earned, or advances made, or losses or liabilities incurred, in the course of the agency, or otherwise arising in the course of the agency,[428] provided—

(a) that the possession of the goods or chattels was lawfully obtained by him

---

[422] This may carry with it the right to direct movement. Thus a shipping agent who had a lien over a bill of lading was held justified in having the goods brought back home: *Edwards v Southgate* (1862) 10 W.R. 528.

[423] *Smart v Sandars* (1848) 5 C.B. 895. Nor, of itself, does it confer the right of stoppage in transit: see Article 69.

[424] *Sibel v Springfield* (1863) 8 New Rep. 36.

[425] *Rogers v Kennay* (1846) 9 Q.B. 592; *Dicas v Stockley* (1836) 7 C. & P. 587; *Bryans v Nix* (1839) 4 M. & W. 775.

[426] *Gladstone v Birley* (1817) 2 Mer. 401 at 404.

[427] *Houghton v Matthews* (1803) 3 B. & P. 485 at 494; *Rushforth v Hadfield* (1805) 6 East 519; (1806) 7 East 224; *Bock v Gorrissen* (1860) 2 De G.F. & J. 434 at 443.

[428] Illustrations 1 and 2; and see Comment. For a discussion of choice of law problems, see Chesterman (1973) 22 I.C.L.Q. 213; *Benjamin's Sale of Goods* (9th edn), para.26-190 onwards.

in the course of the agency, and in the same capacity as that in which he claims the lien[429];

(b) that there is no agreement inconsistent with the right of lien; and

(c) that the goods or chattels were not delivered to him with express directions, or for a special purpose, inconsistent with the right of lien.[430]

(2) The possessory lien of an agent is a particular lien only, except where he has a general lien by agreement, express or implied, with his principal. Such an agreement may be implied from a course of dealing between the principal and agent, or from an established custom or usage.[431]

Comment

Clear authority for the general proposition as to the lien of an agent is difficult to find. This is not surprising, for the word agent can be applied in many situations, and no doubt some persons to whom the word could be applied would have no lien. For example, an estate agent will not normally hold property of his principal upon which he could exercise a lien.[432] Equally, there will be many cases where a person who has agency powers holds his principal's property in circumstances quite inconsistent with his having a lien over it.[433] But in general it is established by the cases that an agent is entitled to a lien over the property of his principal in respect of payments, liabilities, etc., relating to matters connected with that property. This seems in many cases to be a development of the older lien of a craftsman who makes repairs to a chattel[434]; but it was developed by cases on factors, brokers, auctioneers and other undoubted agents.

7-075

When exercisable There is little authority on when the lien is exercisable, and in particular on whether it can only be exercised when the principal's breach is repudiatory in nature. It does not seem that the contract must be brought to an end before the remedy can be exercised. Where the lien is a particular lien over something worked on or produced by the agent (e.g., documents produced by a solicitor) the analogy of the unpaid seller's lien suggests that the existence of the lien will in many situations indicate no more than that the agent need not deliver except against payment, unless he has granted credit. It seems likely however that most agents work on a credit basis; and such reasoning is in any case much more difficult to apply in the case of a general lien. The exercise of the lien requires that payment is due and has not been made.[435] Although late payment is not of itself repudiatory, it has been said that:

7-076

"common sense suggests that where the agency is of a continuing nature, it will not usu-

---

[429] Illustrations 3 and 4; and see Comment.

[430] Illustrations 5–9.

[431] *Bock v Gorrissen*, above; *Rushforth v Hadfield*, above; *Holderness v Collinson* (1827) 7 B. & C. 212; *Langley, Beldon & Gaunt Ltd v Morley* [1965] 1 Lloyd's Rep. 297. Custom is not easy to establish: see Article 31.

[432] But he may hold a deposit: see below, para.7-077. For an attempt by an estate agent to claim rights over proceeds of sale held by his principal's solicitor, see *W.A. Ellis Services Ltd v Stuart Wood* [1993] 2 E.G.L.R. 43.

[433] See *Ariston Products Pty Ltd v Egan* (1977) 3 A.C.L.R. 418 (accountant).

[434] See *Woodworth v Conroy* [1976] Q.B. 884 at 890 (accountant); but cf. *Ariston Products Pty Ltd v Egan*, above. See also *R. v South Devon Ry Co* (1850) 15 Q.B. 1043 (arbitrator); *Ridgway v Ley* (1856) 25 L.J.Ch. 584 (Parliamentary agent); *Fraser v Equitorial Shipping Co Ltd (The Ijaolo)* [1979] 1 Lloyd's Rep. 103 (consulting marine engineer).

[435] *Crawshay v Homfray* (1820) 4 B. & Ald. 50; *Fisher v Smith* (1878) 4 App.Cas. 1.

ally survive the exercise by the agent of rights inconsistent with those of the principal over goods which are the very subject-matter of the agency; and this would appear to indicate that the principal's conduct must at least be of a repudiatory nature, even if not formally treated by the agent as such."[436]

In general it would seem that the fiduciary relationship between principal and agent will require the agent to exercise the right with consideration for his principal, and that the agency relationship will not survive its exercise.[437]

7-077 **Goods and chattels** In principle, a lien operates over goods and chattels only, including those choses in action which are represented by documents, often called securities, which can themselves be treated as goods and chattels—for example, insurance policies, share certificates, bills of exchange. It is sometimes said that the lien extends to funds or money held: thus in connection with bankers it has been said that "[a]ll moneys paid into a bank are subject to a lien,"[438] and the auctioneer's lien has been said to be over goods and their proceeds. It is however difficult to see how a lien can be exercised over money, which will normally be the actual property of the holder subject to an obligation to account for it. It seems that reference to a lien over money should in many cases be explained as references to the agent's right to set-off and counterclaim when sued by the principal for the money.[439] In the case of an auctioneer it may also refer to the auctioneer's right to sue for the price upon a separate contract, and then retain it; or to the rule that the third party may not, to the extent of the auctioneer's lien, set off against the auctioneer claims which he has against the vendor.[440] In other circumstances it may refer to an equitable assignment by way of charge[441]; or to an equitable lien arising out of the position of the parties towards each other, as in the case of solicitor and client.[442] In so far as an estate agent has a lien, it is likely to be over a deposit held for his client's account.[443]

7-078 **Possession** The agent must possess the goods: "there can be no lien upon any

[436] *Compania Financiera "Soleada" SA v Hamoor Tanker Corp Inc (The Borag)* [1980] 1 Lloyd's Rep. 111 at 122, per Mustill J (where the agents arrested the principal's ship: reversed on a different point [1981] 1 W.L.R. 274).
[437] See *Restatement, Second*, comment b to § 464.
[438] *Misa v Currie* (1876) 1 App.Cas. 554 at 569.
[439] See Paget, *Law of Banking* (14th edn), Ch.14, esp. para.14.6; *Halesowen Presswork and Assemblies Ltd v Westminster Bank Ltd* [1971] 1 Q.B. 1 at 33–34, 46; the decision was reversed by the House of Lords on another point ([1972] A.C. 785), but see the judgments of Viscount Dilhorne at 802 and of Lord Cross at 810; *Eide UK Ltd v Lowndes Lambert Group Ltd* [1999] Q.B. 199. See also *Richmond Shipping Ltd v D/S and A/S Vestland (The Vestland)* [1980] 2 Lloyd's Rep. 171 at 181.
[440] See Illustration 1; below, para.9-023.
[441] See *Re Welsh Irish Ferries Ltd (The Ugland Trailer)* [1986] Ch. 471; *The Annangel Glory* [1988] 1 Lloyd's Rep. 45; *Itex Italgrani Export SA v Care Shipping Corp (The Cebu (No.2))* [1990] 2 Lloyd's Rep. 316; *Kingscroft Insurance Co v H.S. Weavers (Underwriting) Agencies Ltd* [1993] 1 Lloyd's Rep. 187 at 194–195. These cases refer to the lien on sub-freights in maritime law. This is now said to be "a contractual non-possessory right of a kind which is sui generis": *Agnew v Commissioner of Inland Revenue* [2001] UKPC 28; [2001] 2 A.C. 710 at [41], per Lord Millett.
[442] See Snell, *Equity* (33rd edn), Ch.44; *Hewett v Court* (1983) 149 C.L.R. 639, esp. at 663.
[443] See Murdoch, *Law of Estate Agency* (5th edn), pp.152–153. This would usually only be so on completion. His right to exercise the "lien" could be affected by failure to comply with the information requirements of the Estate Agents Act 1979 and statutory instruments made thereunder: see above, para.7-007. As to auctioneers, see ibid.; Harvey and Meisel, *Auctions: Law and Practice* (2006).

property unless it is in the possession of the party who claims the lien".[444] But the possession may be held for the agent by another: thus in *Bryans v Nix*[445] an agent's lien was held to arise where the principal delivered a cargo to a bargemaster employed by him together with documents indicating that the bargemaster was to hold the cargo for the agent. And it has been held that an agreement, made for valuable consideration, to hand over a bill of lading to an agent for the purpose of giving him security over the goods represented by it gives the agent the right in equity to the bill of lading and possession of the goods, as against the principal and his creditors.[446] Further, the lien is not lost by giving the goods to be held by another specifically on behalf of the person entitled to the lien.[447] On the other hand, even though the goods are in the agent's custody and control, they may not be in his possession unless he performs some overt act taking them into his possession, and hence there may be no lien.[448]

Lawfully obtained   A lien cannot be acquired by a wrongful act. Thus if an agent obtains goods from his principal by misrepresentation, he has no lien over them, though the circumstances in other respects are such that he would have been a lien if the goods had been obtained lawfully.[449] And where the agent takes goods without authority, or is given goods by the principal after the latter's bankruptcy,[450] he acquires no lien. In general, an agent's claim to a lien cannot be more extensive than his principal's powers in relation to the relevant property; hence, it will not be enough if the principal owns the property but is subject to court restrictions as to its use.[451]

7-079

In the same capacity   Even a general lien will not extend to the retaining of goods by an agent in satisfaction of debts incurred previous to or outside the agency.[452] Thus a factor's general lien did not entitle him to retain goods in respect of rent that was owing to him but which was unconnected with his operations as factor,[453] or in respect of transactions performed by him in some other capacity.[454] This requirement to some extent overlaps with those next referred to.

7-080

[444] *Shaw v Neale* (1858) 6 H.L.Cas. 581 at 601.
[445] (1839) 4 M. & W. 775, distinguishing *Kinloch v Craig* (1789) 3 T.R. 119; (1790) 3 T.R. 783. See also *Evans & Evans v Nichol & Nichol* (1841) 3 M. & G. 614; *Hammonds v Barclay* (1802) 2 East 227; cf. *Kruger v Wilcox* (1755) Amb. 252; *Taylor v Robinson* (1818) 2 Moo. 730, Illustration 5; *Nichols v Clent* (1817) 3 Price 547.
[446] *Re Evans Ex p. Barber* (1843) 3 M.D. & De G. 174; *Lutscher v Comptoir d'Escompte de Paris* (1876) 1 Q.B.D. 709. This is an equitable charge: see *Benjamin's Sale of Goods* (9th edn), para.18-278.
[447] *McCombie v Davis* (1805) 7 East 5; see Article 67. A more modern example is the trust receipt. Aliter if the delivery is a conversion.
[448] See *Hatton v Car Maintenance Co Ltd* [1915] 1 Ch. 621 (owner could remove car from company's premises at will: company had no lien); cf. *Rose v CMS Operations* [2002] EWHC 59 (Ch).
[449] cf. *Madden v Kempster* (1807) 1 Camp. 12.
[450] *Nichols v Clent* (1817) 3 Price 547; *Copland v Stein* (1799) 8 T.R. 199.
[451] See *Withers LLP v Langbar International Ltd* [2011] EWCA Civ 1419 at [53].
[452] *Houghton v Matthews* (1803) 3 B. & P. 485, Illustration 4. See also *Tellrite Ltd v London Confirmers Ltd* [1962] 1 Lloyd's Rep. 236.
[453] *Houghton v Matthews*, above, at pp.494–495.
[454] *Dixon v Stansfield* (1850) 10 C.B. 398, Illustration 5.

7-081 **No inconsistent agreement and goods not delivered in circumstances inconsistent with lien** The scope of these two requirements, which overlap, will be apparent from the Illustrations.[455] It should be noted that the lien will not easily be displaced.[456]

7-082 **General liens** Factors,[457] marine insurance brokers,[458] stockbrokers,[459] solicitors,[460] bankers,[461] wharfingers[462] and packers[463] are among those who have been held to have a general lien by implication from custom. On the other hand it has been held that a confirming house was not a modern version of the factor, and had no such lien[464]; and the old cases on the packer's lien were based on the packer being to some extent a factor and again may not avail those who conduct for different sorts of business in a modern context, e.g. a freight forwarder[465] or a consolidator[466] in the absence of proof of custom. Further details should be sought in specialised works.

7-083 **Solicitors' charging lien** A solicitor has a lien on the property of the client in his possession and an equitable lien on property recovered or preserved through his instrumentality.[467] Once a solicitor notifies a party to litigation with his client that the other is not to pay direct to the client any moneys payable under judgment or a compromise in favour of the client because the client is indebted to the solicitor for fees in respect of the litigation, the other should respect the notification, either by paying over the money owed to the solicitor, or by paying the moneys into court in the case of dispute between solicitor and client.[468] Under s.73 of the Solicitors' Act 1974 a court may also declare a solicitor entitled to a charge upon property

---

[455] See Illustrations 8–11.
[456] See, e.g. *Brandao v Barnett* (1846) 12 C. & F. 787, Illustration 6; *London Chartered Bank of Australia v White* (1879) 4 App.Cas. 413; *Re London & Globe Finance Corp* [1902] 2 Ch. 416.
[457] *Kruger v Wilcox* (1755) Amb. 252; *Godin v London Assurance Co* (1758) 1 W.Bl. 103; *Baring v Corrie* (1818) 2 B. & A. 137; *Re Fawcus Ex p. Buck* (1876) 3 Ch.D. 795; Illustrations 3, 4 and 5.
[458] *Mann v Forrester* (1814) 4 Camp. 60; *Westwood v Bell* (1815) 4 Camp. 349; *Fisher v Smith* (1878) 4 App.Cas. 1.
[459] *Jones v Peppercorne* (1858) John. 430; *Re London & Globe Finance Corp* [1902] 2 Ch. 416; *John D. Hope & Co v Glendinning* [1911] A.C. 419.
[460] *Barratt v Gough-Thomas* [1951] Ch. 242. Money-laundering legislation makes it increasingly unlikely that solicitors will possess a general lien in relation to client money: *Withers LLP v Langbar International Ltd* [2011] EWCA Civ 1419 at [51].
[461] *Brandao v Barnett* (1846) 12 C. & F. 787; *London Chartered Bank of Australia v White* (1879) 4 App.Cas. 413; *Misa v Currie* (1876) 1 App.Cas. 554.
[462] *Naylor v Mangles* (1794) 1 Esp. 109; *Spears v Hartly* (1800) 3 Esp. 81; cf. *Holderness v Collinson* (1827) 7 B. & C. 212; *Jowitt & Sons v Union Cold Storage Co* [1913] 3 K.B. 1 (lien by contract only).
[463] *Re Witt Ex p. Shubrook* (1876) 2 Ch.D. 489. But in *Toll Logistics (NZ) Ltd v McKay* [2011] 2 N.Z.L.R. 601 at [61] it was held that any custom favouring packers with a general lien has not survived in New Zealand, and that, alternatively, the lien was excluded on the facts by the detailed contractual lien.
[464] *Tellrite Ltd v London Confirmers Ltd* [1962] 1 Lloyd's Rep. 236. See also *Ahlers v Broome & Greene Ltd* (1938) 62 Ll.Rep. 163; *Rolls Razor Ltd v Cox* [1967] 1 Q.B. 552.
[465] See *Langley, Beldon & Gaunt Ltd v Morley* [1965] 1 Lloyd's Rep. 297 at 305.
[466] *Chellaram & Sons (London) Ltd v Butlers Warehousing and Distribution Ltd* [1978] 2 Lloyd's Rep. 412. As to warehousemen, see *Majeau Carrying Co Pty Ltd v Coastal Rutile Ltd* (1973) 129 C.L.R. 48.
[467] See Snell, *Equity* (33rd edn), Ch.44; Cordery, *Solicitors* (9th edn), E [691] onwards; (8th edn), Ch.8; *French v Carter Lemon Camerons LLP* [2012] EWCA Civ 1180 at [27]. But cf. the position where a solicitor is acting as stakeholder: *Rockeagle Ltd v Alsop Wilkinson (a firm)* [1992] Ch. 47.
[468] *Khans Solicitor (A Firm) v Chifuntwe* [2013] EWCA Civ 481; [2014] 1 W.L.R. 1185.

recovered or preserved through his instrumentality, and conveyances done or operating to defeat that charge are valid except against a bona fide purchaser for value. This latter is often referred to as a "charging lien", but it depends upon the order of the court.[469]

Maritime liens   A shipmaster has a maritime lien over the ship and freight[470] for their wages and for disbursements and liabilities properly made or incurred by him on account of the ship.[471] Maritime liens, which are enforced by Admiralty action in rem, do not depend on possession, and attach to the ship from the moment when the claim arises: they can have effect even against a bona fide purchaser for value.[472]   **7-084**

"Statutory liens"   Certain Admiralty claims can be enforced by proceeding in rem against the ship: by virtue of s.20(2)(p) of the Senior Courts Act 1981 this includes "any claim by a master, shipper, charterer or agent in respect of disbursements made on account of the ship". This procedure in certain respects creates claims enforceable against the ship, and the result is sometimes referred to as a "statutory lien": but the procedure is a special one and connected neither with the general law of liens nor with that of agency.[473]   **7-085**

Illustrations

(1) An auctioneer who is employed to sell goods has a lien on the goods for his charges and commission.[474]   **7-086**
(2) An agent was appointed by a company to sell goods on their behalf in a shop taken for that purpose, and it was agreed that he should from time to time accept bills representing the value of the goods in his hands for sale. Goods were consigned to the agent, and he accepted a bill for their value. Before the bill became due, the company was wound up, and the liquidators took possession of and sold the goods. Held, that the agent, having paid the bill, had a lien upon the goods for the amount, and was entitled to be repaid out of the proceeds thereof in preference to the other creditors of the company.[475]
(3) A bought goods as a factor for and on behalf of B, and it was agreed that the goods should remain upon the premises of the seller at a rent to be paid by B. After a time A was requested by the seller to remove the goods, but did not do so. Subsequently, without B's authority or instructions, A removed the goods to his own premises, and about the same time a petition in bankruptcy

---

[469] See further Cordery, *Solicitors* (9th edn), E [776] onwards.
[470] See above, para.7-077.
[471] Merchant Shipping Act 1995 s.41. See *The Ever Success* [1999] 1 Lloyd's Rep. 824.
[472] See further Thomas, *Maritime Liens* (1980). An insurance broker's claim for the cost of hull insurance was held not covered in *Bain Clarkson Ltd v Owners of the Ship "Sea Friends"* [1991] 2 Lloyd's Rep. 322. A managing agent may perhaps be an agent for the purposes of this section: see *The Corona Energy* Unreported 1977, folio no.174. See also *The Westport (No.3)* [1966] 1 Lloyd's Rep. 342.
[473] See in general Thomas, above; Meeson, *Admiralty Jurisdiction and Practice* (4th edn). For an example in the agency context see *The Ohm Mariana* [1993] 2 Singapore L.R. 698.
[474] *Williams v Millington* (1788) 1 H.Bl. 81; *Robinson v Rutter* (1855) 4 E. & B. 954; *Webb v Smith* (1885) 30 Ch.D. 192. (The lien does not apply to land.) As to his lien over any deposit paid, see *Skinner v Trustee of the Property of Reed* [1967] Ch. 1194; and above, para.7-077. In *Skinner's* case the amount outstanding on the mortgage exceeded the purchase price, so the auctioneer had no lien. See in general Murdoch, *Law of Estate Agency* (5th edn), p.153.
[475] *Re Pavy's Patent Felted Fabric Co* (1876) 1 Ch.D. 631.

was presented against B. Held, that the possession of the goods continued in B, and that A had therefore no lien upon them.[476]

(4) A, a factor, sold goods in his own name on B's behalf to C. C subsequently sent goods to A for sale, never having employed him as a factor before. C became bankrupt. A had no lien upon C's goods for the price of the goods sold by him on B's behalf.[477]

(5) A factor insures a ship on his principal's behalf as insurance broker, the transaction being quite distinct and separate from his duties as factor. His general lien does not extend to the policy of insurance, because he did not acquire it in the capacity of factor.[478] So, if a policy is left merely for safe custody in an agent's hands, he has no general lien over it for advances.[479] Where a partner deposited a lease with a banker to secure a particular advance to himself personally, it was held that the banker had no lien over it for the general balance due from the firm.[480]

(6) A life policy was deposited at a bank, with a memorandum charging it with overdrafts not exceeding a specified amount. Held, that the banker's general lien was excluded by the special contract, such contract being inconsistent with the existence of a general lien on the policy.[481] If a factor expressly agrees to deal in a particular way with the proceeds of goods deposited with him for sale, his general lien is excluded.[482] But the lien is not excluded unless the contract is clearly inconsistent with its existence.[483] Thus, where certain securities were deposited with stockbrokers for a specific loan, and they were given a power of sale, it was held that their general lien extended to such securities.[484] So, an agreement that there shall be monthly settlements does not affect the lien of an insurance broker for premiums upon policies in his hands.[485] And the general lien of a factor is not excluded merely because he acts under special instructions to sell in his principal's name and at a particular price.[486]

(7) A consigns goods to B, who transfers the bill of lading to his factor C, to secure £1,000. B becomes bankrupt. C has no lien on the bill of lading for a general balance due from B, and A may stop the goods in transit, subject to C's claim for £1,000.[487]

(8) Certain exchequer bills were deposited at a bank, to be kept in a box under lock and key, the key being kept by the customer. The bills were subsequently

---

476 *Taylor v Robinson* (1818) 2 Moo.C.P. 730.
477 *Houghton v Matthews* (1803) 3 B. & P. 485.
478 *Dixon v Stansfeld* (1850) 10 C.B. 398.
479 *Muir v Fleming* (1822) D. & R.N.P. 29.
480 *Wolstenholm v Sheffield Union Banking Co Ltd* (1886) 54 L.T. 746; *Withers LLP v Langbar International Ltd* [2011] EWHC 1151 (Ch) (solicitor's lien).
481 *Re Bowes, Strathmore v Vane* (1886) 33 Ch.D. 586. See also *Re Laurence Ex p. M'Kenna, City Bank Case* (1861) 3 De G.F. & J. 629.
482 *Walker v Birch* (1795) 6 T.R. 258; See also *Buchanan v Findlay* (1829) 9 B. & C. 738; *Bock v Gorrissen* (1860) 2 De G.F. & J. 434; *Frith v Forbes* (1862) 4 De G.F. & J. 409; *Rolls Razor Ltd v Cox* [1967] 1 Q.B. 552.
483 *Brandao v Barnett* (1846) 12 C. & F. 787; *Re European Bank, Agra Bank Claim* (1872) L.R. 8 Ch.App. 41; *Davis v Bowsher* (1794) 5 T.R. 488.
484 *Jones v Peppercorne* (1858) John. 430. See also *Re London & Globe Finance Corp* [1902] 2 Ch. 416.
485 *Fisher v Smith* (1878) 4 App.Cas. 1.
486 *Stevens v Biller* (1883) 25 Ch.D. 31; *König v Brandt* (1901) 84 L.T. 748.
487 *Spalding v Ruding* (1843) 6 Beav. 376.

entrusted to the bank, with instructions to obtain the interest on them, and get them exchanged for new bills, and to deposit the new bills in the box as before. Held, that the banker's lien did not attach to the original bills or to those for which they were exchanged, the special purpose for which they were placed in his hands being inconsistent with a right of general lien.[488]

(9) A factor, who acted as such for the owners of a ship, asked the master to let him have the certificate of registry for the purpose of paying certain duties at the custom house. Held, that his general lien as a factor did not attach to the certificate.[489]

Article 66

CONFINED TO RIGHTS OF PRINCIPAL, EXCEPT IN THE CASE OF MONEY OR NEGOTIABLE SECURITIES

(1) The possessory lien of an agent attaches only upon goods or chattels in respect of which the principal has, as against third parties, the power to create the lien, and except in the case of money or negotiable securities, and subject to any statutory provision to the contrary,[490] is confined to the rights of the principal in the goods or chattels at the time when the lien attaches, and is subject to all rights and equities of third parties available against the principal at that time.[491]   **7-087**

(2) The lien of an agent over negotiable securities deposited with him by or in the name of the principal is not affected by the rights or equities of third parties, and is as effectual as if the principal were the absolute owner of such money or securities, provided that at the time when the lien of the agent attaches he has no notice of any defect in the title of the principal to them.[492]

Comment

No one can create a lien beyond his own interest.[493] This means that not only does a lien take effect subject to the interests existing in the property concerned at the time that any money first becomes due in respect of which it may be exercised, but also that a subsequent disposition of the goods by the owner, in principle and subject to the circumstances of the disposition, freezes the lien at the sum due at that time: notice of such interests or dispositions to the person having the lien is (in the case of legal interests in ordinary chattels) irrelevant.[494] On the other hand, to the extent to which dispositions are subject to the lien, it is equally irrelevant whether or not   **7-088**

---

[488] *Brandao v Barnett* (1846) 12 C. & F. 787.

[489] *Burn v Brown* (1817) 2 Stark. 272.

[490] e.g. Factors Act 1889; Sale of Goods Act 1979 ss.24–26. (See Article 87.)

[491] See Illustrations; *Att.-Gen. v Trueman* (1843) 11 M. & W. 694; *Cuthbert v Robarts, Lubbock & Co* [1909] 2 Ch. 226 at 233.

[492] See Illustration 9.

[493] See e.g. *Eide UK Ltd v Lowndes Lambert Group Ltd* [1999] Q.B. 199. See too *Rockeagle Ltd v Alsop Wilkinson (a firm)* [1992] Ch. 47 (stakeholder).

[494] *Blunden v Desart* (1842) (Ir.) 59 R.R. 753, Illustration 8 (authorities reviewed); see also *Watson v Lyon* (1855) 7 De G.M. & G. 288; *Young v English* (1843) 7 Beav. 10; *Jeffryes v Agra & Masterman's Bank* (1866) L.R. 2 Eq. 674; cases cited at Illustration 4. As to equitable interests see, e.g. *Re Gross Ex p. Kingston* (1871) L.R. 6 Ch.App. 632.

the person taking under such disposition had notice of the lien: nor can he acquire priority to it by giving notice.[495]

The position as regards negotiable instruments depends not on special rules as to liens, but on the normal rules of negotiability. Notice of previous interests in or subsequent dealings as to the goods is therefore relevant, in so far as it may prevent the person claiming the lien from being a holder in due course.[496]

Illustrations

7-089   (1)   A solicitor or other agent can have no lien on the share register or minute book of a company, because the directors have no power to create any lien that could interfere with the use of such register or book for the purposes of the company. So, no lien can attach upon such books of a company as, under the articles of association or the Companies Acts, ought to be kept at the registered office of the company.[497] And where documents come into the hands of a solicitor pending the winding-up of a company, he cannot claim any lien on them that would interfere with the winding-up.[498] But the fact that a company has issued debentures as a floating security does not prevent an agent from acquiring a lien on the title deeds of the company, and such a lien has priority to the claims of the debenture holders.[499]

       (2)   The directors of a building society, which has no borrowing powers, overdraw the banking account of the society, and agree that certain deeds deposited at the bank shall be held as security for the general balance. The transaction is ultra vires, and the banker has no lien on the deeds for the overdraft. He is, however, in equity, entitled to hold them as security for so much of the money advanced as he can show to have been actually applied in payment of the debts and liabilities of the society.[500]

       (3)   A solicitor or other agent is employed by trustees. He normally has no lien on the trust funds for his expenses.[501]

       (4)   Deeds are deposited with a solicitor by a tenant for life. The solicitor has no lien on the deeds as against the remainderman.[502] The lien of a solicitor upon deeds and papers deposited with him by a client is confined to the rights of the client in them, and is subject to all rights and equities of third persons available against the client.[503] So, a solicitor or other agent has no lien, as such, on the separate property of a partner for the obligations of the firm.[504]

---

[495] *West of England Bank v Batchelor* (1882) 51 L.J.Ch. 199.

[496] See Bills of Exchange Act 1882 ss.27(3) and 29.

[497] *Re Capital Fire Ins. Assn* (1883) 24 Ch.D. 408; *Re Rapid Road Transit Co* [1909] 1 Ch. 96; Companies Act 2006 ss.113 and 114.

[498] *Re Anglo-Maltese Hydraulic Dock Co Ltd* (1885) 54 L.J.Ch. 730.

[499] *Brunton v Electrical Engineering Corp* [1892] 1 Ch. 434. See also *Re Dee Estates Ltd, Wright v Dee Estates Ltd* [1911] 2 Ch. 85.

[500] *Blackburn Benefit Building Society v Cunliffe* (1884) 9 App.Cas. 857; see Article 93; Goff and Jones, *Law of Unjust Enrichment* (9th edn), para.15-42.

[501] *Staniar v Evans* (1886) 3 T.L.R. 215; *Worrall v Harford* (1802) 8 Ves. 4; *Lightfoot v Keane* (1836) 1 M. & W. 745; *Hall v Laver* (1842) 1 Hare 571; *Francis v Francis* (1854) 5 De G.M. & G. 108; Cordery, *Solicitors* (8th edn), pp.60–61. See too *Heslop v Cousins* [2007] 3 N.Z.L.R. 679 at [190] (solicitor no lien or set-off on moneys given him for a particular purpose).

[502] *Turner v Letts* (1855) 20 Beav. 185; 7 De G.M. & G. 243; *Ex p. Nesbitt* (1805) 2 Sch. & Lef. 279.

[503] *Hollis v Claridge* (1813) 4 Taunt. 807; *Furlong v Howard* (1804) 2 Sch. & Lef. 115; *Pelly v Wathen* (1851) 1 De G.M. & G. 16; Cordery, *Solicitors* (8th edn), pp.236–238.

[504] *Turner v Deane* (1849) 3 Exch. 836; *Watts v Christie* (1849) 11 Beav. 546.

(5) A mortgage is paid off, and the property is reconveyed to the mortgagor. The mortgagee's solicitor has no lien as against the mortgagor on the title deeds for costs due from the mortgagee, except the cost of the reconveyance, even if such costs were incurred in respect of the mortgaged property, e.g. the costs of an attempted sale by the mortgagee.[505] Where a mortgagor borrowed the title deeds from the mortgagee and sold the property, it was held that the solicitor of the mortgagor, to whom the deeds were handed for the purpose of completing the sale, had no lien over them for costs due from the mortgagor in respect of other transactions.[506]

(6) A sells goods to B, and ships them to B's order. Before the goods arrive, A and B agree to rescind the contract for sale. The wharfinger cannot, on the arrival of the goods at his wharf, claim a lien on them as against A, for a general balance due from B.[507] So, a wharfinger has no lien on goods, as against a buyer, for charges becoming due from the seller after the sale.[508]

(7) A, an owner of land, deposits the title deeds at a bank as security for his general balance, and subsequently contracts to sell the land to B, who has notice of the terms of the deposit. The banker has notice of the sale, but continues to account, and makes fresh advances to A, who pays in sums from time to time. B pays the purchase money to A, by instalments, without notice of such advances. A having paid into the bank sums exceeding in the aggregate the amount owing to the bank at the time of the contract of sale, the banker has no lien on the title deeds or charge on the land as against B, though on the general balance there was always a debt due to the bank.[509]

(8) A client deposits deeds with a solicitor. Judgment is subsequently obtained against the client. The solicitor's lien does not extend to costs becoming due after the date of the judgment.[510]

(9) A banker borrowed a specific sum of money from a stockbroker, with whom he deposited, as security, negotiable instruments belonging to third persons. The banker dealt as a principal with the broker, having had many previous transactions with him, and there was nothing to lead the broker to believe that the securities were not the property of the banker. Held, that the broker's general lien for the balance due to him from the banker attached upon the securities, although the banker had been guilty of gross fraud.[511] So, the general lien of a banker upon negotiable instruments deposited with him is not affected by the circumstance that the customer who deposits them is acting as agent for a third person,[512] nor by equities between the customer and third persons.[513] But an agent has no lien upon a negotiable instrument, as against

---

[505] *Re Llewellin* [1891] 3 Ch. 145; *Wakefield v Newbon* (1844) 6 Q.B. 276. See also *Franicevich v Strong* [1997] 1 N.Z.L.R. 460.
[506] *Young v English* (1843) 7 Beav. 10.
[507] *Richardson v Goss* (1802) 3 B. & P. 119.
[508] *Barry v Longmore* (1840) 12 A. & E. 639.
[509] *London and County Banking Co Ltd v Ratcliffe* (1881) 6 App.Cas. 722 (a case on mortgage: see now Law of Property Act 1925 s.94. But Lord Blackburn refers also to lien). See Paget, *Law of Banking* (14th edn), para.4.2.
[510] *Blunden v Desart* (1842) (Ir.) 59 R.R. 753.
[511] *Jones v Peppercorne* (1858) John. 430.
[512] *Brandao v Barnett* (1846) 12 C. & F. 787; *Baker v Nottingham & Nottinghamshire Banking Co Ltd* (1891) 60 L.J.Q.B. 542.
[513] *Misa v Currie* (1876) 1 App.Cas. 554; *Johnson v Robarts* (1875) L.R. 10 Ch.App. 505.

the true owner, for advances made after notice of a defect in the title of the principal.[514]

Article 67

HOW LIEN EXTINGUISHED OR LOST

7-090 (1) The lien of an agent is extinguished or lost—
   (a) by tender to him of the sum due[515];
   (b) by his entering into any agreement,[516] or acting in any capacity,[517] which is inconsistent with the continuance of the lien;
   (c) by waiver.[518]
(2) The lien of an agent is extinguished by his voluntarily[519] parting with the possession of the goods or chattels subject to it,[520] except where the circumstances in which he parts with possession are consistent with the continuance of the lien and are such as to show that he intends to retain the lien.[521]
(3) The lien of an agent is not affected by the fact that the claim secured by it becomes barred by limitation,[522] or that the principal becomes insolvent, or sells or otherwise deals with the goods or chattels subject to the lien, after the lien has attached.[523]

Comment

7-091 **Tender** Acceptance or refusal of a valid tender extinguishes the lien. But a lien is not necessarily lost by a claim for more than the sum due, unless the claimant gives no details from which the correct sum can be calculated, or makes it clear that he insists on an incorrect sum.[524]

7-092 **Waiver** A waiver is implied whenever the conduct of the agent is such as to indicate an intention to abandon the lien, or is inconsistent with the continuance of it.[525] The situations referred to in Rule (1)(b) are in fact no more than examples of implied waiver. Questions of tender are also sometimes expressed in terms of waiver.[526]

---

[514] *Solomons v Bank of England* (1791) 13 East 135 (but this is hardly clear authority); Bills of Exchange Act 1882 ss.27(3) and 29.

[515] See Comment.

[516] Illustration 1; *How v Kirchner* (1857) 11 Moo.P.C. 21.

[517] Illustrations 2 and 3.

[518] See Comment; Illustrations 4, 5, 6 and 7; Sale of Goods Act 1979 s.43(1)(c).

[519] See *Tibmor Pty Ltd v Nashlyn Pty Ltd* [1989] 1 Qd.R. 610 (obligatory payment into court did not extinguish lien).

[520] Illustration 8; *Kruger v Wilcox* (1755) Amb. 252; *Bligh v Davies* (1860) 28 Beav. 211.

[521] Illustrations 9, 10 and 11.

[522] *Spears v Hartly* (1800) 3 Esp. 81; *Re Broomhead* (1847) 5 D. & L. 52; *Curwen v Milburn* (1889) 42 Ch.D. 424; *Re Carter, Carter v Carter* (1885) 55 L.J.Ch. 230; *Coshott v Barry* [2016] FCAFC 173 at [14]. The statute can be said to bar the remedy, not the right.

[523] The last two propositions follow from the nature of the lien as a right in rem.

[524] *Albemarle Supply Co Ltd v Hind & Co* [1928] 1 K.B. 307; *Coshott v Barry* [2016] FCAFC 173 at [5].

[525] e.g. Illustrations 4 and 5.

[526] e.g. *Scarfe v Morgan* (1838) 4 M. & W. 270. The principle seems to be similar to that of election: a person may waive a contract term which is to his benefit. Obviously there can also be estoppels as

Parting with possession The lien of an agent is not affected where he was **7-093**
induced to part with possession of the goods by fraud,[527] or possession was obtained
from him unlawfully or without his consent.[528] In such cases, the lien continues, and
the person entitled to it can sue in conversion, whether or not he has recovered possession, and if he has recovered possession, even where he did so by a trick[529]: nor
is the lien affected by the fact that the goods are given by the agent to another to
hold on his behalf,[530] even where that other is himself the principal, if the agreement to retain the lien is clear: an example where this occurs is the commercial situation covered by the trust receipt.[531] Where the agent simply delivers the goods with
a purported unilateral reservation of the lien to which the receiver has not agreed,
it is arguable that the lien is lost, on the grounds that such terms of receipt cannot
be unilaterally imposed. It has however been decided that the lien is maintained,
and that if the receiver does not agree to the terms under which the goods are
delivered he must give notice to the lienor to remove them.[532] It appears that in some
cases, where the subject-matter of the lien comes lawfully back into the claimant's
hands after he has voluntarily parted with it, the lien revives, even for sums due
before possession was lost.[533]

Illustrations

(1) The holder of a lien allows the owner of the goods free access to the goods **7-094**
for the purpose of using and returning them: he may be held to have lost his
lien.[534]

(2) A solicitor acts for both mortgagor and mortgagee in carrying out a mortgage.
The solicitor thereby loses his lien on the title deeds of the mortgaged
property for costs due from the mortgagor, even if the costs were incurred
prior to the mortgage, and even if the deeds are not permitted to be taken out
of the solicitor's possession.[535]

(3) A solicitor prepares a marriage settlement, on the instructions of the intended
husband, and retains it in his possession after the marriage. He has no lien on
the settlement as against the trustees, the cost of preparing it being payable
by the husband.[536]

(4) An agent causes goods upon which he has a lien to be taken in execution at

---

to whether there has been or will be a waiver.

[527] *Wallace v Woodgate* (1824) R. & M. 193.

[528] *Dicas v Stockley* (1836) 7 C. & P. 587; *Re Carter, Carter v Carter* (1885) 55 L.J.Ch. 230.

[529] *Bristol (Earl) v Wilsmore* (1823) 1 B. & C. 514.

[530] *Wilson v Kymer* (1813) 1 M. & S. 157; *McCombie v Davis* (1805) 7 East 5.

[531] See Illustration 10; *Benjamin's Sale of Goods* (9th edn), para.18-279 onwards.

[532] *Caldwell v Sumpters* [1972] Ch. 478, Illustration 11. See also *Bentley v Gaisford* [1997] Q.B. 627,
where copying the documents was held a breach of the second holder's duty.

[533] *Levy v Barnard* (1818) 8 Taunt. 149 (marine insurance policy); *Caldwell v Sumpters* [1972] Ch. 478
at 488. But a general lien, at any rate, does not do so where he has meanwhile discovered that the
person with whom he is dealing is only an agent, or where dispositions of the goods have meanwhile
been made: see *Near East Relief v King, Chasseur & Co Ltd* [1930] 2 K.B. 40 at 44–45; Article 70.

[534] *Forth v Simpson* (1849) 13 Q.B. 680; cf. *Albermarle Supply Co Ltd v Hind & Co* [1928] 1 K.B. 307.
See also *Hatton v Car Maintenance Co Ltd* [1915] 1 Ch. 621.

[535] *Re Nicholson Ex p. Quinn* (1883) 53 L.J.Ch. 302; *Re Snell* (1877) 6 Ch.D. 105; *Re Mason and Taylor*
(1878) 10 Ch.D. 729.

[536] *Re Lawrance, Bowker v Austin* [1894] 1 Ch. 556.

his own suit. He thereby waives the lien, though the goods are sold to him under the execution, and are never removed from his premises.[537]

(5)   Upon a demand being made against an agent by his principal for a chattel upon which the agent has a lien, the agent claims to retain the chattel on some other ground, without mentioning the lien. He thereby waives the lien.[538]

(6)   A solicitor, having a lien for costs, takes a security for them, and does not tell the client that he intends to reserve the lien. He is deemed to waive the lien, it being the duty of a solicitor, if he intends to reserve his lien in such a case, to explain to the client that such is his intention.[539]

(7)   An agent entitled to a lien takes other security for the claim. He may be deemed to waive the lien,[540] but only if the nature of the security,[541] or the circumstances in which it is taken,[542] are inconsistent with the continuance of the lien, or indicate an intention to abandon it. The taking of a bill of exchange will usually be no more than conditional acceptance of a particular mode of payment.[543]

(8)   An agent delivers goods, on which he has a lien, on board a ship, to be conveyed on account and at the risk of the principal. The agent thereby surrenders his lien on the goods, and he has no power to revive it by stopping the goods in transit.[544]

(9)   A, as a solicitor, on the instructions of a mortgagor, prepares and engrosses a reconveyance, which he sends to the solicitor of the mortgagee with a request that he will hold it on A's account, he having a lien thereon. The mortgagee executes the reconveyance. A's lien is not, in the circumstances, prejudiced by his parting with the possession of the engrossment, nor by its being executed by the mortgagee as a deed, and he can restrain the mortgagee's solicitor from transferring the deed to a subsequent purchaser of the land.[545]

(10)   An agent gives up a chattel in order that the principal may sell it and account for the proceeds to the agent; he does not thereby lose his lien on the chattel.[546]

(11)   The intending vendor of property changes her solicitor during negotiations. The former solicitor claims a lien on the deeds. The new solicitor requires the

---

[537] *Jacobs v Latour* (1828) 5 Bing. 130.

[538] *Weeks v Goode* (1859) 6 C.B.(N.S.) 367; *Boardman v Sill* (1808) 1 Camp. 410n. The rule is different from that applicable to discharge of contract by breach, where a person who gives an invalid reason for treating the contract as discharged may subsequently justify his conduct by a valid reason.

[539] *Re Morris* [1908] 1 K.B. 473; *Re Taylor, Stileman & Underwood* [1891] 1 Ch. 590; *Bissill v Bradford & District Tramway Co Ltd* (1893) 9 T.L.R. 337; *Re Douglas Norman & Co* [1898] 1 Ch. 199. It seems, therefore, that the solicitor's position is somewhat unfavourable. See Cordery, *Solicitors* (8th edn), p.249.

[540] *Cowell v Simpson* (1809) 16 Ves. 275 (note payable three years later); *Hewison v Guthrie* (1836) 2 Bing.N.C. 755 (bill at 12 months); *Mason v Morley (No.1)* (1865) 34 Beav. 471.

[541] *Angus v McLachlan* (1883) 23 Ch.D. 330.

[542] See *The Albion* (1872) 27 L.T. 723.

[543] *Gunn v Bolckow, Vaughan & Co* (1875) L.R. 10 Ch.App. 491; cf. *Tamvaco v Simpson* (1866) L.R. 1 C.P. 363; *W.J. Alan & Co Ltd v El Nasr Export & Import Co* [1972] 1 Q.B. 189.

[544] *Sweet v Pym* (1800) 1 East 4; *Hathesing v Laing* (1873) 17 Eq. 92. See, however, Article 69.

[545] *Watson v Lyon* (1855) 7 De G.M. & G. 288.

[546] *North Western Bank Ltd v Poynter, Son & Macdonalds* [1895] A.C. 56; see also *Albemarle Supply Co Ltd v Hind & Co* [1928] 1 K.B. 307; *Rose v CMS Operations* [2002] EWHC 59 (Ch); See too *Coshott v Barry* [2016] FCAFC 173 at [4].

deeds in connection with the sale. At the request of the new solicitor, the former solicitor gives them up, accompanying them by a letter saying that they are sent "on the understanding that you will hold them to our order". The new solicitor immediately writes refusing to agree to these terms, but does not offer the deeds back. The former solicitor's lien continues: if the new solicitors were not willing to hold the deeds on these terms they should have told the former solicitors to come and take them back.[547]

Article 68

LIEN OF SUB-AGENTS

(1) Except where otherwise expressly provided by statute,[548] a sub-agent who is employed by an agent in circumstances where the agent has no actual or apparent authority to delegate his functions has no lien over the goods or chattels of the principal as against the principal.[549]

7-095

(2) Where a sub-agent is employed by an agent in circumstances where the agent has actual or apparent authority to delegate without creating privity of contract between principal and sub-agent, the sub-agent—

(a) has the same right of lien, general or particular, against the principal, over the goods and chattels of the principal, in respect of claims arising in the course of the sub-agency, as he would have had against the agent if the agent had been the owner of the goods and chattels; and such right of lien is not liable to be defeated by any settlement between the principal and the agent to which the sub-agent is not a party[550];

(b) has the same right of general lien over the goods and chattels of the principal in respect of all claims, whether arising in the course of the sub-agency or not, as he would have had against the agent if the agent had been the owner of the goods and chattels; provided that, as against the principal, such right of lien is available only to the extent of the lien, if any, to which the agent would have been entitled if the goods and chattels had been in his possession[551]; and

(c) has the same right of lien, general or particular, over the goods and chattels of the principal, as he would have had against the agent if the agent had been the owner of the goods and chattels, where that at the time when the lien attaches he believes on reasonable grounds that the agent is the owner of the goods and chattels and is acting in the matter on his own behalf.[552]

---

[547] *Caldwell v Sumpters* [1972] Ch. 478. See Comment.

[548] See Article 87 as to the Factors Act.

[549] Illustration 1. As to when the agent has the power to affect the legal position of his principal, see Ch.3. And see in general *Restatement, Second*, § 465. As to cases where bailees have authority to place goods in the hands of persons who may subsequently claim a lien against the owner, see *Cassils & Co v Holden Wood Bleaching Co* (1914) 84 L.J.K.B. 834; *Tappenden v Artus* [1964] 2 Q.B. 185; *Chellaram & Sons (London) Ltd v Butlers Warehousing and Distribution Ltd* [1978] 2 Lloyd's Rep. 412; Article 27, Illustration 10.

[550] Illustration 2.

[551] Illustration 3.

[552] Illustration 4–6.

Comment

7-096 Unauthorised delegation Where the agent for a disclosed principal delegates his duties but has no authority, actual or apparent, to do so, it is obvious that the principal's position cannot be affected.[553] The remainder of the Article applies to cases where delegated performance is authorised, but the creation of privity between principal and sub-agent is not.[554] In cases where such privity does exist, the so-called sub-agent is actually an agent of the principal and entitled to an agent's normal remedies against him.[555]

7-097 General rule But where delegation to a sub-agent is authorised by virtue of actual or apparent authority, the principal can be regarded as having authorised the agent to subject the property to a lien. The general rule, therefore, set out in Rule (2)(a), is that the sub-agent's lien against the principal is confined to claims arising in the course of performance of the duties properly delegated to him. However, where the agent himself has an interest in the principal's property by way of lien,[556] the sub-agent is entitled to exercise a lien to that extent against the principal, as stated in Rule (2)(b). Both these rules can be regarded as applications of the principle that no one can create a lien beyond his own interest.[557]

Against the agent, of course, the sub-agent has the normal rights of an agent against his principal.

7-098 Undisclosed principal It has long been established that, as stated in Rule (2)(c), when the agent does not disclose the existence of his principal, the subagent may exercise against such principal the full lien that would have been available against the agent had that agent in fact been principal, to the extent that such lien had accrued up to the time of discovery of the principal[558] provided, of course, that the delegation was within the authority of the agent. The basis of this rule seems to be the notion that an undisclosed principal intervenes on the contract of his agent subject to equities already accrued,[559] and there is no tendency in the cases regarding lien to require some fault in the principal that could be treated as raising an estoppel.[560] However, since the agent is authorised, it would seem that on discovery of the principal the sub-agent is remitted to his position under Rule (2)(a).

Although a lien revives, at any rate in some cases, where possession of the goods is recovered,[561] it has been held that the general lien of a marine insurance broker on a policy does not revive when at the time that he recovers possession he has notice that the person with whom he had dealt was only an agent,[562] and this seems to be a rule applicable to all general liens, based on the fact that the regained pos-

---

[553] Illustration 1.
[554] See Article 35.
[555] See Article 35.
[556] Illustration 3.
[557] See Comment to Article 66.
[558] *Westwood v Bell* (1815) 4 Camp. 349; Marine Insurance Act 1906 s.53(2).
[559] *Montagu v Forwood* [1893] 2 Q.B. 350 at 355–356.
[560] Compare the position as regards set-off: see Comment to Article 81.
[561] *Levy v Barnard* (1818) 2 Moo.C.P. 34 (marine insurance policy).
[562] *Near East Relief v King, Chasseur & Co Ltd* [1930] 2 K.B. 40; *Eide UK Ltd v Lowndes Lambert Group Ltd* [1999] Q.B. 199 at 209–210 and see Marine Insurance Act 1906 s.53.

session is a new possession.[563] It would not, however, apply where the first possession is lost not voluntarily, but by fraud or a trick.[564]

Illustrations

(1) A factor delegated his authority to a sub-agent, without the assent of the principal. The sub-agent, who knew that the goods did not belong to the factor, had no lien on the principal's goods, even for duties paid in respect of those goods.[565]   **7-099**

(2) An agent, with the authority of his principal, employs an insurance broker to effect a policy for his principal, the broker being aware that the agent is acting for a principal. The principal pays the agent the amount of the premiums due in respect of the policy. Notwithstanding such payment, the broker has a lien upon the policy for premiums paid by him in respect of it, or for which he is liable.[566] But he has no lien, as against the principal, for a general balance due from the agent in respect of other transactions.[567]

(3) As against the country solicitor employing him, a London agent has a general lien upon all moneys received and documents deposited with him in the course of his employment,[568] but as against the client, his general lien is limited to the amount due from the client to the country solicitor.[569] As against both the country solicitor and the client, he has a lien upon money recovered and documents deposited with him in a particular suit, for the amount of his agency charges and disbursements in connection with that suit.[570]

(4) An agent, on behalf, and with the authority, of his principal, employs an insurance broker to effect a policy, the broker having no notice, and being unaware, that he is dealing with an agent. The broker has a lien on the policy for the general balance due to him from the agent, and is entitled to apply the proceeds of the policy in payment of such balance, notwithstanding that he has, in the meantime, received notice of the principal's rights.[571]

(5) A, a commission agent, employed B, a broker, to buy certain goods, B having no knowledge that A was acting as an agent. B bought and paid for the goods and retained the warrants relating to them. A was in fact acting for C, and C paid A for the goods. B, on A's instructions, resold the goods, and applied the proceeds in reduction of a running account between himself and A. In an action by C against B for converting the goods, it was held that B was

---

[563] Powell, pp.375–376.

[564] See Comment to Article 67.

[565] *Solly v Rathbone* (1814) 2 M. & S. 298; *Snook v Davidson* (1809) 2 Camp. 218. And see *Chellaram & Sons (London) Ltd v Butlers Warehousing and Distribution Ltd* [1978] 2 Lloyd's Rep. 412 (uncontemplated sub-bailment).

[566] *Fisher v Smith* (1878) 4 App.Cas. 1; Marine Insurance Act 1906 s.53(2).

[567] *Mildred v Maspons* (1883) 8 App.Cas. 874; *Maanss v Henderson* (1801) 1 East 335; *Man v Shiffner* (1802) 2 East 523; Marine Insurance Act 1906 s.53(2); *Fairfield Shipbuilding & Engineering Co Ltd v Gardner Mountain & Co Ltd* (1911) 104 L.T. 288.

[568] *Lawrence v Fletcher* (1879) 12 Ch.D. 858; *Bray v Hine & Fox* (1818) 6 Price 203; *Re Jones and Roberts* [1905] 2 Ch. 219.

[569] *Ex p. Edwards* (1881) 8 Q.B.D. 262; *Moody v Spencer* (1822) 2 D. & R. 6; *Waller v Holmes* (1860) 1 John. & H. 239; *Peatfield v Barlow* (1869) L.R. 8 Eq. 61.

[570] *Dicas v Stockley* (1836) 7 C. & P. 587; *Lawrence v Fletcher* (1879) 12 Ch.D. 858. See Cordery, *Solicitors* (8th edn), p.242.

[571] *Mann v Forrester* (1814) 4 Camp. 60; *Westwood v Bell* (1815) 4 Camp. 349; Marine Insurance Act 1906 s.53(2).

not liable, because at the time of the sale he had a lien on goods for the balance due to him from A.[572]

(6) A employed B to collect general average contributions under an insurance policy. B, in the ordinary course of business, employed C, an insurance broker, to collect the contributions, C being unaware that B was acting as an agent. C collected the contributions, and B became bankrupt. Held, in an action by A against C for the contributions, as money had and received to his use, that C was entitled to set off the amount of a debt due to him from B.[573]

4. OTHER MISCELLANEOUS RIGHTS

Article 69

RIGHTS IN RESPECT OF GOODS BOUGHT IN OWN NAME

7-100 Where an agent, by contracting personally,[574] renders himself solely liable for the price of goods bought on behalf of his principal, the property in the goods, as between the principal and the agent, vests in the agent, and does not pass to the principal until he pays for the goods, or the agent intends that it shall pass[575]; and the agent has the same rights with regard to the disposal of the goods, and with regard to stopping them in transit, as he would have had if the relation between him and his principal had been that of seller and buyer.[576]

Comment

7-101 A person who is in general an agent and obtains goods for his principal may on a particular occasion genuinely buy them from the third party and resell them to the principal.[577] In such a case he has all the normal remedies of a seller, and is under the liabilities of a seller, except in so far as circumstances indicate otherwise.

But another interpretation of his functions is possible: he may deal with the third party as principal, while remaining in the status of agent towards his own principal—i.e. his remuneration will (normally[578]) be by commission rather than by profit on resale, and his duty would not be the absolute one of a seller, but rather that of an agent to exercise due diligence in carrying out the principal's instructions.[579] This is one of the interpretations put on the function of a commission merchant in the leading case of *Ireland v Livingston*.[580] It is referred to elsewhere in this book as "indirect representation" and associated with the civil law

---

[572] *Taylor v Kymer* (1832) 3 B. & Ad. 320.
[573] *Montagu v Forwood* [1893] 2 Q.B. 350. And see *New Zealand, etc., Land Co v Watson* (1881) 7 Q.B.D. 374; Article 81.
[574] See Comment and Article 98.
[575] *Cassaboglou v Gibb* (1883) 11 Q.B.D. 797 at 803–804, 806–806, Illustration 4.
[576] Sale of Goods Act 1979 s.38(2); and see Comment; *Restatement, Second*, § 466.
[577] See above, para.1-036 onwards. Provided that he is not in breach of his fiduciary duties in doing so: see Article 31, Illustration 9; Articles 45 and 47.
[578] See above, para.1-036.
[579] See *Cassaboglou v Gibb* (1883) 11 Q.B.D. 797; *Bolus & Co Ltd v Inglis Bros Ltd* [1924] N.Z.L.R. 164 at 174; *Witt & Scott Ltd v Blumenreich* [1949] N.Z.L.R. 806; *Anglo-African Shipping Co of New York Inc v J. Mortner Ltd* [1962] 1 Lloyd's Rep. 610 (but note the dissenting opinion of Diplock LJ). See above, para.1-017.
[580] (1872) L.R. 5 H.L. 395 at 404–405, 412, 416 (Illustration 1 to Article 26).

notion of *commissionnaire*.[581] The specialised group of cases on which this Article is based concern nineteenth-century examples of (what appears to be) this situation: they are indeed among the only cases which can be said to concern it, and so are of considerable importance. The assumptions behind them are not easy to get into.

In such a case the agent may nevertheless have, as against his principal, some of the remedies regarding the goods which are available to unpaid vendors. It has long been established that the right of stoppage in transit could apply, not being confined to genuine vendors[582]: the unpaid vendor's lien has also been extended to such a case.[583] In any case the agent has a lien as such, but the unpaid vendor's rights may be exercised by a person who has never acquired property or possession.[584] The effect of these cases was put into statutory form in s.38(2) of the Sale of Goods Act 1979 which extends the rights of the unpaid seller against the goods to "any person who is in the position of a seller, as, for instance … a consignor or agent who has himself paid, or is directly responsible for, the price". This indicates that such a person has not only the rights of lien and stoppage in transit but also that of resale.

Whether an agent in such a position can reserve property so as to be able to exercise the right of withholding delivery, as opposed to a lien, is open to argument. It used to be said that the normal rule for agents is that the goods become the property of the principal as soon as they are consigned to him.[585] On one view, an agent who does something that would normally reserve property, e.g. takes a bill of lading to his own order, reserves a lien only: if he is to reserve property he must be acting not as agent but as seller, as it is difficult to see under what transaction the goods would otherwise eventually become the property of the principal.[586] On another view, he may in appropriate cases still be an agent, but may reserve and subsequently transmit property nevertheless.[587] There may be little difference in practice, for even where an agent would be for the above purposes treated as a seller, it is clear that he cannot act as a seller to the exclusion of his instructions and sue his principal for non-acceptance of goods bought[588]; he cannot sue for the price of goods as on a sale[589]; the measure of damages for breach of contract is not that of a contract of sale[590]; and the agent will often not answer for breach of warranty of quality.[591] Property will presumably pass by intention,[592] but not in accordance with the rules for sales laid down in the Sale of Goods Act 1979 as such. In view of these

[581] See above, para.1-021. But compare expressions used elsewhere; and see *Ex p. Miles* (1885) 15 Q.B.D. 39 at 42; *Brown & Gracie v F.W. Green Pty Ltd* [1960] 1 Lloyd's Rep. 289, per Lord Denning. See further Hill (1972) 3 J. Maritime Law and Commerce, 307, esp. at 318–324 (a valuable article); (1968) 31 M.L.R. 623.
[582] *Feise v Wray* (1802) 3 East 93, Illustration 1; cf. *Siffken v Wray* (1805) 6 East 371. See also *The Tigress* (1863) 32 L.J.Ad. 97; *Hawkes v Dunn* (1831) 1 C. & J. 519.
[583] See *Imperial Bank v London & St. Katharine Docks Co* (1877) 5 Ch.D. 195, Illustration 2.
[584] *Jenkyns v Usborne* (1844) 7 M. & G. 678.
[585] *Hathesing v Laing* (1873) L.R. 17 Eq. 92 at 101; *Re Tappenbeck Ex p. Banner* (1876) 2 Ch.D. 278 at 287, Illustration 3. And see Article 89.
[586] See *Benjamin's Sale of Goods* (9th edn), para.18-273 onwards; Blackburn, *Contract of Sale* (3rd edn), p.352.
[587] See *Cassaboglou v Gibb* (1883) 11 Q.B.D. 797 at 804, 806 (Illustration 4); see also *Jenkyns v Brown* (1849) 14 Q.B. 496; *Schuster v McKellar* (1857) 7 E. & B. 704; *Falk v Fletcher* (1865) 18 C.B.(N.S.) 403; *Re Tappenbeck Ex p. Banner*, above; *The Prinz Adelbert* [1917] A.C. 586 at 590; Sale of Goods Act 1979 s.38(2).
[588] *Tetley v Shand* (1871) 25 L.T. 658, Illustration 5; *White v Benekendorff* (1873) 29 L.T. 475; cf. *Robinson v Mollett* (1875) L.R. 7 H.L. 802, Illustration 8 to Article 31.
[589] *Seymour v Pychlau* (1817) 1 B. & A. 14.
[590] *Cassaboglou v Gibb* (1883) 11 Q.B.D. 797.
[591] See *J.S. Robertson (Australia) Pty Ltd v Martin* (1950) 94 C.L.R. 30.

points, it is doubtful whether there is much utility in calling the agent a seller, and it is submitted that the second view is preferable.

A third way in which an agent who contracts personally may act is by making a contract between his principal and the third party and adding his own liability to it: the possibilities in this respect are discussed elsewhere.[593] The cases cited for the propositions above do not apply to such a situation. If appropriate, he can here presumably reserve property, and may certainly exercise his agent's lien. If he discharges his principal's liability, it seems that he also has the unpaid vendor's rights.[594] It is not clear whether or not he has these rights when he is simply liable but has not been called upon to pay, e.g. where his principal is insolvent.[595]

Illustrations

7-102
(1) P instructs A, a factor in Hamburg, to procure and ship wax for him. A buys wax in his own name, ships to P's order, and draws on P for the price. P becomes insolvent. A can stop in transit.[596]
(2) D, a broker, buys goods lying in a warehouse from C for unnamed principals. D obtains a delivery order, and delivers it to Z, his principals. Z pledge their interest in the goods to X and indorse the order to X. X requests the warehouse to attorn to him. Before the warehouse has done so Z becomes insolvent, and D, knowing nothing of X, pays C and obtains another delivery order. D can exercise the unpaid vendor's lien against X and Z.[597]
(3) P employs A in South America to buy goods. A buys goods in his own name using money raised by bills drawn on P. A ships the goods, taking a bill of lading to P's order. The bills of exchange are not all paid. A has the right to stop in transit, but no further rights against the goods once the transit is ended.[598]
(4) P requests A in Hong Kong to buy and ship a certain kind of opium. A ships the wrong kind of opium. P sues A. The measure of damages is not the difference between the value of the opium ordered and that shipped, as on a sale, but the loss actually sustained by P in consequence of the opium not being as ordered, the contract being one of agency.[599]
(5) P requests A, a cotton broker, to buy cotton gradually at eight-and-a-quarter d if A cannot do better. A purchases in his own name at 81/16d and 713/15d and sends P a bought note for the cotton at eight and a quarter d. P discovers what has happened and repudiates the transaction. The contract is not one of sale and A cannot sue for non-acceptance: also, he is in breach of his duties as agent.[600]

[592] See *Cassaboglou v Gibb* (1883) 11 Q.B.D. 797 at 803–804.
[593] See Comment to Article 98.
[594] See Sale of Goods Act 1979 s.38(2); *Imperial Bank v London & St Katharine Docks Co* (1877) 5 Ch.D. 195. See further as to this case, and especially as to the reference to the Mercantile Law Amendment Act, *Benjamin's Sale of Goods* (9th edn), pp.912–913.
[595] See Blackburn, *Contract of Sale* (3rd edn), p.352; *Cassaboglou v Gibb* (1883) 11 Q.B.D. 797 at 804; Sale of Goods Act 1979 s.38(2).
[596] *Feise v Wray* (1802) 3 East 93.
[597] *Imperial Bank v London & St Katharine Docks Co* (1877) 5 Ch.D. 195.
[598] *Re Tappenbeck, Ex p. Banner* (1876) 2 Ch.D. 278.
[599] *Cassaboglou v Gibb* (1883) 11 Q.B.D. 797.
[600] *Tetley v Shand* (1871) 25 L.T. 658.

Article 70

Right to Interplead

(1) Where adverse claims whether legal or equitable, are made upon an agent in respect of any money, goods, or chattels in his possession, and he claims no interest in the subject-matter of the dispute other than for costs or charges, he may claim relief by way of interpleader,[601] even as against his own principal whose title he has acknowledged,[602] provided that he had no notice of the adverse claim at the time of the acknowledgment.[603]   **7-103**

(2) Where the agent claims a lien on property as against the owner, whoever he may be, the lien is not such an interest as deprives him of the right to interplead in respect of the ownership of the property[604]; but where he claims a lien or any other interest in the property, or part of it, other than for costs or charges, as against a particular claimant, he is not permitted to interplead.[605]

Illustrations

(1) An agent has funds in his hands, upon which a third person claims to have been given a lien by the principal. The agent may interplead as against his principal and the third person.[606]   **7-104**

(2) A instructs a stockbroker to sell shares, and sends him the share certificate and blank transfers. The shares are claimed by B, who alleges that they were obtained from him by fraud. A sues the broker, claiming the return of the certificate and transfers. The broker may interplead.[607]

(3) A, a part-owner of a vessel, instructs B, a broker, to insure the vessel. B receives an amount due under the policy in respect of a loss, and the whole of the amount is claimed by A. A sues B for the whole amount, and certain other part-owners sue him for part thereof. B may interplead.[608]

(4) A deposits goods with B, a wharfinger, and afterwards requests him to transfer them to the name of C, reserving to himself a right to draw samples. B enters the goods in C's name. D then claims them as paramount owner, and A acquiesces in his claim. C also claims them. B may interplead as against C and D.[609]

(5) A entrusted a policy to B for a specified purpose. C, who had pledged the

---

[601] See PD RSC 17 (CPR Sch. 1).

[602] *Tanner v European Bank Ltd* (1866) L.R. 1 Ex. 261; *Attenborough v St Katharine Docks Co* (1878) 3 C.P.D. 450; *Ex p. Mersey Docks and Harbour Board* [1899] 1 Q.B. 546; Illustrations 1 to 6. As to interpleader on claims by agent and undisclosed principal, see *Meynell v Angell* (1863) 32 L.J.Q.B. 14.

[603] *Re Sadler Ex p. Davies* (1881) 19 Ch.D. 86. If he had such notice he would formerly have been estopped from denying his principal's title. But by virtue of s.8(1) of the Torts (Interference with Goods) Act 1977 he may now apply for joinder of the third party in such a situation. See Article 56 and Comment.

[604] *Attenborough v St Katharine's Dock Co* above; *Cotter v Bank of England* (1833) 3 Moo. & S. 180.

[605] *Mitchell v Hayne* (1824) 2 Sim. & S. 63; *Moore v Usher* (1835) 7 Sim. 383. But cf. *Best v Hayes* (1863) 1 H. & C. 718, Illustration 6.

[606] *Smith v Hammond* (1833) 6 Sim. 10.

[607] *Robinson v Jenkins* (1890) 24 Q.B.D. 275.

[608] *Suart v Welch* (1839) 4 My. & C. 305.

[609] *Mason v Hamilton* (1831) 5 Sim. 19; *Pearson v Cardon* (1831) 2 Russ. & M. 606; *Ex p. Mersey Docks and Harbour Board* [1899] 1 Q.B. 546.

policy with A, and A each brought an action against B for the policy. Held, that B was entitled to interplead.[610]

(6) A, an auctioneer, sells goods on behalf of B, and whilst a portion of the proceeds is still in his hands, receives notice of a claim by C. B sues A for the balance of the proceeds. A may deduct his expenses and charges and interplead as to the residue.[611]

(7) Two estate agents claim commission in respect of the sale of the same property. There is a possibility that the vendor may be under an obligation to pay commission to both. He may not interplead.[612]

---

[610] *Tanner v European Bank* (1866) L.R. 1 Ex. 261.
[611] *Best v Hayes* (1863) 1 H. & C. 718; cf. *Mitchell v Hayne* (1824) 2 Sim. & S. 63; *Wright v Freeman* (1879) 48 L.J.Q.B. 276; *Ingham v Walker* (1887) 3 T.L.R. 448 (claims against auctioneer not co-extensive; seller claims price paid, buyer claims damages).
[612] *Greatorex & Co v Shackle* [1895] 2 Q.B. 249; *Dominion Factors Pty Ltd v L.J. Hooker Ltd* [1963] N.S.W.R. 573.

CHAPTER 8

RELATIONS BETWEEN PRINCIPALS AND THIRD PARTIES

1. CONTRACT

Article 71

DISCLOSED PRINCIPAL: GENERAL RULE

(1) A disclosed principal, whether identified or unidentified, may sue or be sued **8-001**
on any contract made on his behalf by his agent acting within the scope of his
actual authority or whose acts are validly ratified.[1]

(2) So far as concerns deeds, bills of exchange, promissory notes and cheques, this
Article must be read subject to Articles 77 and 78.

Comment

Rule (1) This Article states the basic principle of contractual agency—that an **8-002**
agent acting within the scope of his actual authority, express or implied, binds and
entitles his principal. As such it does no more than link up this section with Chapter
3, where many relevant authorities will be found. Ratification will also, subject to
the rules peculiar to that branch of the law, achieve the same result.[2] The usual
explanation of the rights and liabilities of the principal is that on an objective
interpretation of the dealings involved he has in fact made the contract, and this
explanation is, if the action used be regarded as contractual, indeed made necessary by the doctrine of consideration and the related rules of privity of contract.[3]
But it is by no means clear that it disposes of all the difficulties. The plain fact is
that business convenience requires that one person be in some cases liable and
entitled on the contract of another; it is potentially to the benefit of both parties that
the dealings of an authorised agent are mutually binding. The historical evolution
of the above rule has been complex.[4]

Written evidence: Statute of Frauds. The old law   Under s.40 of the Law of **8-003**
Property Act 1925, contracts for the sale of land and certain similar contracts were
unenforceable without a note or memorandum, signed by the party to be charged.
Such a document might instead be signed by an agent "thereunto by him lawfully

---

[1]   cf. *Restatement, Third*, § 6.01. See also Article 92. In the case of an unidentified principal, there may
occasionally be difficulty in determining for whom the agent acted. The problem is referred to under
the heading of "Ratification", above, para.2-067.

[2]   See Ch.2, Section 3.

[3]   See *Freeman & Lockyer v Buckhurst Park Properties (Mangal) Ltd* [1964] 2 Q.B. 480 at 502.

[4]   See Ch.1; Powell, pp.148–150; Stoljar, pp.32–41.

authorised".[5] The cases on this provision and its predecessor, s.4 of the Statute of Frauds 1677, "decide that to satisfy the statute the agreement or memorandum must name or identify two parties who are contractually bound to each other".[6] Therefore, if an agent made an agreement in such terms that he was himself liable as a contracting party, the memorandum would satisfy the statute,[7] and would not cease to do so because the other party knew that the agent was acting as an agent.[8] In such a case, and also in the case where the principal was undisclosed, the contract was enforceable by or against either principal or agent, for the effect of the introduction of the principal was to add the liability of a new party to the agent's already existing liability.[9] But where the agreement was made by the agent in such terms that he was not himself liable as a contracting party, the principal could sue or be sued only if his name appeared in the memorandum, or if, from the description of him therein, his identity as a party was clear.[10] Thus where an agent signed as agent for an unnamed principal, there might be no memorandum satisfying the statute, unless a custom existed making the agent personally liable in a manner not inconsistent with the form of signature, so that his signature alone could suffice.[11]

The same rules presumably applied and still apply to contracts of guarantee, which were also governed by the Statute of Frauds, and remain so governed, the wording of which regarding authorisation is the same as that later reproduced in s.40.[12]

8-004   **The new law**   Section 40 of the 1925 Act was however repealed and replaced by s.2 of the Law of Property (Miscellaneous Provisions) Act 1989, which requires that such contracts actually be in writing, signed by each party. This provision also allows signature by agents, but in different words: it requires that the signature be "by or on behalf of each party to the contract". It does not require that the agent himself has written authority.[13] Although the Law Commission Working Paper which eventually led to the Act avowed an intention to "let the ordinary principles of agency operate"[14] it is not clear how they do so. If the agent signs for a principal whom he names, the matter is straightforward.[15] At the other extreme, if he signs "as agent only" and no principal is named in or identifiable from the document, the contract is presumably not in writing, the name of one of the parties being missing.

---

[5]   As to authorisation of such an agent, see above, para.2-019.
[6]   *Basma v Weekes* [1950] A.C. 441 at 454, per Lord Reid.
[7]   *Filby v Hounsell* [1896] 2 Ch. 737, as interpreted by Younger LJ in *Lovesey v Palmer* [1916] 2 Ch. 233.
[8]   *Basma v Weekes*, above; disapproving dicta of Luxmoore LJ in *Smith-Bird v Blower* [1939] 2 All E.R. 406; *Davies v Sweet* [1962] 2 Q.B. 300.
[9]   *Higgins v Senior* (1841) 8 M. & W. 834; *Calder v Dobell* (1871) L.R. 6 C.P. 486; *Basma v Weekes*, above. See also *Morris v Wilson* (1859) 5 Jur.(N.S.) 168.
[10]   *Lovesey v Palmer* [1916] 2 Ch. 233.
[11]   See *Dale v Humfrey* (1857) 7 E. & B. 266; affd (1858) E.B. & E. 1004; Article 100.
[12]   See *Bateman v Phillips* (1812) 15 East 272; *Garrett v Handley* (1825) 4 B. & C. 664. See also *Marginson v Ian Potter & Co* (1976) 136 C.L.R. 161 (where principal already liable, his promise to pay was not a guarantee). An agent may have authority to sign for both parties: above, para.2-014. As to a solicitor's authority see above, para.3-023, Illustration 9 and para.3-032, Illustrations 5 and 6; as to estate agents, para.3-032, Illustration 7.
[13]   See *McLaughlin v Duffill* [2008] EWCA Civ 1627; [2010] Ch.1.
[14]   *Law Com.W.P. No. 92* (1985), s.5.16.
[15]   For the position where an agent signs on behalf of a company not yet formed and is liable under s.51 of the Companies Act 2006, see *Braymist Ltd v Wise Finance Ltd* [2002] EWCA Civ 127; [2002] Ch. 273. A signature as agent was held sufficient to enable the agent (a solicitor) to sign: the agent was the "statutory deemed vendor". See below, para.9-086.

But if the agent signs in such a way as to make himself personally liable, but is also stated to be acting on behalf of an unidentified principal, or is in fact acting on behalf of a completely undisclosed principal, situations where the memorandum may have been adequate under the previous law, the situation is more difficult of analysis. It can be said that the change from a mere requirement of authorisation to the wording "by or on behalf of" means that the signature must now be avowedly "on behalf of" the party concerned, and hence that in neither of the above cases can the principal now sue or be sued. This seems consonant with the policy of the Act of requiring that the full terms of the contract be in writing, rather than merely evidenced by a note or memorandum.[16] But it can be argued alternatively that an agent signs "on behalf of" the principal whenever he signs with authority to do so and intending to act for his principal. On this basis the previous law remains valid, and the unnamed or undisclosed principal may enforce the contract or have it enforced against him. If that is so, it is then, however, necessary to inquire whether or not the unnamed or undisclosed principal is a party to the contract entered into by the agent, or to some other contract: for if it was to some other contract, writing and his signature would be required for that. It seems clear that the undisclosed principal is a party to the same contract as the agent[17]; and although doubt may now be cast on whether the unnamed principal of an agent who undertakes personal liability is a person alternatively as opposed to cumulatively liable, as older cases suggest, it is clear that his liability, whether joint or joint and several, is normally on the same contract as that of the agent.[18] The view that the law has been changed (albeit without this being stated in the relevant Law Commission reports[19]) seems the more natural reading of the provision, but that result could cause considerable inconvenience, since purchasers of land often wish to remain incognito.

Auctions   The provisions of s.2 do not apply to sales by public auction[20] and hence it appears that no writing is needed for such sales.[21]   **8-005**

Cases where agent also liable and entitled   In this context, the fact that the   **8-006**
principal instructs an agent who operates in a market by the rules or customs of which the agent is personally liable and entitled on contracts which he makes within it does not of itself exclude the principal's right to sue and be sued, for the agent's rights and duties are simply additional to those of the principal and not inconsistent with them.[22] If the rules or customs require that the agent be solely liable and entitled, and the principal knows of them, he may be regarded as instructing the agent on that basis.[23] If, however, he does not know of them, he only assents to such

---

[16]   *Spiro v Glencrown Properties Ltd* [1991] Ch. 537 at 541. The requirements for satisfying s.2 are laid down in *Commission for the New Towns v Cooper (GB) Ltd* [1995] Ch. 259.
[17]   Article 76.
[18]   See Comment to Article 98.
[19]   See *Law Com.W.P. No.92* (1985); *Law Com. No. 164* (1987).
[20]   s.2(5)(b).
[21]   It is arguable that s.40 of the 1925 Act is not repealed in the case of public auctions, since the repealing provision (s.2(8)) appears in s.2, which by its own wording does not apply to sales by public auction. But s.2(8) also states in brackets that it supersedes s.40 and this is probably enough to prevent what would be a surprising result.
[22]   See, e.g. *Levitt v Hamblet* [1901] 2 K.B. 53 as an example of many cases concerning the former rules of the London Stock Exchange. And see in general below, para.9-016.
[23]   As in *Morrison, Kekewich & Co v Mendel* (1888) 5 T.L.R. 153.

rules or customs as are reasonable,[24] and such a rule may as against an outsider sometimes not be.[25]

8-007   **Foreign principal**   Certain nineteenth-century cases held that a foreign principal could neither sue nor be sued on his agent's contracts. The rule was based on the notions that such a principal did not authorise his English agent to establish privity of contract between him and English contracting parties; and that the English contracting party did not authorise its agent to establish privity of contract with foreign dealers. Therefore the agent was himself the contracting party and there was not in form any exception to normal agency principles. The rule, if such it was, is now obsolete, though the fact that the principal is foreign may be relevant to the question whether the agent is liable in addition to his principal. Since the case law was, and what remains still is, principally relevant to the liability of the agent rather than that of the principal, it is dealt with under Article 98.

8-008   **Knowledge of third party that agent not authorised**   If the principal does something indicating that he withdraws the authority, but does not communicate this to the agent, between himself and the principal the agent still has actual authority and is not liable to the principal for exercising it. But if in such circumstances that withdrawal of authority comes to the notice of the third party, the third party probably cannot hold the principal liable, not only as regards apparent authority[26] but also on principles of actual authority.[27]

8-009   **Rule (2)**   The general rule is displaced in the case of deeds and negotiable instruments, where special significance is attached to the wording of the documents used. These are therefore dealt with separately in Articles 77 and 78.

Article 72

APPARENT (OR OSTENSIBLE) AUTHORITY

8-010   Where a person, by words or conduct, represents or permits it to be represented that another person has authority to act on his behalf, he is bound by the acts of that other person with respect to anyone dealing with him as an agent on the faith of any such representation, to the same extent as if such other person had the authority that he was represented to have, even though he had no such actual authority.[28]

---

[24]   Article 31.
[25]   See *Morrison, Kekewich & Co v Mendel*, above. But cf. *Cunliffe-Owen v Teather & Greenwood* [1967] 1 W.L.R. 1421 (usage that only members can declare options reasonable).
[26]   Article 72.
[27]   See Wright (1937) 15 Can.B.R. 196, criticising *Robert Simpson Co v Godson* [1937] 1 D.L.R. 454 (to the contrary effect); *Restatement, Second*, § 7, Comment *d*, § 144, Comment *e*. (cf. *Restatement, Third*, § 3.11). See also above, para.2-032.
[28]   See *Pickering v Busk* (1812) 15 East 38; *Pickard v Sears* (1837) 6 A. & E. 469; *Reynell v Lewis* (1846) 15 M. & W. 517; *Freeman v Cooke* (1848) 2 Exch. 654; *Smith v M'Guire* (1858) 3 H. & N. 554; *Robinson v Tyson* (1888) 9 L.R. (N.S.W.) 297; *International Paper Co v Spicer* (1906) 4 C.L.R. 739; *Freeman & Lockyer v Buckhurst Park Properties (Mangal) Ltd* [1964] 2 Q.B. 480; *Hely-Hutchinson v Brayhead Ltd* [1968] 1 Q.B. 549; *R. v Charles* [1977] A.C. 177 at 183; *Armagas Ltd v Mundogas SA (The Ocean Frost)* [1986] A.C. 717 at 777. For consideration of policy issues, see Hetherington (1966) 19 Stanford L.Rev. 76; Rubenstein (1958) 44 A.B.A.J. 849; Lipson (1999) 33 Georgia L.Rev. 1219; Watts [2015] L.M.C.L.Q. 36.

[380]

Comment

Doctrine of apparent authority   This Article seeks to formulate the general   **8-011**
doctrine of apparent (sometimes called alternatively ostensible) authority. It should
be read together with the three Articles following, and with Article 121 that deals
with apparent authority lingering after an agent's authority has been terminated.
Under this doctrine a principal may be bound by the acts of an agent which he has
not authorised, and has even forbidden. Most western systems of law have found
the necessity for some type of reasoning which at least imposes liability, if it does
not confer the right to sue, in situations such as those covered by this doctrine. The
English version is plainly based on the notion of a representation by the principal.
The leading case, which is constantly cited, is *Freeman & Lockyer v Buckhurst Park
Properties (Mangal) Ltd*,[29] in which Diplock LJ said:

> "An 'apparent' or 'ostensible' authority ... is a legal relationship between the principal
> and the contractor created by a representation, made by the principal to the contractor,
> intended to be and in fact acted upon by the contractor, that the agent has authority to enter
> on behalf of the principal into a contract of a kind within the scope of the 'apparent' author-
> ity, so as to render the principal liable to perform any obligations imposed upon him by
> such contract. To the relationship so created the agent is a stranger. He need not be
> (although he generally is) aware of the existence of the representation but he must not
> purport to make the agreement as principal himself. The representation, when acted upon
> by the contractor by entering into a contract with the agent, operates as an estoppel,
> preventing the principal from asserting that he is not bound by the contract. It is ir-
> relevant whether the agent had actual authority to enter into the contract."[30]

Restatement, Third distances itself from the notion of representation used above by
referring to situations "where the third party reasonably believes that the actor has
authority to act on behalf of the principal and that belief is traceable to the
principal's manifestations".[31] This, with its use of the more neutral word "manifestation"[32] is probably, because it is less specific, a better formulation of the notion,
common to most legal systems but uneasy in its justification, that apparent authority stems in some way from the principal's conduct.[33]

Applicable outside contract   The dictum concerns contract, where the main ap-   **8-012**
plication of the doctrine is to be found. While the operation of the doctrine arises
most often in connection with the formation of contracts, it also arises in relation
to the performance of an existing contract.[34] The doctrine also applies in respect of

---

[29] [1964] 2 Q.B. 480, Illustration 31.
[30] At 503.
[31] §§ 2.03 and 3.03.
[32] Discussed in § 1.03.
[33] See below, para.8-028. See PECL, art.3:201; UNIDROIT Principles, art.2.2.5(2); DCFR, II, 6:103.
As to the UNIDROIT Principles, see *Commentary on the UNIDROIT PICC* (Vogenauer and
Kleinhesterkamp eds, 2009), Ch.2, Section 2; *The Unauthorised Agent* (Busch and Macgregor eds,
2009); and Reynolds (2009) 13 Eur. Rev. Private Law 975.
[34] See, e.g. *Martin v Artyork Investments Ltd* [1997] 2 S.C.R. 290 (apparent authority to borrow, but
lender needs also to ensure that draw down is by an authorised person); *Acute Property Developments Ltd v Apostolou* [2013] EWHC 200 (Ch) (manager's authority to direct payment of debt owed
to principal to other person); *Pourzand v Telstra Corp Ltd* [2014] WASCA 14 (lessee's property
manager authorising lessor to make building alterations); *Lo v Russell* [2016] VSCA 323 (estate
agent's apparent authority to receive cooling-off notice).

transfers of property[35]; and sometimes in other contexts as well, such as tort[36] and questions of notification.[37]

8-013 **Liability only**   Normally, of course, the actual and apparent authority will coincide, and it will be unnecessary for the doctrine of apparent authority to be invoked. But when it is, the full consequences of the agency relationship do not flow, for the doctrine is primarily concerned with the question whether the principal is bound,[38] and the burden of proof is on the person alleging it.[39] Apparent authority is not therefore the same as implied authority, though older cases did not always make the distinction now recognised, or at least in the form in which it is now recognised: in the judgments, recourse was more often had to the notion of the wide implied authority of a general agent.[40] Even some more recent cases have tended to confuse the two.[41] Therefore, although apparent authority has twice been mentioned, and juxtaposed with actual authority, in the discussion of the agent's authority,[42] its main treatment is here. It is further developed in the specialised context of dispositions of property by the agent in Article 83. Reference should also be made to Article 121, where the application of the doctrine in cases of termination of authority is discussed.

It will be seen also that the formulation is redolent of estoppel, and that this explanation of the doctrine receives articulate support from the dictum of Diplock LJ quoted. There are however some difficulties with this explanation in modern times, as will appear: the matter is reverted to after the formulation has been analysed.[43]

8-014 **Represents by words or conduct**   There must be a representation, or in *Restatement, Third* terms, a manifestation.[44] This seems to occur in three main ways. It may be express (whether orally or in writing)[45]; or implied from a course of dealing[46]; or it may be made "by permitting the agent to act in some way in the conduct of the principal's business with other persons".[47] There is a statement of Lord Cranworth in *Pole v Leask*,[48] and another of Robert Goff LJ in *Armagas Ltd v*

---

[35]   Article 83.
[36]   Article 90.
[37]   Article 94.
[38]   But see below, para.8-030.
[39]   See above, para.3-007.
[40]   See above, para.1-045.
[41]   See, e.g. *Ryan v Pilkington* [1959] 1 W.L.R. 403, and explanations of that case in *Burt v Claude Cousins & Co Ltd* [1971] 2 Q.B. 426 at 438, 448–449, 454; *Barrington v Lee* [1972] 1 Q.B. 326 at 336, 341; and *Sorrell v Finch* [1977] A.C. 728.
[42]   Comments to Articles 1 and 22.
[43]   Below, para.8-028.
[44]   See above, para.8-011. See also Dal Pont, para.20.18 onwards.
[45]   Illustrations 13 and 22.
[46]   Illustrations 7 and 21. See too *International Sponge Importers Ltd v Watt & Sons* [1911] A.C. 279 at 285; *Pharmed Medicare Private Ltd v Univar Ltd* [2002] EWCA Civ 1569; [2003] 1 All E.R. (Comm) 321 (larger order than usual: principal still liable); *Lovett v Carson Country Homes Ltd* [2009] EWHC 1143 (Ch); [2009] 2 B.C.L.C. 19; *Russell Gould Pty Ltd v Ramangkura (No.2)* [2015] NSWCA 14 at [10].
[47]   *Freeman & Lockyer v Buckhurst Park Properties (Mangal) Ltd* [1964] 2 Q.B. 480 at 503 (managing director). See, e.g. *Collen v Gardner* (1856) 21 Beav. 540 (steward); *Howard v Sheward* (1886) 2 C.P. 148; *Baldry v Bates* (1885) 52 L.T. 620 (horse dealers).
[48]   (1863) 33 L.J. Ch. 155 at 162 (HL).

Mundogas SA,[49] which suggest that a mere course of dealing is not sufficient to establish apparent authority (at least with an agent who is not an employee). Lord Cranworth's judgment in *Pole v Leask* is undoubtedly an important one in the development of agency law, but on this issue (crucial to the outcome of the case) the judgment was a dissenting one. The remarks of Robert Goff LJ on the point were certainly obiter dicta. The weight of authority supports a course of dealing being sufficient to create apparent authority, at least where it can be inferred that the principal must have become aware of the earlier transactions.[50] But the position may be different where it is known that the agent is too junior to be making the contract and is a mere conduit for acceptances.[51] A further way in which such a representation may be made (or at least contributed to), by entrusting the agent with the indicia of ownership of property, is dealt with in connection with dispositions of property.[52]

Two types of case If the doctrine is based on the idea of representation, it may **8-015** be suggested that the cases can be divided into two types. First, and this category embraces the first two types of representation above, cases where there is something that can be said to be something like a genuine representation (orally, in writing, by course of dealing or by allowing the agent to act in certain ways, e.g. entrusting him with the conduct of particular negotiations[53] or allowing him to run a business that appears to be the principal's business[54]) by the principal of the agent's authority, on which the third party relies: such cases could be called cases of "genuine apparent authority" and more easily (but not always perfectly) based on estoppel. Secondly, cases where the representation is only of a very general nature, and arises only from the principal's putting the agent in a specific position carrying with it a usual authority,[55] e.g. placing him in a certain physical position on the principal's business premises, or making him a partner[56] or managing director,[57] or using the services of a professional agent, viz. someone whose occupation normally gives him a usual authority to do things of a certain type, e.g. a solicitor.[58] It is said that:

"by so doing the principal represents to anyone who becomes aware that the agent is so acting that the agent has authority to enter on behalf of the principal into contracts with other persons of the kind which an agent so acting in the course of his principal's business has usually 'actual' authority to enter into."[59]

Here the notion of representation to the third party is more tenuous and the connec-

---

[49] [1986] A.C. 717 at 732–733.
[50] See too Article 121 (effect of termination of authority on apparent authority); and Watts [2015] L.M.C.L.Q. 36.
[51] See *Spooner v Browning* [1898] 1 Q.B. 528, Article 75, Illustration 1 (mere authority of junior clerk to communicate acceptance did not by repeat dealings away from principal's premises create representation that there had in fact been a further acceptance).
[52] See Articles 83–85.
[53] *Crabb v Arun DC* [1976] Ch. 179 at 183; *IRC v Ufitec Group Ltd* [1977] 3 All E.R. 924; *Egyptian International Foreign Trade Co v P.S. Refson & Co Ltd (The Raffaella)* [1985] 1 Lloyd's Rep. 36 at 41 (Illustration 11); *Magripilis v Baird* [1926] St.R.Qd. 89 at 96 (HC of A.: "accredited as his legal agents and medium of communication").
[54] *Gurtner v Beaton* [1993] 2 Lloyd's Rep. 369, Illustration 5.
[55] See Articles 29 and 30.
[56] Partnership Act 1890 ss.5 and 14.
[57] *Hely-Hutchinson v Brayhead Ltd* [1968] 1 Q.B. 549 at 583.
[58] *Waugh v H.B. Clifford & Sons Ltd* [1982] Ch. 374, Illustration 16; *Seiwa Australia Pty Ltd v Beard* (2010) 75 N.S.W.L.R. 74 at [257] (usual business of accountancy partnership).
[59] *Freeman & Lockyer v Buckhurst Park Properties (Mangal) Ltd* [1964] 2 Q.B. 480 at 503, per

tion of the principal's liability with estoppel more difficult to maintain.[60] It seems further that in this category the authority which the third party is entitled to infer is that which would normally be implied between principal and agent, and it is of this that the court receives evidence. But the third party may be quite ignorant of what authority would be so implied, e.g. of what authority a "branch manager" of an insurance company normally has,[61] and is not required to adduce any evidence of his own knowledge.

8-016 **Representation need not be deliberate** The foregoing analysis suggests that the words of Diplock LJ, which appear to require that the representation be deliberate, and certainly say that it must be actually intended to be acted on, are too narrow. This wording does not appear elsewhere in the judgment.

8-017 **Categories not mutually exclusive** It is important to note that the above two categories are not mutually exclusive. There may be additional representations by the principal, peculiar to the case in question, over and above the putting into a position carrying usual authority. Where it is not clear what authority a person in the particular position would normally have, such factors may be crucial:

> "But where, as in the present case, the holding out is alleged to consist of a course of conduct wider than merely describing the agent as holding a particular office, although the authority normally found in the holder of such an office is very material, it must be looked at as part and parcel of the whole course of the principal's conduct in order to decide whether the totality of the principal's actions constitute a holding out of the agent as possessing the necessary authority."[62]

The representation will normally be of an authority of some generality: although there is no reason why there should not be a representation of authority to enter into a specific transaction only, such a case would be rare, especially where the third party knows of the lack of general authority.[63]

8-018 **Ingredients of representation must be sufficient to warrant reliance** It has been seen in the preceding paragraphs that the range of facts that might be used to establish a representation of authority is very broad indeed. It has also been seen that more than one indicium of authority may be needed to constitute an effective representation. What is implicit in that conclusion is that the evidence used to justify an assertion of authority in an agent must be adequate, which carries the further implication that reliance on that evidence must have been reasonable: "[T]he starting point is that the principal must be shown to have made a representation, which

---

Diplock LJ.
[60] See below. See further as to this distinction above, para.3-005.
[61] See *British Bank of the Middle East v Sun Life Insurance Co of Canada (UK) Ltd* [1983] 2 Lloyd's Rep. 9 (HL) (Illustration 10 to Article 75), a harsh decision for this reason. See also *Restatement, Third*, § 3.03 Comment *d*; *Cleveland Manufacturing Co v Muslim Commercial Bank Ltd* [1981] 2 Lloyd's Rep. 646 (shipping agent); *Ricci Burns Ltd v Toole* [1989] 1 W.L.R. 993 at 1007.
[62] *Egyptian International Foreign Trade Co v Soplex Wholesale Supplies Ltd (The Raffaella)* [1985] 2 Lloyd's Rep. 36, Illustration 11; *Pacific Carriers Ltd v BNP Paribas* (2004) 218 C.L.R. 451 at [35], Illustration 2 to Article 21 (a case that on the facts took a very generous view of what was a holding out—see above, para.2-106).
[63] See *Armagas Ltd v Mundogas SA (The Ocean Frost)* [1986] A.C. 717 at 777.

the third party could and did reasonably rely on, that the agent had the necessary authority".[64]

Beyond the criterion of adequacy or reasonableness, much will turn on the facts of the particular case. Guidance is best obtained by examples and a wide range of Illustrations is provided at the end of this Article. However, the case law has thrown up a number of issues of broad application. Hence, mere possession of a principal's property, even by someone who has some agency functions, does not amount to a holding out of any right to deal with the property. This issue and a number of others are dealt with in the paragraphs which follow. The incremental way in which the common law develops has meant that there are other issues that remain unsettled. Some of these involve written communications. The ubiquity of letterhead (paper or electronic) within most businesses means that it would not normally be safe to rely on letterhead alone as representing that the writer has authority to bind the principal whose letterhead it is.[65] A business card that is genuine and gives an agent's status may, however, be an adequate representation.[66] Less clarity attends the issue of a document (paper or electronic) which has been written by the principal or by someone who had actual authority to write it but that is then sent off or handed over prematurely (by accident or design) by another agent without actual authority to deliver it.[67] Modern technology will throw up other new issues. So, it has been held that the mere fact that someone has access to one's password for the purpose of effecting electronic signatures does not create a representation that the person with access to the password has authority to apply the signature.[68]

Authority to make representations as to authority of others The representation as to authority need not be made by the principal himself: it may obviously be made by an intermediate agent with actual authority to do so. More difficulties arise if the authority is apparent. It seems correct in principle to say that an agent can have apparent authority to make representations as to the authority of other agents, provided that his own authority can finally be traced back to a representation by the principal or to a person with actual authority from the principal to make it.[69] However, such apparent authority would in general only be attributed to a person

8-019

---

[64] *Egyptian International Foreign Trade Co v Soplex Wholesale Supplies Ltd (The Raffaella)* [1985] 2 Lloyd's Rep. 36 at 41; *Pourzand v Telstra Corp Ltd* [2014] WASCA 14 at [83].

[65] *Kooragang Investments Pty Ltd v Richardson & Wrench Ltd* [1982] 1 A.C. 462 at 475; *Harvey v State of New South Wales* [2006] NSWSC 1436 at [176] (government stationery); *Quikfund (Australia) Pty Ltd v Chatswood Appliance Spare Parts Pty Ltd* [2013] NSWSC 646 (possession of lender's blank loan forms with authority to distribute them did not confer any authority to make representations) cf. *F. Mildner & Sons v Noble* [1956] C.L.Y. 32; *The Times,* March 8, 1956, Illustration 2, where other cases are collected.

[66] *Martin v Britannia Life Ltd* [2000] Lloyd's Rep. P.N. 412 at [5.3.4]; *Derham v Amev Life Insurance Co Ltd* (1981) 56 F.L.R. 34; *Moneyworld NZ 2000 Ltd v Lee* (2005) N.Z. Business L.C. 101,638; *Heperu Pty Ltd v Morgan Brooks Pty Ltd (No.2)* [2007] NSWSC 1438, reversed on other points in *Perpetual Trustees Australia Ltd v Heperu Pty Ltd* [2009] NSWCA 84 (holding out by webpage, letterhead and business cards).

[67] Compare *Smith v Prosser* [1907] 2 K.B. 735 (attorney in possession of promissory notes signed in blank but with instructions not to use them without telegraphed instructions, confers no rights when he fraudulently negotiates them) with the dicta in *Shearson Lehman Hutton Inc v Maclaine Watson & Co Ltd* [1988] 1 W.L.R. 16 at 28 (HL).

[68] See *Williams Group Australia Pty Ltd v Crocker* [2016] NSWCA 265.

[69] There are, however, dicta appearing to require actual authority in the agent whose representation is relied on as creating apparent authority, in cases connected with companies. It is submitted that *Crabtree-Vickers Pty Ltd v Australian Direct Mail Advertising Co Ltd* (1975) 133 C.L.R. 72 may

who would normally have actual authority to act within that particular sphere of activity.[70] An agent would, therefore, not usually be regarded as having apparent authority, simply because he is or appears to be permitted to answer inquiries, or to attribute authority to another agent, unless he was or appeared to be authorised to involve himself in the conduct of that business, or that part of the business to which the transaction related.[71]

8-020   **Permits it to be represented: representation by agent himself**   As already stated, the essence of apparent authority is an appearance emanating from the principal. Therefore the representation must be made by the principal, or by another agent authorised to act for the principal, as described above. It is usually said that a representation by the agent himself that he has authority cannot create apparent authority in him, unless the principal can be regarded as having in some way instigated or permitted it, or put the agent in a position where he appears to be authorised to make it.[72]

> "All 'ostensible' authority involves a representation by the principal as to the extent of the agent's authority. No representation by the agent as to the extent of his authority can amount to a 'holding out' by the principal."[73]

Thus in *Armagas Ltd v Mundogas SA (The Ocean Frost)*[74] where a person was known to have no relevant authority and did not claim to have it, but wrongly stated that he had obtained authority from his managing director, it was held that there was no apparent authority. But there will be situations where the agent has usual authority to communicate that those with actual authority have exercised that authority.[75] In such cases there will have been a holding out by the principal.

---

go too far in following these and requiring such actual authority, which need not exist except at the ultimate level: see [1983] J.B.L. 409; *Cromwell Corp Ltd v Sofrana Immobilier (NZ) Ltd* (1992) N.Z. Company L.C. 67,997; *AJU Remicon Co Ltd v Alida Shipping Co Ltd* [2007] EWHC 2246 (Comm); and below, para.8-020.

[70] This seems clear from *British Bank of the Middle East v Sun Life Assurance Co of Canada Ltd* [1983] 2 Lloyd's Rep. 9 (HL) (Illustration 10 to Article 75); see esp. 17. See, however, *Canadian Laboratory Supplies Ltd v Engelhard Industries of Canada Ltd* [1979] 2 S.C.R. 787; (1979) 97 D.L.R. (3d) 1, where the Supreme Court of Canada differed as to the effect of an inquiry as to an employee's authority to sell, made to a company's purchasing agent, while agreeing on the effect of that made to a Vice-President (Operations).

[71] See also below, paras 8-020 and 8-021; *BP Oil International Ltd v Target Shipping Ltd* [2012] EWHC 1590 (Comm) at [222]. But cf. *Kelly v Fraser* [2012] UKPC 25; [2013] 1 A.C. 450 (trustees of company pension fund hold out company as their messenger for their decisions).

[72] *Colonial Bank v Cady and Williams* (1890) 15 App.Cas. 267 at 273; *De Tchihatchef v Salerni Coupling Ltd* [1932] 1 Ch. 330 at 342; *Fay v Miller, Wilkins & Co* [1941] Ch. 360 at 365; *Freeman & Lockyer v Buckhurst Park Properties (Mangal) Ltd* [1964] 2 Q.B. 480 at 505. cf. Partnership Act 1890 s.14(1). But see *Hely-Hutchinson v Brayhead Ltd* [1968] 1 Q.B. 549 at 563–564 (affd on another ground at 573); *Canadian Laboratory Supplies Ltd v Engelhard Industries of Canada Ltd* [1979] 2 S.C.R. 787 at 800; (1979) 97 D.L.R. (3d) 1 at 10. The latter dictum is discussed by Fridman (1983) 13 Manitoba L.J. 1.

[73] *Att.-Gen. for Ceylon v Silva* [1953] A.C. 461 at 479, per Mr. L.M.D. de Silva. See also *Lanyon v Blanchard* (1811) 2 Camp. 597; *New Zealand Tenancy Bonds Ltd v Mooney* [1986] 1 N.Z.L.R. 280; *Essfood v Crown Shipping (Ireland) Ltd* [1991] I.L.R.M. 97.

[74] [1986] A.C. 717, Illustration 11 to Article 75. See too *Spooner v Browning* [1898] 1 Q.B. 528, Article 75, Illustration 1.

[75] See *Kelly v Fraser* [2012] UKPC 25; [2013] 1 A.C. 450 at [12]; *Australia and New Zealand Banking Group Ltd v Frenmast Pty Ltd* [2013] NSWCA 459. See further, Watts [2015] L.M.C.L.Q. 36. cf. *Allco Finance Group Ltd v Gothard* [2014] FCAFC 6 (director has no apparent authority to com-

Qualifications and exceptions Qualifications, and perhaps exceptions, can be   **8-021**
said to eat into such an apparently clear principle as that just addressed. Hence, there
will be cases where an agent would normally have authority but only if certain facts
were true, and the agent gives the impression that they are. The agent may have apparent authority to confirm that the preconditions are met. Some examples follow:

(1) The master of a ship has authority to sign bills of lading, but frequently only
     if they are in accordance with mate's receipts, in particular as to date of ship-
     ment and condition on loading. A third party holder of the bill is entitled to
     rely on the master's signature as to such matters.[76] Equally, the master is
     only entitled to sign for goods that are on board: but his attestation that they
     were can be relied on.[77]
(2) A manager of a business directs one of its debtors to pay a third party rather
     than the owner of the business. The debtor might be expected to ask for a
     reason why he is being asked not to pay the owner, but is entitled to believe
     the manager when a plausible answer is given.[78]
(3) A solicitor may have actual authority to enter into a guarantee on behalf of
     his partners or employers if the firm holds the client's money or has good
     reason to expect that it will do so: the third party cannot know whether the
     underlying facts are true, yet may be able to rely on the solicitor's appar-
     ent authority if a reasonably careful and competent lender would have
     concluded that there was an appropriate underlying transaction.[79] There is
     also authority that finds that it is not usually necessary to go behind a
     solicitor's representation in the conduct of litigation, including as to whether
     the principal has agreed to a compromise of it.[80]
(4) More generally, there are cases that have found that an agent who has no
     authority to contract may sometimes have authority to say whether
     particular contract terms will be enforced,[81] or even to say whether the

---

municate more than receivers of company actually decided). See further in relation to companies,
    para.8-039 below.
[76] *The Starsin* [2000] 1 Lloyd's Rep. 85 at 93–98 (point not considered on appeal [2001] 1 Lloyd's Rep.
    437). cf. *George Whitechurch Ltd v Cavanagh* [1902] A.C. 117 (company secretary's authority to
    certify share transfers conditional on sighting share certificates; false certification by fraudulent
    secretary not binding on company).
[77] Carriage of Goods by Sea Act 1992 s.4. But it was not always so: see below, para.8-067, Illustra-
    tion 2.
[78] *Acute Property Developments Ltd v Apostolou* [2013] EWHC 200 (Ch) at [38].
[79] *United Bank of Kuwait Ltd v Hammoud* [1988] 1 W.L.R. 1051, Illustration 10; but cf. *Hirst v
    Etheringtons* [1999] Lloyd's Rep. P.N. 938, where it is suggested (against the background of a
    transaction needing inquiry) that some of the dicta in the first case may go too far in suggesting that
    a solicitor must normally be believed; and that a mere inquiry whether the transaction is within the
    course of business may not be enough. Another example of the same problem (a serious one) may
    be found in connection with officials the normal authority of whom would not necessarily be known
    to a third party: see *British Bank of the Middle East v Sun Life Assurance Co of Canada (UK) Ltd*
    [1983] 2 Lloyd's Rep. 9 (HL), Illustration 10 to Article 75; cf. Article 21, Illustration 2.
[80] *Waugh v H.B. Clifford & Sons Ltd* [1982] Ch. 374, Article 30, Illustration 5. For commentary on this
    case and for other authorities, see above, paras 3-004 and 3-030.
[81] *State Rail Authority of New South Wales v Heath Outdoor Pty Ltd* (1987) 7 N.S.W.L.R. 170 at 184,
    per McHugh JA (albeit in a dissenting judgment). See also *Legione v Hateley* (1983) 152 C.L.R. 406;
    compare different reasoning in *Waltons Stores (Interstate) Ltd v Maher* (1988) 164 C.L.R. 387. But
    cf. *New Zealand Tenancy Bonds Ltd v Mooney* [1986] 1 N.Z.L.R. 280 (no authority to accept deposit
    late).

principal is performing the contract, or whether or not a proposal is accepted.[82]

(5) An agent may be found to have sufficient apparent authority to bind his purported principal to a collateral contract of arbitration, or to a collateral contract designating a jurisdiction for determining disputes, without necessarily having such authority to conclude the main contract.[83]

From these examples it might be argued that it is only a small step to say that the agent may have authority to say whether he has been authorised. But it is this final step which is not approved in *The Ocean Frost*.[84] The case *First Energy (UK) Ltd v Hungarian International Bank Ltd*,[85] the facts of which are summarised in Illustration 12, gets quite near to taking this step. The case involved a misstatement that the agent's superiors had approved a contract. The result was supported in the leading judgment of Steyn LJ on the basis of the importance of protecting third parties. It is submitted that the decision can be supported without invoking any exception to general principle (it was only the manager in question who had qualified the usual authority he otherwise would have had and in such circumstances he should be able to reinstate it; it appears that the third party had attended at the manager's office, and there had been a course of dealing).[86] Any ready admission of the agent's statement of his own authority as creating apparent authority involves a departure from the basic principles of apparent authority, for which no general justifying principle seems ready to hand. Although cases where an agent is authorised to say whether facts which confer authority on him can occur and have occurred, situations where this reasoning is legitimate should be specialised and unusual.[87]

8-022   **Representation of law**   Until recently it would have been said on general grounds that the representation must be one of fact: a pure representation of law would not be sufficient to create apparent authority. A situation in which there was such a representation may be unlikely to arise in this context,[88] but the decision of the House of Lords in *Kleinwort Benson Ltd v Lincoln CC*,[89] allowing recovery in

---

[82] See *International Paper Co v Spicer* (1906) 4 C.L.R. 739.

[83] See *Premium Nafta Products Ltd v Fili Shipping Co Ltd* [2007] UKHL 40; [2007] 4 All E.R. 951; [2007] 2 All E.R. (Comm) 1053; [2008] 1 Lloyd's Rep. 254 (arbitration clause); and *Deutsche Bank AG v Asia Pacific Broadband Wireless Communications Inc* [2008] EWCA Civ 1091; [2008] 2 Lloyd's Rep. 619 at [25] (jurisdiction clause). See Rushworth (2008) 124 L.Q.R. 195.

[84] Above, para.8-020. See especially per Robert Goff LJ in the Court of Appeal, [1986] A.C. at pp.730–735; quoted by Lord Keith of Kinkel in the House of Lords: ibid. at 777.

[85] [1993] 2 Lloyd's Rep. 194, Illustration 12: applied in *HSBC Ltd v Jurong Engineering Ltd* [2000] 2 Singapore L.R. 54. See also *Dale v Govt of Manitoba* (1997) 147 D.L.R. (4th) 605. cf. *Kilcran v Gothard* [2014] FCAFC 6 at [78] (receiver's limited delegation to superseded manager not extendable by manager); Watts [2015] L.M.C.L.Q. 36.

[86] See *Sun Life Assurance Co of Canada v CX Reinsurance Co Ltd* [2003] EWCA Civ 283; [2004] Lloyd's Rep I.R. 58 at [39].

[87] See *Armagas Ltd v Mundogas SA* [1986] A.C. 717, at 777; *Restatement, Third*, § 3.03. See also *Berryere v Firemans Fund Insurance Co* (1965) 51 D.L.R. (2d) 603 (doubted in *The Ocean Frost*); *Jensen v South Trail Mobile Ltd* (1972) 28 D.L.R. (3d) 233; *Cypress Disposal Ltd v Inland Kenworth Sales (Nanaimo) Ltd* (1975) 54 D.L.R. (3d) 598; *Savill v Chase Holdings (Wellington) Ltd* [1989] 1 N.Z.L.R. 257 at 304–306, 313–314; *AJU Remicon Co Ltd v Alida Shipping Co Ltd* [2007] EWHC 2246 (Comm) at [16].

[88] See *De Tchihatchef v Salerni Coupling Ltd* [1932] 1 Ch. 330; below, para.9-066.

[89] [1999] 2 A.C. 349.

restitution of money paid under mistake of law, prompts reconsideration of all situations in which the distinction arises.[90]

No estoppel through simple negligence   It is plain that if the third party does not   **8-023**
know of the existence of any principal, there cannot be apparent authority, as when
the agent purports to deal as principal.[91] A representation that does not come to the
notice of the third party is no representation. The mere fact that the principal enables
the agent to commit fraud by putting him in a position where he can do so is not,
without more, decisive.[92] The common law has avoided, so far at least, a concept
of estoppel by negligence.[93] The mere possession of another's goods or documents (including those of title) creates no representation of entitlement to deal with
them, since there can be any number of reasons why a bailment of them subsists.
The doctrine does not apply even if the principal represents that the agent is the
owner of goods or of a business where the third party was unaware of the
representation, though in many such cases the related doctrine of apparent ownership[94] may apply, or there may be evidence that permits an inference of a grant of
actual authority by the undisclosed principal.[95]

On the faith of any such representations   This involves three elements: **8-024**

(1) The representation must be made to a third party or to a number of third
parties. Old cases speak of holding out to the world,[96] but this is a loose
expression[97]:

> "the 'holding out' must be to the particular individual who says he relied on it,
> or under such circumstances of publicity as to justify the inference that he knew
> of it and acted upon it."[98]

Nevertheless, the holding out may be quite general. If the analogy of estoppel were followed strictly, it is arguable that there could be no apparent
authority where the principal at the time of making the representation by his
words or his conduct had no third party or parties in contemplation, for it
would be difficult to say that he had made a representation with the intent
that it should be acted on, as the dictum of Diplock LJ quoted above seems

---

[90] Contra in this context Treitel, *Law of Contract* (14th edn), para.16-023.
[91] *A.L. Underwood Ltd v Bank of Liverpool* [1924] 1 K.B. 775; *Farquharson Brothers & Co v King & Co* [1902] A.C. 325, Illustration 6 to Article 84; *Freeman & Lockyer v Buckhurst Park Properties (Mangal) Ltd* [1964] 2 Q.B. 480 at 503. But it is possible that the doctrine of undisclosed principal may apply: see Article 76. As to the possibility of a principal's being unable to deny the authority of a sub-agent who has relied on the head agent's apparent authority to appoint him, see *AJU Remicon Co Ltd v Alida Shipping Co Ltd* [2007] EWHC 2246 (Comm).
[92] *Farquharson Brothers & Co v King & Co*, above; *Morris v C.W. Martin & Sons Ltd* [1966] 1 Q.B. 716; Article 74.
[93] *Johnson Matthey (Aust.) Ltd v Dascorp Pty Ltd* (2003) 9 V.R. 171 at 185 (negligent failure to detect employee's theft of gold); *Williams Group Australia Pty Ltd v Crocker* [2016] NSWCA 265 at [69]. See Watts (2005) 26 Aust. Bar Rev. 185.
[94] Article 84.
[95] Article 76.
[96] e.g. *Whitehead v Tuckett* (1812) 15 East 400 at 411.
[97] *Dickinson v Valpy* (1829) 10 B. & C. 128 at 140.
[98] *Farquharson Brothers & Co v King & Co* [1902] A.C. 325 at 341, per Lord Lindley. A third party cannot rely on a representation that he knows was meant solely for others: *Ing Re (UK) Ltd v R & V Versicherung AG* [2006] EWHC 1544 (Comm); [2006] Lloyd's Rep. I.R. 653 at [119].

to require[99]: it is clear however, that in many cases a third party can simply rely on the agent's having the authority usual to a person in his position (usual authority[100]), unless that third party knew that the agent had no such authority. It is not therefore necessary, though it is sufficient, that the representation be to a specific person. In relation to partnerships, the Partnership Act 1890 s.14(1) specifies that the person holding himself out, or knowingly allowing himself to be held out, as a partner does not need to know who among the firm's creditors has relied on the representation.[101]

(2) The third party must have relied on the representation. This is of course another aspect of the same point. Thus the third party cannot hold the principal liable if he did not believe that the agent had authority or knew that the agent did not have authority,[102] despite the appearance of authority,[103] or if he was not aware of the circumstances giving rise to apparent authority.[104] He may also be unable to do so if he has notice of the terms of the agent's authority: this is discussed under Article 73.[105] A third party cannot rely on a document as creating a representation of apparent authority when he knows that he was not supposed to have seen the document.[106]

Further, it is often said that he must in some way have acted on the representation. Again, if the analogy of common law estoppel by representation is followed, the acting must have been to his detriment, and this requirement is stated in several cases.[107] Others, however, speak simply of alteration of position, or acting on the faith of the representation,[108] and it seems in fact that there need be no more than an entering into a contract in reliance on the representation.[109] This tends to make this aspect of the doctrine merge with the previous one.

---

[99] See Comment to Article 21.

[100] See above, para.8-018; Powell, p.37; Articles 22, 29 and 30.

[101] See further, *Lindley and Banks on Partnership* (19th edn), para.12-05; *UCB Home Loans Corp Ltd v Soni* [2013] EWCA Civ 62.

[102] *Home Owners Loan Corp v Thornburgh* 106 P. 2d 511 at 512 (SC Okl., 1940): "Apparent authority loses all of its apparency when the third party knows that actual authority is lacking".

[103] See *Bloomenthal v Ford* [1897] A.C. 156; *Galaxy Aviation v Sayegh Group Aviation* [2015] EWHC 3478 (Comm) at [101]. Reliance is not precluded by the fact that the third party subsequently attempts to get the principal also to sign a memorandum of the agreement, out of precaution: see below, para.8-060.

[104] See e.g. *Farquharson Brothers & Co v King & Co* [1902] A.C. 325; *Technology Leasing Ltd v Lennmar Pty Ltd* [2012] FCA 709 at [153]; *UCB Home Loans Corp Ltd v Soni* [2013] EWCA Civ 62. See further above, para.8-022.

[105] Where the third party has written notice from the principal as to the extent of the agent's authority, it requires a strong case to establish an apparent authority beyond this: *Australian Bank of Commerce v Perel* [1926] A.C. 737.

[106] *Ing Re (UK) Ltd v R & V Versicherung AG* [2006] EWHC 1544 (Comm); [2006] Lloyd's Rep. I.R. 653 at [118].

[107] *Howard v Hudson* (1853) 2 E. & B. 1; *George Whitechurch Ltd v Cavanagh* [1902] A.C. 117; *Farquharson Brothers & Co v King & Co* [1902] A.C. 325; *Mac Fisheries Ltd v Harrison* (1924) 93 L.J.K.B. 811; *Wilson & Meeson v Pickering* [1946] K.B. 422; *Norfolk County Council v Secretary of State for the Environment* [1973] 1 W.L.R. 1400. The situation seems to be similar in the United States: see *Restatement, Third*, § 2.03, reporter's note a.

[108] *Pickard v Sears* (1837) 6 A. & E. 469; *Freeman v Cooke* (1848) 2 Exch. 654; *Cornish v Abington* (1859) 4 H. & N. 549; *Rama Corp v Proved Tin and General Investments* [1952] 2 Q.B. 147; *Freeman & Lockyer v Buckhurst Park Properties (Mangal) Ltd* [1964] 2 Q.B. 480 at 503; *Kelly v Fraser* [2012] UKPC 25; [2013] 1 A.C. 450 at [17].

[109] *Freeman & Lockyer v Buckhurst Park Properties (Mangal) Ltd*, above; *Cleveland Mfg. Co Ltd v*

(3) The reliance must have been reasonable. There are in turn, two aspects to this. First, as already discussed, the grounds used to establish the representation of authority must be adequate to justify a belief that the agent had authority.[110] Secondly, even where there are such grounds, there may be other evidence that undermines what would otherwise be an adequate representation of authority. The latter class of case is dealt with in Article 73.

Effect of representations where third party also acts through agents The **8-025**
foregoing paragraphs are premised on a third party who acts directly. It is, however, part of regular commerce for both sides to the transaction to act through agents, and this will necessarily be the case where the third party is a company. It is obvious that for the purposes of those paragraphs it is sufficient if the agent acting for the third party was aware of the existence of the representations even if his own principal was not. It will not normally matter that the third party's agent gained the relevant knowledge before he was appointed agent.[111] Equally, if the third party is aware of the representation, it will not matter if the agent he appoints to effect the transaction is not. The key principle is that the third party needs to show reliance on the representation, and one cannot rely if one does not know. That principle will need to guide the situation where a third party uses multiple agents in a transaction (as will be common where the third party is a company). It follows that it would not normally be sufficient that an agent of the third party who was not in any way engaged in the transaction was aware of the representation, if the parties so engaged were not. As to the position where the third party's agent knows that the other agent lacks actual authority, see below, para.8-051.

Scope of the doctrine The general doctrine here stated applies to cases where the **8-026**
person concerned is not, apart from the estoppel, an agent at all (an unusual situation)[112]; to cases where he has some authority, but not authority to do what he has in fact done; to cases where he would have such authority but for the existence of reservations unknown to the third party; and to cases where he previously had authority, but this has, unknown to the third party, been terminated.[113] There is no reason of principle why it should not apply to the agent of an unidentified principal. If the principal appoints an agent who acts as such but does not reveal his principal's identity and the third party is willing to deal on this basis, apparent authority may be created.[114]

Muslim Commercial Bank Ltd [1981] 2 Lloyd's Rep. 646 at 650; *Polish SS Co v A.J. Williams Fuels (Overseas Sales) Ltd (The Suwalki)* [1989] 1 Lloyd's Rep. 511 at 514; *Arctic Shipping Co Ltd v Mobilia AB (The Tatra)* [1990] 2 Lloyd's Rep. 51 at 59. In *Silver v Ocean Steamship Co Ltd* [1930] 1 K.B. 416 it was held that the taking up of a bill of lading was sufficient evidence of reliance on it to raise an estoppel: see at 428, 434, 441. See also *Thanakharn Kasikorn Thai Chamchat v Akai Holdings Ltd (In Liquidation)* (2010) 13 H.K.C.F.A.R. 479 at [75].

[110] See above, para.8-018.

[111] *Racing UK Ltd v Doncaster Metropolitan District Council* [2005] EWCA Civ 999; [2005] L.L.R. 701 at [33]. See too *Cramaso LLP v Ogilvie-Grant, Earl of Seafield* [2014] UKSC 9; [2014] A.C. 1093; noted Macgregor (2014) 19 Edin. L.R. 112 (representation as to facts relevant to subject matter of contract made to agent of third party before appointment).

[112] See Illustrations 1–6; Article 121.

[113] As to hidden reservations, see Illustrations 13–23, 26; as to termination of authority, see Illustrations 24 and 25 and Article 121.

[114] The problem can arise in connection with ship's agents. See *Lake Charles Stevedores v M/V Profes-*

8-027 **Doctrine does not validate act for all purposes** The doctrine of apparent authority validates the agent's act as regards the third party.[115] But it does not necessarily make it valid as regards the agent himself, who may be liable to his principal for breach of duty if the breach is not waived.[116]

8-028 **Relationship of apparent authority with estoppel** There is much argument as to whether apparent authority should be regarded as based on estoppel or not.[117] The passage from Diplock LJ cited at the beginning of this Comment indicates that it should, and there are other judicial statements to the same effect. An example is:

> "Ostensible or apparent authority ... is merely a form of estoppel, indeed, it has been termed agency by estoppel, and you cannot call in aid an estoppel unless you have three ingredients: (i) a representation, (ii) a reliance on the representation, and (iii) an alteration of your position resulting from such reliance."[118]

The main difficulties with this approach have already been referred to. They are, first, the fact that the representation giving rise to the estoppel is in this area permitted to be very general indeed,[119] and second, that the detriment incurred by the representee may be small.[120] Of these, the first is clearly the more important. The idea that by allowing his agent to act in certain ways the principal is making representations to third parties is an artificial one, especially where the "representation" simply amounts to putting someone in a position which carries usual authority, or using the services of a professional person whose activities carry a usual authority.[121] If a genuine estoppel is looked for, the category would indeed be even narrower than that marked off above as "genuine apparent authority".[122] In the editions of this work edited by Bowstead himself it can be said that a distinction between two types of case was in fact made, though later writings have enabled it to be more clearly stated. The Article above, which now stands for all apparent authority, by its reference to "representations" may be regarded as having been intended to refer to "genuine" estoppel cases. The broader notion was dealt with in Article 80 of the eighth edition of 1932 (the last edited by Bowstead himself) as follows:

> "Every act done by an agent in the course of his employment on behalf of his principal,

---

sor *Vladimir Popov* 199 F. 3d 220 (5th Cir., 1999); cf. *N. & J. Vlassopulos Ltd v Ney Shipping Ltd (The Santa Carina)* [1977] 1 Lloyd's Rep. 478, Illustration 3 to Article 101; *Restatement, Third*, § 2.13, Comment *f* and reporter's notes thereto.

[115] It does not simply give rise to liability for the reliance interest on the basis of *culpa in contrahendo*, as, it appears, may sometimes be the case in German law.

[116] See Comments to Articles 20 and 36.

[117] Powell, pp.68–72; Stoljar, pp.25–36; Seavey (1920) 29 Yale L.J. 859; Montrose (1938) 16 Can.B.R. 757; Mechem, *Principles of Agency* (4th edn), §§ 84 onwards.

[118] *Rama Corp v Proved Tin and General Investments* [1952] 2 Q.B. 147 at 149–150, per Slade J; see also *R. v Charles* [1977] A.C. 177 at 183; *Egyptian International Foreign Trade Co v Soplex Wholesale Supplies Ltd (The Raffaella)* [1985] 2 Lloyd's Rep. 36 at 41; *Armagas Ltd v Mundogas SA (The Ocean Frost)* [1986] A.C. 717 at 777; *Lloyd's Bank v Independent Insurance* [2000] Q.B. 110 at 122; *The Starsin* [2000] 1 Lloyd's Rep. 85 at 95 (unconscionability: final proceedings [2004] 1 A.C. 715); *AMB Generali, etc. v SEB Trygg, etc.* [2005] EWCA Civ 1237; [2006] 1 Lloyd's Rep. 318 at [31]; Ewart, *Estoppel* (1900), Ch.XXVI; Spencer Bower, *Reliance-Based Estoppel* (5th edn), para.9.2 onwards; Mechem, *Outlines of Agency* (4th edn), §§ 86 onwards.

[119] See above, para.8-015.

[120] See above, para.8-024; Dal Pont, pp.549–550.

[121] See Articles 29 and 30; e.g. *Waugh v H.B. Clifford & Sons Ltd* [1982] Ch. 374, Illustration 16, where the dicta go some way towards attributing an independent position to the agent.

[122] See above, para.8-015.

and within the apparent scope of his authority, binds the principal, unless the agent is in fact unauthorised to do the particular act, and the person dealing with him has notice that in doing such act he is exceeding his authority."[123]

It will be noted that this last formulation approaches the terminology now reserved for the liability of an employer for the torts of his employee. Though it can be connected with the notion of usual authority,[124] it is not in accord with current thinking in contract law.

Alternative analyses   Those common lawyers who reject the idea of estoppel   **8-029**
have indeed mostly argued for some sort of extension of the tort principles of this type[125]; or based themselves on the objective analysis applicable to the formation of contract and argued that it applies equally to the formation of contracts through agents.[126] The former view is certainly one that could be adopted, but is not in accord with the present accepted approach to common law agency, at least in England.[127] The latter has much to commend it. It explains the weak requirements as to representation and reliance in respect of authority, which are difficult to reconcile with the requirements of common law estoppel by representation as normally stated, which are usually taken to require an unequivocal representation[128] and action in reliance on it.[129] Recent developments in estoppel have also tended to stress that the consequences of the estoppel should only be sufficient to satisfy the equity raised[130] which if applied to apparent authority would create serious uncertainties in a doctrine designed to satisfy commercial certainty. Finally, to explain apparent authority in a different way would enable true estoppel situations, which can certainly be found in this area and are discussed under Article 21, to be separated off.[131] The distinction between objective interpretation and estoppel is in fact made in connection with formation of contract situations, where sometimes the normal objective interpretation techniques, which were themselves once attributed to estoppel,[132] give way to true estoppel reasoning.[133] In the United

---

[123] cf. Partnership Act 1890 s.5. This Article, in the form in which it appeared in the 4th edn, was relied on by counsel in *Lloyd v Grace, Smith & Co* [1912] A.C. 716. It was also cited with approval by the Court of Appeal in *Navarro v Moregrand Ltd* [1951] 2 T.L.R. 674 and *Ryan v Pilkington* [1959] 1 W.L.R. 403. But it was severely criticised by Falconbridge in (1939) 17 Can. B.R. 248 at 255–256; and see *Armagas Ltd v Mundogas SA (The Ocean Frost)* [1986] A.C. 717 at 779 onwards; cf. Brown [2004] J.B.L. 391.
[124] See above, para.3-005.
[125] Wright (1935) 1 U. Toronto L.J. 40; Mearns (1962) 48 Va.L.Rev. 50; Bester (1972) 89 S.A.L.J. 49; Comment to Article 22.
[126] Cook (1905) 5 Col.L.R. 36; (1906) 6 Col.L.R. 34; Conant (1968) 47 Neb.L.Rev. 678; Krebs, in Burrows and Peel (eds), *Contract Formation and Parties* (2010), Ch.10.
[127] See above, para.1-026.
[128] *Low v Bouverie* [1891] 3 Ch. 82 at 106.
[129] *Carr v L & NW Ry* (1875) L.R. 10 C.P. 307 at 317.
[130] See, e.g. *Commonwealth v Verwayen* (1990) 170 C.L.R. 394, per Brennan J; Dal Pont, pp.520–521 (paras 20.12–20.13).
[131] See para.2-105 above. Contra, Mechem, *Outlines of Agency* (4th edn), § 90.
[132] See, e.g. Hughes (1930) 54 L.Q.R. 370. See also Lord Bingham in *The Starsin* [2003] UKHL 12; [2004] 1 A.C. 715 at [8], suggesting that in commercial contracts a process of reasoning similar to that used for interpretation should be used for questions of who was a contracting party.
[133] See Treitel, *Law of Contract* (14th edn), paras 2-043–2-045 (estoppel where offer met by silence).

States the distinction was taken in *Restatement, Second*[134] and is emphasised in *Restatement, Third*.[135]

As to English law, it is certainly true that cases on master and servant and cases on principal and agent have not always been clearly separated, that some of the old cases on what is now called apparent authority reached their results without reference to estoppel, on broader notions such as that of the implied authority of a general agent.[136] But cases on agency and the related notion of apparent ownership which use what would now be called estoppel reasoning can also be traced back many years, and indeed some of them even seem to figure among the origins of the general doctrine of estoppel.[137] There can be little doubt that the prevailing approach in England has been in terms of representation and estoppel, at any rate as regards the agent's contracts.

But there are also difficulties with the alternative theory mentioned, that of the objective basis of contract. It is not easy to see how this can avoid the conclusion that not only has the principal made a manifestation to the third party by means of the agent, but also that the third party who contracts has made a (usually much clearer) manifestation to the principal. This logically requires that the principal must be able, without subjecting himself to the ratification rules and their safeguards, to sue the third party for non-performance of an executory contract, simply because the third party could sue on it under the doctrine of apparent authority. This logical conclusion was indeed adopted in *Restatement, Second*,[138] and is continued in *Restatement, Third*,[139] though the sole case cited is hardly strong authority.[140] It seems preferable therefore, and in accordance with English authority, to retain the estoppel justification; but to treat it as invoking a special (and weak) type of estoppel relevant only in the agency context.[141] This still enables what may be called true estoppels (where the full requirements as normally stated are complied with) in the agency context to be separated off, though not so clearly as the *Restatement* position allows. If it is unsatisfactory, it is probably no more so than solutions found elsewhere for a problem which causes difficulty in many legal systems.

It has already been pointed out under Article 21 that true estoppel reasoning can

---

[134] See §§ 140 and 141; 8 and Comment *d*; 8B and Comment.

[135] § 2.05, Comment *d* ("Estoppel does not require as close a fit between affirmative acts of the principal and the third party's belief"). Contra, Mechem, above, § 90 ("The distinction is relatively unimportant").

[136] See *Smith v M'Guire* (1858) 3 H. & N. 554; Stoljar, Ch.3. See also Partnership Act 1890 s.5; Thomas (1971) 6 Victoria U. of Wellington L.Rev. 1. Development on the continent of Europe was certainly not based on any principle like that of estoppel: Müller-Freienfels (1964) 13 Am.J.Comp.L. 193 at 341. See also Articles 2 and 29.

[137] See, e.g. *Pickering v Busk* (1812) 15 East 38 (a case on actual authority); *Pickard v Sears* (1837) 6 A. & E. 469; *Freeman v Cooke* (1848) 2 Exch. 654. See also *VLM Holdings Ltd v Ravensworth Digital Services Ltd* [2013] EWHC 228 (Ch) at [69].

[138] § 292.

[139] § 2.03, Comment and reporter's notes thereto.

[140] *Equitable Variable Life Insurance Co v Wood* 362 S.E.2d 741 (Va., 1987), where an assured cancelled a life insurance policy, notifying only a person with apparent but (as it transpired) not actual authority to receive the notice. She was killed in an air crash one day later. It was held that the policy had been cancelled.

[141] In *Pole v Leask* (1863) 33 L.J.Ch. 155 at 162, Lord Cranworth refers to "this agency by estoppel, if I may so designate it". See too the 2nd edn of *Anson on Contract* (1882). As to the variety of estoppels, see Hon. K. Handley, *Estoppel by Conduct and Election* (2nd edn, 2016), p.20: "Each form of estoppel has its own elements, although some are common to others. The similarities warrant their recognition as a form of estoppel but the differences make each a distinct form with its own history and requirements".

be used in agency situations, outside the doctrine of apparent authority. Examples of such cases are there given.

Can the principal sue on the contract?   No doubt where the principal is sued on   **8-030**
a contract within the apparent authority of an agent, he can make counterclaims as well as adduce defences. But if the doctrine of apparent authority is based on any form of estoppel, it seems clear that he cannot of his own motion sue on such a contract without ratifying it.[142] As stated above, this view is not however taken in the United States, where it seems to be assumed that the principal can sue independently of ratification.[143] If the doctrine is based on estoppel, this view is impossible. Even if it is not, the juristic basis of this analysis is not easy to see. Ratification, which would solve the problem, would not in any case normally be a difficult matter, and could presumably be inferred from the bringing of a counterclaim. The question will only be of practical significance where ratification is for some reason impossible, e.g. because of difficulties about ratification in part[144] or as to the time of ratification.[145] The present law is that ratification is possible though the third party has meanwhile purported to withdraw from the contract.[146] Were it otherwise, the question whether the principal can sue on a contract binding him under the doctrine of apparent authority might assume more practical significance. In general it seems appropriate to apply the safeguards on ratification[147] to such actions by principals; and if this is correct, it provides also a practical reason for adhering to the rule that the doctrine of itself only operates against the principal.

Some special cases are now discussed.

Agents of companies[148]   In general, companies can only act through agents, except   **8-031**
in the comparatively rare situations where a contractual or statutory provision by its wording precludes the operation of attribution through agency.[149] Yet it may be extremely difficult for a person dealing with another who purports to be the agent of a company to know whether that person can be or is in fact authorised to do what he purports to do. The question of the apparent authority of agents of companies is therefore correspondingly important. But it is, not surprisingly, complicated by special factors peculiar to company law. The complications which previously existed have now been reduced, but not eliminated, by statutory provisions. Full

---

[142] Contra, Powell, p.70. Different views were expressed on the point by the Ontario Court of Appeal in *Canadian Laboratory Supplies Ltd v Engelhard Industries of Canada Ltd* (1977) 78 D.L.R. (3d) 232. On appeal the case was decided on different grounds: [1979] 2 S.C.R. 787; (1979) 97 D.L.R. (3d) 1.
[143] See above, para.8-028.
[144] As in the *Canadian Laboratory Supplies* case, above.
[145] Above, para.2-092; Article 19.
[146] *Bolton Partners v Lambert* (1889) 41 Ch.D. 295; see Article 18.
[147] See Article 19.
[148] See above, para.1-028; and *Gower's Modern Company Law* (10th edn), Ch.7. See also the leading cases *Freeman & Lockyer v Buckhurst Park Properties (Mangal) Ltd* [1964] 2 Q.B. 480 and *Hely-Hutchinson v Brayhead Ltd* [1968] 1 Q.B. 549. Compare the situation with that in partnerships, where every partner is an agent of the firm for carrying on the partnership business in the normal way: Partnership Act 1890 s.5.
[149] See above, para.1-028. See too *Stone & Rolls Ltd v Moore Stephens Ltd* [2009] UKHL 39; [2009] 1 A.C. 1391 (noted by Watts (2010) 126 L.Q.R. 14; Halpern (2010) 73 M.L.R. 487).

guidance should be sought in works on company law: what follows seeks only to give general indications as to the impact on agency law of these special factors.[150]

8-032 **Ultra vires doctrine** The first complication is the doctrine of ultra vires. Under this doctrine a company was not bound by a contract or (in some cases) other act into which by virtue of the objects clause in its memorandum it had no capacity to enter, or which it similarly had no capacity to perform.[151] This doctrine was sometimes interpreted rather widely so as to cover situations where the activity was not precluded but the motive for the doing of it was improper, or where the exercise of a power was in the circumstances illegal, or where delegation to particular officers was not authorised by the memorandum or articles. More recent case law, however, confined the ultra vires doctrine to strict questions of capacity—that is to say, to matters outside the actual objects clause in the company's memorandum; the other matters go rather to questions of authority of an agent and notice to the third party.[152] Nevertheless, even in a limited form it remained a trap in respect of the apparent authority of a company's agent: the activity in which he was engaged might be ultra vires in the narrower sense and hence his act simply void as against the company, whatever the appearance of authority to the third party (though it was never clear that third parties were affected if it was not possible even if they had read the memorandum to know whether there had been an infraction of the company's powers). The EC First Directive on Company Law[153] required member states to abolish this doctrine in order to ensure security of transactions between companies and those with whom they deal.

The doctrine remains of relevance for other types of corporation, and is dealt with elsewhere.[154]

8-033 **Constructive notice of company's public documents** There was also a doctrine, of rather uncertain scope, under which a person dealing with a company was deemed to have constructive notice of what appeared in its public documents. It was not clear exactly what these documents were, but they certainly included its memorandum and articles. Thus he might in particular be deemed to know not only of limitations on the company's authorised activities but also of restrictions on delegation contained in its articles. As stated above, sometimes such matters of delegation had been taken into the ultra vires rule; but if it was wrong to do so, the significance of the constructive notice rule for such situations became greater. The third party might not be able to rely on what would otherwise be apparent authority under agency law because he was deemed to have constructive notice of the company's objects and of restrictions on the power to delegate to agents. The rule only applied against the third party: it did not apply in his favour.[155]

8-034 **Common law: the rule in Turquand's case** The public documents of a company

---

[150] There are special rules with respect to charitable companies: see Charities Act 1993 ss.63, 65, 67 and 68. See also Companies Act 2006 s.42, in relation to charities incorporated under that Act.

[151] *Ashbury Railway Carriage and Iron Co v Riche* (1875) L.R. 7 H.L. 653 (unanimous vote of ratification by the shareholders could not validate an ultra vires transaction).

[152] *Rolled Steel Products (Holdings) Ltd v British Steel Corp* [1986] Ch. 246; *Charles Terence Estates Ltd v Cornwall Council* [2012] EWCA Civ 1439; [2013] 1 W.L.R. 466 at [47].

[153] Directive 68/151, art.9.

[154] See above, para.2-021.

[155] *Rama Corp Ltd v Proved Tin & General Investments Ltd* [1952] 2 Q.B. 147 at 149; *Freeman & Lockyer v Buckhurst Park Properties (Mangal) Ltd* [1964] 2 Q.B. 480 at 504, 508.

may provide that a power can be delegated: but they may require some special procedure, for example a resolution of a general meeting; or special procedures may be laid down by the directors for the exercise of ordinary powers, for example a requirement that a cheque on the company's account needs signatures of persons authorised in particular ways.[156] The third party may have no way of finding out whether or not these procedures may have been followed. This problem was dealt with, after the introduction of the system of incorporation by registration, by judicial decision. Under the rule in *Royal British Bank v Turquand*[157] a third party acting in good faith is entitled to assume that the relevant procedures of "indoor management", the details of which were not available to him, have been complied with. He is not, however, entitled to assume from the mere fact that authority was possible that it had actually been conferred.[158] This could only be assumed where under the general principles of agency there would normally be apparent authority. This requires that the company, by a representation traceable back to an authorised officer,[159] has held out the agent as having authority: either by appointing him to a position which would normally carry such authority, or by representing that he has been appointed to it, or by some more specific holding out.[160] If this was so, compliance with internal procedures might be assumed. In other words, the rule is not designed to eliminate the need to deal with persons of sufficient standing to make the relevant contract, but only to protect against failure by such persons to comply with procedural rules.[161]

Statutory reforms: ultra vires Limited provisions protecting third parties dealing with companies in s.9(1) of the European Communities Act 1972, later re-enacted as s.35 of the Companies Act 1985, proved inadequate to abolish the ultra vires doctrine completely,[162] particularly in that they failed to distinguish between issues of corporate capacity and directors' authority. Further reform in 1989 has now been carried through into the Companies Act 2006. Section 39 of the 2006 Act provides that "the validity of an act done by a company shall not be called in question on the ground of lack of capacity by reason of anything in the company's constitution".[163] This provision effectively removes ultra vires as a relevant factor in the company's external relations in this context, and hence from questions of ap-

8-035

---

[156] e.g. *Mahony v East Holyford Mining Co* (1875) L.R. 7 H.L. 869.
[157] (1856) 6 E. & B. 327, Illustration 27; *Mahony v East Holyford Mining Co*, above. A director might in some circumstances rank as a third party for the purposes of this rule: *Hely-Hutchinson v Brayhead Ltd* [1968] 1 Q.B. 549; affd on other grounds [1968] 1 Q.B. 549 at 573.
[158] See *Houghton & Co v Nothard, Lowe & Wills Ltd* [1927] 1 K.B. 246 at 266–267, affd on other grounds [1928] A.C. 1; *Northside Developments Ltd v Registrar-General* (1990) 170 C.L.R. 146 at 195–198.
[159] *Freeman & Lockyer v Buckhurst Park Properties (Mangal) Ltd*, above, at 506 (representation) must be made by person possessing "actual authority to manage the affairs of the company generally or with respect to the matter to which the contract relates". See also below, para.8-040.
[160] cf. above, para.8-015.
[161] *Northside Developments Pty Ltd v Registrar-General* (1990) 170 C.L.R. 146 at 198.
[162] For discussion of s.9(1), see Prentice (1973) 89 L.Q.R. 518; Sealy [1973] C.L.J. 1; Farrar and Powles (1973) 36 M.L.R. 270; Hirtenstein (1973) 123 N.L.J. 312. Special provisions apply to ultra vires acts by companies that are charities: Companies Act 2006 s.42.
[163] This could be interpreted as directed only towards a specific limitation in the memorandum. Such an interpretation would not be justified. The leading cases made it clear that the objects of a company not only positively conferred capacity but also negatively restricted the company from acting outside its powers. Further, such an interpretation would be contrary to the obligation to implement the First Directive. On the obligation to interpret national law in a way which harmonises with the wording and purpose of relevant directives, see *Litster v Forth Dry Dock and Engineering Co Ltd* [1990] 1

parent authority; though internally, as between the company and its directors ultra vires acts are not permissible and may give rise to the directors being liable for breach of duty.[164] To preclude the ultra vires doctrine being reintroduced by the back door, the 2006 Act provides that "the power of the directors to bind the company, or authorise others to do so, is deemed to be free of any limitation under the company's constitution",[165] and goes on to provide that the rights of shareholders are curtailed: no proceedings lie by a shareholder against a company to make it comply with the provisions of the constitution where the act to be restrained is in fulfilment of a legal obligation of the company, including one binding only by virtue of s.39.[166]

8-036 **Constructive notice** As indicated above, mere abolition of the ultra vires rule would not protect third parties adequately unless the constructive notice rule was also abolished, for that could lead to the conclusion that the third party was deemed to know that the act was outside the objects and could not be authorised. Protection was also needed against the constructive notice rule for cases where the articles gave no power to delegate, or actually prohibited delegation, either at all or to particular persons. Provisions protecting third parties were first enacted in s.9(1) of the European Communities Act 1972, but these proved not only inadequate to abolish the ultra vires rule, as stated above, but also unsatisfactory in general. Improved provisions were inserted in the Companies Act 1985 in 1989, and have in turn been replaced by s.40 of the 2006 Act.

8-037 **Companies Act 2006 section 40** Section 40(1) overrides constructive notice by providing that "the power of the directors to bind the company, or authorise others to do so", shall be deemed, in the case of a person "dealing" with a company in "good faith" to be "free of any limitation under the company's constitution". It has been held by the Court of Appeal that a quorum requirement with respect to a board meeting constitutes a "limitation under the company's constitution", and that failure of the necessary quorum did not preclude a third party from relying on the predecessor of s.40.[167] This conclusion must be regarded as authoritative unless and until the Supreme Court reviews it, even though on its face s.40 seems directed to limitations on the power of the board as a whole, that is when constituted by a quorum; the section refers to "the directors", not to individual directors, who ordinarily have little status except at a properly constituted board meeting. It remains doubtful whether directors who themselves do not purport to be acting as the board, but only as delegates, are within the purview of s.40.[168]

The company's constitution for the purposes of the section includes not only its articles, but also any resolution of the shareholders or agreement between the

---

A.C. 546; and in the context of company law *Marleasing SA v La Comercial Internacional de Alimentación SA* (C-106/89) [1990] E.C.R. I-4135.

[164] See s.40(5).

[165] See s.40(1).

[166] See s.40(4). The company must, however, be under a legal obligation; thus, the exercise of a mere option imposing no obligation could be restrained.

[167] *Smith v Henniker-Major & Co* [2002] EWCA Civ 762; [2003] Ch. 182. The Court of Appeal arrived at its conclusion by different routes. See also *Ford v Polymer Vision Ltd* [2009] EWHC 945 (Ch) (failure to notify all directors of meeting, and meeting held in wrong country).

[168] *Wrexham Associated Football Club Ltd v Crucialmove Ltd* [2006] EWCA Civ 237; [2008] 1 B.C.L.C. 508 at [47].

members of the company (or relevant class)[169] Section 40(1) applies to a "person" dealing with a company, but it has been held that this does not cover directors.[170]

Central to the operation of the section are the concepts of dealing and good faith. Both these concepts are defined. As regards dealing, the definition is framed broadly so as to cover any transaction or other act to which the company is a party.[171] However, it has been held that a bonus issue of shares did not constitute a dealing as there was no bilateral transaction.[172] The definition of good faith is not so straightforward. First, a person will be presumed to be acting in good faith.[173] Secondly, a person will not be regarded as acting in bad faith by reason only that he knows that the act is beyond the powers of the directors.[174] The adverb "only" is critical. It is intended to distinguish situations where the directors are exceeding their authority from those where they are actually abusing it, a not altogether easy dichotomy. In the first situation mere knowledge of this fact will not result in a person dealing with the company being unable to enforce his transaction; and this goes further than the normal rules of apparent authority. But where he knows or is to be taken to know that the directors are abusing their authority, there will be no such protection.[175] There are also provisions curtailing a shareholder's internal right to enforce the memorandum and articles against the directors.[176] However, if one of the third parties is a director of the company or its holding company, or is associated with such a director, or is a company with which such a director is associated, the transaction is in certain circumstances voidable against him.[177] In this respect, it can be said that the ultra vires doctrine survives. This provision gives effect to a policy that the protection against ultra vires given to third parties in general should normally not be extended to third parties who are also directors or otherwise involved with the company.

The overall position: dealing with directors Where the third party deals with the board of directors, or with a person actually authorised by it, his position is well protected by s.40. This is further reinforced by s.161 of the 2006 Act, under which "The acts of a director or manager are valid notwithstanding any defect that may afterwards be discovered in his appointment or qualification".[178] Where a company

8-038

---

[169] s.40(3). And see ss.17 and 29 of the 2006 Act. See, e.g. *Cane v Jones* [1980] 1 W.L.R. 1451.

[170] *Smith v Henniker-Major & Co* [2002] EWCA Civ 762; [2003] Ch. 182, (a majority decision). This replicates the common law as expressed in *Morris v Kanssen* [1946] A.C. 459.

[171] s.40(2).

[172] *EIC Services Ltd v Phipps* [2004] EWCA Civ 1069; [2005] 1 W.L.R. 1377. This is open to doubt: see Payne and Prentice [2005] L.M.C.L.Q. 447.

[173] s.40(2)(b)(ii). But on the authority of *International Sales and Agencies Ltd v Marcus* [1982] 3 All E.R. 551, on the 1972 wording, the burden is on the third party to establish that he dealt with the company within the wording.

[174] s.40(2)(b)(iii). A person acts in good faith if he acts genuinely and honestly in the circumstances, i.e. the test is subjective; *Barclays Bank Ltd v TOSG Trust Fund Ltd* [1984] B.C.L.C. 1 at 18 (on the predecessor provision to the current s.40).

[175] This distinction is required by art.9(2) of the First Directive.

[176] s.40(4).

[177] s.41 (superseding Companies Act 1985 s.322A).

[178] This provision is not excluded by s.160 (void resolution to appoint), replacing s.292 of the 1985 Act. However, it only applies where there is a defect in an appointment made by persons who had the ability to make the appointment had they complied with proper procedures, and does not apply to appointments made by persons without the ability to make the appointment: *Morris v Kanssen* [1946] A.C. 459; *Re Northwestern Autoservices Ltd* [1980] 2 N.Z.L.R. 302; *OBG Ltd v Allan* [2007] UKHL

has only one director, he will have authority orally to override earlier general instructions to a bank that it is to act on written instructions only.[179]

8-039 Dealings with other agents of the company   In respect of other agents, including individual directors, the agreement will be enforceable by the application of the normal rules of agency. The third party cannot be affected by anything in the company's constitution. He is also entitled, if acting in good faith, to assume by virtue of s.40 that the board of directors has power to authorise others to bind the company. But he can only assume that it has actually exercised this power by virtue of the common law rules. In particular there must, as before, be a holding out by the company, which might then be reinforced by the indoor management rule.[180] This may be by appointing a person to an office carrying a usual authority,[181] e.g. managing director, or representing that it has done so.[182] In such a case all acts within that authority will bind the company,[183] but not acts outside it. The holding out may also, as in apparent authority generally, be by more specific conduct, as by granting powers of attorney without restriction,[184] or regularly accepting the acts of the agent in question.[185] But pursuant to the general doctrine, there is no protection, even in such a case, for a third party who has notice of the lack of authority[186] or is put on inquiry by the facts of the transaction.[187]

In the leading case on apparent authority, which also relates to the agents of companies, Diplock LJ said that in such cases:

"the representation must be made by a person or persons who had 'actual' authority to manage the business of the company either generally or in respect of those matters to which the contract relates."[188]

This must now be read subject to s.40 of the Companies Act 2006, above. But on the general principle, the High Court of Australia has followed this wording and refused to find apparent authority in a person whose authority was represented by a person who only had apparent authority to do so.[189] It is submitted, however, that whether or not the decision is correct on the facts, this goes too far: so long as the

21; [2008] 1 A.C. 1 at [91]; *New Falmouth Resorts Ltd v International Hotels Jamaica Ltd* [2013] UKPC 11 at [25].
179 *Hill Street Services Co Ltd v National Westminster Bank Plc* [2007] EWHC 2379 (Ch) at [17].
180 See *Kreditbank Cassel GmbH v Schenkers* [1927] 1 K.B. 826 at 842–843; *Wrexham Associated Football Club Ltd v Crucialmove Ltd* [2006] EWCA Civ 237; [2008] 1 B.C.L.C. 508 at [47].
181 See Articles 22 and 29.
182 *Freeman & Lockyer v Buckhurst Park Properties (Mangal) Ltd* [1964] 2 Q.B. 480, Illustration 28.
183 *Mahony v East Holyford Mining Co* (1875) L.R. 7 H.L. 869; *Biggerstaff v Rowatt's Wharf* [1896] 2 Ch. 93, Illustration 25; *British Thomson-Houston Co Ltd v Federated European Bank Ltd* [1932] 2 K.B. 176, as explained in *Freeman & Lockyer v Buckhurst Park Properties (Mangal) Ltd*, above; *Clay Hill Brick & Tile Co Ltd v Rawlings* [1938] 4 All E.R. 100; *Freeman & Lockyer v Buckhurst Park Properties (Mangal) Ltd*, above (Illustration 31); *Panorama Developments (Guildford) Ltd v Fidelis Furnishing Fabrics Ltd* [1971] 2 Q.B. 711, Illustration 30. cf. *Kreditbank Cassel GmbH v Schenkers* [1927] 1 K.B. 826; *Rama Corp Ltd v Proved Tin and General Investments Ltd* [1952] 2 Q.B. 147.
184 *Mercantile Bank of India Ltd v Central Bank of India Ltd* [1938] 1 All E.R. 52.
185 See *First Energy (UK) Ltd v Hungarian International Bank Ltd* [1993] 2 Lloyd's Rep. 194, Illustration 12.
186 *Morris v Kanssen* [1946] A.C. 459; *Howard v Patent Ivory Co* (1888) 38 Ch.D. 156. cf. *Hely-Hutchinson v Brayhead Ltd* [1968] 1 Q.B. 549; affd on other grounds at 573.
187 *A.L. Underwood Ltd v Bank of Liverpool* [1924] 1 K.B. 775; *Liggett v Barclays Bank* [1928] 1 K.B. 48; *Houghton & Co v Nothard, Lowe & Wills* [1927] 1 K.B. 246, Illustration 26; and see Article 75.
188 *Freeman & Lockyer v Buckhurst Park Properties (Mangal) Ltd* [1964] 2 Q.B. 480 at 506.
189 *Crabtree-Vickers Pty Ltd v Australian Direct Mail Advertising and Addressing Co Pty Ltd* (1975)

authority ultimately traces back to a person with actual authority (subject to s.40), that should be sufficient.[190]

Case law as to what usual authority should be attributed to the various company officials other than directors is limited and mostly out of date. As in the case of solicitors, accountants and the like, modern evidence should be required as to what can be regarded as normal.[191] Old cases tended to attribute limited authority to persons designated as "managers", and to company secretaries. But more recent decisions recognise greater authority in such persons[192]; and the role of the chairman of the directors has developed since the nineteenth century, though it varies from company to company.[193]

Execution of documents   Section 44 of the Companies Act 2006, which re-enacts earlier legislation abolishing the necessity for a corporate seal,[194] further provides that in favour of a purchaser (defined as a "purchaser in good faith for valuable consideration ... who ... acquires an interest in property") a document shall[195] be deemed to be duly executed if it purports to be signed by a director and the secretary or by two directors, or by a single director whose signature is witnessed.[196] It is strongly arguable that at common law the unauthorised use of the company seal is a special matter of indoor management of the company and does not turn on the relevant agents' possession of actual or apparent authority to enter into the transaction in question (the deed, however, would have to be correct in form and the signatures those of genuine officers, even if unauthorised).[197] On this basis, a company's deed can be binding without the normal requirements of the law of agency being met, as indeed may deeds generally.[198] Whatever the position at common law, s.44 does appear to give prima facie validity in favour of "purchasers"[199] to company documents executed in accordance with the section whether or not with   **8-040**

---

133 C.L.R. 72.

[190] See *British Bank of the Middle East v Sun Life Assurance Co of Canada (UK) Ltd* [1983] 2 Lloyd's Rep. 9, Illustration 10 to Article 75, where the apparent authority of an intermediate agent was discussed. See also above, para.8-019.

[191] See above, para.3-031.

[192] e.g. *Panorama Developments (Guildford) Ltd v Fidelis Furnishing Fabrics Ltd* [1971] 2 Q.B. 711, Illustration 30 (company secretary); *First Energy (UK) Ltd v Hungarian International Bank Ltd* [1993] B.C.L.C. 1409 at 1422; *Kelly v Fraser* [2012] UKPC 25; [2013] 1 A.C. 450 at [13]; *Australia and New Zealand Banking Group Ltd v Frenmast Pty Ltd* [2013] NSWCA 459. See too *Montreal and St Lawrence Light and Power Co v Robert* [1906] A.C. 196 at 203 (joint representation of president and secretary).

[193] See *Hely-Hutchinson v Brayhead Ltd* [1968] 1 Q.B. 549; *Deutsche Bank AG v Asia Pacific Broadband Wireless Communications Inc* [2008] EWCA Civ 1091; [2008] 2 Lloyd's Rep. 619 at [27].

[194] Companies Act 1985 s.36A, which was superseded on October 1, 2008.

[195] As to good faith in this context, see *LNOC Ltd v Watford Association Football Club Ltd* [2013] EWHC 3615 (Comm) at [91].

[196] See s.44(2). See further *Buckley on the Companies Acts* (2006); *Re Armstrong Brands Ltd* [2015] EWHC 3303 (Ch). In relation to contracts and the execution of documents by overseas companies, see the Overseas Companies (Execution of Documents and Registration of Charges) Regulations 2009 (SI 2009/1917) promulgated under Companies Act 2006 s.1045. As to Scottish companies, see s.48 of the 2006 Act.

[197] See *South Yorkshire Railway and River Dun Co v Great Northern Railway* (1853) 9 Ex. 55 at 84; *Northside Developments Ltd v Registrar-General* (1990) 170 C.L.R. 146 at 164, per Mason CJ.

[198] See Watts (2002) 2 O.U. Commonwealth L.J. 93; *Burkinshaw v Nicolls* (1878) 3 App. Cas. 1004. But see the majority view in the *Northside* case, above.

[199] As to which, see *Lovett v Carson Country Homes Ltd* [2009] EWHC 1143 (Ch); [2009] 2 B.C.L.C. 196; noted by Payne [2010] L.M.C.L.Q. 197.

proper authority. As to the use of powers of attorney by corporations, see below, para.8-087.

8-041 **Forgery** As under apparent authority generally,[200] the company can be bound, though the agent effects a forgery in the sense of executing an unauthorised signature. But an actual counterfeit signature would simply be a nullity.[201] There may, however, be an estoppel against setting up a forgery in either sense, if the elements of a holding out and reliance can be established.[202] It has also been suggested, in relation to companies, that s.44 of the Companies Act 2006 might give effect to forged signatures.[203] In particular, s.44(5) provides: "[i]n favour of a purchaser a document is deemed to have been duly executed by a company if it purports to be signed in accordance with subsection (2)". Forged directors' signatures do *purport* to be official signatures. However, this would lead to the most surprising, and not very just, conclusion that a company could be bound by forged signatures that were placed on a document by persons who had no connection whatsoever with the company. It is difficult to believe that this outcome was contemplated by the section.[204]

8-042 **The Crown** Employees of the Crown are all servants of the Crown and do not employ each other.[205] Apparent authority may be extremely difficult to prove in a Crown or other public agent, for in *Att.-Gen. for Ceylon v Silva*[206] it was said that:

"no public officer, unless he possesses some special power, can hold out on behalf of the Crown that he or some other public officer has the right to enter into a contract in respect of the property of the Crown when in fact no such right exists."[207]

However, this was a clear case, inasmuch as the agent's powers were limited by delegated legislation, and to hold otherwise would have been to give a Crown official a dispensing power to validate ultra vires acts. Apparent authority in a Crown agent, even a Minister of Finance, cannot be established in the face of a constitutional restriction on powers,[208] unless infraction of the restriction was not

---

[200] See Article 74.
[201] *Northside Developments Pty Ltd v Registrar-General* (1990) 170 C.L.R. 146 at 199.
[202] *Greenwood v Martin's Bank Ltd* [1933] A.C. 51; *M'Kenzie v British Linen Co* (1881) 6 App.Cas. 82; *Fung Kai Sun v Chan Fui Hing* [1951] A.C. 489; *Rowe v B. & R. Nominees Pty Ltd* [1964] V.R. 477; *Welch v Bank of England* [1955] Ch. 508; *Spiro v Lintern* [1973] 1 W.L.R. 1002.
[203] *Lovett v Carson Country Homes Ltd* [2009] EWHC 1143 (Ch); [2009] 2 B.C.L.C. 196 at [99], where, however, the forging party was also a real director. He was also held to have had apparent authority to bind the company. cf. *Skandinaviska Enskilda Banken v Asia Pacific Breweries* [2009] 4 Singapore L.R. 788; affd [2011] SGCA 22.
[204] cf. *Kreditbank Cassel GmbH v Schenkers* [1927] 1 K.B. 826 at 842–843, per Atkin LJ.
[205] *Raleigh v Goschen* [1898] 1 Ch. 73; *Bainbridge v Postmaster-General* [1906] 1 K.B. 178; *Moukataff v BOAC* [1967] 1 Lloyd's Rep. 396 at 423–424.
[206] [1953] A.C. 461. See also *Comeau v Province of New Brunswick* (1973) 36 D.L.R. (3d) 763 (welfare official); *Director of Posts and Telegraphs v Abbott* (1974) 22 F.L.R. 157 (clerk in telephone office); *Donegal International Ltd v Republic of Zambia* [2007] EWHC 197 (Comm); [2007] 1 Lloyd's Rep. 397 at [450]; *Tipperary Developments Pty Ltd v The State of Western Australia* (2009) 38 W.A.R. 488.
[207] At 479, per Mr L.M.D. de Silva. cf. *Robertson v Minister of Pensions* [1949] 1 K.B. 227; see as to this case *Howell v Falmouth Boat Construction Co* [1951] A.C. 837 at 845, 849 and *Commissioners of Crown Lands v Page* [1960] 2 Q.B. 274.
[208] *Donegal International Ltd v Republic of Zambia* [2007] EWHC 197 (Comm); [2007] 1 Lloyd's Rep. 397 at [451].

apparent.[209] Another clear case occurs where to bind the Crown would be to permit an officer of the Crown to fetter the Crown's freedom of action to do its public duty.[210] Subject to these important reservations, however, it may be possible to establish apparent authority, including usual authority,[211] in the normal way[212]; though where it is argued that one officer held out another as having authority, it will be necessary to establish the actual (or sometimes apparent) authority of that officer to do so.[213] It may also be difficult to distinguish this form of estoppel from other estoppels, e.g. as to whether the relevant authority has taken a decision or an immunity has been waived.[214] The interaction of public and private law principles makes the area a difficult one.

Illustrations[215]

Creation of an agent

(1) A was in B's counting-house, apparently entrusted with the conduct of B's business. Held, that a payment to A on B's account operated as a payment to B, although A was not, in fact, employed by B.[216]   **8-043**

---

[209] See *Law Debenture Trust Corporation Plc v Ukraine* [2017] EWHC 655 (Comm) at [164].
[210] See *Southend-on-Sea Corp v Hodgson (Wickford) Ltd* [1962] 1 Q.B. 416; *Union SS Co of New Zealand Ltd v CIR* [1962] N.Z.L.R. 656; *Director of Posts and Telegraphs v Abbott*, above.
[211] There are a number of cases involving foreign governments where usual authority has been found to exist or been considered: see *Marubeni Hong Kong & South China Ltd v Government of Mongolia* [2004] EWHC 472 (Comm); [2004] 2 Lloyd's Rep. 198; affirmed on other grounds [2005] EWCA Civ 395; [2005] 2 Lloyd's Rep. 231; *Donegal International Ltd v Republic of Zambia* [2007] EWHC 197 (Comm); [2007] 1 Lloyd's Rep. 397 at [450]; *Charles Terence Estates Ltd v Cornwall Council* [2012] EWCA Civ 1439; [2013] 1 W.L.R. 466 at [49]; *Law Debenture Trust Corporation Plc v Ukraine* [2017] EWHC 655 (Comm) at [161]. As to usual authority separate from apparent authority, see Treitel [1957] P.L. 335, suggesting that *Robertson v Minister of Pensions* [1949] 1 K.B. 227 may be an example of this. The possibility of usual authority was ignored in *Miles v McIlwraith* (1883) 8 App.Cas. 120 but that was a criminal case.
[212] Liability of the Crown in contract was facilitated by the Crown Proceedings Act 1947 s.1. See *J.E. Verreault et Fils Ltée v Att.-Gen. for Quebec* [1977] 1 S.C.R. 41; (1975) 57 D.L.R. (3d) 403; Hilliard (1976) 54 Can.B.R. 401; *Commonwealth v Crothall Hospital Services (Aust.) Ltd* (1981) 54 F.L.R. 439; *PEC Ltd v Asia Golden Rice Co Ltd* [2014] EWHC 1583 (Comm) at [57]; *Pascoe Properties Ltd v Att.-Gen.* [2014] NZCA 616 at [54]. cf. *Director of Posts and Telegraphs v Abbott*, above. As to the apparent authority of a Consul-General, see *Tasita Pty Ltd v Sovereign State of Papua New Guinea* (1991) 34 N.S.W.L.R. 691.
[213] See above, para.8-030.
[214] See *Miles v McIlwraith* (1883) 8 App.Cas. 120; *Att.-Gen. for Ceylon v Silva* [1953] A.C. 461 at 480; *P. v P.* [1957] N.Z.L.R. 854; *P. v P. (No.2)* [1958] N.Z.L.R. 349; *Wells v Minister of Housing and Local Government* [1967] 1 W.L.R. 1000; *Lever Finance Ltd v Westminster (City) London BC* [1971] 1 Q.B. 222; *Norfolk CC v Secretary of State for the Environment* [1973] 1 W.L.R. 1400; *Co-operative Retail Services Ltd v Taff-Ely BC* (1979) 39 P. & C.R. 223; *Rootkin v Kent CC* [1981] 1 W.L.R. 1186; *Western Fish Products Ltd v Penwith DC* [1981] 2 All E.R. 204; Craig, *Administrative Law* (7th edn), para.22-027 onwards.
[215] See further Illustrations to Article 75 for examples of situations where principals are not bound, and the Illustrations to Article 121 for examples of apparent authority operating after the termination of an agent's authority. For discussion of other situations where an agent has no existing actual authority, see DeMott, in Busch, Macgregor and Watts (eds), *Agency Law in Commercial Practice* (2016), Ch.3.
[216] *Barrett v Deere* (1828) Moo. & M. 200. The situation is obviously an unusual one. See also *Galbraith & Grant v Block* [1922] 2 K.B. 155; *Bocking Garage v Mazurk, The Times,* February 4, 1954; *Hoddesdon v Koos Bros* 135 A.2d 702 (N.J., 1957) (Illustration 1 to Article 21) (bogus salesman in shop); *Luken v Buckeye Parking Corp* 68 N.E.2d 217 (Ohio, 1945) (bogus parking attendant: cf. *Mendelssohn v Normand Ltd* [1970] 1 Q.B. 177). Some of these cases come close to contravening the

(2) A professional organiser of fairs and exhibitions ordered supplies for a fair using note paper on which the defendant's names appeared as an "executive committee". They were held liable for the supplies notwithstanding that the fair was a proprietary concern belonging to the organiser, since the suppliers were led to believe that the committee was responsible for the management of the fair.[217]

(3) Goods are ordered for an unincorporated charitable institution on behalf of the person who first managed the institution. A committee of governors is later formed which tacitly acquiesces in the continued supply of goods. A member of the committee is liable.[218]

(4) A, the tenant and licensee of a public house, agreed with B and the owners of the public house that B should become tenant in place of A, but the licence was not transferred to B, and A's name remained painted over the doorway. C, not knowing that A was the licensee, supplied goods at the public house to B; and afterwards discovered that A was the licensee and sued him for the price of the goods. Held, that the agreement that B should occupy a position as tenant which could only be lawfully occupied by A did not make B the agent of A in relation to C; and that there was no estoppel in the matter between A and C, because whatever misrepresentations had been made, they had not reached C nor caused him to act to his detriment.[219]

(5) A person is employed by a company to service their aircraft and teach some of its employees to fly. The company permits him to run an air taxi business under a name which gives the impression that the business is part of theirs. Neither the company nor the person concerned is licensed to do such work. An aircraft crashes while on such work. The company has held out the person concerned as its agent and is the carrier.[220]

(6) The holder of a stolen cheque card and cheque book may, by virtue of the statements on the card, have apparent authority to communicate to a third party the offer of the card issuer to honour a cheque supported by it.[221]

Extension of existing authority

8-044 (7) A occasionally employed B to purchase goods from C and duly recognised

---

principle that one does not become liable merely because one provides facilities within which others can commit fraud: see Comment to Article 21.

[217] *F. Mildner & Sons v Noble* [1956] C.L.Y. 32; *The Times,* March 8, 1956; see also *Pilot v Craze* (1888) 52 J.P. 311; *Royal Albert Hall Corp v Winchilsea* (1891) 7 T.L.R. 362; *Povey v Taylor* (1966) 116 New L.J. 1656.

[218] *Glenester v Hunter* (1831) 5 C. & P. 62; *Luckombe v Ashton* (1862) 2 F. & F. 705; *Harper v Granville-Smith* (1891) 7 T.L.R. 284. cf. *Royal Albert Hall Corp v Winchilsea,* above; *Draper v Earl Manvers* (1892) 9 T.L.R. 73. See further Article 107; Keeler (1971) 34 M.L.R. 615; Fletcher (1979) 11 U.Qd.L.J. 53 and material there cited.

[219] *Mac Fisheries Ltd v Harrison* (1924) 93 L.J.K.B. 811; cf. *Smith v M'Guire* (1858) 3 H. & N. 554; *Dunn v Shanks* [1932] N.I. 66. See also *Charrington Fuel Oils Ltd v Parvant Co, The Times,* December 28, 1988, CA (property changes hands; new owners request previous suppliers, who have no notice of change, to continue; no apparent authority to bind former owners).

[220] *Gurtner v Beaton* [1993] 2 Lloyd's Rep. 369. See also *Lease Management Services Ltd v Purnell Secretarial Services Ltd* [1994] C.C.L.R. 127 (finance company estopped from saying employee of supplying company not its agent). Such an explanation could be applied to the famous but puzzling case of *Watteau v Fenwick* [1893] 1 Q.B. 346, considered below, para.8-077. See Tettenborn [1998] C.L.J. 274.

[221] *First Sport Ltd v Barclays Bank Plc* [1993] 1 W.L.R. 1229.

such purchases. Subsequently, B purchased goods from C for his own use, C believing him to be buying them on behalf of A, and giving credit to A. Held, that it was a question of fact whether A had, by his conduct, held out B as his agent to purchase the goods.[222]

(8) The assignee of a life policy which was voidable if the assured went beyond Europe, in paying the premiums to the local agent of the assurance company, told him that the assured was in Canada. The agent said that that would not avoid the policy, and continued to receive the premiums until the death of the assured. Held, that the company was estopped by the representation of its agent from saying that the policy was avoided by the absence of the assured.[223] So, where a shipmaster signed a bill of lading containing a statement that the freight had been paid, it was held that the owners were estopped from claiming the freight from an indorsee for value of the bill of lading.[224]

(9) A was in debt to a company for goods supplied by its branch at X, and also for goods supplied by its branch at Y. He entered into a deed of assignment for the benefit of his creditors. The company's agent at X branch assented to the deed, but its agent at Y branch refused to assent. The company sued A for the debt incurred at Y branch. Held, that the company was bound by the first assent given by its agent at X branch as to all debts due from A, and was precluded from maintaining the action.[225]

(10) E, in one case as a salaried partner of a firm of solicitors, and in the other as an employed solicitor of a different firm, makes representations that funds becoming available to his firm will be transferred to a bank or to a customer of the bank: on the security of these undertakings the bank makes loans. The firms are bound.[226]

(11) The documentary credits manager of a trading bank signs a guarantee without, as he should have done, obtaining a director's assent and a counter-signature. Evidence indicates that practice regarding the authority of such officials is varied, but there are other indications from which it appears that the

---

[222] *Todd v Robinson* (1825) 1 Ry. & M. 217; *Gilman v Robinson* (1825) 1 Ry. & M. 226. See also *International Paper Co v Spicer* (1906) 4 C.L.R. 739; *International Sponge Importers Ltd v Watt & Sons* [1911] A.C. 279; *Swiss Air Transport Co Ltd v Palmer* [1976] 2 Lloyd's Rep. 604; *Pharmed Medicare Private Ltd v Univar Ltd* [2002] EWCA Civ 1569; [2003] 1 All E.R. (Comm) 321; *Lovett v Carson Country Homes Ltd* [2009] EWHC 1143 (Ch); [2009] 2 B.C.L.C. 19; *CRJ Services Ltd v Lanstar Ltd (t/a CSG Lanstar)* [2011] EWHC 972 (TCC) (agent regularly hiring equipment short term for principal has apparent authority to hire larger capital items for longer periods); cf. *Spooner v Browning* [1898] 1 Q.B. 528 (Article 75, Illustration 1; junior clerk was messenger for conveying written orders and acceptances, but did not thereby obtain apparent authority to represent that order had been accepted); *Bailey & Whites Ltd v House* (1915) 31 T.L.R. 583 (carelessness over paying for unordered goods did not constitute a course of dealing); *Slingsby v District Bank Ltd* [1932] 1 K.B. 544 at 566; *PEC Ltd v Asia Golden Rice Co Ltd* [2014] EWHC 1583 (Comm) at [67] (relevant contract on a grander scale than any previous dealings).
[223] *Wing v Harvey* (1854) 5 De G.M. & G. 265. See Clarke, *Law of Insurance Contracts* (6th edn), paras 8-2A1 and 20-7C. cf. Article 75, Illustration 8.
[224] *Howard v Tucker* (1831) 1 B. & Ad. 712. See also *Compania Naviera Vasconzada v Churchill & Sim* [1906] 1 K.B. 237; *Silver v Ocean Steamship Co Ltd* [1930] 1 K.B. 416 (statements as to apparent order and condition of goods shipped); *The Nea Tyhi* [1982] 1 Lloyd's Rep. 606 (shipment under deck); Article 75, Illustration 2.
[225] *Dunlop Rubber Co Ltd v Haigh & Sons* [1937] 1 K.B. 347.
[226] *United Bank of Kuwait Ltd v Hammoud* [1988] 1 W.L.R. 1051; see [1989] J.B.L. 63 and above, para.8-021. But cf. *Hirst v Etheringtons* [1999] Lloyd's Rep. P.N. 938; and see *Hammoud*'s case criticised in Lindley and Banks, *Partnership* (19th edn), para.12-05.

bank has entrusted the handling of this particular matter to the manager. The bank is bound.[227]

(12) The senior manager in charge of the Manchester office of a foreign bank operating in London who would have usual authority to enter into debt contracts of the type requested, but in fact did not have actual authority, informs the borrower of the fact that any facilities would need to be approved by head office. Pending approval of a loan facility, a valid ad hoc hire purchase agreement was entered into between the parties. The manager writes a letter accepting the borrower's request for further hire purchase finance. He has apparent authority to notify the prospective borrower that his superiors in London have approved the finance and is interpreted as having done so: the bank is bound.[228]

Reservations in authority not known to third party

8-045

(13) An agent was entrusted by his principal with a document containing a written consent signed by the principal to do a particular act, but the agent was told not to give the consent, except on certain conditions which were not specified in the document. The agent consented unconditionally. Held, that the principal was bound, though he had signed the document without having read it.[229] So, where A gave B a power of attorney to charge and transfer in any form whatever any estate, etc., "following A's letters of instructions and private advices which, if necessary," should "considered part of these presents," it was held that A was bound by a mortgage on his property executed by B, although as between A and B the mortgage was not authorised.[230] So, where a principal wrote: "I have authorised A to see you, and, if possible, to come to some amicable arrangement" and gave A private instructions not to settle for less than a certain amount, it was held that he was bound by A's settlement for less than that amount, the instructions not having been communicated to the other party.[231]

(14) A gives B a signed form of promissory note or acceptance in blank, with authority on certain conditions to fill it up and convert it into a bill of exchange or promissory note for a certain amount. B fills it up in breach of the conditions and for a larger amount than was authorised, and negotiates it to C, who takes it in good faith and for value, without notice of the circumstances. A is liable to C on the bill or note as filled up, for he is estopped from denying its validity as between himself and C.[232] It would be otherwise if C had had notice of the circumstances in which the document was issued[233] or if B had not been authorised to issue the document as a

---

[227] *Egyptian International Foreign Trade Co v Soplex Wholesale Supplies Ltd (The Raffaella)* [1985] 2 Lloyd's Rep. 36. cf. Article 21, Illustration 2.

[228] *First Energy (UK) Ltd v Hungarian International Bank Ltd* [1993] 2 Lloyd's Rep. 194.

[229] *Duke of Beaufort v Neeld* (1845) 12 C. & F. 248.

[230] *Davy v Waller* (1899) 81 L.T. 107.

[231] *Trickett v Tomlinson* (1863) 13 C.B.(N.S.) 663.

[232] *Lloyd's Bank Ltd v Cooke* [1907] 1 K.B. 794. But quaere whether this and related cases should be regarded as agency cases: they are more properly to be attributed to general estoppel principles. See also Bills of Exchange Act 1882 s.20. See further Chalmers and Guest, *Bills of Exchange* (18th edn), para.2-139; below, para.8-134; *General & Finance Facilities Ltd v Hughes* (1966) 110 S.J. 847.

[233] *Hatch v Searles* (1854) 24 L.J.Ch. 22.

negotiable instrument except on the receipt of instructions from A on that behalf.[234]

(15) An agent was given authority, in cases of emergency, to borrow money on exceptional terms outside the ordinary course of business. A third person, in good faith and without notice that the agent was exceeding his authority, lent money to him on such exceptional terms. Held, that the principal was bound, although in the particular case the emergency had not arisen.[235]

(16) A solicitor is entrusted with the conduct of litigation for clients who are defendants. A compromise is contemplated involving the purchase of property by the defendants at a valuation. The clients tell him not to agree to the appointment of a valuer, but these instructions do not reach the person handling the matter, who agrees the terms of the compromise and the appointment of a valuer. The client is bound.[236]

(17) An auctioneer is instructed to sell goods by auction, a reserve price being fixed. By mistake he sells without reserve. The principal is bound by the sale,[237] unless the conditions of sale expressly provide that the lot is offered subject to a reserve price.[238]

(18) A solicitor is authorised to sue for a debt. A tender of the debt to his managing clerk operates as a tender to the client, although the clerk was instructed not to receive payment of the particular debt, unless at the time of the tender the clerk disclaims any authority to receive the money.[239]

(19) At a meeting of the provisional directors of a proposed company it was resolved that the company should be advertised, and the secretary was directed to take the necessary steps for that purpose. The secretary employed an advertising agent and upon being asked on what authority he was acting, showed the agent the prospectus and resolution. Held, that the jury were justified in finding the directors who were parties to the resolution liable for the expenses of the advertising agent, though they had allowed their names to appear as provisional directors on the faith of a promise by the secretary to find all the preliminary expenses.[240]

(20) A charterparty provides that the master, who is appointed by the owners, shall sign bills of lading as the agent of the charterers only. The owners are liable on a bill of lading signed on their behalf by the master, to a person who ships goods with notice of the charterparty but without notice of its terms.[241]

---

[234] *Smith v Prosser* [1907] 2 K.B. 735; see also *Baxendale v Bennett* (1878) 3 Q.B.D. 525; *Perpetual Trustees Australia Ltd v Heperu Pty Ltd* [2009] NSWCA 84.

[235] *Montaignac v Shitta* (1890) 15 App.Cas. 357.

[236] *Waugh v H.B. Clifford & Sons Ltd* [1982] Ch. 374. But this may not always be so: see above, para.3-005. See also *Thompson v Howley* [1977] 1 N.Z.L.R. 16; Kenny (1982) 126 S.J. 663; Foskett (1982) 79 L.S.Gaz. 57.

[237] *Rainbow v Howkins* [1904] 2 K.B. 322.

[238] *McManus v Fortescue* [1907] 2 K.B. 1. See also *Fay v Miller, Wilkins & Co* [1941] Ch. 360. cf. *Szembrener v Pepper (New Zealand) Custodians Ltd* [2014] NZHC 324 (vendor ratified auctioneer's action by signing memorandum of sale).

[239] *Moffat v Parsons* (1814) 1 Marsh. 55; *Kirton v Braithwaite* (1836) 1 M. & W. 310; *Finch v Boning* (1879) 4 C.P.D. 143. cf. *Bingham v Allport* (1833) 1 N. & M. 398. And see *Re Buckley and Bienefelt* (1976) 13 A.L.R. 291; Cordery, *Solicitors* (8th edn), p.82.

[240] *Maddick v Marshall* (1864) 17 C.B.(N.S.) 829; *Riley v Packington* (1867) L.R. 2 C.P. 536; cf. *Burbidge v Morris* (1865) 3 H. & C. 664. As to company promoters, see further *Gower's Principles of Modern Company Law* (10th edn), Ch.5.

[241] *Manchester Trust v Furness* [1895] 2 Q.B. 539; cf. *Baumwoll Manufactur von Carl Scheibler v Fur-*

(21) A man who has regularly paid bills in respect of contracts made by his wife[242] or otherwise shown his acquiescence in such contracts, as by directing alterations to goods supplied,[243] revokes his wife's authority to pledge his credit. His wife nevertheless orders further goods from a supplier who does not know of the prohibition. The man is liable. The same would be true if the debt was incurred in similar circumstances by a person who lived with him but was not his wife.[244] But apparent authority does not necessarily arise merely because he has met one bill,[245] or accompanied the person concerned shopping,[246] nor did it arise where the goods were supplied to a different address from that originally used.[247]

(22) A signs an underwriting agreement purporting to give B authority to apply for shares in a company in A's name and on his behalf, and hands it to an agent of the promoters, with a letter stating that the agreement was signed, and is only to hold good, on certain conditions. The agreement is delivered to B, who applies for the shares, and they are duly allotted to A, neither B nor the company having any notice of the letter or conditions. A is bound as a shareholder, though the conditions were not complied with.[248]

(23) A ship requires salvage services. Its owners arrange for a salvage tug. Coincidentally, another tug appears and offers assistance. The master takes it to be the tug ordered by the owners and signs a salvage agreement. He would normally have actual authority to do so, but on this occasion has not because other arrangements have been made. The owners are bound.[249]

Agents of companies

8-046
(24) By the articles of association of a company, the directors are authorised to borrow on bond as may from time to time be authorised by general resolution of the company. The directors borrow £1,000 on a bond, no such resolution having been passed. Held, that the company is liable on the bond, the lender having no notice of the irregularity.[250]

(25) The directors of a company had power, by the articles of association, to delegate such of their powers as they thought fit to a managing director. Held, that the company was bound by the acts, with the scope of such powers, of a person who acted to their knowledge as managing director, though there was no evidence that he had been duly appointed or that the powers of the directors had been delegated to him, the person dealing with him having acted in good faith and without notice of any want of authority.[251]

(26) By the articles of a fruit importing company the directors were authorised to

ness [1893] A.C. 8, where the master was appointed by the demise charterer.
[242] *Debenham v Mellon* (1880) 16 App.Cas. 24 at 36; *Drew v Nunn* (1879) 4 Q.B.D. 661; *Hawthorne Bros v Reilly* [1949] V.L.R. 137.
[243] *Jetley v Hill* (1884) C. & E. 239.
[244] *Ryan v Sams* (1848) 12 Q.B. 460.
[245] *Durrant v Holdsworth* (1886) 2 T.L.R. 763.
[246] *Seymour v Kingscote* (1922) 38 T.L.R. 586.
[247] *Swan & Edgar Ltd v Mathieson* (1910) 103 L.T. 832; cf. *Filmer v Lynn* (1835) 4 N. & M. 559. See also Illustration 7; Article 75, Illustration 1.
[248] *Ex p. Harrison, re Bentley & Co & Yorkshire Breweries Ltd* (1893) 69 L.T. 204.
[249] *The Unique Mariner* [1978] 1 Lloyd's Rep. 438. See above, para.4-008.
[250] *Royal British Bank v Turquand* (1856) 6 E. & B. 327.
[251] *Biggerstaff v Rowatt's Wharf Ltd* [1896] 2 Ch. 93.

delegate their powers. One of the directors, acting without authority, purported to make an agreement on behalf of the company whereby a loan was made (by a fruit broker) to another fruit importing company of which he was also a director, and the lender was granted the right to sell on commission the fruit imported by both companies, retaining the commission against the loan to the second company. The lender required confirmation from the secretary of the first company, who, also acting without authority, gave it. The first company was not bound by the agreement, as the acts concerned were not within the usual authority of a director and a secretary, and the articles not having been read by the lender, no apparent authority arose.[252]

(27) A trading company, having power by its memorandum of association to borrow money and give security and to act through agents, gave a power of attorney to an agent empowering him to borrow and give security. Held, that the company was bound by the acts of the agent acting within the apparent scope of the authority so constituted, notwithstanding that the agent may have exceeded the authority actually given to him as between himself and the company, provided that (as the law then stood) nothing in the articles of association prohibited the company from borrowing through such an agent.[253]

(28) A and B formed a company to purchase and resell a large estate. A and B, together with a nominee of each of them were the directors of the company. A agreed to pay the running expenses of the company and to reimburse himself out of profits. A instructed architects to apply for planning permission and to do other work in connection with the estate. The company was held liable for the architects' fees, though A had never been appointed managing director.[254]

(29) Directors of a company accept a loan and execute a guarantee and a debenture over all the company's assets for an inadmissible purpose. The execution of the guarantee and the debenture come within the company's corporate capacity, but the directors have no authority to enter into the guarantee for such a purpose. The third party is aware of this. The transaction is void.[255]

(30) A company secretary hires cars, saying that they are needed to meet customers of the company at London Airport and drive them to the company's factory at Leeds. He uses the cars for purposes of his own. The company is bound by the contracts of hire, since the secretary has apparent authority to act in such matters of administration.[256]

(31) The chairperson and head of the company's remuneration committee authorises the chief executive to instruct solicitors to prepare remuneration

---

[252] *Houghton & Co v Nothard, Lowe & Wills* [1927] 1 K.B. 246; affd on other grounds [1928] A.C. 1.
[253] *Mercantile Bank of India Ltd v Chartered Bank of India, Australia and China* [1937] 1 All E.R. 231. The headnote is misleading in suggesting that the estoppel arose from the articles rather than the power of attorney: see Gower's *Modern Company Law* (10th edn), para.7-26, fn.79. For the present position see above, para.8-033.
[254] *Freeman & Lockyer v Buckhurst Park Properties (Mangal) Ltd* [1964] 2 Q.B. 480.
[255] *Rolled Steel Products (Holdings) Ltd v British Steel Corp* [1986] Ch. 246. See further Payne and Prentice [2005] L.M.C.L.Q. 447; Article 23.
[256] *Panorama Developments (Guildford) Ltd v Fidelis Furnishing Fabrics Ltd* [1971] 2 Q.B. 711. Earlier decisions giving a very limited authority to a company secretary were said to be obsolete in view of changed practice: see *Barnett, Hoares & Co v South London Tramways Co* (1887) 18 Q.B.D. 815; *Ruben v Great Fingall Consolidated* [1905] A.C. 439; *Kleinwort, Sons & Co v Associated Automatic Machine Corp* (1934) 50 T.L.R. 244. See [1972A] C.L.J. 44; cf. Article 75, Illustration 3. See other cases referred to above, para.8-039.

contracts for himself and an executive colleague. The chief executive includes in his instructions to the solicitors terms that would confer large bonuses to be paid to the executives on the occurrence of certain events. The solicitors act on those instructions and send the prepared contracts to the chairperson for approval and signature. There was a holding out of the chief executive to give instructions to the solicitors in relation to drafting the terms of his own remuneration given that the final version of the contract would go before the remuneration committee.[257]

Article 73

NO UNAUTHORISED ACT BINDING WITH RESPECT TO PERSONS WITH NOTICE

8-047   No act done by an agent in excess of his actual authority is binding on the principal with respect to persons having notice that in doing the act the agent is exceeding his authority.[258]

Comment

8-048   This proposition is mainly relevant to apparent authority: but it seems also true of the perfectly possible situation where the third party knows that the agent's authority has been withdrawn but the agent does not.[259] It arises naturally from the formulation of the doctrine of apparent authority, which requires that the third party deal with the agent on the faith of the principal's representation.[260] Situations of express notice cause no difficulty.[261] The problem is to know what constitutes notice, and when there is a duty to inquire. It is often said that neither constructive[262] nor presumed[263] notice apply in commercial transactions. This certainly excludes the full doctrine of constructive notice of equitable interests in land, whereby a person is expected to take the initiative and make inquiries, being deemed to have notice of property interests which would have come to his knowledge if such inquiries and inspections had been made as ought reasonably to have been made.[264] But there can be no doubt that in many situations where it is relevant to know whether one person has knowledge of facts, including those raising the doctrine of apparent authority, the court may infer from the circumstances that the person concerned must have

---

[257] *Newcastle International Airport Ltd v Eversheds LLP* [2013] EWCA Civ 1514; [2014] 1 W.L.R. 3073.

[258] cf. Partnership Act 1890 s.5. See *Lysaght Bros & Co Ltd v Falk* (1905) 2 C.L.R. 421; *Combulk Pty Ltd v TNT Management Pty Ltd* (1993) 113 A.L.R. 214. This Article and the following Article are cited with approval in *Albright & Wilson UK Ltd v Biachem Ltd* [2001] EWCA 301; [2001] 2 All E.R. (Comm) 537 at [16] (on appeal [2002] UKHL 37; [2002] 2 All E.R. (Comm) 753).

[259] See above, para.8-008.

[260] See above, para.8-024. Continental European systems, from a different starting-point, may tend towards a different result and may even conclude that a third party can hold the principal liable though he knows of the lack of authority, simply because of the position of the agent. The principal's remedy is to remove the agent. But efforts may also be made to avoid such results by the use of other doctrines such as that of good faith. See Schmitthoff, 1970 *I Hague Recueil des Cours*, pp.120–121; Müller-Freienfels (1964) 13 Am.J. Comp.L. 192 at 211 onwards and 341 onwards. See too *The Unauthorised Agent* (Busch and Macgregor eds, 2009).

[261] See Illustration 1.

[262] *Manchester Trust v Furness* [1897] 2 Q.B. 539.

[263] *Eagle Star Insurance Co Ltd v Spratt* [1971] 2 Lloyd's Rep. 116 at 128.

[264] See Law of Property Act 1925, s.199(1).

known of the facts in question or at least must have been suspicious to the extent that further inquiries would have been appropriate in the context.[265]

It seems that the proper approach in commercial cases is to apply the objective interpretation which one person is entitled to put on another's words and conduct in the light of the facts known to the former. The matter was well elucidated in a judgment of Neill J relating to the imposition of a constructive trust on a person who buys goods which are being sold in breach of duty at undervalue—admittedly a different context.[266] He said:

> "In deciding whether a person in the position of the defendants had actual notice, (a) the court will apply an objective test and look at all the circumstances; (b) if by an objective test clear notice was given liability cannot be avoided by proof merely of the absence of actual knowledge; (c) a person will be deemed to have had notice of any fact to which it can be shown that he deliberately turned a blind eye ... ; (d) on the other hand, the court will not expect the recipient of goods to scrutinise commercial documents such as delivery notes with great care; (3) there is no general duty on the buyer of goods in an ordinary commercial transaction to make inquiries as to the right of the seller to dispose of the goods; (f) the question becomes, looking objectively at the circumstances which are alleged to constitute notice, do those circumstances constitute notice? This must be a matter of fact and degree to be determined in the particular circumstances of the case .... The burden of proving a bona fide purchase for value without notice rests on the person who asserts it."

This particular dictum is cited here because, although uttered in the context of the constructive trust where later case law has intervened,[267] it remains appropriate to the sort of commercial situations in which the doctrines of apparent authority and apparent ownership are relied on. It is plain that the demands of commerce are a very significant factor in determining what a reasonable third party would do (note, not "might do") given the information available to him.[268] However, in another case concerned with liability in equity it has been pointed out that the exigencies of commerce cannot be an excuse for tolerating conduct regarded as unreasonable by persons in the same market or line of business[269]:

---

[265] This passage was approved and applied in *Combulk Pty Ltd v TNT Management Pty Ltd* (1993) 113 A.L.R. 214. See also *Macmillan Inc v Bishopsgate Investment Trust Plc* [1993] 1 W.L.R. 837 at 1000 and 1014–1015; *Alliance & Leicester BS v Edgestop Ltd* [1993] 1 W.L.R. 1462; and *Skandinaviska Enskilda Banken v Asia Pacific Breweries* [2009] 4 Singapore L.R. 788; affd [2011] SGCA 22. In *Hirst v Etheringtons* [1999] Lloyd's Rep. P.N. 938, Smedley J refers to "a reasonably acute, experienced and suspicious banker"; but in *Waugh v H.B. Clifford & Sons Ltd* [1982] Ch. 374 at 387, Brightman LJ points out that in some situations an inquiry by one solicitor of another might be "officious". This shows the variable nature of the duty. It appears that in French law the approach tends to concentrate on the reasonableness of the behaviour of the third party rather than the manifestations of the principal, which may enable a more careful scrutiny of questions such as these than the common law might allow: See Saintier in *The Unauthorised Agent* (Busch and Macgregor eds, 2009) Ch.2. But as to equity see below. See also Dal Pont, above, p.539 onwards.

[266] *Feuer Leather Corp v Frank Johnston & Sons Ltd* [1981] Com.L.Rep. 251, Illustration 7; and see *Standard Bank v Bank of Tokyo* [1995] 2 Lloyd's Rep. 167 at 175; *Macmillan Inc v Bishopsgate Investment Trust Plc* [1995] 1 W.L.R. 978 at 1000 and 1014–1015.

[267] See below, para.9-136.

[268] See e.g. *Lexi Holdings Plc v Pannone & Partners* [2009] EWHC 2590 (Ch) at [98] (solicitor not expected to question instructions of managing director of client).

[269] *Baden Delvaux v Société Générale & Co SA* [1993] 1 W.L.R. 509 at 581, per Peter Gibson J; affd [1985] B.C.L.C. 258; below, para.9-132. See also *London Joint Stock Bank v Simmons* [1892] A.C. 201 at 223, per Lord Herschell: "And I do not think the law lays upon [the purchaser of bills] the obligation of making any inquiry into the title of the person whom he finds in possession of them;

"The good sense of the general rule in relation to ordinary commercial transactions where there is no time or opportunity to make inquiries is obvious. But it would be very surprising if the law today was that the mere fact that a transaction was a commercial transaction was sufficient to prevent any duty of inquiry ever arising whatever the circumstances, particularly so many years after the confluence of the separate streams of equity and common law."

8-049 **Recent developments** The foregoing paragraph retains, with small additions, the text of previous editions.[270] Recently, Lord Neuberger of Abbotsbury in the Hong Kong Court of Final Appeal in *Akai Holdings Ltd v Thanakharn Kasikorn Thai Chamchat ("Akai")*[271] was persuaded by an argument that once apparent authority is established, the ability to rely on the representation so made out will be lost only if the third party has actual knowledge of the lack of actual authority or if that party's belief in the agent's authority was dishonest or irrational. The new concept, in this context anyway, of "irrationality" was preferred to the older test of unreasonable reliance on the holding out. Lord Neuberger distinguished a line of cases supporting the unreasonable reliance test on the basis that the cases involved promisors that were companies, and dated from a time when the law was especially protective of companies (since changed by statute). His Lordship then relied upon the idea that at common law it is no defence to a claim founded on a representation to show that the representee might have discovered its falsity by the exercise of reasonable care. The reasoning in *Akai* has now been followed in a number of English cases.[272]

8-050 It is respectfully suggested that this development is based on a misunderstanding of prior authorities and of general principle. For most practical purposes, what is at issue is whether the principal is bound to a contract with the third party. In principal-to-principal contracting it is very clear that the issue whether the parties have intended to contract, and the terms on which they have contracted, are judged from the position of the reasonable person, with such person's knowledge of observable facts, not the unreasonable yet rational person.[273] The same approach, as we have seen, is taken in establishing a representation of authority.[274] It would be surprising to look for reasonableness in assessing whether a representation was made in the first place, but throw that over when assessing whether there were

---

of course, if there is anything to arouse suspicion, to lead to a doubt whether the person purporting to transfer them is justified in entering into the contemplated transaction the case would be different, the existence of such suspicion or doubt would be inconsistent with good faith. And if no inquiry were made, or if on inquiry the doubt were not removed and the suspicion dissipated, I should have no hesitation in holding that good faith was wanting in a person thus acting".

[270] See further Watts [2015] L.M.C.L.Q. 36.

[271] (2010) 13 H.K.C.F.A.R. 479 at [51] onwards (noted Lee and Ho (2012) 75 M.L.R. 91) (absence of apparent benefit and known conflict of interest meant the irrationality test was met on the facts).

[272] *Quinn v CC Automotive Group Ltd* [2010] EWCA Civ 1412; [2011] 2 All E.R. (Comm) 584 at [23(ii)] (noted Roberts [2011] L.M.C.L.Q. 457), Article 73, Illustration 10; *Newcastle International Airport Ltd v Eversheds LLP* [2012] EWHC 2648 (Ch) at [109]; reversed on other points [2013] EWCA Civ 1514; [2014] 1 W.L.R. 3073; *Gaydamak v Leviev* [2012] EWHC 1740 (Ch) at [252]; *Acute Property Developments Ltd v Apostolou* [2013] EWHC 200 (Ch) at [39]; *LNOC Ltd v Watford Association Football Club Ltd* [2013] EWHC 3615 (Comm) at [92]; *PEC Ltd v Asia Golden Rice Co Ltd* [2014] EWHC 1583 (Comm) at [73].

[273] See *Smith v Hughes* (1871) L.R. 6 Q.B. 597 at 607; *Gissing v Gissing* [1971] A.C. 886 at 906; *Rainy Sky SA v Kookmin Bank* [2011] UKSC 50; [2011] 1 W.L.R. 2900 at [14]; *Toll (FGCT) Pty Ltd v Alphapharm Pty Ltd* (2004) 219 C.L.R. 165 at [40].

[274] *Egyptian International Foreign Trade Co v Soplex Wholesale Supplies Ltd (The Raffaella)* [1985] 2 Lloyd's Rep. 36 at 41. See further above, para.8-018.

counter-signs. The cases prior to *Akai* drew no such distinction.[275] In so far as many of these cases involve companies, it is not the case that the courts were taking a stricter stance (in favour of companies) than they would with individuals, but rather the opposite. The courts were insisting that companies cannot be made more readily liable in contract than an individual on the basis of a simplistic reliance by third parties on the rule in *Turquand*'s case.[276] As is explained above, that rule is concerned only with procedural irregularity and does not affect the ordinary requirement that the third party show that he dealt with someone with actual or apparent authority from the company to make the contract. The company cases, therefore, are mainstream agency cases. Nor is there a universal principle that a representee is not required to look behind a representation. If there were, it would be inconsistent with the rules for contract formation. Indeed, the notion of not needing to look behind a representation operates mainly in the law of misrepresentation, where the representee is using the representation to deny or alter what might otherwise be a contractual obligation, not to create a contractual obligation. This is the position with most of the cases on which Lord Neuberger relied in the *Akai* case.[277] Otherwise, in the absence of evidence of actual intention that a representation be relied upon, as in cases of fraud,[278] reliance on a representation needs to be reasonable.[279] In short, the no-inquiries rule operates at common law only where what is sought is rescission (or other form of restitution), or, in cases of fraud, damages for reliance loss.[280] It cannot be relied upon to make a contract. Even within the sphere of its operation, the cases conclude that, in the absence of obfuscation, the no-inquiries rule applies only to unequivocal representations, not to ones where there is ambiguity or a series of inconsistent statements.[281]

Finally, it should be recalled that the operation of estoppel by representation

---

[275] *Houghton & Co v Nothard, Lowe & Wills* [1927] 2 K.B. 28 at 36; *AL Underwood Ltd v Bank of Liverpool & Martins* [1924] 1 K.B. 775 at 788–789; *Morris v Kanssen* [1946] A.C. 459 at 475; *Rolled Steel Products (Holdings) Ltd v British Steel Corp* [1986] 1 Ch. 246 at 30. See too *Egyptian International Foreign Trade Co v Soplex Wholesale Supplies Ltd (The Raffaella)* [1985] 2 Lloyd's Rep. 36 at 44; *Hopkins v TL Dallas Group Ltd* [2004] EWHC 1379 (Ch); [2005] 1 B.C.L.C. 543 at [94]; *Pharmed Medicare Private Ltd v Univar Ltd* [2002] EWCA Civ 1569; [2003] 1 All E.R. (Comm) 321 at [7]; *Wrexham Association Football Club Ltd v Crucialmove Ltd* [2006] EWCA Civ 237; [2008] 1 B.C.L.C. 508 at [45]; *Smith v Peter & Diana Hubbard Pty Ltd* [2006] NSWCA 109 at [74] (transaction pursuant to power of attorney); *Pourzand v Telstra Corp Ltd* [2014] WASCA 14 at [115].

[276] As to which rule, see above, para.8-034.

[277] *Greer v Downs Supply Co* [1927] 2 K.B. 28 at 36; *Bloomenthal v Ford* [1897] A.C. 156. See too *Redgrave v Hurd* (1881) 20 Ch.D. 1; and *Versloot Dredging BV v HDI Gerling Industrie Versicherung AG* [2014] EWCA Civ 1349; [2015] Q.B. 608 (misrepresentation by agent in insurance claim).

[278] See, e.g. *Standard Chartered Bank v Pakistan National Shipping Corp (No.2)* [2002] UKHL 43; [2003] 1 A.C. 959 at [14].

[279] See *Jorden v Money* (1854) 5 H.L.C. 185 at 212; *Sidney Bolsom Investment Trust Ltd v E Karmios & Co (London) Ltd* [1956] 1 Q.B. 529 at 540–541; *Thornton Springer v NEM Ins Co Ltd* [2000] 2 All E.R. 489 at 518. See, more generally, Spencer Bower, *Reliance-Based Estoppel* (5th edn), pp.195–196.

[280] As to damages under the Misrepresentation Act 1967, see *Peekay Intermark Ltd v Australia and New Zealand Banking Group Ltd* [2006] EWCA Civ 386; [2006] 2 Lloyd's Rep. 511.

[281] See *Smith v Chadwick* (1884) 9 App.Cas. 187 at 200, per Lord Blackburn: "I should think that a reasonable man reading this prospectus would hardly act on the faith of such an obscure statement without further inquiry". See too an earlier passage at p.199; *Capel & Co v Sim's Composition Co* (1888) 58 L.T. 808 at 808–809; *Peekay Intermark Ltd v Australia and New Zealand Banking Group Ltd* [2006] EWCA Civ 386 at [25]–[28] and [52].

[413]

within the concept of apparent authority is a somewhat tenuous one.[282] It would be remarkable, therefore, if the law were to treat a representation founded solely on the principal's conduct—there being no verbal communication directly between the principal and third party—as virtually conclusive even though a reasonable person would have spotted counter-signals and inquired about them. This point was well made by Brennan J in *Northside Developments Pty Ltd v Registrar-General*[283]:

> "Although such representations by the company seem a slender foundation on which to build an estoppel, the indoor management rule treats them as sufficient unless the party relying on the rule is put on notice to inquire into the authority of the officers or agents to do what they did in the transaction. The slenderness of the foundation enhances the importance of the qualification."

In this regard, it is suggested that the process of determining whether apparent authority is made out is ultimately a single process, rather than a rigid two-step process of finding a holding out, and then inquiring as to the third party's state of knowledge.

8-051   **Knowledge of agent of third party**   The knowledge of an agent of the third party will often be attributed to the third party himself: this is dealt with in Article 96. If however the third party knows of the lack of authority, he cannot sue even if the agent does not know of it.

8-052   **Powers of attorney**   In the case of a disposition of land by an agent stating that he acts under a power of attorney, there will doubtless be a duty to examine the power. But even in other situations the power itself will often constitute the only holding out by the principal; therefore the third party who knows of it can only rely on it if he has examined it,[284] unless there are other circumstances creating apparent authority, such as the position or profession of the agent, or other acts by the principal indicating authority, e.g. acceptance of similar acts by the agent in the past.[285] However, where such an inspection would not reveal the want of authority, failure to make it has been held not to be fatal. It is not clear that this conclusion is consistent with the general reluctance of the law to let parties avoid making standard inquiries on the basis that if they had made them they would not have learned the truth.[286] However, where there is otherwise a basis for believing the act to be authorised, the third party cannot be expected to inquire further into the agent's

---

[282]   See above, paras 8-015 and 8-027.
[283]   See (1990) 170 C.L.R. 146 at 178.
[284]   See *Jacobs v Morris* [1902] 1 Ch. 816, Illustration 3; *National Bolivian Navigation Co v Wilson* (1880) 5 App.Cas. 176 at 209; *Xie v Huang* [2012] NZHC 960 at [43]. There used to be statutory requirements for the filing of powers of attorney: see Law of Property Act 1925 s.125(1); Trustee Act 1925 s.25. By virtue of s.2 of the Powers of Attorney Act 1971 filing is no longer possible, but lasting powers of attorney made under the Mental Capacity Act 2005 must be registered: see below, para.10-009. As to less formal written authority, see *Suncorp Insurance & Finance v Milano Assecurazioni SpA* [1993] 2 Lloyd's Rep. 225 at 233 ("onus on the third party to ask to see that authority where the agent is acting close to the border of what is usual": per Waller J) It would seem that where a third party has seen the authorising document once, he should, if active over a period, ask to see it again if there is a serious possibility of its terms being changed.
[285]   See, e.g. Article 72, Illustration 7.
[286]   See *Jones v Williams* (1857) 24 Beav. 47 at 62. See further above, para.3-011.

motives for doing it unless there are special reasons (e.g. some irregular practice) for doubt.[287]

Acts within usual authority Where the agent is acting within the usual authority of a person holding the position which he holds, e.g. that of managing director,[288] or of a professional agent exercising such functions as the agent is exercising, e.g. in former days, a factor,[289] or where he exercises functions combining the two, e.g. a solicitor conducting litigation[290] there will not normally be any duty to inquire[291] unless the transaction is abnormal or there are further circumstances giving grounds for suspicion—for instance, in the area of banking practice, where the agent pays the principal's money into his own personal bank account,[292] or uses a signed blank transfer for what might well, to an outsider, be his own purposes.[293]

8-053

Acts outside usual authority An agent acting outside such authority as that indicated above is acting abnormally, and in the absence of other indications of authority there may well be a duty to inquire. Thus a contract of sale of goods by a commodity broker in his own name would not, at any rate according to former usage, normally be authorised, and apparent authority might not be easy to establish.[294] So also where it is notorious that usual authority is specially limited by trade usage, e.g. in particular markets, there may be no apparent authority, though some of the cases applying such reasoning are open to criticism.[295]

8-054

Representation of limited authority only If the representation is of limited authority only, there will obviously be no liability where that authority is exceeded.[296]

8-055

Bills of exchange In the case of bills of exchange, promissory notes and cheques, it has been long established that a signature per procurationem operates as notice that the agent has but a limited authority to sign, and the principal is only bound if the agent in so signing was acting within the limits of his actual authority.[297]

8-056

Public documents: companies It was formerly possible to say that registration of the public documents of a company was notice of limitations of authority

8-057

---

[287] *Hambro v Burnand* [1904] 2 K.B. 10, Illustration 1 to Article 74.
[288] See Articles 29 and 72.
[289] See Articles 2 and 30.
[290] *Waugh v H.B. Clifford & Sons Ltd* [1982] Ch. 374, Illustration 16 to Article 72 (compromise: "officious" of other side to demand to be satisfied as to authority).
[291] *Borries v Imperial Ottoman Bank* (1873) L.R. 9 C.P. 38; see also *Smith v M'Guire* (1855) 3 H. & N. 554; *Knight v Matson & Co* (1902) 22 N.Z.L.R. 293 (horse dealer); *Lexi Holdings Plc v Pannone & Partners* [2009] EWHC 2590 (Ch) (managing director). Some of the cases used the concept of general agent in this connection: see Comments to Articles 2 and 29.
[292] *Midland Bank Ltd v Reckitt* [1933] A.C. 1, Illustration 3 to Article 74.
[293] *Sheffield v London Joint Stock Bank Ltd* (1888) 13 App.Cas. 333; *Levy v Richardson* (1890) 5 T.L.R. 236; *Colonial Bank v Cady and Williams* (1890) 15 App.Cas. 267.
[294] *Cooke & Sons v Eshelby* (1887) 12 App.Cas. 271, Illustration 7 to Article 81; *Baring v Corrie* (1818) 2 B. & A. 137.
[295] See Article 75, Illustration 2. See also the cases on solicitors, above, para.8-021.
[296] *Forman & Co Pty Ltd v The Liddesdale* [1900] A.C. 190; *Russo-Chinese Bank v Li Yau Sam* [1910] A.C. 174; *Doey v L & NW Ry Co* [1919] 1 K.B. 623.
[297] Bills of Exchange Act 1882 s.25. See Chalmers and Guest, *Bills of Exchange* (18th edn), para.3-095 onwards. See *Bryant, Powis & Bryant v Quebec Bank* [1893] A.C. 170; Article 21; Article 74, Illustration 1.

contained in them. The matter is a specialist part of company law now regulated by statute.[298]

8-058 **Agents of the Crown** A person dealing with an agent whose powers are fixed by statute or statutory instrument or other delegated legislation ought to inquire into them, for such an agent can by law have no authority to contract beyond such limits; unless there is some holding out, which can only be effected by an official with power to do so, and would be difficult to establish.[299]

8-059 **Statutes** The inquiries made by a third party may also be relevant to the application of statutes, under which the third party may need to establish that he acted in good faith.[300]

8-060 **Response to inquiries** Sometimes the response to an inquiry may be indecisive. For example, the person of whom the inquiry as to the authority of an agent is made may, if he is not himself the principal (as in the case of a company), say that he will investigate and make further contact but may not do so.[301] In such a case there may be apparent authority if his conduct is such as to give the impression that the authority questioned exists. Any response, whether indirect in this way or direct, will however only bind the principal if given by the principal himself or by an agent with authority to make it. Such authority will normally only be attributed to a person authorised to act in connection with the particular business in question[302]: it is difficult to believe that authority to give answers to inquiries which bind the employer will easily be inferred.[303] Where apparent authority is otherwise established, the mere fact that the third party seeks unsuccessfully to get confirmation from the principal of the agent's authority, and does not renew its efforts, will not remove its ability to rely on the apparent authority.[304]

Illustrations

8-061 (1) General conditions of sale state that auctioneers have no authority to make representations in relation to the property sold. Contrary to this, the auctioneers state that no schemes for compulsory purchase or the like affect the property. Such representations are not within their apparent authority.[305]

(2) A authorised his son to take delivery of a mare, provided that a certain warranty was given, and told the owner so. The son took away the mare without

---

[298] See above, para.8-031 onwards.

[299] See *Att.-Gen. for Ceylon v Silva* [1953] A.C. 461; above, para.8-042.

[300] e.g. Sale of Goods Act 1979 ss.25 and 26; Factors Act 1889 s.2 (see Article 89); Bills of Exchange Act 1882 s.29. As to the Companies Act 2006, see above, para.8-039.

[301] See *Canadian Laboratory Supplies Ltd v Engelhard Industries of Canada Ltd* [1979] 2 S.C.R. 787; (1979) 97 D.L.R. (3d) 1.

[302] See *British Bank of the Middle East v Sun Life Assurance Co of Canada (UK) Ltd* [1983] 2 Lloyd's Rep. 9, Illustration 10 to Article 75; above, para.8-020.

[303] But see Grönfors [1962] *Scandinavian Studies in Law* 97 at 104, discussing the position of a person "to whom telephone customers are referred".

[304] See *Flexirent Capital Pty Ltd v EBS Consulting Pty Ltd* [2007] VSC 158 at [219]; *Golden Ocean Group Ltd v Salgaocar Mining Industries PVT Ltd* [2011] EWHC 56 (Comm); [2011] 1 W.L.R. 2575 at [128]; affd [2012] EWCA Civ 265; [2012] 1 W.L.R. 3674.

[305] *Overbrooke Estates v Glencombe Properties Ltd* [1974] 1 W.L.R. 1335, holding also that such a clause is not within Misrepresentation Act 1967 s.3. *Mendelssohn v Normand Ltd* [1970] 1 Q.B. 177 is somewhat difficult to reconcile with this decision: see Coote [1975] C.L.J. 17. It was followed in *Collins v Howell-Jones* [1981] E.G.D. 207.

the warranty in question. Held, that the son's act did not amount to an acceptance of the mare, so as to bind the father.[306]

(3)   An agent, purporting to act under a power of attorney, which he represented gave him full power to borrow, borrowed money from A, and misapplied it. The agent produced the power, which did not in fact authorise the loan, but A acted on his representation, and did not read the power. Held, that A must be taken to have had notice of the terms of the power, and that the principal was not bound by the loan.[307]

(4)   Cattle are brought to an auctioneer for sale by a dealer who normally buys and resells on his own account, but has on one previous occasion, to the auctioneer's knowledge, sold on account of another. The auctioneer is not fixed with notice that on this occasion the dealer is again acting for that other.[308]

(5)   A accepts a bill of exchange drawn by B, and delivers it to B to be held by him for A's use. B indorses the bill to C for a loan, having told C that it belongs to A, and that he (B) has no authority to deal with it. A is entitled to recover the bill or its value from C.[309]

(6)   A indorses a bill of exchange "pay B or order for my use". B's bankers discount the bill and pay the proceeds to B's account. The bankers are liable to A for the amount, because the restrictive indorsement operated as notice that the bill did not belong to B.[310]

(7)   A dealer in an established market buys goods which are sold at undervalue in circumstances suggesting that the seller is in difficulties. The dealer is not thereby fixed with notice that the seller is selling goods which are not his own in breach of his obligations to the owner.[311]

(8)   A lender which has been approached by A for a large personal loan, agrees to make the loan to the company in which A is a director. The company then asserts that the borrowing was unauthorised. The lender knew (through one of its own directors and its solicitor) who the directors of the company were, but was requested by the company treasurer to prepare a board minute that named as those to be present only half the board, all of whom were family members related to A. Held, that although ordinarily the lender might be able to rely on the company treasurer's certificate that a proper board meeting had been held, it was put on inquiry by the oddity that only a conflicted quorum was expected to be present.[312]

(9)   A, the manager of property-owning company C Ltd, has general authority to engage letting agents. He re-engages D Ltd as agent when its manager, X, knows that the directors of C Ltd had previously terminated its agency for dis-

---

[306]   *Jordan v Norton* (1838) 4 M. & W. 155.

[307]   *Jacobs v Morris* [1902] 1 Ch. 816.

[308]   *Knight v Matson & Co* (1902) 22 N.Z.L.R. 293; see also *Curlewis v Birkbeck* (1863) 3 F. & F. 894.

[309]   *Evans v Kymer* (1830) 1 B. & Ad. 528.

[310]   *Lloyd v Sigourney* (1829) 5 Bing. 525; Bills of Exchange Act 1882 s.35. See Chalmers and Guest, *Bills of Exchange* (18th edn), para.5-031 onwards.

[311]   *Feuer Leather Corp v Frank Johnston & Sons Ltd* [1981] Com.L.Rep. 251 (a case on constructive trust: see above, para.8-048 and Comment to Article 115). See also *Re Funduk and Horncastle* (1973) 39 D.L.R. (3d) 94 (car).

[312]   *Re Moulin Global Eyecare Holdings Ltd, Active Base Ltd v Sutton* [2009] HKCFA 14. See too *Acute Property Developments Ltd v Apostolou* [2013] EWHC 200 (Ch) (put on inquiry by manager's direction to debtor to pay not his principal but his wife).

satisfaction with X's services. Somewhat surprised, X asks A to confirm that his superiors are happy for D Ltd to be reappointed, which A does. Held, D Ltd cannot rely on A's usual authority.[313]

(10) Claimants seeking to buy a new red Jaguar car are persuaded by a sales agent at the defendant's showrooms to agree to buy, on hire purchase, a blue one (not yet in the showroom) in exchange for the claimants' existing silver Jaguar. Later the same day, the agent contacts the claimants to say that he has located a red Jaguar in another town. Some days later, he arranges to meet the claimants at a motorway service station, closer to the claimants' home, in order formally to cancel the agreement for the blue car and substitute new documentation for the red one. A further week later, the agent meets the claimants at the same service station and the silver Jaguar is exchanged for the red one together with a sum of money. The agent is fraudulent; neither he nor the defendant has authority to sell the red car, and the agent on-sells the silver one without arranging for discharge of the outstanding hire purchase debt. The defendant is held vicariously liable for the deceits; the agent's apparent authority was not lost by the off-premises dealings.[314]

Article 74

FRAUD OF AGENT IS NOT INCOMPATIBLE WITH APPARENT AUTHORITY

8-062   An act of an agent within the scope of his apparent authority does not cease to bind his principal merely because the agent was acting fraudulently and in furtherance of his own interests.

Comment

8-063   This principle is applicable to cases of contract[315]; in tort[316]; in the disposition of property[317]; a similar result even appears in criminal cases.[318] But for the principal to be responsible under agency principles the agent must normally have been acting within the scope of his actual or apparent authority.[319] It is a well-known proposition that the mere fact that the principal by appointing an agent gives that agent the opportunity to steal or otherwise to behave fraudulently does not without

---

[313] *IH Wedding & Sons Ltd v Buy-Sell Realty NZ Ltd* [2009] NZHC 1717.

[314] *Quinn v CC Automotive Group Ltd* [2010] EWCA Civ 1412; [2011] 2 All E.R. (Comm) 584.

[315] Illustrations 1 and 2; *Bryant, Powis & Bryant v Quebec Bank* [1893] A.C. 170 at 180; *A.L. Underwood Ltd v Bank of Liverpool* [1924] 1 K.B. 775 at 791–792; *Lloyds Bank v Chartered Bank of India, Australia & China* [1929] 1 K.B. 40; *Uxbridge Permanent Benefit Building Society v Pickard* [1939] 2 K.B. 248; *Alliance and Leicester BS v Edgestop Ltd* [1993] 1 W.L.R. 1462.

[316] *Lloyd v Grace, Smith & Co* [1912] A.C. 716; *Uxbridge Permanent Benefit Building Society v Pickard*, above; *Morris v C.W. Martin & Sons Ltd* [1966] 1 Q.B. 716.

[317] Many of the cases involve fraud on the part of the agent: see, e.g. *Oppenheimer v Attenborough & Son* [1908] 1 K.B. 221; *Canadian Laboratory Supplies Ltd v Engelhard Industries of Canada Ltd* [1979] 2 S.C.R. 787; (1979) 97 D.L.R. (3d) 1; *Lexi Holdings Plc v Pannone & Partners* [2009] EWHC 2590 (Ch); cf. *De Gorter v Attenborough & Son* (1904) 21 T.L.R. 19.

[318] See *Moore v Bresler Ltd* [1944] 2 All E.R. 515.

[319] See *Ruben v Great Fingall Consolidated* [1906] A.C. 439; *Morris v C.W. Martin & Sons Ltd* [1966] 1 Q.B. 716; *Polkinghorne v Holland* (1934) 51 C.L.R. 143 (partner). But see the next paragraph and also Articles 72 and 83–85. As to vicarious liability in tort, see Article 90.

more make him liable.[320] Furthermore, the fact that an agent is acting in furtherance of his own interests may negative actual authority[321] and may, if known to him
or such that he ought to know it, put the third party on notice as regards apparent
authority.[322] As regards forgery, a forger may profess not to act for but as the person
whose document he forges[323]; and a counterfeit document may of itself be
ineffective. The forger may nonetheless have apparent authority to warrant the
genuineness of the document, but the normal requirements for a holding out must
to that effect be established.[324]

Illustrations

(1) A is authorised in writing to act as the agent of B for the purpose of underwrit-   **8-064**
    ing policies of insurance, and carrying on the ordinary business of underwrit-
    ing, at Lloyd's, in the name and on behalf of B, in accordance with the usual
    custom of Lloyd's. A, in his own interests, and in abuse of his authority,
    underwrites a guarantee policy in B's name, the assured acting in good faith,
    but having no knowledge of the existence of the written authority or of its
    terms. It is in the ordinary course of business at Lloyd's to underwrite such
    policies, and A was therefore acting within the scope of his apparent author-
    ity, though in fraud of B. B is bound by the policy.[325]

(2) A was entrusted by B with the letting of B's flat. A, as a condition of granting
    C a tenancy of the flat, demanded an illegal premium which C paid to A. The
    premium was recoverable by C by virtue of the Landlord and Tenant (Rent
    Control) Act 1949 s.2(5). Held, that C could recover the premium from B.[326]

(3) A gave B a power of attorney authorising him to draw cheques on A's bank-
    ing account and apply the money for A's purposes. B fraudulently drew
    cheques on A's account, signing the cheques "A by B his attorney", and paid
    the cheques into his own banking account to meet an overdraft. B's bankers
    applied the cheques in reduction of the overdraft without making inquiries as
    to B's authority. Held, that B's bankers were bound by the terms of B's actual
    authority, which did not extend to paying B's debts with A's money; that they
    had converted the cheques; and as, from the form of the cheques, they had
    notice that the money was not B's money, they were negligent in not making

---

[320] *Farquharson Bros & Co v King & Co* [1902] A.C. 325, Illustration 6 to Article 84; *Ruben v Great
Fingall Consolidated* [1906] A.C. 439; *Morris v C.W. Martin & Sons Ltd* [1966] 1 Q.B. 716 at 726,
737, 740–741; *Leesh River Tea Co v British India Steam Navigation Co* [1967] 2 Q.B. 250;
Koorangang Investments Pty Ltd v Richardson & Wrench Ltd [1982] A.C. 462, Illustration 4.

[321] See Article 23; Article 95, Illustration 11. Especially when the agent is practising a fraud on the
principal himself: *Kwei Tek Chao v British Traders and Shippers Ltd* [1954] 2 Q.B. 459; below,
para.8-213.

[322] Illustration 3; and see Article 73.

[323] A possible explanation of *Ruben v Great Fingall Consolidated* [1906] A.C. 439.

[324] For the ways in which forgery may be committed, see Forgery and Counterfeiting Act 1981 ss.1 and
2–5; also above, para.2-057. As to estoppel against setting up a forgery, see cases cited above, para.8-
041.

[325] *Hambro v Burnand* [1904] 2 K.B. 10, a famous and controversial case which can be and has been
taken to refer also to actual authority. See Comment to Article 23 for further discussion; see (1903)
17 Harv.L.Rev. 56; (1934) 50 L.Q.R. 228–230; (1935) 1 U Toronto L.J. 42–43; (1972) 89 S.A.L.J.
60; Watts (2002) 2 O.U. Commonwealth L.J. 93 at 96–98; Watts [2017] J.B.L. 269; see also *Refuge
Ass. Co Ltd v Kettlewell* [1909] A.C. 243.

[326] *Navarro v Moregrand Ltd* [1951] 2 T.L.R. 674; cf. *Barker v Levinson* [1951] 1 K.B. 342. See also
Credit Services Investments Ltd v Evans [1974] 2 N.Z.L.R. 683; *Gordon v Selico Co Ltd* [1986] 1
E.G.L.R. 71.

inquiry as to B's authority and therefore could not avail themselves of the protection of the Bills of Exchange Act 1882 s.82, and were liable to A for the amount of the cheques.[327]

(4) An employee of valuers is told not to issue valuations for a particular group of companies. He nevertheless does so, on his employer's headed notepaper, and signs it with his employer's name, it not appearing on the valuation who prepared it. The valuation is negligent. His employers are not liable.[328]

(5) The company secretary of the claimant funds manager, and authorised signatory on its bank account, in fraud of the company, drew cheques in favour of a futures trader, using the funds thereby obtained for his personal futures trading with the trader. The paying and collecting bank was the same bank. The trader was not told by the bank who the drawer of the cheques was. The bank was protected from liability in conversion by the apparent authority of the secretary, but not the trader which was put on inquiry because it was deemed to know through the collecting bank, as its agent, that the cheques were drawn on the claimant, rather than its client, and thus had the means of knowing that the client was using other people's money to fund personal dealing.[329]

Article 75

DISCLOSED PRINCIPAL NOT BOUND BY ACTS OUTSIDE ACTUAL OR APPARENT AUTHORITY

8-065   A disclosed principal is not bound by an act of his agent which is outside the scope of the agent's implied or apparent authority unless the principal in fact authorised the agent to do the particular act or ratified it. This Article is subject to the provisions of Articles 79 and 84 to 87.[330]

Comment

8-066   This Article simply completes the account of actual and apparent authority by further examples of principals who are not bound. It should be read in conjunction with Article 23 and with the Article following, Article 76, concerning the doctrine of the undisclosed principal. It should also be noted that the common law reasoning that an act that is unauthorised makes it a nullity, i.e. void, will not usually preclude recourse by the principal to equitable causes of action and remedies against the third party.[331] Where money or other property is transferred under a void transaction, the principal will usually have a choice of common law or equitable remedies.

---

[327] *Midland Bank Ltd v Reckitt* [1933] A.C. 1; *John v Dodwell and Co Ltd* [1918] A.C. 563; *Nelson v Larholt* [1948] 1 K.B. 339. See Article 73; Cheques Act 1957 s.4 as amended.

[328] *Kooragang Investments Pty Ltd v Richardson & Wrench Ltd* [1982] A.C. 462; criticised, [1982] C.L.J. 36.

[329] *NIML Ltd v Man Financial Australia Ltd* (2006) 15 V.R. 156 (Vic CA).

[330] cf. Partnership Act 1890 s.7. As to ratification see Ch.2, section 3. See too para.8-097 below, indicating that the position may be different where it is a question of the rights of the principal, rather than his liabilities.

[331] See *John v Dodwell & Co* [1918] A.C. 563 at 569; *Rolled Steel Products (Holdings) Ltd v British Steel Corp* [1986] Ch. 246 at 298; *Guinness Plc v Saunders* [1990] 2 A.C. 663 at 702, Illustration 13. cf. *Trustee of the Property of F.C. Jones & Sons v Jones* [1997] Ch. 159 at 164. As to actions, both real and personal, to recover money or other assets transferred without authority or in bad faith, see Articles 88 and 116. As to equitable remedies in general against third parties, see Article 96, and

Illustrations

(1)　A, a stockbroker, employed B, a clerk, to whom he allowed a commission on **8-067** orders obtained by him and accepted by A. B was not authorised to accept orders on A's behalf. On three occasions C gave orders to B away from A's premises, which were passed on to A, and executed by him, A sending contract notes to C. C made payment in respect of the first two orders by cheques payable to A's order, and in respect of the third order by a cheques payable to B's order. The cheques were delivered to B, and passed on to A, who duly credited C. Subsequently, C gave orders to B, who did not transmit them to A, but made out bought notes on which he forged A's signature, and handed them to C. C gave cheques in payment to B, who misapplied them. It was held that there was no evidence that A had held out B as authorised to accept orders on his behalf, and that A was under no liability in respect of the orders subsequent to the first three.[332]

(2)　The master of a ship signs a bill of lading on behalf of the owner stating that goods of a particular mercantile quality have been received on board. The goods are of a different quality. The owner is not bound by the statement; for to ascertain such matters is outside the scope of the functions and capacities of a ship's master.[333]

(3)　The secretary of a company fraudulently, and without the knowledge of the directors, represented to A that if he took certain shares he would be appointed solicitor to the company, and subsequently that he had been so appointed. A, on the faith of the representations, applied for the shares, which were allotted to him. Held, that A was bound by the contract to take the shares, the representations being outside the scope of the secretary's authority.[334] So, where the secretary of a tramway company made a representation as to the financial relations of the company, and it was not shown that he was authorised to make the representation, it was held that the company was not bound, it not being part of the ordinary duties of such an official to make such representations on behalf of the company.[335]

(4)　Where an estate agent who is employed to procure a purchaser at a certain price enters into a contract of sale, the principal is not bound unless he in fact

---

esp. para.8-221.

[332] *Spooner v Browning* [1898] 1 Q.B. 528. As to course of dealing generally, see also para.8-014 and Article 72, Illustrations 7 and 21.

[333] *Cox, Patterson & Co v Bruce & Co* (1886) 18 Q.B.D. 147. The reasoning seems valid despite the fact that the case on which this decision was based, *Grant v Norway* (1851) 10 C.B.(N.S.) 665, which held that a master did not bind his owner if he signed for goods not on board, was reversed in England by s.4 of the Carriage of Goods by Sea Act 1992. The reasoning of that case had appeared obsolete for a long time; yet there was substantial authority which made it difficult for any tribunal but the House of Lords to establish this. The application of the decision could however be restricted to its facts, i.e. signature when goods not on board. See *The Nea Tyhi* [1982] 1 Lloyd's Rep. 606; *The Starsin* [2000] 1 Lloyd's Rep. 85 at 93–98 ("aberrant reasoning": point not considered on appeal [2003] UKHL 12; [2004] 1 A.C. 715).

[334] *Newlands v National Employers' Accident Association Ltd* (1885) 54 L.J.Q.B. 428.

[335] *Barnett, Hoares & Co v South London Tramways Co* (1887) 18 Q.B.D. 815; *Ruben v Great Fingall Consolidated* [1906] A.C. 439. The authority of a company secretary in administrative matters was, however, considerably enlarged by *Panorama Developments (Guildford) Ltd v Fidelis Furnishing Fabrics Ltd* [1971] 2 Q.B. 711, Illustration 30 to Article 72; and though these examples do not concern administration they may require reconsideration in view of what was said in that case as to changing practice.

authorised the agent to make the contract on his behalf, because it is not within the ordinary scope of such an agent's authority to enter into binding contracts on his principal's behalf.[336]

(5) An estate agent, not being authorised to do so, takes a deposit from a prospective purchaser of land in a transaction "subject to contract". The prospective vendor is not liable.[337]

(6) The manager of a tied public-house, who had authority to deal with particular persons only, bought spirits from a person with whom he had no authority to deal. Held, that the principal was not bound, it being usual for such managers to be restricted to particular persons from whom to purchase spirits.[338]

(7) A bank manager guaranteed the payment of a draft. It was not within the ordinary scope of a bank manager's authority to give such a guarantee, and the bank therefore was not liable on it unless he was expressly authorised to give it.[339]

(8) The local agent of an insurance company contracted on behalf of the company to grant a policy. Held, that it was not within the ordinary scope of the authority of such an agent to make such a contract (as opposed to issuing a cover note[340]), and that the company was not bound unless it could be shown that the agent had actual authority.[341] So an insurance company has been held not bound by the acceptance of a premium by its agent after the time for payment of the premium had expired.[342]

(9) An insurance broker, being authorised to effect an insurance, agreed with a company for a policy on certain terms. The policy was duly executed by the company and the broker was debited with the amount of the premium. The broker, having been paid the premium by his principal, told the company that the insurance was a mistake, and fraudulently cancelled without the principal's authority. The principal was entitled to enforce the contract against the company, it being no part of a broker's usual authority to cancel contracts made by him.[343]

(10) The "unit manager" of an insurance company, whose only authority is to transmit proposals for life assurance or loans on mortgage to higher officers of the company, purports to bind the company to guarantee a loan. The lender writes to the "general manager" of the company asking whether the "unit manager" is authorised to do this. There is no "general manager": the letter is answered by a "branch manager", who describes himself as such, and whose authority is similar to that of a unit manager. He purports to confirm the authority. He has neither actual nor apparent authority to do so and the company is not bound.[344]

See Article 30, Illustration 6.
[337] *Sorrell v Finch* [1977] A.C. 728. See Articles 92 and 111; below, para.9-026.
[338] *Daun v Simmins* (1879) 41 L.T. 783.
[339] *Re Southport & West Lancashire Banking Co* (1885) 1 T.L.R. 204.
[340] See, e.g. *Wilkinson v General Accident Fire and Life Assurance Corp Ltd* [1967] 2 Lloyd's Rep. 182; and see *Stockton v Mason* [1978] 2 Lloyd's Rep. 430 (broker) (a puzzling case: see [1979] J.B.L. 169).
[341] *Linford v Provincial, etc., Ins Co* (1864) 34 Beav. 291.
[342] *Acey v Fernie* (1840) 7 M. & W. 151. See Clarke, *Law of Insurance Contracts* (6th edn), para.8-2A1 onwards.
[343] *Xenos v Wickham* (1866) L.R. 2 H.L. 296.
[344] *British Bank of the Middle East v Sun Life Assurance Co of Canada (UK) Ltd* [1983] 2 Lloyd's Rep.

(11) The Chartering Manager and Vice-President (Transportation) of a company, authorised to negotiate the sale of a ship belonging to the company, purports to enter into a simultaneous agreement to take it back on charter, the charter containing unusual terms. The third party knows that the Vice-President has no authority to enter into such a charter without approval from higher in the company. The Vice-President falsely states that he has obtained such approval. The company is not bound.[345]

(12) A shipping agent is authorised to arrange for the shipment of goods and prepare the necessary documents, including those to be presented under a letter of credit. An employee prepares a draft, signs and indorses it in blank on behalf of the customer, and the money is paid to the agency firm. The authority to prepare the documents does not represent that the firm has authority to receive payment under the credit, and payment to the firm is invalid: the bank must pay again.[346]

(13) A committee of directors of a company agreed that the company would pay one of their number £5.2 million for his services in connection with a takeover bid being made by the company, and made the payment. The articles of association required any such contract to be made by the whole board, and not by a committee. The contract was void, and the money held recoverable in equity.[347]

Article 76

UNDISCLOSED PRINCIPAL: RIGHTS AND LIABILITIES

(1) An undisclosed principal may sue or be sued on a contract made on his behalf,   **8-068**
or in respect of money paid or received on his behalf, by his agent acting within the scope of his actual authority. Where a contract is involved, the agent on entering into it must have intended to act on the principal's behalf.[348]

(2) (Perhaps), an undisclosed principal may also be sued on any contract made on his behalf, or in respect of money received on his behalf, by his agent acting within the authority usually confided to an agent of that character, notwithstanding limitations put upon that authority as between principal and agent.[349]

---

9 (HL) (a harsh decision). See above, para.8-019.

[345] *Armagas Ltd v Mundogas SA (The Ocean Frost)* [1986] A.C. 717. But cf. *Egyptian International Foreign Trade Co v Soplex Wholesale Supplies Ltd* [1985] 2 Lloyd's Rep. 36, Illustration 11 to Article 72; cf. *First Energy (UK) Ltd v Hungarian International Bank Ltd* [1993] 2 Lloyd's Rep. 194, Illustration 12 to Article 72.

[346] *Cleveland Mfg. Co Ltd v Muslim Commercial Bank Ltd* [1981] 2 Lloyd's Rep. 646.

[347] *Guinness Plc v Saunders* [1990] 2 A.C. 663.

[348] *Siu Yin Kwan v Eastern Insurance Co Ltd* [1994] 2 A.C. 199 at 207 (Illustration 12), per Lord Lloyd of Berwick. See Comment; Illustrations 1, 2 and 3; *Thomson v Davenport* (1829) 9 B. & C. 78 at 90; *Sims v Bond* (1833) 5 B. & Ad. 389; *Browning v Provincial Insurance Co of Canada* (1873) L.R. 5 P.C. 263 at 272; *Moto Vespa SA v Mat (Britannia Express) Ltd* [1979] 1 Lloyd's Rep. 175. cf. *Restatement, Third*, § 6.03. As to what is an undisclosed principal in this context, see below, para.8-071. As to money paid, see *Duke of Norfolk v Worthy* (1808) 1 Camp. 337, Illustration 3 (action by principal); *Transvaal & Delagoa Bay Investment Co v Atkinson* [1944] 1 All E.R. 579 (liability of principal); Articles 92, 93 and 111. The doctrine is considered against the background of the unsatisfactory drafting of s.14(5) of the Sale of Goods Act 1979 in *Boyter v Thomson* [1995] 2 A.C. 628: see Brown (1996) 112 L.Q.R. 225.

[349] *Watteau v Fenwick* [1893] 1 Q.B. 346 at 348. See Comment; Illustrations 4, 5 and 6; cf. *Restatement, Third*, § 2.06.

(3) Where an agent enters into a contract, oral or written, without reference to agency, evidence is admissible to show who is the real principal, in order to charge the principal or entitle him to sue on the contract.[350]

(4) The terms of the contract may, expressly or impliedly, exclude the principal's right to sue and his liability to be sued. The contract itself, or the circumstances surrounding the contract, may show that the agent is the true and only principal.[351]

(5) So far as concerns deeds, bills of exchange, promissory notes and cheques, this Article must be read subject to Articles 77 and 78.[352]

Comment

8-069 **Rule (1): Undisclosed principal doctrine**   This is a statement of the common law doctrine of undisclosed principal. The leading modern formulation of the features of the doctrine is that of Lord Lloyd of Berwick in *Siu Yin Kwan v Eastern Insurance Co Ltd*[353]:

> "For present purposes the law can be summarised shortly. (1) An undisclosed principal may sue and be sued on a contract made by an agent on his behalf, acting within the scope of his actual authority. (2) In entering into the contract, the agent must intend to act on the principal's behalf. (3) The agent of an undisclosed principal may also sue and be sued on the contract. (4) Any defence which the third party may have against the agent is available against his principal. (5) The terms of the contract may, expressly or by implication, exclude the principal's right to sue, and his liability to be sued. The contract itself, or the circumstances surrounding the contract, may show that the agent is the true and only principal."

The proposition that a principal, someone of whose existence or connection with the transaction the third party was totally unaware, can in appropriate circumstances sue and be sued on a contract made by his agent may be surprising, but is well established. Its origin is said to lie in the right of the principal of a factor to intervene in the factor's bankruptcy, to claim his goods or the unpaid price of them; and later to sue in respect of the whole contract.[354] This somehow led to more generalised reasoning whereby such a principal was entitled to sue on his agent's contracts in general; and it became established that he was liable also. Such a conclusion is certainly difficult to accommodate within standard theories of contract, which emphasise, even though under objective criteria, the consent of the parties. It should be remembered however that the doctrine was formed before such theories had acquired prominence.[355] There are judicial dicta to the effect that the contract is that of the undisclosed principal, just as in cases of disclosed principal,[356] and some deci-

---

[350] See Comment; Illustrations 7 and 8.

[351] *Siu Yin Kwan v Eastern Insurance Co Ltd* [1994] 2 A.C. 199 at 207 (Illustration 12), per Lord Lloyd of Berwick.

[352] For the position as between agent and undisclosed principal, see above, para.6-082.

[353] *Siu Yin Kwan v Eastern Insurance Co Ltd* [1994] A.C. 199 at 207.

[354] Stoljar, pp.203–211; Goodhart and Hamson (1932) 4 C.L.J. 320. As to factors, see above, para.1-045.

[355] Müller-Freienfels (1953) 16 M.L.R. 299.

[356] *Keighley, Maxsted & Co v Durant* [1901] A.C. 240 at 261; *Said v Butt* [1920] 3 K.B. 497 at 500 (Illustration 11).

sions can only be justified on this reasoning.[357] But, subject to the intervention of the principal, it seems that the agent also can sue on such a contract and even recover the principal's loss by way of damages; and can be sued on it.[358] There are also special rules whereby a third party cannot be prevented by the intervention of the principal from exercising his rights against the agent[359] nor (normally) from using against the principal defences which he had against the agent.[360] These cast doubt on such dicta and decisions[361] and highlight an uneasy tension between two organising theories, that the contract is that of the agent and that the contract is that of the principal. It is difficult to deny that the undisclosed principal is really a third party intervening on a contract which he did not make, and this view has been accepted in the Court of Appeal.[362]

If it were treated as an exception to the rules of privity of contract, the doctrine would still be unusual, since the third party is not mentioned, nor indeed contemplated by one of the parties, and furthermore takes liabilities as well as rights. Another suggestion is that the basis of the doctrine is similar to that of assignment[363]: but there is no evidenced transfer, formal or informal, nor are the rights of the agent extinguished; and the principal receives liabilities as well as rights. It can be said further that the undisclosed principal takes burdens because he receives benefits: but this does not explain why he receives benefits. Sometimes it is argued that the agent is trustee for the undisclosed principal, but it has been held in the context of the res judicata doctrine that, as regards the third party, the agent is not to be so regarded,[364] and in any case the principal who intervenes has control over litigation in a way that a trust beneficiary would not.[365] Nevertheless, some aspects of the relation between principal and agent are undoubtedly to be accounted for, here as elsewhere, on the basis of trust, or at least of analogous fiduciary duties.[366] The doctrine is probably best explained simply as one of commercial convenience, and its justice is disputable.[367] "It has often been doubted" said Blackburn J "whether it was originally right so to hold: but doubts of this kind come now too late".[368] The Privy Council has in recent years rejected the analogy of

---

[357] e.g. *Cooke & Sons v Eshelby* (1887) 12 App.Cas. 271, Illustration 7 to Article 81; below, para.8-112.

[358] See below, para.9-012; as to measure of damages, see below, para.9-013.

[359] *O'Herlihy v Hedges* (1803) 1 Sch. & Lef. 123 (specific performance in favour of a principal may be refused unless the agent will enter into or continue personal covenants with third party); *Montgomerie v United Kingdom Mutual Steamship Assn* [1891] 1 Q.B. 370 at 372; *Mooney v Williams* (1906) 3 C.L.R. 1 at 8. See below, paras 8-098 and 9-012.

[360] *Siu Yin Kwan v Eastern Insurance Co Ltd* [1994] 2 A.C. 199 at 207 (Illustration 12); Article 79.

[361] See Comments to Articles 80 and 81.

[362] *Welsh Development Agency v Export Finance Co Ltd* [1992] B.C.L.C. 148.

[363] Goodhart and Hamson (1932) 4 C.L.J. 320.

[364] *Pople v Evans* [1969] 2 Ch. 255; and see *Allen v F. O'Hearn & Co* [1937] A.C. 213.

[365] See below, para.9-012.

[366] Higgins (1965) 28 M.L.R. 167; and see Comment to Article 43.

[367] See Pollock (1887) 3 L.Q.R. 358; (1896) 12 L.Q.R. 204; (1898) 14 L.Q.R. 2; Ames (1909) 18 Yale L.J. 443; Lewis (1909) 9 Col.L.Rev. 116; Mechem (1910) 23 HarvL.Rev. 513; Seavey (1920) 29 Yale L.J. 859; Montrose (1938) 16 Can.B.Rev. 770–771; Weinrib (1975) 21 McGill L.J. 298; Barak (1976) 2 Tel Aviv U. Studies in Law 45; Geva (1979) 25 McGill L.J. 32; Stoljar, pp.228–233; Rochvarg (1989) 34 McGill L.J. 286; Barnett (1987) 75 Calif. L.Rev. 1969; Tan Cheng Han (2004) 120 L.Q.R. 480.

[368] *Armstrong v Stokes* (1872) L.R. 7 Q.B. 598 at 604; *VTB Capital Plc v Nutritek International Corp* [2013] UKSC 5; [2013] 2 W.L.R. 398 at [141].

assignment.[369] This throws the law back on the tensions between the two approaches described above—that the contract is that of the principal, or that the principal intervenes on the agent's contract. Reasoning based on the notion, at first glance straightforward, that the contract is that of the principal should however be regarded with caution.

It has been suggested in a leading judgment on apparent authority that the rule "can be rationalised as avoiding circuity of action".[370] It is true that in continental systems similar results can sometimes be achieved by circuitous routes: the principal may sue as assignee of the agent's rights, or directly, and the third party may exercise the agent's right of indemnity against the principal.[371] It is said indeed that the simplicity of the common law doctrine is admired by some continental jurists.[372] But the principal's right to sue is perhaps more easily justified on this basis than his liability to be sued.[373] Indeed, the generalisation of what was apparently in origin a limited right of intervention into an arm of general agency principle causes serious problems, many of which are in England at least still unsolved.[374]

8-070   **Authority and ratification**   The agent must have actual authority to act so as to bind and entitle his principal,[375] though this may of course be express or implied. It has been held that the doctrine of ratification does not apply to undisclosed principals.[376] The reason usually given is that if it did, one person could too easily intervene on the contracts of another. This is certainly true where the person whose acts another seeks to ratify initially had no authority at all. Indeed, in such a case there would be no one who could be called an undisclosed principal, and the proposition would simply mean that a person cannot make himself an undisclosed principal by ratifying the act of another, which is doubtless correct. It is not clear however that such reasoning is so appropriate where the agent already has some authority, but exceeds it. It is arguable that in such a situation a principal who chooses to ratify should be liable; and that he should also be able to sue, the third party being protected by the various safeguards against unfair operation of the doctrine of ratification.[377] Of these, the case for the liability of the principal, which can hurt no one but the principal, is obviously the stronger. The leading case,[378]

[369] *Siu Yin Kwan v Eastern Insurance Co Ltd* [1994] 2 A.C. 199, Illustration 12.
[370] *Freeman & Lockyer v Buckhurst Park Properties (Mangal) Ltd* [1964] 2 Q.B. 480 at 503, per Diplock LJ. cf. Ames, above; Higgins, above.
[371] Müller-Freienfels (1955) 18 M.L.R. 33: Schmitthoff, 1970 I *Hague Recueil des Cours* 115 at 114–145. cf. UNIDROIT Principles, art.2.2.4; criticised by Krebs [2009] L.M.C.L.Q. 57.
[372] Müller-Freienfels (1953) 16 M.L.R. 299.
[373] Zweigert and Kötz, *Introduction to Comparative Law* (tr. Weir) (3rd edn), p.439 onwards; cf. Ames (1909) 18 Yale L.J. 443 at 449; Geva (1975) 25 McGill L.J. 32.
[374] e.g. as to capacity, see below, para.8-074; in connection with indirect representation, para.8-071; connection with unidentified principal, para.8-073; exclusion of the doctrine, para.8-079 onwards; and in connection with dispositions of property, see Article 89.
[375] See further below, para.8-071.
[376] *Keighley, Maxsted & Co v Durant* [1901] A.C. 240, Illustration 3 to Article 15. Schmitthoff calls this a "remarkable restriction": 1970 I *Hague Recueil des Cours* at p.148. See also Seavey (1954) 21 U.Chi.L.Rev. 248; Rochvarg (1989) 34 McGill L.J. 286. As to ratification in general, see Ch.2, section 3.
[377] Article 19.
[378] *Keighley, Maxsted & Co v Durant* above: see above, para.2-063.

however, which is a decision of the House of Lords, concerns just this situation and holds the principal not liable.[379]

Undisclosed principal doctrine compared with indirect representation　It is **8-071** necessary to keep the concept of the undisclosed principal separate from that of indirect representation. The latter concept has already been outlined.[380] It is not uncommon for civil law trained comparative lawyers to assume that the concept of the undisclosed principal is a version of indirect representation.[381] For the undisclosed principal doctrine to operate the principal must have authorised the agent to bring him into contractual privity with the third party. So long as that basic requirement is met, it does not matter whose ends are being pursued by concealing the existence of the principal from the third party. Sometimes, it is the principal who wishes to conceal that he is a party to the contract, perhaps because he does not wish it to be known that he has entered the market.[382] Otherwise, it might be the agent who does not tell the third party who is his principal because he does not wish the third party on the next transaction to bypass him and go direct to the principal; and the principal either acquiesces in this or makes no inquiry as to the agent's practice.[383] These examples are far from exhaustive. Once the conferral of authority is established, the principal can both sue and be sued on any resulting contract. On this basis, the liability of the undisclosed principal is one that is voluntarily assumed, as in agency generally.[384] Subject to the doubtful deployment of the concept of usual authority in *Watteau v Fenwick*,[385] discussed below, an undisclosed principal cannot be liable for the unauthorised acts of the agent, including by a wrongful delegation by the agent to another.[386] Equally, the mere fact that a person "operates" a company does not make him undisclosed principal to its transactions.[387]

In contrast, under the concept of indirect representation, although the intermediary works on an "agency" basis in respect to the principal, viz. undertakes only to use his best endeavours, does not act as an independent merchant or supplier of services but takes a commission on the transaction arranged, and so forth,[388] he nonetheless has no authority to bring his principal into contractual privity with the

---

[379] Ratification by an undisclosed principal is envisaged by the wording of *Restatement, Third*, Agency: § 4.01 and reporter's note a.

[380] See above, paras 1-021 and 1-022.

[381] See e.g. Hamel, *Le Contrat de Commission* (Paris, 1949), pp.310–327.

[382] This is particularly the case with land transactions. As to the United States, see Hynes and Loewenstein, *Agency, Partnership and the LLC* (7th edn, Charlottesville, Va.) p.361.

[383] There may even be cases where the agent acts contrary to instructions in not disclosing his principal's name: *Ex p. Dixon, re Henley* (1876) 4 Ch. D. 133. Swedish law differentiates between cases where the principal is undisclosed in his own interest and cases where he is undisclosed in the interests of the agent. In the former case it seems that he will be liable and entitled; in the latter, entitled but not liable: Grönfors [1962] Scandinavian Studies in Law 97 at 100, 122–123.

[384] For arguments that agency liability can be imposed, see above, paras 1-025 and 1-026.

[385] [1893] 1 Q.B. 346, discussed below, para.8-077.

[386] See *Hutton v Bulloch* (1874) L.R. 9 Q.B. 572; *New Zealand and Australian Land Co v Watson* (1881) 7 Q.B.D. 374; *Kaltenbach, Fischer & Co v Lewis and Peat* (1885) 10 App.Cas. 617, Illustration 9 to Article 81; Goodhart and Hamson (1932) 4 C.L.J. 320 at 330–335. See also *The Astyanax* [1985] 2 Lloyd's Rep. 109.

[387] See *Yukong Line Ltd v Rendsburg Investments Corp (The Rialto) (No.2)* [1998] 1 W.L.R. 294; and see *Atlas Maritime Co SA v Avalon Maritime Ltd (The Coral Rose) (No.1)* [1991] 1 Lloyd's Rep. 563; *Peterson Farms Inc v C&M Farming Ltd* [2004] EWHC 121 (Comm); [2004] 1 Lloyd's Rep. 603 at [62]; *Magellan Spirit ApS v Vitol SA* [2016] EWHC 454 (Comm) at [27], [28].

[388] See above, paras 1-020 and 1-021.

third party and he does not do so. Under European legal systems, despite the lack of privity, the principal is in certain circumstances, mainly upon the insolvency of the intermediary, entitled to intervene to claim the price of goods or services directly from the third party. In some jurisdictions there is a (more controversial) reciprocal right given the third party against the principal.[389] These entitlements are, however, introduced ab extra, and do not depend, as does the common law doctrine, on normal principles of authority.

Some dicta suggest that a category of indirect representation does not exist at all in English law: either there is true agency or a contract (usually of sale) between principals.[390] However, other dicta, including the formidable authority of Lord Blackburn,[391] have been willing to recognise the notion of indirect representation.[392] Lord Blackburn was also clear that where such an analysis was not appropriate, the undisclosed principal doctrine might still operate where its requirements were met.[393] The now obsolete cases on foreign principals[394] also operated on a concept of indirect representation; they are based on the idea that a foreign principal does not authorise his English agent to bring himself into contractual privity with English third parties (and the converse). They recognise clearly, as did Lord Blackburn,[395] that a person acting in such a way does not rank as an undisclosed principal. But the absence of contractual privity in such circumstances precludes the principal from intervening directly on the contracts made by the intermediary or "commissionnaire".

8-072   Intention of the agent   Although the intention of one party not communicated to the other is not usually relevant to the legal effect of a transaction, it is plain that if the agent has, as is required for the doctrine to operate, actual authority, the agent's subjective intention will frequently be relevant to the question whether in this particular situation he has acted for the principal, or for some other principal, or for himself.[396] In particular, where the agent's instructions do not relate to a unique transaction, or the agent has not undertaken to act exclusively for the principal (when an estoppel may run in favour of the principal), it may not be possible, without the agent's personal testimony, to tell whether he intended to exercise his mandate for the principal in relation to the transaction in dispute. The other possibilities are that he was intending to act for himself or for some other principal who has given authority under similar instructions. Whether the agent so intended is a

[389] Kortmann and Kortmann, in *Agency Law in Commercial Practice* (Busch, Macgregor and Watts (eds)), Ch.6. See also PECL, art.3.3-1(b).

[390] e.g. *Anglo-African Shipping Co of New York Ltd v J. Mortner Ltd* [1962] 1 Lloyd's Rep. 610, per Diplock LJ; *Scrimshire v Alderton* (1743) 2 Str. 1182.

[391] *Armstrong v Stokes* (1872) L.R. 7 Q.B. 598, Illustration 7 to Article 80; also *Elbinger Actiengesells-chaft v Claye* (1873) L.R. 8 Q.B. 313.

[392] See *Robinson v Mollett* (1875) L.R. 7 H.L. 802 at 809–810 (but the majority regarded the arrangement as inconsistent with the nature of agency: see Article 31, Illustration 8); *Ireland v Livingston* (1872) L.R. 5 H.L. 395.

[393] *Armstrong v Stokes*, above, at 605–606. But cf. *Maspons y Hermano v Mildred, Goyeneche & Co* (1882) 9 Q.B.D. 530; affd on other grounds (1883) 8 App.Cas. 874 which could be said to apply ordinary agency analysis to such a situation. See Reynolds [1983] C.L.P. 119 at 128–133.

[394] See below, para.9-020.

[395] See *Armstrong v Stokes*, above, at 605–606.

[396] *Siu Yin Kwan v Eastern Insurance Co Ltd* [1994] 2 A.C. 199 at 207 (Illustration 12); *Rolls Royce Power Engineering Plc v Ricardo Consulting Engineers Ltd* [2003] EWHC 2871 (TCC); [2004] 2 All E.R. (Comm) 129; *Gray v Smith* [2013] EWHC 4136 (Comm); [2014] 2 All E.R. (Comm) 359 at [34]. cf. *Restatement, Third*, § 6.03, Comment *d*.

matter of evidence.[397] There are recent dicta doubting this position and suggesting that objective evidence is always required.[398] It might be accepted that objective evidence of the *existence* of an undisclosed principal might be necessary, but it ought not to be necessary that in addition there be objective evidence, contemporary or otherwise, that there has been an *exercise* of the authority.[399] Similar issues arise where it is an unidentified principal that is at issue, rather than an undisclosed principal.[400] If it were necessary in such cases that there be objective evidence of the party for whom the agent was acting in the particular transaction, it would follow that in the absence of such evidence there would be no contract at all. Naturally, where objective evidence is available (such as communications between principal and agent, business records, evidence of past practice) it is likely to be preferred over contradictory personal testimony from the agent at trial. In the last resort, however, the question will turn on whether the trier of fact believes the agent when he or she asserts that in this particular instance he was acting for the principal or on his own account or for a different principal.

Degree of knowledge of the third party Many decisions on the undisclosed principal doctrine could be analysed as, or as very close to, cases of disclosed but unidentified principals, and it is useful to bear this in mind when they are considered. The obvious situation for the operation of the doctrine is that where the third party does not know of the involvement of any principal. Many cases suggest or imply that a third party dealing with an apparent principal has no duty of inquiry as to whether that person has anyone behind him[401]; that he need not establish that he had no knowledge of a principal's existence[402]; and that constructive notice of it is not to be attributed to him.[403] But there are several decisions which go further and apply the undisclosed principal doctrine to situations where the third party is actually aware that the agent sometimes deals for himself and sometimes on behalf of others but does not know which is true on this occasion[404]; to situations where the third party is aware of the existence (possibly even the name) and involvement of the principal, but is not clear as to his exact relationship with the agent,[405] and even to situations where he is aware that the principal is using the intermediary's services on an agency basis and that the principal does not wish to

8-073

---

[397] See above, para.2-067. For examples of the sort of evidence that may be used, see *National Oilwell (UK) Ltd v Davy Offshore Ltd* [1993] 2 Lloyd's Rep. 582 at 596–597.

[398] See *Magellan Spirit ApS v Vitol SA* [2016] EWHC 454 (Comm) at [17] and [19], per Leggatt J.

[399] For example, in the leading case of *Keighley Maxsted & Co v Durant* [1901] A.C. 240 the agent certainly had authority, and had he stayed within it there would surely (in the absence of other indications) have been no need to communicate to the principal or otherwise manifest an intention that he intended to exercise it.

[400] See *National Oilwell (UK) Ltd v Davy Offshore Ltd* [1993] 2 Lloyd's Rep. 582 at 597; above, para.2-067. See also *A. Tomlinson (Hauliers) Ltd v Hepburn* [1966] A.C. 451; and *Lai Wo Heung v Cheung Kong Fur Pty Co Ltd* [2004] 1 H.K.L.R.D. 959 (subjective intention of agent important where principal unidentified).

[401] *Fish v Kempton* (1849) 7 C.B. 687; *Ex p. Dixon, re Henley* (1876) 4 Ch.D. 133; *Gothard v Davey* [2010] FCA 1163 at [236].

[402] *Borries v Imperial Ottoman Bank* (1873) L.R. 9 C.P. 38. See also *Semenza v Brinsley* (1865) 18 C.B. (N.S.) 467; *Knight v Matson & Co* (1902) 22 N.Z.L.R. 293.

[403] *Greer v Downs Supply Co* [1927] 2 K.B. 28.

[404] *Baring v Corrie* (1818) 2 B. & A. 137; *Cooke & Sons v Eshelby* (1887) 12 App.Cas. 271, Illustration 7 to Article 81; and perhaps *Armstrong v Stokes* (1872) L.R. 7 Q.B. 598, Illustration 7 to Article 80.

[405] *Addison v Gandassequi* (1812) 4 Taunt. 574; *Paterson v Gandasequi* (1812) 15 East 62; *Teheran-Europe Co Ltd v S.T. Belton (Tractors) Ltd* [1986] 2 Q.B. 545 (where the Court of Appeal was

become a party to the agent's contract.[406] In all these cases the first requisite would of course be that the agent was liable as a contracting party: otherwise the transaction would lack certainty.[407] It is possible that the first two situations would really be better analysed as involving disclosed but unidentified principals, if a rule that the agent of such a principal was prima facie personally liable could be adopted, for they seem to be brought within the undisclosed principal doctrine by the desire to hold the agent liable and entitled as well as the principal, or otherwise to use reasoning applicable to undisclosed rather than fully disclosed principals.[408] Whether the third situation invokes the undisclosed principal rules has already been discussed.[409] Here again there are significant uncertainties as to the application of the doctrine.

8-074   Capacity of agent   Although the doctrine is here explained on the general basis that the principal intervenes on the agent's contract, this need not mean that the agent who acts for an undisclosed principal must, contrary to the normal rule for agents,[410] have capacity. There are sufficient inelegancies in the doctrine for it to be appropriate to examine each situation on its merits rather than by reference to formulae. If the agent's contract is unenforceable for lack of capacity, it is possible that the principal may nevertheless be able to intervene, and is liable, although the agent could not sue or be sued.[411]

8-075   Contract in writing   The question whether an undisclosed principal can intervene on a contract signed only by his agent and the third party is undetermined. He certainly was able to do so under s.40 of the Law of Property Act 1925, which re-enacting the Statute of Frauds 1677 required a note or memorandum of the contract. But s.2 of the Law of Property (Miscellaneous Provisions) Act 1989 requires that the contract actually be in writing and signed by or on behalf of the parties. The matter is discussed elsewhere.[412]

8-076   Merger and election   It seems to have been at least in part unease about the justifiability of the doctrine which led to the application of rules as to merger and election, whereby the third party may be able to sue principal or agent, but not both.[413] These are separately discussed under Article 82. They operate in one direction only: the third party cannot elect as to by whom he is sued; though he may be

---

undecided whether the case was one of unidentified or of undisclosed principal); and perhaps *Pyxis Special Shipping Co Ltd v Dritsis & Kaglis Bros Ltd (The Scaplake)* [1978] 2 Lloyd's Rep. 380.

[406]   *Maspons y Hermano v Mildred, Goyeneche & Co* (1882) 9 Q.B.D. 530; affd on other grounds (1883) 8 App.Cas. 874. *Browning v Provincial Insurance Co of Canada* (1873) L.R. 5 P.C. 263 also seems to concern such a person. See Busch, *Indirect Representation in European Contract Law* (2005), pp.171–172.

[407]   See *Public Trustee v Taylor* [1978] V.R. 289 ("for himself or as agent for an undisclosed principal"— agent personally liable so transaction valid).

[408]   See below, para.9-016.

[409]   See above, para.8-071.

[410]   Article 5.

[411]   See Weinrib (1975) 21 McGill L.J. 298, criticising *Commonwealth Trust Co v De Witt* (1973) 40 D.L.R. (3d) 113, in which the fact that it acted for an undisclosed principal was held actually to confer capacity on a corporate agent. The case is also criticised in (1976) 40 Sask.L.Rev. 291. In *Danziger v Thompson* [1944] K.B. 654, Illustration 8, specific performance was decreed against an undisclosed principal whose agent was a minor: but the facts and decision are not clear, and the contract was probably one of those binding minors.

[412]   See Comment to Article 71.

[413]   e.g. *Kendall v Hamilton* (1879) 4 App.Cas. 504 at 544.

able to insist on exercising rights against the agent despite the principal's intervention,[414] and, as explained below, there are cases where the principal may not be permitted to intervene at all.[415]

Rule (2): Watteau v Fenwick   This Rule represents the proposition to be derived **8-077** from a Divisional Court case of 1893 which has achieved a surprising prominence. The interest that it has generated among commentators, and the fact that its result is regarded as acceptable doctrine in the United States,[416] justify its continued statement here. Its correctness is however most doubtful.

In *Watteau v Fenwick*[417] the owner of a hotel sold his business to a firm of brewers, who retained him as their manager. The licence was taken out in his name and his name was painted over the door. It was agreed that he should buy all supplies other than bottled ales and mineral waters from the brewers. In breach of this stipulation he bought cigars on credit from the plaintiffs, and the brewers were held liable on this contract. The case cannot be explained on the basis of apparent authority, since the principal was undisclosed,[418] and there was no actual authority. It was in fact based on a wider principle. Wills J said[419]:

> "Once it is established that the defendant was the real principal, the ordinary doctrine as to principal and agent applies—that the principal is liable for all the acts of the agent which are within the authority usually confided to an agent of that character, notwithstanding limitations, as between the principal and the agent, put upon that authority. It is said that it is only so where there has been a holding out of authority—which cannot be said where the person supplying the goods knew nothing of the existence of a principal. But I do not think so. Otherwise in every case of undisclosed principal, or at least in every case where the fact of there being a principal was undisclosed, the secret limitation of authority would prevail and defeat the action of the person dealing with the agent and then discovering that he was an agent and had a principal."

This proposition, which can be regarded as suggesting a special form of usual authority,[420] is however extremely dubious. It was supported by two arguments: an analogy with the law of partnership, and an earlier case in the Queen's Bench, *Edmunds v Bushell and Jones*.[421] The analogy with the law of partnership has long since been shown to be wrong.[422] *Edmunds v Bushell and Jones* is a case where the facts are not clear[423] and there may have been apparent authority: in any case the

---

[414] See *O'Herlihy v Hedges*, above, para.8-069; *Finmoon Ltd v Baltic Reefers Management Ltd* [2012] EWHC 920 (Comm); [2012] 2 Lloyd's Rep. 388 at [76] (undisclosed principal entitled to join arbitration action).

[415] See below, para.8-079.

[416] See below, text to fn.436.

[417] [1893] 1 Q.B. 346, Illustration 5; criticised (1893) 9 L.Q.R. 111; (1893) 7 HarvL.Rev. 49; (1893) 37 S.J. 280; Ewart, *Estoppel* (1900), p.246 onwards.

[418] Though Goodhart and Hamson seek so to explain it: see (1932) 4 C.L.J. 320 at 336, but cf. Wright (1935) 13 Can.B.R. 116 at 120; Montrose (1939) 17 Can.B.R. 693 at 696; Powell, pp.75–76.

[419] At 348–349.

[420] See Comment to Article 22.

[421] (1865) L.R. 1 Q.B. 97, Illustration 4.

[422] See Lindley and Banks, *Partnership* (19th edn), para.12-11; Pollock (1893) 9 L.Q.R. 111; Montrose (1939) 17 Can.B.R. 693 at 699 onwards (but as to some of the points made, see Thomas (1971) Vic.U. of Wellington L.R. 1); Powell, pp.76–77; *Construction Engineering (Aust.) Pty Ltd v Hexyl Pty Ltd* (1985) 155 C.L.R. 541.

[423] See Montrose (1939) 17 Can.B.R. 693 at pp.697–699; (1893) 37 S.J. 280.

dicta in the short judgments cast doubt on the reasoning employed. Thus Shee J said[424]:

"The natural inference when a person allows an agent to carry on a particular business as an ostensible principal, is that he clothes him with every authority incidental to a principal in the business."

But this involves confusion: a principal has no authority and deals on his own account.[425]

The case was followed, and indeed preferred to other authority which might appear contrary,[426] by the Divisional Court in a case subsequently reversed on other grounds,[427] and it has been distinguished.[428] The supposed doctrine of *Watteau v Fenwick*[429] is therefore tentatively reproduced here. But the Supreme Court of Ontario[430] and the Court of Appeal of British Columbia[431] have refused to follow it; and doubt has been cast on it in the High Court of Australia[432] and in England.[433] It may be that a careful study of the facts would enable a conclusion that the case was really one of unidentified principal. It is submitted that it is in fact inconsistent with the basic principles of agency law as subsequently established.[434] If the doctrine is adopted, therefore, this should only be done on the basis of a conscious advance on the previous accepted theories of agency, made for the purpose of extending liability.[435]

Restatement, Second regarded this as an example of "inherent agency power": that is to say, as a rule not justifiable on orthodox linking theory, but creating a satisfactory result.[436] In *Restatement, Third* the notion of "inherent agency power" is eliminated, but a rule similar to the effect of *Watteau v Fenwick* is retained under the heading of "Estoppel of Undisclosed Principal". Article 2.06 reads:

"An undisclosed principal may not rely on instructions given to an agent that qualify or reduce the agent's authority to less than the authority a third party would reasonably believe the agent to have under the same circumstances if the principal had been disclosed."

The Comment states that:

"Liability will result only when a third party deals with an agent but has no notice that

---

[424] At 100.
[425] cf. Ewart, *Estoppel* (1900), Ch.XVII.
[426] *Daun v Simmins* (1879) 41 L.T. 783.
[427] *Kinahan & Co v Parry* [1910] 2 K.B. 389; reversed [1911] 1 K.B. 459, Illustration 6.
[428] See *Johnston v Reading* (1893) 9 T.L.R. 200; *Lloyd's Bank Ltd v Swiss Bankverein* (1912) 107 L.T. 309 (affd 108 L.T. 143); *Jerome v Bentley* [1952] 2 All E.R. 114.
[429] [1893] 1 Q.B. 346.
[430] *McLaughlin v Gentles* (1919) 51 D.L.R. 383; see also *Becherer v Asher* (1896) 23 Ont.App. 202.
[431] *Sign-o-Lite Plastics Ltd v Metropolitan Life Insurance Co* (1990) 73 D.L.R. (4th) 541.
[432] *International Paper Co v Spicer* (1906) 4 C.L.R. 739 at 763. The Privy Council made no attempt to use such reasoning in the earlier case of *Miles v McIlwraith* (1883) 8 App.Cas. 120.
[433] See *The Rhodian River* [1984] 1 Lloyd's Rep. 373. See also *Re Att.-Gen.'s Reference (No.1 of 1985)* [1986] Q.B. 491 at 506.
[434] See Comment to Article 22; Hornby [1961] C.L.J. 239. In *A.L. Underwood Ltd v Bank of Liverpool* [1924] 1 K.B. 775 at 792, Scrutton LJ said: "Just as you cannot ratify the act of an agent who did not profess to act for you ... so in my view you cannot rely on the apparent authority of an agent who did not profess in dealing with you to act as agent". See also above, para.1-026.
[435] Montrose (1939) 17 Can.B.R. 693; Bester (1972) 89 S.A.L.J. 49.
[436] § 8A: "the power of an agent which is derived not from authority, apparent authority or estoppel, but solely from the agency relation, and exists for the protection of persons harmed by or dealing with a servant or other agent". See also above, para.3-005.

the agent represents the interests of another and when the third party would not have reason to inquire into the scope of the agent's authority if the third party knew the agent acted on behalf of a principal."

In justifying the rule, the injustice of allowing a principal who has chosen to deal through an agent but to remain undisclosed to have the benefit of restrictions on an agent's authority is stressed, and also the fact that the third party would not think to inquire. Although the UNIDROIT Principles in general abolish the doctrine of the undisclosed principal altogether, an exception is puzzlingly retained for cases where the owner of a business sells the business but continues as manager while appearing as owner and enters into a contract which would not be queried were he still the owner.[437] Some protection for third parties in such situations may well be justified; and indeed for any case where a person disposes of assets to which his creditors might expect recourse. But it is not easy to see why this should be obtained by applying rules of agency to a person who has indeed changed the capacity in which he acts to that of agent, yet as such has neither actual nor apparent authority. If relief is to be given under the law of contract, it should rather be under the law of mistake as to the person.[438]

Although such an extension of liability such as that which could be taken to follow from *Watteau v Fenwick* might on the face of it appear progressive, it is not easy to justify a rule of liability on such a loose basis. Contemporary decisions of the House of Lords[439] and Privy Council,[440] while not adverting expressly to the point, are not consistent with any trend to extend liability beyond situations where authority exists or appears to exist. In a fairly recent case Bingham J said that the argument advanced for the unsuccessful defendant in *Watteau v Fenwick* seemed to him in principle correct.[441] It is submitted that the supposed doctrine is too vague to be satisfactorily employed.[442] It is sometimes suggested that the actual decision in *Watteau v Fenwick* can be explained on the basis of apparent ownership[443]: but this would be an extension of that doctrine, which only applies to dispositions of property and perhaps to contracts to dispose of property, and which requires not only that the owner of property must have given another possession of the property, but also done something more, so as to raise an estoppel against him.[444] Had execution been sought against the property, that doctrine might conceivably have applied: but it would not (again unless the case indicates an extension of the doctrine) make the brewer liable for the money.[445] Other explanations of the decision, e.g. that the

---

[437] Article 2.2.4(2): "However, where such an agent, when contracting with the third party on behalf of a business, represents itself to be the owner of that business the third party, upon discovery of the real owner of the business, may also exercise against the owner the rights it has against the agent".

[438] cf. *Lake v Simmons* [1927] A.C. 487.

[439] *Moorgate Mercantile Co Ltd v Twitchings* [1977] A.C. 890, Illustration 7 to Article 84; *British Bank of the Middle East v Sun Life Assurance Co of Canada (UK) Ltd* [1983] 2 Lloyd's Rep. 9, Illustration 10 to Article 77.

[440] *Kooragang Investments Pty Ltd v Richardson & Wrench Ltd* [1982] A.C. 462, Illustration 4 to Article 74.

[441] *Rhodian River Shipping Co SA v Holla Maritime Corp (The Rhodian River)* [1984] 1 Lloyd's Rep. 373 at 379.

[442] See also Comment to Article 22.

[443] Hornby [1961] C.L.J. 239; Conant (1968) 47 Neb.L.Rev. 678; Mechem, *Outlines of Agency* (4th edn), §§ 173–176. This receives some support from the cases dealing with set-off against the agent: see Article 81.

[444] Article 84.

[445] Ewart, *Estoppel* (1900), p.247.

brewer had received and used the goods and was liable on that basis only,[446] or that the owners were estopped from establishing that they were a separate entity from the person with whom the supplier did business,[447] are possible, should they be thought necessary.

It does not appear that the supposed doctrine of this case enables the principal to sue, any more than does that of apparent authority: and the principal being undisclosed, there can be no ratification.[448]

8-078   **Rule (3): Contract in writing: evidence to show who is the real principal**   In *Humble v Hunter*[449] the argument was accepted that where the contract was in writing, the intervention of the undisclosed principal might be prevented under the parol evidence rule, as being inconsistent with the written contract.[450] This was contrary to the rationale of the cases on the Statute of Frauds, referred to above, which is that where the effect of the principal's intervention is to add a contracting party, not to exclude one, the writing is adequate.[451] Though the case has been followed,[452] it has more often been distinguished,[453] and it has also been judicially questioned.[454] It is obvious that if such a view was readily taken, the intervention of an undisclosed principal would be almost impossible. It is therefore submitted that the undisclosed principal can only be excluded from intervening under the proposition stated in Rule (4) of this Article, and that evidence of such a principal will be admitted unless the exclusion of such a principal is expressed or implied by the terms of the contract, written or unwritten, as explained below.[455] Indeed the dicta of Lord Denman CJ

---

[446] Ferson (1951) 4 Vand.L.Rev. 260 at 280.

[447] Tettenborn [1998] C.L.J. 274. Such reasoning would be similar to that in *Gurtner v Beaton* [1993] 2 Lloyd's Rep. 369, Illustration 5 to Article 72, and *Lease Management Services v Purnell Secretarial Services* [1994] C.C.L.R. 127. See the discussion of other estoppels, above, para.8-028.

[448] See above, para.8-070.

[449] (1848) 12 Q.B. 310, Illustration 7.

[450] But compare the arguments of counsel with the judgment given. However, such was the interpretation put on the case in *Formby Brothers v Formby* (1910) 102 L.T. 116. The argument had been rejected in *Wilson v Hart* (1817) 1 Moo.C.P. 45.

[451] See above, para.8-075; Comment to Article 71.

[452] *Formby Brothers v Formby* (1910) 102 L.T. 116 ("proprietor"), where the court would have followed *Humble v Hunter* but was prevented by the fact that the matter had not been raised in the lower court (and see on this case Stoljar, p.223, fn.25); *Rederiaktiebolaget Argonaut v Hani* [1918] 2 K.B. 247 ("as charterer") (but see Lord Shaw in *Drughorn v Rederiaktiebolaget Transatlantic* [1919] A.C. 203); *Fawcett v Star Car Sales Ltd* [1960] N.Z.L.R. 406 at 420–425.

[453] *Killick & Co v Price & Co & Lingfield SS Co Ltd* (1896) 12 T.L.R. 263; *Drughorn Ltd v Rederiaktiebolaget Transatlantic* [1919] A.C. 203 ("charterer"); *Danziger v Thompson* [1944] K.B. 654, Illustration 8 ("tenant"); *Epps v Rothnie* [1945] K.B. 562 ("landlord"); *O/Y Wasa SS Co & N.V Stoomschip Hannah v Newspaper Pulp & Wood Export* (1949) 82 Ll.L.Rep. 936 ("disponent owner") (where there is a full review of the authorities); *Murphy v Rae* [1967] N.Z.L.R. 103 ("vendor"); *The Astyanax* [1985] 2 Lloyd's Rep. 109 ("disponent owner"; held to act personally); *White v Baycorp Advantage Business Information Services Ltd* (2006) 200 F.L.R. 125 at [83] (plaintiff claimed that defendant credit reference bureau incorrectly listed it as a defaulting debtor in relation to certain creditors; defendant countered that named creditors were undisclosed principals of parties with whom plaintiff had contracted).

[454] *Killick & Co v Price & Lingfield SS Co Ltd*, above, at 264 (but see *Formby Brothers v Formby*, above); *Drughorn Ltd v Rederiaktiebolaget Transatlantic*, above, at 209; *Epps v Rothnie*, above, at 565; *Diamond Stud Ltd v New Zealand Bloodstock Finance Ltd* [2010] NZCA 423 (para.8-078 expressly approved).

[455] *Finzel, Berry & Co v Eastcheap Dried Fruit Co* [1962] 1 Lloyd's Rep. 370 at 375; *Murphy v Rae* [1967] N.Z.L.R. 103; *Teheran-Europe Co Ltd v S.T. Belton (Tractors) Ltd* [1968] 2 Q.B. 545 at 552;

in *Humble v Hunter* itself afford some support for this view,[456] and *Humble v Hunter* may be explained as an example, if a curious one, of such exclusion. This would be a true application of the parol evidence rule to this situation. The relation between the two rules—the rule of law dealing with exclusion of the principal by the express or implied terms of the contract, and the rule of evidence against variation of written contracts by extrinsic evidence—has often been misunderstood.[457]

Rule (4): Express or implied exclusion of undisclosed principals[458] It is to be expected that there should be some limitations on the principal's intervention, but it is not clear what these are. First, older case law finds that where the agent contracts for a named principal, no other principal may intervene.[459]But this may not be a rigid rule. Companies, for instance, must act through agents but there seems no reason why a company could not be undisclosed principal for another party.[460] Secondly, where there is an express term of the contract that the agent is the only party to it, there can be no intervention by an undisclosed principal.[461] It may indeed be prudent to insert such clauses into contracts where it is desired to exclude the possibility of intervention.[462] As Rule (4) states, there can however be cases where the agent impliedly contracts that he is principal, or that no other party is directly involved.[463] Sometimes this implication is derived from the interpretation of words descriptive of the agent himself, and of the contract as a whole, that he alone answers the description in question: this is probably the best interpretation of the cases cited in the preceding paragraph, and it seems that (if the cases are all to be treated as correct) whereas the words "owner" or "proprietor" may perhaps raise

8-079

Davies (1968) 8 U. of W.A.L.Rev. 534; Fridman (1968) 84 L.Q.R. 224 at 239–244; McLauchlan, *The Parol Evidence Rule* (Wellington, NZ, 1976), Ch.13.

[456] See the case explained by a court containing two of the same judges in *Schmaltz v Avery* (1851) 12 Q.B. 655 at 660. See also *Drughorn Ltd v Rederiaktiebolaget Transatlantic* [1919] A.C. 203 at 207 ("a term of the contract that he should contract as owner of that property"); *O/Y Wasa SS Co v Newspaper Pulp & Wood Export* (1949) 82 Ll. L. Rep. 936.

[457] See Landon (1945) 61 L.Q.R. 130; (1946) 62 L.Q.R. 20; McLauchlan, above.

[458] Ivamy (1951) 18 *Solicitor* 245; Goodhart and Hamson (1932) 4 C.L.J. 320; Powell, pp.154–166; Glanville Williams (1945) 23 Can.B.R. 397–416; *Restatement, Third*, § 6.03, Comment *d*; Dal Pont, para.19.34 onwards.

[459] *Phillips v Duke of Bucks* (1683) 1 Vern. 227; cf. *M'Auliffe v Bicknell* (1835) 2 Cr.M. & R. 263. But see Article 108.

[460] See *Foster v Action Aviation Ltd* [2014] EWCA Civ 1368 (but parent company of seller was disclosed principal).

[461] *United Kingdom, etc., Assn v Neville* (1887) 19 Q.B.D. 110, Illustration 9; *J.A. Rayner (Mincing Lane) Ltd v Department of Trade and Industry* [1990] 2 A.C. 418 at 516 ("The contract is made between ourselves and yourselves as principals, we alone being liable to you for its performance"). This exception was criticised as illogical by Williston, *Contracts* (rev. ed.), § 286. See also *Bart v British West Indian Airways* [1967] 1 Lloyd's Rep. 239 at 243–249, 284–287 (contract regulated by Warsaw Convention).

[462] A non-assignment clause would not necessarily be effective: see below, para.8-079.

[463] See *Finzel, Berry & Co v Eastcheap Dried Fruit Co* [1962] 1 Lloyd's Rep. 370 at 375; *Foster v Action Aviation Ltd* [2014] EWCA Civ 1368 at [38] (legal owner disclosed principal; no room for beneficial owner as undisclosed principal); *Aspen Underwriting Ltd v Kairos Shipping Ltd* [2017] EWHC 1904 (Comm) at [43]. It is possible that *Greer v Downs Supply Co* [1927] 2 K.B. 28 and *Collins v Associated Greyhound Racecourses* [1930] 1 Ch. 1 could be so explained, but see fnn.479 and 475 below. See *Talbot Underwriting Ltd v Nausch, Hogan & Murray Inc (The Jascon 5)* [2006] EWCA Civ 889; [2006] 2 Lloyd's Rep. 195, finding the undisclosed principal doctrine excluded, distinguishing *Siu Yin Kwan v Eastern Insurance Co Ltd* [1994] 2 A.C. 199. For argument that the undisclosed principal doctrine is readily excluded in insurance contracts, see Merkin (2006) 17 K.C.L.J. 111.

such an implication,[464] descriptions of the agent as "landlord", "tenant", "disponent owner", "charterer" or "vendor" are less likely to do so.[465] In these cases intervention by an undisclosed principal would be inconsistent with the contract on which he seeks to intervene. "The principle applied is clearly sound, whether or not as a matter of interpretation the contracts were properly construed."[466]

It was formerly arguable that further guidance could be obtained by applying the analogy of the assignment rules, and that it could be said that where the benefit of a contract is not assignable or its burden could not be vicariously performed[467] the undisclosed principal cannot intervene.[468] This view however was rejected by the Privy Council in the leading modern case of *Siu Yin Kwan v Eastern Insurance Co Ltd*,[469] which concerned the (perhaps unusual) situation of an insurance policy which was unassignable, but where it was found that the identity of the assured was at the time of contract a matter of indifference to the insurer. The mere fact that the contract by its terms excluded subsequent assignment was not crucial as to whether an undisclosed principal already existing at that time could intervene.[470]

Other guidance is therefore needed as to when the terms of the contract are to be regarded as expressly or impliedly excluding the principal's intervention. It is clear that this will not occur often, for the Privy Council approved a dictum of Diplock LJ that in an "ordinary commercial contract" it may be assumed that a person is:

"willing to treat as a party to the contract anyone on whose behalf the agent may have been authorised to contract ... unless either the other party manifests his unwillingness or there are other circumstances which would lead the agent to realise that the other party was not so willing."[471]

This is described by Lord Lloyd of Berwick as a "beneficial assumption".[472] But it is an assumption rather than a prescription: unwillingness does not have to be manifested by a term in the contract.[473] Commercial contracts must be scrutinised as to their purpose and terms. Even if these prohibit assignment (which was true

---

[464] e.g. *Davis v Capel* [1959] N.Z.L.R. 825; *Construction Engineering (Aust.) Pty Ltd v Hexyl Pty Ltd* (1985) 155 C.L.R. 541 at 546–547; *White v Baycorp Advantage Business Information Services Ltd* (2006) 200 F.L.R. 125 at [83] (see above, para.8-078).

[465] See above, para.8-078. Goodhart and Hamson describe such implied exclusion as arising only in "highly peculiar circumstances": (1932) 4 C.L.J. 320 at 356. But the decision as to "tenant" can be criticised: see fn.492 below.

[466] *Restatement, Second*, Appendix, p.520 (Seavey).

[467] See Chitty, *Contracts* (32nd edn) para.19-043 onwards and para.19-082 onwards. Intervention on a sale would under this rule rarely be disallowed, for both in the case of assignment and in the case of undisclosed principal, the liability of the original contracting party to the third party remains. But intervention on a loan would rarely be permitted.

[468] This was the view of Goodhart and Hamson (1932) 4 C.L.J. 320.

[469] [1994] 2 A.C. 199, Illustration 12. Had it not been for findings of fact, the case would be a straightforward one of unidentified principal: the insurers knew the occupation of the agents and that they did not own the ship. The case may in fact be another where facts appropriate to unidentified principals distort the rules for undisclosed principals: see Reynolds, in *Consensus ad Idem* (Rose ed., 1997), pp.92–95; and above, para.8-073.

[470] See *Restatement, Third*, § 6.03, Comment *d*.

[471] *Teheran-Europe Co Ltd v S.T. Belton (Tractors) Ltd* [1968] 2 Q.B. 545 at 555.

[472] [1994] 2 A.C. at 209. See too *Diamond Stud Ltd v New Zealand Bloodstock Finance Ltd* [2010] NZCA 423 (term expressly making bidder at auction liable despite any undisclosed agency did not impliedly exclude liability of undisclosed principal).

[473] *Rolls Royce Power Engineering Plc v Ricardo Consulting Engineers Ltd* [2003] EWHC 2871 (TCC); [2004] 2 All E.R. (Comm) 129.

in the case itself). It may nevertheless be inferred that obligations of a personal nature, which could not be vicariously performed, will not permit intervention.

Other approaches to the problem have been suggested. In *Said v Butt*[474] a theatre critic bought, as undisclosed principal through an agent, a ticket for a first night performance. He was refused admission. He was held not entitled to sue for breach of contract, apparently on the ground that the formation of the contract was affected by mistake. But this reasoning involves the assumption that the contract is between third party and undisclosed principal, and as we have seen the validity of this reasoning is limited.[475] Further, it does not provide useful guidance: if the contract is made (as this was) with a named person, on such reasoning no other person can ever be a party to it. Since the first night was largely by invitation, this may have been a case where an implied exclusion of the, or any, principal was appropriate: and this may be the best explanation of the decision.

It has also been suggested that there should be a simple rule that the undisclosed principal cannot intervene when he knew or should have known at the time of the contract that the third party would not have dealt with him[476]: this rule may be a fair one, but it can only be justified on grounds of being an exception to an admitted anomaly, designed to prevent that anomaly from going too far and interfering with the commercial convenience for which it arose. It would be easier to refuse an order of specific performance in such a case than to refuse an action in damages. But there seems to be no case in which intervention has clearly been prevented on the basis of such a rule and no more, and it would therefore seem that such knowledge by the third party, as a feature present at its formation, is only to be treated as relevant to the express or implied terms of the contract.

The question whether a principal could, if sued, himself plead that the contract was one excluding intervention does not appear to have been considered; but if the question depends on the terms of the contract there seems no reason why he should not. If a misrepresentation was involved, as discussed below, the matter would be different.

Intervention is not permitted in respect of deeds and negotiable instruments for reasons connected with the nature of those documents. These are discussed in the following two Articles.

It is unlikely that there is any role for the concept of the undisclosed principal in relation to the tort of negligent misstatement.[477] The absence of reciprocity would not encourage an assumption that the utterer of a statement was content for unknown parties to rely upon it.

---

[474] [1920] 3 K.B. 497, Illustration 11. The action was actually against the manager of the theatre for inducing breach of contract. See also *Smith v Wheatcroft* (1878) 9 Ch.D. 223 at 230; *Nelthorpe v Holgate* (1844) 1 Col.C.C. 203.

[475] See above, para.8-069; Glanville Williams (1945) 23 Can.B.R. 397–414; Goodhart and Hamson (1932) 4 C.L.J. 320. *Said v Butt* is to some extent supported by *Greer v Downs Supply Co* [1927] 2 K.B. 28, where a third party made a contract with an agent because the agent owed him money which could be set off, and the undisclosed principal was not permitted to intervene. But the judgments in the case are unsatisfactory (see (1945) 23 Can.B.Rev. 411) since it is clear that the setoff could have been used against the principal in any case: see Article 81. See also *Collins v Associated Greyhound Racecourses Ltd* [1930] 1 Ch. 1, below, para.8-099; *Campbellville Gravel Supply Ltd v Cook Paving Co Ltd* (1968) 70 D.L.R. (2d) 354.

[476] Treitel, *Law of Contract* (14th edn), para.16-061; see also *Smith v Wheatcroft* (1878) 9 Ch.D. 223 at 230; *Humble v Hunter* (1848) 12 Q.B. 310 at 313 (the undisclosed principal "shall not come forward so as unfairly to prejudice the party sued"). It derives some support from the judgment of Diplock LJ in *Teheran-Europe Co Ltd v S.T. Belton (Tractors) Ltd*, quoted above.

[477] *Playboy Club London Ltd v Banca Nazionale del Lavoro SpA* [2016] EWCA Civ 457; [2016] 1 W.L.R. 3169 at [22].

8-080   **Misrepresentation**   Where the contract is procured by misrepresentation by the agent, whether fraudulent or innocent, on general principles the contract can be rescinded if it is not too late to do so; and specific performance may be refused. The representation must be material to the representee.[478] Where the agent or the principal, or both, knew or must have known that the third party would not deal with the particular principal, or would only deal with the agent, a specific representation that that principal was not involved, or that no one else but the agent was involved, could be material.[479] Greater difficulties arise if the agent simply does not disclose the principal's involvement. Rescission should only be available where the situation is one of those in which non-disclosure constitutes a misrepresentation[480]; though there are cases in this context where specific performance has been refused though rescission might not perhaps have been granted.[481] It would seem however that an innocent misrepresentation or non-disclosure is not to be regarded as material if the only facts are that the agent was thereby seeking to secure better terms for his principal.[482]

8-081   **Discovery against principal**   It has been held that where it is alleged that the claimant agent acted for an undisclosed principal, proceedings by him may be stayed unless the principal discloses documents (or the agent procures that the principal does so) which he would be required to do if he were a party to the contract.[483] As a matter of disclosure this may be correct, for what is revealed may well be relevant to the claimant's damages. But it seems to have been assumed that the agent in such a case had no interest in the proceedings other than the right to bring them in his own name. In view of the interest of the agent of an undisclosed principal in the contract made, as explained above, this seems doubtful.[484]

Illustrations

8-082   (1)   S, a solicitor, practised in the name of S and C (which was not a partnership). C was also a solicitor, but acted as clerk to S. Held, that S, being the real principal, was entitled to sue alone upon a contract made in the name of the firm.[485]

(2)   Gunpowder is bought by a person who appears to be acting on his own

---

[478] See Treitel, above, paras 9-020–9-023.
[479] See *Restatement, Third,* § 6.03, Comment *d*; (1931) 44 Harvard L.R. 1271.
[480] See Chitty, *Contracts* (32nd edn), para.7-017 onwards; (1927) 75 U.Pa.L.R. 761 at 764.
[481] e.g. *Archer v Stone* (1898) 78 L.T. 34; *Phillips v Duke of Bucks* (1683) 1 Vern. 227.
[482] e.g. *Dyster v Randall & Sons* [1926] Ch. 932, Illustration 10 (criticised, *Restatement, Second*, Appendix, p.524); *Smith v Wheatcroft* (1878) 9 Ch.D. 223; and see the well known judgment of Cardozo J in *Kelly Asphalt Block Co v Barber Asphalt Paving Co* 105 N.E. 88 (Ct.App.N.Y. 1914). cf. *Nash v Dix* (1898) 78 L.T. 445, where it was held that there was no agency but a purchase for resale. See J.C. Smith [1972B] C.L.J. 197 at 219 onwards, considering the relationship between these cases and *Berg v Sadler and Moore* [1937] 2 K.B. 158. See also *Garnac Grain Co Inc v H.M.F. Faure & Fairclough Ltd* [1966] 1 Q.B. 650 (at first instance); [1966] 1 Q.B. 650 at 685–686 (in CA); affd by HL [1968] A.C. 1130 (fraud of undisclosed principal: below, para.8-096).
[483] *Abu Dhabi National Tanker Co v Product Star Shipping Co (The Product Star)* [1992] 2 All E.R. 20. And see below, para.9-015.
[484] See above, para.8-069.
[485] *Spurr v Cass, Cass v Spurr* (1870) L.R. 5 Q.B. 656. See also *Cothay v Fennell* (1830) 10 B. & C. 671.

account. At a later stage the seller discovers that the buyer was agent for certain mineowners. He may sue the mine-owners.[486]

(3) An agent entered into a contract in his own name for the purchase of property, and paid a deposit. Held, that on the default of the vendor, the agent's principal was entitled to sue for the return of the deposit.[487]

(4) A owned a business, which was carried on in the name of B with B as manager. B appeared to be the principal. The drawing and accepting of bills of exchange were incidental to the ordinary conduct of such a business. A forbade B to draw or accept bills. B accepted a bill in the name in which the business was carried on. Held, A was liable on the bill.[488] Sed quaere.

(5) The owner of a hotel sold it but continued to act as manager and licensee, and dealt as such in his own name, the new owner being undisclosed. The manager was forbidden by the new owner to buy cigars on credit, but he bought cigars on credit. Held, the new owner was liable as undisclosed principal for the price of the cigars, it being within the authority usually confided to the manager of a hotel to buy such goods on credit.[489] Sed quaere.

(6) A appointed B as the manager of an hotel owned by A, and the licence was taken out in the name of B, who appeared to be the principal. A told B to order spirits from a certain brewery only, but B disregarded this instruction and ordered whisky from C. Held, A was liable to C for the price of the whisky.[490] Sed quaere.

(7) An agent executed a charterparty in his own name, and was described in the contract as the owner of the vessel. It was held that the principal was not entitled to give evidence to show that the agent contracted on his behalf, so as to enable him to maintain an action on the contract, because such evidence was inconsistent with the statement that the agent was the owner of the vessel.[491]

(8) The expression "tenant" does not negative agency, and oral evidence has been held admissible to show that a person described in a tenancy agreement as the tenant in fact entered into the agreement as agent for another.[492]

(9) A is the managing part-owner of a ship. He becomes a member of a mutual insurance association, and insures the ship under the rules and regulations of that association. By the terms of the policy and rules of the association, the right to recover in respect of losses, and the liability for contributions in the nature of premiums, are confined to members of the association. The other partowners, not being members of the association, cannot, as undisclosed principals of A, sue for any losses, nor can they be sued for contributions due in respect of the policy, even if A fails to pay them, because the right and li-

---

[486] See *Curtis v Williamson* (1874) L.R. 10 Q.B. 57.

[487] *Duke of Norfolk v Worthy* (1808) 1 Camp. 337.

[488] *Edmunds v Bushell and Jones* (1865) L.R. 1 Q.B. 97. See Comment.

[489] *Watteau v Fenwick* [1893] 1 Q.B. 346. See Comment.

[490] *Kinahan & Co v Parry* [1910] 2 K.B. 389. See Comment. But the decision was reversed [1911] 1 K.B. 459, on the ground that there was no evidence that the manager had not bought the goods for his own use.

[491] *Humble v Hunter* (1848) 12 Q.B. 310.

[492] *Danziger v Thompson* [1944] K.B. 654; *Hanstown Properties Ltd v Green* (1977) 246 E.G. 917, CA. The reasoning is criticised by McLauchlan, *The Parol Evidence Rule* (Wellington, NZ, 1976), p.137 on the grounds that the identity of a tenant is likely to be of importance. cf. *Carberry v Gardiner* (1936) 36 S.R. (N.S.W.) 559 (assignment of lease).

ability of the principals to sue and be sued are excluded by the terms of the contract.[493] It would be otherwise, if the liability for contributions is thrown by the policy on the persons assured, without reference to whether or not they are members of the association; or if it is provided that the persons assured shall be liable therefore as if they were members.[494]

(10) P, a developer, knew that T would not sell land to him, and therefore bought it through A, who did not disclose that he was acting as agent. A later requested T to cancel the contract, but P sued for specific performance. Held, he was entitled to succeed.[495] So also when in a similar case the persons wishing to buy the land (a committee of Roman Catholics) knew that the sellers (trustees of a Congregational chapel) would not sell to them, and offered an intermediary a commission to buy the land and resell it to them: but here there was no agency.[496]

(11) P wished to see the first night of a play at a theatre of which T was managing director, but knew that T would not allow a ticket to be sold to him on account of allegations he had previously made about T. He bought a ticket through an intermediary, but when he appeared at the theatre he was refused admission on T's instructions. Held, he could not sue T for inducing a breach of contract by the company that owned the theatre, for there was no breach of contract in refusing him admission: the contract was one on which he had no right to intervene as undisclosed principal.[497]

(12) Shipping agents take out workmen's compensation insurance on the crew of a vessel owned by others. The policy is not assignable, but it is not established that the insurers knew that the agents were not the employers of the crew, and it is found as a fact that the identity of the employers of the crew is a matter of indifference to them. The owners of the vessel can claim under the policy.[498]

(13) A demise charterer sues the defendant alleging it is liable for causing the death of a senior crewman. The defendant defends by arguing that the claimant was not the employer of the crewman and not entitled to damages. It was held that the charterer was the undisclosed principal of the employment agency which was the nominal employer of the crewman.[499]

---

[493] *United Kingdom Mutual Steamship Assurance Assn v Nevill* (1887) 19 Q.B.D. 110; *Montgomerie v United Kingdom Mutual Steamship Assn* [1891] 1 Q.B. 370.

[494] *Ocean Iron Steamship Insurance Assn Ltd v Leslie* (1889) 22 Q.B.D. 722n; *Great Britain 100 A1 Steamship Insurance Assn v Wyllie* (1889) 22 Q.B.D. 710; *British Marine Mutual Insurance Co v Jenkins* [1900] 1 Q.B. 299.

[495] *Dyster v Randall & Sons* [1926] Ch. 932; criticised, *Restatement, Second*, Appendix, at p.524; *Williams v Bulat* [1992] 2 Qd.R. 566.

[496] *Nash v Dix* (1898) 78 L.T. 445.

[497] *Said v Butt* [1920] 3 K.B. 497. See Comment. As to the tort liability, see below, para.9-121.

[498] *Siu Yin Kwan v Eastern Insurance Co Ltd* [1994] 2 A.C. 199, a case on Third Parties (Rights against Insurers) legislation. See fn.469 above; Reynolds, in *Consensus ad Idem* (Rose ed., 1997), pp.92–95. See also *Ferryways NV v Associated British Ports* [2008] EWHC 225 (Comm); [2008] 1 Lloyd's Rep. 639.

[499] *Ferryways NV v Associated British Ports* [2008] EWHC 225 (Comm); [2008] 1 Lloyd's Rep. 639; affd on appeal on other points [2009] EWCA Civ 189; [2009] 1 Lloyd's Rep. 595.

Article 77

DEEDS

(1) Subject to the following exceptions, a principal may not sue or be sued on any **8-083** deed inter partes, even if it is expressed to be executed on his behalf, unless he is described as a party to it and it is executed in his name.[500]

(2) Where an agent who has entered into a deed in his own name is a trustee for his principal of the rights under the deed, the principal may enforce such rights in proceedings to which the agent is a party as plaintiff or defendant.[501]

(3) By virtue of the Law Property Act 1925 s.56(1), a person may take an immediate interest in land or other property, or the benefit of any condition, right of entry, covenant or agreement over or respecting land or other property, although he is not named as a party to the conveyance or other instrument.

(4) By virtue of the Contracts (Rights of Third Parties) Act 1999 a person who is not a party to a contract may in his own right enforce a term of the contract if (a) the contract expressly provides that he may, or (b) the term purports to confer a benefit on him.[502]

(5) By virtue of the Powers of Attorney Act 1971 s.7(1),[503] if the donee of a power of attorney is an individual he may, if he thinks fit, execute any instrument with his own signature, and, where sealing is required, with his own seal, by the authority of the donor of the power; and every document executed in that manner shall be as effective as if executed or done by the donee with the signature and seal of the donor of the power.

Comment

Rule (1)   Rule (1) is an exception to the general principles stated in Articles 71 **8-084** and 72, and to the rules as to undisclosed principal stated in Article 76, and results from the strict rules concerning deeds. It requires signature in a form such as "A, by B his attorney".[504] But the exact form might not matter, for example "B for A" is acceptable.[505] The rules are to some extent modified by statute: and where the deed is not inter partes the principal may, if a covenantee, sue in any case.[506] And in general a right of action may be assigned by the normal procedures. *Restatement, Third* makes no reference to such a rule, which has been abolished by statute in many American states, judicial decisions having taken the view that abolition was not within the judicial function.[507] But the Supreme Court of Canada has affirmed the rule on the same grounds, though not without casting doubt on it.[508] It can be

---

[500] Illustrations 1–4. The formalities required for deeds are now laid down by the Law of Property (Miscellaneous Provisions) Act 1989 s.1.

[501] *Harmer v Armstrong* [1934] Ch. 65, Illustration 5.

[502] s.1.

[503] As amended by Law of Property (Miscellaneous Provisions) Act 1989.

[504] *Combe's Case* (1613) 9 Co.Rep. 75a; *Frontin v Small* (1726) 2 Ld.Raym. 1418; *White v Cuyler* (1795) 6 T.R. 176; *Wilks v Back* (1802) 2 East 142; cf. above, para.2-020.

[505] *Wilks v Back*, above; and see *Lawrie v Lees* (1880) 14 Ch. D. 249.

[506] *Cooker v Child* (1673) 2 Lev. 74; *Sunderland Marine Insurance Co v Kearney* (1851) 16 Q.B. 925.

[507] § 6.03: see Comment *f.*

[508] *Friedmann Equity Developments Inc v Final Note Ltd* [2000] 1 S.C.R. 842; (2005) 188 D.L.R. (4th) 269 ("to effect such a change would have unwarranted, far-reaching and complex consequences both in the law of contract and the law of property": per Bastarache J at [48]).

argued that a party wishing to exclude undisclosed principals can do so by the terms of the document.

8-085 **Rule (2)** Rule (2) is straightforward from the point of view of principle: if the trustee will not sue, the beneficiary may, joining the trustee as co-defendant. The question when a trust arises, of course, causes more difficulty.[509] When the beneficiary sues, he does not do so as beneficiary, but to enforce the agreement according to its tenor in favour of the trustee.[510]

8-086 **Rules (3) and (4)** Rules (3) and (4) embody the effect of s.56 of the Law of Property Act 1925 and the general effect of the Contracts (Rights of Third Parties) Act 1999. Their details are beyond the scope of this book[511] but they may clearly entitle the principal to sue on the agent's deed in some situations.

8-087 **Rule (4): Powers of attorney** The effect of s.7(1) of the Powers of Attorney Act 1971[512] is not clear. The previous rule was that the holder of a power of attorney should exercise it in the principal's name, i.e. sign the principal's name and use his seal.[513] Otherwise the principal, at any rate, would not at common law be bound or entitled, though in some cases the agent himself might be bound.[514] It is clear that the agent may now in certain circumstances use his own name and seal and nevertheless render the principal liable and entitled. The first problem is as to whether the section by its words requires that he should have specific authority to act in his own name. Earlier editions of this book took the view (on the former legislation) that it does, but the wording of the section is not clear and it seems unlikely that such authority is required.[515] The second problem is whether the principal must in such a case be named in the deed. It seems likely that he must, as otherwise the rule that an undisclosed principal cannot intervene on a deed would have been abolished, yet in *Harmer v Armstrong*[516] it was clearly assumed to exist, apart from the exception as to trust beneficiaries recognised in that case. The effect of the section is therefore to allow execution by an attorney in his own name: but the principal should be mentioned in the body of the deed, and though it may not be strictly necessary,[517] it is highly desirable that the attorney should express that he executes as attorney or on behalf of the principal, though he need not be so care-

---

[509] See Snell, *Equity* (33rd edn), para.21-003.

[510] See *Harmer v Armstrong* [1934] Ch. 65 at 88 (Illustration 5), as explained in the *Friedmann Equity Developments*, above.

[511] As to s.56, see *Beswick v Beswick* [1968] A.C. 58; Chitty, *Contracts* (32nd edn), para.18-127 onwards. As to the 1999 Act, see ibid., para.18-091, reaching the conclusion that the Act probably applies to contracts by deed. The 1999 Act operates without prejudice to s.56: s.7(1). Section 56 is narrower in that it requires that the instrument purport to contain a grant to or covenant with the third party. As to the agent's liability on a deed, see below, para.9-047.

[512] Superseding s.123(1) of the Law of Property Act 1925, itself re-enacting Conveyancing Act 1881 s.46.

[513] The requirement of sealing was abolished by the Law of Property (Miscellaneous Provisions) Act 1989 s.1, which also provides that in certain circumstances solicitors and licensed conveyancers are conclusively presumed to be authorised to deliver the instrument.

[514] See *Appleton v Binks* (1804) 5 East 148, Illustration 1 to Article 102. It would be more difficult for him to show that he was entitled to sue: see *Frontin v Small* (1726) 2 Ld.Raym. 1418.

[515] Powell, p.178; *Davidson's Concise Precedents in Conveyancing* (21st edn), Vol.2, p.447.

[516] [1934] Ch. 65, Illustration 5. (Though in that case the authority had in any case not been given by deed.)

[517] See *Re Whitley Partners Ltd* (1886) 32 Ch.D. 337 at 338; but cf. Wolstenholme and Turner, *The Conveyancing Acts* (3rd edn, 1883), p.99.

ful in the formula used as under the old law. It is not clear whether the agent is himself discharged from liability in cases where he would hitherto have been bound. The former provision said that the deed "shall be as effectual to all intents" as if the agent had executed it in the principal's name. This made it arguable that the agent was discharged. The removal of these words may be thought to make such a construction less likely. If the provision does have this effect, it would assimilate the law as to deeds with that as to other written contracts.

The provision operates without prejudice to any statutory direction that an instrument is to be executed in the name of an estate owner, and is an alternative to the procedure prescribed by s.74(3) and (4) of the Law of Property Act 1925 (as amended), which deal with execution of conveyances by or on behalf of corporations.[518]

Illustrations

(1) An agent entered into a contract by deed in his own name, the principal not being named in it. It was held that the principal was not liable to be sued on the contract.[519]   **8-088**

(2) A shipmaster executed a charterparty by deed in his own name "as agent for the owners". Held, that the owners were not entitled to sue for the freight, because they were not parties to the deed.[520]

(3) An attorney, who was authorised in writing to execute a lease, signed and sealed the lease in and with his own name and seal. It was held that the principal was not entitled to sue on the covenants in the lease, though they were expressed to be made by the tenant with the landlord, because the deed was not executed in his name.[521]

(4) A by deed transferred shares to B. In consequence of the winding up of the company, the transfer could not be registered, and A was compelled to pay a call. A had no right of action for indemnity against B's principal, for whom B acted in taking the transfer.[522]

(5) By a contract under seal made between A and B, A agreed to purchase the copyright in certain periodicals from B. A in fact entered into the contract as agent and trustee for himself and C. Held, in an action brought by C against A and B for a declaration that A was agent and trustee as stated above and for specific performance, that as the agency and trusteeship of A had been established and all necessary parties were before the court, there was jurisdiction to decree specific performance.[523]

Article 78

BILLS, NOTES AND CHEQUES

(1) A principal is not liable on a bill of exchange, promissory note or cheque un-   **8-089**

---

[518] s.7(2), as amended, s.7(3). As to s.74 of the Law of Property Act 1925, see *Skelwith (Leisure) Ltd v Armstrong* [2015] EWHC 2830 (Ch); [2016] Ch. 345 at [73].

[519] *Re International Contract Co, Pickering's Claim* (1871) L.R. 6 Ch.App. 525.

[520] *Schack v Anthony* (1813) 1 M. & S. 573. A charterparty would not be made by deed nowadays.

[521] *Berkeley v Hardy* (1826) 5 B. & C. 355; *Lord Southampton v Brown* (1827) 6 B. & C. 718. But the result might now be different by virtue of s.56 of the Law of Property Act 1925.

[522] *Viscount Torrington v Lowe* (1868) L.R. 4 C.P. 26.

[523] *Harmer v Armstrong* [1934] Ch. 65.

less his signature appears on it[524]: but it is not necessary that he should sign with his own hand, it is sufficient if his signature is written by some person by or under his authority.[525]

(2) No person can be liable as acceptor of a bill except the person on whom it is drawn, except where it is accepted for honour.[526]

Comment

8-090   These rules can be justified on the ground that negotiable instruments are likely to come into the hands of persons who have no knowledge of the circumstances in which they were issued. Such persons must be able to rely on what appears on the face of the instrument. Hence undisclosed principals are not liable.

8-091   **Rule (1)**   Rule (1) provides another exception to the general rules as to the liability of a principal on his agent's transactions stated in Articles 71, 72 and 76: he cannot be liable on a bill when his name does not appear on it, although his signature may be effected by an agent. If the agent simply writes the principal's name, there is no difficulty. In other cases, the form of representative signature is regulated by s.26 of the Bills of Exchange Act 1882, which reads:

"(1)   Where a person signs a bill as drawer indorser or acceptor, and adds words to his signature, indicating that he signs for or on behalf of a principal, or in a representative character, he is not personally liable thereon; but the mere addition to his signature of words describing him as an agent, or as filling a representative character, does not exempt him from personal liability.

(2)   In determining whether a signature on a bill is that of the principal or that of the agent by whose hand it is written, the construction most favourable to the validity of the instrument shall be adopted."

Subsection (1) lays down the standard rule for representative signatures. In cases of drawing or indorsing the question is usually as to whether the principal or the agent is the drawer or indorser; to this subsection (2) is not normally relevant, and the matter is decided by application of the main rule, which is discussed elsewhere.[527]

It should be noted that forged and unauthorised signatures do not bind principals,[528] though a principal may be precluded from setting up the forgery,[529] and may ratify an unauthorised signature.[530] A signature by procuration operates as notice that

---

[524] Bills of Exchange Act 1882 ss.23 and 89.
[525] Bills of Exchange Act 1882 s.91(1).
[526] Bills of Exchange Act 1882 s.17(1); *Polhill v Walter* (1832) 3 B. & Ad. 114; *Steele v M'Kinlay* (1880) 5 App.Cas. 754. As to acceptance for honour, see Bills of Exchange Act 1882 ss.65–68. Section 1 of the Contracts (Rights of Third Parties) Act 1999 confers no rights in respect of such instruments: s.6(1).
[527] See Article 103. For full citation of the many cases relevant to this section, see Byles, *Bills of Exchange* (29th edn), para.7-007 onwards; Chalmers and Guest, *Bills of Exchange* (18th edn), para.3-105 onwards.
[528] Bills of Exchange Act 1882 s.24. But as to the meaning of this provision, see Chalmers and Guest, above, para.3-043 onwards.
[529] *Greenwood v Martins Bank Ltd* [1933] A.C. 51. See further above, para.8-041.
[530] Ch.2, Section 3.

the agent has but a limited authority to sign, and the principal is only bound by such signature if the agent in so signing was acting within the limits of his authority.[531]

Rule (2) Since only the drawee can be liable as acceptor, it may be important to know whether or not a signature is valid as an acceptance; and here s.26(2) may be more often relevant. It seems that where the bill is drawn on an agent, the principal cannot be liable on the agent's acceptance, even though the agent accepts in the principal's name or in a representative character, and with his authority.[532] Where the bill is drawn on the principal, if the agent accepts in the principal's name or using representative words the principal will be liable: but if he accepts in his own name or using descriptive words, the principal will not be liable (and nor will the agent). In either case s.26(2), with its presumption of validity, assists in doubtful cases only: it does not reverse the rule as to representative signatures, nor does it prevent clearly inappropriate signatures from being inoperative.[533]

As regards partnerships, the signature of the firm is equivalent to those of the partners[534]: otherwise, the names of all partners sought to be held liable would have to appear in accordance with s.23 of the Bills of Exchange Act 1882.

The above rules relate to the suing of the principal: whether or not he can sue depends on whether he is the payee, or a holder of the bill, in accordance with the general law.

8-092

Illustrations

(1) A bill of exchange is drawn on "Artitalia", a partnership. One partner accepts it with the authority of the other but signs her own name. The other partner is not liable on the bill.[535]
(2) A duly authorised agent draws or indorses a bill, or indorses a note or cheque, in his own name. The principal is not liable on it.[536]
(3) A promissory note is signed "The JS Laundry Ltd, JS, Managing Director". JS is not liable; the company would be.[537]
(4) A promissory note in the form "We promise to pay ... etc." is signed "C D, Director, E F, Secretary, The FE Ltd". The signatories are personally liable and the company is not.[538]
(5) A bill of exchange is addressed to A B, and is accepted "A B for and on behalf of C D". C D is not liable as acceptor, even if A B was expressly authorised to accept the bill on his behalf.[539]

8-093

[531] Bills of Exchange Act 1882 s.25.
[532] Bills of Exchange Act 1882 s.17; *Polhill v Walter* (1832) 3 B. & Ad. 114; *Steele v M'Kinlay* (1880) 5 App.Cas. 754. For the liability of the agent in this case, see Article 103.
[533] *Britannia Electric Lamp Works v D. Mandler & Co Ltd* [1939] 2 K.B. 129.
[534] Partnership Act 1890 s.6. As regards companies, see Companies Act 2006 s.52.
[535] *Geo. Thompson (Aust.) Pty Ltd v Vitadello* [1978] V.R. 199.
[536] *Ducarrey v Gill* (1830) M. & M. 450. And see *Leadbitter v Farrow* (1816) 5 M. & S. 345 at 350.
[537] *Chapman v Smethurst* [1909] 1 K.B. 927. See also *Britannia Electric Lamp Works Ltd v D. Mandler & Co Ltd* [1939] 2 K.B. 129.
[538] *Brebner v Henderson* 1925 S.C. 643.
[539] *Polhill v Walter* (1832) 3 B. & Ad. 114.

Article 79

DEFENCES TO ACTION BY OR AGAINST PRINCIPAL

8-094   (1)   Where a principal, whether disclosed or undisclosed, sues the other party to a contract made by the principal through an agent, the other party has all the defences which he would have had against the principal if the principal had himself made the contract in the same circumstances.[540]

    (2)   Where an undisclosed principal sues the other party to a contract, the other party may, in addition to the defences mentioned above, plead all defences which had accrued against the agent before he had reasonable notice that the agent was not acting for himself.[541]

    (3)   Where the other contracting party sues the principal, the principal, whether disclosed or undisclosed, can plead against him all defences arising out of the other party's transaction with the agent, and defences personal to himself, but not defences personal to the agent.[542]

Comment

8-095   There is little direct English authority for these rules, which followed some of the wording of *Restatement, Second*[543] but it is submitted that they are logically correct, though many points of detail remain unsettled. The propositions in Article 81 should be taken as an elaboration of these rules in a specific context.

8-096   **Rule (1): General rule**   The third party should be able to use all defences arising out of the contract itself, and all defences available against the principal himself (e.g. set-off, the fact that he is an alien enemy)[544] but not defences and set-offs[545] which he may have against the agent but which are not connected with the instant transaction. It is clear that he can allege fraud,[546] misrepresentation,[547] non-performance, illegality and mistake, where these are attributable to the agent, just as he could if the agent were a contracting party. And where he has such a defence, he can also take proceedings for rescission and restitution.[548] Where there is fraud or misrepresentation by the principal himself, a fortiori this will be a[549] defence to

---

[540] See Comment. cf. *Restatement*, §§ 298, 299 and 308.

[541] See Comment; *Siu Yin Kwan v Eastern Insurance Co Ltd* [1994] 2 A.C. 199 at 207.

[542] See Comment.

[543] §§ 179, 203, 299, 300, 333 and 371. See now *Restatement, Third*, § 6.06 and Comment (much simpler than *Restatement, Second*).

[544] The application of this rule to undisclosed principals is criticised by Busch (1999) 3 Eur.Rev. Private Law 319 at 332–333 on the basis that in such cases the third party never expected the benefit of such defences. The criticism is however made against the background of the action directe of the civil law in the case of indirect representation, which is more closely linked to the agent's contract than is the common law action of the principal.

[545] As to payment to or set-off with agent on the same transaction, see Article 81.

[546] *Archer v Stone* (1898) 78 L.T. 34 (action by agent); *Raphael v Goodman* (1838) 8 A. & E. 565; *Foster v Green* (1862) 7 H. & N. 881; *Ludgater v Love* (1881) 44 L.T. 694.

[547] *Mullens v Miller* (1882) 22 Ch.D. 194; *Winch v Winchester* (1812) 1 V. & B. 375; *Myers v Watson* (1851) 1 Sim.(N.S.) 523. As to liability in tort, see below, para.8-185.

[548] *Wilde v Gibson* (1848) 1 H.L. Cas. 605; *Stevens v Legh* (1853) 2 C.L.R. 251; *Wauton v Coppard* [1899] 1 Ch. 92; *Whurr v Devenish* (1904) 20 T.L.R. 385.

[549] But see above, para.8-077.

the third party.[550] It was held at first instance in *Garnac Grain Co Inc v HMF Faure and Fairclough Ltd*[551] that where an agent sued on a contract made on behalf of an undisclosed principal, it would be a defence to prove that the contract was induced by the fraud of the undisclosed principal. The decision was reversed on other grounds, but this view was accepted in the Court of Appeal.[552] A fortiori such fraud could be pleaded if the undisclosed principal was himself plaintiff.

Rescission for misrepresentation   It is not yet clear whether the third party's   **8-097** defence under Rule (1), where based on an agent's misrepresentation, requires that the misrepresentation have been made within the agent's actual or apparent authority, so long as the agent had some authorised role in the transaction.[553] If the relevant contract was entirely negotiated by the agent, the principal may find it difficult to deny the agent's apparent authority to make the statements that induced it if he wishes to enforce the contract. In such circumstances, it is unlikely to matter that at the time the misrepresentation was made the agent had not yet been appointed, so long as the representation can be regarded as continuing after the appointment.[554] Obviously, the third party will be in a weaker position where the misrepresenting agent had a lesser role to play in the process. However, it has been suggested that there is a general principle that "no person can take advantage of the fraud of his agent",[555] which precludes the principal from enforcing a contract induced by deceit whether or not the agent had express or apparent authority to have made the statement.[556] In *New Brunswick Railway v Conybeare*,[557] both Lord Westbury and Lord Chelmsford adverted to the possibility of a contract procured by the fraud of an agent being rescindable even though no action for damages would lie against the principal (actual or apparent authority normally being required before tortious liability for an agent's misstatements arises[558]) There are other dicta,[559] although it is difficult to find a case which has in fact turned on this point.[560] The principle being advocated appears to be an example of the idea that a principal should not be

---

[550] See *Mullens v Miller*, above.

[551] [1966] 1 Q.B. 650.

[552] See pp.685–686. See also [1968] A.C. 1130n.

[553] As to rescission by a principal on the basis of a bribe paid or promised by an unauthorised agent of the third party to the principal's agent, see below, para.8-221.

[554] See *Briess v Woolley* [1954] A.C. 333. cf. *Cramaso LLP v Ogilvie-Grant, Earl of Seafield* [2014] UKSC 9; [2014] 1 A.C. 1093.

[555] *Mair v Rio Grande Rubber Estates Ltd* [1913] A.C. 853 at 872–873, per Lord Moulton.

[556] See Hon. K. Handley (2003) 117 L.Q.R. 537.

[557] (1862) 9 H.L. Cas. 711 at 726 and 749.

[558] See below, para.8-180. See too *Savash v CIS General Insurance Ltd* [2014] EWHC 375 (TCC) at [59] (father makes fraudulent insurance claim on behalf of son).

[559] See *Swift v Jewsbury* (1874) L.R. 9 Q.B. 301 at 312–313; *Weir v Bell* (1878) 3 Ex.D. 238 at 245; *Mackay v Commercial Bank of New Brunswick* (1874) L.R. 5 P.C. 394 at 416; *Refuge Assurance Co Ltd v Kettlewell* [1909] A.C. 243 at 244; *Hughes v Liverpool Victoria Legal Friendly Society* [1916] 2 K.B. 482 at 493–494; *Briess v Woolley* [1954] A.C. 333 at 348–349; less clearly, *Bradford Third Equitable Building Society v Borders* [1941] 2 All E.R. 205 at 228. See too *Armagas Ltd v Mundogas SA* [1986] A.C. 717 at 745, per Robert Goff LJ; and *Bank of Credit and Commerce International SA v Aboody* [1990] 1 Q.B. 923 at 972. See also Watts [2017] L.M.C.L.Q. 385 at 405.

[560] *Refuge Assurance Co Ltd v Kettlewell* [1909] A.C. 243 comes closest, but the House of Lords simply affirmed the Court of Appeal ([1908] 1 K.B. 545), where two of the three judges thought that damages would have been available against the principal had they been sought. But see [1907] 2 K.B. 242 at 246–247, per Phillimore J.

permitted to approbate and reprobate.[561] Although the cases relied upon involve fraud, it is not clear why the principle, if it exists, should be confined to fraud.[562] On the other hand, where the agent had no actual or apparent authority to make the statement, and neither the principal nor any agent whose approval was needed for the making of the contract knew of the misrepresentation, it seems likely that rescission would be permitted only where the principal could adequately be put back in his pre-contractual position.[563]

8-098   **Rule (2): Undisclosed principal**   As a starting-point, the same position as pertains under rule (1) should apply where the principal is undisclosed, mutatis mutandis. But as the contract is initially made between third party and agent, the third party should not be prejudiced by the intervention of the undisclosed principal. Therefore the third party should in addition be able to plead against the principal all defences against the agent, including personal defences such as set-offs which accrued before he had reasonable notice of the principal's existence.[564] In the case of settlement with the agent and set-off against the agent, however, some English cases indicate that these can only be pleaded against the principal where he was in some way at fault in misleading the third party: the matter is dealt with in Article 81.

8-099   **Rule (3): Defences available to principal**   The principal should be able to plead defences arising out of the transaction, and defences personal to himself (e.g. that he is a minor, set-off in his favour)[565] but not defences personal to the agent (e.g. that the agent is a minor, set-off in favour of the agent), which only the agent could plead.[566]

In *Collins v Associated Greyhound Racecourses Ltd*[567] it was held that an undisclosed principal could not rescind, for misrepresentation in the prospectus, a contract to underwrite part of an issue of shares when he alone, and not the agent, was proved to have relied on the misrepresentation. This seems correct, and probably follows from the proposition that the third party cannot by the principal's intervention be deprived of his rights against the agent should he desire to exercise them[568]: the principal cannot therefore deprive him of them by rescinding the whole contract unless it is clear that the agent could do so, or at least that the agent would have a valid defence to proceedings against him.[569]

---

[561] See *Lloyd v Grace, Smith & Co* [1912] A.C. 716 at 738, per Lord Macnaghten. See too above, para.2-081.

[562] cf. *Versloot Dredging BV v HDI Gerling Industrie Versicherung AG* [2014] EWCA Civ 1349; [2015] Q.B. 608 (avoidance of otherwise valid insurance claim by reason of agent's misrepresentation on incidental matter).

[563] For discussion of cognate issues, see Watts, [2002] C.L.J. 301.

[564] *Siu Yin Kwan v Eastern Insurance Ltd* [1994] 2 A.C. 199; *Sims v Bond* (1833) 5 B. & Ad. 389 at 393; *Browning v Provincial Insurance Co of Canada* (1873) L.R. 5 P.C. 263 at 272–273; *Rabone v Williams* (1785) 7 T.R. 360. And see above, para.8-069; below, para.9-012.

[565] See *Restatement, Second*, § 203.

[566] The exclusion of defences personal to the agent is criticised in respect of undisclosed principals by Busch (1999) 3 Eur.Rev. Private Law 319 at 333–334 as unduly favourable to the third party.

[567] [1930] 1 Ch. 1.

[568] See above, para.8-098; *O'Herlihy v Hedges* (1803) 1 Sch. & Lef. 123; see also *Montgomerie v United Kingdom etc., Ass.* [1891] 1 Q.B. 370 at 372.

[569] See Goodhart and Hamson (1932) 4 C.L.J. 320 at 353 onwards. Despite dicta in the case to the contrary, it is however doubtful whether this was correctly assessed as a situation where the undisclosed principal could not intervene, for shares are transferable, and the agent would be liable

Article 80

(1) Except as provided in this Article, a principal is not discharged by the **8-100**
circumstances that he has paid or settled or otherwise dealt to his prejudice
with the agent.

(2) Where a debt or obligation has been contracted through an agent, and the
principal is induced by the conduct of the creditor reasonably to believe that
the agent has paid the debt or discharged the obligation or that the creditor has
elected to look to the agent alone for its payment or discharge, and in
consequence of such belief pays, or settles or otherwise deals to his prejudice
with the agent, the creditor is not permitted to deny, as between himself and
the principal, that the debt has been paid or the obligation discharged or that
he has elected to give exclusive credit to the agent so as to discharge the
principal.[570]

(3) (Perhaps) where an undisclosed principal settles with his agent at a time when
the third party still does not know that the agent acted for a principal, the
principal is discharged.[571]

Comment

General rule   In general, the right of a third party is not affected by the fact that **8-101**
the principal has paid or otherwise adjusted his accounts with the agent[572]: this is a
transaction with which the third party has no concern, and the mere fact that the
third party delays in enforcing his claim, or in making application to the principal
for payment of the debt or discharge of the obligation, is irrelevant, unless there are
special circumstances rendering the delay misleading.[573]

Exceptions   But there may be cases where such third party is precluded from su-   **8-102**
ing the principal, other than under the rules relating to merger and election (though
the two overlap).[574] Two different lines of reasoning are to be found in the cases:
(i) the principal may be discharged in such a case where the third party has led him
to suppose that he should settle with the agent; (ii) the principal is discharged where
hardship would be caused to him if he were forced to pay the third party.

First view: estoppel   The first view, a form of estoppel, has been more generally   **8-103**
accepted. Thus the principal is discharged from liability by paying the agent where
the third party requests payment by the agent,[575] or leads the principal to believe that

---

for any loss.
[570] See Comment; *Restatement, Third*, § 6.07; as to election, see Article 82.
[571] See Comment.
[572] *Kymer v Suwercropp* (1807) 1 Camp. 109; *Waring v Favenck* (1807) 1 Camp. 85; *Heald v Kenworthy*
(1855) 10 Exch. 739; *Macfarlane v Giannacopulo* (1858) 3 H. & N. 860; *Irvine & Co v Watson &
Sons* (1880) 5 Q.B.D. 414.
[573] See *Davison v Donaldson* (1882) 9 Q.B.D. 623, Illustration 6.
[574] See Article 82, esp. at para.8-119.
[575] *Smyth v Anderson* (1849) 7 C.B. 21. When the agent paid by the principal is also the agent of the
third party, normal principles of agency law must be invoked to ascertain whether the agent has
authority to receive payment for the third party. See *Miller v Douglas* (1886) 56 L.J.Ch. 91.

the agent has paid,[576] or that he looks to the agent alone for payment.[577] If this view is correct, since the discharge of the principal is based on the action of the third party in misleading him,[578] it is difficult to see how there can be such discharge while the principal is undisclosed, for the third party could not make any representation to someone of whose existence he was ignorant at the time of making the supposed representation.[579] The argument is however not found to be conclusive in other situations.[580] *Restatement, Third* applies it to undisclosed principals as a matter of policy—that the principal should take the risk.[581]

8-104 **Second view: prejudice of principal** The second view is that the third party cannot sue the principal where the principal would be unfairly prejudiced were he to do so.[582] This is a looser formulation which stresses the position of the principal rather than that of the third party and has its origin in old cases,[583] some of which can now be, and have been, re-explained in terms of the first view.[584] But this second view, if correct, could of course apply to undisclosed principals, and it was so applied in *Armstrong v Stokes*,[585] where it was held that a third party could not sue an undisclosed principal who had in good faith paid the agent at a time when the third party still knew of no principal. In that case a reconciliation of the two views previously attempted by Parke B,[586] that it would only be an unfair prejudice to the principal for the third party to sue him where that third party had by his conduct induced the principal to believe that a settlement had been made with the agent, was specifically rejected by Blackburn J.

But in the leading cases of *Irvine & Co v Watson & Sons*[587] and *Davison v Donaldson*[588] the views of Parke B were preferred, and *Armstrong v Stokes* was explained as a special case where the third party, by virtue of local usage,[589] dealt

---

[576] *Horsfall v Fauntleroy* (1830) 10 B. & C. 755; *Wyatt v Hertford* (1802) 3 East 147, Illustration 1; *MacClure v Schemeil* (1871) 20 W.R. 168, Illustration 3; but cf. *Irvine & Co v Watson & Sons* (1880) 5 Q.B.D. 414, Illustration 5.
[577] *Smith v Ferrand* (1827) 7 B. & C. 19, Illustration 2; *Smethurst v Mitchell* (1859) 1 E. & E. 623, as explained in *Davison v Donaldson* (1882) 9 Q.B.D. 623; cf. *Hopkins v Ware* (1869) L.R. 4 Ex. 268, Illustration 4. A further line of reasoning appears here which is not clearly distinguished: that of taking the agent's bill in satisfaction of the principal's debt. See below, para.8-121.
[578] *Kymer v Suwercropp* (1807) 1 Camp. 109; *Heald v Kenworthy* (1855) 10 Exch. 739; *Irvine & Co v Watson & Sons* (1880) 5 Q.B.D. 414; *Davison v Donaldson* (1882) 9 Q.B.D. 623.
[579] See *Campbell v Hicks* (1858) 28 L.J.Ex. 70. cf. below, para.8-109. It is possible that this could be said to occur where a document is issued which might come into the hands of third parties, e.g. a freight prepaid bill of lading. See *Restatement, Third*, § 6.07, Comment *b*.
[580] See Articles 76(2), 81, 84 and 85.
[581] § 6.07; see Comments *b* and *d*.
[582] Some cases even refer to an alteration of the accounts between principal and agent as avoiding the principal's liability: *Thomson v Davenport* (1829) 9 B. & C. 78; *Curtis v Williamson* (1874) L.R. 10 Q.B. 57. But this must be too wide: see, e.g. *Waring v Favenck* (1807) 1 Camp. 85 (principal cannot set off against third party money owed to him by agent).
[583] Principally the judgment of Bayley J in *Thomson v Davenport* (1829) 9 B. & C. 78.
[584] See *Smyth v Anderson* (1849) 7 C.B. 21 and *Wyatt v Hertford* (1802) 3 East 147, Illustration 1, explained in *Heald v Kenworthy* (1855) 10 Ex. 739; *Smethurst v Mitchell* (1859) 1 E. & E. 623, explained in *Davison v Donaldson* (1882) 9 Q.B.D. 623.
[585] (1872) L.R. 7 Q.B. 598, Illustration 7.
[586] In *Heald v Kenworthy* (1855) 10 Exch. 739.
[587] (1880) 5 Q.B.D. 414, Illustration 5.
[588] (1882) 9 Q.B.D. 623, Illustration 6.
[589] Among Manchester commission merchants: see above, para.1-021 as to commission agents and indirect representation; also Article 69.

with the agent as sole principal and it was reasonable for the principal to believe that he had so dealt.

Different rule for undisclosed principals   It is submitted that any difficulty there **8-105** may be is caused by an assumption that the same rule should be applied to disclosed and to undisclosed principal cases, and in particular by a failure to distinguish between disclosed but unidentified principals and true undisclosed principals. As has already been pointed out, the true undisclosed principal's position is a very special one.[590] Where the principal is disclosed, the first, or estoppel view is clearly appropriate: and this is so whether he is identified or unidentified. It seems to be the latter situation which *Irvine & Co v Watson & Sons*[591] and *Davison v Donaldson*[592] concern. In a true undisclosed principal situation, however, the third party deals on the credit of the agent alone and reasoning based on the notion that the contract is that of the principal (the estoppel view) is inappropriate. Rather it may be said that the principal "has done his duty to customers of the agent if he has seen to it that the agent is properly kept in funds to meet his obligations".[593] Thus where at the time of payment the third party still gave credit to the agent and knew of no principal, it may be right to hold the principal discharged. This was in fact the situation to which Blackburn J confined his decision in *Armstrong v Stokes*[594]; he specifically excluded "the case of the broker, who avowedly acts for a principal (though not necessarily named)". Of the three judges in *Irvine & Co v Watson & Sons*[595] only one, Bramwell LJ, doubted whether the undisclosed principal case was rightly distinguished from the general rule.[596] A special rule for undisclosed principal situations is therefore tentatively formulated above.

Illustrations

(1)   A creditor takes a security from the agent of his debtor, and gives the agent a **8-106** receipt for the debt. The principal deals to his detriment with the agent on the faith of the receipt. The principal is discharged from liability to the creditor.[597]
(2)   An agent of a debtor offers to pay the debt either in cash or by a bill of exchange. The creditor takes a bill in payment, and it is dishonoured. If the agent had funds of the principal's with which to pay the debt, or if the principal deals to his prejudice with the agent on the faith of his having paid it, the principal is discharged from liability to the creditor.[598]
(3)   Goods were sold, on the terms that they should be paid for cash on delivery, to an agent who appeared to be buying on his own account. The seller omitted to enforce cash payment, and the principal, not knowing that the seller had

[590]   See above, para.8-071 onwards.
[591]   (1880) 5 Q.B.D. 414.
[592]   (1882) 9 Q.B.D. 623. Also *Thomson v Davenport* (1829) 9 B. & C. 78. See further *Sopwith Aviation & Engineering Co Ltd v Magnus Motors Ltd* [1928] N.Z.L.R. 433 (principal disclosed).
[593]   Mechem, *Principles of Agency* (4th edn), § 186. See Reynolds [1983] C.L.P. 119 at 133–135. See also (1947) 18 Mississippi L.J. 436.
[594]   *Armstrong v Stokes* (1872) L.R. 7 Q.B. 598. But cf. Higgins (1965) 28 M.L.R. 167 at 175–178.
[595]   *Irvine & Co v Watson & Sons* (1880) 5 Q.B.D. 414.
[596]   See pp.417–418; cf. Baggallay LJ at 419 and Brett LJ at 421. See also the judgment of Jessel MR in *Davison v Donaldson* (1892) 9 Q.B.D. 623 at 628.
[597]   *Wyatt v Hertford* (1802) 3 East at 147; *Smyth v Anderson* (1849) 7 C.B. 21.
[598]   *Smith v Ferrand* (1827) 7 B. & C. 19. But see fn.577 above.

not been paid, paid the agent for the goods. Held, that the principal was discharged.[599]

(4) The agent of a debtor paid the debt by means of his own cheque, and the creditor neglected to present the cheque for four weeks, when it was dishonoured and the agent absconded. There was a reasonable chance that the cheque would have been honoured if it had been presented within three weeks, and the principal had dealt to his detriment with the agent on the faith of the payment. Held, that the principal was discharged.[600]

(5) A employed a broker to buy oil. The broker bought from B, telling him that he was acting for a principal, the terms being that the oil should be paid for by "cash on or before delivery". B delivered the oil without payment, and A, not knowing that B had not been paid, in good faith paid the broker. The broker soon afterwards became insolvent, and B sued A for the price of the oil. It was proved that it was not the invariable custom in the oil trade to insist on prepayment in the case of a sale for "cash on or before delivery". Held, that, in the absence of such an invariable custom, the mere omission to insist on prepayment was not such conduct as would reasonably induce A to believe that the broker had paid for the oil, and that, therefore, A was liable to B for the price.[601]

(6) Stores are sold to the managing owner of a ship. The supplier applies for payment but does not obtain it. The managing owner's principal settles accounts with his agent three months after the goods were supplied, and again two years later. More than three years after the supply of the goods, the agent becomes bankrupt. There has been no such conduct on the part of the supplier as to prevent his suing the principal.[602]

(7) Commission merchants, who act sometimes for themselves and sometimes as agents, regularly buy shirting from X on credit. X never inquires whether the commission merchants are acting for themselves or not. They subsequently stop payment. It is discovered that the shirting was bought for Y on a commission basis and sent to him after being bleached. Y had paid for the shirtings the day after receipt and before the commission merchant stopped payment. Y is not liable to pay again.[603]

Article 81

SETTLEMENT WITH OR SET-OFF AGAINST AGENT AFFECTING RIGHTS OF PRINCIPAL

8-107 (1) Except as provided in this Article, the third party, in an action by the principal, has no right to set off any claim he may have against the agent personally[604]; and the principal is not bound by a payment to or settlement with the agent unless that payment or settlement was made in the ordinary course of business and in a manner actually or apparently authorised by him.[605]

(2) A person who, in dealing with an agent, reasonably believes that the agent is

---

[599] *MacClure v Schemeil* (1871) 20 W.R. 168 (but the judgments proceed principally on the basis of election); cf. *Kymer v Suwercropp* (1807) 1 Camp. 109.

[600] *Hopkins v Ware* (1869) L.R. 4 Ex. 268; cf. *Everett v Collins* (1810) 2 Camp. 515.

[601] *Irvine & Co v Watson & Sons* (1880) 5 Q.B.D. 414.

[602] See *Davison v Donaldson* (1882) 9 Q.B.D. 623.

[603] *Armstrong v Stokes* (1872) L.R. 7 Q.B. 598. But see discussion above.

[604] i.e. unconnected with the instant transaction. See Illustrations 6–10.

[605] See Comment and Illustrations 1–3. See also *Mooney v Williams* (1905) 3 C.L.R. 1.

the principal in the transaction is discharged from liability by payment to or settlement with the agent in any manner which would have operated as a discharge if the agent had been the principal, and is entitled, as against the principal, to the same right of set-off in respect of any debt due from the agent personally as he would have been entitled to if the agent had been the principal; provided that he had not, at the time when the payment to or settlement took place, or the set-off accrued, received notice that the agent was not in fact the principal.[606]

Comment

Rule (1): General rule A set-off against an agent is a defence against him personally: therefore the third party cannot use it against a disclosed principal by virtue of the rules stated in Article 79, unless this is authorised by the principal.[607] And the third party is only discharged by settlement with the agent if the latter had authority, actual or apparent, to receive it, in accordance with the principles explained in Chapter 3.[608] Hence payment by set-off, under which the money is not readily available to the payee, is normally unauthorised.[609] However, if the money is paid over to the principal the third party is, obviously, discharged. And there are cases where an agent, for example an auctioneer, may be regarded as contracting independently with the third party.[610] In such a case, the right of the principal to sue on the contract is subservient to that of the agent: and a payment to or settlement with the agent may operate as a discharge, notwithstanding that the person making the payment or settlement has had notice from the principal or trustee in bankruptcy not to pay the agent; and such payment or settlement may be by way of set-off or settlement of accounts between the agent and the person making the settlement.[611]

8-108

Rule (2): Undisclosed principal[612] Where the principal is undisclosed, and the third party therefore believes that the agent is dealing on his own account, the third party may use all the defences, including set-offs and other matters personal to the agent,[613] which had already arisen[614] (whether or not on the original account, and

8-109

---

[606] See Comment; *Restatement, Third*, § 6.07. § 6.07(3)(a) provides that a third party who receives notice of the principal's existence may demand reasonable proof of the principal's identity, and is in general not affected until it is given.
[607] As in *Barker v Greenwood* (1837) 2 Y. & C.Ex. 414, Illustration 2 to Article 28; *Stewart v Aberdein* (1838) 4 M. & W. 211; cf. *Young v White* (1844) 7 Beav. 506.
[608] See especially Article 28.
[609] See *Pearson v Scott* (1878) 9 Ch.D. 198, Illustration 3 to Article 28.
[610] See below, paras 9-009 and 9-023.
[611] Illustrations 4 and 5. See also below, para.10-010.
[612] See valuable discussions in Derham, *Law of Set-Off* (4th edn), para.13.79 onwards; Wood, *English and International Set-Off* (1989), Ch.19.
[613] See Article 79, Illustrations 1 and 3; *Rabone v Williams* (1785) 7 T.R. 360n.; *George v Clagett* (1979) 7 T.R. 359; *Ex p. Dixon, re Henley* (1876) 4 Ch.D. 133. Where there are mutual credits between the agent and the other contracting party, in order to constitute a right of set-off as against the principal, each of the debts must be liquidated: *Turner v Thomas* (1871) L.R. 6 C.P. 610.
[614] As to the meaning of this word see Derham, *Law of Set-Off* (4th edn), para.13.84; cf. Wood, *English and International Set-off* (1989), p.985 onwards. It seems likely that the debt need not be payable, but perhaps it must be payable by the time the money is actually demanded, or the third party would be able to get satisfaction in respect of a debt not yet payable.

whether previously or subsequently to the original transaction[615]) against the agent prior to the discovery of the principal,[616] and is discharged by payment to the agent prior to such time.[617] So also the third party, before he has notice of the principal's existence, may vary the contract by agreement with the agent.[618] But if the principal intervenes, the third party should no longer pay the agent.[619]

All this is obviously reasonable, but the principle justifying it is not certain, and there may be differences of application, depending upon what that principle is. One approach, which, it is submitted, is the better, concentrates on the position of the third party, and holds him entitled to take advantage of such defences provided he believed the agent to be principal, on the ground that the principal intervenes on the agent's contract and must do so, like an assignee, subject to equities.[620] This would be contrary to the Privy Council's rejection of the assignment analogy in *Siu Yin Kwan v Eastern Insurance Co Ltd*,[621] but in its favouring of the third party is in accord with modern approaches to agency.

The other approach concentrates on the position of the principal[622] and only holds him bound by such defences if he has done something towards misleading the third party, as by giving the agent possession of goods. The fact that he is bound is said to depend on estoppel.[623] This reasoning seems to arise to some extent from a confusion with the rules as to apparent ownership,[624] where the validity of a disposition of property is in issue and an estoppel is required to displace the operation of the property—protecting *maxim nemo dat quod non habet*. In the present case, however, the validity of the contract is not disputed and no special reasoning is therefore required: a person contracting with another is surely entitled to assume that the other contracts for himself and that he can therefore safely pay the other or plead set-off against him unless he has reason to believe the contrary, and to this the fault, or lack of it, of a person unknown to him is not conclusive. Further, as with the situation of the third party indicating that he has received payment, discussed above,[625] it is difficult to see how a person can ever rely on the representation of someone of whom he has not heard. The same criticism applies to the doctrine of apparent ownership, and this has therefore to receive a special and somewhat involved justification in terms of estoppel by conduct,[626] which can here be avoided. It also seems clear that the supposed estoppel can arise even where the

---

[615] It is submitted that this is the best view, though there seems to be no clear authority. For an exhaustive, though now dated, summary of English and American cases on this and related topics, see 53 A.L.R. Annotated 414 (1928).

[616] Illustrations 9 and 10; *Mann v Forrester* (1814) 4 Camp. 60.

[617] *Coates v Lewes* (1808) 1 Camp. 444; *Curlewis v Birkbeck* (1863) 3 F. & F. 894.

[618] *Blackburn v Scholes* (1810) 2 Camp. 341. See *Restatement, Third*, § 6.08.

[619] See below, para.9-012.

[620] cf. *Rabone v Williams* (1785) 7 T.R. 360n.; *George v Clagett* (1797) 7 T.R. 359; *Ramazotti v Bowring* (1859) 7 C.B.(N.S.) 851 at 856; *Turner v Thomas* (1871) L.R. 6 C.P. 610 at 613; *Montgomerie v UK Mutual Steamship Assn* [1891] 1 Q.B. 370 at 372. And see Article 79(2).

[621] [1994] 2 A.C. 199; above, para.8-079.

[622] See *Baring v Corrie* (1818) 2 B. & A. 137.

[623] *Cooke & Sons v Eshelby* (1887) 12 App.Cas. 271 at 278 (Illustration 7); cf. p.283. See also *Fish v Kempton* (1849) 7 C.B. 687; *Ramazotti v Bowring* (1859) 7 C.B.(N.S.) 851; *Drakeford v Piercy* (1866) 7 B. & S. 515.

[624] Article 84. See the same confusion in *Lloyds & Scottish Finance Ltd v Williamson* [1965] 1 W.L.R. 404. But cf. Mechem, *Outlines of Agency* (4th edn), §§ 177–183.

[625] Para.8-103.

[626] See Article 84 and Comment.

principal told the agent to disclose the agency.[627] Finally, the conditions giving rise to estoppel in this case appear to fall short of those required to give rise to apparent ownership: it is now settled that apparent ownership is not created by merely giving the possession of goods to another,[628] whereas it seems that the estoppel in this situation can be raised by such conduct without more.[629]

Notice as to principal's existence Under each approach it is clear that, while it is said that the doctrine of constructive notice is not applicable in commercial transactions,[630] the third party may be taken to have notice that the agent has or may have a principal, e.g. by the nature of the agent's occupation[631] or because the fact or possibility is known to his own agent.[632] Under the first approach there would not be an equity in favour of the third party: under the second, this prejudice would not have been caused by the principal's conduct.   **8-110**

Preferable approach Although the second approach was adopted by the House of Lords in *Cooke & Sons v Eshelby*[633] it is submitted that, as in the case of settlement by the principal with the agent, previously discussed,[634] the difficulty arises partly from the failure to distinguish between disclosed principal cases and undisclosed principal cases. The latter type of case is a very special one and may not be rightly subsumed under normal agency principles.[635] The estoppel approach is based on the notion that the contract is that of the principal, and hence is again only appropriate to the case of the disclosed principal, whether named or unnamed.   **8-111**

Where the third party knows of no principal and this is reasonable in the circumstances it seems inappropriate and indeed unfair to him to require fault in the

---

[627] *Ex p. Dixon, re Henley* (1876) 4 Ch.D. 133; *Knight v Matson & Co* (1903) 22 N.Z.L.R. 293.

[628] See Article 84.

[629] *Borries v Imperial Ottoman Bank* (1873) L.R. 9 C.P. 38; *Rabone v Williams* (1785) 7 T.R. 360n; *George v Clagett* (1797) 7 T.R. 359; *Ex p. Dixon, re Henley*, above; *Knight v Matson & Co*, above. The old cases usually required that possession be given to a factor, who had authority to and often did sell in his own name, as opposed to a broker who should not—indeed the distinction between them was largely worked out in this connection: see *Baring v Corrie* (1818) 2 B. & Ald. 137; *Semenza v Brinsley* (1865) 18 C.B.(N.S.) 467; *Drakeford v Piercy* (1866) 7 B. & S. 515; *Cooke & Sons v Eshelby* (1887) 12 App.Cas. 271 above; above, para.1-046. If these were the only cases, this could rank as an extra feature over and above delivery of possession (see Comment to Article 84). But the doctrine was also applied to brokers; see *Coates v Lewes* (1808) 1 Camp. 444; *Blackburn v Scholes* (1810) 2 Camp. 341; and in any case, decisions could not turn on that distinction today. This difference seems to have been ignored in *Lloyds & Scottish Finance v Williamson* [1965] 1 W.L.R. 404, where these cases were cited, but passing of property was in issue.

[630] *Manchester Trust v Furness* [1895] 2 Q.B. 539; *Greer v Downs Supply Co* [1927] 2 K.B. 28; *Borries v Imperial Ottoman Bank* (1873) L.R. 9 C.P. 38; but see Article 73 and above, para.8-073.

[631] Notably if he is a broker: *Baring v Corrie* (1818) 2 B. & A. 137, which was a leading case on the position of brokers as opposed to factors; *Cooke & Sons v Eshelby* (1887) 12 App.Cas. 271. It is not, of course, necessary that the actual principal is known: *Maanss v Henderson* (1801) 1 East 335; *Semenza v Brinsley* (1865) 18 C.B. N.S. 467; *Mildred v Maspons* (1883) 8 App.Cas. 874.

[632] *Dresser v Norwood* (1864) 17 C.B.(N.S.) 446, Illustration 6. See the cases discussed in Derham, *Law of Set-Off* (4th edn), para.13.85 onwards.

[633] (1887) 12 App.Cas. 271, Illustration 7: treated as correct in *Cooper v Strauss & Co* (1898) 14 T.L.R. 233 and *Wester Moffat Colliery v Jeffrey* 1911 S.C. 346. See also *Owens v Harris Bros* (1932) 34 W.A.L.R. 110. In *Montagu v Forwood* [1893] 2 Q.B. 350, Illustration 10, the emphasis on fault is not so strong, and indeed on the facts stated in the official report it is not easy to see how the principal was at fault. But further facts appear in the report at 69 L.T. 371. See also Powell, pp.174–178.

[634] Article 80.

[635] See Comment to Article 76.

principal before set-off against the agent may be valid or settlement with the agent effective. The third party may have dealt with the agent precisely because the agent was indebted to him. Where the principal cannot be said to have been at fault, his intervention could on the estoppel approach only be prevented under the rules preventing an intervention which is inconsistent with the express or implied terms of the contract,[636] rules which are of rare application.[637] It is therefore submitted that in the case of undisclosed principals, the analogy of the assignee intervening subject to equities should again be followed, and Rule (2) has been modified to permit this.[638] *Cooke & Sons v Eshelby*[639] is a marginal decision (albeit a common fact situation) where the agent (a broker) sometimes dealt on his own account and sometimes as an agent: the third party said that he had no belief one way or the other as to which was the case on this occasion. It is thus not clear whether the principal should have been treated as undisclosed or merely as unidentified. The decision against the third party may or may not have been a fair one on the facts.[640]

The two approaches will normally yield the same result: for a principal who uses the services of an agent whom he directs not to disclose his name, or who he knows does not disclose the existence of his principals, can be regarded as leading the third party to suppose that the agent acts for himself.[641] The same is true where, as often, he gives the agent possession of goods. But there can be a difference. Where he does not transfer such possession, and does not do anything that facilitates the deception of the third party, but simply tells the agent to contract in his (the principal's) name, and the agent disobeys and contracts in his own name, the principal might on the estoppel view not be bound by set-offs against, and payments to, the agent.[642]

Illustrations

8-112 (1) A traveller offers a sample of goods to a tradesman with whom he has had previous dealings: the tradesman knows that the traveller is probably acting for someone else. The tradesman orders coats as per sample, and they are sent to him by the supplier. The traveller was working for the supplier on this occasion only, having represented to the supplier that he could obtain an order from the tradesman. Payment to the traveller, there being an invoice bearing the supplier's name, is no discharge to the tradesman.[643]

(2) A firm employed A, a traveller, to carry with him for sale parcels of sponges. It was A's duty, on concluding a bargain, to forward particulars of the transaction to the firm. The firm would then send to the customer an invoice and (monthly) a statement of account. The statement of account contained three notices: (1) "Cheques to be crossed". (2) "All cheques to be made payable to the firm". (3) "No receipt valid unless on firm's printed form to be attached hereto". B dealt thus with the firm for some years. Between 1905 and

---

[636] As in *Greer v Downs Supply Co* [1927] 2 K.B. 28.

[637] See above, para.8-079.

[638] The wording in earlier editions was "A person who, in dealing with an agent, is led by the conduct of the principal to believe, and does in fact believe … etc." But Derham, *Law of Set-Off* (4th edn), simply regards this as an anomaly upon a doctrine already anomalous: see para.13.99.

[639] (1887) 12 App.Cas. 271, Illustration 7.

[640] It was criticised by Pollock (1887) 3 L.Q.R. 358. See also Reynolds [1983] C.L.P. 119 at 122–125.

[641] See *Semenza v Brinsley* (1865) 18 C.B.(N.S.) 467; *Ex p. Dixon, re Henley* (1876) 4 Ch.D. 133 (where the agent acted contrary to instructions).

[642] *Restatement*, § 306, Comment *a*, rejected in *Restatement, Third*, § 6.06, Comment *a* and reporter's notes thereto. But cf. *Ex p. Dixon, re Henley*, above.

[643] *Butwick v Grant* [1924] 2 K.B. 483. See also Article 28.

1908 A sold three parcels of sponges to B. In respect of two of these sales A induced B to pay by cheque payable to him. For the third parcel B paid A in cash. A had no authority to receive in payment anything except crossed cheques in favour of the firm. A fraudulently appropriated the three sums to himself. Held, that the payments to A were valid against the firm, for the notices in the statements of accounts did not contain sufficient intimation to their customer that A was not authorised to receive payment for goods delivered in cash or by a cheque in his favour cashable at once.[644]

(3)   A broker sells goods in the name of his principal to A, who pays the broker for them. The broker absconds without paying over the money to the principal. A is liable to the principal for the price of the goods, unless the broker had authority, or was held out by the principal as having authority, to receive payment, and the mere fact that the principal had on previous occasions authorised him to receive payment for goods sold on his behalf is not sufficient evidence of such authority or holding out.[645]

(4)   A factor who has a lien on goods for advances sells the goods in his own name. The buyer, though he knew that the factor was acting as an agent, is, to the extent of the factor's lien, discharged by a payment to him, even if the payment be by way of set-off,[646] or be made after the bankruptcy of the principal, and after notice from the trustee in bankruptcy not to pay the factor.[647]

(5)   A factor who had a lien on goods in excess of the value sold the goods to A, to whom he was indebted. The factor became bankrupt. A gave credit for the price of the goods, and proved in the bankruptcy for the residue of his debts against the factor. Held, that this settlement was a good answer to an action by the principal against A for the price.[648]

(6)   A broker bought goods on behalf of A from a factor who sold them on behalf of B. The broker knew that the factor sold the goods on behalf of a principal, but A thought that he was selling his own goods. B sued A for the price. Held, that A was bound by the knowledge of his broker, and therefore had no right to set off a debt to him from the factor.[649]

(7)   A broker who was entrusted by his principal with the possession of goods sold them in his own name without disclosing the principal. The buyer knew that the broker sometimes sold goods in his own name, though acting as a broker, and sometimes sold goods of his own, and in this case had no particular belief one way or the other. Held, that the buyer was not entitled, in an action by the principal for the price, to set off a debt due from the broker personally.[650]

(8)   A, who acted as shipping agent for B, a merchant in Havana, consigned in his own name to C a cargo of tobacco C, according to his instructions, insured the cargo for the benefit of all concerned, having had notice that there was a principal. The cargo was lost, and the insurance money was paid to C after

---

[644] *International Sponge Importers Ltd v Andrew Watt & Sons* [1911] A.C. 279. See also Article 28.

[645] *Linck, Moeller & Co v Jameson & Co* (1885) 2 T.L.R. 206.

[646] *Warner v M'Kay* (1836) 1 M. & W. 591.

[647] *Drinkwater v Goodwin* (1775) Cowp. 251.

[648] *Hudson v Granger* (1821) 5 B. & A. 27. These cases, like that of the auctioneer, are nowadays best explained as involving collateral contracts. See below, paras 9-009 and 9-021.

[649] *Dresser v Norwood* (1864) 17 C.B.(N.S.) 466. See the same case, Article 95, Illustration 3.

[650] *Cooke & Sons v Eshelby* (1887) 12 App.Cas. 271.

he had received notice that B claimed it. Held, that C was not entitled to set off, as against B, debts due to him from A personally.[651]

(9)   Goods were consigned to an agent for sale. The agent pledged the goods to brokers as security for a specific advance, and authorised them to sell. The broker sold the goods, but before receiving the proceeds had notice that the principal was the owner, and that he claimed the proceeds. Held, that the principal was entitled to the balance of the proceeds after deducting the amount of the advance, and that the brokers were not entitled to set off such balance against a general account due to them from the agent.[652] It would be otherwise, if they had received the proceeds in the bona fide belief that they belonged to the agent, and had credited the amount in the account with the agent before receiving notice of the principal's claim.[653]

(10)   A employed B to collect general average contributions under an insurance policy. B instructed a broker to collect the contributions, the broker believing him to be the principal. B became bankrupt. In an action by A against the broker for the contributions, as money received to his use, it was held that the broker was entitled to set off a debt due from B.[654]

Article 82

MERGER AND ELECTION: RELEASE OF PRINCIPAL

8-113   (1)   Where an agent enters into a contract on which he is personally liable, and judgment is obtained against him on it, the judgment, though unsatisfied is, so long as it subsists,[655] a bar to any proceedings against the principal, undisclosed or (perhaps) disclosed, on the contract.[656]

(2)   (Perhaps), where an agent enters into a contract on behalf of an undisclosed principal or on such terms that he is personally liable on it together with his principal, and the other contracting party, knowing or discovering who is the real principal, elects to pursue his rights against the agent, he is bound by his election and cannot afterwards sue the principal on the contract. The question whether or not he has so elected is a question of fact.

(3)   Except as provided in this Article, the liability of the principal, whether disclosed or undisclosed, upon a contract made on his behalf is not affected by fact that the agent is personally liable on the contract.[657]

---

[651] *Mildred, Goyeneche & Co v Maspons y Hermano* (1883) 8 App.Cas. 874.

[652] *Kaltenbach, Fischer & Co v Lewis and Peat* (1885) 10 App.Cas. 617. See on this case (1932) 4 C.L.J. 320 at 333–334.

[653] ibid.; *New Zealand and Australian Land Co v Watson* (1881) 7 Q.B.D. 374.

[654] *Montagu v Forwood* [1893] 2 Q.B. 350. See also *Knight v Matson & Co* (1903) 22 N.Z.L.R. 293; *Curlewis v Birkbeck* (1863) 3 F. & F. 894.

[655] As to the position where the first judgment is set aside, see *C Inc Plc v L* [2001] 2 Lloyd's Rep. 459 at [107].

[656] But see below, paras 8-116 and 8-117.

[657] See Comment. For an extended treatment of the problems in this area, see Reynolds (1970) 86 L.Q.R. 318 (on which, however, the present text represents some advance). See also Clayton (1925) 3 Texas L. Rev. 384; Merrill (1933) 12 Nebr.L.Bull. 100; (1953) 34 Nebr.L.Rev. 613; Hill [1967] J.B.L. 125–128; Sargent and Rochvarg (1982) 36 U. Miami.L.Rev. 411; Richmond (1983) 66 Marq.L.Rev. 745; Seavey, *Studies in Agency* (1949), pp.215–219 and 330–331; Stoljar, pp.216–219. cf. Indian Contract Act s.233, the interpretation of which has caused difficulties: Pollock and Mulla, *Indian Contract and Specific Relief Acts* (14th edn). As to the position in Scotland, see Phillips, 1993 J.R. 133.

Comment

Questions of principle The propositions stated above represent a conservative at- **8-114**
tempt to state the law emerging from the many and rather confused decisions on
this topic. They are, however, difficult propositions to justify in principle.[658] It is difficult to see in principle why, where principal and agent are both liable on a contract,
any doctrine of merger or election should bar a person who has proceeded against
one from proceeding against the other. Only satisfaction of the claim should
normally be a bar.

The real basis of such notions of merger and election seems to be an assumption, common in older cases, that the contract was either with the principal or with
the agent. In cases of disclosed principal these were in effect alternative interpretations of the facts: but it seems to have been applied also to undisclosed principals
and their agents on the basis that there was alternative liability as a matter of
substantive law. But it is now clear that there can be cases where the agent is liable together with the disclosed principal[659]: and there seems no real reason why
this should not be so in the case of the undisclosed principal also. To such analysis,
the idea of merger or election in respect of alternative liabilities seems
inappropriate.

Only three lines of reasoning appear available to justify the results stated in the
Article as formulated. The first is that the principal and the agent are liable jointly.
If there is only one obligation, it can be said that judgment against one can release
the other. This would be solely a doctrine of merger: any notion of election would
be irrelevant. This is certainly a possible interpretation of some cases where
disclosed principal and agent are both liable on a contract. But it is by no means
the only one: indeed, it is an unlikely one.[660] Further, there seems no reason at all
to apply it to undisclosed principals and their agents, and indeed it has not been applied to them. In any case, the rule that judgment against one person jointly liable
releases the other was abolished in England by statute in 1978, so that the reasoning now fails, at any rate in England.[661]

The second possible justification is that the liability of principal and agent is,
where they are both liable to the third party, as a matter of substance an alternative
liability. The leading case of *United Australia Ltd v Barclays Bank Ltd*,[662] concerning waiver of tort, accepts a distinction as to choice between inconsistent rights and
choice between alternative remedies. In the first, election is required; but in the
second the right to proceed is (probably[663]) only lost by satisfaction of the claim.
The standard example of the first is the right to treat a contract as discharged for
breach, or to forfeit a lease: once this is done, the party concerned cannot proceed
on the basis that the contract or lease subsists. An example in the context of agency
is the right or power to ratify.[664] It is possible, and indeed is assumed in the *United*

---

[658] See a valuable discussion of this topic by Thomas J in *L.C. Fowler & Sons Ltd v St Stephen's College Board of Governors* [1991] 3 N.Z.L.R. 304.
[659] See below, para.9-006.
[660] See below, para.9-006.
[661] Civil Liability (Contribution) Act 1978 s.3.
[662] [1941] A.C. 1.
[663] cf. [1941] A.C. 1 at 3, 21 and 30.
[664] See Article 17; *Verschures Creameries Ltd v Hull and Netherlands SS Co Ltd* [1921] 2 K.B. 608,
Illustration 6 to Article 20. But this is probably distinct from election.

Australia case itself,[665] that the liabilities of agent and undisclosed principal are inconsistent in such a way as to require election between rights. This can only really be justified as a special analysis applicable in this context to situations of undisclosed principals. But as to disclosed principals, although a third party could enter into a contract with a disclosed principal and agent on the basis that their liability was alternative, it is difficult to see that in normal situations there would be any reason for doing so,[666] and hence for a court to put such an interpretation on the facts. The problem in the disclosed principal situation seems rather to be one of alternative remedies against persons who are both liable. Modern analysis of the situation where the agent is liable together with the principal has made this clearer than it was before.[667] As stated above, older cases tended to assume that either the principal or the agent was liable. Such reasoning more easily raises the possibility of an argument that the third party must choose. There has also sometimes been, as in other areas, a lack of clarity in distinguishing a true undisclosed principal from a mere unidentified though disclosed principal,[668] which may have added to the confusion.

It does, however, seem that the liability of agent and undisclosed principal is on present authority to be regarded as an alternative one: and since the whole doctrine of the undisclosed principal can be said to be anomalous anyway,[669] it cannot be said that such a view is demonstrably wrong, even if there is not much to commend it.[670] If this is so, the governing principle could be regarded either as one of merger or as one of election. If it is one of merger, manifestation of choice to sue one or the other would have no relevance; but a judgment against one would discharge the other, and where it is against the agent, even where it was taken without knowledge of the principal. If the principle is the broader one of election, the third party has an election or choice as to with whom he wishes to regard the contract as having been. When he has manifested this choice he cannot thereafter change course. Until he realises the existence of the undisclosed principal, of course, he is not able to make a valid election, for on general principles a choice cannot be exercised by one who does not know that he has it.[671] Though the narrower, merger principle predominates, the election approach has been taken in some cases, including the *United Australia* case itself.[672] A compromise position is that judgment is the only true election.[673]

The third justification is this. There are many situations where a person does not allege that both agent and principal were liable to him, but cannot decide on the correct interpretation of the facts whether his contract was with one or the other; and therefore sues both in the alternative and leaves the court to decide the question. Or again, he may allege one interpretation and the other party may in defence allege another. Here the court is asked to decide between two mutually inconsistent legal interpretations of the facts. Once a final judgment has been obtained on this issue of fact, the matter is res judicata. This is obviously not a matter of merger;

---

[665] See [1941] A.C. at 30.
[666] But see below, para.9-023 as to certain types of brokerage arrangements.
[667] See Comment to Article 98.
[668] See above, para.8-073.
[669] See Comment to Article 76.
[670] See *L.C. Fowler & Sons Ltd v St Stephen's College Board of Governors* [1991] 3 N.Z.L.R. 304.
[671] See below, para.8-121.
[672] See [1941] A.C. at 30.
[673] See cases cited below, para.8-119.

but neither is it one of election between inconsistent rights. In this situation, at least in theory, one interpretation is right and the other simply wrong. The matter is rather one of finality of decision as to the proper legal analysis of facts; or sometimes as to restrictions on the advancing of mutually inconsistent allegations. Difficulties arise in particular when it is sought to reopen the issue in connection with judgments subject to appeal, and as to default and summary judgments, and some of the leading cases concern procedural problems arising in such situations.[674] In such situations there is an element of choice in a rather special sense. The third party may choose which interpretation to allege, and sue on that basis. If the action is undefended, or summary judgment is given, that interpretation is in theory adopted by the court. But this happened merely at the choice of the plaintiff. Had the case proceeded to trial the court might have decided on a different interpretation of the facts. So the third party has certainly made a choice of a sort; but it is not an election between inconsistent rights, to each of which he is entitled, it is, rather, a pragmatic choice as to against whom to start proceedings in an uncertain situation. However, the dicta in these cases are sometimes uncompromisingly general. Both for default and summary judgments, the procedural decisions are given on the apparent basis that the liability in issue is alternative. This, it is submitted, is not correct. It is these cases which are productive of the most confusion.[675]

It may be added that there are other situations where the third party may do an act which is relevant to the establishment of liability at a much earlier stage, e.g. enter principal or agent in his books as debtor. This is even less an election in respect of legal rights: it is simply an act which may assist in interpreting the initial intentions of all possible parties with respect to any contractual position between them.[676]

The last technique which may be applied is that of estoppel. By the principle of equitable estoppel, a person who represents that he intends to take a particular course of action may be debarred from going back on that representation if there is some element of reliance making it inequitable to do so.[677] By other forms of estoppel, for example estoppel by convention, a person who acts on the basis of a

---

[674] e.g. *Morel Bros & Co Ltd v Earl of Westmorland* [1904] A.C. 11; *Moore v Flanagan* [1920] 1 K.B. 919. See also the cases on default judgments cited below, para.8-118. The leading Australian case of *Petersen v Moloney* (1958) 84 C.L.R. 91 may be of this type. Here the purchaser of land paid the vendor's estate agent and the question was whether the agent had authority to receive payment: the eventual answer was "no". The vendor sued the purchaser and his agent in the alternative: and it was held that a judgment against the agent which was subject to appeal did not prevent judgment against the purchaser. Here the inconsistent interpretations were that the purchaser had paid and the agent was liable to the vendor; or that the purchaser had not paid and was still liable to pay, and hence the agent not liable to the vendor. However, it can be said that the action against the agent was a ratification of the agent's act in receiving the money, which would have involved a need to elect between inconsistent rights. But ratification was not argued: see p.93. In any case, the decision concerns an action by a principal against his own agent—not by the third party (despite some argument to the contrary: see pp.93 and 97–98). It accepts the view that judgment alone constitutes election. It was followed in *Bain Securities Ltd v Curmi* (1990) 1 A.C.S.R. 794, which was a true case of a third party suing agent and undisclosed principal. See also *Con-Stan Industries of Australia Pty Ltd v Norwich Winterthur Insurance (Australia) Ltd* (1986) 160 C.L.R. 226.

[675] In *Lang Transport Ltd v Plus Factor International Trucking Ltd* (1997) 143 D.L.R. (4th) 672, the Ontario Court of Appeal by a majority held that where a default judgment was obtained against an agent who was not liable at all, it could be set aside.

[676] See below, para.8-120.

[677] See *Société Italo-Belge, etc. v Palm and Vegetable Oils (M) Sdn Bhd (The Post Chaser)* [1982] 1 All E.R. 19; note the reference to election reasoning (though in a different context) at the end of the judgment.

particular assumption of facts or interpretation may be debarred from going back on it.[678] These and similar lines of reasoning may sometimes debar a person who has taken one course of action in such a dispute from going back on it. They are not, however, the same as election.

8-115   **The Restatements**   It will be seen that the clearest case for the application of some doctrine of merger or election is the specialised one of the undisclosed principal, where the view that the liability is substantively alternative certainly can, though it need not, be taken. The alternative liability can, as has been stated, be attributed either to a merger rule, or to a wider rule of election. *Restatement, Second*, of 1958 accordingly provided, in deference to the case law of the time, but contrary to the inclinations of the Reporter, Professor Seavey,[679] for release of the agent of an undisclosed principal by judgment against the principal.[680] This was a rule of merger only: no role was left for election.[681] But it only provided for release of the undisclosed principal by judgment against the agent where it was taken with knowledge of the principal's connection with the transaction[682]—an exception which, as the Reporter recognised[683] could be justified under a principle of election, but is contrary to the principle of merger on an alternative liability. It is nevertheless a gloss which can readily be understood. The *Restatement* also preserved the application of estoppel.[684] In the area of disclosed principal it allowed for loss of the right of action only if the parties contracted jointly, in which case there was a merger once judgment is given.[685] This is not now relevant in English law. It also again allowed for estoppel.[686] *Restatement, Third*,[687] by reference to more recent case law,[688] simply provides that judgment against principal or agent does not discharge the liability unless satisfied. Estoppel is again preserved.[689] However, the English cases are such and so numerous as to require special treatment: it is (unfortunately) difficult to say that they at present justify the formulation in this Article of rules even such as those of either *Restatement*.[690]

These general points being made, discussion follows of the case law on which the actual wording of the Article is based.

8-116   **Rule (1): Judgment. Undisclosed principal**   It is well established in England that if the third party obtains judgment against the agent of an undisclosed principal, he can no longer sue the principal, even though he obtained judgment in ignorance of the fact that the agent had been acting for another, and so of his full rights, and even

---

[678] See above, para.8-028.
[679] See Comment to § 210; 7 Proc. Am. Law Inst. 257 (1929) (on the first *Restatement*): "We do not think that it is a sound theory, sound common sense or good justice".
[680] § 337.
[681] §§ 209 and 237.
[682] § 210.
[683] See Comment to § 210.
[684] § 337.
[685] § 184(1).
[686] § 336.
[687] § 6.09.
[688] Especially *Grinder v Bryans Road Building and Supply Co* 432 A.2d 453 (Md. 1981), where it is said (at 463) that "The foregoing reasoning is unassailable on any ground other than its lack of strict adherence to the precedents". See also fn.696 below.
[689] See § 6.09, Comment *d*.
[690] See Rix J in *The Nea Tyhi* [1999] 2 Lloyd's Rep. 497 at 534.

though the judgment is unsatisfied.[691] The rule seems to be based on two arguments. The first is that there is only one obligation, which is merged in the judgment.[692] The analogy is with the case of joint debtors[693]; but the reasoning seems rather that the obligation is an alternative one. This is reinforced by a rather rough and ready argument, that the liability of the undisclosed principal involves an interpretation of the facts inconsistent with that involving the agent's liability, and the third party cannot have it both ways: the principal's liability is in a sense a windfall, and the third party cannot complain if the windfall turns out to be of limited value.[694] But, as stated above, this rule relating to joint debtors has been changed by statute.[695] And what may be called the "windfall" argument can be regarded as reneging on the doctrine of undisclosed principal itself. It seems that in the late nineteenth century the doctrine came to be thought of as inconsistent with basic contract theory, and limitations were consequently placed on it. Such inconsistency was not of itself a valid reason for the limitations imposed. It seems clear, however, that the present rule for undisclosed principals, that the obligation is alternative, can only be changed by the Supreme Court. There is now considerable authority in the United States rejecting such a rule.[696]

Disclosed principal   The cases indicate that the same doctrine of merger applies   **8-117**
to situations where both agent and principal are liable on the contract, but where the existence of the principal is disclosed: it has been applied to cases of identified principals[697] and a fortiori would apply to cases of unidentified principals, who are in any case nearer to undisclosed principals. It has also been applied to recovery of judgment for part only of an undivided debt.[698] In the disclosed principal situation, however, the doctrine is even more difficult to justify. The "windfall" argument is completely inapplicable. The "one obligation" argument, though relied on,[699] is as regards joint obligations again now rendered obsolete by statute,[700] and there seems in the case of a disclosed principal little reason to regard the obliga-

---

[691] *Priestly v Fernie* (1863) 3 H. & C. 977, Illustration 1 (not a convincing case, nor a case on a true undisclosed principal, since ships are known to have owners); *Kendall v Hamilton* (1879) 4 App.Cas. 504 at 513–515. See too *Antonio Gramsci Shipping Corp v Stepanovs* [2011] EWHC 333 (Comm); [2011] C.L.C. 396 at [28].

[692] *Kendall v Hamilton*, above, at 515; *M. Brennen & Sons Mfg. Co Ltd v Thompson* (1915) 33 Ont.L.T. 465 at 471–472; *Marginson v Ian Potter & Co* (1976) 136 C.L.R. 161.

[693] *Kendall v Hamilton*, above, was in fact the leading case on joint debtors, though paradoxically it takes the position of the undisclosed principal as a paradigm.

[694] *Kendall v Hamilton*, above, at 544.

[695] Civil Liability Contribution Act 1978 s.3.

[696] A leading case is *Grinder v Bryans Road Building and Supply Co* 432 A.2d 453 (CA Md., 1981); see also *Crown Controls Inc v Smiley* 756 P.2d 717 (Wash., 1988); *Engelstat v Cargill Inc* 336 N.W. 2d 284 (Minn., 1983); *Tower Cranes of America v Public Service Co* 702 F.Supp.371 (DNH, 1988). See above, para.8-115.

[697] *Morel Bros & Co Ltd v Earl of Westmorland* [1904] A.C. 11, Illustration 2; *Sullivan v Sullivan* [1912] 2 I.R. 116 at 127–128; *Moore v Flanagan* [1920] 1 K.B. 919; *RMKRM (A Firm) v MRM VL (A Firm)* [1926] A.C. 761, Illustration 3; *Debenhams Ltd v Perkins* (1925) 133 L.T. 252 at 254; *Barrington v Lee* [1972] 1 Q.B. 326. See also the leading Australian case of *Petersen v Moloney* (1958) 84 C.L.R. 91; as to which see fn.674 above.

[698] *French v Howie* [1906] 2 K.B. 674.

[699] *Moore v Flanagan* [1920] 1 K.B. 919 at 925–926.

[700] See Civil Liability (Contribution) Act 1978. See too *1196303 Inc v Glen Grove Suites Inc* 2015 ONCA 580.

tion as alternative.[701] In those circumstances where the third party may be regarded as having stipulated for the liability of both agent and principal, it may be thought that he does so in order to make sure of satisfaction: the dual liability would be of much reduced utility if lost by a mere unsatisfied judgment against one party. It has been suggested above that the extension of the merger doctrine to disclosed principal situations is due to two things: a failure, as in other contexts,[702] to distinguish an unidentified principal situation from a true undisclosed principal situation[703]; and a failure to analyse adequately the nature of the agent's liability in cases where he is liable together with his principal.

Older cases tended to assume that either the principal or the agent was liable. But modern analysis[704] indicates that an agent liable together with his principal may in principle be liable jointly, jointly and severally, as surety, on a separate contract, or in the alternative. Joint liability, with its technical rules, is rarely appropriate: it applies to partners,[705] but not normally to husband and wife.[706] The possibilities of suretyship[707] and separate contracts[708] are also recognised. But in this context of the taking of proceedings against one or the other, there are a surprising number of assertions against joint and several liability and in favour of alternative liability.[709] Indeed the doctrine of merger has in some cases been applied where it might appear that the agent against whom judgment was obtained was in fact not liable at all,[710] so that the judgment should have been regarded as abortive and as being no bar to subsequent proceedings against a person who was liable.[711] It has also been extended to actions in restitution in respect of deposits paid to estate agents in

---

[701] See *L.C. Fowler & Sons Ltd v St Stephen's College Board of Governors* [1991] 3 N.Z.L.R. 304 at 311–312 (Illustration 7); and above, para.8-114.

[702] cf. above, paras 8-073, 8-105 and 8-111.

[703] cf. above, para.8-114. See also *Priestly v Fernie* (1863) 3 Hurl. & C. 977.

[704] See Comment to Article 98.

[705] Partnership Act 1890 s.9.

[706] *Morel Bros & Co Ltd v Earl of Westmorland* [1904] A.C. 11. cf. *Swanton Seed Service Ltd v Kulba* (1968) 68 D.L.R. (2d) 38.

[707] *Imperial Bank v London & St Katharine Docks Co* (1877) 5 Ch.D. 195 at 200; *Fleet v Murton* (1871) L.R. 7 Q.B. 126 at 132. See also *Young v Schuler* (1883) 11 Q.B.D. 651; *Rutherford v Ounan* [1913] 2 I.R. 265 at 268.

[708] *Barclays Bank Ltd v Williams* (1971) 115 S.J. 674 (breach of warranty of authority); *M. Brennen & Son Mfg Co Ltd v Thompson* (1915) 33 Ont.L.R. 465 at 469–470; *1196303 Inc v Glen Grove Suites Inc* 2015 ONCA 580. But cf. *Benton v Campbell, Parker & Co* [1925] 2 K.B. 410 at 414, where it is contemplated that election may apply between the separate causes of action against the auctioneer and his vendor. Sometimes the agent's liability comes to an end by its terms on the acceptance of a contract by the third party with the principal. This could formerly occur on the Stock Exchange: see *Grissell v Bristowe* (1868) L.R. 4 C.P. 36; *Maxted v Paine* (1869) L.R. 4 Ex. 203; affd (1871) L.R. 6 Ex. 132; (1929) 39 Yale L.J. 265; below, para.9-023.

[709] See cases cited in notes to para.8-117 above; *Murray v Delta Copper Co Ltd* [1925] 4 D.L.R. 1061 at 1067; *Lang Transport Ltd v Plus Factor International Trucking Ltd* (1997) 143 D.L.R. (4th) 672.

[710] See the (then) RSC Ord.14 cases cited on the liability of husband and wife: *Morel Bros & Co Ltd v Earl of Westmorland* [1904] A.C. 11 (discussed (1970) 86 L.Q.R. at 338–340); *French v Howie* [1906] 2 K.B. 674; *Sullivan v Sullivan* [1912] 2 I.R. 116; *Moore v Flanagan* [1920] 1 K.B. 919. See also *Cross & Co v Matthews and Wallace* (1904) 91 L.T. 500 (default judgment: discussed (1970) 86 L.Q.R. at 341–342); *Cyril Lord (Carpet Sales) v Browne* (1966) 111 S.J. 51 (default summons: discussed at 342–343). But cf. *Longman v Hill* (1891) 7 T.L.R. 639; *Petersen v Moloney* (1951) 84 C.L.R. 91; *Goodey v Garriock* [1972] 2 Lloyd's Rep. 369 (Ord. 14).

[711] On the basis of *Isaacs & Sons v Salbstein* [1916] 2 K.B. 139, discussed below; *Longman v Hill*, above.

"subject to contract" situations.[712] But many cases[713] where the doctrine of merger has been held to operate should probably be explained by the proposition that where claims are made against principal and agent in the alternative, on the basis that the facts justify the liability of one or the other, but not both, judgment against one, unless set aside, involves res judicata in favour of the other. Whatever the arguments, the true interpretation of the facts is now settled.[714] This is based on the idea, not that both are substantively liable in the alternative, but that one is and the other is not. But it is submitted that the law urgently requires clarification. There should be no scope for merger in most disclosed principal cases. But it may be that in England, because of the weight of authority, again only the Supreme Court can say so.[715]

There can, of course, be cases where on any criterion the agent's liability is separate. Thus a wife may order goods for herself, and other, identifiably different, goods as agent for her husband.[716] In another case an agent negotiated a sale of patents by his principal, and received the price, which he retained. The principal later agreed to repurchase the patents and gave the third party a cheque, which was dishonoured. It was held that the third party had separate causes of action against the agent as stakeholder, and against the principal on the cheque and the agreement to repurchase.[717] It has also been held that where judgment had been obtained against a firm (Salbstein Bros) which was never proved to exist or to be liable, this was no bar to a subsequent action on the same facts against a person (H. Salbstein) who was liable.[718] And where the actions are in tort the position is different: principal and agent are joint tortfeasors.[719]

Setting aside of judgments   It seems in principle correct to say that where a judgment against the agent is set aside on the merits, i.e. as being wrong, it is no bar to another action against the principal[720]; but that a judgment may not simply be set aside by consent for this purpose.[721] But the cases are not clear.[722]   **8-118**

Rule (2): Election. Undisclosed principal   Some cases state the doctrine under   **8-119**

---

[712] *Barrington v Lee* [1972] 1 Q.B. 326, Illustration 6. But on this fact situation see *Sorrell v Finch* [1977] A.C. 728, Illustration 4 to Article 92.

[713] Perhaps the Ord.14 cases on husband and wife, cited above.

[714] See above, para.8-114; *Reardon Smith Line Ltd v Cayzer, Irvine & Co Ltd* (1929) 35 Com.Cas. 270; see also *Beadon v Capital Syndicate* (1912) 28 T.L.R. 427; *Clark v Urquhart* [1930] A.C. 28. As to setting aside of judgments, see below.

[715] But see *L.C. Fowler & Sons Ltd v St Stephen's College Board of Governors* [1991] 3 N.Z.L.R. 304, where a bold line was taken.

[716] *Debenham's Ltd v Perkins* (1925) 133 L.T. 252.

[717] *B.O. Morris Ltd v Perrott & Bolton* [1945] 1 All E.R. 567. See also *Bucknell v O'Donnell* (1922) 31 C.L.R. 40; *Goldrei Foucard & Son v Russian Chamber of Commerce* [1918] 1 K.B. 180.

[718] *Isaacs & Sons v Salbstein* [1916] 2 K.B. 139; followed in *Maxform SpA v Mariani and Goodville* [1979] 2 Lloyd's Rep. 385; affd [1981] 2 Lloyd's Rep. 54.

[719] See below, para.8-191; *Derham v Amev Life Assurance Co Ltd* (1981) 56 F.L.R. 34.

[720] See *Partington v Hawthorne* (1888) 52 J.P. 807 (explained in *Brennen & Sons Mfg Co Ltd v Thompson* (1915) 33 Ont. L.R. 465 at 470–471); *Buckingham v Trotter* (1901) I.S.R.(N.S.W.) 253; *Petersen v Moloney* (1951) 84 C.L.R. 91; *Goodey v Garriock* [1972] 2 Lloyd's Rep. 369 (Ord.14); *Lang Transport Ltd v Plus Factor International Trucking Ltd* (1997) 143 D.L.R. (4th) 672.

[721] *Hammond v Schofield* [1891] 1 Q.B. 453 (Ord. 14).

[722] Difficulty is caused by *Cross & Co Ltd v Matthews & Wallace* (1904) 91 L.T. 500 (default summons: discussed (1970) 86 L.Q.R. at 341–342); *Cyril Lord (Carpet Sales) v Browne* (1966) 111 S.J. 51 (default summons: discussed (1970) 86 L.Q.R. at 342–343); and the cases on husband and wife cited above. A default judgment was set aside in *Kohn v Devon Mortgage Ltd* (1983) 3 D.L.R. (4th) 466 (reversed on other grounds (1985) 20 D.L.R. (4th) 480).

which the third party may not sue both agent and undisclosed principal as applying to situations short of judgment.[723] If this is correct, the bar must be caused by the notion of election, or manifestation of choice, rather than merger. The basis of such a doctrine must again be that the obligations of agent and principal are as a matter of substantive law alternative at the election of the third party. There are, however, cases which speak of judgment as the only proof of election.[724] Here also the famous case of *Scarf v Jardine*,[725] which requires election between inconsistent liabilities in partnership law, is sometimes invoked. But, as in the case of judgment against joint debtors, the situation here is not quite the same and need not be treated in the same way.[726] "Elective liability" between two parties is a strange concept for the law. The problem is made easier, however, by the fact that though many cases speak of election, virtually every case in the field of undisclosed principal holds that the acts in question are insufficient to constitute election.[727] Only two have been traced which purport to hold that there has been a binding election short of judgment, and both can also be explained on the basis that the third party, after learning of the principal's existence, did an act which induced the principal to settle with, or alter his position as to the agent, and thereby debarred himself from looking to the principal.[728] Such cases are part of a well-established group which is not normally associated with the idea of election at all,[729] but rather with estoppel, the hallmark of which is some form of reliance. It is submitted therefore that though there is in a Court of Appeal case concerning an undisclosed principal[730] extensive discussion on the basis that the rights against principal and agent are inconsistent and subject to election (though the decision was that there had been no election), a third party should only be debarred from suing an undisclosed principal, short of an actual judgment against the agent, by an act which raises an estoppel against him, e.g. where after discovery of the principal he does an act leading the principal to suppose that he relied on the agent, or has been paid by the agent, or in some other way waives the liability of the principal in a manner relied on.[731] There are, however, fairly recent dicta in the Court of Appeal maintaining the notion of election.[732]

[723] *Curtis v Williamson* (1874) L.R. 10 Q.B. 57, Illustration 4; *United Australia Ltd v Barclays Bank Ltd* [1941] A.C. 1 at 30; *Clarkson Booker Ltd v Andjel* [1964] 2 Q.B. 775 at 794, Illustration to Article 104; *Chestertons v Barone* [1987] 1 E.G.L.R. 15 at 17; *Adams v Atlas International Property Services Ltd* [2016] EWHC 2680 (QB); [2017] Bus. L.R. 287 (but claimant also pleading agent solely liable).
[724] *Priestly v Fernie* (1863) 3 Hurl. & C. 977 at 983–984; *Buckingham v Trotter* (1901) 1 S.R.(N.S.W.) 253, at 259, 261; *Petersen v Moloney* (1951) 84 C.L.R. 91; *Morgan v Lifetime Building Supplies Ltd* (1967) 61 D.L.R. (2d) 178; *Bain Securities Ltd v Curmi* (1990) 1 A.C.S.R. 794.
[725] (1882) 7 App.Cas. 345; see also *Fell v Parkin* (1882) 52 L.J.Q.B. 99.
[726] See (1970) 86 L.Q.R. at 321–322, 327; Spencer Bower, *Reliance-Based Estoppel* (5th edn), para.13.44 onwards.
[727] *Nelson v Powell* (1784) 3 Doug. 410; *Taylor v Sheppard* (1835) 1 Y. & C.Ex. 271; *Curtis v Williamson* (1874) L.R. 10 Q.B. 57, Illustration 4; *Clarkson Booker Ltd v Andjel* [1964] 2 Q.B. 775, Illustration to Article 104.
[728] *MacClure v Schemeil* (1871) 20 W.R. 168, Illustration 3 to Article 82; *Smethurst v Mitchell* (1859) 1 E. & E. 622 (explained in *Davison v Donaldson* (1882) 9 Q.B.D. 623).
[729] See Article 80.
[730] *Clarkson Booker Ltd v Andjel* [1964] 2 Q.B. 775.
[731] See *MacClure v Schemeil*, and the other cases, above. But the taking of a bill or cheque from the agent will not normally produce such an estoppel: see cases cited in fn.747 below; cf. *Restatement, Third*, § 6.09, Comment *d*; see also Corbin (1909) 19 Yale L.J. 221 at 239.
[732] *Chestertons v Barone* [1987] 1 E.G.L.R. 15 at 17, per May LJ. See also *Adams v Atlas International*

Disclosed principal   Again, in the case of disclosed principal there are clear dicta   **8-120**
that where both principal and agent are liable, the third party must elect.[733] The criticisms made above of the merger doctrine for such cases apply a fortiori to any
requirement of election. Only if the liabilities are in the alternative does the idea
of election make sense[734]; and of the many possible interpretations which can be
given to the situation where agent and principal are liable, alternative liability is an
unlikely one.[735] In this area however most of the cases appear fairly obviously not
to be based on election between two liabilities on an alternative contract at all, but
on problems of formation of contract. The typical situation is that discussed in
several nineteenth-century cases, where a third party deals with an agent in
circumstances where either agent or principal might reasonably be regarded as the
other contracting party. In principle the law of agency assumes that he is dealing
with the principal, unless there are clear indications to the contrary,[736] but these there
may be.[737] It is also clear that the third party may contract on the basis that both are
liable to him.[738] Thus invoicing and debiting the agent or the like, which are
sometimes spoken in terms of election, should perhaps really be classified in terms
of offer or counter-offer.[739] There are many cases dealing with this point where the
idea of election is not employed at all.[740] Such situations may of course give rise
to estoppels as in the case of undisclosed principals. It is therefore submitted that
in this area also a supposed election (short of judgment) to have recourse to the
agent does not bind the third party unless it again gives rise to some form of
estoppel.[741] This does not, of course, remove any authority from the cases referred
to above dealing with the question with whom the contract was made.

What constitutes election?   If, however, contrary to what is suggested above, any   **8-121**

Property Services Ltd [2016] EWHC 2680 (QB); [2017] Bus. L.R. 287.

[733] *Calder v Dobell* (1871) L.R. 6 C.P. 486 at 499 (Illustration 5); *Benton v Campbell Parker & Co*
[1925] 2 K.B. 410 at 414; *Murray v Delta Copper Co* [1925] 4 D.L.R. 1061 at 1067; *Tedrick v Big
T Restaurants of Canada Ltd* [1983] 2 W.W.R. 135.

[734] *L.C. Fowler & Sons Ltd v St Stephen's College Board of Governors* [1991] 3 N.Z.L.R. 304 at 309
(Illustration 7).

[735] See above, para.8-114.

[736] *Thomson v Davenport* (1829) 9 B. & C. 78 at 90.

[737] e.g. *Addison v Gandassequi* (1812) 4 Taunt. 574; cf. *Paterson v Gandasequi* (1812) 15 East 62.

[738] *Calder v Dobell* (1871) L.R. 6 C.P. 486 at 494; Comment to Article 98.

[739] e.g. *Thomson v Davenport* (1829) 9 B. & C. 78. See also cases on building subcontracts: *Young &
Co v White* (1911) 28 T.L.R. 87; *Beigtheil & Young v Stewart* (1900) 16 T.L.R. 177; cases on husband
and wife: *Jewsbury v Newbold* (1857) 26 L.J.Ex. 247; *Bentley v Griffin* (1814) 5 Taunt. 356; *Metcalfe
v Shaw* (1811) 3 Camp. 22; *Callot v Nash* (1923) 39 T.L.R. 292; shipping cases of various sorts: *Eastman v Harry* (1875) 33 L.T. 800; *Whitwell v Perrin* (1858) 4 C.B.(N.S.) 412; *Lamont v Hamilton*
1907 S.C. 628; *Beliard, Crighton (Belgium) & Co Ltd v Charles Lowe & Partners Ltd* (1922) 13
Ll. L. Rep. 567; *The Huntsman* [1894] P. 214; and other cases regularly cited in this connection: *Bottomley v Nuttall* (1858) 5 C.B.(N.S.) 122; *Dramburg v Pollitzer* (1873) 28 L.T. 470; *Re Bowerman
Ex p. Vining* (1836) 1 Deac. 555.

[740] e.g. as to husband and wife: *Lea Bridge District Gas Co v Malvern* [1917] 1 K.B. 803; as to ship
stores: *Dawson (Ship Stores) v Atlantica Co Ltd* (1931) 40 Ll. L. Rep. 63; *Evans & Reid Coal Co v
McNabb, Rougier & Co Ltd* (1924) 18 Ll. L. Rep. 471; *Fraser-Johnston Engineering, etc., Co v Sam
Isaacs (Aberdeen) Ltd* (1922) 12 Ll. L. Rep. 233; *Freimuller (Ships Stores) Ltd v Ocean Carriers
(London) Ltd* [1961] 2 Lloyd's Rep. 309; *Pearson v Nell* (1860) 12 L.T. 607; *Thompson v Finden*
(1829) 4 C. & P. 158. See also *Williamson v Barton* (1862) 7 H. & N. 899; *Gardiner v Heading*
[1928] 2 K.B. 284; *Pennell v Alexander* (1854) 3 E. & B. 283; *Thomas v Edwards* (1836) 2 M. &
W. 215; *Mortimer v M'Callan* (1840) 6 M. & W. 58 (cf. *Stoneham v Wyman* (1901) 6 Com.Cas. 174);
Format International Security Printers Ltd v Mosden [1975] 1 Lloyd's Rep. 37. As to ship repairs
and stores see Article 99, Illustration 8; Article 101, Illustration 2.

[741] cf. *Restatement, Third*, reporter's notes to § 6.09.

doctrine of election (as opposed to one of estoppel) is applicable, on general grounds the person electing must know the facts,[742] and the election must be clear and unequivocal[743] and voluntary.[744] It may also be that it must occur within a reasonable time,[745] though cases on this point seem better attributed to estoppel.[746] The question is certainly one of fact.[747] The following have been held not to constitute election: debiting the agent in the third party's books,[748] demanding payment of the agent,[749] receipt of part payment from the agent[750]; taking a bill of exchange or cheque from the agent[751]; proving in the agent's bankruptcy[752]; pursuing a claim in arbitration against the agent[753]; serving a writ on the agent[754]; or obtaining leave to sign judgment against him under the then RSC Ord.14.[755] It has, however, recently been said that "the clearest evidence of election is at least the commencement of proceedings against one or other of the two relevant parties".[756]

8-122 **Rule (3)** The strength of this residual rule obviously varies in accordance with the validity of the doctrine of election above discussed. But the cases deciding that there has been no election far outnumber those holding that there has been.

8-123 **Substance or procedure?** A difficult question is whether the above rules are to be classified as rules of substance or procedure for the purposes of the conflict of laws. In general, the rules for undisclosed principal do appear to represent rules of substance whereby the principal is liable alternatively with the agent. Much of the law as to disclosed principals, on the other hand, seems to derive from procedural considerations concerning summary and default judgments; though questions of guarantee and joint and several liability would be substantive. The question which

---

[742] *Dunn v Newton* (1884) C. & E. 278; *Clarkson Booker Ltd v Andjel* [1964] 2 Q.B. 775 at 792; *Pyxis Special Shipping Co Ltd v Dritsas & Kaglis Bros Ltd (The Scaplake)* [1978] 2 Lloyd's Rep. 380; *Kammins Ballrooms Co Ltd v Zenith Investments (Torquay) Ltd* [1971] A.C. 850 at 882–883; *Peyman v Lanjani* [1985] Ch. 457; *L.C. Fowler & Sons v St Stephen's College Board of Governors* [1991] 3 N.Z.L.R. 304.
[743] *Clarkson Booker Ltd v Andjel* [1964] 2 Q.B. 775 at 792.
[744] *L.C. Fowler & Sons Ltd v St Stephen's College Board of Governors* [1951] 3 N.Z.L.R. 304.
[745] Powell, p.272.
[746] e.g. *Smethurst v Mitchell* (1859) 1 E. & E. 622.
[747] *Clarkson Booker Ltd v Andjel* [1964] 2 Q.B. 775.
[748] *Thomson v Davenport* (1829) 9 B. & C. 78; *Calder v Dobell* (1871) L.R. 6 C.P. 486, Illustration 5; *Eastman v Harry* (1875) 33 L.T. 800; *Young & Co v White* (1911) 28 T.L.R. 87. This is really a matter of formation of contract: see above.
[749] *Calder v Dobell*, above; *Beigtheil & Young v Stewart* (1900) 16 T.L.R. 177; *Eastman v Harry*, above; cf. *MacClure v Schemeil* (1871) 20 W.R. 168, Illustration 3 to Article 80.
[750] *Ex p. Pitt* (1923) 40 T.L.R. 5.
[751] *Robinson v Read* (1829) 9 B. & C. 449. Unless it is received in full satisfaction, which would be difficult to establish. See *Everett v Collins* (1810) 2 Camp. 515; *Marsh v Pedder* (1815) 4 Camp. 257; *Strong v Hart* (1827) 6 B. & C. 160; *Smith v Ferrand* (1827) 7 B. & C. 191; *The Huntsman* [1894] P. 214.
[752] *Curtis v Williamson* (1874) L.R. 10 Q.B. 57, Illustration 4; cf. *MacClure v Schemeil* (1871) 20 W.R. 168; *Scarf v Jardine* (1882) 7 App.Cas. 345; *Fell v Parkin* (1882) 52 L.J.Q.B. 99; *Con-Stan Industries of Australia Pty Ltd v Norwich Winterthur Insurance (Australia) Ltd* (1986) 160 C.L.R. 226.
[753] *Pyxis Special Shipping Co Ltd v Dritsas & Kaglis Bros Ltd (The Scaplake)* [1978] 2 Lloyd's Rep. 380.
[754] *Clarkson Booker Ltd v Andjel* [1964] 2 Q.B. 775 (actually here served on principal).
[755] *C. Christopher (Hove) Ltd v Williams* [1936] 3 All E.R. 68.
[756] *Chestertons v Barone* [1987] 1 E.G.L.R. 15 at 17, per May LJ. Contrast *Bain Securities Ltd v Curmi* (1990) 1 A.C.S.R. 794.

of two persons is a party to a contract is of course one of substance. The confused bases of the rules make generalisation extremely difficult.

Illustrations

(1) The master of a ship signs a bill of lading in his own name. The consignee **8-124** obtains judgment against him on it, but the judgment is not satisfied. The consignee cannot thereafter sue the shipowner.[757]

(2) The Earl and Countess of Westmorland are sued jointly by a tradesman for wines and provisions ordered by the Countess. The Countess submits to summary judgment but the Earl obtains leave to defend. It is held that there is no evidence of joint liability; and that having signed judgment against the wife the plaintiff cannot sue the husband as her principal.[758]

(3) The agent of a moneylender sues the agent of another moneylender on a debt and obtains judgment. Later the first moneylender sues the second moneylender on the same debt. The action is barred.[759]

(4) A bought goods in his own name on behalf of B. The seller discovered that B was the principal, and subsequently, A having filed a liquidation petition, a clerk of the seller, for the purpose of proving in the liquidation, made an affidavit treating A as the debtor, and the affidavit was duly filed. The seller could still sue B for the price of the goods.[760]

(5) A broker is authorised to buy cotton, but not to disclose his principal's name. Being unable to obtain a contract on his own credit, he reveals the principal's name and bought and sold notes are exchanged between him and the seller naming the principal as the buyer. The goods are invoiced to the broker, but, the market falling, he refuses to accept the goods. The seller threatens both with legal proceedings, but subsequently sues the principal. He is not precluded from doing so.[761]

(6) The seller of a house instructs two estate agents. B makes an offer subject to contract and pays a deposit to each agent. The sale does not proceed. One estate agent returns the deposit, the other does not. B obtains judgment against the second agent, but it is unsatisfied. Even if the principal is liable in respect of the deposit, an action against him is barred by the judgment against the agent.[762]

(7) An agent acting for a school contracts on the school's behalf, with a firm which

---

[757] *Priestly v Fernie* (1863) 3 Hurl. & C. 977. This leading case reads strangely to modern eyes. In present times the master (who appears to have been imprisoned for the debt in Melbourne) would not be liable at all. The assumption seems to have been that he was the sole contracting party; the argument put was that in the case of shipmasters the owners were, by maritime law and contrary to principle, liable also. The court applied what it said was a general rule that principal and agent were liable in the alternative.

[758] *Morel Bros & Co Ltd v Earl of Westmorland* [1904] A.C. 11 (where the husband's liability was affected by the rules as to presumptions of authority: see above, para.3-040). See also *Sullivan v Sullivan* [1912] 2 I.R. 116, where the court regretted the conclusion to which it regarded itself as bound to come; *Moore v Flanagan* [1920] 1 K.B. 919, a claim by a milliner and dressmaker, where Scrutton LJ said that the rule was "extremely technical" but Atkin LJ robustly said that "[a]ny ill result to the plaintiff arises from her abuse of the procedure under Order XIV".

[759] *RMKRM (A Firm) v MRMVL (A Firm)* [1926] A.C. 761 (discussed (1970) 86 L.Q.R. at 337–338).

[760] *Curtis v Williamson* (1874) L.R. 10 Q.B. 57.

[761] *Calder v Dobell* (1871) L.R. 6 C.P. 486.

[762] *Barrington v Lee* [1972] 1 Q.B. 326 (noted (1972) 88 L.Q.R. 184). But as to the principal's liability, see *Sorrell v Finch* [1977] A.C. 728, Illustration 4 to Article 92.

arranges such tours, for a sporting tour for the school. The school pays its agent, who passes on some of the money to the firm and disappears. The firm obtains a default judgment against the agent for the remainder, but it is not satisfied. Later the firm sues the school. The school is liable and the firm's action is not barred by election or judgment, the judgment against the agent being against one who was not liable to the firm at all.[763]

2. DISPOSITIONS OF PROPERTY AND RESTITUTIONARY CLAIMS

Article 83

DISPOSITIONS OF PRINCIPAL'S PROPERTY BY AGENT ACTING WITHIN ACTUAL OR APPARENT AUTHORITY

8-125   A principal is bound by dispositions of property made by his agent acting within the scope of such agent's actual or apparent authority or which are ratified.[764]

Comment

8-126   It is obvious that a disposition within an agent's actual authority, express or implied, transfers property, whether the principal is disclosed or not[765]; and that an unauthorised disposition can be ratified, the ratification ranking as a transfer from the time at which it occurs.[766] It is difficult therefore to resist the conclusion that the doctrine of apparent authority as stated in Article 72 must in principle, apply here, as in other parts of the law of agency. However, considerable difficulties arise.

First, the general theoretical underpinning of the doctrine of apparent authority in this area is not clear. It has been pointed out earlier that although the doctrine is often said to be based on estoppel, the normal requirements for estoppel appear only in very weak form.[767] From this doctrine true estoppel situations, which require inter alia clear representations or negligent conduct, causal connection and action in reliance, are to be distinguished.[768] Yet some of the oldest cases on apparent authority arising where the agent is put in a position where there is normally authority of the requisite type (usual authority)[769] actually relate to property situations: the person concerned would normally have authority to make dispositions of property, and hence the disposition he makes is valid though unauthorised.[770] And it is difficult to see why the other type of apparent authority, that arising where the principal is

---

[763] *L.C. Fowler & Sons Ltd v St Stephen's College Board of Governors* [1991] 3 N.Z.L.R. 304.

[764] See Comment. The rules as to principal and agent are preserved by s.62(2) of the Sale of Goods Act 1979. As to actual authority, see Ch.2; as to apparent authority, see Article 72; as to ratification, see Articles 13–20. For extended discussion of this difficult topic, see Powell, pp.80–97; Stoljar, Ch.5; Fridman, Ch.7.

[765] An example would be a distributor of goods which he holds under a "Romalpa" clause: he is generally authorised to resell them. Such a person is not usually however a true agent. See above; below, para.8-165.

[766] For examples, see Illustrations to Article 17. On principle, the ratification should operate from the time of the act ratified: see Article 20. But in any case there could often be an estoppel from alleging that an act had not been ratified: see Article 21.

[767] See above, para.8-024.

[768] See Article 21.

[769] See above, para.8-015.

[770] e.g. *Pickering v Busk* (1812) 15 East 38, Illustration 1; *Quinn v CC Automotive Group Ltd* [2010] EWCA Civ 1412; [2011] 2 All E.R. (Comm) 584.

taken as making a representation to the third party, which indeed is normally mentioned as the first example of such authority[771] cannot exist in connection with property transfers. For example, the agent may not be one who would normally have authority to make such transfers, but the principal may regularly acquiesce in them, which could create apparent authority in contract. It seems therefore, and indeed is generally assumed, that the doctrine of apparent authority applies to property transfers. But it is no surprise that vague notions such as that of general agent were formerly and still occasionally are employed in this context.[772]

There follows a further problem. In so far as estoppel is relied on, an estoppel in general only operates between two parties and their privies. Yet the result of a disposition which is effective under estoppel is apparently to confer "a real title and not merely a metaphorical title by estoppel",[773] viz. a title which can be transmitted to a person unable to rely on the estoppel, and which will bind not only a volunteer but also a bona fide purchaser from the person estopped.[774] This is recognised in s.21(1) of the Sale of Goods Act 1979, which gives as an exception to the maxim *nemo dat quod non habet* the case where "the owner of goods is by his conduct precluded from denying the seller's authority to sell".[775] This again causes difficulties of theory, at least where there is no abstract transfer by deed, where the notion of apparent authority may validate the document itself.[776]

A third general point should be noted, though this is a point of application rather than theory. A basic tenet of this part of the law is that the mere entrusting of goods or documents of title to an agent does not confer apparent authority to make a disposition of them, for otherwise "no one would be safe in parting with possession of anything".[777] Even carelessness in an owner is not fatal; it would, in any event, be an unsafe assumption that the third party dealing with the non-owner is more innocent of blame than the owner. As Lord Macnaghten put the matter in one of the leading cases:

---

[771] See above, para.8-015.
[772] See above, para.1-045.
[773] *Eastern Distributors Ltd v Goldring* [1957] 2 Q.B. 600 at 611, per Devlin J (Illustration 4 to Article 84). cf. W.H. Goodhart (1957) 73 L.Q.R. 455.
[774] *Eastern Distributors Ltd v Goldring*, above, at 611. But where the interests of the person concerned are adverse to those of the person estopped, e.g. as a creditor, he may not be bound by the estoppel; see *Heane v Rogers* (1820) 9 B. & C. 577; *Richards v Johnston* (1859) 4 H. & N. 660; *Richards v Jenkins* (1887) 18 Q.B.D. 451; *Geddes v M'Donnell* (1896) 22 V.L.R. 330; *Curtis v Perth & Fremantle Bottle Exchange Co Ltd* (1914) 18 C.L.R. 17 at 23, 28; Ewart, *Estoppel* (1900), pp.196–221; Spencer Bower, *Reliance-Based Estoppel* (5th edn), Ch.6. The solution to this difficulty turns on the extent to which apparent ownership and apparent authority are separate from the general rules of estoppel.
[775] This provision only applies to a sale as opposed to an agreement to sell: *Shaw v Commissioner of Police of the Metropolis* [1987] 1 W.L.R. 1332.
[776] See *Northside Developments Pty Ltd v Registrar-General* (1990) 170 C.L.R. 146; Watts (2002) 2 O.U. Commonwealth L.J. 93; and see Companies Act 2006 ss.44 and 45.
[777] *Weiner v Gill* [1905] 2 K.B. 172 at 182; *Cole v North Western Bank* (1872) L.R. 10 C.P. 354 at 362; *Farquharson Brothers & Co v King & Co* [1902] A.C. 325, Illustration 6 to Article 84; *Johnson v Crédit Lyonnais* (1877) 3 C.P.D. 32; *Fry v Smellie* [1912] 3 K.B. 282, Illustration 3 to Article 85; *Jerome v Bentley & Co* [1952] 2 All E.R. 114; *Central Newbury Car Auctions Ltd v Unity Finance Ltd* [1957] 1 Q.B. 371, Illustration 3 to Article 84; *Moorgate Mercantile Co Ltd v Twitchings* [1977] A.C. 890 at 902–904 (Illustration 7 to Article 84); *Yu v Brownvalley Investments Pty Ltd* [2010] NSWSC 253 at [22] (possession of signed guarantee but without authority to deliver it, did not give any entitlement to lender upon wrongful delivery); *Bassano v Toft* [2014] EWHC 377 (QB) at [56] (pledgee does not lose pledge by delivering to an agent); *Ramsay v Love* [2015] EWHC 65 (Ch) at [117].

"If it were permissible it would be interesting to inquire which of the two firms parties to this litigation was the more blameworthy in a moral point of view. The plaintiffs trusted a man whom they had long known and whom they believed to be honest. The defendants trusted a man they had never seen, whom a breath of suspicion and the most ordinary inquiries would have unmasked. But we have nothing to do with this matter ... The right of the true owner is not prejudiced or affected by his carelessness in losing the chattel, however gross it may have been."[778]

A person in possession of goods may be a bailee; a person in possession of documents of title may be a mortgagee or a mere depositary. The cases therefore constantly indicate the necessity for some further act on the part of the owner beyond the mere parting with possession.

Returning to apparent authority,[779] an agent may have such authority by virtue of a representation by his principal. This can occur in the property context where the principal regularly acquiesces in transfers by an agent; or where the agent is entrusted with goods or documents of title together with a further indication that he has authority to dispose of them. It is difficult to find a clear case of this where the disposition is not binding by virtue of a contract,[780] but if an agent is given goods and a written authority to pledge them, his disposition would surely be valid notwithstanding that there are secret limits on his authority which he does not disclose.[781] Again, in the second category the entrusting of goods to an agent, e.g. in former times a factor, who in the way of business normally had authority to sell, will create apparent authority,[782] and a disposition in the ordinary course of business of such an agent will be effective: but here a clear modern case is difficult to find because such an agent would normally come under the wider protections of the Factors Act.[783]

8-127   There are two other ways in which the courts have sought to validate unauthorised dispositions by agents in possession of goods or documents of title.

(1)   *Apparent ownership.* Where the owner has allowed his agent to have possession of goods or documents of title and also in some further way let him appear to be *owner* of the goods or the property represented by the document of title, the agent's unauthorised disposition may be valid. This is not really a rule of agency, inasmuch as the person concerned is not thought to be an agent and need not in fact be such: but the reasoning in the cases is virtually identical to

---

[778]   *Farquharson Brothers & Co v King & Co* [1902] A.C. 325 at 335–336. See also *Shogun Finance Ltd v Hudson* [2003] UKHL 62; [2004] 1 A.C. 919 at [192], per Lord Walker of Gestingthorpe.

[779]   See above, para.8-015.

[780]   A possible example is *Davy v Waller* (1899) 81 L.T. 107, but the case does not distinguish clearly between actual and apparent authority as now understood. See also *Robinson v Montgomeryshire Brewery Co Ltd* [1896] 2 Ch. 841; cf. *Jameson v Union Bank of Scotland* (1913) 109 L.T. 850. The third party must of course rely on the appearance of authority: see *Raffoul v Esanda Ltd* [1970] 3 N.S.W.R. 8.

[781]   See Illustration 2.

[782]   *Pickering v Busk* (1812) 15 East 38, Illustration 1 (actually a case on a broker). As to the distinction between brokers and factors see above, para.1-046.

[783]   Article 87. A possible modern example is *Fuller v Glyn, Mills, Currie & Co* [1914] 2 K.B. 168, as explained in *Mercantile Bank of India Ltd v Central Bank of India Ltd* [1938] A.C. 287 and in *Tobin v Broadbent* (1947) 75 C.L.R. 378. In *Shearson Lehman Brothers Inc v Maclaine, Watson & Co Ltd* [1988] 1 W.L.R. 16 at 28 it was said that authority to pass property may be more easily inferred than authority to enter into an obligation: "business would come to a standstill if persons who receive documents from clerks and secretaries, acting in the course of their employment, were not entitled to assume that these documents were sent with the authority of the employer": per Lord Bridge of Harwich.

that relating to apparent authority and indeed the majority of the cases on property dispositions by agents lie in this area rather than in that of true apparent authority. The interconnection between the two is shown by the fact that Chalmers, in his first commentary on the Sale of Goods Act,[784] cited cases on apparent ownership as cases where the owner is under s.21 precluded from denying the seller's authority to sell.[785] One difference however should be noted. The fact that a sale is not in the ordinary course of business may be evidence that it is not within the apparent authority: but this point would not be relevant where the agent actually appeared to own the goods.[786] The doctrine of apparent ownership is dealt with in the following Article.

(2) *Delivery plus some actual authority to make a disposition.* A number of cases, mostly dealing with land, tend to suggest a proposition that where the principal delivers possession of documents of title, and authorises the agent to make certain property dispositions, he may in certain circumstances be bound when the agent makes other, unauthorised dispositions. Though this may be a reasonable idea, it does not accord with central agency doctrines, inasmuch as there is in these cases no actual or apparent authority (or apparent ownership), and the position between principal and agent should not be relevant to the position of the third party (though references to that position tend to creep into cases in all categories). It seems to be based on reasoning applicable to problems of priority in land law, and any more general validity is doubtful. It is dealt with in Article 85.

Other estoppels   It should be noted finally that even though a disposition is not valid under any of the above rules, the principal may by his conduct subsequent to it be estopped from alleging its invalidity; or from alleging in general that the property is his. This conduct may take the form of a positive representation; in other cases there must be a duty to speak or disclose.[787]

Illustrations

(1) The purchaser of hemp lying at wharves in London has, at the time of the purchase, the hemp transferred into the wharfinger's books in the name of the broker who effected the purchase, and whose ordinary business it is to buy and sell hemp. An unauthorised sale by the broker passes property.[788]

8-128

(2) Stockbrokers have a loan account with their bankers, with whom they deposit stocks, shares and bonds belonging to various clients en bloc as security for the bankers' advances. These are transferred to and held by trustees for the bank. A client alleges that the authority which he had given to the brokers to

---

[784] *Sale of Goods* (2nd edn, 1894).

[785] A common root for both doctrines is *Pickering v Busk* (1812) 15 East 38: see Stoljar, p.113 onwards; *Eastern Distributors Ltd v Goldring* [1957] 2 Q.B. 600, Illustration 4 to Article 84 likewise is relevant to both doctrines. The relevant section of the Sale of Goods Act is sometimes cited in apparent ownership cases: see *J. Sargent (Garages) Ltd v Motor Auctions (West Bromwich) Ltd* [1977] R.T.R. 121.

[786] *Motor Credits (Hire Finance) Ltd v Pacific Motor Auctions Pty Ltd* (1963) 109 C.L.R. 87, reversed on other grounds [1965] A.C. 867; but cf. *General Distributors Ltd v Paramotors Ltd* [1962] S.A.S.R. 1.

[787] See above, Article 21.

[788] *Pickering v Busk* (1812) 15 East 38, really a case on implied authority, though a root for both implied and apparent authority. See Stoljar, p.113 onwards.

repledge his securities authorised them to do so only for an amount not exceeding what was due from him to them. On the evidence of Stock Exchange practice there was nothing to make the bank think that the stocks and shares were not the broker's own property, and a pledge for a greater sum was valid.[789]

(3) A person purports to sell a leasehold interest in land, and the agreement is signed for him by a land agent. The agent has no authority to sign, but the owner knows of the sale, and allows the purchaser to pay rent and rates on the land. It is held that whether he had assented or not, he is estopped by his conduct from denying that he had so assented, and he is ordered to do what is necessary to give effect to the rights of the purchaser.[790]

Article 84

DOCTRINE OF APPARENT OWNERSHIP

8-129   Where a principal, by words or conduct, represents or permits it to be represented that his agent is the owner of any property, any sale, pledge, mortgage or other disposition for value of the property by the agent is as valid against the principal as if the agent were its owner, with respect to anyone dealing with him on the faith of such representation.[791]

Comment

8-130   Where, in such a case, the agent's disposition is authorised, it is valid under ordinary doctrine; if necessary, the principal can be referred to as undisclosed.[792] But the above proposition embraces also more complex cases which do not strictly depend on agency principles, for there is no actual authority, and the third party does not think that the agent is an agent, but the owner. The proposition in the Article is in fact a specific formulation of a more general proposition which is not confined to disposition by persons who are already agents. But the cases are usually confused with cases on agency, and agency terminology used.[793]

The rule is regarded, by longer pedigree than that of apparent authority in contract, as based on estoppel,[794] though it is an even looser application, for, apart

---

[789] *Bentinck v London Joint Stock Bank* [1893] 2 Ch 120. See this case explained by Dixon J in *Tobin v Broadbent* (1947) 75 C.L.R. 378 at 404–407 (a useful discussion).

[790] *West v Dillicar* [1920] N.Z.L.R. 139; [1921] N.Z.L.R. 617; see also *Fung Kai Sun v Chan Fui Hing* [1951] A.C. 489; *Spiro v Lintern* [1973] 1 W.L.R. 1002; *Worboys v Carter* [1987] 2 E.G.L.R. 1; *M'Kenzie v British Linen Co* (1881) 6 App.Cas. 82; *Greenwood v Martin's Bank Ltd* [1933] A.C. 51. See in general Article 21; above, para.8-028.

[791] See Comment.

[792] See *VLM Holdings Ltd v Ravensworth Digital Services Ltd* [2013] EWHC 228 (Ch) at [65] (grant of copyright licence).

[793] See *Rimmer v Webster* [1902] 2 Ch. 163, Illustration 5; *Central Newbury Car Auctions Ltd v Unity Finance Ltd* [1957] 1 Q.B. 371, Illustration 3; *Eastern Distributors Ltd v Goldring* [1957] 2 Q.B. 600, Illustration 4; *Jerome v Bentley & Co* [1952] 2 All E.R. 114; *Stoneleigh Finance Ltd v Phillips* [1965] 2 Q.B. 537; above, para.8-127; Sale of Goods Act 1979 s.21 (referred to in such a situation in *J. Sargent (Garages) Ltd v Motor Auctions (West Bromwich) Ltd* [1977] R.T.R. 121).

[794] See cases cited below, fnn.798 and 803; indeed some of these cases are seminal for the doctrine of estoppel in general. But cf. *Eastern Distributors Ltd v Goldring*, above, at 611.

from the fact that the estoppel confers title,[795] it is difficult to see that a third party can rely on the representation of someone of whose existence he may not be aware. The estoppel is therefore usually said to be based on representation in a very loose sense, or on negligent conduct. Although the two are often difficult to distinguish, e.g. in the case of signature of a document, the latter is usually more appropriate, since the word "representation" implies a manifestation or communication from the principal to the third party, and, as stated above, in many cases the third party does not know of the principal at all. The rules seem to be effectively the same whichever is relied on.[796] Where the notion of representation is employed, it is said that it must be made to a person or group of persons,[797] though as the group can apparently be quite a wide one this is necessarily vague in its application. Where negligent conduct is relied on, it is often said that there must be a duty of care,[798] breach of which is the proximate cause of the deception of the third party,[799] and detrimental reliance. But again it seems that the duty can be owed to a wide class of persons, and indeed some cases speak of it being owed to all the world.[800] The loss must however be foreseeable, and one which the principal is culpable in failing to guard against: there cannot be negligence in the air. Moreover, it seems that negligence is not of itself sufficient to create apparent ownership, because the common law has long taken the view that mere negligence in parting with possession of goods does not imperil one's ownership.[801]

Hence, the principal is not bound merely because he has let the agent have goods and/or documents of title[802]: he must have done something more, e.g. allowed property to stand in the agent's name,[803] given the agent an acknowledgment that

---

[795] But see Comment to Article 83, esp. para.8-126.

[796] *Mercantile Bank of India Ltd v Central Bank of India Ltd* [1938] A.C. 287 at 298–299. See also *Bell v Marsh* [1903] 1 Ch. 528 at 541; Dal Pont, paras 21.18–21.19.

[797] "The 'holding out' must be to the particular individual who says he relied on it, or under such circumstances of publicity as to justify the inference that he knew of it and acted upon it": *Dickinson v Valpy* (1829) 10 B. & C. 128 at 140, approved in *Farquharson Bros & Co v King & Co* [1902] A.C. 325 at 341 (Illustration 6). As to representation through an agent, see *Moorgate Mercantile Co Ltd v Twitchings* [1977] A.C. 890, Illustration 7.

[798] *Swan v North British Australasian Co Ltd* (1863) 2 Hurl. & C. 175 at 182; *R.E. Jones Ltd v Waring & Gillow Ltd* [1926] A.C. 670 at 693; *Mercantile Bank of India Ltd v Central Bank of India Ltd* [1938] A.C. 287, disapproving dicta in *Commonwealth Trust v Akotey* [1926] A.C. 72; *Wilson & Meeson v Pickering* [1946] K.B. 422 at 425; *Mercantile Credit Co Ltd v Hamblin* [1965] 2 Q.B. 242 at 271; *Moorgate Mercantile Co Ltd v Twitchings* [1977] A.C. 890; *Beverley Acceptances Ltd v Oakley* [1982] R.T.R. 434 at 439 (Illustration 8); *Haines Bros Earthmoving Pty Ltd v Rosecell Pty Ltd* [2016] NSWCA 112 (manager of owner victim of duress to the person).

[799] *Swan v North British Australasian Co Ltd*, above, where this was not so because the agent stole share certificates from the principal.

[800] *Swan v North British Australasian Co Ltd*, above; *Gallie v Lee* [1969] 2 Ch. 17 at 36, 48; (affd sub nom. *Saunders v Anglia Building Society* [1971] A.C. 1004). But see *Thomas Australia Wholesale Vehicle Trading Co Pty Ltd v Marac Finance Australia Ltd* (1985) 3 N.S.W.L.R. 452 esp. at 458–459, per Kirby P. (dissenting); *Leonard v Ielassi* (1987) 46 S.A.S.R. 495.

[801] See the cases in fn.777 above.

[802] cf. Illustrations 6–8; *Motor Credits (Hire Finance) Ltd v Pacific Motor Auctions Pty Ltd* (1963) 109 C.L.R. 87 at 99 (reversed on other grounds [1965] A.C. 867). A car registration document is not such a document of title: *J. Sargent (Garages) Ltd v Motor Auctions (West Bromwich) Ltd* [1977] R.T.R. 121; *Beverley Acceptances Ltd v Oakley* [1982] R.T.R. 417, Illustration 8. Lord Denning MR consistently took a different view: ibid.

[803] Illustration 2; *Dyer v Pearson* (1824) 3 B. & C. 38; *Pickard v Sears* (1837) 6 A. & E. 469; *Freeman v Cooke* (1848) 2 Exch. 654; *Henderson & Co v Williams* [1895] 1 Q.B. 521; *Leonard v Ielassi* (1987) 46 S.A.S.R. 495. See also *Lloyds & Scottish Finance v Williamson* [1965] 1 W.L.R. 404; sed

the agent has bought and paid for the goods,[804] signed a document offering to buy the goods from the agent or a third party[805]; or (perhaps) entrusted the goods to a person who in the normal course of business sells goods that are his own.[806] Further, in all these cases the representation must be relied on: a person who did not believe that the agent was owner cannot found on this doctrine.[807] But it is not at all clear how far this goes: in particular, the question of the duty of care owed by those who sign documents in blank, which is not of course confined to agency situations, is a vexed one.[808] It seems that no estoppel will normally arise against a person who gives his agent share certificates accompanied by signed blank transfers,[809] for this could be used as a method of effecting a mortgage. It has been suggested that, apart from cases of specific representation and (possibly) entrusting to a person who normally sells goods that are his own, any estoppel is confined to the case of negotiable instruments,[810] viz. (presumably), instruments intended to become negotiable instruments[811]: where incomplete documents are deposited merely for custody there is apparently no actionable negligence.[812] More recent authority however indicates doubt as to whether it should be so limited, even if cases in other areas would be rare.[813] The formulation of principles is so difficult that the courts have frequently been forced back on the famous dictum of Ashurst J: "Whenever one of two innocent persons must suffer by the acts of a third, he who has enabled

---

quaere what was the extra feature in that case. The court seems to have applied the rules as to settlement with an agent discussed in Article 80; but these do not require more than possession of goods, and the principal seeks to affirm the transfer and require a second payment. Unless the case can be justified on the basis of *Brocklesby v Temperance Building Society*, discussed under Article 85, it is probably best treated, as it seems to have been at first instance, as a case of actual authority.

[804] Illustration 5.

[805] Illustrations 3 and 4.

[806] *Motor Credits (Hire Finance) Ltd v Pacific Motor Auctions Pty Ltd* (1963) 109 C.L.R. 87.

[807] *Motor Credits (Hire Finance) Ltd v Pacific Motor Auctions Pty Ltd*, above; *Pickering v Busk* (1812) 15 East 38; *Motor Finance and Trading Co Ltd v Brown* [1928] S.A.S.R. 153. Sed quaere.

[808] See Pickering (1939) 55 L.Q.R. 400; Ewart, *Estoppel* (1900), p.438 onwards.

[809] *France v Clark* (1884) 26 Ch.D. 257; *Hutchison v Colorado Mining Co* (1886) 3 T.L.R. 265; *Fox v Martin* (1895) 64 L.J.Ch. 473, Illustration 2 to Article 85; cf. cases on the negligent custody of company seals: *Bank of Ireland v Evans' Trustees* (1855) 5 H.L. Cas. 389; *Merchants of Staple v Bank of England* (1888) 21 Q.B.D. 160; *Lewes Sanitary Steam Laundry v Barclay & Co Ltd* (1906) 22 T.L.R. 737. But a duty of care was held to exist in *Fuller v Glyn, Mills, Currie & Co* [1914] 2 K.B. 168. This case is difficult to reconcile with *Fox v Martin*, above, and the matter turns on the correct propositions to be derived from *Colonial Bank v Cady and Williams* (1890) 15 App.Cas. 267. It was explained in *Mercantile Bank of India Ltd v Central Bank of India Ltd* [1938] A.C. 287 at 302–303 as a case where the agent, a stockbroker, had a usual authority to pledge: this explanation was accepted by Starke and Dixon JJ in *Tobin v Broadbent* (1947) 75 C.L.R. 378, but Latham CJ thought the case "not satisfactorily supported by authority". See further *Chomley v Union Bank of Australia Ltd* [1951] S.A.S.R. 152; *Pan-Electric Industries Ltd v Sim Lim Finance Ltd* [1993] 3 Singapore L.R. 242 (authorities reviewed).

[810] *Wilson & Meeson v Pickering* [1946] K.B. 422 at 427; *Swan v North British Australasian Co Ltd* (1863) 2 Hurl. & C. 175. This, if correct, would explain *Lloyds Bank v Cooke* [1907] 1 K.B. 794; but cf. (1945) 9 M.L.R. 298. That case can also be based on the doctrine of *Brocklesby v Temperance Building Society*, but this doctrine is itself doubtful: see Article 85. See also Bills of Exchange Act 1882 s.20; Article 72, Illustration 14.

[811] Powell, p.90.

[812] *Smith v Prosser* [1907] 2 K.B. 735, Illustration 14 to Article 72; *Perpetual Trustees Australia Ltd v Heperu Pty Ltd* [2009] NSWCA 84.

[813] *Mercantile Credit Co Ltd v Hamblin* [1965] 2 Q.B. 242 at 279; *Gallie v Lee* [1967] 2 Ch. 17 at 48; affd sub nom. *Saunders v Anglia Building Society* [1971] A.C. 1004; *Union Credit Bank Ltd v Mersey Docks and Harbour Board* [1899] 2 Q.B. 205 at 210; *United Dominions Trust Ltd v Western* [1976] Q.B. 513; *Gator Shipping Corp v Trans-Asiatic Oil Ltd SA (The Odenfeld)* [1978] 2 Lloyd's Rep 357 at 375–378.

such third person to occasion the loss must sustain it".[814] But this hardly furnishes a precise guide: whether a person has "enabled" seems to turn on the criteria indicated above.[815]

Agent as trustee   The doctrine is inapplicable where the principal vests property in the agent as trustee,[816] for "a person is entitled to leave his property, whatever it may be, in the name of a trustee".[817] But in such a case the principal's interest could of course be defeated by a bona fide purchaser for value of the legal estate without notice.[818]   **8-131**

Notice   The question of notice is discussed under Article 73.   **8-132**

Illustrations

(1)   A, though the agency of B, a broker, obtained a loan on a mortgage of stock, and afterwards permitted the security to be transferred to B's banker, who had no notice of A's title and believed that B was the owner of the stock. B sold the stock, which was transferred by the banker to the purchaser, and, having paid off the loan, converted the balance to his own use. Held, that A had no remedy against the banker.[819]   **8-133**

(2)   A broker, having effected an insurance policy in his own name, was permitted to retain possession of it for the purpose of receiving the proceeds. The broker pledged the policy. Held, that the pledgee was entitled, as against the principal, to retain the advance out of the proceeds of the policy.[820]

(3)   B agrees to buy A's car on hire-purchase and signs documents proposing to buy it from a finance company. A lets B have car and registration document and drive away. Later B sells the car, with the registration document, to a third party who is ignorant of B's lack of title. The third party does not acquire title, since possession of the car is not apparent ownership of it and the registration document contains a warning that the person holding it may or may not be the owner.[821]

(4)   A wishes to borrow money on the security of his car. He agrees to a dealer representing to a finance company that he (the dealer) owns the car, and signs in blank documents agreeing to buy the car on hire-purchase from the finance company. The dealer fills in the documents and purports to sell the car to the

---

[814]   *Lickbarrow v Mason* (1787) 2 T.R. 63 at 70.

[815]   *Farquharson Bros & Co v King & Co* [1902] A.C. 325 at 342 (Illustration 6); *R.E. Jones Ltd v Waring & Gillow Ltd* [1926] A.C. 670 at 693; *Jerome v Bentley & Co* [1952] 2 All E.R. 114 at 118; *Central Newbury Car Auctions Ltd v Unity Finance Ltd* [1957] 1 Q.B. 371 at 389 (Illustration 4); *Johnson Matthey (Aust.) Ltd v Dascorp Pty Ltd* (2003) 9 V.R. 171 at 185 (see above, para.8-023).

[816]   *Shropshire Union Railways and Canal Co v R.* (1875) L.R. 7 H.L. 496; *Burgis v Constantine* [1908] 2 K.B. 484.

[817]   *Burgis v Constantine*, above, at 498.

[818]   The above cases involved subsequent equitable mortgagees, who were postponed to the equitable owners.

[819]   *Marshall v National Provincial Bank* (1892) 61 L.J.Ch. 465; cf. *Tobin v Broadbent* (1947) 75 C.L.R. 378.

[820]   *Callow v Kelson* (1862) 10 W.R. 193. See also *Williams v Allsup* (1861) 10 C.B.(N.S.) 417.

[821]   *Central Newbury Car Auctions Ltd v Unity Finance Ltd* [1957] 1 Q.B. 371 (see (1957) 73 L.Q.R. 309); *Astley Industrial Trust Ltd v Miller* [1968] 2 All E.R. 36; *J. Sargent (Garages) Ltd v Motor Auctions (West Bromwich) Ltd* [1977] R.T.R. 121.

company, who duly hire it to A. A is estopped from denying the dealer's authority to sell the car to the finance company.[822]

(5) R gives a broker a mortgage bond and instructs him to sell it. The broker induces R to execute transfers of the bond to him, acknowledging receipt of purchase money (though R has received nothing). The broker sub-mortgages the bond to W. The sub-mortgage binds R.[823]

(6) F, timber merchants, warehouse timber with a dock company and instruct the company to accept all orders signed by their clerk. The clerk gives orders transferring timber to himself under an assumed name and under that name fraudulently sells it to K. F would be estopped against the warehouse company but not against K. He can recover the timber from K.[824]

(7) A finance company transferring a car on hire purchase negligently fails to register the transaction with H.P. Information Ltd, an independent organisation to which 95 per cent of such finance companies belong and which maintains a central register of hire-purchase agreements. The hirer offers it to a motor dealer who is also a member. That dealer inquires as to the existence of any agreement on the car, and on being told none is recorded, buys it. Held by a majority that there was no estoppel. The first company can assert its interest because (a) the answer does not allege that there is no such agreement; (b) H.P.I. are independent suppliers of information and not agents for their members (in this case the finance company); (c) the members owe no duty to each other to register agreements.[825]

(8) The pledgee of two valuable motor cars who keeps them in a shed in the yard of his premises lends the owner the keys, and the registration document of one, supposedly to enable the owner to show the cars to insurers. The owner executes bills of sale on the cars. The first pledgee is not estopped from setting up his prior interest.[826]

Article 85

DISPOSITIONS BY AGENTS ENTRUSTED WITH INDICIA OF PROPERTY

8-134   (Perhaps) where a principal entrusts his agent with the possession of the indicia of title to property, and authorises him to raise money on their security, any security given by the agent on the property for money advanced, though for a higher amount than he was authorised to raise, is valid against the principal, provided that the

---

[822] *Eastern Distributors Ltd v Goldring* [1957] 2 Q.B. 600, a leading case on apparent authority also; *Stoneleigh Finance Ltd v Phillips* [1965] 2 Q.B. 537; *Snook v London & West Riding Investments Ltd* [1967] 2 Q.B. 786; cf. *Mercantile Credit Co Ltd v Hamblin* [1965] 2 Q.B. 242.

[823] *Rimmer v Webster* [1902] 2 Ch. 163; *Abigail v Lapin* [1934] A.C. 491. See also *Shaw v Commissioner of Police of the Metropolis* [1987] 1 W.L.R. 1332. Contrast *Debs v Sibec Developments Ltd* [1990] R.T.R. 91 (document signed under duress does not found estoppel by representation).

[824] *Farquharson Bros & Co v King & Co* [1902] A.C. 325; see (1902) 18 L.Q.R. 18 and 159. See also *Mercantile Bank of India Ltd v Central Bank of India Ltd* [1938] A.C. 287; cf. *Canadian Laboratory Supplies Ltd v Engelhard Industries of Canada Ltd* [1979] 2 S.C.R. 787; (1979) 97 D.L.R. (3d) 1.

[825] *Moorgate Mercantile Co Ltd v Twitchings* [1977] A.C. 890. See also *Cadogan Finance Ltd v Lavery* [1982] Com.L.Rep. 248 (aircraft); *Leonard v Ielassi* (1987) 46 S.A.S.R. 495; *Debs v Sibec Developments Ltd* [1990] R.T.R. 91 (failure to report robbery to police).

[826] *Beverley Acceptances Ltd v Oakley* [1982] R.T.R. 417 (Lord Denning MR dissenting). See also *McManus v Eastern Ford Sales Ltd* (1981) 128 D.L.R. (3d) 246.

person taking the security acts in good faith, and without notice that the agent is exceeding his authority.[827]

Comment

A person who holds the indicia of title to another's property has no apparent **8-135** authority to sell or mortgage it from his holding alone, for he may well, for example, be a mortgagee; nor has he apparent ownership.[828] The cases on which this Article is based seek to find an additional element that validates an unauthorised disposition in the fact that the principal has, unknown to the third party, given the agent authority to effect some sort of disposition of the property in the agent's possession. It is however difficult to justify such a proposition on principle. The underlying notion seems to be that where a person is given documents of title with authority to use them for the purpose of raising money, the owner of the documents cannot take advantage of any limitation in point of amount placed on the agent's authority as against a lender who had no notice of such limitation.[829] This may be a reasonable idea, but it is not in accord with well-established rules of agency to the effect that where an agent acts outside his actual authority, his principal is only bound where there is apparent authority, or where the contract is ratified.[830] The fact that the agent, unknown to the third party, has some limited authority in the relevant direction should, if principle were adhered to, make no difference in the absence of ratification, apparent authority, or apparent ownership. The cases seem to have developed a pragmatic exception based on an aggregation of possession and a limited degree of actual authority to dispose of the property.

One of the leading cases, *Brocklesby v Temperance Building Society*,[831] could be explained on the ground that the agent had, in addition to the deeds, a document conferring on him an apparent authority to pledge them,[832] but the relevance of this was discounted in the judgments and emphasis placed on the existence of some initial authority, and the possible injustice to third parties if the unauthorised pledge was not valid. In another leading case, *Fry v Smellie*,[833] an agent who was given share certificates and a signed blank transfer, and instructed to borrow not less than a certain sum, borrowed less than the stipulated sum, and the owner of the shares was held bound. It could be argued that the deposit of share certificates together with such a transfer gives apparent ownership, or gives an apparent authority to bor-

---

[827] *Brocklesby v Temperance Building Society* [1895] A.C. 173, Illustration 1; *Perry-Herrick v Attwood* (1857) 2 De G. & J. 21; *Rimmer v Webster* [1902] 2 Ch. 163; *Fry v Smellie* [1912] 3 K.B. 282, Illustration 3. *Brocklesby*'s case was followed in *Lloyd's Bank v Cooke* [1907] 1 K.B. 794, but this difficult case should probably be explained on the grounds of estoppel by conduct. (See *Wilson & Meeson v Pickering* [1946] K.B. 422; above, para.8-130.) It was also referred to with approval by the Court of Appeal in *Abbey National BS v Cann* [1989] 2 F.L.R. 265; affd on other grounds [1991] 1 A.C. 56.

[828] Articles 83 and 84.

[829] *Brocklesby v Temperance Building Society* [1895] A.C. 173 at 180–181.

[830] cf. *Keighley Maxsted & Co v Durant* [1901] A.C. 240. And the distinction between exceeding authority and doing an act right outside the authority would be difficult to operate. It is, however, defended by Atiyah [1965] J.B.L. 130 at 136; Sale of Goods (12th edn). cf. Ewart, *Estoppel* (1900), pp.244–246. It could never apply to an agent to sell goods.

[831] [1895] A.C. 173, Illustration 1.

[832] Powell, p.84.

[833] [1912] 3 K.B. 282, Illustration 3; criticised by Powell, pp.82–83.

row on their security,[834] but there was authority against this,[835] based on a practice of effecting mortgages by the use of such documents. Again the initial authority was held to make the difference. It is indeed difficult to escape the significance of the initial authority if this line of cases is to be accepted. The rule seems to originate from cases of priority of mortgages of land,[836] where it takes the form that if a mortgagee of property permits the mortgagor to have possession of the title deeds for the purpose of giving a security on the property, any security given for value by the mortgagor thereon has priority to the claim of the mortgagee, provided that the person taking the security acts in good faith and without notice of the mortgage.[837] But in this rather different area, priority is largely regulated by conduct rendering the equities unequal as between the parties, or displacing the superiority of the legal estate, and it is obvious that conduct of one party, even where unknown to the other, could be taken into account in this sort of inquiry.[838] Thus gross negligence with regard to the deeds has been said to displace the claim of a prior or legal mortgagee.[839] Although it is said that the cases involving agents are not based on negligence,[840] their rationale is most imprecisely stated,[841] and their relation to agency cases not fully worked out.[842] Further, many mortgage cases can also be explained on the ground of apparent ownership, in that the mortgagee, by returning the mortgagor's own deeds to him (or allowing him to hold them), whether

---

[834] See per Farwell LJ at p.296. See also *Tobin v Broadbent* (1947) 75 C.L.R. 378 at 405–406.

[835] *Fox v Martin* (1895) 64 L.J.Ch. 473, Illustration 2.

[836] See the doctrine discussed by Millett J in *Macmillan Inc v Bishopsgate Investment Trust Plc (No.3)* [1995] 1 W.L.R. 978 (where counsel had described it as "the arming principle"). Millett J said that it was "indeed part of the law of priorities and not of agency" (at 1012).

[837] *Perry-Herrick v Attwood* (1857) 2 De G. & J. 21; *Briggs v Jones* (1870) L.R. 10 Eq. 92; *Clarke v Palmer* (1882) 21 Ch.D. 124; cf. *Colyer v Finch* (1856) 5 H.L.Cas. 905; *Northern Counties Insurance Co v Whipp* (1884) 26 Ch.D. 482; *Hunt v Elmes* (1861) 30 L.J.Ch. 255; *Cottey v National Provincial Bank Ltd* (1904) 20 T.L.R. 607. The connection between the rule and these mortgage cases is supported by the fact that in *Northern Counties Insurance Co v Whipp*, above, at 492–493 it is suggested that it is only where the delivery was for the purpose of raising money that a prior mortgagee who fails to retain the deeds (as opposed to one who fails to obtain them) is postponed.

[838] "To hold that a person who advances money on an estate, the title deeds of which are under such circumstances left in the hands of the mortgagor, is not to have preference would be to shut our eyes to the plainest equity": *Perry-Herrick v Attwood* (1857) 2 De G. & J. 21 at 39, per Lord Cranworth LC "A person who puts it in the power of another to deceive and to raise money must take the consequences; he cannot afterwards rely on a particular or a different equity": *Briggs v Jones* (1870) L.R. 10 Eq. 92 at 98, per Lord Romilly MR.

[839] See in general Waldock, *Law of Mortgages* (2nd edn), p.392 onwards and 420 onwards (though the interpretation given of the cases here discussed at p.393 is, it is submitted, erroneous). Quaere to what extent this differs from estoppel by conduct: see, e.g. *Rimmer v Webster* [1902] 2 Ch. 163 at 172; Ashburner, *Principles of Equity* (2nd edn), p.453 onwards. For an argument that the weight of authority does not support gross negligence as being sufficient to disturb equitable priorities, see Watts (1998) 18 N.Z.U.L.R. 46.

[840] *Perry-Herrick v Attwood*, above at 37 and 39.

[841] See *Perry-Herrick v Attwood* above, discussed in *Briggs v Jones*, above at 98; *Hunter v Walters* (1870) L.R. 11 Eq. 292 at 318; *Clarke v Palmer* (1882) 21 Ch.D. 124 at 129; *Manners v Mew* (1885) 29 Ch.D. 725 at 732; *Northern Counties Insurance Co v Whipp* (1884) 26 Ch.D. 482 at 492–493; *Fox v Hawks* (1879) 13 Ch.D. 822 at 834; *National Provincial Bank v Jackson* (1886) 33 Ch.D. 1 at 12; *Jones v Rhind* (1869) 17 W.R. 1091; *Lloyds Bank v Bullock* [1896] 2 Ch. 193 at 198.

[842] In land cases the tendency is to think in terms of priority of estates and to consider what conduct will displace the holder of an earlier title. In chattel cases, the reasoning used is more likely to follow the maxim *nemo dat quod non habet* unless there is apparent authority or apparent ownership. Cases involving shares may employ either type of reasoning.

simpliciter or with some false acknowledgment of receipt of the mortgage debt,[843] has enabled the mortgagor to appear as the owner of unencumbered property. Similar reasoning can be applied to other mortgage cases.[844]

The leading cases contain dicta which are very difficult to reconcile with the normal principles of agency law.[845] One case, *Rimmer v Webster*,[846] suggests that where the agent has authority to sell, an unauthorised pledge may be effective. This is however even more difficult to reconcile with other authority,[847] and the case is probably best explained on its other ground of decision, that of apparent ownership.[848] Another view, however, is that the cases referred to in this Article and in Article 84 constitute pragmatic qualifications to the generality of the *nemo dat* rule and to the general principles of agency law.[849] They do not in themselves justify reopening those principles, nor do they support the result in *Watteau v Fenwick*.[850]

Forgery   Forged instruments do not confer rights, and if the agent counterfeits a   **8-136**
signature, seal or document in a situation such as those above, no rights are transferred by the forged document.[851] But if the forgery consists only in signing or sealing as agent but without authority it may be ratified.[852]

Notice   The question of notice is discussed under Article 73.   **8-137**

Illustrations

(1)   The owner of deeds entrusts them to an agent, with authority to pledge them   **8-138**
for a certain sum. The agent pledges them for a larger sum to a person who takes them in good faith and without notice of the limit on the agent's

---

[843]   e.g. *Rice v Rice* (1854) 2 Drew. 73; cf. *Martinez v Cooper* (1826) 2 Russ. 198.
[844]   e.g. *Robinson v Montgomeryshire Brewery Co* [1896] 2 Ch. 841; cf. *Jameson v Union Bank of Scotland* (1913) 109 L.T. 850.
[845]   Including references to "equitable estoppel": *Fry v Smellie* [1912] 3 K.B. 282 at 299; cf. *Eastern Distributors Ltd v Goldring* [1957] 2 Q.B. 600 at 611. The doctrine seems to have been nurtured by Farwell LJ, who sat in most of the cases.
[846]   [1902] 2 Ch. 163, Illustration 5 to Article 84. See also *Wishart v Credit & Mercantile Plc* [2015] EWCA Civ 655; [2015] 2 P. & C.R. 15. Here, the disposition was also outside the class of transactions authorised. This again makes the case difficult to square with general principle, but the result may be justified by the fact that the claimant's rights were equitable only and he was relying on an exception to override a legal interest. See the critical notes by Sampson [2016] C.L.J. 21 and Televantos [2016] Conv. 181.
[847]   See *Fox v Martin* (1895) 64 L.J.Ch. 473, Illustration 2; *Hutchison v Colorado Mining Co* (1886) 3 T.L.R. 265. This situation will often be covered by s.2 of the Factors Act 1889; see *Lloyd's Bank Ltd v Bank of America, etc.* [1938] 2 K.B. 147, Illustration 6 to Article 87, and this seems to be the proper approach to it.
[848]   See *Tsang Chuen v Li Po Kwai* [1932] A.C. 715 at 728–729; *Abigail v Lapin* [1934] A.C. 491 at 508; Article 84. The case was distinguished in *Jerome v Bentley & Co* [1952] 2 All E.R. 114; and there are signs of a similar approach in *Lloyds & Scottish Finance v Williamson* [1965] 1 W.L.R. 404. This case was, however, treated also as a case of apparent authority, and is probably even better explained as a case of actual authority. There are similar suggestions in *Mercantile Credit Co Ltd v Hamblin* [1965] 2 Q.B. 242 at 276, 277. See also *Union Credit Bank Ltd v Mersey Docks & Harbour Board* [1899] 2 Q.B. 205.
[849]   See Watts (2002) 2 O.U. Commonwealth L.J. 93 at 99–100. Compare Seavey's notion of inherent agency power, above, para.3-005.
[850]   [1893] 1 Q.B. 346, fully discussed above, para.8-077.
[851]   Illustration 4.
[852]   See above, para.2-059. And a person may be estopped from setting up forgery: ibid.

authority. The owner is not entitled to recover the deeds except on repayment of the full amount advanced on them.[853]

(2) A authorises B, stockbroker, to sell certain shares and entrusts him with the certificates and a blank transfer of the shares for that purpose. B deposits the blank transfer and certificates with his banker as security for an advance to himself. The banker has no title to the shares as against A.[854]

(3) A gives B share certificates and a signed blank transfer, authorising him to borrow not less than £250. B borrows £100. The mortgage is valid, because B was authorised to borrow.[855]

(4) A solicitor is employed to obtain a loan of £100 on a mortgage of certain property, and is entrusted with the title deeds for that purpose. He forges a mortgage deed for £400, and misappropriates the whole sum. The mortgage is void, and the client is not liable to the mortgagee, even to the extent of £100.[856]

Article 86

DEALINGS WITH MONEY AND NEGOTIABLE SECURITIES

8-139 (1) Where an agent, in consideration of an antecedent debt or liability, or for any other valuable consideration, pays or negotiates money or negotiable securities in his possession to a person who receives the same in good faith and without notice that the agent has not authority so to pay, title in the money or negotiable securities passes that person.

(2) A thing is deemed to be done in good faith within the meaning of this Article when it is in fact done honestly, whether it is done negligently or not.

Comment

8-140 **Bills of exchange** The position is here regulated by statute: the holder in due course of a negotiable instrument, i.e. a person who receives it in the circumstances specified in Rule (1) of this Article, acquires title to it free from defects in title of prior parties,[857] and subsequent transferees deriving title through a holder in due course have the same rights unless parties to fraud or illegality affecting the bill.[858] The doctrine of constructive notice does not apply in this branch of the law.[859]

---

[853] *Brocklesby v Temperance Building Society* [1895] A.C. 173.

[854] *Fox v Martin* (1895) 64 L.J.Ch. 473; *Hutchison v Colorado Mining Co* (1886) 3 T.L.R. 265. But cf. *Rimmer v Webster* [1902] 2 Ch. 163, Illustration 5 to Article 84; *Fuller v Glyn, Mills, Currie & Co* [1914] 2 K.B. 168 (see above, para.8-126). See also *Tobin v Broadbent* (1947) 75 C.L.R. 378.

[855] *Fry v Smellie* [1912] 3 K.B. 282.

[856] *Painter v Abel* (1863) 2 H. & C. 113; see also *Fox v Hawks* (1879) 13 Ch.D. 822.

[857] Bills of Exchange Act 1882 ss.38 and 29(2); but see s.81 ("not negotiable" crossing). For definition of "holder in due course", see s.29(1) (2); for definition of "valuable consideration", see s.27(1). For special rules as to bankers, see ss.60, 80, 81A and 82; Cheques Act 1957 s.4 (all as amended by Cheques Act 1992).

[858] Bills of Exchange Act 1882 s.29(3).

[859] Bills of Exchange Act 1882 s.90; see Rule (2) above; *Goodman v Harvey* (1836) 4 A. & E. 870; *Raphael v Bank of England* (1855) 17 C.B. 161; *Jones v Gordon* (1877) 2 App.Cas. 616; Illustration 2. But this simply means that there is no duty to inquire: it may be found as a fact that a person must have been suspicious: cf. Article 73.

Money   Money has been called a "negotiable chattel",[860] and partakes both of the   **8-141**
nature of chattels and of the nature of negotiable instruments. When the principal's
money is transferred by the agent to a third party but has not yet passed into currency (e.g. coins of a set kept in a case), and the agent has no actual or apparent
authority to transfer the property, and none of the exceptions to the maxim *nemo
dat quod non habet* apply, it can be recovered at common law, no property having
passed.[861] But where it is paid as money for valuable consideration to a person having no notice of the lack of authority (both of these requirements applying in the
modified form laid down for bills of exchange[862]), it cannot be recovered, because
it has passed into currency.[863] Such money could not normally be identified in any
case: but even if it could, the rule would apply.[864]

Illustrations

(1)   A, having bought on the Stock Exchange scrip which was issued in England   **8-142**
      by the agent of a foreign government, and which purported to entitle the bearer,
      on payment of £100, to receive a bond for that amount, entrusted the scrip to
      a broker. The broker pledged the scrip as security for a debt owing by himself,
      the pledgee taking it in good faith and without notice that the broker was not
      authorised so to pledge it. Held, that the scrip being negotiable in the same
      manner as the bond which it represented would be, the pledgee acquired a
      good title, as against A, to the extent of the pledge.[865]
(2)   A broker fraudulently pledged with a banker negotiable securities belonging
      to various principals, as security for an advance. The banker acted in good
      faith, but had no knowledge whether the securities were the property of the
      broker, or whether he had authority to pledge them, or not, and made no
      inquiries. Held, that the banker had a good title to the securities, as against the
      principals, to the extent of the advance.[866]
(3)   An agent fraudulently applies moneys of his principal in the purchase of
      overdue bills, which he sells to a company. The company has no title to the
      bills as against the principal, overdue bills not being negotiable instruments.[867]

---

[860]   *Banque Belge pour l'Etranger v Hambrouck* [1921] 1 K.B. 321 at 329. See Proctor, *Mann on the Legal Aspect of Money* (7th edn), Ch.1.
[861]   See Article 88.
[862]   As to consideration, see Rule (1) above. As to notice, see Rule (2); *Raphael v Bank of England* (1855) 17 C.B. 161; *Lloyds Bank Ltd v Swiss Bankverein* (1913) 108 L.T. 143; *Nelson v Larholt* [1948] 1 K.B. 339 at 343–344.
[863]   *Miller v Race* (1758) 1 Burr. 452 at 457; *Clarke v Shee & Johnson* (1774) 1 Cowp. 197 at 200; *Wookey v Pole* (1820) 4 B. & A. 1 at 7; *Lipkin Gorman v Karpnale Ltd* [1991] 2 A.C. 548. But its proceeds may be recovered from the agent if they are identifiable: see Article 88.
[864]   *Miller v Race* (1758) 1 Burr. 452 at 457.
[865]   *Goodwin v Robarts* (1876) 1 App.Cas. 476; *Rumball v Metropolitan Bank* (1877) 2 Q.B.D. 194; *Edelstein v Schuler* [1902] 2 K.B. 144; *Bechuanaland Exploration Co v London Trading Bank Ltd* [1898] 2 Q.B. 658.
[866]   *London Joint Stock Bank v Simmons* [1892] A.C. 201; *Bentinck v London Joint Stock Bank* [1893] 2 Ch. 120; *Mutton v Peat* [1900] 2 Ch. 79; *Lloyds Bank Ltd v Swiss Bankverein* (1913) 108 L.T. 143; cf. *Sheffield v London Joint Stock Bank* (1888) 13 App.Cas. 333.
[867]   *Re European Bank Ex p. Oriental Commercial Bank* (1870) L.R. 5 Ch.App. 358. And see Article 90.

Article 87

DISPOSITIONS PROTECTED BY THE FACTORS ACT 1889

8-143   Where a mercantile agent is, with the consent of the owner, in possession of goods, or of the documents of title to goods, any sale, pledge or other disposition of the goods made by him when acting in the ordinary course of business of a mercantile agent is as valid as if he were expressly authorised by the owner of the goods to make the same: provided that the person taking under the disposition acts in good faith and has not, at the time of the disposition, notice that the agent has not authority to make the same.[868]

Comment

8-144   **Historical**   The Factors Act 1889 is a consolidation, with changes and improvements, of a series of Acts dating from 1823, the general purpose of which was to protect bona fide purchasers in mercantile transactions.[869] It should be noted that it involves making a distinction between such transactions and nonmercantile transactions, a distinction familiar in civil law countries but not prominent in the common law. In general it may be said that the Act both confirmed and altered the law, the latter principally by validating not only unauthorised sales by agents, which would often have been effective at common law if the agent was a person in the business of selling,[870] but also unauthorised pledges, which would not normally be effective under the common law rules.[871] The Acts take their name from the factor, a well-known type of commercial agent of the nineteenth century who regularly dealt with goods in his own name,[872] though that operation was not confined to factors. But the operations of business intermediaries are now conducted in different ways from those in use in the nineteenth century, and the main application of the Act seems nowadays to be in respect of situations of much more casual agency, such as that of a motor car dealer obtaining offers for a customer, or a commercial traveller carrying samples. The term "Factors Act" is therefore in some ways misleading[873]: "Mercantile Agents Act" would give a better indication of the ambit of the legislation, and in some common law jurisdictions titles of this sort are adopted.

It is tempting to think of this provision as a statutory form of the doctrine of apparent authority. This is only true in the most general sense, as it contains specific requirements, connected with a need for fault in the owner, compliance with which would usually be outside the knowledge of the third party. (The same is true of the traditional doctrine of agency of necessity, except that here the requirements do not link to fault in the principal, but rather, to the existence of necessity: this is one of the reasons for doubting it.[874]) The protection conferred by the Act is detailed and specific, and even when combined with the doctrines of apparent authority, apparent ownership and other possible lines of reasoning do not constitute a complete protection for bona fide purchasers such as is found in the laws of some countries.

---

[868] Factors Act 1889 s.2(1). cf. Uniform Commercial Code s.2-403(2), a much simpler and wider provision.
[869] See Munday (1977) 6 Anglo-Am.L.Rev. 221 at 243 onwards.
[870] Under the doctrines of apparent authority and apparent ownership: see Articles 83 and 84.
[871] See Stoljar, Ch.5; *Cole v North Western Bank* (1875) L.R. 10 C.P. 354.
[872] See above, para.1-046; *Heyman v Flewker* (1863) 13 C.B.(N.S.) 519 at 527–528.
[873] See *Rolls Razor Ltd v Cox* [1967] 1 Q.B. 552 at 578.
[874] See above, para.4-007.

Alongside the Factors Act existed the common law concept of "market overt". Under this concept a bona fide purchaser in certain markets could acquire title to goods even though they were stolen. It was of very limited application and has now been abolished by statute.[875]

Mercantile agent   The term was introduced by the 1889 Act.[876] The notion of "mercantile agent" is defined in partly circular terms as "a mercantile agent having, in the customary course of his business as such agent, authority either to sell goods, or to consign goods for the purpose of sale, or to buy goods, or to raise money on the security of goods".[877] This excludes, e.g. mere servants of the owner (such as shop assistants), carriers and warehousemen.[878] But it does not appear that such a person need follow a recognised occupation as commercial agent of a known sort,[879] and a person may be a mercantile agent though he acts for one principal only, or for an isolated transaction.[880] However, a person who agrees to find a purchaser for goods for another as a friend is not a mercantile agent on these facts alone,[881] nor is a person who only buys and sells on his own behalf.[882] If a person receives goods when not a mercantile agent and subsequently becomes one, the section will not apply unless there is further consent to his possession of the goods subsequent to his acquisition of the character of mercantile agent.[883]   **8-145**

With the consent of the owner   Such consent is presumed in the absence of evidence to the contrary.[884] Where the agent has, with such consent, been in possession of the goods themselves or documents, a disposition which would have been valid if the consent had continued is valid notwithstanding determination of the consent, provided that the person taking under the disposition had not, at the time thereof, notice that the consent had been determined.[885] Where the agent has obtained possession of documents of title through being or having been, with such consent, in possession of the goods themselves or of other documents of title to   **8-146**

---

[875] Sale of Goods (Amendment) Act 1994. For the old law see *Benjamin's Sale of Goods* (4th edn), para.7-016 onwards.

[876] Previous statutes used the words "agent entrusted". Therefore cases on such statutes should be viewed with caution, though it has been said that the wording of the 1889 Act represents the results of decisions on the earlier wording: *Oppenheimer v Attenborough & Son* [1907] 1 K.B. 510 at 514. Statutes in other jurisdictions also may use the older wording.

[877] s.1(1).

[878] *Lowther v Harris* [1927] 1 K.B. 393, Illustration 3; *Cole v North Western Bank* (1875) L.R. 10 C.P. 354; *Lamb v Attenborough* (1862) 1 B. & S. 831, Illustration 1; *Heyman v Flewker* (1863) 13 C.B.(N.S.) 519.

[879] There are dicta to the contrary in *Heyman v Flewker*, above, and *Hastings Ltd v Pearson* [1893] 1 Q.B. 62, but the latter case was disapproved in *Weiner v Harris* [1910] 1 K.B. 285. See also *Davey v Paine Bros (Motors) Ltd* [1954] N.Z.L.R. 1122.

[880] *Lowther v Harris* [1927] 1 K.B. 393; *Weiner v Harris*, above; *Heyman v Flewker*; *Mortgage Loan & Finance Co of Australia Ltd v Richards* (1932) 32 S.R.(N.S.W.) 50; *Thoresen v Capital Credit Corp Ltd* (1962) 37 D.L.R. (2d) 317 at 327 (decision reversed (1964) 43 D.L.R. (2d) 94); *Fairfax Gerrard Holdings Ltd v Capital Bank Plc* [2006] EWHC 3439 (Comm); [2007] 1 Lloyd's Rep. 171 at [31]; reversed on other grounds [2007] EWCA Civ 1226; [2008] 1 Lloyd's Rep. 297; [2008] 1 All E.R. (Comm) 632.

[881] *Budberg v Jerwood & Ward* (1934) 51 T.L.R. 99; *Kendrick v Sotheby & Co* (1967) 111 S.J. 470.

[882] *Belvoir Finance Co Ltd v Harold G. Cole & Co Ltd* [1969] 1 W.L.R. 1877; *Fadallah v Pollak* [2013] EWHC 3159 (QB) at [35].

[883] *Heap v Motorists Advisory Agency Ltd* [1923] 1 K.B. 577 at 588.

[884] s.2(4).

[885] See s.2(2); cf. Article 121.

them, his possession of the former documents is deemed to be with such consent.[886] Where the owner consents to possession by the agent, the operation of the Act is not defeated by the fact that the consent was obtained by deception or fraud,[887] unless the owner did not intend the agent to have possession at all.[888]

The word "owner" may cover a person who would not strictly be so called, but without whose concurrence the goods cannot be sold even by the true owner, e.g. a pledgee whose right of sale has not arisen who returns documents of title to the pledgor under a trust receipt.[889]

8-147 **In possession** It is provided that a person is deemed to be in possession of goods or documents when they are in his actual custody, or are held by any other person subject to his control, or for him, or on his behalf.[890] It has been held that a person who pledges goods for less than their value retains sufficient control to make a further pledge for the balance valid against the principal.[891] But if he simply pledges the goods twice and the first pledgee has possession, this provision cannot be used to validate the second pledge against the first pledgee.[892] The possession must be held by the agent in his capacity as a mercantile agent: the fact that the person in possession is a mercantile agent makes no difference if he is not in possession of the goods for a purpose in some way connected with his business as a mercantile agent, e.g. where goods are deposited for repair with a person who is also a dealer, or let to a dealer on hirepurchase.[893] This is a strong limitation: but if it were not so, when a furnished house was let to an auctioneer he might acquire power to dispose of the furniture.[894] But it does not seem that it is necessary for the owner to have contemplated that the agent would dispose of all the goods: thus where pictures were sent to the owner of a gallery, some for sale but some for display only, the Act was held to apply to all.[895]

---

[886] s.2(3).

[887] *Whitehorn Bros v Davison* [1911] 1 K.B. 463; *Pearson v Rose & Young Ltd* [1951] 1 K.B. 275; *Folkes v King* [1923] 1 K.B. 282; *Du Jardin v Beadman Bros* [1952] 2 Q.B. 712; *Ingram v Little* [1961] 1 Q.B. 31 at 70.

[888] *Pearson v Rose & Young Ltd*, above; *Stadium Finance Ltd v Robbins* [1962] 2 Q.B. 664. This might be the case where the agent obtains the goods as the result of a mistake on the part of the owner as to the agent's identity, where such identity is material: see *Lake v Simmons* [1927] A.C. 487. See also Illustration 4.

[889] *Lloyds Bank Ltd v Bank of America National Trust and Savings Association* [1938] 2 K.B. 147, Illustration 6; see also *Beverley Acceptances Ltd v Oakley* [1982] R.T.R. 417, Illustration 10.

[890] s.1(2). See *Brown & Co v Bedford Pantechnicon Co* (1889) 5 T.L.R. 449.

[891] *Portalis v Tetley* (1867) L.R. 5 Eq. 140.

[892] *Beverley Acceptances Ltd v Oakley* above.

[893] *Staffs Motor Guarantee Ltd v British Motor Wagon Co Ltd* [1934] 2 K.B. 305; *Lowther v Harris* [1927] 1 K.B. 393; *Pearson v Rose & Young Ltd* [1951] 1 K.B. 275; *Stadium Finance Ltd v Robbins* [1962] 2 Q.B. 664 above; *Astley Industrial Trust Ltd v Miller* [1968] 2 All E.R. 36; *Belvoir Finance Co Ltd v Harold G. Cole & Co Ltd* [1969] 1 W.L.R. 1877; *Henderson v Prosser* [1982] C.L.Y. 21 (car left for valeting); *Schafhauser v Shaffer and National Finance Co* [1943] 3 D.L.R. 656; *Universal Guarantee Pty Ltd v Metters* [1966] W.A.R. 74 ("display or return"); *McManus v Eastern Ford Sales Ltd* (1981) 128 D.L.R. (3d) 246; *Fadallah v Pollak* [2013] EWHC 3159 (QB) at [53]. The criticism of the *Staffs Motor Guarantee* case in *Pacific Motor Auctions Pty Ltd v Motor Credits (Hire Finance) Ltd* [1965] A.C. 867 applies only to the point in relation to s.25(1) of the Sale of Goods Act 1893 (now s.24 of 1979 Act).

[894] See *Cole v North Western Bank* (1875) L.R. 10 C.P. 354 at 369, per Blackburn J.

[895] *Moody v Pall Mall Deposit & Fowarding Co Ltd* (1917) 33 T.L.R. 306; sed quaere (an inadequately reported case). See also *Fuentes v Montis* (1868) L.R. 3 C.P. 268 at 284; *Turner v Sampson* (1911) 27 T.L.R. 200, Illustration 5; *Pearson v Rose & Young Ltd* [1951] 1 K.B. 275 at 288. But cf. *Stadium*

Goods   The term includes wares and merchandise,[896] but not certificates of   **8-148**
stock.[897] It was suggested in *Pearson v Rose & Young Ltd*[898] that where a person
obtained possession of a car with the consent of the owner but of the registration
document without such consent, he had not obtained "goods" with the owner's
consent because "goods" in the Act means in this connection the car together with
the registration document.[899] But this reasoning was not accepted in *Stadium
Finance Ltd v Robbins*[900] and *Pearson v Rose & Young Ltd* can be otherwise
explained (though the alternative explanation is equally unsatisfactory).[901]

Documents of title to goods   This expression includes any bill of lading, dock   **8-149**
warrant, warehouse keeper's certificate, and warrant or order for the delivery of
goods, and any other document used in the ordinary course of business as proof of
the possession or control of goods, or authorising, or purporting to authorise, either
by indorsement or by delivery, the possessor of the document to transfer to receive
the goods thereby represented.[902] This is wider than the notion of "document of title"
at common law, which is effectively confined to bills of lading, in that it could cover
documents incapable of transferring constructive possession even by attornment.[903]
A motor vehicle registration document is in England not a document of title.[904]

Sale, pledge or other disposition   The meaning of "sale" is clear from the Sale   **8-150**
of Goods Act 1979.[905] It should be noted that there is not, as there is in other provisions,[906] any requirement of delivery.[907] "Pledge" includes any contract pledging or
giving a lien or security on goods, whether in consideration of an original advance,
or of any further or continuing advance, or of any pecuniary liability.[908] A pledge
of the documents of title to goods is deemed to be a pledge of the goods.[909] The Act
thus applies to pledges for antecedent debts: but where the goods are pledged,
without authority, for an antecedent debt or liability of the pledgor, the pledgee
acquires no further right to the goods than could have been enforced by the pledgor

---

Finance Ltd v Robbins [1962] 2 Q.B. 664 at 674, on which see Hornby (1962) 25 M.L.R. 719.
[896] s.1(3).
[897] *Freeman v Appleyard* (1862) 32 L.J.Ex. 175.
[898] [1951] 1 K.B. 275.
[899] See esp. at 290.
[900] [1962] 2 Q.B. 664. See also (1951) 67 L.Q.R. 3; Powell, pp.228–229; *Paris v Goodwin* [1954] N.Z.L.R. 823.
[901] See below, para.8-153.
[902] s.1(4).
[903] See *Benjamin's Sale of Goods* (9th edn), para.7-036.
[904] *Joblin v Watkins & Roseveare Motors Ltd* [1949] 1 All E.R. 47; see also *Pearson v Rose & Young Ltd* [1951] 1 K.B. 275; *Central Newbury Car Auctions Ltd v Unity Finance Ltd* [1957] 1 Q.B. 371, Illustration 3 to Article 84; *Moorgate Mercantile Co Ltd v Twitchings* [1977] A.C. 890, Illustration 7 to Article 84; *J. Sargent (Garages) Ltd v Motor Auctions (West Bromwich) Ltd* [1977] R.T.R. 121; *Beverley Acceptances Ltd v Oakley* [1982] R.T.R. 417. Lord Denning MR consistently took a different view: ibid.
[905] s.2.
[906] e.g. Sale of Goods Act 1979 ss.24 and 25.
[907] But it may be that the property would only pass by delivery: *Benjamin's Sale of Goods* (9th edn), para.7-048.
[908] s.1(5).
[909] s.3; Illustration 8. The transfer of a document may be by indorsement, or where the document is by custom or by its express terms transferable by delivery, or makes the goods deliverable to the bearer, then by delivery: s.11.

at the time of the pledge.[910] Where the goods are pledged without authority in consideration of the delivery or transfer of other goods or documents of title to goods, or of a negotiable security, the pledgee acquires no right or interest in the goods so pledged in excess of the value of the goods, documents or security when so delivered or transferred in exchange.[911] It has been held in Canada that the Act applies where the goods are pledged along with other goods to secure a loan based on the total value of all the goods so pledged.[912]

8-151   **Other disposition**   Sales and pledges have consideration: but it seems that "other dispositions" must equally not be gratuitous, for it is provided that the consideration necessary for the validity of a sale, pledge or other disposition may be any valuable consideration.[913] But it would in any case be rare for a gratuitous transfer to be in the normal course of business of a mercantile agent. Entrusting goods to an auctioneer for sale is not a pledge or other disposition within the meaning of the Act, though the auctioneer makes advances on the goods.[914]

8-152   **Time and effect of disposition**   It seems that the sale, pledge or other disposition must occur at the same time as the possession is held.[915] It also seems that the effect of the Act is only to transfer such title as the person who entrusted the goods had.[916]

8-153   **Acting in the ordinary course of business of a mercantile agent**[917]   This requirement must be distinguished from the requirement that the agent have authority to deal with goods in the customary course of his business as a mercantile agent. If he has no such authority, he is not a mercantile agent within the Act: but even if he is, the section may not apply, because he acts outside the ordinary course of business, e.g. by selling outside business premises, or out of business hours.[918] But it is irrelevant whether or not he sells in his own name, and it seems that provided the general requirements relating to sales by mercantile agents are fulfilled, it is not relevant whether the agent is acting within the ordinary course of business of his particular type of mercantile agent, nor whether the circumstances of the transaction in question are normal.[919] Thus a diamond broker may be acting in the ordinary course of business of a mercantile agent within the meaning of the Act in pledging

---

[910] s.4; Illustration 8.

[911] s.5.

[912] *Thoresen v Capital Credit Corp* (1964) 43 D.L.R. (2d) 94; and see *Kaltenbach, Fischer & Co v Lewis and Peat* (1885) 10 App.Cas. 617; but cf. *City Bank of Sydney v Barden* (1908) 9 S.R. (N.S.W.) 41. See further *Benjamin's Sale of Goods* (9th edn), para.7-049 onwards.

[913] See s.5. "Consideration" includes exchange: ibid. As to "disposition", see *Worcester Works Finance Ltd v Cooden Engineering Co Ltd* [1972] 1 Q.B. 210.

[914] *Waddington & Sons v Neale & Sons* (1907) 96 L.T. 786; *Roache v Australian Mercantile Land & Finance Co Ltd (No.2)* [1966] 1 N.S.W.L.R. 384.

[915] *Beverley Acceptances Ltd v Oakley* [1982] R.T.R. 417, Illustration 10; *Fairfax Gerrard Holdings Ltd v Capital Bank Plc* [2006] EWHC 3439 (Comm); [2007] 1 Lloyd's Rep. 171 at [31]; reversed on other grounds [2007] EWCA Civ 1226; [2008] 1 Lloyd's Rep. 297; *Fadallah v Pollak* [2013] EWHC 3159 (QB) at [55].

[916] cf. *National Employers' Mutual General Insurance Ltd v Jones* [1990] 1 A.C. 24, a case on s.25(1) of the Sale of Goods Act 1979; *Cook v Rodgers* (1946) 46 S.R.(N.S.W.) 229.

[917] Ivamy (1951) 18 *Solicitor* 28 at 31; Dal Pont, para.21.26 onwards.

[918] *Oppenheimer v Attenborough & Son* [1908] 1 K.B. 221 at 230–231 (Illustration 7). But see *Newtons of Wembley Ltd v Williams* [1965] 1 Q.B. 560, where the sale of a second-hand car in Warren Street in London was held to be within the ordinary course of business.

[919] *Janesich v Attenborough & Son* (1910) 102 L.T. 605; *Ceres Orchard Partnership v Fiatagri Australia*

diamonds entrusted to him for sale, although by the custom of the trade such a broker has no authority to pledge diamonds so entrusted to him.[920] But it is not in the ordinary course of business for a mercantile agent to ask a friend to pawn goods entrusted to him: in order that the pledgee may be protected, the agent must pledge the goods himself, or by a servant or agent employed in the ordinary course of business.[921] A sale by a dealer on terms that the price is to be paid direct to one of the dealer's creditors would probably not be in the ordinary course of business[922] nor a forced sale to provide security for a debt owed by the agent,[923] nor a sale the profits of which went to the agent,[924] nor a sale of an entire stock-in-trade[925]; nor, perhaps, in some cases, the sale of a car in England without the registration document.[926]

In each case the special facts of the transaction may, however, be evidence that the receiver did not act in good faith, e.g. if there is an unduly high rate of interest,[927] the price was unduly low,[928] or it is well known that such an agent has not authority to make the type of disposition involved.[929] Indeed, the demarcation between matters of ordinary course of business and good faith is not clear, and they do not always operate as separate requirements.

In *Pearson v Rose & Young Ltd*[930] it was suggested that where a car dealer obtains possession of a car with the consent of the owner, but obtains the registration document without such consent, a sale by him of car and registration document is not in the ordinary course of business. This is dubious: provided the book was supplied to the buyer, its provenance should be irrelevant, for the sale is perfectly regular on its face.[931] The case can be explained on other grounds, but these are equally unsatisfactory.[932] It was followed in *Stadium Finance Ltd v Robbins*,[933] but in this case it appears that the buyer was given neither the registration document

Pty Ltd [1995] 1 N.Z.L.R. 112 (citing further authority).
[920] *Oppenheimer v Attenborough & Son* [1908] 1 K.B. 221.
[921] s.6; *De Gorter v Attenborough & Son* (1904) 21 T.L.R. 19.
[922] See *Lloyds & Scottish Finance Ltd v Williamson* [1965] 1 W.L.R. 404; *Biggs v Evans* [1894] 1 Q.B. 88 (the other point on which the Act was excluded was doubted in *Turner v Sampson* (1911) 27 T.L.R. 200). But a sale on credit could be: *Tingey v Chambers* [1967] N.Z.L.R. 785.
[923] *Motor Credits (Hire Finance) Ltd v Pacific Motor Auctions Pty Ltd* (1963) 109 C.L.R. 87 (reversed on other grounds [1965] A.C. 867); *Nash v Barnes* [1922] N.Z.L.R. 303.
[924] *Raffoul v Esanda Ltd* [1970] 3 N.S.W.R. 8.
[925] *Mortimer-Rae v Barthel* (1979) 105 D.L.R. (3d) 289.
[926] *Pearson v Rose & Young Ltd* [1951] 1 K.B. 275; *Stadium Finance Ltd v Robbins* [1962] 2 Q.B. 664; *Lambert v G. & C. Finance Corp* (1963) 107 S.J. 666. Sed quaere: should this be a matter relevant to the buyer's good faith? cf. *Folkes v King* [1923] 1 K.B. 282; *Oppenheimer v Attenborough & Son*, above; *Janesich v Attenborough & Son*, above; *Durham v Asser* (1968) 67 D.L.R. (2d) 574; *Astley Industrial Trust v Miller* [1968] 2 All E.R. 36 (document left with licensing authority for taxing purposes). As to different practice in Australia, see *Magnussen v Flanagan* [1981] 2 N.S.W.L.R. 926. As to sale on part-exchange basis, see *Davey v Paine Bros (Motors) Ltd* [1954] N.Z.L.R. 1122.
[927] *Janesich v Attenborough & Son* (1910) 102 L.T. 605.
[928] *Heap v Motorists Advisory Agency Ltd* [1923] 1 K.B. 577 at 591; *Davey v Paine Bros (Motors) Ltd* [1954] N.Z.L.R. 1122 at 1130; *Summers v Havard* [2011] EWCA Civ 764; [2011] 2 Lloyd's Rep. 283.
[929] *Oppenheimer v Attenborough & Son* [1908] 1 K.B. 221, Illustration 7.
[930] [1951] 1 K.B. 275.
[931] See (1951) 67 L.Q.R. 3.
[932] See above, para.8-148.
[933] [1962] 2 Q.B. 664. See Hornby (1962) 25 M.L.R. 719; Thornely [1962] C.L.Y. 139; (1972) 78 L.Q.R. 468.

nor the ignition key (which the owner had retained) when he bought the car, which might perhaps indicate that the sale was not in the ordinary course of business.[934]

8-154   **Good faith and absence of notice**   This must be proved by the third party.[935] "Good faith" is not defined, but on the analogy of the Sale of Goods Act[936] it may be assumed that the standard is one of honesty: a thing is done in good faith if it is done honestly, whether or not negligently. It is often said that constructive notice is not relevant in commercial transactions.[937] The court may, however, infer that the third party must have known of the lack of authority, e.g. in the circumstances discussed above; and in general the courts have in other contexts, especially that of constructive trust, imposed something akin to a duty to inquire.[938] In the case of a disposition by two or more persons who are acting in the transaction as partners, want of good faith on the part of any one of them may deprive all of the protection of the statute.[939] It has been held that if the disponee has had possession of documents that would, if read, have pointed to a lack of authority in the disponor, the disponee will not get the protection of the Act.[940]

8-155   **Undisclosed principal**   It should be noted that the Act applies notwithstanding that the third party believes the agent to be the owner of the goods: what is relevant is that the agent is a mercantile agent in possession, etc., not that the third party thinks he is.[941] Thus the Act applies to agents of undisclosed as well as disclosed principals.

8-156   **Miscellaneous**   An agreement made with a mercantile agent through a clerk or other person authorised in the ordinary course of business to make contracts of sale or pledge on his behalf is deemed to be an agreement with the agent.[942] The Act is in amplification and not in derogation of other powers of an agent.[943] But nothing in it authorises an agent to exceed or depart from his authority as between him and

---

[934] See above, fn.926 and text.

[935] *Heap v Motorists Advisory Agency Ltd* [1923] 1 K.B. 577; *Stadium Finance Ltd v Robbins* [1962] 2 Q.B. 664 at 673. Yet under s.23 of the Sale of Goods Act 1979, the burden is on the original owner: *Whitehorn Bros v Davison* [1911] 1 K.B. 463. See in general Dal Pont, para.21.30; *Fairfax Gerrard Holdings Ltd v Capital Bank Plc* [2006] EWHC 3439 (Comm); [2007] 1 Lloyd's Rep. 171 at [31]; reversed on other grounds [2007] EWCA Civ 1226; [2008] 1 Lloyd's Rep. 297; [2008] 1 All E.R. (Comm) 632.

[936] s.61(3). See also *Barclays Bank Ltd v TOSG Trust Fund Ltd* [1984] B.C.L.C. 1 at 18 ("genuinely and honestly in the circumstances of the case"); *Ceres Orchard Partnership v Fiatagri Australia Pty Ltd* [1995] 1 N.Z.L.R. 112 at 117 ("must have known or must have suspected and wilfully shut his eyes to the means of knowledge available").

[937] See Article 73; *Re Funduk and Horncastle* (1973) 39 D.L.R. (3d) 94.

[938] See *Summers v Havard* [2011] EWCA Civ 764; [2011] 2 Lloyd's Rep. 283. Comments to Articles 73 and 116. As to knowledge of adverse claims as preventing bona fides see *Carl Zeiss Stiftung v Herbert Smith & Co (No.2)* [1969] 2 Ch. 276.

[939] *Oppenheimer v Frazer & Wyatt* [1907] 2 K.B. 50.

[940] *Fairfax Gerrard Holdings Ltd v Capital Bank Plc* [2006] EWHC 3439 (Comm): [2007] 1 Lloyd's Rep. 171 at [31], reversed on other grounds [2007] EWCA Civ 1226; [2008] 1 Lloyd's Rep. 297.

[941] *Oppenheimer v Attenborough & Son* [1908] 1 K.B. 221 at 229 (Illustration 7); cf. *Boyter v Thomson* [1995] 2 A.C. 628. *Greer v Downs* [1927] 2 K.B. 28 might have been another example, had the defendant chosen to rely on the Factors Act 1889.

[942] s.6.

[943] s.13.

his principal, or exempts him from any liability, civil or criminal, for so doing[944]; or prevents the owner from recovering goods from an agent or his trustee in bankruptcy before a sale or pledge; or from redeeming pledged goods, before sale, on satisfying the claim for which they were pledged and paying to the agent, if required, money in respect of which he would have a lien; or from recovering from a pledgee any balance in his hands as the proceeds of sale, after deducting the amount of his lien[945]; or from recovering the price agreed to be paid by the buyer.[946]

The protection given by ss.24 and 25 of the Sale of Goods Act 1979 to dispositions by sellers and buyers in possession after sale extends to dispositions by them through mercantile agents; and the peculiar wording of s.25(1) leads to the apparent conclusion that where a buyer is in possession after sale, advantage can only be taken of its provisions if he sells, though a private person, in the ordinary course of business of a mercantile agent.[947] Therefore cases on the application of this section may be relevant to the interpretation of s.2 of the Factors Act 1889.[948]

Where an owner of goods has given possession of the goods to an agent for the purpose of consignment or sale, or has shipped goods in the name of the agent, and the consignee of the goods has not had knowledge that the agent is not the owner of the goods, the consignee, in respect of advances made to or for the use of the agent, has the same lien on the goods as if the agent were the owner of the goods, and may transfer any such lien to another person; but this does not limit or affect the validity of any sale, pledge or other disposition by a mercantile agent.[949]

Exclusion of the Act   It is not possible to contract out of the provisions of the Factors Act; but if a mercantile agent is in possession as buyer of the goods and not as mercantile agent they will not apply.[950]   **8-157**

Illustrations

(1)   A wine merchant's clerk, permitted to have the possession for the purpose of his master's business of dock warrants for wine belonging to his master, fraudulently pledges the warrants for an advance to himself. The transaction is not protected by the Factors Act, because the clerk is not a mercantile agent within the meaning of the Act.[951]   **8-158**

(2)   A, a manufacturing jeweller, supplies jewellery to B, a retail jeweller, on sale or return, on the terms that it is to remain the property of A until it is sold or paid for—B, after selling it, to retain half the difference between the cost price and selling price, by way of remuneration, and to remit the balance of the

---

[944] s.12(1).

[945] s.12(2).

[946] s.12(3).

[947] See *Newtons of Wembley Ltd v Williams* [1965] 1 Q.B. 560, a case on s.9 of the Factors Act 1889, which is largely reproduced in s.25(1) of the Sale of Goods Act 1979. But cf. *Langmead v Thyer Rubber Co Ltd* [1947] S.A.S.R. 29; *Jeffcott v Andrew Motors Ltd* [1960] N.Z.L.R. 721.

[948] e.g. *Newtons of Wembley Ltd v Williams*, above (sale of second-hand car in street market); *Pacific Motor Auctions Pty Ltd v Motor Credits (Hire Finance) Ltd* [1965] A.C. 867; *Fadallah v Pollak* [2013] EWHC 3159 (QB) at [49]. See in general *Benjamin's Sale of Goods* (9th edn), para.7-055 onwards.

[949] Factors Act 1889 s.7. See *Mildred, Goyeneche & Co v Maspons y Hermano* (1883) 8 App.Cas. 874 at 883; see Article 69.

[950] See *Weiner v Gill* [1906] 2 K.B. 574; *Kempler v Bravingtons* (1925) 41 T.L.R. 519; cf. *Weiner v Harris* [1910] 1 K.B. 285, Illustration 2. This distinction can be criticised: see Stoljar, p.124.

[951] *Lamb v Attenborough* (1862) 1 B. & S. 831. See also *Farquharson Bros & Co v King & Co* [1902] A.C. 325, Illustration 6 to Article 84.

proceeds to A. B is merely A's agent for sale, and therefore a mercantile agent within the meaning of the Act.[952]

(3) L wishes to sell furniture and a tapestry. He stores it in a house and engages P, an art dealer who has a shop nearby, to sell it on commission: he permits P to occupy a flat in the house and to show the items to customers. P is a mercantile agent but is not in possession of the goods. P pretends that he has sold the tapestry to W, and L permits him to remove it. P sells it to H. He was at the time of sale in possession of the tapestry with L's consent and the sale is valid.[953]

(4) An agent employed by a foreign principal to negotiate sales in London obtains an offer from A, which the principal accepts. The principal specially indorses to A the bill of lading for the goods, and sends it to the agent to be exchanged for A's acceptance. The agent, without the principal's authority, agrees with A to cancel the contract, and subsequently induces him to indorse the bill of lading by representing that it was specially indorsed by mistake, and then, having obtained possession of the goods by means of the bill of lading, pledges them for an advance. The pledge is not protected by the Factors Act, because the agent did not obtain possession of the goods with the consent of the principal. The principal, therefore, is entitled to recover the goods from the pledgee.[954]

(5) The owner of a picture asks a dealer to hang it in his gallery and report any offers he may receive for it. The dealer sells it and disappears. The sale is valid.[955]

(6) A company pledged bills of lading with A, a bank, as security for bills of exchange or advances. A handed the bills of lading back to the company upon terms contained in trust receipts, whereby the company was authorised to sell the goods and undertook to hold the proceeds in trust for A. The company pledged the bills of lading with B, a bank, to secure advances. B acted in good faith and without notice that the company was not entitled so to pledge the bills of lading. A claimed the bills of lading from B. Held, that A was owner of the goods represented by the bills of lading within the meaning of the Factors Act; but that the company was a mercantile agent in possession of the bills of lading within the meaning of the Act and that the pledge to B was valid.[956]

(7) A diamond broker asks a diamond dealer to let him have some diamonds to show to two firms of diamond merchants to whom he says he thinks he can sell them. The dealer lets him have diamonds for this purpose, but the broker, instead of showing them to any merchant, pledges them. The pledge is valid.[957]

(8) A broker is authorised to sell goods, and is entrusted with the bill of lading for them by their owner. By means of the bill of lading he obtains dock war-

---

[952] *Weiner v Harris* [1910] 1 K.B. 285; cf. *Weiner v Gill* [1906] 2 K.B. 574; *Universal Guarantee Pty Ltd v Metters Ltd* [1966] W.A.R. 74 (electrical goods "on consignment").
[953] *Lowther v Harris* [1927] 1 K.B. 393.
[954] *Vaughan v Moffatt* (1868) 38 L.J.Ch. 144.
[955] *Turner v Sampson* (1911) 27 T.L.R. 200.
[956] *Lloyds Bank Ltd v Bank of America National Trust and Savings Association* [1938] 2 K.B. 147. See *Benjamin's Sale of Goods* (9th edn), para.18-281.
[957] *Oppenheimer v Attenborough & Son* [1908] 1 K.B. 221.

rants for the goods, and without the authority of the principal, pledges the warrants with his banker as security for an overdraft, the banker taking them in good faith, and without notice that in so pledging them he is exceeding his authority. Before receiving notice of the want of authority, the banker, on the faith of the pledge, permits the overdraft to be increased. So far as concerns the overdraft existing at the time of the pledge, the principal is only bound by the pledge to the extent of any lien the broker had on the goods at that time, and may redeem the goods upon payment to that extent, and payment of the amount overdrawn since the date of the pledge. If the broker has a lien in excess of the full amount of the overdraft, the principal must, if required, also pay to the broker the amount of the excess before he is entitled to redeem the goods.[958]

(9) A factor is entrusted with the possession of goods for sale. The principal revokes his authority, and demands the return of the goods. The factor refuses to return the goods, and then fraudulently sells and delivers them to a person who purchases them in good faith, and without notice that the factor has no authority to sell them, or that he is in possession of the goods without the consent of the owner. The principal is bound by the sale, but may sue in his own name for the price, subject to any right of set-off the purchaser may have against the factor.[959]

(10) A person pledges two cars and possession is transferred to the pledgee. He subsequently asks to borrow the keys and one registration document (the other not being available), ostensibly to show them to insurance representatives. He actually shows the car to representatives of a finance house; and by virtue of having done so he is later able to execute a bill of sale in favour of the finance house. The disposition is not protected by the Factors Act as (a) he never regained possession of the goods; (b) the registration document is not a document of title; (c) the disposition did not occur at the same time as any possession that he might have had.[960]

Article 88

PRINCIPAL'S RIGHTS TO RECOVER PROPERTY AND MONEY—RESTITUTIONARY CLAIMS

(1) Subject to the provisions of Articles 83 to 87, where an agent disposes of the property or money of his principal in a manner not authorised, ratified or otherwise valid, the principal is entitled, as against the agent and third parties, to recover that property or money, or the proceeds of that property or money, wherever they may be found, provided that they can be traced in accordance with the rules of common law and equity.[961] **8-159**

(2) Subject again to Articles 83 to 87, where an agent otherwise disposes of

---

958 s.12(2).
959 s.12(3).
960 *Beverley Acceptances Ltd v Oakley* [1982] R.T.R. 417.
961 See Comment. The literature on this topic is extensive. See Lewin, *Trusts* (19th edn), Ch.41; Goff and Jones, *Law of Unjust Enrichment* (9th edn), Ch.7; Burrows, *Law of Restitution* (3rd edn), Chs 6 and 7; Lionel Smith, *Law of Tracing* (1997); Birks, "The Necessity of a Unitary Law of Tracing", in *Making Commercial Law* (Cranston ed., 1997), p.239; Lionel Smith (2009) 125 L.Q.R. 338; Burrows (2001) 117 L.Q.R. 412. As to the distinction between "following" and "tracing", see *Foskett v McKeown* [2001] 1 A.C. 102 at 127.

property or money on behalf of his principal under circumstances that, if made by the principal, would give rise to a restitutionary claim in the principal, the principal may assert such a claim against the third party.

Comment

8-160   The subject matter of this Article is very wide and connects to areas of law that have historically been very complex, and which are undergoing much development. It is not practicable to treat in any depth the substantive requirements of the range of claims that might be relevant to the recovery of property or money by a principal. Nor is it possible to engage with all the terminological and substantive controversies that attend the subject matter.[962] The use of the phrase "restitutionary claims" to cover the group of claims available for the recovery of both property and money is itself controversial, since not all commentators treat property claims as restitutionary, but it is a convenient expression and there are undoubted connections between them.[963] No attempt is made here to engage with the idea that a concept of unjust enrichment can be used to claim mere increases in a defendant's general wealth causally connected with the claimant, without the claimant needing to show a particular transfer of property or a particular payment made by or on behalf of the claimant and a corresponding receipt by the defendant.[964] Reflecting the underlying analytical controversies of the field, the material in this Article should be read with that in Article 96, dealing with particular aspects of the rights of a principal where third parties become implicated in an agent's breach of duty. Finally by way of introduction, it should be noted that previous editions of this book addressed in this section the risks that principals were exposed to when their agents became subject to the law of distress. All this law in relation to commercial tenancies has, from April 6, 2014, been swept away by the Tribunals, Courts and Enforcement Act 2007 s.71, and the replacement regime does not permit the seizure of goods not owned by the tenant.

8-161   **Rule (1): Common law**   Where an agent holds the property or money of his principal and disposes of it in a manner authorised, title passes. So also it passes by virtue of the special rules of the law of agency in cases of apparent authority,[965] and where one of the exceptions to the rule *nemo dat quod non habet* applies.[966] Otherwise where the dealing is unauthorised the property or money remains the property of the principal, who may have the right to recover it (and in some circumstances its traceable substitutes) at common law not only from the original recipient but from subsequent recipients.[967] It matters not whether the agent exceeds

---

[962] See the sources in the preceding footnote.

[963] See Watts [2016] C.L.P. 289.

[964] See Birks, *Unjust Enrichment* (2nd edn), Ch.4; and *Menelaou v Bank of Cyprus UK Ltd* [2015] UKSC 66; [2016] A.C. 176.

[965] Articles 72 and 83.

[966] Articles 83–87.

[967] *Lang v Smyth* (1831) 7 Bing. 284 at 292; *Farquharson Bros & Co v King & Co* [1902] A.C. 325. The principal may have sufficient title to trace where the agent draws money from the principal's bank account, for the bank's indebtedness is a chose in action belonging to the principal: see *Lipkin Gorman v Karpnale Ltd* [1991] 2 A.C. 548. Where the transfer is authorised or ratified, the principal may of course sometimes be able to trace against the *agent*; but that is not relevant in this context. See Article 43.

his mandate dishonestly or mistakenly.[968] The principal's rights to reclaim remain so long as the property remains identifiable,[969] whether tangible[970] or intangible,[971] and in some cases if it is converted into a different form of property,[972] provided that there is no admixture of other property or money (when it may be necessary to have recourse to equity[973]). The primary action for enforcing the principal's rights in relation to chattels is that of conversion,[974] and in the case of money an action in money had and received, though this latter action really affirms property in the defendant, because money is not normally identifiable.[975] Either of these actions lies against a recipient who has parted with what he has received; but in the case of the restitutionary action a defence of change of position is available to a recipient who has changed his position in good faith in such a way that it would be inequitable to require him to make restitution in whole or in part.[976] In the past there have been doubts in relation to money claims as to whether they can lie against a recipient subsequent to the first.[977] If they do, as now seems likely in relation to unauthorised payments, they should not lie against a person who gave value in good faith[978] or against such a recipient who was only a conduit of the funds.[979] Nor should there be an entitlement to profits made. Recent authority however suggests that profits can be recovered, at least where these result from a mere increase in the value of

---

[968] For instances of mistaken excess of authority, see *R v Vincent* (1852) 16 Jur. 457; and *J.S. Brooksbank & Co (Australasia) Ltd v EXFTX Ltd* (2009) 10 N.Z.C.L.C. 264,520, Illustration 8.

[969] *Taylor v Plumer* (1815) 3 M. & S. 562 at 575 (Illustration 1). (It is by no means clear that this is really a common law case, though it is normally treated as such.) See Smith [1995] L.M.C.L.Q. 240.

[970] e.g. coins in a bag: *Taylor v Plumer*, above, at p.565.

[971] *Banque Belge pour l'Etranger v Hambrouck* [1921] 1 K.B. 321 (unmixed bank balance); *Agip (Africa) Ltd v Jackson* [1990] Ch. 265; [1991] Ch. 547 (effect of bank clearing mechanisms).

[972] e.g. *Taylor v Plumer* above (draft converted into stock and bullion). An unpaid debt in respect of the sale of the property would presumably be recoverable: cf. *Re Wood Ex p. Boden* (1873) 28 L.T. 174; and see Illustration 8.

[973] See below, para.8-162.

[974] e.g. *Farquharson Bros & Co v King & Co* [1902] A.C. 325; *Gompertz v Cook* (1903) 20 T.L.R. 106.

[975] See *Calland v Lloyd* (1840) 6 M. & W. 26; *Marsh v Keating* (1834) 1 Bing.N.C. 198; *Scott v Surman* (1742) Willes 400; *Banque Belge pour l'Etranger v Hambrouck* [1921] 1 K.B. 321, per Atkin L.J.; *Primlake Ltd v Matthews Associates* [2006] EWHC 1227 (Ch); [2007] 1 B.C.L.C. 666 at [335]; *Napier v Torbay Holdings Ltd* [2016] NZCA 608. In *Relfo Ltd v Varsani* [2012] EWHC 2168 (Ch) at [88] it was accepted that money had and received might be available against a downstream recipient of the claimant's funds on the basis of but-for causation without using the rules of tracing. This is a surprising conclusion, and the subsequent reasoning in the Court of Appeal is somewhat more cautious: [2014] EWCA Civ 360; [2015] 1 B.C.L.C. 14, noted Nolan (2015) 131 L.Q.R. 8. This case needs now to be considered in the light of *Investment Trust Companies (In Liquidation) v Revenue and Customs Commissioners* [2017] UKSC 29; [2017] 2 W.L.R. 1200 at [37] and [48].

[976] *Lipkin Gorman v Karpnale Ltd* [1991] 2 A.C. 548. See McKendrick (1992) 55 M.L.R. 377; Goff and Jones, *Law of Unjust Enrichment* (9th edn), Chs 27 and 30; Burrows, *Law of Restitution* (3rd edn), Chs 21 and 22; Bant, *Change of Position* (2009), pp.204–209.

[977] See the Rt Hon. Lord Millett (1991) 107 L.Q.R. 71 at 77–79; and McKendrick [1991] L.M.C.L.Q. 378 at 384–386; Goff and Jones, *Law of Unjust Enrichment* (9th edn), para.6-63. See the controversial case, *Banque Belge*, above; and the discussion in *Agip (Africa) Ltd v Jackson* [1990] Ch. 265 and [1991] Ch. 547. The case seems to be regarded as correct in *Lipkin Gorman v Karpnale Ltd*, above. See too *Shalson v Russo* [2003] EWHC 1637; [2005] Ch. 281; *Spangaro v Corporation Investment Funds Management Ltd* (2003) 47 A.C.S.R. 285 at [50].

[978] Unless this is to be regarded as a manifestation of the change of position defence, as to which see Birks [1989] L.M.C.L.Q. 296 at 301–302; [1991] L.M.C.L.Q. 473 at 490–492; the Rt Hon. Lord Millett (1991) 107 L.Q.R. 71 at 82.

[979] *Agip (Africa) Ltd v Jackson* [1990] 1 Ch. 265 at 287.

what is traced.[980] It is easier to justify such a result against a knowing recipient than an innocent volunteer who by having to account for profits or capital gains may be deprived of the benefits of his skill (or luck).

Claims more readily classifiable as in rem may also be asserted in other ways, such as bankruptcy proceedings, in an action for a declaration,[981] by way of defence to an action in conversion[982] and in proceedings regarding the registration of shares.[983] There is however no general common law action of a proprietary nature, and many of the problems here discussed arise from the difference between the right vindicated and the common law remedies available to support it.

8-162 **Equity** In equity there is a historically separate right to recover unauthorised distributions of property or money, and to trace into substitute property, and the significance of the latter is greater because equity's mechanisms, which include a lien, can be applied to a mixed fund. It has often been said that equitable restitutionary claims are only triggered by a breach of trust or fiduciary duty. Although that may at first sight seem reasonable, such a requirement is paradoxical, since it attributes greater force to the principal's equitable title than his legal ownership, though equity always recognised legal ownership. However, fiduciary relationships have been detected on extremely slender bases[984] and it seems likely that the need to find such a relationship will disappear as the historically distinct tracing rules of common law and equity are assimilated.[985] In the agency context the matter is of less importance, since where an agent holds property entrusted to him by his principal he often does so as fiduciary and an unauthorised disposition may involve a breach of the equitable duties of loyalty[986]; and in other cases he may have control over his principal's money as fiduciary in a way that gives equal access to the right to trace.[987] Plainly, where the principal's title to an asset is only equitable, the principal's rights to follow and trace the asset will only be equitable (whether or not the agent has the legal title).[988]

The principal's right in equity consists of an entitlement at the claimant's option to assert beneficial ownership of the property concerned or a proportionate share of it, even where it has increased in value[989]; or to enforce a lien (sometimes referred to as a charge) for the amount of misapplied money[990] against the fund or

---

[980] *Trustee of the Property of F. C. Jones & Co v Jones* [1997] Ch. 159; see Andrews and Beatson (1997) 113 L.Q.R. 21. See too Rt Hon. Lord Millett, in Degeling and Edelman (eds.), *Equity in Commercial Law* (2005), at p.305.

[981] e.g. *Banque Belge pour l'Etranger v Hambrouck* [1921] 1 K.B. 321.

[982] e.g. *Taylor v Plumer* (1815) 3 M. & S. 562, Illustration 1.

[983] e.g. *France v Clark* (1884) 26 Ch.D. 257; *Hutchison v Colorado United Mining Co & Hamill, Hamill v Lilley* (1887) 3 T.L.R. 265; *Colonial Bank v Cady and Williams* (1890) 15 App.Cas. 267; *Fox v Martin* (1895) 64 L.J.Ch. 473, Illustration 2 to Article 85.

[984] e.g. the right to rescind for fraud: see *El Ajou v Dollar Land Holdings Plc* [1993] 3 All E.R. 717 at 734; *National Crime Agency v Robb* [2014] EWHC 4384 (Ch); [2015] Ch. 520 (post-formation fraud); noted Turner [2016] C.L.J. 206. cf. *Twinsectra Ltd v Yardley* [1999] Lloyd's Rep. Bank 438 at 461–462; [2000] Lloyd's Rep.P.N. 239; *Chase Manhattan Bank NA v Israel British Bank (London) Ltd* [1981] Ch. 105; cf. *Bank of America v Arnell* [1999] Lloyd's Rep. Bank, 399.

[985] See material cited at fn.961 above. See also *Bank of New Zealand v Elders Pastoral Ltd* [1992] 1 N.Z.L.R. 536.

[986] See Comment to Article 43.

[987] *Agip (Africa) Ltd v Jackson* [1990] Ch. 265.

[988] See, e.g. *Gray v Smith* [2013] EWHC 4136 (Comm); [2014] 2 All E.R. (Comm) 359.

[989] *Foskett v McKeown* [2001] 1 A.C. 102 at 131–132.

[990] *Foskett v McKeown*, above, at 131–132, *Re Hallett's Estate* (1880) 13 Ch.D. 696 at 709; *Clark v*

property, whether mixed or not,[991] held by the agent or by a subsequent holder. The right operates against one who takes with notice[992] or a volunteer,[993] but not against a bona fide purchaser for value without notice,[994] nor where the property or (more usually) money sought to be traced has ceased to be identifiable, e.g. because, being money, it has been spent without identifiable proceeds,[995] or has passed into an overdrawn bank account.[996]

Constructive trust/knowing receipt Whether or not there exists a proprietary **8-163** claim and an accompanying right to trace, a person receiving trust property or property affected by some other fiduciary interest with knowledge of the trust or fiduciary interest may nevertheless be liable to account as constructive trustee.[997] It is usually assumed that this is a separate head of liability, effectively in personam, based on different principles, and it might be thought that it is only on this ground that a recipient who has parted with the property would still be liable, and could be required to account for profits made. The action is usually called one for "knowing receipt". The relationship of this part of the law with that of tracing is however controversial at present.[998] The matter is discussed in connection with the liability of the agent to his principal[999] and again in connection with the liability of the agent to third parties[1000]; but of course the principles apply equally to third parties who receive money *from* agents, and some aspects of this type of liability are dealt with in Article 96.[1001]

Bankruptcy Bankruptcy of the agent involves the clearest case where a claim in **8-164** rem may be needed. The principal will seek to assert that money or goods are his and, the agent's authority to deal with them having ceased, he is entitled to extricate them from the agent's bankruptcy. The basic rule is that property held by the bankrupt the legal title to which is in his principal, and property held by him in trust, or as a fiduciary, is not liable to be seized: this extends to property that can be traced

---

Cutland [2003] EWCA Civ 810; [2004] 1 W.L.R. 783; *Primlake Ltd v Matthews Associates* [2006] EWHC 1227 (Ch); [2007] 1 B.C.L.C. 666 at [334].

[991] See *Lupton v White* (1808) 15 Ves. Jun. 432.

[992] *Re Diplock, Diplock v Wintle* [1948] Ch. 465 at 539; affd [1951] A.C. 251; *Crédit Agricole Corp and Investment Bank v Papadimitriou* [2015] UKPC 13; [2015] 2 All E.R. 974; noted Watts (2015) 131 L.Q.R. 511.

[993] *Re Diplock, Diplock v Wintle*, above, at 539.

[994] *Re Diplock, Diplock v Wintle*, above, at 539; *Thorndike v Hunt* (1859) 3 De G. & J. 563. As to the meaning of "notice" in this context, see *Polly Peck International Plc v Nadir (No.2)* [1992] 4 All E.R. 769 at 781–782 (but see Bryan (1993) 109 L.Q.R. 368); *Gray v Smith* [2013] EWHC 4136 (Comm); [2014] 2 All E.R. (Comm) 359.

[995] *Re Diplock, Diplock v Wintle*, above, at 546–550.

[996] *Bishopsgate Investment Management Ltd v Homan* [1995] Ch. 211; *Moriarty v Various Customers of BA Peters Plc* [2008] EWCA Civ 1604; *Federal Republic of Brazil v Durant International Corp* [2015] UKPC 35; [2016] A.C. 297. See Smith [1995] C.L.J. 290; cf. Conaglen (2011) 127 L.Q.R. 432.

[997] See, e.g. *Vernon v Public Trustee* [2016] NZCA 388 (receipt of funds misapplied by holder of power of attorney). See further below, para.9-136.

[998] See *Re Montagu's Settlement Trusts* [1987] Ch. 264 at 285; but cf. the Rt Hon. Lord Millett (1991) 107 L.Q.R. 71 at 80–81; and by the same author (1998) 114 L.Q.R. 399.

[999] Article 43.

[1000] Article 116.

[1001] See below, para.9-138 as to the duties and liabilities of banks.

at law or in equity.[1002] But once the property can no longer be traced, the principal becomes an ordinary creditor with the rest. Debts owed to the principal are not owed to the agent and so can be recovered by the principal.[1003] Some debts owed to the agent could be regarded as held in trust for the principal and so rank as property held on trust.

8-165 **"Romalpa" clauses** Considerable difficulties can be caused by the use of so-called "Romalpa" clauses, whereby a supplier of goods may seek to protect himself against the bankruptcy of the person to whom he supplies them by reserving title not only in the goods themselves, but also sometimes in the proceeds of their resale, and even into the product of mixing and manufacturing processes to which they may be subjected. Sometimes such provisions contain a "current account" clause, which reserves title not only pending payment in respect of the goods concerned, but also so long as any debt is outstanding between the parties. Apart from problems of identification of goods and appropriation of payments to particular consignments, the main danger from the point of view of the supplier is that they may be held to create some sort of charge and hence be void for non-registration. Therefore, though such arrangements are not normally related to agency relationships at all but rather to that of seller and buyer, attempts may be made to draft or interpret them as creating agency features, even though the transaction concerned is inappropriate to such interpretation. Thus it may be suggested that a buyer of goods under such a clause resells as agent and holds the proceeds as trustee. The concept of agency can be made to work in this context, but the generally arm's-length nature of the sales setting makes it a marginal case, and its invocation may create unexpected and unsatisfactory side-effects. For example, the supplier may be liable as undisclosed principal on a resale by his purchaser.[1004]

8-166 **Rule (2): Other restitutionary claims** A principal, disclosed or undisclosed, is entitled to sue for the recovery of money paid by an agent on the principal's behalf where the payment is made under a mistake of fact or any other circumstances ordinarily entitling a person paying money to recover it from the payee.[1005] It is sufficient that the payment is made on the principal's behalf even if not with money belonging to the principal.[1006]

The question has arisen of the effect on the principal's right to recover money paid by an agent under a mistake of fact of the circumstance that, when the payment is made, some other agent has knowledge of the true facts. It has been said that:

"where ... a limited liability company is concerned and payments are made under a bona fide mistake ... by an authorised agent of the company, the fact that some other agent of the company may have had full knowledge of all the facts does not disentitle the company

---

[1002] See Insolvency Act 1986 s.283(3); Williams and Muir Hunter, *Bankruptcy* (19th edn), pp.260–280 (not reproduced in the subsequent *Muir Hunter on Personal Insolvency* (looseleaf)). A number of old illustrations concerning bankruptcy of agents were collected in the 15th edition of the present work (1985).

[1003] See *Angove's Pty Ltd v Bailey* [2016] UKSC 47; [2016] 1 W.L.R. 3179.

[1004] See further above, para.1-035. More generally, see general Chitty, *Contracts* (32nd edn), para.44-174 onwards; *Benjamin's Sale of Goods* (9th edn), para.5-141 onwards; Watts (1986) 6 O.J.L.S. 456.

[1005] See Goff and Jones, *Law of Unjust Enrichment* (9th edn); Mitchell, "Banks, Agency and Unjust Enrichment" in *Commercial Law: Perspectives and Practice* (Lowry and Mistelis eds, 2006), Ch.8.

[1006] See *Agip (Africa) Ltd v Jackson* [1991] Ch. 547.

to recover the money so paid, provided that the agent with the full knowledge does not know that the payments are being made on an erroneous basis."[1007]

Presumably this principle applies also where the payment is made on behalf of any other kind of corporation or natural person. It seems likely that not only the state of knowledge of the other agent but the scope of his authority, actual or apparent, will be relevant since what the recipient will essentially be asserting against the principal is some sort of estoppel.[1008] It has been suggested that (in the absence of estoppel) so long as the paying agent is mistaken, the mere fact that other, even more senior agents, are aware of the facts and of the payment will not be fatal to a restitutionary action.[1009]

Illustrations

(1) A broker misapplied his principal's money by purchasing stock and bullion, **8-167** and absconded. He was adjudicated bankrupt on the day upon which he received and misapplied the money. On being arrested he surrendered the securities for the stock and bullion to the principal. Held, that the principal was entitled to retain the securities as against the trustee in bankruptcy.[1010]

(2) An agent who was entrusted with bills to get discounted mixed them with his own property, absconded, and became bankrupt. He was arrested with money in his possession which was the produce of portions of the mixed property. Held, that the principal was entitled, in preference to the other creditors, to a first charge on such money for the amount of the bills.[1011]

(3) Money is paid to a broker by his principal for application in a particular way. The broker pays the money into his own account at a bank, and becomes bankrupt before applying it as directed. The principal is entitled to the money as against the broker's trustee in bankruptcy.[1012] If, in such a case, the agent has drawn on the account, the principal has a charge on the balance in the banker's hands, the amounts so drawn being deemed to be drawn out of the agent's own moneys, whenever they were paid in,[1013] so long as the balance exceeds the trust moneys.[1014] Where the moneys of several principals have

---

[1007] See *Turvey v Dentons (1923) Ltd* [1953] 1 Q.B. 218 at 224; and *BP Oil International Ltd v Target Shipping Ltd* [2012] EWHC 1590 (Comm) at [226]. For the right of the agent to recover money, see Article 110.

[1008] *Turvey v Dentons* (1923) Ltd [1953] 1 Q.B. 218 at 224, per Pilcher J; applying the stronger case of *Anglo-Scottish Beet Sugar Corp Ltd v Spalding UDC* [1937] 2 K.B. 607, where "the carelessness of the various officials of the company was more pronounced than any carelessness" existing in the later case; *BP Oil International Ltd v Target Shipping Ltd* [2012] EWHC 1590 (Comm) at [239]; *Astex Therapeutics Ltd v Astrazeneca AB* [2017] EWHC 1442 (Ch) at [392] (person inducing mistaken view need not be agent making the payment). See also below, para.8-185.

[1009] See *HKSAR v Luk Kin* [2016] HKCFA 81 at [36], per Lord Hoffmann.

[1010] *Taylor v Plumer* (1815) 3 M. & S. 562; *Re Hulton Ex p. Manchester and County Bank* (1891) 39 W.R. 303. See also *Marsh v Keating* (1834) 1 Bing. (N.C.) 198.

[1011] *Frith v Cartland* (1865) 34 L.J.Ch. 301.

[1012] *Re Strachan Ex p. Cooke* (1876) 4 Ch.D. 123; *Hancock v Smith* (1889) 41 Ch.D. 456; *Re Arthur Wheeler* (1933) 102 L.J.Ch. 341. See also *Re Cotton Ex p. Cooke* (1913) 108 L.T. 310 (auctioneer); cf. *Re Hallett & Co, Ex p. Blane* [1894] 2 Q.B. 237; *Re Mawson Ex p. Hardcastle* (1881) 44 L.T. 523; *King v Hutton* [1900] 2 Q.B. 504; *Wilsons & Furness-Leyland Line Ltd v British & Continental Shipping Co Ltd* (1907) 23 T.L.R. 397.

[1013] *Re Hallett's Estate* (1880) 13 Ch.D. 696; *Re Wreford* (1897) 13 T.L.R. 153; *Banque Belge pour l'Etranger v Hambrouck* [1921] 1 K.B. 321. See also *Re Oatway* [1903] 2 Ch. 356.

[1014] *James Roscoe (Bolton) Ltd v Winder* [1915] 1 Ch. 62; and see *Campden Hill Ltd v Chakrani* [2005] EWHC 911; [2005] N.P.C. 65.

been paid into the account, their charges have priority in the inverse order of the payments, the balance being deemed to consist of the trust moneys most recently paid in.[1015]

(4) An agent who was employed to sell certain goods mixed them with goods of his own, and consigned the whole of the goods together to a factor for sale, representing to his principal that he had sold his goods, and debiting himself with the amount of the supposed prices. The agent having become bankrupt, the principal was held entitled to have the proceeds of the mixed property marshalled, so as to throw advances made by the factor, as far as possible, on to the agent's own goods.[1016]

(5) A factor becomes bankrupt. Goods in his hand for sale, fresh goods directly bought with the proceeds of sale of such goods, and unmatured bills and notes received by him as the price of goods sold, must, subject to his lien, be returned to the principal, and may be recovered by him from the trustee in bankruptcy.[1017] The price of goods already sold may, subject to the agent's lien, be recovered by the principal from the purchaser,[1018] and, if paid to the trustee in bankruptcy, may be recovered from him by the principal.[1019]

(6) The chief accountant of a company fraudulently alters a cheque duly signed on the company's behalf, with the effect that it is credited to another company with which the paying company has no connection, and from there the money is paid out on instructions. It is assumed that the directors of the latter company have no knowledge of the reason behind the transaction. They are liable for money still in their possession.[1020]

(7) A partner in a firm of solicitors fraudulently draws money from the company's account and spends it gambling at a casino. The firm may recover the money from the casino subject to a defence of change of position.[1021]

(8) A warehouse holding wool on behalf of a seller with strict instructions not to deliver it to the buyer without express confirmation from the seller of receipt of payment, mistakenly delivers the wool to the buyer when it has not been paid for. The seller is entitled to recover the wool or its value in conversion from the buyer (and its receivers).[1022]

(9) A custom-house officer took exorbitant fees from a shipmaster. Held, that the owner of the vessel had a right to sue to recover the amount paid in excess of the proper fees.[1023]

[1015] *Re Stenning* [1895] 2 Ch. 433. See also *Re Diplock* [1948] Ch. 465; affd [1951] A.C. 251. This is subject to contrary intention: see *Barlow Clowes International Ltd v Vaughan* [1992] 4 All E.R. 22; *Commerzbank Aktiengesellschaft v IMB Morgan Plc* [2004] EWHC 2771 (Ch); [2005] 1 Lloyd's Rep. 298.

[1016] *Broadbent v Barlow* (1861) 3 De G.F. & J. 570; *Re Holland Ex p. Alston* (1868) L.R. 4 Ch.App. 168; *Re Burge, Woodall & Co Ex p. Skyrme* [1912] 1 K.B. 393.

[1017] *Scott v Surman* (1742) Wiles 400 (see as to this case *Triffit Nurseries v Salads Etcetera Ltd* [2000] 1 All E.R. (Comm) 737 at 742–743); *Whitecomb v Jacob* (1710) 1 Salk. 160; *Godfrey v Furzo* (1733) 3 P. Wms. 186. See also *Ex p. Sayers* (1800) 5 Ves. 169.

[1018] *Scott v Surman*; *Re Wood Ex p. Boden* (1873) 28 L.T. 174.

[1019] See *Scott v Surman* (1742) Wiles 400 and the other cases cited with it, above.

[1020] *Agip (Africa) Ltd v Jackson* [1990] Ch. 265; [1991] Ch. 247.

[1021] *Lipkin Gorman v Karpnale Ltd* [1991] 2 A.C. 548.

[1022] *J.S. Brooksbank & Co (Australasia) Ltd v EXFTX Ltd* (2009) 10 N.Z.C.L.C. 264,520.

[1023] *Stevenson v Mortimer* (1778) Cowp. 805; see also *Holt v Ely* (1853) 1 E. & B. 795; *Taylor v Smith* (1926) 38 C.L.R. 48.

Article 89

DISPOSITIONS AND PAYMENTS TO AGENT

(1) Where a purported transfer of property in goods[1024] is made to the agent of a disclosed principal, and the agent receives it as such acting within his actual or apparent authority, the property in the goods is transferred to the principal if such is the intention of the parties to the transfer.

(2) (Perhaps) where a purported transfer of property in goods is made to the agent of an undisclosed principal and the agent is authorised to receive it and does so intending to act as agent, the property in the goods is transferred to the undisclosed principal if such is the intention of the agent and the principal, unless the principal knows that the transferor would not have transferred the property in the goods to him.

(3) (Perhaps), where there is an attornment by the holder of goods to the agent of an undisclosed principal and the agent is authorised to receive it and does so intending to act as agent, the principal has the right to treat the attornment as being to him unless the principal knows that the holder of the goods would not have attorned to him.[1025]

(4) A disclosed principal can be subject to restitutionary claims brought in respect of money paid (and sometimes other property transferred) to his agent in connection with transactions effected within the agent's actual or apparent authority, even though the principal has not personally received it.

8-168

Comment

The question of the effect of dispositions *by* an agent of his principal's property raises problems of transfer of property by a non-owner. That of the effect of dispositions *in favour* of the agent, on the other hand, raises quite different problems regarding the relevance of the intention of the parties to the transfer of property and possession, and in some circumstances, the law of restitution.

8-169

Disclosed principal   Property in goods is transferred by delivery, and in some cases (particularly contracts of sale of goods[1026]) by intention. There is no objection to the acquisition of property through an agent. Hence a transfer of goods, whether by delivery or mere intention, to an agent who in receiving possession or assenting to receive property without possession acts for a disclosed principal, named or unnamed, will pass property to the principal, provided that all the other conditions normally required for the passing of property[1027] are satisfied. It would of course be necessary that the agent was acting within his actual or apparent authority: since the acquisition of property is usually an advantage, cases where there was no authority of either sort would be the exception rather than the rule. Where *possession* is also transferred to the agent, however, this rests with him,

8-170

[1024] The position as to land would be different: see above, para.2-037.

[1025] See Comment; Goode, *Proprietary Rights and Insolvency in Sales Transactions* (3rd edn), Ch.III.

[1026] Sale of Goods Act 1979 s.17.

[1027] e.g. that the goods are ascertained: see Sale of Goods Act 1979 s.16 (as modified by Sale of Goods (Amendment) Act 1995).

though by a pre-existing intention he may immediately constitute himself bailee for his principal. As bailee he possesses: his principal does not.[1028]

8-171 **Undisclosed principal** When however there is a transfer to a person who is acting as agent for an undisclosed principal and intends to receive for his principal, the position becomes very difficult to analyse. The operation of the undisclosed principal doctrine outside the realm of pure contract raises many problems, the solutions to which have hardly been considered. On one view, transfer of property is not the same as contract, and the passage of property does not necessarily occur in pursuance of a contract. Hence the intentions of the parties must be looked at in isolation from any contractual implications. On this basis the intention of the transferor is only to transfer to the agent, and a concealed intention of the agent to acquire for another should not be able to produce a different effect. If the agent wishes to make a further transfer to his principal this can be instantly effected, as regards property, by intention alone (at least where there is consideration for the disposition): but the property will have passed through the agent for a *scintilla temporis*, which may have legal significance, e.g. for bankruptcy or tax purposes. Again, *possession* will pass to the agent, though he may immediately, by virtue of his intention, become bailee to the principal.

It may furthermore be argued that in a contract situation the undisclosed principal doctrine involves an element of intervention. The undisclosed principal intervenes on a transaction entered into by the agent which is valid in itself; and the third party may elect to sue the principal on such a transaction, but need not do so. Such an element of choice can be said to be inappropriate in property transactions: there cannot be a right to possess in both principal and agent. It is also true that agents taking conveyances of land are held to act as trustees for their principals and not to vest property in their principals directly[1029]: but these cases seem to depend on the fact that written instruments are used which by their words purport to vest the land in the agent.

As against these arguments it may be said that the formation of obligation is, at least prima facie, of an even more personal nature than the transfer of property. The latter rids the transferor of obligations rather than creates them, and does not produce a continuing relationship: it is often, perhaps usually, a matter of indifference to a transferor who receives the goods with which he intends to part. If an undisclosed principal can intervene on an obligation, a fortiori he should be able to intervene on a transfer of property, which usually occurs in pursuance of an obligation. It may even be argued that in the case of sale of goods the requirement of intention of the parties[1030] is supplied by the transferor's intention to transfer and the undisclosed principal's intention to receive, though these have no reference to each other. These propositions are strengthened by the usual view that the origin of the undisclosed principal doctrine lay in the desire to protect the principal in the agent's bankruptcy.[1031] For that purpose it is obviously important that the principal's title should be protected from the moment of acquisition of goods for the principal by the agent.

[1028] See Paton, *Bailment in the Common Law* (1952), pp.6–9; Pollock and Wright, *Possession in the Common Law* (1888), pp.57–60. As to possession of documents by an agent for the purpose of subpoena *duces tecum*, see *Rochfort v Trade Practices Commission* (1982) 153 C.L.R. 134 and cases there cited.

[1029] Article 53.

[1030] Sale of Goods Act 1979 s.17.

[1031] See above, para.8-069.

If the principal has the right to intervene and claim property, that right is presumably subject to the exception to which intervention on a contract is subject: that it must not be excluded by the express or implied terms of the transaction.[1032] It is arguable also that the exception goes further than this and that he cannot claim that property vested in him automatically (rather than by a further transfer from the agent) where he knows that the transferor would not have transferred to him.[1033]

An agent who has no authority to create privity with the third party, but nevertheless acts for a principal (the *commissionnaire* of the civil law)[1034] may probably (though the question is unsolved) receive and transmit the property to his principal. A group of old cases involving this problem is considered in Article 71.

Attornment   An attornment in respect of goods occurs where the possessor of   **8-172**
goods, whether himself the transferor or the bailee of the transferor, acknowledges that he holds, and possesses, for another. There is authority that such an attornment creates a fresh bailment by means of a constructive delivery and redelivery.[1035] It may be used to pass property to a buyer: but it may instead create a pledge in favour of the attornee. Attornment to the agent of a disclosed principal acting as such may plainly rank as attornment to the principal. If intention is the key to the effect of attornment, the intention where the agent's principal is undisclosed is, however, only to attorn to the agent. Indeed, any other conclusion could be said to lead to there being a constructive delivery to two persons, each of whom effects a redelivery. But again it can be argued that, since attornment will usually occur in pursuance of a contract, the undisclosed principal's intervention should not be disallowed in such a case when it is allowed in the case of contract; and that not only should attornment be capable of passing property to an undisclosed principal, it should also (subject to the same provisos regarding cases where the attornor did not or would not have attorned to the principal) be capable of constituting him a pledgee. Such a conclusion has been reached by the Court of Appeal of New South Wales in *Maynegrain Pty Ltd v Compafina Bank*,[1036] the facts of which are summarised below.

Estoppel   In the above case there was an additional complication: the goods in   **8-173**
respect of which an attornment (for the purposes of creating a security) was made were part of an undivided bulk, and the court assumed[1037] that there can be no possession, and hence no bailment, of such unascertained goods. Therefore as a pure attornment, viz. a constructive delivery and redelivery, the act concerned (the issue of a warehouse receipt) was ineffective. In such cases however there is authority that an attornment also operates by way of estoppel, in that it prevents the person

---

[1032] See above, para.8-078; *Maynegrain Pty Ltd v Compafina Bank Ltd* [1982] 2 N.S.W.L.R. 141 at 153: "unless the terms of the attornment or of the arrangements for the making of that attornment require A.N.Z. to be treated as the only attornee".

[1033] See above, para.8-078.

[1034] See above, para.1-029.

[1035] *Dublin City Distillery Ltd v Doherty* [1914] A.C. 823 at 852; *Official Assignee of Madras v Mercantile Bank of India Ltd* [1935] A.C. 53 at 58.

[1036] [1982] 2 N.S.W.L.R. 141, Illustration 1; reversed on the facts (1984) 58 A.L.J.R. 389, (PC). See Goode, *Proprietary Rights and Insolvency in Sales Transactions* (3rd edn), at pp.11–12.

[1037] But see *Hayman & Son v M'Lintock* (1907) S.C. 936; *Benjamin's Sale of Goods* (9th edn), para.18-339. It is possible that the position is altered by the Sale of Goods (Amendment) Act 1995, which allows ownership of part of a bulk to arise in new circumstances: see *Benjamin's Sale of Goods*, para.18-335 onwards. The position as regards possession is unsolved. See Gullifer [1999] L.M.C.L.Q. 93.

attorning from denying that he in fact holds goods as described for the attornee.[1038] A further doctrinal point therefore arises: can a warehouseman be estopped against someone whose existence he has not contemplated? This turns on the scope of his representation, not on any notion of intervention. Again there is a choice. On one view, it may be immaterial to a holder of goods to whom they are transferred, for whom he holds or to whom the receipt which he has signed is shown. On another, estoppel raises the question of who is contemplated as likely to rely on the representation, and a statement specifically addressed to one person may well not be intended to be relied on by another, at any rate where a document of title is not involved.[1039] The analogy of share certificates,[1040] which are not documents of title, suggests the adoption of the first view, and indeed to differentiate in result between cases where the goods are specific and cases where they are part of a bulk seems wrong. The court not surprisingly held that the estoppel applied likewise: granted the first decision, it would have been unsatisfactory to decide differently on this issue.

8-174   Rule (4): Restitutionary claims in relation to payments to agent   Rule (4) touches on a wide subject, the law of restitution, a close scrutiny of which is beyond this book.[1041] Plainly, where a claimant wishes to assert a restitutionary right, he may often prefer to sue the principal of the actual recipient of the money, or other property, for the usual reason that there are stronger chances of enforcing judgment against him. As with many other areas of the law of restitution, the precise bounds of a principal's liability in such circumstances are still being settled. It is reasonably clear that if the payment was made to a person who received the payment for a principal, disclosed or undisclosed, within his actual authority, or for a disclosed principal within the agent's apparent authority, the principal will be prima facie liable.[1042] If the money is in fact accounted for by the agent to the principal, and accepted as such, the principal is also likely to be liable to a restitutionary claim, if only on the basis of ratification, even when the initial receipt was without authority. Where the claimant has a proprietary claim, the mere receipt by the principal may well be sufficient to expose the principal to an action, even without ratification. Less clear are the circumstances in which the principal might be able to raise defences such as change of position and bona fide purchase for value without notice, especially where the receiving agent was aware of the circumstances that might give rise to a claim but the principal was not. Another defence that might arise to protect the principal is the defence of "ministerial receipt", arising where an agent on a frolic of his own has simply used his principal as a receiving box, and the money has merely gone in and out of the principal's accounts. In cases of that sort the agent will usually have initiated the transaction, and relevant commentary and cases are found in Article 92.

[1038] *Knights v Wiffen* (1870) L.R. 5 Q.B. 660; *Coventry, Sheppard & Co v GE Ry Co* (1883) 11 Q.B.D. 776. See also *Alicia Hosiery Ltd v Brown, Shipley & Co Ltd* [1970] 1 Q.B. 195 at 206.
[1039] cf. *V/O Rasnoimport v Guthrie & Co* [1966] 1 Lloyd's Rep 1, where a signature as agent was held to constitute a contractual offer of authority to persons taking up the document.
[1040] *Re Bahia and San Francisco Ry Co Ltd* (1868) L.R. 3 Q.B. 584; see *Gower's Principles of Modern Company Law* (10th edn), paras 27-5–27-6; Spencer Bower, *Reliance-Based Estoppel* (5th edn), Ch.6.
[1041] See Goff and Jones, *Law of Unjust Enrichment* (9th edn); Watts [2017] L.M.C.L.Q. 385.
[1042] *Coulthurst v Sweet* (1866) L.R. 1 C.P. 649, Illustration 2; *Portman Building Society v Hamlyn Taylor Neck* [1998] 4 All E.R. 202 at 207; *Marsfield Automotive Inc v Siddiqi* [2017] EWHC 187 (Comm).

Illustrations

(1) A warehouseman, holding imported goods for a customer at the customer's **8-175**
request, for purposes of creating a security, issues a warehouse receipt for a
quantity of goods, part of an undivided mass, for the account of a local bank.
He subsequently delivers some of the goods at the customer's direction. The
local bank to whom he issued the receipt was in fact agent for another bank
which has actually advanced money to the owner of the goods. The lending
bank can intervene and, as bailor, sue the warehouseman in conversion.[1043]
(2) An agent appointed by the managing owner of a ship demanded too much
freight from the consignees of certain goods, and refused to deliver the goods
until payment. The consignees paid the amount demanded, under protest, and
sued one of the part-owners of the ship for the excess. Held, that he was liable, though no portion of the money had come to his hands.[1044]

3. WRONGS

Introductory Note

Torts The primary application of the principles of agency is in the fields of **8-176**
contract, dispositions of property and the law of restitution. The law of tort, in
general, uses different techniques. Anyone considering the application of agency
principles in the law of tort is initially faced with the fact that when that branch of
the law deals with liability of one person for the acts of another, the question
normally turns not on the authority of the person who committed the tort, but on
whether he was the servant (or employee) of the person sought to be held liable,
or an independent contractor. An agent may be either (or indeed, in some situations, such as the case of a gratuitous agent, neither). A very rough summary of the
usual view would be to say that a person is liable for torts committed by another
which he specifically instigates or authorises, or which are committed by his servant acting within the course of employment, or which involve a breach of a non-
delegable duty owed by him, though the acts leading to such breach were actually
performed by another (usually an independent contractor). Vicarious liability in the
law of tort seems also to have a different basis from agency in contract, and
elsewhere. In contract, the agent is not liable as a matter of course, and the effect
of agency rules is, in the majority of cases, to establish the primary liability of the
person with whom the third party intended to deal. But with most torts the actual
tortfeasor is in principle liable, and the effect of vicarious liability is to add a defendant, often unknown to and uncontemplated by the victim; on one view its purpose
is simply to find a defendant who can pay.[1045]
However, the law of agency appears to be important in the operation of some

---

[1043] *Maynegrain Pty Ltd v Compafina Bank* [1982] 2 N.S.W.L.R. 141. But the decision was reversed on
the facts on the basis that the local bank had assented to the delivery: (1984) 58 A.L.J.R. 389 (PC).
[1044] *Coulthurst v Sweet* (1866) L.R. 1 C.P. 649.
[1045] Atiyah, *Vicarious Liability in the Law of Torts* (1967), Chs 1, 2; and see *Rose v Plenty* [1976] 1
W.L.R. 141 at 147. See too *Dubai Aluminium Co Ltd v Salaam* [2002] UKHL 48; [2003] A.C. 366
at [107], per Lord Millett; *Majrowski v Guy's & St. Thomas's NHS Trust* [2006] UKHL 34; [2007]
1 A.C. 224 at [9], per Lord Nicholls of Birkenhead. The orthodox view is that vicarious liability
works by making the employer (or, in some cases, principal) secondarily liable for the tort or other
wrong of the employee (or agent): *Majrowski v Guy's & St. Thomas's NHS Trust*, above, at [15], [56],
[68], and [81]. But cf. Stevens (2007) 123 L.Q.R. 30; and Stevens, *Torts and Rights* (2007), Ch.11.

torts, especially those involving liability for statements, including deceit, negligent misstatement and, possibly, defamation.[1046] It may also be relevant to tortious claims for negligent performance of services, where, as with negligent misstatement, the underlying explanation is, arguably anyway, the near-contractual one of assumption of responsibility.[1047] The deployment of agency law in these torts may have both a narrowing and a broadening effect compared to other torts. On the one hand, a claimant may need to show that the agent's conduct was authorised or appeared to be authorised (rather than simply that the conduct took place "in the course of employment"). On the other hand, in such cases it would not usually matter that the agent was not an employee of the defendant.

Moreover, there are various ways in which considerable interrelation with the law of agency exists and these prevent a total separation between agency in contract and vicarious liability in tort. They may be enumerated as follows, with the reservation that, as is obvious, the categories are not mutually exclusive:

(a) Parallels from one part of the law have long been cited in the other[1048] and the terminologies of master and servant and principal and agent have been and still are readily interchanged: the same applies to the phrases "course of employment" and "scope of authority".[1049]

(b) The clear dichotomy between contract and tort which was made from the late nineteenth century was not made in earlier times,[1050] and is now again subject to considerable reservations and qualifications.

(c) Ancillary notions primarily related, according to modern ideas, to contractual agency, e.g. ratification, have on occasion been useful in the field of tort.[1051] Another example arises where a party instigates or authorises a third party, not necessarily an employee, to commit a tort on its behalf.[1052]

See too Neyers (2005) 43 Alberta L.R. 287.

[1046] See *Mercantile Credit Co v Garrod* [1962] 3 All E.R. 1103 (a case on partnership); *Armagas Ltd v Mundogas SA (The Ocean Frost)* [1986] A.C. 717 (deceit); *Williams v Natural Life Health Foods Ltd* [1998] 1 W.L.R. 830 (negligent misstatement); *Colonial Mutual Life Assurance Society Ltd v Producers and Citizens Cooperative Co of Australia Ltd* (1931) 46 C.L.R. 41 (defamation). The latter three cases are discussed below. For general discussion, see Ferson (1948) 2 Vand.L.Rev. 1; Watts (2012) 128 L.Q.R. 260. cf. liability under the Misrepresentation Act 1967 s.2(1); and as to the tort of inducement of breach of contract, see below, para.9-121; *Kallang Shipping SA Panama v Axa Assurances Senegal* [2008] EWHC 2761 (Comm) at [92]; *New South Wales v Lepore* (2003) 212 C.L.R. 511.

[1047] See *Williams v Natural Life Health Foods Ltd* [1998] 1 W.L.R. 830 at 834; *Sainsbury's Supermarkets Ltd v Condek Holdings Ltd* [2014] EWHC 2016 (TCC); [2014] B.L.R. 574 at [17].

[1048] "There has never been a time when cases on master and servant were not cited as authority in the law of principal and agent, and vice versa": Street, *Foundations of Legal Liability* (1906), Vol.2, p.454.

[1049] Had there been separate commercial courts, the result might have been otherwise; the terminology of agency is a commercial one, but that of master and servant has long been rooted in the common law. See Holdsworth, *H.E.L. VIII*, p.227. See also e.g. Pollock, *Contracts* (15th edn), p.58 onwards; *Barwick v English Joint Stock Bank* (1867) L.R. 2 Ex. 259 at 266; *Swire v Francis* (1877) 3 App.Cas. 106; *Holdsworth v City of Glasgow Bank* (1880) 5 App.Cas. 317 at 326–327; *Lloyd v Grace, Smith & Co* [1912] A.C. 716 at 734–735; *Uxbridge Permanent Benefit Building Society v Pickard* [1939] 2 K.B. 248 at 254; *Navarro v Moregrand Ltd* [1951] 2 T.L.R. 674; *Morris v C.W. Martin & Sons Ltd* [1966] 1 Q.B. 716 at 726; *Heaton Transport (St Helen) Ltd v T&GWU* [1973] A.C. 15 at 99; *Rose v Plenty* [1976] 1 W.L.R. 141. Statutes relating to tort may use the term "agent": see Crown Proceedings Act 1947 s.2(1)(a).

[1050] Especially as regards representations: Stoljar, pp.64–67.

[1051] Indeed ratification may be older than the idea of agency. But it is probably now confined to cases

(d) Certain persons whom the law of tort, as expounded above, might for the sake of consistency describe as servants seem in common speech more appropriately described as agents, especially where their duties involve commercial matters such as the making of contracts, dispositions of property, etc. Thus a shipmaster who sells the cargo wrongfully,[1053] a solicitor's managing clerk dealing with a mortgage who defrauds the person with whom he is dealing,[1054] or a bailiff levying distress wrongfully[1055] may well be servants (or independent contractors), but the term "agent" may nevertheless be used when the principal is made liable for their torts committed in the course of their professional activities. On the other hand though a bus driver could be an agent for buying petrol, he is certainly more likely to be called a servant if he is involved in a collision on the way to get it.[1056] In some cases the term used may depend simply on whether a tort leading to personal injuries is involved, or an economic tort, e.g. deceit.

(e) In one unique line of cases one person is held liable for the tort of another who is certainly neither his servant nor his independent contractor, but who can be said in some sense to be acting for him—in most cases by driving a car. These cases, often referred to as involving the notion of casual delegation, are sometimes explained as based on agency.[1057]

(f) Some statutory sources of civil liability are drafted using the concepts of the law of agency, rather than vicarious liability.[1058]

Attempts can be and have been made to unify all agency in contract and tort into one set of principles,[1059] and even, abandoning the terminology of master and servant, to seek to establish the types of authority as the guiding criteria in tort as well as contract.[1060] If there is a separate notion of usual authority,[1061] it is plainly of much assistance for this: some of the rules relating to independent contractors would be incorporated here and some related to the personal duty of the principal. Though there is plenty of useful material in the cases,[1062] such an exercise is a creative and theoretical one involving a development of the law beyond the form in which it is at present stated and understood in England and Wales. It has already been sug-

---

of conversion and trespass: see Comment to Article 14. Agency terminology may also be used where a servant does acts upon which the tortiousness of further acts may depend, e.g. invites persons on to land where they would otherwise be trespassers: *Hillen & Pettigrew v ICI Alkall Ltd* [1936] A.C. 65; *Young v Box & Co* [1951] 1 T.L.R. 789.

[1052] See below,para.8-177.

[1053] *Ewbank v Nutting* (1849) 7 C.B. 797.

[1054] *Lloyd v Grace, Smith & Co* [1912] A.C. 716, Illustration 12 to Article 90; *Uxbridge Permanent Benefit Building Society v Pickard* [1939] 2 K.B. 248, Illustration 13 to Article 90.

[1055] Article 90, Illustration 17.

[1056] *Limpus v London General Omnibus Co Ltd* (1862) 1 H. & C. 526.

[1057] See below, para.8-187.

[1058] See, e.g. *Giltrap City Ltd v The Commerce Commission* [2004] 1 N.Z.L.R. 608 (price-fixing); *Alfred v Wakelin (No.2)* [2008] FCA 1543 (proscribed industrial action).

[1059] cf. *Restatement, Second*, § 2. And see above, para.1-026 onwards.

[1060] See Powell, pp.184–194; Fridman, Ch.7; cf. Ferson (1951) 4 Vand.L.Rev. 260; Conant (1968) 48 Neb.L.Rev. 42; Tedeschi (1969) 4 Israel L.Rev. 1; Atiyah, *Vicarious Liability in the Law of Torts* (1967), Ch.9.

[1061] See Comment to Article 22; above, para.8-077.

[1062] See material cited at fn.1049 above; cases relating to false imprisonment cited at Article 90, Illustration 5; cases on solicitors and bailiffs cited at Article 90, Illustration 18. cf. Partnership Act 1890 s.10.

gested that such attempts are of doubtful validity in pure contract situations,[1063] and they do not seem to illuminate tort situations either.

For the elucidation of the law as at present applied it is more appropriate to set out briefly an indication of the basic rules as to liability in tort, based on the distinction between servants and independent contractors, and to suggest the ways in which agency reasoning may arguably be regarded as modifying the results which the orthodox tort reasoning might reach. More attention is then given to those torts where the use of agency reasoning, arguably at least, performs a more substantive role.

Article 90

LIABILITY OF PRINCIPAL FOR TORTS COMMITTED BY AGENT

8-177   (1)   In general,[1064] if an agent is the servant of his principal, the principal is liable for loss, damage or injury caused by the wrongful act of the agent when acting in the course of his employment.[1065] Partners are similarly liable for wrongful acts of one another.[1066]

(2)   A principal is liable in tort for loss or injury caused by his agent, whether or not his servant, and if not his servant, whether or not he can be called an independent contractor, in the following cases:

(a)   if the wrongful act was specifically instigated, authorised[1067] or ratified[1068] by the principal.

(b)   (semble) in the case of a statement made in the course of representing the principal within the actual or apparent authority of the agent: and for such a statement the principal may be liable notwithstanding that it was made for the benefit of the agent alone and not for that of the principal.[1069]

(c)   where the principal can be taken to have assumed a responsibility for the actions of the agent.[1070]

(3)   In some circumstances, the owner of a business or organisation may owe duties of care, usually in relation to the personal safety and wellbeing of others, that apply whether or not the owner performs the services personally or through servants, or by engaging independent contractors. Such duties are

---

[1063] See Comment to Article 22.

[1064] This is an important qualification; see, for instance, torts based on statements, discussed below, para.8-180.

[1065] See Comment: Salmond and Heuston, *Torts* (21st edn), Ch.21; Clerk and Lindsell, *Torts* (21st edn), Ch.6; Atiyah, *Vicarious Liability in the Law of Torts* (1967); Giliker, *Vicarious Liability in Tort* (2010). See a not dissimilar formulation in *Restatement, Third*, §7.03. In *New South Wales v Ibbett* (2006) 231 A.L.R. 485 (HCA) exemplary damages were awarded against an employer who was vicariously liable only, see para.8-192, Illustration 7. In *S v Att.-Gen.* [2003] 3 N.Z.L.R. 450 at 472–475 (CA) (abuse of foster children by foster parents under state control) exemplary damages were held to be generally inappropriate where liability was only vicarious, but the case of abuse of official status was left open. cf. *Kuddus v Chief Constable of Leicestershire Constabulary* [2002] 2 A.C. 122; and *Blackwater v Plint* (2005) 258 D.L.R. (4th) 275 (SCC) (noted by Neyers (2006) 122 L.Q.R. 195).

[1066] See Partnership Act 1890 s.10. See Lindley and Banks, *Partnership* (19th edn), Ch.12.

[1067] Illustrations 14 to 16; Atiyah, above, Ch.27. See *C. Evans & Sons Ltd v Spritebrand Ltd* [1985] 1 W.L.R. 317 (director) and the collection of cases below, para.8-194.

[1068] See Article 14.

[1069] See Comment; Article 74. cf. Partnership Act 1890 s.10. As to apparent authority, see Article 72.

[1070] See Comment.

termed "non-delegable". These duties do not necessarily invoke agency concepts.

(4)   Where principal and agent are both liable for a wrongful act committed by the agent they are joint tortfeasors.[1071]

(5)   In this Article, save where the context requires, "act" includes "omission".

Comment

Rule (1): Servants and partners   This gives a brief indication of the liability of   **8-178**
a principal for the acts of his servant, and of one partner for the acts of another. A definition of "servant" is given in Article 2. In the context of the present article it should be taken to embrace company directors, who as officers will not necessarily also be employees. The usual corollary is that a party, P, is not liable for torts committed by persons who do not fit into the categories of servant, director or partner.[1072] This would generally be so even if, apart from the actions constituting the tort, the tortfeasor were for some purposes an agent of P.[1073] Recent extensions of vicarious liability outside the traditional categories, but not generally involving the use of agency concepts, are discussed below.

As for liability for the acts of servants, the traditional view is that a servant acts in the course of his employment if he commits any wrongful act authorised by the employer or does an act within the scope of his duties as a servant in a wrongful and unauthorised manner.[1074] It is established that he may act in the course of his employment notwithstanding that the employer has expressly prohibited the act done[1075]: whether the prohibited act is or is not in the course of the servant's employment depends upon whether the prohibition is such as merely regulates the conduct of the servant within the scope of his employment or is such as limits the sphere of that employment itself.[1076] A servant may act in the course of his employment notwithstanding that the act is done for the benefit of the servant alone and not for that of the employer.[1077] But the leading modern case of *Lister v Hesley Hall Ltd*[1078] uses a looser test of connection between the acts in question and the employment in the context of the liability of the employer of a warden of a school for sexual abuse of the pupils by the warden. Lord Steyn said that "The test is whether the [person concerned's] torts are so closely connected with his employment that it

---

[1071] *Jones v Manchester Corp* [1952] 2 Q.B. 852 at 869. See below, para.8-191.

[1072] The leading case is *Quarman v Burnett* (1840) 6 M.&W. 499. See also *Emmanuel v DBS Management Plc* [1999] Lloyd's Rep P.N. 593 at 594; *Woodland v Swimming Teachers Association* [2013] UKSC 66; [2014] A.C. 537 at [3]; *Scott v Davis* (2000) 204 C.L.R. 333 at [18] and [301]; *Hollis v Vabu Pty Ltd* (2001) 207 C.L.R. 21 at [40].

[1073] See *Holdnerness v Goslin* [1975] 2 N.Z.L.R. 46 at 50–51; *Emmanuel v DBS Management Plc* [1999] Lloyd's Rep P.N. 593 at 594. As to Scotland, see *M v Hendron* [2007] CSIH 27 at [132].

[1074] See *Poland v John Parr & Sons Ltd* [1927] 1 K.B. 236 at 240; *Bugge v Brown* (1919) 26 C.L.R. 110; Salmond and Heuston, above, p.443; *Stevens v Brodribb Sawmilling Company Pty Ltd* (1986) 160 C.L.R. 16.

[1075] Illustrations 7–10.

[1076] See *Plumb v Cobden Flour Mills Co Ltd* [1914] A.C. 62 at 66–67; *Canadian Pacific Ry Co v Lockhart* [1942] A.C. 591 at 599; *Rose v Plenty* [1976] 1 W.L.R. 141; *Harrison v Michelin Tyre Co Ltd* [1985] 1 All E.R. 918; *Kooragang Investments Pty Ltd v Richardson & Wrench Ltd* [1982] A.C. 462, Illustration 9.

[1077] Illustrations 11–13. cf. Article 74.

[1078] [2001] UKHL 22; [2002] 1 A.C. 215. See also not dissimilar discussion in the High Court of Australia in *New South Wales v Lepore* (2003) 212 C.L.R. 511. But cf. *Prince Alfred College Inc v ADC* [2016] HCA 37.

would be fair and just to hold the employers vicariously liable".[1079] This was said in the context of intentional torts, and of torts performed for the tortfeasor's benefit. However, similar reasoning has been used more recently in the context of the lesser, but still basically intentional, equitable wrong of accessory liability to breach of trust ("knowing assistance"[1080]). A firm of solicitors was held liable under s.10 of the Partnership Act 1890 in respect of "any wrongful act or omission" of a partner acting in such a way.[1081] It was said that:

> "[i]f regard is paid to the closeness of the connection between the employee's wrongdoing and the class of acts which he was employed to perform or to the underlying rationale of vicarious liability, there is no relevant distinction to be made between performing an act in an improper manner and performing it for an improper purpose or by improper means."[1082]

Such reasoning now seems likely to be deployed in respect of vicarious liability generally It was applied but the test held not to be satisfied (again for the purposes of s.10 of the Partnership Act) where the act of a partner in indorsing an unlikely investment plan was quite outside the normal function of a solicitor.[1083]

Recent case law, generally in the context of liability for sexual molestation of minors, has extended the application of vicarious liability beyond employees and partners in the technical sense. This has seen liability imposed on parties that share co-membership of an unincorporated association,[1084] and on a church notwithstanding the absence of an employment relationship between the relevant bishop and the tortfeasor and indeed where the bishop, having appointed the tortfeasor, was without powers of control over him.[1085] It was held sufficient that the tortfeasor was appointed by the bishop in order that the tortfeasor could represent the church in the exercise of its mission. The Supreme Court in *Cox v Ministry of Justice* has now made clear that the expansion in the scope of vicarious liability is not confined to

---

[1079] At [28]. See also *Majrowski v Guy's & St. Thomas's NHS Trust* [2006] UKHL 34; [2007] 1 A.C. 224 at [10], per Lord Nicholls of Birkenhead; *Maga v The Trustees of the Birmingham Archdiocese of the Roman Catholic Church* [2010] EWCA Civ 256; [2010] 1 W.L.R. 1441; *Brink's Global Services Inc v Igrox Ltd* [2010] EWCA Civ 1207; [2011] I.R.L.R. 343 (employer vicariously liable for theft by employee whilst fumigating claimant's containers); noted Morgan [2011] L.M.C.L.Q 172; *Weddall v Barchester Healthcare Ltd* [2012] EWCA Civ 25 (assault by junior employee on more senior); *Bellman v Northampton Recruitment Ltd* [2016] EWHC 3104 (QB); [2017] I.C.R. 543 (company not liable for managing director's assault of employee outside work hours); *Mohamud v Wm Morrison Supermarkets Plc* [2016] UKSC 11; [2016] A.C. 677 (assault by employee on supermarket forecourt). *Axon v Ministry of Defence* [2016] EWHC 787 (QB); [2016] E.M.L.R. 20 at [95] (potential breach of privacy by employee in respect of information available only through employer). See also *Hickey v McGowan* [2017] IESC 6.

[1080] See Article 116.

[1081] *Dubai Aluminium Co Ltd v Salaam* [2002] UKHL 48; [2003] 2 A.C. 366. (It should be noted that the liability of the actual solicitor was posited in the context of the matter in dispute and had never been admitted.)

[1082] At [124], per Lord Millett.

[1083] *J.J. Coughlan Ltd v Ruparelia* [2003] EWCA Civ 1057; [2004] P.N.L.R. 4. See too *The Northampton Regional Livestock Centre Co Ltd v Cowling* [2015] EWCA Civ 651; [2016] 1 B.C.L.C. 431 at [96] (vicarious liability found).

[1084] *Various Claimants v The Catholic Child Welfare Society* [2010] EWCA Civ 1106 at [41] and [76]; reversed on other points [2012] UKSC 56; [2013] 2 A.C. 1; noted Bell [2013] C.L.J. 17; Morgan (2013) 129 L.Q.R. 139. See too Rt Hon. Lord Hope of Craighead (2013) 129 L.Q.R. 514; Rt Hon. Lord Phillips (2015) 45 H.K.L.J. 29. See too *Armes v Nottinghamshire CC* [2017] UKSC 60; *S v Attorney General* [2003] 3 N.Z.L.R. 450.

[1085] *E v English Province of Our Lady of Charity* [2012] EWCA Civ 938; [2013] Q.B. 722 (noted Tan (2013) 129 L.Q.R. 30.

assaults,[1086] nor need there be a close degree of control or supervision.[1087] It is relevant to look to the degree of integration of the occupation of the tortfeasor with the defendant's business, and conversely liability will not generally arise "where the tortfeasor has a recognisably independent business of his own or of a third party."[1088] It is not yet clear whether it is sufficient that the business be independent in structure or whether it needs also to be economically independent of the defendant's business.

These recent developments have not required the invocation of agency law,[1089] and it is suggested that it would be unsafe to assume that they represent the start of a general broadening of the scope of vicarious liability based on powers of appointment. *Kuwait Asia Bank EC v National Mutual Life Nominees Ltd*,[1090] for instance, remains authority for the proposition that a shareholder of a company is not vicariously liable for the wrongs of its appointees as directors of a company, even when those appointees are its employees, so long as there is no attempt to direct them in that capacity. In that context, the employees exercise their powers qua directors independently of their employer.

Transferred employment[1091]   A servant may be in the general employment of A,   **8-179** but, as the result of arrangements made between A and B, he may be acting as the servant of B, so as to make B, and not A, responsible for his tort at the relevant time.[1092] The test is whether the servant is transferred, or only the use and benefit of his work,[1093] and this depends upon the extent to which A places the servant under the control and at the disposition of B.[1094] The question of control will be determined by deciding where the authority lies to direct, or to delegate to, the servant the manner in which the work is to be done.[1095] Where a servant is lent with a machine, such as a crane, "it is easier to infer that the general employer continues to control the method of performance", since the driver remains responsible to him for the safe keeping of the machine.[1096] The agreement between the principals does not determine the question, although it may help to determine such relevant matters as, e.g. who pays the servant or can dismiss him, how long the alternative service is

---

[1086] *Cox v Ministry of Justice* [2016] UKSC 10; [2016] A.C. 660 at [29] (Crown liable for personal injury caused by the negligence of prisoners while working in prison); noted Morgan [2016] C.L.J. 202.

[1087] *Cox v Ministry of Justice* [2016] UKSC 10; [2016] A.C. 660 at [21].

[1088] *Cox v Ministry of Justice* [2016] UKSC 10; [2016] A.C. 660 at [26] and [29]. See also *Various Claimants v Barclays Bank Plc* [2017] EWHC 1929 (QB).

[1089] But cf. *Heaton's Transport (St Helens) v Transport and General Workers Union* [1973] A.C. 15; and *S v Attorney General* [2003] 3 N.Z.L.R. 450 (CA) (abuse of foster children by foster parents under state control; arguably better analysed as an example of non-delegable duty).

[1090] [1991] 1 A.C. 187 (PC).

[1091] See Clerk and Lindsell, *Torts* (21st edn), paras 6-03 and 6-23.

[1092] *Century Insurance Co Ltd v Northern Ireland Road Transport Board* [1942] A.C. 509 at 513.

[1093] *Century Insurance v Northern Ireland RTB*, above, pp.509, 513 and 516.

[1094] *Cameron v Nystrom* [1893] A.C. 308 at 312; *Century Insurance Co Ltd v Northern Ireland Road Transport Board*, above at 517. See also *Chua Chye Leong Alan v Grand Palace De-luxe Nite Club Pte Ltd* [1993] 3 Singapore L.R. 449 ("parking jockey" supplied by independent contractor to night club for valet parking held "servant or agent" of night club).

[1095] *Mersey Docks and Harbour Board v Coggins & Griffith* [1947] A.C. 1 at 12.

[1096] *Mersey Docks and Harbour Board v Coggins & Griffith*, above, at 17; *Ready Mixed Concrete (East Midlands) Ltd v Yorkshire Traffic Area Licensing Authority* [1970] 2 Q.B. 397 at 404. See also *Garrard v A.E. Southey & Co* [1952] 2 Q.B. 174; *Denham v Midland Employers Mutual Ass. Ltd* [1955] 2 Q.B. 437; *Bhoomidas v Port of Singapore Authority* [1978] 1 All E.R. 956 (PC); *Royal Bank of Scotland v Bannerman Johnstone Maclay* 2005 S.C. 437 (financial controller).

to last, and (where relevant) what machinery is to be employed.[1097] Each case must depend on its own circumstances.[1098] Prima facie, responsibility for the negligence of the servant rests upon the master who engaged him and generally employs him, and the burden upon the general employer to shift that responsibility to the hirer is a heavy one.[1099] But the Supreme Court has now confirmed that two different levels of employer may each be liable for a person transferred to their control.[1100]

8-180 **Torts involving misstatements** Torts of misrepresentation involve reliance by the plaintiff. This suggests that the principal should not be liable for the misstatements of his agent who is also a servant unless the third party was justified in relying on them, viz. unless they were made within the agent's actual or apparent authority, which of course they may be.[1101] This approach, consistent with that employed in *Lloyd v Grace, Smith & Co*,[1102] was adopted by the House of Lords in *Armagas Ltd v Mundogas SA* as regards the tort of deceit.[1103] On this approach it will not matter whether or not the agent is a servant; liability arises if, but only if, the relevant misstatement was made within the agent's actual or apparent authority.

However, the Court of Appeal in *So v HSBC Bank Plc*[1104] held that the reasoning in *Armagas* on the issue of vicarious liability is confined to deceit, and that the standard "course of employment" test applies to an action in negligent misstatement. It is difficult to see on what basis an employer should be more readily liable for an employee's negligent statements than for his deceits, and cases prior to *So v HSBC* provide no support for such a conclusion. Hence, in *Kooragang Investments Pty Ltd v Richardson & Wrench Ltd*,[1105] not cited in *So v HSBC*, the Privy Council declined to make an employer liable for an employee's negligent valuations of land expressly on the basis that the employee had no actual or apparent authority to furnish them to the particular claimant, even though it was part of the employee's general functions to provide valuations. In *Williams v Natural Life*

[1097] *Mersey Docks and Harbour Board v Coggins & Griffith*, above.

[1098] *Ready Mixed Concrete (East Midlands) Ltd v Yorkshire Traffic Area Licensing Authority*, above, at 406.

[1099] *Mersey Docks and Harbour Board v Coggins&Griffith*, above, at 10; *Ready Mixed Concrete (East Midlands) Ltd v Yorkshire Traffic Area Licensing Authority*, above, at 404; *Biffa Waste Services Ltd v Maschinenfabrik Ernst Hese GmbH* [2008] EWCA Civ 1257; [2009] Q.B. 725.

[1100] *Various Claimants v The Catholic Child Welfare Society* [2012] UKSC 56; [2013] 2 A.C. 1; approving *Viasystems (Tyneside) Ltd v Thermal Transfer (Northern) Ltd* [2005] EWCA Civ 1151; [2005] 4 All E.R. 181 (sub-contractor and sub-sub-contractor liable for negligence of employee of subsubcontractor). cf. *Day v The Ocean Beach Hotel Shellharbour Pty Ltd* [2013] NSWCA 250; (2013) 85 N.S.W.L.R. 335.

[1101] e.g. Illustration 20. cf. *Bank of Montreal v Young* (1966) 60 D.L.R. (2d) 220 (bank manager not authorised to advise on investments).

[1102] *Lloyd v Grace, Smith & Co* [1912] A.C. 716 at 725, 736 and 742.

[1103] *Armagas Ltd v Mundogas SA (The Ocean Frost)* [1986] A.C. 717, Illustration 26. See also *Kleinwort, Sons & Co v Associated Automatic Machine Corp Ltd* (1934) 151 L.T. 1 (authority needed before liability for deceit, but company secretary not an employee); *Quinn v CC Automotive Group Ltd* [2010] EWCA Civ 1412; [2011] 2 All E.R. (Comm) 584; *Pioneer Mortgage Services Pty Ltd v Columbus Capital Pty Ltd* [2016] FCAFC 78 at [66].

[1104] [2009] EWCA Civ 296; [2009] 1 C.L.C. 503. See Watts (2012) 128 L.Q.R. 260 for critique of this case and for more detailed analysis of the relevant principles and authorities; Watts [2015] L.M.C.L.Q. 36. See too Tan Cheng Han [2012] S.J.L.S. 92. cf. *Skandinaviska Enskilda Banken AB v Asia Pacific Breweries (Singapore) Pte Ltd* [2011] SGCA 22 (noted Chan and Tjio (2012) 128 L.Q.R. 27), where, however, the Singapore court's recognition of a plea of contributory negligence makes the case hard to square with English law.

[1105] [1982] A.C. 462.

Health Foods Ltd,[1106] a case also not referred to in *So v HSBC*, the House of Lords held that an employee is himself not liable for his negligent statements made in the course of employment without an assumption of responsibility for their accuracy, and the court went on to conclude that the employer can be liable only on the same basis.[1107] These holdings reinforce the view that, if an employer is to be liable for an employee's statements, some form of authorisation of the relevant statement, including by way of holding out, is needed. Such reasoning is as applicable to principals and agents who are not in an employment relationship as to those who are. Under this approach, the liability of the employer is direct, not vicarious.[1108] Dicta in the House of Lords in *Dubai Aluminium Co Ltd v Salaam*[1109] also support the view that the rules governing employer liability are not uniform for all torts, and in particular that torts founded on reliance on an agent's statements require that those statements be made with actual or apparent authority before a principal, including an employer, can be liable for them. Liability for other wrongs committed in connection with authorised activities where the claimant has less control over events (e.g. assault, negligent driving) remains; in this respect the course of employment test is wider than "authority" reasoning.[1110]

Rule (2)(a): Authorising and procuring wrongs The principal's liability where the tort is specifically authorised or ratified is obvious: he has effectively committed the tort himself, and the liability is not truly vicarious.[1111] **8-181**

Rule (2)(b): Liability for statements based only on agency reasoning The second category causes more difficulty. The formula suggested here is put forward tentatively. As has been seen above, where an agent commits a tort involving misstatements, the terminology of authority is appropriate: he renders his principal liable when he makes the misstatement within the scope of his authority and the statement is acted on. In the case of a servant it has been argued above that this authority terminology controls the normal tort "course of employment" test, which cannot be used to invoke a wider vicarious liability.[1112] But it is almost the corollary of that reasoning that "authority" may also be used to *create* liability in one person for another who is not his servant, and for whom there is no liability under the normal principles of non-delegable duty[1113] relating to independent contractors. The reasoning is somewhat limited. It should apply to an agent: **8-182**

[1106] [1998] 1 W.L.R. 830. See too *Standard Chartered Bank v Pakistan National Shipping Corp (No.2)* [2002] UKHL 43; [2003] 1 A.C. 959 at [21]. cf. *Customs and Excise Commissioners v Barclays Bank Plc* [2006] UKHL 28; [2007] 1 A.C. 181.

[1107] [1998] 1 W.L.R. 830 at 838. See also *Foster v Action Aviation Ltd* [2014] EWCA Civ 1368 (company that legally owned aeroplane being sold was sole party liable for negligent misrepresentation by chairman and beneficial owner of company). cf. *Playboy Club London Ltd v Banca Nazionale del Lavoro SpA* [2016] EWCA Civ 457; [2016] 1 W.L.R. 3169 at [23]; *CGL Group Ltd v The Royal Bank of Scotland Plc* [2017] EWCA Civ 1073 at [82].

[1108] See Roberts [2013] N.Z. Law Rev. 625, arguing that even for deceit a principal's liability, being based on authorisation, should be direct not vicarious.

[1109] [2002] UKHL 48; [2003] 2 A.C. 366 at [29]–[30] and [127].

[1110] See *Navarro v Moregrand Ltd* [1951] 2 T.L.R. 674 at 680, Illustration 21, per Denning LJ. But cf. *Heaton Transport Ltd (St Helen) v T&GWU* [1973] A.C. 15 at 99. See also Illustrations 3, 4, 11 and 12. As to defamation, see *Riddick v Thames Board Mills Ltd* [1977] Q.B. 881.

[1111] Illustrations 15 and 16. See further below, para.9-120.

[1112] *Armagas Ltd v Mundogas SA (The Ocean Frost)* [1986] A.C. 717; see above, para.8-180. See also *Brockway v Pando* (2000) 22 W.A.R. 405.

[1113] See Clerk and Lindsell, *Torts* (21st edn), para.6-60 onwards; *Gladman Commercial Properties v* "when the function entrusted is that of representing the person who requests his performance in a transaction with others, so that the very service to be performed consists in standing in his place and assuming to act in his right and not in an independent capacity."[1114]

Thus it has been held that an estate agent, who is not a servant, may have authority to make representations about property for which he is seeking a buyer or tenant, so that his principal is liable for their falsity.[1115] So also the vendor of land may be liable for false statements wilfully or negligently made by his solicitor in answer to inquiries.[1116] Cases involving negligent representations seem relatively straightforward, at least where there has been a holding out of authority by the principal to make them. The tortious liability, based on an assumption of responsibility, closely parallels contractual liability. The liability is also direct, and frequently the agent who made the statements will not be personally liable unless he too can be taken as undertaking an assumption of responsibility.[1117] So much is apparent from *Williams v Natural Life Health Foods*,[1118] discussed above. But such reasoning may perhaps be extendable further. In *Colonial Mutual Life Assurance Society Ltd v Producers' and Citizens' Cooperative Co of Australia Ltd*,[1119] from which the above quotation is taken, the High Court of Australia held an insurance company liable for defamation of another company committed by its agent (not a servant) in the course of soliciting business. The victim of the defamation will not usually have relied on the agent as having had authority to make the defamatory statement, and there will not normally be an assumption of responsibility by the agent, or the principal, for its accuracy. An English case in which similar suggestions appear is *Uxbridge Permanent Benefit Building Society v Pickard*,[1120] where a solicitor was held liable for the fraud (involving forgery) of his managing clerk, though this could be explained on the basis of the established rules as to master and servant. There are also cases where the agent was not a servant, and the possibility

---

Fisher Hargreaves Proctor [2013] EWHC 25 (Ch) at [125]; affd [2013] EWCA Civ 1466.

[1114] *Colonial Mutual Life Assurance Society Ltd v Producers and Citizens Cooperative Co of Australia Ltd* (1931) 46 C.L.R. 41, per Dixon J. See also *The Litsion Pride* [1985] 1 Lloyd's Rep. 437 at 513–514; *NZ Guardian Trust Ltd v Brooks* [1995] 1 W.L.R. 4 (PC).

[1115] See Illustrations 19–22.

[1116] *Cemp Properties (UK) Ltd v Dentsply Research and Development Corp* [1989] 2 E.G.L.R. 196, Illustration 22 (Misrepresentation Act 1967 s.2(1)); *Gran Gelato Ltd v Richcliff Group Ltd* [1992] Ch. 560 (Misrepresentation Act 1967 s.2(1)); criticised Cane (1992) 108 L.Q.R. 539; and see *Derham v Amev Life Insurance Co Ltd* (1981) 56 F.L.R. 34 (fraud of insurance agent).

[1117] See *Gran Gelato*, above. cf. *McCullagh v Lane Fox & Partners Ltd* [1996] 1 E.G.L.R. 35 at 41–44; *Punjab National Bank Ltd v de Boinville* [1992] 1 W.L.R. 1138, where employees of insurance brokers were held to owe a duty of care to an assignee of the policy brokered; and cf. *NRAM Plc v Steel* [2016] CSIH 11; [2016] P.N.L.R. 20 (solicitor acting without authority). In *Dean v Allin & Watts* [2001] EWCA Civ 758; [2001] 2 Lloyd's Rep. 249 the *Gran Gelato* case was accepted as laying down a general rule for solicitors, though the solicitor was in fact held liable to the third party. For further discussion, see below, para.9-117.

[1118] [1998] 1 W.L.R. 830. See too *Challinor v Juliet Bellis & Co* [2013] EWHC 347 (Ch) at [732]; reversed on other points, sub nom. *Bellis v Challinor* [2015] EWCA Civ 59.

[1119] (1931) 46 C.L.R. 41, Illustration 23. See also cases there cited and *Thiessen v Clarica Law Reinsurance Co* (2002) 219 D.L.R. (4th) 98 (insurance agent steals money given to him for investment); *Cornwall v Rowan* (2004) 90 S.A.S.R. 269 (consultant responsible for report issued by others not liable for defamation). The principle has been held not to apply to make the client of a solicitor conducting litigation liable for contempt of court by the solicitor: *Forestview Nominees Pty Ltd v Perron Investments Pty Ltd* (1999) 93 F.C.R. 117 (Aus.)—see valuable discussion at pp.134–140, per R.D. Nicholson J.

[1120] [1939] 2 K.B. 248, Illustration 12.

of his nevertheless having acted within his authority so as to render his principal liable was discussed, but negatived on the facts.[1121]

Notwithstanding the questions that attend the *Colonial Mutual* case, it has been suggested that a person should be liable in respect of all tortious statements, whether in deceit, negligence, defamation or injurious falsehood, made by his agent (not being a servant) in the course of representing him, provided that the statement made was within a category which the agent had actual or apparent authority to make.[1122] This formulation would still exclude loss caused by acts to which such "authority" reasoning cannot be related. Thus it has been held in South Africa that an insurance company was not liable for the negligent driving of its agent who was taking a doctor to examine a prospective client.[1123]

Rule (2)(c): Wider use of the concept of an assumption of responsibility The **8-183** concept of an assumption of responsibility, which, as seen, has had a prominent role in the development of tortious liability for negligent misstatement, has gradually been invoked in a wider range of circumstances, particularly where services have been performed negligently. However pragmatic the development has been as a method of avoiding perceived shortcomings in the law of contract,[1124] especially when there is concurrent contractual liability, its role seems established.[1125] Difficult questions remain as to whether the assumption of legal responsibility is a necessary, as opposed to a sufficient,[1126] element in tortious liability for causing loss that is exclusively economic, and, if so, whether the assumption needs to be a genuine one.[1127] In many cases where a genuine assumption exists, it will be appropriate to regard as agents those employees and independent contractors who are engaged by the principal to perform the relevant tasks. It is not so obvious that all persons whose tasks are merely part of the process by which the principal intends to perform his undertaking, for example a contractor engaged to make technical drawings or to make a valuation, would be regarded as an agent, in the strict sense. The mere performance of work by such persons may not, for instance, itself change their principals' legal position, since at the time it was performed it may not be certain that the product of their work will ever be delivered to the third party. There

---

[1121] *Bradford Third Equitable BS v Borders* [1941] 2 All E.R. 205; *Kwei Tek Chao v British Traders and Shippers Ltd* [1954] 2 Q.B. 459; *Strover v Harrington* [1988] Ch. 390, Illustration 8 to Article 94 (Misrepresentation Act 1967 s.2(1)).

[1122] See Atiyah, *Vicarious Liability in the Law of Torts* (1967), Chs 9 and 10. See also *Sweeney v Boylan Nominees Pty Ltd* [2006] HCA 19; (2006) 226 C.L.R. 161 at [24].

[1123] *Colonial Mutual Life Assurance Society Ltd v Macdonald* [1931] A.D. 412, Illustration 24. See also *Eggington v Reader* [1936] 1 All E.R. 7, Illustration 6; and *Sweeney v Boylan Nominees Pty Ltd* (2006) 226 C.L.R. 161 (defendant owner of commercial refrigerator not vicariously liable for negligent repair by repairman who was an independent contractor). But cf. *Dobson v Holderness* [1975] 2 N.Z.L.R. 749; *Nelson v Raphael* [1979] R.T.R. 437, cases, however, which move into the area of "casual delegation": see below, para.8-187.

[1124] See *Cramaso LLP v Ogilvie-Grant, Earl of Seafield* [2014] UKSC 9; [2014] A.C. 1093. cf. *Robinson v PE Jones (Contractors) Ltd* [2011] EWCA Civ 9; [2011] 3 W.L.R. 815; [2012] Q.B. 44.

[1125] See *Hedley Byrne & Co Ltd v Heller & Partners Ltd* [1964] A.C. 465; *Kooragang Investments Pty Ltd v Richardson & Wrench Ltd* [1982] A.C. 462; *Henderson v Merrett Syndicates Ltd* [1995] 2 A.C. 145; *Dunlop Haywards Ltd v Erinaceous Insurance Services Ltd* [2008] EWHC 520 (Comm); [2008] Lloyd's Rep. I.R. 676 at [66], reversed on other points [2009] EWCA Civ 354. See further above, para.6-016.

[1126] *Caparo Industries Plc v Dickman* [1990] 2 A.C. 605 at 628 and 637; *Customs and Excise Commissioners v Barclays Bank Plc* [2006] UKHL 28; [2007] 1 A.C. 181; *CGL Group Ltd v The Royal Bank of Scotland Plc* [2017] EWCA Civ 1073 at [82].

[1127] See, e.g. *Chandler v Cape Plc* [2012] EWCA Civ 525; [2012] 1 W.L.R. 3111 at [64].

may also not be much room of the application of fiduciary obligations in some of these cases. It can be expected, nonetheless, that the label agent will often be applied to such persons, particularly those who are not employees.

8-184 **Non-delegable duties**[1128] The concept of assumption of responsibility to take due care is potentially capable of resulting in direct liability on the owners of businesses in a wide range of circumstances. Such liability can run in parallel with express or implied contractual duties of care. Having connections to assumption of responsibility, but not exclusively explained by that rationale, is a body of law that turns on a person being liable as principal for what is called a "non-delegable duty of care". The performance of that duty may be delegated to others who need not be employees, but the principal remains responsible for injury or damage caused by the actions of the delegate. The leading case is now the decision of the Supreme Court in *Woodland v Essex County Council*.[1129] In this case Lord Sumption referred to the long recognition of a non-delegable duty of care in "a large, varied and anomalous class of case" concerned with physical harm resulting from the operation of hazardous activities, especially in public places. A second line of cases has developed within the law of nuisance to impose liability on a building owner for the negligent actions of his independent contractors in damaging the claimant's property, whether or not the activities were inherently dangerous. *Woodland* confirms that there is another category of case—that where there is an antecedent relationship between claimant and defendant, but where, for one reason or another, a contractual route to finding a duty of care does not exist.[1130] The relevant services (in *Woodland*, school swimming lessons) may, for example, be provided by the state or a local authority without a contract with the claimant. This category of case is based on an assumption of responsibility for the exercise of due care in relation to the relevant activity.[1131] The claimant will usually have been in the custody, charge or care of the defendant, and will have had little control over the way in which the care was discharged. As with other cases based on a voluntary assumption of responsibility, it is probably not necessary to regard the independent contractor as the agent of the defendant, although some of the cases concerned with the duties of an employer to his own workforce have used the language of agency.[1132] In *Woodland*, Lord Sumption cautioned about finding an assumption of a non-delegable duty too readily, lest it swallow the general rule that one is not liable for the tortious actions of others.[1133]

8-185 **Deceit: division of ingredients**[1134] The tort of deceit, where because of its connection with contract situations agency terminology is frequently used, raises

---

[1128] See Stevens, in *Emerging Issues in Tort Law* (Neyers, Chamberlain and Pitel, eds, 2007), Ch.13; Beuermann (2013) 20 Torts L.J. 265; Foster in *Divergences in Private Law* (Robertson and Tilbury, eds, 2016), Ch.7; Todd (2016) 23 Torts LJ 105.
[1129] [2013] UKSC 66; [2014] A.C. 537; noted Morgan [2015] C.L.J. 109. See also *Riverstone Meat Co Pty Ltd v Lancashire Shipping Co Ltd (The Muncaster Castle)* [1961] A.C. 807; *Biffa Waste Services Ltd v Maschinenfabrik Ernst Hese GmbH* [2008] EWCA Civ 1257; [2009] Q.B. 725; *Central Darling Shire Council v Greeney* [2015] NSWCA 51.
[1130] For a comparable situation where a contractual action was available, see *Wong Mee Wan v Kwan Kin Travel Services* [1996] 1 W.L.R. 38 (package tour operator liable for negligence of sub-contractors).
[1131] *Woodland v Swimming Teachers Association* [2013] UKSC 66; [2014] A.C. 537 at [7].
[1132] *Wilsons & Clyde Coal Co Ltd v English* [1938] A.C. 57 at 75.
[1133] *Woodland v Swimming Teachers Association* [2013] UKSC 66; [2014] 1 A.C. 537 at [22].
[1134] Powell, pp.200–207; Salmond and Heuston, *Torts* (21st edn), pp.376–377; Devlin (1937) 53 L.Q.R.

special problems where agents are involved, in so far as it requires a false statement made, with the intention that it should be acted on, "knowingly, or without
belief in its truth, or recklessly, careless whether it be true or false".[1135] Is the
principal to be liable to a third party where (for instance) the agent made a
representation innocently, believing it to be true, and the principal knew of the
untruth of the statement but did not know that it was being made? In such case no
individual is guilty of personal fraud: there is an "innocent division of
ingredients".[1136] But are the acts and minds of principal and agent to be regarded
as so far one that, by taking the agent's statement and the principal's knowledge
together, the principal can be held liable to the third party in deceit? There was some
authority that they were[1137]: but the law was later clarified by the decision of the
Court of Appeal in *Armstrong v Strain*[1138] and is best stated in a series of
propositions.

(a)   The principal is liable if he authorised the agent to make the false
      representation which he (the principal) knew to be untrue (or did not believe
      to be true), whether or not the agent knew the truth.[1139]
(b)   The principal is liable if, while not expressly authorising the agent to make
      the false representation, he knew it to be untrue and was guilty of some posi-
      tive wrongful conduct, as by consciously permitting the agent to remain
      ignorant of the true facts, so as to prevent the disclosure of the truth to the
      third party, if the third party should ask the agent for information, or in the
      hope that the agent would make some false representation.[1140] The agent's
      representation when made would of course require to be within the scope
      of his actual or apparent authority.[1141]
(c)   The principal is liable if the agent made the false representation fraudulently,
      it being within the scope of his actual or apparent authority and within the
      course of his employment, to make such a representation,[1142] sometimes
      even where the representation reached the third party by way of another in-

---

344; Wright (1937) 15 Can.B.R. 716; Gower (1952) 15 M.L.R. 232; Unger (1952) 15 M.L.R. 508;
Müller-Freienfels in *Civil Law in the Modern World* (Yiannapoulos ed., 1965), pp.77 and 120–124.
See also Article 21, Illustration 2; Dugdale (2006) 12 N.Z. Business L.Q. 3.
[1135] *Derry v Peek* (1889) 14 App.Cas. 337 at 374, per Lord Herschell.
[1136] The language of Devlin J in (1937) 53 L.Q.R. 344 and in *Armstrong v Strain* [1951] 1 T.L.R. 856
(at first instance).
[1137] See the confusing discussion in *Woyka & Co v London & Northern Trading Co* (1922) 10 Ll. L. Rep.
110.
[1138] [1952] 1 K.B. 232; affirming [1951] 1 T.L.R. 856, Illustration 20 (not considering the *Woyka* case,
above).
[1139] If the agent knew the truth, they are jointly and severally liable; if not, the principal is alone liable
for his own tort committed through the agent as an innocent instrument.
[1140] *Ludgater v Love* (1881) 44 L.T. 694; *Cornfoot v Fowke* (1840) 6 M. & W. 358 at 370, 372 and 373–
374; *Gordon Hill Trust Ltd v Segall* [1941] 2 All E.R. 379 at 390; *Awaroa Holdings Ltd v Commercial Securities & Finance Ltd* [1976] 1 N.Z.L.R. 19; *The Siboen and The Sibotre* [1976] 1 Lloyd's
Rep. 293 at 320–321. Presumably this would be equally so if the wrongful conduct was of another
agent of the principal acting in the course of his employment, the principal being innocent: *UBS AG
(London Branch) v Kommunale Wasserwerke Leipzig GmbH* [2014] EWHC 3615 (Comm) at [757]
(affd [2017] EWCA Civ 1567).
[1141] See *MCI WorldCom International Inc v Primus Telecommunications Inc* [2003] EWHC 2182; [2004]
1 All E.R. (Comm) 138 at [58], [59]; reversed on other grounds [2004] EWCA Civ 957; [2004] 2
All E.R. (Comm) 833.
[1142] *Barwick v English Joint Stock Bank* (1867) L.R. 2 Ex. 259; *Briess v Woolley* [1954] A.C. 333, Illustration 19; *Egger v Viscount Chelmsford* [1965] 1 Q.B. 248 at 261; *Mackay v Commercial Bank
of New Brunswick* (1874) L.R. 5 P.C. 394. See also *Hern v Nichols* (1701) 1 Salk. 289; *Udell v*

nocent agent,[1143] or by way of the innocent principal himself,[1144] because in such a case the innocent second agent or principal may be no more than a conduit pipe for the fraud of the guilty agent.[1145]

(d) The principal is not liable if the agent made the false representation innocently, the principal knowing the true facts but not having authorised the agent to make the representation, nor knowing that it would be made, nor being guilty of fraudulent conduct as in (b) above.[1146]

(e) Conversely, the principal is not liable if he himself made the false representation innocently, notwithstanding that an agent knew the true facts.[1147]

The question whether the principal can exclude liability for his agent's fraud has only recently been articulately addressed. It is normally assumed that he cannot exclude liability for his own fraud; and that he can provide that the agent has no authority to speak for him.[1148] It appears that liability for an agent's fraud in the making of the contract can probably be excluded, but the wording would need to be very clear.[1149] Such a clause would however be subject to the unfair contract terms legislation in so far as that applied in the context.[1150]

8-186   **Negligence**   The problems centred around *Armstrong v Strain* arose from attempts to invoke the tort of deceit in respect of actions that were in substance in respect of negligent misrepresentation—largely in respect of misrepresentations made by the agents of companies. Since 1964[1151] it has been established that an action in negligence may in principle lie in such cases (at least where the agents had apparent authority to be making the statements), and the rules stated above are therefore of less importance. It is possible in appropriate cases to sue the principal

---

Atherton (1861) 7 H. & N. 172, per Pollock CB and Wilde B. Unless perhaps the fraud of the agent is primarily practised on the principal himself: *Kwei Tek Chao v British Traders & Shippers Ltd* [1954] 2 Q.B. 459. See also *Credit Lyonnais Bank Nederland NV v ECGD* [2000] 1 A.C. 486 (no liability for employee not himself committing deceit but assisting external tortfeasor to do so; liability in conspiracy not relied upon).

[1143] *London County Freehold & Leasehold Properties Ltd v Berkeley Property & Investment Co Ltd* [1936] 2 All E.R. 1039; as explained in *Anglo-Scottish Beet Sugar Corp Ltd v Spalding UDC* [1937] 2 K.B. 607; approved by the Court of Appeal in *Armstrong v Strain* [1952] 1 K.B. 232. See also *UBS AG (London Branch) v Kommunale Wasserwerke Leipzig GmbH* [2014] EWHC 3615 (Comm) at [757] (affd [2017] EWCA Civ 1567).

[1144] *S. Pearson & Son Ltd v Dublin Corp* [1907] A.C. 351; as explained in *Anglo-Scottish Beet Sugar Corp Ltd v Spalding UDC*, above.

[1145] *S. Pearson & Son Ltd v Dublin Corp*, above, at 367.

[1146] *Armstrong v Strain*, above; *Cornfoot v Fowke* (1840) 6 M. & W. 358; *Gordon Hill Trust v Segall* [1941] 2 All E.R. 379.

[1147] See *Anglo-Scottish Beet Sugar Corp Ltd v Spalding UDC*, above. "You cannot add an innocent state of mind to an innocent state of mind and get as a result a dishonest state of mind": per Devlin J in *Armstrong v Strain* [1951] 1 T.L.R. 856 at 872. The same reasoning would apply where the relevant knowledge was possessed by another agent.

[1148] cf. *Overbrooke Estates Ltd v Glencombe Properties Ltd* [1974] 1 W.L.R. 1335.

[1149] *HIH Casualty and General Insurance Ltd v Chase Manhattan Bank* [2003] UKHL 6; [2003] 1 All E.R. (Comm) 349; but see Lord Hobhouse of Woodborough at [98]. Previous authority (*S. Pearson & Son Ltd v Dublin Corp* [1907] A.C. 351; *Mair v Rio Grande Rubber Estates Ltd* 1913 S.C.(H.L.) 74; and *Boyd and Forrest v Glasgow & SW Ry Co* 1915 S.C.(H.L.) 20 was regarded as inconclusive. See also *Satyam Computer Services Ltd v Upaid Systems Ltd* [2008] EWCA Civ 487; [2008] 2 All E.R. (Comm) 465 at [82].

[1150] See Chitty, *Contracts* (32nd edn), Chs 15 and 38.

[1151] *Hedley Byrne & Co Ltd v Heller & Partners Ltd* [1964] A.C. 465.

where the statement was negligently made by an agent[1152]; or where, though no one person can be said to have been negligent, the totality of the operations of the principal in the particular respect can be regarded as negligent.[1153] The same is true of actions under s.2 of the Misrepresentation Act 1967.[1154] Exclusion clauses raise the same considerations as elsewhere in the law.[1155]

Casual delegation   A distinct line of tort cases holds the owner or bailee of a mo-   **8-187** tor car or other conveyance, and sometimes some other type of chattel, liable for the negligence of one whom he permits to use it. The cases mostly concern cars, and from the policy point of view there is obviously some relevance in the owner's or bailee's insurance. The cases have been the subject of numerous explanations, each of which imposes its own limits on the doctrine: one of them has been that the driver or user is in some sense an agent of the owner or bailee in that he is carrying out that person's purposes: though in the leading English case[1156] Lord Wilberforce said that in the present context agency "is merely a concept, the meaning and purpose of which is to say 'is vicariously liable'".[1157] In an Australian leading case Dixon J said that "it is easier to see the direction in which the branch grows than to understand the support it derives from the main trunk of traditional doctrine governing vicarious responsibility".[1158] The doctrine and its history have recently been exhaustively reconsidered by the High Court of Australia in a case involving a private aeroplane, the owner of which was held not liable.[1159] What seems to emerge clearly from the decision is that the cases do not link to agency, at least in the central sense of that word.[1160] Further details should therefore be sought in works on tort.[1161]

Contributory negligence   The attribution to a principal of acts, omissions and   **8-188** knowledge that might be relevant to a defence of contributory negligence remains a subject of considerable uncertainty. It is widely assumed that attribution ought to occur in the same way as for liability.[1162] It is not yet clear that this is the correct approach. For many torts, a principal is vicariously liable only for the acts and omis-

---

[1152] Thus in *Mutual Life and Citizen's Assurance Co v Evatt* [1971] A.C. 793 it was alleged that the defendant company gave advice "by itself, its servants and agents". See also *Ministry of Housing and Local Government v Sharp* [1970] 2 Q.B. 223; *Esso Petroleum Co Ltd v Mardon* [1976] Q.B. 801; *Box v Midland Bank Ltd* [1979] 2 Lloyd's Rep. 391.

[1153] See *W.B. Anderson & Sons v Rhodes (Liverpool) Ltd* [1967] 2 All E.R. 850; *McInerny v Lloyd's Bank Ltd* [1974] 1 Lloyd's Rep. 246. See also Article 21, Illustration 2.

[1154] *Howard Marine and Dredging Co Ltd v A. Ogden & Sons (Excavations) Ltd* [1978] Q.B. 574. But the state of mind of the "reasonable belief" defence must be that of the principal: see *MCI WorldCom International Inc v Primus Telecommunications Inc* [2003] EWHC 2182; [2004] 1 All E.R. (Comm) 138 at [58], [59]; reversed on other grounds [2004] EWCA Civ 957; [2004] 2 All E.R. (Comm) 833. See also *Gosling v Anderson* (1972) 223 E.G. 1743 at 1745, per Lord Denning MR Although this section uses the analogy of fraud in imposing liability, it seems that the fraud rules as to division of ingredients will not be applied: cf. Atiyah and Treitel (1967) 30 M.L.R. 369 at 374.

[1155] See Chitty, *Contracts* (32nd edn), Chs 15 and 38.

[1156] *Launchbury v Morgans* [1973] A.C. 127.

[1157] At 135.

[1158] *Soblusky v Egan* (1960) 103 C.L.R. 215 at 229.

[1159] *Scott v Davis* (2000) 204 C.L.R. 333.

[1160] See especially para.227 onwards (Gummow J) and 299 onwards (Hayne J). See too *Lloyd v Borg* [2013] NSWCA 245; (2013) 84 N.S.W.L.R. 652 (control held necessary).

[1161] See Clerk and Lindsell, *Torts* (21st edn), paras 6-78–6-80.

[1162] See a valuable article by Bartlett (1998) 114 L.Q.R. 460. See also *Daniels v Anderson* (1995) 37 N.S.W.L.R. 438 at 569–570.

sions of employees, and not liable for the acts and omissions of independent contractors even if they are agents.[1163] On the other hand, to the extent that a principal is expected to take due care of its own interests, it could be argued that if it uses an independent contractor to do that, it carries the risk of that party's failures. Some of the cases concern claims in negligent misstatement and for pure economic loss, where there is, in any event, more room for the operation of agency models.[1164] Otherwise, there are some cases that have in relation to companies used *alter ego* reasoning for the attribution of contributory negligence[1165]; or whether in relation to companies or not, have used the supposed fraud exception to the rules as to imputation of the agent's knowledge to the principal, whereby such an imputation is not made where the agent is acting in fraud of his principal.[1166] The resolution of the difficulties in this area is unlikely to be assisted by creating special rules for companies. As for the fraud exception, this is difficult to reconcile with the principle that makes the principal liable for the agent's fraud.[1167] The problems in this area are of fairly recent development and await clarification.

8-189 **Corporations** Corporate principals can be liable in tort like individuals, though the torts must necessarily be committed through servants or agents. Arguments based on the notion of ultra vires have long been rejected or evaded in the tort context,[1168] and are now removed by legislation which has primary applicability in contract but is also relevant to torts.[1169] Thus corporations can be sued for conversion,[1170] wrongful distress,[1171] false imprisonment,[1172] trespass to land or goods[1173] and, as regards cases where a specific mental element may be involved, defamation,[1174] malicious prosecution,[1175] fraud[1176] and conspiracy.[1177] In general, corporations are liable for the torts of their servants, independent contractors and agents in accordance with the principles already discussed above. The difficulties caused

---

[1163] See above, para.8-178.

[1164] See, e.g. *O'Hagan v Body Corp 189855* [2010] 3 N.Z.L.R. 445 at [141] (claimants suing local authority found contributorily negligent on basis of their solicitor's failure to undertake proper search of property records); *Zurich Australian Insurance Ltd v Withers* [2016] NZCA 618; [2017] 2 N.Z.L.R. 745 at [58] (contributory negligence of non-employee agent under statutory liability for "misleading conduct in trade").

[1165] See *British Racing Drivers' Club Ltd v Hextall Erskine & Co* [1996] 3 All E.R. 667.

[1166] This may be the explanation of *Dairy Containers Ltd v NZI Bank Ltd* [1995] 2 N.Z.L.R. 30: see criticism by Bartlett, above. See also *Edwards Karwacki Smith & Co Pty Ltd v Jacka Nominees Pty Ltd* (1994) 15 A.C.S.R. 502.

[1167] *Lloyd v Grace Smith & Co* [1912] A.C. 716. As to the fraud exception, see below, para.8-214.

[1168] e.g. *Campbell v Paddington Corp* [1911] 1 K.B. 869.

[1169] Companies Act 2006 ss.39 and 40, considered above, para.8-035 onwards.

[1170] *Yarborough v Bank of England* (1812) 16 East 6; *Giles v Taff Vale Ry* (1853) 2 E. & B. 822; *Barnett v Crystal Palace Co* (1861) 4 L.T. 403.

[1171] *Eastern Counties Ry Co v Broom* (1851) 6 Exch. 314; *Smith v Birmingham Gas Co* (1834) 3 L.J.K.B. 165.

[1172] Illustration 5.

[1173] *Maund v Monmouthshire Canal Co* (1842) 4 Man. & G. 452.

[1174] Illustration 23.

[1175] *Cornford v Carlton Bank* [1899] 1 Q.B. 392.

[1176] *Ranger v Great Western Ry Co* (1854) 5 H.L.Cas. 72; *Barwick v English Joint Stock Bank* (1867) L.R. 2 Ex. 259; *Mackay v Commercial Bank of New Brunswick* (1874) L.R. 5 P.C. 394.

[1177] See *Barclay Pharmaceuticals Ltd v Waypharm LP* [2012] EWHC 306 (Comm); [2013] 2 B.C.L.C. 551 at [229]; *Muduroglu v Reddish LLP* [2015] EWHC 1044 (Ch). But see Watts in Busch, Macgregor and Watts, eds, *Agency Law in Commercial Practice* (2016), p.109.

by the use of reasoning that the acts of certain persons may rank as the acts of the corporation itself ("*alter ego*" reasoning) have already been referred to.[1178]

The Crown   The Crown Proceedings Act 1947 provides that the Crown is subject   **8-190**
to all those liabilities in tort to which, if it were a private person of full age and capacity, it would be subject in respect of torts committed by its servants or agents: provided that no proceedings lie against the Crown by virtue of this provision in respect of any act or omission of a servant or agent of the Crown unless the act or omission would apart from the provisions of the Act give rise to a cause of action in tort against that servant or agent or his estate.[1179] The words "servant or agent" cause some difficulty. It is arguable that there is nowadays no such person as a servant of the Crown in the strict sense, but it has been said that there is a large category of persons, including civil servants, whom "the Crown (through or with the advice of a Minister) controls ... and directs their activities in a way which ... makes the term 'servant' quite appropriate".[1180] As regards agents, it is provided that "agent ... includes an independent contractor",[1181] but the inference from this is that the word covers also persons other than independent contractors. It is submitted that the effect of the use of the word is to leave it in no doubt that the Crown is to be liable in those cases in which an ordinary person would be liable for the torts of his agent. It seems that the word covers also those public bodies that act on behalf of the Crown, though there is little authority on which bodies are to be regarded as agents of the Crown for this purpose.[1182] Further discussion should be sought in specialised works.[1183]

Rule (3): Judgment against principal or agent: contribution[1184]   Where the   **8-191**
principal is liable for the torts of his agent, or the master for those of his servant, they are in principle to be regarded as joint tortfeasors.[1185] At common law judgment against one such tortfeasor released the others[1186] and there was no general right of contribution between them.[1187] The Law Reform (Married Women and Tortfeasors) Act 1935[1188] abolished the first rule; and also made provision for contribution between such tortfeasors. The Civil Liability (Contribution) Act

---

[1178] See above, paras 1-028 and 8-184.

[1179] Crown Proceedings Act 1947 s.2(1)(b) and proviso. See *New South Wales v Ibbett* (2006) 231 A.L.R. 485 (exemplary damages for unlawful acts of police officers); *Cox v Ministry of Justice* [2016] UKSC 10; [2016] A.C. 660; *Axon v Ministry of Defence* [2016] EWHC 787 (QB) at [81].

[1180] *Bank voor Handel en Scheepvaart NV v Administrator of Hungarian Property* [1954] A.C. 584 at 616, per Lord Reid, rejecting dicta of Devlin J at first instance, [1952] 1 All E.R. 314 at 319.

[1181] s.38(2).

[1182] Treitel [1957] P.L. 320 at 327 onwards. See also Griffith (1952) 9 U. Toronto L.J. 169; *Moukataff v BOAC* [1967] 1 Lloyd's Rep. 396.

[1183] e.g. Clerk and Lindsell, *Torts* (21st edn), para.5-03 onwards.

[1184] See in general a valuable article by Mitchell [1997] Restitution L.R. 27; Glanville Williams, *Joint Torts and Contributory Negligence* (1951); Salmond and Heuston, *Torts* (21st edn), p.423 onwards; Clerk and Lindsell, *Torts* (21st edn), para.5-02 onwards; *NZ Guardian Trust Ltd v Brooks* [1995] 1 W.L.R. 96 (PC).

[1185] *Jones v Manchester Corp* [1952] 2 Q.B. 852 at 869.

[1186] *Merryweather v Nixan* (1788) S.T.R. 186. As to release as a result of settlement with one of the parties, see *Gladman Commercial Properties v Fisher Hargreaves Proctor* [2013] EWCA Civ 1466; *Starlight Shipping Co v Allianz Marine and Aviation Versicherungs AG* [2014] EWHC 3068 (Comm); [2015] 2 All E.R. (Comm) 747 at [58].

[1187] *Brinsmead v Harrison* (1872) L.R. 7 C.P. 547.

[1188] s.6.

1978[1189] repealed the relevant part of the 1935 Act, extending the right to contribution to situations where one wrongdoer was not liable in tort (but rather for breach of contract or in equity)[1190] and also making improved provision for the right to contribution,[1191] dealing with two cases which previously had been controversial. These were whether a tortfeasor who had settled a claim against him was entitled to contribution: and whether contribution could be recovered from a person who had been sued to judgment and held not liable in circumstances in which he would have been liable had he been sued at some other time or in some other way.[1192] The Act binds the Crown.[1193]

The master can often, however, recover an indemnity at common law apart from statute,[1194] for a servant is under a duty to take reasonable care in the execution of his duties, and if he breaks this duty the measure of damages may be the loss he has caused his master, who has had to answer for his tort.[1195] Where an agent can be brought under this reasoning, he may similarly be liable.[1196] But if his master or principal is himself at fault, the agent or servant may not be liable under this head.[1197] However, even if the master or principal was at fault, he may be able to recover such sum as the court considers just and equitable by way of contribution under the Act: and where he is not at fault he can equally sue under the statute, instead of at common law, and may recover 100 per cent contribution.[1198] But he has no right to recover contribution where the agent is completely innocent, for here he is himself under a duty to indemnify the agent.[1199]

Illustrations

The course of the servant's employment

8-192   (1)   The driver of a tanker, whose duty included the delivery of petrol into storage tanks, while transporting petrol from the tanker to a storage tank at a garage, struck a match to light a cigarette and threw the lighted match on the floor, thereby causing a fire. Held, that his employer was liable for the damage so caused by the negligent act of the driver, which was done in the course of his employment.[1200]

(2)   An assistant storekeeper at a warehouse is inconvenienced by a lorry belong-

---

[1189] See *Law Com. No.79* (1977).

[1190] ss.2, 4 and 6. But release of one joint tortfeasor still releases the others. For application of the Act to equitable wrongs, see *Dubai Aluminium Co Ltd v Salaam* [2002] UKHL 48; [2003] 2 A.C. 366.

[1191] ss.1, 2 and 7(3).

[1192] The Act creates, however, considerable difficulties; see Clerk and Lindsell, above.

[1193] s.5.

[1194] The right to do so is preserved by s.7(3).

[1195] *Lister v Romford Ice & Cold Storage Co* [1957] A.C. 555. But the effect of this case has been circumvented in practice: see Gardiner (1959) 22 M.L.R. 652; Clerk and Lindsell, *Torts* (21st edn), para.4-36 onwards.

[1196] See Articles 40 and 42 as to the duties owed by contractual and non-contractual agents.

[1197] See *Jones v Manchester Corp* [1952] 2 Q.B. 852 at 865. But cf. Atiyah, *Vicarious Liability in the Law of Torts* (1967), pp.428–430. See also *Adamson v Jarvis* (1827) 4 Bing. 66, Illustration 9 to Article 63 for the converse case where an agent recovers indemnity because innocent.

[1198] *Ryan v Fildes* [1938] 3 All E.R. 517; *Semtex v Gladstone* [1954] 1 W.L.R. 945; *Harvey v R.G. O'Dell* [1958] 2 Q.B. 78. This may be useful where for some reason the common law action is not available, as in *Harvey v R.G. O'Dell*.

[1199] See *Adamson v Jarvis* (1827) 4 Bing. 66; and Article 63 generally.

[1200] *Century Insurance Co Ltd v Northern Ireland Road Transport Board* [1942] A.C. 509; *Jefferson v Derbyshire Farmers Ltd* [1921] 2 K.B. 281; *Staton v National Coal Board* [1957] 1 W.L.R. 893.

ing to a customer, which is blocking the entrance. Without making any inquiries of anyone he attempts to move the lorry and causes personal injuries to another. His employers are liable.[1201]

(3) The manager of a branch of a furniture business, while repossessing goods under a hire-purchase contract, assaults the hirer. His employer is liable.[1202]

(4) An employee of a garage, after serving a customer with petrol, incorrectly thinking that the customer was about to depart without paying or giving up the necessary coupons, pursued him and abused him. The customer paid and delivered the coupons and then said that he would report the employee to his employers. The employee struck the customer. Held, the assault had no connection with the discharge of the employee's duty to his employers, who were therefore not liable.[1203]

(5) The manager of a shop detains a person suspected of shoplifting. The person detained is innocent. The manager's employer may be liable for false imprisonment.[1204]

(6) A commission agent uses his own car for the purpose of getting orders for his principal. The principal is not liable for damage caused by the agent's negligent driving. The agent was not the servant of the principal.[1205]

(7) Two non-uniformed and armed police officers pursuing someone against whom only a driving offence can be charged enter without lawful right private property waking the pursued's mother at 2 a.m. and brandishing a pistol at her. Held, Crown vicariously liable for aggravated damages and exemplary damages for assault and trespass.[1206]

Prohibited acts

(8) A bus driver, in order to prevent a rival bus from overtaking him, drove his **8-193** bus across the road and caused the rival bus to overturn. The driver had instructions from his employers not to race with or obstruct other buses. Held, that the employers were liable, the wrongful act being done in the course of the driver's employment.[1207]

(9) The driver of a vehicle had authority to carry his employer's servants, but had

[1201] *Kay v ITW Ltd* [1968] 1 Q.B. 140; cf. *Beard v London General Omnibus Co* [1900] 2 Q.B. 530; and see *Ilkiw v Samuels* [1963] 1 W.L.R. 991; *Nelson v Raphael* [1979] R.T.R. 437 (person demonstrating controls of car to buyer).
[1202] *Dyer v Munday* [1895] 1 Q.B. 742. cf. Illustration 17. And see *Hamlyn v John Houston & Co* [1903] 1 K.B. 81 (bribery).
[1203] *Warren v Henlys* [1948] 2 All E.R. 935; cf. *Pettersson v Royal Oak Hotel Ltd* [1948] N.Z.L.R. 136; *Deatons Pty Ltd v Flew* (1949) 79 C.L.R. 370; *Keppel Bus Co Ltd v Salad bin Ahmed* [1974] 1 W.L.R. 1082; *Auckland Workingmen's Club v Rennie* [1976] 1 N.Z.L.R. 278; *Brown v Robinson* [2004] UKPC 56. See further as to assaults by servants and agents Rose (1977) 40 M.L.R. 420; Clerk and Lindsell, *Torts* (21st edn), para.6-47; Atiyah, *Vicarious Liability in the Law of Torts* (1967), pp.276–280.
[1204] See *Neville v C & A Modes Ltd* 1945 S.C. 175 (a case of slander). An account of such a case heard in York is reported in *The Times* on September 30, 1983. The older cases often concerned the giving of a person into custody, and drew a distinction between preservation of the employer's property and a mere desire to punish. See e.g. *Bank of New South Wales v Owston* (1879) 4 App.Cas. 270; *Abrahams v Deakin* [1891] 1 Q.B. 516. Police officers are more likely nowadays to arrest on their own responsibility: see *Meering v Graham-White Aviation Co Ltd* (1919) 122 L.T. 44; but cf. *Martin v Watson* [1996] A.C. 74 (malicious prosecution). See further Atiyah, above, at pp.266–267.
[1205] *Eggington v Reader* [1936] 1 All E.R. 7; cf. Illustration 24.
[1206] *New South Wales v Ibbett* (2006) 231 A.L.R. 485. See, however, para.8-177, above.
[1207] *Limpus v London General Omnibus Co* (1862) 1 H. & C. 526.

been expressly forbidden to carry other persons, and a notice to this effect was displayed in the vehicle. The driver gave a lift to a person who was not a fellow employee and who, in dismounting, suffered injury. Held, the driver acted outside the course of his employment, so that the employer was not liable.[1208]

(10) The employee of a firm of valuers is instructed not to make valuations for certain companies. He nevertheless does so on the vendor's headed notepaper, it not appearing who made the valuation. The valuation is negligent. The valuers are not liable for it.[1209]

(11) An employee of A, in disregard of a written notice issued to A's employees prohibiting the use of privately owned cars for the purpose of A's business unless adequately protected by insurance, used his own uninsured car for the purpose of ordinary work, and by negligent driving injured the plaintiff. Held, that the means of transport was incidental to the execution of what the servant was employed to do; that the prohibition merely limited the way in which, or means by which, the servant was to execute the work; and that A was liable to the plaintiff.[1210]

Wrong of servant or agent committed for his own benefit

8-194 (12) A solicitor's managing clerk who had a general authority to conduct conveyancing business induced a widow to give him instructions to realise properties with a view to reinvestment of the proceeds. For that purpose she handed him her title deeds, for which he gave her a receipt in his principal's name; and, at his request, she signed two documents, which were not read over or explained to her, and which were in fact conveyances of the properties to the clerk. He afterwards disposed of the properties for his own benefit. The principal was liable for the fraud.[1211]

(13) A solicitor's managing clerk was authorised to carry out conveyancing business and to borrow money from building societies, on behalf of clients, upon security of mortgage. He obtained an advance from a building society by producing a deed which he knew to be forged. Held, he was acting within the scope of his apparent authority and his principal was liable for the fraud, despite the fact that it involved a forgery.[1212]

(14) A, at the request of B, a transport contractor, committed goods to B's servants for carriage by road. In the course of their employment B's servants stole the goods so received. Held, B was liable to A for the value of the goods.[1213]

[1208] *Conway v George Wimpey & Co (No.2)* [1951] 2 K.B. 266; *Twine v Bean's Express Ltd* [1946] 1 All E.R. 202. cf. *Young v Edward Box & Co Ltd* [1951] 1 T.L.R. 789.

[1209] *Kooragang Investments Pty Ltd v Richardson & Wrench Ltd* [1982] A.C. 462 (criticised, [1982] C.L.J. 36; but see Watts (2012) 128 L.Q.R. 260).

[1210] *Canadian Pacific Ry Co v Lockhart* [1942] A.C. 591; *LCC v Cattermoles (Garages) Ltd* [1953] 1 W.L.R. 997.

[1211] *Lloyd v Grace, Smith & Co* [1912] A.C. 716.

[1212] *Uxbridge Permanent Benefit Building Soc. v Pickard* [1939] 2 K.B. 248. As to the liability of a solicitor to the disciplinary action of the court for the misdeeds of his clerk, see *Myers v Elman* [1940] A.C. 282.

[1213] *United Africa Co Ltd v Saka Owoade* [1955] A.C. 130; *Morris v C.W. Martin & Sons* [1966] 1 Q.B. 716, overruling *Cheshire v Bailey* [1905] 1 K.B. 237; *Mendelssohn v Normand Ltd* [1970] 1 Q.B. 177.

Authority to commit the wrongful act

(15)   A, the chairman at a meeting, at the request of B, who took part in the meet-   **8-195**
ing, made a defamatory statement concerning C, and both A and B expressed
a desire that the reporters present would take notice of "this very scandalous
case". Correct reports having been published, it was held, in an action by C
for libel, that there was evidence for the jury of publication by A and B
through the reporters, whom they had made their agents.[1214]

(16)   A, being hired to sing at a music hall, and being permitted to choose his own
song, sang a song infringing B's copyright. No control was exercised by the
proprietor of the music hall to prevent infringement of copyright. Held, that
there was sufficient evidence of authority to sing the song complained of to
justify a verdict for B in an action against the proprietor for the
infringement.[1215]

Liability for acts of agent

(17)   An unnecessary sale by a shipmaster of any part of the cargo, where the sale,   **8-196**
though unauthorised, is within the general scope of the authority conferred
upon the master by the owners of the ship, is a conversion for which the owners are liable.[1216]

(18)   A landlord is liable for wrongful distress committed by a bailiff acting on the
landlord's behalf and within the scope of the bailiff's authority.[1217] But he is
not liable for an unauthorised assault committed by the bailiff in levying a
distress, at any rate if the person assaulted was not interfering with the
distress.[1218]

(19)   A principal is liable for infringement by his employee or agent, acting in the

---

[1214] *Parkes v Prescott* (1869) L.R. 4 Ex. 169. cf. *Lucas v Mason* (1875) L.R. 10 Ex. 251. See Gatley,
Libel and Slander (12th edn), para.6-52 onwards. See too *Body Corporate 366611 v Wu* [2012]
NZCA 614; [2013] 3 N.Z.L.R. 522 (liability for authorised nuisance), varied on appeal [2014] NZSC
137; [2015] 1 N.Z.L.R. 215 (liability for trespass).

[1215] *Monaghan v Taylor* (1886) 2 T.L.R. 685; *Marsh v Conquest* (1864) 17 C.B. 418; cf. *Performing
Rights Society Ltd v Ciryl Theatrical Syndicate Ltd* [1924] 1 K.B. 1; *Fish & Fish Ltd v Sea Shepherd
UK* [2015] UKSC 10; [2015] A.C. 1229; and further cases cited below, para.9-120. For com-
mentary, see Cornish and Llewelyn, *Intellectual Property* (7th edn), paras 12-18–12-20.

[1216] *Ewbank v Nutting* (1849) 7 C.B. 797. And see Illustration 18.

[1217] See, e.g. *Hurry v Richman and Sutcliffe* (1831) 1 M. & Rob. 126; *Freeman v Rosher* (1849) 13 Q.B.
780; *Hasseler v Lemoyne* (1858) 5 C.B.(N.S.) 530. But the basis of liability is not clear: some cases
put it on the basis of express authorisation or ratification only, also sheriffs are liable for the acts of
their officers: *Hooper v Lane* (1857) 6 H.L.Cas 443. But the sheriff himself is the agent of the court
and the execution creditor is not liable for his acts unless he specifically authorised them: *Barclays
Bank v Roberts* [1954] 1 W.L.R. 1212. However, a solicitor is the agent of the execution creditor,
so that if he by indorsement of the writ directs the sheriff to seize the goods of the wrong party, the
client is liable for the acts of the sheriff as so directed: *Jarmain v Hooper* (1843) 6 Man. & G. 827;
Morris v Salberg (1889) 22 Q.B.D. 614; *Lee v Rumilly* (1891) 55 J.P. 519; cf. *Condy v Blaiberg*
(1891) 55 J.P. 580. The same applies if the solicitor issues execution after the debt has been paid:
Bates v Pilling (1826) 6 B. & C. 38; *Clissold v Cratchley* [1910] 2 K.B. 244. But he has no authority to direct the seizure of particular chattels, and the client will not be liable if he does this: *Smith
v Keal* (1882) 9 Q.B.D. 340; *Hewitt v Spiers & Pond* (1896) 13 T.L.R. 64; and see *Williams v Williams & Nathan* [1937] 2 All E.R. 559; *Barclays Bank v Roberts*, above. These lines of cases are
well established, but their basis and their reconciliation with more recent authorities on vicarious
liability are a difficult matter. See Atiyah, *Vicarious Liability in the Law of Torts* (1967), pp.136–
142. Note that the right of distraint in relation to commercial tenancies has been abolished by the
Tribunals, Courts and Enforcement Act 2007 s.71.

[1218] *Richards v West Middlesex Waterworks Co* (1885) 15 Q.B.D. 660. See Illustrations 3 and 4 above.

course of his employment or within the scope of his authority, of a patent,[1219] trade mark[1220] or copyright.[1221]

(20) A director starts negotiations to sell the shares in the company without authority, and makes fraudulent misrepresentations. He is later authorised to negotiate by the shareholders in general meeting, and takes no steps to correct the misrepresentations. The shareholders are liable.[1222]

(21) An estate agent tells a prospective purchaser of a bungalow that any building society will lend £1,200 on a mortgage of it. The bungalow is in fact structurally unsound, but the estate agent was not fraudulent in making such statements. The owners of the bungalow, for whom the estate agent was acting, knew of the unsoundness, but not that the estate agent had made such a representation. The owner is not liable in deceit for the agent's false statement, it not having been proved that he deliberately kept the agent in ignorance of the facts.[1223]

(22) An estate agent demands a premium from a person who wishes to acquire the tenancy of a flat. The premium is illegal. It is recoverable from the landlord though the agent kept the money himself and the taking of the premium was not within his actual authority.[1224]

(23) A solicitor acting for the vendor in a conveyancing transaction negligently makes false statements in answer to inquiries. The vendor is liable in respect of the statements but the solicitor is not.[1225]

(24) A canvasser and agent was engaged by an insurance company under an agreement one of the terms of which prohibited him from defaming any other person or institution. While attempting to obtain business, he made defamatory statements concerning another assurance company. It was held that in doing so he was acting not independently but as a representative of the first assurance company conducting negotiations for that company, and that the company was liable for his statements.[1226]

[1219] *Betts v Neilson* (1868) L.R. 3 Ch.App. 429.

[1220] *Tonge v Ward* (1869) 21 L.T. 480.

[1221] Illustration 15 above.

[1222] *Briess v Woolley* [1954] A.C. 333.

[1223] *Armstrong v Strain* [1952] 1 K.B. 232. See above, para.8-185.

[1224] *Navarro v Moregrand Ltd* [1951] 2 T.L.R. 674. See also *Credit Services Investments Ltd v Evans* [1974] 2 N.Z.L.R. 653. cf. *Kabel v Ronald Lyon Espanola SA* (1968) 208 E.G. 265.

[1225] *Cemp Properties (UK) Ltd v Dentsply Research and Development Corp* [1989] 2 E.G.L.R. 196 (Misrepresentation Act 1967 s.2(1)); see also *Strover v Harrington* [1988] Ch. 390 (Misrepresentation Act 1967 s.2(1), Illustration 8 to Article 94; no liability on facts); *Gran Gelato Ltd v Richliff Group Ltd* [1992] Ch. 560 (Misrepresentation Act and common law negligence: see above, para.8-180); as to surveyors *Thompson v Henderson & Partners Pty Ltd* (1989) 51 S.A.S.R. 43 (negligence); and as to insurance agents *Derham v Amev Life Insurance Co Ltd* (1981) 56 F.L.R. 34 (fraud).

[1226] *Colonial Mutual Life Assurance Society Ltd v Producers' and Citizens Co-operative Assurance Co Ltd of Australia* (1931) 46 C.L.R. 41; *Citizens Life Assurance Co Ltd v Brown* [1904] A.C. 423 (PC). See the first case discussed by McHugh J in *Scott v Davis* (2000) 204 C.L.R. 333, para.56 onwards. See also *Derham v Amev Life Assurance Co Ltd* (1981) 56 F.L.R. 34. See further as to defamation *Whitfield v SE Ry Co* (1858) E.B. & E. 115; *Nevill v Fine Arts Assurance Co* [1895] 2 Q.B. 156; [1897] A.C. 68; *Ellis v National Free Labour Assn* (1905) 7 F. 629; *Finburgh v Moss Empires Ltd* 1908 S.C. 928; *Fitzsimons v Duncan and Kemp & Co* [1908] 2 I.R. 483; *Glasgow Corp v Lorimer* [1911] A.C. 209; *Aiken v Caledonian Ry Co* 1913 S.C. 66; *Egger v Viscount Chelmsford* [1965] 1 Q.B. 248; Atiyah, *Vicarious Liability in the Law of Torts* (1967), pp.274–276. As to partners see *Meekins v Henson* [1964] 1 Q.B. 472. Liability was imposed on a person employing a debt collec-

(25) An agent employed by an assurance company drives a doctor to make the necessary examination of a person who wishes to propose for life insurance. He drives negligently and the doctor is injured. The company is not liable.[1227]

(26) The Chartering Manager and Vice-President (Transportation) of a company, authorised to negotiate the sale of a ship belonging to the company, purports to enter into a simultaneous agreement to take it back on charter. The third party knows that the Vice-President has no authority to enter into such a charter without approval from higher in the company, but believes the Vice-President when he falsely says that he has obtained such approval. There is no apparent authority; nor therefore is the company vicariously liable for the deceit of its agent.[1228]

Article 91

MISREPRESENTATIONS BY AGENT AS TO CREDIT OF THIRD PARTIES

No action can be maintained against a principal in deceit or under s.2(1) of the Misrepresentation Act 1967 in respect of any representation as to the character, conduct, credit, ability, trade or dealings of another person, to the intent that such other person may obtain credit, unless such representation is in writing signed by the principal[1229]; the signature of an agent is not sufficient, even if expressly authorised by the principal, except in the case of a limited company.[1230] **8-197**

Comment

This Article reproduces the effect of the Statute of Frauds Amendment 1828 (Lord Tenterden's Act), the purpose of which was to prevent a person against whom the Statute of Frauds was pleaded in respect of a guarantee evading the protection of the Statute by suing in tort.[1231] It was subsequently established that it applied only to actions in deceit, the form of action which would have been used at the time, and not to those in negligence, where the gist of the tort is said to lie not in the representation but in the breach of a duty of care.[1232] It is also confined to representations as to creditworthiness.[1233] However, the wording of s.2(1) of the Misrepresen- **8-198**

---

tion agency which used extremely threatening methods in *Wong Wai Hing v Hui Wei Lee* [2001] 1 H.K.L.R.D. 736.

[1227] *Colonial Mutual Life Assurance Society Ltd v Macdonald* [1931] A.D. 412.

[1228] *Armagas Ltd v Mundogas SA (The Ocean Frost)* [1986] A.C. 717.

[1229] Statute of Frauds Amendment Act 1828 (Lord Tenterden's Act) s.6. The actual wording reads: "May obtain credit, money or goods upon, unless etc,": see *Lyde v Barnard* (1836) 1 M. & W. 101 at 104 (explaining the background of the Act). For a case on similar Scottish legislation, see *Clydesdale Bank Ltd v Paton* [1896] A.C. 381. See *Contex Drouzhba Ltd v Wiseman* [2007] EWCA Civ 1201; [2008] 1 B.C.L.C. 631. The representation may be made in an email provided that the email includes a written indication of who is sending it: *Lindsay v O'Loughnane* [2010] EWHC 529 (QB) at [95].

[1230] See Comment. There is a useful discussion of this provision (which led to its repeal in New South Wales) in Report LRC 57 of the *New South Wales Law Reform Commission* (1988).

[1231] See *Williams v Mason* (1873) 28 L.T. 232. See further below, para.9-119.

[1232] *Banbury v Bank of Montreal* [1918] A.C. 626; *W.B. Anderson & Sons v Rhodes (Liverpool) Ltd* [1967] 2 All E.R. 850; *Diamond v Bank of London and Montreal Ltd* [1979] Q.B. 333.

[1233] *Diamond v Bank of London and Montreal Ltd*, above; *Roder UK Ltd v West* [2011] EWCA Civ 1126; [2012] Q.B. 752 (statute does not extend to renewals of existing credit). See discussion in Clerk and Lindsell, *Torts* (21st edn), paras 18-52–18-53.

tation Act 1967, which uses the referent of fraud liability, appears to produce the result that s.6 applies also to claims under that provision.[1234]

It was held in *Swift v Jewsbury and Goddard*[1235] that signature of an agent was not sufficient under the Act:

> "If you mean to charge a person with a fraudulent act ... you shall not charge that person unless you can produce his own handwriting for the statement of fraud by which you say you have been misled."[1236]

However, this caused difficulties with the emerging doctrine of corporate personality. A corporation can only sign by agents, and hence it might appear that a fraudulent misrepresentation signed by the agent of a corporation would never render the corporation liable. In *Hirst v West Riding Union Banking Co Ltd*[1237] it was therefore argued that the Act only applied to natural persons and not to corporations at all. The proposition was rejected, but the Act held effective to protect the Bank against liability for a fraudulent representation as to credit signed by a local manager. On this basis companies would not be liable except perhaps where reasoning that the signature ranks as that of the company itself can be deployed. This was done in *UBAF Ltd v European American Banking Corp Ltd*,[1238] where a company was held liable for a fraudulent misrepresentation as to credit signed by its assistant secretary. As to the relevance of Lord Tenterden's Act to an agent's liability in deceit for misrepresentation as to his principal's creditworthiness, see below, para.9-114.

Article 92

MONEY, ETC., MISAPPROPRIATED BY AGENT

8-199   Where the money of a third party is received by an agent while acting within the scope of his authority or in respect of a transaction ratified by the principal, and misapplied by him, or is received by the principal and misapplied by the agent, the principal is liable to repay the third party.[1239]

Comment

8-200   The authority of the agent may of course be actual or apparent.[1240] This rule, which is based on s.11 of the Partnership Act 1890, is placed here for convenience, since it relates to the liability of a principal for the wrongs of his agent, but it does not follow that the liability is always in tort. Sometimes situations arise where the liability of the principal is indeed in tort for the fraud or conversion of his

---

[1234] *UBAF v European American Banking Corp* [1984] Q.B. 713; *LBI HF v Stanford* [2014] EWHC 3921 (Ch) at [184].

[1235] (1874) L.R. 9 Q.B. 301.

[1236] Per Lord Coleridge CJ at 312.

[1237] [1901] 2 K.B. 560.

[1238] [1984] Q.B. 713; *Contex Drouzhba Ltd v Wiseman* [2007] EWCA Civ 1201; [2008] 1 B.C.L.C. 631, treated further below, para.9-119. See also above, paras 1-028 and 8-189.

[1239] See Illustrations. cf. Partnership Act 1890 s.11, which refers to "money or property", as to which see Atiyah, *Vicarious Liability in the Law of Torts* (1967), pp.119–121. As to the agent's liability, see Article 111.

[1240] *Trott v National Discount Co* (1900) 17 T.L.R. 37.

agent[1241]: but sometimes the action may be in restitution, whether in money had and received, or at equity in the form of the constructive trust and the action for knowing receipt,[1242] and sometimes it is sufficient to say that a payment made in respect of a contract is binding whatever may have happened to it,[1243] or that there is a breach of contract, whether or not the facts also constitute a tort.[1244] Liability will not arise in respect of receipts of money paid by an agent into a principal's bank account then withdrawn where the agent had no actual or apparent authority to pay the money into the account.[1245]

Illustrations

(1) A local manager, acting as agent for a bank, induced a lady to invest money **8-201** in paying off a certain mortgage. The money was paid to him for that purpose, and he misappropriated it. Held, that he was acting within the scope of his apparent authority in receiving the money, which must therefore be deemed to have been received by the bank, and that the bank was liable to repay it.[1246]

(2) An agent, acting apparently in the ordinary course of business, sent an account to A, representing that certain advances had been made on his account, and drew on him for the amount. It was within the scope of the agent's authority to make advances of that kind, but he had in fact misappropriated the money, and had not made the advances. A accepted and paid the bill. Held, that the principal was liable to A for the amount.[1247]

(3) An auctioneer receives a deposit in connection with a concluded contract, and does not pay it over to the vendor. The vendor is liable whether the auctioneer received it as agent for the vendor or as stakeholder.[1248]

(4) An estate agent receives a deposit on a transaction "subject to contract," whether expressly "as stakeholder" or without any indication of the capacity in which he was to hold it, and does not pay it over to the prospective vendor. The vendor is not liable unless the agent received it as agent for him, having authority to do so.[1249]

(5) A husband has signing authority on his wife's bank accounts, and uses those accounts for temporary lodgement of funds obtained by him by fraud. The wife is unaware of the movement of the funds through her accounts and has given

---

[1241] *Swire v Francis* (1877) 3 App.Cas. 106, Illustration 2.
[1242] *Thompson v Bell* (1854) 10 Exch. 10, Illustration 1; cf. *Russo-Chinese Bank v Li Yau Sam* [1910] A.C. 174. Again, the principal may be a trustee: see *Hackney v Knight* (1891) 7 T.L.R. 254. See also Article 71, Illustration 2; Article 111. More detailed treatment of equitable claims, including that for knowing receipt, is found in Article 116.
[1243] *Thompson v Bell*, above, at 14 ("the money is still in the hands of the bank").
[1244] *National Bank of Lahore v Sohan Lal, A.I.R.* 1965 S.C. 1663.
[1245] *General Accident Fire & Life Assurance Corp Ltd v Midland Bank Ltd* [1940] 2 K.B. 388 at 415–416; *National Commercial Banking Corporation of Australia Ltd v Batty* (1986) 160 C.L.R. 251; *Heperu Pty Ltd v Belle* (2009) 76 N.S.W.L.R. 230, Illustration 5; *Jones v Churcher* [2009] EWHC 722 (QB); [2009] 2 Lloyd's Rep. 94; *Perpetual Trustee Co Ltd v El-Bayeh* [2010] NSWSC 1487. cf. *Law Society of England and Wales v Habitable Concepts Ltd* [2010] EWHC 1449 (Ch) at [14] (beneficial receipt as principal).
[1246] *Thompson v Bell* (1854) 10 Exch. 10. cf. *Bishop v Jersey (Countess)* (1854) 2 Drew. 143; *Russo-Chinese Bank v Li Yau Sam* [1910] A.C. 174. See also *Royal Globe Life Assurance Co Ltd v Kovacevic* (1979) 22 S.A.S.R. 78.
[1247] *Swire v Francis* (1877) 3 App.Cas. 106.
[1248] See Article 111, Illustrations 2 and 3 and cases cited.
[1249] *Sorrell v Finch* [1977] A.C. 728. cf. *Branwhite v Worcester Works Finance Ltd* [1969] 1 A.C. 552. See Article 111, Illustration 3 and cases cited.

no authority to her husband to use them for purposes unrelated to her own finances. She is not liable at law or in equity for the receipt or withdrawal of the funds.[1250]

Article 93

MONEY APPLIED BY AGENT FOR BENEFIT OF PRINCIPAL

8-202 Where, by any wrongful act of an agent, or by an unauthorised act which is not ratified, the money of the third party is obtained and applied for the benefit of the principal, the principal is liable in equity to restore such money to the extent that it has been so applied.[1251]

Comment

8-203 This applies notwithstanding that the third party knew that the agent was not authorised to obtain or receive money,[1252] for its basis is not liability for the acts of the agent, but a wider principle akin to a doctrine of subrogation, whereby the third party is entitled to stand in the same position as the principal's creditor when the money has been paid over. There is no full subrogation, however, because the third party is not entitled to the benefit of the securities of the creditor,[1253] at least where the third party intended itself to be a secured creditor. It has been suggested that the true basis of the principle is rather, that an unauthorised loan is adopted or validated pro tanto.[1254] The main application of the wider principle lay in cases of ultra vires borrowing by companies, where the view could have been taken that the transaction, though ultra vires, had not added to the liabilities of the company, which remained unchanged[1255]: but there is a similar rule in the case of loans for necessaries purchased by minors[1256] and in some cases the doctrine, or a similar doctrine, has been applied to situations of money obtained by fraud.[1257] The money must be used by the defendant himself or his authorised agent: the principle does not apply where a third party discharges the defendant's debt without authority.[1258] It is uncertain how far the words "for his benefit" in this Article should be stretched: the cases concern discharge of his legal liabilities, but it is possible that the principle can apply wherever the money is used on any purpose authorised by the defendant,[1259] e.g. in making authorised but gratuitous payments.

It should be noted that a similar result may sometimes be obtained without the

---

[1250] *Heperu Pty Ltd v Belle* (2009) 76 N.S.W.L.R. 230.

[1251] See Comment.

[1252] *Reversion Fund & Insurance Co v Maison Cosway Ltd* [1913] 1 K.B. 364, Illustration 1, interpreting *Bannatyne v D. & C. McIver* [1906] 1 K.B. 103; accepted in *Rolled Steel Products (Holdings) Ltd v British Steel Corp* [1986] Ch. 246 at 300 and 307.

[1253] *Reversion Fund & Insurance Co v Maison Cosway Ltd* [1913] 1 K.B. 364 at 377.

[1254] See *Hazlewood v West Coast Securities Ltd* (1974) 49 D.L.R. (3d) 46; affd (1976) 68 D.L.R. (3d) 172; and cf. *Orakpo v Manson Investments Ltd* [1978] A.C. 95.

[1255] *Blackburn Building Society v Cunliffe, Brookes & Co* (1882) 22 Ch.D. 61 at 71 (see also (1884) 9 App.Cas. 857). The scope of this doctrine is now much reduced: see above, para.8-035 onwards.

[1256] *Marlow v Pitfield* (1719) 1 P.Wms. 558. See also *City Bank of Sydney v McLaughlin* (1909) 9 C.L.R. 615 (person of unsound mind).

[1257] Illustration 2. See also *Barrow v Bank of New South Wales* [1931] V.R. 323, deriving a wider doctrine from *Refuge Assurance Co Ltd v Kettlewell* [1909] A.C. 243.

[1258] *Re Cleadon Trust Ltd* [1939] Ch. 286.

[1259] See Lindley and Banks, *Partnership* (19th edn), paras 12–178.

aid of equity, by invoking the doctrine of tracing at common law. If the money has been paid into the principal's bank account, he may be liable to an action in restitution.[1260]

Illustrations

(1) The managing director of a company borrows money on the company's behalf **8-204** without authority. The lender knows that he has no authority, but expects that the company will adopt the loan. The company does not·do so, but the money is spent by the managing director in discharging existing legal debts of the company. The company must repay the money.[1261]

(2) The secretary of a company forges and discounts certain bills of exchange, and pays the proceeds to his own account, upon which he draws cheques in favour of the company. The company is liable to the discounter to the extent that the proceeds of the bills have been applied for its benefit.[1262]

(3) A manager who had no authority to borrow money or overdraw his principal's account, having overdrawn the account and misapplied the money, borrowed £20 for the alleged purpose of paying the principal's workmen (but really to make up the defalcations), paid it into the principal's account, and drew on the account to pay the workmen. Held, that the £20 having been applied for the benefit of the principal, he was liable to repay the amount to the lender.[1263]

4. NOTIFICATION TO AND KNOWLEDGE ACQUIRED THROUGH AGENT[1264]

Article 94

NOTIFICATION TO AGENT

A notification given to an agent is effective as such if the agent receives it within **8-205** the scope of his actual or apparent authority,[1265] whether or not it is subsequently transmitted to the principal, unless the person seeking to charge the principal with notice knew that the agent intended to conceal the notification from the principal.[1266]

[1260] Illustration 3; see Article 88.

[1261] *Reversion Fund & Insurance Co v Maison Cosway Ltd* [1913] 1 K.B. 364. See also *Bannatyne v D. & C. McIver* [1906] 1 K.B. 103; and *Campden Hill Ltd v Chakrani* [2005] EWHC 911; [2005] N.P.C. 65 at [90].

[1262] *Ex p. Shoolbred* (1880) 28 W.R. 339. See also *Hazlewood v West Coast Securities Ltd* (1974) 49 D.L.R. (3d) 46; affd (1976) 68 D.L.R. (3d) 172.

[1263] *Reid v Rigby & Co* [1894] 2 Q.B. 40.

[1264] Some older editions contained an Article on the question when admissions by agents were evidence against the principal. The case law on this constituted, as did the rules as to admissions by the principal himself, an exception to the Hearsay Rule. Since the abolition of that rule by the Civil Evidence Act 1995 this body of authority is of little relevance in civil law in England, the matter being now one of reliability and weight of evidence. They may sometimes be relevant in criminal cases, and similar reasoning may apply in some other common law jurisdictions (e.g. Australian Evidence Act 1995 (Cth.) s.87; Singapore Evidence Act s.18). A full account was given in the 16th edition of this work, and an abbreviated account is given in *Cross and Tapper on Evidence* (12th edn), p.582 onwards. Problems may arise in connection with admissions by solicitor and counsel in litigation: an account is given in Phipson, *Evidence* (18th edn), para.4-23 onwards.

[1265] *Tanham v Nicholson* (1872) L.R. 5 H.L. 561, Illustration 3; and see Comment.

[1266] *Restatement, Third*, § 5.02; *Blackley v National Mutual Life Assn of Australasia Ltd* [1972] N.Z.L.R. 1038, Illustration 7. See also *Norwegian American Cruises A/S v Paul Mundy Ltd (The Vistafjord)*

Comment

8-206   The notion that the knowledge of an agent is that of the principal is frequently invoked in cases of varying types and its full applications are not clearly determined: "When a question of notice, or knowledge, arises, we find ourselves overwhelmed in a sea of authorities, not altogether reconcilable with each other".[1267] *Restatement, Second* sought to lay down exhaustive rules,[1268] but *Restatement, Third* adopts a more general approach.[1269] This Article is the first part of an initial division between cases of notification and mere notice or knowledge. This distinction has been forcefully argued by academic writers,[1270] is adopted in both Restatements,[1271] and has received judicial support in England[1272] and New Zealand.[1273] It is based on the fact that in some cases of the formal giving of information, use of the notion of authority to receive it, not only actual but also apparent, seems natural and appropriate.

Restatement, Third[1274] defines notification as:

> "a manifestation that is made in the form required by agreement among parties or applicable law, or in a reasonable manner in the absence of any agreement or applicable law, with the intention of affecting the legal rights and duties of the notifier in relation to rights and duties of persons to whom the notification is given."

An obvious example is the notice to quit, and this and other examples appear in the Illustrations. In England Hoffmann LJ referred to a category of cases:

> "in which the agent has actual or ostensible authority to receive communications, whether informative (such as the state of health of an insured) or performative (such as a notice to quit)."[1275]

Whether something is intended as a notice is generally to be assessed using objective criteria.[1276] A notice, once communicated, is not normally permitted to be forgotten, whereas mere knowledge it seems can be forgotten.[1277] While a notice will normally be intended to take immediate effect, it is possible that the parties anticipate that some passage of time will be needed for the agent to communicate the information to the principal before it is effective.

[1988] 2 Lloyd's Rep. 343 at 354.

[1267] *Taylor v Yorkshire Insurance Co Ltd* [1913] 2 Ir.R. 1 at 21, per Palles CB.

[1268] See §§ 9–11 and 268–282.

[1269] §§ 5.01–5.04.

[1270] Powell, pp.236–244; Wright (1935) 1 U. Toronto L.J. 17 at 52, fn.5; Falconbridge (1939) 17 Can.B.R. 248 at 259; Seavey (1916) 65 U.Pa.L.Rev. 1 (a valuable article); but cf. Fridman, para.10.6, who rejects the distinction.

[1271] *Restatement, Second*, §§ 9 and 268–271; *Restatement, Third*, § 5.01(1)(3).

[1272] *El Ajou v Dollar Land Holdings Ltd* [1994] 2 All E.R. 685; see below.

[1273] *Blackley v National Mutual Life Assn of Australasia Ltd* [1972] N.Z.L.R. 1038, per Turner P. (Illustration 7).

[1274] § 5.01(1).

[1275] *El Ajou v Dollar Land Holdings Ltd* [1994] 2 All E.R. 685, at 703. See too *Ng Hock Kon v Sembawang Capital Pte Ltd* [2010] 1 S.L.R. 307.

[1276] But cf. *HLB Kidsons (a firm) v Lloyd's Underwriters Subscribing To Lloyd's Policy No. 621/PK1D00101* [2008] EWCA Civ 1206 at [64] and [137].

[1277] See *MCP Pension Trustees Ltd v Aon Pension Trustees Ltd* [2010] EWCA Civ 377; [2012] Ch. 1 (this case was concerned with the concept of "notice" within the Trustee Act 1925 s.27, which may be broader than that of notification, but the reasoning therein would apply, with perhaps more force, to the common law concept of notification). As to knowledge, see below, para.8-209.

The fact that cases involving notification, notice or knowledge have until fairly recently been run together does however mean that the sort of reasoning applied in knowledge cases, for example a presumption that information has been passed on, is sometimes found in notification cases.[1278] The leading case of *Blackley v National Mutual Life Association of Australasia Ltd*,[1279] the facts of which are given in Illustration 7, depends for its distinction from the insurance cases referred to in Illustrations 1 and 2 to Article 96 on the interpretation that the assured's wife gave the agent notification of new information as to the assured's health in accordance with the requirements of the policy.[1280]

It is clear on principle that where the third party *knows* (as opposed to merely suspects) that the information will not be passed on by the agent, the notification is ineffective.[1281] Whether under apparent or even authority reasoning, the agent is simply disclaiming that he is exercising any agency authority in receiving the notification, and there is no justification for reliance on him.

Illustrations

(1) An underwriter sought to avoid a policy on the ground of the non-disclosure **8-207** of a material fact. The fact had been disclosed to his solicitor, but had not been communicated to him. Held, that he was not bound by the disclosure to his solicitor, it not being in the ordinary course of a solicitor's employment to receive notice as to mercantile business.[1282]

(2) Notice of withdrawal of an application for shares was given during business hours to a clerk at the registered office of the company, the clerk stating that the secretary was out. Held, that it operated as notice to the company.[1283]

(3) A notice to quit is served at the house of a tenant upon a servant whose duty it is to deliver it to the tenant. That is good service on the tenant though the servant does not deliver the notice to him.[1284]

(4) Notice of a bankruptcy petition against an execution debtor is given to a man left in possession by the sheriff. That does not operate as notice to the sheriff, because the man in possession is only his agent for the purpose of levying, selling the goods, and handing over the proceeds.[1285]

(5) Notice of an incumbrance was given to a solicitor who had been employed by trustees in all matters relating to the trust in which professional assistance was required, but who had not been authorised to receive notices on their behalf, and the solicitor wrote formally acknowledging receipt on behalf of the trustees. Held, that the notice to the solicitor did not operate as notice

---

[1278] See, e.g. the speeches of Lord Westbury and Lord Colonsay in *Tanham v Nicholson* (1872) L.R. 5 H.L. 561, Illustration 3; *A/S Rendal v Arcos Ltd* [1937] 3 All E.R. 577 (HL); and see below, para.8-210.

[1279] [1972] N.Z.L.R. 1038, Illustration 7.

[1280] [1972] N.Z.L.R. 1038 at 1051.

[1281] *Blackley*'s case, above, at 1049, citing *Sharpe v Foy* (1868) L.R. 4 Ch.App. 35; *Re Fitzroy Bessemer Steel Co Ltd* (1884) 50 L.T. 144, Illustration 9 to Article 95—neither of them notification cases however. See also *The Vistafjord* [1988] 2 Lloyd's Rep. 343.

[1282] *Tate v Hyslop* (1885) 15 Q.B.D. 368. See too *JL Builders & Son v Naylor and Naylor* [2008] EWCA Civ 1621 (notice to quantity surveyor).

[1283] *Re Brewery Assets Corp, Truman's Case* [1894] 3 Ch. 272.

[1284] *Tanham v Nicholson* (1872) L.R. 5 H.L. 561. See also *Townsend Carriers Ltd v Pfizer Ltd* (1977) 33 P. & C.R. 361.

[1285] *Re Holland Ex p. Warren* (1885) 1 T.L.R. 430.

to the trustees, solicitors not being, as such, standing agents of their clients to receive notices on their behalf.[1286]

(6) A car dealer may be the agent of the finance company for whom he acts, to receive notification of revocation of offer from a prospective hirer.[1287]

(7) B proposes for life insurance. After a medical examination the company accepts the proposal, acceptance not to be completed till the first premium is paid and a banker's order signed. The agent who communicates this acceptance knows at the time of doing so, and is also told by B's wife, that B has just been admitted to hospital and has undergone an apparently successful operation. The premium is paid and a banker's order signed (by B's wife). The agent does not tell the company of the operation. Later B's situation deteriorates. The company cannot repudiate the policy for non-disclosure, there having been notification of circumstances affecting the risk, in accordance with the policy terms, to the agent, who had apparent authority to receive it. Suspicion, short of actual knowledge or positive belief, by B's wife that the information would not be passed on does not vitiate the notification.[1288]

(8) In negotiations for the sale of a house, a misrepresentation is made in the particulars that it is on main drainage. This is subsequently corrected by the vendor's agent in a letter to the purchaser's solicitor. The solicitor does not pass on the information. The purchaser is deemed to have notice for the purposes of an action by him under s.2(1) of the Misrepresentation Act 1967: his loss was caused not by reliance on the continuing representation but by his solicitor's failure to communicate the correction to him.[1289]

(9) An agent with a power of attorney for several principals to purchase racehorses borrows money for the purpose from a bank. The bank makes disclosures requisite under credit contract legislation to the attorney. It has made the disclosure to his principals thereby.[1290]

(10) A vendor's solicitor receives tender of a personal cheque as deposit on a land transaction. He does not have implied authority to accept payment by that method, but he does have implied authority to receive it for the purposes of communicating to the vendor the fact of its tender. The purchaser can as-

---

[1286] *Saffron Walden Second Benefit Building Society v Rayner* (1880) 14 Ch.D. 406. See also *IVI Pty Ltd v Baycrown Pty Ltd* [2005] QCA 205 at [33] (notice of revocation of offer given to purchaser's solicitor ineffective where negotiations had principally been face-to-face and otherwise solicitor had not been appointed to receive notices); and *Vaughan v Von Essen Hotels 5 Ltd* [2007] EWCA Civ 1349 (notice had to be to firm of solicitors expressly stipulated; it was hence not sufficient to give notice to a different firm that was acting in relation to some matters under the contract); *Nakanishi Marine Co Ltd v Gora Shipping Ltd* [2012] EWHC 3383 (Comm) at [16].

[1287] *Financings Ltd v Stimson* [1962] 1 W.L.R. 1184; *CF Asset Finance Ltd v Okonji* [2014] EWCA Civ 870 at [22]. See Consumer Credit Act 1974 ss.57, 69 and 102. See also *HLB Kidsons (a firm) v Lloyd's Underwriters Subscribing to Lloyd's Policy No.621/PK1D00101* [2007] EWHC 1951 (Comm) at [89]; and see clarification judgment [2007] EWHC 2699 (Comm) (partnership was held in default under insurance policy by failing to file in time notice of claim when secretary to partnership had, within authority, received notice of circumstances that could justify claim); varied on appeal [2008] EWCA Civ 1206; [2009] 1 Lloyd's Rep. 8.

[1288] *Blackley v National Mutual Life Association of Australasia Ltd* [1972] N.Z.L.R. 1038. The distinction between this case and cases such as those discussed under Illustration 2 to Article 95 is explained at 1051. As to notice of insurance claims, see also *Marsden v City and County Assurance Co* (1865) L.R. 1 C.P. 232.

[1289] *Strover v Harrington* [1988] Ch. 390, See too *Gabriel v Little* [2013] EWCA Civ 1513 at [37] (affd on other issues sub nom. *Hughes-Holland v BPE Solicitors* [2017] UKSC 21; [2017] 2 W.L.R. 1029).

[1290] *National Australia Finance Ltd v Fahey* [1990] 2 N.Z.L.R. 482.

sume that that fact has been communicated and can further assume that the tender has been accepted if a prompt rejection does not follow.[1291]

(11) An insurer is prepared to renew a policy only on the basis of adding a terrorism exclusion to the policy, and communicates that fact to the broker acting for the insured, the latter not communicating this change to the insured. Held, the insured is bound by the notification to the broker of the change of terms.[1292]

Article 95

KNOWLEDGE ACQUIRED THROUGH AGENT

(1) A principal is generally imputed with knowledge relating to the subject matter of the agency which an agent acquired while acting for the principal.[1293]   **8-208**

(2) Where an agent is authorised to enter into a transaction in which his own knowledge is material, knowledge which he acquired before his appointment or outside the scope of his authority may also be imputed to the principal.[1294]

(3) Where the principal has a duty to investigate and make disclosure, he may have imputed to him not only facts which he knows but also material facts of which he might expect to have been told by his agents.[1295]

(4) Knowledge is not attributed to the principal where the principal is claiming in respect of a breach of duty of his own agent that relates to the information in question.[1296] Otherwise, whether a fraudulent or miscreant agent's knowledge is imputable to the principal depends upon the type of legal issue that arises.[1297] There is, therefore, no general fraud exception to imputation to the principal of the knowledge, or the acts, of an agent.

Comment

Introduction   The law on this topic is constituted by a plethora of cases in different contexts, which are extremely difficult to reduce to any order. It may be useful therefore to draw attention initially to some main points that may be found lying within them.[1298] Assuming as a starting point that the knowledge of an agent can   **8-209**

[1291] *Southbourne Investments Ltd v Greenmount Manufacturing Ltd* [2008] 1 N.Z.L.R. 30 (NZSC) at [20].

[1292] *Axa Corporate Solutions SA v National Westminster Bank Plc* [2010] EWHC 1915 (Comm).

[1293] *Taylor v Yorkshire Insurance Co Ltd* [1913] 2 Ir.R. 1 at 21, per Palles CB. See also *Merry v Abney* (1663) 1 Ch. Cas. 38; *Jennings v Moore* (1708) 2 Vern. 609; affd sub nom. *Blenkarne v Jennens* (1709) 2 Bro. P.C. 278 (HL); *Le Neve v Le Neve* (1748) 1 Ves. Sen. 64, Illustration 22; (1748) 3 Atk. 646; *Doe d. Willis v Martin* (1790) 4 T.R. 39; *Boursot v Savage* (1866) L.R. 2 Eq. 134; *Rolland v Hart* (1871) L.R. 6 Ch.App. 678; *Real Estate Opportunities Ltd v Aberdeen Asset Managers Jersey Ltd* [2007] EWCA Civ 197; [2007] 2 All E.R. 791 at [49]; *UBS AG (London Branch) v Kommunale Wasserwerke Leipzig GmbH* [2014] EWHC 3615 (Comm) at [762].

[1294] See *El Ajou v Dollar Land Holdings Ltd* [1994] 2 All E.R. 685 at 702; but see Comment.

[1295] See *El Ajou v Dollar Land Holdings Ltd*, above; but see Comment.

[1296] See, e.g. *Belmont Finance Corp Ltd v Williams Furniture Ltd* [1979] 1 Ch. 250 at 261–262. See *Bilta (UK) Ltd v Nazir (No.2)* [2015] UKSC 23; [2016] A.C. 1 at [7], [202] and for more detail, below, para.8-214.

[1297] *Bilta (UK) Ltd v Nazir (No.2)* [2015] UKSC 23; [2016] A.C. 1 at [9], [41]–[45], [181]–[182], [191], [202], [207]. See further below, para.8-214.

[1298] See Watts, in *Unjust Enrichment in Commercial Law* (Degeling and Edelman eds, 2008), Ch.21. For the US position, see DeMott, (2003) 13 Duke J.Comp. and Int.L. 291; Scordato (2004) 10 Fordham and must sometimes be imputed to the principal, and for the present simply cutting through the undergrowth of the cases, the main points that need to be considered are as follows.

(a) It is always necessary to consider the context of the particular legal issue to which imputation of knowledge might be pertinent. There is no overarching principle that a principal is deemed to know at all times and for all purposes that which his agent knows. In this regard the rules of imputation do not exist in a state of nature, such that some reason has to be found to disapply them.[1299] Hence, a principal might be deemed to possess an agent's knowledge for the purpose of liability to outside parties, but not deemed to know those same facts (let alone have condoned any action by the agent) for the purpose of action by the principal against the agent himself.[1300] Further, a distinction needs to be drawn between imputation of knowledge in the context of the formation or execution of a contract between arm's length parties, and imputation in the context of the imposition of tortious or restitutionary liability. Cases of the former sort turn on the express or implied understandings between the parties, and, in the absence of express agreement, can usually be reduced to determining what a party could reasonably expect the counterparty to know, given the state of knowledge of their respective agents.[1301] This type of case is always very fact specific. Cases of the latter sort involve *imposed* obligations, and require the law to formulate relatively firm principles. Questions of knowledge play a particularly prominent role in restitutionary liability, either as an element of the cause of action or as a factor in the application of defences.[1302] There can be cases of a third sort, where the operation of a statutory rule turns on the state of a party's knowledge. There, it is a question of statutory construction what rules of imputation were intended; the context of the provision will be highly relevant, as in the contractual context, but the inference may also be that the legislature intended to borrow the rules used in tortious and restitutionary situations.[1303] Normally, however, it is unsatisfactory to borrow case law from one context for use in another.

(b) Is knowledge acquired outside the agency attributed to the principal? Again, this issue is dependent on context. Where the only relevant parties are those negotiating a contract, whether it is reasonable to expect a principal to be burdened by an agent's pre-mandate knowledge will very much turn on the

---

J. Corporate and Financial L. 129; Loewenstein (2013) 85 U. Colorado L.R. 305.

[1299] A passage approved in *Bilta (UK) Ltd v Nazir (No.2)* [2015] UKSC 23; [2016] A.C. 1 at [44] and [191]. See also *Moulin Global Eyecare Trading Ltd v CIR* [2014] HKCFA 22 at [106], per Lord Walker of Gestingthorpe; *HKSAR v Luk Kin* [2016] HKCFA 81 at [41], per Lord Hoffmann.

[1300] See *Bilta (UK) Ltd v Nazir (No.2)* [2015] UKSC 23; [2016] A.C. 1 at [7], [43], and [208]; *Mobile Sourcing Ltd v Revenue and Customs Commissioners* [2016] UKUT 274 (TCC) at [48].

[1301] See *Jafari-Fini v Skillglass Ltd* [2007] EWCA Civ 261 at [97], per Moore-Bick LJ, Illustration 20; *Bilta (UK) Ltd v Nazir (No.2)* [2015] UKSC 23; [2016] A.C. 1 at [198]; *Hut Group Ltd v Nobahar-Cookson* [2014] EWHC 3842 (QB) at [226]; affd on other points [2016] EWCA Civ 128. For an example where, as a matter of construction, imputation was found inapplicable, see *Infiniteland Ltd v Artisan Contracting Ltd* [2005] EWCA Civ 758; [2006] 1 B.C.L.C. 632.

[1302] On this, see Watts [2017] L.M.C.L.Q. 385.

[1303] See, e.g. *Meridian Global Funds Management Asia Ltd v Securities Commission* [1995] 2 A.C. 500; *G-Star Raw CV v Rhodi Ltd* [2015] EWHC 216 (Ch) at [167] (civil liability for knowingly importing items that infringe copyright); *Jeanswest Corp (New Zealand) Ltd v G-Star Raw CV* [2015] NZCA 14 at [111] (copyright).

context. It is perhaps less likely to be reasonable to burden a principal with imposed obligations (i.e. those owed to outside parties) on the basis of knowledge acquired by an agent before appointment. In the latter context, English law tends to utilise the notion of the agent's authority and not impute pre-mandate knowledge; but it can recognise exceptions which prove extremely difficult to formulate. *Restatement, Third*, follows the view (which was held by Seavey[1304]) that how the knowledge was acquired is irrelevant, provided that it is "material to the agent's duties to the principal".[1305] It will be seen below that much is likely to turn on the scope of the agent's mandate. Sometimes an intermediary may be found not to be agent at all but rather agent for another party to the transaction,[1306] while at the other end of the spectrum the agent may have been delegated the whole carriage of the transaction, with solicitors and canvassing agents often performing roles lying between these two extremes.

(c)   Should there be an exception for cases where the agent is acting in fraud of the principal in the very transaction in which the knowledge is sought to be imputed, with the result that the agent is unlikely, or certain not, to pass on the knowledge? This is often referred to as the "fraud exception". Until recently it had been thought that there should be such an exception. In fact, despite many references to it in the case law, it had always been open to serious question, especially as a defence to tortious or restitutionary claims.[1307] It is undoubtedly true that where an agent has acted in breach of duty to his principal, the law needs to preclude the agent and parties associated with him from asserting that they cannot be sued by the principal because the principal must be deemed to know what his miscreant agent knew. But imputation of knowledge simply does not operate in such circumstances. No exception is therefore necessary there, and even if it were it would need to cover any breach of duty owed the principal by the agent, and not just fraud. For that reason it would be misleading to refer to it as "the *fraud* exception".[1308] The judgments in *Bilta (UK) Ltd v Nazir (No.2)* now establish, in England at least, that there is no general fraud exception to imputation.[1309]

(d)   It is not clear how to deal with situations where the agent (and through him the principal) may claim to have forgotten the information in question. In some circumstances it might seem reasonable to plead forgetfulness, if the knowledge came to the agent a long time before, or he dealt with sufficient such transactions to confound them. It is not just a problem of the law of agency, but it has seldom been addressed specifically.[1310] Sometimes recourse might be had to the burden of proof. Many of the old cases concern

---

[1304] The Reporter for *Restatement, Second*: (1916) 65 U.Pa.L.Rev. 1 at 23 onwards.

[1305] § 5.03.

[1306] *Salkeld Investments Ltd v West One Loans Ltd* [2012] EWHC 2701 (QB) at [45]; *Cassegrain v Gerard Cassegrain & Co Pty Ltd* [2015] HCA 2; (2015) 254 C.L.R. 425 at [41] (husband not agent for wife in fraudulent transfer of property to her).

[1307] See below, para.8-214.

[1308] See further below, para.8-214.

[1309] [2015] UKSC 23; [2016] A.C. 1. For details, see below, para.8-214.

[1310] There is some discussion of the question in the corporate context in *Beach Petroleum NL v Johnson* (1993) 115 A.L.R. 411 at para.22.36. See also, albeit in a slightly different context, *Re Montagu's ST* [1987] Ch. 264.

solicitors dealing with mortgages in their locality in a way that is less common nowadays.[1311] Similar unsettled questions arise in relation to the knowledge of an agent who has ceased to work for the principal before the relevant transaction arises. If the relevant transaction takes place after the departure, the knowledge may no longer be imputed.[1312]

(e) In what circumstances can the knowledge of more than one agent be aggregated in the principal? In causes of action where it is necessary to establish dishonesty in the defendant, it is not, in general, possible to aggregate in the defendant bits of knowledge held separately by the defendant's otherwise innocent agents. The main exemplars are the torts of deceit, and interference with contractual relations, and the equitable action for dishonest assistance in a breach of fiduciary duty.[1313] The position may be different if there is evidence that the principal deliberately structured its business to avoid being affected by inconvenient knowledge.[1314] Aggregation is, it seems, possible where the cause of action does not require proof of dishonesty, as in actions for knowing receipt of trust property in breach of trust.[1315] But again the position may be different where what is at issue are discrete transactions with different employees acting for the principal on each occasion, with no single transaction in itself sufficiently indicating anything amiss.[1316]

Issues of imputed knowledge need to be kept separate from constructive knowledge. Imputed knowledge is concerned with deeming a principal to know that which an agent actually knows. Constructive knowledge is concerned not with things that the principal and his agents know but with things the principal ought to have known about by reason of being put on inquiry. The two concepts can, however, operate in tandem. Such actual knowledge as an agent has can generate in the principal a duty to make further inquiry. Whether the agent's actual knowledge triggers a duty of further inquiry turns on the facts and on the source of the duty to inquire. [1317]

[1311] See e.g. *Warrick v Warrick* (1745) 3 Atk. 291; *Worsley v Earl of Scarborough* (1746) 3 Atk. 392.

[1312] *Crossco No.4 Unltd v Jolan Ltd* [2011] EWHC 803 (Ch) at [172]; affd [2011] EWCA Civ 1619.

[1313] cf. *Real Estate Opportunities Ltd v Aberdeen Asset Managers Jersey Ltd* [2007] EWCA Civ 197; [2007] 2 All E.R. 791 at [50]. As to deceit, see above, para.8-185. See generally Dugdale (2006) 12 N.Z. Business L.Q. 3. See too *Progressive Enterprises Ltd v Commerce Commission* (2009) 9 N.Z. Business L.C. 102,485 (no aggregation for offence requiring mens rea); affd (2010) 9 N.Z. Business L.C. 103,060 at [38]; *McNamara v Auckland City Council* [2012] 3 N.Z.L.R. 701 at [161] and [176] (NZSC) (defence of good faith not circumventable by aggregating knowledge).

[1314] See *Australian Competition and Consumer Commission v Radio Rentals Ltd* (2006) 146 F.C.R. 292 at [179].

[1315] See *National Provincial Bank of England v Jackson* (1886) 33 Ch.D. 1 at 12; *Efploia Shipping Corp Ltd v Canadian Transport Co Ltd* [1958] 2 Ll. L. Rep. 449 at 457; *Krakowski v Eurolynx Properties Ltd* (1995) 183 C.L.R. 563 at 583; *NIML Ltd v Man Financial Australia Ltd* (2006) 15 V.R. 156 at [38]; *Public Trustee v Guardian Trust & Executors Co of New Zealand Ltd* [1939] N.Z.L.R. 613 at 644; affd [1942] N.Z.L.R. 115 (PC). cf. *Commonwealth Bank of Australia v Kojic* [2016] FCAFC 186.

[1316] *Australian Competition and Consumer Commission v Radio Rentals Ltd* (2006) 146 F.C.R. 292 at [179] (no unconscionability in retailer where mildly mentally impaired man buys many items of electrical goods on different visits to the retailer's two stores, dealing with a range of sales people, none of whom appreciates the extent of his disability); *Glencore International AG v MSC Mediterranean Shipping Co SA* [2015] EWHC 1989 (Comm); [2015] 2 Lloyd's Rep. 508 at [23] (knowledge on part of prior agents of third party's practices not imputed for purpose of construction of contract made by later agents).

[1317] For further discussion, see Watts, *Unjust Enrichment in Commercial Law* (Degeling and Edelman

What follows is intended as an account of the English cases. The Article is based in part on the judgment of Hoffmann LJ in *El Ajou v Dollar Land Holdings Ltd*.[1318] This appears to accept the separation off of notification cases as stated in Article 94 above, and to lay down the two categories of cases for the imputation of knowledge stated in Rules (2) and (3) above. It would be misleading in a practitioner's work not to state these categories, which are stated in other books also[1319]; but some reservations are expressed about them below. Rule (1), which did not figure in Hoffmann LJ's account, preserves a general rule of imputation for the reasons stated below; and Rule (4) addresses the relevance of fraud in an agent.

Rule (1): Rationales for imputation   This gives a general indication of an often **8-210** stated approach to this part of the law. Apart from general pragmatic justifications,[1320] two main reasons are given for imputing knowledge to the principal for the purposes of a common law rule. The first is that of the identity of principal and agent. This rather conceptual approach can be explained on the basis that a principal should not be able by using an agent to put himself in a better position than that in which he would have been if he had dealt personally. This is a very old idea in the case law, well illustrated by a dictum of Lord Northington LC's in *Sheldon v Cox*: "[It] is a fixed and settled principle that notice to an agent is notice to the principal. If it were otherwise it would cause great inconvenience, and notice would be avoided in every case by employing agents".[1321] Consistently, knowledge acquired by an agent after the relevant contract has been completed will no more bind the principal than if the principal had itself acquired the knowledge at that stage.[1322] *Aliter*, where the knowledge is acquired before the contract becomes unconditional.[1323] The position is less clear where knowledge is acquired before the principal has provided its consideration and the principal can withdraw from the contract.[1324]

The second explanation is that where an agent receives information which it would be his duty to pass on to his principal, it may be assumed or presumed in favour of the third party, at least in the absence of explicit indications to the contrary, that he has done so.[1325] This explanation may permit the imputation of knowledge acquired outside the agency, which is a key problem of this part of the law. It has been said that such reasoning is "rather a justification of the rule than a reason for it".[1326] It links with the so-called fraud exception discussed below.[1327] With varying indications as to the strength of the supposed presumption, it has a

eds, 2008), Ch.21.
[1318] [1994] 2 All E.R. 685.
[1319] e.g. *Lewin on Trusts* (19th edn), para.42-065.
[1320] e.g. "Policy and the safety of the public": per Lord Brougham LC in *Kennedy v Green* (1834) 3 Myl. & K. 699 at 719.
[1321] (1764) 2 Eden 224 at 228. See too *Boursot v Savage* (1866) L.R. 2 Eq. 134 at 142, per Kindersley VC: "I confess my own impression is, that the principle on which the doctrine rests is this: that my solicitor is alter ego; he is myself; I stand in precisely the same position as he does in the transaction, and therefore his knowledge is my knowledge; and it would be a monstrous injustice that I should have the advantage of what he knows without the disadvantage."; *Vane v Vane* (1873) L.R. 8 Ch.App. 383 at 400. See further Watts (2001) 117 L.Q.R. 300 at 301.
[1322] *Kettlewell v Watson* (1882) 21 Ch.D. 685 at 712.
[1323] *MBF Australia Ltd v Malouf* [2008] NSWCA 214. See also *Forsyth v Blundell* (1973) 129 C.L.R. 477.
[1324] See *Atterbury v Wallis* (1856) 8 De G.M. & G. 454 at 466.
[1325] See, e.g. *Boursot v Savage* (1866) L.R. 2 Eq. 134 at 142; *Rolland v Hart* (1871) L.R. 6 Ch.App. 678.
[1326] Mechem, *Law of Agency* (2nd edn), § 1806.

long history in the cases, but there are as many cases that do not support it, and it was rejected in *El Ajou*.[1328] Hoffmann LJ admitted that there were situations in which a weak presumption that information had been passed on might be applied, but no more, and he treated the reasoning as primarily applicable to notification cases.[1329] On analysis, it is an unsatisfactory explanation for imputation. In the first place, it is apparent from the case law that imputation can occur even though it is clear beyond doubt that the principal was personally unaware of the relevant fact, and that therefore there has not been any communication by the agent. In such circumstances, the rationale would have to work as an irrebuttable presumption,[1330] which is an artifice. Secondly, it is not obvious how obligations as between principal and agent can confer rights on third parties, who are strangers to that relationship. Thirdly, it is unrealistic to assume that there is in fact a duty as between principal and agent that the agent will inform the principal of all matters of relevance to the principal's business that the agent learns; one of the reasons for using agents is to free the principal's time for other things. The first rationale is, therefore, the more satisfactory one.

8-211   **Only knowledge acquired while performing mandate prima facie imputed**   It is implicit in Rule (1) that only knowledge acquired by an agent whilst carrying out tasks for the principal will be imputed.[1331] Knowledge acquired when not acting for the principal, whether acquired before or even during the period of appointment, would not be imputed. Such an approach has been taken in decisions over many years[1332]; though it is rejected by both *Restatement, Second* and *Restatement, Third*.[1333] Rule (1) is consistent with either general rationale discussed in the previous paragraph, but arguably not dictated by them. Another explanation that has been given from time to time, particularly in priority disputes and other restitutionary contexts, is that it is unreasonable to expect a busy agent, such as a solicitor, to recall all information that might be relevant to a client's affairs when it was learned while acting for other clients. This rationale emerged early in judgments of Lord Harwicke LC, in particular *Warrick v Warrick*[1334]:

> "[N]otice should be in the same transaction: this rule ought to be adhered to, otherwise it

---

[1327] See below, para.8-214.

[1328] See *Espin v Pemberton* (1859) 3 De G. & J. 547 at 555; *Rolland v Hart* (1871) L.R. 6 Ch.App. 678 at 681–682; *Boursot v Savage* (1866) L.R. 2 Eq. 134 at 142. For other cases not supporting the presumption as the basis of imputation, see (2001) 117 L.Q.R. 300 at 304–308.

[1329] [1994] 2 All E.R. 685 at 703–704. *Mobile Sourcing Ltd v Revenue and Customs Commissioners* [2016] UKUT 274 (TCC) at [51].

[1330] See *Kettlewell v Watson* (1882) 21 Ch.D. 685 at 705 (presumption irrebuttable).

[1331] For discussion, see Watts [2005] N.Z.L. Rev. 307; Watts [2017] L.M.C.L.Q. 385.

[1332] See, e.g. *Taylor v Yorkshire Insurance Co Ltd* [1913] 2 Ir.R. 1 at 21 and other cases there cited; *Mountford v Scott* (1818) 3 Madd. 34 at 40; *Williamson v Barbour* (1877) 9 Ch.D. 529 (knowledge of new partner that defendant had been defrauding firm not imputed); *Farah Constructions Pty Ltd v Say-Dee Pty Ltd* (2007) 236 C.L.R. 89 at [125] (assumption by court that only knowledge acquired within mandate is imputable); *Hickman v Turn and Wave Ltd* [2011] 3 N.Z.L.R. 318 at [192], reversed on other grounds [2013] 1 N.Z.L.R. 741; *Steel Co Ltd v Pipes NZ Ltd* [2016] NZCA 175 at [28] (knowledge of counterparty's standard terms acquired when agent was acting for former owner of business not carried forward to new owner).

[1333] See *Restatement, Third*, § 5.03.

[1334] (1745) 3 Atk. 291 at 293. See also *Preston v Tubbin* (1684) 1 Vern. 286; *Worsley v The Earl of Scarborough* (1746) 3 Atk. 392: "It is settled, that notice to an agent or counsel who was employed in the thing by another person, or in another business, and at another time, is no notice to his client, who employs him afterwards; and it would be very mischievous if was so, for the man of most practice and greatest eminence would then be the most dangerous to employ."

would make purchasers and mortgagees' titles depend altogether on the memory of their counsellors and agents, and oblige them to apply to persons of less eminence as counsel, as not being so likely to have notice of former transactions."

This led some later judges to suggest that if two matters for separate principals took place so close to one another that the knowledge acquired in the first matter must have been still present in the agent's mind, imputation could occur. So, Lord Eldon LC stated in *Mountfort v Scott*[1335]:

"The Vice-Chancellor in this case appears to have proceeded upon the notion that notice to a man in one transaction is not to be taken as notice to him in another transaction; in that view of the case it might fall to be considered, whether one transaction might not follow so close upon the other, as to render it impossible to give a man credit for having forgotten it. I should be unwilling to go so far as to say, that if an attorney has notice of a transaction in the morning, he shall be held in a Court of Equity to have forgotten it in the evening; it must in all cases depend upon the circumstances."

The tendency nonetheless has been to conform to the understanding that knowledge needs to have been acquired by the agent whilst acting for the principal.[1336] There are, however, some very important notes and qualifications that need to be made about Rule (1). First, the rule is about knowledge acquired by an agent outside any agency for the principal, so that imputation could still occur where the knowledge was acquired while acting for the same principal, albeit in an earlier transaction (subject to issues of forgetfulness).[1337] It will be seen below that there is an important statutory exception to that position. Secondly, the knowledge of an agent who is acting for more than one party to the same transaction is not generally compartmentalised, and is likely to be imputed to both (or more) principals.[1338] There may be circumstances where the agent's duties of confidentiality might provide a reason for not imputing the knowledge to both principals,[1339] but where the knowledge relates to the position of some outside claimant (e.g. possession of an equitable interest in an asset) it is unlikely that the agent's duties of confidentiality could justify prejudicing the position of that party. Thirdly, courts will be resistant to arguments that two connected transactions were nonetheless discrete for the purposes of the rules of imputation. Fourthly, the rule is, in any event, only a starting point. Most of the cases that created the rule have involved solicitors, the scope of whose authority is normally limited. Other case law suggests that where an agent is given responsibility for the carriage of the transaction at issue, the principal may be burdened with whatever knowledge the agent possesses wherever acquired. For

---

[1335] (1818) 3 Madd. 34. See also *Hargreaves v Rothwell* (1836) 1 Keen 154; *Williamson v Barbour* (1877) 9 Ch.D. 529 at 535; *Burnard v Lysnar* [1927] N.Z.L.R. 757.

[1336] See *Fuller v Benett* (1843) 2 Hare 394; *O'Keefe v London & Edinburgh Insurance Co Ltd* [1928] N.I. 85 at 97, per Andrews LJ: "The danger of making the agent's memory of bygone transactions a jury question is obvious, and recollection or forgetfulness by the agent of matters known to him previous to that relation is not allowed to affect the liability of the principal except in certain well-recognised cases."

[1337] See *Brotherton v Hatt* (1706) 2 Vern. 574; *Jennings v Moore* (1708) 2 Vern. 609; affd sub nom. *Blenkarne v Jennens* (1709) 2 Bro. P.C. 278 (HL); *Le Neve v Le Neve* (1748) 1 Ves. Sen. 64; (1748) 3 Atk. 646; *Doe d. Willis v Martin* (1790) 4 T.R. 39; *Rolland v Hart* (1871) L.R. 6 Ch.App. 678.

[1338] In addition to the cases in the preceding footnote, see *Dresser v Norwood* (1864) 17 C.B.(N.S.) 466; *Boursot v Savage* (1866) L.R. 2 Eq. 134; *Belmont Finance Corp v Williams Furniture Ltd (No.2)* [1980] 1 All E.R. 393 at 404 (common director); *Bank of Credit and Commerce International SA v Aboody* [1990] 1 Q.B. 923 at 974–975. See also the cases in fn.1343 below.

[1339] See *Harkness v Commonwealth Bank of Australia Ltd* (1993) 32 N.S.W.L.R. 543 at 555.

example, if it is only through the auspices of the agent that the principal could have obtained the property or rights that are now contested by the claimant, it would be wrong to allow the principal to adopt the agent's actions whilst disowning the agent's knowledge of the claimant's prior rights.[1340] The well-known dictum of Lord Halsbury LC in *Blackburn, Low & Co v Vigors* provides support for such an approach[1341]:

"Some agents so far represent the principal that in all respects their acts and intentions and their knowledge may truly be said to be the acts, intentions, and knowledge of the principal. Other agents may have so limited and narrow an authority both in fact and in the common understanding of their form of employment that it would be quite inaccurate to say that such an agent's knowledge or intentions are the knowledge or intentions of his principal …".

This would provide an explanation for the actual result in the *El Ajou* case, itself a case concerned with knowledge acquired outside the agency, and more convincing than the reasoning actually used in that case, which was to fashion a special rule for companies.[1342] Hoffmann LJ alluded to other situations where a principal can be affected by his agent's knowledge acquired before or outside the agency. These are also somewhat problematic and are the subject of Rules (2) and (3).[1343]

There is relatively little case law on the somewhat different situation where a principal has agents who hold knowledge relevant to a transaction (and acquired that knowledge while acting for the principal) but who are not involved in it. Again, where the only parties involved are those negotiating a contract, the issue will be governed by the reasonable expectations of the parties.[1344] Where, however, what is at issue is the rights of outside parties, the law is less likely to tolerate a situation where a principal would be advantaged by a mere change of personnel.[1345] Plainly, no tolerance is likely to be shown if there were evidence that the principal had deliberately excluded an agent with prior knowledge from participating in the transaction. The position is also different where it is a defendant who is resisting an otherwise valid claim on the basis that the claimant had agents not involved in the transaction who knew the truth as to some matter. So, a principal may bring an action in deceit so long as the agent acting for it was deceived by the defendant,

---

[1340] See, e.g. *Jessett Properties Ltd v UDC Finance Ltd* [1992] 1 N.Z.L.R. 138; *Permanent Trustee Australia Co Ltd v FAI General Insurance Co Ltd* (2001) 50 N.S.W.L.R. 679 at 692–697 (reversed on other issues (2003) 214 C.L.R. 514). cf. *Cassegrain v Gerard Cassegrain & Co Pty Ltd* [2015] HCA 2; (2015) 254 C.L.R. 425 at [41] (where the defendant was (puzzlingly) held to be the purely passive recipient of property, deputing no agency tasks to obtain it).

[1341] (1887) 12 App.Cas. 531 at 537–538. See too *Brittain v Brown* (1871) 24 L.T. 504 at 506, per Cockburn CJ: "I quite agree that where a man employs an attorney or agent, and places him in his own place and treats him as alter ego, there the doctrine contended for would apply, viz., that a principal is bound by the knowledge of his agent. But it is very different when the contract itself is not placed in the hands of an agent, but the agent is, as here, employed about a matter entirely subsidiary and accessory to the contract"; *Grand Trunk Railway Co of Canada v Robinson* [1915] A.C. 740 at 747.

[1342] [1994] 2 All E.R. 685 at 705, Illustration 16. See further below, para.8-215.

[1343] e.g. Illustrations 7–11 and 15; and *Bank of Credit and Commerce International SA v Aboody* [1990] 1 Q.B. 923 at 974–975. But see Law of Property Act 1925 s.199(i)(ii), below, para.8-216.

[1344] See, e.g. *Aste v Montague* (1858) 1 F.&F. 264 (principal able to rely on apparent authority even though some employees not involved in transaction aware of termination of authority). See too the discussion in para.8-215, below.

[1345] See the discussion in para.8-214, below.

even though another of the principal's agents knew the truth.[1346] Similarly, it has already been seen that a principal may have a restitutionary claim to recover a mistaken payment when the paying agent made a mistake, even though some other agent was aware of the true facts.[1347]

Rule (2): Agent's own knowledge material This category, the first mentioned **8-212** by Hoffmann LJ in which previously acquired knowledge or knowledge acquired outside the agency is attributed to the principal, is said to refer to situations where the agent's knowledge affects "the terms or performance" of an authorised contract.[1348] It is said not to rest on imputation, but rather on a special duty resting on agents to insure, who are apparently treated as central examples of the category. This duty is derived from a dictum of Lord Macnaghten in *Blackburn, Low & Co v Vigors*[1349] but although a category of this nature has much to commend it, difficulties of detail were subsequently pointed out by Handley JA in the Court of Appeal of New South Wales in a case in which knowledge of agents acquired outside the agency was imputed to the principal.[1350] First, the view of Lord Macnaghten was a minority view and the majority proceeded by more traditional reasoning in not treating the knowledge of a former agent as that of the principal.[1351] Too much should not however be read into the wording of short judgments in a dispute the answer to which was fairly obvious. Secondly, and more important, non-disclosure by an agent to insure does not affect the "terms or performance" of the contract of insurance, but rather its validity.[1352] Thirdly, one of two other (and older) cases cited[1353] can be said plainly to have been based on general imputation of knowledge rather than on any more limited principle; and neither, though both are in fact examples of an agent entrusted with carrying through a transaction, relates to the agent to insure first mentioned.[1354] In the Australian case the principal was in the end held liable on the basis of an exception where the agent was an "agent to know" or that his knowledge had been purchased.[1355] This however seems rather a vague formula and it may be that a better analysis of this category would base it more generally

---

[1346] See *Nationwide Building Society v Dunlop Haywards Ltd* [2007] EWHC 1374 (Comm); *Baturina v Chistyakov* [2017] EWHC 1049 (Comm) at [149].

[1347] See above, para.8-166.

[1348] See the *El Ajou* case [1994] 2 All E.R. 685 at 702.

[1349] (1887) 12 App.Cas. 531 at 542–543 (Illustration 5), cited in the *El Ajou* case, above, at 703. cf. *Blackburn, Low & Co v Haslam* (1888) 21 Q.B.D. 144. This speech is often said to be the basis of s.19 of the Marine Insurance Act 1906 (replaced from August 2016 by the Insurance Act 2015).

[1350] *Permanent Trustee Australia Co Ltd v FAI General Insurance Co Ltd* (2001) 50 N.S.W.L.R. 679: see esp. para.76 onwards; reversed on other grounds (2003) 214 C.L.R. 514.

[1351] See pp.537–538 and 540–541. This was accepted by Phillips J in *Deutsche Ruckversicherung AG v Walbrook Insurance Co Ltd* [1995] 1 W.L.R. 1017 at 1034, though not as a central point of his judgment. But in *SA d'Intermediaries Luxembourgeois v Farex Gie* [1995] L.R.L.R. 116, Hoffmann LJ adhered to his earlier view: see also Dillon LJ at 142–143, but cf. Saville LJ at 156.

[1352] See *Banque Keyser Ullmann SA v Skandia (UK) Insurance Co Ltd* [1990] 1 Q.B. 665 at 777–781; [1991] 2 A.C. 249 at 280.

[1353] *Dresser v Norwood* (1864) 17 C.B.(N.S.) 466 at 481 (Illustration 3).

[1354] The other is *Turton v L & NW Ry Co* (1850) 15 L.T. (O.S.) 92 (agent to conclude contract of carriage).

[1355] See (2001) 50 N.S.W.L.R. 679 at [94]–[96]; below, para.8-212. This is based on the *Blackburn, Low* case (1887) 12 App.Cas. 531 at 537. See also *Taylor v Yorkshire Insurance Co Ltd* [1913] 2 I.R. 1 at 20–21 (a valuable judgment of Palles CB); *Jessett Properties Ltd v UDC Finance Ltd* [1992] 1 N.Z.L.R. 138; *Body Corporate 398983 v Zurich Australian Insurance Ltd* [2013] NZHC 1109 (reversed on other points [2014] NZSC 147). cf. *Stevenson Brown Ltd v Montecillo Trust* [2017] NZCA 57 at [30].

on the idea that the making of a contract is entrusted to an agent—an instance of the argument raised in the previous paragraph. In such a case the agent's entire knowledge would be relevant, whether acquired during the agency or not. It can also be said that in such situations it is simply the knowledge of the agent that is relevant to the transaction: there is no need to assume it communicated with the principal.[1356] However, it has since been said in the English Court of Appeal that knowledge of an agent to insure acquired otherwise than in his capacity as such agent was not attributable to his principal.[1357] The variation of result and reasoning in these cases can in some cases be explained by the fact that many of them fall into the category of case, alluded to above, concerned with the scope of the obligations of disclosure undertaken between parties to a contract; imputation in such a setting is ultimately a matter of determining what the parties reasonably expected of one another.[1358]

8-213   **Rule (3): Duty to investigate**   Hoffmann LJ's second category is addressed to situations where the principal "has a duty to investigate or make disclosure": if he employs an agent to discharge such a duty, the agent's knowledge will be imputed to him.[1359] The cases on which this category is based however are disparate and raise considerable difficulties. The first case cited is part of a group concerning knowledge of the dangerous characteristics of animals for the purposes of the *scienter* action in tort.[1360] A scrutiny of them does not suggest any principle useful for the other types of case mentioned.

The second type of case covers situations where "there may be something about a transaction by which the principal is 'put on inquiry'".[1361] This can be taken to refer to a very long line of cases involving solicitors. These cases (mostly in the context of priority disputes) have taken the view that if a principal engages the same solicitor as his counterparty, then he can be affected by the solicitor's knowledge of an extraneous party's interests acquired by the solicitor whilst acting for the counterparty even if acquired in an earlier retainer for that counterparty.[1362] The application of these cases in relation to land transactions has now been confined by statute law, because the positive duties of inquiry formerly applied to such transactions were, when coupled with imputation of knowledge, regarded as leading to harsh results.[1363] The standards of inquiry expected of persons dealing in assets other than land are lower, so the mere fact that the solicitor has some relevant knowledge would not necessarily adversely affect the principal. On the other hand, where the solicitor's knowledge is sufficient, for instance, to mean that proceeding with the

---

[1356] See *Permanent Trustee Australia Ltd v Fai General Insurance Co Ltd* (2001) 50 N.S.W.L.R. 679 at [88]–[89].

[1357] *PCW Syndicates v PCW Reinsurers* [1996] 1 W.L.R. 1136 at 1145; see also at 1148; cf. at 1151–1152. But the matter largely turned on s.19 of the Marine Insurance Act 1906, referred to above, which deals with agents to insure, replaced from August 2016 by the Insurance Act 2015. See Macgregor, in Busch, Macgregor and Watts (eds), *Agency Law in Commercial Practice* (2016), Ch.11; Merkin and Gürses (2016) 132 L.Q.R. 445.

[1358] See above, para.8-209; and (2001) 117 L.Q.R. 300, discussing *Arab Bank Plc v Zurich Insurance Co* [1999] 1 Lloyd's Rep. 262, and a number of the other cases referred to above.

[1359] See [1994] 2 All E.R. at 702.

[1360] *Baldwin v Casella* (1872) L.R. 7 Ex. 325; see Illustration 6.

[1361] [1994] 2 All E.R. at 703.

[1362] *Brotherton v Hatt* (1706) 2 Vern. 574; *Jennings v Moore* (1708) 2 Vern. 609; affd sub nom. *Blenkarne v Jennens* (1709) 2 Bro. P.C. 278 (HL); *Le Neve v Le Neve* (1748) 1 Ves. Sen. 64; (1748) 3 Atk. 646; *Doe d. Willis v Martin* (1790) 4 T.R. 39; *Fuller v Benett* (1843) 2 Hare 394; *Rolland v Hart* (1871) L.R. 6 Ch.App. 678, Illustration 8.

[1363] See below, para.8-216.

transaction would involve wilful blindness to a third party's protected interests, imputation may still occur.[1364] The duty of loyalty the agent owes his clients does not extend to suppressing knowledge that, if held by the principal, would involve the dishonest destruction of the property interest of a third party. As for the rationale for imputing knowledge acquired for the other client in an earlier matter, it seems to turn on the difficulty, if not the absurdity, of requiring a claimant to prove that the agent re-acquired knowledge in the current transaction of something the agent well knew from the prior transaction for that same client.[1365]

The third type of case is that of disclosure in connection with insurance: where the principal is under a duty to make disclosure, he may have to disclose not only facts which he himself knows, but also facts "which he could expect to have been told by his agent", for example the master of the ship to be insured.[1366] But, again as pointed out by Handley JA, "the imputation to the principal ... has hitherto been based on the agent's duty to communicate his knowledge to the principal and not the latter's duty of disclosure"[1367]; though for the reasons given above this reasoning is itself unsatisfactory. Cases of this sort,[1368] usually involve only the principal and the insurer, and are essentially cases of construction; the question is, do the parties expect that the insured will have systems in place for receiving information relevant to the insurance and the risks to be insured against? Whether this should extend to knowledge acquired before, or otherwise outside, the agency is problematic. The general assumption in this area seems again to be that it should not do so[1369] unless the agent's knowledge can be said to have been "bought", or he is an "agent to know",[1370] as where a shipmaster is engaged who has prior knowledge of the ship.

Rule (4): Claims by principal against own agent, and fraud of agent   Rule (4)   **8-214** is a modification of the wording that has appeared in editions of this work before the 20th. The earlier wording spoke of a single "fraud exception" to the imputation of knowledge. However, it is clear that the so-called exception has been raised, if not actually applied, in some four different types of situation, in none of which is it straightforward.[1371] The judgments in *Bilta (UK) Ltd v Nazir (No.2)* now make it clear, in England at least, that there is no general fraud exception to imputation.[1372]

The first relates to complaints by the principal himself that his agent has caused

---

[1364] *Bank of Credit and Commerce International SA v Aboody* [1990] 1 Q.B. 923.
[1365] *Dresser v Norwood* (1864) 17 C.B. (N.S.) 466 at 481.
[1366] [1994] 2 All E.R. at 703.
[1367] (2001) 50 N.S.W.L.R. at [76].
[1368] An example given by Hoffmann LJ is *Gladstone v King* (1813) 1 M. & S. 35, Illustration 4; but see this case criticised in the House of Lords in *Blackburn, Low & Co v Vigors* (1887) 12 App.Cas. 531, and by Lord Esher MR in the Court of Appeal (1886) 17 Q.B.D. 553 at 567. A better example is perhaps *Proudfoot v Montefiore* (1867) L.R. 2 Q.B. 511, also summarised in Illustration 4. See in general Marine Insurance Act 1906 ss.18 and 19; *MacGillivray on Insurance Law* (13th edn), para.18-009 onwards. These sections were replaced from August 2016 by the Insurance Act 2015. But the situation must be one where there is a duty to pass on information: see *Australia and New Zealand Bank Ltd v Colonial and Eagle Wharves Ltd* [1960] 2 Lloyd's Rep. 241; *Simner v New India Assurance Co Ltd* [1995] L.R.L.R. 240. See also *Det Danske Hedeselskabet v KDM International Plc* [1994] 2 Lloyd's Rep. 534 (relevance of knowledge in the answer of interrogatories: reference to a person "for whose knowledge" the interrogated party "is responsible", at 538).
[1369] See the *Permanent Trustee* case (2001) 50 N.S.W.L.R. 679 at [87].
[1370] See cases cited in fn.1355 above.
[1371] See in general *Moulin Global Eyecare Trading Ltd v CIR* [2014] HKCFA 22 at [106].
[1372] See *Bilta (UK) Ltd v Nazir (No.2)* [2015] UKSC 23; [2016] A.C. 1 at [9], [41]–[45], [181]–[182], [191], [202], [207].

loss to him by breach of duty; the claim may be against the agent, or a third party which has promoted[1373] or otherwise assisted in, or benefited from, the breach.[1374] The principal is then met with an allegation that he must be deemed to have known what his agent knew or has done, and by inference to have condoned the agent's actions. The fraud exception has been used to reject this argument. This version of the exception is often associated with *Re Hampshire Land Co*,[1375] although the facts of the case do not in fact furnish a good example of it. It is not surprising that defences of this sort have been routinely rejected,[1376] for they have no merit. However, it is suggested that to invoke a fraud exception to deal with them is misconceived. First, there is no reason to limit the "exception" to fraudulent breaches of duty. If this defensive argument had had any merit it would have been equally applicable to honest breaches of duty. The simple point is that, were the principal deemed to possess the agent's knowledge of his own breaches of duty, and thereby to have condoned them, the principal could never successfully vindicate his rights.[1377] Secondly, there is no need for an exception as such. The putative defence that the exception is used to rebut is premised on the fallacy that a principal is prima facie deemed to know at all times and for all purposes that which his agents know. As observed already, imputation has never operated in such a way.[1378] Before imputation occurs, there needs to be some purpose for deeming the principal to know what the agent knows. There is none in this type of case. Reasoning of this sort has now been adopted in the *Bilta* case; there is no exception, rather there is no reason to impute knowledge in these cases.[1379]

The second situation where a fraud exception has appeared is as a defence to property-based claims, including those involving conflicting priorities, and to

---

[1373] See *Wells v Smith* [1914] 3 K.B. 722 at 726, per Scrutton J: "[A] man who tells a lie to another cannot protect himself by saying 'Your agent should have warned you of my lie'" (defendant to deceit action cannot rely on fact one dishonest agent of claimant knew of the untruth); *Renault UK Ltd v Fleetpro Technical Services Ltd* [2007] EWHC 2541 (QB); [2008] Bus. L.R. D17 at [124]; *OMV Petrom SA v Glencore International AG* [2015] EWHC 666 (Comm) at [152] (affd on different points, [2016] EWCA Civ 778).

[1374] See *Brinks-Mat Ltd v Noye* [1991] 1 Bank L.R. 68; *Nationwide Building Society v Dunlop Haywards Ltd* [2007] EWHC 1374 (Comm) (action in deceit); *Bilta (UK) Ltd v Nazir (No.2)* [2015] UKSC 23; [2016] A.C. 1 at [95], [207]; *Burnden Holdings (UK) Ltd v Fielding* [2016] EWCA Civ 557; [2017] 1 W.L.R. 39 at [49] (knowledge of dishonest agents not imputed for purposes of limitation period in action by principal); *Singularis Holdings Ltd v Daiwa Capital Markets Europe Ltd* [2017] EWHC 257 (Ch); [2017] 1 Lloyd's Rep. 226 at [215].

[1375] [1896] 2 Ch. 743, Illustration 21. See note to Illustration 21 below, and Watts (2001) 117 L.Q.R. 300 at 319–320 and in *Unjust Enrichment in Commercial Law* (Degeling and Edelman eds, 2008), Ch.21.

[1376] See *Sharpe v Foy* (1868) L.R. 4 Ch.App. 35; *Re Fitzroy Bessemer Steel Co Ltd* (1884) 50 L.T. 144, Illustration 9; *Houghton v Nothard, Lowe & Wills* [1928] A.C. 1; *Belmont Finance Corp v Williams Furniture Ltd* [1979] Ch. 250; *Nationwide Building Society v Dunlop Haywards Ltd* [2007] EWHC 1374 (Comm) at [75]; *Moore Stephens v Stone & Rolls Ltd* [2008] EWCA Civ 644; [2009] 1 A.C. 1391; [2008] 2 Lloyd's Rep. 319; [2008] 2 B.C.L.C. 461 at [71]–[72]; affd [2009] UKHL 39; [2009] 1 A.C. 1391; *Soods Solicitors v Dormer* [2010] EWHC 502 (QB); *Moulin Global Eyecare Trading Ltd v CIR* [2014] HKCFA 22 at [106]; *Grimaldi v Chameleon Mining NL (No.2)* (2012) 287 A.L.R. 22 at [285]; *JSC BTA Bank v Ablyazov* [2013] EWHC 510 (Comm) at [166].

[1377] See *Stone & Rolls Ltd v Moore Stephens Ltd* [2009] UKHL 39; [2009] 1 A.C. 1391 at [198]; *Tonto Home Loans Australia Pty Ltd v Tavares* [2011] NSWCA 389 at [209]. See further Watts (2001) 117 L.Q.R. 300 at 316–318. See now *Bilta (UK) Ltd v Nazir (No.2)* [2015] UKSC 23; [2016] A.C. 1 at [7], [202].

[1378] cf. *El Ajou v Dollar Land Holdings Plc* [1994] 2 All E.R. 685 at 715, per Hoffmann LJ: "English law has never taken the view that the knowledge of a director [is] ipso facto imputed to the company—see *Powles v Page* (1846) 3 C.B. 16".

[1379] *Bilta (UK) Ltd v Nazir (No.2)* [2015] UKSC 23; [2016] A.C. 1 at [9], [37], [181].

restitutionary claims.[1380] Where the defendant has himself been the victim of his agent's fraud, he invokes the exception to deny being burdened with his agent's knowledge of the claimant's rights. However, it is most doubtful whether such a defence should be allowed in such circumstances. In very few cases has such a defence been decisive, and as far as England and Wales is concerned, anyway, it is not supported by the weight of authority,[1381] nor is it consistent in that context with the principles of vicarious liability.[1382] In this fact pattern, the claimant will usually know nothing of the transaction which might defeat his interests, but the agent of the acquiring party, the defendant, does know of the claimant's interests. There, the mere fact that the recipient's agent was intending also to defraud his principal cannot justify the principal's taking advantage of the agent's actions whilst disowning the agent's knowledge. The principal cannot approbate and reprobate.[1383] It makes no difference that the dishonest agent might be aiming to benefit some third party and not himself. Where, however, the principal has simply been a post-box for the agent's fraud, the principal may be permitted to disown the transaction altogether by invoking the concept of "ministerial receipt".[1384]

The third type of case arises in the context of duties of disclosure in the formation and performance of contracts. As noted above,[1385] in this type of case the courts are essentially attempting to provide a solution to issues the parties might themselves have expressly provided for. The court's task is one of construction, and in such circumstances it might well be appropriate to conclude that it was unreasonable for one party to expect the other to know about something that his agent was deliberately keeping from him.[1386] Each example needs to be decided on its facts, and the cases are strictly of no application outside the contractual context.[1387]

[1380] *Kennedy v Green* (1834) 3 My. & K. 699; *Thompson v Cartwright* (1863) 33 Beav. 178 at 185 (but see the better reasoning on appeal: (1863) 2 De G.J. & S. 10); *Waldy v Gray* (1875) L.R. 20 Eq. 238 at 251–252; *Cave v Cave* (1880) 15 Ch.D. 639 at 644; *Re European Bank Ex p. Oriental Commercial Bank* (1870) L.R. 5 Ch.App. 358 (exception not decisive); *Kwei Tek Chao v British Traders & Shippers Ltd* [1954] 2 Q.B. 459; *Stoneleigh Finance Ltd v Phillips* [1965] 2 Q.B. 537; *Abbey National Plc v Tufts* [1999] 2 F.L.R. 399. See each of these cases criticised or explained: (2001) 117 L.Q.R. 300.

[1381] See *Jennings v Moore* (1708) 2 Vern. 609; affd sub nom. *Blenkarne v Jennens* (1709) 2 Bro. P.C. 278 (HL); *Le Neve v Le Neve* (1747) 1 Ves. Sen. 64; *Doe d. Willis v Martin* (1790) 4 T.R. 39; *Atterbury v Wallis* (1856) 25 L.J.Ch. 792; *Boursot v Savage* (1866) L.R. 2 Eq. 134; *Bradley v Riches* (1878) 9 Ch.D. 189; *Rolland v Hart* (1871) L.R. 6 Ch.App. 678; *Kettlewell v Watson* (1882) 21 Ch.D. 685; *Ex p. Batham* (1888) 6 N.Z.L.R. 342; *Bank of Credit and Commerce International SA v Aboody* [1990] 1 Q.B. 923; *Nathan v Dollars & Sense Ltd* [2008] 2 N.Z.L.R. 557 (noted Watts (2008) 124 L.Q.R. 529); *Permanent Trustee Co Ltd v O'Donnell* [2009] NSWSC 902 at [369], reversed, but not on this point, sub nom. *Tonto Home Loans Australia Pty Ltd v Tavares* [2011] NSWCA 389; *UBS AG (London Branch) v Kommunale Wasserwerke Leipzig GmbH* [2014] EWHC 3615 (Comm) at [616] and [639] (affd [2017] EWCA Civ 1567).

[1382] See *Doe d. Willis v Martin* (1790) 4 T.R. 39 ("without imputing any fraud to Martin, and indeed it is negatived by the verdict, the maxim, that the principal is civilly responsible for the acts of his agent, universally prevails both in Courts of Law and Equity").

[1383] See *Lloyd v Grace, Smith & Co* [1912] A.C. 716 at 738, per Lord Macnaghten; *Nathan v Dollars & Sense Ltd* [2008] 2 N.Z.L.R. 557 at [48]; *Mobile Sourcing Ltd v Revenue and Customs Commissioners* [2016] UKUT 274 (TCC); [2016] B.V.C. 524 at [49].

[1384] See above, para.8-174, and Article 92.

[1385] See above, para.8-209.

[1386] See, e.g. *Group Josi Re v Walbrook Insurance Co Ltd* [1996] 1 Lloyd's Rep. 345; *PCW Syndicates v PCW Reinsurers* [1996] 1 Lloyd's Rep. 241; *SA d'Intermediaries Luxembourgeois v Farex Gie* [1995] L.R.L.R. 116; *Arab Bank Plc v Zurich Insurance Co* [1999] 1 Lloyd's Rep. 262. But cf. *Moore Stephens v Stone & Rolls Ltd* [2008] EWCA Civ 644; [2009] 1 A.C. 1391; [2008] 2 Lloyd's

The fourth type of case embraces those where an agent's knowledge is potentially relevant in the operation of a statutory provision. This type of case raises the same issue as the last category, namely it is impossible to know whether knowledge should be imputed or not without considering the purpose of the provision and how it was intended to operate.[1388] Because the answer turns on the construction of particular statutory wording, which in turn requires regard to statutory context, it is doubtful whether there is utility in invoking a generalised "fraud exception".

Each of the foregoing categories poses a discrete problem. To the extent that in each category there might be grounds for not burdening a principal with his agent's knowledge, it is necessary in each case to determine whether it is only actual dishonesty that suffices to avoid imputation or other degrees of wrongdoing. In the first category, as seen, dishonesty is not necessary. In the second, it is argued that even dishonesty should not preclude imputation of knowledge, but, in any event, the cases make clear that mere suppression of information by the agent will not suffice,[1389] and that one should look to the effect of the acts when committed and not to the result once the fraud is revealed.[1390] In the third and fourth categories, everything turns on the particular contractual or statutory context. It can be said that no exception is likely to be accepted in relation to a company where its sole director and shareholder holds the knowledge.[1391]

8-215   **Agents of companies and large organisations**   The lines of reasoning found in the previous paragraphs may obviously cause special difficulty in the case of agents of companies,[1392] or large organisations, for there may be situations where the information relevant to a transaction is available to some employees or other agents in the company or business but not to others; it may perhaps also have been acquired at an earlier time although still while an agent was engaged for the organisation. It is difficult yet to see clear answers emerging from the case law on these points. In some such cases it may, because of a time gap or a gap between departments (for example, as to renewals of insurance and new proposals), not be appropriate to attribute the information to the organisation when the person handling the particular matter on its behalf was ignorant of it.[1393] Some assistance in such cases may be derived from the cases that have held that a principal is entitled in some

---

Rep. 319; [2008] 2 B.C.L.C. 461 at [72], doubting *Arab Bank Plc v Zurich* on this point (upheld [2009] 1 A.C. 1391).

[1387] For recognition of this, see *Re Bank of Credit and Commerce International SA (No.15); Morris v Bank of India* [2005] EWCA Civ 693; [2005] 2 B.C.L.C. 328 at [124]; *Bilta (UK) Ltd v Nazir (No.2)* [2015] UKSC 23; [2016] A.C. 1 at [198]; *Hut Group Ltd v Nobahar-Cookson* [2014] EWHC 3842 (QB) at [226]; affd on other points [2016] EWCA Civ 128.

[1388] See, e.g. *McNicholas Construction Co Ltd v Customs and Excise Commissioners* [2000] S.T.C. 553 at [55]; *Greener Solutions Ltd v HMRC* [2012] S.T.C. 1056 at [41]; *Moulin Global Eyecare Trading Ltd v CIR* [2014] HKCFA 22 at [106].

[1389] *Atterbury v Wallis* (1856) 25 L.J.Ch. 792; *Rolland v Hart* (1871) L.R. 6 Ch.App. 678 at 682–683; *Espin v Pemberton* (1859) 3 De G. & J. 547 at 555; *Bunbury v Hibernian Bank* [1908] 1 I.R. 261; *Beach Petroleum NL v Johnson* (1993) 115 A.L.R. 411 at [22.34]; *Lebon v Aqua Salt Co Ltd* [2009] UKPC 2; [2009] 1 B.C.L.C. 549 at [26]. See too *Kirschner v KPMG LLP* (2010) 15 N.Y.3d 446.

[1390] *McNicholas Construction Ltd v HMRC* [2000] S.T.C. 523 at [55]; *Greener Solutions Ltd v HMRC* [2012] S.T.C. 1056 at [41].

[1391] *Stone & Rolls Ltd v Moore Stephens Ltd* [2009] UKHL 39; [2009] 1 A.C. 1391 (noted by Watts (2010) 126 L.Q.R. 14; Halpern (2010) 73 M.L.R. 487).

[1392] For application of the basic rules to companies see Illustrations 9, 12, 13 and 14.

[1393] *Malhi v Abbey Life Assurance Co Ltd* [1996] L.R.L.R. 237; distinguishing *Evans v Employers Mutual Life Assn Ltd* [1936] 1 K.B. 505 and other authority; see also *FAME Ins. Co Ltd v Spence* [1958] N.Z.L.R. 735; *Grimaldi v Chameleon Mining NL (No. 2)* (2012) 287 A.L.R. 22 at [675]. See circumstances to have forgotten facts.[1394] There may also be cases where one part of the organisation may have a duty not to disclose to the other.[1395] On the other hand, it has been held that the mere fact that an employee or other agent has left the organisation will not necessarily terminate imputation.[1396] It is again likely to be useful to bear in mind the distinction between imputation in the context of the formation and performance of contracts, and imputation in law the law of property and restitution.[1397]

An issue that has arisen quite frequently, but once more without clear resolution, is the situation where one director of a company knows a relevant fact but others do not. The same issue could arise with other organisations. The starting point seems to be that knowledge held by one director relevant to the position of a third party will generally be imputed to the company.[1398] This may reflect the general idea that the more senior the agent the less appropriate it is to permit the principal to disown inconvenient knowledge. But this is only a starting point, and as usual the question turns on the issue at stake. The same categories of case as are discussed in the preceding paragraph need to be considered. Hence, where it is an issue of a wrong done to a company in respect of which the company is now claiming, the knowledge of a director implicated in the wrongdoing would not be imputed for the purposes of defeating the claim; imputation in such circumstances would operate as a rogue's charter. Similarly, in the context of the creation and performance of contracts, it may in the particular context be unreasonable for one party to assert that the other knew something, let alone agreed to something, by reason of one director's knowledge.[1399] There can be other reasons for not imputing the knowledge of one or more directors. In two well-known cases where imputation did not occur the knowledge related to a matter that was only tangential to a claim being brought by the relevant company. In particular, the defendant, also a company, wanted to deny liability on a contract of loan because it asserted that its management was intending to use the proceeds for ultra vires activity, and that one of the lender's directors, being also a director of the borrower, was aware of the intended use of

---

in general Clarke, *Law of Insurance Contracts* (6th edn), para.20-7C1.

[1394] See above, para.8-209.

[1395] See above, para.6-047 onwards. As to partnerships, see ibid.; Partnership Act 1890 s.16; Lindley and Banks, *Partnership* (19th edn), para.12-24 onwards.

[1396] *Real Estate Opportunities Ltd v Aberdeen Asset Managers Jersey Ltd* [2007] EWCA Civ 197; [2007] 2 All E.R. 791 at [50]. cf. *Crossco No.4 Unltd v Jolan Ltd* [2011] EWHC 803 (Ch) at [172]; affd [2011] EWCA Civ 1619 (knowledge not imputed when director left company before relevant transaction took place); *Premier Motorauctions Ltd v Pricewaterhousecoopers LLP* [2016] EWHC 2610 (Ch); [2017] Bus. L.R. 490 at [54] (company in liquidation negotiating insurance contract not affected by knowledge of ex-director).

[1397] See above, para.8-209.

[1398] See *Belmont Finance Corp v Williams Furniture Ltd (No.2)* [1980] 1 All E.R. 393 at 404; *Marr v Arabco Traders Ltd* (1987) 1 N.Z. Business L.C. 102,732; *ZBB (Australia) Ltd v Allen* (1991) 4 A.C.S.R. 495 at 506–507; *Farrow Finance Co Ltd v Farrow Properties Pty Ltd* (1998) 26 A.C.S.R. 544 at 587; *Jafari-Fini v Skillglass Ltd* [2007] EWCA Civ 261 at [98]; *Lebon v Aqua Salt Co Ltd* [2009] UKPC 2 at [26]; *Tonto Home Loans Australia Pty Ltd v Tavares* [2011] NSWCA 389 at [212].

[1399] See, e.g. *Sycamore Bidco Ltd v Breslin* [2012] EWHC 3443 (Ch) at [388] (directors of company the shares of which were being sold became directors of purchaser; knowledge of transferred directors not imputed to preclude purchaser from complaining about breaches of warranty and misrepresentations made by and on behalf of seller); *Jafari-Fini v Skillglass Ltd* [2007] EWCA Civ 261 at [97]; *PEC Ltd v Asia Golden Rice Co Ltd* [2014] EWHC 1583 (Comm) at [58] (majority of board's knowledge of more junior employee's actions did not bind company where formal resolution of board needed for actual authority).

the funds.[1400] It is, perhaps, not surprising that imputation did not occur in those circumstances. These cases do not create a general principle, contrary to the assumption made in *El Ajou*. In a third case, the issue of law related to the giving of notice, not knowledge, and it was held that no notice was given to a company, Co B, which shared a common officer with the party that might have given notice, Co A, in circumstances where Co A had no wish to give a notice.[1401]

Another approach, applicable only to companies involves asking whether the company *itself* has information. For this purpose the "directing mind" reasoning[1402] has been used and it may be held that since a person of sufficient significance in the company's operations is aware of something, the company itself is. It has been held that the "directing mind" need not (as earlier cases had suggested) be a person with general management and control: it may be necessary only to identify the person who had management and control in relation to the act or omission in point.[1403] But as was suggested earlier in this book, recourse to this sort of reasoning should only be required when construing statutes and other documents[1404]; there may be specific contractual or statutory wording which will work only if a company is identified with particular actors.[1405]

As noted already, the deployment of directing-mind reasoning in the *El Ajou* case was unnecessary because the court assumed that the ultra vires cases, above, were of more general application than they were.

8-216 **Law of Property Act 1925 s.199(1)(II)**[1406]   This section provides that a purchaser of property[1407] for valuable consideration shall not be prejudicially affected by notice of any instrument, fact or thing unless it is within his own knowledge, or would have come to his knowledge if such inquiries or inspections had been made as ought reasonably to have been made by him; or *in the same transaction*[1408] with respect to which a question of notice to the purchaser arises, it has come to the

---

[1400] *Re Marseilles Extension Railway Co Ex p. Crédit Foncier and Mobilier of England* (1871) L.R. 7 Ch.App. 161; *Re David Payne & Co Ltd* [1904] 2 Ch. 608. See the discussion in Watts [2005] N.Z.L. Rev. 307 at 329. As for *Re Hampshire Land Co* [1896] 2 Ch. 743, Illustration 21, see fn.1440, below.

[1401] *Re Fenwick, Stobart & Co, Deep Sea Fishery Co's Claim* [1902] 1 Ch. 507 (notice of dishonour of a bill of exchange).

[1402] See above, paras 1-028 and 8-184. See too *The Dolphina* [2012] 1 Lloyd's Rep. 304 at 341 (Sing. HC).

[1403] *Meridian Global Funds Management Asia Ltd* [1995] 2 A.C. 500 at 507; *El Ajou v Dollar Land Holdings Plc* [1994] 2 All E.R. 685 at 706; *Lebon v Aqua Salt Co Ltd* [2009] UKPC 2; [2009] 1 B.C.L.C. 549 (knowledge of single director imputed) See too *Stone & Rolls Ltd v Moore Stephens Ltd* [2009] UKHL 39; [2009] 1 A.C. 1391.

[1404] See above, paras 1-028 and 8-210. See now *Moulin Global Eyecare Trading Ltd v CIR* [2014] HKCFA 22 at [106]; and *Bunnings Group Ltd v CHEP Australia Ltd* [2011] NSWCA 342 at [110] (knowledge relevant to aspects of company's liability in tort of conversion did not require knowledge in a "directing mind and will").

[1405] See, e.g. *Meridian Global Funds Management Asia Ltd v Securities Commission* [1995] 2 A.C. 500; *Re BCCI (No.15): Morris v Bank of India* [2005] EWCA Civ 836; [2005] 2 B.C.L.C. 328; *Man Nutsfahrzeuge AG v Ernst & Young* [2005] EWHC 2347 at [154]; affd on other points [2007] EWCA Civ 910; [2007] B.C.C. 986; [2008] 2 B.C.L.C. 22; *Jafari-Fini v Skillglass Ltd* [2007] EWCA Civ 261; *Lebon v Aqua Salt Co Ltd* [2009] UKPC 2; [2009] 1 B.C.L.C. 549; and *Regent Leisuretime Ltd v NatWest Finance Ltd* [2003] EWCA Civ 391 at [105].

[1406] Re-enacting Conveyancing Act 1882 s.3. See Nield [2000] Conv. 196; and Watts in *Unjust Enrichment in Commercial Law* (Degeling and Edelman eds, 2008), p.431.

[1407] Unless the context otherwise requires, "property" includes any thing in action and any interest in real or personal property: s.205(1)(xx).

[1408] Emphasis added.

knowledge of his counsel, as such[1409]; or of his solicitor, or other agent, as such, or would have come to the knowledge of his solicitor or other agent, as such, if such inquiries and inspections had been made as ought reasonably to have been made by the solicitor or other agent.[1410] In its own context, particularly of land, it very clearly adopts the traditional position that knowledge acquired outside the scope of the agency will not be imputed.[1411] In one respect it goes further than the common law, since at common law knowledge acquired by an agent in an earlier transaction could be imputed if the agent was acting for the same principal in both transactions.[1412] The rule in the 1925 Act puts the principal who uses agents in a better position than if he acted personally. If he acted personally he would not be permitted to disown knowledge acquired in an earlier transaction, but his agent's knowledge is not carried forward even when the agent was acting for the same principal both times and indubitably has not forgotten the relevant information. This seems insupportable but a remedy would require statutory amendment.

Illustrations

(1) An agent of an insurance company negotiated a contract of insurance with a man who had lost the sight of an eye. Held, that company must be deemed to have had notice that the assured had lost the sight of an eye, and that it could not avoid the contract on the ground of non-disclosure by him of that fact.[1413] **8-217**

(2) An insurance proposal form signed by the proposer contained untrue answers which were warranted to be true and which formed the basis of the contract. The answers were filled in by the insurance company's agent, whom the proposer had required or permitted to fill in the form after informing him of the true facts. Held, that the company were entitled to repudiate liability on the ground of the untrue answers. The agent, in filling in the form, was the agent of the proposer. If the agent knew that the answers were untrue, he was committing a fraud which prevented his knowledge being the knowledge of the company; if he did not know, he had no knowledge to be imputed to the company.[1414]

(3) A broker bought goods from a factor, knowing from other experience that he

---

[1409] i.e. as his agent; see *Re Cousins* (1886) 31 Ch.D. 671; *Taylor v London & County Banking Co* [1901] 2 Ch. 231; cf. *Meyer v Charters* (1918) 34 T.L.R. 589.

[1410] See *Maxfield v Burton* (1873) L.R. 17 Eq. 15.

[1411] See the provision applied in *Halifax Mortgage Services Ltd v Stepsky* [1996] Ch. 207; and *Barclays Bank Plc v Thomson* [1997] 4 All E.R. 816.

[1412] See, e.g. *Le Neve v Le Neve* (1747) 1 Ves. Sen. 64.

[1413] *Bawden v London, Edinburgh & Glasgow Ass. Co* [1892] 2 Q.B. 534. And see *Hough v Guardian Fire & Life Ass. Co* (1902) 18 T.L.R. 273; *Holdsworth v Lancashire & Yorkshire Insurance Company* (1907) 23 T.L.R. 521; *Thornton-Smith v Motor Union Insurance Co Ltd* (1913) 30 T.L.R. 139; *Golding v Royal London Auxiliary Insurance Co Ltd* (1914) 30 T.L.R. 350; *Keeling v Pearl Life Ass. Co Ltd* (1923) 129 L.T. 573. But these cases became doubtful after *Newsholme Bros v Road Transport & General Ins. Co Ltd* [1929] 2 K.B. 356, Illustration 2, and represent a view of the facts which was subsequently less easily taken. Thus in *Newsholme*'s case Scrutton LJ said: "The decision in *Bawden*'s case is not applicable to a case where the agent himself, at the request of the proposer, fills up the answers in purported conformity with information supplied by the proposer". See Clarke, *Law of Insurance Contracts* (6th edn), para.10-2 onwards; *MacGillivray on Insurance Law* (13th edn), para.18-022 onwards.

[1414] *Newsholme Bros v Road Transport & General Ins. Co Ltd* [1929] 2 K.B. 356 (where there is a full review of the authorities); *Biggar v Rock Life Ass. Co* [1902] 1 K.B. 516; *Jumna Khan v Bankers and Traders Insurance Co Ltd* (1925) 37 C.L.R. 451; *Dunn v Ocean Accident & Guarantee Ltd* was selling on behalf of a principal. Held, that the principal for whom the broker acted must be deemed to have had notice that the factor was not selling his own goods.[1415]

(4)   A ship was driven on a rock and damaged. The master afterwards wrote a letter to the owner, but did not communicate the fact of the ship having been damaged, and, subsequent to the receipt of the letter, the owner insured the ship. Held, that the master ought to have communicated the fact, and that therefore the owner must be deemed to have had knowledge of it at the time of the insurance.[1416] So, where an agent shipped goods, and, having heard of a loss, purposely refrained from telegraphing to the principal because he thought it might prevent him from insuring, it was held that it was his duty to have telegraphed, and that an insurance effected by the principal after the time when he would have received the telegram was void on the ground of non-disclosure of material facts.[1417]

(5)   A broker was employed to effect an insurance, but did not effect it. Subsequently, another broker effected a policy in respect of the same risk on behalf of the same principal. It was sought to avoid the policy on the ground of the non-disclosure of material fact which had come to the knowledge of the firstmentioned broker in the course of his employment, but which he had not communicated to the principal, and which was not known either to the principal or to the broker who effected the policy. Held, that the policy was valid, there being no duty on the first broker to communicate the knowledge he had acquired.[1418]

(6)   A had a dog, which was kept at his stables under the care and control of his coachman. The coachman's knowledge of the ferocity of the dog was

---

(1933) 50 T.L.R. 32; *Facer v Vehicle & General Insurance Co* [1965] 1 Lloyd's Rep. 113; *O'Connor v BDB Kirby & Co* [1972] 1 Q.B. 90. This is perhaps the prevailing view. But it does not always yield just results, and in some contexts and countries, e.g. where illiteracy is prevalent, it must yield most unfair results. Attempts are sometimes therefore made to evade it, on grounds which are not very clear: see *Stone v Reliance Mutual Insurance Society Ltd* [1972] 1 Lloyd's Rep. 469 (noted (1972) 88 L.Q.R. 462; Tan Lee Meng (1975) 17 Malaya L.Rev. 104); *Blanchette v CIS Ltd* [1973] S.C.R. 833, following *Stone*'s case; *Woolcott v Excess Insurance Co Ltd* [1979] 1 Lloyd's Rep. 231; *Deaves v CML Fire & General Insurance Co Ltd* (1978) 143 C.L.R. 24; *Moxness v Cooperative Fire and Casualty Co* (1979) 95 D.L.R. (3d) 365; Jeyeretnam [1991] 2 M.L.J. lxvii, suggesting a distinction between situations where the information disclosed to the agent is contradicted by the signed proposal form and situations where the information supplements or clarifies the contents of the form; Clarke, above; Adams [1999] J.B.L. 215. Clauses providing that the person filling in the form is the agent of the proposer are probably not caught by s.3 of the Misrepresentation Act 1967, which gives the court discretion to disallow reliance on certain exemption clauses: cf. *Overbrooke Estates Ltd v Glencombe Properties Ltd* [1974] 1 W.L.R. 1335; *Collins v Howell-Jones* [1981] E.G.D. 207. It is not yet clear just how much reform of this older law has resulted from the Insurance Act 2015 ss.3 to 6.

[1415] *Dresser v Norwood* (1864) 17 C.B.(N.S.) 466. See this case explained in *El Ajou v Dollar Land Holdings Plc* [1994] 2 All E.R. 685 at 702. See also *Apthorp v Neville & Co* (1909) 23 T.L.R. 575 (printing contract: agent knew manuscript defamatory).

[1416] *Gladstone v King* (1813) 1 M. & S. 35 But see para.8-213 above.

[1417] *Proudfoot v Montefiore* (1867) L.R. 2 Q.B. 511.

[1418] *Blackburn, Low & Co v Vigors* (1887) 12 App.Cas. 531; cf. *Blackburn, Low & Co v Haslam* (1888) 21 Q.B.D. 144. See Comment above. See also *Wilson v Salamandra Ass. Co of St Petersburg* (1903) 88 L.T. 96 (knowledge of Lloyd's agents not imputed to underwriters); *Glencore International AG v MSC Mediterranean Shipping Co SA* [2015] EWHC 1989 (Comm); [2015] 2 Lloyd's Rep. 508 at [23].

equivalent to A's knowledge.[1419] So, where the wife of A occasionally attended to his business, which was carried on upon premises where a dog was kept, and B made a complaint to her, for the purpose of its being communicated to A, that the dog had bitten B's nephew, it was held that that was evidence of scienter on the part of A.[1420] So also, where complaints were made of a publican's dog to his barman.[1421] But the mere fact that a servant knows a dog to be dangerous is no evidence of scienter on the part of the master, where the servant has nothing to do with the care or control of the dog, and has not the control of the premises or place where it is kept.[1422]

(7)   The solicitor of a judgment creditor, having issued execution against the debtor, instructed A, a solicitor at the place where the execution was levied, to take an assignment of the goods seized from the sheriff. A did so, after having received notice of an act of bankruptcy by the debtor. Held, that the creditor must be deemed to have taken the assignment with notice of the act of bankruptcy.[1423] So, if a solicitor, with the consent of his client, puts his managing clerk in his place to conduct and manage a matter, notice of an act of bankruptcy to the clerk operates as notice to the solicitor and to the client.[1424]

(8)   A solicitor induced a client to advance money on a mortgage of land which he held as trustee and afterwards induced another client to advance money on the same land. Held, that the last-mentioned client must be deemed to have had notice of the prior mortgage.[1425]

(9)   Where the directors of a company took part in a misfeasance against the company, it was held that their knowledge did not operate as notice to the company of the misfeasance.[1426]

(10)   A solicitor sells or mortgages property, and himself draws the purchase or mortgage deed and carries the transaction through on behalf, and with the consent, of the purchaser or mortgagee. The purchaser or mortgagee is deemed to have notice of all incumbrances known to the solicitor, even if the solicitor fraudulently conceals them.[1427] But the mere fact that the purchaser or mortgagee employs no solicitor does not mean that, when the vendor or

---

[1419] *Baldwin v Casella* (1872) L.R. 7 Ex. 325; Animals Act 1971 s.2(2). See North, *The Modern Law of Animals* (1972), p.58 onwards.

[1420] *Gladman v Johnson* (1867) 36 L.J.C.P. 153. It seems that this and the following case are still relevant despite the wording of s.2(2) of the Animals Act 1971; North, above, p.66 onwards.

[1421] *Applebee v Percy* (1874) L.R. 9 C.P. 647.

[1422] *Stiles v Cardiff Steam Navigation Co* (1864) 33 L.J.Q.B. 310; *Cleverton v Uffernel* (1887) 3 T.L.R. 509; *Colget v Norrish* (1886) 2 T.L.R. 471; North, above, p.62 onwards. See also *The Cawood III* [1951] P. 270 (knowledge of lightermen as to warning notice on jetty not attributed to employers); *Diment v N.H. Foot Ltd* [1974] 1 W.L.R. 1927 (knowledge of agents regarding user of right of way not attributed to absent owner of land). cf. *The Gudermes* [1991] 1 Lloyd's Rep. 456 (knowledge of appointed inspectors that ship had no cargo heating arrangements attributed to principals: decision reversed [1993] 1 Lloyd's Rep. 311).

[1423] *Brewin v Briscoe* (1859) 2 E. & E. 116; *Rothwell v Timbrell* (1842) 1 Dowl.(N.S.) 778.

[1424] *Re Ashton Ex p. McGowan* (1891) 64 L.T. 28; *Pike v Stephens* (1848) 12 Q.B. 465; *Pennell v Stephens* (1849) 7 C.B. 987.

[1425] *Rolland v Hart* (1871) L.R. 6 Ch.App. 678.

[1426] *Re Fitzroy Bessemer Steel Co Ltd* (1884) 50 L.T. 144.

[1427] *Atterbury v Wallis* (1856) 25 L.J.Ch. 792; *Re Weir, Hollingworth v Willing* (1888) 58 L.T. 792; *Boursot v Savage* (1866) L.R. 2 Eq. 134 (see (1916) 65 U. Pa.L.Rev. 34); *Dryden v Frost* (1837) 3 M. & C. 670; *Sheldon v Cox* (1764) 2 Eden 224; *Dixon v Winch* [1900] 1 Ch. 736. Some of the distinctions taken are not convincing. See also *Burnard v Lysnar* [1927] N.Z.L.R. 757 (knowledge by solicitor of true nature of transaction).

mortgagor is a solicitor and prepares the documents, he constitutes such vendor or mortgagor his solicitor.[1428]

(11) A solicitor who was employed to transfer a mortgage knew that there were incumbrances on the property subsequent to such mortgage. Held, that his knowledge did not operate as notice of the incumbrances to the transferee, because the incumbrances were not material to the transfer, for which alone the solicitor was employed.[1429]

(12) The secretary of a company, while attending a funeral as a relative of the deceased, acquires at a subsequent meeting of relatives at which the will and other documents are read out by a solicitor, knowledge of an equitable assignment relevant to the company's business. That does not operate as notice to the company of such facts.[1430]

(13) A company, X Ltd, buys assets from Y at an overvalue in order that Y would thereby have funds that could be used to buy shares in X Ltd. It is illegal for X Ltd to give financial assistance in the purchase of its shares in this way. Y uses the money received to buy shares in X Ltd from Z Ltd. Z Ltd is sued as a knowing receiver of the X Ltd's money under an illegal scheme. Z Ltd was held imputed with the knowledge of J, who was one of the directors of both X Ltd and Z Ltd. X Ltd is not, however, deemed to have consented to J's actions.[1431]

(14) Directors of a banking company who had no voice in the management of the accounts acquired knowledge of certain circumstances relating to the accounts. Held, that this did not operate as notice of such circumstances to the company.[1432]

(15) On the sale of land, one firm of solicitors acts for the vendor, another for the purchaser. The two firms are in fact constituted by the same two partners. Knowledge acquired by one firm in acting for the vendor is not to be attributed via the other firm to the purchaser.[1433]

(16) Money which in fact consists of misappropriated trust funds is lent to a company. It is sought to charge the company with knowing receipt of trust property.[1434] The fact that the funds were misappropriated is known for other reasons to a Swiss "fiduciary agent" who acts as broker in the transaction. He is also a director and chairman of the company, is claimed to be the ultimate beneficial owner of the company and signed the relevant agreement regarding the loan. Although as broker he has a duty to disclose the facts to the company and does not do so, the company itself has no duty to inquire into their provenance and hence has no notice through him as their broker in the

---

[1428] *Espin v Pemberton* (1859) 3 De G. & J. 547; *Hewitt v Loosemore* (1851) 9 Hare 449. But he may be affected by such notice as he would have had had he employed a solicitor: *Kennedy v Green* (1834) 3 Myl. & K. 699; *Boursot v Savage*, above.

[1429] *Wyllie v Pollen* (1863) 32 L.J.Ch. 782; *Brittain v Brown & Millar* (1871) 24 L.T. 504. See also *Wythes v Labouchere* (1859) 3 De G. & J. 593; *Wells v Smith* [1914] 3 K.B. 722; *Wilkinson v General Accident, etc., Corp* [1967] 2 Lloyd's Rep. 182; *The Hayle* [1929] P. 275.

[1430] *Société Générale de Paris v Tramways Union Co* (1884) 14 Q.B.D. 424.

[1431] *Belmont Finance Corp v Williams (No.2)* [1980] 1 All E.R. 393. See too *Lebon v Aqua Salt Co Ltd* [2009] UKPC 2; [2009] 1 B.C.L.C. 549.

[1432] *Powles v Page* (1846) 3 C.B. 16; *Re Carew's Estate Act* (1862) 31 Beav. 39. cf. *Ex p. Agra Bank, Re Worcester* (1868) L.R. 3 Ch.App. 555.

[1433] *Campbell v M'Creath* 1975 S.C. 81.

[1434] See Article 116.

matter. But his position as a director and chairman of the company acting in connection with this transaction means that he is for this purpose the "directing mind and will" of the company, and the company itself has direct knowledge, not through an agent, that trust funds are involved, sufficient to make it liable for knowing receipt.[1435]

(17) A barrister's knowledge that the judge hearing a case was the brother of a partner of a law firm that was party to indirectly connected proceedings was imputed to the client, precluding the client from later raising an issue of bias against the judge.[1436]

(18) A building society lends on the basis of property valuations that proved fraudulent. One of the society's employees, but not the person who approved the loans, may have been aware of the fraudulent basis to the valuations. The knowledge of that employee was not imputed to the society, which remained able to sue the company that prepared the valuations in the tort of deceit.[1437]

(19) An employer is sued for breach of a duty of care to take reasonable steps to prevent psychiatric injury to an employee. Such injury results from severe racial harassment and intimidatory conduct by a colleague. Knowledge of other employees who were not, however, in the chain of command that the harassment was taking place was not imputed to the employer. Vicarious liability for intentional infliction of emotional harm was, however, upheld, in relation to which imputation was not a requirement.[1438]

(20) A loan contract required the borrower to disclose all facts relevant to the fulfilment of conditions attached to the contract. A bribe was found to have been paid by an employee of the borrower to get officers of the lender to waive certain conditions. The sole director of the borrower was aware of the bribe, and his knowledge entailed that the borrower was in breach of its contractual disclosure obligations. The issue of imputation was a question of construction of the contract.[1439]

(21) A loan made between related companies, which had four directors and a company secretary in common, was challenged some 12 years later on the basis that the borrowing had not been formally approved by the shareholders of the borrower as its articles of association required. The secretary's knowledge of the failure to follow correct procedures was not imputed to the lending company.[1440]

(22) X makes a marriage settlement under which the children of the marriage will inherit upon X's death. Twenty-five years' later, following the death of X's

---

[1435] *El Ajou v Dollar Land Holdings Plc* [1994] 2 All E.R. 685; following on the first point *Re David Payne & Co Ltd* [1904] 2 Ch. 608. See above, para.8-215.

[1436] *Smits v Roach* (2006) 228 A.L.R. 262 (HCA). The case may simply have raised issues of a barrister's apparent authority to waive objections to the composition of the tribunal.

[1437] *Nationwide Building Society v Dunlop Haywards Ltd* [2007] EWHC 1374 (Comm).

[1438] *Nationwide News Pty Ltd v Naidu* (2007) 71 N.S.W.L.R. 471.

[1439] *Jafari-Fini v Skillglass Ltd* [2007] EWCA Civ 261.

[1440] *Re Hampshire Land Co* [1896] 2 Ch. 743. This is treated as a leading authority on the fraud exception to imputation, above, para.8-215, though it is difficult to see how the company's secretary's failures were fraudulent in any way, nor was he the only officer in common between the companies. A better explanation of the case would seem to be that after some 12 years all shareholders in the borrower had become aware of, and informally approved, the loan. The borrower could also have been subject to a restitutionary claim.

wife, X marries Y purporting to settle the same property on the same terms. This may have been a fraud on Y by X, as well as on the children of the first marriage, X hoping no one would know of the double settlement before he died. It was held that Y was bound by her solicitor's knowledge of the first settlement, she having used the same solicitor as her husband.[1441]

(23) A son residing in London uses his father, resident in Leicestershire, to negotiate the purchase of land in the county. The father learns that the vendor has already agreed to sell the land to C. In action by C to restrain the sale, the father's knowledge is imputed to the son.[1442]

5. INTERFERENCE WITH AGENT BY THIRD PARTY AND INVOLVEMENT IN AGENT'S BREACH OF DUTY

Article 96

RIGHTS OF PRINCIPAL WHERE THIRD PARTY IMPLICATED IN AGENT'S BREACH OF DUTIES

8-218 (1) A contract made or act done by an agent which is, to the knowledge of the other party involved, in violation of the agent's equitable duties to his principal entitles the principal to equitable remedies against the third party.[1443]

(2) Where an agent is induced by bribery (or a secret commission) to depart from his duty to his principal, the third party who bribed or promised the bribe to the agent is liable at common law and equity jointly and severally with the agent to the principal

  (a) in restitution, for the bribe; or

  (b) in tort, for any loss sustained by the principal from entering into the transaction in respect of which the bribe was given.[1444]

Comment

8-219 **Relationship with common law claims** The material covered in this Article is mainly addressed to aspects of the equitable liability of third parties for involvement in breaches of duty by an agent. It should be observed that many of the cases where equity intervenes are ones where there will also be common law liability. This is apparent from Rule (2), addressed to bribes. It is obvious too that where an agent acts in breach of his duty of loyalty he may also act without authority, including by reason of dishonesty.[1445] In such circumstances, the relevant dealing will, in

---

[1441] *Le Neve v Le Neve* (1748) 1 Ves. Sen. 64.

[1442] *Merry v Abney* (1663) 1 Ch. Cas. 38.

[1443] *Panama & South Pacific Telegraph Co v India Rubber, etc., Co* (1875) L.R. 10 Ch.App. 515. See Comment and Illustrations 1–4. There are terse but similar provisions entitling the principal to avoid the contract in the PECL art.3:205 (where part of the statement about common law on p.211 is incorrect), in the UNIDROIT Principles art.2.2.7; and in the DCFR, II, 6:109.

[1444] *Mahesan v Malaysian Government Officers' Co-operative Housing Society Ltd* [1979] A.C. 374; see below. Much litigation on bribery has occurred in the context of the conflict of laws. See, e.g. *Lemenda Trading Co Ltd v African Middle East Petroleum Co Ltd* [1988] Q.B. 448; *Arab Monetary Fund v Hashim* [1996] 1 Lloyd's Rep. 589; *Dubai Aluminium Co Ltd v Salaam* [2002] UKHL 48; [2003] 2 A.C. 366; *Grupo Torras SA v Al Sabah (No.5)* [2001] Lloyd's Rep. Bank. 36. For a valuable survey of civil liability in respect of bribery, see Berg [2001] L.M.C.L.Q. 27.

[1445] See Article 23.

the absence of apparent authority or some other exception, be ineffective either to create a contract or to pass property at law in assets intended to be subject to the dealing. The principal may have claims against a third party in conversion or money had and received.[1446] Another potentially relevant common law claim against a third party is the action for inducing a breach of contract, in this case the contract between principal and agent. But the development over time of parallel claims in equity has assumed increasing importance. So, in many cases where there have been dispositions without authority, the principal may prefer to use equitable claims to follow the property, or to sue the third party in what is usually called "knowing receipt". Commonly, the basis of equity's intervention in such cases has been breach of fiduciary duty, but breach of fiduciary duty is probably not essential to equitable intervention, except perhaps where the most that can be alleged against the third party is dishonest assistance in the agent's wrongdoing. More is said on these topics in Article 88 and in Article 116, the latter Article being concerned with an agent's liabilities, but in circumstances where the agent is that of the third party, not of the original principal. Much of this material is as applicable to third parties as to agents, but for convenience, it is treated in the next chapter.

Rule (1): Equitable claims   Apart from those just addressed, there are a number   **8-220**
of circumstances in which third parties can find themselves implicated in an agent's breach of equitable duty. The most serious of these is involvement in an agent's breach of the duty of loyalty—a failure (not merely one of negligence) to act in the principal's best interests.[1447] A transaction, not necessarily disloyal but affected by a conflict of interest, including one under which an agent receives an incidental benefit, is another example. A third type of case has traditionally been called a "fraud on a power", although again dishonesty need not be shown.[1448] This concept responds to an exercise of powers that is not disloyal but which involves action that equity concludes is contrary to the purposes for which the relevant power was given (hence, the alternative label, "proper purposes doctrine"). The concept of authority, the central focus of agency, turns on the terms of the mandate given by the principal, and on honesty in the exercise of the mandate, whereas the duty of loyalty and the proper purposes doctrine seek to control the use of the mandate for purposes not expressly precluded by the mandate but foreign to what is perceived as its underlying purposes.[1449] Clear distinctions between the two concepts are not always easy to draw, and certainly conscious failure to act in the principal's best interests will usually involve a finding of dishonesty, thereby triggering liability at common law as well.[1450] Historically, the principal applications of the proper purposes

---

[1446] See e.g. *Matthews v Gibbs* (1860) 30 L.J.Q.B. 55; *Heinl v Jyske Bank (Gibraltar) Ltd* [1999] Lloyd's Rep. Bank. 511 at 521, per Nourse LJ; citing dicta of Slade and Browne-Wilkinson LJJ in *Rolled Steel Products (Holdings) Ltd v British Steel Corp Ltd* [1986] Ch. 246 at 295, 297 and 304. See also Article 88.

[1447] See above, para.6-034. As to dishonesty not being an essential element, see *State of South Australia v Clark* (1996) 66 S.A.S.R. 199; *Bishopsgate Investment Management Ltd v Maxwell (No.2)* [1994] 1 All E.R. 261.

[1448] See *Farwell on Powers* (Farwell and Archer eds, 3rd edn); Thomas, *Powers* (2nd edn); Nolan [2009] C.L.J. 293; Devonshire (2007) 22 N.Z.U.L.R. 496 (trustee powers only).

[1449] See the valuable discussion by Nolan in [2009] C.L.J. 293 at 297 onwards. See too above, para.3-011; *Senex Holdings Ltd v National Westminster Bank Plc* [2012] EWHC 131 (Comm); [2012] 1 All E.R. (Comm) 1130, Illustration 9.

[1450] See, e.g. *Criterion Properties Plc v Stratford UK Properties LLC* [2004] UKHL 28; [2004] 1 W.L.R. 1846 at [2] and [30]; noted by Watts (2005) 120 L.Q.R. 4. At first instance this case was argued on doctrine have involved trustees and company directors.[1451] In principle, the doctrine could apply to any fiduciary, although in practice the issue is most likely to arise with those in positions that confer broad discretionary powers.[1452] The onus of proving an improper purpose lies on the claimant.[1453] Where there are co-agents, such as a board of directors, it seems that the improper purpose must have actuated a majority of the board.[1454] The necessary causative connection between the improper purpose and the transaction being impugned remains unsettled.[1455]

8-221   Effect of breach of equitable duty   Although it is common to say that a contract affected by a breach of equitable duty is voidable, it seems that something may turn on the type of duty infringed by the agent. While a simple undisclosed conflict of interest makes the contract merely voidable,[1456] active disloyalty in the agent,[1457] and, it seems, fraud on a power, make the contract void at equity.[1458] In the latter situations, it would normally be possible for the claimant to follow money or other property transferred, or to sue for knowing receipt, without first needing to rescind any contract with the third party.[1459] Apart from declaring a contract void, or setting it aside,[1460] equity can respond in a variety of ways against third parties who involve themselves in an agent's breaches of equitable duty, including withhold-

---

the basis of fraud on a power, but in the House of Lords it became apparent that questions of actual authority were at issue.

[1451] In relation to directors, the leading cases are *Howard Smith Ltd v Ampol Petroleum Ltd* [1974] A.C. 821, Illustration 8; and *Eclairs Group Ltd v JKX Oil & Gas Plc* [2015] UKSC 71; [2016] 1 B.C.L.C. 1; noted Nolan (2016) 132 L.Q.R. 369; Worthington [2016] C.L.J. 213. See too *Re Sherborne Park Co Ltd* [1987] B.C.L.C. 82; *Roadchef (Employee Benefits Trustees) Ltd v Hill* [2014] EWHC 109 (Ch) at [123] (directors of trustee company transfer shares to another company for purpose foreign to trust). For further detail, see *Gower's Principles of Modern Company Law* (10th edn), at para.16-22 onwards; Nolan, in *The Realm of Company Law* (Rider ed., 1998).

[1452] For the possible application of the doctrine to others than fiduciaries, see Nolan [2009] C.L.J. 293 at 313.

[1453] *Australian Metropolitan Life Assurance Co Ltd v Ure* (1923) 33 C.L.R. 199 at 206 and 219.

[1454] *Howard Smith Ltd v Ampol Petroleum Ltd* [1974] A.C. 821 at 831; *Roadchef (Employee Benefits Trustees) Ltd v Hill* [2014] EWHC 109 (Ch) at [129]. cf. the position at common law in relation to conflict of interest: *Benson v Heathorn* (1842) 1 Y. & C. Ch. Cas. 326.

[1455] See *Eclairs Group Ltd v JKX Oil & Gas Plc* [2015] UKSC 71; [2016] 1 B.C.L.C. 1.

[1456] *Hely-Hutchinson v Brayhead Ltd* [1968] 1 Q.B. 549 at 595; *Guinness Plc v Saunders* [1990] 2 A.C. 663 at 697; *Charles Terence Estates Ltd v Cornwall Council* [2012] EWCA Civ 1439; [2013] 1 W.L.R. 466 at [47] (exercise of local authority powers).

[1457] *Rolled Steel Products (Holdings) Ltd v British Steel Corp* [1986] Ch. 246; *Guinness Plc v Saunders* [1990] 2 A.C. 663 at 702, Illustration 13 to Article 75; *Houghton v Fayers* [2000] 1 B.C.L.C. 511; *J.J. Harrison (Properties) Ltd v Harrison* [2001] EWCA Civ 1467; [2002] 1 B.C.L.C. 162; *GHLM Trading Ltd v Maroo* [2012] EWHC 61 (Ch) at [171].

[1458] For authorities and discussion, see Nolan [2009] C.L.J. 293 at 316 onwards; *Roadchef (Employee Benefits Trustees) Ltd v Hill* [2014] EWHC 109 (Ch) at [131]. The position in relation to issues of company shares appears to be different: see *Bamford v Bamford* [1970] Ch. 212 (voidable only); cf. *Residues Treatment & Trading Co Ltd v Southern Resources Ltd (No.4)* (1989) 14 A.C.L.R. 569; and the discussion in Nolan [2009] C.L.J. 293 at 319–320.

[1459] See, e.g. *Belmont Finance Corp v Williams Furniture Ltd (No.2)* [1980] 1 All E.R. 393; *Rolled Steel Products (Holdings) Ltd v British Steel Corp* [1986] Ch. 246; *Houghton v Fayers* [2000] 1 B.C.L.C. 511.

[1460] *Re Panama and South Pacific Telegraph Co v India Rubber, Gutta Percha and Telegraph Works Co* (1875) L.R. 10 Ch.App. 515; *Smith v Sorby* (1875) 3 Q.B.D. 552n, Illustration 2; *Taylor v Walker* [1958] 1 Lloyd's Rep. 490, Illustration 4; *Armagas Ltd v Mundogas SA (The Ocean Frost)* [1986] A.C. 717 at 742–743; *Logicrose Ltd v Southend United Football Club* [1988] 1 W.L.R. 1256 at 1260 (Illustration 6); *Hurstanger Ltd v Wilson* [2007] EWCA Civ 299; [2007] 1 W.L.R. 2351 at [47]. This can be done even though it has previously been treated as discharged on inadequate grounds: *Alexander v Webber* [1922] 1 K.B. 642, and perhaps the *Panama* case, above. But the person seeking specific performance of a contract,[1461] permitting a set-off against debts owed the third party,[1462] declaring a constructive trust of assets in the third party's possession,[1463] imposing liability for knowing receipt[1464] and imposing compensatory liability for dishonest assistance in the agent's breach of duty.[1465] In all cases, a third party is unlikely to be affected by an agent's breach of equitable duty unless that third party has a sufficient degree of knowledge of the breach to warrant equity's attention.[1466] It is clear now that only dishonesty, in an objective sense (itself a difficult concept), is sufficient for liability for dishonest assistance,[1467] but there remains uncertainty as to the applicable tests for liability to rescission, for the invocation of the defence of bona fide purchaser for value in relation to proprietary actions and for liability for knowing receipt.[1468]

Rule (2): Bribery and secret commissions   Bribery is a particularly obvious form   **8-222**
of corruption, and one that has attracted much attention since the nineteenth century from both common law and equity. A small group of core cases before and after the beginning of the twentieth century lay down and repeat stern rules in respect of bribery, which dominate the area and appear to have had some element of deterrent purpose. Definitions of bribery and of the wider concept of a secret commission, together with an account of the internal effect of the applicable rules as between principal and agent have been addressed in Article 49. This Article concerns the external effect, but should be read in conjunction with the commentary to Article 49. The breadth of the concept of a secret commission means that a third party who offers or confers money or some other personal benefit on an agent cannot escape legal repercussions merely because he avers that he thought that the agent would tell or had told the principal of the payment[1469]; or where he was unaware of the agent's exact intention but aware that the agent did not intend to disclose the dealing to the principal.[1470] He is also liable where he originally arranged for the payment not knowing of the agency, but continued and entered into

---

ing to do so must of course come in time. See Lewin, *Trusts* (19th edn), para.20-067.

[1461] *Galloway v Pedersen* (1915) 34 N.Z.L.R. 513. cf. *Odessa Tramways Co v Mendel* (1878) 8 Ch.D. 235.

[1462] *Clark v Cutland* [2003] EWCA Civ 810; [2004] 1 W.L.R. 783.

[1463] See the cases referred to in commentary to Article 88.

[1464] See, e.g. *Aerostar Maintenance International Ltd v Wilson* [2010] EWHC 2032 (Ch) at [194]. See also the cases in fn.1460, above, and the discussion in Article 116. In cases of receipt of corporate opportunities, as opposed to receipt of existing assets of the principal, it seems that a higher test of knowledge is required for liability: see *Satnam Investments Ltd v Dunlop Heywood* [1999] 3 All E.R. 652; *Farah Constructions Pty Ltd v Say-Dee Pty Ltd* (2007) 230 C.L.R. 89 at [118]; and as to Scotland, *Commonwealth Oil & Gas Co Ltd v Baxter* [2009] CSIH 75 at [95].

[1465] *Aerostar Maintenance International Ltd v Wilson* [2010] EWHC 2032 (Ch) at [185] and [197] (recipient of corporate opportunity (and others) also liable for dishonestly assisting director to divert opportunity). See too below, para.8-225. For general discussion of the dishonest assistance action, see Article 116.

[1466] See *Chancery Client Partners Ltd v MRC 957 Ltd* [2016] EWHC 2142 (Ch) at [22].

[1467] See *Royal Brunei Airlines Sdn Bhd v Tan* [1995] 2 A.C. 378.

[1468] For discussion, see commentary to Article 116.

[1469] *Shipway v Broadwood* [1899] 1 Q.B. 369 at 373 (Illustration 3); *Grant v Gold Exploration and Development Syndicate Ltd* [1900] 1 Q.B. 233 at 248–250; *Taylor v Walker* [1958] 1 Lloyd's Rep. 490, Illustration 4, at 509–513; *Otkritie International Investment Management Ltd v Urumov* [2014] EWHC 191 (Comm) at [68].

[1470] *Logicrose Ltd v Southend United FC* [1988] 1 W.L.R. 1256 at 1260–1262.

the contract with the principal after he had learned of it.[1471] Although it is true that the objectionable feature of bribery is the general one that it gives rise to a conflict of interest,[1472] factors such as those above distinguish bribes from the more general idea of undisclosed profit, which need not involve the complicity of a third party.[1473]

8-223   **Forms of relief and remedy**   The principal who learns of a bribe or secret commission is presented with a wide range of legal options against the bribing third party. The principal has the right to rescind, or cancel, any contract with the third party. Such rights arise at common law and equity, but with equity taking a wider view of what constitutes a conflicting interest sufficient to warrant curial intervention. Relevant case law is found under Rule (1) above, and in the commentary to Article 49. In cases where the agent is not dishonest, albeit receiving a secret commission, the contract may be voidable only, and this may be so too where the agent has disclosed the inducement but not given as complete an account as should have been given.[1474] Where bribery is involved, it will not generally be necessary that the briber be placed back in its pre-contract position.[1475]

Otherwise, the principal may, at common law, claim from the third party the amount of the bribe or damages for loss flowing from the agent's involvement with the bribing party. These are alternative remedies: "(1) to recover from [the third party] the amount of the bribe as money had and received, or (2) to recover, as damages for tort, the actual loss which he has sustained as a result of entering into the transaction in respect of which the bribe was given".[1476] Older case law suggested that the third party's liability was without taking into account any sum recovered from the agent.[1477] Such a rule was almost penal in operation and surprising, inasmuch as it seemed to allow double recovery[1478] and its origin may have been influenced by the rule, applicable at the time of the leading case, that judgment against one tortfeasor released the others[1479]: it was important to establish the briber's liability as separate from the restitutionary liability of the agent for the bribe. The law however was clarified in *Mahesan v Malaysian Government Officers' Co-operative Housing Society Ltd*[1480] in which it was held that the notion that there could be cumulation was unjustified and inconsistent with the principle as to

---

[1471] *Grant v Gold Exploration and Development Syndicate Ltd*, above.
[1472] *Anangel Atlas Cla. Naviera SA v Ishikawajima-Harima Heavy Industries Co Ltd* [1990] 1 Lloyd's Rep. 167 at 171.
[1473] As to secret profits, see Articles 45–47.
[1474] See *Hurstanger Ltd v Wilson* [2007] EWCA Civ 299; [2007] 1 W.L.R. 2351; [2007] 4 All E.R. 1118 at [47]. See too above, para.6-085.
[1475] See *UBS AG (London Branch) v Kommunale Wasserwerke Leipzig GmbH* [2014] EWHC 3615 (Comm) at [792] (affd [2017] EWCA Civ 1567).
[1476] *Mahesan v Malaysian Government Officers' Co-operative Housing Society Ltd* [1979] A.C. 374 at 383, per Lord Diplock. As to money had and received, see *Hovenden & Sons v Millhoff* (1900) 83 L.T. 41.
[1477] *Salford Corp v Lever* [1891] 1 Q.B. 168; *Morgan v Elford* (1876) 4 Ch.D. 352; *Phosphate Sewage Co v Hartmont* (1877) 5 Ch.D. 394; cf. *Lands Allotment Co v Broad* (1895) 13 R. 699; *Grant v Gold Exploration & Development Syndicate Ltd* [1900] 1 Q.B. 233; *Cohen v Kuschke & Co and Koenig* (1900) 83 L.T. 102.
[1478] Pollock (1891) 7 L.Q.R. 99. But there does not seem to have been actual double recovery in any of the cases; cf. however Tettenborn (1979) 95 L.Q.R. 68, who defends this possibility.
[1479] *Brinsmead v Harrison* (1872) L.R. 7 C.P. 547 (abolished by the Law Reform (Married Women and Tortfeasors) Act 1935). See the argument in *Salford Corp v Lever* [1891] 1 Q.B. 168.
[1480] [1979] A.C. 374, Illustration 8 to Article 49; see Needham (1979) 95 L.Q.R. 536; (1978) 94 L.Q.R. 344; (1978) 41 M.L.R. 603. cf., however, Tettenborn, above.

election laid down in *United Australia Ltd v Barclays Bank Ltd*.[1481] It has since been held, however, that the principal may rescind the contract with the third party, whilst maintaining his rights to strip the agent of the benefits received by way of bribe; otherwise the agent would remain unjustly enriched.[1482] In other cases, the principal will be required to elect between alternative remedies, but the election need not be made before judgment has been entered in his favour in one or other of them.[1483]

Some difficulties have arisen in categorising the rights of the principal against the third party, especially those at common law. One view has been that the action for damages should be regarded as lying in deceit, and that that cause of action might also embrace liability for the amount of the bribe. Where no clear loss could be proved, such liability was to be explained on the basis that the damages would be presumed to be at least the amount of the bribe.[1484] This would however involve tort liability without actual loss or damage and is contrary to principle. Further, this analysis involves a claim in deceit without representation (except at best by inference) or reliance on a representation; hence the suggestion that the relevant tort is the broader one of "fraud".[1485] Then, in relation to the third party's liability for the amount of the bribe in an action for money had and received, the difficulty is that the third party will have paid the bribe, not received it. The action seems to be based on the proposition that "he is entitled to treat the benefit obtained by or promised to the agent as part of the consideration which should have been received by the principal (if he is a vendor) or as excess consideration provided by the principal (if he is a purchaser)".[1486] A conclusive presumption of enrichment appears to be in operation. The cause of action in tort will be advantageous where there is loss which exceeds the amount of the bribe. It might also be more easily available when the bribe has not been paid but merely promised: though it appears that the action in money had and received may still lie in such a case.[1487]

Where the payment is made or agreed upon (or, when originally unauthorised, adopted) after the making of the contract, the effect of a bribe probably turns on the general principles of breach of contract, viz. the payment will be a breach of contract and the consequences of that fact will turn in the ordinary way on what significance the arrangement had for the due performance of the contract.[1488] The

---

[1481] [1941] A.C. 1. The agent is also liable on a proprietary basis: see above, para.6-085. But there is no indication that this extinguishes the personal liability of agent or third party.

[1482] *Logicrose Ltd v Southend United FC* [1988] 1 W.L.R. 1256. See too *Grant v Gold Exploration and Development Syndicate Ltd* [1900] 1 Q.B. 233.

[1483] *Mahesan* [1979] A.C. 374 at 383.

[1484] See *Hovenden & Sons v Millhoff* (1900) 83 L.T. 41; *Industries & General Mortgage Co v Lewis* [1949] 2 All E.R. 573; *Grant v Gold Exploration and Development Syndicate Ltd* [1900] 1 Q.B. 233.

[1485] See *Petrotrade Inc v Smith* [2000] 1 Lloyd's Rep. 486 at [19], per David Steel J. But cf. *Kensington International Ltd v Republic of Congo* [2007] EWCA Civ 1128; [2008] 1 Lloyd's Rep. 161 at [62]–[63] (the offering and receiving of bribes involves deception of the principal); and *Cavell USA Inc v Seaton Insurance Co* [2009] EWCA Civ 1363 at [25]. See too Mitchell (2001) 117 L.Q.R. 207; but contra the Hon. Justice K.R. Handley, ibid., 536.

[1486] *Logicrose Ltd v Southend United FC* [1988] 1 W.L.R. 1256 at 1263, per Millett J.

[1487] See too *Nelmes v NRAM Plc* [2016] EWCA Civ 491; [2016] C.T.L.C. 106 at [36] (relief under Consumer Credit Act 1974 s.140A). *Grant v Gold Exploration and Development Syndicate*, above (but see on this case *Mahesan*'s case [1979] A.C. 374 at 382–383); and the dictum of Millett J quoted above ("or promised to"). As to mere promises to pay a bribe or attempts to suborn, see also *Whaley Bridge Calico Printing Co v Green* (1879) 5 Q.B.D. 109; *Donegal International Ltd v Republic of Zambia* [2007] EWHC 197 (Comm); [2007] 1 Lloyd's Rep. 397; and *Nayyar v Sapte* [2009] EWHC 3218 (QB).

[1488] *Armagas Ltd v Mundogas SA (The Ocean Frost)* [1985] 1 Lloyd's Rep. 1 at 18–22, following the appropriate remedy in such circumstances may be cancellation of the contract rather than rescission ab initio.[1489]

The foregoing describes the main claims used by the principal against the third party. A range of other options have been invoked in particular circumstances, including declaring the contract between the parties to be inoperative for failure of a required condition,[1490] or discharged for breach,[1491] holding a promissory note not provable in a bankruptcy[1492] and determining that a particular transaction was not for the best rent under the Settled Land Act.[1493] In these latter situations, common law and equity reasoning is not always distinguished. A transaction involving some forms of corruption may also be unenforceable under the rules for illegal contracts.[1494]

8-224 **Bribery by agent of third party** The discussion so far has been concerned with bribes paid or promised by third parties themselves, or readily imputable to such third parties. Where a bribe is paid or promised by an *agent*[1495] of the third party without that party's knowledge, the position is likely to be affected by the remedy being sought by the third party. If only rescission is being sought, it may be that the third party cannot maintain the contract because that would be both to adopt and disown the agent's conduct.[1496] If damages are being sought, then probably the standard tort rules should be applied, meaning that usually the principal would be liable only if the agent were an employee, or cognate and the conduct took place in "the course of employment".[1497] There may also be cases where the third party uses an intermediary but does not know exactly what the intermediary will do. In

---

view of Mellish LJ in *Panama & South Pacific Telegraph Co v India Rubber, etc., Co* (1875) L.R. 10 Ch.App. 515 at 531–532 and applying *Hong Kong Fir Shipping Co Ltd v Kawasaki Kisen Kaisha Ltd* [1962] 2 Q.B. 26. The decision was reversed on other grounds: [1986] A.C. 717 (CA and HL). See also *Tigris International NV v China Southern Airlines Company Ltd* [2014] EWCA Civ 1649 at [143] (third party innocently thought agency for claimant had terminated).

[1489] *Panama & South Pacific Telegraph Co v India Rubber, etc., Co* (1875) L.R. 10 Ch.App. 515 to the contrary, may need reconsideration in the light of the now favoured principle that post-contract breaches permit cancellation *de futuro* only: see, e.g. *Thornton Hall v Wembley Electrical Appliances Ltd* [1947] 2 All E.R. 630 at 634; *Manifest Shipping Co Ltd v Uni-Polaris Insurance Co Ltd* [2001] UKHL 1; [2003] 1 A.C. 469 at [52]; *Tigris International NV v China Southern Airlines Company Ltd* [2014] EWCA Civ 1649 at [143]. See Watts (2009) 125 L.Q.R. 369 at 372.

[1490] *Shipway v Broadwood* [1899] 1 Q.B. 369, Illustration 3.

[1491] *Bartram & Sons v Lloyd* (1904) 90 L.T. 357.

[1492] *Re a Debtor* [1927] 2 Ch. 367.

[1493] *Chandler v Bradley* [1897] 1 Ch. 315.

[1494] For the general law, see Chitty, *Contracts* (32nd edn), Ch.16. For particular difficulties in this context, see Berg [2001] L.M.C.L.Q. 27 at 41 onwards. See too *Hurstanger Ltd v Wilson* [2007] EWCA Civ 299; [2007] 1 W.L.R. 2351; [2007] 4 All E.R. 1118. cf. *Honeywell International Middle East Ltd v Meydan Group LLC* [2014] EWHC 1344 (TCC); [2014] 2 Lloyd's Rep. 133 at [185]; and *Medsted Associates Ltd v Canaccord Genuity Wealth (International) Ltd* [2017] EWHC 1815 (Comm) at [135].

[1495] See the discussion above, para.6-087.

[1496] See above, paras 8-097 and 8-222.

[1497] See *Armagas Ltd v Mundogas SA* [1986] A.C. 717 at 744–745 (in CA, bribing party a joint venturer, perhaps partner), following *Barry v Stoney Point Canning Co* (1917) 55 S.C.R. 51. See also *Hamlyn v John Houston & Co* [1903] 1 K.B. 81; *UBS AG (London Branch) v Kommunale Wasserwerke Leipzig GmbH* [2014] EWHC 3615 (Comm) at [589] (affd [2017] EWCA Civ 1567). The payment of bribes is normally outside the authority of the agent: *E. Hannibal & Co Ltd v Frost* (1988) 4 B.C.C. 3, Illustration 4 to Article 29; see further above, para.2-026. But that would not preclude the operation of vicarious liability in appropriate cases.

such cases the act of such party may still be attributed to him[1498]; or he may at least be subject to the rescissionary remedy on the grounds that it would be inequitable for him to insist on the transaction in the circumstances.[1499] It will not usually matter that the agent also performs some role for the other party; the party whose agent received the bribe is nonetheless entitled to rescind the transaction.[1500] This liability would not preclude the third party suing its agent for having embroiled it in corrupt activity.[1501] Conversely, where the third party knows that his own agent is attempting to bribe the agents of the principal, he is likely to find himself unable to plead any default against his agent by reason of the principle ex turpi causa non oritur action.[1502]

Action for dishonest assistance   Now that the basis of accessory liability in   **8-225** respect of breach of fiduciary duty has been clarified,[1503] it is possible that claimants, apprised of their agents' corruption, may prefer to rely on the action for dishonest assistance in a breach of fiduciary duty than rely on the law of tort and the action for money had and received, though the remedies would be slightly different; it has been said that "the difference lies not in the factual background but in the remedy sought".[1504] An unsettled issue is whether accessory liability can apply where there is no misappropriation of existing trust assets.[1505] However, there is some authority that it can,[1506] and it seems that the action can extend to stripping the briber of profits.[1507] The use of this action would also enable use of the more generalised principles as to the knowledge required, recently developed in connection with accessory liability, instead of some of the awkward quasi-presumptions which dicta in the common law cases have sometimes seemed to apply.

Illustrations

(1)   A company awards to another company a sub-contract for the laying of cable.   **8-226** The performance of the sub-contract is subject to certification by an engineer

---

[1498] See Berg [2001] L.M.C.L.Q. 27 at 46–47.

[1499] *Armagas Ltd v Mundogas SA*, above, at 745, per Robert Goff LJ.

[1500] *UBS AG (London Branch) v Kommunale Wasserwerke Leipzig GmbH* [2014] EWHC 3615 (Comm) at [616] (affd [2017] EWCA Civ 1567).

[1501] *Ho Kang Peng v Scintronix Corp Ltd* [2014] SGCA 22.

[1502] *Nayyar v Sapte* [2009] EWHC 3218 (QB).

[1503] See *Royal Brunei Airlines Sdn Bhd v Tan* [1995] 2 A.C. 378; *Secretary of State for Justice v Topland Group Plc* [2011] EWHC 983 (QB) at [94]; and Article 116.

[1504] *Logicrose Ltd v Southend United FC* [1988] 1 W.L.R. 1256 at 1261, per Millett J. As to the monetary remedies available in equity, see Comment to Article 115.

[1505] See Comment to Article 116; Lewin, *Trusts* (19th edn), para.40-027.

[1506] See ibid.; *Fyffes Group Ltd v Templeman* [2000] 2 Lloyd's Rep. 643, per Toulson J; *Secretary of State for Justice v Topland Group Plc* [2011] EWHC 983 QB. cf. *Petrotrade Inc v Smith* [2000] 1 Lloyd's Rep. 486 to the contrary; and see Lewin, above, para.20-069; Mitchell (2001) 118 L.Q.R. 207.

[1507] See *Novoship (UK) Ltd v Mikhaylyuk* [2012] EWHC 3586 (Comm) at [99]; affd [2014] EWCA Civ 908 at [84]; *Australian Careers Institute Pty Ltd v Australian Institute of Fitness Pty Ltd* [2016] NSWCA 34; (2017) 340 A.L.R. 580; *Lifeplan Australia Friendly Society Ltd v Ancient Order of Foresters in Victoria Friendly Society Ltd* [2017] FCAFC 74. In *Sinclair Investment Holdings SA v Versailles Trade Finance Ltd* [2007] EWHC 915 (Ch); [2007] 2 All E.R. (Comm) 993 at [133]–[134] affd [2011] EWCA Civ 347; [2012] Ch. 453 it was doubted whether the liability of the briber would extend to liability for incidental profits gained beyond the amount of the bribe itself, and the view was strongly expressed that, if it did, the profits would not be held on trust for the claimant. The third party is unlikely to be liable to the principal for remuneration forfeited by an agent as a result of an improper conflict of interest: *Electrosteel Castings (UK) Ltd v Metalpol Ltd* [2014] EWHC 2017 (Ch) at [65].

appointed by the first company. The sub-contractor employs the same engineer as sub-sub-contractor to lay the cable. The financing of the project goes wrong. The first company discovers the involvement of its engineer in the sub-contract and claims that it should be set aside. The company is successful.[1508]

(2)   A person who dealt with an agent gave him a gratuity in order to influence him generally in favour of the giver. The agent was in fact so influenced in making a contract with the giver on the principal's behalf. Held, that the contract was voidable by the principal, although the gratuity was not given in direct relation to the particular contract.[1509]

(3)   A agreed to buy a pair of horses from B, provided a veterinary surgeon who had been employed by A to find such horses certified that they were sound. B secretly offered the vet a certain sum if the horses were sold, and the vet accepted the offer. The vet certified that the horses were sound. Held, that A was not bound by the contract whether the vet was in fact biased by the offer made to and accepted by him or not.[1510]

(4)   A person injured in a road accident employs a "claims service" to negotiate a tort claim. The service uses an assessor, who tells the insurer that he will recommend acceptance of the insurer's offer if the insurer pays his fee. The claimant settles. The sum is a bribe and he can rescind the settlement and pursue his claim for damages.[1511]

(5)   By paying a bribe of $18,000, third parties sell land to a Government and make a profit of $67,940. They are liable for the latter sum, but the $18,000 is subsumed into it. The fact that the Government resold the land at prices whereby it recovered its costs is irrelevant.[1512]

(6)   An agent accepts a bribe in connection with the grant of a licence to operate a market on his principal's land. On learning of this the principal rescinds the contract. He need not give credit for the amount of the bribe, which he is entitled to recover from the agent whether or not he adopts the transaction, and which he can treat as a gift to him.[1513]

(7)   A director bought land from his company not revealing his knowledge that the land had the potential to be re-zoned and indeed that he had already taken steps to apply for planning permission. Held, that the director held the proceeds of on-sale of the relevant property on constructive trust.[1514]

(8)   Company directors exercise their powers to allot unissued shares in the company in favour of shareholder X for the purpose of thereby diluting the voting power of shareholder Y. They act in good faith, believing that Y's business intentions are inimical to the company's best interests. Held, that the allotment was made for an improper purpose and was voidable in equity.[1515]

[1508] *Panama and South Pacific Telegraph Co v India Rubber, Gutta Percha and Telegraph Works Co* (1875) L.R. 10 Ch.App. 515.

[1509] *Smith v Sorby* (1875) 3 Q.B.D. 552n; *Hough v Bolton* (1885) 1 T.L.R. 606. See also *Galloway v Pedersen* (1915) 34 N.Z.L.R. 513 (specific performance refused).

[1510] *Shipway v Broadwood* [1899] 1 Q.B. 369.

[1511] *Taylor v Walker* [1958] 1 Lloyd's Rep. 490.

[1512] *Att.-Gen. for Nova Scotia v Christian* (1974) 49 D.L.R. (3d) 742.

[1513] *Logicrose v Southend United FC* [1988] 1 W.L.R. 1256.

[1514] *J.J. Harrison (Properties) Ltd v Harrison* [2001] EWCA Civ 1467; [2002] 1 B.C.L.C. 162.

[1515] *Howard Smith Ltd v Ampol Petroleum Ltd* [1974] A.C. 821. See too *Hogg v Cramphorn* [1967] Ch. 254; *Whitehouse v Carlton Hotel Pty Ltd* (1987) 162 C.L.R. 285.

(9)   A claimant, company A, is one of the holders of a joint account at the defend-
        ant bank, a local authority being the other joint holder. The sole director of
        company A gives a direction to the bank to change the party to the joint ac-
        count from company A to its parent company, company B, and the bank does
        so. Company A is arguably insolvent at the time. Held, the bank was entitled
        to rely on the instructions of the director, who had actual authority to give
        them, even if the director had failed to comply with equitable duties to take
        account of the interests of creditors of company A upon its insolvency. He had
        acted honestly, and in what he thought were the interests of company A.[1516]

(10)   Directors of a company sign a "poison pill" agreement with another company,
        under which the other company can demand to be bought out from an inter-
        est in a joint venture company on terms that are deliberately highly favour-
        able to it. The agreement may be voidable as having been made for an
        improper purpose.[1517] But if the directors had neither actual nor apparent
        authority to make the agreement, the transaction would be void. The third
        party's liability in such circumstances does not turn on unconscionability in
        equity.[1518]

[1516] *Senex Holdings Ltd v National Westminster Bank Plc* [2012] EWHC 131 (Comm); [2012] 1 All E.R.
(Comm) 1130.
[1517] *Criterion Properties Plc v Stratford UK Properties LLC* [2002] EWHC 496 (Ch); [2002] 2 B.C.L.C.
151.
[1518] *Criterion Properties Plc v Stratford UK Properties LLC* [2004] UKHL 28; [2004] 1 W.L.R. 1846.

CHAPTER 9

RELATIONS BETWEEN AGENTS AND THIRD PARTIES

1. CONTRACT

Article 97

GENERAL RULE

In the absence of other indications, when an agent makes a contract, purporting to act solely on behalf of a disclosed principal, whether identified or unidentified, he is not liable to the third party on it. Nor can he sue the third party on it.[1]

9-001

Comment

"There is no doubt whatever as to the general rule as regards an agent, that where a person contracts as agent for a principal, the contract is the contract of the principal and not that of the agent; and, prima facie, at common law the only person who may sue is the principal and the only person who can be sued is the principal."[2]

9-002

This is so even where the principal himself is not in fact bound because the agent was not authorised; and even where the agent is a *del credere* agent and as such liable to the principal for the third party's debt.[3] This basic prima facie result is often expressed in the maxim that the agent "drops out" of the transaction, an expression which, though convenient, may be seriously misleading if pushed too far,[4] and certainly if pushed beyond contract. In truth, the reason why the agent is not liable or entitled, when this is so, is that the objective interpretation of the dealings between the between the parties indicate a contract between principal and third party only.

When actual authority is present, the contract may be seen as the principal's contract. Where the authority is merely apparent, the principal (unless he ratifies) is only liable, on the basis of a form of estoppel.[5]

Thus, the mere fact that a person acts as agent and is known to do so does not

---

[1] See Comment.
[2] *Montgomerie v UK Mutual SS Assn Ltd* [1891] 1 Q.B. 370 at 371, per Wright J. (But see the continuation of this passage quoted below, para.9-005.) See also *Paquin v Beauclerk* [1906] A.C. 148; *Restatement, Third*, § 6.01. For the apparently different starting point in Scots law, at least where the principal is disclosed but unidentified, see *Ruddy v Marco* [2008] CSIH 47 at [21]. PECL art.3:202; UNIDROIT Principles art.2.2.3; DCFR, II, 6:105 all appear to have the same starting point as the common law.
[3] *Bramwell v Spiller* (1870) 21 L.T. 672. See above, para.1-042.
[4] See Müller-Freienfels (1963) 12 Am.J.Comp.L. 272 at 278.
[5] See above, para.8-028.

necessarily negate his involvement in the transaction. It has been said that:

"it is not the case that, if a principal is liable, his agent cannot be. The true principle of law is that a person is liable for his engagements (as for his torts) even though he acts for another, unless he can show that by the law of agency he is to be held to have expressly or impliedly negatived his personal liability."[6]

The possibilities had in fact earlier been listed as follows:

"An agent can conclude a contract on behalf of his principal in one of three ways:

(a) *By creating privity of contract between the third party and his principal without himself becoming a party to the contract.* The principal need not be named but the contract must show clearly that the agent was acting as such. Familiar examples are contracts made by X as agents and signed by X, the signature being claused 'as agents only. The consequence of such an arrangement is that the third party can only sue, and be sued by, the principal.

(b) *By creating privity of contract between the third party and his principal, whilst also himself becoming a party to the contract.* The consequence of this arrangement is that the third party has an option whether to sue the agent or the principal, although this is of little practical value if he does not know of the principal's existence ...

(c) *By creating privity of contract between himself and the third party, but no such privity between the third party and his principal.* In other words, in relation to the third party he is a principal, but in relation to his principal he is an agent.

The consequence of this arrangement is that the only person who can sue the third party or be sued by him is the agent."[7]

Thus it is possible for an agent to be a contracting party instead of or in addition to his principal, as explained in the next Article. Agents are also normally held by a separate contract to warrant their authority to act even when they are not liable on the main contract itself[8]; and they may be liable on other collateral contracts.[9] Agents may also of course be liable in tort.[10] Sometimes agents seek advice as to their own duties, and in so doing would normally contract as principals; their principals would not normally have any right to rely on that advice.[11]

Illustrations

9-003   (1)   A solicitor is prima facie not personally liable for the expenses of skilled or

---

[6]   *Yeung Kai Yung v Hong Kong and Shanghai Banking Corp* [1981] A.C. 787 at 795, per Lord Scarman. See also *The Swan* [1968] 1 Lloyd's Rep. 5, Illustration 6 to Article 98; *Ex p. Hartop* (1806) 12 Ves. Jun. 349 at 352: "for the application of that rule, the agent must name his principal as the person to be responsible", per Lord Erskine LC. This quotation makes the same point; but it should not be taken to require that the agent actually give the name of the principal, merely that he indicate that he acts as agent for a principal.

[7]   *Teheran-Europe Co Ltd v S.T. Belton (Tractors) Ltd* [1968] 2 Q.B. 53 at 59–60, per Donaldson J; decision affd on this point ibid., 545; approved in *Australian Trade Commission v Goodman Fielder Industries Ltd* (1992) 36 F.C.R. 517.

[8]   Articles 105 and 106.

[9]   See *Yeung Kai Yung v Hong Kong and Shanghai Banking Corp*, above, Illustration 5 to Article 98.

[10]   Article 113.

[11]   See e.g. *Edenwest Ltd v CMS Cameron McKenna (A Firm)* [2012] EWHC 1258 (Ch) at [77] (receiver not agent of company in obtaining advice in personal capacity).

other witnesses retained or subpoenaed by him.[12] Nor is he personally liable for sheriff's fees merely because in the course of his duty he lodges a writ at the sheriff's office for execution.[13] In such matters he is deemed to act merely as the agent of his client, unless he expressly pledges his personal credit. But a solicitor who employs a particular bailiff to levy execution may be prima facie personally liable to the bailiff for the fees, if it is the usual course of business for the solicitor to pledge his personal credit in such a case.[14] The same is true where he employs another solicitor.[15]

(2) A broker sent a contract note in the following form: "I have this day sold you, on account of B, etc." (signed) "A B, broker". Held, that the broker had no right of action in his own name against the buyer for refusing to accept the goods.[16] So, where a broker sent a contract note as follows: "Mr. L, I have this day bought in my own name for your account, of AKT, etc." (signed) "A B, broker," it was held that he was acting as agent of AKT; that the words "bought in my own name" were inserted to inform the purchaser that the broker was liable to the vendor; and that the broker had no right to sue L for the price.[17]

(3) A shipmaster signs bills of lading as agent for the owners. He can sue for freight neither under the bills nor on an implied contract.[18] Nor can he sue on an implied contract to pay demurrage.[19]

(4) The manager of a mutual insurance association subscribes a policy on behalf of the members of the association. He cannot sue in his own name for contributions due from the member effecting the policy, though the rules of the association purport to give him such a power.[20]

Article 98

WHEN AGENT HAS RIGHTS AND LIABILITIES

An agent who makes a contract on his principal's behalf is liable to or entitled to sue the third party in accordance with the terms of any contractual engagement, whether upon the same contract or upon some independent contract, into which he has entered.[21]   **9-004**

---

[12] *Robins v Bridge* (1837) 3 M. & W. 114; *Lee v Everest* (1857) 2 H. & N. 285; *Wakefield v Duckworth* [1915] 1 K.B. 218 (order for photographs to be used in connection with a trial). cf. *Cocks v Bruce, Searl and Good* (1904) 21 T.L.R. 62 (shorthand writer: solicitor liable).
[13] *Royle v Busby* (1880) 6 Q.B.D. 171, following *Mayberry v Mansfield* (1846) 9 Q.B. 754.
[14] *Newton v Chambers* (1844) 13 L.J.Q.B. 141; *Maile v Mann* (1848) 2 Exch. 608 as explained in *Royle v Busby*, above. See further Cordery, *Solicitors* (8th edn), p.98–99.
[15] *Scrace v Whittington* (1823) 2 B. & C. 11; and see *Porter v Kirtlan* [1917] 2 I.R. 138.
[16] *Fairlie v Fenton* (1870) L.R. 5 Ex. 169.
[17] *Fawkes v Lamb* (1862) 31 L.J.Q.B. 98.
[18] *Repetto v Millar's Karri and Jarrah Forests Ltd* [1901] 2 K.B. 306. A signature without qualification anywhere else in the document (see Article 101) could perhaps still make the master a contracting party: see p.310 and *Atkinson v Cotesworth* (1825) 3 B. & C. 647. But such a signature would be rare in a commercial context today. See also *Smith v Plummer* (1818) 1 B. & A. 575; cf. *Cawthron v Trickett* (1864) 15 C.B.(N.S.) 754.
[19] *Brouncker v Scott* (1811) 4 Taunt. 1; *Evans v Forster* (1830) 1 B. & Ad. 118; cf. *Jesson v Solly* (1811) 4 Taunt. 52.
[20] *Evans v Hooper* (1875) 1 Q.B.D. 45; *Gray v Pearson* (1870) L.R. 5 C.P. 568.
[21] See Comment.

Comment

9-005 **Agent may be liable or entitled**   As has been stated in the Comment to the previous Article, there is no reason why an agent should not be entitled and/or liable on the contract which he has made for his principal, or upon a separate but related contract. "In all cases the parties can by the express contract provide that the agent shall be the person liable either concurrently with or to the exclusion of the principal."[22] The question whether an agent who has made a contract on behalf of his principal is to be deemed to have contracted personally, and, if so the extent of his liability, depends on the intention of the parties, to be deduced from the nature and terms of the particular contract and the surrounding circumstances, including any binding custom.[23] As in all matters of formation of contract, the test is objective.[24] The rules can be most easily articulated in relation to written contracts, where the use of a particular form of words may constitute an agent a contracting party though it is on the underlying facts doubtful whether he intended to become such.[25]

It is sometimes said that an agent can be liable to the third party without being entitled to sue, but cannot be entitled to sue without being liable, for then there would be no consideration to support his right to sue.[26] This is true in the sense that a collateral contract can more easily be constructed on the basis that the agent, in return for the third party's dealing with his principal, undertakes also personal liability on the main contract. But the converse position can also exist, though it may be less likely: a third party may, in return for being introduced to the principal or for some other benefit, be held to make the same promise to the agent as he does to the principal. Thus a person buying goods at auction is liable to the auctioneer for the price: but the auctioneer's reciprocal promise to him may be extremely limited and certainly does not involve liability on the contract of sale itself.[27]

9-006 **Agent's liability**   Where an agent is potentially liable, the terms of his liability

---

[22] *Montgomerie v UK Mutual SS Assn* [1891] 1 Q.B. 370 at 372, per Wright J (in a later part of the judgment some of which is cited in para.9-002 above). See also *Fawkes v Lamb* (1862) 31 L.J.Q.B. 98 at 100; *The Swan* [1968] 1 Lloyd's Rep. 5, Illustration 6; *Carminco Gold & Resources Ltd v Findlay & Co Stockbrokers (Underwriters) Pty Ltd* (2007) 243 A.L.R. 472, Illustration 24 to Article 98; *Felty v Ernst & Young LLP* [2015] BCCA 445.

[23] This sentence was quoted with approval in *Maritime Stores Ltd v H.P. Marshall & Co Ltd* [1963] 1 Lloyd's Rep. 602 at 608. See too *Temple Legal Protection Ltd v QBE Insurance (Europe) Ltd* [2009] EWCA Civ 453; [2009] Lloyd's Rep. I.R. 544; *CIFAL Groupe SA v Meridian Securities (UK) Ltd* [2013] EWHC 3553 (Comm). In some cases statutory provisions may make the position of the agent different to that of the principal: see, e.g. *Domsalla (t/a Domsalla Buildings Services) v Dyason* [2007] EWHC 1174 (T.C.C.); (2007) 112 Con. L.R. 95 (construction contract entered into by owner on instructions of insurer, found to bind insurer and owner, but owner entitled to invoke the Unfair Terms in Consumer Contracts Regulations 1999).

[24] *The Swan* [1968] 1 Lloyd's Rep. 5 at 12; *Carminco Gold & Resources Ltd v Findlay & Co Stockbrokers (Underwriters) Pty Ltd* (2007) 243 A.L.R. 472 at [23], Illustration 24 to Article 98.

[25] See *Fisher v Marsh* (1865) 6 B. & S. 411; *Sika Contracts Ltd v B.S. Gill* (1978) 9 Build. L.R. 11, Illustration 10 to Article 99; *Foxtons Ltd v Thesleff* [2005] EWCA Civ 514, [2005] 2 E.G.L.R. 29 (estate agent's contract by its wording made signatory of contract liable though in fact an agent); Articles 99–101 and 102–103.

[26] *Fawkes v Lamb* (1862) 31 L.J.K.B. 98 at 101; *Fairlie v Fenton* (1870) L.R. 5 Ex. 169 at 172. See criticism of the dicta in these cases by Stoljar, pp.245–247.

[27] In some cases the consideration would seem to be the release by the auctioneer of his lien when he delivers the goods; see *Chelmsford Auctions v Poole* [1973] Q.B. 542, Illustration 17; below, para.9-023.

may require careful analysis. Except as regards the undisclosed principal, discussed below, no specific rules have been laid down by the courts. The possibilities seem to be as follows.

(1) Sole liability of agent   The agent may be solely liable, i.e. although perhaps authorised to do so, he has not created any contract binding his principal at all but has made the contract himself. The majority of the cases seem to assume this as the main interpretation of a situation involving the agent's personal liability[28]: other interpretations have often been justified by reference to special circumstances such as trade custom,[29] or (as in the case of the auctioneer) lien or special property.[30] In such a case the agent's position vis-á-vis his principal may still be regulated by the general part of the law of agency, viz. he is remunerated on a commission basis, undertakes only to use his best endeavours, must not accept discounts or bribes, etc.; this is the position of the *commissionnaire* of civil law, referred to earlier.[31] Alternatively, it may be regulated by some other set of rules, e.g. those governing the relationship of buyer and seller or consignor and carrier. This is not the concern of the third party.

There are however other possibilities. "There is nothing to prevent an agent entering into a contract on the basis that he is himself to be liable to perform it as well as his principal."[32] Other possibilities may have been too easily overlooked in the past,[33] though there are signs that they may be more readily recognised in the future.[34] It is suggested below that they may be particularly relevant in considering unidentified principal situations. The remainder of this list enumerates them.

---

[28]   See in general *Parker v Winslow* (1857) 7 E. & B. 942 at 947 ("An agent is liable personally if he is the contracting party; and he may be so though he names his principal"); *Gadd v Houghton* (1876) 1 Ex.D. 357 at 360 ("It seems extraordinary that there should be any doubt whether this binds the principal or the agent"); *H.O. Brandt & Co v H.N. Morris & Co Ltd* [1917] 2 K.B. 784 at 793 ("Prima facie when a person signs a document in his own name ... he is the person liable on the contract"). For specific examples may be cited cases on solicitors: *Hall v Ashurst* (1883) 1 C. & M. 714 at 718; *Iveson v Conington* (1823) 1 B. & C. 160 at 162; *Tanner v Christian* (1855) 4 E. & B. 591 at 597–598, all of which should be considered with *Lavan v Walsh* [1964] I.R. 87; and cases on ship repairs and stores, where the contract is often with the local agent placing the order. See Article 101, Illustration 2. See also *Salsi v Jetspeed Air Services Ltd* [1977] 2 Lloyd's Rep. 57 (air freightage broker); *Tranton v Astor* (1917) 33 T.L.R. 383 (advertising agent), not followed by *CFTO-TV Ltd v Mr Submarine Ltd* (1994) 108 D.L.R. (4th) 517; affd (1997) 151 D.L.R. (4th) 382. There are also cases involving companies, where it has been concluded that a shareholder or director has in fact undertaken personal responsibility but not the company: see, e.g. *Hamid v Francis Bradshaw Partnership* [2013] EWCA Civ 470.

[29]   See below, para.9-016.

[30]   As to which see below, para.9-009.

[31]   See above, para.1-021 onwards.

[32]   *International Ry v Niagara Parks Commission* [1941] A.C. 328 at 342, per Luxmoore LJ. See also *Young v Schuler* (1887) 11 Q.B.D. 651; *Elbinger Actiengesellschaft v Claye* (1873) L.R. 8 Q.B. 313 at 317; *Calder v Dobell* (1871) L.R. 6 C.P. 486 at 494; *Montgomerie v UK Mutual SS Assn* [1891] 1 Q.B. 370 at 372; *The Swan* [1968] 1 Lloyd's Rep. 5; *Scottish and Newcastle International Ltd v Othon Ghalanos Ltd* [2008] UKHL 11; [2008] 1 Lloyd's Rep. 462 at [45].

[33]   Stoljar, p.234–238. And see Blackburn, *Contract of Sale* (3rd edn), p.352.

[34]   See *The Swan* [1968] 1 Lloyd's Rep. 5, Illustration 6; *Gardiner v Heading* [1928] 2 K.B. 284; *Teheran-Europe Co Ltd v S.T. Belton (Tractors) Ltd* [1968] 2 Q.B. 53 at 59–60; [1968] 2 Q.B. 545 at 558; *Wolfe Stevedores (1968) Ltd v Joseph Salter's Sons Ltd* (1971) 16 D.L.R. (3d) 334; *Burt v Claude Cousins & Co Ltd* [1971] 2 Q.B. 426 at 455; *Format International Security Printers Ltd v Mosden* [1975] 1 Lloyd's Rep. 37; *Et Biret Cie SA v Yukiteru Kaiun KK (The Sun Happiness)* [1984] 1 Lloyd's Rep. 381; *Stag Line Ltd v Tyne Shiprepair Group Ltd (The Zinnia)* [1984] 2 Lloyd's Rep. 211; *The Starsin* [2001] 1 Lloyd's Rep. 437 at 452. But cf. *Wilson v Avec Audio-Visual Equipment Ltd* [1974] 1 Lloyd's Rep. 81 at 83, where such liability is said to require "clear and precise evidence

(2) Joint or joint and several obligation The agent may be held to contract jointly or jointly and severally together with his principal.[35] Joint liability applies to partners,[36] but not normally to husband and wife.[37] Joint liability is subject to certain technical rules which may make it inappropriate to an agency relationship[38]: so, though to a lesser degree, is joint and several liability.[39]

(3) Suretyship He may be a surety for his principal, that is to say he may guarantee the principal's obligation; or contract to indemnify the third party in respect of its non-performance. This is to be distinguished from *del credere* agency, where the agent's liability is to his principal, not to the third party. Here again suretyship in general, and guarantee in particular, are subject to special rules which may not be appropriate to the particular situation.[40] The possibility is however occasionally referred to.[41]

(4) Collateral contract He may undertake a separate liability on a separate or collateral contract which is not one of suretyship. A contract of indemnity is of course a specialised form of such a contract. Consideration can often be found by the entry into the main contract with the principal. Examples of such contract are found in cases of warranty of authority[42] and auctioneers.[43] It has been held that a stockbroker may warrant the genuineness of a share transfer which he presents for registration.[44]

(5) Alternative liability He may undertake a liability alternative to that of the principal, the choice to lie with the third party. Though this interpretation seems to be assumed by some of the cases on election, it is submitted that there is little to

---

of a very special relationship"; *N. & J. Vlassopulos Ltd v Ney Shipping Ltd (The Santa Carina)* [1977] 1 Lloyd's Rep. 478, Illustration 3 to Article 101; *Foalquest Ltd v Roberts* [1990] 1 E.G.L.R. 50; *Belleli SpA v AIG (Europe) Ltd*, QBD (Rix J), May 22, 1996. See also below, para.9-016.

35 See, e.g. *Middle East Tankers and Freighters Bunker Services SA v Abu Dhabi Container Lines* [2002] EWHC 957 (Comm); [2002] 2 Lloyd's Rep. 643; *Savills (UK) Ltd v Blacker* [2017] EWCA Civ 68 at [46], Illustration 15. See too *Air Tahiti Nui Pty Ltd v McKenzie* [2009] NSWCA 429 (subsidiary company agent of parent; both liable); *Rabiu v Marlbray Ltd* [2016] EWCA Civ 476; [2016] 1 W.L.R. 514 (husband severally liable on contract of purchase when lacked authority also to bind wife).

36 Partnership Act 1890 s.9.

37 *Morel Bros & Co Ltd v Earl of Westmorland* [1904] A.C. 11; cf. *Hoare v Niblett* [1891] 1 Q.B. 781; *Swanton Seed Service Ltd v Kulba* (1968) 68 D.L.R. (2d) 38; *Rabiu v Marlbray Ltd* [2016] EWCA Civ 476; [2016] 1 W.L.R. 514.

38 See Glanville Williams, *Joint Obligations* (1949); but see Civil Liability (Contribution) Act 1978 s.3; and *David Moore Builders Ltd v Preddy* Unreported October 24, 1995 CA); *Goei Tsusho Co Ltd v Leader Engineering & Construction Ltd* [2010] 2 H.K.L.R.D. 1084.

39 e.g. release of one debtor releases all: see Glanville Williams, above, p.135.

40 e.g. giving time to the principal debtor releases the surety: Chitty, *Contracts* (32nd edn), para.44-104 onwards. See also Rowlatt, *Principal and Surety* (6th edn); Glanville Williams, above, p.121 onwards. Guarantees may require written evidence under the Statute of Frauds.

41 *Imperial Bank v London and St Katharine Docks Co* (1877) 5 Ch.D. 195 at 200; *Fleet v Murton* (1871) L.R. 7 Q.B. 126 at 132; see also *Young v Schuler* (1883) 11 Q.B.D. 651; *Rutherford v Ounan* [1913] 2 I.R. 265 at 268.

42 Article 105.

43 Below, paras 9-009 and 9-023; Illustrations 11–14 and 18–20. It may be that the position of the nineteenth-century factor would today be explicable in such terms, but it is no longer relevant to seek to explain it.

44 *Yeung Kai Yung v Hong Kong & Shanghai Banking Corp* [1981] A.C. 787, Illustration 5.

commend it.[45] Such cases as do recognise the liability of the agent do not usually consider further the nature of that liability, because the question is not relevant. Many old cases raise questions of the Statute of Frauds or of parol evidence, and concern the question whether the fact that a written contract mentions only principal or agent necessarily excludes the other.[46] Others are simply concerned with the question whether the agent can be sued, regardless of whether the principal can, or whether the agent who has paid on a contract is entitled to indemnity as having discharged a legal liability resting on him: they go no further than is necessary for the particular decision. The area is therefore not yet fully mapped.

Election When principal and agent are both liable, the doctrines of merger and election may apply, and the third party may be debarred from suing one by obtaining judgment against, or even perhaps simply electing to look to, the other. But this only operates where the two remedies available to the third party are inconsistent, and this may not be so in all cases. The nature of the liability assumed by the agent may therefore be crucial, but it has received insufficient attention in the cases. The value of the doctrine is also doubtful.[47]

9-007

Agent's right to sue The question of the agent's right to sue certainly arises less frequently than that of his liability,[48] and it seems that the incorporation of the agent into the contract has more normally the purpose of securing his liability. In any case, the right to sue can often be specifically assigned to the agent when this is thought desirable. On the analysis given above of the possible interpretations of the agent's liability, headings (1), (2) and (4) could also involve the right to sue. Plainly, the agent who makes the contract as sole contracting party can sue on it as well as be held liable.[49] An agent who is a party to a joint or joint and several obligation can sue on it, subject to the technical rules applicable.[50]

9-008

And a collateral contract made by agent with the third party may give the agent the right to sue on it: a conspicuous example is that of the auctioneer, who can sue for the price of the goods or land sold.[51] On the other hand, a contract of suretyship does not, and a contract of indemnity would not normally, confer a right to sue; and the cases suggesting alternative liability do so in connection with the *third party's* right to choose between principal and agent. In so far as any question arises between these two as to who should sue, it would probably be solved by reference to the subordinate position of the agent vis-á-vis the principal.[52] Where a party has

---

[45] See Comment to Article 82.
[46] See Article 102; *Higgins v Senior* (1841) 8 M. & W. 834; *Calder v Dobell* (1871) L.R. 6 C.P. 486; *Basma v Weekes* [1950] A.C. 441; *Davies v Sweet* [1962] 2 Q.B. 300.
[47] See Articles 82 and 104.
[48] See above, para.9-006. It has arisen where the principal is fictitious or non-existent, or where the agent is his own principal: see Articles 107 and 108.
[49] e.g. *Short v Spackman* (1851) 2 B. & Ad. 962. For a more modern example where this was probably the case, see *Anglo-African Shipping Co of New York Inc v J. Mortner Ltd* [1962] 1 Lloyd's Rep. 610; *Carminco Gold & Resources Ltd v Findlay & Co Stockbrokers (Underwriters) Pty Ltd* (2007) 243 A.L.R. 472, Illustration 24.
[50] e.g. a partner: cf. Co Litt. 182A. See also *Jung v Phosphate of Lime Co Ltd* (1868) L.R. 3 C.P. 139; *Perpetual Trustee Co Ltd v Nebo Road Pty Ltd* [2011] QSC 283 (contract recognises lead lender as having power to sue for all lenders).
[51] See below, para.9-023; Illustrations 11–14 and 18–20.
[52] See below, para.9-012.

assigned absolutely his contractual rights, he cannot usually avoid the rule requiring the assignee to be joined by asserting that he is suing as agent of the assignee.[53]

9-009 **Lien and special property** A number of cases, mostly on nineteenth-century factors and auctioneers, suggested that certain types of agent could sue because they have a special property in or lien upon the subject-matter of the contract or a beneficial interest in the completion thereof.[54] It is however clear that the mere fact that an agent has an interest in the completion of the contract, e.g. because he hopes to earn commission on it, does not entitle him to sue upon it.[55] The cases are in the modern context best explained as particular collateral contracts, upon which there is long-standing authority conferring specific rights and imposing specific duties upon these types of agent. The case law on the factor may be obsolete, but the auctioneer's contract is still of importance.[56] The possibility of detecting such contracts in new circumstances is not of course closed.

9-010 **Agent suing on behalf of principal** A further group of old cases can be read as suggesting that the agent can in general sue on behalf of his disclosed principal and recover his principal's loss.[57] They should be viewed with extreme caution. Many date from a time when there was no method of assigning legal choses in action, communications did not make it easy for foreign contracting parties to sue in England, contract rights under bills of lading were not transferable,[58] and the central contractual doctrines now accepted had not been fully worked out. The distinction between a right of suit and a right to recover substantial damages was not taken in some of these early cases. However the matter would have been viewed at the time, it is submitted that most of them would not now be followed or would be otherwise explained. An action brought for another by an agent authorised to do so should nowadays be brought in the name of the principal.[59]

9-011 **Insurance cases** There are also cases in the context of insurance law in which an assured is held entitled to recover loss though another party has actually suffered it; and agency reasoning has sometimes been invoked to justify this.[60] However, it is not clear that this is the correct analysis for such cases. Where the assured is a bailee of goods, his right can be explained by reference to his interest in them. The

---

53 *Bexhill UK Ltd v Razzaq* [2012] EWCA Civ 1376 at [58] (no evidence of authority).
54 The wording of Article 119 of the 1st edition of this book.
55 e.g. *Bramwell v Spiller* (1870) 21 L.T. 672 (*del credere* agent); *Fairlie v Fenton* (1870) L.R. 5 Ex. 169; *Turnbull & Jones Ltd v Amner & Sons* [1923] N.Z.L.R. 673.
56 See below, para.9-023; also above, para.1-046; Reynolds, in *Contemporary Issues in Commercial Law* (Lomnicka and Morse eds, 1997), p.161 onwards.
57 *Davis v James* (1770) 5 Burr. 2680; *Moore v Wilson* (1787) 1 T.R. 659; *Joseph v Knox* (1813) 3 Camp. 320; *Atkinson v Cotesworth* (1825) 3 B. & C. 647; *Dunlop v Lambert* (1839) 6 Cl. & F. 600; *Mead v SE Ry* (1870) 18 W.R. 735. The nearest to a strong case is *Joseph v Knox*. Also cases indicating that admissions by principal or agent are admissible against the other: *Bauerman v Radenius* (1792) 7 T.R. 663; *Smith v Lyon* (1813) 3 Camp. 465; *Welstead v Levy* (1831) 1 M. & Rob. 138; and on discovery: *Willis & Co v Baddeley* [1892] 2 Q.B. 324 (but cf. *James Nelson & Sons Ltd v Nelson Line (Liverpool) Ltd* [1906] 2 K.B. 217); *Abu Dhabi National Tanker Co v Product Star Shipping Ltd* [1992] 2 All E.R. 20.
58 A problem dealt with by the Bills of Lading Act 1855 (now replaced by the Carriage of Goods by Sea Act 1992).
59 *Jones v Gurney* [1913] W.N. 72; *PM Law Ltd & Motorplus Ltd* [2016] EWHC 193 (QB); [2016] 1 Costs L.R. 143 at [45]. See too *Moores v Hopper* (1807) 2 B. & P.N.R. 411.
60 See, e.g. *Waters v Monarch Fire and Life Insurance Co* (1856) 5 E. & B. 870.

leading case on such facts is *A. Tomlinson (Hauliers) Ltd v Hepburn*[61] where it was stressed that goods may be insured by a person with an interest in them so as to cover the interests of others. In such a case the assured would have an insurable interest in the full value of the goods, and would recover on *his own* contract; he would then be under an obligation to account to any person actually suffering loss.[62] Where actions are brought by agents and brokers, reliance is often placed on wide dicta regarding actions by agents on insurance policies in *Provincial Insurance Co of Canada v Leduc*[63]; but the case itself still concerned insurance by a part-owner for the other part-owner. Other situations and dicta can be explained on the basis that the agent is in some circumstances a *trustee* for others[64]; but this is by no means true of every agency situation.[65] The person suffering loss may also be able to sue under the Contracts (Rights of Third Parties) Act 1999. But though it has been held at first instance that the principle permitting actions by agents and brokers is a general one[66] it is not in fact clear that there is such a principle, or that it is needed.[67] If it existed it might also make such agents liable, as well as entitled on the contract, which may be contrary to expectation. Where normal agency requirements are satisfied, the principal can of course sue.[68] If however the principal is undisclosed and does not wish to sue, or was excluded by the terms of the contract,[69] the agent as the ostensible contracting party would be able to sue (and also liable).[70] In this special case it may be that he could recover the principal's loss as an exception to the normal rules for *damages*: the problem is discussed below.[71] Some special situations are now discussed.

Undisclosed principal   Where the principal is undisclosed at the time of contract-ing, the contract is made with the agent, and he is personally liable and entitled on it. There is no need for the agent to join the principal as a party. However, the principal also may intervene to sue, and may be sued, but the latter only subject to the general rule that nothing must prejudice the right of the third party to sue the agent if he so wishes.[72] This is therefore a case where both agent and principal are liable and entitled. The doctrine of election, referred to above, may raise problems when the agent is sued.

9-012

In this context it is often said that the right of the principal is superior to that of

---

[61] [1966] A.C. 451. The principle can be extended beyond bailment: see *Petrofina (UK) Ltd v Magnaload Ltd* [1984] Q.B. 127 (multi-participant construction project).

[62] See *Re E. Dibbens & Sons Ltd* [1990] B.C.L.C. 577.

[63] (1874) L.R. 6 P.C. 224 at 244.

[64] See *Woodar Investment Development Ltd v Wimpey Construction UK Ltd* [1980] 1 W.L.R. 277 at 294 (HL), referring to *Lloyd's v Harper* (1880) 16 Ch.D. 290.

[65] See *Allen v F. O'Hearn & Co* [1937] A.C. 213 at 218.

[66] *Transcontinental Underwriting Agency SRL v Grand Union Insurance Co Ltd* [1987] 2 Lloyd's Rep. 409 at 415.

[67] See Lord Millett in *Alfred McAlpine Construction Ltd v Panatown Ltd* [2001] 1 A.C. 518 at 582; Reynolds, in *Consensus ad Idem* (Rose ed., 1996), pp.84–88. Insurance textbooks do not clearly commit themselves: see *MacGillivray on Insurance Law* (13th edn), para.38–003.; Clarke, *Law of Insurance Contracts* (6th edn), para.5-5 onwards.

[68] See *National Oilwell (UK) Ltd v Davy Offshore Ltd* [1993] 2 Lloyd's Rep. 582 (unidentified principal).

[69] See above, para.8-081.

[70] See below, para.9-012.

[71] See below, para.9-013.

[72] See Comment to Article 76; *O'Herlihy v Hedges* (1803) 1 Sch. & Lef. 123; *Montgomerie v UK Mutual SS Assn* [1891] 1 Q.B. 370 at 372. See also *Sargent v Morris* (1820) 3 B. & Ald. 277 at 281. As to principal's liability where agent lacks capacity, see above, para.8-074.

the agent, and it is a defence for the third party to prove that the principal has intervened and claimed payment or damages, or that the agent's authority to sue is otherwise terminated. On principle this seems correct[73]; though some of the cases usually cited for the proposition would now be otherwise explained.[74] This subordination may also apply where the agent of a *disclosed* principal is a joint and several creditor of the third party; his right is presumably secondary to that of the principal.[75]

9-013   **Damages**[76]   The fact that the agent of the *undisclosed* principal appears to be and is regarded as a party to the contract can raise serious problems in the law of damages. The agent can certainly sue for specific performance, at any rate in his own favour[77]: but if he sues for damages he may be met by the fact that in general the victim of a breach of contract (or indeed a tort) can in general only recover his own loss.[78] In the case under consideration, any loss may be suffered by the agent's principal. If the agent was a trustee, he could recover his beneficiary's loss; but it has been held that the agent of an undisclosed principal cannot be regarded as a trustee for this purpose.[79]

Exceptions to the main rule have long existed, and were recognised in the leading case of *The Albazero*,[80] which concerned an action by a person who was the shipper of goods and charterer of a vessel to recover the loss of the consignee. The exceptions were principally identified in the context of goods in transit which were likely to pass into hands other than those of the original contracting party.[81] More recently decisions in the context of construction have permitted contracting parties to sue for loss suffered by others. The first case involved land changing hands in a way that had parallels with goods in transit,[82] but the next case did not.[83] The matter came to a head in *Alfred McAlpine Construction Ltd v Panatown Ltd*,[84] where the House of Lords accepted in principle[85] the availability of an action for defective performance by the party engaging a construction firm where the person doing so was in effect a nominee and the loss was suffered by another, associated firm which owned the land on which the building was erected.

Unfortunately the reason for permitting such recovery was not agreed. The majority view was that the contracting party had an interest in the performance which

---

73   cf. *Restatement, Second*, § 302, Comment c; § 368, Comments d, e, f; § 370; *Maynegrain Pty Ltd v Compafina Bank Ltd* [1982] 2 N.S.W.L.R. 141 at 150 (reversed without reference to this point (1984) 58 A.L.J.R. 389, PC). See Dal Pont, para.19.2.

74   e.g. *Rogers v Hadley* (1821) 2 H. & C. 227.

75   cf. *Restatement, Second*, § 370.

76   See Tan Cheng Han [2013] J.B.L. 799.

77   A claim for an order in favour of another might be met by the defence that the third party had not promised to perform in favour of that party.

78   A proposition accepted in the leading case, *Alfred McAlpine Construction Ltd v Panatown Ltd* [2001] 1 A.C. 518 at 522–523, 575, 580–581, discussed below.

79   *Allen v F. O'Hearn & Co* [1937] A.C. 213 at 218 ("the supposed agent's rights would be to recover the damage suffered by him on the footing that he had been principal"): but this is a puzzling passage.

80   [1977] A.C. 774.

81   See p.847, per Lord Diplock.

82   *Linden Gardens Trust Ltd v Lenesta Sludge Disposals Ltd* [1994] 1 A.C. 85.

83   *Darlington BC v Wiltshire Northern Ltd* [1995] 1 W.L.R. 68.

84   [2001] 1 A.C. 518. See in general Chitty, *Contracts* (32nd edn), para.18-049 onwards. See also Unberath, *Transferred Loss* (2003), Ch.7, indicating (at p.178) similar difficulties in German law.

85   The majority also held the action excluded because of the presence of a separate contract between contractor and site owner.

enabled him to sue when it was defective.[86] The minority view was that the loss was that of a third party but that in this and other exceptional cases the contracting party could sue for loss suffered by another. He would then be accountable to that other[87]; which would not be so (in the absence of other special arrangements) under the first view. Either view, but especially the first, can encounter difficulties with the basic rule of remoteness of damage in contract, which confines damages to what had been in the contemplation of the parties when the contract was made. Where the contract has a value which can be assessed objectively, its breach, whether by way of supply of inferior goods or services, can be assessed on the basis of that value and the problem can be met.[88] Similarly, the costs of obtaining alternative performance of what was promised will usually be reasonably apparent to the promisee. But when what is claimed is loss idiosyncratic to the third party, it may be difficult to say that such loss was in the contemplation of the parties. There are nevertheless in the *Panatown* case suggestions that, whichever view is adopted, the rule is one of law, and that such loss can be taken in on an objective basis.[89] In the context of undisclosed principal such theoretical problems are acute, as the third party has no contemplation of the existence of another party to the contract, let alone of special losses which that party might suffer. It is however assumed that some sort of objective assessment is to be applied as a matter of law,[90] though it cannot be said that the matter is exhaustively argued. There is Scottish authority to that effect, albeit conditioned by procedural considerations.[91]

Indirect representation[92]   In this situation the principal specifically did not   **9-014**
authorise the agent to bring him into privity with the third party (as with the old foreign principal rule[93]) or the contract with the third party excluded the intervention of anyone else.[94] Here again the agent may wish to sue for the principal's loss. In this context a rather vague reference to agency has been used to give the same result as that above.[95] The proper analysis of both situations awaits further development.

Interrogatories as to existence of undisclosed principal   It has been held that   **9-015**

---

[86] A view strongly put forward by Coote [1997] C.L.J. 537; (2001) 117 L.Q.R. 81; see also Ian Duncan Wallace QC (1999) 115 L.Q.R. 394; and Friedmann (1995) 111 L.Q.R. 628.
[87] A proposition for which there is surprisingly little authority. See however *The Albazero* [1977] A.C. 774 at 846; *Joseph v Knox* (1813) 3 Camp. 320; *Allen v F. O'Hearn & Co*, above, at 218.
[88] See *Leif Hoegh & Co v Petrolsea Inc (The World Era)* [1992] 1 Lloyd's Rep. 45 at 52–53, per Hobhouse J.
[89] See pp.535–536 (Lord Clyde), 554–555 (Lord Goff), 591 (Lord Millett).
[90] See pp.530 and 535–536 (Lord Clyde), 555–556 (Lord Goff), 591–592 (Lord Millett). See also p.581, where Lord Millett cites the *Bovis* case, fn.95 below, as authority for the undisclosed principal situation. Despite this, in *Rolls-Royce Power Engineering Plc v Ricardo Consulting Engineers Ltd* [2003] EWHC 2871 (TCC): [2004] 2 All E.R. (Comm) 129 it was held that recovery was limited to situations where the third party was aware of the interest of the principal. This seems doubtful: see Tettenborn, *Amicus Curiae*, Issue 60, July/August 2005. See also *Welburn v Dibb Lupton Broomhead* [2002] EWCA Civ 1601; [2003] P.N.L.R. 28; *Family Food Court v Seah Boon Lock* [2008] SGCA 31.
[91] *Craig & Co v Blackater* 1923 S.C. 472; *James Laidlaw & Sons v Griffin* 1968 S.L.T. 278; and see *Corfield v Grant* (1992) 29 Con.L.R. 58.
[92] See above, paras 1-021 and 1-022.
[93] See below, para.9-020.
[94] See above, para.8-079.
[95] See *L/M International Construction Inc (now Bovis International Inc) v The Circle Ltd Partnership* (1995) 49 Con.L.R. 12 at 23–24 (Staughton LJ), 32–33 (Millett LJ). In the *Panatown* case, Lord Millett referred to the *Bovis* case as a case of undisclosed principal: [2001] 1 A.C. 518 at 581.

in an action by the vendor for specific performance of a contract of sale of land, the plaintiff is not entitled to interrogate the defendant for the purpose of ascertaining whether he was acting as agent for an undisclosed principal.[96] And in general it would seem that, the contract being that of the agent, he is under no duty when suing or sued to disclose the existence of his principal.[97]

9-016   **Unidentified principal**   Difficult problems must frequently occur in the case of unidentified principals. Where the agent gives the third party to understand that he acts for another, as by reference to "our principals", "our clients", "the trustees" etc., there may indeed be cases where the third party can be regarded as being willing to deal with the principal, whoever he is. Indeed it has been said that in an ordinary commercial transaction such willingness may be assumed by the agent in the absence of other indications.[98] But this may sometimes be an improbable construction to put on the situation; at the other end of the scale, therefore, such facts may give rise, or assist in giving rise, to the inference that the third party deals only with the agent (the problem of the agent's position vis-à-vis his principal being irrelevant to the third party). But there is a middle course. The *Restatement, Third*[99] provides that when the agent acts for a principal whose existence is known but who is not identified at the time of contracting, the agent is unless otherwise agreed a party to the contract, and the inference is that he is liable in addition to and not in substitution for the principal (though sometimes his liability may cease on disclosure of the principal's identity). Though the fact that the agent does not name his principal is obviously relevant in determining whether he contracts personally, such a general proposition has actually been rejected in England in respect of unwritten contracts,[100] and in the Supreme Court of Canada in respect of a written contract.[101] In view of the weakness, or at least uncertainty, of the law as to demanding to know the identity of the principal,[102] this is perhaps unfortunate. But the wording of written contracts may certainly give rise to the agent being a party to the contract in such a case.[103] And there are many cases showing that in such situations the court will recognise a trade usage that a commercial agent, e.g. a broker, is personally liable, particularly if his principal is unidentified.[104] Here again the exact terms of the agent's engagement with the third party require careful analysis.

---

[96] *Sebright v Hanbury* [1916] 2 Ch. 245. But as to discovery against the principal, see above, para.8-081.

[97] See below, para.9-017; *IVI Pty Ltd v Baycrown Pty Ltd* [2007] 1 Qd R. 428 at [26] and [98] (no duty to reveal identity of undisclosed principal in pleadings, nor during trial).

[98] *Teheran-Europe Co Ltd v S.T. Belton (Tractors) Ltd* [1968] 2 Q.B. 545 at 555, per Diplock LJ, referred to as a "beneficial assumption in commercial cases" by Lord Lloyd of Berwick in *Siu Yin Kwan v Eastern Insurance Co Ltd* [1994] 2 A.C. 199 at 209. See also *Thomson v Davenport* (1829) 9 B. & C. 78.

[99] § 6.02.

[100] *N. & J. Vlassopulos Ltd v Ney Shipping Co (The Santa Carina)* [1977] 1 Lloyd's Rep. 478, Illustration 3 to Article 101. But equally it may make clear that he acts as agent: see the *Chartwell Shipping* case, below; *Southwell v Bowditch* (1876) 1 C.P.D. 374.

[101] *Chartwell Shipping Ltd v Q.N.S. Paper Co Ltd* [1989] 2 S.C.R. 683; (1989) 62 D.L.R. (4th) 36, Illustration 9 to Article 99, on the basis that "to add a burden of proof on the mandatary would blur the focus of analysis: the goal is to identify the intentions of the parties" (per L'Heureux Dubé J at pp.745 and 78).

[102] See below, para.9-017.

[103] e.g. *Tudor Marine Ltd v Tradax Export SA (The Virgo)* [1976] 2 Lloyd's Rep. 135, Illustration 6 to Article 99; *Seatrade Groningen BV v Geest Industries Ltd (The Frost Express)* [1996] 2 Lloyd's Rep. 375, Illustration 7 to Article 99.

[104] *Dale v Humfrey* (1858) E.B. & E. 1004 (oil); *Cropper v Cook* (1868) L.R. 3 C.P. 194 (wool); *Fleet*

The trade custom cases, which arise mostly in the context of the rules of evidence, on the whole do seem to assume that the agent's liability is additional to that of his principal[105]: a collateral contract[106] and suretyship[107] are also sometimes suggested. The doctrine of election, referred to above,[108] may again cause problems.

The most difficult cases may perhaps be those where the third party deals with an agent who is known normally to act for principals or in a situation where persons dealing frequently act for principals, but there is no indication as to whether or not that is so on this occasion. This was of course a common situation with the nineteenth-century factor, who was distinguished from a broker on the basis that a broker could be *assumed* to be dealing on behalf of a principal[109]; and cases of this type are associated with the growth of the undisclosed principal doctrine.[110] Problems may also arise in connection with bidders at auction sales.[111] Such cases may indeed fall to be considered under the undisclosed principal doctrine, in which case the contract is with the agent, subject to the principal's right to intervene and liability to be sued. But more rigorous analysis may require them to be considered in connection with the possible rules for unidentified principal cases.[112]

If there is in unidentified principal cases not even a prima facie rule that the agent is liable together with the principal, the agent may sometimes appear to be free from liability in cases where he should arguably be regarded as undertaking it. In such cases the courts have sometimes classified the principal as undisclosed rather than unidentified in order to secure the liability of the agent. The undisclosed principal rules may then themselves be confused by considerations which are really relevant to the unidentified principal situation. For example, it has been held that a third party cannot set off against the principal a debt accruing before he had notice of the principal's existence unless the principal was in some way at fault in misleading him[113]—a rule appropriate to unidentified principal situations where the existence of a principal is from the start envisaged, but not to true undisclosed principals. It is therefore submitted that the courts should be willing to adopt a rule of at least prima facie liability together with an unidentified principal unless it is absolutely clear that the person concerned acted as agent only.[114]

An action by the agent of an unidentified principal, where available, would be

---

v Murton (1871) L.R. 7 Q.B. 126 (fruit); *Hutchinson v Tatham* (1873) L.R. 8 C.P. 482 (charterparty); *Imperial Bank v London & St Katharine Docks Co* (1877) 5 Ch.D. 195 (fruit); *Bacmeister v Fenton, Levy & Co* (1883) C. & E. 121 (rice); *Pike v Ongley* (1887) 18 Q.B.D. 708 (hops); *Thornton v Fehr & Co* (1935) 51 Ll. L. Rep. 330 (tallow); *Anglo Overseas Transport Ltd v Titan Industrial Corp (United Kingdom) Ltd* [1959] 2 Lloyd's Rep. 152; *Perishables Transport Co v N. Spyropoulos (London) Ltd* [1964] 2 Lloyd's Rep. 379; *Cory Bros Shipping Ltd v Baldan* [1997] 2 Lloyd's Rep. 58 (forwarding agents); cf. *Wilson v Avec Audio-Visual Equipment Ltd* [1974] 1 Lloyd's Rep. 81 (no such custom as to insurance brokers). See further Article 98.

[105] See, e.g. *Pike v Ongley*, above.

[106] *Hutchinson v Tatham*, above (collateral contract coming into effect if name of principal not given; *Reid v Dreaper* (1861) 6 H. & N. 813.

[107] *Imperial Bank v London and St Katharine Docks Co*, above.

[108] Para.9-007.

[109] *Baring v Corrie* (1818) 2 B. & A. 137. The factor's contract could perhaps also be treated as collateral: above, para.9-009.

[110] e.g. *Armstrong v Stokes* (1872) L.R. 7 Q.B. 598; see Articles 76 and 80.

[111] See Illustration 4.

[112] See the differing views taken by Lord Denning MR and Diplock LJ in *Teheran-Europe Co Ltd v S.T. Belton (Tractors) Ltd* [1968] 2 Q.B. 545; *Marsh & McLennan Pty Ltd v Stanyers Transport Pty Ltd* [1994] 2 V.R. 232; Comment to Article 76.

[113] *Cooke & Sons v Eshelby* (1887) 12 App.Cas. 271: see Comment to Article 80.

[114] See Reynolds [1983] C.L.P. 119. See *Ferryways NV v Associated British Ports* [2008] EWHC 225

an action in accordance with the contract into which he had entered. It would not involve the problems of recovery of another's loss discussed in connection with undisclosed principals.[115]

9-017   **Interrogatories as to name of unidentified principal**   It is not clear whether an agent acting for an unidentified principal can be compelled to disclose his principal's name by interrogatory.[116] In some countries an agent who does not name his principal becomes personally liable[117]; but outside trade custom this would in England require legislation. Even if the question can usually be answered in practice, the lack of a proper formal mechanism for ascertaining the principal of a person who acts "for principals" or equivalent is a weakness of English common law, particularly in view of the lack of any presumption that such a person contracts together with his principal.[118]

9-018   **Fictitious or non-existent principal**   Such situations have given rise to specialised case law in the context of companies in the course of formation and unincorporated associations. This is discussed separately.[119]

9-019   **Agent his own principal**   Some cases suggest that where the agent has no principal, viz. is his own principal, he is personally liable and entitled. This seems contrary to general principle; but since such a proposition is not infrequently put forward, this topic also is separately discussed.[120] It may certainly assist in providing a remedy in situations where the name of the principal is difficult or impossible to discover.

9-020   **Foreign principal**[121]   There long existed a strong presumption of fact[122] (so strong that a court was "justified in treating it as a matter of law"[123]) that in the context of sale where an agent in England contracted on behalf of a foreign principal, disclosed

---

(Comm); [2008] 2 All E.R. (Comm) 504; [2008] 1 Lloyd's Rep. 639 at [69]; cf. *Lundie v Rowena Nominees Pty Ltd* (2007) 32 W.A.R. 404 (standard form loan agreement was expressed as an agreement to lend money to the plaintiff by defendant as agent for unnamed lender pursuant to a power of attorney; it was held that the defendant could itself be the lender where there was no principal in fact, nor valid power of attorney from any principal).

[115] See above, para.9-013.
[116] See *Hersom v Bernett* [1955] 1 Q.B. 98; *Thöl v Leask* (1855) 10 Exch. 704; *Hancocks v Leblache* (1878) 3 C.P.D. 197; *Sebright v Hanbury* [1916] 2 Ch. 245; *McBride v Christie's Australia Pty Ltd* [2014] NSWSC 1729 at [131]. See also *Santander UK Plc v National Westminster Bank Plc* [2014] EWHC 2626 (Ch) (duty on receiving bank to reveal who account holder is where claimant makes mistaken payment). But cf. *Santander UK Plc v Royal Bank of Scotland Plc* [2015] EWHC 2560 (Ch).
[117] See PECL art.3:203 and material there cited.
[118] See above, para.9-016.
[119] See Article 107.
[120] See Article 108.
[121] Hudson (1957) 35 Can.B.Rev. 336; (1960) 23 M.L.R. 695; (1966) 29 M.L.R. 353; (1969) 32 M.L.R. 207. The term "foreign principal" does not seem to be a very precise one, but it is normally taken to mean a principal who does not reside or carry on business in England or Wales. However, the purpose of the rule indicates what sort of person might be regarded as a foreign principal, and it is very doubtful whether principals in Scotland, Northern Ireland or even the Irish Republic should be treated as foreign.
[122] *Paterson v Gandasequi* (1812) 15 East 62; *Smyth v Anderson* (1849) 7 C.B. 21; *Dramburg v Pollitzer* (1872) 28 L.T. 470; *Glover v Langford* (1892) 8 T.L.R. 628; *Malcolm Finn & Co v Hoyle* (1893) 63 L.J.Q.B. 1; *Harper & Sons v Keller, Bryant and Co Ltd* (1915) 84 L.J.K.B. 1696.
[123] *Armstrong v Stokes* (1872) L.R. 7 Q.B. 598 at 605.

or undisclosed, the agent assumed personal liability to his English suppliers and had no authority to pledge the principal's credit by establishing privity of contract between the principal and the third party[124]; and conversely, where a merchant in England contracted for a principal abroad, that merchant was not to be regarded as having authority to bring his principal into privity of contract with the home supplier. Several of the cases associate this rule with the "commission merchant", in some respects an equivalent of the civil law *commissionnaire*.[125] The presumption could be displaced by clear evidence of authority. Further the effect of the presumption was to render the agent alone liable and entitled on the contract; so that when it was clear that the agent contracted only as agent, and that it was not intended that he should be personally liable, there was no room for the presumption, which could not operate inconsistently with the clear purport of the contract.[126] The presumption was not affected by the fact that the contract was in writing: most, if not all, of the cases concern such contracts.

The status of this presumption was discussed in many cases, and though it could be questioned,[127] it was said to reflect both a preference by foreign merchants to use an intermediary who did not bring them into privity of contract with a merchant in another country, especially where the contract involved bulk supplies from several foreign sources; and also the reluctance of English merchants to enter into transactions which might involve them in problems of the conflict of laws or the possibility of having to sue in a foreign jurisdiction, or both,[128] especially where the contract concerned bulk supplies from overseas sources. The latter reasoning seems more significant to modern eyes, since the foreign merchant's contract with his English intermediary may not be governed by English law. The banker's commercial credit system performs a similar function in to some extent localising the transaction. Later cases tended to treat the fact that the principal was foreign as one to be taken into account but no more.[129] In *Teheran-Europe Co Ltd v S. T. Belton (Tractors) Ltd*,[130] where air compressors were ordered for use in Iran, the Court of Appeal finally held that the presumption itself no longer exists, for "the usages of the law merchant are not immutable". But the fact that the principal is foreign is not irrelevant. Diplock LJ said[131]:

> "The fact that the principal is a foreigner is one of the circumstances to be taken into account in determining whether or not the other party to the contract was willing, or led 'the agent to believe' that he was willing, to treat as a party to the contract the agent's principal, and, if he was so willing, whether the mutual intention of the other party and the agent was that the agent should be personally entitled to sue and liable to be sued on the contract

---

124 *Armstrong v Stokes*, above; *Elbinger, etc. v Claye* (1873) L.R. 8 Q.B. 313; *Hutton v Bulloch* (1874) L.R. 9 Q.B. 572; and see cases cited in fn.122 above.
125 See above, paras 1-021 and 1-022; and the cases cited in fnn.123 and 124 above. See also Munday (1977) 6 Anglo-Am.L.Rev. 221 at 232–242.
126 *Miller, Gibb & Co v Smith & Tyrer Ltd* [1917] 2 K.B. 141.
127 See *Miller, Gibb & Co v Smith & Tyrer Ltd*, above, at 162; *Holt & Moseley v Cunningham & Partners* (1949) 83 Ll.Rep. 141.
128 See *Armstrong v Stokes* (1872) L.R. 7 Q.B. 598 at 605; Hill (1968) 31 M.L.R. 623 at 637–639; Munday (1977) 6 Anglo-Am.L.Rev. 221 at 235 onwards.
129 *H.O. Brandt & Co v Morris & Co* [1917] 2 K.B. 784; *Rusholme and Bolton and Roberts Hadfield v S.G. Read & Co* [1955] 1 W.L.R. 146; *Cox v Sorrell* [1960] 1 Lloyd's Rep. 471; *Anglo African Shipping Co of New York Inc v J. Mortner Ltd* [1962] 1 Lloyd's Rep. 610 at 617, 621; *Maritime Stores v H.P. Marshall & Co Ltd* [1963] 1 Lloyd's Rep. 602.
130 [1968] 2 Q.B. 545.
131 At 558.

as well as his principal. But it is only one of many circumstances, and as respects the creation of privity of contract between the other party and the principal its weight may be minimal, particularly in a case such as the present where the terms of payment are cash before delivery and no credit is extended by the other party to the principal. It may have considerably more weight in determining whether the mutual intention of the other party and the agent was that the agent should be personally liable to be sued as well as the principal, particularly if credit has been extended by the other party."[132]

9-021 **Confirming houses in international sales**[133] A confirming house provides specialised agency functions for an overseas buyer who wishes to import goods. The normal purpose of the intervention of a confirming house is so that the seller, in a transaction between himself and an overseas buyer, shall have someone in his own country to look to in respect of performance of the contract: like the banker's commercial credit, it performs the function of reducing the possibility of becoming involved in questions of the conflict of laws or of suing in foreign jurisdictions. A confirming house may, on instructions, act for the buyer as agent only, and if so is not liable to the seller.[134] Alternatively, it may act as merchant, viz. by buying from the seller and reselling to its principal, the buyer.[135] Neither of these arrangements really involves confirmation. A transaction involving confirmation will normally be intended to result in privity of contract being established between seller and confirming house.[136] In some cases the confirming house may be liable on a collateral contract whereby it answers in some way for the performance of the buyer's contract.[137] In other cases the confirming house may be solely liable to the seller, creating no privity between buyer and seller, but still remaining as an agent in relation to the buyer rather than a seller to its own principal: this possibility, which again involves the notion of what is sometimes called the commission merchant or *commissionnaire*, has not been fully explored.[138] It is clear that the fact that a confirming house acts as principal in one respect does not mean that it cannot act as agent in another, e.g. as a forwarding agent, and vice versa.[139] A confirming house that does undertake liability to the seller may answer for more than the mere solvency of the buyer: subject to the terms of the particular contract and to the commercial understanding of the transaction, it is subject to litigation on the contract in general.[140] So also it may sue the seller, or assign its rights of action to the buyer.

9-022 **Del credere agents** The position of a *del credere* agent is to be contrasted with

---

[132] As to which see *Fraser v Equitorial Shipping Co Ltd (The Ijaolo)* [1979] 1 Lloyd's Rep. 103.
[133] Hill (1972) 3 J. Maritime Law and Commerce 307; Schmitthoff (1970) 1 *Hague Recueil des Cours* at p.154–157; *The Export Trade* (12th edn), para.27-018 onwards; [1957] J.B.L. 17.
[134] cf. *Bolus & Co Ltd v Inglis Bros Ltd* [1924] N.Z.L.R. 164; *Stunzi Sons Ltd v House of Youth Pty Ltd* [1960] S.R.(N.S.W.) 220.
[135] See the dissenting judgment of Diplock LJ in *Anglo-African Shipping Co of New York Inc v J. Mortner Ltd* [1962] 1 Lloyd's Rep. 610.
[136] *Sobell Industries Ltd v Cory Bros & Co* [1955] 2 Lloyd's Rep. 82 at 89.
[137] *Sobell Industries Ltd v Cory Bros & Co*, above (Illustration 7).
[138] *Rusholme and Bolton and Roberts Hadfield v S.G. Read & Co* [1955] 1 W.L.R. 146 and *Anglo-African Shipping Co of New York Inc v J. Mortner Ltd* [1962] 1 Lloyd's Rep. 610, may be examples of this. See paras 1-021 and 1-022 above; Hill, above, at 318–324; (1968) 31 M.L.R. 623; *Bolus & Co Ltd v Inglis Bros Ltd*, above, at 174–175; *Downie Bros v Henry Oakley & Sons* [1923] N.Z.L.R. 734; *Scott v Geoghegan & Sons Pty Ltd* (1969) 43 A.L.J.R. 243; *Isaac Gundle v Mohanlal Sunderji* (1939) 18 Kenya L.Rep. 137; Comment to Article 69.
[139] *Anglo-African Shipping Co of New York Inc v J. Mortner Ltd*, above, at 616–617; *Sobell Industries Ltd v Cory Bros & Co*, above, at 90.
[140] *Sobell Industries Ltd v Cory Bros & Co*, above (Illustration 7); *Rusholme, etc., v Read*, above.

that of a confirming house. A *del credere* agent is normally the agent of the seller, not of the buyer. Thus, though he answers to the seller, he is not undertaking to the third party that his principal will perform a contract, but is undertaking to his principal that the third party will.[141] Equally, he cannot sue the third party.[142] A confirming house on the other hand is normally agent of the buyer, and thus answers to the seller not as agent but as a party to a contract with him.[143] Its duty to the buyer is therefore usually greater than that of a *del credere* agent, whose obligation is confined to answering for the failure by the other contracting parties, owing to insolvency or the like, to pay ascertained sums which may become due from them as debts.[144] However, situations may occur where it is difficult to distinguish between the two.[145]

Auctioneers Auctioneers provide examples of liability on what must be explained in modern terms (however the matter is put in old cases) as collateral contracts.[146] Where an auctioneer sells a specific chattel by auction for a disclosed principal, he is not liable upon the contract of sale,[147] nor does he impliedly warrant the title of his principal, although the name of the principal has not been disclosed to the buyer.[148] But he warrants that he has authority to sell, and that he knows of no defect in the title of his principal.[149] His contract with the buyer entitles him to sue for the price,[150] and is independent of the contract of sale, which he makes on behalf of the seller and to which he is not a party.[151] It is traditionally said to be based on his lien over or special property in the goods, and for this reason seems inappropriate to the sale of land,[152] though no doubt in such cases he may still be subject to contractual duties.[153] Liability of an auctioneer on a collateral contract has also arisen where an auctioneer declines to knock down an item to the highest bidder when the item was said to be without reserve.[154]

9-023

Another example was provided by the jobber on the Stock Exchange, who contracted, through the broker, with the seller of shares, to find a purchaser to whom no legitimate objection could be taken. When he had done so, he effected a contract

---

[141] *Churchill & Sim v Goddard* [1937] 1 K.B. 92.

[142] *Bramwell v Spiller* (1871) 21 L.T. 672; Article 2. But sometimes a *del credere* agent may by special arrangement or by the usage of trade answer to both parties to a sale: see Hill (1968) 31 M.L.R. 623 at 639 note 64. And see Illustration 23.

[143] See above, para.9-021.

[144] *Thomas Gabriel & Sons v Churchill & Sim* [1914] 3 K.B. 1272; *Rusholme, etc., v Read*, above.

[145] See Hill, above. See further as to *del credere* agents, Comment to Article 2.

[146] See above, para.9-009.

[147] *Elder Smith Goldsbrough Mort Ltd v McBride* [1976] 2 N.S.W.L.R. 631, Illustration 14; cf. *Fraser v Dalgety & Co Ltd* [1953] N.Z.L.R. 126.

[148] *Benton v Campbell, Parker & Co* [1925] 2 K.B. 410; *Chelmsford Auctions Ltd v Poole* [1973] Q.B. 542. The special situation where a sale merely goes through an auctioneer's books was analysed as a sale to the auctioneer and a resale by him in *Murphy v Howlett* [1960] E.G.D. 231.

[149] *Peto v Blades* (1814) 5 Taunt. 657; *Pollway Ltd v Abdullah* [1974] 1 W.L.R. 493 (warranty of authority to sign memorandum and accept deposit entitled auctioneer to sue upon cheque for deposit). See further below, para.9-029; Illustrations 11–14 and 18–20; Murdoch, *Law of Estate Agency* (5th edn), pp.172–173; Reynolds, in *Contemporary Issues in Commercial Law* (Lomnicka and Morse eds, 1997), p.161 onwards.

[150] See Illustration 18.

[151] *Benton v Campbell, Parker & Co*, above, at 416.

[152] See *Cherry v Anderson* (1876) I.R. 10 C.L. 204; *Fisher v Marsh* (1865) 6 B. & S. 411; *Evans v Evans* (1834) 3 A. & E. 132; cf. *Cleave v Moore* (1857) 3 Jur.(N.S.) 48.

[153] See *Pollway Ltd v Abdullah* [1974] 1 W.L.R. 493.

[154] *Barry v Davies* [2000] 1 W.L.R. 1962; noted by Coote [2001] NZ Law Rev. 277; Scott [2001] L.M.C.L.Q. 334. See Illustration 11.

between seller and buyer and his own collateral undertaking was performed.[155] This method of trading is no longer used in England.

9-024 **Freight forwarders**[156]   The obvious function of freight forwarders is to make contracts of carriage, often several, on behalf of a shipper. For this reason they were often formerly called "forwarding agents". There is however no objection to a person conducting business of this sort acting as carrier, i.e. undertaking to carry and actually performing by means of employees or independent subcontractors, and many do so (and indeed perform various other related functions also). The difficulty is then to determine exactly what is the appropriate legal analysis of what has been arranged.[157] Although in 1920 it was said that a forwarding agent was not a carrier,[158] and in 1965 it was said that the interpretation under which the freight forwarder was a carrier as opposed to an agent was exceptional,[159] this seems no longer to be so.[160] No doubt this is at least in part connected with the increased possibility of consolidating consignments which was created by the use of containers. The matter is not assisted however by many sets of standard terms the meaning (and sometimes application) of which is not clear, and an alleged tendency of freight forwarders to fight cases seeking to impose responsibility on them.[161] There certainly can be freight forwarders who act as agents for the main contract of carriage but also undertake liability towards the carrier.[162] Beyond the roles of agent and carrier, however, there is at least in theory a third possibility for analysis, based on the notion of indirect representation explained elsewhere in this book[163]: the forwarder is as regards his client an agent, working on an agency basis and owing a duty of best endeavours only, but as regards the carrier a principal. This reduces the forwarder's liability and also makes it difficult for the client to proceed against the carrier. One unreported case accepts this interpretation in the context of the CMR.[164] A more recent case,[165] while casting doubt on some of the reasoning in the earlier case,[166] accepts such an interpretation as a possibility, but states that clear evidence (not present in the case) would be required regarding the assumption of such a role.[167] In some countries, notably Germany, there is recent legislation

---

[155] *Grissell v Bristowe* (1868) L.R. 4 C.P. 36; *Maxted v Paine* (1869) L.R. 4 Ex. 203; affd (1871) L.R. 6 Ex. 132. See on these cases (1929) 39 Yale L.J. 265–271.

[156] See in general Reynolds, "The Liability of Freight Forwarders", Ch.14 in Soyer and Tettenborn (eds), *Carriage of Goods by Land, Sea and Air: Unimodal and Multimodal Transport in the 21st Century* (2014).

[157] For a case where both forwarder and actual carrier issued a bill of lading for the same goods, and the effect of the forwarder's document was not clear, see *Carrington Slipways Pty Ltd v Patrick Operations Pty Ltd (The Cape Comorin)* (1991) 24 N.S.W.L.R. 745.

[158] *Jones v European & General Express Co Ltd* (1920) 4 Ll.L.Rep. 127 per Rowlatt J.

[159] *Lengley, Beldon & Gaunt Ltd v Morley* [1965] 1 Lloyd's Rep. 297 at 306 per Mocatta J.

[160] For examples of freight forwarders as carriers, see *Ulster-Swift Ltd v Taunton Meat Haulage Ltd* [1977] 1 Lloyd's Rep. 346; *Elektronska Industrija Oour v Transped Oour Kontinentalna Spedicna* [1986] 1 Lloyd's Rep. 49; *Vastfame Camera Ltd v Birkart Glogistics* [2005] 4 H.K.C. 117.

[161] See Tetley, *Marine Cargo Claims* (4th edn, 2008), Vol.2. Ch.33.

[162] *Anglo Overseas Transport Ltd v Titan Industrial Corp (UK) Ltd* [1959] 2 Lloyd's Rep. 152 (liable for dead freight); *Perishables Transport Co Ltd v N. Spyropoulos (London) Ltd* [1964] 2 Lloyd's Rep. 379; *Cory Bros Shipping Ltd v Baldan Ltd* [1997] 2 Lloyd's Rep. 58.

[163] See above, para.1-021.

[164] *Bardiger v Halberg Spedition Aps*, Evans J, Unreported October 26, 1990, only available on LEXIS.

[165] *Aqualon (UK) Ltd v Vallana Shipping Corp* [1994] 1 Lloyd's Rep. 669.

[166] See at p.664 per Mance J.

[167] A possible example is *Salsi v Jetspeed Air Services Ltd* [1977] 2 Lloyd's Rep. 57. See also *Royal &*

determining the status and duties of freight forwarders.[168] Such an approach would have many advantages, but is not very likely to be adopted in large common law countries, where an opportunity for such legislation is unlikely to arise.

Deposits: receipt as agent for vendor   An agent, particularly an estate agent, auctioneer or solicitor acting in connection with the sale of land, may receive money from a third party to hold by way of deposit. Sometimes he receives this as agent for the vendor: this is the assumption in the case of solicitors[169] and estate agents[170] unless there are indications to the contrary. Old cases suggest that auctioneers, on the other hand, prima facie receive money in such circumstances not as agents but as stakeholders[171] though it is not clear why the rule for them should be different, and hence whether this interpretation is still correct. The consequence of receipt as agent is that it is the vendor who is liable if the sale goes off and the money is not returned.[172] Statute law may, in some circumstances, govern the use of deposits, and make agents liable for non-compliance with those requirements.[173]

9-025

Agent as stakeholder   Whatever the prima facie rule, circumstances frequently arise where persons in these categories receive money as stakeholders. A person receiving money as stakeholder must hold or at least account for it pending the occurrence of the relevant event, and when this has occurred, pay it across in accordance with his instructions. He must not accede to the unilateral instructions of one of the parties to do otherwise, though he must accept the instructions of both of them, for example, to transfer the deposit to another stakeholder.[174] He does not, as a general rule, hold the deposit in trust[175] and must pay it to one of the parties, usually the vendor, when the relevant event occurs. If he takes the view that it has occurred, but his view is wrong, he is liable, but in personam.[176] It is sometimes said that in such a case he is agent of both parties[177]; but it seems rather that he receives the money from the purchaser under a specific and separate obligation as

9-026

Sun Alliance Insurance Plc v MK Dgital (Cyprus) Ltd [2006] EWCA Civ 629 (interpretation as commissionaire de transport).
[168] See Reynolds, "The Liability of Freight Forwarders", Ch.14 in Soyer and Tettenborn (eds), *Carriage of Goods by Land, Sea and Air: Unimodal and Multimodal Transport in the 21st Century* (2014) at 257–258.
[169] *Ellis v Goulton* [1893] 1 Q.B. 350 at 352–353 (Illustration 1 to Article 111); *Tudor v Hamid* [1988] 1 E.G.L.R. 251 at 255. This has the advantage for the purchaser that he has a lien on the property to the extent of the deposit: *Whitehead & Co Ltd v Watt* [1902] 1 Ch. 835; cf. *Combe v Lord Swaythling* [1947] Ch. 625. See also *Skinner v Trustee of the Property of Reed* [1967] Ch. 1194.
[170] *Ojelay v Neosale Ltd* [1987] 2 E.G.L.R. 167 at 168.
[171] *Harington v Hoggart* (1830) 1 B. & Ad. 577; *Furtado v Lumley* (1890) 6 T.L.R. 168.
[172] See Article 111.
[173] See in relation to tenancies of houses, the liabilities of landlords' agents under the Housing Act 2004 ss.214–215, considered in *Draycott v Hannells Letting Ltd (t/a Hannells Letting Agents)* [2010] EWHC 217 (QB); [2011] 1 W.L.R. 1606.
[174] *Rockeagle Ltd v Alsop Wilkinson* [1992] Ch. 47 (despite solicitors having an interest in retaining it against debts owed by vendor). His lien is confined to so much as becomes the property of the vendor: *Skinner v Trustee of the Property of Reed*, above. As to interest, see Article 52.
[175] *Hastingwood Property Ltd v Saunders Bearman Anselm* [1991] Ch. 114; *Potters (A Firm) v Loppert* [1973] Ch. 399.
[176] *Hastingwood Property Ltd v Saunders Bearman Anselm*, above; *Merchant International Co Ltd v Natsionalna Aktsionerna Kompaniia Naftogaz Ukrainy* [2014] EWHC 391 (Comm); [2014] 1 C.L.C. 271 at [34].
[177] *Collins v Stimson* (1883) 11 Q.B.D. 142 at 144.

principal.[178] It appears from the auctioneer cases that the vendor also is liable if the stakeholder defaults[179]: but the agent's obligation is clearly a separate one from that of his principal. The obligation is probably contractual, the consideration for his promise being that he has the use of the money without accounting for interest[180]; but alternatively it may lie in restitution, though this head of restitution is not yet well worked out in English law.[181]

Where the agent receives money under a pre-contract situation in the sale of land "subject to contract", as estate agents sometimes do, he is often also said to hold as stakeholder, and it has indeed been said that this is the appropriate interpretation where there are no other indications.[182] In this context the term "stakeholder" has at best a specialised meaning, however, and would be better avoided,[183] for the holder is under a duty to return the money to the prospective purchaser on demand at any time before he has paid it away on the completion of the contract in accordance with instructions.[184] Such a person is probably better described as agent of the purchaser, authorised to hold and pay away the money unless that authority is revoked. Here the fact that the agent must be ready to return the money on mere demand is more plausibly treated as consideration for his entitlement to interest.[185] In such cases the vendor is not liable if the estate agent defaults.[186]

9-027 **Express restriction of liability** Where an agent contracts personally, his liability may be expressly restricted to certain events. The cesser clause in a charterparty may be cited as an example.[187] Older forms of the clause provide that the charterer signs as agent for others, and that his liability to the shipowner is to cease as soon as the cargo is shipped, the shipowner holding a lien for unpaid charges. Under it the charterer's liability may cease as specified and be superseded

---

[178] *Hastingwood Property case*, above, at 123. See also *Berry v Hodson* [1989] 1 Qd.R. 361 (knowledge of stakeholder not imputed to vendor); *Bank of Scotland v Truman* [2005] EWHC 583 (QB) at [54]; *Bristol Alliance Nominee No.1 v Bennett* [2013] EWCA Civ 1626 at [24].

[179] *Fenton v Browne* (1807) 14 Ves. 144; *Annesley v Muggridge* (1816) 1 Madd. 593 at 596; *Rowe v May* (1854) 18 Beav. 613; *Christie v Robinson* (1907) 4 C.L.R. 1338; *Swindle v Knibb* (1929) 29 S.R.(N.S.W.) 325; *Grant v O'Leary* (1955) 93 C.L.R. 587; *Goding v Frazer* [1967] 1 W.L.R. 286 at 290–291; *Barrington v Lee* [1972] 1 Q.B. 326 at 335; *Ojelay v Neosale Ltd* [1987] 2 E.G.L.R. 167 at 168; *Thomson Hill Pte. Ltd v Chang Erh* [1992] 2 Singapore L.R. 769; Murdoch, *Law of Estate Agency* (5th edn), p.235 onwards. The rule seems to be based on the idea that the vendor appoints the stakeholder: quaere whether it should apply when he cannot easily be said to have done so, as where it is the purchaser's solicitor who holds the money. But in the *Thomson Hill* case, above, it was held that the same result ensued because the parties in such a case have by mutual consent made the purchaser's solicitor the stakeholder.

[180] *Potters (A Firm) v Loppert* [1973] Ch. 399, following *Harington v Hoggart* (1830) 1 B. & Ad. 577; and see *Smith v Hamilton* [1951] Ch. 174 at 184. See also Article 52.

[181] See *Chillingworth v Esche* [1924] 1 Ch. 97. See also as to this point *Burt v Claude Cousins & Co Ltd* [1975] 1 Q.B. 426 at 449; *Barrington v Lee* [1972] 1 Q.B. 326 at 337; *Potters (A Firm) v Loppert* above; (1976) 92 L.Q.R. 484; Article 111, Illustration 2.

[182] *Burt v Claude Cousins & Co Ltd*, above, per Lord Denning MR and Sachs LJ. But see *Desmond v Brophy* [1985] I.R. 449, where it was held on the facts that a solicitor received such a deposit as agent for the prospective vendor.

[183] *Maloney v Hardy and Moorsehead* [1971] 2 Q.B. 442n.

[184] *Sorrell v Finch* [1977] A.C. 728 at 749 (Illustration 4 to Article 92). See a recent but rather inconclusive discussion of the role of stakeholders and of vendors and purchaser in a pre-contract situation in *Gribbon v Lutton* [2001] EWCA Civ 1956; [2002] Q.B. 902.

[185] See *Potters (A Firm) v Loppert*, above, at 414–415.

[186] *Sorrell v Finch*, above. See also Article 111, Illustration 3.

[187] See below, para.9-096.

by the liability of the holders of the bills of lading.[188] Such clauses, which are the subject of extensive case law,[189] do not necessarily involve true agency by the charterer, for he may not at the time of contracting have a principal or principals as required. He may simply intend to procure that other shippers fill the ship with general cargo and pay the freight between them. Indeed he may in the end ship himself. Later forms of the clause do not refer to agency.

Agents of the Crown Prior to 1947, no action for breach of contract lay against the Crown, except where permitted by statute. However, as the Crown was to all intents and purposes liable in contract by Petition of Right, no special rule was avowedly applied to agents of the Crown, who were therefore, like other agents, not liable unless they had contracted personally. But they would rarely be held to do so,[190] which is doubtless fair when the magnitude of commitment involved in some government contracts is considered. Cases of personal liability are however not impossible,[191] and indeed where the "agent" is a public body there is no particular difficulty about them: in such a case at any rate it is also possible for the Crown and the agent to be liable together.[192] The Crown can now be sued directly by virtue of the Crown Proceedings Act 1947, but the rules as to the liability and entitlement to sue an agent of the Crown remain unchanged.

9-028

Defences[193] Where the agent, being liable on it, is sued on the main contract, he can presumably plead defences arising out of the contract, and defences personal to himself, but not defences personal to the principal. Where the agent sues, the third party can likewise plead defences on the main transaction, but not defences against the agent personally unless the principal was undisclosed.

9-029

But where the agent sues on a separate or collateral contract, defences available on the main contract may not be available against him, depending on the terms of his contract as interpreted by the court. The best example of this is the case of auctioneers.[194] Auctioneers, as stated above, make a separate and quite independent contract with the buyer which renders them subject to certain liabilities and also entitles them to sue. Payment to or set-off against the principal are therefore normally no defence to the auctioneer's claim.[195] But it may sometimes be a defence if the auctioneer knew of such a set-off, for then the contract with him may be otherwise interpreted, or if the auctioneer apparently waived his right by allowing

---

[188] *Oglesby v Yglesias* (1858) E.B. & E. 930; *Milvain v Perez* (1861) 3 E. & E. 495.
[189] See in general Scrutton, *Charterparties* (23nd edn), para.9-168 onwards.
[190] See *Palmer v Hutchinson* (1881) 6 App.Cas. 619; *Macbeath v Haldimand* (1786) 7 T.R. 172; also *Kenny v Cosgrave* [1926] I.R. 517. As to the liability of agents of the Crown for breach of warranty of authority, see below, para.9-074.
[191] Illustrations 8–10. But these are special cases: a private individual contracting on behalf of the Crown (as opposed to a public body specially incorporated by statute, or a private person making arrangements on his own behalf) does not seem to be liable, and dicta that he is free from liability have been couched in strong terms: see, e.g. *Gidley v Palmerston* (1822) 3 B. & B. 275 at 286–287.
[192] *International Ry Co v Niagara Parks Commission* [1941] A.C. 328 (again a case on a public body, incorporated by statute with the power to sue and be sued).
[193] See Derham [1985] C.L.J. 384; *Law of Set-Off* (4th edn), para.13-75; Wood, *English and International Set-Off* (1989), Ch.19.
[194] See Derham, above at [13.93], [13.94]; Reynolds, in *Contemporary Issues in Commercial Law* (Lomnicka and Morse eds, 1997), p.161 onwards.
[195] Illustration 19.

goods to be taken away contrary to normal practice without asking for payment.[196] And if the auctioneer's principal did not own the goods, the auctioneer has no one from whom he can derive an interest in the goods, and payment to the true owner will discharge a purchaser.[197] Further, the auctioneer's right to sue may sometimes be extinguished if he has received his commission, for here an equity may be raised against him.[198] Similar reasoning was applied to nineteenth-century factors, who likewise had a lien, and sometimes (less obviously) to brokers.[199]

The contract on which the agent sues may be independent of the main contract to such an extent that defences against him may be pleaded though he effectively sues for his principal. Thus it has been held that an underwriter may set off, in an action by a broker for insurance money due to a client, debts owed by the broker to the underwriter.[200]

9-030 **Estoppel as to whether a party to contract**   There may be circumstances when, although he is not on true analysis a party to the contract, an agent conducts himself towards the third party as though he is. In such circumstances an estoppel may be raised against him. This has been held to occur in connection with the demise or "identity of carrier" clause, a bill of lading clause which purports to create a contract with the shipowner where the ship is not owned by or chartered by demise to the party issuing the bill of lading.[201] Under such clauses the party issuing the bill of lading acts as agent only. But where such a party conducted himself as if he was the contracting party, and the third party proceeded on this basis with the result that his action against the true principal became time-barred, it was held that the party issuing the bill was estopped from alleging that he was not a party to the contract.[202]

9-031 **Warranty of authority**   An agent who contracts on behalf of his principal is normally regarded as warranting his authority to do so. This special collateral contract is treated separately in Article 105.

9-032 **Tort**   An agent may of course be liable to the third party in deceit. There may also be circumstances in which the agent assumes a duty of care towards the third party. This would not involve liability on the promise, but in respect of negligent representation, or sometimes negligent conduct.[203]

9-033 **Statute**   Section 21 of the Estate Agents Act 1979, in combination with regulations made under the Act,[204] impose on estate agents certain duties of disclosure to third parties of any personal interest in a transaction.[205] These have, however, no civil sanction and are only enforceable in so far as they may trigger the enforce-

---

[196] Illustration 20.
[197] *Dickenson v Naul* (1833) 4 B. & Ad. 638; and see *Fraser v Dalgety & Co Ltd* [1953] N.Z.L.R. 126.
[198] Illustration 20; but cf. Illustration 19.
[199] See Illustrations 21 and 22; Reynolds, above; para.9-009 above.
[200] *Gibson v Winter* (1833) 5 B. & Ad. 96.
[201] See Scrutton, *Charterparties* (23rd edn), para.6-046 onwards.
[202] *Pacol Ltd v Trades Lines Ltd (The Henrik Sif)* [1982] 1 Lloyd's Rep. 456, applying reasoning in *Amalgamated Investment & Property Co Ltd v Texas Commerce International Bank Ltd* [1982] Q.B. 84; *Taylors Fashions Ltd v Liverpool Victoria Trustee Co Ltd*, ibid. 133n. See further *The Stolt Loyalty* [1993] 2 Lloyd's Rep. 281 at 289–291; [1995] 1 Lloyd's Rep. 598; above, para.8-028.
[203] See Article 113.
[204] Estate Agents (Undesirable Practices) (No.2) Order 1991 (SI 1991/1032).
[205] See Murdoch, *Law of Estate Agency* (5th edn), p.297 onwards; *The Estate Agents and Property Misdescriptions Acts* (3rd edn), Ch.3C.

ment powers of the Director General of Fair Trading. The legal position of travel agents who act as intermediaries, but do not expressly undertake contractual liability, for package holidays offered by principals under the Package Travel, Package Holidays and Package Tours Regulations 1992,[206] is unclear, but some authority suggests that liability under those Regulations does turn on the defendant being in a contractual relationship with the claimant,[207] or the organiser of the package.

Illustrations

Liability of agent

(1) A acted as the London agent of C & Co, who were paper manufacturers in Vienna. B, by letter, ordered paper from A, who in his own name acknowledged the letter, and promised to supply the paper in certain quantities at certain times. A portion of the paper was delivered, and on B complaining to A respecting the non-delivery of the remainder, A stated that it was the default of C & Co B then wrote to C & Co telling them of the position of affairs, and the excuses made by A. Subsequently B sued A for breach of contract. Held, that A, having contracted personally, was liable, and that B's letter to C & Co did not amount to an election by B to substitute C & Co for A as the contracting parties.[208] Some weight was attached to the circumstance that the principals were foreign.[209]

(2) Where solicitors instructed stockbrokers to sell stock belonging to A, and enclosed a blank transfer signed by A, it was held that the instructions to sell were given by the solicitors as principals and that they were liable when A objected to the registration of the transfer.[210]

(3) An agent signed in his own name, without mentioning his principal, an undertaking to accept shares in a company, and the shares were allotted to him. Subsequently, the principal took a larger number of shares, in satisfaction, as the agent said, of his undertaking. Held, that the agent, having personally accepted the shares, was liable as a contributory.[211]

(4) An agent buys goods at a sale by auction, and gives his own name, which is entered as that of the buyer. He is personally liable, unless it is clearly proved that he did not intend to bind himself, and that the auctioneer knew that.[212]

(5) A stockbroker in Hong Kong presenting share transfers for registration has been held to promise that he will indemnify the person to whom he presents

9-034

---

[206] SI 1992/3288.
[207] See *Hone v Going Places Leisure Travel Ltd* Unreported November 16, 2000, QBD; affd [2001] EWCA Civ 947; and *Titshall v Qwerty Travel Ltd* [2011] EWCA Civ 1569 at [16]; [2012] 2 All E.R. 627.
[208] *Dramburg v Pollitzer* (1873) 28 L.T. 470; cf. *J.S. Robertson (Aust.) Pty Ltd v Martin* (1956) 94 C.L.R. 30. See Articles 82 and 104. The "election" reasoning would not be so expressed today: see above, paras 8-119 and 9-030.
[209] See above, para.9-020.
[210] *Hichens, Harrison Woolston & Co v Jackson & Sons* [1943] A.C. 266; and see *Lavan v Walsh* [1964] I.R. 87; *Saxon v Blake* (1861) 29 Beav. 438; *Hobhouse v Hamilton* (1826) 1 Hog. 401 (Ir.); and see Article 97. As to the enforcement of solicitors' undertakings, see *Geoffrey Silver & Drake v Baines* [1971] 1 Q.B. 396 at 402; Cordery, *Solicitors* (8th edn).
[211] *Re Southampton, Bird's Case* (1864) 4 De G.J. & S. 200.
[212] *Williamson v Barton* (1862) 7 H. & N. 899; *Chadwick v Maden* (1851) 9 Hare 188. Presumably commercial usage in the type of auction sale in question would be relevant.

them against the consequences of registering them; and may also be held to warrant their genuineness.[213]

(6)   A fishing vessel is owned by R, who forms a company to hire it from him and operate it. Repairs are ordered by R on the company's notepaper, signed "R, Director". Although R undoubtedly contracts as agent for the company, he also, as owner of the vessel, undertakes personal liability.[214]

(7)   A buyer in Turkey orders radio sets from an English manufacturer. The order is confirmed by an English confirming house and accepted by the seller. The buyer fails to accept full delivery. The confirming house is liable for the buyer's breach of contract.[215]

(8)   A naval commander, when employing a cook, undertook to pay him a certain sum per annum in addition to the government pay. Held, that the commander was personally liable to pay that sum, he having contracted personally, and not as an agent for the government.[216]

(9)   A clerk of a county court gave orders for the fitting up, etc., of the courthouse. Held, that it was properly left to the jury to say whether he had contracted personally, and that, if he had, he was personally liable on the contract.[217]

(10)   The Commissioners of Public Works and Buildings entered into a contract with certain builders for the erection of public buildings. It was held that the Commissioners must be taken to have contracted for themselves, and not merely as agents for the Crown, and that they were liable to be sued by the builders for damages for breach of the contract.[218]

(11)   An auctioneer sold goods on behalf of a disclosed principal, the conditions of sale providing that the lots should be cleared within three days, and that if from any cause the auctioneer was unable to deliver, etc., the purchaser should accept compensation. Held, that the auctioneer, being in possession of the goods, and having contracted to deliver, was personally liable to the purchaser for nondelivery.[219]

(12)   In a case of a sale of standing corn with straw, to be removed at the

---

213 *Yeung Kai Yung v Hong Kong and Shanghai Banking Corp* [1981] A.C. 787; cf. *Guaranty Trust Corp of New York v Hannay & Co* [1918] 2 K.B. 623. And see below, para.9-062.

214 *The Swan* [1968] 1 Lloyd's Rep. 5; see also *R. & J. Bow Ltd v Hill* (1930) 37 Ll.Rep. 46; *Format International Security Printers Ltd v Mosden* [1975] 1 Lloyd's Rep. 37; cf. *Badgerhill Properties Ltd v Cottrell* [1991] B.C.L.C. 805, Illustration 16 to Article 99. Compare comments by Legh-Jones (1969) 32 M.L.R. 325 and Reynolds (1969) 85 L.Q.R. 92. See also Prentice (1973) 89 L.Q.R. 518 at 531, suggesting that the case is inconsistent with *Newborne v Sensolid (Great Britain) Ltd* [1954] 1 Q.B. 45, Illustration 6 to Article 107 and *Henry Browne & Sons Ltd v Smith* [1964] 2 Lloyd's Rep. 276. It could also be said that some of the dicta are inconsistent with what was subsequently said in *N. & J. Vlassopulos Ltd v Ney Shipping Co (The Santa Carina)* [1977] 1 Lloyd's Rep. 478. Illustration 3 to Article 101. As regards repairs to and stores for ships, see further cases cited above; Article 99, Illustration 7; Article 101, Illustration 2; *H.J. Lyons & Sando Ltd v Houlson* [1963] S.A.S.R. 29; *Stag Line Ltd v Tyne Shiprepair Group Ltd (The Zinnia)* [1984] 2 Lloyd's Rep. 211. For a case where there was express provision for joint and several liability, see *Middle East Tankers and Freighters Bunker Services SA v Abu Dhabi Container Lines* [2002] EWHC 957 (Comm); [2002] 2 Lloyd's Rep. 643.

215 *Sobell Industries Ltd v Cory Bros & Co Ltd* [1955] 2 Lloyd's Rep. 82; see above, para.9-021.

216 *Clutterbuck v Coffin* (1842) 3 M. & G. 842. See also *Cunningham v Collier* (1785) 4 Doug. 233; cf. *Unwin v Wolseley* (1787) 1 T.R. 674 (cases on deeds); *Rice v Chute* (1801) 1 East 579.

217 *Auty v Hutchinson* (1848) 6 C.B. 266.

218 *Graham v Public Works Commrs* [1901] 2 K.B. 781; *Roper v Public Works Commrs* [1915] 1 K.B. 45. The Commissioners were a public body incorporated by statute.

219 *Woolfe v Horne* (1877) 2 Q.B.D. 355.

purchaser's expense, it was held that the auctioneer contracted to give proper authority to enter and carry away the corn and straw, and undertook that he was in fact authorised to sell, but that he did not warrant the title.[220] Upon a sale of shares, which required transfer by deed, the auctioneers, who were acting on behalf of an unnamed principal, were held liable in damages for failure to procure a transfer of the shares, upon the ground that they had agreed to do so.[221]

(13) Where a sale by auction is advertised as being "without reserve" it may be that the auctioneer impliedly contracts to accept the offer of the highest bona fide bidder, and is liable in damages for breach of such implied contract if he accepts a bid from the vendor.[222] But an advertisement to the effect that certain goods will be sold on certain days does not amount to a contract to sell them, so as to entitle a person who acts on the advertisement to recover damages for loss of time or expense if the goods are not put up at all.[223]

(14) An auctioneer sells a bull at an auction of stud cattle. The bull proves infertile. The auctioneer is not liable for breach of the implied condition as to description and may sue for the price.[224]

(15) A director instructs estate agents to sell land, most of which is owned by his company but part of which he owns personally. Both he and his company are jointly and severally liable for the agents' commission.[225]

Agent's right to sue

(16) A contract was made in the following form: "It is mutually agreed between J. & R. W., of the one part, and S J C, on behalf of G. & M. Rail Co, of the other part, etc." (signed) "J & R W, S J C". Held, that S J C was entitled to sue in his own name for breach of the contract, he having contracted personally.[226] **9-035**

(17) A broker contracted in writing in his own name to buy goods, the seller being told that there was a principal. The broker then, under a general authority from the principal, contracted to resell. On hearing of the last-mentioned contract, the principal refused to have anything to do with the goods, and the broker acquiesced. The seller then refused to deliver. Held, that the broker, having contracted personally, had a right to recover damages for the non-delivery, and that the principal's renunciation of the contract did not affect that right.[227]

(18) An auctioneer sells A's goods to a buyer who knows that they are A's property.

---

[220] *Wood v Baxter* (1883) 49 L.T. 45; *Benton v Campbell Parker & Co* [1925] 2 K.B. 410.

[221] *Franklyn v Lamond* (1847) 4 C.B. 637; *Hanson v Roberdeau* (1792) Peake 163.

[222] *Warlow v Harrison* (1858) 1 E. & E. 295 at 309; followed in *Barry v Davies* [2000] 1 W.L.R. 1962. See Slade (1952) 68 L.Q.R. 238; (1953) 69 L.Q.R. 21; Gower (1952) 68 L.Q.R. 457; *Johnston v Boyes* [1899] 2 Ch. 73. See also *Wright v Madden* [1992] 1 Qd. R. 343; cf. *Rainbow v Howkins* [1904] 2 K.B. 322; *McManus v Fortescue* [1907] 2 K.B. 1; *Richards v Phillips* [1969] 1 Ch. 39. Compare the auctioneer's liability for breach of warranty of authority: Article 105.

[223] *Harris v Nickerson* (1873) L.R. 8 Q.B. 286. On these auctioneer cases see in general Murdoch, *Law of Estate Agency* (5th edn), p.167 onwards.

[224] *Elder Smith Goldsbrough Mort Ltd v McBride* [1976] 2 N.S.W.L.R. 631; cf. *Fraser v Dalgety & Co Ltd* [1953] N.Z.L.R. 126.

[225] *Savills (UK) Ltd v Blacker* [2017] EWCA Civ 68.

[226] *Cooke v Wilson* (1856) 1 C.B.(N.S.) 153; *Clay & Newman v Southern* (1852) 7 Exch. 717; *H.O. Brandt & Co v H.N. Morris & Co* [1917] 2 K.B. 784; cf. *Sharman v Brandt* (1871) L.R. 6 Q.B. 720.

[227] *Short v Spackman* (1831) 2 B. & Ad. 962.

The auctioneer may, nevertheless, sue in his own name for the price,[228] even where he has already been paid a sum sufficient to cover his commission and charges.[229] But if the contract can be treated by the buyer, who has not paid, as discharged for breach, it may be that the auctioneer cannot sue.[230]

(19)   An auctioneer sued for the price of goods sold and delivered. The defendant pleaded that the plaintiff acted as an auctioneer, and that the defendant had paid the principal for the goods before action. Held, that the plea was bad, because the auctioneer would have had, as against the principal, a lien on the proceeds for charges, etc.[231] The defendant should have shown that, either by the conditions of sale or by facts accruing subsequently, payment to the principal was permitted in discharge of the plaintiff's claim.

(20)   An auctioneer, on behalf of A, sold goods to B. A was indebted to B, and there was an agreement between them before the sale that the price of any goods bought by B should be set off against the debt, but the auctioneer had no notice of the agreement. The auctioneer permitted B to take away the goods, thinking that he was going to pay for them, B thinking that he was taking them in pursuance of his agreement with A. The auctioneer paid A on account and after receiving notice of the agreement between A and B, paid A the balance of the proceeds of the sale, such balance exceeding the amount of B's purchases. The auctioneer subsequently sued B for the price of the goods. Held, that the auctioneer's charges having been paid before action, and he having had notice of the agreement between A and B at the time of his payment to A (exceeding the amount for which he was suing B), the settlement between A and B constituted a good defence.[232] Here, the auctioneer was not really prejudiced by the settlement with the principal.

(21)   A factor sold, in his own name, goods on which he had a lien for advances. While the advances were unpaid, the factor's right to sue the purchaser and compel payment had priority to that of the principal or his trustee in bankruptcy.[233]

(22)   A broker sold, in his own name, goods on which he had made advances. The buyer had no right, in an action by the broker for the price, to set off a debt due to him from the principal.[234]

(23)   A, acting as *del credere* agent on behalf of B, a timber exporter, sold a cargo of timber to C. A, in accordance with the contract of agency, paid to B the price of the timber, less A's commission; and, in accordance with the contract of sale, C accepted bills of exchange drawn by A for the price of the timber. When the timber arrived, C rejected it on the ground that it was not as speci-

---

[228]   *Williams v Millington* (1788) 1 H.Bl. 81.
[229]   *Chelmsford Auctions Ltd v Poole* [1973] Q.B. 542. See also *Fisher v Marsh* (1865) 6 B. & S. 411. But this does not apply to the sale of land: above, para.9-023.
[230]   See *Dickenson v Naul* (1833) 4 B. & Ad. 638; see also discussion in *Elder Smith Goldsbrough Mort Ltd v McBride* [1976] 2 N.S.W.L.R. 631 at 648; above, para.9-023.
[231]   *Robinson v Rutter* (1855) 4 E. & B. 954.
[232]   *Grice v Kenrick* (1870) L.R. 5 Q.B. 340; *Holmes v Tutton* (1855) 5 E. & B. 65; see explanation of these cases in *Chelmsford Auctions Ltd v Poole*, above, at 549; cf. *Manley & Sons Ltd v Berkett* [1912] 2 K.B. 329. On these auctioneer cases, see in general Murdoch, *Law of Estate Agency* (5th edn), p.167 onwards; Derham, *Law of Set-Off* (4th edn), paras 13.101–13.102.
[233]   *Drinkwater v Goodwin* (1775) 1 Cowp. 251. See above, para.1-046.
[234]   *Atkyns and Batten v Amber* (1796) 2 Esp. 493. But this case was doubted in *Bramwell v Spiller* (1870) 21 L.T. 672.

fied, and it was found that he was entitled so to do. C dishonoured his acceptances. Held, that A was not the trustee or agent of B in respect of A's rights as holder of the bills of exchange; that there was no failure of consideration for the bills, which were separate contracts between A and C, and were not affected by the failure of consideration under the contract for sale of the timber; and that C was liable to A for the amount of the bills.[235]

(24) A stockbroking company as agent for unidentified and unascertained principals ("clients of the company") made a contract to lend money on conditions including that the borrower would make an Initial Public Offering ("IPO") by set date. The money was advanced but the IPO did not occur. Properly construed, the agent alone was party to the contract (its principals each to provide part of the funds), and hence entitled to sue to recover the loan funds.[236]

Article 99

WRITTEN CONTRACTS

The question whether the agent is to be deemed to have contracted personally, in the case of a contract in writing other than a deed, bill of exchange, promissory note or cheque, depends upon the intention of the parties, as appearing from the terms of the written agreement as a whole, the construction of which is a matter of law.[237] The party concerned may act as agent in some respects and as principal (including as trustee) in others.[238]   **9-036**

Comment

In the context of a written contract, an agent may be held liable and entitled rather more easily than in unwritten contracts, because of the interpretation put by the court on words used. There is also a sizeable body of case law in this area which can be cited as precedent in disputes. This is particularly the case in relation to small companies, the owner-managers of which frequently fail to make clear whether they are signing personally or on behalf of their company.[239]   **9-037**

The cases on this topic should only be treated as single instances exemplifying the application of a rather imprecise principle; much turns on the particular context of each contract. Some of the older cases have been overruled,[240] and some may not be able to stand—in particular those which turned on the assumption, at one time

---

[235] *Churchill & Sim v Goddard* [1937] 1 K.B. 92; *Hindle v Brown* (1908) 98 L.T. 791; *Pollway Ltd v Abdullah* [1974] 1 W.L.R. 493; *Pendergrast v Chapman* [1988] 2 N.Z.L.R. 177. cf. *Barton, Thompson & Co v Vigers Bros* (1906) 19 Com.Cas. 175; *Jordeson & Co v London Hardwood Co* (1913) 110 L.T. 666; *Flatau, Dick & Co v Keeping* (1931) 39 Ll.L.Rep. 42; *Turnbull & Jones Ltd v Amner & Sons* [1923] N.Z.L.R. 673.

[236] *Carminco Gold & Resources Ltd v Findlay & Co Stockbrokers (Underwriters) Pty Ltd* (2007) 243 A.L.R. 472.

[237] See *Universal Steam Navigation Co v McKelvie* [1923] A.C. 492; *Bowes v Shand* (1877) 2 App.Cas. 455; *The Swan* [1968] 1 Lloyd's Rep. 5, Illustration 6 to Article 98; Illustrations. See also criticism of the decisions in Stoljar, pp.251–256.

[238] *British Energy Power & Trading Ltd v Credit Suisse* [2008] EWCA Civ 413; [2008] 1 Lloyd's Rep. 413 ("as agent and security trustee" in context of syndicated loan agreement).

[239] See, e.g. *Badgerhill Properties Ltd v Cottrell* [1991] B.C.L.C. 805, Illustration 16 to Article 99; *Hamid v Francis Bradshaw Partnership* [2013] EWCA Civ 470.

[240] e.g. *Lennard v Robinson* (1855) 5 E. & B. 125; overruled in *Universal Steam Navigation Co v*

held, that the agent must be liable if the principal was not,[241] for it has been clear that in such cases his liability is based on a separate contract,[242] a warranty of authority.[243] Generalisations about particular formulae are dangerous.[244]

The following rules have, however, appeared in previous editions and still seem valid starting points.

(a) If the contract is signed by the agent in his own name without qualifica-tion, he is deemed to have contracted personally[245] unless a contrary inten-tion plainly appears from other portions of the document.[246]

(b) The mere fact that the agent is described as an agent, director, secretary, manager, broker, etc., whether by words connected with or forming part of the signature,[247] or in the body of the contract,[248] and whether or not the principal is named, raises no presumption that the agent did not intend to contract personally; but here again an intention to contract as agent only may be gathered from the whole document and surrounding circumstances.[249]

(c) But if the agent adds words to his signature, indicating that he signs as agent, or for or on behalf or on account of a principal, he is deemed not to have contracted personally,[250] unless it is plain from other portions of the docu-ment that, notwithstanding such qualified signature, he intended to bind himself.[251] This is so even though he does not name his principal.[252] But this

---

McKelvie [1923] A.C. 492; *Paice v Walker* (1870) L.R. 5 Ex. 173; disapproved in *Gadd v Houghton* (1876) 1 Ex.D. 357. It was formerly thought that the form of the signature was conclusive.

[241] *Downman v Williams* (1845) 7 Q.B. 103, Illustration 2; *Harper v Williams* (1843) 4 Q.B. 219.

[242] *Lewis v Nicholson* (1852) 18 Q.B. 503; *Jenkins v Hutchinson* (1849) 13 Q.B. 744.

[243] Article 105.

[244] Two cases worth particular study are *Gadd v Houghton* (above), Illustration 11 and *Universal Steam Navigation Co v McKelvie* (above), Illustration 13.

[245] Illustration 5. And see *Lavan v Walsh* [1964] I.R. 87 and *Transcontinental Underwriting Agencies Srl v Grand Union Insurance Co Ltd* [1987] 2 Lloyd's Rep. 409, where this formulation is ap-proved; *Farncombe v Sperling* (1922) 66 S.J. 312; *Ernest Scragg & Son Ltd v Perserverance Bank-ing and Trust Co Ltd* [1973] 2 Lloyd's Rep. 101; *Sika Contracts Ltd v B.S. Gill* (1978) 9 Build. L.R. 11, Illustration 10.

[246] Illustrations 6 and 11; *Concordia Chemische Fabrik auf Actien v Squire* (1876) 34 L.T. 824. But cf. Illustration 12, where the indications in the document were not sufficiently clear.

[247] *Hutcheson v Eaton* (1884) 13 Q.B.D. 861 ("brokers"). As to the term "agent", see *Universal Steam Navigation Co v McKelvie*, above, at 501: "When people add 'agent' to a signature to a contract, they are trying to escape personal liability, but are unaware that the attempt will fail". But see Com-ment to Article 100(1).

[248] Illustrations 1, 2 (first part), 4 and 5.

[249] Illustrations 2 (second part) and 3.

[250] Illustrations 12 and 13. In *Gadd v Houghton* (1876) 1 Ex.D. 357 at 359 James LJ said: "When a man says that he is making a contract 'on account of' someone else, it seems to me that he uses the very strongest terms the English language affords to shew that he is not binding himself, but is binding his principal".

[251] Illustration 14; *Paice v Walker* (1870) L.R. 5 Ex. 173 (but this case was disapproved in *Gadd v Houghton*, above); *Weidner v Hoggett* (1876) 1 C.P.D. 533. But such a contingency is unlikely: see *Universal Steam Navigation Co v McKelvie* [1923] A.C. 492 at 499, per Lord Shaw: "But I desire to say that in my opinion the appending of the word 'agents' to the signature of a party to a mercantile contract is, in all cases, the dominating factor in the solution of the problem of principal or agent. A highly improbable and conjectural case (in which this dominating factor might be overcome by other parts of the contract) may by an effort of the imagination be figured, but, apart from that, the appending of the word 'agent' to the signature is a conclusive assertion of agency, and a conclusive rejection of the responsibility of a principal, and is and must be accepted in that twofold sense by the other contracting party".

proposition should be read subject to Article 102(2) regarding the liability of agents under trade custom.

As in other cases, care should be taken to ascertain exactly what liability an agent undertakes, if he does appear to contract personally.[252] Although most of the cases assume that the agent is the only party to the contract, this need not necessarily be so.[254] Extrinsic evidence is admissible to clarify a written contract,[255] provided that it is not inconsistent with the contract.[256] It is not impossible for a person to sign both for himself and also as agent of another.[257]

In the case of signatures for companies, a further distinction must be taken between cases where an agent signs as agent, which are governed by the above rules, and those where he signs as the company, viz. simply purports to authenticate the company's signature and so does not even sign as agent. In this latter case the agent's liability or right to sue will be difficult to establish.[258]

Illustrations

(1)   An agent entered into a written agreement to grant a lease of certain premises.   **9-038**
He was described in the agreement as making it on behalf of the principal, but in a subsequent portion of the document it was provided that he (the agent) would execute the lease. Held, that the agent was liable for a breach of the agreement, though the premises belonged to the principal.[259]

(2)   The directors of a company signed a contract in the following terms: "We, the undersigned, three of the directors, agree to repay £500 advanced by A to the company", and at the same time assigned to A, as security, certain property belonging to the company. Held, that the directors were personally liable.[260] But when an agent signed a contract in the following form: "I undertake, on behalf of A [the principal], to pay, etc." it was held that he was not personally liable.[261]

(3)   A broker sent a contract note in the following terms: "Messrs. S.—I have this day sold by your order and for your account to my principal, etc., one per cent. brokerage"; (signed) "W A B". Held, that W A B was not personally liable in an action for goods sold.[262]

---

[252] *Southwell v Bowditch* (1876) 1 C.P.D. 374, Illustration 3; *Chartwell Shipping Ltd v Q.N.S. Paper Co Ltd* [1989] 2 S.C.R. 683; (1989) 62 D.L.R. (4th) 36, Illustration 9.

[253] *Universal Steam Navigation Co v McKelvie*, above, at 501. See Comment to Article 100.

[254] See, e.g. *Stag Line Ltd v Tyne Shiprepair Group Ltd (The Zinnia)* [1984] 2 Lloyd's Rep. 211 at 216; *Seatrade Groningen BV v Geest Industries Ltd (The Frost Express)* [1996] 2 Lloyd's Rep. 375, Illustration 7; above, para.9-006.

[255] See *McCollin v Gilpin* (1881) 6 Q.B.D. 516, Illustration 2; *Young v Schuler* (1883) 11 Q.B.D. 651; *Automobiles Renault Canada Ltd v Maritime Import Autos Ltd* (1961) 31 D.L.R. (2d) 592.

[256] See Article 100.

[257] See Illustration 14; Article 98.

[258] See *Newborne v Sensolid (Great Britain) Ltd* [1954] 1 Q.B. 45, Illustration 6 to Article 107; *Black v Smallwood* (1966) 117 C.L.R. 52 at 61–62 (Illustration 7 to Article 107); above, para.1-029; below, para.9-082.

[259] *Norton v Herron* (1825) 1 C. & P. 648; *Tanner v Christian* (1855) 4 E. & B. 591; cf. *Spittle v Lavender* (1821) 5 Moo.C.P. 270.

[260] *McCollin v Gilpin* (1881) 6 Q.B.D. 516. See also *H.O. Brandt & Co v H.N. Morris & Co* [1917] 2 K.B. 784.

[261] *Downman v Williams* (1845) 7 Q.B. 103; *Glover v Langford* (1892) 8 T.L.R. 628; *W.T. Avery Ltd v Charlesworth* (1914) 31 T.L.R. 52.

[262] *Southwell v Bowditch* (1876) 1 C.P.D. 374; *Sunnyvale Property Trust v Liu* [2015] NZHC 2804

(4)   A solicitor wrote: "I hereby undertake to pay on behalf of these creditors [his clients] two-thirds" of certain expenses. Held, that he was personally liable.[263] So, the solicitor of the assignees of a bankrupt tenant was held personally liable on an undertaking as follows: "I, as solicitor to the assignees, undertake to pay the landlord his rent, provided it does not exceed the value of the effects distrained".[264]

(5)   A charterparty was expressed to be made between A B and C D, agent for E F & Son, and was signed by C D, without qualification. Held, that C D was personally liable, though the principals were named, there being nothing in the terms of the contract clearly inconsistent with an intention to contract personally.[265]

(6)   A charterparty states that it is entered into between "A, owners" and "B, charterers". A clause in it provides "This vessel was chartered on behalf of C". B is liable as charterer.[266]

(7)   A charterparty is signed "SG as agents to owners or as disponent owners". SG is personally liable; the actual vessel owners may be also.[267]

(8)   Repairs are arranged for a vessel by telex and a document is signed headed "Agreement between 'Cape Hatteras' and 'Astican'" (the repairers). The contract is with the owners of the Cape Hatteras, whoever they may be.[268]

(9)   Ship's agents write to two firms "As Managing Operators for the charterers we are again pleased to appoint you as agents for the vessel's forthcoming call"; "On behalf of our principals we are again pleased to appoint you as agent for the above-mentioned vessel". The first letter is signed by them "C Shipping Ltd", the second "C Shipping Ltd as agents". They are not personally liable on either contract.[269]

(10)   A tender is accepted in these words: "We have pleasure in informing you that

---

(agent not liable on contract for sale of land between named parties when signed for principal without reference to his being an agent).

[263]   *Hall v Ashurst* (1833) 1 C. & M. 714; *Lavan v Walsh* [1964] I.R. 87 ("sale to the writer in trust for a client"). See also *Weidner v Hoggett* (1876) 1 C.P.D. 533; cf. *Allaway v Duncan* (1867) 16 L.T. 264.

[264]   *Burrell v Jones* (1819) 3 B. & A. 47; *Harper v Williams* (1843) 4 Q.B. 219; cf. *Lewis v Nicholson* (1852) 18 Q.B. 503.

[265]   *Parker v Winslow* (1857) 7 E. & B. 942. See also *Cooke v Wilson* (1856) 1 C.B.(N.S.) 153; *Hick v Tweedy* (1890) 63 L.T. 765. cf. Illustration 12. See also *The Elikon* [2003] EWCA Civ 812; [2003] 2 Lloyd's Rep. 430 (charterparty named owners as "A c/o B": signed by B without qualification: B, but not A, party to contract).

[266]   *Tudor Marine Ltd v Tradax Export SA (The Virgo)* [1976] 2 Lloyd's Rep. 135. See also *Pyxis Special Shipping Co Ltd v Dritas & Kaglis Bros Ltd (The Scaplake)* [1978] 2 Lloyd's Rep. 380 (noted [1979] J.B.L. 150); *Jugoslavenska Linijska Plovidba v Hulsman (The Primorje)* [1980] 2 Lloyd's Rep. 74; *Et. Biret et Cie SA v Yukiteru Kaiun KK (The Sun Happiness)* [1984] 1 Lloyd's Rep. 381. See also *Electrosteel Castings Ltd v Scan-Trans Shipping and Chartering Sdn. Bhd* [2002] EWHC 1993 (Comm); [2003] 1 Lloyd's Rep. 190 (chartering: later booking note signed as agents superseded earlier recap telex).

[267]   *Seatrade Groningen BV v Geest Industries Ltd (The Frost Express)* [1996] 2 Lloyd's Rep. 375.

[268]   *Astilleros Canarios SA v Cape Hatteras Shipping Co Inc (The Cape Hatteras)* [1982] 1 Lloyd's Rep. 518; *Armour v Duff & Co* 1912 S.C. 120. Importance may be attached to the fact that if the contract is with the owner, it will often be possible to arrest a ship; cf. *Dawson (Ship Stores) v Atlantica Co Ltd* (1931) 40 Ll.Rep. 63 (contract with agent); *The Swan* [1968] 1 Lloyd's Rep. 5, Illustration 6 to Article 98 (contract with both: above, para.9-006). As to oral contracts see Article 101, Illustration 3.

[269]   *Chartwell Shipping Ltd v Q.N.S. Paper Co Ltd* [1989] 2 S.C.R. 683; (1989) 62 D.L.R. (4th) 36.

your tender dated 19th July 1974 has been accepted ... Yours faithfully, BS, Chartered Civil Engineer". The signer is personally liable.[270]

(11) Fruit brokers in Liverpool signed in their own names without qualification a contract in the following form: "We have this day sold to you on account of J M & Co, Valencia, etc.". Held, the brokers were not personally liable, the word "on account" clearly showing that there was no intention to contract personally.[271]

(12) A charterparty is signed "for A B, of L, C Bros, as agents". C Bros are not liable, unless it clearly appears from the body of the contract that they intended to bind themselves.[272] So, where a contract was signed "G W, J L, for C J M & Co", it was held that G W and J L were not personally liable.[273]

(13) A charterparty was signed "For and on behalf of James McKelvie and Co as agents, J.A. McKelvie", but James McKelvie & Co were described in the body of the agreement as charterers. Held, that James McKelvie & Co were not personally liable, the qualified signature indicating an intention to exclude personal liability.[274]

(14) An agent signed a contract—"p p A, J A & Co, A B". The contract contained a clause providing that A B should guarantee moneys due from his principal to the other contracting party. Parol evidence was admitted to show that A B intended to sign, not only as an agent, but also as a surety. Held, that such evidence was rightly admitted, and that he must be taken to have signed in both capacities.[275]

(15) An insurance policy is issued to "PN Bank, a/c E (Commodities) Ltd". The contract is with the bank.[276]

(16) A contract is signed "The Plumbing Centre, BT, Director". "The Plumbing Centre" is in fact the trade name of BP Ltd, whose name appears (inaccurately) at the foot of the page. The contract is with BP Ltd under its trade name and BT is not liable on it.[277]

[270] *Sika Contracts Ltd v B.S. Gill* (1978) 9 Build. L.R. 11. See also *Fraser v Equitorial Shipping Co Ltd (The Ijaola)* [1979] 1 Lloyd's Rep. 103.
[271] *Gadd v Houghton* (1876) 1 Ex.D. 357; disapproving *Paice v Walker* (1870) L.R. 5 Ex. 173 (but see *Hough & Co v Manzanos & Co* (1874) 4 Ex.D. 104); *Ogden v Hall* (1879) 40 L.T. 751; *Mercer v Wright, Graham & Co* (1917) 33 T.L.R. 343, *Lester v Balfour Williamson & Co* [1953] 2 Q.B. 168; cf. *H.O. Brandt & Co v H.N. Morris & Co* [1917] 2 K.B. 784.
[272] *Deslandes v Gregory* (1860) 30 L.J.Q.B. 36; *Green v Kopke* (1856) 18 C.B. 549; *Miller, Gibb & Co v Smith & Tyrer* [1917] 2 K.B. 141.
[273] *Redpath v Wigg* (1866) L.R. 1 Ex. 335; *Mahony v Kekulé* (1854) 14 C.B. 390.
[274] *Universal S.N. Co v McKelvie* [1923] A.C. 492; overruling *Lennard v Robinson* (1855) 5 E. & B. 125. See also *Kimber Coal Co v Stone & Rolfe Ltd* [1926] A.C. 414; *Dragages et Travaux Publics v Gladhover Ltd* [1988] 1 H.K.L.R. 298 ("between G for and on behalf of N and the contractors").
[275] *Young v Schuler* (1883) 11 Q.B.D. 651; *Ontario Marble Co Ltd v Creative Memorials Ltd* (1963) 39 D.L.R. (2d) 149; affd (1964) 45 D.L.R. (2d) 244; *VSH Ltd v BKS Air Transport Ltd* [1964] 1 Lloyd's Rep. 460; *Sun Alliance Pensions Life & Investments Services Ltd v Webster* [1991] 2 Lloyd's Rep. 410; *Elpis Maritime Co Ltd v Marti Chartering Co Inc (The Maria D)* [1992] 1 A.C. 21.
[276] *Punjab National Bank v de Boinville* [1992] 1 W.L.R. 1138.
[277] *Badgerhill Properties Ltd v Cottrell* [1991] B.C.L.C. 805. See also *Vic Spence Associates v Balchin* 1990 S.L.T. 10.

Article 100

ADMISSIBILITY OF EXTRINSIC EVIDENCE

9-039   (1) Where it is clear from the terms of a written contract made by an agent that he contracted personally, extrinsic evidence is not admissible to show that, notwithstanding the terms of the contract, it was the intention of the parties that he should not be personally liable on it, because such evidence would be contradictory to the written contract.[278]

   (2) But where it appears from the terms of a written contract made by an agent that he contracted as agent, extrinsic evidence is nevertheless admissible to show that, by custom or usage in the particular trade or business, an agent so contracting is liable either absolutely or conditionally in addition to the principal,[279] provided that such custom or usage is not inconsistent with nor repugnant to the express terms of the written contract.[280]

Comment

9-040   **Rule (1)**   It is sometimes said that parol or other extrinsic evidence may not be admitted to add to, vary or contradict a deed or written contract.[281] Such evidence may therefore not be adduced to delete an apparent contracting party (though it may be adduced to *add* a party, e.g. to establish the liability of the principal as well as the agent[282]). But this reasoning is only appropriate where the contract is exclusively contained in a document or documents: there may be documents (e.g. invoices) which do not purport to constitute the complete contract, and in such cases extrinsic evidence will certainly be admissible.[283]

Further, where a written document can be established not to represent the intention of the parties as clearly agreed, it can be rectified in equity: and there are a few cases holding that the fact that it would be rectified could be pleaded as a defence to a common law action.[284] This can apparently be pleaded even by a plaintiff,[285] and a party can plead that he is not liable, even though it is not established who, if

---

[278] *Higgins v Senior* (1841) 8 M. & W. 834, Illustration 1; *Magee v Atkinson* (1837) 2 M. & W. 440; *Sobell Industries v Cory Bros* [1955] 2 Lloyd's Rep. 82 Illustration 7 to Article 98; *Sika Contracts Ltd v B.S. Gill* (1978) 9 Build. L.R. 11, Illustration 10 to Article 99; *Transcontinental Underwriting Agency Srl v General Union Insurance Co Ltd* [1987] 2 Lloyd's Rep. 409; *K v S* [2015] EWHC 1945 (Comm). But see Comment.

[279] Illustrations 2 to 4.

[280] Illustrations 5 and 6. And see Article 31.

[281] *Jacobs v Batavia & General Plantations Trust Ltd* [1924] 1 Ch. 287 at 295 (an extreme formulation). See Chitty, *Contracts* (32nd edn), para.13-099 onwards; McLauchlan, *The Parol Evidence Rule* (Wellington, NZ, 1976); *Law Com. No.154* (1986) for full discussion of this often misunderstood topic.

[282] *Higgins v Senior* (1841) 8 M. & W. 834 at 844. See further Comment to Article 71. As to cases where the principal is undisclosed, see Comment to Article 76.

[283] *Rogers v Hadley* (1861) 2 H. & C. 227; *Holding v Elliott* (1860) 5 H. & N. 117.

[284] *Wake v Harrop* (1862) 1 H. & C. 202; affirming 6 H. & N. 768; *Cowie v Witt* (1874) 23 W.R. 76. And see *Breslauer v Barwick* (1876) 36 L.T. 52; *Mostyn v West Mostyn Coal & Iron Co* (1876) 1 C.P.D. 145; Senior Courts Act 1981 s.49. The possibility of a collateral contract to the same effect is discussed in a note on *Farncombe v Sperling* (1922) 66 S.J. 312; it is possible that breach of a collateral contract might bar an action on the main contract (see *Benjamin's Sale of Goods* (9th edn), para.10-014). *Wake v Harrop* was applied at first instance in Australia in *Alliance Acceptance Co Ltd v Oakley* (1987) 45 S.A.S.R. 148; but on appeal the decision was reversed on grounds which made *Wake v Harrop* irrelevant: (1988) 48 S.A.S.R. 337.

[285] *Breslauer v Barwick*, above.

anyone, is liable, provided it is clear that the true intention of the parties was that the person concerned should not be. Thus where an agent made a charterparty and signed it "for X Co A, agents" on the express undertaking that he was acting only as agent and that the use of this formula was the correct way of expressing this, he was held to have a good defence to an action on the charterparty.[286] Even if these cases are correct, situations where such clear evidence is available will be rare. It is not clear to what extent the defence is subject to the normal rules relating to the availability of rectification (e.g. that a third party must not be prejudiced), and, of course, the extent to which equity will relieve against mistakes of law as opposed to fact is in general by no means clear.[287] On general principles, any operative mistake would have to be common to the parties, or there would have to be some unconscionable conduct on the part of the person not mistaken.[288]

Rule (2) Where the agent signs a contract as agent only, he is prima facie not liable. However, the rules referred to above do not prevent evidence being adduced to establish who the principal is (though if the case is one regulated by the Statute of Frauds, the principal's identity must be clear from the memorandum[289]); or to establish that, notwithstanding the fact that the agent signed as agent, it was intended that he should in fact additionally be liable to some extent not inconsistent with the primary liability of the principal (in which case the agent's signature would satisfy the Statute of Frauds[290]). The cases in this area suggest that the agent may fairly readily be held liable together with, as opposed to instead of, his principal: usages that hold the agent liable have always been common[291] and may be increasing.[292]

9-041

Illustrations

(1) An iron commission agent receives an order to purchase iron from a named company but sends in return a sold note saying "We have this day sold ... to Messrs H & Sons ... " and signs it "JB & Co, WS". Although JB & Co are "notoriously an agent" they are in this instance personally liable.[293]

9-042

(2) An agent signed a charterparty expressly "as agent to merchants", the principals being unnamed. It was held that, although it plainly appeared that he did not intend to contract as principal, it might nevertheless be proved that, by a general custom, an agent so signing was, in the ordinary course of trade, personally liable on the contract in the event of his not identifying the principals within a reasonable time. Such a custom was not inconsistent with

---

[286] *Wake v Harrop*, above.
[287] See Kerr, *Fraud and Mistake* (7th edn), p.133 onwards; uncertainty now arises as to the reach of the decision of the House of Lords in *Kleinwort Benson Ltd v Lincoln CC* [1999] 2 A.C. 349, concerning money paid under mistake of law.
[288] As to rectification in general, see Snell, *Equity* (33rd edn), Ch.16.
[289] See *Lovesy v Palmer* [1916] 2 Ch. 233; above, paras 8-003 and 8-004.
[290] See *Dale v Humfrey* (1858) E.B. & E. 1004.
[291] See Illustrations; Marine Insurance Act 1906 ss.53 and 54. As to proof of custom or usage, see Article 31. Sometime the agent's liability ceases on naming a principal. As to the 1906 Act, see Hon. Mrs Justice Gloster [2007] L.M.C.L.Q. 302.
[292] See Comment to Article 98.
[293] *Higgins v Senior* (1841) 8 M. & W. 834.

the terms of the contract as the primary liability was that of the unnamed principals.[294]

(3) A broker entered into a contract in the following terms: "Sold by A to Messrs. B, for and on account of owner, 100 bales of hops". An action was brought against A for not delivering the hops according to sample. Evidence of a custom in the hop trade, whereby a broker who does not identify his principal at the time of the contract is personally liable, was admitted, and the broker was held liable on the contract.[295]

(4) A and B, who were brokers, contracted in the following terms: "We have this day sold for your account to our principal, etc." (signed) "A and B, brokers". Some of the goods were accepted by the principal, whose name was declared by A and B before delivery, and an action was subsequently brought against A and B for not accepting the residue. Held, that they were personally liable, it being proved that by a custom in the particular trade, the broker was personally liable for his principal's default unless the name of the principal was inserted in the written contract.[296] So, by the usage of the London dry goods market, where a broker bought goods for an unnamed principal, he was personally liable for the price.[297]

(5) Brokers entered, as such, into a contract which contained a clause providing that they should act as arbitrators in the event of any dispute between the parties. Held, that evidence of a custom rendering them personally liable on the contract was inadmissible, because the custom was inconsistent with the clause appointing them arbitrators.[298]

(6) Agents sign a contract in a clearly representative capacity. It is argued that since their principals are foreign, they are personally liable. Even when such a custom existed, it would here be inconsistent with the contract.[299]

Article 101

ORAL CONTRACTS

9-043   Where an agent makes a contract which is not reduced to writing, the question whether he contracted personally, together with his principal or solely in his capacity as an agent is a question of fact.[300]

---

[294] *Hutchinson v Tatham* (1873) L.R. 8 C.P. 482 (collateral contract).

[295] *Pike v Ongley* (1887) 18 Q.B.D. 708; *Dale v Humfrey* (1858) E.B. & E. 1004 (similar custom in fruit trade); *Thornton v Fehr* (1935) 51 Ll. L. Rep. 330 (tallow trade); *Anglo Overseas Transport Ltd v Titan Industrial Corp* [1959] 2 Lloyd's Rep. 152 (forwarding agents); *Perishables Transport Co v Spyropoulos* [1964] 2 Lloyd's Rep. 379 (air forwarding agents); cf. *Wilson v Avec Audio-Visual Equipment Ltd* [1974] 1 Lloyd's Rep. 81 (no such usage for insurance broker).

[296] *Fleet v Murton* (1871) L.R. 7 Q.B. 126 (fruit trade and colonial market). Similar custom in the rice trade: *Bacmeister v Fenton Levy & Co* (1883) Cab. & El. 121.

[297] *Imperial Bank v London & St Katharine Docks Co* (1877) 5 Ch.D. 195 (agent held a surety).

[298] *Barrow & Bros v Dyster, Nalder & Co* (1884) 13 Q.B.D. 635.

[299] *Miller, Gibb & Co v Smith & Tyrer Ltd* [1917] 2 K.B. 141. As to the alleged custom, see above, para.9-020.

[300] See Illustrations; *Castle v Duke* (1832) 5 C. & P. 359; *Gurney v Womersley* (1854) 4 E. & B. 133; *Lakeman v Mountstephen* (1874) L.R. 7 H.L. 17; *Blake v Melrose* [1950] N.Z.L.R. 781.

Comment

The proposition contained in this Article means nowadays little more than that general rules or presumptions cannot be laid down for such cases, whereas precedents can be cited on the interpretation of documents.[301] An appellate tribunal may also be more reluctant to interfere with findings of fact as to oral contracts[302]; and in many cases an appeal only lies on point of law.

9-044

Unidentified principals One area in which a rule might be thought to exist is that of unidentified principals. *Restatement, Third* provides that where an agent acts for an unidentified principal the principal and the third party are parties to the contract and the agent is (also) a party to the contract unless the agent and the third party agree otherwise.[303] Such a rule would to some extent avoid problems about the third party's right to ascertain the name of the principal.[304] In *The Santa Carina* (Illustration 2), however, the Court of Appeal refused to accept such a proposed rule formulated in similar terms to those of *Restatement, Second*[305] and said that the question was entirely one of fact; and that for the agent's additional liability there would have to be some indication, whether from trade custom[306] or special facts,[307] which did not exist in that case. This means that the presumption is that the agent is not liable unless there are indications to displace it.[308] It has already been suggested, however,[309] that the close connection of such cases with undisclosed principal cases, where the agent is liable and entitled, mean that there is a good case for a prima facie rule as in the *Restatement*.

9-045

Illustrations

(1) Brokers sell goods by auction and invoice them in their own names as sellers. It is a question of fact whether the invoice was intended to be the contract. If it was, the brokers are personally liable. If not, it is a question of fact whether they intended to contract personally.[310]

9-046

(2) Stores are supplied to, or repairs effected on, a ship on the oral orders of the ship's agent. In appropriate cases the agent may be held to have assumed personal liability.[311]

(3) Brokers on the Baltic Exchange order bunkers from other brokers, also

---

[301] *The Swan* [1968] 1 Lloyd's Rep. 5 at 12.
[302] e.g. *Gardiner v Heading* [1928] 2 K.B. 284.
[303] § 6.02(2).
[304] See above, para.9-017.
[305] § 321, to similar effect to *Restatement, Third*, § 6.02(2), above.
[306] See Article 100.
[307] e.g. that the principal is foreign: see *Fraser v Equitorial Shipping Co Ltd (The Ijaolo)* [1979] 1 Lloyd's Rep. 103; above, para.9-020.
[308] See also *Wilson v Avec Audio-Visual Equipment Ltd* [1974] 1 Lloyd's Rep. 81 at 83.
[309] See above, para.9-016.
[310] *Holding v Elliott* (1860) 5 H. & N. 117.
[311] See *Fraser-Johnston Engineering, etc., Co v Sam Isaacs (Aberdeen) Ltd* (1922) 12 Ll. L. Rep. 233; *Beliard, Crighton (Belgium) Ltd v Charles Lowe & Partners Ltd* (1922) 13 Ll. L. Rep. 567; *Evans & Reid Coal Co Ltd v McNabb, Rougier & Co (Italy) Ltd* (1924) 18 Ll. L. Rep. 471; *J.D. McLaren & Co v Nomikos* [1961] 1 Lloyd's Rep. 318; *Freimuller (Ship Stores) v Ocean Carriers (London) Ltd* [1961] 2 Lloyd's Rep. 309; *Victory Shipchandlers v Leslie & Anderson Ltd* [1972] E. Africa L.Rep. 42. Sometimes the agent is made liable by statute: see New Zealand Carriage of Goods Act 1979 s.29 (ship's agents). See also *Lamont v Hamilton* 1907 S.C. 628 (insurance); *H.J. Lyons & Sando Ltd v Houlson* [1963] S.A.S.R. 29 (car repairs); cf. *Whitwell v Perrin* (1858) 4 C.B.(N.S.) 412;

members of the Baltic, for a ship at Penang. The order is given on the telephone without indication of the capacity in which either party is acting. The bunkers are not paid for. The first broker does not expect the second broker to effect the bunkering himself: the second broker knows that the first broker does not own ships. The first broker is not personally liable.[312]

Article 102

DEEDS

9-047   Where an agent is a party to a deed and executes it in his own name, he is personally liable and entitled on it, even when he is described in the deed as acting for and on behalf of a named principal.[313]

Comment

9-048   This rule, which is an application of the strict rules relating to deeds, applies even though he executes it specifically on behalf of the principal: a fortiori if he executes it personally, merely adding descriptive words. To escape liability the agent must purport to execute the deed as the principal's deed.[314] However, by virtue of s.7(1) of the Powers of Attorney Act 1971[315] an agent with a power of attorney may execute a deed with his own signature, and it may be that he is exempt from liability if he does so, at least so long as he indicates that he signs in a representative capacity. If so, the rules for deeds are now in these circumstances the same as for other written contracts. The matter is discussed elsewhere.[316]

Illustrations

9-049   (1)   A, on behalf of B, contracted by deed to purchase certain houses, and covenanted that he (A) would pay £800 for them. The houses were destroyed. Held, that A was personally liable to pay the £800, although he had no effects in his hands belonging to B.[317] If A covenants under his own hand and seal for the act of B, A is personally liable, though he describes himself as covenanting for and on behalf of B.[318]

(2)   A person signs a deed "signed as agent for and on behalf of CIC". CIC is a

---

Eastman v Harry (1875) 33 L.T. 800. As to written contracts see Article 99, Illustration 8. The liability of a local agent may be an advantage: on the other hand where the contract is with the shipowner there may be a right to arrest a ship; cf. Article 98, Illustration 6; Article 99, Illustration 8.

[312] *N. & J. Vlassopulos Ltd v Ney Shipping Ltd (The Santa Carina)* [1977] 1 Lloyd's Rep. 478. See also *Marina Shipping Ltd v Laughton* [1982] Q.B. 1127; *A/S Hansen-Tangens Rederi III v Total Transport Corp (The Sagona)* [1984] 1 Lloyd's Rep. 194 at 198–199 (shipping agent arranging port facilities acts for charterer); *Shipping Co Uniform Inc v Intl Transport Workers' Fedn (The Uniform Star)* [1985] 1 Lloyd's Rep. 173.

[313] See Illustrations; *Plant Engineers (Sales) Ltd v Davies* (1969) 113 S.J. 484 (liquidator); Article 77.

[314] See Article 77; *Lundie v Rowena Nominees Pty Ltd* (2007) 32 W.A.R. 404 (see para.9-016, above).

[315] Replacing Law of Property Act 1925 s.123; as amended by Law of Property (Miscellaneous Provisions) Act 1989.

[316] Article 77.

[317] *Cass v Rudele* (1692) 2 Vern. 280.

[318] *Appleton v Binks* (1804) 5 East 148; *Bacon v Dubarry* (1697) 1 Ld.Raym. 246.

French company, but its corporate title is not given. The signer is personally liable.[319]

(3) A mortgagee by deed contracted for a tenancy of the mortgaged property, the contract being expressed to be made between the mortgagee "as agent, hereinafter called the landlord", and the tenant. Held, that it was a question of construction who was the lessor, and on the true construction the contract was that of the mortgagee, and that the mere use of the words "as agent" was not sufficient to prevent the demise operating on the legal estate of the mortgagee.[320]

Article 103

BILLS, NOTES AND CHEQUES

(1) An agent is not personally liable on a bill of exchange, promissory note or cheque unless his name appears on it.[321]   **9-050**

(2) Where a person signs a bill as drawer, indorser or acceptor, and adds words to his signature indicating that he signs for or on behalf of a principal, or in a representative character, he is not personally liable on it; but the mere addition to his signature of words describing him as an agent, or as filling a representative character, does not exempt him from personal liability.[322]

(3) But no person can be liable as acceptor of a bill except the person on whom it is drawn, except where it is accepted for honour.[323]

(4) In determining whether the signature on a bill is that of the principal or that of the agent by whose hand it is written, the construction most favourable to the validity of the instrument will be adopted.[324]

Comment

Rule (1)   These rules are to be justified on the ground that negotiable instruments are likely to come into the hands of persons who have no knowledge of the circumstances in which they were issued; such persons must be able to rely on what appears on the fact of the instrument.   **9-051**

Rule (2)   In this case the Bills of Exchange Act 1882 provides when the agent contracts personally and when for his principal. In cases of drawing or indorsement the question is usually merely whether principal or agent is liable, and the problem therefore is as to whether additional words are merely descriptive or indicate that the agent signs solely in a representative capacity for another, viz. "says plainly 'I am the mere scribe'"[325] If the agent signs solely in such a capacity and   **9-052**

---

[319] *Bailey v de Kerangat*, CA, December 7, 1993 (but the case was actually decided on general agency principles).

[320] *Chapman v Smith* [1907] 2 Ch. 97.

[321] Bills of Exchange Act 1882, ss.23 and 89. See e.g. *Maxform SpA v Mariani and Goodville* [1981] 2 Lloyd's Rep. 54. But see also Companies Act 2006 ss.82 and 84, and regulations made thereunder.

[322] Bills of Exchange Act 1882 s.26(2). See *Rolfe Lubbell & Co v Keith* [1979] 1 All E.R. 80.

[323] Bills of Exchange Act 1882 s.17(1). As to acceptance for honour, see ss.65–68.

[324] Bills of Exchange Act 1882 s.26(2).

[325] *Leadbitter v Farrow* (1816) 5 M. & S. 345 at 349. For full citation of the main cases on signatures, see Byles, *Bills of Exchange* (29th edn); Chalmers and Guest, *Bills of Exchange* (18th edn).

has authority, his principal is bound; if he has no authority, his principal is not bound, and the agent is liable for breach of warranty of authority.

9-053 **Rule (3)**   Rule (3) raises difficulties. Where a bill is drawn on an agent but accepted by him in the principal's name and with his authority, the principal nevertheless cannot be bound[326]; but since the agent has not purported to act for himself, it seems that he cannot be bound either.[327] Where the bill is drawn on the principal and accepted by the agent in his own name without qualification, equally the agent cannot be liable.[328]

9-054 **Rule (4)**   Where however in acceptance cases such as those above it is not clear how the signature should be regarded, the presumption in favour of validity may assist in construing it as the signature of the drawee. The presumption only operates in cases of ambiguity,[329] and it is difficult to see that it can have much relevance in cases of drawing or indorsement, where the question is simply as to whether principal or agent is liable, for in both cases the signature will normally (i.e. in the absence or incapacity of one of the parties or the like) be operative.[330]

9-055 **Trade, firm and company names**   Where an agent signs in a trade or assumed name, he is liable as if he had signed his own name[331]; and the signature of a firm is equivalent to the signature by the person so signing of the names of all the persons liable as partners in that firm.[332] Whether the director or other officer of a company who signs on behalf of the company is personally liable depends on ordinary principles of construction.[333] Under former companies legislation,[334] if an officer of a company or a person on its behalf signed or authorised to be signed on behalf of the company any bill of exchange, promissory note, endorsement, cheque or order for money or goods in which the name of the company was not mentioned in legible characters, he was liable to a fine and became personally liable on it unless payment was made by the company.[335] Only the criminal consequences were preserved in the Companies Act 2006 ss.82 to 84, leaving the civil law consequences to be determined by the common law.

Illustrations

9-056 (1)   An agent draws a bill in his own name. He is personally liable as drawer, even

---

[326] Bills of Exchange Act 1882 s.17(1); *Polhill v Walter* (1832) 3 B. & Ad. 114; *Steele v M'Kinlay* (1880) 5 App.Cas. 754.
[327] Bills of Exchange Act 1882 s.26(1).
[328] Bills of Exchange Act 1882 s.17(1).
[329] See *Britannia Electric Lamp Works Ltd v D. Mandler & Co Ltd* [1939] 2 K.B. 129.
[330] But see *Elliott v Bax-Ironside* [1925] 2 K.B. 301, Illustration 4, for an example where the presumption was invoked in such a case.
[331] Bills of Exchange Act 1882 s.23(1).
[332] Bills of Exchange Act 1882 s.23(2). See *Ringham v Hackett* [1980] C.L.Y. 158.
[333] See *Ferguson v Wilson* (1866) L.R. 2 Ch.App. 77.
[334] See Companies Act 1985 s.349, now repealed.
[335] As to liability as a matter of contract construction, see *Badgerhill Properties Ltd v Cottrell* [1991] B.C.L.C. 805, Illustration 16 to Article 99; *Hamid v Francis Bradshaw Partnership* [2013] EWCA Civ 470.

to a holder who knows that he is merely an agent, unless words are added to the signature, indicating that he signs merely as an agent.[336]

(2) A shipmaster draws a bill on his owners in payment for necessaries, the bill concluding with the words "value received in 300 tons coal and disbursements ... supplied to my vessel to enable her to complete her voyage ... for which I hold my vessel, owners and freight responsible". The master is personally liable as drawer, there being nothing in the concluding words excluding such liability.[337]

(3) An agent draws a bill in the name of his principal. The agent is not liable on the bill as drawer.[338]

(4) A bill directed to a company was accepted in the following form: "Accepted ... A B and C D, directors—F F E Ltd". This was the acceptance of the company. The drawer, however, required the bill to be indorsed by the company's directors. Accordingly, A B and C D signed on the back of the bill, "F F E Ltd, A B and C D, directors". Held, A B and C D were personally liable on the indorsement, because unless the indorsement was read as the personal indorsement of the directors, it added nothing to the validity of the bill.[339]

(5) Directors have been held personally liable on promissory notes in the following forms:
   (a) "We, directors of A B Company Limited, do promise to pay J D, etc ...";
      sealed and signed by four directors without qualification.[340]
   (b) "We, directors of A B Company, for ourselves and other shareholders of the company, jointly and severally promise to pay, etc., on account of the company", signed without qualification.[341]
   (c) "We promise to pay ... C D, Director, E F, Secretary, the F E Ltd ... "[342]
   (d) "We, being members of the executive committee, on behalf of X Cooperative Society, do jointly promise to pay ... "[343]

(6) The secretary of a company signed a note in the following form: "I promise to pay, etc ... (signed)—For M T and W Railway Company, J S, secretary ...". Held, that he was not personally liable.[344]

(7) A note was signed "The J S Laundry Ltd, J S, Managing Director ... " J S was not personally liable: the company would have been.[345]

---

[336] *Leadbitter v Farrow* (1816) 5 M. & S. 345; *Sowerby v Butcher* (1834) 4 Tyr. 320.

[337] *The Elmville* [1904] P. 319.

[338] *Wilson v Barthrop* (1837) 2 M. & W. 863.

[339] *Elliott v Bax-Ironside* [1925] 2 K.B. 301, applying Bills of Exchange Act 1882 s.26(2). See also *Rolfe, Lubell & Co v Keith* [1979] 1 All E.R. 860, where parol evidence was admitted to displace the operation of s.26(1) in case of ambiguity. cf. *Kettle v Dunster and Wakefield* (1927) 43 T.L.R. 770.

[340] *Dutton v Marsh* (1871) L.R. 6 Q.B. 361; *Courtauld v Saunders* (1867) 16 L.T. 562.

[341] *Penkivil v Connell* (1850) 5 Exch. 381.

[342] *Brebner v Henderson* 1925 S.C. 643. See also *Landes v Bradwell* (1909) 25 T.L.R. 478.

[343] *Gray v Raper* (1861) L.R. 1 C.P. 694.

[344] *Alexander v Sizer* (1869) L.R. 4 Ex. 102.

[345] *Chapman v Smethurst* [1909] 1 K.B. 927; see also *Britannia Electric Lamp Works Ltd v D. Mandler & Co Ltd* [1939] 2 K.B. 129; *Bondina Ltd v Rollaway Shower Blinds Ltd* [1986] 1 W.L.R. 517.

Article 104

MERGER AND ELECTION: RELEASE OF AGENT

9-057   Any liability of an agent on any contract made by an agent on behalf of his principal is discharged by the obtaining of judgment against the principal, and may perhaps be discharged where the third party elects to pursue his rights against the principal, in accordance with the principles stated in Article 82.

Comment

9-058   The situations in which an agent may be liable on a contract made for him by his principal are discussed under Article 98. The relevant authorities mainly concern the release of the principal by the obtaining of judgment against, or electing to look to the agent, and are discussed critically under Article 82, where considerable doubts are expressed as to their correctness. But the considerations applicable where the agent seeks to be discharged are obviously the same; thus, subject to the reservations there expressed, the obtaining of judgment against the principal releases the agent,[346] and a clear manifestation of an intention to hold the principal liable might perhaps have the same effect.[347] But where there are separate causes of action, the rule would not apply,[348] for it is based on there being two inconsistent rights.[349] And, of course, where the principal is not liable at all, the agent cannot be released by any attempt to make the principal liable.

Illustration

9-059   Travel agents supply and credit A with tickets, which he buys in his own name. Subsequently they are informed by B Ltd that A was B Ltd's agent in the transaction. They write to both demanding payment, and threatening proceedings, and subsequently issue a writ against B Ltd. Hearing that B Ltd is going into liquidation, they discontinue these proceedings and sue A. A is liable, there having been no election on these facts.[350]

Article 105

WARRANTY OF AUTHORITY

9-060   (1)   Where a person, by words or conduct, represents that he has actual authority to act on behalf of another, and a third party is induced by such representation to act in a manner in which he would not have acted if that representation had not been made, the first-mentioned person is deemed to warrant that the representation is true, and is liable for any loss caused to such third party

---

[346] *LGOC v Pope* (1922) 38 T.L.R. 270.

[347] *Clarkson Booker Ltd v Andjel* [1964] 2 Q.B. 775, Illustration.

[348] See for the nature of the possible causes of action, Comment to Article 98.

[349] See Comment to Article 82.

[350] *Clarkson Booker Ltd v Andjel* [1964] 2 Q.B. 775; cf. *Beigtheil & Young v Stewart* (1900) 16 T.L.R. 177. See also *Format International Security Printers Ltd v Mosden* [1975] 1 Lloyd's Rep. 37.

by a breach of that implied warranty, even if he acted in good faith, under a mistaken belief that he had such authority.[351]

(2) Every person who purports to act as an agent is deemed by his conduct to represent that he is in fact duly authorised so to act,[352] except where the purported agent expressly disclaims authority[353] or where the nature and extent of his authority, or the material facts from which its nature and extent may be inferred, are known to the other contracting party.[354]

Comment

Historical background   Early nineteenth-century cases found great difficulty in   **9-061** identifying a basis of liability for the agent who acted without authority, and there was at one time a tendency to hold that the agent had contracted personally wherever it turned out that he had no authority.[355] This solution was not sustainable in principle,[356] except where the agent could genuinely be regarded as undertaking personal liability on the contract,[357] or conceivably where the agent was really acting for himself.[358] An agent who fraudulently professed authority would always be liable in deceit,[359] but the basis of an innocent agent's liability was not settled till *Collen v Wright*,[360] where it was decided by a majority that he was liable on a separate, implied warranty of authority.

Willes J said:

"I am of the opinion that a person, who induces another to contract with him as the agent of a third party by an unqualified assertion of his being authorised to act as such agent, is answerable to the person who so contracts for any damages which he may sustain by reason of the assertion of authority being untrue ... The fact that the professed agent honestly thinks that he has authority affects the moral character of his act; but his moral innocence, so far as the person whom he has induced to contract is concerned, in no way aids such person or alleviates the inconvenience and damage which he sustains. The obligation which arises in such a case is well expressed by saying that a person, professing to contract as agent for another, impliedly, if not expressly, undertakes to or promises

---

[351] *Collen v Wright* (1857) 7 E. & B. 301; affd (1857) 8 E. & B. 647; *Yonge v Toynbee* [1910] 1 K.B. 215; and see Comment; *Restatement, Third*, § 6.10. But see below as to powers of attorney.

[352] *Collen v Wright*, above.

[353] *Halbot v Lens* [1901] 1 Ch. 344, Illustration 10.

[354] Illustrations 8 and 9; see also *Beattie v Ebury* (1872) L.R. 7 Ch.App. 777 at 810; affd L.R. 7 H.L. 102.

[355] *Downman v Williams* (1845) 7 Q.B. 103; *Thomas v Hewes* (1834) 2 C. & M. 519 at 530n. See also the cases on contracts made on behalf of companies in the course of formation, below, para.9-085; Radcliffe (1902) 18 L.Q.R. 364; *Randell v Trimen* (1856) 18 C.B. 786; the judgment of Cockburn CJ, dissenting, in *Collen v Wright* (1857) 8 E. & B. 647; discussion in *Black v Smallwood* (1966) 117 C.L.R. 52.

[356] *Lewis v Nicholson* (1852) 18 Q.B. 503; *Jenkins v Hutchinson* (1849) 13 Q.B. 744; see Article 108. For a modern example of what could be taken as similar reasoning, see *Savills v Scott* [1988] 1 E.G.L.R. 20, as to which see also [1989] J.B.L. 62.

[357] See Articles 98 and 107.

[358] See Article 108.

[359] *Randell v Trimen*, above; *Polhill v Walter* (1832) 3 B. & Ad. 114; *West London Commercial Bank v Kitson* (1884) 13 Q.B.D. 360. And he may commit the offence of obtaining a pecuniary advantage by deception: *R. v Charles* [1977] A.C. 177.

[360] (1857) 7 E. & B. 301; affd (1857) 8 E. & B. 647.

the person who enters into such contract, upon the faith of the professed agent being duly authorised, that the authority which he professes to have does in point of fact exist."[361]

Where the agent is entirely innocent, this action is the only one available: where he is fraudulent, the plaintiff can sue for deceit or breach of warranty of authority at his option. Where he is negligent, it might be thought that a similar choice obtains in those cases where the negligence gives rise to liability in tort.[362] But the Court of Appeal of New Zealand has ruled against the existence of a duty of care in such circumstances,[363] on the ground that the contractual remedy is adequate and that to permit a tort remedy would create a vicarious liability in a principal who had not authorised the agent.[364] But it seems appropriate to conclude that an agent assumes a responsibility to be careful in representing the extent of his authority, which liability need not also lead to vicarious liability in the principal. Granted therefore the general co-existence of actions in contract and tort, it seems doubtful whether the complete denial of a duty of care is necessary or appropriate, bearing in mind that there may be other advantages of tort actions.

9-062 **Nature of liability** The nature of the liability arising under this rule has been much discussed.[365] There are dicta in many of the cases which to modern eyes leave it doubtful whether the cause of action is to be classified as contractual or tortious. But in the absence of fraud an action in tort did not seem appropriate at the time: indeed, the possibility of an action for negligent misstatement has only become apparent comparatively recently. The assumption in the later nineteenth century that all actions must be classifiable into one group or the other eventually led to these actions being regarded as contractual, and contractual rules being applied.[366] The contract is normally unilateral, viz., the agent offers to warrant his authority in exchange for the third party entering into a contract with the principal or otherwise acting as requested; the offer is accepted by the third party acting accordingly.[367] The result of the cause of action being classified as contractual is the strict liability customarily placed on parties who make contractual promises: the agent is in effect a guarantor of his authority. There are repercussions as regards the damages obtainable, which are not limited to reliance loss.[368] Perhaps surprisingly, international codifications appear to take the same view.[369]

9-063 **Cessation of authority unbeknown to agent** There was at one time a tendency

---

[361] At 657–658.
[362] On the basis of *Hedley Byrne & Co Ltd v Heller & Partners Ltd* [1964] A.C. 465. See further para.9-061.
[363] *Kavanagh v Continental Shelf (No. 46) Ltd* [1993] 2 N.Z.L.R. 648. See however *Fong Maun Yee v Yoong Weng Ho* [1997] 2 Singapore L.R. 297, where a different view appears to have been taken.
[364] See too *Heskell v Continental Express Ltd* [1950] 1 All E.R. 1033, Illustration 5 to Article 106. But cf. *Hedley Byrne & Co Ltd v Heller & Partners Ltd* [1964] A.C. 465 at 532.
[365] Radcliffe (1902) 18 L.Q.R. 364; Holdsworth (1924) 40 L.Q.R. 1 (suggesting that the liability is quasi-contractual); Seavey (1920) 29 Yale L.J. 859 at 886 onwards; *Edwards v Porter* [1923] 2 K.B. 538 at 545–546 (but cf. on appeal, [1925] A.C. 1 at 23, 45); *Leggo v Brown & Dureau Ltd* (1923) 32 C.L.R. 95. See too Reynolds [2012] L.M.C.L.Q. 189.
[366] See *Dickson v Reuter's Telegram Co Ltd* (1877) 3 C.P.D. 1 at 5; *The Piraeus* [1974] 2 Lloyd's Rep. 266 (action contractual for the purposes of RSC Ord.11 r.1(f) (g)); *Commonwealth Bank of Australia v Hamilton* [2012] NSWSC 242 at [304] (plea of contributory negligence not available); *Zoya Ltd v Sheikh Nasir Ahmed (t/a Property Mart)* [2016] EWHC 2249 (Ch); [2016] 4 W.L.R. 174 at [30].
[367] See *Yonge v Toynbee* [1910] 1 K.B. 215 at 227–228, discussed further below, para.9-063; *Permanent Custodians Ltd v Geagea* [2014] NSWSC 562.
[368] See Article 106.
[369] *Restatement, Third, Agency*, § 6.10; PECL art.3:024; UNIDROIT Principles art.2.2.6; DCFR, II,

to confine the remedy for false profession of agency, as if on a tort, to cases where the agent was negligent[370]: but this, as stated above, does not square with the supposed contractual nature of the liability. The premise of strict liability has been applied in cases where, unknown to the agent, the agent's authority has terminated. The leading case has been *Yonge v Toynbee*.[371] That case was concerned with supervening mental incapacity, and it is now in doubt whether the mere intervention of mental incapacity does automatically terminate an agent's authority.[372] But it is likely that the general premise still applies, and that it could lead to an agent's liability on the warranty in cases of death and, in the case of a company, its dissolution.[373] There remains a degree of flexibility in the implication of the warranty,[374] and in relation to powers of attorney, the position has been mitigated by statute.[375]

Warranty not confined to misrepresentation resulting in contract   The   **9-064** implication of a warranty is not confined to cases where the transaction with the person representing himself as having authority results in a contract with the principal[376]:

> "The rule to be deduced is, that where a person by asserting that he has the authority of the principal induces another person to enter into any transaction which he would not have entered into but for that assertion, and the assertion turns out to be untrue, to the injury of the person to whom it is made, it must be taken that the person making it undertook that it was true, and he is liable personally for the damage that has occurred."[377]

Thus the doctrine has been applied where directors purported to pay a creditor by the use of debentures which the company had no power to issue, and to the presentation of a transfer under a forged power of attorney.[378] Nor is the rule confined to cases where the person sought to be held liable is the person who was thought to have authority: there may be liability for a representation that another person has

---

6:107(2). See also *The Unauthorised Agent* (Busch and Macgregor eds, 2009); and Verhagen (2009) 6 *European Review of Private Law* 1003. For a view that the whole issue requires reconsideration, see Faulkner (2000) 74 A.L.J. 465. See also below, paras 12-026 and 12-027.

[370] *Salton v New Beeston Cycle Co* [1900] 1 Ch. 43; following *Smout v Ilbery* (1842) 10 M. & W. 1. In relation of *Smout* itself, the case may perhaps be supported on the grounds that on the facts there was no warranty: "the continuance of the life of the principal was ... a fact equally within the knowledge of both contracting parties": at 11. See *Yonge v Toynbee* [1910] 1 K.B. 215 at 227–228; *Randall v Trimen* (1856) 18 C.B. 786 at 793.

[371] [1910] 1 K.B. 215, Illustration 12. See also *Starkey v Bank of England* [1903] A.C. 114 at 119.

[372] See *Blankley v Central Manchester and Manchester Children's University Hospitals NHS Trust* [2015] EWCA Civ 18; [2015] 1 W.L.R. 4307, and para.10-020.

[373] See *Yonge v Toynbee* [1910] 1 K.B. 215 at 227–228; below, para.10-032. This was the situation dealt with in *Salton v New Beeston Cycle Co* [1900] 1 Ch. 43, the actual decision in which has not been questioned; see also *Schlieske v Overseas Construction Co Pty Ltd* [1960] V.R. 195; *Babury Ltd v London Industrial Plc* (1989) 139 N.L.J. 1596.

[374] See below, para.9-070.

[375] See below, Article 122 (the legislation dating back to Law of Property Amendment Act 1859 s.26).

[376] See Illustrations 3 and 6; *Brown v Law* (1895) 72 L.T. 779; *British Russian Gazette Ltd v Associated Newspapers Ltd* [1933] 2 K.B. 616; *Heskell v Continental Express Ltd* [1950] 1 All E.R. 1033 at 1042, where an attempt to put a limit on the rule was rejected.

[377] *Firbank's Exors v Humphreys* (1886) 18 Q.B.D. 54 at 60, per Lord Esher MR; but cf. the slightly narrower formulation by Lindley LJ at 62.

[378] See Illustrations 3 and 6.

authority.[379] And there may be liability to a person unknown to the defendant who relies on the warranty, e.g. the indorsee of a bill of exchange or bill of lading containing a false representation of authority.[380] But there are limits: the mere fact that a person misrepresents a fact relevant to a third party does not mean that he asserts that he has authority to do so.[381]

9-065   **Warranty to third persons**   It has further been held in England by the Court of Appeal that the warranty can also be given to a third party other than the purchaser of land; the party concerned was a prospective lender under a mortgage by the purchaser.[382] It was said that such a party would certainly not have proceeded had he known that the vendor's solicitor was not authorised by the vendor (in fact by one of two co-vendors). It can certainly be said that the dictum of Lord Esher cited above, and other dicta,[383] do not require that the third party actually enter into a contract with the vendor, but refer only to a "transaction": but they do suggest directness of relationship and it is probably going too far to say that the whole scenario of purchase funded by mortgage is one transaction,[384] for events may happen at different times. The reasoning was in fact based on general warranty reasoning of a broader nature than that which justified the basic type of breach of warranty of authority,[385] supported by reference to the bill of lading case referred to above[386] (where the agent was necessarily aware of the fact that the contract was transferable by statute) and the well-known case of *Carlill v Carbolic Smoke Ball Co*,[387] concerning reliance on an advertisement expressed in general terms. Such an extension does not seem to be envisaged by *Restatement, Third*, or the various European codifications referred to above.[388] Though it is well established in England it may be doubted whether such an extension of strict liability is appropriate. As it stands, however, such reasoning can be applied also to purchasers' solicitors acting on behalf of them as borrowers,[389] or in general, to solicitors acting for both borrower and lender,[390] despite the fact that in other respects the latter may be under a

---

[379] Illustrations 1, 4 and 9 can be so explained.

[380] *V/O Rasnoimport v Guthrie & Co Ltd* [1966] 1 Lloyd's Rep. 1, Illustration 11; following wide dicta in textbooks (mostly to be justified by reference to the words used in *Starkey v Bank of England* [1903] A.C. 114) and dicta of A.L. Smith J at first instance in *West London Commercial Bank v Kitson* (1883) 12 Q.B.D. 157 at 161 (treated by the Court of Appeal as a case of fraud: (1884) 13 Q.B.D. 360). However, the result seems correct, for the agent knows that such a contract is transferable. See also *New Georgia National Bank v Lippman* 249 N.Y. 307, 164 N.E. 108 (1928); Reynolds (1967) 80 L.Q.R. 189.

[381] *Salvesen v Rederi A/B Nordstjernan* [1905] A.C. 302; *Jones v Still* [1965] N.Z.L.R. 1071.

[382] *Penn v Bristol & West BS* [1997] 1 W.L.R. 1356 (leave to appeal to House of Lords was refused). See Reynolds [2012] L.M.C.L.Q. 189.

[383] See *Starkey v Bank of England* [1903] A.C. 114 at 119, per Lord Davey.

[384] Despite Lord Diplock's reference to the "real-property-mortgaged-to-a-building-society-owning democracy": *Pettitt v Pettitt* [1970] A.C. 777 at 824 (we are grateful to Mark West QC for this reference).

[385] [1997] 1 W.L.R. at 1363.

[386] *V/O Rasnoimport v Guthrie & Co Ltd* [1966] 1 Lloyd's Rep. 1.

[387] [1893] 1 Q.B. 156.

[388] See above, para.9-062.

[389] See *Bristol & West B.S. v Fancy & Jackson* [1997] 4 All E.R. 582. In such a case the warranty might be of authorisation of certain conveyancing procedures, but there would be little difference: see at 613. But solicitors may sign contracts themselves, as in *Suleman v Shahsavari* [1988] 1 W.L.R. 1181.

[390] See *Excel Securities Plc v Masood*, Mercantile Court, Manchester, June 10, 2009, HH Judge Hegarty QC, below, para.9-068.

retainer to the lender which on normal practice makes them liable for negligence only.[391]

The question that would then arise is as to the test for determining when such a warranty is deemed to be given. It is submitted that this should only be so where, in accordance with normal contractual principles, the warranty of authority can be regarded as inducing an act[392]; and there must then be corresponding reliance on it.[393] Mere knowledge in the warrantor that certain persons can be foreseen as relying on the warranty is redolent of tort liability and should not be sufficient in this context. Thus some flexibility can be derived from this feature.

Nature of liability   The basic warranty is only that the agent has authority from his principal: this is something peculiarly within the agent's knowledge. If the principal proves unreliable, that is something in respect of which the third party could have made inquiries. Merely as agent, therefore, the agent does not warrant that his principal is solvent,[394] or will perform the contract (if any). As can be seen below, in the context of litigation, the warranty is similarly limited in that the agent (normally a solicitor) does not promise that a claim is valid. The difficulty arises however when the cause of lack of authority is that the principal has never existed, no longer exists, or lacks capacity. In England the leading case has been *Yonge v Toynbee*,[395] where the agent was held liable in the context of litigation when his principal had without his knowledge become incapable. As stated above, there is now considerable doubt that the mere intervention of mental incapacity automatically terminates an agent's authority (with the result that the agent's warranty would not be broken), but an agent might remain exposed should his principal have died, or ceased to exist.[396] If the agent warrants that his principal still exists, a fortiori he may be held to warrant that his principal has at some time existed.[397] Hence problems of the liability of promoters of companies not yet formed could sometimes perhaps be solved by the implication of this warranty.[398] In many situations where the principal, whether supposedly human or corporate, is non-existent, however, there is some degree of knowledge on both sides, so that the warranty may be

    9-066

---

[391] A case sometimes cited in this context is *Midland Bank Plc v Cox McQueen* [1999] P.N.L.R. 593, where, however, the relevance of a warranty was rejected.

[392] See the dictum of Lord Esher MR quoted above, para.9-064.

[393] See *Leggo v Brown & Dureau Ltd* (1923) 32 C.L.R. 95 at 106: "The essentials are (1) assertion of authority; (2) inducement by asserting; (3) transaction which but for that assertion the other party would not have entered into"; *Zoya Ltd v Sheikh Nasir Ahmed (t/a Property Mart)* [2016] EWHC 2249 (Ch); [2016] 4 W.L.R. 174 at [39]. See on the whole topic, West (2009) 25 J. Prof. Negligence 131; Reynolds, ibid., 142.

[394] See Article 106.

[395] [1910] 1 K.B. 215, Illustration 12. See also *Scott v J.B. Livingston & Nicol* 1990 S.L.T. 305; cf. *Nelson v Nelson* [1997] 1 W.L.R. 233, where the principal was an undischarged bankrupt, with the result that the cause of action vested in his trustee. This went to its validity, which the solicitor did not warrant.

[396] See above, para.9-063.

[397] See *Simmons v Liberal Opinion Ltd* [1911] 1 K.B. 966; *Russian & English Bank v Baring Bros & Co Ltd* [1935] Ch. 120; *Salter v Cormie* (1993) 108 D.L.R. (4th) 372.

[398] Such an action was successful in *Delta Construction Co Ltd v Lidstone* (1979) 96 D.L.R. (3d) 457; but failed on the issue of damages. See Article 106; Article 107; *Brownett v Newton* (1941) 64 C.L.R. 439 (company not entitled to commence business); *Black v Smallwood* (1966) 117 C.L.R. 52 at 64; *Fernée v Gorlitz* [1915] 1 Ch. 177 (principal a minor); cf. *Newborne v Sensolid (Great Britain) Ltd* [1954] 1 Q.B. 45 at 47; *Hawke's Bay Milk Corp Ltd v Watson* [1974] 1 N.Z.L.R. 236. The argument was successful in *Lomax v Dankel* (1981) 29 S.A.S.R. 68. But there can be problems as to damages. See below, para.9-085.

excluded,[399] and in some cases, e.g. unformed companies and unincorporated associations, the agent has in fact been held liable on the contract itself.[400]

Cases holding the agent liable where the contract would be ultra vires the corporate principal, and certain other cases such as that of the non-existent principal, may require to be analysed as an extension of the warranty of authority. For in some of them the agent is held liable though the act would, even if authorised by the supposed principal, be a nullity, with the result that there would be no loss caused by the lack of authority.[401] Though *Collen v Wright*[402] is frequently cited in these cases, it may sometimes be necessary to say that what is warranted is that, e.g. there is a power to issue debentures, that the document presented is genuine, and so forth.[403] In the absence of evidence, an agent would not ordinarily be taken to warrant that he has named his principal correctly, but only that he existed and had given authority.[404]

9-067 **Warranty in litigation** A specialised application of the warranty of authority is that given by a solicitor or other representative who issues process in litigation. It has been truly said that "this contractual theory presents some conceptual problems in the case of a solicitor conducting litigation".[405] In general, the solicitor only warrants that he has been authorised by a client who exists[406]; it has been held that he does not warrant that the name given by him for that client is correct,[407] and he certainly does not warrant the client's solvency or the validity, or even arguability, of the client's claim.

9-068 **Cases of identity fraud** The narrow warranty applied to solicitors in litigation has recently been applied to the warranty given by the solicitor for a prospective mortgagor of land to the prospective mortgage lender. These cases have held solicitors against whom identity fraud has been practised by the prospective mortgagor not liable, on the basis that the warranty which they give is in such situations very limited, namely that they have been authorised by a person who reasonably appears to them to be the person whom he alleges that he is.[408] So, agents will not normally promise that a named principal is not impersonating another or that he has

---

[399] See below, para.9-070.
[400] Article 107.
[401] Article 106; *Heskell v Continental Express Ltd* [1950] 1 All E.R. 1033; Radcliffe (1902) 18 L.Q.R. 364; cf. *British Russian Gazette v Associated Newspapers Ltd* [1933] 2 K.B. 616 at 649.
[402] (1857) 8 E. & B. 647.
[403] See Illustrations 2–5; *Sheffield Corp v Barclay* [1905] A.C. 392. But as to the presentation of bills of exchange, see *Guaranty Trust Co of New York v Hannay & Co* [1918] 2 K.B. 623; *Greenwood v Martins Bank Ltd* [1933] A.C. 51 at 59–60; cf. *Yeung Kai Yung v Hong Kong and Shanghai Banking Corp* [1981] A.C. 787, Illustration 5 to Article 98.
[404] *Knight Frank LLP v Du Haney* [2011] EWCA Civ 404.
[405] *AMB Generali Holding AG v SEB Trygg Liv* [2005] EWCA Civ 1237; [2006] 1 Lloyd's Rep. 318 at [60], per Buxton LJ. The matter is commonly relevant to the court's jurisdiction to award costs: see e.g. *Bank of Scotland v Qutb* [2012] EWCA Civ 1661; *Re Sherlock Holmes International Society Ltd* [2016] EWHC 1392 (Ch); [2016] 4 W.L.R. 173; *Zoya Ltd v Sheikh Nasir Ahmed (t/a Property Mart)* [2016] EWHC 2249 (Ch); [2016] 4 W.L.R. 174.
[406] See *Nelson v Nelson* [1997] 1 W.L.R. 233.
[407] *AMB Generali Holding AG v SEB Trygg Liv* [2005] EWCA Civ 1237; [2006] 1 Lloyd's Rep. 31. See too *Knight Frank LLP v Du Haney* [2011] EWCA Civ 404.
[408] *Excel Securities Plc v Masood* [2010] Lloyd's Rep. P.N. 165; *Cheshire Mortgage Corp Ltd v Grandison* [2012] CSIH 66, noted Macgregor (2013) 17 Edin. L.R. 398; *Stevenson v Singh* [2012] EWHC 2880 (QB), Illustration 14. cf. *Knight Frank LLP v Du Haney* [2011] EWCA Civ 404, Illustration 14; *P&P Property Ltd v Owen White & Catlin LLP* [2016] EWHC 2276 (Ch); [2016] Bus.

a particular qualification, e.g. owns the property concerned,[409] though this could also be so for an unnamed principal, for example on whose behalf a car is sold.[410] There may also be difficulty in finding that an agent, including a solicitor, has undertaken a duty of care to a non-client in cases such as this.[411]

Mistake of law   The traditional view has been that the warranty will not be implied where the representation is one of law.[412] There may however be difficulty in distinguishing representations of fact from representations of law.[413] Thus a representation that a company has power to borrow may be one of law if on the true construction of its memorandum it has no such power: but if the power could have been conferred by resolution, the representation may be of fact, that such a resolution has been passed.[414] Again, there may be a representation of the fact that the borrowing limit has not been exceeded.[415] Though there is no clear authority, it seems on principle that a wilfully false statement of law would give rise to liability in deceit, provided the other requirements (e.g. that the statement is likely to be acted on) were satisfied.[416]

9-069

Rebuttal of the warranty   The circumstances in which the warranty is implied create the possibility of considerable flexibility, and the strictness of the liability placed on the agent is in effect tempered by this technique. Thus where the agent disclaims authority, he avoids such liability,[417] unless the case is one where he contracts to obtain authority.[418] If the third party does not think that authority can be obtained, this may be a ground for negativing the implication of a warranty, though the fact that A does not think that B can perform his contract with A does not usually affect B's liability.[419] In some cases the third party may be taken to know of the limitation or lack of authority, so that there are no grounds for implying a war-

9-070

L.R. 1337 (where there is a good discussion by Dicker QC of the earlier authorities). See Reynolds [2012] L.M.C.L.Q. 189; Tan Cheng Han (2012) 30 J.C.L. 92.
[409] *Houlgate Investment Co Ltd v Biggart Baillie LLP* [2011] CSOH 160; [2012] P.N.L.R. 2; *P&P Property Ltd v Owen White & Catlin LLP* [2016] EWHC 2276 (Ch); [2016] Bus L.R. 1337 at [126]. cf. *LSC Finance Ltd v Abensons Law Ltd* [2015] EWHC 1163 (Ch).
[410] See two notes doubting a South African decision to the contrary, (1985) 102 S.A.L.J. 596 and 603. See also *Scott v J.B. Livingston & Nicol* 1990 S.L.T. 305 at 307.
[411] See *P&P Property Ltd v Owen White & Catlin LLP* [2016] EWHC 2276 (Ch); [2016] Bus. L.R. 1337 at [176]. See further below, para.9-117.
[412] Illustration 5; *Beattie v Ebury* (1872) L.R. 7 Ch.App. 777; affd L.R. 7 H.L. 102; *Saffron Walden Second Benefit Building Society v Rayner* (1880) 14 Ch.D. 406.
[413] See *Eaglesfield v Londonderry* (1876) 4 Ch.D. 693 at 703 (affd (1876) 38 L.T. 303), Illustration 5.
[414] See *Beattie v Ebury* above at 800–803.
[415] *Weeks v Propert* (1873) L.R. 8 C.P. 427.
[416] See *Beattie v Ebury*, above; *Eaglesfield v Londonderry*, above; *Hirschfeld v London, Brighton & South Coast Ry Co* (1876) 2 Q.B.D. 1; *West London Commercial Bank v Kitson* (1884) 13 Q.B.D. 360 (but none of these are clear authorities).
[417] *Halbot v Lens* [1901] 1 Ch. 344, Illustration 10; *Re Sherlock Holmes International Society Ltd* [2016] EWHC 1392 (Ch); [2016] 4 W.L.R. 173; *Zoya Ltd v Sheikh Nasir Ahmed (t/a Property Mart)* [2016] EWHC 2249 (Ch); [2016] 4 W.L.R. 174 at [50] (no warranty in litigation where authority to bring the proceedings was the very matter in contention). In *McManus v Fortescue* [1907] 2 K.B. 1 it was held that if the purchaser had notice that there might be a reserve the auctioneer who knocked down an item short of the reserve was not liable for breach of warranty of authority when he refused to sign a memorandum of the sale. Sed quaere: see Murdoch, *Law of Estate Agency* (5th edn), pp.174–178.
[418] *Halbot v Lens*, above, at 351.
[419] Powell, pp.256–257.

ranty by the agent.[420] There will not, however, usually be any duty on a third party to inquire,[421] for he is entitled to assume that a person purporting to act as agent promises that he is so authorised.

9-071   **Apparent authority**   Where the agent has no actual authority, but contracts in circumstances in which the principal would be bound under the doctrine of apparent authority, it seems that the agent should be prima facie liable, for he has no authority: the fact that the principal could be held liable, however, would mean that the third party could prove no loss. However, the expense of proving this could perhaps be recoverable: certainly, the costs of an abortive action in which apparent authority is *not* established can.[422] Even if the principal were insolvent, the agent would not be liable, for he is only liable for loss arising out of the fact that he has no authority.[423] However, there are dicta that in a case of apparent authority there is no breach of warranty of authority at all.[424] These can only be justified on the rather doubtful ground that the agent warrants that he has actual *or apparent* authority.[425]

9-072   **Ratification**   It may be assumed that the agent is not liable where the principal ratifies. Here again there is no loss to the third party, but it may be more plausibly argued that there was no breach of warranty at all,[426] on the basis that the agent warrants that he has authority or that the principal will ratify.

9-073   **Powers of attorney**   There is statutory protection for the agent where he acts in pursuance of a power of attorney which has been revoked: this is set out in Article 122.

9-074   **Agents of the Crown**   It was held in *Dunn v Macdonald*[427] that an agent of the Crown was not liable for breach of warranty of authority where he purported to engage an employee on behalf of the Crown for a fixed period of three years and the plaintiff was dismissed, in accordance with the powers of the Crown to dismiss,

---

[420] Illustrations 8 and 9; and see *Beattie v Ebury*, above; *Dillon v Macdonald* (1902) 21 N.Z.L.R. 45 (third party ought to have assumed authority expired); *Cook v Williams* (1897) 14 T.L.R. 31 (third party ought to have known estate agent had no authority to sell); *Zoya Ltd v Sheikh Nasir Ahmed (t/a Property Mart)* [2016] EWHC 2249 (Ch). cf. *Austin v Real Estate Listing Exchange* (1912) 2 D.L.R. 324 (list of properties for sale guaranteed by issuers).

[421] See *V/O Rasnoimport v Guthrie & Co Ltd* [1966] 1 Lloyd's Rep. 1, esp. at 11: though there are dicta to the contrary concerning the public documents of companies. And see *Schlieske v Overseas Construction Co Pty Ltd* [1960] V.R. 195 where it was held that solicitors should have realised that the defendant company might have been dissolved. cf., however, *Leggo v Brown & Dureau Ltd* (1923) 32 C.L.R. 95 (plaintiff need not affirmatively establish reliance).

[422] See below, para.9-081. Contra, *Restatement, Third*, § 6.10, Comment b.

[423] See Article 106. It is difficult to see why this point was not considered in *Yonge v Toynbee* [1910] 1 K.B. 215 in view of *Drew v Nunn* (1879) 4 Q.B.D. 661, in which it had been held that there was apparent authority in an agent whose principal had become incapable: see Article 121. cf. Powers of Attorney Act 1971 s.5(1) and (2); see Article 122.

[424] See *Rainbow v Howkins* [1904] 2 K.B. 322 at 326. Some doubt was cast on this case in *McManus v Fortescue* [1907] 2 K.B. 1, but as regards the apparent authority of an auctioneer to sell without reserve, and in the later case there was notice that there might be a reserve. See also *V/O Rasnoimport v Guthrie*, above at 10; *Mitsui & Co Ltd v Marpro Industrial Ltd* [1974] 1 Lloyd's Rep. 386.

[425] See *Restatement, Second*, § 329, Comment f; *Restatement, Third*, § 6.10, Comment b.

[426] Unless perhaps the principal initially refused to ratify, thereby causing expense to the third party.

[427] [1897] 1 Q.B. 401; ibid., 555; followed in *The Prometheus* (1949) 82 Ll. L. Rep. 859. See also *Kenny v Cosgrave* [1926] I.R. 517. See Street, *Governmental Liability* (1953), p.93; Nettheim [1975] C.L.J. 253.

within this period. This case is usually taken as authority for a general exemption from liability for breach of warranty of authority on the part of such agents on grounds of public policy: the implication of a warranty is "utterly inconsistent with the facts".[428] Though the majority of the judges involved in the case[429] took this view, the case can be explained as one involving a mistake of law.[430] Further, it could be argued that the defendant had in fact authority to engage the plaintiff, that the contract was impliedly subject to the Crown's right of dismissal, and that all that was held was that the agent did not warrant that the right of dismissal would not be exercised[431] not a matter of authority at all. However, though an agent of the Crown can no doubt expressly warrant his authority, it is very doubtful whether he should be regarded as impliedly doing so in the same circumstances as other agents. His non-liability may be explained as based on the other party's being presumed to know of this; but such a presumption is somewhat artificial, and public policy may provide the best explanation.

Procedure   Where the authority of the agent is disputed by the person on whose behalf the contract is made, the person who made the contract may be joined with him as co-defendant and relief claimed against them alternatively.[432]   **9-075**

Illustrations

(1)   The directors of a company wrote a letter to the company's bankers representing that A had been appointed manager and had authority to draw cheques on the company's account, which, to the knowledge of the directors, was already overdrawn. A further overdrew the account, the directors having, in fact, no authority to overdraw. Held, that the directors were liable to the bankers for breach of an implied warranty that they had authority to overdraw.[433] But the mere fact that directors of a company in that capacity sign cheques drawn on the company's bankers after the account is overdrawn does not amount to a representation that they have authority to overdraw the account, or to borrow money on the company's behalf.[434]   **9-076**

(2)   A lent £70 to a building society, and received a certificate of the deposit, signed by two directors. The society had no borrowing powers. Held, that the directors were personally liable to A on an implied warranty that they had authority to borrow on behalf of the society.[435]

(3)   The directors of a company issued a certificate for debenture stock, which A agreed to accept in lieu of cash due to him from the company, all the debenture stock that the company had power to issue having already been issued. Held, that the directors were liable to A on an implied warranty that they had authority to issue valid debenture stock, although they had acted in

[428]   [1897] 1 Q.B. 401 at 558.
[429]   Charles J at first instance; Lopes and Chitty LJJ in the Court of Appeal.
[430]   See arguments before Charles J.
[431]   See the judgment of Lord Esher MR.
[432]   *Honduras Inter-Oceanic Ry Co v Lefevre & Tucker* (1877) 2 Ex.D. 301; *Massey v Heynes* (1888) 21 Q.B.D. 330; *Bennetts v McIlwraith* [1896] 2 Q.B. 464; *Sanderson v Blyth Theatre Co* [1903] 2 K.B. 533. In such a case the court would, in the exercise of its discretion, normally order the unsuccessful defendant to pay the successful defendant's costs by making either a "Bullock Order" or a "Sanderson Order": see *Civil Procedure 2010*, Vol.1, § 44.3.8.
[433]   *Cherry & M'Dougall v Colonial Bank of Australasia* (1869) 38 L.J.P.C. 49.
[434]   *Beattie v Ebury* (1872) L.R. 7 Ch.App. 777; affd L.R. 7 H.L. 102.
[435]   *Richardson v Williamson* (1871) L.R. 6 Q.B. 276.

good faith, not knowing that all the stock had been issued.[436] So, where directors of a company which had already fully exercised its borrowing powers issued a debenture bond, it was held that the directors thereby impliedly warranted that they had authority to issue a valid debenture.[437]

(4)   The directors of an unincorporated society held out the secretary as having authority to borrow in excess of the amount prescribed by the rules of the society. The secretary borrowed in excess of such amount, and misappropriated the money. Held, that the directors were personally liable to the lenders on an implied warranty of authority, though they had not acted fraudulently.[438]

(5)   The directors of a company having no borrowing powers induce A to advance money on the security of a Lloyd's bond, which they in good faith represent to be a valid security, A being aware that the company has no borrowing powers. The directors are not liable on an implied warranty of authority, though the bond is invalid, because its validity is a question of law.[439] So, where directors issued certain stock and described it as No.1 Preference Stock, in the erroneous belief that they had power to issue stock to rank with the No.1 Preference Stock already issued, and A purchased some of the new stock, knowing that it was new stock, but believing that it would rank with the No.1 Preference, it was held that the directors were not liable to make good the misrepresentation, because it was a misrepresentation as to a matter of law, and A had not been deceived by any misrepresentation of fact.[440]

(6)   A stockbroker, acting in good faith, induces the Bank of England to transfer consols to a purchaser under a forged power of attorney. He is liable, in an action for breach of warranty of authority, to indemnify the Bank against the claim of the stockholder for restitution.[441]

(7)   A acts as broker for both buyer and seller. He impliedly warrants to each that he is duly authorised to act on behalf of the other.[442]

(8)   A ship-broker signs a charterparty—"by telegraphic authority; as agent". It is proved that such a form of signature is commonly adopted to negative the implication of any further warranty by the agent than that he has received a telegram which, if correct, authorises such a charterparty as he is signing. The ship-broker is not answerable for a mistake in the telegram.[443]

(9)   H, a ship-broker, professes to make a charterparty on behalf of A, and signs it—"by telegraphic authority of B, G H as agent". B is A's agent, but A did not authorise the charterparty. H is liable for breach of an implied warranty that he has authority to make the charterparty on behalf of A, though he acted in good faith, believing that the telegram from B gave him such authority.[444]

---

[436] *Firbank's Exors v Humphreys* (1886) 18 Q.B.D. 54; criticised (1902) 18 L.Q.R. 364; cf. *Elkington & Co v Hürter* [1892] 2 Ch. 452 and Illustration 5.

[437] *Weeks v Propert* (1873) L.R. 8 C.P. 427; *Whitehaven Joint Stock Banking Co v Reed* (1886) 2 T.L.R. 353. cf. Illustration 5.

[438] *Chapleo v Brunswick Building Society* (1881) 6 Q.B.D. 696. cf. *Smith v Reed* (1886) 2 T.L.R. 442.

[439] *Rashdall v Ford* (1866) L.R. 2 Eq. 750.

[440] *Eaglesfield v Londonderry* (1876) 38 L.T. 303; affirming (1874) 4 Ch.D. 693.

[441] *Starkey v Bank of England* [1903] A.C. 114; affirming decision of CA sub nom. *Oliver v Bank of England* [1902] 1 Ch. 610; *Commonwealth Bank of Australia v Hamilton* [2012] NSWSC 242 at [296].

[442] *Hughes v Graeme* (1864) 33 L.J.Q.B. 335. See above, paras 2-013, 6-046 and 6-060.

[443] *Lilly, Wilson & Co v Smales, Eeles & Co* [1892] 1 Q.B. 456.

[444] *Suart v Haigh* (1893) 9 T.L.R. 488.

(10) A signs a composition agreement with B on behalf of X, both A and B being aware that X has refused to enter into such an agreement, and taking the risk that X would again refuse to be bound. A does not warrant that X will accept the agreement.[445]

(11) A loading broker signed a bill of lading covering goods some of which were never shipped. As regards the goods not shipped his principal, the shipowner, was as the law then stood not bound. The loading broker was liable for breach of warranty of authority.[446]

(12) Solicitors enter an appearance in an action on behalf of a client who has unknown to them become mentally incapable and hence lacks capacity to instruct them. They are liable for the claimant's costs (which their client could not be) as having warranted their authority to act.[447] A solicitor warrants that he has a client who has instructed him. He does not however warrant that he has correctly named the client, nor that the client is solvent or has a good cause of action.[448]

(13) Where a solicitor, without authority, prosecutes or defends an action, the action will in general be dismissed or the defences struck out on the motion of either the plaintiff or the defendant, and the solicitor so acting without authority will be ordered to pay all the costs occasioned thereby.[449]

(14) A solicitor has a client who is impersonating the owner of land. The client engages the solicitor to act in a purported sale of the land, which is naturally ineffective. The purchasers sue the solicitor asserting a warranty of authority. It is held that the solicitor warrants only that he has a client who has authorised him to assist in the sale of the land, not that the client does in fact own the land or otherwise has power to sell it.[450]

Article 106

MEASURE OF DAMAGES FOR BREACH OF WARRANTY OF AUTHORITY

(1) The measure of damages for breach of warranty of authority is the loss which the parties should reasonably have contemplated as liable to result from the breach of warranty.[451] **9-077**

[445] *Halbot v Lens* [1901] 1 Ch. 344.

[446] *V/O Rasnoimport v Guthrie & Co Ltd* [1966] 1 Lloyd's Rep. 1; noted (1967) 83 L.Q.R. 189. cf. Article 106, Illustration 5. The principal could now be bound by virtue of Carriage of Goods by Sea Act 1992 s.4.

[447] *Yonge v Toynbee* [1910] 1 K.B. 215—actually a case on the summary jurisdiction in respect of solicitors. This is a different way of raising the same issue: no formal action is required and hence expense is saved, but the considerations taken into account appear to be the same. See *Civil Procedure 2010*, Vol.2, 7C-208; Cordery, *Solicitors* (8th edn), p.113 onwards, 9th (looseleaf) edn, F2A; *Skylight Maritime SA v Ascot Underwriting* [2005] EWHC 15 (Comm).

[448] *AMB Generali Holding AG v SEB Trygg Liv Holding, etc.* [2005] EWCA Civ 1237; [2006] 1 Lloyd's Rep. 318 at [56] onwards, explaining *Nelson v Nelson* [1977] 1 W.L.R. 233, above, para.9-066. See also below, para.10-032.

[449] *Hubbart v Phillips* (1845) 13 M. & W. 702; *Simmons v Liberal Opinion Ltd* [1911] 1 K.B. 966; *Babury Ltd v London Industrial Plc* (1989) 139 N.L.J. 1596. And see Cordery, above. cf. *Zoya Ltd v Sheikh Nasir Ahmed (t/a Property Mart)* [2016] EWHC 2249 (Ch); [2016] 4 W.L.R. 174 (litigation to contest right to sue on behalf of company).

[450] *Stevenson v Singh* [2012] EWHC 2880 (QB). See also *P&P Property Ltd v Owen White & Catlin LLP* [2016] EWHC 2276 (Ch).

[451] See *C. Czarnikow Ltd v Koufos (The Heron II)* [1969] 1 A.C. 350; Illustrations; *Restatement, Third,*

(2) Where a contract is repudiated by the person on whose behalf it was made on the ground that it was made without his authority, such loss is prima facie the amount of damages that could have been recovered from him in an action if he had duly authorised and subsequently refused to perform the contract, together with the costs and expenses (if any) incurred in respect of any legal proceedings reasonably taken against him on the contract.[452]

Comment

9-078 **Contractual principle** The cause of action for breach of warranty of authority being eventually classified as contractual, the damages were eventually settled as those required to put the plaintiff in the position in which he would have been had the warranty been made good, viz. had the representation of authority been true.

> "The damages, under the general rule, are arrived at by considering the difference in the position [the plaintiff] would have been in had the representation been true and the position he is actually in consequence of it being untrue."[453]

The claimant must establish loss and not leave it to the court to infer it.[454] Where an agent only warrants that he has authority to negotiate a contract, the damages may be confined to the third party's wasted expenditure.[455]

9-079 **Insolvent principal** Thus it has often been stated that when the principal is insolvent only nominal damages may be given, for a successful action against him would have produced no money.[456] However, the fact that the principal is insolvent does not necessarily mean that there will be no damages, if the result of the transaction would, if the agent had had authority, have been to make the third party a preferred creditor of the principal. In *Firbank's Executors v Humphreys*[457] the plaintiffs were induced by the directors of a company to accept debenture stock in lieu of payment for services rendered, but such stock was null because the amount which the company had power to borrow had been exceeded. Had the company been solvent, the loss recoverable from the directors would probably have been

---

§ 6.10; McGregor, *Damages* (19th edn), Ch.33.

[452] See Comment and Illustrations. But cf. *Chitholie v Nash & Co* (1973) 229 E.G. 786 (measure of damages available in lieu of specific performance in an action against principal under Lord Cairns' Act not applicable to claim against agent: but see McGregor, *Damages* (19th edn), para.34-007 and Illustration 10).

[453] *Firbank's Executors v Humphreys* (1886) 18 Q.B.D. 54 at 60, per Lord Esher MR. But cf. *Doyle v Olby (Ironmongers) Ltd* [1969] 2 Q.B. 158 at 168, where Winn LJ used this passage to distinguish liability for breach of warranty of authority from liability for breach of contract and to liken it to liability in deceit. This does not seem to be correct, though of course in actions in respect of statements the question of loss actually incurred often has more prominence than the expectation interest, viz. the profit that might have been made: see, e.g. *Kwei Tek Chao v British Traders and Shippers Ltd* [1954] 2 Q.B. 459; *McRae v Commonwealth Disposals Commission* (1951) 84 C.L.R. 377. *Salvesen v Rederi A/B Nordstjernan* [1905] A.C. 302 seems contrary to Winn LJ's suggestion. The statement above is in accord with the PECL art.3:204 and the UNIDROIT Principles art.2.2.6.

[454] *McIntosh v Linke Nominees Pty Ltd* [2008] QCA 275 at [20].

[455] *Stevenson v Singh* [2012] EWHC 2880 (QB) at [101].

[456] *Simons v Patchett* (1857) 7 E. & B. 568 at 574; *Spedding v Nevell* (1869) L.R. 4 C.P. 212 at 226; *Goodwin v Francis* (1870) L.R. 5 C.P. 295 at 308; *Richardson v Williamson* (1871) L.R. 6 Q.B. 276 at 279–280; *Weeks v Propert* (1873) L.R. 8 C.P. 427 at 439; *Re National Coffee Palace Co Ex p. Panmure* (1883) 24 Ch.D. 367 at 372; *Skylight Maritime SA v Ascot Underwriting* [2005] EWHC 15 (Comm).

[457] (1886) 18 Q.B.D. 54, Illustration 3 to Article 105.

nothing, as the plaintiffs could have sued the company on the original debt: but as it was insolvent, this right was valueless, so that the loss was the par value of the debentures, since valid stock of this type retained its value.[458]

Transaction unenforceable against principal   Where no redress could be obtained from the principal even if the agent had been authorised, there is again no loss.[459] Thus in *Heskell v Continental Express Ltd*[460] (Illustration 5) even express authorisation of the signature by the principal would not have created a contract with the principal, since no goods had ever been shipped. The same result could follow where the contract is unenforceable against the principal because the principal is a company not yet formed,[461] or for lack of writing under the Statute of Frauds. The latter point arose in *Fay v Miller, Wilkins & Co*[462] and the agent was held liable specifically because it could be held that there was a sufficient memorandum, the argument that if there had been no such memorandum no damage could be shown being apparently accepted. However, the absence of a memorandum could between the contracting parties be outweighed by an act or acts of part performance. Can these be pleaded against the agent, to show that the contract with the principal would have been enforceable? It was held in 1876 that this could not be pleaded because the notion of part performance is one that affects the equities between two parties to a suit for specific performance.[463] This is a narrow view; but in England the Statute of Frauds now only applies to guarantees, so the matter is not of importance. It has also been held that if the third party repudiates the obligation, he may suffer no loss and thus not be entitled to damages.[464]

9-080

Costs of legal proceedings   The costs of unsuccessful legal proceedings may also be recovered, provided that they were reasonable[465] and the fact that they might be brought was within the contemplation of the parties.[466] These will usually be proceedings against the principal, but the costs of defending proceedings brought by an unauthorised agent may also be recovered,[467] as may the cost of defending

9-081

---

[458]   cf. *Weeks v Propert*, above; *Whitehaven Joint Stock Banking Co v Reed* (1886) 2 T.L.R. 353. In neither case was there a pre-existing debt. See also *Alvin's Auto Service Ltd v Clew Holdings Ltd* (1997) 3 B.L.R. (2d) 11 (Canada), where the supposed principal, though insolvent, was amenable to a decree of specific performance.

[459]   Quaere whether out-of-pocket expenses could be recovered. On general principle they should: see Chitty, *Contracts* (32nd edn), para.26-089 onwards.

[460]   [1950] 1 All E.R. 1033.

[461]   *Delta Construction Co Ltd v Lidstone* (1979) 96 D.L.R. (3d) 457. See above, para.9-066; below, para.9-085.

[462]   [1941] Ch. 360. See also *Pow v Davies* (1861) 1 B. & S. 220 (seven-year lease without deed: defence of ejectment action held unreasonable). But cf. *British Russian Gazette Ltd v Associated Newspapers Ltd* [1933] 2 K.B. 616 at 649.

[463]   *Warr v Jones* (1876) 24 W.R. 695; but in land contracts the doctrine of part performance is no longer relevant in England by virtue of the Law of Property (Miscellaneous Provisions) Act 1989.

[464]   *Charan Singh v Sardar Investments Ltd* [2002] EWHC 380 ("on principle an agent suing for breach of warranty of authority ought to be able to rely on any defences which would have been available to his principal had the contract in fact been authorised") (at [58]: claimant had refused to complete); cf. *Habton Farms v Nimmo*, Illustration 11 below.

[465]   See *Hughes v Graeme* (1864) 33 L.J.Q.B. 355, Illustration 7; cf. *Godwin v Francis* (1870) L.R. 5 C.P. 295, Illustration 9. See also *Hammond & Co v Bussey* (1887) 20 Q.B.D. 79.

[466]   See *Spedding v Nevell* (1869) L.R. 4 C.P. 212, Illustration 8.

[467]   *Yonge v Toynbee* [1910] 1 K.B. 215, Illustration 12 to Article 105; *Fernée v Gorlitz* [1915] 1 Ch. 177.

proceedings brought by the supposed principal.[468] Persisting with proceedings after it has become clear that the agent was unauthorised may not however be reasonable.[469] The cost of establishing liability of the principal under the doctrine of apparent authority would not however be recoverable (though it should be recoverable from the principal). It is not clear whether such expenses can be recovered in those cases where the transaction is unenforceable against the principal. In the case of an insolvent principal, it is submitted that they might be, on the basis that a plaintiff in an action for breach of contract may abandon his claim for the expectation interest and claim his expenses only.[470] In the other two cases discussed above, those of the purported transaction that is a nullity and of the contract unenforceable for lack of writing, it is submitted that expenses will not often be regarded as reasonably incurred. An attempt under the same principles to obtain the full loss caused to the plaintiff in such situations would be met by the defence that the loss was too remote,[471] for otherwise the rules as to the contractual measure of damages would be circumvented.

9-082 **Other warranties** These propositions concern the warranty of authority. If the agent is held liable on some *other* warranty, as is suggested in the comment to the previous Article,[472] the damages would require to be calculated by reference to that warranty.

Illustrations

9-083 (1) Directors of a building society represent that they have authority to borrow money on behalf of the society, and A is induced to lend £70. The society being solvent, the measure of damages for breach of warranty of authority is £70, with interest at the rate agreed upon.[473]

(2) A contracted, on behalf of B, to buy a ship. A was not authorised so to do, and B repudiated the contract. The seller having resold the ship at a lower price (which was the best price that, acting reasonably, he could get), it was held that the measure of damages recoverable against A was the difference between the contract price and the price at which the vessel was resold.[474]

(3) A instructed B to apply for shares in a certain company. B by mistake applied for shares in another company, and they were duly allotted to A. The lastmentioned company was ordered to be wound up, and A's name was removed from the list of contributories on the ground that he had not authorised the application for shares. Held, that, A being solvent and the

---

[468] *Pow v Davis* (1861) 1 B. & S. 220; *Oliver v Bank of England* [1901] 1 Ch. 562; affd on different grounds sub nom. *Starkey v Bank of England* [1903] A.C. 114.

[469] Illustration 9. In *Greenglade Estates v Chana* [2012] EWHC 1913 (Ch) it was held that pursuing proceedings against both the agent and the supposed principal had been reasonable. The costs of such proceedings are not discussed, but it was held that the property concerned must be valued at the date of trial.

[470] See *Anglia Television Ltd v Reed* [1972] 1 Q.B. 60; *Collen v Wright* (1857) 7 E. & B. 301; affd (1857) 8 E. & B. 647; *Pow v Davis* (1861) 1 B. & S. 220 (seven-year lease not under seal: cost of repairs allowed); *Lloyd v Stanbury* [1971] 1 W.L.R. 535; McGregor, *Damages* (19th edn), para.2-018 onwards and Ch.31; *CCC Films (London) Ltd v Impact Quadrant Films Ltd* [1985] Q.B. 616.

[471] cf. *Heskell v Continental Express Ltd*, para.9-080 above (Illustration 5).

[472] See above, para.9-066; below, para.9-085.

[473] *Richardson v Williamson* (1871) L.R. 6 Q.B. 276.

[474] *Simons v Patchett* (1857) 7 E. & B. 568.

shares unsaleable, the liquidator of the company was entitled to recover from B the full amount payable on the shares.[475]

(4) A brought an action against a company in the United States, and recovered judgment for £1,000. An agent of the company in good faith represented that he had authority to settle for £300, and A agreed to accept that sum. The agent was, in fact, not authorised to settle. Held, that, the judgment against the company being, in the circumstances, unenforceable, A was entitled to recover £300 from the agent for the breach of warranty of authority.[476]

(5) Under a contract to sell goods to a foreign buyer, A, the seller, had to procure shipment of the goods. He registered cargo space for the goods, but did not enter into a contract of carriage. He arranged for the dispatch of the goods to the ship, but they were not dispatched. A did not know this, and applied for a bill of lading. A bill of lading was negligently issued by B, the shipowners' broker, the goods never having been received. A later had to pay damages to the buyer for non-delivery. A claimed damages against B for breach of warranty of authority to issue the bill of lading. Held, that A could not have recovered against the shipowners even if the bill of lading had been issued with their authority, for only receipt of the goods on behalf of the shipowner would here have concluded a contract; as they had never been received, there was no contract of carriage and the bill was a nullity. A's rights upon the bill was therefore not affected by B's lack of authority, and he could recover nothing against B.[477]

(6) A bought goods, professedly on behalf of B. The seller brought an action for the price against B, which was dismissed with costs, on the ground that A was not authorised by B. Held, that the seller was entitled to recover from A the price of the goods, and also the costs incurred in the action against B.[478]

(7) A professed to sell property on behalf of B. Held, that A, not being authorised to sell, was liable to the purchaser for the taxed costs of a suit for specific performance against B, as well as for the value of the contract.[479]

(8) Where an agent without authority granted a lease, and the lessee agreed to sell his interest, it was held that damages and costs recovered against the lessee for breach of such agreement to sell could not be recovered by him in an action against the agent for breach of warranty of authority; but that the lessee was entitled to recover the value of the lease, and the costs of a suit for specific performance against the principal.[480]

(9) A contracted to sell an estate to B, and sent him an abstract of title, representing that he had the authority of the owners to sell. The owners repudiated the

---

[475] *Re National Coffee Palace Co Ex p. Panmure* (1883) 24 Ch.D. 367. See also *Habton Farms v Nimmo*, Illustration 11 below.
[476] *Meek v Wendt* (1888) 21 Q.B.D. 126. As to an unauthorised settlement, see further *British Russian Gazette Ltd v Associated Newspapers Ltd* [1933] 2 K.B. 616.
[477] *Heskell v Continental Express Ltd* [1950] 1 All E.R. 1033 (on which see Grunfeld (1950) 13 M.L.R. 516); said to require reconsideration as regards the decision on negligence in *Hedley Byrne & Co Ltd v Heller & Partners Ltd* [1964] A.C. 465 at 532; cf. *V/O Rasnoimport v Guthrie & Co Ltd* [1966] 1 Lloyd's Rep. 1, Illustration 11 to Article 105, where there was a contract of carriage and the plaintiff recovered the value of the goods not delivered plus interest.
[478] *Randall v Trimen* (1856) 18 C.B. 786. See also *Farley Health Products v Babylon Trading Co* [1987] C.L.Y. 1126 (damages included cost of manufacturing, packing and shipping goods not paid for).
[479] *Hughes v Graeme* (1864) 33 L.J.Q.B. 335; *Collen v Wright* (1857) 8 E. & B. 647.
[480] *Spedding v Nevell* (1869) L.R. 4 C.P. 212.

contract and sold the estate at a higher price to C. B sued the owners, continued the action after they had sworn answers to interrogatories that A had no authority, and was nonsuited. In an action by B against A, it was held that the measure of damages for the breach of warranty of authority was (a) the costs of investigating the title; (b) the costs of the action up to the time when the answers to the interrogatories had been received and considered by the plaintiff's legal advisers; and (c) the difference between the contract and market prices of the estate, the price at which it was resold to C being prima facie evidence of the market price; but that the loss on a resale of horses, which were bought to stock the land before the investigation of the title and without notice to A, was too remote, it not appearing that the purchase of stock was contemplated by the parties when the contract was made.[481]

(10) A solicitor falsely warrants that he has authority to sell land, and the vendor refuses to complete. The land rises in value between the date for completion and the date of the action against the solicitor. He is liable for the difference in value between the purchase price and the value of the property at the date of judgment.[482]

(11) A bloodstock agent purported to buy a racehorse on behalf of his principal for £70,000, subject to certain tests. The tests proved satisfactory and the horse was made available for collection. The agent was not authorised and principal refused to proceed; but the third party seller refrained from selling the horse to anyone else and continued to demand the price. The horse then contracted peritonitis and had to be destroyed. The agent was liable for the full price which the third party would have received without deduction of the value of the horse, since the third party's decision to refrain from reselling the horse on the ground that it was already sold was caused by the agent's breach of warranty of authority.[483]

(12) A co-owner of land, A, has authority to sell land on behalf of both owners, but has no actual authority to make a commission agreement with real estate agent that would bind both owners. A is found to warrant to the real estate agent his authority to engage the agent on behalf of both owners and is liable for the full commission on the sale of the land.[484]

Article 107

PRINCIPAL FICTITIOUS OR NON-EXISTENT

9-084 (1) At common law, where a person purports to contract on behalf of a principal, and the principal is a fictitious or non-existent person or entity, the person so

---

[481] *Godwin v Francis* (1870) L.R. 5 C.P. 295. See also *Schlieske v Overseas Construction Co Pty Ltd* [1960] V.R. 195 (action continued after indications received that principal, a company, dissolved); *McDonnell v McGuinness* [1939] I.R. 223 (principal unable to make title: damages against agent limited by rule (no longer applicable in England) in *Bain v Fothergill* (1874) L.R. 7 H.L. 158).

[482] *Suleman v Shahsavari* [1988] 1 W.L.R. 1181, distinguishing and in part not following *Chitholie v Nash & Co* (1973) 229 E.G. 786. *Suleman* was doubted in *Greenglade Estates Ltd v Chana* [2012] EWHC 1913 (Ch); [2012] 42 E.G. 138 at [12].

[483] *Habton Farms v Nimmo* [2003] EWCA Civ 68; [2004] Q.B. 1.

[484] *Mathews v CD Realty (PN) Ltd* [2010] NZHC 1881.

purporting to contract may sometimes be regarded as having contracted personally.[485]

(2) By statute, where a contract purports to be made by or on behalf of a company at a time when the company has not been formed, then subject to any agreement to the contrary, the contract has effect as a contract made with the person purporting to act for the company or as agent for it, and he is personally liable on the contract and entitled to enforce it accordingly.[486]

Comment

Rule (1)   The situation referred to in this Article normally arises where a person purports to act for a company not yet formed, or for an unincorporated association, which has no legal existence, neither of which can be bound. Where both parties were aware of the position at the time of contracting, it may sometimes be appropriate to conclude that the transaction was intended to have legal effect[487] and hence that the agent contracted personally, viz. is liable, and also entitled to sue. The only alternative interpretation would be that the third party knowingly entered into a transaction of the "subject to contract" or "subject to ratification" type.[488] Where the parties are not aware of the true position there will be more difficulty in applying either of these interpretations,[489] and in any case the agent cannot be treated as contracting personally where he clearly contracts as agent only.[490] The cases on companies to be formed[491] have perhaps been more lenient towards allowing the third party to establish liability than those on unincorporated associations.[492] But even in the case of companies there is no actual rule of law that a person purporting to contract for an unformed company is necessarily (as opposed to by interpretation) personally liable on the contract[493]; it is all a matter of interpretation, sometimes said to be aided by a presumption,[494] of law in the case of a written contract, and of fact in the case of an oral contract.[495] Much of the force of a presumption in these circumstances is derived from the fact that the purporting

9-085

---

[485]   See Comment; *Kelner v Baxter* (1866) L.R. 2 C.P. 174, Illustration 1; *Black v Smallwood* (1966) 117 C.L.R. 52, Illustration 7; *Marblestone Industries Ltd v Fairchild* [1975] 1 N.Z.L.R. 529; Gross (1971) 87 L.Q.R. 367; (1972) 18 McGill L.J. 512; Shapira (1975) 3 Otago L.Rev. 309.

[486]   Companies Act 2006 s.51, replacing Companies Act 1985 s.36C(1) (inserted by Companies Act 1989 s.130(4)). See Comment; Prentice (1973) 89 L.Q.R. 518 at 530–533; Farrar and Powles (1973) 36 M.L.R. 270; Collier and Sealy [1973] C.L.J. 1; Griffiths [1993] L.S. 241; *Gower's Principles of Modern Company Law* (10th edn), paras 5-23–5-28.

[487]   See *Kelner v Baxter* (1866) L.R. 2 C.P. 174 at 85.

[488]   As to which see Article 18.

[489]   See *Wickberg v Shatsky* (1969) 4 D.L.R. (3d) 540; *Jones v Hope* (1880) 3 T.L.R. 247n., Illustration 4; *Coral (UK) Ltd v Rechtman* [1996] 1 Lloyd's Rep. 235; *Restatement, Third*, § 6.04.

[490]   *Hollman v Pullin* (1884) C. & E. 254, Illustration 5; *Coral (UK) Ltd v Rechtman*, above.

[491]   Illustrations 1 and 2. But cf. *Re Banque du Marchands de Moscou* [1952] 1 All E.R. 1269 as to a company that had been dissolved.

[492]   Illustrations 3, 4 and 5. See Powell, pp.263–265; Lloyd, *Law of Unincorporated Associations* (1938); Keeler (1971) 34 M.L.R. 615; Fletcher (1979) 11 U. Qd.L.J. 53 and material there cited.

[493]   *Newborne v Sensolid (Great Britain) Ltd* [1954] 1 Q.B. 45 at 50; *Black v Smallwood* (1966) 117 C.L.R. 52; *Stott Land Development Corp v Dean* [1967] W.A.R. 86; *Re Whiteley Insurance Consultants* [2008] EWHC 1782 (Ch). For cases where there was no liability, see e.g. *Dairy Supplies Ltd v Fuchs* (1959) 18 D.L.R. (2d) 408; *Hawke's Bay Milk Corp Ltd v Watson* [1974] 1 N.Z.L.R. 236; *Lomax v Dankel* (1981) 29 S.A.S.R. 68.

[494]   See *Marblestone Industries Ltd v Fairchild* [1975] 1 N.Z.L.R. 529 at 539–540; *Vickery v Woods* (1952) 85 C.L.R. 336. But presumptions are perhaps out of fashion nowadays, and the tendency is to rely on interpretation only. See Oliver LJ in *Phonogram Ltd v Lane* [1982] Q.B. 938 at 945–946.

[495]   *Summergreene v Parker* (1950) 80 C.L.R. 304 at 323–324.

agent is leading the third party to believe that it is bound; reciprocity suggests that the agent should also be bound. There is some suggestion that this reasoning applies only to a person who purports to act *for* the company: if he purports to act *as* the unformed company, his act is simply a nullity and he cannot be held personally liable on it.[496] But where in the latter situation that person knows that the company does not exist, and the third party does not, it may be a more compelling conclusion to find a contractual obligation than one in deceit.

The alternative analysis, that the party acting is liable only on a warranty of authority, is scarcely more satisfactory.[497] Such an action would probably yield no more than the cost of any abortive proceedings brought against the principal, because since the company has no existence and so no funds it might well not be possible affirmatively to prove further loss arising from the lack of authority.[498] In the case of a signature not on behalf of the company but as the company, to authenticate the company's signature, there is the further difficulty that the signer arguably does not profess agency. It may however be possible in either case to imply some sort of warranty that there is or is still an extent company as described, on the analogy of the cases in which directors were held liable in respect of transactions which even if authorised would have been ultra vires their companies.[499] This depends on the scope of the agent's warranty, which is discussed elsewhere[500]; and would again raise problems of proof of loss.[501] But in the leading case of *Kelner v Baxter*[502] Willes J did not suggest using the reasoning he had employed nine years earlier in *Collen v Wright*,[503] the leading case on warranty of authority.

Should it transpire that the agent is in fact his own principal, he might perhaps be held liable under the anomalous rule stated in the next Article. But it would be necessary to prove that he was his own principal: such a conclusion would not follow from the mere fact that the supposed principal was not liable.[504]

---

[496] *Newborne v Sensolid (Great Britain) Ltd* [1954] 1 Q.B. 45, Illustration 6; *Black v Smallwood* (1966) 117 C.L.R. 52, Illustration 7; *Miller Associates (Australia) Pty Ltd v Bennington Pty Ltd* (1975) 7 A.L.R. 144; *Western Radio Group Ltd v McIsaac* (1989) 63 D.L.R. (4th) 433. See Fridman (1966) 116 New L.J. 1605; Baxt (1967) 30 M.L.R. 328. But a company can only act through agents, and *Newborne v Sensolid* is open to criticism as turning on a technicality: see Gray (1953) 17 Conv. 217–219; Shapira (1975) 3 Otago L.Rev. 309; the judgment of Windeyer J in *Black v Smallwood*; and cf. *Elliott v Bax-Ironside* [1925] 2 K.B. 301.

[497] For this approach, see *Black v Smallwood* (1966) 117 C.L.R. 52 at 64–65, per Windeyer J; above, para.9-066. See also *Scott v J.B. Livingston & Nichol* 1990 S.L.T. 305 at 307.

[498] See Article 105. This argument was accepted in *Delta Construction Co Ltd v Lidstone* (1979) 96 D.L.R. (3d) 457 in a case where the principal came into existence but was insolvent; see also *Wickberg v Shatsky* (1969) 4 D.L.R. (3d) 540; *General Motors Acceptance Corp of Canada Ltd v Weisman* (1979) 96 D.L.R. (3d) 159. An action succeeded in *Lomax v Dankel* (1981) 29 S.A.S.R. 68 but damages were not in issue. It also succeeded in *Alvin's Auto Service Ltd v Clew Holdings Ltd* (1997) 33 B.L.R. (2d) 11 (Canada); but although the supposed principal was insolvent it was amenable to an order of specific performance.

[499] See Article 105, Illustrations 2, 3, 4 and 5; *Black v Smallwood*, above, at 64–65; Palmer (1975) 9 U.Qd.L.J. 123. But cf. *Newborne v Sensolid (Great Britain) Ltd*, above, at 47; *Hawke's Bay Milk Corp Ltd v Watson* [1974] 1 N.Z.L.R. 236; cf. the warranties by solicitors commencing proceedings described in Article 106, Illustration 12.

[500] See above, para.9-066.

[501] The cases referred to in fn.498 above do not touch on this, as they concern situations where the insolvency of the supposed principal was accepted. They tend also to be concerned with the availability of the action rather than the damages recoverable.

[502] (1866) L.R. 2 C.P. 174, Illustration 1.

[503] (1857) 8 E. & B. 647; see Article 105.

[504] *Newborne v Sensolid (Great Britain) Ltd* [1954] 1 Q.B. 45, Illustration 6.

Rule (2) reproduces s.51(1) of the Companies Act 2006,[505] the successor section **9-086** to that which originally gave effect to a provision of the first EEC directive on company law. The purport of this directive was that any person who enters into a transaction on behalf of a company not yet formed[506] shall be personally liable on it unless the company on formation assumes the obligation, or there is "a clear exclusion of personal liability".[507] It is now clear that the words "person purporting to act for the company or as agent for it" impose liability regardless of whether at common law the agent might have been held to sign as agent for the company or as authenticating the company's own signature.[508] It does not apply when a contract is made on behalf of a company which exists but is in the process of changing its name to that used[509]; nor when the company existed but has been dissolved[510]; and it applies only to companies formed and registered under the Companies Act 2006, or its predecessors.[511] In some such cases, the company, though mis-named, may as a matter of fact be a party to the contract.[512]

Section 51(1) by virtue of its final words "and he is personally liable on the contract accordingly" may be interpreted as referring only to the agent's liability. However, the words immediately preceding state that the contract has effect as a contract made with the person concerned, which suggests that he can sue also; and it has been held that he can. In the case concerned, *Braymist Ltd v Wise Finance Co Ltd*,[513] which involved signature by a solicitor as agent for a company not formed, two of the judges derived this effect from the statute, with the result that the solicitor could sue on a contract for the sale of land. The third judge, Arden LJ, however, was of the opinion that the statute could not be given this effect, and that the matter must be solved by the applicable common law principles, and that these made the agent entitled to sue. It is however not clear on what basis they did so. If the interpretation of the contract led to the inference that the solicitor was a party to it, then the solicitor could sue: but it is not easy without more to derive support for such an interpretation from a signature "as agents". The only other available reasoning was that the solicitor was his own principal; but this is not an easy interpretation of the situation. It is considered in Article 108 below. Statutory provi-

---

[505] The original provision was s.9(2) of the European Communities Act 1972. See *Gower's Principles of Modern Company Law* (10th edn), paras 5-23–5-28.
[506] The relevant EC Directive refers to a company "en formation", i.e. already in the process of formation, which would by English law be liable and entitled in any case. In *Phonogram Ltd v Lane* [1982] Q.B. 938, Illustration 8, the Court of Appeal noted the different wording of the then English statute and followed it.
[507] *Phonogram Ltd v Lane*, above, at 944. An argument that the provision only applies to a person who is the "alter ego" of the company (see above, para.1-029) was rejected in *Braymist Ltd v Wise Finance Co Ltd* [2002] EWCA Civ 127; [2002] Ch. 273; *Royal Mail Estates Ltd v Maple Teesdale* [2015] EWHC 1890 (Ch); [2016] 1 W.L.R. 942 (the contract stating that it is "personal to the company" did not preclude agent being bound by, and able to enforce, the contract).
[508] *Phonogram Ltd v Lane*, above.
[509] *Oshkosh B'Gosh Inc v Dan Marbel Inc Ltd* [1989] B.C.L.C. 507; *Vic Spence Associates v Balchin* 1990 S.L.T. 10. See also *Badgerhill Properties Ltd v Cottrell* [1991] B.C.L.C. 805 (company not properly named).
[510] *Cotronic (UK) Ltd v Dezonie* [1991] B.C.L.C. 721.
[511] *Rover International Ltd v Cannon Film Sales Ltd* [1987] B.C.L.C. 540; decision varied on other grounds [1989] 1 W.L.R. 912.
[512] See *Coral (UK) Ltd v Rechtman* [1996] 1 Lloyd's Rep. 235 at 238–239.
[513] [2002] EWCA Civ 127; [2002] Ch. 273 (holding also that the agent's signature was sufficient for the purposes of the Law Reform (Miscellaneous Provisions) Act 1989 s.2). This is subject to the common law restrictions applicable where other party can assert that he would not have entered into the contract: at [62].

sions drafted to meet this problem in other common law jurisdictions are often more clearly formulated, and may deal also with the problem of ratification by the company when it is formed,[514] which is not possible under English law.[515]

Illustrations

9-087   (1)   A enters into a written contract on behalf of a company not yet incorporated. A is personally liable on the contract, even if he expresses himself as contracting on behalf of the future company; and parol evidence is not admissible to show that he did not intend to contract personally, because it is only by holding him personally liable that any effect at all can be given to the contract, which refers to "the proposed company".[516]

(2)   The promoters of a future company borrowed money from a bank, to be repaid out of calls on shares. Held, that the promoters must be taken to have contracted that the money would be repaid out of calls, if the calls should prove sufficient, and if not, to pay personally.[517]

(3)   The managing committee of a club authorises the steward to order provisions for the use of the club. A supplies provisions on his orders, and invoices them to the club. If A looked to the funds of the club alone for payment, and contracted on the terms that if there were no such funds he should not be paid, the committee is not personally liable. But it is personally liable if he gave credit to them. Whether A gave credit to the committee or looked to the funds of the club alone is a question of fact.[518]

(4)   A, a colonel of a volunteer corps, contracts on behalf of the corps with B. A does not intend to pledge nor does B intend to accept, his personal credit, but both think that the corps as an entity may be bound. The corps cannot be bound. A is not personally liable on the contract.[519]

(5)   H makes a contract with P and signs it "on behalf of the Tunbridge Wells

---

[514]   e.g. Singapore Companies Act (cap. 50) s.41; Companies Ordinance (Hong Kong) s.32A. For discussion under comparable Ontario legislation of the phrase "RS in trust for a company to be incorporated and not in his personal capacity", see Ziegel (2002) 37 Can.Bar Rev. 445. See too Companies Act 1993 (NZ) ss.182–185.

[515]   See above, para.2-069.

[516]   *Kelner v Baxter* (1866) L.R. 2 C.P. 174 (further facts, 36 L.J.C.P. 94); *Wilson & Co v Baker Lees & Co* (1901) 17 T.L.R. 473; *Rita Joan Dairies Ltd v Thompson* [1974] 1 N.Z.L.R. 285; *Marblestone Industries Ltd v Fairchild* [1975] 1 N.Z.L.R. 529. But cf. *Black v Smallwood* (1966) 117 C.L.R. 52, Illustration 7. A company cannot ratify a contract made on its behalf before its incorporation: see Article 15.

[517]   *Scott v Ebury* (1867) L.R. 2 C.P. 255; *Coutts & Co v Irish Exhibition in London* (1891) 7 T.L.R. 313; *Drew, Wood & Son v Heath* (1899) 8 T.L.R. 111. cf. *Royal Albert Hall Corp v Winchilsea* (1891) 7 T.L.R. 362.

[518]   *Steele v Gourley* (1887) 3 T.L.R. 772; *Collingridge v Gladstone* (1890) 7 T.L.R. 60; *Harper v Granville-Smith* (1891) 7 T.L.R. 284; *Bradley Egg Farm Ltd v Clifford* [1943] 2 All E.R. 378. See also *Carlton Cricket and Football Social Club v Joseph* [1970] V.R. 487; cf. *Peckham v Moore* [1975] 1 N.S.W.L.R. 353. The members of the committee do not normally act as agents for the members: *Flemyng v Hector* (1836) 2 M. & W. 172; *Todd v Emly* (1841) 8 M. & W. 505; *Wise v Perpetual Trustee Co Ltd* [1903] A.C. 139; cf. *Cockerell v Aucompte* (1857) 2 C.B.(N.S.) 440; *Ideal Films Ltd v Richards* [1927] 1 K.B. 374; *Campbell v Thompson* [1953] 1 Q.B. 445. See in general Keeler (1971) 34 M.L.R. 615; Fletcher (1979) 11 U.Qd.L.J. 53; *Davies v Barnes Webster & Sons Ltd* [2011] EWHC 2560 (Ch).

[519]   *Jones v Hope* (1880) 3 T.L.R. 247n; and as to clubs see *Overton v Hewett* (1887) 3 T.L.R. 246; cf. *Cross v Williams* (1862) 31 L.J.Ex. 145; *Samuel Bros Ltd v Whetherly* [1908] 1 K.B. 184; *Lascelles v Rathbun* (1919) 35 T.L.R. 347.

Medical Association, H". The association is un-registered at the time of the contract. H cannot sue on the contract since he contracted as agent only.[520] Nor can he be sued upon it.[521]

(6) N enters into a contract for the sale of goods to S and signs the contract: "LN (London) Ltd, LN". LN (London) Ltd was not incorporated at the date of the contract. LN cannot sue on this contract, since he made it neither as agent nor as principal.[522] Nor can he be sued on it.[523]

(7) S and C enter into a contract for the sale of land. They sign the contract: "Western Suburbs Holdings Pty Ltd S, C, Directors". The company was not incorporated at the date of the contract. They cannot be sued personally on the contract.[524]

(8) A written letter of contract is signed by the recipient "Signed by BL for and on behalf of Fragile Management Ltd". The company is never formed and the contract never performed. BL is personally liable by virtue of s.9(2) of the European Communities Act 1972 (now s.51 of the Companies Act 2006).[525]

Article 108

AGENT SHOWN TO BE THE REAL PRINCIPAL

(1) Where a person professes to contract as agent, whether in writing or orally, and it is shown that he is, in fact, himself the principal, and was acting on his own behalf, he is (perhaps) personally liable on the contract.[526] **9-088**

(2) Where a person who enters into a contract professedly as an agent is in fact the real principal, he may (perhaps) sue on the contract:
   (a) where the identity of the contracting party is not a material element in the making of the contract, provided that he gives notice to the other contracting party, before action, that he is the real principal;
   (b) where it has been partly performed or otherwise affirmed by the other contracting party with knowledge that he is the real principal.[527]

Comment

These propositions have appeared in all editions of this book and are probably generally accepted[528] despite the slender authority in their support. **9-089**

---

[520] *Hollman v Pullin* (1884) C. & E. 254 at 257.
[521] Semble; but see the judgment in *Hollman v Pullin*, above, at 257.
[522] *Newborne v Sensolid (Great Britain) Ltd* [1954] 1 Q.B. 45.
[523] *Newborne v Sensolid*, above, at 47; Illustration 7. But see *Hollman v Pullin*, above, at 257.
[524] *Black v Smallwood* (1966) 117 C.L.R. 52, discussed by Fridman (1966) 116 N.L.J. 1605; *Hawke's Bay Milk Corp Ltd v Watson* [1974] 1 N.Z.L.R. 236.
[525] *Phonogram Ltd v Lane* [1982] Q.B. 938. See above, para.9-086.
[526] See Comment.
[527] See Comment.
[528] See *Leigh and Sillivan Ltd v Aliakmon Shipping Ltd (The Aliakmon)* [1983] 1 Lloyd's Rep. 203 at 207 (where counsel accepted the agent's right to sue in such a case) (for further proceedings see [1986] A.C. 785); *Fraser v Thames Television Ltd* [1984] Q.B. 44 at 54–55 (where Hirst J appears to accept it). But in *Electrosteel Castings Ltd v Scan-Trans Shipping and Chartering Sdn. Bhd* [2002] EWHC 1993 (Comm); [2003] 1 Lloyd's Rep. 190 Gross J, though clear that he should follow a relevant decision, referred to the view here expressed as raising "very cogent doubts". See too *Lundie v Rowena Nominees Pty Ltd* (2007) 32 W.A.R. 404 (see above, para.8-087).

9-090   **Rule (1): Liability**   The cases usually cited in support of the agent's liability date from a time when the courts were searching for a way of holding the unauthorised agent personally liable.[529] At one time it was thought that if he had no authority he was always to be regarded as having contracted personally[530]: but this was not supportable,[531] and later decisions made it clear that his liability, where it could not be regarded as being a second, parallel liability on the contract itself,[532] was on a collateral warranty of authority.[533] However, when it could be established that the agent was the real principal, the case was naturally a simpler one, and views were sometimes expressed, even after the establishment of an action for breach of warranty of authority, that in such a case he was personally liable.[534]

9-091   **Identified principal**   If the agent in fact acts for himself, but outwardly for a named principal from whom he has no authority, and that principal is not liable on the basis of apparent authority,[535] any liability of the agent (unless the principal ratifies[536]) ought prima facie to be for breach of warranty of authority or in tort (most obviously, deceit if the representation is false to his knowledge). If he has not expressly undertaken personal liability on the contract, it is contrary to the principle of objective interpretation in contract to find the agent a party. The main possible justification of the agent's liability on the contract is that an undisclosed principal can be sued when discovered.[537] But the anomalies of the undisclosed principal rules could be cited as authority for many breaches of principle, and this situation comes under no established rule relating to the undisclosed principal, whose liability is additional to the agent's: the analogy can go no further than providing another case where facts initially unknown to the third party can be invoked in his aid.

     In *Gardiner v Heading*[538] a builder did work on the orders of H, the director of a company for which the builder had previously done work on H's order. The builder addressed estimates to the company and after completing the work was paid some of his charges by the company. He was then told that the work was not for the company but for other principals. He sued H. H was held liable as the person who

---

[529] They are *Railton v Hodgson* (1804) 4 Taunt. 576n; *Jenkins v Hutchinson* (1849) 13 Q.B. 744; *Carr v Jackson* (1852) 7 Exch. 382; *Adams v Hall* (1877) 37 L.T. 70; and *Gardiner v Heading* [1928] 2 K.B. 284. In *Railton v Hodgson* there seems to have been no clear indication of agency, and it appears that the liability of the agent might have been together with that of the supposed principal, the example of a factor being cited. The relevance of *Jenkins v Hutchinson* is confined to the words "unless it be shown that he was the real principal". *Carr v Jackson* contains similar dicta, but concerns a foreign principal (see above, para.9-020) and a cesser clause (below, para.9-096). These dicta are perhaps the strongest: but they seem contrary to later dicta of Brett J in *Hutchinson v Tatham* (1873) L.R. 8 C.P. 482 (which were only partly withdrawn by him in *Pike v Ongley* (1887) 18 Q.B.D. 708). In any case the agent was held not liable. *Adams v Hall* seems to be a straightforward case of the personal liability of an agent. *Gardiner v Heading* is a case where it was not clear that the agent did contract as agent, though the third party thought that he was doing so: it contains dicta discussed below.

[530] *Thomas v Hewes* (1834) 2 Cr. & M. 519 at 530n; *Downman v Williams* (1845) 7 Q.B. 103. And see discussion in *Black v Smallwood* (1966) 117 C.L.R. 52.

[531] See *Lewis v Nicholson* (1852) 18 Q.B. 503; *Jenkins v Hutchinson*, above; *Black v Smallwood*, above.

[532] See Comment to Article 98.

[533] *Collen v Wright* (1857) 8 E. & B. 647; see Article 105.

[534] See cases cited at fn.529 above.

[535] Article 72.

[536] *Re Tiedemann and Ledermann Freres* [1899] 2 Q.B. 66, Illustration 4 to Article 15.

[537] See *Gardiner v Heading* [1928] 2 K.B. 284 at 290; Article 76.

[538] Above.

ordered the work, on the facts found by the judge of first instance. Scrutton LJ asked[539]:

> "If a man who contracts with another thinking he is a principal may, on finding he is in truth an agent, sue the real principal, why should not the reverse hold good also? Why should not a man who contracts with another, thinking he is an agent, sue him when he finds out that he is the real principal?"

But it should be noted that the reference is to "the real principal", and the passage goes on to exclude where "the supposed agent … has expressly contracted as agent so as to exclude his liability as a principal party to that contract" and the dicta seem wider than was necessary for the decision of the case, which may be regarded as a straightforward decision on the objective interpretation of the facts surrounding the formation of the contract.[540]

The only other justification for the agent's liability seems to be his right to sue in such a situation, but this is equally disputable, as appears below.

From the third party's point of view there are of course advantages in the agent's personal liability on the contract. Where the purported principal is bankrupt, an action for breach of warranty of authority would produce limited damages, for the loss caused to the third party by the agent's lack of authority is small.[541] If the agent is really himself the principal, it seems unfair that he should be able to take advantage of such a fortuitous circumstance.[542] But it can be argued that the third party's reliance was on the financial standing of the supposed principal, not on that of the agent.[543] If the fact that the agent was acting for himself can be genuinely established, however, liability would normally lie in deceit, which would be immune from the limits of the action for breach of warranty of authority.

Unidentified principal   If the agent does not name a principal, there is a possibil-   **9-092** ity that he will be held to have contracted personally. This is another situation where, as previously suggested,[544] a rule of prima facie liability of the agent in such situations would, by reason of the unsatisfactory nature of the authorities on demanding to know the name of the principal,[545] yield fairer results. However that be, where there is a trade usage to that effect this may override his appearing to contract as agent only.[546] But where he clearly does contract as agent only, and has no principal, analytically his liability should again be on a collateral contract that he has a principal fitting the description (if any) given,[547] and the danger of his producing an insolvent person is met by the fact that he would have to prove that he was in fact acting as agent for such person—otherwise he would be presumed to have acted for a solvent principal. Analogies from the law as to undisclosed principal are again unconvincing. Alternatively, he may be liable in tort (most obviously again, deceit).

The notion that an agent would be liable on the contract in such a case was

---

[539] At 290.
[540] The case was followed by the majority in *Salim v Ingham Enterprises Pty Ltd* (1998) 55 N.S.W.L.R. 7, a case concerning the personal liability of the operator of a one-person company.
[541] See Article 106.
[542] See *Railton v Hodgson* (1804) 4 Taunt. 576n, where this situation arose: but see fn.524 above.
[543] cf. Mechem, *Outlines of Agency* (4th edn), p.221.
[544] See Article 98, esp. at para.9-016.
[545] See above, paras 9-016 and 9-017.
[546] Article 100(2).
[547] *Restatement, Second*, § 329, Comment e.

however apparently accepted in *Hersom v Bernett*,[548] where a defendant gave evidence that his principal was X: this was rejected as false and he himself was held liable. Roxburgh J said that[549]:

> "a fundamental principle of justice requires that a defendant who has given false evidence that his principal was X should not be heard to say ... that his principal may have been somebody else, but must thereafter be treated as having no principal; or, in other words, as being himself the principal."

The latter two propositions are not, with respect, equivalent, and it is submitted that the first proposition is the one properly applicable. The judge however seems to have applied the second: although he was not willing to find as a fact that the defendant was himself the principal,[550] he held that he should be treated as such because of his conduct. If the liability of the agent on the contract is to be accepted, this can only be on the somewhat tenuous basis that it provides a quick route to a desired result.[551] But the mere fact that the agent's act does not bind his purported principal does not mean that he is to be regarded as acting for himself[552]: there must be evidence that he actually is doing so, or (as in *Hersom v Bernett*[553]) other circumstances preventing him from denying this. There is now obiter support for the view that ordinarily an agent who contracts on behalf of a non-existent principal will be liable on a warranty that he has a principal, rather than directly liable for the contract purportedly made.[554]

9-093   **Rule (2): Right to sue**   Whereas the liability on the contract itself of the agent who is his own principal is an advantage to the third party, the agent's right to sue in such a case is not so and is even more difficult to justify.

9-094   **Identified principal**   Although there is a strong dictum by Lord Ellenborough that "Where a man assigns to himself the character of agent to another whom he names, I am not aware that the law will permit him to shift his situation, and to declare himself the principal, and the other to be a mere creature of straw",[555] it was held in *Rayner v Grote*[556] that a person who had purported to sell goods as agent for such a principal but who was really himself the seller could sue for nonacceptance where the third party had become aware of the true position and nevertheless continued with the contract. On this basis it might be argued that such a person can do so in any case, if he gives notice that he is the principal,[557] and provided that the third

---

[548] [1955] 1 Q.B. 98, following a dictum in *Owen v Gooch* (1797) 2 Esp. 567 at 568.
[549] At 103.
[550] At 100.
[551] "I am sure it is justice. It is probably the law for that reason": *Gardiner v Heading* [1928] 2 K.B. 284 at 290, per Scrutton LJ; "It is not worth while to be learned on very plain matters": *Layng v Stewart*, 1 Watts & S. (Pa.) 222 (1841), quoted by Mechem, *Outlines of Agency* (4th edn), p.221. See, however, above, para.9-017.
[552] cf. *Newborne v Sensolid (Great Britain) Ltd* [1954] 1 Q.B. 45, Illustration 6 to Article 107; *Black v Smallwood* (1966) 117 C.L.R. 52, Illustration 7 to Article 107.
[553] [1955] 1 Q.B. 98.
[554] See *Knight Frank LLP v Du Haney* [2011] EWCA Civ 404 at [27]. See also above, para.9-066.
[555] *Bickerton v Burrell* (1816) 5 M. & S. 383 at 386; *Galaxy Aviation v Sayegh Group Aviation* [2015] EWHC 3478 (Comm) at [76].
[556] (1846) 15 M. & W. 359, Illustration 2. See also *Fellowes v Lord Gwydyr* (1829) 1 Russ. & M. 83.
[557] *Bickerton v Burrell*, above; *Fellowes v Lord Gwydyr*, above. But cf. *Rogers v Hadley* (1861) 2 H. & C. 227.

party is not clearly prejudiced.[558] But in such a case the contract is with the named principal, an identified person different from the agent, the agent being by the wording of the contract excluded from being a party, and it is extremely difficult to see how the agent can then intervene and claim the benefit of such a contract. For although mistake is not relevant in the formation of contract where it is not material, it should not be difficult for the third party to show that he intended to contract with the named principal only.[559] He should not be left to establish prejudice, which, in view of the fact that the benefit of contracts is usually assignable, might not be easy. It is submitted therefore that the case itself should be explained on the basis of novation. The agent having disclosed his own interest in the transaction, the third party accepted him as seller. In other circumstances it is highly doubtful whether the purported agent could intervene as principal: this is supported by a dictum of Alderson B in the case,[560] which has since been cited with approval[561]:

> "In many such cases, such as, for instance, the case of contracts in which the skill or solvency of the person who is named as the principal may reasonably be considered as a material ingredient in the contract, it is clear that the agent cannot then shew himself to be the real principal, and sue in his own name; and perhaps it may be fairly urged that this, in all executory contracts, if wholly unperformed, or if partly performed without the knowledge of who is the real principal, may be the general rule."

Unidentified principal   It was decided in *Schmaltz v Avery*[562] that an agent who   **9-095**
signed a charterparty containing a cesser clause purportedly as agent for an unidentified principal could show that he was himself the principal and sue on the contract, on the grounds that it was not of moment to the third party who contracted on such terms to whom he was liable, and that the agent could say that he was his own principal. Such a right is in danger of being inconsistent with the terms of the contract, especially where the contract can be said to be embodied in a document.[563] It is therefore submitted that, even on the most favourable view of the situation, the true analysis is that the contract in such cases is with the unidentified principal,[564] and that the agent can only intervene if he fits such description (if any) as has been given of the supposed principal.[565] Further, if the third party can establish that, with whomsoever he was willing to contract, he was not willing to contract with the agent, he should equally be able to say that he had no agreement with the agent.[566] In *Harper & Co v Vigers Bros*[567] the plaintiff was allowed to sue on a charterparty which he had signed "as agent for owner", though the third party gave evidence that

---

[558] *Rayner v Grote* (1846) 15 M. & W. 359. This view appears to be accepted by Arden LJ in *Braymist v Wise Finance Co Ltd* [2002] EWCA Civ 127; [2002] Ch. 273 at [60]–[63]. But the case was one where there was no principal, and was dealt with by the other members of the court in a different way: see above, para.9-086.

[559] cf. *Hardman v Booth* (1863) 1 H. & C. 803.

[560] (1846) 15 M. & W. 359 at 365.

[561] In *Gewa Chartering BV v Remco Shipping Lines Ltd (The Remco)* [1984] 2 Lloyd's Rep. 205, Illustration 3.

[562] (1851) 16 Q.B. 655, Illustration 1.

[563] See Article 100.

[564] See Glanville Williams (1945) 23 Can.B.R. at 397 onwards; cf. *Hardman v Booth* (1863) 1 H. & C. 803.

[565] cf. *Restatement, Second*, § 369, Comment b. See too *Carminco Gold & Resources Ltd v Findlay & Co Stockbrokers (Underwriters) Pty Ltd* (2007) 243 A.L.R. 472, Illustration 24 to Article 98.

[566] cf. *Sowler v Potter* [1940] 1 K.B. 271 (but this case is often criticised); *Hill SS Co Ltd v Hugo Stinnes Ltd* 1941 S.C. 324 at 337.

[567] [1909] 2 K.B. 549. See criticism by Parker J at first instance in *Newborne v Sensolid (Great Britain)*

he would not have made the contract had he known that the agent was acting on his own behalf. Although the plaintiff was refused costs, it is submitted that the case goes further than necessary in following *Schmaltz v Avery*. In both cases it is arguable that the agent was excluded by the terms of the contract, at least unless a trade usage was proved whereby persons so contracting could nevertheless declare themselves their own principals.[568]

9-096 **Supposed rule doubtful** *Schmaltz v Avery* is a case arising in the context of a particular form of the cesser clause, a very specialised charterparty provision on which there is much case law. The purpose of such a clause is that the charterer can substitute for himself shippers or consignees of cargo whose positions are regulated by bills of lading and against whom the shipowner can recover outstanding charges by the exercise of his lien.[569] A charterer who uses such a clause may well have no principals: he may hope to procure others to ship or receive goods on bill of lading terms. Indeed, modern forms of the clause make no reference to agency. If the charterer cannot achieve his object, he may ship himself and/or consign to himself[570] in the absence of indications that he would not be an acceptable shipper or receiver of the cargo on bill of lading terms (which is unlikely if he is acceptable as charterer). Even if the clause contains a reference to agency, it implies initial involvement of the charterer. In *Schmaltz v Avery* itself the dispute arose because the cargo was not taken on board, so that the question of the charterer's initial liability did not arise: but it was held that he could sue. The general reasoning of the case has been criticised in Scotland[571] as being obsolete in view of the restatement of the rules as to interpretation of written contracts by the House of Lords in *Universal Steam Navigation Co v McKelvie*,[572] and is difficult to reconcile with the principles of law established since that time. The right to sue of an agent purporting to act for a *disclosed* principal is even more difficult to justify. It is equally difficult to support the agent's liability in such cases: indeed in the context of the cesser clause that liability can be regarded as contrary to other authority.[573] Analogies to the case of the undisclosed principal are misleading, as in that case the third party thinks that he is dealing with the agent, and the effect of the doctrine is to add a further right and liability of a further person.[574] The whole of this Article should therefore be viewed with caution and even suspicion, and the cases approached on the basis that in many if not all of them different reasoning would be used today.[575] In view of the existing case law, however, it does not seem appropriate to omit these propositions at present.

Even if the third party cannot plead that he made no contract with the agent, he

---

Ltd [1954] 1 Q.B. 45 at 48.
[568] See *Hill SS Co Ltd v Hugo Stinnes Ltd* 1941 S.C. 324 at 333; cf. Article 100.
[569] See Scrutton, *Charterparties* (23rd edn), Article 108. The more modern form there given makes no reference to agency. See also above, para.9-027.
[570] See *Gullischen v Stewart Bros* (1884) 13 Q.B.D. 317; *Hill SS Co v Hugo Stinnes Ltd* 1941 S.C. 324.
[571] *Hill SS Co Ltd v Hugo Stinnes Ltd* 1941 S.C. 324. And see *Sharman v Brandt* (1871) L.R. 6 Q.B. 720. But it has been followed in Australia: see *MacCormac v Bradford* [1927] S.A.S.R. 152; *Marzo v Land and Homes (W.A.) Ltd* (1931) 34 W.A.L.R. 62.
[572] [1923] A.C. 492; see Article 99.
[573] *Oglesby v Yglesias* (1858) E.B. & E. 930; see Scrutton, above, para.9-175.
[574] Article 76.
[575] But see *Restatement, Second,* § 372 and Comment.

can presumably plead misrepresentation in appropriate cases[576]; and all authorities agree that the agent cannot intervene when such intervention would prejudice the third party,[577] e.g. where the third party could show that he relied on liability of both agent and principal, or where the agent's liability as principal is by the terms of the contract less onerous than his liability as agent.[578] But this is similar to the rule preventing the intervention of the undisclosed principal in some situations,[579] and it might well be more difficult for the third party to establish such prejudice than merely to plead that the contract was made with the supposed principal and not with the agent. *Harper & Co v Vigers Bros*,[580] indeed, shows clearly the difficulty of establishing prejudice.

Whatever the correct view on this matter, the agent can only sue if he purported to contract as agent: if he purported to contract, e.g. as a company which was in fact not yet formed, he cannot sue as principal.[581]

Application in other contexts   In *Braymist v Wise Finance Ltd*[582] this reasoning was extended by Arden LJ (but not by the other members of the court) to solicitors who signed as agents for a company which had not been incorporated, and allowed them to sue on the contract. Although it is true that the solicitors had, for technical reasons, no principals, it does not follow that they were their own principals. The purported contract was between two purported parties, one of whom did not exist. It is not easy to see why there was a contract at all, unless the agent could be interpreted as being a party to it: but any use of such an interpretation, which would accord with the view taken in *Restatement, Third*,[583] was not discussed. The reasoning seems to have been that unless there was a reason why the identity of the contracting counterparty was material to the third party, a party who had only signed as agent could sue. But considerations of materiality of mistake in contract, and questions of assignability of the right of action, only arise where there is a party to the contract the materiality of whose actual identity may be considered. Where there is no such party, there is simply no transaction, and the rights and liabilities of the agent must be dealt with by asking the question what he has undertaken. The dictum of Diplock LJ as to the assumption that the identity of the counterparty is irrelevant in an ordinary commercial contract[584] applies to an agent who acts for an unidentified principal, and also to an agent who purports to act on his own account but has an undisclosed principal. It is far from clear that it should apply to an agent who actually gives the name of a principal, even if the name given is not that of a legal entity. If there is no principal, such a person may well be liable for breach of warranty of authority or otherwise, but that does not confer a right to sue. Furthermore, the reasoning that the agent is his own principal is only appropriate to an agent who had no authority, actual or apparent, from any principal and simply

---

[576]   See *Newborne v Sensolid (Great Britain) Ltd* [1954] 1 Q.B. 45 at 48.
[577]   *Rayner v Grote* (1846) 15 M. & W. 359; *Hill SS Co Ltd v Hugo Stinnes Ltd*, above.
[578]   *Hill SS Co Ltd v Hugo Stinnes Ltd*, above.
[579]   See above, para.8-079.
[580]   [1909] 2 K.B. 549; above.
[581]   *Newborne v Sensolid (Great Britain) Ltd*, above, Illustration 6 to Article 107.
[582]   [2002] EWCA Civ 127; [2003] Ch. 273; above, para.9-086.
[583]   § 6.02. The position is similar to that as to whether an undisclosed principal should be treated as a party to the contract: see above, para.8-079.
[584]   See *Teheran-Europe Co Ltd v S.T. Belton (Tractors) Ltd* [1968] 2 Q.B. 545 at 555: above, para.8-079.

contracted as agent, perhaps because he believed that the third party would not contract with him personally.

Illustrations

9-097 (1) A signed a charterparty "as agent for the freighter", a cesser clause being inserted therein limiting A's liability to certain events in view of his being an agent. A was himself the freighter. Held, that he might sue on the contract (the clause limiting his liability would be inoperative). It would be otherwise, if the other contracting party had relied on his character as agent, and would not have contracted with him had he known him to be the principal. The freighter, whoever he might have been, would have had a right to sue.[585]

(2) A, professedly as agent for a named principal, contracted in writing to sell certain goods. The buyer, with notice that A was the real principal, accepted and paid for part of the goods. Held, that A might sue for non-acceptance of the residue.[586]

(3) The chartering broker of a firm conducting various maritime commercial activities charters a vessel, the owners of which are given the impression that the charterers are a large trading group known to the owners' broker. The chartering broker actually intended to charter for his own firm and arrange by back-to-back charters a recharter to the trading group. The chartering broker's firm is not a party to the contract, which is between the owners and the trading group.[587]

Article 109

NO RIGHT OF ACTION FOR PROMISED BRIBES OR SECRET COMMISSIONS

9-098 No action can be maintained by an agent for recovery of any property or money promised to be given to him by way of a bribe whether he was in fact induced by such promise to depart from his duty or not.[588]

2. RESTITUTION

Article 110

RIGHT OF AGENT TO SUE FOR MONEY PAID BY MISTAKE, ETC

9-099 Where an agent pays money on his principal's behalf under a mistake of fact, or in respect of a consideration which fails, or in consequence of some fraud or wrong-

---

[585] *Schmaltz v Avery* (1851) 15 Q.B. 655. But see Comment.
[586] *Rayner v Grote* (1846) 15 M. & W. 359. But see Comment.
[587] *Gewa Chartering BV v Remco Shipping Lines Ltd (The Remco)* [1984] 2 Lloyd's Rep. 205.
[588] *Harrington v Victoria Graving Dock Co* (1878) 3 Q.B.D. 549; *Laughland v Millar* (1904) 6 F. 413; *Lemenda Trading Co Ltd v African Middle East Petroleum Co Ltd* [1988] Q.B. 448. But cf. *Meadow Schama & Co v C. Mitchell & Co Ltd* (1973) 228 E.G. 1571 (sum promised after commission earned: not a bribe). And see Articles 48, 49 and 96. Nor, of course, can the agent be sued for not performing the act which he was bribed to do: nor (normally) for return of the bribe to its donor. These are applications of the rules as to illegal contracts. See Chitty, *Contracts* (32nd edn), Ch.16.

ful act of the payee or otherwise under such circumstances that the payee is liable to repay the money, the agent may sue the payee for its recovery.[589]

Comment

In such cases the proper plaintiff is normally the principal[590]: but the agent can sue also.[591] There is some authority that suggests that where the restitutionary claim is for a failure of consideration, whether brought by an innocent party or a party who was in breach of contract, the agent may not sue even where he provided the consideration, but only the principal.[592] There is also older authority that where the agent is mistaken as to his authority to pay, but the money was owed by the principal, the agent would not be able to recover, as the mistake was not one as between plaintiff and defendant[593]: nor, of course, could the principal recover. But if the principal did not ratify the payment the debt would not be discharged and the principal would still be liable: in such a case it would be strange if the agent could not recover, and authority now takes the view that he can.[594]

9-100

Article 111

DUTY OF AGENT TO REPAY MONEY RECEIVED FOR USE OF PRINCIPAL

(1) Except as provided below, an agent is not personally liable to repay money received by him for the use of his principal.[595]

9-101

(2) Where money is paid to an agent for the use of his principal, and the circumstances are such that the person paying the money is entitled to recover it back, the agent is personally liable to repay such money in the following cases:

    (a) Where the agent contracts or acts personally, and the money is paid to him in respect of or pursuant to that contract or transaction.[596]

    (b) Where the money is obtained by duress or by means of any fraud or wrongful act to which the agent is party or privy.[597]

    (c) Where the money is paid under a mistake of fact, or under duress or in consequence of some fraud or wrongful act to which the agent is not party, or generally under circumstances in which an immediate right of recovery arises, and repayment is demanded of the agent, or notice is

---

[589] *Stevenson v Mortimer* (1778) 2 Cowp. 805; *Langstroth v Toulmin* (1822) 3 Stark. 145; *Holt v Ely* (1853) 1 E. & B. 795; *Colonial Bank v Exchange Bank of Yarmouth, Nova Scotia* (1885) 11 App.Cas. 84; *Royal Securities Corp v Montreal Trust Co* (1966) 59 D.L.R. (2d) 666 (citing this Article) (affd (1967) 63 D.L.R. (2d) 15). As to the principal's right to sue, see Article 71.

[590] See above, para.8-166; and Article 88.

[591] *Duke of Norfolk v Worthy* (1808) 1 Camp. 337.

[592] *Hepworht Group Ltd v Stockley* [2006] EWHC 3626 (Ch); [2007] 2 All E.R. (Comm) 82 (consideration took the form of land, not money).

[593] *Barclay & Co Ltd v Malcolm & Co* (1925) 133 L.T. 512.

[594] See *Barclays Bank Ltd v W. J. Simms Son & Cooke (Southern) Ltd* [1980] Q.B. 677, doubting *Barclay & Co Ltd v Malcolm*, above; *Agip (Africa) Ltd v Jackson* [1990] Ch. 265 at 283–284; affd [1991] Ch. 547 at 561–562; *Customs & Excise Commissioners v National Westminster Bank* [2002] EWHC 2204 (QB); [2003] 1 All E.R. (Comm) 327. See Goff and Jones, *Law of Unjust Enrichment* (9th edn), para.5-59. See too *Walter v James* (1871) L.R. 6 Ex. 124; *Colonial Bank v Exchange Bank of Yarmouth, Nova Scotia* (1885) 11 App.Cas. 84.

[595] See Comment. As to the principal's liability, see Articles 71, 92 and 93.

[596] See Comment; Article 98.

[597] See Comment.

given to him of the intention of the payer to demand repayment, before he has in good faith paid the money over to, or otherwise dealt to his detriment with, the principal in the belief that the payment was a good and valid payment.[598]

(d) Where the receipt of the money is outside the actual and apparent authority of the agent and is not ratified by the principal.[599]

Comment

9-102 **Questions of principle** The cases on this subject indicate two different and possibly inconsistent lines of reasoning which could be taken in respect of recovery of money from an agent.[600] The first uses the notion that payment to an agent for the principal in respect of a matter on which the agent has actual or apparent authority to receive it is payment to the principal. Under this reasoning, unless there is a separate liability in the agent (as where the principal is undisclosed,[601] or where he is liable together with his principal, or where he himself commits a wrong), the proper defendant is the principal and the agent is not liable even where he has not passed the money on to the principal.[602] The money is in contemplation of law in the hands of the principal: for example, in the case of a deposit.

The second line of reasoning uses the notion that where the agent holds money to which neither he nor his principal is entitled, it can be intercepted and recovered at this stage unless without knowledge of the claim the agent has paid it over to his principal. The case law on payment over is of considerable antiquity and has developed its own rules. It was formerly criticisable on the basis that if the agent was liable in personam, the fact that he no longer had the money should make no difference. It could now be justified as an example of the notion of change of position now recognised in restitution cases[603]; but the cases certainly have their own, and anterior, existence and it seems that they should still be treated separately.[604]

The two lines of reasoning can, however, be reconciled. Where there was no basis for the payment, as where it was paid under mistake or duress, the money may be recovered from the agent before there has been any accounting to the principal.[605] Where, however, the ground of restitution is simply a failure of consideration, and

---

[598] See Comment.

[599] See, e.g. *Sorrell v Finch* [1977] A.C. 728, Illustration 4 to Article 94. With slight modifications and a change of order this Article dates from the 2nd edition of this work (1898).

[600] Mechem, *Treatise on the Law of Agency* (2nd edn), §§ 1432–1433. See in general Goff and Jones, *Law of Unjust Enrichment* (9th edn), Ch.27.; Burrows, *Law of Restitution* (3rd edn), p.558 onwards; Virgo, *Principles of the Law of Restitution* (3rd edn), p.674 onwards; Stevens [2005] L.M.C.L.Q. 101 at 109 onwards (a careful study of the area). See also Mitchell, in Lowry and Mistelis *Commercial Law: Perspectives and Practice* (2006), Ch.6; Bant [2007] L.M.C.L.Q. 225.

[601] See *Agip (Africa) Ltd v Jackson* [1990] 2 Ch. 265 at 289; affd [1991] Ch. 547; the Rt Hon. Lord Millett (1991) 107 L.Q.R. 71 at 77. But the defence succeeded in *Transvaal and Delagoa Bay Investment Co v Atkinson* [1944] 1 All E.R. 579.

[602] *Ellis v Goulton* [1893] 1 Q.B. 350, Illustration 1.

[603] *Lipkin Gorman v Karpnale Ltd* [1991] 2 A.C. 548; see Goff and Jones, *Law of Unjust Enrichment* (9th edn), Ch.27; Burrows, *Law of Restitution* (3rd edn), Ch.21. Virgo, *Principles of the Law of Restitution* (3rd edn), p.674 onwards.

[604] See below, para.9-107; *Australia and New Zealand Banking Group Ltd v Westpac Banking* (1988) 164 C.L.R. 662 at 684; Burrows, above, p.558 onwards.

[605] *Buller v Harrison* (1777) 2 Cowp. 565; *Kleinwort, Sons & Co v Dunlop Rubber Co* (1907) 97 L.T. 263; *Kerrison v Glyn, Mills, Currie & Co* (1911) 81 L.J.K.B. 465 (HL); *Santander UK Plc v National Westminster Bank Plc* [2014] EWHC 2626 (Ch). See also *Owen & Co v Cronk* [1895] 1 Q.B. 265 (receiver not involved in duress by company).

the agent received as a disclosed agent, the action is against the principal only. Here the money is rightly regarded as paid to the principal (even if the agent still has it) because he may be permanently entitled to it; but by virtue of subsequent events it becomes repayable, as where a deposit correctly paid is justifiably reclaimed, or there is a total failure of consideration on a contract.[606] The matter should therefore be disputed between the principal and the third party.[607] It is sometimes sought to solve such problems on the basis of a supposed principle of agency that the agent "drops out".[608] This is a serious oversimplification in the context of restitution: even in respect of contract, it is not always so[609]; and in tort it is not so at all.[610]

Rule (1)   It is most convenient to start with the general agency-based rule that money paid to an agent for his principal and received within the agent's actual or apparent authority, or the receipt of which is ratified, is regarded as having been paid to the principal and is recoverable from the principal, for "in contemplation of law the payment is made to the principal and not to his agent".[611] It will normally still be recoverable from the principal even when it is also recoverable from the agent. Thus where a deposit is paid to an agent and the transaction falls through, the money must be recovered from the principal even though the agent has not paid it across,[612] unless the agent was a stakeholder, in which case he assumes personal liability.[613]   **9-103**

Rule (2)(a)   Where the agent acts personally, however, he is obviously liable to repay,[614] and his liability is not confined to cases of contract.[615] The question of when he contracts personally is discussed in Article 98. In particular, an agent acting for an undisclosed principal contracts personally and so is liable.[616] So also a stakeholder is personally liable unless he has paid money away in accordance with his instructions.[617] But where both agent and principal are liable, the third party may sometimes be prevented from suing the agent by reason of merger or election[618]; and the agent may in appropriate cases have a defence of change of position. A recipient of money paid into a joint bank account will be assumed to receive personally, and not as agent or conduit, in the absence of evidence to the contrary.[619]   **9-104**

---

[606] *Ellis v Goulton*, above; *Marsfield Automotive Inc v Siddiqi* [2017] EWHC 187 (Comm).

[607] Mechem, *Treatise on the Law of Agency* (2nd edn), § 438.

[608] See Birks (ed.), *English Private Law* (1st edn, 2000), Vol.1, paras 15.259 and 15.310.

[609] See above, para.9-002.

[610] See Article 113. See Stevens, [2005] L.M.C.L.Q. 101.

[611] *Portman B.S. v Hamlyn Taylor Neck* [1998] 4 All E.R. 202 at 207, per Millett LJ.

[612] See *Ellis v Goulton* [1893] 1 Q.B. 350, Illustration 1; *Sadler v Evans* (1766) 4 Burr. 1984; *Duke of Norfolk v Worthy* (1808) 1 Camp. 337.

[613] See Illustrations 2 and 3; above, paras 9-025 and 9-026.

[614] Illustrations 4 and 5; *Continental Caoutchouc & Gutta Percha Co v Kleinwort, Sons & Co* (1904) 90 L.T. 474.

[615] See *Baylis v Bishop of London* [1913] 1 Ch. 127; *Wakefield v Newbon* (1844) 6 Q.B. 276.

[616] Illustration 5 (though the principal here may have been unnamed rather than undisclosed). But see *Transvaal and Delagoa Bay Investment Co v Atkinson* [1944] 1 All E.R. 579, where the point was not argued. A trustee also acts personally: *King v Stewart* (1892) 66 L.T. 339.

[617] See above, para.9-026.

[618] Article 104.

[619] *OEM Plc v Schneider* [2005] EWHC 1072 (Ch).

9-105   Rule (2)(b)

"If any person gets money into his hands illegally, he cannot discharge himself by paying it over to another."[620]

Therefore, where the agent is a party or privy to a wrong in respect of which money is paid to him, the action lies against him and it is no defence to allege that he has paid the money over to his principal.[621] This applies whether he receives the money on his own account[622] or on behalf of the principal.[623] In *Snowdon v Davis*,[624] Mansfield CJ said that the reason that the agent was liable in that case (a case of duress of goods) was that the third party did not pay the money for the purpose of its being paid over to the principal, but "under the terror of process, to redeem his goods". But this would be so in a case where the agent was not the party applying the duress, yet in such cases recovery is barred where the agent has paid the money over.[625] The true explanation is therefore that quoted at the beginning of this paragraph, that the agent as a party to the wrong is himself liable.[626] The principal may also be liable to effect restitution, at least where the agent has accounted for the money to the principal, subject to the rules of merger and election.[627]

9-106   Rule (2)(c)

"Where money has been paid under a mistake of fact to an agent, it may be recovered back from that agent, unless he has in the meantime paid it to his principal, or done something equivalent to payment to him, in which cases the recourse of the party who has paid the money is against the principal only."[628]

This rule has been applied to a wide variety of agents.[629] Although the majority of the decisions and dicta concern money paid under mistake, the formulation of this Article has been extended to all cases where the very fact of payment creates an im-

---

[620] *Townson v Wilson* (1808) 1 Camp. 396 at 397, per Lord Ellenborough.
[621] See Illustrations 6–9; *Steele v Williams* (1853) 8 Exch. 625; *Wakefield v Newbon* (1844) 6 Q.B. 276; *Chappell v Poles* (1837) 2 M. & W. 867; *Keegan v Palmer* [1961] 2 Lloyd's Rep. 449.
[622] *Smith v Sleap* (1844) 12 M. & W. 585, Illustration 9.
[623] *Oates v Hudson* (1851) 6 Exch. 346.
[624] (1808) 1 Taunt. 359, Illustration 6. See also *Steele v Williams*, above, at 632; *Oates v Hudson*, above, at 348.
[625] e.g. *Owen & Co v Cronk* [1895] 1 Q.B. 265.
[626] The statement by Baggallay LJ in *Ex p. Edwards, re Chapman* (1884) 13 Q.B.D. 747 at 751 (Illustration 7) is also probably too wide.
[627] Article 104.
[628] *Pollard v Bank of England* (1871) L.R. 6 Q.B. 623 at 630, per Blackburn J; and see *Portman BS v Hamlyn Taylor Neck* [1998] 4 All E.R. 202 at 207, per Millett LJ. See also *Buller v Harrison* (1777) 2 Cowp. 565; *Continental Caoutchouc and Gutta Percha Co v Kleinwort, Sons & Co* (1904) 90 L.T. 474; *Kleinwort, Sons & Co v Dunlop Rubber Co* (1907) 97 L.T. 263; *Kerrison v Glyn, Mills, Currie & Co* (1911) 81 L.J.K.B. 465; *Transvaal and Delagoa Bay Investment Co Ltd v Atkinson* [1944] 1 All E.R. 579; *Australia and New Zealand Banking Group Ltd v Westpac Banking Corp* (1988) 164 C.L.R. 662; *Agip (Africa) Ltd v Jackson* [1990] Ch. 265 at 288–289.
[629] e.g. clerks: *Cary v Webster* (1721) 1 Str. 480; solicitors: *Davys v Richardson* (1888) 21 Q.B.D. 202; bankers: *Gowers v Lloyds, etc., Foreign Bank* [1938] 1 All E.R. 766, Illustration 12; *Egyptian Intl Foreign Trade Co v Soplex Wholesale Supplies Ltd (The Raffaella)* [1984] 1 Lloyd's Rep. 102; affd on other grounds [1985] 2 Lloyd's Rep. 36; *B.M.P. Global Distribution Inc v Bank of Nova Scotia* [2009] 1 S.C.R. 504; (2009) 304 D.L.R. (4th) 292; auctioneers: *Galland v Hall* (1888) 4 T.L.R. 761, Illustration 11 (but cf. Illustration 2); one railway company collecting money for another: *Taylor v Metropolitan Ry* [1906] 2 K.B. 55; cotton brokers: *Re Bourne, Ex p. Bird* (1851) 4 De G. & S. 273; excise collectors: *Greenway v Hurd* (1792) 4 T.R. 553; churchwardens: *Horsfall v Handley* (1818) 8 Taunt. 136. See also Illustrations.

mediate liability to repay; in such cases, the agent is liable, and can only escape by proving payment over in the circumstances mentioned.[630] The principal is however also liable, subject to the rules of merger and election.[631] Where the liability to repay arises subsequently, however, e.g. because of breach of contract, it seems that the more general rule (Rule (1)) applies and the agent is not liable even though he still has the money.[632] A recent case has exonerated a bank on the basis of an argument that a bank (or other agent) is not enriched when it receives money for a customer.[633] This decision is *per incuriam*.[634] A preferable analysis might have been that a payment made to a disclosed agent is intended as a payment only to the principal, but the convenience of being able to sue the agent (particularly where the principal is foreign) has meant that this has never been the law. It remains possible that where the agent acts in a merely ministerial capacity, e.g. as a bank cashier, he is not the proper defendant in an action.[635] Rule 2(c) does not enable an action to be maintained against the agent in a situation where the principal, as a foreign sovereign, is immune from suit.[636]

Payment over   It could be said that this should now be regarded as an example   **9-107**
of the defence of change of position[637]; but the rules are long-established and quite fully worked out, and there is recent authority that this view is not correct.[638] For the agent to be immune from suit by reason of payment over, the mere fact that he has credited the principal with the amount is not sufficient to discharge him from liability: he must have:

> "paid over the money which he received to the principal, or settled such an account with the principal as amounts to payment, or done something which so prejudiced his position that it would be inequitable to require him to refund."[639]

---

[630] cf. Goff and Jones, *Law of Unjust Enrichment* (9th edn), para.9-128 onwards. See *Cox v Prentice* (1815) 3 M. & S. 344 at 348; *Davys v Richardson*, above; *Galland v Hall*, above; *Owen & Co v Cronk* [1895] 1 Q.B. 265. But the agent may sometimes be liable in conversion in any case, e.g. in respect of a cheque: see Article 114.

[631] Article 104.

[632] See cases cited at fn.606 above; *North Eastern Timber Importers v Ch. Arendt & Sons* [1952] 2 Lloyd's Rep. 513.

[633] *Jeremy D. Stone Consultants Ltd v National Westminster Bank Plc* [2013] EWHC 208 (Ch) at [243] (criticised Watts, [2016] C.L.P. 289 at 315). See too *Bellis v Challinor* [2015] EWCA Civ 59 at [114] (but point conceded).

[634] cf. *Investment Trust Companies v Revenue and Customs Commissioners* [2017] UKSC 29; [2017] 2 W.L.R. 1200 at [40].

[635] cf. *Restatement, Second*, § 339, Comment g.

[636] *Rahimtoola v Nizam of Hyderabad* [1958] A.C. 379.

[637] See *Lipkin Gorman v Karpnale Ltd* [1991] 2 A.C. 548; cf. *Australia and New Zealand Banking Group Ltd v Westpac Banking Corp* (1988) 164 C.L.R. 662; Goff and Jones, *Law of Unjust Enrichment* (9th edn), Ch.27. cf. Burrows, *Law of Restitution* (3rd edn), Ch.21; Virgo, *Principles of the Law of Restitution* (3rd edn), p.678 onwards. In *Abou-Rahmah v Abacha* [2006] EWCA Civ 1492; [2007] 1 All E.R. (Comm) 827; [2007] 1 Lloyd's Rep. 115 the defendant bank relied only on the change of position defence.

[638] *Portman BS v Hamlyn Taylor Neck* [1998] 4 All E.R. 202 at 207, per Millett LJ. See too *Citigroup Pty Ltd v National Australia Bank Ltd* [2012] NSWCA 381; (2012) 82 N.S.W.L.R. 391.

[639] *Kleinwort, Sons & Co v Dunlop Rubber Co* (1907) 97 L.T. 263 at 265, per Lord Atkinson. See *Australia and New Zealand Banking Group Ltd v Westpac Banking Corp*, above, at 682–684; Watts (1991) 107 L.Q.R. 521 at 525. And see *Buller v Harrison* (1777) 2 Cowp. 565; *Cox v Prentice* (1815) 3 M. & S. 344; *Scottish Met. Ass. Co v P. Samuel & Co* [1923] 1 K.B. 348: *Bavins, Jnr. & Sims v London & South Western Bank* [1900] 1 Q.B. 270; *Jones v Churcher* [2009] EWHC 722 (QB); [2009] 2 Lloyd's Rep. 94; *Citigroup Pty Ltd v National Australia Bank Ltd* [2012] NSWCA 381;

Thus he may have given new credit,[640] or credited the sum to his principal in a settled account, or spent it on the instructions of his principal.[641] But where the agent has paid the money to the principal and received it back again for the very purpose of returning it to the claimant, he again becomes liable.[642]

9-108   **Rule (2)(d)**   If the agent is not authorised to receive the money and the principal is not bound under the doctrine of apparent authority and does not ratify the payment, even though it is said to be received for the principal, there is no way in which the principal can be liable, and it is the agent who must be sued.

Illustrations

9-109   (1)   The solicitor of the vendor at a sale by auction receives a contract deposit as agent for the vendor.[643] The sale goes off through the vendor's default. The purchaser cannot maintain an action against the solicitor for its return whether or not it has been paid over to the vendor. The purchaser's action is against the vendor.[644]

    (2)   The auctioneer at a sale by auction receives a deposit as stakeholder[645] and pays it over to the vendor. He is personally liable to refund the amount on the default of the vendor, because it was his duty to hold it until the completion of the contract.[646] In such a case the principal is liable also.[647]

    (3)   An estate agent arranges an agreement for the sale of land "subject to contract" and takes a deposit. The sale never comes into effect and thus no contract is ever made. If he expressly took the deposit as stakeholder he is liable to the payer for its return,[648] and if he accepts it without indication as to the capacity in which he has taken it he is likewise liable,[649] though in both cases the term "stakeholder" is an unsatisfactory one.[650] It is irrelevant that he has paid the deposit over to his principal, for he would act wrongly if he did so. His liability is a personal one to the payor, whether in contract or in restitution. If he defaults, the principal is in such a case not liable.[651]

(2012) 82 N.S.W.L.R. 391. See also *M'Carthy v Colvin* (1839) 9 A. & E. 607.

[640] See *Buller v Harrison*, above.

[641] See *Holland v Russell* (1861) 1 B. & S. 424; affd (1863) 4 B. & S. 14, Illustration 10: see also Illustrations 11–12.

[642] *British American Continental Bank v British Bank of Foreign Trade* [1926] 1 K.B. 328.

[643] The prima facie rule is that he does so: see the cases cited in the next footnote and *Tudor v Hamid* [1988] 1 E.G.L.R. 251 at 255. This is also true of estate agents: *Ojelay v Neosale Ltd* [1987] 2 E.G.L.R. 167 at 168 as regards contract deposits. See also above, para.9-025.

[644] *Ellis v Goulton* [1893] 1 Q.B. 350; *Bamford v Shuttleworth* (1840) 11 A. & E. 926; *Edgell v Day* (1865) L.R. 1 C.P. 80; *Burt v Claude Cousins & Co Ltd* [1971] 2 Q.B. 426 at 435 (estate agent); *Goodey v Garriock* [1972] 2 Lloyd's Rep. 369; *Arnhem Technology Ltd v Dudley Joiner*, ChD, January 31, 2001; but cf. *Wilder v Pilkington* [1956] J.P.L. 739, where *Ellis v Goulton* was distinguished on grounds that are not clear.

[645] The prima facie rule seems to be that he does so, though quaere whether this is appropriate: see the cases cited below; and above, paras 9-025 and 9-026.

[646] *Burrough v Skinner* (1770) 5 Burr. 2639; *Edwards v Hodding* (1814) 5 Taunt. 815; *Gray v Gutteridge* (1828) 3 C. & P. 40; *Furtado v Lumley* (1890) 6 T.L.R. 168.

[647] cf. Illustration 3; see also above, para.9-026.

[648] See *Burt v Claude Cousins & Co Ltd* [1971] 2 Q.B. 426 at 435–436; *Rayner v Paskell and Cann*, ibid., 439n; *Brodard v Pilkington*, ibid., 442n; *Barrington v Lee* [1972] 1 Q.B. 326.

[649] *Burt v Claude Cousins & Co Ltd*, above, per Lord Denning MR and Sachs LJ.

[650] See *Maloney v Hardy and Moorsehead* [1971] 2 Q.B. 442n; above, para.9-026.

[651] *Sorrell v Finch* [1977] A.C. 728, Illustration 4 to Article 92.

(4)   An agent discounts certain bills, and in good faith pays over the proceeds to his principal. The bills turn out to be forgeries. The discounter has no remedy against the agent unless he indorsed or guaranteed the bills, or dealt as a principal with the discounter.[652] But the agent is personally liable to repay the amount, as upon a total failure of consideration, if he dealt as a principal with the discounter.[653]

(5)   A bought goods from B, a broker acting for an undisclosed principal, and by mistake paid him too much. B gave his principal, who was largely indebted to him, credit for the amount received. Held, that B was liable to repay to A the amount paid in excess, on the grounds (a) that B dealt as principal with A, and (b) that the mistake accrued to B's personal benefit.[654]

(6)   A sheriff issued a warrant of distress against A. The bailiff levied the debt on the goods of B, and, under pressure of the illegal distress, B paid the debt. Held, that the bailiff was personally liable to repay B, though he had paid the amount over to the sheriff.[655]

(7)   Pending a bankruptcy petition, and with notice of the act of bankruptcy, a solicitor, as the agent of the petitioning creditor, received from the debtor various sums of money in consideration of the adjournment of the petition, and paid such sums over to his principal. Held, that the solicitor was personally liable to repay the amount to the trustee in bankruptcy, notwithstanding the payment over, because the money was obtained wrongfully.[656]

(8)   An agent who acts for an executor de son tort is himself an executor de son tort and personally liable to account for assets collected by him, even after he has paid them over to his principal. Payment over is no defence in the case of wrongdoers.[657]

(9)   An agent demands more money than is due, and wrongfully withholds documents from T, who pays him the amount demanded, under protest, in order to recover the documents. The agent is personally liable to T in respect of the amount overpaid, even after he has paid the money over to the principal.[658]

(10)   An insurance broker received money from an underwriter in respect of a voidable policy, and settled with his principal for the amount, amongst other matters, without notice of the underwriter's intention to dispute the policy, and without fraud. Held, that the agent was not liable to repay the amount to the underwriter, who had paid it to him under a mistake of fact.[659]

(11)   An auctioneer sold certain shares by private contract, and received a deposit. The purchaser declined to complete, on the ground that the contract was void as not complying with the provisions of Leeman's Act,[660] and sued the auctioneer for the return of the deposit. Held, that, the auctioneer having paid over the amount of the deposit to the vendor before the repudiation of the contract, the purchaser was not entitled to recover, because the auctioneer was

---

[652] *Re Bourne Ex p. Bird* (1851) 4 De G. & S. 273.

[653] *Gurney v Womersley* (1854) 4 E. & B. 133; *Royal Exchange Ass. v Moore* (1863) 8 L.T. 242.

[654] *Newall v Tomlinson* (1871) L.R. 6 C.P. 405.

[655] *Snowdon v Davis* (1808) 1 Taunt. 359; cf. *Goodall v Lowndes* (1844) 6 Q.B. 464.

[656] *Ex p. Edwards, re Chapman* (1884) 13 Q.B.D. 747.

[657] *Sharland v Mildon*, Sharland v Loosemore (1846) 5 Hare 469; *Padget v Priest* (1787) 2 T.R. 97. See Williams, Mortimer and Sunnucks, *Executors, Administrators and Probate* (20th edn), para.7-12.

[658] *Smith v Sleap* (1844) 12 M. & W. 585; *Oates v Hudson* (1851) 6 Exch. 346.

[659] *Holland v Russell* (1863) 4 B. & S. 14; *Shand v Grant* (1863) 15 C.B.(N.S.) 324.

[660] Banking Companies (Shares) Act 1867; repealed by Statute Law Revision Act 1966.

authorised to pay over the deposit to the vendor either on the completion of the contract or on the purchaser's refusal to complete, and such authority had not been revoked.[661]

(12) A, a pensioner, collected his pension from the Crown Agents for the Colonies through the defendant bank by means of receipt forms sent to him by the Crown Agents. Each receipt form contained a certificate that A was still alive. The forms when completed were sent by A to the bank, who obtained payment on A's behalf from the Crown Agents and credited A's account with the amount so obtained. A died. Thereafter, receipt forms containing a forged signature, purporting to be that of A, and a false certificate that A was still living, were sent to the bank by a person pretending to be A, and the bank, believing that the signatures and certificates were genuine and that A was still alive, collected the pension from the Crown Agents and credited the amount to A's account, from which it was withdrawn. The Crown Agents, having discovered that A was dead, sued the bank for the amount of the pension so collected after A's death. Held, that the money could not be recovered as money paid under a mistake of fact, as the bank had paid it over to a person who was their principal, and their belief that such person was A made no difference in this respect.[662]

Article 112

MONEY HELD TO USE OF THIRD PARTIES

9-110 (1) Except as is provided in this Article, an agent is not liable or accountable to any third party in respect of money in his hands which he has been directed or authorised by his principal to pay to any third party.[663]

(2) Where a specific fund existing or accruing in the hands of an agent to the use of his principal is assigned or charged by the principal to or in favour of a third party, the agent is bound, upon receiving notice of the assignment or charge, to hold the fund, or so much thereof as is necessary to satisfy the charge, to the use of such third party.[664]

(3) Where an agent is directed or authorised by his principal to pay to a third party money out of a fund existing or accruing in his hands to the use of the principal, and he expressly or impliedly promises such third party to pay him, or to receive or hold such money on his behalf or for his use, he is personally liable to pay such third party, or to receive or hold such money on his behalf or for his use, as the case may be, even if he has had fresh instructions from the principal not to pay such third party.[665]

---

[661] *Galland v Hall* (1888) 4 T.L.R. 761.

[662] *Gowers v Lloyds, etc., Foreign Bank* [1938] 1 All E.R. 766; *Vella v Permanent Mortgages Pty Ltd* [2008] NSWSC 505 at [460]; *Citigroup Pty Ltd v National Australia Bank Ltd* [2012] NSWCA 381; (2012) 82 N.S.W.L.R. 391 at [121].

[663] See Comment; Illustration 5; *Gibson v Minet* (1824) 2 Bing. 7.

[664] Illustration 1.

[665] See Comment and Illustrations 2–4.

Comment

Rule (1)   Rule (1) is the general rule: there is no privity of contract with such third   **9-111**
party, and therefore no third party can sue.

Rule (2)   This rule refers to cases where the chose in action has been assigned,   **9-112**
whether simpliciter or by way of charge. The same rule would therefore apply to
mere debts owed by the agent to the principal, though here of course the money
could not be regarded as held to the use of the third person, whose action would
be contractual. The reference to a "specific fund" in this rule is therefore dictated
only by the subject of this section of the chapter: although the assignment must of
course be of a specific chose in action[666]; it is not necessary that the chose in action be a fund as opposed to a debt (though the distinction is probably relevant for
the purposes of Rule (3)). The complexities of the law of assignment of choses in
action are beyond the scope of this work, but once an assignment has been duly
made the assignee can sue for the money and the debtor must not pay the assignor,
and is not discharged by doing so.[667] But an assignee takes subject to equities, and
therefore the agent can plead against the third party set-offs he had against the
principal before the assignment.[668] An assignment should be sharply distinguished
from a mere authority to pay money out of a fund, which is revocable and gives no
right to any third party[669] except as provided in Rule (3).

Rule (3)   This refers to an "intractable mass of conflicting authority ... contradic-   **9-113**
tory and unintelligible".[670] A large group of mainly nineteenth-century cases
establishes that where an agent holds a fund for his principal and is directed by that
principal to pay it to a third party, and notifies the third party that he is willing to
do so, he becomes liable to the third party, and the principal's authority becomes
irrevocable. It is now clear that the liability is in restitution, and it is submitted that
the only way in which the cases can be justified in the light of modern notions is
as a sort of attornment of money,[671] whereby the agent holds a fund for the principal
and then attorns to the third party, this being evidenced by his promising to pay the
third party. And it seems that such was the original doctrine: but the rule was
extended in *Israel v Douglas* (1789)[672] to cases where the agent was merely a debtor
to the principal. This, of course, causes theoretical complications regarding what
is now called privity of contract: but the modern notions of consideration, privity
and assignment were not then fully worked out, and there followed a large number
of cases purporting to explain the rule on the basis of novation,[673] assignment,[674]

---

[666]   See *Citizens' Bank of Louisiana v First National Bank* (1874) L.R. 6 H.L. 352.
[667]   *Brandt's Sons & Co v Dunlop Rubber Co* [1905] A.C. 454; *Brice v Bannister* (1878) 3 Q.B.D. 569.
[668]   *Roxburghe v Cox* (1881) 17 Ch.D. 520, Illustration 1.
[669]   *Brandt's Sons & Co v Dunlop Rubber Co*, above; *Ex p. Hall, Re Whitting* (1879) 10 Ch.D. 615;
       Rodick v Gandell (1852) 1 De G.M. & G. 763. And see Illustrations 1 and 5 and cases there cited.
[670]   Jackson, *History of Quasi-Contract* (1936), pp.99 and 103. See ibid., p.31 onwards and p.93
       onwards; Davies (1959) 75 L.Q.R. 220; Winfield, *Province of the Law of Tort* (1931), p.135 onwards;
       Yates (1977) 41 Conv. 49; Comment to Article 118.
[671]   See Goff and Jones, *Law of Unjust Enrichment* (9th edn); *FTV Holdings Cairns Pty Ltd v Smith*
       [2014] QCA 217 at [32].
[672]   1 H.Bl. 239.
[673]   *Walker v Rostron* (1842) 9 M. & W. 411, Illustration 3; *Hodgson v Anderson* (1825) 3 B. & C. 842;
       Hamilton v Spottiswoode (1849) 4 Exch. 200.
[674]   *Crowfoot v Gurney* (1832) 9 Bing. 372, Illustration 2; *Hutchinson v Heyworth* (1838) 9 A. & E. 375;

trust[675] or declaration of agency in favour of the third party.[676] The rule was in the mid-nineteenth century again confined to the case of a fund, and recognised as involving an action not in contract but in restitution, in *Liversidge v Broadbent*[677] and *Griffin v Weatherby*.[678] More than a century later it was discussed in *Shamia v Joory*,[679] where the full complexities were apparently not cited to Barry J, who decided that there was for this purpose no difference between a debt and a fund. But it is only this distinction, unsatisfactory though it may be, that prevents the rule from subverting many of the fundamental principles of the law of contract as now understood. It is submitted that the rule should therefore be confined to the case of a fund: but if it were extended to the case of a debt, it would provide a rather curious type of appropriation or quasi-assignment operating at common law. It does not follow logically that the arrangement should be irrevocable by the principal, especially where the third party is a mere donee, but this irrevocability seems too firmly rooted in the cases to be questioned.

The illustrations that follow have been left, apart from the addition of *Shamia v Joory*, in the arrangement in which they appeared in the second edition of this work (1898), though a few that seem to have no modern relevance have been omitted. But it should be noted that the proper assessment of the cases cited is today a doubtful matter. The doctrine of privity of contract and the rules of assignment and consideration are now established with reasonable clarity: therefore the issues should be looked at as being of principle, and the old cases viewed critically. In particular, cases that refuse to distinguish between a debt and a fund could be regarded as wrong in view of *Liversidge v Broadbent* and *Griffin v Weatherby* were it not for the authority of *Shamia v Joory*. Many cases purporting to find an assignment[680] or a novation[681] can now be regarded as outdated: and cases refusing to allow a third party to sue unless there is consideration or assignment[682] should probably be regarded as wrong where a fund is involved, and possibly, if *Shamia v Joory* is correct, where a debt is involved.

The Article, however, which also dates from the second edition, is submitted as being a correct reconciliation of the cases as they stand.[683]

Illustrations

9-114   (1)   A principal assigns to another money held by his agent to his use, and the assignee gives notice to the agent of the assignment. The agent is bound to account for the money to the assignee,[684] subject to any right of lien or set-off the agent may have against the principal at the time when he receives notice

---

    Gardner v Lachlan (1838) 4 Myl. & C. 129; *Burn v Carvalho* (1839) 4 Myl. & C. 690.

[675] See *Re Douglass Ex p. Cotterill* (1837) 3 Mont. & Ayr. 376 at 385.

[676] See *Lilly v Hays* (1836) 5 A. & E. 548 at 551.

[677] (1859) 4 H. & N. 603. Of course, the term "restitution" is of modern usage.

[678] (1869) L.R. 3 Q.B. 753.

[679] [1958] 1 Q.B. 448, Illustration 6; followed in a case involving a fund in *Dellas v Kourtessis* [1962] V.R. 456.

[680] e.g. *Crowfoot v Gurney* (1832) 9 Bing. 372, Illustration 2; *Hutchinson v Heyworth* (1838) 9 A. & E. 375; *Gardner v Lachlan* (1838) 4 Myl. & C. 129; *Burn v Carvalho* (1839) 4 Myl. & C. 690.

[681] e.g. *Walker v Rostron* (1842) 9 M. & W. 411, Illustration 3; *Hodgson v Anderson* (1825) 3 B. & C. 842; *Hamilton v Spottiswoode* (1849) 4 Exch. 200.

[682] e.g. *Wharton v Walker* (1825) 4 B. & C. 163.

[683] The formulation in the first edition was in terms of the third party suing in contract.

[684] *Webb v Smith* (1885) 30 Ch.D. 192; *Row Ex p. South* (1818) 3 Swan. 392; *Rodick v Gandell* (1852) 1 De G.M. & G. 763; *Greenway v Atkinson* (1881) 29 W.R. 560.

of the assignment.[685] So, if a debtor charges money in the hands of his agent with payment of the debt, the agent is liable to the creditor upon receiving notice of the charge.[686]

(2)   A principal gives his agent authority to pay money to T, a third person. The agent promises T that he will pay him when the amount is ascertained. The agent is liable to T for the amount when it is ascertained, though in the meantime the principal has become bankrupt,[687] or has countermanded his authority.[688]

(3)   A principal writes a letter authorising his agent to pay to A the amounts of certain acceptances, as they become due, out of the proceeds of certain assignments. A shows the letter to the agent, who assents to the terms of it. Before the acceptances fall due, the principal becomes bankrupt, and the agent pays the proceeds of the assignments to the trustee in bankruptcy. The agent is personally liable to A for the amounts of the acceptances as they become due.[689]

(4)   A bill drawn on an agent is made payable out of a particular fund, and the agent promises to pay the holder when he receives money for the principal. The agent is liable to the holder, if he subsequently receives the money.[690]

(5)   An acceptor of a bill pays money to a banker for the purpose of taking up the bill, and the banker promises to apply the money accordingly. The banker refuses to take up the bill, and claims to retain the money for a balance due to him from the acceptor. The drawer of the bill has no right of action, either at law or in equity, against the banker to compel him to apply the money to the payment of the bill, there being no privity of contract between them.[691] So, where an agent is authorised to pay a debt out of moneys in his hands, and there is no assignment of or charge on such moneys to or in favour of the creditor, the agent is not liable to the creditor, unless he expressly or impliedly contracts to pay him, or agrees to hold the money to his use.[692]

(6)   A owes P money. Ps who lives abroad, wishes to make a gift to T, and instructs A to pay some of the debt to T. A agrees, tells T that he will do so, and sends him a cheque, which is, however, incorrectly drawn. The cheque is returned by T to A for correction, but A makes no further effort to pay T. T can sue A in restitution.[693]

---

[685] *Roxburghe v Cox* (1881) 17 Ch.D. 520; *Webb v Smith*, above.

[686] See *Webb v Smith*, and the other cases, above.

[687] *Crowfoot v Gurney* (1832) 9 Bing. 372.

[688] *Robertson v Fauntleroy* (1823) 8 Moo. C.P. 10.

[689] *Walker v Rostron* (1842) 9 M. & W. 411; *Fruhling v Schroder* (1835) 7 C. & P. 103; *Hamilton v Spottiswoode* (1849) 4 Exch. 200; *Noble v National Discount Co* (1860) 5 H. & N. 225.

[690] *Stevens v Hill* (1805) 5 Esp. 247; *Langston v Corney* (1815) 4 Camp. 176.

[691] *Moore v Bushell* (1857) 27 L.J.Ex. 3; *Hill v Royds* (1869) L.R. 8 Eq. 290; *Johnson v Robarts* (1875) L.R. 10 Ch.App. 505.

[692] *Williams v Everett* (1811) 14 East 582; *Howell v Batt* (1833) 5 B. & Ad. 504; *Malcolm v Scott* (1850) 5 Exch. 601; *Brind v Hampshire* (1836) 1 M. & W. 365; *Wedlake v Hurley* (1830) 1 C. & J. 83; *Bell v London & Northern Western Ry Co* (1852) 15 Beav. 548; *Morrell v Wotten* (1852) 16 Beav. 197; *Scott v Porcher* (1817) 3 Meriv. 652.

[693] *Shamia v Joory* [1958] 1 Q.B. 448; *Dellas v Kourtessis* [1962] V.R. 456. But see Comment above.

3. TORTS

Article 113

AGENT PERSONALLY LIABLE FOR TORTS AND OTHER WRONGS

9-115   Where loss, damage or injury is caused to any third party by any act or omission of an agent that constitutes a civil wrong[694] while the agent is acting on behalf of his principal, the agent is, in general, personally liable, whether or not he was acting with the authority of the principal, to the same extent as if he was acting on his own behalf,[695] unless the authority of the principal justifies the wrong.[696]

Comment

9-116   **General**   It is in general no defence to an action against a tortfeasor for the tortfeasor to prove that he acted under the authority, instructions or orders of another.[697] In this respect liability for most torts differs from contract liability, where it is sometimes (misleadingly[698]) said that the agent "drops out". But, of course, where such authority, instructions or orders make legal what might otherwise be tortious, there will be no liability; and ratification also may make non-tortious what was tortious when it was done.[699] Again, there are many cases where a person who follows the instructions or orders of a person who has superior status or skill may for that reason, not be negligent,[700] and a person who acts purely ministerially may sometimes not be liable.[701] It must also be borne in mind that the text of art.113 refers to acts and omissions that are sufficient to constitute a wrong that the law recognises. Mere fault or carelessness in a person, including an agent, where there is no duty of care will not found liability, even if there were liability in others. Hence, some forms of tortious liability turn not merely on fault but on the presence of an assumption of responsibility for the outcomes of the conduct. In such cases, a careless agent who has assumed no responsibility to the claimant commits no wrong, even where he had authority to make his principal liable for the same conduct. In the next paragraph it will be seen that liability for negligent statements

---

[694] Civil liability of an agent for a criminal wrong in the tort of breach of statutory duty will usually turn on statutory intention: see *Campbell v Peter Gordon Joiners Ltd* [2016] UKSC 38; [2016] A.C. 1513.

[695] See Illustrations; *Restatement, Third*, § 7.01: "An agent is subject to liability to a third party harmed by the agent's tortious conduct. Conduct otherwise tortious is not privileged simply because an actor acts as an agent or an employee, with actual or apparent authority, or within the scope of employment". He may be liable as joint tortfeasor with the principal: see below, para.9-123.

[696] Illustrations 9 and 10.

[697] *Bennett v Bayes* (1860) 5 H. & N. 391, Illustration 1; *Heugh v Earl of Abergavenny* (1874) 23 W.R. 40; *Carey v Laiken* 2015 SCC 17; [2015] 2 S.C.R. 79 (solicitor liable for contempt of court for releasing frozen fund on client's instructions).

[698] See above, para.9-002.

[699] Illustrations 9 and 10. The reverse does not apply: an agent sued for defamation who pleads qualified privilege is not affected by the malice of his principal: *Egger v Viscount Chelmsford* [1965] 1 Q.B. 248. State immunity under the State Immunity Act 1978 extends to the agents of a foreign state party: *Koo Golden East Mongolia v Bank of Nova Scotia* [2007] EWCA Civ 1443; [2008] Q.B. 717 (bank, as agent of central bank of Mongolia, not subject to order for disclosure of details of its customer's affairs, in relation to alleged tort by the central bank).

[700] See *Gold v Essex CC* [1942] 2 K.B. 293.

[701] See Article 114 (conversion).

that are made on behalf of a disclosed principal within the agent's actual or apparent authority and are intended to create legal responsibility rests directly with the principal, rather than with the agent, unless the agent has also assumed responsibility for their accuracy. English law has also been more resistant than some other jurisdictions to the imposition of liability in tort for economic loss, for example in relation to liability for defective products,[702] but should such liability develop it too may result in direct liability on the owner of the relevant business without liability on the part of the employees and others who are responsible for the actual manufacture of the products.[703] This is not centrally an issue of agency law, and it is not further treated here.

Torts connected with contract—deceit and negligent misstatement In contractual situations it is clear that an agent may be liable to the third party in deceit, e.g. when he deliberately misrepresents his authority[704] or knowingly signs a false bill of lading.[705] It is also now clear that an action in negligence may be brought within a pre-contractual[706] and also a contractual situation[707] against a contracting party himself. By the same token, the existence of a contractual situation does not bar an action against the agent of one of the contracting parties. The mere fact that the agent acts for one party does not prevent his owing, in appropriate cases, a duty of care to the other. Such liability is most likely to occur in connection with negligent misrepresentation.[708] Although earlier authority on the leading case of *Hedley Byrne & Co Ltd v Heller & Partners Ltd*[709] suggested a narrow scope for the duty of care in respect of statements,[710] later authority expanded this.[711] In Commonwealth cases, estate agents have been held liable for negligent misrepresentations, not made within the scope of their authority on behalf of the vendor, to prospective purchasers of land.[712] Beyond this specialised context, other decisions have found agents liable to third parties for misstatements.[713] However, except to the extent that these authorities rest on a finding that the agent assumed

9-117

[702] See, e.g. *Murphy v Brentwood District Council* [1991] 1 A.C. 398.
[703] See, e.g. *Body Corporate 202254 v Taylor* [2009] 2 N.Z.L.R. 17.
[704] *Polhill v Walter* (1832) 3 B. & Ad. 114; *Randell v Trimen* (1856) 18 C.B. 786; *West London Commercial Bank v Kitson* (1884) 13 Q.B.D. 360.
[705] *Standard Chartered Bank v Pakistan National Shipping Corp* [2002] UKHL 43; [2003] 1 A.C. 959.
[706] *Esso Petroleum Co Ltd v Mardon* [1976] Q.B. 801.
[707] *Henderson v Merrett Syndicates Ltd* [1995] 2 A.C. 145; *Midland Bank Trust Co Ltd v Hett, Stubbs & Kemp* [1979] Ch. 384.
[708] But as to Misrepresentation Act 1967, see below, para.9-118.
[709] [1964] A.C. 465.
[710] *Mutual Life and Citizens' Assurance Co Ltd v Evatt* [1971] A.C. 793 (PC).
[711] *Esso Petroleum Co Ltd v Mardon* [1976] Q.B. 801.
[712] *Dodds v Dodds and Millman* (1964) 45 D.L.R. (2d) 472; *Bango v Holt* (1971) 21 D.L.R. (3d) 66; *Avery v Salie* (1972) 25 D.L.R. (3d) 495; *Olsen v Poirier* (1978) 91 D.L.R. (3d) 123; *Chand v Sabo Bros Realty Ltd* (1979) 96 D.L.R. (3d) 445; *Komarniski v Marien* (1979) 100 D.L.R. (3d) 81; *Roberts v Montex Development Corp* 100 D.L.R. (3d) 660; *Barrett v J.R. West Ltd* [1970] N.Z.L.R. 789; *Richardson v Norris Smith Real Estate Ltd* [1977] 1 N.Z.L.R. 152; *Roots v Oentory Pty Ltd* [1983] 2 Qd.R. 745. But cf. *Alessio v Jovica* (1973) 34 D.L.R. (3d) 107, reversed in part (1973) 42 D.L.R. (3d) 242; *Jones v Still* [1965] N.Z.L.R. 1071; *Presser v Caldwell Estates Pty Ltd* [1971] 2 N.S.W.L.R. 471; *Shing v Ashcroft* [1987] 2 N.Z.L.R. 154. As to the possibility that an agent may undertake no duty beyond that of passing on what the principal wishes to communicate, see *Butcher v Lachlan Realty Pty. Ltd* (2004) 218 C.L.R. 592.
[713] *Allied Finance and Investments Ltd v Haddow & Co* [1983] N.Z.L.R. 22, Illustration 13 (solicitor); *Computastaff Ltd v Ingledew Brown Bennison & Garrett* (1983) 268 E.G. 906 (solicitors and estate agents); *Garland v Ralph Pay & Ransom* (1984) 271 E.G. 106 (selling agent employed by mortgagee liable to mortgagor); *Al-Kandari v J.R. Brown & Co* [1988] Q.B. 665, Illustration 13; *Punjab*

responsibility for a statement's accuracy, they would need, in England and Wales, to be reviewed in the light of the decision of the House of Lords in *Williams v Natural Life Health Foods Ltd*.[714] Here the principal director of a small company was held not liable for negligent projections in an advisory memorandum to a third party on the basis that the director himself had assumed no responsibility to the claimant. The basis of the case was the orthodox one that no tort is committed by the agent, because, as in the case of the solicitor answering inquiries,[715] there is in the particular case no personal assumption of responsibility for the purposes of a duty of care in respect of pure economic loss.[716] The principal might be liable in such circumstances, though this itself may give rise to difficulties.[717] No assumption of responsibility is, however, necessary for liability in deceit.[718] As regards actions under s.2(1) of the Misrepresentation Act 1967, its wording is confined to representations made by a party to a contract and does not cover misrepresentations by their agents, unless they also are parties to the contract.[719] The position with

---

National Bank Ltd v de Boinville [1992] 1 W.L.R. 1138 (insurance broker liable to assignee of policy); *McCullagh v Lane Fox & Partners Ltd* [1996] 1 E.G.L.R. 35 (estate agent); *Woodward v Wolferstans* [1997] N.P.C. 51, *The Times*, April 8, 1997 (solicitor); *BCCI (Overseas) Ltd v Price Waterhouse (No.2)* [1998] Lloyd's Rep. Bank. 85 (auditor); *J. Jarvis & Sons Ltd v Castle Wharf Developments Ltd* [2001] EWCA Civ 19; [2001] Lloyd's Rep. P.N. 308 (quantity surveyor); *Dean v Allin & Watts* [2001] 2 Lloyd's Rep. 249, Illustration 16 (solicitor); *European International Reinsurance Co v Curzon Insurance Ltd* [2003] EWCA Civ 1074; [2003] Lloyd's Rep. I.R. 793 (insurance intermediary); *Crowson v HSBC Insurance Brokers Ltd* Unreported January 26, 2010, ChD; cf. *James McNaughton Paper Group Ltd v Hicks Anderson & Co* [1991] 2 Q.B. 113 (accountant); *Connolly-Martin v Davis* [1999] Lloyd's Rep. P.N. 790; *A. & J. Fabrications (Batley) Ltd v Grant Thornton* [1997] T.L.R. 588 (solicitor); *BDG Roof-Bond v Douglas* [2000] 1 B.C.L.C. 401 (solicitor); *Noel v Poland* [2001] 2 B.C.L.C. 645 (director of Lloyd's underwriting firm); *Avrora Fine Arts Investment Ltd v Christie, Manson & Woods Ltd* [2012] EWHC 2198 (Ch) at [123] (auctioneer, but disclaimer effective); *Smith v Eric S. Bush* [1990] 1 A.C. 831 (valuer); *Merrett v Babb* [2001] EWCA Civ 214; [2001] Q.B. 1174; *Propell National Valuers (WA) Pty Ltd v Australian Executor Trustees Ltd* [2012] FCAFC 31 (valuer).

[714] [1998] 1 W.L.R. 830 (HL). See also *Gran Gelato Ltd v Richcliff (Group) Ltd* [1992] Ch. 560 at 569; and *Spring v Guardian Assurance Plc* [1995] 2 A.C. 296 at 316, per Lord Goff of Chieveley; *Foster v Action Aviation Ltd* [2014] EWCA Civ 1368 (fact director was beneficial owner of asset being sold by his company not important). The relationship between *Williams* and the reasoning of the Court of Appeal in *So v HSBC Bank* [2009] EWCA Civ 296 is, however, not straightforward—see further above, paras 8-180 and 8-182.

[715] *Gran Gelato v Richcliff (Group) Ltd* [1992] Ch. 560, Illustration 15 (criticised Cane (1992) 108 L.Q.R. 539); *P&P Property Ltd v Owen White & Catlin LLP* [2016] EWHC 2276 (Ch); [2016] Bus. L.R. 1337 at [144]; *NRAM Plc v Steel* [2016] CSIH 11; [2016] P.N.L.R. 20. cf. *McCullagh v Lane Fox & Partners Ltd* [1996] 1 E.G.L.R. 35 at 43–44, per Hobhouse LJ.

[716] Quaere whether the same reasoning could be applied to cases of negligence causing physical damage, as is suggested in the judgment of LaForest J in *London Drugs Ltd v Kuehne & Nagel International Ltd* [1992] 3 S.C.R. 299; but McLachlin J did not agree: see p.461. A lone English case is *Fairline Shipping Corp v Adamson* [1975] Q.B. 180, Illustration 12.

[717] See above, paras 8-180 and 8-182.

[718] See *Standard Chartered Bank v Pakistan National Shipping Corp (No.4)* [2002] UKHL 43; [2003] 1 A.C. 959.

[719] *Resolute Maritime Inc v Nippon Kaiji Kyokai (The Skopas)* [1983] 1 W.L.R. 857, Illustration 16; and see *MCI WorldCom International Inc v Primus Telecommunications Inc* [2003] EWHC 2182 (Comm); [2004] 1 All E.R. (Comm) 138, reversed on a different point [2004] EWCA Civ 957; [2004] 2 All E.R. (Comm) 833. But an agent may be a genuine party to the contract: see Article 98; and *Avrora Fine Arts Investment Ltd v Christie, Manson & Woods Ltd* [2012] EWHC 2198 (Ch) at [134] where potential liability under the Act was conceded. For a case where a principal was held liable under the Act, see *Gosling v Anderson* (1972) 223 E.G. 1743.

claims for pure economic loss not founded on an alleged misstatement is less clear.[720]

Statute law may also in some cases provide a basis for suit against an agent for misstatement or for failing to reveal relevant information known to the agent, and for other misconduct (such as failure to comply with codes of conduct). In particular, the Consumer Protection from Unfair Trading Regulations 2008[721] are apt to impose wide-ranging duties on businesses and individuals, including estate agents, engaged in the sale of property, including an active duty to reveal material adverse information about the property known to the agent. Liability can be both criminal and civil.

Misrepresentation as to another's creditworthiness   In relation to representa- **9-118** tions as to another's creditworthiness, an agent may be protected by the Statute of Frauds Amendment Act 1828 s.6 ("Lord Tenterden's Act"), which requires a representation as to another's creditworthiness to be in writing in order to be actionable. In *Contex Drouzhba Ltd v Wiseman*,[722] however, it was held that the section did not protect a director and principal controller of a company where the director purported to be speaking on behalf of the company as to its own state of credit; the representation was treated as the company's own, albeit procured by the director. This decision was upheld on appeal but on the narrower basis that the director's signature to relevant documents on the company's behalf met both the representation and writing requirements of the 1828 Act.[723] No comment was offered on the broader ground adopted by Irwin J at first instance, a ground which perhaps places undue weight on the particular words the director adopts in contracting on the company's behalf. It has been held that the writing requirement of the 1828 Act could be established by a document that impliedly represented that a third party was creditworthy.[724]

Companies   For a short period, it was thought that the position of company direc- **9-119** tors was different to that of agents in general in relation to torts and other wrongs; they were to be identified with the company and not personally liable.[725] There was, however, no reason to privilege directors over employees and other agents,[726] and it has been affirmed that the general principles applicable to unincorporated

---

See *Henderson v Merrett Syndicates Ltd* [1995] 2 A.C. 145, assumption of responsibility necessary for liability for negligent performance of services. But cf. *Customs and Excise Commissioners v Barclays Bank Plc* [2006] UKHL 28; [2007] 1 A.C. 181 at [37], per Lord Hoffmann. The other judgments in *Customs and Excise v Barclays* also suggest that an assumption of responsibility is not necessary in all cases, particularly those not involving misstatement. See too *CGL Group Ltd v The Royal Bank of Scotland Plc* [2017] EWCA Civ 1073 at [82].

[721] These Regulations have replaced, and go beyond, the Property Misdescriptions Act 1991, which has now been repealed. In relation to estate agents engaged in transactions involving residential property, see also ss.23A to 23C of the Estate Agents Act 1979, inserted by the Consumers, Estate Agents and Redress Act 2007 Sch.6. For an illustrative case under the Property Misdescriptions Act 1991, see *Norfolk County Trading Standards Service v Bycroft* [2012] EWHC 4417 (Admin); [2012] 45 E.G. 95 (C.S.).

[722] [2006] EWHC 2708 (Comm); [2007] 1 B.C.L.C. 758.

[723] [2007] EWCA Civ 1201; [2008] 1 B.C.L.C. 631.

[724] *Lindsay v O'Loughnane* [2010] EWHC 529 (QB).

[725] See *Trevor Ivory Ltd v Anderson* [1992] 2 N.Z.L.R. 517 at 524, 528; *Standard Chartered Bank v Pakistan National Shipping Corp (No.2)* [2000] 1 Lloyd's Rep. 218 (CA); reversed [2002] UKHL 43; [2003] 1 A.C. 959.

[726] See above, para.1-029; and Watts (2001) 116 L.Q.R. 525; Flannigan (2002) 81 Can.Bar Rev. 247; Campbell and Armour [2003] C.L.J. 290; Reynolds (2003) 33 H.K.L.J. 51; Stevens [2005]

principals and their agents are as applicable to companies and directors.[727] Where tortious liability turns on an assumption of responsibility, it may be found that directors, like other agents, have not assumed any personal liability, but rather have acted solely on behalf of the company, their principal.[728] Otherwise, directors can be liable in tort in the same way as anyone else. They may, however, be liable for procuring the commission of a tort or other wrong by the company or one of its employees, a subject discussed next. There is some authority that a company may commit the tort of conspiracy by conspiring with its sole director.[729] This is a difficult notion. At the least, it would require that the director (or directors, if more than one is involved) purport to perform some acts necessary for the tort in his personal capacity and not merely as agent of the company, since conspiracy requires not only agreement between two or more persons but acts performed by, or perhaps on behalf of, each of them.[730] Further, if a company were to be a direct party to the common design, as opposed to merely vicariously liable for the acts of others, it would need to be shown that the relevant director had authority to commit the wrongful conduct on the company's behalf.[731]

9-120   **Procuring of, and other involvement in, wrongs**   Agents, including directors, can be liable for procuring or authorising the commission of torts or other wrongs by others.[732] Again, this is simply part of the general law, and by no means limited to agents. Many of the leading cases, however, have involved directors who have directed more junior agents to do things which are actionable.[733] There are numerous cases on each side of the line in relation to patent and copyright infringement.[734] Where the agent has actually committed the central acts constituting the wrong,

---

L.M.C.L.Q. 101.

[727] *Standard Chartered Bank v Pakistan National Shipping Corp (No.2)* [2002] UKHL 43; [2003] 1 A.C. 959 (deceit); *Lewis v Yeeles* [2010] EWCA Civ 326 at [26] (procuring a breach of contract by a third party); *Body Corporate 202254 v Taylor* [2009] 2 N.Z.L.R. 17; *Eco3 Capital Ltd v Ludsin Overseas Ltd* [2013] EWCA Civ 413 at [125].

[728] *Williams v Natural Life Health Foods Ltd* [1998] 1 W.L.R. 830; *Foster v Action Aviation Ltd* [2014] EWCA Civ 1368.

[729] *Barclay Pharmaceuticals Ltd v Waypharm LP* [2012] EWHC 306 (Comm); [2013] 2 B.C.L.C. 551 at [229] (criticised by Watts, in Busch, Macgregor and Watts (eds), *Agency Law in Commercial Practice* (2016), pp.108–113).

[730] See Carty, *An Analysis of the Economic Torts* (2010), Ch.6; Carty (1999) 19 L.S. 489.

[731] As to authority to act illegally, see above, paras 2-026 and 6-023. See also *Digicel (St Lucia) Ltd v Cable & Wireless Plc* [2010] EWHC 774 (Ch), Annex I at [77] (alleged conspiracy as between related companies).

[732] See Clerk & Lindsell, *Torts* (21st edn), para.5-76 onwards; Carty, above; Stevens, *Torts and Rights* (2007), Ch.7; Davies [2011] C.L.J. 353; Davies, *Accessory Liability* (2015).

[733] e.g. *Yuille v B&B Fisheries (Leigh) Ltd* [1958] 2 Lloyd's Rep. 596 (sending unseaworthy vessels to sea); *Wah Tat Bank Ltd v Chan Cheng Kum* [1975] A.C. 507 (PC) (conversion for delivery of goods without bill of lading); *Anderson Antiques (UK) Ltd v Anderson Wharf (Hull) Ltd* [2007] EWHC 2086 (Ch) (procuring company to wrongly register notices against registered title); cf. *Rainham Chemical Works v Belvedere Fish Guano Ltd* [1921] 2 A.C. 465 (no liability for factory explosion); *CBS Songs Ltd v Amstrad Consumer Electronics Plc* [1988] A.C. 1013. As to the concept of "authorising" infringement, see the cases cited in para.8-195; and *Ellis v Sheffield Gas Consumers Co* (1853) 2 E. & B. 767; *Southwark LBC v Mills* [2001] 1 A.C. 1 at 22; *Twentieth Century Fox Film Corp v Newzbin Ltd* [2010] EWHC 608 (Ch); [2010] F.S.R. 21; *Body Corporate 366611 v Wu* [2014] NZSC 137; [2015] 1 N.Z.L.R. 215 (owner of property authorised agent to commit trespass), varied on appeal [2014] NZSC 137; [2015] 1 N.Z.L.R. 215 (liability for trespass); *Twentieth Century Fox Film Corp v Sky UK Ltd* [2015] EWHC 1082 (Ch); cf. *Coventry v Lawrence (No.2)* [2014] UKSC 46; [2015] A.C. 106 (landlord did not authorise nuisance merely by collecting rent from known tortfeasor).

[734] e.g. *Performing Rights Society v Ciryl Theatrical Syndicate Ltd* [1924] 1 K.B. 1; *British Thomson-*

thereby making his employer liable, it will not normally be appropriate to plead that the agent has procured the employer to commit the wrong; the agent will be a primary tortfeasor not a secondary one in such cases.[735] It would also be unnecessary, as a rule, to use the concept of procurement where the defendant uttered a fraudulent, or defamatory, statement intending that some other party, innocent or not, would pass on the inaccurate information to the claimant; the utterer would be directly liable in deceit, or defamation.[736] Apart from liability for procurement or authorisation, agents can also find themselves subject to liability for participating in a common design to commit a tort or other wrong.[737] Where there is an intention to injure there is also the possibility of liability in the separate tort of conspiracy.[738] In English law, there is, at present anyway, no concept of merely facilitating the commission of the tort of another.[739]

Inducement of breach of contract? In *Said v Butt*[740] it was held that an agent could not be liable for inducing a breach of contract by his principal. A major reason given was that the liability of the principal, for whom the agent acted, and who would be responsible, could not lie in tort but would rather be for breach of contract. This ground is not convincing.[741] It would be equally unconvincing, however, **9-121**

Houston Co Ltd v Stirling Accessories Ltd [1924] 2 Ch 33; *Mentmore Manufacturing Co Ltd v National Merchandising Co Ltd* (1978) 89 D.L.R. (3d) 195; *Hoover Plc v George Hulme (Stockport) Ltd* [1992] F.S.R. 565; *White Horse Distillers Ltd v Gregson Associates Ltd* [1984] R.P.C. 61; *C. Evans & Sons Ltd v Spritebrand Ltd* [1985] 1 W.L.R. 317; *PLG Research Ltd v Ardon International Ltd* [1993] F.S.R. 197; *Root Quality Pty Ltd v Root Control Technologies Pty Ltd* (2001) 177 A.L.R. 231; *MCA Records Inc v Charly Records Ltd* [2001] EWCA Civ 1441; [2002] F.S.R. 26; [2003] 1 B.C.L.C. 93; *Societa Esplosivi Industriali Spa v Ordnance Technologies (UK) Ltd* [2007] EWHC 2875 (Ch); [2008] 2 B.C.L.C. 428; *Football Association Premier League Ltd v QC Leisure* [2008] EWHC 1411 (Ch); *JR Consulting & Drafting Pty Ltd v Cummings* [2016] FCAFC 20; *Phonographic Performance Ltd v CGK Trading Ltd* [2016] EWHC 2642 (Ch). See Hon. R. Arnold and P. Davies (2017) 133 L.Q.R. 442.
[735] *Williams v Natural Life Health Foods Ltd* [1998] 1 W.L.R. 830 at 838–839; *Standard Chartered Bank v Pakistan National Shipping Corp (No.2)* [2002] UKHL 43; [2003] 1 A.C. 959 at [38]. cf. *Watson v Dolmark Industries Ltd* [1992] 3 N.Z.L.R. 311.
[736] See, e.g. *Cornfoot v Fowke* (1840) 6 M. & W. 358 at 373–374; *Egger v Viscount Chelmsford* [1965] 1 Q.B. 248 at 261; *Clef Aquitaine Sarl v Laporte Materials (Barrow) Ltd* [2001] Q.B. 488 at 502–503.
[737] *The Koursk* [1924] P. 140; *Brooke v Bool* [1928] 2 K.B. 578; *Unilever Plc v Chefaro* [1994] F.S.R. 135; *Fish & Fish Ltd v Sea Shepherd UK* [2015] UKSC 10; [2015] A.C. 1229; noted McMeel [2016] L.M.C.L.Q. 29; *Glaxo Wellcome UK Ltd (t/a Allen & Hanburys) v Sandoz Ltd* [2017] EWCA Civ 227.
[738] See, in general, *Kuwait Oil Tanker Co SAK v Al Bader* [2000] 2 All E.R. (Comm) 271; *OBG Ltd v Allan* [2007] UKHL 21; [2008] 1 A.C. 1; *Meretz Investments NV v ACP Ltd* [2007] EWCA Civ 1303; [2008] Ch. 244; *Revenue and Customs Commissioners v Total Network SL* [2008] UKHL 19; [2008] A.C. 1174. For recent cases involving directors and agents, see *Digicel (St Lucia) Ltd v Cable & Wireless Plc* [2010] EWHC 774 (Ch) at Annex I; *Baldwin v Berryland Books* [2010] EWCA Civ 1440; *Stevenson v Singh* [2012] EWHC 2880 (QB) at [18]; *Alpstream AG v PK Airfinance Sarl* [2013] EWHC 2370 (Comm) at [110]; *Emerald Supplies Ltd v British Airways Plc* [2015] EWCA Civ 1024; [2016] Bus. L.R. 145. cf. Stevens, *Torts and Rights* (2007), Ch.7.
[739] See, e.g. *Credit Lyonnais v Export Credit Guarantee Department* [1998] 1 Lloyd's Rep. 19; affd [2000] 1 A.C. 486; *Fish & Fish Ltd v Sea Shepherd UK* [2015] UKSC 10; [2015] A.C. 1229.
[740] *Said v Butt* [1920] 3 K.B. 497; *Welsh Development Agency v Export Finance Co Ltd* [1992] B.C.L.C. 148 at 171–173, 179–182 and 191. See Oditah [1992] J.B.L. 541 at 565–569; Tan (2011) 23 Sing. Ac. L.J. 816.
[741] See *Welsh Development Agency v Export Finance Co Ltd*, above at 173, 191.

simply to conclude that all torts must be governed by the same rules.[742] The tort of inducing breach of contract is itself problematic, given that deliberate breach of contract does not itself engage the law of tort. Imposing liability on agents for inducing breach of contract would be to place them in an invidious position when their duty is to act in the best interests of their principal and they conclude that breaching the contract is in their principal's interests. Principals should not be disadvantaged because they have employed agents and relied on them to assess their interests. *Said v Butt* has been assumed to be correct in later decisions.[743] It may however be possible to claim where the defendant did not purport to act as agent or acted in breach of his duty to his principal or employer[744] or not in good faith.[745] A parent company is not precluded from liability for inducing a breach of contract by its subsidiary or for causing loss by unlawful means,[746] but where the two companies share directors regard must be had to the capacity in which they have acted.[747] It is also possible for a contract between the parties to exclude the possibility of suit against agents for inducing a breach by any of the parties.[748]

9-122   Vicarious immunity[749]   It might be expected that where a principal has an immunity conferred upon him by contract, an agent working for him in respect of that contract would be entitled to the same immunity towards the third party.[750] The notion of privity of contract, however, has prevented this result being easily achieved. It was held by the House of Lords in 1962 that there is no general doctrine of vicari-

---

[742] See in respect of conversion, below para.9-126. The first basis for the decision concerned the doctrine of the undisclosed principal: see above, para.8-079. The use of "alter ego" reasoning is also not satisfactory: see above, paras 1-030, 8-188 and 9-119.

[743] *G. Scammell & Nephew Ltd v Hurley* [1929] 1 K.B. 419 at 443 and 449; *D.C. Thomson & Co Ltd v Deakin* [1952] Ch. 646 at 680, 681; *O'Brien v Dawson* (1942) 66 C.L.R. 18 at 32, 34; *Rutherford v Poole* [1953] V.L.R. 130 at 135–136; *Official Assignee v Dowling* [1964] N.Z.L.R. 578 at 580–581; *Telemetrix Plc v Modern Engineers of Bristol (Holdings) Plc* [1985] B.C.L.C. 213 at 217; *Holding Oil Finance Inc v Marc Rich & Co AG* [1996] C.L.Y. 1085; *Cook Strait Skyferry Ltd v Dennis Thompson International Ltd* [1993] 2 N.Z.L.R. 72; *Ridgeway Maritime Inc v Beulah Wings Ltd* [1991] 2 Lloyd's Rep. 611; *Goodacre v Meyer* [2002] EWHC 1785 (Ch) (no liability for procurement of alleged breach of commission-sharing agreement); *Johnson Matthey (Aust.) Ltd v Dascorp Pty Ltd* (2003) 9 V.R. 171. But cf. *Thames Valley Housing Association Ltd v Elegant (Guernsey) Ltd* [2011] EWHC 1288 (Ch) at [110], where, however, *Said v Butt* and the foregoing cases were not referred to. It was suggested therein that the position may be different for directors who are performing their constitutional role in good faith. But, there is, it is submitted, no good reason to protect directors at the expense of employees and other agents who are also attempting to do their best for their principal; they are all immune from action.

[744] See *The Leon* [1991] 2 Lloyd's Rep. 611 at 624–625, per Waller J; *SPL Private Finance (PF1) IC Ltd v Arch Financial Products LLP* [2014] EWHC 4268 (Comm) at [288]. See also *Official Assignee v Dowling* [1964] N.Z.L.R. 578 at 580–581; Clerk & Lindsell, *Torts* (21st edn), para.24-36.

[745] *Official Assignee v Dowling* [1964] N.Z.L.R. 578 at 580–581; *Bromley Industries Ltd v Martin & Judith Fitzsimons Ltd* [2009] NZHC 1992; *Knights Capital Group Ltd v Bajada and Associates Pty Ltd* [2016] WASC 69 at [76].

[746] See *Esso Petroleum Co Ltd v Kingswood Motors (Addleston) Ltd* [1974] Q.B. 142 at 155; *Stocznia Gdanska SA v Latvian Shipping Co (No.3)* [2002] EWCA Civ 889; [2002] 2 All E.R. (Comm) 768; [2002] 2 Lloyd's Rep. 436 (parent company liable for inducing subsidiary's breach), noted by Edmundson (2008) 30 M.U.L.R. 62. See too *Lewis v Yeeles* [2010] EWCA Civ 326 at [26] (director of third party company not immune from personal liability for inducing breach of contract by a fourth party).

[747] *LMI Australasia Pty Ltd v Baulderstone Hornibrook Pty Ltd* [2003] NSWCA 74.

[748] *Mir Steel UK Ltd v Morris* [2012] EWCA Civ 1397 at [39].

[749] Treitel, *Law of Contract* (14th edn), para.14-022 onwards; Chitty, *Contracts* (32nd edn), para.15-042 onwards.

[750] *Restatement, Second*, § 347, esp. Comment *b*.

ous immunity in English law.[751] On the other hand the agent will be protected where a contract can be construed between agent and third party under which the agent is entitled to the immunities conferred by the main contract on the principal,[752] and the principal can sometimes be regarded as having, acting in the capacity of agent for his own agent, negotiated such a contract of immunity for the agent.[753] Although difficulties might be expected in finding the consideration supplied by the agent, the Privy Council brushed these aside and held that there was an implied contract between a consignor of goods and the stevedore at the port of discharge entitling the stevedore to the limitations and immunities of the bill of lading.[754] There may also be other ways of conferring immunity on the agent. In particular, the principal can contract to indemnify the agent against claims made on him, and insert into the main contract a clause whereby the third party promises not to sue the agent. If the third party is made aware of the indemnity provision, the liability under it will become the measure of loss caused to the principal if the third party does sue the agent. In such a case the principal may be able to have the third party's action against the agent stayed,[755] or even, if all the parties are before the court, dismissed.[756] A broader rule still is to say that the agent, when sued in tort, owes a duty no higher than that prescribed in the main contract, and perhaps in some circumstances no duty at all.[757]

Similar considerations apply where the agent seeks to rely as against the third party on an immunity conferred by his contract with the principal. If a contract with the third party on such terms can be inferred, he will be protected.[758] And here there is more recent authority that if the owner of goods expressly or impliedly authorises sub-bailment of them on the sub-bailee's terms (as where he authorises sub-bailment "on any terms") and the sub-bailee has sufficient notice that a person other than the bailee (his bailor) is interested in the goods, the subbailee's terms may be invoked against the owner.[759]

For England and Wales the law is now changed by the Contract (Rights of Third Parties) Act 1999, which allows a third party to sue on contracts where the contract

---

751 *Scruttons Ltd v Midland Silicones Ltd* [1962] A.C. 446; *Dunlop Pneumatic Tyre Co v Selfridge* [1915] A.C. 847.
752 This is a possible explanation of *Elder Dempster & Co v Paterson Zochonis & Co* [1924] A.C. 522; discussed in *Scruttons v Midland Silicones*, above; but see *The Pioneer Container* [1994] 2 A.C. 324.
753 *Hall v North Eastern Ry Co* (1875) L.R. 10 Q.B. 437; *Starlight Shipping Co v Allianz Marine and Aviation Versicherungs AG* [2014] EWHC 3068 (Comm); [2015] 2 All E.R. (Comm) 747 at [72].
754 *New Zealand Shipping Co Ltd v A.M. Satterthwaite & Co Ltd (The Eurymedon)* [1975] A.C. 154; *Port Jackson Stevedoring Pty Ltd v Salmond & Spraggon (Australia) Pty Ltd (The New York Star)* [1981] 1 W.L.R. 138. See too *Sheehan v Watson* [2011] 1 N.Z.L.R. 314 (statutory immunity for lessees impliedly extended to agents of lessees).
755 cf. *Gore v Van Der Lann* [1967] 2 Q.B. 31; and see *Nippon Yusen Kaisha v Intl Import and Export Co Ltd (The Elbe Maru)* [1978] 1 Lloyd's Rep. 206.
756 *Snelling v John G. Snelling Ltd* [1973] Q.B. 87. Quaere whether the agent himself could plead the promise as a defence by virtue of the reasoning in *Hirachand Punamchand v Temple* [1911] 2 K.B. 330; Birks (1975) 1 Poly.L.Rev. 39.
757 See *London Drugs Ltd v Kuehne & Nagel International Ltd* [1992] 3 S.C.R. 299; (1992) 97 D.L.R. (4th) 261.
758 *Pyrene Co Ltd v Scindia Navigation Co Ltd* [1954] 2 Q.B. 402, as explained in *Scruttons Ltd v Midland Silicones Ltd* [1962] A.C. 446 at 471.
759 *The Pioneer Container* [1994] 2 A.C. 324; following dicta in *Morris v C.W. Martin & Sons* [1966] 1 Q.B. 716 at 730. See also *The Mahkutai* [1996] A.C. 650, where there was no decision on an argument based on the terms of the main contract.

expressly provides that he may, or the term purports to confer a benefit on him.[760] The third party must be expressly identified in the contract by name, as a member of a class or as answering a particular description, but need not be in existence when the contract is entered into.[761] Where a term in a contract excludes or limits liability, references to enforcement are to be construed as references to his availing himself of the exclusion or limitation.[762] In effect therefore a properly drafted clause protecting servants and/or agents can now be effective without reference to the devices mentioned above.

9-123 **Effect of judgment against principal or agent: contribution** Where the principal is liable for the torts of his agent they are in principle joint tortfeasors. Questions relating to the effect of judgment and contribution have been considered in Chapter 8.[763]

9-124 **The Crown** Agents of the Crown are liable for their torts[764]; indeed, until the Crown Proceedings Act 1947, they alone were liable, and the Crown was not, and an action could only be brought against the tortfeasor in his private capacity. Orders from the Crown, without more, do not justify torts.[765] To this there is one exception, that of Act of State. Where an agent of the Crown, whose act is duly authorised or ratified by the Crown, commits what would otherwise be a tort to an alien not resident in British territory, and the act is committed outside British territory, Act of State will be a defence to any action against him.[766] It may also be a defence in respect of an act against an enemy alien within British territory.[767] Whether it can be pleaded as a defence in respect of acts against British subjects outside British territory is not clear.[768] In view of the many changes within the Commonwealth over recent years there is much connected with the doctrine that may require reconsideration.[769]

Illustrations

9-125 (1) An agent signed a distress warrant, and after the warrant was issued, but

---

[760] s.1(1). See, e.g. *Laemthong International Lines Company Ltd v Abdullah Mohammed Fahem & Co* [2005] EWCA Civ 519; [2005] 1 Lloyd's Rep. 688; *Far East Chartering Ltd v Great Eastern Shipping Co Ltd* [2012] EWCA Civ 180; [2012] 2 All E.R. (Comm) 707; *Starlight Shipping Co v Allianz Marine and Aviation Versicherungs AG* [2014] EWHC 3068 (Comm); [2015] 2 All E.R. (Comm) 747 at [88]. See in general Chitty, *Contracts* (32nd edn), paras 15-046–15-047; Treitel, *Law of Contract* (14th edn), para.14-090 onwards; *Privity of Contract: the Impact of the Contract (Rights of Third Parties) Act 1999* (Merkin ed., 2000).
[761] s.1(3).
[762] s.1(7).
[763] See Comment to Article 90.
[764] See Wade (1991) 107 L.Q.R. 4.
[765] *Entick v Carrington* (1765) 19 St.Tr. 1029.
[766] *Burton v Denman* (1848) 2 Exch. 167; *Sinclair v Broughton and Government of India* (1882) 47 L.T. 170; *Walker v Baird* [1892] A.C. 491; *Salaman v Secretary of State for India* [1906] 1 K.B. 613; *Johnstone v Pedlar* [1921] 2 A.C. 262; *Commercial & Estates Co of Egypt v Board of Trade* [1925] 1 K.B. 271; *Nissan v Att.-Gen.* [1970] A.C. 179.
[767] *Netz v Ede* [1946] Ch. 224; *R. v Bottrill Ex p. Kuechenmeister* [1947] K.B. 41.
[768] See *Nissan v Att.-Gen.* [1970] A.C. 179.
[769] See Collier [1968] C.L.J. 102; [1969] C.L.J. 166; de Smith (1969) 32 M.L.R. 427.

before it was executed, refused a tender of the rent. Held, that the agent was personally liable for the illegal distress.[770]

(2) The manager of a bank signed a letter, as such, falsely and fraudulently representing that the credit of a certain person was good. Held, that the manager was personally liable in an action for deceit.[771]

(3) A solicitor who is employed to conduct the sale of an estate advises trustees to conceal an incumbrance from a mortgagee. He is personally liable with the trustees for the concealment.[772]

(4) A solicitor, on his client's instructions, presents a bankruptcy petition against A, knowing that A has not committed any act of bankruptcy. An action is maintainable against the solicitor for maliciously, and without reasonable and probable cause, presenting such petition, and causing A to be adjudged bankrupt.[773]

(5) A, a printer, is employed to print pictures which are an infringement of copyright. A, though not aware of the infringement of copyright, is liable, as well as his employers, for penalties for the infringement.[774]

(6) A ship is fitted with pumps which are an infringement of a patent. An injunction may be granted[775] against the master, restraining his from using the pumps, or otherwise infringing the patent.[776] But where a custom-house agent merely passed through the custom-house an article infringing a patent, and obtained permission for landing and storing it in magazines belonging to the principals, who were the importers, it was held that the acts of the agent did not amount to an exercise or user of the patent, and that therefore no action could be maintained against him in respect of the infringement.[777]

(7) An agent converts goods of a third person to his principal's use. He is liable to the true owner for their value, even if he acted in good faith and in the belief that his principal was the owner.[778] If, in such a case, the owner elects to adopt the transaction and proceed against the agent for an account, the agent is only liable to account for so much of the proceeds of the converted property as still remains in his hands, and not for what he has duly handed over in the course of his agency to the principal.[779]

(8) An agent of an executor *de son tort* collects assets, and pays them over to his principal. The agent is personally liable to account for the assets to the right executor or administrator, or to the beneficiaries.[780] But an agent who acts by

---

[770] *Bennett v Bayes* (1860) 5 H. & N. 391.

[771] *Swift v Jewsbury & Goddard* (1874) L.R. 9 Q.B. 301. See Article 91. See also *Standard Chartered Bank v Pakistan International Shipping Corp (No.2)* [2002] UKHL 43; [2003] 1 A.C. 959 (director procured signature of false bill of lading).

[772] *Arnot v Briscoe* (1748) 1 Ves. 95; *Clark v Hoskins* (1867) 36 L.J.Ch. 689.

[773] *Johnson v Emerson & Sparrow* (1871) L.R. 6 Ex. 329. And see *Stevens v Midland Counties Ry Co* (1854) 10 Exch. 352.

[774] *Baschet v London Illustrated Standard Co* [1900] 1 Ch. 73; cf. *Kelly's Directories Ltd v Gavin & Lloyds* [1902] 1 Ch. 631.

[775] s.2; *Lowe v Dorling* [1906] 2 K.B. 772: affirming [1905] 2 K.B. 501, decided under the Lodgers Goods Protection Act 1871. See also *Interoven Stove Co Ltd v Hibbard, etc.* [1946] 1 All E.R. 263.

[776] *Adair v Young* (1879) 12 Ch.D. 13.

[777] *Nobel's Explosives Co v Jones & Co* (1882) 8 App.Cas. 5.

[778] *Stephens v Elwall* (1815) 4 M. & S. 259; *Hollins v Fowler* (1874) L.R. 7 H.L. 757; *Wilson v New Brighton Panelbeaters* [1989] 1 N.Z.L.R. 74. But see Article 114.

[779] *Re Ely Ex p. Trustee* (1900) 48 W.R. 693. See Article 111.

[780] *Sharland v Mildon* (1846) 5 Hare 468; *Hill v Curtis* (1865) L.R. 1 Eq. 90. See also *Padget v Priest*

the authority of an executor (even before probate) or of a person who is subsequently granted letters of administration is not liable to account as an executor *de son tort*, because the title of the executor dates from, and that of the administrator relates back to, the time of the death.[781]

(9)   An agent, on behalf of his principal, but without the principal's authority, distrains the goods of a third person. The principal ratifies the distress, which is justifiable at his instance. The agent ceases to be liable, his act being justified by the ratification.[782]

(10)   A solicitor, being retained to sue for a debt, by mistake and without malice takes all the proceedings to judgment and execution against another person of the same name as the debtor; or, having obtained judgment against the debtor, by mistake and without malice issues execution against another person of the same name. The solicitor is not liable, for the tort of wrongful process of law requires malice.[783] But liability in trespass is strict. So where a solicitor directs the seizure of particular goods, so as to make the seizure his act rather than one done as part of a public duty,[784] he is personally liable if the seizure turns out to be wrongful.[785] So, where a solicitor directs or personally takes part in the execution of a warrant for arrest, he is liable in an action for false imprisonment if the warrant is illegal.[786]

(11)   Owners of ship's provisions agree with a company to store their goods in a warehouse which is owned by the managing director of the company but leased to the company. The contract is entered into by a director on behalf of the company; but a confirming letter from the managing director and an invoice indicate that the managing director is treating the storage of the goods as his own venture. Because of negligence in supervising the refrigeration the goods are damaged. The managing director is personally liable in negligence, though there is no contract with him and he is not bailee of the goods.[787]

(12)   In a matrimonial dispute, solicitors for the husband agree to hold the husband's passport to the order of the court. With the agreement of the wife they allow it to be lodged with the embassy of the husband's country, but negligently fail to inform her of facts creating risks that the husband will obtain it, and they also fail to take practicable steps to prevent this. The husband does obtain it, kidnaps the children and takes them abroad: the wife is injured in the kidnapping. The solicitors are liable to the wife in tort.[788]

(13)   Solicitors for a borrower on the security of a yacht certify to the lender that an instrument of security is fully binding on the borrower and that there are no charges on the yacht. In fact the yacht does not belong to the borrower but

---

(1787) 2 T.R. 97; Williams, Mortimer and Sunnucks, *Executors, Administrators and Probate* (20th edn), para.7-12.

[781] *Sykes v Sykes* (1870) L.R. 5 C.P. 113. See Williams, Mortimer and Sunnucks, above.

[782] *Hull v Pickersgill* (1819) 1 B. & B. 282.

[783] *Davies v Jenkins* (1843) 11 M. & W. 745; cf. *Clissold v Cratchley* [1910] 2 K.B. 244.

[784] See *Wilson v Tunman and Fretson* (1843) 6 M. & W. 236; *Smith v Keal* (1882) 9 Q.B.D. 340; *Morris v Salberg* (1889) 22 Q.B.D. 614.

[785] *Rowles v Senior* (1846) 8 Q.B. 677; *Davies v Jenkins*, above; *Clissold v Cratchley*, above.

[786] *Green v Elgie* (1843) 5 Q.B. 99; *Codrington v Lloyd* (1838) 8 A. & E. 449.

[787] *Fairline Shipping Corp v Adamson* [1975] Q.B. 180. See also *C. Evans & Sons Ltd v Spritebrand Ltd* [1985] 1 W.L.R. 317 (liability of director for breach of copyright). *Fairline* was doubted in *Mitsui & Co Ltd v Novorossiysk Shipping Co Ltd (The Kilmun)* [1993] 1 Lloyd's Rep. 311 at 328.

[788] *Al-Kandari v J.R. Brown & Co* [1988] Q.B. 665.

is being purchased by a company of which he is a shareholder, and the money was not intended to be used to enable the borrower to purchase the yacht. The solicitors knew this. They are liable to the lender.[789]

(14) Solicitors for vendors of an underlease negligently and incorrectly answer questions as to the terms of a superior lease. They are not liable to the purchaser who suffered loss thereby.[790]

(15) Solicitors acting for a borrower on the security of land negligently fail to ensure that the security intended by both parties is valid. They are liable to the lender.[791]

(16) Brokers acting for the seller of a vessel make representations which are not true. They are not parties to the contract and hence cannot be sued under s.2(1) of the Misrepresentation Act 1967, which only applies to a party to a contract.[792]

Article 114

CONVERSION BY INNOCENT AGENT

(1) Where an agent holds possession or control of goods for his principal, and: **9-126**

(a) sells and delivers or otherwise deals with the possession of and assumes to deal with the property in the goods without the authority of the true owner[793]; or

(b) refuses without qualification to deliver possession to the true owner on demand[794]; or

(c) transfers possession to his principal or any other person except the true owner, with notice of the claim of the true owner,[795]

he is liable in conversion to the true owner for the value of the goods, even if he obtained possession from his principal, reasonably believing that such principal owned the goods or had the right to dispose of them, and acted in good faith on the authority of such principal.

(2) But an agent is not guilty of conversion who in good faith merely:

(a) receives or holds goods on behalf of his principal without dealing with them[796];

(b) refuses to deliver to the true owner goods which he holds for his principal in such terms that the refusal does not amount to a repudiation of the title of the true owner[797];

[789] *Allied Finance and Investments Ltd v Haddow & Co* [1983] N.Z.L.R. 22.

[790] *Gran Gelato Ltd v Richcliff (Group) Ltd* [1992] Ch. 560; but see Cane (1991) 108 L.Q.R. 539 and discussion of this decision in *McCullagh v Lane Fox & Partners Ltd* [1996] 1 E.G.L.R. 35 at 43–44, per Hobhouse LJ.

[791] *Dean v Allin and Watts* [2001] EWCA Civ 758; [2001] 2 Lloyd's Rep. 249.

[792] *Resolute Maritime Inc v Nippon Kaiji Kyokai (The Skopas)* [1983] 1 W.L.R. 857; followed in *MCI WorldCom International Inc v Primus Telecommunications Inc* [2003] EWHC 2182 (Comm); [2004] 1 All E.R. (Comm) 138 (reversed [2004] EWCA Civ 957; [2004] 2 All E.R. (Comm) 833).

[793] Illustrations 1 to 4.

[794] Illustration 7 and cases cited.

[795] Illustration 5; *Powell v Hoyland* (1851) 6 Exch. 67; *Union Credit Bank v Mersey Docks & Harbour Board* [1899] 2 Q.B. 205. As to agent's right to interplead, see Article 70.

[796] *Caxton Publishing Co v Sutherland Publishing Co* [1939] A.C. 178 at 202.

[797] Illustration 7 and cases cited.

(c) contracts on behalf of his principal to sell goods of which he has neither possession nor control[798];

(d) by the authority of his principal, and without notice of the claim of the true owner, deals with the possession of, without assuming to deal with the property in, the goods.[799]

Comment

9-127 The tort of conversion raises special problems in connection with agents, in so far as it does not apply where the relevant act is purely ministerial. It therefore requires special treatment.

9-128 Rule (1) Conversion may be called:

"an act or complex series of acts of wilful interference, without lawful justification, with any chattel in a manner inconsistent with the right of another, whereby that other is deprived of the use and possession of it."[800]

It is a tort of strict liability, and, as stated in Article 113, the authority of the principal cannot provide immunity from liability for a tort committed by an agent against a third party. Therefore any act performed by an agent which amounts to a conversion is actionable against him, and it is no defence to the agent to prove that he was authorised to perform the act by a person who appeared to be the owner, or to have the authority to perform, or authorise the performance of, such acts.[801]

It is not clear whether or not this rule applies to acts done in good faith, and without notice of the claim of the true owner, on the authority of a mercantile agent, or of a buyer or seller, in possession of the goods or of the documents of title thereto with the consent of the true owner within the meaning of the Factors Act. The authorities are conflicting.[802] But the relevant sections refer only to the validity of the disposition made by the mercantile agent himself and do not seem, on their wording, to legalise what would otherwise be conversions by persons assisting in the making of such dispositions.

9-129 Rule (2) Merely to hold goods is however no conversion unless there is refusal to deliver up, or a dealing with the goods inconsistent with the owner's right.[803] And an agent may refuse to deliver goods while he makes reasonable inquiries, without rendering himself liable in conversion.[804] Further, there are some cases where, although there is a dealing with the goods to which the agent is a party, he is said to have acted as a mere conduit pipe[805] and therefore not to have performed any act amounting to a conversion. Thus an agent who negotiates a sale of goods of which

---

[798] See Comment. And see in general Clerk and Lindsell, *Torts* (21st edn), paras 17-17 and 17-73 onwards.
[799] Illustration 6.
[800] Salmond and Heuston, *Torts* (21st edn), pp.97–98 and in general pp.103–105. And see *Restatement, Second*, Appendix, reporter's note to § 349; *18th Report of Law Reform Committee (on Conversion and Detinue)*, Cmnd. 4774 (1971), esp. pp.14–18.
[801] See Article 113, Illustration 8; *Consolidated Co v Curtis & Son* [1892] 1 Q.B. 495, Illustration 1.
[802] See *Waddington & Sons v Neale & Sons* (1907) 96 L.T. 786; *Shenstone & Co v Hilton* [1894] 2 Q.B. 452; Article 89.
[803] See *Caxton Publishing Co v Sutherland Publishing Co* [1939] A.C. 178 at 202.
[804] Illustration 7 and cases cited.
[805] *Barker v Furlong* [1891] 2 Ch. 172 at 181, 183; *Consolidated Co v Curtis & Son* [1892] 1 Q.B. 495

he has neither possession nor control between two persons who contract directly does not himself interfere with the goods and so cannot be held liable for conversion.[806] So also an agent who performs acts with relation to goods, authorised by his principal, which are no more than a bailee or finder of goods could lawfully authorise, does not commit acts of conversion,[807] e.g. where he merely stores or carries goods,[808] transfers them to another agent,[809] or, not knowing of any adverse claim, returns them to his principal.[810] It is also probable that he does not convert if he performs acts in a transaction that actually transfers the title, provided that he does not know that such a transaction is involved; and even if he does know of it, there is authority that he does not commit conversion provided that he does not himself participate in the transaction, but acts only ministerially.[811] The general rule is significant as an analogy in other contexts where it is sought to argue that an agent only acted ministerially.[812]

Cheques   In principle, a bank which collects for a customer a cheque to which the customer has no title commits conversion.[813] But banks have statutory protection. By s.4 of the Cheques Act 1957, where a banker in good faith and without negligence[814] receives payment for a customer of a cheque,[815] or, having credited a customer's account with the amount of a cheque, receives payment thereof for himself, and the customer has no title, or a defective title, to the cheque, the banker does not incur any liability to the true owner of the cheque by reason only of having received payment thereof. This provision extends to uncrossed cheques the protection previously afforded to bankers in respect of crossed cheques.[816] It seems **9-130**

---

at 502; *Greenway v Fisher* (1824) 1 C. & P. 190 at 192.

[806] *Turner v Hockey* (1887) 56 L.J.Q.B. 301, as explained in *Barker v Furlong*, above, and *Consolidated Co v Curtis & Son*, above; *Cochrane v Rymill* (1879) 40 L.T. 744 at 746. *Turner v Hockey* was, however, doubted by the Court of Appeal in *R.H. Willis & Son v British Car Auctions Ltd* [1978] 1 W.L.R. 438.

[807] *Hollins v Fowler* (1875) L.R. 7 H.L. 757 at 766–767.

[808] *Union Credit Bank v Mersey Docks & Harbour Board* [1899] 2 Q.B. 205 at 216; *Barker v Furlong*, above, at 182 (carriers and packing agents "merely purport to change the position of the goods and not the property in them"). And see *Greenway v Fisher* (1824) 1 C. & P. 190 (packer).

[809] *Re Samuel (No.2)* [1945] Ch. 408, Illustration 8.

[810] *Union Credit Bank v Mersey Docks & Harbour Board*, above; *Marcq v Christie, Manson and Woods* [2004] EWCA Civ 731; [2004] Q.B. 286, Illustration 7. cf. Illustration 5.

[811] *National Mercantile Bank v Rymill* (1881) 44 L.T. 767, Illustration 6; queried by Salmond and Heuston, *Torts* (21st edn), p.109, in view of the opinion of Blackburn J in *Hollins v Fowler*, above and *Stephens v Elwall* (1815) 4 M. & S. 259. The case was approved in *Consolidated Co v Curtis & Son* [1892] 1 Q.B. 495, where it was pointed out at 501 that the decision is "a long step in the direction which Brett J invited the House of Lords to take in *Hollins v Fowler*" but doubted by the Court of Appeal in *R.H. Willis & Son v British Car Auctions Ltd* [1978] 1 W.L.R. 438. But see *Marcq v Christie, Manson and Woods*, above. See also *Wilson v New Brighton Panelbeaters* [1989] 1 N.Z.L.R. 74.

[812] See, e.g. below, para.9-139.

[813] *Arnold v Cheque Bank* (1876) 1 C.P.D. 578.

[814] On good faith, see Bills of Exchange Act 1882 s.90. On negligence, see Cheques Act 1957 s.4(3); *Thackwell v Barclays Bank Plc* [1986] 1 All E.R. 676. See in general Byles, *Bills of Exchange* (29th edn), Ch.22; Chalmers and Guest, *Bills of Exchange* (17th edn), para.17-002 onwards; Paget, *Law of Banking* (14th edn), para.27-11.

[815] The protection is not in fact limited to cheques, but applies to certain other instruments: see Cheques Act 1957 s.4(2) as amended.

[816] Bills of Exchange Act 1882 s.82, as amended by Bills of Exchange (Crossed Cheques) Act 1906, both repealed by Cheques Act 1957.

possible that the Law Reform (Contributory Negligence) Act 1945 may apply in this context,[817] though it is not applicable to the tort of conversion.[818]

Illustrations

9-131   (1)   An auctioneer was instructed to sell by auction furniture which the possessor and apparent owner had assigned by bill of sale to a third person. The auctioneer, who had no notice of the assignment, sold the furniture at the residence of the assignor, and, in the ordinary course of business, delivered it to the purchaser. Held, that the auctioneer was liable to the assignee for the value of the furniture.[819]

(2)   A obtained certain goods by fraud. B, a broker, bought the goods in his own name from A, thinking that they would suit C, a customer of his. B, having sold the goods to C at the same price at which he had bought them from A, merely charging the usual commission, took delivery and conveyed the goods to the railway station, whence they were conveyed to C. The jury found that B bought the goods merely as an agent, in the ordinary course of his business. Held, that B was liable to the true owner for the value of the goods.[820]

(3)   A hired cabs from B, and obtained advances on them from an auctioneer. The auctioneer, on A's instructions, and without notice of B's title, in good faith sold the cabs, and after deducting the advances and his expenses, paid the proceeds to A. Held, that the auctioneer was liable to B for the value of the cabs, having had control of them, and having sold them in such a way as to pass the property in them. It would be otherwise, if he had not possession or control of the cabs, and had merely contracted to sell, without delivering them.[821]

(4)   An insurance broker effected a policy on behalf of A. A became bankrupt, and after the adjudication instructed the broker to collect money due under the policy and pay it to him. The broker, without notice of the bankruptcy, collected the money and paid it to A. Held, that the broker was liable to the trustee in bankruptcy for the amount.[822]

(5)   A husband entrusted goods, which were the property of his wife, to an auctioneer for sale. The auctioneer received notice of the wife's claim, but nevertheless subsequently sold a portion of the goods, and permitted the husband to remove the remainder. Held, that the auctioneer was liable to the wife for the value of the goods removed by the husband, as well as of those which had been sold.[823]

(6)   An auctioneer receives goods for sale from one who has not title to them. The

---

[817] *Lumsden & Co v London Trustee Savings Bank* [1971] 1 Lloyd's Rep. 114.

[818] Torts (Interference with Goods) Act 1977 s.11(1).

[819] *Consolidated Co v Curtis & Son* [1892] 1 Q.B. 405; *Barker v Furlong* [1891] 2 Ch. 172; *Brown v Hickinbotham* (1881) 50 L.J.Q.B. 426.

[820] *Hollins v Fowler* (1872) L.R. 7 Q.B. 616; affd L.R. 7 H.L. 757; *Union Transport Finance Ltd v British Car Auctions Ltd* [1978] 2 All E.R. 385; *R.H. Willis & Son v British Car Auctions Ltd* [1978] 1 W.L.R. 438 (where a "provisional bid" procedure was used).

[821] *Cochrane v Rymill* (1879) 40 L.T. 744.

[822] *McEntire v Potter & Co* (1889) 22 Q.B.D. 438.

[823] *Davis v Artingstall* (1880) 49 L.J.Ch. 609. See also *Winter v Bancks* (1901) 84 L.T. 504.

goods are offered at public auction but not sold. They are returned to the person who sent them. The auctioneer is not liable in conversion.[824]

(7) A held a bill of sale over horses in the possession of B. B took the horses to C's repository for sale by auction, and they were entered in the catalogue for sale. Before the sale took place, B sold the horses by private contract in C's yard. The price was paid to C, who deducted his commission and charges, and handed the balance to B, and the horses, on B's instructions, were delivered by C to the purchaser. Held, that C, having merely delivered the horses according to B's orders, and not having himself sold or otherwise assumed to deal with the property in them, was not guilty of a conversion.[825]

(8) An agent in possession of goods by the authority of his principal, on demand by the true owner refuses to deliver them up without an order from the principal, or requires a reasonable time to ascertain whether the person demanding the goods is the true owner. Such a qualified refusal is not a conversion. It is otherwise, where the refusal is absolute, or amounts to a setting-up of the principal's title to the goods.[826]

(9) The solicitor of a bankrupt receives after-acquired property on behalf of his client and on his client's instruction transfers it to another agent, knowing that that agent has been instructed to sell it and use the proceeds to educate the bankrupt's son. The solicitor is not liable in conversion.[827]

Article 115

AGENT NOT LIABLE FOR WRONGS OF CO-AGENTS OR SUB-AGENTS WORKING FOR PRINCIPAL

An agent is not liable as such to any third person for loss or injury caused by the wrongful act or omission of a co-agent not being a partner, or of a sub-agent in privity of contract with the principal, unless he authorised or was otherwise party or privy to such wrongful act or omission.[828]   **9-132**

Comment

The relationship of employer and employee or of principal and agent does not exist between co-agents: therefore an agent is not, as such, liable to third parties for wrongs committed by co-agents acting as such.[829] This applies as much to company directors as others. Nor is an agent liable for a sub-agent whom he appointed to act for the principal, creating privity of contract between them[830]: indeed such a sub-agent might, but for the fact that he often holds a position of lower status than the   **9-133**

---

[824] *Marcq v Christie, Manson and Woods* [2003] EWCA Civ 731; [2004] Q.B. 286.
[825] *National Mercantile Bank v Rymill* (1881) 44 L.T. 767. But this case was doubted by the Court of Appeal in *R.H. Willis & Son v British Car Auctions Ltd* [1978] 1 W.L.R. 438. See Clerk and Lindsell, *Torts* (21st edn), para.17-74 onwards.
[826] *Alexander v Southey* (1821) 5 B. & A. 247; *Wilson v Anderton* (1830) 1 B. & Ad. 450; *Lee v Bayes and Robinson* (1856) 18 C.B. 599; *Pillott v Wilkinson* (1864) 3 H. & C. 345.
[827] *Re Samuel (No.2)* [1945] Ch. 408.
[828] See Comment.
[829] *Cargill v Bower* (1878) 10 Ch.D. 502; *Re Denham & Co* (1883) 25 Ch.D. 752; cf. *Dovey v Cory* [1901] A.C. 477 (cases on directors).
[830] See Ch.5.

appointing agent, be called a co-agent. Thus in *Stone v Cartwright*[831] the manager of a colliery was held not liable for the negligence of a colliery employee. But an agent could be liable in accordance with normal principles for the wrongs of a sub-agent whom he himself employs, and who has privity of contract with him alone.[832] And the agent is of course liable for his own personal negligence; delegation to another agent may be evidence of such negligence.[833]

4. EQUITY

Article 116

ACCESSORY LIABILITY TO BREACH OF TRUST OR FIDUCIARY OBLIGATION AND KNOWING RECEIPT OF PROPERTY SUBJECT TO TRUST OR FIDUCIARY OBLIGATION

9-134   (1)   Where an agent dishonestly procures or assists in a breach of trust or fiduciary obligation by his principal he is liable to account to the beneficiary or beneficiaries of the trust or fiduciary obligation to restore the assets, the loss of which he has caused.

(2)   Where an agent receives money or property for his own benefit and (perhaps) with knowledge that it is subject to a trust or fiduciary obligation and that it has been transferred to him in breach of such obligation, or discovers this after it has been transferred to him, he is liable to account for that money or property to the person for whom the property is held in trust or to whom the fiduciary obligation is owed.

(3)   Where an agent lawfully holds money or property which he knows to be subject to a trust or fiduciary obligation, and deals with that money or property in a manner inconsistent with that trust or fiduciary obligation, he is liable to the person for whom the property is held in trust or to whom the obligation is owed.

(4)   But an agent who has no knowledge that a breach of trust or fiduciary obligation has been or is being committed is not liable merely because he acts as agent in a transaction which constitutes or involves such a breach.[834]

Comment

9-135   **Rule (1): Accessory liability in respect of breach of trust**[835]   This area of equity, and that of "knowing receipt" which follows, are not part of the law of agency as such, but involve situations in which agents (particularly solicitors, banks, and directors of companies) are likely to become involved. This liability, often referred to as "knowing" or "dishonest assistance", first emerged in connection with trusts, and its components became established during the nineteenth century. Its greater

---

[831]   (1795) 6 T.R. 411. See also *Bear v Stevenson* (1874) 30 L.T. 177; *Weir v Bell* (1878) 3 Ex.D. 238 (directors not liable for torts committed by persons working for the company).

[832]   This is the more normal position of a sub-agent: see Article 35.

[833]   See *Re City Equitable Fire Insurance Co* [1925] Ch. 407; cf. *Dovey v Cory* [1901] A.C. 477 and Article 35.

[834]   See Comment.

[835]   For full discussion see Lewin, *Trusts* (19th edn), para.40-014 onwards; *Snell's Equity* (33rd edn), para.30-687; Davies, *Accessory Liability* (2015); Dietrich and Ridge, *Accessories in Private Law* (2015). As to issues of limitation affecting both the action for dishonest assistance, and that for knowing receipt, see *Williams v Central Bank of Nigeria* [2014] UKSC 10; [2014] A.C. 1189.

significance at the present time is in relation to funds impressed with a fiduciary obligation. Such situations can arise in the agency context (in the broad sense), though they are of course not confined to that context. The action for dishonest assistance is also frequently pursued against directors of companies who cause the company to breach fiduciary duties owed by it to the claimant or who involve themselves, through their company, in breaches of fiduciary duty owed by others to the claimant.[836] In such cases, the subject of the litigation may not be money but property (or a "corporate opportunity") that has been wrongly diverted away from the claimant to other parties.[837]

To be liable under this head the agent must have contributed in a material way to the commission by his principal of a breach of his trust or fiduciary[838] obligations: a mere receipt of assets will not suffice, nor is a mere failure to act (at least unless the agent is a manager who knows that colleagues and subordinates are operating dishonestly).[839] The action is also not available where the principal's conduct does not involve a breach of fiduciary duty.[840] It is not necessary that there should be a trust in the formal sense: it is sufficient if there is a fiduciary relationship in relation to another's property,[841] but it must have arisen before the acts complained of.[842] In acting, the agent must have appreciated that he was assisting in such breach.[843] Generally, however, no appreciation of the full nature of the obligation, nor of the details of the breach is required.[844] It seems also that liability can be incurred without there having been a diversion or illegitimate manipulation of a fund or other distinct item of property subject to a fiduciary obligation.[845] It may even be that acts done which assist in the breach of the equitable wrong of breach of confidence are actionable under this head, though no fiduciary obligation is involved at all.[846] What may in fact be emerging from the cases is a form of accessory liability for assistance in connection with equitable wrongdoing more generally, a liability which

---

[836] See, e.g. *JD Wetherspoon Plc v Van De Berg & Co Ltd* [2009] EWHC 639 (Ch), Illustration 7; *Law Society of England and Wales v Habitable Concepts Ltd* [2010] EWHC 1449 (Ch).

[837] See, e.g. *Satnam Investments Ltd v Dunlop Heywood & Co Ltd* [1999] 3 All E.R. 652.

[838] Where the obligation is a common law one this reasoning would not apply: see *Bristol and West BS v Mothew* [1998] Ch. 1 at 16 onwards.

[839] *Baden Delvaux v Société Générale, etc., SA* (1983) [1993] 1 W.L.R. 509 at 574–575; *Gregson v HAE Trustees Ltd* [2008] EWHC 1006 (Ch); [2008] 2 B.C.L.C. 542; [2009] 1 All E.R. (Comm) 457. cf. *Otkritie International Investment Management Ltd v Urumov* [2014] EWHC 191 (Comm); [2014] 1 W.L.R. 748 at [455].

[840] *Fitzalan-Howard (Norfolk) v Hibbert* [2009] EWHC 2855 (QB); [2010] P.N.L.R. 11(manager not liable for dishonest assistance merely for failing to procure his employing company to repay a simple mistaken payment received by it).

[841] *Baden Delvaux*, above, at 573.

[842] *Goose v Wilson Sandford & Co* [2001] Lloyd's Rep. P.N. 189.

[843] See *Bank of America v Arnell* [1999] Lloyd's Rep. Bank 399 at 406–407 (actually a knowing receipt case, but the two types of case remain very intertwined on such points: see Lewin, *Trusts* (19th edn), para.40-49); *Alpstream AG v PK Airfinance Sarl* [2013] EWHC 2370 (Comm).

[844] *Barlow Clowes International Ltd v Eurotrust International Ltd* [2005] UKPC 37; [2006] 1 W.L.R. 1476: see also *Agip (Africa) Ltd v Jackson* [1990] Ch. 265 at 293–294 (but the defendant did not call evidence); *Att.-Gen. of Zambia v Meer Care & Desai (a firm)* [2007] EWHC 952 (Ch) at [340].

[845] See *Banque National de Paris v Credit Agricole Indosuez* [2001] 1 Singapore L.R. 300 at 331–339; in England the matter is certainly arguable: see *Brown v Bennett* [1999] 1 B.C.L.C. 649 at 658–659; *Gencor ACP Ltd v Dalby* [2000] 2 B.C.L.C. 734; Lewin, *Trusts* (19th edn), para.40-027. If the proposition is correct, this reasoning might apply in the context of bribery: see *Petrotrade Inc v Smith* [2000] 1 Lloyd's Rep. 486; Mitchell (2001) 117 L.Q.R. 207; above, para.8-222.

[846] See *Thomas v Pearce* [2000] F.S.R. 718. But see Lewin, above, para.40-012.

would run parallel and analogous to, while not based on, accessory liability to common law wrongs, as in the tort of interference with contract.[847]

The liability was reshaped in the advice of the Privy Council delivered by Lord Nicholls of Birkenhead in *Royal Brunei Airlines Sdn Bhd v Tan*,[848] from which case the phrases "accessory liability" and "dishonest assistance" emanate. Until that time the liability normally went under the name of "knowing assistance" and it was thought that the state of mind of the fiduciary was relevant as well as that of the accessory.[849] But Lord Nicholls indicated that it was only the state of mind of the accessory that was crucial, and it is highly probable that this has been accepted into English law. As to the state of mind required of the accessory (agent), Lord Nicholls indicated that what was required was "objective dishonesty".[850] This has not proved an easy criterion to apply, however, and appeared subsequently to have been interpreted in the House of Lords as prescribing that a defendant was not dishonest unless he appreciated that what he was doing would be regarded by honest men as dishonest,[851] which introduced a subjective element. However, it has recently been explained in the Privy Council that the passage in question:

"meant only that his knowledge of the transaction had to be such as to render his participation contrary to normally acceptable standards of honest conduct. It did not require that he should have had reflections about what those normally acceptable standards were."[852]

The person concerned need not have been consciously dishonest: it is likely to be sufficient for liability that he had solid grounds for suspicion which he consciously ignored.[853] Nor was it necessary that he knew the full details of the wrongdoing:

"someone can know, and can certainly suspect, that he is assisting in a misappropriation without knowing that the money was held on trust or what a trust means."[854]

The application of these dicta make it easier to fix the dishonest with liability, but

---

[847] See *Royal Brunei Airlines Sdn Bhd v Tan* [1995] 2 A.C. 378 at 386–387; *Markel International Insurance Co Ltd v Surety Guarantee Consultants Ltd* [2008] EWHC 1135 (Comm); affd [2009] EWCA Civ 790.

[848] Above. See criticism of the decision by Berg (1996) 59 M.L.R. 443 and Birks [1996] L.M.C.L.Q. 1; cf. Harpum (1995) 111 L.Q.R. 545.

[849] At 384 onwards. Where the defaulting fiduciary is honest, and he is also the only agent of a putative assisting party, then no liability in that party can arise since there will be no dishonesty: *Roadchef (Employee Benefits Trustees) Ltd v Hill* [2014] EWHC 109 (Ch).

[850] At 389–390. It is not necessary, it seems, to show that all reasonable people would regard the relevant conduct as dishonest: *Starglade Properties Ltd v Nash* [2010] EWCA Civ 1314 at [32] (it is "irrelevant that there may be a body of opinion which regards the ordinary standard of honest behaviour as being set too high").

[851] See *Twinsectra Ltd v Yardley* [2002] UKHL 12; [2002] 2 A.C. 164 at [35], per Lord Hutton.

[852] *Barlow Clowes International Ltd v Eurotrust Ltd* [2005] UKPC 37; [2006] 1 All E.R. 333 at [15], per Lord Hoffmann; see Yeo (2006) 122 L.Q.R. 171. See also *US International Marketing Ltd v National Bank of New Zealand Ltd* [2004] 1 N.Z.L.R. 589; *Central Bank of Ecuador v Conticorp SA* [2015] UKPC 11; [2016] 1 B.C.L.C. 26 at [9].

[853] Lord Hoffmann's views, though expressed in an opinion of the Privy Council, are applied as representing English law in *Abou-Rahmah v Abacha* [2006] EWCA Civ 1492; [2007] 1 All E.R. (Comm) 827; [2007] 1 Lloyd's Rep. 115, where a claimant in a knowing assistance claim was however unable to show that a bank employee had a clear enough suspicion that transactions with which he was engaged were wrongful. See also *City Index Ltd v Gawler* [2007] EWCA Civ 1382; [2008] 3 All E.R. 126; [2008] 2 All E.R. (Comm) 425; [2008] Ch. 213; *Att.-Gen. of Zambia v Meer Care & Desai (a firm)* [2008] EWCA Civ 1007 at [21].

[854] *Barlow Clowes International Ltd v Eurotrust International Ltd* [2005] UKPC 37; [2006] 1 W.L.R. 1476 at [28], per Lord Hoffmann; see also at [20].

may create difficulties for professionals who handle money. Such are the problems of formulating objective standards in equity. It is at least clear that a defendant who can show that he was duped or merely naïve will escape liability.[855]

The remedy available to a successful claimant, while sometimes said to treat him as a constructive trustee, is in fact an in personam one for compensation in monetary terms. This category of constructive trusteeship:

"is nothing more than a formula for equitable relief. The court is saying that the defendant shall be liable in equity as though he were a trustee".[856]

It is calculated by reference to equity's willingness to restore fully funds that can be shown to have suffered a loss by reason of the breach. This could perhaps include profits made by the wrongdoer.[857] Contributory negligence should not be relevant.[858] Where there are several wrongdoers, each is liable for the full loss, subject to the requirements of contribution inter se under the Civil Liability (Contribution) Act 1978,[859] which need not take account of the relative gravity of fault but may be affected by the continuing existence of the profit in the hands of some parties.[860] It seems possible that the reasoning of the leading House of Lords decision on equitable compensation for breach of trust, *Target Holdings Ltd v Redferns*,[861] will provide a guide. Despite this more generous measure than the common law provides, however, it would seem that the liability has totally outgrown its origin in the law of trusts. It bears little or no resemblance to a constructive trust as regards the requirements for liability or the remedy available for breach. Even Lord Nicholls in his judgment in the Privy Council spoke of the liability as involving a "duty of care".[862] The relationship of this liability to the tort of interference with contract remains open to argument and possibly development.[863]

---

[855] See *Brinks Ltd v Abu-Saleh (No.3)* [1996] C.L.C. 133 (accompanying husband on money laundering trips to Zurich did not create liability). The onus of proving both breach of trust and dishonesty lies with the claimant: *Attorney General of Zambia v Meer Care & Desai (a firm)* [2008] EWCA Civ 1007 at [147] and [256].

[856] *Selangor United Rubber Estates Ltd v Cradock (No.3)* [1968] 1 W.L.R. 1555 at 1582, per Ungoed-Thomas J; see further *Dubai Aluminium Co Ltd v Salaam* [2002] UKHL 48; [2003] 2 A.C. 366 at [140]–[142], per Lord Millett. And see Lewin, *Trusts* (19th edn), paras 40-014 and 40-053. For limitation issues applicable to claims against accessories to a breach of trust or fiduciary obligation, see *Williams v Central Bank of Nigeria* [2014] UKSC 10; [2014] A.C. 1189. See too *Halton International Inc v Guernroy Ltd* [2006] EWCA Civ 801.

[857] See Article 96; *Fyffes Group Ltd v Templeman* [2000] 2 Lloyd's Rep. 643 (bribes: see above, para.8-222); *Ultraframe (UK) Ltd v Fielding* [2005] EWHC 1638 (QB) at [1594]; *Novoship (UK) Ltd v Nikitin* [2014] EWCA Civ 908; [2015] 1 Q.B. 499 at [84], noted Davies (2015) 131 L.Q.R. 173, Gummow [2015] C.L.J. 405; *Central Bank of Ecuador v Conticorp SA* [2015] UKPC 11; [2016] 1 B.C.L.C. 26 addendum at [9]. But cf. *Royal Brunei Airlines Sdn Bhd v Tan* [1995] 2 A.C. 378 at 386 (accessory liability not restitution based). See further, para.8-225.

[858] See *Corporacion Nacional del Cobre de Chile v Sogemin Metals Ltd* [1997] 1 W.L.R. 1396; *Standard Chartered Bank v Pakistan National Shipping Corp (No.2)* [2002] UKHL 43; [2003] 1 A.C. 959.

[859] See above, para.8-191.

[860] *Dubai Aluminium Co Ltd v Salaam* [2002] UKHL 48; [2003] 2 A.C. 366. It has been held that there is no necessary inconsistency between a party's being liable in knowing receipt of a claimant's funds and that party having a right of contribution under the Civil Liability (Contribution) Act 1978 against the agents (including directors) of the claimant who caused the misapplication of the funds. The court, however, left open the issue whether the liability would be for the "same damage" within s.1(1): *City Index Ltd v Gawler* [2007] EWCA Civ 1382; [2008] 3 All E.R. 126.

[861] [1996] A.C. 421. See above, para.6-043.

[862] [1995] 2 A.C. at 391–339.

[863] In *Metall und Rohstoff AG v Donaldson Lufkin & Jenrette Inc* [1990] 1 Q.B. 391 at 481 the Court

9-136   **Rule (2): Receipt of trust property**[864]   Traditionally linked with what was formerly called "knowing assistance" is the liability that can be imposed upon a person who (on the orthodox formulation) knowingly receives trust property, or having received it unknowingly becomes aware that it is trust property and that it has been transferred in breach of duty. This liability is plainly less likely to be applicable to agents as such and it is mentioned here largely for completeness. It is more likely to be applied to principals, but its historic pairing with dishonest assistance liability makes this a convenient place to offer a brief treatment of the key issues that arise.

Liability arises from receipt alone and requires no acts of assistance of another performed by the receiver: but it is confined to beneficial receipt. It, therefore, does not apply to receipt as a mere conduit.[865] On the other hand, it has been held as a matter of the application of limitation provisions that receipt by a company which the fraudulent agent controls can be treated as receipt by the agent.[866]

The basis of such liability has long been and remains controversial. Formerly, consistent with normal equity terminology, especially as applicable to property interests, it was often said to be based on notice. The word "knowledge" might more properly be employed. In *Baden Delvaux v Société Générale, etc., SA*[867] Peter Gibson J formulated the possible degrees of knowledge for the purposes of the operation of equity as follows:

> "(i) Actual knowledge; (ii) wilfully shutting one's eyes to the obvious; (iii) wilfully and recklessly failing to make such inquiries as an honest and reasonable man would make; (iv) knowledge of circumstances which would indicate the facts to an honest and reasonable man; (v) knowledge of circumstances which would put an honest and reasonable man on inquiry."

The meticulous discriminations of this passage have been criticised,[868] and it is not always easy to know which part to apply in a particular fact situation. It is also true that the passage occurs in a judgment on *accessory* liability (formerly knowing assistance), a part of the law that is, as stated above, now separating itself off; and that in the *Royal Brunei* case Lord Nicholls said that in the context of that liability "the *Baden* scale is best forgotten".[869] It remains nevertheless useful, here and elsewhere[870] as a starting point which draws attention to the problems likely to be encountered. On this basis it is clear that the constructive notice of conveyancers,

---

of Appeal rejected the existence of a tort of procuring a breach of trust. See however the Rt Hon. Lord Hoffmann in *The Frontiers of Liability* (Birks ed., 1994), Vol.1, p.28. A claim under this head was held to lie in "tort, delict or quasi-delict" for the purposes of art.5(3) of the Brussels Convention on Jurisdiction and the Enforcement of Judgments in *Casio Computer Co Ltd v Sayo* [2001] EWCA Civ 661; [2001] I.L.Pr. 43; see also *Grupo Torras SA v Al Sabbah (No.5)* [2001] Lloyd's Rep. Bank 36. cf. *OBG Ltd v Allan* [2007] UKHL 21; [2008] 1 A.C. 1 at [192] and [202].

[864] For full discussion see Lewin, *Trusts* (19th edn), para.42-022 onwards; Snell.

[865] See, e.g. *Heperu Pty Ltd v Belle* (2009) 258 A.L.R. 727 (very brief receipt into joint account without knowledge does not lead to liability). For other cases, see commentary and illustrations to Article 92.

[866] *Burnden Holdings (UK) Ltd v Fielding* [2016] EWCA Civ 557; [2017] 1 W.L.R. 39.

[867] [1993] 1 W.L.R. 509 at 575–576.

[868] Jacobs, *Law of Trusts in Australia* (7th edn, Heydon and Leeming eds), para.1335; *Agip (Africa) Ltd v Jackson* [1990] Ch. 265 at 293.

[869] [1995] 2 A.C. at 762.

[870] See, e.g. Article 73. See too *Farah Constructions Pty Ltd v Say-Dee Pty Ltd* [2007] HCA 22; (2007) 230 C.L.R. 89 at [175]; *Armstrong DLW GmbH v Winnington Networks Ltd* [2012] EWHC 10 (Ch); [2013] Ch. 156.

whereby a person is deemed to have notice of property interests in respect of which he ought to have made inquiry, is not relevant.[871] It has then been said that the approach should be to ask whether the conscience of the recipient is affected, which will involve looking for knowledge or appreciation of relevant circumstances—category (iv), running in appropriate contexts into (v) on the *Baden* scale,[872] both of which are addressed to facts rather than adverse property interests (to which the first three are more appropriate). Subsequently, it was said that:

> "It may well be that the underlying broad principle which runs through the authorities regarding commercial transactions is that the court will impute knowledge, on the basis of what a reasonable person would have learnt, to a person who is guilty of commercially unacceptable conduct in the particular context involved."[873]

More recently it has been held in the Court of Appeal that, in contrast to accessory liability, where "dishonest assistance" is required, there is in this context no requirement of dishonesty.[874] In the case in question a more general formulation is adopted, the single test is simply that "the recipient's state of knowledge must be such as to make it unconscionable to retain the benefit of the receipt".[875]

Most of the modern cases have involved breaches of duty by agents, rather than trustees in the strict sense. In such circumstances, if the recipient cannot establish that the agent had apparent authority liability will usually follow.[876] The position is more complex where the breach is merely of an equitable duty; for some breaches, such as where the contract is affected by a mere conflict of interest, it may be necessary for the claimant to be able to rescind the contract with the recipient before any liability arises.[877] The property must be subject to an equitable interest in the claimant's favour at the moment of receipt. The measure of liability is sometimes described as that of a constructive trustee,[878] but again the action is in effect in personam for the replacement of the value lost, even if the receiver has paid it away. It is therefore not clear whether it should include profits made from the property.

Knowing receipt liability is usually treated as distinct from tracing in equity, where knowledge of the trust interest is not required, profits may be recoverable,[879] but liability ceases when the property is transmitted away, lying against the

---

[871] *Re Montagu's ST* [1987] Ch. 264 at 285.

[872] *Re Montagu's ST* [1987] Ch. 264 at 285.

[873] *Cowan de Groot Properties Ltd v Eagle Trust Plc* [1992] 4 All E.R. 700 at 761, per Knox J, on knowing receipt, but approved also in the *Royal Brunei* case, [1995] 2 A.C. at 390.

[874] *BCCI (Overseas) Ltd v Akindele* [2001] Ch. 437; *Uzinterimpex JSC v Standard Bank Plc* [2008] EWCA Civ 819; [2008] 2 Lloyd's Rep. 456; *Despot v Registrar-General of NSW* [2013] NSWCA 313.

[875] At 439, per Nourse LJ. On this basis, perhaps not only the awareness issue in dishonest assistance resembles a jury question, as Millett J perceived at first instance in *Agip (Africa) Ltd v Jackson* [1990] Ch. 265, but the receipt issue also. cf. the Rt Hon. Lord Walker (2005) 27 Sydney L.Rev. 187. On the other hand, it is arguable that *Akindele* gave insufficient weight to the test of constructive knowledge favoured in *Belmont Finance Corp v Williams Furniture Ltd (No.2)* [1980] 1 All E.R. 393 at 404 and 412. See too *Credit Agricole Corp and Investment Bank v Papadimitriou* [2015] UKPC 13; [2015] 1 W.L.R. 4265 at [16] and [33] (noted Watts (2015) 131 L.Q.R. 511).

[876] *Thanakharn Kasikorn Thai Chamchat v Akai Holdings Ltd (In Liquidation)* (2010) 13 HKCFAR 479 at [136]. See Conaglen and Nolan (2013) 129 L.Q.R. 359.

[877] See further above, paras 8-219–8-221.

[878] See the *Akai Holdings* case, above, at [156].

[879] As to recovery of profits against a party receiving money in breach of trust, see *Akita Holdings Ltd*

new holder, subject always to the defence of bona fide purchase for value without notice, or in some circumstances, change of position.[880] The formulations above do no more than escape the old generalised concept of notice in equity and require in this context something which affects the conscience of the receiver.[881] A second possibility is however that the similarity with accessory liability should be abandoned, and the duty analysed as a strict one, based squarely on no more than receipt. If this is correct, the receiver is liable unless he can plead the defence of change of position or bona fide purchase[882]; and the burden of proof is reversed.[883] This would involve a development in equity which could be seen as paralleling or assimilating to current developments in restitutionary liability, and be in some ways parallel to the tort of conversion. As such it has authoritative extra-judicial support.[884] There is also some support for it in the *Royal Brunei* case referred to above,[885] and this approach has the advantage of avoiding the difficult questions of proof which arise under any of the tests for knowledge (and indeed notice) so far discussed. But the decision of the English Court of Appeal referred to above casts doubt on the possibility,[886] and it has been rejected by the High Court of Australia.[887]

9-137   **Rule (3): Inconsistent dealing by agent**[888]   A further group of cases, much more relevant to agency, holds an agent who lawfully, but not for his own benefit, holds property which he knows to be impressed with a trust or fiduciary interest, liable if without the authority of the trustees he deals with it inconsistently with the trust.[889] This is not a "knowing receipt" situation, for the receipt does not generate liability: it is rather the dealing which does so. In such cases the liability is not based on dishonesty (though this may exist), but rather on the inconsistent dealing following the lawful receipt and knowledge of the trust; and since the holder received the property lawfully he appears to be a genuine constructive trustee rather than one of the sort created by the previous two categories.[890]

---

v *Attorney General of the Turks and Caicos Islands* [2017] UKPC 7; [2017] A.C. 590.

[880] See *Credit Agricole Corp and Investment Bank v Papadimitriou* [2015] UKPC 13; *Heperu Pty Ltd v Belle* (2009) 258 A.L.R. 727.

[881] *Re Montagu's S.T.* [1987] Ch. 264 at 285; *Cowan de Groot Properties Ltd v Eagle Trust Plc* [1992] 4 All E.R. 700; *Eagle Trust Plc v SBC Securities Ltd* [1993] 1 W.L.R. 484; *Eagle Trust Plc v SBC Securities Ltd (No.2)* [1996] 1 B.C.L.C. 121. But cf. the Rt Hon. Lord Millett (1991) 107 L.Q.R. 71 at 78 ("profoundly mistaken").

[882] As established in *Lipkin Gorman v Karpnale Ltd* [1991] 2 A.C. 548: see Goff and Jones, *Law of Unjust Enrichment* (9th edn), Ch.27.

[883] See *Credit Agricole Corp and Investment Bank v Papadimitriou*, above; and Harpum in *Frontiers of Liability* (Birks edn, 1994), Vol.1, Ch.1.

[884] See Birks, *Introduction to the Law of Restitution* (1985), p.439 onwards; the Rt Hon. Lord Millett (1991) 107 L.Q.R. 71; the Rt Hon. Lord Nicholls in *Restitution Past, Present and Future* (Cornish ed., 1998), Ch.15; Birks in *Breach of Trust* (Birks and Pretto eds, 2002), Ch.7.

[885] See esp. [1995] 2 A.C. at 386 ("recipient liability is restitution based"), 387 ("strict liability"); *El Ajou v Dollar Land Holdings Plc* [1994] 2 All E.R. 685.

[886] *BCCI (Overseas) Ltd v Akindele* [2001] Ch. 437 at 455, per Nourse LJ. See also *Citadel General Assurance Co v Lloyd's Bank Canada* [1997] 3 S.C.R. 805; (1997) 152 D.L.R. (4th) 411, noted by L.D. Smith (1998) 114 L.Q.R. 394 ("equity's conversion"); L.D. Smith (2000) 116 L.Q.R. 412.

[887] *Farah Constructions Pty Ltd v Say-Dee Pty Ltd* (2007) 236 C.L.R. 89 (noted by Ridge and Dietrich (2008) 124 L.Q.R. 26).

[888] See Lewin, *Trusts* (19th edn), para.42-111 onwards.

[889] e.g. *Lee v Sankey* (1873) L.R. 15 Eq. 204; *Purrunsing v A'Court & Co (a firm)* [2016] EWHC 789 (Ch); and see Illustrations below.

[890] See Lewin, above, paras 7-017 and 44-061 onwards.

Trustee de son tort[891]   Similar to, but not the same as, the above, an agent may   **9-138**
also incur liability as trustee *de son tort* by assuming to act as trustee when he is
not. Thus an agent who holds trust money for trustees, and administers and takes
decisions as to what is to be done with it without reference to them could become
liable to account under this head as if an express trustee. Although technically a
constructive trustee, as a trustee *de son tort* he is in a very similar position to that
of a trustee duly appointed.[892] In general however an agent for trustees holds for and
is accountable to the trustees only.[893]

Rule (4): Agent performs ministerial functions only   An argument can also be   **9-139**
made that, on the analogy of cases on innocent handling in the law of conversion,[894] an agent who acts only ministerially and does no more than carry out
instructions cannot be liable at all.[895] Though such a proposition must be correct in
principle, the circumstances where it is actually needed to exclude the agent's liability are few. Accessory liability only exists in cases where the agent is dishonest; knowing receipt liability operates only where he holds beneficially and thus not
ministerially. In inconsistent dealing cases, where the agent is free of liability the
reasoning that this is because he acts ministerially is rarely needed: the reasoning
simply constitutes a denial of the lack of authority or of the dealing. But it is true
that an agent acting on the instructions of trustees or fiduciaries is in general not
liable for mere inadvertence, or even (under the heads discussed above) for
negligence. For example, he is not liable to account if he pays over the trust money
to the trustee in circumstances in which he might suspect (but no more) that the
trustee will apply it inconsistently with the trust.[896] The adoption of strict liability
for what is now called "knowing receipt" would make a "ministerial function"
defence more significant, as it is in conversion.

Solicitors[897]   Some of these questions have arisen in connection with solicitors: a   **9-140**
solicitor may become a constructive trustee, e.g. by improperly applying trust
funds[898] or by paying such funds to one trustee only.[899] On the other hand a solicitor was held not liable when he invested trust funds, on the instructions of the
trustee, in unauthorised mortgages: he was acting as agent only.[900] Similar reason-

---

[891] See Lewin, above, para.42-101 onwards.
[892] See Lewin, above, para.7-017; *Dubai Aluminium Co Ltd v Salaam* [2002] UKHL 48; [2003] 2 A.C.
      366 at [132] onwards, per Lord Millett.
[893] *Bath v Standard Land Co Ltd* [1911] 1 Ch. 618; *Gregson v HAE Trustees Ltd* [2008] EWHC 1006
      (Ch); [2008] 2 B.C.L.C. 542; [2009] 1 All E.R. (Comm) 457.
[894] See Article 114.
[895] See in general Swadling, in *Laundering and Tracing* (Birks ed., 1995), p.243. See also above, para.8-
      199.
[896] *Adams v Bank of New South Wales* [1984] 1 N.S.W.L.R. 285 and other cases cited in Lewin, *Trusts*
      (19th edn), para.42-117.
[897] See Cordery, *Solicitors* (9th (looseleaf) edn), F[409] onwards.
[898] See *Att.-Gen. v Leicester Corp* (1844) 7 Beav. 176 (town clerk); *Morgan v Stephens* (1861) 3 Giff.
      226; *Hardy v Caley* (1864) 33 Beav. 365; *Blyth v Fladgate* [1891] 1 Ch. 337; *Soar v Ashwell* [1893]
      2 Q.B. 390, Illustration 5; *Cooper v Stoneham* (1893) 68 L.T. 18; *Purrunsing v A'Court & Co (a
      firm)* [2016] EWHC 789 (Ch). See also Illustration 3.
[899] *Lee v Sankey* (1873) L.R. 15 Eq. 204. As to the liability of the partner of such a solicitor, see *Re Bell's
      Indenture* [1980] 1 W.L.R. 1217; *Dubai Aluminium Co Ltd v Salaam* [2001] Q.B. 113.
[900] *Mara v Browne* [1896] 1 Ch. 199 as explained in *Williams-Ashman v Price and Williams* [1942] Ch.
      219 and *Dubai Aluminium Co Ltd v Salaam* [2002] UKHL 48; [2003] 2 A.C. 366 at [132], per Lord
      Millett; see also Illustration 3; Illustration 4.

ing applies to solicitors acting in connection with fiduciaries. But such cases may require reassessment in the light of the recent developments referred to above.

9-141   **Banks**[901]   The question has also arisen in connection with banks, who may become constructive trustees, for example by seeking to apply trust money to a fiduciary's personal overdraft,[902] transferring money deposited with them to the personal account of the trustee, honouring cheques drawn on trust accounts for improper purposes, or by facilitating an inadmissible transaction, such as where a company uses its money to purchase its own shares. Unless the account is overdrawn, they are not easily regarded as "receiving" money as agents for their customers; but they can of course be on risk for "accessory" liability.[903] The duties of bankers in such cases are difficult to define. They have an obligation to comply with their customers' instructions in relation to moneys in their customers' accounts.[904] On the other hand they have responsibilities to prevent misuse of trust funds, and evasion of statutory provisions, again such as those that prevent companies from buying their own shares.[905] They are often therefore the subject of conflicting duties.[906] Older dicta can be cited to the effect that a banker was not liable unless he was privy to the breach of trust,[907] or where an element of personal benefit was involved.[908] But other authority has placed a stricter duty on banks.[909]

Illustrations

9-142   (1) An agent of an executor applies a fund, which he knows to be part of the estate of the testator, in satisfaction of advances made to the executor for his own business. He is personally liable to account for the fund to the beneficiaries under the will.[910]

  (2) A director is passively involved in transactions arranged by a stranger who

---

[901] See Lewin, *Trusts* (19th edn), paras 40-050 and 42-085 onwards; Bryan, in *Restitution and Banking Law* (Rose ed., 1998) at 161; Mitchell, in *Commercial Law: Perspectives and Practice* (Lowry and Mistelis eds, 2006), Ch.6.
[902] cf. *Neste Oy v Lloyd's Bank Plc* [1983] 2 Lloyd's Rep. 658 at 666; approved in *Kingscroft Ins. Co Ltd v H.S. Weavers (Underwriting Agencies) Ltd* [1993] 1 Lloyd's Rep. 187 at 195.
[903] *Uzinterimpex JSC v Standard Bank Plc* [2008] EWCA Civ 819 (bank ceased to be agent when it had entitlement to ring-fence funds for its own benefit).
[904] *Baden Delvaux v Société Générale, etc., SA* (1983) [1993] 1 W.L.R. 509 at 585–586; affd [1985] B.C.L.C. 258; *US International Marketing Ltd v National Bank of New Zealand Ltd* [2004] 1 N.Z.L.R. 589 (NZCA) (bank not permitted to decline right of customer to withdraw funds simply on basis that a third party had informed the bank that it had claimed the funds and was intending to seek a court order freezing the moneys); *Westpac New Zealand Ltd v Map & Associates Ltd* [2011] 3 N.Z.L.R. 751 (NZSC).
[905] See Companies Act 2006 Pt. 18.
[906] *Gray v Johnston* (1868) L.R. 3 H.L. 1 at 11.
[907] *Gray v Johnston*, above.
[908] *Foxton v Manchester and Liverpool District Banking Co* (1881) 44 L.T. 406; cf. *Coleman v Bucks and Oxon Union Bank* [1897] 2 Ch. 243.
[909] See *Selangor United Rubber Estates Ltd v Cradock (No.3)* [1968] 1 W.L.R. 1555; *Karak Rubber Co Ltd v Burden (No.2)* [1972] 1 W.L.R. 602; *Belmont Finance Corp v Williams Furniture Ltd (No.2)* [1980] 1 All E.R. 393; (1981) 44 M.L.R. 107; *Baden Delvaux v Société Générale, etc., SA*, above (authorities reviewed); and in general cases cited at Illustration 6. See too *Nicholson v Morgan (No.3)* [2013] WASC 110.
[910] *Wilson v Moore* (1834) 1 Myl. & K. 126 and 337.

purchased the majority of the company's shares, whereby the company's money is used to finance the purchase. The director is liable.[911]

(3) A trustee allows his solicitor to retain costs out of the trust estate. The solicitor knows that the trustee has secretly bought for himself part of the trust estate. The solicitor is not a trustee of the sums received out of the estate.[912]

(4) A solicitor receives money from a client in respect of costs and expenses in defending an action under which a third party is claiming that the client is constructive trustee of all the client's assets. The solicitor is not liable as a constructive trustee.[913]

(5) The solicitor to a trust invests trust money mixed with moneys of other trusts, in an equitable mortgage. When the mortgage is redeemed he distributes half the proceeds to beneficiaries who have by that time become absolutely entitled to the same. He retains the other half, to which others are entitled. He holds the retained money on constructive trust.[914]

(6) A bank transfers trust money from a trust account to the personal account of the trustees or otherwise participates in a transfer of trust money in circumstances which would put a reasonable bank on inquiry as to the nature of the transaction being conducted. The bank is liable to the beneficiaries for the amount so transferred, whether it acquired a personal benefit from the transaction or not.[915]

(7) Directors of a company which is an agent to identify suitable public houses for acquisition by the claimant cause the company to breach its fiduciary duties to the claimant, inter alia, by procuring for the claimant leases only of a number of houses and suppressing the availability of freehold interests for them. The directors were held liable for dishonest assistance in their company's breaches of duty.[916]

---

[911] *Selangor United Rubber Estates Ltd v Cradock (No.3)*, above; see also *Belmont Finance Corp v Williams (No.2)*, above.

[912] *Re Blundell, Blundell v Blundell* (1888) 40 Ch.D. 370; *Williams v Williams* (1881) 17 Ch.D. 437; *Competitive Insurance Co Ltd v Davies Investments Ltd* [1975] 1 W.L.R. 1240 (liquidator); cf. *Blyth v Fladgate* [1891] 1 Ch. 337.

[913] *Carl Zeiss Stiftung v Herbert Smith & Co (No.2)* [1969] 2 Ch. 276.

[914] *Soar v Ashwell* [1893] 2 Q.B. 390. See also *Gathergood v Blundell & Brown Ltd* [1992] 3 N.Z.L.R. 643; *Nimmo v Westpac Banking Corp* [1993] 3 N.Z.L.R. 218.

[915] See *Baden Delvaux v Société Générale, etc., SA* [1993] 1 W.L.R. 509; *Selangor United Rubber Estates Ltd v Cradock (No.3)* [1968] 1 W.L.R. 1555; *Karak Rubber Co Ltd v Burden (No.2)* [1972] 1 W.L.R. 602; *Rowlandson v National Westminster Bank Ltd* [1978] 1 W.L.R. 798; *Barclays Bank Plc v Quincecare Ltd* (1988) [1992] 4 All E.R. 363. These cases concern accessory liability. As to knowing receipt, where liability will arise less often, see *Gray v Johnston* (1868) L.R. 3 H.L. 1; *Thomson v Clydesdale Bank* [1893] A.C. 282; *Coleman v Bucks and Oxon Union Bank* [1897] 2 Ch. 243; *Union Bank of Australia v Murray-Aynsley; Shields v Bank of Ireland* [1901] 1 I.R. 222; *Bank of New South Wales v Goulburn Valley Butter Co Pty Ltd* [1902] A.C. 543; *Westpac Banking Corp v Savin* [1985] 2 N.Z.L.R. 41. See in general Lewin, *Trusts* (19th edn), paras 40-050 and 42-085 onwards and 42-093; Ellinger and Lomnicka, *Modern Banking Law* (5th edn), p.291 onwards.

[916] *JD Wetherspoon Plc v Van De Berg & Co Ltd* [2009] EWHC 639 (Ch).

Chapter 10

TERMINATION OF AUTHORITY

Introductory Note

The propositions collected in this chapter, like those in Chapter 3, straddle the **10-001** three main aspects of agency, the relations between principal and agent, principal and third party, and agent and third party. Therefore careful attention should be paid to determining which aspects of an agency situation are affected by each rule. Thus the termination of authority between principal and agent may not affect a third party who has no notice of such termination: Article 121 (which deals with apparent authority where actual authority is determined) must be regarded as qualifying some of the earlier Articles in the Chapter. And although a termination of authority may as between principal and agent be operative in some respects, e.g. in making further actions by the agent on the principal's behalf ineffective, and terminating his right to remuneration or indemnity, it may also be wrongful as a breach of contract and give rise to a right to damages.[1] Furthermore, the fiduciary obligation and in some cases that as to commission may continue.

Article 117

Termination of Actual Authority

(1) The actual authority of an agent is terminated— **10-002**
  (a) by agreement between principal and agent;
  (b) if given for a particular transaction, by the completion of that transaction[2];
  (c) if given for a limited period, by the expiration of that period, or in any case after the elapsing of a period which is reasonable in all the circumstances[3];
  (d) by the happening of any event upon the happening of which it is agreed between the principal and the agent that the authority shall terminate,[4] or upon the happening of which the agent should reasonably infer that the principal does not or would not wish the authority to continue[5];
  (e) by the destruction of the subject-matter of the agency[6];

---

[1] See Article 120.
[2] Illustrations 1–4.
[3] Illustration 5; *Danby v Coutts & Co* (1885) 29 Ch.D. 550, Illustration 1 to Article 22.
[4] See *Restatement, Third*, § 3.09.
[5] See Comment. Mere cessation of the agent's business does not of itself terminate his authority: *Trif-fit Nurseries v Salads Etcetera Ltd* [1999] 1 All E.R. (Comm) 110; [2000] 1 All E.R. (Comm) 737. cf. *Angove's Pty Ltd v Bailey* [2016] UKSC 47; [2016] 1 W.L.R. 3179.
[6] *Rhodes v Forwood* (1876) 1 App.Cas. 256, Illustration 1 to Article 123; *Northey v Trevillion* (1902) 7 Com.Cas. 201. See Article 123.

(f) by the happening of any event rendering the agency or its objects unlawful, impossible or otherwise frustrating the agency or its objects.[7]

(2) The actual authority of an agent is also terminated, unless it is irrevocable in
accordance with the provisions of Article 120—

(a) (prima facie) by the death, mental incapacity or (in some situations)
insolvency of the principal or the agent; or where the principal or agent
is a body corporate, by its dissolution[8];

(b) by notice of revocation given, whether or not in breach of contract, by the
principal to the agent[9];

(c) by notice of renunciation given, whether or not in breach of contract, by
the agent to the principal and accepted by the principal.[10]

Comment

10-003 Rule (1)   The circumstances stated in Rule (1) above are relevant to the agreement, whether contractual or not, between principal and agent, and relate to implied
(or express) terms of it. They are no more than illustrations of situations in which
the agent is not justified in thinking that his authority continues. It should be noted
however that the third party may still be able to rely in some cases on the doctrine
of apparent authority.[11] The propositions contained in (a) to (c) are self-evident. The
second part of (d) is derived from a suggestion in *Restatement, Third*[12] that
circumstances may occur in which at the time the agent comes to act it is no longer
reasonable for him to believe that the principal would wish him to do so. Where
however the agent is in reasonable doubt as to whether his authority persists, his
actions are to be treated as authorised if reasonable in the circumstances.[13] Rule
(1)(e) is again self-evident for cases where a subject-matter can be readily identified, though here the correct analysis of the contractual position, and hence whether
the principal is liable to the agent, is open to much argument.[14] In both these cases
it is a matter of interpretation whether the actual authority ends on the happening
of the event or on the agent's receiving notice of the happening of the event.

Rule 1(f) involves a more general application of the doctrine of frustration to
agency contracts and agreements. An agent's authority has been held to terminate
when the operation of Military Service Acts made it illegal or impossible for him
to perform his duties.[15] Where the contract of agency may require intercourse with
the enemy during a war, the agency is normally terminated by the outbreak of war.[16]

---

7   See Comment.
8   Article 119. The dissolution of a partnership may have the same effect: ibid.
9   Article 120.
10   Article 120.
11   See Article 121.
12   See Comment *b* to § 3.06.
13   cf. Articles 26 and 38.
14   See Article 123.
15   *Marshall v Glanvill* [1917] 2 K.B. 87; and see *Morgan v Manser* [1948] 1 K.B. 184.
16   *Sovfracht, etc., v Van Udens, etc.* [1943] A.C. 203 at 253–255; *Hugh Stevenson & Sons Ltd v
     Aktiengesellschaft für Cartonnagen Industrie* [1918] A.C. 239; *Nordisk Insulin-laboratorium v
     Gorgate Products Ltd* [1953] Ch. 430 (in all of which the principal became an enemy); *Kuenigl v
     Donnersmarck* [1955] 1 Q.B. 515 (where the agent became an enemy). See also *Daimler Co Ltd v
     Continental Tyre & Rubber Co Ltd* [1916] 2 A.C. 307; Webber, *Effect of War on Contracts* (2nd edn);
     McNair, *Legal Effects of War* (4th edn).

Thus the retainer of a solicitor ceases when his client becomes an alien enemy,[17] though it has been held that while the solicitor remains on the record, service upon him of an application to strike out the statement of claim is sufficient.[18] It has also been held that a purportedly irrevocable power of attorney to sell land and give a receipt for the purchase money was not avoided by the donor subsequently becoming an alien enemy.[19] This case has however been criticised, and should at least be regarded as turning on special facts: ordinarily the relationship of principal and agent necessitates communication between the parties,[20] which would not be possible in such a situation. But the occurrence of war does not of itself determine the authority of an enemy alien resident in this country who acts for a principal also resident in this country.[21] In general each case of this type must turn on its facts: "the general grounds of abrogation are, broadly speaking, the danger of intercourse and the desire not to enhance, but to cripple, the resources of the enemy".[22]

Rule (2) The circumstances stated in Rule (2) have a different operation. Those **10-004** in (a) relate to the capacity of the principal to have an agent at all, or of the agent to act as such. The law in this area is still in a state of development. In particular, it is not yet fully settled whether an agent's actual authority is terminated automatically by the principal's mental incapacity, or whether the agent needs to have become aware (or ought to have become aware) of the occurrence of the incapacity. Nor is the position with apparent authority settled.[23] In relation to mental incapacity, there are also certain protections provided by statute.[24] Renunciation by either party, referred to in (b) and (c), terminates authority because as a matter of policy such a rule seems appropriate to the relationship[25]; but there may be repercussions both between principal and agent (where the renunciation may be a breach of contract by one or the other) and as regards third parties (who may be able to rely on the doctrine of apparent authority if they had no notice of the renunciation).[26]

For the *authority* to be terminated, a revocation by the principal does not require to be accepted by the agent. But where there is a contract between them, on general principles a repudiatory breach of it is ineffective unless accepted by the innocent party. Thus any *contract* may in some respects be regarded as subsisting, even though the authority is revoked, if the revocation is a breach by the principal and is not accepted by the agent.[27] Even where it is accepted, some contractual duties operating beyond the end of the contract service may continue, as may some fiduci-

---

[17] *Sovfracht, etc., v Van Udens, etc.*, above.
[18] *Eichengruen v Mond* [1940] Ch. 785 (claim frivolous and vexatious).
[19] *Tingley v Müller* [1917] 2 Ch. 144.
[20] See *Sovfracht, etc., v Van Udens, etc.* [1943] A.C. 203 at 236, 254; *Hangkam Kwingtong Woo v Liu Lan Fong* [1951] A.C. 707 at 720. But cf. *Perpetual Trustee Co Ltd v Aroney* (1944) 44 S.R.(N.S.W.) 313.
[21] *Nordman v Rayner and Sturges* (1916) 33 T.L.R. 87 (where the alien was actually interned for a short period); *Schostall v Johnson* (1919) 36 T.L.R. 75.
[22] *Hangkam Kwingtong Woo v Liu Lan Fong*, above, at 179, per Lord Simonds (a case where the principal was in a country allied to the United Kingdom and the agent in Japanese-occupied Hong Kong). See also *Ottoman Bank v Jebara* [1928] A.C. 269; *Sovfracht, etc., v Van Udens*, above.
[23] See below, Articles 119 and 121.
[24] See below, para.10-020; Article 122.
[25] Article 120.
[26] Articles 121 and 122.
[27] See *Atlantic Underwriting Agencies Ltd v Cia. di Assicurazione di Milano SpA* [1979] 2 Lloyd's Rep. 240; *Paper Reclaim Ltd v Aotearoa International Ltd* [2007] 3 N.Z.L.R. 169 (N.Z.S.C.) at [22] (see para.7-046, above); *Société Générale, London Branch v Geys* [2012] UKSC 63; [2013] 1 A.C. 523;

ary duties.[28] On the other hand, since the conferring or withdrawal of authority is within the power of the principal, a renunciation by the *agent* does not terminate his authority (quite apart from the question of the contractual position between them) unless the principal indicates that it should. It may however be a breach of contract, and may also release the principal from the duty to give notice of the termination of authority.

Illustrations

10-005
(1) A broker is employed to sell goods. As soon as the contract of sale is completed, he is functus officio, and cannot subsequently alter the terms of the contract without fresh authority from the principal.[29]

(2) A solicitor is retained to conduct an action. His authority to act for the client prima facie ceases at the judgment, though it may be renewed by any act showing the client's intention that the solicitor shall continue to act.[30]

(3) An auctioneer is authorised to sell property. He has no authority to sign a memorandum of the sale a week after the sale.[31]

(4) An estate agent was employed to let or sell a house. Having let the house, he negotiated for a sale, and subsequently found a purchaser. Held, that he had no authority to sell after having let the house, and that he was not entitled to commission on the sale.[32]

(5) A broker is authorised to sell goods. It may be shown that by the custom of the particular trade such an authority expires with the expiration of the day on which it is given.[33]

Article 118

WHEN AUTHORITY CANNOT BE TERMINATED (IRREVOCABLE AUTHORITY)

10-006
(1) At common law, where the authority of an agent is given by deed,[34] or for valuable consideration,[35] for the purpose of supporting or effectuating any security, or of protecting or securing an interest of parties other than the principal, it is irrevocable during the subsistence of such security or interest.[36] But authority is not irrevocable merely because an agent would be prejudiced by its revoca-

---

Treitel, *Law of Contract* (14th edn), para.18-005 onwards.

[28] *Thomas Marshall (Exports) Ltd v Guinle* [1979] Ch. 227; as to fiduciary duties, see Article 43.

[29] *Blackburn v Scholes* (1810) 2 Camp. 341.

[30] *Butler v Knight* (1867) L.R. 2 Ex 109; but cf. *Re Newen, Carruthers v Newen* [1903] 1 Ch. 812. No doubt it covers matters ancillary to the judgment. See in general Cordery, *Solicitors* (8th edn), Ch.4.

[31] *Bell v Balls* [1897] 1 Ch. 663. The situation could not now arise in exactly this form because of the effect of the Law of Property (Miscellaneous Provisions) Act 1989 s.2.

[32] *Gillow & Co v Lord Aberdare* (1892) 9 T.L.R. 12.

[33] *Dickinson v Lilwall* (1815) 4 Camp. 279.

[34] Illustration 1; *Walsh v Whitcomb* (1797) 2 Esp. 565.

[35] Illustrations 2–4.

[36] See Illustrations. For the wording see *Clerk v Laurie* (1857) 2 H. & N. 199 at 200 ("for the purpose of securing some benefit to the donee of the authority": per Williams J), cited in *Carmichael's* case, Illustration 4. See also *Slatter v Railway Commissioners (New South Wales)* (1931) 45 C.L.R. 68; *Griffin v Clark* (1940) 40 S.R.(N.S.W.) 409; *Re Hartt Group and Land Securities Ltd* (1984) 7 D.L.R. (4th) 89 (landlord's right to re-enter and take custody as agent of tenant). Revocation may probably be restrained by injunction: see *Knight v Bulkeley* (1859) 5 Jur.(N.S.) 817. See also below, para.12-024.

tion, as by loss of commission,[37] or has a special property in, or lien for advances upon, the subject-matter of it,[38] unless the authority was given expressly for the purpose of securing such interest or advances.

(2) By statute, where a power of attorney, whenever created, is expressed to be irrevocable and is given to secure a proprietary interest of the donee of the power, or the performance of an obligation owed to the donee,[39] then, so long as the donee has that interest, or the obligation remains undischarged, the power is irrevocable.[40]

(3) Authority expressed by this Article to be irrevocable is not determined by the death,[41] mental incapacity or insolvency[42] of the principal, nor, where the principal is a body corporate, by its winding-up or dissolution.[43]

(4) A lasting power of attorney as defined in the Mental Capacity Act 2005 is not revoked by the subsequent mental incapacity of the donor, and is exercisable thereafter in accordance with the provisions of that Act.[44]

Comment

Rule (1): Irrevocability at common law   The dominant assumption in the cases   **10-007**
is that a grant of authority is of its nature revocable.[45] The mere fact that a power is declared in the instrument granting it to be irrevocable does not make it so, even if that instrument is a deed. Authority *can* be irrevocable; but this is only where the notion of agency is employed as a legal device for a different purpose from that of normal agency, to confer a security or other interest on the "agent". In such a case it is intended that the agent use the authority not for the benefit of his principal but for his own benefit, to achieve the objects of the arrangement.

The last two sentences of the immediately preceding paragraph were disapproved in an obiter dictum of Lord Sumption in *Angove's Pty Ltd v Bailey*,[46] as being too narrow a description of the circumstances when authority might be irrevocable. The judge did not provide an alternative formulation but he did make a number of points. First, he rejected the idea that irrevocability must exist solely in order to secure the agent's financial interest. Secondly, he took the view that irrevocability was not incompatible with the agent's being able to promote both his

---

[37]   Illustrations 3 and 5; *Frith v Frith* [1906] A.C. 254; *Angove's Pty Ltd v Bailey* [2016] UKSC 47; [2016] 1 W.L.R. 3179 at [9].

[38]   Illustration 5; below, para.10-010.

[39]   See Comment.

[40]   Powers of Attorney Act 1971 s.4(1). Such a power may be given to the person entitled to the interest and persons deriving title under him to that interest: s.4(2). See in general *Law Com. No.30*, Cmnd. 4473 (1970).

[41]   See *Lepard v Vernon* (1813) 2 V. & B. 51; *Spooner v Sandilands* (1842) 1 Y. & C.Ch.Cas. 390; *Carter v White* (1883) 25 Ch.D. 666 (completion of blanks in bill of exchange after death of drawer). But these are not strong cases: see Comment.

[42]   *Alley v Hotson* (1815) 4 Camp. 325 (a case on mutual credit under the law of bankruptcy setoff); cf. *Bristow and Porter v Taylor* (1817) 2 Stark. 50 (a case on the then recently changed law on fraudulent releases).

[43]   See Powers of Attorney Act 1971 s.4(1). It is normally assumed that the same is true at common law: see Comment. See too *Wellington Steam Ferry Co Ltd (In Liquidation) v Wellington Deposit, Mortgage, and Building Assoc. Ltd* (1915) 34 N.Z.L.R. 913; *Lim Eng Chuan Sdn Bhd v United Malayan Banking Corp* [2011] 1 M.L.J. 486 (Malaysia CA).

[44]   See Comment.

[45]   See *Angove's Pty Ltd v Bailey* [2016] UKSC 47; [2016] 1 W.L.R. 3179 at [6].

[46]   *Angove's Pty Ltd v Bailey* [2016] UKSC 47 at [9].

own interests as well as the principal's. Thirdly, it would be possible to infer irrevocability in a clear enough case.[47]

It can be accepted, with respect, that the first of Lord Sumption's points is valid. In cases where a company promoter or an issuer of company shares takes an irrevocable authority to ensure that underwriters or subscribers for shares do not renege on a subscription,[48] it can be readily accepted that the collective interests of the other subscribers are being protected as much as the promoter's or the company's. Similarly, the cases upholding an irrevocable authority given to an auctioneer of land to sign a memorandum in writing on behalf of the successful, but now regretful, bidder are protecting the interests of the vendor as much as the auctioneer.[49] These examples were referred to by Lord Sumption, but, surprisingly, treated as special cases and not relied upon by him for his criticism. More is said about these types of case, below para.10-010. There will be other cases where the interest to be protected is not the agent's; an authority given, for example, to a receiver will usually be given to promote the interests of debentureholders, not the receiver personally.[50]

Lord Sumption's second point is, with respect, less easy to accept. It seems hard to reconcile with the reasons for the existence of a general principle that authority can always be revoked even when doing so puts the principal in breach of his contract with the agent. Those reasons were stated by the judge as follows:

"An agent is empowered to commit his principal within the limits of his authority as if the principal had agreed personally. This is a confidential relationship importing a duty of loyalty, and normally of undivided loyalty, on the part of the agent."[51]

The judge went on to indicate that, while an agent could not have irrevocable authority in order to maintain a right to future commissions, he might to secure payment of past commissions. This example, and the judge's broader dicta, cut against the idea that the exercise of authority is indissolubly connected with the principal's autonomy and the article of faith that the principal's confidence in the agent is paramount. This is not to say that agents must place themselves in peril of not being paid by their principal, but if their rights of lien are inadequate they must take a security of some sort, whereby their rights are circumscribed by the property interest they have taken from their principal.[52]

Lord Sumption's third point, as to the possibility of inferring irrevocability must, with respect, be sound. But it will be very rare when it is appropriate to do so, especially given that only damages are available for breach of an express clause.[53] *Angove's case* itself involved an attempt, unsuccessful, to imply irrevocability.

The principle of revocability and its exceptions have a very long history. The wording of Rule 1 remains closely based on that written by Bowstead in the first

---

[47] *Angove's Pty Ltd v Bailey* [2016] UKSC 47 at [8] and [16].
[48] See, e.g. *Re Hannan's Empress Gold Mining & Development Co, Carmichael's Case* [1896] 2 Ch. 643, Illustration 5.
[49] See, e.g. *Van Praagh v Everidge* [1902] 2 Ch. 266, reversed on other grounds [1903] 1 Ch. 434.
[50] See *Sowman v David Samuel Trust Ltd* [1978] 1 W.L.R. 22 at 31, per Goulding J: followed in *Re Leslie Homes (Aust.) Pty Ltd* (1984) 8 A.C.L.R. 1020; and see Millett (1977) 41 Conv. 83. Contra, *Barrows v Chief Land Registrar*, *Times* October 18, 1977 Ch.D. See Goode, *Principles of Corporate Insolvency Law* (4th edn), para.10-41.
[51] *Angove's Pty Ltd v Bailey* [2016] UKSC 47; [2016] 1 W.L.R. 3179 at [6].
[52] See *Smith v Plummer* (1818) 1 B. & A. 575 at 579 (Parke in argument).
[53] See, e.g. *Schindler v Brie* [2003] EWHC 1804 (Ch); [2003] W.T.L.R. 1361 (power of attorney to apply for letters of administration).

edition of this work in 1896. He himself derived it from dicta of Lord Kenyon in *Walsh v Whitcomb*[54] in 1797 and the decision in *Smart v Sandars*, in the context of factors, in 1848.[55] These cases date from a time of what one might call experimentation between legal doctrines (not all of which survive),[56] experimentation that also drew on ancient doctrines.[57] By the time Bowstead wrote many of the cases he cited were obsolete by reason of the property, insolvency, commercial and judicature reforms of the nineteenth century. They have not yet been set in order. On any basis, *Angove's* shows that there is still some way to go before the bounds of irrevocability are settled.

Angove's case accepts that cases where an irrevocable authority accompanies a security or proprietary interest and is part of it or a means of achieving it remain central examples of the phenomenon of irrevocability. The fact that the agent subsequently acquires an interest in the property is irrelevant: the authority must be conferred as part of, or as protection of the agent's interest.[58] The authority is referred to as "authority" or "power" "coupled with an interest", a phrase not unconnected with the nineteenth-century notion in a different context of a licence coupled with an interest.[59] The mere right to earn commission is not such an interest[60]; nor is an agent's lien, unless the power was conferred specifically to protect it or sums due under it.[61] Subject to what is said in *Angove's case*, the central cases are different from normal agency, in which the agent must act in the interests of the principal: here the agent acts in his own interests. Agency is here a device for supporting or conferring a property interest (a power of attorney to sue on another's behalf and a power of sale are ways of enforcing a security). Although exposition of this area of law in textbooks on the law of agency is traditional, both in England and the United States,[62] it is not really within the bounds of general agency reasoning.

The idea that an irrevocable power survives death and other losses of capacity, stated in Rule 3, is in fact not really supported by the old cases. In particular, it was difficult to see how a power of attorney to be exercised in the donor's name could

---

[54] (1797) 2 Esp. 565: see McGaw, below, at pp.246–257.
[55] (1848) 5 C.B. 895, Illustration 8.
[56] This article draws on the unpublished doctoral thesis of Dr Mark McGaw, "*A History of the Common Law of Agency with Particular Reference to the Concept of Irrevocable Authority Coupled with an Interest*" (2005). Most if not all of the cases cited in the text and Illustrations are there analysed in considerable detail, much more than is possible here. See also on this topic, Reynolds, in *Making Commercial Law* (Cranston ed., 1994), Ch.10 (itself criticised in the above thesis at pp.335–337).
[57] McGaw (above) mentions the wider pattern of articulation of recognisably modern principles in place of practitioners' rules of pleading and practice and various fictions and estoppels, the recognition of an equitable jurisdiction in the common law courts encouraged by acute delays in Chancery and the experimentation in special pleading associated with the Hilary Rules of 1835 eventually superseded by the judicature reforms of 1852–1875.
[58] See *Smart v Sandars* (1848) 5 C.B. 895; *Despot v Registrar-General of NSW* [2013] NSWCA 313.
[59] As to which see *Wood v Leadbitter* (1845) 13 M.& W. 838. Aspects of this concept affect the role of receiver in company law—see, in general, Lightman and Moss, *Law of Administrators and Receivers of Companies* (5th edn).
[60] *Doward, Dickson & Co v Williams & Co* (1890) 6 T.L.R. 316; *Temple Legal Protection Ltd v QBE Insurance (Europe) Ltd* [2009] EWCA Civ 453; [2009] Lloyd's Rep I.R. 544 at [50].
[61] See Illustration 4.
[62] *Restatement*, §§ 3.12 and 3.13 (dealing also with irrevocable proxies: below, para.10-013). As to § 3.12, it provides: "A power given as security is a power to affect the legal relations of its creator that is created in the form of a manifestation of actual authority and held for the benefit of the holder or a third person. This power is given to protect a legal or equitable title, or so secure the performance of a duty apart from any duties owed the holder by its creator that are incident to a relationship of agency ...". See too DeMott on irrevocable proxies in American law (2008) 82 A.L.J. 516.

be exercised after his death.[63] The rule has to be justified on the general basis that what is in issue is a property right, which is (obviously) once granted, unaffected by loss of capacity of the grantor. This justification would not be available for cases of irrevocable authority that do not involve proprietary interests. The general proposition is now confirmed by statute, as appears below: but despite the problems it has been assumed for a considerable time that the same was and is true at common law.[64] Problems of corporate insolvency remain to be worked out.

10-008   **Rule (2): Statute: powers of attorney**   Special provisions as to the irrevocability of powers of attorney in like situations (for which they might well be used) are laid down in the Powers of Attorney Act 1971 s.4, and the general effect of this provision is reproduced in Rules (2) and (3) of this Article. It may be that the Act aims to declare the common law in this respect, and hence can be cited as an indication of the common law position. But it should be noted that, to be irrevocable, the authority must be contained in a power of attorney, and so witnessed[65]; and it must also be expressed to be irrevocable. Neither is true at common law. On the other hand, by its reference to securing the performance of an obligation owed to the donee, it is drafted, no doubt in accordance with formulations of the law current at the time,[66] to take in more than security interests. By contrast, it has been suggested above that at common law, in the case of a grant of authority coupled with an interest, the interest need not be that of the donee of the power: but the statutory wording seems to exclude this possibility.[67] Finally, in the corporate sphere it only applies to winding up or dissolution, which leaves questions not only about these procedures but also about other insolvency procedures. It is sometimes argued that the provision was intended to replace the common law; but there is no indication of this, and it will often be more convenient to rely on the possibly wider common law rules. The Act however contains protection for third parties where the power was expressed to be given by way of security but was in fact not so given,[68] protection which might be difficult to establish at common law.

10-009   **Rule (4): Lasting Powers of Attorney**   From October 1, 2007,[69] the Mental Capacity Act 2005 has made available a new type of registrable instrument that

---

[63] See *Watson v King* (1815) 4 Camp. 272, concerning ship mortgages. Now however a power of attorney can be executed in the attorney's name: Powers of Attorney Act 1971 s.7: see Article 77.

[64] In the United States a famous decision of Marshall CJ in *Hunt v Rousmanier's Administrators* 21 U.S. 174 (1823), again in the context of ship mortgages, distinguished between cases where the power accompanied a proprietary security interest and those where it stood alone: in the latter case it was revoked by death. This led to an unsatisfactory distinction, probably not justified from the case itself, between powers coupled with an interest and powers given as security. Only in the first was the power not revoked by death. The distinction was not taken in England and is not accepted in the *Restatement*, in which "power given as security" is the general test for irrevocable authority and is defined as in the previous paragraph. There is discussion in McGaw, above, at p.260 onwards.

[65] Powers of Attorney Act 1971 s.1(1): see above, para.2-039.

[66] See *Law Com. No.30* (1970), para.33, where the provision is stated to "restate the common law position when a power is given by way of security". Introducing his first Bill into the House of Lords, Lord Diplock said "Clause 4 deals with a special case on which I need not linger": 315 HL Debs col.1206 (February 25, 1971).

[67] But see Millett (1977) 41 Conv. 83 at 86.

[68] See Article 122.

[69] SI 2007/1897. Some parts of the Act had already been brought into effect on April 1 by SI 2007/563. Minor amendments are made by the Mental Health Act 2007. See in general Bartlett, *Blackstone's Guide to the Mental Capacity Act 2005* (2nd edn, 2008); *Cretney and Lush on Lasting and Enduring Powers of Attorney* (6th edn); Aldridge, *Powers of Attorney* (10th edn); Thurston,

endures where the donor has lost mental capacity, the Lasting Power of Attorney.[70] Powers of attorney under the Act can be revoked by the donor both before and after registration, but only where the donor retains capacity.[71] Bankruptcy of the donor will revoke the power in relation to the donor's property and affairs.[72] The Act, surprisingly perhaps, does not expressly provide for revocation by the death of the donor, although regulations assume that death does revoke powers of attorney made under the Act, and provide for deregistration accordingly.[73] The Act does provide for termination upon the death of, and other circumstances, relating to the donee.[74] The Act replaces the Enduring Power of Attorney which had been introduced by the Enduring Powers of Attorney Act 1985, now repealed. The Lasting Power is a wider type of power than the Enduring Power, under which the donee, or different donees, can be given authority to act in respect of the donor's personal welfare as well as his or her property and affairs,[75] though limited powers can of course be conferred in either respect. Such powers require two separate documents, one for each power, in prescribed form.[76] The 2005 Act begins with elaborate "principles" regarding what constitutes mental incapacity,[77] and what constitutes the "best interests" of the incapacitated person.[78] Even without such a document, a person may sometimes be justified in acting reasonably in the interests of another in respect of care or treatment,[79] and may in other circumstances be entitled to pledge that other's credit, use that other's money and obtain reimbursement.[80] These powers are not dissimilar from the more limited authority applicable in cases of agency of necessity and are referred to above under that head.[81] Lasting Powers of Attorney require a "certificate of capacity" that the donor acts voluntarily and understands the purpose of the document.[82] The power is invalid unless registered,[83] but registration can be effected before the onset of incapacity. The court may control the exercise of the power,[84] or appoint a "deputy" to take decisions for the incapacitated person.[85] The Court of Protection is reconstituted by the Act as part of the reforms. There are provisions protecting the donee and bona fide third parties where no power was created or the power has been revoked.[86] Regulations supplement the provisions of Schs 1 and 4 to the Act regarding registration and revocation of pow-

---

Powers of Attorney (6th edn).

[70] ss.9–29; stemming from recommendations contained in *Law Com. No.231* (1995), 94.

[71] s.13(1)(2).

[72] s.13(3), but see s.13(4).

[73] See Lasting Powers of Attorney, Enduring Powers of Attorney and Public Guardian Regulations (SI 2007/1253) reg.22.

[74] s.13(5)–(11).

[75] ss.9, 11 and 12. As to property held by the donor on trust for others, see *Godfrey v Marshall* [2017] NZHC 420.

[76] Lasting Powers of Attorney, Enduring Powers of Attorney and Public Guardian Regulations (SI 2007/1253) cl.5 (setting out forms for use).

[77] ss.1–3.

[78] s.4 (specifying criteria for establishing reasonable belief).

[79] ss.5 and 6.

[80] s.8 (the person lacking capacity is liable for necessaries supplied by virtue of s.7).

[81] See above, para.4-012.

[82] Sch.1 cl.2(1)(e).

[83] s.9(2)(b).

[84] ss.22–23.

[85] s.16.

[86] s.14, in terms similar to s.9 of the Enduring Powers of Attorney Act 1985 and similarly modifying s.5 of the Powers of Attorney Act 1971.

ers of the new, and also of the former, types.[87] The Act is supported by a Code of Practice issued by the Lord Chancellor.[88] Enduring Powers of Attorney created under the 1985 Act before the 2005 Act came into operation are still valid (as regards property and affairs),[89] but such powers may no longer be created.[90] An attorney holding a lasting power of attorney may, depending on the principal's intention, continue to exercise powers granted before and outside the power, including drawing on bank accounts for personal benefit where so authorised.[91]

10-010 **Reference to irrevocable authority in other contexts** Where in the execution of his authority the agent incurs a personal liability to a third party, such that he would be entitled to reimbursement or indemnity in respect of it, the principal cannot, by purporting to revoke the agent's authority to discharge it, destroy that right. Thus where in the pursuance of his authority the agent incurs contractual liability to pay money to a third party, he is entitled to reimbursement in respect of payments which he makes even though the principal has subsequently forbidden them.[92] The principle applies also where the agent incurs a liability in respect of an authorised transaction which it is proper for him to discharge even though it could not be legally enforced, e.g. a liability to pay wagering debts,[93] or barrister's fees.[94] It may also be that this principle extends to the agent's right to take positive action, e.g. initiate proceedings, in respect of matters occurring while he had authority, even though, again, the principal forbids such action.[95] It would not, however, extend to prevent revocation merely because the agent has incurred other liabilities, for example given a personal undertaking that he would have authority at a certain time in the future.

These propositions are sometimes expressed as propositions relating to irrevocable authority.[96] But they do not relate to authority in the sense of the power

---

[87] See Lasting Powers of Attorney, Enduring Powers of Attorney and Public Guardian Regulations (SI 2007/1253).

[88] In accordance with ss.42 and 43 of the Act, and published by TSO.

[89] s.66(3); they are regulated by Sch.4 to the new Act, which in substance reproduces the 1985 Act. Quaere, whether the "Principles" of ss.1 and 2 of the Act should be applied under Sch.4.

[90] s.66(1) (2). Nor can they be converted.

[91] See *Day v Harris* [2013] EWCA Civ 191; [2014] Ch. 211 (a case under the 1985 legislation).

[92] See, e.g. *Chappell v Bray* (1860) 6 H. & N. 145; *Warlow v Harrison* (1859) 1 E. & E. 309. See in general Article 62. Where the principal indemnifies the agent in advance, the same rule applies: *Yates v Hoppe* (1850) 9 C.B. 541.

[93] *Read v Anderson* (1884) 13 Q.B.D. 779; and see *Seymour v Bridge* (1885) 14 Q.B.D. 460.

[94] *Rhodes v Fielder* (1919) 89 L.J.K.B. 15.

[95] See *Daly v Lime Street Underwriting Agencies Ltd* [1987] 2 F.T.L.R. 277, where a former member of a Lloyd's syndicate failed in an action for a declaration that there was no authority to continue an action brought by the managing agents of his syndicate, in respect of matters occurring while he was a member. The power of the agent was described in the agreement conferring it as "irrevocable", but there is no discussion whether there was any proprietary interest, or (more likely in the circumstances) obligation, to protect. There had, however, been no attempt to revoke the authority before it was exercised, and this may be the best explanation. See Reynolds, fn.48 above. See also *Yasuda Fire and Marine Insurance Co Ltd v Orion Marine Insurance Underwriting Agency Ltd* [1995] Q.B. 174 (relationship of principal and agent continued despite termination of contract by repudiatory breach, to entitle principal to see agent's books; *Mortgage Express v Sawali* [2010] EWHC 3054 (Ch); [2010] N.P.C. 114; [2011] 7 E.G. 98; [2011] P.N.L.R. 11 (solicitor common to borrower and lender obliged to hand over client files to lender where borrower's contract with lender irrevocably authorised delivery of such files).

[96] See, e.g. *Chappell v Bray* (1860) 6 H. & N. 145 at 162; and early editions of this book.

of an agent to affect the legal position of his principal[97]: their relevance is to authority in the context of the rule that the right to reimbursement and indemnity does not extend to unauthorised acts.[98] The rules as to reimbursement and indemnity, however, are not confined to agents at all, and the common use of the term "authority" in this context can be confusing. Therefore it is submitted that the rule in question is better expressed as in the above paragraph, and without reference to any idea of irrevocable authority.[99] Similar reasoning may apply to cases where the agent is entitled to remuneration: (subject to any contract term) the principal may not, by purporting to revoke authority, deprive the agent of the right to remuneration earned but not yet paid.[100] Such propositions are sometimes also cited in connection with a supposed general rule that authority cannot be revoked once acted on. This is true in the sense that once the act authorised has been done, a purported revocation of authority to do it is ex hypothesi ineffective to prevent the agent carrying it through, and to obtaining reimbursement, indemnity and if appropriate, remuneration in respect of it. As regards authority the proposition can go no further.

In another group of cases, where an agent holds money for his principal, and the principal directs him to pay it to a third party, and the agent notifies the third party that he holds the money for the third party, the agent becomes liable to the third party in restitution, and the principal becomes unable to cancel his instructions: the principal's trustee in bankruptcy is in the same position.[101] Here again it can be said that the authority is irrevocable. But these cases seem really to depend on the idea of attornment of money, the irrevocability being like that of a property disposition: the agent is authorised to participate in such a disposition in favour of a third party, and once he has done so it cannot be recalled.[102]

A further rule which can be expressed in terms of revocation of authority is that which provides that where an agent who contracts personally has an unsatisfied lien on the subject-matter of a contract, he may have the right to sue for the price, and payment to and set-off against him is normally a discharge to the third party to the extent of the lien.[103] In such cases it can be said that the principal to this extent cannot revoke the authority to receive payment.[104] But this is a rule as to performance of contract, relating to payment to or settlement with an agent, whereby the right of the principal to intervene and require payment to himself is inapplicable to the extent to which the agent has a lien. It is accompanied by, and to some extent stems from, the agent's right to sue for the price. A lien, which constitutes the agent a secured creditor, obviously cannot be unilaterally terminated by the principal, even by his bankruptcy,[105] but this is not a rule as to revocation of authority. Irrevocable authority would prevent the revocation of the actual power to sell.

The idea of irrevocable authority can also be used to explain cases more properly

---

[97]   See Article 1.
[98]   Article 63. See *Pacific and General Insurance Co Ltd v Hazell* [1997] L.R.L.R. 65, per Moore-Bick J; and *Temple Legal Protection Ltd v QBE Insurance (Europe) Ltd* [2009] EWCA Civ 453; [2009] Lloyd's Rep I.R. 544 at [59].
[99]   See *Warlow v Harrison* (1859) 1 E. & E. 309, 317; *Read v Anderson* (1884) 13 Q.B.D. 779 (Bowen LJ); Powell, p.395.
[100] See Articles 56–58.
[101] See, e.g. *Walker v Rostron* (1842) 9 M. & W. 441; *Griffin v Weatherby* (1868) L.R. 3 Q.B. 753.
[102] The cases are fully discussed under Article 112.
[103] The examples concern factors and auctioneers. See above, paras 8-112 and 9-009.
[104] See *Drinkwater v Goodwin* (1775) 1 Cowp. 251, Illustration 5 to Article 81; *Robson v Kemp* (1802) 4 Esp. 233.
[105] See Article 67. And see above, paras 8-108, 9-009 and 9-023.

to be considered in connection with the rule in *Milroy v Lord*,[106] which relates to the perfection of gifts and the declaration of trusts. Indeed the whole subject touches the fringes of assignment of choses in action and transfer of property generally, and many of the old cases date from a time when no proper method of assignment had been evolved, and powers of attorney and the like were used to effect what would now be an assignment.

Finally, it is arguable that in some situations equity may intervene to restrain a revocation of authority which is in breach of contract. This point is considered under Article 120.

10-011 **Completion of transactions** It might plausibly be thought that there was in some cases an authority to complete transactions commenced before revocation of authority or death or incapacity of the principal.[107] As already stated, an agent can certainly discharge matters in respect of which he has incurred a personal liability. There is a relevant provision in the Partnership Act 1890 s.38, which on dissolution gives the remaining partners authority to "complete transactions begun but unfinished at the time of the dissolution".[108] Outside this area, though the *contract* between principal and agent may continue, it is difficult to see that there can be any such continuing *authority* where the mandate has clearly been terminated, even though it might be useful, for example, in connection with practices at Lloyd's.[109] If an interest sufficient to secure irrevocability could be found, it would be under the category of "securing an obligation of the principal", as in the case of underwriting agreements[110]; but this is for most such situations far from certain.

In *Trifft Nurseries v Salads Etcetera Ltd* it was held that, on the appointment by debenture holders of a receiver in respect of an agent for sale, the authority of the agent, and hence the receiver, to call in debts in respect of sales made by the agent was not terminated in a situation where it was intended that the agent should not keep the money received separate but should be free to mix it with his normal cashflow.[111] If the debts are owed to the principal, there seems no reason why the authority to collect them should not, however, be revocable before execution in the normal way if a clear revocation occurs. Robert Walker LJ said that "the debt belonged to [the agent] while it was trading, subject to the charge in favour of the bank".[112] If the case was one of true agency it would seem that the chose in action arose on the sale and belonged to the principal, who could revoke the agent's author-

---

[106] (1862) 4 De G.F. & J. 264. See also *Re Williams, Williams v Ball* [1917] 1 Ch. 1; *Ex p. Pye* (1811) 18 Ves. Jur. 140; *Kiddill v Farnell* (1857) 3 Sn. & G. 428; and more generally Snell, *Equity* (33rd edn), paras 22-049 and 24-012–24-015.

[107] See Reynolds, in *Making Commercial Law* (Cranston, ed, 1994), Ch.10, at p.266 onwards.

[108] See *Inland Revenue v Graham's Trustees* 1971 S.C.(H.L.) 1 at 21.

[109] See *Daly v Lime Street Underwriting Agencies Ltd* [1987] 2 F.T.L.R. 277; discussed by Reynolds, above, at p.271 onwards; *Society of Lloyd's v Leighs*, QBD (Colman J), February 20, 1997; decided by CA on other grounds [1997] T.L.R. 449. See also *Temple Legal Protection Ltd v QBE Insurance (Europe) Ltd* [2009] EWCA Civ 453; [2009] Lloyd's Rep I.R. 544.

[110] See above, paras 10-007 and 10-008. PECL art.3:209(3), the UNIDROIT Principles art.2.2.10, and DCFR, II, 6:112(4) all provide for authority to act after termination of (normal) authority, to preserve the principal's interests (of which completion of a transaction or transactions would simply be an example) in such a case: but this can be more easily achieved by (quasi) legislation than by development of general theory. DCFR, II, 6.112 provides for authority to continue where the principal is under an obligation to the third party not to terminate the agency.

[111] *Trifft Nurseries v Salads Etcetera Ltd* [2000] 1 All E.R. (Comm) 737.

[112] At 747.

ity to collect the money[113]; and that the permission to merge the proceeds with the agent's funds did not extend to permission to charge the proceeds before the merger. Subsequent authority confirms this.[114] It seems likely that *Triffit*'s case was not one of pure agency, but rather of the equivalent of indirect representation,[115] and this may be the route to an explanation of it.[116]

Statute of Frauds   A group of cases holds authority to sign a note or memoran- **10-012** dum under the Statute of Frauds irrevocable in the context of auctions.[117] As such they are no longer relevant in England[118]; and they seem in any case best explained as based on considerations of the well-known policy of preventing the Statute being used itself as an instrument of fraud. Before the law was changed, it would certainly have undermined the efficacy of sales by auction were the auctioneer unable to consummate the sale by completing the necessary memorandum. In relation to a buyer, there would be no repose of confidence that an irrevocable authority would intrude upon, but it seems that such an authority also binds the vendor once the property has been knocked down to a successful bidder.[119]

Proxies   Special problems can arise in connection with voting proxies in company **10-013** law. An agent to negotiate for shareholders may acquire proxies from individual members of the group, but the earlier proxies may be revoked before he has completed the securing of the number required.[120] In the United States statutes deal with this problem in various ways.[121] The agent may well have no interest of his own to prevent revocation. In England the only reasoning available to prevent revocation would seem to be the notion of fraud on the other proxy grantors, on the analogy of the law as to compositions with creditors.[122]

Illustrations

(1) A, being indebted to B, gives him a power of attorney to sell certain land and **10-014** discharge his debt out of the purchase money. The power is irrevocable.[123]
(2) Goods are consigned to a factor for sale, and he later makes advances to the principal on the credit of them. Subsequently, the principal instructs the fac-

[113] Counsel relied on *Re Farrow's Bank Ltd* [1923] 1 Ch. 41, in which it was held that a bank's authority to collect a cheque ceased on the bank's suspending payment.
[114] See *Angove's Pty Ltd v Bailey* [2016] UKSC 47; [2016] 1 W.L.R. 3179.
[115] See above, paras 1-021 and 1-022.
[116] This appears more clearly from the first instance judgment of Longmore J: [1999] 1 All E.R. (Comm) 110 at 115. The argument of counsel appears in general to have been that when authority was revoked even a debt owed to the agent must now be held on trust for the principal, which seems to go too far.
[117] *Van Praagh v Everidge* [1902] 2 Ch. 266, reversed on other grounds [1903] 1 Ch. 434; *Chaney v Maclow* [1929] 1 Ch. 461; *Phillips v Butler* [1945] Ch. 358. See Reynolds, above, at pp.265–266.
[118] See Law of Property (Miscellaneous Provisions) Act 1989 s.2(5)(b).
[119] See *Nguyen v SM & T Homes Ltd* [2016] NZCA 581.
[120] See Reynolds, in *Making Commercial Law* (Cranston, ed, 1994), at pp.273–275.
[121] Details are given in *Restatement, Third*, § 3-12, Comment and reporter's notes.
[122] See *Cook v Lister* (1863) 13 C.B.(N.S.) 543; *West Yorkshire Darracq Agency Ltd v Coleridge* [1911] 2 K.B. 326; Treitel, *Law of Contract* (14th edn), para.3-109.
[123] *Gaussen v Morton* (1830) 10 B. & C. 731: see McGaw, fn.56 above, at pp.278–283. See also *Re Rose Ex p. Hasluck & Garrard* (1894) 1 Manson 218.

tor not to sell. The factor's authority is revocable, not being given for valuable consideration.[124]

(3) Goods are consigned to a factor for sale. He makes advances, in consideration of an agreement by the principal that his authority to sell shall be irrevocable. The authority is irrevocable.[125] It is a question of fact whether such an agreement was made, and it may be inferred from the circumstances.[126] In the absence of such an agreement for valuable consideration, the authority of a factor to sell does not become irrevocable by the failure of the principal duly to repay advances made on the security of the goods.[127]

(4) An auctioneer was authorised to sell goods, and after he had incurred expenses in respect of them, the principal revoked his authority. Held, that the authority of the auctioneer was not irrevocable merely by reason of his special property in the goods and his lien on them for advances, and that he was liable to the principal in trespass for going to the premises to sell the goods after notice of the revocation.[128]

(5) A signs and addresses to B an underwriting letter by which he agrees, in consideration of a commission, to subscribe for a certain number of shares in a company, and authorises B to apply for the shares in his name and on his behalf. B, being a vendor to the company, and therefore having an interest in the raising of the capital, by letter accepts the terms of A's agreement. The authority given to B to apply for the shares is irrevocable, and A is bound to take the shares applied for and allotted in pursuance of the underwriting letter, although in the meantime he has given notice to B and to the company repudiating the agreement.[129]

Article 119

TERMINATION OF AUTHORITY BY DEATH, MENTAL INCAPACITY OR INSOLVENCY

10-015   The actual authority of an agent, whether or not conferred by deed and whether or not expressed to be irrevocable, is determined by the death[130] of either the principal or the agent. The intervention of mental incapacity in the principal or agent

---

[124] *Smart v Sandars* (1848) 5 C.B. 895: see McGaw, above, at p.289 onwards; *Raleigh v Atkinson* (1840) 6 M. & W. 670.

[125] See *Smart v Sandars*, above; *De Comas v Prost* (1865) 3 Moo.P.C.(N.S.) 158.

[126] *De Comas v Prost*, above.

[127] *Smart v Sandars*, above.

[128] *Taplin v Florence* (1851) 10 C.B. 744.

[129] *Re Hannan's Empress Gold Mining & Development Co, Carmichael's Case* [1896] 2 Ch. 643 (see McGaw, fn.56 above, at pp.323–325: the proceedings were for rectification of the register under the Companies Act 1862, which required the court to be "satisfied of the justice of the case". A comment in (1896) 102 L.T.Jo. refers to "a portion of the security for the benefit conferred". One in (1897) 13 L.Q.R.11, presumably by F.P., says the arrangement was "part and parcel of the bargain": "a lawyer's defence—no layman would ever have thought of it"). The case was followed in *Re Olympic Reinsurance Co, Pole's Case* [1920] 2 Ch. 341. cf. *Re Consort Deep Level Gold Mines Ltd, Ex p. Stark* [1897] 1 Ch. 575; *Re Bultfontein Sun Diamond Mine Ltd, Ex p. Cox, Hughes and Norman* (1897) 75 L.T. 669. See also *Schindler v Brie* [2003] EWHC 1804 (Ch); [2003] W.T.L.R. 1361.

[130] Illustrations 1 to 3; *Houstoun v Robertson* (1816) 6 Taunt. 448; *Carr v Levingston* (1865) 35 Beav. 41; *Farrow v Wilson* (1860) L.R. 4 C.P. 744; *Phillips v Jones* (1888) 4 T.L.R. 401; *Lodgepower Ltd v Taylor* [2004] EWCA Civ 1367; [2005] 1 E.G.L.R. 1.

would normally terminate actual authority, but at least in the case of an incapax principal only where the agent is aware or ought to be aware of the fact.

Comment

Death   The death of the agent obviously terminates his authority, for the relation-   **10-016**
ship is a personal one.[131] And the death of the principal deprives the agent of anyone for whom he can act.[132] Therefore it is normally said that on the principal's death the actual authority terminates unless it comes under the category of irrevocable authority[133]; not only can the agent not sue for remuneration, reimbursement or indemnity in respect of acts committed after his principal dies,[134] but he may, if he continues to act, be liable for loss caused to the estate.[135] It may also be that the principal's estate cannot be bound under the doctrine of apparent authority[136]; and that the agent may consequently be liable to the third party for breach of warranty of authority.[137] The question is discussed under Article 121. There is some statutory protection in the case of powers of attorney.[138] It has been suggested that it might be possible for the agent to take a special term in his agency agreement that he is to be protected against personal liability arising after the principal's death.[139] In principle, this should be possible, but there is no authority on the validity of such an arrangement. It would in any case only operate inter partes.

Restatement, Third[140] takes the view that actual authority should not terminate until the agent knows of the principal's death. This approach is principally supported by the analogy of existing legislation in the United States. Although there is some discussion in connection with revocation of offer by death which might be of assistance,[141] the extremely limited English authority cannot be said to support such a view. It could however be supported on the general basis that actual authority does not terminate until the agent knows, or ought to know, of the termination, by whatever means.[142] It may be that only statutory reform could achieve such a result.

Ratification   It is not clear whether the executors or administrators of the deceased   **10-017**
can ratify a contract made on behalf of the deceased: it seems that in the case usually cited for the proposition that they can, the contract was made on behalf of the

---

[131] See *Farrow v Wilson*, above, at 746. As regards joint agents, see *Adams v Buckland* (1705) 2 Vern. 514; *Friend v Young* [1897] 2 Ch. 421 and Article 11. The termination of authority may affect the position of sub-agents: see Ch.5. Commission may continue payable after the death of the agent: see *Wilson v Harper, Son & Co* [1908] 2 Ch. 370; above, para.7-041.
[132] See *Drew v Nunn* (1874) 4 Q.B.D. 661 at 666.
[133] See Article 118 and Comment.
[134] Illustration 3.
[135] Illustration 2.
[136] See Comment to Article 121.
[137] *Yonge v Toynbee* [1910] 1 K.B. 215; Article 105. But see Article 122 as to powers of attorney. See also *Bank of Scotland v Qutb* [2012] EWCA Civ 1661.
[138] See Article 122. See also Seavey (1930) 44 HarvL.Rev. 265.
[139] Powell, p.389. As to the possibility of deliberately creating authority which does not terminate on the death of the principal, see Wolff (1946) 62 L.Q.R. 272; Fitzgerald (1946) 13 *Solicitor* 224 (which should be read now in the light of the provisions dealt with in Article 122).
[140] § 3.07.
[141] e.g. *Coulthart v Clementson* (1879) 5 Q.B.D. 42.
[142] See para.10-020 and fn.214 below.

administrators.[143] A person who purported to contract with a person who is, unknown to him, already dead, might well not have been willing to contract with the personal representatives, and the permissibility of ratification therefore seems doubtful.[144] That would certainly be the position where the contract was one that contemplated the personal services of the person now deceased. The third party may, of course, make a fresh contract with the executors or administrators.

10-018 **Companies** The actual dissolution of a company is analogous to the death of a non-corporate principal or agent and arguments similar to those above are applicable. Authorities on the point are surprisingly sparse, and in the case usually cited for automatic termination of actual authority, the point was simply assumed by both counsel and the court.[145] The position is in any event different where a company has simply been placed in liquidation. The company does not cease to exist merely by going into liquidation, and indeed a liquidator generally becomes the agent of the company.[146] However, the authority of its directors to act will in most respects cease, and as a result so will that of those agents who derive their authority from a delegation by the directors.[147] The liquidator might nonetheless ratify action by directors or other agents.[148] The directors would also normally retain authority to challenge the actual appointment of a liquidator or other supplanting authority.[149] It is also possible to restore a dissolved company to the register.[150] Special consequences may follow the appointment of liquidators,[151] receivers and administrators. For instance, an agency for a company which arises on the appointment of administrators to the company does not make the agent the agent of the administrators, nor are the expenses of the agent the expenses of the administration.[152] Reference should be made to specialised works.[153]

10-019 **Partnerships** The rule stated in this Article also applies to cases where the

---

[143] *Foster v Bates* (1843) 12 M. & W. 226. See also Powell, p.388, fn.7.
[144] But see *Alexander Ward & Co Ltd v Samyang Navigation Ltd* [1975] 1 W.L.R. 673 (liquidator: not a contract case, however).
[145] *Salton v New Beeston Cycle Co* [1900] 1 Ch. 43, Illustration 4. See also *Selfe v Colonial Ice Co* (1894) 10 W.N.(N.S.W.) 153; *Wellington Steam Ferry Co Ltd v Wellington Deposit, Mortgage and Building Association Ltd* (1915) 34 N.Z.L.R. 913 at 916–917. As regards partnerships, see Comment. As regards a possible authority to complete transactions, see above, para.10-011.
[146] See, e.g. *Knowles v Scott* [1891] 1 Ch. 717; *Dunphy v Sleephead Manufacturing Co Ltd* [2007] 3 N.Z.L.R. 602 at [22]; *DVB Bank SE v Isim Amin Ltd* [2014] EWHC 2156 (Comm) (agency for service not terminated by liquidation). For further discussion, see Tan Cheng Han and Wee Mee Seng, in Busch, Macgregor and Watts (eds), *Agency Law in Commercial Practice* (2016), Ch. 6.
[147] See *Pacific and General Insurance Co Ltd v Hazell* [1997] L.R.L.R. 65. Here the appointment was only of a provisional liquidator but it was still considered that the authority of agents appointed by the directors ceased.
[148] *Re Mawcon Ltd* [1969] 1 W.L.R. 78.
[149] *Re Union Accident Insurance Co Ltd* [1972] 1 W.L.R. 640.
[150] See Companies Act 2006 Pt 31 Ch.3.
[151] See *Pacific and General Insurance Co Ltd v Hazell* [1997] L.R.L.R. 65 (appointment of provisional liquidator revoked authority of agents of company). A liquidator will usually himself act as agent of the relevant company: see, e.g. *Dunphy v Sleephead Manufacturing Co Ltd* [2007] 3 N.Z.L.R. 602 (CA) at [22].
[152] *Centre Reinsurance International Co v Freakley* [2006] UKHL 45; [2006] 1 W.L.R. 2863; [2006] 4 All E.R. 1153 (insurers authorised to conduct litigation upon administration in relation to insured claims retained authority, but were not entitled to have expenses treated as administration expenses).
[153] See *Palmer's Corporate Insolvency* (looseleaf); Goode, *Principles of Corporate Insolvency* (4th edn); Lightman and Moss, *Law of Administrators and Receivers of Companies* (5th edn).

principal[154] or agent[155] is a partnership, and there is by death or retirement a change in the partnership, which thereby technically becomes a new partnership.[156] If the contract is regarded as personal to the particular partners, and an agency contract usually is so regarded,[157] the agency is frustrated. A fortiori the same rule applies where the partnership is dissolved.[158]

Mental incapacity   Mental incapacity in this context means inability to appreci-   **10-020**
ate the nature and quality of the act done,[159] but plainly there can be varying degrees of incapacity. In such circumstances, it is perhaps not surprising that the blunt rule assumed to apply to cases of death, viz. that actual authority automatically ceases, probably does not apply to cases of incapacity. As with the position in respect of mental incapacity in a principal existing at the date of appointment,[160] the law is currently unsettled on the effect on an agent's actual authority of supervening incapacity in the principal. It is submitted that the better view is that supervening mental incapacity does not terminate an agent's actual authority until the agent becomes aware, or at least ought to have become aware, of the incapacity, unless the parties have expressly agreed that incapacity is to terminate the mandate.[161] Recent authority has confirmed that where the agent has a contract of appointment, that contract at least is not automatically determined by supervening incapacity.[162] This paragraph was quoted by the Court with apparent sympathy for the views expressed in it. The Court also indicated that even once an incapax party's solicitor becomes aware of supervening incapacity the solicitor may have a residual authority to take steps to ensure that the interests of the client are properly attended to.[163] In the relatively few other relevant cases, the notion of automatic termination has generally been assumed by the parties rather than contested and decided, or it appears that the agent was aware of the incapacity.[164] The agent may also continue to have apparent authority.[165] Statute law has also intervened to some extent. Hence, the agent's authority may continue if the provisions of the Mental Capacity Act 2005 are applicable and complied with.[166] By virtue of the Civil Procedure Rules, compromises of litigation entered into by a party who loses capacity are invalid if that party does

---

[154] *Tasker v Shepherd* (1861) 6 H. & N. 575; *Brace v Calder* [1895] 2 Q.B. 253.
[155] *Friend v Young* [1897] 2 Ch. 421.
[156] Lindley and Banks, *Partnership* (19th edn), paras 3-38–3-40.
[157] See *Tasker v Shepherd*, above; *Brace v Calder*, above; *Friend v Young*, above.
[158] See *Bovine Ltd v Dent & Wilkinson* (1904) 21 T.L.R. 82. But there may in the case of dissolution or retirement be liability for breach of contract: see *Brace v Calder*, above; *Hurst v Bryk* [2002] 1 A.C. 185; Article 58; Lindley and Banks, above, para.3-40.
[159] *Boughton v Knight* (1873) L.R. 3 P. & D. 64 at 72. Elaborate criteria are specified by the Mental Capacity Act 2005 ss.1–4, for matters within its scope: see *Ali v Caton* [2014] EWCA Civ 1313 at [55].
[160] See above, para.2-009. As to the law in Scotland, see Macgregor, para.10-06.
[161] cf. *Restatement, Third*, § 3.08; above, para.10-016.
[162] *Blankley v Central Manchester and Manchester Children's University Hospitals NHS Trust* [2015] EWCA Civ 18; [2015] 1 W.L.R. 4307 at [36]; *Mole v Parkdean Holiday Parks Ltd* [2017] EWHC B10 (Costs). See further, Watts [2015] C.L.J. 140.
[163] *Blankley v Central Manchester and Manchester Children's University Hospitals NHS Trust* [2015] EWCA Civ 18; [2015] 1 W.L.R. 4307 at [36], citing *Fore Street Warehouse Co Ltd v Durrant & Co* (1883) 10 Q.B.D. 471. See too *Johnston v Schurr* [2015] NZSC 82; [2016] 1 N.Z.L.R. 403 at [93].
[164] *Drew v Nunn* (1874) 4 Q.B.D. 661; *Yonge v Toynbee* [1910] 1 K.B. 215; *Re Coleman* (1929) 24 Tas. L.R. 77 (power of attorney); *Evans v James* [2000] 3 E.G.L.R. 1 (client had stroke, but illness known to agent).
[165] *Drew v Nunn* (1874) 4 Q.B.D. 661.
[166] See above, para.10-009.

not have a litigation friend appointed to assist them and the compromise is not approved by the court.[167]

The position where it is the agent who has become mentally incapable is also not settled. The case for automatic termination of actual authority seems stronger in such a case.[168] The agent is the party who is actively altering the principal's legal position and loss of capacity in the agent could lead to unfortunate consequences, whereas with supervening incapacity in the principal the initial instructions will have been given at a time when the principal was capable and the agent retains his sanity. Express provision at the time of appointment for termination in such circumstances should also be effective. Where the agent had apparent authority, this might continue so long as the supervening incapacity were not obvious to the third party.[169] In other circumstances, the incapax agent might be liable to the third party on a warranty of authority, again so long as the incapacity had not been apparent to the third party.

10-021 **Personal insolvency**[170] It seems that the formal declaration of bankruptcy would usually terminate the actual authority[171] of any agent of the bankrupt, unless the agent's authority met the criteria for irrevocability.[172] Once a person is adjudicated bankrupt, dispositions of his estate between the date of the presentation of the petition and the taking effect of the appointment of a trustee are void,[173] with exceptions in favour of a bona fide purchaser.[174] When the appointment of the trustee in bankruptcy takes effect the property vests in him[175]: "property" is defined to include things in action and obligations.[176] Therefore an agent of the bankrupt cannot in general,[177] unless authorised by the trustee, dispose of the bankrupt's property; and if he receives property he receives it for the trustee, who may claim[178] or disclaim[179] it. Similar reasoning applies to contracts. He can enter into a contract on behalf of the principal in cases where the principal can contract himself: but some contracts may be claimed or disclaimed by the trustee. The bankruptcy does not however of itself frustrate, or constitute a repudiatory breach of any, agency contract, though it sometimes may have this effect; and the bankrupt may retain a solicitor.[180]

---

[167] See *Dunhill v Burgin* [2014] UKSC 18; [2014] 1 W.L.R. 933. See further above, para.2-009.
[168] But see *Probus Ltd v Treble & Triple Ltd* [2010] HKCU 2485; affd on other points CACV270/2010, where it was held, largely on pragmatic grounds, that the mental incapacity of an agent did not terminate his actual authority. See further above, Article 5.
[169] See Article 121.
[170] See Chitty, *Contracts* (32nd edn), Ch.20; *Muir Hunter on Personal Insolvency* (looseleaf).
[171] See Story, *Agency* (9th edn), § 482.
[172] Article 118.
[173] Insolvency Act 1986 s.284(1). See too *Estate of F Jones & Sons v Jones* [1997] Ch. 159.
[174] Insolvency Act 1986, s.284(4).
[175] Insolvency Act 1986 s.306.
[176] Insolvency Act 1986 s.436. If a trustee seeks to ratify an act done on behalf of the bankrupt, it might seem that he cannot, for the same reason as the executors or administrators of a deceased person ratify: above, para.10-017. But the wide wording of s.436 may pass the power to ratify. For an example of ratification, see *Alexander Ward & Co Ltd v Samyang Navigation Co Ltd* [1975] 1 W.L.R. 673.
[177] There are exceptions to what the bankrupt's estate includes: Insolvency Act 1986 s.283.
[178] Insolvency Act 1986 s.307: with exceptions for bona fide purchasers: s.307(4).
[179] Insolvency Act 1986 s.315.
[180] See *Nelson v Nelson* [1997] 1 W.L.R. 233.

Likewise the bankruptcy of the agent may or may not frustrate or constitute a repudiation or grounds for termination of any agency contract.[181]

Illustrations

(1) A undertakes to pay B £100 if B succeeds in selling a picture at a certain price—"no sale, no pay". B endeavours to sell the picture, and after A's death succeeds in doing so. The representatives of A's estate are not bound by the contract of sale,[182] but they may ratify it if they think fit, at any rate if it purported to be made on their behalf.[183] Even if the representatives ratify the sale, they are not liable to pay B the £100 unless they ratify his contract with A, but they are liable to pay him a reasonable sum for the services performed.[184]   **10-022**

(2) A stockbroker had a continuation account open with a client. The client died, and the broker, failing to get instructions from his representatives, carried over the transactions instead of closing them on or before settling day, and ultimately sold the shares at a loss. It was held that the representatives were entitled to stand by the carrying-over sale on the first settling day after the death, and that the broker was liable for the subsequent loss.[185]

(3) A solicitor is retained to conduct a divorce suit. The retainer ceases on the death of the client pending the proceedings, and the solicitor cannot recover costs subsequently incurred, even when he had no knowledge of his client's death.[186]

(4) While an action against a company was pending, the company was dissolved under the Companies Acts. It was assumed by the parties and the court that the authority of the company's solicitor was determined by the dissolution, though he had no knowledge of it.[187]

Article 120

TERMINATION OF AUTHORITY BY NOTICE OF REVOCATION OR RENUNCIATION

Subject to the provisions of Articles 118 and 122, the authority of an agent, whether or not conferred by deed, and whether or not expressed to be irrevocable, is terminated by the principal giving to the agent notice of revocation at any time before the authority has been completely exercised,[188] or by the agent giving to the principal notice of renunciation accepted by the principal[189]; but without prejudice   **10-023**

---

[181] See *McCall v Australian Meat Co Ltd* (1870) 19 W.R. 188; *Hudson v Granger* (1821) 5 B. & A. 27. A lasting power of attorney is revoked by the insolvency of the attorney, except so far as the power relates to the donor's personal welfare: Mental Capacity Act 2005 s.13.

[182] *Blades v Free* (1829) 9 B. & C. 167.

[183] *Foster v Bates* (1843) 12 M. & W. 226.

[184] *Campanari v Woodburn* (1854) 15 C.B. 400.

[185] *Re Overweg, Haas v Durant* [1900] 1 Ch. 209, referring of course to former practices.

[186] *Pool v Pool* (1889) 58 L.J.P. 67 (little more than a ruling); *Whitehead v Lord* (1852) 7 Exch. 691.

[187] *Salton v New Beeston Cycle Co* [1900] 1 Ch. 43.

[188] See Illustrations.

[189] See above, para.10-004. For the power of a solicitor to decline to continue to act, see Cordery, *Solicitors* (looseleaf edn), J2; and *Richard Buxton (Solicitors) v Mills-Owens* [2010] EWCA Civ 122; [2010] 1 W.L.R. 1997.

to any claims for damages that the principal or agent may have against the other for breach of any contract between them.[190]

Comment

10-024 **General rule** The general rule, which is perhaps not widely understood, is that the *authority* of an agent, whether given by power of attorney,[191] or informally, even if for consideration,[192] and whether or not expressed to be irrevocable,[193] is revocable, without prejudice to the fact that such revocation may be wrongful as between principal and agent. It is a very longstanding rule: "a man cannot by his act make such an authority, power or warrant not countermandable, which is by the law and of its own nature countermandable."[194] The revocation may be oral whether or not the authority was conferred in writing.[195] There is a power to revoke: but there is not necessarily a privilege to exercise the power—there may indeed be a duty not to do so, with the result that the revocation is a breach of contract. This is subject to the rules as to irrevocable authority set out in Article 118.

The rule is based on policy, and is the same as that relating to dismissal of persons working under contracts of service: "the proper conduct of the affairs of life necessitates that this should be so".[196] It is reinforced by the separate rule that a contract of agency will not usually be enforced by a decree of specific performance.[197] Frequently, of course, the revocation or renunciation constitutes the acceptance of a repudiatory breach by the other party.

The application of these general principles to the position of sub-agents has yet to be worked out. In principle, the sub-agent's actual authority terminates with that of the agent. *Restatement, Third* takes the view, however, that a principal who withdraws authority from an agent owes a duty to known sub-agents to communicate that fact to them and that until that occurs their authority continues.[198] The basis given is that, having approved of the appointment of subagents and having ultimate control over chains of command, the principal should bear the risk of the agent's not having communicated with the sub-agents. It is not clear, nonetheless, that English law would take this view. It is one thing to have consented to a delegation, it is another to bear responsibility for the agent's defaults in respect of his delegates (whose contact details the principal may not even possess). Nor, where the agent is not an employee, is there an obvious basis for the imposition of a duty on the principal (direct or vicarious) to indemnify a sub-agent in respect of his liability to third parties resulting from the termination of his authority. As between

---

[190] See further, Article 123; *Restatement, Third*, § 3.10 (using "manifestation" for what is here described as notice). See too *Temple Legal Protection Ltd v QBE Insurance (Europe) Ltd* [2009] EWCA Civ 453; [2009] Lloyd's Rep I.R. 544 at [49]; *Gu v Du* [2011] NZCA 577 (real estate agent terminates agency without giving reasonable notice, liable to damages).

[191] *Walsh v Whitcomb* (1797) 2 Esp. 565; *Frith v Frith* [1906] A.C. 254; *Sinfra Aktiengesellschaft v Sinfra Ltd* [1939] 2 All E.R. 675.

[192] *Doward, Dickson & Co v Williams & Co* (1889) 6 T.L.R. 316.

[193] See *Vynior's Case* (1609) 8 CoRep. 81b.

[194] ibid.

[195] *The Margaret Mitchell* (1858) Sw. 382; *R. v Wait* (1823) 11 Price 518.

[196] *Frith v Frith* [1906] A.C. 254 at 259, per Lord Atkinson. See also, in the sphere of public law, *Huth v Clarke* (1890) 25 Q.B.D. 391 at 394 ("delegation does not imply a denudation of power and authority"); followed in *Manton v Brighton Corp* [1951] 2 All E.R. 101. See also below, para.12-009, 12-023.

[197] See Article 59.

[198] Comment (e) to § 3.15.

principal and the agent, there may a duty, sounding in damages, to indemnify the agent if, in terminating authority, the principal does not give the agent sufficient time to communicate the fact of termination to any sub-agents. Of course, the foregoing does not affect the position of any apparent authority that the sub-agent may retain following termination of the agent's mandate.

Effect of equity   Equity will sometimes restrain breach of a negative covenant by   **10-025**
injunction.[199] A well-known example is revocation of a licence to enter upon land, which would make the licensee a trespasser. Unless the licence is coupled with an interest,[200] the revocation is effective as regards the land even if it involves a breach of contract. But where there is a contract to permit such access covering a fixed period, revocation of the licence may be restrained by injunction, with the result that the licensee cannot be treated as a trespasser.[201] Equity also sometimes restrains termination of employment contracts[202] and distributorship contracts,[203] and in an unreported but well-reasoned decision, the Court of Appeal granted an interim injunction restraining the termination of a company from management of the Dorchester Hotel in London.[204] All of these have some affinity with agency situations. It seems unlikely that a court would grant such a remedy in what may be called a "pure agency" situation, for example one involving no more than the authority of a broker or a person acting as an agent for sale, because of the overriding interest of the principal of such an agent in determining how and by whom he is represented.[205] But many situations brought under the general umbrella of agency in fact bring in other elements, such as employment, distributorship or general management; and when agency functions are undertaken by companies there may be some element of joint venture.[206] Any of these may make the grant of an injunction appropriate.

Reliance   Finally, it may be said that when the agent has foreseeably relied on an   **10-026**
assurance that the authority would not be revoked, the principal may be restrained from revoking where revocation would be inequitable or unconscionable. There are certainly dicta which if quoted out of context suggest that there is a rule to this effect.[207] They relate, however, to agents who have done exactly what was authorised and who seek no more than reimbursement or indemnity.[208] The significance of estoppel reasoning such as this in general contract law is undoubtedly increasing. But this reasoning should on principle only operate between the

---

[199] *Doherty v Allman* (1878) 3 App.Cas. 709 at 719–720.
[200] cf. above, para.10-007.
[201] See *Hurst v Picture Theatres Ltd* [1915] 1 K.B. 1; *Winter Garden Theatre (London) Ltd v Millennium Productions Ltd* [1948] A.C. 173; Hanbury and Martin, *Modern Equity* (19th edn), Ch.27.
[202] See *Hill v C.A. Parsons & Co Ltd* [1972] 1 Ch 305; Freedland, *The Personal Employment Contract* (2006), p.372 onwards; Article 59.
[203] e.g. *Decro-Wall SA v Practitioners in Marketing Ltd* [1971] 1 W.L.R. 361 (see esp. at 372 and 388); *Evans Marshall v Bertola SA* [1973] 1 W.L.R. 349 (see esp. at 379–380, 382); *Thomas Borthwick & Sons v SOFCO* [1978] N.Z.L.R. 538 per Cooke J; *Dietrichsen v Cabburn* (1846) 2 Ph. 52.
[204] *Re Regent International Hotels (UK) Ltd v Pageguide Ltd*, CA, *The Times,* May 13, 1985 (Ackner and Robert Goff LJJ and Sir Roualeyn Cumming-Bruce); referred to with approval in *Lauritzencool AB v Lady Navigation Inc* [2005] EWCA Civ 579; [2005] 2 Lloyd's Rep. 63.
[205] See Mechem, *Outlines of Agency* (1952), § 262. cf. Article 59. See further, above, para.7-045.
[206] See, e.g. *Shell (Petroleum Mining) Co Ltd v Todd Petroleum Mining Co Ltd* [2008] 2 N.Z.L.R. 418 (parties all companies).
[207] e.g. *Read v Anderson* (1884) 13 Q.B.D. 779 at 781.
[208] See above, para.10-010.

parties: it should not affect the authority of the agent where the only reliance is that of the agent. Where there is reliance by the third party, the doctrine of apparent authority will give such protection as is appropriate.

10-027 **Notice**   As between principal and agent, the agent's authority does not cease until he receives notice of the revocation[209]: but there may be implied revocation by an act clearly[210] inconsistent with the continuation of the agency, coming to the notice of the agent,[211] and in some cases the agent may be employed on the basis that no notice of revocation is required.[212] It was suggested in *Restatement, Second*[213] that a repudiatory breach of his duties by the agent, as by taking a bribe, would terminate his authority automatically; but in England at any rate it seems that the better view is that this would entitle the principal to terminate the authority and no more. As regards third parties, however, revocation should be effective to remove actual authority even if unknown to the agent; but apparent authority will continue until the third party has notice.[214]

10-028 **Joint principals and joint agents**   Where the authority is conferred by two or more principals jointly, unless the terms of appointment otherwise provide, it is sufficient if the notice is given by or to any one of the principals,[215] and the same rule presumably applies in respect of notice given to one agent where co-agents are appointed to act jointly.[216] Where authority is conferred as a result of a resolution of a board or committee of a corporation (including a company), authority would not normally terminate unless the resolution were properly rescinded by a further resolution. A board may generally rescind a resolution at any time until it is communicated to a third party by someone with actual or apparent authority to communicate it.[217]

Illustrations

10-029   (1)   An indenture of lease provided that an agent named in it should have authority to receive the rent on behalf of the lessor, and that his receipt should be a sufficient discharge, during the term thereby granted. Held, that the lessor

---

[209] See *Re Oriental Bank Corp Ex p. Guillemin* (1884) 28 Ch.D. 634 at 640. This problem should not be confused with the question whether the agent can or cannot be dismissed without notice, under the terms of his contract: see Article 123.

[210] See *Re E (Enduring Power of Attorney)* [2001] Ch. 364 at 373 ("unambiguous"); *Houston v Houston* 2012 BCCA 300; [2012] 12 W.W.R. 215.

[211] See *Smith v Jenning's Case* (1610) Lane 97; *Cousins v International Brick Co Ltd* [1931] 2 Ch. 90; *Heaton's Transport (St Helen's) Ltd v TGWU* [1973] A.C. 15 at 110.

[212] e.g. an estate agent: *E.P. Nelson & Co v Rolfe* [1950] 1 K.B. 139. But in some cases the proper explanation may be that agency never arises, since what is revoked is the offer to appoint an agent. See Comment to Article 123.

[213] Comment to § 112.

[214] In *Robert Simpson Co v Godson* [1937] 1 D.L.R. 454 it was held that notice to a third party, but not to the agent, did not terminate the agent's actual authority. The decision was criticised by Wright (1937) 15 Can.B.R. 196. See also above, para.8-008. See too *Dry Bulk Handy Holding Inc v Fayette International Holdings Ltd* [2013] EWCA Civ 184; [2013] 1 W.L.R. 3440.

[215] *Bristow and Porter v Taylor* (1817) 2 Stark. 50.

[216] See Article 11.

[217] See *Powell v Lee* (1908) 99 L.T. 284 (revocation by board of school of resolution appointing headmaster); *Lagunas Nitrate Co Ltd v Schroeder & Co* (1901) 85 L.T. 22 (revocation of dividend); *Potel v IRC* [1971] 2 All E.R. 504 at 511; *Brookton Co-op Society Ltd v FCT* (1981) 147 C.L.R. 441 at 455.

might revoke the authority during the term, the agent having no interest in the rent.[218]

(2) An auctioneer is authorised to sell certain goods by auction. His authority may be revoked by the principal at any time before the goods are knocked down to a purchaser, though the auctioneer may be liable to a bidder in consequence of withdrawing the goods.[219]

(3) Money is deposited with A, to be applied for the use of the poor. The authority may be countermanded at any time before the application of the money, and the money recovered by the principal from A.[220]

(4) Money is deposited with a stakeholder, to be paid to the winner of a wager. The authority of the stakeholder may be revoked at any time before he has actually paid over the money to the winner, and if he pays it over after notice of revocation he is personally liable to the depositor for the amount.[221]

(5) A authorised his banker to hold £20 at the disposal of B. The authority of the banker may be countermanded, provided that he has not paid the money to B, nor attorned to him to hold it on his behalf.[222]

Article 121

APPARENT AUTHORITY WHERE ACTUAL AUTHORITY TERMINATED

Where a principal, by words or conduct, represents or permits it to be represented **10-030** that an agent is authorised to act on his behalf, he is bound by the acts of the agent, notwithstanding the termination of authority (unless perhaps by the death or insolvency of the principal[223]), to the same extent as he would have been if the authority had not been terminated, when it was reasonable for the third party to deal with the agent on the faith of any such representation, without notice of the termination of his authority.[224]

Comment

This is an application of the doctrine of apparent authority in the specific context **10-031** of revocation. It has earlier been pointed out that the doctrine of apparent authority covers two types of case: situations where there is some specific representation, and cases where the representation arises only from the agent's being permit-

[218] *Venning v Bray* (1862) 2 B. & S. 502; and see *Doward & Co v Williams & Co* (1890) 6 T.L.R. 316; *Frith v Frith* [1906] A.C. 254.

[219] *Warlow v Harrison* (1859) 1 E. & E. 309.

[220] *Taylor v Lendey* (1807) 9 East 49.

[221] *Hampden v Walsh* (1876) 1 Q.B.D. 189; *Diggle v Higgs* (1877) 2 Ex.D. 422; *Trimble v Hill* (1879) 5 App.Cas. 342. These cases were not affected by the Gaming Act 1892, now repealed.

[222] *Gibson v Minet* (1824) 9 Moo.C.P. 31; *Brummell v M'Pherson* (1828) 5 Russ. 263. See Article 112(3).

[223] See below, para.10-032.

[224] See Illustrations 1–4; *Pole v Leask* (1862) 33 L.J.Ch. 155 at 162–163; *Ryan v Sams* (1848) 12 Q.B. 460; *Aste v Montague* (1858) 1 F. & F. 264; *Stavely v Uzielli* (1860) 2 F. & F. 30; *Curlewis v Birkbeck* (1863) 3 F. & F. 894; *Debenham v Mellon* (1880) 6 App.Cas. 24 at 33; *Scarf v Jardine* (1882) 7 App.Cas. 345 at 349; *Willis, Faber & Co Ltd v Joyce* (1911) L.T. 576; *Morgan v Lifetime Building Supplies Ltd* (1967) 61 D.L.R. (2d) 178; *Restatement, Third*, § 3.11: "Apparent authority ends when it is no longer reasonable for the third party with whom the agent deals to believe that the agent continues to act with actual authority"; cf. Partnership Act 1890 s.36(1); Factors Act 1889 s.2(2); Articles 21 and 72.

ted to assume a position carrying with it a usual authority.[225] Similar ideas operate where the principal holds the agent out as owner.[226] The question whether apparent authority persists where the principal gives the agent instructions limited to a particular period, or unexpectedly revokes his instructions, has not yet been fully worked out, because most apparent authority cases refer to the extent of authority rather than its duration.[227] It is certainly clear that a third party does not need to point to fresh evidence of a holding out occurring at or after the time that the agent's authority was terminated; such an argument has been expressly rejected.[228] In many circumstances, it will be reasonable for the third party to assume that an express representation as to an agent's authority, or an agent's usual authority, continues unless and until the principal takes steps to notify the third party that the authority has been terminated.[229] In earlier editions of this work it was almost stated as a rule that a holding out would continue to be effective unless and until the third party had been notified of the termination. There are dicta in *Scarf v Jardine*[230] which can be read as supporting that view, but the references there to authority continuing until the third party has "notice" could equally, and it is submitted, should, be taken as references to the third party's state of mind, and then to the reasonableness of that belief, rather than to express notification. To the extent that a requirement of notification, in reliance on (a misreading of) the dicta in *Scarf v Jardine*, was incorporated into the Partnership Act 1890,[231] there is at least room for argument that that requirement does not apply outside partnerships. It seems contrary to the general principles of apparent authority to permit a third party to rely on an absence of notification that a past representation of authority has been withdrawn when no reasonable person would have assumed its continuance.[232] In *Stavely v Uzielli*,[233] a case brought for payment for services performed, Erle CJ is reported as saying to the jury:

> "The lapse of time makes a difference in this case ... there may be notice by other means than by express or actual notice. And here you have the fact, that no accounts were sent, even to the servant (and none to the master), for four years before the servant's death."

Hence, in some cases, the principal's representation may itself indicate the dura-

---

[225] See Comments to Articles 22 and 72.
[226] *Curlewis v Birkbeck* (1863) 3 F. & F. 894. See Article 84.
[227] Stoljar, pp.166–168.
[228] See *SEB Trygg Liv Holding AB v Manches* [2005] EWCA Civ 1237; [2006] 1 W.L.R. 2276 at [32]. See, generally, Powell, pp.399–402; and Comment to Article 22.
[229] See *SEB Trygg Liv Holding AB v Manches*, above; *Rockland Industries Ltd v Amerada Minerals Corp of Canada* [1980] 2 S.C.R. 2: (1980) 108 D.L.R. (3d) 513, Illustration 4. The proposition in the text was in earlier editions of this work almost treated as a rule.
[230] *Scarf v Jardine* (1882) 7 App. Cas. 345 at 349–350 per Lord Selborne LC, and at 356–357 per Lord Blackburn (principles not confined to partnership). See too *Drew v Nunn* (1879) 4 Q.B. 661 at 668; *Willis, Faber & Co Ltd v Joyce* (1911) 104 L.T. 576. Movement of a director from one company to another in a group may not terminate apparent authority to act for the former company unless the significance of the move is itself apparent to the third party: see *Benourad v Compass Group Plc* [2010] EWHC 1882 (QB) at [113] (on facts, director himself had made clear to third party termination of actual authority).
[231] Partnership Act 1890 s.36.
[232] See above, paras 8-018 and 8-050.
[233] (1860) 2 F. & F. 30, Illustration 7. See too *Farrar v Definne* (1844) 1 Car. & K. 580 at 581 (reference to surmise that partner has left partnership being sufficient).

tion for which the authority is to continue,[234] and in others the circumstances may make it inappropriate for the third party to assume that the mandate is continuing. So, if, as in *Stavely*, a long period has elapsed since any earlier dealings with the agent, or there is otherwise something that would alert a reasonable person to the fact that the agent's appointment or authority had ended, it may be unreasonable for the third party to rely on an earlier holding out of authority. The position is put in the following way in the *Restatement, Third*:

> "Apparent authority ends when it is no longer reasonable for the third party with whom the agent deals to believe that the agent continues to act with actual authority."[235]

Application to cases of death or incapacity   Special problems arise in cases of **10-032** incapacity. Where the principal dies, it is arguable on a purely theoretical basis that no apparent authority can continue, for "[h]ow can a valid act be done in the name of a dead man?"[236] A similar argument can be put forward on dissolution of a company, or in personal insolvency.[237] It can also be put forward, though less strongly, in cases of mental incapacity, for the principal becomes incapable of continuing his consent to the relation, or of making or continuing representations to the third party.

In *Drew v Nunn*,[238] however, a strong Court of Appeal decided that a principal who became mentally incapable could be bound under the doctrine of apparent authority. The decision is clearly based on the desirability of protecting third parties: "insanity is not a privilege, but a misfortune which must not be allowed to injure innocent persons".[239] One of the judgments contains suggestions that the reasoning should be extended also to cases of the principal's death.[240] The decision is said to be inconsistent with *Yonge v Toynbee*,[241] in which a solicitor who took steps in litigation on behalf of a defendant client who had unknown to him become mentally incapable was held liable to pay costs incurred by the claimant: it is argued that if the solicitor had apparent authority there would be no loss to the third party.[242] It is, however, difficult to see how the doctrine of apparent authority could have helped the claimant in that case, who seems to have acted reasonably in discontinuing the action after negotiations regarding the appointment of a guardian ad litem had fallen through.[243] The decision was in any case one on the court's summary jurisdiction over solicitors.[244] There is authority therefore that the doctrine may protect the contracts of the agent of a principal who subsequently becomes mentally incapable; and possibly one who dies.

---

[234] See *Pole v Leask* (1862) 33 L.J.Ch.155 at 162.

[235] *Restatement, Third*, § 3.11.

[236] *Watson v King* (1815) 4 Camp. 272 at 274, per Lord Ellenborough (possibly a case on a power coupled with an interest, but no distinction taken).

[237] See above, paras 10-018 and 10-020. See also Partnership Act 1890 s.36(3).

[238] (1879) 4 Q.B.D. 661. See also *Re Parks* (1956) 8 D.L.R. (2d) 155 (adopting a test of constructive notice).

[239] per Bramwell LJ at p.668; see also Brett LJ at pp.667–668.

[240] See Brett LJ at p.668.

[241] [1910] 1 K.B. 215.

[242] Powell, p.390; Treitel, *Law of Contract* (13th edn), para.16-110.

[243] See Higgins (1961) 1 U.Tas.L.Rev. 569. *Drew v Nunn* was not cited to the court in *Yonge v Toynbee*. It seems in fact to have been an early case on apparent authority as we know it now, and was cited with approval in this connection by the Court of Appeal in *Republic of Chili v London and River Plate Bank* (1894) 10 T.L.R. 658 and by Scrutton J in *Willis, Faber & Co v Joyce* (1911) 104 L.T. 576.

[244] It is difficult to see how an implied contract of warranty of authority could arise in such a case.

It is submitted that this is the better view. It might even be argued that there is a stronger case for the continuation of apparent authority in the case of death than in that of mental incapacity, for in the latter case there may be a legitimate interest in protecting the mentally incapable.[245] The policy of protection of innocent third parties appears also in statutes.[246] The authority for cessation of apparent authority is not strong and some of it antedates the development of modern doctrine[247]; such reasoning has also been strongly criticised.[248] It also antedates the strict liability for breach of warranty of authority, which dates from 1857,[249] and which is arguably the real cause of the difficulties in this situation.[250] *Restatement, Third* confines the revocation of authority by incapacity to actual authority and applies the general principles of apparent authority in such situations.[251]

Where the third party knows of the mental incapacity of the principal, it is submitted that the transaction should be void for lack of authority rather than merely voidable.[252] Where the principal's property is, under the Mental Capacity Act 2005, under the control of the court, the analogy seems rather to be with bankruptcy: but the matter is too specialised for consideration here. There is again statutory protection in the case of powers of attorney.[253]

Illustrations

10-033 (1) A authorises B to purchase goods on his credit, and holds him out to C as his agent for that purpose. C supplies goods to B, on A's credit, after revocation by A of B's authority to act on his behalf, C having had no notice of such revocation. A is liable to C for the price of the goods, even if B contracted on his own behalf, and did not intend to bind A.[254]

(2) A husband holds out his wife as having authority to pledge his credit, and subsequently becomes mentally incapable. A tradesman, on the faith of such holding out, supplies goods to the orders of the wife, without notice of the husband's incapacity. The husband is liable for the price of the goods.[255]

(3) A policy was effected through the local agent of an insurance company and notice of a loss was given to him after the branch of business concerned had been transferred to another company. The agent in fact reported the loss to the other company. Held, that that was notice to "a known agent of the company"

---

[245] See Müller-Frienfels in *Civil Law in the Modern World* (Yiannopoulos ed., 1965), 77 at 111–115 (citing comparative material); (1957) 6 Am.J.Comp.L. 165 at 184–185.

[246] As in the case of powers of attorney: see Article 122. See also Partnership Act 1890 s.14(2). For broader protections found overseas, see Powers of Attorney and Agency Act 1984 (South Australia); and Power of Attorney Act 1996 (British Columbia).

[247] e.g. *Blades v Free* (1829) 9 B. & C. 167, Illustration 5.

[248] See *Restatement, Second*, § 120, Comments *a* and *c* and Appendix, Reporter's Note to § 120; (1933) 11 Proc. Am. Law Inst. p.85 onwards ("shocking result"); Seavey (1921) 29 Yale L.J. 859 at 893–895 ("shockingly inequitable").

[249] See Article 105.

[250] See McGaw, fn.56 above, at 331–332. It is noteworthy that statutory protection of persons acting under powers of attorney followed shortly in the Law of Property Amendment Act 1859.

[251] See §§ 3-07, 3-08 and 3-11.

[252] See Powell, pp.390–391; Ashley (1928) 3 Wash.L.Rev. 133; Thomson (1951) 25 Tulane L.Rev. 249; McCormick (1960) 22 Mont.L.Rev. 74.

[253] Article 122.

[254] *Trueman v Loder* (1840) 11 A. & E. 589; *Summers v Solomon* (1857) 7 E. & B. 879, Illustration 8.

[255] *Drew v Nunn* (1879) 4 Q.B.D. 661. But see Comment; above, para.3-042.

within the meaning of the policy, the assured having no knowledge of the change of company.[256]

(4) A manager has general authority to make sales. He negotiates for a substantial contract. His superior decides that higher approval is needed for a particular transaction into which the manager would previously have been authorised to enter. This new restriction is not communicated to the third party and the manager subsequently ends a telephone conversation "we have a deal". His company is bound.[257]

(5) A woman lived with a man as his wife for some years and ordered necessaries from a tradesman to whom she had been held out by the man as having authority to pledge his credit. The man went abroad and died there, the woman continuing to order necessaries for herself and children, the tradesman having had no notice of the death. Held, that the woman had the same authority as a wife to bind the man, but that his estate was not liable for the price of the goods.[258]

(6) For some years P had A in his employ as a coachman who with actual authority ordered corn from T. A went into business on his own account as a stable keeper leasing premises from P. He (casually) continued to wear the livery of P, and continued to order corn from T. When the corn was not paid for, T sued P. Held, P was liable not having brought the termination of A's employ to T's notice, nor intervened when late in the piece P became aware that T was under the impression that A was still P's employee.[259]

(7) For 12 years P employed A as a groom, who for the first eight of those years regularly engaged T as a farrier and veterinary surgeon. P restricted A's authority, but some four years' later A purported to engage T again. Held, that T could not rely on A's prior authority continuing after such a gap.[260]

(8) A had for some years managed a shop belonging to B and ordered goods in B's name from C, and B had duly paid for them. A absconded, called on C and bought goods in B's name, and took them away. Held, that B was liable for the price of the goods.[261]

Article 122

STATUTORY PROTECTION OF THIRD PARTIES AND AGENTS IN RESPECT OF ACTS DONE UNDER POWERS OF ATTORNEY

(1) Where a power of attorney has been revoked and a person, without knowledge of the revocation, deals with the donee of the power, the transaction between them is, in favour of that person, as valid as if the power had then been in existence.[262] **10-034**

(2) Where a power of attorney is expressed in the instrument creating it to be ir-

---

[256] *Marsden v City and County Ass. Co* (1865) L.R. 1 C.P. 232. See also Article 21.
[257] *Rockland Industries Inc v Amerada Minerals Corp of Canada Ltd* [1980] 2 S.C.R. 2; (1980) 108 D.L.R. (3d) 513.
[258] *Blades v Free* (1829) 9 B. & C. 167. But see Comment.
[259] *Aste v Montague* (1858) 1 F. & F. 264.
[260] *Stavely v Uzielli* (1860) 2 F. & F. 30.
[261] *Summers v Solomon* (1857) 7 E. & B. 879. See also *Trueman v Loder* (1840) 11 A. & E. 589.
[262] Powers of Attorney Act 1971 s.5(2). Further protection in respect of Stock Exchange transactions is given by s.6.

revocable and to be given by way of security, then, unless the person dealing with the donee knows that it was not in fact given by way of security, he is entitled to assume that the power is incapable of revocation except by the donor acting with the consent of the donee, and will accordingly be treated for the purposes of Rule (1) above as having knowledge of the revocation only if he knows that it has been revoked in that manner.[263]

(3) Where the interest of a purchaser depends on whether a transaction between the donee of a power of attorney and another person was valid by virtue of Rule (1) above, it will be conclusively presumed in favour of the purchaser that that person did not at the material time know of the revocation of the power if—(a) the transaction between that person and the donee was completed within 12 months of the date on which the power came into operation, or (b) that person makes a statutory declaration, before or within three months after the completion of the purchase, that he did not at the material time know of the revocation of the power.[264]

(4) A donee of a power of attorney who acts in pursuance of the power at a time when it has been revoked does not, by reason of the revocation, incur any liability (either to the donor or to any other person) if at that time he did not know that the power had been revoked.[265]

Comment

10-035   This Article paraphrases the provisions of s.5(1) to (4) of the Powers of Attorney Act 1971,[266] which protect third parties and the donee of the power where the power has, unknown to them, been revoked.[267] The 1971 provisions replace ss.124, 127 and 128 of the Law of Property Act 1925, which were directed towards achieving the same sort of protection, but which were notoriously obscure and unsatisfactory. Rules (1), (2) and (3) therefore represent statutory formulations, in their particular context, of the doctrine of apparent authority. Rule (4) affects the doctrine of warranty of authority.

10-036   **Revocation**   It seems clear that revocation includes not only express or implied revocation but also death, mental incapacity and insolvency: for by s.5(5) it is provided that knowledge of the revocation of the power includes knowledge of the occurrence of any event (such as the death of the donor) which has the effect of revoking the power.[268]

10-037   **Lasting powers of attorney**   These provisions also apply to lasting powers of attorney governed by the Mental Capacity Act 2005, with special variants.[269] That Act also contains provisions protecting the attorney and bona fide third parties in the case of transactions under instruments which did not create valid powers of at-

---

[263] Powers of Attorney Act 1971 s.5(3).
[264] Powers of Attorney Act 1971 s.5(4).
[265] Powers of Attorney Act 1971 s.5(1).
[266] See in general *Law Com. No.30*, Cmnd. 4473 (1970); (1971) 121 New L.J. 746 at 751, 764, 771, 795; (1971) 115 S.J. 596; (1971) 35 Conv (N.S.) 310; (1971) 68 L.S.Gaz. 434 at 437.
[267] The section applies whenever the power was created, but only to acts and transactions after the commencement of the Act: s.5(7).
[268] As to revocation, see in general Article 117.
[269] s.14(5).

torney but have nevertheless been registered[270]; there are presumptions similar to those of the 1971 Act.[271]

Article 123

COMPENSATION AT COMMON LAW ON TERMINATION OF AUTHORITY

The termination of the authority of an agent, while valid as such—   **10-038**

(1) may entitle the agent to compensation in accordance with the require-ments of statute or delegated legislation; or
(2) may constitute a breach by the principal of the express terms of any contract of agency or of implied terms or contractual promises, in respect of any of which the principal may be liable in damages or subject to other remedies.[272]

Comment

The question whether a principal is liable to an agent for terminating his author-   **10-039**
ity turns on the type of contract or other arrangement under which the agent is employed.

Agent an employee If the agent is an employee he may be entitled to compensa-   **10-040**
tion for unfair dismissal or redundancy in accordance with the relevant statutory provisions of employment law.[273] He may also be entitled to damages at common law for wrongful dismissal, viz. dismissal in breach of contract.[274]

Agent a commercial agent Where the agent is a commercial agent as defined by   **10-041**
the Commercial Agents (Council Directive) Regulations 1993, the circumstances in which he may be dismissed and special compensation payable on dismissal are regulated by statutory instrument. Then provisions are discussed in Chapter 11.[275]

Agent engaged under bilateral contract for services If the agent is engaged, not   **10-042**
as an employee but as an independent intermediary, his rights will turn on whether he acts under a bilateral contract or under a unilateral one. If he himself undertakes duties towards his principal, e.g. to use his best endeavours, as seems to be a normal implication of a sole or exclusive agency,[276] his contract is a bilateral one involv-ing reciprocal obligations. Usually such contracts make their own provision for

---

[270] s.14(1).
[271] s.14(3). See in general Cretney and Lush, *Enduring Powers of Attorney* (5th edn), Ch.8; Aldridge, *Powers of Attorney* (10th edn); Thurston, *Powers of Attorney* (5th edn).
[272] See Comment: Powell, pp.380–385. As to continuing commission and repayment of overpaid com-mission, see above, paras 7-025 and 7-041.
[273] See e.g. Deakin and Morris, *Labour Law* (6th edn); Chitty, *Contracts* (32nd edn), Ch.40. Special considerations apply when a company alters its articles. See *Southern Foundries Ltd v Shirlaw* [1940] A.C. 701; *Shindler v Northern Raincoat Co Ltd* [1960] 1 W.L.R. 1038; *Russell v Northern Bank Development Corp Ltd* [1992] 1 W.L.R. 588; Davenport (1993) 109 L.Q.R. 553; *Gower's Principles of Modern Company Law* (10th edn), (paras 14-52 and 19-25–19-28). See also *Micklefield v SAC Technology Ltd* [1990] 1 W.L.R. 1002.
[274] See Chitty, above, para.40-200 onwards.
[275] See esp. below, para.11-045 onwards.
[276] See above, para.7-036. Contra, Murdoch (1975) 91 L.Q.R. 357 at 373–375, who treats this as involv-ing the offer of a unilateral contract also. See also McConnell (1983) 265 E.G. 547.

termination[277]; but unless carefully drafted these may not always be as efficacious as might have been hoped.[278] Questions regarding the termination of such a contract depend on whether it has or has not a time limit specified in it.

(1) No time limit[279] If there is no time limit referred to in the contract, three interpretations are possible as to termination.

A. terminable at will Decisions[280] and dicta[281] can be found suggesting that the confidential nature of the contract of agency means that where there are no provisions relating to termination such a contract can be terminated at will by the principal. The authority for this approach mostly derives however from unilateral contract cases, where it is the *offer* which is terminated[282]; and there is sometimes confusion with the proposition that the termination of authority is *effective* whether a breach of contract or not. It is submitted that such an approach will rarely if ever be appropriate for a binding bilateral contract, which of its nature involves the likely expenditure of time and effort by the agent.

B. not terminable at all Conversely, dicta can also be produced for the proposition that such a contract is (in the absence of special provision for termination) not terminable at all (other than on breach or frustration), at least if the express terms provide any support for such a construction.[283] It is submitted however that although there are cases where there is in effect the grant of a perpetual benefit in return for consideration,[284] in the commercial situation of representation such an interpretation would rarely be appropriate.[285]

C. terminable on notice The third and most likely possibility is that the parties are interpreted as having at the time of the contract intended that the contract is terminable on reasonable notice, taking into account the expenditure and time incurred by the agent, the desirability of a period for readjustment of business and so forth.[286] This is so even where the contract itself makes other provision for

---

[277] e.g. *Christie & Vesey Ltd v Maatschappij, etc., Helvetia NV (The Helvetia-S)* [1960] 1 Lloyd's Rep. 540. See also *Sport International Bussum BV v Inter-Footwear Ltd* [1984] 1 W.L.R. 776.

[278] e.g. *Wickman Machine Tool Sales Ltd v L. Schuler AG* [1974] A.C. 235, where the use of the word "condition" was not sufficient.

[279] See Carnegie (1969) 85 L.Q.R. 392; Lücke (1973) 5 Adelaide L.Rev. 32 at 48 onwards.

[280] e.g. *Alexander v Davis & Son* (1885) 2 T.L.R. 142 (where the contract appears bilateral); followed in *Henry v Lowson* (1885) 2 T.L.R. 199.

[281] e.g. *Martin-Baker Aircraft Co Ltd v Canadian Flight Equipment Ltd* [1955] 2 Q.B. 556 at 582.

[282] e.g. *Motion v Michaud* (1892) 8 T.L.R. 253; affd ibid. at 447: see below.

[283] e.g. *Llanelly Ry and Dock Co v L & NW Ry Co* (1873) L.R. 8 Ch.App. 942 at 949; (1873) L.R. 7 H.L. 550 at 567.

[284] See explanation of the *Llanelly* case by Goff LJ in *Staffordshire Area Health Authority v South Staffordshire Waterworks Co* [1978] 1 W.L.R. 1387 at 1402.

[285] See *Martin-Baker Aircraft Co Ltd v Canadian Flight Equipment Ltd* [1955] 2 Q.B. 556 at 577. See also *Tower Hamlets LBC v British Gas Corp, The Times,* December 14, 1984 (no implication of reasonable duration).

[286] e.g. *Bauman v Hulton Press Ltd* [1952] 2 All E.R. 1121 (six months); *Martin-Baker* case, above (12 months: one contract a licence to manufacture); *Decro-Wall International SA v Practitioners in Marketing Ltd* [1971] 1 W.L.R. 361 (distributorship: 12 months); *Crawford Fitting Co v Sydney Valve and Fittings Pty Ltd* (1988) 14 N.S.W.L.R. 438 (stressing in a distributorship contract the notion that "the relationship of the parties should continue long enough to enable the distributor to recoup extraordinary expenditure or effort"; particularly when that was incurred "with the actual or tacit

termination,[287] unless such provision can be treated as exclusive.[288] The matter is sometimes said to turn on whether the contract is similar to an employment contract.[289] It is submitted that this interpretation will nearly always be appropriate in bilateral contract cases. Plainly, misconduct by the agent may still justify summary dismissal.[290]

(2) Time limit If there is a time limit contained in the contract, as where the contract provides for the agent to act for a specified period of years, it might be thought that the agent was by such a term entitled to continue to act for that period unless the contract was discharged by frustration, and that if his authority was terminated before the end of the period he would be entitled to damages. There are however many cases which hold that the principal may terminate without breach by simply going out of business[291] or disposing of the subject-matter of the agency.[292] The reasoning is that the promise is only conditional on the business being carried on, which itself is not promised[293]; or that

"a person is entitled to deal with his property as he chooses, and a person is entitled either to carry on his business or to give up carrying on his business, as he wishes."[294]

Other cases however hold that the principal may not do so and that there is a right to serve for a particular period,[295] sometimes explained as a right to a "continuing benefit".[296] These cases make very fine distinctions.[297] They are often explained as

authority of the principal"); *Alpha Lettings Ltd v Neptune Research and Development Inc* [2003] EWCA Civ 704 (distributorship: four months); *Concourse Initiatives Ltd v Maiden Outdoor Advertising Ltd* [2005] EWHC 2995 (advertising); *W Nagel (a firm) v Pluczenik Diamond Company NV* [2017] EWHC 1750 (Comm) at [89]. "Reasonableness" is ascertained at the time of the notice given; ibid.; *Ogilvy & Mather (NZ) Ltd v Turner* [1996] 1 N.Z.L.R. 641 at 646; and see in general the *Staffordshire Area Health Authority* case, above.

[287] As it did in the *Martin-Baker* case, above (see esp. at 573).

[288] As in *Re Barker Sportcraft Ltd's Agreements* (1947) 177 L.T. 420.

[289] e.g. the *Martin-Baker* case, above, at 582; see also *Paper Sales Corp Ltd v Miller Bros Co Ltd* (1975) 55 D.L.R. (3d) 492; *Knight v Calderlodge Developments* (1978) 238 E.G. 117.

[290] See, e.g. *Gledhill v Bentley Designs (UK) Ltd* [2010] EWHC B8 (dismissal for abusive language).

[291] *Ex p. Maclure* (1870) L.R. 5 Ch.App. 737; *Rhodes v Forwood* (1876) 1 App.Cas. 256, Illustration 1 (even though the contract itself provided for termination); *Hamlyn & Co v Wood & Co* [1891] 2 Q.B. 488 (sale contract); *Northey v Trevillion* (1902) 7 Com.Cas. 201; *Lazarus v Cairn Line Ltd* (1912) 106 L.T. 378; *In Re R.S. Newman Ltd* [1916] 2 Ch. 309; *Leak v Charles & Sons Ltd* (1948) 92 S.J. 154. As to changes in partnerships, see *Tasker v Shepherd* (1861) 6 H. & N. 575; *Cowasjee Nanabhoy v Llallbhoy Vullubhoy* (1876) L.R. 3 Ind.App. 200; *Brace v Calder* [1895] 2 Q.B. 253; Lindley and Banks, *Partnership* (18th edn), para.3-40.

[292] *Lazarus v Cairn Line Ltd*, above; *L. French & Co Ltd v Leeston Shipping Co Ltd* [1922] 1 A.C. 451, Illustration 2 to Article 58; *Howard Houlder & Partners Ltd v Manx Islands SS Co* [1923] 1 K.B. 110 (all cases on ships); *Shackleton Aviation Ltd v Maitland Drewery Aviation Ltd* [1964] 1 Lloyd's Rep. 293 (aircraft).

[293] *Warren & Co v Agdeshman* (1922) 38 T.L.R. 588 at 590.

[294] *Alpha Trading Ltd v Dunnshaw-Patten* [1981] Q.B. 290 at 304, per Brandon LJ. See also *Lazarus v Cairn Line Ltd* (1912) 106 L.T. 378 at 380 (Scrutton LJ).

[295] *Re London & Colonial Co Ex p. Clark* (1869) L.R. 7 Eq. 550; *Re Patent Floor Cloth Co Ltd* (1872) 26 L.T. 467; *Turner v Goldsmith* [1891] 1 Q.B. 544, Illustration 2; *Mutzenbecher v La Aseguradora Española SA* [1906] 1 K.B. 254; *Reigate v Union Manufacturing Co (Ramsbottom) Ltd* [1918] 1 K.B. 592; *General Publicity Services Ltd v Best's Brewery Co Ltd* [1951] 2 T.L.R. 875; *Re Premier Products Ltd* [1965] N.Z.L.R. 50 (full analysis of case law: partly distributorship contract).

[296] *Lazarus v Cairn Line Ltd*, above, at 380.

[297] *Bauman v Hulton Press Ltd* [1952] 2 All E.R. 1121 at 1124; Burrows (1968) 31 M.L.R. 390 at 399.

turning on the existence or non-existence of an implied term,[298] which is in general rarely found by the courts unless necessary to give business efficacy to the contract.[299] But in truth the question of implication of a term does not arise until the initial promise has been interpreted as absolute or non-absolute.[300] Thus in one such case[301] one member of a divided Court of Appeal posed the question whether there was any indication that a two-year contract could be ended in less than two years, and another whether there was a term that the business would be continued for two years.[302] All this emphasises the need for careful drafting of such contracts in order to avoid disputes.

The question may arise whether, if the principal is entitled to cease business, he must nevertheless give the agent reasonable notice. On the whole this seems unlikely: a cancellation of authority "from today" has been held valid.[303] The agent will however doubtless be entitled to a reasonable packing-up period before, e.g. he becomes a trespasser.[304]

This whole question interlocks very considerably with the question whether the principal is in breach of contract if he prevents the agent from earning commission. Such prevention may of course occur during the course of the agency arrangement (as when he sells himself or through another agent, or refuses to complete a negotiated transaction[305]) as well as by complete termination of it. Reference should therefore be made also to the discussion of prevention of earning of commission under Article 58.[306]

10-043 Agent's rights derive only from offer of unilateral contract   In some cases the rights of an agent will be based only on a single or continuing offer by the principal to pay commission, which is best interpreted as an offer of a unilateral contract, under which the agent is not obliged to do anything but simply qualifies for commission if he does. It has been submitted elsewhere[307] that this is the best explanation of the estate agent's contractual position where he is not a sole or exclusive agent[308] and the same may be true of other canvassing agents.[309] In such a case the question of termination of authority depends on the rules for the revocation of contractual offers[310]; and although the courts have sometimes sought to answer the questions by considering the implication of a *term* it is submitted that the question is here better put as one whether there is an implied *contract* not to revoke the offer.[311] The principal might promise not to withdraw the offer in consideration of

[298] e.g. *Mutzenbecher v La Aseguradora Española SA* [1906] 1 Q.B. 254; *Alpha Trading Ltd v Dunnshaw-Patten Ltd* [1981] Q.B. 290.
[299] cf. *The Moorcock* (1889) 14 P.D. 64; above, para.7-001.
[300] See *Re Premier Products Ltd* [1965] N.Z.L.R. 50.
[301] *Brace v Calder* [1895] 2 Q.B. 253; see Burrows (1968) 31 M.L.R. 390.
[302] See pp.262 and 259.
[303] *Lazarus v Cairn Line Ltd* (1912) 106 L.T. 378.
[304] See *Winter Garden Theatre (London) Ltd v Millenium Productions Ltd* [1948] A.C. 173.
[305] e.g. *Alpha Trading Ltd v Dunnshaw-Patten Ltd* [1981] Q.B. 290, Illustration 3 to Article 58.
[306] See also Article 59 on specific performance.
[307] See Comment to Article 58; *Luxor (Eastbourne) Ltd v Cooper* [1941] A.C. 108, esp. at 124–125; Murdoch (1975) 91 L.Q.R. 357.
[308] Murdoch, above, treats sole agencies on the same basis.
[309] As to canvassing agents, see above, para.1-020.
[310] See *Luxor (Eastbourne) Ltd v Cooper*, above, at 128–129.
[311] But see Treitel, *Law of Contract* (14th edn), paras 2-051–2-057.

the agent commencing or maintaining activities within a reasonable time.[312] Put this way, it is obvious that such a promise will rarely be detected, and that the offer can normally be withdrawn without warning. This seems the true explanation of cases holding that an agent's authority may be withdrawn summarily.[313] This is now the accepted explanation of the position of an estate agent who is not a sole agent, unless he succeeds in securing other terms.[314] Wide dicta regarding the irrevocability of offers in such situations should be treated with caution.[315]

Gratuitous agency An agent who has no contractual relationship, actual or   **10-044**
potential, with his principal can be dismissed (in so far as that term is appropriate) without liability on the principal's part, except in so far as he has rights under the law of restitution.

Remedies for wrongful termination In principle a wrongful termination of   **10-045**
authority will not terminate the contract also unless the agent accepts the breach as doing so.[316] The usual remedy for wrongful termination will however (apart from the statutory provisions of employment law and the regulations governing commercial agents) be an action for damages; though there may be cases where an injunction or a declaration can be obtained.[317] The damages will normally be calculated by reference to what would have been earned by way of commission if the term of the agency had run its full course,[318] or if reasonable notice had been given,[319] as appropriate in the circumstances, less expenses which would have been incurred, and subject to the duty to mitigate damages.[320]

Illustrations

(1) A and B agree that for seven years or so long as A shall continue to carry on a   **10-046**
business at the town of Liverpool, A shall be sole agent at Liverpool for the sale of B's coals. After four years B sells his colliery. He is not liable to A, for

---

[312] cf. *Errington v Errington* [1952] 1 K.B. 290.

[313] e.g. *Motion v Michaud* (1892) 8 T.L.R. 253; affd ibid. at 447; *Joynson v Hunt & Son* (1905) 93 L.T. 470; *Levy v Goldhill* [1917] 2 Ch. 297. See also *Keshen v S. Lipsky Co Ltd* (1956) 3 D.L.R. (2d) 438; *Lowe v Rutherford Thompson McRae Ltd* (1970) 14 D.L.R. (3d) 772.

[314] See above, paras 7-035–7-036.

[315] e.g. that of Goff LJ in *Daulia Ltd v Millbank Nominees Ltd* [1978] Ch. 231 at 239.

[316] *Atlantic Underwriting Agencies Ltd v Cia. di Assicurazione di Milano SpA* [1979] 2 Lloyd's Rep. 240, following *Thomas Marshall (Exports) Ltd v Guinle* [1979] Ch. 227; *Société Générale, London Branch v Geys* [2012] UKSC 63; [2013] 1 A.C. 523; See Chitty, *Contracts* (32nd edn), para.40-193. In any case, ancillary duties survive breach, e.g. a valid exclusive dealing clause (the *Thomas Marshall* case, above) and a clause permitting inspection of books (*Yasuda Fire Ins. Co v Orion Marine Insurance Underwriting Agency Ltd* [1995] Q.B. 174).

[317] Article 59.

[318] e.g. *Reigate v Union Manufacturing Co (Ramsbottom Ltd)* [1918] 1 K.B. 592.

[319] *W Nagel (a firm) v Pluczenik Diamond Company NV* [2017] EWHC 1750 (Comm) at [85] (detailed assessment of lost revenue and avoided costs). e.g. *Bauman v Hilton Press Ltd* [1952] 2 All E.R. 1121; *Roberts v Elwells Engineers Ltd* [1972] 2 Q.B. 586 (account not an appropriate remedy); *Paper Reclaim Ltd v Aotearoa International Ltd* [2007] 3 N.Z.L.R. 169 (SC) (compensation for wrongful termination of agency to be calculated on the basis that the repudiation had the same effect as the giving of proper notice).

[320] Account must be taken of the probabilities of a sale taking place: *Hampton & Sons Ltd v George* [1939] 3 All E.R. 627; and see also *G. Trollope & Sons v Caplan* [1936] 2 K.B. 382 (overruled on another point in *Luxor (Eastbourne) Ltd v Cooper* [1941] A.C. 108). See in general McGregor, *Damages* (19th edn), paras 33-002—33-004.

the contract does not bind him to keep the colliery, nor to send coals to Liverpool.[321]

(2) A shirt manufacturer agreed with the plaintiff to employ him as "agent canvasser and traveller" for five years. After two years the manufacturer's shirt factory burnt down. The business was closed down and he ceased to employ the plaintiff. Held, the plaintiff was entitled to substantial damages, it being an implied term of the particular contract in question that in employing the plaintiff for five years, the manufacturer must be taken to have agreed to continue to send him samples so that he could earn his commission.[322]

---

[321] *Rhodes v Forwood* (1876) 1 App.Cas. 256. See also Article 58, Illustration 2; *Groves v Stirling Bonding Co* [1935] 3 D.L.R. 481.
[322] *Turner v Goldsmith* [1891] 1 Q.B. 544. See also *Comet Group Plc v British Sky Broadcasting Ltd*, QBD, *The Times,* April 26, 1991.

CHAPTER 11

COMMERCIAL AGENTS[1]

1. INTRODUCTION

Background   In continental European countries agents are often placed in named   **11-001**
categories which are the subject of special rules. These may require particular
qualifications in the agent, and sometimes registration as a person authorised to
conduct the commercial activity concerned. It has also been the case that certain
categories of agent have been regarded as requiring protection against their
principals, in a manner not unlike that in which employees are often, and nowadays
in developed countries usually, regarded as requiring protection against their
employers. In particular, it has in some countries been made legally requisite for a
principal who wishes to terminate the services of an agent in certain categories to,
in effect, buy the agent out by the payment of a sum which can be justified on the
basis of the expense he has incurred and/or customer connection which he has
generated—a notion sometimes referred to by the French phrase *indemnité de
cessation*. It is thought that there is a danger that after the agent has built up a market
for his principal the principal may intervene and deal direct with the customers
before the agent has recovered his outlay and legitimate profit. Agents are also
perceived as requiring, and have been given, protection against their principals in
other ways, for example as regards the supply of information as to transactions
entered into by the principal as a result of the agency and (a related question) as to
payment of commission.

   A directive seeking to generalise and harmonise among the EC countries the effect of such legislation, so far as it is applied to commercial agents, a category
generally understood in civil law countries, was in the offing from 1976. The
proposed directive[2] aimed at coordinating national laws on independent commercial agents in order to reduce legal differences that were thought to impede the

---

[1]   Randolph and Davey, *European Law of Commercial Agency* (3rd edn, 2010); Saintier and Scholes,
Commercial Agents and the Law (2005); Christou, *International Agency, Distribution and Licensing Agreements* (6th edn, 2011) (covering other topics also, but containing valuable insights and
drafting examples); Singleton, *Commercial Agency Agreements: Law and Practice* (4th edn, 2015).
Valuable insights appear in Bennett, *Principles of the Law of Agency* (2013). Some insights can also
be obtained from the Draft Common Frame of Reference (2009), IVE 3:101 onwards, and from the
ICC Model Commercial Agency Contract.

[2]   Proposal for a Council Directive to Coordinate the Laws of Member States relating to (Self-
Employed) Commercial Agents [1977] OJ C13/2. On the background, see Commission des Com-
munautés Européennes, *Egalité des droits pour les agents commerciaux: Proposition de directive
relative à la coordination des droits des Etats membres concernant les agents commerciaux
(indépendants)*, Bull.Cté.eur., suppl. 1/77. The proposal was submitted to the Economic and Social
Committee on November 24, 1977 (see [1978] OJ C59/31). The modified proposal was published
in 1979: [1979] OJ C56/5.

functioning of the common market and to affect the conditions of competition in Europe. At the same time the proposal aimed at actually improving the protection of commercial agents throughout the Community. Commercial agents were thought to suffer from the uncertainties of their legal position within the Member States. The scope of the proposed directive was therefore broader than the fundamental freedoms laid down by the EC Treaty because the harmonisation of the laws of the Member States governing commercial agency was advanced irrespective of any cross-border elements.[3]

For some countries such legislation was of a familiar type and the need was only to harmonise details. For the common law countries in the EC, however, the category, and indeed (with some exceptions) the categorisation of agents in general did not exist; and the type of legal control introduced was of a completely new type. The common law rules as to the relationship between any principal and any agent are based on the assumption that freedom of contract prevails. In so far as any protection has been perceived as necessary, it is protection of the principal against misuse of his powers by the agent, as by taking a bribe, making a secret profit and in general assuming a position in which his own interests or those of others for whom he acts are adverse to those of his principal.[4] It was against the context of such perceived dangers that the fiduciary duties of the agent have developed. Their potential breadth is related to the breadth of the common law of agency itself, which does not in general utilise categories, and applies to many types of representative, some of which (e.g. solicitors) would hardly be regarded in some other countries as within the law of agency at all. Where detailed control of types of agent has been introduced, as in the case of estate agents,[5] this has been done in the interest of protecting the principal against the agent, not the reverse; or even (as in the case of financial intermediaries[6]) in the interest of protecting the public.

Thus it was perhaps not surprising that the Law Commission for England and Wales in 1977 reported rather hysterically that the proposed directive "in many respects offend[s] against basic principles of the English law of agency"[7]: but this was not so. It also stated that it was "unable to identify such a social group [as commercial agents] in England"[8]: a claim that was speedily rebutted in the press at the time and, after a gap, by litigation. A more measured report of a committee of the House of Lords assessed the proposal as one to introduce detailed regulation in an area in which it did not exist in the United Kingdom,[9] and this was correct. It may also be true that in the United Kingdom agents of the type regulated by the Directive are less frequently used as instruments of market penetration than in some other countries.

11-002   **The EC Directive**   The Council Directive on the Co-ordination of the Laws of the Member States Relating to Self-Employed Commercial Agents[10] was adopted in 1986, but the United Kingdom and Ireland were given more time to bring it into

---

3   *Centrosteel srl v Adipol GmbH* (C-456/98) [2000] E.C.R. I-6007, para.13.
4   See Article 43 onwards.
5   See, e.g., above, paras 7-020 and 7-038.
6   See Financial Services and Markets Act 2000.
7   *Law Com. No.84* (1977) (reproduced in Randolph and Davey, fn.1 above, Appendix 4), p.32.
8   *Law Com. No.84* (1977), p.6.
9   *Select Committee on the European Communities*, 51st Report, Session 1976–1977 (reproduced in Randolph and Davey, fn.1 above, Appendix 5).
10   Directive 86/653 [1986] OJ L382/17. Its protective function is stressed in *Bellone v Yokohama SpA* (C-215/97) [1998] E.C.R. I-2191, where it was held that a national law requiring such an agent to

force, on the (rather dubious) grounds, stated in the preamble to the Directive, that "a particular effort" had to be made in those countries. In the United Kingdom the "particular effort" proved to be confined to copying out the Directive almost verbatim (with two minor errors) and leaving others to interpret it as best they could. In Ireland the Directive was put into effect as it stood, with only a few special provisions at the beginning of the regulation. A second regulation was later promulgated there to make the choice required by the Directive between indemnity and compensation. Time was also granted to Italy, where such protection of the agent existed, but was in fact more elaborate and complex than elsewhere. The Directive has considerable similarities with German law,[11] and reference to German law in particular may therefore sometimes assist in elucidating its likely intention, though it is obviously not to be presumed that the Directive simply intended to generalise the results obtained in any one national system of law. There is no objection to the protection being extended more widely than the Directive requires, i.e. to services, and it should be noted that in some countries (e.g. Germany, France) this has been done.[12]

2. THE COMMERCIAL AGENTS REGULATIONS

The Commercial Agents (Council Directive) Regulations 1993   The Directive   **11-003**
was implemented in Great Britain by the Commercial Agents (Council Directive) Regulations 1993,[13] made under s.2(2) of the European Communities Act 1972. These came into effect on January 1, 1994. They were not confined to contracts made after that date, and hence contracts of agency whenever made were subject to them, save in respect of rights and liabilities accrued before that date.[14]

Interpretation   On general principles of EU law the Regulations must be   **11-004**
interpreted against the background of the Directive itself.[15] Since the wording of the Regulations follows the Directive extremely closely, the Directive is relevant not only as to general purpose but also as to matters of detail. As will be seen, however, the Directive, and hence the Regulations, contain many obscurities and

---

register cannot prevent the application of the Directive. See also regarding registration *Centrosteel Srl v Adipol GmbH* (C-456/98) [2000] E.C.R. I-6007; *Caprini v Conservatore Camera di Commercio, etc.* (C-485/01) [2003] E.C.R. I-2371.

[11] For a brief account of the relevant German law in English, see Reiling, in Randolph and Davey, fn.1 above, Ch.10. As to French law, see Saintier, in Randolph and Davey, fn.1 above, Ch.11; Saintier and Scholes, fn.1 above, esp. Ch.6.

[12] For example, in connection with services: see below para.11-016.

[13] SI 1993/3053, as amended by Commercial Agents (Council: Directive) (Amendment) Regulations 1993 (SI 1993/3173) and Commercial Agents (Council Directive) (Amendment) Regulations 1998 (SI 1998/2868). Effect was given to the Directive in Northern Ireland by the Commercial Agents (Council Directive) Regulations (Northern Ireland) 1993 (SR 1993/483), which was effective on a different date, January 13, 1994. See Schrire (1994) 15 B.L.R. 171; Hodgkinson (1994) 5 E.B.L.Rev 119; Singleton [1994] Tr. L. 26; Bell and O'Toole (1994) 138 S.J. 10; Davis (1994) 144 N.L.J. 388. The Directive applies also to countries in the European Economic Area.

[14] reg.23. The Regulations therefore permitted calculation of indemnity in respect of events occurring before that date, because no right or liability in respect of them accrued at the time of those events but rather, the right to indemnity accrued after that date: *Moore v Piretta PTA Ltd* [1999] 1 All E.R. 174 at 180.

[15] See, e.g., *Von Colson v Land Nordrhein-Westfalen* [1984] E.C.R. 1891; [1986] 2 C.M.L.R. 430; *Litster v Forth Dry Dock & Engineering Co Ltd* [1990] 1 A.C. 546; *Marleasing v La Comercial Internacional de Alimentacion SA* (C-106/89) [1990] 1 E.C.R. 4135; [1992] 1 C.M.L.R. 305; *Moore v Piretta PTA Ltd*, above.

uncertainties. Some of these derive from the structure of the Directive itself: for example, the extent to which particular provisions are *ius cogens*, i.e. cannot be derogated from, as opposed to *ius dispositivum*, i.e. provisions which only apply in the absence of other agreement, is far from clear.[16] Other problems derive from words selected by translators.[17] It is sometimes appropriate to look at the original proposals for a Directive and the Explanatory Memorandum and see what changes were made in the final form of the Directive.[18] It should be noted that the individual Regulations are preceded by headings. These do not (apart from the chapter headings) appear in the Directive itself. While instructive as to the beliefs of the English drafter, therefore, they provide no certain guide to the intentions of the Directive. The same is true of material issued by the Department of Trade and Industry at the time.[19] Standard English methods of statutory interpretation, or assumptions that common law techniques will fill gaps, will in many cases of dispute, however convenient, be not at all appropriate. The point that what is required is development of "Euro-law" in this context (as in others) is often made.[20] Many problems will eventually require resolution, in the last resort by the Court of Justice of the European Union, formerly European Court of Justice, which already has several decisions on the Convention.[21] There are certainly areas in which different decisions may be given in different countries; and there are several areas in which the interaction with domestic law is not clear.[22]

3. APPLICATION OF THE REGULATIONS

11-005 **Coverage** By reg.1(2) the Regulations cover the relations between commercial agents and their principals. They therefore apply only to the internal agency relationship between principal and agent. They do not affect the external authority of the agent, nor the result of transactions entered into by him with third parties.

11-006 **Applicability: conflict of laws**[23] Regulation 1(2) states that the Regulations "apply in relation to the activities of commercial agents in Great Britain". It appears therefore that the test for application of the British[24] regulations is principally based on where the activities are conducted, i.e. is geographical. There is no requirement that the agent maintain any place of business in Great Britain. There is no

---

[16] See, e.g., below, paras 11-033, 11-035 and 11-041.
[17] See, e.g., below, paras 11-024, 11-025, 11-034 and 11-048. A much larger number was listed by the Law Commission, fn.7 above: see Randolph and Davey, fn.1 above, Appendix 4, Annex C (actually omitted).
[18] See Randolph and Davey, fn.1 above, Appendix 4, Annex A.
[19] These are printed in Randolph and Davey, fn.1 above, Appendices 2 and 3.
[20] See, e.g. Tosato (2016) 36 O.JL.S. 661.
[21] The authority of the court's rulings is based largely on its power, when a national court refers the matter to it, to determine by means of a "preliminary ruling" the meaning of the Directive, the extent to which national law complies with it and (where this is possible) how national law should be interpreted so as to comply with it. The power may also arise incidentally in other proceedings lawfully brought before the court, including in some cases proceedings by private individuals. Finally, the court can also entertain direct proceedings against a Member State based on failure properly to implement the Directive (the so-called "Francovich action", in which an aggrieved party may recover damages from the state in question), though none has so far been brought against the United Kingdom in the present context.
[22] An obvious example is provided by regs 16 and 18, below, paras 11-039 and 11-056.
[23] See Dicey, Morris and Collins, *The Conflict of Laws* (15th edn), Vol.2, para.33-420 onwards. Some of this discussion concerns applicability and does not rank as within the conflict of laws.
[24] Northern Ireland is separately provided for: see SI 1993/483 (NI).

definition of "activities" but the word presumably refers to the typical acts of such an agent, as defined in the Regulations, in soliciting and introducing business and in general acting on the principal's behalf.[25] Since the criterion of application is geographical, many questions of how far this can be done from outside by electronic means remain to be settled. It will be seen from the illustrations below that this basic requirement does not always fit neatly with the choice of law applicable to the internal relationship between principal and agent by virtue of the (later) Rome I Regulation on the Law Applicable to Contractual Obligations ("Rome I").[26]

Under the Rome I Regulation, which is discussed in more detail in Chapter 12, the parties may choose a law governing the contract of agency. If they do not, the Regulation provides that a contract for the provision of services shall be governed by the law of the country in which the service provider (in our context the commercial agent[27]) had his habitual residence[28]; or, if this category is not applicable, by the law of the country in which the person rendering the characteristic performance of the contract (in our context, plainly the agent)[29] had his habitual residence.[30]

The general scheme of the British Commercial Agents Regulations is that their operation is territorial: they govern the relations between commercial agents and their principals and apply in relation to activities of such agents in Great Britain. There is no statement specifically directed towards the conflict of laws position, but the starting point has to be the normal one, that the Regulations, being part of English law,[31] should only apply where English law is the governing law. But they may also be superimposed as a matter of public policy on contracts governed by other laws where they involve activities in Great Britain: arts 9.1 and 2 of the Rome I Regulation allow a court to apply overriding mandatory provisions of the law of the forum to a contract governed by another law,[32] and it seems clear, as is stated below, that the Commercial Agents Regulations, or at any rate their unexcludable

---

[25] See the description in the opinion of Advocate General Trstenjak referred to in fn.27 below.

[26] Regulation 593/2008 [2008] OJ L177/6, which applies to contracts concluded as from December 17, 2009.

[27] In *Wood Floor Solutions Andreas Domberger GmbH v Silvo Trade SA* (C-19/09) [2010] 1 W.L.R. 1900, the ECJ treated a commercial agency contract as one for the provision of services under art.5(1)(b) of Council Regulation 44/2001 on jurisdiction and the enforcement of judgments. See the judgment, and in more detail the opinion of Advocate General Trstenjak at [53] onwards. See above, para.1-035.

[28] art.4(1)(b). In so far as the agent is also a franchisee or distributor, the same criterion is applied by art.4(1)(e) and (f).

[29] arts 3 and 4: see below; *Lawlor v Sandvik Mining and Construction Mobile Crushers and Screens Ltd* [2012] EWHC 1188 (QB); [2012] 2 Lloyd's Rep. 25 (art.4(2) applied: governed by Spanish law). Some agency contracts might rank as consumer contracts (the principal being the consumer) and be governed by art.6.

[30] "Habitual residence" is defined broadly in art.19 (see below, para.12-005) and in general in the commercial context denotes something like establishment, which word will be used in the rest of this chapter.

[31] References to English law are hereafter for the purpose of simplicity of exposition, and cover England and Wales. Where Scots law is relevant parallel reasoning will usually apply.

[32] See Dicey, Morris and Collins, *The Conflict of Laws* (15th edn), Vol.2, para.32-092 onwards. A possibly relevant provision is art.23, similar to but not identical with art.20 of the Rome Convention, which provides that the Regulation does not prejudice the application of provisions of Community law which, in relation to particular matters, lay down conflict of laws rules relating to contractual obligations. But it is not clear to what extent reg.1(2) and (3) are to be so regarded, and in any case it is only the operation of the Rome I Regulation which is potentially displaced. There are also provisions permitting the application of overriding law where all other elements relevant to the situation at the time of choice of law are located other than in a country whose law has been chosen, or one

part, rank as such. One way of achieving this overriding application in connection with international instruments has been to provide an enacting statute that enables them to have the "force of law". This was done with the Hague-Visby Rules,[33] which contain within them a provision which prevents contracting out in certain circumstances.[34] This has enabled striking out of clauses indirectly inconsistent with the regime of the Rules, for example a jurisdiction clause for a country which would not apply them.[35] The jurisdiction clause in question was embedded in a choice of law clause, and it is possible that the choice of law clause was intended by the court to be void also, which would have necessitated, had a relevant issue arisen, a fresh search for the applicable law. It is submitted that this should not have been so, as the Hague and Hague-Visby Rules do not supersede a whole contract (for example, they have no application to freight) but simply declare invalid certain types of terms within it. There is no such drafting technique used in the Commercial Agents Regulations, but they implement an EU policy directed to the protection of agents so should be regarded as overriding before courts within the EU.[36] They may also justify declaring void particular clauses in the governing law which might indirectly interfere with the operation of the Regulations: for example a jurisdiction or arbitration clause requiring proceedings in a country where the Regulations would, or might, not be applied. To negate a choice of law clause would however be to produce a need for a governing law for the unobjectionable provisions of the contract.

The geographical application of the Regulations has two exceptions. First, if the parties to a contract involving activity of a commercial agent in Great Britain have agreed that the agency contract is to be governed by the law of another Member State,[37] the provisions of the law of that Member State corresponding to the operative part of the Regulations apply.[38] The Regulations stop there, but as regards other matters within the agency contract, the law of that state applies by virtue of the choice of law rules of the Rome I Regulation.

Secondly, they apply to the activities of an English established agent in another Member State where the law of that State enables the parties so to agree that the contract is governed by a foreign law, and they agree that it is governed by English law.[39] Presumably, the Rome I Regulation as applicable in that state, with its ac-

---

or more Member States: arts 3.3 and 4; as to which see Dicey, Morris and Collins, *The Conflict of Laws* (15th edn), Vol.2, Rule 224.

[33] Carriage of Goods by Sea Act 1971 s.1(2).

[34] art.III.8.

[35] *The Hollandia* [1983] 1 A.C. 565 (Dutch jurisdiction clause: Dutch law had not at that time adopted the Visby Protocol to the Hague Rules and retained the Hague Rules, which gave less protection to cargo claimants than the Hague-Visby Rules: clause invalid at least in part).

[36] See *Accentuate Ltd v Asigra Inc* [2009] EWHC 2655 (QB); [2009] 2 Lloyd's Rep. 599 (considered below) at [97] onwards.

[37] "Member State" means a State which is a contracting party to the EEA agreement signed at Oporto on May 2, 1992, as adjusted by the Protocol signed at Brussels on March 18, 1993: reg.2(1), inserted by Commercial Agents (Council Directive) (Amendment) Regulations 1998 (SI 1998/2868).

[38] reg.1(3)(a). But this would not be so merely because the contract was governed by the law of that Member State by virtue of art.4 of the Rome I Regulation, because of the place of establishment of the agent.

[39] reg.1(3)(b). It is believed that this must be the intended effect of these two provisions, which are by no means easy to understand. A different view is put forward in Randolph and Davey, *The European Law of Commercial Agency* (3rd edn, 2010), pp.29–31. Their exposition is doubted by Mann J in *Fern Computer Consultancy Ltd v Intergraph Cadworx & Analysis Solutions Inc* [2014] EWHC

ceptance of the principle of choice (and the specific provisions of art.4), would normally do so. This is in a sense the reciprocal of the previous provision.[40]

If however there is no choice of law, but English law applies by virtue of the Rome I Regulation, the British Regulations, which apply only to activities in England, do not in the above case apply.[41] It might be hoped that the law of the place of acting would do so.

A more controversial matter is whether the overriding mandatory nature of much of the Regulations applies (especially arts 17 and 18 on indemnity and compensation) where the contract is expressed to be governed by the law of another country (outside the EU), which may know no such protection of agents; or where the law of such a country applies by virtue of the Rome I provisions on the applicable law in the absence of choice because the agent is established[42] in that country. It might be thought not, on the ground that the preamble to the Commercial Agents Directive refers to the mischief potentially occurring "where principal and agent are domiciled in different Member States". The European Court of Justice, on a reference from the Court of Appeal for England and Wales, held however in *Ingmar GB Ltd v Eaton Leonard Technologies Ltd*[43] that the provisions apply on two grounds: that the parties should not be able to evade the Directive by "the simple expedient of a choice-of-law clause", and that "the purpose served by the provisions in question requires that they be applied where the situation is closely connected with the Community, in particular where the commercial agent carries on his activity in the territory of a Member State, irrespective of the law by which the parties intended the contract to be governed".[44] This means that the Regulations should certainly be regarded as overriding mandatory rules of the forum and before an English court should (it is submitted) be superimposed on a contract involving activities of a commercial agent in England, by whatever law the agency contract is governed.[45]

This has was confirmed in an English case where the agent's activities were subject to an express choice of the law of Ontario, and furthermore an arbitral

---

2908 (Ch); [2015] 1 Lloyd's Rep. 1 at [114]–[119], though the judge reaches no firm conclusion as to the meaning of reg.1(2) and 1(3), relying on the fact that whatever their purport, they only have effect if the agreement governing the agency is expressly subject to English law or the law of another Member State, which was not so (at [119]).

[40] It was added by the Commercial Agents (Council Directive) Regulations 1998 (SI 1998/2868).

[41] cf. *Agro Foreign Trade Agency v Petersime NV* (C-507/15) where it was held that Belgian law was entitled to limit its own application to commercial agents whose principal place of business is in Belgium, with the result that the Directive did not apply to activities in Turkey under a commercial agency contract governed by Belgian law.

[42] This word is used here in a loose sense.

[43] *Ingmar GB Ltd v Eaton Leonard Technologies Inc* (C-381/98) [2000] E.C.R. I-9305; [2001] 1 All E.R. (Comm) 329; criticised by Verhagen (2002) 51 I.C.L.Q. 135; see also Idot (2001) 90 Rev Crit. de Droit Int.Privé 107; Kruger (2002) 18 Col. J.Eur. Law 85; Roth (2002) 3 C.M.L. Rev 369. For a list of further notes and articles on the point see Rühl, (2007) 15 Eur.Rev Private Law 891 at fn.3. It is possible that some such situations might be soluble on the basis of art.3.3 and 3.4, referred to above.

[44] See the judgment at [25].

[45] Where legislation under the Directive is in a particular Member State wider than is required by the Directive, e.g. in applying to services, and the governing law is that of another State which has correctly implemented the minimum protection required by the Directive, the additional protection provided by the first State is only to be applied in a court in the first State if it finds that it is crucial in its legal order to give protection beyond that provided by the Directive: *United Antwerp Maritime Agencies (Unamar) NV v Navigation Maritime Bulgaria* (C-184/12) [2014] 1 Lloyd's Rep. 161(concerning an arbitration clause in a contract governed by Bulgarian law which a Dutch court had held invalid).

tribunal in Canada had rendered an award applying that law and not taking into account the Regulations.[46] On general conflict of laws principles the arbitral tribunal must have been correct: (subject to different considerations within the EU) one country does not apply the public policy of another unless the law of that country is the governing law. But before an English court the result would not be acceptable by reason of EU-based regulations. It was therefore held that the arbitration clause was void before an English court, and this is similar to the refusal, referred to above, to accept a Dutch jurisdiction clause where the Hague-Visby Rules were mandatory for shipments out of the United Kingdom, and a Dutch court, applying Dutch law, would have rendered a decision different to that required by those Rules.[47]

The court however went on to grant leave to serve out of the jurisdiction on the basis that the contract was governed by English law, arguing that there was no other candidate to govern the compensation claim under the Regulations than English law. But the requirement is that the contract be governed by English law, not merely a part of it, albeit a discrete part.[48] The Commercial Agents Regulations are not all mandatory, nor do they apply to all parts of a contract involving the activities of a commercial agent, as is shown by the extensive issues in the dispute itself. In the *Ingmar* case referred to above the ECJ simply said that it should not be possible to evade the Regulations by the simple expedient of a choice-of-law clause[49]: but that does not mean that the only way to prevent evasion is to nullify a choice of law altogether. It is submitted that the contract was still governed by the law of Ontario[50] even if parts of it were unenforceable or inoperative and subjected to different terms[51] before an English court by reason of English (EU-originating) public policy. This view, that the overriding provisions of the Regulations do not necessarily affect choice of law clauses themselves, has recently been accepted.[52]

Some illustrations may be of assistance.

1. *Agent established in Great Britain acts in Great Britain*

11-007
    (i)   The contract contains a choice of English law. English law is the governing law. The acts are performed in England and the Regulations apply as part of the governing law.

    (ii)   The contract contains no choice of law. In most cases art.4 of the Rome I Regulation, referred to above, would require to be invoked,

---

[46] *Accentuate Ltd v Asigra Inc* [2009] EWHC 2655 (QB); [2009] 2 Lloyd's Rep. 599. A German court rendered a very similar decision in 2006: OLG München, May 17, 2006—7 U.1781/06, though perhaps going too far in looking to see only if it was "likely" that the designated tribunal would not apply arts 17 and 18, See Rühl, fn.43 above.

[47] *The Hollandia* [1983] 1 A.C. 565: see above.

[48] CPR r.6.20(5).

[49] See the judgment at [25].

[50] There is some reference to invalidity of the choice of law, however, in [88].

[51] This of course is different from the Hague and Hague-Visby Rules, which simply proscribe certain types of contract clause.

[52] *Fern Computer Consultancy Ltd v Intergraph Cadworx & Analysis Solutions Inc* [2014] EWHC 2908 (Ch); [2015] 1 Lloyd's Rep. 1 at [34]. The court went on to say (in the context of service out of the jurisdiction) that the cause of action under the Regulations was not in any case to be classified as contractual, but rather, as statutory (see at [38], [39]), and possibly in the nature of a tort (at [55]). The proposition that the cause of action is statutory would still have permitted a claim "in respect of a contract where the contract ... is governed by English law" for the purposes of CPR Pt 6 had the contract been governed by English law, but it was not. On the other hand, jurisdiction "in respect of a breach of contract committed within the jurisdiction" would not be available at all, because the claim was not for breach of a contract (at [47]). See further below, para.11-040, fn.198.

leading to the result that the governing law is English because the agent is established in England. The result will therefore be the same as that in (i).

(iii) The contract contains a choice of the law of a Member State, for example Dutch law, perhaps because the firm acted for is Dutch. By English law, Dutch law is the governing law of the contract of agency. The choice excludes the British regulations by virtue of reg.1(3)(a)above. Dutch law, and its application of the Directive, will apply.

(iv) The contract contains a choice of the law of a non-Member State, for example that of California, perhaps because the principal operates in California. English law will accept the chosen law as governing the contract unless all its elements are connected with another country, when non-derogable provisions of that country's law may apply, or all the other relevant elements are located in one or more Member States, in which case non-derogable provisions of Community law may apply.[53] Beyond this, the question arises as to whether the British regulations apply. On their (territorial based) wording they clearly do. And it appears that the application of them to commercial agents acting in Great Britain is an overriding mandatory rule of English law which an English court should apply whatever the governing law.[54] The British regulations therefore apply, but in other respects the contract remains governed by the law of California.

2. *Agent established in the Netherlands acts in Great Britain*

(i) The contract contains a choice of English law. The governing law is English and the Regulations apply both as part of the governing law and because of their territorial application. It might be arguable that this is only so if Dutch law agrees that English law may govern, under the wording of reg.1(3)(b), but it is difficult to see any reason why this should be required before an English court. **11-008**

(ii) The contract contains no choice of law. The governing law will probably be Dutch under art.4 of the Rome I Regulation, as the law of the agent's place of establishment. It might then be argued that the Dutch rules would apply as part of the governing law: but it seems preferable to say that the territorial application of the British regulations means that before an English court they apply to the contract as overriding policy of the forum, and that the parties have not agreed otherwise, which is what reg.1(3)(a) of the Regulations requires. In other respects the contract is governed by Dutch law.

(iii) The contract contains a choice of Dutch law. Dutch law is the governing law. The British regulations do not apply: reg.1(3)(a). The Dutch implementation of the Directive applies.

(iv) The contract contains a choice of German law (perhaps because the principal is German). By the same reasoning as that in (iii) above, German law is the governing law and the German implementation of

---

[53] arts 3.3 and 3.4 of the Rome I Regulation, above, para.11-006.

[54] *Ingmar GB Ltd v Easton Leonard Technologies Ltd* (C-381/98) [2001] 1 All E.R. (Comm) 329; *Accentuate Ltd v Asigra Inc* [2009] EWHC 2655; [2009] 2 Lloyd's Rep. 599, both discussed above, para.11-006.

the Directive applies as part of the governing law under reg.1(3)(a). If the Dutch law would (before a Dutch court) have regarded itself as applicable and is different, the English court would not apply it, as not being part of the governing law nor of that of the forum.

(v) The contract contains a choice of the law of California (perhaps because the principal is from California). The law of California is the governing law. The reasoning of the *Ingmar* case, discussed above, would again lead to the conclusion that the British regulations should be superimposed on the contract.

3. *Agent established in England or Wales acts in the Netherlands*

11-009

(i) The contract contains a choice of English law. English law is the governing law. Under reg.1(3)(b) the English regulations apply if Dutch law allows the choice of law. If not (which is no doubt unlikely), they do not. The English court could, however, apply Dutch law as overriding mandatory provisions of the law of the place of performance, by virtue of art.9.3 of the Rome I Regulation.[55]

(ii) The contract contains no choice of law. The governing law is likely to be English, as that of the place of establishment of the agent, but the British regulations apply only to activities in Great Britain. An English court could however again apply the Dutch law by virtue of art.9.3 of the Rome I Regulation.

(iii) The contract contains a choice of German law (the principal may be German). German law is the governing law. With their territorial basis, the British regulations do not apply. The German version may.[56]

(iv) The contract contains a choice of the law of California. The governing law is the law of California. With their territorial basis, the English regulations do not apply. An English court could again however apply the Dutch law by virtue of art.9.3 of the Rome I Regulation.

4. *Agent established in California acts in England*

11-010

(i) The contract contains a choice of English law. English law is the governing law and on the territorial basis also the Regulations apply.

(ii) The contract contains a choice of the law of California. That law governs. On a territorial basis however the Regulations apply even though there might have been justification for the choice of law. The regulations apply on the basis of the *Ingmar* and *Accentuate* cases, discussed above.

(iii) The contract contains no choice of law. The law of California will probably govern as that of the place of establishment of the agent. It could be argued that the law of California alone should apply, but it seems that the relevant parts of the Regulations should again apply on a territorial basis.

11-011 **Regulations applicable by agreement of the parties** The Regulations largely operate by implying terms into or imposing them upon contracts. There seems no

---

[55] See Dicey Morris and Collins, *The Conflict of Laws* (15th edn), Vol.2, para.32-094 onwards.
[56] It is difficult to believe that this can be by virtue of reg.1(3)(a) of the Regulations: despite reg.4(2) being made subject to para.(3), reg.1(3)(a) surely applies only where the activities are conducted in Great Britain.

reason why parties should not expressly or impliedly incorporate the Regulations even when they are not compulsorily applicable, though problems of interpretation would arise in respect of the provisions against derogation.[57] Conversely, they do not exclude law applicable overall, except where they are mandatory, and although the common law is not clear on some of the matters covered, a common law claim should often be considered, for example where it is not clear that the claimant ranks within the definition of a commercial agent.

Activities   This word has already been discussed. It remains to note that since   **11-012**
nothing in the Regulations requires the presence of the agent at the place where the activities are conducted, problems will arise as to where the activities of an agent who operates from one country into another by means of telephone, telex, fax or the internet are to be regarded as taking place. Where an agent conducts activities in several jurisdictions, the Regulations presumably apply only in respect of the activities in Great Britain.

What is a commercial agent?   The term "commercial agent" is, as stated above,   **11-013**
unknown to the common law; and the definition in the Regulations is therefore crucial. A designation by the contract itself, or by the parties, cannot be conclusive.[58] Such an agent is defined in reg.2(1) as:

"a self-employed intermediary who has continuing authority to negotiate the sale or purchase of goods on behalf of another person (the 'principal'), or to negotiate and conclude the sale or purchase of goods on behalf of and in the name of that principal."[59]

There are specific exceptions which are dealt with below. Since "the terms and content of an agent's authority may, change or reduce during the course of an agency as the result of agreement by words or conduct, or sometimes as a result of external events", it has been held that "the relevant time at which to determine the scope of the agent's retainer is…the date on which it is necessary to determine whether it is or is not a commercial agent for the purposes of the relief being claimed."[60]

It is, however, clear that the Directive and Regulations refer to an *agent*. A person who has not function but to transmit the goods in question on predetermined terms and at predetermined prices is not covered. A *distributor* of goods, though often

---

[57] This is accepted in *Tamarind International Ltd v Eastern Natural Gas (Retail) Ltd* [2000] C.L.C. 1397; [2000] Eu. L.R. 708; and in *McQuillan v McCormick* [2010] EWHC 1112 (QB); [2011] E.C.C. 18.

[58] See *Blanc Canet v Europcar France SA* [2005] E.C.C. 34 (French Cour de Cassation).

[59] The Regulations appear to envisage agents acting for multiple principals, and that they do so was held in *Rossetti Marketing Ltd v Diamond Sofa Co Ltd* [2011] EWHC 2482 (QB); [2011] E.C.C. 28, the point being made that the obligation under art.3 to act "dutifully and in good faith", together with the normal fiduciary duties applicable under English law should protect the principal against abuse by the agent by preferring one customer over another and so forth. On appeal the general possibility was not doubted, but it was held that the normal fiduciary rules and the rules as to implied terms operated to prevent the agent acting without the principal's consent for competitors whose products clashed with those of the principal: see [2012] EWCA Civ 1021; [2013] 1 All E.R. (Comm) 308, esp. at [27] and [42].

[60] *W Nagel (A Firm) v Pluczenik Diamond Co NV* [2017] EWHC 1750 (Comm); [2017] 2 Lloyd's Rep. 215 at [43] per Popplewell J. But cf. [44]; also the position as regards secondary activity, below, para.11-020, fn.116.

described as an "agent", buys for resale and, unlike an agent, takes a financial risk.[61] Although in some countries distributors and sometimes franchisees may be entitled to protections similar to those afforded to agents, the Directive and regulations are not intended to cover distributors.[62] It is of course possible for a distributor to perform an appropriate agency function also. This would raise a question of whether the activity is secondary or not.[63] A broker acting independently of both parties is not a commercial agent.[64]

11-014 Sub-agency   The Regulations appear to be drafted on the basis of a contract of agency.[65] Thus it has been held that if an agent appoints a sub-agent or sub-agents, and if there is no privity of contract between them and the principal (which is the normal interpretation in English law[66]) the sub-agents are not agents of the principal so as to be entitled to claim compensation under the Regulations even though they negotiate, and/or sell the goods.[67] Nor are they commercial agents of the main agent, since they do not sell on his behalf.[68] It has been suggested that they might be able to "establish a stake" in the compensation due to the main agent,[69] and perhaps this is an indication that the result described above is unlikely to have been intended.[70] The position of sub-agents who have no privity with the principal is in fact controversial in other contexts of agency law as well.[71] A practical solution for the present situation could be to determine on the facts that in such cases they have privity with the principal.[72]

11-015 Self-employed   This phrase to a common lawyer contains echoes of employ-

---

[61] See above, para.1-035.
[62] *AMB Imballaggi Plastici Srl v Pacflex Ltd* [1999] 2 All E.R. (Comm) 249; [1999] C.L.C. 1391; *Mercantile International Group Plc v Chuan Soon Huat Industrial Group Ltd* [2002] EWCA Civ 288; [2002] 1 All E.R. (Comm) 788 (remuneration partly by mark-up to which principal did not object: sale plainly on an agency basis): cf. *Umbro International Ltd v Revenue & Customs Commissioners* [2009] EWHC 438 (Ch); [2009] S.T.C. 1345 (purchase for resale to "principal"); *Crane v Sky In-Home Service Ltd* [2007] EWHC 66 (Ch); [2007] 2 All E.R. (Comm) 599 (agent supplied digital boxes, but acted as agent for digital services: held commercial agent in respect of boxes); *Sagal v Atelier Bunz GmbH* [2009] EWCA Civ 700; [2009] 2 Lloyd's Rep. 303 (agent who acts in own name is not a commercial agent). This appears to exclude cases of indirect representation (above, para.1-020), which seems correct. The actual nature of the contract between the parties is not considered, but it does not appear to have been a sale and resale. (See also the *Mavrona* case regarding indirect agents, fn.99 below, not referred to in the *Sagal* case). Agreements between principal and an agent who does not bear any significant risk in relation to the contracts concluded and/or negotiated on behalf of the principal will normally not be subject to art.101 TFEU (Treaty on the Functions of the European Union) (formerly art.81 EC). The relevant principles, in particular in relation to relevant risks, are discussed in paras 12–21 of the European Commission's Guidelines on Vertical Restraints [2010] OJ C 130/1, replacing the Commission's earlier Guidelines on Vertical Restraints [2000] OJ C 291/1.
[63] See below, para.11-020.
[64] *Ferro v Santoro OJ 2002* (C-323/24); cf. above, para.1-035.
[65] See regs 13, 17(1).
[66] See Article 35.
[67] *Light v Ty Europe Ltd* [2003] EWCA Civ 1238; [2004] 1 Lloyd's Rep. 693.
[68] *Light v Ty Europe Ltd* [2003] EWCA Civ 1238 at [26].
[69] *Light v Ty Europe Ltd* [2003] EWCA Civ 1238 at [26], per Tuckey LJ.
[70] See Tosato [2013] L.M.C.L.Q. 544, arguing in general that insufficient attention has been paid, at any rate in English courts, to the European dimension of the Regulations. cf. above, para.11-004. The relevant discussion of the present point is at pp.561–565. Such a restriction does not operate in France: Saintier, in Randolph and Davey, fn.1 above, p.161.
[71] See above, paras 5-011 and 5-012.
[72] See above, para.5-010.

ment law. An employee must be a natural person; hence it might be thought that the reference to self-employment carried the same implication. It seems clear that in this context that is a wrong inference and that the reference is rather to what at common law might be called an independent contractor. Hence a company or partnership can be a commercial agent.[73] In a useful case where an employee agent changed his status to that of an independent commercial agent[74] the court applied English notions of employment law in considering the effect of the change; but it has been argued that primary recourse should have been had to European materials.[75]

Sale or purchase of goods It is convenient next to note that the protection only **11-016** applies to agents who act in connection with sale or purchase of goods, and does not cover agents whose principal activity lies in the provision of services, though similar legislation in other countries (e.g. France and Germany) does so, thus extending the protection. The fact, however, that an agent for sale provides ancillary servicing facilities does not prevent his being a commercial agent. But when it is the selling which is subsidiary, this activity could in Great Britain rank as merely "secondary" under another provision of the Regulations, and they might not then apply.[76] It seems likely that the question whether a contract for work and materials involves a sale of goods will require solution on the basis of asking which element is predominant, as under current English law.[77] There is no definition of "goods".[78] The main problem regularly arising in this connection in the modern context is whether computer software ranks as "goods".[79] Contracts relating to such software are often, however, drafted in other ways, in particular as licences, and this raises special problems.[80]

---

[73] The Regulations were applied to a corporate agent in the *Imballaggi* case, fn.58 above. See *Bell Electric Ltd v Aweco Appliances Systems GmbH & Co KG* [2002] EWHC 872 (QB); [2002] Eu.L.R. 443 at [50] (argument to the contrary "wholly unsustainable") (proceedings on appeal [2002] EWCA Civ 1501; [2003] 1 All E.R. 344).

[74] *Smith v Reliance Water Controls Ltd* [2003] EWCA Civ 1153; [2003] Eu.L.R. 874.

[75] See Tosato [2013] L.M.C.L.Q. 544 at 551–553.

[76] See below, para.11-020 onwards.

[77] The question is discussed in connection with a firm supplying and erecting conservatories in *Marjandi Ltd v Bon Accord Glass Ltd* (Sheriff J.K. Tierney, 2007 WL 4947410). The contract was held to be one for the building of an extension, with the result that the Regulations were not relevant. Tosato [2013] L.M.C.L.Q. 544 at 558–561 suggests the use of a phrase "focal point".

[78] In *Commission of the European Communities v Italy* (7/68) [1968] E.C.R. 423, the ECJ gave a meaning for "goods" for the purposes of art.9 of the Treaty: "By goods, within the meaning of that provision, there must be understood products which can be valued in money and which are capable, as such, of forming the subject of commercial transactions". This gives general guidance, but the differing contexts in which the notion has been considered mean that analysis in a specific context is required. Tosato [2013] L.M.C.L.Q. 544, again argues that European criteria should be employed. In *Tamarind International Ltd v Eastern Natural Gas (Retail) Ltd* [2000] Eur.L.R. 708, gas (and perhaps electricity) were assumed to be "goods".

[79] See *St Albans City and District Council v International Computers Ltd* [1996] 4 All E.R. 481; Schmidt 1996 S.L.T. 13 at 17–18. See *Benjamin's Sale of Goods* (9th edn, 2014), paras 1-078 onwards. There is useful recent discussion concerning software supplied on CDs in *Fern Computer Consultancy Ltd v Intergraph Cadworx & Analysis Solutions Inc* [2014] EWHC 2908 (Ch); [2015] 1 Lloyd's Rep. 1 at [62] onwards. See also *Software Incubator UK Ltd v Computer Association UK Ltd* [2016] EWHC 1587 (QB); [2017] Bus. L.R. 245.

[80] See *London Borough of Southwark v IBM UK Ltd* [2011] EWHC 549 (TCC); 135 Con. L.R. 136. See also *Fern Computer Consultancy Ltd v Intergraph Cadworx & Analysis Solutions Inc* [2014] EWHC 2908 (Ch); [2015] 1 Lloyd's Rep. 1 at [88].

11-017 **Continuing authority**   The authority must be continuing; an agent appointed for a single transaction would not be covered, for if he were, there would be no force in the word "continuing". But it would seem that the phrase "continuing authority" could cover an agent appointed for a number of transactions, definite or indefinite, for a period or for a season (e.g. Christmas),[81] or an agent whose activities are repeatedly accepted by the principal.[82] It has been held, though in the context of legislation applying the provisions to services (chartering), that this covers an agent who negotiates one contract which is then renewed over a period.[83] It has been said that "the question whether an agent has continuing authority to negotiate is a question which is to be determined by the terms of the contract with the principal, not by the extent or frequency of the exercise of that authority."[84]

11-018 **Negotiate the sale or purchase of goods on behalf of another person: canvassing agents**   These words cover agents who are entrusted with negotiation of terms, even though they are not authorised to enter into the final contract itself.[85] It may be questioned whether the wording also covers agents who simply introduce business and leave the principal to negotiate, as in the case (outside the contract of sale of goods and hence outside this context) of estate agents. The category is referred to in this book as one of "canvassing" or "introducing agents".[86] Since in such a case the agent plays a fairly active role on behalf of another it would seem on the wording that the Regulations ought to apply. It seems that actual bargaining is not required[87] and, so long as the agent is not merely passive, he may be regarded as "negotiating".[88] In a recent case an agent was held to rank within these words where what could principally be said was that "the generation and maintenance of [the agent's] goodwill with [the principal was at the heart of the services which [the agent] was engaged to perform."[89] But some such intermediaries would not be regarded as commercial agents in at least some continental European countries accepting the notion of commercial agent,[90] and of course an estate agent is not likely to be classified as a commercial agent either, quite apart from the fact that he acts in connection with land and not goods. It seems likely that a key lies in the requirement of continuing authority referred to above. A canvassing agent who holds himself out as available to anyone would not be a commercial agent; but one who canvasses on what one could call a "retained" basis could, at least unless he is actu-

---

[81]   See Saintier and Scholes, fn.1 above, at pp.31–32.
[82]   See *Mercantile International Group Plc v Chuan Soon Huat Industrial Group Plc* [2002] EWCA Civ 288; [2002] 1 All E.R. (Comm) 788 at [33]; *W Nagel (A Firm) v Pluczenik Diamond Co NV* [2017] EWHC 1750 (Comm); [2017] 2 Lloyd's Rep. 215 at [55].
[83]   See the opinion of Advocate General Geelhoed in *Poseidon Chartering BV v Marianne Zeeschip VOF* (C-3/04) [2007] Bus. L.R. 446; [2006] 2 Lloyd's Rep. 105 (referred to at [25]: but on services—chartering).
[84]   *W Nagel (A Firm) v Pluczenik Diamond Co NV* [2017] EWHC 1750 (Comm); [2017] 2 Lloyd's Rep. 215 adding that "An agent may have authority to carry out functions which he never performs or performs only occasionally": per Popplewell J at [44].
[85]   See *Sagal v Atelier Bunz GmbH* [2009] EWCA Civ 700; [2009] 2 Lloyd's Rep. 303 at [12].
[86]   See above, para.1-020. The term "marketing agent" is also used.
[87]   *Parks v Esso Petroleum Co Ltd* [2000] Eu. L.R. 25 at 32, quoting the Oxford English Dictionary definition "deal with, manage or conduct".
[88]   See the cases cited in fn.91 above.
[89]   *W Nagel (A Firm) v Pluczenik Diamond Co NV* [2017] EWHC 1750 (Comm); [2017] 2 Lloyd's Rep. 215 at [54] (diamond broking: indicating functions performed).
[90]   Where such an intermediary may be called "courtier", "makler", "mediatore", etc. See *Ferro v Santoro OJ 2002* (C-323/24).

ally forbidden to solicit contractual offers.[91] Where it can be said that he has no duty to act, problems may arise as to whether he has a *contract* of agency at all.[92]

Negotiate and conclude the sale or purchase of goods on behalf of and in the name of the principal   This obviously covers agents who are actually authorised to contract on behalf of their principals, including those who acquire repeat orders.[93] The requirement that the agent do so "in the name of", as well as "on behalf of", the principal raises problems, as this phrase can be used in civil law but (although it was sometimes used in nineteenth-century cases, usually to differentiate undisclosed principals) has no specific meaning in common law.   **11-019**

Three categories which require consideration in the above context are agents acting for identified principals, agents acting for unidentified principals, and agents acting for undisclosed principals.[94] Clearly, an agent acting for a named principal can be said to act in the principal's name. At common law it is, however, possible that such an agent undertakes personal liability on the contract as well as his principal.[95] Should the agent do this, civil law parallels suggest that he should not be regarded as acting in his own name for the purpose of these regulations in those cases where the agent's liability is upon the same contract; i.e. the words "acts in the name of the principal" should be taken as referring only to an agent who, to use the traditional words, "drops out" of the transaction; but the matter is not at all clear. More difficult is the case of the agent acting for an unidentified principal, for he is more likely (though far from certain) to be regarded at common law as undertaking personal liability.[96] The best view seems to be that here again, if he undertakes no personal liability, but the third party deals solely with the principal, whoever he is, the agent acts in his principal's name: but if the agent undertakes personal liability on the same contract also, it is arguable that he does not do so "in the name of" the principal. The nature of any liability undertaken by the agent may therefore be crucial.[97]

It is, however, difficult to see that an agent acting for an *undisclosed* principal ever acts in the principal's name, for he clearly acts in his own; and indeed the doctrine of the undisclosed principal is a difficult doctrine of common law which those responsible for the Directive are not likely to have had fully in mind. And an agent acting under a contract of *commission*[98] clearly acts in his own name.[99]

Commercial agency a secondary activity   The Regulations do not apply to   **11-020**

---

[91] An agent who effected introductions and played a significant role in persuading third parties to be interested but had no authority to agree terms or prices was held a commercial agent in *PJ Pipe and Valve Co Ltd v Audco India Ltd* [2005] EWHC 1904 (QB); [2006] Eu.L.R. 368 and *Nigel Fryer Joinery Services Ltd v Ian Firth Hardware Ltd* [2008] EWHC 767 (Ch); [2008] 2 Lloyd's Rep. 108; see also *Kenny v Ireland Roc Ltd* 2005 IEHC 241 (Ireland), supporting the argument, but doubting the result in *Parks v Esso Petroleum Co Ltd* [2000] E.C.C. 45; [2000] Eu. L.R. 25 (petrol retailer: as to which see Saintier and Scholes, fn.1 above, at pp.39–40). A useful recent discussion is to be found in *Invicta UK v International Brands Ltd* [2013] EWHC 1564 (QB); [2013] E.C.C. 30: see at [31]–[32] (sale of wine to supermarkets).
[92] See above, para.7-016; though this may be a specific common law problem.
[93] See *Invicta UK v International Brands Ltd* [2013] EWHC 1564 (QB); [2013] E.C.C. 30.
[94] For indications of the meaning of these terms, see Article 2.
[95] See Article 98.
[96] See above, para.9-016.
[97] cf. above, para.9-006 onwards. A *del credere* agent (above, para.1-042) only undertakes as such a subsidiary liability and hence should be covered.
[98] Above, para.1-021.
[99] *Mavrona & Sia OE v Delta Etaireia Symmetochon AE* (C-85/03) [2004] E.C.R. I-1573. This is in

persons whose activities as commercial agents are to be considered secondary.[100] The meaning of this notion is elaborated for Great Britain[101] by an extensive Schedule to the Regulations which is intended to give further elucidation to the notion of commercial agency and states that where it may reasonably be taken that the primary purpose of the arrangement with the principal is *other than* as set out, the activities of the commercial agent as such are to be considered secondary only. The indications in this schedule are so important to a legal system that has no category of commercial agent that they require to be set out almost in full. They are stated in para.2 of the Schedule as follows:

"(a)   the business of the principal is the sale, or as the case may be purchase, of goods of a particular kind[102]; and

(b)   the goods concerned are such that—

(i)   transactions are normally individually negotiated and concluded on a commercial basis, and

(ii)   procuring a transaction on one occasion is likely to lead to further transactions in those goods with that customer on future occasions, or to transactions in those goods with other customers in the same geographical area or among the same group of customers and

that accordingly it is in the commercial interests of the principal in developing the market in those goods to appoint a representative to such customers with a view to the representative devoting effort, skill and expenditure from his own resources to that end."

There follow in para.3 more specific indications of when an arrangement falls within the above criteria, the absence of any of which is some indication that it does not. They are that:

"(a)   the principal is the manufacturer, importer or distributor of the goods;

(b)   the goods are specifically identified with the principal in the market in question rather than, or to a greater extent than, with any other person;

(c)   the agent devotes substantially the whole of his time to representative activities (whether for one principal or a number of principals whose interests are not conflicting);

(d)   the goods are not normally available in the market in question other than by means of the agent;

(e)   the arrangement is described as one of commercial agency."

Three points may be noted. First, the title or label used by the parties is relevant but not conclusive.[103] Secondly, the method of remuneration used is not one of the

---

accord with the later decision taken on other grounds in *Sagal v Atelier Bunz GmbH* [2009] EWCA Civ 700; [2009] 2 Lloyd's Rep. 303. See also *Royal & Sun Alliance Plc v MK Digitial FZE (Cyprus) Ltd* [2006] EWCA Civ 629; [2006] 2 Lloyd's Rep. 110 (interpretation as commissionnaire de transport).

[100] reg.2(4). This exception, and the ways in which it has been utilised in France, Germany and the United Kingdom, is convincingly criticised by Saintier [2012] J.B.L. 128. An account of how it operates in France is given by Saintier in Randolph and Davey, fn.1 above, Ch.11.

[101] The application of such a limitation is authorised by art.2(2) of the Directive. This limit was only adopted in some countries. An argument that the implementing provisions were ultra vires was rejected in *Crane v Sky In-Home Service Ltd*, below.

[102] For an example where this was not so see *Crane v Sky In-Home Service Ltd* [2007] EWHC 66 (Ch); [2007] 2 All E.R. (Comm) 599 (sale of digital box: main purpose was to attract subscribers to television services: agency for sale a secondary activity). Further proceedings [2008] EWCA Civ 978.

[103] cf. above, para.1-036.

features mentioned as relevant,[104] though it plainly is not irrelevant inasmuch as agents are typically remunerated by commission. Third, what is looked at is the initial primary purpose of the arrangement, not an incidental purpose nor its later operation.

Indications that commercial agency is not involved at all or is secondary are stated in para.4, as being that:

"(a)   promotional material is supplied direct to potential customers;
(b)   persons are granted agencies without reference to existing agents in a particular area or in relation to a particular group;
(c)   customers normally select the goods for themselves and merely place their orders through the agent."

This Schedule has been described in the Court of Appeal as "an almost impenetrable piece of drafting".[105] The first difficulty which it creates is that whereas the Directive can be taken to authorise Member States to disapply the Directive where the activities of the agent are secondary *as compared with the rest of the agent's business* (sometimes called the "horizontal approach"), the Schedule itself "seems to contemplate an assessment not of the activities of the agent as a 'commercial agent' as compared with his other business, but an assessment of the agent's arrangement with a principal",[106] which may be called the "vertical approach". Thus it would appear that if the agent has an arrangement with a principal that falls within the wording of the first set of criteria set out above (para.2 of the Schedule), interpreted with the aid of the criteria subsequently mentioned (paras 3 and 4), his activity in that respect is not secondary, however it may appear against the background of his activities generally.[107] Whatever the intention of the Directive, this approach certainly favours protection of the agent. **11-021**

The second and principal problem is highlighted by the dictum of Waller LJ in the Court of Appeal referred to above. It being accepted that, whatever the original intention, the investigation must be into whether the particular arrangement between principal and agent is secondary, the drafting largely proceeds on the basis of simply seeking to define the commercial agency arrangement which is presumably primary. Several of the requirements listed above seem fairly obvious, for example that the principal must be the manufacturer, importer or distributor of the goods. Others may be unduly restrictive in this context, for example the reference to goods of a particular kind, and the requirements that transactions are normally individually negotiated and that the agent devotes substantially the whole of his time to representative activities. Further, it seems likely that though the intermediary is a commercial agent, a principal may sometimes supply promotional material direct, and the customer may sometimes select the goods themselves and place their orders through the agent. The current trend of overall interpretation of this unsatisfactory Schedule seems to be to concentrate on the final words of para.2 and use them as a tool for an emphasis on the interest of the principal in developing a market for the **11-022**

---

[104] And indeed, reg.6(3) envisages that a commercial agent need not be remunerated by commission: see below, para.11-027. Some agents are paid by retainer alone, without being employees.
[105] *AMB Imballaggi v Pacflex Ltd* [1999] 2 All E.R. (Comm) 249 at 254, per Waller LJ.
[106] *AMB Imballaggi v Pacflex Ltd* [1999] 2 All E.R. (Comm) 249 at 254.
[107] See at 254. The matter was expressly decided by Morison J in *Tamarind International Ltd v Eastern Natural Gas (Retail) Ltd* [2000] Eu.L.R. 708.

goods by means of an agent generating the goodwill which is the basis of the entitlement to indemnity or compensation on the termination of the contract.[108]

If this is so, "secondary" seems to mean "not goodwill-generating", which is unusual, since the word suggests the existence of something else "primary" to which the activity, while still a commercial agency, is secondary. It had however previously been said that "Because there is no easily recognizable way of measuring whether activities are secondary or not, it is ... unnecessary and perhaps misleading to seek to find an antithesis to the word 'secondary'. The contrast is simply between agents who are covered and the agents who are not".[109] The result can be however that a person performing extensive agency functions in marketing the principal's goods and even occupying a dominant market position may find that he is not a commercial agent at all because his activity, even if full-time, is found to have been secondary in the sense of not generating goodwill.[110]

The Directive permits States to disapply it in respect of "commercial agents whose activities are considered secondary by the law of that Member State". The law of the United Kingdom does not know the notion of a commercial agent, so the only relevant provision of it must be the Schedule itself, which certainly does not reproduce already existing law. The Schedule so interpreted must have the effect of reducing considerably for the United Kingdom the number of persons within the basic definition of art.1(2), on the ground that though they are commercial agents their activities can be described as "secondary" without any indication of what they are secondary to.[111] It has even been said that "The concept of activities as a commercial agent which are considered secondary is fundamental to the scheme of the legislation. It distinguishes commercial agents who are affected by the mischief at which the ... Directive is aimed from those who are not".[112] It is difficult to believe that such a result was what the Directive envisaged when it permitted such a limitation on the general wording of art.1(2), in an exception which has only been taken up, and by different means, in some countries.[113] The history of the reservation has however been traced back more than once in judgments, and it has been held in England in a case where this was done that the course taken in the Schedule is consistent with the Directive and so not ultra vires.[114]

At present there are some not very conclusive decisions, many of which are case-

---

[108] See *Gailey v Environmental Waste Controls* 2004 Scot SC 300 (OH); [2004] Eu. L.R. 708, accepted in *McAdam v Boxpak Ltd* [2006] CSIH 9; 2006 S.L.T. 217.

[109] *Tamarind International Ltd v Eastern Natural Gas (Retail) Ltd* [2000] C.L.C. 1397 at [21], per Morison J.

[110] As in *MacAdam v Boxpak Ltd*, above, where the agent had a dominant position (70–80 per cent of the market for aluminium foil containers: see judgment of the Sheriff at [11], quoted in the judgment of the Extra Division at [7]) but it was held that his activities were secondary.

[111] Two cases where the agent performed functions that were fairly clearly separate are *Crane v Sky In-Home Service Ltd* [2007] EWHC 66 (Ch), where the agent marketed subscriptions to a digital broadcasting services and also sold box packages and dish packages to receive them. Another is *Gailey v Environmental Waste Controls*, fn.112 below.

[112] See *Gailey v Environmental Waste Controls* 2004 Scot SC 300 (OH); [2004] Eu.L.R.423 at [40], per Lord Drummond Young (agent for firm selling waste handling equipment and providing administrative facilities).

[113] See Saintier, fn.1 above, stating that in France the option was taken up to deal with the position of car dealers whose main business is selling, and in Germany to protect the insurance sector.

[114] *Crane v Sky In-Home Service Ltd* [2007] EWHC 66 (Ch); [2007] 1 C.L.C. 389, per Briggs J (further proceedings [2008] EWCA Civ 978).

specific, and some of which, it has been argued, should be reconsidered.[115] It appears however from the cases decided so far that the matter must be assessed at the time of inception of the contract,[116] with the result that a contract where the activity is secondary cannot from the legal point of view metamorphose by reason of successful operation into a contract where the activity is primary.[117] It has been held that where the main activity, while goodwill-generating, was outside the scope of the Regulations (because it involved the commodity market), a lesser activity in the same context that might not be caught by the exclusion is secondary; and that the effect of this is to exclude it altogether rather than create a separate part of the contract governed by the Regulations.[118] Finally, it has been held that the onus of proof is on the agent to prove that his activities were secondary,[119] though this has subsequently been doubted.[120]

Specific exceptions The activities of mail order catalogue agents for consumer goods and consumer credit agents are presumed, unless the contrary is established, not to be within the definition of commercial agency. The term "commercial agent" excludes officers of companies or associations who are authorised to bind the company or organisation, partners authorised to bind their partners and persons acting as insolvency practitioners as defined in the Insolvency Act 1986[121] or its equivalent in other jurisdictions.[122] Nor do the Regulations apply to commercial agents whose activities are unpaid, commercial agents where they operate on commodity exchanges or in the commodity market,[123] or to the Crown Agents.[124]   **11-023**

4. RELATIONS BETWEEN AGENT AND PRINCIPAL

Duties of agent to principal The Regulations then turn to the mutual duties of principal and agent. By reg.3(1) a commercial agent must "in performing his activities look after the interests of his principal and act dutifully[125] and in good faith." In particular he must "(a) make proper efforts to negotiate and where appropriate   **11-024**

---

[115] See Randolph and Davey, fn.1 above, para.6.13.
[116] *McAdam v Boxpak Ltd* [2006] CSIH 9; 2006 S.L.T. 217; *Crane v Sky In-Home Service Ltd*, fn.108 above [2007] EWHC 66 (Ch); [2007] E.C.C. 25 (Ch); *Invicta UK v International Brands Ltd* [2013] EWHC 1564 (QB); [2013] E.C.C. 30 (wine for supermarkets). But cf. in the context of the agent's retainer *W Nagel (A Firm) v Pluczenik Diamond Co NV* [2017] EWHC 1750 (Comm); [2017] 2 Lloyd's Rep. 215, above, para.11-013.
[117] A point made by Randolph and Davey, fn.1 above, at para.5.9; and it appears that Mr Randolph QC may have argued it in the *Invicta* case, above.
[118] *W Nagel (A Firm) v Pluczenic Diamond Co NV* [2017] EWHC 1750 (Comm); [2017] 2 Lloyd's Rep. 215 (see at [71]–[74]) (further proof that the Schedule was not well-conceived).
[119] *Gailey v Environmental Waste Controls* fn.106 above, at [40]; *Crane v Sky In-Home Service Ltd* [2007] EWHC 66 (Ch) at [51].
[120] *Edwards v International Connection (UK) Ltd* [2006] EWCA Civ 662, per Arden LJ (leave to appeal proceedings, available on BAILII).
[121] s.388 (amended).
[122] reg.2(1)(i) (ii) (iii). In respect of (iii) the Directive (art.1.3) uses the words "a receiver, a receiver and manager, a liquidator or a trustee in bankruptcy".
[123] The rationale of this exclusion is considered in *W Nagel (A Firm) v Pluczenik Diamond Company NV* [2017] EWHC 1750 (Comm); [2017] 2 Lloyd's Rep. 215, where sales of diamonds were held (after consideration of the commercial framework of such sales) to be sales on the commodity market and in a commodity exchange. Some sales were of a different nature, but were regarded as secondary within reg.2(3) (see above, para.11-020).
[124] reg.2(2).
[125] This unusual word for English legal drafting is selected by translators to correspond with the French "loyalement" and German "treu". See *Rossetti Marketing Ltd v Diamond Sofa Co Ltd* [2011] EWHC

conclude the transactions he is instructed to take care of; (b) communicate to his principal all the necessary information available to him"[126] and "(c) comply with reasonable instructions given by his principal".[127] These duties are by reg.5(1) non-derogatable, and the consequences of their breach are by reg.5(2) governed by the normal principles of the law applicable to the contract between principal and agent, which for the purposes of this book is assumed to be English law. Although the terminology of the general duties, with its invocation of the notion of good faith, is different from that which a common lawyer would use, these or similar duties already exist to quite a considerable extent as implied terms at common law or as fiduciary duties in equity.[128] However, dealing in competing products where there is no clause forbidding this would perhaps more easily be caught by reg.3(1) than by the normal rules of equity.[129] The duties will be remediable by actions for damages, sometimes proprietary claims and injunctions; and sometimes a breach will entitle the principal to terminate the contract. They call for no special comment, save that whereas there is controversy as to the extent to which such duties may at common law or in equity be modified or excluded,[130] the duties here laid down for commercial agents in this context plainly may not.

11-025 **Duties of principal to agent** The common law contains, however, no general law on the implied duties of principal to agent, and here therefore the Regulations break a certain amount of new ground. Regulation 4(1) which, like reg.3, is, by virtue of reg.5(1), non-derogatable, requires that the principal in his relations with the agent in his turn act "dutifully[131] and in good faith". The notion of good faith has been little developed in the common law, and a principal is not normally regarded as owing fiduciary duties to his agent.[132] There is scope here therefore for the development of implied terms of fair treatment, co-operation and disclosure of relevant information; and contract terms in which the principal retains the right to act in a manner contrary to these requirements will not be valid.

As has been stated above,[133] for the purposes of the implication of terms, contracts come into two categories: standardised contracts of a recognisable type, where the implication may be regarded as drawing the purpose out of the contract, and non-standardised contracts, where terms will only be applied to give business efficacy to the contract. It would seem that in common law contracts involving agency powers are too varied to be dealt with under the first category, and the case law, which is parsimonious on implication of terms in favour of the agent, bears this out. However, in the present context it could be said that the effect of the Regulations is to create a new type of standardised contract to which the first technique

---

2482 (QB); [2011] E.C.C. 28 at [41]; on appeal [2012] EWCA Civ 1021; [2013] 1 All E.R. (Comm) 308. See also the extended discussion by Tosato (2016) 36 O.J.L.S. 661.

[126] A principal was held to have the right to delivery up of documents in order that he could inspect and copy them in *Fairstar Heavy Transport NV v Adkins* [2013] EWCA 886 (order for inspection: not a commercial agency case).

[127] McGee [2013] J.B.L. 534 at 540, draws attention to problems in applying this where the agent prefers to operate on his own but the principal is keen to supervise what he is doing.

[128] See Articles 36 onwards; *Crane v Sky In-Home Service Ltd* [2007] EWHC 66 (Ch); [2007] 2 All E.R. (Comm) 599 at [82]. But cf. Tosato (2016) 36 O.J.L.S. 661.

[129] See above, para.6-015.

[130] See above, para.6-056 onwards.

[131] See fn.125 above. The duty of good faith is specifically referred to in *Chavassus-Marche v Groupe Danone* (C-19/07) [2008] 2 All E.R. (Comm) 1093 at [22].

[132] But see above, para.7-001.

[133] See above, para.7-001.

can apply, thus creating a vessel to carry new law. It is said that in French law the commercial agency contract is regarded as an enterprise of common interest between principal and agent[134]; and it is certainly true that even in common law the relationship is not commercially adverse, and that this is a way of distinguishing agency from distributorship[135] and justifying the rules about secret profits.[136] Parallels providing reasoning may sometimes be drawn from partnership law and from some modern developments in employment law.[137] Decisions in France[138] and Italy[139] respectively, useful as providing examples, have concerned a principal who sends another person to solicit offers into the area where the agent is sole representative and one who systematically refuses to conclude the contracts negotiated by the agent; in Germany, inducing the agent's customers to deal with the principal directly.[140] Other examples where such reasoning was deployed have concerned changes in pricing policy or in the list of products entrusted to the agent, the allowing of parallel sales by another agent or distributor of the principal and the unfair exercise of a power to vary the contract.[141] There is certainly considerable potential for advancing arguments under the Regulations which might not be acceptable under the general common law. It has however been held (after most elaborate argument including reference to bona fides[142]) that the Regulations cannot qualify an express right of termination on the principal's part, in respect of which the situation remains as at common law, which is that the right may be an absolute contractual right.[143]

The duty is to some extent filled out with specific indications by reg.4(2) and (3), though it seems unlikely that these are intended to be exhaustive. A principal must "provide [the] agent with the necessary documentation relating to the goods concerned", "obtain for his commercial agent the information necessary for the performance of the agency contract, and in particular notify the commercial agent within a reasonable period once he anticipates that the volume of commercial transactions will be significantly lower than that which the commercial agent could normally have expected" and "inform the commercial agent within a reasonable period of his acceptance or refusal of, and of any non-execution by him of a commercial transaction which the commercial agent has procured for him".[144] The second requirement in particular, in its reference to notification of change of volume of transactions, may involve more than some principals would be in the habit of doing. Again, the consequences of breach of duty are covered by the normal

---

[134] Saintier and Scholes, fn.1 above, at pp.80-81 and 84 onwards.

[135] See above, para.1-035.

[136] Article 47.

[137] Freedland, *The Personal Employment Contract* (2005), Ch.3; Brodie (2001) 117 L.Q.R. 604.

[138] Cour d'appel de Rennes, December 1, 1993, Dalloz 1994, *informations rapides*, 127.

[139] Corte di cassazione, December 18, 1985, fn.6475, Giur.it. 1986, I, 1, 1649 note di Loreto.

[140] See e.g. BGH, WM 2003, 255; BGH, NJW 2014, 155.

[141] A number of such claims against a principal were however rejected in *Simpson v Grant & Bowman* [2006] Eu. L.R. 933.

[142] Particularly the case of *Mediterranean Shipping Co SA v Cottonex Anstalt* [2015] EWHC 283 (Comm); [2015] 1 Lloyd's Rep. 359.

[143] *Monk v Largo Foods Ltd* [2016] EWHC 1837 (Comm) (where the right arose from a "term of arrangement" under which the operation of the contract was said to be "for a three year period subject to the completion of a successful review", which was held to be at common law an absolute contractual right rather than a contractual discretion: at [64]. It was then held that reg.4(1) did not qualify the operation of the clause. The judgment contains extensive discussion of both issues).

[144] reg.22 makes provision as to how a "notice, statement or other document" is to be given or supplied. It is not clear that it covers merely "informing".

principles of law applicable to the contract, which for the purposes of this book is assumed to be English law.

11-026 **Right to written statement of terms of contract** By reg.13, which appears in the section entitled "Conclusion and Termination of the Agency Contract", each party is "entitled to receive from the other, on request, a signed written document setting out the terms of the agency contract including any terms subsequently agreed".[145] Any purported waiver of this right is void. It seems that many such arrangements are entered into and varied on an informal basis.[146] In view of the disputes that can arise it is in the interests of both parties to have such a document. But it is not clear what the remedy is for failure to comply with the duty to supply such a document. In principle, there must be a right to damages; but loss arising from breach of the duty might not be easy to prove, and this is in any case too much of a common law approach. In labour law in the United Kingdom, there are similar requirements to supply a statement of terms of the contract of employment, but breach of this duty is cognisable in industrial tribunals. A mandatory injunction, an order of the court or a declaration would seem to be necessary. A party who does not receive such a document may perhaps refuse to commence performance; but at least on the side of the agent this may not always be prudent.

5. REMUNERATION AND COMMISSION

11-027 **Cases where no agreement on remuneration** Part III of the Regulations deals with remuneration in some detail. Regulation 6 provides that where no remuneration is agreed, the agent shall be entitled to "the remuneration that commercial agents appointed for the goods forming the subject of his agency contract are customarily allowed in the place where he carries on his activities", and in the absence of such practice to "reasonable remuneration taking into account all the aspects of the transaction".[147] This seems straightforward, but there is no reason to think that reasoning such as that already employed at common law[148] will not be equally valid under the Regulations. The provision is excludable in that specific remuneration can be agreed and so prevent its application; and if it is agreed that the activities of the agent shall be unpaid, the person concerned is not a commercial agent at all.[149] However, the Regulations, and the Directive, appear also to assume that a commercial agent need not be remunerated by commission, for by reg.6(3), regs 7 to 12 do not apply "where a commercial agent is not remunerated (wholly or in part) by commission"—an odd way of putting it, which is rendered in the enactments of some other countries in positive form, i.e. that the following rules apply where the agent *is* remunerated by commission. Either way, remunera-

---

[145] Provisions as to how the giving or supply of such documents is to be effected are to be found in reg.22. It is likely that in due course an electronic document will be permitted. According to *Bellone v Yokohama SpA* (C-215/97) [1998] E.C.R. I-2191, since writing is the only requirement of form mentioned by art.13(2) of the Directive and the Community legislature had dealt exhaustively with the matter, the Member States cannot impose any formal condition for the validity of the contract other than requiring that a written document be drawn up.

[146] e.g. the *Imballaggi* case, fn.62 above, and the *Mercantile International Group* case, fn.150 below.

[147] For an example of its application see *PJ Pipe and Valve Co Ltd v Audco India Ltd* [2005] EWHC 1904 (QB); [2006] Eu.L.R. 368, where the fact that the parties had intended a higher commission than usual was taken into account.

[148] See Article 55.

[149] reg.2(2); above, para.11-023.

tion by commission is not part of the definition of commercial agents, and some agents may be remunerated by markups, shares of profits and similar arrangements.[150] There is a danger that a commercial agent remunerated by salary (as opposed to a retainer) may in some situations and/or countries be regarded as an employee and not a commercial agent at all.

Commission The remainder of Pt III deals with the agent's commission, defined **11-028** in reg.2(1) as "any part of the remuneration of a commercial agent which varies with the number or value of business transactions". It seeks to protect the agent against situations which have been perceived as unfair to him. These particular words prevent the dressing up of commission as, for instance, expenses. As will be seen, the Regulations distinguish between *entitlement* to commission, when commission is *due*, when commission shall be *paid*, and the *right* to commission: though the last phrase may be an oversight of a translator and hence equivalent to "entitlement".[151] There seems no reason why commission agreed should not vary between types of transaction or in particular situations such as where sales targets are exceeded.

Entitlement to commission Under reg.7(1) the agent is "entitled to commis- **11-029** sion" on "commercial transactions concluded during the period covered by the agency contract—(a) where the transaction has been concluded as a result of his action". In considering this provision it should be borne in mind that the term "commercial agent" covers not only one who concludes transactions, but also one who negotiates them.[152] Where he actually *concludes* them there is no difficulty in seeing that he is entitled to commission. Where he merely *negotiates* them, the reference to the transaction being concluded as the result of his action will give something very like (but not necessarily the same as) the existing "effective cause" rule of English law.[153] There is nothing in the Regulations which would render ineffective an entitlement to commission at an earlier stage, as for example when a customer is introduced: unlike the English estate agent cases, the concern in the Regulations is not about agents providing that they are entitled to commission when there is no sale, but for agents failing to obtain commission despite there having been a sale. Furthermore, it would seem that, subject to the requirement of good faith,[154] the principal can deprive the agent of commission by refusing to conclude a transaction negotiated by the agent. Existing English cases would allow the agent to protect himself against this if the clause is sufficiently clear in making commission due despite the non-conclusion of the contract.[155] Some such clauses may now perhaps be contrary to the good faith requirement; though equally some forms of conduct by the principal may themselves be contrary to good faith.

Repeat orders By reg.7(1)(b) the agent is entitled to commission "where the **11-030**

---

[150] See above, para.11-013. An agent remunerated partly by mark-up was held a commercial agent in *Mercantile International Group Plc v Chuan Soon Huat Industrial Group Plc* [2002] EWCA Civ 288; [2002] 1 All E.R. (Comm) 788. See also the *Imballaggi* case, fn.62 above. As to share in profit, see *Mar-Train Heavy Haulage Ltd v Shipping DK Chartering A/S* [2014] EWHC 355 (Comm) at [38] onwards (context: freight forwarding).
[151] See below, para.11-034.
[152] Above, para.11-018.
[153] Article 57. This rule has largely been developed in connection with estate agents, who are certainly not commercial agents.
[154] Above, para.11-025.
[155] See Article 58.

transaction is concluded with a third party whom he has previously acquired as a customer for transactions of the same kind", i.e. on what is sometimes called a "repeat order" placed without any further intervention of the agent.[156] This is an area where the English law is far from clear.[157] In other legal systems the notion of a customer whom the agent has previously acquired for transactions of a similar kind is held to be similar to that emerging from the distinction between new customers and old customers in the context of the provisions concerning the agent's right to indemnity on termination of the agency contract under reg.17(3)(a).[158] There may be dispute as to what is a transaction "of the same kind".

11-031   **Geographical zone or customer group**   Finally, by reg.7(2) the agent is entitled to commission on transactions concluded during the period of the contract "where he has an exclusive right to a specific geographical area or to a specific group of customers and where the transaction has been entered into with a customer belonging to that area or group", and require no specific activity from the agent. Here there is even less of anything corresponding to a requirement of "effective cause" for the particular transaction; the entitlement is to commission on transactions which do no more than emanate from the agent's area or customer group.[159] However, commission is not due if the transaction not only did not involve action by the agent, but also did not involve action by the principal, direct or indirect, in the conclusion of the transaction. Although art.7(2) might appear to apply, art.10(1) and (2) require or imply execution by the principal.[160] The meaning of "exclusive right" may require determination, in particular on the question whether the principal can himself sell. For this the common law estate agency distinction between "sole" and "exclusive" agency[161] may provide useful argument, though there is no reason whatever to think that the Regulations were drafted with this in mind.

11-032   **Commission on transactions after agency contract terminated**   Regulation 8 deals with this problem, on which English law is again not clear.[162] It provides that the agent is "entitled to commission" in such cases if:

"(a)   The transaction is mainly attributable to his efforts during the period covered by the agency contract and if the transaction was entered into within a reasonable period after that contract terminated; or

(b)   in accordance with the conditions mentioned in regulation 7 above, the order of the third party reached the principal or the commercial agent before the agency contract terminated."

The requirements of (a) are somewhat imprecise and may give rise to difficulties

---

[156]   See *Moore v Piretta Pte Ltd* [1999] 1 All E.R. 174 at 178 ("the first paragraph requires some action on the part of the agent to earn the commission, the second does not").

[157]   See above, para.7-042.

[158]   See below, para.11-044. cf. Hopt, *Handelsvertreterrecht* (4th edn, München 2009) § 87, No.17, at p.71.

[159]   An example is provided by *McQuillan v McCormick* [2010] EWHC 1112 (QB); [2011] E.C.C. 18. See also *Kontogeorgas v Kartonpak AE* (C-104/95) [1996] E.C.R. I-6643; [1997] 1 C.M.L.R. 1093 as to the word "belonging". Quaere whether the principal can exclude named customers.

[160]   *Chevassus-Marche's Heirs v Groupe Danone* (C-19/07) [2008] 2 All E.R. (Comm) 1093 (where the goods were purchased from other dealers outside the control of the principal). But if the customer is within the area, the fact that delivery is actually made to a party outside the area may be irrelevant: *Edwards v International Connection (UK) Ltd*, Central London County Court, Judge Knight QC, November 25, 2005 (subsequent Court of Appeal proceedings [2006] EWCA Civ 662).

[161]   See above, para.7-037.

[162]   See above, para.7-042.

of application. It has been held that "the words 'mainly attributable' impose a heightened causation requirement beyond simply being an effective cause", and this is justified on the basis that anything else would have a detrimental effect on the rights of a replacement agent.[163] The following provision, (b), appears to refer to situations where the order has come in at the time the agency contract terminated, but not been accepted. Regulation 9 then deals with situations where an agent claims under reg.7 and commission is payable to his predecessor by virtue of reg.8: the later agent does not qualify for commission "unless it is equitable because of the circumstances for the commission to be shared between the commercial agents"—a provision which could require adjudication if there was a dispute under it.

When commission due and date for payment By reg.10(1) a further refine-   **11-033** ment is introduced. Commission is actually *due*[164] in one of three situations: when the principal has "executed" the transaction (which presumably means performed it), or according to his agreement with the third party ought to have done so, or the third party has executed the transaction. The first two provisions are facultative only in the sense that other arrangements may be made. But the third provides a final limit which cannot, by para.(4), be derogated from to the detriment of the agent. This provides that commission becomes due *at the latest* when "(2) the third party has executed his part of the transaction or should have done so if the principal had executed his part of the transaction as he should have".[165] Paragraph (3), also non-derogatable, provides that commission shall be *paid* "not later than on the last day of the month following the quarter in which it became due".[166] There follows a provision for determining quarter periods, which may be varied by agreement. Paragraph (2) may raise problems of application when there is no time set for the principal to perform the contract.

"Right" to commission The effect of the above provisions is reinforced by   **11-034** reg.11(1), which provides that:

"the right to commission can be extinguished only if and to the extent that (a) it is established that the contract between the third party and the principal will not be performed; and (b) that fact is due to a reason for which the principal is *not to blame*."[167]

This provision cannot be derogated from to the detriment of the commercial

---

[163] *Monk v Largo Foods Ltd* [2016] EWHC 1837 (Comm), following dicta in *Tigana Ltd v Decoro Ltd* [2003] EWHC 23 (QB); [2003] Eu. L.R. 189, where the reasonable period was set at nine months. See discussion by McGee [2011] J.B.L. 782 at 783, stressing difficulties caused by "attributable" and "reasonable period". It is not clear whether or not reg.8(b) applies to all the situations referred to in reg.7. It is suggested in *Monk v Largo Foods* that it applies neither to repeat orders covered by reg.7(b) nor to orders originating as prescribed in reg.(2): see [109]–[110]. The main reason seems to be inconsistency with the provision for apportioning commission provided by reg.9. But it is not clear that the wording of reg.8(b) permits such a conclusion, and attention should perhaps be directed to the words "order of the third party reached the principal."

[164] French "acquise".

[165] In *ERGO Poist'ovna a.s.* (C-48/16), CJEU, May 17, 2017 the agent was paid before this date, and a provision that if the contract was not performed she would refund part on a pro rata basis in the event of partial non-execution of the contract was held not (without more) a derogation to her detriment caught by reg.11(3), because it complied with the scheme of reg.11(a) and (2).

[166] For a similar distinction in common law, see *Explora Group Plc v Hesco Bastion Ltd* [2005] EWCA Civ 646 at [59], [60].

[167] Emphasis supplied. The agent must in such cases refund any commission he has received: reg.11(2).

agent.[168] It seems unlikely that any special significance is to be attached to the word "right" as opposed to "entitlement" in regs 7, 8 and 9, as the same French word ("droit") appears in all these provisions in the French text of the Directive. The word "extinguished" appears to envisage the effect of a specific contract term. The overall result is that the agent only actually earns commission on business entitling him to it where the contract is in fact performed, or not performed for reasons in some way not attributable to the principal—unless of course the contract gives the agent a more generous entitlement, which it may. Although the wording of the provision could be taken to suggest that the right can be extinguished only if it is established that the whole contract will not be performed, it has been held that it covers also partial non-execution of the contract: in the particular case, where the contract provided for the procurement of separate insurance contracts and payment of commission on each.[169]

It should be noted that the reference is actually to non-performance for a reason for which the principal is not to *blame*. At common law a principal can be liable for non-performance even where no blame attaches to him, if the circumstances are such that he is to be regarded as having undertaken responsibility for them. The French text of the Directive uses the word "imputable" and other foreign texts are similar: the variation seems to arise in translation only and it might be thought that it was not intended to convey any effect substantially different from that which would be expected under English law, but to refer to legal reasons which led directly to the termination of the contract between the principal and the third party (for which the word "attributable" would be appropriate). However, it has been held in the same case that such an interpretation is not consistent with the objectives of the Directive in protecting agents, and that the court should make a broad factual assessment as to whether the principal was to blame for the circumstances leading to the termination. In the particular case the principal, an insurer, had treated the clients badly by asking them to reply to numerous questions and sending letters seeking payment of sums already paid, which was said to make the customers lose confidence in the insurer and terminate their contracts, to the disadvantage of the agent who had secured them.[170] This decision introduces an element of uncertainty that is not even linked to the notion of negligence.

If the principal sues the third party for non-performance, the agent should normally be entitled to commission.[171] Problems could arise if the principal refuses or fails to do so. This could lead to the inference that it is not established that the third party will not perform; or perhaps be a breach of the principal's duty of good faith.

11-035 **Exclusion or modification of commission rules by contract terms** There is certainly nothing in the Regulations preventing an entitlement to commission at an *earlier* stage than they prescribe: the prohibitions on derogation are on derogation to the detriment of the agent. Equally, there is no need for an agent to be allocated a specific geographical area or group of customers. The question whether the provisions as to remuneration may be modified or in some respect altogether excluded,

[168] reg.11(3).
[169] *ERGO Poist'ovna a.s.* (C-48/16), CJEU, May 17, 2017. The party in question was not a commercial agent but negotiated and concluded contracts for insurance services. The reasons why the court nevertheless determined the case are to be found at paras 26 to 32 of the judgment.
[170] *GO Poist'ovna a.s.* (C-48/16), CJEU, May 17, 2017.
[171] See above, para.7-018

in particular as regards commission on what may loosely be called repeat orders, or in cases where the agent does have a geographical area or group of customers, or where a transaction is concluded after the end of the agency contract, is more difficult.

The obvious answer might appear to be that they may, since only some of the provisions of reg.10, those as to the time at which commission is due and must be paid, and of reg.11, as to extinction of the right to commission if the contract will not be executed for reasons not attributable to the principal, are specifically made non-derogatable to the agent's detriment. If this interpretation is correct, it can be argued that as regs 7 and 8 are not, as are other provisions, specifically made unexcludable, the entitlements which they prescribe are merely *ius dispositivum* and only operate if there are no contract terms providing otherwise. On this basis it is possible to exclude the other situations of entitlement to commission and provide that commission only arises on transactions actually concluded as a result of the agent's actions. It would be difficult (but perhaps not impossible) to go further and reduce the right to commission on *concluded* transactions, but an attempt to extinguish the right to commission would be caught by reg.11, and if it is provided that no commission at all is due on such sales, the agency would be gratuitous and not covered by the Regulations at all. On the other hand, as already pointed out, it is also contemplated that the agent may not be remunerated by commission at all, but rather by retainer or salary.

As against this it may be said that it is odd to provide in such firm terms when the entitlement to commission arises, if the rules only operate where there is no provision to the contrary; and that there are other provisions in the Regulations which must be unexcludable, yet where this is not stated.[172] Further, the general wording of reg.11(1), quoted above, which provides that the "right to commission" is extinguished "only if and to the extent that" certain circumstances connected with non-performance of the contract occur, and which cannot be derogated from to the detriment of the agent, could be taken to suggest that where the circumstances indicated in reg.7 apply, commission must be due as there prescribed unless the contract is not carried out in accordance with what is prescribed in reg.11. More generally, it is difficult to see why there should be an unexcludable right to commission in all situations where contracts are not performed bar specific exceptions, while the actual initial entitlement to commission in respect of contracts can itself be modified.

The only English judicial authority is a dictum of Morland J:

> "It should be noted that there is no non-derogation article equivalent to Article 19 applicable to Articles 7 and 8. In my judgment the absence of such a specific nonderogation article means that commercial agents and principals may derogate contractually from Articles 7 and 8 but only in so far as they do not thwart the purpose of the Council Directive."[173]

One English book gives an argued view that the provisions cannot be excluded or

---

[172] regs 3, 4, 14, 15(3), 15(5), 20. It should be noted also that when Member States can modify a rule, the Directive says so.

[173] *Ingmar GB Ltd v Eaton Leonard Ltd*, at first instance [2001] EWHC 3 (QB); [2001] Eur. L.R. 755 at [30] (assessment of compensation: for main proceedings see above, para.11-006). There is no reference to art.9. As to frustrating the purpose of the Directive, see *Bellone v Yokohama Spa* (215/97) [1998] E.C.L.R. I-291. Another example might be a clause providing that the intermediary did not act as a commercial agent, when by the definition given in the Regulations he did.

modified.[174] The leading German book (significant because the Directive was inspired by German law) takes the view that they can, though some support is derived from the German law before the Directive.[175] An English book, which contains much discussion on French law, is of the same view for both English and French law,[176] as is the leading English specialised work on the subject.[177] The Italian legislation implementing the Directive actually permits the exclusion of arts 7(1)(b) and 7(2),[178] indicating that the Italian legislator understood the Directive in that way. The dominant view seems to be that the remuneration provisions can be excluded save in so far as the Regulations specifically provide. This does however much reduce the importance of what appear at first sight to be carefully thought-out rules.

It is important to note what this means. It may, as already suggested, be difficult, whatever the scope of the provisions of the Regulations, to exclude completely the right to commission on transactions concluded as a result of the agent's action (reg.7(1)(a)), unless there is remuneration by some other means, as is possible.[179] It is not difficult to accept as a matter of policy that the contract can exclude or restrict commission on (what may loosely be called) "repeat orders" (reg.7(1)(b)), or on orders from particular zone or group of customers (reg.7(2)), orders which may come in without further action by the agent.[180] But if these provisions are excludable, the rules in regs 8 and 9 must be regarded as modifiable also: there is no reason for distinguishing them. This means that it is also permissible to make different provision concluded after the agency contract has terminated, or to modify the rules about apportionment of commission between new and previous agents (reg.9).[181] The only thing that cannot be modified is the rule that the commission, if earned in accordance with what is said above, is due as soon as, or not later than, the contract has been executed,[182] unless it can be established that it will not be executed for a reason not attributable to the principal.[183]

11-036 **Supply of information** Regulation 12 deals with the supply of information by principal to agent with a view to the calculation of commission earned. The background is plainly, like that of the previous regulation, a perception that the agent is in danger of not getting all the commission to which he is entitled. It provides in paras (1) and (2) that the principal shall supply the agent with a statement of the commission due not later than the last day of the month following the quarter in which the commission has become due, setting out the main components used in calculating it; and that the agent "shall be entitled to demand that he be provided with all the information (and in particular an extract from the books)

---

[174] Christou, fn.1 above, at para.3-227 onwards.
[175] Hopt, *Handelsvertreterrecht* (4th edn, München 2009) § 87, No.48, making the point also that such exclusion or modification cannot affect the calculation of the indemnity, which is non-derogatable.
[176] Saintier and Scholes, fn.1 above, pp.115–116; though it is true that the French legislation does not list the relevant provisions as being non-derogatable. A generally helpful discussion in Bennett, fn.1 above, uses the ICC Model Commercial Agency Contract as an example where this is done: see para.8.47.
[177] Randolph and Davey, n.1 above, at p.80.
[178] Italian CC art.1748, para.2.
[179] See above. The right to commission could of course be formulated more advantageously to the agent than this: see above, para.11-029.
[180] See *Kontogeorgas v Kartonpak AE* (C-104/95) [1997] 1 C.M.L.R. 1093.
[181] See *Explora Group Plc v Hesco Bastion Ltd* [2005] EWCA Civ 646 at [59], per Rix LJ.
[182] As to "execution" see above, para.11-033.
[183] Article 11(1), above, para.11-034.

which is available to his principal and which he needs in order to check the amount of the commission due to him".[184] In this case an agreement to derogate from these provisions is by para.(3) stated to be void. This is without prejudice to other enactments or rules of law permitting agents to inspect their principals' books.[185]

It is, however, not clear how the duty is to be enforced. An action for damages, which seems the most obvious remedy at common law, would seem to be of limited utility. Some sort of order of the court, for instance a mandatory injunction, or a declaration, would be required.[186]

6. TERMINATION OF THE AGENCY[187]

Fixed period contract which continues to be performed   Where there is an   **11-037**
agency contract for a fixed period, and it continues to be performed by both parties after the expiry of the period, reg.14 provides that it "shall be deemed to be converted" into an agency contract for an indefinite period. It then attracts the provisions for the termination of agency contracts concluded for indefinite periods, which follow in reg.15. While this is reasonable, there is obviously here a danger for principals who allow what may be intended to be only a slight run-over, or allow a run-over by inadvertence.

Argument is possible that this provision also is not mandatory, and that the result prescribed can be avoided by an appropriate term in the original contract. As with regs 7 to 9, it is true that there is no express indication that the regulation cannot be derogated from, whereas non-derogation provisions appear in various forms in respect of regs 13, 15, 17 and 18.[188] On the other hand the wording of the Regulations appears to the English reader firm, and it appears that a provision in the original draft of the Directive allowing derogation was deleted.[189] Perhaps the best solution is that a contract for a fixed period containing a clause providing for what happens if the parties continue performance at the end of the period is not, at any rate at the moment when the clause first comes into operation, for the purposes of the Regulations, a contract for a fixed period.

Termination of contract concluded for an indefinite period   The Regulations   **11-038**
here provide specific rules for a situation on which English law has, at any rate in the context of agency, not been at all clear.[190] Under reg.15(1) in all such situations either party may terminate the contract by notice: this for English law avoids possible arguments that the contract is not terminable at all.[191] Regulation 15(2) provides that the minimum period of notice is one month for the first year of the

---

[184]   reg.22 makes provision for how such statements are to be supplied.

[185]   reg.12(4). The right to information does not require that it be given where disclosure would be contrary to public policy: reg.21. For an example of a corresponding right in the principal (though not in a commercial agency context), see fn.126 above.

[186]   The Access to Medical Reports Act 1988 confers a right to inspect such reports in certain circumstances: but here a special power is given by s.8 to the court to order compliance. In *Yasuda Fire Insurance Co v Orion Marine Insurance Underwriting Agency* [1995] Q.B. 174 a contractual term allowing such inspection was enforced by an order of specific performance, and declarations were also made.

[187]   For a very thorough discussion of this topic with strong reference to French law, see Saintier and Scholes, fn.1 above, Ch.5. See also McGee [2011] J.B.L. 782.

[188]   See regs 13(2), 15(2), 19.

[189]   See Randolph and Davey, fn.1 above, at p.89.

[190]   See Article 123.

[191]   Provisions as to how the giving of notice is to be effected are to be found in reg.22.

contract, two months "for the second year commenced", and three months "for the third year commenced and for the subsequent years". Presumably this means that the two-month period becomes necessary as soon as the agent has commenced his second year of operation under the contract. The parties may agree on longer but not on shorter periods. Unless otherwise agreed, "the end of the period of notice must coincide with the end of a calendar month", which may add nearly a further month to the period of notice. Where a fixed period contract is converted into an indefinite period contract under reg.14, discussed above, the fixed period must be taken into account in calculating the period of notice; since this refers back to unexcludable entitlements, it may be assumed that this rule is unexcludable also. No remedies or special time bars are prescribed for noncompliance with these requirements, and it seems that the general law is applicable.[192]

11-039 **Savings for the domestic law** By reg.16 the Regulations do not "affect the application of any enactment or rule of law which provides for immediate[193] termination of the agency contract—(a) because of the failure of one party to carry out all or part of his obligations under that contract; or (b) where exceptional circumstances arise". This provision, which links forward to reg.18,[194] appears intended to preserve the normal rules of domestic[195] law regarding what a common lawyer would call discharge of contract by breach, and frustration, and it may be assumed that the right to damages is unaffected. Paragraph (a) could in fact refer to the operation of both doctrines; paragraph (b) no doubt refers to situations where the contract might be automatically discharged by frustration, though a common lawyer would not express himself in this way. It could cover situations where the principal is by reason of exceptional circumstances unable to continue the contract, for example if his factory is destroyed by an earthquake, or he is affected by unforeseeable personal circumstances. The wording of (a) would presumably cover a wrongful repudiation by the principal accepted by the agent (including repudiation of a fixed term contract): that indemnity or compensation is then due is made clear by reg.18(b)(i). It would also cover wrongful repudiation by the agent accepted by the principal. A force majeure clause would however be a specific contract term and would not come within the words "enactment or rule of law". It is submitted that the common law "rule of law" as to termination for breach takes in that part of it which enables justification of a termination for which an inadequate reason is given where an adequate reason actually existed at the time of termination, a rule usually based on *Boston Deep Sea Fishing and Ice Co v Ansell*.[196]

11-040 **Entitlement to indemnity or compensation** The most significant provision in

---

[192] See *Roy v MR Pearlman Ltd* 1999 S.C. 459; 2000 S.L.T. 727, rejecting an argument that the Regulations must here be viewed as completely outside the general law. It should however be noted that whereas normal legal remedies are preserved in respect of the mutual duties of principal and agent by reg.5(2), there is no such specific provision here. See further discussion by McGee [2011] J.B.L. 782 at 785.
[193] This word (French "sans délai") appears to be inserted to distinguish the provisions as to notice in the immediately preceding reg.15.
[194] Below, para.11-056.
[195] See the Directive itself, art.16.
[196] *Boston Deep Sea Fishing & Ice Co v Ansell* (1888) 39 Ch. D. 339. See, e.g. *Crocs Europe BV v Anderson (t/a Spectrum Agencies (A Partnership))* [2012] EWCA Civ 1400; [2013] 1 Lloyd's Rep. 1 (principal terminated agency on insufficient grounds: compensation due); *Dadin Habitat (Société) v Constructions Traditionelles du Val de Loire* [2015] E.C.C. 27 the French Cour de Cassation held that compensation for termination was due when the principal terminated the agreement during a "trial period".

this part of the Regulations, and indeed, from the common law point of view, in the Regulations as a whole, is reg.17, which together with reg.18 seeks to secure that "after termination of the agency contract"[197] the commercial agent is entitled to be "indemnified … or compensated for damage" (reg.17(1)). As has been explained above, this idea results from a perception (which takes various forms) that an agent may establish a market and goodwill for a principal, and then be deprived of the benefit of his investment, both in money and in labour, by termination of his authority by a principal who may then seek to deal direct with customers, or perhaps use the services of another agent at a cheaper rate of commission, though the payment of indemnity or compensation is by no means limited to these cases. The agent is in effect to be "bought out", as is sometimes the case in employment law. The sum due in this respect is over and above money contractually due in other respects, for example in respect of unpaid arrears of commission or "repeat orders".[198]

The alternative between compensation and indemnity derives from art.17 of the Directive, and was intended to avoid the clash between the German and the French approaches to the issue, approaches which had developed some time before the harmonisation procedure was set in motion. The choice between the two regimes was to be left open. The indemnity regulated by art.17 of the Directive reproduced almost literally the then para.89b of the German Commercial Code (HGB). The compensation provision was inspired by French law and practice based originally on decree n.58—1345 of December 23, 1958.[199] The Directive did not eliminate these differences, but rather, limited the number of options available on this point to Member States. The divergence is quite great: in the most general terms it seems that compensation under French law can be about double the indemnity paid under German law.[200]

Provisions cannot be derogated from   The provisions of regs 17 and 18 can-   **11-041** not, by virtue of reg.19, be derogated from to the detriment of the agent "before the agency contract[201] expires". The provision against derogation is not difficult to understand. A recent example of a clause held to be an inadmissible derogation concerns a clause providing for an indemnity, but for compensation if the amount of it would be less than the amount payable by way of indemnity.[202] It may be asked why derogation may nevertheless be permitted after the expiry of the contract. This

---

[197] In *Scottish Energy Retail Ltd v Taskforce Contracts Ltd* [2008] CSOH 110; [2009] Eu.L.R. 62 it was held that partial termination of the contract (in regard to part of the services required) did not give rise to a right to indemnity or compensation.

[198] See above, para.11-030. In the context of CPR Pt 6 (service out of the jurisdiction) it has been said that this is not a contractual but a statutory action, possibly in the nature of a tort: *Fern Computer Consultancy Ltd v Intergraph Cadworx & Analysis Solutions Inc* [2014] EWHC 2908 (Ch); [2015] 1 Lloyd's Rep. 1 at [38], [39] and [47]. Although the contexts are different, this does not accord with the reasoning adopted concerning jurisdiction under what is now the Brussels I Regulation in *Arcado v Haviland SA* (C-9/87) [1988] E.C.R. 1539, which is clear that the action is contractual, reasoning which, it is submitted, should apply also under the Rome I Regulation on choice of law. It must be questioned whether domestic reasoning should be employed in connection with CPR Pt 6 when the cause of action is of EU origin (the *Arcado* case does not appear have been cited). For an example of a successful claim, see *McQuilllan v McCormick* [2010] EWHC 1112 (QB); [2011] E.C.C. 18 (jewellery). The possibility of amalgamating the two notions is considered by Saintier in *Commercial Contract Law: Transatlantic Perspectives* (Di Matteo and others, eds, 2003), Ch.12.

[199] See in general European Commission, report of July 23, 1996, The Application of the Commercial Agents Directive, COM 96/364 FINAL (reproduced in Randolph and Davey, fn.1 above).

[200] See below, para.11-053.

[201] As to this phrase see regs 16 and 17(1), paras 11-039 and 11-040, above.

[202] *Shearman (t/a Charles Shearman Agencies) v Hunter Boot Ltd* [2014] EWHC 47 (QB); [2014]

seems to be because after such expiry the principal's power to exercise pressure on the agent may be assumed to be no longer operative. However, the surprising opinion of Advocate General Léger in *Ingmar GB Ltd v Eaton Leonard Technologies Ltd*[203] suggests that art.19 of the Directive, which corresponds to reg.19, does not allow derogation of the indemnity and compensation provisions even *after* the contract has expired. This argument, not commented on by the court, is partly based on the notion that the provisions are of a special mandatory nature in so far as they protect competition policy and commercial agents within the community; and partly on the idea that the agent would have no interest in giving up his rights when he is freed of any obligation to the principal, whereas if he was in negotiation to renew the contract the regime would be valueless if derogatable.[204]

11-042 When does the entitlement arise? Indefinite period contracts Assuming that no breach of contract by principal or agent is involved, the obvious case of entitlement occurs where a contract for an indefinite period is terminated by the principal. An abrupt termination, even though notice is given within the minimum periods specified,[205] may obviously deprive the agent of expected benefits. Although English law has not recognised any rights in the agent in such circumstances, the object of the Directive plainly requires it. Perhaps more surprising, however, is the fact that reg.17(8) provides that the right to indemnity or compensation also arises where the agent dies, and reg.18(b)(ii)[206] assumes that it exists also where he himself terminates the agency contract "on grounds of the age, infirmity or illness of the commercial agent in consequence of which he cannot reasonably be required to continue his activities". This transfers the risk of those events to the principal, but is in accordance with the objects of the Directive as recompensing the agent (or his estate) for connections built up, or more generally his interest in the agency. It has been held that this covers normal retirement of the agent even if his physical condition would permit him to continue.[207] The entitlement may seem on the generous side: one might think that the agent could at the time of contracting have taken into account the fact that he might be prevented from continuing, at any rate if the infirmity was foreseeable or the age at which he might retire was known.

Problems may arise if the agent does a wrongful act which entitles the principal to terminate the contract and then dies. The common law analysis is that the contract is not terminated for breach until the innocent party to the breach elects to exercise the power to do so, and the principal may not have done this. Hence the right to compensation may sometimes be said to have accrued before the innocent party can terminate, though if the parties had agreed for an indemnity it might be possible to say that the payment of it was not (in whole or in part) "equitable" in accordance with reg.17(3)(b). Otherwise, it might sometimes be possible to argue that the agent

E.C.C. 12. The invalidity of the clause led to the operation of the basic rule for compensation rather than indemnity. cf. *Brand Studio Ltd v St John Knits Inc* [2015] EWHC 3143 (QB); [2015] Bus. L.R. 1421, where a similar clause was held severable from the choice of an indemnity, which therefore remained valid.

[203] *Ingmar GB Ltd v Eaton Leonard Technologies Inc* (C-381/98) [2000] E.C.R. I-9305; [2001] 1 All E.R. (Comm) 329.
[204] See paras 77–91, with discussion of the legislative history of art.19 of the Directive.
[205] In *Fadin Habitat (Société) v Constructions Traditionelles du Val de Loire* [2015] E.C.C.27 it was held that compensation was due when the contract was terminated during a trial period.
[206] Below, para.11-056.
[207] *Abbott v Condici Ltd* [2005] 2 Lloyd's Rep. 450 (reaching age of 65).

had by his (wrongful) conduct terminated the contract himself, though this argument is not usually attractive.[208]

Fixed period contracts   In the case of agency for a fixed period, or to a certain **11-043** age, however, it might be thought that (unless the agency is allowed to run on after the period), just as the periods of notice are inapplicable, so also is the requirement of payment of indemnity or compensation, for here the agent has taken on a fixed period contract and in doing so might be expected to have calculated whether or not he would receive adequate recompense for his outlay; though perhaps there should be a provision for termination before the end of the period by death, illness, etc., of the agent. Such an interpretation receives some support from the wording of the UK Regulations, which refer to entitlement on "termination" of the agency contract[209]; though the terminology used in the versions in other languages does not seem to give guidance here. The word "terminate" is used elsewhere in common law of a voluntary act of termination, and one might argue that it does not apply where the contract simply *expires*, or if renewable is not renewed, which is the word used in reg.14 in connection with fixed terms. Further, even if the idea of *indemnity* on expiry of a fixed term contract might be accepted, it is not easy to see why compensable *damage* should follow the (pre-arranged) expiry of a fixed term contract. In this sense, the wording of reg.17(6), which refers to "the damage he suffers as a result of the termination of his relations with his principal" may cause surprise on first reading: if the contract ends by the expiry of time, it might be thought that damage is not suffered thereby, but (if at all) by the agent's wrong estimation of the period of contract needed to recover his outlay or realise his investment. Without further background, therefore, a common lawyer might come to the conclusion that there was nothing due on the regular expiry of a fixed term contract.

It is however clear that not only indemnity, if otherwise available, but also compensation, where there is no indemnity, is available in this case, and that the word "terminates" in reg.17 is used in an intransitive sense meaning no more than "comes to an end".[210] For a start, one might say that although the agent regarded himself as needing a longer period of the contract to recover his outlay, he might not have been able to negotiate this: hence he requires some sort of protection against the results of failure to do so. It could also be said that a fixed term contract can be renewed: when the principal fails to renew such a contract he is doing something very similar to termination, which is only not termination because he has been prudent or commercially strong enough to secure a short term renewable contract.[211] Both these arguments are suggestive of a notion of good faith in the exercise of the power to terminate or not to renew. There are analogies in UK labour

---

[208] See *Geys v Société Générale* [2012] UKSC 63; [2013] 1 A.C. 623 (employment).

[209] reg.17(1).

[210] *Light v Ty Europe Ltd* [2003] EWCA Civ 1238; [2004] 1 Lloyd's Rep. 693 at [32]; *Tigana Ltd v Decoro Ltd* [2003] EWHC 23 (QB); [2003] Eu.L.R. 189; *Frape v Emreco International Ltd* 2002 S.L.T. 371; 2001 S.C.L.R. 997, though the matter was uncertain in the United Kingdom before these cases. This applies even to non-renewal where the principal thinks that he has grounds to terminate for the agent's default but does not seek to do so: *Cooper v Pure Fishing (UK) Ltd (formerly Outdoor Technology Group (UK) Ltd)* [2004] EWCA Civ 375; [2004] 2 Lloyd's Rep. 518.

[211] But this argument is rejected, albeit in a slightly different context, in *Cooper v Pure Fishing (UK) Ltd* [2004] EWCA Civ 375; [2004] 2 Lloyd's Rep. 518.

law.[212] Finally, the thinking that entitles the agent to compensation on death or retirement suggests that there should be a right on termination of a fixed term contract.[213] This preferred interpretation requires, however, a special meaning to be attributed to the phrase "compensation for damage", and this is discussed below.

11-044 **Indemnity**[214] In some countries an indemnity is payable as a matter of course. The directive in its final form, however, allowed countries to choose between indemnity and compensation; and for Great Britain, reg.17(2) provides that "except where the agency contract[215] otherwise provides, the commercial agent shall be entitled to be compensated rather than indemnified". The principal does not have to agree to such an arrangement, therefore, but it has been held that a reference in the contract to "compensation after termination" on the particular facts envisaged an indemnity.[216] Where indemnity is chosen, reg.17(3) provides that:

> "the commercial agent shall be entitled to an indemnity if and to the extent that—
>
> (a) he has brought[217] the principal new customers or has significantly increased the volume of business with existing customers and the principal continues to derive substantial benefits from the business with such customers; and
>
> (b) the payment of this indemnity is equitable having regard to all the circumstances and, in particular, the commission lost by the commercial agent on the business transactions with such customers." [218]

This indemnity has been described for German law (where it is called "Ausgleich") as "capitalised remuneration for the continued performance". Regulation 17(4) limits it to "a figure equivalent to an indemnity for one year calculated from the

---

[212] There are also analogies in land law. At common law a tenant for life was entitled to emblements provided that the determination of the tenancy was not caused by his own act: see Megarry and Wade, *Law of Real Property* (8th edn, 2012), para.3-105.

[213] The matter had been raised, but not decided, in *Whitehead v Jenks & Caitell Engineering Ltd* [1999] Eu. L.R. 827.

[214] See in general European Commission, Report of July 23, 1996, COM 96/364 FINAL, where the method of calculation of indemnity is discussed. There is an exhaustive consideration, going up to 2010, of indemnity and compensation in Randolph and Davey, fn.1 above, containing in Ch.9 comparisons with the original proposal for a Directive, the 1996 Report, and in Chs 10 and 11 expositions of German and French law by Reiling and Saintier respectively. Since the UK Regulations created something new for the countries affected, some knowledge of the German and French laws is a help in comprehension. In general, the German law is more valuable, because it is of longer standing and formed the basis of the Directive. The French law developed later, but is essential for the understanding of the notion of compensation. A further chapter by Dr Ruth Bender, Ch.12, addresses business valuation, which is relevant in the context of the right to compensation.

[215] The original text used the word "contact". This was corrected by SI 1998/2868. Where the parties have a series of agency contracts it can be said that the rights arise at the end of each. It has however been held that the words should normally be taken to apply at the end of the agency in general: *Moore v Piretta PTA Ltd* [1999] 1 All E.R. 173 at 179.

[216] *Hardie Polymers Ltd v Polymerland Ltd* 2002 S.C.L.R. 64.

[217] It has been held that this word simply means that the agent was instrumental in obtaining new customers; specific introduction is not required: *Moore v Piretta PTA Ltd*, above, at 179. In *Marchon Germany GmbH v Karaskiewicz* (C-315/14) [2016] Bus.L.R. 694 the CJEU held that where an agent was responsible for certain of the principal's brands only, the other brands being entrusted to other commercial agents, the principal gave the agent a list of customers for other brands and the agent secured orders from some of those on the list, the agent ranked for the purpose of the indemnity as having brought new customers.

[218] See *Honyvem Informazioni Commerciali Srl v De Zotti* (C-465-04) [2006] E.C.R. I-02789 as to the impact (in Italy) of collective indemnity agreements.

commercial agent's average annual remuneration over the preceding five years and if the contract goes back less than five years the indemnity shall be calculated on the average for the period in question". This limit, which is in substantial accord with German law,[219] gives the principal some advantage in use of the indemnity, and it is not necessarily true that principals would be best advised to avoid such an arrangement. The essence of the indemnity arrangement may therefore be regarded as a buy-out on one year's remuneration, but only "if and to the extent that" the agent has brought the business and the principal continues to receive substantial benefits, and the payment is equitable. The burden of proof of these requirements appears to lie on the agent.[220]

Usually, the first step in the calculation is to ascertain the commission earned by the agent in the last year, whether in respect of new customers or additional value of business generated with existing customers. This is however only a starting point. Another feature is the estimated benefit that will accrue to the principal through business relationships with customers originally acquired by the agent or developed by the agent.[221] Of course, after the agency contract terminates a proportion of such relationships will be lost over the years. Therefore, the estimated benefit to the principal must be discounted in this respect. The period considered for this purpose ranges from two to five years. The capital sum due on this basis represents a prospective income which must be discounted at a standard interest rate to reflect the value of the indemnity. The outcome is subject to an equitable adjustment to take into account all the circumstances of the case. This seldom seems necessary, but may take into account matters such as whether the agent worked for several principals; whether he was himself in breach of contract in any respect; and whether he received high commissions in respect of customers whom he might not have introduced. It appears that the "cap" is comparatively seldom reached: it is definitely not a method of calculating the indemnity.

It appears that in Germany equitable considerations may displace the rule denying the right to indemnity where the agent's behaviour would justify immediate dismissal.[222] It is however difficult to extract such possibilities from the UK Regulations, and equally from at least the English version of the Directive itself, with which the Regulations are identical at this point save for a slight difference in punctuation.

---

[219] However, it appears that German courts interpreted the equivalent of reg.17(2)(a) on the basis that the amount of commission lost represented an upper limit for indemnity. This was held wrong by the ECJ in *Semen v Deutsche Tamoil GmbH* (C-348/07) [2009] 1 Lloyd's Rep. 653. Consequent on this, art.89B of the HGB was changed. The case also holds that where the principal is part of a group of companies, benefits accruing to other companies in the group are not to be taken into account.

[220] See the indemnity provision applied in the only English case, *Moore v Piretta PTA Ltd* [1999] 1 All E.R. 174 (fashion clothing): see Segal (1998) 142 S.J. 376 (German law was referred to). The value of the business brought in was taken and deductions were made for the existing customer base, the agent's expenses and accelerated payment. The balance exceeded the cap, and only the cap was therefore awarded (the assessment is questioned by Randolph and Davey, fn.1 above, at pp.105–106). Matters of mitigation of loss (e.g. that the agent could have taken paid employment) were held not relevant. But these, and perhaps the eventual effect of a restraint of trade clause, could perhaps be relevant in some situations. See also discussion by McGee [2011] J.B.L. 782 at 796.

[221] Where there have been several contracts in succession, the period covered by the words "the agency contract" is not confined to the contract operative at the date of termination, but the "agency" can be regarded as operative further back: *Moore v Piretta PTA Ltd* [1999] 1 All E.R. 714.

[222] See brief reference to such considerations in *Volvo Car Germany GmbH v Autohof Weidensdorf GmbH* (C-203/09) [2011] 1 All E.R. (Comm) 906 at [44].

11-045 **Non-derogation** The indemnity is not compulsory. But the provision against derogation in reg.19[223] seems to mean that if an indemnity is adopted to the exclusion of compensation it must be adopted as specified in the Regulations, or under a scheme more favourable to the agent.[224]

11-046 **Time limit** By virtue of reg.17(9) the agent loses his entitlement "if within one year following termination of his agency contract he has not notified his principal that he intends pursuing his entitlement".[225] Although informal notice may well be sufficient,[226] a formal notice is a safer procedure.

11-047 **Damages** But by reg.17(5) "the grant of an indemnity ... shall not prevent the commercial agent from seeking damages". This follows from the nature of the indemnity. Such damages would be over and above the indemnity, and granted on normal principles of domestic law in respect of a breach of contract, where there was one; but it has been held that such an award must not allow double recovery by combining the indemnity with compensation for loss resulting in particular from loss of commission.[227] Unpaid commission could also be recoverable, whether by way of damages or debt.[228]

11-048 **Compensation**[229] In Great Britain the indemnity is a voluntary arrangement. If, however, there is no indemnity provided for, the agent has, as stated above, a right to be what is called "compensated for damage", a right which again by reg.19 cannot be derogated from to the agent's detriment. The question then arises as to what this "compensation" is and how far it is different from ordinary damages under domestic law for wrongful termination of the contract. It is clear that it is different, for in accordance with what is said in para.11-043 above, it can arise where there is no breach of the contract at all; and further, paras (5) and (6) of reg.17 imply a distinction between "damages" (para.(5)) and "compensation for the damage he suffers as a result of the termination of his relations with his principal" (para.(6)).

---

[223] See above, para.11-041.

[224] cf. *Shearman v Hunter Boot Ltd* [2013] EWHC 47 (QB); [2014] E.C.C. 12, above, para.11-041.

[225] The position when a termination by notice occurs is considered in *Claramoda Ltd v Zoomphase Ltd* [2009] EWHC 2857 (Comm) (primary agency duties had ended but secondary duties continued, with the result that termination occurred at a later date).

[226] A letter from a solicitor was held to be adequate notice in *Hackett v Advanced Medical Computer Systems Ltd* [1999] C.L.Y. 111. But in *Cerascope Ltd v Todagres SA* [2008] EWHC 1502 (Ch); [2010] E.C.C. 1 a letter from lawyers was held to be insufficiently specific under Spanish law (which governed the contract and also the question of interruption of the limitation period).

[227] See *Quenon K SPRL v Beobank SA* (C-338/14) [2016] Bus. L.R. 264. Here Belgian legislation was more specific and provided that where the amount of the indemnity does not fully indemnify the commercial agent for the loss actually incurred, the agent can (in effect) claim damages for proved additional loss. It was held that since the Directive does not give clear guidance as to the circumstances in which damages can be claimed it is for Member States "in the exercise of their discretion, to determine those circumstances and the procedural rules" (at [32]). However, the Directive requires that an initial choice be made between the indemnity and compensation schemes, and "[t]he award of damages may not result in double recovery by combining the indemnity for customers with the compensation for loss resulting, in particular, from the loss of commission following termination of the contract" (at [34]).

[228] The possible overlap is considered by McGee [2011] J.B.L. 782 at 790.

[229] The United Kingdom is alone in providing a choice for the parties instead of making the choice itself, and it is not certain that this was a proper implementation of the Directive. All countries chose indemnity except France, Ireland and Iceland, where compensation was chosen; and the United Kingdom, which takes in both.

The French text of the Directive uses, indeed, a different word here—"*réparation*"—from that used in art.17(5) (equivalent to reg.17(6))—"*dommages-interêts*": though the German text uses the same ("*Schadensersatz*"). This notion of compensation under the Directive seems therefore a special one, in effect compensation which is payable even though no breach of contract may have occurred. It may be that, before implementation of the Directive in the Member States, there was no exact parallel to it (as opposed to the indemnity) in the domestic law of any European country.[230]

Calculation   Regulation 17(7) provides that: **11-049**

"For the purpose of these Regulations such damage shall be deemed to occur *particularly* when the termination takes place in *either or both* of the following circumstances, namely circumstances which—

(a)   deprive the commercial agent of the commission which proper performance of the agency contract would have procured for him whilst providing his principal with substantial benefits linked to the activities of the commercial agent; or

(b)   have not enabled the commercial agent to amortize the costs and expenses that he had incurred in the performance of the agency contract on the advice of his principal." [231]

French law[232]   It has already been said that the compensation method is known   **11-050**
to be derived from French law. Under French law it seems that compensation is in principle due to the agent when the contract was wrongfully terminated by the principal, or it expired for other reasons, provided that the agent suffered a loss from the termination of the relationship. The commercial agency is regarded as a matter of common interest of which the agent is (in cases where he does not assign it) deprived: his claim is quasi-proprietary.[233] This seems to be a controlling feature.[234] However, the right to compensation is excluded if the principal terminated the contract because of a serious breach by the agent ("*faute grave de l'agent*"), such as dealing in competing products; or if the agent himself terminated the contract, unless he did so for justifiable reasons such as breach by the principal, or an unjustified reduction of the agent's area of operation; or unless the agent terminated because of age, infirmity, illness and so forth. It should be noted that the French law is drafted to refer to loss ("*indemnité compensatrice du préjudice subi*" because the relationship between the parties came to an end) and does not refer to the accrual

---

[230]   Though the similarity is with the French approach, French law before the implementation of the Directive (by law 91-593 of June 25, 1991) did not award compensation in case of expiration of fixed term contracts, nor for termination due to the agent's death. It appears that the new legislation transformed the French approach on these points, thus making clear that the principal's obligation to compensate the agent is not necessarily linked to a wrongful termination of the agency relationship.

[231]   Emphasis supplied.

[232]   French law has remained unchanged on this point since law 91-593 of June 25, 1991, referred to in McGee [2011] J.B.L. 782, now incorporated into the Code de Commerce as arts L134-1-16. See an authoritative account in Saintier and Scholes, fn.1 above, at p.170 onwards; Christou, fn.1 above, para.3-135 onwards.

[233]   See Saintier and Scholes, fn.1 above, at pp.81–82.

[234]   Article L134-4(i) of the Code de Commerce states that "Les contrats entre les agents commerciaux et leurs mandants sont conclus dans l'interêt commun des parties".

of substantial benefits to the principal mentioned in art.17(3) of the Directive(reg.17(3)).

In contrast with the German law on indemnity the principal owes compensation to the agent even if the agent did not acquire new customers. The emphasis is on whether the agent suffered a loss because the agency contract ended, rather than whether the principal benefited from the agent's activity. The loss is the loss of an asset, his interest in the common enterprise of himself and the principal.[235] There is of course no "cap" as under German law. In France the calculation of the award does not involve the application of a structured formula, though in fact as regards indefinite period contracts, it appears that the agent usually obtains something like the total of two average years' commissions, calculated on the basis of earnings over the last two or three years; and it may be that further sums can be added if the agent's loss is above the average. On the other hand, French courts do have the power to reduce the standard amount of compensation if it exceeds the agent's loss, because reference to that standard is not required by the applicable legislation. It appears that French judges seem reluctant to resort to this power, at least in some contexts, e.g. where the agency was terminated suddenly by reason of the principal's breach, if that breach was completely unjustified in the light of the agent's performance. It appears also that the parties may not determine in advance the amount of compensation to be paid on termination.

11-051 **British cases** The method of assessment for the United Kingdom[236] is now laid down by the House of Lords' decision in *Lonsdale v Howard & Hallam Ltd*,[237] which supersedes all earlier authority, of which a considerable amount (of varied quality) had been accumulating.[238] Such an idea of compensation has so far been unique to French law. The opinion of Lord Hoffmann accepts the French notion that the agent is regarded "as having had a share in the goodwill of the principal's business which he has helped to create".[239] "This means, primarily, the right to future commissions 'which proper performance of the agency contract would have

---

[235] See Saintier and Scholes, fn.1 above, at pp.185–186.
[236] The Regulations apply in Scotland as well as England and Wales, and there are parallel Regulations in Northern Ireland. The Supreme Court (formerly House of Lords) is the final appellate tribunal for all three jurisdictions. But see Macgregor (2008) 12 Edin.L.Rev 86.
[237] *Lonsdale (t/a Lonsdale Agencies) v Howard & Hallam Ltd* [2007] UKHL 32; [2007] 1 W.L.R. 2055 (shoes), in substantial accord with the judgment of Moore-Bick LJ in the Court of Appeal: [2006] EWCA 63; [2006] 1 W.L.R. 1281. Noted by Saintier (2008) 124 L.Q.R. 31; Macgregor (2008) 12 Edin.L.Rev 86 (both suggesting that the method laid down makes too much use of criteria relevant to indemnity).
[238] Principally the decision of the Inner House of the Court of Session in *King v T Tunnock Ltd* 2000 S.C. 424; 2000 S.L.T. 744 (cakes and biscuits), which was not accepted in the House of Lords, though it may remain valid in Scotland. Other cases prior to *Lonsdale* are also considered in the opinion of Lord Hoffmann and in Randolph and Davey, fn.1 above, pp.111–117. Cases decided since the judgment in *Lonsdale*'s case include *McQuillan v McCormick* [2010] EWHC 1112 (QB); [2011] E.C.C. 18 (jewellery) and *Invicta UK Ltd v International Brands Ltd* [2013] EWHC 1564 (QB); [2013] E.C.C. 30 (wine for supermarkets); *Alan Ramsay Sales & Marketing Ltd v Typhoo Tea Ltd* [2016] EWHC 486 (Comm) (food sector, especially cash and carry and wholesale); *Monk v Largo Foods Ltd* [2016] EWHC 1387 (Comm) (agent for marketing of crisps and similar products); *W Nagel (A Firm) v Pluczenik Diamond Co NV* [2017] EWHC 1750 (Comm); [2017] 2 Lloyd's Rep. 215 (diamond dealings; where the discussion is obiter since the judge had decided that the Regulations did not apply). In each of these cases specialist advice was received by the court.
[239] At [9].

procured him'."[240] As already stated, in its implementation French courts have regularly awarded, though not by way of applying a rule, a sum equivalent to twice the average annual gross commission over the previous three years. It is clear however that other countries are not under any obligation to follow any one state's method of calculation.[241] The French practice appears to be based on the assumption that agencies in France change hands at the sort of valuation mentioned above, whereas there is no such market in the United Kingdom.[242] The courts of the United Kingdom are entitled, therefore, to use their own methods of calculating the loss for which the compensation is payable. "What has to be valued is the income stream which the agency would have generated."[243] This should be done "by reference to the value of the agency on the assumption that it continued: the amount which the agent could reasonably expect to receive for the right to stand in his shoes, continue to perform the duties of the agency and receive the commission which he would have received".[244] If the agency was unassignable, it must be assumed that a purchaser would have been entitled to take it over, but not that he would thereby acquire an assignable asset.[245] The court would require information about "the standard methodology for the valuation of such businesses", though there might be cases where courts could eventually take judicial notice of the "standard case".[246] In the case in question the business concerned was declining, and the agency would not be likely to change hands at any considerable value. The court would therefore have been justified in awarding nothing,[247] and this is a significant part of the decision. However, a small award made by the judge (much less than the amount claimed) was approved. By the same reasoning, the converse might have been the case had the business been increasing. The earlier judgment of the Court of Appeal in *Lonsdale* had previously been considered in another case[248] in which the judge said that he would only have made a nominal award of £2 on a claim unsupported by evidence, and doubted whether the court should simply "make the best estimate it can".

However, loss of goodwill is not the only damage in respect of which there may **11-052** be recovery. On this issue, the judgment of Moore-Bick LJ in the Court of Appeal in *Lonsdale* remains significant. When the agency is terminated in circumstances which deprive him of the commission which proper performance of the contract would have enabled him to earn:

[240] At [10].
[241] *Honyvem Informazioni Commerciali SrL v Mariella de Zotti* (C-465/04) [2006] E.C.R. I-02879; and for this reason the House of Lords in Lonsdale declined to make a reference to the ECJ.
[242] At [18]. See also at [26]: "the French practice is of no evidential value whatever". For a critique of the method used, see McGee [2011] J.B.L. 782 at 791 onwards. As to valuation methods, see Randolph and Davey, fn.1 above, Ch.12.
[243] At [12].
[244] At [21]. It may be assumed that where the agency has been covered by more than one contract, its general value rather than that referable to the last contract in time will be taken into account, as has been held in the case of indemnity in *Moore v Piretta PTA Ltd* [1999] 1 All E.R. 174, fn.215 above: see Randolph and Davey, fn.1 above, at p.89.
[245] At [13].
[246] At [35], [36].
[247] At [34]. See also *Warren (t/a On-line Cartons and Print v Drukkeri)* [2014] EWCA Civ 993; [2015] 1 Lloyd's Rep. 111.
[248] *Vick v Vogle-Gapes Ltd* [2006] EWHC 1665 (QB); (2006) 150 S.J.L.B. 917 (Richard Seymour QC).

"the value of the business at the date of termination ought to reflect the agent's future earnings which are the rewards he was entitled to receive in respect of any benefit that his principal might obtain from his activities. In this type of situation, therefore, the agent should be adequately compensated if he is paid the value at the date of termination of the business he has built up."

But:

"if the agency is terminated in circumstances where the agent has not been able to amortise expenses which he has incurred on the advice of the principal in setting up the agency, the value attaching to the business may or may not provide sufficient compensation ... the agent is entitled to recover whatever loss he can show he has suffered which in a case of this kind might consist in whole or in part of the amount of the unamortised expenses."[249]

This latter point is not adverted to in the opinion of Lord Hoffmann, but there seems no reason why it should not be regarded as correct.

11-053 It remains to ask whether an action in damages for breach of contract might also be available for loss suffered (assuming that double recovery could be avoided) in appropriate circumstances. It would of course not normally apply where the agency determined by death, retirement or expiry of a fixed term; though it might sometimes if appropriate notice is not given. The fact that such an action is expressly preserved by reg.17(5) in respect of the indemnity is some indication that it is not available where the remedy is compensation. It is also possible that in French law some such elements could be taken in under the compensation award, though it would seem likely that a remedy for termination in bad faith might be separate. But there is no indication that the Directive supersedes other remedies, let alone of which remedies would be superseded, and as a matter of principle other remedies for breach of contract should survive if relevant, and if the elements of loss could be separated out.[250] In particular, it is clear that sums due as commission, but payable at a later date, under reg.8(a)[251] would be a separate matter. Overall, though there is undoubtedly overlap in the methods of calculation, that for compensation, which starts by looking to the past, tends the favour the agent more than that for indemnity, which tends to look to future prospects and is subject to a cap of one year's average remuneration.

11-054 Non-derogation As has been stated, reg.19 provides that the parties may not derogate from the compensation provisions before the agency contract expires.[252]

11-055 Time limit Like the indemnity, the right to compensation is by virtue of reg.17(9) lost if the agent does not notify his principal within one year that he intends pursuing the entitlement.[253]

---

[249] *Lonsdale v Howard & Hallam Ltd* [2006] EWCA Civ 760; [2006] 1 W.L.R. 1281 at [29].
[250] See Moore-Bick LJ in the *Lonsdale* case, above, at [28] (compensation for damage caused by breach of duty could be claimed outside the Regulations); *McQuillan v McCormick* [2010] EWHC 11123 (QB); [2011] E.C.C. 18 (outstanding commission and damages for noncompliance with notice requirements); Saintier and Scholes, fn.1 above, at p.160. This point was not discussed in the House of Lords.
[251] See above, para.11-032.
[252] See above, paras 11-041 and 11-045.
[253] See above, para.11-046.

Cases where no indemnity or compensation due Regulation 18 provides that **11-056**
the indemnity or[254] compensation is not payable where:

> "(a)   the principal has terminated the agency contract because of default attributable to
> the commercial agent which would justify immediate termination of the agency
> contract pursuant to Regulation 16 above."[255]

This refers straight back to reg.16[256] and is not difficult to understand: the agent
loses the right to these benefits if he commits a breach entitling the principal in effect to dismiss him by virtue of general rules of law.[257] It does not however apply
where the principal simply does not renew the agency, even though he may fail to
do so because he believes that the agent's conduct justifies termination.[258] Nor, by
reason of general common law principles as to discharge by breach, does it apply
where the principal does not accept the agent's repudiation.[259] The phrase "attributable to the agent" is preferable for a common lawyer to the reference to "blame"
in reg.11(1), which as stated above can be given a rather imprecise meaning.[260]
Equally it obviously will not apply if the commercial agent has himself terminated
the contract without justification.

Regulation 18(b) thus provides that indemnity or compensation is not payable **11-057**
where:

> "the commercial agent has himself terminated the agency contract, unless such termina-
> tion is justified
>
> (i)   by circumstances attributable to the principal, or

---

[254] These words, which appear in the Directive, seem to have been omitted in error and were added to
the Regulations by SI 1993/3173.

[255] As to which see above, para.11-039. For examples see *Vick v Vogle-Gapes Ltd* [2006] EWHC 1665
(TCC) (uncooperative behaviour); *Crane v Sky In-Home Service Ltd* [2007] EWHC 66 (Ch); [2007]
2 All E.R. (Comm) 599 (passing off main supplier's warranty service as agent's own); *Nigel Fryer
Joinery Services Ltd v Ian Firth Hardware Ltd* [2008] EWHC 767 (Ch); [2008] 2 Lloyd's Rep. 108
(failure to notify working for other companies, and to make appropriate reports); *Gledhill v Bentley
Designs Ltd* [2010] EWHC 1965 (QB); [2011] 1 Lloyd's Rep. 270 (rude behaviour: not stated that
the agent was a commercial agent: see above, para.10-042). The question whether this covers
termination for an invalid reason when a valid reason operative at the time of the termination is
subsequently discovered which is effective at common law) is briefly considered in *Rossetti Marketing Ltd v Diamond Sofa Co Ltd* [2012] EWCA Civ 1021; [2013] 1 All E.R. (Comm) 308. It was common ground in the *Nigel Fryer* case, above, that this could not be done; but Lord Neuberger in *Rossetti* is doubtful, as was Bean J in *Cureton v Mark Insulations Ltd* [2006] EWHC 2279 (Admin), cited
by Lord Neuberger at [59].

[256] Above, para.11-039.

[257] The policy is however questioned, as involving an unjustified forfeiture, by Bennett, fn.1 above,
para.11.48.

[258] *Cooper v Pure Fishing (UK) Ltd* [2003] EWCA Civ 375; [2004] 2 Lloyd's Rep. 518. It must be
doubtful to what extent the contract can be drafted so as to create such a "default". See *Laboratoires
Arkopharma SA v Gravier* [2003] E.C.C. 333, where a contract designated failure to meet targets
in such terminology, but the French Cour de Cassation held the question to be subject to the general
law. Nor will it apply where the relevant conduct, which would otherwise justify immediate termination, occurs after the giving of notice but before the contract expired: *Volvo Car Germany GmbH v
Autohof Weidensdorf GmbH* (C-203/09) [2011] 1 All E.R. (Comm) 906, suggesting however, in the
case of an indemnity, that the agent's conduct might sometimes be taken into account in determining what sum was "equitable".

[259] *Alan Ramsay Sales & Marketing Ltd v Typhoo Tea Ltd* [2016] EWHC 486 (Comm); [2016] 4 W.L.R.
59.The agent was however held entitled to damages for termination not consistent with the normal
notice period.

[260] See above, para.11-034.

(ii) on grounds of age, infirmity or illness of the commercial agent in consequence of which he cannot reasonably be required to continue his activities."

Plainly, if it is the agent that terminates the contract without justification he is not entitled to commission. On the face of it (i) is not surprising: if the principal commits a repudiatory breach entitling the agent to terminate the contract, the agent remains entitled to compensation. However, there are differences. The first is that where the "circumstances attributable to the principal" involve a breach of contract by him, the normal common law rules referred to in art.16 would regard the repudiation as requiring acceptance by the agent.[261] This does not appear to be envisaged by the Directive and could cause difficulties if it were argued that the breach had not been accepted, but rather, waived.[262] Secondly, it has been held that *"circumstances attributable to the principal"* include situations where there has been no breach at all, as where the principal ceases to manufacture such goods but no breach of contract by him is involved and there is no frustration.[263] This to some extent fits with the third point, that reg.18(1)(b) makes no reference to "immediate" termination, a word which is obviously more appropriate to termination for breach, nor to "default" as opposed to "circumstances". Although it has been said that reg.18(1)(a) and (b) are "two sides of the same coin"[264] this is not perhaps completely true.

The reference in (ii) to age, infirmity or illness is consistent with the fact that the right to compensation survives the death of the agent, and it has been held that it applies to an agent who simply reaches the retiring age, being still capable of carrying on.[265]

Lastly, under sub-para.(c), the right to indemnity or compensation is excluded where:

"the commercial agent, with the agreement of his principal, assigns his rights and duties under the agency contract to another person."

The assumption seems to be that in such a case the agent has obtained the value of the goodwill and so forth in the purchase price of his business; or has given it to another, for example a son or daughter. If the principal does not consent, the assignment may be ineffective under the general law of assignment, and the attempt to achieve it might be a repudiatory breach of contract by the agent. On the other hand failure to consent might be a breach of the requirement of good faith.[266]

---

[261] See *Roy v MR Pearlman Ltd* 1999 S.C. 459; 2000 S.L.T. 727 at [24]. See also the *Bell Electric* case, below. In *Alan Ramsay Sales & Marketing Ltd v Typhoo Tea Ltd* [2016] EWHC 486 (Comm) the rule is applied to breach by the *agent*.

[262] There are difficulties in this connection in respect of employment contracts: see *Chitty on Contracts* (32nd edn), Vol.2, para.40-192; *Geys v Société Générale* [2012] UKSC 63; [2013] 1 A.C. 523. The agency context could be considered analogous: but see *Atlantic Underwriting Agencies Ltd v Cia di Assicurazioni di Milano SpA* [1979] 2 Lloyd's Rep. 240 and discussion in *Roy v MR Pearlman Ltd* 1999 S.C. 459; 2000 S.L.T. 727.

[263] *King v T Tunnock Ltd* 2000 S.C. 424; 2000 S.L.T. 744.

[264] See *Bell Electric Ltd v Aweco Appliance Systems Gmbh* [2002] EWHC 872 (QB); [2002] Eu.L.R. 443 at [48] onwards, per Elias J (non-payment of commission: the case was appealed on a different point [2002] EWCA Civ 1501; [2003] 1 All E.R. 344).

[265] *Abbott v Condici Ltd* [2005] 2 Lloyd's Rep. 450.

[266] See above, para.11-025. On assignment see Saintier and Scholes, fn.1 above, at pp.176–177. In *Rossetti Marketing Ltd v Diamond Sofa Co Ltd* [2012] EWCA Civ 1021; [2013] 1 All E.R. (Comm) 308 it was held that the Regulation envisages the new agent having taken both the principal's rights and

Restraint of trade clauses   A restraint of trade clause is defined as "an agree-   **11-058**
ment restricting the business activities of a commercial agent following termination of the agency contract".[267] Such clauses are dealt with in reg.20, under which
a restraint of trade clause is valid:

> "only if and to the extent that:
>
> (a)   it is concluded in writing; and
> (b)   it relates to the geographical area or the group of customers and the geographi-
>   cal area entrusted to the commercial agent and to the kind of goods covered by
>   his agency under the contract."

By para.(2) it shall be valid for not more than two years after termination of the
agency contract.

This provision appears to provide a substitute for the normal common law rules
in this context. In practice it probably varies little from the common law on
contracts in restraint of trade, except for the requirement of writing, and the fact that
where a legislative provision uses, as it must, specific wording, the result might not
be exactly the same as would be expected in a system only using case law in the
area.[268] There is no such requirement at common law, but it does not seem likely
that an agreement of this nature, which requires some precision in its drafting,
would easily be entered into orally. The restriction to two years is a fixed limit, but
it may be that restrictions on agents of this type for longer than two years might not
easily be held reasonable at common law. The restrictions to certain types of
customers and goods are likewise broadly in accord with the common law rules,
though differences of detail could well occur.[269] Paragraph (3) preserves the effect
of domestic enactments or rules of law which restrict the enforceability of restraint
of trade clauses to a greater extent than the Regulations or enables the court to
reduce the obligations on the parties resulting from such clauses. It is in fact
conceivable that the common law rules would operate more strictly than this regulation in some instances. The English courts have, however, no specific power to
reduce the obligations under such contracts; but the power to sever invalid portions of contracts, which they have, can also come under the words.[270]

---

duties: see at [55] and [56]. This analysis is accepted in *Invicta UK v International Brands Ltd* [2013]
EWHC 1564 (QB); [2013] E.C.C. 30. A possible assignment situation is also analysed (with the
conclusion that there was no assignment) in *Barnett Fashion Agency Ltd v Nigel Hall Menswear Ltd*
[2011] EWHC 978 (QB).

[267]   reg.2(1).
[268]   See however *BCM Group Ltd v Visualmark Ltd* [2006] EWHC 1831 (QB), where the wording of
the Regulations (which covered others than customers "entrusted to" the agent) was applied to make
the restriction too wide.
[269]   As to the common law on contracts in restraint of trade see *Chitty on Contracts* (32nd edn), Vol.I,
paras 16-085 onwards.
[270]   This seems to be assumed in the *Visualmark* case, above.

CHAPTER 12

CONFLICT OF LAWS[1]

INTRODUCTION

The first 16 editions of this work did not refer to the conflict of laws at all. The **12-001** next two contained a "Note on the Conflict of Laws" suggesting that the number of separate topics deployed within the general law of agency, and within the book, made considering each separately from the point of view of the conflict of laws impracticable; and that the central problems of dealing through another, and the exiguous English case law on the topic, were, like the more specific topics, already adequately dealt with in books on the conflict of laws in general.

However, English decisions involving points of basic agency law in a foreign context have become more frequent; also, an early version of the European Commission's proposal for a Regulation on the Law Applicable to Contractual Obligations (Rome I) actually contained a (somewhat unsatisfactory) provision purporting to deal with the topic specifically. This was dropped before adoption of the final version,[2] which excludes, as did its predecessor the Rome Convention on the Law Applicable to Contractual Obligations,[3] "the question whether an agent is able to bind a principal ... in relation to a third party".[4] The scope and significance of this exclusion are by no means as straightforward as may appear: this will be considered below.[5] But while the English case law is scant, it seems worthwhile putting forward what, because of the paucity of authority, are bound to be mostly not much more than suggestions and pointers as to the law which should apply to the salient separate topics within the law of agency in connection with contractual obligations, both under and outside the Rome I Regulation.

Most of the inquiry is directed towards whether an agent can enter into contractual obligations binding and entitling his principal, but the question can also

---

[1] See Dicey, Morris and Collins, *The Conflict of Laws* (15th edn, 2012), Vol.2, para.33R-407 onwards, containing much valuable new discussion and material; Verhagen, *Agency in Private International Law* (1995), containing much discussion of the Hague Convention on the Law Applicable to Agency of 1978, which received little support; Breslauer, "Agency in Private International Law" (1938) 50 Jur.Rev 282; Rees and Flesch, "Agency and Vicarious Liability in Conflict of Laws" (1960) 60 Col.L.Rev 75. For comparative approaches in the English language, see Wolff, *Private International Law* (1944), para.424; Rabel, *The Conflict of Laws: a Comparative Study* (2nd edn), Vol.3, Chs 39–41; Rigaux, *International Encyclopedia of Comparative Law*, Vol.III, Ch.29. The writer of this chapter is much indebted to discussions on this topic with Professor Michele Graziadei.

[2] Regulation 593/2008 [2008] OJ L177/6, taken with Corrigendum 593/2008, which applies to contracts concluded as from December 17, 2009.

[3] Formerly applicable under the Contracts (Applicable Law) Act 1990.

[4] art.I.2(g): see below, para.12-011.

[5] See para.12-012.

arise during the performance of contractual obligations by an agent. Such questions are normally to be solved by the law governing the main obligation.[6] No attempt is made to consider situations where agency reasoning may be deployed in other contexts, for example tort, property, restitution or statutory representation in connection with guardianship.

12-002 **The internal and external aspects of the law of agency** It is a fundamental of the law of agency that it has two aspects, the internal relationship between principal and agent, and the external relationship between principal and third party created by the agent.[7] Any consideration of the law of agency under the conflict of laws must start from this distinction. As in the substantive law of agency, there is in the conflict of laws an ongoing tension between the notion that a principal should not be held for more than what he has authorised and that which seeks to protect a third party who had no practicable way of discovering whether or not an agent was authorised. On the basis of this general distinction, it might seem appropriate to say that the relationship between principal and agent is governed by the law governing that internal relationship, whereas the relationship between principal and third party is governed by the law governing the external relationship, each of which would under common law involve questions of ascertaining the intentions of the parties to it. In several recent English cases this distinction seems to have been taken and accepted,[8] indeed this is the only major point emerging from most of the recent case law. It seems likely however that it is too simplistic.

12-003 **The internal law: the Rome I Regulation** If one takes first, therefore, the law governing the relationship between principal and agent, this relationship normally involves some form of contract. As such the law applicable to it is now controlled in the United Kingdom by the Rome I Regulation.[9] This starts by providing that the contract is governed by the law chosen by the parties.[10] Failing that, recourse is to be had to a list of rules concerning specific types of contract laid down in art.4. Under these, if the agency contract is to be regarded as one for the provision of services, the contract is governed by the law of the country where the service

---

[6] See *Lexington Ins Co v Multinacional de Seguros SA* [2008] EWHC 1170 (Comm); [2009] 1 All E.R. (Comm) 35. A case in which a different law was applied may be the *Ruby SS Co* case, discussed below, para.12-018.

[7] See above, para.1-019.

[8] See *Merrill Lynch Capital Services Inc v Municipality of Piraeus (No.2)* [1997] C.L.C. 1214; *Marubeni Hong Kong and South China Ltd v Government of Mongolia* [2004] EWHC 472 (Comm); [2004] 2 Lloyd's Rep. 198; *AMB Generali Holding AG v SEB Trygg Liv, etc.* [2005] EWCA Civ 1237; [2006] 1 Lloyd's Rep. 318; *Donegal International Ltd v Zambia* [2007] EWHC 197 (Comm); [2007] 1 Lloyd's Rep. 397; *Sea Emerald SA v Prominvestbank* [2008] EWHC 1979 (Comm); *Novus Aviation Ltd v Onur Air Tasimacilik AS* [2009] EWCA Civ 122; [2009] 1 Lloyd's Rep. 576; *Calyon v Wytwornia Sprxetu Komunikacynego Pzl AS* [2009] EWHC 1914 (Comm); [2009] 2 All E.R. (Comm) 603; *Rimpacific Navigation Inc v Daehan Shipbuilding Ltd* [2009] EWHC 2941 (Comm); [2010] 2 Lloyd's Rep. 236; *Emeraldian Ltd v Wellmix Shipping Ltd (The Vine)* [2010] EWHC 1411 (Comm); [2011] 1 Lloyd's Rep. 301 at [165]; *Standard Chartered Bank v Ceylon Petroleum Corp* [2011] EWHC 1785 (Comm); affd without reference to this point [2012] EWCA Civ 1049; *Haugesund Kommune v Depfa ACS Bank* [2010] EWCA Civ 579; [2012] Q.B. 549 at [7], fn.3 and [47]; *Spar Shipping AS v Grand China Logistics Holding (Group) Co Ltd* [2015] EWHC 718 (Comm); [2015] 2 Lloyd's Rep. 407.

[9] EC 593/2008, effective December 17, 2009. See in general Dicey Morris and Collins, fn.1 above, Vol.2, Ch.32.

[10] art.3.1.

provider has his habitual residence[11]; a distribution contract, which may sometimes involve agency functions,[12] is governed by the law of the distributor's habitual residence.[13] An agent's contract would often be one for the provision of services. If that classification is inapplicable, or if the elements of the contract would be covered by more than one of these rules, the contract is governed by the law of the country where the party required to effect the characteristic performance of the contract has his habitual residence. In general it may be assumed that it is normally the agent's performance which ranks as characteristic.[14] However, if it is clear from the circumstances of the case that the contract is manifestly more closely connected with another country, the law of that country applies[15]; and if the law applicable cannot be determined by the criteria laid down, a contract is governed by the law of the country with which it is most closely connected.[16] As will be seen, there may be cause to invoke these variants in certain agency situations.

Nature of relationship between principal and agent under the internal law A **12-004** question may arise in this context as to whether the Rome I Regulation also applies where the relationship between principal and agent is not, or may not be, contractual in common law terms. This might occur, for example, where an agent simply acts under a power of attorney. From a common law point of view there may be no supporting contractual relationship between principal and agent, or at best an exiguous one.[17] It is submitted that the idea of contract referred in the Regulation must be an autonomous and(to a common lawyer) loose one[18] which takes in mandate, a civil law notion under which one person is mandated to act on behalf of another, an arrangement which has been classified as a consensual contract from Roman times; and that on this basis the Regulation should at any rate usually be applied to the internal relationship arising under a power of attorney or otherwise, whether or not a common lawyer would recognise it as contractual.[19] As to *how* the

---

[11] art.4.1(f). In *Wood Floor Solutions Andreas Domberger GmbH v Silvo Trade SA (C-19/09)* [2010] 1 W.L.R.1900 the ECJ treated a *commercial agency* contract (a specialised institution) as one for the provision of services under art.5(1)(b) of Council Regulation 44/2001 on jurisdiction and the enforcement of judgments. See the judgment, and in more detail the opinion of Advocate General Trstenjak at [53] onwards, where the nature of the contract is considered.

[12] See above, para.1-035.

[13] art.4(1)(c). Likewise a franchise contract is governed by the law of the place of residence of the franchisee: art.4.1(e). A contract for the sale of goods by auction is governed by the law of the country where the auction takes place, if such a place can be determined: art.4(1)(g).

[14] In *Hogg Insurance Brokers Ltd v Guardian Insurance Co Inc* [1997] 1 Lloyd's Rep. 412 it was held under the original Rome Convention that the employment of an English insurance broker evidenced an intention that the broker should perform his professional services and if possible obtain reinsurance in England. See also (under the original Convention) *Bank of Baroda v Vysya Bank Ltd* [1994] 2 Lloyd's Rep. 87 (confirming bank); *Albon v Naza Motor Trading Sdn Bhd* [2007] EWHC 9 (Ch); [2007] 1 W.L.R. 2489 at [30]; *Lawlor v Sandvik Mining and Construction Mobile Crushers and Screens Ltd* [2012] EWHC 1188 (QB); [2012] 2 Lloyd's Rep. 25 (commercial agency: governed by Spanish law).

[15] art.4.3. See *Intercontainer Interfrigo (ICF) SC v Balkenende Oosthuizen BV* (C-133/080) [2010] Q.B. 411; noted by Dickinson [2010] L.M.C.L.Q. 27.

[16] art.4.4.

[17] See below, para.12-010.

[18] What is required can be said to be an "obligation freely assumed by one party towards another"; *Jakob Handte & Co GmbH v Traitments Mecano-Chimniques des Surfaces SA* (C-26/91) [1992] E.C.R. I-3967; Dicey, Morris and Collins, fn.1 above, Vol.2, para.32-016.

[19] There is recent discussion of the point in *Pan Oceanic Chartering Inc v UNIPEC UK Co Ltd* [2016] EWHC 2774 (Comm); [2017] 2 All E.R.(Comm) 196 at [151] and following.

Regulation applies in such cases, the relevant categories seem to be those of a service provider or more simply an agent rendering characteristic performance as such. It is suggested however that this is an area in which the specific contractual categories may sometimes require displacement under art.4.3 or 4.4 on the ground that the contract is more closely connected with another country—which might, where exercise of authority in another country is contemplated, be that country, or the principal country in which the power is to be or is exercised.[20]

12-005 Concepts used by the Rome I Regulation: habitual residence The notion of habitual residence, used in several of the specific rules referred to above, is developed in art.19 of the Rome I Regulation. The habitual residence of companies and other bodies, corporate or unincorporated, is their place of central administration; of an individual, it is his or her principal place of business. Where a contract is concluded in the course of operations of an agency, branch or any other establishment, the place where it is located[21] is the place of habitual residence. The relevant time is that of conclusion of the contract.

12-006 Consumer contracts There are special provisions for consumer contracts, directed to protection of the consumer, in art.6 of the Rome I Regulation, and these also may affect the law applicable to the internal relationship. Under these it is likely to be the principal who is the consumer. These will be relevant, for example, to contracts between clients and auctioneers, real estate agents, lawyers, or stockbrokers who do not operate solely in the client's country, and they may entitle the consumer to the protection of the law of the country of his own residence.[22] Real estate agents, however, though they may attract the provisions of Rome I in some respects, normally act as canvassing agents only: as such they are considered below.[23] Lawyers perform different functions, of which agency is only one.

12-007 Employment contracts Where the agent is also an employee of the principal, the internal position is likely to be governed by art.8 of the Rome I Regulation, which contains special provisions for choice of law, in this case directed at protection of the employee.[24]

12-008 Agent's fiduciary duties to principal In so far as general fiduciary duties apply between principal and agent, it could be said that these are non-contractual. There are certainly dicta that fiduciary duties are separate from any related contract. There are also indications that the duty is or can be contractual.[25] In the United Kingdom, if the duty is regarded as contractual, the Rome I Regulation would apply. In so far as the duty is characterised as non-contractual this might bring such duties under the (Rome II) Regulation on the Law Applicable to Non-Contractual Obligations.[26]

---

[20] As in *Chatenay v Brazilian Submarine Telegraph Co Ltd* [1891] 1 Q.B. 79, referred to below, para.12-010.
[21] In *Etablissements Somafer SA v Saar-Ferngas AG* (C-33/78) [1979] 1 C.M.L.R. 490 the ECJ held that the place of business "must have the appearance of permanency": at [12].
[22] See Dicey, Morris and Collins, fn.1 above, Vol.2, Rule 235.
[23] See below, para.12-031.
[24] See Dicey, Morris and Collins, fn.1 above, Vol.2, Rule 238.
[25] See discussion above, para.6-034.
[26] Regulation 864/2007 [2007] OJ L199/40, effective January 11, 2009: see below, paras 12-034 and 12-036.

However, the effect of that Regulation seems to be that such duties should often be regarded as arising in connection with the contract between principal and agent for the purposes of that Regulation and hence governed by the law governing that contract.[27]So by one means or another (but more probably by virtue of Rome I) the law governing the contract seems likely normally to apply to such duties.[28]

Conferral of authority separate from accompanying contract   It must be noted **12-009** next that even if there is an internal contract between principal and agent in the loose sense referred to above, it is not easy to consider that contract as of itself constituting the source of the agent's authority. As is stated earlier in this book, the conferral of authority is and must be, at least from an analytical point of view, a separate unilateral manifestation of will.[29] This is demonstrated by at least three features. First, it is generally accepted that the authority may in most cases be withdrawn notwithstanding that doing so may create a breach of any internal contract between principal and agent.[30] Secondly, the relationship between principal and agent may vary: it may be a contract for the hire of services, or the equivalent of a mandate but, as is said above, it may, at least at common law, not be contractual at all—the agent may act gratuitously, and/or may have no duty to act. Thirdly, in civilian jurisdictions it is often pointed out that the capacity to act as agent may be different from that required of principal or agent for the contract made to be effective.[31] The conferring of authority is therefore analytically best regarded as something separate, whether prior to, simultaneous with or subsequent to any accompanying contract. Although it appears that in some legal systems the mandate can, though a contract, itself be thought of as a source of authority, this is not easy to justify analytically.[32] The distinction is better made in those systems which differentiate between mandate and the notion of representation. The question then arises: what law should govern the matter?[33]

It is true however that if the law governing the relationship between supposed agent and principal does not permit an agency interpretation of it *at all*, there is no scope for a conferral of authority, unless there is, by virtue of other facts, apparent authority. There is thus no scope for considering a main transaction under which the principal is said to be bound to the third party. This could be so where the principal does not authorise the agent to bind him at all, but seeks to operate under the system of indirect representation only. This is discussed below.[34]

Powers of attorney   The separate nature of conferral of authority is demonstrated **12-010** by the institution of a power of attorney. In the important case of *Chatenay v Brazil-*

---

[27]   art.4.3.

[28]   See Dickinson, *The Rome II Regulation* (2008), paras 3.141–3.142. Directors' fiduciary duties would seem to be outside the scope of the Rome I and Rome II Regulations by virtue of art.1.2(f) and 1.2(d) respectively, and governed by the law of the place of incorporation (*Base Metal Trading Ltd v Shamurin* [2004] EWCA Civ 1316; [2005] 1 W.L.R. 1157).

[29]   See above, para.1-006; and especially Müller-Freienfels, "Legal Relations in the Law of Agency" (1964) 13 Am.J. Comp. Law 193 at 203.

[30]   See Articles 117 and 120.

[31]   See above, Articles 4 and 5.

[32]   See Graziadei, Mattei and Smith, *Commercial Trusts in European Private Law* (2005), pp.48–52: "A Note on Terminology".

[33]   See below, paras 12-011–12-014.

[34]   See para.12-029.

ian Submarine Telegraph Co[35] a power of attorney was said to be a "one-sided instrument ... not in any sense a contract".[36] It is simply evidence of a grant of authority as described above; but its separate and tangible nature certainly makes it easier to look for a separate law governing it, and hence, pursuant to what is said above, for a law governing the grant of authority in general. Internally, in some cases the attorney will operate under a mutual contract, whether mandate or some other, entitling him to remuneration and indemnification, but in others there may be no obligation to act at all nor entitlement to any remuneration against his principal (though there could be a right to indemnification[37]). The absence of a contract of mandate in common law means that the nature of the internal arrangements supporting a power of attorney may require careful analysis.

12-011 **The external relationship: conferral of authority**　When one comes to the external contractual relationship between principal and third party, it might be thought that this, a separate contract, was also governed by the Rome I Regulation and hence by the law chosen by the parties to that contract in question, or failing that the law indicated under the various additional criteria indicated in the Regulation.[38] This is of course true. But art.1(2)(g) of the Regulation excludes altogether from its scope "the question whether an agent is able to bind a principal, or an organ to bind a company or other body corporate, in relation to a third party". The Giuliano/Lagarde Report attached to the original Rome Convention on the Law Applicable to Contractual Obligations,[39] which initiated the exclusion, says that the reason for this is that "it is difficult to accept the principle of freedom of contract on this point". To the matters excluded other rules must then apply. The question as to exactly what is for this reason excluded from the scope of the Regulation, and why, is however not straightforward.

12-012 **The exclusion of authority questions from the Rome I Regulation**　It seems likely that what is intended to be excluded by the reference to agents in the Regulation[40] is simply the rules for determining the law governing the conferring of authority (as opposed to any contract accompanying the conferral) referred to above.[41] If so, once it is established that authority has been conferred, any *external* contract made thereunder is governed like any other (including any internal contract) by the law prescribed by the Rome I Regulation.[42] This approach therefore regards the granting of authority, including the principal's manifestation leading to apparent authority or ratification, as a separate notion, entitled to its own choice of law rule, and seeks an indication for what that rule is. A rule actually utilising the notion of choice of the parties is said to be unacceptable for this purpose, perhaps because it may be thought to create a danger of one party in effect choosing himself into a law

---

[35] *Chatenay v Brazilian Submarine Telegraph Co Ltd* [1891] 1 Q.B. 79 (governed by law of country in which to be acted on).

[36] At 85, per Lindley LJ. The case is one much approved by those advancing such an approach. See Rabel, fn.1 above, Vol.3, p.153: "While numerous other English decisions are elusive or confusing, this Court of Appeal decision is outstanding".

[37] See above, Article 62.

[38] See Dicey, Morris and Collins, fn.1 above, Vol.2, Ch.32.

[39] [1980] OJ C282, comment to art.1 at para.7.

[40] As to corporations, see below, para.12-020.

[41] Above, para.1-006.

[42] See Verhagen, fn.1 above, para.6.3.4.

that suits his purposes.[43] An obvious possibility for the applicable rule is the law of the place where the authority is to be (or perhaps is) exercised[44] (assuming that this is only in one jurisdiction); but there are other possibilities, for example the law of the agent's place of habitual residence, place of business of a company or the like. To separate off authority of all types from the contractual arrangements associated with it in this way fits with the distinction made in the nineteenth century by Laband between the internal and external aspects of agency: the authority goes to the external element,[45] though some of the words selected by translators (particularly as regards the notions of agency and representation) in the various versions of the Rome I Regulation suggest a degree of imprecision in the original intentions of some of those involved. Whether or not there is or should be such a separate choice of law rule, as the Regulation plainly envisages, is one of the central problems of this area.

Problems with such an exclusion It may be suggested that, however correct in   **12-013**
theory, the isolating of the conferring of authority for the purposes of choice of law encounters practical problems in duly differentiating between questions relating to the authority itself and questions arising out of its exercise, the latter of which would be dealt with by the law governing the contract entered into.[46] And from a common lawyer's point of view the reference to the place where the authority is to be or is exercised introduces an undesirable geographical criterion open to the same objection in days of rapid communication in commerce as the old reliance on *lex loci contractus*. Further, where the authority may be exercised in more than one jurisdiction, a problem arises as to whether there can be different applicable laws.[47] On the other hand, if criteria relating to the residence or place of residence or business of the agent are to be used, as they often are in international instruments,[48] the selection of the applicable law, while no doubt intended to give fair and predictable results in as many cases as possible, is likely to create more potentially arbitrary consequences of a sort to which common lawyers are again not usually sympathetic. Therefore while such an approach, which is probably conceptually correct, may be acceptable in principle, and assist in the perception of agency

---

[43] See Dicey, Morris and Collins, fn.1 above, Vol.2, para.33-447.
[44] See Rabel, fn.1 above, Vol.3, p.167.
[45] See above, para.1-025; Rabel, fn.1 above, Ch.40, esp. at pp.123–127: "The German, and to a certain degree the English, courts have recognised that the power of an agent to affect the rights and duties of the principal constitutes an independent institution and ought to have its own proper law, not necessarily coincident with those governing either of the two other relationships". The Hague Convention on the Law Applicable to Agency of 1978 states that among matters governed by the internal law are "the existence and extent of the authority of the agent" (art.8(a)), and that a different law governs "the existence and extent of the agent's authority" as regards third parties (art.11(d)). The internal rule presumably governs, for example, the question whether the agent is liable to the principal for exceeding his authority, the external, whether the principal is liable to the third party where the agent was unauthorised but had apparent authority: see Verhagen, fn.1 above, paras 5.2.2, 5.2.3 and 5.2.18.
[46] See Rabel, fn.1 above, at pp.140–142; Verhagen, fn.1 above, Ch.6.
[47] This seems unlikely. See for example *Intercontainer Interfrigo (ICF) SC v Balkenende Oosthuizen BV* (C-133/08) [2010] Q.B. 411, noted by Dickinson [2010] L.M.C.L.Q. 27, on this point at 31.
[48] As in the Hague Convention, above, art.6, and in an unsuccessful proposal made in connection with Rome I.

phenomena, the special choice of law rule or rules which it is likely to entail makes it less easy to accept fully for the purposes of the conflict of laws.[49]

Where there is a power of attorney it is, as indicated above, often easier easy to seek to fix this with its own governing law, which may be that of the place of exercise.[50] The two English cases usually cited, however, can also be explained on the basis, not of the place of exercise, but that the power was regulated by the law of the transaction in connection with which it was to be exercised.[51]

Despite the above, proposals were at one time put forward for dealing with this matter in the Rome I Regulation; and in 2017 provisions dealing with the matter were adopted in Germany in a new art.8 of the Introductory Law to the German Civil Code (EGBGB) which utilises notions of choice, habitual residence and the country in which the agent exercises his powers.[52] For the present, however, subject to the problems of interpretation, certain questions of agency are excluded from the scope of the Regulation and where this is so a common law court, at any rate, is entitled to proceed in the excluded area on the basis of what it regards as the existing law as indicated below. If the result of this involves the application of German law, the provisions referred to above would be excluded by the rule that there is no *renvoi* in contract situations.[53]

12-014 **The common law approach to the exclusion** With the possible exception of situations involving a power of attorney mentioned above, common law commentaries tend to assume that the exclusion from the scope of the Regulation leaves the court free to apply the law which it would normally apply to this question—in so far as the issue excluded can be isolated. To apply a special common law rule, whatever it might be, to this highly restricted question would however be difficult and probably sometimes inappropriate in result. At the other extreme, the view can be taken that the exclusion leaves the court free to apply to the entire contract between principal and third party the rules for choice of law that it would otherwise have applied. On this interpretation, simply because of the intervention of an agency element, the law applicable to the whole relationship between principal and third party is determined by existing principles of the common law conflict of laws, unaffected by the Regulation. Although the English books do not always make completely clear what they envisage, this would have a very wide effect and hence seems an unlikely approach.[54] The better, and certainly more convenient, approach would seem to be that the court should take the view that, the question excluded not being a separate one under common law, the court should apply to it the law which it would otherwise apply, that is to say the law governing the external contract, but as determined by the Rome I Regulation, as indicated below. There may also be some role for the internal law between principal and agent: this is dealt with below.[55] Overall, this is undoubtedly somewhat paradoxical, in that the Regulation specifically excludes the questions identified from its scope. But it is submit-

---

[49] See below, para.12-016; Rabel, fn.1 above, at 161–162.
[50] See above, para.12-010.
[51] *Chatenay v Brazilian Submarine Telegraph Co* [1891] 1 Q.B. 79 and *Sinfra Aktiengesellschaft v Sinfra AG* [1939] 2 All E.R. 675.
[52] The background to this approach is usefully considered (in English) by Gebauer, in Leible (ed), *Principles of European Private International Law*, (2016) Ch.16.
[53] Art.20 of the Rome I Regulation; and this would be so in common law anyway.
[54] See Dicey, Morris and Collins, fn.1 above, para.33-434.
[55] See below, para.12-017.

ted that where the Regulation makes an exclusion of something that a particular system of law does not necessarily recognise as a discrete topic, it is not inappropriate to allow that system of law to bring the Regulation back in where appropriate, as it were, by incorporation and without its exclusions.[56] This in fact already links easily with the common law view as to the law governing questions of apparent authority explained below.[57]

Which law governs the main contract between principal and third party? This should be the law designated in the various provisions of the Rome I Regulation referred to above.[58] If there is doubt as to whether a contract has been formed, the putative governing law will determine whether or not a contractual relationship exists.[59]   **12-015**

Questions of apparent authority arising in connection with the main contract It is well established, and independently of the approach which seeks a special choice of law rule for authority, that questions of *apparent* authority are governed by the law governing the main contract entered into.[60] It is submitted that this entails that the apparent authority of an agent extends in appropriate cases to subjecting the contract, whether directly or indirectly,[61] to a particular system of law.[62] It can be argued, however, that when the applicable law for the main contract under the Rome I Regulation is based on an express choice of law, rather than on a test of substantial connection, such a rule should not apply, on the ground that it enables an agent who has not been authorised, or has even been forbidden to do so, to choose a law for the contract. In such a case, it has been suggested that the choice should only be valid if it coincides with the law applicable in the absence of choice.[63] This view is similar to, and partly based on, one sometimes put forward   **12-016**

---

[56] For a slightly different view, see Dicey, Morris and Collins, fn.1 above, Vol.2, para.33-434.

[57] See paras 12-016 and 21-017.

[58] See para.12-003.

[59] See art.10, which deals with formation of contract; Dicey, Morris and Collins, fn.1 above, Vol.2, Rule 225. But as to agreement on choice of law, see below, fn.66. See also Rome II art.12, dealing with *culpa in contrahendo*, considered by Dickinson, *The Rome II Regulation* (2008), Ch.12. Questions of capacity are specifically excluded: see below, para.12-019.

[60] The point is specifically decided by David Steel J in *Rimpacific Navigation Inc v Daehan Shipbuilding Co Ltd* [2009] EWHC 2941 (Comm); [2010] 2 Lloyd's Rep. 236 and cases there cited (further proceedings before Teare J [2011] EWHC 2618 (Comm)), rejecting an argument, previously rejected elsewhere, that Regulations modifying s.36 of the Companies Act 1985 excluded the rules of apparent authority as applicable to companies. See also *Britannia SS Ins Assn v Ausonia Assecurazioni SpA* [1984] 2 Lloyd's Rep. 98; *Azov Shipping Co v Baltic Shipping Co* [1999] 2 Lloyd's Rep. 159; *Sea Emerald SA v Prominvestbank* [2008] EWHC 1979 (Comm) at [106]; *Donegal International Ltd v Zambia* [2007] EWHC 197 (Comm); [2007] 1 Lloyd's Rep. 397 (applying English law's reluctance to find apparent authority in a governmental agent: see at [844]–[845] and distinguishing on this point *Marubeni Hong Kong and South China Ltd v Mongolia* [2004] EWHC 472 (Comm); [2004] 2 Lloyd's Rep. 198; *Standard Chartered Bank v Ceylon Petroleum Corp* [2011] EWHC 1785 (Comm); affd without reference to this point [2012] EWCA Civ 1049; *Spar Shipping AS v Grand China Logistics Holding (Group) Co Ltd* [2015] EWHC 718 (Comm); [2015] 2 Lloyd's Rep. 407.

[61] An example of "indirectly" would be agreeing to an arbitration clause which is held to be relevant to the choice of law issue. See *Habas Sinai Ve Tibbi Gaziar Isthisal Endustrisi AS v VSC Steel Co Ltd* [2013] EWHC 4071 (Comm); [2014] 1 Lloyd's Rep. 479.

[62] This statement, in a slightly different form, was approved by Hamblen J in *Habas Sinai Ve Tibbi Gaziar Isthisal Endustrisi AS v VSC Steel Co Ltd*, above at [113].

[63] See Dicey, Morris and Collins, fn.1 above, Vol.2, para.33-447. In the *Habas* case, above, such an

in connection with capacity.[64] Whatever its value there (which is open to doubt) it is a negation of the principles of choice and of the putative proper law as now understood[65] to apply it here.[66]

That law will determine questions of how such authority can be established, its extent, when the third party is put on inquiry and the degree of inquiry required[67] and so forth. This is despite the fact that on one account, accepted elsewhere in this book,[68] apparent authority is based on estoppel, and the possibility of arguing that estoppel is, at least in some contexts, a matter of evidence or procedure.[69] It seems clear that apparent authority is one of the areas in which it must be regarded as having a substantive character.[70]

12-017   **Actual authority**   It seems fairly clear that the exclusion of agency matters from the scope of the Regulation (and previously the Convention) was to a considerable extent directed to the point that the law applicable to the internal contract between principal and agent, which can be based on choice by the parties, is not appropriate to the question of conferral of actual authority, which for the reasons given above is analytically separate from any accompanying contract and should not depend on criteria which permit such choice. If one accepts the conceptual separateness of the conferral of authority, it requires a different law from that governing the contract between principal and agent (which may not always exist anyway). The idea mentioned above, namely that that different law should be the law of the place where the authority is to be exercised, has hardly been considered in the English cases,[71] and without reform to the Regulation probably will not be.

---

argument was put forward in connection with an arbitration clause alleged not to be authorised, for which there is an even weaker case. These are not subject to Rome I, so the question had to be resolved at common law. The matter is discussed in some detail. It was argued that the matter would have triggered off art.8(2) of the Rome Convention, now art.10(2) of the Rome I Regulation (concerning situations where it is not reasonable to hold a party bound in accordance with the main principles of the Convention) and that such a rule should apply at common law. This was rejected. A similar argument was rejected by Andrew Smith J in *PEC Ltd v Asia Golden Rice Co Ltd* [2014] EWHC 1583 (Comm) at [73]–[74]. This is a case where the adoption of a special rule for the law governing conferral of authority might have made a difference.

[64]   See Dicey, Morris and Collins, fn.1 above, Vol.2, para.32-176, cited in *Habas*, above, at [105].
[65]   As to which see Dicey, Morris and Collins, fn.1 above, Vol.2, Rule 225.
[66]   That the putative proper law governing the contract in question covers the existence of apparent authority to conclude such a contract is expressly decided in *Habas Sinai Ve Tibbi Gaziar Isthisal Endustrisi AS v VSC Steel Co Ltd* [2013] EWHC 4071 (Comm); [2014] 1 Lloyd's Rep. 479, rejecting a contrary view expressed in Dicey Morris and Collins, fn.1 above, Vol.1, para.33-447 and citing, in addition to several of the cases in fn.8 above, *The Parouth* [1982] 2 Lloyd's Rep 351 and *The Atlantic Emperor* [1989] 1 Lloyd's Rep 548. It is however arguable that the actual question of consent to a choice of law, express or implied, should be dealt with by the *lex fori* as a connecting factor, rather than by the putative proper law. See Dicey, Morris and Collins, fn.1 above, Vol.2, para.32-066. This would not have made a difference in the present case. (I am grateful to Professor Andrew Dickinson for this point.)
[67]   See (for powers of attorney) *Jacobs v Morris* [1902] 1 Ch. 816, above, para.8-052; and for the general rules above, Article 73.
[68]   See above, para.8-028.
[69]   See Yeo, *Choice of Law for Equitable Doctrines* (2004), para.7.118 onwards.
[70]   See Handley, *Estoppel by Conduct and Election* (2nd edn, 2016) para.1-015; *The Amazonia* [1990] 1 Lloyd's Rep. 236 at 247; *First Laser Ltd v Fujian Enterprises (Holdings) Co Ltd* [2012] HKEC 946 (HKCFA, judgment delivered by Lord Collins). It would seem that cases of true estoppel in a contractual agency situation, as in *Spiro v Lintern* [1973] 1 W.L.R. 1002 (see above, Article 21) should also be governed by the same law as the relevant contract.
[71]   See *Chatenay v Brazilian Submarine Telegraph Co Ltd* [1891] 1 Q.B. 79 and *Sinfra Aktiengesells-*

But as already stated, the existing English case law tends to assume, sometimes by simple concession, that the law applicable to the question of the actual (as opposed to the apparent) authority of an agent is still that governing the internal relationship between principal and agent[72]—a solution which, it is submitted, the exclusion of agency matters was designed to modify. However, on the law as it stands it is possible to argue that the other available law, the law governing the main contract, should apply to this question. This would have considerable advantages. If, as at present, the third party is entitled to rely on the main putative contract that he has with the principal where the question is (as it very frequently is) one of appearance of authority (apparent authority), then where apparent authority under that law cannot be established, the third party may reasonably seek to rely on actual authority. It is surely unsatisfactory to require the third party to transfer to a law which he may have had no means of knowing and may find it difficult to prove— bearing in mind that it is the principal who, by giving authority to the agent, can usually be regarded as having taken the risk of his activities.[73] The agent may be liable to his principal under any internal contract for exceeding his authority: but whether he *has* exceeded that authority should arguably be a question for the main contract (in the absence of problems of formality or capacity, or a situation where there had never been any authority granted at all). A problem then arises, that to expose the principal to the law of the main contract is still to expose him to matters of choice, this time under the contract between principal and third party. But in view of the present common law solution that the law governs questions of apparent authority, it can be said that that drawback should be accepted.

---

chaft v Sinfra Ltd [1939] 2 All E.R. 675, above, para.12-010.

[72] This seems to be true of most of the cases referred to in fn.8 above, where the matter is usually conceded or agreed. However, several of these appear to turn on the law governing a public entity or the law governing the incorporation of a private company rather than the law governing the relationship between principal and agent, which is frequently one of employment by the entity. The two might often be the same; but it is submitted that in most cases at least it is the law governing the entity that is applied to the internal relationship. This fits with the policy of the Companies Act 2006 s.43(1)(b) (as substituted by Overseas Companies (Execution of Documents and Registration of Charges) Regulations 2009 (SI 2009/1917)): see below, para.12-020. In any case, the courts tend to fall back quite easily on applying English rules of interpretation for ascertaining actual authority: for recent examples in the cases cited in fn.8 above, see the *Sea Emerald* case, the *Ceylon Petroleum* case (though in the latter it appears that some evidence was given that the law of Sri Lanka was similar to English law in relevant respects), and *Golden Ocean Group Ltd v Salgaocar Mining Industries PVT Ltd* [2011] EWHC 56 (Comm); [2011] 1 W.L.R. 2575 at [161]; affd on other grounds [2012] EWCA Civ 265; [2012] 1 W.L.R. 3674.

[73] "There is no sense in differentiating in conflicts law powers conferred by the principal on the agent directly, or by declaration or conduct on which the third party relies": Rabel, fn.1 above, Vol.3, pp.139–140. See also at p.145: "Where a principal constitutes authorisation by an ordinary, private, voluntary act, intending its use in a foreign state, the law of this state is justifiedly considered competent to construe the validity and effects of the authorisation". In *Habas Sinai Ve Tibbi Gaziar Isthisal Endustrisi AS v VSC Steel Co Ltd* [2013] EWHC 4071 (Comm); [2014] 1 Lloyd's Rep. 479 the unsuccessful argument entailed an assumption that in some contexts lack of actual authority could have a function of "trumping" apparent authority. The context was of agreement to an arbitration clause relevant to the ascertainment of the putative governing law: see above. The general view advanced above receives some support from the judgment of Hamblen J at [110]: "As between the principal and the third party there is no difference between actual and ostensible authority"; and in *PEC Ltd v Asia Golden Rice Co Ltd* [2014] EWHC 1583 (Comm) at [4], Andrew Smith J said that he saw some force in it; see also *Credit Suisse International v Stichting Vestia Group* [2014] EWHC 3103 (Comm); [2015] Bus.L.R. D5 at [280]. Briggs, *Private International Law in English Courts* (2014), paras 7.279–7.280 can be read as taking a similar view.

12-018 **Reservations** To the above point about actual authority there are two reservations. First, in interpreting the actual authority, the court should take account of the understandings which might attach to the conferral of authority according to the internal law. Thus in the *Chatenay* case, referred to above,[74] English law governed the effect of a power of attorney executed in Brazil in the Portuguese language, intended to be executed by a London stockbroker, but subject to the taking into consideration of the sense likely to have been intended for the document in Brazil. The same technique could be applied to persons exercising a usual authority: it can be asked what the understandings as to their authority would be in the place where they operate.[75]

A second possible reservation is that where the law governing the internal relationship confers authority but the law governing the main contract does not because it finds no apparent authority (obviously the principal situation in which actual authority may be significant), the contract is in any case to be regarded as authorised: that is to say that the internal law should have a validating but not an invalidating effect and can be relied on by the third party as such. This is a possible interpretation of a notorious (difficult to interpret) decision of a not undistinguished tribunal in 1933, *Ruby SS Corp v Commercial Union Assurance Ltd*,[76] in which actual authority under the law operative between principal and agent was held effective despite the fact that under the law governing the contract between third party and principal it would seem that by reason of the usages of the London insurance market the agent had no such authority. It was held that an agent had power to cancel an insurance policy under American law, which governed the agent's relationship with its principal, because the principal had not paid the premiums; though the law governing the policies, English law, would regard the premiums as paid by virtue of its own special rule regarding the payment of the premium by broker to insurer. The reasoning in the case is however far from clear[77] and its significance seems largely to be due to the fact that there are so few other cases.[78] A simple rule that questions of actual authority as well as those of apparent authority are governed by the law governing the main contract seems the best solution.

12-019 **Capacity** By art.I.2(a) the Rome I Regulation does not apply to "Questions involving the status or legal capacity of natural persons, without prejudice to Article 13". This exclusion applies to any contract accompanying the conferral of authority between principal and agent, and also to the main contract entered into between principal and third party. Such questions are therefore a matter for the conflict of laws rules of the forum,[79] but subject to art.13, which provides certain restrictions

---

[74] The rejection of *renvoi* in contract prevents the court asking what view the law of the contract would take of capacity conferred by a different law.

[75] See *Sea Emerald SA v Prominvestbank* [2008] EWHC 1979 (Comm) (Ukrainian bank employee). As to usual authority see above, para.3-005.

[76] *Ruby SS Corp v Commercial Union Assurance Ltd* (1933) 39 Com.Cas. 48 (Scrutton, Greer and Romer LJJ).

[77] Rabel, fn.1 above, describes it as "scantily equipped": p.154.

[78] For another explanation of this case see Dicey, Morris and Collins, fn.1 above, Vol.2, paras 33-441–33-445.

[79] Dicey, Morris and Collins, fn.1 above, Vol.2, Rule 228(1) (objective proper law of main contract plus personal law as an additional validating factor). The view that the relevant law should be the governing law of the contract objectively ascertained is to avoid the possibility that a choice of law might

on a plea of incapacity.[80] As regards English law, the special questions relevant to this chapter concern capacity to act as principal and capacity to act as agent, i.e. capacity to confer authority and capacity to act on it. As to principals, it is stated above in this book,[81] that "Capacity to contract or do any other act by means of an agent is co-extensive with the capacity of the principal himself to make the contract or do the act which the agent is authorised to make or do". For the purposes of the conflict of laws, this refers the question of the law governing the principal's capacity to act as such to the law governing the main, external contract, and the normally accepted rules on capacity add the possibility that the principal's personal law may enlarge but not diminish the capacity.[82] As to the agent's capacity to act as such, the rules simply require soundness of mind and ability to understand what the person concerned is doing.[83] The rather limited requirements for capacity to act as agent operative in most legal systems mean that the matter will not often arise except in the context of public law controls on the operation of certain types of agent, e.g. stockbrokers, freight forwarders, which would raise questions of interpretation of scope. But in general it is submitted that, like formalities, they need not affect capacity under the main contract. The question of corporate capacity is separate and is dealt with below.

Corporations   The Rome I Regulation likewise excludes in art.1.2(f) various matters governed by the law governing corporations, and in art.1.2(g) excludes the question whether "an organ" can "bind a company or other body corporate or unincorporated, in relation to a third party." The proposition that capacity is regulated by the law governing the contract entered into must therefore be modified in relation to corporations, which only exist under a particular system of law. Obviously, though the law governing the contract is still applicable, the law governing the incorporation must have considerable say in what bodies incorporated (or otherwise associated) under it can do and how they can do it. This will necessarily raise questions of the limits of the notion of capacity, for it is in this context primarily to matters of capacity that the law governing the corporation (the law of the place of incorporation) should apply.[84] In English law, the initial starting point has been that companies can only do what is authorised by their memorandum of association and articles. Anything outside this would be void as ultra vires. The rule was established as one of capacity: a result was that if an act within the company's capacity was done for improper motives it was not invalid under the ultra vires doctrine.[85] Such constitutional limits have long been circumvented by wide objects clauses; and the ultra vires doctrine has for most purposes been abolished in the United Kingdom by statute.[86] There are related provisions dealing with agency arguments directed to the authority of company directors, whereby a third party may be **12-020**

---

enable a person to confer capacity on himself: see para.32-176. Such a rule is however not immune from question.

[80]   See Dicey, Morris and Collins, fn.1 above, Vol.2, Rule 228(2) (situations where both parties in same country and one unaware of incapacity of the other under an applicable law).

[81]   Article 4.

[82]   Dicey, Morris and Collins, fn.1 above, Vol.2, Rule 228(1)(b).

[83]   See Article 5.

[84]   See Dicey, Morris and Collins, fn.1 above, Vol.2, Rule 175.

[85]   *Rolled Steel Products (Holdings) Ltd v British Steel Corp* [1986] Ch. 246.

[86]   For the present day, see Companies Act 2006 s.39.

entitled to assume that internal procedural rules have been complied with.[87] But this statutory modification and protection only applies to UK registered companies.

When one comes to consideration of the position of *foreign* companies under a contract governed by English law, it must be arguable that something like an ultra vires analysis is to be applied where the foreign company can be said to have no power to act.[88] Rule 175 of *Dicey, Morris & Collins on the Conflict of Laws* provides that the capacity of a corporation to enter into any legal transaction is governed both by the constitution of the corporation and by the law of the country which governs the transaction in question, but that all matters concerning the constitution of a corporation are governed by the law of the place of incorporation. To the latter extent the law governing the contract entered into must yield to the law governing the incorporation.

This matter is considered in a leading case concerning the power of a Norwegian municipality to enter into a "swap" agreement, in which it was clear that the analysis of the position adopted by Norwegian law would be quite different from that which a common lawyer would apply.[89] By English law such a question would be regarded as one of the capacity of the corporation; and this question being one of characterisation it was therefore before an English court governed by English law.[90] It was said that the notion of capacity should not be interpreted in the normal domestic sense, but in a broad internationalist way that accommodates different notions as to capacity and also as to what constitutes the constitution of the corporation; though both of these led to the conclusion that a question of capacity was involved and the transaction void.[91] More recently it has been held that such reasoning also applies to provisions of the foreign law as to the procedures by which the corporation can act: these may be regarded as relating to the corporation itself rather than the contract into which it enters.[92] But where there is no question of lack of power, the matter is likely to be one of authority only and governed by the law applicable to that topic.[93] A general provision, applicable both to corporations and to

---

[87] For the present day, see Companies Act 2006 ss.40 and 41.

[88] See Dicey, Morris and Collins, fn.1 above, Vol.2, Rule 175 and para.33-451. The Giuliano/Lagarde Report, the official commentary on the Rome Convention and the Rome I Regulation, mentions ultra vires in connection with the scope of art.1(f), which excludes most corporate matters from the scope of the Regulation. This reasoning is not to be applied to foreign states even where an inability to act in certain ways can be represented as arising from its constitution, for a state has unlimited capacity in public international law: *Law Debenture Trust Corp Plc v Ukraine* [2017] EWHC 655 (Comm); [2017] 3 W.L.R. 667 (where it was in fact held that the Minister of Finance had apparent (in the sense of usual: above, para.3-005) authority to sign). See also *Standard Chartered Bank v Ceylon Petroleum Corp* [2012] EWCA Civ 1049 at [24] (Sri Lankan statutory corporation); *Credit Suisse International v Stichting Vestia Groep* [2014] EWHC 3103 (Comm); [2015] Bus.L.R. D5 at [254].

[89] *Haugesund Kommune v Depfa ACS Bank* [2010] EWCA Civ 579; [2012] Q.B. 549.

[90] See at [40]. Article I(g) of the Rome I Regulation, referred to above, also excludes "capacity", thus leaving this to national laws.

[91] See at [47] and [48]. See also *Credit Suisse International v Stichting Vestia Groep* [2014] EWHC 3103 (Comm); [2015] Bus.L.R. D5 at [254]; *Law Debenture Trust Plc v Ukraine* [2017] EWHC 655 (Comm); [2017] 3 W.L.R. 667.

[92] *Integral Petroleum SA v SCU-Finanz AG* [2015] EWCA Civ 144; [2015] Bus.L.R. 640 (Swiss law required signature by two *prokurists* for validity of transaction by corporation: transaction void). See also *Janred Properties Ltd v ENIT* [1989] 2 All E.R. 444 (purchase of land in London requiring assent of Italian Ministry of Tourism); *Rimpacific Navigation Inc v Daehan Shipbuilding Ltd* [2009] EWHC 2941 (Comm); [2010] 2 Lloyd's Rep. 236 at [36] (further proceedings [2011] EWHC 2618).

[93] See above paras 12-016 and 12-017 and *Law Debenture Trust Corp Plc v Ukraine* [2017] EWHC 655 (Comm); [2017] 3 W.L.R. 667.

individuals, requiring certain formalities for all contracts (or documents) of a certain type (e.g. relating to land) would however attach to the contract and hence to the law governing formalities for it.[94]

English law also has special rules for *how* contracts are made *by* companies and *for* companies, and for the execution of documents by companies[95]: these again only apply to UK registered companies. But it also has corresponding provisions for the making of contracts and the execution of documents by overseas companies where business is done "under the law of England and Wales",[96] i.e. the contract is governed by English law.[97] They contain provisions permitting in some cases that the signatory have authority under the laws of the territory in which the company is incorporated.[98] It has been held however that these provisions relate to formal validity, where they are not exclusive,[99] and that they do not exclude the English law rules of apparent authority, which will apply where the contract is governed by English law.[100]

If the governing law of the transaction is foreign, it will be appropriate to ask, over and above the law governing the incorporation, what the foreign law would do on the question of corporate capacity; but though the provisions as to the execution of documents only apply to business done under the law of England and Wales it seems that the rules of English law as to what constitutes the capacity to which the law of the place of incorporation is relevant should prevail, *renvoi* reasoning being normally irrelevant in contract.[101]

Form   The law governing the relationship between principal and agent may **12-021** sometimes require formalities for the validity or efficacy of an agency relationship. In so far as the relationship is a contract, art.11 of the Rome I Regulation (which contains detailed provisions on the topic) applies. But the Regulation excludes, as stated above, from its scope, the question of whether an agent is able to bind a principal. For example, in England an agent authorised to contract by deed must be

---

[94]   See Rome I Regulation, art.11.

[95]   Companies Act 2006 ss.43 and 44 (for Scotland, s.48. Not all provisions apply in Scotland).

[96]   Overseas Companies (Execution of Documents and Registration of Charges) Regulations 2009 (SI 2009/1917), amending ss.43, 44 and 46 of the Companies Act 2006 for overseas companies. Equivalent provisions apply to limited liability partnerships by virtue of the Limited Liability Partnerships (Application of Companies Act 2006) Regulations 2009 (SI 2009/1804).

[97]   Difficulty is raised by the wording of s.44(4) of the original Act and its amended version s.44(5) which is applicable to overseas companies. Both provide that a document which "purports to be signed" in accordance with provisions earlier in the section are valid in favour of a good faith purchaser. But s.44(4) is drafted in such a way that might apply even to forged documents, and this is even more so of s.44(5), part of the modification of the rules in respect of overseas companies, the wording of which is not identical. See above, para.8-040.

[98]   s.43(1)(b) and s.43(2)(a). As to whether authority to affix a corporate seal is needed, see above, para.8-039.

[99]   *Integral Petroleum SA v SCU-Finanz AG* [2015] EWCA Civ 144; [2015] Bus.L.R. 640.

[100]   See *Habas Sinai Ve Tibbi Gaziar Isthisal Endustrisi v VSC Steel Co Ltd* [2013] EWHC 4071 (Comm); [2014] 1 Lloyd's Rep. 479 at [125]; *Rimpacific Navigation Inc v Daehan Shipbuilding Ltd* [2009] EWHC 2941 (Comm); [2010] 2 Lloyd's Rep. 236 at [30]–[31]: further proceedings [2011] EWHC 2618. See also *Azov v Baltic Shipping Co (No.3)* [1999] 2 Lloyd's Rep. 159 at 170; *Golden Ocean Group v Salgaocar Mining Industries PVT Ltd* [2011] EWHC 56 (Comm); [2011] 1 W.L.R. 2575 at [160], [161] (further proceedings [2012] EWCA Civ 265; [2012] 1 W.L.R. 3674). In the *Rimpacific* case there was no actual authority because board approval was required for such a transaction: see at [36]. This would in fact acceptably bring in the rules of the law of the place of incorporation, as to which see above, text to fn.98.

[101]   See Dicey, Morris and Collins, fn.1 above, Vol.2, para.32-029.

authorised by deed,[102] but this need not be so everywhere. It is submitted that lack of formalities for creation of agency by any law operating internally need not affect the external contract between principal and third party, though such lack under the law governing the main contract will (subject to interpretation of the scope of art.11, and any relevant statute or similar provision) be relevant.

12-022 **Public law** There can be little doubt that if there are public law restrictions on an agent's authority, as in the case of public officials, these should be effective as against the law governing the main transaction. As regards public officials, it seems to be accepted that constitutional and other public restrictions of a disabling nature on their actual authority should be effective, and the interpretation of such restrictions is a matter for the law imposing them[103]; though in the absence of clear evidence the court falls back fairly easily on English interpretation techniques, at least where the governing law of the main transaction is English,[104] and similarly estoppel, apparently under English law, has been applied to later conduct relevant to earlier authorisation.[105] The reluctance of English law to find apparent authority in public officials has recently been applied in the context of foreign officials.[106]

12-023 **Revocation of authority** It is submitted that authority is of its nature revocable in the absence of relevant rules making it irrevocable. This follows from the law's recognition of the dangers of conferring on another a power to bind oneself.[107] The question whether authority has actually been revoked as between principal and agent must depend on the internal law operating between them and governing the grant of authority, unaffected by any contract between them and hence by the Rome I Regulation. This is an example of the help afforded by the recognition of the independence of the grant of authority from the accompanying contract.[108] The revocation may or may not be a breach of such a contract. However, the revocation need not affect third parties. Thus apparent authority under the law governing the external transaction may persist despite internal revocation of authority as between principal and agent (unless the third party has notice of it), and the existence of apparent authority comes under the normal rules applicable to such authority in a case between principal and third party.[109] This is arguably also so if the

---

[102] See above, Article 10.
[103] See *Janred Properties Ltd v ENIT* [1989] 2 All E.R. 444 (consent of Minister of Tourism required for taking lease); *Merrill Lynch Capital Services Inc v Municipality of Piraeus* [1997] C.L.C. 214 (authority of Mayor to raise loans); *Marubeni Hong Kong and South China Ltd v Mongolia* [2004] EWHC 472 (Comm); [2004] 2 Lloyd's Rep. 198 (authority of Minister of Finance, rejecting a distinction between public and private entities); cf. *Donegal International Ltd v Zambia* [2007] EWHC 197 (Comm); [2007] 1 Lloyd's Rep. 397 (authority of Minister of Finance: constitutional provisions).
[104] See the *Zambia* case, above, at [436]–[437].
[105] See *Janred Properties Ltd v Ente Nazionale Italiano per il Turismo (ENIT) (No.2)* [1989] 2 All E.R. 444.
[106] Above, para.8-042; *Donegal International Ltd v Zambia* [2007] EWHC 197 (Comm); [2007] 1 Lloyd's Rep. 397. But cf. *Law Debenture Trust Corp Plc v Ukraine* [2017] EWHC 655 (Comm); [2017] 3 W.L.R. 667 (Minister of Finance had apparent authority (in the sense of usual authority: above, para.3-005), to enter into a transaction involving borrowing under Eurobonds.)
[107] See above, para.10-024.
[108] See above, para.12-009.
[109] See above, Article 121; e.g. *AMB Generali Holding AG v SEB Trygg Liv, etc.* [2005] EWCA Civ 1237; [2006] 1 Lloyd's Rep. 318.

authority relied on is actual.[110] Under English law at any rate it is arguable that if the authority is revoked by death, it cannot survive even within a doctrine of apparent authority, for the principal has simply been removed.[111] It is submitted elsewhere in this book[112] that this reasoning should in any case no longer be permitted to affect the normal operation of the doctrine of apparent authority. In any case it is a rule of English law, applicable where English law applies.

Termination of authority by lack of mental capacity, insolvency or bankruptcy is apt to be dealt with specifically by statute, though questions of the conflict of laws application of such statutes could undoubtedly arise. In England and Wales the law applicable to certain aspects of a lasting power of attorney[113] is now governed by the Hague Convention of 2000 on the International Protection of Adults,[114] which attributes jurisdiction primarily to the authorities of the adult's habitual residence,[115] but art.15 of which permits the designation of an applicable law in certain circumstances.

Irrevocable authority   There can be cases where authority is, under some relevant **12-024** system of law, not revocable, either at all or for a particular period. At common law this occurs where a power is given as security or (perhaps) to protect some other interest of the agent.[116] Obviously other legal systems could provide differently, though there seems some unanimity in the use in this context of the idea of protecting an interest of the agent. For common law at least, such an arrangement is not really agency at all, because the agent, as the holder of a security, is entitled and indeed expected to act in his own interest, which is not true of agents in general. It could also be said that it is contrary to the nature of authority that it should be irrevocable. The problem is (again) easier to deal with if the creation of authority is regarded as governed by its own law, for it can be said that the governing law may make the authority revocable or irrevocable. But again[117] it is possible alternatively to say that the (internal) actual authority is in fact regulated by the law governing the main external transaction, and that will determine the question of revocability. Consistently with what is suggested, the effect of such irrevocability was in *Sinfra Aktiengesellschaft v Sinfra AG*[118] held to be governed by the law governing the document used, a power of attorney, which was said to be the law of the country where the power was to operate. In the case in question this was English law, though the document had been prepared under German law.[119] It was held that whatever the position under German law, the power under English law was not such as to create the type of authority that would be irrevocable.[120] It is submit-

---

[110] See above, para.12-017.
[111] See above, Article 119.
[112] See above, para.10-032.
[113] See above, para.10-009.
[114] This Convention was apparently enacted into law for England and Wales by s.63 of and Sch.3 to the Mental Capacity Act 2005, which took effect on October 1, 2007 by virtue of the Mental Capacity Act 2005 (Commencement No.2) Order (SI 2007/1897), though the Convention itself (to which the United Kingdom had only acceded on behalf of Scotland) did not take effect until January 1, 2009.
[115] art.5: but see also arts 7-10.
[116] See above, Article 118.
[117] See above, para.12-017.
[118] *Sinfra Aktiengesellschaft v Sinfra AG* [1939] 2 All E.R. 675.
[119] Under which it was in fact probably not irrevocable: but the matter did not require decision.
[120] Apparent authority was not arguable, as the third party was aware of the purported revocation.

ted however that the law governing the *transaction* in which it is used or to be used, i.e. the main contract, might be more appropriate. Where security is created by such arrangements, it is possible that some forms of such authority might be classified as assignments or the creation of a specific security interest or as part of a multiparty transaction, to which other choice of law rules might be appropriate.[121]

12-025 Ratification   It seems to be generally accepted that ratification is likewise governed by the law governing the relationship between principal and third party.[122] If it is accepted that questions of actual authority are also so governed, this creates no problems, being explicable on the basis that ratification is equivalent to antecedent authority. If however the view is accepted that *actual* authority is regulated by the law governing the internal relationship, the ratification would require to be isolated from the authority, as a separate event occurring after the formation of the contract, and related specifically to the contract ratified. Questions of estoppel from proving that one has not ratified[123] would probably come under the same law as that governing the putative ratification itself. Ratification seems to be an almost universal concept, but it should be noted that it may have slightly different applications in different legal systems. Thus under the American Restatement, Third, Agency,[124] an undisclosed principal may ratify, which is not so in English law. It also it seems that in some legal systems the notion can apply where the third party actually knows the agent to be unauthorised but anticipates ratification. This latter is a situation to which common law (at any rate outside the United States) might apply a completely different analysis.[125]

12-026 The unauthorised agent (falsus procurator): warranty of authority   The common law approach to the problem of a person who purports to act as agent without having any authority to do so, either at all or in the particular respect, is to say that he has made a contract with the third party under which he promises absolutely that he has authority and will be liable to the third party for the consequences of the lack of authority if this proves not to be so.[126] The liability covers the positive or expectation interest, i.e. it seeks to put the claimant in the position in which he would have been had there been authority.[127] On this interpretation there is a contract freestanding from that between principal and third party. Such a contract does not seem to come within the "agency" exception in the Rome I Regulation referred to above, because the question whether the agent can bind the principal to a third party would

---

[121] See Dicey, Morris and Collins, fn.1 above, Vol.2, Ch.24.
[122] See *Britannia SS Ins Assn v Ausonia Assecurazioni SpA* [1984] 2 Lloyd's Rep. 98; *Merrill Lynch Capital Services Inc v Municipality of Piraeus* [1997] C.L.C. 1214; *Sea Emerald SA v Prominvestbank* [2008] EWHC 1979 (Comm) at [100]; *Law Debenture Trust Corp Plc v Ukraine* [2017] EWHC 655 (Comm); [2017] 3 W.L.R. 667. The matter is raised in *Presentaciones Musicales SA v Secunda* [1994] Ch. 271, but only in connection with ratification of English proceedings commenced by an English solicitor whose retainer was governed by English law; in this context see also *Grupo Torras SA v Al-Sabah (No.5)* [1999] C.L.C. 1469 at 1505–1506 (reversed on other grounds [2001] C.L.C. 221); *Bao Xiang International Garment Centre v British Airways Plc* [2015] EWHC 3071 (Ch); [2016] C.P. Rep. 8 (ratification of English proceedings, as opposed to of solicitor's retainer, governed by English law).
[123] Above, para.2-080.
[124] See above, para.2-063.
[125] See above, para.2-051.
[126] See above, Article 105.
[127] See above, Article 106.

not appear to cover the (secondary) consequences of not doing so. Hence Rome I applies. In this case the contract usually arises by implication, and it is not likely to contain a choice of law. It has been suggested that the characteristic performance is not the provision of the warranty but, rather, the seeing to it that the agent has authority.[128] In the Court of Appeal however it was said that there was in such a case no characteristic performance.[129] It will presumably often come within the residual provisions of arts 4.3 or 4.4[130] and as it is clearly a contract ancillary to the proposed contract between principal and third party, albeit such a contract did not come into force, it is arguable that it should be governed by that law, or what it would have been, by attraction. Such a result has recently been reached in a case applying the Rome Convention, applicable under the Contracts (Applicable Law) Act 1990 but now superseded by the Rome I Regulation, the relevant wording of which is not however quite the same.[131]

Other classifications of the above situation The above assumes that the agent's **12-027** liability is contractual and for the expectation interest, which seems to be the majority view.[132] However, the situations involved certainly could be classified as giving rise to an action in tort, which would almost certainly require negligence and would limit recovery to the reliance, or negative, interest. This seems to be true in some countries[133] and would, where it operated, bring the Rome II Regulation[134] into operation. Other analyses are possible, for example that the liability arises as a matter of law.

Undisclosed principal The doctrine of the undisclosed principal only applies in **12-028** its typical form in common law countries and may contain differences of detail between even them. It is submitted that it is best to regard it as starting from the proposition that the undisclosed principal intervenes on, or is the subject of intervention in respect of, the contract between agent and third party.[135] This means that standard discussion of agency in the conflict of laws is unlikely to be helpful. On this basis, it is necessary to look first at the contract between agent and third party, which is crucial to this inquiry in a way which is not so for identified and unidentified principal situations. There must in fact as a starting point be such a contract, and its governing law and existence will be ascertained in the same way as is applicable to contracts in general (i.e. applying the Rome I Regulation in countries where this applies). Such a contract being established, it will be necessary to know whether it as such permits intervention by an undisclosed principal. If it does not,

---

[128] See *Golden Ocean Group Ltd v Salgaocar Mining Industries PVT Ltd* [2011] EWHC 56 (Comm); [2011] 1 W.L.R. 2575 at [133].
[129] *Golden Ocean Group Ltd v Salgaocar Mining Industries PVT Ltd* [2012] EWCA Civ 265; [2012] 1 W.L.R. 3674 at [52].
[130] See also the Hague Convention on the Law Applicable to Agency 1978 art.15.
[131] *Golden Ocean Group Ltd v Salgaocar Mining Industries PVT Ltd* [2012] EWCA Civ 265; [2012] 1 W.L.R. 3674.
[132] Rabel, fn.1 above, Vol.3, p.142 says that "common law has led the way in this construction". See *The Unauthorised Agent* (Busch and Macgregor, eds, 2008), considering the law of eight countries, the Principles of European Contract Law and the UNIDROIT Principles of International Commercial Contracts: most appear to give the expectation interest and hence to adopt the contractual basis. The Draft Common Frame of Reference, para.II.6-107 appears to make the same assumption.
[133] See Dickinson, *The Rome II Regulation* (2008), para.12.10.
[134] Below, para.12-034.
[135] See above, para.8-069.

that is probably the end of the matter.[136] It may be assumed that this is not so (at any rate in such a simple form) for any contract not governed by the law of a common law country. If a common law regime governs, intervention probably will be permitted, but there may be some slight differences between jurisdictions as to situations where the undisclosed principal cannot intervene to sue, or be sued.[137] Assuming these do not make a difference, the doctrine, at least in English law, is normally taken as requiring that there was actual authority to enter into a contract binding the principal.[138] It is tempting to suggest that the application of this rule and the establishment of such internal authority must come outside the law governing the contract itself by reason of the "agency" exception of art.1(2)(g) of the Rome I Regulation. This would lead to an unnecessary complication, and it is submitted that the question should be governed by the law governing the external contract.[139] In effect this requires that that contract be governed by the law of a common law jurisdiction.

12-029   **Indirect representation**   As has been already explained elsewhere in this book,[140] indirect representation is a civil law notion, the facts constituting which can perfectly well occur in respect of a dispute regulated by common law, but which are not normally analysed under that system on the basis that a special type of agency or representation is involved. The arrangement is sometimes referred to as operation under a contract of *commission*. The notion represents a way of dealing whereby an agent (frequently pursuing a known occupation such as freight forwarder) deals on his own account with the third party: but internally accounts to his principal on an agency basis, e.g. (in common law terms) promising reasonable endeavours, not guaranteeing a result, typically remunerated on commission, owing fiduciary duties, and (a more controversial element) subject to the principal's control.[141] The few common law cases dealing with such situations have often assumed that either the relationship is one of normal agency, or that there are two back-to-back contracts, such as a purchase for resale.[142] In England, only Lord Blackburn paid articulate attention to such a method of commercial operation.[143]

This is not dissimilar to the undisclosed principal situation of which an analysis has been given above, but it is in fact not the same because the English undisclosed principal doctrine requires that the agent be actually authorised to contract so as to bind the principal,[144] but does not disclose the principal's existence or connection with the transaction. The principal under a contract of *commission* does not grant authority for the creation of privity of contract with himself at all; conversely, the

---

[136] cf. above, para.12-009.

[137] For the English position see above, para.8-079.

[138] See above, paras 8-071 and 8-072.

[139] cf. above, para.12-016. *Mildred Goyeneche & Co v Maspons y Hermano* (1882) 9 Q.B.D. 530 (CA) can be taken as authority for this: but the case went to the House of Lords, which decided it on other grounds. The judgments of the Court of Appeal, are considered below, para.12-030.

[140] See above, paras 1-021 and 1-022.

[141] See above, para.1-018.

[142] e.g. *Anglo-African Shipping Co of New York Inc v J.Mortner Ltd* [1962] 1 Lloyd's Rep. 610.

[143] See *Ireland v Livingston* (1871–72) L.R. 5 H.L. 395; *Armstrong v Stokes* (1871–72) L.R. 7 Q.B. 598; *Die Elbinger Actien Gesellschaft für Fabricatien von Eisenbahn Materiel v Claye* (1872-73) L.R. 8 Q.B. 313; *Hutton v Bulloch* (1873) L.R. 8 Q.B. 312; affd (1874) L.R. 9 Q.B. 572; and *Mildred Goyeneche & Co v Maspons y Hermano*, fn.150 below. There is discussion of this interpretation in relation to freight forwarders above, para.9-024.

[144] Above, para.8-071.

third party may be well aware that the agent, who may specialise in acting in this way, has a principal.

This has no connection with most of rules for agency considered above.[145] If such an arrangement is entered into, there is no grant of authority and the relationship between principal and agent is presumably governed by the transaction between them, and that between agent and third party by the law governing that contract (for example, a sale), in both cases subject to the Rome I Regulation. Assuming that that law does not recognise an undisclosed principal doctrine, and there is no apparent authority, the principal is not affected.[146] In some civil law countries the principal may, especially in insolvency situations, in fact sometimes intervene to sue, and may less commonly even be sued.[147] Whether or not this is so in conflict of laws situations is not within the scope of this chapter, but may perhaps be governed by the law governing the principal-agent relationship.[148] The question of whether the third party may sometimes sue the principal instead of the agent, on the other hand, might be attributed to the contract between principal and agent.

However, as discussed both above[149] and below, it appears that English courts have tended to override this difference and simply classified an indirect principal as coming under the undisclosed principal rules; though perhaps this should not happen if the court is adequately briefed as to the foreign law. A leading case now discussed bears this out.

A leading case: Mildred v Maspons The above context requires specific discus- **12-030**
sion of another of the few, and hence celebrated, English cases specifically dealing with agency in the conflict of laws, *Mildred, Goyeneche & Co v Maspons y Hermano*.[150] This deserves attention because in it the Court of Appeal at least addresses agency issues specifically. In that case agents in Cuba, Demestre Chia, consigned tobacco to Messrs Mildred & Co in London, who were to sell it and account for the proceeds as agents. Demestre chartered a vessel, took out a bill of lading in their own name, and arranged for Mildred to insure the goods. The vessel was lost. Demestre became insolvent and Maspons, the actual exporter, intervened to claim the insurance money from Mildred as having still been the owner of the goods insured. During the dealings between Mildred and Demestre there had been frequent references to the "*interesado*", i.e. the person interested, and it must have been clear to Mildred that Demestre was only some sort of agent. To the question "did [Mildred] know or have reason to believe that Demestre & Co were acting as agents for some other person or persons not named?" the jury answered "yes; they knew or had reason to believe it".[151] On the insolvency of Demestre, Mildred claimed a lien (or right of set-off[152]) over the policy money in respect of the general balance of account between themselves and Demestre under a contract between

---

[145] But see Kortmann and Kortmann, "Undisclosed indirect representation—protecting the principal, the third party or both?", Ch.6 in Busch, Macgregor and Watts (eds), *Agency Law in Commercial Practice* (2016).

[146] cf. above, para.12-009.

[147] See above, para.1-021.

[148] See Verhagen, fn.1 above, p.380 onwards, esp. p.386.

[149] See above paras 1-021, 1-022.

[150] *Mildred, Goyeneche & Co v Maspons y Hermano* (1882) 9 Q.B.D. 530 (CA); (1883) 8 App.Cas. 874 (HL).

[151] See (1883) 8 App.Cas. at 883.

[152] See above, para.7-077.

them, itself one of agency and presumably governed by English law. It was held that this did not attach because at the time the insurance was effected Mildred knew that another party was involved.

If Mildred knew this, the contract with Demestre would appear in common law terms to have been made for unidentified principals; but the court treated the case as one of undisclosed principal (a confusion not unknown at the time and subsequently[153]). The result must have been much the same in either case, as Maspons intervened to sue on a marine policy in favour of "every other person or persons to whom the same doth may or shall appertain", and the general lien or right of set-off of Mildred against Demestre in respect of the policy money, presumably governed by English law, would not have applied against an identified or unidentified principal, nor against an undisclosed principal who intervened before a sum had attached to the lien.[154]

If however Demestre was an agent acting as an indirect agent (as seems not unlikely) the dealing was by virtue of the internal arrangements between Demestre and Maspons entirely between Demestre and Mildred, and the fact that Mildred was aware that there was an *interesado* should have been irrelevant. The Spanish law quoted appears to create a *commission* situation: such appears likely to have been the explanation given by an expert witness from the Spanish bar.[155] The Court of Appeal however said that the Spanish law was to be taken into account in considering the nature and extent of the authority given by Maspons to Demestre, but that the overall question was to be determined by English law, not the law of Spain. The contract conferring the lien or right of set-off was between Demestre and Mildred: and the law governing that contract determined whether an undisclosed principal could intervene. He could do so since Mildred already knew of him when the lien attached.[156]

The case is therefore one where the Court of Appeal imposed its own domestic analysis on the situation, and this fits with the proposition that the law governing the main contract between agent and third party determines whether an undisclosed principal can intervene.[157] However, the English law of undisclosed principal requires that the principal has authorised the agent to create privity of contract with the third party.[158] In so far as that requirement is disregarded, and the Spanish law on indirect representation not taken into account at all, the statements of doctrine in the case seem doubtful.[159] The court said that it would do no more than take the Spanish law into account, and this is consistent with other cases[160]: but it is surely going too far to override an intention not to authorise a contract at all under the

---

[153] See above, para.8-105.

[154] See above, Article 81.

[155] See reference to this evidence at p.539.

[156] See above, Article 81. An attempt to apply the foreign principal rule (above, para.9-020) was rejected.

[157] See the judgment of the Court of Appeal at 541–543, where it was said by Lindley LJ that the English law as to undisclosed principals is known to differ from that of other countries, whose law is similar to the law of Spain, but that it was now too late to reconsider the matter.

[158] See above, para.8-071.

[159] But that the doctrine of undisclosed principal was correctly applied is argued by Busch, *Indirect Representation in European Contract Law* (2005), pp.171–172.

[160] Especially the later case of *Chatenay*, fn.20 above.

internal law, especially when the law applicable to the main transaction actually requires such an intention.[161]

The House of Lords affirmed the decision without reliance on the agency point, Lord Blackburn saying that the provisions cited went so far as to show that the Spanish law differed from the English, but that the matter did not turn on privity of contract: the goods had belonged to Maspons and he had the same right to demand the insurance money as the goods.[162] He refused to follow Lindley LJ in discussing matters which did not arise.[163]

Canvassing agents   A canvassing agent[164] normally has no power, or very limited **12-031** power, to create a contract between principal and third party: he simply introduces business. As such his only relationship is internal, and if this is, as is likely, contractual, whether in common law terms unilateral or bilateral (either of which is possible) it is governed by the law governing that contract, as regulated by the Rome I Regulation. As with indirect representation, the grant of authority does not (normally) arise. Such agents may owe fiduciary duties, which may, as is said above of fiduciary duties in general,[165] in principle come within the scope of the Rome I or II Regulations but would probably usually be regarded under the latter Regulation as governed by the same law as the contract anyway.[166] Some such agents, for example estate agents acting for private clients, will be affected by the consumer provisions of art.7 of Rome I.[167]

Agency of necessity   It is submitted elsewhere in this book that the clearest agency **12-032** applications of this doctrine, under which an agent may in certain situations of emergency make contracts binding his principal, ought now to be assimilated into ordinary notions of actual and apparent authority,[168] in which case as a separate category it would disappear. The traditional formulation of the rules in common law, however, regards them as a separate matter of law.[169] In their best-known form they confer authority on shipmasters to act for ship and/or cargo, for example when a salvage agreement is entered into; and a traditional argument, apparently accepted in many countries, is in fact that the matter, being related to a maritime venture, is generally known as being subject to the law of the flag of the vessel.[170] It is not clear that such an analysis is still required.[171] In so far as it involves the law of property (where ship or cargo are mortgaged or sold) the situation would be controlled by the *lex situs* of the property at the relevant time.[172] There is however another aspect

---

[161] It is however worth noting that the Court of Appeal was in about its strongest possible constitution even for the present day: Jessel MR and Lindley and Bowen LJJ.
[162] See Lord Blackburn at 887. He also based his judgment (with some acerbity) on the Factors Acts.
[163] At 888.
[164] See above, para.1-020.
[165] See above, para.12-008.
[166] See Dicey, Morris and Collins, fn.1 above, Vol.2, para.34-087; Dickinson, *The Rome II Regulation* (2008), paras 3.141–142.
[167] See Dicey, Morris and Collins, fn.1 above, Vol.2, Rule 235.
[168] See above, para.4-008.
[169] See *Industrie Chimiche Italia Centrale and Cerealfin SA v Alexander G Tsavliris & Sons Maritime Co (The Choko Star) (1990)* [1990] 1 Lloyd's Rep. 516.
[170] See Rabel, fn.1 above, Vol.3, pp.146–148.
[171] See Dicey, Morris and Collins, fn.1 above, Vol.2, para.33-108.
[172] As in the leading case of *Cammell v Sewell* (1860) 5 H. & N. 728. See Dicey, Morris and Collins, fn.1 above, Vol.2, Ch.24.

of the doctrine operating only internally between principal and agent, which may justify the agent's intervention and sometimes entitling him to compensation or indemnity.[173] These latter entitlements seem restitutionary in character and, at least unless there is already an agency relationship in operation, may be linked to the Roman and civil law concept of *negotiorum gestio* and the choice of law rules applicable for such cases under the Rome II Regulation.[174] Some of the powers conferred by the Mental Capacity Act 2005 enabling persons to act on behalf of others in certain circumstances are similar to one or the other of the two categories of agency of necessity,[175] and their conflict of laws aspects may be governed by the Hague Convention on the Protection of Adults.[176]

12-033 **Commercial agents** The category of commercial agent was unknown to the common law. Regulations on such agents implementing an EC Directive were introduced in 1993. The Regulations contain indications of their own application and certain choice of law provisions, which are discussed in Chapter 11.[177]

12-034 **Torts** Where it is claimed that an agent is in any respect liable in tort, or that his principal is liable for his acts, as is perfectly possible,[178] the normal rules for torts in the conflict of laws, now laid down by the Rome II Regulation on the Law Applicable to Non-Contractual Obligations, will apply.[179] Within those rules, the connection with a contract may sometimes be a reason for adopting the law governing that contract. The equitable wrongs (often applicable to persons who can be called agents) of accessory liability to breach of trust or fiduciary obligation and knowing receipt of property subject to such obligation,[180] or at least the first of them, may require treating on the analogy of torts and hence brought within Rome II under that head.[181]

12-035 **Property** Where a question of property arises,[182] as with an agent for sale or purchase of goods, the normal rules for property in the conflict of laws, viz. usually the *lex situs* of the property at the time of the disposition, will apply.[183]

---

[173] A leading case is *China-Pacific SA v Food Corp of India (The Winson)* [1982] A.C. 939: above, Illustration 2 to Article 33.

[174] As to restitutionary liability, see below. As to *negotiorum gestio*, dealt with in art.11 of the Rome II Regulation, see below and Dickinson, *The Rome II Regulation* (2008), paras 11.13–11.14.

[175] Above, para.4-012.

[176] This Convention was enacted into law for England and Wales by s.63 of and Sch.3 to the Mental Health Act 2005, which took effect on October 1, 2007 by virtue of the Mental Capacity Act 2005 (Commencement No.2) Order (SI 2007/1987).

[177] Above, paras 11-006–11-010.

[178] The main instances occur in Articles 42, 48, 90, 91 and 113–115 above.

[179] Regulation 864/2007, effective January 11, 2009. See Dicey, Morris and Collins, fn.1 above, Vol.2, Ch.35; Dickinson, *The Rome II Regulation* (2008), Ch.4. For an example of the rules applied to bribery (of an agent), treated as a tort, see *Fiona Trust & Holding Corp v Skarga* [2013] EWCA Civ 275, where the law governing the relevant contracts was not applied.

[180] Above, Article 116.

[181] As to this topic, see above, Article 116. See Dicey Morris and Collins, fn.1 above, Vol.2, para.36-057 onwards; cf. Dickinson, *The Rome II Regulation* (2008); 4.101, 102 (accessory liability), 103–105 (knowing receipt); Yeo, *Choice of Law for Equitable Doctrines* (2004), p.272 onwards.

[182] See esp. Articles 33, 69 and Ch.8.2.

[183] See Dicey, Morris and Collins, fn.1 above, Vol.2, Ch.24.

Restitution and unjust enrichment The question whether an issue should be **12-036**
classified as restitutionary or related to the principle of unjust enrichment is of itself
difficult,[184] and the allocation of appropriate laws to the issues so identified is also
controversial. Such problems certainly arise in the context of agency.[185] Both
problems continue after the Rome II Regulation, which (in so far as they are seen
to fall within the category of non-contractual obligations) deals with them in arts
10 and 11.[186] Questions of the law applicable where the common law uses trust
reasoning in an agency context may also arise.[187] Article 1.2(e) excludes from the
scope of the Regulation "non-contractual obligations arising out of the relations
between the settlors, trustees and beneficiaries of a trust created voluntarily". This
refers to (what may be called) express trusts, which are the subject of the Hague
Convention on the Law Applicable to Trusts, which was implemented in the United
Kingdom by the Recognition of Trusts Act 1987; but the exception may go further.
Beyond this, situations where trust reasoning is used, especially in a remedial
context, may be capable of giving rise to non-contractual obligations within the
scope of Rome II. The impact of that Regulation on such cases is a matter of some
complexity outside the scope of this chapter.[188]

---

[184] See in general Goff and Jones, *Law of Unjust Enrichment* (9th edn).
[185] Issues which are arguably of this type arise in Articles 46, 48, 50, 51, 62, 88, 92, 92, 96 and 111–112.
[186] See Dicey, Morris and Collins, fn.1 above, Vol.2, Ch.36; Dickinson, *The Rome II Regulation* (2008), Chs 10 (Restitution), 11 (Negotiorum Gestio); Yeo, *Choice of Law for Equitable Doctrines* (2004).
[187] Questions involving trust reasoning of one sort and another appear in Articles 45–49, 50 and 53.
[188] On the application of the Regulation to such issues, see Dicey, Morris and Collins, fn.1 above, Vol.2, para.36-075 onwards; Dickinson, *The Rome II Regulation* (2008), paras 3.173–3.207 (saying, at para.3.174, that at least from an English law perspective, art.1.2(e) is probably the most complex in the Rome II Regulation).

THE COMMERCIAL AGENTS (COUNCIL DIRECTIVE) REGULATIONS 1993[1]

(SI 1993/3053)

Made 7 December 1993.
Laid before Parliament 8 December 1993.
Coming into Force 1 January 1994.

ARRANGEMENT OF REGULATIONS

PART I

General

Regulation
1   Citation, commencement and applicable law
2   Interpretation, application and extent

PART II

Rights and Obligations

3   Duties of a commercial agent to his principal
4   Duties of a principal to his commercial agent
5   Prohibition on derogation from regulations 3 and 4 and consequence of breach

PART III

Remuneration

6   Form and amount of remuneration in absence of agreement
7   Entitlement to commission on transactions concluded during agency contract
8   Entitlement to commission on transactions concluded after agency contract has terminated
9   Apportionment of commission between new and previous commercial agents
10   When commission due and date for payment
11   Extinction of right to commission
12   Periodic supply of information as to commission due and right of inspection of principal's books

PART IV

Conclusion and Termination of the Agency Contract

13   Right to signed written statement of terms of agency contract
14   Conversion of agency contract after expiry of fixed period
15   Minimum periods of notice for termination of agency contract
16   Savings with regard to immediate termination
17   Entitlement of commercial agent to indemnity or compensation on termination of agency contract

---

[1]   This S.I. is printed as amended by the Commercial Agents (Council Directive) (Amendment) Regulations 1993 (S.I. 1993 No. 3173) and 1998 (S.I. 1998 No. 2868).

18	Grounds for excluding payment of indemnity or compensation under regulation 17
19	Prohibition on derogation from regulations 17 and 18
20	Restraint of trade clauses

Part V

Miscellaneous and Supplemental

21	Disclosure of information
22	Service of notice etc
23	Transitional provisions

The Secretary of State, being a Minister designated[2] for the purposes of section 2(2)of the European Communities Act 1972[3] in relation to measures relating to relations between commercial agents and their principals, in the exercise of the powers conferred by him by that section, hereby makes the following Regulations:

Part I

General

Citation, commencement and applicable law

1.—(1)   These Regulations may be cited as the Commercial Agents (Council Directive) Regulations 1993 and shall come into force on 1st January 1994.

(2)   These Regulations govern the relations between commercial agents and their principals and, subject to paragraph (3), apply in relation to the activities of commercial agents in Great Britain.

(3)   A court or tribunal shall:

(a)   apply the law of the other member State concerned in place of regulations 3 to 22 where the parties have agreed that the agency contract is to be governed by the law of that member State;

(b)   (whether or not it would otherwise be required to do so) apply these regulations where the law of another member State corresponding to these regulations enables the parties to agree that the agency contract is to be governed by the law of a different member State and the parties have agreed that it is to be governed by the law of England and Wales or Scotland.

Interpretation, application and extent

2.—(1)   In these Regulations—

"commercial agent" means a self-employed intermediary who has continuing authority to negotiate the sale or purchase of goods on behalf of another person (the "principal"), or to negotiate and conclude the sale or purchase of goods on behalf of and in the name of that principal; but shall be understood as not including in particular:

(i)   a person who, in his capacity as an officer of a company or association, is empowered to enter into commitments binding on that company or association;

---

2   S.I. 1989/1327.
3   1972 c.68.

> > (ii)   a partner who is lawfully authorised to enter into commitments binding on his partners;
> > (iii)   a person who acts as an insolvency practitioner (as that expression is defined in section 388 of the Insolvency Act 1986[4]) or the equivalent in any other jurisdiction;
>
> "commission" means any part of the remuneration of a commercial agent which varies with the number or value of business transactions;
>
> "EEA Agreement" means the Agreement on the European Economic Area signed at Oporto on 2nd May 1992 as adjusted by the Protocol signed at Brussels on 17th March 1993;
>
> "member State" includes a State which is a contracting party to the EEA Agreement;
>
> "restraint of trade clause" means an agreement restricting the business activities of a commercial agent following termination of the agency contract.

(2)   These Regulations do not apply to—
> (a)   commercial agents whose activities are unpaid;
> (b)   commercial agents when they operate on commodity exchanges or in the commodity market;
> (c)   the Crown Agents for Overseas Governments and Administrations, as set up under the Crown Agents Act 1979[5], or its subsidiaries.

(3)   The provisions of the Schedule to these Regulations have effect for the purpose of determining the persons whose activities as commercial agents are to be considered secondary.

(4)   These Regulations shall not apply to the persons referred to in paragraph (3) above.

(5)   These Regulations do not extend to Northern Ireland.[6]

PART II

RIGHTS AND OBLIGATIONS

Duties of a commercial agent to his principal

3.—(1)   In performing his activities a commercial agent must look after the interests of his principal and act dutifully and in good faith.

(2)   In particular, a commercial agent must—
> (a)   make proper efforts to negotiate and, where appropriate, conclude the transactions he is instructed to take care of;
> (b)   communicate to his principal all the necessary information available to him;
> (c)   comply with reasonable instructions given by his principal.

---

[4]   1986 c.45.
[5]   1979 c.43.
[6]   But similar regulations apply there; above, para. 11-003.

Duties of a principal to his commercial agent

4.—(1) In his relations with his commercial agent a principal must act dutifully and in good faith.

(2) In particular, a principal must—

    (a) provide his commercial agent with the necessary documentation relating to the goods concerned;

    (b) obtain for his commercial agent the information necessary for the performance of the agency contract, and in particular notify his commercial agent within a reasonable period once he anticipates that the volume of commercial transactions will be significantly lower than that which the commercial agent could normally have expected.

(3) A principal shall, in addition, inform his commercial agent within a reasonable period of his acceptance or refusal of, and of any non-execution by him of, a commercial transaction which the commercial agent has procured for him.

Prohibition on derogation from regulations 3 and 4 and consequence of Breach

5.—(1) The parties may not derogate from regulations 3 and 4 above.

(2) The law applicable to the contract shall govern the consequence of breach of the rights and obligations under regulations 3 and 4 above.

PART III

REMUNERATION

Form and amount of remuneration in absence of agreement

6.—(1) In the absence of any agreement as to remuneration between the parties, a commercial agent shall be entitled to the remuneration that commercial agents appointed for the goods forming the subject of his agency contract are customarily allowed in the place where he carries on his activities and, if there is no such customary practice, a commercial agent shall be entitled to reasonable remuneration taking into account all the aspects of the transaction.

(2) This regulation is without prejudice to the application of any enactment or rule of law concerning the level of remuneration.

(3) Where a commercial agent is not remunerated (wholly or in part) by commission, regulations 7 to 12 below shall not apply.

Entitlement to commission on transactions concluded during agency contract

7.—(1) A commercial agent shall be entitled to commission on commercial transactions concluded during the period covered by the agency contract—

    (a) where the transaction has been concluded as a result of his action; or

    (b) where the transaction is concluded with a third party whom he has previously acquired as a customer for transactions of the same kind.

(2) A commercial agent shall also be entitled to commission on transactions concluded during the period covered by the agency contract where he has an exclusive right to a specific geographical area or to a specific group of customers

and where the transaction has been entered into with a customer belonging to that area or group.

Entitlement to commission on transactions concluded after agency contract has terminated

8. Subject to regulation 9 below, a commercial agent shall be entitled to commission on commercial transactions concluded after the agency contract has terminated if—

    (a)   the transaction is mainly attributable to his efforts during the period covered by the agency contract and if the transaction was entered into within a reasonable period after that contract terminated; or

    (b)   in accordance with the conditions mentioned in regulation 7 above, the order of the third party reached the principal or the commercial agent before the agency contract terminated.

Apportionment of commission between new and previous commercial agents

9.—(1)   A commercial agent shall not be entitled to the commission referred to in regulation 7 above if that commission is payable, by virtue of regulation 8 above, to the previous commercial agent, unless it is equitable because of the circumstances for the commission to be shared between the commercial agents.

(2)   The principal shall be liable for any sum due under paragraph (1) above to the person entitled to it in accordance with that paragraph, and any sum which the other commercial agent receives to which he is not entitled shall be refunded to the principal.

When commission due and date for payment

10.—(1)   Commission shall become due as soon as, and to the extent that, one of the following circumstances occurs:

    (a)   the principal has executed the transaction; or

    (b)   the principal should, according to his agreement with the third party, have executed the transaction; or

    (c)   the third party has executed the transaction.

(2)   Commission shall become due at the latest when the third party has executed his part of the transaction or should have done so if the principal had executed his part of the transaction, as he should have.

(3)   The commission shall be paid not later than on the last day of the month following the quarter in which it became due, and, for the purposes of these Regulations, unless otherwise agreed between the parties, the first quarter period shall run from the date the agency contract takes effect, and subsequent periods shall run from that date in the third month thereafter or the beginning of the fourth month, whichever is the sooner.

(4)   Any agreement to derogate from paragraphs (2) and (3) above to the detriment of the commercial agent shall be void.

Extinction of right to commission

11.—(1)   The right to commission can be extinguished only if and to the extent that—

(a) it is established that the contract between the third party and the principal will not be executed; and

(b) that fact is due to a reason for which the principal is not to blame.

(2) Any commission which the commercial agent has already received shall be refunded if the right to it is extinguished.

(3) Any agreement to derogate from paragraph (1) above to the detriment of the commercial agent shall be void.

Periodic supply of information as to commission due and right of inspection of principal's books

12.—(1) The principal shall supply his commercial agent with a statement of the commission due, not later than the last day of the month following the quarter in which the commission has become due, and such statement shall set out the main components used in calculating the amount of the commission.

(2) A commercial agent shall be entitled to demand that he be provided with all the information (and in particular an extract from the books) which is available to his principal and which he needs in order to check the amount of the commission due to him.

(3) Any agreement to derogate from paragraphs (1) and (2) above shall be void.

(4) Nothing in this regulation shall remove or restrict the effect of, or prevent reliance upon, any enactment or rule of law which recognises the right of an agent to inspect the books of a principal.

PART IV

CONCLUSION AND TERMINATION OF THE AGENCY CONTRACT

Right to signed written statement of terms of agency contract

13.—(1) The commercial agent and principal shall each be entitled to receive from the other, on request, a signed written document setting out the terms of the agency contract including any terms subsequently agreed.

(2) Any purported waiver of the right referred to in paragraph (1) above shall be void.

Conversion of agency contract after expiry of fixed period

14. An agency contract for a fixed period which continues to be performed by both parties after that period has expired shall be deemed to be converted into an agency contract for an indefinite period.

Minimum periods of notice for termination of agency contract

15.—(1) Where an agency contract is concluded for an indefinite period either party may terminate it by notice.

(2) The period of notice shall be—

(a) 1 month for the first year of the contract;

(b) 2 months for the second year commenced;

(c) 3 months for the third year commenced and for the subsequent years;

and the parties may not agree on any shorter periods of notice.

(3)   If the parties agree on longer periods than those laid down in paragraph (2) above, the period of notice to be observed by the principal must not be shorter than that to be observed by the commercial agent.

(4)   Unless otherwise agreed by the parties, the end of the period of notice must coincide with the end of a calendar month.

(5)   The provisions of this regulation shall also apply to an agency contract for a fixed period where it is converted under regulation 14 above into an agency contract for an indefinite period subject to the proviso that the earlier fixed period must be taken into account in the calculation of the period of notice.

Savings with regard to immediate termination

16.   These Regulations shall not affect the application of any enactment or rule of law which provides for the immediate termination of the agency contract—

- (a)   because of the failure of one party to carry out all or part of his obligations under that contract; or
- (b)   where exceptional circumstances arise.

Entitlement of commercial agent to indemnity or compensation on termination of agency contract

17.—(1)   This regulation has effect for the purpose of ensuring that the commercial agent is, after termination of the agency contract, indemnified in accordance with paragraphs (3) to (5) below or compensated for damage in accordance with paragraphs (6) and (7) below.

(2)   Except where the agency contract otherwise provides, the commercial agent shall be entitled to be compensated rather than indemnified.

(3)   Subject to paragraph (9) and to regulation 18 below, the commercial agent shall be entitled to an indemnity if and to the extent that—

- (a)   he has brought the principal new customers or has significantly increased the volume of business with existing customers and the principal continues to derive substantial benefits from the business with such customers; and
- (b)   the payment of this indemnity is equitable having regard to all the circumstances and, in particular, the commission lost by the commercial agent on the business transacted with such customers.

(4)   The amount of the indemnity shall not exceed a figure equivalent to an indemnity for one year calculated from the commercial agent's average annual remuneration over the preceding five years and if the contract goes back less than five years the indemnity shall be calculated on the average for the period in question.

(5)   The grant of an indemnity as mentioned above shall not prevent the commercial agent from seeking damages.

(6)   Subject to paragraph (9) and to regulation 18 below, the commercial agent shall be entitled to compensation for the damage he suffers as a result of the termination of his relations with his principal.

(7)   For the purpose of these Regulations such damage shall be deemed to occur particularly when the termination takes place in either or both of the following circumstances, namely circumstances which—

(a) deprive the commercial agent of the commission which proper performance of the agency contract would have procured for him whilst providing his principal with substantial benefits linked to the activities of the commercial agent; or

(b) have not enabled the commercial agent to amortize the costs and expenses that he had incurred in the performance of the agency contract on the advice of his principal.

(8) Entitlement to the indemnity or compensation for damage as provided for under paragraphs (2) to (7) above shall also arise where the agency contract is terminated as a result of the death of the commercial agent.

(9) The commercial agent shall lose his entitlement to the indemnity or compensation for damage in the instances provided for in paragraphs (2) to (8) above if within one year following termination of his agency contract he has not notified his principal that he intends pursuing his entitlement.

Grounds for excluding payment of indemnity or compensation under regulation 17

18. The indemnity or compensation referred to in regulation 17 above shall not be payable to the commercial agent where—

(a) the principal has terminated the agency contract because of default attributable to the commercial agent which would justify immediate termination of the agency contract pursuant to regulation 16 above; or

(b) the commercial agent has himself terminated the agency contract, unless such termination is justified—

(i) by circumstances attributable to the principal, or

(ii) on grounds of the age, infirmity or illness of the commercial agent in consequence of which he cannot reasonably be required to continue his activities; or

(c) the commercial agent, with the agreement of his principal, assigns his rights and duties under the agency contract to another person.

Prohibition on derogation from regulations 17 and 18

19. The parties may not derogate from regulations 17 and 18 to the detriment of the commercial agent before the agency contract expires.

Restraint of trade clauses

20.—(1) A restraint of trade clause shall be valid only if and to the extent that—

(a) it is concluded in writing; and

(b) it relates to the geographical area or the group of customers and the geographical area entrusted to the commercial agent and to the kind of goods covered by his agency under the contract.

(2) A restraint of trade clause shall be valid for not more than two years after termination of the agency contract.

(3) Nothing in this regulation shall affect any enactment or rule of law which imposes other restrictions on the validity or enforceability of restraint of trade

clauses or which enables a court to reduce the obligations on the parties resulting from such clauses.

PART V

MISCELLANEOUS AND SUPPLEMENTAL

Disclosure of information

21. Nothing in these Regulations shall require information to be given where such disclosure would be contrary to public policy.

Service of notice etc

22.—(1) Any notice, statement or other document to be given or supplied to a commercial agent or to be given or supplied to the principal under these Regulations may be so given or supplied:

    (a) by delivering it to him;

    (b) by leaving it at his proper address addressed to him by name;

    (c) by sending it by post to him addressed either to his registered address or to the address to his registered or principal office;

or by any other means provided for in the agency contract.

    (2) Any such notice, statement or document may—

    (a) in the case of a body corporate, be given or served on the secretary or clerk of that body;

    (b) in the case of a partnership, be given to or served on any partner or on any person having the control or management of the partnership business.

Transitional provisions

23.—(1) Notwithstanding any provision in an agency contract made before 1st January 1994, these Regulations shall apply to that contract after that date and, accordingly any provision which is inconsistent with these Regulations shall have effect subject to them.

    (2) Nothing in these Regulations shall affect the rights and liabilities of a commercial agent or a principal which have accrued before 1st January 1994.

THE SCHEDULE

Regulation 2(3)

1. The activities of a person as a commercial agent are to be considered secondary where it may reasonably be taken that the primary purpose of the arrangement with his principal is other than as set out in paragraph 2 below.

  2. An arrangement falls within this paragraph if—

    (a) the business of the principal is the sale, or as the case may be purchase, of goods of a particular kind; and

    (b) the goods concerned are such that—

      (i) transactions are normally individually negotiated and concluded on a commercial basis, and

      (ii) procuring a transaction on one occasion is likely to lead to further transactions in those goods with that customer on future occasions, or to transactions in those goods with other customers in the same geographical area or among the same group of customers and

    that accordingly it is in the commercial interests of the principal in developing the market in those goods to appoint a representative to such customers with a view to the representative devoting effort, skill and expenditure from his own resources to that end.

3. The following are indications that an arrangement falls within paragraph 2 above, and the absence of any of them is an indication to the contrary—

    (a)   the principal is the manufacturer, importer or distributor of the goods;

    (b)   the goods are specifically identified with the principal in the market in question rather than, or to a greater extent than, with any other person;

    (c)   the agent devotes substantially the whole of his time to representative activities (whether for one principal or for a number of principals whose interests are not conflicting);

    (d)   the goods are not normally available in the market in question other than by means of the agent;

    (e)   the arrangement is described as one of commercial agency.

4. The following are indications that an arrangement does not fall within paragraph 2 above—

    (a)   promotional material is supplied direct to potential customers;

    (b)   persons are granted agencies without reference to existing agents in a particular area or in relation to a particular group;

    (c)   customers normally select the goods for themselves and merely place their orders through the agent.

5. The activities of the following categories of persons are presumed, unless the contrary is established, not to fall within paragraph 2 above—

Mail order catalogue agents for consumer goods

Consumer credit agents.

INDEX

This index has been prepared using Sweet and Maxwell's Legal Taxonomy. Main index entries conform to keywords provided by the Legal Taxonomy except where references to specific documents or non-standard terms (denoted by quotation marks) have been included. These keywords provide a means of identifying similar concepts in other Sweet & Maxwell publications and online services to which keywords from the Legal Taxonomy have been applied. Readers may find some minor differences between terms used in the text and those which appear in the index. Suggestions to *sweetandmaxwell.taxonomy@tr.com*.

Acceptor for honour
agency of necessity
generally, 4–003, 4–006
restitution, 4–010
Accessory liability
banks, 9–141
breach of trust, 9–135
examples, 9–142
generally, 9–134
inconsistent dealing, 9–137
knowing receipt, 9–136
ministerial agents, 9–139
receipt of trust property, 9–136
solicitors, 9–140
trustees de son tort, 9–138
Account
action of
account stated, 6–098
benefits derived, 6–097
expenses, 6–097
history, 6–095
illegal transactions, 6–098
duty to account
account of profits, 6–045
account, the, 6–097
co-principals, 2–046
estoppel as to principal's title,
6–110—6–112
general duty, 6–095
sub-agents, 5–012, 5–016
substantive significance, 6–096
profits, of
conflict of interest, 6–047
duty to account, 6–045
fiduciary duty, 6–042, 6–073—6–074
Account stated
use of in action of account, 6–098
Accountants
gratuitous agents, liability of, 6–032
inspection of books by, 2–026
misappropriation, liability for, 6–101
paying over money held for principal, 6–101
production of documents by, 6–093
same matter conflict, 6–049
Accounts
agent bound by, 6–097
delivery of, 6–093

duty to keep, 6–091—6–093
presumption against agent, 6–092
separation of property, 6–091
Acknowledgement for Limitation Acts
debts, 2–026, 2–034
Acquiescence
ratification, 2–079
Act of state
agent not liable for, 9–124
ratification, 2–053
Actual authority
see also Apparent authority; Authority
acts outside
principal/third party relations,
8–065—8–067
conflict of laws, 12–017
dispositions of property by agent,
8–125—8–128
express actual authority
ambiguous terms, 3–019—3–020
not given by deed, 3–016—3–018
powers of attorney, 3–013—3–015
implied actual authority
course of dealing, 3–041—3–042
customary authority, 3–033—3–040
incidental authority, 3–021—3–023
managerial agents, 3–027—3–029
professional agents, 3–030—3–032
receiving payment of money,
3–024—3–026
usual authority, 3–027—3–032
meaning, 1–014, 3–001, 3–003
termination, 10–002—10–005
Administrative law
delegation to sub-agents, 2–024, 5–006
Administrators
ratification, 2–070
Admiralty claims
liens, 7–085
Admissibility of evidence
agents' liabilities, 9–039—9–042
Adverse possession
agents' powers, 2–026
Agency
see also Agency of necessity; Estoppel
actual authority, 1–014
apparent authority

meaning, 1–011, 1–014
commercial function, no requirement for, 1–010
companies, 1–028—1–030
consensual agency
  creation of, 2–003
  fundamental role of, 1–005
  paradigm case, 1–012
contract of
  implied terms, 6–002—6–024
control, 1–018
creation
  apparent authority, 2–005
  contract relevance, 2–003
  estoppel, 2–005
  express agreements, 2–027—2–028
  general rule, 2–001—2–002
  implied agreements, 2–029—2–034
  ratification, 2–004
definition
  further, 1–039
  limits of, 1–003
  purpose of, 1–002
distinction from other relationships
  bailees, 1–033
  borrowers, 1–037
  buyers, 1–036, 1–043
  concessionaires, 1–035
  distributors, 1–035
  franchisees, 1–035
  generally, 1–031
  independent contractors, 1–034
  sellers, 1–036
  servants, 1–034
  supplier of services, 1–038
  trustees, 1–032
diverse use of reasoning, 1–027
due diligence, 1–017
essence of, 1–024
external aspects, 1–019
externalised theories, 1–025
features of, 1–016—1–018
generally, 1–001
incomplete agency
  canvassing agents, 1–020
  indirect representation, 1–021—1–022
  introducing agents, 1–020
internal aspects, 1–019
purporting to act for principal, no requirement for, 1–009
remuneration, 1–016
tort, 1–026
unilateral manifestation, arising from, 1–006—1–008
Agency of necessity
acceptor for honour
  generally, 4–003, 4–006
  restitution, 4–010
benefit of principal, 4–005
communications with principal, 4–005
competence, 4–005
conflict of laws, 12–032
deserted wives, 4–011

doctrine, 4–001
express instructions, and, 4–005
good faith, 4–005
impossibility of communications, 4–005
impracticality of communications, 4–005
inconvenience, and, 4–005
introduction, 4–002
meaning, 4–002
mentally incapacitated persons, 4–012
restitution, 4–010
rules of, determining, 4–005
salvage contracts
  cargo, 4–008
  examples, 4–013
  generally, 4–008
  present law, 4–009
shipmasters
  apparent authority, 4–007
  communications with shipowners, 4–007, 4–013
  generally, 4–003
  salvage contracts, 4–008, 4–009, 4–013
  scope of authority, 4–004
  vicarious liability, 4–007
Agents
  see also Actual authority; Agents' duties; Agents' liabilities; Agents' powers; Agents' rights; Apparent authority; Authority
appointments
  formalities, 2–035—2–036
  powers of attorney, 2–039
  purchase of land, 2–037
breach of duty
  third party involvement with, 8–218—8–226
brokers, 1–039, 1–046
capacity
  acting for both parties, 2–013
  examples, 2–016
  general rule, 2–011—2–012
  minors, 2–015
  one party as agent for other, 2–014
co-agents, 2–043—2–044
commercial agents, 1–039, 1–044
consent to agency, 2–032
dealings with money and negotiable instruments
  bills of exchange, 8–140
  examples, 8–142
  generally, 8–139
  money, 8–141
del credere agent, 1–039, 1–042, 1–043
discretion, 6–020
dispositions of property by
  actual authority, 8–125—8–128
  apparent authority, 8–125—8–128
  apparent ownership, 8–129—8–133
  Factors Act 1889, protection by, 8–143—8–158
  indicia of property, agent entrusted with, 8–134—8–138
  restitutionary claims, 8–159—8–167

dispositions of property to
  attornment, 8–172
  disclosed principals, 8–170
  estoppel, 8–173
  examples, 8–175
  general rule, 8–168—8–169
  restitutionary claims, 8–174
  undisclosed principals, 8–171
distinction from other relationships
  bailees, 1–033
  borrowers, 1–037
  buyers, 1–036, 1–043
  concessionaires, 1–035
  distributors, 1–035
  franchisees, 1–035
  generally, 1–031
  independent contractors, 1–034
  sellers, 1–036
  servants, 1–034
  supplier of services, 1–038
  trustees, 1–032
dual agency, 2–033
factors, 1–039, 1–046
fiduciary relationship, 1–015
general agents, 1–039, 1–045
implied agreements, 2–032
knowledge acquired through
  agent's own knowledge, 8–212
  claims by principal against agent, 8–214
  companies' agents, 8–215
  duty to investigate, 8–213
  examples, 8–217
  fraud of agent, 8–214
  general rule, 8–208—8–209
  large organisations, 8–215
  Law of Property Act 1925, 8–216
  rationale for imputation, 8–210
  scope of, 8–211
meaning, 1–023
messenger, 1–039, 1–047
nuntius, 1–039, 1–047
principal, relationship with
  conferral of authority, 12–009
  consumer contracts, 12–006
  employment contracts, 12–007
  fiduciary duties, 12–008
  generally, 12–004
  habitual residence, 12–005
  powers of attorney, 12–010
sale
  conflict of interest, 6–061
special agents, 1–039, 1–045
types, 1–039—1–040
Agents' duties
commercial agents
  agent to principal, 6–006
common law, 6–003—6–039
duty of care
  contract, 6–113
  degree of skill and care, 6–019
  discretion, 6–020
  examples, 6–024
  generally, 6–017

illegal conduct, 6–023
information, 6–021
special skill, 6–022
tort, 6–018
duty to account
  account, 6–097
  account of profits, 6–045
  account stated, 6–098
  action of account, 6–095
  co-principals, 2–046
  estoppel as to principal's title,
    6–110—6–112
  general duty, 6–095
  sub-agents, 5–012, 5–016
  substantive significance, 6–096
fiduciary duties
  see also Fiduciary duty
  account, duty to, 6–094—6–098
  accounts, duty to keep, 6–090—6–093
  acquiring benefits in breach of duty,
    6–079—6–083
  attribution of, 6–037—6–038
  breach of, 6–005, 6–079—6–083
  bribes, 6–084—6–089
  conflict of interest, 6–046—6–061
  consent, 6–039
  dealing with principal, 6–062—6–072
  development of, 6–036
  disclosure, 6–039
  general principle, 6–033
  interest, liability for, 6–102—6–109
  introduction, 6–001
  loyalty, 6–039—6–045
  meaning, 6–034
  nature of, 6–035
  pay over money held for principal,
    6–099—6–101
  position, use of, 6–079—6–083
  principal's property, use of, 6–075—6–078
  profits made, 6–073—6–074
  remedies, 6–040—6–045
  secret profits, 6–084—6–089
introduction, 6–001
performance
  ambiguous instructions, 6–010—6–011
  authority, not to exceed, 6–002—6–007
  diligence, 6–012—6–016
  due skill and care, 6–017—6–024
  further instructions from principal,
    6–008—6–009
restitution
  repayment of money received for use of
    principal, 9–101—9–109
  third parties, money held for,
    9–110—9–114
Agents' liabilities
admissibility of evidence, 9–039—9–042
alternative liability, 9–006
attornment, 9–113
auctioneers, 9–023
bills of exchange, 9–050—9–056
breach of trust
  accessory liability, 9–134—9–135

banks, 9–141
  examples, 9–142
  inconsistent dealing, 9–134, 9–137
  ministerial acts, 9–134, 9–139
  receipt of trust property, 9–134, 9–136
  solicitors, 9–140
  trustees de son tort, 9–138
cheques, 9–050—9–056
collateral contracts, 9–006
confirming houses in international sales,
  9–021
conflict of laws, 12–027
Crown agents, 9–028
damages, 9–013
deeds, 9–047—9–049
defences, 9–029
del credere agents, 9–022
deposits, 9–025
election, 9–007, 9–057—9–059
entitlement, 9–005
estoppel as to parties to contract, 9–030
examples, 9–034
express restriction of, 9–027
fictitious principals, 9–018, 9–084—9–087
foreign principals, 9–020
freight forwarders, 9–024
general rule, 6–025—6–026, 9–004—9–005
gratuitous agents, 6–001, 6–027—6–032
identified principals, 9–091, 9–094
indirect representation, 9–014
insurance cases, 9–011
interrogatories
  existence of principal, 9–015
  name of principal, 9–017
joint and several liability, 9–006
joint liability, 9–006
liens, 9–009
merger, 9–057—9–059
non-existent principals, 9–018, 9–084—9–087
oral contracts, 9–043—9–046
own principal, 9–019, 9–088—9–097
promissory notes, 9–050—9–056
sole liability, 9–006
special property, 9–009
stakeholders, agent as, 9–026
statute, 9–033
strict liability, 6–001
suretyship, 9–006
tort
  co-agents, 9–132—9–133
  conversion by innocent agent,
    9–126—9–131
  generally, 9–032
  personal liability, 9–115—9–125
  sub-agents, 9–132—9–133
undisclosed principals, 9–012
unidentified principals, 9–016, 9–092, 9–095
warranty of authority, 9–031, 9–060—9–083
written contracts, 9–036—9–038
Agents' powers
adverse possession, 2–026
bills of sale, 2–026
breach

sub-agent's liability, 5–008
contract, 2–019
corporations, 2–020
deeds, execution of
  generally, 2–019, 2–040—2–041
  powers of attorney, 2–042
discretionary powers, 2–021
distress, 2–026
exercise of options, 2–026
generally, 2–017—2–018
illegality, 2–025
notices to quit, 2–026
right to representation, 2–024
sampling officers, 2–026
signature by proxy, 2–022—2–023
trade unions, inspection of books of, 2–026
trustees, 2–021
valuer, signing for, 2–026
Agents' rights
commercial agents, 7–002
co-operation, 7–001, 7–002, 7–041
goods bought in own name, 7–100—7–102
indemnity
  liabilities incurred during agency,
    7–057—7–062
  non-availability, 7–063—7–070
interplead, 7–103—7–104
liens
  agents, of, 7–074—7–086
  definitions, 7–071—7–073
  extinguishment, 7–090—7–094
  loss of, 7–090—7–094
  principal, confined to rights of,
    7–087—7–089
  sub-agents, of, 7–095—7–099
reimbursement
  expenses incurred during agency,
    7–057—7–062
  non-availability, 7–063—7–070
remuneration
  breach of duty, 7–048—7–051
  effective cause of transaction,
    7–027—7–032
  entitlement to, 7–003—7–012
  implied terms, 7–005
  misconduct, 7–048—7–051
  on happening of event, 7–013—7–026
  principal preventing agent from earning,
    7–033—7–044
  scale, 7–005
  specific performance, 7–045—7–047
  unauthorised transactions, 7–048—7–051
  unlawful transactions, 7–052—7–056
restitution
  money paid by mistake, 9–099—9–100
suing on behalf of principal, 9–010
title to sue, 9–008, 9–035, 9–093, 9–098
Alien enemies
agency of necessity, 4–005
capacity
  to act as agent, 2–012
  to act as principal, 2–010
principal as, 6–070, 10–003

ratification, 2–066, 2–070
Allotment of shares
ratification, limits on, 2–094
Ambiguity
agents' duties, 6–010—6–011
express actual authority, 3–019—3–020
Apparent authority
see also Actual authority; Authority
conflict of laws, 12–016
creation of agency, 2–005
dispositions of property by agent,
8–125—8–128
exceeding authority, and, 6–004
meaning, 1–011, 1–014, 3–001, 3–004
principal/third party relations
acts outside, 8–065—8–067
generally, 8–010—8–046
shipmasters, 4–007
sub-agents
delegation to, 5–005
principal, relationship with, 5–015
termination
death, 10–032
examples, 10–033
general rule, 10–030—10–031
incapacity, 10–032
warranty of authority, 9–071
Apparent ownership
dispositions of property by agent,
8–129—8–133
Appointments
agents
express appointment, 2–027—2–028
formalities, 2–035—2–036
powers of attorney, 2–039
purchase of land, 2–037
Arbitration clauses
authority, types of, 3–012
Architects
plans, claim to, 6–091
production of documents, 6–091
Assault
ratification, 2–061
Assent
see Consent
Assumption of responsibility
agents' liabilities, 6–005
tortious liability of principal, 8–183
Attornment
agents' liabilities, 9–113
dispositions of property to agent, 8–172
Attribution
fiduciary duty, 6–037—6–038
Auctioneers
agents' liabilities, 9–023, 9–034
cash, sales for
authority to accept other forms of payment,
6–007
clerks, authority of, 5–007
collateral contracts, 9–006
dealing with principal, 6–070
defences, 9–029
delegation, 5–002, 5–007

deposits, 9–025
disposition of property, 8–147, 8–151
duty of care, 6–024
estoppel as to principal's title, 6–112
liens, 7–075, 7–077, 7–086, 9–009
misappropriation, 8–201
reimbursement, 7–062, 7–070
remuneration
effective cause of transaction, 7–032
entitlement to, 7–012
unauthorised transactions, 7–051
reservation of authority, 8–045
special property, 9–009
unauthorised acts, 7–051, 8–061
Auctions
acquiring benefit in breach of duty, 6–083
Auditors
implied agency, 2–034
Authorisation
tortious liability of principal, 8–181
Authority
see also Actual authority; Apparent authority; Irrevocable authority; Usual authority
act illegally, to, 2–025
arbitration clauses, 3–012
basis of power, 1–013
burden of proof, 3–007
co-agents, 2–043—2–044
companies, exercise of authority on behalf of, 2–038
conflict of laws, 12–009
co-principals, 2–045—2–046
delegation
administrative law, 5–006
apparent authority, 5–005, 5–015
examples, 5–007
general rule, 5–002
introduction, 5–001
ministerial acts, 5–003
unauthorised, effect of, 5–004
jurisdiction clauses, 3–012
meaning, 3–001—3–002
necessity, 3–006
powers of attorney, construction of,
3–013—3–015
principal retaining right to act personally,
3–008—3–009
principal's benefit, not acting in
comment, 3–011
general rule, 3–010
sub agents' liens, 7–097
types of
actual authority, 3–001, 3–003
apparent authority, 3–001, 3–004
arbitration clauses, 3–012
jurisdiction clauses, 3–012
necessity, 3–006
principal's benefit, acting in, 3–010—3–011
usual authority, 3–005
Bailees
agency of necessity, 4–004, 4–006—4–008, 4–013

distinction from agents, 1–033
estoppel as to principal's title, 6–110, 6–111
liability of
  conversion, in, 4–006
Bailiffs
fees of, liability for, 9–003
liabilities
  repayment of money, 9–106
Bank managers
acts outside authority, 8–067
extension of existing authority, 8–044
notification to agent, 8–207
Bankers
bankers' drafts, ratification of, 2–083
dispositions of principal's property, 8–128
documentary credit managers, 2–109
fraud of agent, 8–064
unauthorised acts, 8–061
Bankruptcy
agent, of, 8–164
conversion by innocent agent, 9–131
dispositions and payments to agent, 8–171
dispositions of property, 8–156
election, 8–121
knowledge acquired through agent, 8–217
money held to use of third parties, 9–114
notice of, 8–207
petition
  malicious presentation, 9–125
priority in, 9–035, 9–136
repayment of money received for principal,
  9–109
restitution, 8–164, 8–165, 8–167
settlement, 8–109, 8–112
third party implicated in agent's breach,
  8–223
trustees in, 2–083
undisclosed principals, 8–069
Banks
breach of trust, 9–141
instructions by sole directors, 6–009
Barristers
agency duties
  compromising actions, 6–003
  warn and advise, 6–003
Beneficiaries
ratification of acts on behalf of unknown,
  2–070
Bets
see Wagering contracts
Bilateral contracts
agents' liabilities, 6–005
compensation for termination of authority,
  10–042
Bills of exchange
acceptance for honour, 4–003
agents' dealings with, 8–140
agents' liabilities, 9–050—9–056
authority
  false representation of, 9–064
delegation by agent, 5–007
principal/third party relations, 8–089—8–093

Bills of lading
agents' duties
  on indorsing, 6–007
  sending within reasonable time, 6–014
agents' rights to sue, 9–010
charterparties, 9–096
estoppel
  denying agency, 2–109
  parties to contract, 9–030
false representation of authority, 9–064,
  9–117
freight forwarders, 9–024
loading broker, 9–076
negligent issue of, 9–083
restriction of liability, 9–027
vicarious immunity, 9–122
warranty of authority, 9–065, 9–076
Bills of sale
agents' powers, 2–026
Books
inspection of by agent, 2–026
production of by agent, 6–090, 6–093
Borrowers
distinction from agents, 1–037
Breach of contract
inducement
  personal liability of agent, 9–121
Breach of duty
agents
  third party involvement with,
    8–218—8–226
  remuneration, 7–048, 7–050—7–051
Breach of trust
agents' liabilities
  accessory liability, 9–134—9–135
  banks, 9–141
  examples, 9–142
  inconsistent dealing, 9–134, 9–137
  ministerial agents, 9–134, 9–139
  receipt of trust property, 9–134, 9–136
  solicitors, 9–140
  trustees de son tort, 9–138
Breach of warranty of authority
see also Warranty of authority
measure of damages for, 9–077—9–083
Bribery
breach of duty
  third party involvement, 8–222, 8–224
sub-agents, 5–012
Bribes
benefits in breach of duty, 6–080
criminal law, 6–088
disclosure, 6–086
examples, 6–089
general duty, 6–084
meaning, 6–085
remedies of principal, 6–042, 6–044, 6–087
Brokers
see also Insurance brokers
dealing with principal, 6–070, 6–071
delegation by, 5–002
duty of care, 6–019, 6–024

information to principal, duty to supply,
  6–021
sale to principal, 6–071
standard of care, 6–024
types of agents, 1–039, 1–046
Building societies
dissolution, 2–022, 2–036
Burden of proof
authority, 3–007
Buyers
distinction from agents, 1–036, 1–043
Canvassers
confidential information, 6–078
Canvassing agents
agents' duties, 6–001
agents' liabilities, 6–005
conflict of laws, 12–031
fiduciaries, as, 6–035, 6–038
incomplete agency, 1–020
misconduct, 6–001
principal's property, use of, 6–078
Capacity
agents
  acting for both parties, 2–013
  examples, 2–016
  general rule, 2–011—2–012
  minors, 2–015
  one party as agent for other, 2–014
conflict of laws, 12–019
principals
  alien enemies, 2–010
  general rule, 2–006—2–007
  mentally disordered persons, 2–009
  minors, 2–008
Care and skill
see Agents' duties; Reasonable skill and care
Cargo
insurance
  duty to carry out instructions with dispatch,
    6–014
salvage
  communication with owners, 4–008, 4–009,
    4–013
shipmasters' authority over, 4–004,
  4–007—4–009, 4–013
Carriers
agency of necessity, 4–004
ratification, effect of, 2–100
uncollected goods, 4–006
Cessation of authority unbeknown to agent
warranty of authority, 9–063
Charterparties
evidence of, 9–040, 9–042
express restriction of liability, 9–027
unidentified principals, 9–095—9–097
warranty of authority, 9–076
written contracts, 9–038
Chattels
liens, 7–077
ratification
  unauthorised sales, 2–061

Cheques
agents' liabilities
  contract, 9–050—9–056
  tort, 9–130
principal/third party relations, 8–089—8–093
Chinese walls
conflict of interest, 6–049—6–053
Clerks
auctioneers, of, 2–014, 5–007
leases, signature on, 5–007
signatures, 2–014, 2–034
Co-agents
authority, 2–043—2–044
liability for wrongs of, 9–132—9–133
Cocoa options
purchase from principal, 6–070
Collateral contracts
agents' liabilities, 6–005, 9–006
Commencement of proceedings
ratification following, 2–057, 2–086
solicitors' warranty of authority, 9–067
Commercial agents
activities of, 11–012
background, 11–001
canvassing agents, 11–018
commodity exchanges, 11–023
compensation
  British cases, 11–051—11–053
  calculation, 11–049
  entitlement to, 11–040
  French law, 11–050
  generally, 11–048
  non-derogation, 11–054
  not due, 11–056—11–057
  termination of authority, 10–041
  time limit, 11–055
conflict of laws, 11–006, 12–033
consumer credit agents, 11–023
continuing authority, 11–017
Crown agents, 11–023
duties
  agent to principal, 6–006, 11–024
  principal to agent, 11–025
EU law
  Directive, 11–002
  implementation into UK law, 11–003
  interpretation, 11–004
indemnity
  damages, 11–047
  entitlement to, 11–040
  generally, 11–044
  non-derogation, 11–045
  not due, 11–056—11–057
  time limit, 11–046
mail order catalogue agents, 11–023
meaning of, 11–013
negotiating sales or purchases, 11–018,
  11–019
purchase of goods, 11–016, 11–018, 11–019
Regulations
  applicability, 11–006—11–011
  conflict of laws, 11–006
  coverage, 11–005

illustrations, 11–007—11–010
implementation of, 11–003
interpretation, 11–004
remuneration
    commission, 11–028—11–029
    date for payment, 11–033
    due date, 11–033
    effective cause of transaction, 7–031
    entitlement to, 7–011
    exclusion by contract terms, 11–035
    geographical zone, 11–031
    happening of event, on, 7–026
    modification by contract terms, 11–035
    no agreement, 11–027
    principal preventing agent from earning,
        7–043
    repeat orders, 11–030
    right to, 11–034
    supply of information, 11–036
    transactions after agency terminated,
        11–032
sale of goods, 11–016, 11–018, 11–019
secondary activity, as, 11–020—11–022
self-employment, 11–015
sub-agents, 11–014
termination of agency
    compensation, 10–041, 11–038, 11–040,
        11–048—11–057
    fixed period contracts, 11–037, 11–043
    indefinite period contracts, 11–038, 11–042
    indemnity, 11–040, 11–044—11–048,
        11–056—11–057
    non-derogation from provisions, 11–041,
        11–045, 11–054
    restraint of trade, 11–058
    savings for general law, 11–039
    written statement of terms of contract,
        11–026
types of agents, 1–039, 1–044
Commission
    see also Remuneration
    commercial agents, 11–028—11–029
    sub-agents, 5–004
Committees
    acting by majority, 2–043, 2–044
    co-agents' authority, 2–044
Commodity exchanges
    commercial agents, 11–023
Commodore
    ratification, effect of, 2–100
Common law
    irrevocable authority, 10–007
Companies
    acquiring benefits in breach of fiduciary duty,
        6–081
    attributing acts, omissions and states of mind
        to, 1–028
    conflict of interest, 6–049
    directing mind and will of, 1–029
    exercise of authority on behalf of, 2–038
    name, 9–055
    promoters
        fictitious principals, 9–087

fiduciary duty, 6–035, 6–036
ratification, 2–064
warranty of authority, 9–066
ratification
    company secretaries, 2–100
    goods ordered and used by company, 2–083
    pre-incorporation acts, 2–064
right to sue, 9–008, 9–087, 9–096
secretaries
    bribes, 6–089
    promissory notes, liability re, 9–056
    ratification, effect of, 2–100
    warranty of authority, 9–076
shareholders as agents, 1–030
subsidiary as agent, 1–030
termination of authority on death, 10–018
unincorporated
    fictitious principals, 9–087
    right to sue, 9–087, 9–096
    warranty of authority, 9–066, 9–076
Company agents
    knowledge acquired through agent, 8–214
Compensation
    commercial agents
        British cases, 11–051—11–053
        calculation, 11–049
        entitlement to, 11–040
        French law, 11–050
        generally, 11–048
        non-derogation, 11–054
        not due, 11–056—11–057
        termination of agency, 10–041, 11–038,
            11–040, 11–048—11–057
        time limit, 11–055
    equitable compensation, 6–043
    remedies for breach of fiduciary duty, 6–042
    termination of authority
        bilateral contract for services, 10–042
        commercial agents, 10–041
        employees, 10–040
        examples, 10–046
        general rule, 10–038—10–039
        gratuitous agents, 10–044
        unilateral contracts, 10–043
        wrongful termination, 10–045
Competence
    agency of necessity, 4–005
    ratification
        competence at time act done, 2–065
        competence at time of ratification, 2–066
Concessionaires
    distinction from agents, 1–035
Conduct
    estoppel from denying agency, 2–105
Confidential information
    compensation for losses, 6–043
    fiduciary duty
        acquiring benefit from use of principal's
            property, 6–075
        generally, 6–077
        not to profit from position, 6–074
    former client conflicts, 6–051

Confirming houses in international sales
agents' liabilities, 9–021
Conflict of interest
account for profits, liability to, 6–047
Chinese walls, 6–049—6–053
companies, 6–049
contractual modification of duty, 6–056
custom or usage, 6–057
examples, 6–061
"fair dealing" conflict, 6–049, 6–053
financial considerations, 6–047
Financial Services and Markets Act 2000, 6–060
former client" conflict, 6–049, 6–051
"future client" conflict, 6–047
general duty, 6–046
material conflict, 6–047
partnerships, 6–049
positive obligation to inform, 6–054
principals with conflicting interests, 6–048
public law, 6–060
same matter" conflict, 6–049, 6–050
separate matter" conflict, 6–049, 6–052
statutory disclosure requirements, 6–055
unfair contract terms, 6–058—6–059
Conflict of laws
actual authority, 12–017
agency of necessity, 12–032
agent/principal relationship
conferral of authority, 12–009
consumer contracts, 12–006
employment contracts, 12–007
fiduciary duties, 12–008
generally, 12–004
habitual residence, 12–005
powers of attorney, 12–010
apparent authority, 12–016
canvassing agents, 12–031
capacity, 12–019
commercial agents, 11–006, 12–033
corporations, 12–020
external aspects of agency, 12–002
formalities of relationship, 12–021
indirect representation, 12–029—12–030
internal aspects of agency
agent/principal relationship, 12–004
generally, 12–002
Rome I Regulation, 12–003
introduction, 12–001
irrevocable authority, 12–024
powers of attorney, 12–010
principal/third party relationships
authority, and, 12–012—12–013
common law approach, 12–014
generally, 12–011
law governing, 12–015
property, 12–035
public law, 12–022
ratification, 12–025
reservations, 12–018
restitution, 12–036
revocation of authority, 12–023
Rome I Regulation

agent's fiduciary duties, 12–008
consumer contracts, 12–006
employment contracts, 12–007
generally, 12–003
habitual residence, 12–005
tortious liability, 12–027, 12–034
unauthorised agents, 12–026
undisclosed principals, 12–028
unjust enrichment, 12–036
Consensual agency
fundamental role of, 1–005
paradigm case, 1–012
Consent
consensual agency
creation of, 2–003
creation of agency
contract relevance, 2–003
express agreements, 2–027—2–028
implied agreements, 2–029—2–034
fiduciary duty, 6–039
principals, of, 6–039
Consumer contracts
conflict of laws
agent/principal relationship, 12–006
Consumer credit agents
role of, 11–023
Consumer credit agreements
implied agency, 2–034
Consumer protection
unfair contract terms, 6–059
Continuing authority
commercial agents, 11–017
Contracts
agents' liabilities
admissibility of evidence, 9–039—9–042
alternative liability, 9–006
auctioneers, 9–023
bills of exchange, 9–050—9–056
cheques, 9–050—9–056
collateral contracts, 9–006
confirming houses in international sales, 9–021
Crown agents, 9–028
damages, 9–013
deeds, 9–047—9–049
defences, 9–029
del credere agents, 9–022
deposits, 9–025
election, 9–007, 9–057—9–059
entitlement, 9–005
estoppel as to parties to contract, 9–030
examples, 9–034
express restriction of liability, 9–027
fictitious principals, 9–018, 9–084—9–087
foreign principals, 9–020
freight forwarders, 9–024
general rule, 9–004—9–005
identified principals, 9–091, 9–094
indirect representation, 9–014
insurance cases, 9–011
interrogatories on existence of undisclosed principal, 9–015
interrogatories on name of unidentified

principal, 9–017
joint and several liability, 9–006
joint liability, 9–006
liens, 9–009
merger, 9–057—9–059
non-existent principals, 9–018,
9–084—9–087
oral contracts, 9–043—9–046
own principal, 9–019, 9–088—9–097
personal liability, 9–117
promissory notes, 9–050—9–056
sole liability, 9–006
special property, 9–009
stakeholders, agent as, 9–026
statute, 9–033
suretyship, 9–006
tort, 9–032
undisclosed principals, 9–012, 9–015
unidentified principals, 9–016, 9–017,
9–092, 9–095
warranty of authority, 9–031,
9–060—9–083
written contracts, 9–036—9–038
agents' powers, 2–019
agents' rights
right to sue, 9–008, 9–035, 9–093, 9–098
suing on behalf of principal, 9–010
duty of skill and care, 6–016
estoppel from denying agency, 2–106
general rule, 9–001—9–003
principal/third party relations
acts outside actual or apparent authority,
8–065—8–067
apparent authority, 8–010—8–046
bills of exchange, 8–089—8–093
cheques, 8–089—8–093
deeds, 8–083—8–088
defences to action, 8–094—8–099
disclosed principals, 8–001—8–009
fraud of agent, 8–062—8–064
merger and election, 8–113—8–124
promissory notes, 8–089—8–093
set-off affecting rights of principal,
8–107—8–112
settlement affecting recourse to principal,
8–100—8–106
settlement affecting rights of principal,
8–107—8–112
unauthorised acts where third party aware,
8–047—8–061
undisclosed principals, 8–068—8–082
ratification
acts capable of, 2–055
generally, 2–053
reimbursement of expenses, 7–059
remuneration, 7–004, 7–010
sub-agents, by, 5–009
tortious liability of agents, 6–003
Contracts of employment
agents' duties, 6–001
conflict of laws
agent/principal relationship, 12–007

Contribution
personal liability of agent, 9–123
tortious liability of principal, 8–191
Contributory negligence
fiduciaries, 6–043
tortious liability of principal, 8–188
Control
features of agency, 1–018, 6–009
Conversion
acceptor for honour, 4–006
agents' liabilities, 6–003, 9–126—9–131
bailees' liabilities, 4–006
ratification, 2–048, 2–056, 2–061
stoppage of goods in transit, 2–091
Co-principals
authority, 2–045—2–046, 6–100
disclosure to, 6–039
money held for principal, 6–100
Corporate opportunities
disclosure and consent, 6–039
Corporations
conflict of laws, 12–020
tortious liability of principal, 8–189
Costs
breach of warranty of authority, 9–081
Cotton brokers
duty to carry out instructions with dispatch,
6–014
Course of dealing
implied authority, 3–041—3–042
Crown
tortious liability of principal, 8–190
Crown agents
agents' liabilities, 9–028
apparent authority of Crown agents, 8–042
personal liability, 9–124
ratification, 2–053
role of, 11–023
warranty of authority, 9–074
Custom
conflict of interest, 6–057
Customary authority
implied authority, 3–033—3–040
Damages
see also Measure of damages
agents' liabilities, 9–013
commercial agents
indemnity, 11–047
Dealing with principal
basis of principle, 6–063
examples, 6–070—6–072
former agents, 6–067
general duty, 6–062
gifts, 6–069
purchase from principal, 6–064, 6–070
remedies of principal, 6–068
sale to principal, 6–065, 6–071
specific instructions, agent with, 6–066
Death
ratification following, 2–088
termination of authority
apparent authority, 10–032
companies, 10–018

examples, 10–022
general rule, 10–015—10–016
indemnity, 10–016
partnerships, 10–019
ratification by executors, 10–017
reimbursement, 10–016
remuneration, 10–016
Debts
payment by non-debtor
ratification following, 2–088
Deceit
liability of agent, 9–117
liability of principal, 8–185
Declarations
remedies for breach of fiduciary duty, 6–044
Declarations of trust
irrevocable authority, 10–010
Decrees
sale under, 2–034
Deeds
agents' liabilities, 9–047—9–049
authority to execute, 2–040
execution
agents' powers, 2–019, 2–040—2–042
principal/third party relations, 8–083—8–088
Deeds of arrangement
execution by agent, 2–026
Defences
agents' liabilities, 9–029
principal/third party relations, 8–094—8–099
Del credere agents
agents' liabilities, 9–022
liability of, 6–026
types of agents, 1–039, 1–042, 1–043
Del credere commission
sub-agents, use of, 5–016
Delegation
agents' powers, 2–021
authority
administrative law, 5–006
apparent authority, 5–005, 5–015
examples, 5–007
general rule, 5–002
introduction, 5–001
ministerial acts, 5–003
unauthorised, effect of, 5–004
tortious liability of principal
casual delegation, 8–187
non-delegable duties, 8–184
unauthorised
authority, effect of, 5–004
sub agents' liens, 7–096
Delegatus non potest delegare
general rule, 5–002
Deposits
agents' liabilities, 9–025
interest, 6–109
receipts
estate agent, by, 2–083
stakeholders, 6–104
Diligence
duty of
canvassing agents, 6–014

dealing for competitors, 6–015
estate agents, 6–014
examples, 6–016
generally, 6–012—6–013
Directors
accessory liability, 9–135, 9–142
acquiring benefit in breach of duty, 6–083
bank instructions by sole director, 6–009
breach of fiduciary duty, liability for, 6–045
bribes, 6–089
co-agents' authority, 2–044
conflict of interest, 6–039, 6–061
dealing with principal, 6–071
deceit, 9–117
delegation by, 5–002
disclosure, 6–039
fictitious principals, 9–087
liability for authorised purchase of failing
business, 6–007
managing director, 3–029
misrepresentation, 9–117, 9–119, 9–120
personal liability of agent, 9–119
principal's property, use of, 6–078
ratification, effect of, 2–100
signatures
company name, 9–055, 9–056
warranty of authority, 9–064, 9–076, 9–079,
9–083
Disclosed principals
dispositions of property to agent, 8–170
meaning, 1–039, 1–041
principal/third party relations, 8–001—8–009
Disclosure
bribes, 6–086
conflict of interest, 6–048—6–056
dealing with principal
former agents, 6–067
generally, 6–062
purchases from, 6–064, 6–070
remedies, 6–068
sales to, 6–065, 6–071
fiduciary duty, 6–039
insurance broker, 6–021
joint principals, 6–039
secret profits, 6–076
ship's agent, 6–021
Discounts
bribes, and, 6–085, 6–089
Discretion
agents' liabilities, 6–003
agents' powers, 2–021
duty of care, and, 6–020
stockbrokers, 6–007
Dishonest assistance
breach of duty
third party involvement, 8–225
Dismissal
remuneration, 7–040
Dispositions of property
by agent
actual authority, 8–125—8–128
apparent authority, 8–125—8–128
apparent ownership, 8–129—8–133

Factors Act 1889, protection by,
  8–143—8–158
indicia of property, agent entrusted with,
  8–134—8–138
restitutionary claims, 8–159—8–167
to agent
  attornment, 8–172
  disclosed principals, 8–170
  estoppel, 8–173
  examples, 8–175
  general rule, 8–168—8–169
  restitutionary claims, 8–174
  undisclosed principals, 8–171
Distress
agents' powers, 2–026
ratification
  acts capable of, 2–061
  effect of, 2–100
  example, 2–083
  knowledge required, 2–073
Distributors
agents' duties, 6–001
distinction from agents, 1–035
Documents
production of, 6–090, 6–093
Due diligence
features of agency, 1–017
Duties of agents
see Agents' duties
Election
agents' liabilities, 9–007, 9–057—9–059
principal/third party relations, 8–113—8–124
ratification, 2–050
Emergencies
see also Agency of necessity
restitution for expenses incurred in, 4–010
Employees
compensation for termination of authority,
  10–040
fidelity, 6–054
Employment contracts
see Contracts of employment
Equity
agents' liabilities
  breach of trust, 9–134—9–142
breach of trust
  accessory liability, 9–134—9–135
  banks, 9–141
  examples, 9–142
  inconsistent dealing, 9–134, 9–137
  ministerial agents, 9–134, 9–139
  receipt of trust property, 9–134, 9–136
  solicitors, 9–140
  trustees de son tort, 9–138
irrevocable authority, 10–010
revocation of authority, 10–025
Estate agents
agents' duties
  regulation, and, 6–001
agents' liabilities, 6–005
client accounts, 6–041
conflict of interest, 6–048, 6–052, 6–071
dealing with principal, 6–071

delegation by, 5–002
duty of care, 6–019, 6–024
exclusive agency, 6–005
information to principal, duty to supply,
  6–021, 6–045
ratification
  knowledge required, 2–073
  scope of, 2–083
regulation of, 6–001
remuneration
  conclusion, 7–023
  custom, 7–022
  entitlement to, 7–007, 7–017
  generally, 7–015
  introduction to person ready to purchase,
    7–019
  introduction to purchaser, 7–018
  nature of contract, 7–016
  other types of contract, 7–021
  principal preventing agent from earning,
    7–036—7–038
  Regulations, 7–020
sale to principal, 6–071
sole agency, 6–005
stakeholders, as, 6–104
unilateral contracts, 6–005
Estoppel
agents' liabilities, 9–030
creation of agency, 2–005, 2–102
denying existence of agency
  agency situations, 2–103
  bills of lading, 2–109
  by representation, 2–104
  conduct of principal, 2–105
  contract, 2–106
  documentary credit managers, 2–109
  extensions of time, 2–109
  general rule, 2–101
  guarantee with illegible signature, 2–109
  ratification, 2–108
  sale of goods by impostor, 2–109
  sale of land under power of attorney, 2–109
  spouses, 2–109
  tort, 2–107
dispositions of property to agent, 8–173
gratuitous agents, 6–030
principal's title, as to
  examples, 6–112
  general rule, 6–110
  scope of, 6–111
ratification, and, 2–080, 2–108
Ethics
further instructions, duty to follow, 6–009
EU law
commercial agents
  Directive, 11–002
  implementation into UK law, 11–003
  interpretation, 11–004
ratification, 2–052
European zone controllers
conflict of interest, 6–061
Exclusive agents
agents' liabilities, 6–005, 7–016

Execution
deeds
agents' powers, 2–019, 2–040—2–042
Executors
ratification by, 2–021, 10–017
Exercise of options
agents' powers, 2–026
Express actual authority
ambiguous terms, 3–019—3–020
not given by deed, 3–016—3–018
powers of attorney, 3–013—3–015
Express agreement
creation of agency, 2–027—2–028
Express authority
agency of necessity, 4–005
Extensions of time
estoppel from denying agency, 2–109
Factors
delegation by, 5–002
dispositions of property by agent,
8–143—8–158
paying over money held for principal, 6–101
ratification, effect of, 2–100
sub-agents, use of, 5–016
types of agents, 1–039, 1–046
Fair dealing
agents dealing with principal, 6–063
conflict of interest, 6–049, 6–053
Fictitious principals
agents' liabilities, 9–018, 9–084—9–087
Fiduciary duty
account, duty to
account, 6–097
account stated, 6–098
action of account, 6–095
general duty, 6–094
substantive significance, 6–096
accounts, duty to keep
accounts, 6–092
documents, 6–093
general rule, 6–090
separation of property, 6–091
acquiring benefits in breach of duty
acquiring asset in own name, 6–082
corporate opportunities, 6–081
examples, 6–083
general duty, 6–079
scope of principal, 6–080
attribution of, 6–037—6–038
breach of, 6–005, 6–079—6–083
bribes
criminal law, 6–088
disclosure, 6–086
examples, 6–089
general duty, 6–084
meaning, 6–085
remedies of principal, 6–087
conflict of interest
account for profits, liability to, 6–047
agent/principal relationship, 12–008
Chinese walls, 6–049—6–053
companies, 6–049
contractual modification of duty, 6–056

custom or usage, 6–057
examples, 6–061
fair dealing" conflict, 6–049, 6–053
financial considerations, 6–047
Financial Services and Markets Act 2000,
6–060
former client" conflict, 6–049, 6–051
general duty, 6–046
generally, 6–039
material conflict, 6–047
partnerships, 6–049
positive obligation to inform, 6–054
principals with conflicting interests, 6–048
public law, 6–060
same matter" conflict, 6–049, 6–050
separate matter" conflict, 6–049, 6–052
statutory disclosure requirements, 6–055
unfair contract terms, 6–058—6–059
consent, 6–039
dealing with principal
basis of principle, 6–063
examples, 6–070—6–072
former agents, 6–067
general duty, 6–062
gifts, 6–069
purchase from principal, 6–064, 6–070
remedies of principal, 6–068
sale to principal, 6–065, 6–071
specific instructions, agent with, 6–066
development of, 6–036
disclosure, 6–039
general principle, 6–033
interest, liability for
examples, 6–109
financial services, 6–106
general rule, 6–102—6–103
proceedings, following, 6–108
rate of interest, 6–107
solicitors, 6–105, 6–109
stakeholders, 6–104
introduction, 6–001
loyalty, 6–039—6–045
meaning, 6–034
nature of, 6–035
paying over money held for principal
common law duty, 6–099
examples, 6–101
illegal transactions, 6–100
joint principals, 6–100
payments to third parties, 6–100
remedies, 6–041
restitution, and, 6–100
position, use of, 6–079—6–083
principal's property, use of
confidential information, 6–077
examples, 6–078
general duty, 6–075
property, meaning of, 6–076
profits made, 6–042, 6–073—6–074
remedies of principal
agent holding money for principal, 6–041
declarations, 6–044

equitable compensation for losses caused, 6–043
examples, 6–045
injunctions, 6–044
profits made in breach of duty to principal, 6–042
proprietary or personal, 6–040
rescission, 6–044
remuneration, 7–006
secret commissions, 6–084—6–089
Fiduciary relationship
agents, 1–015
sub-agent and principal, 5–012
Finance companies
dealer as agent of, 2–034, 8–207
Financial limits
ratification
exceeding limit set by principal, 2–061, 2–072, 2–083, 2–100
Financial Services and Markets Act 2000
conflict of interest, 6–060
Fisherman's co-operative
gratuitous agents, liability of, 6–032
Fixed term contracts
termination of agency
commercial agents, 11–037, 11–043
Food safety
samples obtained by agents, 2–026
Foreign principals
see Overseas principals
Forgery
ratification, 2–059, 2–061
Forwarding agents
duty of care, 6–024
further instructions, duty to follow, 6–009
Franchisees
distinction from agents, 1–035
Fraud
duty to account, 6–098
ratification, 2–061
Fraud of agent
knowledge acquired through agent, 8–214
principal/third party relations, 8–062—8–064
Fraud on a power
application of concept, 6–036
Freight forwarders
agents' liabilities, 9–024
Funeral expenses
restitution, 4–010
Furniture salesmen
estoppel from denying existence of agency, 2–109
Gambling
reimbursement of expenses, 7–069
remuneration, 7–055
General agents
types of agents, 1–039, 1–045
Gifts
dealing with principal, 6–067
irrevocable authority, 10–010
Good faith
agency of necessity, 4–005
commercial agents, 6–006

Goods
liens, 7–077
Goods in own name
breach of fiduciary duty, and, 6–082
Gratuitous agents
agents' liabilities
examples, 6–032
exclusions of liability, 6–030
generally, 6–001, 6–003, 6–005, 6–027
non-feasance, 6–029
standard of care, 6–031
tort, 6–028
compensation for termination of authority, 10–044
duty of skill and care, 6–016
Guarantees
estoppel from denying agency, 2–109
Habitual residence
conflict of laws
agent/principal relationship, 12–005
Hotel broker
conflict of interest, 6–048
Housing society
bribery, 6–089
Identified principals
agents' liabilities, 9–091, 9–094
meaning, 1–039, 1–041
Identity fraud
solicitors' warranty of authority, 9–068
Illegality
agent's duties to principal in respect of, 6–023
agents' liabilities, 6–003
agents' powers, 2–025
duty to account, 6–098
further instructions, duty to follow, 6–009
money held for principal, 6–100
ratification, 2–060
remuneration, 7–054
unlawful customs, 3–038
Implied actual authority
course of dealing, 3–041—3–042
customary authority, 3–033—3–040
incidental authority, 3–021—3–023
managerial agents, 3–027—3–029
professional agents, 3–030—3–032
receiving payment of money, 3–024—3–026
usual authority, 3–027—3–032
Implied agreements
creation of agency
assent of agent, 2–032
assent of principal, 2–031
examples, 2–034
general rule, 2–029—2–030
Implied authority
shipmasters
emergency powers, 4–007
inference from conduct, 4–008
Implied terms
remuneration, 7–005
Impossibility
agency of necessity, 4–005
Impracticality
agency of necessity, 4–005

Incapacity
remuneration, 7–053
termination of authority, 10–015, 10–020,
10–022, 10–032
Incidental authority
implied authority, 3–021—3–023
Incomplete agency
canvassing agents, 1–020
indirect representation, 1–021—1–022
introducing agents, 1–020
Inconsistent dealing
breach of trust, 9–134, 9–137
Inconvenience
agency of necessity, 4–005
Indefinite period contracts
termination of agency
commercial agents, 11–038, 11–042
Indemnities
commercial agents
damages, 11–047
entitlement to, 11–040
generally, 11–044
non-derogation, 11–045
not due, 11–056—11–057
time limit, 11–046
irrevocable authority, 10–010
termination of authority on death, 10–016
Indicia of property
dispositions of property by agent,
8–134—8–138
Indirect representation
agents' liabilities, 9–014
conflict of laws, 12–029—12–030
incomplete agency, 1–021—1–022, 8–071
Inducement of breach of contract
personal liability of agent, 9–121
Information
supply of
duty of care, 6–021
estate agents, 6–021, 6–045
insurance brokers, 6–021
Injunctions
breach of fiduciary duty, 6–044
Insolvency
termination of authority, 10–015, 10–021,
10–022
warranty of authority, 9–079
Instructions
agents' duties
further instructions from principal,
6–008—6–009
Insurance brokers
agents' duties, 6–112
agents' liabilities, 9–011
conflict of interest, 6–048
contracts, liability for, 6–026
duty of care, 6–024
duty to carry out instructions with dispatch,
6–014
gratuitous agents, liability of, 6–032
implied agency, 2–034
information to principal, duty to supply,
6–021

non-feasance, 6–029
Insurance companies
authorised repairs
implied agency, 2–034
sub-agents, liability of, 5–016
Insurance intermediaries
bribes, 6–089
Insurance policies
gratuitous arrangement, 6–032
marine insurance policy, 6–032
ratification
acts capable of, 2–100
following loss, 2–093
generally, 2–053
sub-agents, by, 5–009, 5–016
Interest
liability for
examples, 6–109
financial services, 6–106
general rule, 6–102—6–103
proceedings, following, 6–108
rate of interest, 6–107
solicitors, 6–105
stakeholders, 6–104
Interplead
agents' rights, 7–103—7–104
Interrogatories
existence of principal, 9–015
name of principal, 9–017
Intestacy
estoppel as to principal's title, 6–112
Introducing agents
incomplete agency, 1–020
Involvement in wrongs
personal liability of agent, 9–120
Irrevocable authority
common law, 10–007
completion of transactions, 10–011
conflict of laws, 12–024
declaration of trust, 10–010
equity, 10–010
examples, 10–014
general rule, 10–006
gifts, perfection of, 10–010
indemnities, 10–010
lasting powers of attorney, 10–009
payments to third parties, 10–010
powers of attorney, 10–008
proxies, 10–013
references in other contexts, 10–010
reimbursement of personal liability, 10–010
Statute of Frauds, 10–012
unsatisfied liens, 10–010
Issue of proceedings
ratification, limits on, 2–094
sub-agents, by, 5–009
Joint agents
revocation of authority, 10–028
Joint and several liability
agents' liabilities, 9–006
bribes, 6–087
Joint liability
agents' liabilities, 9–006

Joint principals
revocation of authority, 10–028
Joint tortfeasors
reimbursement of expenses, 7–068
Joint ventures
acquiring benefit in breach of duty, 6–083
Judgment against principal
personal liability of agent, 9–123
Jurisdiction clauses
authority, types of, 3–012
Knowledge
acquisition through agent
agent's own knowledge, 8–212
claims by principal against agent, 8–214
companies' agents, 8–215
duty to investigate, 8–213
examples, 8–217
fraud of agent, 8–214
general rule, 8–208—8–209
large organisations, 8–215
Law of Property Act 1925, 8–216
rationale for imputation, 8–210
scope of, 8–211
ratification, 2–071—2–073
sub-agents, acquired via, 5–009
Land agents
production of documents, 6–093
Lasting powers of attorney
irrevocable authority, 10–009
termination of authority, 10–037
Leases
agents' clerks, signature by, 5–007
dealing with principal, 6–064
Letters of credit
implied agency, 2–034
Liens
admiralty claims, 7–085
agents' liabilities, 9–009
definitions, 7–071—7–073
examples, 7–086
extinguishment or loss of
examples, 7–094
generally, 7–090
parting with possession, 7–093
tenders, 7–091
waiver, 7–092
general liens, 7–082
general rule, 7–074—7–075
goods and chattels, 7–077
inconsistent agreement, 7–081
irrevocable authority, 10–010
lawfully obtained, 7–079
maritime liens, 7–084
money, over, 7–077
non-delivery of goods, 7–081
possession, 7–078
principal, confined to rights of, 7–087—7–089
same capacity, 7–080
solicitors' charging liens, 7–083
statutory liens, 7–085
sub-agents
authority, 7–097
examples, 7–099

generally, 5–004, 5–014, 7–095
unauthorised delegation, 7–096
undisclosed principal, 7–098
when exercisable, 7–076
Limitation periods
acknowledgement and, 2–026, 2–034
agents' powers, 2–026
duty of skill and care, 6–016
Liquidators
delegation by, 5–002, 5–007
ratification, 2–061
Literacy
agents, ability to act as, 2–012
Lloyd's
brokers
capacity, 2–016
names, 5–016
Open Form, 4–008
Local authorities
inspection of accounts of, 2–026
Loyalty
fiduciary duty, 6–039—6–045
Mail order catalogue agents
role of, 11–023
Managing agents
usual authority, 3–027—3–029
Maritime liens
agents' rights, 7–084
Marriage
conditional gifts on
estoppel as to principal's title, 6–112
Married women
deserted wives
agency of necessity, 4–011
Measure of damages
breach of warranty of authority
contractual principle, 9–078
costs, 9–081
examples, 9–083
generally, 9–077
insolvent principal, 9–079
other warranties, 9–082
transactions unenforceable against
principal, 9–080
Mental incapacity
termination of authority, 10–015, 10–020,
10–022, 10–032
Mentally disordered persons
agency of necessity, 4–012
capacity
to act as agent, 2–012
to act as principal, 2–009
ratification, 2–066
Merchants
gratuitous agents, liability of, 6–032
Merger
agents' liabilities, 9–057—9–059
principal/third party relations, 8–113—8–124
Messenger
types of agents, 1–039, 1–047
Military personnel
see Service personnel

Property
conflict of laws, 12–035
principal's property, use of
confidential information, 6–077
examples, 6–078
general duty, 6–075
property, meaning of, 6–076
separation of, 6–091
Proprietary rights
ratification, limits on, 2–091
Provisional committees
see Committees
Proxies
irrevocable authority, 10–013
signature by, 2–022—2–023
Public law
conflict of interest, 6–060
conflict of laws, 12–022
Purchase of goods
commercial agents, 11–016, 11–018, 11–019
dealing with principal, 6–064, 6–070
Purchase of land
appointment of agent, 2–037
dealing with principal, 6–064, 6–070
ratification
following, 2–088
knowledge required, 2–071
Quantity surveyors
production of documents, 6–093
Quantum meruit
remuneration, 7–009
Ratification
acts capable of ratification
contract, 2–055
examples, 2–061
forgery, 2–059
general rule, 2–054
illegality, 2–060
notices, 2–057
tort, 2–056
ultra vires acts, 2–058
advance ratification, 2–049
conflict of laws, 12–025
contract, 2–053
creation of agency by
general principle, 2–047—2–048
introduction, 2–004
Crown Agents, 2–053
effect of
binding nature, 2–099
breach of unauthorised contract, 2–100
carriers, 2–100
company secretaries, 2–100
confinement to act done, 2–098
directors, 2–100
distress, 2–100
factors, 2–100
generally, 2–095—2–096
insurance policies, 2–100
shipmasters, 2–100
time limits, 2–097
entitlement
agents, 2–068

companies, 2–069
competence at time act done, 2–065
competence at time of ratification, 2–066
examples, 2–070
general rule, 2–062
person acted for, 2–063
pre-registration companies, 2–064
purported authority to bind principal, 2–063
unidentified principals, 2–067
estoppel from denying agency, 2–108
EU law, 2–052
events not preventing
commencement of proceedings, 2–086
death of principal, 2–088
examples, 2–088
generally, 2–084
payment of debt, 2–088
purchase of land, 2–088
reluctance to ratify, 2–085
retrospective effect, 2–087, 2–088
uncommunicated refusal, 2–085
exceeding authority, and, 6–004
insurance policies, 2–053
juristic nature of, 2–050
knowledge required, 2–071—2–073
limits on
general rule, 2–089—2–090
insurance policies following loss, 2–093
issue of writ without authority, 2–094
notices to quit, 2–094
options to purchase partnership share following death, 2–094
property rights, 2–091
reasonable time, 2–092
share allotments, 2–094
stoppage in transit, 2–094
tenders, errors in, 2–094
tug services, liability for, 2–094
Restatements, 2–051
scope of
acquiescence, 2–079
communication, need for, 2–078
estoppel, 2–080
evidence of, 2–082
examples, 2–083
express ratification, 2–076
generally, 2–074—2–075
implied ratification, 2–077
inactivity, 2–079
partial ratification, 2–081
sub-agents, appointment of, 5–004
termination of authority on death, 10–017
tortious liability of principal, 8–181
warranty of authority, 9–072
Reasonable skill and care
agents' duties
basis of duty, 6–018
degree of skill and care, 6–019
discretion, 6–020
examples, 6–024
generally, 6–017
illegal conduct, 6–023
information, 6–021

special skill, 6–022
Reasonable time
ratification, limits on, 2–092
Rebuttal
warranty of authority, 9–070
Receipt of trust property
breach of trust, 9–134, 9–136
Refusal
ratification following uncommunicated, 2–085
Reimbursement
expenses incurred during agency
contract, 7–059
examples, 7–062
general rule, 7–057—7–058
remuneration, right to superseded by,
7–061
restitution, 7–060
irrevocable authority, 10–010
non-availability
agent at fault, 7–066
examples, 7–070
general rule, 7–063—7–064
joint tortfeasors, 7–068
unauthorised acts, 7–065
unlawful transactions, 7–067
wagering transactions, 7–069
termination of authority on death, 10–016
Reliefs
breach of duty
third party involvement, 8–223
Remedies
breach of duty
third party involvement, 8–223
bribes, 6–087
dealing with principal, 6–068
declarations, 6–044
equitable compensation for losses caused,
6–043
examples, 6–045
injunctions, 6–044
money held for principal, 6–041
profits made in breach of duty to principal,
6–042
proprietary or personal, 6–040
rescission, 6–044
Remuneration
breach of duty, 7–048, 7–050—7–051
bribes, and, 6–087
commercial agents
commission, 11–028—11–029
date for payment, 11–033
due date, 11–033
effective cause of transaction, 7–031
entitlement to, 7–011
exclusion by contract terms, 11–035
geographical zone, 11–031
happening of event, on, 7–026
modification by contract terms, 11–035
no agreement, 11–027
principal preventing agent from earning,
7–043
repeat orders, 11–030
right to, 11–034

supply of information, 11–036
transactions after agency terminated,
11–032
effective cause of transaction
commercial agents, 7–031
examples, 7–032
general rule, 7–027—7–028
scope of rule, 7–029—7–030
entitlement to
commercial agents, 7–011
contractual claims, 7–004
contractual rights, 7–010
custom, 7–005
estate agents, 7–007
examples, 7–012
fiduciaries, 7–006
general rule, 7–003
implied terms, 7–005
quantum meruit, 7–009
scales, 7–005
unfair contract terms, 7–008
expenses incurred during agency, 7–061
generally, 1–016
happening of event, on
commercial agents, 7–026
estate agents, 7–015—7–023
general rule, 7–013—7–014
overpaid commission, 7–025
work done when commission not earned,
7–024
misconduct, 7–048—7–051
overpaid commission, 7–025
principal preventing agent from earning
case law, 7–035
commercial agents, 7–043
dismissal, 7–040
estate agents, 7–036—7–038
examples, 7–044
exclusive agency, 7–037
general rule, 7–033—7–034
prevention by other means, 7–041
principles of general application, 7–039
sole agency, 7–037
termination of authority, 7–040, 7–042
specific performance
exceptional use, 7–046
general rule, 7–045
subsistence of contract, 7–047
sub-agents, 5–012, 7–017
termination of authority on death, 10–016
unauthorised transactions
examples, 7–051
general rule, 7–048
wrongful withdrawal of authority, 7–049
unlawful transactions
examples, 7–056
general rule, 7–052
illegality, 7–054
incapacity to act, 7–053
wagering transactions, 7–055
Rent collectors
ratification
action for account of rent and profits, 2–083

Repeat orders
commercial agents
remuneration, 11–030
Rescission
remedies for breach of fiduciary duty, 6–044
Reservations
conflict of laws, 12–018
Restitution
agency of necessity, 4–010
agents' duties
repayment of money received for use of
principal, 6–100, 9–101—9–109
third parties, money held for,
9–110—9–114
agents' rights
money paid by mistake, 9–099—9–100
bribes, 6–084, 6–085, 6–087
conflict of laws, 12–036
money held for principal, 6–100
reimbursement of expenses, 7–060
sub-agents, 5–012
Restitutionary claims
dispositions of property by agent,
8–159—8–167
dispositions of property to agent, 8–174
Restraint of trade
termination of agency
commercial agents, 11–058
Retrospective effect
ratification, 2–087—2–088
Revocation of authority
conflict of laws, 12–023
equity, effect of, 10–025
examples, 10–029
general rule, 10–023—10–024
joint agents, 10–028
joint principals, 10–028
notice, 10–027
powers of attorney, 10–036
reliance, 10–026
Right to representation
agents' powers, 2–024
Romalpa clauses
restitution, 8–165
Rome I Regulation
conflict of laws
agent's fiduciary duties, 12–008
consumer contracts, 12–006
employment contracts, 12–007
generally, 12–003
habitual residence, 12–005
Sale of goods
commercial agents, 11–016, 11–018, 11–019
dealing with principal, 6–065, 6–071
estoppel from denying agency, 2–109
ratification, 2–070, 2–083
Sale of land
dealing with principal, 6–065, 6–071
estoppel from denying agency, 2–109
Salvors
warehousing of goods, 4–006, 4–008, 4–013
Same matter
conflict of interest, 6–049, 6–050

Sampling officers
agents' powers, 2–026
Secret commission
breach of duty
third party involvement, 8–222
Secret profits
fiduciary duty, 6–042, 6–084—6–089
position from, 6–079—6–083
property, from use of, 6–075—6–078
purchases from principal, 6–070
right of action concerning, 9–098
sub-agents, by, 5–012
Seized goods
ratification, 2–070
Self-employment
commercial agents, 11–015
Sellers
distinction from agents, 1–036
Separate matter
conflict of interest, 6–049, 6–052
Sergeant
fiduciary duty, 6–083
Servants
distinction from agents, 1–034
tortious liability of principal, 8–178
Service personnel
acquiring benefit in breach of duty, 6–083
Set-off
assignment, and, 9–112, 9–114
principal/third party relations, 8–107—8–112
sub-agents, 5–013
third party, against
pleaded by agent, 9–029, 9–112
Settlement
principal/third party relations
affecting recourse to principal,
8–100—8–106
affecting rights of principal, 8–107—8–112
Shareholders
as agent of company, 1–030
Sheriffs
ratification of act of, 2–070
Shipbrokers
bribes, 6–089
Shipmasters
see also Bills of lading
agency of necessity
apparent authority, 4–007
communications with shipowners, 4–007,
4–013
generally, 4–003
salvage contracts, 4–008, 4–009, 4–013
scope of authority, 4–004
vicarious liability, 4–007
bribes, 6–089
cargo, authority over 4–004, 4–007—4–009,
4–013
delegation by, 5–007
hypothecating ship
consultation, requirement for, 4–008
general authority, 4–004
indemnity of, 4–004
principal's property, use of, 6–078

ratification
 effect of, 2–100
 knowledge required, 2–071
 scope of, 2–083
sale of ship
 consultation, requirement for, 4–008
 general authority, 4–004
salvage, 4–006, 4–008—4–010, 4–013
Shipowners
 communication with, 4–007, 4–017
 ratification
 sale of ship, 2–083
 unauthorised repairs to ship, 2–083
 sub-agents, recovery from, 5–016
Ships
 estoppel as to principal's title, 6–112
Ship's agent
 delegation by, 5–007, 5–016
 duty to account, 5–016, 6–045
 gratuitous agents, liability of, 6–032
 information to principal, duty to supply,
 6–021
Shop stewards
 implied agency, 2–034
Signatures
 agents' powers
 by proxy, 2–022—2–023
 for valuers, 2–026
 charterparties, 9–076
 deeds, 9–048
 firm name, 9–055
 forgery, 9–109
 form of, 2–124, 8–004, 8–086, 9–084
 misrepresentation, 9–119
 non-existent principals, 9–086
 qualified, 9–038
 unenforceable transactions, and, 9–080
 written contracts, 9–037, 9–038
Skill and care
 see Reasonable skill and care
Sole agents
 agents' liabilities, 6–005
Solicitors
 acquiring benefit in breach of duty, 6–083
 agents' duties
 account of profits, 6–045
 compromising actions, 6–003
 conflict of interest, 6–048—6–052, 6–061
 duty of care, 6–020, 6–024
 duty to account, 6–045
 warn and advise, 6–003
 breach of trust, 9–140
 charging liens, 7–083
 dealing with principal
 former agents, 6–067
 gifts, 6–069
 mortgage from client, 6–072
 purchases from client, 6–064, 6–070
 delegation by, 5–002, 5–007
 estoppel as to principal's title, 6–112
 gratuitous agents, liability of, 6–032
 implied agency
 sale under degree, 2–034

information to principal, duty to supply,
 6–021
interest, liability for, 6, 105, 6–109
London agent, 5–007, 5–016
reimbursement, 7–056, 7–062, 7–070
sub-agents, 5–016
warranty of authority
 identity fraud, 9–068
 issue of proceedings, 9–067
Special agents
 types of agents, 1–039, 1–045
Special property
 agents' liabilities, 9–009
Specific performance
 exceptional use, 7–046
 general rule, 7–045
 subsistence of contract, 7–047
Sports agents
 acquiring benefit in breach of duty, 6–083
 conflict of interest, 6–048
Spouses
 deserted wives, 4–011
 estoppel from denying agency, 2–109
 presumed authority, 3–043
 ratification of agreement giving title to sue,
 2–070
Stakeholders
 agents' liabilities, 9–026
Standard of care
 gratuitous agents, 6–031
Statute of Frauds
 irrevocable authority, 10–012
Statutory liens
 agents' rights, 7–085
Stewards
 dealing with principal, 6–072
Stockbrokers
 conflict of interest, 6–061
 dealing with principal, 6–067, 6–070, 6–071
 discretion, 6–007
 duty of care, 6–024
 duty to carry out instructions with dispatch,
 6–014
 principal's property, use of, 6–078
Stoppage in transit
 ratification, limits on, 2–094
Stray animals
 restitution, 4–010
Strict liability
 agents' liabilities, 6–001
Sub-agents
 breach of agent's duties, 5–008
 bribes, 6–087
 commercial agents, 11–014
 delegation to
 administrative law, 5–006
 apparent authority, 5–005
 examples, 5–007
 fiduciary duties, 5–008, 5–011, 5–015
 general rule, 5–002
 introduction, 5–001
 ministerial acts, 5–003
 unauthorised, effect of, 5–004

dishonest assistance by, 5–008
liability for wrongs of, 9–132—9–133
liens
  authority, 7–097
  examples, 7–099
  generally, 5–004, 5–014, 7–095
  unauthorised delegation, 7–096
  undisclosed principal, 7–098
principal, relationship with
  apparent authority, 5–015
  binding nature of acts, 5–009
  equitable liability, 5–012
  examples, 5–016
  generally, 5–008
  lien, 5–014
  no privity of contract, 5–011
  privity of contract, 5–008, 5–010
  set-off, 5–013
purchasing from principal, 6–064
Subsidiaries
as agent of company, 1–030
Supply of goods
ratification, 2–070
Supply of information
commercial agents
  remuneration, 11–036
Supply of services
distinction from agents, 1–038
Suretyship
agents' liabilities, 9–006
Surveyors
conflict of interest, 6–061
Tenders
extinguishment of liens, 7–091
ratification, limits on, 2–094
Termination
actual authority, 10–002—10–005
apparent authority
  death, 10–032
  examples, 10–033
  general rule, 10–030—10–031
  incapacity, 10–032
commercial agents
  compensation, 11–038, 11–040,
    11–048—11–057
  fixed period contracts, 11–037, 11–043
  indefinite period contracts, 11–038, 11–042
  indemnity, 11–040, 11–044—11–048,
    11–056—11–057
  non-derogation from provisions, 11–041,
    11–045, 11–054
  remuneration for transactions after, 11–032
  restraint of trade, 11–058
  savings for general law, 11–039
  written statement of terms of contract,
    11–026
compensation
  bilateral contract for services, 10–042
  commercial agents, 10–041
  employees, 10–040
  examples, 10–046
  general rule, 10–038—10–039
  gratuitous agents, 10–044

unilateral contracts, 10–043
wrongful termination, 10–045
death
  apparent authority, 10–032
  companies, 10–018
  examples, 10–022
  general rule, 10–015—10–016
  partnerships, 10–019
  ratification by executors, 10–017
insolvency, 10–015, 10–021, 10–022
introduction, 10–001
irrevocable authority
  common law, 10–007
  completion of transactions, 10–011
  declaration of trust, 10–010
  equity, 10–010
  examples, 10–014
  general rule, 10–006
  gifts, perfection of, 10–010
  indemnities, 10–010
  lasting powers of attorney, 10–009
  payments to third parties, 10–010
  powers of attorney, 10–008
  proxies, 10–013
  references in other contexts, 10–010
  reimbursement of personal liability, 10–010
  Statute of Frauds, 10–012
  unsatisfied liens, 10–010
mental incapacity, 10–015, 10–020, 10–022
powers of attorney
  general rule, 10–034—10–035
  lasting powers of attorney, 10–037
  revocation, 10–036
remuneration, 7–040, 7–042
renunciation, 10–023
revocation
  equity, effect of, 10–025
  examples, 10–029
  general rule, 10–023—10–024
  joint agents, 10–028
  joint principals, 10–028
  notice, 10–027
  reliance, 10–026
Third parties
agents relationship with
  contract, 9–001—9–098
  equity, 9–135—9–142
  restitution, 9–099—9–114
  torts, 9–115—9–133
involvement with agent's breach of duty
  breach of equitable duty, 8–221
  bribery, 8–222, 8–224
  common law claims, 8–219
  dishonest assistance, 8–225
  equitable claims, 8–220
  examples, 8–226
  generally, 8–218
  reliefs, 8–223
  remedies, 8–223
  secret commission, 8–222
money held for principal, 6–100
payments to
  irrevocable authority, 10–010

principals' relationship with
    conflict of laws, 12–011—12–015
    contract, 8–001—8–124
    dispositions of property, 8–125—8–175
    generally, 1–004
    knowledge acquired through agent,
        8–208—8–217
    notification to agent, 8–205—8–207
    wrongful acts of agent, 8–176—8–204
  warranty of authority, 9–065
Timber
  restitution for securing of, 4–010
Time limits
  commercial agents
    compensation, 11–055
    indemnity, 11–046
  ratification, effect of, 2–097
Title to sue
  bribes, 9–098
  secret commission, 9–098
Tortious liability
  conflict of laws, 12–027, 12–034
Torts
  agents' duties, 6–003
  agents' liabilities
    co-agents, 9–132—9–133
    conversion by innocent agent,
        9–126—9–131
    generally, 9–032
    personal liability, 9–115—9–125
    sub-agents, 9–132—9–133
  approach in, 1–026
  cheques, 9–130
  co-agents, 9–132—9–133
  conversion by innocent agent, 9–126—9–131
  duty of skill and care, 6–016
  estoppel from denying agency, 2–107
  gratuitous agents, 6–028
  introduction, 8–176
  liability of principal
    assumption of responsibility, 8–183
    authorising wrongs, 8–181
    casual delegation, 8–187
    contribution, 8–191
    contributory negligence, 8–188
    corporations, 8–189
    Crown, 8–190
    deceit, 8–185
    examples, 8–192—8–196
    generally, 8–177
    misstatements, 8–180
    negligence, 8–186
    non-delegable duties, 8–184
    partners, 8–178
    procuring wrongs, 8–181
    servants, 8–178
    statements based only on agency reasoning,
        8–182
    transferred employment, 8–179
  personal liability
    contract, 9–117
    contribution, 9–123
    Crown, 9–124

    deceit, 9–117
    directors, 9–119
    effect of judgment against principal, 9–123
    examples, 9–125
    general rule, 9–115—9–116
    inducement of breach of contract, 9–121
    involvement in wrongs, 9–120
    misrepresentation, 9–118
    misstatements, 9–117
    procuring wrongs, 9–120
    vicarious immunity, 9–122
  ratification
    acts capable of, 2–056
  sub-agents
    liability for wrongs of, 9–132—9–133
    liability of, 5–012
Trade unions
  implied agency
    shop stewards, 2–034
  inspection of books
    agents' powers, 2–026
Tribunals
  agents' powers, 2–024
Trust management
  dealing with principal, 6–070
Trust property
  receipt of
    breach of trust, 9–134, 9–136
Trustees
  accessory liability, 9–135—9–142
  agents' powers, 2–021
  co-agents' authority, 2–044
  constructive, 9–135, 9–140
  conversion, 9–131
  damages, 9–013
  dealing with principal, 6–064
  distinction from agents, 1–032
  fiduciary duty
    equitable compensation for loss, 6–043
    profits, account of, 6–042
  personal liability, 9–036
Trustees de son tort
  breach of trust, 9–138
Trustees in bankruptcy
  priority, 9–035
  ratification, scope of, 2–083
  repayment to, 9–109, 9–114
Trusts
  irrevocable authority, 10–010
Tug services
  shipmasters' powers as agent
    agency of necessity, and, 4–013
    ratification, limits on, 2–094
Turf commission agent
  see also Wagering contracts
  payment of winnings by, 6–099
Ultra vires
  fictitious principals, 9–087
  ratification, acts capable of, 2–058
  warranty of authority, 9–066
Unauthorised acts
  principal/third party relations, 8–047—8–061
  reimbursement of expenses, 7–065

remuneration
    examples, 7–051
    general rule, 7–048
    wrongful withdrawal of authority, 7–049

Unauthorised agents
    conflict of laws, 12–026

Underwriters
    bribes, 6–089
    brokers
        as agents of, 2–016
    disclosure to, 6–021
    duty of care owed to, 6–024

Undisclosed principals
    agents' liabilities, 9–006, 9–012, 9–013,
        9–015
    conflict of laws, 12–028
    damages, 9–013
    dispositions of property to agent, 8–171
    identified principals, and, 9–091
    interrogatories as to existence of, 9–015
    meaning, 1–041
    oral contracts, 9–045
    principal/third party relations, 8–068—8–082
    ratification, 2–063, 8–072
    repayment of money, and, 9–104, 9–109
    sub agents' liens, 7–098
    unidentified principals, and, 9–016, 9–092,
        9–096

Undue influence
    dealing with principal, 6–063, 6–069

Unenforceable transactions
    warranty of authority, 9–080

Unfair contract terms
    conflict of interest, 6–058—6–059
    remuneration, 7–008

Unidentified principals
    agents' liabilities, 9–016, 9–092, 9–095
    meaning, 1–039, 1–041
    ratification, 2–067

Unilateral contracts
    agents' liabilities, 6–005
    compensation for termination of authority,
        10–043

Unincorporated associations
    fictitious principals, 9–018, 9–085
    liability for torts, 9–120
    principal's liability, 8–179
    warranty of authority, 9–076

Unjust enrichment
    conflict of laws, 12–036

Unlawful transactions
    see also Illegality
    reimbursement of expenses, 7–067
    remuneration
        examples, 7–056
        general rule, 7–052
        illegality, 7–054
        incapacity to act, 7–053
        wagering transactions, 7–055

Unsatisfied liens
    irrevocable authority, 10–010

Use of position
    fiduciary duty, 6–079—6–083

Usual authority
    generally, 3–005
    managerial agents, 3–027—3–029
    professional agents, 3–030—3–032

Valuers
    negligence, 6–024
    production of documents, 6–093
    signing for, 2–026

Vicarious liability
    personal liability of agent, 9–122
    shipmasters, 4–007

Void transactions
    further instructions, duty to follow, 6–009

Voluntary organisations
    ratification, 2–070

Wagering contracts
    reimbursement of expenses, 7–069
    remuneration, 7–055

Waiver
    extinguishment of liens, 7–092

War
    agency, effect on, 2–010, 2–012, 2–066,
        2–070

Warehousing
    salvor's authority, 4–006, 4–008, 4–013

Warranty of authority
    apparent authority, 9–071
    breach of
        measure of damages for, 9–077—9–083
    cessation of authority unbeknown to agent,
        9–063
    Crown agents, 9–074
    examples, 9–076
    general rule, 9–031, 9–060
    historical background, 9–061
    measure of damages for breach
        contractual principle, 9–078
        costs, 9–081
        examples, 9–083
        generally, 9–077
        insolvent principal, 9–079
        other warranties, 9–082
        transactions unenforceable against
            principal, 9–080
    misrepresentation, not confined to, 9–064
    mistake of law, 9–069
    nature of liability, 9–062
    powers of attorney, 9–073
    procedure, 9–075
    ratification, 9–072
    rebuttal, 9–070
    scope of, 9–066
    solicitors
        identity fraud, 9–068
        issue of proceedings, 9–067
    third parties, to, 9–065

Winding-up
    ratification, 2–061

Wives
    see Spouses

Writer to the signet
    gratuitous agents, liability of, 6–032

Written contracts
agents' liabilities, 9–036—9–038
Wrongful acts of agent
agent's liability
companies, 9–120
contribution, 9–123
Crown liability, 9–124
deceit, 9–1117
examples, 9–125
generally, 9–115—9–116
inducement of breach of contract, 9–121
misrepresentation, 9–118—9–119

misstatements, 9–117
vicarious immunity, 9–122
principal's liability
misappropriation, 8–199—8–201
misrepresentations as to credit of third
parties, 8–197—8–198
money applied for benefit of principal,
8–202—8–204
torts, 8–176—8–196
Wrongful termination
compensation, 10–045